CHILTON'S
Foreign Car Repair Manual

French, British, Japanese Cars Edition
Volume II

Managing Editor
John D. Kelly

Assistant Managing Editor
Peter J. Meyer

Senior Technical Editor
Kerry A. Freeman

Technical Editors

Zane C. Binder
Stephen J. Davis
Jon C. Jay
James H. Johnson
Howard L. Kenig
George S. Rizzo
N Banks Spence Jr
William J. Wartman

CHILTON BOOK COMPANY
401 Walnut St., Philadelphia, Pennsylvania 19106
PHILADELPHIA NEW YORK

Published in Philadelphia by Chilton Book Company and simultaneously in Ontario, Canada, by Thomas Nelson & Sons, Ltd.
ISBN: 0-8019-5637-4 Library of Congress Catalog Card No. 73-168562 Manufactured in the United States of America

Contents

Acknowledgments

The Chilton Book Company expresses appreciation to the following firms for their assistance: A Pierburg Auto-& Luftfahrt-Geratebau KG (Zenith Carburetors); Arnolt Corporation (Solex Carburetors), Warsaw, Indiana; Bob Carl Incorporated (Subaru), Media, Pennsylvania; British Leyland Motors (Austin-Healey, Jaguar, MG, Triumph), Leonia, New Jersey; Chalmers Import Restorations (Austin-Healey), West Chester, Pennsylvania; Champion Spark Plug Company, Toledo, Ohio; Chrysler Corporation (Colt), Center Line, Michigan; Chrysler-Plymouth (Cricket), Bala-Cynwyd, Pennsylvania; Devon Datsun, Division of DiSimone Imports, Devon, Pennsylvania; Ed Fisher Motors (Toyota), Parkesburg, Pennsylvania; Joseph Lucas North America, Englewood, New Jersey; Lincoln Mercury (Capri), Dearborn, Michigan; Midway Motors (Triumph), Atlantic City, New Jersey; Nissan Motor Corporation (Datsun), Secaucus, New Jersey; Peugeot Incorporated, Clifton, New Jersey; Renault Incorporated, Englewood Cliffs, New Jersey; Robert Bosch Corporation, Long Island City, New York; Royston Distributors (Jaguar), Jessup, Maryland; Speedcraft Enterprises (Jaguar, MG, Toyota), Devon, Pennsylvania; Subaru of North America, Pennsauken, New Jersey; Toyota Motor Distributors Incorporated, Torrance, California.

AUSTIN-HEALEY SECTION

Index

Introduction

Austin dates back as one of the oldest English manufacturers of economy cars. In the 1930's attempts were made to assemble the Austin in the U.S., but these failed. It was not until after W.W. II that the Austin was imported into the U.S. on a large scale. The first Austin-Healey, the 100-4 appeared in 1952. Designed by Donald Healey, it was originally powered by a four-cylinder engine of Austin design. In the late 1950's a six-cylinder engine was introduced, and the design of the car was updated. Also, in the late 1950's the first Austin-Healey Sprite, now known as the Bugeye, was produced. The larger Healey continued until the end of its production, in 1967, basically unchanged. The Sprite body became identical, except for trim, with the MG Midget in 1962. The Sprite ceased being imported in 1970.

Year and Model Identification

Austin-Healey 100-6

Austin-Healey 3000 Mk. I

Austin-Healey 3000 Mks. II and III

Austin-Healey Sprite Mk. I Bugeye

Austin-Healey Sprite Mks. II, III, and IV

Austin America 1968-70

Austin America 1971

Vehicle and Engine Serial Number Identification

Vehicle number identification

The Austin-Healey vehicle number is located on a plate at the rear of the engine compartment. The Austin-Healey Sprite has its number stamped on a plate attached to the left front wheel arch, inside, under the hood. Locating the vehicle number of the Austin America presents more of a problem than either of the above cars. On the early models the number is on a plate that is mounted on the right-hand side of the hood lock platform. Later cars in the series have *two* vehicle number plates. One is mounted on the left-hand windshield pillar; the other plate is to the right of hood lock platform, or on the left-hand door pillar.

Engine number identification

The engine number of the Sprite and the Austin America is on a plate attached to the right side of the cylinder block. The engine number of the 3000 is at the left side of the cylinder block.

Vehicle Identification—Austin-Healey

Year	*Model*	*Serial Number*
1956-57	100-6 (2-port)	H-BN4/* 22,598-48,863
1957-59	100-6 (6-port)	H-BN4/* 48,864-77,766
1958-59	100-6 (6-port)	H-BN6/* 501-4,650
1959-61	3000 Mk. I	H-BN7/* H-BT7/* 101-13,750
1961-62	3000 Mk. II (3-carb.)	H-BN7/* 18,888 H-BT7/* 101-19,853
1962-64	3000 Mk. II (2-carb.)	H-BJ7/* 17,551-25,314
1964-67	3000 Mk.III	H-BJ8/* 25,315-43,026

* An L in the serial number denotes left-hand drive.

Vehicle Identification—Sprite

Year	*Model*	*Serial Number*
1958-61	Mk. I	H-AN5/* 501-50,116
1961-62	Mk. II (948 cc.)	H-AN6/* 101-24,731
1963-64	Mk. II (1,098 cc.)	H-AN7/* 24,732-38,828
1965-66	Mk. III	H-AN8/* 38,829-64,734
1967-70	Mk. IV	H-AN9/* 64,735-***

* An L in the serial number denotes left-hand drive.

*** Finishing serial numbers for North American models not known.

Vehicle Identification—Austin America

Year	*Model*	*Serial Number*
1968-71	America	AA-25DUB 101-**

**—Series still in production.

Engine Identification—Austin-Healey

Number of Cylinders	*Displacement*	*Type*	*Serial Number*
6-inline	2,639 cc.	OHV	26C/R/U/H 101-60,984
6-inline	2,639 cc.	OHV	26D/R/U/H 60,949-77,766
6-inline	2,912 cc.	OHV	29D/R/U/H 101-26,212
6-inline	2,912 cc.	OHV	29E/R/U/H 101-5,799
6-inline	2,912 cc.	OHV	29F/R/U/H 101-6,188
6-inline	2,912 cc.	OHV	29K/R/U/H 101-17,636

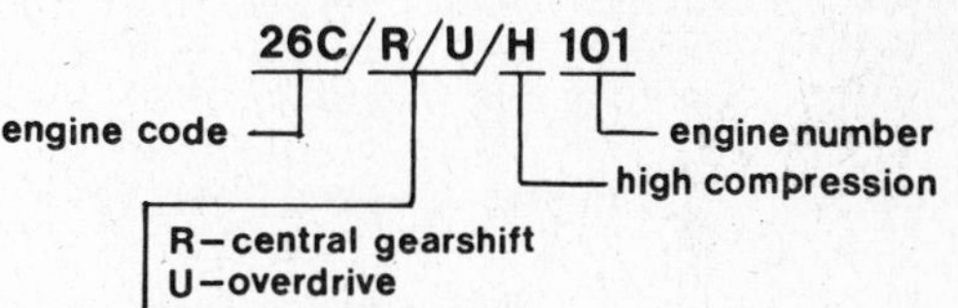

Engine Identification—Sprite

Number of Cylinders	Displacement	Type	Serial Number
4-inline	948 cc.	OHV	9C/U/H 101-49,201
4-inline	948 cc.	OHV	9CG/Da/H 101-36,711
4-inline	1,098 cc.	OHV	10CG/Da/H 101-21,048
4-inline	1,098 cc.	OHV	10CC/Da/H 101-16,300
4-inline	1,275 cc.	OHV	12CC/Da/H 101-16,300
4-inline	1,275 cc.	OHV	12CD/Da/H 101-N.A.

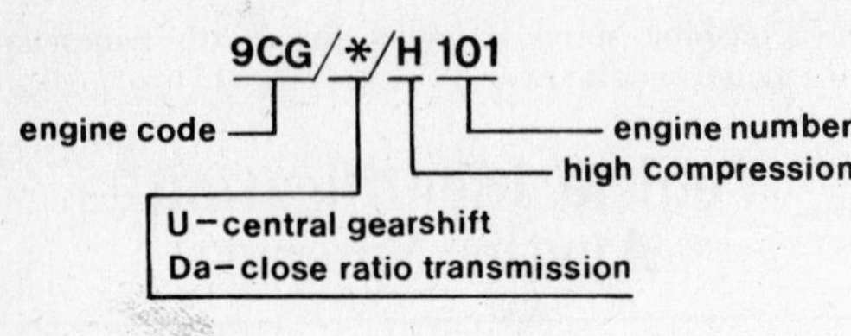

Engine Identification—Austin America

Number of Cylinders	Displacement	Type	Serial Number
4-inline	1,275 cc.	OHV	12H/157
4-inline	1,275 cc.	OHV	12H/185
4-inline	1,275 cc.	OHV	12H/291
4-inline	1,275 cc.	OHV	12H/292
4-inline	1,275 cc.	OHV	12H/393
4-inline	1,275 cc.	OHV	12H/394
4-inline	1,275 cc.	OHV	12H/451
4-inline	1,275 cc.	OHV	12H/452

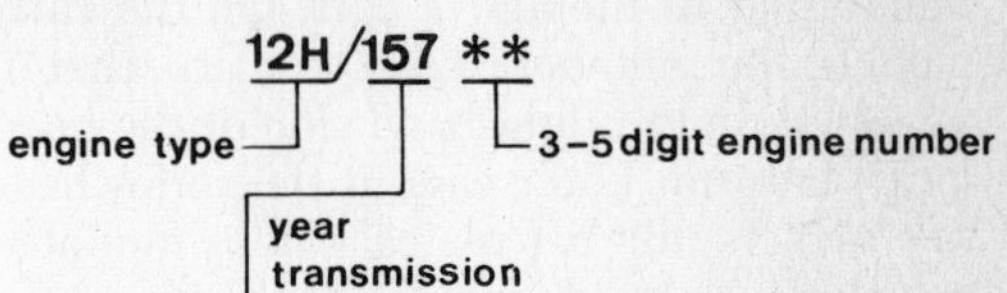

General Engine Specifications

Model/Year	Engine Code	Dis-placement	S.U. Carburetor Type (No. of carbs.)	Advertized Horse-power @RPM	Advertized Torque @RPM (ft. lbs.)	Bore and Stroke (in.)	Com-pression Ratio	Oil Pressure (psi)
Austin-Healey 100-6								
1957-59	26C	2,639 cc.	H4 (2)	102@4,600	142@2,400	3.125x3.500	8.25:1	55-60
1957-59 (6-port)	26D	2,639 cc.	HD6 (2)	117@5,000	150@3,000	3.125x3.500	8.70:1	55-60
Austin-Healey 3000								
1959-61 (Mk. I)	29D	2,912 cc.	HD6 (2)	130@4,600	167@3,000	3.280x3.500	9.03:1	50@40mph
1961-62 (Mk. II)	29E	2,912 cc.	HS4 (3)	136@4,750	167@3,000	3.280x3.500	9.03:1	50@40mph
1963-64 (Mk. II)	29F	2,912 cc.	HS6 (2)	136@4,750	167@3,000	3.280x3.500	9.03:1	50@40mph
1964-67 (Mk. III)	29K	2,912 cc.	HS8 (2)	150@5,250	167@3,000	3.280x3.500	9.03:1	50@40mph
Sprite Mk. I								
1958-61	9C	948 cc.	H1 (2)	43@5,000	52@3,300	2.478x3.000	9.00:1	30-60
Sprite Mk. II								
1961-62	9CG	948 cc.	HS2 (2)	46@5,500	53@3,000	2.478x3.000	8.90:1	30-60
1963-64	10CG	1,098 cc.	HS2 (2)	55@5,500	62@3,250	2.543x3.296	8.90:1	30-60
Sprite Mk. III								
1965-66	10CC	1,098 cc.	HS2 (2)	59@5,750	65@3,500	2.543x3.296	8.90:1	30-60
Sprite Mk. IV								
1967	12CC	1,275 cc.	HS2 (2)	65@6,000	72@3,000	2.780x3.200	8.80:1	40-70
1968-70	12CD*	1,275 cc.	HS2 (2)	62@6,000	72@3,000	2.780x3.200	8.80:1	40-70
Austin America								
1968-70	12H**	1,275 cc.	HS4 (1)	58@5,250	69@3,000	2.780x3.200	8.80:1	40-70

*—Exhaust emission control system fitted.
**—Exhaust emission control, and evaporative loss control systems fitted.

Tune-up Specifications

Model/Year	Engine Code	Spark Plugs Champion	Spark Plugs Gap (in.)	Distributor Dwell (deg.)	Distributor Gap (in.)	Timing Static (deg. BTDC)	Compression Pressure (psi)	Valves Clearance (in.) Intake	Valves Clearance (in.) Exhaust	Valves Intake Opens (deg.)	Idle Speed (rpm)
Austin-Healey 100-6											
1957-59	26C	UN12Y	.025	35	.015	6	190	.012H	.012H	5B	1,100
1957-59	26D	UN12Y	.025	35	.015	6	190	.012H	.012H	5B	1,100
Austin-Healey 3000											
1959-61	29D	UN12Y	.025	35	.015	5	190	.012C	.012C	5B	1,100
1961-62	29E	UN12Y	.025	35	.015	5	190	.012C	.012C	5B	1,100
1963-64	29F	UN12Y	.025	35	.015	10	190	.012C	.012C	10B*	1,100
1964-67	29K	UN12Y	.025	35	.015	10	190	.012C	.012C	16B	1,100
Sprite Mk. I											
1958-61	9C	N5	.025	60	.015	5	165	.012C	.012C	5B	1,000
Sprite Mk. II											
1961-62	9CG	N5	.025	60	.015	4	165	.012C	.012C	5B	1,000
1963-64	10CG	N5	.025	60	.015	5	165	.012C	.012C	5B	1,000
Sprite Mk. III											
1965-66	10CC	N5	.025	60	.015	5	165	.012C	.012C	5B	1,000
Sprite Mk. IV											
1967	12CC	N9Y	.025	60	.015	7	120	.012C	.012C	5B	700
1968-70	12CD	N9Y	.025	60	.015	4	120	.012C	.012C	5B	1,000
Austin America											
1968-71	12H	N9Y	.025	60	.015	TDC	120	.012C	.012C	5B	850

*—Mk. II BJ7 from engine number 29F/2286, earlier numbers opened at 5° BTDC.
B—Before top dead center.
C—Engine cold.
H—Engine hot.

CAUTION: *General adoption of anti-pollution laws has changed the tune-up specifications of almost all engines to reduce crankcase emissions and terminal exhaust products. Timing and idle speed are of particular importance, and the manufacturer's recommendations should be strictly adhered to. This information is clearly displayed in the engine compartment of any vehicle equipped with emission control systems.*

Firing Order

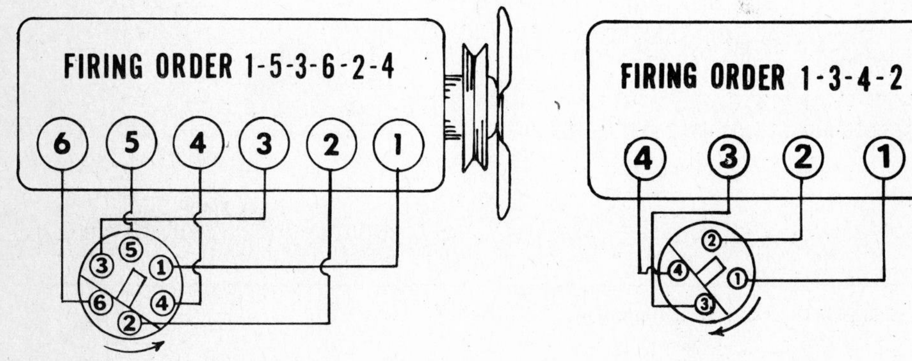

Austin-Healey 100-6 and 3000 firing order: 1, 5, 3, 6, 2, 4

Sprite Mk. I firing order: 1, 3, 4, 2 (rotor clockwise)

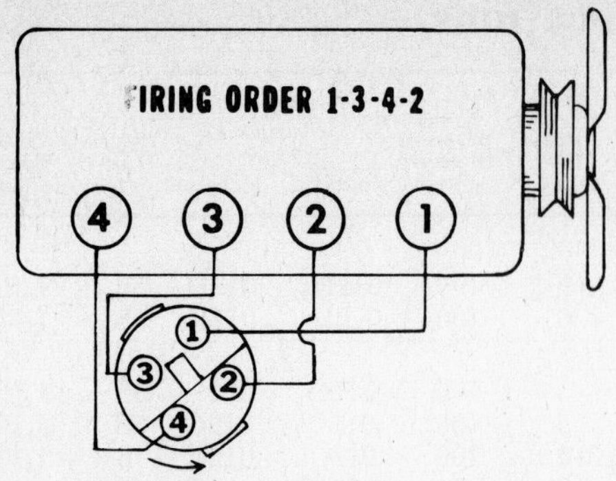

Sprite Mks. II, III, and IV firing order 1, 3, 4, 2 (rotor counter-clockwise)

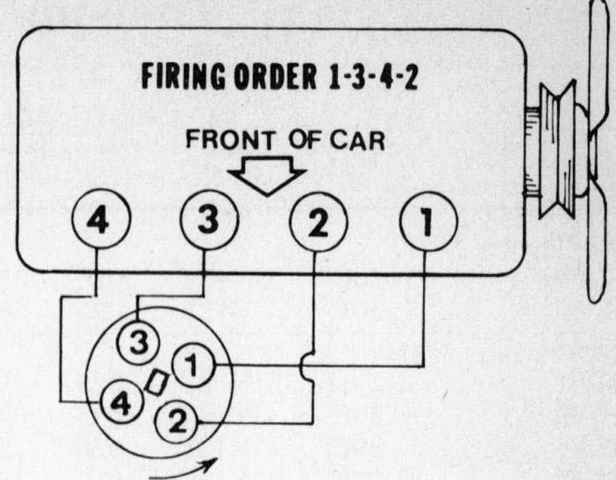

Austin America firing order: 1, 3, 4, 2

Engine Rebuilding Specifications

Crankshaft Specifications										
	Main Bearing Journals (in.)					*Connecting Rod Bearing Journals (in.)*				
Model & Engine	*Journal Diameter New*	*Journal Diameter Minimum*	*Oil Clearance*	*Shaft End-play*	*Thrust On No.*	*Journal Diameter New*	*Journal Diameter Minimum*	*Oil Clearance*	*End-play*
Austin-Healey 26C/26D	2.3742-2.3747	-.040	.0013-.0028	.0025-.0055	2	2.00-2.0005	-.040	.0005-.002	.007-.004
29D/29E/ 29F/29K	2.3742-2.3747	-.020	.0013-.0028	.0025-.0055	2	2.00-2.0005	-.020	.002-.0035	.005-.009
Sprite 9C/9CG/ 10CG	1.7505-1.7510	-.040	.001-.0025	.002-.003	2	1.6254-1.6259	-.040	.001-.0025	.008-.012
10CC	2.0005-2.0010	-.040	.001-.0025	.002-.003	2	1.6254-1.6259	-.040	.001-.0025	.008-.012
12CC/ 12CD	2.0005-2.0010	-.010*	.001-.0027	.002-.003	2	1.6254-1.6259	-.010*	.001-.0025	.006-.010
Austin America 12H	2.0005-2.0010	-.040	.001-.0027	.002-.003	2	1.7504-1.7509	-.040	.001-.0025	.006-.010

*—Maximum permissible without heat treatment.

Engine Rebuilding Specifications

Valve Specifications

Model & Engine	Seat Angle (deg.)	Valve Lift (in.)		Valve Head Diameter (in.)		Valve Spring Free Length (in.)		Spring Pressure (lbs.)**		Stem Diameter (in.)		Stem to Guide Clearance (in.)		Guide Height Above Head (in.)	
		Intake	Exhaust	Intake	Exhaust	Inner	Outer	Intake	Exhaust	Intake	Exhaust	Intake	Exhaust	Intake	Exhaust
Austin-Healey															
26C	30/45*	.3145	.3145	1.693-1.683	1.420-1.415	1.969	2.047	79.5	79.5	.34175-.34225	.34175-.34225	.0025-.0015	.002-.001	N.A.	N.A.
26D	45	.3145	.3145	1.750-1.745	1.5625-1.5575	1.969	2.047	81.7	81.7	.34175-.34225	.34175-.34225	.0025-.0015	.002-.001	N.A.	N.A.
29D	45	.3145	.3145	1.750-1.745	1.5625-1.5575	1.969	2.047	81.7	81.7	.34175-.34225	.34175-.34225	.0025-.0015	.002-.001	1.348	1.036
29E/29F/29K	45	.368	.368	1.750-1.745	1.5625-1.5575	1.969	2.031	93.5	93.5	.34175-.34225	.34175-.34225	.0025-.0015	.002-.001	1.348	1.036
Sprite															
9C	45	.28	.28	1.094	1.000	1.672	1.750	105	105	.2793-.2798	.2788-.2793	.0015-.0025	.002-.003	.594	.594
9CG	45	.312	.312	1.151-1.156	1.000-1.005	1.672	1.750	118	118	.2793-.2798	.2788-.2793	.0015-.C025	.002-.003	.594	.594
10CG/10CC	45	.312	.312	1.213-1.218	1.000-1.005	1.672	1.750	118	118	.2793-.2798	.2788-.2793	.0015-.0025	.002-.003	.594	.594
12CC/12CD	45	.318	.318	1.307-1.312	1.152-1.156	1.703	1.750	131	131	.2793-.2798	.2788-.2793	.0015-.0025	.0015-.0025	.594	.594
Austin America															
12H	45	.318	.318	1.307-1.312	1.152-1.156	1.950	1.950	124	124	.2793-.2798	.2788-.2793	.0015-.0025	.0015-.0025	.540	.540

*—Intake and exhaust seat angles respectively.
**—Combined pressure of inner and outer valve springs with valve fully open.

Engine Rebuilding Specifications

Model & Engine	Piston Specifications (in.)				Ring Specifications (in.)			
			Skirt Clearance		Compression		Oil Control	
	Oversize Maximum	Wrist Pin Diameter	Top	Bottom	End-Gap	Side Clearance	End-Gap	Side Clearance
Austin-Healey 26C/26D	+.040	.8748-.8750	.0008-.0226*	.0008-.0226*	.009-.014	.0034-.0014	.009-.014	.0015-.0035
29D/29E 29F/29K	+.040	.8748-.8750	.0032-.0043	.0010-.0016	.013-.018	.0015-.0035	.013-.018	.0015-.0035
Sprite 9C	+.040	.6244-.6246	.0010-.0016*	.0010-.0016*	.007-.012	.0015-.0035	.007-.012	.0015-.0025
9CG	+.040	.6244-.6246	.0036-.0042	.0016-.0022	.007-.012	.0015-.0035	.007-.012	.0015-.0025
10CG/10CC	+.020	.6244-.6246	.0021-.0037	.0005-.0011	.007-.012	.002-.004	.012-.028	.0015-.0025
12CC/12CD	+.020	.8123-.8125	.0029-.0037	.0015-.0021	.008-.013**	.0015-.0035	.012-.028	.0015-.0025
Austin America 12H	+.020	.8123-.8125	.0029-.0037	.0015-.0021	.011-.016	.0015-.0035	.008-.013	.0015-.0035

*—The clearance is measured at right angles to the wrist pin.
**—Top compression ring—.011-.016 in.

Torque Specifications

Model & Engine	Head Bolts (ft. lbs.)	Main Bearing Bolts (ft. lbs.)	Rod Bearing Bolts (ft. lbs.)	Crankshaft Balancer* Bolt(s) (ft. lbs.)	Flywheel to Crankshaft Bolt(s) (ft. lbs.)	Manifold Nuts (ft. lbs.)	
						Intake	Exhaust
Austin-Healey All series	75	75	50	N.A.	50	N.A.	N.A.
Sprite 9C/9CG/ 10CG/10CC	40	60	35	70	40	15	15
12CC/12CD	42**	60	45***	70	40	15	15
Austin America 12H	50	60	31-35	70	110-115	15	15

*—Torque figure given applies to crankshaft pulley on cars not equipped with balancer.
**—Studs stamped 22 or with a small drill point—50 ft. lbs.
***—Nylon type self-locking nut—32-34 ft. lb.

Tightening Sequences

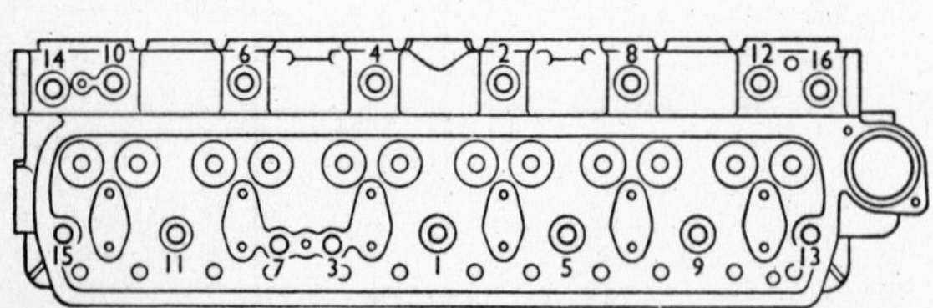

Cylinder-head nut tightening sequence, six-cylinder engine.

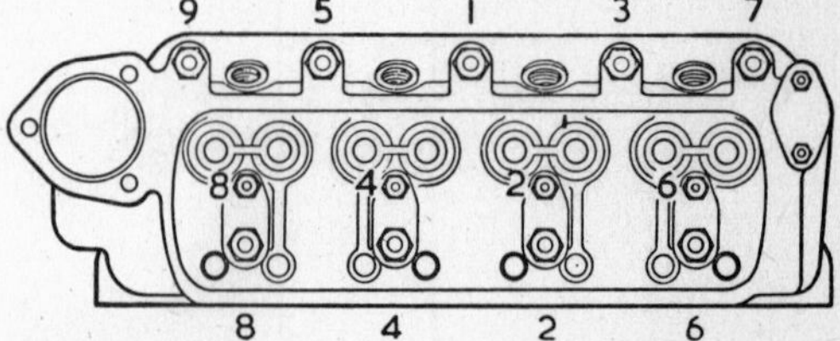

Order of loosening and tightening cylinder-head nuts, four-cylinder engine.

Battery and Starter Specifications

Model & Engine	Battery** Capacity (amp. hrs.)	Volts	Grounded Terminal	Type	Lock Test Amps	Volts	Torque (ft. lbs.)	No Load Test Amps	Volts	rpm	Brush Spring Tension (oz.)
Austin-Healey (All series)	58	12	Pos.	M418G	440-460	7.2	17	45	11.5	7,400-8,500	30-40
Sprite 9C/9CG/10CG/10CC	43	12	Pos.	M35G	250-365	7	6.7	60	11.5	8,000-11,500	25
12CC/12CD	50	12	Neg.*	M35J	250-375	7	7.0	65	11.5	8,000-10,000	28
Austin America 12H***	40	12	Pos.	M35G	250-365	7	6.7	60	11.5	8,000-11,500	15-20
12H	50	12	Neg.	M35J	250-375	7	7.0	65	11.5	8,000-10,000	28

*—Positive ground up to car number H-AN9/72,041. Positive ground cars (12CC engine only) use the M35G starter.

**—Austin Healey series BN7 cars have two 6-volt batteries wired in series. The same specifications apply.

***—1968-69 Austin Americas equipped with a positive ground electrical system and a generator.

Generator and Regulator Specifications

Model & Engine	Generator (Lucas) Type	Max. Output (Amps)	Brush Pressure (oz.)	Resistance (Ohms)	Regulator (Lucas) Type	Cut-Out Relay Points Close (Volts)	Reverse Current (Amps)	Points Air Gap (in.)	Maximum Current (Amps)	Points Air Gap (in.)	Stop Arm Height (in.)
Austin-Healey 26C/26D	C45PV5	22	N.A.	6.0	RB106/2	12.7-13.3	5.0	.010-.020	19	.015	.025-.040
29D/29E/29F	C45PV6	25	34-44	6.0	RB106/2	12.7-13.3	5.0	.010-.020	19	.015	.025-.040
29K	C42	30	24-44	4.5	RB340	12.7-13.3	5.0	**	22	.015	.018
Sprite 9C/9CG	C39	19	18-26	6.0-6.3	RB106/2	12.7-13.3	5.0	.010-.020	19	.015	.025-.040
10CG/10CC	C40/1	22	22-25	6.0	RB106/2	12.7-13.3	5.0	.010-.020	19	.015	.025-.040
12CG/12CD	C40/1	22	22-25	6.0	RB340*	12.7-13.3	8.0	**	22	.015	.018
Austin America 12H (1968-9)	C40/1	22	22-25	6.0	RB340	12.7-13.3	8.0	**	22	.015	.018

*—Early cars (12CC engine with positive ground) use the RB106/2 regulator.

**—See text.

Alternator and AC Regulator Specifications

Model & Engine	Alternator (Lucas)					AC Regulator (Lucas)					
	Type	Output (amps.) @ Engine rpm 850 rpm	Output (amps.) @ Engine rpm 3,300 rpm	Field Current Draw (Amps @12V)	Brush Tension (oz.)	Type	Field Relay Air Gap (in.)	Field Relay Point Gap (in.)	Points Close (Volts)	Air Gap (in.)	Volts @ 125 deg.
Austin America 12H (1970-71)	16ACR	12-15	34	3	7-10	8TR	Integral with alternator, trans-				14.0-14.4
						11TR	sistor type—no adjustment.				14.0-14.4

Capacities and Pressures

Model & Engine	Crankcase (qts.) With Filter	Crankcase (qts.) Without Filter	Transmission (pts.) 4-Speed	Transmission (pts.) 4-Speed with O.D.	Transmission (pts.) Auto.	Drive Axle (pts.)	Fuel Tank (gals.)	Coolant w/Heater (qts.)	Fuel Pressure (psi)	Coolant Pressure (max. psi)
Austin-Healey 26C	7.6	6.9	6	7.5	—	3.6	14.4	12	1.5-2.0	7
26D	7.6	6.9	6	7.5	—	3.6	14.4	12	3.2	7
29D/29E/29F 29K	7.6	6.9	6	7.5	—	3.6	14.4	12	3.2	7
Sprite 9C	4.0	3.5	2.8	—	—	2.1	7.2	6.3	1.5-2.5	7
9CG/10CG	4.0	3.5	2.7	—	—	2.1	7.2	6.3	1.5-2.5	7
10CC/12CC	4.0	3.5	2.7	—	—	2.1	7.2	6.3	2.5-3.0	7
12CD	4.0	3.5	2.7	—	—	2.1	7.2	6.3	2.5-3.0	15
Austin America 12H (Man.)	5.12	4.9	*	—	—	*	9	4**	2.5-3.0	13
12H (Auto.)	8	5.5	—	—	*	*	9	4**	2.5-3.0	13

*—Transmission and drive axle located in engine sump.
**—Includes expansion tank.

Brake Specifications

Model	Type Front	Type Rear	Brake Cylinder Bore (in.) Master Cylinder	Brake Cylinder Bore (in.) Wheel Cylinder Front	Brake Cylinder Bore (in.) Wheel Cylinder Rear	Disc/Drum Diameter (in.) Front	Disc/Drum Diameter (in.) Rear
Austin-Healey 100-6	drum	drum	3/4	1.00	1.00	11.0	11.0
Austin Healey 3000 Mk. I/Mk. II	disc	drum	9/16	2 1/8	N.A.	11.0	11.0
Mk. II/Mk. III*	disc	drum	N.A.	2 1/8	N.A.	11.0	11.0
Sprite Mk. I/Mk. II (9CG)	drum	drum	7/8	15/16	3/4	7.0	7.0
Mk. II (10CG)/ Mk. III	disc	drum	3/4	2 1/4	3/4	8.25	7.0
Mk. IV	disc	drum	11/16**	2 1/4	3/4	8.25	7.0
Austin America	disc	drum	11/16	N.A.	3/4	8.40	8.0

*—Power brakes optional on Mk. II; standard on Mk. III.
**—3/4 (in) up to vehicle number H-AN9/72,034.

Chassis and Wheel Alignment Specifications

Model & Year	Wheelbase (in.)	Track (in.) Front	Track (in.) Rear	Caster (deg.) Range	Caster (deg.) Ideal	Camber (deg.) Range	Camber (deg.) Ideal	Toe-In (in.)	King-Pin Inclination (deg.)	Wheel Pivot Ratio (deg.) Inner	Wheel Pivot Ratio (deg.) Outer
Austin-Healey All Series	92	48¾	50	—	2P	—	1N	⅛	6½	21	20
Sprite 9C	80	45¾	44¾	—	3P	—	1N	⅛	6½	20	18½
9CG/10CG/ 10CC	80	45¾	44¾	—	3P	—	¾N	⅛	6¾	20	18½
12CC/12CD	80	46⁵⁄₁₆	45¼	—	3P	—	¾N	⅛	6¾	20	19¾
Austin America 12H	92½	51½	50⅞	4½P-6½P	5½P	¼N-1¾P	¾P	1/16*	10	21½	20

*—1/16″ front wheel *toe-out.*

Fuses

Model	Circuit	Amps
Austin-Healey All Series	A1-A2. Auxiliary circuits not controlled by the ignition switch. (Horn, interior lamps, etc.)	50
	A3-A4. Auxiliary circuits wired through the ignition switch. (Fuel gauge, wiper motor, etc.)	35
Sprite All Series	A1-A2. Protects circuits not controlled by the ignition switch. (Horn, lights, etc.)	35
	A3-A4. Auxiliary circuits wired through the ignition switch. (Direction indicators, wipers, gauges etc.)	35
Austin America 12H	1-2. Interior lights, and horn.	35
	3-4. Brake/stop lights, heater blower, wiper motor.	35
	Line fuse. Parking lights and tail lights.	35
	Line fuse. Hazard warning flasher.	35

Distributor Specifications

Model & Engine	Distributor Type (Lucas)	Serial Number	Centrifugal Advance** Start (deg. @ rpm)	Centrifugal Advance** Intermediate (deg. @ rpm)	Centrifugal Advance** Finish (deg. @ rpm)	Vacuum Advance Start (in. Hg.)	Vacuum Advance Finish (in. Hg.)	Vacuum Advance Maximum (deg.)	Maximum Distributor Advance (deg. @ rpm)
Austin-Healey									
26C	DM6A	N.A.	N.A.	N.A.	N.A.	N.A.	N.A.	N.A.	35@N.A.
26D	DM6	N.A.	N.A.	N.A.	N.A.	N.A.	N.A.	N.A.	36@N.A.
29D/29E	DM6A	N.A.	N.A.	N.A.	N.A.	N.A.	N.A.	N.A.	36@N.A.
29F/29K	25D6	40966B	2-8@1,100	17@2,000	30@4,400	5	12	16	36@6,400
Sprite									
9C	DM2P4H	N.A.	N.A.	N.A.	N.A.	N.A.	N.A.	N.A.	N.A.
9CG	DM2P4	40752A	0-3@750	16@1,800	26@5,000	5	12	12	28@5,000
10CG/10CC	25D4	40919	0-3@800	16@1,800	32@5,500	4	13	20	32@5,000
12CC	23D4	40818*	0-3@600	15@2,000	27@6,000	—	—	—	27@6,000
	25D4	41198	1@600	14@2,000	24@5,600	5	8	4-8	24@5,600
12CD	25D4	41229	4@600	19@2,500	30@4,300	5	8	4-8	30@5,000
Austin America									
12H	25D4	40897/ 41155	10 @500	24@1,625	31@3,000	5	13	20-22	32@5,000

*—Centrifugal advance only.
**—Lucas distributor advance should be checked while the distributor is *decelerating*, except for the Austin America, which conforms to standard U.S. practice.

Carburetor Specifications

Model & Engine	S.U. Type	Venturi (in.)	Main Jet Size (in.)	Jet Needle*** Identification No. Standard	Rich	Lean	Piston Spring Strength (Color Identification)
Austin-Healey							
26C	H4	1.50	.090	AJ	N.A.	N.A.	N.A.
26D/29D	HD6	1.75	.100	CV	N.A.	N.A.	yellow
29E	HS4	1.50	.090	DJ	DK	DH	red
29F	HS6	1.75	.100	BC	RD	TZ	red
29K	HD8	2.00	.125	UH	UN	UL	red and green
Sprite							
9C	H1	1.25	N.A.	GG	N.A.	N.A.	N.A.
9CG	HS2	1.25	.090	V3	V2	GX	light blue
10CG	HS2	1.25	.090	GY	M	GG	blue
10CC	HS2	1.25	.090	AN	H6	GG	blue
12CC	HS2	1.25	.090	AN	H6	GG	light blue
12CD	HS2	1.25	.090	AAC*	—	—	blue
Austin America	HS4	1.50	.090	AAG**	—	—	red

*—Fixed needle—AN.
**—Fixed needle—DZ.
***—Most emission control engines are fitted with spring-loaded jet needles.

Light Bulb Specifications

Year	Model	Usage	Type	Number	Wattage
1956-67	Austin-Healey	Parking/turn signal, stop/tail light.	594	4	21/6
		License plate illumination.	467/2	1	4
		Turn signal, high beam, ignition warning lights.	4732	3	2.2
		Panel lights.	4817	4	2.2
1958-61	Sprite	Parking/turn signal, stop/tail lights.	380	4	21/6
		Rear turn signals.	382	2	21
		License plate illumination.	989	1	6
		Panel, turn signal, high beam lights.	987	7	2.2
1961-67	Sprite	Parking, stop/tail lights.	380	4	21/6
		Front and rear turn signals.	382	4	21
		License plate illumination.	989	1	6
		Back-up lights.	382	2	21
		Panel lights, map light, engine warning lights, high beam indicator light.	987	6	2.2
		Turn signal indicator light.	280	1	1.5
1968-69	Sprite	Parking/turn signal, stop/tail lights.	380	4	5/21
		Rear turn signal lights.	382	2	21
		Back-up lights.	273	2	18
		License plate illumination, side marker lights.	989	6	6
		Panel lights, map light, turn signal, engine, emergency flasher warning lights.	987	8	2.2
		Brake warning light.	280	1	1.5
1970	Sprite	The light bulb specifications are the same as those for the 1968-69 Sprite, except for the following:			
		Turn signal indicator light.	280	2	1.5
		Emergency flasher warning light.	281	1	2
		Brake warning light.	987	1	2.2
1968-71	Austin America	Parking, side marker, license plate illuminating lights.	989	7	6
		Front and rear turn signals.	382	4	21
		Stop/tail lights.	380	2	6/21
		Back-up lights.	273	2	21
		Warning lights.	281	3	2
		Brake warning light.	290	1	2
		Panel lights.	987	4	2.2
		Courtesy light.	254	1	6

Wiring Diagrams

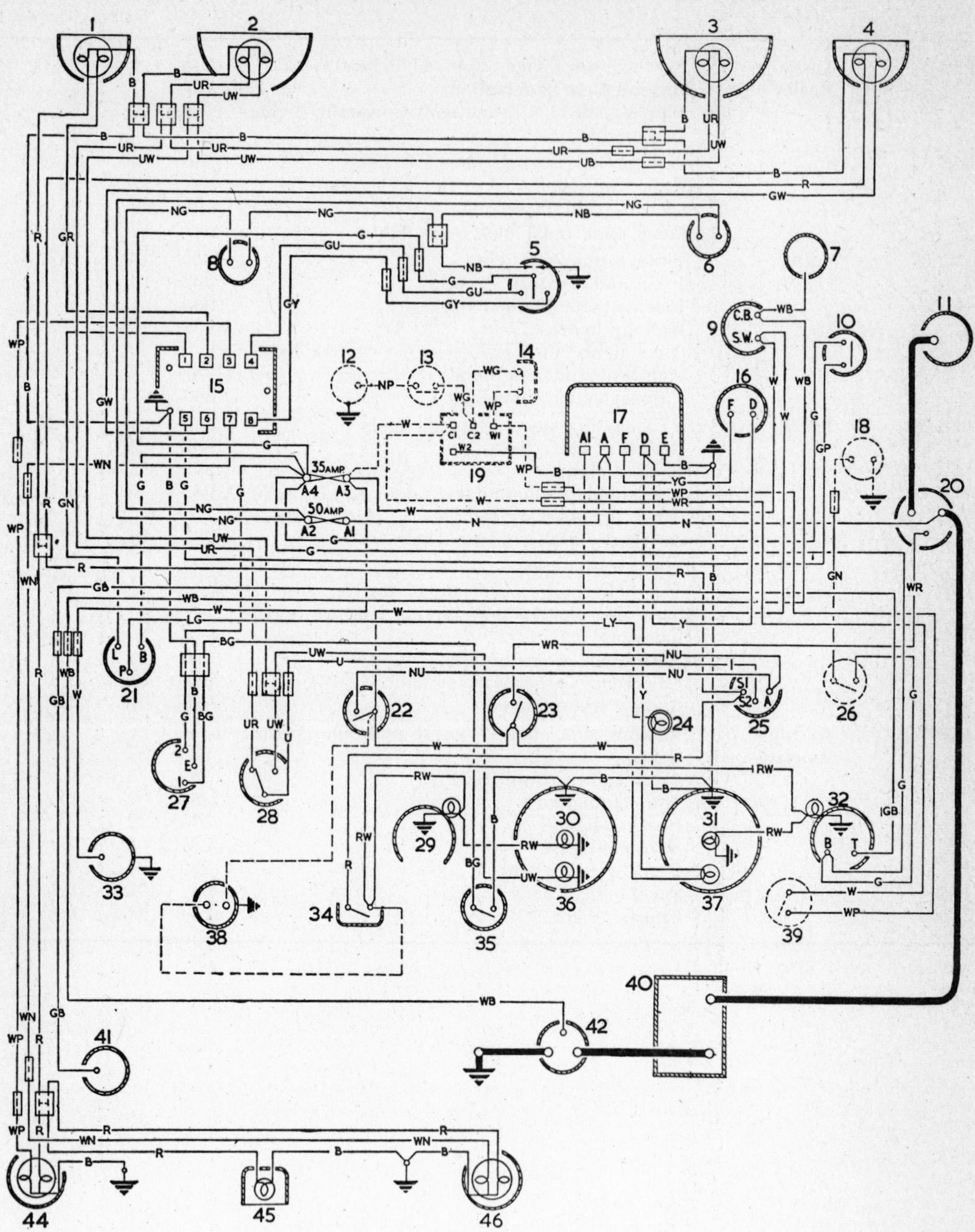

Wiring diagram for the Austin-Healey 100-6

Wiring diagram for the Austin-Healey 100-6

1 L.H. pilot light and front flasher light
2 L.H. head light
3 R.H. head light
4 R.H. pilot light and front flasher
5 Direction switch and horn push button
6 R.H. horn
7 Distributor
8 L.H. horn
9 Ignition coil
10 Stop light switch
11 Starter
12 Overdrive solenoid (when fitted)
13 Gearbox switch
14 Throttle switch (when fitted)
15 Flasher relay
16 Generator
17 Regulator
18 Heater motor (when fitted)
19 Overdrive relay (when fitted)
20 Starter solenoid
21 Flasher unit
22 Ignition switch
23 Starter switch
24 Flasher warning light
25 Lighting switch
26 Heater switch (when fitted)
27 Wiper motor
28 Head light beam switch
29 Panel light
30 Panel light
31 Panel light
32 Fuel gauge
33 Fuel pump
34 Panel light switch
35 Wiper motor switch
36 High beam warning light
37 No charge warning light
38 Cigar lighter (when fitted)
39 Overdrive switch (when fitted)
40 12 volt battery
41 Tank unit
42 Battery master switch
44 L.H. stop and tail lamp and rear flasher
45 License plate lamp
46 R.H. stop and tail lamp and rear flasher

COLOR CODE

U	Blue	GN	Green with brown
UR	Blue with red	GB	Green with black
UW	Blue with white	Y	Yellow
W	White	YG	Yellow with green
WR	White with red	N	Brown
WG	White with green	NU	Brown with blue
WP	White with purple	NG	Brown with green
WN	White with brown	NP	Brown with purple
WB	White with black	NB	Brown with black
G	Green	R	Red
GR	Green with red	RW	Red with white
GY	Green with yellow	B	Black
GU	Green with blue	BG	Black with green
GW	Green with white	LG	Light green
GP	Green with purple	WU	White with blue

Wiring diagram for the Austin-Healey 3000—Mks. I and II

1 Generator
2 Voltage regulator
3 Battery
4 Starter solenoid
5 Starter motor
6 Lighting switch
7 Headlight high/low beam switch
8 R.H. Headlight
9 L.H. Headlight
10 Main-beam warning light
11 R.H. pilot light
12 L.H. pilot light
13 Panel light switch
14 Panel lights
15 License-plate illumination
16 R.H. Stop and tail light
17 L.H. Stop and tail light
18 Stop light switch
19 Fuse unit (50 amps. 1-2, 35 amps. 3-4)
23 Horns
24 Horn switch
25 Flasher unit
26 Direction indicator switch
27 Direction indicator warning lights
28 R.H. Front flasher light
29 L.H. Front flasher light
30 L.H. Rear flasher light
31 L.H. Rear flasher light
32 Heater motor switch
33 Heater motor
34 Fuel gauge
35 Fuel gauge tank unit
36 Windshield wiper motor switch
37 Windshield wiper motor
38 Ignition/starter switch
39 Ignition coil
40 Distributor
41 Fuel pump
43 Oil pressure gauge
44 Ignition warning light
45 Speedometer
46 Water temperature gauge
57 Cigar lighter
60 Radio
63 Flasher relay
67 Line fuse
68 Overdrive relay (25-amp. fuse)
71 Overdrive solenoid
72 Overdrive manual control switch
73 Overdrive gear switch
74 Overdrive throttle switch
92 Battery cut off switch
95 Tachometer

CABLE COLOR CODE

B	Black	R	Red
U	Blue	W	White
N	Brown	Y	Yellow
G	Green	L.G	Light Green
P	Purple		

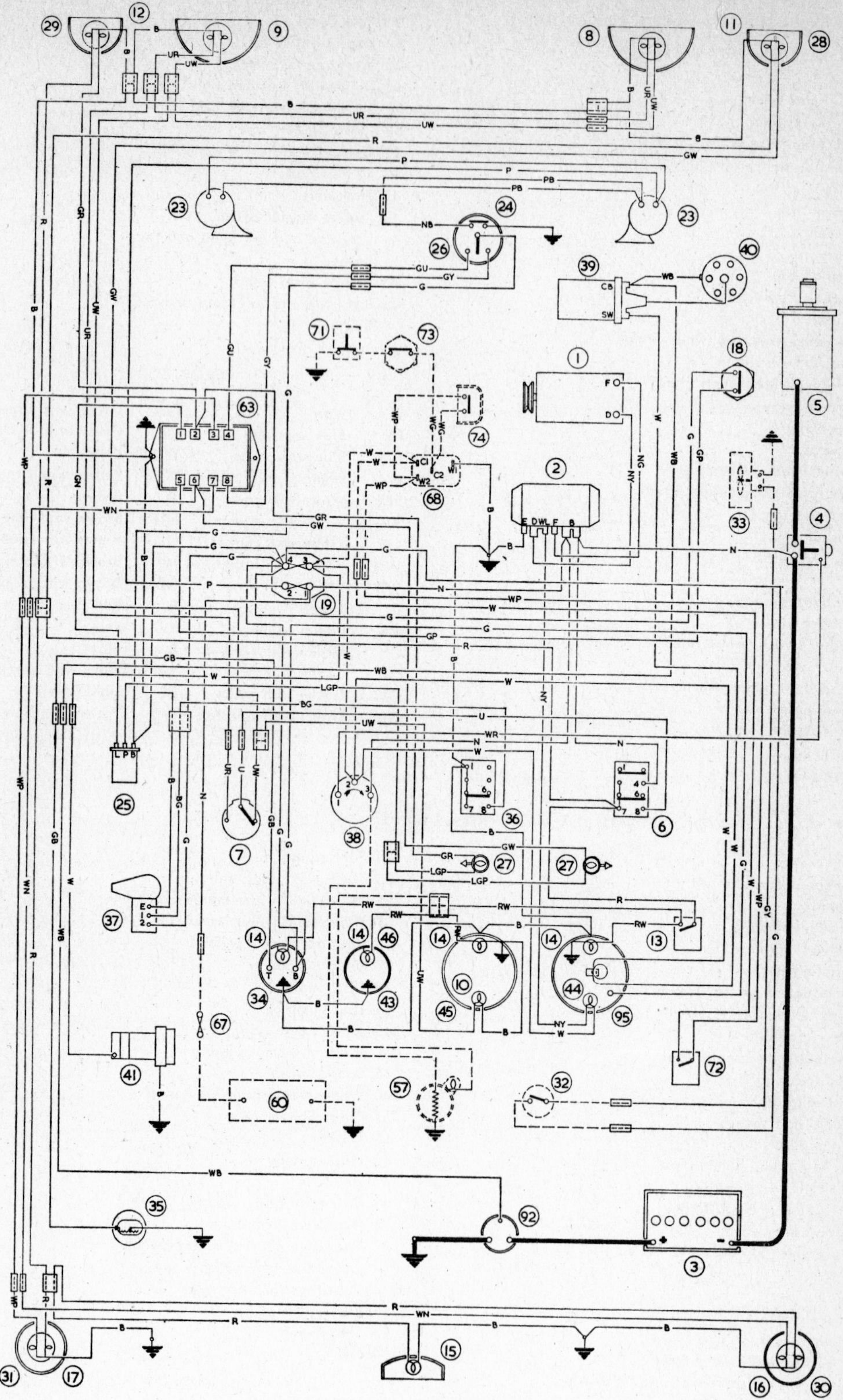

Wiring diagram for the Austin-Healey 3000—Mks. I and II

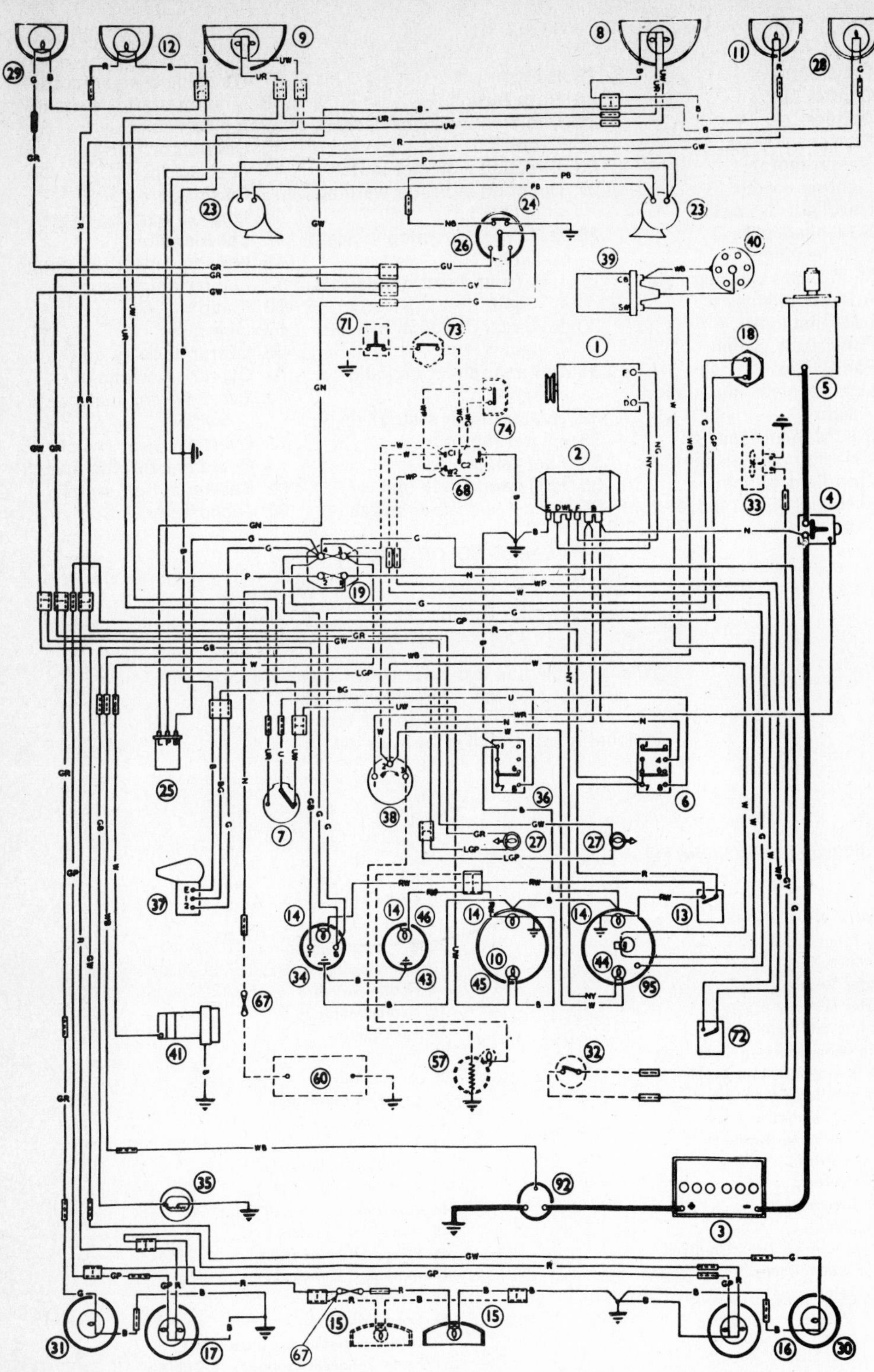

Wiring diagram for the Austin-Healey 3000 Mk. III

Wiring diagram for the Austin-Healey 3000 Mk. III

1 Generator
2 Control box
3 Battery
4 Starter solenoid
5 Starter motor
6 Lighting switch
7 Headlight dip switch
8 R.H. headlight
9 L.H. headlight
10 Main beam warning light
11 R.H. pilot light
12 L.H. pilot light
13 Panel light switch
14 Panel light
15 License plate illumnation light
16 R.H. stop and tail light
17 L.H. stop and tail light
18 Stop light switch
19 Fuse unit (50 amps. 1–2, 35 amps. 3–4)
23 Horns
24 Horn button
25 Direction indicator flasher unit
26 Direction indicator switch
27 Direction indicator warning light
28 R.H. front direction indicator light
29 L.H. front direction indicator light
30 R.H. rear direction indicator light
31 L.H. rear direction indicator light
32 Heater motor switch*
33 Heater motor*
34 Fuel gauge
35 Fuel gauge tank unit
36 Windshield wiper switch
37 Windshield wiper motor
38 Ignition/starter switch
39 Ignition coil
40 Distributor
41 Fuel pump
43 Oil pressure gauge
44 Ignition warning light
45 Speedometer
46 Water temperature gauge
57 Cigarette lighter
60 Radio*
67 Line fuse
68 Overdrive relay unit*
71 Overdrive solenoid*
72 Overdrive manual control switch
73 Overdrive gear switch*
74 Overdrive throttle switch
92 Battery cut-off switch
95 Tachometer

CABLE COLOR CODE

N. Brown	P. Purple	W. White
U. Blue	G. Green	Y. Yellow
R. Red	L.G. Light Green	B. Black

When a cable has two color code letters the first denotes the main color and the second denotes the tracer color.
* Optional extra, circuit shown dotted.

Wiring diagram for the Sprite Mk. I

1 Generator
2 Ignition Warning Light
3 Regulator
4 12-volt Battery
5 Starter Switch
6 Starter Motor
7 Lighting and Ignition Switch
8 Main Beam Warning Light
9 R/H Headlamp Main Beam
10 L/H Headlamp Main Beam
11 L/H Headlamp Dip Beam
12 R/H Headlamp Dip Beam
13 Dipper Switch
14 L/H Sidelamp
15 R/H Sidelamp
16 Fuse Unit
17 Connections for Twin Windtone Horns (when fitted)
18 Horn Relay
19 Horn switch
20 Horn switch
21 Horn
22 Cigar Lighter & Illumination
23 Panel Light Switch
24 Panel Light
25 Speedometer Light
26 Panel Light
27 Tachometer Light (when fitted)
28 R/H Tail Lamp
29 License Plate Lamp
30 L/H Tail Lamp
31 Stop Lamp Switch
32 R/H Stop light
33 L/H Stop light
34 Heater Switch } when fitted
35 Heater Motor } when fitted
36 Fuel Gauge
37 Fuel Gauge Tank Unit
38 Flasher Unit
39 L/H Front turn signal
40 L/H Rear turn signal
41 Flasher Switch
42 R/H Rear turn signal
43 R/H Front turn signal
44 Turn signal Warning Light
45 Windshield Switch
46 Windshield Wipers
47 Ignition Coil
48 Distributor
49 Snap Connectors
50 Terminal Blocks or Junction Box
51 Earth Connections made via Cable or
52 Via Fixing Bolts

CABLE COLOR CODE

B	Black	P	Purple	Y	Yellow
U	Blue	R	Red	L	Light
N	Brown	S	Slate	D	Dark
G	Green	W	White	M	Medium

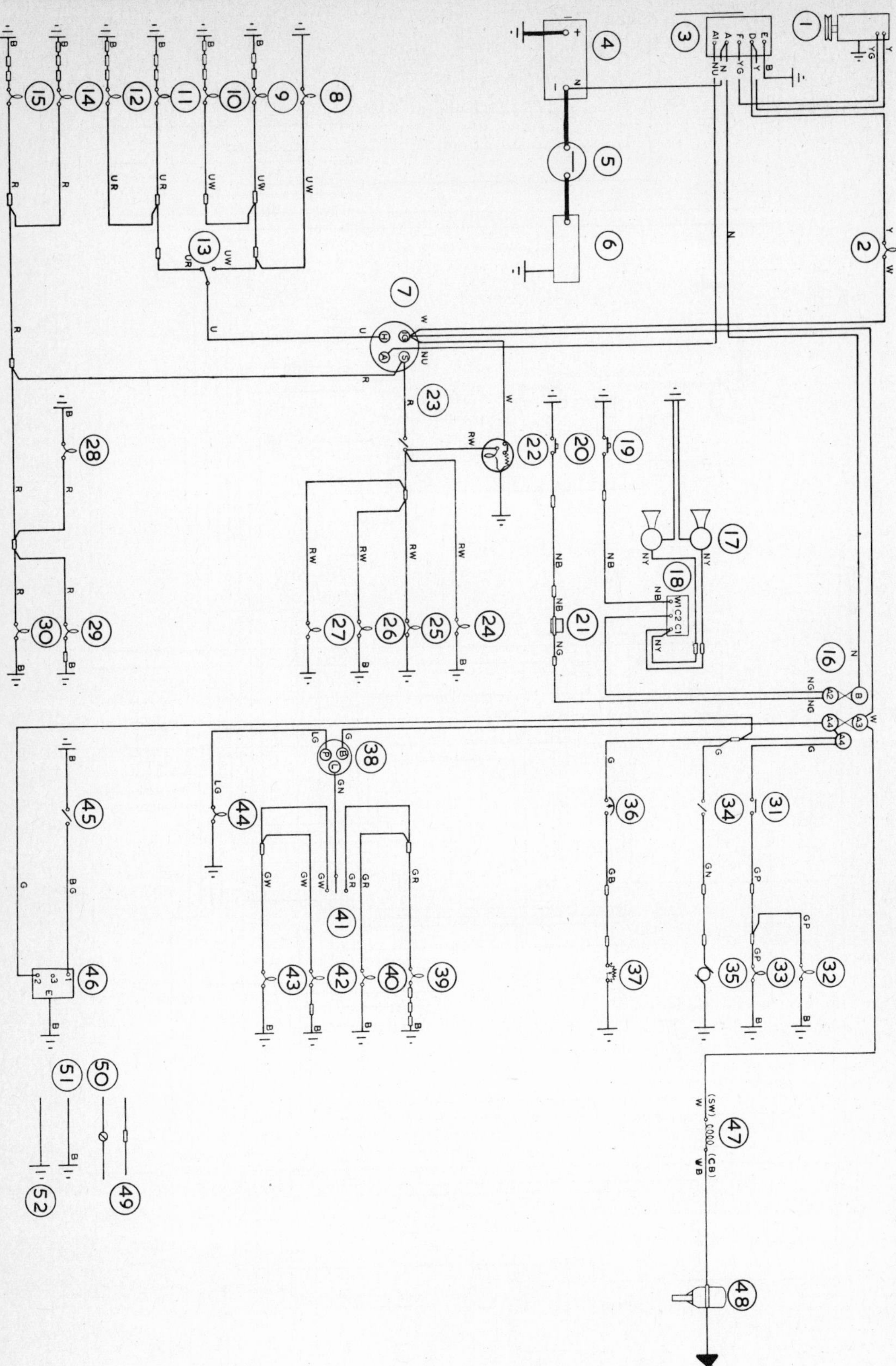

Wiring diagram for the Sprite Mk. I

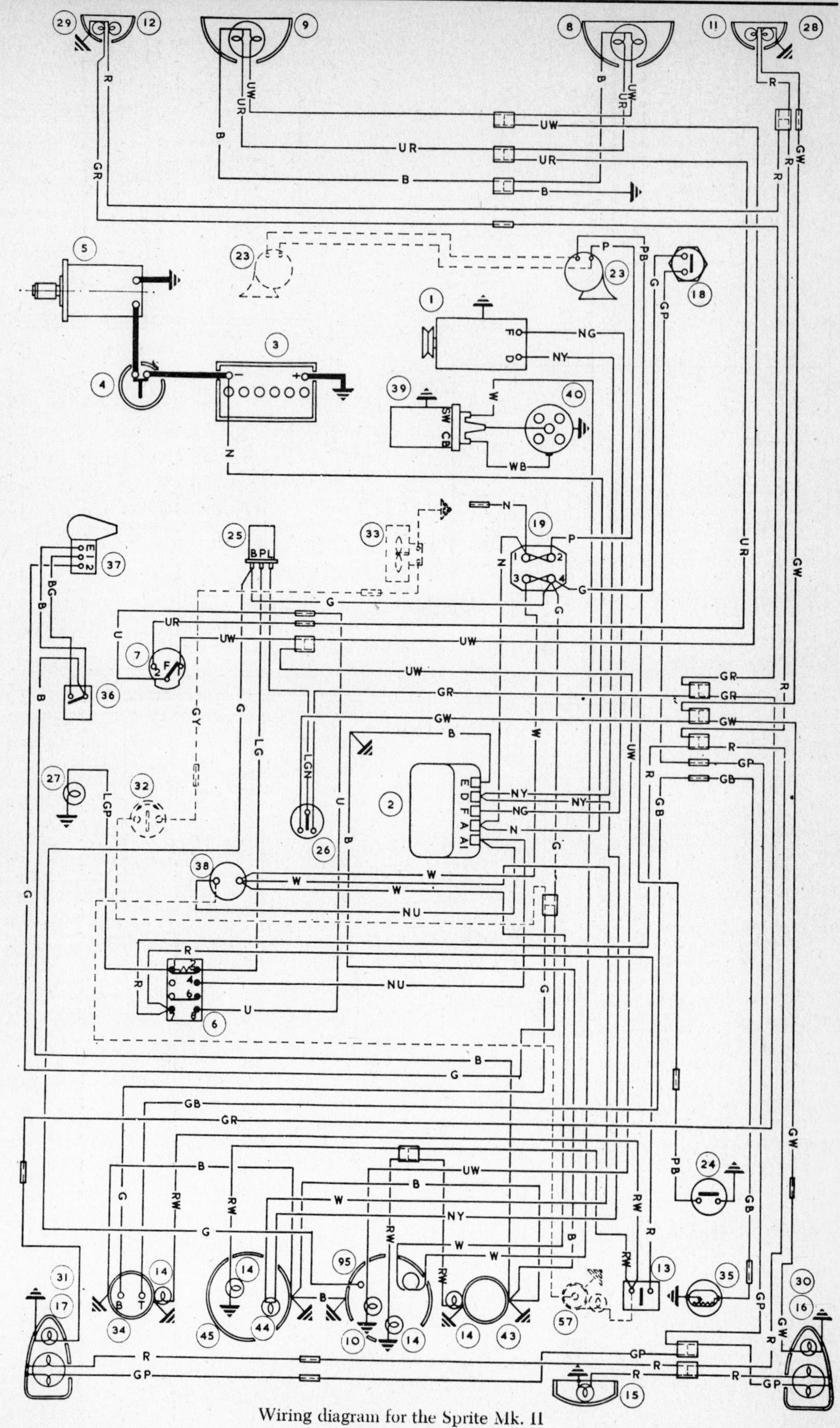

Wiring diagram for the Sprite Mk. II

Wiring diagram for the Sprite Mk. II

1 Generator
2 Regulator
3 Battery—12-volt
4 Starter switch
5 Starter motor
6 Lighting switch
7 Headlamp dip switch
8 Headlamp—R.H.
9 Headlamp—L.H.
10 Main-beam warning light
11 Parking light—R.H.
12 Parking light—L.H.
13 Panel light switch
14 Panel lights
15 License-plate illumination lamp
16 Stop and tail lamp—R.H.
17 Stop and tail lamp—L.H.
18 Stop light switch
19 Fuse unit
23 Horn (twin horns when fitted)
24 Horn-push button
25 Flasher unit
26 Direction indicator switch
27 Direction indicator warning light
28 Front flasher light—R.H.
29 Front flasher light—L.H.
30 Rear flasher light—R.H.
31 Rear flasher light—L.H.
32 Heater or fresh-air motor switch (when fitted)
33 Heater or fresh-air motor (when fitted)
34 Fuel gauge
35 Fuel gauge tank unit
36 Windshield wiper switch
37 Windshield wiper motor
38 Ignition switch
39 Ignition coil
40 Distributor
43 Oil pressure gauge
44 Ignition warning light
45 Speedometer
57 Cigar-lighter (when fitted)
95 Tachometer (impulse) (later cars)

CABLE COLOR CODE

N	Brown	P	Purple	W	White
U	Blue	G	Green	Y	Yellow
R	Red	LG	Light Green	B	Black

Wiring diagram for the Sprite Mk. III

1 Generator
2 Control box
3 Battery (12 volt)
4 Starter solenoid
5 Starter motor
6 Lighting switch
7 Headlight dip switch
8 R.H. headlight
9 L.H. headlight
10 High beam warning light
11 R.H. sidelight
12 L.H. sidelight
13 Panel light switch
14 Panel lights
15 License-plate illumination
16 R.H. stop and tail light
17 L.H. stop and tail light
18 Stop light switch
19 Fuse unit (35 amps.)
23 Horn (twin horns when fitted)
24 Horn button
25 Flasher unit
26 Direction indicator switch
27 Direction indicator warning lights
28 R.H. front flasher light
29 L.H. front flasher light
30 R.H. rear flasher light
31 L.H. rear flasher light
32 Heater or fresh-air motor switch (when installed)
33 Heater or fresh-air motor (when installed)
34 Fuel gauge
35 Fuel gauge tank unit
36 Windshield wiper switch
37 Windshield wiper motor
38 Ignition/starter switch
39 Ignition coil
40 Distributor
41 Fuel pump
43 Oil pressure gauge
44 Ignition warning light
45 Speedometer
57 Cigarette lighter (illuminated)
60 Radio
94 Oil filter switch
95 Tachometer
105 Lubrication warning light

CABLE COLOR CODE

N. Brown	P. Purple	W. White
U. Blue	G. Green	Y. Yellow
R. Red	L.G. Light green	B. Black

When a cable has two color code letters the first denotes the main color and the second denotes the tracer color.

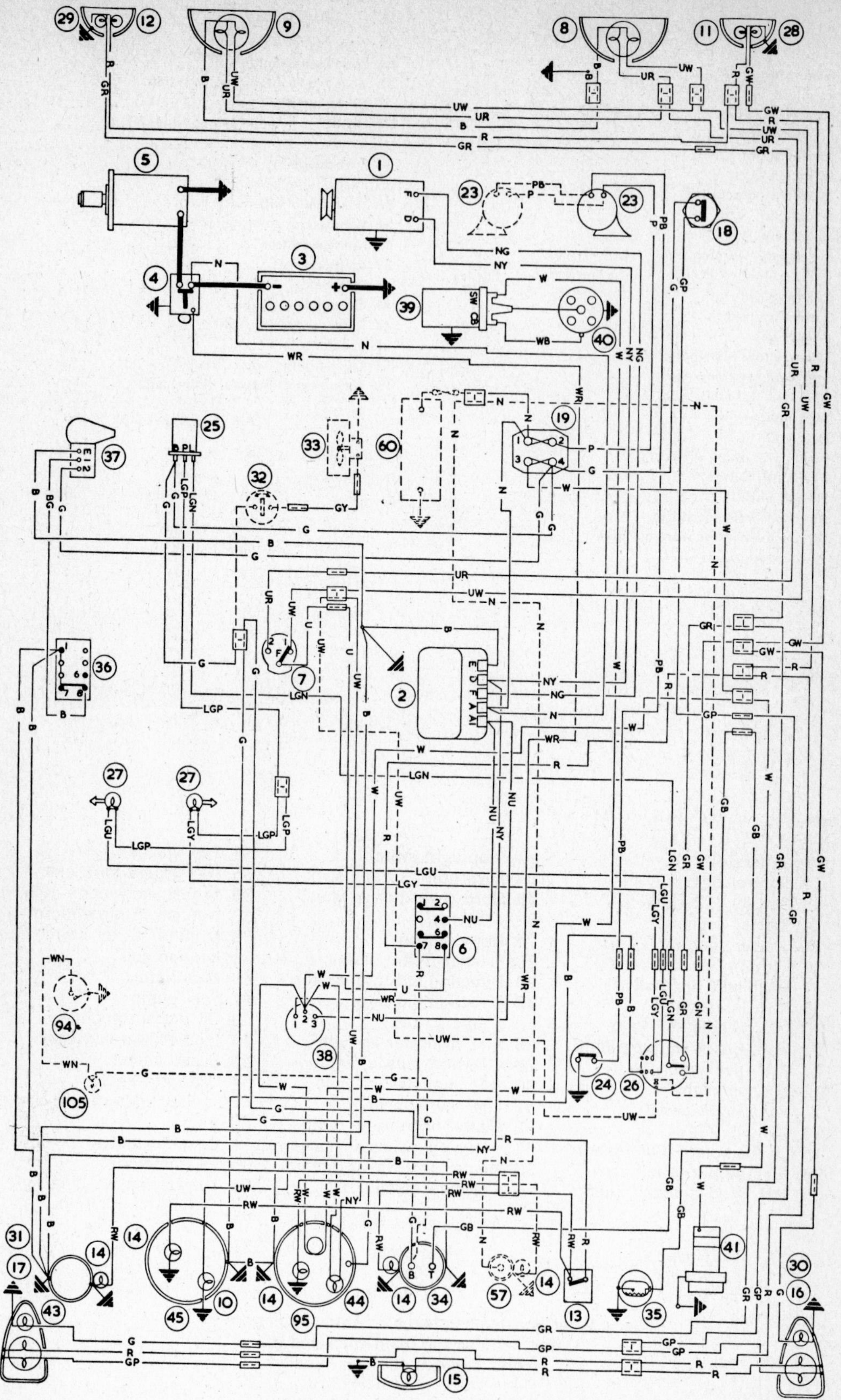

Wiring diagram for the Sprite Mk. III

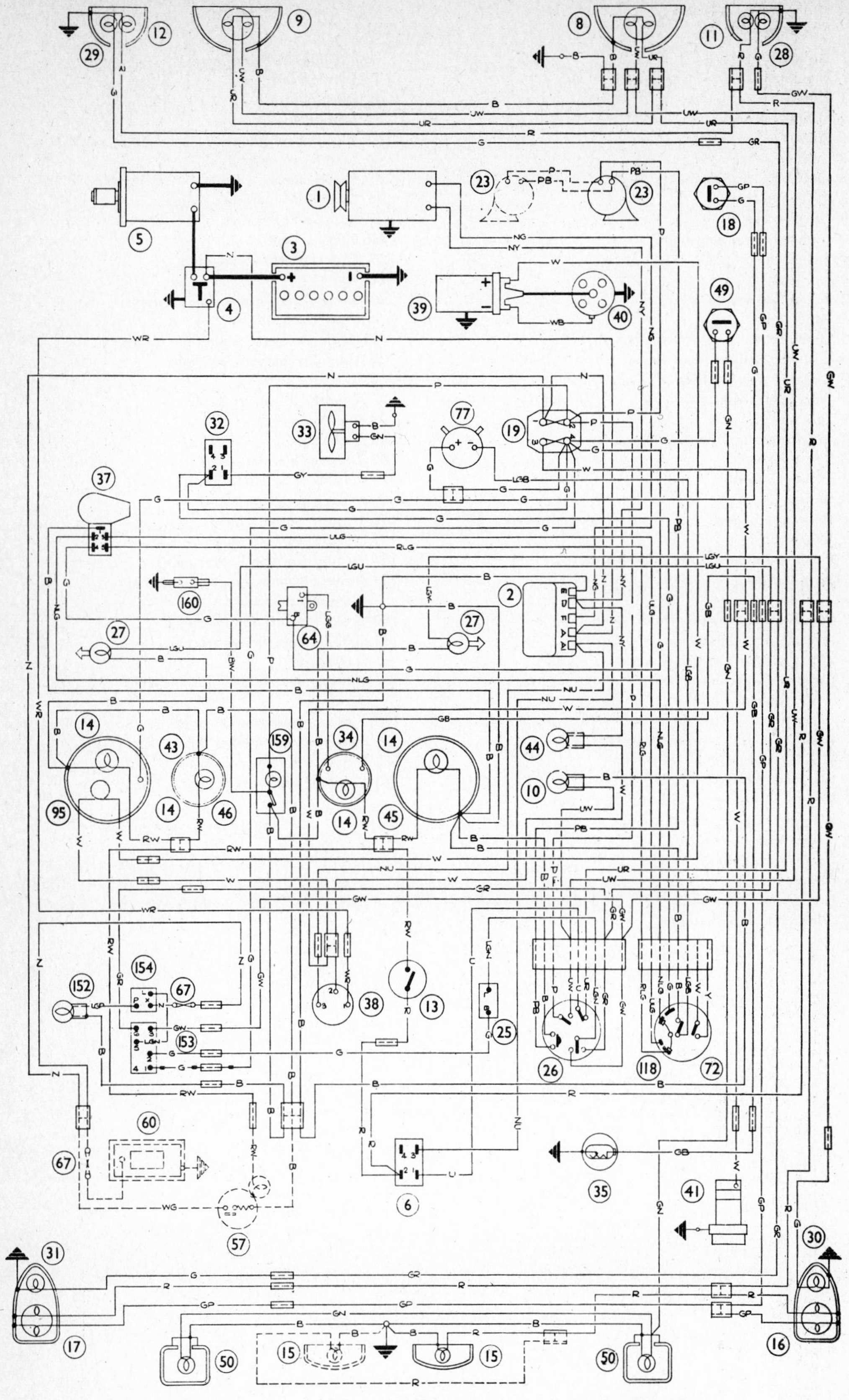

Wiring diagram for the Sprite Mk. IV (from car H-AN9/72041)

Wiring diagram for the Sprite Mk. IV (from car H-AN9/72041)

1 Generator
2 Regulator
3 Battery
4 Starter solenoid
5 Starter motor
6 Lighting switch
7 Headlamp dip switch
8 R.H. headlamp
9 L.H. headlamp
10 High-beam warning light
11 R.H. parking light
12 L.H. parking light
13 Panel light switch
14 Panel lights
15 License plate illumination lamp
16 R.H. stop and tail light
17 L.H. stop and tail light
18 Stop light switch
19 Fuse unit
20 Interior courtesy light
21 R.H. door switch
22 L.H. door switch
23 Horns
24 Horn-push button
25 Flasher unit
26 Combined direction indicator/head-lamp flasher

or

26 Combined direction indicator/head-lamp flasher/headlamp highglow beam/hornpush switch
26 Combined direction indicator, head-lamp flasher, headlamp highlow-beam switch
27 Direction indicator warning light
28 R.H. front turn signal light
29 L.H. front turn signal light
30 R.H. rear turn signal light
31 L.H. rear turn signal light
32 Heater fan motor switch
33 Heater fan motor
34 Fuel gauge
35 Fuel gauge tank unit
37 Windshield wiper motor
38 Ignition/starter switch
39 Ignition coil
40 Distributor
41 Fuel pump
43 Oil pressure gauge
44 Ignition warning light
45 Speedometer
46 Coolant temperature gauge
49 Back-up light switch
50 Back-up light
57 Cigar-lighter—illuminated
60 Radio
64 Bi-metal instrument voltage stabi-lizer
65 Luggage compartment light switch
66 Luggage compartment light
67 Line fuse
77 Windshield washer pump
94 Oil filter switch
95 Tachometer
105 Oil filter warning lamp
118 Combined windshield washer and wiper switch
152 Hazard warning lamp
153 Hazard warning switch
154 Hazard warning flasher unit
159 Brake pressure warning lamp and lamp test push button
160 Brake pressure failure switch
168 Ignition key audible warning buzzer
169 Ignition key audible warning door switch
170 R.H. front side-marker light
171 L.H. front side-marker light
172 R.H. rear side-marker light
173 L.H. rear side-marker light

CABLE COLOR CODE

N	Brown	P	Purple	W	White
U	Blue	G	Green	Y	Yellow
R	Red	LG	Light Green	B	Black

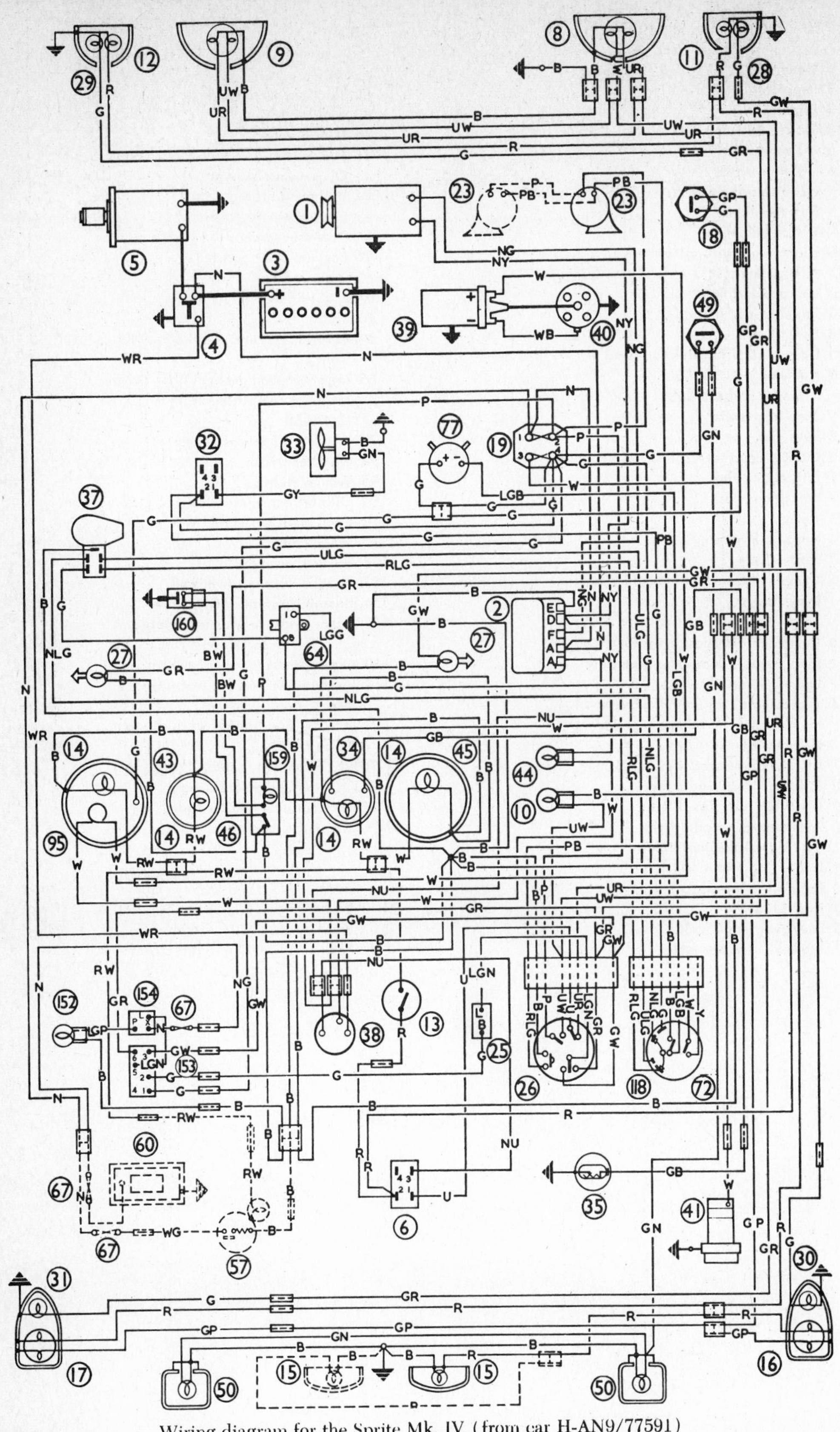

Wiring diagram for the Sprite Mk. IV (from car H-AN9/77591)

Wiring diagram for the Sprite Mk. IV (from car H-AN9/77591)

1 Generator
2 Regulator
3 Battery
4 Starter solenoid
5 Starter motor
6 Lighting switch
7 Headlamp dip switch
8 R.H. headlamp
9 L.H. headlamp
10 Highbeam warning light
11 R.H. parking light
12 L.H. parking light
13 Panel switch light
14 Panel lights
15 License plate illumination lamp
16 R.H. stop and tail light
17 L.H. stop and tail light
18 Stop light switch
19 Fuse unit
20 Interior courtesy light
21 R.H. door switch
22 L.H. door switch
23 Horns
24 Horn-push button
25 Flasher unit
26 Combined direction indicator/headlamp flasher
or
26 Combined direction indicator/headlamp flasher/headlamp highglow beam/ hornpush switch
26 Combined direction indicator, headlamp flasher, headlamp high-low beam switch
27 Direction indicator warning light
28 R.H. front turn signal light
29 L.H. front turn signal light
30 R.H. rear turn signal light
31 L.H. rear turn signal light
32 Heater fan motor switch
33 Heater fan motor
34 Fuel gauge
35 Fuel gauge tank unit
37 Windshield wiper motor
38 Ignition/starter switch
39 Ignition coil
40 Distributor
41 Fuel pump
43 Oil pressure gauge
44 Ignition warning light
45 Speedometer
46 Coolant temperature gauge
49 Back-up light switch
50 Back-up light
57 Cigar-lighter—illuminated
60 Radio
64 Bi-metal instrument voltage stabilizer
65 Luggage compartment light switch
66 Luggage compartment light
67 Line fuse
77 Windshield washer pump
94 Oil filter switch
95 Tachometer
105 Oil filter warning lamp
118 Combined windshield washer and wiper switch
152 Hazard warning lamp
153 Hazard warning switch
154 Hazard warning flasher unit
159 Brake pressure warning lamp and lamp test push button
160 Brake pressure failure switch
168 Ignition key audible warning buzzer
169 Ignition key audible warning door switch
170 R.H. front side-marker light
171 L.H. front side-marker light
172 R.H. rear side-marker light
173 L.H. rear side-marker light

CABLE COLOR CODE

N	Brown	P	Purple	W	White
U	Blue	G	Green	Y	Yellow
R	Red	LG	Light Green	B	Black

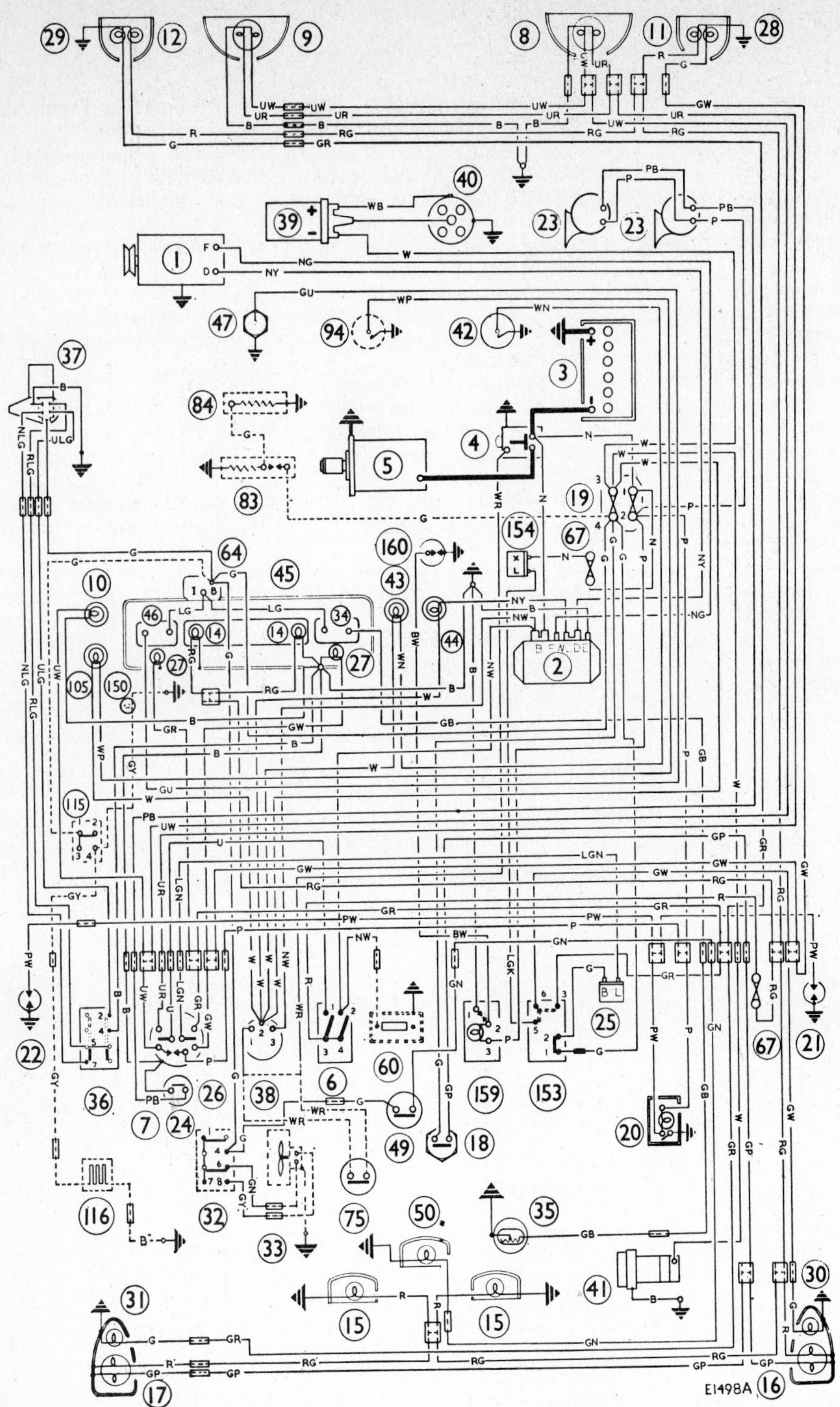

Wiring diagram for the Austin America 1968-69

Wiring diagram for the Austin America 1968-69

1 Generator
2 Control box
3 Battery 12-volt
4 Starter solenoid
5 Starter motor
6 Lighting switch
7 Headlight dimmer switch
8 R.H. headlight
9 L.H. headlight
10 Main-beam warning light
11 R.H. parking light
12 L.H. parking light
14 Panel light
15 License-plate illumination light
16 R.H. stop and tail light
17 L.H. stop and tail light
18 Stop light switch
19 Fuse unit, 35-amp. 1–2; 35-amp. 3–4
20 Interior light
21 R.H. door switch
22 L.H. door switch
23 Horns
24 Horn button
25 Flasher unit
26 Direction indicator switch
27 Direction indicator warning lights
28 R.H. front flasher light
29 L.H. front flasher light
30 R.H. rear flasher light
31 L.H. rear flasher light
32 Heater or fresh-air motor switch (when fitted)
33 Heater or fresh-air motor (when fitted)
34 Fuel gauge
35 Fuel gauge tank unit
36 Windshield wiper switch
37 Windshield wiper motor
38 Ignition/starter switch
39 Ignition coil
40 Distributor
41 Fuel pump
42 Oil pressure switch
43 Oil pressure warning light
44 Ignition warning light
45 Speedometer
46 Water temperature gauge
47 Water temperature transmitter
49 Reverse light switch
50 Reverse light
60 Radio (when installed)
64 Bi-metal instrument voltage stabilizer
67 Line fuse, 35-amp.
75 Automatic transmission safety switch
83 Induction heater and thermostat
84 Suction chamber heater
94 Oil filter switch } Syncro-mesh transmission only
105 Oil filter warning light } Syncro-mesh transmission only
115 Rear window defroster switch
116 Rear window defroster unit
150 Rear window defroster warning light
153 Hazard warning switch
154 Hazard warning flasher unit
159 Brake pressure warning light and button
160 Brake pressure failure switch

CABLE COLOR CODE

N. Brown	P. Purple	W. White
U. Blue	K. Pink	Y. Yellow
R. Red	G. Green	B. Black
	L.G. Light Green	

When a cable has two color code letters the first denotes the main color and the second denotes the tracer color.

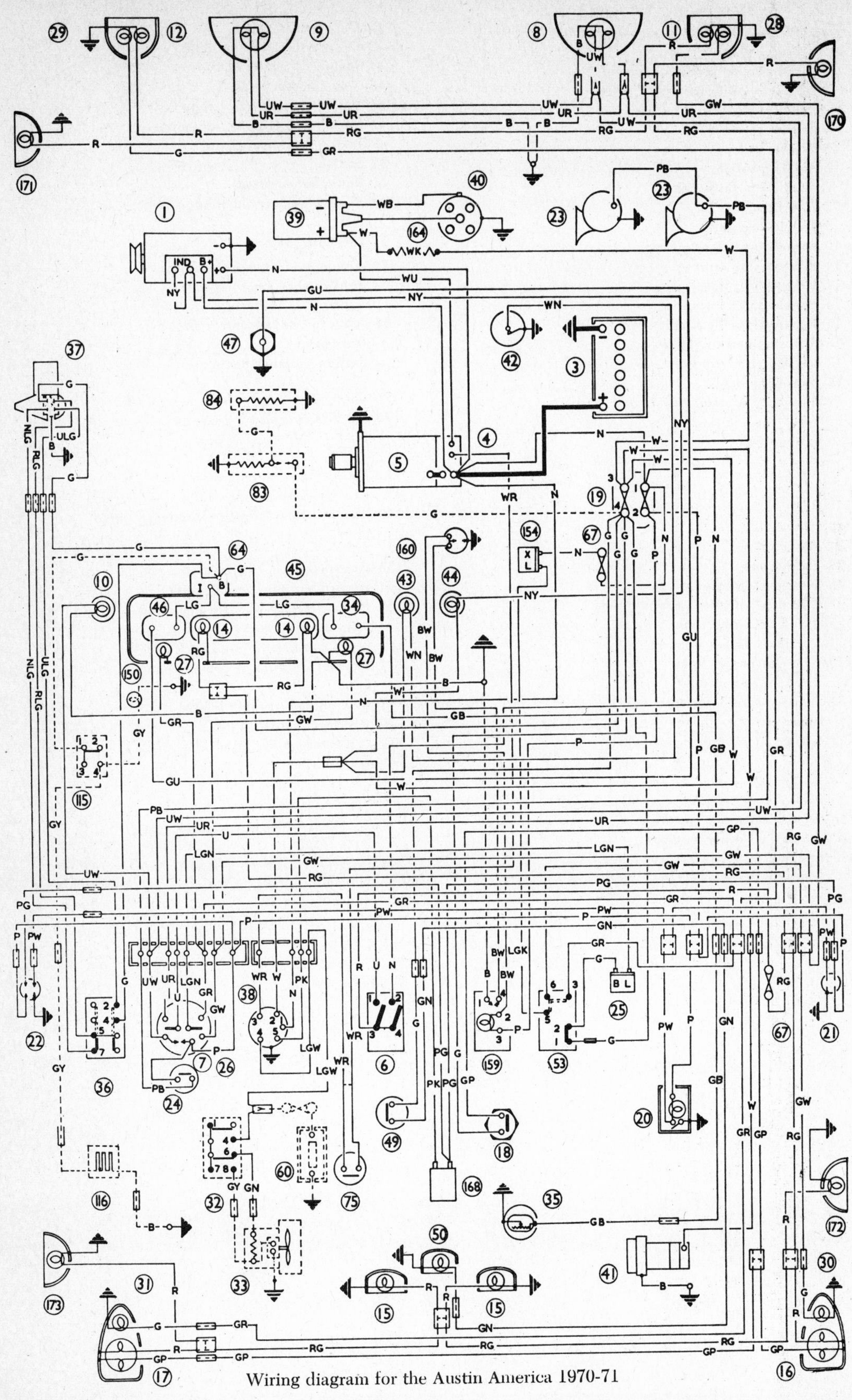

Wiring diagram for the Austin America 1970-71

Wiring diagram for the Austin America 1970-71

1 Generator or 16ACR alternator
2 Regulator (with generator only)
3 Battery—12-volt
4 Starter solenoid
5 Starter motor
6 Lighting switch
7 Headlamp dip switch
8 R.H. headlamp
9 L.H. headlamp
10 Main-beam warning lamp
11 R.H. parking light
12 L.H. parking light
14 Panel lights
15 License-plate illumination lamps
16 R.H. stop and tail light
17 L.H. stop and tail light
18 Stop light switch
19 Fuse unit, 35-amp. 1-2; 35-amp. 3-4
20 Interior light
21 R.H. door switch } Combined with Ignition key buzzer—1970-71 models.
22 L.H. door switch } Combined with Ignition key buzzer—1970-71 models.
23 Horns
24 Horn switch
25 Flasher unit
26 Direction indicator switch
27 Direction indicator warning lights
28 R.H. front flasher light
29 L.H. front flasher light
30 R.H. rear flasher light
31 L.H. rear flasher light
32 Heater or fresh-air motor switch (when fitted)
33 Heater or fresh-air motor (when fitted)
34 Fuel gauge
35 Fuel gauge tank unit
36 Windshield wiper switch
37 Windshield wiper motor
38 Ignition/starter switch (combined with steering lock—1970-71 models)
39 Ignition coil
40 Distributor
41 Fuel pump
42 Oil pressure switch
43 Oil pressure warning light
44 Ignition warning light
45 Speedometer
46 Water temperature gauge
47 Water temperature transmitter
49 Back-up light switch
50 Back-up light
60 Radio (when fitted)
64 Bi-metal instrument voltage stabilizer
67 Line fuse, 35-amp
75 Automatic transmission safety switch (when fitted)
83 Induction heater and thermostat } when fitted
84 Suction chamber heater } when fitted
94 Oil filter switch } synchromesh transmission, early cars only
105 Oil filter warning lamp } synchromesh transmission, early cars only
115 Rear window defogger switch } when fitted
116 Rear window defogger unit } when fitted
150 Rear window defogger warning light } when fitted
153 Hazard warning switch
154 Hazard warning flasher unit
159 Brake pressure warning lamp and lamp push button
160 Brake pressure failure switch
164 Ballast resistance or cable (when fitted)
168 Ignition key warning buzzer
170 R.H. front marker light
171 L.H. front marker light
172 R.H. rear marker light
173 L.H. rear marker light

CABLE COLOR CODE

N	Brown	P	Purple	W	White
U	Blue	K	Pink	Y	Yellow
R	Red	G	Green	B	Black
		LG	Light Green		

Engine Electrical

Distributor

Removal

The removal procedures for the distributors on all Austin lines are similar. Two exceptions are: there is no vacuum line on certain Sprite models, and not all models have tachometer fittings.

The first thing to do, is rotate the engine so that the rotor arm is pointing toward the segment for the number one plug lead. This is done to have a reference-point when replacing the distributor.

Once this has been done, detach the spring clips, remove the distributor cap, low and high tension wires, and the vacuum connection. Remove the screws holding the tachometer drive, on cars so equipped. Next, remove the bolts securing the distributor clamp to the cylinder block and lift the distributor out. Do not loosen the pinch bolt, unless the timing is to be reset.

If the pinch bolt has not been disturbed, the replacement of the distributor is the opposite of the removal procedure and the clamping bolt tightened after the distributor camshaft has engaged the driveshaft. In order to avoid difficulties in installation, the distributor should be replaced with the rotor pointing in the same direction as before removal.

Breaker Points

Removal and Installation

If the contact points are badly burned or pitted, they should be replaced. Remove the wires from the connections at the post which retains the spring of the moveable point and, keeping track of the spacers and washers, lift off the moveable point. Remove the screws which secure the fixed-point plate and remove the fixed point and plate.

Before replacing, clean the surfaces of the contact points with a non-oily solvent, such as alcohol, to remove any dirt or preservative coating. Replacement of the points is the opposite of their removal. Set the gap to the proper specification when they are open fully. Recheck the point gap after tightening the securing screw.

Apply a drop or two of engine oil to the felt in the top of the distributor shaft. Lightly smear the cam with engine oil or distributor cam lubricant. Be careful not to get any lubricant on the points themselves. Replace the rotor.

Replace the distributor, making sure that the cap is clean and crack-free. Check the wiring and replace any that shows signs of aging; making sure that all connections are tight and moisture-proof.

Distributor Installation—If Timing Has Been Disturbed

Remove the valve cover so that valve action may be observed. Turn the engine over

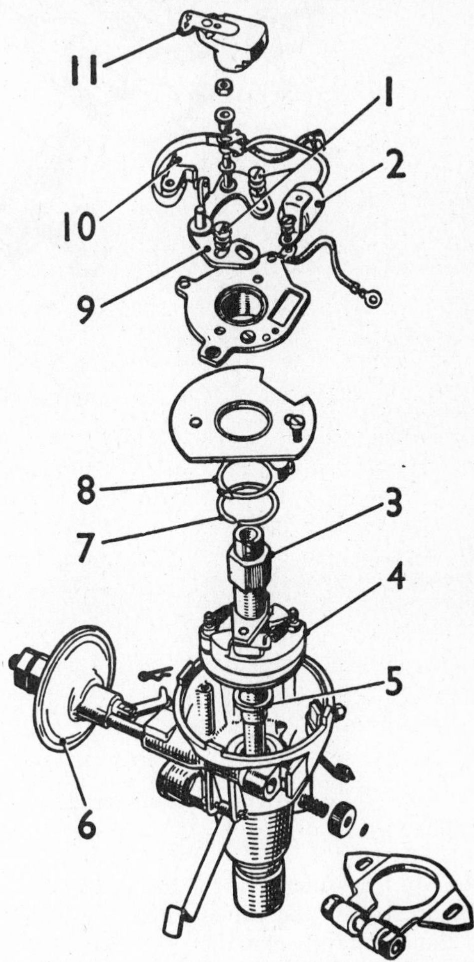

The distributor for the Austin-Healey 100-6 and 3000 Mk. I

1 Screws for contact plate
2 Condenser
3 Cam
4 Automatic timing contact
5 Distance collar
6 Vacuum control
7 Felt ring
8 Spring
9 Fixed contact plate
10 Moving contact
11 Rotor

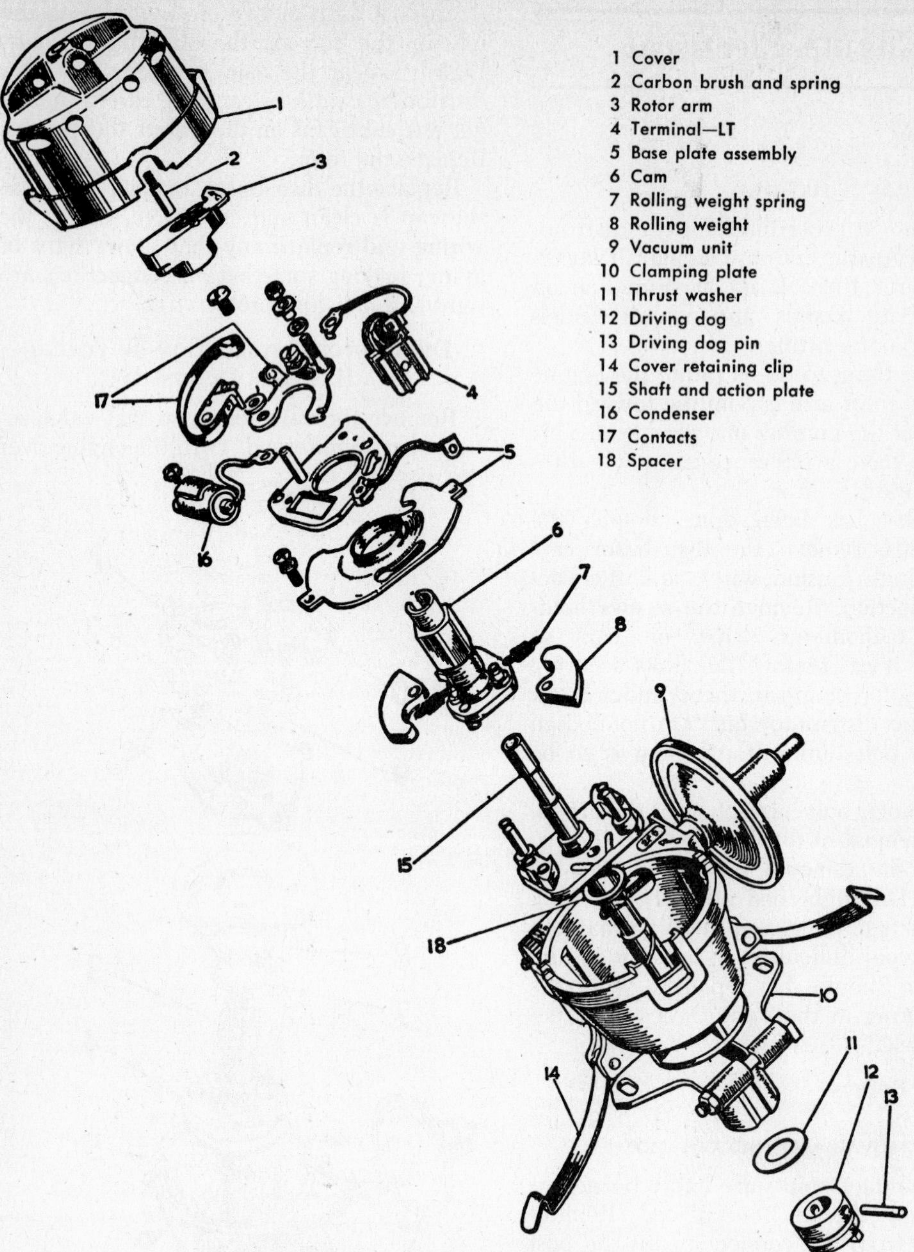

The distributor for the Austin-Healey 300 Mk. II and Mk. III

until No. 1 cylinder is at the top of its compression stroke (the valves for No. 1 cylinder should be fully closed).

Install the distributor. Tighten the clamp pinch bolt, and align the shaft with the clamp. Insert, and tighten the clamp hold-down bolts, and loosen the pinch bolt so that the distributor can be rotated. Rotate the distributor until it is positioned in the same manner as it was before removal. The ignition timing can now be set exactly.

Ignition Timing

Static Timing Procedure

The static timing procedures for the Austin-Healey and the Sprite are both the same. The Austin America differs only in the location of the timing marks, and the method of turning the crankshaft. For America models equipped with manual transmissions, remove the spark plugs, put the car into 4th gear and push it forward

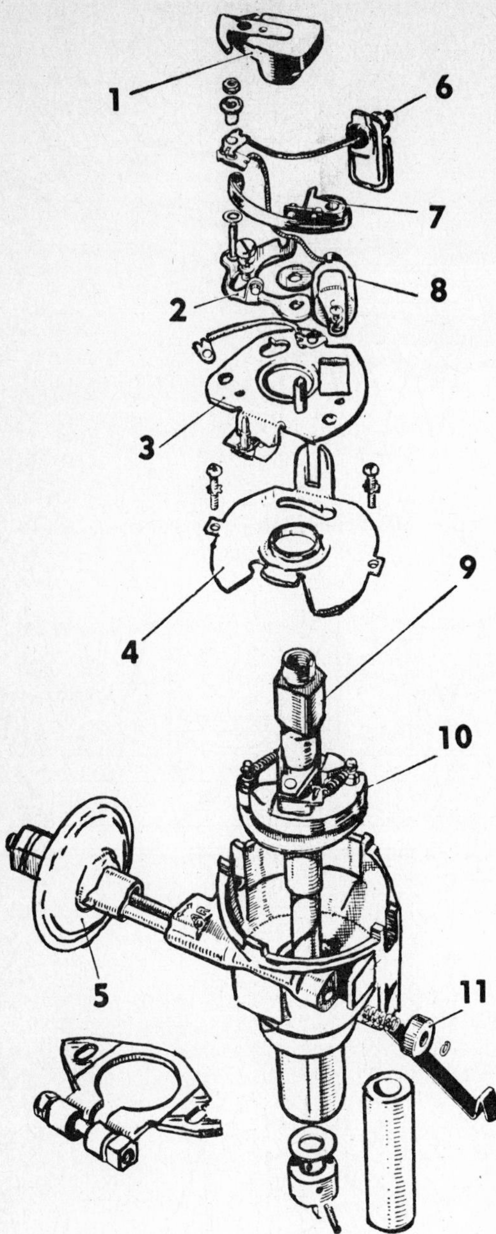

The distributor for the Sprite Mk. I

1 Rotor
2 Fixed contact plate
3 Moving conatact breaker plate
4 Vacuum advance unit
6 Low tension terminal
7 Conatact breaker lever
8 Capacitor
9 Cam
10 Centrifugal timing control
11 Octane selector

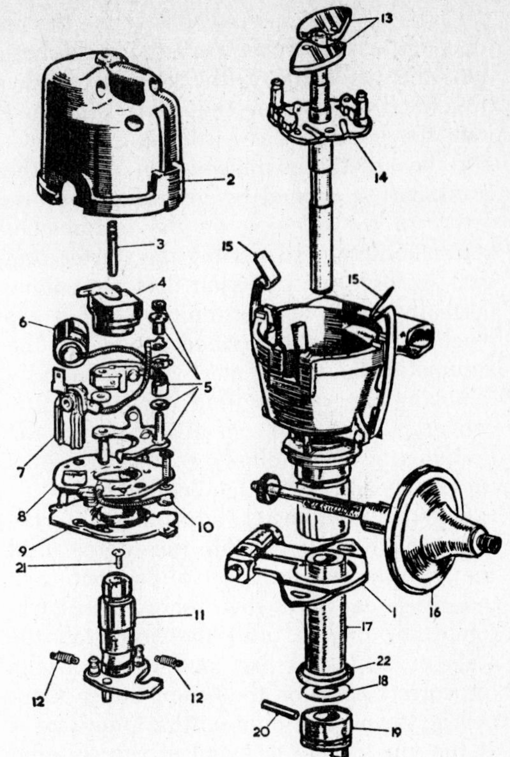

The distributor for the Sprite Mks. II-IV and the America

1 Clamping plate
2 Moulded cap
3 Brush and spring
4 Rotor arm
5 Contacts (set)
6 Capacitor
7 Terminal and lead (low-tension)
8 Moving contact breaker plate*
9 Contact breaker base plate
10 Ground lead
11 Cam
12 Automatic advance springs
13 Weight assembly
14 Shaft and action plate
15 Cap-retaining clips
16 Vacuum unit
17 Bush
18 Thrust washer
19 Driving dog
20 Parallel pin
21 Cam screw (Sprite)
22 O-ring oil seal (Sprite)
*Except early Sprite Mk IV.

until the number one piston is at the top of its compression stroke. Turn the crankshaft until the 1/4 mark on the flywheel, under the clutch cover inspection plate is aligned with the pointer. The piston is now TDC. For the automatic transmission model the crankshaft is rotated by inserting a screwdriver in the opening on the torque-converter housing, and turning the starter ring gear in the same direction that the engine normally turns, when running, until it has reached the point described above. On the automatics the timing mark can be seen by removing the rubber plug on the torque-converter housing. From this point on, the timing procedure follows that of the Austin-Healey and Sprite detailed below.

Set the micrometer adjustment in the center of the scale. Rotate the engine until the rotor approaches the No. 1 (front) cylinder segment in the distributor cap. Slowly rotate the engine until the notch on the scale of the crankshaft pulley is opposite the correct point on the timing cover. Connect a 12-volt test light so that one wire is at the low-tension terminal of the coil and the other is grounded. Loosen the distributor clamping bolt and rotate the distributor body slowly clockwise until the test light is illuminated, then tighten the distributor plate clamping bolt. After the bolt is tightened, recheck the timing by rotating the engine by hand and noting if the test light is illuminated at the proper position of the crankshaft.

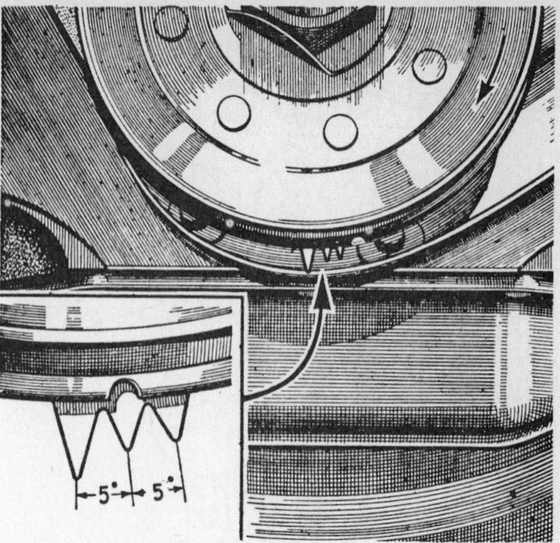

Sprite Mk. I crankshaft pulley and timing marks

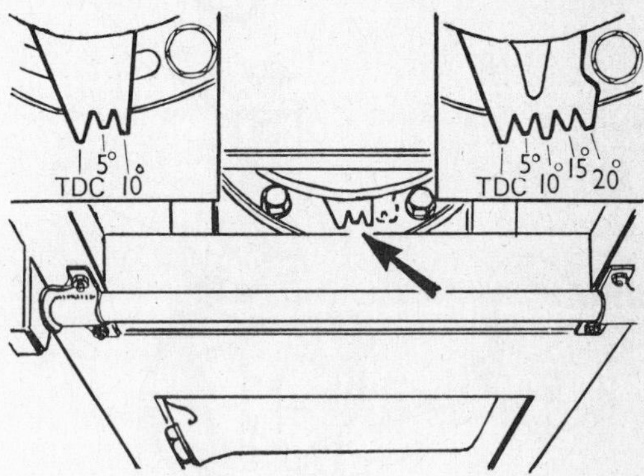

Sprite Mks. II-IV crankshaft pulley and timing marks

The Austin-Healey crankshaft pulley—showing the timing pointer and notch with No. 1 piston at TDC

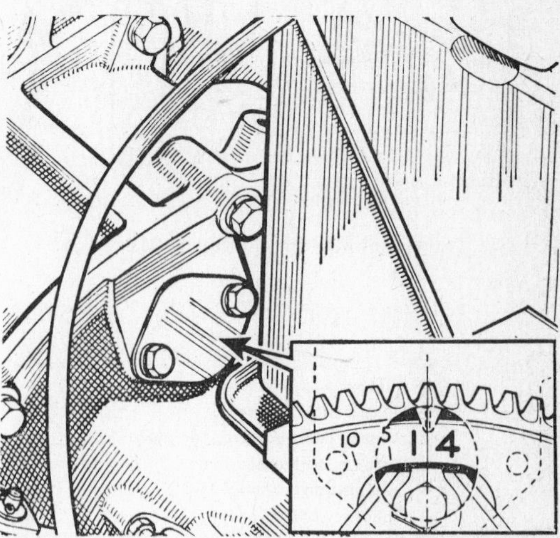

A mirror must be used to see the timing marks on the manual transmission America models. The inspection hole is located under the plate on the clutch housing. TDC is indicated by 1/4.

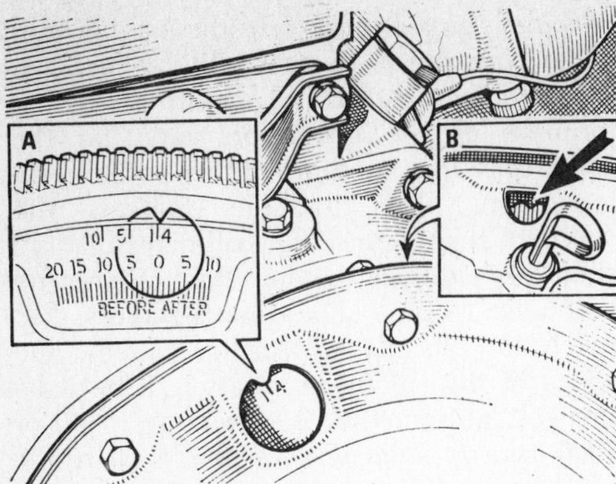

On the Austin America automatic models the timing marks are on the torque converter. TDC is indicated by 1/4 on the early models; on later models by 0. Insert B: The hole in the converter housing that is used to insert a screwdriver to turn the converter.

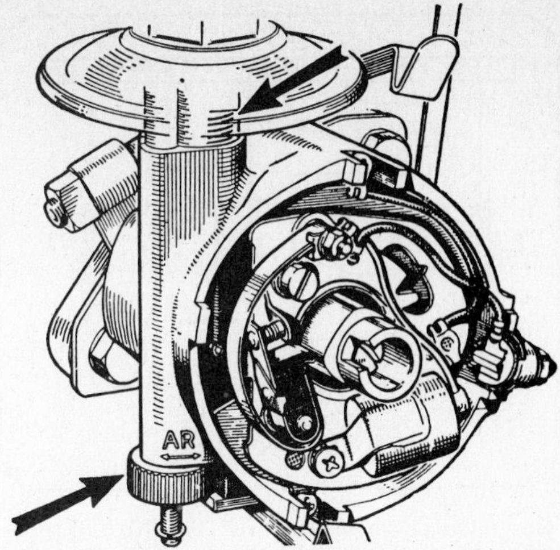

A Lucas distributor showing the fine timing, or octane selector (bottom arrow); and the vernier scale (upper arrow). Turn the nut to the left to advance the ignition, to the right to retard it.

A fine manual adjustment is also possible on the distributor in order to allow for slight differences in gasolines used. The adjustment nut is indicated by the arrow in the illustration. Each graduation point on the scale indicates approximately 5° of timing variation and is equal to 55 clicks of the adjustment nut. Turning the nut in the clockwise direction will retard the ignition, turning counterclockwise will advance. This manual adjustment should not be used for major timing changes which can better be handled by moving the distributor itself, but is useful for fine adjustments of 5° or less.

Timing Specifications

Model & Engine	*Deg. BTDC @ rpm*
Austin-Healey 29D/29E/29F/ 29K	15@600
Sprite 12CC	22@1,000
12CD	10@1,000
Austin America 12H	33@1,000

Dynamic Timing Procedure

Connect the timing light in the manner shown in the manufacturer's instructions. Mark the notch in the crankshaft pulley with a bright color so that it can be seen easily. Disconnect and plug the vacuum advance line from the intake manifold. Also, care should be taken to see that the centrifugal advance weights are not engaged from over-reving. Failure to observe either of the above will result in improper timing.

The engine should be warm, and running steadily at the correct rpm when the timing check is made. If the timing is 5° off, or less, correction may be made with the fine manual adjustment on the vacuum advance unit of the distributor. If a greater adjustment is needed, the distributor pinch bolt must be loosened, and the distributor rotated to the correct position. Check the timing again after the pinch bolt has been tightened, and then reconnect the vacuum line.

Charging System

Testing the Generator and the Generator Regulator

If the charging system is not functioning properly, the following procedure should be followed to evaluate the circuitry and components: Be sure the generator belt is properly adjusted. It should be possible to deflect the belt about 1/2 in. (13 mm.) with hand pressure at the longest run. Be sure that the generator and regulator are properly connected. With all lights and ac-

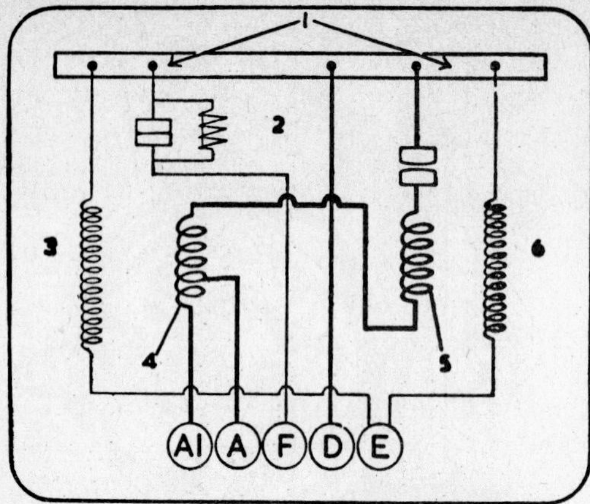

The internal connections for the RB106 series regulator—Austin-Healey 100-6 and Sprite Mks. I-II

1 Regulator and cut-out frame	4 Tapped series coil
2 Field resistance	5 Series coil
3 Shunt coil	6 Shunt coil

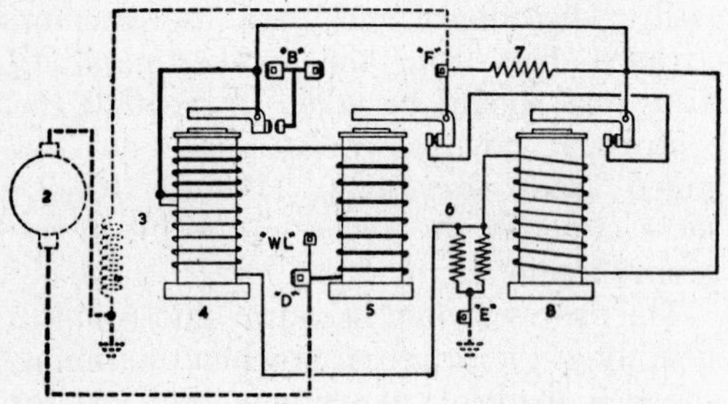

Generator charging circuit used on the Austin-Healey 3000, Sprite Mks. III and IV, and early America

1 Generator	5 Current regulator
2 Armature	6 Swamp resistor
3 Field	7 Field resistor
4 Cut-out relay	8 Voltage regulator

cessories turned off, start the engine and allow it to run at normal idling speed. Attach the negative lead of a voltmeter to one terminal of the generator, and clip the other lead to a good grounding point on the generator yoke. Gradually increase the speed of the engine. The voltmeter reading should rise quickly without fluctuation. The voltmeter reading should not be allowed to reach 20 volts; do not further increase the speed of the engine in an attempt to make the voltage increase. A generator speed of 1000 rpm is sufficient for this test. If the highest reading obtained is 0 volt, the brushes may be defective; 1/2-1 volt, the field winding may be faulty; and 4-5 volts, the armature winding is suspect.

NOTE: *If there is excessive sparking at the commutator while conducting the above test, the armature is defective and should be replaced.*

A good reading would point to a faulty regulator as the cause for the charging system failure. If this is the case, the proper adjustment may restore its operating efficiency; however, in most cases, it will be found that replacement of the defective regulator is the simplest and cheapest cure. The time involved in adjustment of the regulator can cost more than the price of a new unit.

Servicing the Generator and the Generator Regulator

Generator Removal and Replacement

To remove the generator, disconnect the two wires from their terminals, and then

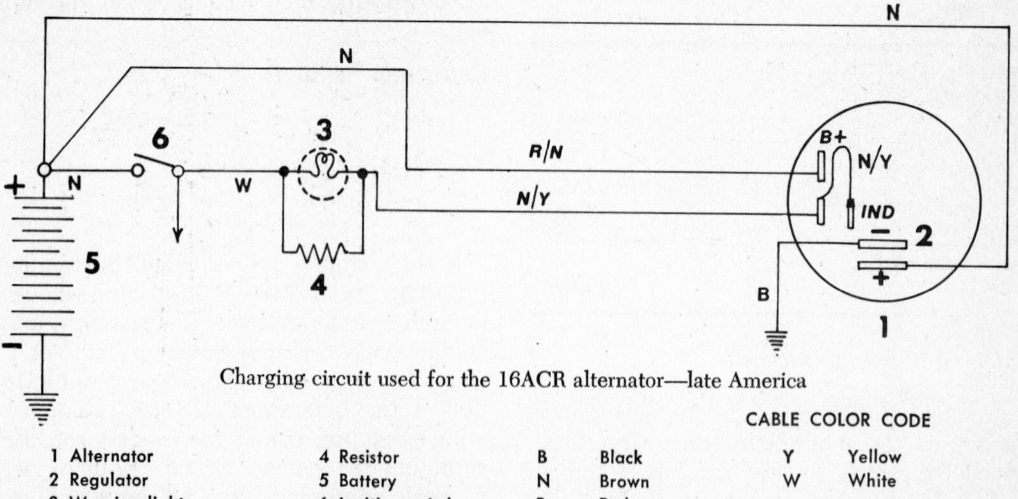

Charging circuit used for the 16ACR alternator—late America

				CABLE COLOR CODE	
1 Alternator	4 Resistor	B	Black	Y	Yellow
2 Regulator	5 Battery	N	Brown	W	White
3 Warning light	6 Ignition switch	R	Red		

disconnect the high and low tension cables to the coil. Next, loosen the attachment bolts that secure the generator to its mounting bracket. Push it downward (towards the engine on the America) to slacken the fanbelt so that it can be removed. Remove the mounting bolts, lift the generator away from the engine block, and then remove the coil from its bracket on the generator.

To remove the voltage regulator, first disconnect, at the battery, the battery cable that leads to the starter. This should be done to protect the wiring harness. Next, disconnect the wires on the regulator, being careful to mark them if unsure of positions on the terminal block. Finally, remove the two screws at the base of the regulator and remove it.

The generator and the regulator may be polarized at the same time that they are installed in the car. Reconnect the battery. Disconnect the wire from the regulator terminal F (field) and touch it momentarily to regulator terminal B or AI (battery). Do not hold the wire to the terminal for more than a second. Reconnect the wire to terminal F. The polarity of the generator and regulator will then be in line with the polarity of the vehicle electrical system.

Generator Maintenance

On older Austin-Healey and Sprite models, lubricate the generator by unscrewing the cap of the lubricator, which is located on the side of the bearing housing. Withdraw the felt pad and spring, and fill the lubricator about half-full with grease. On newer cars, put two drops of motor oil in the lubricating hole that is located at the center of the rear end bearing plate.

The only service that can be performed on the generator, in the event of failure, without using special tools, is polishing the commutator and replacing the brushes. The brushes and commutator are accessible after the commutator end bracket is removed. Older models have inspection windows for the brushes. To gain access to these, remove the metal band from around the yoke. On newer generators there are no inspection windows, so the generator must be removed, and the two long through-bolts withdrawn, to inspect the brushes.

To replace the brushes, lift the brush springs out of the way and slide the brushes out of their holders. Unscrew the brush wire ends and install the new ones. Make sure that the brushes move freely in their holder. If they display a tendency to stick, their sides should be smoothed with a file.

Inspect the commutator for smoothness and freedom from burned spots. It may be polished by using a fine emery or sandpaper while rotating the armature. If the commutator segments are too badly burnt, the generator should be replaced.

Before replacing the commutator end bracket, the brush spring tension should be checked by means of a spring scale. Mini-

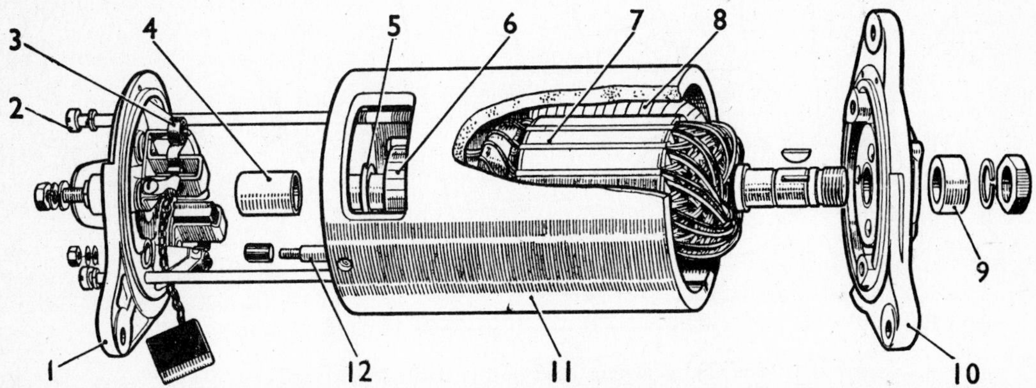

The C45PV5/6 generator use on the Healey 100-6 and 3000 Mks. I-II

1 Commutator end bracket
2 Through bolt
3 Brush spring
4 Brush
5 Thrust collar
6 Commutator
7 Armature
8 Field coil
9 Distance collar
10 Drive end bracket
11 Yoke
12 Field terminal post

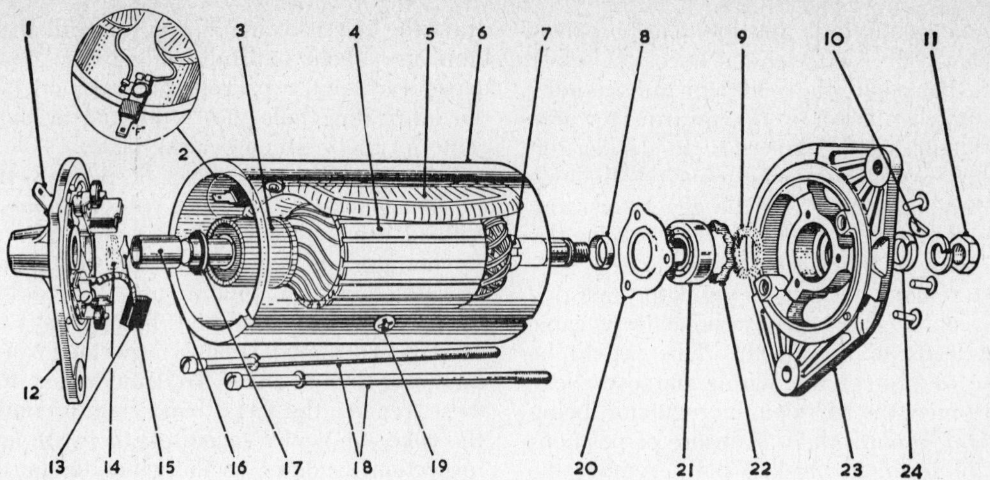

The C42 generator used on the Healey 3000 Mk. III

1 Output terminal D
2 Field terminal connections
3 Commutator
4 Armature
5 Field coils
6 Yoke
7 Shaft collar
8 Shaft collar retaining
9 Felt ring
10 Shaft key
11 Shaft nut
12 Commutator end bracket
13 Brushes
14 Felt ring
15 Felt ring retainer
16 Porous bronze bush
17 Fiber thrust washer
18 Thru-bolts
19 Pole-shoe securing screws
20 Bearing retaining plate
21 Ball bearing
22 Corrugated washer
23 Drive end bracket
24 Pulley spacer

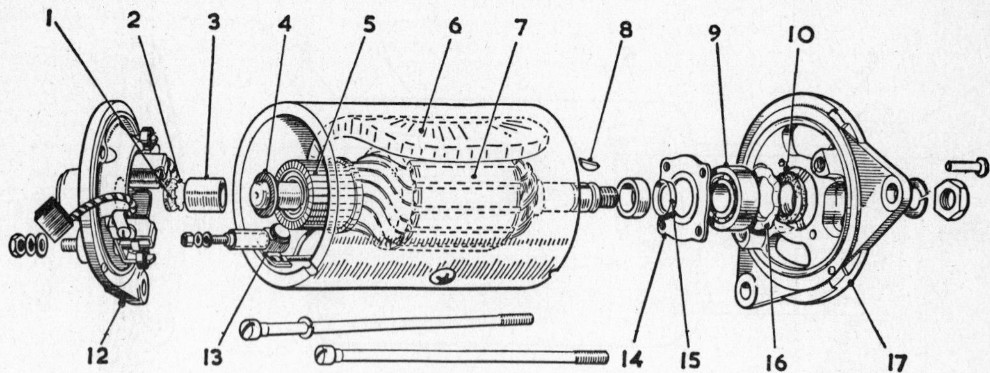

The C39 generator used on the Sprite Mks. I and II

1 Felt pad
2 Aluminum disc
3 Bronze bushing
4 Fiber washer
5 Commutator
6 Field coils
7 Armature
8 Shaft key
9 Bearing
10 Felt washer
12 Commutator end bracket
13 Field terminal post
14 Bearing retaining plate
15 Cup washer
16 Corrugated washer
17 Driving end bracket

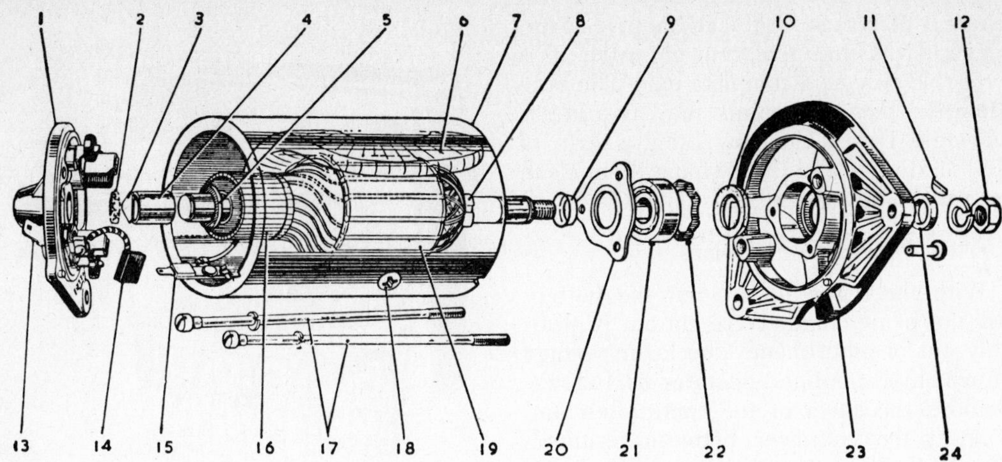

The C40/1 generator used on the Sprite Mks. III-IV and the early America models

1 Commutator end bracket	9 Shaft collar retaining cup	17 Through bolts
2 Felt ring	10 Felt ring	18 Pole-shoe securing screws
3 Felt ring retainer	11 Shaft key	19 Armature
4 Bronze bush	12 Shaft nut	20 Bearing retaining plate
5 Thrust washer	13 Output terminal 'D'.	21 Ball bearing
6 Field coils	14 Brushes	22 Corrugated washer
7 Yoke	15 Field terminal 'F'.	23 Driving end bracket
8 Shaft collar	16 Commutator	24 Pulley spacer

mum acceptable tension is 15 oz. Replace the end bracket and reinstall the generator. Generator output should then be checked.

Adjusting the RB106 Series Regulator

Both the Austin-Healey 100-6 and the majority of Sprites are equipped with the RB106/2 regulator. This regulator contains two units: the voltage regulator, and the cut-out switch. The voltage regulator controls the generator output in accordance with demands on the battery, and its state of charge. The cut-out switch connects and disconnects the battery with the generator in order that the battery will not discharge through the generator when the engine is stopped or running slowly.

Electrical Setting—Voltage

The regulator electrical setting can be checked without the cover of the control box being removed, and is carried out as follows: Remove the wires from the terminals marked A and A1 at the control box and connect them together. Connect the negative lead of a voltmeter to terminal D and the other lead to terminal E. Slowly increase the speed of the engine until the voltmeter needle flutters, and then becomes steady. This should occur at the following range of voltages depending on the temperature:

Ambient Temperature	*Voltage*
10° C (50°F)	16.1-16.7
20° C (68° F)	16.0-16.6
30° C (86° F)	15.9-16.5
40° C (104° F)	15.8-16.4

If the voltage indicated is outside of the above limits for the ambient temperature, the electrical setting must be adjusted as follows: Turn off the engine and remove the cover of the control box. Release the locknut which secures the regulator-adjusting screw and turn the screw clockwise to raise the setting or counterclockwise to lower. The adjusting screw should be rotated only a fraction of a turn at a time until the correct setting is achieved. During adjustment, do not speed the engine to more than half-throttle and make all adjustments as quickly as possible to guard against false readings due to temperature increases.

The settings of the voltage regulator and the cut-out relay contact points should not be disturbed. These were accurately set at the factory, and should not need adjustment unless they have been disturbed.

There is no reason for this to happen, as the regulator has no replacement parts; it is available only as a complete unit. The only attention that the points may require, is cleaning. This is done by using a strip of fine sandpaper and then wiping them clean with a non-oily solvent.

Electrical Cut-out Adjustment

With the regulator set, but the battery still not being charged, the cut-out is probably out of adjustment. Check the voltage at which the cut-out operates as follows: Remove the cover of the control box and connect the voltmeter between terminals D and E. Start the engine and slowly increase its speed until the cut-out contacts are observed to close, noting the voltage at which this occurs. The voltage observed should be between 12.7 and 13.3 volts. If it is not, adjust the setting as follows:

1. Loosen the locknut that secures the cut-out adjusting screw and turn the screw clockwise to raise the setting, or counterclockwise to lower. (Turn the screw only a fraction of a turn at a time.) Tighten the locknut.
2. Test after each adjustment by following the checking procedure outlined above, being careful to operate as quickly as possible to avoid false readings caused by increases in temperature.
3. Adjust the drop-off voltage, if necessary, to the range of 8.5–11.0 volts by carefully bending the fixed contact blade. If the cut-out does not operate, remove the box for further examination.

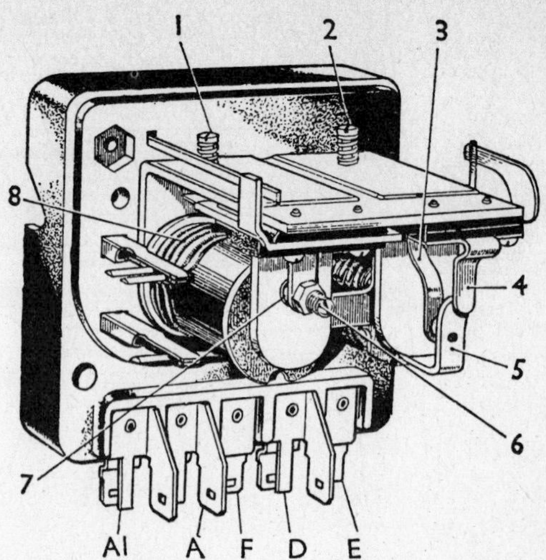

The RB 106/2 control box used in the Sprite and 100-Six models.

1 Regulator adjusting screw
2 Cut-out adjusting screw
3 Fixed contact blade
4 Stop arm
5 Armature tongue and moving contact
6 Regulator fixed contact screw
7 Regulator moving contact
8 Regulator series windings

Adjusting the RB340 Regulator

This regulator is found in the Austin-Healey 3000 series, in the later Sprites, and in the Austin Americas that are equipped with a generator. It contains, in addition to the cut-out relay and voltage regulator, a current regulator which further monitors generator output.

As with the RB106 regulator, none of the settings of the contact breaker points should be adjusted or tampered with (see above.). However, the electrical settings of the two regulators and the cut-out relay can be adjusted.

Electrical Adjustment—Voltage Regulator

The voltage regulator segment of the RB

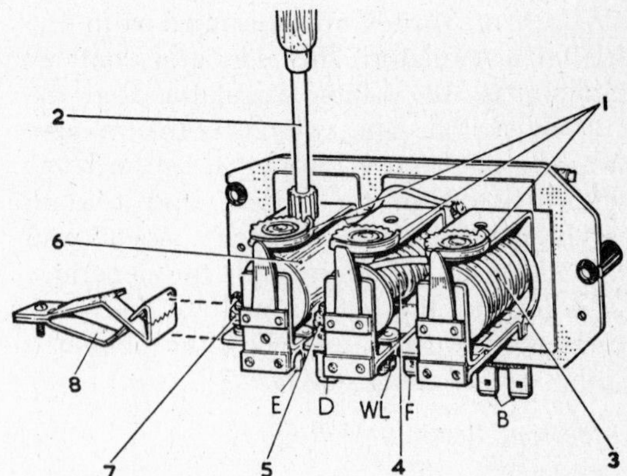

The RB340 regulator used on the Austin-Healey 3000, late Sprites, and early America models (generator)

1 Adjustment cams
2 Setting tool
3 Cut-out relay
4 Correct regulator
5 Current regulator contacts
6 Voltage regulator
7 Voltage regulator contacts
8 Bulldog dip

340 is adjusted as follows: Disconnect the wires from the control box terminal B and connect a voltmeter between terminal D and a good ground. Start the engine and run the generator at a speed of 4.500 rpm. The reading of the voltmeter should be steady and should lie within the following limits, which vary according to the temperature:

Ambient Temperature	*Voltage*
10° C (50° F)	14.9-15.5
20° C (68° F)	14.7-15.3
30° C (86° F)	14.5-15.1
40° C (104° F)	14.3-14.9

If the reading of the voltmeter is outside the range specified, adjust as follows: Rotate the voltage adjustment cam clockwise to raise the setting, and counterclockwise to lower it. After adjusting the voltage, turn the engine off, restart, repeat the measurement procedure and make final adjustments as necessary.
CAUTION: *The voltage regulator adjustment should not be carried out for longer than 30 seconds or heating of the shunt coil may cause false readings.*

Electrical Setting—Current Regulator

In order to conduct the current regulator test, the voltage regulator contact must be short-circuited by a clip placed between the insulated fixed contact bracket and the voltage regulator frame, as shown in the illustration. This will make the voltage regulator inoperative and allow the generator to develop its full output independent of the condition of the battery. Disconnect the wires from terminal B and connect an ammeter between the wires disconnected and terminal B. Start the engine and speed it up until the generator is turning about 4000 rpm. At this speed, the generator should be producing its maximum output of 30 amperes. If the ammeter reading is significantly greater or less than 30, turn the current-adjusting cam clockwise to raise the setting and counterclockwise to lower.
CAUTION: *Limit this test to 30 seconds.*

Electrical Setting—Cut-In

The cut-in voltage, which is approximately 12.7-13.3 volts, is checked and adjusted as follows: Connect a voltmeter between terminal D and ground. Start the engine and slowly increase the speed, at the same time observing the voltmeter needle. The voltage should rise steadily and then drop slightly when the contacts close. The cut-in voltage is the figure reached just before the voltmeter pointer drops. If the instant of contact closure is not distinct (due to the cut-in and battery voltages being approximately equal), turn on the headlights in order to reduce the battery voltage and make the drop easier to spot. If the cut-in voltage is outside the specified limits, adjust by turning the cam clockwise to raise and counterclockwise to lower the setting. After each adjustment, repeat the test and complete within 30 seconds each time.

Testing the Alternator

Precautions

1. Do not run the engine with battery or any of the charging circuit wires disconnected (except as indicated in a test procedure.)
2. All charging circuit electrical connections must be clean and tight.
3. Correct battery and alternator polarity (negative ground) must be maintained or the alternator will be destroyed.
4. If arc-welding equipment is used on the car, the alternator and the regulator leads must be disconnected.
5. The cable that connects the battery to the alternator is hot even if the engine is not running; so do not ground this cable, or either of the terminals that it runs to.

16ACR Alternator—on Vehicle Testing

The 16ACR alternator is used on the 1970-71 Austin America. The voltage regulator used with it (8TR or 11TR) is a micro-circuit that is integral with the alternator. The regulator is located on the slip-ring bracket which may be found inside the plastic end-cover of the alternator.

Before proceeding with any testing, be sure that the fanbelt is correctly tensioned, and that all of the electrical connections are clean and tight. All the tests should be carried out on an engine that has reached normal operating temperature. If possible, the battery should be fully charged.

Disconnect the wires from the alternator. Remove the plastic end-cover. Turn the ignition on and ground the wire that connects to terminal F on the alternator (the brown and yellow wire). The ignition warning light should come on. If it does not, check

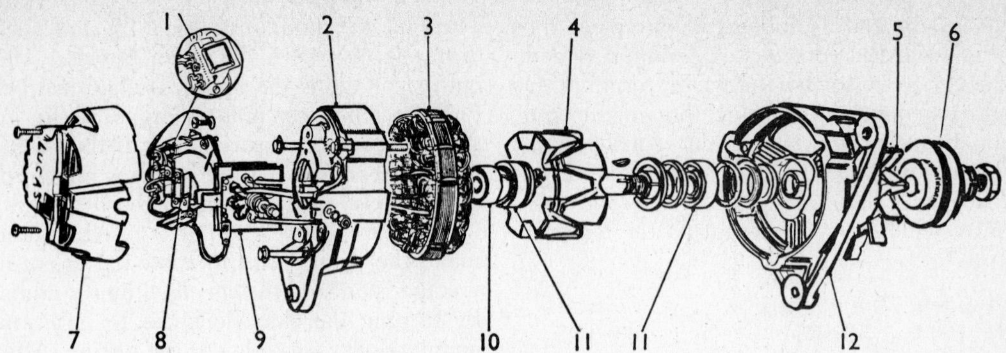

The 16ACR alternator—later Austin America

1 Regulator pack
2 Slip-ring end bracket
3 Stator
4 Rotor
5 Fan
6 Pulley
7 End cover
8 Brush box moulding
9 Rectifier pack
10 Slip-rings
11 Rotor bearings
12 Drive end bracket

the continuity of wiring between the ignition switch and the alternator, as well as, the bulb itself. Correct any faults if they exist, then continue with the testing.

Reconnect the wires as originally found. Failure to connect the wires to the terminals correctly will destroy the alternator. If unsure of the connections refer to the charging system diagrams.

Connect one end of a jumper wire to terminal F on the alternator, and ground the other end. Connect an ammeter between the (+) terminal at the alternator and the battery terminal of the starter solenoid. Start the engine; switch on the headlights and the other electrical accessories to load the battery. The ammeter should show a charge of approximately 15 amps at 1,000 rpm, and 30 amps at 2,000 rpm (engine speed).

NOTE: *Do not run the engine above 2,000 rpm with the regulator out of the circuit.*

If the ammeter indicates that a deficiency exists in the alternator proceed with the section on Bench Testing the alternator.

If the alternator is producing a sufficient charge, shut the engine off and leave the headlights on for three to five minutes. Remove the jumper wire. Leave the ammeter connected. Start the engine, and, with the lights and accessories on, check the alternator output. It should produce about 15 amps at 1,000 rpm and at least 25 amps at 3,000 rpm.

If the output is good, the alternator and regulator are functioning normally and any fault existing in the charging system will be found in the battery wiring, or in the battery itself. If the output is insufficient, replace the regulator, with a new one, and run the final test again as a check.

16ACR—Bench Testing

Disconnect the wires from the alternator, being careful not to let the wire that connects the (+) terminals of the battery and the alternator touch ground. Remove the alternator mounting bolts, slip the belt from the pulley, and remove the alternator. Installation is the reverse of the removal procedure.

Remove the plastic end-cover. Unsolder the three wires from the rectifier pack, noting their positions.

CAUTION: *When soldering or unsoldering the connections, a pair of long-nose pliers must be used as a heat-sink on the diode pins, or the diodes will be destroyed. Be careful not to bend or break the pins with the pliers.*

Remove the brush holder box retaining screws; loosen the rectifier pack retaining nuts and remove the rectifier pack, brush holder box, and the regulator.

The rectifier pack may be tested by connecting a 12 volt battery and a test light in turn to each of the nine diodes and its corresponding heat-sink, and then reversing the connections. The lamp should light with the current flowing in only one direction. If the lamp lights in both directions, indicating an open diode, or if it fails to light at all, the entire rectifier pack must be replaced. If there are any defects in the pack, install a new one. Replace the alternator in the car, and retest it.

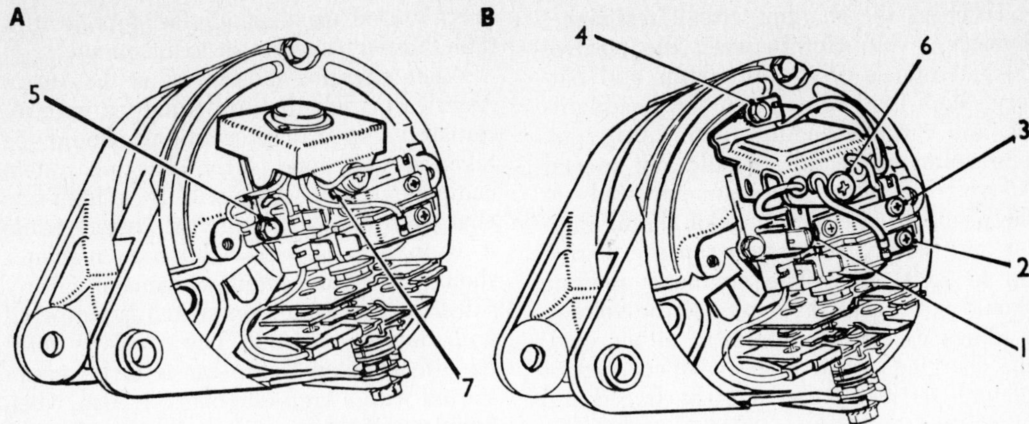

A. 11TR regulator; B. 8TR regulator—both are used with the 16ACR alternator

1 B+ (both types)
2 Positive (+) (both types)
3 Field (F) (both types)
4 Ground (—) and lower mounting screw (8TR type)
5 Ground (—) and brush box securing screw (11TR type)
6 Upper mounting screw (both types)
7 Spacer (11TR type)

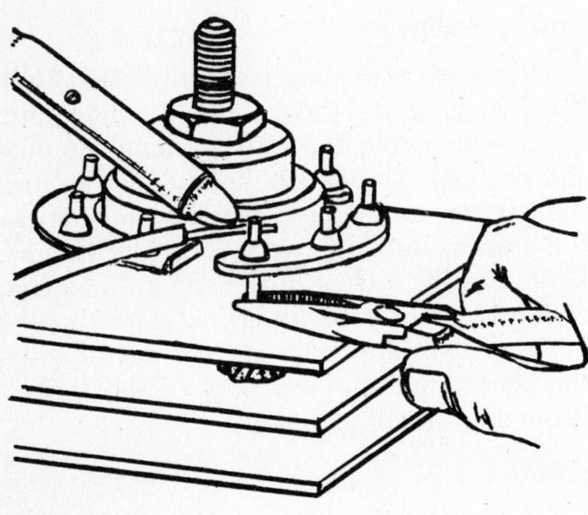

Pliers may be used as a heat-sink when soldering diodes

If the rectifier pack test indicates that it is functioning properly, the alternator brushes should be checked. The brushes should protrude at least 0.20″ from the holder, and spring pressure should be a minimum of 7 oz. Replace the brush assemblies, if necessary. This is done by removing the pair of screws that hold the brush assembly in, and withdrawing it from its holder. If the brushes do not move freely in their holders, polish them with a fine file, and wash them off with gasoline.

Be sure that the slip-rings are clean and free of burn marks. Remove the burn marks with fine sandpaper, do *not* use emery cloth, and clean them with gasoline.

Any other repair work that must be done to the alternator requires special tools and equipment. Thus, if the rectifier pack and the brush assemblies appear to be in good condition, and a major internal fault is indicated; the simplest method of repair is replacement of the alternator unit.

Testing The Alternator Regulators—8TR and 11TR

The 8TR and the 11TR regulators are used interchangeably in the 16ACR alternator. They are located *inside of the alternator.* If they are to be removed, the alternator must be taken off the car. When the plastic end-cover is removed, the regulator is accessible. Note the position of, and remove, the regulator leads. Take out the lower mounting screw and the regulator will be free.

With the alternator and regulator in place on the car, connect an ammeter between the (+) terminals on the alternator and starter solenoid. Connect a voltmeter across the battery terminals. Start the engine and run it at 2,000 rpm. If the ammeter reads zero, the regulator must be replaced.

If the ammeter registers a current flow, adjust the engine speed until the ammeter reads approximately 5 amps. The voltmeter reading should be between 14.0 and 14.4 volts. If the reading is outside these limits there is either a high resistance in the charging circuit wires, or the regulator is bad.

To check the charging circuit resistance, connect a voltmeter between the positive (+) terminals of the alternator and battery. Start the engine, turn the headlights on, and run the engine up to 2,000 rpm. The voltmeter reading should not exceed 0.5 volts. Transfer the voltmeter leads to the negative (−) terminals of the alternator and battery, and again run the engine up to 2,000 rpm. The voltmeter reading should not exceed 0.25 volts. If the voltage readings exceed the limits in either case, the charging circuit has developed an area of high resistance that must be traced and eliminated.

If the charging cicuit is normal, with respect to resistance, the regulator unit must be replaced with a new one, and the alternator output checked.

Battery and Starter

Once a month—more frequently in hot weather—the battery (batteries, in the case of some 3000 models) should be topped up with distilled or demineralized water to a level just above the separators between the cells.

The condition of the battery may be tested reliably with the use of a hydrometer, which measures the specific gravity of the acid in each cell. All cells should read approximately the same, and the readings should be adjusted (corrected) to reflect the specific gravity at 60° F. (16° C.). For every 5° F. above 60° F., add .002 to the observed reading of the hydrometer. For each 5° F. below the 60° F. level, subtract .002 from the observed reading. The temperature measured should not be that of the ambient air, but that of the electrolyte itself. The corrected specific gravity of the electrolyte should then be compared with values given in the following table:

State of Battery	*Specific Gravity*
Fully charged	1.270-1.290
Half discharged	1.190-1.210
Fully discharged	1.110-1.130

If the battery proves to be discharged, it should be charged either by daytime driving or by removal and charging with an external source of electricity. If a battery is several years old and has trouble holding a charge for short periods of time, it should be replaced. Battery deterioration is more a function of time than of mileage, and, as a matter of fact, batteries in cars that are frequently used are generally far more healthy than those in cars that sit in the garage.

When charging the battery in the Austin America models that are equipped with alternators, special precautions should be taken so that none of the charging system components are damaged. If a high-rate charger is used to charge the battery while it is in the car, the alternator regulator should be disconnected, as damage will result to it if the ignition switch is tampered with during charging. The regulator *must* be disconnected if the car is to be jump-started with a high-rate charger. Also, when jump-starting, proper polarity must be observed. Do not reconnect the regulator until the charger is disconnected, and the engine is idling. Under no circumstances disconnect the battery while the engine is running.

Starter Removal and Replacement

Austin-Healey

To remove the starter on all of the Austin-Healey series, begin by disconnecting the starter cable from its terminal on the starter. Take the two bolts out that secure the starter to the flywheel housing. Slide the starter forward, work it below the oil filter, and lift it clear of the engine. In some instances, it may be found necessary to remove the oil filter housing in order to slide the starter out. Replacement of the starter is the opposite of its removal.

Sprite

On the Sprite, remove the distributor, being careful not to disturb the pinch bolt, and then undo the cable from its terminal on the starter. Unscrew the top fastening bolt from the starter. From underneath the car, take off the dirt deflector that is located below the starter motor. Undo the bottom bolt, pull the starter forward, and lift it away from the engine. It may be helpful to take off the oil filter, as an aid to starter removal. Installation of the starter is the reverse of its removal.

Austin America

The starter on the America is located on the right-hand side of the car, at the front of the tranverse engine. The procedure for its removal is the same as that for the Sprite, above; except that the oil filter should not have to be removed to get the starter out.

Fuel System

Fuel Pumps

Location

With two exceptions (both early Sprites), the fuel pumps used on the Austin-Healey, America, and the later Sprites are of the S.U. electric type. These pumps may be hidden in various places around the car. For example, in the early Healeys the fuel pump is located in one of two places. On the BT series it is located under the left rear seat pan, while on the BN series, access to it is gained through a hinged door in the left-hand side of the trunk. But starting with car number 17547 (BN7) and 17352 (BT7), the pump was moved so that it is on the *right-hand* side of the car, but in the same corresponding location, i.e., under the rear seat pan or trunk floor respectively. On all subsequent series, it is under the right rear seat pan.

On the later Sprites that are equipped with an S.U. electric fuel pump, it is located at the rear of the car on the passenger's side. Access to it is from underneath the car.

The Austin America has its fuel pump located on the right-hand side of the trunk.

Troubleshooting The S.U. Electric Fuel Pump

In the case of a fuel system failure, where the pump is suspected to be the cause, the first thing to do, is to determine whether the pump is working or not. The surest method to determine pump operation is to listen for its characteristic ticking sound. If no sound is heard, when the ignition is turned on, the pump is not operating. There can be two basic causes for this.

First, check to see that the pump is getting power. Make sure that all of the electrical connections are clean and tight. If they are, and the pump still is not working, unscrew the lead from the pump. With the ignition on, strike the lead against the metal pump housing, and look for a spark. If there is none, then a fault exists in the wiring that requires attention.

If there is a sufficient spark, then the problem probably lies in the pump's points. To get at these, remove the plastic top cover by undoing the brass terminal nut.

NOTE: *Care should be taken to see that the electrical system is not accidently grounded out. It may be a good idea to disconnect the battery leads, or on cars so equipped, to turn the master switch off.*

Some pumps may have a tape seal that must be pulled off before the plastic cover can be removed. Next, take out the condenser, if the pump has one, and the blade that holds the top point in place. Clean the top point with sandpaper and wipe it off with trichloroethylene. The bottom point should be cleaned in the same manner; but care should be taken so that the adjustment of the bottom point is not disturbed. Assembly is the reverse of the dismantling procedure.

If the pump ticks, but still is not pumping fuel, the most likely cause is a clogged fuel line. Check the line for leaks and make sure that all of the fittings are tight. If, when the intake line is disconnected, the pump operates, then the line has a restriction in it. After removing the gas cap, the line can be cleaned by forcing compressed air through it. Under no circumstances, should compressed air be forced through the pump, as it will damage its mechanism.

Be sure that the fuel tank is properly vented, if it is not the pump will run slowly and burn its points up. A clogged filter may also cause restricted flow; be sure that they are clean and clear of obstructions. A stiff brush is recommended for this job; never use a cloth or rag.

On Austin America models that are equipped with evaporative loss control systems be sure that the fuel line filter is renewed every 12,000 miles. At the same time, replace the air filter element in the absortion canister. Every 50,000 miles the complete canister must be replaced. Because the fuel tank is not vented, if any of the above systems become clogged or damaged the fuel pump will behave exactly as though the fuel tank were *improperly* vented, i.e., the pump will slow down and burn up its points. *Under no circumstances* should compressed air be forced through the fuel system to clean it; nor should a vented filler cap be used. Either of these will cause the fuel system to work improperly, and can lead to unnecessary damage and expense.

If the fuel still is not being pumped after the above checks and repairs, there is probably a major fault in the fuel pump.

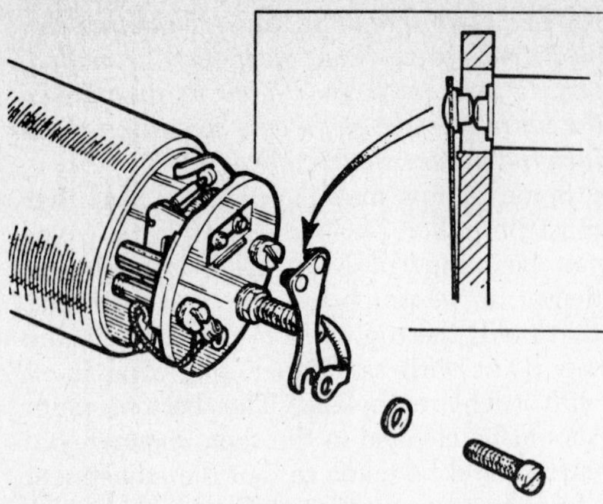

Inset shows the correct position of the blade and rocker contact points.

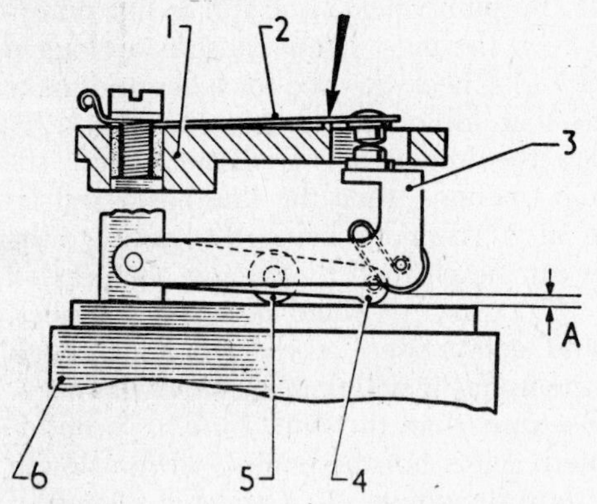

Contact gap setting, earlier rocker assemblies.

1 Pedestal	4 Inner rocker
2 Contact blade	5 Trunnion
3 Outer rocker	6 Coil housing

A = .030 in. (.8 mm.)

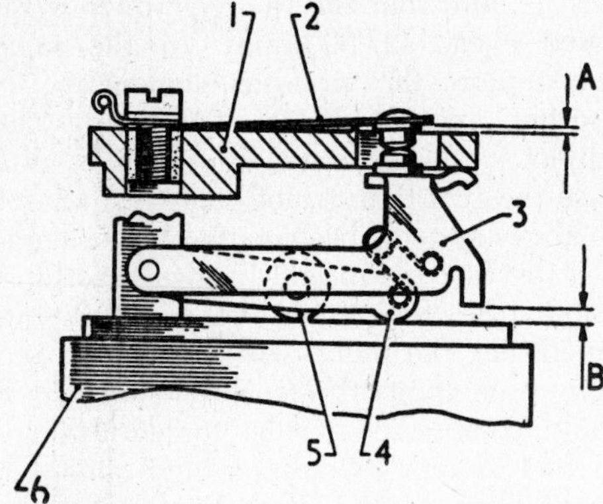

Contact gap setting on later modified rocker assemblies.

1 Pedestal	4 Inner rocker
2 Contact blade	5 Trunnion
3 Outer rocker	6 Coil housing

A = .035 in. (.9 mm.) B = .070 in. (1.8 mm.)

The cheapest method of repair is to have the pump replaced; either with a new or a reconditioned unit. Many dealers will accept the old pump as a trade-in, so it would be wise to save the defective one when it is removed.

The AC Mechanical Fuel Pump

The AC Y type mechanical fuel pump is used on the Mk. I and Mk. II Sprites. It is activated by an eccentric on the engine camshaft. Remove the pump by removing the fuel line connections, removing the two retaining bolts holding the pump to the crankcase, and lifting the pump from its position.

Disassemble the mechanical pump as follows: Remove the retaining bolt and lift off the top cover. Remove the filter and sealing washer. Take out the screws which secure the upper chamber, then separate the halves of the pump body. For reassembly purposes, it is helpful if the halves are marked before being separated. Remove the securing screws, valve plate, intake and delivery valve assemblies, and gasket. Rotate the diaphragm and pull rod assembly 90°, then withdraw the diaphragm, spring, and metal and fiber washers. Remove the retaining circlip and washer from one side of the rocker arm pivot pin and withdraw the pin, at the same time releasing the rocker arm, connecting link, washers, and anti-rattle spring.

Reassembly of the mechanical fuel pump is the reverse of the disassembly operation, except that the following points should be noted:

1. The installation of the rocker arm pin can be simplified by first inserting a piece of .240 in. (6.1 mm.) diameter rod through the pin hole far enough to engage the rocker arm washers and link, then pushing in the rocker arm pin from the opposite side and removing the guide rod as the pin assumes its position. It is sometimes possible to insert the diaphragm pull rod too far through the slot in the operating link, resulting in the connecting link riding on the pull rod shoulder instead of engaging the two small slots in the pull rod.
2. Check correct assembly by measuring the distance from the top of the pump body to the upper diaphragm protector when the diaphragm is held at the top

of its stroke by the return spring. Correct assembly will result in a measurement of approximately 9/16 in. (14.3 mm.), whereas unsatisfactory assembly leads to a measurement of 3/16 in. (4.8 mm.).

3. The rocker arm should be pushed toward the pump until the diaphragm is level with the body flanges.
4. Install the upper half of the pump into the original position, as indicated by the marks made on the two flanges prior to disassembly.

The installation of the pump is the reverse of the removal operation, except for the following precautions: Be sure that the rocker arm is properly located against the eccentric on the camshaft, because it is possible to accidentally position the rocker arm under or to one side of the eccentric. If the rocker arm is not correctly positioned, tightening the securing bolts may cause damage to the pump. After replacing the pump on the engine, the engine should be run for a short period and the fuel line connections and pump examined for gasoline leakage.

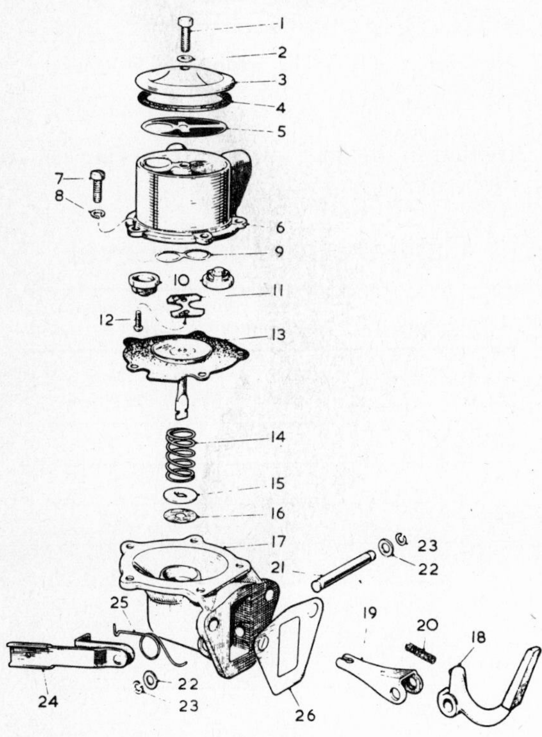

The AC Y mechanical fuel pump used in earlier Sprites.

1 Cover screw
2 Gasket
3 Filter cover
4 Filter cover gasket
5 Filter gauze
6 Upper casting
7 Screw
8 Lock washer
9 Valve gasket
10 Valve assembly
11 Valve retainer
12 Screw
13 Diaphragm
14 Spring
15 Metal washer
16 Fabric washer
17 Pump body
18 Rocker arm
19 Rocker arm link
20 Rocker arm spring
21 Rocker arm pin
22 Washer
23 Clip
24 Priming lever
25 Spring
26 Gasket

Carburetor

The Austin-Healey, Sprite, and America all use S.U. constant vacuum carburetors. The Healey and Sprite models have twin carburetors (except for the Healey 3000 Mk. II, BN7/BJ7, which have three), and the America has only a single carburetor. The basic design of all S.U. carburetors is similar; it is also quite simple. Because of their simplicity, they require much less attention than more complex designs, and when they must have work done to them it is easier to do.

The fuel and air mixture is determined by a tapered needle in the jet. The needle is attached to, and moved by, a piston in the vacuum chamber. The needle is moved upward and downward according to the vacuum pressure that exists above the suction disc, which forms part of the top of the piston. As the vacuum increases, the piston rises and exposes a smaller cross-section of the needle to the jet, thereby allowing more gasoline to enter and enrich the mixture. A damper mounted on the upper portion of the vacuum chamber guide bore delays the upward motion of the piston during acceleration; thus enriching the mixture and preventing piston flutter.

Removal and Installation

Austin-Healey and Sprite

The Austin-Healey and the Sprite use basically the same procedure for removal and replacement of the carburetor. This holds true, even for the Healey models fitted with three carburetors instead of the usual two.

On the Austin-Healey, turn off the battery master switch before proceeding. Remove the air cleaners and, on the later Sprites, disconnect any attendant emission control hoses. Remove the fuel line from the front carburetor, the snap-lock ball joint from the accelerator relay shaft, and the two (or three) throttle return springs. Remove the mixture control cables from their carburetor levers. Take off the connector for the vacuum control line that is located on the top of the back carburetor.

Undo the four nuts (or in some cases, bolts), and washers that attach each carburetor flange. Then remove the two (or three) carburetors as a single unit, including the float chamber overflow pipes.

Installation is the reverse of removal. Be sure, though, to check and adjust the throttle linkage where necessary.

Austin America

Because it has only one carburetor, and also, an evaporative emission control system, the procedure for carburetor removal on the Austin America is somewhat different than that of the Healey or Sprite. Remove the air cleaner and emission control system hoses. Take off the control cables for both throttle and mixture. Next, remove the vacuum advance line and the fuel line. On cars that have automatic transmissions the governor control rod should be disconnected from the throttle lever. Unscrew the nuts and take off the spring washers that hold the carburetor on to the manifold flanges. Withdraw the carburetor and the cable abutment plate.

Replacement is the reverse of the above. Be sure to check the carburetor gaskets, and replace any that may have become damaged during carburetor removal.

Adjusting the Float Level

The float level setting of the S.U. carburetor, though not as critical as that of the fixed jet carb, should still be closely adhered to so that the car will perform as well as intended. When the float level is correct, a test bar will slide between the float lever face and the inside curve of the float lever fork when the needle valve is in the closed position. If the float level is such that the test bar does not fit snugly, the float lever will have to be bent in the necessary direction to bring about the proper level. The lever should be bent at the intersection of the curved and straight portions, as shown in the illustration. Both prongs of the fork should be kept level, and the straight portion kept perfectly flat. Once the float level has been set correctly, chances are that it won't have to be changed very often, if at all. For this reason, flooding is more likely to be the result of a leaky float, excessive

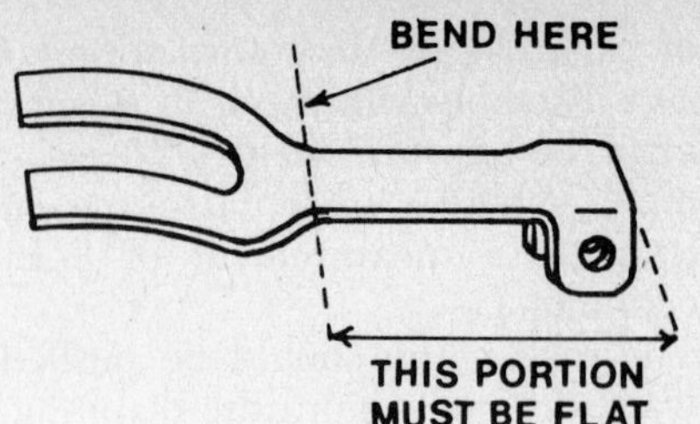

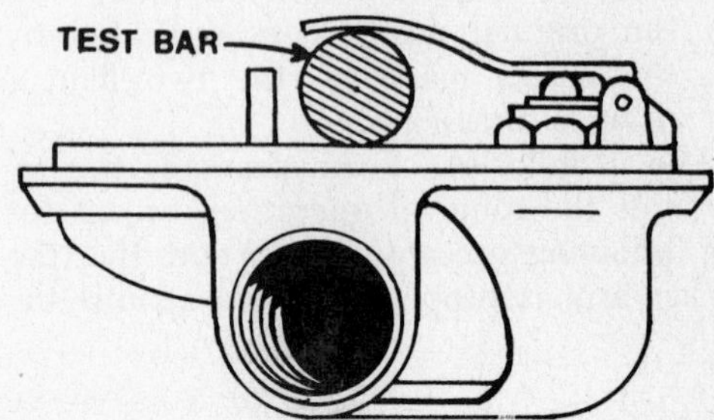

The correct method of setting the float level—S.U. carburetor

friction in the float lever, or a sticking needle valve.

Carburetor Float Level

Model & Engine	Carburetor	Float Level (in.)
Austin-Healey 26C	H4 (2)	7/16
26D/29D	HD6 (2)	7/16
29E	HS4 (3)	5/16
29F	HS6 (2)	7/16
29K	HD8 (2)	1/8
Sprite 9C	H1 (2)	7/16
All others	HS2 (2)	5/16
Austin America 12H	HS4 (1)	1/8

Centering the Jet

Centering the jet is an operation which can ensure trouble-free operation of the S.U. carburetor. However, when centering the jet, be very careful not to bend the needle. Remove the connection between the jet lever and the jet head. Unscrew the connection and remove the nylon feed tube and jet from the carburetor. Unscrew the jet-adjusting nut and remove the lock spring. Replace the adjusting nut and screw it to its uppermost position. Replace the jet and feed tube. Loosen the large jet-locking nut until the jet bearing is free to rotate by finger pressure. With the piston damper removed, use a pencil and gently press the piston and needle down on to the jet bridge. Tighten the jet-locking nut, keeping the jet in position. Check to see if the jet is centered properly. When the jet is correctly centered, the piston should be able to fall freely and hit the jet bridge with a metallic click. If the piston does not fall, repeat the operation, pushing the jet upward and pressing the piston downward, then tighten the locking nut.

On the HS2 carburetor of the Sprite, there is no diaphragm attached to the jet, but the 100-Six and 3000 carburetor is equipped with a diaphragm, which must be replaced in its original position relative to the carburetor body. Otherwise, the centering adjustment, if correct, will be lost.

Check the centering of the jet by noting the difference in sounds when: (1) the piston drops on to the jet when the jet is in its highest position, and (2) when the piston is dropped when the jet is in its lowest position. If there is any difference in sound between conditions (1) and (2), the adjustment process will have to be repeated. When the operation is complete, adjust the mixture setting of the carburetors.

On some of the Austin Americas, the needle used is of the spring-loaded variety. This kind of needle is self-centering, and requires no adjustment. No attempt should be made to use fixed needles and spring-loaded needles interchangeably; nor should the position of the spring seat be altered in any way.

Replacement of a spring-loaded needle is as follows: install the jet bearing, replace

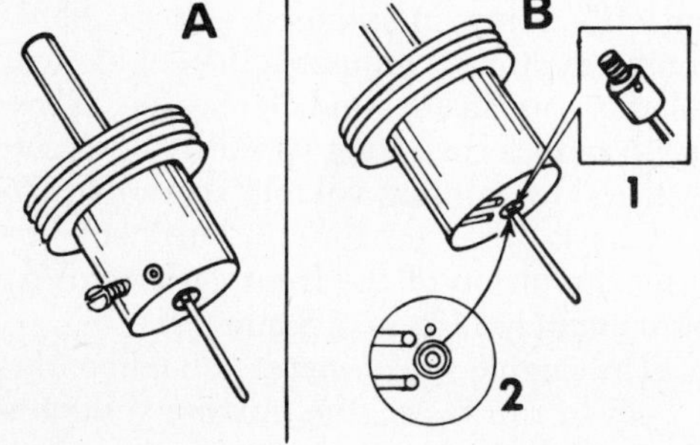

A fixed needle and piston (A); a spring-loaded needle and piston (B)—1. The needle spring and top; 2. The correct alignment of the mark on the needle guide

and tighten the jet locking nut. Replace the jet nut spring and the jet travel restrictor. (Do not attempt to adjust the travel restrictor.) Screw the adjusting nut as far up as possible. Slip the jet into its bearing. Put the sleeve nut, washer, and gasket on the end of the flexible tube. The tube must project at least 3/16 in. beyond the gasket. Tighten the sleeve nut until the washer is compressed; do not overtighten, as this may cause leakage. Position the spring in the jet needle assembly, making sure that it is properly seated. Fit the needle assembly into the guide, and fit this into the piston. The lower edge of the guide should be flush with face of the edge of the piston. The etched mark on the guide should be midway between the two piston transfer holes.

Auxiliary Starting Carburetor

Adjustment

The early Austin-Healey 3000 Mk. I, has a thermo-electrically controlled auxiliary carburetor. A small carburetor, mounted next to the two main ones, is used to enrich the mixture during starting and cold running. It is engaged by a solenoid, which is in turn controlled by a thermostatic switch housed in the water jacket of the cylinder head. When the temperature in the water jacket drops below 86°-95° F. the switch closes, which completes the circuit, thus opening the solenoid on the top of the auxiliary carburetor. The richer mixture is allowed to flow to the intake manifold via an external feed line.

The adjustment operation is limited to turning the stop screw, which moves the needle in the jet. Because this adjustment must be carried out at normal running temperatures, the solenoid must be activated by grounding the thermostatic switch to open the throttles. If a hissing noise is heard the solenoid is operating properly. Rotating the stop screw counterclockwise makes the mixture richer; while rotating it clockwise makes the mixture leaner. The idea is to make the mixture rich but not overly so. The exhaust gas should be distinctively black, but the mixture not so rich as to cause the engine to run with noticeable irregularity. Once the adjustments are made, return the circuit to normal by removing the ground from the thermostatic switch.

Repair

Several things can go wrong with the auxiliary carburetor's electrical system. The simplest of these is a stuck solenoid. This can usually be cured by tapping on the plastic cover of the auxiliary carburetor with a non-metallic object. This should cure the problem, if it does not, or if the problem persists, the solenoid will have to be replaced.

The other problem concerns the thermostatic switch. If the auxiliary carburetor remains on (or off) and the solenoid is working properly, the thermostatic switch is at fault. There are two solutions to this problem. One is to replace the switch and its gasket. Because the thermostatic switches are fragile, and not always readily available, it may be easier to replace it with a manual control.

Mount a single pole-single throw (SPST) toggle switch in a position on, or under the dash where it may be conveniently reached by the driver. Run a wire from one terminal of the switch to a suitable ground. Disconnect the wire from the thermostatic switch and splice it to a longer wire. Run this wire to the other terminal of the toggle switch. Tape up the connections; both the splice and the loose wire to the thermostatic switch. For cold starting the choke may now be operated manually by means of the toggle switch. After the car warms up (coolant above 96° F.) turn the switch off, thus deactivating the auxiliary carburetor.

Carburetor Tuning

Pre-emission Control—Healey and Early Sprite

Before tuning the carburetors, it should be ascertained that all other engine adjustments, and the engine itself, are up to specifications. If one cylinder has a compression pressure 40 psi less than the others, it will be impossible to achieve a smooth running engine merely by manipulating the carburetors. The carburetor tuning will be only as good as the engine adjustments which precede it. Tuning of the Austin-Healey carburetor is limited to the adjustment of the slow-speed mixture, slow-speed synchronization, and the fast-idle speed.

The piston damper should be filled with engine oil to within 1/2 in. of the top of the hollow piston rod. This prevents piston flutter and insures proper operation of the piston.

Before tuning the carburetors, the engine should be warmed to operating temperature and the air cleaners removed. Release the clamping bolts on the couplings between the throttle spindles in order to make the carburetors mechanically independent. Now, working on one carburetor at a time fully close each throttle butterfly valve by rotating the throttle spindle clockwise, as seen from the front. With the throttles held closed, tighten the clamp bolts in turn, then operate the accelerator linkage to see if the throttles are opening at the same time by noting the movement of the full throttle stops at the side of the throttle spindles.

Screw the slow-running screws down to their seatings, then unscrew two full turns for an initial setting. Remove the piston and suction chambers and unscrew the mixture-adjusting screws until each jet is flush with the bridge of its carburetor. Replace the pistons and suction chambers and check that each piston falls freely onto the bridge of its carburetor after being lifted by the piston-lifting pin. Screw the mixture-adjusting nuts down two and one-half turns. Start the engine and adjust to the desired idling speed of 1000 rpm by moving each slow-running-volume screw by an equal amount. By listening to the hiss of the carburetors (or observing the level of a Uni-syn indicator) adjust the slow-running-volume screws so that the intensity of the hiss (or the level of the Uni-syn indicator) is the same for all carburetors. This will synchronize the volume of air flowing through the carburetors.

When the air flow has been synchronized, adjust the mixture by screwing all the mixture-adjusting nuts (or screws) up or down by the same amount until the fastest idle speed is obtained with even running still being maintained. As the slow-running mixture is adjusted, the engine will probably run faster, and it may be necessary to reduce the idling speed by unscrewing the slow-running-volume screws equally. Check the mixture adjustment by lifting the piston of the front carburetor by approximately 1/32 in. (.8 mm). If:

1. The engine speed increases and continues to run faster, the mixture setting is too rich
2. The engine speed immediately decreases, the mixture setting is too lean
3. The engine speed momentarily in-

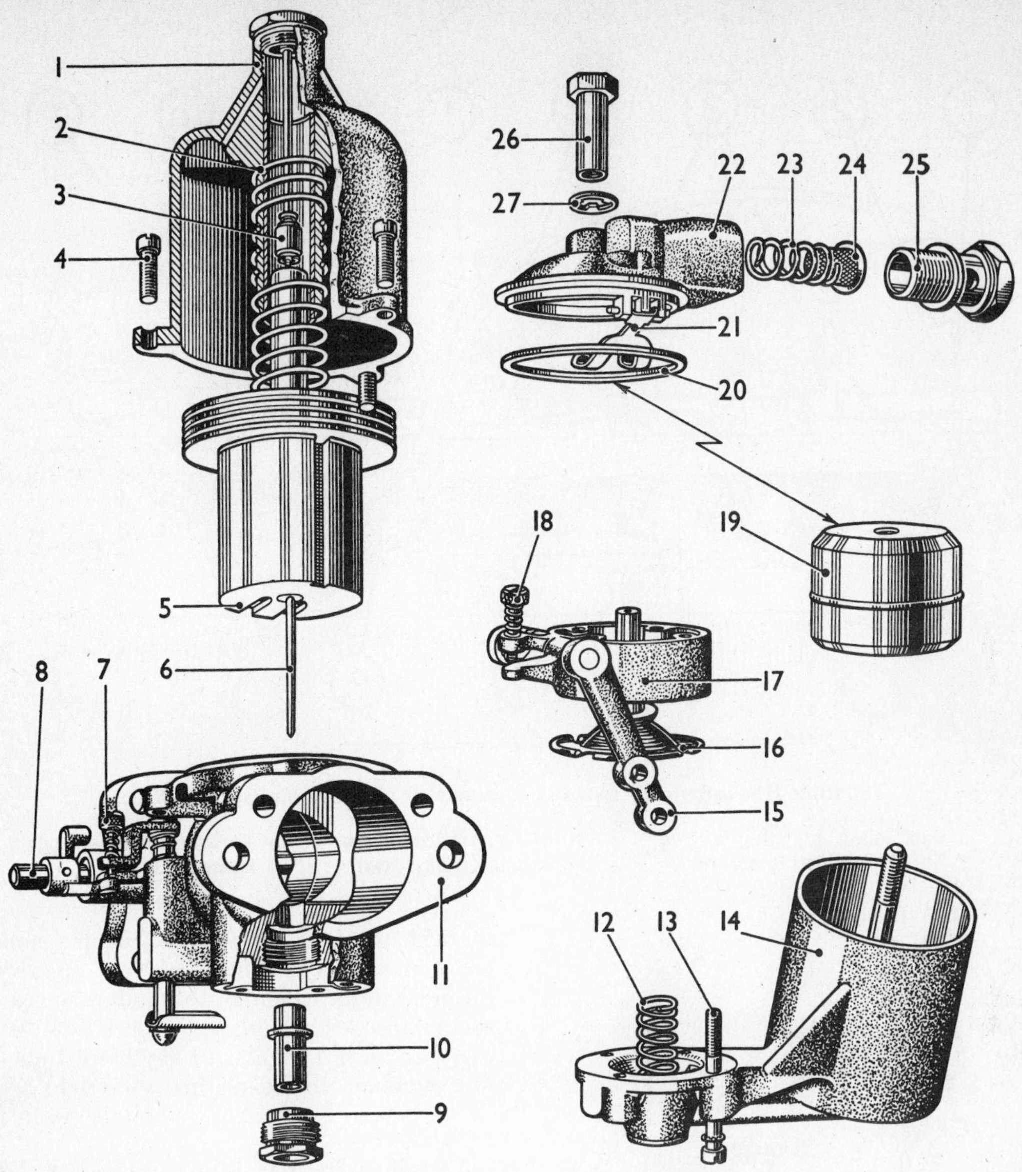

Exploded view of a typical S.U. carburetor—the 406 used in the Austin-Healey 100-Six.

1 Suction chamber
2 Piston spring
3 Hydraulic damper
4 Suction chamber screw
5 Piston
6 Needle
7 Throttle stop lever adjusting screw
8 Throttle spindle
9 Jet screw
10 Jet bearing
11 Carburetor body
12 Jet return spring
13 Float chamber securing screw
14 Float chamber
15 Jet control lever
16 Jet and diaphragm
17 Diaphragm casing
18 Jet adjusting screw
19 Float
20 Cover gasket
21 Float lever
22 Float chamber cover
23 Filter spring
24 Filter
25 Inlet connection
26 Float chamber cover screw
27 Fiber washer

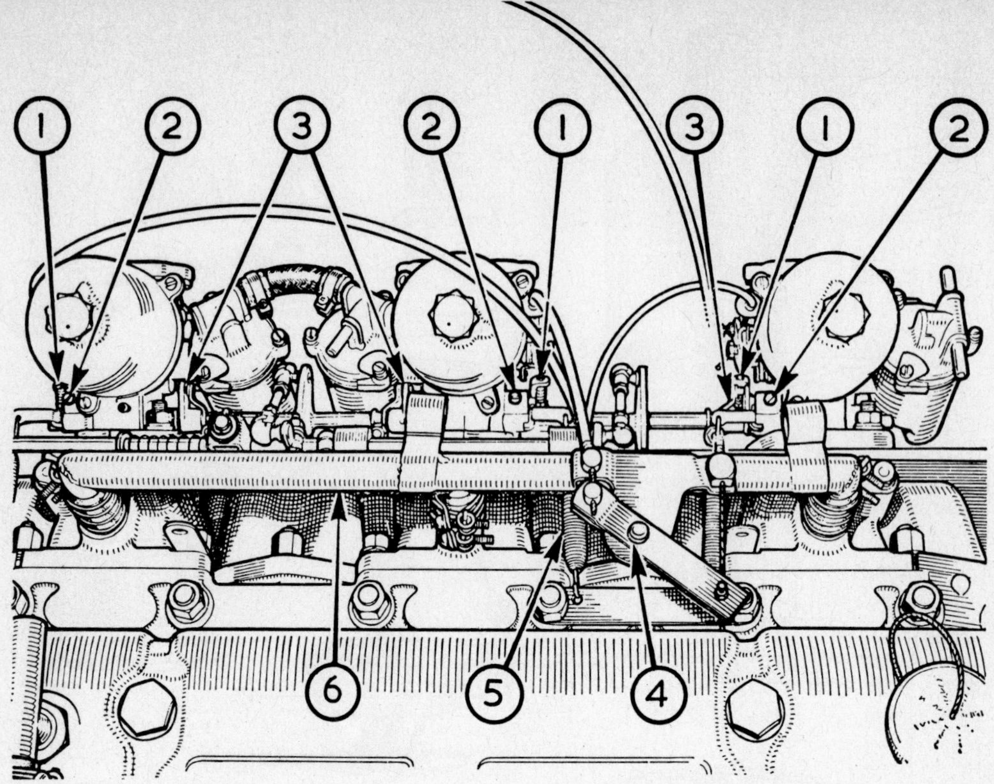

The triple HS4 carburetors found in some models of the Austin-Healey 3000.

1 Fast idling adjusting screws
2 Throttle adjusting screws
3 Throttle operating levers
4 Choke cable relay lever
5 Throttle return spring
6 Balance tube

Arrow shows the needle stop screw that adjusts the mixture strength of the auxiliary enrichment carburetor of the 3000.

creases, then returns to the previous level, the mixture setting is correct.

Repeat this operation on the remaining carburetor(s), and after adjustment, recheck them all, since the carburetors are interdependent. When the mixture is correct, the exhaust note should be regular and even. A colorless exhaust with a splashy misfire and an irregular note indicates that the mixture is too lean, while black exhaust, together with a regular or rhythmical misfire, is a clue that the mixture is too rich.

Fast Idle Adjustment

To adjust the fast idling, reconnect the jet-operating cable so that there is 1/16 in. (1.5 mm.) free travel at the panel control before the jet levers begin to move. Set the mixture-control knob on the dashboard short of the position at which the adjusting-screw levers begin to move. This will be approximately at the halfway position of the control knob. Adjust the fast-idle screws on the throttle stops so that an idle speed of about 1100-1200 rpm is attained when the engine is at normal operating temperature.

Emission Controlled Engines—America and Late Sprite

Before tuning is attempted on these 1968 and subsequent engines, the engine should be warmed to normal operating temperature and run for at least 5 minutes after the thermostat has opened. After the engine has been run for another minute at 2500 rpm under no load, the tuning operations may be immediately begun and carried out as quickly as possible. If the time for the tuning operation exceeds 3 minutes, the 2500 rpm, 1-minute procedure must be repeated before tuning is resumed and after every 3-minute period.

Emission-controlled carburetors are equipped with jet-adjustment restrictors, and it is not advisable that these be removed or repositioned. Only mixture adjustments within the limits of the restrictor are available for tuning. Before tuning, top up the piston damper with the recommended engine oil until the level is 1/2 in. above the top of the hollow piston rod.

NOTE: *On dust-proof carburetors—identified by a transverse hole drilled in the neck of the suction chambers and no vent hole in the damper cap—the oil level must be 1/2 in.* below *the top of the hollow piston rod.*

After the engine has been warmed up and run for 1 minute at 2500 rpm under no load, turn the throttle-adjusting screw on each carburetor until the correct idling speed of 1000 rpm is obtained. Using a suitable air-flow-balancing meter, balance the carburetors by turning the throttle-adjusting screws, maintaining the correct idling speed of 1000 rpm.

NOTE: *During the following operation, gently tap the neck of each suction chamber lightly with a screwdriver handle or other non-metallic instrument.*

Turn the jet-adjusting nuts an equal amount upward (to lean) or downward (to enrich) until the rpm reading on the tachometer is as high as possible. Now, turn both adjusting nuts slowly upward (to weaken the mixture) until the engine speed begins to drop, then turn the adjusting nuts down by a single flat. Check the idling speed and adjust to 1000 rpm if necessary, by moving the adjusting screws the same amount. Use the balance meter to check the balance of air flow through the carburetors.

If an exhaust-gas analyzer indicates that the percentage of carbon monoxide in the exhaust is greater than 3-4 per cent, the jet-adjusting nuts will have to be reset by the minimum amount necessary to bring the percentage within the limits. If this adjustment requires more than a two-flat rotation of the adjusting nuts, it is advisable to check the exhaust-gas analyzer for correct calibration.

With the jet-adjusting nut held stationary, rotate the adjustment restrictor until the vertical tag contacts the carburetor body on the left side when seen from the air cleaner flange. Bend the small tag on the restrictor so that it will lock to the nut. The small tag may then be painted to identify the locking position. Set the throttle interconnection clamping levers so that the link pin is .012 in. (.31 mm.) away from the lower edge of the fork. Tighten the clamping bolts, ensuring that there is a slight end float on the interconnection rod (about 1/32 in.). With both jet levers in their lowest position, set the jet interconnection lever clamping bolts so that both jets begin to open at the same time. With the engine running at 1500 rpm, check to see that the air flow through the carburetors is still balanced.

Reconnect the mixture-control wire so that there is approximately 1/16 in. free movement before it begins pulling on the jet levers. Pull the mixture-control knob on the dashboard until the linkage is about to move the carburetor jets. Use the air-flow meter to ensure equal adjustment and turn

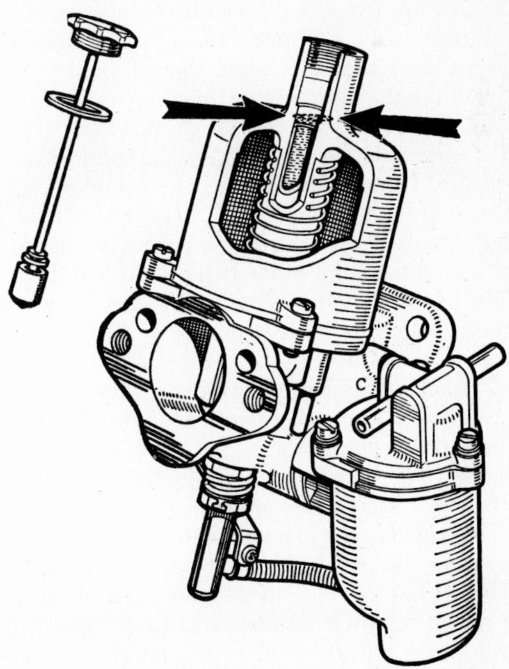

The arrows indicate the oil level of the piston damper on single carburetor, emission controlled engines.

the fast-idle screws to obtain the correct fast-idling speed of 1100-1200 rpm. Replace the air cleaners.

The procedure for the Austin America is similar to the above, except there is no need for carburetor synchronization, as there is only one carburetor. All other operations are the same, except they are only done once.

Exhaust System

For the most part, the exhaust systems on the Austin-Healey, Sprite, and Austin America are very conventional. Thus, replacing and repairing them should pose little or no problem.

Most Healey models have dual exhaust systems. The only exception is the older two-port engine, type 26C. The pipes run down the left side of the car, through a single two chamber muffler. Late Healeys have resonators mounted transversely with the tailpipe coming out at the right of the car.

The Sprite's exhaust system is on the left side of the car. On certain models it is one piece, thus if any part becomes defective, the whole system must be replaced. On Sprites made before 1968, only pinch clamps are used at the manifold; no gasket is fitted, only a flange. Therefore, muffler sealer and a new clamp should be used when the downpipe is removed or replaced. And always be sure that the joint is tight.

To remove the exhaust system undo the manifold pinch clamp, and the retainer on the clutch housing. Next, loosen the two hangers under the car, one is located on a crossmember, the other behind the muffler. The entire exhaust system may now be removed. Installation is the reverse of the removal procedure.

The exhaust system used on the Austin America is a one piece unit that runs down the center of the car. The exhaust system used on the automatic is slightly different than that used on the manual.

To remove the exhaust system, loosen the clamp that holds it on to the manifold. Undo the U-bolt and remove it from the bracket on the transmission casing. Remove the pinch bolts from the two clamps underneath the car. Spread the clamps apart and release the tailpipe. The system can now be removed altogether from the car.

Reinstallation is the reverse of removal. Remember to leave the U-bolt and the manifold clamp loose until the whole system is fitted. The rear hanger can be adjusted vertically to aid in alignment of the exhaust pipe.

When installing any exhaust system, care should be taken so that none of it touches the underpan of the car, otherwise noise and vibration will result. Also, be sure that all joints are tight and leak free; carbon monoxide is a *deadly* poison! To this end, always use muffler sealer and new clamps at any joint where there is no gasket. Be sure to let the car stand for two hours before it is driven, so that the sealer can harden.

Cooling System

CAUTION: *Any operation on the cooling system should be carried out only when the engine is cold. A hot cooling system builds up high pressure. Thus, injury may result, if work is done on it when it is hot.*

Radiator

Removal and Installation

Austin-Healey 100-6 and 3000

Drain the cooling system. Remove the upper water hose from the thermostat housing extension. Remove the radiator bottom hose by releasing the clamps on the water pump and heater outlet pipe. Disconnect the temperature sending element from the radiator header tank. Take off the six nuts which secure the radiator to the mounting flanges. Remove the radiator.

Inspect the radiator core for damage and test for water leaks. Points at which leakage occurs should be soldered if possible, otherwise replace the core. Inspect the flexible mountings for wear and the drain tap for leakage. Test the condition of the pressure-sealing filler cap. Examine hoses for deterioration and replace if necessary. Install the radiator by reversing the removal procedure.

Sprite

There are two different types of cooling system used on the Sprite. Early models are equipped with a conventional open cooling system, while later models have a closed system with an expansion tank.

To remove the radiator from the early cars, first take off the radiator cap and drain the system. Remove the hose clamp and hose from the thermostat housing. Remove the bottom hose and its clamps from the radiator. Disconnect the fresh air induction pipe from its fitting on the cowl (when fitted). Take the temperature gauge sender out from the right side of the radiator, being careful not to damage the unit, as this would mean replacement. Undo the bolts that attach the radiator to its bracket, and take out the radiator. Installation is the reverse of removal.

The radiator on later cars is removed in the following manner: remove the caps from the radiator and the expansion tank, when the engine is cold. Drain the cooling system. Take the car's grille off; reach behind the opening to remove the top, bottom, and expansion hose clamps and then remove the hoses themselves from the radiator. Loosen the nuts that attach the bottom radiator shroud to the body. Undo the four bolts that hold the radiator on to its bracket. Remove the radiator and the bottom shroud as a unit. Disconnect the hose clamps and the return hose from the cylinder block. Take out the bottom return pipe bolts, then withdraw the pipe and its attendant hoses. Reinstallation is the reverse of removal; after it is complete refill the system as detailed below.

To refill the cooling system, replace both drain plugs and open the heater valve. Fill the cooling system through the radiator; then replace the radiator cap. Fill up the expansion tank to the half-way point, and put the expansion tank cap back on. Run the engine for 30 seconds. Stop the engine and remove the radiator cap; fill the radiator if it needs it. Replace the cap and run the engine until it reaches normal operating temperature. Turn the car off and allow the engine to cool down. After the system has cooled off, remove the cap, and check the coolant level in the expansion tank. Fill it half-way up, if necessary.

Austin America

Cooling on the Austin America is accomplished by means of a closed circuit system. Only remove the caps from the radiator and the expansion tank when the engine is cool. Never do any work on the cooling system when it is hot. When the caps are removed, be sure that they are not mixed up; as they are different types. Care should be taken when removing the radiator cap; it is not a pressure-release type.

Drain the cooling system. Take off the fan shroud's upper support bracket. Undo the bolt that secures the bottom radiator support bracket to the transmission housing. Remove the hose clamps from the upper and lower radiator hoses; then remove the hoses themselves. Disconnect the heater hose. Take off the hose that runs from the radiator to the expansion tank, and remove its attendant clip. Unscrew the screws that attach the fan shroud to the radiator, withdraw the upper section of the shroud, and lift out the radiator. Replacement of the radiator is the reverse of its removal.

To refill the system, close the heater valve and disconnect the heater hose. Using a funnel, fill the cooling system until the radiator is filled all the way to the top. Check the coolant level in the expansion tank, it should be 2-1/4 in. deep. Reconnect the heater hose and open the heater valve. Replace both radiator cap and the expansion tank cap. Run the engine until it reaches normal operating temperature. Shut the engine off and allow it to cool; serious injury could result if the cap is removed with engine hot! Remove the radiator cap and check the coolant level, adding water if necessary.

Water Pump

Removal and Installation

Austin-Healey

Remove the radiator and the generator. Remove the water pump from the crankcase by undoing the four bolts that hold it in place. Lift the fan and the pump out together, then remove the fan belt.

Reinstallation is the reverse of removal. Be sure to replace the gasket between the pump body and the block. Adjust the fan belt so that it is properly tensioned. Lubricate the pump by removing the lubrication plug on the pump housing, and adding a *small* quantity of grease. Using too much grease will cause the carbon sealing ring to operate inefficiently.

Sprite

The procedure for removing the water pump from the Mk. I (Bugeye) Sprite is similar to that for the Austin-Healey 100-6, and 3000. The later series, especially those that have emission equipment, require a slightly different procedure.

Drain the cooling system and take out the radiator. Unscrew the fan retaining bolts and remove the fan. On cars with an air pump installation, loosen the bolts that mount the air pump, and remove the drive belt from it. The air pump's adjusting link bolt should be removed and the air pump lifted as high as the hoses will allow. Retighten the mounting bolts so that the pump is held in place out of the way.

Loosen the generator (or alternator) mounting bolts, and remove the fan belt. Remove the top mounting bolts from the generator; swing the generator down so that it rests on the wheel arch.

Disconnect the bypass hose, and the bottom hose of the radiator, from the water pump and heater tube. Undo the four bolts that attach the water pump to the cylinder block, and lift out the water pump. Reinstallation is the reverse of the above. Be sure to use a new gasket between the pump and the block. Adjust the tension on all of the drive belts.

Austin America

Drain the water from the cooling system; then remove the radiator. Remove the hose that goes to the water pump intake, and loosen the top clamp on the thermostat bypass hose. Remove the generator (or alternator), and the air pump, along with their attendant drive belts. Undo the four bolts that hold the fan blades on to the hub of the water pump. Remove the blades and the hub.

Remove the four bolts that attach the pump to the block; withdraw the pump and the hose together. Remounting is the reverse of removal. Fit a new gasket between the pump and the block. Adjust all drive belts so that they are tensioned properly.

Maintenance

Aside from lubrication, any repair work that must be done to the water pump presents certain difficulties. Special tools are required, and the cost of replacement parts

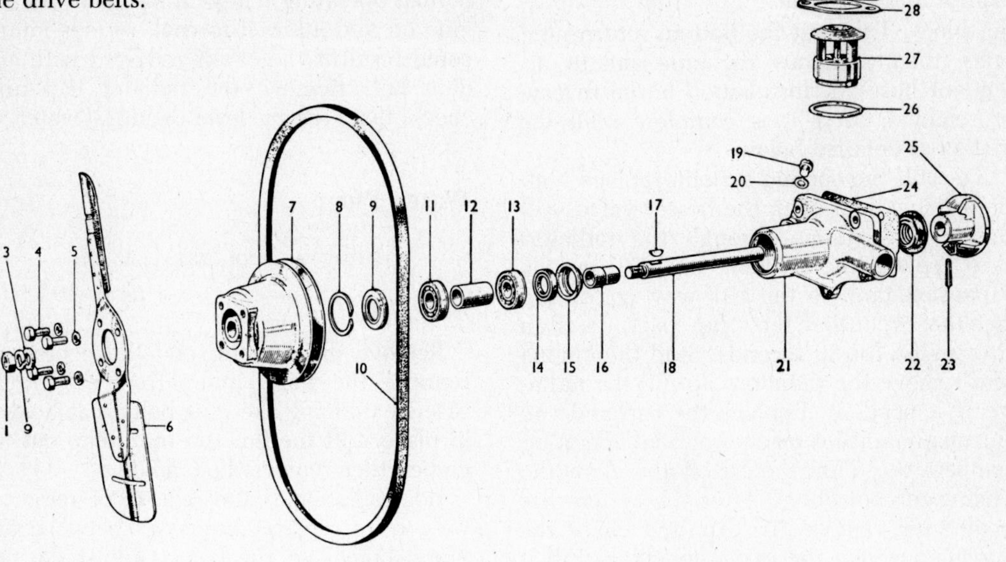

The Austin-Healey water pump

1 Spindle nut
2 Spring washer
3 Plain washer
4 Fan blade bolts
5 Spring washer
6 Fan (some early models have 2 blades)
7 Fan pulley
8 Snap-ring
9 Grease retainer
10 Fan belt
11 Ball race
12 Spacer
13 Ball race
14 Rubber seal
15 Seal housing
16 Spacer
17 Key
18 Spindle
19 Oil plug
20 Fiber washer
21 Pump body
22 Water seal
23 Locking pin
24 Gasket
25 Impeller
26 Gasket
27 Thermostat
28 Gasket
29 Thermostat cover

is as much as a rebuilt pump, with an old pump in exchange.

Lubricate the water pump by removing the lubrication plug and filling the fitting with lubricant. Do not over lubricate the pump or use a grease gun on it, as this forces grease past the bearings, which tends to interfere with the operation of the carbon seal. On late Sprites there is no lubrication plug; the pump is sealed and requires no attention.

Thermostat

To remove the thermostat, drain the cooling system. Undo the hose clamp and disconnect the top hose. Remove the nuts and washers that hold the thermostat cover in place. Lift the cover off the mounting studs, and remove the old paper gasket. Be sure that all surfaces are clean and free from pieces of old gasket. Lift out the thermostat, being careful to note which side of it goes up, and inspect it for damage.

Test the thermostat by immersing it in water of the proper temperature (see chart). If the valve fails to open, or if it sticks open, replace the thermostat. Do not attempt to repair it.

Installation is the reverse of removal. CAUTION: *The threaded stem goes up.* IF *the thermostat is improperly installed it may destroy the engine.* Install a new paper gasket to prevent leaks.

Thermostat Usage

Model & Engine	*Thermostat (deg. F.)*
Austin-Healey	
26C/26D/29D/29E/	
29F (early)	158°
All cars from 29F 2592	182°
Sprite	
9C	154°-157°
9CG	149°-158°
	180° (Standard)
10CG/10CC/12CC/12CD	165° (Hot climates)
	190° (Cold climates)
Austin America	180° (Standard)
12H	165° (Hot climates)
	190° (Cold climates)

Exhaust Emission Controls

Any automobile imported to the U.S.A. from 1968 on, must be equipped with an exhaust emission control system to reduce engine emissions to a specified level. As the Austin-Healey was not imported after 1967, the only emission control found on it is a positive crankcase ventilation (PCV) valve. In addition to the PCV valve, the Sprites and Austin Americas imported since 1968, have an exhaust port air injection system. The 1971 Austin America has the required evaporative loss control system, as well. This is not found on the Sprite, as importation ceased after 1970. In addition to the air injection system, the America uses engine modifications to control exhaust emissions.

Positive Crankcase Ventilation (PCV)

The positive crankcase ventilation system incorporates a control valve and an oil separator which are connected by a hose that runs to the intake manifold and the crankcase respectively. The four-cylinder engines are equipped with a filtered, restricted orifice oil breather cap. Six-cylinder engines have a standard breather cap; a line connects the oil filler pipe on the rocker cover with the air cleaner to supply fresh air to the engine.

The pressure changes in the intake manifold act upon the PCV valve causing the opening to the crankcase to vary in size. A positive pressure in the intake manifold causes the valve to open, thus allowing crankcase vapors to be drawn into the manifold. At low engine speeds and loads a vacuum is formed; the diaphragm closes the valve, and the flow into the intake manifold is restricted. This prevents the fuel mixture from becoming too lean. The oil separator keeps engine oil from being pulled in to the intake manifold along with the crankcase vapors.

Testing and Servicing the PCV System

The PCV valve should be checked frequently. At the least, its failure can lead to a build-up of deposits in the crankcase; at worst it can burn a valve or piston.

Allow the engine to warm-up to normal running temperature. With the engine at idle, remove the breather cap; if engine speed rises, then the valve is working properly. If there is no change in engine speed the valve is stuck open. If the valve appears to be working normally replace the breather cap, and with the engine still running at idle, place a finger over the vent hole on the valve. Again listen to a rise in engine speed; if none occurs, service or replace the valve. Another indication that the valve is stuck open is a loud hissing sound, if this is present, then there is a hole in the diaphragm. If the hiss is heard, proceed with the two tests given above.

Dirt and deposits may cause the valve to stick closed. If this is suspected, remove the hose that runs from the oil separator to the PCV valve, at the oil separator's end. Run the engine up to about 2,500 rpm; if no suction is felt, the valve is stuck closed. It must be dismantled and cleaned to free it.

To begin dismantling the valve, first disconnect the hoses. Remove the spring-clip, cover plate, metering valve, and spring. Clean all metal parts in a non-oily solvent; *never use an abrasive.* If the deposits are stubborn, boil the metal parts in water, then use the solvent again.

Inspect the diaphragm for holes or cracks, if any are present it must be replaced. If it is in good condition clean it off with a detergent; do not use fuel or alchohol, as this will cause the diaphagm to deteriorate.

Check the other parts for wear and replace them where necessary. If most of the parts are worn it will be cheaper to replace the whole PCV valve assembly with a new unit.

Reassembly and replacement are the reverse of the above. Be sure that the metering valve is correctly positioned in its guides, and that the diaphragm is properly seated. Run the test procedures to make sure that the PCV valve is functioning in the proper manner.

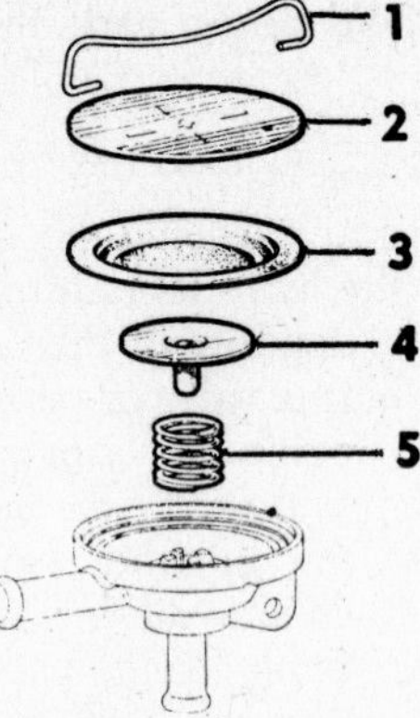

The positive crankcase valve (PCV)—emission controlled engines

1 Spring clip
2 Cover
3 Diaphragm
4 Metering valve
5 Valve spring

Exhaust Port Air Injection

Operation

Air is drawn through a dry element air filter into a rotary vane air pump, which is driven by a belt from the water pump pulley. The air is routed from these, through a manifold, to an air injection nozzle in the cylinder head exhaust port of each cylinder. A check valve placed in the air delivery line prevents exhaust gases from flowing back into the pump. If pressure from the pump stops, e.g., the drive belt breaks, the check valve closes.

The pump also supplies air to the intake manifold via a gulp (anti-backfire) valve. This is done to make the mixture leaner during deceleration. A sensing line runs from the gulp valve to the intake manifold to meter manifold pressure. A rapid increase in manifold vacuum, because of throttle closure, opens the valve, causing air to enter the intake manifold.

Some engines have a restrictor in the line from the air pump to the gulp valve, to prevent a surge from occurring when the gulp valve opens.

Testing and Servicing

Air Pump

It must be remembered that the air injection system will not work properly if the engine is not tuned to the manufacturer's exact specifications. Not only should the system be maintained so that it works properly; but valve clearance, spark plug gaps, carburetor settings, etc., must be correct as well. This is done not only to control emissions, but also to insure proper running and a long life for the engine.

The air pump drive belt tension should be checked regularly, along with the fan belt tension. The belt should deflect 1/2 in. with moderate hand pressure. If it does not, proceed as follows: loosen the mounting bolt and the link bolt. With only hand pressure, slide the pump in the proper direction• the bolts to 10 ft. lbs. of torque; do not overtighten.

To test the air pump circuit, a tachometer and pressure gauge (showing psi) are needed. Connect the tachometer according to the manufacturer's instructions. Remove the air hose that goes to the gulp valve, at the gulp valve end, and plug up the hose. Undo the air manifold hose, at the check valve end, and connect the pressure gauge

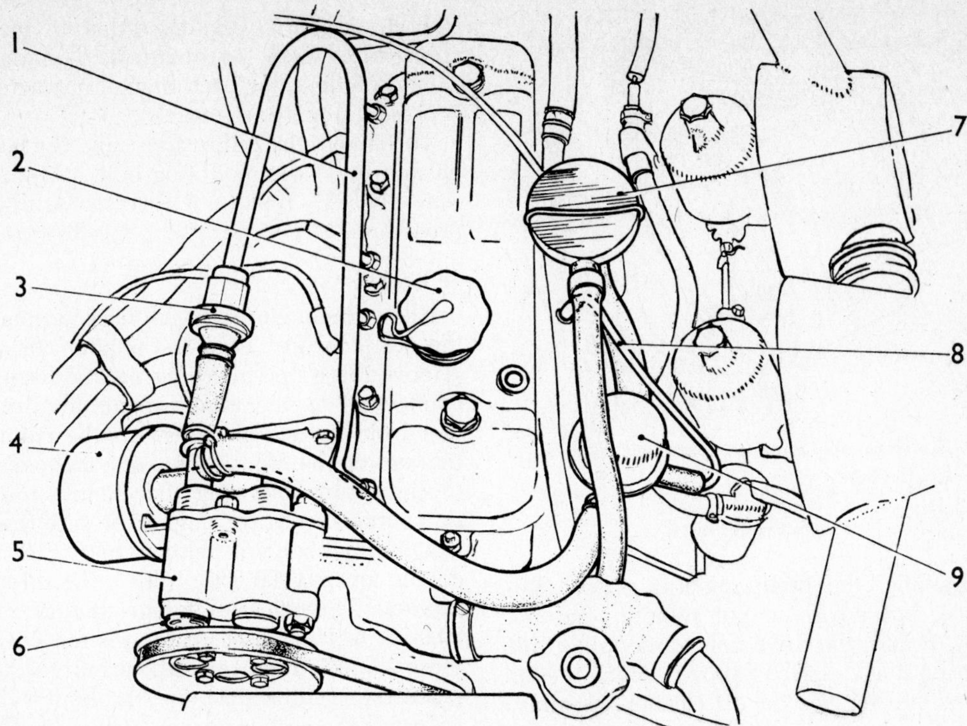

The air injection system—emission controlled engines

1 Air manifold
2 Filtered oil filler cap
3 Check valve
4 Emission air cleaner
5 Air pump
6 Relief valve
7 Crankcase emission valve
8 Vacuum sensing tube
9 Gulp (anti-backfire) valve

to the hose. Start the engine and run it up to 1,200 rpm. The gauge should read, at least, 2.75 psi. If it does not, replace the pump air cleaner element. Retest the system. If the reading is still too low, plug the pump relief valve. CAUTION: *Do not use a finger to stop the air flow from the relief valve.*

Repeat the test. If the reading is correct, the check valve is at fault, and must be replaced.

If the reading is still too low, the pump is defective, and it must be repaired or replaced.

To remove the air pump for servicing or replacement, first take off the pump air cleaner assembly. Remove all of the air hoses. Loosen the mounting and link bolts; slide the drive belt off of the pump pulley. Finish taking off the adjusting link bolt and the mounting nut. Support the pump with one hand; with the other, remove the mounting bolt. Lift the pump clear of the engine.

CAUTION: *Never use a tool to grip the pump, nor put it in a vise; the case will become distorted and the pump will be destroyed.*

Servicing the pump requires special tools and lubricants. Great care must be taken not to damage the pump housing. Because of this, service of the pump should be left to qualified technicians.

Reinstall the pump by replacing it in its mounting bracket and inserting, but not

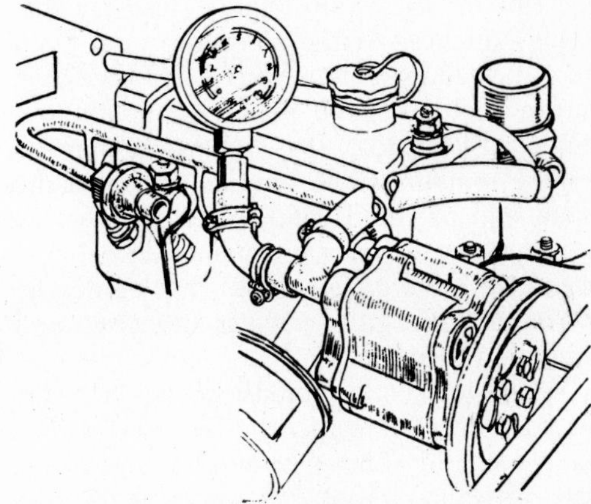

Using a pressure gauge to test an air pump

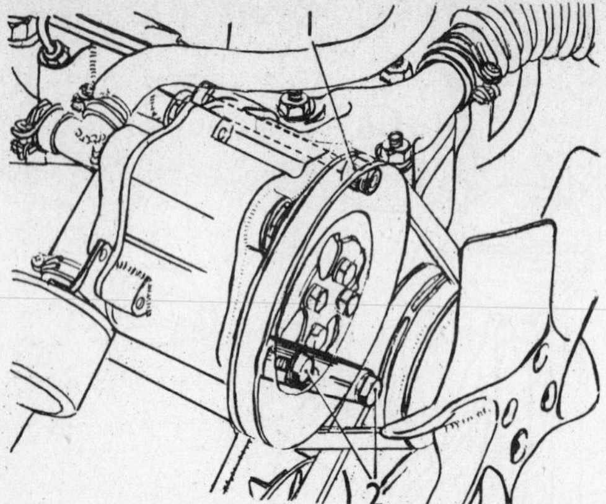

The air pump—emission controlled engines

1 Pump mounting bolt
2 Adjusting link bolts

tightening, the pump mounting bolt. Replace, but again do not tighten, the link bolt. Return the drive belt to its pulley and tension it as described above. Attach the air hoses and replace the air cleaner assembly.

Check Valve

Remove the air hose from the check valve connection; then while holding the air manifold connection so that it doesn't twist, unscrew the check valve.

Try to blow through the valve orally from each connection.

CAUTION: *Do not use compressed air to test the valve; the valve will be destroyed.*

If air passes through the air manifold connection, the valve is defective and it must be replaced. Air should only pass through the check valve from the air hose connection.

Gulp Valve

Remove the gulp vale (anti-backfire valve) air hose at the air pump end. Connect a vacuum gauge with a T connector, to the free end of the air hose. Start the engine and let it idle. It is important that the engine remain at idle for this test. Seal the open end of the T, and check to see if a reading of zero can be maintained for 15 seconds. If the gauge shows that a vacuum is present, the gulp valve is defective and must be replaced.

With the T connector still sealed, accelerate and decelerate the engine rapidly. The gauge should show a vacuum. Repeat the test, unsealing the open end of the T momentarily before acceleration each time. This destroys the vacuum so that an accurate reading may be obtained. The result should be the same each time, if no vacuum is present, replace the valve.

To remove the gulp valve, take the hoses off and undo the mounting bolt. Withdraw the valve. To replace it reverse the above procedure.

Limit Valve

Allow the engine to reach normal operating temperature. Turn the engine off, and remove the gulp valve sensing line from its connection to the intake manifold. Run a line from a vacuum gauge to the connection on the manifold. Connect a tachometer to engine by following the manufacturer's instructions. Start the engine, be sure that it is at normal running temperature. Run the engine up to 3,000 rpm; release the throttle rapidly. The vacuum gauge should read 20.5-22 in. Hg. If the reading is not within these limits, remove the carburetor; replace the throttle disc and the limit valve. Reinstall the carburetor and retune it. (See the section on carburetors.)

Engine Modifications—Austin America

In addition to the air injection system, the Austin America has several other modifications made to the engine to reduce the level of exhaust emissions. These consist of a throttle damper, and an adjustable intake on the air cleaner.

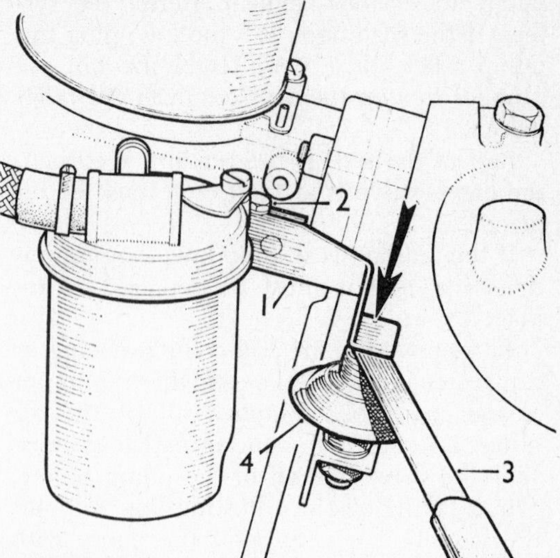

Throttle damper adjustment—emission controlled engines

1 Throttle lever
2 Clamp screw
3 Feeler gauge
4 Throttle damper

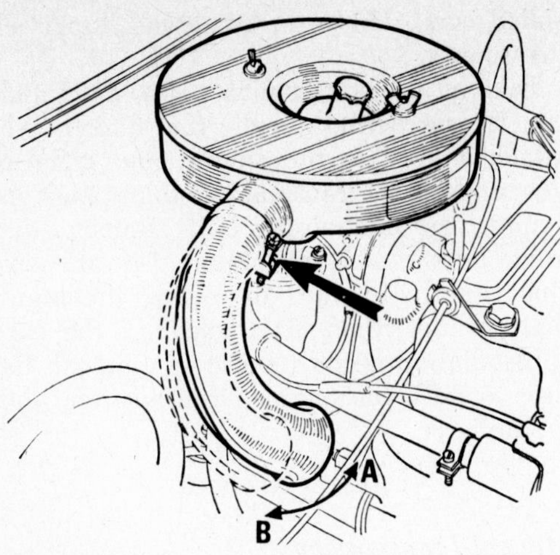

The Austin America carburetor air intake can be rotated for either winter (A) or summer (B) driving.

The damper is installed on the throttle lever to slow down throttle closure during deceleration. The damper occasionally needs to be adjusted.

To do this, loosen the clamp nut on the damper lever. Place a 0.10 in. feeler gauge between the plunger and the operating arm. Press the lever down all the way, with the carburetor butterfly completely closed. With the lever being held in this position, tighten the clamp nut. Slide the feeler gauge out from between the plunger and arm.

To adjust the intake on the air cleaner for high and low temperature ranges, loosen the wing nuts, on top of the air cleaner, and the intake fastening clamp. Remove the intake from the air cleaner. Depending upon the temperature, reposition the intake near the rocker cover (hot weather) or in the manifold shroud (cold weather). Retighten the intake clamp and the wing nuts.

Engine

Removal and Installation

Austin-Healey

Turn off the battery master switch, which is found inside the trunk. Drain the oil from the engine sump. Remove the hood by undoing the nuts and bolts on each hood bracket, and lifting the hood off. Drain the cooling system and remove the radiator. Unscrew the four bolts that hold the fan in place, and remove the fan.

Detach the throttle linkage by unclamping the control rod at the firewall. Remove the air cleaners. Take the fuel line off at the carburetor union. Detach the high tension cables at both the coil and the spark plugs. Undo the low tension cables that run to the generator, coil, and the distributor; lay these aside as one unit. Remove the tachometer drive from the distributor. Unclamp the heater intake and outlet hoses. Remove the distributor (see the section on ignition) and the generator, along with its coil (see the generator section). Take off the oil filter; then remove the oil pressure line at its upper connection. Detach the starter motor. Undo the four bolts which attach each engine mounting bracket to the frame. NOTE: *Removal of the left-side bracket is made easier by a slot provided in the carburetor heat shield.*

Remove the six brass nuts that hold the exhaust headpipe on to the exhaust manifold, then lower it from the manifold studs. Take the valve rocker assembly out by removing the twelve nuts that attach its brackets to the head. Using two suitable lifting brackets, and a hoist, support the engine so that its mounting brackets are slightly clear of the chassis mounts. Remove the four bolts that fix the right-hand engine mounting bracket to the cylinder block, and remove the bracket.

With a suitable support placed under the transmission bellhousing, remove the nuts and bolts that attach the bellhousing to the engine. Lift the engine to provide clearance between the crankshaft damper and the frame crossmember. Pull the engine forward so that the clutch disc slides off the input shaft splines. The engine may now be lifted through the hood opening and clear of the car.

Installation is the reverse of removal. Be sure to refill the engine and radiator, and see that all lines and cables are securely connected.

Sprite

To remove the engine from the Sprite, disconnect the battery and drain the crankcase. Remove the hood from its hinges. On the Mk. I Sprite (Bugeye) this requires some extra steps:

First, disconnect the wiring harness that runs to the headlights and parking lights, at

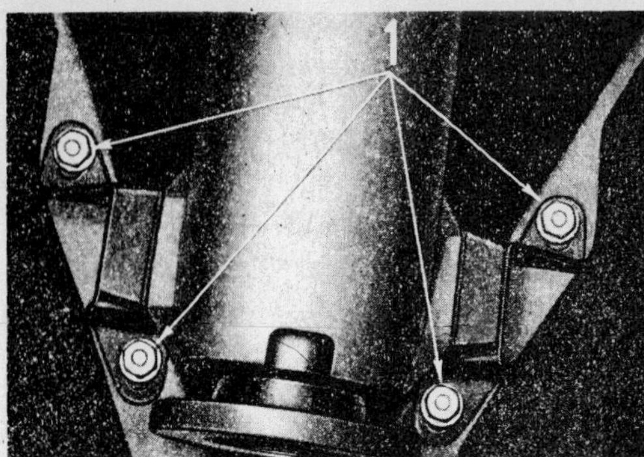

The Austin-Healey 3000 transmission rear upper support bracket with four securing bolts (1).

Austin-Healey 3000 lower transmission securing points: (1) bolts, (2) stabilizer adjusting nut, and (3) securing pin.

the snap connectors that are located by the right-hand hinge. Then remove the harness from the hinge, itself, by undoing the bolt at the top of the hood support. Undo the four bolts that attach each hinge to the hood; lift the hood clear of the car.

On later Sprites, remove the bolts that hold the hood on the hinges. Drain the cooling system, disconnect the heater hose and remove the radiator. On late models undo the oil cooler lines. Disconnect the choke and throttle cables. On Mk. I and Mk. II models remove the tachometer cable. Disconnect the oil pressure gauge line from the engine. Disconnect all of the electrical connections, and mark them, to make reassembly easier. Undo the high tension wires from the coil and spark plugs; remove the distributor cap.

Unbolt the exhaust header pipe from the manifold, and tie the pipe out of the way. Remove the air cleaner and fuel line from the carburetors. On exhaust emission controlled cars, remove any lines necessary at this time.

Take off the starter motor. On Mk. I and Mk. II cars, withdraw the fuel filter bowl. Attach a hoist to the engine, and place a jack under the transmission to support it. Remove the bellhousing bolts. Remove the front, left-side engine mount. Lift the engine slightly forward to release the input shaft splines, then lift it clear of the car.

Installation is the reverse of removal. Be sure to refill the engine, transmission, and the radiator.

Austin America

Manual Transmission

Drain the cooling system and the sump. Take off the hood. Remove the ground cable from the clutch housing, and the cables from the distributor, coil, and generator (alternator). Take off the starter motor. Remove the air cleaner, emission control hoses and the carburetor. Remove the control cable and water hose from the heater valve on the cylinder head. Unfasten the heater hose from the return pipe.

Take the tension spring off of the clutch lever, remove the mounting bolts from the slave cylinder. Attach the cylinder unit on the suspension so that it is clear of the engine. Under *no* circumstances disconnect the fluid line. Remove the clamp that attaches the exhaust pipe to the manifold. Unfasten the overflow hose from the radiator and its shroud.

On early cars disconnect the speedometer cable from the transmission housing. On later cars disconnect it at the cable coupling.

Remove the boot from the gearshift and unscrew the retaining plate screws; pull out the gearshift lever. Remove the two bolts that attach the shift linkage housing to the floor tunnel.

Using a jack, lift up the front of the car and place supports under the frame rails. Detach the exhaust pipe from the transmission housing. Undo the bolts (two on each side) that attach the shift linkage housing to the differential housing; then remove the linkage housing.

Remove the U-bolts which join the axle shafts to the inner universal joint trunnions. Slide the axles away to provide adequate clearance when removing the engine.

Undo the nuts that hold the left-side engine mount to the mounting plate. Remove the two right-side cylinder head nuts, slip a chain link over the studs and replace the bolts. Support the engine weight using the hoist, and unbolt the right engine mounting bracket to the sub-frame. Lift the power unit from the car (this includes the engine/transmission, and the radiator). Be sure that the wiring, hoses, and lines are clear of the engine.

Reinstallation is the reverse of removal. Refill the cooling system as detailed in the section that deals with it above.

Austin America

Automatic Transmission

Disconnect the battery and remove the battery tray.

To perform the next few operations, it is necessary to crawl underneath the car. Remove the coverplate from the bell-crank lever, or, on early cars pull back the rubber boot. Detach the yoke that holds the selector cable to the bell-crank lever. Loosen the clamp nut and take off the yoke, the rubber ferrules and the sleeve. Undo the cable adjusting nut, at the front of the cable, and free the cable from the transmission. Remove the cable clamp, and tie the cable out of the way. Take the exhaust bracket off the transmission housing. Using a jack or some other suitable and *safe* means, lift the front of the car so that the wheels may be rotated. Undo the nuts that attach the driveshaft flanges. Detach the lower engine brace. Remove the nuts that hold the rear engine mount on the sub-frame. Drain the cooling system; remove the heater hoses, the control cable for the water valve, and the water valve return line.

The next series of operations are performed from above the car. Disconnect the hood support and tie back the hood, out of the way. Disconnect the speedometer cable. Remove the ground cable from its body mount; disconnect the cables from the coil, starter, and generator (alternator). Remove the distributor cap. Undo the wing nuts that attach the air cleaner and remove it. Remove the emission control hoses, the choke and accelerator cables and the fuel line.

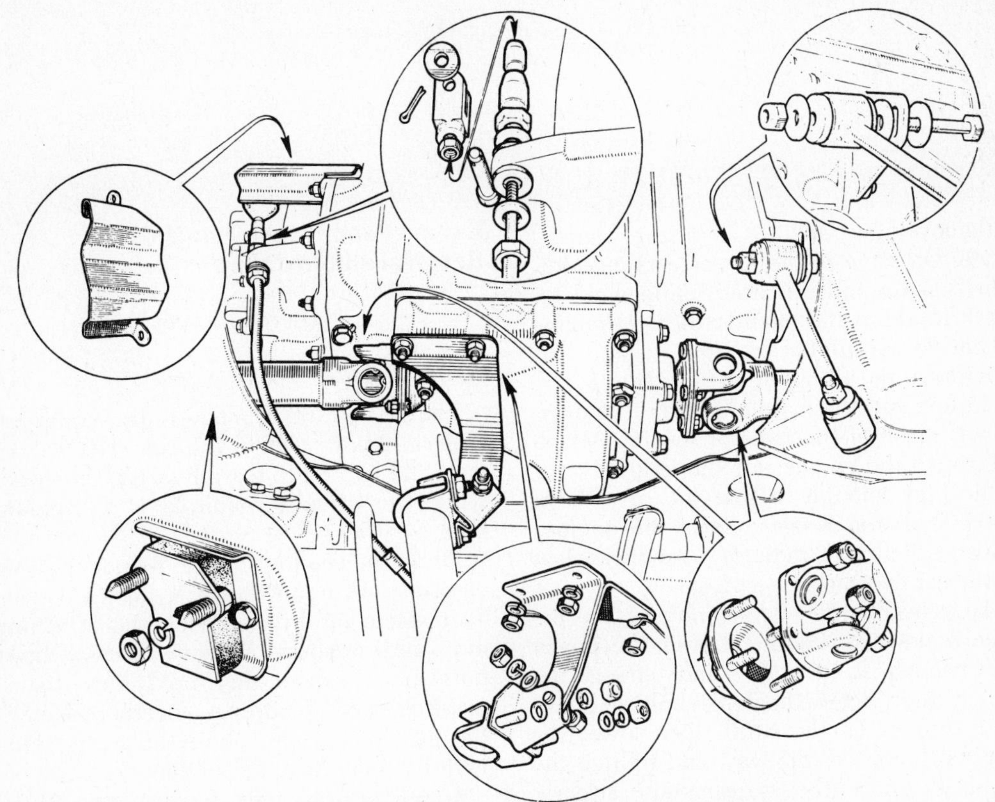

Remove these items from underneath the engine—America

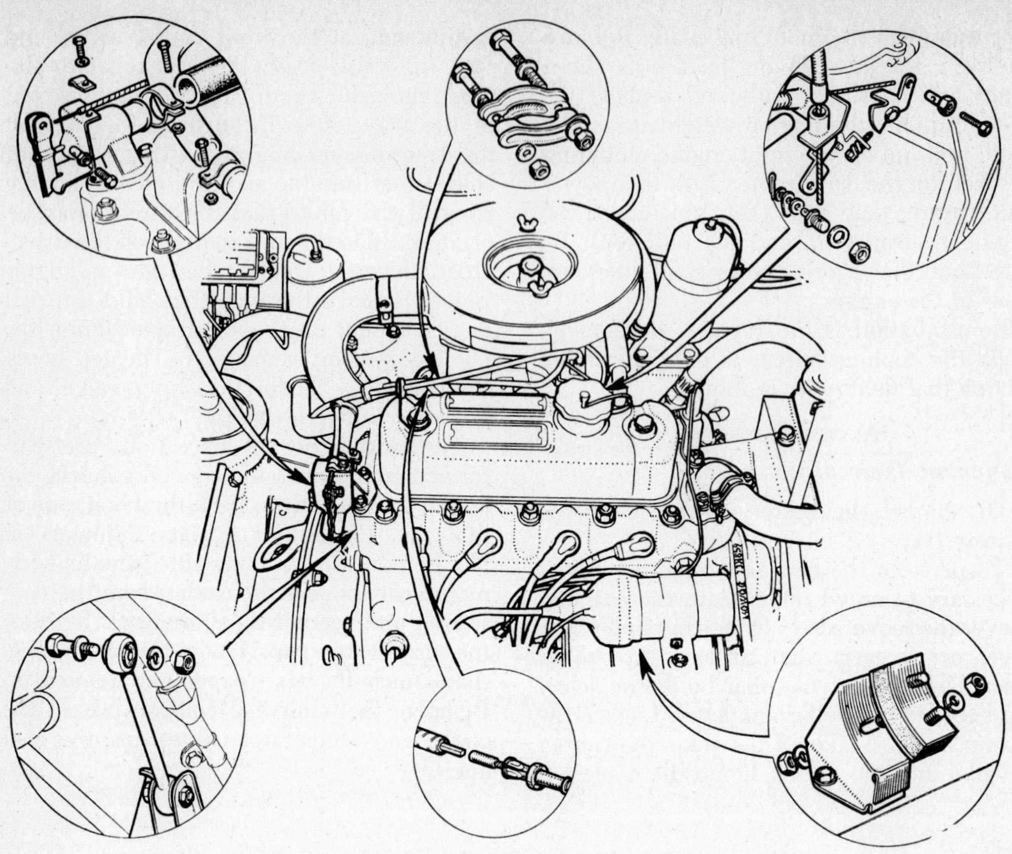

Remove these items from the top of the engine—America

Remove the engine stabilizer support brace. On some of the newer cars an additional engine brace is used; unbolt and remove it. Undo the nuts on the two engine mounts at the front of the car.

Remove the clamp at the junction of the headpipe and the manifold. Take the overflow hose off of the radiator shroud. Attach a hoist to the engine; lift the engine vertically, high enough so that the driveshafts are free of the flanges. Raise the engine/transmission and radiator assembly clear of the car to remove it.

To reinstall the engine, reverse the engine removal procedure. Lower the power unit enough, so that driveshafts engage the flange studs. Screw the flange bolts in about four threads on the studs; then lower the engine the rest of the way, and tighten the nuts. Readjust the transmission selector cable and rod. Refill the cooling system.

Exhaust and Intake Manifold Removal and Installation

Austin-Healey

2-Port Cylinder Head

The early 100-6 models are equipped with a 2-port cylinder head. The intake manifold is cast integrally with the head, while the exhaust manifold is a separate unit.

Drain the cooling system. Remove the air cleaners and undo the PCV line. Take the heat shield off by removing the attaching nuts and washers. Remove the six brass nuts and washers that hold the exhaust manifold and headpipes together. Detach the accelerator and choke linkages; along with the vacuum and fuel lines.

Undo the four nuts and washers on the carburetor flanges, and the ten nuts on the

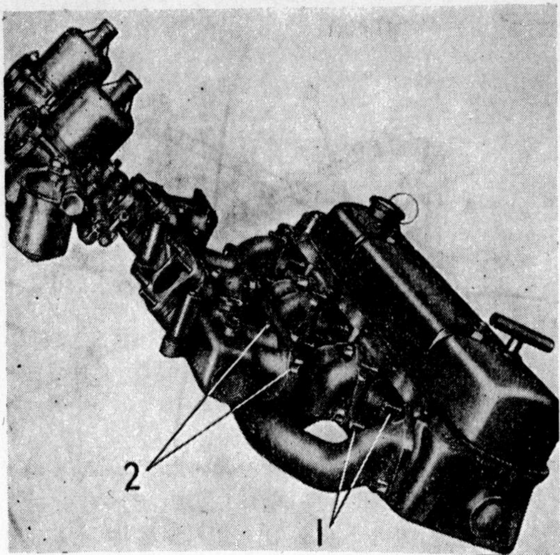

The 6-port cylinder head, from an Austin-Healey, with the intake manifold detached

1 Intake manifold mounting studs
2 Mounting holes in the intake manifold

exhaust manifold. Withdraw the manifold and carburetor assembly from the studs.

Reinstallation is the reverse of the above. Remember to use a new manifold gasket, and to refill the cooling system.

6-Port Cylinder Head

Later 100-6 models and all 3000 models have a 6-port cylinder head which uses separate exhaust and intake manifolds.

Remove the air cleaners and the attendant PCV line from the carburetors. Next, remove the linkages, and the fuel line from the carburetors. Take the heat shield off the intake manifold. Remove the intake manifold by undoing the nine nuts that attach it to the cylinder head.

The exhaust manifold is detached by removing the six brass nuts and washers that attach the head pipes to it. Next, undo the eight nuts that attach the manifold to the head. It may now be withdrawn from the studs and lifted clear of the engine.

Reinstallation is the reverse of removal. Be sure to replace the manifold gaskets to keep the manifolds from leaking.

SPRITE

Drain the cooling system. Remove the air cleaners and PCV lines from the carburetors. Remove the carburetors, the fuel lines, the carburetor linkages, and the emission control system lines (if present). Also, remove the lines that run from the gulp valve to the manifold, on cars that have an air injection system. Detach the water line bracket from the intake manifold. Remove the six nuts and washers that hold the exhaust and intake manifolds on to the head. NOTE: *The four center washers are different from the two outside washers; care should be taken so that they are not mixed.*

Withdraw the intake and exhaust manifold assembly from the mounting studs. Lift the assembly clear of the engine.

To take apart the exhaust and intake manifold assembly; remove the four bolts that hold the manifolds together. Be sure to note the position of the special gasket that goes between them.

Reassembly and reinstallation are the reverse of the above. New gaskets should be used to prevent any chance of leaks.

AUSTIN AMERICA

Remove the air cleaner and the PCV line. Remove the emission system lines, throttle linkages, fuel lines, and the carburetor. Detach the gulp valve lines from the intake manifold. Undo the nuts, that attach the manifolds. Removal of the manifolds is similar to that of the Sprite above.

Reinstallation is the reverse of removal. Be sure to replace the old manifold gasket with a new one.

Cylinder Head

REMOVAL

The basic removal procedures for the cylinder heads used on the Austin-Healey, the Sprite, and the America are the same. However, there are some minor differences; these will be noted where necessary. There are a few important points to remember when removing any cylinder head:

The cylinder head nuts should be loosened gradually, and in the same sequence that they are tightened, to prevent the head from warping (see Tightening Sequences). For this same reason, the head should be removed only when the engine is *cold.* With the nuts and all of the accessories unbolted from the head, it may be necessary to tap each side of the head with a *rubber* mallet to break the head gasket seal. When the head is free, lift it off the studs evenly. If any water is present in the cylinders, it should be removed immediately, and the cylinder walls coated with oil. If the head is to be left off for more than a day, clean towels should be stuffed into the cylinders to protect them.

To remove the cylinder head on the Healey, the Sprite and the America proceed as follows: Drain the cooling system. On the Austin-Healey turn the battery master switch off; on the Sprite and the America, disconnect the negative side of the battery. Detach the radiator and heater hoses from the head. Remove the vacuum advance line from its clamp on the head. Remove the heater control valve. On the America unbolt the top radiator bracket. Remove the air cleaner(s), the carburetor(s), and their attendant assemblies. Remove the manifolds as detailed in the section that deals with them above. Remove the rocker cover, and unbolt the cylinder head nuts in the *proper* sequence (see Tightening Sequences).

Lift the rocker shaft assembly off, and remove the pushrods. It is important to keep the pushrods in their correct order. Remove the spark plugs and disconnect the water temperature sending unit from the head. On cars equipped with an air injection system, disconnect the air supply hose from the check valve; also, remove the air pump from its mount on the head. Lift the head from the cylinder block.

Installation

Installation is the reverse of the removal procedure. There are some important points to be noted, however. Clean the surfaces of the cylinder block and head thoroughly. Always replace the head gasket with a new one. The gasket is marked front and/or top to make installation easier. Gasket sealing compound is not necessary, but may be used. Return the vacuum advance line and its clamp to the proper position on the head. Replace the washers on the studs in the correct order. Cylinder head nuts should be tightened gradually, in the *proper* sequence (see Tightening Sequences), and to the proper torque value (see Torque Specifications). The pushrods must be installed in the same positions from which they were taken.

When the head has been tightened the valves must be adjusted to specifications. After the engine has been run for 100 to 200 miles the head should be retorqued and the valves readjusted. When retorquing the head, back off on each nut slightly, and retighten them, one at a time, in the proper sequence.

Valve Train

Valve Adjustment

The valve clearances for the Austin-Healey, the Sprite, and the America may be found in Tune-Up Specifications. Adjustments should be performed at every tune-up, or when excessive valve train noise is present. Loose clearances will only cause over-abundant valve train noise, as a rule; while over-tight adjustment can cause rough idling, and will lead to burnt valves.

To adjust the valves on all models, remove the valve covers, and provide some means of rotating the engine slowly. The engine may be rotated by hand, by use of the ignition switch, or by means of a remote control starter switch, attached by following the manufacturer's instructions. On all of the models, except the Austin-Healey 100-6 and the Mk. I Sprite (Bugeye), the valves are adjusted when the engine is *cold.* On the Mk. I Sprite and the 100-6 the valves are adjusted when the engine is *hot.* With the valve fully closed, insert a feeler gauge of the proper size between the valve stem and the adjustment screw tip (see Tune-Up Specifications).

If adjustment is needed, loosen the locknut while applying pressure to the adjustment screw with a screw driver. Reinsert the proper size feeler gauge in place, and raise or lower the adjustment screw until the clearance is correct. Tighten the locknut; but be sure to check the valve clearance again after the locknut has been tightened, in case the adjustment was disturbed. Check each valve when it is fully closed by following the same procedure.

Replace the valve cover. Use a new gasket if the old one is damaged, be sure that it is correctly seated to prevent any damage.

Removal and Installation of the Valve Rocker Shaft Assembly

The removal and reinstallation procedure for the rocker shaft assembly on the Healey, the Sprite, and the America is the same. On cars equipped with air injection, it may be necessary to remove some of the lines to get the valve cover off. On the America the air cleaner must be removed in order to gain access to the valve cover.

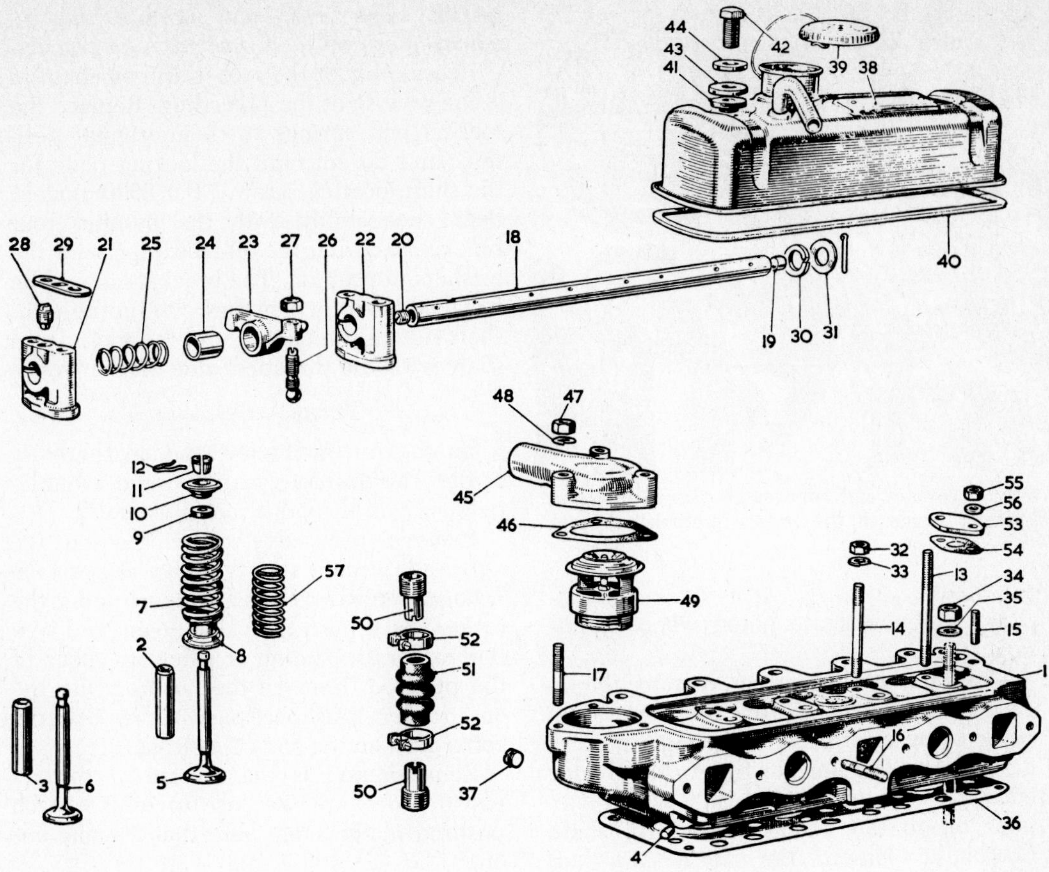

Sprite cylinder head and valve gear components.

1 Cylinder head with valve guides
2 Intake valve guide
3 Exhaust valve guide
4 Oil hole plug
5 Intake valve
6 Exhaust valve
7 Outer valve spring
8 Shroud for valve guide
9 Valve packing ring
10 Valve spring cup
11 Valve cotter
12 Valve cotter circlip
13 Rocker bracket stud (long)
14 Rocker bracket stud (short)
15 Cover-plate stud
16 Manifold stud
17 Water outlet elbow stud
18 Valve rocker shaft (plugged)
19 Rocker shaft plug (plain)
20 Rocker shaft plug (screwed)
21 Rocker shaft bracket (tapped)
22 Rocker shaft bracket (plain)
23 Rocker (bushed)
24 Rocker bushing
25 Rocker spacing spring
26 Tappet adjusting screw
27 Locknut
28 Rocker shaft locating screw
29 Rocker shaft bracket plate
30 Spring washer
31 Washer
32 Nut
33 Spring washer
34 Cylinder head nut
35 Washer
36 Cylinder head gasket
37 Temperature indicator plug
38 Valve rocker cover
39 Oil filler cap
40 Cover gasket
41 Cover bushing
42 Nut
43 Spacer
44 Cup washer
45 Water outlet elbow
46 Gasket
47 Nut
48 Spring washer
49 Thermostat
50 By-pass adaptor
51 By-pass connector (rubber)
52 By-pass clip
53 Cover-plate
54 Gasket (plate to cylinder head)
55 Cover nut
56 Spring washer
57 Inner valve spring

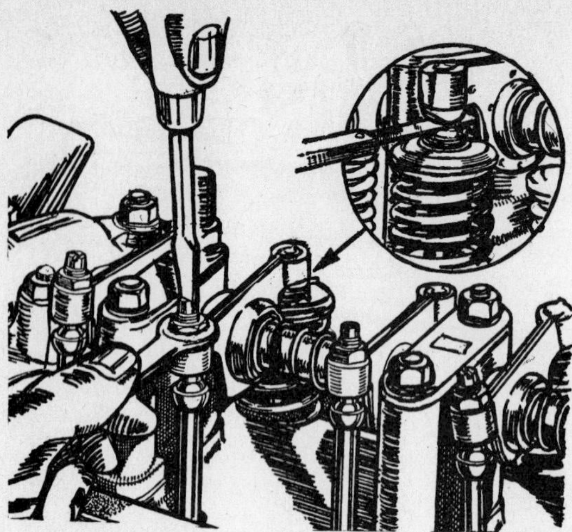

Valve clearance and adjustment—the insert shows a feeler gauge in the proper position to check valve clearance.

Other differences are noted where necessary.

Drain the cooling system. Remove the securing bolts and lift off the rocker-arm cover being careful not to damage the cork gasket. At this point, for the Austin-Healey 3000, remove the oil-feed pipe which supplies oil to the hollow rocker-arm shaft. Gradually loosen the rocker-arm-shaft bracket securing nuts and external cylinder-head nuts until tension is released on the studs. The order of loosening is the same as that in which the cylinder head is tightened down. The cylinder-head nuts must be loosened along with the bracket nuts because four of the nuts holding the rocker-arm shaft to the cylinder head also serve to retain the head itself. If the bracket and cylinder-head nuts are not slackened gradually in the proper order, distortion could result by water being able to enter the cylinder bores. Remove the bracket securing nuts completely and lift off the rocker assembly, complete with brackets. Withdraw the push rods and store them carefully so that they may be replaced to their original positions.

Disassembly of the rocker-arm shaft is as follows: Remove the set screw which locates the shaft at the rear mounting bracket. Remove the cotter pins, flat washers, and spring washers from both ends of the shaft. Slide the rocker arms, brackets, and springs from the shaft. Remove the plug at the end of the shaft so that the interior of the shaft may be cleaned.

NOTE: *The 3000 will require the removal of the oil-feed pipe from its bracket.*

Reassembly of the rocker-arm mechanism is the reverse of the preceding. Replace the rockers and springs to their original positions and do not omit the locking plate for the shaft-locating screw. (For 3000 models, begin reassembly with the number four bracket, securing the oil-feed pipe with the washers in position. The brackets should be installed with their highest lug on the camshaft side of the engine, and the rocker-arm shaft with the threaded plug to the front.)

Pushrod Removal

On the Austin-Healey, and on the early Sprites the pushrods may be removed independently of the valve rocker assembly.

Remove the valve cover. Loosen the valve adjustment screws as far as possible. Using a screwdriver as a support under the rocker shaft, push the valve down, and free the rocker by sliding it sideways clear of the pushrod. Remove the pushrod. On the end rocker it is necessary to remove the cotter pins on the end of each shaft.

Reinstallation is the reverse of the removal procedure. Be sure to replace each pushrod in the same bore that it came out of.

Valves

For valve removal, resurfacing, and other types of work to the valve train, see the general section on Engine Rebuilding.

Camshaft and Timing Chain Assembly

Timing Gear Cover Removal and Installation

Austin-Healey

Drain the cooling system and remove the radiator. Loosen the generator attaching bolts. Knock back the tab washer and unscrew the nut provided for hand-cranking the engine. If possible, remove the crankshaft damper and pulley as one unit. If this is not possible, the pulley is probably tight on the crankshaft, and it will be necessary to remove the six nuts securing the damper. With the damper removed, withdraw the pulley. Remove the five 1/4 in. and the seven 5/16 in. bolts from the timing cover flange, being careful not to lose the special elongated washers installed under the bolt heads. Remove the timing cover and oil thrower.

Clean and examine the surfaces of the timing cover and the front mounting plate. Check the felt oil seal for wear, hardening, or damage. If it is worn, the timing cover must be replaced with it, as it is a single assembly.

When replacing the timing cover, be sure that the oil seal is concentric with the crankshaft. Lubricate the hub, and rotate it into the seal. On later engines, fill the groove between the lips of the rubber seal with grease. Next, slide the pulley on to the crankshaft, aligning the pulley keyway with the key on the crankshaft. Without exerting any stress on the seal, turn the timing cover to line up the bolt holes with those on the crankcase. Install a new gasket between the timing cover and the front mounting plate.

America and Early Sprite

Drain the cooling system and remove the radiator. Loosen the generator or alternator bolts and remove the fanbelt. On the America, loosen the air pump bolts and remove the drive belt. Tap the tab back on the pulley lockwasher. Remove the pulley nut (or bolt) and carefully lever the pulley off the crankshaft.

On emission controlled engines, detach the crankcase breather pipe from the oil separator. Remove the timing gear cover bolts, and lift off the cover.

Check the oil seal for signs of wear or damage. If these are present, replace the oil seal.

Reinstallation is the reverse of removal. Always use a new cover gasket. If the engine is equipped with the newer type of cover, be sure that the side marked F on the oil thrower, is installed away from the engine.

NOTE: *The older covers and oil throwers must be used together; they are not interchangeable with the new ones. When using them be sure that the concave side of the oil thrower faces away from the engine.*

The crankshaft pulley should be attached to the timing gear cover before the cover is reinstalled on the engine. If this is not done, the oil seal will not be centered properly and will leak. Fill the groove between the lips of the oil seal with grease; lubricate the hub of the pulley. Insert the hub into the oil seal, while rotating it in a clockwise direction, so as not to damage the lip of the seal. Next, press both the pulley and the cover on to the crankshaft. Be sure that the keyway on the pulley is aligned with the key on the crankshaft; then drift the pulley into place. Bolt the cover back on, by tightening each bolt a little at a time, so that the cover goes on evenly. Reattach the oil breather pipe and oil separator.

Sprites Equipped With Air Injection

Drain the cooling system, remove the radiator and the return line. Loosen the air pump and generator (alternator) mounting bolts, and remove their respective drive belts. Remove the fan and its pulley.

Undo the three bolts that attach the right engine mount to the body. Undo the two nuts that hold the left engine mount. Remove the headpipe flange bolts, disconnect the headpipe and the manifold.

Lift the front of the engine just enough so that the crankshaft pulley will slide off over the crossmember. Tap the lockwasher tab back on the pulley bolt. Using a puller remove the bolt. Carefully lever the pulley off of the crankshaft.

Detach the crankcase breather pipe from the oil separator. Unbolt the cover and remove it. Check the seal in the cover for wear or damage. If there is any present, replace the seal.

Reinstallation is the reverse of removal. To center the seal on the crankshaft, use the procedure detailed in the America/Sprite section above. Remember to connect the engine mounts, and the exhaust headpipe.

Camshaft Removal

Austin-Healey

Drain the oil pan and remove it from the engine. Remove the oil pump. Remove the rocker-arm assembly. Take out the push rods and tappets. Remove the timing cover, timing-chain tensioner, chain and sprockets. Remove the distributor and its drive (do not loosen the clamping plate bolt or the ignition setting will be disturbed). Remove the two bolts which secure the camshaft locating plate to the cylinder block. Withdraw the camshaft forward, rotating it slightly to assist removal. Inspect the camshaft bearing journals and cams for signs of scoring. Examine the camshaft bearings for scores, pits, or other evidence of damage. If the bearings must be replaced, special tools are needed. Therefore, it is not advisable for the mechanic-owner to attempt this job himself. However, because of the relatively light loads carried by the camshaft bearings (as opposed, for example, to the heavier forces acting on the crankshaft bearings), the installation of new camshaft bearings is definitely not a common operation. In an engine as rugged as that of the Austin-Healey, it is quite likely that the camshaft bearings, properly lubricated with clean oil, will easily last the life of the engine.

Sprite–MKS. I, II, III

Drain the oil pan and remove it. Remove the rocker arm assembly, and the pushrods. Take off the side and front covers to remove the tappets. Life them out, being sure to keep them in sequence, so that they are returned to the bore that they came out of. Remove the timing cover, the chain assembly, and the oil pump. Remove the distributor, and its drive, being careful not to disturb the pinchbolt. Undo the bolts that attach the camshaft mounting plate. Bring the camshaft forward, by rotating it slowly as it is eased out.

Inspect the camshaft journals; replace the camshaft if they are scored or worn. If there are any signs of unusual wear, replace the tappets.

Sprite MK. IV and America

Drain the sump and the cooling system. Follow the engine removal procedure. The transmission should remain in the car on the Sprite; as the transmission on the America is integral with the sump it must be removed with the engine. Once the engine/transmission assembly is out, the transmission should be separated from the engine.

Take out the rocker shaft and the pushrods. Take off the cover and withdraw the timing gear assembly. Detach the distributor assembly.

Remove the oil pan from the Sprite. Undo its bolts and remove the camshaft locating plate. Turn the engine upside down, so that the tappets fall clear of the camshaft. Rotate the camshaft slowly to disengage the distributor drive.

NOTE: *If the oil pump drive flange comes out with the camshaft as it is withdrawn, replace it with the drive lug side facing the oil pump.*

If it is not possible to invert the engine, remove the camshaft by holding the tappets up with a magnet assembly. Be careful not to gall the camshaft when removing it. Because of this possibility, it is advisable to invert the engine where possible.

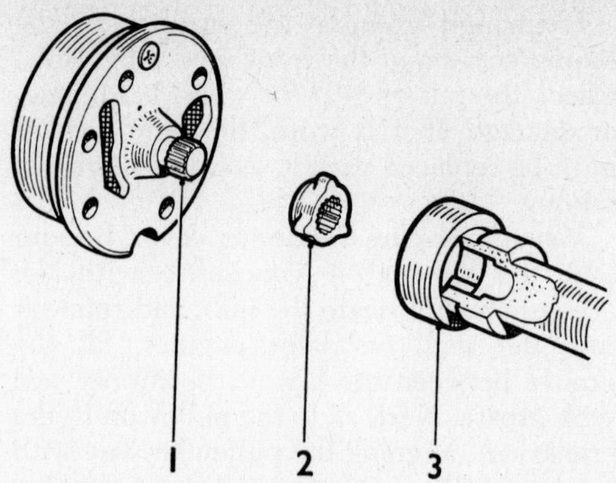

The oil pump drive of the Sprite Mk. IV and the America

1 The oil pump driveshaft
2 The correct position of the drive flange
3 Camshaft

Inspect the camshaft journals. Replace the camshaft if they are scored or worn. If there are any signs of wear, replace the tappets by removing them from their bores with a magnet.

Camshaft Installation—all Models

The basic procedure for camshaft replacement of each model, is the reverse of that model's removal procedure. There are several things to remember when reinstalling the camshaft, however. Always lubricate the camshaft journals with engine oil when replacing them.

When the camshaft is removed, it disturbs the positioning of the distributor drive spindle. To achieve correct valve timing, it is important to return the spindle to its proper position. To do this, turn the No. 1 piston to TDC of its compression stroke. Check to see that the timing marks are properly aligned. Screw a 5/16 in. bolt into the threaded end of the drive. Position the drive in its housing so that it is pointing to "twenty-of-two" with the large end of the offset facing upward.

The Healey is equipped with a mechanical tachometer, with its housing over the distributor drive; engage its external drive member in the distributor drive slot with the small segment pointing downward. Replace and tighten the three bolts that attach it to the distributor drive housing.

Engage the distributor drive gear. Replace the distributor. If the distributor

The distributor drive in the correct position for distributor replacement

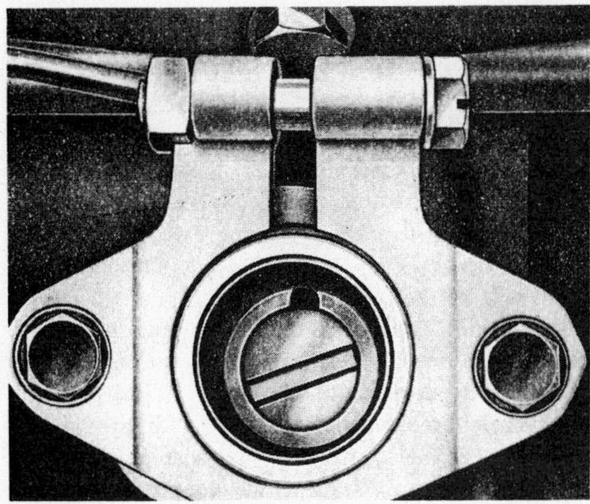

The tachometer drive in the Healey; the large offset is facing upward

pinchbolt has not been disturbed, the timing will not have to be reset.

Timing Chain and Sprocket Removal—all Models

Follow the procedures for the removal of the oil thrower assembly and the timing cover as outlined above. Bend back the tab on the camshaft sprocket lockwasher. Remove it and the nut, being sure to note how the locking tab on the lockwasher fits into the keyway on the camshaft chain sprocket.

Both of the timing chain sprockets, and the timing chain itself, may now be removed by using small levers to ease each sprocket off, a little at a time. Be careful not to lose any of the washers that fit behind the crankshaft sprocket.

Timing Chain and Sprocket Installation

Austin-Healey

Unless the camshaft or the crankshaft has been replaced, use exactly the same number of washers that were removed from behind the crankshaft sprocket. If either of these components were replaced, it is necessary to determine the proper number of washers required to align the crankshaft sprocket with the camshaft sprocket. To do this, lay a straightedge across the sides of the camshaft sprocket teeth and, using a feeler gauge, measure the size of the gap between the straightedge and the crankshaft sprocket.

Set the keyways of the two sprockets at TDC, as seen from the front. Bring the two bright links together, by doubling the timing chain. If this has been done correctly, the chain should be longer on one side of the links than the other. With the short part of the chain on the *right* (bright links facing forward) and the long part on the *left*, place the upper bright link over the marking on the camshaft sprocket, and the lower bright mark over the mark on the crankshaft sprocket.

Place the chain and sprocket assembly in their proper positions on the camshaft and the crankshaft. Press the assembly on, keeping the sprockets in line, so that the chain is not over-tensioned. Replace the lockwasher and nut on the camshaft sprocket. Lubricate the assembly with engine oil. The re-

The Austin-Healey timing chain with the bright links and the marks aligned correctly: showing the short length of chain between the bright links (A)

mainder of the procedure is the reverse of removal.

Sprite and America

Replace the same number of washers as were taken out during disassembly if the same components are to be replaced. If, however, new camshaft or crankshaft components are used, a different number of washers will probably be required to retain the alignment of the two sprockets. To determine the thickness of the washers required, place a straightedge across the sides of the camshaft sprocket teeth and measure with a feeler gauge the distance between the straightedge and the crankshaft sprocket.

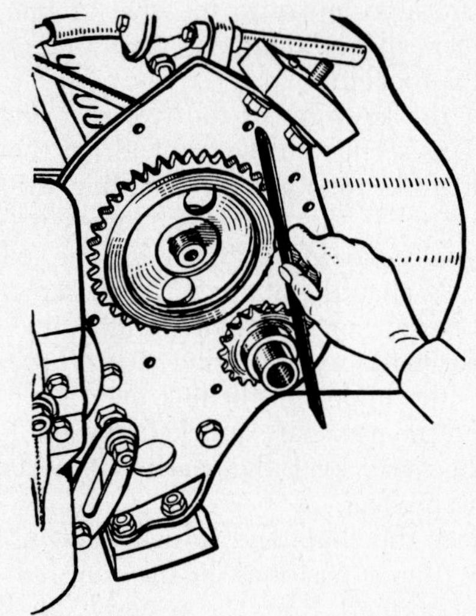

Aligning the crankshaft and the camshaft sprockets using a straight-edge

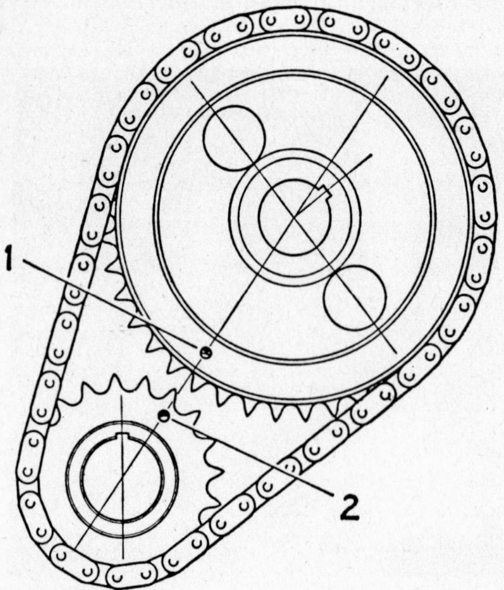

When the Sprite timing chain is installed, the sprockets should be positioned with the two marks on the center-to-center line, as shown.

Set the crankshaft keyway at TDC, and the camshaft keyway at "one o'clock" as seen from the front. Place the two marks on the sprockets across from each other, and fit the sprockets into the chain. Keep the gears in this position, fit the crankshaft sprocket keyway over the key on the crankshaft key. Turn the camshaft until its key and the keyway on the camshaft sprocket are aligned. Press the assembly on to the shafts as far as it will go. Replace the lockwasher and nut on the camshaft sprocket. The remainder of the procedure is the reverse of removal.

Timing Chain Tensioner

Austin Healey

The Austin-Healey is equipped with an automatic timing chain tensioner which is secured at the engine front-mounting plate by two bolts and a locking plate. When the engine is running, oil enters the back face of the tensioner and flows to the load-bearing surface through a hole provided in the slipper pad. The tensioner is self-adjusting to compensate for wear of either the rubber slipper or the timing chain itself.

To remove the chain tensioner unlock the tab washer at the bottom plug. Insert a 1/8 in. Allen wrench into the plug hole, engage the cylinder, and turn the wrench clockwise until the slipper is completely free of spring pressure. Approximately one and one-half turns will be necessary. Unlock and remove the securing bolts and detach the tensioner assembly and backing plate. To disassemble the tensioner, first withdraw the plunger and slipper assembly from the body, then engage the lower end of the cylinder with the Allen wrench. Turn the key counterclockwise until the cylinder and spring are released from the inside of the plunger.

Clean all components in gasoline, and use compressed air to blow out the oil holes before reassembly. Check the tensioner spring and examine the slipper pad for wear. If all components are satisfactory for reuse, reassemble and replace the tensioner as follows:

Insert the spring into the plunger and position the cylinder at the other end of the spring. Compress the spring until the cylinder enters the bore of the plunger and engages the limiting pin. With the assembly compressed in this position, engage the Allen wrench and turn the cylinder clockwise until the end of the cylinder is below the pin. This will fully compress the spring and locking cylinder. Remove the Allen wrench and insert the plunger assembly into the body. Position the backing plate and secure the tensioner assembly to the cylinder block. Move the timing chain into position, then release the tensioner by inserting the Allen wrench and turning it counterclockwise as far as possible. NOTE: *It may be necessary to use hand pressure to initially move the rubber slipper.*

Tighten the bolts into the locking plate; replace the bottom plug and lock with the tab washer.

Timing Chain Vibration Damper

Austin-Healey

With the introduction of the Mk. II model of the Austin-Healey 3000, a timing-chain vibration damper was installed in addition to the automatic tensioner already used. This damper consists of an angle bracket bolted to the cylinder block and located on the engine front-mounting plate by means of a dowel. The oil-resistant rubber pad is bonded to the bracket and maintains a light rubbing contact with the timing chain and serves to dampen chain vibration under light-load running conditions. Because of this modification, the Mk. II models have a new cylinder block, front mounting plate and gasket which are *not* interchangeable with those of previous 3000's.

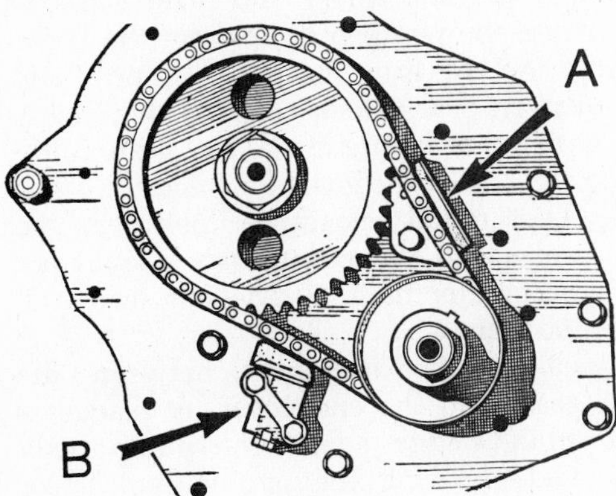

The Austin-Healey 3000 Mk. II incorporates a vibration damper (A), as well as, a chain tensioner (B).

Engine Lubrication

General Description

The Austin-Healey, the Sprite, and the America have pressurized, pump-fed, wet sump, lubrication systems. The pressure in the system varies from model to model, as does the type of pump used. The only major difference appears on the Austin America models, where the same sump supplies both engine and transmission. Because of this, the America lacks a conventional oil pan; the transmission casing serves this function, as well. All of the models are equipped with an external full-flow oil filter, which may be either a replaceable element type, or a spin off canister type.

Relief Valve Maintenance

All models are equipped with an oil pressure relief valve, of a non-adjustable type. If oil pressure becomes excessive, the valve allows an extra oil passage to come into service.

The relief valve is located on the right, rear side of the engine block. It is held in place by a hexagonal nut and several washers. Its spring maintains valve cup pressure against the valve seat. The cup may be removed and reground into the seat if neces-

The oil relief valve is located on the right side of the engine on all models

sary. The spring should be replaced with a new one, in the event that it becomes weak.

Oil pan and Strainer Removal and Installation

Austin-Healey

Drain the engine oil. Remove the bolts and washers securing the oil pan, and lower the pan. Remove the bottom of the oil strainer by removing the nut, washer, and spacer. Remove the three bolts holding the strainer to the oil pump. Clean the pump and strainer with gasoline and dry with a lint-free rag. Inspect the two gaskets and replace if necessary.

Clean the oil pan with kerosene, removing all traces of cleaner before replacing the pan to the engine. Clean the joining faces of the oil pan and crankcase, and remove all traces of old gasket material. Install a *new* gasket. Smear the joining surfaces with grease and apply the gasket. Lift the oil pan into position, insert the securing bolts and tighten evenly.

Sprite

Drain the engine oil, remove the bolts and spring washers and lower the oil pan. Unscrew the oil suction pipe at its connection with the crankcase. Remove the two bolts which secure the oil strainer support bracket to the main bearing cap. Remove the strainer and support bracket from the engine. Clean the strainer in gasoline and dry with a lint-free rag.

Replace the strainer and its securing bracket, being sure that the oil suction pipe is properly located at its connection in the crankcase. Tighten down the suction pipe connection and support bracket. Clean the oil pan and joining surfaces, remove all traces of cleaning fluid, use a new gasket if necessary, and replace the oil pan to the bottom of the crankcase.

Oil Cooler

Sprite

The later Sprites are equipped with an oil cooler. To remove it, drain the sump, and undo the lines that run to it. Remove the bolts that hold it in place.

Installation is the reverse of removal. Be careful to start the line fittings by hand, so that their threads are not stripped. Refill the sump, run the engine, and check for leaks.

Oil Pump

Austin-Healey 100-6

Remove the oil pan and strainer. Remove the oil pump by unscrewing the nuts and spring washers from the three studs holding the oil pump assembly to the crankcase.

NOTE: *If the pump is removed while the engine is still in the car, the driveshaft will be free to disengage from the camshaft. Therefore care must be taken to prevent its falling out. Also note the thrust washer installed on the driveshaft above the gear.*

Once removed, the oil pump may be disassembled by separating the body from the bottom flange, then lifting the outer rotor out of the body. The flange and the pump body should be marked to facilitate reassembly. When replacing the pump, insert from below and push the shaft home until the driving gear is in mesh with the camshaft gear.

Austin-Healey 3000

These models are equipped with a gear-type oil pump to replace the earlier, Hobourn-Eaton rotary vane type. Remove the oil pan and strainer. Remove the nuts and spring washers from the studs securing the oil pump assembly to the crankcase, then withdraw the pump.

NOTE: *Be careful of the driveshaft, which is free to fall from the camshaft gear, and note the thrust washer above the driveshaft gear.*

Once removed, the gear-type oil pump is disassembled as follows: Mark the flange and the pump body to facilitate reassembly, then remove the four retaining bolts along with their spring and plain washers. Separate the pump pick-up from the body, withdraw the drive gear and spindle and the driven gear. Clean all parts thoroughly in gasoline or kerosene and dry with a lint-free rag. Check the gears for wear.

1. The radial clearance between the gears and the pump body should not be greater than .00125-.0025 in. (.032-.063 mm.)
2. Check the clearance between the gears and the end cover by placing a straight-edge across the pump body and checking the gap with a feeler gauge. The end float of the gears should be within the limits of .0005-.002 in. (.013-.051 mm.).

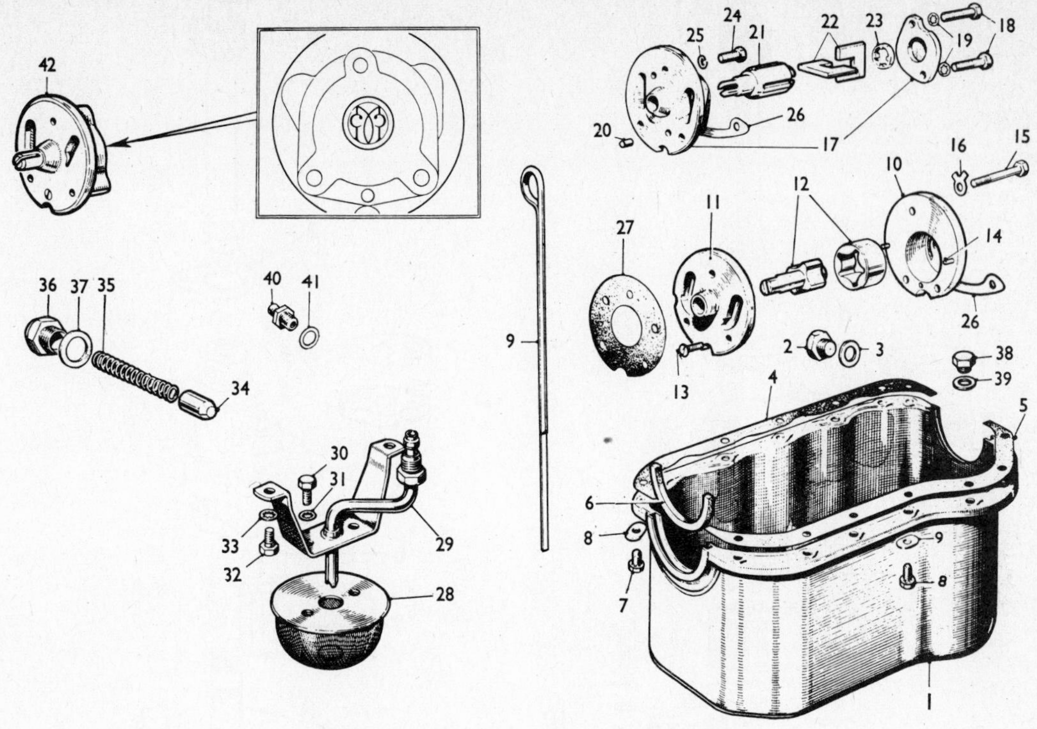

Oil pump and oil pan components, Austin-Healey Sprite.

1 Oil pan
2 Drain plug
3 Washer
4 Oil pan gasket—right side
5 Oil pan gasket—left side
6 Main bearing cap oil seal
7 Screw and washer
8 Washer
9 Dipstick

Hobourn-Eaton Type:
10 Oil pump body
11 Cover (plain hole)
12 Driving shaft with inner and outer rotors
13 Cover to body screws
14 Dowel
15 Pump to crankcase
16 Lock washer

Burman Type:
17 Body and cover assembly
18 Bolt
19 Shakeproof washer
20 Dowel
21 Rotor
22 Vane
23 Sleeve
24 Pump to crankcase bolt
25 Spring washer

26 Lock plate (for all pumps)
27 Pump to crankcase gasket
28 Oil strainer
29 Suction pipe with oil strainer bracket
30 Bolt
31 Shakeproof washer
32 Bolt (bracket to bearing cap)
33 Shakeproof washer
34 Oil relief valve
35 Spring for oil relief valve
36 Cap nut
37 Washer
38 Oil priming plug
39 Washer (copper)
40 Oil pressure connector
41 Washer (fiber)
42 Pump assembly—concentric type

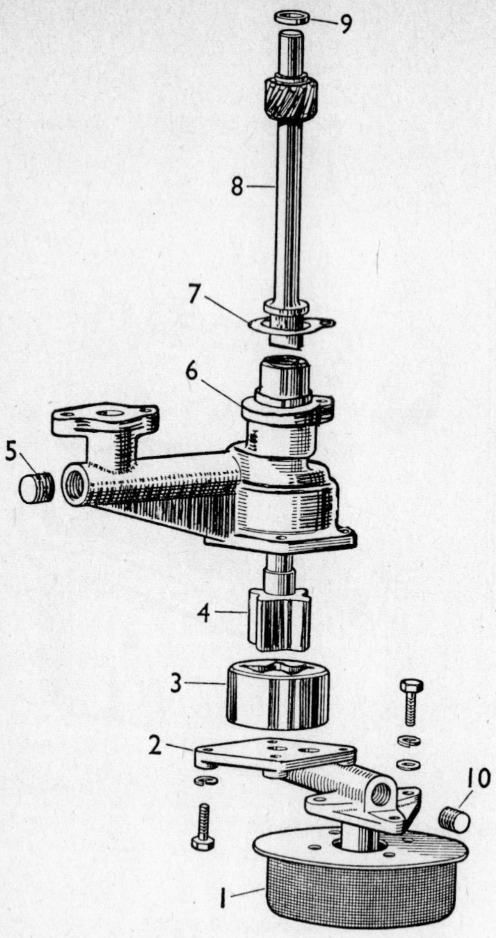

The oil pump used on the Austin-Healey 100-6

1 Pick-up strainer
2 Bottom lower plate
3 Outer rotor
4 Inner rotor
5 Plug
6 Pump body
7 Gasket
8 Drive spindle
9 Drive spindle thrust washer
10 Plug

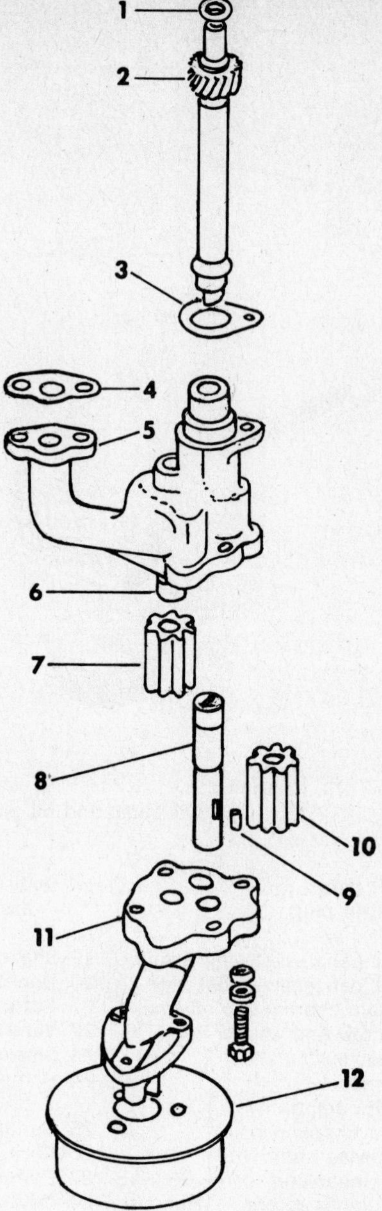

The oil pump used on the Austin-Healey 3000

1 Thrust washer
2 Drive spindle
3 Gasket
4 Gasket
5 Pump body
6 Driven gear spindle
7 Driven gear
8 Drive gear spindle
9 Key
10 Drive gear
11 Pick-up
12 Pickup-up strainer

Replace worn parts and reassemble. The pump driving gear is a press fit on its shaft and is keyed in position. After assembly, the spindle should protrude .312 in. (7.94 mm.) from the gear face.

In replacing the pump, be sure that the joining surfaces of the cylinder block and oil pump are clean and that the gaskets are in good condition. Insert the pump from below, and ensure that the driving gear is in mesh with the camshaft gear. Secure the pump, replace the pick-up strainer and install the oil pan.

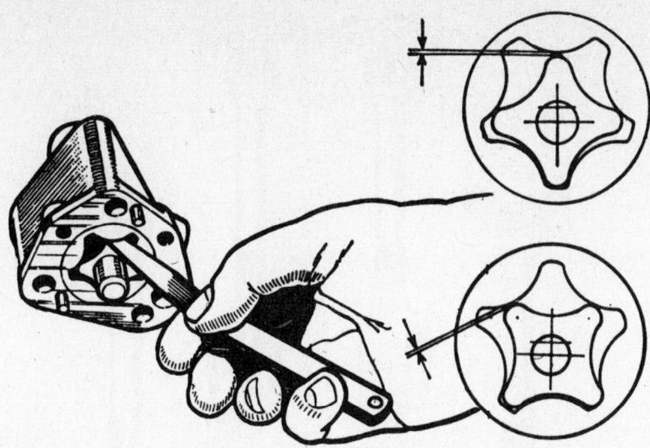

The Holbourn-Eaton oil pump used on some Sprite and America models—Insert A shows the lobe positions used when checking clearances.

Sprite

Remove the engine, flywheel, clutch assembly, and engine back-plate. Unscrew the oil pump retaining screws and withdraw the pump. Disassembly and reassembly is different for the three types of pumps used, and is as follows:

Concentric type. The Concentric-type pump is serviced only as a complete assembly.

Burman type. Unscrew the cover bolts, remove the cover, and withdraw the rotor and vane assembly. Remove the retaining sleeve from the end of the rotor, then withdraw the vanes. Reassembly is the opposite of the preceding.

Hobourn-Eaton type. Remove the cover securing bolt, withdraw the cover and remove the inner and outer rotors complete with drive shaft. Clean all parts thoroughly and inspect for wear. The diametrical clearance between the outer rotor and the pump body should not exceed .010 in. (.254 mm.). If the clearance exceeds this limit, the rotors, pump body, or complete assembly must be replaced. Place a straight-edge across the joint face of the pump body and measure the clearance between the edge and the face of the rotors. If this clearance exceeds .005 in. (.127 mm.) the cover locating dowels may be removed and the joint face carefully shaved. Check the minimum clearance between the stationary and movable rotor lobes. If the clearance exceeds .006 in. (.152 mm.) the rotors should be replaced. Reassembly is the reverse of the preceding.

While replacement of the oil pump to the cylinder block is primarily the reverse of the removal operation, attention should be paid to the following points:

1. Be sure that all components are perfectly clean prior to reassembly
2. In positioning the paper gasket, be sure that the intake and delivery ports are not obstructed
3. Use a new paper gasket if the condition of the old one appears to be marginal.

America—Manual Transmission

Drain the sump, the cooling system, and remove the engine/transmission assembly. Disconnect the clutch and flywheel from the engine. Remove the flywheel housing. Undo its mounting bolts and remove the pump.

The pumps used in the manually equipped Americas are either the Holbourn-Eaton, or the Concentic type; service for them is the same as for the Sprite (see above).

Reassembly and reinstallation are the reverse of the removal procedures. Be careful not to block the intake and outlet ports on the pump with the paper gasket. Always use a new gasket and tab washer.

America—Automatic Transmission

Follow the procedure for removing the engine/transmission unit. Separate the torque converter and its housing from the engine. Unbolt and remove the oil pump.

The automatic transmission America models use the Holbourn-Eaton pump only. Service for it is the same as for the Sprite models that use the Holbourn-Eaton pump; for the correct teardown procedure see the Sprite section, above.

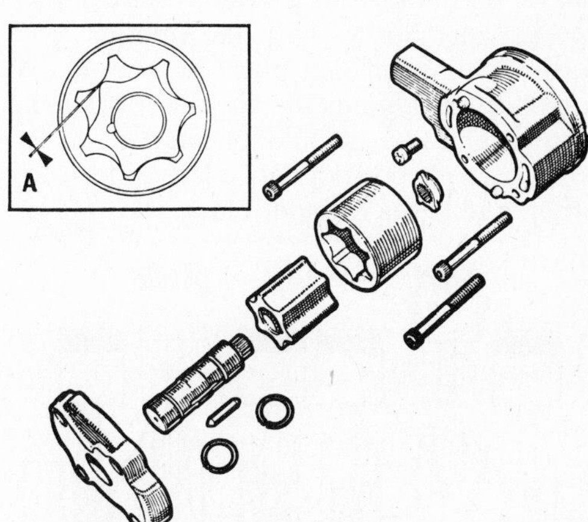

The Holburn-Eaton oil pump used on some Sprite and America models—Insert A shows inner rotor to outer rotor clearance.

Installation procedures are the reverse of removal. Always remember to use a new paper gasket for leak-free operation.

Pistons and Connecting Rods

Identification

NOTE: *For information regarding piston and connecting rod removal, and installation procedures, see the section that deals with general engine rebuilding operations.*

The Austin-Healey, the Sprite, and the America do not have identifying marks for placement on their rods and pistons. Because of this, it is a good idea to mark each connecting rod, cap, bearing, and piston with the cylinder number from which it was removed, and with an arrow denoting front. A water-proof felt pen is ideal for this; as it is non-abrasive.

The connecting rod ends are offset on the Healey. Rods in cylinders 1, 3, and 5 are offset toward the front, while those in cylinders 2, 4, and 6 are offset toward the rear. In the Sprite and the America, the connecting rod bearings 1, and 3 are offset toward the rear, while bearings 2, and 4 are offset toward the front.

On the early Healey models, the split on the piston skirt should be adjacent to the split on the top of the connecting rod, when assembling the piston and the rod. On the engines from No. 40501, connecting rods with fully floating pins were used. The slot in the piston goes on the opposite side from the camshaft, when they are fitted into the cylinder block.

The early Sprite pistons and rods are correctly installed when the piston pin clampbolt is on the camshaft side of the cylinder block. Later Sprites and the America have fully floating piston pins, so the above methods of alignment do not work; the pistons and rods should be marked to insure correct positioning relative to each other, and to the cylinder block.

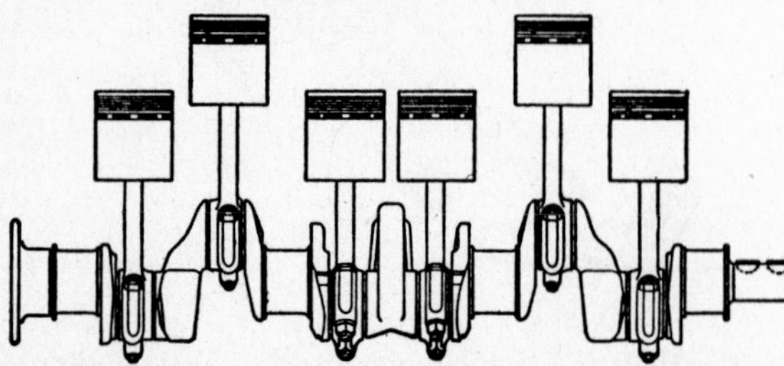

The correct position for connecting rod offsets in the Austin-Healey engine

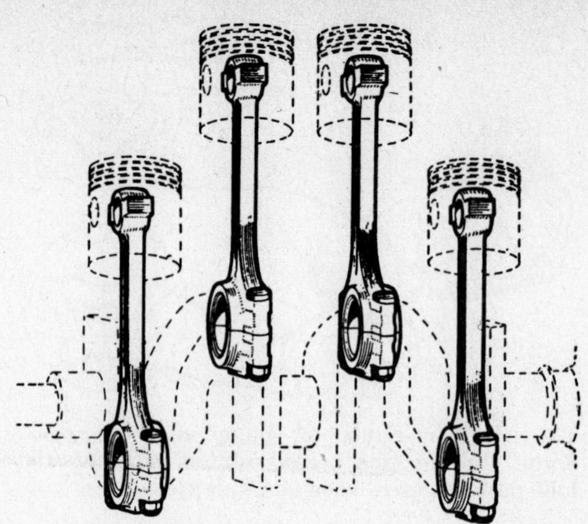

The correct position for the connecting rods and pistons in relation to the crankshaft—Sprite and America

The Sprite Mk. IV, and the America require a special tool to remove and install a piston pin. If it is not used the piston will be crushed or damaged. Therefore, this job should be entrusted to an Austin service center.

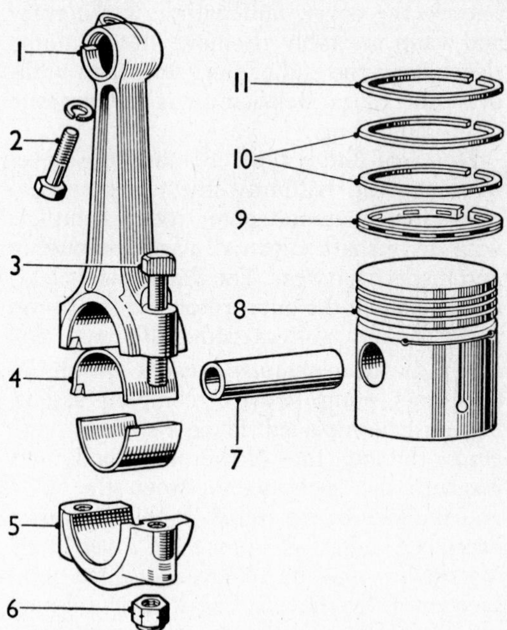

Connecting rod and piston assembly for the Healey 100-6, showing the clamped piston pin

1 Connecting rod
2 Small end clamping screw
3 Big-end bolt
4 Shell bearing
5 Big-end cap
6 Big-end nut
7 Piston pin
8 Piston
9 Oil control ring
10 Taper compression rings
11 Plain compression ring

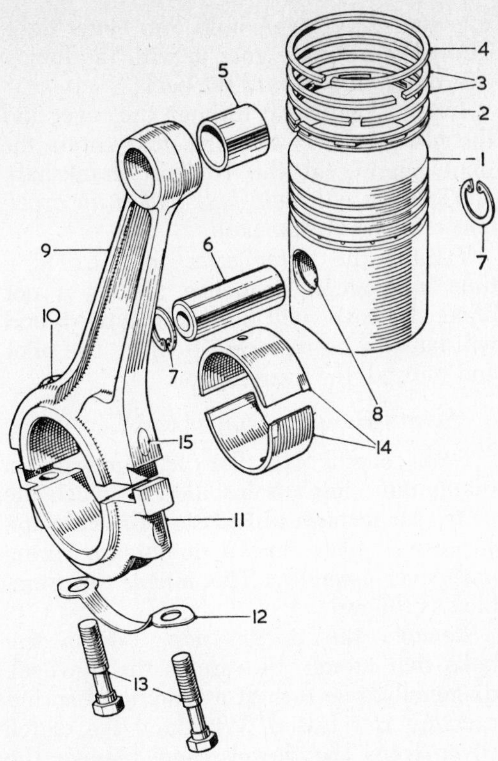

Connecting rod and piston assembly from the late Sprite, showing the free-floating piston pin

1 Piston
2 Piston ring—scraper
3 Piston rings—taper
4 Piston ring—parallel
5 Small-end bushing
6 Piston pin
7 Circlip
8 Piston pin lubricating hole
9 Connecting rod
10 Cylinder wall lubricating jet
11 Connecting rod cap
12 Lock washer
13 Bolts
14 Connecting rod bearings
15 Connecting rod and cap marking

Oversized Pistons

Oversized pistons are available for all models; see the chart in the front of the section for oversize maximums. The oversize gradings are stamped on the crown of the pistons. This number is enclosed in an ellipse, and should not be confused with the production size grading which is stamped in a diamond.

Clutch and Transmission

Removal and Installation

Transmission

Austin-Healey

Turn off the battery master switch, which is located in the trunk. Remove the seat cushions and the center armrest. Expose the bolts that hold the transmission tunnel on the car, by unclipping and rolling back the rug. Undo the twelve mounting bolts and remove the tunnel and the rug. Take out the bulkhead, along with its carpet, by undoing the six bolts that hold it in place.

Bend the tabs back on their washers and unfasten the six driveshaft flange bolts. Remove the four bolts from the gearbox mounting bracket. Detach the speedometer cable from its drive on the transmission. If the car is equipped with overdrive, disconnect the cable at the transmission switch.

The next series of operations is performed from underneath the car. Undo the nuts and bolts that attach the rear transmission bracket, and withdraw the bracket.

The clutch slave cylinder is removed from the clutch housing by undoing the two bolts that attach it. Remove the pushrod from the clutch operating lever by taking out the pivot pin.

Remove the starter motor. Support the transmission bell housing, and the engine oil pan. Remove the nuts and bolts that attach the bell housing to the cylinder block. Gently ease the input shaft off of the flywheel bearing and clutch. If the transmission does not slide off easily the back of the engine will have to be raised.

Installation is the reverse of the removal procedure.

Sprite

Remove the engine, as shown in the section that deals with engine removal. Undo the four self-tapping screws from the gearshift cover, and remove the cover. Take the anti-rattle plunger, spring, and cap out of the shift lever housing. Withdraw the lever by undoing the bolts that attach it. Pull the carpet away from the transmission cover; undo the two bolts that attach the transmission to the rear mount. Detach the speedometer drive cable at the transmission extension housing.

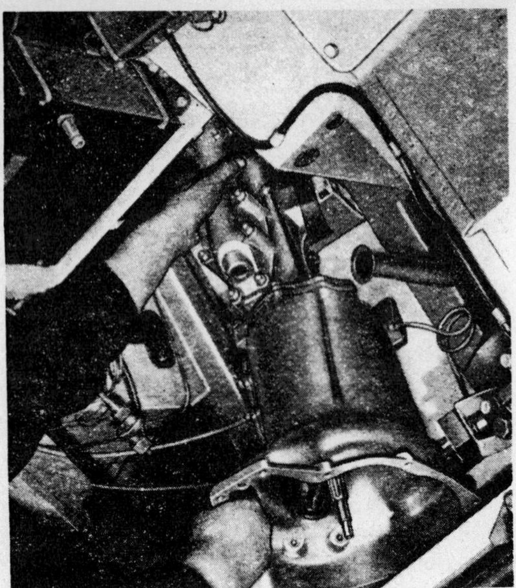

Removal of the transmission and driveshaft from the Sprite

Remove the slave cylinder from the clutch housing, by removing the two bolts that attach it, and detaching the pushrod at the rear of the cylinder. Take the driveshaft off at the differential. Remove the rest of the rear mounting bolts. Remove the gearbox and the driveshaft as a unit.

Installation is the reverse of removal. The driveshaft must be reconnected to the transmission *before* installation.

America

Because the transmission is located in the sump, it is naturally removed with the engine (see Engine Removal). The engine and transmission can only be removed as a unit; they must be separated *after* removal.

Clutch

Austin-Healey—Finger-type Clutch

NOTE: *If the cover assembly is to be replaced, mark the cover, pressure plate lugs, and release so that they are replaced in the same positions during reassembly.*

Remove the transmission. Loosen the clutch cover bolts, one turn at a time, by diagonal selection until spring pressure is released. Remove the bolts the rest of the way; lift the clutch cover off of the flywheel assembly. Check the flywheel for any signs of damage or misalignment.

To install, hold the cover assembly and the pressure plate on the flywheel, while screwing the cover bolts on finger-tight. The pressure plate goes in with the longer side of the hub toward the back.

Insert a pilot shaft through the cover and the plate hub, so that the drift enters the pilot bearing at the back of crankshaft. NOTE: *An old mainshaft makes an excellent pilot for this purpose.*

Tighten the cover bolts one turn at a time in diagonal sequence. If this is not done, the cover will become distorted, and will have to be replaced. Remove the pilot and reinstall the transmission.

Austin-Healey—Diaphragm Clutch

From engine No. 29F/4898 onward, a diaphragm clutch is installed in which the clutch mechanism consists of a driven plate, a pressure plate, and a diaphragm spring and cover assembly. This unit is disassembled as follows:

Remove the transmission. Loosen the bolts that attach the case to the flywheel, diagonally, one turn at a time, until spring pressure is released. Withdraw the clutch cover from the dowels, and remove the clutch assembly. Remove the circlip which secures the release plate to the diaphragm, then lift the plate from the diaphragm. Unscrew the three screws that secure the clips to the pressure plate, a turn at a time, until the diaphragm contacts the cover. Remove the bolts, clips, washers, and pressure plate. Turn the release-bearing-spring retainers through an arc of 90° , then withdraw the bearing from the fork of the withdrawal lever.

Assembly is the reverse of the preceding, but be certain that the release-bearing retainers are located correctly and that the spring clip bolts are tightened to the correct torque.

Sprite Mk. I, Mk. II, and Mk. III.

The clutches used in the Sprite prior to the Mk. IV are of the single dry plate type. There are two variations used, one on early cars and one for the later cars. Basically they are the same, and the procedures used for removal and installation are the same as those used for the Austin-Healey models equipped with dry plate clutch assemblies. See the section above for these procedures.

Sprite Mk. IV.

The clutch used in the Sprite Mk. IV is correspondent to the diaphragm clutch

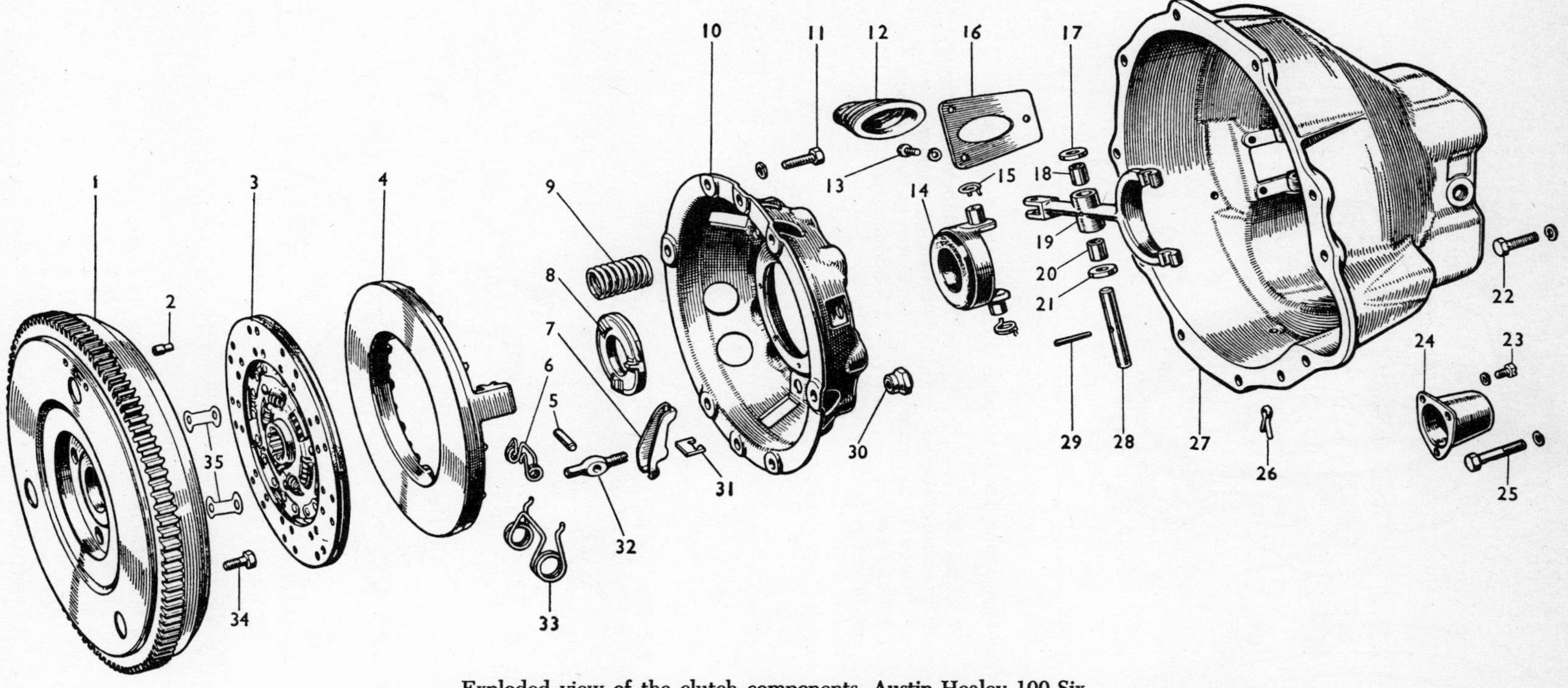

Exploded view of the clutch components, Austin-Healey 100-Six.

1 Flywheel
2 Locating peg
3 Clutch plate with lining
4 Pressure plate
5 Release lever pin
6 Release lever retainer
7 Release lever
8 Release lever plate
9 Pressure plate spring
10 Clutch cover
11 Cover bolt
12 Fork and lever seal
13 Retaining plate screw
14 Release bearing
15 Release bearing retainer spring
16 Seal retaining plate
17 Fork and lever thrust washer
18 Fork and lever shaft bushing
19 Clutch fork and lever
20 Fork and lever shaft bushing
21 Fork and lever thrust washer
22 Clutch to transmission bolt
23 Starter cover screw
24 Cover
25 Clutch to transmission bolt
26 Cotter pin for drain hole
27 Clutch housing
28 Fork and lever shaft
29 Taper pin
30 Eye bolt nut
31 Release lever strut
32 Eye bolt
33 Anti-rattle spring
34 Flywheel to crankshaft bolt
35 Lockwashers

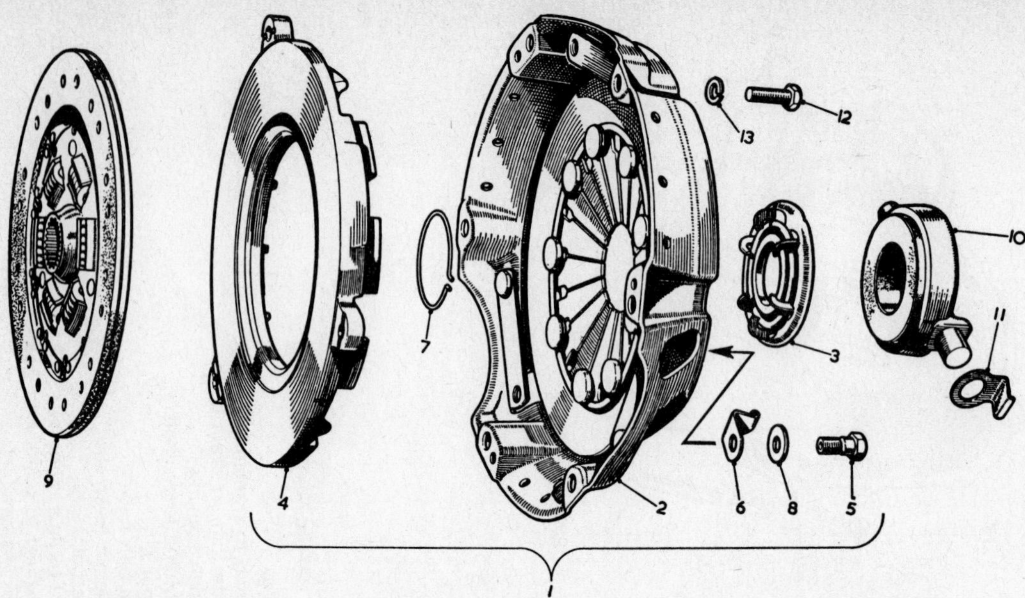

Exploded view of the diaphragm spring clutch components of the Austin-Healey 3000.

1 Cover assembly
2 Cover with straps and diaphragm spring
3 Release plate
4 Pressure plate
5 Strap bolt
6 Pressure plate dip
7 Release plate circlip
8 Strap washer
9 Driven plate assembly
10 Release bearing assembly
11 Bearing retainer
12 Clutch to flywheel bolt
13 Spring washer

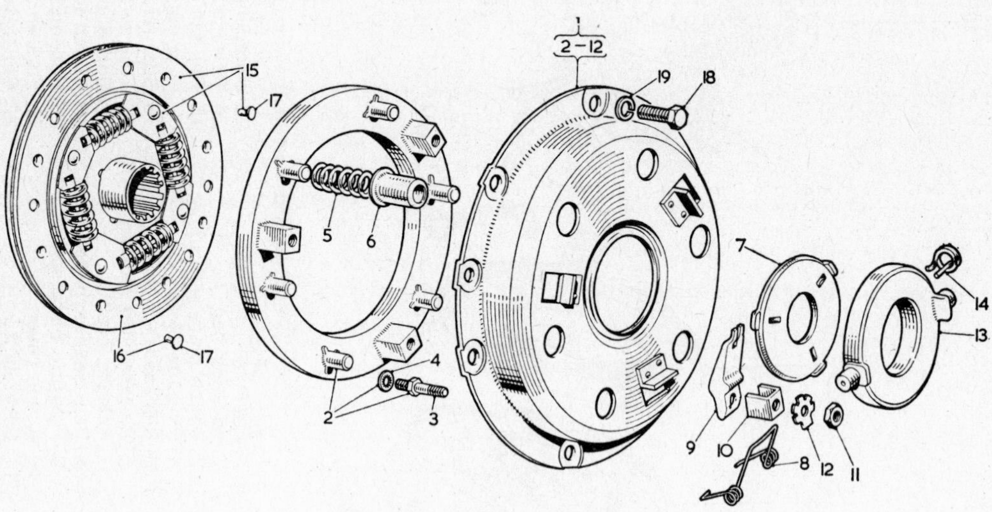

The clutch assembly for the early Sprite

1 Cover assembly
2 Pressure plate
3 Pressure plate stud
4 Washer
5 Thrust spring
6 Thrust spring cup
7 Thrust plate
8 Thrust plate retainer
9 Release lever
10 Release lever bearing plate
11 Nut
12 Tab washer
13 Throwout bearing and cap assembly
14 Bearing retainer
15 Driven plate
16 Linings
17 Rivets
18 Bolt
19 Washer

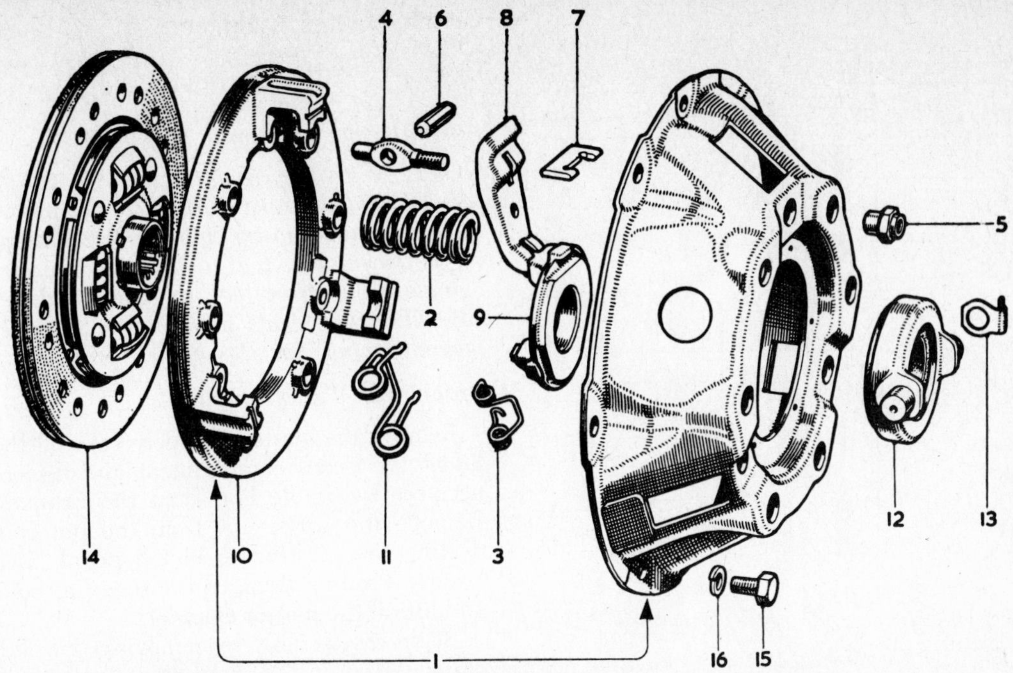

Components of the clutch used in later Sprites prior to the Mk. IV model.

1 Clutch assembly
2 Thrust spring
3 Release lever retainer
4 Eyebolt
5 Eyebolt nut
6 Release lever pin
7 Strut
8 Release lever
9 Bearing thrust plate
10 Pressure plate
11 Anti-rattle spring
12 Release bearing
13 Retainer
14 Driven plate assembly
15 Clutch to flywheel bolt
16 Spring washer

used in the later Healey models. The removal and installation procedures are the same as those given above for the Healey, except that, the Sprite engine must be removed in order to take the transmission out.

America

The clutch and flywheel may be removed from the America without having to pull the engine/transmission unit out of the car.

Remove the battery and its holder. Detach the starter from the side of the flywheel housing. Take out the spark plugs to facilitate turning the engine over by hand. Remove the pin from clutch release lever pivot, and remove the spring. Unbolt the slave cylinder from the clutch housing, and place it out of the way. Detach the top radiator mounting bracket from the cylinder head. Unbolt the rear, right side engine mount from the sub-frame. Lift the engine just enough so that the clutch cover may be removed.

CAUTION: *Be careful not to allow the fan blades to make contact with the radiator; if they do, it may be damaged.*

Unbolt and remove the clutch cover housing. Bend back the locking tab. On the flywheel bolt, remove the locking tab, bolt and washer. The clutch and flywheel assembly may now be removed.

The flywheel and clutch are difficult to remove because their hubs and the crankshaft end are tapered. There is a special service tool to remove them. If it is not available, a carefully used hammer will suffice. A soft piece of metal, such as a brass drift or a lead block, must be used to absorb the impact, so that the flywheel is not damaged. Be careful not to hit the pressure plate or the starter gear. Turn the flywheel slightly, now and then, to distribute the impact force around the hub.

When the flywheel gives an indication of breaking loose, turn it until the "1/4" mark is at TDC (The No. 1 piston is also at TDC.), to prevent the C-washer on the primary gear from dropping down behind the flywheel oil seal. Keep the flywheel vertical

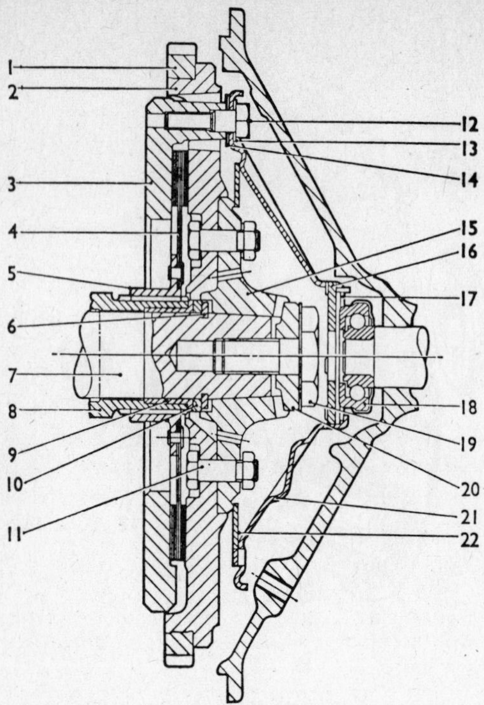

A sectional view of the diaphragm clutch used in the America

1 Starter ring
2 Flywheel
3 Pressure plate
4 Driven plate
5 Driven plate hub
6 Circlip
7 Crankshaft
8 Crankshaft primary gear
9 Primary gear bearing
10 Thrust washer
11 Flywheel hub bolt
12 Driving pin
13 Lock washer
14 Driving strap
15 Flywheel hub
16 Thrust plate
17 Plate retaining spring
18 Thrust bearing
19 Flywheel screw
20 Keyed washer
21 Cover
22 Diaphragm spring

during removal from the crankshaft, to prevent oil, which is drawn past the seal, from wetting the surface of the clutch disc. A small amount of leakage during removal is normal; however, make sure that the oil was not there before removal, due to a faulty oil seal.

Remove the pressure plate bolts, and separate the pressure plate, the disc, the flywheel, and the cover. Replace the disc, and examine the flywheel, the pressure plate, and diaphragm spring for wear or damage.

If the throwout bearing is worn, remove it with a gear puller, and press a replacement on to the shaft.

Installation is the reverse of removal. Lubricate the lips of the oil seal, and wipe the crankshaft and flywheel tapers clean before reinstallation. Tighten the flywheel bolt to a 110-115 ft. lbs. torque figure.

Clutch Master Cylinder

Reconditioning

Austin-Healey and Sprite Mks. I-III

NOTE: *With the exceptions of the Sprite Mk. IV, and the Austin America, the procedure for clutch master cylinder reconditioning is the same as that for the brake master cylinder. Therefore, see the section under* BRAKES *that deals with master cylinder reconditioning, for the proper procedures.*

Sprite Mk. IV and America

Remove the master cylinder. Take off the lid of the pedal compartment and disconnect the hydraulic line from the cylinder. Remove the cotter pin from the pin connecting the pushrod to clutch pedal, then remove the pin. Remove the securing bolts and lift off the master cylinder.

Begin disassembly by removing the filler cap and draining the fluid. Remove the rubber dust cover from the body and slide it up the push rod. Remove the circlip which retains the push rod and withdraw the push rod complete with the rubber dust cover and dished washer. Withdraw the piston, secondary cup, piston washer, main cup, spring retainer and spring from the cylinder body. Remove the secondary cup from the piston by carefully stretching it over the end of the piston. Use finger pressure only.

Prior to reassembling the master cylinder components, dip all parts into clutch fluid and assemble them while they are still wet. Stretch the secondary cup over the piston so that the lip of the cup is facing toward the head of the piston. After the cup is in its groove, work it gently with the fingers to ensure that it is correctly seated. Install the spring retainer into the small diameter end of the spring and insert the spring into the body, large diameter end first. Install the main cup, cup washer, piston and push rod. The lip end of the cups should be inserted into the barrel first. Install the circlip and rubber boot and replace the master cylinder to its position in the car. Fill with clutch fluid and bleed the hydraulic system.

Slave Cylinder

Reconditioning

The typical Austin clutch slave cylinder is bolted to the clutch housing and consists of a piston, rubber cup, cup filler, spring, pushrod, and bleeder screw. To remove, place a container to catch the fluid and remove the hydraulic line from the slave cylinder. Remove the retaining pins from the withdrawal lever to free the slave cylinder pushrod. Remove the two bolts and spring washers securing the cylinder to the clutch housing and lift off the assembly.

Begin disassembly by removing the rubber cover, pushrod and circlip. If compressed air is available, the piston and seal should be blown out. Remove the spring. Clean the main casting with any available cleaning fluids, but use only hydraulic fluid as a cleaning agent for the slave cylinder components. Prior to reassembly, remove all traces of cleaning fluid, lubricate the slave cylinder bore and components with hydraulic fluid and replace all rubber parts. Reassembly and replacement of the unit are opposite the instructions which precede, but the hydraulic unit should be bled before the car is operated.

Transmission

Disassembly and Assembly

Austin-Healey 100-6, 3000 Mk. I, and Mk. II (early)

Disassembly of the transmission used in these models is as follows:

Remove the dipstick and unscrew the breather from the overdrive unit, if installed. Drain the oil from the transmission and overdrive units, using the separate drain plugs provided for each. Unscrew the speedometer drive from the right side of the rear extension. Remove the seven short bolts and single long bolt and remove the clutch housing. Unscrew the nuts from the three studs mounted on the gear lever cup. After these nuts are removed, the cup may be withdrawn along with the three washers and spacers on the studs. Withdraw the gear lever from the transmission. Remove the thirteen bolts which secure the side cover to the transmission housing and remove the cover.

NOTE: *There are two dowels which locate the cover. Be careful not to lose the three selector balls and springs which will be released when the cover is withdrawn.*

Unscrew the eight bolts and remove the rear extension.

Overdrive-equipped models. Separate the overdrive unit from the transmission by removing the nuts from the six 5/16 in. studs. There are two long studs and four shorter ones and the nuts should be removed from the shorter studs before the long-stud nuts are disturbed. The remaining two nuts should be unscrewed together to gradually and evenly release the pressure of the clutch springs. After the six nuts have been removed, the overdrive unit can be withdrawn from the mainshaft, leaving only the adapter plate attached to the transmission. After the overdrive unit is removed, the adapter plate may be detached by unscrewing the eight nuts in the recess of the plate.

The overdrive pump cam should slide freely along the third motion shaft, providing access to the circlip which holds the spacer to the rear adapter plate. Remove the circlip and slide the spacer off the shaft, then pull the adapter plate and rear main bearing from the transmission. It may be necessary for a helper to hold the transmission vertically, by the adapter plate, while the third motion shaft is tapped slightly until the bearing race in the adapter plate is free of the shaft.

Cut the locking wires and remove the fork retaining bolts. Remove the shafts and forks in the following order:

1. Reverse shaft and fork along with the selector and detent plungers and springs.
2. Fourth gear shifter shaft.
3. First and second shaft and fork.
4. Fourth gear shift fork.

In removing the above components, be careful not to drop the two interlock balls which are normally located one at each side of the center-shifter shaft. Remove the reverse-shaft locating bolt and push out the shaft. Lift the reverse gear from the transmission. Tap out the countershaft and allow the cluster gear to rest at the bottom of the transmission case. Withdraw the clutchshaft assembly, noting that there are 16 rollers. Withdraw the mainshaft to the rear and lift out the cluster gear and thrust washers.

Dismantle the mainshaft as follows: Slide the third-fourth gear hub off the mainshaft from the forward end. Depress the plunger which locates the third gear locking plate, then rotate the plate to line up the splines and slide it from the shaft. Remove the plunger and spring and slide off the third gear and its 32 rollers. Unscrew and remove the mainshaft nut, locking washer, speedometer drive gear, bearing with housing,

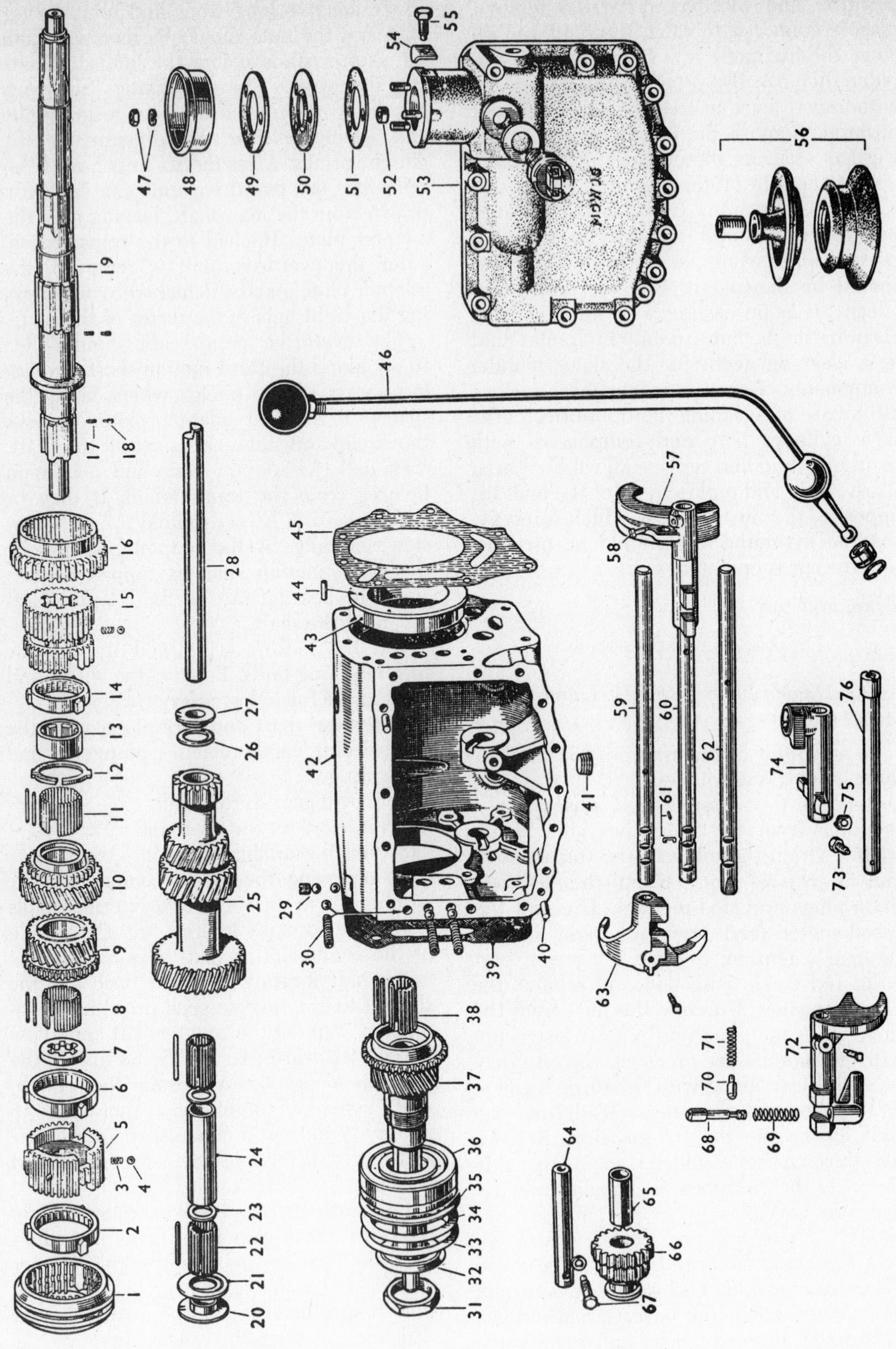

An exploded view of the transmission used in the Healey 100-6; 3000 Mk. I and Mk. II (early)

An exploded view of the transmission used in the Healey 100-6; 3000 Mk. I and Mk. II (early)

1 Synchromesh sleeve
2 Blocker ring
3 Synchronizer spring
4 Synchronizer ball
5 Third and fourth gear synchronizer
6 Blocker ring
7 Locking plate
8 Needle rollers
9 Third gear
10 Second gear
11 Needle rollers
12 Gear washer
13 Locking plate
14 Blocker ring
15 Second gear synchronizer
16 First gear
17 Plunger spring
18 Gear plunger
19 Main shaft
20 Thrust plate
21 Thrust washer
22 Needle rollers
23 Washer, roller
24 Spacer, roller
25 Cluster gear
26 Washer
27 Thrust plate
28 Countershaft
29 Interlocking balls
30 Selector ball and spring
31 Bearing nut
32 Bearing nut lockwasher
33 Bearing spring plate
34 Bearing plate
35 Bearing circlip
36 Clutch shaft bearing
37 Clutch shaft
38 Needle rollers
39 Gasket
40 Side cover dowel
41 Drain plug
42 Transmission case
43 Bearing housing
44 Locating peg
45 Gasket
46 Gear lever
47 Nut and washer
48 Cup
49 Rubber washer (thick)
50 Steel washer
51 Rubber washer (thin)
52 Spacer
53 Side cover
54 Washer
55 Gear lever locating bolt
56 Rubber dust covers
57 First and second gear fork
58 Screw for fork
59 Third and fourth fork rod
60 First and second fork rod
61 Interlocking pin and rivet
62 Reverse fork rod
63 Third and fourth gear fork
64 Reverse shaft
65 Bushing
66 Reverse gear
67 Locking screw
68 Selector plunger
69 Selector plunger spring
70 Detent plunger
71 Detent plunger spring
72 Reverse fork
73 Control shaft locating bolt
74 Locking washer
75 Control shaft
76 Control lever

and spacing collar. Slide the first-second gear hub and first gear to the rear and remove the shaft. If the first gear has been withdrawn from its hub, be careful to retain the balls and springs located in the holes of the hub. Depress the second gear locking collar plunger and rotate the collar in order to line up the splines. Slide the collar from the shaft and remove the halves of the second gear washer, being careful not to lose the spring and plunger. The second gear and its 33 rollers may now be withdrawn from the shaft. Dismantle the clutch-shaft assembly by straightening the locking tab, unscrewing the nut and removing the bearing.

In assembling the transmission, keep in mind that the method of disassembling and assembling the overdrive transmission is the same as the standard transmission except that no speedometer drive gear or locking washer and nut is installed.

Assemble the mainshaft. Smear the shaft with grease and install the 33 second gear rollers. Slide the gear into position. Replace the plunger and spring, install the halves of the second gear washer and slide the collar on to the splines. Depress the plunger and push the collar into position, locating the lugs of the washer in the cut-outs of the collar. Rotate the collar until the splines are not in line. Replace the balls and springs in the first-second gear hub. Depress the balls and slide the first gear on to the hub. Install the assembly to the shaft. Replace the bearing spacer collar, bearing and housing, speedometer drive gear key and gear, locking washer and nut. Tighten the nut and secure with the locking washer. Install the third gear and its 32 rollers to the shaft. Replace the plunger and spring and the third gear locking plate, rotating the plate so that the splines are not in line. Install the balls and springs to the third-fourth hub and replace the hub to the shaft.

Assemble the countershaft. Install the spacer tube to the cluster gear so that a washer is at each end of the tube. After smearing the rollers with grease, position them in the gear, then place the thrust washers and plates in position at each end of the gear.

NOTE: *In order to hold the rollers in position, a round bar of countershaft diameter may be inserted into the gear assembly.*

Place the cluster gear in the bottom of the transmission case.

Assemble the transmission. Insert the mainshaft assembly from the rear of the case and position the clutch shaft rollers and shaft assembly into the case. Lift the cluster gear into position, locating the thrust washer tags in the grooves provided. Push the countershaft through the housing and cluster gear, then withdraw the countershaft-size bar as the countershaft pushes through the gear. The cut-away portion of the countershaft should be aligned to fit the groove in the bell housing. Replace the reverse gear and shaft and tighten the securing bolt. Position the fourth gear shifter fork in the case and replace the first-second shift fork and shaft. Install one interlock ball above the first-second shifter shaft and insert the fourth gear shifter shaft. Position the remaining interlock ball by holding it in place with grease. Replace the reverse fork and shaft along with the selector, detent plungers, and springs. Tighten the fork securing bolts and lock with wire. Bolt the rear extension into place, using a new gasket. Note that the plain bearing plate is installed against the bearing.

Overdrive models. Slide the adapter plate bearing, and gasket along the third motion shaft. Insert and tighten the eight bolts which secure the adapter plate to the transmission. Install the spacer which fits between the rear main bearing and the circlip groove and install the circlip. Replace the overdrive unit.

Replace the selector balls to the holes in the transmission housing and install the springs into the holes in the side cover. Attach the gear lever, along with its cup, washers, and spacers, to the side cover. Be sure that the lever ball fits properly into the socket. Replace the cover, using a new gasket if necessary. (Note that the top bolt on the right side is longer than the other twelve.) Replace the clutch housing so that the plain bearing plate is against the bearing. Replace the speedometer drive, breather, and dipstick.

Austin-Healey 3000 Mk. II (Late), and Mk. III.

The transmission of later 3000 Mk. II and Mk. III cars is of a revised design and was installed beginning with car numbers BN7 16039 and BT7 15881 for BN7 and BT7 engines.

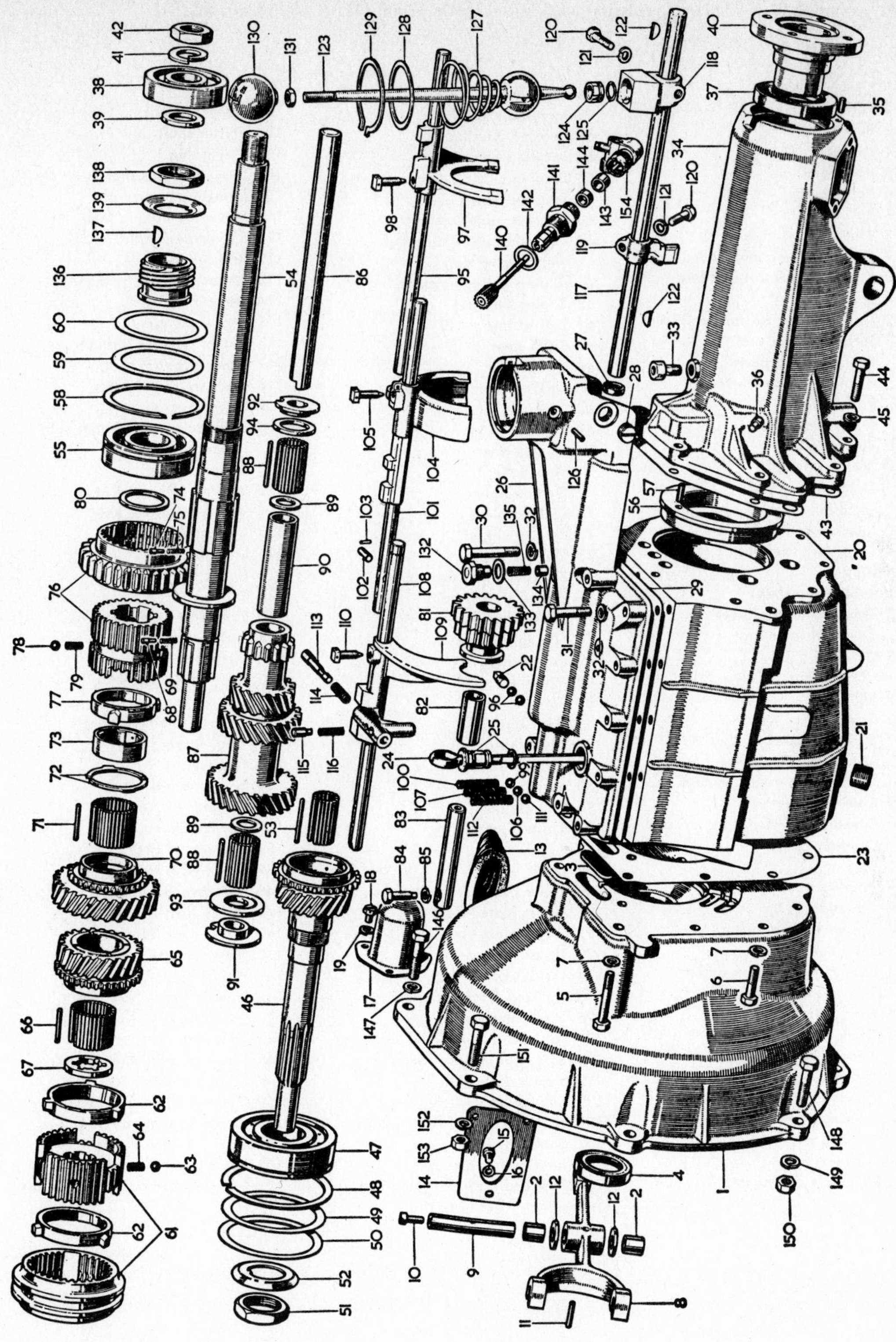

An exploded view of the transmission used in the Healey 3000 Mk. II (late) and Mk. III

An exploded view of the transmission used in the Healey 3000 Mk. II (late) and Mk. III

1 Clutch housing
2 Fork and lever shaft bushing
3 Buffer pad
4 Oil seal
5 Bolt—long
6 Bolt—short
7 Spring washer
8 Clutch fork and lever
9 Fork and lever shaft
10 Clutch withdrawal fork screw
11 Taper pin
12 Thrust washer for fork and lever
13 Fork and lever seal
14 Seal retaining plate
15 Retaining plate screw
16 Spring washer
17 Starter end cover
18 End cover bolt
19 Spring washer
20 Transmission case
21 Oil drain plug
22 Interlock ball hole plug
23 Case to clutch housing gasket
24 Dipstick
25 Rubber grommet
26 Transmission top cover
27 Cover oil seal
28 Cover plug
29 Cover to transmission gasket
30 Bolt—long
31 Bolt—short
32 Spring washer
33 Transmission breather
34 Transmission extension case
35 Case taper plug
36 Speedometer pinion thrust button
37 Oil seal
38 Bearing
39 Bearing washer
40 Coupling flange
41 Spring washer
42 Flange nut
43 Case to transmission gasket
44 Bolt—case to transmission
45 Spring washer
46 Drive gear
47 Bearing for drive gear
48 Bearing circlip
49 Bearing plate
50 Bearing plate (spring)
51 Bearing nut
52 Lock washer
53 Roller for drive gear
54 Mainshaft
55 Mainshaft bearing
56 Bearing housing
57 Locating peg
58 Bearing circlip
59 Bearing plate
60 Bearing plate (spring)
61 Top and third sliding hub with striking dog
62 Sliding hub interceptor
63 Sliding hub ball
64 Ball spring
65 Third gear
66 Gear roller
67 Locking plate
68 Gear plunger
69 Plunger spring
70 Second gear
71 Gear roller
72 Gear washer
73 Locking plate
74 Gear plunger
75 Plunger spring
76 First gear with first and second sliding hub
77 Sliding hub interceptor
78 Sliding hub ball
79 Ball spring
80 Mainshaft spacer collar
81 Reverse gear
82 Gear bushing
83 Gear shaft
84 Shaft retaining screw
85 Spring washer
86 Countershaft
87 Cluster gear
88 Roller
89 Roller washer
90 Roller spacer
91 Thrust plate—front
92 Thrust plate—rear
93 Thrust washer—front
94 Thrust washer—rear
95 Top and third shifter shaft
96 Shaft interlocking ball
97 Top and third striking fork
98 Screw for striking fork
99 Shifter shaft ball
100 Ball spring
101 First and second shifter shaft
102 Shaft interlocking pin
103 Interlocking pin rivet
104 First and second striking fork
105 Screw for striking fork
106 Shifter shaft ball
107 Ball spring
108 Reverse shifter shaft
109 Reverse striking fork
110 Screw for striking fork
111 Shifter shaft ball
112 Ball spring
113 Reverse selector plunger
114 Plunger spring
115 Detent plunger
116 Detent plunger spring
117 Remote control shaft
118 Gear shift lever shaft
119 Selector lever
120 Selector lever and gear shift lever socket screw
121 Spring washer
122 Selector lever and gear shift lever socket key
123 Gear shift lever
124 Lever bushing
125 Circlip for bushing
126 Pin
127 Ball end retaining spring
128 Spring washer
129 Circlip
130 Gear shift lever knob
131 Locknut for knob
132 Plunger retaining plug
133 Plug washer
134 Plunger
135 Plunger spring
136 Speedometer gear
137 Key for gear
138 Locknut for gear
139 Lockwasher for gear
140 Speedometer pinion
141 Pinion bearing
142 Washer for bearing
143 Pinion spacer collar
144 Pinion oil seal
145 Reverse switch hole plug
146 Clutch housing bolt—long
147 Spring washer
148 Clutch housing bolt—short
149 Spring washer
150 Nut
151 Clutch housing dowel bolt
152 Spring washer for dowel bolt
153 Nut for dowel bolt
154 Speedometer drive adapter box

Disassembly of this transmission is as follows: Remove the nine bolts (eight short, one long) and remove the clutch housing complete with clutch operating mechanism. Withdraw the drive gear bearing along with the plain and spring plates. Remove the dipstick from the top of the transmission cover, unscrew the 12 bolts securing the cover to the transmission and lift off the cover. (Note that the two cover bolts nearest the shift lever are longer than the others.) Be careful not to lose the three detent springs which are located in the transmission case under the front edge of the cover.

If it is necessary to remove the gear shift lever from the top cover, proceed as follows: Release the circlip, washer and conical spring from the shift lever turret, then use a punch to drive the two securing pins into the 3/16 in. holes on each side. Lift out the lever and retrieve the pins.

Remove the three detent springs, cut the locking wire and unscrew the bolts which secure the striking fork. With the shifter shafts in the neutral position (to prevent the interlock balls from operating), withdraw the third-fourth gear shifter shaft, being careful not to lose the detent ball which will drop down into the shaft bore at the front of the transmission case. Withdraw the remaining shifter shafts, at the same time retaining the detent balls and the two interlocking balls located between the shafts at the front of the case. Lift out the three striking forks.

If it is necessary to remove the reverse selector plunger from the reverse striking fork, do so by extracting the cotter pin to release the plunger and spring.

Unscrew the driveshaft nut and pull the flange from the mainshaft splines of the transmission. Unscrew and remove the speedometer pinion housing and pinion from the rear extension of the case. Remove the eight securing bolts and remove the transmission rear extension case from the main case. Withdraw the spring and plain plates of the mainshaft bearing.

Overdrive transmission. Remove the eight nuts holding the overdrive adapter plate to the rear of the transmission, being careful not to disturb the joint between the overdrive and the adapter plate. Pull the overdrive and adapter plate away from the transmission and over the mainshaft. Slide the overdrive oil-pump cam from the mainshaft, thus exposing the mainshaft-bearing spacer collar and circlip, which may be left in position during disassembly of the transmission. The circlip and spacer collar need not be removed unless it is desired to remove the mainshaft bearing from the shaft. Withdraw the plain and spring plates of the mainshaft bearing.

Remove the reverse idler gear shaft locating bolt, withdraw the shaft and lift out the idler gear. Push the countershaft forward and pull it from the front of the transmission case. Lower the cluster gear unit to the bottom of the case. Mark the position of the mainshaft-bearing housing locating peg in relation to the transmission case for reassembly purposes. Withdraw the mainshaft assembly from the rear of the transmission case. Remove the 18 rollers from the rear of the drive gear. Use a suitable punch to drive the bearing forward from its housing, then withdraw the drive gear assembly from the front of the case. Lift out the cluster gear unit and thrust washers.

Disassembly and assembly of the mainshaft is as described in the preceding section dealing with the older 100-6 and early Mk. II transmissions. The remainder of the assembly process is as follows:

Install the spacer to the cluster gear unit so that there is a roller washer at each end. Smear the rollers with grease and position them in the ends of the gear unit. There will be 23 rollers at each end. After assembling the front and rear thrust washers and plates of the gear unit, position them in the transmission with grease and be sure that the tags engage the grooves in the transmission case. Place the cluster gear unit at the bottom of the case. Grease the 18 mainshaft rollers and place them in the drive gear. With the drive gear inserted through the front of the case, press the bearing into position. Install the mainshaft assembly from the rear of the case, being careful that the sliding dog and interceptors are in position on the third-fourth gear synchronizing hub. Line up the mainshaft-bearing housing locating peg with the mark made on the transmission case during disassembly. Press the bearing housing into position. Lift the cluster gear unit into position and insert the countershaft through the front of the case. Be sure that the thrust washers and rollers remain in their correct locations. With the reverse idler gear in place, push the shaft into its housing and secure with the locating bolt and washer. Install the mainshaft-bearing plates with the plain plate against the bearing. Ensure that the rear bearing washer is in the correct position on the mainshaft, then bolt the transmission rear extension into place. Install the speedometer pinion and housing. Position the flange of the driveshaft onto the splines of the mainshaft and secure with washer and nut.

If the reverse selector plunger assembly has been removed from the reverse gear striking fork, replace the detent plunger and spring to the fork. Press the detent plunger and push in the selector plunger and spring. Install a new cotter pin in the end of the plunger and make sure that the selector plunger, when pressed into the fork, returns freely. Position the three gear striking forks, then install the reverse gear shifter shaft and secure to the reverse gear striking fork. Be sure that the dowelled end of the locating bolt engages in the hole in the shaft. Position the shifter shaft interlock ball between the reverse gear and the first-second gear shifter shaft bores at the front of the case. With the reverse striking fork in the neutral position, install the first-second shifter shaft, noting that this shaft is provided with an interlocking pin. Install the fork locating screw and place the second interlock ball into its location between the first-second gear and the third-fourth gear. With the first-second gear striking fork held in the neutral position, install the third-fourth gear shifter shaft and the fork locating bolt. Tighten down the three striking fork locating bolts and secure with new locking wires.

Install the gear lever to the transmission top cover by installing the two pins into the diametrically opposed holes on each side of the lever turret. Before the pins are driven in too far, the gear lever should be placed into its seating with the ball notches opposite the holes. The pins should be driven in until their ends are even with the bottom of the counterbores on each side. Install the conical spring, washer, and circlip over the gear lever and secure by pressing the spring and engaging the circlip into its groove. Place the shifter shaft detent balls and springs into their bores, then replace the transmission top cover. The remote-control-rod selector arm should be properly located in the striking forks. Replace the dipstick.

Overdrive transmissions. Check the components of the overdrive unit for alignment before attempting to install the unit to the transmission. A long, thin screwdriver may be used to align by eye the splines of the uni-directional clutch with those of the planet carrier. If the splines are not aligned, the splined hub of the uni-directional clutch may be turned counterclockwise by the screwdriver until the correct position is obtained.

Insert a dummy mainshaft (an old mainshaft works well), and gently turn the coupling flange back and forth, while holding the dummy mainshaft, to assist in engaging it with the splines of the planet carrier and uni-directional clutch. Using a screwdriver as a depth gauge, make sure that the dummy shaft has penetrated as far as possible into the bushing. Position the oil pump operating cam on the central bushing of the body with the lowest part of the dam in contact with the oil pump plunger. NOTE: *A smear of grease will help in retaining the cam in the correct position.*

Install the mainshaft-bearing spring and plain plates into the recess in the adapter plate with the plain plate towards the bearing. With fourth gear engaged in the transmission, carefully install the overdrive and adapter plate over the mainshaft. The mainshaft should be threaded through the oil-pump cam and into the center bushing of the body in such a way that the pump cam is not disturbed from its proper position relative to the pump plunger. The clutch shaft should be gently turned back and forth to help engage the mainshaft splines into the planet carrier, uni-directional clutch and oil-pump cam. If the parts are properly aligned, the studs on the rear face of the transmission will readily enter the holes in the adapter plate. Press the overdrive unit into position, tapping the driveshaft flange, if necessary, with a hammer while at the same time turning the clutch shaft of the transmission.

NOTE: *If difficulty in installing the overdrive unit occurs, it is likely that one or more components have become misaligned. If this is the case, the overdrive must be removed and the components re-aligned with a dummy mainshaft.*

Turn the countershaft so that its stepped end will be aligned to engage the groove in the clutch housing. Position the plain and spring plates of the drive-gear bearing into the recess in the rear face of the clutch housing. (The plain plate should be toward the bearing.) Replace the clutch housing to the main case, being careful not to damage the oil seal on the clutch shaft splines.

Sprite

Disassembly of the transmission of the Sprite is as follows:

Remove the filler plug and drain plug and drain the oil from the transmission. Unscrew and remove the speedometer pinion sleeve from the left side of the rear extension and withdraw the speedometer pinion. Remove the nuts which secure the remote-control housing and lift the housing from the rear cover. Remove the bolts and washers which attach the rear cover to the transmission. Pull back slightly on the rear cover and turn it counterclockwise until the control lever is able to clear the ends of the fork rods, then remove the rear cover. Remove the control shaft locating bolt and screw it into the tapped front end of the control shaft. A slight pressure on the bolt will facilitate removal of the control shaft, which is a push fit in the rear cover. As the shaft is removed, the control lever will slip off the end. Remove the one-piece control lever bushing from the lever. Remove the bolts which secure the bottom cover to the tower of the gear shift lever. If the paper gasket is undamaged, retain it for use during assembly. Unscrew and remove the gear lever locating peg and the anti-rattle springs. (The latter are removed by unscrewing the caps, then tilting the remote-control housing until the springs and plungers drop out.)

Remove the bolts which secure the gear shift lever cover to the top of the tower, then remove the lever, being careful to retain the thrust button and spring. Remove the bolts in the front and rear selector levers, remove the core plugs at the ends of the remove-control housing, and tap out the remote-control shaft. Remove the front and rear selector levers. Unscrew the reverse plunger cap, remove the detent spring, ball, and locating pin, then remove the reverse selector plunger. Remove the two retaining springs and withdraw the clutch release bearing. Remove the clutch withdrawal lever by straightening the locking washer, removing the retaining nut and washer, and unscrewing the bolt which is threaded into the support bracket. Remove the nuts and washers from the front cover within the clutch bell housing. Withdraw the front cover by pulling on the clutch withdrawal lever brackets. Remove the paper gaskets and the packing shim.

Release the bolts in the side cover and remove the side cover and gasket. Remove the two springs which are located at the front edge of the side cover joining face. Turn the transmission over on to its side to let the plungers fall out of the holes from which the springs were removed. Remove the plugs which are located near the clutch bell housing on the side cover side of the transmission case. Note that each plug is provided with a fiber washer. The lower plug covers the reverse plunger and springs. These may be removed by turning the transmission on its side. The other plug blocks the hole through which the interlock ball between the first-second and third-fourth selector rods is inserted. Place the transmission in neutral by lining up the slots in the rear ends of the selector rods. With the side cover of the transmission in the upward position, unlock and remove the reverse fork locating bolt, locknut and washer through the drain plug hole. Also remove the locating bolt locknut and washer from the first-second and third-fourth selector forks. Tap the third-fourth selector rod from the front end and withdraw it from the back of the transmission. Remove the first-second and reverse selector rods in the same manner.

NOTE: *As the selector rods are withdrawn, be sure to remove the two interlock balls from the front of the transmission case.*

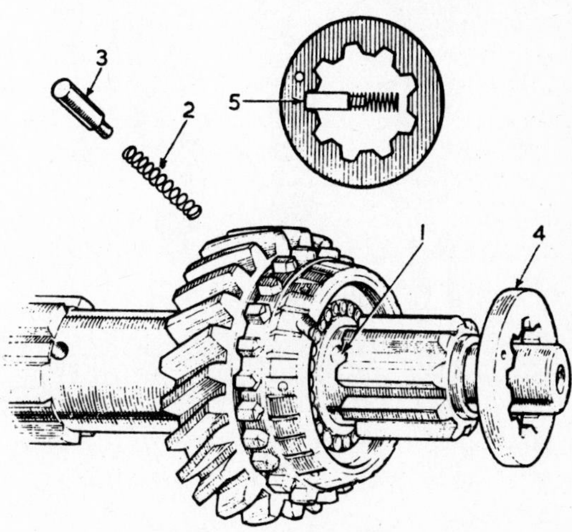

The output shaft of the Sprite transmission

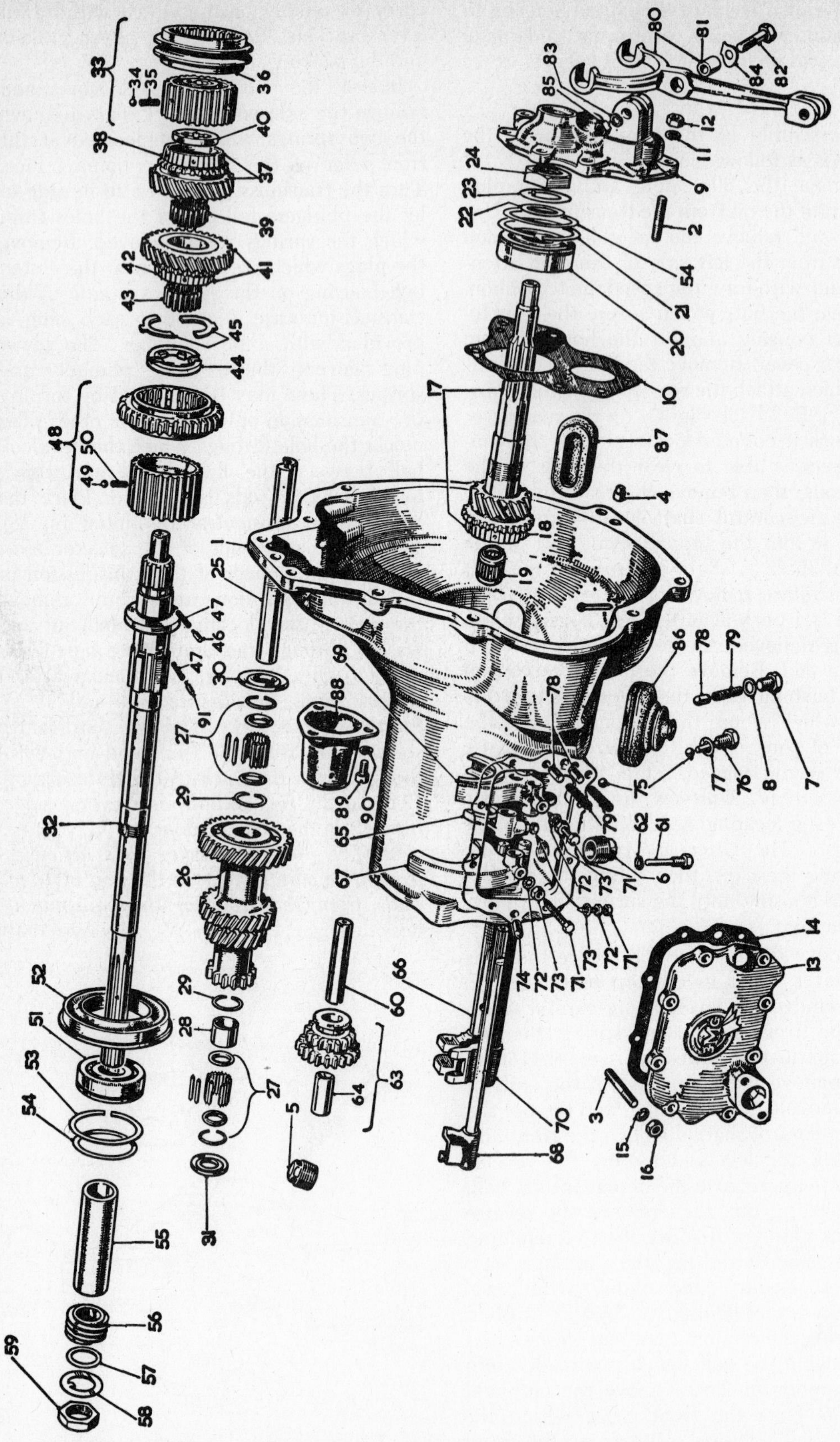

The components of the Sprite transmission

The components of the Sprite transmission

1 Case assembly
2 Stud for front cover
3 Stud for side cover
4 Dowel
5 Filler plug
6 Drain plug
7 Plug for reverse plunger spring
8 Gasket
9 Front cover
10 Front cover gasket
11 Spring washer
12 Nut
13 Side cover
14 Gasket for side cover
15 Spring washer
16 Nut
17 Clutch shaft with cone
18 Synchronizing cone
19 Needle-roller bearing
20 Clutch shaft journal ball bearing
21 Spring ring
22 Washer
23 Lock washer
24 Nut
25 Countershaft
26 Cluster gear
27 Needle-roller bearing with spring ring
28 Spacer
29 Spring ring
30 Thrust washer (front)
31 Thrust washer (rear)
32 Main shaft
33 Third and fourth gear synchronizer
34 Ball
35 Spring
36 Sleeve
37 Third gear with cone
38 Synchronizng cone
39 Needle roller
40 Third gear locking collar
41 Second gear with cone
42 Synchronizing cone
43 Needle roller
44 Second speed locking collar
45 Washer
46 Peg for locking collar
47 Springs for pegs
48 First gear assembly
49 Ball
50 Spring for ball
51 Third motion shaft journal ball bearing
52 Bearing housing
53 Spring ring
54 Bearing packing washer
55 Third motion shaft spacer
56 Speedometer gear
57 Plain washer
58 Locking washer
59 Third motion shaft nut
60 Reverse shaft
61 Screw
62 Spring washer
63 Reverse wheel and bushing
64 Bushing
65 Reverse fork
66 Reverse fork rod
67 First and second gear fork
68 First and second gear fork rod
69 Third and fourth gear fork
70 Third and fourth gear fork rod
71 Fork locating bolt
72 Shakeproof washer
73 Nut
74 Interlock plunger
75 Interlock ball
76 Plug
77 Washer
78 Plunger for fork rod
79 Spring
80 Clutch fork with bushing
81 Bushing
82 Bolt
83 Spring washer
84 Locking washer
85 Nut
86 Dust cover
87 Dust cover for bell housing
88 Starter pinion cover
89 Slot headed bolt
90 Washer
91 Peg for locking collar

Remove the double-end interlock plunger from the rear end of the case. Lift the three selector forks from the transmission. Tap the countershaft from the front of the transmission; the cluster gear and thrust washers will drop to the bottom of the case. Withdraw the third motion shaft assembly from the rear of the transmission case. Drive the clutch shaft forward out of the case and remove the cluster gear and thrust washers. Remove the reverse shaft locking bolt. Place a screwdriver at the slotted end of the reverse shaft and push it into the transmission with a turning motion. The reverse shaft and gear may now be removed.

Disassemble the third motion shaft. Remove the third-fourth synchronizer assemblies. Depress the spring-loaded plunger which locks the front splined ring at the end of the third motion shaft. Rotate the ring until one of its splines covers the plunger and slide the ring and the third gear off the end of the shaft. Remove the plunger and spring. Remove the locking washer at the other end of the shaft and unscrew the securing nut. Remove the lockwasher, plain washer, speedometer gear, and spacer. Withdraw the ball bearing and its housing from the end of the shaft and remove the bearing from the housing. Withdraw the first gear and synchronizer assembly from the shaft. Depress the spring-loaded plunger locking the splined ring at the end of the third motion shaft. Rotate the ring until one of its splines covers the plunger, then slide the ring from the shaft. Remove the plunger and spring, then remove the two halves of the splined ring from the shaft. Slide the second gear from the shaft, being careful to retain the rollers.

Disassemble the clutch shaft. Unlock and remove the securing nut. Withdraw the lockwasher and packing shim. Press the bearing from the shaft and detach the circlip from the bearing.

Disassemble the cluster gear assembly. Remove the locking rings from their grooves at each end of the assembly. Withdraw the outer race rollers and inner race, then remove the inner locking ring from its groove in the large end of the cluster gear and remove the spacer and locking ring from the small end.

Assembly of the Sprite transmission begins with the assembly of the main-shaft.

NOTE: *In reassembling the main-shaft of later Sprites, the second gear and third-fourth gear synchronizers are provided with baulk rings, as indicated in the illustration. The correct position of the gear on the hub is important. The position of the gear should be such that the plunger in the hub lines up the cut-away tooth.*

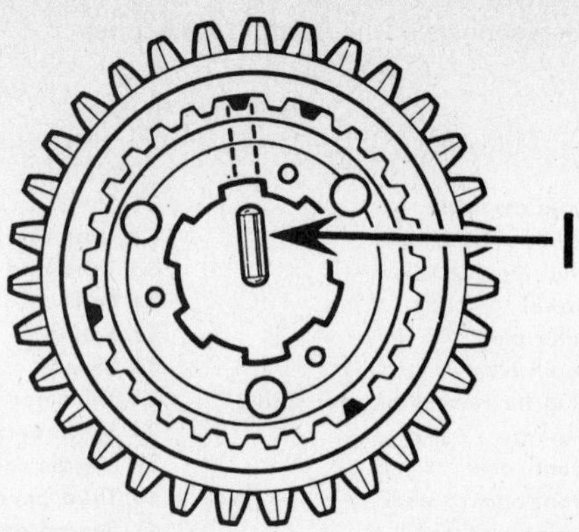

The first and second gear assembly of later Sprites, showing the correct positioning of the gear and hub with the plunger (1).

In reassembling, note that the outer race of the mainshaft bearing is grooved to accommodate a locking ring. The ring also rests in a recess of the bearing housing. Press the bearing into the flanged end of the housing so that the ring end of the bearing is last. Install the rollers on to the shaft and replace the second gear. Position the two halves of the splined ring washer on to the shaft so that the locking pegs are properly located in the splined ring. Install the spring and plunger into the hole in the shaft and replace the splined ring. Slide the first gear and synchronizer assembly on to the shaft so that the protruding end of the synchronizer is toward the bearing. Press the bearing and its housing on to the shaft so that the bearing housing flange will be toward the rear of the shaft. Replace the spacer, speedometer drive gear, plain and lock washers and tighten the locknut. At the other end of the shaft, assemble the needle-roller bearing and install the third gear assembly. Replace the spring and plunger into the hole in the shaft and install the splined ring. The third-fourth synchronizer should then be replaced to the shaft so that the boss of the synchronizer hub is away from the splined ring.

Assemble the clutch shaft by reversing the removal procedure and being careful that the inner tag of the lockwasher, which

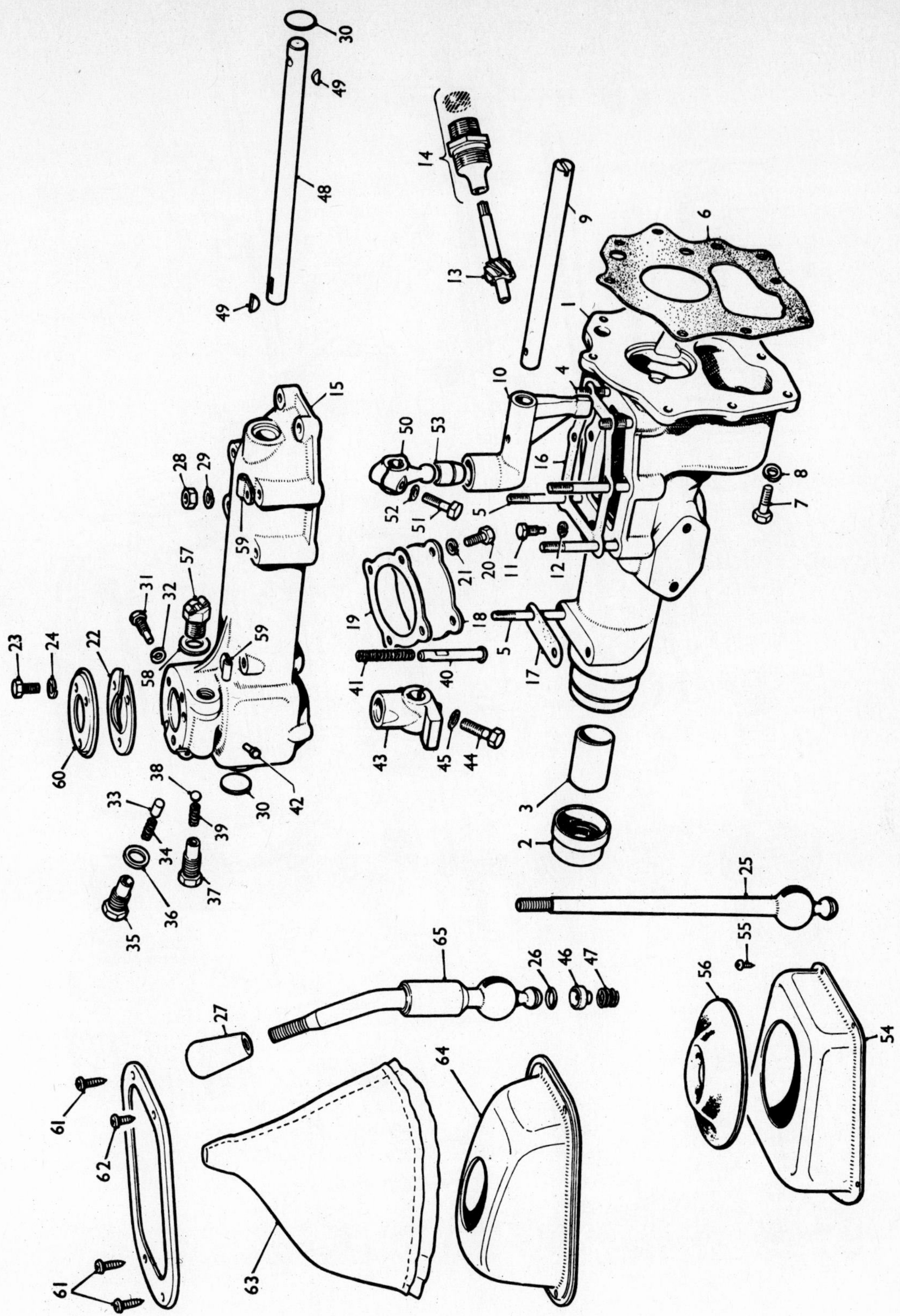

The extension housings used on the Sprite transmissions

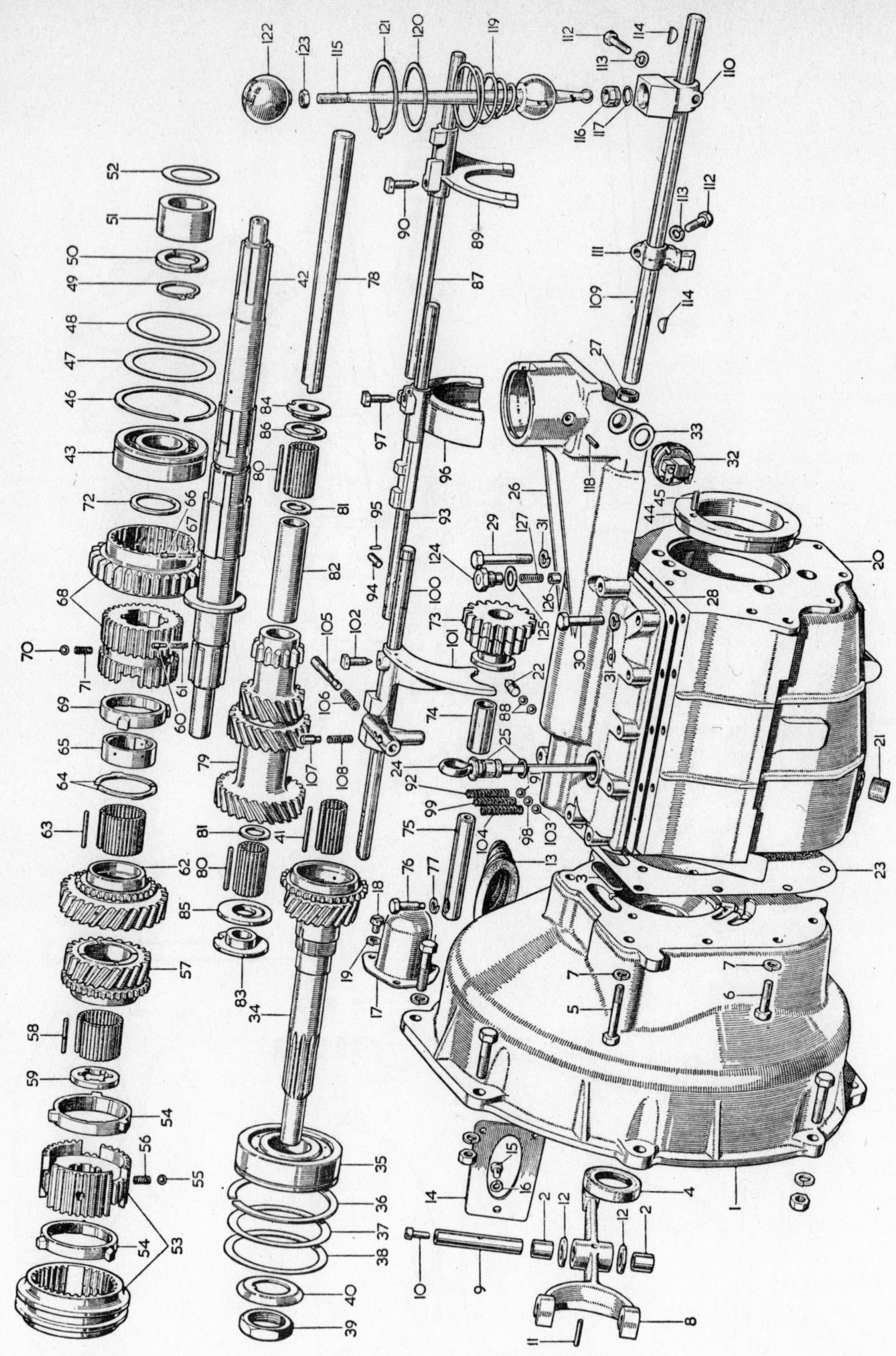

The later Austin-Healey 3000 transmission with overdrive

The later Austin-Healey 3000 transmission with overdrive

1 Clutch housing
2 Fork and lever shaft bushing
3 Buffer pad
4 Oil seal
5 Bolt—long
6 Bolt—short
7 Spring washer
8 Clutch fork and lever
9 Fork and lever shaft
10 Clutch withdrawal fork, screw
11 Taper pin
12 Thrust washer for fork and lever
13 Fork and lever seal
14 Seal retaining plate
15 Retaining plate screw
16 Spring washer
17 Starter end cover
18 End cover screw
19 Spring washer
20 Gearbox case
21 Oil drain plug
22 Interlock ball hole plug
23 Case to clutch housing gasket
24 Oil level indicator
25 Rubber grommet
26 Gearbox top cover
27 Cover oil seal
28 Cover to gearbox gasket
29 Bolt—long
30 Bolt—short
31 Spring washer
32 Overdrive switch
33 Gasket for switch
34 Drive gear
35 Bearing for drive gear
36 Circlip for bearing
37 Plate for bearing
38 Plate for bearing (spring)
39 Nut for bearing
40 Lockwasher
41 Drive gear roller
42 Mainshaft
43 Mainshaft bearing
44 Bearing housing
45 Locating peg
46 Bearing circlip
47 Plate for bearing
48 Plate or bearing (spring)
49 Mainshaft circlip
50 Bearing abutment collar
51 Abutment collar retaining ring
52 Shim
53 Top and third sliding hub with striking dog
54 Sliding hub interceptor
55 Sliding hub ball
56 Ball spring
57 Third gear
58 Roller for gear
59 Locking plate
60 Gear plunger
61 Plunger spring
62 Second gear
63 Roller for gear
64 Gear washer
65 Locking plate
66 Gear plunger
67 Plunger spring
68 First gear with first and second sliding hub
69 Sliding hub interceptor
70 Sliding hub ball
71 Ball spring
72 Mainshaft spacer collar
73 Reverse gear
74 Gear bush
75 Gear shaft
76 Shaft retaining bolt
77 Spring washer
78 Countershaft
79 Cluster gear
80 Roller
81 Roller washer
82 Roller spacer
83 Thrust plate—front
84 Thrust plate—rear
85 Thrust washer—front
86 Thrust washer—rear
87 Top and third shifter shaft
88 Shaft interlocking ball
89 Top and third striking fork
90 Bolt
91 Shifter shaft ball
92 Ball spring
93 First and second shifter shaft
94 Shaft interlocking pin
95 Interlocking pin rivet
96 First and second striking fork
97 Bolt
98 Shifter shaft ball
99 Ball spring
100 Reverse shifter shaft
101 Reverse striking fork
102 Bolt
103 Shifter shaft ball
104 Ball spring
105 Reverse selector plunger
106 Plunger spring
107 Detent plunger
108 Detent plunger spring
109 Remote control shaft
110 Gearshift shaft
111 Selector lever
112 Bolt
113 Spring washer
114 Key
115 Gearshift
116 Lever bushing
117 Circlip for bushing
118 Rollpin
119 Ball end retaining spring
120 Washer for spring
121 Circlip
122 Gearshift knob
123 Locknut for knob
124 Plunger retaining plug
125 Plug washer
126 Plunger
127 Plunger spring

The extension housings used on the Sprite transmissions

1 Rear extension
2 Oil seal
3 Bushing
4 Extension short stud
5 Extension long stud
6 Gasket
7 Bolt
8 Spring washer
9 Control shaft
10 Control lever
11 Control lever locating peg
12 Spring washer
13 Speedometer pinion
14 Speedometer pinion oil seal assembly
15 Remote control casing
16 Gasket
17 Gasket
18 Lever tower bottom cover
19 Gasket
20 Bolt
21 Spring washer
22 Lever seat cover
23 Bolt
24 Spring washer
25 Gearshift lever
26 Ring (rubber)
27 Knob
28 Nut
29 Spring washer
30 Welch plug
31 Lever locating peg
32 Spring washer
33 Control shaft damper plunger
34 Spring
35 Spring retaining cap
36 Washer
37 Reverse selector detent plug
38 Ball
39 Spring
40 Reverse selector plunger
41 Spring
42 Reverse selector plunger locating pin
43 Rear selector lever
44 Bolt
45 Spring washer
46 Thrust button
47 Spring
48 Remote control shaft
49 Key
50 Front selector lever
51 Bolt
52 Spring washer
53 Bushing
54 Remote control cover
55 Screw
56 Dust cover
57 Back-up light switch
58 Washer for switch
59 Clip, back-up light switch lead
60 Retaining plate, boot support
61 Self-tapping screw (long)
62 Self-tapping screw (short)
63 Boot
64 Boot support
65 Gearshift lever

Sprite Mk IV (HAN10) cars

engages the keyway in the shaft, is turned away from the bearing.

Assemble the cluster-gear assembly, replacing or varying the thrust washers used. The cluster-gear end-float should be approximately .001-.003 in. (.0254-.0762 mm.) and is obtained by installing the proper thrust washer at the rear. The rear thrust washer (the smaller of the two) is manufactured in the following thicknesses:

.123-.124 in. (3.124-3.150 mm.)
.125-.126 in. (3.175-3.200 mm.)
.127-.129 in. (3.226-3.250 mm.)
.130-.131 in. (3.302-3.327 mm.)

Reassembly of the transmission is the reverse of the disassembly operation, except for the following points:

If a new front or rear gasket is to be installed, it should be compressed by bolting the cover and gasket into position before the other components are installed. The cover and gasket should then be removed. A dummy countershaft should be used to align the gear cluster components. The correct thickness of the end cover shims is determined as follows:

Measure the depth of the recess in the front cover and the distance which the bearing outer race protrudes from the casing. Tighten the cover (with only the paper gasket in position), then remove the cover and measure the thickness of the paper gasket. The thickness of the shims to be used may then be calculated from the following formula: (Required Thickness of Shims) = (Thickness of Paper Gasket after Compression) + (Depth of Cover Recess) − (Distance which Bearing Race Protrudes from Casing). Use the smallest number of shims which will give the required thickness. Shims are available in thicknesses of .004 in. (.10 mm.), .006 in. (.15 mm.), and .010 in. (.25 mm.). A .006 in. (.15 mm.) shim will usually be sufficient. Tighten the bolts of the rear cover evenly by diagonal selection. Shimming for front and rear covers is carried out in the same manner.

The remainder of the assembly of the Sprite transmission is the reverse of the disassembly operation.

America

Remove the engine from the car. Remove the bolts that retain the clutch cover plate; remove the clutch and flywheel assembly, as detailed in the section that deals with them above. Remove the bolts from the flange of the transmission case. Hoist the engine clear of the transmission. Remove the idler gear and thrust washers.

Take out the differential assembly in the following manner:

Remove the extension housing. Detach the remote control lever from the upper side of the remote control shaft. Remove the shaft.

Remove the cotter pins from the nuts that attach both drive flanges to the output shafts, and remove the nuts. Use a pinion flange wrench to hold the drive flanges during this operation.

CAUTION: *Do not use the transmission housing as a brace when removing the flanges, or other drive components; damage to the case will result if this is done.*

Undo the five bolts from each of the end covers, and remove the covers. Check the number of shims used between the bearing and the housing.

Undo the nuts that attach the transmission housing to the differential housing; remove the differential housing and take out the differential assembly.

Remove the back-up light switch and plunger. Detach the clamp and key from the inside end of the gearshift shaft, and slide out the shaft. Undo the setscrew on the speedometer pinion bushing and withdraw the complete speedometer gear assembly.

Detach the front cover, along with the radiator mounting bracket assembly. Withdraw the selector interlock arm.

Unclip the oil line from its bracket and flange. Remove the line from the strainer being careful not to damage the gasket.

Remove the snap ring and take out the input shaft roller bearing with a puller.

Lock the first and third gears by using the shifter shafts. Bend back the lockwasher tabs and remove the input shaft nut. Undo the nut that attaches the ouput gear and remove both the output and the input gears.

Bend back the lockplates on the four bolts that attach the input shaft bearing retainer. Remove the bolts, the retainer, and the shims. Detach the locating plate that serves for both the countershaft and the reverse idler shaft; push the countershaft out from the clutch housing side of the transmission. Remove the counter gear cluster along with its thrust washers.

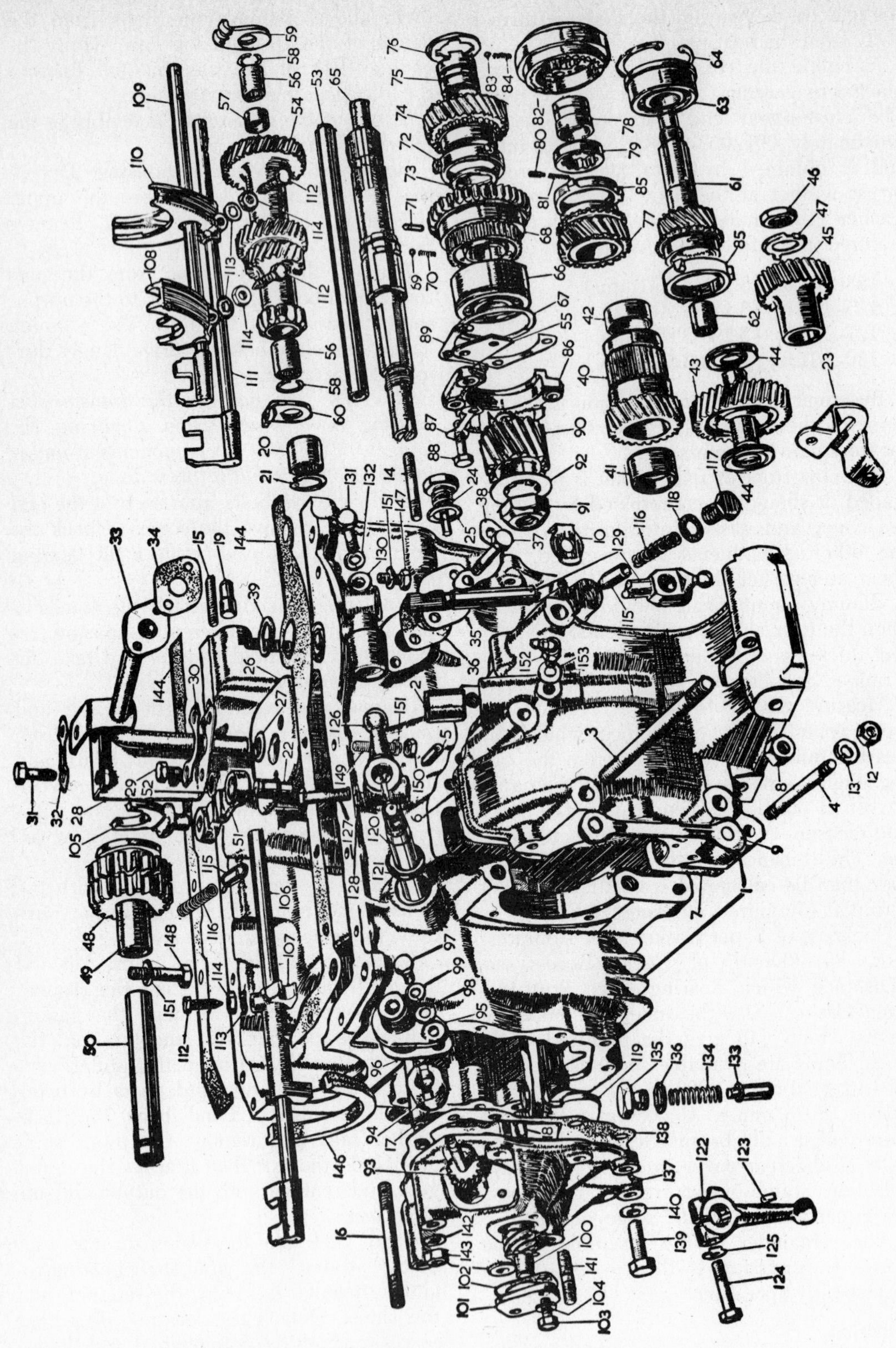

The transmission components of the America

The transmission components of the America

1 Transmission case
2 Control shaft bushing
3 Differential cover stud
4 Differential cover stud
5 Differential cover dowel
6 Differential cover gasket (upper)
7 Differential cover gasket (lower)
8 Differential cover stud nut
9 Washer
10 Washer
12 Differential cover stud nut
13 Washer
14 Flywheel housing stud
15 Flywheel housing stud
16 Front cover stud (long)
17 Front cover stud (short)
18 Front cover dowel
19 Flywheel housing dowel
20 Idler gear bearing
21 Bearing circlip
22 Operating lever pin
23 Exhaust pipe bracket
24 Drain plug
25 Gasket
26 Oil strainer
27 Sealing ring
28 Strainer bracket
29 Bolt to strainer
30 Washer
31 Bolt to casing
32 Washer
33 Oil suction pipe
34 Gasket washer
35 Pipe flange
36 Gasket washer
37 Gasket
38 Washer
39 Sealing ring
40 Primary gear
41 Gear bushing (front)
42 Gear bushing (rear)
43 Idler gear
44 Idler gear thrust washer
45 Input shaft gear
46 Nut
47 Lock washer
48 Reverse gear
49 Bushing
50 Reverse shaft
51 Reverse operating lever
52 Pivot pin circlip
53 Countershaft
54 Countergear
55 Locating plate
56 Bearing
57 Spacer
58 Retaining ring
59 Thrust washer (rear)
60 Thrust washer (front)
61 Input shaft
62 Input shaft roller bearing
63 Input ball bearing
64 Circlip
65 Output shaft
66 Output shaft bearing
67 Circlip
68 First gear
69 Synchronizer ball
70 Spring
71 Second gear synchronizer plunger
72 Blocker ring
73 Second gear thrust washer
74 Second gear
75 Bushing
76 Interlocking ring
77 Third Bushing gear
78 Bush
79 Output shaft thrust washer
80 Thrust washer peg
81 Spring
82 Third/fourth synchronizer
83 Ball
84 Spring
85 Blocker ring
86 Bearing retainer
87 Lock washer
88 Bolt
89 Bearing shim
90 Final drive pinion
91 Nut
92 Washer
93 Speedometer pinion
94 Bushing
95 Bushing assembly
96 Gasket
97 Bolt
98 Washer
99 Washer
100 Speedometer spindle and gear
101 End plate
102 Gasket
103 Bolt
104 Washer
105 Reverse fork
106 Reverse fork rod
107 Fork rod shifter
108 First and second speed fork
109 First and second speed fork rod
110 Third and fourth speed fork
111 Third and fourth speed fork rod
112 Selector bolt
113 Washer
114 Locknut
115 Plunger fork end
116 Plunger spring
117 Plug
118 Plug washer
119 Gearshift gate
120 Gearshift shaft
121 Oil seal
122 Operating lever
123 Key
124 Lever bolt
125 Washer
126 Change shaft lever
127 Lever bolt
128 Washer
129 Remote-control shaft
130 Shaft lever
131 Lever bolt
132 Washer
133 Reverse check plunger
134 Plunger spring
135 Spring plug
136 Plug gasket
137 Front cover
138 Gasket
139 Cover bolt
140 Washer
141 Mounting adaptor stud
142 Washer
143 Nut
144 Crankcase gasket—R.H.
145 Crankcase gasket—L.H.
146 Bearing cap oil seal
147 Transmission to crankcase bolt
148 Transmission to crankcase bolt (long)
149 Transmission to crankcase stud
150 Nut
151 Washer
152 Gearshift remote control shaft lubricator
153 Lubricator washer

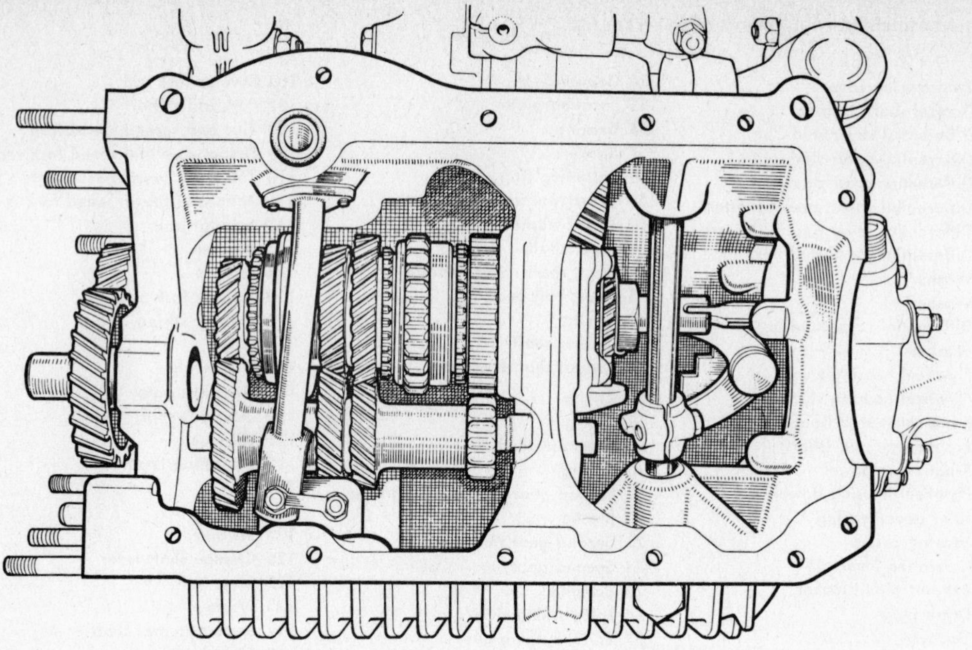

The America four-speed synchromesh transmission viewed from the top

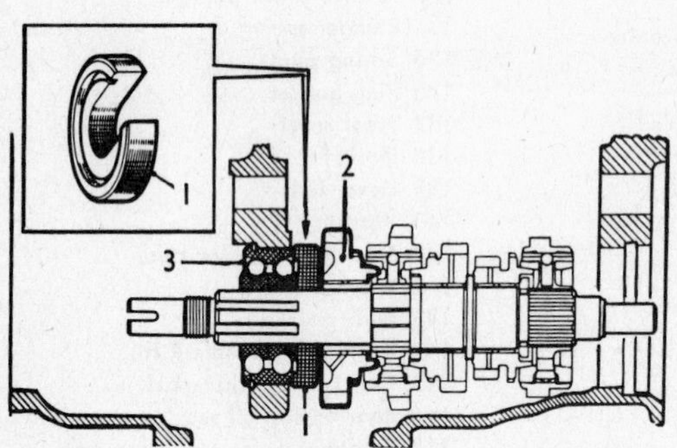

Removal of the output shaft bearing on the America

1 Spacing collar
2 First gear
3 Bearing

Remove the plugs from the outside of the housing. Take out the shifter rod springs and plungers. Take the snap-ring off the input shaft bearing, and remove the bearing and shaft by careful use of a slidehammer.

Drift the output shaft backwards, until a spacing collar of the same O.D. as the output shaft bearing can be placed between first gear and the bearing. The spacer can be fabricated from a piece of pipe having the same O.D. as the output shaft bearing. Care should be taken to see that neither the bearing nor the housing are damaged. Drift the output shaft out of the housing until the bearing is almost clear, then slide the bearing off of the shaft and out of the housing. Finish drifting the shaft out of the housing. CAUTION: *Care should be taken to see that the shifter forks are not damaged.*

Remove the oil strainer, its bracket, the reverse shaft, gear and the shifter fork.

If the transmission is to be completely removed from its housing, remove the screws from the shifter forks and shafts. Remove the shafts and forks themselves. Remove the snap-ring from the pin on the reverse gear operating lever; and withdraw the lever.

The procedure for dismantling the output shaft, if necessary, is as follows; remove the third and fourth gear synchromesh hub and blocker rings, which are positioned in the front of the shaft.

Push down the plunger on the front thrust washer, and rotate the washer until its splines engage those on the shaft; remove it, along with the plunger and spring. Remove the third gear and its bearing.

Remove the first gear, the blocker ring and the bearing in a similar manner from the opposite end of the output shaft. Lever the bearing journal backward and use a puller to remove it from the shaft. Remove reverse gear. Take off the synchronizer assembly and the blocker ring.

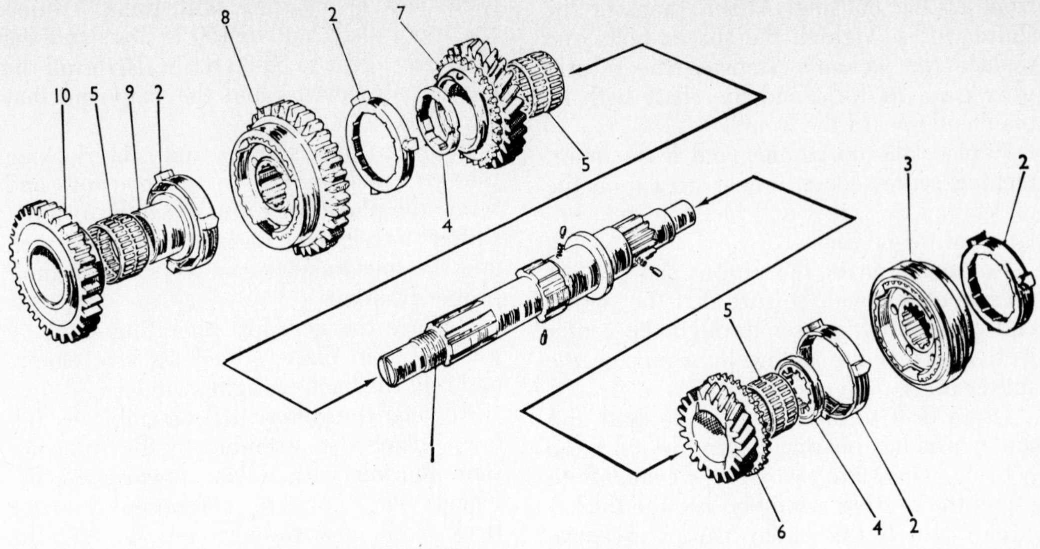

The output shaft assembly on the America transmission

1 Output shaft
2 Blocker rings
3 3rd and 4th gear synchronizer
4 Thrust washers
5 Roller bearings
6 Third gear
7 Second gear
8 Reverse gear/1st and 2nd gear synchronizer
9 Roller bearing journal
10 First gear

Depress the two plungers on the rear thrust washer, turn it to engage the splines on the shaft and remove it. Remove second gear and its roller bearing.

Reassembly of the output shaft is the reverse of disassembly. Be careful to replace the synchronizers in the correct positions; the third and fourth speed synchronizer flange faces the output shaft bearing. The first and second gear synchronizer flange faces first gear; otherwise synchromesh will be lost on second gear. Use a drift to replace the bearing journal on the output shaft.

If the rest of the transmission has been completely dismantled, begin reassembly by replacing the reverse operating lever and pin. Push the shifter rods in from the

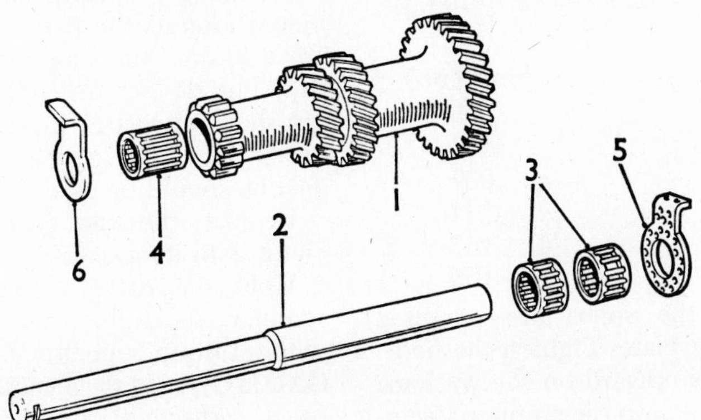

The countergear assembly for the America transmission

1 Countergear
2 Countershaft
3 Roller bearings
4 Roller bearing
5 Large thrust washer
6 Small (variable size) thrust washer

front of the housing. Attach them to the shifter forks. Tighten the shifter bolts and replace the locknuts. Replace the reverse idler gear, its fork, and the shaft with its plain end toward the front.

Replace the oil strainer and leave its attaching screws loose. Smear grease on the oil sealing ring; this will facilitate reinstallation of the oil line.

Reinstallation of the output shaft is the reverse of removal; be sure that the slotted end of the shaft passes through the center web, and that the sliding hubs engage the shifter forks.

Use a drift to install the input shaft and the attendant bearing assembly into the housing. There are two circlips available to retain the bearing assembly; use the thicker circlip first. If this circlip causes excessive binding when the shaft is rotated, replace it with the thinner circlip. Drift the output shaft bearing, and spacer into place.

Replace the countergear assembly with the standard sized thrust washer at the large end. The small end thrust washer is available in several sizes, the correct size should be selected to give .002-.006 in. end-play.

Use a dummy countershaft to properly place the thrust washer. Replace the countershaft from the clutch side, with its slotted end pointing toward that of the reverse shaft. Replace the locating plate which serves for both the countershaft and the reverse shaft.

Replace the output shaft bearing retainer without the shims, tighten the bolts lightly. Measure the gap, and use the proper number of shims required, as shown in the following table:

Gap (in.)	Shims (in.)
.005-.006	.005
.006-.008	.007
.008-.010	.009
.010-.012	.011
.012-.014	.013
.014-.015	.015

Be sure that the shims are mounted *under* the locating plate. Tighten the bolts, and bend the tabs upward on the washers.

Insert the oil line into the strainer assembly, and tighten the flange attachment bolts. Finish tightening the bracket bolts. Care should be taken not to disturb the oil seal.

Replace the input and final drive gears, using new lockwashers with them. Torque the input shaft nut to 150 ft. lbs., and the final drive gear to 55-60 ft. lbs. Reinstall the input shaft bearing and the snap-ring that retains it.

Replace the shifter rod interlocking plungers and springs in the housing, and screw the plugs back into place. Return the shifter interlocking arm, the front cover, and the speedometer gear assembly to their proper positions.

Replace the gearshift operating shaft by pushing it in place. Attach its key, clamp, and refit the back-up light switch.

Replace the differential assembly as follows: place the assembly in the transmission housing with a bias toward the flywheel side. Put the differential housing back on, along with its gaskets. Tighten the nuts enough to hold the bearings in place, while still allowing sideways motion of the assembly. Replace the right-side end cover and gasket. Tighten the bolts *evenly*, this allows the differential to move away from the flywheel side, and the bearing to make proper contact with the inner surface of the cover.

Replace the left-side end cover *without* its gasket. Tighten the bolts enough for the cover surface to contact the outer race of the bearing. NOTE: *The word* THRUST, *on the bearing, should be facing outside.*

If the cover is overtightened it will distort. The necessary preload for the bearings is .004 in. The compressed thickness of the gasket is .007 in., thus the gap between the cover flange and the differential housing should be .011 in. Using a feeler gauge, make measurements several places around the flange, if they vary, the cover has not been tightened evenly. Adjust this, but do not overtighten the bolts. To get the proper .011 in. gap, shims must be used, i.e., if the gap is .008 in. a shim of .003 in. should be used.

Remove the end cover, and replace it along with its gasket and the proper shims.

Hold the drive flanges with a pinion spanner, and tighten the nuts to 70 ft. lbs. with a torque wrench.

CAUTION: *Both driveshafts must rotate freely, otherwise the car will pull to one side.*

From underneath the car, reposition the remote control lever on the ball end of the gearshift, and engage the splined end of the remote control lever with the remote con-

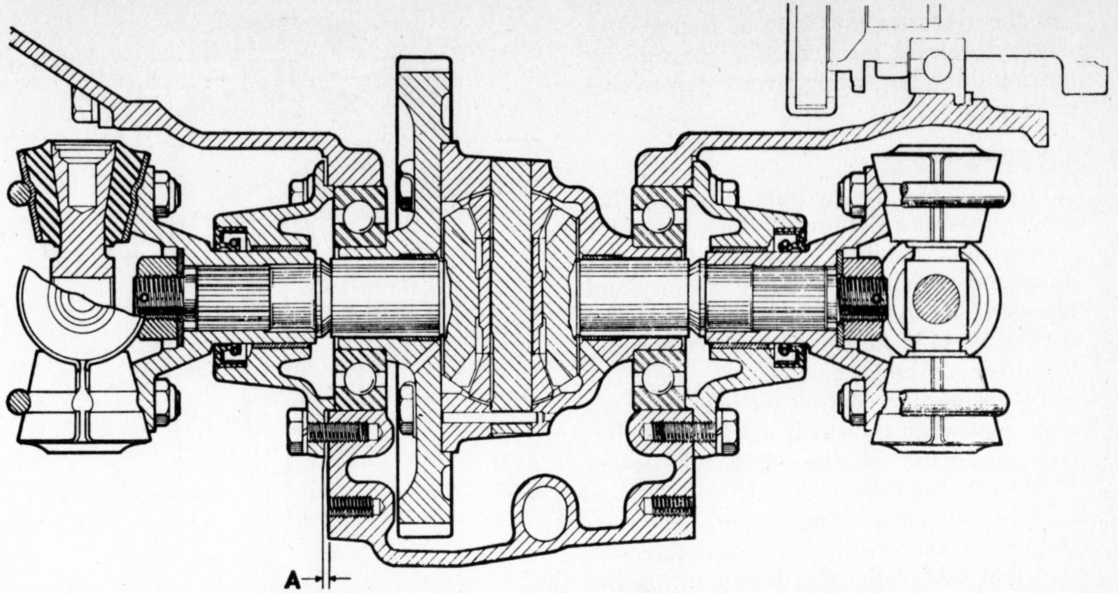

Measure the gap at A with the left end cover in place; but without the gasket. Fit shims between the cover and the bearing to get the proper preload.

trol shaft. Align the hole in the flange with the one in the shaft, and replace the bolt that goes in it. Replace the extension housing.

Reinstall the idler gear with its thrust washers; the chamfered side of each washer goes against the gear.

Put a new gasket on the flywheel housing, and replace the housing, using a torque figure of 18 ft. lbs. for the nuts and bolts that attach it.

The end-play of the idler gear should be .003-.008 in.; thrust washers of different thicknesses are available to compensate for this.

Take the flywheel housing and gasket off again; reassemble the engine and transmission, which is the reverse of the procedure for separating them.

Tighten the nuts and the bolts on the transmission housing finger tight, and then tighten them with a torque wrench, one turn at a time, to a torque figure of 6 ft. lbs. Use a new gasket on the flywheel to replace the one used for checking the idler gear end-play. Be sure that all gaskets and seals are correctly positioned and leak-free.

Overdrive

Adjustments and Maintenance

Some Austin-Healey models are equipped with an overdrive unit as an option. It is an electrically controlled unit, which acts on the third and fourth gears; it is engaged by operating a switch on the instrument panel.

The oil supply, for both the overdrive and the transmission, is common. Check the oil level of the overdrive unit with the transmission dipstick. If the overdrive unit is not acting properly, check the oil level before making other adjustments. If the oil is low, add clean oil of the proper type, and retest the unit.

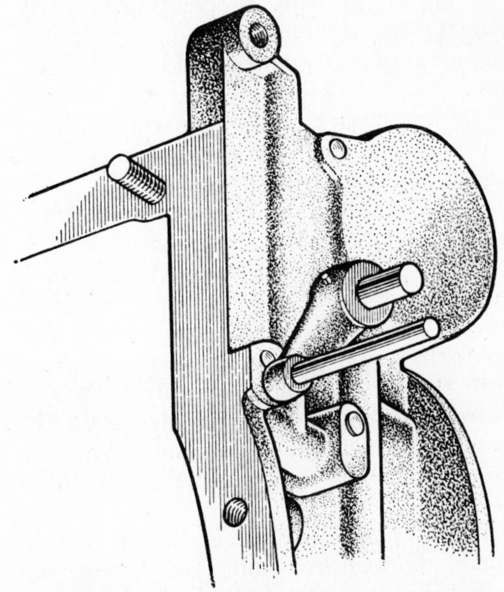

Overdrive valve setting lever on the Austin-Healey

If the overdrive unit is to be removed or serviced, release the hydraulic pressure by moving the valve setting lever ten or twelve times.

Operating Valve

Depressurize the hydraulic system. Remove the carpet and tunnel, the same as for transmission removal. Unscrew the valve plug and remove the valve spring and plunger. The ball inside the valve chamber should lift 1/32 in. from its seat when the overdrive control is engaged.

To operate the control, for overdrive engagement when the car is not running, bypass the parts of the electrical system which are responsive to speed.

If the ball is not lifting properly, the control lever must be adjusted. It is located on the right side of the overdrive unit, on the valve crossshaft. In the outer end of it there is a 3/16 in. hole, which should correspond to a similar hole in the housing when the overdrive unit is engaged.

If the holes do not align, adjust the control assembly until a 3/16 in. rod can be inserted through both holes, simultaneously, from the lever side.

Using a magnet, withdraw the ball from the chamber. Remove the valve with a 1/8 in. rod, being careful not to damage the valve seat. Clear the small hole at the bottom of the valve, of restrictions. Clean and reinstall the ball, plunger, and spring.

Hydraulics

If the control valve is operating properly and the overdrive is not functioning, the operation of the pump should be checked out.

To do this, jack up the rear wheels of the car. With the engine at idle in fourth gear, remove the valve plug to see if oil is being pumped into the valve chamber. Lack of oil indicates that the pump is not working.

If this is the case, either the pump return valve needs attention, i.e. it is clogged or has a broken spring; or the spring that holds the pump plunger in place is broken.

If the pump won't self-prime, the air bleed is clogged, trapping air inside the pump. Remove the pump and clean the bore into which it fits, and the flat on its body.

If the pump is suspect, drain the oil out of the overdrive unit, and remove the solenoid. Loosen the bolt on the operating lever; remove the lever along with the solenoid plunger.

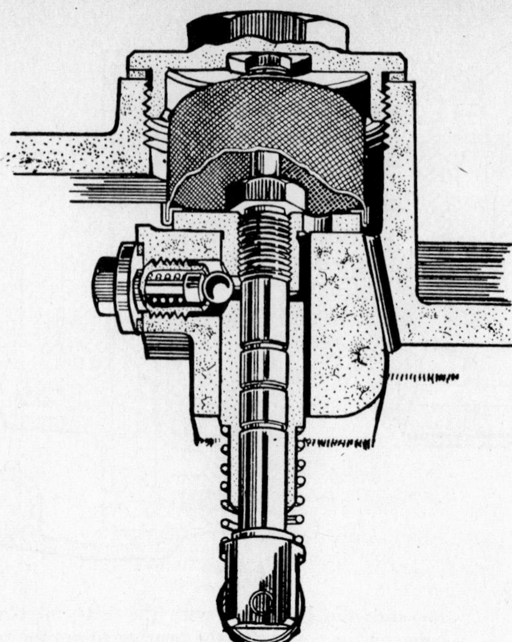

Cut-away view of the oil pump used for the Healey overdrive

The spacer on the valve shaft should be removed next. The bracket that attaches the solenoid has two bolts and two studs attaching it, which must be removed in the proper sequence, in order to take the bracket off. CAUTION: *The heads of the bolts are painted red. Remove the nuts from the studs first. Do not touch the bolts until this is done; then loosen the bolts together, to release the tension on the accumulator spring.*

Remove the bracket. Take the cap off of the valve and withdraw the spring, plunger, and ball. Clean the ball and its seat with a lint-free rag. Drift the ball back into the seat gently. Reassembly is the reverse of teardown.

To remove the pump, drain the overdrive unit and remove the pump valve, as above. Remove the filter. Undo the two screws that attach the pump flange, and withdraw the pump body. A threaded bar that screws in, in place of the drain plug, is useful for this. Clean the pump and check it for wear or damage.

Replace the pump body so that its intake port and screw holes correspond with those in the housing. Tap the body home, using a wood block to absorb some of the impact.

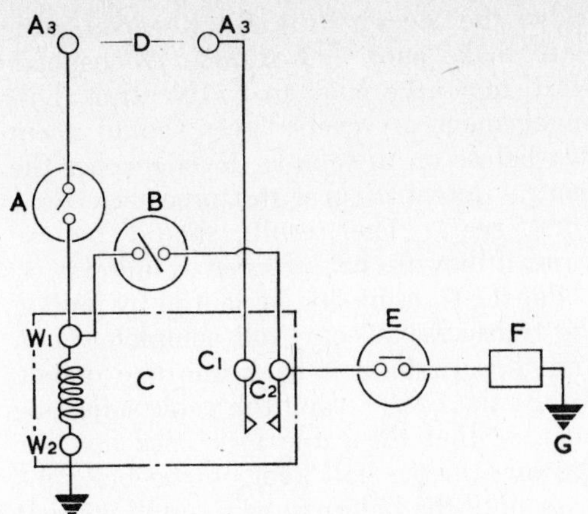

Schematic diagram for the electrical system used to operate the Healey overdrive

A Toggle switch
B Throttle switch
C Relay
D Fuse block
F Solenoid
G Ground

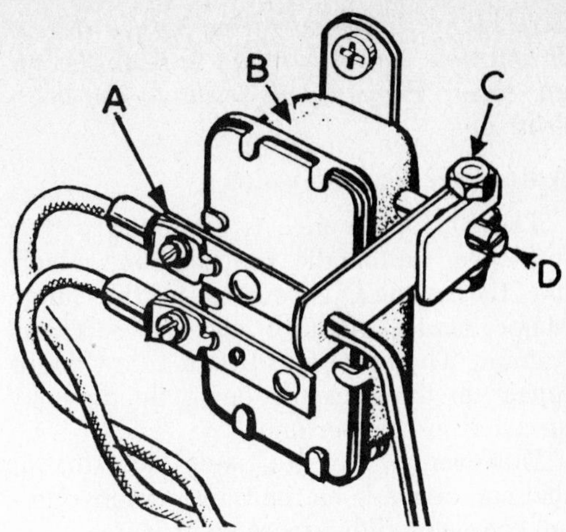

The Healey overdrive throttle switch

A Switch terminal
B Switch body
C Clamp bolt
D Operating shaft

The plunger is inserted into the body with the flat side of the head facing rearward. Guide the plunger past the anti-rotation peg, by using a screwdriver inserted in the side of the housing. Replace the plug.

Relay System Testing

To check the operation of the solenoid, engage neutral, with the ignition switch on, the engine off, and the solenoid disconnected. Momentarily jump the solenoid to fuse terminal A3. The solenoid should operate; failure to do so, indicates a defective solenoid, or an incorrectly adjusted operating linkage. Reconnect the solenoid.

With the ignition and engine set up in the same manner as above, engage fourth gear, and momentarily jump terminals C2 and A3. If the solenoid does not operate, the transmission switch is defective. Return the transmission to neutral.

Next, test the relay coil. Jump relay terminal W1 to fuse terminal A3, if the relay does not operate, the relay coil is defective, and the relay must be replaced.

Turn the toggle switch on and off; if the relay does not work, the toggle switch is defective.

Engage fourth gear, close the toggle switch and open the accelerator switch. The solenoid should operate; if it does not, the relay should be replaced.

With fourth gear still engaged, and starting with the toggle switch closed, open the toggle switch while slowly depressing the accelerator. The solenoid should remain engaged from zero to one-fifth of the way down. If it releases before one-fifth throttle is reached, the accelerator switch should be checked and adjusted.

When driving the car, early release of the switch will appear as a pronounced braking effect, when the car slows down with the throttle closed.

If any of these symptoms occur, or if the carburetor and accelerator linkages have been adjusted, the switch will require adjustment.

Connect a 12 volt low draw (2 watt) bulb between the switch's upper terminal and a ground.

The bulb should light when the overdrive and the ignition are on at the same time, with the gearshift in third or fourth gear. Switch the overdrive off and leave the throttle closed; the bulb should remain lit.

Depress the accelerator pedal, slowly until the light goes out. Check the position of the throttle at this point, it should be one-fifth of the way open. This may be determined by insertion of a 3/16 in. diameter rod between the stop screw and the stop. On the HD type of carburetor it should just clear them. On the H4 carburetor, use a .048 in. feeler gauge between the stop screw and the stop to determine a one-fifth throttle opening.

To adjust the switch, loosen the lever clamp bolt, and turn the operating shaft with a screwdriver until the correct setting is reached.

CAUTION: *If the overdrive fails to release at any time, do not attempt to back the car up; severe damage will result to the overdrive unit.*

Automatic Transmission

The Austin America is equipped with a four-speed automatic transmission, which, like the manual, is located in the sump. Major service requires special tools and training. Therefore, it is best to allow major repair on the transmission to be done by qualified service personnel.

However, there are some adjustments that can be made on the transmission, without too much difficulty. Also, it is necessary to remove the transmission from the engine, in order to perform some of the repairs to the engine, covered in this section.

Adjustments

Linkage

To check the selector linkage, apply the emergency brake and start the engine. Move the lever to the R (Reverse) position; make sure that reverse is engaged. Next, move the lever to N (Neutral). Disengagement of reverse gear should occur just before or, as soon as, lever reaches the neutral detent. Repeat this procedure for 1 (first gear). The results should be the same, if they are not, proceed as follows:

Put the transmission in neutral by pulling the transverse selector rod completely out, and then pushing it back into one detent. Adjust the cable, using the cable adjusting nuts, so that the cable fork lines up with the bore in the ball joint on the bellcrank lever until the bolt may be inserted without difficulty.

NOTE: *Be sure that the yoke end of the selector cable is attached squarely to the bellcrank before it is reconnected.*

Recheck the gear engagement as described above. Some readjustment may be needed, so that amount of lever movement to engage or disengage gears is the same in both directions.

Neutral Safety Switch

The neutral safety switch is located on the back end of the gear selector housing. Its function is to prevent the transmission from being started in any gear, other than neutral.

Check to see that the car will start only when the gear selector is in N (Neutral) and that the back-up lights come on only if R (Reverse) is selected. If not, then adjust the switch as follows:

Place the selector lever in neutral, and remove the electrical connections from the switch. Loosen the locknut and unscrew the

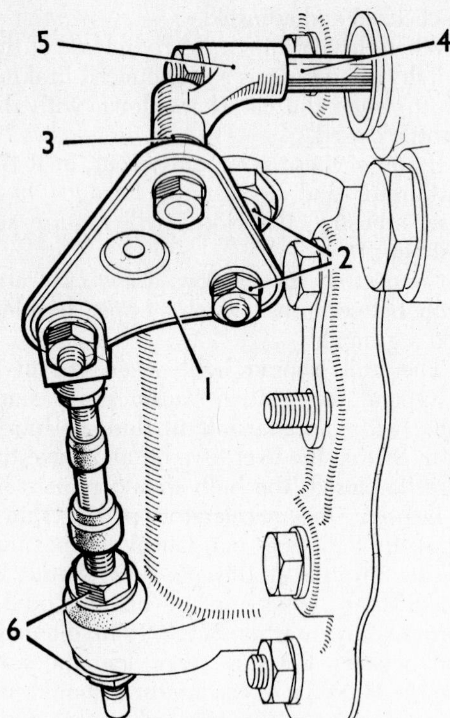

The America's bellcrank assembly

1 Bellcrank arm
2 Pivot and attachment nut
3 Joint
4 Transverse rod
5 Bracket
6 Cable adjustment nuts

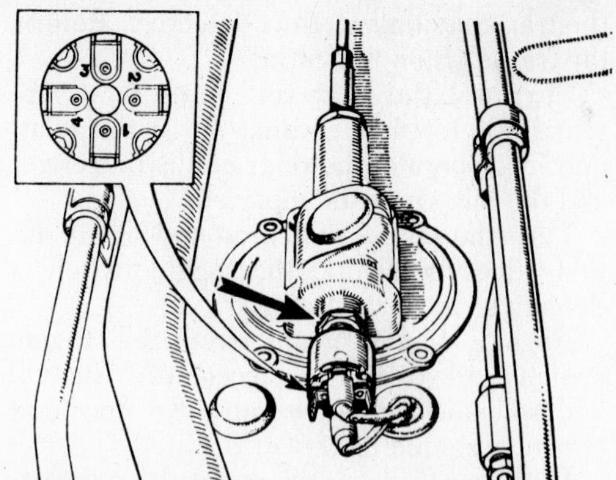

The neutral safety switch on the America automatic; poles 1-3 back-up lights, and poles 2-4 ignition/starter

switch until it is almost entirely out of the housing. Connect a test light across the ignition interlock terminals.

Screw the switch back into the housing until the light comes on; mark the switch body at this point. Count the turns while continuing to screw the switch in, until the light goes out. Disconnect the light. Unscrew the switch, out half the number of turns counted. Retighten the locknut and connect the leads to the proper terminals. If the switch is still not working correctly, it is defective and must be replaced.

Kick-Down Adjustment

Run the engine until it reaches normal operating temperature. Connect a tachometer to see that the engine has a 650 rpm idle speed.

Remove the governor control rod, at the carburetor end. Insert a 1/4 in. rod through the bellcrank lever hole to locate the hole in the transmission housing. See if the control rod can now be reconnected to the carburetor. The pin should slide easily throughout the forked end and the carburetor linkage.

If this cannot be done; adjust the linkage. Loosen the locknut on the control rod. Detach the fork end at the carburetor linkage. Rotate the rod until its length is correct. Reconnect the forked end, tighten the locknut, and withdraw the 1/4 in. rod.

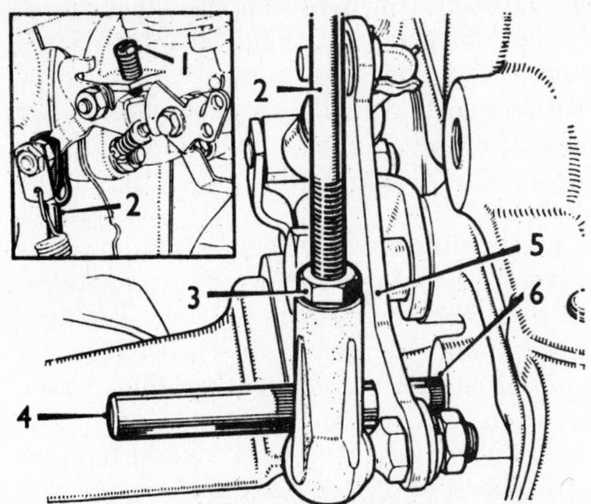

Kick-down adjustment—America automatic

1 Throttle adjustment screw
2 Governor control rod
3 Locknut
4 ¼ in. diameter rod
5 Intermedate bellcrank lever
6 Transmission case hole

Road test the car, and see that the kick-down occurs as indicated in the table below:

Gear	mph
Second to first	22
Third to second	34
Fourth to third	43

If kick-down speeds are too *low*, disconnect the forked end, loosen the locknut and make the rod shorter. If the kickdown speeds are too *high*, proceed as above, but rotate the rod counterclockwise to make it slightly longer. Retest the car.

Removal and Installation

Remove the engine/transmission assembly from the car. Remove the radiator bracket from the transmission housing, as well as, the starter, and the converter cover. Drain the transmission. Knock the tab back on the converter center bolt. Insert a screwdriver through the hole in the converter housing to prevent it from rotating. Use a socket wrench to remove the center bolt.

Bend back the lock tabs, and undo three equally spaced bolts from the center of the converter. Be sure that the slot at the end of the crankshaft is horizontal. Use a hub puller by attaching it to the converter with the three equally spaced bolts.

Undo the low pressure valve from the converter housing, being careful *not* to remove the screw plug from the valve.

Hold the converter output gear with a spanner; and remove input gear nut.

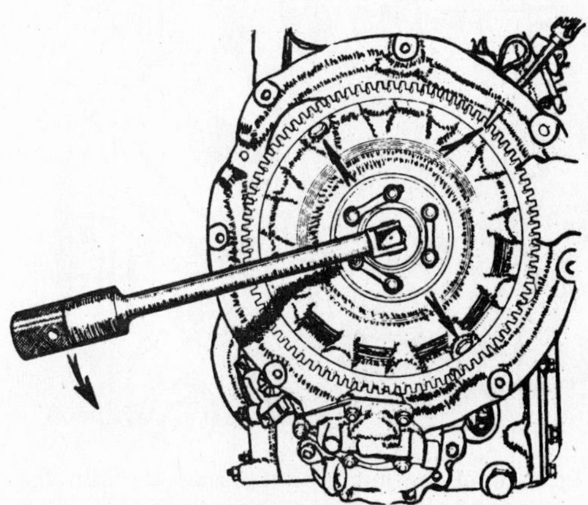

The center bolt removal procedure on the America automatic—use a screwdriver inserted through the converter housing hole to keep the converter from turning. Arrows indicate drain plugs.

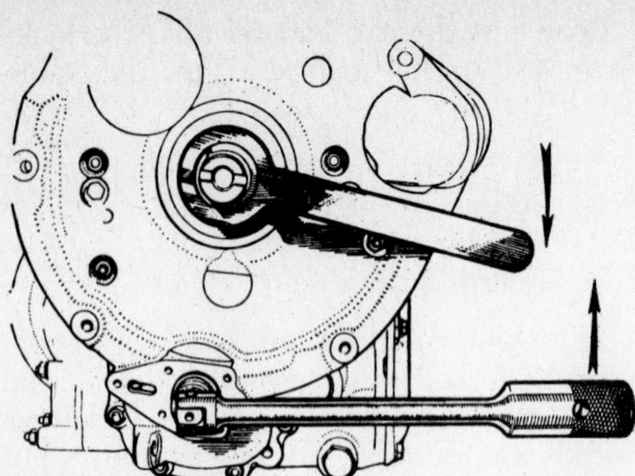

Hold the converter output gear with a spanner while the input gear nut is removed.

Remove the transverse rod from the bell-crank. Undo the nut that attached the bell-crank to its pivot; remove the bellcrank. Bend back the lockwasher tab on the pivot, and unscrew the pivot.

Cover the converter output gear, to protect it during the next operation. Undo the nuts and bolts that attach the converter housing and remove the housing. Remove the oil outlet line for the converter from the housing.

Remove the main oil line from the transmission to the oil pump by levering it off.

Withdraw the idler gear along with its thrust washers. It is important to save the

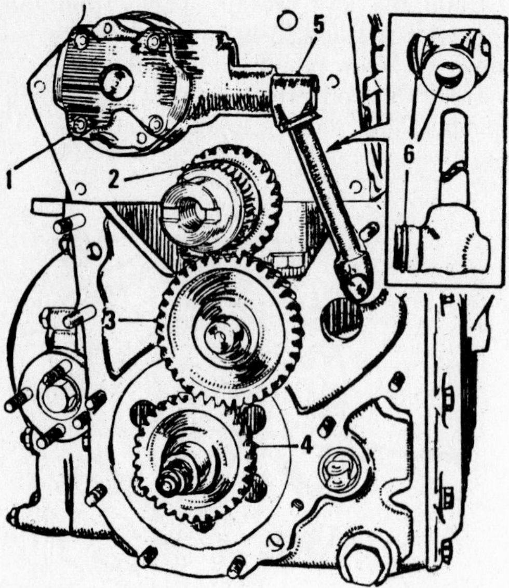

The view of the automatic transmission with the converter housing removed

1 Main oil pump
2 Converter output gear
3 Idler gear
4 Input gear
5 Oil line
6 Sealing rings

thrust washers for reassembly. Remove the output gear.

CAUTION: *Do not remove the input gear, as replacing it requires special tools.*

Detach the governor control rod from the carburetor. Remove the oil filter and its assembly along with the engine oil line.

Undo the nuts and bolts that attach the engine to the transmission assembly. Using a hoist, lift the engine clear of the transmission.

Begin reassembly by immersing the rubber oil seal, for the main bearing cap, in oil. Replace it with the lip facing the back of the engine. Use a new rubber sealing ring on the main oil strainer line; also, replace the gaskets on the transmission case with new ones.

Reassemble the engine and transmission by lowering the engine onto the transmission, checking that the rubber oil seal is properly positioned, and tightening the nuts and bolts *while* the transmission is being lowered.

Replace the engine oil line. Attach the oil filter assembly, being careful not to cover any oil passages with the gasket. Attach the main oil pump.

Remove any excess gasket from the back of the transmission. Be sure that the surfaces are clean, and free of old gasket, and replace the converter housing gasket with a new one.

When replacing the converter output gear observe the correct running clearance of .0035-.0065 in. between the inner thrust washer and the gear. If the clearance is not within the specified limits, various sized washers are available to compensate for any difference. Be sure that the chamfered inner edge of the washer faces the crankshaft.

Reassemble the idler gear using the *same* washers that were removed. If any transmission components have been replaced this cannot be done; the procedure for computing the correct washer thickness is involved, and requires the use of special tools. In this case, the work should be done by authorized service personnel.

NOTE: *If the idler gear fails to mesh with the input gear, the thrust washer has come off one of the gears inside the geartrain assembly; the assembly must be torn down and rebuilt. This should be left to qualified service personnel only.*

Align and replace the converter outlet

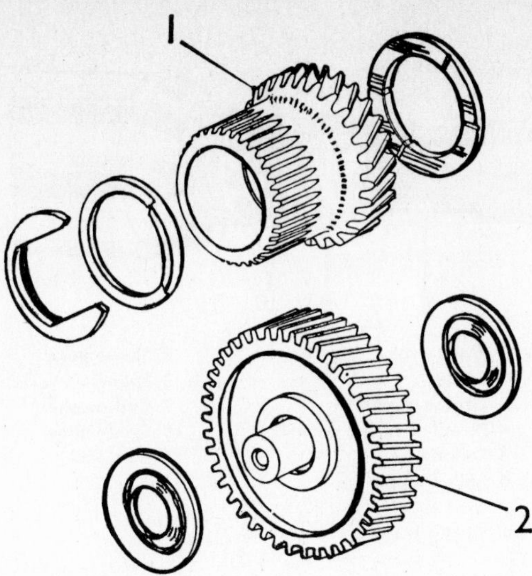

The converter output (1) and the idler gears (2) showing their thrust washer assemblies

line. Put the converter housing back on, using a new gasket for it. Tighten the converter housing bolts to 18 ft. lbs. Replace the input gear nut and tighten it to 70 ft. lbs., using a spanner to hold the output gear.

Remove each pair of bolts, in sequence, from the torque converter; fit new lock-plates. Tighten each bolt to 22-24 ft. lbs., and bend the lock tabs upward.

CAUTION: *Do not remove all six bolts from the converter center at the same time.*

Lubricate the oil seal for the converter. Reinstall the converter in its housing. Replace the gasket. Replace the center bolt and lockwasher. Tighten the center bolt to 110-115 ft. lbs. Refit the low pressure valve and gasket.

Replace the gear selector bellcrank and pivot. Attach it to the transverse rod. Replace the guard.

Reassemble the converter cover, starter motor and the back engine mount.

Install the engine/transmission assembly in the car.

Driveshaft and U-Joints

Type

The driveshafts used on the Austin-Healey and Sprite are basically alike. They consist of a sliding spline between the transmission, and two universal joints, each of which has a center spider, four needle-roller bearings, and two yokes.

Lubrication

Austin-Healey

Each center spider has a nipple for lubrication of the bearings. The needle-roller bearings are pre-filled with lubrication when they are assembled, and fed by reservoirs that are connected to the central lubrication chambers of the spiders. There is also a nipple on the sliding spline sleeve yoke for lubrication of the splines.

If the cork seals leak large amounts of grease, the joint should be taken apart, and the seals replaced with new ones. Before reassembly, smear the sleeve yoke splines with grease.

Sprite

The early Sprites have lubrication nipples on both front and rear joints. To gain access to the front nipple, remove the rubber plug on the left side of the tunnel, after first, having lifted the carpet.

Later Sprites have sealed, pre-packed U-joints that do not require attention.

The sliding joint, between the driveshaft and the transmission, receives its lubrication from the transmission.

Overhaul

Austin-Healey and Sprite

The removal, repair, and reassembly of the driveshafts for the Austin-Healey and the Sprite are similar

On the Mk. I Sprite it is easier to remove and reinstall the driveshaft if the engine and transmission are removed first. The later Sprites require someone in the car to guide the driveshaft into position with a screwdriver inserted through the lubrication hole in the tunnel. Otherwise, the procedures below are to be followed for removal and overhaul.

Remove the transmission tunnel (100-Six and 3000 only). Mark the driveshaft and the transmission and rear axle flanges to facilitate replacement in the same position. With the driveshaft supported near the sliding joint, remove the bolts at the transmission flange. Unscrew the dust cap at the rear of the sliding joint and slide the splined sleeve yoke about a half-inch to the

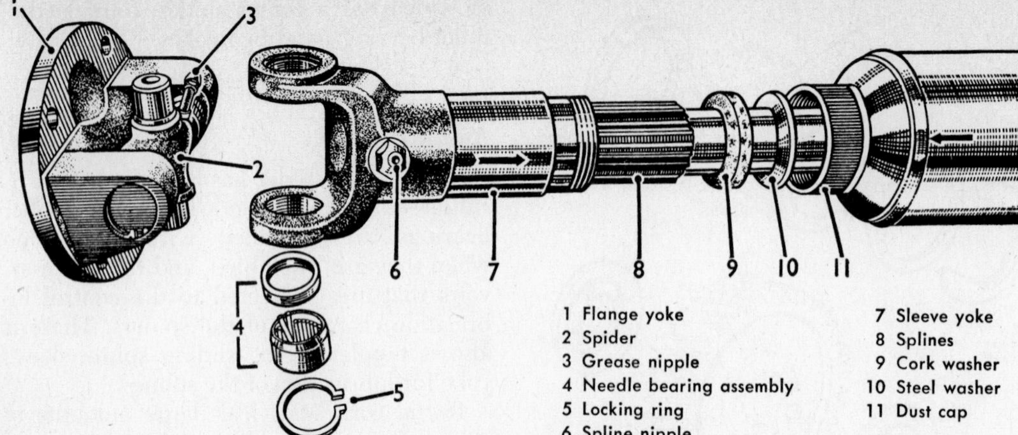

Exploded view of the front U-joint used on the Healey

rear in order to disengage the pilot flanges. Remove the four nuts and bolts which attach the rear flange yoke to the rear axle flange and lower the driveshaft.

Disassemble the driveshaft as follows: Remove the enamel from the locking rings and bearing faces in order to facilitate the removal of the bearings. Remove the locking rings by pressing the ends together. If a ring is difficult to remove, tap the bearing face lightly in order to relieve the pressure exerted on the ring. With the splined end of the shaft in one hand, tap the radius of the yoke with a soft-head hammer to remove the bearing. If the bearing is difficult to remove, carefully tap it from the inside, being careful not to damage the race. Turn the yoke over and be careful not to lose any of the rollers when extracting the bearing. Repeat the preceding operation for the other bearing and remove the splined yoke from the spider. Remove the spider from the yoke in similar fashion.

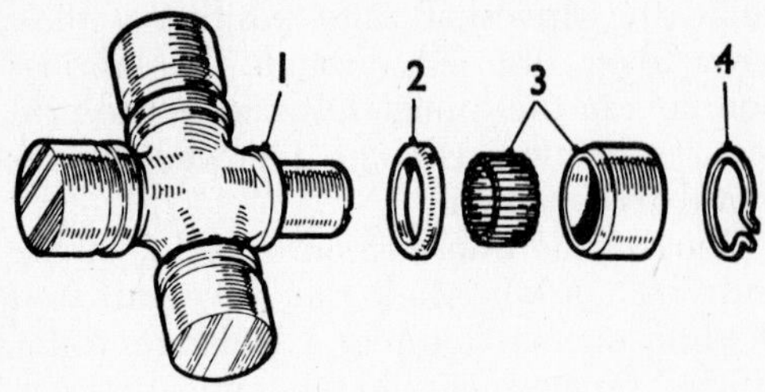

The sealed U-joint bearing used on the late Sprites

1 Journal spider
2 Rubber seal
3 Needle rollers and bearings
4 Snap-ring

Check the components for damage and wear. The parts most likely to show wear after long service are the bearing races and the spider journals of the universal joints. If looseness or stress signs are observed, the complete assembly should be replaced, as neither oversize journals nor bearings are manufactured. The bearing races should be a light drive fit in the yoke. If there is ovality evident in the bearing holes, new yokes must be installed. There is permitted a total of .004 in. (.1 mm.) of free circumferential movement, measured on the outside diameter of the spline. If this figure is exceeded, a new tubular shaft assembly or other components may be required.

Reassemble the driveshaft. Be sure that all drilled holes in the journals of the universal joints are thoroughly cleaned and filled with lubricant. Assemble the needle rollers into the bearing races and fill with grease.

NOTE: *Smearing the walls of the races with grease may help to keep the rollers in place.*

Insert the spider into the flange yoke and tap the bearing into position. It is important that the bearing races be a light drive fit into the yoke. Repeat the preceding operation for the other bearings. In order to achieve a good seal, the spider journal shoulders may be coated with shellac prior to the installation of the retainers. If the joint binds, tap lightly with a wooden mallet to relieve any pressure which the bearings might be exerting on the end of the journals. When installing the sliding joint on the shaft, be sure that the components are properly lined up. Alignment can be checked by noting whether the arrows marked on the splined sleeve yoke and on the splined stub shaft are in line. It is advisable to replace the cork washers and washer retainers on the spider journals. Install the dust cover, steel washer and cork washer over the splines of the shaft. When sliding the splined sleeve onto the shaft, be sure that the front and rear universal joint spiders are lying in the same plane. This condition will be achieved if the arrows on the sleeve and the shaft are in line.

Replace the driveshaft assembly. Wipe the joining flange faces clean. Be sure that the sliding joint is at the transmission end of the shaft. Align the marks which were made on the flanges during the removal operation. Tighten the securing nuts evenly and lock.

Lubrication points for the Healey and Sprite rear axles: (1) filler plug, (2) drain plug, and (3) U-joint nipple

Drive Axle, Suspension, and Steering

Drive Axle

Type and Lubrication

Austin-Healey and Sprite

The Austin-Healey and Sprite rear axle is a fully-floating type which uses hypoid gears. Lubrication is supplied by adding hypoid gear lubricant through a filler plug located on the back of the axle. After the axle has been filled the surplus should have time to run out. If this is not done, the axle will be overfilled, and this could possibly cause brake failure.

America

The differential of the Austin America is located in the engine sump along with the transmission. The two short driveshafts from it are fitted with bell joints. These joints are protected by a rubber boot; if it becomes damaged through wear or deterioration, it must be replaced. Otherwise, the lubrication for the joint will be lost, and dirt may enter it, as well. The differential is lubricated from the engine sump, and the bell joints should be packed with a special grease, available from the dealer.

Any work done to the driveshafts requires that the suspension system be depressurized. To do this a special suspension service unit is necessary; therefore, repair should be left to authorized service facilities.

Removal and Installation

Austin-Healey

Loosen the wheel nuts or center hubs (wire wheels), and raise the car using a jack. Place supports under the frame members forward of the front anchorage point of the rear springs. Remove both wheels.

From underneath the car, remove the four locknuts and bolts that attach the driveshaft flange to the pinion flange.

Detach the handbrake cable from the axle, by unscrewing it from the brake balance lever link, and the nut fixing its outer casing to the axle.

Disconnect the hydraulic brake line from the flexible union, which is located forward of the right shock absorber. Remove the nuts from the shock absorber links that attach them to the axle mounts.

NOTE: *Removal of the links themselves is much easier, if done when the axle is being freed.*

Remove the locknuts from the U-bolts that attach the rear axle to the springs. Note the fiber pad between the axle and the spring. Unscrew the nuts that hold the shackle to the axle anchoring point.

Now that the axle is free, disconnect the shock absorber links. Remove the rubber block from between the axle and the frame member on the left side; the right block does not have to be removed.

Remove the axle from the right side of the car. Be careful not to damage other components underneath the car.

Installation is the reverse of removal. Jack the springs up so that they meet the axle, in order to locate the spring center bolt. Replace the fiber pad between the axle and spring. Adjust the handbrake and bleed the hydraulic brake system.

Sprite

Raise the car by placing a jack under the differential housing. Place supports under the rear spring anchoring points on the body. Remove the wheels and the exhaust system.

Keep the jack under the differential, and undo the retaining strap at the point at which it attaches to the body. Take the shock absorber arm off of its connecting linkage. Detach the upper suspension link from the bracket on the rear axle by undoing the nut and tapping the bolt from its bracket. Remove the emergency brake cable at its cable adjustment point.

From underneath the car, unscrew the four nuts and bolts that attach the driveshaft and pinion flanges. Detach the brake line at the union in front of the differential housing.

Be sure that the weight of the rear axle is *fully* on the jack, then undo the bolts that attach the shackles. Lower and remove the axle.

Reinstallation is the reverse of removal. If the suspension upper link has been removed at the same time that the axle is out of the car, do not tighten the shackle bolts until *after* the upper link is in place.

America

The front drive axle cannot be removed without the use of special equipment. Therefore, this should be done by an authorized service center only.

Reconditioning

Austin-Healey

NOTE: *The following operation does not require the use of special factory tools or*

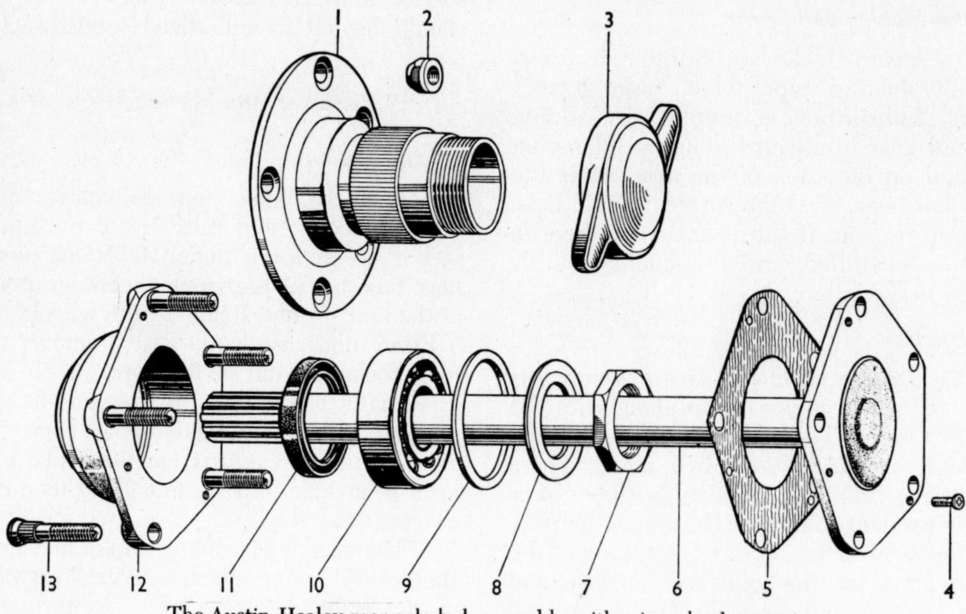

The Austin-Healey rear axle hub assembly with wire wheel extension

1 Hub extension
2 Nut
3 Knock-off hub
4 Screw
5 Gasket
6 Half shaft
7 Hub locknut
8 Hub lockwasher
9 Bearing spacer
10 Hub bearing
11 Oil seal
12 Casing
13 Extension stud

procedures. Anybody who has done differential work before, should encounter little difficulty; but the inexperienced would do well to seek aid from their dealer or someone familiar with this type of work.

Drain and remove the rear axle. Remove the shafts by undoing the brake drum locating screws. On cars with wire wheels remove the hub extensions by removing the five locknuts first. If the brake shoes are not binding the drum, and the handbrake is off, tap the drum off. If the drum is held in place by the shoes, loosen the adjuster a few notches first.

Undo the screw that holds the axle shaft in place, and remove the shaft. If the paper gasket is damaged, it must be replaced.

The driveshaft and pinion flanges should be marked so that they can be returned to their original positions during replacement. Detach the driveshaft.

Remove the complete carrier assembly by removing the twelve nuts and washers that attach it to the axle housing. Mark the differential bearing caps for replacement, undo their four nuts, and remove the washers. Remove the caps and the differential case from the carrier. Be careful to note the thickness of the spacers located between the *outer* ring of each bearing and the carrier.

Tap out the 3/16 in. dowel that positions the differential pinion shaft. This must be done from the ring gear side of the differential case, as the dowel fits into a tapered bore. If the dowel is difficult to remove, clean out the metal which has been peened over the entrance of the bore, with a 3/16 in. drill.

Drift out the pinion shaft and remove the pinions and thrust washers from the differential case. Examine the pinions and the thrust washers; replace them if they are worn.

Take the lockplates and the bolts off, then withdraw the ring gear. If the ball races at each end of the differential case are loose, the case will have to be replaced.

Keep the pinion from turning by using a pipe wrench and remove the nut and washer from it. Use an extractor to remove the flange.

Drive the pinion out toward the rear with a *soft* metal drift. The pinion will bring the inner race and rollers off the rear bearing, the spacer and the shims along with it. The front bearing and oil seal will remain in the carrier. Use an extractor to remove the rear inner race and rollers from the pinion. Save the pinion head washer.

Remove the oil seal from the carrier. Take the front bearing inner race and rollers out by hand. Use an extractor to remove the outer races of both bearings. Replace all worn or defective oil seals, and gaskets. Check all gears for wear or dammage.

If any new parts, such as a ring gear and pinion assembly, bearings etc., are installed, the following assembly and adjustment procedures must be used.

NOTE: *If either the ring gear or pinion requires replacement, a matched set of both gears must be used; they cannot be installed separately.*

When reassembling, variations in pinion head thickness must be accounted for. This appears as an unbracketed number etched on the pinion head. It will always be preceeded by a minus (—) sign. If there is no unbracketed number on the pinion head, it is of nominal thickness.

Replace the bearing outer races in the carrier, using a suitable sized pipe as a drift. Care should be used to see that the races are not cocked when mounted. Use an oil stone to smooth the pinion head, but do not remove any of the figures that are etched on it.

If the pinion and ring gear have not been replaced use the old head washer to shim the pinion. If this cannot be used, i.e., the pinion has been replaced, select another head washer.

Using the markings on the old pinion as a guide, compare the markings on the new pinion. If the new pinion marking is larger (numerically) than the old pinion marking, use a washer of the appropriate added thickness to the original washer. If the marking is smaller (numerically), subtract thickness. This will provide a convenient starting point.

Press the inner race of the rear bearings on the pinion shaft, carefully. Place the pinion in the carrier, using the shims, the bearing spacer, and the oil seal. Replace the inner race of the front bearing.

Replace the U-joint drive flange. Gradually tighten its nut until a preload of 18 in. lbs. is reached. If the proper figure cannot be attained, shims should be added or removed, as required.

NOTE: *To obtain a proper preload, an excessively large torque figure may be re-*

quired (140 ft. lbs.) Also, preload must be achieved when tightening the nut; if the preload figure is surpassed, the nut must be completely loosened and gradually retightened.

Assemble the pinions in the differential case in the reverse manner in which they were removed. Install the differential assembly in the carrier with a spacer on each side.

Using the trial and error method, find spacers that allow the differential, with its bearings, and the spacers, to fit into the carrier; without being loose and without interfering with the bearings.

Remove the assembly, and add .002 in. thickness to *each* collar to obtain the required preload.

Arrows indicate the matching tolerance markings for the Healey and Sprite differential bearing housings

Replace the bearings on the differential case with the word Thrust facing outward from the case. Without bending the locking tabs upward, bolt the ring gear on to the differential case. Tighten the nuts to 60 ft. lbs.

Mount the assembly on two V-blocks. Using a dial indicator, check the amount of runout of the ring gear as it is turned. The maximum runout is .002 in. If it is greater than this, rotate it 90° on its mount; also, check for dirt on the faces of the flange. Retighten the bolts to the proper torque figure, and bend the locking tabs upward.

Mount the differential case back in the carrier, using the spacers the thickness of which were calculated above. Use a torque wrench setting of 65 ft. lbs. to tighten the bearing caps. Mount the dial indicator so that a measurement of backlash may be taken. NOTE: *The correct backlash for the ring gear and pinion assembly is stamped on the back face of the ring gear; it must be strictly adhered to.*

Backlash is varied by increasing the thickness of the spacer on one side, while simultaneously decreasing the thickness on the other side by *exactly* the same amount. CAUTION: *Do not change the total thickness of the two spacers.*

Coat eight to ten teeth of the ring gear with red lead, and rock the pinion back and forth evenly. Check the tooth contact pattern against the illustration. Make the adjustments indicated in the illustration, by replacing the pinion thrust washer with one of a different thickness. A thicker or thinner washer may be used, depending upon the direction in which the pinion is to be moved. Remember, if this operation is necessary, the entire assembly and adjustment process will have to be repeated. NOTE: *If the pinion depth is altered by changing the thickness of the washer, backlash must be checked again and kept within limits.*

The hub bearing assembly cannot be adjusted. It is replaced as a unit by pressing it into place, being careful to see that it protrudes .001-.004 in. beyond the hub's outer face. Otherwise, reinstallation is the reverse of removal.

Sprite

The procedure for drive axle removal and reconditioning is almost the same for the Sprite as it is for the Austin-Healey. For this procedure, reference should be made to the preceeding section. The following are differences to be noted when working on the Sprite differential:

1. The dowel pin that positions the differential pinion shaft is 1/8 in. diameter. The entry hole should be cleaned out, if necessary, with a 1/8 in. drill.
2. The maximum preload for the pinion bearing is 13 in. lbs.

NOTE: *The spacer used on the Sprite Mk. II, III, and VI is of the collapsible type. When the nut is tightened to the correct torque figure of 135-140 ft. lbs., the spacer is collapsed to give the proper preload. This only happens once, thus, when the pinion is reassembled, or if the nut is overtightened, a new spacer must be used.*

3. Repack the hub bearings with grease. The paper washer between the axle shaft and hub should be compressed

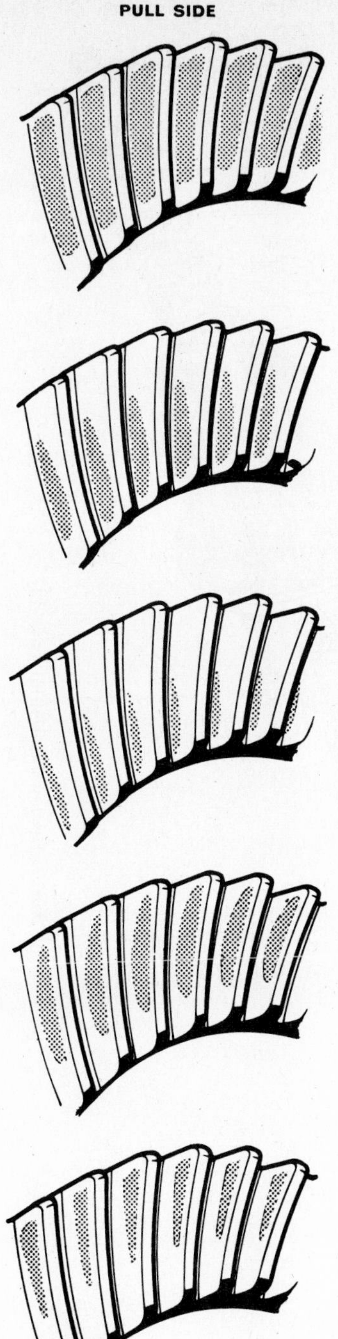

Correct tooth contact.

Contact pattern should be evenly spread over ring gear teeth, on both pull and coast sides.

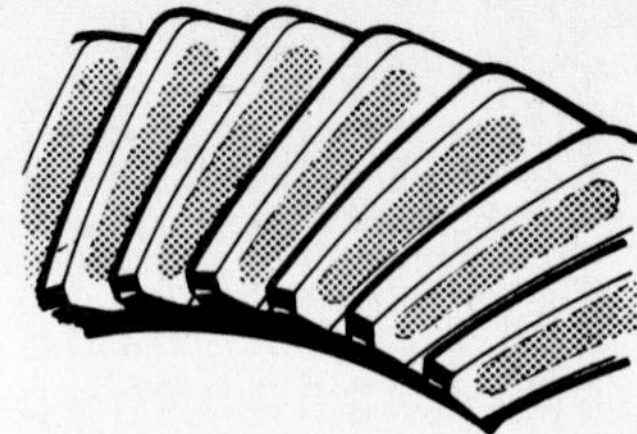

Incorrect contact.

Pull side: heavy contact at tooth toe, toward the center.

Coast side: heavy contact at tooth heel, toward the center.

Move pinion away from ring gear by reducing thrust washer thickness.

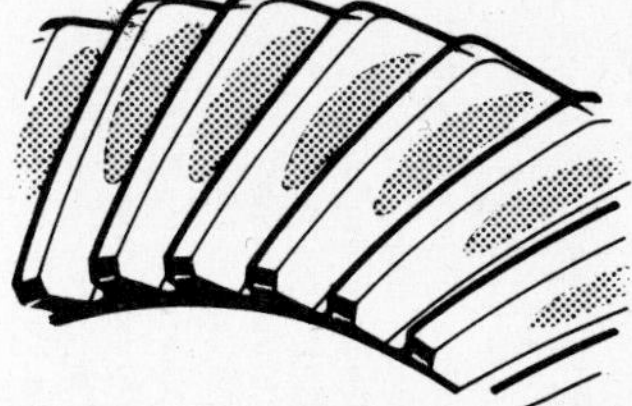

Incorrect contact.

Pull side: heavy contact on toe, at tooth flank bottom.

Coast side: heavy contact on heel, at tooth flank bottom.

Move pinion away from ring gear by reducing thrust washer thickness.

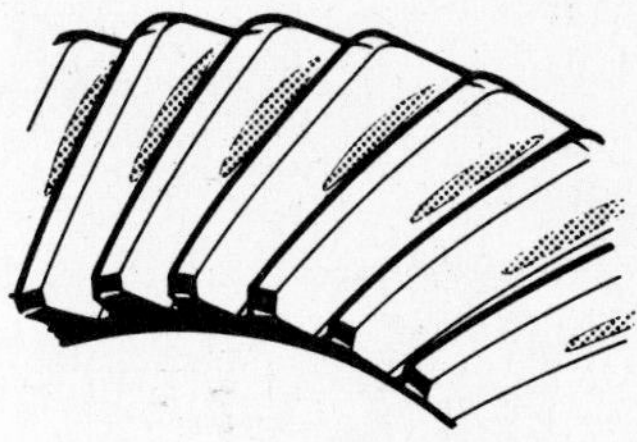

Incorrect contact.

Pull side: heavy contact at tooth heel and toward the center.

Coast side: heavy contact at tooth toe and toward the center.

Move the pinion toward ring gear by increasing thrust washer thickness.

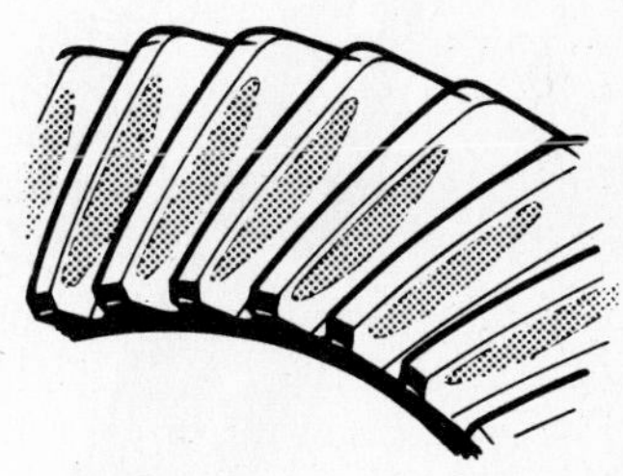

Incorrect contact.

Pull side: heavy contact on heel, at tooth face.

Coast side: heavy contact on toe, at tooth face.

Move the pinion toward ring gear by increasing thrust washer thickness.

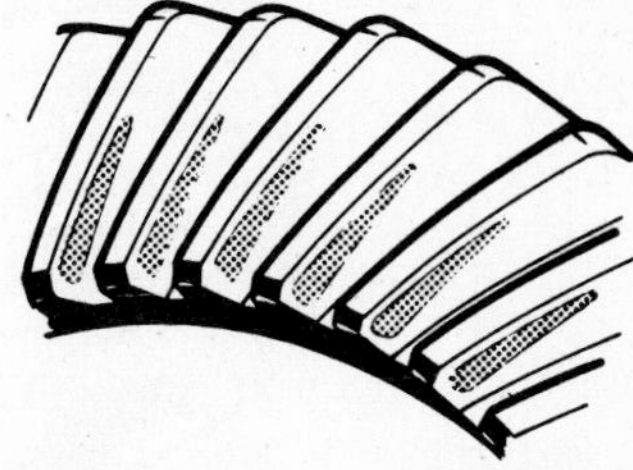

Ring gear tooth contact patterns and adjustments.

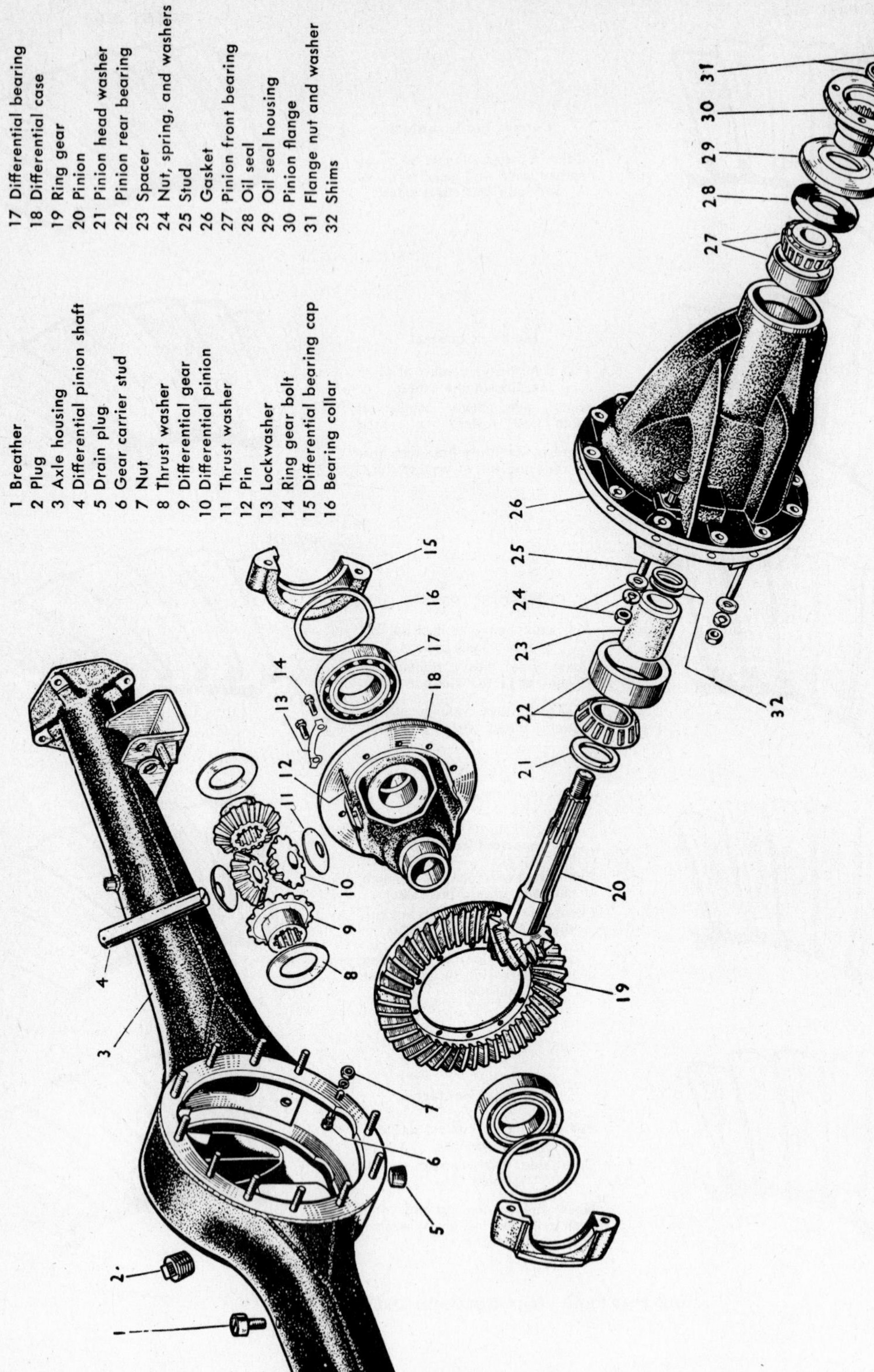
1 Breather
2 Plug
3 Axle housing
4 Differential pinion shaft
5 Drain plug
6 Gear carrier stud
7 Nut
8 Thrust washer
9 Differential gear
10 Differential pinion
11 Thrust washer
12 Pin
13 Lockwasher
14 Ring gear bolt
15 Differential bearing cap
16 Bearing collar
17 Differential bearing
18 Differential case
19 Ring gear
20 Pinion
21 Pinion head washer
22 Pinion rear bearing
23 Spacer
24 Nut, spring, and washers
25 Stud
26 Gasket
27 Pinion front bearing
28 Oil seal
29 Oil seal housing
30 Pinion flange
31 Flange nut and washer
32 Shims

The Austin-Healey differential assembly

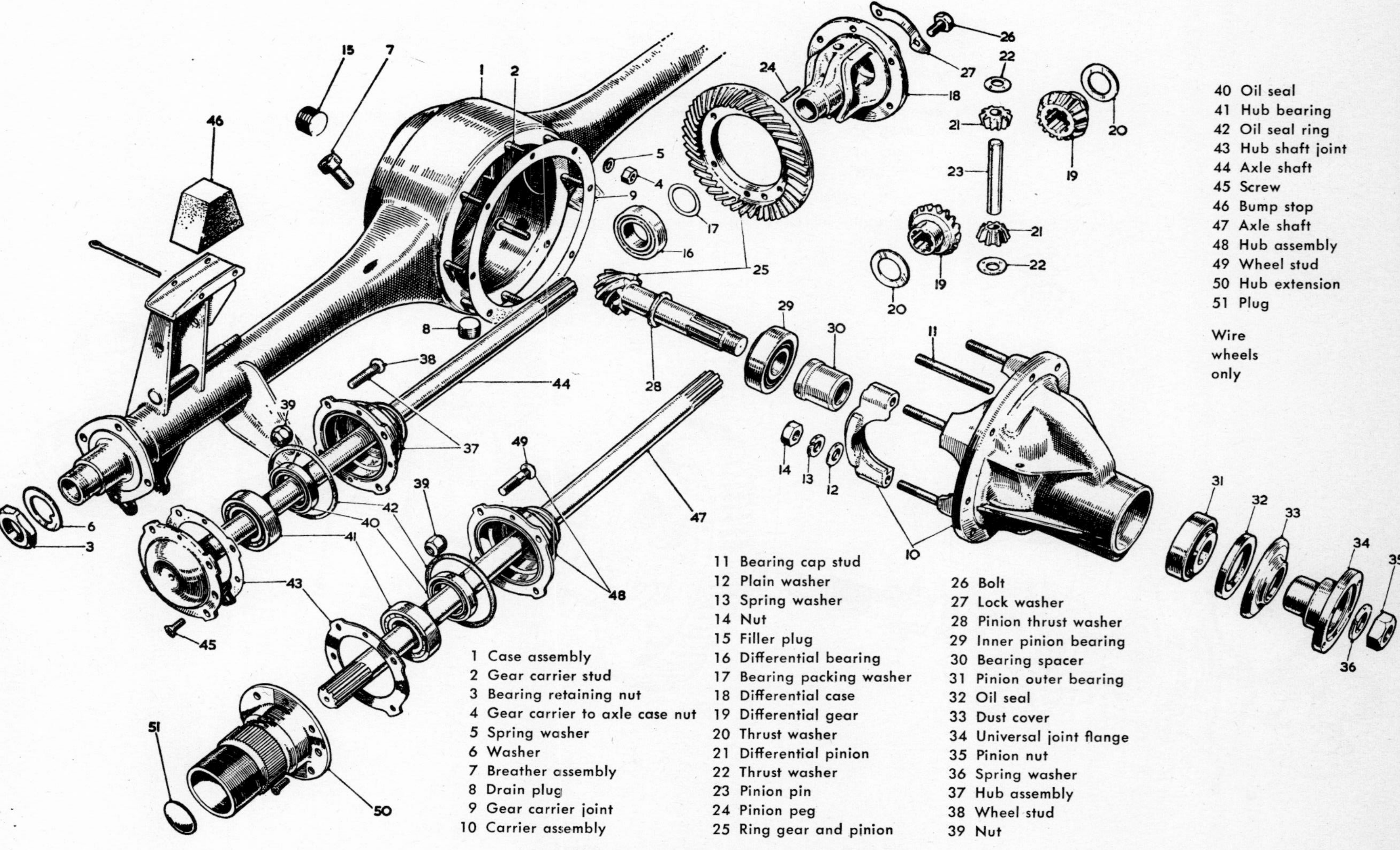
1 Case assembly
2 Gear carrier stud
3 Bearing retaining nut
4 Gear carrier to axle case nut
5 Spring washer
6 Washer
7 Breather assembly
8 Drain plug
9 Gear carrier joint
10 Carrier assembly
11 Bearing cap stud
12 Plain washer
13 Spring washer
14 Nut
15 Filler plug
16 Differential bearing
17 Bearing packing washer
18 Differential case
19 Differential gear
20 Thrust washer
21 Differential pinion
22 Thrust washer
23 Pinion pin
24 Pinion peg
25 Ring gear and pinion
26 Bolt
27 Lock washer
28 Pinion thrust washer
29 Inner pinion bearing
30 Bearing spacer
31 Pinion outer bearing
32 Oil seal
33 Dust cover
34 Universal joint flange
35 Pinion nut
36 Spring washer
37 Hub assembly
38 Wheel stud
39 Nut
40 Oil seal
41 Hub bearing
42 Oil seal ring
43 Hub shaft joint
44 Axle shaft
45 Screw
46 Bump stop
47 Axle shaft
48 Hub assembly
49 Wheel stud
50 Hub extension
51 Plug
Wire wheels only

The Sprite differential assembly

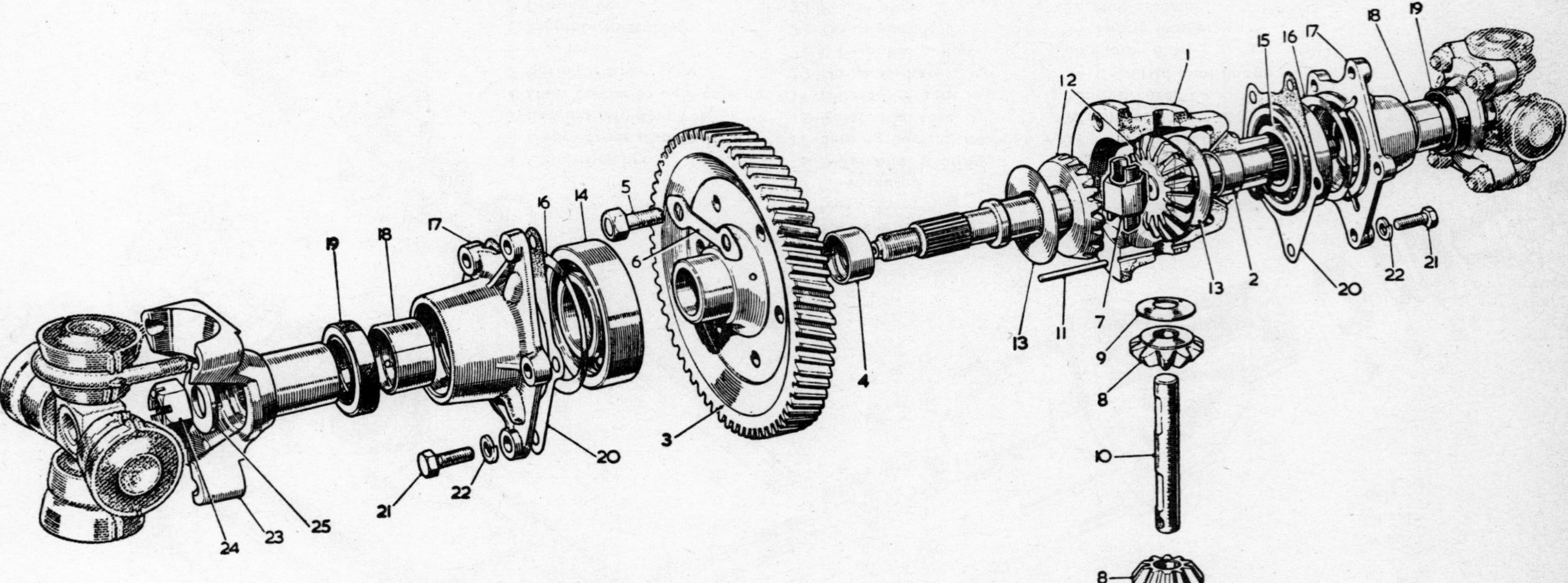

The differential assembly for the America—manual

1 Differential case
2 Case bushing
3 Drive gear
4 Gear bushing
5 Gear bolt
6 Lock washer
7 Thrust block
8 Differential pinion
9 Pinion thrust washer
10 Center pin
11 Pin peg
12 Differential gear
13 Gear thrust washer
14 Drive gear bearing
15 Case bearing
16 Bearing shim
17 End cover
18 Cover bushing
19 Oil seal
20 Cover gasket
21 End cover bolt
22 Washer
23 Driving flange
24 Flange nut
25 Washer

before the shoulder of the shaft rests against the bearing races.

The rest of the specifications and procedures are the same as for the Healey.

America—Manual Transmission

The procedure for removal, servicing, and reinstallation of the differential used in the Austin America equipped with a manual transmission, is given in the TRANSMISSION section, as the differential must be removed in order to remove the transmission.

Check the differential for worn or damaged parts, and replace whatever is necessary. Use the tolerances and specifications given in the TRANSMISSION section.

America—Automatic Transmission

The differential assembly in the America automatic transmission models is, unlike the manual, removed separately from the transmission. This requires a slightly different procedure than the manual.

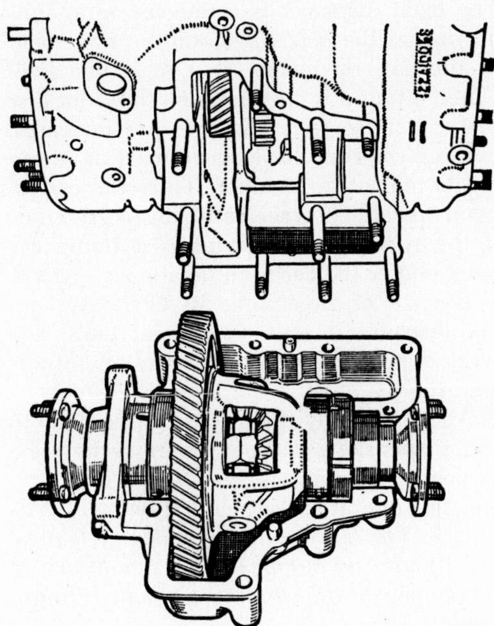

The differential assembly being removed from the America automatic

Remove the engine/transmission unit from the car, and drain it. Use a pinion flange spanner to hold the drive flanges while removing the center bolts. Remove the flanges from their splined shafts. Bend the lockwasher back and undo the nuts on the final drive housing.

Undo the bolts that attach the kickdown linkage, and pull it free of the transmission case. Remove the final drive components and housing by undoing the two bolts that hold the end cover down. Finish removing the bolts from the end cover, and remove it along with its adjustment shims.

Withdraw the differential from its case. Remove the oil seal housing, and, using an extractor, the bearings.

Bend back the lockplate tabs, and undo the bolts that attach the drive gear to the case. Mark the drive gear and the case for reassembly, then detach the drive gear from the case.

Separate the differential gear and thrust washer from the drive gear. Knock out the roll pin. Remove both pinions, their thrust washers, the pinion spacer, the second differential gear and thrust washer.

Clean all parts and examine them for wear. Replace any parts that are worn or damaged.

CAUTION: *If any parts are damaged so that chips from them can enter the lubrication system, the transmission must be removed, and torn down, otherwise it may be severely damaged. This job should be entrusted to an authorized service facility.*

Because of the possibility of transmission damage, cleanliness is essential.

Assembly is the reverse of teardown. Care should be taken to replace the differential gear thrust washer with the cham-

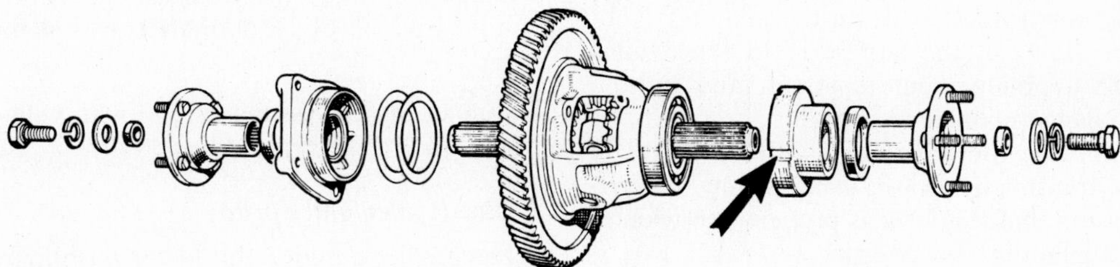

The components for the America differential—automatic; the arrow indicates the alignment of the spacer

fered bore *against* the machined faces of the gears. All parts must be replaced in their original positions.

Replace the differential in the transmission case. Push the differential assembly toward the torque converter, being sure to align the slot in the spacer with the dowel in the transmission case. Replace the gasket after coating it with commercial sealer. Press the oil seal squarely against the face of the spacer. Reinstall the differential housing, using new lockplates. Tighten the nuts lightly.

Replace the end cover without a gasket, but using the original adjusting shims; tighten the cover bolts evenly. CAUTION: *The bolts should be tight enough for the cover face to touch the outer race of the bearing; if they are overtightened the flange will become distorted.*

Measure the distance in several places, between the side cover flange and the differential housing, using a feeler gauge. If there are any variations in measurement, the cover bolts have not been evenly tightened. Make the necessary adjustments, so that identical measurements may be obtained.

The compressed thickness of a new gasket is .007 in.; the required preload on the bearings is .004 in.; thus, the correct gap is .011 in. If this cannot be reached, shims should be added or subtracted as necessary. NOTE: *The word Thrust faces outward, toward the end cover.*

Remove the end cover. Using the required shims and a new gasket, coated with commercial sealer, reinstall the end cover. Tighten the differential housing nuts and the end cover bolts to 18 ft. lbs. Bend the lockplate tabs upward; except for the one to which the exhaust pipe bracket is attached. This is done once the engine has been installed in the car.

Lubricate the drive flange oil seals. Reinstall the flanges, being sure the split collars are properly positioned inside the flanges. Use new rubber seals on the center attachment bolts of the flange. Hold the flanges with a pinion flange spanner, and tighten the flange bolts to 40-50 ft. lbs.

Replace the governor control linkage on the transmission case, using a new washer. Be sure that the lever is properly positioned in relation to the governor.

Reinstall the engine/transmission assembly in the car.

Front Suspension

Description

Austin-Healey and Sprite

The fron suspension on the Austin-Healey and the Sprite, uses independent upper and lower wishbones. These hold the stub axles, the coil springs, and the shock absorbers in place.

America

The front suspension consists of upper and lower control arms of unequal length. These are positioned in the side members of the subframe; the outer ends are attached to the stub axle by means of ball joints.

The unusual feature of this suspension is, that, instead of springs and shock absorbers, Hydrolastic® displacer units are used. The front displacer is connected to a similar unit at the rear wheel, on the same side of the car, by means of a hydraulic line. When a bump is encountered, the front displacer acts so that line pressure increases, causing the rear displacer to react in an opposite and equal manner. Thus, the car remains level. The reverse of this is true, i.e., if the rear wheel encounters a bump the front end of the car is automatically leveled.

Because of the complexity of this system, and because it requires special tools, any work done to it should be left to an authorized service facility.

About the only thing that can be done to the suspension, without depressuring Hydrolastic® system, is wheel bearing service; this operation is included below. CAUTION: *The system works under high pressure; under no circumstances should any of the valves on the system be touched. Injury could result.*

If, for any reason, the system loses fluid, the car may be driven at speeds below 30 mph over surfaced roads, to the nearest dealer. The suspension rests on rubber bumpers which give adequate travel at this speed.

Front Shock Absorber Removal and Installation

Austin-Healey and Sprite

Place a jack under the lower wishbones, and raise the wheel. Place stands under the chassis members, and remove the wheel.

Remove the top kingpin pivot bolt and swing the wheel down, being careful not to strain the brake line. NOTE: *The clamp bolt must be removed before the pivot bolt can be withdrawn.*

Unbolt and remove the shock absorber, being careful to note the number of bolts and washers removed from the suspension system. CAUTION: *The jack must be left under the suspension wishbone, while the upper link is disconnected. If this is not done, the coil spring and steering linkage may be damaged.*

Check all of the bushings for wear, and replace them if necessary.

Installation is the reverse of removal. Tighten the pivot bolt only where there is a load on the suspension; i.e., with the jack under the lower suspension arm.

Shock Absorber Maintenance

Austin-Healey and Sprite

The anchoring points for the shock absorbers should be checked periodically, and their nuts and bolts tightened when needed.

The screws that attach the cover plates should be kept tight, or the fluid will tend to leak out.

The fluid level should also be checked periodically. The fluid level should come just below the threads of the filler plug. CAUTION: *Clean all the dirt away from the area around the filler plugs before they are removed. No dirt should be allowed to enter the chamber. Use the proper shock absorber fluid; do not use engine oil or engine oil additives—severe suspension damage will result.*

Anti-Roll Bar

On cars equipped with an anti-roll bar, the rubber bushings should be inspected and lubricated periodically. Engine oil and other types of oil that attack rubber, must be avoided, as they will cause the bushings to deteriorate.

Competition anti-roll bars are available to fit both the Healey and the Sprite.

Kingpin Replacement

Austin-Healey and Sprite

Place a jack under the lower wishbone; raise the car and remove the wheel. Disconnect the tie-rod from the steering arm. On cars that are equipped with disc brakes, unbolt the brake caliper; support it clear of the hub. Remove the hub and brake assembly. Undo the top kingpin pivot bolt, and swing the stub axle down.

Remove the nut from the lower pivot locating pin, and drive the pin completely out. Unscrew the pivot end plug (core plug on later Sprites), and unscrew the pivot using a large screwdriver.

Withdraw the stub axle and kingpin assembly from the lower control arm. Unscrew the nut from the top of the stub axle and kingpin assembly. Remove the kingpin washers and seals. Press the bushings out from the bottom of the axle.

Install new bushings, being careful that the open end of the oil groove enters first, and, also, that the hole in the bushing is in line with the lubrication channel in the axle.

On the Austin-Healey, the lower bushing should be flush with the recessed housing, and should stick out 1/8 in. beyond the upper bore of the lower housing. Ream the bushings, as required, on the Austin-Healey.

On the Sprite the kingpin bushings do not require reaming. Install the kingpin, and lubricate it, in order to check its fit. If excessive effort is required to rotate the kingpin, the inner surfaces should be refinished, by using a brake cylinder hone.

Install the kingpin in the axle body along with the washers, and seals, as removed, and tighten the nut. Lubricate the bushings, using the grease fittings, with a high-pressure grease gun. Check the kingpin for resistance to rotation. If excessively stiff, remove the nut, and substitute a thinner floating thrust washer on the Healey. Use a feeler gauge to see that the maximum lift does not exceed .002 in.

For the Sprite, replace the adjustment shim so that there is only a slight amount of resistance felt when the stub axle is moved from lock to lock. To adjust the resistance, increase the thickness of the shims to loosen, and decrease the thickness to tighten.

From this point, the installation procedure is the reverse of removal.

Coil Spring Removal and Installation

Austin-Healey and Sprite

Raise the car, by placing a jack under

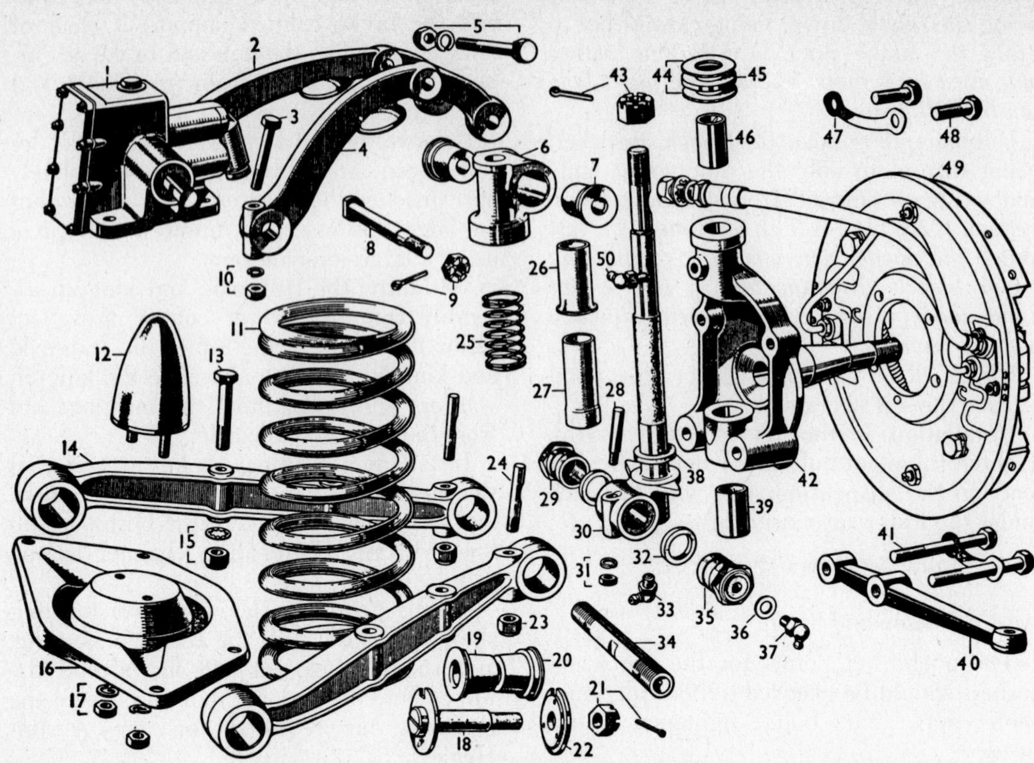

Exploded view of 100-Six and 3000 front suspension.

1 Shock absorber
2 Rear top control arm
3 Clamping bolt for front control arm
4 Front top control arm
5 Joining bolt for top wishbone arms
6 Upper trunnion link
7 Trunnion rubber bearing
8 Upper trunnion pivot pin
9 Pivot locking nut and cotter pin
10 Nut and washer for clamping bolt
11 Coil spring
12 Rebound rubber bumper
13 Spring plate bolt
14 Rear lower control arm
15 Nut and lockwasher
16 Spring plate
17 Rebound bumper nut and washer
18 Pivot pin for inner lower bearing
19 An inner lower rubber bearing
20 An outer lower rubber bearing
21 Pivot pin nut and cotter pin
22 Pivot pin washer
23 Nut for bushing cotter
24 Bushing cotter
25 Kingpin dust cover spring
26 Upper dust cover
27 Lower dust cover
28 Cotter for pivot pin
29 Rear screwed bushing
30 Kingpin and lower trunnion
31 Nut and washer
32 Cork ring
33 Trunnion oil nipple
34 Screwed pivot pin
35 Front screw bushing
36 Flat washer
37 Oil nipple
38 Cork ring
39 Stub axle lower bushing
40 Steering arm
41 Steering arm bolt
42 Stub axle
43 Kingpin nut and cotter pin
44 Washers
45 Washer
46 Stub axle upper bushings
47 Back plate bolt lockwasher
48 Back plate bolt
49 Back plate assembly
50 Kingpin oil nipple

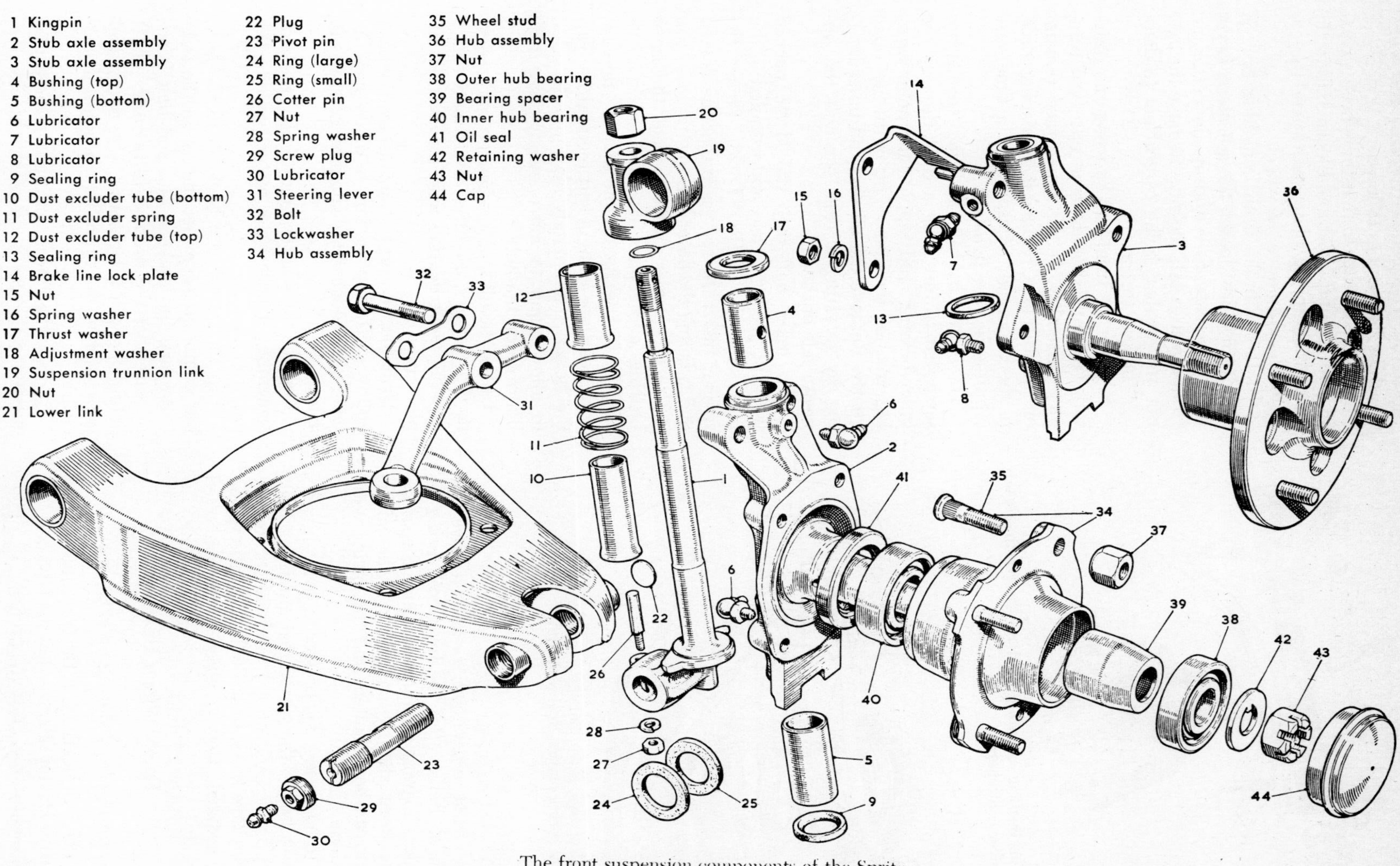
1 Kingpin
2 Stub axle assembly
3 Stub axle assembly
4 Bushing (top)
5 Bushing (bottom)
6 Lubricator
7 Lubricator
8 Lubricator
9 Sealing ring
10 Dust excluder tube (bottom)
11 Dust excluder spring
12 Dust excluder tube (top)
13 Sealing ring
14 Brake line lock plate
15 Nut
16 Spring washer
17 Thrust washer
18 Adjustment washer
19 Suspension trunnion link
20 Nut
21 Lower link
22 Plug
23 Pivot pin
24 Ring (large)
25 Ring (small)
26 Cotter pin
27 Nut
28 Spring washer
29 Screw plug
30 Lubricator
31 Steering lever
32 Bolt
33 Lockwasher
34 Hub assembly
35 Wheel stud
36 Hub assembly
37 Nut
38 Outer hub bearing
39 Bearing spacer
40 Inner hub bearing
41 Oil seal
42 Retaining washer
43 Nut
44 Cap

The front suspension components of the Sprite

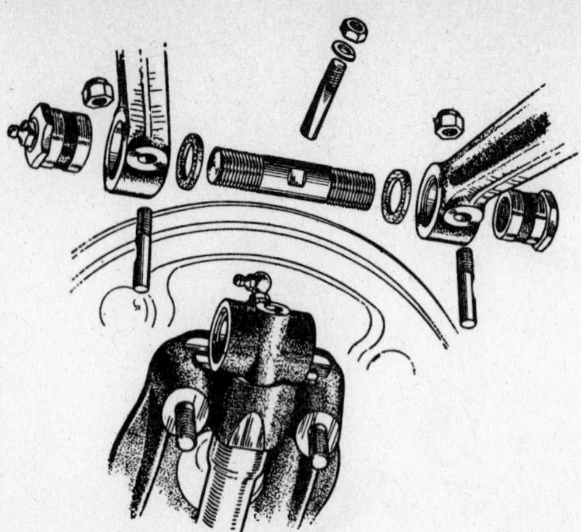

The bushing assembly used on the Austin-Healey lower control arm

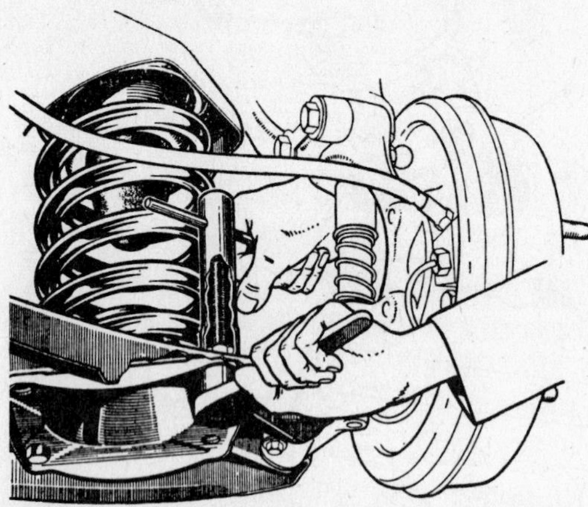

Using two slave bolts to remove and replace a coil spring on the Healey or Sprite

the front crossmember, and remove the wheel. Removal of the front coil spring requires a spring compressor. Once the spring has been slightly compressed, the spring seat can be unbolted, and the spring withdrawn.

If no spring compressor is available, remove two of the spring seat mounting bolts (opposite each other), and substitute two long slave bolts, which will allow the spring to expand slowly when it is unbolted evenly.

Front Wheel Bearings

Austin-Healey 100-6—Steel Wheels

The ball bearings in the front hubs of the Austin-Healey 100-6 with steel wheels are not adjustable; rather, preload is determined by a spacer. To replace the wheel bearings, proceed as follows:

Jack the car up, so that the wheel is clear of the ground. Position blocks under the suspension spring plate, and lower the car onto them. Remove the wheel.

Undo the brake drum attaching bolt. If the drum binds, loosen the adjusters. Lever the grease cap off. Withdraw the cotter pin from the stub axle locknut. Remove the axle nut and washer, being careful not to damage the axle thread.

Remove the front hub by using an extractor. The hub should come out as a complete assembly. If the inner race remains on the stub axle, remove it by placing a rod in the two small holes, one at a time, and tapping the race *lightly*.

The outer bearing and the spacer are separated by inserting a drift through the inner bearing, and tapping the outer bearing free of the hub. This must be done gently. Remove the oil seal and inner bearing by inserting a drift through the opposite side of the hub.

The inner ball race should be packed with the proper grease, and installed in the hub with the THRUST side facing the spacer. Insert the spacer so that the domed end is facing the outer bearing.

Use the proper grease to pack the outer bearing, and replace it in the hub with its THRUST side facing the spacer. Replace both bearings, using a soft metal drift. Tap the bearings alternately, on opposite sides, to allow them to move evenly into their housings on the hub.

Check the oil seal for damage, and renew it, if necessary. Fill the cavity between it and the inner bearing with grease, then replace it.

Drift the hub on to the stub axle, with a hollow drift. Tap the hub in place until the inner race touches the shoulder of the stub axle.

Replace the washers and tighten the nut; remember to insert the cotter pin into the nut.

Tap the grease cap back on to the hub; but do not grease either the cap or the hub.

Replace the brake drum, and bolt it on. Be sure that the drum is fully on the shaft before the bolt is tightened. Use two wheel nuts to press the drum into position if necessary.

Replace the wheel, and tighten the wheel nuts once the car is off of the blocks. Re-

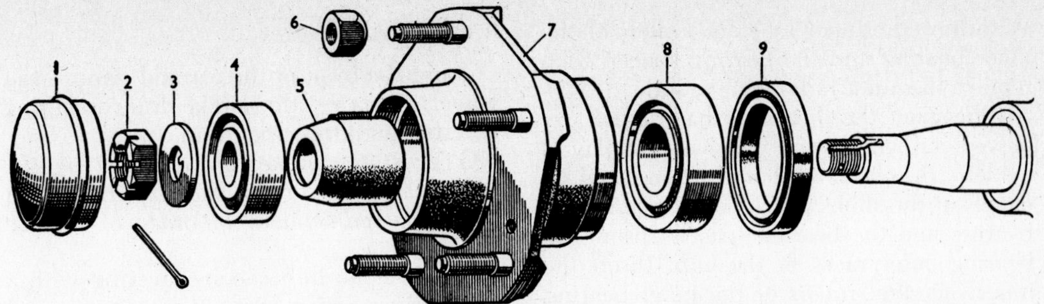

The front hub assembly—Austin-Healey 100-6 (steel wheels)

1 Grease cap
2 Nut
3 Washer
4 Outer bearing
5 Spacer
6 Wheel nut
7 Hub
8 Inner bearing
9 Oil seal

member to readjust the brake shoes *before* lowering the car.

Austin-Healey 3000 (and 100-6—Wire Wheels)

Removal, replacement and adjustment of the front wheel bearings is as follows: Raise the car until the wheel is clear of the ground, then position a block under the spring plate for safety. If equipped with wire wheels, remove the knock-off hub cap by hitting in the direction of rotation indicated on the cap. Pull the wheel off the splines. Disc wheels may be removed from the wheel studs in the conventional manner. Remove the brake caliper unit. Extract the grease-retaining cap from the wheel hub. Straighten the end of the cotter pin and remove it from the hole in the hub. Remove the nut and washer from the axle. Withdraw the front hub complete with the inner and outer bearings and oil seal.

NOTE: *Do not attempt to remove the hub by pulling on the brake disc.*

After the hub is removed, withdraw the inner race and rollers of the outer bearing along with the shims installed between the bearing and spacer. Remove the oil seal.

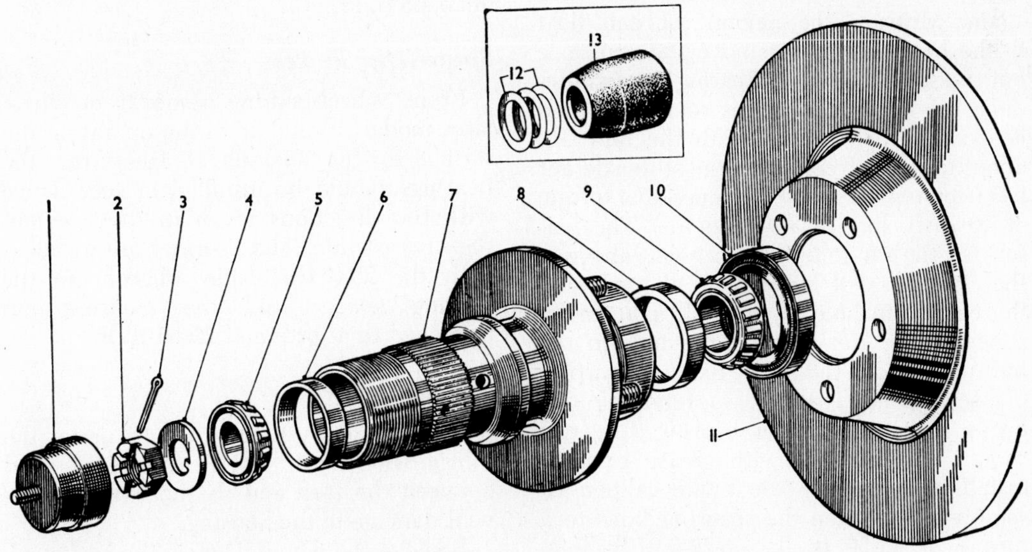

Exploded view of front hub and brake disc. Austin-Healey 3000.

1 Grease cup
2 Axle nut
3 Cotter pin
4 Washer
5 Outer bearing
6 Bearing outer race
7 Hub
8 Bearing outer race
9 Inner bearing
10 Oil seal
11 Brake disc
12 Shims
13 Spacer

Withdraw the inner race and rollers of the inner bearing and the bearing spacer, then remove the outer race from the hub.

Whenever the bearings have been removed, or whenever excessive end-play is evident, the end float should be adjusted by means of the shims provided between outer bearing and the bearing spacer. Install the bearing outer races to the hub. Insert the inner race and rollers of the inner bearing and the bearing spacer into the hub.
NOTE: *The bearing and the space between the inner bearing and the oil seal should be packed with grease.*

Install the oil seal to the hub and mount the hub assembly onto the stub axle. Pack the inner race and rollers of the outer bearing with grease and install them into the hub. Do not install shims at this stage. Install the stub axle nut and washer and tighten the nut while at the same time rotating the hub back and forth. The nut should be tightened until there is a noticeable drag. This will ensure that the bearing cones are properly seated. Unscrew and remove the stub axle nut and extract the washer and the center of the outer bearing. Insert a thickness of shims which will produce an *excessive* amount of end float, and note the thickness of the shims used. Replace the bearing center and washer and tighten the stub axle nut once again. Measure the amount of end float in the bearings, then remove the stub axle nut, washer and outer bearing center. Reduce the number of shims so that all end float will be eliminated with the hub still about to rotate freely after the stub axle nut has been replaced and tightened to a torque of 40-70 ft. lb. (5.53-9.68 kg.m.) The reason for the range of torque given above is that the nut will have to be aligned with the cotter pin hole in the stub axle. Insert a new cotter pin through the hole in the hub and lock the nut. Remove surplus grease and tap the grease retaining cap firmly against the outer bearing. The cap should not be filled with grease prior to installation. Replace the brake caliper assembly and tighten the securing bolts to a torque of 45-50 ft. lb. (6.22-6.91 kg.m.). If wire wheels are installed, grease the hub splines before replacing the wheel and the knock-off hub cap. If equipped with disc wheels, replace the wheel and tighten the wheel nuts to 60–63.5 ft. lb.

Sprite—Drum Brakes

Raise the front of the car and remove the wheel. Remove the brake-drum securing bolt and withdraw the drum.
NOTE: *If the brakes are adjusted tightly, it may be necessary to back off slightly on the brake adjustment in order to remove the drum.*

Remove the hub cap by levering with a screwdriver. Wipe away excess grease and remove the cotter pin. Remove the slotted nut and washer, and withdraw the complete hub assembly from the axle. If the inner bearing remains on the axle, it should be removed very carefully. With the hub removed, tap out the outer bearing and spacer. Remove the inner bearing and oil seal from the other side of the hub.

Before replacing the bearings, pack both the bearings and the cavity between them with grease. In order to allow for expansion, remove surplus grease after the hub has been installed. Do not fill the grease retaining cap with lubricant. When installing the bearings, be sure that the inner and outer bearings are positioned with the sides marked THRUST toward the center of the hub. The oil seal should be pressed in so that its lipped end is toward the inner bearing. Install the washer and nut and tighten the nut to a torque of 25–65 ft. lb.

Sprite—Disc Brakes

Front wheel-bearing removal on these later models is similar to the operation described for the 3000 model, except that the bearings should be installed in accordance with the directions given in the previous (Sprite) section. The bearings are installed with the THRUST side adjacent to the bearing spacer and the securing nut tightened to a torque of 25-65 ft. lb.

America

Lift the car by placing a jack under the transmission housing. Put a piece of wood between the jack and the housing, to prevent damage to the housing.

Remove the wheel. Detach the brake caliper assembly. Support the assembly; do not allow it to hang by the hydraulic line.

Remove the cotter pin and nut. Withdraw the hub and brake disc assembly, using an extractor. Unbolt the brake disc from the hub. Pack the bearings with grease.

When installing the bearings in the hub, be sure that the word THRUST on the bearings, is against the spacer.

If the runout at the outer edge of the brake disc exceeds .006 in. after installation, remove it and reposition it on the splines. The rest of the installation is the reverse of the removal procedure.

Rear Suspension

DESCRIPTION

Austin-Healey

The rear springs used on the Healey are of the semi-elliptic, in this case, half-elliptic, type. The back spring ends are mounted on shackles, which allow for variations in their lengths as they flex. The fronts of the springs are attached to rigid brackets which, in turn, are mounted to the chassis members. Two rubber stops attached to the axle, prevent too much upward movement of it.

The shock absorbers are also mounted on the chassis members at one end, while their arms are fixed to brackets on the axle.

Sprite

The rear axle of the Sprite is located by quarter-elliptic springs, and hydraulic shock absorbers. The springs and their shackles are both mounted on rubber bushings.

America

The rear suspension of the Austin America is located on a sub-frame. The suspension uses Hydrolastic® displacer units, instead of coil springs and shocks. In addition to the displacer units, independent trailing arms, helper springs and stablizer bars are used.

NOTE: *For an explanation of the operation of the America's suspension system, and precautions concerning it see Front Suspension.*

REAR SHOCK ABSORBER REMOVAL AND INSTALLATION

Austin-Healey and Sprite

Undo the nut, and remove the washer that attaches the shock absorber lever to the link. Remove the bolts from the body of the shock and the chassis bracket. Thread the lever over the bolt in the link, and withdraw the shock absorber. Be careful to keep the unit upright, as air may otherwise enter the chamber.

If the connecting link bushings are worn, the entire arm must be replaced as a single unit. The rubber bushings are not available separately.

Reinstallation of the shocks is the reverse of removal. For maintenance procedures see the FRONT SUSPENSION section.

REAR SPRING REMOVAL

Austin-Healey

Raise the car, using a jack on the side from which the spring is to be removed. Support the rear chassis crossmember, as near the rear spring attachment point as possible.

Use a screw jack under the center section of the spring, as a support, to relieve tension. Remove the wheel.

Remove the four self-locking nuts from the U-bolts, that attach the spring to the axle. Undo the nut and remove the washer from the inside of the upper rear shackle.

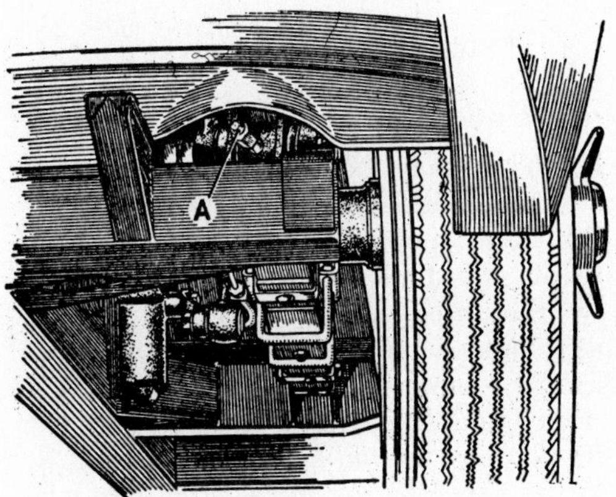

The Austin-Healey rear spring lubricator (A) is located in the trunk

The Healey rear spring rear shackle assembly

Do the same thing to the locknut, nut, and washer on the lower rear shackle.

Detach the inside connecting link from the shackle, along with the outside link.

Remove the anchor bolt from the front end of the spring, by removing the nut and washer. Drift the pin free of the assembly. Take the support jack from under the spring. Remove the spring from the car.

Place the spring in a vise, gripping the top and the bottom leaves in the jaws near the center bolt of the spring. Undo the clips. Remove the nut from the center bolt and extract the bolt.

Open the vise, allowing the spring leaves and the zinc interleaves to separate. Examine the components for wear and cracks.

Put the springs back into the vise. Use a tapered rod, of about the same diameter as the center bolt, to position the leaves. The bolt may now be replaced without damage to its thread. Replace the bolt, its nut and washer. Put the leaf clips back on.

Installation is the reverse of removal.

Sprite

Jack up the car, by placing a jack under the differential housing; use supports under the body. CAUTION: *Be sure that the weight of the axle is completely on the jack. The springs must have no load on them.*

Remove the wheels. Undo the shackle bolts. On the older Sprites, remove the bolts at the front attachment plate, and remove the U-bolt. The spring is free to be withdrawn.

The rear spring mount for the Sprite

1 Spring attachment bolts
2 Shock absorber nuts
3 U-bolt nuts

On the newer Sprites the front bracket bolts must be removed from behind the seats, inside of the car. From underneath of the car, remove the four U-bolt nuts, and the shock absorber attachment plate. Detach the nuts, bolts, and plates from the rear shackle. Withdraw the spring assembly.

Installation is the reverse of removal. On the newer Sprite models, remove the axle retaining strap to aid in U-bolt replacement. Tighten the spring bolt, only when the spring has a normal working load on it.

Rear Wheel Bearings

Austin-Healey and Sprite

For the rear wheel bearing removal and installation procedures, see the Drive Axle section, above.

America

Place a jack under the rear frame crossmember, and raise the car. Remove the wheel. Withdraw the grease cap. Remove the cotter pin, undo the hub nut, and remove the washer. Pull the hub assembly off by means of an extractor.

Pack both bearings with grease. There should be a small amount of grease showing on either side of each bearing. Pack the cavity between the inner bearing and the oil seal; lightly smear grease on the spacer. NOTE: *Do not fill the cavity between the bearings, or the cap with grease.*

Replacement is the reverse of removal. Be sure that the side marked THRUST on the bearings, goes next to the spacer. The inner chamfered edge of the flat washer should go next to the bearing.

Steering

Steering Wheel Removal

Austin-Healey

Undo the snap-lock connector located at the bottom of the steering column.

On those models which are equipped with an adjustable steering column, withdraw the three screws from the steering wheel hub. Remove the horn/turn signal assembly, complete with the short section of tube, and the cables. NOTE: *Do not twist the horn assembly while removing it. If this is done, the slot in the long tube will become enlarged, allowing excessive play in the horn assembly.*

If the car has a non-adjustable steering wheel, the nut and plug must be removed from the bottom end of the steering box. The tube is now free to slide out of the column, from inside of the car. Plug the hole in the bottom of the steering gear box to prevent the oil from leaking out of it. Undo the steering wheel nut, and slide the steering wheel off of the column. Assembly is the reverse of removal.

Sprite

Remove the press fit emblem assembly from the steering wheel hub, undo the center bolt and slide the wheel off.

On later cars, once the emblem is removed, the wheel may be withdrawn, by undoing the bolts that attach it to the hub. The nut in the center does not have to be removed, unless the steering wheel hub is to be removed. Installation is the reverse of removal.

America

The steering wheel removal procedure is essentially the same as that for the later Sprites.

STEERING GEAR REMOVAL AND INSTALLATION

Austin-Healey

Remove the horn and steering wheel assembly as detailed above. On cars equipped with adjustable steering columns, remove the telescopic spring, and the locating collar.

Remove the bracket, which supports the steering column, from behind the instrument panel.

Remove the radiator and the grille. Undo the screws from the two plates, on either side of the firewall, through which the steering column passes.

Raise the front of the car, and remove the wheels. Disconnect the tie rods from the steering arm, by removing the cotter pins, and nuts from the ends of the tie-rods. Detach the ball and socket assembly from the steering lever.

Remove the nuts and the bolts that attach the steering box bracket to the chassis. Slide the steering column and box assembly out through the grille opening.

Installation is the reverse of removal. Be careful to see that no bending stresses are applied to the column, before its support brackets are tightened. When the tie-rod is installel, be sure that the steering wheel and front wheels are in a centered, straight-ahead position. Tighten the steering wheel nut to 480 in. lbs.

Sprite

Remove the radiator. Undo the clamp nut and bolt at the splined lower end of the steering column; withdraw the column from the splines.

Remove the cotter pins and nuts from the ball and socket assembly; detach the assembly from the tie-rods.

Undo the bolts from the steering rack mounting brackets, which attach them to the front crossmember. The entire rack assembly may now be removed.

Installation is the reverse of removal. Do not fully tighten the rack housing bolts until the assembly has been replaced. This aids in correct pinion alignment with the steering column.

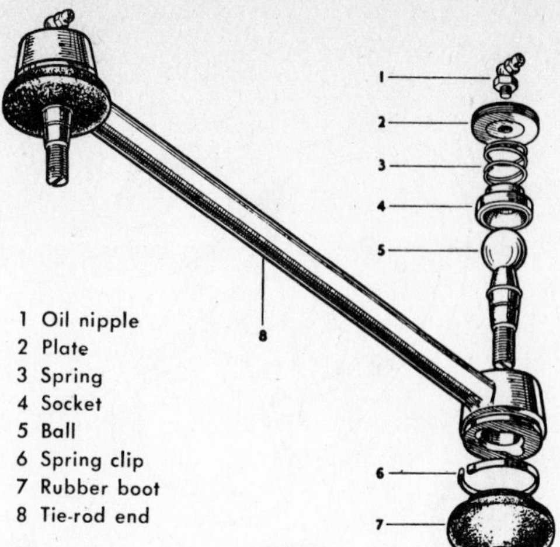

The tie-rod ball joint assembly—Austin-Healey

The steering column being removed through the grille opening on the Austin-Healey

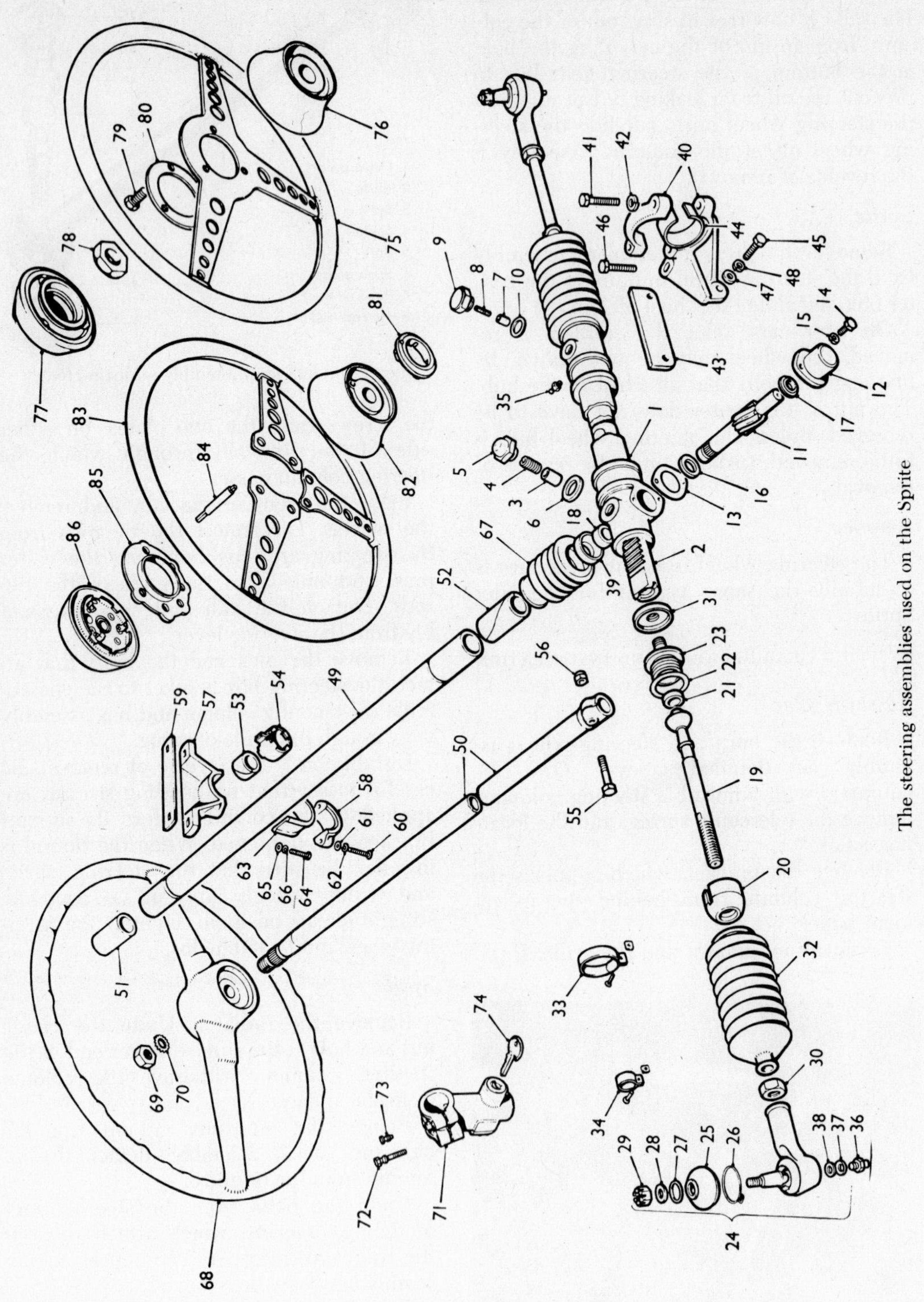

The steering assemblies used on the Sprite

The steering assemblies used on the Sprite

1 Rack housing
2 Rack
3 Damper pad
4 Damper pad spring
5 Damper pad housing
6 Shim
7 Secondary damper pad
8 Secondary damper spring
9 Secondary damper housing
10 Housing washer
11 Pinion
12 Pinion thrust bearing
13 Shim
14 Bolt
15 Spring washer
16 Pinion thrust washer (top)
17 Pinion thrust washer (bottom)
18 Pinion seal
19 Tie-rod
20 Ball housing (female)
21 Ball seat
22 Shim
23 Ball housing (male)
24 Ball socket assembly
25 Boot
26 Clip
27 Ring
28 Washer
29 Nut
30 Locknut
31 Lockwasher
32 Seal
33 Clip (inner)
34 Clip (outer)
35 Lubricator
36 Lubricator
37 Dished washer
38 Fiber washer
39 Retainer
40 Bracket and cap assembly
41 Bolt
42 Spring washer
43 Seating
44 Packing
45 Bolt
46 Bolt
47 Plain washer
48 Spring washer
49 Outer column
50 Inner column tube
51 Felt bearing (top)
52 Felt bearing (bottom)
53 Felt bearing (bottom)
54 Clip
55 Bolt
56 Nut
57 Bracket
58 Bracket cap
59 Shim
60 Bolt
61 Plain washer
62 Spring washer
63 Seating
64 Bolt
65 Plain washer
66 Spring washer
67 Boot
68 Steering-wheel
69 Nut
70 Shakeproof washer
71 Steering-column lock
72 Shear bolt
73 Locating screw
74 Key
75 Steering-wheel
76 Steering-wheel nut
77 Emblem
78 Nut
79 Bolt
80 Locking ring

(75–80: Sprite Mk. IV (HAN 10))

81 Slip ring
82 Steering wheel hub
83 Steering wheel
84 Horn contact
85 Lock ring
86 Horn button

(81–86: Sprite Mk. IV (HAN 10) from car number 86303)

Sprite—Energy Absorbing Steering Column

Remove the radiator. Take the cotter pins out, and the nuts off of the ball and socket assembly. Disengage the tie-rod ball joints from the arms, by using an extractor.

Undo the steering column pinch bolt. Loosen and remove the six nuts which attach the rack assembly to the crossmember.

Slide the rack assembly forward, as far as possible. Collect all of the shims, which are located between the right mounting bracket and the front of the crossmember. CAUTION: *It is important that exactly the same number of shims be replaced as were removed; if not, the steering column will have to be aligned, as detailed below.*

Remove the three bolts from the floorboard. Loosen the upper attachment bolts from the steering column, and pull the column back, to detach the splines from the pinion.

Take off the right front wheel and extract the rack assembly.

Installation is the reverse of removal. Be sure to replace the same number of shims, as were removed.

If new parts have been used, or if the shims have been lost, the column must be aligned as follows:

The column U-joint should be completely free to move, before the rack mounting bolts are tightened. If the joint is offset during installation, the steering will be stiff, and the upper pinion bearing will wear prematurely.

If any binding is apparent, adjust the shim thickness by trial and error, until the binding stops. Also, the column support bracket and plate may be shifted to aid in alignment.

America

Disconnect the snap-lock connectors for the horn and turn signals, which are located below the parcel shelf.

Pull back the rubber shroud, then remove the nut, bolt, and washer which clamp the steering column to the pinion shaft. Undo the column support bracket screws, from underneath of the instrument panel. Disengage the steering column from the pinion splines.

Raise the front of the car, by placing a jack under the front subframe. Remove both wheels. Detach the steering tie-rod ball joints.

Support the engine, either from above or by placing a jack under the transmission housing.

From inside of the car, undo the U-bolt nuts, that attach the rack housing to the floor boards.

Lower the engine slightly, just enough so that rack assembly clears the floor pan, and remove rack assembly from the driver's side. CAUTION: *Do not lower the engine more than necessary. The suspension hydraulic lines, fuel lines, and the linkages have not been disconnected from the engine; if it is lowered too far, damage to them will result.*

Installing is the reverse of removal. Leave the support nuts loosened until the steering column clamp bolt has been tightened to 8-9 ft. lbs. Be sure that the slot in the steering column clamp is pointing upward, with the wheels in a straight ahead-position; otherwise the turn signals will not fit.

Steering Gear Reconditioning

Austin-Healey

Remove the steering gear from the car as described above. Extract the cotter pin, and unscrew the nut at the bottom of the Pitman arm. Use an extractor to pull the Pitman arm off of the splines. Remove the cover-plate by undoing its four attachment bolts.

Turn the gear over, support the top, and drift the rocker shaft out, by tapping it lightly. NOTE: *Do not remove the peg from the rocker shaft, unless it is worn and needs replacement.*

Remove the nut and the plug on the end of the steering box, and allow the oil to drain out. If the car has a non-adjustable steering column, this has already been done during the steering gear removal procedure. On cars with an adjustable column, remove the long tube, at this point.

Remove the four bolts that attach the end cover and remove the cover. Rotate the unit, so that the steering box is pointing upward. Remove the worm and both ball bearings by *lightly* striking the end of the inner shaft against a piece of wood placed on the floor. Remove the complete inner column through the open end of the box.

Withdraw the ball race from the top of the outer casing by lifting it out by hand. If it is in the casing too tightly to do this,

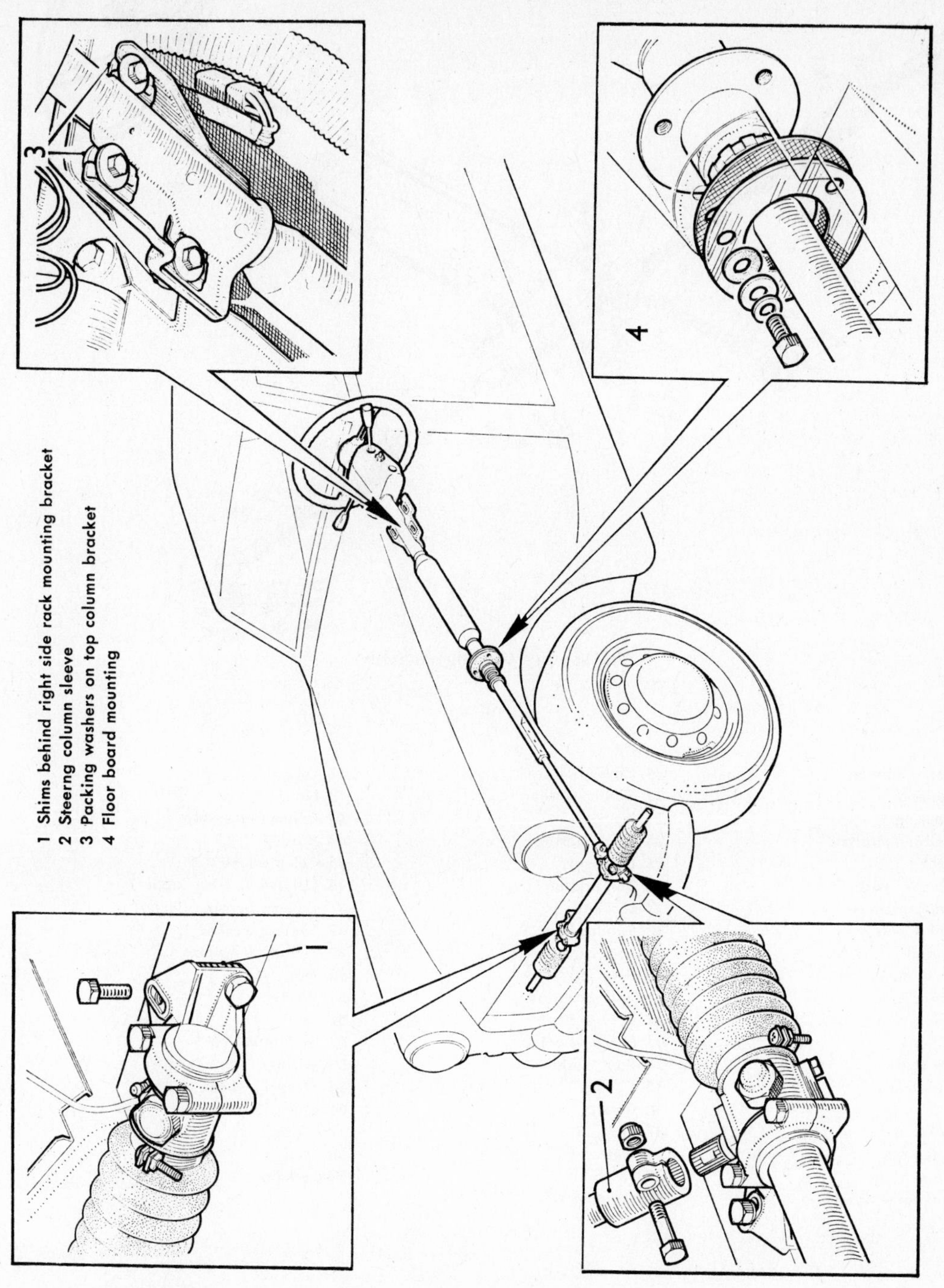

Steering alignment used on the Sprite with an energy absorbing steering column

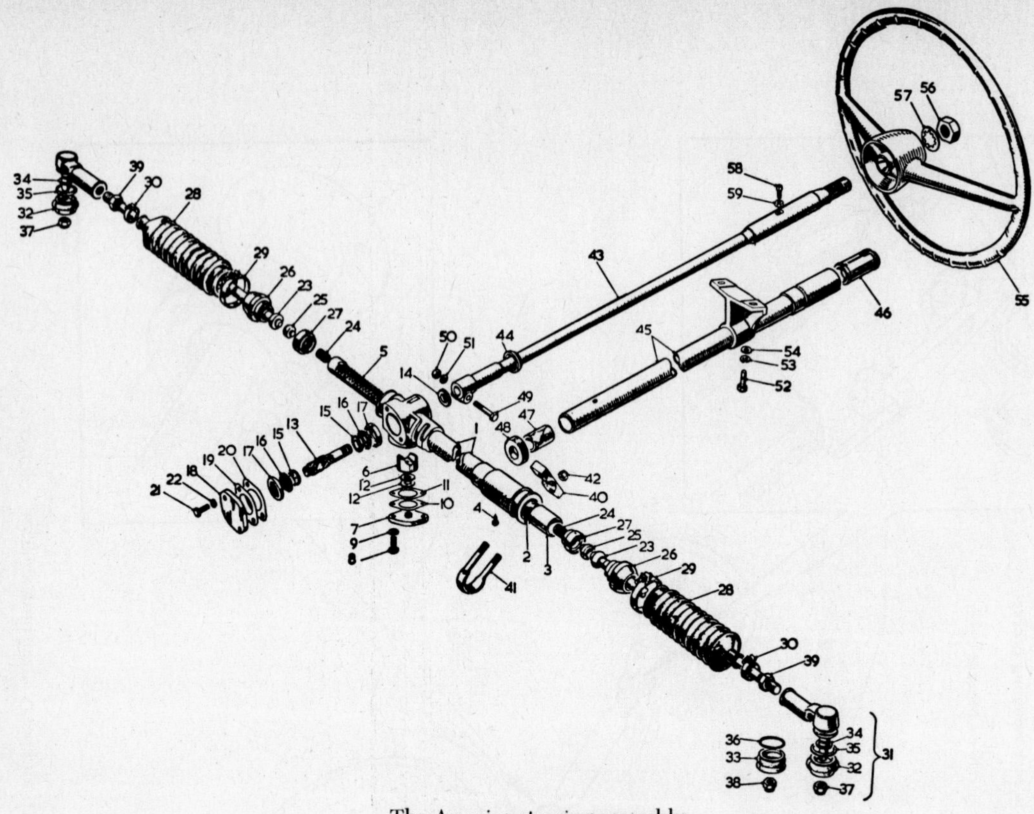

The America steering assembly

1 Rack housing
2 Bushing
3 Housing
4 Housing screws
5 Rack
6 Damper yoke
7 Damper cover
8 Cover bolt
9 Spring washer
10 Yoke shim
11 Cover joint
12 Disc spring
13 Pinion
14 Oil seal
15 Ball cone
16 Ball cage
17 Ball cup
18 End cover
19 Cover shim
20 End cover gasket
21 Cover bolt
22 Spring washer
23 Tie-rod
24 Thrust spring
25 Ball seat
26 Ball housing
27 Locknut
28 Rubber boot
29 Seal clip (inner)
30 Seal clip (outer)
31 Ball socket assembly
32 Rubber boot
33 Rubber boot
34 Boot washer
35 Circlip
36 Circlip
37 Nut
38 Nut
39 Locknut
40 Clamp base
41 U-bolt
42 Nut
43 Column assembly
44 Washer
45 Column tube
46 Column bearing (upper)
47 Column bearing (lower)
48 Sealing washer
49 Pinion clamp bolt
50 Nut
51 Washer
52 Bolt
53 Spring washer
54 Washer
55 Steering-wheel
56 Steering-wheel nut
57 Washer
58 Stud
59 Locknut

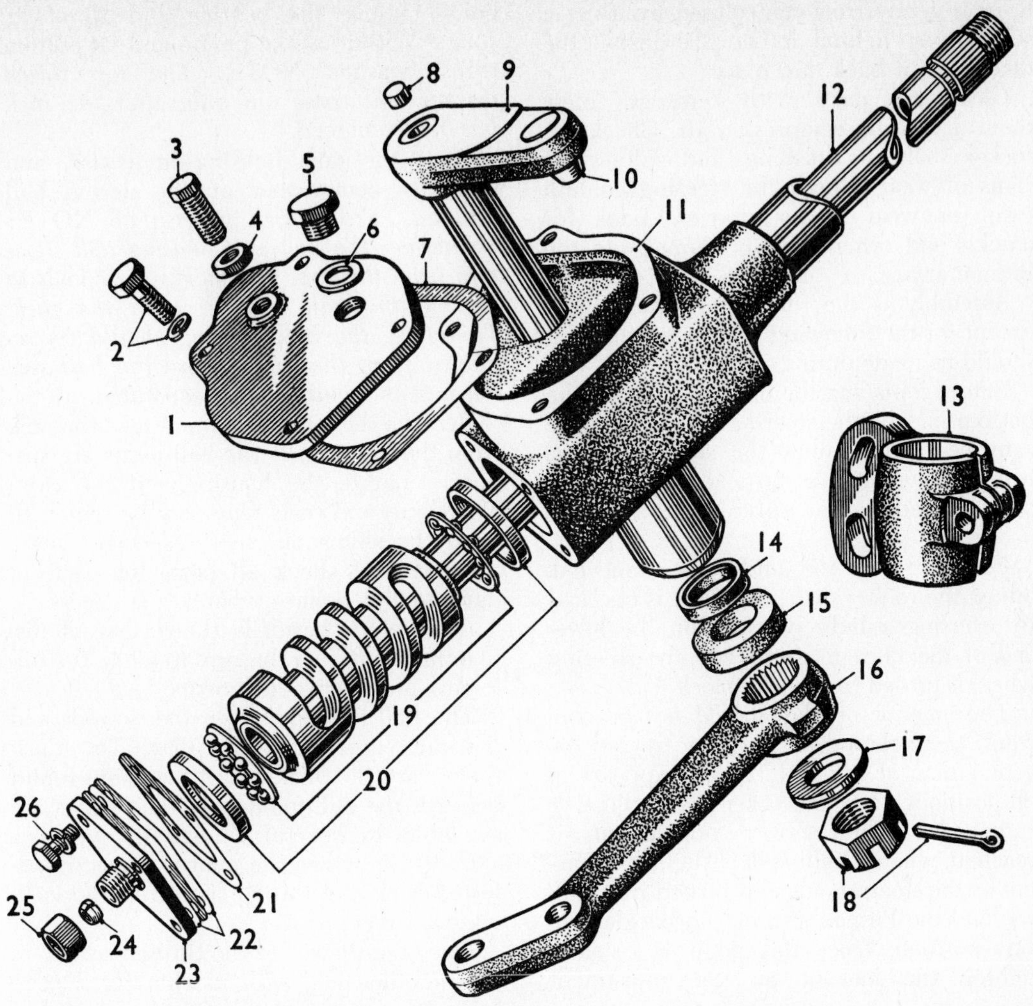

The Austin-Healey steering box assembly

1 Top cover
2 Bolt and washer
3 Adjusting screw
4 Locknut
5 Filler plug
6 Washer
7 Gasket
8 Adjusting screw stop
9 Follower peg screw
10 Follower peg
11 Steering box
12 Inner column
13 Steering box bracket
14 Oil seal
15 Gasket
16 Steering lever
17 Washer
18 Nut and washer
19 Inner races
20 Outer races
21 Gasket
22 Adjusting shims
23 End cover
24 Plug
25 Stator tube nut
26 Gasket and washer

lever it gently from the column by using a screwdriver behind its lip. To install the race, push it back into place.

Clean the parts with kerosene; blow them dry, using compressed air. Check the rocker shaft, its bushing, and splines for signs of wear. Check the steering column cam for wear in its grooves. Look for cracks, and other signs of damage to the Pitman arm.

Assembly is the reverse of dismantling, except for the following adjustments, which should be made during assembly:

Before replacing the nut and plug on the bottom end of the steering box, adjust the cam bearings so that the steering wheel turns freely, but has no end play. This is done by adding or subtracting shims as necessary.

Before the tie-rod ends are connected, adjust the rocker shaft. Backlash is checked by exerting a light pressure on the lower end of the Pitman arm, while the steering wheel is turned from lock to lock.

The amount of play should not be constant; there should be less play toward the center than at full lock. If play appears in all positions, turn the rocker shaft adjusting screw in. The correct adjustment is reached, when a tight spot is slightly apparent as the steering wheel is turned past center, and the Pitman arm has no backlash in this position. Once this point is reached, tighten the locknut on the adjustment screw.

Remember to refill the steering box with SAE 90 gear oil, after the nut and plug are replaced.

Sprite

Remove the rack and pinion assembly from the car as outlined above. NOTE: *Before dismantling the assembly, measure and note the distance from the wrench flats on the tie-rod to each of the ball joint locknuts; this will aid in reassembly.*

Loosen the locknuts and unscrew the ball joint assemblies. After placing a container under the rack housing to catch the oil from it, undo the boot clips from the rack housing and tie-rods. Remove the boots.

Undo the hexagonal cap which is next to the oil nipple on the housing, and remove the washer, pressure-pad and spring. Perform the same operation on the damper pad housing, being careful to collect all of the shims. Remove the shaft thrust bearing bolts; remove the bearing and all of its shims. Withdraw the pinion and its bottom thrust washer. NOTE: *The top thrust washer will come out only after the rack has been removed.*

Place the rack housing in a vise, and undo the lockwasher on the tie-rod ball housing. Take the ball joint cap off. NOTE: *Sometimes the ball seat housing will separate from the cap; this makes it difficult to remove the ball housing from the rack. Therefore, the ball housing should be removed from the rack before the ball seat housing and joint caps are separated.*

Remove the lockwasher and take the rack from the housing. If the ball joints are suspect, separate the housing and the caps. The shims and seats may now be removed; keep the shims on their respective sides.

Clean and check all parts for wear or damage and replace whatever is necessary.

Assembly is basically the reverse of dismantling, however, be sure to make the following necessary adjustments:

The ball joints between the tie-rods and the rack must have no play. To adjust them, vary the thickness of the shims found beneath the ball joint seats. The shims are available in several thicknesses between .002–.010 in. Once the joint is correctly adjusted, lock it in three places with the lockwasher flange.

Place the thicker of the thrust washers in the rack housing, with its chamfered edge facing the rack. The thinner thrust washer goes on the plain end of the pinion shaft with its chamfered edge facing the pinion teeth.

Align the center tooth on the rack with the mark on the splined end of the pinion shaft, while replacing the pinion.

The end-play of the pinion is adjusted by using shims. Use a dial indicator to check the end-play, which should be between .002–.005 in. Shims are available in several thicknesses to adjust this.

Replace the ball joint locknuts and ball joints in their original positions by using the measurements made before the rack was dismantled.

With the plunger in place, screw down the cap until it is possible to rotate the pinion shaft by drawing the rack through its housing. Use a feeler gauge to measure the clearance between the hexagon of the damper cap and its seating in the rack housing. Add .002-.005 in. to the measurement ob-

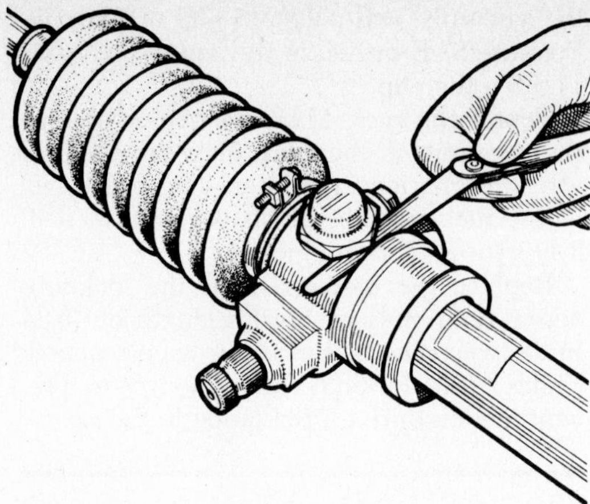

Checking the damper cap adjustments on the Sprite

tained. The result is the thickness of shims which should be placed under the damper cap. Adjusting shims are available in thicknesses of .003 and .010 in. Remove the damper cap and plunger and install the spring beneath the plunger and assembly along with the required thickness of shims to provide the proper clearance.

Use a new pinion shaft oil seal and pump 10 fl. oz. of oil into the rack housing through the nipple.

America

Undo the locknuts; remove the ball and socket assemblies from the tie-rods.

Unclip the boots from the rack housing and the tie-rods. Drain the oil, and take the boots completely off.

Undo the damper housing mounting bolts. Remove the damper cover, packing shims, and extract the damper complete with spring.

Remove the two bolts which attach the cover-plate for the pinion thrust bearing. Take off the plate and packing shims. Withdraw the lower thrust washer, bearing, and bearing race. Remove the pinion. NOTE: *The upper thrust washer, bearing, and bearing race are trapped behind the rack teeth; they can be removed once the rack is removed.*

Extract the pinion shaft oil seal. Remove the ball joint housing. Pry up the indentations in the lock-ring, so that they are clear of the slots in the rack and ball housings. Loosen the lock-ring; unscrew the housing which, in turn, will release the tie-rod, ball seat and ball seat spring.

Remove the rack from the pinion end of the housing; to prevent damage to the plastic bushings, which are located in the other end of the housing.

Remove the attachment screw from the bushing; extract the bushing from the housing. Remove the metal sleeve that the bushing fits into.

Clean, and check all parts for damage and wear. Any fractures or roughness in either the rack or pinion teeth will make them useless; they will have to be replaced. Check the rubber boots for wear. Replace any other worn or defective parts.

If any part of the outer ball socket is found to be defective, it must be replaced as an entire assembly, since there are no replacement components available.

Install the plastic bushing and sleeve in the rack housing. Put the upper bearing assembly back in the housing, also. Next, replace the rack, and then the pinion.

Bolt the pinion thrust bearing cover on without its shims; but do not overtighten it. Use a feeler gauge to measure the distance between the cover and the housing.

To obtain the proper preload, remove the cover and replace the packing shims to the value of the feeler gauge reading less .001-.003 in. Use gasket sealer on the faces of the joint to prevent leakage.

Use a new lock-ring on the ball housing; screw it on the rack end to limit of the threads. Install the spring, seat, tie-rod, and ball housing; tighten it until the tie-rod is

A The distance between the ball pins is 45.34 in
B Rack travel from the center position is 2.5 in
C Rack travel from the center position is 2.5 in.
D The length of the tie-rod when threaded

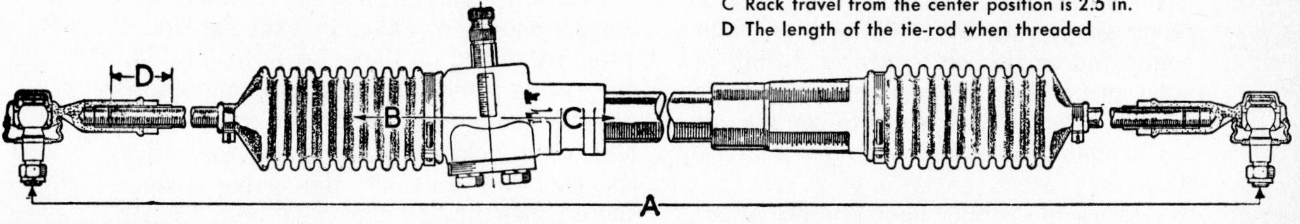

The steering rack dimensions on the America

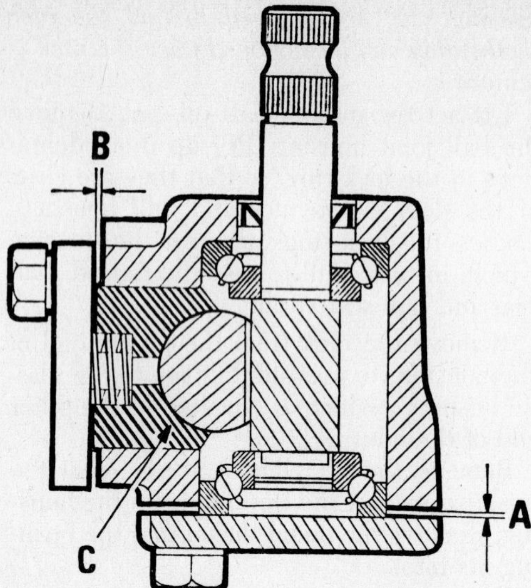

A sectional view of the steering damper used on the America

A Feeler gauge measurement minus .001-.003 in., is the correct thickness for shims to be used at this point
B Measure this gap to fit shims
C The damper yoke

secure. Bring the lock-ring over to meet the bell housing; be sure that the tie-rod remains secured. Loosen the ball housing 1/8 of a turn. This allows the tie-rod to move freely.

Lock the housing by tightening the lock-ring to 33–37 ft. lbs. Do not allow the housing to rotate. The preload should be such that a torque of 32-52 in. lbs. is required on the tie-rods to move them.

Install the damper assembly; lock it in place by pinching the lips of the ring into the slots on the ball housing and the rack.

Replace the damper yoke and cover-plate, without the springs or the shims. With the rack in the dead center position, tighten the attachment bolts until the pinion shaft just rotates with a torque wrench setting of 15 in. lbs. Measure the gap between the cover-plate and the surface of the rack housing.

Remove the cover-plate, and replace the shims to the thickness obtained with the feeler guage plus .002–.005 in. Use sealing compound on the joint surfaces. Install the yoke spring, cover-plate, and the shims.
NOTE: *The load required to set the pinion assembly in motion should not exceed 35 in. lbs.*

Replace the rubber boots. Before attaching the boot clip on the tie-rod end, upright the assembly, and pour 2/5 pint of Extreme Pressure SAE 140 oil in the end of the boot. Tighten the clip.

Center the rack. Mark the pinion so that the position of the rack may be checked after installation in the car. The full travel of the rack is 5 in.; this is accomplished in 3-1/3 turns of the pinion.

Replace the ball end, and the locknuts. Screw both ends in, until a length of 45.34 in. between the ball pins has been reached. Tighten the locknuts only enough to prevent motion during installation in the car.

Brakes

Master Cylinder

Reconditioning

Austin-Healey 100-6

The procedures for servicing the clutch and brake master cylinders are exactly the same. Therefore, the procedures given in this section may be used to recondition the clutch master cylinder as well.

The brake master cylinder, which consists of an alloy body with a polished bore and capped reservoir, is disassembled as follows:

Release the master cylinder push rod from the brake pedal. Disconnect the pressure pipe from the cylinder and remove the securing bolts. Withdraw the master cylinder and its fluid supply from the car. Remove the filler cap and drain the fluid from the reservoir. Pull back the rubber dust cover and remove the circlip. Remove the pushrod and dished washer. Remove the plunger assembly. Depress the plunger return spring and remove the thimble, valve, and spring as a unit. Detach the valve spacer. Be careful not to lose the spring washer under the valve head. Remove the seal. Examine all parts for wear or distortion and replace where necessary.

In assembling the master cylinder, first replace the valve seal so that the flat side is properly seated on the valve head. Position the spring washer so that its dome side is against the underside of the valve head and it is held in position by the valve spacer. The legs of the valve spacer should face toward the valve seal. Center the plunger return spring on the spacer,

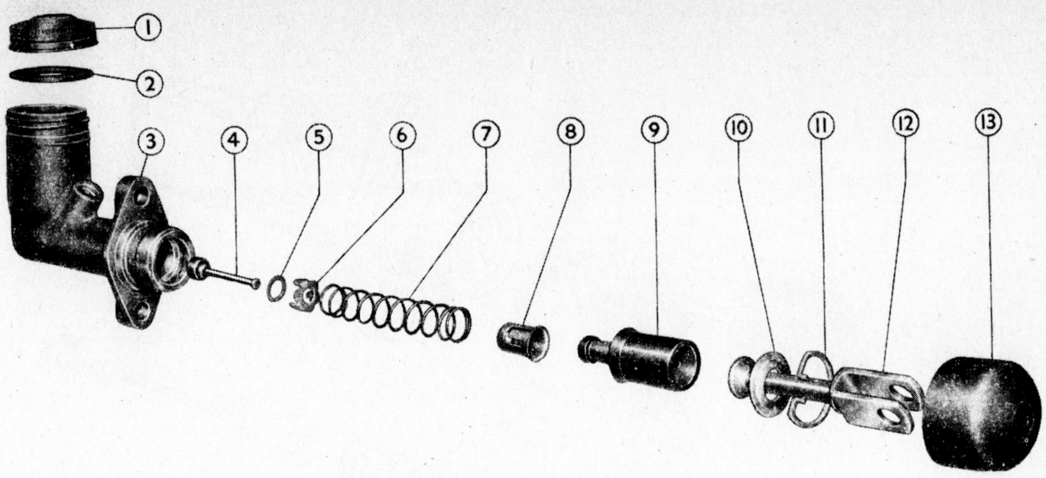

The brake (or clutch) master cylinder components
—Austin-Healey 100-6

1 Filler cap
2 Washer
3 Master cylinder
4 Valve stem
5 Spring washer
6 Valve spacer
7 Return spring
8 Thimble
9 Plunger
10 Dished washer
11 Circlip
12 Fork
13 Dust cover

then insert the thimble into the spring and depress until the valve stem engages through the elongated hole of the thimble. Be sure that the stem is correctly located in the center of the thimble. Check to see that the spring is still centered on the spacer. Install a new plunger seal so that the flat of the seal is seated against the face of the plunger. Insert the small end of the plunger into the thimble until the thimble leaf is engaged under the shoulder of the plunger. Press the thimble leaf home. Smear the cylinder assembly with brake fluid, then insert into the bore of the cylinder valve. Replace the push rod so that the dished side of the washer is under the spherical head. Install the circlip into the groove machined in the cylinder body. Replace the rubber dust cover and install the master cylinder to its original position. (Do not omit the packing washer.) Secure with the two bolts on the flange and replace the pressure pipe to its connection at the cylinder. Reconnect the pushrod fork to the pedal lever and secure with the circlip. Bleed the brake hydraulic system.

Austin-Healey 3000

Since the procedure for servicing the brake and clutch master cylinders is the same, the following may be used for either operation.

Release the master cylinder push rod from the pedal. Disconnect the intake and pressure pipe attachments from the cylinder and remove the securing bolts. Withdraw the master cylinder. Drain the fluid from the cylinder, pull back the dust cover and remove the circlip. Remove the pushrod and dished washer. Remove the plunger assembly, which is released by lifting the thimble leaf over the shouldered end of the plunger. Press the plunger return spring and remove the thimble, spring and valve. Detach the valve spacer, noting the spacer washer under the valve head. Remove the seal. Examine all parts for wear and distortion and replace where necessary.

Begin assembly by replacing the valve seal so that the flat side is correctly seated on the valve head. Position the spring washer with its domed side against the underside of the valve head, then hold it in position with the valve spacer. The valve spacer legs should face toward the valve seal. The remainder of the assembly operation is as set forth for the master cylinder of the 100-6.

Sprite Mks. I-III

The master cylinder of the Sprite Mk. I, Mk. II, and Mk. III is responsible for the operation of both the brakes and the clutch. It contains two bores which are side by

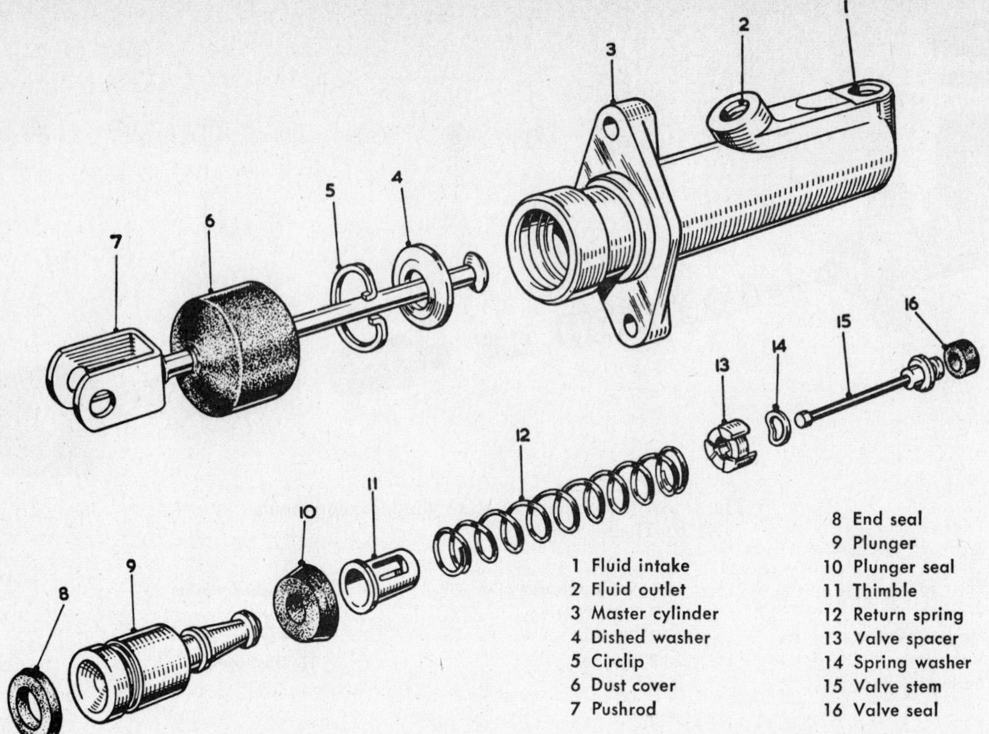

The Healey 3000 brake (or clutch) master cylinder components

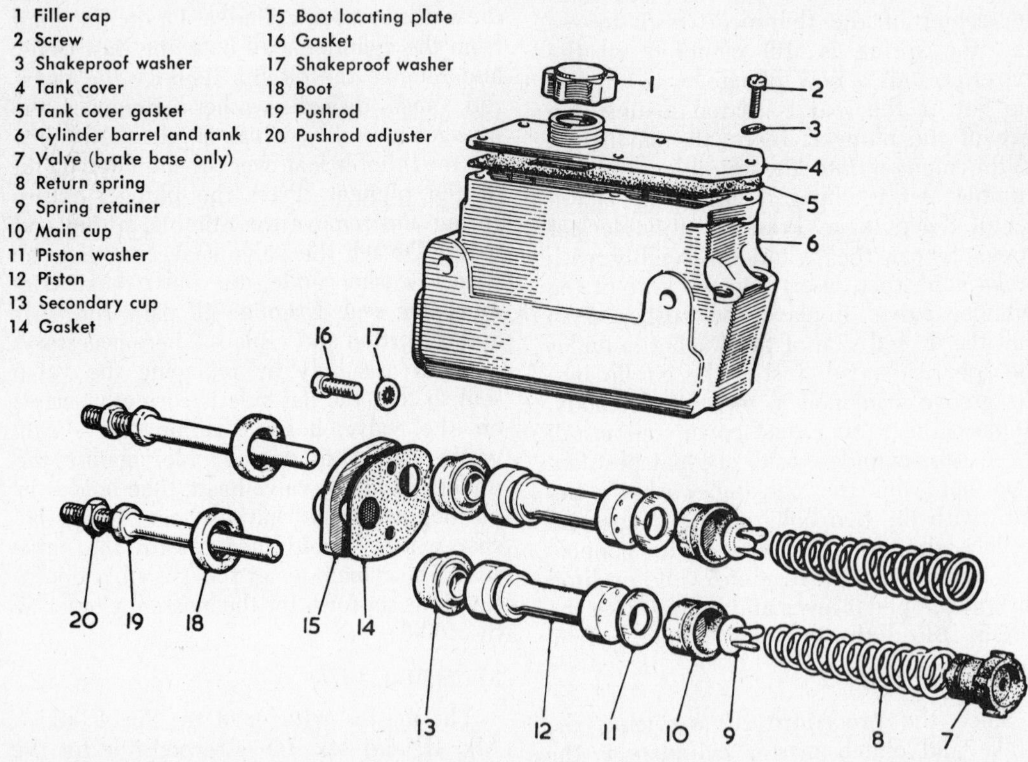

The master cylinder used on the Sprite Mks. I-III. A single master cylinder serves both the clutch and brake systems.

side, both of which consist of normal master cylinder parts. The bore which contains the check valve serves the brakes, the other transmits hydraulic pressure to the clutch slave cylinder.

Remove the heater blower unit. Remove the bracket of the heater blower and unscrew the bolts securing the master cylinder mounting plate to the engine bulkhead.

NOTE: *Before disconnecting the master cylinder, ascertain which bore of the cylinder serves the clutch and which the brakes.*

Disconnect the two hydraulic lines from the master cylinder. Withdraw the master cylinder by lifting upward and at the same time manipulating the clutch and brake pedals through the opening in the bulkhead. The cylinder and pedals are removed as an assembly.

Begin disassembly of the unit by disconnecting each pedal from its master cylinder pushrod by removing the spring clips and securing pins. Remove the bolts securing the master cylinder to its mounting plate and withdraw the unit. Remove the bolts which secure the dust cover plate to the body of the master cylinder. Remove the plate from the master cylinder and remove the dust covers and pushrods. Remove the common filler cap and drain out the fluid. Withdraw the piston, piston washer, main cup, spring retainer, and return spring. Remove the secondary cup by stretching it over the end flange of the piston. Examine all parts for wear and distortion and replace where necessary.

Reassembly of the unit is the reverse of the dismantling procedure, except that special attention should be paid to the installation of the rubber dust covers. The vent hole in each dust cover should be at the bottom when the cylinder is mounted in the car. After reassembly and installation, bleed the hydraulic system.

Sprite Mk. IV

While the earlier Sprite had the brake master cylinder combined with the clutch master cylinder as a single casting, the Mk. I is equipped with a separate master cylinder for the braking system. This unit is removed from the car as follows:

Remove the front hood and remove the lid of the pedal compartment. Disconnect the hydraulic pipe from the brake master-cylinder. Withdraw the cotter pin from the pin which connects the push rod to the brake pedal, and remove the pin. Remove the two bolts securing the master cylinder to the pedal compartment and remove the master cylinder.

Disassembly is as follows: Remove the filler cap and drain the hydraulic fluid. Detach the rubber boot from the body and slide it up the push rod. Remove the circlip which retains the push rod and withdraw the push rod complete with rubber boot and dished washer. Withdraw the piston complete with secondary cup. Withdraw the piston washer, main cup, and spring complete with spring retainer and valve. Stretch the secondary cup over the end flange of the piston, using finger pressure only, and remove the cup. Clean all components with brake fluid and dry with a lint-free cloth. Examine metal parts for wear or damage, and the rubber parts for swelling and other deterioration, and replace all worn or suspect parts.

Reassemble the master cylinder. Dip all components into brake fluid and assemble while wet. Install the secondary cup by stretching over the piston with the lip of the cup facing towards the head of the piston. When the cup is in its groove, it should be worked gently to ensure that it is properly seated. Install the spring retainer and valve to the spring, then install the spring, valve end first, into the body. Install the main cup, cup washer, piston, and push rod. When the cups are being installed, the lip edge should be carefully entered into the barrel first. Install the circlip and the rubber boot.

Replace the master cylinder to the car by reversing the removal procedure, then fill the cylinder with brake fluid and bleed the brake system.

America

The America is equipped with a tandem type master cylinder. Thus, if the hydraulic system to one set of wheels fails, the other set will remain operative. Servicing the master cylinder is as follows:

Unfasten the lines from the master cylinder. To prevent fluid loss, and to keep dirt from entering the system, plug up the line ends.

Undo the two nuts which attach the master cylinder to the firewall. Lift the master cylinder clear, but leave the pushrod connected to the brake pedal.

Drain the fluid and replace the cap. Replug the hydraulic line connections. Clean the outside of the unit and take off its rubber boot.

Use a vise that has soft jaws to hold the cylinder body. The mouth of the bore should face upward. Remove the ring from the piston groove by compressing the spring.

CAUTION: *Care should be taken not to distort the coils of the ring; nor should the bore of the cylinder be scored.*

Remove the snap-ring which retains the piston. Move the piston up and down in the bore; this will free the nylon guide bearing and cap seal. Remove them once that they have been freed. Remove the washer and withdraw the inner circlip.

Withdraw the roll pin which retains the piston link, by compressing the spring that separates the pistons.

Using the indentation in the caps, note the position of the caps before removal. Next, remove the cups and washers from the pistons. Remove the plastic reservoir from the body, by undoing the four bolts which hold it in place. Unfasten the two sealing rings from the reservoir.

Remove the connection adapters, the disposable copper gaskets, the spring and the trap valve.

Clean all of the parts with brake fluid, using a clean, lint-free cloth.

Check all of the metal parts for wear or damage. Examine the rubber and plastic parts for signs of deterioration. Replace any parts necessary. NOTE: *All internal parts should be placed in brake fluid before assembly, and assembled while still wet.*

Position the piston washer on the head of the secondary piston, convex surface down. Ease the main cup, lip last, over the piston end and seat in the groove next to the washer. All of this is done with the fingers. Repeat the above procedure with the primary piston.

The rest of the assembly and installation is the reverse of the teardown and removal procedures. Refill the system with brake fluid, and bleed it.

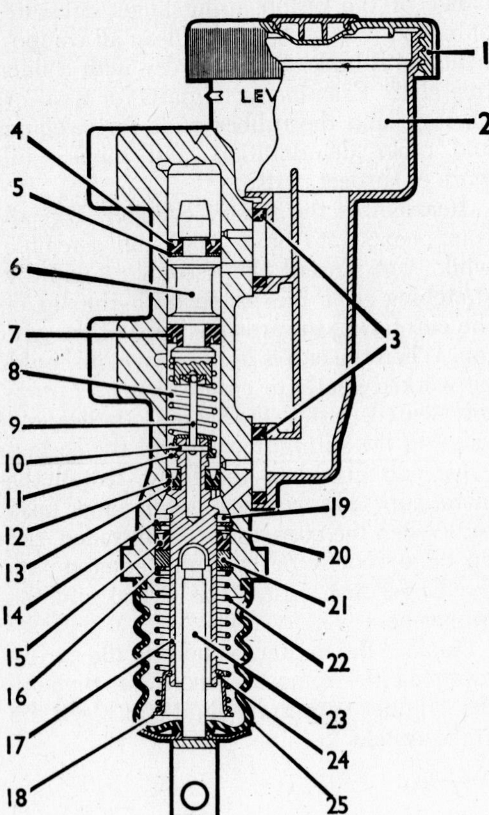

The dual tandem master brake cylinder used in the America

1 Filler cap
2 Plastic reservoir
3 Reservoir seals
4 Main cup
5 Piston washer
6 Piston
7 Main cup
8 Spring
9 Piston link
10 Pin
11 Pin retainer
12 Main cup
13 Piston washer
14 Circlip
15 Cup
16 Circlip
17 Piston
18 Spring retainer
19 Stop washer
20 Washer
21 Bearing
22 Spring
23 Pushrod
24 Ring
25 Rubber boot

Bleeding the Hydraulic Brake System

Bleeding of the hydraulic system must be done after most of the service operations which have preceded and when air has entered the hydraulic system. During the bleeding operation it is important that the brake fluid reservoir be kept at least half full to avoid drawing air into the system. Check to see that all connections are secure and that all bleed screws are closed.

Fill the reservoir with brake fluid, then remove the cap from the rear bleed screw on the wheel cylinder which is farthest away from the master cylinder, and install a bleed tube to the screw. With the free end of the tube submerged in a clean container partially filled with brake fluid, loosen the bleed screw and depress the brake pedal slowly through its full length of travel. Allow the pedal to return without assistance, then repeat the pumping action, pausing slightly before each depression of the pedal. When the fluid leaving the tube is completely free of air bubbles, hold the pedal down firmly and tighten the bleed screw. Repeat the bleeding operation on all remaining wheel cylinders, finishing at the wheel which is nearest the master cylinder. Top up the fluid reservoir to the correct level, apply a normal force to the brake pedal for 3 minutes, then examine the entire hydraulic system for leaks.

Front Brakes—Drum

Inspection

NOTE: *Wheel bearing removal and service are given in the* Suspension, Drive Axle, and Steering *chapter.*

Austin-Healey and Sprite (Early)

The Austin-Healey and the early Sprites are equipped with drum brakes in the front. Examine the brake shoes for wear and replace them, if necessary. Also, examine the drums for signs of scoring and distortion; have them turned if either of these are apparent.

The procedure for drum removal may be found with wheel bearing service; see the note above.

Front Brakes—Disc

Caliper Removal and Inspection

Austin-Healey 3000

Jack up the car and remove the wheels. Undo the brake line nut, which is found in front of the brake line support bracket. Detach and plug the line. Remove the support bracket by undoing the two nuts that attach it.

Unfasten the bolts which attach the caliper and remove it. Remove the brake pads (see below), but do not depress the pistons fully in their bores.

Clean the caliper assembly before proceeding any further. Next, being careful not to damage the groove or the surface of the piston, extract the piston by pushing back the dust seal, and inserting two levers in the seal groove.

Detach the dust cover. Withdraw the internal seal by inserting a blunt blade beside it, and then ease it out. If signs of wear are apparent, replace the seal and dust cover with new ones.

Clean the internal metal parts with denatured alcohol. Use brake fluid on the rubber parts; do not use alcohol.

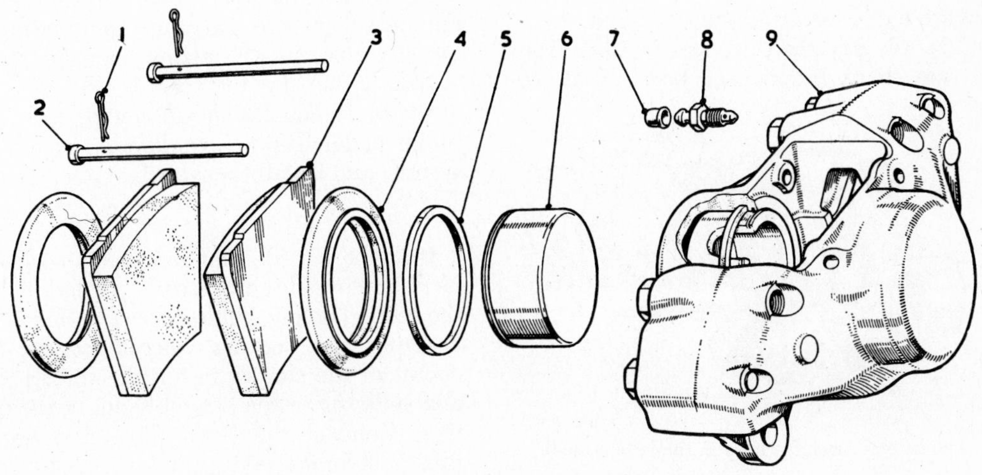

Exploded view of an Austin-Healey front disc brake caliper.

1 Wire clip
2 Retaining pin
3 Lining pad and steel backplate
4 Dust cover
5 Sealing ring
6 Pistons
7 Bleed nipple dust cover
8 Bleed nipple
9 Caliper body

CAUTION: *Under no circumstances, should the through-bolts that hold the two halves of the caliper together, be removed.*

Assemble the caliper as follows: replace the internal seal with the smaller diameter on the inside. Position the lip of the dust cover in the outer groove. Smear the piston with brake fluid, and insert it, closed end first, into the bore. Push the piston fully home. Position the outer edge of the dust cover in the groove on the piston body.

Install the pads. Lock them in place by using the retaining pins. Replace the caliper assembly on the car; be sure that the disc is between the two pads. Connect the brake lines and bleed the system. Check for leaks. Tighten the caliper retaining bolts to 45-50 ft. lbs.

Sprite

The later Sprites are equipped with disc brakes in the front. Jack up the front of the car; remove the wheel. Remove the pads (see below). Detach the hydraulic line. Unfasten the bolts which attach the caliper assembly, and withdraw it.

Clean the outside of the caliper. Be careful to note the position of the relieved section on the piston face. Reconnect the hydraulic lines, being careful to support the caliper, so that the line is not strained.

Using a C clamp, clamp the piston on the mounted side of the caliper assembly, in place. Put a container underneath the caliper to catch the fluid. Depress the brake pedal until piston in the rim section is far enough out to be withdrawn by hand.

Carefully pry the dust seal retainer from the mouth of the caliper bore. Next, remove the dust seal. Extract the fluid seal, using care not to damage any of the inner surfaces.

To remove the piston from the mounted half of the caliper, repeat the above procedure, but with the piston replaced and clamped in the lip half of the caliper. First, remove the bleeder screw. CAUTION: *Do not separate the two halves of the caliper.*

Remove any traces of dirt or rust from the pad recesses. Clean the faces of the pistons and their bores. Use only brake fluid or denatured alcohol to clean the caliper assembly. Do not use alcohol to clean any of the rubber parts. Clear the fluid passages with compressed air.

Replace the bleeder screw. Coat the fluid seal with brake fluid, then ease it into the groove in the caliper bore. Seat it, by using the fingers. Loosen the bleeder screw one turn.

Coat the piston with brake fluid, then place it in the mouth of the bore. Be sure that the cut-away section of the piston face is facing downward. Press the piston into the bore until the piston just protrudes 5/16 in. from the assembly. Be sure that the piston does not lift.

Coat the dust seal with brake fluid and insert it into its retainer. Place the seal assembly over the protruding portion of the piston, with the seal facing inward. Use a C clamp to push the assembly fully home. Tighten the bleeder screw.

Replace the seals and the piston in the mounted half of the caliper in the same manner, but disconnecting the hydraulic line so that the C clamp can be used.

Installation in the car is the reverse order of removal; but do not depress the brake pedal during installation. Bleed the system, and install the wheels.

America

Jack the car up, and remove the wheels. Next, remove the brake pads, as detailed in the section below. Undo the brake line.

Swing the floating caliper toward the center of the car. Unfasten the spring clip, and slide the piston assembly out of the caliper. Connect the brake line, and gently press the brake pedal until the piston can be withdrawn by hand.

Proceed as outlined in the Sprite section, but for only one piston, until the piston assembly has been fully dismantled, cleaned, and reassembled.

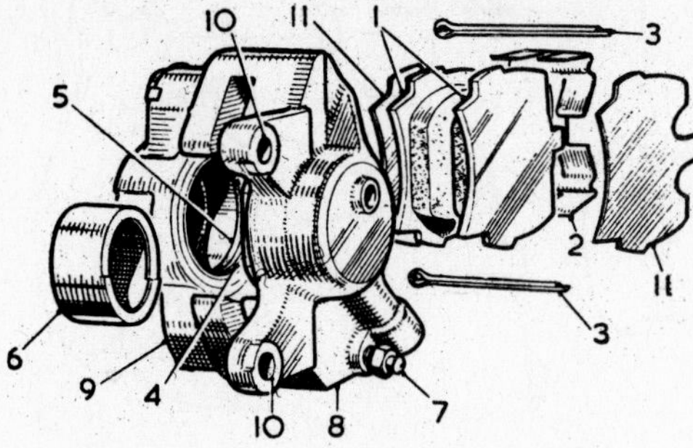

The caliper assembly used in the later Sprites

1 Pads
2 Pad retaining spring
3 Retaining pin
4 Piston dust seal
5 Piston fluid seal
6 Piston
7 Bleeder screw
8 Caliper (mouting half)
9 Caliper (rim half)
10 Caliper mounting point
11 Anti-squeak shims

Next, clean the slots in the piston and the caliper edges. With the bleed nipple facing the rear, install the piston assembly in the caliper. Fasten the retaining clip. Reconnect the brake line, and install the pads. Bleed the system, and replace the wheel.

Brake Pads

Friction pads which have worn down to a thickness of approximately 1/16 in. (1.6 mm.) should be replaced. Wear can easily be checked by observing the pads through the openings in the calipers. Remove the retaining pins and withdraw the worn pads from the calipers. In order to insert the new pads, it will be necessary to use a lever to force the pistons back into their cylinder bores. Before doing this, however, drain the brake fluid reservoir to one-half of the full level so that forcing the pistons back will not result in displaced fluid being ejected from the reservoir and on to the paint. Insert the new friction pads and secure with retaining pins. Be sure that the pads are free to move slightly to allow for automatic adjustment. Top up the brake fluid reservoir and apply the brakes several times until the pedal feels solid. Some mechanics recommend that new friction pads not be subjected to hard braking for at least the first few hundred miles.

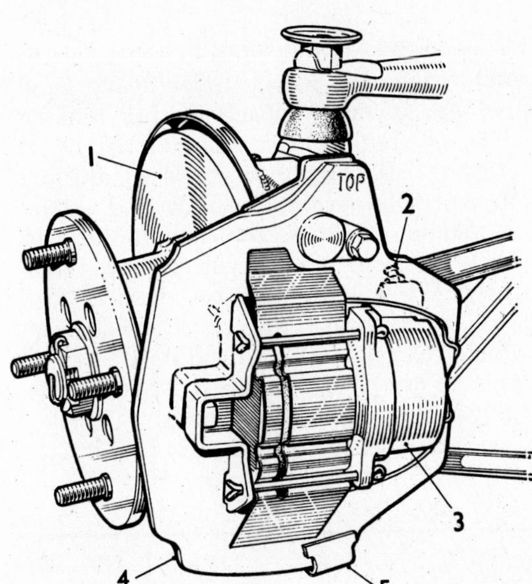

The floating caliper assembly used on the America

1 Brake disc
2 Bleeder screw
3 Piston assembly
4 Swinging caliper
5 Fixed to swinging caliper securing clip

NOTE: *On the Sprite, remove and install the anti-rattle shims along with the pads. On the America the pad should be centered. To do this, loosen the bolt on the top of the caliper, depress the brake pedal several times and retighten the bolt to 65–80 in. lbs.*

Disc Inspection

To check runout, clamp a dial indicator to a fixed point on the car. Take a reading; the figure for the Healey should not exceed .004 in., while that for the Sprite and the America should be no greater than .006 in. NOTE: *Excessive runout could also be the result of worn wheel bearings; these should be checked also.*

Examine the discs for erratic or excessive scoring; if either of these are present, replace them.

Be sure that the disc is centered between the calipers. To check this, remove the pads, and insert a feeler gauge between the pad abutments and the disc surface. The gap on the opposite side of the disc may differ by no more than .015 in. There should be no differences betwen the abutments on the same side of the caliper; to correct any differences use shims at the caliper mounting points.

Rear Brakes—Drum Type

Inspection

NOTE: *The inspection procedure of rear brake drums is the same as that for the front (see above). Wheel bearing procedure is listed in the suspension chapter.*

Adjustments

The procedure for adjusting the drum brakes, front and rear, is similar for all models. The adjustments are made with a screwdriver, or a wrench depending upon the model. Some cars have adjusting screws, while others have a single square headed adjustment bolt protruding from each rear backplate.

In each case, turn the adjuster until the wheel cannot be turned. Then back off, just enough so that the shoe no longer contacts the drum when the wheel is turned.

Handbrake

The handbrake lever, for all models, is located on the tunnel between the seats, and is of the pull-up type. The handbrake

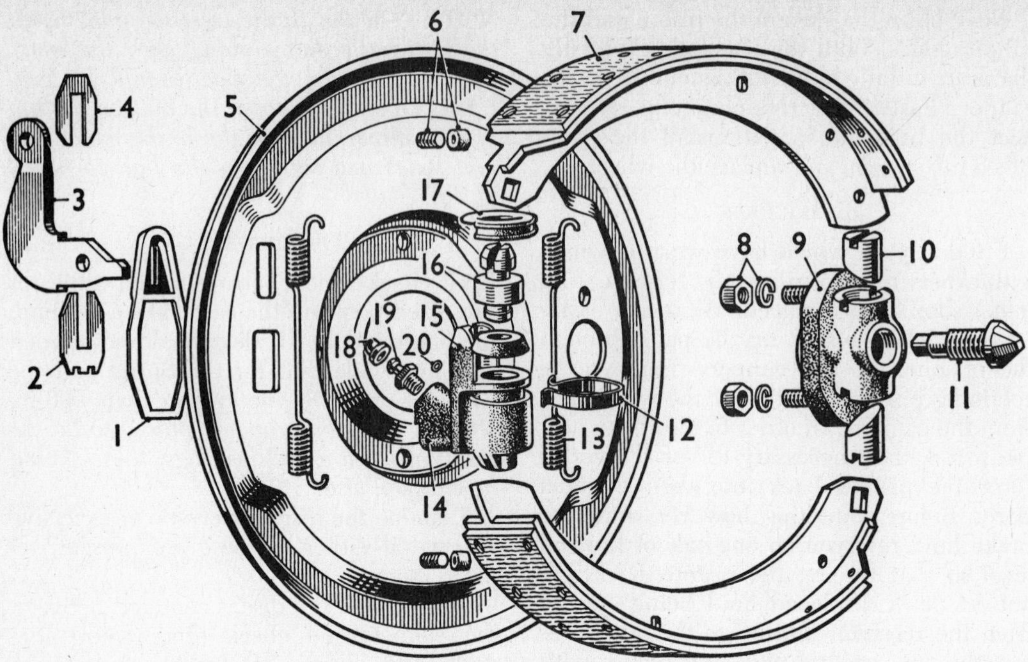

The rear brake assembly used on the Austin-Healey 100-6 and 3000

1 Rubber seal
2 Wheel cylinder locking plate
3 Handbrake lever
4 Wheel cylinder locking plate
5 Backplate
6 Anchoring post
7 Brake shoe
8 Nut and spring washer
9 Adjuster body
10 Adjuster tappets
11 Adjuster wedge
12 Dust cover clip
13 Shoe return spring
14 Orifice
15 Cylinder body
16 Piston
17 Dust cover
18 Bleed nipple dust cover
19 Bleed nipple
20 Bleed valve ball

works on the rear wheels. When the rear brakes are adjusted properly, so is the handbrake. The only adjustment, aside from this, that can be made to the handbrake, is that for cable tension.

Cable Adjustment

Austin-Healey

Be sure that the rear brake shoes are adjusted properly. When the handbrake is correctly adjusted, the shoes should be tight against the drum, with no slack in the cable, and lever slightly on.

The cable is tensioned by an adjustment sleeve nut at the front of the cable.

Sprite and America

The cable adjustment linkage is beneath the car, attached to the rear axle, and is adjusted in the following manner: With the rear brake shoes adjusted properly, block the front wheels and jack up the rear of the car. Apply the handbrake to the third notch on the ratchet. Adjust the handbrake cable, by means of the nut, until it is possible to rotate each rear wheel under heavy hand pressure. In order to achieve full braking efficiency, both wheels should offer equal resistance. If not, the brake-shoe adjusting job was not performed evenly and should be redone. Release the handbrake and check to see that both wheels now rotate freely. While under the car, it is a good idea to lubricate the pivot mechanism which transfers the handbrake cable's force to the two individual wheels, especially during the winter months.

Heater

Core

Removal and Installation

Austin-Healey and Sprite

The heater core is located in the heater box which, in turn, is found in the engine

The heater used in the Sprite; note the hose clamp (insert)

compartment of the car. On the Healey it is attached to the firewall; in the Sprite the battery carrier. To remove the core, proceed in the following manner:

Drain the cooling system. Disconnect the butterfly control wire, and on the Sprite, the battery. Unfasten the water hoses from the heater box. Remove the bolts (or screws) which attach the heater box to its mounting point.

Release the clamp that holds the flexible hose to the heater box. The heater box may now be withdrawn from the car as a complete unit.

The core is fastened in the heater box by means of sheet metal screws. Remove the screws and lift out the core assembly.

Assembly and installation are the reverse of dismantling and removal. Bleed the system, if necessary, by removing the water return hose from its connector. Extend the return hose with an additional piece of hose, so that the water may be returned to the radiator via the filler cap. Temporarily plug the lower connection.

Run the engine. When the water flow into the radiator is not erratic, and is free of bubbles; reconnect and fasten the hose as quickly as possible.

America

In order to remove the heater from the America, the entire dashboard and parcel shelf must be removed as follows:

Detach the ground lead from the battery. Remove the four screws *which hold the padded top of the dashboard in place.* NOTE: *It is necessary to bend back the tabs covering the two outer screws.* Lift off the top.

Remove the six screws that hold the front of the dash in place. Ease the door trim out of the way, and pull the front panel toward the interior.

Detach the choke cable at the carburetor end. Unfasten the electrical connectors from the switches. Disconnect the speedometer drive and ground lead.

Lift the entire dashboard assembly out of the car. Remove the parcel shelf, by undoing the nine screws that attach it to the car, and lower it to the floor.

The heater box and its connections are now accessible. Drain the cooling system. Remove the heater fan as outlined below. Disconnect the control cable that operates the butterfly valve. Detach the heater hoses at the engine, draining as much residual water from them as possible. Unfasten the bolts that attach the heater box to the car, and carefully lift the box out.

Take the sheetmetal screws out of the heater box, and withdraw the core.

Assembly and installation are the reverse of removal and dismantling. Feed the water hoses through the firewall before mounting the heater box.

Blower

Removal and Installation

Austin-Healey and Sprite

The heater blower is found in the engine compartment. On the Healey it is attached to the right fender; on the Sprite it is adjacent to the heater box. To remove it proceed as follows:

Undo the hose clamps on either side of it, and withdraw the flexible hoses. Unfasten the ground lug, and the snap connector for the hot wire which comes from the harness. Remove the sheet metal screws that attach the blower to the car and lift it out.

Installation is the reverse of removal.

America

From underneath the parcel shelf, unfasten the snap connector in the power lead, and undo the ground lug. Remove the screws that attach the fan mounting bracket to the heater box, and lower the fan clear of the box.

Installation is the reverse of removal.

Windshield Wipers

Motor and Transmission

Removal and Installation

Austin-Healey and Sprite

Disconnect or turn off the battery. Undo the electrical connections at the motor. Remove the wiper arms by sliding them off of the splined shaft. Remove the setscrew, first, on the Sprite. Unfasten the connector tube at the wiper transmission.

Remove the nuts and bolts that attach the motor. Lift out the motor assembly, complete with the drive cable.

Installation is the reverse of removal.

America

Disconnect the battery. Unfasten the electrical connections at the motor. Remove the wiper arms, by sliding them off of their splined shaft. Withdraw the outer case from the wiper transmission housing.

Undo the bolts which attach the wiper motor to the radiator shroud. Lift out the motor and the inner drive cable.

Installation is the reverse of removal.

Radio

The radios used in the Austin line are usually dealer installed options; therefore they may differ from unit to unit. In the older models the radios are mounted below the instrument panel, while newer models have them mounted in the center console or in the dash panel.

Removal is basically a matter of finding the mounting screws and unfastening them; then disconnecting the power and ground leads, and unplugging the antenna connector.

Installation, especially if it is initial, requires attention to several points. Care should be used not to reverse the ground and power leads, as severe damage to the radio will result. The power lead can usually be identified by the in-line fuse holder attached to it, while the ground lead is plain.

The older Austin cars, with Lucas electrical systems, are positive (+) ground, and require a radio that may be used for positive ground operation. This includes positive ground radios, or those which are adjustable to either ground. Under no circumstances should a radio be used, which is designed for negative ground (—) only operation. Be sure which side of the electrical system is grounded before installing the radio. Also, be sure that those radios which may be used with either ground are properly adjusted before installation in the car. CAUTION: *A radio which is designed for negative ground only operation cannot be used with a positive ground electrical system by isolating it from the rest of the car. This practice will lead to a severe shock hazard, and destruction of the electrical system.*

If a new antenna has been installed, or a new antenna cable, the radio trimmer must be adjusted. Tune in a fairly weak station around 1400 kc; adjust the small screw protruding from behind the set until the strongest signal is heard.

Should the speaker require replacement, it should be replaced with one of the same impedance. This is especially important with transistorized units; failure to observe proper impedance can result in rapid transistor failure. CAUTION: *Never operate a radio without a load; i.e., with no speaker, or with the speaker leads shorted together. Doing either of these will lead to instant output tube or transistor failure.*

CAPRI SECTION

Index

Introduction

Available in one model since 1970-71, Capri is Lincoln-Mercury's entry into the growing small car market. Capri is powered by a four-cylinder (1.6 liter), OHV engine, with a 2.0 liter, OHC four-cylinder engine as an option. Three types of transmissions are available; a three-speed manual, a fully synchronized four-speed, and an automatic, all operated by a floor mounted shifter. Other noteworthy Capri features include power front disc brakes, rack and pinion steering and an aluminized exhaust system.

Vehicle and Engine Serial Number Identification

Vehicle Identification Plate

The identification plate is found under the hood, riveted to the inner fender panel. Interpretation of the plate is as follows:

A type drive (1 = left-hand drive)
B type engine (L1 = 1600 cc.)
C type transmission (5 = four-speed floorshift)
D axle ratio (V = 3.89:1)
E paint code
  B = ermine white
  7 = amber gold metallic
  1 = blue mink metallic
  5 = fern green metallic
  6 = aquatic jade metallic
  H = red

Year and Model Identification

1970 Capri

Vehicle Identification Plate

F trim code
G S.V.C. reference (indicates date of manufacture when car is shipped elsewhere for final assembly)
H vehicle serial number

Vehicle Serial Number

The serial number consists of eleven digits, both letters and numbers, arranged in five sections.

1st digit: letter–product source (G = Germany)
2nd digit: letter–assembly plant (A = Cologne, B = Genk)
3rd & 4th digits: letters–body type (EC = two-door sedan)
5th & 6th digits: letters–assembly code (The first letter denotes year of manufacture, the second the month. See chart following.)
7th to 11th digits: sequential serial number (from 00001-99999)

Assembly Code

YEAR CODE

Month	*K-1970*	*L-1971*
Jan.	L	C
Feb.	Y	K
Mar.	S	D
Apr.	T	E
May	J	L
June	U	Y
July	M	S
Aug.	P	T
Sept.	B	J
Oct.	R	U
Nov.	A	M
Dec.	G	P

General Engine Specifications

Year	*Cu. In. Displacement*	*Carburetor*	*Developed Horsepower @ Rpm*	*Developed Torque @ Rpm (Ft. Lbs.)*	*A.M.A. Horsepower*	*Bore & Stroke (In.)*	*Compression Ratio*	*Valve Lifter Type*	*Normal Oil Pressure (Psi)*
1970-71	97.51	Autolite, 1-BBL.	71 @ 5000	91 @ 2800	16.1	3.188 x 3.056	8:1	Mech.	35-40
1970-71	122.0	Weber, 2-BBL.	100 @ 5600	120 @ 3600	20.4	3.575 x 3.029	8.6:1	–	N.A.

Tune-Up Specifications

Year	Model	Spark Plugs Type	Spark Plugs Gap (In.)	Distributor Point Dwell (Deg.)	Distributor Point Gap (In.)	Ignition Timing (Deg.) ▲	Cranking Comp. Pressure (Psi)	Valves Tappet (Hot) Clearance (In.) Intake	Valves Tappet (Hot) Clearance (In.) Exhaust	Valves Intake Opens (Deg.)	Fuel Pump Pressure (Psi)	Idle Speed (Rpm) *
1970-71	1,600 cc.	Autolite AG22	.025	38-40	.025	12B	165	.010[2]	.017[2]	17B	3½-5	830-870[1]
1970-71	2,000 cc.	BRF 32	.034	48-52	.025	12B	•	.008	.010	18B	3.8-5.0	750**
1972	All Models	See engine compartment stickers for tune-up specifications.										

▲—With vacuum advance disconnected. Add 50 rpm when equipped with air conditioning.
•—Lowest reading within 75% of highest.
*—650 rpm with automatic transmission.

B—Before top dead center.
1—Fast idle = 1,775 rpm.
2—Cold = intake .008″-.010″.
exhaust .018″-.020″.

CAUTION

General adoption of anti-pollution laws has changed the design of almost all car engine production to effectively reduce crankcase emission and terminal exhaust products. It has been necessary to adopt stricter tune-up rules, especially timing and idle speed procedures. Both of these values are peculiar to the engine and to its application, rather than to the engine alone. With this in mind, car manufacturers supply idle speed data for the engine and application involved. This information is clearly displayed in the engine compartment of each vehicle.

Firing Order

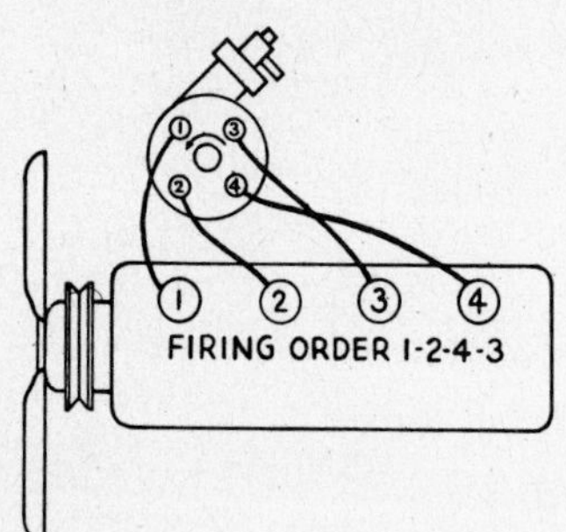

Capri 1,600 cc. firing order

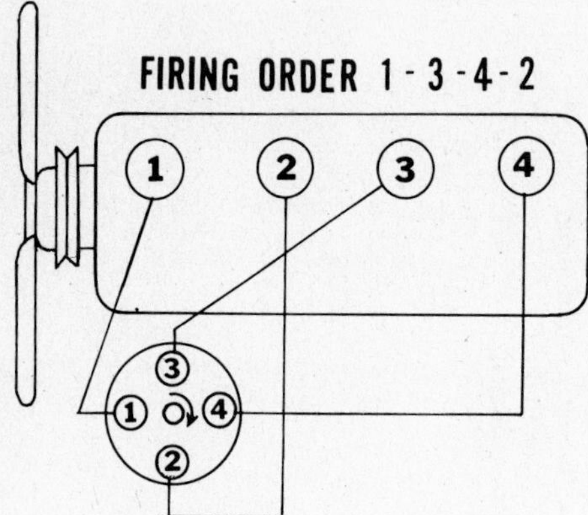

Capri 2,000 cc. firing order

Engine Rebuilding Specifications

		Block		Pistons			Rings		
		Bore (In.)		Piston Diameter (In.)					
Year	*Model*	*New*	*Maximum Oversize*	*New*	*Maximum Oversize*	*Wrist Pin Diameter (Fit)*	*Side Clearance (ring-to-groove) (In.)*	*End-Gap (In.)*	*Piston Clearance (In.)*
1970-71	1,600 cc.	3.1881	3.2181[4]	2.314	2.344	.0002-.0004	.0016-.0036[1]	.009-.014[2]	.0013-.0019
	2,000 cc.	3.5748-3.5763	3.615	3.5740-3.5749	3.6134-3.6143	(light slip)	.0019-.0038	.0189-.021[3]	.001-.002

1—Oil control ring to groove clearance—.0018"-.0038".
2—Oil control ring gap faces rear, all others staggered 90°.
3—Oil control ring gap—.016"-.055".
4—

Engine Rebuilding Specifications

Year and Model		Main Bearing Journals (In.)				Connecting Rod Bearing Journals (In.)		
		Journal Diameter	Oil Clearance	Shaft End-Play	Thrust On No.	Journal Diameter	Oil Clearance	End-Play
1970-71	1600 cc.	[1]	.001-.002	.003-.011	3	1.9368-1.9376	.0004-.0024	.004-.010
1970-71	2000 cc.	2.432-2.440	.0005-.0015	.004-.008	3	2.0464-2.0772	.001-.0015	.010-.024

1—Blue color code—2.1257-2.1261
Red color code—2.1253-2.1257

Year and Model		Seat Angle (Deg.)	Intake Valve Lift (In.)	Exhaust Valve Lift (In.)	Valve Spring Pressure Intake & Exhaust		Stem to Guide Clearance (In.)		Stem Diameter (In.)	Valve Guide Removable
					Outer	Inner	Intake	Exhaust		
1970-71	1,600 cc.	45	.315	.319	44-49 @ 1.263″	—	.0008-.003	.0017-.0039	[2]	No[1]
1970-71	2,000 cc.	44[3]	.3993	.3993	60-64 @ 1.417″	—	.0007-.002	.0018-.0035	[4]	No[1]

1—Sleeves available for repairs.
2—Intake—0.3095-0.3105.
Exhaust—0.3086-0.3096.
3—Valve face angle—45°.
4—Intake—.3159″-.3166″
Exhaust—.3156″-.3163″ } available in .003″, .015″ and .030″ O/S.

Distributor Advance Characteristics

Year	Model	Distributor Identification	Centrifugal Advance: Start Degrees @ rpm	Centrifugal Advance: Intermediate Degrees @ rpm	Centrifugal Advance: End Degrees @ rpm	Vacuum Advance: Start Degrees @ ins./Hg	Vacuum Advance: Intermediate Degrees @ ins./Hg	Vacuum Advance: End Degrees @ ins./Hg	Vacuum Retard: Start Degrees @ ins./Hg	Vacuum Retard: Intermediate Degrees @ ins./Hg	Vacuum Retard: End Degrees @ ins./Hg
1970-71	1,600 cc.	Autolite① 70AB-DA	+½ to −½ @ 450 and below	8.6-10.6 @ 1,500	13.2-15.2 @ 2,500	0° @ 2.5	2-5 @ 6.5	5-8 @ 10 and above	0° @ 5 and below	0 to -1.5 @ 10	-5 to -7 @ 17 and above
	2,000 cc.	Bosch② D1FZ-A	0-½ @ 350	7.5-9.5 @ 1,500	9.75-11.75 @ 2,500	2 @ 5	5.5-7.5 @ 15	7.5 @ 25	0° @ 5	2-4 @ 15	4 @ 20
	2,000 cc.	Bosch② D1FZ-C	0-½ @ 350	8.5-10.5 @ 1,500	10.5-12.5 @ 2,500	0° @ 5	7-10 @ 15	10 @ 25	0° @ 5	2-4 @ 15	4 @ 20

①—Autolite specifications given in distributor degrees and distributor speed.

②—Bosch specifications given in camshaft degrees and distributor speed.

Carburetor Specifications

Year	Model	Carburetor Identification	Throttle Bore Diameter		Venturi Diameter		Main Metering Jet		Idle Jet		High Speed Air Bleed		Float Setting		Float Drop (ins.)	Choke Plate Pull-Down (ins.)	Dechoke (ins.)	Idle Speed (rpm)	Accelerator Pump Stroke (ins.)
			Primary (ins.)	Secondary (ins.)	Primary (ins.)	Secondary (ins.)	Primary	Secondary	Primary	Secondary	Primary	Secondary	Up (ins.)	Down (ins.)					
1970-71	1,600 cc.	Auto-lite 1-V 9510 w/IMCO	1.42	—	1.10	—	N.A.	N.A.	N.A.	N.A.	N.A.	N.A.	1.09-1.11	1.35-1.37	N.A.	.08-.10	.19-.23	780-820	.08-.09
	2,000 cc.	Weber-② Auto-lite 5200	1.26	1.417	1.02	1.06	137	145	19①	19①	71	67	N.A.	31/64	1.875	.221-.251	.295-.335	700-750 ③	N.A.

①—With automatic transmission—Primary—21
Secondary—19

②—Carburetor identification number—D12F-9510-BA with automatic transmission
D12F-9510-AA with manual transmission

③—500-650 rpm with automatic transmission

Chassis and Wheel Alignment Specifications

Year and Model	Wheelbase	Track		Caster		Camber		Toe-In (In.)	King-Pin Inclination (Deg.)	Wheel Pivot Ratio	
		Front	Rear	Range (Deg.)	Pref. Setting (Deg.)	Range (Deg.)	Pref. Setting (Deg.)			Inner Wheel	Outer Wheel
1970-71 Two-door sedan	100.8″	53.0″	52.0″	0°30′-1°30′①	—	0°30′-0°30′①	—	.09-.15	7°30′-8°30′①	N.A.	N.A.

①—Not adjustable.
N.A.—Not available.

Torque Specifications

Year	Model	Cylinder Head Bolts (Ft. Lbs.)	Rod Bearing Bolts (Ft. Lbs.)	Main Bearing Bolts (Ft. Lbs.)	Crank-shaft Balancer Bolt (Ft. Lbs.)	Flywheel to Crank-shaft Bolts (Ft. Lbs.)	Manifold (Ft. Lbs.)	
							Intake	Exhaust
1970-71	1,600 cc.	65-70	30-35	65-70	24-28	50-55	15-18	15-18
1970-71	2,000 cc.	39-43	29-34	65-75	39-43	47-51	12-15	12-15

Tightening Sequences

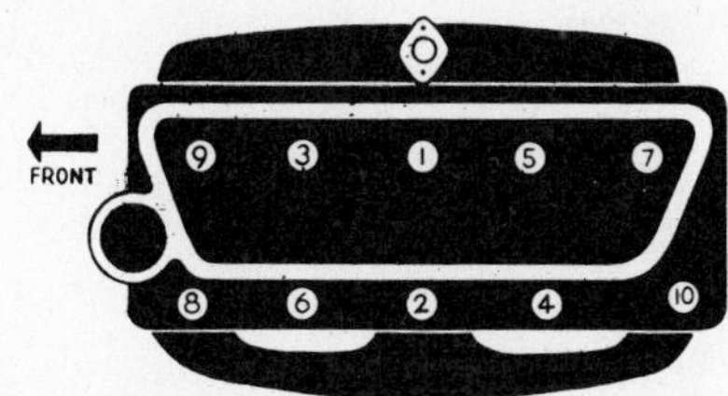

1,600 cc. cylinder head bolt tightening sequence

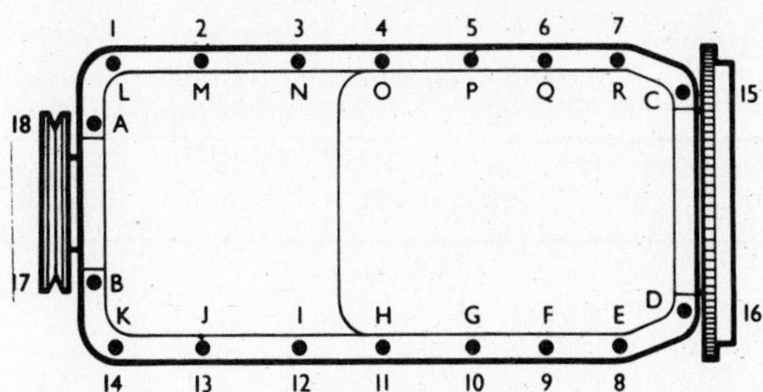

1,600 cc. oil pan bolt tightening sequence. Tighten, first in alphabetical, then in numerical, order.

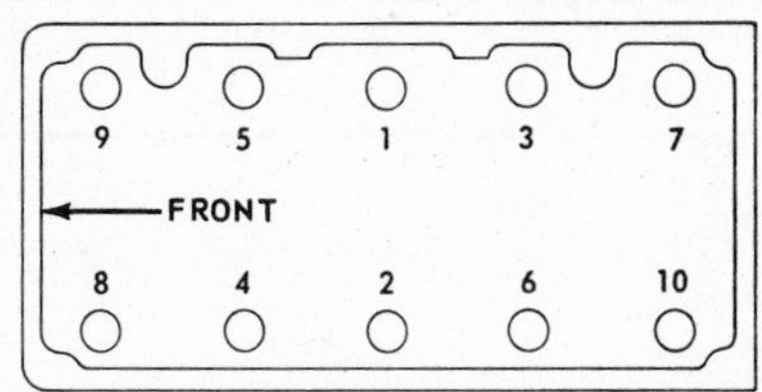

2,000 cc. cylinder head bolt tightening sequence

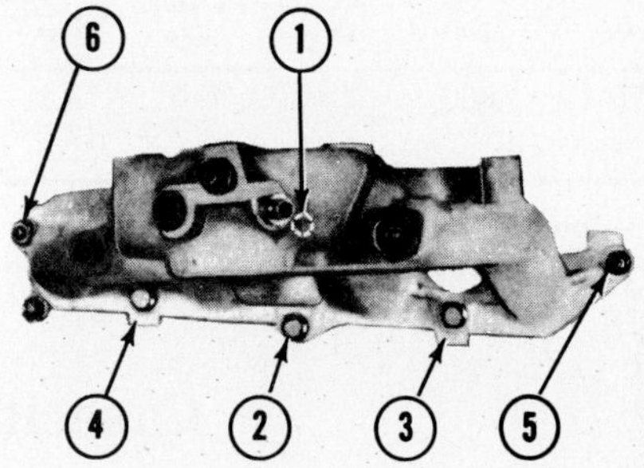

2,000 cc. intake manifold bolt tightening sequence

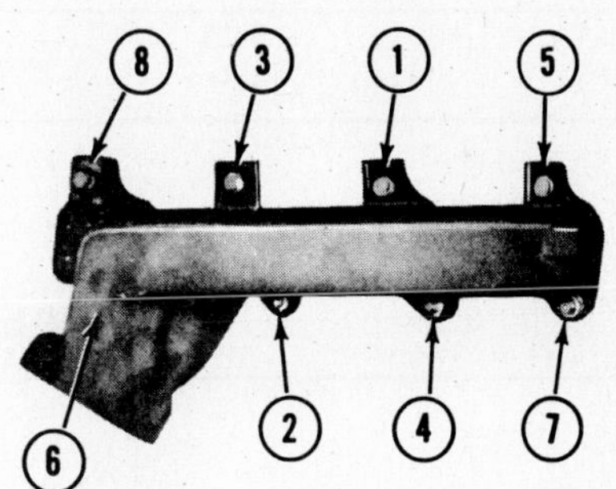

2,000 cc. exhaust manifold bolt tightening sequence

Electrical Specifications

Year	Model	Battery: Capacity (Amp. hours)	Battery: Volts	Battery: Grounded Terminal	Starter: Brush Spring Tension (Oz.)
1970-71	1,600 cc.	55	12	Neg.	28
	2,000 cc.	55	12	Neg.	40

Year	Model	Alternator: Type	Alternator: Brush Spring Pressure (Oz.)	Alternator: Output Volts	Alternator: Output Amps.	Regulator: Type	Regulator: Volts @ 5000 RPM-②
1970-71	1,600 cc.	17ACR	7-10	14.1-14.5	35	17ACR ①	14.1-14.5

①—Integral with alternator.
②—Alternator rpm. Alternator speed is 1.88 x engine speed.

Capacities and Pressures

Year and Model		Engine Crankcase (Qts.) Incl. Filter	Transmissions Pts. To Refill After Draining: Manual 3-Speed	Manual 4-Speed	Automatic	Drive Axle (Pts.)	Gasoline (Gals.)	Cooling System (Qts.) with Heater	Normal Fuel Pressure (Psi)
1970-71	1,600 cc.	4.25	—	2⅞①	—	2.4	12	7.25	3.5-5
1970-71	2,000 cc.	5.0	—	2⅞①	16	2.2	12	N.A.	3.8-5.0

①–SAE 80 E.P.

Brake Specifications

Year	Model	Type: Front	Type: Rear	Brake Cylinder Bore: Master Cylinder (ins.)	Piston Diameter (ins.): Front	Piston Diameter (ins.): Rear	Brake Drum or Disc Diameter (ins.): Front	Brake Drum or Disc Diameter (ins.): Rear
1970-71	1,600 cc. 2,000 cc.	Disc	Drum	N.A.	①	.75	9.625	9.0

①—Disc brake piston cylinder bore—2.125″

Fuses and Circuit Breakers

Year	*Circuit*	*Amperage*
1970-71	Back-up lights	8
	All others	10

Light Bulb Specifications

Year	*Usage*	*Wattage*
1970-71	Headlights	2x 50 watts
	Side lights	2x 5 watts
	Rear turn signals	2x 28 watts
	License plate	2x 5 watts
	Indicators	4x 2.2 watts
	Side markers	4x 5 watts
	Clock	1x 1.2 watts
	Front turn signals	2 x 7/28 watts
	Tail and stop	2 x 7/28 watts
	Interior	1x 6 watts
	Instrument panel	4x 2.2 watts

Wiring Diagrams

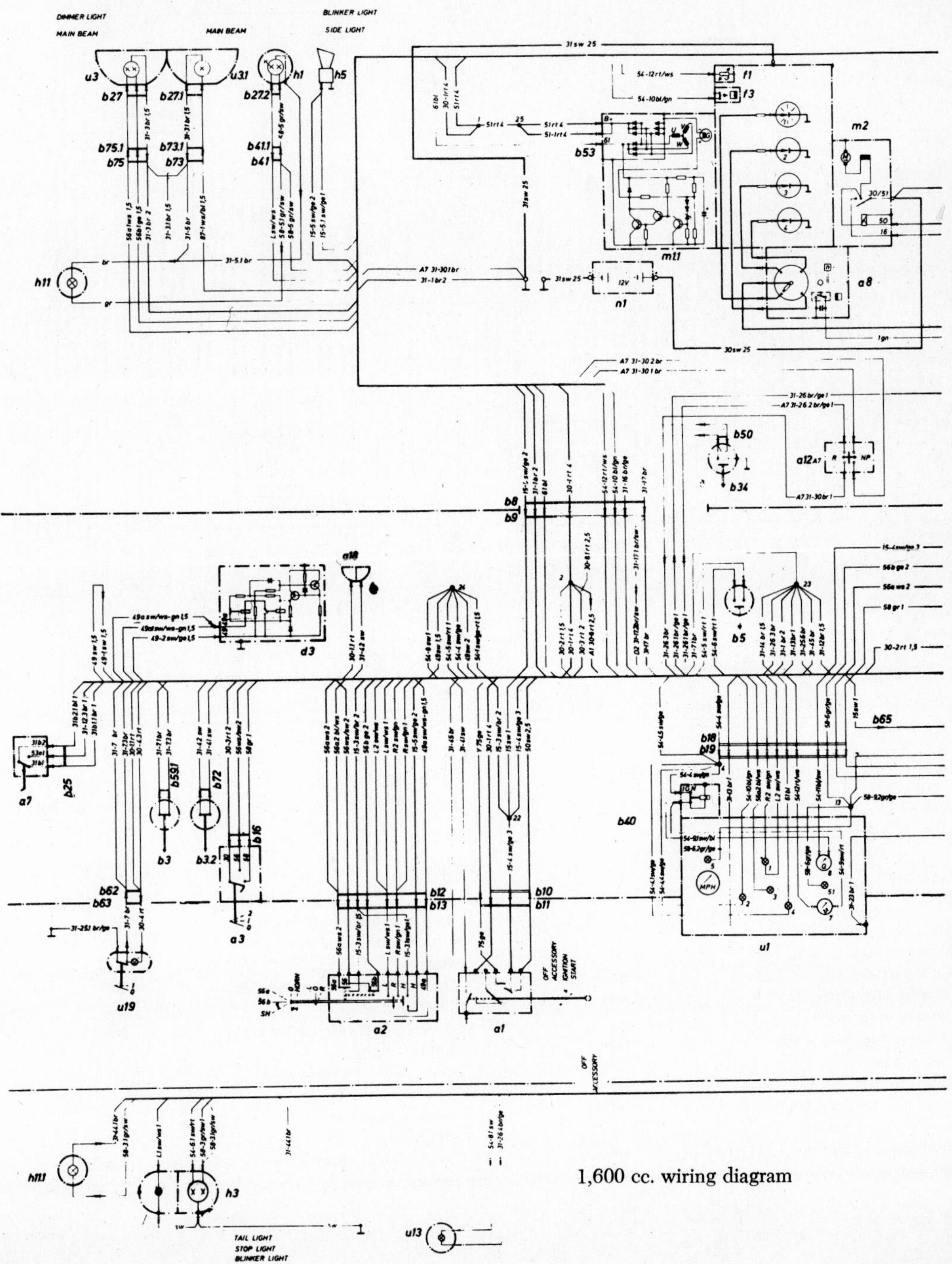

1,600 cc. wiring diagram

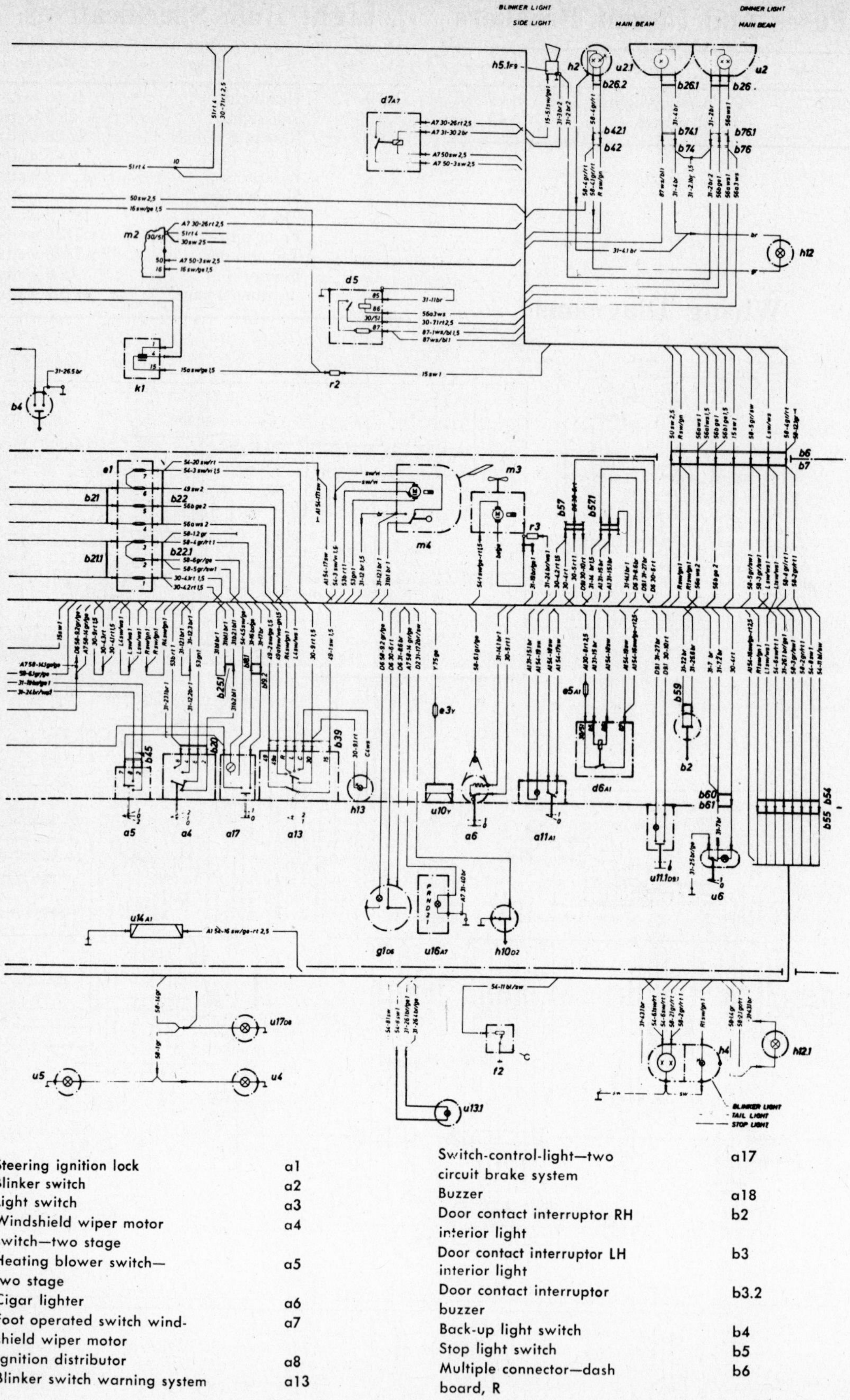

Steering ignition lock	a1
Blinker switch	a2
Light switch	a3
Windshield wiper motor switch—two stage	a4
Heating blower switch—two stage	a5
Cigar lighter	a6
Foot operated switch windshield wiper motor	a7
Ignition distributor	a8
Blinker switch warning system	a13
Switch-control-light—two circuit brake system	a17
Buzzer	a18
Door contact interruptor RH interior light	b2
Door contact interruptor LH interior light	b3
Door contact interruptor buzzer	b3.2
Back-up light switch	b4
Stop light switch	b5
Multiple connector—dash board, R	b6

Description	Code
Multiple connector—dash board, R	b7
Multiple connector—dash board, L	b8
Multiple connector—dash board, L	b9
Multiple connector—steering/ ignition lock	b10
Multiple connector—steering/ ignition lock	b11
Multiple connector—blinker switch	b12
Multiple connector—blinker switch	b13
Multiple connector—light switch	b16
Multiple connector—instrument cluster	b18
Multiple connector—switch-control light—two circuit brake system	b18.1
Multiple connector—instrument cluster	b19
Multiple connector—switch-control light—two circuit brake system	b19.2
Multiple connector—windshield wiper motor switch	b20
Multiple connector—fuse box	b21
Multiple connector—fuse box	b21.1
Multiple connector—fuse box	b22
Multiple connector—fuse box	b22.1
Multiple connector foot operated switch windshield wiper motor	b25
Multiple connector wiper wash system	b25.1
Multiple connector main beam headlight, R	b26
Multiple connector remote headlight, R	b26.1
Multiple connector blinker —side light, R	b26.2
Multiple connector main beam headlight, L	b27
Multiple connector remote headlight, L	b27.1
Multiple connector blinker —side light, L	b41.1
Multiple connector blinker —side light, R	b42
Multiple connector blinker —side light, R	b42.1
Multiple connector heating blower switch	b45

Code	Description
b50	Multiple connector warning light switch—two circuit brake system
b53	Multiple connector alternator
b54	Multiple connector—instrument panel, R
b55	Multiple connector—instrument panel, R
b57	Multiple connector
b57.1	Multiple connector
b59	Door contact switch, R
b59.1	Door contact switch, L
b60	Multiple connector—interior light, R
b61	Multiple connector—interior light, R

Code	Description
b62	Multiple connector—interior light, L
b63	Multiple connector—interior light, L
b65	Connector wire 15
b72	Multiple connector buzzer switch
b73	Multiple connector remote headlight, L
b73.1	Multiple connector remote headlight, L
b74	Multiple connector remote headlight, R
b74.1	Multiple connector remote headlight, R
b75	Multiple connector main beam headlight, L
b75.1	Multiple connector main beam headlight, L
b76	Multiple connector main beam headlight, R
b76.1	Multiple connector main beam headlight, R
d3	Blinker unit
d5	Relay remote headlights
e1	Fuse box
f1	Transmitter water temperature gauge
f2	Transmitter fuel gauge
f3	Oil pressure control switch
h1	Blinker—side light, L
h2	Blinker—side light, R
h3	Combined tail light, L
h4	Combined tail light, R
h5	Horn, L
h11	Side marker front, L
h11.1	Side marker back, L
h12	Side marker front, R
h12.1	Side marker back, R
h13	Warning indicator—control light
k1	Ignition coil
m1.1	Alternator
m2	Starter
m3	Heating blower motor
m4	Windshield wiper motor
n1	Battery
r2	Series resistance wire ignition
r3	Series resistor heating blower
u1	Instrument cluster
u2	Main beam headlight, R
u2.1	Remote headlight, R
u3	Main beam headlight, L
u3.1	Remote headlight, L
u4	License plate light, R
u5	License plate light, L
u6	Interior light, R
u13	Back up light, L
u13.1	Back up light, R
u19	Interior light, L
a11	Heating plate switch
d6	Working current relay heating plate
e5	Fuse heating plate
u14	Heating plate
a12	Blocking—switch automatic transmission
u16	Transmission control selector dial

d7	Working current relay automatic transmission
h10	Hand brake warning switch
g1	Clock
u17	Luggage compartment light
u11.1	Reading light
h5.1	Horn, R
e3	Fuse radio
u10	Radio
b27.2	Multiple connector blinker—side light, L
b34	Warning light switch two circuit brake system
b39	Multiple connector blinker switch warning system
b40	Voltage divider
b41	Multiple connector blinker—side light, L
30	Interior lights Reading lights Four way hazard flasher Clock Buzzer Cigar lighter
58	Tail light, L Side light front and back, L Illumination—instrument cluster Illumination—cigar lighter Illumination—transmission control selector dial Illumination—clock Tail light, R Side light front and back, R Luggage compartment lights License plate lights
56a	Main beam Relay remote headlights
56b	Low beam
15	Back-up lights Heating blower motor Blinker system Stop light Voltage divider Control light—two circuit brake system Control light charging current Control light oil pressure
15	Windshield wiper motor Curren circuit heating plate

Interior wiring diagram and symbol according to DIN. A. IEC.

A1	In combination with heating plate
A7	In combination with automatic gear
D2	In combination with two circuit brake system
D6	In combination with clock
D8	In combination with luggage compartment light
D9	In combination with interior light, L
D9.1	In combination with reading light
F9	In combination with horn, R
Y	In combination with radio

R . . . Red
Bk . . . Black
Bi . . . Blue
W . . . White
Br . . . Brown
G . . . Green
Y . . . Yellow
LG . . . Light Green
P . . . Purple
O . . . Orange
Pk . . . Pink

Engine Electrical

Distributor

1,600 cc.

The Autolite distributor is mounted on the right-hand side of the engine and is gear-driven by the camshaft. It incorporates both centrifugal and vacuum advance mechanisms. The vacuum *advance* action is controlled by carburetor vacuum, while the vacuum *retard* action is controlled by intake manifold vacuum. The IMCO system is used to control exhaust emissions.

Removal

1. Unsnap the two clips and remove the distributor cap.

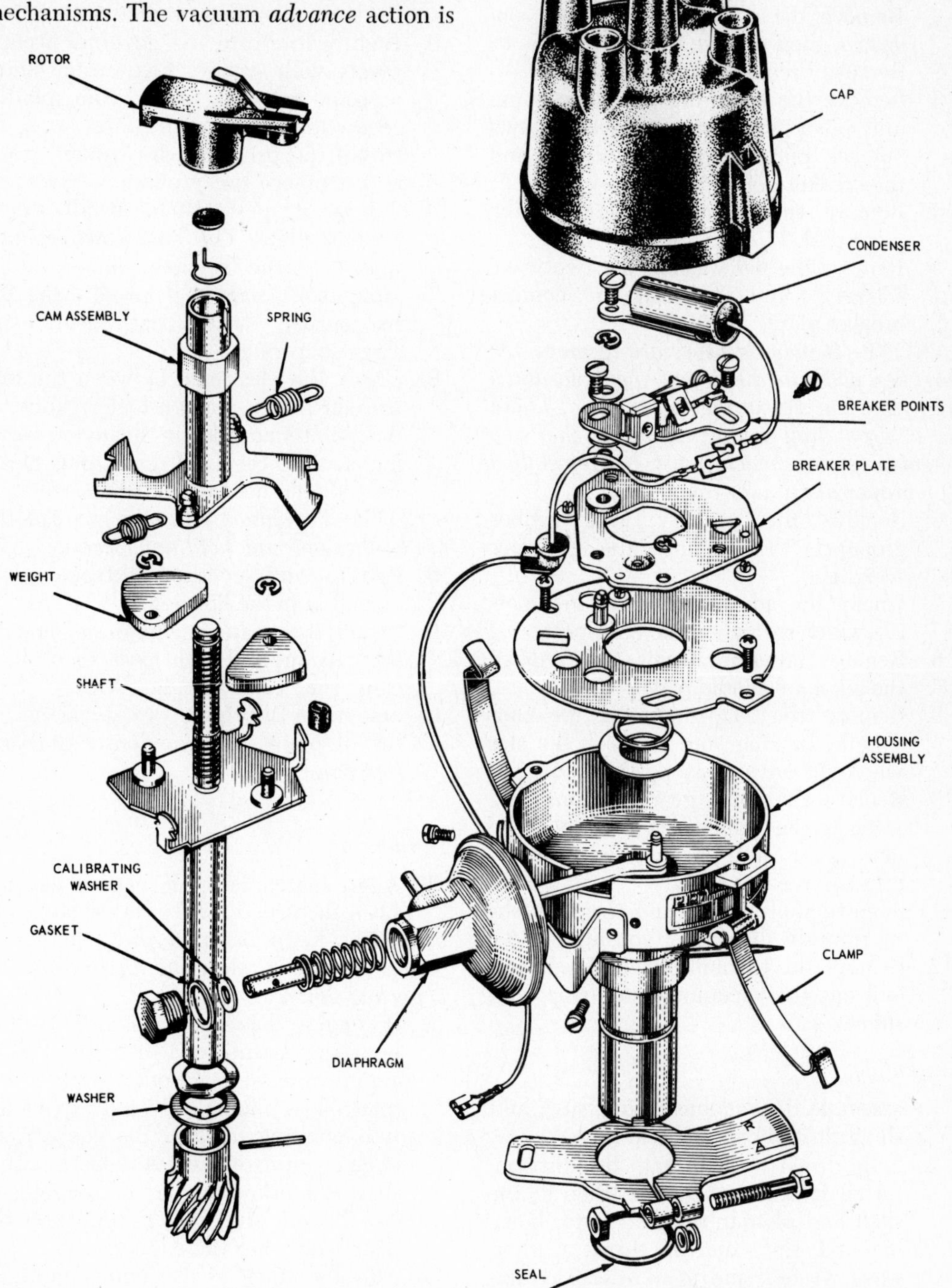

Exploded view—1,600 cc. distributor

2. Disconnect the vacuum lines from the distributor.
3. Matchmark the distributor housing and the engine block, then scribe another mark on the housing to indicate the rotor position.
4. Remove the bolt that holds the distributor, then carefully pull out the unit.

Disassembly

1. Remove the condenser lead and condenser, then remove wires from points.
2. Remove breaker point assembly.
3. Remove the snap-ring on the vacuum unit pivot post, then remove the two breaker plate hold-down screws and the breaker plate.
4. Remove the large snap-ring on the pivot post.
5. Remove the flat washer, the two wave washers, and the upper contact breaker plate.

NOTE: *It may be necessary to move the breaker plate to disengage the hold-down pin from the slot in the lower plate. There is a grounding spring between the two breaker plates which must be reinstalled for proper distributor operation.*

6. Remove the primary wire rubber grommet, then remove the governor weights.
7. Unclip the advance springs, first noting which spring goes to each post.
8. Remove the vacuum unit, then remove the felt cam spindle pad.
9. Remove the snap-ring and the cam spindle, making sure to mark the slot where the advance stop is located.
10. Remove the drive gear retaining pin, using a pin punch, then remove the drive gear and the two washers located above it.
11. Remove shaft, plate, and thrust washers from the distributor housing.
12. Remove the vacuum unit end bolt and pull out the vacuum spring, stop, and shims.

Assembly

1. Assemble the vacuum spring, stop, and shims; install bolt and seal ring.
2. Slide thrust washers onto the distributor shaft below the plate, then fit the shaft and plate to the distributor housing and slide on the thrust washer, wave washer, and gear. Install retaining pin.

NOTE: *If a new gear or shaft is installed, a new retaining pin hole must be drilled. The new gear has a pilot hole as supplied.*

3. Install the distributor cam spindle, making sure the advance stop is in the correct slot, and secure with snap-ring. Place a new felt wick, moistened with oil, in the cam spindle top.
4. Install vacuum unit, then reconnect the springs to their original posts.
5. Lightly lubricate the governor weight pivots with grease, then install them with the flat sides toward cam spindle; secure them with spring clips.
6. Install the primary wire rubber grommet, connect the grounding spring to the pivot post, then install upper breaker plate. The hold-down spindle must enter the "keyhole" slot.
7. Hold this assembly in place using the two spring washers, flat washer, and large snap-ring.
8. Check the clearance between the two breaker plates, using a feeler gauge, at the point underneath the nylon bearing nearest the hold-down pin; clearance should not exceed 0.010″.

NOTE: *To reduce clearance, thread the nut further onto the hold-down screw.*

9. Position and secure the breaker plate assembly in the housing.
10. Install the snap-ring onto the end of the vacuum unit pivot post, then lubricate the cam spindle with a tiny amount of Lubriplate or equivalent.
11. Install points and condenser and adjust point gap.

Installation

1. Align matchmarks, if engine has not been disturbed, and install distributor.

NOTE: *Keep in mind that the helical gear will tend to rotate the distributor as it is pushed down.*

2. If engine has been disturbed, turn crankshaft until No. 1 piston is at TDC on compression stroke and timing marks are aligned. With the vacuum unit pointing towards the back of the engine approximately 45° from crankshaft centerline, and rotor pointing to No. 2 spark plug wire tower, insert the distributor into the engine.
3. Adjust contact breaker points and ignition timing.

2,000 cc.

The Bosch distributor is mounted on the left side of the engine at the front and is driven by the oil pump. The distributor incorporates a centrifugal and vacuum advance, the vacuum advance controlled by carburetor vacuum and the vacuum retard controlled by intake manifold vacuum.

Removal

1. Remove the distributor cap and disconnect the vacuum lines from the distributor.
2. Rotate the engine until the crankshaft pulley timing marks are aligned. Remove the oil filler cup and make sure that No. 1 cylinder is on the compression stroke. The distributor rotor should point at the No. 1 cylinder mark on the distributor body.
3. Remove the distributor retaining bolt and remove the distributor.

Disassembly

NOTE: *Service parts are not available for replacement of distributor driveshaft, drive gear, bushing or cam on the Bosch distributor.*

1. Disconnect the condenser lead from the contact breaker. Remove the condenser attaching screw and remove the condenser.
2. Remove the snap ring which holds the diaphragm rod to the advance plate and remove the diaphragm.
3. Remove the breaker points.
4. Remove the screws attaching the distributor cap hold-down clips (these clips also retain the advance plate). Through the diaphragm mounting

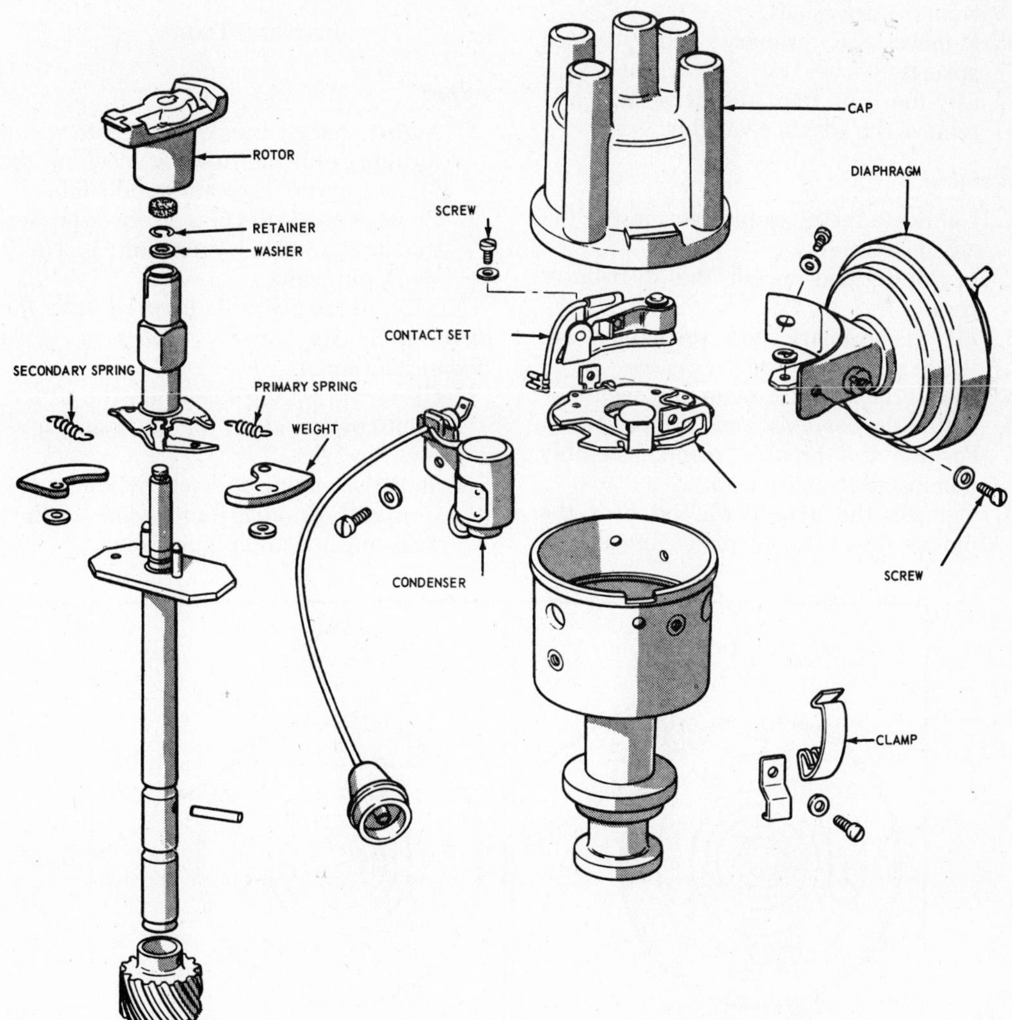

Exploded view—Bosch distributor for 2,000 cc. engine

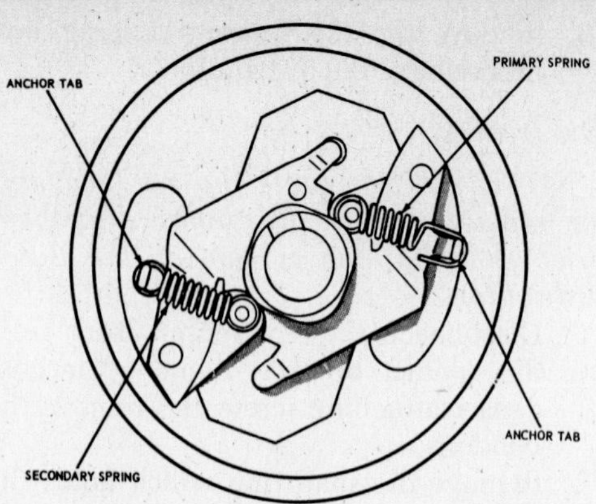

Bosch mechanical advance assembly

hole, use a screwdriver to wedge the advance plate from the distributor body.
5. Remove the felt pad from the top of the cam and remove the snap-ring from the driveshaft.
6. Remove the primary and advance springs.
7. Lift the cam from the driveshaft and remove the advance weights.

Assembly

1. Lubricate the pivot pins and install the advance weights.
2. Lubricate and install the distributor cam.
3. Fit the primary and secondary advance springs.
4. Install the advance plate and secure.
5. Install the condenser and grommet.
6. Position the breaker points assembly and install the wire lead.
7. Connect the diaphragm rod over the pin in the advance plate. Install the mounting screws and the snap-ring on the advance plate pin.
8. Adjust the breaker points to specification.

Installation

1. Make sure the crankshaft is positioned correctly (see Distributor, Removal).
2. If the oil pump driveshaft was removed with the distributor, coat one end with heavy grease and insert this end into the recess in the distributor driveshaft.
3. Insert the distributor, making sure that the rotor aligns with the No. 1 cylinder mark on the distributor housing. Be sure that the oil pump driveshaft seats properly in the pump.
4. Install the distributor clamp bolt and the distributor cap.
5. Adjust the ignition timing.

Ignition Timing

Adjust

1. Adjust contact breaker points to specification, with the rubbing block on the highest part of the cam spindle lobe.
2. Connect the leads of a strobe-type timing light to the battery and to No. 1 spark plug wire.

NOTE: *A small nail, inserted into the distributor cap tower, makes a good hook-up terminal.*

3. Clean the timing marks on the timing front cover and on the crankshaft pulley.
4. Start the engine and set the idle at 600 rpm with the distributor vacuum lines disconnected and plugged.

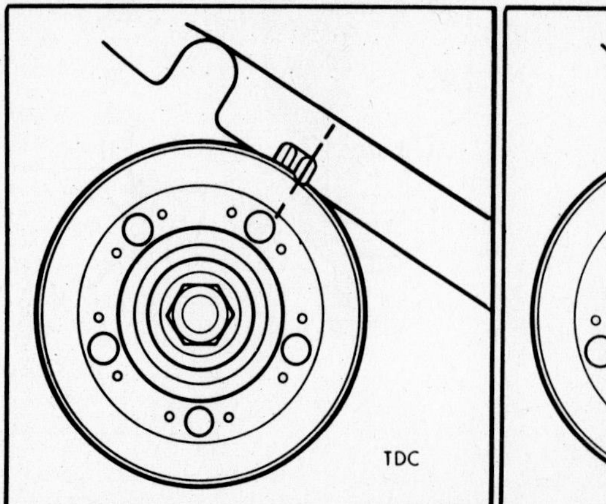

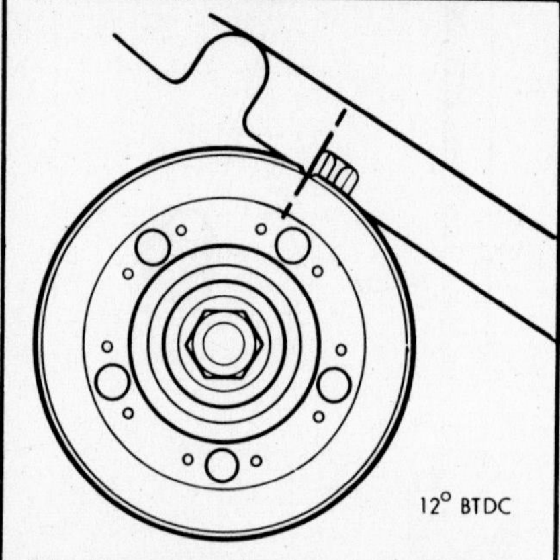

Timing marks—1,600 cc. engine

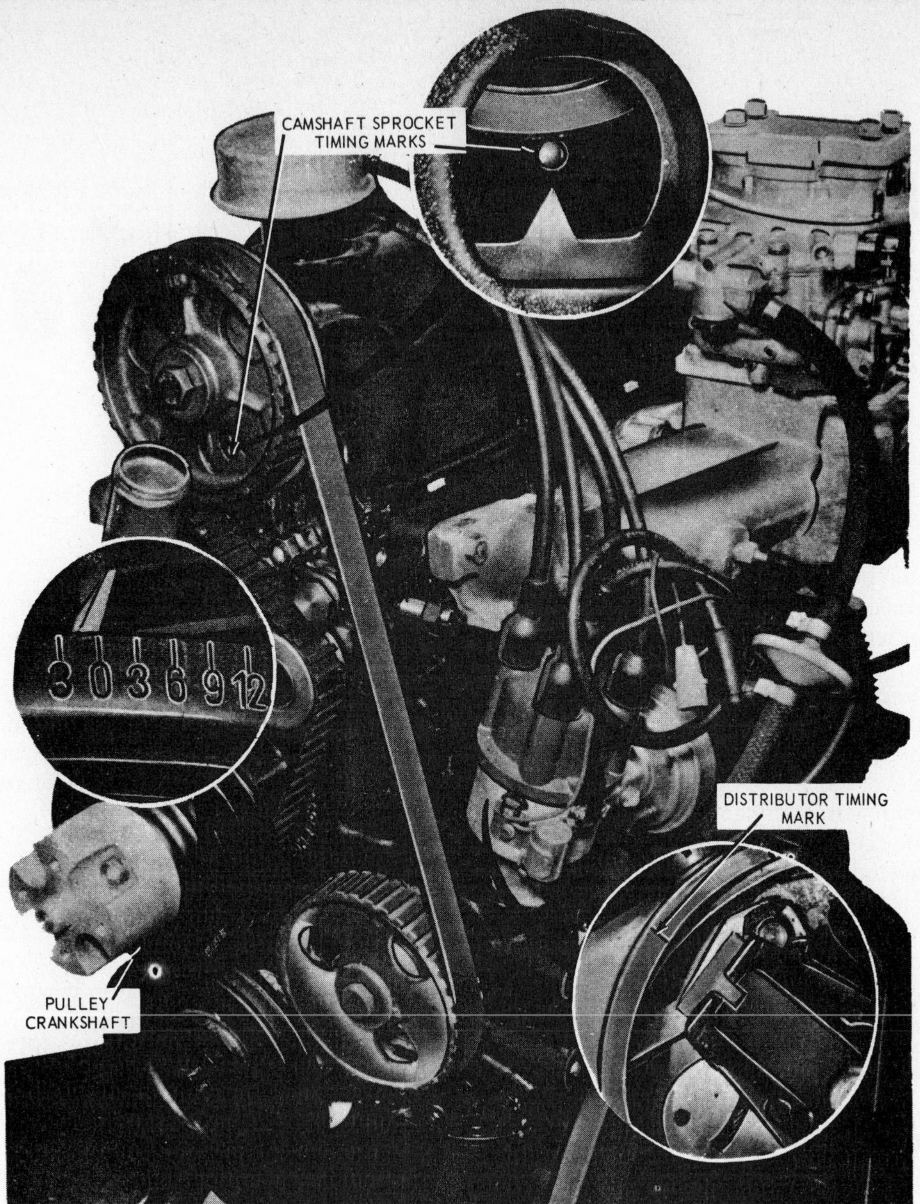

Timing marks—2,000 cc. engine

5. Shine the timing light on the index area. The timing should be set at 12° BTDC for both the 1,600 cc. and the 2,000 cc. engine.

NOTE: *To advance the timing on the 1,600 cc. engine, loosen the distributor clamp and rotate the distributor in a direction opposite to normal distributor rotation. To retard the timing, rotate the distributor in the normal rotation direction. On the 2000 cc. engine rotate the distributor in a counterclockwise direction to advance the timing; to retard the timing, rotate the distributor clockwise.*

Alternator

1,600 CC.

The charging system consists of the battery, the alternator, the regulator and the wires and cables required to connect these units. The alternator used is an English Lucas unit, model 17ACR, having a 35 amp. output. The alternator is driven by a V-belt from the engine at 1.88 times engine speed.

The regulator is integral with the alternator and is non-adjustable.

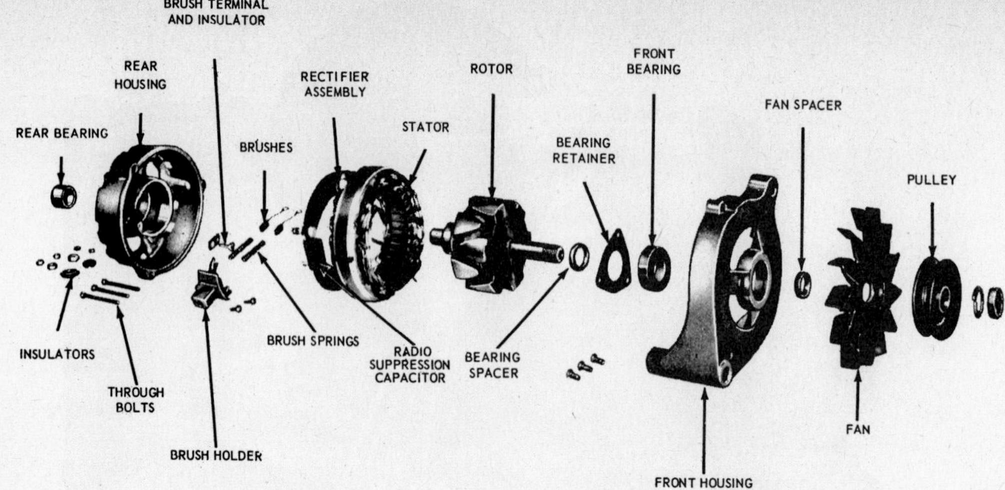

Exploded view of alternator for 2,000 cc. engine

Some precautions that should be taken into consideration when working on this, or any other, AC charging system are as follows:

1. Never switch battery polarity.
2. When installing a battery, always connect the grounded terminal first.
3. Never disconnect the battery while the engine is running.
4. If the molded connector is disconnected from the alternator, do not ground the hot wire.
5. Never run the alternator with the main output cable disconnected.
6. Never electric weld around the car without disconnecting the alternator.
7. Never apply any voltage in excess of battery voltage during testing.
8. Never "jump" a battery for starting purposes with more than 12 volts.

Removal

1. Disconnect the battery negative cable.
2. Unplug the alternator connectors.
3. Loosen the three mounting bolts and tilt the alternator in towards the engine.
4. Remove the fanbelt, then remove the mounting bolts and the alternator.

Installation

1. Position the alternator and loosely install the mounting bolts.
2. Install fanbelt, hold alternator so as to place tension on the belt (½" deflection at belt midpoint), then tighten mounting bolts.
3. Connect alternator plugs and the battery cable.

2,000 cc.

The 2,000 cc. Capri engine uses an Autolite alternator and a separate regulator. The alternator is a negative ground unit, belt driven. The Autolite electro-mechanical regulator is factory calibrated and not to be adjusted. If the unit is proved to be improperly calibrated, it must be replaced.

Removal

1. Disconnect the battery ground cable.
2. Loosen the alternator mounting bolts and remove the adjusting arm. Detach the alternator belt.
3. Disconnect the alternator wiring connectors and wiring harness.
4. Remove the mounting bolt and alternator.

Disassembly

NOTE: *If the alternator rectifier has an exposed diode circuit board, remove the screws from the rectifier by turning the bolts clockwise to unlock them. Push the stator terminal screw out of the rectifier with the diodes built into the circuit board. Do not remove the grounded screw and avoid turning the screw while removing, to make sure that the straight knurl will engage the insulators when installing.*

1. Scribe alignment marks on both end housings and the stator.
2. Remove the three through-bolts and separate the front housing and rotor from the stator and rear housing.
3. Remove the rear housing from the stator and rectifier assembly.
4. Remove the brush holders, brushes, brush springs, insulators and terminals.

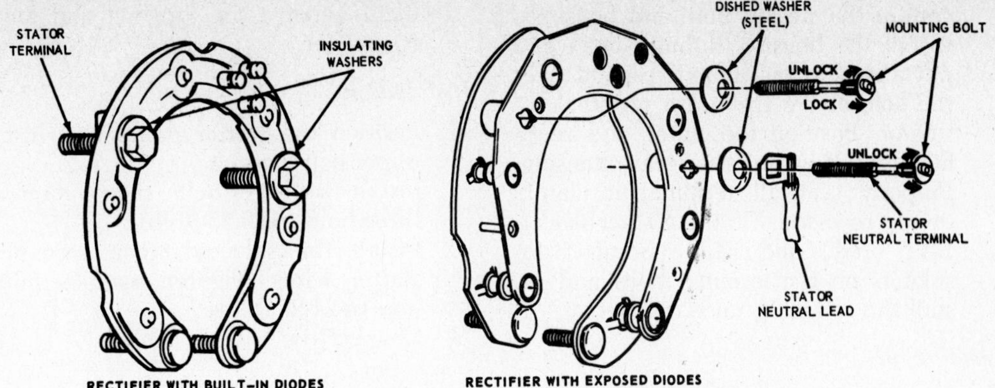

Two types of circuit boards for 2,000 cc. engine alternators

5. If replacement is necessary, press the bearing from the rear housing, supporting the bearing on the inner boss.
6. If the rectifier assembly is being replaced, unsolder the stator leads from the printed circuit board terminals. CAUTION: *Use only a 100 Watt soldering iron.*
7. Original production alternators have two types of rectifier circuit boards; an exposed diode type with the circuit board spaced away from the diode plates and a single circuit board with built in diodes.
8. Remove the drive pulley nut and the components from the rotor shaft.
9. Remove the front end bearing retainer, support the housing close to the bearing boss and press out the bearing.

Inspection

1. Wipe the rotor, stator and bearings with a clean cloth. *Do not clean with solvent.*
2. Check the rotor driveshaft bearing for excessive wear or lubricant leakage.
3. Inspect the rotor shaft bearing surfaces for roughness or chatter marks.
4. Place the rear bearing on the slip ring end of the shaft and check for excessive wear or lubricant leakage.
5. Check the pulley, fan and rotor shaft for looseness or stripped threads.
6. Check all wire leads on stator and rotor connections and resolder those that are loose.
7. Check the brushes, brush springs, rotor shaft and slip rings.

Assembly

1. Install the front bearing in the front housing (apply pressure to the outer race only) and fit the bearing retainer.
2. Push the snap-ring onto the shaft and into the groove. *Do not open the snap-ring with pliers.*
3. Fit the rotor stop on the driveshaft with the recessed side against the snap-ring.
4. Position the front housing, fan spacer, fan, pulley and lockwasher on the driveshaft and tighten the retaining nut.
5. If the rear bearing housing was removed, press in a new bearing from the inside until it is flush with the outer end surface.
6. Place the brush springs, brushes, brush terminal and insulator in the brush holder. Position the brush holder assembly in the rear housing and tighten the retaining screws.
7. Wrap the three stator winding leads around the circuit board terminals and solder them. *Use only a 100 Watt iron and resin core solder.*
8. For an exposed diode rectifier, insert the special screws through the wire lug, dished washers and circuit board. *The dished washers are to be used on molded circuit boards only.*
9. Position the radio noise suppressor on the rectifier terminals. On the molded circuit board, install the STA and BAT terminal insulators. On fiber circuit boards, install the square terminal insulator in the square hole in the rectifier assembly.
10. Wipe the rear end bearing surface of the rotor shaft with a clean lint-free cloth.
11. Position the rear end housing over the rotor and match the alignment marks. Seat the machined portion of the stator

core in the step in both end housings. Install the housing through bolts and put a dab of waterproof cement over the hole above the brush terminal insulator. Position the stator and rectifier assembly in the rear housing. Properly seat all terminal insulators in the recesses. Fit the STA (black), BAT (red) and FLD (orange) insulators on the terminal bolts and install the retaining nuts.

Installation

1. Installation is the reverse of removal.

Battery

The battery is a standard lead acid unit with a capacity of 55 amp/hrs. Be sure that the battery is kept full of distilled water and that the terminals are clean and lightly coated with vaseline.

Starter

1,600 cc.

The Lucas starter motor used is very similar to American-made units of the same type.

Removal

1. Disconnect the battery.
2. Disconnect the motor wires from the starter motor.
3. Remove the solenoid hold-down nuts, then remove the solenoid.
4. Set the parking brake, jack up the front of the car and support on axle stands.
5. Remove the two lower starter hold-down bolts, then loosen the upper bolt.
6. While supporting the starter with one hand, remove the top bolt and lower the starter.

Installation

1. Position the starter motor and install upper bolt loosely.
2. Install two lower bolts, then tighten all three bolts to 20-25 ft. lbs.
3. Install the solenoid, then reconnect starter wires. Tighten main terminal nuts to 24-26 ft. lbs.
4. Connect the battery cables.

2,000 cc.

The 2,000 cc. engine uses an Autolite positive engagement starter, very similar to the Lucas starter used on the 1,600 cc. engine.

Removal

1. Jack the vehicle.
2. Disconnect the starter cable from the starter terminal.
3. Remove the mounting bolts and move the starter over the steering linkage to remove it.

Installation

1. Fit the starter in the flywheel housing and insert the mounting bolts, but do not tighten.
2. Fully insert the starter into the pilot hole, and hold the starter squarely against the mounting surface.
3. Connect the starter cable to the starter and lower the vehicle to the ground.

Disassembly—Lucas and Autolite

The disassembly and assembly procedures for these starters will vary slightly,

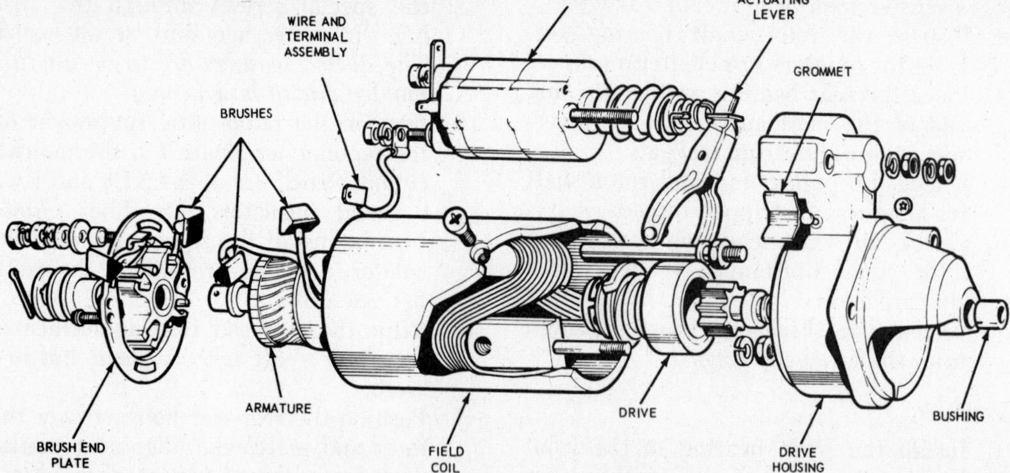

Cross-sectional view of Lucas starter motor

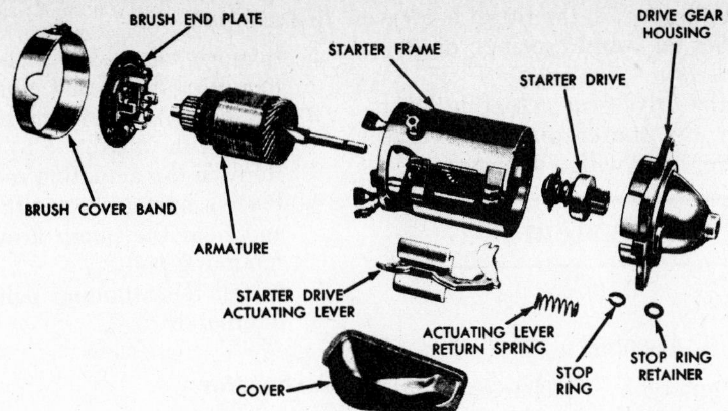

Exploded view of Autolite starter motor

although they are basically alike in design and operation.

1. Remove brush cover band and starter drive gear actuating lever cover. Observe the brush lead locations for reassembly, then remove the brushes from their holders.
2. Remove the through-bolts, starter drive gear housing and the drive gear actuating lever return spring.
3. Remove the pivot pin retaining the starter gear actuating lever and remove the lever and the armature.
4. Remove the stop ring retainer. Remove and discard the stop ring holding the drive gear to the armature shaft; then remove the drive gear assembly.
5. Remove the brush end plate.
6. Remove the two screws holding the ground brushes to the frame.
7. On the field coil that operates the starter drive gear actuating lever, bend the tab up on the field retainer and remove the field coil retainer.
8. Remove the three coil retaining screws. Unsolder the field coil leads from the terminal screw, then remove the pole shoes and coils from the frame (use a 300 watt iron).
9. Remove the starter terminal nut, washer, insulator and terminal from the starter frame.

Assembly

1. Install starter terminal, insulator, washers and retaining nut in the frame. (Be sure to position the slot in the screw perpendicular to the frame end surface.)
2. Position coils and pole pieces, with the coil leads in the terminal screw slot, then install the retaining screws. As the pole screws are tightened, strike the frame several sharp hammer blows to align the pole shoes. Tighten, then stake the screws.
3. Install solenoid coil and retainer and bend the tabs to hold the coils in the frame.
4. Solder the field coils and solenoid wire to the starter terminal, using resin-core solder and a 300-watt iron.
5. Check for continuity and ground connections in the assembled coils.
6. Position the solenoid coil ground terminal over the nearest ground screw hole.
7. Position the ground brushes to the starter frame and install retaining screws.
8. Position the brush end plate to the frame, with the end plate boss in the frame slot.
9. Lightly Lubriplate the armature shaft splines and install the starter drive gear assembly on the shaft. Install a new retaining stop-ring and stop-ring retainer.
10. Position the fiber thrust washer on the commutator end of the armature shaft, then position the armature in the starter frame.
11. Position the starter drive gear actuating lever to the frame and starter drive assembly, and install the pivot pin.
12. Position the drive actuating lever return spring and the drive gear housing to the frame, then install and tighten the through-bolts. Do not pinch brush leads between brush plate and frame. Be sure that the top-ring retainer is properly seated in the drive housing.

13. Install the brushes in the brush holders and center the brush springs on the brushes.
14. Position the drive gear actuating lever cover on the starter and install the brush cover band with a new gasket.

Fuel System

Fuel Pump

1,600 cc.

A diaphragm-type mechanical fuel pump, mounted on the right-hand side of the engine, supplies fuel to the carburetor. The fuel pump has a gauze screen and a glass sediment bowl which must be cleaned periodically.

Removal

1. Lift the hood, then disconnect the fuel lines at the pump.

NOTE: *Plug the lines, as gas may siphon from tank.*

2. Remove the two bolts and washers that hold the pump to the block.
3. Remove the fuel pump, carefully lifting the lever to clear the cam eccentric.

Installation

1. To install, reverse the removal procedure. Torque the bolts to 12-15 ft. lbs.

Fuel pump and actuating rod—2,000 cc. engine

2,000 cc.

The 2,000 cc. engine fuel pump is a permanently sealed diaphragm type mounted on the left front side of the cylinder block. The pump is actuated by a rod driven from an eccentric on the auxilliary shaft.

Removal

1. Disconnect both fuel lines at the fuel pump.
2. Remove the fuel pump and pump gasket from the block. Discard the gasket.
3. Remove the actuating rod.

Installation

1. Remove all gasket material from the mounting flange and pump.
2. Apply an oil resistant sealant to both sides of the gasket.
3. Replace the actuating rod in the block.
4. Place a new gasket on the pump flange and hold the pump firmly against the mounting pad.
5. Install the retaining bolts and tighten alternately.

Carburetor

Autolite 1-v

The carburetor used on the 1600 cc. engine is an Autolite single-barrel downdraft unit having idle, main, power valve, and accelerator pump systems. Cars equipped with exhaust emission controls (all those imported) have a tamper-proof slow-running volume screw that limits the rich mixture setting. All carburetors have an automatic choke.

Removal

1. Lift the hood and remove the air cleaner.
2. Disconnect fuel and vacuum lines at the carburetor.
3. Disconnect decel valve line at carburetor.
4. Disconnect accelerator linkage, drain cooling system, and disconnect automatic choke.
5. Remove carburetor hold-down nuts and washers and the carburetor.

Disassembly

NOTE: *Carburetor repair kits are available for servicing this particular type of carburetor.*

1. Remove the shoulder screw retaining the fast idle cam and rod assembly to the lower body.
2. Remove the upper body from the lower body. The gasket should come away with the upper body, and care should be used to be sure it does not adhere to the lower body.
3. Remove the needle valve and remove the gasket from the upper body.
4. Remove the weight and accelerator pump discharge ball valve.
5. Remove the needle valve housing and the gauze screen.
6. Remove the main jet.

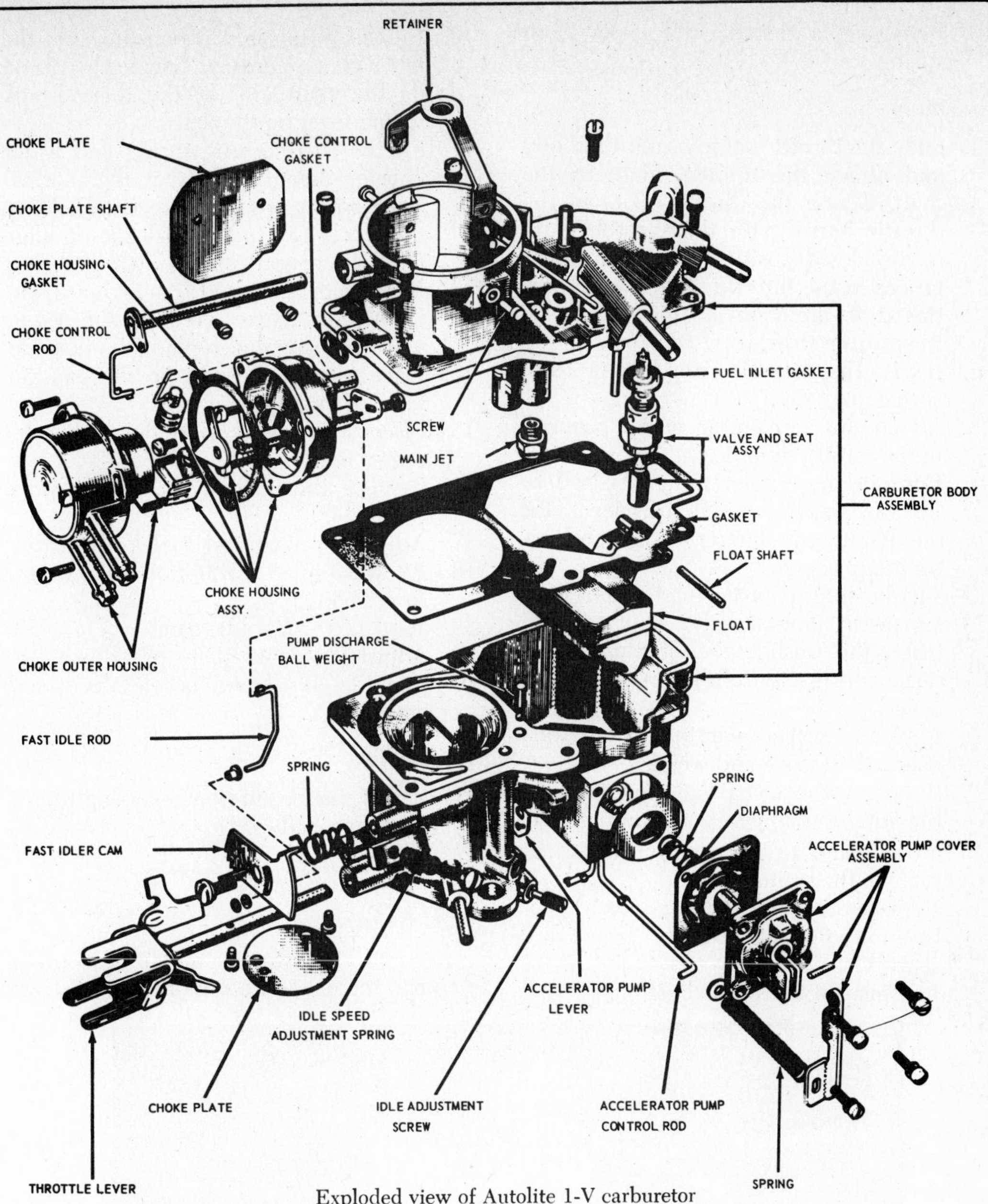

Exploded view of Autolite 1-V carburetor

7. Remove the thermostatic spring and water housing.
8. Detach the thermostatic spring lever, choke piston lever, choke piston link and choke piston from the housing.
9. Withdraw the choke inner housing and gasket.
10. Remove the choke control lever assembly and choke control rod from the inner housing. Carefully, remove the Teflon bushing.
11. Remove the air cleaner retainer if removal of the choke plate and shaft is desired.
12. Remove the choke plate from the shaft. Clean any burrs from around the choke plate screw holes, and remove the choke plate shaft.
13. Remove the accelerator pump body, operating arm, diaphragm and return spring. Also remove the fuel shut-off washer and return spring.
14. Detach the accelerator pump pushrod arm from the throttle spindle. Remove the throttle plate from the spindle.
15. Clean burrs from around throttle plate screw holes, and remove the throttle spindle from the body.

16. Remove the throttle stop screw and spring.

Assembly

1. Slide the throttle spindle into the body and attach the throttle plate to the shaft. Center the throttle plate in the throttle barrel with the throttle plate in the closed position. The two indentations in the throttle plate should face the same direction as the recesses in the throttle shaft.
2. Insert the throttle stop screw and spring.
3. Attach the accelerator pump pushrod to the throttle spindle.
4. Connect the accelerator pump rod to the arm and pump operating lever. Fit the diaphragm plunger to the accelerator pump cover.
5. Fit the return spring for the accelerator pump shut-off valve in its socket. Insert the washer and diaphragm return spring. Carefully replace the cover.
6. Replace the accelerator pump discharge ball valve and weight.
7. Insert the choke shaft and lever assembly into the upper body and fit the choke plate to the shaft. Center the plate in the venturi.
8. Replace the air cleaner retainer.
9. Insert the choke control lever and shaft assembly into the inner choke housing. Fit the Teflon bushing.
10. Fit the piston and piston link into the inner choke housing. Locate the piston on the shaft and fit the thermostatic spring lever on the shaft.
11. Fit the thermostatic spring and water housing assembly so that the thermostatic spring engages the central slot in the lever. The index mark should align with the central mark on the housing.
12. Replace the main jet.
13. Locate the gauze screen in the needle valve housing and replace the housing.
14. Place the needle valve in the housing, tapered end upward.
15. Place a new gasket on the carburetor upper body.
16. Replace the float and float arm pivot pin.
17. Adjust the float and fuel level setting.
18. Fit the upper carburetor body to the lower body.
19. Replace the fast idle cam.
20. Adjust the choke plate pull-down, fast idle, de-choke and accelerator pump stroke.

Installation

1. Install the carburetor, reversing the removal procedures.

ADJUSTMENTS

Slow-Running

Accurate adjustment of the carburetor requires the use of an exhaust gas analyzer.

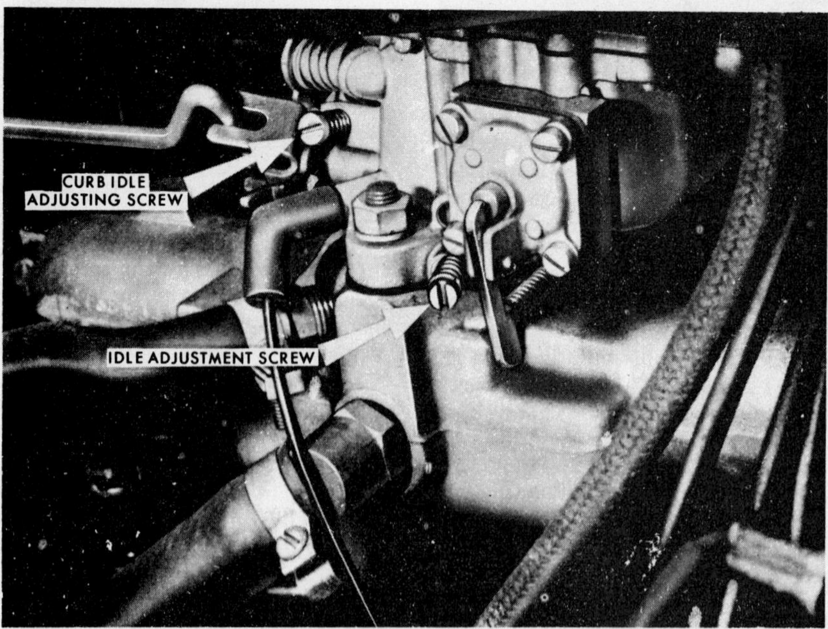

Slow-running adjustment screws (Autolite 1-V)

Using the analyzer, adjust for a 13.4-13.9 air/fuel ratio at 780-820 rpm.

If an analyzer is not available, the carburetor can be roughly adjusted in the following manner:

1. Connect a tachometer between coil-to-distributor primary wire and ground. Adjust idle to 820 rpm, turning the curb idle screw.
2. Adjust the lower idle screw to obtain maximum rpm—do not break the limit stop.
3. Screw in the lower idle screw to obtain a 20-40 rpm drop from the maximum idle speed.
4. Reset the idle speed, if necessary, using the curb idle screw to obtain 870 rpm.

Choke Plate Pull-Down

1. Remove the air cleaner assembly.
2. Remove the thermostatic spring and water housing.
3. Depress the vacuum piston until the vacuum bleed port is revealed. Insert a piece of wire .040″ diameter (suitably bent) into this port. Raise the piston to trap the wire.
4. Close the choke plate until its movement is stopped by the linkage (partially open the throttle for the fast idle tab to clear the cam).
5. The bottom of the choke plate should be .08″-.10″ from the carburetor body. This can be measured with a proper size drill.
6. Bend the extension of the choke thermostat lever to adjust the clearance.

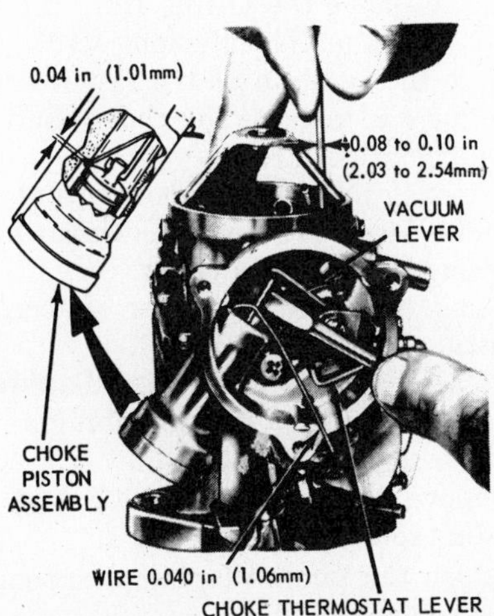

Choke plate pull-down adjustment (Autolite 1-V)

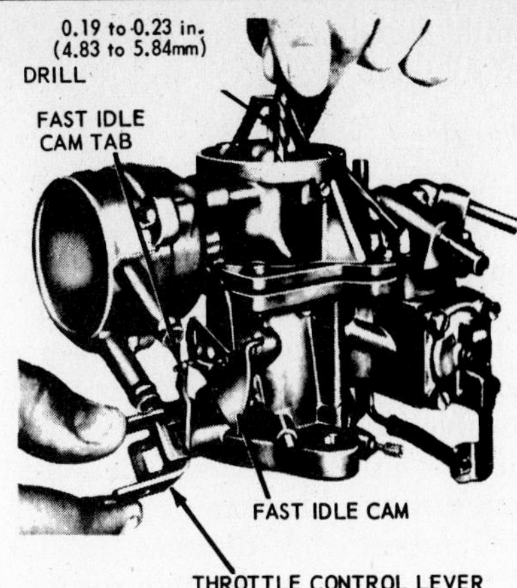

De-choke adjustment (Autolite 1-V)

De-choke

1. Open the throttle fully and hold it against the stop.
2. Check the clearance between the bottom of the choke plate and the carburetor body. It should measure .19″-.23″.
3. Adjust the clearance by bending the projection on the fast idle cam.

Accelerator Pump Stroke

1. Unscrew the throttle stop screw until the throttle plate is fully closed.
2. Depress the accelerator pump plunger and check the clearance between the operating lever and the plunger. This should be .08″-.09″.
3. Bend the gooseneck of the pump push-rod to adjust the stroke.
4. Reset the throttle stop screw to its original position.
5. Replace the air cleaner.

Fast Idle

1. With the choke plate pull-down correctly adjusted, and held in the pull-down position, check that throttle lever fast idle tab is in the first, or high speed, step of the fast idle cam. If necessary, bend the fast idle rod at its existing bend to achieve this result.
2. Fit the thermostatic spring and water housing, in the center slot, and align the marks before tightening the screws.
3. Run the engine to normal operating temperature, and connect a tachometer.
4. Position the throttle lever fast idle tab on the first step of the cam and check the engine speed. Adjust to 2,000-2,200

rpm by bending the tab contacting the fast idle cam.

Float Level

1. Remove the carburetor upper body.
2. Hold the upper body in a vertical position, with the float hanging down.
3. Measure the distance from the bottom of the float to the upper body gasket and adjust to 1.09"-1.11", by bending the tab contacting the needle valve.
4. Turn the upper body and measure the same distance (bottom of float to gasket). Adjust this distance to 1.35"-1.37" by bending the tab resting on the needle valve housing.
5. Replace the upper body and adjust the carburetor mixture and idle speed.

Weber-Autolite 5200

The Weber-Autolite 5200 is a two stage, two venturi carburetor with a smaller primary stage connected to the secondary stage by mechanical linkage. The primary stage consists of a transfer system, idle system, main metering system and power enrichment system. The secondary stage includes a metering, transfer and power system, drawing fuel from the same bowl as the primary stage.

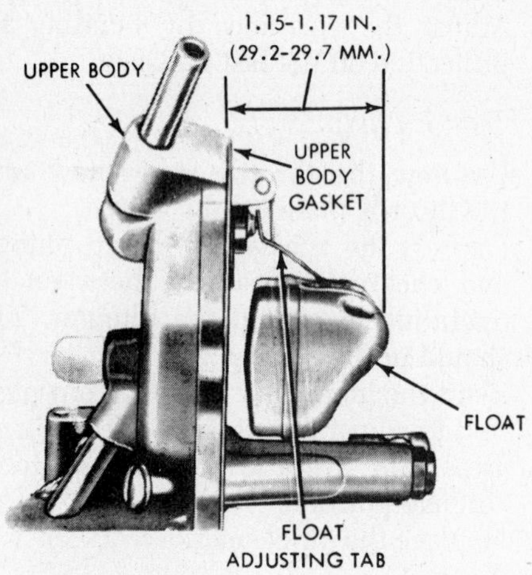

Float level setting (Autolite 1-V)

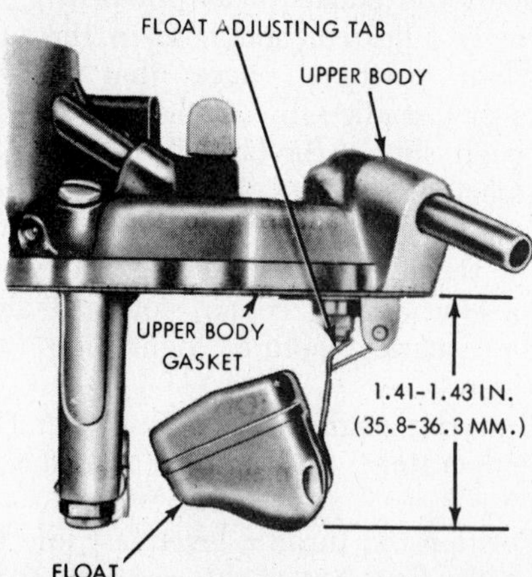

Float level setting (Autolite 1-V)

Removal

1. Remove the air cleaner.
2. Disconnect the fuel supply and vacuum pipes at the carburetor.
3. Disconnect the fuel-air supply pipe for the decel valve at the carburetor.
4. Disconnect the throttle control shaft from the throttle shaft.
5. Partially drain the cooling system and disconnect the automatic choke hoses.
6. Remove the retaining nuts and spring washers and remove the carburetor from the manifold.

Disassembly

1. Remove the fuel intake filter plug and filter screen.
2. Disconnect the choke rod (retaining clips) and carefully remove the bowl cover. Remove the choke rod seal plug and seal.
3. Remove the float shaft, float and intake needle.
4. Remove the diaphragm.
5. Remove the choke water cover and gasket.
6. Remove the ring, choke thermostatic spring housing and gasket.
7. Slip the choke housing away from the main body and disengage the fast idle rod. Remove the O-ring from the vacuum passage. Note the long screw.
8. Note the position of the fast idle cam spring and remove the choke shaft nut and lockwasher.
9. Remove the spring loop from the choke lever. Remove the choke lever, spring and spring retainer.
10. Remove the fast idle lever, spacer, adjusting screw and spring.
11. Detach and remove the diaphragm cover, return spring, diaphragm and rod assembly.
12. Remove the diaphragm plug and adjusting screw.
13. Detach the pump diaphragm assembly and return spring.
14. Remove the accelerator pump dis-

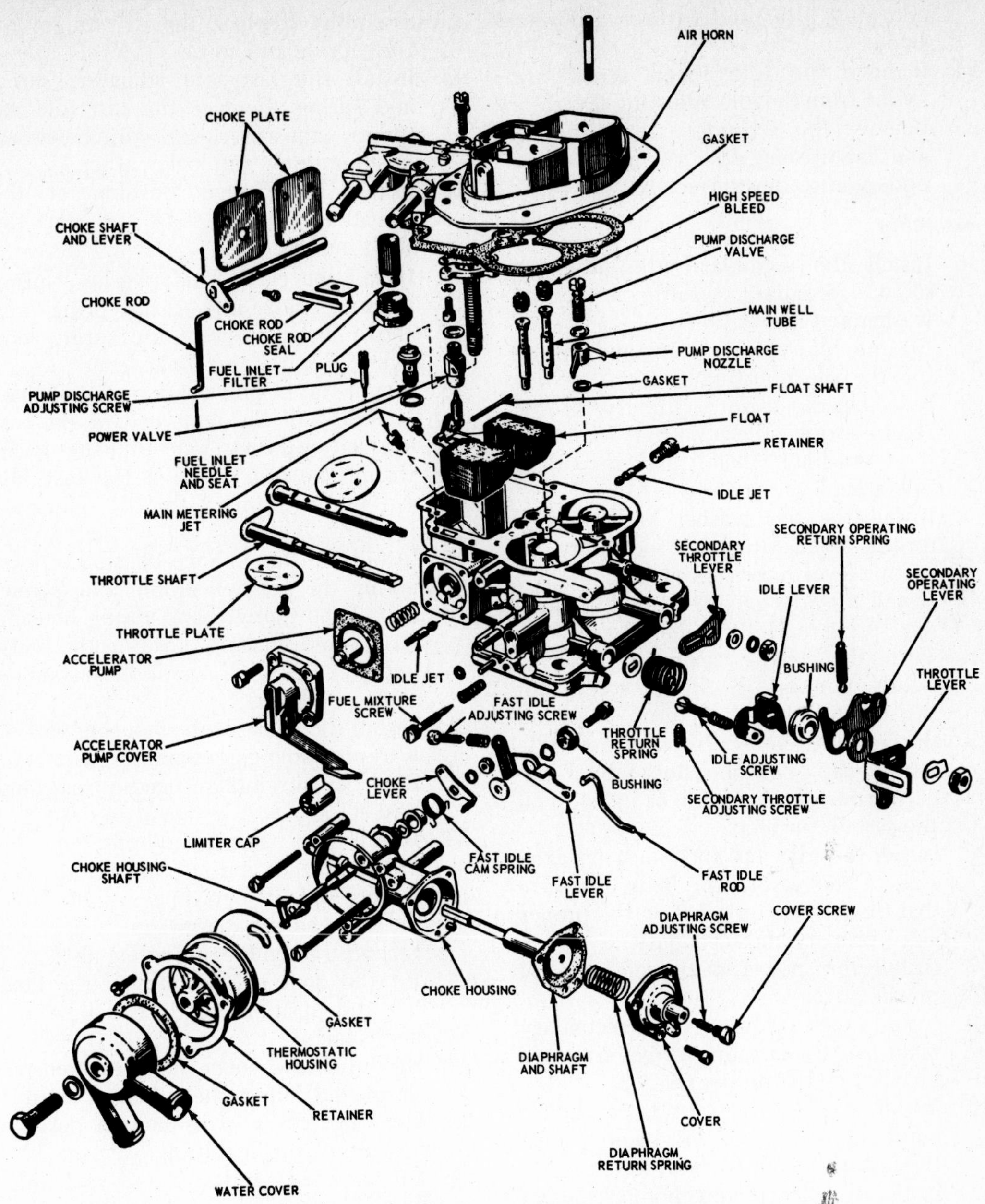

Exploded view of Weber-Autolite 5200 carburetor

charge valve assembly, discharge nozzle, two gaskets and pump channel plug screw.

15. Remove the primary main well air bleed plug and emission tube.
16. Remove the secondary main well air bleed plug and emulsion tube.
17. Remove the primary and secondary main metering jets.
18. Remove the power valve and gasket, primary and secondary idle jet retaining plugs and idle jets (located on sides of carburetors).
19. Turn the idle limiter cap in to stop and remove it. To the nearest 1/16th of a turn, count the turns needed to lightly seat the idle adjustment needle.
20. Remove the idle needle and spring.
21. Remove the secondary operating lever return spring.
22. Remove the primary lever, flat washer, secondary operating lever and lever bushing.
23. Remove the idle adjusting lever and spring, noting how the primary throttle return spring is attached to the idle

adjusting lever and to the carburetor body.

24. Remove the idle speed screw and spring from the idle adjusting lever.
25. Remove the secondary throttle lever and flat washer. Also, remove the secondary idle adjusting screw.

Assembly

1. Install the secondary idle adjusting screw, secondary throttle lever, flat washer and lockwasher.
2. Fit the idle speed screw and spring into the idle adjusting lever.
3. Assemble the washer, primary throttle return spring, idle adjusting lever and lever bushing. Install the secondary operating lever assembly.
4. Install the flat washer and primary throttle lever. Attach the secondary operating lever return spring.
5. Install the idle mixture needle adjusting spring and the adjusting needle. Turn the needle screw in until it lightly bottoms. Back the screw out the exact number of turns, recorded during disassembly. Install a new idle limiter cap with the stop tab of the cap against the lean side of the stop on the carburetor body.
6. Install the idle jets and plugs on each side of the carburetor body. Be sure that the jets are installed on the proper side (primary and secondary).
7. Install the power valve gasket and power valve.
9. Install the primary and secondary main jets. Be sure the correct sizes are installed on the proper side.
10. Install the primary and secondary emulsion tubes and air bleed plugs. Be sure to install the correct sizes.
11. Install the accelerator pump channel plug screw. Install the pump discharge nozzle, with a gasket on top and bottom. Install the pump discharge valve assembly.
12. Install the accelerator pump return spring and diaphragm assembly. Start the pump cover screws and hold the pump operating lever partially open to align the diaphragm gasket. Tighten the four cover screws evenly.
13. Seat the diaphragm adjusting screw so that the threads are flush with the inside of the cover. Install the adjusting screw plug.
14. Install the choke diaphragm and rod assembly. Replace the diaphragm return spring and cover.
15. Install the fast idle adjusting screw and spring. Replace the fast idle flat spacer, adjusting lever, spring washer, bushing screw and lock washer.
16. Install the Teflon bushing at the thread end of the shaft and start the shaft into the bore.
17. Install the choke shaft washer, spring retainer, fast idle cam spring and choke lever. Position the spring loop over the end of the choke lever.
18. Install the O-ring on the vacuum passage. Install the bent end of the fast idle rod in the fast idle adjusting lever. Install the other end of the fast idle rod in the primary throttle operating lever.
19. Install the three choke housing screws, noting the position of the long screw.
20. Install the thermostatic spring housing gasket and housing. Position the housing at index and install the retaining screws and ring.
21. Install the choke water housing gasket, water housing gasket and screw.
22. Replace the intake needle seat and gasket.
23. Install the vacuum diaphragm, depressing the spring to install the screws and washers finger tight. Hold the stem so the diaphragm is horizontal and tighten the screws evenly.
24. Fit the float needle clip on the float tab and position the float, needle and float shaft.
25. Hold the bowl cover in an inverted position and adjust the dry float setting.
26. Hold the cover in its normal position and adjust the float drop.
27. Fit the choke rod seal and seal plug. Install the choke rod through the seal and attach it to the choke lever with the retaining clip.
28. Install the bowl cover gasket.
29. Fit the choke link to the choke lever with the retaining clip.
30. Tighten the five bowl screws evenly.
31. Install the fuel filter screen, open end in. Fit the filter screen plug.

Installation

1. Installation is the reverse of removal.

ADJUSTMENTS

Idle Speed and Fuel Mixture

All Weber-Autolite 5200 carburetors are equipped with idle limiter caps over the

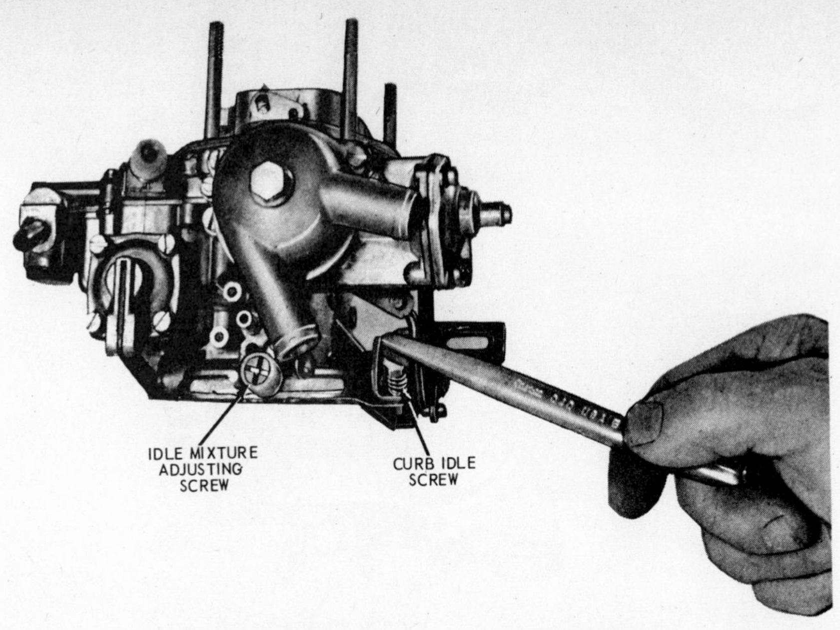

Idle mixture, speed adjustments (Weber-Autolite 5200)

idle mixture screw, to prevent an overly rich idle adjustment. An exhaust gas analyzer should be used to determine the proper adjustment; however, if no analyzer is available, use the following procedure.

1. Stabilize the engine temperature by running the engine for twenty minutes at 1,500 rpm. This can be done by positioning the fast idle cam follower on the kickdown step of the fast idle cam.
2. Check and properly set distributor advance and ignition timing. Manual transmissions must be in Neutral, while automatic transmissions must be in Drive, except when using exhaust gas analyzer.
3. Adjust the engine idle to specifications, with the air cleaner installed.
4. Turn the idle mixture screws to obtain the smoothest possible idle. If the idle limiter cap precludes a satisfactory idle, the idle limiter cap should be removed and the proper idle set.
5. After a satisfactory idle has been obtained, a service idle limiter cap should be installed.

Fast Idle Cam Clearance

1. Insert a 5/32″ drill between the lower edge of the choke plate and the air horn well. With the fast idle screw held on the second step of the fast idle cam, the clearance between the tang of the choke lever and the arm on the fast idle cam should be .010″-.030″.
2. Adjust the clearance by bending the choke lever tang up or down.

Choke Plate Pull-Down

1. Remove the screws and ring retaining the choke thermostatic spring cover. *Do not remove the water cover screw.*
2. Pull the water cover and thermostatic spring assembly out of the way.
3. Use a screwdriver to push the diaphragm stem back against its stop. Place a .260″ gauge rod or C size drill

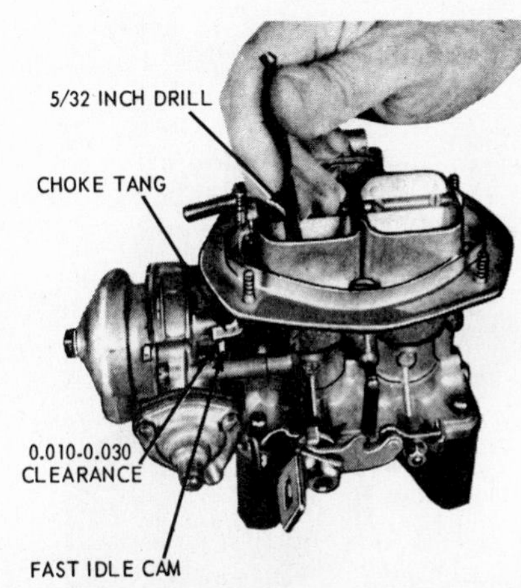

Fast idle cam clearance adjustment (Weber-Autolite 5200)

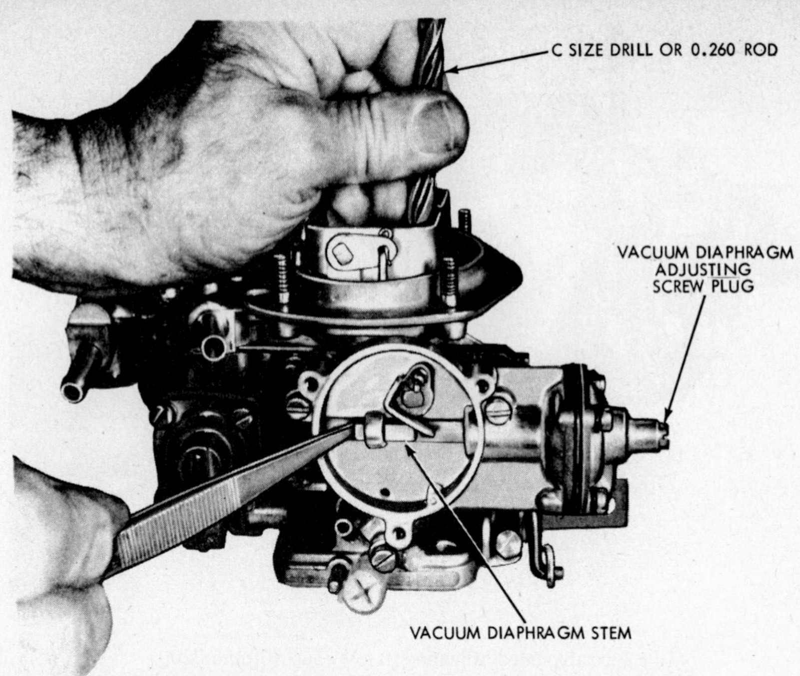

Choke plate pull-down adjustment (Weber-Autolite 5200)

between the lower edge of the choke plate and the air horn wall.

4. Apply finger pressure to the choke linkage at the top edge of the choke plate to remove all slack from the linkage.
5. To adjust the clearance between the choke plate and air horn, remove the plug from the diaphragm and turn the screw in or out. Replace the plug.

De-choke

1. Hold the throttle lever wide open.
2. Remove the slack from the choke linkage by applying pressure to the top edge of the choke plate.
3. The clearance between the lower edge of the choke plate and the air horn wall should be .320″.
4. Adjust the clearance by bending the tab on the fast idle lever where it touches the fast idle cam.

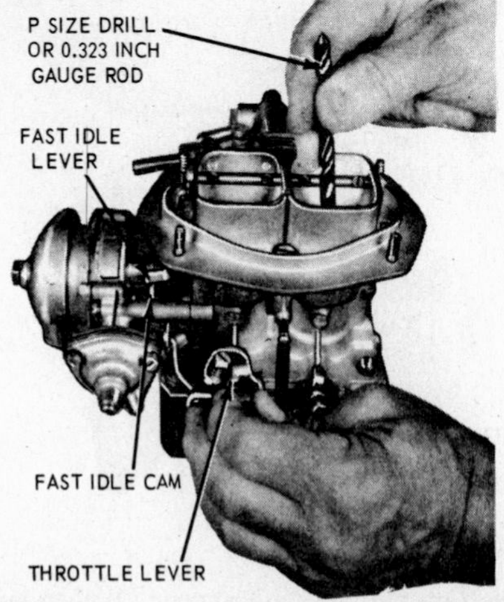

De-choke adjustment (Weber-Autolite 5200)

Fast Idle

1. With the engine at operating temperature and the fast idle screw on the second step of the fast idle cam (against the shoulder of the first step), adjust the fast idle speed to 1,800 rpm, by turning the adjusting screw in or out.

Dry Float Setting

1. Remove the bowl cover.
2. Hold the bowl cover in an inverted position, with the float tang resting lightly on the fuel intake needle. The clearance between the top of the float and the bottom of the bowl cover casting should be .450″ (Z size drill).
3. Bend the float tang up or down to adjust the clearance. NOTE: *Do not damage the tang. Both floats must be adjusted equally.*

Float Drop

1. Hold the bowl cover in its normal po-

Fast idle adjustment (Weber-Autolite 5200)

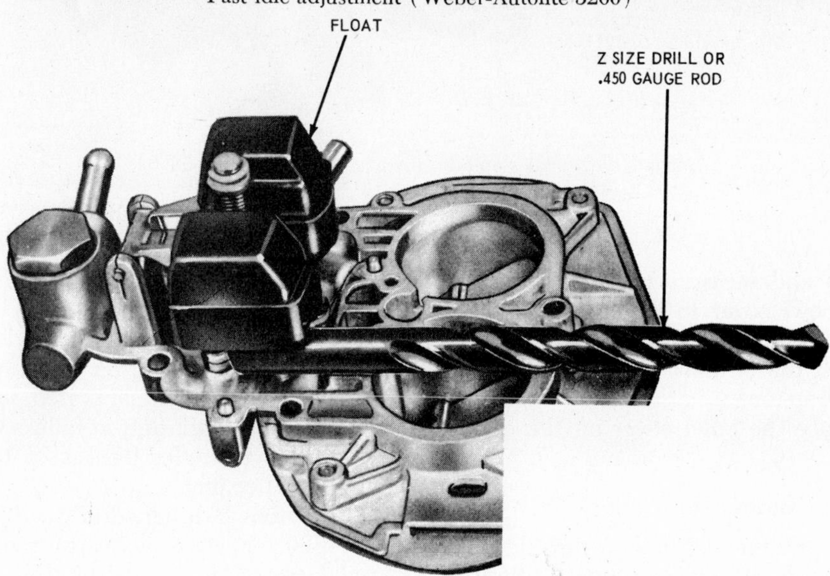

Dry float setting (Weber-Autolite 5200)

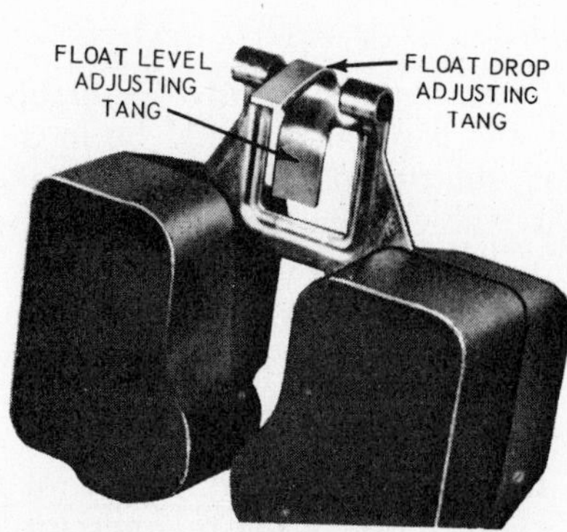

Float adjustment (Weber-Autolite 5200)

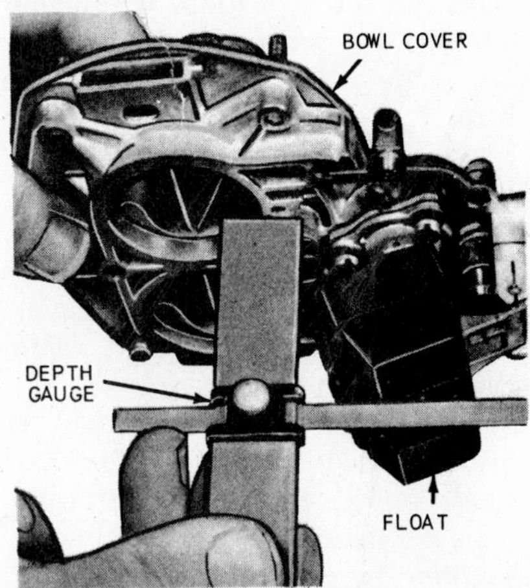

Float drop adjustment (Weber-Autolite 5200)

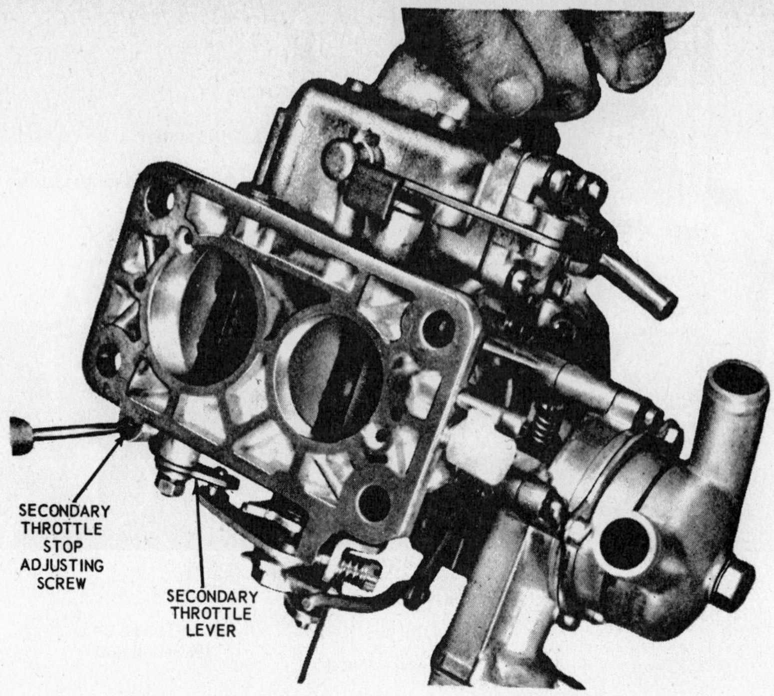

Secondary throttle stop adjustment (Weber-Autolite 5200)

sition and measure the distance from the bowl cover to the lowest point of the float.

2. Adjust the distance to 1.9" by bending the drop tang up or down.
3. Replace the bowl cover on the carburetor.

Secondary Throttle Stop Screw

1. Back off the secondary throttle stop screw until the secondary throttle plate seats in its bore.
2. Turn the screw in until it touches the tab on the secondary throttle lever. Turn the screw in an additional ¼ turn.

Choke Thermostatic Spring Housing

1. Remove the air cleaner.
2. Loosen (do not remove) the choke cover retaining screws. The cover can be rotated slightly without removing the water cover.
3. Set the choke cover to ⅛" lean (counterclockwise) from the index mark. A small punch mark will indicate the proper location.
4. Tighten the cover retaining screws and replace the air cleaner.

Air Cleaner

1,600 cc.

The air cleaner used on the Capri 1,600 cc. has a temperature-operated valve and duct assembly built-in, the failure of which will reduce the effectiveness of the emission control system.

The system is designed to provide heated air (+90° F.) to the carburetor during normal operation. A thermostatic bulb is connected through a spring-loaded linkage to a flap valve. This valve is designed to shut off the flow of hot air when underhood temperatures approach 110° F.

Testing

With the duct and valve assembly installed, the flap valve should be in the *up* position, shutting off the cold air intake, so long as ambient air temperature is below 85°F. If the valve is not in the *up* position, check for valve wear or breakage in the duct. The entire duct and valve assembly must be replaced as a unit if wear is in evidence.

To further test the unit, remove it from the car and immerse the thermostatic bulb in water. Heat the water to 85°F., allow the temperature to stabilize for about five minutes, then observe valve—it should be in the *up* position. Increase water temperature to 110°F. and again wait five minutes. The flap valve should be in the *down* position to shut off the hot air. If the flap does not work as indicated, the thermostatic bulb must be replaced as a unit.

Evaporative Emission Control System

1970–71

All cars imported into the U.S. are equipped with a fuel vapor control system. The system has four major components—the fuel tank, the vapor separator, the three-way control valve, and the vapor absorbing charcoal canister. The fuel tank is equipped with a non-vented filler cap and has the vapor separator welded to its top side. The vapor separator cannot be serviced separately if defective—the entire fuel tank must be replaced.

The tank fuel filler neck is double-sealed and, in addition to fulfilling its primary function of receiving fuel, vents air through a secondary chamber and indicates fuel level.

The vapor separator serves to prevent the entry of liquid fuel into the three-way control valve supply line.

The three-way control valve has three internal valves—a check valve to regulate fuel control (0.3-0.65 psi), a safety pressure relief valve to permit vapor blow-off in case of a plugged vapor line, and a vacuum relief air valve to replace air in the tank as fuel is consumed (to prevent tank collapse).

The primary function of the three-way control valve is the control of fuel fill level. As fuel level rises, vapor is discharged into the atmosphere through the fill control tube and the space between the inner filler tube and the outer neck. When the fuel level is high enough to cover the fill control tube orifice, vapor can no longer escape and the filler tube begins to fill up. At this point, neither vapor nor fuel can flow through the system to the check valve, since at least 0.3 psi is required to open the valve and the pressure head in the filler is still insufficient. The tank level is therefore controlled by the level in the fill control tube and is maintained, when full, at approximately 90% of full tank volume to allow for thermal expansion.

When thermal expansion takes place, vapor flows when a vapor pressure of 0.3 to 0.65 psi is developed in the line from the separator unit. The vapor passes through the now open three-way control valve, through the system, to the charcoal canister in the engine compartment. Vapor is there

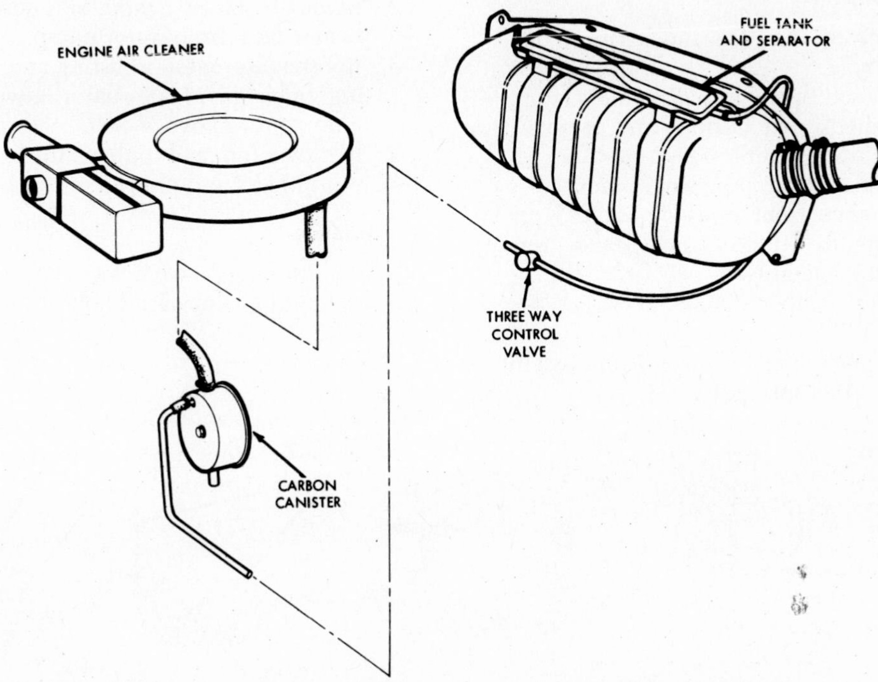

1,600 cc. engine evaporative emission control system schematic

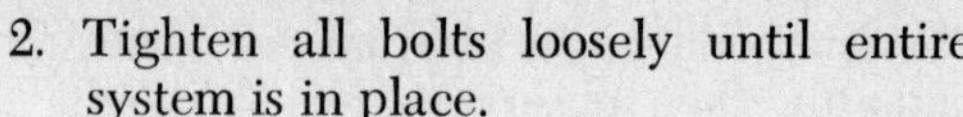

absorbed by the activated charcoal until the car is started, whereupon the "stored" vapor is sucked through a connecting hose into the air cleaner and burned.

If the line should become restricted (between charcoal canister and check valve), the vapor pressure is permitted to rise to 0.7 to 1.5 psi, at which point the pressure relief valve portion of the three-way control valve opens to allow the vapor to pass into the atmosphere.

The vacuum relief valve portion of the three-way control valve always remains closed until a pressure differential of 0.25 psi is reached (between atmospheric pressure and vacuum in tank). When this point is reached, the valve opens to the atmosphere and air is allowed to pass into the tank, through a filter, until pressure balance is achieved.

Exhaust System

The exhaust system consists of two parts—a front pipe, resonator and front muffler assembly; and a rear muffler and tailpipe assembly. The exhaust system is clamped together and suspended on four rubber O-rings, in addition to a bracket from the transmission that holds the front pipe.

Removal

1. Jack up the car and support on axle stands.
2. Loosen the rear muffler inlet clamp.
3. Unhook rear O-rings and remove rear muffler assembly.
4. Release front pipe from bracket.
5. Remove front pipe-to-manifold clamp.
6. Unhook front O-rings and remove front assembly.

Installation

1. To install, first position front assembly, then rear assembly.
2. Tighten all bolts loosely until entire system is in place.
3. Tighten manifold clamp nuts to 15-20 ft. lbs., rear assembly clamp to 10-12 ft. lbs., and bracket to 12-15 ft. lbs.
4. Start engine and check for exhaust leaks, then lower car to floor.

Cooling System

1,600 cc.

The cooling system consists of the water pump, fan, thermostat, radiator, and connecting lines. Coolant is circulated from the bottom of the radiator up through the water pump and into the cylinder block and cylinder head to the thermostat. If the engine is at operating temperature (or hotter), the coolant is returned to the radiator top tank, from where it flows down through the radiator tubes to be cooled by air. If the engine is cold, the coolant flows through a bypass hose to allow the coolant in the block and head to warm up quickly.

WATER PUMP

Removal

1. Lift the hood, then drain the cooling system.
2. Remove lower radiator hose and heater hose from water pump.
3. Loosen alternator adjusting and mounting bolts, pivot alternator toward engine, and remove V-belt.
4. Remove fan and pulley, then remove pump bolts and pump.

Installation

1. To install, reverse removal procedure, tightening alternator bolt to 15-18 ft. lbs.

NOTE: *Use a new gasket, with Permatex.*

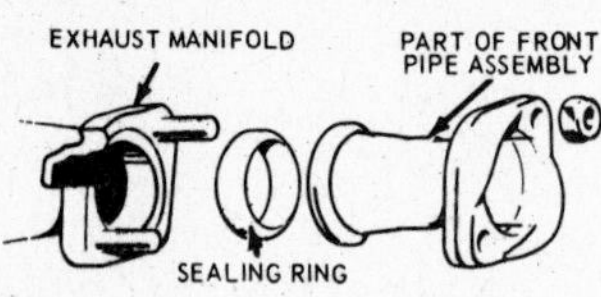

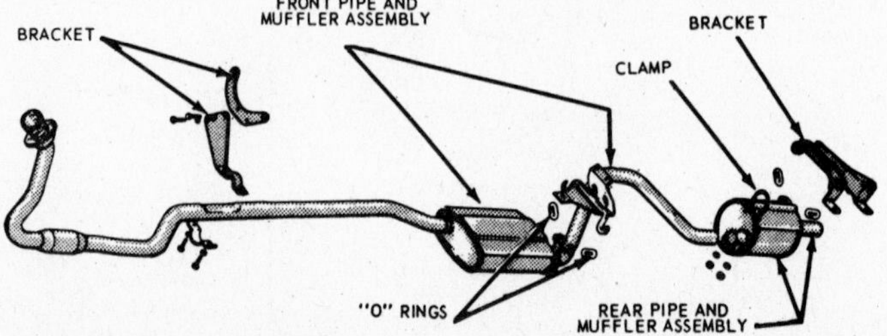

Exhaust system (1,600 cc.)

Radiator

Removal

1. Lift the hood and drain the cooling system.

NOTE: *Radiator cap should be opened to allow pressure release.*

2. Disconnect radiator top and bottom hoses, remove hold-down bolts, and lift out radiator.
3. Remove the overflow hose from the filler neck.

Installation

1. To install, reverse removal procedure.

NOTE: *Cap should be left off with engine running to allow air to bleed out of system.*

2,000 cc.

The 2,000 cc. engine is water cooled with full length water jackets. Coolant is circulated through the system by a belt driven water pump. At 183°-190°, the thermostat is closed preventing coolant circulation through the radiator. As the engine temperature rises above 183°-190°, the thermostat opens and permits coolant to reach the radiator to control engine temperatures.

An oil cooler core, for cooling the automatic transmission fluid is built into the bottom of the radiator.

Thermostat

Removal

1. Drain the radiator so that the coolant level is below the thermostat.
2. Remove the thermostat housing retaining bolts and pull the housing away from the engine.
3. Remove the retaining ring, thermostat and seal from the housing.

Testing

1. Immerse the thermostat in boiling water. If it does not open ¼″ or more, it must be replaced.
2. If the problem is insufficient heat the thermostat should be checked for leakage. Hold the thermostat up to a lighted background. With the thermostat at room temperature, there should be no more than slight light leakage at one or two locations on the perimeter of the valve. More than slight light leakage indicates a defective valve.

Installation

1. Clean the thermostat and engine gasket surfaces.
2. Assemble the thermostat, seal and retaining ring in the thermostat housing.
3. Install the thermostat housing on the engine.
4. Fill the cooling system with the recommended anti-freeze and water mixture. When the engine reaches operating temperature, check the coolant level.

Radiator

Removal

1. Drain the cooling system. Disconnect the upper and lower hoses from the radiator. If the vehicle is equipped with an automatic transmission, disconnect the intake for the automatic transmission fluid cooler.
2. If the vehicle is equipped with a radiator shroud, remove the shroud. Remove the retaining bolts from the radiator support brackets and remove the radiator.

Installation

1. If a new radiator is being installed, transfer the drain cock from the old radiator. Transfer the oil cooler fittings from the old radiator to the new one, attaching them with an oil resistant sealant. When tightening the fittings, do not exceed 12 ft. lbs. of torque.
2. Installation is the reverse of removal.

Water Pump

Removal

1. Drain the cooling system.
2. Disconnect the heater hose and radiator lower hose from the pump.
3. Remove the alternator drive belt.
4. Remove the fan, fan spacer and pulley.
5. Remove the camshaft drive belt cover.
6. Remove the water pump and clean all gasket material from the cylinder block.

Installation

1. Use a new gasket and torque the water pump retaining bolts to 5-7 ft. lbs. (¼″ bolts) and to 12-15 ft. lbs. (5/16″ bolts).
2. Further installation is the reverse of removal.

Engine

Exhaust Emission Control 1970-71

The IMCO (improved combustion) system is used on the 1,600 and 2,000 cc. Capri engines. With this system, exhaust emissions are controlled by improving combustion efficiency during deceleration from the higher speed ranges.

The system, as used on these models, consists of three major components—the deceleration valve, the dual-diaphragm distributor, and a modified carburetor.

Deceleration Valve

The deceleration valve is connected to the intake manifold by a nut and tapered adapter. The valve itself is controlled by two springs, the tension of which is set at the factory by the nylon screw on the cap. Basically, it operates like a power brake vacuum servo. One side of a diaphragm is subject to atmospheric pressure, while the other side is open to intake manifold vacuum. When the valve is opened by the strong vacuum in the intake manifold, an air/fuel mixture is drawn, at the same time, from the carburetor into the manifold. When this occurs, pressure in the manifold rises slightly and increases the volume of mixture into the cylinders. This greater volume results in better burning and reduced hydrocarbon emissions.

Dual-Diaphragm Distributor

The distributor has a normal set of centrifugal advance weights and vacuum diaphragm advance, with the addition of another diaphragm controlled by manifold vacuum. This second diaphragm acts to retard the spark under deceleration and idle, when manifold vacuum is greatest. While this decreases the power of the engine at these times, there is an increase in the braking effect of the engine and hydrocarbon emissions are reduced further.

Carburetor

The Autolite single-barrel carburetor is calibrated for use with the IMCO system. Major differences between this and other carburetors of the same type are the limit stop on the mixture screw and a modified carburetor float.

Adjustment

Deceleration Valve

1. Run the engine at idle for five minutes.
2. Connect a tachometer and vacuum gauge to the engine, using a T-fitting so that the valve remains operational.
3. Remove the fuel/air mixture hose from the decel valve.
4. With the transmission in Neutral (Park for automatic transmission) raise the engine rpm to 3,000 and hold it stable for two seconds.
5. Release the throttle suddenly and immediately observe the reading on the vacuum gauge.
6. Record the elapsed time from when the throttle was released until the vacuum reading reaches O. If the elapsed time is more than five seconds, turn the nylon adjuster approximately ½ turn clockwise. If the time is less than three seconds (1,600 cc.) or less than 1½ seconds (2,000 c.c.), turn the adjuster ½ turn counterclockwise and recheck the operation.

NOTE: *Fabricate an adjustment tool as illustrated to prevent damaging the nylon adjuster.*

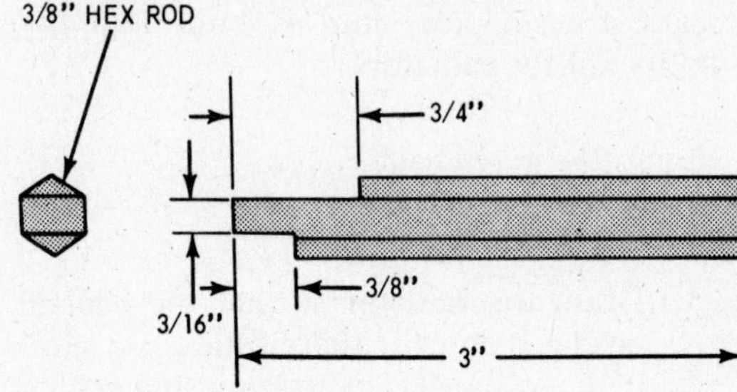

1,600 cc. Engine

The 1,600 cc. Capri engine is a four-cylinder, inline overhead valve unit having a cross-flow cylinder head and piston shaped combustion chambers. The cylinder bores are machined in the cast-iron block and are cooled by full-length water jackets.

The crankshaft is made of cast iron and runs in five main bearings having steel backed copper/lead or lead/bronze inserts. End-play is controlled by half thrust washers on each side of the center main bearing.

The connecting rods are forged H-section units having steel backed copper/lead or aluminum/tin big end inserts and steel backed bronze piston pin bushings. Pistons are solid skirt aluminum alloy having two compression rings and one oil ring. Piston pins are full-floating, being retained by snap-rings.

The camshaft is driven in a conventional manner, at one-half engine speed, by a single-row roller chain. A helical gear on the cam drives the distributor and oil pump, while an eccentric operates the fuel pump.

The cast-iron cylinder head is machined flat on the down side, having no cast-in combustion chambers. Valve guides are integral, although guide replacement is possible and sleeves are available from the dealer.

Removal

1. Remove hood, after scribing matchmarks around hinges.
2. Disconnect battery cables.
3. Drain the cooling system.

NOTE: *Drain engine block as well as radiator.*

4. Disconnect radiator hoses and remove radiator.
5. Remove air cleaner assembly.
6. Disconnect heater hoses from water pump and intake manifold.
7. Disconnect throttle linkage.
8. Disconnect oil pressure and temperature sender wires, then disconnect alternator wires.

NOTE: *It is a good idea to tag these wires.*

9. Disconnect exhaust pipe from manifold and remove hot air tubes.
10. Disconnect fuel inlet line at fuel pump.

NOTE: *Plug the line so that gas does not siphon from tank.*

11. Disconnect coil wires, then remove spark plug wires and distributor cap.
12. Jack up the front of the car and support on axle stands.
13. Disconnect starter wires, remove starter and oil pan shield.
14. Remove clutch cover.
15. Lower the car to the floor.
16. Remove clutch housing-to-engine bolts, then install lifting brackets and chain hoist.
17. Disconnect the front motor mounts, while supporting engine with chain hoist.
18. Place an axle stand or wooden block under the transmission.
19. Raise the engine slightly, while pulling forward to separate the transmission driveshaft from the clutch; lift engine out of car.

Installation

20. To install, reverse removal procedure.

NOTE: *Don't forget to attach engine ground strap.*

Cylinder Head

Removal

1. Remove the air cleaner, then disconnect the fuel line at the pump and the carburetor.
2. Drain the cooling system.
3. Disconnect spark plug wires, then disconnect heater and vacuum hoses from the intake manifold and choke housing.
4. Disconnect temperature sender wire, then disconnect exhaust pipe at manifold flange.
5. Disconnect throttle linkage and distributor vacuum line at carburetor.
6. Remove thermostat housing and thermostat.
7. Remove rocker arm cover and gasket, then remove the rocker shaft bolts, evenly, and the rocker shaft assembly.
8. Remove pushrods and place them aside in proper order for correct installation.
9. Remove cylinder head bolts, head, and gasket.

Cleaning and Inspection

1. Use a scraper and a wire brush to clean carbon deposits from head, following up with a kerosene-soaked rag.
2. Remove the valves and springs.
3. Remove spark plugs and manifolds, then carefully clean the gasket surfaces of the head and manifolds.
4. Inspect the head for cracks or burned areas around the valves and ports.
5. With the gasket surface completely clean, check the straightness of the head using a straightedge and feeler gauges. Generally, 0.001″ per inch of head length is acceptable.

Installation

1. Place head gasket on the block.
2. Position the cylinder head and install the bolts. Tighten evenly in sequence (see illustration under *Torque Specifications* table) to proper torque.

NOTE: *Manifolds may be installed prior to placing head on block.*

3. Install pushrods in correct order, then place rocker arms and shaft assembly on head and locate pushrods in rocker arm screws. Tighten rocker arm bolts to 25-30 ft. lbs.
4. Adjust valve clearance, then install rocker arm cover and gasket.
5. Continue installation by reversing Steps 1-6 of removal procedure.

Valves

The valves are mounted vertically in the cylinder head, the intake valve heads being larger than the exhaust valve heads. The exhaust valves are stellite-coated for better heat and wear resistance, while the intake valves are coated with diffused aluminum for the same reason. The factory does not recommend grinding the intake valves or lapping the intake valve seats, because the grinding operation removes the coating and shortens the life of the valve. Exhaust valves, on the other hand, may be ground if necessary.

Valve stems are phosphate-coated for better wear resistance. Valve guides are cast integral with the head, although sleeves are available if guides become worn. In addition, valves are available with 0.003 and 0.015 in. oversize stem diameters.

The valve keepers do not grip the stem, allowing the valves to rotate freely during operation.

Removal

1. Remove cylinder head, as previously described.
2. Compress valve springs, using valve spring compressor.
3. Remove valve locks or keys.
4. Release valve springs.
5. Remove valve springs, retainers, oil seals, and valves. Check valve spring squareness—5/64 in. is maximum permissible tolerance.

NOTE: *If a valve does not slide out of the guide easily, check end of stem for mushrooming or heading over. If head is mushroomed, file off excess material, remove and discard valve. If valve is not mushroomed, lubricate stem, remove valve and check guide for galling. Valve seat width (minimum and desirable) is 1/16 in. for intakes, 5/64 in. for exhausts.*

Installation

1. Installation is the reverse of removal.

Valve Clearance Adjustment

Consulting the chart, rotate the engine in the normal direction of rotation until the valves in the first column are fully open. At this point, the valves in the second column can be checked and adjusted, using a 7/16″ box wrench and feeler gauges. Clearance should be 0.008-0.010″ for intake valves, 0.018-0.020″ for exhaust valves when using this method.

Adjusting valve clearance—1,600 cc. engine

The valves also can be adjusted with the engine running. In this case, clearance should be set to specifications found in the *Tune-up Specifications* table.

Valves Open	*Valves to Adjust*
1 and 6	3 and 8
2 and 4	5 and 7
3 and 8	1 and 6
5 and 7	2 and 4

Timing Cover

Removal

1. Drain the coolant.
2. Disconnect radiator hoses at the engine, then remove radiator.
3. Remove fanbelt, fan, and water pump pulley.
4. Remove the water pump.
5. Remove the crankshaft pulley, using a puller only.
6. Remove the front cover.

NOTE: *Cover is secured by four oil pan bolts as well.*

Installation

1. Remove the old oil seal by driving out to the rear.
2. Install new seal by driving in from the rear.
3. Position a new gasket, new cork seal, and new front portion of oil pan seal (if necessary) using Permatex, then align the cover and install the bolts. Front cover bolts are tightened to 5-7 ft. lbs., oil pan bolts to 7-9 ft. lbs.

NOTE: *Make sure oil seal is concentric with crankshaft.*

4. Position crankshaft pulley, making sure keyway is properly aligned, then draw into place and tighten bolt to 24-28 ft. lbs.
5. Continue installation by reversing Steps 1-4 of removal procedure.

Camshaft and Timing Chain

The camshaft runs in three bearings in the block. The front and rear camshaft bearings are approximately ¾″ wide, the front bearing having an oil hole for the rocker arm oil feed, while the center camshaft bearing is approximately ⅝″ wide.

The camshaft is retained by an iron thrust plate bolted to the front face of the block. A single-row timing chain, with tensioner, operates the camshaft. The timing chain runs across a synthetic rubber pad on the tensioner arm. This pad wears in service so that the chain runs in two grooves. These grooves are essential to the life of the timing chain and never should be removed.

Timing chain tensioner—1,600 cc. engine

Timing Chain

Removal

1. Remove the front cover.
2. Remove the crankshaft oil slinger.
3. Remove the camshaft sprocket and disconnect the timing chain.

Installation

1. To install, position the timing chain on the sprockets so that the sprocket marks will face each other when the chain is installed.
2. Place the sprocket in position, with chain in place, and tighten bolts to 12-15 ft. lbs. Bend up the lock tabs.
3. Install the oil slinger and front cover.

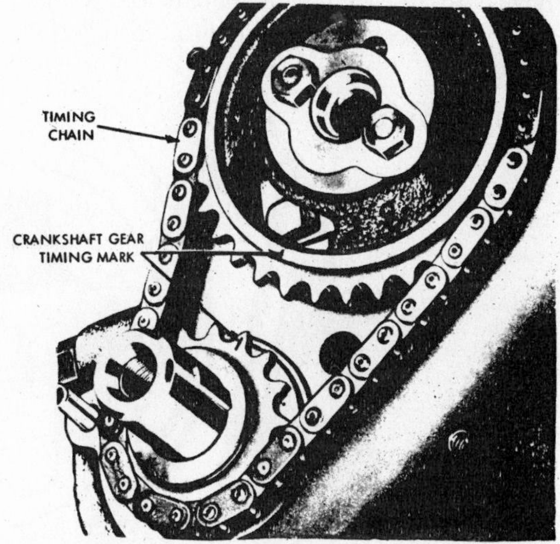

Valve timing marks—1,600 cc. engine

Lubrication

Oil Pan

Removal

1. Drain the engine oil and disconnect the battery cables.
2. Disconnect throttle linkage at the carburetor.
3. Set the parking brake, jack up the front of the car and support on axle stands.
4. Place a jack under the transmission.
5. Remove the front motor mount bolts.
6. Remove oil pan shield.
7. Remove the starter motor.
8. Remove the oil pan and gasket, jacking up the transmission to gain clearance.
9. Remove cork packing strips, then clean block surface.
10. Remove oil pump pickup tube screen and soak it in gasoline or kerosene, then blow dry with compressed air.

Installation

1. To install, first position gaskets with Permatex, then place the cork packing strips in place with the chamfered ends in the grooves and install the oil pan and bolts. Tighten bolts to 7-9 ft. lbs., following the torque sequence illustrated (first the letters, then the numbers).
2. Continue installation by reversing Steps 1-7.

Oil Pump

The oil pump and filter assembly is bolted to the right side of the block and can be serviced with the engine installed in the car.

Two types of oil pump have been installed during production—an eccentric bi-rotor type and a sliding vane type. These pumps are readily identified by their end covers—the eccentric bi-rotor type has four recesses cast into its cover while the sliding vane type has a flat cover. These two pumps are interchangeable, although their internal parts are not.

Removal

1. Lift the hood and place a drain pan under the oil pump.
2. Remove the three bolts which hold the pump and filter assembly.

NOTE: *Tighten these bolts to 13-15 ft. lbs. when installing pump.*

3. Remove filter from pump.

Disassembly—Bi-Rotor Type

1. Remove oil filter and seal ring.
2. Remove end plate and O-ring from groove in pump body.
3. Check clearance between inner and outer rotor lobes; it should not exceed 0.006″.

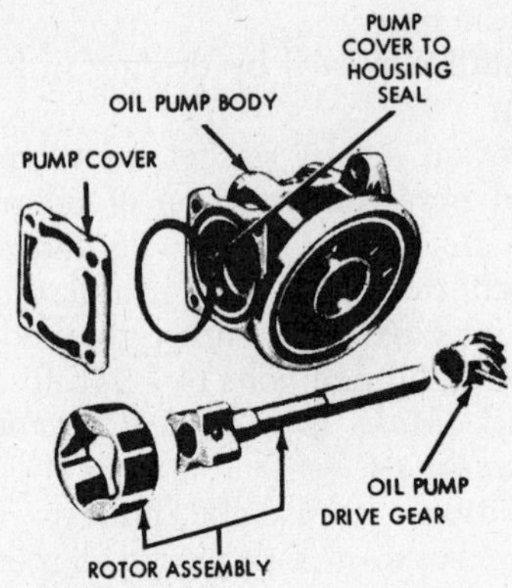

Exploded view of eccentric bi-rotor oil pump—1,600 cc. engine

Checking rotor clearance—bi-rotor type oil pump

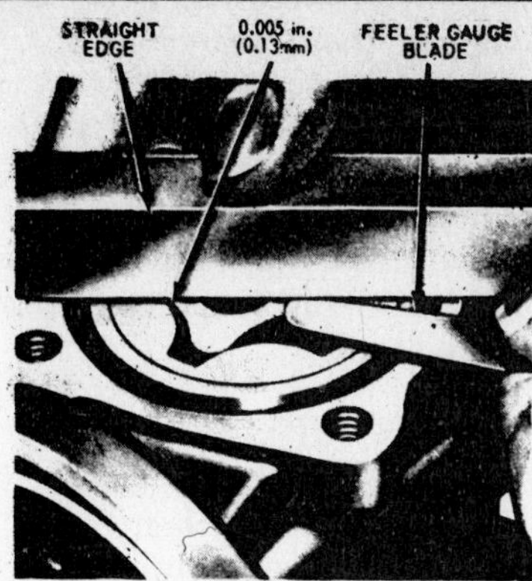

Checking rotor end-play—bi-rotor type oil pump

NOTE: *Rotors are sold only in matched pairs.*

4. Check clearance between outer rotor and housing; it should not exceed 0.010″.

NOTE: *If clearance is excessive, a new rotor assembly and/or pump body must be installed.*

5. Check the clearance between the rotor faces and the pump housing, using a straightedge; clearance should not exceed 0.005″.

NOTE: *Pump body face can be lapped on a glass plate, using fine valve grinding compound, to correct clearance.*

6. If necessary, remove the outer rotor, drive out the pin that holds the drive gear to the shaft, and pull off the gear.
7. Pull out the inner rotor and drive shaft.

Assembly—Bi-Rotor Type

1. Place inner rotor and shaft into pump body.
2. Press the drive gear onto the shaft until the gear teeth are 2¼″ from mounting flange. Drill a 0.125″ hole at right angles to the shaft through the gear shoulder 1.3″ from the mounting flange, then insert a retaining pin and peen the ends.
3. Install the outer rotor, with the chamfered face towards the pump body.
4. Install O-ring into pump body groove, then position the end plate with the machined face towards the rotors.
5. Install filter and seal ring, tightening center bolt to 12-15 ft. lbs.

NOTE: *Use a new aluminum seal washer on the center bolt.*

Disassembly—Vane Type

1. Remove the filter body and seal ring.
2. Remove the end plate, keeping drive shaft vertical, then remove the O-ring from the groove in the pump body.
3. Place a straightedge across the face of the pump body and check the clearance between the face of the vanes and rotor assembly and the straightedge; it should not exceed 0.005″.

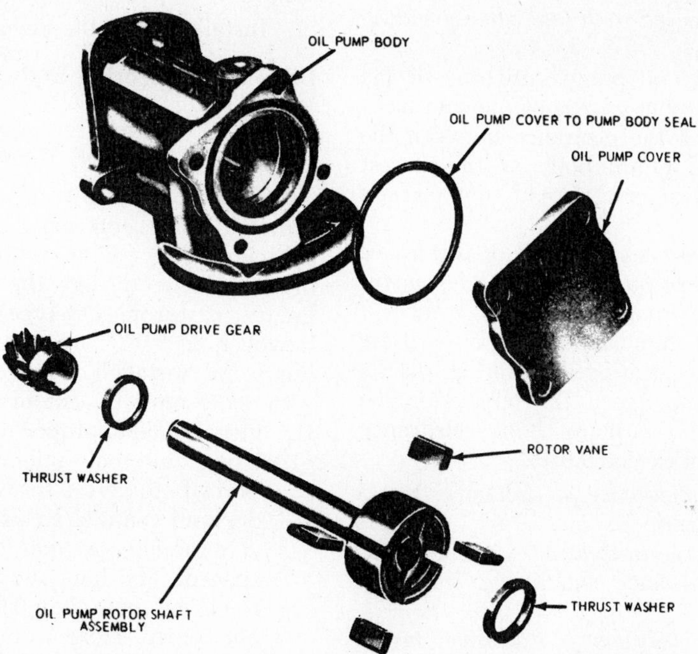

Exploded view of sliding vane type oil pump—1,600 cc. engine

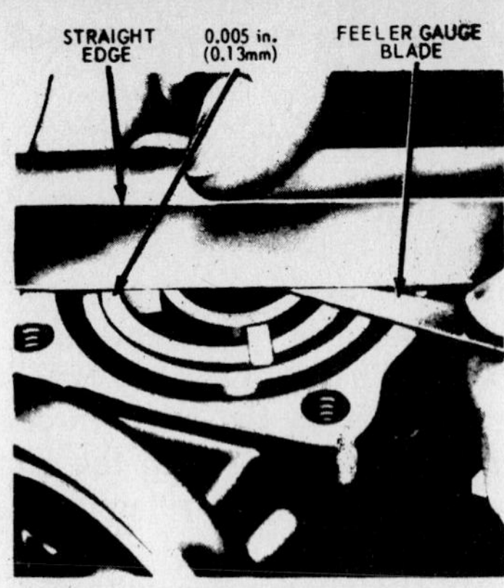

Checking rotor end-play—sliding vane type oil pump

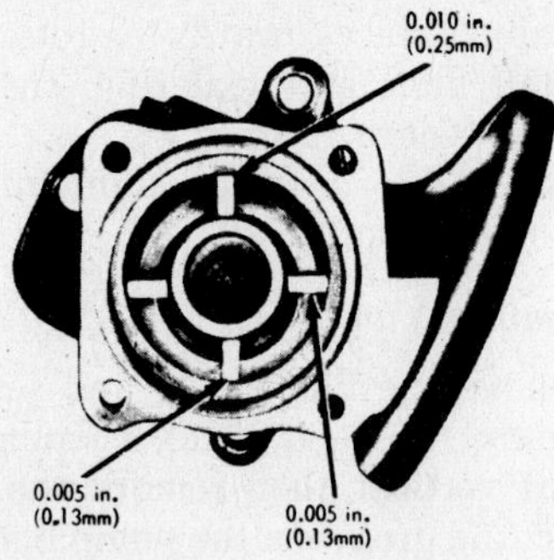

Checking vane and rotor clearance—sliding vane type oil pump

NOTE: *Clearance can be adjusted by lapping the face of the pump body on a glass plate covered with fine valve grinding compound.*

4. Rotate the oil pump until one of the vanes is in the middle of the cam base, then check the clearance between the rotor and pump body at the closest point; clearance should not exceed 0.005″.

NOTE: *Clearance in excess of this figure indicates a worn pump body, which means that the entire pump must be replaced.*

5. With the rotor in the same position, center the locating ring and check the clearance between the opposite vane edge and the pump body; clearance should not exceed 0.010″.

NOTE: *If clearance is excessive, vanes must be replaced.*

6. Check vane-to-locating groove clearance; clearance should be less than 0.005″.

NOTE: *If clearance is excessive, install new vanes and recheck; if clearance is still excessive, the rotor grooves are worn and a new rotor and shaft assembly must be installed.*

7. If necessary, remove the vanes and outer locating ring, drive out the gear retaining pin, and pull off the gear. Remove drive shaft and rotor arm assembly, and the inner ring, from the pump housing.

Assembly—Vane Type

1. Place the vane locating inner ring in the pump housing, then install drive shaft and rotor assembly.
2. Press the drive gear onto the shaft until the far end of the gear teeth are 2¼″ from the mounting flange. Drill a 0.125″ hole, at right angles to the shaft, through the gear shoulder 1.3″ from the mounting flange. Insert a retaining pin and peen the ends.
3. Install the vane locating outer ring, then locate the vanes in the rotor grooves with the curved edges outwards.
4. Install an O-ring in the groove of the pump body, then install the end plate with the machined face towards the rotor.
5. Install new filter and seal, install a new aluminum washer on the center bolt and tighten the center bolt to 12-15 ft. lbs.

Installation

1. Installation is the reverse of removal.

Pistons, Connecting Rods and Main Bearings

Piston Rings

Engine disassembly is entirely conventional. Before replacing rings, inspect the cylinder bores. The cylinder bores are machined directly into the block. Cylinder liners (cast-iron, dry-type) are available, however, in 0.020″ oversize (O.D.). When liners are installed, connecting rod clearance slots must be cut in their bases and the liners honed to proper size.

1. Using internal micrometer measure bores both across thrust faces of cylinder and parallel to axis of crankshaft at minimum of four locations equally spaced. The bore must not be out of round by more than 0.005″ and it must not "taper" more than 0.010″. "Taper" is the difference in wear between two bore measurements in any cylinder.

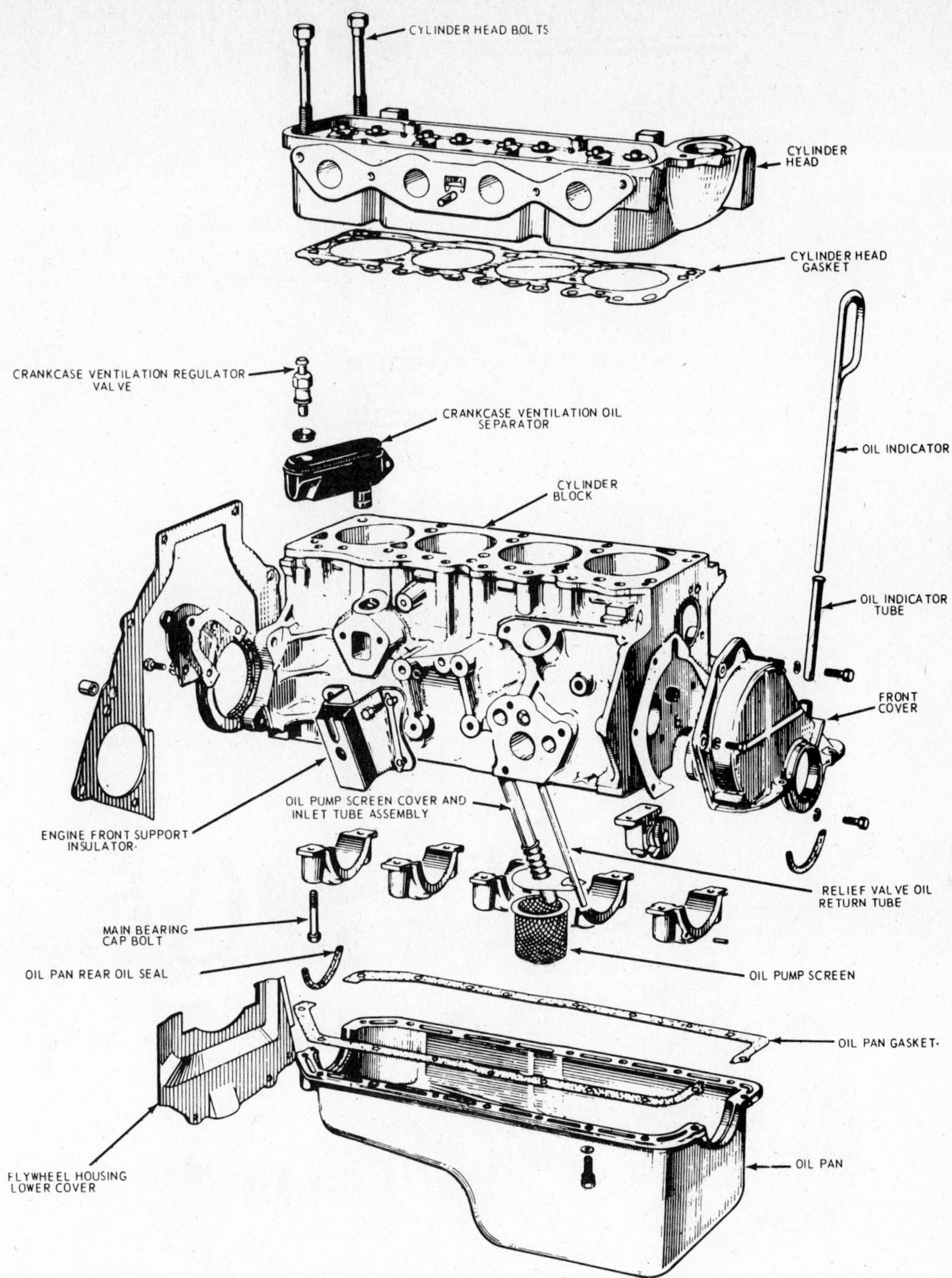

1,600 cc. engine block, cylinder head and related parts

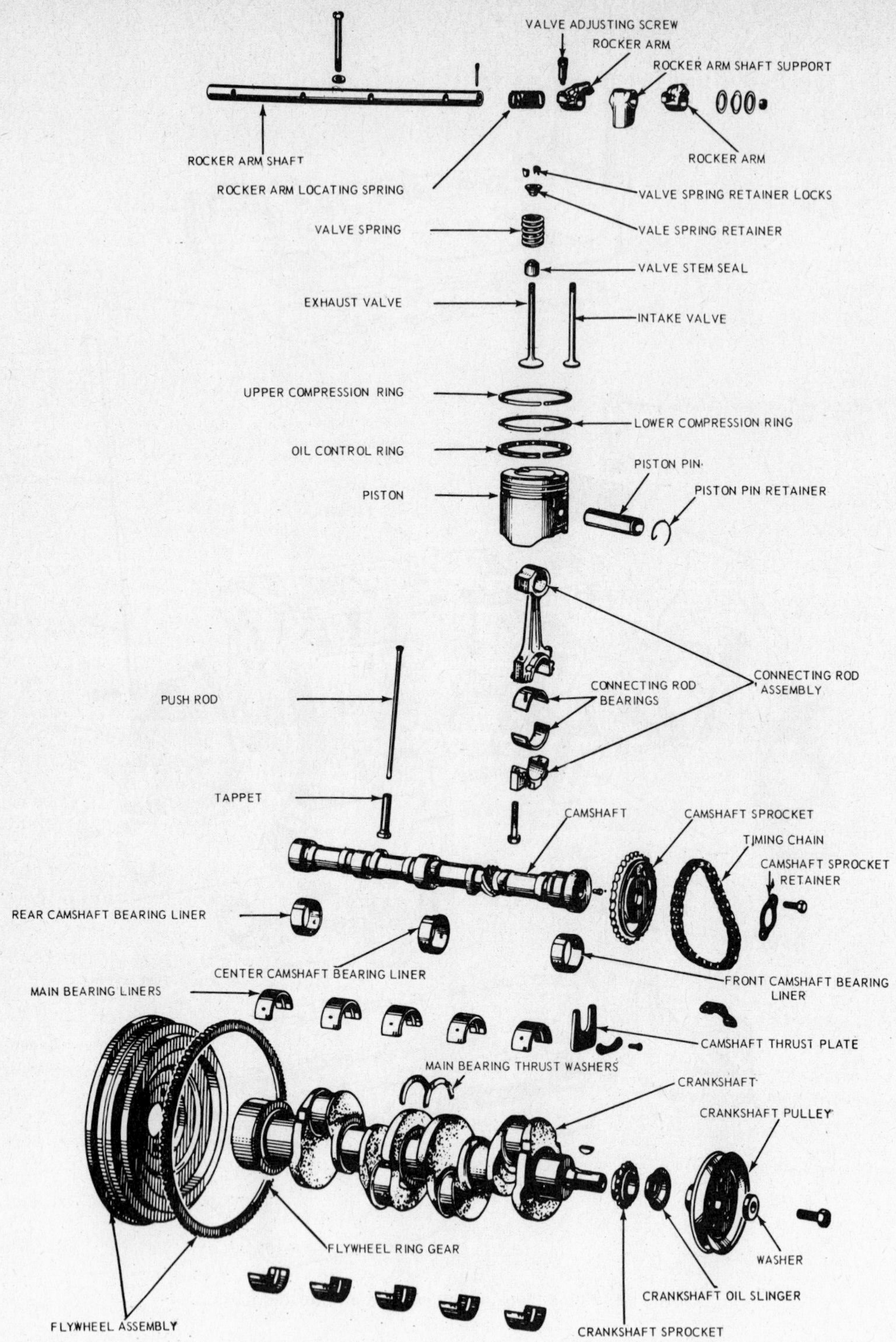
VALVE ADJUSTING SCREW
ROCKER ARM
ROCKER ARM SHAFT SUPPORT
ROCKER ARM SHAFT
ROCKER ARM
ROCKER ARM LOCATING SPRING
VALVE SPRING RETAINER LOCKS
VALVE SPRING
VALE SPRING RETAINER
VALVE STEM SEAL
EXHAUST VALVE
INTAKE VALVE
UPPER COMPRESSION RING
LOWER COMPRESSION RING
OIL CONTROL RING
PISTON PIN
PISTON
PISTON PIN RETAINER
CONNECTING ROD ASSEMBLY
CONNECTING ROD BEARINGS
PUSH ROD
TAPPET
CAMSHAFT
CAMSHAFT SPROCKET
TIMING CHAIN
CAMSHAFT SPROCKET RETAINER
REAR CAMSHAFT BEARING LINER
CENTER CAMSHAFT BEARING LINER
FRONT CAMSHAFT BEARING LINER
MAIN BEARING LINERS
CAMSHAFT THRUST PLATE
MAIN BEARING THRUST WASHERS
CRANKSHAFT
CRANKSHAFT PULLEY
FLYWHEEL RING GEAR
WASHER
CRANKSHAFT OIL SLINGER
FLYWHEEL ASSEMBLY
CRANKSHAFT SPROCKET

1,600 cc. engine internal components

Bore any cylinder beyond limits of out of roundness or taper to diameter of next available oversize piston that will clean up wear. Recommended clearance for new pistons (in bore) is 0.0013-0.0019″. Clearance between block face and piston top at TDC should be 0.085-0.103″.

2. If bore is within limits dimensionally, examine bore visually. It should be dull silver in color and exhibit a pattern of machining cross hatching intersecting at about 30°. There should be no scratches, tool marks, nicks, or other damage. If any such damage exists, bore cylinder to clean up damage and then to next oversize. Pistons are available in 0.0025″, 0.015″, and 0.030″ oversizes. Identification of pistons is found in the specifications.

   Polished or shiny places in the bore are known as glazing. Glazing causes poor lubrication, high oil consumption and ring damage. Remove glazing by honing cylinders with clean, sharp stones of No. 180-220 grit to obtain a surface finish of 15-35 RMS. Use a hone also to obtain correct piston clearance and surface finish in any cylinder that has been bored.
3. If cylinder bore is in satisfactory condition, place each ring in bore in turn and square it in bore with head of piston. Measure ring gap; it should be 0.009-0.014″. If ring gap is greater than limit, get new ring. If ring gap is less than limit, file end of ring to obtain correct gap.
4. Check ring side clearance by installing rings on piston, and inserting feeler gauge of correct dimension between ring and lower land. Clearance for compression rings is 0.0016-0.0036″, for oil rings 0.0018-0.0038″. Gauge should slide freely around ring circumference without binding. Any wear will form a step on lower land. Replace any pistons having high steps. Before checking ring side clearance be sure ring grooves are clean and free of carbon, sludge, or grit.

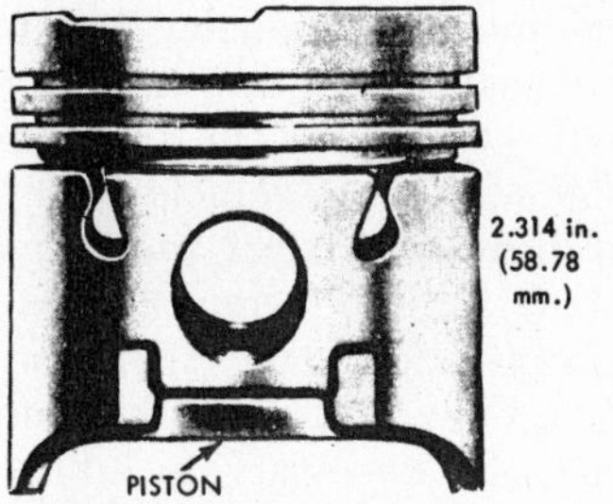

Piston gauging point

5. Space ring gaps at equidistant intervals around piston circumference. Be sure to install piston in its original bore. Install short lengths of rubber tubing over connecting rod bolts to prevent damage to rod journal. Install ring compressor over rings on piston. Lower piston, and rod assembly into bore until ring compressor contacts block. Using wooden handle of hammer, push piston into bore while guiding rod onto journal.

NOTE: *Arrows on pistons must point forward.*

Main Bearings

Replace

1. Remove oil pan.
2. Remove one main bearing cap and lower bearing insert.
3. With a "roll out" pin inserted into the oil hole in the crankshaft, rotate crankshaft in normal direction of rotation (clockwise seen from front) to remove top bearing insert.
4. Oil the new upper bearing insert and place un-notched end of shell between crankshaft and notched upper bearing web.
5. With "roll out" pin positioned in oil hole, rotate new upper bearing insert into place.
6. Install new lower bearing insert into bearing cap, with a 0.002″ strip of brass shim stock between insert and cap. Do not oil this bearing.
7. Place a strip of Plastigage (available from automotive parts jobbers) on the lower bearing insert, then install main cap, tightening bolts to specification.

NOTE: *Do not rotate crankshaft. Arrows on caps must point forward.*

8. Remove bearing cap and, using the scale on the envelope, measure the width of the compressed Plastigage; this is the oil clearance for this main bearing.
9. If clearance is satisfactory, remove brass shim stock and install lower cap and new bearing; if clearance is unsatisfactory, undersize bearing inserts are available to correct.

Measuring crankshaft end-play

NOTE: *Never file main caps to adjust clearance.*

10. Replace the remaining main bearings in the engine by following Steps 2-9, then install oil pan.

NOTE: *Don't forget to check crankshaft end-play—it may be necessary to replace thrust washers on center main bearing to correct for this.*

Connecting Rods and Bearings

Replace

The connecting rods usually are numbered for proper assembly sequence. When removing the rod caps, make sure such numbers exist. If not, punchmark the caps and rods for proper assembly. If stock numbers are in evidence, they go together, facing the camshaft side of the block, during assembly. Never switch caps to other rods. The connecting rod web has the word "front" embossed on it.

Connecting rod bearing clearance is measured in the same manner as is main bearing clearance.

2,000 cc. Engine

This is an overhead camshaft, four-cylinder engine with a cast iron block. The crankshaft runs in five main bearings, while the camshaft runs in three. The camshaft is belt driven with adjustable tension by means of a spring loaded idler pulley.

Removal

1. Drain the engine of coolant and oil.
2. Remove the air cleaner and the exhaust manifold shroud.
3. Disconnect the battery ground cable.
4. Remove the upper and lower hoses from the radiator.
5. Remove the radiator and fan.
6. Disconnect the heater hose from the water pump and carburetor choke fitting.
7. Disconnect the wires from the alternator and starter. It is good practice to tag these wires to prevent confusion during installation.
8. Disconnect the carburetor accelerator cable. If the vehicle is equipped with air conditioning, remove the compressor from the mounting bracket and lay it aside. NOTE: *Leave the refrigerant lines attached.*
9. Disconnect the flexible fuel line from the fuel tank line and plug the fuel tank line.
10. Disconnect the coil primary wire and the water temperature and oil temperature sending units.
11. Jack the vehicle and remove the starter.
12. Remove the flywheel (or converter housing) upper mounting bolts.
13. Disconnect the exhaust pipe at the exhaust manifold. Unbolt the engine right and left mount at the underbody bracket. Remove the flywheel (or converter housing) cover.
14. On vehicles equipped with manual transmissions, remove the flywheel housing lower mounting bolts. On automatic transmission vehicles, disconnect the converter from the flywheel and remove the converter housing lower mounting bolts.
15. Lower the vehicle and support the transmission or converter housing with a hydraulic jack.
16. Attach the engine lifting apparatus and carefully pull the engine from the engine compartment.

Installation

1. Place a new gasket over the exhaust pipe.
2. Carefully, lower the engine into the engine compartment. Be sure that the exhaust manifold studs are aligned with the holes in the exhaust pipe flange. On a vehicle with automatic transmission, start the converter pilot shaft into the crankshaft. On manual transmission cars, start the transmission drive gear into the clutch disc. It may be necessary to adjust the position of the transmission with relation to the engine if the input shaft fails to

enter the clutch disc. If the engine hangs up after the shaft enters, turn the crankshaft slowly with the transmission in gear, until the input shaft splines mesh with the clutch disc splines.
3. Remove the lifting apparatus and install the flywheel (or converter housing) upper mounting bolts.
4. Remove the jack from the transmission and jack the vehicle.
5. Install the flywheel (or converter housing) lower mounting bolts. On an automatic transmission car, attach the converter to the flywheel and torque to 23-28 ft. lbs.
6. Install the flywheel (or converter housing) dust cover.
7. Install the engine left and right mounting brackets to the underbody.
8. Unplug the fuel tank line and connect it to the flexible line. Tighten the exhaust pipe and exhaust manifold.
9. Lower the vehicle and connect the water and oil temperature sending units, coil primary wire and accelerator cable.
10. Install and connect the starter. Connect the alternator wires and heater hose to the water pump and carburetor choke fitting.
11. Install the fan pulley, fan and drive belt. On vehicles equipped with air conditioning, install the compressor on the mounting bracket and adjust the belt tension. Drive belt should sag approximately ½″ under thumb pressure at the middle of the longest side.
12. Install the radiator and connect the upper and lower hoses. Fill and bleed the cooling system. Fill the engine with the proper amount and grade of engine oil.
13. Connect the battery ground cable and operate the engine at fast idle, checking all gaskets and hoses for leaks.
14. On automatic transmission vehicles, adjust the transmission control linkage.
15. Install the air cleaner and connect the crankcase ventilation hose.

Intake Manifold

Removal

1. Remove the air cleaner and disconnect the fuel line from the carburetor.
2. Disconnect the two distributor vacuum lines from the intake manifold.
3. Disconnect the crankcase ventilation hose at the intake manifold.
4. Disconnect the accelerator cable from the carburetor.
5. Remove the intake manifold, carburetor and decel valve as an assembly.

Installation

1. Clean the cylinder head and intake manifold mating surfaces thoroughly.
2. Carefully coat the mating surfaces with sealer and position a new gasket on the studs. Install the manifold and torque the nuts to specification.
3. Further installation is the reverse of removal.

Exhaust Manifold

Removal

1. Remove the air cleaner and exhaust manifold shroud.
2. Disconnect the exhaust pipe from the manifold.
3. Remove the manifold from the cylinder head.

Installation

1. Clean all mating surfaces and carefully coat the mating surfaces with sealer.
2. Position a new gasket and install the exhaust manifold. Torque the mounting nuts according to specifications.
3. Install a new exhaust flange gasket.
4. Install the exhaust manifold shroud and the carburetor air cleaner.

Cylinder Head

Removal

1. Drain the cooling system.
2. Remove the air cleaner and the valve rocker cover.
3. Remove the intake and exhaust manifolds. The intake manifold, decel valve and carburetor can be removed as an assembly.
4. Remove the camshaft drive belt cover.
5. Loosen the drivebelt tensioner and remove the drive belt.
6. Remove the water outlet from the cylinder head.
7. Remove the cylinder head bolts evenly, and remove the cylinder head.

Cleaning

1. Clean the cylinder head gasket surfaces on the head and on the block.

2. Clean carbon deposits from the top of the pistons.
3. Clean the mating parts of the cylinder head, water outlet and manifolds.
4. If a new cylinder head is to be installed, transfer the valves, camshaft and spark plugs to the new head.

Installation

1. Position a new cylinder head gasket on the block.
2. Position the cylinder head and camshaft assembly on the block. Install the bolts finger tight, then torque according to specifications.
3. Set the crankshaft at TDC and be sure that the camshaft drive gear and distributor are positioned correctly.
4. Install the camshaft drive belt and release the tensioner. Rotate the crankshaft two full turns to remove all slack from the belt. The timing marks should again be aligned. Tighten the tensioner lockbolt and pivot bolt.
5. Install the camshaft drive belt cover.
6. Apply sealer to the water outlet and new gasket, and install.
7. Install the intake and exhaust manifolds.
8. Adjust the valve clearance.
9. Install a new valve cover gasket and install the valve cover.
10. Install the air cleaner and crankcase ventilation hose.
11. Refill the cooling system.

Valves

Removal

Valve removal and cylinder head service are covered in the Engine Rebuilding Section.

Rocker Arm

Removal

1. Remove the air cleaner and valve rocker cover.
2. Rotate the crankshaft to bring the heel (low side) of the camshaft lobe next to the rocker arm being replaced.
3. Remove the rocker arm retaining spring.
4. Depress the valve spring just enough to remove the rocker arm.

Installation

1. Position the rocker arm on the valve and adjustment screw.
2. Secure the rocker arm to the adjustment screw with the retaining spring.
3. Adjust the valve clearance.
4. Install the rocker cover and air cleaner. Do not forget to connect the crankcase ventilation hose.

Valve Clearance

Adjust

1. Remove the air cleaner and valve rocker arm cover.
2. Rotate the crankshaft until the toe (high point) of No. 1 camshaft lobe is in the uppermost position.
3. Check the clearance between the cam lobe and rocker arm. Intake valves should show a clearance of .008″, while exhaust valve clearance should be .010″. NOTE: *Valve clearance may be checked on a hot or cold engine.*

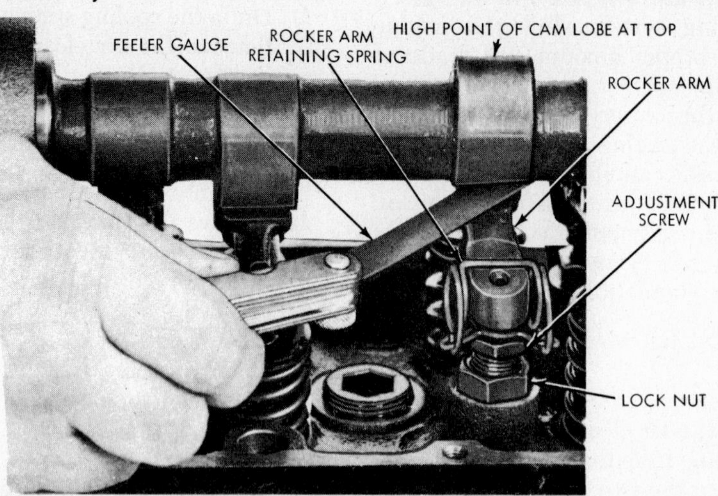

Adjusting valve clearance—2,000 cc. engine

4. If the clearance is not as specified, loosen the locknut and turn the adjusting screw to obtain the specified clearance. When the proper clearance is obtained, tighten the locknut.
5. Repeat the above procedure for all valves.
6. Clean away all old gasket material and install a new gasket. Install the valve cover with the two screws with rubber coated washers at the front and vertical attaching points.
7. Install and connect the air cleaner.

Camshaft, Auxiliary Shaft and Timing Belt

Removal

1. Rotate the crankshaft until No. 1 cylinder is at TDC.
2. Remove the cover from the camshaft drive belt.
3. Loosen the drive belt tensioner adjustment and force the tensioner toward the exhaust manifold side of the engine. Tighten the adjustment bolt again.
4. Remove the belt from the sprockets. NOTE: *Do not rotate the crankshaft or camshaft after the drive belt is removed. Any rotation will alter valve timing.*

Installation

1. Be sure that the valve timing marks are properly aligned.
2. Place the belt over the sprockets and loosen the tensioner to put tension on the belt. Rotate the belt two full turns to remove slack from the belt. The timing marks should be aligned after two complete crankshaft revolutions.
3. Tighten the tensioner adjustment bolt.
4. Install the camshaft drive belt cover.
5. Run the engine and check the ignition timing.

Camshaft

Removal

1. Position No. 1 cylinder at TDC.
2. Remove the air cleaner and the rocker cover.
3. Remove the camshaft drive belt.
4. Remove the rocker arms from the cylinder head.
5. Remove the camshaft gear mounting bolt. Slide off the camshaft gear and belt guide plate.
6. Remove the camshaft thrust plate from the rear of the cylinder head and remove the camshaft. Be sure that the bearings are not damaged during the removal process.

Installation

1. Oil the camshaft journals with heavy engine oil MS, and install the camshaft in the head.
2. Insert the camshaft thrust washer.
3. Install the camshaft gear and check the camshaft end-play, which must be .0025″-.0075″.
4. Install the valve rocker arms.
5. Be sure that the timing marks are aligned, and install the camshaft drive belt.
6. Check and adjust the valves.
7. Install the drive belt cover, valve rocker cover and air cleaner.
8. Run the engine and time the ignition.

Auxiliary Shaft

Removal

1. Remove the camshaft drive belt cover.
2. Remove the drive belt and auxiliary shaft sprocket.
3. Remove the distributor and fuel pump.
4. Remove the auxiliary shaft cover and thrust plate.
5. Withdraw the auxiliary shaft from the block.

Installation

1. Slide the auxiliary shaft into the husing and insert the thrust plate to hold the shaft.
2. Install a new gasket and auxiliary shaft cover.
3. Fit a new gasket to the fuel pump and install the pump.
4. Insert the distributor and install the auxiliary shaft sprocket.
5. Align the timing marks and install the drive belt.
6. Install the drive belt cover.
7. Check the ignition timing.

Oil Seals

The cylinder front cover, camshaft and auxiliary shaft seals are replaced in the same manner after removing the respective gear.

Crankshaft Oil Seal

Removal

1. Remove the alternator drive belt.
2. Remove the crankshaft pulley from the crankshaft.
3. Remove the camshaft drive belt.
4. Slide the drive belt sprocket and belt guide off the crankshaft. It may have to be removed with a gear puller.
5. Remove the old oil seal.

Installation

1. Install a new seal.
2. Slide the drive belt sprocket guide plate onto the crankshaft, followed by the sprocket (large chamfer toward the engine) and the crankshaft pulley.
3. Install the camshaft drive belt, making sure that the timing marks are aligned.
4. Install the drive belt cover.
5. Install the alternator drive belt.
6. Check the ignition timing.

Lubrication

Lubrication is of the force feed type using a full flow oil filter. The five crankshaft main bearings, camshaft bearings and auxiliary shaft bearings are in direct connection with the main oil gallery. Connecting rod bearings are supplied by the front and rear main bearings, through inclined passages. A squirt hole in each connecting rod crankpin supplies oil to the piston thrust side.

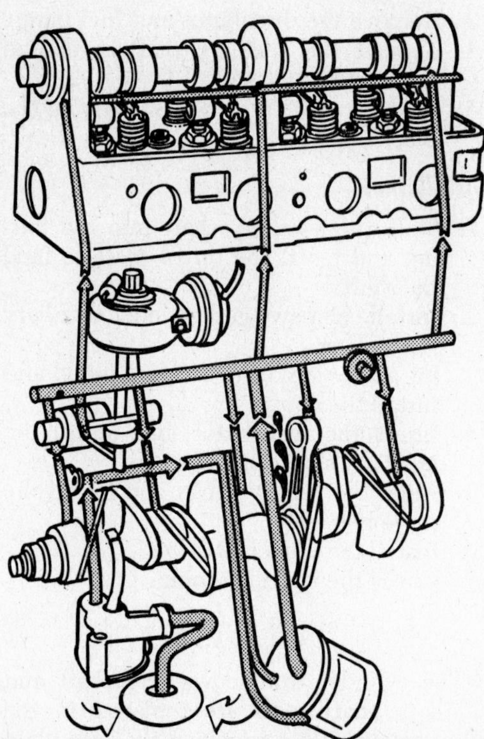

2,000 cc. engine lubrication system

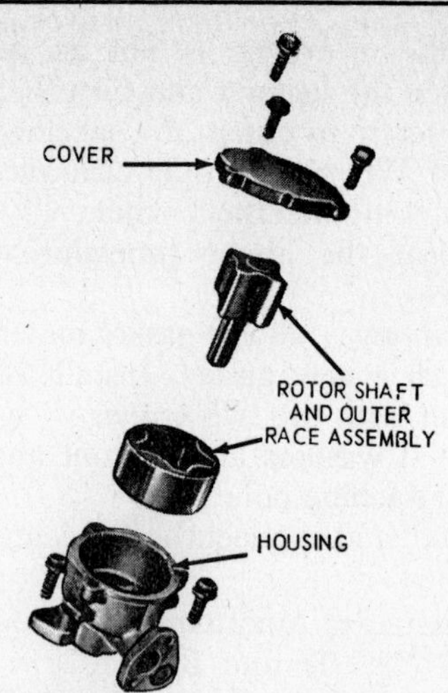

Exploded view of oil pump—2,000 cc. engine

Oil Filter

There are no maintenance procedures associated with the oil filter other than a regular replacement at the time of oil change. When installing the oil filter, coat the gasket with oil and hand tighten the filter until it contacts the adapter face. Tighten it 1/2 turn farther.

Oil Pan Removal

1. Drain the crankcase.
2. Remove the oil dipstick and the flywheel housing inspection cover.
3. Disconnect the steering cable from the rack and pinion.
4. Disconnect the rack and pinion from the crossmember to provide clearance.
5. Remove the oil pan and gasket.

Oil Pan Installation

1. Clean the gasket surfaces of the block and oil pan. Be sure to clean the seal retainer grooves in the cylinder front cover and rear main bearing cap.
2. The oil pan has a two piece gasket. Coat the oil pan surface and gasket with an oil resistant sealer. Position the gaskets on the cylinder block.
3. Install the rear seal on the rear main bearing cap. Coat all seal joints with sealer.
4. Position the oil pan and torque the bolts to 4-6 ft. lbs.

5. Position the rack and pinion and secure it to the crossmember.
6. Connect the steering cable to the rack and pinion.
7. Fill the crankcase with 5 qts. of oil and run the engine, checking for leaks.

Oil Pump Removal

1. Remove the oil pan.
2. Remove the two retaining bolts and remove the oil pump and tube assembly.

Oil Pump Disassembly

1. Separate the pick-up tube and screen from the body.
2. Remove the three screws and the cover.
3. Lift the rotor assembly from the housing.

Oil Pump Assembly

1. Check the inside of the pump housing and outer race for wear. Check the mating surface of the pump cover for wear.
2. Install the inner rotor, outer race and shaft assembly. The identification mark on the rotor and outer race must face the bottom of the pump. NOTE: *Rotor and outer race may only be replaced as a set.*
3. Measure the outer race to housing clearance (.005″-.011″) and the rotor end-play (.001″-.004″). If these measurements do not conform to specifications, replace the rotor and outer race assembly.
4. Install the cover.
5. Install a new gasket and the oil intake tube on the pump and install the oil pump.

Oil Pump Installation

1. Installation is the reverse of removal. NOTE: *Prime the oil pump by filling with oil and rotating shaft until oil emerges from outlet.*

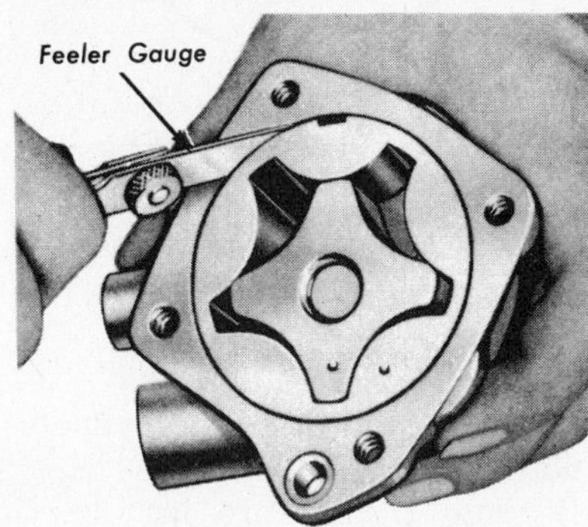

Checking outer race to housing clearance on 2,000 cc. oil pump

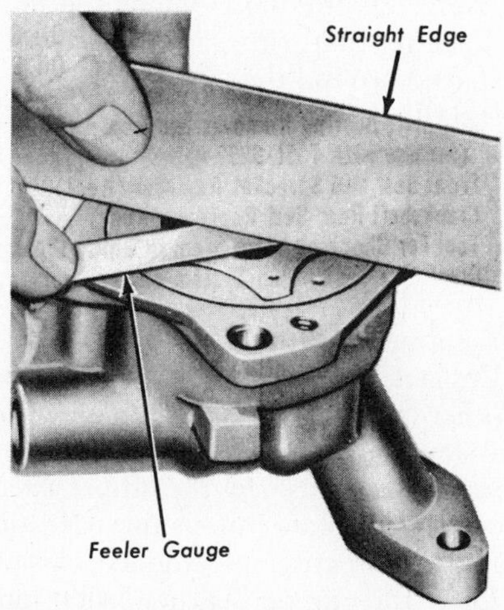

Checking rotor end-play on 2,000 cc. oil pump

Pistons, Connecting Rods and Main Bearings

Pistons and Connecting Rods Removal

1. Drain the cooling system and the crankcase.
2. Remove the cylinder head and manifold assemblies as a unit.
3. Remove the oil pan and oil pump.
4. Turn the crankshaft until the piston to be removed is at the bottom of its stroke.
5. Place a cloth on the head of the piston being serviced and ridge (deposits) at the upper end of the cylinder bore, using a ridge reamer. Follow the manufacturer's instructions. NOTE: *Never remove more than 1/32″ from the ring travel area, when removing ridges.*
6. Make certain that all connecting rod caps are marked, to facilitate installation in the original position.
7. Remove the connecting rod cap.
8. Push the connecting rod and piston out through the top of the cylinder with the handle end of a hammer. Be careful not to damage the cylinder wall or crankshaft journal.

Connecting Rod Bearing Replacement

1. Remove the bearing inserts from the rod and bearing cap.

2. Be sure that the bearing inserts and the bearing bore in the connecting rod and cap are clean. Foreign material under the bearing insert will cause premature bearing failure.
3. Clean the crankshaft journal.
4. Install the bearing inserts in the cap and rod with the tangs fitted to the slots provided.
5. Pull the rod down firmly on the crankshaft journal. NOTE: *Connecting rods and bearing caps are numbered (1-4 beginning at front of engine). Cap and rod number must be on same side when installed.*
6. Since connecting rod bearings are selectively fitted, it will be necessary to check the clearance using Plastigage (available from local parts dealers).
7. Place a piece of Plastigage across the full width of the bearing cap about 1/4″ off center. Install the bearing cap and torque bolts to specification. NOTE: *Do not turn crankshaft or connecting rod with Plastigage in place.*
8. Remove the cap and use the Plastigage scale to check the width of compressed Plastigage at widest and narrowest point. The difference between the two is the journal taper.
9. If clearance exceeds specifications, try a .002″ undersize bearing half, in combination with a standard bearing half. NOTE: *Always install the undersize bearing half on the cylinder block side.*
10. If this combination does not bring clearance within specified limits, refinish the crankshaft journal and install under size bearings. NOTE: *When replacing standard bearings with new bearings it is good practice to obtain minimum specified clearance.*
    NOTE: *Be sure to check crankshaft end-play (.004″-.008″) and correct, if necessary, with thrust washers.*
11. After the bearing has been fitted, apply a light coat of engine oil to bearings and journal.
12. Install the bearing cap and torque bolts to specification.
13. Replace the oil pan and oil pump.
14. Replace the cylinder head and manifold assembly.
15. Fill the crankcase and cooling system.

Pistons

The following information should be adhered to when fitting pistons.

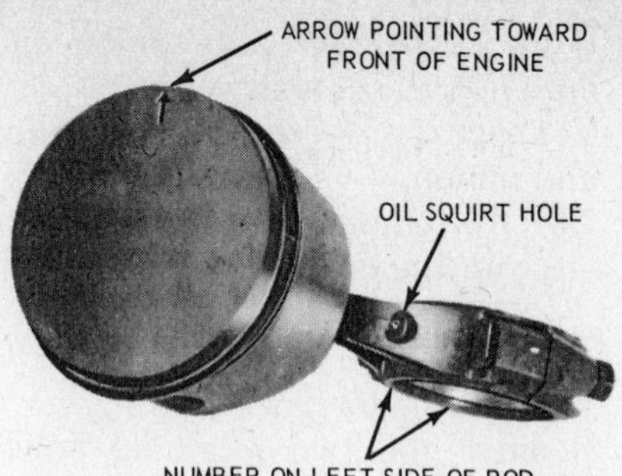

Correct position of piston and connecting rod

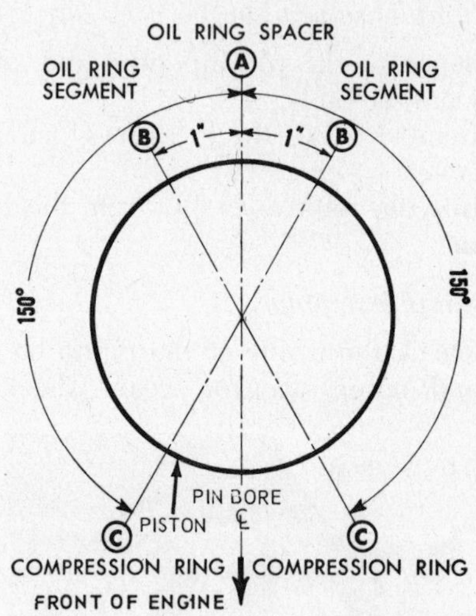

Correct piston ring end gap position

1. Oil the piston rings and cylinder walls with light engine oil.
2. Be sure pistons are installed in the same cylinder from which they were removed.
3. Install the piston with the arrow in the piston toward the front of the engine.
4. Be sure that ring gaps are properly spaced around the piston.
5. Install a piston ring compressor and push the piston into the cylinder with a wooden hammer handle.

Main Bearing Replacement

1. Drain the crankcase.
2. Remove the oil pan and oil pump.
3. Replace one bearing at a time, leaving other bearings securely in place.
4. Remove the main bearing cap.
5. Insert "rollpins" in the upper bearing oil hole. Rotate the crankshaft slowly in the direction of engine rotation to force the upper bearing insert out of the block.

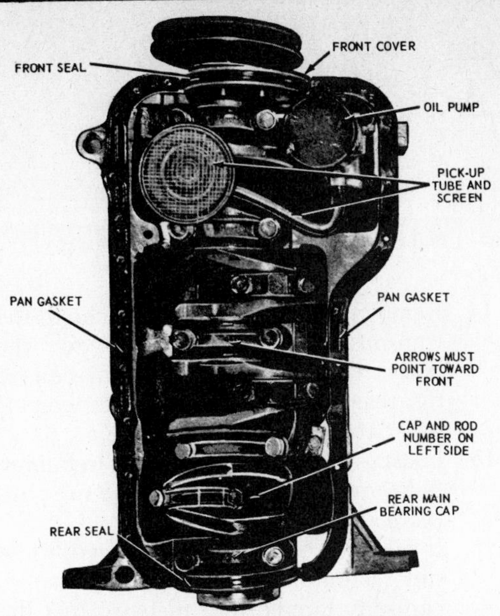

2,000 cc. engine as seen from lower end

6. Clean and inspect the crankshaft journals and thrust washers.
7. Selectively fit the new bearing to the minimum specified clearance. Use the same procedure detailed under connecting rod bearing replacement.
8. When installing the bearing, position a jack under the counterweight adjoining the bearing being serviced. Support the crankshaft so that its weight will not compress the Plastigage and give a false reading.
9. To install the upper main bearing shell, lubricate the bearing with heavy engine oil MS. Place the plain end of the bearing over the shaft on the locking tang side of the block. Partially insert the bearing so that the "rollpins" can be inserted. Rotate the crankshaft in the direction of engine rotation until the bearing is seated. Remove the tool.
10. Coat the lower bearing insert with heavy engine oil MS and fit it to the bearing cap. Install the cap and torque to specification. NOTE: *Be sure to check crankshaft end-play (.004"-.008")*
11. Install the oil pan and oil pump and fill the crankcase with oil.

Clutch and Transmission

Clutch

1,600 CC. AND 2,000 CC.

The clutch used is 7.5" diameter unit using a diaphragm spring pressure plate. The clutch is cable activated and operates in the conventional manner.

Adjustment

1. Remove release lever boot and lubricate the ball end of the cable with MS_2 grease. Replace boot.
2. Loosen locknut and, with the clutch pedal pulled back to its stop on the pedal bracket, adjust the nut to give 0.138-0.144" clearance between the nut and the shoulder of the fitting.

NOTE: *This should result in 1/2-3/4" free-play at clutch pedal.*

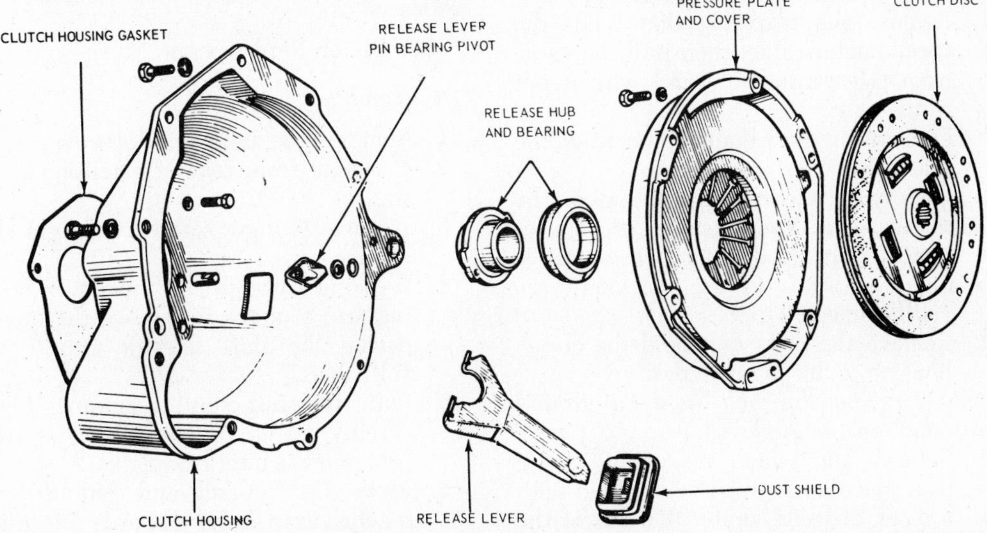

Clutch components—1,600 cc. engine

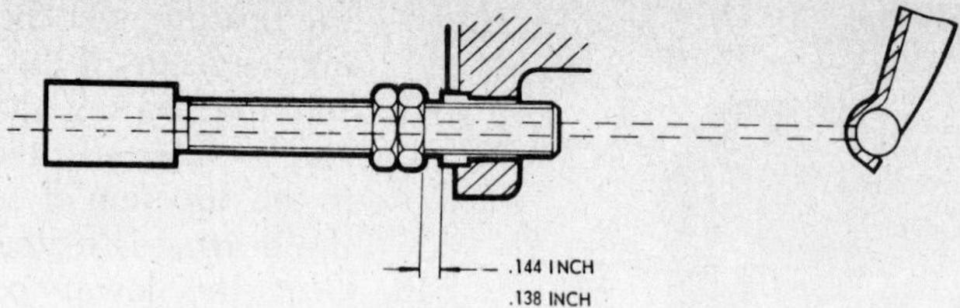

Clutch adjustment—1,600 cc.

3. Tighten the locknut, then grease the pedal end of the cable.

Replacement

1. Lift the hood and disconnect the battery cables.
2. Disconnect throttle linkage at the carburetor.
3. Loosen gearshift knob locknut, then remove knob and locknut.
4. Remove the seven screws that hold the console to the floor, then remove the console.
5. Bend up the lock tab and unscrew the plastic nut, then remove gearshift lever.
6. Jack up the car at all corners and support on axle stands.
7. Matchmark the rear U-joint where it connects to the pinion flange, then remove the four bolts and separate the U-joint.
8. Remove the two bolts that hold the center driveshaft bearing carrier, then slide the driveshaft to the rear to pull the front splined yoke from the transmission extension housing.

NOTE: *Plug the opening in the transmission with rags to prevent oil loss.*

9. Remove the snap-ring that holds the speedometer cable, then pull the cable from the transmission and wire it out of the way.
10. Disconnect the exhaust pipe from the manifold.
11. Disconnect the clutch cable from the release lever, then remove the starter motor bolts and swing the starter motor away from the working area (still connected to its wires).
12. Remove the bolts that hold the clutch housing to the engine block.

NOTE: *The top bolt holds a ground strap that must be replaced.*

13. Remove the clutch inspection cover, then place a screw jack, insulated with a block of wood, under the rear of the engine.
14. Remove the four bolts that hold the transmission crossmembers to the body, then slide the transmission to the rear (while supporting its weight) and detach it from the engine.
15. Loosen the six pressure plate retaining bolts, evenly, then remove the pressure plate and clutch disc.
16. If pilot bearing is to be removed, use a slide hammer. New bearing must be carefully tapped into place so that the bearing is seated 0.156″-0.175″ below crankshaft flange level.
17. Place new clutch disc in position on flywheel, after coating splines with MS_2 grease, and center it using a dummy pilot shaft or old transmission mainshaft. Place pressure plate on flywheel and install bolts, tightening them evenly all around to 12-15 ft. lbs.
18. Remove pilot shaft, then install clutch housing by reversing Steps 1-14.

NOTE: *The two lower clutch housing bolts are longer than the others. Tighten all clutch housing bolts to 40-45 ft. lbs.*

Transmission

1,600 CC.

Removal

See Clutch Replacement.

Disassembly

1. Remove four bolts and top cover plate.
2. Pry plug from rear of extension housing.
3. Remove plunger screw from right side of case.
4. Working through the top cover opening, use a punch to remove the pin securing the shift selector arm to the shift shaft.
5. Pull the shift shaft rearward, being careful not to drop the shift selector arm and the interlock plate.
6. Move the 1st-2nd and 3rd-4th gear synchronizer hubs toward the input shaft bearing.

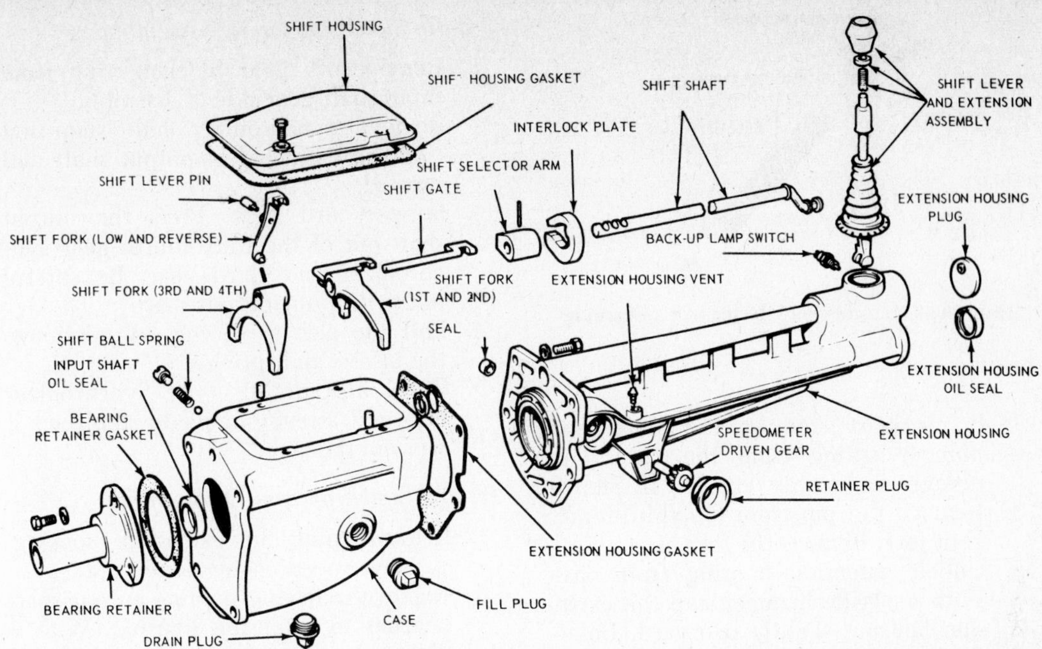

Exploded view of Dagenham transmission external parts

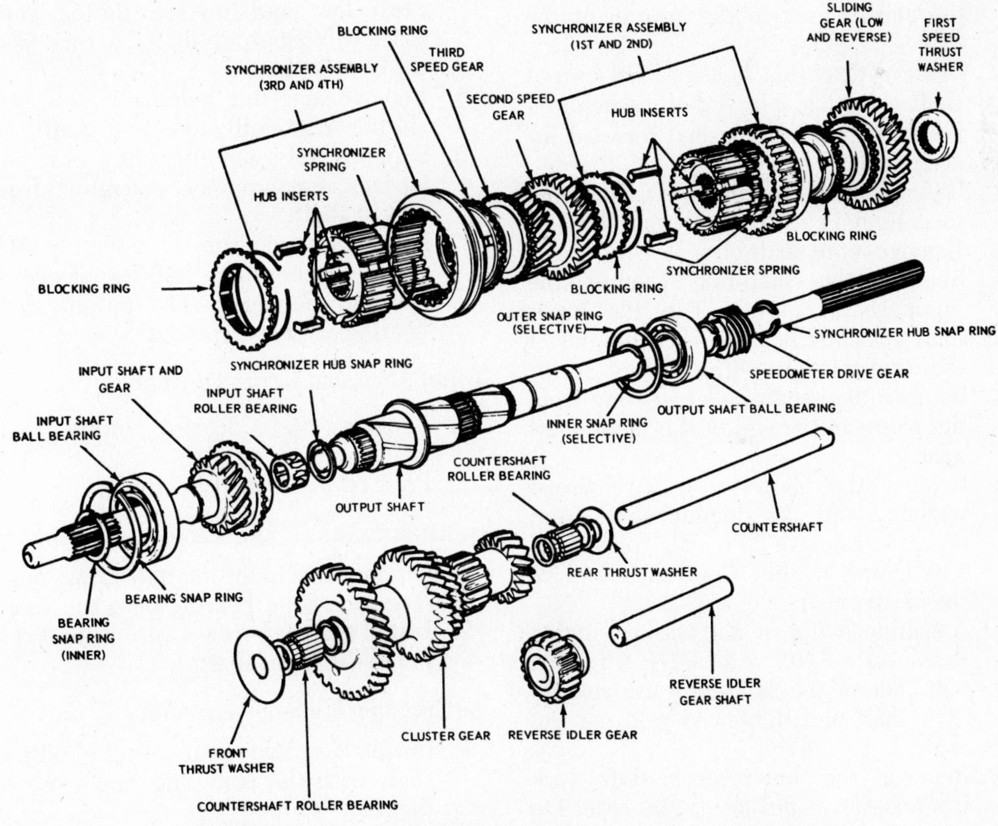

Exploded view of Dagenham transmission internal components

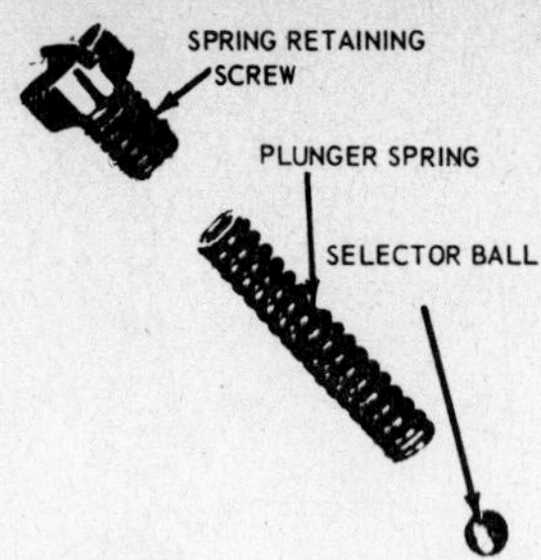

Dagenham transmission selector ball and spring

7. If necessary, remove the shift shaft plunger spring from the case. The plunger screw was removed in Step 3.
8. Remove the pin from the third-fourth shift fork. Remove the fork.
9. Unbolt extension housing from case. With a plastic hammer, tap the extension housing slightly rearward. Rotate the housing until the countershaft lines up with the notch in the housing flange.
10. Tap the countershaft rearward with a brass drift until it is just clear of the front of the case. Push the countershaft out with a dummy shaft. Lower the cluster gear to the bottom of the case.
11. Remove extension housing and output shaft assembly. The 3rd-4th synchronizer sleeve must be pushed forward for clearance.
12. Unbolt front bearing retainer from case. Remove retainer and gasket.
13. Remove input shaft oil seal.
14. Remove the snap-ring around the input shaft bearing. Tap the input shaft gear and bearing assembly out of the transmission with a brass drift. Remove the needle roller bearing from the recess in the end of the input shaft gear.
15. Remove the cluster gear, two thrust washers, and the dummy shaft from the case. Remove 20 needle rollers and a retaining washer from each end of the cluster gear.
16. Assemble a nut, a flat washer, and a sleeve on a 5/16″ x 24 UNF threaded bolt. Screw the bolt into the reverse idler shaft and tighten to pull out the shaft.
17. Remove the low-reverse shift fork from the lever pin inside the case. Do not remove the pin.

3rd-4th Synchronizer—Disassembly

1. Remove 4th gear blocking ring from input shaft gear side of assembly.
2. Remove synchronizer hub snap-ring from forward end of output shaft and discard.
3. Support 3rd gear. Press the output shaft out of the third-fourth gear synchronizer and third gear. Be careful not to drop the output shaft.
4. Pull the sleeve off the hub. Remove the inserts and springs.
5. Check all parts for wear. Synchronizer hub and sleeve should be replaced if worn or damaged.

1st-2nd Synchronizer—Disassembly

1. Remove plug in extension housing. Remove speedometer driven gear.
2. Remove snap-ring holding output shaft bearing to extension housing. With a plastic hammer, tap output shaft assembly out of housing.
3. Remove snap-ring holding speedometer drive gear. Pull off gear. Remove snap-ring holding output shaft bearing.
4. Support low and reverse sliding gear. Press low and reverse sliding gear, spacer, and output shaft bearing from the output shaft.
5. Remove snap-ring holding 1st-2nd synchronizer assembly to output shaft.
6. Support 2nd gear. Press 2nd gear and 1st-2nd synchronizer assembly from output shaft.
7. Dismantle synchronizer assembly. Replace synchronizer hub or sleeve if worn or damaged. The output shaft bearing must be replaced.

Input Shaft and Gear—Disassembly

1. Remove and discard input shaft snap-ring.
2. Press off input shaft bearing.

INPUT SHAFT AND GEAR—ASSEMBLY

1. Support the input shaft bearing inner race. Press the bearing onto the shaft.
2. Install the snap-ring securing the bearing to the input shaft.

1st-2nd Synchronizer—Assembly

1. Install the 2nd gear on the output shaft with the cone and dog teeth to the rear.
2. Slide the synchronizer sleeve over the

Replacing 1st-2nd synchronizer assembly (Dagenham transmission)

hub. Place an insert in each of the three slots.

3. Install synchronizer springs as for 3rd-4th synchronizer assembly.
4. Install a blocking ring to cone on 2nd gear.
5. Install synchronizer assembly on output shaft with the gear teeth on the periphery of the synchronizer sleeve forward. Slide low and reverse sliding gear to the rear of the synchronizer hub.
6. Support the sliding gear. Press synchronizer assembly onto output shaft as far as possible.
7. Secure the synchronizer assembly with snap-ring.
8. Place a blocking ring on 1st gear side of 1st-2nd synchronizer assembly on output shaft. Install first gear, cone side forward.
9. Place the spacer with the larger diameter adjacent to first gear.
10. Select a snap-ring of the proper size to hold the output shaft bearing into the bearing recess with no end float.
11. Position the selected snap-ring loosely on the output shaft next to the spacer.
12. Support the bearing inner race. Press the bearing onto the shaft.
13. Select the thickest snap-ring that fits the groove to hold the bearing to the output shaft.
14. Locate output shaft ball bearing in shaft indent, push speedometer drive gear onto output shaft. Install new snap-ring.
15. Heat the end of the extension housing. Do not use a torch. A pan of hot water is recommended.
16. Install the output shaft into the extension housing. Install the snap-ring securing the output shaft bearing to the housing.
17. Replace the speedometer driven gear. Install a new plug, using sealer.

3rd-4th Synchronizer—Assembly

1. Slide gear over hub. Locate an insert in each slot.
2. Install a synchronizer spring inside the sleeve beneath the inserts; the spring tang should fit into an insert. Install the other spring on the opposite side, fitting the tang into the same insert. When viewed from the edge, the springs should run in opposite directions.
3. Place the 3rd gear on the output shaft with the dog teeth forward. Assemble the blocking ring on the 3rd gear cone.
4. Place the synchronizer assembly on the output shaft with the boss forward.

Replacing output shaft bearing (Dagenham transmission)

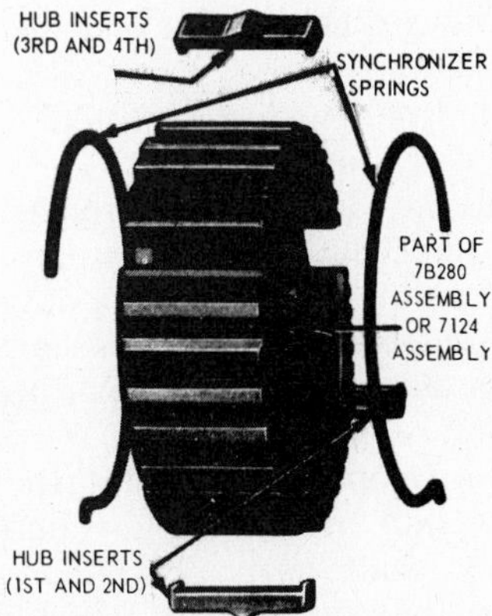

Installation position of synchronizer springs (Dagenham transmission)

5. Support the hub. Press the hub on the output shaft and install a new snap-ring.

Transmission—Assembly

1. Slide the low-reverse lever onto the lever pin inside the case.
2. Push the idler shaft into the case. Place the reverse idler gear on the shaft. Locate the low-reverse lever in the gear groove. Tap the reverse idler shaft into position with a soft hammer.
3. Slide a dummy shaft into the cluster gear. Push a retainer washer into the gear bore. Grease and install 20 needle rollers and the second retaining washer. Install the washers and rollers at the other end of the gear. Grease and install the thrust washers with their convex side into the gear recess.
4. Place the cluster gear in the bottom of the case. Position the thrust washers with the flat upward.
5. Place the input shaft and gear in the case. Using a brass drift, tap bearing outer race into place. Be careful not to damage the dog teeth on the input shaft gear with the cluster gear. Install the bearing snap-ring.
6. Place the input shaft needle bearing in the input shaft gear recess.
7. Drive a new oil seal into the input shaft retainer. Cover the input shaft splines. Install a new gasket on the transmission front face. Check that the retainer oil groove is lined up with the oil passage in the case. Coat the bolts with sealer and install them with lock-washers.
8. Locate the fourth gear blocking ring on the input shaft gear cone.
9. Install a new oil seal in the shift shaft aperture. Drive the seal in with a socket.
10. Install a new sealer coated gasket to the extension housing.
11. Pull the 3rd-4th synchronizer sleeve forward. Slide the extension housing and output shaft into position. Align the cutaway on the extension housing with the countershaft aperture in the rear face of the case.
12. Using loops of cord, lift the cluster gear into mesh with the output and input shaft gears. Take care not to drop the countershaft thrust washers.
13. Tap the countershaft into place, driving out the dummy shaft, ensuring that the lug on the rear of the countershaft fits into the recess on the extension housing flange.
14. Push the extension housing onto the transmission case. Apply sealer to bolts. Torque to 30-35 ft. lbs.
15. Replace both shift forks. Secure 3rd-4th fork with a new pin.
16. Position shift forks to synchronizer sleeves. Move synchronizer hubs into neutral positions.
17. Grease shift shaft oil seal in rear of case. Slide shift shaft through extension housing. Position shift selector arm and interlock plate so that interlock plate locates in cutouts in shift forks. Pass the shift shaft through the shift selector arm and forks until the pin holes are aligned.
18. Replace the plunger ball and spring. Replace the retaining screw, using sealer.
19. Install the pin through the shift selector arm and shift shaft.
20. Apply sealer to plug. Tap plug into rear of extension housing.
21. Install top cover and gasket.
22. Refill transmission with 2.8 pints SAE 80 oil.

2,000 cc.

REMOVAL

See 1,600 cc. Clutch Replacement.

Disassembly

1. Remove the clutch release bearing and lever.
2. Remove the clutch housing.
3. Drain the lubricant and remove the cover and gasket from the case.

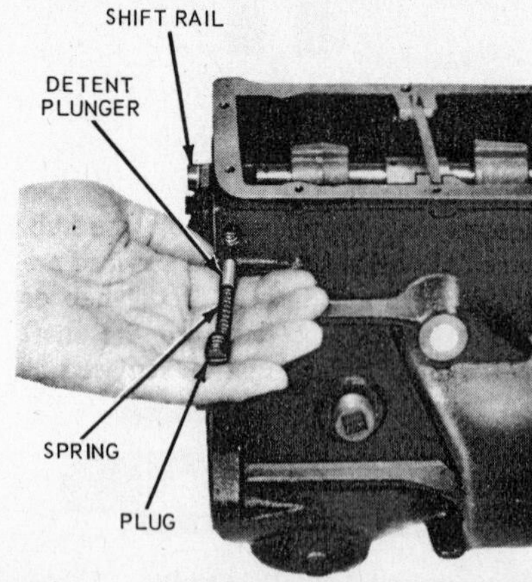

Removing detent plunger spring and plug

4. Remove the threaded plug, spring and shift rail detent plunger from the front of the case.
5. Drive the access plug from the rear of the case.
6. Remove the interlock pin retaining plate from the case and remove the interlock plate.
7. Remove the rollpin from the selector lever arm.
8. Tap the front end of the shift rail to displace the plug at the rear of the extension housing. Withdraw the shift rail from the extension housing and case.
9. Remove the selector arm and shift fork from the case.
10. Unbolt the extension housing. Tap the housing with a plastic hammer to loosen it from the case, so that it can be rotated.
11. Rotate the housing to align the countershaft with the cutaway in the extension housing. With a brass drift, drive the countershaft rearward until the countershaft clears the front of the case. Install a dummy shaft until the countershaft gear can be lowered to the bottom of the case. Remove the countershaft.
12. Remove the extension housing and mainshaft from the case as an assembly.
13. Remove the input shaft and bearing retainer from the case as an assembly.
14. Remove the reverse idler gear shaft from the rear of the case. Remove the reverse idler gear.
15. Remove the bearing retaining washers, bearings (19 from each end), dummy shaft and spacer from the countershaft gear.
16. Remove the input shaft gear bearing retainer and pilot bearing.
17. Do not remove the ball bearing from the input shaft unless replacement is necessary. To remove the ball bearing, remove the snap-ring from the input shaft and remove the ball bearing by pressing it out.
18. Pry the input shaft seal from the bearing retainer.
19. Lift the 4th gear blocker ring from the front of the output shaft.
20. Remove the snap-ring from the forward end of the output shaft and discard it.
21. Place the output shaft and extension housing in a press. Press the output shaft from the 3rd-4th speed synchronizer assembly and 3rd gear, while supporting the extension housing from below. Remove the snap-ring and washer and slide the blocker ring and 2nd gear from the output shaft. Discard the snap-ring.

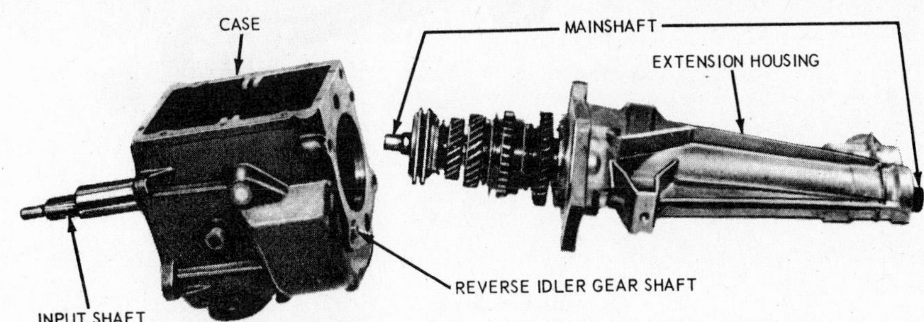

Removing or installing extension housing and mainshaft

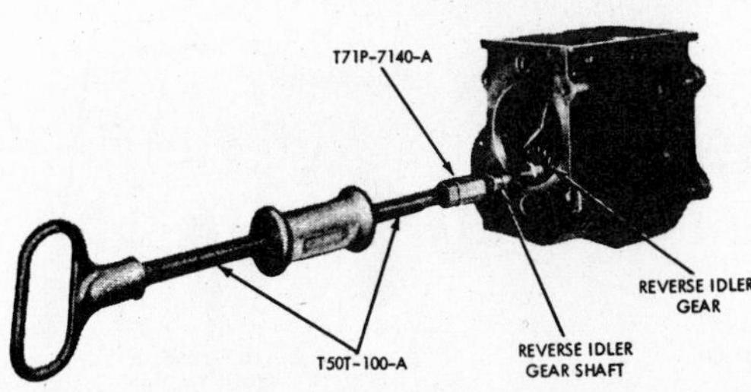

Removing reverse idler gear shaft

22. Pull the synchronizer sleeve from the hub and remove the inserts and springs.
23. Remove the snap-ring retaining the output shaft bearing in the extension housing. Measure the snap-ring thickness, to facilitate assembly.
24. Tap the output shaft assembly out of the extension housing with a plastic hammer.

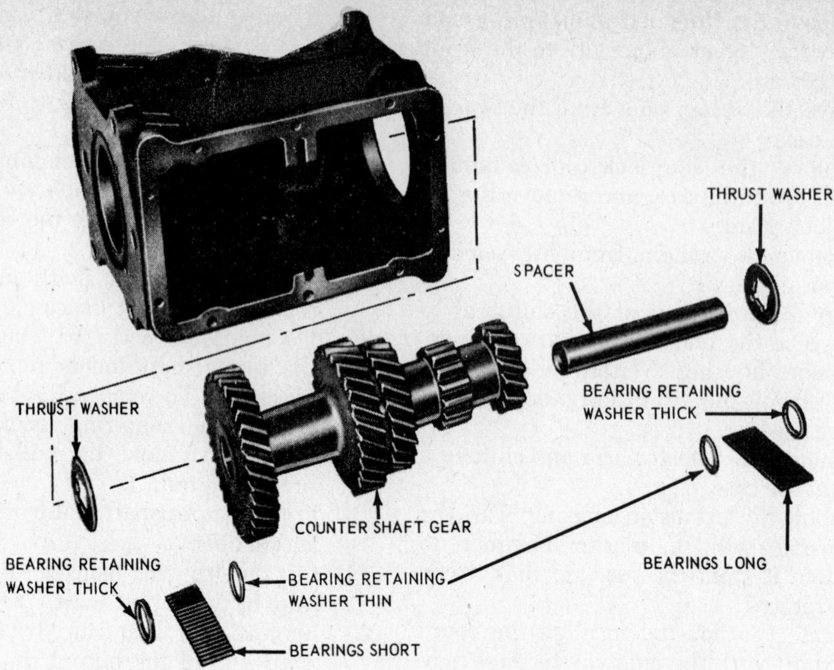

Exploded view of countershaft

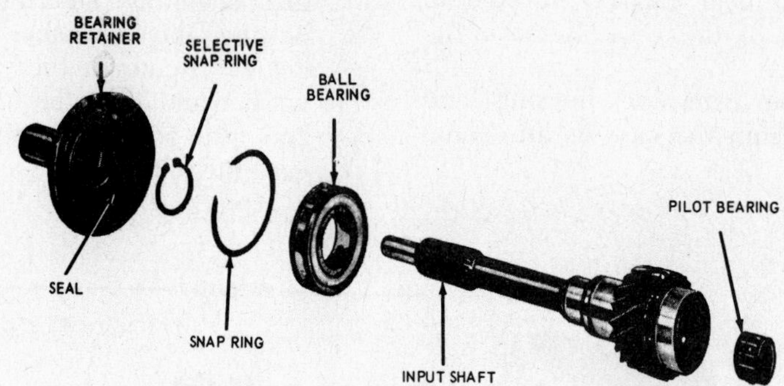

Exploded view of input shaft

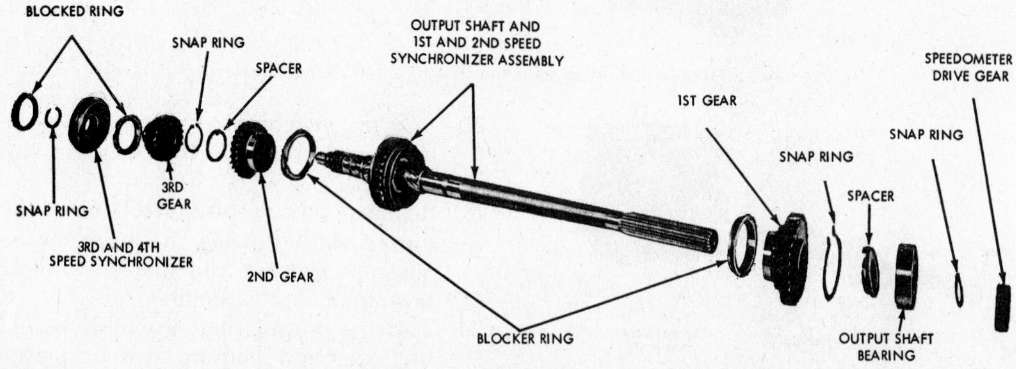

Exploded view of output shaft

25. The 1st and 2nd speed synchronizer is serviced as an assembly. No attempt should be made to separate the hub from the shaft. The sleeves, springs and inserts may be removed from the hub. If the hub or sleeve is worn or damaged, the shaft and synchronizer must be replaced as an assembly.
26. Use a 9/16″ socket and extension to drive the shift rail bushing from the rear of the extension housing. This bushing need not be removed if in good condition.
27. Pry the shift rail seal from the rear of the transmission case.
28. Remove the remaining shift linkage from the case.

Assembly

1. Seat the new shift rail seal in the rear of the transmission case.
2. If the shift rail bushing was removed, drive a new bushing into place with a 9/16″ socket and extension.
3. If the 1st or 2nd speed synchronizer was dismantled, slide the sleeve over the hub, making sure that the shift fork groove is toward the front of the shaft. The sleeve and hub are select fit and must be assembled with the etch mark in the same relative position. Locate an insert in each of the three slots cut in the hub. If a new synchronizer and shaft is being used, clean all traces of preservative from the component parts. Oil all parts at the time of assembly. Install the spring inside the synchronizer sleeve beneath the insert. The tab on the end of the spring must locate in the section of an insert. Fit the other spring to the opposite side of the synchronizer unit. Be sure that both springs locate in the same insert and are installed in the same rotational direction. Looking down on the synchronizer the tab end of one spring should be aligned with the tab of the spring on the opposite side.
4. Assemble a blocker ring to the 1st gear side of the 1st-2nd speed synchronizer. Apply chassis grease or equivalent to the cone surface of 1st gear and slide 1st gear onto the output shaft, so that cone surface engages the blocker ring.
5. Position the spacer on the shaft with the larger diameter toward the rear of the shaft.
6. A new snap-ring must be used to retain the output shaft bearing in the extension housing. The thickness of the snap-ring must be sufficient to remove all end-play from the bearing. (Normally, a snap-ring of original thickness will accomplish this.) Snap-rings are available in the following thicknesses:

Snap-ring Thickness	*Identification*
.0679″	Color coded—copper
.0689″	Letter—W
.0699″	Letter—V
.0709″	Letter—U
.0719″	None
.0728″	Color coded—blue
.0738″	Color coded—black
.0748″	Color coded—brown

7. Position the snap-ring and bearing on the output shaft and press the bearing into place. Secure the bearing with the thickest snap-ring that will fit the groove.
8. Slide the synchronizer over the hub and locate an insert in each of three slots cut in the sleeve. The sleeve and hub are select fit, so they must be assembled with the etch marks in the same relative position. If a new synchronizer assembly is being installed, clean all parts. Be sure to remove all traces of preservative. Lightly oil all parts.
9. Assemble the synchronizer unit as described in Step 3.
10. Position 2nd gear and the blocker ring on the output shaft with the dog teeth facing rearward.
11. Position 3rd gear on the output shaft so that the gear teeth face forward. Apply chassis lubricant to the cones of the gears and assemble the blocker ring on the third gear cone.
12. Position 3rd-4th synchronizer assembly on the output shaft with the hub boss facing forward.
13. Place the entire unit in a press (extension end up) and press the synchronizer assembly on the output shaft as far as possible.
14. Secure the 3rd-4th synchronizer assembly with a snap-ring. Pull up on the assembly so that the snap-ring fits tightly in the groove.
15. Apply chassis lubricant to the gear cone and place the 4th gear blocker ring on the input shaft gear cone.
16. Press the speedometer drive gear onto

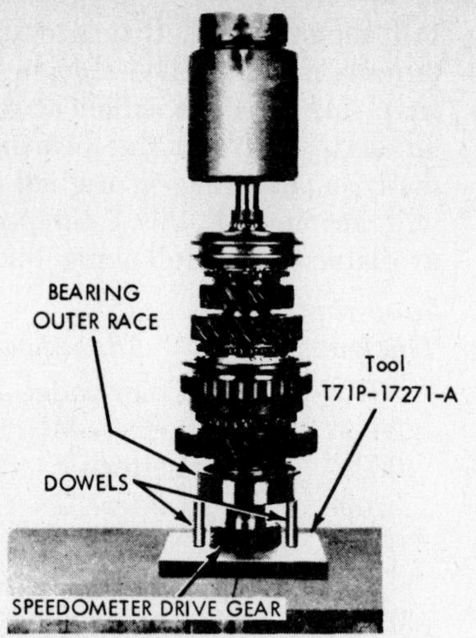

Installing speedometer drive gear

Countershaft gear removal or installation

the shaft as shown. The dowels must contact the bearing outer race to properly locate the speedometer drive gear.

17. Coat the bearing core of the extension housing with chassis grease. Install the output shaft in the extension housing. Tap the shaft with a plastic hammer, while holding the synchronizer sleeves firmly. Secure it to the extension housing with the selective snap-ring previously installed.
18. Slide the spacer and dummy shaft into the countershaft gear. Position a thin bearing retaining washer, one at each end of the dummy shaft. Coat the 38 bearings with chassis lubricant and load 19 long bearings into the small end of the gear, and 19 short bearings into the long end of the gear. Fit a thick retaining washer over each end of the dummy shaft. Coat the thrust washers with chassis lubricant and place one on each end of the dummy shaft. Make sure that the tabs are in the same relative position to engage the slots in the case when the gear is lowered into place. Loop a piece of rope over the countershaft gear as shown and lower the gear into the case, making sure the thrust washer tabs engage the slots.
19. Lubricate the reverse idler gear shaft with chassis lubricant. If the selector lever relay was removed, position it on the pivot pin. Secure the lever to the pin with a spring clip. Hold the gear in the lever with the long hub toward the rear of the case. Seat the shaft in the case with a copper hammer.
20. Install a new seal in the bearing retainer.
21. Assemble the input shaft to the transmission case, using a new O-ring. Tap the outer race of the bearing, evenly, with a copper hammer, until the snap-ring is seated. Do not tap the input shaft, since doing so might damage the bearing.

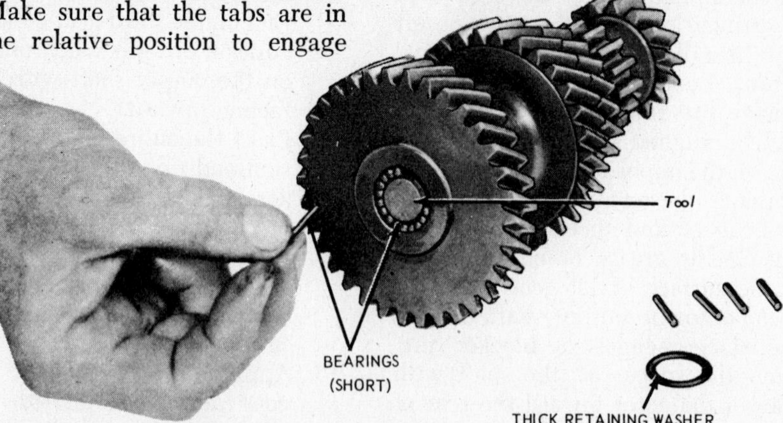

Assembling the countershaft gear

22. Slide the 3rd-4th synchronizer sleeve into 4th gear to provide clearance.
23. Place a new gasket on the extension housing.
24. Lubricate the input shaft pilot bearing and install it in the shaft.
25. Slide the extension housing and output shaft into place without disturbing the 3rd-4th synchronizer.
26. Align the cutaway in the extension housing flange with the countershaft bore in the rear of the case.
27. Lift the countershaft gear into place with the rope previously installed. Be sure that both thrust washers are in place. The flat on the countershaft should face the top of the case and be in a horizontal position. Tap the countershaft into the case with a brass hammer until the front of the shaft is flush with the case.
28. Place the shift forks in the synchronizer sleeves. Position the interlock lever and install a new retaining pin. Lubricate the shift rail oil seal and slide the shift rail through the extension housing, transmission case and 1st and 2nd speed shift fork. Position the selector arm on the rail and slide the rail through the 3rd and 4th speed shift fork until the center detent is aligned with the detent plunger bore. Install a new retaining pin in the selector arm.
29. Install the detent plunger, spring and plug.
30. Install a new access plug in the rear of the case.
31. Rotate the extension housing to align the bolt holes and install the bolts loosely. Before tightening the bolts, be sure that the shift rail slides freely. If it binds, rotate the housing slightly to free the rail and push the housing into the case. Torque the bolts to 30-35 ft. lbs.
32. Position a new oil seal so that the tension spring and sealing element lip face the front of the case.
33. Drive the seal in until it bottoms.
34. Install a new O-ring in the groove in the front of the case. Be careful the seal lip is not damaged.
35. Position the input shaft bearing retainer in the case. Be sure that the oil groove in the retainer is aligned with the oil groove in the case. Apply sealer to the attaching bolts; but do not tighten.
36. Coat the retainer with grease.
37. Install the clutch release arm and bearing.
38. Apply sealer to the new extension housing plug and install it in the housing.
39. Place a new cover gasket on the case and position the cover on the case with the vent facing the rear.
40. Install and tighten the 10 attaching bolts.

INSTALLATION

1. Installation is the reverse of removal.

Automatic Transmission (Ford C-4)

The Ford C4 automatic transmission (see illustration) is a three speed unit that provides automatic upshifts and downshifts through three forward gear ratios and also

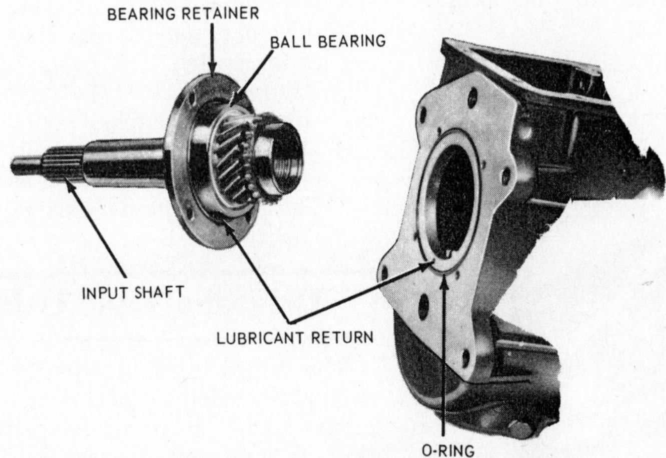

Input shaft gear installation

provides manual selection of first and second gears.

The Ford C4S semi-automatic transmission is a manually operated power shift transmission which does not require a clutch pedal. The transmission is similar to the C4 automatic transmission except for differences in the control valve body and there is no vacuum diaphragm, throttle rod, governor, and the inner and outer downshift lever assemblies.

Both transmissions consist of a torque converter, planetary gear train, two multiple disc clutches, a one-way clutch, and a hydraulic control system. The only adjustments necessary on these transmissions during normal maintenance are band adjustments on the intermediate and low-reverse bands. The transmission fluid is cooled through an oil cooler core in the radiator lower tank when a steel converter is used. If an aluminum converter is used, the transmission fluid is air-cooled.

Removal

See 1,600 cc. clutch replacement.

ADJUSTMENTS

Intermediate Band

1. Clean all the dirt from the adjusting screw and remove and discard the locknut.
2. Install a new locknut on the adjusting screw. Using the tool shown in the illustration, tighten the adjusting screw until the wrench clicks and breaks at 10 ft-lbs. torque.
3. Back off the adjusting screw *Exactly* 1 3/4 turns.
4. Hold the adjusting screw steady and tighten the locknut to the proper torque.

Low-Reverse Band

1. Clean all dirt from around the band adjusting screw, and remove and discard the locknut.

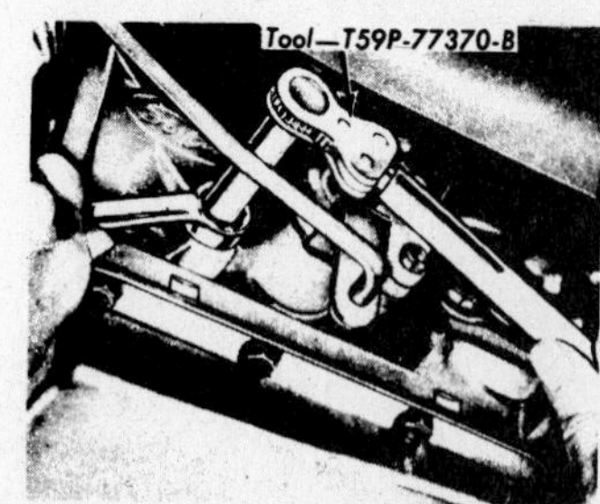

Adjusting intermediate band (Ford C4)

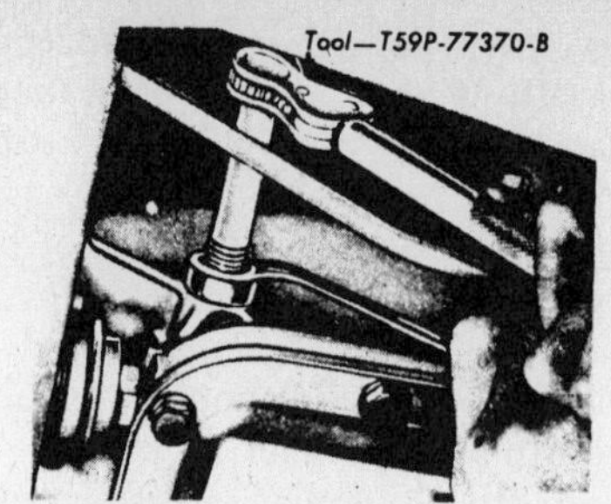

Adjusting low-reverse band (Ford C4)

2. Install a new locknut on the adjusting screw. Using the tool shown in the illustration, tighten the adjusting screw until the wrench clicks and breaks at 10 ft-lbs. torque.
3. Back off the adjusting screw *Exactly 3 full turns.*
4. Hold the adjusting screw steady and tighten the locknut.

Manual Linkage

1. Place the transmission selector lever in D.
2. Raise the vehicle and loosen the shift rod retaining nut.
3. Move the transmission manual lever to D (fourth detent position from the rear of the transmission.)
4. Fit the shift rod and torque the attaching nuts to 10-20 ft. lbs.

Neutral Start Switch

1. With the manual lever properly adjusted, loosen the two switch attaching bolts.
2. With the transmission manual lever in Neutral, rotate the switch and insert the gauge pin into the gauge pin holes in the switch. The gauge pin must be inserted a full 31/64" into the three holes of the switch. Tighten the switch attaching nuts and remove the gauge pin. Check the operation of the switch. The engine should start in Neutral or Park only.

Driveshaft and U-Joints

The Capri uses a tubular, two-piece driveshaft which is splined to the gearbox output shaft. It transmits drive through three U-joints and a center bearing, placed in front of the middle U-joint.

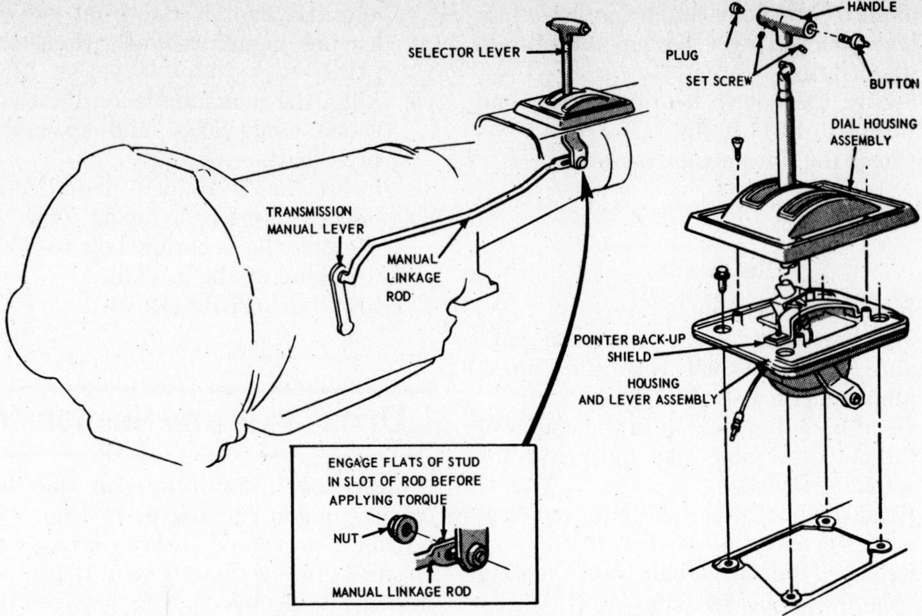

Adjusting manual linkage rod (Ford C4)

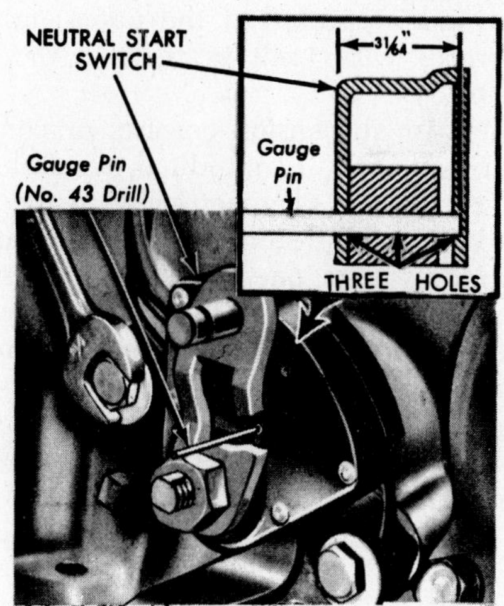

Neutral start switch adjustment (Ford C4)

Driveshaft

Removal

1. Matchmark the driveshaft and pinion flanges.
2. Remove the bolts and spring washers from the pinion flange and center bearing support.
3. Lower the driveshaft and withdraw it from the transmission.

Disassembly

1. Extract each spider bearing snap-ring and remove the bearing cups and rollers by gently tapping the yoke of each bearing.
2. Remove the spider and detach the oil seal and seal retainer from the spider journal.

Assembly

1. Fit new oil seals to the retainers and install them on the spider journals with the oil seals outwards. Locate the spider in the driveshaft yoke and install the needle rollers in each bearing cup. Pack the bearings with lithium base grease and refit the bearings, tapping them into place. Refit the other half of the joint.
2. Refit the circlips to each bearing.

Installation

1. Slide the front yoke into the gearbox and engage the mainshaft splines.
2. Lift the rear of the driveshaft and

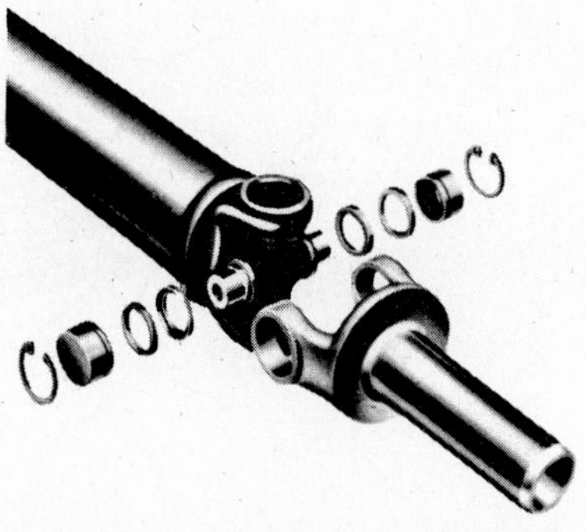

Capri universal joint—exploded view

align the matchmarks on the driveshaft and pinion flange. Torque the nuts to 43-47 ft. lbs.

3. Secure the center bearing carrier and torque to 13-17 ft. lbs.
4. Check the transmission oil level.

Center Bearing

Removal

1. Remove the driveshaft.
2. Matchmark the center universal yoke and front universal yoke for correct alignment on assembly.
3. Bend back the locktab in the center of the universal joint yoke and loosen the retaining bolt.
4. Remove the U shaped plate and separate the halves of the driveshaft.
5. Remove the driveshaft and bearing from the rubber insulator.
6. Bend back the six securing tabs and remove the rubber insulator.
7. Remove the bearing and protective caps from the driveshaft with a two legged puller.

Installation

1. Drive the bearing and protective caps onto the driveshaft with a length of suitable diameter pipe.
2. Insert the rubber insulator into the carrier with the boss upward. Bend the six tabs on the carrier over the beaded edge of the insulator.
3. Slide the carrier and rubber insulator over the bearing assembly.
4. Install the bolt, with a new locktab, into the end of the front driveshaft, leaving enough room for the U shaped plate.
5. Align the matchmarks on the two universal joint yokes, and assemble the driveshaft.
6. Insert the U shaped plate, with the smooth surface facing the fork. Tighten the securing bolt to 25-30 ft. lbs. Bend up the locktab.
7. Install the driveshaft.

Drive Axle and Suspension

Capri uses a Salisbury rear axle, with a driving pinion running in two taper roller bearings, preloaded by a selective tubular spacer between them. Pinion depth is controlled by selective spacers between the pinion head and the rear bearing. The axle shafts are splined to the differential side gears and supported at the outer ends by ball races with built in seals in the axle housing.

The rear suspension consists of conventional three-leaf, longitudinal, semi-elliptic springs, located asymmetrically to the rear axle carrier and fastened by U-bolt clamps. Two radius arms, one on each side, prevent excessive lateral axle movement, while standard telescopic shock absorbers control vertical rebound. The shock absorbers are staggered (front of axle on right-hand side, rear of axle on left-hand side) to provide additional control of axle tramp and wheel hop during acceleration and deceleration.

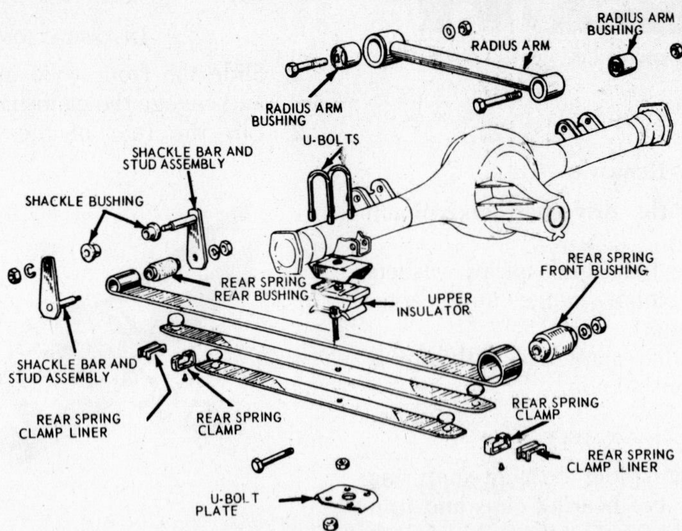

Exploded view of Capri rear suspension

Leaf Springs

Removal

1. Block the front wheels, jack the rear of the car and fit chassis stands.
2. Position a hydraulic jack under the rear axle.
3. Remove the rear shackle nuts and washers and detach the shackle bolt and plate assemblies.
4. Unscrew the nut from the front mounting bracket and withdraw the through-bolt.
5. Remove the U-bolts and attachment plate.
6. Remove the spring assembly.
7. Remove the retaining plate and insulator sleeve.
8. Remove the bushings from the spring mounting tees.

Installation

1. Installation is the reverse of removal.
2. Install all bolts but do not tighten initially. When the installation is complete, lower the car to the ground and tighten all bolts and nuts.

Axle Shafts

Replace

The Salisbury rear end of the Capri is assembled with metric bolts, therefore be sure to use the correct tool when servicing this unit.

1. Jack up car and remove wheels, brake drum retaining screw, and brake drums.
2. Remove the screws that secure the bearing retainer plate to the axle housing. These are accessible through holes in the axle shaft flange.
3. Pull the axle shaft and bearing assembly out of the axle housing.
4. Loosen the inner retaining ring by nicking it with a chisel.
5. Press on new bearing. Do not attempt to press on both bearing and retainer ring at the same time. Before assembling the retainer ring onto the shaft, the inside of the retainer and the shaft journal should be wiped clean. These parts must not be degreased or lubricated.
6. Insert the shaft in the housing, tap home.
7. Install the four bolts and spring washers to secure bearing retainer plate; torque to 15-18 ft. lbs.
8. Replace brake drums, brake drum retaining screw, wheels.

Rear Axle

Removal

1. Jack the rear of the car, fit chassis stands and remove the wheels.
2. Release the parking brake and release the cable from the lever on the axle housing.
3. Disconnect the brake line at the junction on the housing.
4. Matchmark the driveshaft and pinion flange for alignment, on assembly separate the driveshaft from the pinion flange.
5. Jack the center of the axle and disconnect the shock absorber lower mounting bolts.
6. Detach the rear end of the radius arms from the rear axle. If necessary, use a C clamp to remove the load from this bolt.
7. Remove the rear spring U-bolt nuts and remove the bolts and plates.
8. Lift the axle and remove it from the car through a wheel arch.

Installation

1. Installation is the reverse of removal.
2. Be sure to bleed the brake system.

Differential

Removal

1. Jack car and pull axle shafts.
2. Mark driveshaft and pinion flanges for realignment, remove four bolts and washers, the ten retaining bolts, the cover, gasket, and drain the axle.
3. Unscrew differential bearing cap screws, mark and remove caps. Using two pry bars, remove the differential.

Overhaul

1. Remove bearings from each side of differential assembly. Remove shims.
2. Unscrew the ring gear retaining bolts and remove the ring gear from the differential assembly.
3. Remove locking pin which secures the differential pinion shaft in the differential case, remove the pinion shaft, differential pinions, differential side gears and adjusting shims.

4. Hold drive pinion flange and remove nut, pull off pinion flange using suitable puller, remove pinion and bearing spacer from pinion.
5. Pull off large roller bearing from pinion shaft, remove spacer shims from pinion shaft.
6. Remove small taper roller bearing together with radial oil seal from axle housing.
7. Drive bearing races out from axle housing.
8. Install pinion bearing races, pulling races squarely into position.
9. To determine total side play of differential case in the housing, press the taper roller bearings on differential case without shims. Install pressure blocks into axle tubes and install differential into housing. Install bearing caps, tighten, loosen, then retighten finger tight. Mount dial indicator gauge on axle housing so feeler contacts side of ring gear and dial reads zero. By moving the differential, the total side play can be measured. Record this measurement. Remove differential and pressure blocks.
10. To determine the thickness of the pinion bearing spacer, use the trial and error method. Install the pinion with a selected spacer, small taper bearing, drive pinion flange, and the old self-locking nut. Tighten the nut to 72-87 ft. lbs. and rotate the pinion several times using an in. lbs. torque wrench. If the rotating torque required is too high, the spacer is too thin, and should be replaced with a thicker one. If the torque is too low, a thinner spacer should be used. Correct torque is 13-19 in. lbs. Remove the old nut. To check the spacer thickness, use the method described in *Pinion Mesh Markings*.

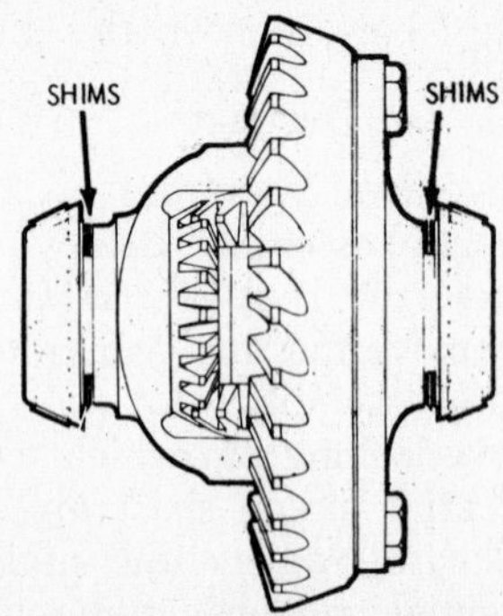

Location of differential case side shims

Measuring ring gear backlash

11. Check that the new radial oil seal has grease between the two sealing lips and coat it with sealing compound, install it and a new self locking nut; torque to 72-87 ft. lbs.
12. Remove differential case bearings. Position shims as indicated by the total side play figure, one half of the required amount on each side, on the differential case. Press the taper roller bearings on the differential case. Insert the case in the axle housing and center. Position the bearing caps as marked. Insert the screws and torque to 43-49 ft. lbs.
13. Position the dial indicator feeler in a vertical position on one ring gear tooth and check the tooth flank backlash. If the backlash is not within 0.005-0.009 in. (0.12-.0.22 mm.) the differential must be removed again. If the backlash is too large, remove shims from the ring gear face side and transfer to ring gear back side. Reverse procedure if backlash is too small. Do not increase or decrease number of shims, but only interchange between one side and the other.
14. For proper tooth contact pattern check, see *Pinion Mesh Markings.*
15. Position a new gasket and the axle case cover on the axle case, secure with bolts and torque to 22-29 ft. lbs.
16. Install driveshaft, axles and wheels.

Pinion Mesh Markings

The following method of determining the relative position of the ring gear and pinion, and whether or not they are in proper mesh, will prove satisfactory for all pinion and ring gears. This should be followed by a final check, even when the pinion depth has been determined by special micrometers. Assemble the pinion in the housing, without preload, and tighten the

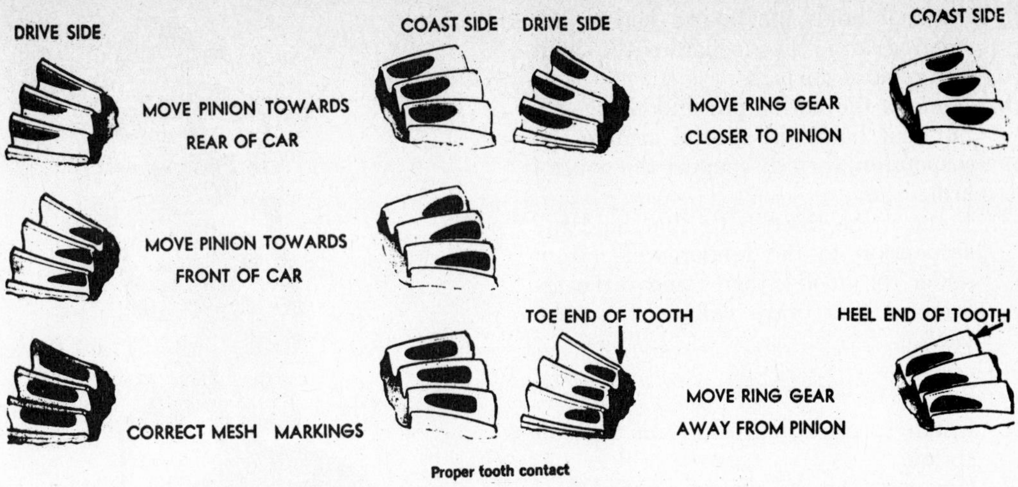

Proper tooth contact

Pinion mesh markings

pinion nut until a preload of about 10 in. lbs. is developed on the bearings to insure that they are completely free of end-play.

This, of course, is not the final bearing preload setting, but is a good one for checking the pinion mesh markings.

Install the differential assembly and adjust it to provide from .004-.008 in. backlash of the ring gear, measured at the rim of the gear.

Paint five or six of the ring gear teeth with red or white lead and, while the helper brakes the ring gear with a piece of wood, slowly turn the pinion until the ring gear makes at least one full revolution. The mesh of the pinion with the ring gear will be indicated as a mark in the red lead on the ring gear teeth. Compare this mark with the accompanying photographs. The caption on each photograph explains whether the mark indicates the pinion is too deep or too shallow, the ring gear too close or too far away.

When the marking is found to be improper, it is customary to make trial changes in increments of .005 or .007″. If changing the shim .005-.007 throws the marking from too deep to too shallow, the proper distance is about half-way between.

If, after changing this increment of shims, the mark still indicates that more must be changed, it is advisable to continue changing in the same increments, that is .005-.007″.

While considerable time is generally required to disassemble the rear, press off the bearings, change the shims, press the bearing back on and reassemble the rear; this is still the only positive method of determining if the rear will operate quietly after it is finally installed in the vehicle.

Installation

1. Place differential in housing. Position bearing caps as marked. Torque screws to 43-49 ft. lbs.
2. Position new gasket, axle case cover, secure with bolts, torque to 22-29 ft. lbs.
3. Attach driveshaft, install axle shafts.

Front Suspension

The independent front suspension, of the McPherson strut type, utilizes variable rate coil springs and hydraulic shock absorbers. Lateral front wheel movement is controlled by a track control arm and front to rear movement by a stabilizer bar.

Downward movement is limited by rebound stops inside the integral suspension unit, while upward movement is restricted by the compression limit of the coil springs. In practice, a rubber bumper is hit before the coil spring is completely compressed.

The front suspension geometry, except toe-in, is not adjustable. Any tolerance deviations require disassembly and repair of the affected part/s.

Removal

1. Lift the hood, then jack up the car and support on chassis stands.
2. Remove the front wheel.
3. Disconnect the brake line from the suspension unit.
4. Place a jack under the control arm and jack up the suspension.
5. Remove the cotter pin and the castle

nut that holds the tie-rod end to the steering arm, then separate the joint and remove the jack.

6. Remove the cotter pin and the castle nut that holds the tie-rod arm to the suspension, then disconnect the control arm.
7. Remove the three bolts that hold the suspension to the fender well (from under the hood), then remove the assembly, with brake caliper, from the car.

Compressing coil spring—out of car

Disassembly

1. Install spring compressors on the coil spring.
2. Compress the coil spring slightly, then unscrew the piston rod nut and remove the retainer.
3. Remove the top mount and the upper spring seat, coil spring, and rubber bumper.
4. Using a large pipe wrench, remove the bumper platform.
5. Remove the O-ring from upper guide assembly.

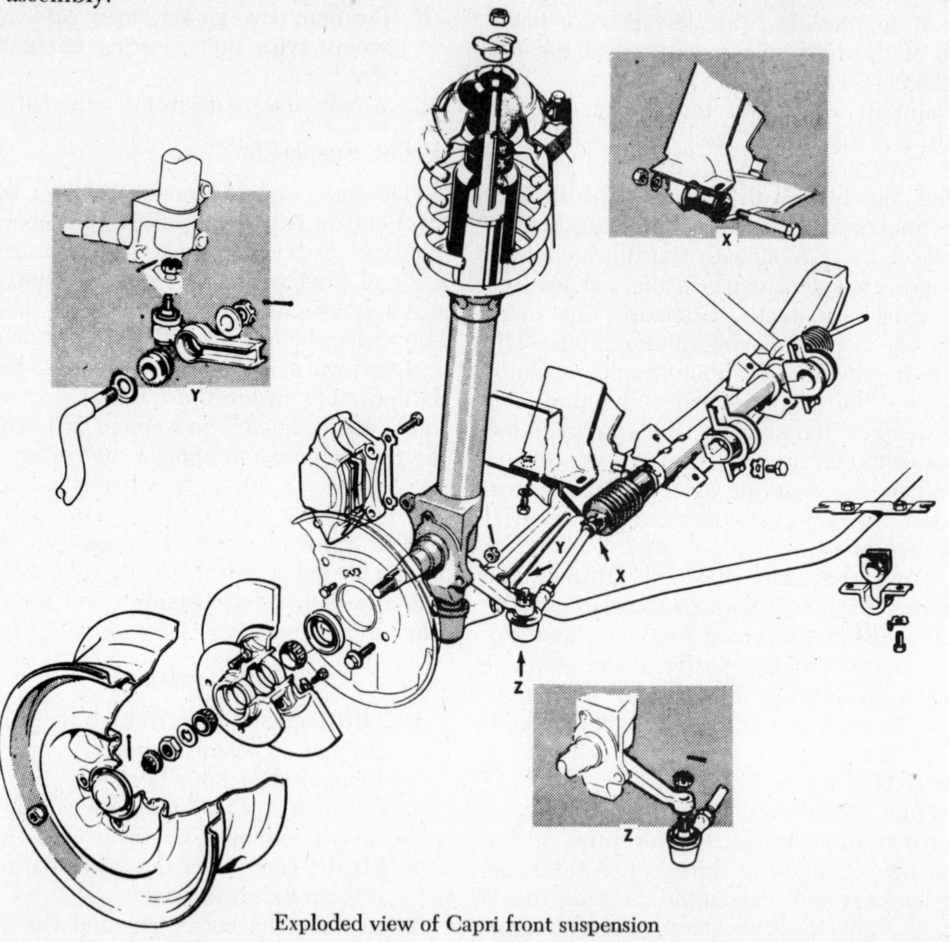

Exploded view of Capri front suspension

6. Check the top edge of the piston rod (machined area); it must be free of burrs and nicks.

NOTE: *Remove any burrs with a fine oil stone. If this is not done, the bushing will be damaged as it is removed.*

7. Lift the piston rod until the gland and bushing assembly is free of the outer casing, then slide the gland assembly from the rod.
8. Empty the fluid into a container. Pull the piston rod—complete with piston, cylinder, and compression valve—from the outer casing.
9. Remove the piston rod from the cylinder by pushing the compression valve out of the base while pushing the rod downwards.
10. Remove the ring from the piston.

Assembly

1. Wash all parts with solvent, then examine for wear and damage. Especially check the spindle body for distortion.

NOTE: *Do not remove the piston from the rod—these parts are replaced as an assembly.*

2. Install a new piston ring.
3. Insert the piston rod into the cylinder and push the compression valve into the base of the cylinder.
4. Insert the cylinder and piston rod assembly into the outer casing.

NOTE: *At this point, the unit must be filled with exactly 326 cc. of fluid.*

5. Slide the gland and bushing onto the end of the piston rod, using care so as not to damage the bushing, until the assembly fits into the end of the cylinder and the complete internal assembly is below the top of the outer casing.
6. Locate a rubber O-ring on top of the gland and bushing assembly.
7. Screw the bumper platform onto the top of the outer casing and tighten it to about 55-60 ft. lbs.
8. Continue assembly of components (coil spring, etc.), making sure dished washer is installed with convex side up.
9. Install piston rod nut, with Loctite on threads, and tighten to 5-10 ft. lbs.
10. Remove coil spring compressors, then loosen the piston rod nut and retorque to 28-32 ft. lbs. when the suspension is fully installed and car on its wheels.

NOTE: *Wheels must be straight ahead and "cranked" retainer must face in towards the engine.*

Installation

1. Lift the suspension into position and secure using the three bolts through the wheel well, tightening bolts to 15-18 ft. lbs.
2. Reconnect the control arm ball stud to the suspension unit, tighten nut to 30-35 ft. lbs., and install a new cotter pin.
3. Reconnect tie-rod end to steering arm and tighten castle nut to 18-22 ft. lbs., then install a new cotter pin.
4. Reconnect brake line to bracket, then bleed brakes.
5. Replace wheel and lower the car.

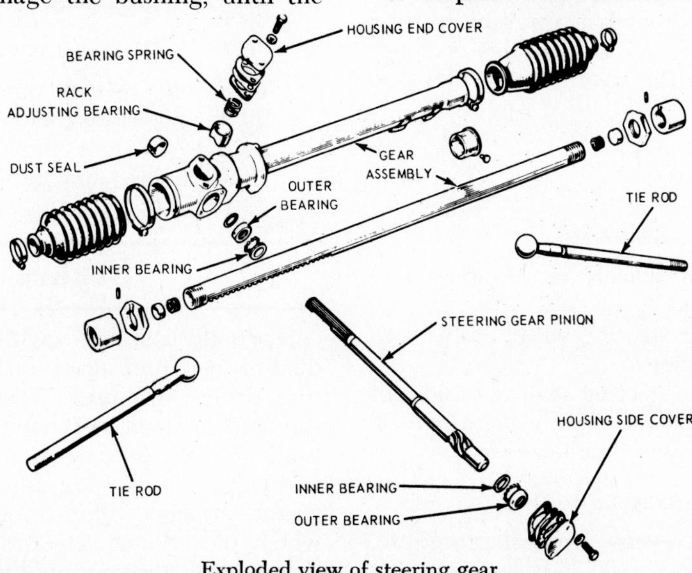

Exploded view of steering gear

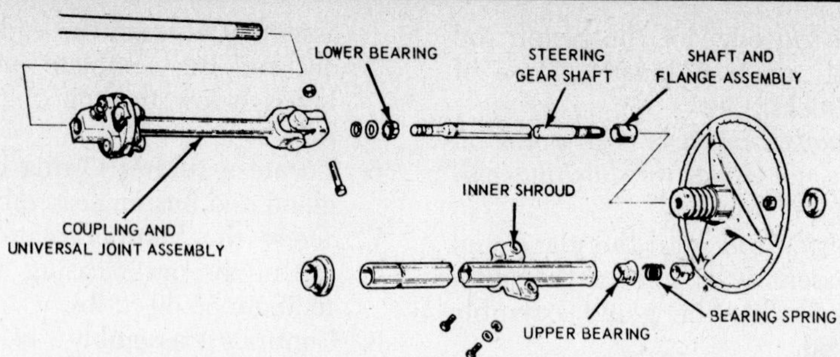

Exploded view of steering column and U-joint

Steering

The rack and pinion steering gear is rubber-mounted to the front crossmember. Movement of the steering wheel is transmitted through a universal joint and flexible coupling to the pinion, which in turn moves the rack laterally to turn the wheels. Steering is approximately 3 1/2 turns lock to lock, with an overall steering ratio of 17.7:1.

There are two possible adjustments to the steering gear—rack damper adjustment and pinion bearing preload adjustment. Both of these adjustments are made by varying the thickness of the shim pack under the steering box cover plate. It is necessary to have the gear removed from the car for these two adjustments.

The tie-rods are adjustable to provide a toe-in adjustment range; caster and camber angles are built-in and are not adjustable.

One caution that should be followed: when the car is jacked up with the front wheels off the ground, never rapidly turn wheels from lock to lock. If this is done, pressure within the steering may blow off the bellows.

Steering Wheel

Removal

1. Align front wheels in straight-ahead position.
2. Pry out the steering wheel emblem to expose the nut.
3. Remove the steering shaft nut and pull the wheel off the shaft, using a universal steering wheel puller.

Installation

1. To install, reverse removal procedure, tightening nut to 20-25 ft. lbs.

Steering Gear

Removal

1. Place wheels in straight-ahead position.
2. Jack up the front of the car and support on axle stands.
3. Remove the nut and bolt that secure the flexible coupling in the pinion splines.
4. Bend back the lock tabs and remove the bolts that hold the gear box to the crossmember.
5. Remove the cotter pins and castle nuts that hold tie-rod ends to steering arms, then separate the ball studs from the tapered fittings.
6. Remove the steering gear from the car.

NOTE: *It is necessary to turn one wheel against the stop to give enough clearance between the steering gear and the sway bar.*

7. Remove the tie-rod ends and locknuts, counting the number of turns required to remove each one.

Installation

1. To install, reverse removal procedure tightening gear box-to-crossmember bolts to 15-18 ft. lbs., tie-rod ends to 18-22 ft. lbs., and flexible coupling to 12-15 ft. lbs.

Brakes

Hydraulic brakes, with fixed-caliper, dual-piston front discs and self-adjusting rear drums, are used. The system is the standard tandem type, having two separate brake circuits. A failure in one brake circuit will cause the pressure differential valve to switch braking effort from that circuit which, in so doing, activates another switch that controls the warning light on the dashboard. The pressure differential valve is similar to American-made units, except for a special centering procedure.

The brake booster is non-serviceable and must be replaced if defective. Vacuum to the booster is supplied via a check valve, and both sides of the diaphragm normally are under equal vacuum. When the brake pedal is depressed, atmospheric pressure is admitted to the rear diaphragm chamber, and the vacuum in the forward chamber pulls the diaphragm forward to apply additional braking force to the master cylinder.

The parking brake is operated through a floor-mounted lever located between the front seats. Pulling the lever transmits force through a two cable linkage to operate the rear drum brakes. A self-adjusting feature operates when there is excessive clearance between the brake shoes and drums.

Master Cylinder

Removal

1. Siphon the fluid from the reservoir.
2. Disconnect brake lines from master cylinder.
3. Remove the master cylinder retaining nuts.
4. Remove the master cylinder, being careful not to damage the vacuum seal.

Installation

1. Position the master cylinder and fluid seal on the pushrod.
2. While holding in this position, thread the brake line fittings a few turns.
3. Bolt the master cylinder to the vacuum booster, then tighten brake lines.
4. Fill the reservoir with an approved type brake fluid.

NOTE: *FoMoCo C6AZ-19542-A is recommended.*

5. Bleed the brake system, both front and rear.
6. Check brake operation.

Power Brake Booster

Removal

1. Disconnect brake pushrod clevis pin from brake pedal, then remove pin.
2. Remove master cylinder retaining nuts and wire cylinder out of the way, being careful not to damage the fluid seal.
3. Remove the vacuum hose from the brake booster.
4. Remove the booster to firewall retaining screws, then remove booster and seal.
5. Remove retaining bracket and gasket from booster.

Installation

1. To install, reverse removal procedure, using new gaskets throughout where possible.

Disc Brakes

Brake Pads

Replace

1. Jack up car and remove tires and wheels.
2. Pull out retaining pin clips, retaining

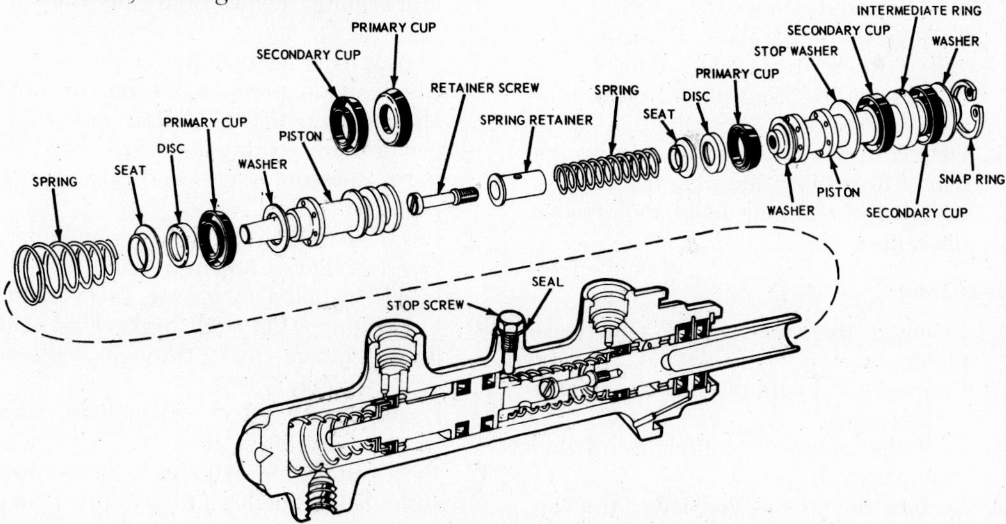

Exploded view of tandem master cylinder

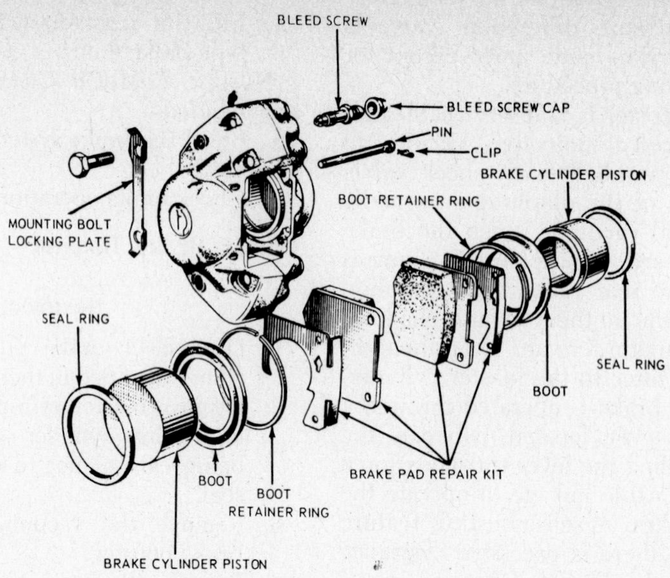

Exploded view of Capri disc brakes

pins and remove pads and shims. If necessary, use needle nosed pliers carefully.

3. Push pistons in cylinders until they seat. If the master cylinder was full, it may overflow, so remove some fluid.
4. Install new shims and pads.
5. Install retaining pins and secure with retaining pin clips.
6. Replace wheels and lower car.

Calipers

Removal

1. Apply the parking brake, jack the front of the car and remove the wheels.
2. Remove the brake pads. If the caliper unit is to be overhauled, depress the brake pedal to bring the piston in contact with the disc.
3. Detach the hydraulic pipe from the rear of the caliper and plug the line.
4. Unbolt the retaining bolts and remove the caliper.

Installation

1. Remount the caliper. Use new lockplates.
2. Connect the hydraulic line to the rear of the caliper.
3. Push the pistons into their bores and insert the pads.
4. Replace the wheels and lower the car. Bleed the brakes.

Piston Seal

Replace

1. Lift car and remove wheels.
2. Remove brake pads. Push brake pedal to bring pistons in contact with disc.
3. Remove brake line from union on rear of caliper and plug ends.
4. Bend lock tabs, remove the two caliper retaining bolts and remove caliper assembly.
5. Partially remove piston, remove retaining ring and remove the bellows from lower point of piston skirt. Remove piston.
6. Pull sealing bellows from ring in cylinder.
7. Repeat for other cylinder.
8. Clean metal parts in alcohol or suitable solvent. Inspect piston and cylinder bore for scoring and wear. Replace parts showing wear and all rubber parts.
9. Insert piston seal in groove in cylinder. Insert bellows to cylinder with lip outwards installed in groove in cylinder.
10. Lubricate piston with brake fluid and insert, crown first, through bellows into cylinder.
11. Install inner edge of bellows into groove in piston skirt.
12. Push piston into cylinder as far as possible. Secure bellows to piston with retaining ring.

13. Repeat for other piston.
14. Using new locking plate, replace caliper assembly and tighten bolts to 40-50 ft. lbs. Bend tabs on locking plate.
15. Attach brake line to caliper.
16. Push pistons into cylinders and insert pads and shims. Secure pads with retaining pins and clips.
17. Replace wheels and lower car, bleed system.

Disc and Hub

Replace

1. Remove the caliper assembly.
2. Remove the grease cap from the end of the hub.
3. Remove cotter pin and adjusting nut retainer, adjusting nut, thrust washer and outer bearing race.
4. Remove hub and disc from spindle.
5. Separate disc from hub by bending lock tabs and removing the bolts. Discard the locking plate and bolts.
6. Clean mating surfaces of hub and disc.
7. Align mating marks, place disc on hub and install new locking plate and bolts. Tighten bolts to 30-34 ft. lbs. and bend lock tabs.
8. Replace hub and disc assembly on spindle. Install outer bearing race, thrust washer and adjusting nut.
9. Tighten nut to 27 ft. lbs. while rotating disc to insure proper seating of the bearings.
10. Slacken nut 90 degrees and install nut retainer so castellations line up with cotter pin hole in wheel spindle. Install new cotter pin.
11. Check runout.
12. Tap grease cap in place in end of hub.

Checking Brake Disc Runout

Disconnect the connecting rod from the steering arm at its outer end, after removing the cotter pin, castellated nut and separating the ball joint. Attach dial indicator to steering arm and check runout. If it exceeds 0.0035″ either cure the problem if it is misalignment of hub or dirt or dust, or replace the disc.

Pressure Differential Valve

Centering Procedure

Remove the dust cover at the bottom of the valve body and insert the centering tool through the opening. The piston can be moved to the center position with this tool, which can be fabricated from a small screwdriver.

Rear Brakes

The rear brakes are self-adjusting drum type brakes similar to the type used in U.S. cars, except that the self-adjustment occurs when the parking brake is applied.

Parking Brake

Adjustment

1. Jack up the rear of the car and support on axle stands.
2. Release the parking brake and make sure primary cable is free and greased.
3. Loosen the primary cable rear locknut and adjust cable length until primary cable has no slack and relay lever is just clear of the rear axle housing.
4. Loosen the locknut on the transverse cable end near the right-hand rear brake and adjust the cable so that there is no slack. The parking brake operating levers must be on their stops.
5. Tighten locknuts and lower car.

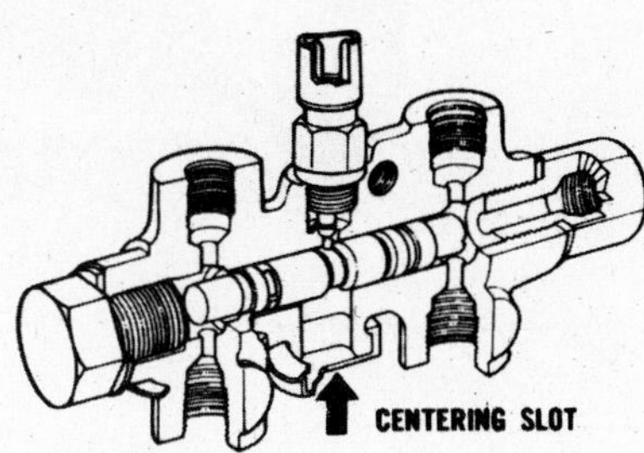

Brake system pressure differential valve

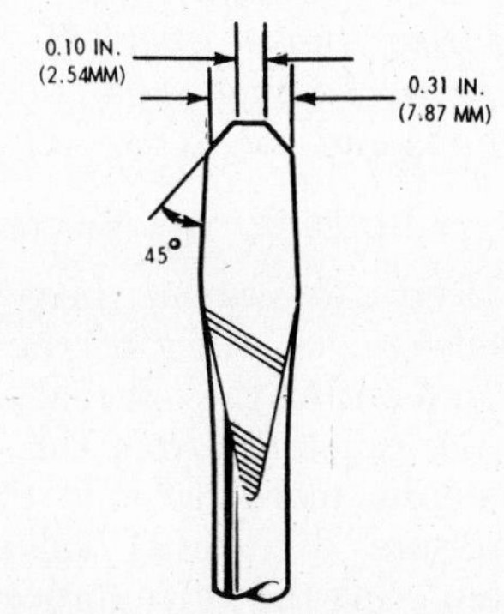

Special centering tool made from screwdriver

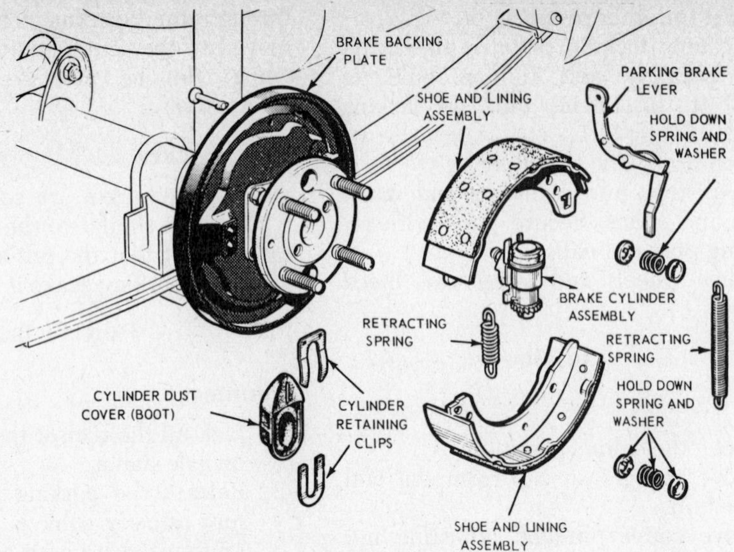

Exploded view of Capri rear brake assembly

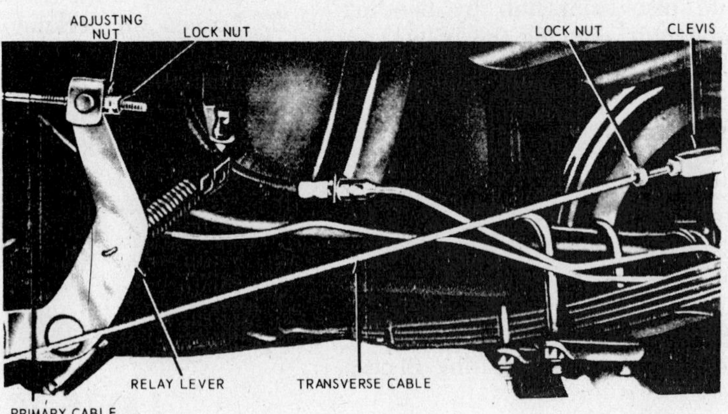

Parking brake adjustment points

NOTE: *Never adjust the cables to take up for rear brake wear. If brake wear seems to be causing cable slack, pull the rear drums and check the self-adjusters.*

Bleeding the Brakes

To bleed the system, three screws are provided—one on each of the front disc brakes and one on the left rear drum brake. The major difference from U.S. cars is that the centering tool must hold the piston in the pressure differential valve centered. After centering the valve, proceed to bleed the brakes as normal.

Accessories

Instruments

The standard instruments consist of two clusters and four warning lights. The left-hand cluster contains a speedometer and an odometer, while the right-hand cluster contains the fuel and temperature gauges. These two gauges are powered through a 5-volt voltage regulator mounted on the rear of the speedometer. The warning lights are for turn signals (green), high beam (blue), alternator (red), and oil pressure (amber). Light bulbs can be replaced without removing the cluster.

A bank of rocker switches is mounted in the center of the instrument panel. These switches control the windshield wipers, emergency flashers, and the tandem brake system test circuit.

Cluster

Removal

1. Remove the two steering column hold-down bolts, then lower the steering column.
2. Remove the five Phillips-head screws, then pull the instrument panel forward.
3. Disconnect the speedometer cable and wiring, remove the four remaining Phillips-head screws, and remove the cluster.
4. To service any one gauge, simply remove it from the cluster.

Installation

1. Installation is the reverse of removal.

Headlight Switch

Removal

1. Disconnect batter ground cable.
2. Pull the connector from the back of the switch.
3. From behind the sub-panel, push the switch to one side and remove.

Installation

1. Installation is the reverse of removal.

Ignition Switch

Removal

1. Disconnect battery ground cable.
2. Remove steering column shroud.
3. Place key on "O" position, then disconnect switch wires.
4. Remove the two screws that hold switch to steering lock, then remove switch.

Installation

1. Installation is the reverse of removal.

Ignition Key Warning Buzzer

Removal

1. Remove parcel tray.
2. Disconnect the two leads to the buzzer.

NOTE: *The buzzer is located beside the flasher unit on the brake pedal support.*

3. Remove buzzer retaining screw and buzzer.

Installation

1. Installation is the reverse of removal.

Steering Lock

Removal

1. Disconnect battery ground cable.
2. Remove steering column shroud, then remove screws that hold upper steering column.

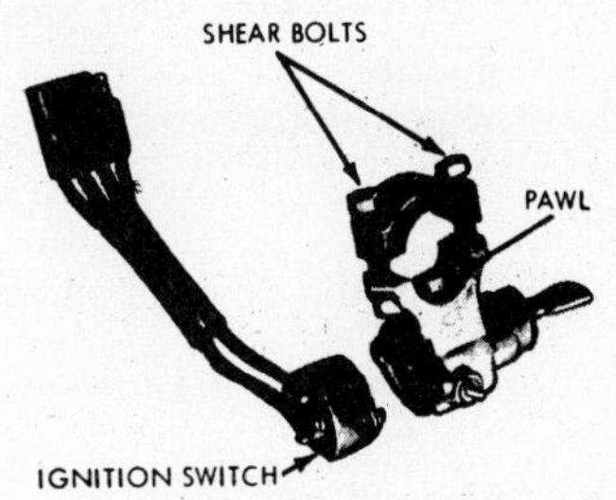

Disassembled view of steering lock

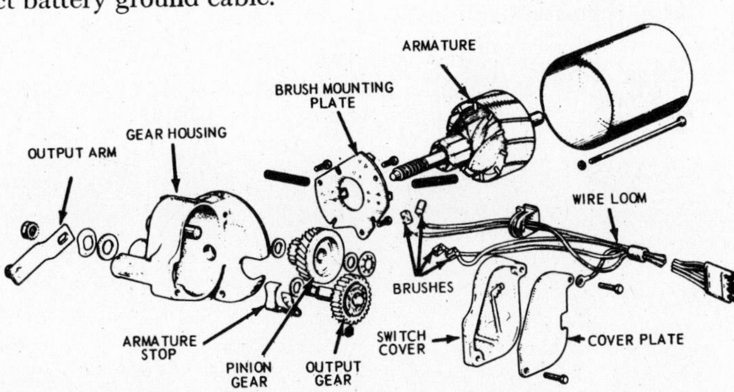

Exploded view of wiper motor

3. Turn steering column to gain access to headless bolts, then disconnect leads to ignition switch and lock.
4. Drill out the headless bolts and remove steering lock.

Installation

1. Position the lock assembly, with ignition key in place, on the steering column.
2. Withdraw lock to allow pawl to enter steering shaft.
3. Place clamp in position, install "shear head" bolts, and tighten bolts until heads break off. Make sure pawl operates freely.
4. Connect wires to switch terminals, reposition steering column, and replace shroud. Tighten upper steering column screws.
5. Connect battery cable.

Windshield Wiper Motor

Removal

1. Disconnect battery ground cable.
2. Remove wiper arms and the two nuts that hold the wiper spindles.
3. Remove front parcel tray.
4. Disconnect defroster vent hose, then disconnect the two control cables.
5. Remove the two screws that hold the motor to its bracket, then disconnect wires to motor.
6. Remove wiper motor assembly.

Installation

1. Installation is the reverse of removal.

Windshield Wiper Linkage

Removal

1. Pry the short wiper link from the motor output arm, then remove plastic pivot bushing.
2. Remove the three screws that hold motor to linkage, then separate linkage.

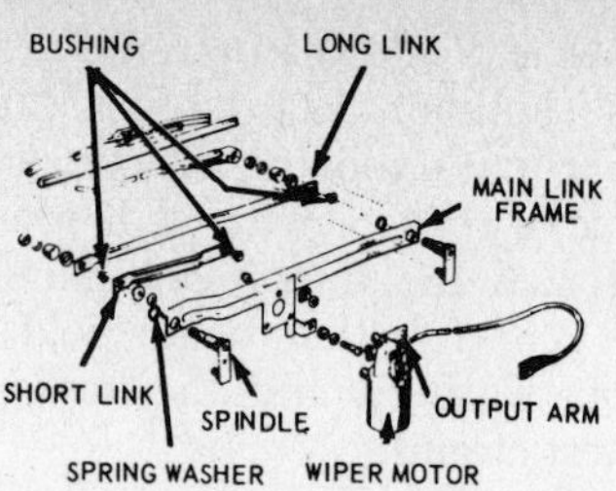

Exploded view of wiper linkage

Installation

1. Installation is the reverse of removal.

Heater

Removal

1. Disconnect battery and drain cooling system.
2. Remove parcel tray, then, from inside engine compartment, disconnect heater hoses from panel.
3. Remove two screws, then heater hose plate and gasket, from panel.
4. Remove heater control cables, then disconnect heater motor wires.
5. Remove ducts from the heater, then remove four bolts and heater.

Installation

1. Installation is the reverse of removal.

COLT SECTION

Index

Introduction

The Dodge Colt is the first combined effort of Dodge and Mitsubishi Heavy Industries, Ltd. It is a descendant of the Mitsubishi Colt, which has been sold in Japan for several years. The Colt joins a growing field of small, low priced, but well equipped economy cars, which are becoming popular in the United States. The Colt is sold and serviced as part of the Dodge dealer network, rather than having its own, and is considered a Dodge product.

Year and Model Identification

1971-72 Colt Sedan

1971-72 Colt Hardtop

1971-72 Colt Station Wagon

Vehicle and Engine Serial Number

Vehicle Number

The vehicle identification plate is mounted on the instrument panel, adjacent to the lower corner of the windshield on

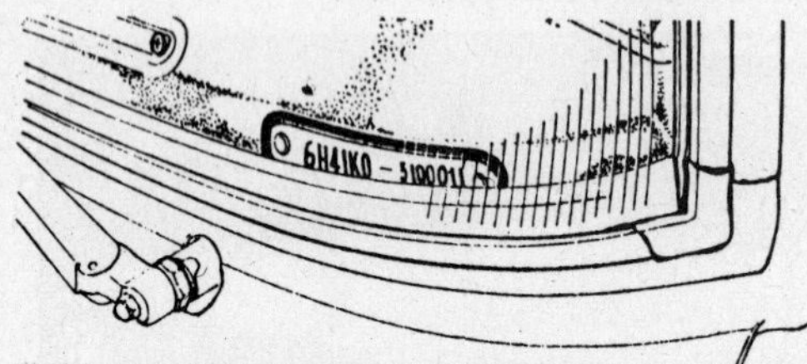

Serial number location

the driver's side, and is visible through the windshield. The thirteen digit vehicle number is composed of a seven digit identification code, and a six digit sequential number. The code is interpreted as follows:

Year	*Code*	*Body Style*	*Transmission Type*
1971	6H21K19	2 Door coupe	Automatic
	6H21K15	2 Door coupe	Manual
	6H23K19	2 Door hardtop	Automatic
	6H23K15	2 Door hardtop	Manual
	6H41K19	4 Door sedan	Automatic
	6H41K15	4 Door sedan	Manual
	6H45K19	Station wagon	Automatic
	6H45K15	Station wagon	Manual

Engine Number

The engine model number is embossed on the lower left side of the block. The sequential engine number is stamped on a pad at the upper right front of the engine, adjacent to the exhaust manifold.

Engine **model** number

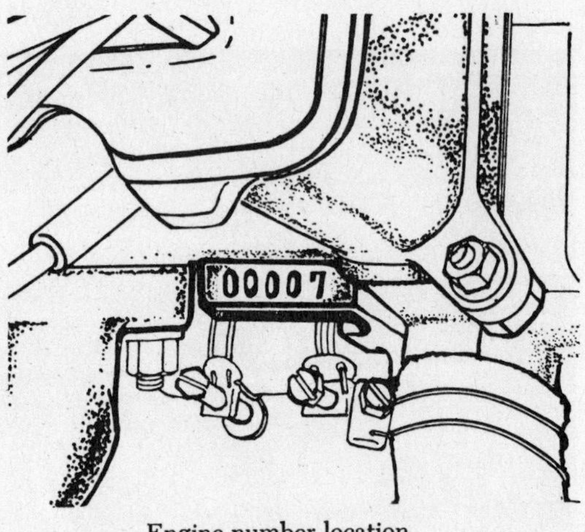

Engine number location

General Engine Specifications

Year	*Type*	*Cu. In. Displacement (cc's.)*	*Carburetor*	*Developed Horsepower @ rpm (SAE)*	*Developed Torque @ rpm (ft. lbs.)*	*Bore and Stroke (in.)*	*Compression Ratio*	*Normal Oil Pressure (psi)*
1971	4 cyl., inline, OHC	97.5 (1600)	1 x 2 bbl.	100@6300	101@4000	3.03 x 3.39	8.5:1	28-57

Tune-Up Specifications

Year	Model	Spark Plugs Make (Type)	Spark Plugs Gap (in.)	Breaker Points Dwell Angle (deg.)	Breaker Points Gap (in.)	Basic Ignition Timing (deg.)	Cranking Compression (psi)	Valves Clearance (in.) Intake	Valves Clearance (in.) Exhaust	Valves Intake Opens (deg.)	Idle Speed (rpm)
1971	All	NGK (B6E, B6ES, BP6ES)	.028-.032	49-55	.018-.022	TDC	149	.006 (hot)	.010 (hot)	32 BTDC	700-750① 1350-1450②
1972	All Models	See engine compartment stickers for tune-up specifications.									

TDC—Top dead center
BTDC—Before top dead center
①—With solenoid off.
②—With solenoid on.

Firing Order

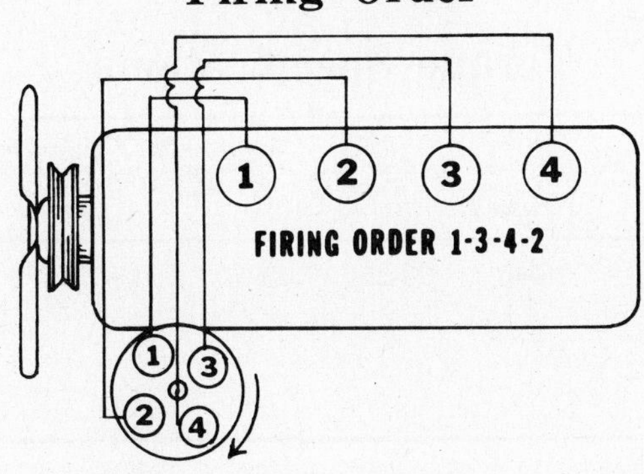

Distributor Advance Specifications

Year	Model	Distributor Identification	Centrifugal Advance ① Degrees Start @ rpm	Centrifugal Advance ① Intermediate Degrees @ rpm	Centrifugal Advance ① Final Degrees @ rpm	Vacuum Advance ① Start Degrees @ in. Hg.	Vacuum Advance ① Intermediate Degrees @ in. Hg.	Vacuum Advance ① Final Degrees @ in. Hg.
1971	All	TVG-4GR	0@1000	13@2000	28@6100	0@6.3	5.5@11.8	8.5@15.7

①—Crankshaft degrees @ crankshaft rpm.

Engine Rebuilding Specifications

Year	Model	Crankshaft: Main Bearing Journals (in.) Journal Diameter New	Journal Diameter Minimum	Oil clearance	Shaft End-Play	Thrust On No.	Connecting Rod Bearing Journals (in.) Journal Diameter New	Journal Diameter Minimum	Oil Clearance	End-Play
1971	All	2.2433-2.2441	2.2087	.00063-.00307	.002-.007	3	1.7709-1.7717	1.7363	.00039-.00283	.0039-.0098

Year	Model	Pistons (in.) Cylinder Bore New	Cylinder Bore Maximum	Piston Diameter New	Piston Diameter Maximum Oversize	Wrist Pin Diameter (Fit)	Rings: Ring No.	Side Clearance (in.)	End-Gap (in.)
1971	All	3.0276-3.0288	3.0758	3.0264-3.0276	3.0315	.748 (Press)	Upper	.0012-.0028	.006-.014
							Middle	.0008-.0024	.006-.014
							Lower	.0010-.0030	.006-.014

Engine Rebuilding Specifications

Year	Model	Valves										
		Seat Angle (deg.)	Minimum Valve Seat Width (in.)	Valve Lift (in.)		Spring Pressure (lbs.)		Spring Installed Height (in.)	Stem Diameter (in.)		Stem to Guide Clearance (in.)	
				Intake	Exhaust	Intake	Exhaust		Intake	Exhaust	Intake	Exhaust
1971	All	45	.035	N.A.	N.A.	① 59-65 ② 130-142		1.47	.3133-.3139	.3121-.3129	.0010-.0022	.0020-.0033

①—Installed
②—Compressed

Torque Specifications

Year	Model	Cylinder Head (ft. lbs.)	Main Bearing Caps (ft. lbs.)	Rod Bearing Caps (ft. lbs.)	Crankshaft Pulley (ft. lbs.)	Flywheel to Crankshaft Bolts (ft. lbs.)	Manifolds (ft. lbs.)	
							Intake	Exhaust
1971	All	① 51-55 (cold) ② 7-9	36-40	23-25	43-51	69-76	11-14	11-14

①—Bolts
②—Nuts

Tightening Sequence

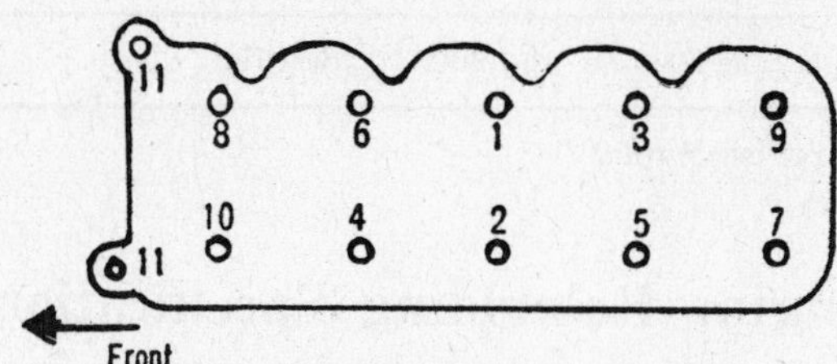

Cylinder head nut tightening sequence

Electrical Specifications

Year	Model	Battery			Starter						
		Capacity (Amp hours)	Volts	Grounded Terminal	Lock Test			No Load Test			Brush Spring Tension (oz)
					Amps	Volts	Torque	Amps	Volts	RPM	
1971	All	60	12	Negative	500	6	11.2	55	11	5500	56

Electrical Specifications

Year	Model	Alternator			Regulator						
		Part Number	Field Current Draw @ 12V	Output (amps) @ Generator rpm	Part Number	Charge Relay		Voltage Regulator			
						Air Gap (in.)	Point Gap (in.)	Volts to Close	Air Gap (in.)	Point Gap (in.)	Volts @ 125°F.
1971	All	AC2040K	N.A.	① 16.5@1300 ② 32@2500	RQB2220D	.035-.047	.030-.043	14.3-15.3	.032-.047	.012-.016	N.A.

①—No Load
②—Loaded

Capacities and Pressures

Year	Model	Crankcase Refill After Draining (qts.)		Transmission Refill After Draining (qts.)		Drive Axle (pts.)	Fuel Tank (gals.)	Cooling System With Heater (qts.)	Normal Fuel Pressure (psi)	Maximum Coolant Pressure (psi)
		With Filter	Without Filter	Manual	Automatic					
1971	All	4.2	3.5	1.8	6.2	2.0	① 13 ② 11	7.2	3.7-5.1	15.6

①—Hardtop and sedan.
②—Station wagon.

Brake Specifications

Year	Model	Type		Brake Cylinder Bore (in.)			Disc Diameter (in.)	Drum Diameter (in.)	
		Front	Rear	Master Cylinder	Wheel Cylinder				
					Front *	Rear		New	Maximum
1971	All	Disc	Drum	11/16	1.8906	¾	N.A.	9.0	9.079

*—Caliper bore diameter

Chassis and Wheel Alignment Specifications

Year	Model	Chassis			Wheel Alignment							
		Wheelbase	Track (in.)		Caster ▲		Camber ▲		Toe-in (in.)	Steering Axis Inclination	Wheel Pivot Ratio	
			Front	Rear	Range (deg.)	Preferred Setting (deg.)	Range (deg.)	Prefered Setting (deg.)			Inner Wheel	Outer Wheel
1971	All	95.3	50.6	50.6	1¼-1½	N.A.	N.A.	1½	.08-.23	8°50′	43°	32°

▲—Caster and camber are not adjustable.

Fuses and Circuit Breakers

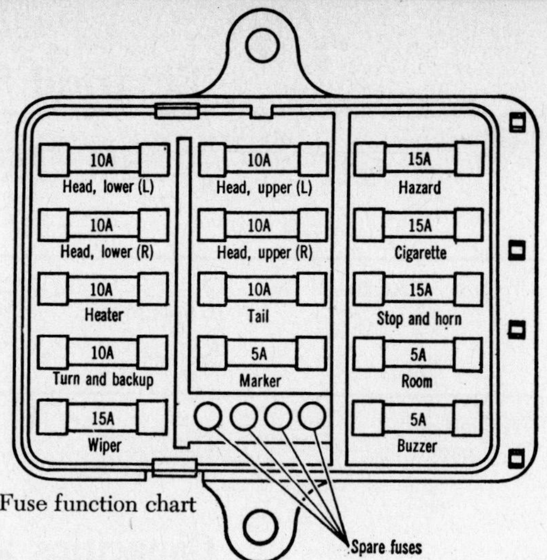

Fuse function chart

Light Bulb Specifications

Year	Model	Usage	Type	Number	Wattage
1971	Sedan and Hardtop	Headlight, low beam	Sealed beam	2	37.5/50
		Headlight, high beam	Sealed beam	2	37.5
		Front turn signal and parking lights	Orange	2	8/27
		Front side marker lights	Orange	2	8
		Tail light, stop and turn signal lights	Red	4	8/27
		Rear side marker lights	Red	2	8
		License plate lights	White	2	8
		Back-up lights	White	2	27
		Dome light	White	1	10
		Shift quadrant light	Green	1	3
		Instrument panel lights	Purple	2	3
		Clock light	Green	1	3
		Combination meter lights:			
		Oil pressure indicator	Red	1	3
		Charge indicator	Red	1	3
		Parking brake indicator	Red	1	3
		Door indicator	Red	1	3
		High beam indicator	Blue	1	3
		Turn signal indicators	Green	2	3
	Station Wagon	Headlight, low beam	Sealed beam	2	37.5/50
		Headlight, high beam	Sealed beam	2	37.5
		Front turn signal and parking lights	Orange	2	8/23
		Front side marker lights	Orange	2	8
		Tail light, stop and turn signal lights	Red	4	8/23
		Rear side marker lights	Red	2	8
		License plate lights	White	2	8
		Back-up lights	White	2	27
		Dome light	White	2	10
		Shift quadrant light	Green	1	3
		Instrument panel lights	Purple	2	3
		Clock light	Green	1	3
		Combination meter lights:			
		Oil pressure indicator	Red	1	3
		Charge indicator	Red	1	3
		Parking brake indicator	Red	1	3
		Door indicator	Red	1	3
		High beam indicator	Blue	1	3
		Turn signal indicator	Green	2	3

Wiring Diagrams

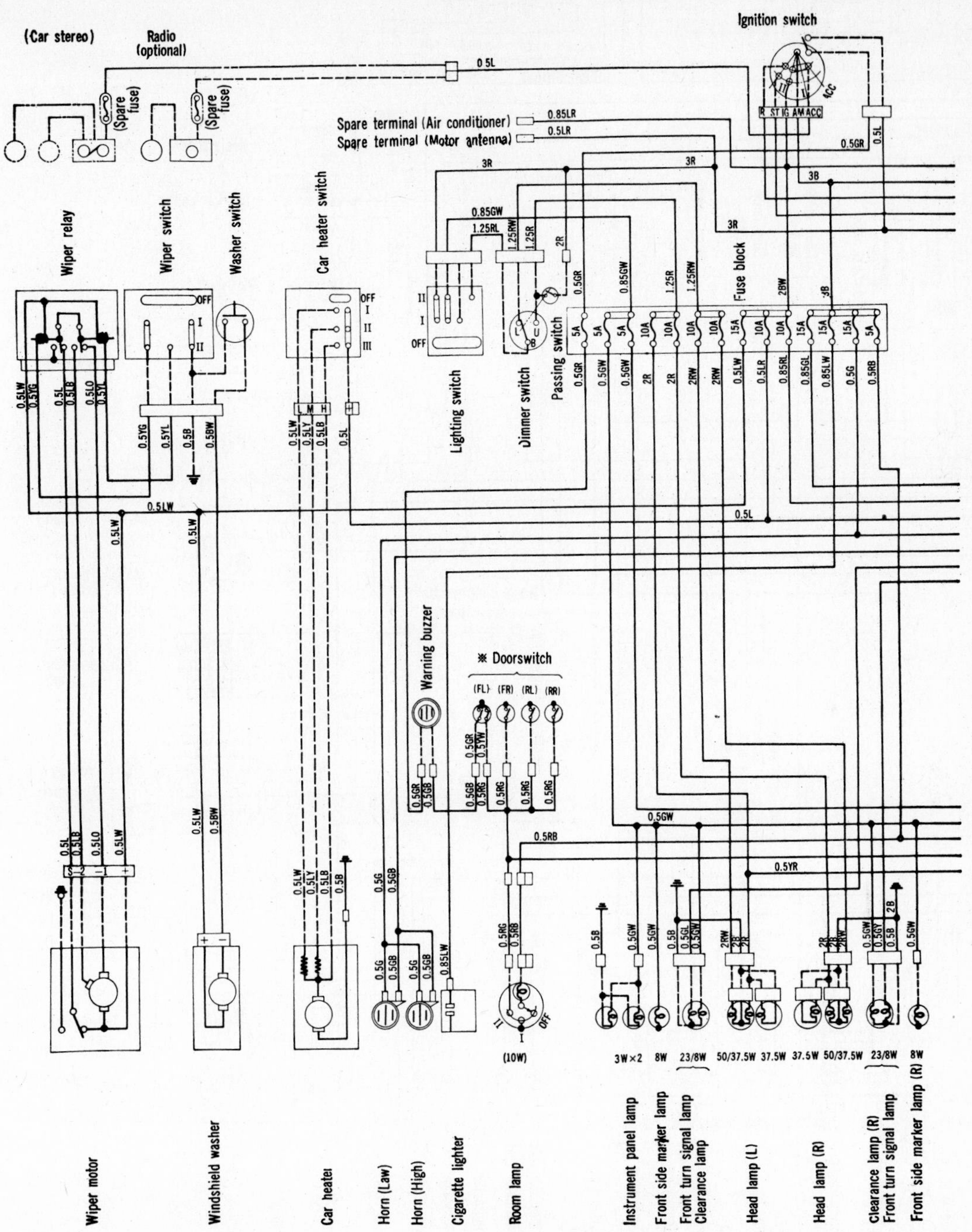

Wiring diagram—Sedan and Hardtop with manual transmission

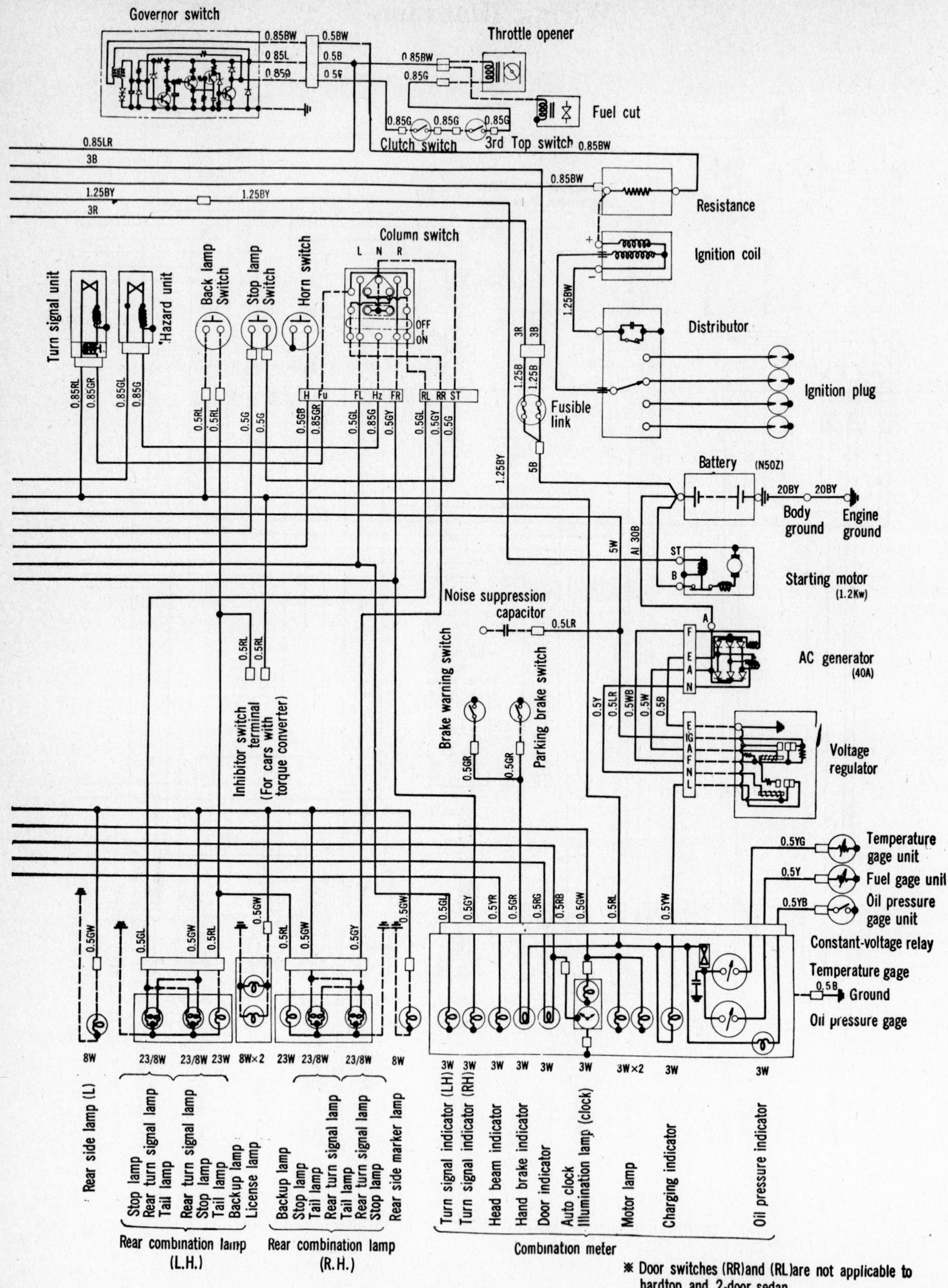

Wiring diagram—Sedan and Hardtop with manual transmission

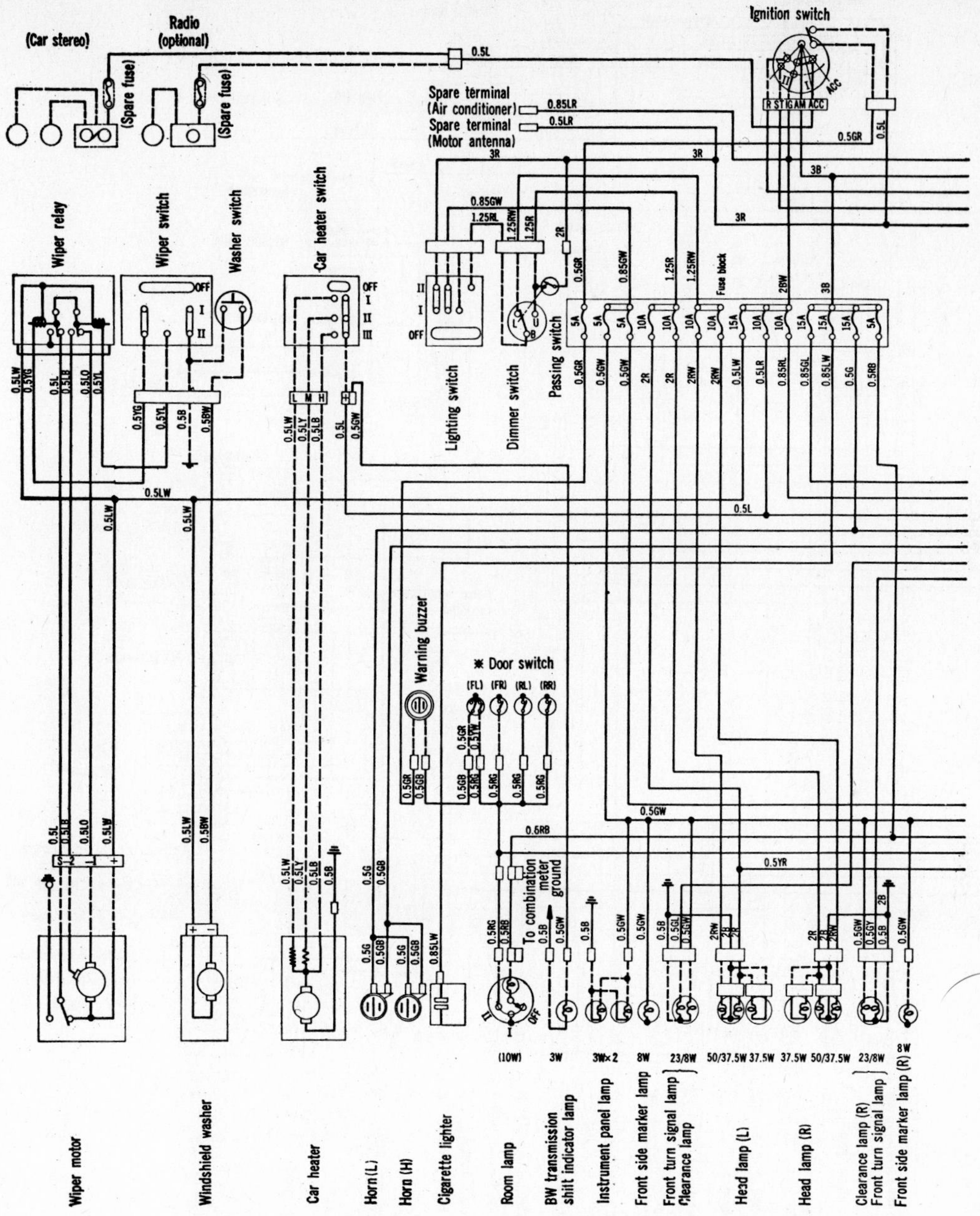

Wiring diagram—Sedan and Hardtop with automatic transmission

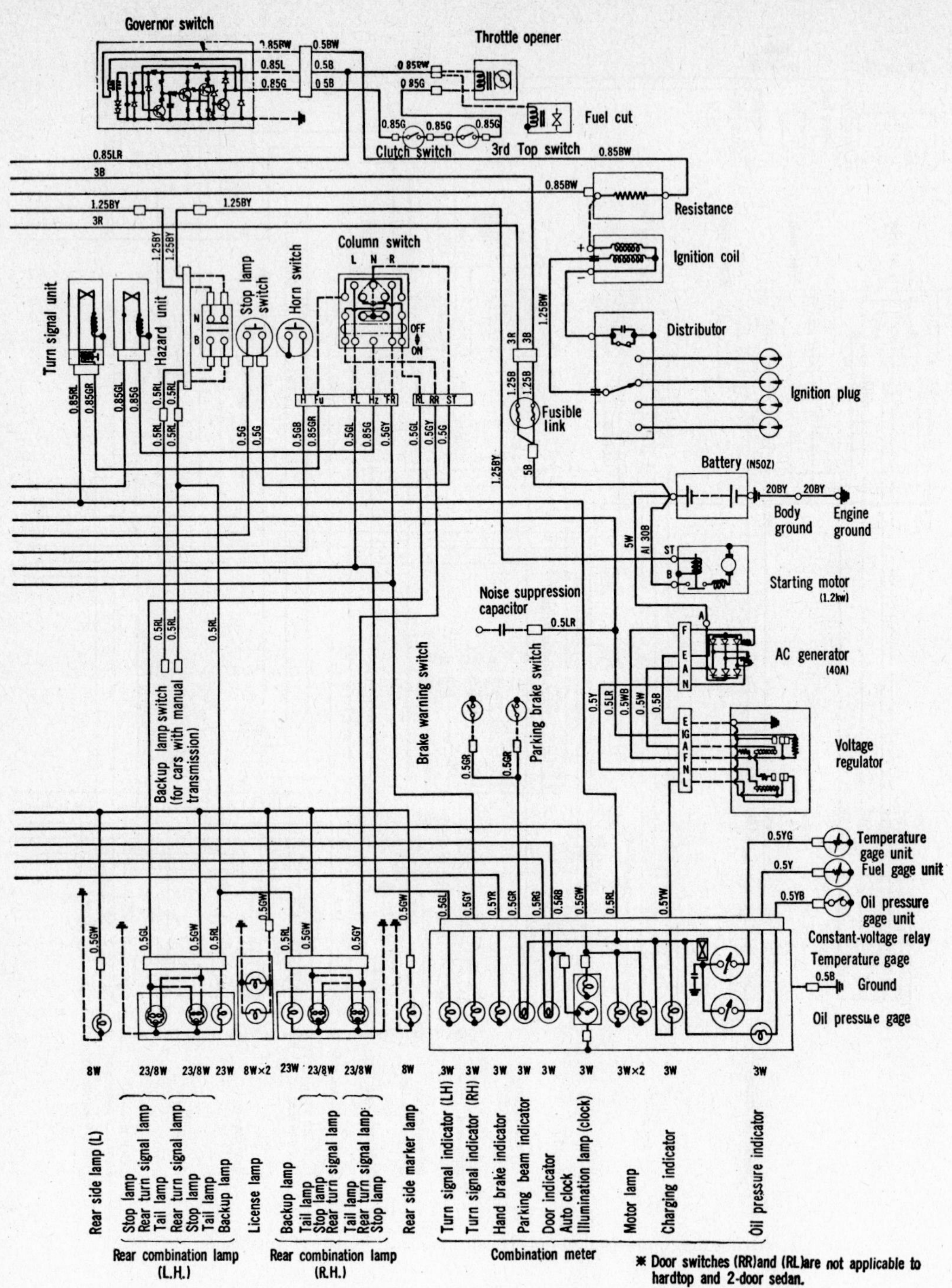

Wiring diagram—Sedan and Hardtop with automatic transmission

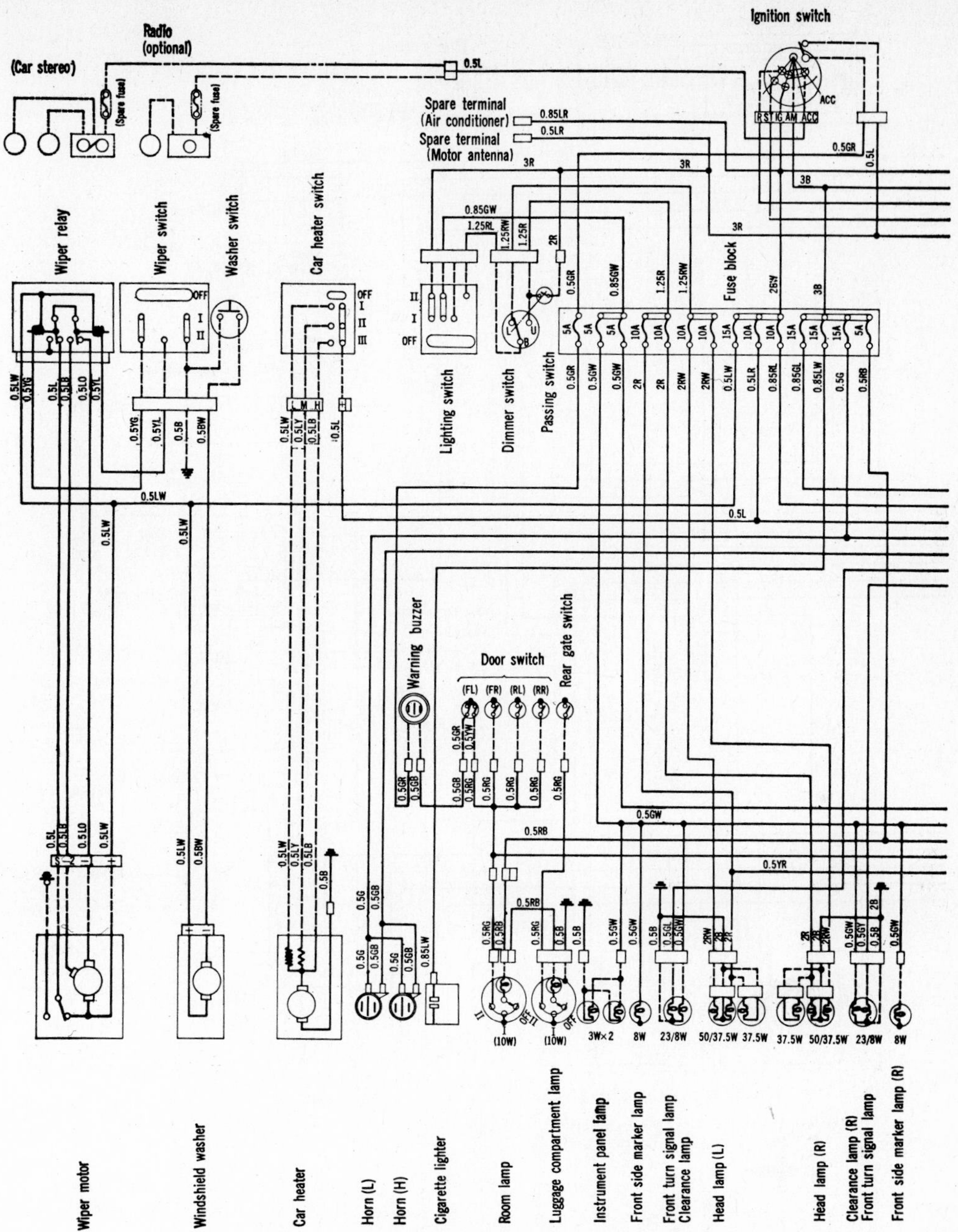

Wiring diagram—Station Wagon with manual transmission

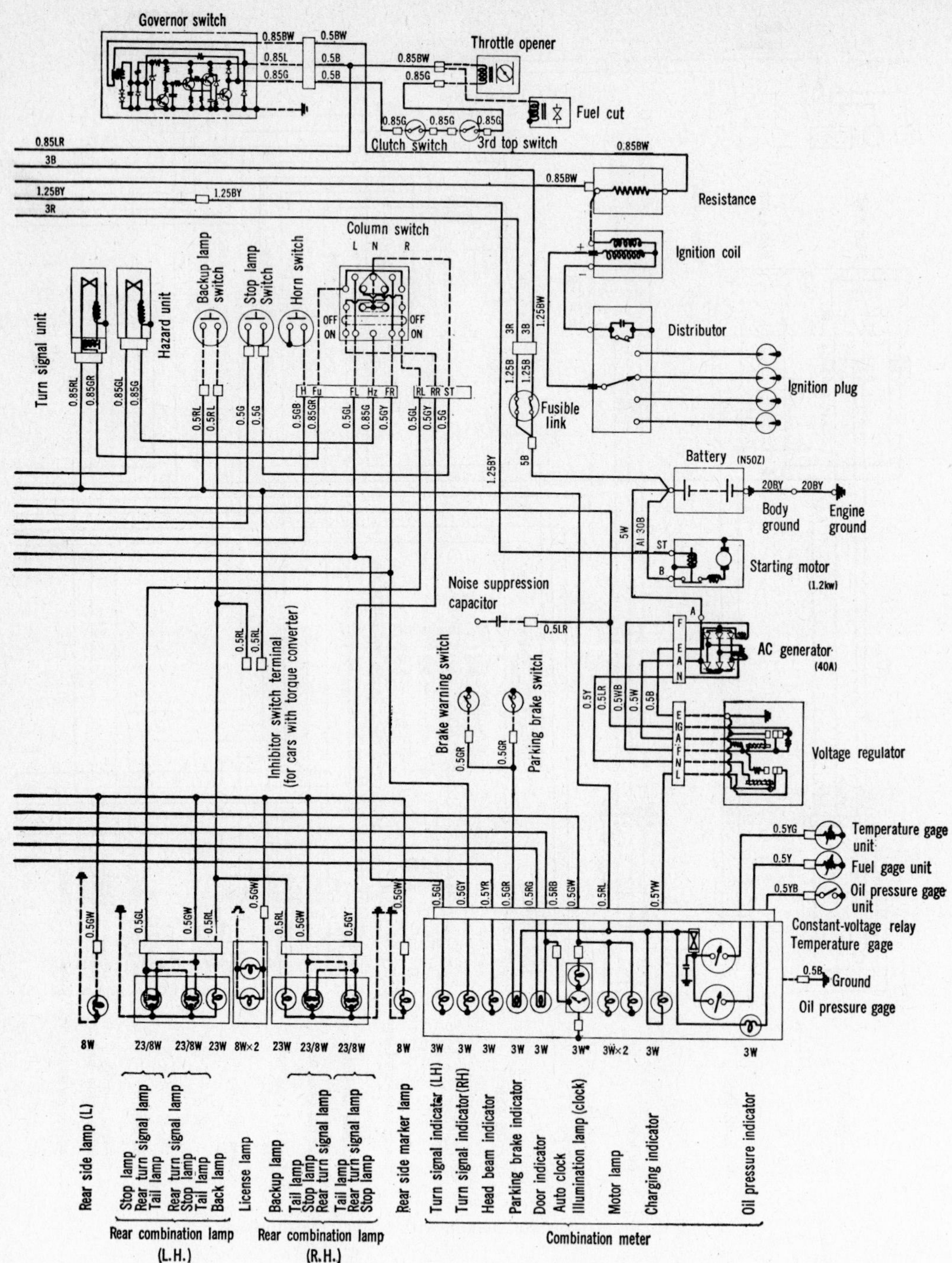

Wiring diagram—Station Wagon with manual transmission

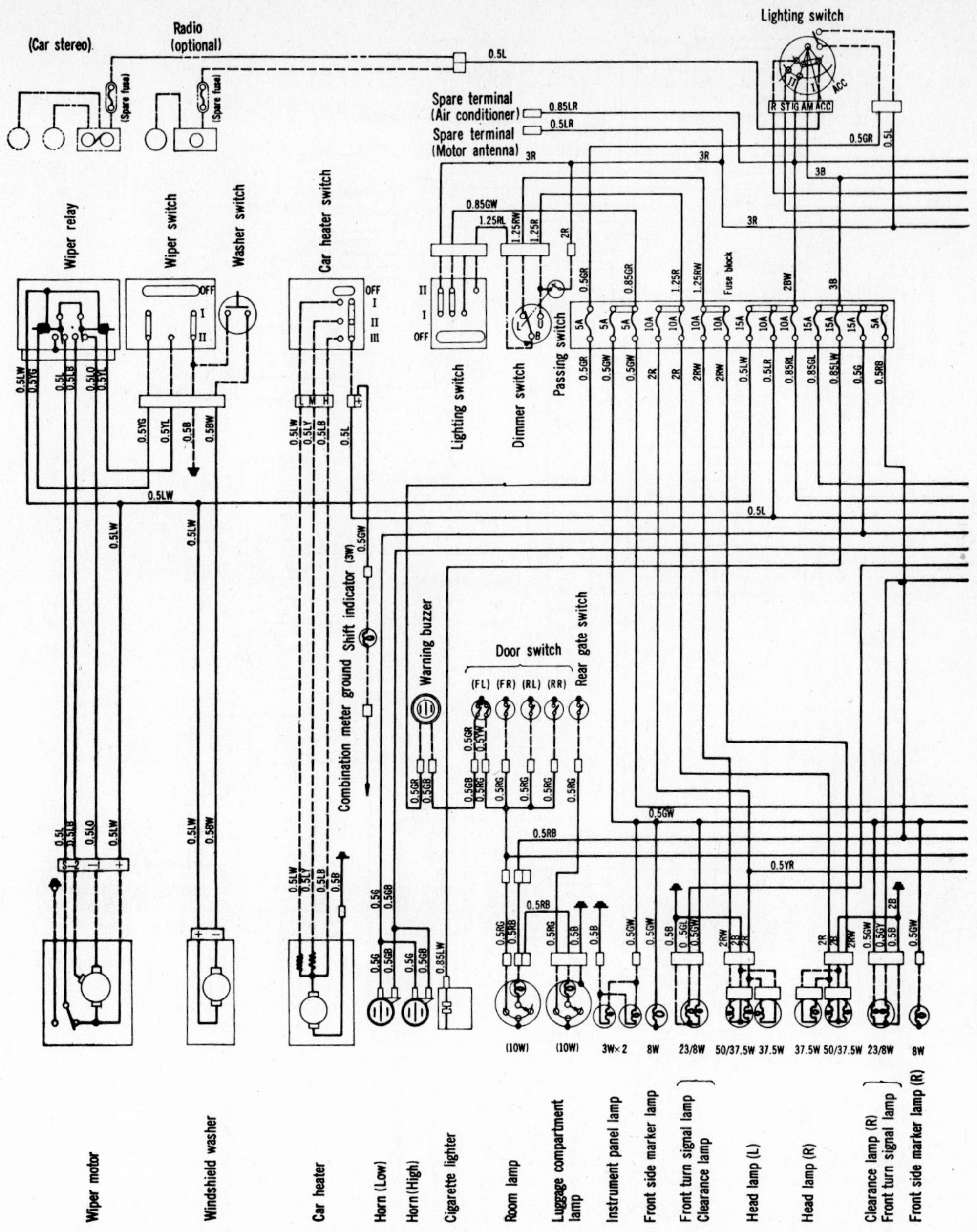

Wiring diagram—Station Wagon with automatic transmission

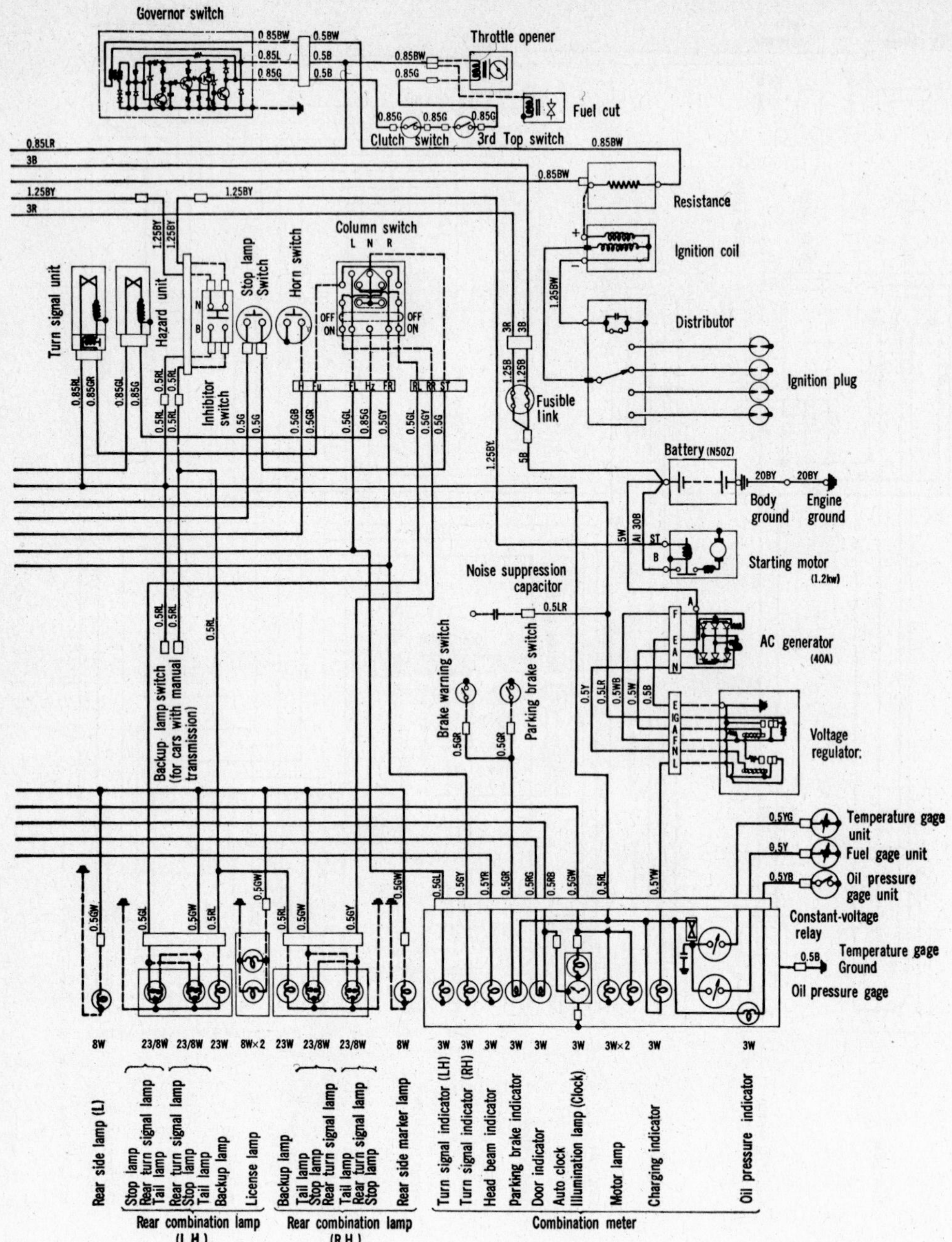

Wiring diagram—Station Wagon with automatic transmission

Carburetor Specifications

1 x 2 bbl.

Throttle Bore (in.)		Venturi (in.) Large		Venturi (in.) Small	Main Jet (in.)		Main Air Jet (in.)		Pilot Jet (in.)	
Prim.	Sec.	Prim.	Sec.	Prim./Sec.	Prim.	Sec.	Prim.	Sec.	Prim.	Sec.
1.102	1.260	.827	1.063	.354-.472	.0374	.0709 (MT) .0748 (AT)	.039	.047	.023	.047

Pilot Jet (in.) Primary (1)	Pilot Jet (in.) Prim. (2)	Pilot Jet (in.) Sec.	Enrichment Jet (in.)	Float Valve Seat (in.)	Fuel Level/ Pressure	Float Chamber Air Vent Hole (in.)	Accel. Pump Diaphragm Diameter (in.)	Pump Jet Length (in.)	Delivery Capacity
.063	.055	.039	.024 (MT) .018 (AT)	.079	①.748 in./ 4.3 psi	.276	.945	.014-.394	②.155 cu. in./stroke

①—Measured above top of throttle body.
②—Throttle valve opening over 70°

Engine Electrical

Distributor

Removal and Installation

Remove the distributor cap and disconnect the distributor primary lead from the coil. Rotate the engine until the rotor points toward the No. 1 tower in the distributor cap, and mark the relative position of the rotor to the distributor body, and the distributor body to the engine block. Remove the retaining nut, and lift out the distributor.

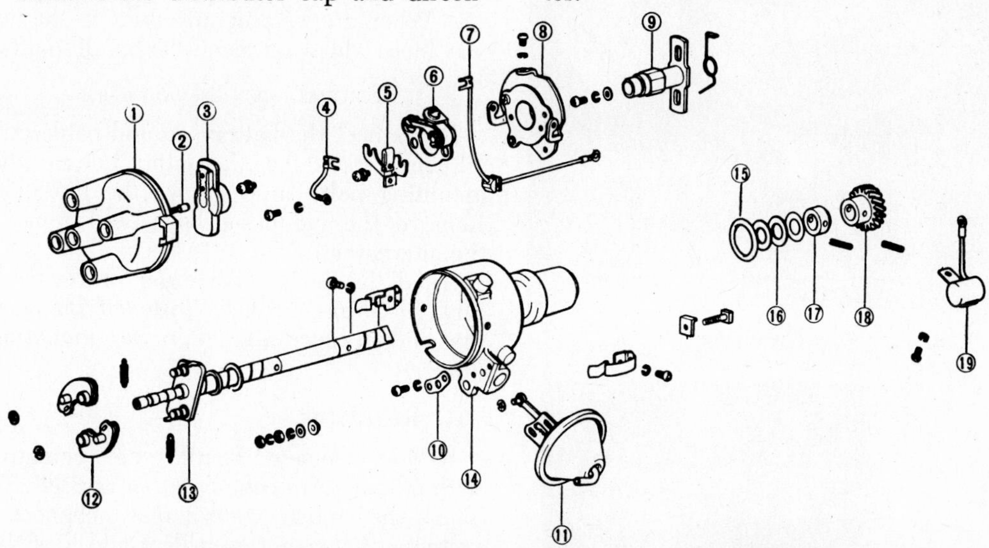

Distributor—exploded view

1 Cap
2 Carbon
3 Rotor
4 Ground wire
5 Cam felt
6 Arm support
7 Lead wire
8 Breaker base
9 Cam
10 Locking plate
11 Vacuum control
12 Governor weight
13 Shaft
14 Housing
15 O-ring
16 Washer
17 Thrust collar
18 Gear
19 Condenser

When installing, rotate the crankshaft so that the No. 1 cylinder is on the compression stroke, and the basic ignition timing is indicated by the timing marks. Point the rotor 15° counterclockwise of the No. 1 tower in the distributor cap, and insert the distributor into the block. If the oil pump drive will not engage (the distributor will not seat), remove the distributor, and turn the pump drive with a long screwdriver, so that it is perpendicular to the crankshaft centerline. Align the distributor body index marks, install and tighten the retaining nut. Check the ignition timing, and adjust if necessary.

Breaker Points

The breaker points are retained in the distributor by two screws. A spring loaded, felt wiper arm, which lubricates the distributor cam, is also retained by the screws. An eccentric screw, positioned in a slot in the base of the stationary point, is used to adjust point gap.

IGNITION TIMING

The ignition timing is adjusted with the vacuum advance hose disconnected and the engine running at idle speed. To adjust the timing, insert a Phillips head screwdriver into the hole provided in the vacuum advance mounting boss. Turning the screwdriver counterclockwise advances timing, clockwise retards timing. If correct ignition timing is outside the range of adjustment provided, loosen the distributor retaining nut, and rotate the distributor body in the appropriate direction to bring the correct timing within the adjustment range.

Adjusting timing

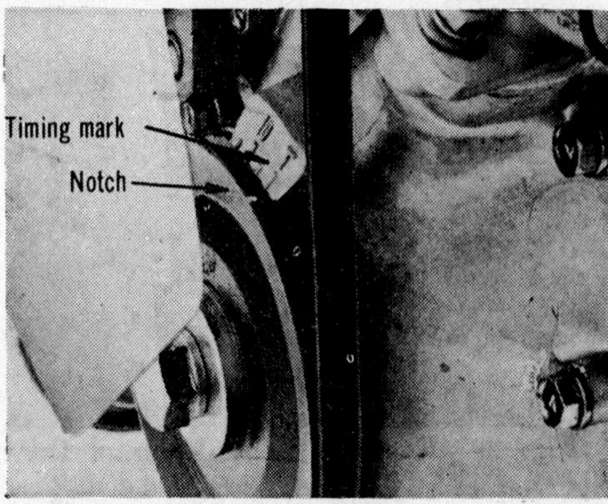

Timing marks

Ignition Timing Marks

The ignition timing marks are located at the front of the engine. A notch on the front edge of the fan pulley aligns with a scale integral with the timing cover. The marks are visible from the right side of the engine.

AC Generator

When servicing the charging system of vehicles equipped with an AC generator, the following precautions should be taken to avoid damaging the system.

1. Never operate the alternator on an open circuit (battery disconnected).
2. When installing a battery, connect the ground terminal (negative) before connecting the positive terminal.
3. When arc welding anywhere in the vehicle, always disconnect the alternator.

REMOVAL AND INSTALLATION

Disconnect the battery ground cable and all wires from the alternator. Loosen the mounting bolts, and remove the fan belt. Remove the mounting bolts, and remove the alternator.

Install in the reverse order of removal. NOTE: *Shims must be installed between the timing cover and alternator mounting bracket.*

AC Regulator

A dual element Tirrill type regulator, with temperature compensation, is used. To check the voltage control relay, connect a voltmeter between terminals A and E of the regulator connector, by inserting clips into the gaps in the connector. NOTE: *Do not disconnect the connector.* Start the engine, run at 2000 rpm and observe the voltage reading. If the reading is outside specifications, remove the regulator cover and adjust the voltage by bending the spring tensioner. Bending the tensioner downward

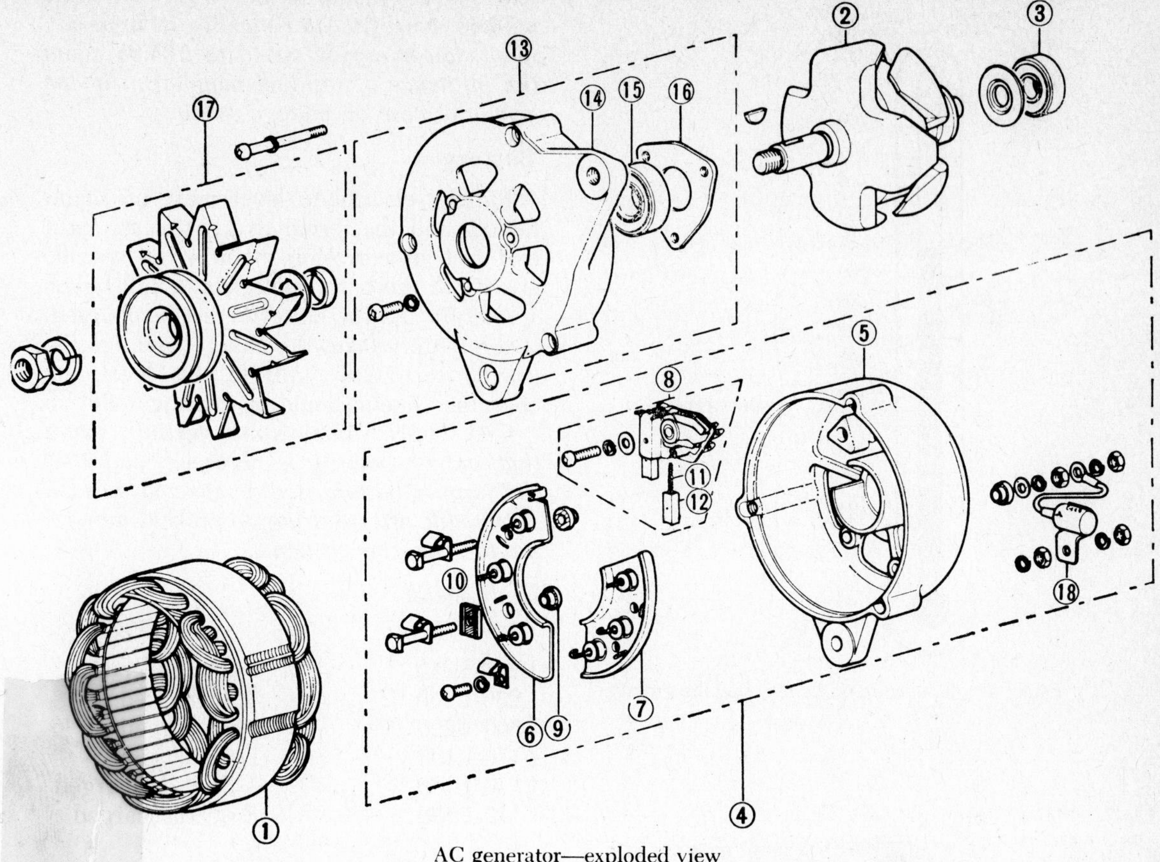

AC generator—exploded view

1 Stator
2 Rotor
3 Ball bearing
4 Rear bracket assembly
5 Rear bracket
6 Heat sink complete (+)
7 Heat sink complete (—)
8 Brush holder assembly
9 Insulator
10 Insulator
11 Brush spring
12 Brush
13 Front backet assembly
14 Front bracket
15 Ball bearing
16 Bearing retainer
17 Pulley
18 Condenser

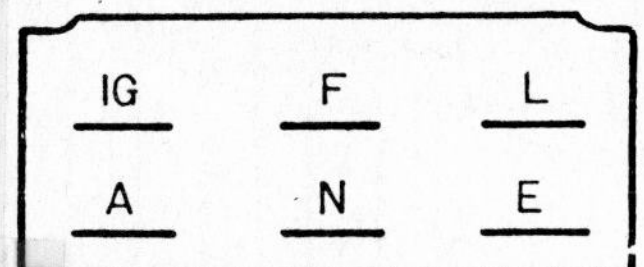

Regulator terminals

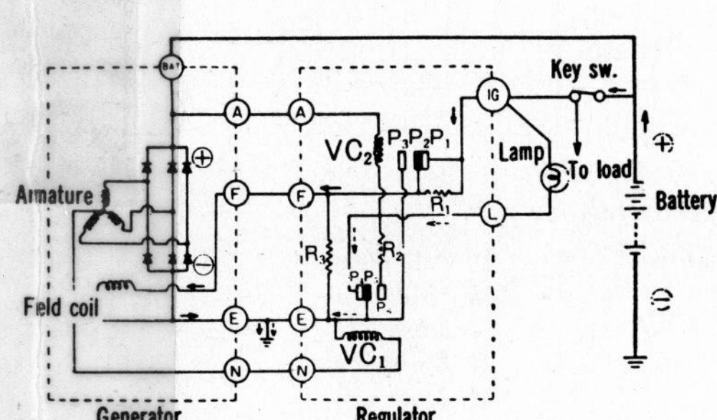

Schematic diagram of regulator

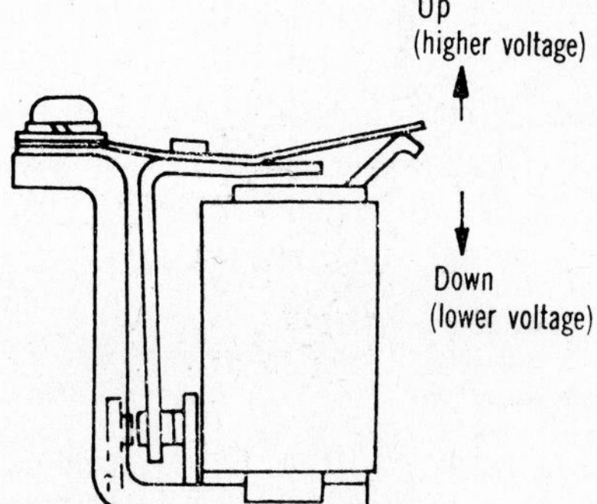

Adjusting the voltage

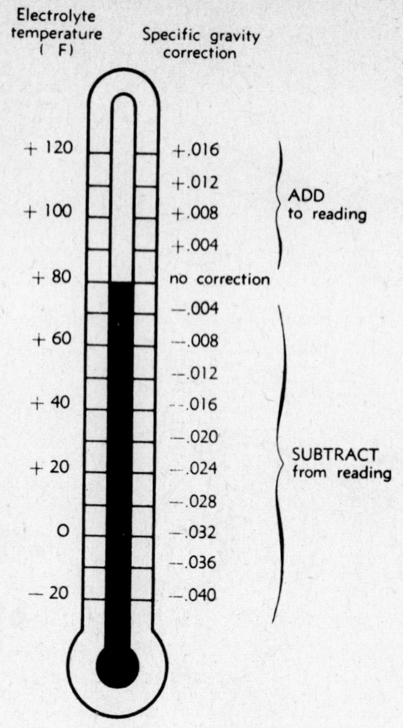

Effect of temperature on battery specific gravity

will lower voltage, and upward will raise voltage. NOTE: *After making each adjustment, lower engine speed to idle to avoid the influence of residual magnetism in the regulator core on voltage readings.*

Battery

Battery electrolyte level must be maintained, and the terminals kept clean, tight and free of corrosion. Should the specific gravity of the battery electrolyte fall below 1.19 at 68° F., the battery must be charged. If the battery takes the charge, and specific gravity repeatedly falls to this level, the charging system should be investigated.

CAUTION: *When jump starting ensure that proper polarity is observed, and that the jumper battery is disconnected as soon as possible after starting, to prevent damaging the charging system.*

Hydrometer Readings	*Condition*
1.260-1.310	Fully charged
1.230-1.250	3/4 charged
1.200-1.220	1/2 charged
1.170-1.190	1/4 charged
1.140-1.160	Almost discharged
1.110-1.130	Fully discharged

Starter—exploded view

1 Lever assembly
2 Lever spring (A)
3 Lever spring (B)
4 Spring retainer
5 Electromagnetic switch
6 Through bolt
7 Front bracket
8 Front bracket bearing
9 Plate
10 Stop ring
11 Overrunning clutch
12 Armature
13 Insulating washer
14 Yoke assembly
15 Pole piece
16 Field coil
17 Brush
18 Brush holder
19 Brush spring
20 Rear bracket
21 Rear backet bearing

Starter

REMOVAL AND INSTALLATION

Disconnect the battery ground cable. Code for identification and remove all starter wires. Remove the starter mounting bolts, and lift out the starter.

Before installing the starter, clean the mating surfaces on the engine and the starter mounting bracket. Install in the reverse order of removal.

Fuel System

Fuel Pump

REMOVAL AND INSTALLATION

Remove the fuel lines from the pump and cover the ends. Unbolt the pump mounting bolts, and remove the pump, insulator, and gasket.

Coat both sides of a new insulator and gasket with sealer, and install the pump in the reverse order of removal.

Rebuilding

Remove the cap and the diaphragm from the upper body. Remove the retaining screws, and separate the upper body from the lower body. Pull out the rocker arm pivot pin, and remove the rocker arm, diaphragm, and diaphragm spring from the lower body. NOTE: *Neither the intake and outlet valves nor the fuel return valve should be removed from the fuel pump body.*

Inspect the diaphragm for cracks and hardening, and replace if necessary. Check the intake and outlet valves for action and sealing.

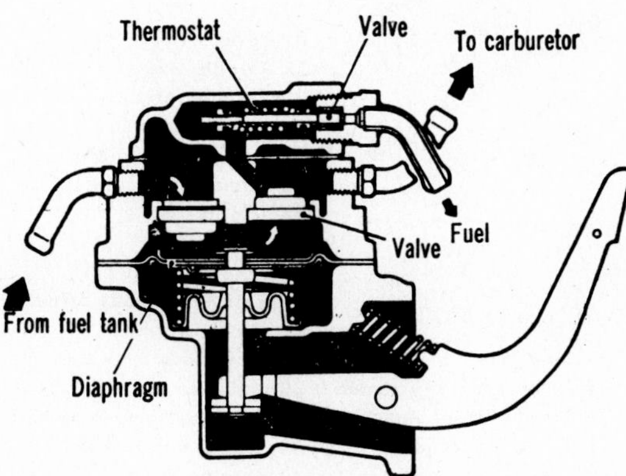

Fuel pump showing internal parts

Carburetors

The carburetor used on all Colt vehicles consists of an emission controlled, downdraft, two barrel unit.

REMOVAL AND INSTALLATION

Remove solenoid valve wiring. Disconnect air cleaner breather hose, air duct and vacuum tube. Loosen wing nuts and remove air cleaner. Unscrew support bolts and remove air cleaner case. Remove accelerator and shift cables (automatic transmission) at carburetor. Disconnect purge valve hose; remove vacuum, compensator, and fuel lines. Loosen drain plug (on right side of block) and drain the water. NOTE: *Water contains anti-freeze and may be reused.*

After block is completely drained, remove water hose between carburetor and cylinder head. Be sure to have some clean, dry rags at hand to catch any overflow. Remove the carburetor.

To replace carburetor, reverse removal procedure. Be sure to use a new gasket and coat with commercial sealer.

Disassembly

Be sure to keep all parts separate to avoid confusion. Disconnect the throttle return spring and intermediate spring. Remove choke rod and depression chamber rod. Pull off water hose. Take off idle compensator. Remove accelerator pump ball and weight. Remove screws holding float chamber cover in place. Lift off cover. Remove accelerator pump lever rod at throttle shaft. Remove Phillips screws holding throttle and main body of carburetor together. Separate the throttle and carburetor main body, and remove packing and insulator. CAUTION: *Under no circumstances remove pump lever rod nut.* Disassemble the main body.

Inspection

Clean all parts in appropriate solvent. Clean all carburetor passages with compressed air. If passages are still dirty, a non-metallic object may be used to loosen dirt. Check all parts for cracking. In addition, check needle and seat for contact. Examine all membranes, screw seats, and linkage for wear, and replace as necessary.

To check accelerator pump, fill float chamber with gasoline and move throttle lever. If a leaking diaphragm is suspected,

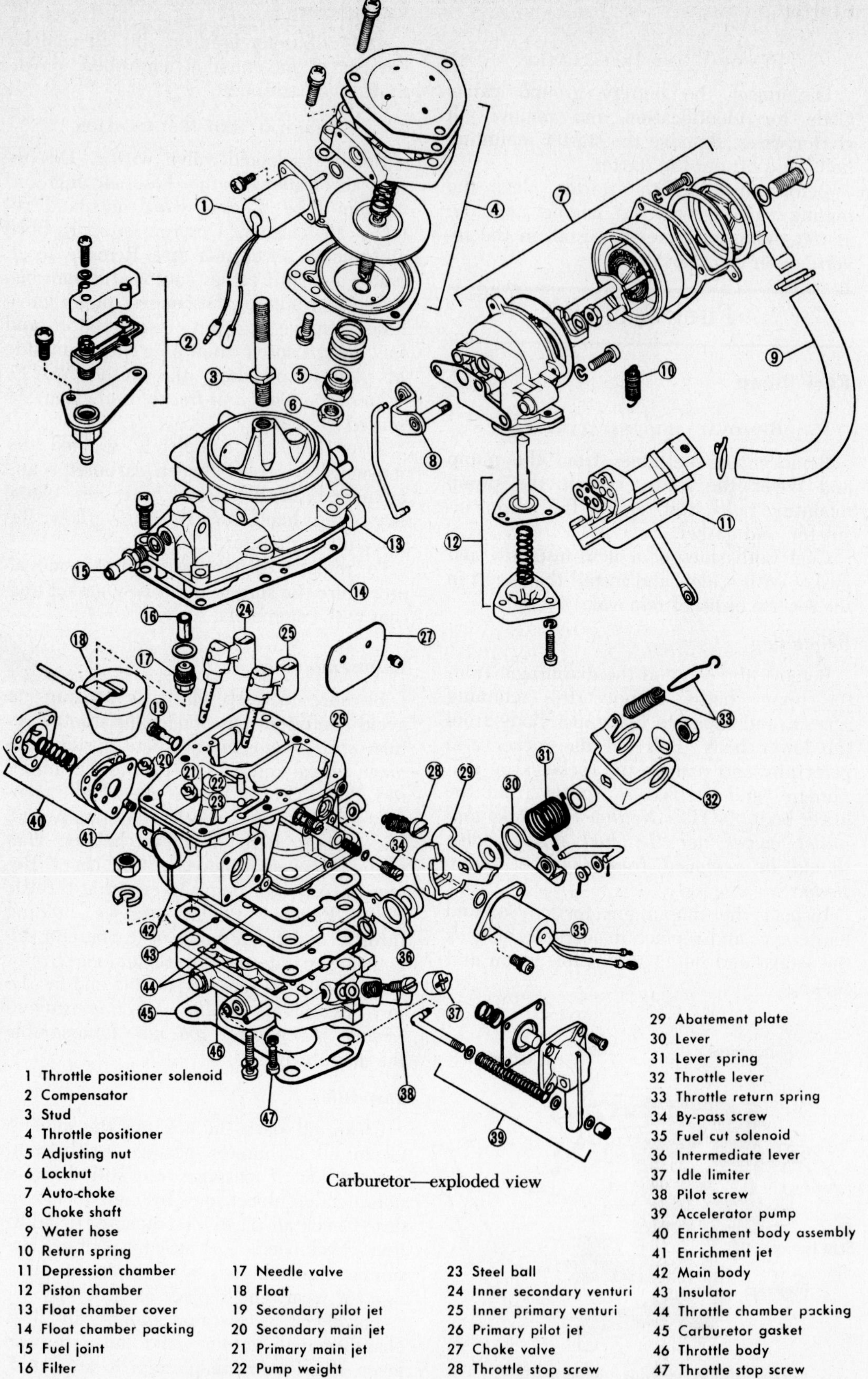

1 Throttle positioner solenoid
2 Compensator
3 Stud
4 Throttle positioner
5 Adjusting nut
6 Locknut
7 Auto-choke
8 Choke shaft
9 Water hose
10 Return spring
11 Depression chamber
12 Piston chamber
13 Float chamber cover
14 Float chamber packing
15 Fuel joint
16 Filter
17 Needle valve
18 Float
19 Secondary pilot jet
20 Secondary main jet
21 Primary main jet
22 Pump weight
23 Steel ball
24 Inner secondary venturi
25 Inner primary venturi
26 Primary pilot jet
27 Choke valve
28 Throttle stop screw
29 Abatement plate
30 Lever
31 Lever spring
32 Throttle lever
33 Throttle return spring
34 By-pass screw
35 Fuel cut solenoid
36 Intermediate lever
37 Idle limiter
38 Pilot screw
39 Accelerator pump
40 Enrichment body assembly
41 Enrichment jet
42 Main body
43 Insulator
44 Throttle chamber packing
45 Carburetor gasket
46 Throttle body
47 Throttle stop screw

Carburetor—exploded view

push down on depression chamber connecting rod, seal vacuum passage with finger, and check for leakage.

Assembly

If the choke and throttle shaft interlocking section are hard to operate, wash in solvent and apply oil before assembly. Be sure to use new gaskets. Make certain they are installed properly. When replacing diaphragms, take care not to distort or damage them. If the throttle body has been disassembled, set the throttle valve stop screw in the fully closed position. Loosen screw 1/4 turn and tighten locknut.

Main Body

Install main and pilot jet. Be sure not to reverse jets by utilizing following code, which is marked on the jet.

Primary Pilot Jet-57.5
Secondary Pilot Jet-70
Primary Main Jet-95
Secondary Main Jet-180

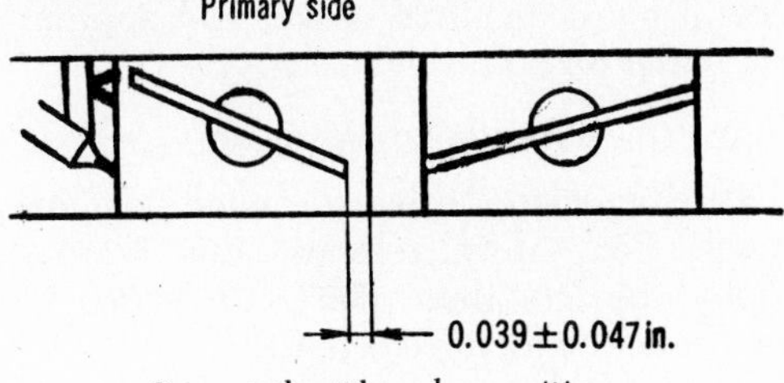

Correct throttle valve position

Be sure that pilot jet O-ring fits properly in groove. Note that the skirt section of the inner venturi (primary side) has a groove cut in it. Replace the enrichment valve and spring. This spring (length, .984″) should not be confused with any others. Install pump cover and accelerator pump (spring length, .512″).

Replace throttle and main body and connect pump rod end to throttle shaft. When installing insulator packing, be sure that all holes are aligned.

Float Chamber Cover Installation

Replace idle compensator and automatic choke case. Install membrane and spring (length 1.299″). Being certain of proper valve side, insert choke shaft and valve. Fit diaphragm ring in body groove (press fit). Assemble the depression chamber so that joint face will fit into the float chamber cover. Be sure shaft on which nylon bearing rides is parallel with joint face and bushing is directed outward.

Assemble the depression and float chamber. Replace strainer and valve seat. When tightening seat, be sure not to crack strainer. Replace needle valve and clip. Hold float upright with pin. Install weight and accelerator pump ball on top side of main body.

Using packing, install float chamber cover. Connect rod and spring. Bend connecting rod section with fast idle cam engaged (fourth position) so that throttle

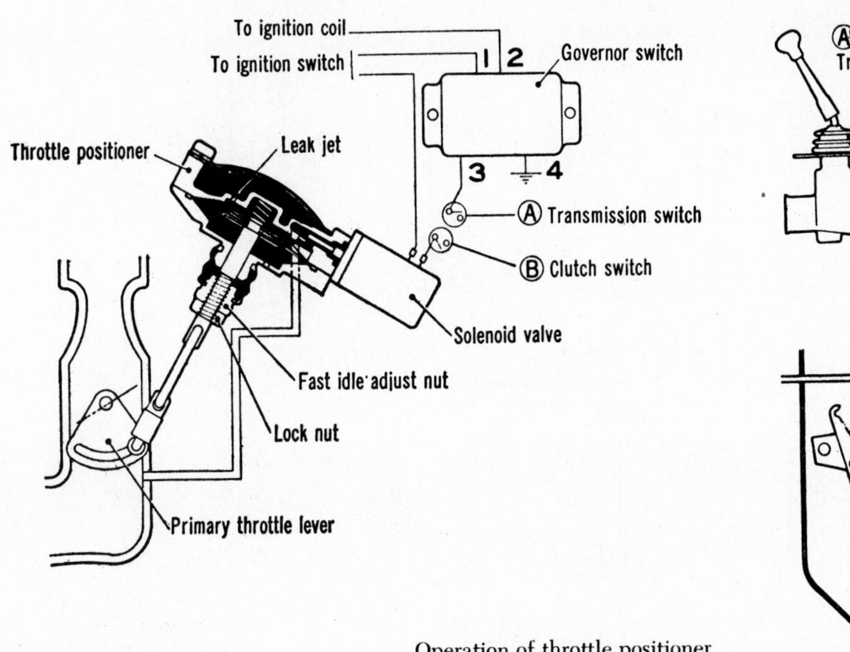

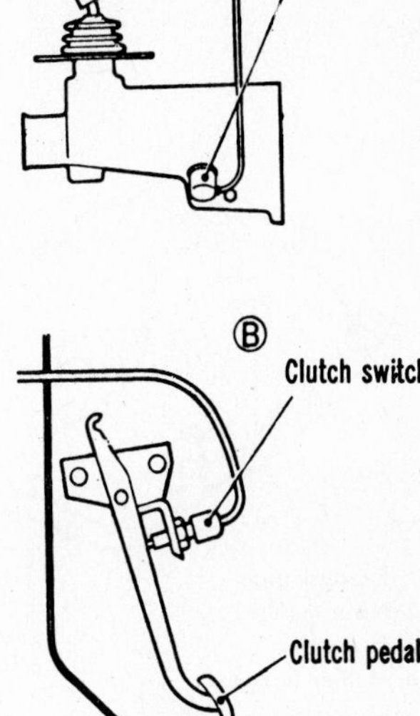

Operation of throttle positioner

opening will be as prescribed (see illustration). Be sure rod is completely engaged and at proper angle.

Replace choke ring and tighten so that red line on case aligns with similar mark on choke case. Set choke valve to fully closed position at 77°.

THROTTLE POSITIONER AND IDLE SPEED ADJUSTMENTS

Run engine at idle speed for two minutes with engine at 170°-190°. Initially operate pilot and primary throttle stop screw. Temporarily adjust idle speed to 700-750 rpm. Carbon monoxide reading should be no higher than 3.5-5%. Place idle limiter cap on top end of pilot screw. CAUTION: *Be sure not to injure screw during this operation.*

Adjust throttle and pilot screw to obtain a reading of *LESS THAN* 3.5-5% CO at 700-750 rpm. Run the engine at idle speed for six minutes. After six minutes of operation, adjust throttle position in the following manner.

Disconnect boost pipe running between intake manifold and air cleaner. Remove air cleaner. Block off boost pipe hole at intake manifold side. Remove green (negative) wire of solenoid at its solenoid juncture. Accelerate engine to 2,500-3,000 rpm. Ground green (negative) wire to carburetor and place solenoid in on position. Release pressure on throttle lever. Be sure throttle positioner is set for 1,350-1,450 rpm. If incorrect, adjust with throttle positioning nut.

Exhaust System

All Colt exhaust manifolds are made from cast iron. Cylinders one and four are grouped together in the manifold as are two and three. This prevents overlapping exhaust pulses from interfering with each other and causing back pressure. A conventional muffler-resonator combination is employed.

Manifold Removal

Disconnect air cleaner and remove all tubing. Remove the air filter and jack the front of vehicle. Disconnect the exhaust pipe at exhaust manifold flange. Loosen bolts and remove manifold.

Installation

Reverse removal procedures and torque bolts to 10.8-14.5 ft.lbs. Be sure to use a new exhaust manifold gasket and appropriate sealer on both sides.

MANIFOLD WARPAGE

On occasion, exhaust manifolds may warp. For safety reasons, this warpage should be less than .006". Under no circumstances may it exceed .012".

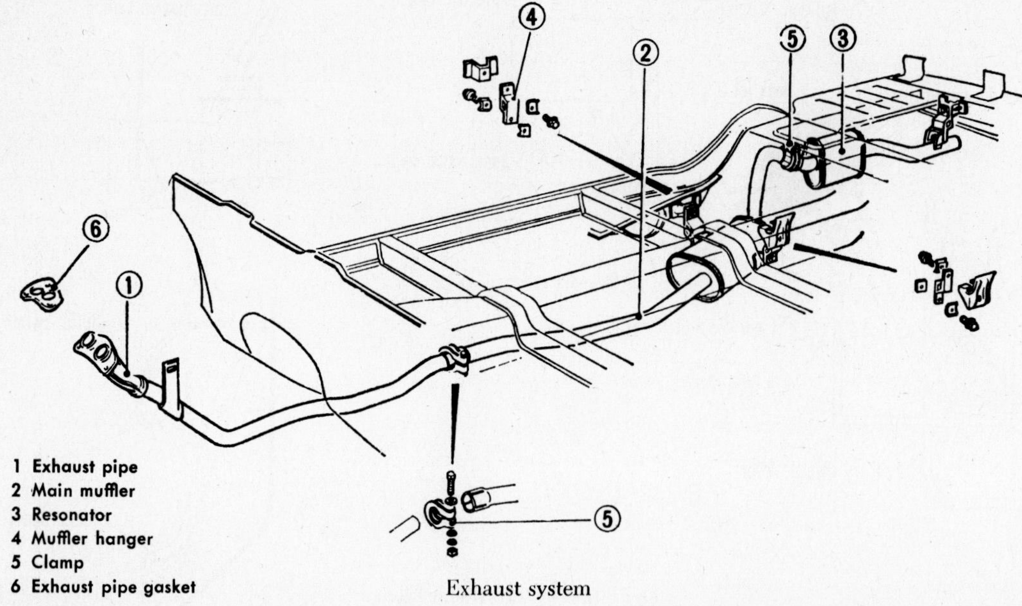

1 Exhaust pipe
2 Main muffler
3 Resonator
4 Muffler hanger
5 Clamp
6 Exhaust pipe gasket

Exhaust system

Cooling System

Radiator

REMOVAL

Loosen drain plug and drain coolant. Remove all radiator hoses at engine end. Take four attaching bolts from radiator sides and lift radiator from vehicle. CAUTION: *If car is equipped with automatic transmission, remove front oil tube. Be aware of possible fluid spillage, when disconnecting cover tube end to prevent entry of foreign matter. Also, when lifting radiator from car, use caution as the core is easily damaged.*

INSTALLATION

When replacing radiator, be sure to align white marks on lower radiator hose. If car is equipped with an automatic transmission, be sure to replace all lost transmission fluid. To replace radiator, reverse removal procedure.

Water Pump

REMOVAL

Drain engine cooling system (the coolant may be used again). Swing alternator from position and remove fan pulley and belt. Remove attachments and lift off water pump.

Disassembly

Remove impeller from the pump body. Using the minimum necessary force, drive seal from body. Heat pump body to 212° and press the shaft assembly towards pulley.

Check bearings for excessive wear. Closely inspect other parts and replace as necessary. If pump has a history of leaking, replace all seals.

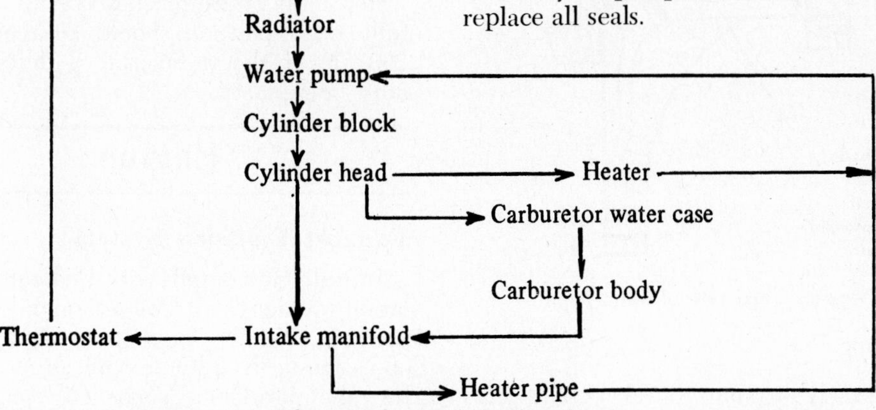

Schematic diagram of coolant flow

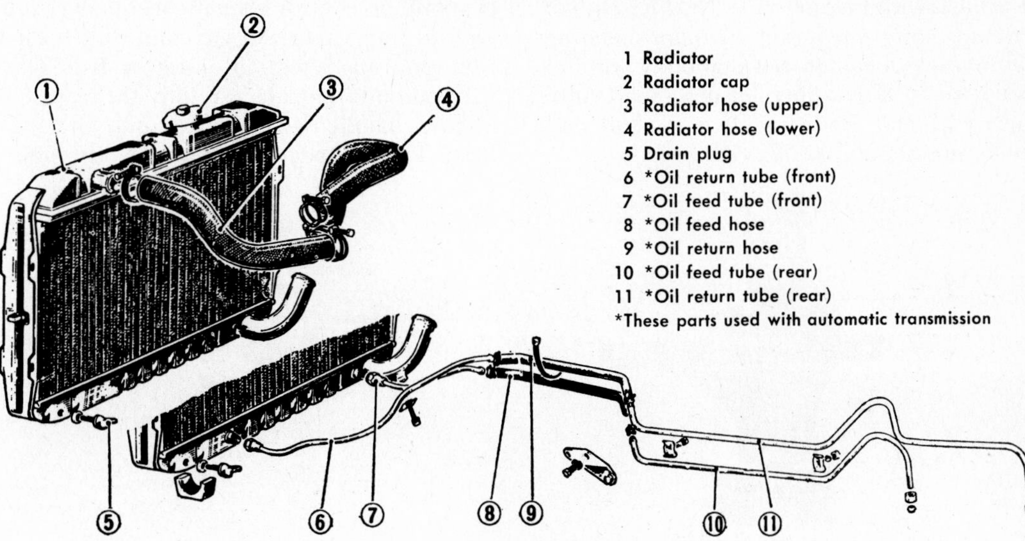

Radiator parts

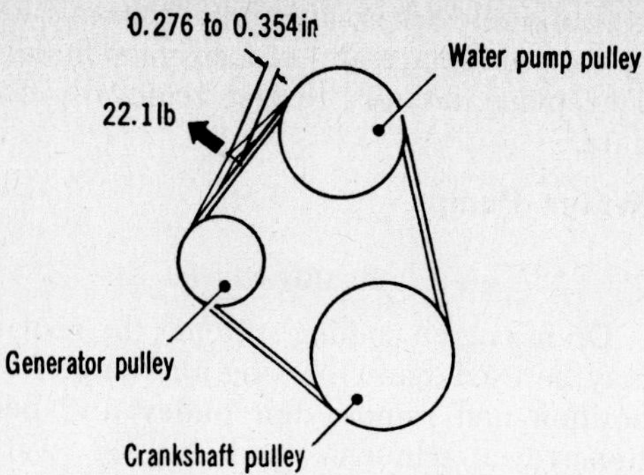

Fan belt adjustment

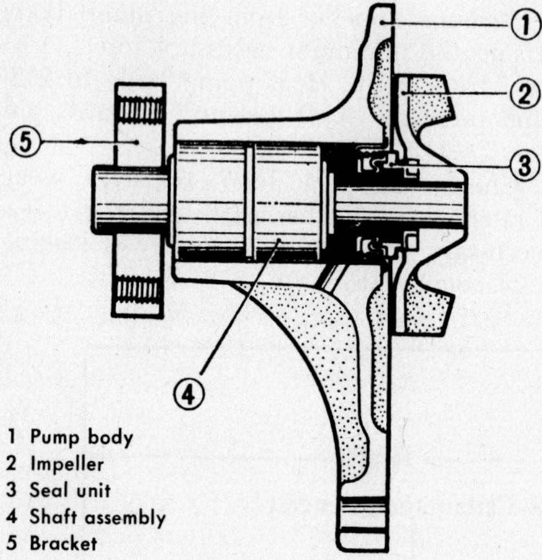

Cross-sectional view of water pump

Assembly

Heat body of pump to 212°. Using press, drive shaft assembly into body unit. Be sure it is flush with bearing face. NOTE: *Do not attempt this operation without heating pump body.* Use new seals on body and impeller sides. Drive impeller onto shaft until flush with end. Body end face to shaft end dimension should be .772-.788″

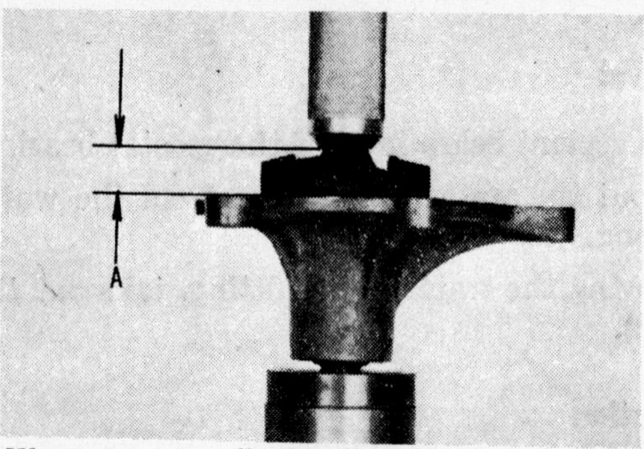

Water pump impeller installation—Dimension A= .772-788″

INSTALLATION

To replace pump, reverse removal procedure. When installing pump body on timing chain case, be sure to use new packing and an adequate amount of sealant. Rotate the shaft to be sure impeller does not interfere with case. Install the fan pulley and belt. Adjust the belt tension using the illustration. Replace coolant and check for leaks with engine running.

Thermostat R&R

Drain coolant from engine. Remove the water outlet hose from fitting, located next to intake manifold. Remove thermostat. To replace, reverse removal procedure. Be sure to use a good sealant on the water outlet fitting.

TESTING

Immerse the thermostat in water. The thermostat should begin to open when the water temperature reaches 179-182° F. The fully open position should be reached at 203° F. If the thermostat is defective, it must be replaced.

Engine

Exhaust Emission System

In order to comply with Federal air pollution standards, all Colt automobiles incorporate a Cleaner Air System. This consists of various carburetor modifications (throttle valve positioner, leaner jets, etc.) and a fuel tank evaporative emission system. The evaporative control system consists of a sub tank to trap vaporized gas and a filter canister equipped with a purge valve. This valve admits outside air into the canister to force condensed gas back into the fuel lines. The charcoal contained in this canis-

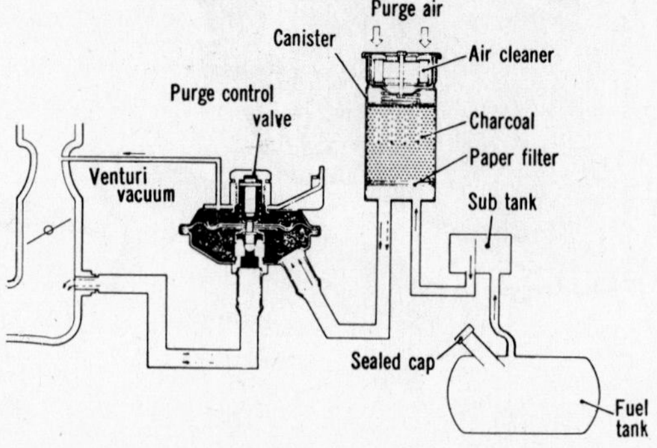

Evaporative emission system schematic diagram

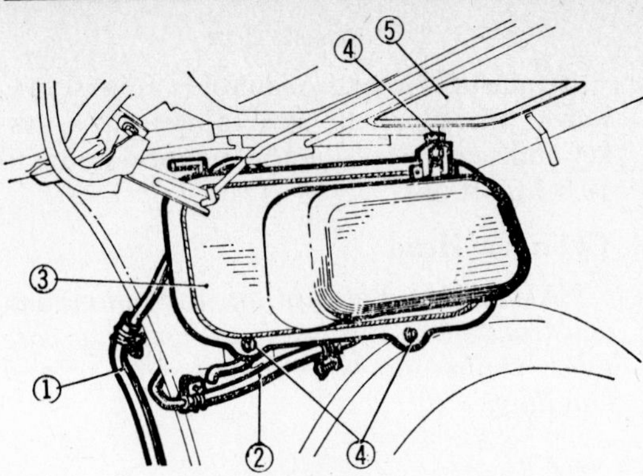

Sub tank schematic diagram

1 Liquid tube
2 Vapor tube
3 Sub tank
4 Attaching bolt
5 Shelf trim

Exploded view of charcoal canister

1 Canister body
2 Filter
3 Strainer
4 Charcoal
5 Plate
6 Spring
7 Plate
8 Spacer
9 Air cleaner element
10 Cup

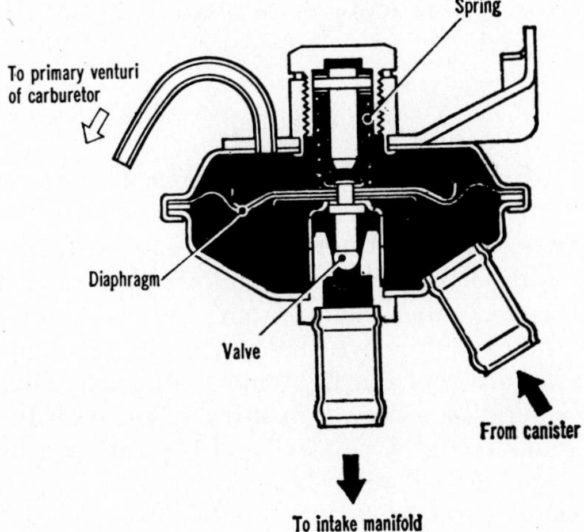

Purge valve schematic diagram

ter must be serviced at 50,000 mile intervals. When replacing charcoal (8.802.), be sure to remove all carbon dust. In addition, this canister contains a filter paper and air cleaner. These must be replaced yearly or at 12,000 mile intervals.

Purge Valve Maintenance

This valve must be checked for proper operation at 24,000 mile intervals. Apply a vacuum of -19.69 in. Hg. to the carburetor side of the intake manifold. If purge valve air flow rate is *less* than .071 cubic feet per minute, valve is operating properly. NOTE: *Poor idle may also be indicative of an inoperative purge valve. Service is by replacement.*

Engine/Transmission Removal

1. Loosen attaching bolts and remove hood. Remove bridge panel and front grill. Drain radiator and remove from vehicle. On automatic transmission equipped vehicles, be sure to use catch pan when removing oil line from radiator. Disconnect and remove battery.
2. Disconnect the ground strap, ignition coil wiring and vacuum and fuel solenoid valves.
3. Disconnect the following: generator, starter, transmission switch, backup light switch, temperature gauge and oil pressure gauge.
4. Disconnect all hoses and remove air cleaner.
5. Disconnect all carburetor linkage at rear of engine. Remove heater hose.
6. Unbolt exhaust pipe at manifold flange and disconnect muffler pipe bracket at transmission.
7. Remove hose between fuel filter and fuel pump return line. Be sure gas spillage is held to a minimum.
8. Remove vacuum hose from purge control valve.
9. Disconnect the speedometer cable, backup light and distributor switches.
10. Disconnect clutch cable and shift lever.
11. Remove cross shaft and control rod from bracket under transmission.
12. Gently take off leatherette cover (inside car) and remove shifter assembly.
13. Attach a hoist to the engine and tension slightly to remove weight from the engine mounts. Remove the attaching bolts from the engine mounts, and lift the engine upward and forward.

Installation

To replace engine, reverse the order of removal. Note the following when installing the engine.

Drape clean rags at rear of cylinder head to prevent damage to firewall when lowering engine in position.

Bolt the front of the engine in place first.

TORQUE SPECIFICATIONS

Engine support bracket nuts: 14-18 ft. lbs.
Front insulator to sub frame bolts: 15-17 ft. lbs.
Front insulator to engine bracket nut 15-17 ft. lbs.
Front bolt, cylinder block to engine bracket: 29-36 ft. lbs.
Rear insulator support bracket bolt: 7-8.5 ft. lbs.
Support bracket to body bolt: 7-8.5 ft. lbs.
Rear insulator to frame bolt:
Manual transmission: 15-17 ft. lbs.
Automatic transmission: 9-11.5 ft. lbs.

Intake Manifold

REMOVAL

Drain cooling system. Be sure to keep water for later use. Remove water outlet and heater hoses. Disconnect accelerator and choke linkages. Remove vacuum, fuel, and water connections at carburetor. Disconnect water temperature gauge. Loosen attaching bolts and remove intake manifold.

Inspection

Check manifold mounting face for distortion. A tolerance of .006-.012″ is permissible. If the distortion exceeds the tolerance, mill the intake manifold mounting face.

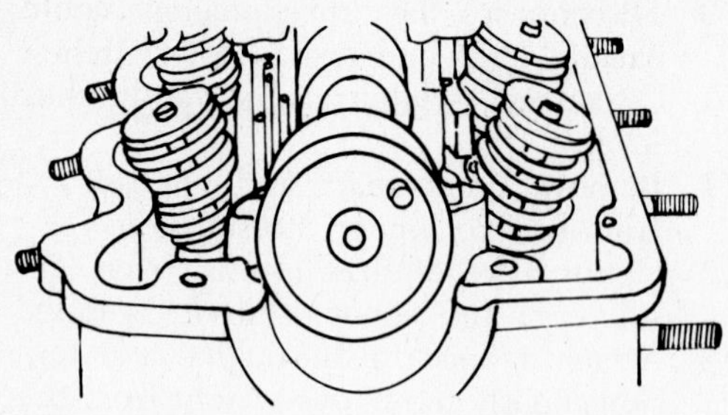

Position of installed camshaft dowel pin

INSTALLATION

To install intake manifold, reverse removal procedure. Be sure to use a new gasket and sealer. Torque the mounting nuts to 10.8-14.5 ft. lbs.

Cylinder Head

CAUTION: *Because of the aluminum construction of the head, use extreme care when tightening bolts and during general handling.*

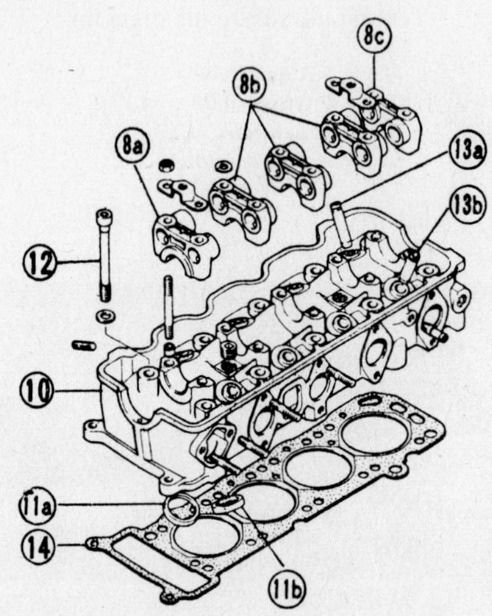

Exploded view of cylinder head

8a Camshaft bearing cap
8b No. 2, 3 and 4 caps
8c Camshaft bearing cap (rear)
10 Cylinder head
11a Intake valve seat ring
11b Exhaust valve seat ring
12 Cylinder head bolt
13a Exhaust valve guide
13b Intake valve guide
14 Cylinder head gasket

REMOVAL

Remove valve cover. Relieve tension on timing chain by turning tensioner lever, located inside timing chain case. Remove camshaft sprocket and timing chain. Do not remove the chain from the crankshaft sprocket. Remove the head bolts reversing the order of the tightening sequence. They should be removed in three stages with the engine cold. Cylinder head is positioned by four dowel pins (two front, two rear). When removing the head from engine deck, lift it straight up to prevent damaging the locating dowels.

Inspection

After removal, visually inspect head for cracks or scoring on the mounting surface. Check the cylinder head face for warpage, which should not exceed .002″. The head may be milled a maximum of .012″ to correct deep scoring.

Disassembly

See the Engine Rebuilding Section of this manual for cylinder head service procedures.

INSTALLATION

Install the gasket on the block with reference to a matchmark on the top of the block. Be sure that the joining surfaces of the chain case and top of the cylinder block are smooth and parallel. Install the cylinder head on the block, making sure that the dowels locate properly. Tighten the bolts in three stages, weakly at first, progressing to the specified torque. Be sure that the timing marks on the chain and camshaft gear are aligned. Install the camshaft sprocket on the camshaft, being sure that the locating pin seats in the hole. If it is hard to install the sprocket loosen the timing chain tensioner.

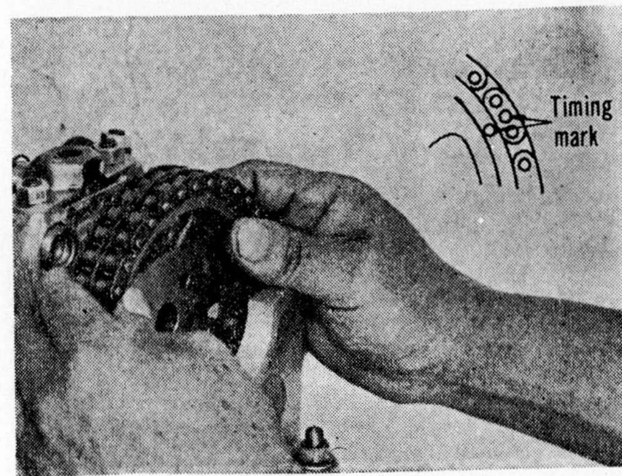

Camshaft sprocket installation

Valve Train

VALVE ADJUSTMENT PROCEDURES

Rotate engine to TDC of each cylinder. Loosen the rocker arm nuts. Adjust valves (cold) to .003 in. intake and .007 in. exhaust. Tighten the adjusting nuts. Start engine and run to operating temperature. Loosen the rocker arm nuts and adjust the valve clearance to the specified hot clearance (see specifications). Tighten the rocker arm nuts and install the valve cover.

CAMSHAFT AND ROCKER ARM

Removal

Remove the valve cover. Relieve tension on the timing chain by turning the tensioner lever, located inside the timing case. Remove the camshaft sprocket and timing chain. Do not remove the chain from the crankshaft sprocket. Support the camshaft gear and chain on the cylinder head. Remove spark plugs. Remove camshaft bearing cap nuts from camshaft bearing caps. While holding front and rear cap, lift off rocker arm assembly. NOTE: *If rocker arms are disassembled, be sure to replace components in the same order: rocker arm no. 1 to cylinder no. 1, etc. Be careful not to lose bearing cap dowel pins.* Lift camshaft from head.

Installation

Installation is the reverse of removal. Be sure to install the camshaft so that the dowel pin on the leading face of the camshaft is positioned at approximately 2 o'clock (see illustration). The front bearing cap has a .079″ mark on the front side which corresponds to a .118″ mark on the rocker arm shaft. Rocker shafts are installed with 8 oil holes to the right and 4 to the left. These marks should be aligned (see illustration). Install the bearing caps with the arrows pointing to the front of the engine. Check the camshaft end-play, which should be .002-.0059″. If camshaft end-play exceeds limits, either the camshaft or the cylinder head must be replaced. Install the rocker arm washers with the bulged side toward the front of the engine. Torque cap nuts in the order of 3, 2, 4, 1, 5 to 13-14.5 ft. lbs.

Engine Lubrication

The Colt lubrication system consists of a full flow canister type oil filter and a Tro-

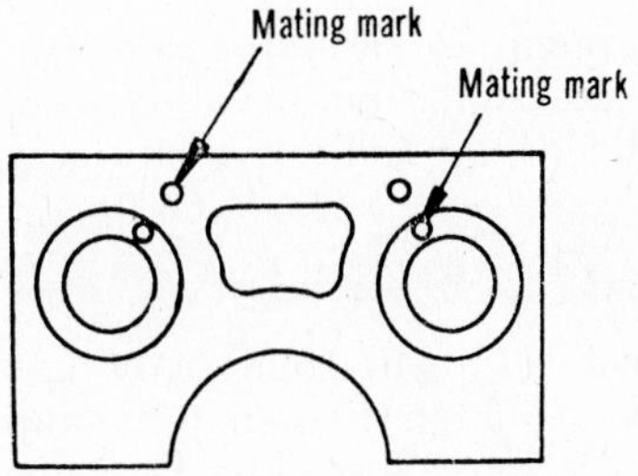

Front bearing cap/rocker arm alignment

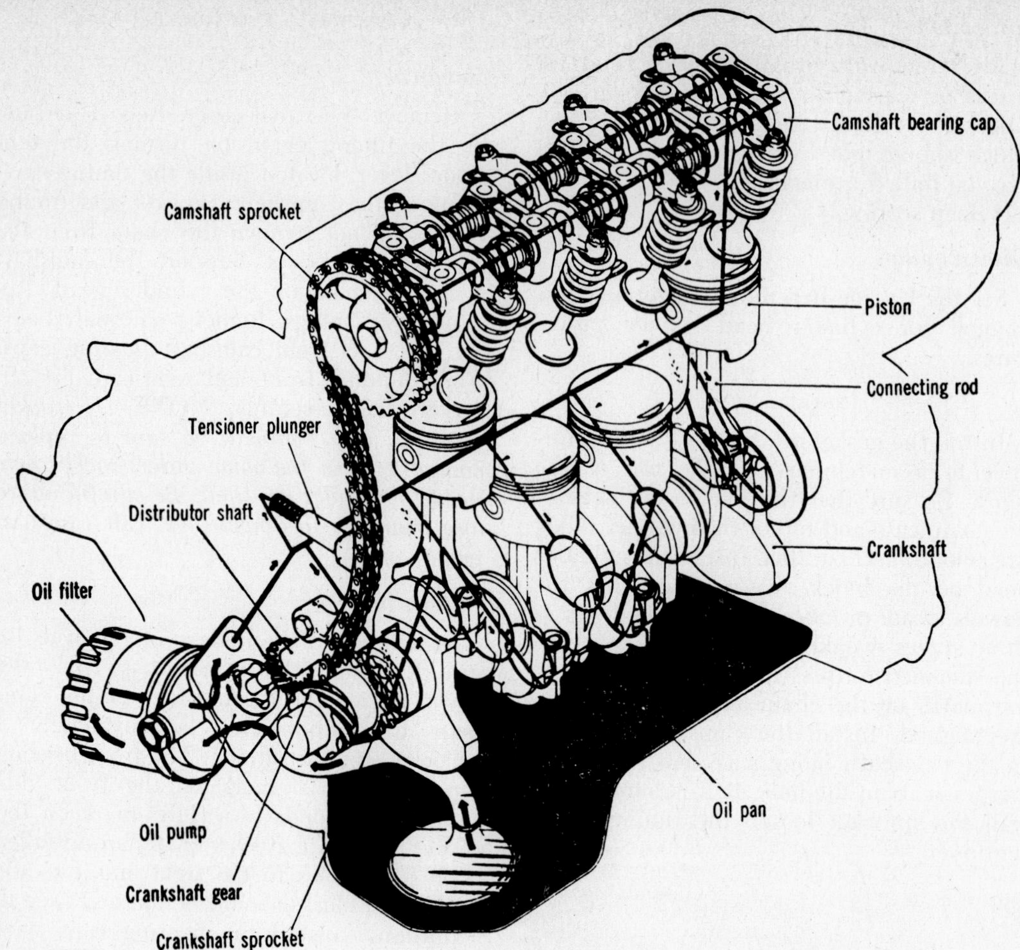

Engine oil circulation

choid gear type oil pump. Only oil graded Api Dg-Ms or higher should be used in this vehicle. Oil change intervals are after the first 600 miles and every 3 months or 4000 miles thereafter. The oil filter must be replaced at every other oil change. If car is driven exceptionally hard, or under adverse conditions, oil and filter changes should be performed more often. Both multi and single weight oils are acceptable for service.

Oil Pump

The pump is located inside the timing chain case at the bottom. Pressures higher than 56.8 psi are indicative of a clogged oil filter.

Removal

Unbolt skid pan from body underside. Remove oil filter. Loosen oil pump cover bolts and rotor assembly fastenings. Remove all above and lift off pump.

Rebuilding

Visually check all parts for defects. Insert rotor assembly into case and tighten to 10.8-14.5 ft. lbs. Apply oil to rotor shaft. When installing pump cover gasket, be sure both faces are entirely clean. Coat gasket with commercial sealant. When assembling, adhere to the following specifications.

Chain case to shaft clearance: .0008-.0022″.

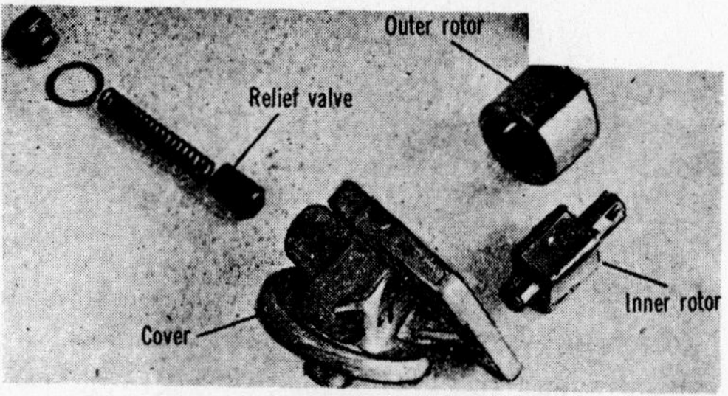

Exploded view of oil pump

Oil pump gear end play

Inner rotor to outer rotor clearance: .0047" or less.
Rotor to cover end-play: .0027-.0051".
Outer rotor to chain case clearance: .0039-.0051".
Oil pump pressure relief spring
Free length: 2.351".
Tension: 16.6-17.8 lbs. at 1.698" length.

Installation

Installation is the reverse of removal.

Pistons, Rings, Connecting Rods

Pistons used in all Colt models are aluminum with press fit, forged pins. In addition, they utilize three cast iron rings: two compression and one oil control. The top and oil rings are hard chromed. Connecting rods are carbon steel forgings. Bearings are copper alloy lined for good wear qualities. NOTE: *When engines are assembled, cylinder/piston matchings are determined by dimensions. Matching piston-bore assemblies are stamped with A, B, or C. When assembling engine, bore-piston letters must agree.*

Cylinder block and piston identification.

Remove engine from vehicle. Drain the oil and remove the oil pan. Remove the manifolds and cylinder head. Remove carbon deposits from the top of the cylinder bore, using a ridge reamer. Unbolt the connecting rod caps and install a short length of rubber hose over the connecting rod bolts. Push the connecting rod and piston assembly out through the top of the block. Remove in the order of 1, 4, 2, 3. See the Engine Rebuilding section of this manual for service procedures associated with pistons, connecting rods or rings.

Installation

Assemble piston and connecting rod unit with front marking facing towards front of

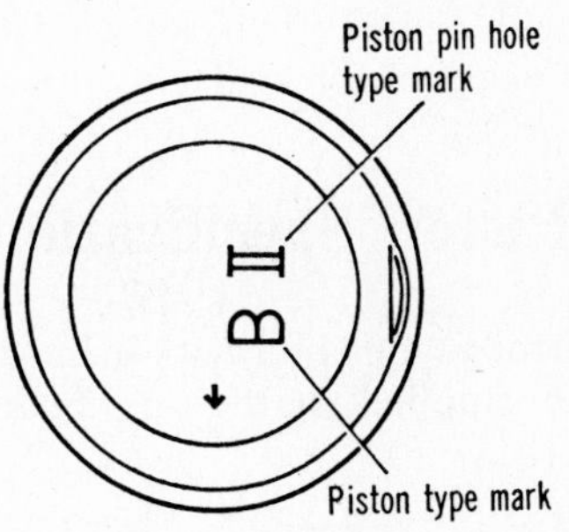

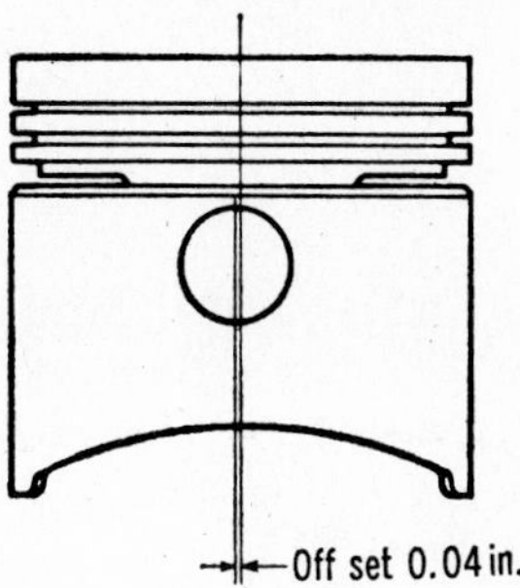

Piston markings and pin offset

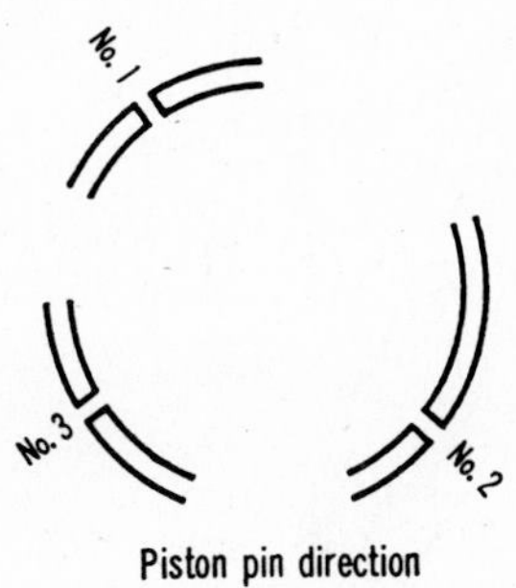

Ring end-gap positioning

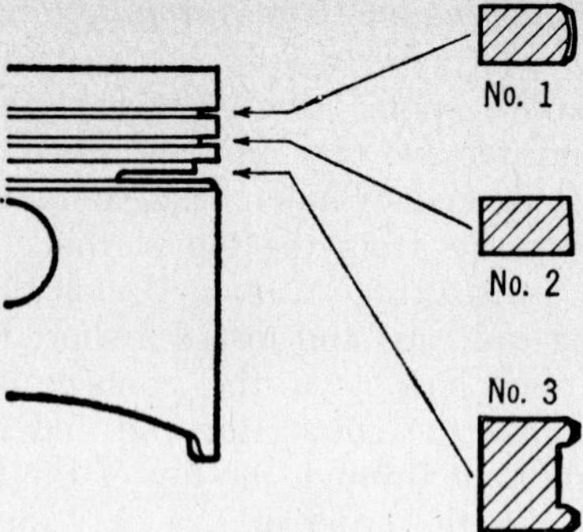

Piston ring installation

engine. Lubricate entire assembly. NOTE: *Front piston mark consists of a small arrow, connecting rod mark is an embossed numeral.* Position assembly in cylinder bore with rings in position. Piston letters must agree with cylinder bore letters. Installation is the reverse of removal.

Piston Specifications

The following information is in addition to that supplied in the specifications section.

Connecting rod side clearance: .0039-.0098″

Piston clearance: .0016-.0079″

Clutch and Transmission

The clutch used in all Colt vehicles is a dry, single disc diaphragm type clutch of conventional design and construction.

Clutch Adjustment

Adjust clutch switch so that distance between toe board and pedal face is 6.7″. Pull outer cable from holder. Turn adjusting wheel so cable holder clearance is .20-.24″ (each turn of wheel is .06″). Check clutch free play. This is the distance between re-

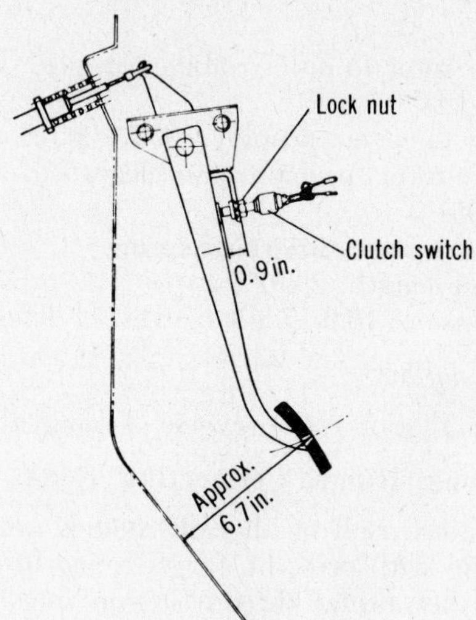

Clutch switch adjustments

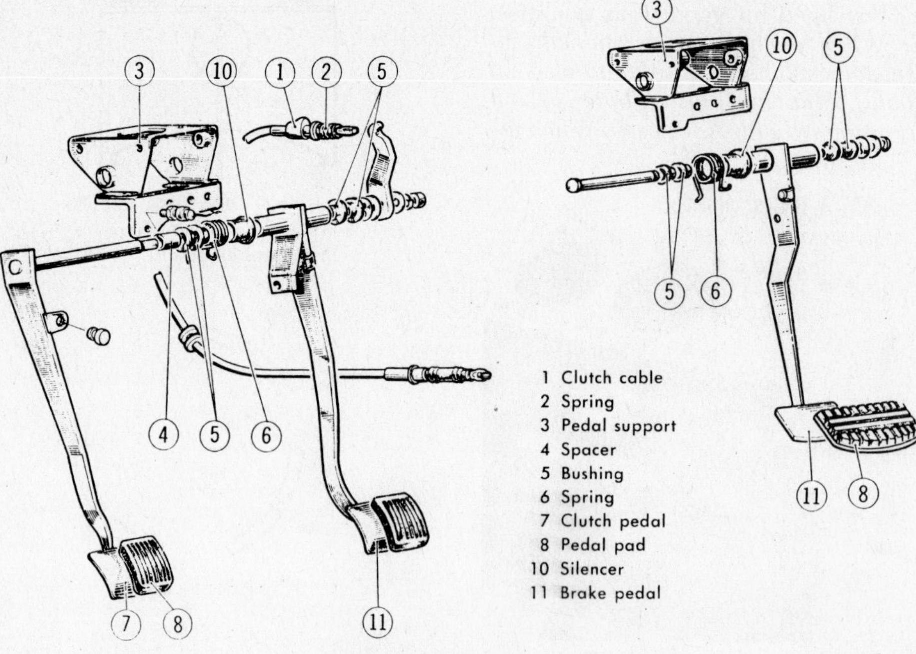

Clutch pedal components

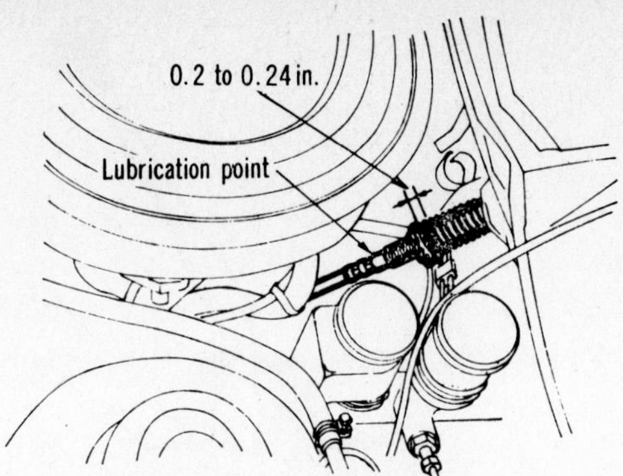

Clutch lubrication and adjustment

lease bearing and diaphragm spring operation. It should be .079". Free pedal play should be .8-1.2".

Clutch Removal

Remove transmission. Loosen six bolts on pressure plate assembly and remove pressure plate. Be certain not to damage clutch components. Lift off return clip on transmission side and remove release bearing and carrier. Utilizing a 3/16" punch, loosen and remove control lever and spring pin. Shift arm and return spring are now free to remove.

Clutch Installation

Insert control lever tongue into transmission with springs and arm. Fill shaft oil seal

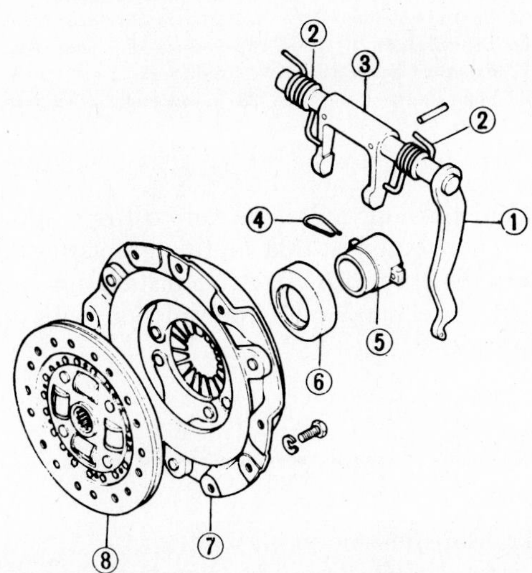
Exploded view of clutch

1 Clutch control shaft
2 Return spring
3 Clutch shift arm
4 Return clip
5 Release bearing carrier
6 Release bearing
7 Pressure plate assembly
8 Clutch disc

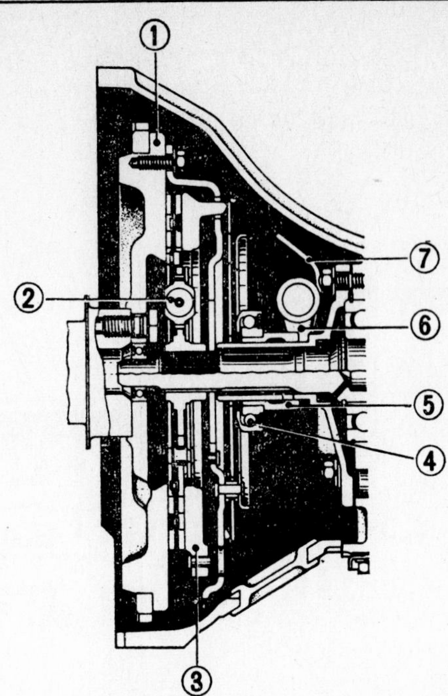
Cross-sectional view of clutch

1 Flywheel
2 Clutch disc
3 Pressure plate
4 Release bearing
5 Release bearing carrier
6 Clutch shift arm
7 Return spring

with lubricant. Be certain spring pins are aligned. See illustration. Install the release bearing, carrier, and return clip. Lubricate carrier groove, inner wall, and clutch disc spine. Place disc and pressure plate on flywheel and center the disc with an old mainshaft. Be certain to install disc with larger boss facing transmission. Install transmission and adjust clutch assembly.

Manual Transmission

All Colt manual transmissions are four speed, fully synchromeshed units. Lubricant to be used in this transmission should be an SAE 80 multipurpose type with a grade of GL4 or higher. This lubricant should be changed after the first 600 miles and at 36,000 mile intervals thereafter.

Removal

1. Disconnect and remove battery. Remove starter. Withdraw two large transmission top bolts (located in engine compartment).
2. Remove gearshift assembly and related parts from inside vehicle.

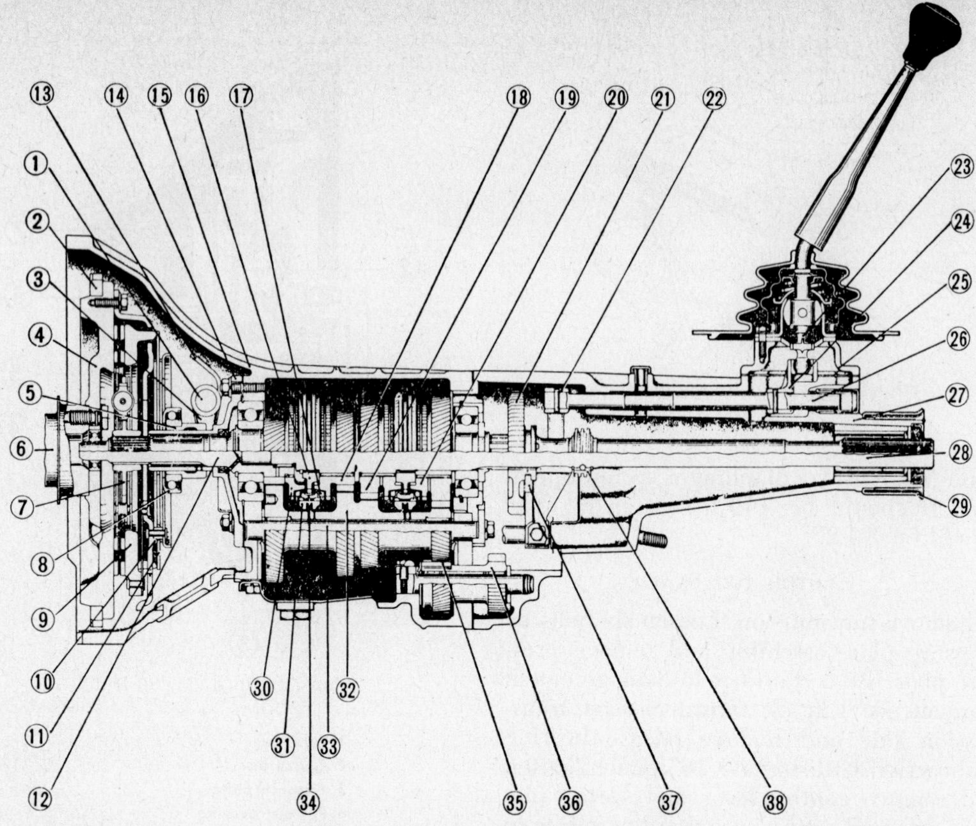

Cross-sectional view of four-speed transmission

1 Clutch shaft
2 Flywheel gear
3 Clutch shift arm
4 Flywheel
5 Release bearing carrier
6 Crankshaft
7 Clutch disc
8 Release bearing
9 Pressure plate
10 Wire
11 Diaphragm spring
12 Main drive gear
13 Return spring
14 Front bearing retainer
15 Transmission case
16 Synchronizer hub
17 Blocking ring
18 Third speed gear
19 Second speed gear
20 First speed gear
21 Reverse gear
22 Shift lever
23 Control housing
24 Shifter
25 Control housing
26 Control shaft
27 Extension housing
28 Main shaft
29 Dust seal guard
30 Clutch gear
31 Synchronizer sleeve
32 Countergear
33 Countergear shaft
34 Synchronizer piece
35 Reverse idler gear front
36 Reverse idler gear rear
37 Shift fork
38 Speedometer drive gear

3. Place vehicle on jack stands and drain transmission. Disconnect speedometer and back-up light switch.
4. Disconnect driveshaft at transmission. Remove muffler pipe and clutch cables.
5. With transmission fully supported, unbolt rear support (insulator).
6. Remove bell housing.
7. Remove remaining nuts and pull transmission rearward.

CAUTION: Be certain not to damage transmission when withdrawing.

Installation

To install transmission, reverse removal procedure. When replacing gearshift assembly, place shifter in first gear. This will align bushing holes. Be sure all operations are performed so that no foreign matter enters the transmission. After installation, adjust clutch and refill transmission with lubricant.

Torque Specifications

Transmission mounting bolts:
18.1-21.7 ft. lbs. (NO. 7 on head of bolt)
8.7-10.8 ft. lbs. (NO. 4 on head of bolt)
Starter bolts: 14.5-21.7 ft. lbs.
Transmission-insulator bolts: 7.2-8.7 ft. lbs
Insulator-frame bolts: 14.5-17.4 ft. lbs.
Frame bolts: 14.5-17.4 ft. lbs.

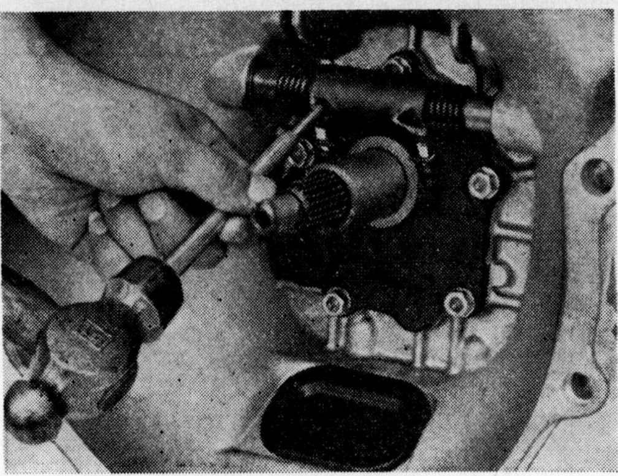

Spring pin removal

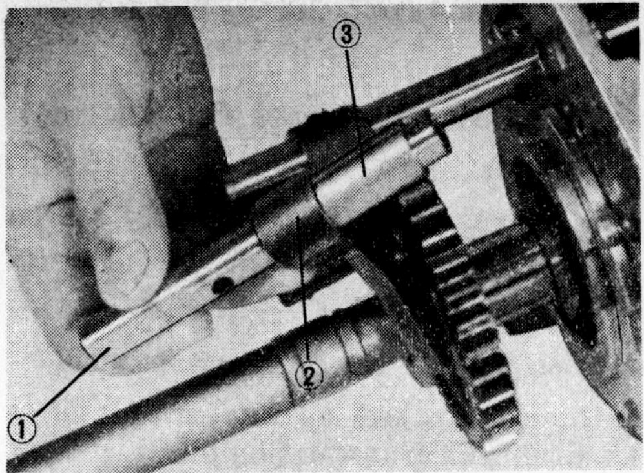

Reverse shifter fork removal

1 Reverse shift bar
2 Reverse shift fork
3 Spacer

Disassembly

Thoroughly clean outside of transmission before disassembly.

1. Using a 3/16″ punch, drive out clutch spring pins. Remove clutch shaft with release fork and springs.
2. Remove speedometer gear assembly and lockplate. Remove clutch and back-up light switches.
3. Extension housing may now be removed by tapping lightly with hammer.
4. With transmission inverted, remove bottom cover. Be sure not to support transmission on mainshaft.
5. Remove speedometer drive snap-rings and gear. Remove main drive gear retainer. Remove countershaft stopper.
6. Remove countershaft rearward. Remove counter gear, 40 roller bearings, spacers, and front and rear washers.
7. Lift out thrust washer, rear idler gear, needle bearings, and spacer located on reverse idler gear shaft.
8. Withdraw gear shaft bolt and pull shaft from case. Remove front idler gear.
9. Locate three plugs on left case side. Remove with poppet springs and balls.
10. Loosen reverse shift bar and reverse locking bolt. Pull out reverse shift bar. Remove reverse shaft fork and spacer.
11. Using a 3/16″ punch, drive fork spring pins and shift bar from mount. Remove shift bar and shaft fork. Do not disassemble shift bar.
12. Remove reverse gear from case.
13. Remove mainshaft and main drive gear synchronizer ring.
14. Pull main drive gear assembly from case front. Remove all snap-rings.
15. Remove shifter assembly.
16. Thoroughly clean inside of case.

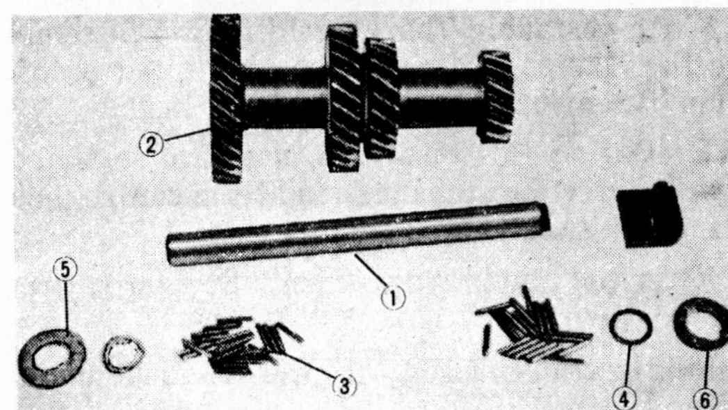

Exploded view of countergear

1 Countershaft
2 Counter gear
3 Needle rollers
4 Spacer
5 Thrust washer
6 Thrust washer

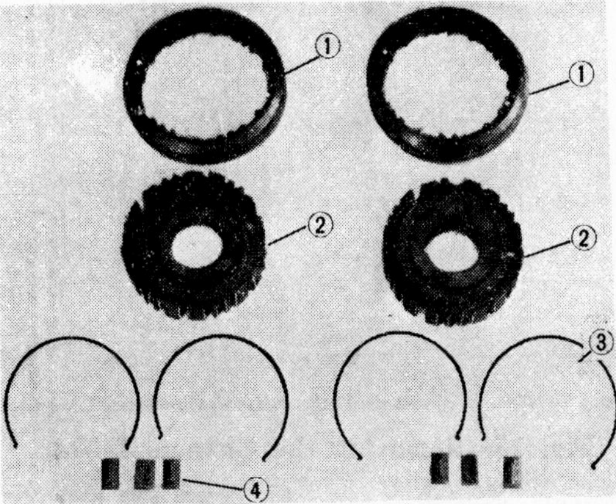

Exploded view of synchronizers

1 Synchronizer sleeve
2 Synchronizer hub
3 Springs
4 Synchronizer pieces

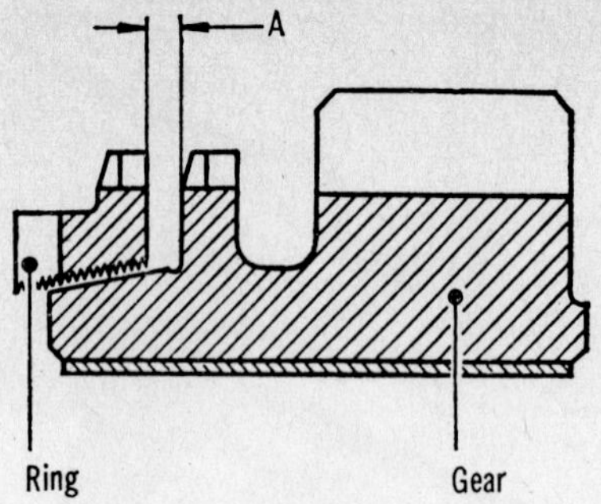

Synchronizer inspection—Dimension A=.059 in.

Rebuilding

Thoroughly wash all components. Check all parts for wear and serviceability. All shims and oil seals must be replaced with new pieces. When assembling, lubricate all parts as necessary.

Four-Speed Transmission Specifications

Helical gear backlash: .002-.006″.
Shift fork to sleeve clearance: .004-.008″.
Spur gear backlash: .004-.008″.
Gear change lever-selector groove clearance: .004-.012″.
Reverse shift fork-reverse gear groove clearance: .004-.012″.

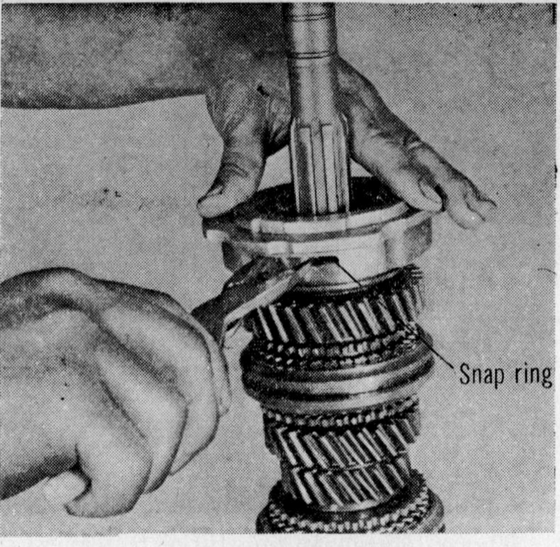

Snap ring installation

Main Drive Gear Unit

Press bearing onto main drive gear. Secure with snap-ring of appropriate thickness to give end-play of .002″.

Snap-Ring Code
White .091″
None .093″
Red .094″
Yellow .098″

Assemble hub and synchronizer ring. Place front and rear springs on shaft in opposite directions. Assemble second gear synchro-

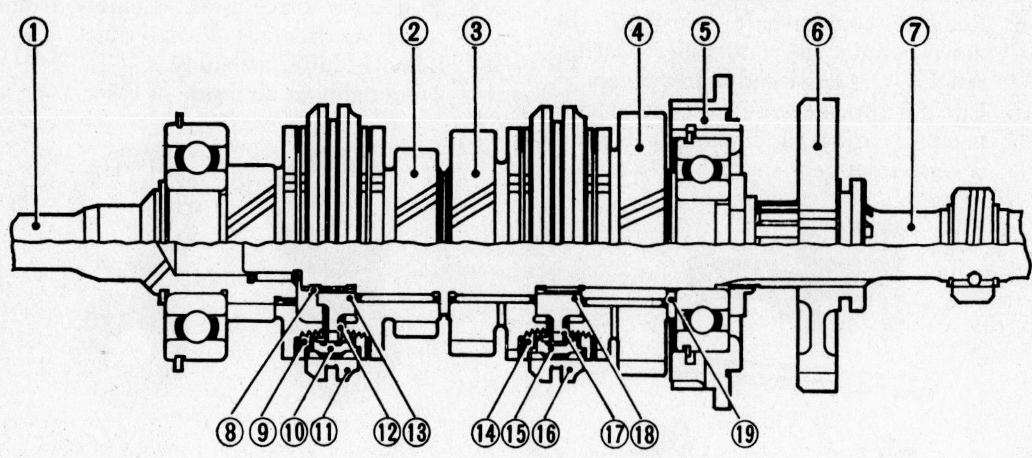

Assembled view of mainshaft

1 Main drive gear
2 Third speed gear
3 Second speed gear
4 First speed gear
5 Rear bearing retainer
6 Reverse gear
7 Mainshaft
8 Snap-ring
9 Synchronizer ring
10 Synchronizer piece
11 Synchronizer sleeve
12 Synchronizer spring
13 Synchronizer hub (third-fourth)
14 Synchronizer ring
15 Synchronizer piece
16 Synchronizer sleeve
17 Synchronizer spring
18 Synchronizer hub (first-second)
19 Spacer

nizer hub with stepped gear end (narrow toothed side) rearward. Install needle bearings and third gear onto mainshaft from front end. Install synchronizer assembly. Assemble first-second synchronizer in the same direction it was removed. Fit snap-rings to give proper end-play of .0012-.0075″. The third-fourth gear hub end-play is 0.00-.0043″.

Snap Ring Code
None .085″
Yellow .087″
Green .090″
Blue .093″

Place needle bearings and second gear on mainshaft from rear. Install synchronizer assembly. Check and adjust end-play to .0012-.0075″.

Place first gear spacer, needle bearings, synchronizer, and first gear on shaft. Adjust end-play to .0012-.0075″. Spacer must be installed with I mark in direction of ball bearing. Install mainshaft bearing with a suitable driver and tighten locknut. Install snap-ring and retainer. Adjust to give mainshaft bearing end-play of 0.00-.006″.

Snap-Rings
None .057″
Red .060″
White .064″
Yellow .067″
Blue .071″

Invert transmission case. Install main drive gear assembly into transmission case. Place needle bearings on main drive gear front end. Install synchronizer ring. Be certain all synchronizer rings are in proper mesh. Install rear bearing retainer in case.

Shifter Fork and Bar Installation

1. Place reverse gear in position on mainshaft. Install shift fork into shift fork groove in synchronizer sleeve. While holding forks, place third-fourth shift bar assembly into case through lower rear hole.
2. Insert first interlock plunger in case; drive plunger in position with use of appropriate driver.
3. Place first-second gear shift bar assembly into case. Position shift forks so that pin holes are aligned with shift bar holes. Secure shift forks to shift bars with spring pins. Be sure to drive spring pins into position with slot on centerline of shift bar.

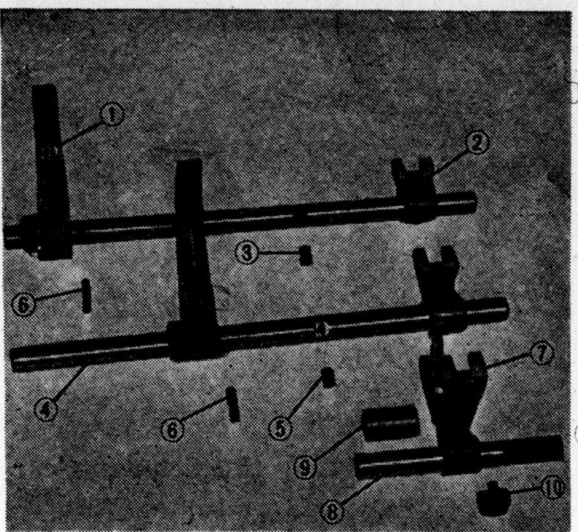

Exploded view of shift bar

1 Shift fork
2 Third-fourth speed shift bar
3 Interlock plunger
4 First-second speed shift bar
5 Interlock plunger
6 Spring pins
7 Reverse shift fork
8 Reverse shift bar
9 Spacer
10 Locking bolt

4. Insert second interlock plunger in case.
5. Place reverse shift fork ends in reverse gear groove. Insert reverse gear bar into fork. Install spacer on shift bar and place reverse shift bar assembly into case. Secure fork to bar with locking bolt.
6. Position poppet balls and springs. Insert plugs with commercial sealant. Be certain to install tapered end of poppet spring towards poppet balls.

Reverse Idler Gear Installation

Place needle bearings and spacers in position on rear reverse idler gear. Insert assembly into rear of case. Place front idler gear with thrust washer onto rear shaft end. Insert gear shaft in case and secure with bolt.

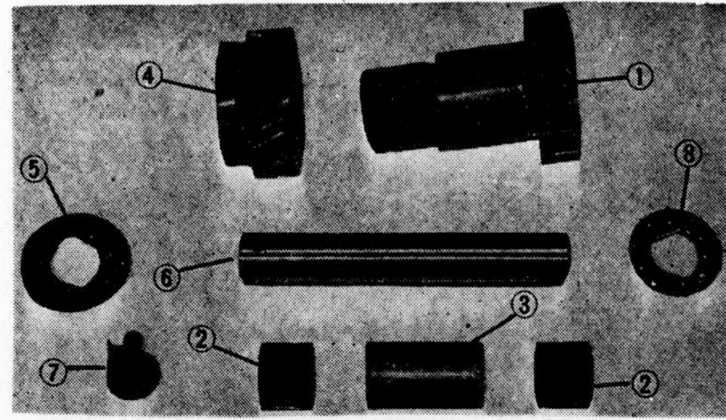

Exploded view of reverse idler gear

1 Reverse idler gear
2 Needle bearing
3 Spacer
4 Front idler gear
5 Thrust washer
6 Gear shaft
7 Bolt
8 Selective rear thrust washer

Rear Thrust Washer Installation

1. Measure size from rear surface of transmission case to rear of reverse idler gear.
2. Measure depth from extension housing end to idler gear shaft end. Add .004″. This figure is extension housing packing thickness.
3. Subtract NO. 2 from NO. 1. Subtract .009-.012″. (thrust washer clearance) from result.

Example

Dimension (1)	.863 in.	
Dimension (2)	–.774 in.	(includes .004 in.)
	.089 in.	
	–.011 in.	(minus .009-.012 in. clearance)
	.078 in.	(This figure is thickness of thrust washer required.)

Thrust Washer Identification
A-.078″
B-.085″
C-.093″
D-.100″

Counter Gear Installation

Insert needle roller bearings (20 front, 20 rear) and spacers in front and rear holes of counter gear. Lubricate as necessary. Be sure spacers are installed on outside of roller bearings. Install a 1.378″ OD thrust washer on front end of counter gear. Install a 1.181″ ID thrust washer on rear end. Holding counter gear cluster inside case, install counter gear shaft from rear and properly mesh gears. Select rear thrust washer to give .002-.007″ counter gear end-play.

Counter gear installation

Needle roller bearing installation

1 Needle rollers
2 Bearing spacers

A-.080″
B-.083″
C-.086″
D-.089″
E-.092″

Secure rear shaft end with stopper plate. Place front bearing retainer in position and install front bearing. Bearing to retainer clearance should be .002-.0012″. Place speedometer driven gear on mainshaft. There should be no clearance between speedometer gear and snap-ring. Shim if necessary.

Connect extension housing to transmission case. Be sure to apply sealant. When installing washers, install with bulged side towards bolt head. Install transmission and back-up light switch. Next, install locking plate and transmission driven gear. Finally, secure under-cover to transmission. Torque bolts to 5.8-7.2 ft. lbs. Tighten in a criss-cross pattern in two stages. Fill transmission with appropriate lubricant.

Shifter Installation

Place gear lever in first gear gate. Be sure nylon bushing is in vertical position. With transmission in car, apply sealant to packings and grease bushings. Insert clutch control shaft into transmission from left-hand side. Assemble shift fork and springs onto shaft. Align shift fork with clutch control shaft. Drive spring pin into pin hole and set spring. Be certain spring pin has its slot on the centerline of the clutch control shaft. Grease all appropriate parts and check operation of shifter.

Automatic Transmission

The automatic transmission used in all Colt models is a Borg Warner, with an aluminum case. This transmission is cooled by a separate cooler/filter assembly located in the radiator bottom. Fluid capacity is 1.4 gallons (plus cooler capacity).

Removal

1. Remove: air cleaner, battery with cables, starter, and upper bolts attaching engine to transmission.
2. Place car on jack stands. Drain transmission. Remove speedometer cable and disconnect driveshaft.
3. Remove exhaust system from connecting pipe rearwards to muffler.
4. Remove transmission oil lines.
5. Remove control rod from its attachment to arm.
6. Loosen and remove bell housing. While rotating torque converter, remove four exposed bolts.
7. Place jack under transmission. *NOTE: Do not support transmission on oil pan.* Remove insulator attaching bolts, ground cable, and spacer. Remove insulator.
8. Remove insulator frame member.
9. Remove torque converter and pull out transmission.

Installation

To install transmission, reverse removal procedure.

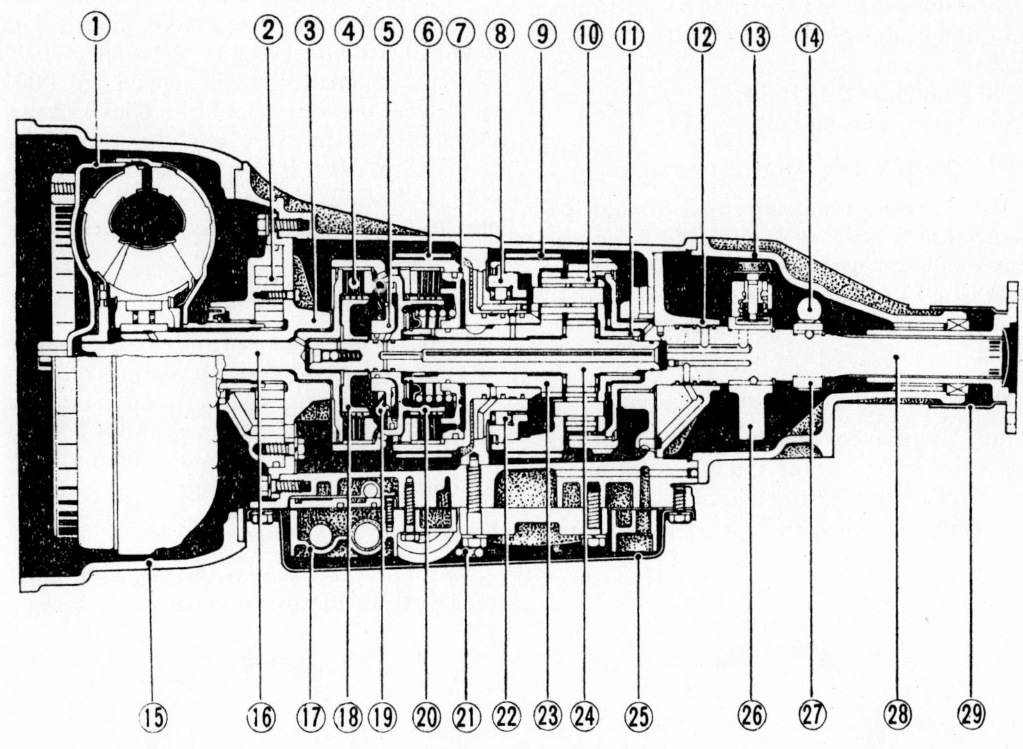

Automatic transmission

1 Torque converter
2 Oil pump gear
3 Pump adapter and converter support
4 Front clutch plate
5 Front clutch piston
6 Front brake band
7 Front drum
8 One-way clutch outer race
9 Rear brake band
10 Long pinion
11 Planet cover
12 Rear adapter
13 Extension housing
14 Speedometer driven gear
15 Converter housing
16 Input shaft
17 Valve body assembly
18 Front clutch hub
19 Front clutch spring
20 Front clutch cylinder
21 Oil tube
22 One-way clutch assembly
23 Reverse sun gear
24 Forward sun gear
25 Oil pan
26 Governor assembly
27 Speedometer drive gear
28 Output shaft
29 Coupling flange

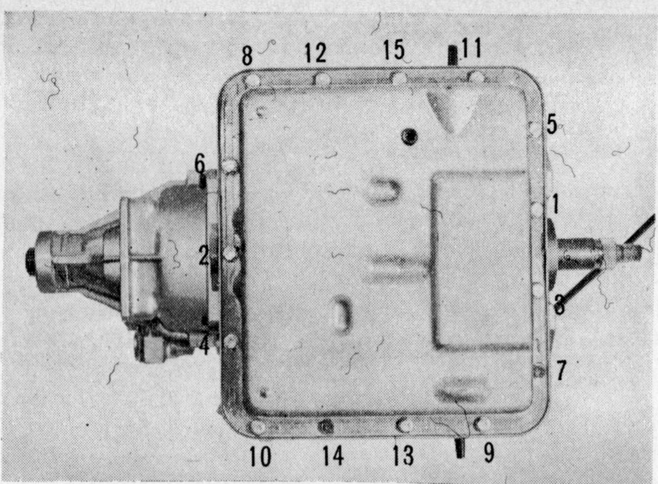

Oil pan bolt removal sequence

Torque Specifications

Insulator attaching bolts: 14.5-17.4 ft. lbs.

Insulator to transmission bolts: 9.4-11.6 ft. lbs.

Oil pan bolts: 8-13 ft. lbs.

Converter housing bolts: 8-13 ft. lbs.

Maintenance and Adjustment

Automatic transmission fluid should be changed at 2 year or 24,000 mile intervals. This should be performed more often if vehicle is used in severe service. When oil is replaced, transmission bands should be adjusted.

Adjusting Downshift Cable

Run engine to operating temperature. Adjust cable by turning the outer adjusting screw till bottom just contacts calked stopper. Adjust to .002-.004″ clearance. If further adjustment is necessary, perform the following: Remove transmission pipe plug with 3/16″ Allen wrench. Connect transmission pressure gauge. Set both parking and foot brake. With engine at idle, place car in gear. Check line pressure. Normal is 49.7-65.3 psi. Increase engine speed to 1,000 rpm. Line pressure should be 65.3-85.2 psi. Difference in pressure readings should be 15.6-19.9 psi. If it is not, tighten outer cable with adjusting screw. This will increase pressure. To decrease pressure, reverse this procedure.

Front Band Adjustment

Remove transmission oil pan. Loosen locknut and move servo lever out of way. Insert .35″ feeler gauge between servo piston pin and adjusting screw. Adjust servo screw to 10.44 in. lbs. torque. Tighten locknut and remove feeler gauge.

Rear Band Adjustment

This screw is located on the right-hand outer wall of the transmission case. Loosen

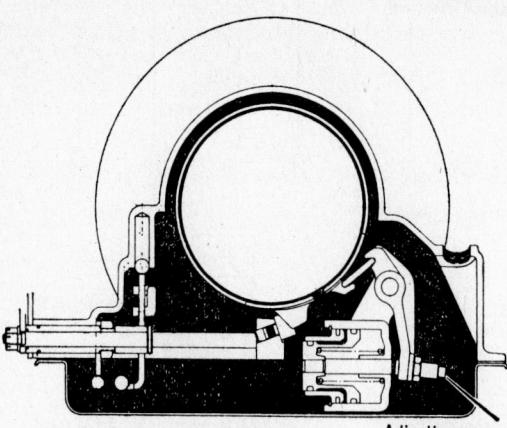

Adjusting screw

Front band adjusting screw location

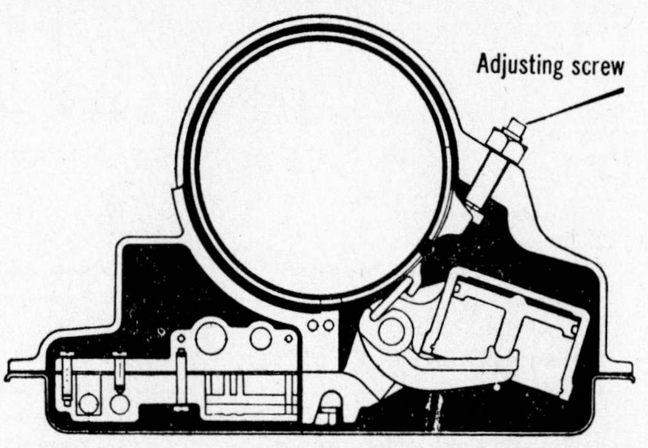

Rear band adjusting screw location

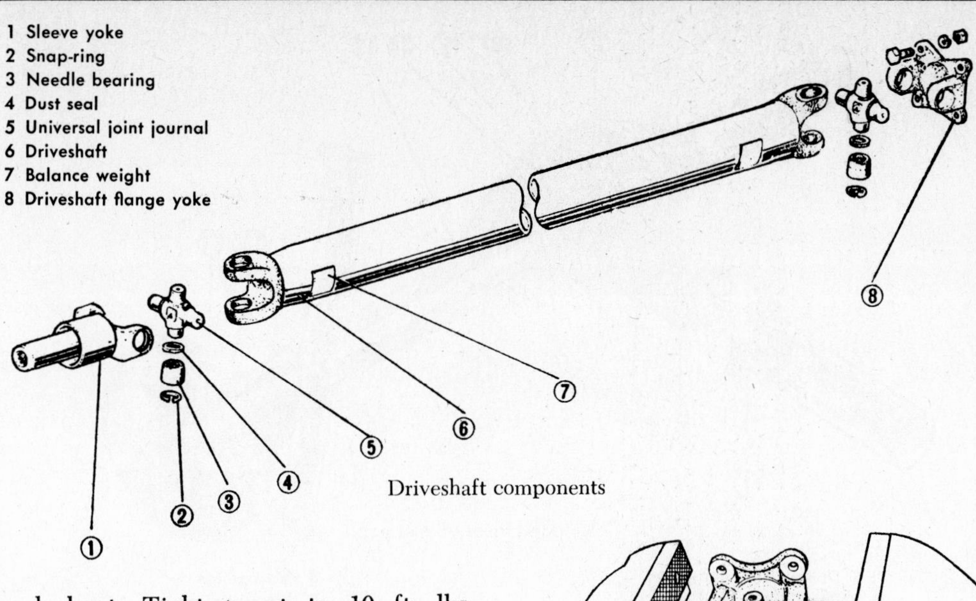

Driveshaft components

the locknut. Tighten nut to 10 ft. lbs. Loosen nut 3/4 turn. Tighten down locknut.

Driveshafts and U-Joints

The driveshaft and U-joints used in all Colt models are of conventional design and construction. Driveshaft length differs between manual and automatic transmission equipped vehicles; therefore, when replacing be sure to specify transmission type. Normally, no maintenance is required of either driveshafts or U-joints.

Driveshaft Removal

Place car on jack stands. Drain transmission fluid. Remove flange yoke bolts at differential pinion flange. Remove driveshaft from transmission end by withdrawing rearward. Be sure not to damage any transmission components.

Driveshaft Installation

To replace driveshaft, reverse removal procedure. Torque the flange yoke bolts to 11-14.5 ft. lbs.

U-Joints and Bearing Removal

Remove the driveshaft. Remove U-joint snap rings. Be sure to note exact position of removed parts. With suitable tools, hold driveshaft flange yoke stationary. Drive out needle bearings. U-joint is now free to remove.

Assembly

Pack U-joint journals, needle bearings, and trunnion with grease. Be sure not to over-lubricate. In addition, apply thin coating of grease to dust seal lips. Install bearings on U-joint journals using vise and appropriate sockets. Be sure to replace exactly as removed. Install snap-rings to give proper bearing to snap-ring clearance. Snap-rings selected must be of the same or nearly the same thickness for both shaft ends. This will guarantee proper shaft balance.

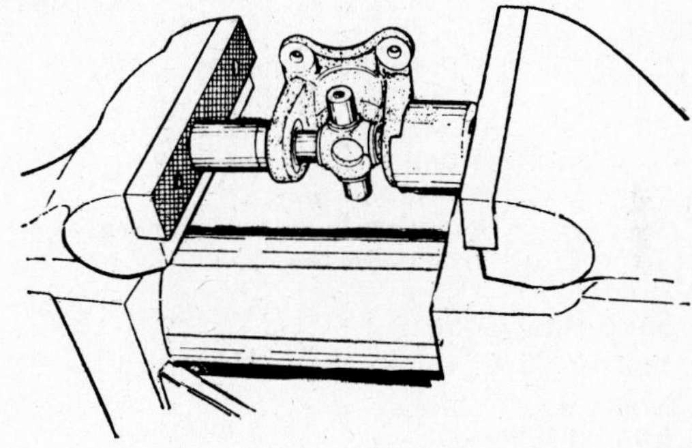
U-Joint bearing removal

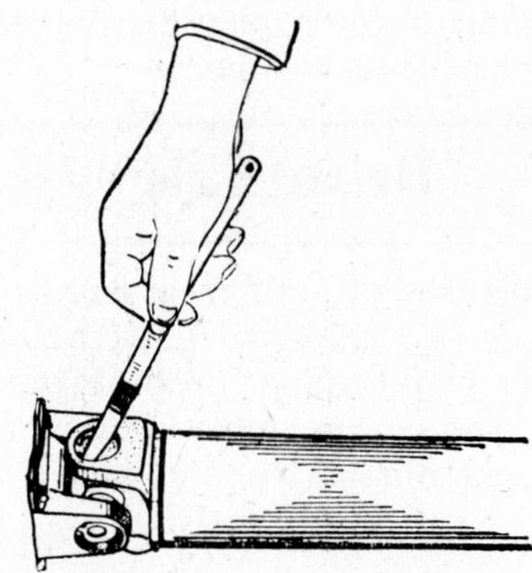
Measuring snap-ring clearance

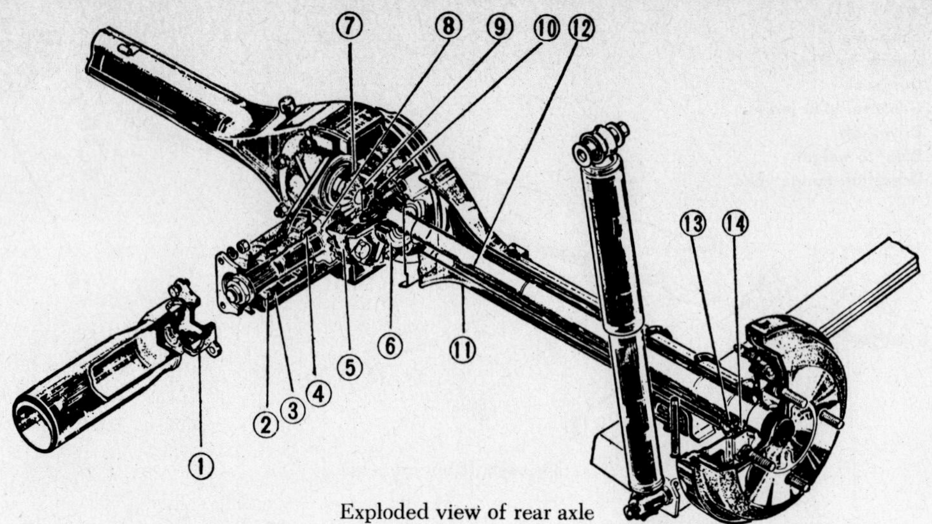

Exploded view of rear axle

1 Driveshaft flange yoke
2 Drive pinion oil seal
3 Drive pinion front bearing
4 Drive pinion rear bearing
5 Final drive gear
6 Differential carrier side bearing
7 Differental case
8 Drive pinion
9 Differential pinion
10 Differential side pinion
11 Rear axle housing
12 Rear axle shaft
13 Rear axle shaft oil seal
14 Rear axle shaft bearing

Snap-Ring Code
Yellow-.0516″ thick
None-.0504″ thick
Blue-.0528″ thick
Purple-.0539″ thick

Bearing to Snap-Ring clearance is 0.00-.001″. When snap-rings are installed, press each bearing towards opposite shaft ends to measure maximum clearance.

Drive Axle

All Colt models utilize a rear axle of banjo type and a hypoid final drive. Axle shafts are semi-floating; pressure type ball bearing retainers are employed at each axle housing end. Final drive ratio is 3.889:1.

Removal

1. Jack the vehicle and remove rear wheels. Place jack stands under rear frame members. With car resting on jack stands, place slight upward pressure on rear axle housing with jack saddle.
2. Remove driveshaft.
3. Disconnect all foot and parking rear brake lines. Be sure not to spill brake fluid.
4. Remove rear U-bolts and shock absorbers.
5. From attachment, remove spring shackle pin nuts and shackle plate. With axle housing resting on jack, remove rear springs. Axle housing is now free. Slowly lower jack with axle housing.

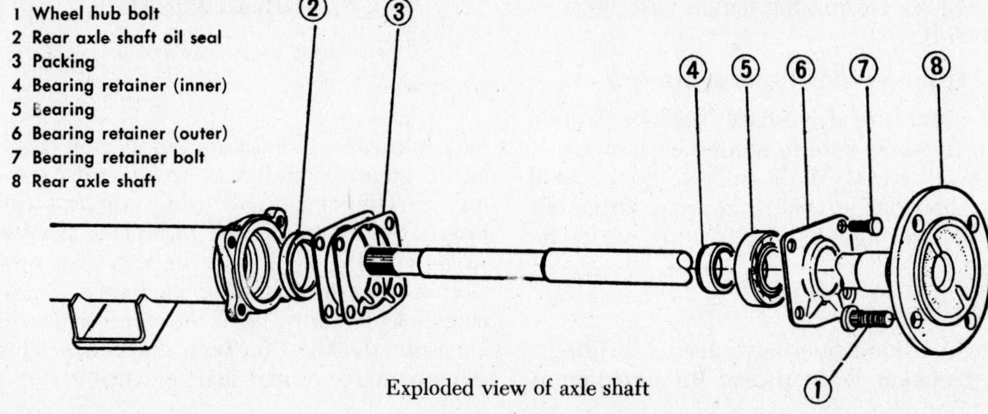

Exploded view of axle shaft

Installation

To replace axle assembly, reverse removal procedure.

Rear Axle Shaft Removal

Jack up vehicle on rear axle housing. Remove rear wheels and brake backing plate. Axle shaft may be pulled out manually or with use of a slide hammer.

Axle Shaft Bearing Removal

Utilizing a grinder, grind a spot on the inner bearing retainer to a depth of about .04-.06″. With a chisel, lightly strike ground portion of inner bearing retainer. When retainer cracks, remove bearing.

Axle Shaft Oil Seal Removal

With rear axle shaft removed, pull out oil seal using appropriate tool.

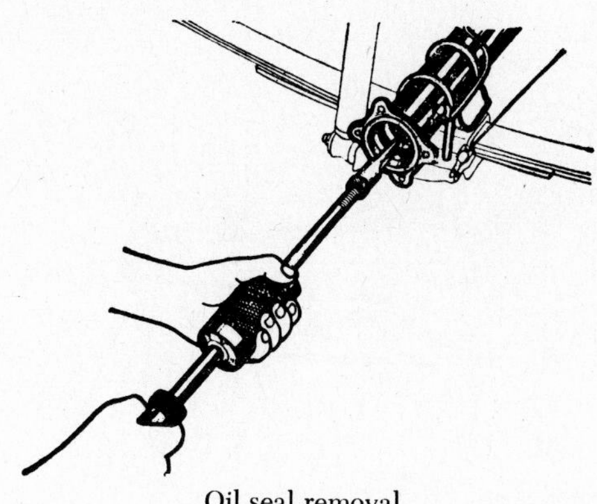

Oil seal removal

Rear Axle Shaft Assembly and Installation

Place outer bearing retainer with raised surface facing wheel hub on axle shaft. Next, install axle shaft bearing and outer retainer on shaft. Locate smaller machined side of inner bearing retainer. With this side facing bearing, install retainer using a hydraulic press, capable of developing at least 13,000 lbs. Be sure the bearing is firmly seated. Clean rear axle oil seal seat and lightly grease. Using appropriate tool, drive oil seal into rear axle housing. Lightly grease oil seal outer lip. Using packings, set clearance between outer bearing retainer and bearing to 0.00-.01″. Install brake backing plate on shaft. Fit shaft assembly into axle housing, making sure the splines align properly. Align packing oil holes with bearing retainer and lightly secure bearing retainer to axle housing flange. Bolts with spring washers should be used. Tighten outer bearing retainer nuts in diagonal sequence to 25-29 ft. lbs.

Differential

Removal

1. Drain the oil from the rear axle.
2. Disconnect and remove the driveshaft.
3. Pull out both axle shafts to disengage the axle shafts from the differential gears. They need only be pulled out about 2″.
4. Unbolt and remove the differential carrier.

Disassembly

1. Remove the bearing caps and gently pry the differential from the carrier. wooden hammer handle does this job well.
2. Using a bearing puller, remove the differential side bearings. Be sure to keep the right and left bearing shims separated to avoid confusion.
3. Pry up the lockwashers on the ring gear bolts. Remove the ring gear bolts in a diagonal sequence and remove the ring gear.
4. Drive out the pinion shaft knockpin from the rear of the ring gear, and remove the pinion shaft.
5. Remove the pinions and side gears with spacers. Note the position of the side gear spacers so that they may be assembled in the same place.
6. Hold the end yoke with a pipe wrench and remove the pinion nut.
7. Remove the end yoke.
8. Tap the drive pinion shaft with a plastic faced mallet and remove the drive pinion with adjusting shim, rear inner race, spacer and preload adjusting shim.
9. Remove the front pinion bearing outer race and oil seal. Discard the oil seal.
10. Remove the pinion bearing rear outer race.

Assembly

NOTE: If the unit is to be assembled using no replacement parts, the same spacers and shims can generally be used. If either pinion bearing or ring gear and drive pinion are being replaced, new shims should be used. Only replace the drive pinion and ring gear in matched sets.

1. Assemble the side gears in the differen-

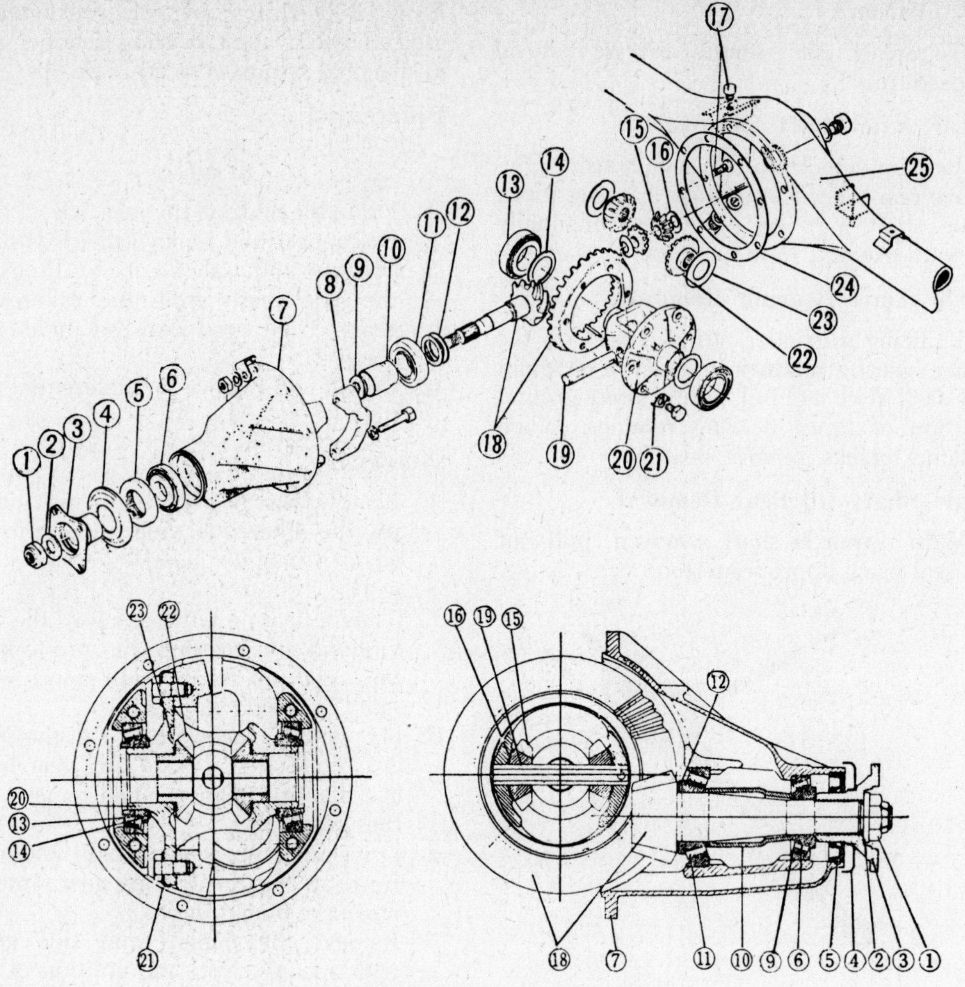

Exploded view of differential

1 Locknut
2 Washer
3 End yoke
4 Slinger
5 Oil seal
6 Drive pinion bearing (front)
7 Gear carrier
8 Carrier cap
9 Preload adjusting shim
10 Drive pinion spacer
11 Drive pinion bearing (rear)
12 Drive pinion adjusting shim
13 Side bearing
14 Side bearing adjusting shim
15 Differential pinion
16 Differential pinion washer
17 Air breather
18 Final drive gear set
19 Differential pinion shaft
20 Differential case
21 Lockwasher
22 Differential side gear
23 Side gear spacer
24 Packing
25 Rear axle housing

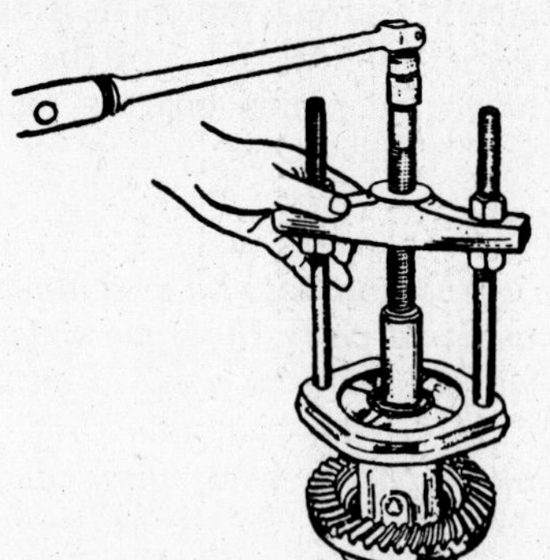

Side bearing removal

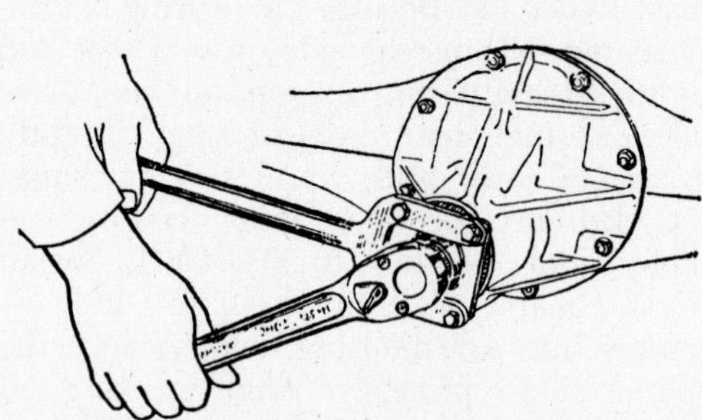

Drive pinion outer race removal

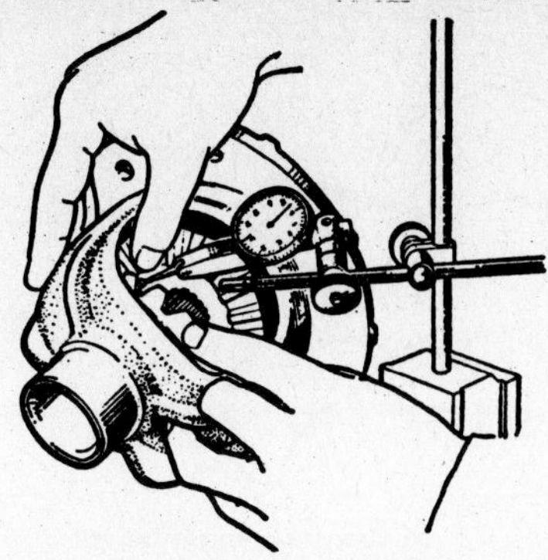

Checking pinion and side gear backlash

tial case. Install the thrust washers in the same place as they were installed.

2. With washers, insert both differential gears at the same time to mesh with the side gears. Insert the pinion shaft.
3. Measure the backlash of the differential gears and side gears. The backlash should be .003-.005″, and can be adjusted with the use of spacers listed below.

Side Gear Spacers

Part No.	Thickness of spacer
MA180860	0.0394 0 / —0.0028″
MA180861	0.0394 —0.0031 / —0.0067″
MA180862	0.0394 —0.0071 / —0.0098″

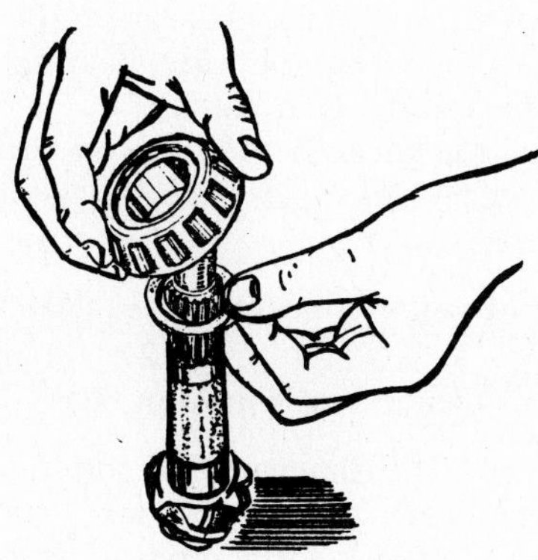

Pinion height shim installation

4. Align the pinion shaft hole with the case and drive the knockpin in.
5. Clean the ring gear mounting surfaces. Install the ring gear on the differential case and tighten the mounting bolts to 50-58 ft. lbs. in a diagonal pattern. Always use new lockplates.
6. To assemble the drive pinion, press the front and rear outer races into the gear carrier with a press or drift. Be sure not to use excessive pressure on the outer races and be sure they are not cocked.
7. Insert a shim between the drive pinion and rear bearing. If the original gear set is being replaced, the original shims may be used. If a new gear set is being installed, calculate the shim dimension in the following manner. Assuming the pinion height before disassembly is correct, subtract the new pinion variation marking (on the pinion head) from the old pinion variation marking. Be careful of positive and negative numbers. If the answer is positive add shims in the corresponding amount. If the answer is negative, subtract shims in the corresponding amount. This will produce a reasonable starting point for assembly. Bear in mind that if the shim is subsequently proved incorrect, the entire pinion must be disassembled, and the shim changed accordingly. The etched marking on the face of the pinion represents a positive or negative variation from the standard in millimeters.
8. Assemble the front bearing, end yoke, pinion spacer and washer and torque the pinion nut gradually. Torque the pinion nut constantly checking the preload, until a preload of 6.1-8.7 in. lbs. is reached (without the oil seal).
9. Mount the pinion height gauge (Colt special tool CT-1096-72) on the side bearing seats of the gear carrier and

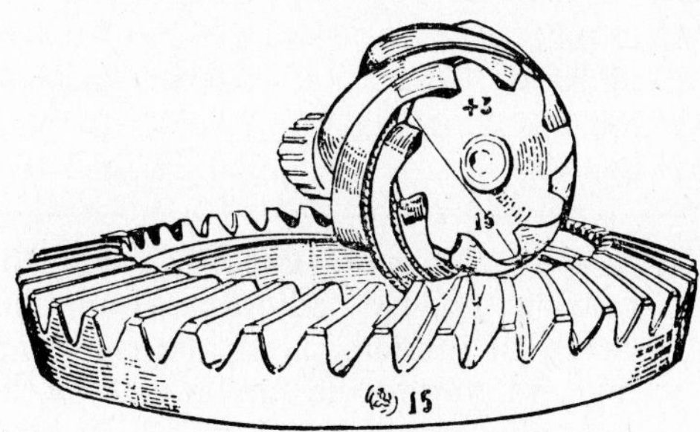

Pinion and ring gear markings

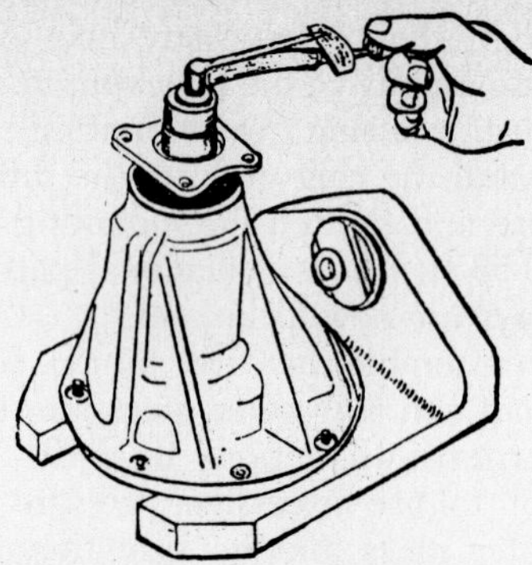

Measuring pinion preload

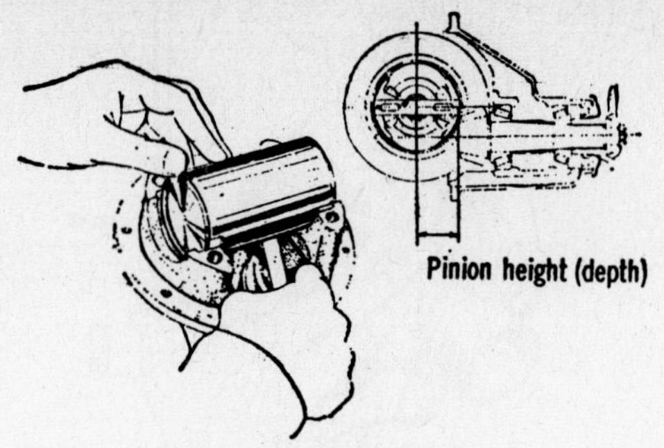

Measuring pinion height

place a block gauge (Colt special tool CT-1096-D16) on the top end of the face of the drive pinion.

10. Measure the clearance between the gauges.
11. The clearance between the two gauges is set at .0118″ if the pinion height is standard. The following formula may be used to determine the thickness of the preload shim thickness:

$$(\text{Feeler gauge reading}) - \frac{\text{Etched value}}{25.4 \times 1000} - .0118 = \text{Thickness of shim to be added}$$

If the answer is positive, add the thickness to the original shim; if negative, subtract the thickness from the original shim. Shims are available in the following sizes:

Pinion Bearing Preload Shims

Part No.	Thickness of shim
MA180842	0.0543±0.0004″
MA180843	0.0555±0.0004″
MA180844	0.0567±0.0004″
MA180845	0.0579±0.0004″
MA180846	0.0591±0.0004″
MA180847	0.0603±0.0004″
MA180848	0.0614±0.0004″
MA180849	0.0626±0.0004″
MA180850	0.0638±0.0004″
MA180851	0.0650±0.0004″
MA180852	0.0118±0.0005″

12. Remove the end yoke and insert the bearing preload adjusting shim between the pinion spacer and the bearing and torque the pinion nut to the prescribed preload (8.7-11.3 in. lbs. with oil seal).

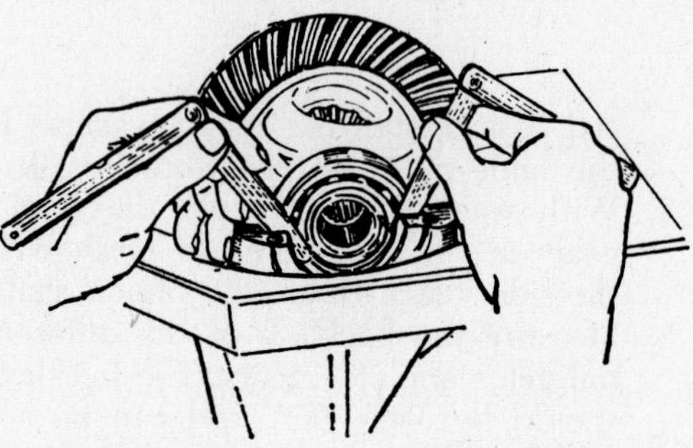

Measuring side bearing to carrier clearance

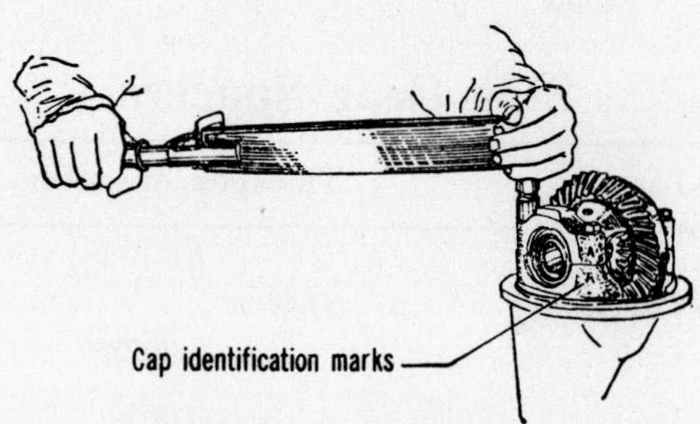

Bearing cap identification marks

13. The pinion nut torque should be 100-145 ft. lbs.
14. Install each side bearing into the differential case without the adjusting shim.
15. Install the differential case assembly on the gear carrier and measure the clearance between the side bearing outer race and the gear carrier.
16. The thickness of the shim on each side is determined by the following formula:

$$\frac{\text{Measured clearance} + .004''}{2} = \text{Thickness of shims on one side.}$$

The .004″ dimension is added as the side bearing preload (.002″ on each side). Side bearing preload shims are available in the following sizes:

Side Bearing Preload Shims

Part No.	Shim thickness
MA180828	0.0787±0.0004″
MA180829	0.0799±0.0004″
MA180830	0.0811±0.0004″
MA180831	0.0823±0.0004″
MA180832	0.0835±0.0004″
MA180833	0.0846±0.0004″
MA180834	0.0858±0.0004″
MA180835	0.0870±0.0004″
MA180836	0.0882±0.0004″
MA180837	0.0894±0.0004″
MA180838	0.0906±0.0004″
MA180839	0.0917±0.0004″

17. Align the gear carrier and bearing cap positioning marks and torque the cap bolts to 25-29 ft. lbs.
18. Mount a dial indicator with the pin registering on the rear face of the ring gear. Zero the dial indicator.
19. Measure the run-out of the ring gear. If the run-out exceeds .002″, change the position of the ring gear on the differential carrier by 90°. If the run-out still exceeds .002″, replace the ring gear or differential carrier.
20. Measure the backlash of the ring gear at four points, 90° apart. Ring gear backlash should not exceed .005-.007″. If the measured backlash is greater than the specification, shift shims in a corresponding thickness from the ring gear tooth side to the rear of the ring gear. If backlash is less than specified, shift shims from the rear side of the ring gear to the tooth side. Side gear adjusting shims are available in the following sizes:

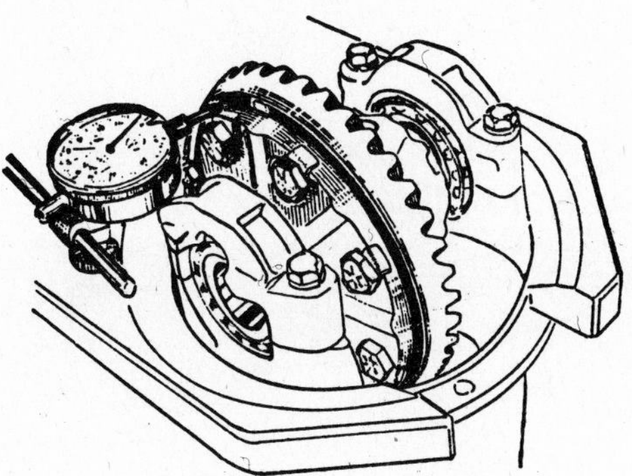

Measuring ring gear run-out

Side Bearing Adjusting Shims

Part No.	Thickness
MA180822	0.0028±0.0004″
MA180823	0.0051±0.0006″
MA180824	0.0098±0.0010″
MA180825	0.0020±0.0002″
MA180826	0.0063±0.0008″
MA180827	0.0157±0.0012″

21. Paint the ring gear teeth with red lead or similar testing compound. Use a socket and breaker bar on the pinion nut and rock the drive pinion back and forth on the ring gear teeth. Compare the results of this test with the following illustrations and note the corrective procedure.
   A. Proper gear tooth contact pattern—a pattern of 50-70% of gear tooth contact on the ring gear, centered or slightly inclined towards the toe.

Proper tooth contact

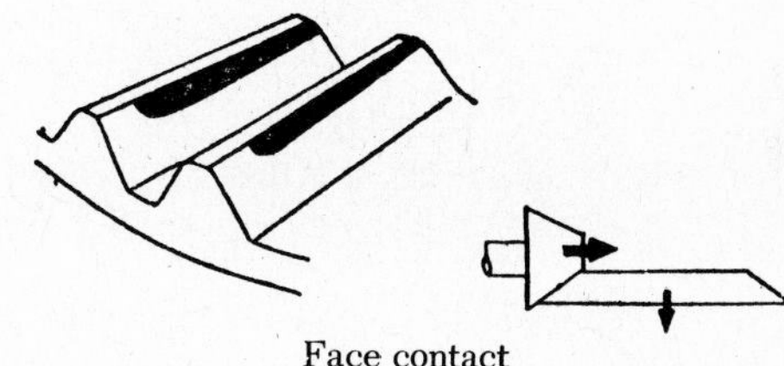

Face contact

   B. Face contact—indicates backlash is too large; increase the shim thickness to move the drive pinion towards the ring gear axis. This will reduce backlash, necessitating side gear shim adjustment to compensate the backlash.
   C. Flank contact—indicates too little backlash; decrease the shim thickness to move pinion away from ring gear axis. Be sure to compensate for backlash changes by altering side gear shim positioning, to bring backlash to specification.

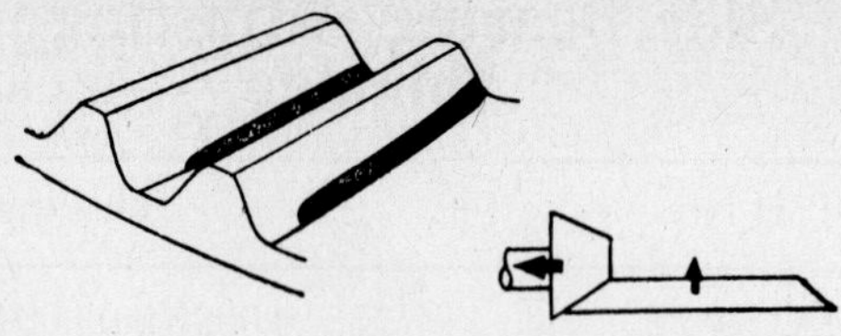

Flank contact

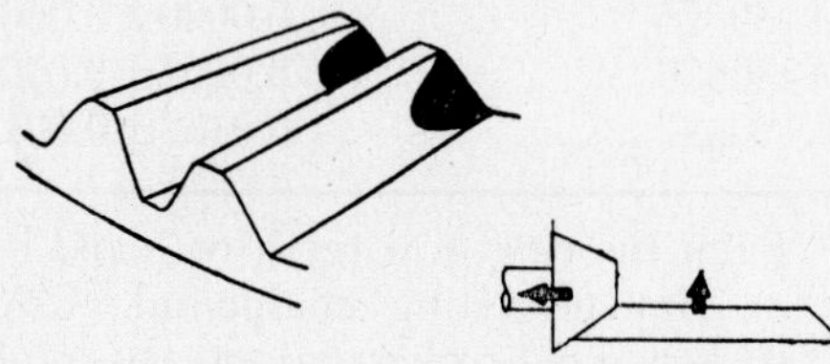

Toe contact

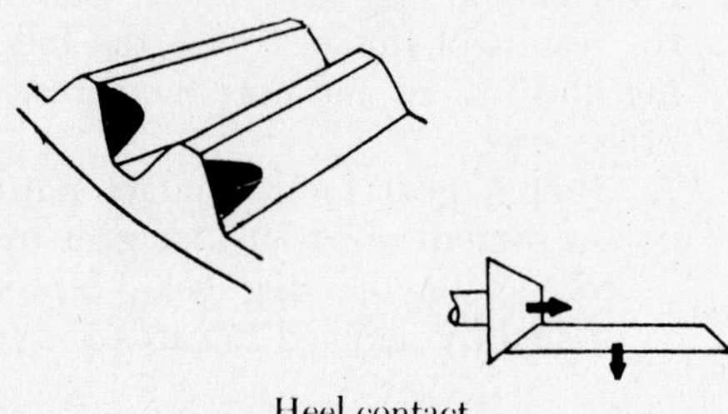

Heel contact

D. Toe contact—too little contact; adjust in the same manner as Step C.
E. Heel contact—too little contact on heel side; adjust in same manner as Step B.

INSTALLATION

Installation is the reverse of removal. Torque the carrier to axle housing bolts to 11-14.5 ft. lbs.

Front Suspension

All Colt models utilize a strut type front suspension, with a coil over shock system and a front stabilizer bar. Caster and camber are factory set; no adjustment should be made.

Lower Arm Disassembly

1. Unscrew bolts from opposite ends of lower arm shaft. Remove lower arm shaft with bushings. Remove rubber stopper and arm bushing.
2. Remove joint cover by wedging screwdriver in lower ball joint ring and gently prying upward.
3. Remove ball joint.

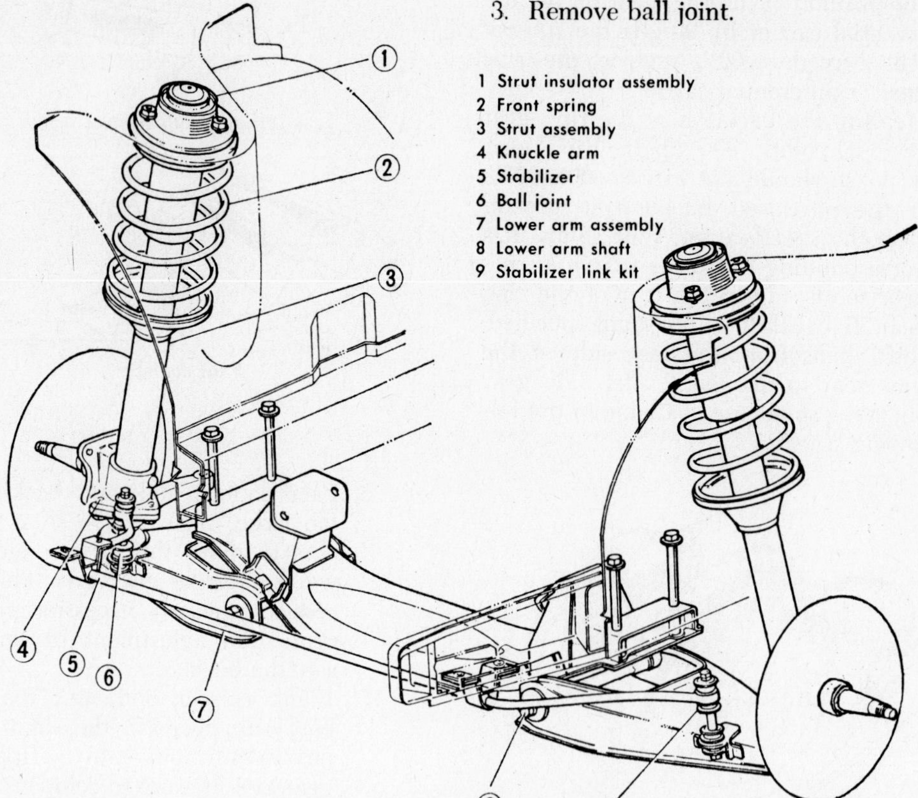

Front suspension

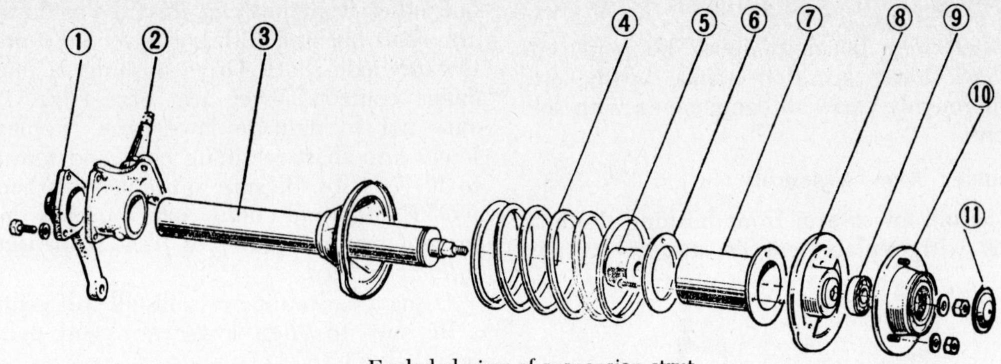

Exploded view of suspension strut

1 Knuckle arm
2 Knuckle
3 Strut sub-assembly (shock absorber)
4 Front suspension spring
5 Rubber bumper
6 Dust cover plate
7 Dust cover
8 Upper spring seat
9 Ball bearing
10 Insulator
11 Dust cover

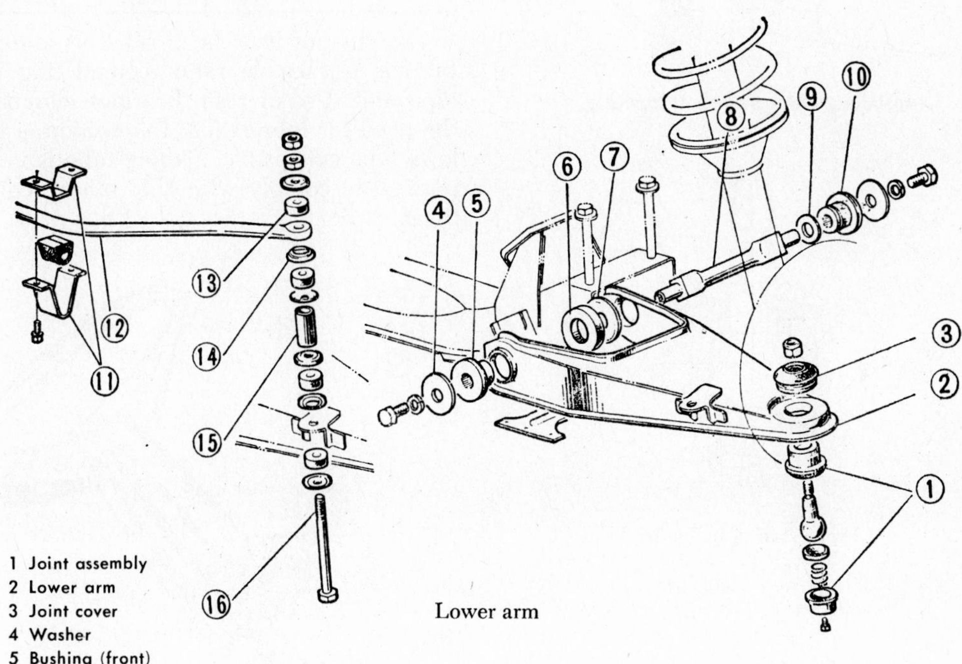

1 Joint assembly
2 Lower arm
3 Joint cover
4 Washer
5 Bushing (front)
6 Stopper rubber
7 Stopper washer
8 Lower arm shaft
9 Spacer
10 Bushing (rear)
11 Stabilizer fixture
12 Stabilizer
13 Rubber bushing
14 Seat
15 Collar
16 Stabilizer bolt

Lower arm

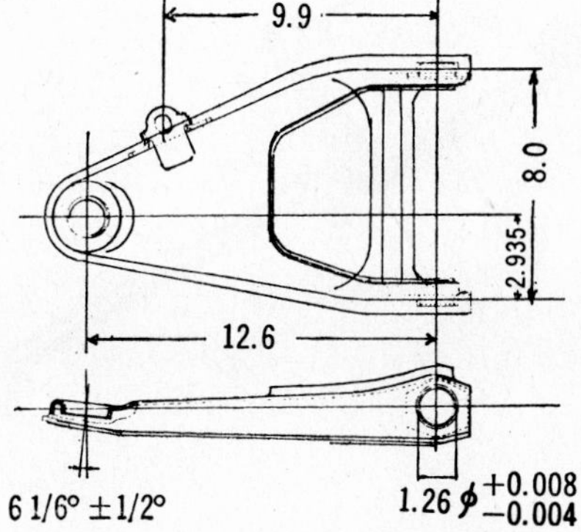

Alignment of lower arm

Rebuilding

Removed bushings must be replaced. Check lower arm for cracks, bends, etc. Thoroughly clean all components with solvent.

Lower Arm Assembly

Install lower arm front bushing. Follow this with replacement of stopper washer and other front bushing. Install rear lower arm shaft bushing with bushing bore center towards axle shaft. Drive bushing in until flange contacts lower arm bore edge. Be sure not to damage lower arm. Replace lower arm shaft retaining bolts and torque to 40-47 ft. lbs. Be sure to use new washers. *NOTE: Torque only with wheels on ground and remainder of front suspension fully assembled.*

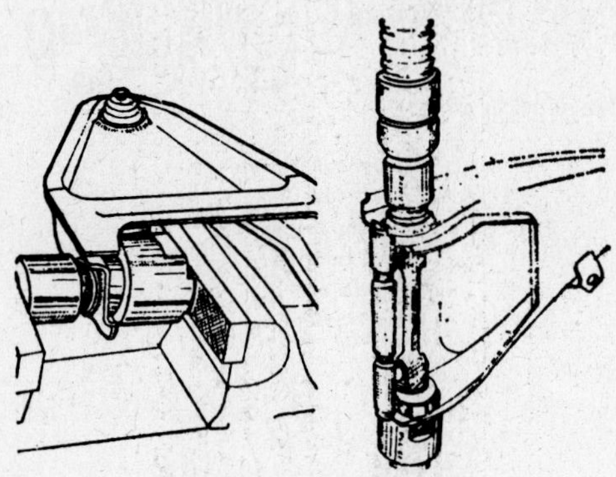

Installing lower arm shaft bushing

Using a hydraulic press, install ball joints. Be sure to align lower arm end mark with ball joint.

Replace joint cover—be sure it contacts lower arm surface. *NOTE: Once removed, a new cover should be installed. Lubricate joint cover with grease.*

Steering

The steering system of all Colt automobiles is a variable ratio recirculating ball type unit. Use of resin bearings eliminates the need for lubrication. In addition, a bellows type collapsible steering tube is incorporated to comply with U.S. safety regulations.

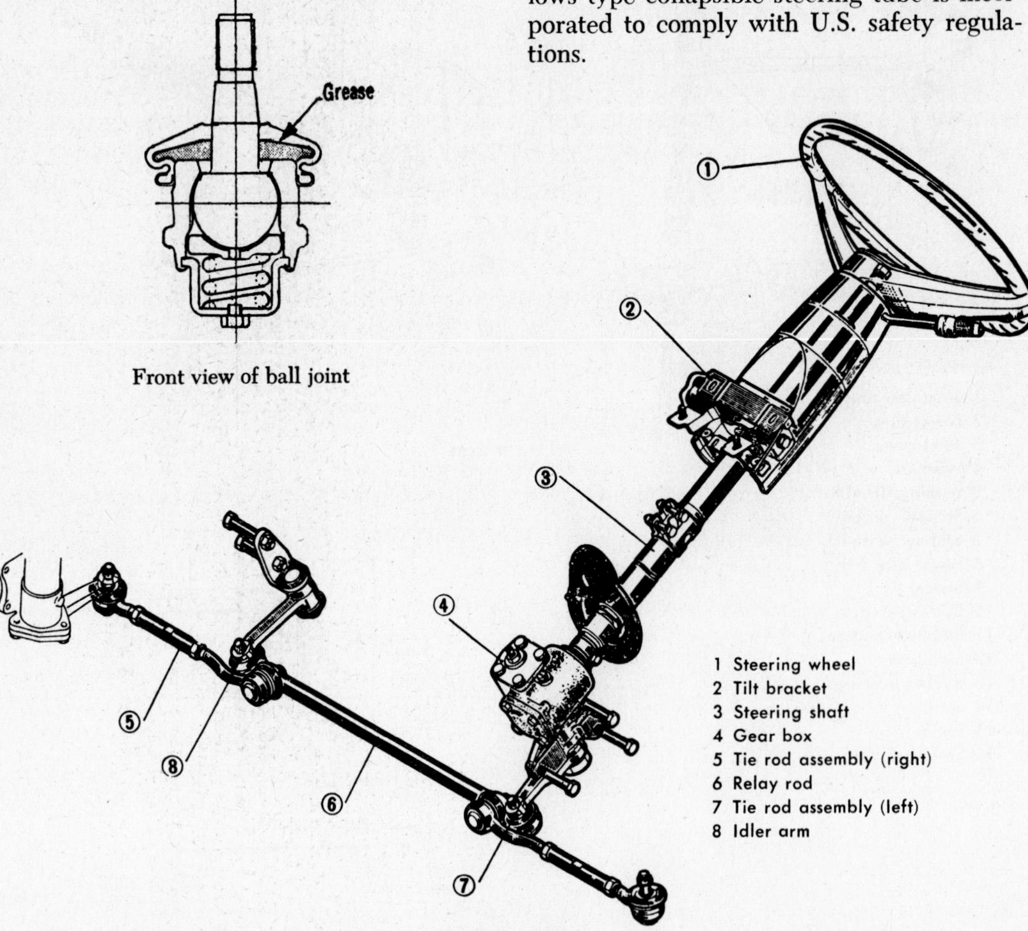

Front view of ball joint

Steering system

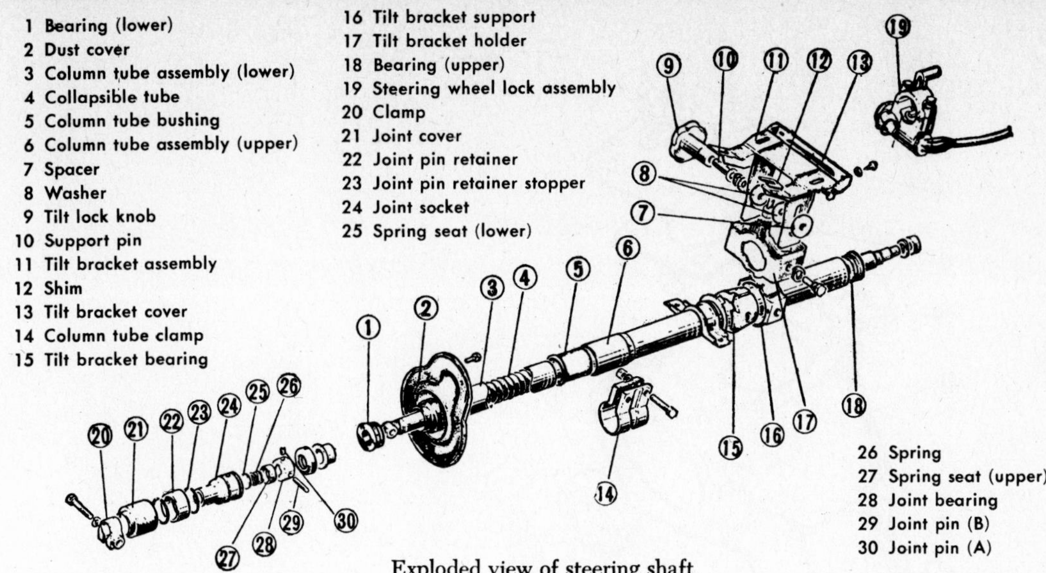

Exploded view of steering shaft

Steering Wheel

Removal

Gently pry off steering wheel central foam pad. Loosen and remove large steering wheel retaining nut. Using steering wheel puller, remove wheel. *CAUTION: Under no conditions should a hammer be used to assist steering wheel removal.*

Installation

Be sure front wheels are in a straight ahead position. Reverse removal procedure. Torque steering wheel nut to 14.5-18.0 ft. lbs.

Steering Box

Removal

1. Remove upper and lower control rods.
2. Disconnect gear box main shaft. Pull out steering shaft.
3. Disconnect, but do not remove, pitman arm and relay rod.

Installation

To install gearbox, note information given below and reverse above procedure. Be sure to align pitman arm and cross shaft. When installing upper control rod, be sure to adjust to proper end clearance (.532-.571").

Torque values
Gear box bolts: 25-29 ft. lbs.
Pitman arm: 94-108 ft. lbs.
Tie rod and relay rod sockets: 29-36 ft. lbs.

Disassembly

Before proceeding, record the main shaft torque and shim height. This will be used as an assembly guide.

1. Unscrew locknut on gear box adjusting bolt and turn bolt counterclockwise until upper cover is free to remove. Lift upper cover from cross-shaft.
2. Remove adjusting bolt from upper cover.
3. Move cross-shaft to straight ahead position and remove main shaft from steering box. *CAUTION: Be gentle in all operations, since cross-shaft serrations and seals damage easily.*
4. Again measure main shaft torque with cross-shaft removed.
5. Remove gear box end cover. Take note of number and thickness of shims.
6. *CAUTION: Remove ball nut assembly, bearing, and main shaft. Do not disassemble main shaft and ballnut assembly.*

Rebuilding

Take note of bushing to cross-shaft clearance. If excessive, replace as necessary. Check main shaft play. Visually inspect other parts for wear and replace as needed. *CAUTION: Do not move ball nut to either end of mainshaft.*

Place gear box in vise. Positioning main shaft horizontally, tighten shim to proper torque. The shim height and torque were recorded during disassembly. As a guide, usual shim used is .020". Apply bonding

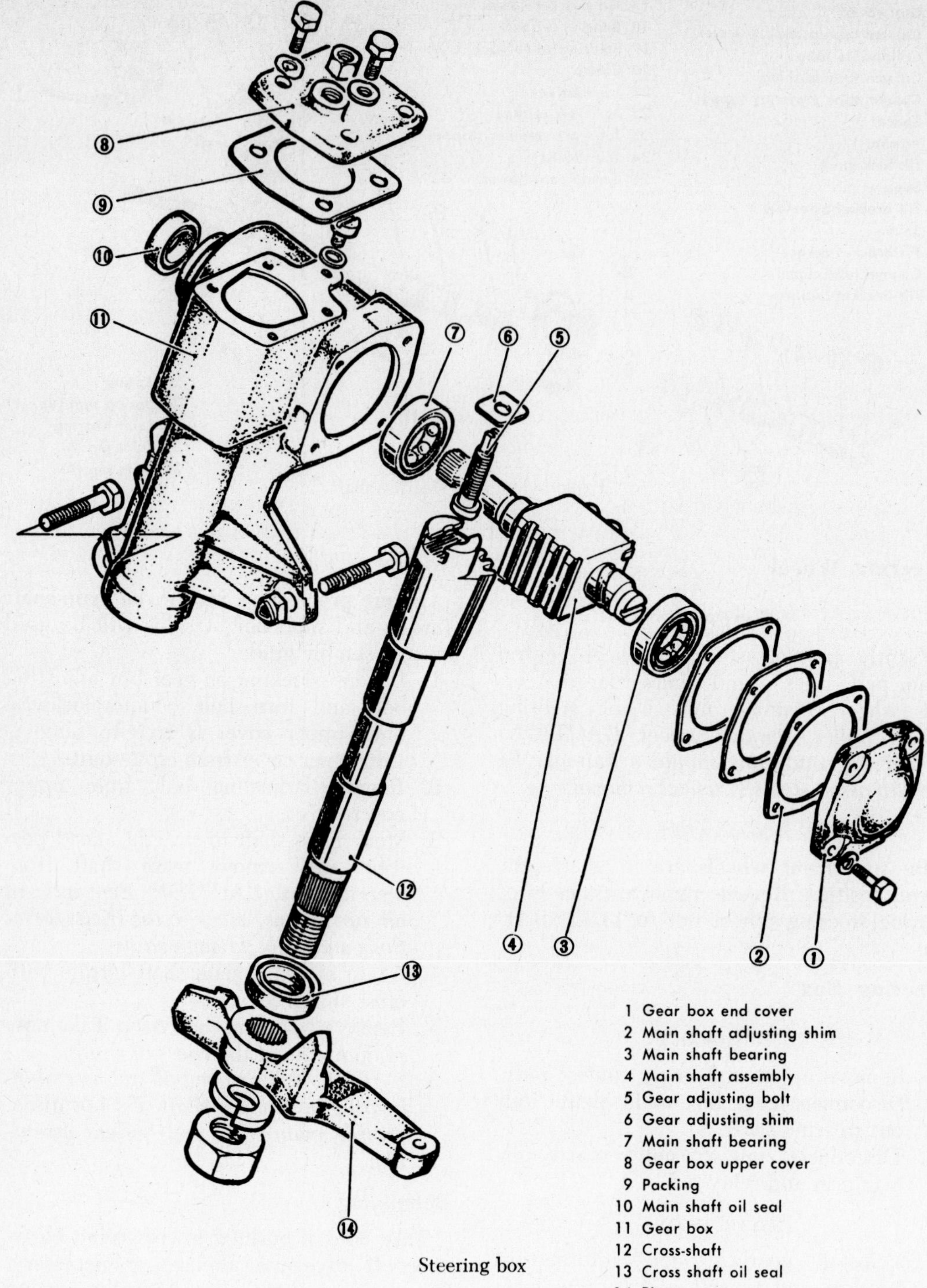
1 Gear box end cover
2 Main shaft adjusting shim
3 Main shaft bearing
4 Main shaft assembly
5 Gear adjusting bolt
6 Gear adjusting shim
7 Main shaft bearing
8 Gear box upper cover
9 Packing
10 Main shaft oil seal
11 Gear box
12 Cross-shaft
13 Cross shaft oil seal
14 Pitman arm

Steering box

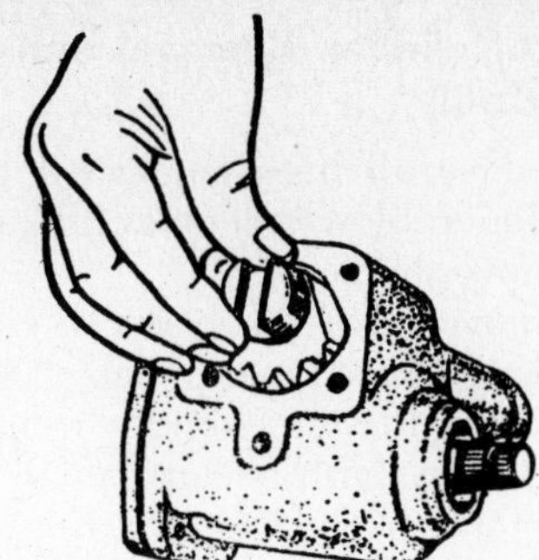
Removing cross-shaft from steering box

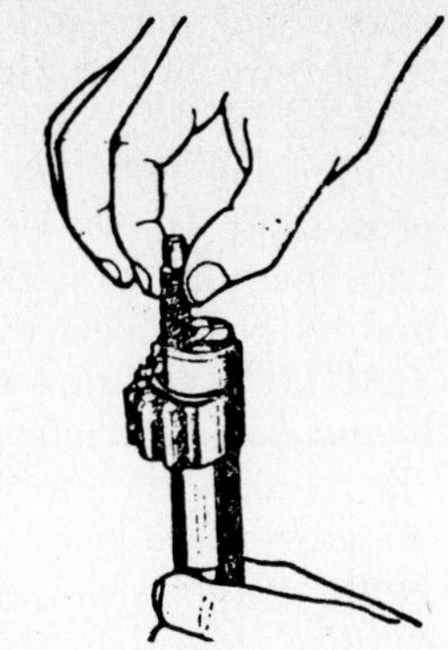
Cross-shaft T groove adjustment

Main shaft removal

Main shaft free play adjustment

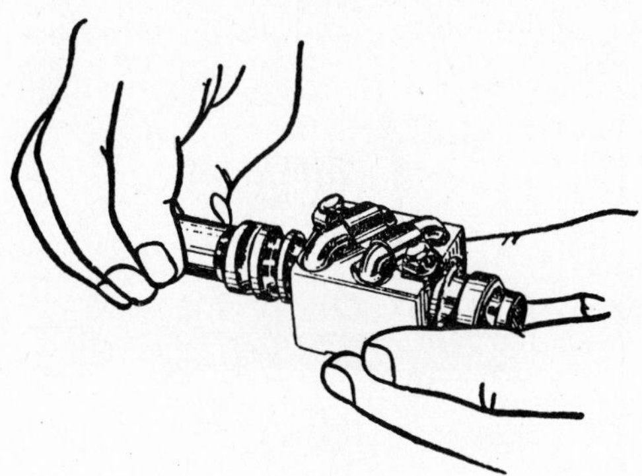
Ball nut removal

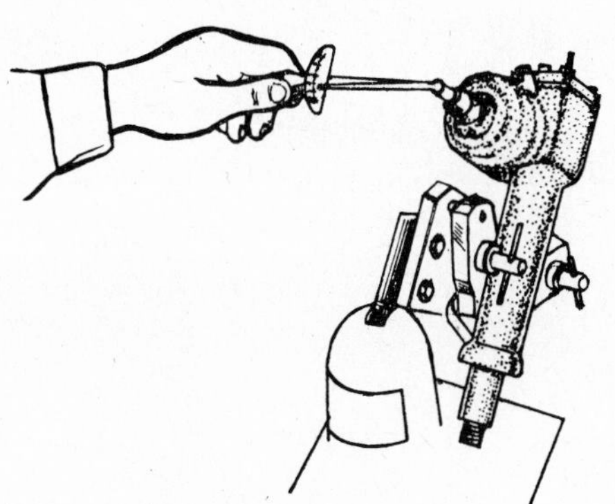
Measuring mainshaft preload

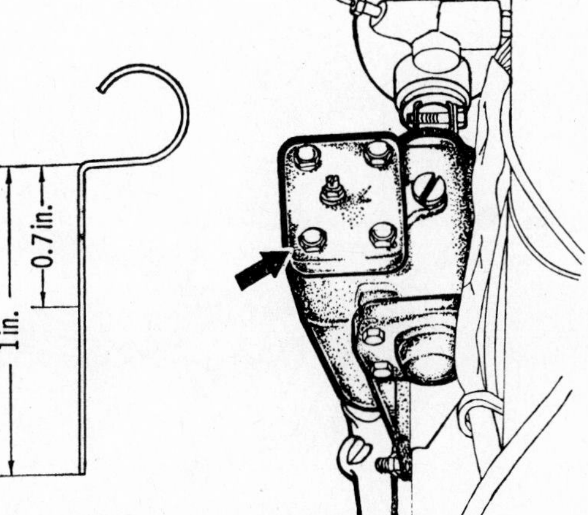

Steering gear oil level check

agent to both sides of shim and bolts when replacing end cover. Check main shaft preload. If not 3.5-4.4 in. lbs., adjust by use of shims. Place adjusting bolt and shim in T groove on cross-shaft (upper end). Adjust shim height to give play of 0-.002″. Install cross-shaft and tighten upper cover to 10.8-14.5 ft. lbs. *CAUTION: Be sure not to damage oil seals and bushings when installing cross-shaft.* Be certain to apply adequate lubrication to cross-shaft gears. Also, coat oil seal lip with grease. Using sealant, install side cover.

Move cross-shaft in housing. Screw adjusting bolt in two to three turns to push cross-shaft into proper mesh. Back off bolt till main shaft shows no free play at center position. Check main shaft preload. If incorrect, be sure that the cross-shaft bushing is not damaged and that the end-cover is installed correctly. Fill unit to proper level with hypoid gear oil NO.90 GS type.

Brakes

All Colt vehicles utilize a front disc and rear drum brake system with a tandem type master cylinder, using independent front and rear cylinders.

1	Reservoir cap complete	16	Cup spacer
2	Fluid reservoir	17	Pressure cup
3	Reservoir band	18	Secondary piston
4	Piston stopper	19	Screw
5	Gasket	20	Spring seat (B)
6	Check valve spring	21	Primary return spring
7	Check valve	22	Spring seat (A)
8	Valve cup gasket	23	Primary cup
9	Valve case	24	Cup spacer
10	Outer pipe seat	25	Primary piston
11	Check valve cap	26	Secondary cup
12	Brake master cylinder body	27	Piston stopper
13	Secondary return spring	28	Stopper ring
14	Spring seat	29	Master cylinder boots
15	Primary cup	30	Pushrod assembly

Master Cylinder Removal and Disassembly

1. Remove all lines connected to master cylinder. Slowly depress brake pedal to remove fluid.
2. Remove clevis pin between master cylinder push rod and pedal.
3. Remove master cylinder from firewall and thoroughly clean.
4. Remove boots, stopper ring, primary and secondary piston assembly. Remove return spring.
5. Loosen valve case and remove check valve and spring. Do not attempt to disassemble primary piston assembly.

Inspection

Visually inspect all parts. Replace as necessary. Check clearance between piston and master cylinder. If it exceeds .001-.006″, replace piston or master cylinder. Check primary spring free length. It should be 1.6-1.75″. Measure secondary spring free length which should be 2.2-2.4″. Replace if not according to specifications.

Assembly

To assemble master cylinder, reverse removal procedure. Lubricate master cylinder

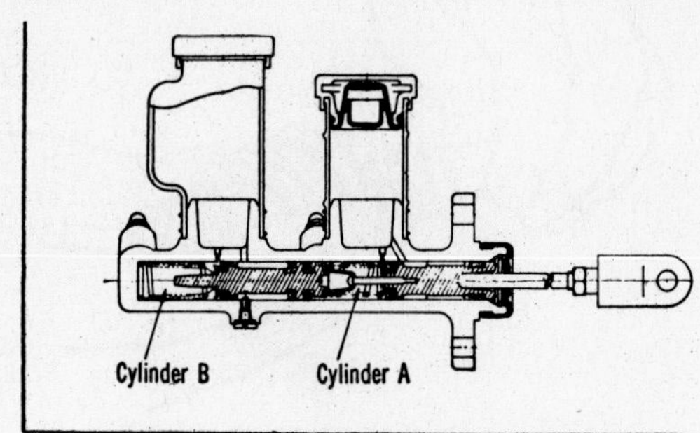

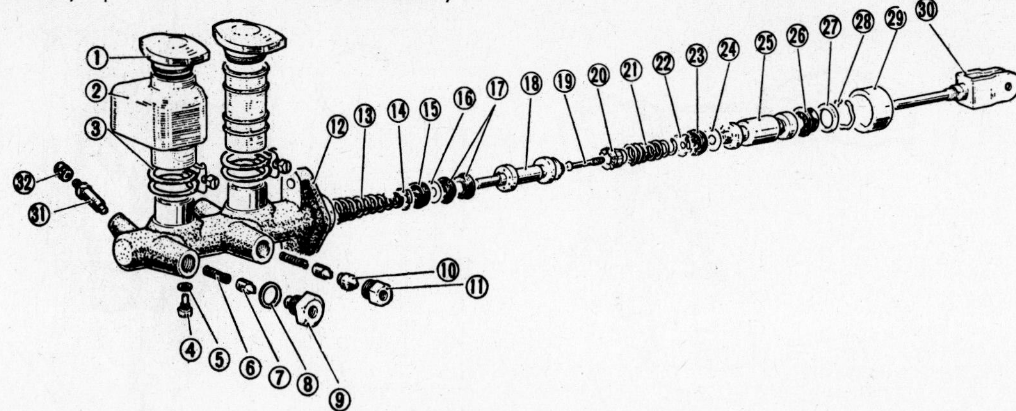

Exploded view of master cylinder

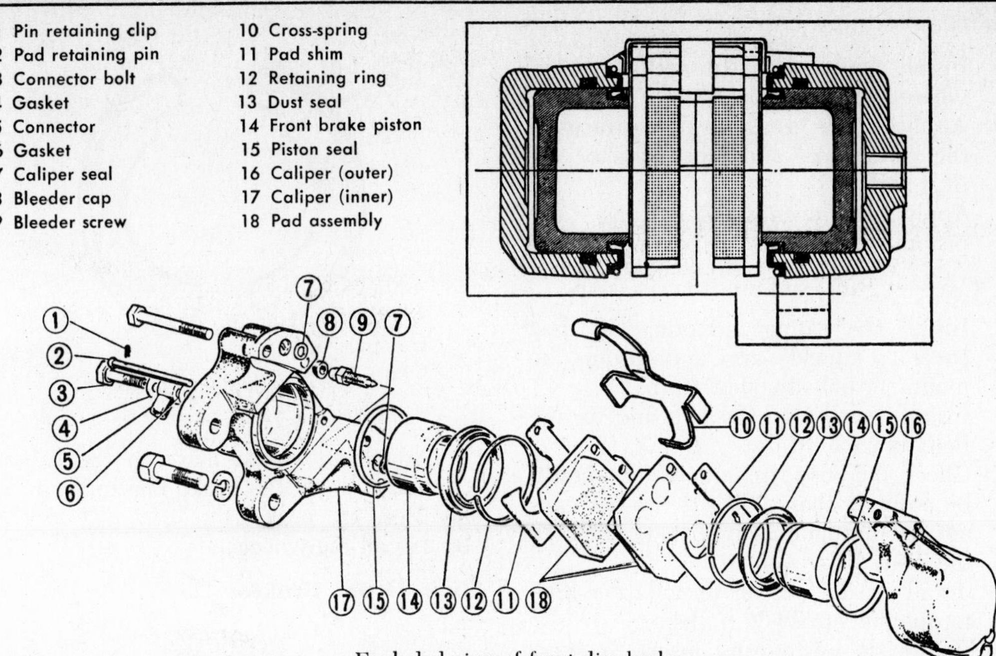

Exploded view of front disc brake

parts (excluding boots) before assembly. Be certain return port is not obstructed by piston cup when in return position. Torque master cylinder to 5.8-8.7 ft. lbs.

Front Disc Brakes

Caliper, Pad and Disc Removal

1. Remove the wheel.
2. Disconnect the brake line from the brake hose.
3. Remove the flexible hose from the caliper.
4. Pull out the clip and remove the retaining pin and cross-spring.
5. Hold the pad backing plate with pliers and remove the pad and shim.
6. Remove the caliper assembly from the disc.

Measuring brake disc run-out

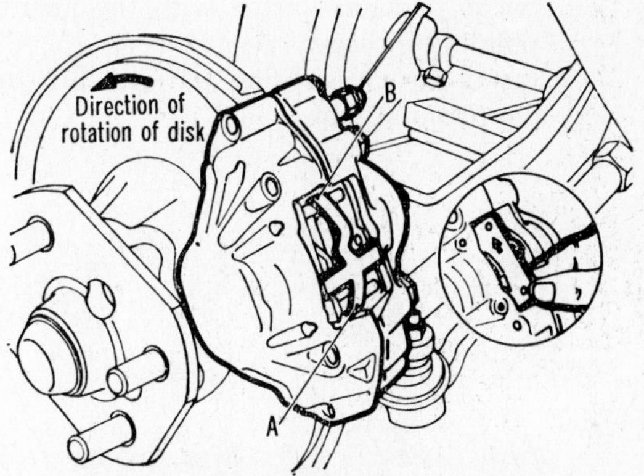

Cross-spring and shim installation

7. Remove the hub assembly and disconnect the hub from the disc. A soft jawed vise should be used for this.

Caliper Disassembly

1. Remove the retaining ring and dust seal.
2. Remove the piston on the outer side holding the inner piston in place. If the piston on one side is not held in place, both pistons may jump out simultaneously, causing injury.
3. *NOTE: Do not loosen the bridge bolts or attempt to separate the calipers.*
4. Remove the inner piston through the cavity by gently tapping with a soft instrument.
5. Carefully remove the piston seal.
6. Clean all parts in brake fluid.

Caliper Assembly

1. Install the piston seal and dust seal where removed.
2. Apply rubber grease to the surfaces of the piston seal and inner side of the dust seal.
3. Apply rust preventive oil and insert the piston. Do not twist the piston.

CALIPER, PAD AND DISC INSTALLATION

1. Install the caliper adapter and dust cover to knuckle arm and torque the mounting bolts to 30-36 ft. lbs.
2. Install the disc on the hub and torque bolts to 25-29 ft. lbs.
3. Check the disc run-out, which should be no more than .006″. If run-out cannot be brought below .006″, replace the disc.
4. Install the caliper on the adapter and torque bolts to 29-36 ft. lbs.
5. Spread the piston and insert the pad and shim. The shim is installed between pad and piston with the arrow pointing forward.
6. Install the cross-spring and attach it to the retaining pin.

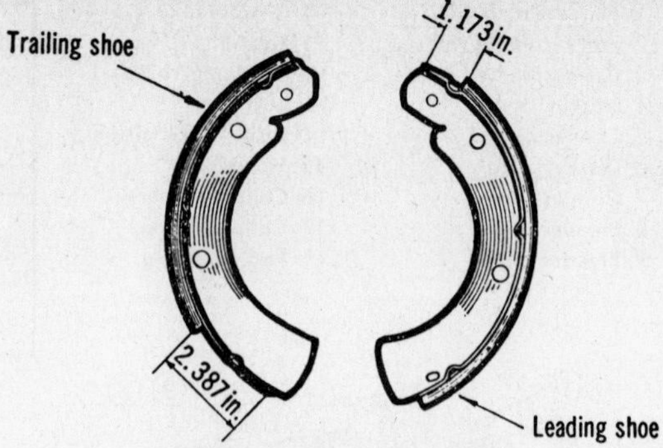

Brake lining installed position

7. Attach the brake hose to the caliper and connect the brake line to the hose.
8. Bleed the brakes.
9. Install the wheels.

Rear Drum Brakes

REMOVAL

1. Remove wheel, brake drum, and hold-down spring.
2. Disassemble shoe return spring.
3. Remove clevis pin between extension lever and parking brake cable. Remove adjusting assembly.
4. Remove brake lines from wheel.
5. Remove the wheel cylinder from the backing plate.

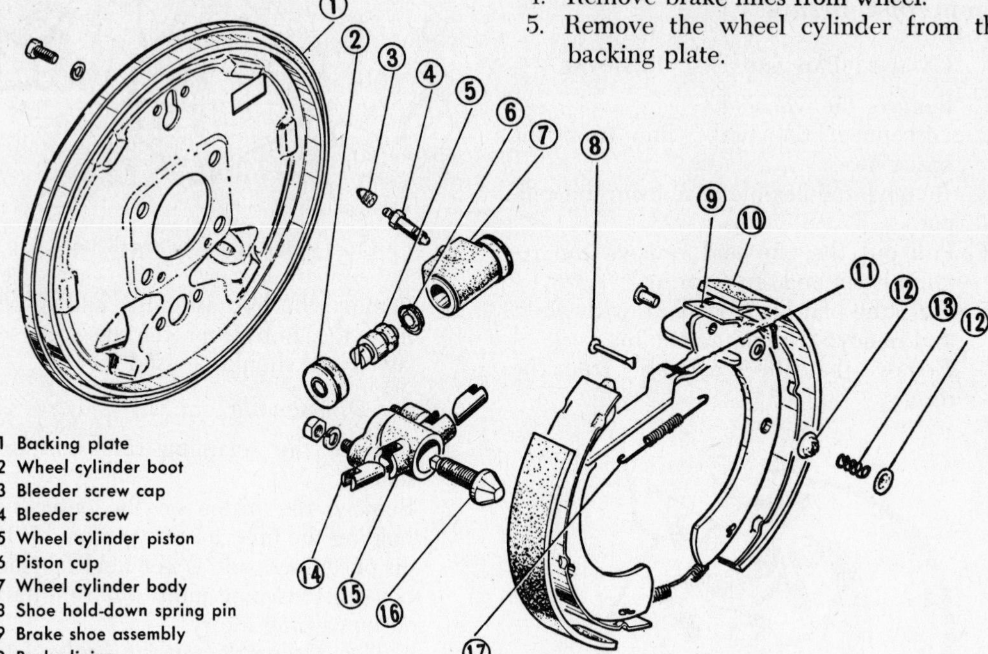

1 Backing plate
2 Wheel cylinder boot
3 Bleeder screw cap
4 Bleeder screw
5 Wheel cylinder piston
6 Piston cup
7 Wheel cylinder body
8 Shoe hold-down spring pin
9 Brake shoe assembly
10 Brake lining
11 Parking brake extension lever
12 Shoe hold-down spring seat
13 Shoe hold-down spring
14 Slack adjuster anchor
15 Slack adjuster body
16 Slack adjuster
17 Shoe return spring

Exploded view of rear brakes

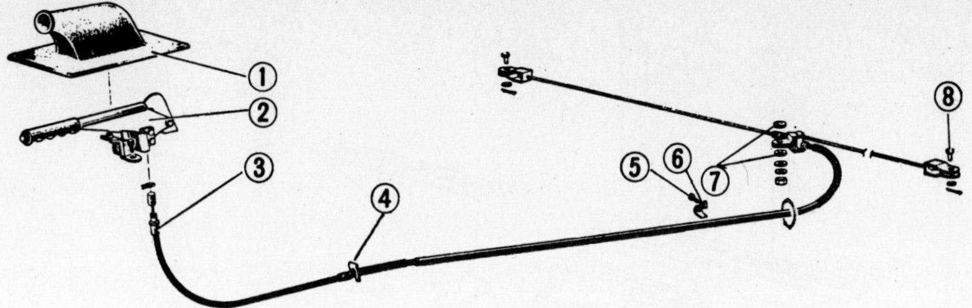

Exploded view of parking brake linkage

1 Parking brake lever cover
2 Parking brake lever assembly
3 Parking brake cable
4 Clip
5 Bolt
6 Clip
7 Bushing
8 Clevis pin

Inspection

Thoroughly clean all components. Brake lining thickness may be no less than .04 in. Check inner wall of brake drum for scoring. Repair limit is 9.079″.

INSTALLATION

Installation is the reverse of removal. Leave the adjuster slack.

Brake Shoe to Drum Clearance Adjustment

Move parking brake lever to release brake cable. Turning clockwise, fully tighten adjuster. Back adjuster off to free linings from contact with brake drum. Maximum brake shoe to drum clearance is .012″.

Parking Brake Adjustment

Release brake cable. Loosen adjusting nuts on either side of the cable. Move cable lever to each side and tighten nuts to tension cable. Cable tightening should provide backing plate and extension lever clearance of *less* than .04″. Be certain drum does not contact lining. Standard parking brake lever travel is 10 notches.

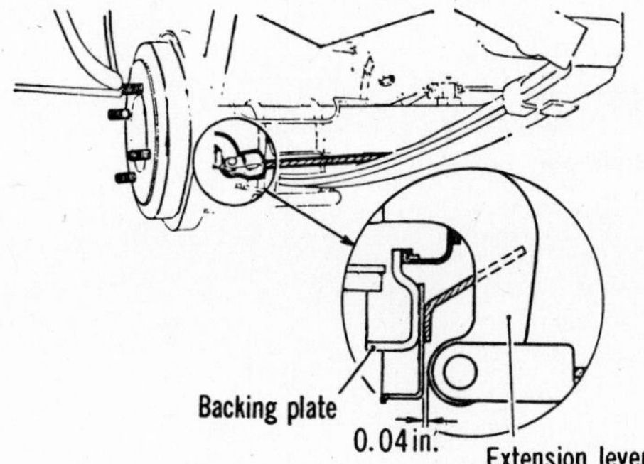

Parking brake adjustment

Heater

Removal

Drain cooling system. Remove center console assembly from car interior. Disconnect all heater wiring. Remove heater control assembly. Disconnect all heater hoses and ducts. Pull heater from car.

Installation

To replace heater, reverse removal procedure. Be sure to adjust screws at heater control assembly bottom. This will prevent control lever from contacting center console indentation.

Windshield Wipers

Motor Removal

1. Remove attaching bolts holding motor to body.
2. Loosen and remove nut on wiper arm shaft on driver's side. Pull motor assembly from position. Motor crank arm and linkage may be removed by extracting bushing.

Installation

To replace wiper motor, reverse removal procedure.

Radio

Removal

1. Remove fastenings and extract padding on top of radio. This may be accomplished by withdrawing screws at radio

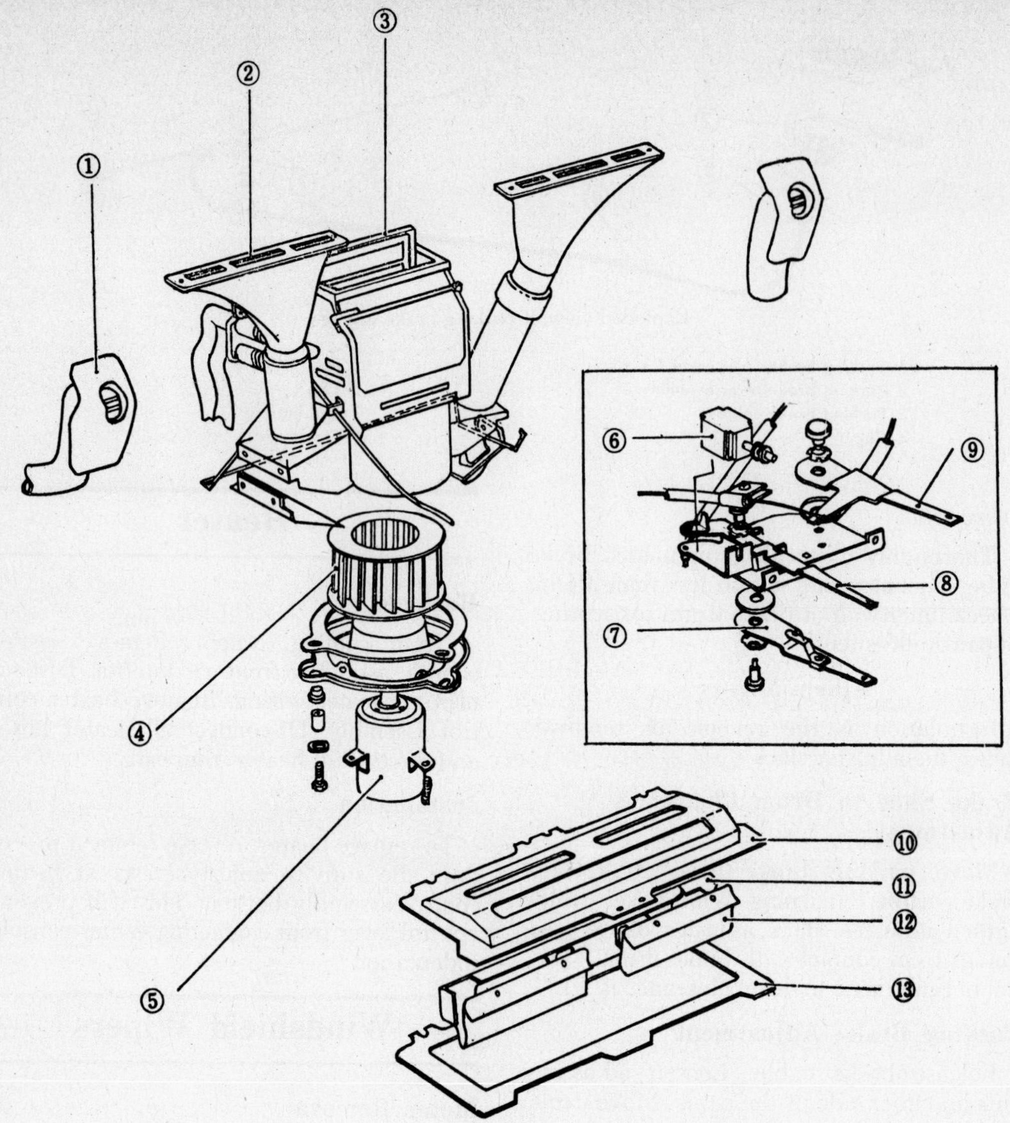

Exploded view of heater

1 Ventilator duct assembly
2 Defroster nozzle
3 Heater assembly
4 Turbo fan
5 Motor
6 Fan motor switch
7 Air control lever
8 Heater-defroster changeover and fan motor switch lever
9 Temperature control lever
10 Upper panel
11 Plate
12 Non-return valve
13 Lower panel

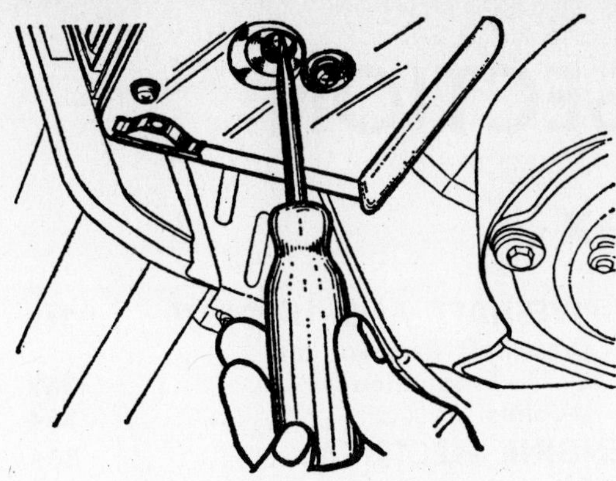
Adjusting heater control position

bottom, which are also connected to the console.

2. Remove all radio switches. In addition, remove all heater control levers and knobs. Remove wing nut on radio right-hand side.
3. Remove screws at bottom of ash tray and console cover.
4. Pull radio slightly forward. Disconnect all wiring and lift out.

Installation

To replace radio, reverse removal procedure.

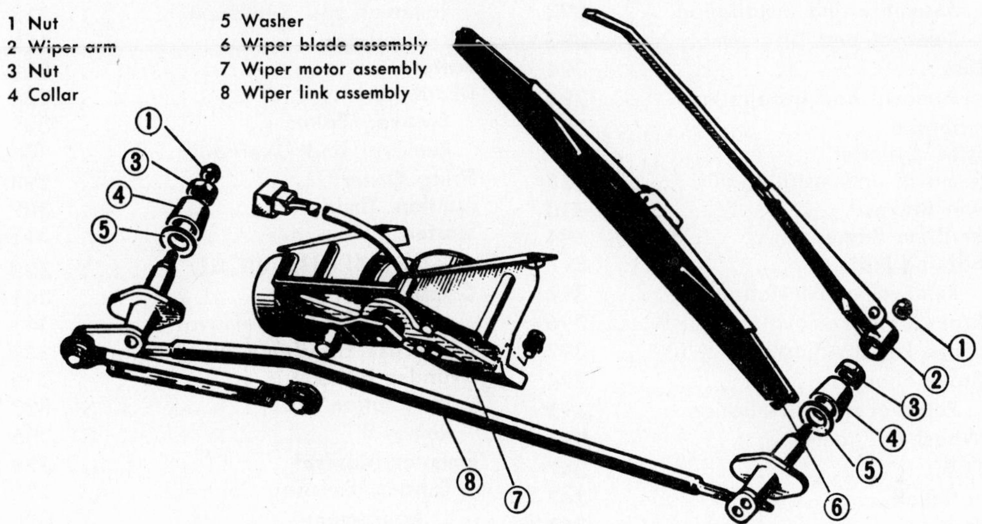

Exploded view of windshield wiper linkage

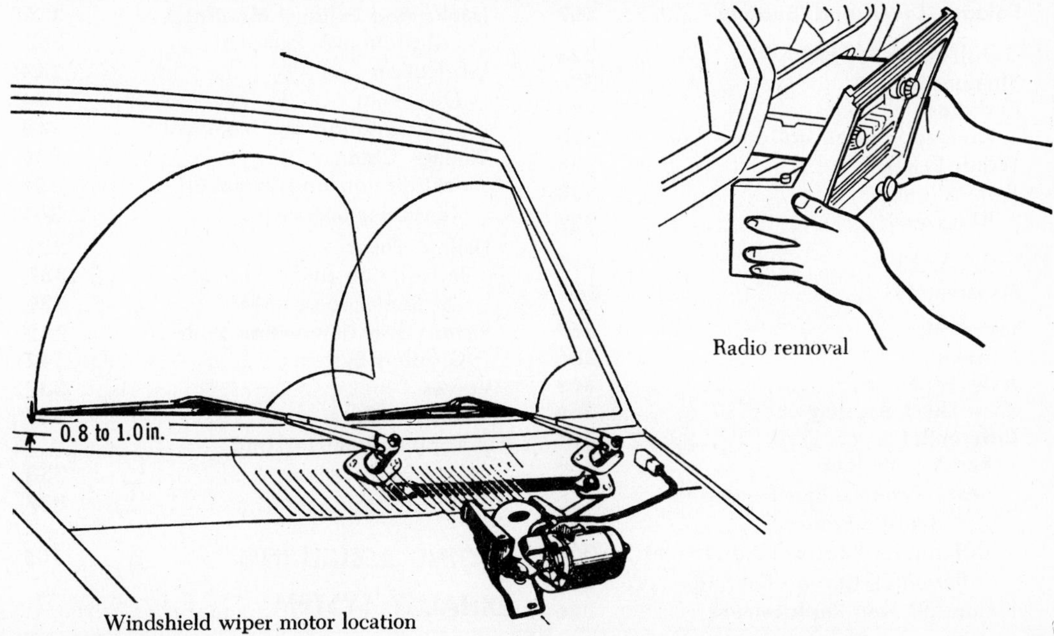

Windshield wiper motor location

Radio removal

CRICKET SECTION

Index

Introduction

The Plymouth Cricket is a four-door economy sedan powered by a four-cylinder, 94.1 cubic inch engine with either a four-speed synchronized manual transmission or a three-speed automatic transmission. The car, first imported to the United States in 1971 from England, is equipped with the required exhaust emission control equipment. The carburetor used with this equipment is the nonadjustable Stromberg 150 CDSE. The carburetor used in other countries is the Stromberg 150 CDS model, which is adjustable. The brake system consists of disc brakes on the front wheels and drum brakes on the rear wheels—all hydraulically-operated. In some cars, a vacuum-assisted power brake cylinder is used to help operate the brakes with less pedal pressure.

The Cricket is available in two basic versions—Cricket and Cricket SE. The Cricket is the basic model (91.4 cu. in. engine and manual transmission) to which various optional equipment may be added. Some of these options are automatic transmission, voltmeter, oil pressure gauge, extra horn, and cigarette lighter. The Cricket SE is the basic Cricket with a special deluxe trim and interior package that includes carpets, adjustable front seat backs, and chrome trim in addition to the gauges, horn and cigarette lighter.

Model Identification

Plymouth Cricket

Vehicle and Engine Serial Number Identification

VEHICLE NUMBER IDENTIFICATION

Vehicle number identification plates

A. Vehicle identification number
B. Certification label showing vehicle identification number and date of manufacture
C. Tire pressure and load plate

Vehicle identification is made by plates attached as follows:

a. The serial number is on a plate located on the instrument panel between the left windshield wiper and the left roof post. It is visible through the windshield from the outside.
b. The certification number and build date is on a plate located on the left door post between the front and rear doors.
c. Tire pressure and load data is on a plate located in the glove compartment.
d. The chassis number plate, containing the chassis number and the paint color code, is located on the hood locking platform at the front of the engine compartment.

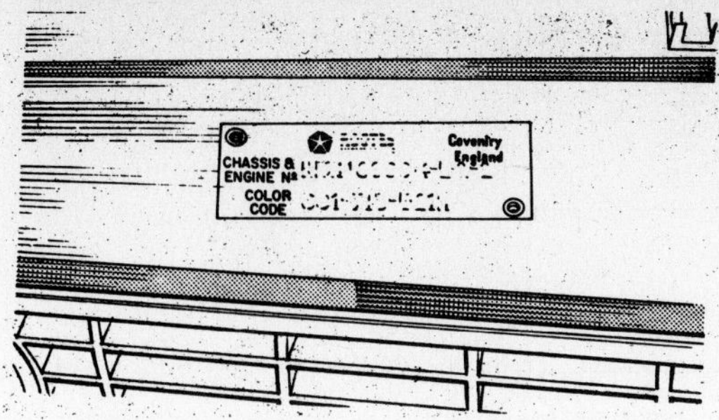

Chassis number identification plate

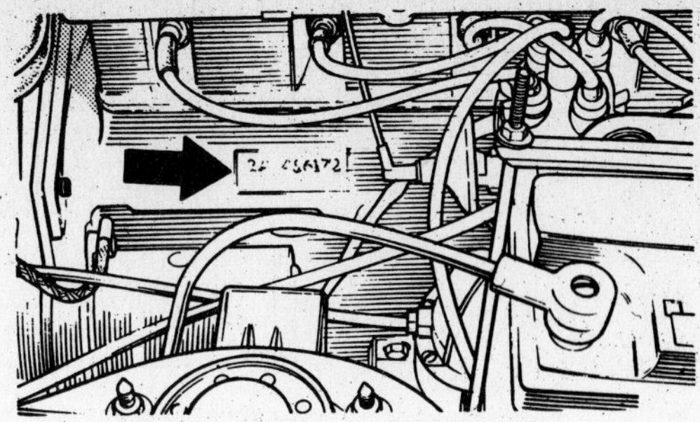

Engine number identification

ENGINE NUMBER IDENTIFICATION

The engine number is stamped on the right side of the engine block directly below the No. 3 spark plug. The engine identification code is cast in the block just above the engine mounting bracket on the exhaust manifold side.

Engine Identification

Number of Cylinders	*Cu. In. Displacement (cc.)*	*Type*	*Code*
4	91.41 (1,498)	OHV-pushrod	LB

General Engine Specifications

Year	*Type*	*Cu. In. Displacement (cc.)*	*Carburetor*	*Developed Horsepower (DIN) @ rpm*	*Developed Torque (ft. lb.) @ rpm*	*Bore and Stroke (in.)*	*Compression Ratio*	*Normal Oil Pressure (hot) psi*
1971	OHV	91.41	One barrel,	57 @5,000	74 @ 3,000	A-3.3908 x 2.53	8.0:1	50-60
		(1,498)	side draft,			B-3.3912 x 2.53		
			constant			C-3.3916 x 2.53		
			depression			D-3.3920 x 2.53		
			(vacuum)					

*—Pistons and cylinder bores are graded A, B, C, and D by size so that the correct piston may be fitted to new cylinter bores having the same grade letters as the piston. Each grade variation is 0.0004".

Tune-up Specifications

Year	*Model*	*Spark Plugs*		*Distributor*		*Basic Ignition Timing (degrees)*	*Cranking Compression Pressure (psi)*	*Valves Clearance (in.)*		*Intake Opens (deg.)*	*Idle Speed rpm*
		Make Type	*Gap*	*Point Dwell*	*Point Gap*			*Intake*	*Exhaust*		
1971	4 cyl.	Champion N9Y	.025	60 + 3	.015	7 BTDC	150-160	.008	.016	35 BTDC	#
1972		All Models	See engine compartment stickers for tune-up specifications.								

#—Refer to Carburetor Specifications Chart for correct idle speed.

Engine Firing Order

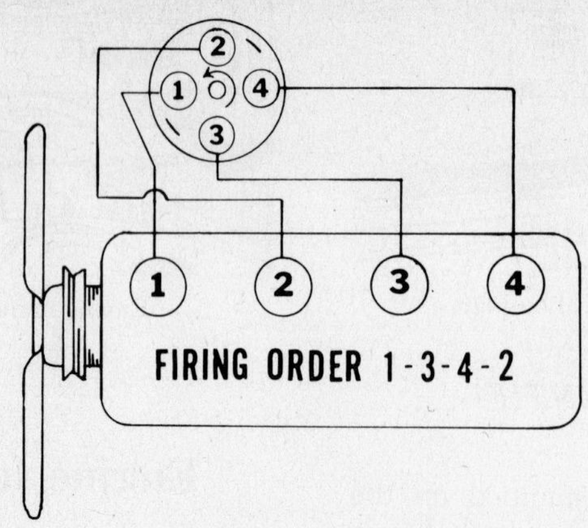

Engine Rebuilding Specifications

Model	Crankshaft: Main Bearing Journals (in.): Journal Diameter New	Max. Oversize	Oil Clearance	Shaft End-play	Thrust on No.	Connecting Rod Bearing Journals (in.): Journal Diameter New	Max. Oversize	Oil Clearance	Side Play
1,498 cc.	2.1245-2.1251	.040	.0005-.0025	.002-.008	rear main[1]	2.1460-2.1465	N.A.	.0009-.0024	.007-.012

Cylinder Bore (in.) New	Max. Oversize	Pistons (in.): Piston Diameter New	Max. Oversize	Wrist Pin Diameter (fit)	Rings (in.): Side Clearance (in.)	End-Gap	Piston-to-Bore Clearance[3]
A-3.3906-3.3910	.030	A-3.3887-3.3891	.030	(Thumb push fit @ 68 degrees F.).	.0015-.0035	top .014-.018	.0015-.0023
B-3.3910-3.3914		B-3.3891-3.3895		Grade:		2nd & scraper .010-.014	
C-3.3914-3.3918		C-3.3895-3.3899		Yellow .9374-.9375			
D-3.3918-3.3922		D-3.3899-3.3903		Green .9375-.9376			
		E-3.3903-3.3907[2]		White .9376-.9377			
				Blue (service) .9377-.9378			

1. End play thrust is adjusted by 2 steel semi-circular, copper, lead faced washers.
2. For service (replacement) use only.
3. Measured at right angles to piston pin hole ⅝" above bottom of piston.

Engine Rebuilding Specifications

Model	Valves										
	Seat Angle (deg.)	Minimum Valve Seat Width (in.)		Valve Lift (in.)		Valve Spring Pressure Intake & Exhaust (lbs. @ in.)		Valve Spring Free Length (in.)	Stem Diameter (in.)		Stem-to-Guide Clearance (in.)
		Intake	Exhaust	Intake	Exhaust	Valve Closed	Valve Open		Intake	Exhaust	Intake	Exhaust
1,498	45	1.418-	1.198-	N.A.	N.A.	71.25-	183.5 @	1.758	Standard	Standard	.001-	.0025-
cc.		1.422	1.202			78.75	1.138″		.3110-.3115	.3095-	.0025	.0045
						@ 1.505″			(+3)	.3100		
									.3140-	(+3)		
									31.45	.3125-		
									(+15)	31.30		
									.3260-	(+15)		
									.3265	.3245-		
									(+30)	.3250		
									.3410-	(+30)		
									.3415	.3395-		
										.3400		

Torque Specifications

Year	Model	Cylinder Head Bolts and Nuts (ft. lbs.)	Main Bearing Bolts (ft. lbs.)	Rod Bearing Nuts (ft. lbs.)	Crankshaft Balancer Bolt (ft. lbs.)	Flywheel to Crankshaft Bolts (ft. lbs.)	Manifold (ft. lbs.) Intake	Manifold (ft. lbs.) Exhaust
1971	1,498 cc.	56	55	29	50	40	16	16

Tightening Sequence

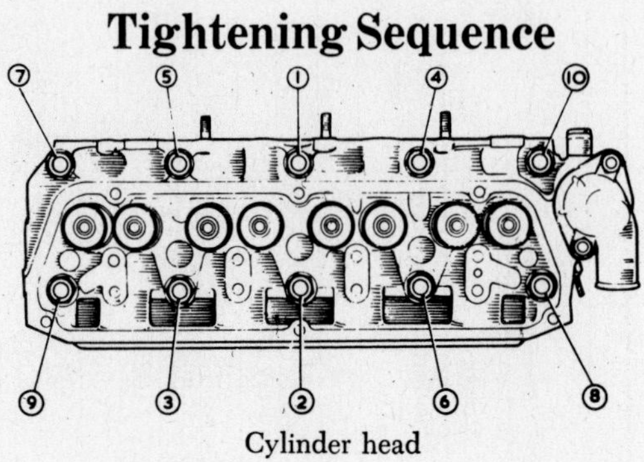

Cylinder head

Electrical Specifications

Year	Model	Battery Capacity (amp. hours)	Battery Volts	Grounded Terminal	Starter Lock Test Amp.	Starter Lock Test Volts	Starter Lock Test Torque (ft. lb.)	Starter No Load Test Amps.	Starter No Load Test Volts	Starter No Load Test rpm	Brush Spring Tension (oz.)
1971	1,498 cc.	38	12	Negative	350-375	N.A.	7	260-275	N.A.	1,000	28

Alternator Part Number	Alternator Field Current Draw @ 12V	Alternator Output @ Alternator RPM	AC Regulator Part Number	Field Relay Air Gap (in.)	Field Relay Point Gap (in.)	Regulator Volts to Close	Regulator Air Gap (in.)	Regulator Point Gap (in.)	Regulator Volts @ 125 deg. F.
16ACR	N.A.	34 @ 6,000	8TR	—	—	14.0-14.4	—	—	—

Distributor Specifications

Year	Model	Distributor Identification	Centrifugal Advance Start Degrees @ dist. rpm	Centrifugal Advance Intermediate Degrees @ dist. rpm	Centrifugal Advance Intermediate Degrees @ dist. rpm	Centrifugal Advance End Degrees @ dist. rpm	Vacuum Advance Start Degrees @ in./Hg	Vacuum Advance Intermediate Degrees @ in./Hg	Vacuum Advance End Degrees @ in./Hg
1971	1,498 cc.	Lucas 25D4	0 @ 400	5-7 @ 750	12-14 @ 2,000	15-17 @ 3,000	0-½ @ 7	1½-4 @ 16	5-7 @ 25

1. These figures are used when testing the distributor, off the engine, on a distributor tester.
2. The ignition static advance angle must be added to these figures when testing the distributor on the engine.
3. On the engine, vacuum advance depends upon the amount of vacuum applied from the intake manifold to the distributor vacuum advance diaphragm, and vacuum advance may be correct on a distributor tester, but incorrect on the engine due to a vacuum problem.

Capacities and Pressures

Year	Model	Engine Crankcase Oil Refill after Draining (qts.)		Transmission Refill after Draining (pts.)		Drive (Rear) Axle (pts.)	Fuel Tank (gals.)	Cooling System with heater (qts.)	Max. Coolant Pressure (psi) Fuel	Normal Pump Pressure (psi)	Steering Gear (pts.)
		With Filter	Without Filter	Manual 4-speed	Auto.						
1971	1,498 cc.	4.25	3.6	3.6	13.5	1.75	10.75	15.5	9	2.75-4.25	.25

*—Transmission capacity given is for complete draining of transmission and converter. If only the transmission is drained, about 6 pints of fluid is needed to refill the transmission. If only the converter is drained, about 6-7 pints of fluid is needed for refill. Refill transmission according to instructions in automatic transmission section.

Brake Specifications

Year	Model	Type		Brake Cylinder Bore			Brake Disc Diameter (in.)	Brake Drum Diameter (in.)
		Front	Rear	Master Cylinder (in.)	Caliper Piston Diameter (in.)	Wheel Cylinder (in.) Rear		
1971	4 dr. Sedan	Disc	Drum	.750	1.893	.700	9.5	8.01

Chassis and Wheel Alignment Specifications

Year	Model	Chassis			Wheel Alignment							
		Wheel-base (in.)	Track (in.)		Caster*		Camber*		Toe-in (in.)	King-pin Inclination (deg.)*	Wheel Pivot Ratio	
			Front	Rear	Range (deg.)	Pref. Setting (deg.)	Range (deg.)	Pref. Setting (deg.)			Inner Wheel (deg.)	Outer Wheel (deg.)
1971	Cricket 4-dr. Sedan	98	51	51.25	N.A.	+1 (+30′)	N.A.	+1 (+45′)	1/32-1/8	11°(−30′+45′) @ +1 camber	N.A.	N.A.

*—With car on alignment checking equipment.

Fuses

Year	Model	Circuit	Rating (amps.)	Type
1971	Cricket 4-door Sedan	#1 Auxiliary circuits controlled through ignition switch—heater, windshield wiper, back-up lights, stoplights, etc.	35	8FJ
		#2 Auxiliary circuits not controlled by system switches—interior lights, courtesy lights.	35	8FJ
		#3 Auxiliary circuits controlled through light switch—headlamps, sidelamps, panel lights, license plate lamp, etc.	35	8FJ

Light Bulb Specifications

Year	Model	Circuit Usage	Type	Voltage	Wattage or Candlepower
1971	Cricket 4-dr. Sedan	Twin headlamp—North America	F575		
		Outer sealed beam No. 2	54521335	12V	37-1/2/50W
		Inner sealed beam No. 1	54521334	12V	37-1/2W
		Turn signals—front and rear	382	12V	21W
		Stop/tail and front parking/turn signals	380	12V	6/21W
		Rear license plate	989	12V	6W
		Back-up lamp	382	12V	21W
		Interior courtesy	254	12V	6W
		Ignition/alternator warning	N.A.	N.A.	N.A.
		High beam warning	N.A.	N.A.	N.A.
		Turn signal warning	504	12V	2.2W
		Oil pressure warning	N.A.	N.A.	N.A.
		Panel illumination	N.A.	N.A.	N.A.
		Glove compartment	989	12V	6W
		Side marker	989	12V	6W
		Bulb, four-way flasher	281	12V	2W

Carburetor Specifications

Year	Model	Carburetor Identification	Idle Speed (rpm)		Fast Idle Speed Adjust. (in.)*	Needle Identification	Spring Identification
			Manual Trans.	Auto. Trans.			
1971	Cricket 4-door Sedan	Stromberg 150 CDS	700-750	—	0.04-0.05	6AG (1,500cc)	RED
		Stromberg 150 CDSE	800	600	0.025-0.035	B5BD	RED

*—Fast idle speed adjustment is made between adjustment screw head and fast idle cam.

Wiring Diagrams

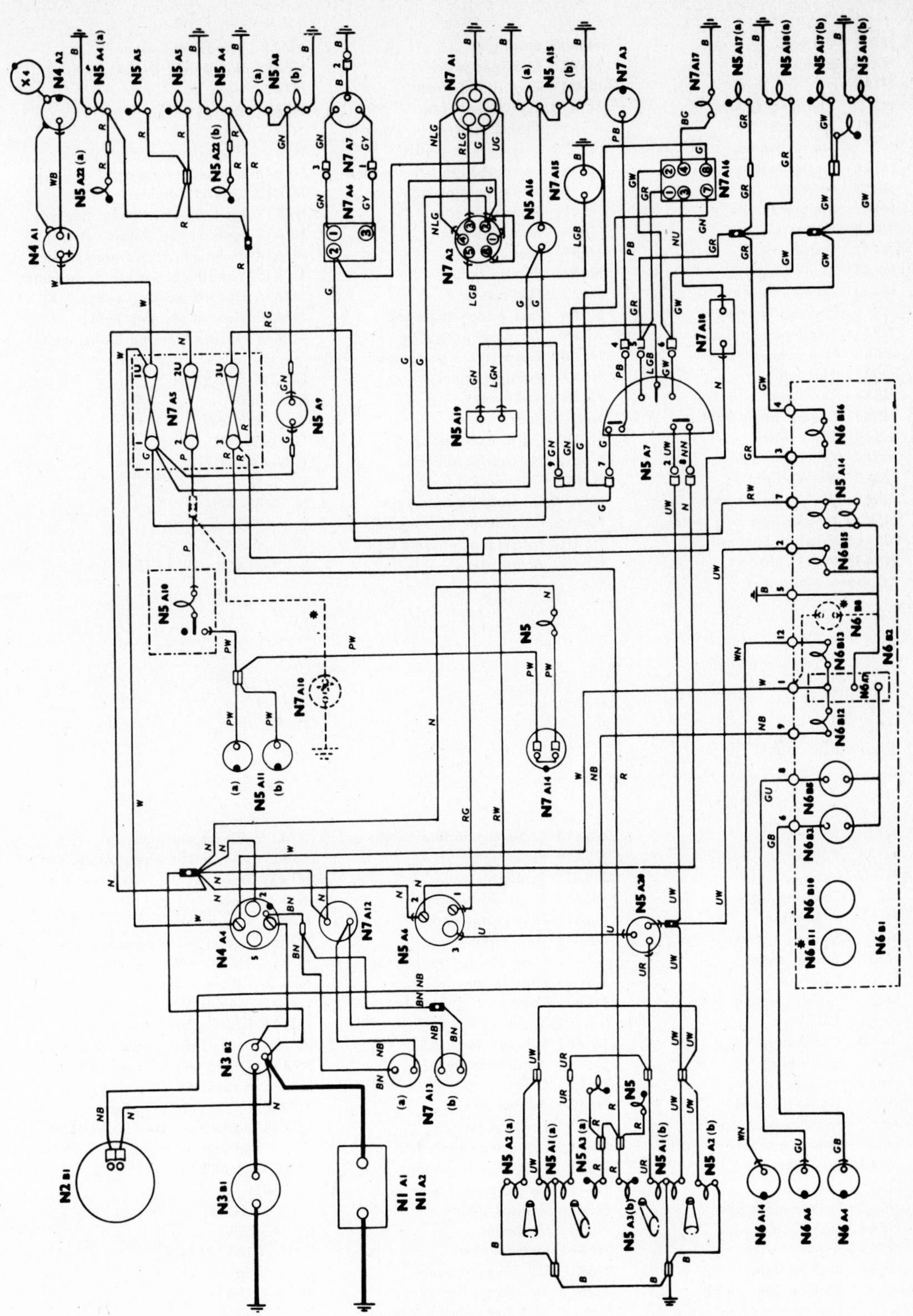

Plymouth Cricket

Plymouth Cricket

N1 Battery
N1A1 Battery
N1A2
N2 Charging system
N2B1 Alternator
N3 Starter system
N3B1 Starter motor
N3B2 Solenoid
N4 Ignition system
N4A1 Coil
N4A2 Distributor
N4A3 Spark plug
N4A4 Ignition switch
N5 Lighting system
N5A1 Headlamp—outer
N5A2 Headlamp—inner
N5A3 Sidelight
N5A4 Tail light
N5A5 License plate light
N5A6 Light switch
N5A7 Column switch
N5A8 Backup light
N5A9 Backup light switch
N5A10 Interior light and switch
N5A11 Courtesy light switch
N5A14 Panel light
*Optional equipment
N5A15 Stoplight
N5A16 Stoplight switch
N5A17 Turn signal—front
N5A18 Turn signal—rear
N5A19 Flasher unit—turn signal
N5A20 Foot dimmer switch
N5A21 Combined ignition key and brake warning light
N5A22 Side marker light
N6 Instrumentation
N6B1 Cluster
N6B2 Printed circuit
N6B3 Fuel gauge
N6A4 Fuel gauge tank unit
N6B5 Temperature gauge
N6A6 Temperature gauge bulb unit
N6A7 Voltage limiter
N6B8 Voltmeter*
N6B10 Speedometer
N6B11 Oil pressure gauge*
N6B12 No charge indicator
N6B13 Oil warning light
N6A14 Oil warning light switch
N6B15 High beam warning light
N6B16 Turn signal warning light
N7 Accessories
N7A1 Windshield wiper
N7A2 Windshield wiper switch
N7A3 Horn
N7A4 Horn*
N7A5 Fuse block
N7A6 Heater blower motor
N7A7 Blower motor switch
N7A10 Cigarette lighter*
N7A12 Ignition key warning buzzer
N7A13 Ignition key warning switch
N7A14 Brake failure warning switch
N7A15 Windshield washer pump motor
N7A16 Hazard warning switch
N7A17 Hazard warning light
N7A18 Hazard warning flasher unit (a) Left (b) Right

COLOR CHART
R —RED
Y —YELLOW
G —GREEN
L/G—LIGHT GREEN
U —BLUE
N —BROWN
P —PURPLE
W —WHITE
B —BLACK

Plymouth Cricket SE

N1 Battery
N1A1 Battery
N1A2
N2 Charging System
N2B1 Alternator
N3 Starting system
N3B1 Starter motor
N3B2 Solenoid
N4 Ignition system
N4A1 Coil
N4A2 Distributor
N4A3 Spark plug
N4A4 Ignition switch
N5 Lighting system
N5A1 Headlamp—outer
N5A2 Headlamp—inner
N5A3 Sidelight
N5A4 Tail light
N5A5 License plate light
N5A6 Light switch
N5A7 Column switch
N5A8 Back-up light
N5A9 Back-up light switch
N5A10 Interior light and switch
N5A11 Courtesy light switch
N5A12 Glove compartment light
N5A13 Glove compartment light switch
N5A14 Panel light
N5A15 Stoplight
N5A16 Stoplight switch
N5A17 Turn signal—front
N5A18 Turn signal—rear
N5A19 Flasher unit—turn signal
N5A20 Foot dimmer switch
N5A21 Combined ignition key and brake warning light
N5A22 Side marker light
N6 Instrumentation
N6B1 Cluster
N6B2 Printed circuit
N6B3 Fuel gauge
N6A4 Fuel gauge tank unit
N6B5 Temperature gauge
N6A6 Temperature gauge bulb unit
N6A7 Voltage limiter
N6B8 Voltmeter
N6B10 Speedometer
N6B11 Oil pressure gauge
N6B12 No charge indicator
N6B15 High beam warning light
N6B16 Turn signal warning light
N7 Accessories
N7A1 Windshield wiper
N7A2 Windshield wiper switch
N7A3 Horn
N7A4 Horn
N7A5 Fuse block
N7A6 Heater blower motor
N7A7 Blower motor switch
N7A10 Cigarette lighter
N7A12 Ignition key warning buzzer
N7A13 Ignition key warning switch
N7A14 Brake failure warning switch
N7A15 Screen washer pump motor
N7A16 Hazard warning switch
N7A17 Hazard warning light
N7A18 Hazard warning flasher unit (a) Left (b) Right

COLOR CHART
R —RED
Y —YELLOW
G —GREEN
L/G—LIGHT GREEN
U —BLUE
N —BROWN
P —PURPLE
W —WHITE
B —BLACK

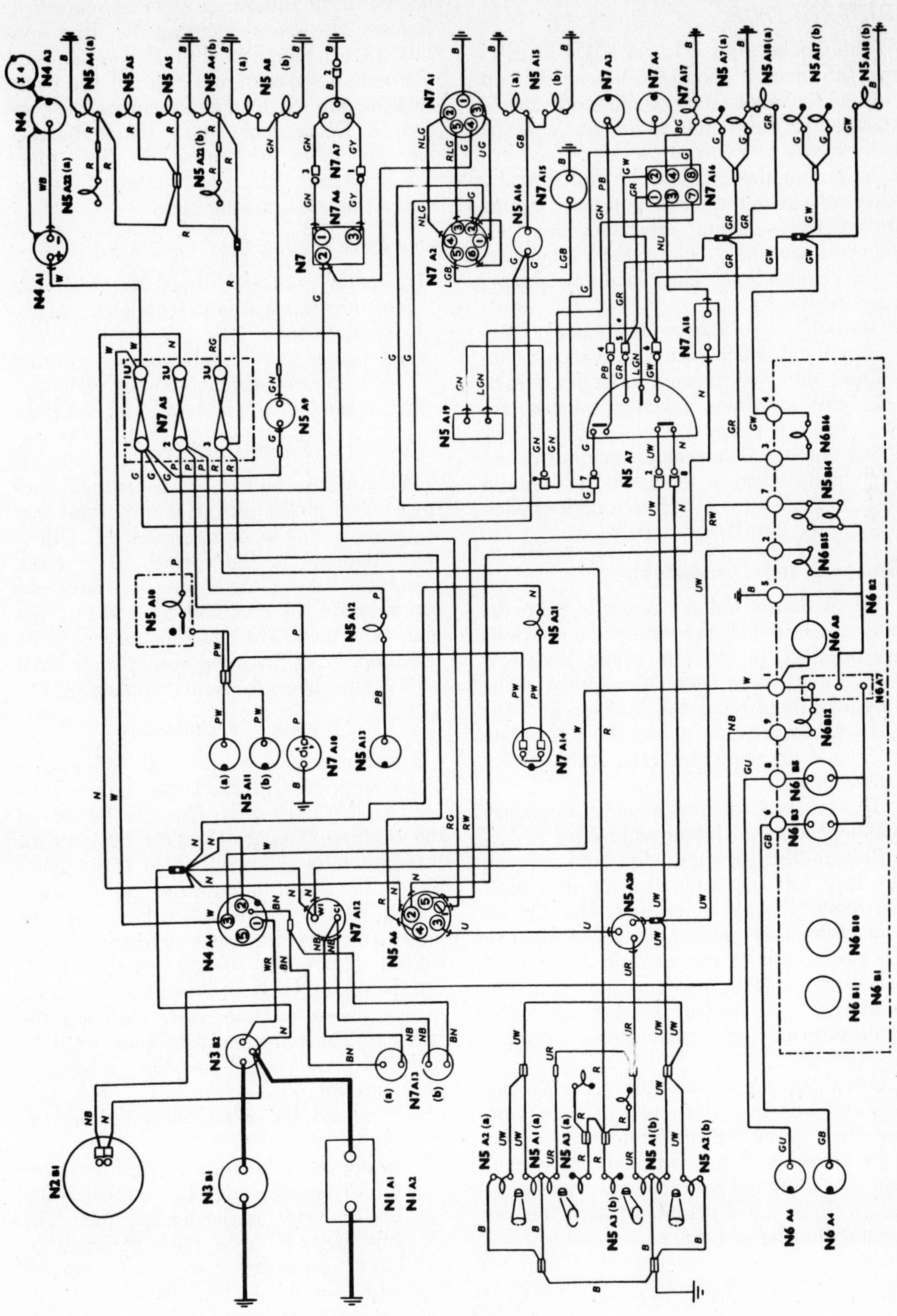

Plymouth Cricket SE

Engine Electrical

DISTRIBUTOR

The Cricket uses a Lucas 25D4 distributor. Information about the amount of centrifugal advance and vacuum advance is stamped on these units as follows: centrifugal advance is stamped on the curved arm extension of the cam spindle and is visible after removing the contact breaker mounting plate; vacuum advance units are stamped externally behind the vacuum advance connection. The vacuum advance markings are:

1st number = vacuum in inches of mercury at which vacuum advance begins
2nd number = vacuum in inches of mercury at which maximum vacuum advance is reached
3rd number = maximum amount of vacuum advance in distributor degrees reached after 11″ of vacuum is applied to the diaphragm unit.

Removal and Disassembly

When disassembling, carefully note the positions in which the various components are installed, in order to insure their correct replacement on reassembly. The tongue of the driving dog is offset; note the relationship between it and the rotor electrode and maintain this relationship when reassembling.

The amount of disassembly necessary will depend on the repair required.

Release the securing clips and remove the cap. Lift the rotor arm off the shaft. Disconnect the vacuum unit link to the contact breaker moving plate and remove the two screws at the edge of the contact breaker baseplate. Disconnect the low tension wire. The contact breaker assembly, along with the external terminal, can now be lifted off.

Drive out the hollow pin securing the vacuum advance and retard unit and remove it from the distributor body. The shaft assembly, along with the centrifugal timing control and cam foot can now be removed from the distributor body after removing the dog securing pin.

Contacts

Separate Contact Set

To disassemble further, remove the nut, insulating piece, and connections from the pillar on which the contact breaker spring is anchored. Lift off the contact breaker lever and the insulating washers beneath it. Remove the screw securing the fixed contact plate, together with the spring and plain steel washers, and take off the plate. Remove the single screw securing the condenser. Disassemble the contact breaker base assembly by turning the base plate clockwise and pulling to release it from the contact breaker moving plate.

One-Piece Contact Set

1. Remove nut and lift off terminal ends of low tension and condenser leads. Replace nut.
2. Remove screw and washer securing contact set to contact moving plate.
3. Lift contact assembly off its pivot post.

Shaft and Plate

When disassembling the centrifugal timing control mechanism, it is important that it be done in the order described. Otherwise, damage to the springs may result. Carefully lift off the springs, remove the screw inside the cam and take off the cam and cam foot. The weights can now be lifted off. Note that a spacer collar is fitted on the shaft beneath the action plate.

Bushing Replacement

The bushing is of sintered copper-iron and is stepped, with the larger diameter extending 3/4″ (19 mm.) from the bottom of the bushing. Prepare the new bushing for installation by allowing it to stand completely immersed in clean medium viscosity (SAE 30-40) engine oil for at least 24 hours. In cases of extreme urgency, this period of soaking may be shortened by heating the oil to 212°F for 2 hours and then allowing the oil to cool before removing the bushing. The following procedure must be followed closely when installing a replacement bushing.

1. Press out the worn bushing from the body end.
2. Insert the replacement bushing from the drive end, with the smaller bushing diameter as the leading part. The bushing will be a push fit until the larger diameter comes into contact with the shank. Push the bushing in with steady pressure, using a press, vise or similar method. When in place, the bushing must be a tight fit, flush

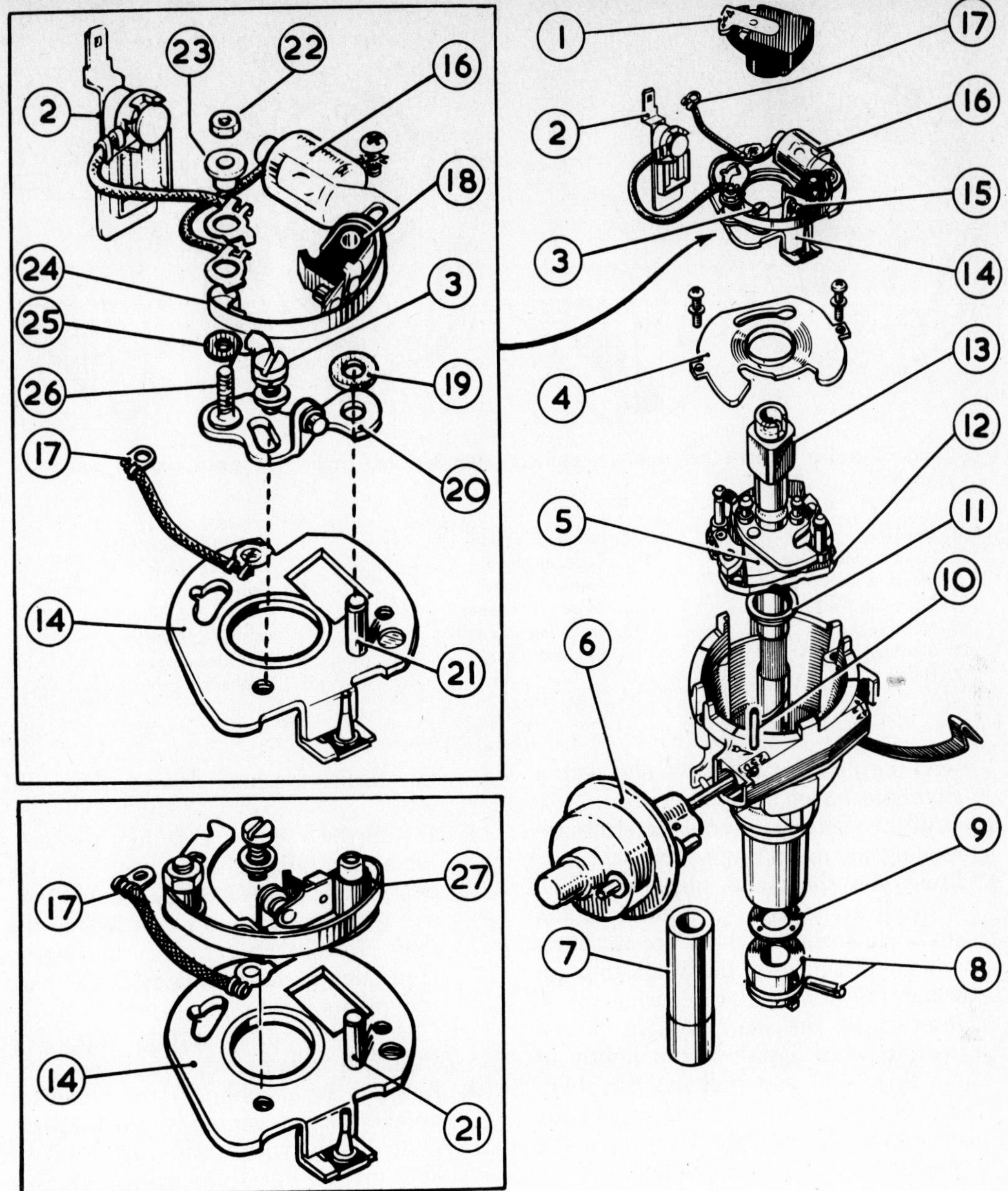

Distributor disassembled

1. Rotor arm
2. Low tension terminal
3. Fixed contact plate securing screw
4. Contact breaker base plate
5. Centrifugal advance control weights and mechanism
6. Vacuum advance and retard unit
7. Bearing bushing
8. Driving dog and pin
9. Thrust washer
10. Hollow pin
11. Spacer collar
12. Action plate
13. Cam
14. Contact breaker moving plate
15. Contacts
16. Condenser
17. Ground connector
18. Contact breaker lever
19. Insulating washer
20. Fixed contact plate
21. Contact breaker pivot post
22. Nut
23. Shouldered insulator
24. Movable contact point spring
25. Insulating washer
26. Terminal pillar
27. One piece contact breaker point assembly

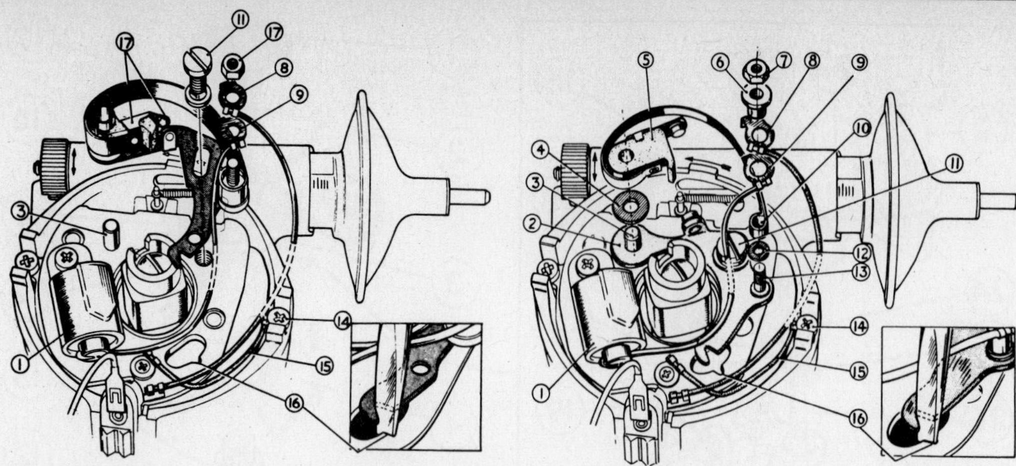

Contact breaker points—(left) separate contact point set, and (right) one piece contact point assembly

1. Capacitor
2. Fixed contact point plate
3. Movable contact pivot
4. Insulating washer
5. Movable contact
6. Shoulder insulator
7. Nut
8. Low tension lead
9. Capacitor lead
10. Contact breaker spring
11. Screw and washer
12. Insulating washer
13. Terminal pillar
14. Contact breaker plate mounting screw
15. Contact breaker ground lead
16. Contact gap adjustment slots for screwdriver
17. One piece contact breaker assembly

with the shank at the drive end with a slight protrusion at the top end.

3. Drill the shaft drain hole, carefully removing any metal fragments.
4. Insert the shaft and plate assembly, with clean engine oil applied to the shaft. Be sure that there are no burrs around the hole in the shaft through which the driving dog securing pin is inserted. If the shaft is tight in the bearing when installed, tap lightly at the drive end and pull out the shaft. Again insert the shaft, and repeat the operation. It is important that the shaft rotates without binding.
5. Run the shaft and body in a test rig or lathe for about 15 minutes, re-lubricate the shaft with clean engine oil, and reassemble the distributor.

Under no circumstances is the bushing to be over-bored by reaming or any other means, since this will impair the porosity of the bushing.

Reassembly

The following instructions assume that the distributor has been completely disassembled.

1. Place the spacer collar over the shaft, smear the shaft with clean engine oil, and install it into its bearing. Install the thrust washer, driving dog, and pin.
2. Install the vacuum unit onto its housing and install the hollow pin.
3. Reassemble the centrifugal timing control weights, cam, and cam foot to the shaft. Install the cam securing screw, then engage the springs with the cam foot pillars.
   Check that the springs are not stretched or damaged.
4. Before reassembling the contact breaker base assembly, smear the base plate lightly with clean engine oil or light grease. Install the contact breaker moving plate to the contact breaker base plate and secure. Install the contact breaker base into the distributor body. Engage the link from the vacuum unit. Insert the two base plate securing screws, one of which also secures one end of the contact breaker grounding wire.
5. Install the condenser. Place the fixed contact plate in position and secure lightly with the screw. One plain and one spring washer must be installed under the screw.
6. Place the insulating washers, etc., on the contact breaker pivot post end of the pillar on which the end of the con-

tact breaker spring is mounted. Install the contact breaker lever and spring.

7. Slide the terminal block into its slot.
8. Thread the low tension connector and condenser eyelets onto the insulating piece, and place these on the pillar which secures the end of the contact breaker spring. Install the washer and securing nut.
9. Set the contact gap to .015″ and tighten the fixed contact plate screw.
10. Install the rotor arm. Reinstall the cap.

Breaker Point Replacement

The contact breaker points can be replaced with either a separate point set or a one piece point set.

Removal—Separate Point Set

Remove nut, shouldered insulator, low tension lead, and condenser lead from the contact breaker spring. Lift off the movable contact, leaving the insulating washer in place. Remove the screw and washer and lift off the fixed contact plate and insulating washer.

Removal—One Piece Point Set

Remove nut, low tension lead, and condenser lead. Remove screw and washer and lift off contact set assembly.

Inpection

Points should be slate grey in color from normal use. Replace the points if burned or worn excessively or unevenly.

Installation—Separate Contacts

1. Place the fixed contact plate into position over the movable contact pivot and secure lightly with its mounting screw.
2. Place the insulating washers on the base of the moving contact pivot, and onto the terminal pillar, on which the movable contact spring end is secured.
3. Oil the movable contact terminal pillar lightly, and place the movable contact lever and spring into position.
4. Thread the eyelets of the leads from the distributor low tension terminal and condenser onto the shouldered insulator. Then, insert the insulator into the eye of the movable contact spring and over the terminal pillar.
5. Install and tighten nut.
6. Adjust contact gap to .015″ and smear a very small amount of vaseline on the cam lobes.

Installation—One Piece Point Set

1. Place point set on pivot post and install the screw and washer, tightening it just enough to prevent the point set from moving.
2. Remove the nut from the plastic terminal, place the condenser lead and low tension lead on top of the looped end of the movable spring and replace the nut. Tighten it about one-half turn more than finger tight.
3. Adjust the point gap and rub a very small amount of lubricant (vaseline or grease) on the cam lobes.

Ignition Timing

The ignition timing should be set after adjusting the point gap to the correct setting. If the timing is adjusted before setting the point gap, the timing will be incorrect after the point gap is adjusted. When adjusting the timing, the timing marks on the crankshaft pulley are used. The timing marks (or notches) are spaced at 5 degree intervals from TDC to 60° BTDC. The engine ignition timing may be adjusted using either the static method or the stroboscopic timing light method.

Checking Ignition Timing—Static Method

1. Rotate the engine in its running direction until it reaches 7° BTDC.
2. Remove the distributor cap and connect a 12 volt bulb between the low tension terminal of the distributor and a good ground. With the ignition switched on, the bulb will light when the points open.
3. Loosen the distributor clamp screw and rotate the body of the distributor counterclockwise enough to close the contact points.
4. Switch on the ignition and, applying light finger pressure to the rotor in a clockwise direction, turn the distributor body clockwise until the bulb just lights.
5. Tighten the distributor clamp screws. Do not overtighten because this distorts the clamp.
6. Check the setting by turning the crankshaft one revolution clockwise until the bulb lights again, and noting which timing mark on the crankshaft

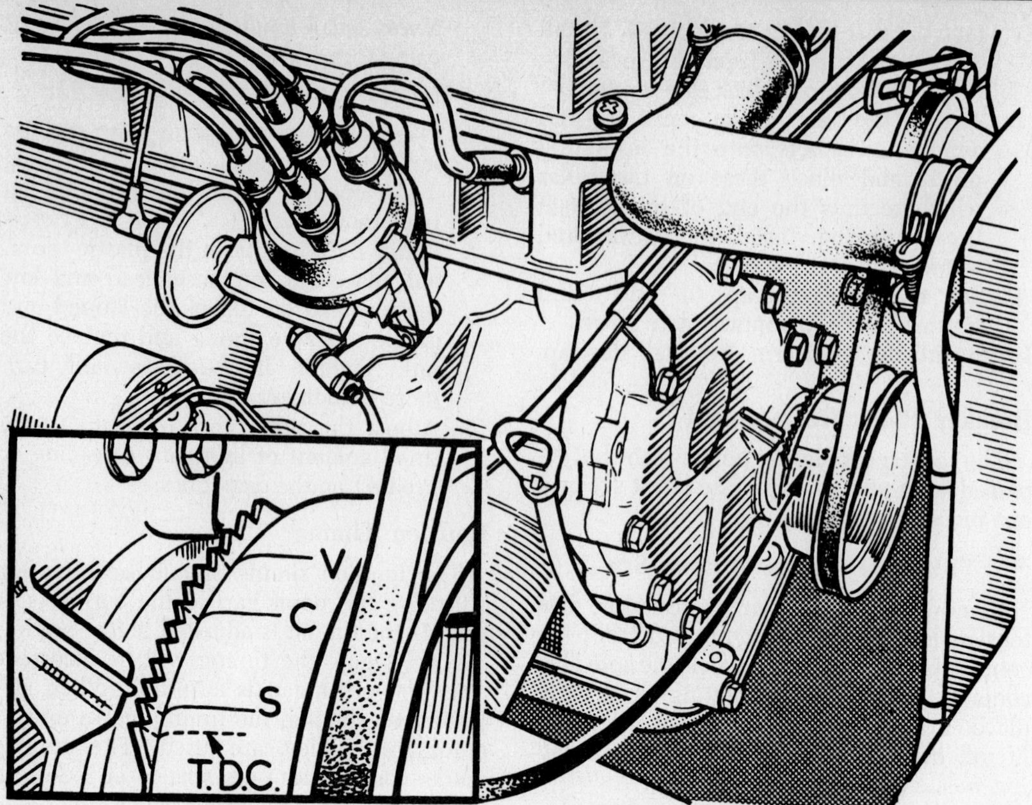

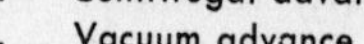

Crankshaft pulley marks

TDC. Top dead center
S. Static ignition setting
C. Centrifugal advance
V. Vacuum advance

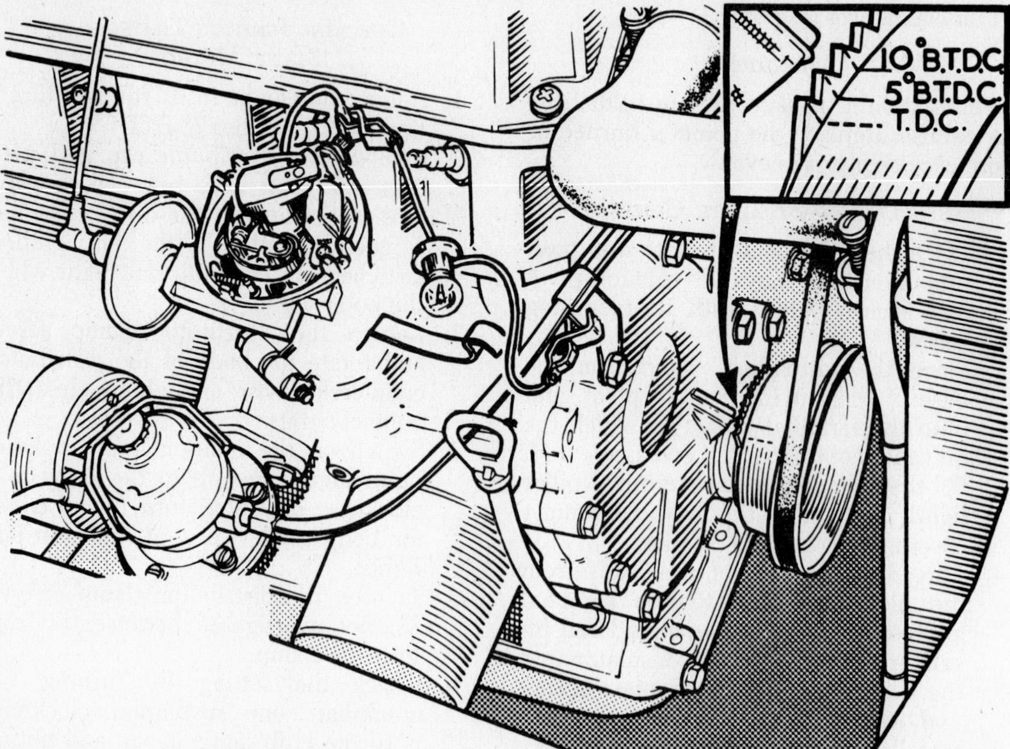

Checking static ignition timing—inset shows timing mark details

pulley is aligned with the mark on the timing cover. This shows the static ignition timing degrees before TDC (top dead center).

7. Switch off the ignition, remove test light, replace distributor cap.

Checking Ignition Timing—with Timing Light

A stroboscopic timing light can be used to check the ignition timing while the engine is running provided the following points and procedure are understood.

1. The static ignition timing, which is set and checked by turning the engine slowly, is not seen in the stroboscopic light flash, because the centrifugal advance begins to operate at a speed below the idling speed.
2. The ignition timing must be adjusted and checked at a known speed at which a known centrifugal advance occurs.
3. The speed used for this purpose is 1,000 rpm. When the engine is running at this speed the ignition timing equals the static advance angle plus the centrifugal advance angle at 1,000 rpm (500 distributor rpm).

Example

These figures are only an example. Refer to the Tune-Up Chart for the correct figures.

Static advance angle ......4°–6°BTDC
Centrifugal advance at 1,000 rpm . . 4°—8°
Therefore advance at 1,000 rpm is
...... 5° static + 6° centrifugal = 11° BTDC

4. 11° BTDC is about two divisions of the 5° timing marks.
5. To check the ignition timing by this method:
   a. Disconnect the vacuum advance from the carburetor so that the vacuum advance unit does not operate.
   b. Clean the TDC line on the timing cover and the crankshaft pulley markings. Using quick drying white paint, paint the TDC line and the correct degree mark on the crankshaft pulley.
   c. Connect a tachometer and adjust the speed to 1,000 rpm. Aim the timing light beam onto the TDC line of the timing cover. When the timing is correct the painted mark on the crankshaft pulley will appear opposite the TDC line on the timing cover. If necessary, the disbutor can be rotated while the engine is running.
   d. Reconnect the vacuum advance line, and readjust the idling speed.

BATTERY

The battery used in the Cricket is a D7/9 type 7 plate lead-acid 12 volt unit with a one-piece manifold venting system. A 9 plate battery (D9) is used on cars with automatic transmission. Maintenance consists of frequent and regular inspections to be sure that the battery top is clean and dry, the vents are clear, the electrolyte level is just above the separator guard, and the case is not cracked or leaking. Cables should be fastened to the posts tightly and the posts lightly coated with vaseline or other suitable grease.

When removing or installing a battery, be sure the battery cables are installed with the correct polarity. Push the cable connectors on by hand and install the clamp screws.

When attempting to jump-start another car or get a jump-start, be sure the jumper cables between the two cars are connected with the correct polarity—negative post of one car battery to the negative post of the other car battery, and the positive post of one car battery to the positive post of the other car battery. Do not try to start the disabled car longer than 10-15 seconds at a time.

STARTER

The starter used in the Cricket is a Lucas M35JPE four-pole four-brush unit with a series field and a solenoid-operated roller clutch drive. Routine maintenance is unnecessary but the electrical connections should be checked for tightness occasionally.

Replacement

1. Disconnect the battery. Then, disconnect the harness cables and the solenoid main feed cable.
2. Remove the mounting bolts and remove the starter assembly from the engine.
3. Install the starter by positioning it on the engine and tightening the mounting bolts. Connect the harness cables,

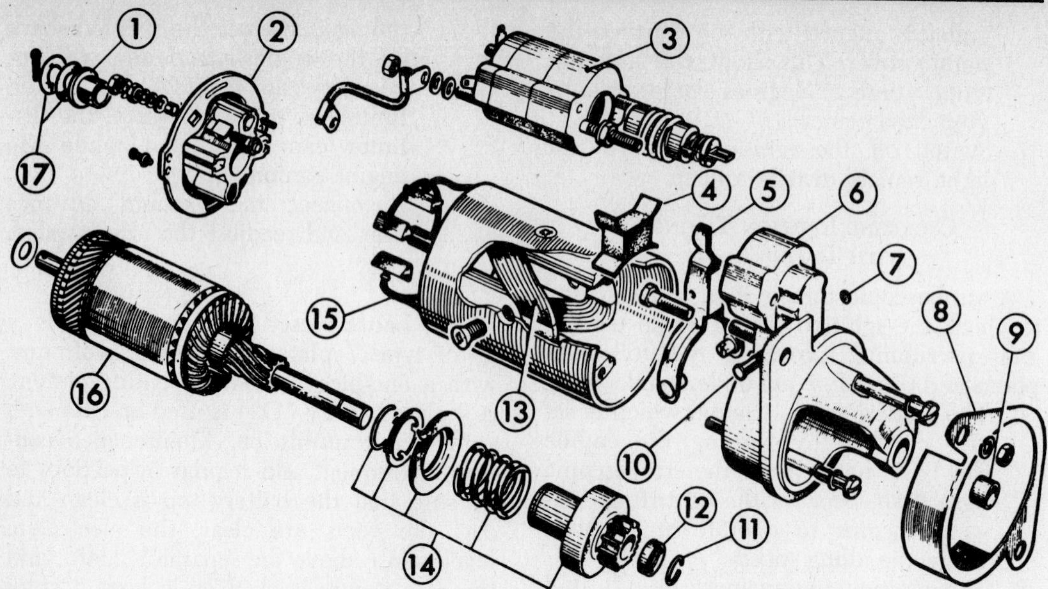

Lucas M35JPE Pre-engaged starter disassembled

1. Bushing, commutator end
2. Commutator end bracket
3. Solenoid
4. Grommet
5. Engagement lever
6. Drive end bracket
7. Pivot pin retainer
8. Dust cover
9. Bushing, drive end
10. Pivot pin
11. Jump ring
12. Thrust collar
13. Field coil set
14. Drive, roller clutch assembly
15. Brush set
16. Armature
17. Thrust washer, shim set

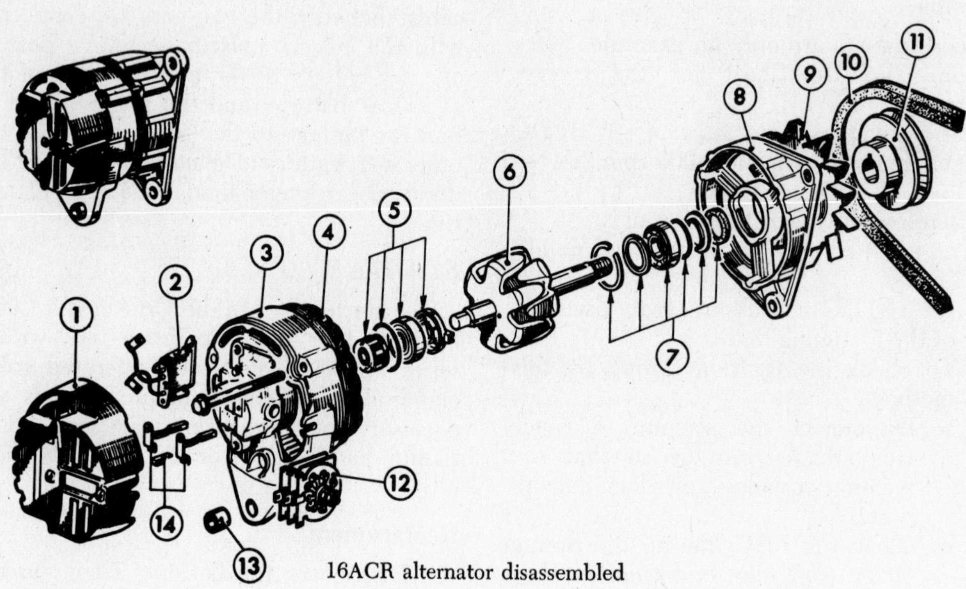

16ACR alternator disassembled

1. Cover
2. Regulator and heat sink
3. Slip-ring end bracket
4. Stator
5. Slip-ring end bearing set
6. Rotor and field winding assembly
7. Drive end bearing set
8. Drive end bracket
9. Fan
10. Driving belt
11. Drive pulley
12. Rectifier
13. Spacer bushing
14. Brush set

solenoid main feed cable, and the ground straps. Connect the battery cables.

ALTERNATOR

The Cricket uses a 16 ACR alternator with a built-in micro-circuit regulator. A warning light is used in the alternator circuit to show when the battery is not being charged. As the alternator speed increases, the light brilliance decreases until the alternator is at full speed and is charging the battery or at least holding the battery charge steady. The light will stay off unless the battery is discharging.

Since the alternator circuit components are sensitive and costly to repair, the following precautions should always be observed to avoid damaging them:

To avoid bearing damage when adjusting alternator belt tension, apply leverage only on the alternator drive-end bracket, not on any other part of the alternator. The lever should be of a soft material, preferably wood.

The alternator bearings are packed with grease during assembly. No further attention is needed.

Care must be taken when connecting either a battery or replacement alternator on a vehicle or in a test circuit, to observe correct polarity matching. Reversed polarity will damage the diodes.

Whenever electric arc welding is carried out on any part of the car, the connector should be removed from the alternator and the battery positive terminal disconnected to avoid any risk of damage. The vehicle must never be started with the welding apparatus connected.

The vehicle must never be started with a charger connected.

Always disconnect both battery cables before connecting a battery charger.

Never run the alternator on open circuit with the field winding energized or the diodes will be damaged.

Do not use a high voltage source to test diodes; a 12-volt DC supply will suffice.

Never use an ohmmeter having a hand driven generator for checking diodes or transistors.

Removal and Installation

1. Release the radiator cap to depressurize the cooling system (this will prevent a water leak when releasing the timing cover strap bolt).
2. Release belt tension and remove belt.
3. Remove bolts, nuts and washers and remove the alternator (do not lose the spacer bushing from the slip-ring end bracket bolt hole).
4. Reverse procedure for installation.

Alternator Testing

Testing the Alternator in Position

Check the belt for condition and tension. The following test procedure should be carried out with the alternator running as near as possible to its normal operating temperature.

1. Disconnect the alternator harness connector.
2. Remove the two screws and remove the cover.
3. Now link together regulator terminals F and negative.
4. Connect an external test circuit as shown. Observe carefully the polarity of battery and alternator terminals—reversed connections will damage the alternator diodes.
5. The variable resistor across the battery terminals must not be left connected any longer than is necessary to carry out the following test:
6. Start the engine and run up to 800 rpm (1,500 alternator rpm); the test circuit bulb should now be unlit.
7. Increase engine speed to 3,200 rpm (alternator speed 6,000 rpm) approximately, and adjust the variable resistance until the voltmeter reads 14 volts. The ammeter reading should be about equal to the rated output—see Electrical Specification Chart. Any deviation from this figure will require removal of the alternator.
8. Failure of one or more of the diodes will be shown in the test by the effect on alternator output and by abnormally high alternator temperature and noise level.

Regulator Test

It is assumed that the alternator has been tested and is satisfactory.

Disconnect the variable resistor and remove the link bridging regulator terminals F and negative.

With the rest of the test circuit connected as for the alternator output test, start the engine and again run the engine

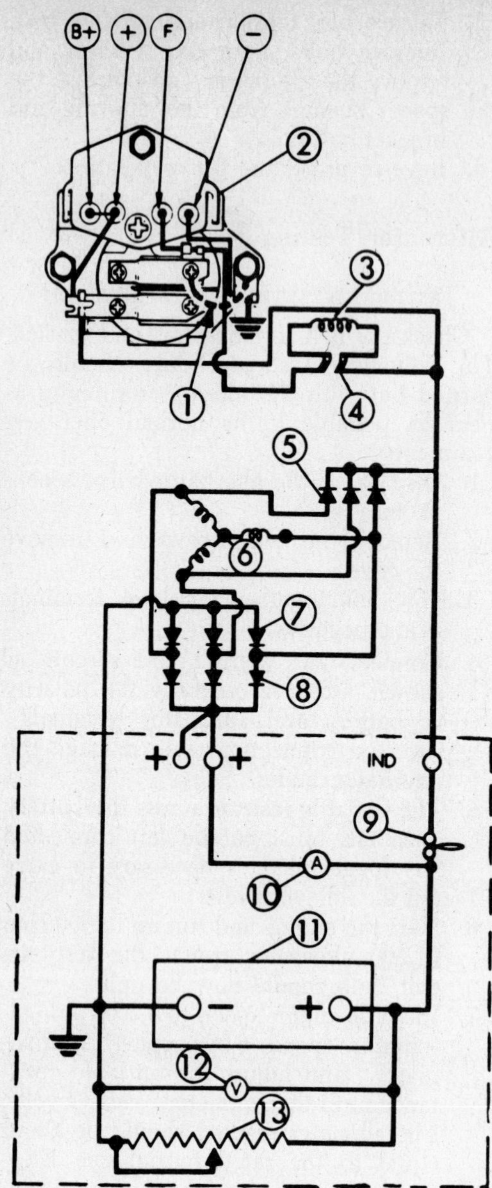

Alternator output test circuit

up to 3,200 rpm (alternator speed approx. 6,000 rpm) until the ammeter registers an output current of less than 10 amps. The voltmeter should then give a reading of 14.0-14.4 volts. Any deviation from this (regulated) voltage means that the regulator is not functioning correctly and must be replaced.

If the above tests show the alternator and regulator to be operating satisfactorily, disconnect the test circuit and reconnect the alternator harness connector.

Now connect a low-range voltmeter between either of the positive (+) terminals of the alternator and the positive (+) terminal of the vehicle battery. Switch on the headlamps, start the engine and increase engine speed to 3,200 rpm (alternator speed approx. 6,000 rpm). Note the voltmeter reading.

Transfer the voltmeter to the frame of the alternator and the negative (−) terminal of the battery, and again note the reading.

If the reading exceeds 0.5 volt on the positive (+) side or 0.25 volt on the negative (−) side, there is a high resistance in the charging circuit which must be traced and corrected.

Electrical Test Procedure (Alternator Removed from Vehicle)

The following instructions cover the disassembly required to test the alternator electrically.

1. Disconnect the battery and alternator harness connection and remove the alternator from the vehicle.
2. Remove the two screws and the cover.
3. Unsolder the three stator connections to the rectifier assembly, noting the order of connection. (See Diode Tests for resoldering procedure).
4. Remove the two brush molding securing screws, loosen the nut on the rectifier assembly bolt, remove the screw securing the regulator to the slip-ring end bracket and detach the suppressor cable at the rectifier. Now withdraw the brush molding and rectifier assembly, together with the short cable which joins them.

Inspection of Brushes

1. The brush length when new is ½″. For a brush to remain serviceable, the amount protruding should be at least 0.2″ (5 mm.). Replace the brush assemblies if the brushes are worn to or below this amount. If brush replacement is necessary, do not lose the leaf spring at the side of the inner brush.
2. Check the brush spring pressure using a push-type spring gauge. The brush should be pushed back until the brush face is flush with the housing.
3. Clean a sticking brush with a suitable solvent, or, if necessary, by lightly polishing the brush sides on a smooth file.

Inspection of Slip-rings

The slip-ring surfaces should be smooth and clean. Clean them using a solvent moistened cloth, or, if there is evidence of burning, very fine glass paper. Do not use emery cloth or abrasive. Do not machine the slip-rings.

Rotor

1. Test the rotor winding by connecting either an ohmmeter or a 12 volt battery and ammeter between the slip-rings. The resistance should be 4.33 ohms or the current approximately 3 amps.
2. Test for defective insulation between the slip rings and the rotor poles using a 110 volt AC supply and a 15 watt test lamp. If the lamp lights, the winding is grounded to the core and a replacement rotor/slip-ring assembly must be installed. Do not try to machine the rotor poles or to straighten a distorted shaft.

Stator

1. Check the continuity of the stator windings by first connecting any two of the three stator cables in series with a 12 volt battery and a test lamp of not less than 36 watts. Repeat the test, replacing one of the two cables by the third cable. Failure of the test lamp to light means that part of the stator winding is open and a replacement stator must be installed.
2. Test for defective insulation between the stator coils and the laminated core-pack using the test lamp. Connect the test probes between any one of the three cable ends and the laminated core-pack. If the lamp lights, the stator coils are shorted and a replacement stator must be installed.

Diodes

If one of the diodes is defective as indicated by the alternator output test, the stator winding connections to the rectifier pack must be unsoldered.

1. To test a diode, connect each of the nine diode pins in turn in series with a 1.5 watt test bulb and one terminal of a 12 volt battery. Connect the other battery terminal to the particular heat sink on the rectifier pack into which the diode under test is soldered. Next, reverse the connections to diode pin and heat sink. The bulb should light in one direction only. Should the bulb light in both tests, or not light in either, the diode is defective and a new rectifier pack must be installed.
2. When resoldering the stator cables to the diode pins, use only M grade 45-55 tin-lead solder. Take great care to avoid overheating the diodes or bending the diode pins. The diode pins should be lightly gripped with a pair of long-nose pliers (which act as a heat sink) and the soldering done as quickly as possible without overheating the diode.

Complete Disassembly

If, as a result of the above electrical tests further disassembly is necessary, proceed as follows:

1. Remove the three through-bolts.
2. Separate the slip-ring end bracket and stator assembly from the rotor and drive end bracket by sleeving a metal tube about 3″ (76 mm.) long over the slip-ring molding so as to engage with the outer ring of the slip-ring end bearing and then carefully drive the bearing from its housing with the alternator positioned vertically, fan down. The tube should be 1.320″ (33.53 mm.) outside diameter and bored to 1.240″ (31.5 mm.) for half its length.

Carefully file away any extra solder from the field winding terminals which may prevent the tubing from sleeving over the slip-ring molding.

An alternate method of separating the slip-ring bracket and stator assembly is to insert a lever between the stator and the drive end bracket and carefully pry the two apart until the slip-ring end bearing is clear of its housing.

If necessary, press out the rotor shaft from the drive-end bracket after removing the shaft nut, washers, pulley, fan, and shaft key.

BEARING REPLACEMENT

Should bearing replacement become necessary, proceed as follows:

1. Disassemble the alternator (it is not necessary to unsolder the rectifier assembly) including separation of the rotor from the drive end bracket.
   The drive end bearing can be removed following the removal of the retaining circlip.

2. To remove slip-ring end bearing, unsolder the field winding connection to the slip-ring molding assembly which can then be removed from the rotor shaft.
3. Extract the bearing from the shaft, noting that the shielded side of the bearing faces towards the slip-ring molding assembly.
4. Pack the new bearing with lubricant. Install the bearing (shielded side toward the slip-ring) insuring that it is fully on the shaft and reinstall the slip-ring molding assembly.

Reassembly

1. Reassembly is the reverse of disassembly. Check that the slip-ring bearing is properly positioned and fully seated on the rotor shaft. Check that the brushes are seated in their housing before installing the brush molding. Tighten the bolts evenly.
2. If the rotor and drive-end bracket have been separated, support the inner ring of the drive-end bearing with the spacer collar for reassembly. Do not use the drive-end as a support for the bearing while installing the rotor.

Alternator Belt Adjustment

The alternator belt must be adjusted for ⅝″ deflection along the longest run while the engine is cold. If the adjustment is done while the engine is hot and under its operating pressure of 9 psi, some coolant may leak out from the water pump body face.

1. Loosen the nuts and bolts at the front and rear bottom mounting brackets and on the slotted adjusting bracket.
2. Pivot the alternator on the bottom mounting bolts for the correct belt tension. Tighten the nut and bolt on the slotted bracket first; then, tighten the bottom mounting bolts and nuts. Do not overtighten the belt.

NOTE: When moving the alternator during the belt adjustment, pull it against the belt by hand. Do not lever it with a bar or pipe since this may damage the alternator bearings.

Fuel System

The carburetor on the Cricket imported to the United States complies with the exhaust emission control standards and is nonadjustable except for the slow running mixture.

FUEL PUMP

The fuel pump is a diaphragm type pump mechanically operated by an eccentric lobe on the camshaft pressing against the pump rocker arm.

Fuel Filter Replacement

1. Move spring clamp off top of glass bowl, loosen the knurled knob, lift off glass bowl.
2. Remove the filter element from the pump. Wash the filter in a suitable cleaning solution and dry with compressed air.
3. Install the clean filter in the pump body, replace the glass bowl, and tighten the knob and the spring clamp. Be sure the washer is in good condition and seated correctly. Do not overtighten the knob or the gasket might be damaged.

Testing Fuel Pump Installed on Engine

Fuel pump operation can be checked while installed on the engine by disconnecting the fuel line between the carburetor and the pump, installing a T connector in the line, and running the engine at 1,500-2,000 rpm. The amount of fuel pumped out should be 1 pint in 1 minute. The fuel pump pressure can be measured by installing a fuel pressure gauge to the T connector and reading the pressure. The pressure should be 2.75-4.25 psi. Disconnect the ignition coil primary wire when cranking the engine with the starter so the engine does not start. Excess fuel pump pressure can be corrected by additional gaskets between the fuel pump flange and the engine block pump mounting face. Do not use too many gaskets since this could cause fuel starvation under full throttle conditions.

Removal

Disconnect the fuel lines at the fuel pump. Plug the fuel line. Remove the two nuts holding the pump to the engine crankcase and remove the pump, noting the number of gaskets used between the pump mounting face and the crankcase face.

Disassembly

1. Before disassembling the pump, thor-

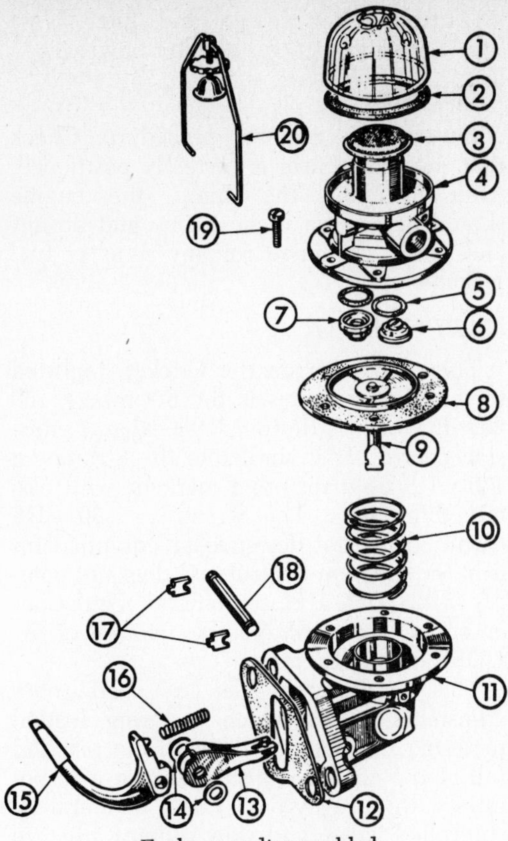
Fuel pump disassembled

1. Cover
2. Gasket
3. Screen
4. Body, upper
5. Gaskets
6. Valve outlet
7. Valve inlet
8. Diaphragm
9. Rod
10. Spring
11. Body, lower
12. Gasket
13. Link
14. Washers
15. Rocker arm
16. Spring
17. Retainer
18. Pin
19. Screw
20. Clip

oughly clean the exterior and make a mark across the two flanges of the pump housing, as a guide for assembly. Remove the six screws and separate the halves of the casting.

2. Turn the diaphragm and pullrod assembly 90° and disconnect it from its securing slot in the connecting link. Remove the diaphragm spring. The diaphragm and pull rod are a permanent assembly and should not be separated.
3. Fasten rocker arm in a vise and tap body mounting flange with a soft mallet until the two retainers are dislodged.
4. The rocker arm and the connecting link spring and washers may now be removed.
5. The valves are a press fit into the valve body. They are also staked in position and should only be removed when they have to be replaced, since they have to be pried out with a screwdriver, which destroys them.

Cleaning and Inspection

1. Thoroughly clean all parts in a safe solvent. All parts should be blown dry.
2. The diaphragm and pull rod assembly should be replaced if there is any sign of hardening or cracking.
3. All badly worn parts must be replaced.
4. The valve assemblies cannot be disassembled and should be replaced when necessary.
5. Check the diaphragm spring, although this seldom requires replacement. When necessary, check that the replacement spring has the same identification color and the same strength as the original. All gaskets should be replaced.

Assembly

1. If new valves have to be installed, new valve gaskets should be put in the bottom of the valve seat bores. The valves must be installed correctly or the pump will not operate.
2. Press the new valves into the valve body with a piece of steel tubing with an outside diameter of 3/4″ (19.0 mm.) and an internal diameter of 9/16″ (14.3 mm.). Then, stake the valve body in six places around each valve with a punch.
3. Assemble the link rocker arm and washers onto the pivot pin. Place this assembly into the main body and then add the rocker arm return spring, making sure that it seats correctly. Tap new retainers into the main body until they press hard against the rocker arm pin and then stake over the open ends of the two grooves to secure the retainers. Place the diaphragm spring in position in the pump body.
4. Place the diaphragm assembly over the spring (the pump rod downward).
5. Press downward on the diaphragm while turning the assembly to the right so that the slots on the pull rod will engage the fork in the link. Then, turn the assembly a complete quarter turn

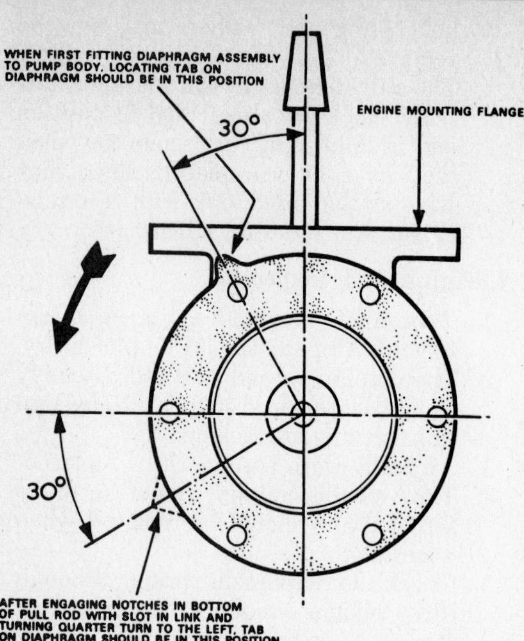
WHEN FIRST FITTING DIAPHRAGM ASSEMBLY TO PUMP BODY, LOCATING TAB ON DIAPHRAGM SHOULD BE IN THIS POSITION
ENGINE MOUNTING FLANGE
30°
30°
AFTER ENGAGING NOTCHES IN BOTTOM OF PULL ROD WITH SLOT IN LINK AND TURNING QUARTER TURN TO THE LEFT, TAB ON DIAPHRAGM SHOULD BE IN THIS POSITION
Installing diaphragm assembly

to the right, which will place the pull rod in the proper working position in the link and align the holes in the diaphragm with those in the pump body flange. When first inserting the diaphragm assembly into the pump body, the locating tab on the outside of the diaphragm should be at the position shown. After turning the diaphragm assembly a quarter turn to the right, the tab should be in the position shown by the dotted line.

6. Push the rocker arm toward the pump until the diaphragm is level with the body flanges. Place the upper half of the pump in the proper position, as shown by the mark made on the flanges before disassembly. Install the cover screws and tighten. Then loosen each screw one turn.
7. Before finally tightening the screws, push the rocker arm toward the pump using about a 4″ (10 cm.) length of tube slipped over the end of the rocker arm to hold the diaphragm at the bottom of its stroke. Hold in this position and tighten screws alternately. After assembly, the edges of the diaphragm should be about flush with the two flanges.
8. If the diaphragm protrudes, repeat Steps 6 and 7. Tighten down the screws.
9. Install filter screen and filter bowl seating gasket. Install filter bowl.

Installation

Reverse the removal procedure. Check that the rocker arm is correctly positioned. After installing the pump, the engine should be run for a short time and fittings and pump examined for any signs of fuel leakage.

CARBURETOR

The carburetor on the Cricket imported to the United States is the Stromberg 150 CDSE which is designed for exhaust emission control. It is similar to the Stromberg 150 CDS used for other markets, with certain differences. The Stromberg 150 CDS carburetor is not designed or equipped for exhaust emission control and does not comply with United States federal regulations on emission control. Notable features of the CDSE carburetor are:

This carburetor has a fixed non-adjustable jet in which a spring loaded metering needle operates with the rise and fall of the air valve piston. It also incorporates a throttle by-pass valve, temperature controlled valve, and slow running mixture air control screw.

An air valve return spring and hydraulic damper are used as in the 150 CDS.

The throttle bypass valve allows a fuel-air mixture to bypass the closed throttle during deceleration. It is operated by intake manifold vacuum whenever the control valve opens.

The temperature controlled valve provides means of weakening the idling and light load mixture when the carburetor is hot.

The idle control screw provides a means of small adjustment of the idle mixture strength.

Carburetor Adjustments

CDSE Adjustments

Idle Speed Adjustment

The idle speed should be 800 rpm for manual transmission and 600 rpm for cars with automatic transmission in Drive. Adjust as follows:

1. Warm engine to operating temperature after connecting a tachometer.
2. With a flat-bladed screwdriver, turn the idle speed (slow running) screw

until the correct idle speed is shown on the tachometer. Do not turn the idle speed screw in too much since this could damage the needle or seat.

3. Stop the engine and remove the tachometer.

If idle speed cannot be set correctly, the idle mixture may need adjustment. If the engine still runs roughly, check the air-fuel ratio for a reading of at least 11.4:1 on an air-fuel meter or check the exhaust gas for a carbon monoxide level of no more than 7.5% on a CO meter.

Idle Mixture Adjustment

If the idle mixture is only slightly rich, it can be made leaner by adjusting the idle air mixture screw. This adjustment is limited in effect and can be turned about four turns from is seated position for full effect.

To make the idle mixture slightly leaner, turn the screw counterclockwise.

Temperature Controlled Valve

1. If the mixture is too rich, remove the plastic cover from the temperature controlled valve and gently feel that the valve is free to move.
2. If the valve appears faulty, remove the valve body from the carburetor. If the valve is sticky, carefully remove the bi-metal spring after unscrewing the adjusting nut and retaining screw. Remove the valve and clean out any foreign matter.
3. Reassemble the valve, taking care not to damage or bend the bi-metal spring. The letters on the bi-metal spring must be up. Be sure that the spring is not causing a twist or side load on the valve. The adjusting nut is set so that the valve is just on its seat at room temperature (about 70°F). This temperature is not critical, but the adjustment must be carefully carried out. Immersion of the valve assembly in hot water (110°–120°F) should cause the valve to open.
4. Replace the valve on the carburetor. Install the cover and recheck the idle.

Throttle Bypass Valve

Check the setting of the throttle bypass valve as follows:

1. Remove the three screws holding the throttle bypass valve to the carburetor and lift off the bypass valve unit.
2. Remove three countersunk screws holding the bypass valve base and cover together, and separate these parts, taking care not to lose the internal parts, which are a spring, adjusting screw, and O-ring.
3. Drive the brass sealing disc out of the valve outer body.
4. Reassemble the valve unit, taking care to ensure that the O-ring is seating in its recess.
5. Turn the valve adjusting screw clockwise as far as possible, and turn counterclockwise one turn. This is the normal setting.
6. Install the bypass valve and check its action by pressing the control valve spindle while the engine is idling. If the engine speed does not increase, change the bypass valve.

CDS Adjustments

Idle Adjustment

This adjustment must be made very carefully because it affects the entire operating range of the carburetor as well as the idle. Excessive fuel consumption or poor performance will occur if the adjustment is made incorrectly.

1. Remove the air valve piston damper.
2. Insert a screwdriver or metal rod into the air valve piston bore from which the damper was removed. Using this tool, hold the air valve piston down, and at the same time, turn the jet adjustment screw clockwise until the jet just contacts the air valve piston. When this occurs, the adjusting screw will become very hard to turn.
3. Remove the tool used to hold the air valve piston down, and with the piston lifting pin, check that the piston falls freely from the raised position. An audible sound should be heard as the piston falls onto the carburetor body when the lifting pin is released.
4. If the piston will not fall freely with the jet fully raised, the jet should be centered.
5. Turn the jet adjustment screw counterclockwise two turns.
6. Fill the air valve piston damper bore, and install the piston damper. Thin oils must not be used for this purpose because they allow too rapid rising of the air valve piston when the throttle is suddenly opened.

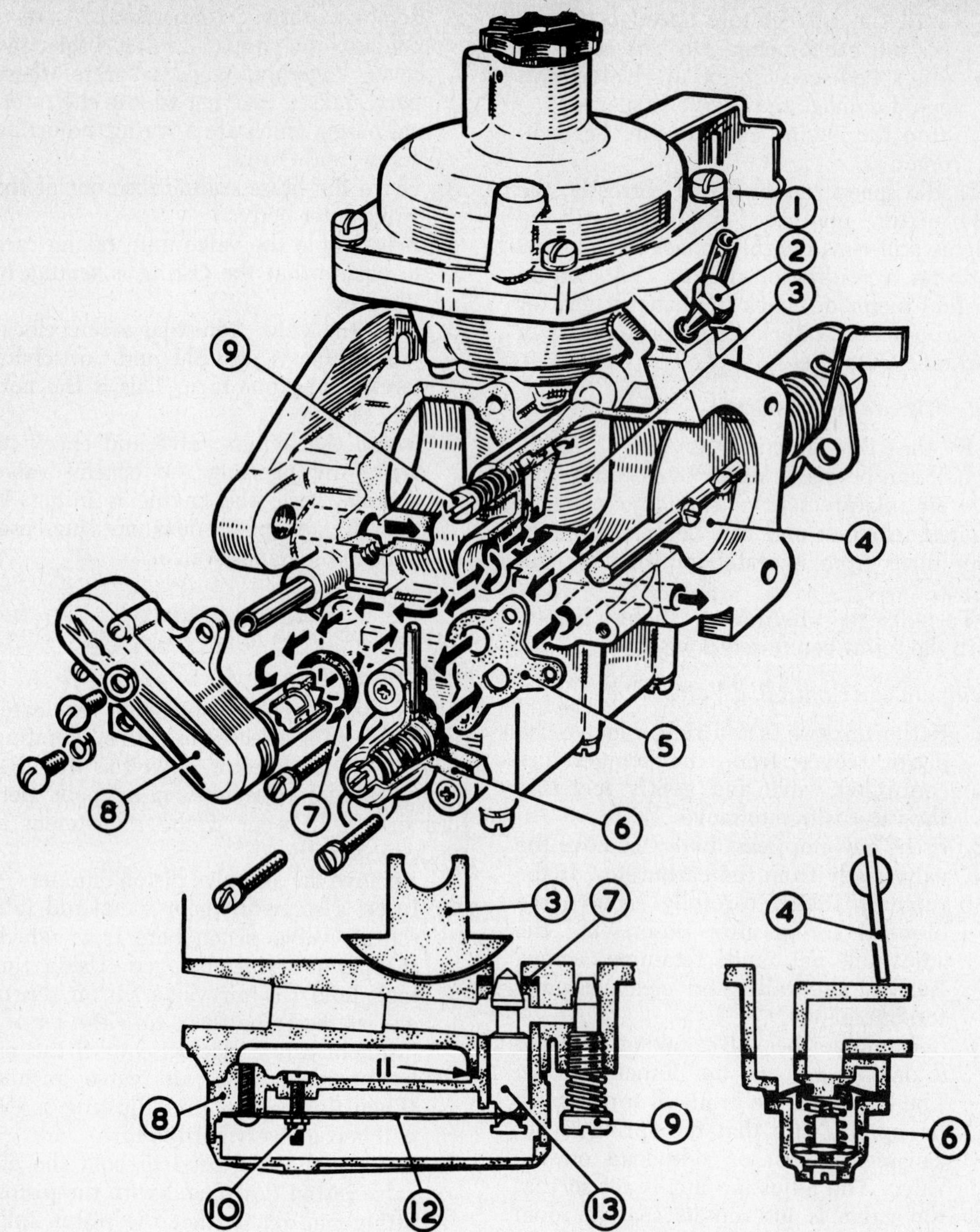

Stromberg 150 CDSE carburetor temperature controlled valve and throttle bypass valve

1. Vacuum advance hose connection
2. Blank plug (do not remove)
3. Air valve piston
4. Throttle
5. Gasket, bypass valve to carburetor body
6. Throttle by-pass valve
7. Rubber valve seat
8. Temperature controlled valve
9. Idle air adjustment screw (limited range)
10. Adjustment for temperature controlled valve spring
11. Rubber O-ring
12. Bimetal spring
13. Valve operated by bimetol spring

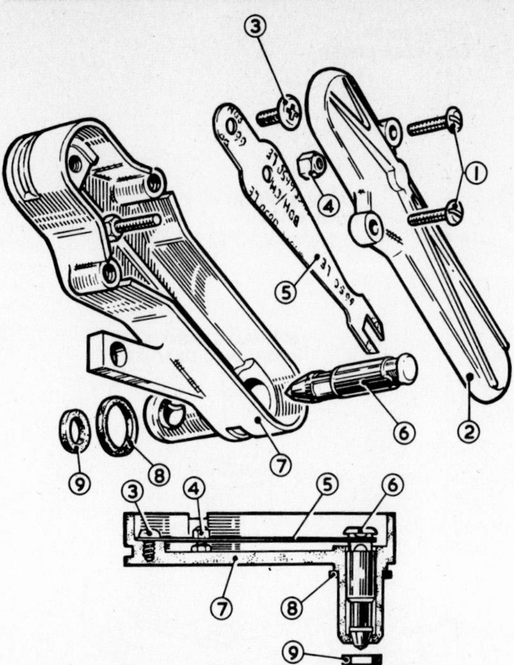

Temperature controlled valve—CDSE

1. Cover retaining screws
2. Plastic cover
3. Retaining screw, bimetal spring plate
4. Adjusting nut, bimetal spring plate
5. Bimetal spring plate
6. Valve operated by (5.)
7. Valve body
8. Rubber seating washer
9. Rubber seating washer

7. Run the engine to normal operating temperature. Adjust the idle speed adjustment screw to give the correct idle speed.
8. If necessary, adjust the jet adjustment screw not more than half a turn up or down from the previously set position to improve idling. Clockwise movement weakens and counterclockwise movement richens the mixture. If the jet cannot be adjusted within these limits, check the needle position in the air valve piston.
9. If movement of the jet adjustment screw has altered the engine speed, adjust the idle speed.

Needle Position

The needle should be level with the air valve piston lower face, after tightening the needle securing screw.

Centering Jet

The jet is correctly centered on the needle if the air valve piston will fall freely onto the carburetor body when the jet is flush with its brass bushing.

The jet will require recentering if it is removed for any reason, and this should be done as follows with the carburetor in position:

1. Check that the needle shoulder is flush with the underside of the air valve piston.
2. Loosen the jet bushing retaining screw one and a half turns.
3. Tighten the jet adjustment screw so that the jet is level with the bridge face on which the air valve piston rests when the engine is not running.
4. Give the retaining screw a sharp tap, on one of its hexagon sides. This helps the jet and its bushing to centralize around the needle, and usually allows the air valve piston to fall freely. Tighten the jet retaining screw.
5. Check that the air valve piston falls freely onto the carburetor body, when it is lifted and released.

Starter Assembly Travel Stop

The normal position for this stop is shown. Under very cold conditions around and below −10°, the stop can be pushed down slightly and turned a quarter of a turn to raise it to the alternate position. This allows the starter assembly to supply additional fuel for cold starting.

Choke Control

The choke control securing screw on the cam should be tightened when the choke control is about ⅛″ (3 mm.) from its normal position. This ensures that the cam rests against its stop when the control is pushed in.

Fast Idle Speed

This adjustment is made by adjusting the gap between the screw head and fast idle cam with the carburetor in position as follows:

1. Check that the cam comes against its back stop when the choke control is pushed in.
2. Check that the idle speed is in correct.
3. With the choke control pushed in, adjust the screw head for the correct clearance between the screw head and fast idle cam.

Float Level

The two highest and two lowest points

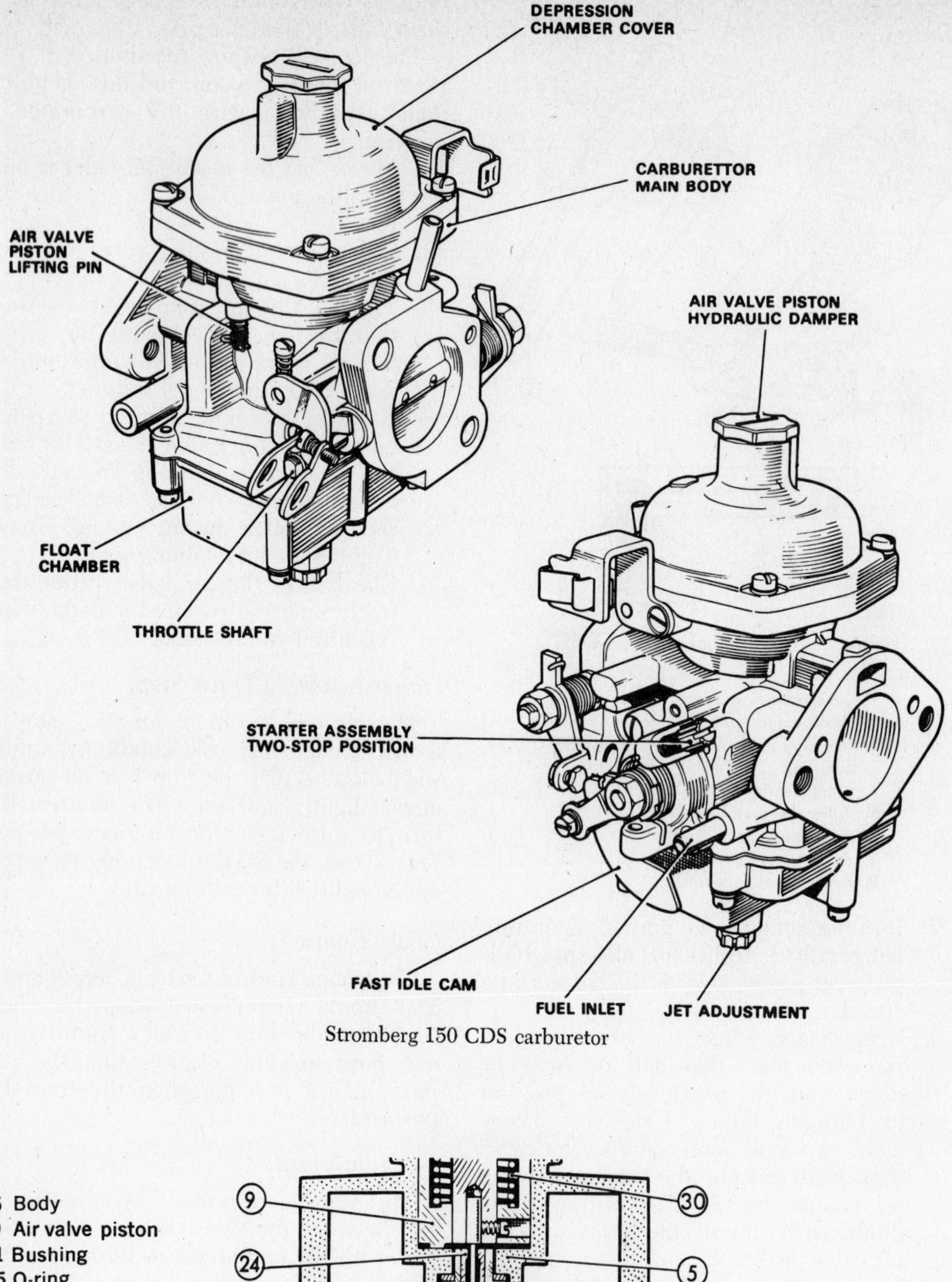

DEPRESSION CHAMBER COVER
CARBURETTOR MAIN BODY
AIR VALVE PISTON LIFTING PIN
AIR VALVE PISTON HYDRAULIC DAMPER
FLOAT CHAMBER
THROTTLE SHAFT
STARTER ASSEMBLY TWO-STOP POSITION
FAST IDLE CAM
FUEL INLET
JET ADJUSTMENT
Stromberg 150 CDS carburetor

5 Body
9 Air valve piston
11 Bushing
15 O-ring
16 O-ring
17 Jet adjusting
18 Retaining screw
21 Needle
22 Jet spring
23 O-ring
24 Jet
30 Return spring

9
24
23
21
18
16
30
5
11
22
15
17
Jet centralization details—CDS

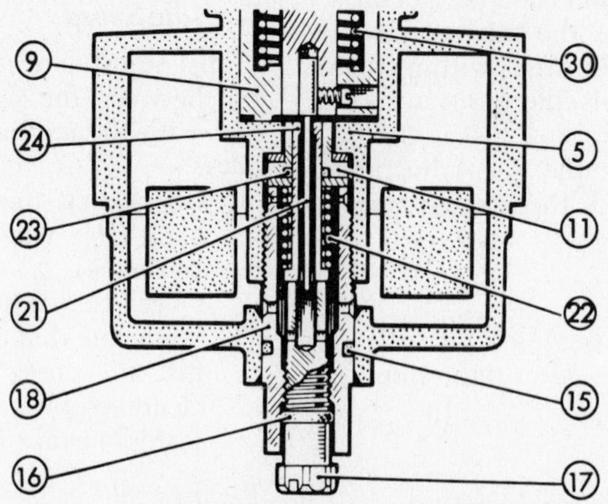

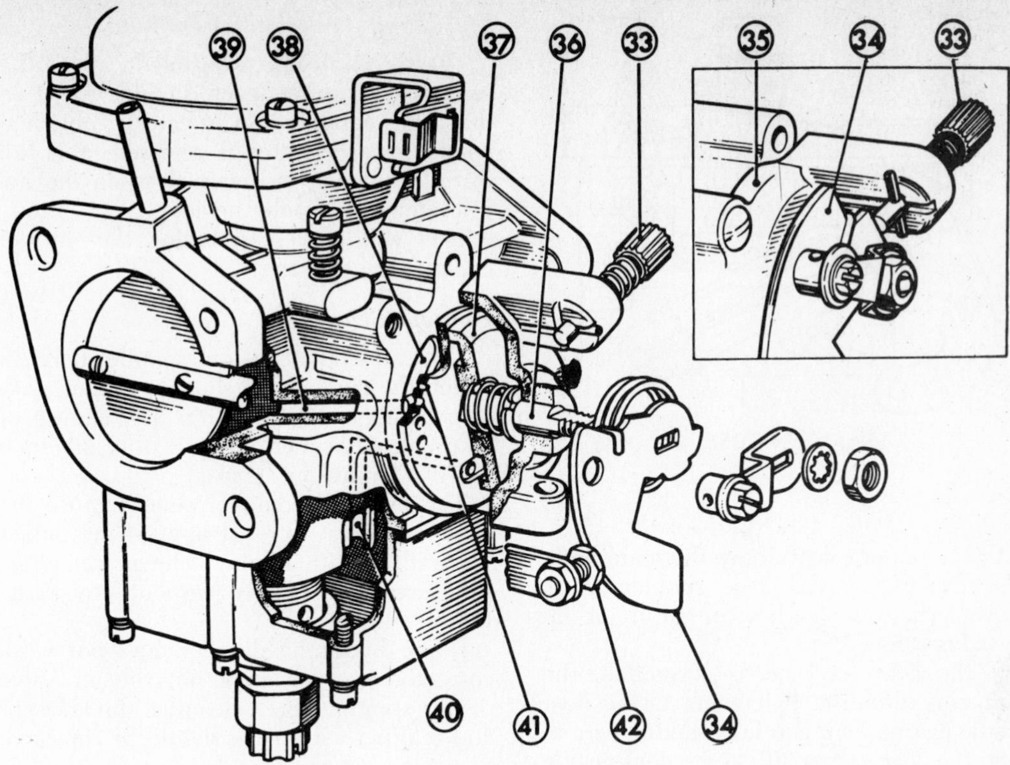

Carburetor starter assembly details

33. Starter assembly two-position stop
34. Fast idle cam
35. Starter assembly outer housing
36. Disc valve spindle
37. Starter assembly disc valve
38. Port feed by metering holes in disc valve
39. Fuel feed from Port 38 to throttle bore
40. Fuel feed drilling to starter assembly
41. Metering holes in disc valve
42. Cold fast idle speed adjustment

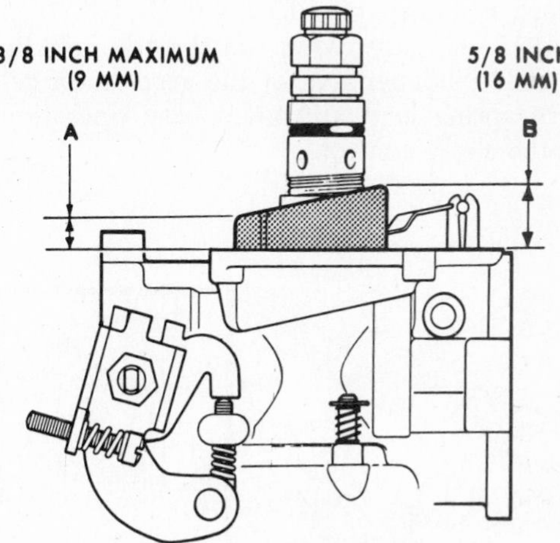

Float setting dimensions

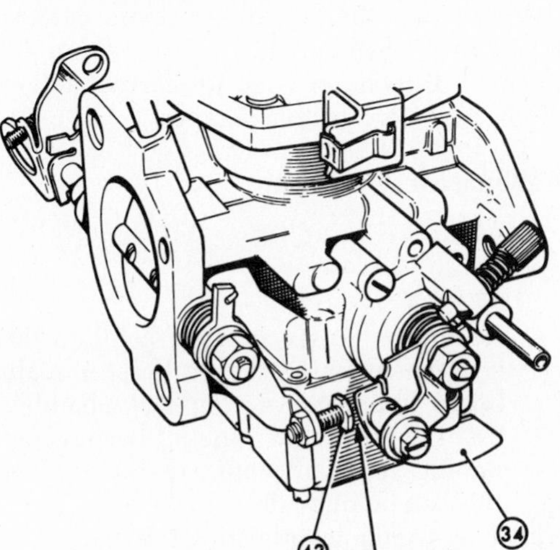

Setting throttle opening for cold starting

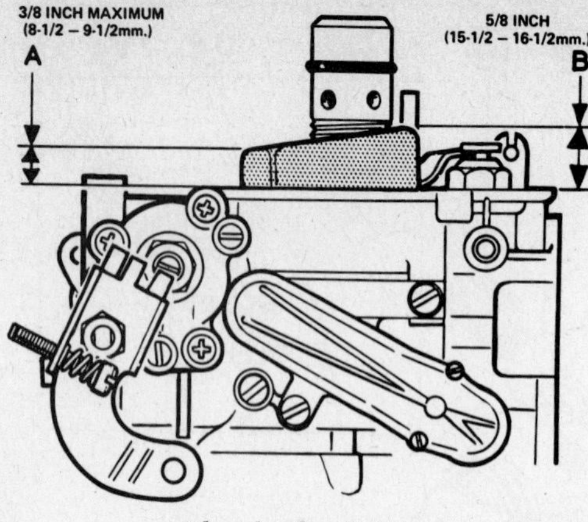

Float level—CDSE

of the carburetor float above the main body float chamber gasket face should be as shown when the carburetor is in an inverted position.

If the float level needs correction, the float arm extension that contacts the float needle can be bent carefully, taking care to keep the float arm at 90° to the float needle valve center. Small corrections can also be made by putting an extra washer under the float needle valve assembly.

Throttle Linkage Adjustment

Check that the idle speed is correct. Adjust the throttle linkage adjustment so that there is a gap of .015 to .020″ (.3 to .5 mm.). The gap allows the throttle spindle to move independent of the accelerator return spring load and gives easy operation of the choke control.

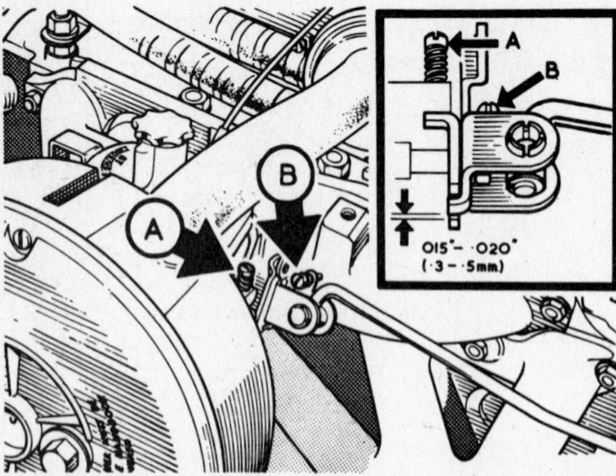

Stromberg 150 CDS carburetor—idle and throttle linkage adjustment. A is adjustment screw; B is throttle linkage adjustment screw.

Full Throttle Accelerator Position

The throttle cable adjustment, above the carburetor throttle lever, should be set so that the correct idle speed is obtained when the accelerator is released, and full throttle opening is obtained when the accelerator is held onto the floor.

This will prevent straining the throttle cable at full throttle.

Hydraulic Damper

The air valve piston spindle bore in which the damper fits should be filled with clean engine oil to within ¼″ (6mm.) of its upper edge. Very low viscosity oils such as 5W/20 must not be used.

The hydraulic damper should cause the air valve piston to resist upward movement when lifted with a finger. The air valve piston should fall freely without any resistance.

If the hydraulic damper does not work correctly after cleaning out the air valve piston spindle bore, cleaning the damper and refilling with oil, it should be replaced.

Carburetor R&R

1. Remove the air cleaner assembly.
2. Disconnect fuel line.
3. Disconnect choke control and throttle cables.
4. Disconnect the vacuum advance line.
5. Remove the carburetor flange retaining nuts and lift off the carburetor.
6. Carburetor installation is the reverse of the removal procedure.

After installing the choke and throttle cables, adjust the idle speed.

Check that the air valve spindle bore is filled with clean engine oil to within ¼″ (6mm.) of its outer edge for correct action of the air valve piston damper.

Carburetor Overhaul

CDS

Disassembly

1. Remove the six screws holding the float chamber to the carburetor main body, and remove the float chamber by drawing it down the jet bushing retaining screw. Because of the O-ring, this can be difficult.
2. Remove the jet adjusting screw.
3. Remove the hydraulic damper and the depression chamber cover.

4. Lift out the air valve piston, needle and diaphragm assembly.
5. Apply compressed air into the fuel inlet hole inside the float chamber and, at the same time, move the starter assembly over the entire range of its movement several times, with the travel stop in its out position.

There is no need to remove the jet bushing retaining screw when only cleaning is required.

Cleaning

A suitable cleaning solvent should be used for cleaning the carburetor parts.

CAUTION: Certain cleaning and degreasing fluids will ruin the diaphragm and O-rings.

The jet, and the space inside the jet bushing retaining screw, should be blown out with compressed air.

Assembly

This is the reverse of the disassembly procedure. If necessary, the float chamber gasket and O-rings should be replaced.

When assembling the diaphragm and air valve piston, the locating lip on the diaphragm must fit in the corresponding locating recess in the carburetor body. Since the jet adjusting screw was removed, it will be necessary to readjust the idle.

CDSE

Each Stromberg 150 CDSE carburetor is factory-tested to ensure that its fuel-air ratio is within very close limits. The jet is pressed into position. Certain parts cannot be renewed or interchanged with another carburetor since this might allow excessive exhaust emissions.

Non-replaceable parts

Jet
Air valve piston
Depression chamber cover
Carburetor body

If any of these items are damaged the carburetor must be replaced.

Replaceable parts

Float
Float needle valve assembly
Gaskets and other small items
Temperature controlled valve
Throttle bypass valve
Metering needle
Diaphragm

The lead seal in one of the depression chamber cover screws can be removed if any of the last three items have to be replaced, or it the top cover has to be removed.

1. Remove the carburetor top cover, noting that the lug on the top cover is farthest away from the engine, because the cover must be installed in this position. A tight fitting cover can be removed by lifting the air valve piston quickly after removing the piston damper, using one hand to prevent it from falling when released. Carefully lift out the air valve and needle assembly. Check that the needle is assembled with the spring bias towards the inlet manifold, and that the shoulder on the needle is exactly level with the piston face when the needle is held square to the face.
2. The needle can be assembled incorrectly in the air valve piston. Correct assembly allows the needle to lean 3°, by spring loading, toward the intake manifold side of the carburetor. Do not overtighten the metering needle retaining screw or the spring casing in which the upper end of the needle is held will be damaged.
3. Reassemble the carburetor, check that the air valve piston falls freely, and readjust idle.

Air Cleaner

Filter Replacement

To replace the filter element:

1. Remove the two bolts which hold the air cleaner to the carburetor flange.
2. Release the tube which connects the air cleaner to the flame trap.

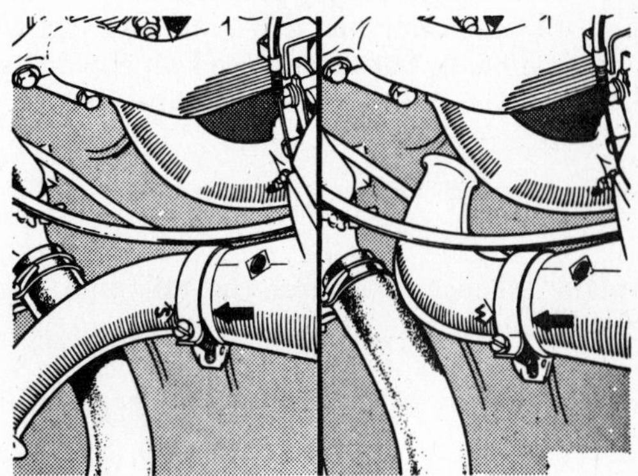

Air cleaner winter and summer positions

3. Note the position of the cover for reassembly. Remove the cover.
4. Clean out the air cleaner body.
5. Check the condition of the rubber sealing rings. Install the new element on the sealing ring followed by the other sealing ring.
6. Replace the cover and fasten with four screws.
7. Reinstall the air cleaner and tighten to 12 ft. lbs.

WINTER/SUMMER POSITIONS

The air intake tube is adjustable for winter or summer conditions. Turn the intake tube so that the W (winter) or S (summer) on the tube is in line with the arrow on the air cleaner body.

Exhaust System

The exhaust system consists of the exhaust pipe and muffler which are a welded assembly and a separate tail pipe. The system is flexibly mounted at the rear ends of the muffler and tail pipe.

TAIL PIPE REPLACEMENT

1. Apply penetrating oil to tail pipe where it enters muffler.
2. Remove nut and washer inside muffler rear flexible support and lift support off the tail pipe clamp bolt.
3. Remove the long hex nut from the tail pipe clamp bolt and remove the bolt.
4. Using a large screwdriver, spread the tail pipe clip so that it can be driven off the pipe.
5. Support muffler.
6. Disconnect tail pipe from its rear flexible mounting and drive tail pipe out of muffler or cut through tail pipe near its muffler end. Remove tail pipe over the rear axle.

MUFFLER REPLACEMENT

The muffler can be removed from the main exhaust pipe after the tail pipe has been removed.

EXHAUST PIPE REPLACEMENT

This can be removed after the tail pipe has been removed.

After installation, the tail pipe end should be centered in the body clearance cutaway.

Cooling System

DRAINING AND REFILLING

When the cooling system is drained, the cylinder block must be drained as well as the radiator.

If the system is only partly drained, other than for a short time, corrosion of the water pump impeller seal face can occur. This causes later failure of the water pump seal and water pump bearing.

Draining

1. First put the heater controls into the HOT position.
2. Remove the radiator cap. If the engine is very hot allow it to cool down.
3. Place a container under each drain plug.
4. Unscrew the drain plug in the radiator bottom tank. Remove the drain plug, or open the drain tap on the left hand side of the cylinder block, to allow coolant to drain.
5. If the drained coolant is rusty, the cooling system should be reverse flushed.

Refilling

1. Set the heater control to the HOT position.
2. Screw in the radiator drain plug and tighten finger tight only. Replace the cylinder block drain plug, or close the drain tap.
3. Pour coolant into radiator slowly to avoid air lock. The correct coolant level is 1" below the radiator filler neck.
4. Run the engine for a few minutes and add coolant as needed.

THERMOSTAT

Removal

1. Drain off enough coolant to bring its level below the thermostat housing on the front of the cylinder head.
2. Remove the two bolts holding the coolant outlet to the cylinder head, and move it aside to allow the thermo-

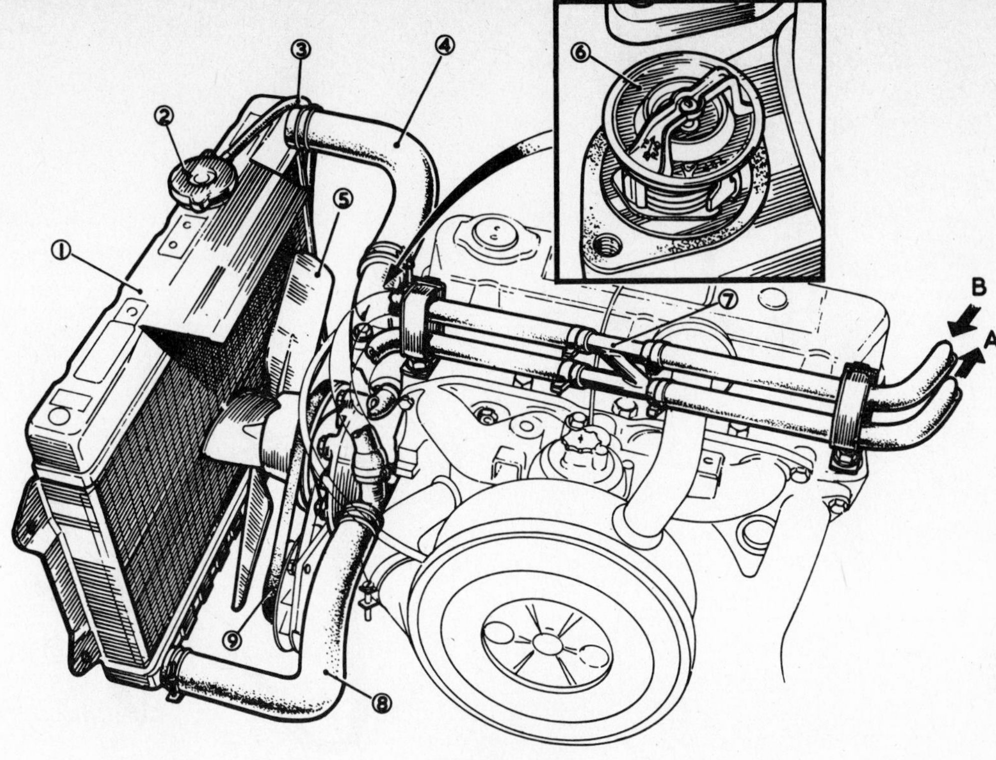

Cooling system

1. Radiator
2. Radiator cap with relief valve
3. Overflow tube
4. Radiator return hose
5. Fan
6. Thermostat
7. Thermostatic mixture control valve
8. Radiator to engine feed hose
9. Fan belt
A. Heater feed hose
B. Heater return hose

stat to be lifted out of the cylinder head.

Installation

1. Place the thermostat into the cylinder head so that the word TOP is up.
2. Install the coolant outlet connection using a new gasket.
3. Refill cooling system.

Testing

1. Check that the riveted and soldered joints are secure.
2. Check that the jiggle pin is in position and free.
3. Check that the wax element is not cracked or leaking.
4. Suspend the thermostat in cold water without touching the bottom or sides of the container.
5. Heat the water to 166—167°F. Stir the water for an even temperature. After about 3 minutes at this temperature, the thermostat should have opened about 1/16″.
6. Raise the water temperature to 203°F. After two or three minutes check that the thermostat has opened 3/8″.
7. While the thermostat is open, check that its seat is clear.
8. Remove the thermostat from the hot water. Submerge it in cold water. The valve should close within 15 or 20 seconds.
9. Replace the thermostat if defective.

WATER PUMP

Removal

1. Drain radiator and cylinder block.
2. Loosen alternator, mountings, and bolts. Remove the fan belt.
3. Remove fan assembly and fan pulley.
4. Remove five bolts holding pump to timing case, noting the position of the two longer, lower bolts.

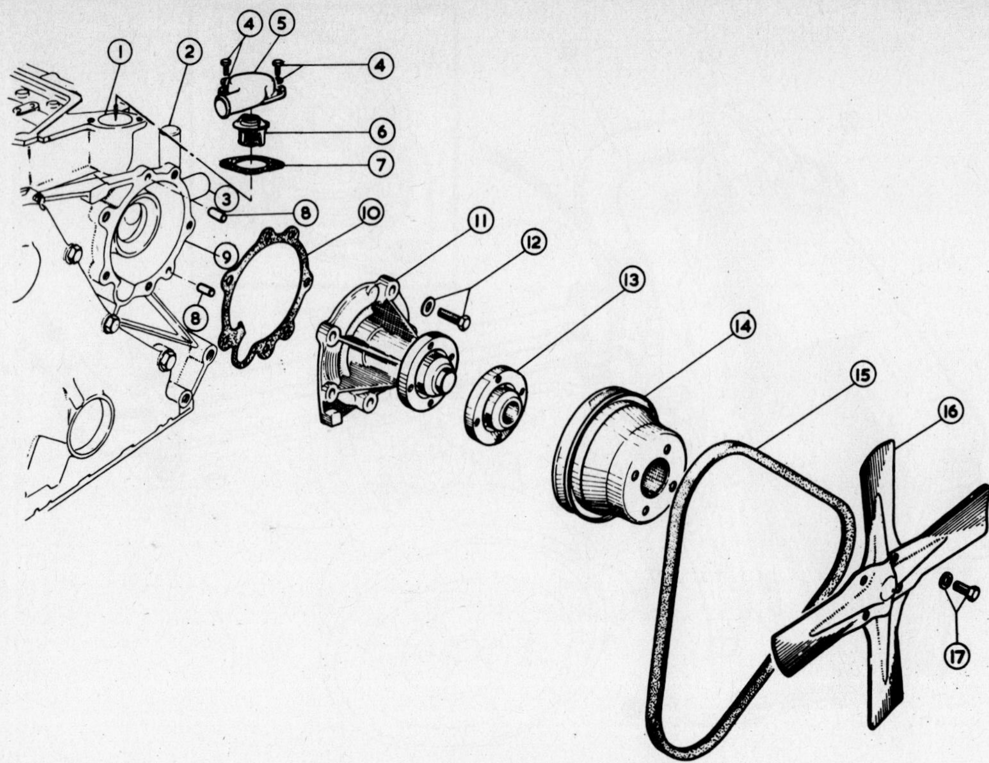

Water pump and thermostat disassembled

1. Thermostat location in cylinder head
2. Bypass return connection
3. Radiator bottom hose connection
4. Water outlet housing bolts
5. Water outlet housing
6. Thermostat
7. Gasket, water outlet to cylinder head
8. Dowels, pump to timing case
9. Pump housing in timing case
10. Gasket, pump to timing case
11. Water pump
12. Bolts, pump to timing case or cylinder block
13. Fan pulley hub
14. Fan pulley
15. Fan belt
16. Fan assembly
17. Bolts, fan and pulley to hub

5. Remove pump from timing case. The pump is located by two dowels and is sometimes tight on these dowels.

Installation

1. A new gasket should always be used between the pump and timing case.
2. Tighten the fan belt to give 5/8″ deflection.

RADIATOR

Removal and Installation

1. Drain the cooling system.
2. Disconnect the top and bottom water hoses at the radiator.
3. Remove the four radiator attaching bolts and lift the radiator clear, making sure that the cooling fins are not damaged.
4. Keep the radiator in its normal upright position to prevent sediment from entering its cooling tubes.
5. Replacement is the reverse of removal.

Engine

Emission Control

The Cricket uses an exhaust emission control system, a crankcase emission control system and an evaporative emission control system to control engine exhaust emissions, and crankcase and fuel vapors.

Exhaust Emission Control

The exhaust emission control system con-

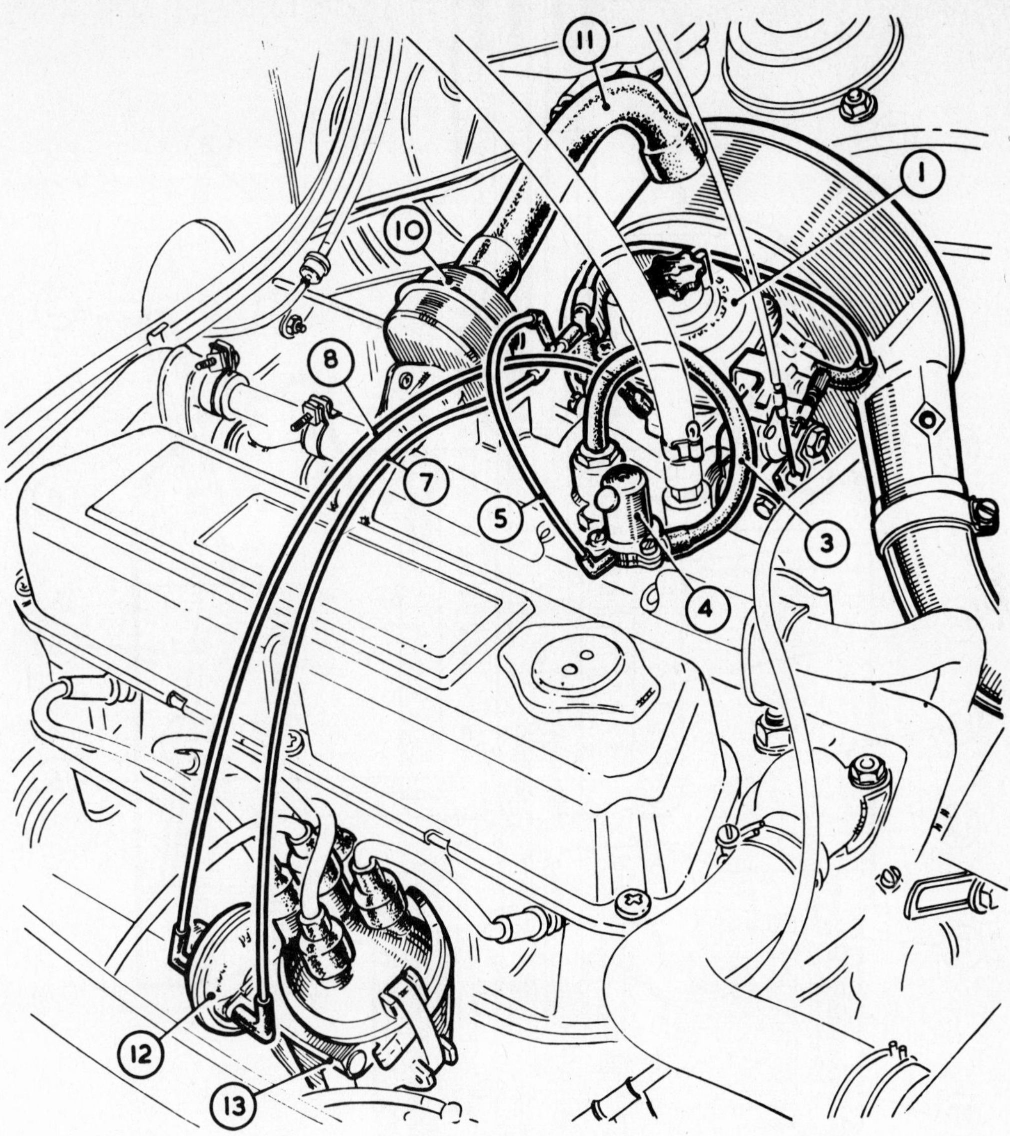

Exhaust emission control system

1. Stromberg 150 CDSE carburetor
3. Intake manifold to control valve hose
4. Control valve
5. Control valve to system hose
7. Vacuum actuator hose (retard)
8. Carburetor to vacuum advance actuator hose
10. Crankcase emission flame trap
11. Flame trap to air filter hose
12. Vacuum advance and retard actuator
13. Distributor

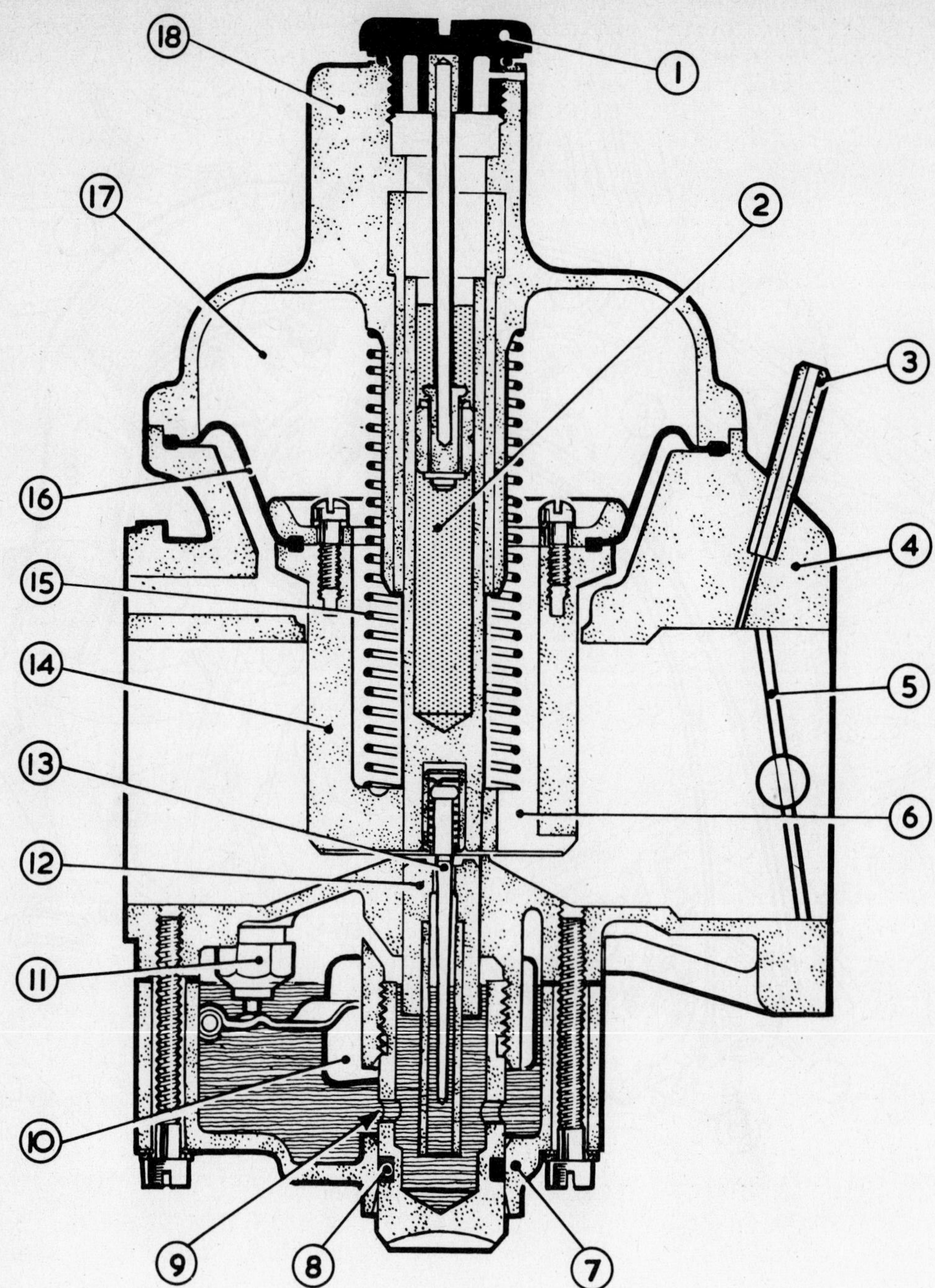

Stromberg 150 CDSE carburetor—sectional view

1. Air valve piston damper assembly
2. Piston damper reservoir
3. Vacuum advance connection
4. Carburetor body
5. Throttle
6. Vacuum feed hole to 17
7. Float chamber
8. O-ring
9. Fuel feed holes to jet
10. Twin float, one shown
11. Float needle valve seat
12. Metering jet and feed tube
13. Metering needle
14. Air valve piston
15. Air valve piston return spring
16. Diaphragm
17. Depression chamber
18. Depression chamber cover

sists of the following components connected by vacuum hoses:

A Stromberg 150 CDSE carburetor.

A control valve.

Distributor with deceleration retard control.

These components give very precise control of the fuel-air mixture so that the hydrocarbon, oxides of nitrogen, and carbon monoxide content in the exhaust gas is well below legal limits.

Control Valve

This valve is operated by intake manifold vacuum and opens under deceleration when intake manifold vacuum exceeds 20 in. Hg. When open it allows intake manifold vacuum to operate the throttle bypass valve and the distributor retard actuator.

Distributor

The distributor used with this system has a tandem vacuum actuator. The extra actuator chamber operates to retard the ignition timing 12 crankshaft degrees during deceleration. The distributor centrifugal and vacuum advance operate in the usual way.

Idling, Part Throttle, & Full Throttle

Under these driving conditions, the carburetor operates in a manner similar to other Stromberg CD and CDS carburetors, except that its fuel metering is controlled more accurately to prevent a rich air fuel mixture.

This is done by the use of a spring biased metering needle and factory adjusted jet. In addition, a lean mixture is provided by opening of the temperature controlled valve when the carburetor is hot.

Deceleration

On the CDSE carburetor, the throttle bypass valve allows enough mixture to be supplied to give proper combustion during deceleration. This causes the engine to produce enough power to reduce the effect of engine braking. To overcome this unwanted feature, the ignition is retarded 12 crankshaft degrees during deceleration by the action of the distributor retard actuator.

Operation of the throttle bypass valve and retarding of the ignition is caused by the opening of the control valve when the intake manifold vacuum exceeds 20 in. Hg. This allows vacuum to open the throttle bypass valve and to operate the ignition retard actuator.

When intake manifold vacuum falls to 17 in. Hg., air entering through the calibrated air bleed allows the throttle bypass valve and ignition retard actuator to return to their normal closed positions, after the control valve closes.

Adjustments

The exhaust emission control equipment depends on the proper operation of the fuel and ignition systems of the engine to be most effective. Therefore, these systems must be adjusted periodically. The adjustments should be made in the order following:

NOTE: The following information is for the 1,500cc engine, with a cast iron cylinder head and a single Stromberg CDSE carburetor.

1. Check valve clearances.
2. Check spark plug gaps.
3. Check distributor breaker point gap.
4. Check static ignition timing.
5. Remove large hose from control valve and plug manifold connection.
6. Check ignition system.
7. Set idle speed.
8. Check idle ignition timing with a timing light.
9. Connect hose to control valve.
10. Recheck idle speed.
11. Check time for engine to decelerate from 2,500 rpm to idle in neutral. This should be 4-6 seconds.
12. If necessary, re-adjust the control valve. Remove the control valve cover to gain access to the adjusting nut.

Crankcase Emission Control

This system consists of a flame trap attached to the engine rocker cover, and connected by an oil resistant rubber hose to the air cleaner.

All crankcase fumes pass through the flame trap and are drawn through the rubber hose into the air cleaner, where they mix with the incoming air. They are then drawn through the filter and are burned by the engine. The flame trap should be removed and washed in a suitable solvent periodically.

The metal tube on the rocker cover and the rubber hose should also be cleaned.

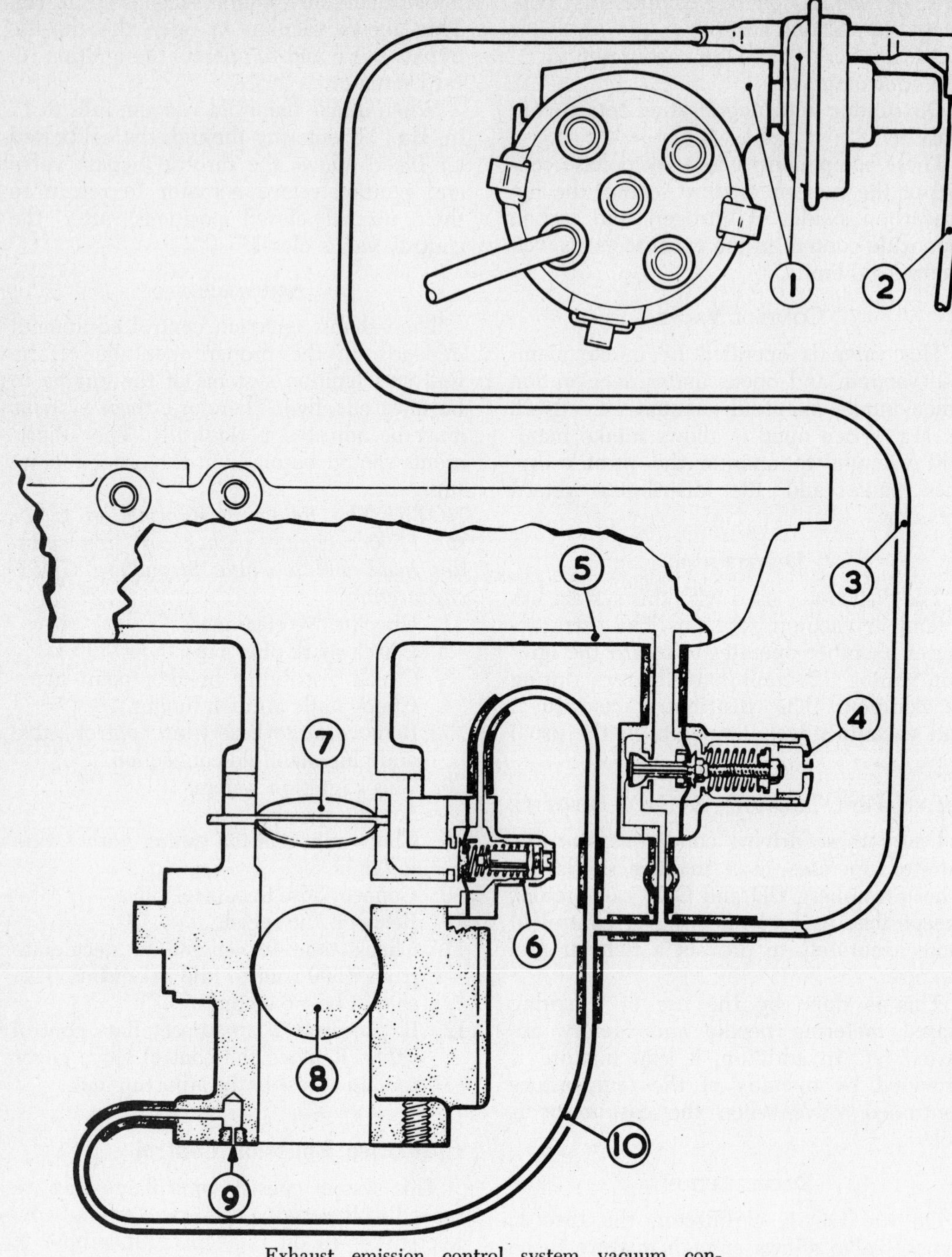

Exhaust emission control system vacuum connections

1. Vacuum advance and retard actuator
2. Vacuum advance hose
3. Vacuum retard hose
4. Control valve
5. Intake manifold
6. Throttle bypass valve
7. Throttle valve
8. Air valve piston
9. Calibrated air bleed

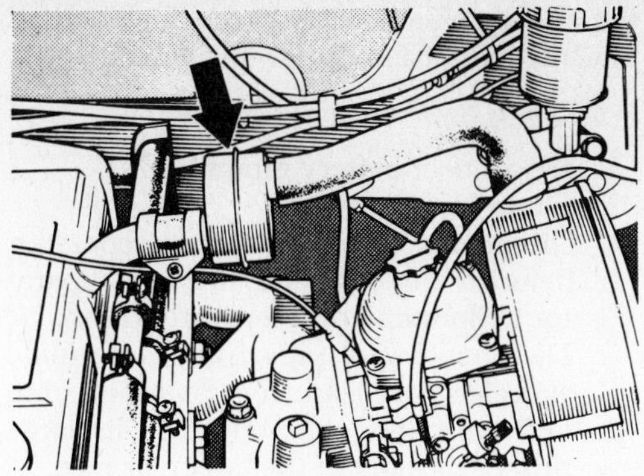

Flame trap

Evaporative Emission Control

This system prevents the escape of fuel vapors into the atmosphere.

The system consists of the following items:

A fuel tank which has a filler cap without a vent.

A fuel tank inner chamber which allows space for fuel expansion.

A separator located above the forward end of the tank and connected by fuel vapor escape tubes and to the four corners of the fuel tank. When the tank is not level, one tube will always be above the fuel level so that there is a vapor escape outlet

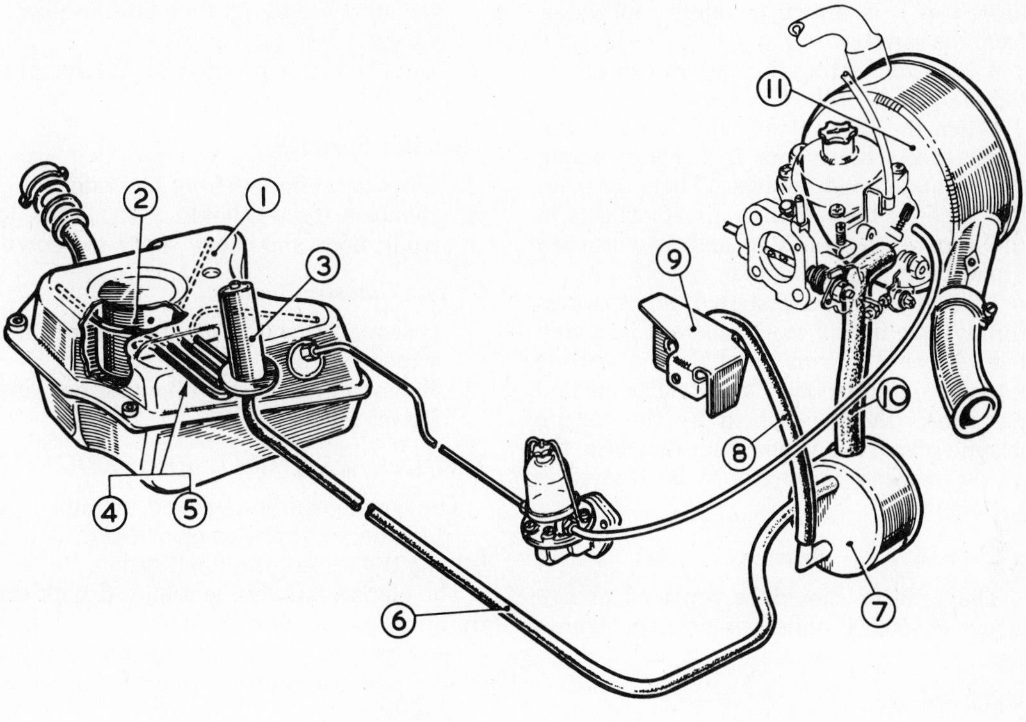

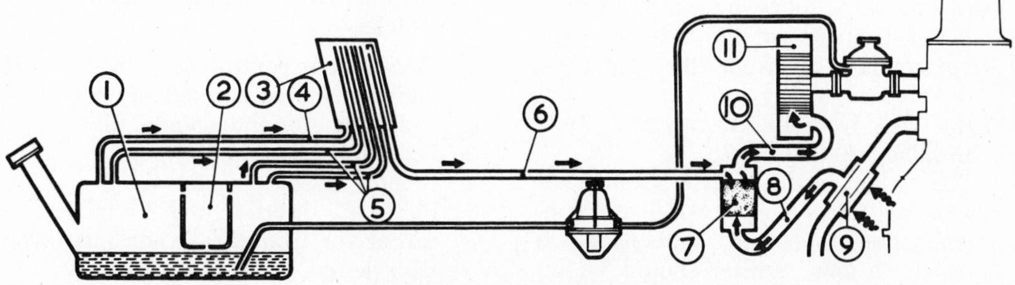

Evaporative emission control system

1. Fuel tank
2. Fuel tank inner chamber
3. Separator
4. Separator drain tube
5. Vent pipes
6. Vapor and tank vent tube
7. Carbon canister
8. Hose
9. Air heating stove
10. Hose
11. Air cleaner

to the separator. One tube also allows condensed fuel vapor to return to the fuel tank from the separator.

A vapor escape and tank vent tube through which fuel vapor can escape to the storage canister. This tube has a .060″ diameter hole, at its upper end inside the separator, to make it difficult for liquid fuel to leave the separator by the tube rather than drain back to the fuel tank. It also vents the fuel tank to prevent a vacuum occurring above the fuel as the fuel level lowers.

A carbon canister which contains carbon granules that can adsorb—not absorb—the fuel vapor.

An air heating stove through which air is heated as it is drawn to purge fuel vapor from the canister.

A hose connecting the carbon canister to the intake side of the air cleaner.

When the fuel in the tank is warm enough, excess fuel vapor is discharged into the separator and canister. Then, because the vapor is heavier than air, it collects in the top of the canister and is adsorbed around the carbon granules.

When the engine is started, air is drawn through the hot air stove where it is heated before being drawn through the carbon granules into the air cleaner. The heated air purges the vapor held by the carbon granules and the vapor is drawn into the air cleaner and carburetor to be burned in the engine.

SERVICE

The canister should be replaced at five years or 50,000 miles, whichever comes first.

Smell of Fuel

A smell of fuel vapor is an indication of one or more of the following conditions:

1. A leak from one of the tubes or their connections, or from the separator unit.
2. Fuel leak from filler neck seal at tank.
3. Leaking fuel tank.
4. The carbon in the canister cannot adsorb fuel vapor due to accidental contamination, such as immersion in water. A new canister should be installed.
5. The hot air stove or tubes are disconnected or damaged.

Engine Stops

If the tube between the separator and the canister is restricted, the fuel tank is unvented and can become air locked.

Fuel Tank Removal and Installation

1. Disconnect battery ground cable.
2. Drain fuel tank.
3. Disconnect outlet tube from separator.
4. Remove three screws holding separator to floor and pull separator down.
5. Disconnect fuel pipe from tank union and electrical lead from fuel tank unit.
6. Pull tank filler tube out from its large rubber bushing in the tank rear face.
7. Remove two nuts and washers and two bolts and washers holding the tank to the body. Lower tank with the separator attached by its four flexible plastic tubes.
8. Installation is reversal of the removal procedure.

Separator Removal

1. Disconnect outlets from separator.
2. Remove screws holding separator to trunk floor and move separator down.

Carbon Canister Removal

1. Disconnect warm air feed tube and vapor feed tube from the canister.
2. Remove the canister retaining bolt and lift off canister.

ENGINE REMOVAL PROCEDURES

The engine can be removed by unbolting it from the transmission and lifting it out, leaving the transmission in position.

The engine can also be removed with the transmission attached.

On cars with automatic transmission, the engine and transmission must be removed as a unit.

Removal, Leaving Transmission in Vehicle

1. Place heater control valve in the HOT position so that the heater will drain.
2. Drain radiator and cylinder block.
3. Disconnect battery.
4. Remove hood.
5. Remove throttle rod retainer in carburetor throttle lever. Lift away throttle rod.
6. Disconnect choke cable.
7. Disconnect alternator leads.
8. Disconnect radiator bottom hose at water pump end.
9. Disconnect radiator top hose at cylinder head end.

10. Disconnect heater hoses at heater end.
11. Remove four radiator attaching bolts and remove radiator.
12. Remove four attaching bolts and remove blades, fan pulley, and fan belt.
13. Disconnect leads from water temperature unit, oil warning light switch, distributor low tension connection, and coil high tension lead at coil end.
14. Disconnect fuel inlet line from fuel pump.
15. Disconnect starter lead from starter terminal. Remove starter top attaching bolt and ground lead from bolt.
16. Remove upper two transmission attaching bolts.
17. Jack up front of car and place two stands in position. Lower car onto stands. When jacking up the front of the car, be sure that the jack platform is under the center of the front crossmember, and not under the engine oil pan.
18. Remove flywheel cover plate bolts and flywheel cover.
19. Remove starter lower attaching bolt and remove starter with its splash guard.
20. Remove lower transmission to engine bolts.
21. Disconnect exhaust pipe from exhaust manifold.
22. Remove two engine front mount securing nuts inside front cross member.
23. Attach lifting gear under two cylinder head nuts that hold heater hose support brackets after detaching heater hoses at their front connections.
24. Support engine weight on lift, and transmission weight with a jack so that the transmission will not drop down after the engine is removed.
25. Lift engine so that threaded studs on front mounts come out of crossmember. Draw engine forward far enough to clear the transmission and lift out.

Installation with Transmission in Vehicle

1. Engage first gear.
2. Check that the two locating dowels are in their correct position in the engine cylinder block transmission face.
3. Lower engine into position, keeping the cylinder block and transmission faces parallel. Guide the engine into position so that the transmission drive shaft splines enter the splines in the clutch driven plate, as the engine is moved backward. The two locating dowels should enter the holes in the transmission face.
4. Reassembly of the remaining items is a reversal of the removal procedure.
5. Refill the engine with oil. Fill the cooling system, with the heater controls fully open. After running the engine for a short while, check coolant level.

Removal with Transmission Attached

In addition to Steps 1-15 and 21-23, under Removal, Leaving Transmission In Vehicle, the following operations are required when removing the engine with the transmission attached:

1. Jack up the car and place axle stands under the rear axle and front crossmember.

When jacking up the rear axle, be sure that the jack is not under the rear cover. A serious oil leak may result.

When jacking up the front of the car, be sure that the jack is under the center of the front cross member, and not under the oil pan.

2. Remove three screws and shift lever.
3. Unbolt the drive shaft from the rear axle flange and remove from the transmission. Plug the transmission end to prevent loss of oil when the engine is lifted out.
4. Disconnect speedometer cable.
5. Disconnect clutch cable at transmission end.
6. Disconnect back-up light switch.
7. Remove four bolts holding the anti-roll bar to body frame underside.
8. Remove engine rear mounting bolts. At the same time, use a jack to lower the transmission.
9. Lift out the unit.

Installation with Transmission Attached

1. The engine, with transmission attached, should hang at about 45° from the vertical when lowered into position. A jack should be used to raise the transmission as needed.
2. Connect all parts previously removed.
3. Fill the engine with oil. Fill the cooling system with the heater controls fully open. After running the engine, check the coolant level.
4. Refill transmission or check its oil level.

INTAKE AND EXHAUST MANIFOLDS

Removal

The intake manifold is bolted to the exhaust manifold and cannot be removed separately.

1. Remove air cleaner.
2. Remove two exhaust flange nuts. Remove flange and lower exhaust pipe.
3. Disconnect throttle linkage, fuel line, choke cable, and vacuum advance hose at the carburetor.
4. Remove seven bolts and washers and three nuts and washers holding manifolds to cylinder head.
5. Remove manifolds with carburetor attached.

Disassembly and Reassembly

To separate the intake manifold from the exhaust manifold, remove the two bolts holding the manifolds together and lift them apart. An exhaust heat deflector plate is placed between the manifolds to control the amount of exhaust heat to the intake manifold. No gaskets are used between the deflector plate and the manifolds. When reassembling the manifolds, the two bolts should be tightened after the manifolds are bolted to the cylinder head.

Installation

This is the reverse of the removal procedure. A new gasket should be used between the manifolds and cylinder head. The attaching bolts and nuts should be retightened when the engine is hot.

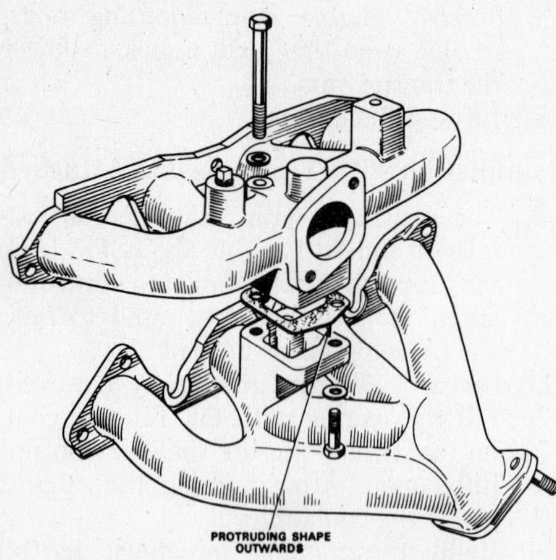

Intake and exhaust manifold disassembled

CYLINDER HEAD

The cast iron cylinder head has the valve guide bores machined directly in the cylinder head. If worn, these guide bores should be reamed out to take valves with .015″ or .030″ oversize stems.

Some engines have valves with .003″ oversize stems. This oversize is used only on new production engines. The cylinder head is stamped to show which size valves are installed. When the valve guide bores are reamed out to take valves with oversize stems, the stamped numbers should be obliterated, and the reamed oversize stamped on as +15 or +30.

All head gaskets are stamped with the word TOP and their identifying part number. They are installed dry. Gaskets are also identified by the letters LB stamped on the top right corner. The letters can be seen when the cylinder head is in place.

The maximum amount that can be machined off the cylinder head gasket surface is .005″.

Removal

1. Drain the radiator and cylinder block. The system must be drained completely because partial draining can damage the water pump seal face on the impeller, causing failure of the water pump seal.
2. Disconnect battery.
3. Remove air cleaner.
4. Disconnect radiator top hose.
5. Remove rocker cover.
6. Disconnect lead from water temperature sensor unit.
7. Disconnect spark plug leads.
8. Disconnect heater hoses.
9. Remove eight bolts holding rocker shaft assembly to cylinder head. These bolts must be released evenly where they are loaded by any compressed valve springs.
10. Lift off rocker shaft assembly.
11. Remove pushrods being careful not to draw the tappets out of the block. The pushrods should be replaced in their original positions.
12. Disconnect fuel line at fuel pump, carburetor, and its clip.
13. Disconnect carburetor controls.
14. Disconnect the exhaust pipe at its flange on the exhaust manifold.
15. Remove eight bolts and two nuts holding the cylinder head to the block.

16. Lift off cylinder head with manifolds and carburetor.
17. While the cylinder head is off, lift each tappet and inspect its bottom face for wear.

Installation

1. Reverse the removal procedure, checking that all gasket surfaces are clean. Always use a new gasket. No sealing compound should be used on either the gasket or gasket surfaces of the cylinder head or cylinder block.
2. The cylinder head bolts should be tightened to 56 ft. lbs. in the correct tightening sequence and retightened after the engine has run 500 miles. When checking cylinder head bolt tightness, each cylinder head bolt should be loosened slightly and tightened to the correct torque.
3. Adjust valve clearances.
4. Run engine until hot and reset the valve clearances.

VALVES

Rocker Cover Removal and Installation

1. Disconnect vacuum advance hose and crankcase breather hose.
2. Remove screws holding rocker cover to cylinder head and lift off cover.
3. When installing, the screws should be tightened down onto the shoulder of their shanks. The gasket should be replaced if the cover screws do not compress it.

Valve Adjustment

This adjustment is made when the engine is hot or cold but never when partly warm. The valve clearances are given in the Tune-Up Specifications Chart. Valve

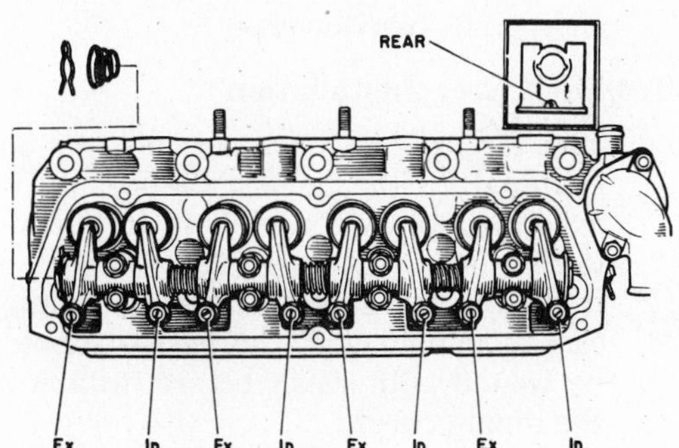

Rocker shaft assembly showing correct position for standard on rocker shaft

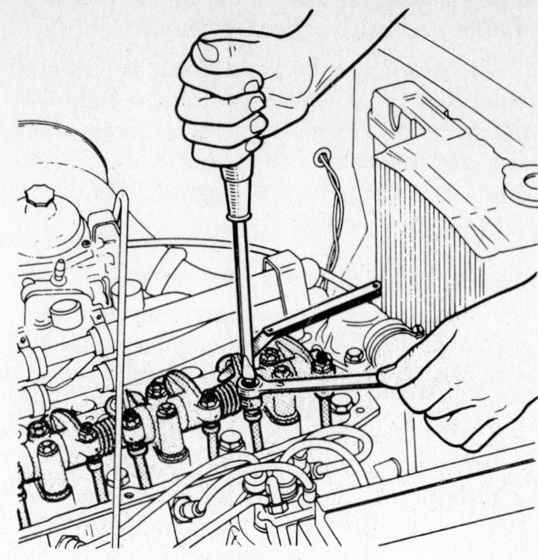

Adjusting valves

clearances should be readjusted when the engine is hot after reassembling any part of the valve mechanism.

1. Remove rocker cover.
2. Turn the engine using a 15/16″ socket on the crankshaft pulley bolt, to bring No. 1 cylinder to the TDC position of its compression stroke. In this position the TDC pointer on the crankshaft pulley will be opposite the TDC line on the timing case when the intake valve of No. 4 cylinder is just beginning to open.

NOTE: Do not turn the engine with the fan blades.

3. Adjust both valve clearances on No. 1 cylinder and turn engine exactly half a turn in the normal direction of rotation.
4. Adjust both valve clearances on No. 3 cylinder. Turn engine half a turn.
5. Adjust both valve clearances on No. 4 cylinder. Turn engine half a turn.
6. Adjust both valve clearances on No. 2 cylinder. Turn engine half a turn.
7. To check clearance, insert a feeler gauge (.008″ intake; .016″ exhaust) between the valve stem and rocker.

When the clearance is correct, the feeler will be held firmly, but not tightly, when moved between the rocker and valve stem end while pushing down on the adjustment screw slot with a screwdriver.

8. To adjust clearance, loosen locknut and turn screw. Tighten lock nut and check clearance.

Valve and Valve Seat Reconditioning

The procedure for resurfacing valves and valve seats is given in the Engine Rebuilding Section. The clearances for both standard and oversize valves and valve guide bores are given in the Engine Rebuilding Specification Tables.

Exhaust Valve Seat Inserts

Exhaust valve seat inserts are not normally installed in new engines but are available in four sizes; standard, +.002″ (.050mm.), +.005″ (.127mm.), and +.010″ (.254mm.).

When inserts are to be used, the valve guides should be reamed oversize and the cylinder head recessed deep enough to take the insert and to a diameter that will give the insert an interference fit of .0025″ (.063mm.) to .0045″ (.0114mm.). The cylinder head should be bored .0035″ (.088mm.) smaller than the diameter of the insert to be installed.

The insert must be pressed in perfectly square until it seats on the entire bottom face of the recess. This is important. If the insert outer bottom radius is greater than the radius in the corner of the recess bore, the insert will not press down onto the bottom face of the recess, and may hammer down under valve action. This reduces the valve clearance and may cause exhaust valve burning.

The exhaust valve guide bore should be reamed oversize before machining the valve seat on the fitted insert.

The valve seat on the newly installed insert should be cut at an angle of 45°. The seat width should be reduced to a width of .075-.095″ with a 75° cutter. The seat must be concentric to within .001″ (.025mm.) of the valve guide bore. Valves should be ground in lightly after the insert seat(s) have been cut.

Tappet Removal and Installation

1. Remove rocker cover, rocker shaft assemblies; and push rods.
2. Remove cylinder head—tappets cannot be removed without removing cylinder head.
3. Lift out tappets. Tappets should be numbered on removal so that they can be replaced in their original positions. The tappet faces that contact the cams should be free from pitting and wear. Regrinding of the tappet faces is not allowable.
4. Installation is the reverse of the above procedure. The tappets should be replaced in the same bores from which they were removed.

Tappets should rotate freely in the cylinder block without any side clearance. Oversize tappets are available.

TIMING COVER AND OIL SEAL

If the following instructions are followed exactly, the timing case can be removed without removing the oil pan. If Steps 7 and 8 are ignored, water will enter the oil pan when the timing cover is removed, and the oil pan will then have to be removed. The timing cover can be removed with the radiator in position.

Timing Cover Removal

1. Drain radiator and cylinder block.
2. Disconnect battery.
3. Remove alternator.
4. Remove fan blades and fan belt.
5. Remove radiator.
6. Remove crankshaft pulley retainer bolt and crankshaft pulley.
7. Remove water pump.
8. Jack up rear of car so that any water in the cylinder block drains forward and runs out of the water pump recess in the timing case. Lower car and wipe cylinder block dry before removing the timing case.
9. Remove four oil pan bolts below front of timing case, and loosen enough oil pan bolts to allow the front of the oil pan to drop clear of the timing case lower face.
10. Remove timing case bolts, placing the bolts through holes in a piece of cardboard with their positions as in the timing case. This saves time on installation as the bolt lengths are different.
11. Remove timing case, which may be tight on its two dowels.

Timing Cover Installation

1. The timing case does not have to be centered on the crankshaft because it is located by two dowels in the cylinder block.
2. If the oil pan gasket below the timing case is undamaged, the gasket should be coated with sealer before installing the timing cover.
3. If the oil pan gasket is damaged, the oil pan should be removed and a new gasket installed before installing the

timing case. Do not tighten the oil pan until the timing case bolts are tight.

4. Install a new seal in the timing cover if necessary.
5. Clean off cylinder block gasket surface behind timing cover and timing cover gasket surface. Position new gasket and install cover.
6. Install water pump.
7. Check that crankshaft pulley journal is polished and undamaged where it runs in the seal. If damaged, a new pulley must be installed. Install pulley. The pulley retaining bolt should be tightened to 50 ft. lbs.
8. Install four oil pan bolts at front of oil pan and tighten all oil pan bolts.
9. Install heater hose and bottom water hose.
10. Install fan pulley and fan blades.
11. Install alternator and fan belt. Adjust fan belt.
12. Refill cooling system.

Timing Cover Oil Seal Replacement

1. The oil seal can be driven out from inside the timing case while the case is supported as close as possible to the seal bore on the outside.
2. The new seal should be pressed into the timing case while the case is supported on its inside face below the seal recess, using a thick flat steel plate between the press arbor and seal.
3. The correct assembly of the seal in the timing case brings the seal contracting spring side of the seal to the inside of the timing case.
4. Apply Multi-Mileage lubricant or the equivalent, not engine oil, to the seal lip before replacing the timing case.
5. If oil was leaking, check the crankshaft pulley diameter that runs inside the seal. This must be polished and free from scratches and burrs. A new pulley should always be installed if the existing one is damaged.

TIMING CHAIN AND SPROCKETS

Removal

1. Remove timing cover. Turn crankshaft to bring the timing marks together.
2. Remove timing chain automatic adjuster.
3. Remove the retainer bolt and plain washer from camshaft.
4. Pull camshaft sprocket off with a suitable puller and then remove both sprockets and chain together. The crankshaft sprocket is not a tight fit on the crankshaft.

Installation

1. When installing, turn No. 1 and 4 pistons to TDC so that the key is at the top of the crankshaft and the camshaft dowel is in the position shown.
2. Push crankshaft sprocket onto crankshaft far enough to allow the timing chain to be installed.
3. Install chain to crankshaft and camshaft sprocket so that the dots on the camshaft and crankshaft sprockets are in line while the chain is in tension on its driving side.

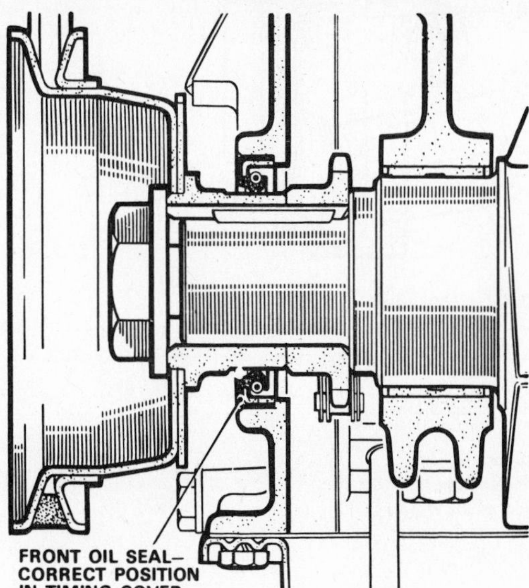

Timing cover oil seal position

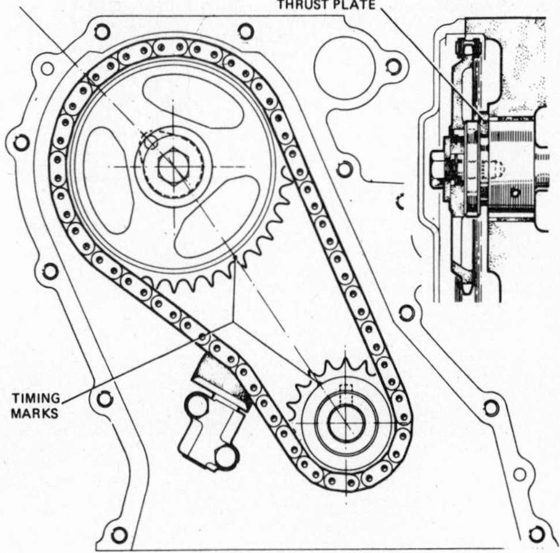

Alignment of timing marks

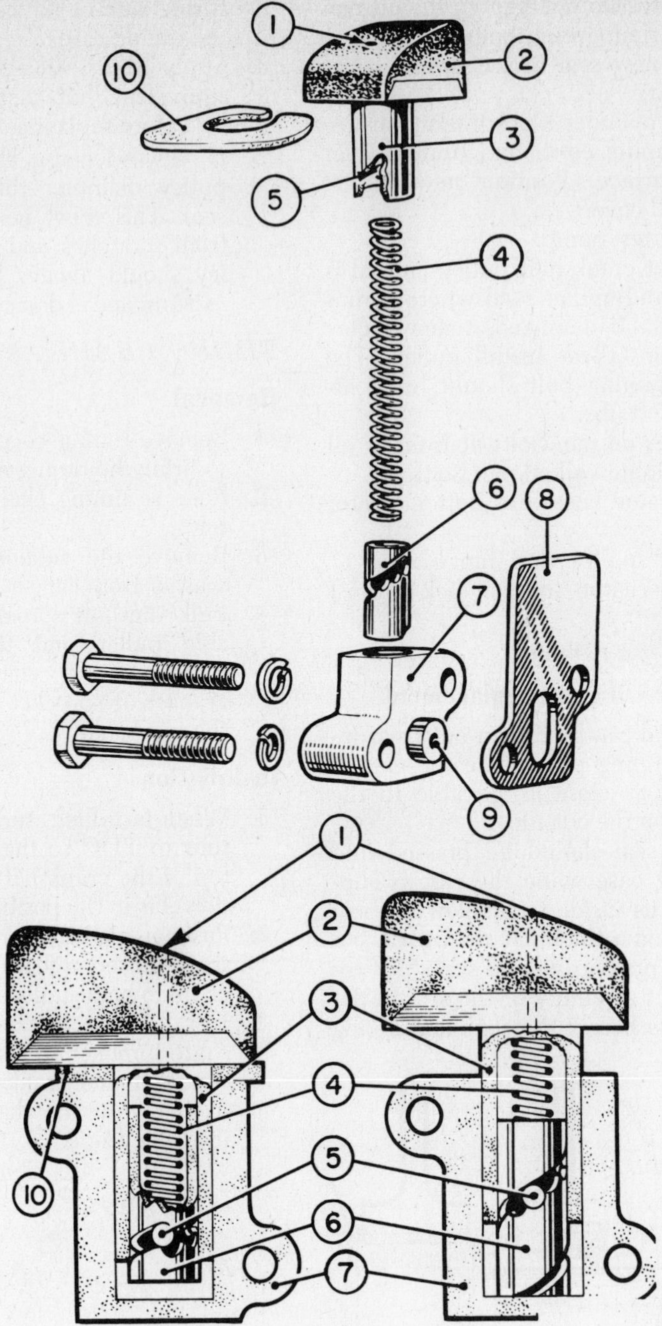

Timing chain automatic tensioner

1. Oil feed hole to timing chain
2. Slipper head
3. Slipper head plunger
4. Spring, compression type
5. Limit peg, inside plunger (3.)
6. Restraint cylinder
7. Chain tensioner body
8. Back plate
9. Oil feed hole
10. Cardboard packer

4. Pull camshaft sprocket into position with its attaching bolt and washer and push the crankshaft sprocket against its shoulder on the crankshaft. The camshaft sprocket must not be driven onto the camshaft because this can damage the camshaft thrust plate.
5. Tighten camshaft sprocket bolt to 34 ft. lbs.
6. Install chain tensioner, timing cover, and crankshaft pulley.

Timing Chain Tensioner

Removal

1. Remove timing cover.
2. Loosen the two bolts holding the tensioner to the engine.
3. Hold the tensioner together with the left thumb and first finger. Remove the two attaching bolts and lift off the tensioner and its back plate.
4. Release tensioner so that its slipper head comes out all the way.

If the rubber slipper head is worn deeper than 0.05″ (1.3mm.) or if there is any sign of the rubber wearing, the tensioner should be replaced.

Disassembly

The tensioner can be disassembled by lifting the slipper head out of the tensioner body and restraint cylinder and the spring out of the slipper head plunger. The restraint cylinder may have to be rotated counterclockwise.

Reassembly

1. Place spring in slipper head plunger.
2. Place restraint cylinder in spring. Push restraint cylinder into plunger, rotating counterclockwise to lock. The restraint cylinder should extend about ⅛″ from the slipper head plunger end.

Installation

Hold the slipper head in position and bolt the tensioner onto the engine. Then, release the slipper head so that it moves outward to tension the chain. Do not lift the chain as this may leave it too tight and cause excessive wear on the slipper head face. The chain will automatically be tensioned when the engine is started.

CAMSHAFT

Removal

The following procedure allows the camshaft to be taken out and replaced, with the engine in place, after removing the oil pan and oil pump. The camshaft cannot be removed while the oil pump is in place.

1. Drain radiator and cylinder block.
2. Disconnect battery.
3. Remove grille.
4. Disconnect throttle and choke cable, temperature sending unit, distributor low tension lead, and alternator leads. Disconnect vacuum advance hose at carburetor.
5. Disconnect water hoses and heater hoses at engine.
6. Remove radiator, fan blades, and fan pulley.
7. Disconnect exhaust pipe at exhaust manifold flange.
8. Remove rocker cover, rocker shaft, push rods, and cylinder head.
9. Drain oil pan.
10. Remove alternator.
11. Turn No. 4 cylinder to TDC on firing stroke and remove distributor. Note position of oil pump distributor drive slots.
12. Remove oil pan and oil pump.
13. Remove engine mounting nuts inside front crossmember.
14. Remove timing cover.
15. Disconnect fuel lines and remove fuel pump.
16. Remove camshaft sprocket bolt and washer.
17. Remove timing chain tensioner.
18. Withdraw camshaft sprocket from camshaft, using a suitable puller. Remove timing sprockets and chain.
19. Remove camshaft thrust washer and tappets.
20. Place a block under the front of the cylinder block oil pan face and, using a jack, raise the front of the engine high enough to allow the camshaft to be withdrawn through the grille opening.
21. Withdraw camshaft. This is easier if a long stud is screwed into the camshaft sprocket bolt thread.

Installation

1. Oil the camshaft journals and cams.
2. Place the camshaft carefully until its thrust face is flush with the cylinder block face against which the thrust plate is bolted. Install camshaft thrust plate.
3. After replacing the camshaft thrust

plate, the camshaft end play should be checked. The end play must not exceed .004-.009″. Oversize thrust plates are available.

4. Install timing sprockets and chain.
5. Install oil pump as under Oil Pump Installation.
6. Install remaining items removed.
7. Adjust ignition timing.
8. Check valve clearance.

Camshaft Bearings

These bearings have a very long life and normally are changed only when the cylinder block is reconditioned. Bearings are prefinished and do not need reaming. They must be pulled out, and pulled in, with a special tool.

The following operations must be performed before the bearings can be pulled out.

1. Remove engine.
2. Remove clutch, flywheel, cylinder head, tappets, timing gears, oil pump and camshaft.
3. Using a long drift, drive out the rear camshaft bearing end cup.
4. Pull out the bearings.

Each camshaft bearing has one or more oil holes. These holes must line up with the oil feed drillings in the camshaft bearing bores after the bearings have been pulled into position. All bearings must be installed with their small notch toward the front of the block.

To install new camshaft bearings with special tool:

1. Place center bearing in tool and install.
2. Remove the tool, check that the bearing oil hole lines up to the oil hole in the cylinder block, and that the oil cross groove points to the center of the tappets adjacent to the center bearing.
3. Install remaining shells the same way. Align the front bearing so its two oil holes line up to the two oil holes in the bearing bore and the rear bearing to the single oil hole in the bearing bore.
4. After the bearings have been installed, a new oil seal cup should be driven into its recess at the rear of the rear camshaft bearing.

PISTONS AND CONNECTING RODS

The pistons and connecting rods must be assembled as shown in order that the .06″ offset piston pin be on the right (thrust) side. The rods are numbered on the camshaft side. If the rod nuts can be screwed on with the fingers, they must be replaced.

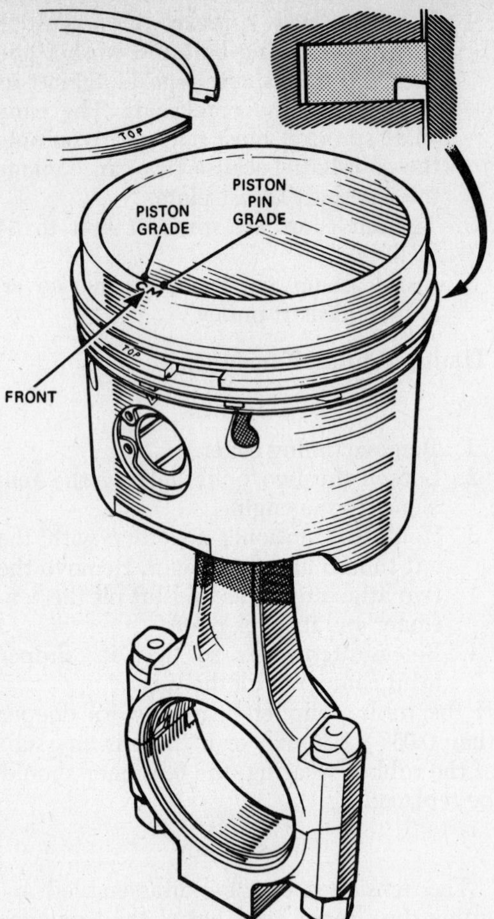

Piston and rings correctly assembled to connecting rod

Piston and Cylinder Bore Grading System

The pistons and cylinder bores are graded A, B, C, or D. The variation between each grade diameter is .0004″ (.010mm.) and the total difference between the highest and lowest cylinder bore limits is .0016″ (.040mm.). By means of the grading system, the correct piston fit is obtained when pistons are installed in new cylinder bores having similar grade letters to the pistons. The difference between similar grade letters for the cylinder block and piston is the required clearance for the piston.

Cylinder bore grade A		*Piston grade A*		*Piston clearance*
3.3910″	less	3.3887″	=	.0023″
(86.131 mm)	less	(86.073 mm)	=	(.058 mm)
3.3906″	less	3.3891″	=	.0015″
(86.121 mm)	less	(86.083 mm)	=	(.038 mm)

Piston clearance is .0019″ (.048mm.) at the piston grade checking diameter which is ⅝″ (16 mm.) above the lowest point of the piston.

The cylinder grade letters are stamped on two vertical machined faces at the front and rear ends of the cylinder block, just below the cylinder head gasket face, on the exhaust manifold side of the engine.

The piston grade is stamped on the top face of each piston.

LUBRICATION SYSTEM

Oil Filter

The throw-away full flow oil filter screws onto a threaded sleeve connected to the main oil gallery on the lower right front of the cylinder block.

Oil from the oil pump enters through eight port holes into the filter body and passes through the filter cartridge from the outside to the center. Then it leaves through the oil filter threaded end to the main oil gallery.

The inlet ports on the underside of the filters are shrouded by a flexible anti-drain valve.

The throw-away filter unit must be changed every 5,000 miles.

Replacement

1. The rubber ring on the filter base tends to stick to the cylinder block. If the filter cannot be removed by hand, it can be unscrewed with a 1″ socket.
2. Clean the cylinder block and lubricate the ring on the bottom of the filter with clean engine oil.
3. Screw the filter into position until it just touches the seat on the cylinder block. Then screw the filter a further two thirds of a turn by hand only.
4. Run the engine and check for oil leaks.

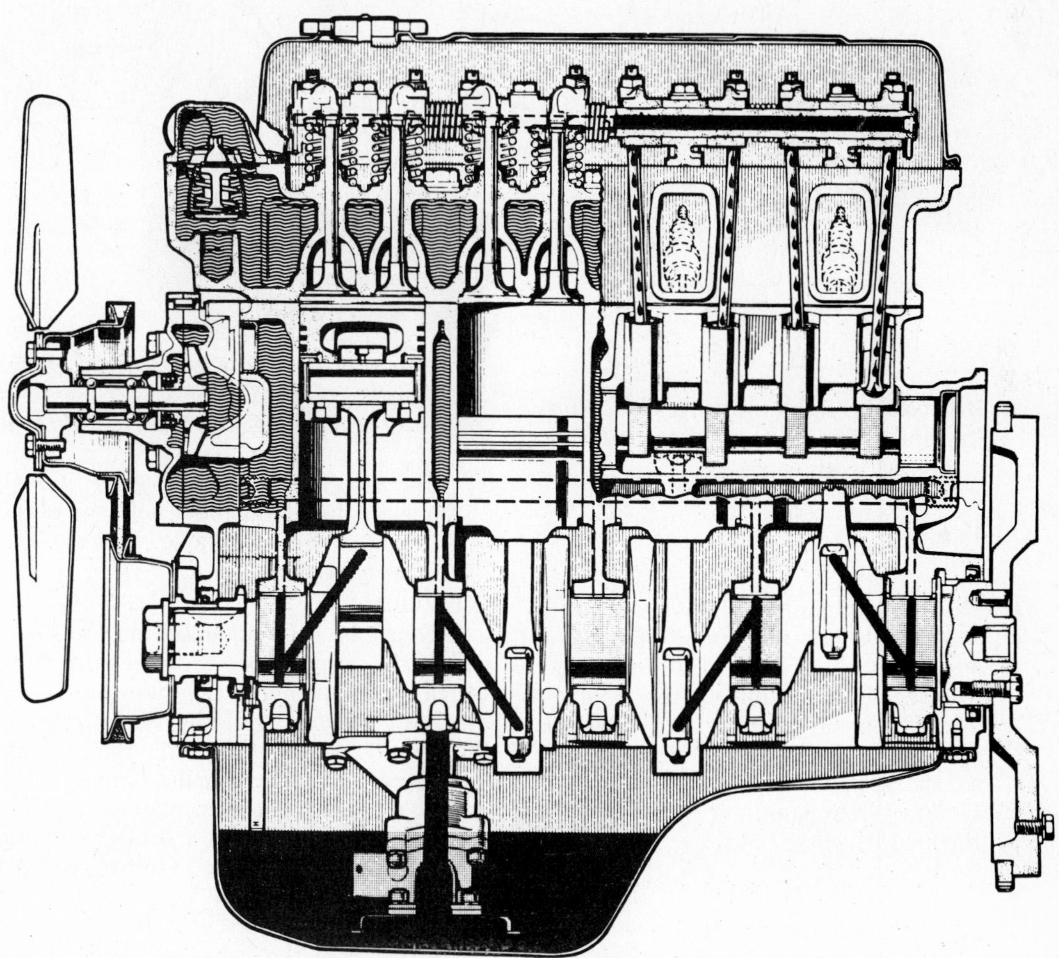

Engine cutaway

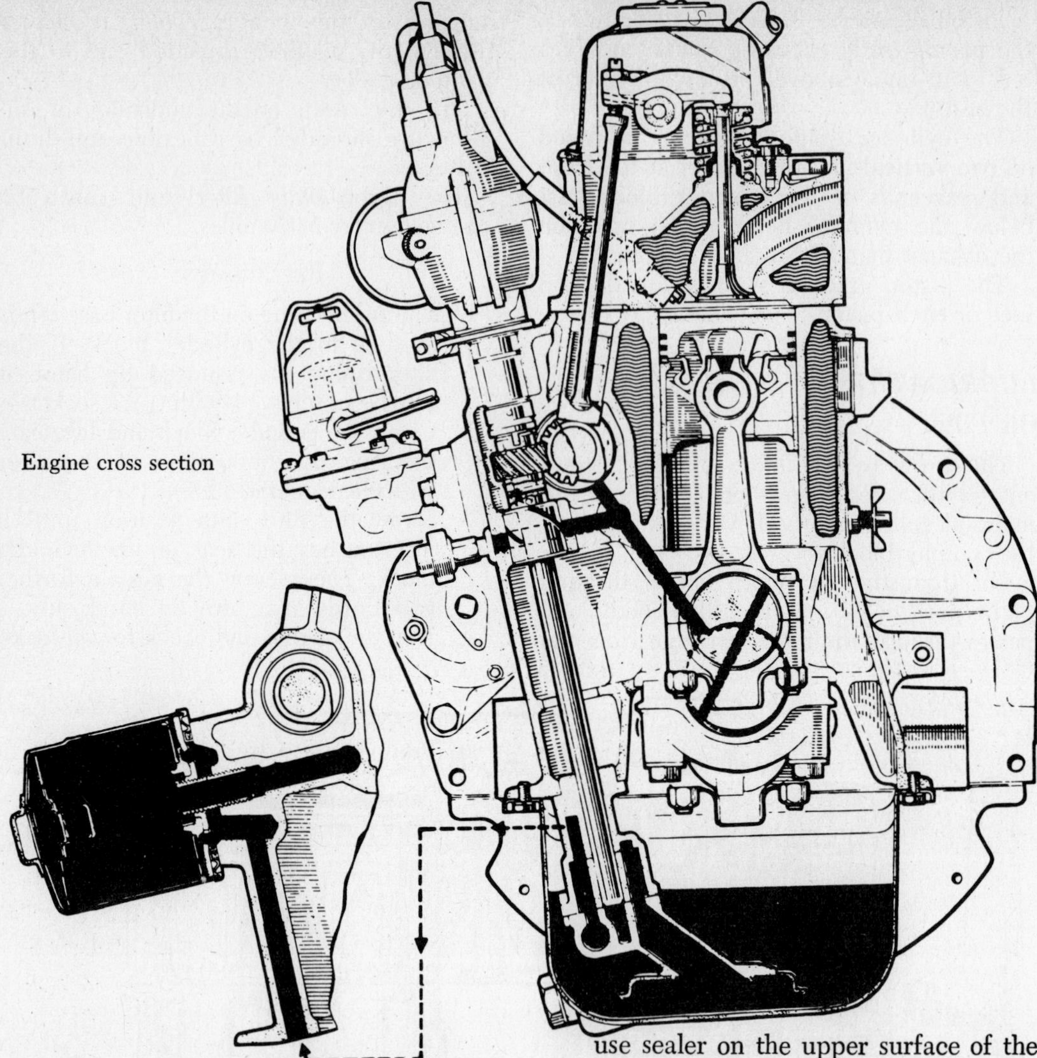

Engine cross section

5. If necessary, tighten filter a little more by hand. The filter must not be tightened with a wrench.

Oil Pan

Removal

1. The front of the car should be raised and stands placed under the body members or blocks placed under the wheels. When jacking up the front of the car, be sure that the jack is under the center of the cross member, and not the oil pan.
2. Drain oil from pan.
3. Remove attaching bolts.

Installation

1. Clean the pan thoroughly.
2. Flatten the pan surface around the bolt holes if the pan surface is bent.
3. Stick a new gasket on oil pan. Do not use sealer on the upper surface of the gasket.
4. Before installing the pan, check that the oil pump intake screen is clean. The screen can be removed by taking out its two attaching bolts, washing the filter in a suitable cleaner, and blowing it dry.

Oil Pump

A four-lobe rotor mounted on the lower end of the oil pump shaft drives a ring into which are machined five internal lobes. The outer diameter of the ring rotates in the circular bore of the oil pump body, which is offset from the main shaft.

The action of the four-lobe rotor inside the five-lobe ring creates a strong pumping force by progressively increasing and decreasing the clearance between each set of lobes. The pump itself is driven by helical gears from the camshaft. These gears are lubricated by oil thrown out from three spiral grooves in the journal below the

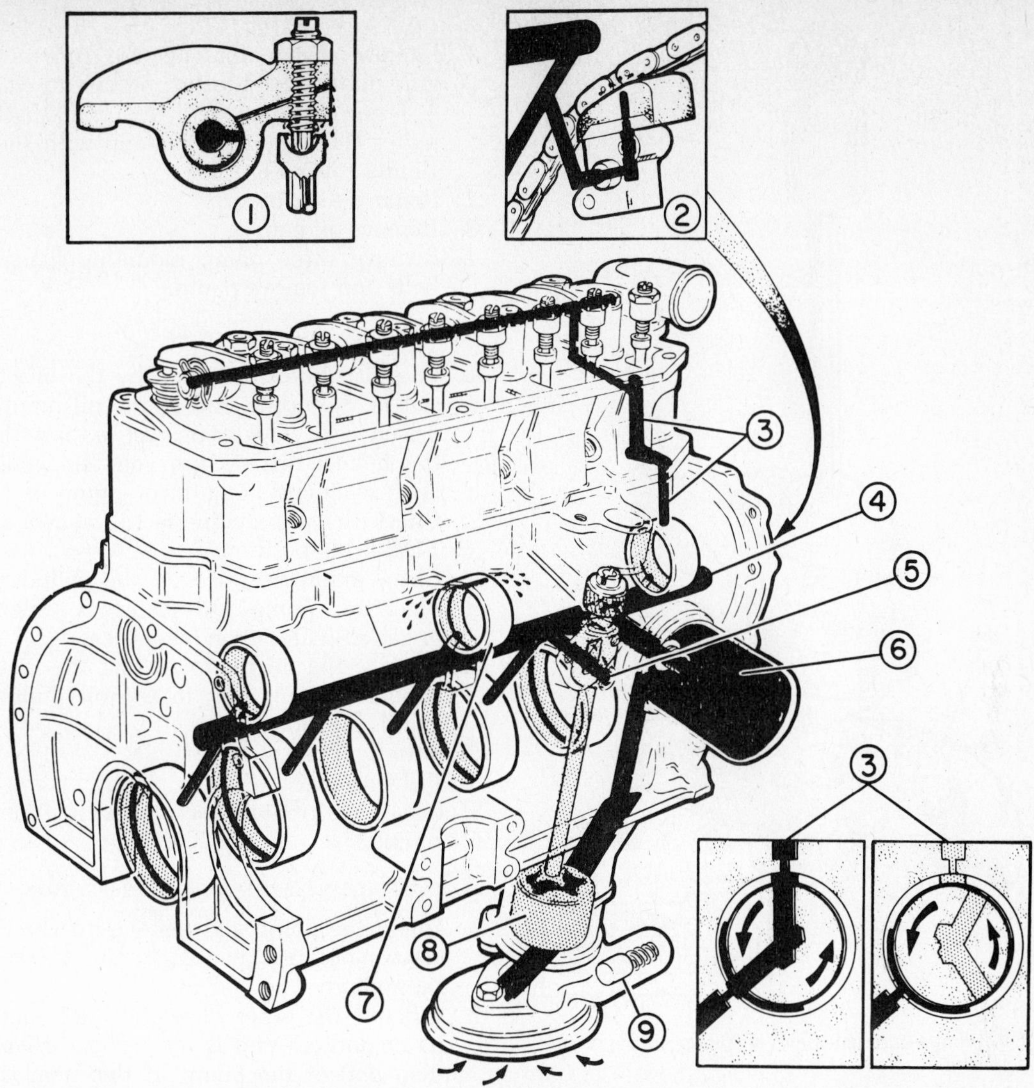

Oil passages in cylinder block and cylinder head

1. Inset—oil feed from rocker shaft to push rod cup
2. Inset—oil feed to timing chain automatic tensioner
3. Oil feed to rocker shaft
4. Oil gallery
5. Oil pressure warning light switch feed
6. Full flow oil filter
7. Oil feed groove in center camshaft bearing to adjacent cams and tappets
8. Oil pump
9. Oil pressure relief valve in pump
10. Inset—oil feeding through front camshaft journal from gallery (4.) to rocker shaft feed drilling (3.)
11. Inset—oil feed to rocker shaft cut off by rotation of front camshaft journal

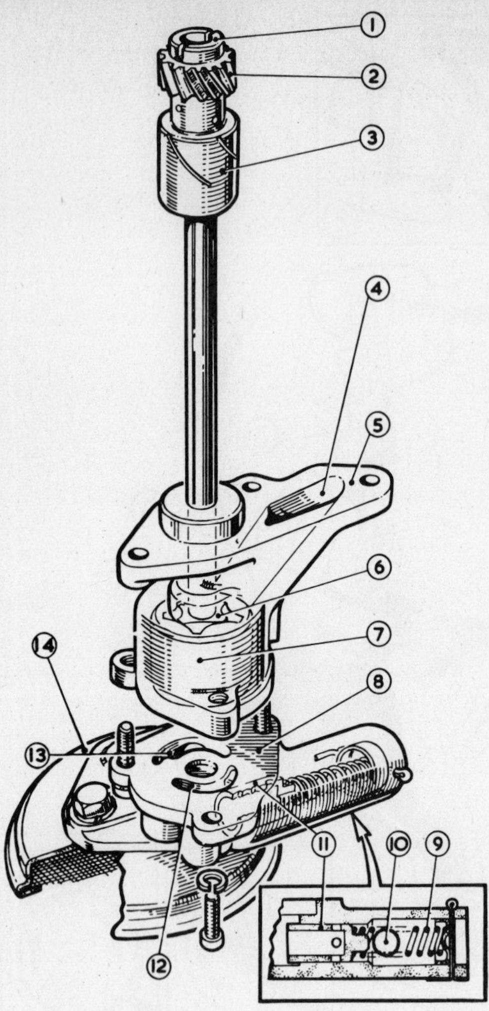

Oil pump—internal view of pump and pressure relief valve

1. Distributor offset drive slot
2. Oil pump driven gear
3. Three oil grooves feeding oil to gear (2.)
4. Oil feed channel to cylinder block oil gallery
5. Oil pump body
6. Four lobe rotor and pump shaft
7. Five lobe driven rotor
8. Oil pump base
9. Oil pressure relief valve spring
10. Oil pressure relief valve discharge hole (shown in this position for illustration only)
11. Oil pressure relief valve piston

pump driven gear. The oil pump intake screen usually does not need cleaning. Whenever the oil pan is removed, inspect and clean this screen, which is held to the pump intake by two bolts.

The screen should be washed in a suitable solvent and blown dry. Do not dry with rags or towels.

Removal

1. Remove distributor cap and turn engine until distributor is pointing to No. 4 firing position and the crankshaft pulley TDC pointer lines up with the timing cover TDC line.
2. Remove distributor.
3. Remove oil pan.
4. Remove three pump mounting flange bolts and remove pump.

Installation

1. The distributor is driven by the offset slot in the upper end of the oil pump driven gear. This gear must mesh with the helical driving gear on the camshaft when installing the oil pump.
2. Check that the engine is still at No. 4 TDC firing position.
3. Clean mating surface on the cylinder block and pump. Do not use a sealer or gasket material on these faces.
4. Replace the oil pump so that the distributor driving slot in the oil pump gear is positioned correctly.
5. Install oil pan.
6. Fill with oil.
7. Install distributor and check ignition timing.

Disassembly, Cleaning and Inspection

1. Invert the pump and remove the three screws holding the base plate to the pump body.
2. Lift out the outer rotor ring. See that its chamfered end is toward the drive gear end of the pump. If this item is dropped, it can crack easily.
3. Remove all oil from the inside of the pump body and both rotors. Replace outer rotor with its chamfered end towards the gear end of the pump.

The following clearances should be checked:

4. End clearance between the inner and outer rotor ring and pump body. The maximum and minimum are .003″ (.075mm.) and .001″ (.025mm.) when measured with a feeler gauge and straight edge.
5. Side clearance between the top of the lobes on the inner and outer rotor. The maximum and minimum clearances are .006″ (.15mm.) and .001″ (.025mm.).
6. Clearance between the outside of the outer rotor and pump body must not be greater than .008″ (.20mm.) and not less than .005″ (.125mm.). If any

of these clearances are larger than the maximum figure, a replacement pump should be installed.

The piston type relief valve and its spring can be removed for cleaning after removing the cotter pin holding the spring retainer in position.

Clutch and Transmission

CLUTCH

The clutch is a cable operated diaphragm spring unit.

Clutch Linkage Free Play

Check that the free play of the clutch linkage is no more than 3/16″. Adjust if necessary. Pedal free play should be .8″.

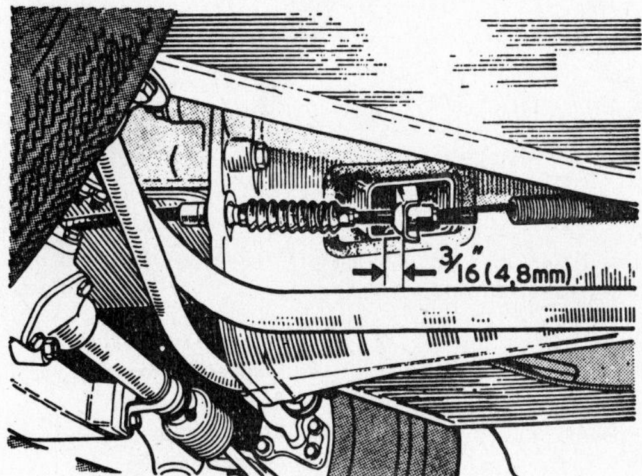

Clutch control linkage free play measurement

Clutch Removal

1. Remove the transmission.
2. Loosen and back off clutch cover attaching bolts one or two turns at a time, in succession, to avoid bending cover flange.
3. Remove the attachment bolts and clutch cover assembly complete with the disc.

Clutch Installation

1. Apply SAE 30 engine oil sparingly to the pilot bushing in the crankshaft.
2. Using a clutch disc aligning arbor or a spare transmission drive pinion, locate the disc in position against the flywheel with the marking "this side to flywheel" inboard.
3. Locate the clutch cover assembly on the dowels. Insert the attaching bolts and tighten evenly and in succession to 16 ft. lb.
4. Remove the centering tool.
5. Install the transmission.

Clutch Cable

REMOVAL

1. Remove the locknut and cable adjuster nut from the release lever end.

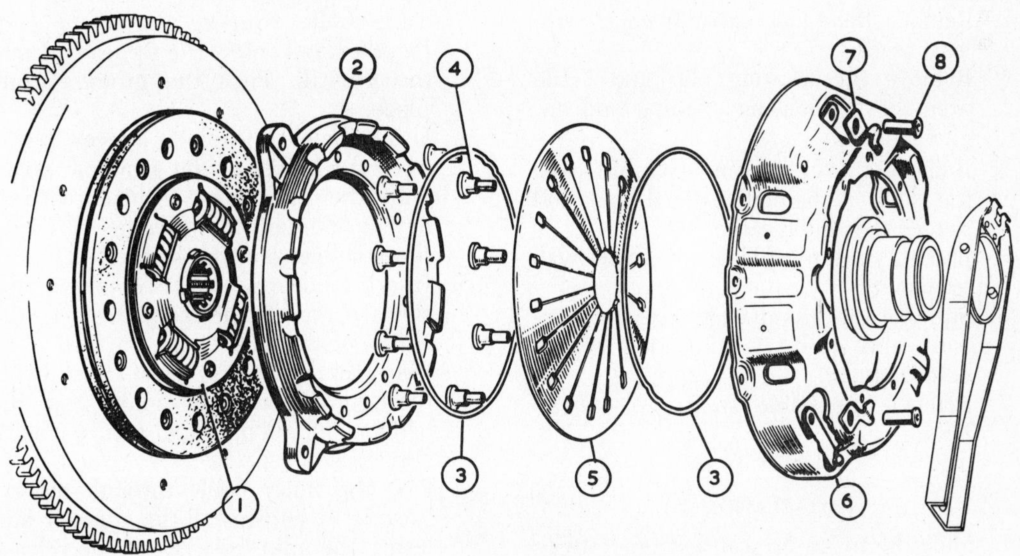

Clutch assembly

1. Driven plate
2. Pressure plate
3. Fulcrum ring
4. Shouldered rivet
5. Diaphragm spring
6. Cover plate
7. Retractor clip
8. Rivet

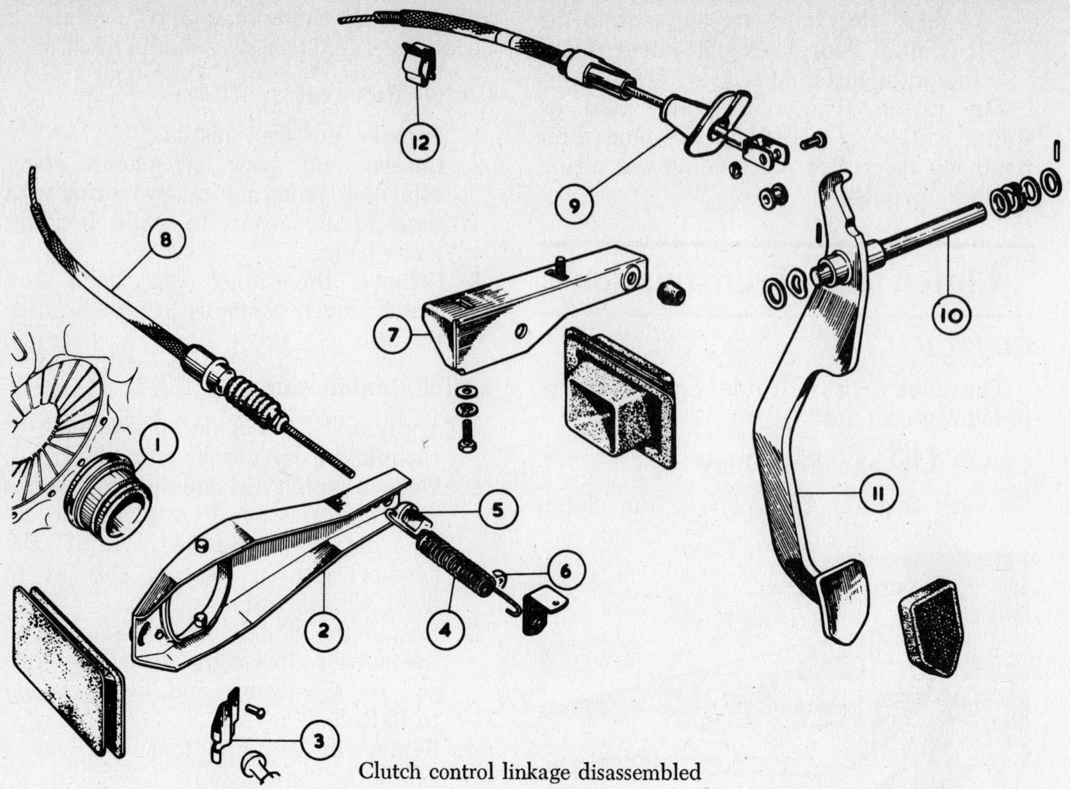

Clutch control linkage disassembled

1. Release bearing
2. Release lever
3. Spring clip
4. Return spring
5. Adjuster nut
6. Locknut
7. Pedal stop plate
8. Clutch cable
9. Bulkhead grommet
10. Pedal cross-shaft
11. Clutch pedal
12. Attachment clip

2. Remove the inner cable from the release lever.
3. Remove the locating clip and cable from the bellhousing opening and engine mounts.
4. Remove the clevis pin assembly from the clevis at the clutch pedal hook and detach the clutch cable.
5. pull the outer cable from the firewall grommet.
6. Squeeze the grommet next to the firewall and pull it into the engine compartment.
7. Remove the cable from the firewall opening.

Installation

1. Slide the nylon firewall grommet away from the outer cable onto the inner cable.
2. From the engine compartment, insert the inner cable through the firewall.
3. With the grommet around the inner cable only, squeeze the lower ends together and insert the upper end into the firewall. Push the grommet into place.
4. Using the outer cable as a lever, gently force the halves of the grommet apart. Slide the outer cable in place with its key in line with the grommet slot until the grommet seats in the firewall.
5. Insert the clevis pin assembly in the clevis to fasten the inner cable to the clutch pedal hook.
6. Pass the lower end of the cable through the engine mount and the bellhousing opening and secure it with clip.
7. Pass the inner cable through the release lever and install the adjuster nut.
8. Using the adjuster nut, set the release lever/pedal free play to 3/16″.
9. Install and tighten the locknut to 3 ft.lb.
10. Check that the free play at the clutch pedal is .8″.

Release Lever and Bearing

REMOVAL AND INSTALLATION

1. Remove the transmission.
2. Disconnect the return spring from the release lever.
3. Move the release lever in the direction illustrated to disconnect the lever and spring clip from the pivot.
4. Remove the release lever and bearing from the drive pinion retainer.
5. Disconnect the release bearing from the release lever.
6. Installation is the reverse of the removal procedure.

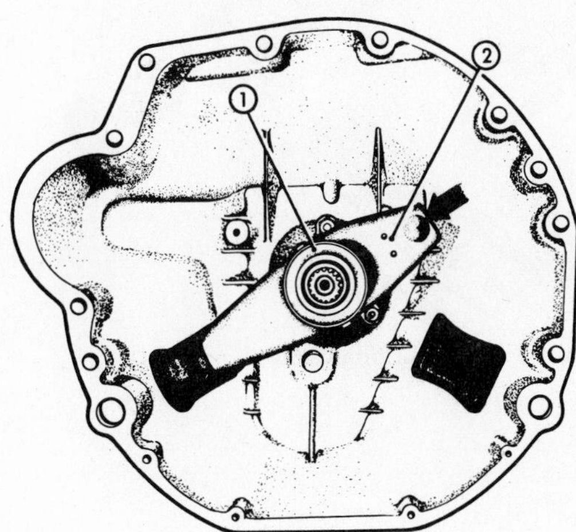

Release lever and bearing removal

1. Release bearing
2. Release lever

Clutch Pedal

REMOVAL AND INSTALLATION

1. Remove the clevis pin from the clevis to disconnect the clutch cable from the pedal assembly.
2. Remove the pedal stop plate along with the stoplight switch to gain access to the pedal cross shaft.
3. Tap out the shaft pin next to the clutch pedal. Remove the washers.
4. Move the cross-shaft through the support bracket toward the brake pedal.
5. Disconnect the clutch pedal from the cross-shaft.
6. Installation is the reverse of the removal procedure. Check that the free play at the clutch pedal is 8″.

MANUAL TRANSMISSION

The unit is built into an aluminum case which is integral with the clutch housing.

There are four synchronized forward gears and a reverse gear, which are selected by a remote control lever integral with the extension housing.

Constant mesh gears are used for 1st, 2nd and 3rd, while 4th gear is direct drive.

The oil filler/level plug is on the left side, about half way down the case, and the drain plug is at the bottom on the same side. The recommended lubricant is SAE 30 oil.

Removal

1. Place the car on a hoist and drain the oil.
2. Disconnect the battery ground cable. Disconnect the throttle rod from the carburetor by removing the retaining clip from the rod and the rod from the coupling.
3. Remove electrical leads and bolts holding the starter motor. Remove the starter motor.
4. Remove the console.
5. Remove the gearshift lever cover and the lever.
6. Remove the driveshaft rear coupling nuts and bolts and ease the flanges apart; then pull the shaft off the mainshaft spline.
7. Disconnect the speedometer drive cable.
8. Disconnect the clutch release cable by removing the locknut and the adjuster nut; then move the cable forward from the release lever.
9. Remove the inspection cover from the forward lower portion of the clutch housing.
10. Disconnect the exhaust pipe flange from the manifold.
11. Disconnect the wires from the backup light switch.
12. Place a small jack under the front of the engine, using a piece of wood as protection for the engine. (This prevents the engine from tilting forward after the transmission has been removed).
13. Remove the rear support mounting from the body and lower the transmission.
14. Remove the nuts and bolts from the upper part of the clutch housing and remove the transmission.

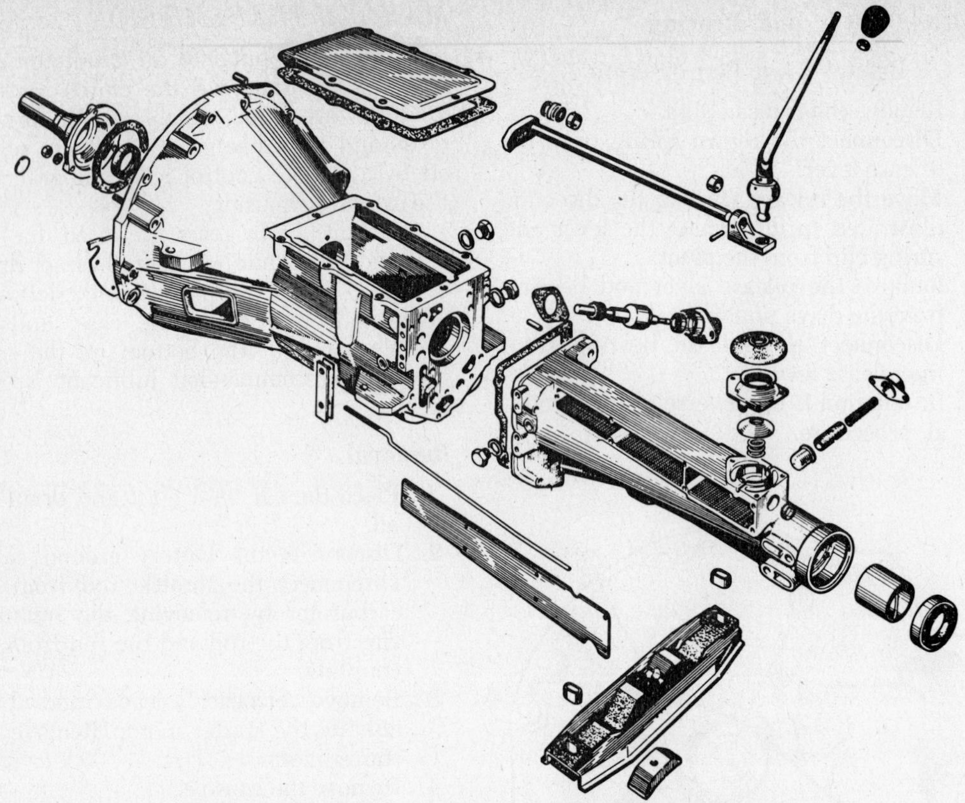

Manual transmission case and gearshift arrangement disassembled

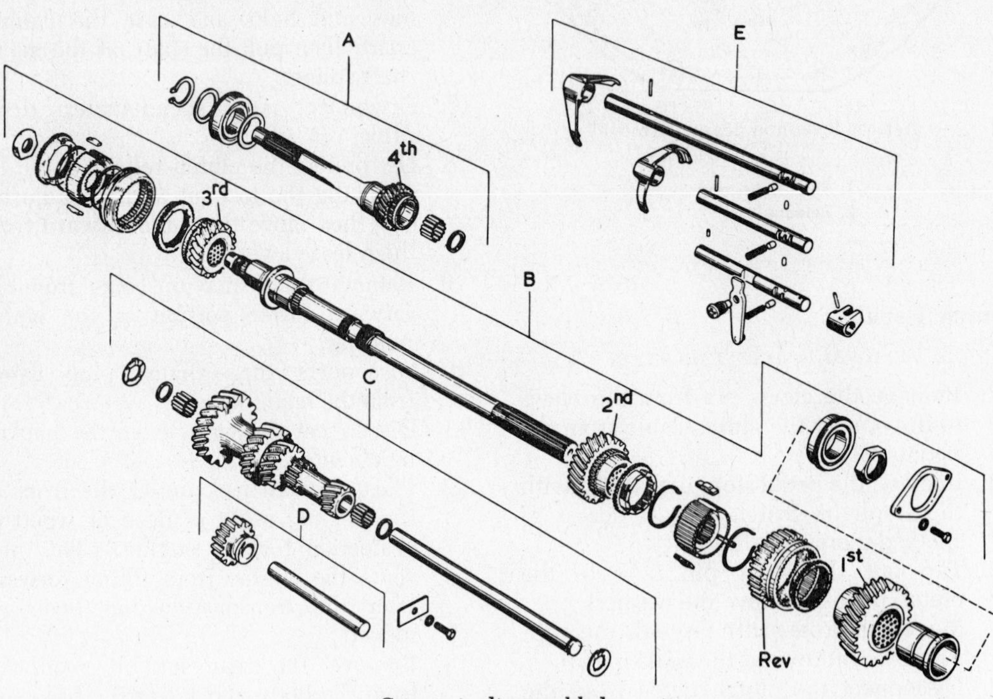

Gear train disassembled

A. Drive pinion assembly
B. Mainshaft assembly
C. Countershaft gear assembly
D. Reverse idler
E. Shift fork and shaft assembly

Installation

1. Installation is the reverse of the removal procedure.
2. If the clutch has been disturbed, the disc must be centered.
3. Raise transmission on a jack until drive pinion is in line with clutch disc.
4. Move transmission forward and turn output shaft, with transmission in gear, to align splines.
5. Install attaching bolts before removing jack.
6. Tighten to 30 ft.lbs.
7. The clutch pedal free travel must be reset to .8".
8. Refill the transmission with SAE 30 oil.

Transmission Disassembly

1. Clean the outside of the transmission.
2. Remove two bolts and remove the reverse gear detent spring and plunger.
3. Take out the two bolts and remove the speedometer gear housing and gear.
4. Remove the five bolts holding the extension housing, noting the location of the longer bolts.
5. The extension housing can be removed after the gearshift lever shaft has been turned counterclockwise to the stop and moved rearward as far as possible to disengage it from the three selector shafts.
6. Unless the extension housing oil seal has been removed, be careful not to damage the seal on the mainshaft spline.
7. Remove the oil feed tube which is a push fit into both the extension housing and the rear of the transmission.
8. Remove the bolts and lift off top cover and gasket.
9. Remove the two bolts holding the detent spring cover plate at the left rear top corner of the transmission case and remove the plate together with the springs and plungers.
10. Using a punch, drive out the roll pin holding 3rd/4th shift fork and remove both.
11. Remove 1st/2nd shift fork and shaft by the same method.
12. Slide out interlock plungers from the case between 3rd/4th and 1st/2nd shift shafts, and from 1st/2nd and reverse.
13. Before removing the mainshaft, check the end-play of the 1st, 2nd and 3rd gears by inserting feelers between the gear and its flange.

Clearances should be:

1st gear	.005- .0085"
2nd gear	.004- .0075"
3rd gear	.004- .0075"

14. Engage any two gears to lock rotation.
15. Remove the mainshaft rear bearing clamp plate.
16. Remove the mainshaft rear self locking nut, and return gears to the neutral position.
17. At the rear of unit, remove the bolt and locking plate holding the countershaft and reverse gear shafts.

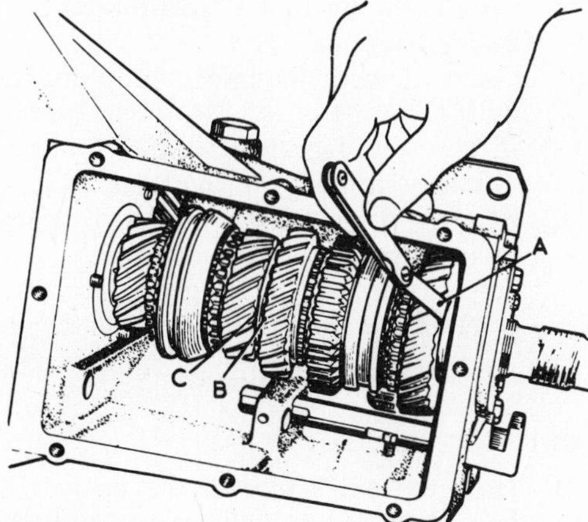

Checking gear end play at points A, B, and C

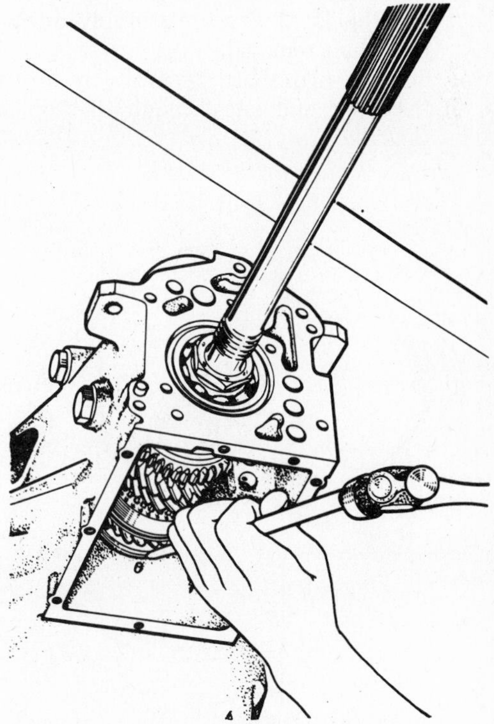
Tapping out the front bearing

18. Engage a long dummy countershaft with the front end of the original shaft and push in, pushing out the original. Then, countershaft gear can be lowered into the bottom of the case.
19. Remove the clutch release lever by sliding it off the pivot post in the direction illustrated under Release Lever and Bearing Removal.
20. Remove the nuts and the front bearing retainer.
21. Tap the drive pinion bearing forward from inside the transmission until there is a gap of 1/8″ (3.2mm.) between the housing face and the bearing retainer ring, taking care not to damage the oil slinger. Place two angled levers behind the retainer ring and pry bearing forward and free from housing.
22. Support the mainshaft at its forward end and, using a mallet, carefully drive it forward until it is free of the bearing.
23. Remove the rear bearing from the case by tapping rearward and prying out with two angled levers.
24. Using any suitable dummy spacer (length 1″ [25.4 mm.] with 1¼″ [31.8 mm.] inside diameter) placed over the rear of the mainshaft, install the original rear nut finger tight to retain the 1st/2nd gear assembly during mainshaft removal.
25. Remove mainshaft assembly by lifting the front end out through the top of the case.

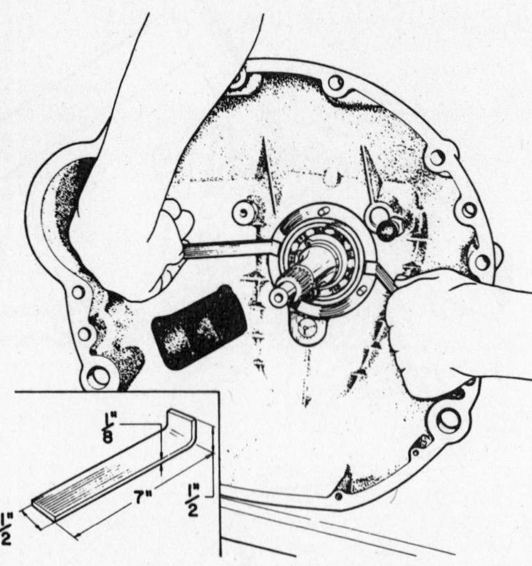

Prying out the front bearing

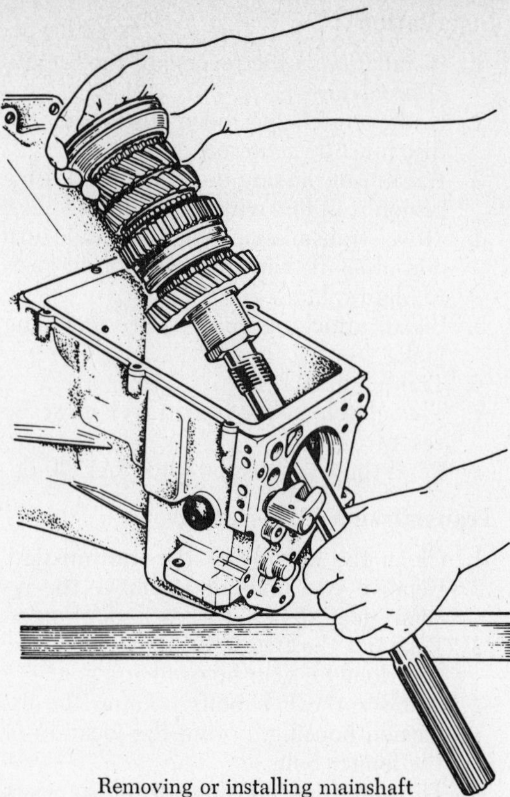
Removing or installing mainshaft

26. Lift out countershaft gear assembly with the two thrust washers.
27. Remove the reverse selector pivot bolt from the left side of the transmission to release the fulcrum lever inside, which can then be lifted out.
28. Slide out the shift shaft.
29. Remove the reverse shift shaft guide peg.
30. Install special tool RG-3072-3 on reverse idler shaft, engaging the locking plate slot. Tighten the tool clamp bolt. Install adapter tool W-313 followed by a slide hammer.
31. Using the slide hammer, bump out the shaft.

CAUTION: Driving out from the front will cause damage to both the shaft and case.

32. Remove drive pinion retainer oil seal by prying out. Push in a new seal. Smear the seal with grease to ease assembly on the drive pinion shaft.

Drive Pinion

Inspection

1. Hold the outer race of the bearing in one hand and spin the shaft with the other. See if there is any roughness.

2. If, for any reason, the bearing has to be removed, it should be replaced.
3. To wash out the bearing, use clean solvent and blow out with compressed air, holding the air line at 90° to the bearing.

CAUTION: Do not allow the air to spin the bearing.

4. Oil the bearing immediately.
5. Check the pinion pilot which fits in the crankshaft pilot bearing.
6. The splines on the shaft should be examined for excessive wear.
7. Examine the 4th gear teeth and cone for wear and pitting.
8. Check the counterbore which houses the needle rollers for wear or pitting.
9. Examine the needle rollers for wear or pitting.
10. If any one needle roller shows signs of either condition, the complete set of (23) rollers must be replaced.
11. If the snap-ring retaining the bearing to the shaft is removed, replace it.

Disassembly

1. Remove the snap-ring and plain washer holding the bearing to the shaft. Press off drive pinion shaft along with oil slinger.

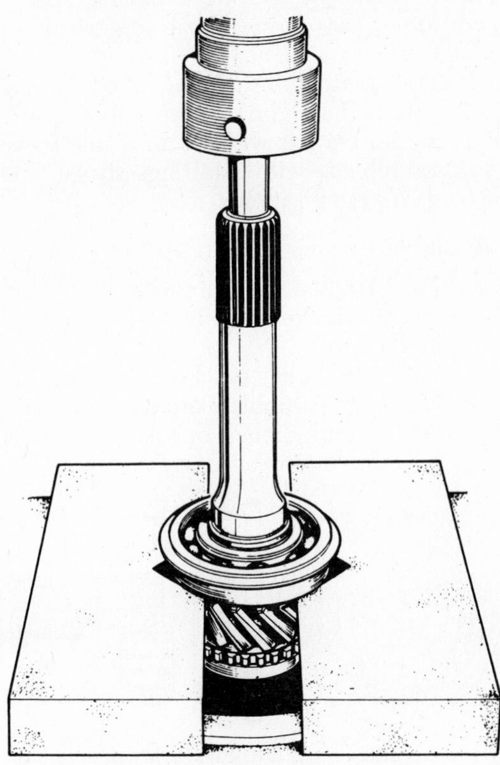

Pressing off the pinion shaft bearing

2. Remove outer retaining ring from bearing.

Assembly

1. Assemble the retaining ring to bearing.
2. Assemble oil slinger to drive pinion shaft followed by the bearing with the retaining ring side up. Press into position.
3. Install a plain (selective fit) washer on the shaft. Then, using the outside of the snap-ring in the groove at one side of the shaft, measure the clearance between the snap-ring and the washer. This should be .006-.010″.
4. If necessary, install a new washer to get the correct clearance, then install a new snap-ring.
5. Apply a small quantity of grease to the counterbore and assemble the 23 needle rollers followed by the spacer ring.

Countershaft Gear

Disassembly

Remove dummy countershaft spacer rings and needle rollers (26 each end).

Inspection

1. Examine gear teeth for wear or pitting.
2. Clean and examine the counterbore at each end for wear or pitting.
3. Examine the needle rollers for wear or pitting. If any needle roller shows signs of either condition, the complete set of rollers must be replaced.
4. Examine spacer rings, thrust washers, and countershaft. Before selecting thrust washers, see Transmission Assembly.

Assembly

1. Apply a small quantity of grease to the counterbore at each end of the countershaft gear.
2. Assemble the 26 needle rollers on each end of the shaft.
3. Install one steel spacer ring to each end. Slide in the dummy countershaft.

Mainshaft

Disassembly

1. Take care that all items removed are replaced in their original positions on assembly.
2. Remove rear nut and dummy spacer

and remove 1st/2nd gear assembly from the mainshaft.

3. Remove the front self locking nut and discard. To aid in the removal and installation of the mainshaft front nut, mount the front coupling of the driveshaft between soft jaws in a vise and insert the mainshaft in the coupling. Do not clamp the shaft directly in a vise.
4. Remove 3rd/4th synchronizer hub assemly and the 3rd gear assembly.

Inspection

1. Check the mainshaft for wear at the pilot, the splines, and the ground surfaces on which 2nd and 3rd gear bushings operate.
2. Examine the bushings for wear and scoring.
3. Check gear teeth for wear and pitting.
4. Examine cones for glazing or ridging.

Assembly

1. With all the parts clean, lightly coat all bearings with oil.
2. Install 2nd gear with the flat side of the gear toward the rear face of the mainshaft flange. Place 2nd gear stop ring on the cone.
3. The 1st/2nd synchronizer assembly is installed with the selector groove in the sliding sleeve to the rear.
4. Place the spacer on 1st gear with the flange to the flat side of the gear. Install both on the mainshaft with the cone and stop ring toward the synchronizer hub.
5. Check that both stop-rings are correctly aligned and held in position with a dummy spacer and the original nut removed earlier.
6. 3rd gear is assembled with the flat side of the gear to the front side of the mainshaft flange. Place 3rd gear stop ring on the cone.
7. The 3rd/4th synchronizer hub is installed on the spline with the wide face boss toward 3rd gear and the selector groove in the sliding sleeve toward 4th gear.
8. Install the self locking nut with the plain side toward the synchronizer hub and tighten to 70 ft.lbs.

Synchronizer Assemblies

Disassembly

1. Before disassembly, mark all parts so they may be reassembled in their original positions.
2. Remove the sliding sleeve, detach the shifting struts and remove the two springs from the hubs.

Inspection

1. Check the stop-rings for concentricity by blueing the corresponding gear cone and rotating the stop-ring on the cone. A blue marking should show evenly on the tops of the grooves in the ring. With the stop-ring engaged on the cone, there should be a minimum clearance of .010″ (.254mm.) between the stop ring gear teeth and the front of the gear dog teeth. Otherwise, a replacement ring should be used.
2. Check the fit of each sliding sleeve on the hub. The sleeve should slide freely, but should not have more than .010″ (.254mm.) play on the splines.
3. Check the condition of the chamfers on the sliding internal teeth. Each face should be flat and smooth.
4. See that the gear dog teeth clear the roots of the sliding sleeve teeth. If contact is made, the tops of the teeth should be carefully filed until a clearance is obtained.
5. Replace any shifting struts (in sets of three) or springs that are weak or worn.
6. Test that the stop-ring slides freely within the sliding sleeve and the hub recess. Do this with the hub and sleeve assembled with shifting struts and springs in position.

Assembly

1. The 1st/2nd synchronizer hub and sliding sleeve can be assembled as marked.
2. The 3rd/4th synchronizer sliding sleeve is assembled on the hub with the selector groove opposite the wide face boss on the hub.

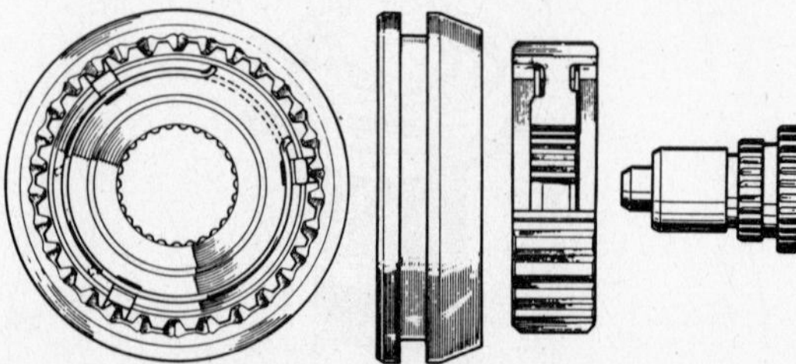

Correct positioning of 3rd/4th synchromesh hub to mainshaft and shift strut springs

3. Install sliding sleeve on hub. Insert the shifting struts and retain with springs installed with the ends evenly spaced between two different shifting struts.

SHIFT FORKS

1. Examine the fork ends for wear. If worn excessively or unevenly, the forks should be replaced.
2. Examine shaft for excessive wear, particularly at the interlock and detent plunger grooves.
3. Inspect the plungers for pitting, wear, and flat spots.
4. Check for any broken or weak springs.

REVERSE GEAR

1. Examine gear teeth for wear or pitting.
2. Check gear shaft and shift lever for serviceability.

EXTENSION HOUSING

Gearshift Lever

1. Check gearshift lever seat and engagement slot for wear.
2. Examine the shift shaft and lever for wear; do not remove unless replacing parts.

SHIFT SHAFT

Removal

1. Remove the screws and the shift shaft cover.
2. Using a small punch, partly drive out the roll pin holding the yoke end to the shaft. Then, line up the protruding end of the pin with the forward screw hole for the reverse plunger assembly to enable the pin to be driven right through the hole, being careful not to damage the threads.

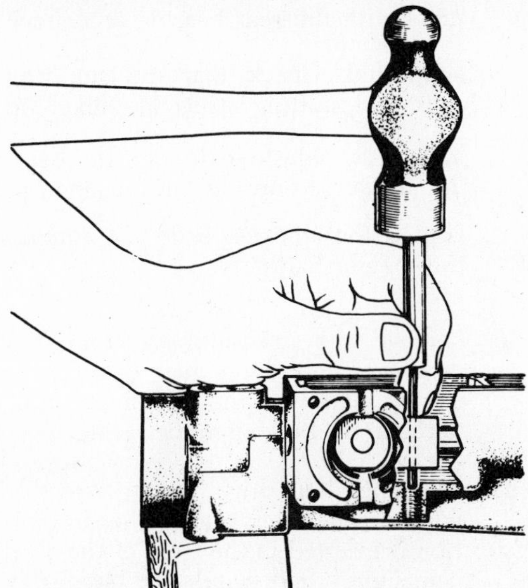

Removing roll pin from gearshift shaft

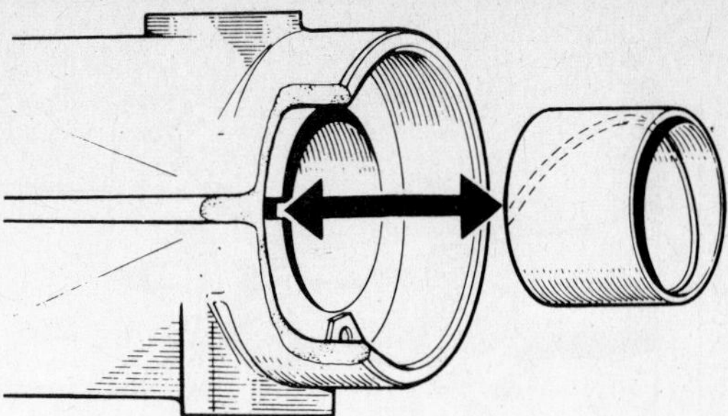

Extension housing bushing alignment

Installation

1. Insert the shaft and locate the yoke end on the shaft with a pin through the forward screw hole of the reverse plunger assembly.
2. Drive the roll pin in flush from the cover side so that the locating pin is driven back through the screw hole.

Housing Bushing

If the rear bushing is worn or scored, a housing with a finished bushing is available. If boring facilities are available, a new bushing may be installed and bored to 1.377-1.376″ (34.98-34.95mm.) within .002″ (.05mm.) total indicator reading at 90° to the front face of the cover. If installing a new bushing in the extension housing, the oil groove must be positioned as shown. This is essential to provide lubrication to the driveshaft sleeve.

Oil Seal

1. If the oil seal needs replacement the original can be removed with the extension housing installed.
2. To remove the oil seal, use a seal extractor.
3. To install oil seal, drive in squarely until flush with the end of the housing.
4. After installing, pack the recess between the two sealing lips with grease.

Transmission Assembly

1. Assemble reverse idler shaft in the transmission and position the idler gear, with the selector groove toward

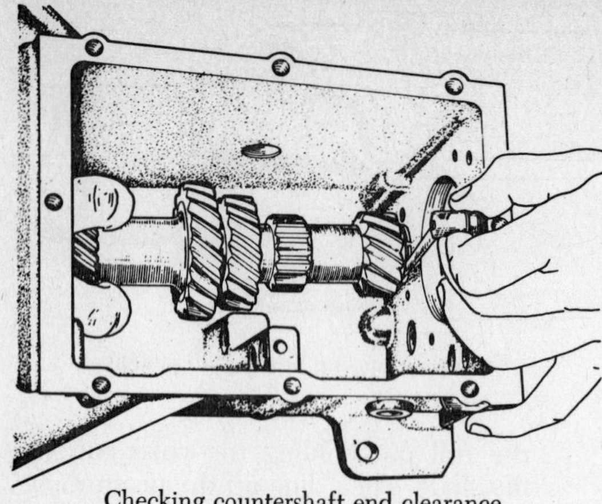
Checking countershaft end clearance

the rear. Tap in the shaft, using the locking plate as a guide to position and depth.

2. Install the countershaft gear in the case to check and, if necessary, select a thrust washer to adjust the end play.
3. Apply grease to the countershaft gear thrust washers and position them with the tangs in the slots in the case.

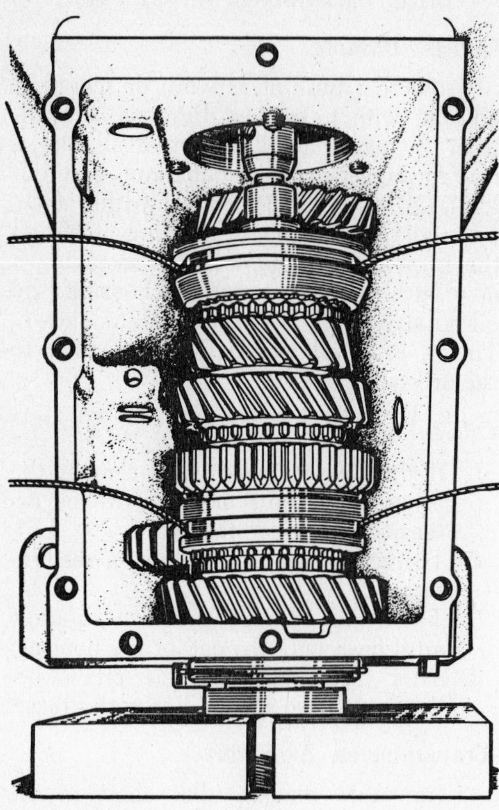
Pressing rear bearing assembly on mainshaft

4. The thinner (selective fit) washer is installed at the front and held in position by inserting a short dummy countershaft until it is flush with the inside face of the washer.
5. The thicker (non-selective) washer, installed at the rear end, is held in position by inserting the countershaft.
6. Place the countershaft gear in position, then slide in the countershaft pushing out both dummy shafts.
7. Check the end-play with feeler gauges.
8. See end-play figures given earlier under Transmission Disassembly.
9. Make any necessary adjustments.
10. After the above check has been carried out, remove the countershaft by reinstalling the dummy shafts.
11. Place two cord slings around the countershaft gear and lower it to the bottom of the case with the ends of the cords hanging over the sides.
12. The complete mainshaft is assembled by lowering the rear end of the shaft through both the top cover and rear bearing openings.
13. Remove the rear nut and dummy spacer, discarding the nut.
14. Slide rear bearing over mainshaft with the retainer ring to the rear, and lightly tap in the bearing until the retainer ring is in contact with the case.
15. Place the transmission, front up, in a press with the rear bearing inner race supported. Check that the stop-ring slots and shifting struts are lined up and press mainshaft through the bearing. Take care during the pressing operation that the gears do not contact the countershaft gear.
16. Remove the transmission from the press and install the rear bearing retaining plate with the bolts finger tight to retain the bearing in the casing.
17. The complete drive pinion assembly with needle rollers and washer in position is inserted in the front of the case. Tap lightly and evenly the outer race until the retainer ring is fully seated

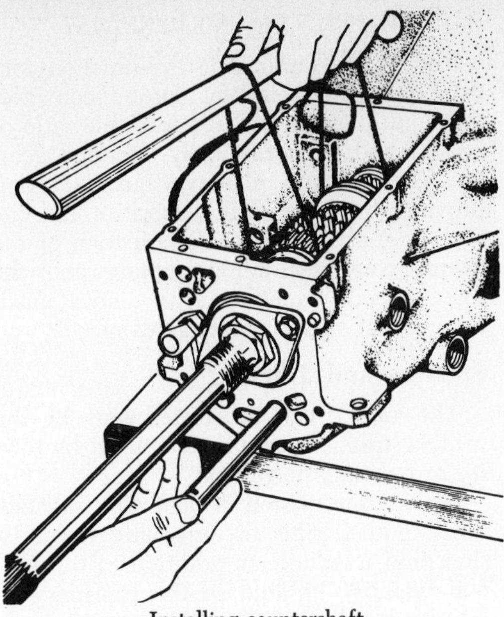

Installing countershaft

against the case. Check at stages to ensure that both shafts turn freely.

18. Install drive pinion bearing retainer using sealing compound on gasket and tighten nuts evenly to 6 ft.lbs.
19. Recheck the end-play of 1st, 2nd and 3rd gears.
20. Tie the ends of the cords at equal lengths and insert a rod to use as a handle. Arrange the cords to pass around the mainshaft in the fork grooves of the synchronizer sliding sleeves.
21. The countershaft gear can be lifted into position and the countershaft pushed in moving the dummy shafts. Remove both cords.
22. Apply sealing compound to the front end of the countershaft.
23. Install and secure the lockplate between the countershaft and reverse idler shaft.
24. Assemble the reverse shift shaft in the case. Using a dab of grease on the end of a thin rod, locate the guide peg in its bore and into the slot at the forward end of the shift shaft.
25. Screw the reverse gear fulcrum lever pivot bolt into the case until the fulcrum lever can be located on the pivot.
26. Continue screwing in and locate the upper end in the slot in the shift shaft, followed by the lower end in the groove in the idler gear.
27. Tighten the pivot bolt to 25 ft.lbs.
28. Check shifting operation.
29. Insert the interlock plunger in the case between reverse and 1st/2nd shift shaft positions.
30. Insert 1st/2nd shift fork shaft through the case and engage the shift fork with the boss facing to the rear. Drive in the roll pin flush.
31. Insert the interlock plunger in the case between 1st/2nd and 3rd/4th shift shaft positions.
32. Insert 3rd/4th shift fork with the boss facing to the rear. Drive in the roll pin flush.
33. Details of the assembly are shown.
34. Remove the rear bearing clamp plate.
35. Engage 4th and reverse gears by hand to lock rotation. Then install and tighten a new rear bearing nut to 69 ft.lbs. Re-engage neutral and install rear bearing clamp plate.
36. Insert detent plungers and springs and install gasket with cover plate, tighten-

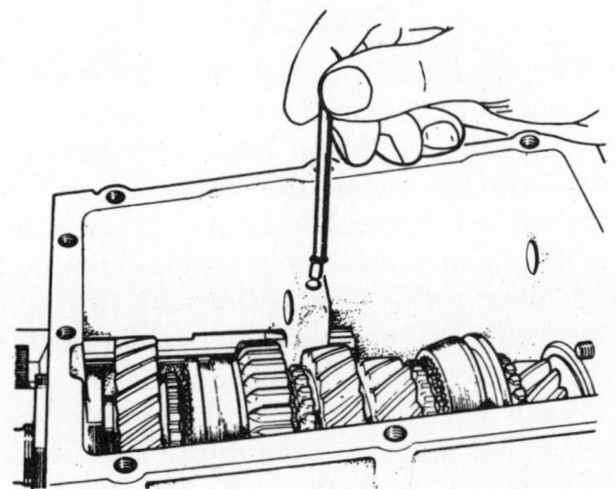

Inserting reverse shift shaft guide peg

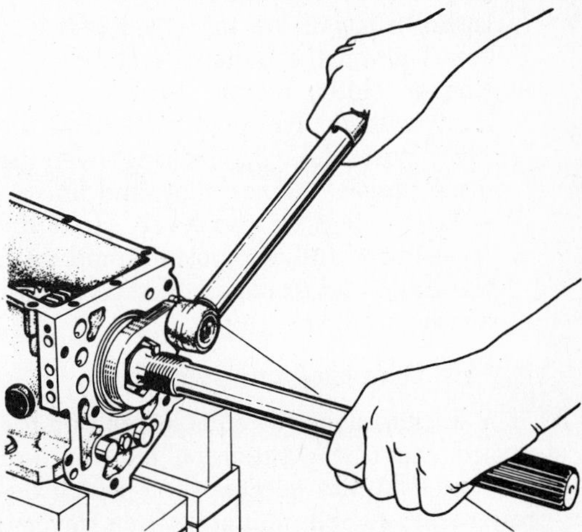

Tightening mainshaft rear nut using special tool RG 544

ing the bolts to 4 ft.lbs. Be sure that the three shift slots are all in neutral and in line.

37. Check that both the extension housing and transmission mating faces are clean and free from burrs. Smear them with sealing compound.
38. Install the oil tube in the extension housing with the double bend facing forward and angled upward towards the top of the transmission.
39. Coat the inside of the rear oil seal with grease.
40. To install the housing, move the gearshift shaft rearward and rotate counterclockwise, as seen from the rear, as far as movement will allow. Hold the shaft at this point while the extension is placed in position, carefully locating the old tube in the hole at the rear of the transmission.
41. Install the housing bolts and, before fully tightening, engage the gearshift by moving forward and turning to locate the shaft lever in the shift shaft slots.
42. Insert and secure the gearshift lever assembly and test the selection of gears.
43. Tighten the extension housing bolts to 14 ft.lbs.
44. Install the reverse gear plunger, spring, and cover, and tighten the bolts evenly to 5 ft.lbs.
45. Install speedometer pinion, bearing, gasket, and cover, and tighten the bolts to 4 ft.lbs.
46. Check the position of the oil feed tube. This should be 1″ (25.4mm.) below the top face of the case.
47. Install transmission top cover and gasket. Tighten the bolts to 4 ft.lbs.
48. Engage clutch release lever by locating it with the ball cup end against the pivot post, slide the bearing over the drive pinion retainer pilot, and line up with the pegs on the lever. Hold the lever in the fully off position and push the cable end to engage the pivot post and bearing.

Back-up Light Switch

The backup light switch is located on the forward end of the extension housing and is operated by the selector shaft which depresses the switch plunger when reverse gear is engaged. Adjustment is made with shims.

AUTOMATIC TRANSMISSION

The Cricket automatic transmission consists of a three-element torque converter that multiplies torque at a variable ratio of 2:1-1:1 and a hydraulically operated gearbox containing a planetary gear set that provides three forward gear ratios and one reverse gear ratio. The combination of the torque converter fluid coupling and the three speed planetary gear allows maximum use of engine power at all speeds.

Starting and Towing

The engine can be started only by the vehicle starter; it cannot be started by towing or pushing the vehicle.

If the transmission is operating satisfactorily, and 4 pints of automatic transmission fluid is added, in addition to the normal quantity of fluid in the transmission, the car can be towed with the engine off, in Neutral up to a maximum distance of 25 miles at speeds below 30 mph. If the transmission is defective, or the car has to be towed more than the maximum distance of 25 miles, the driveshaft must be removed and the rear of the extension housing sealed to prevent entry of dust, mud or water. Also, the car can be towed with the rear wheels raised.

Do not coast in neutral with engine off.

Maintenance

Transmission Fluid

The automatic transmission is filled at the factory with special fluid, and periodic fluid changes are not required.

Dexron automatic transmission fluid must always be used for service. Fluid additives must not be used.

After service, the fluid level must be carefully checked.

Fluid Check

The filler and dipstick is located under the hood just forward of the firewall.

Checking should be done with car on a level surface after the transmission has reached its normal running temperature (after about 5 miles of driving). Select P and allow the engine to idle for two minutes; with the engine idling in P, remove and wipe the dipstick and check level.

When checking the level, be sure that the loop at the top of the dipstick is toward the front of the car.

If necessary, add Dexron automatic

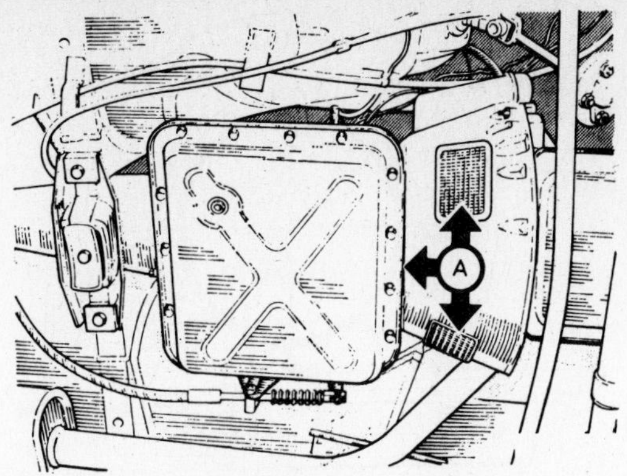

Transmission cooling ducts

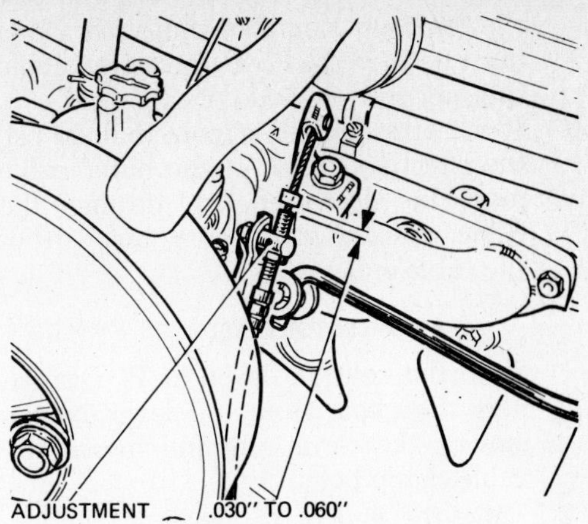

Downshift valve cable adjustment

transmission fluid to bring the level to the HIGH mark while the engine is still idling in P. Do not overfill.

The difference between the LOW and HIGH marks on the dipstick is 1 pint.

Transmission Fluid Capacity

The total fluid capacity of the transmission and converter is 13½ pints, but if the transmission only is drained, approximately 6 pints will be needed to refill the unit. The converter holds 6 pints of fluid, some of which will be lost when the transmission is removed.

CAUTION: The transmission is cooled by air admitted through ducts in the front of the transmission case. The circulated air passes through two grilles on the bottom of the converter housing.

The slots, grilles and transmission pan must be cleared of any accumulated mud or dust during the routine maintenance of the car, especially when operating in very hot temperatures.

Adjustments

Pedal Linkage Full Throttle Adjustment

1. Adjust accelerator pedal so that carburetor is fully open when pedal is 3/8" from floor.
2. Adjustment is made under hood at bellcrank. Adjust top end of vertical rod from accelerator pedal where it fastens to bellcrank.

Downshift Cable

Before adjusting the downshift cable, check that full throttle can be obtained and that the idling speed is set correctly. The cable is prelubricated and requires no service.

1. Normal adjustments to the idling speed do not upset the cable setting.
2. The adjustment is preset by means of a crimped cable stop on the inner cable.
3. With the engine idling at 600 rpm, a gap of .030 to .060" should exist between the crimped stop and the end of the threaded outer cable.
4. The adjustment is made by shortening or lengthening the outer cable by turning the downshift cable adjustment stud up or down on the cable end.
5. If the crimped stop has moved on the cable or if a new cable, on which the stop is not preset, is being installed, set the adjustment as follows:
6. Remove the pressure take-off plug from the rear of the transmission.
7. Screw an adapter into the plug hole.
8. Connect a pressure gauge to the adapter.
9. Connect a tachometer.
10. With P selected, run the engine until the transmission reaches normal operating temperature.
11. Chock the rear wheels, and with the handbrake applied, select D and increase the engine speed to approximately 1,000 rpm to check that the handbrake holds the car.
12. With D selected and the engine idling (600 rpm) note the reading of the tachometer and pressure gauge.
13. Increase the engine speed to 1,100 rpm.
14. Note the pressure gauge reading, which should be 15-20 psi above that in Step 12.
15. If the pressure rise is less than 15 psi,

the effective length of the outer cable must be increased by turning the cable adjuster stud toward the cable end.

16. If the pressure rise is more than 20 psi, the effective length of the outer cable must be decreased by turning the cable adjuster stud down, away from the cable end.

Selector Cable

1. Place the selector lever in P. Disconnect the cable from the lever by removing the clevis pin, and loosen the cable clamp bolts.
2. Move the end of the lever as far forward as possible into its P position.
3. Reconnect cable clevis and clevis pin to the lever.
4. Pull outer cable backward lightly to take up any slack and tighten the two clamp bolts to position the clamp correctly in the slotted holes in the bracket. Check that all the selector positions engage with a distinct click as the control lever is moved into any of its six positions.

Front Band

1. For this adjustment, the transmission oil pan must be removed.

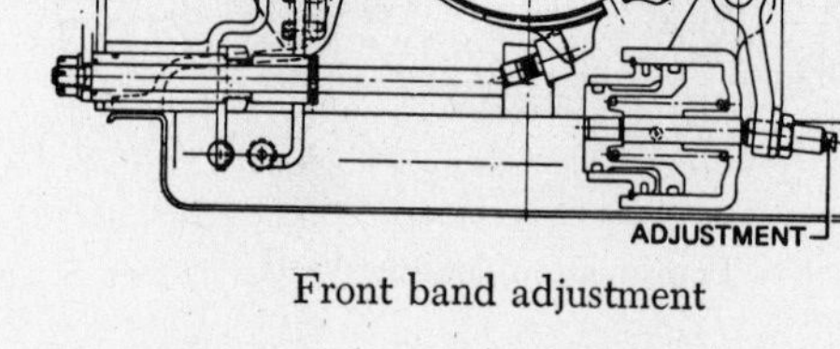

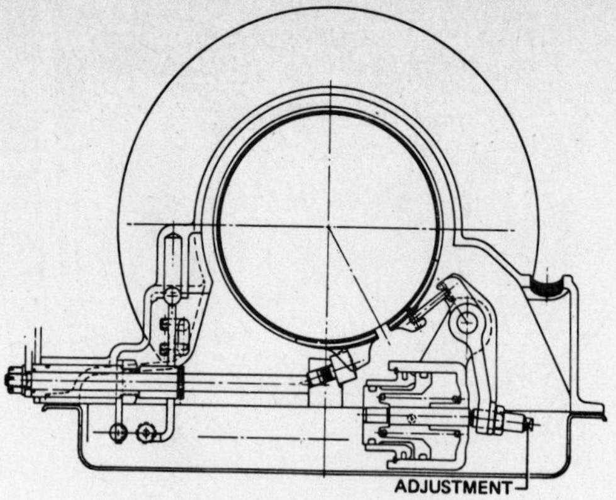

Front band adjustment

2. Loosen the adjuster locknut.
3. Tighten the adjuster screw to 10 in. lbs.
4. Back off the adjuster screw exactly 4 turns.
5. Hold the adjuster screw steady and tighten the locknut to 20-25 ft. lbs.
6. Install the oil pan and refill the transmission.

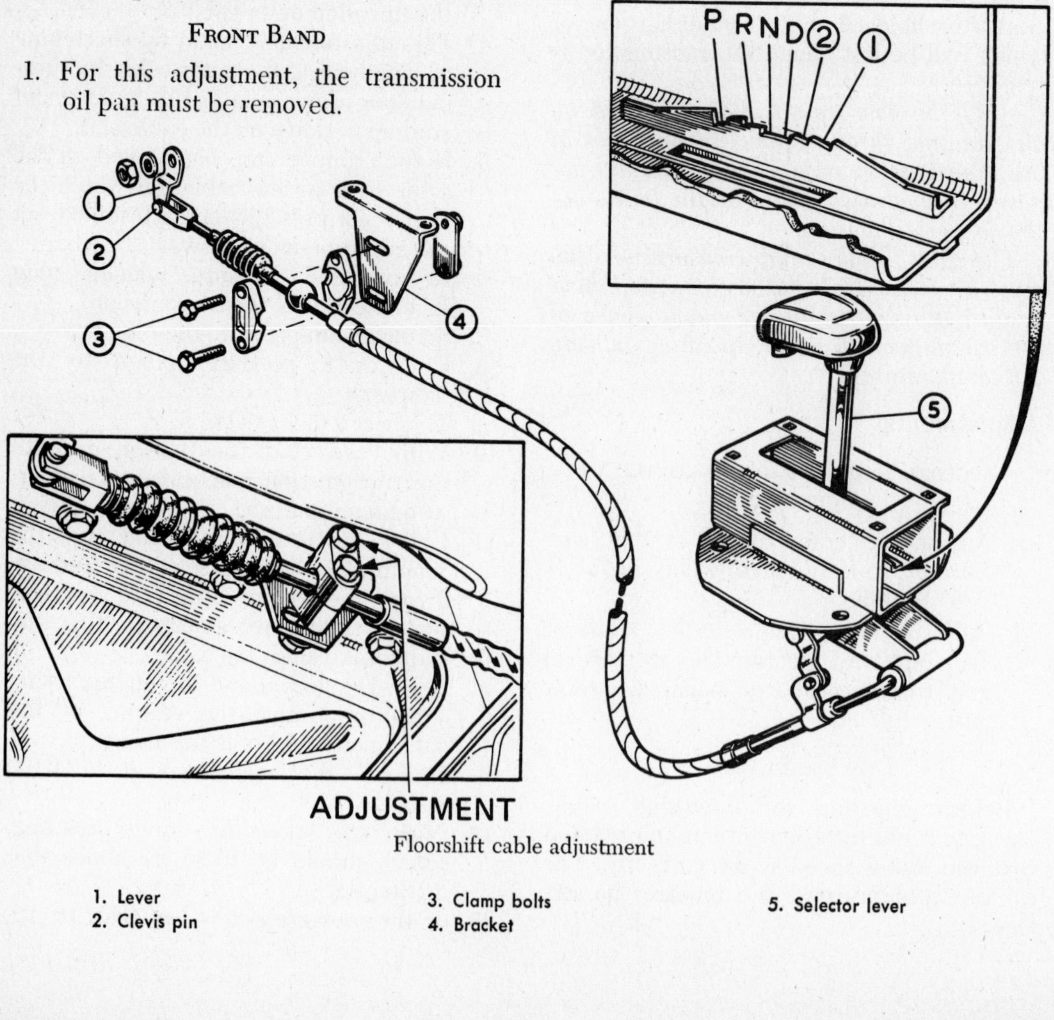

ADJUSTMENT

Floorshift cable adjustment

1. Lever
2. Clevis pin
3. Clamp bolts
4. Bracket
5. Selector lever

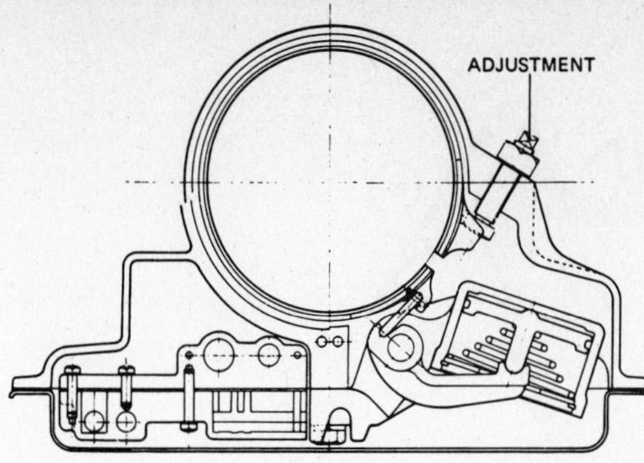

Rear band adjustment

Rear Band

1. The adjustment is normally done with a torque wrench.
2. With transmission installed on the car, it is impossible to use a torque wrench, but the following method will give a satisfactory result.
3. Loosen the locknut.
4. Using a 5/16″ open end wrench, 4″ long, tighten the adjusting screw fully and back off one complete turn.
5. Hold the adjuster screw steady and tighten the locknut.

Neutral Safety Switch

1. This switch also operates the back-up light.
2. Check selector cable adjustment before adjusting switch.
3. Place the selector lever in D.
4. Loosen the locknut and unscrew the switch, with an 11/16″ wrench, 3″ long.
5. Connect a test lamp across the small terminals (Neutral/Park). These terminals are opposite each other. The test lamp should be lit.
6. Screw in the switch until the lamp just goes out.
7. With a pencil, mark the switch body opposite a mark on the transmission housing.
8. Connect the test lamp to the other two larger terminals (back-up). The lamp should not light.
9. Screw the switch in further until the lamp just lights.
10. Make a second mark on the switch opposite the mark on the transmission.
11. Unscrew the switch until the transmission mark is midway between the two marks.
12. Carefully tighten the locknut, using a thin 11/16″ wrench, 3″ long, until it is just tight. The torque figure for the locknut is 5 ft.lbs., but a torque wrench cannot be used while the unit is installed.
13. Reconnect the wiring and check that the starter only operates in P and N and the back-up light only operates in R.

Repairs

Due to the extensive procedures required to repair the various subassemblies of the automatic transmission, only shift linkage repairs and removal and installation procedures for the entire transmission and converter are given. Repairs to the transmission should be made by a qualified repair facility.

Downshift Valve Cable Replacement

1. Disconnect at carburetor.
2. Drain and remove oil pan.
3. Disconnect cable from downshift valve operating cam.
4. Unscrew cable from transmission housing.
5. Installation is the reverse of Steps 1-4.
6. The pan must be carefully filled to avoid overfilling.
7. The cable must be correctly adjusted.

Selector Lever Cable Replacement

1. Disconnect cable from the lever on the transmission by removing the clevis pin.
2. Remove two bolts securing outer cable to its mounting clamps and bracket on the transmission case.
3. Remove clevis pin securing outer cable to the lever and move cable sideways so that its L-shaped end comes out of its locating plastic bushing in the selector fulcrum extension.
4. Installation is the reverse of the removal procedure.
5. After installing, adjust outer cable mounting clamp in the slots in the mounting bracket so that selector lever operates correctly.

Transmission Removal

1. Disconnect the battery.
2. Remove the throttle rod from the carburetor linkage.
3. Disconnect downshift cable from the carburetor linkage. Distance of

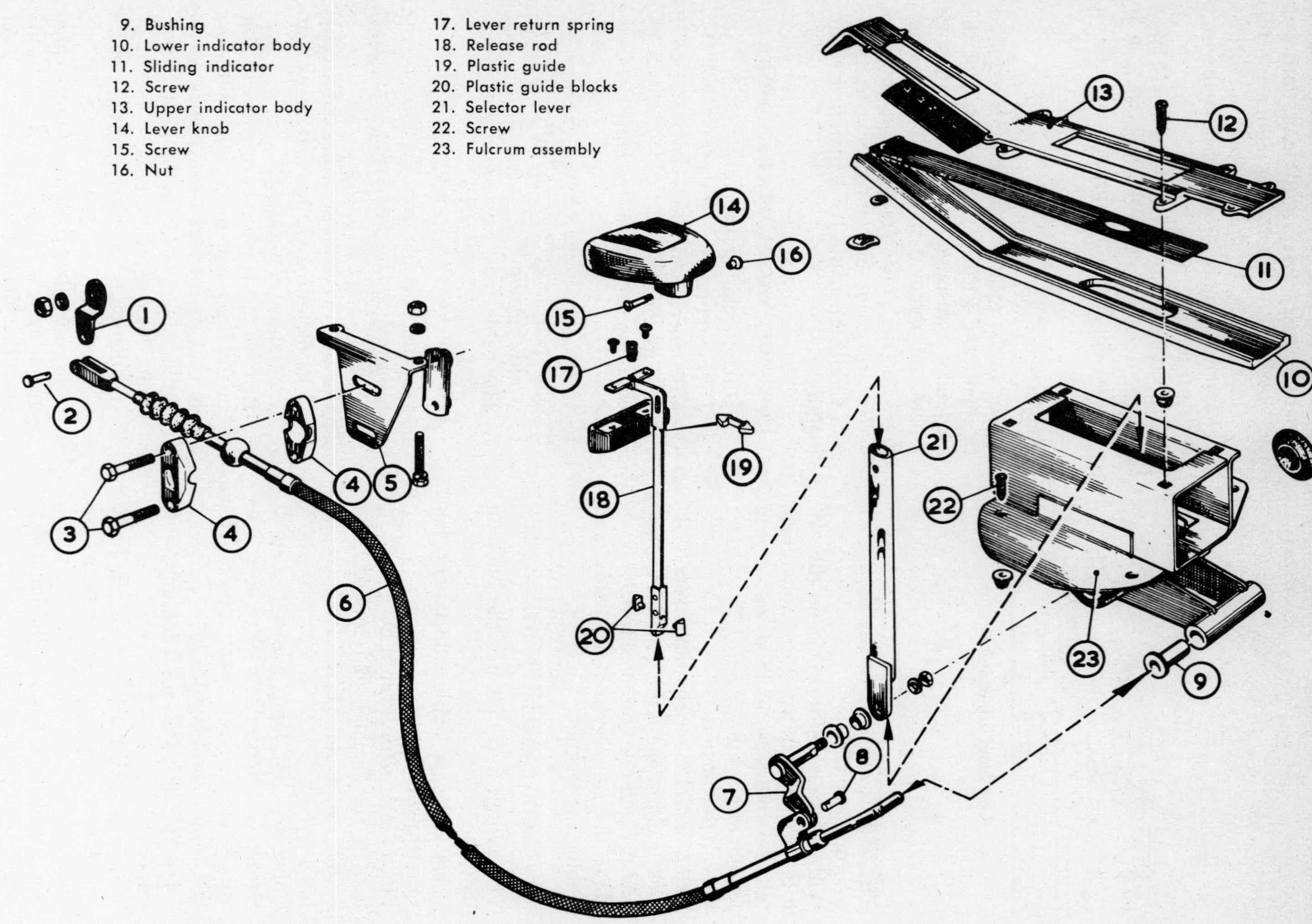

Selector lever and cable disassembled

crimped sleeve from outer cable should be .030-0.60".
4. Remove the starter and the filler tube.
5. Drain the transmission fluid into a clean container.
6. Remove the driveshaft.
7. Disconnect the speedometer cable.
8. Disconnect the gearshift inner cable from the transmission lever, remove the bracket from the transmission, and hang the cable complete with bracket over the exhaust pipe.
9. Disconnect the four wires from the neutral safety and back-up light switch.
10. Place a transmission jack to support the transmission.
11. Remove converter access plate.
12. Rotate engine crankshaft pulley nut to locate converter to drive plate bolts and remove them.
13. Remove rear mount and center cross-member.
14. Place a jack and block of wood under the front of the engine pan to prevent the engine from tipping forward after removal of the transmission.
15. Remove the transmission to engine bolts.
16. Remove the transmission, placing a C-clamp on the converter housing mounting flange to retain the converter.

TORQUE CONVERTER REMOVAL

After removing the transmission, remove the C-clamp from the flange of the converter housing and slide the converter out of the transmission. Some fluid will come out of the converter hub at this time.

DRIVE PLATE REMOVAL

After removing the transmission and torque converter, remove the five drive plate to crankshaft bolts and the drive plate and stiffening plates.

Driveshaft and Universal Joint

The driveshaft is a tubular assembly capped at each end by a universal joint. At one end, a splined sleeve engages with the transmission output shaft, and is lubricated by the oil in the transmission. At the other end, a flange couples the driveshaft to the rear axle. Both universal joints have jour-

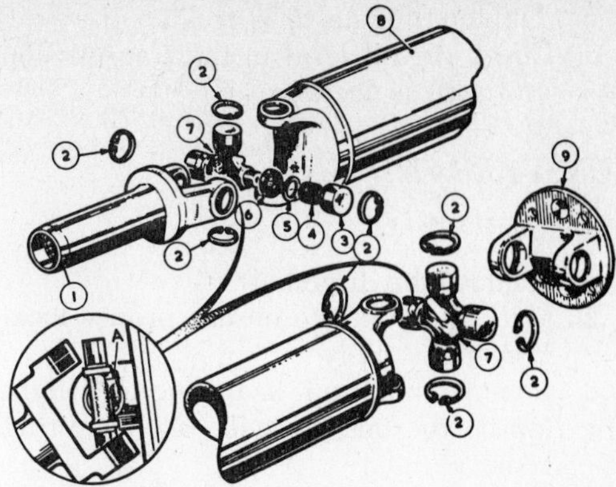

Driveshaft and universal joint disassembled

1. Sleeve yoke assembly
2. Snap ring
3. Bearing cup
4. Needle rollers
5. Bearing washer
6. Seal
7. Universal joint
8. Driveshaft
9. Flange yoke assembly

nals with needle roller bearings which are sealed for life. The universal joints are non-serviceable and must be replaced as an assembly.

DRIVESHAFT

Removal

The driveshaft is balanced as a unit. To remove:

1. Mark the flange for assembly.
2. Remove the four attachment nuts, washers and bolts on the flange.
3. Place a tray under the transmission rear to catch the oil overflow.
4. Move the driveshaft toward the transmission until the flange disengages from the rear axle coupling. Lower the flanged end and remove the splined end from the transmission.

Installation

1. Be sure that the splines and the sliding sleeve are lightly lubricated and free from dirt or damage.
2. Being careful that the oil seal is not damaged, locate and slide the splined end of the driveshaft into the rear of the transmission.
3. Be sure that the mating faces of the shaft flange and the rear axle flange are free from dirt or damage. Position shaft to rear axle and align marks.
4. Insert the attachment bolts and install new lockwashers. Install the nuts and tighten evenly.

5. Tighten the nuts to 17 ft. lbs.
6. Check the oil level in the transmission and refill as necessary.

UNIVERSAL JOINT

Removal

1. Remove the driveshaft.
2. Mark the yokes to ensure proper location on assembly.
3. Remove the four snap-rings. A light tap on the bearing will ease snap-ring removal.
4. With the yoke on a wooden support and using a soft-faced hammer, tap the top of the adjacent side until the bearing cup projects from the underside.
5. Clamp the projecting cup in a vise and tap the fork until the cup disengages from the bore.
6. Remove the opposite cup.
7. Remove the yoke and seals from the cross.
8. Place the exposed joint bearing faces on wooden supports and remove the cups.
9. Remove the joint and seals from the yoke.

Installation

1. Carefully remove the bearing cups from the replacement joint. Be careful that the needle rollers remain in position.
2. Fill the cup one-third full with multi-purpose grease.
3. Place the joint in the yoke.
4. Raise the joint to its limit in the yoke and locate the bearing cup assembly complete with seal over the projecting joint trunnion and into the bearing bore. Press the cup in until its outer face is flush with the face of the yoke.
5. Using an old bearing cup and keeping the joint in its cup to retain the needles, press the replacement cup into the bore until the snap-ring can be installed. Remove the old cup and install the snap-ring.
6. Turn the yoke 180°, keeping the joint in the cup.
7. Raise the joint until the trunnion is

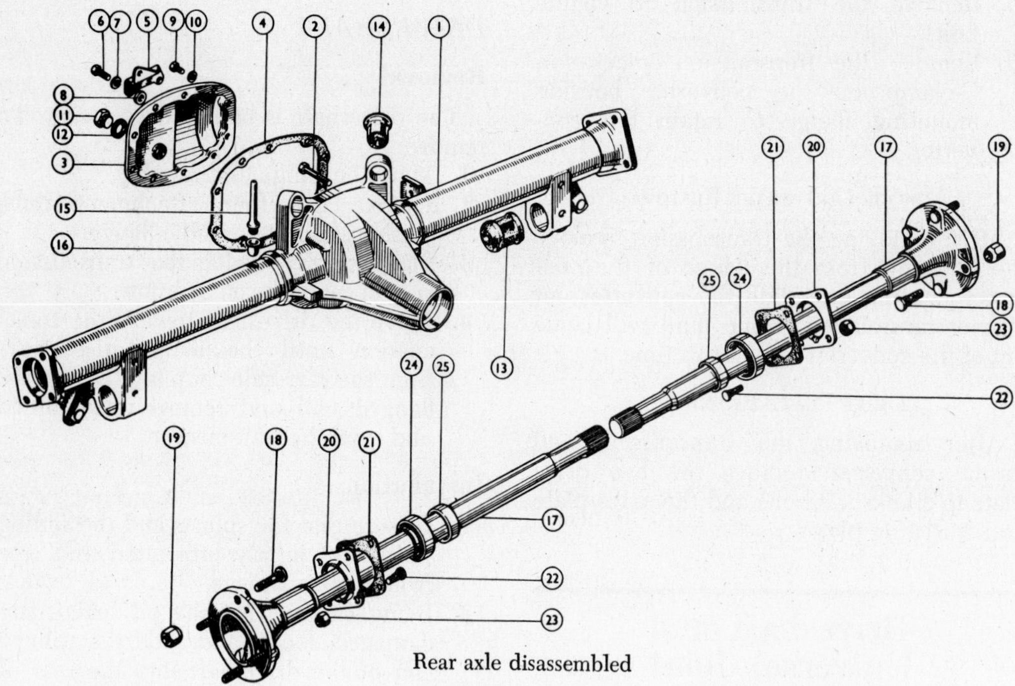

Rear axle disassembled

1. Axle housing
2. Bolt, differential bearing cap
3. Rear cover
4. Gasket, rear cover
5. Bracket, brake tubing
6. Long bolt, rear cover
7. Lock washer
8. Spacer washer
9. Short bolt, rear cover
10. Lock washer
11. Filler plug
12. Washer
13. Mounting bushing, lower
14. Mounting bushing, upper
15. Breather
16. Breather seat
17. Axle shaft
18. Stud, wheel
19. Nut, wheel
20. Retainer plate
21. Gasket, retainer plate
22. Bolt, retainer to housing
23. Nut, retainer to housing
24. Bearing, axle shaft
25. Retaining collar

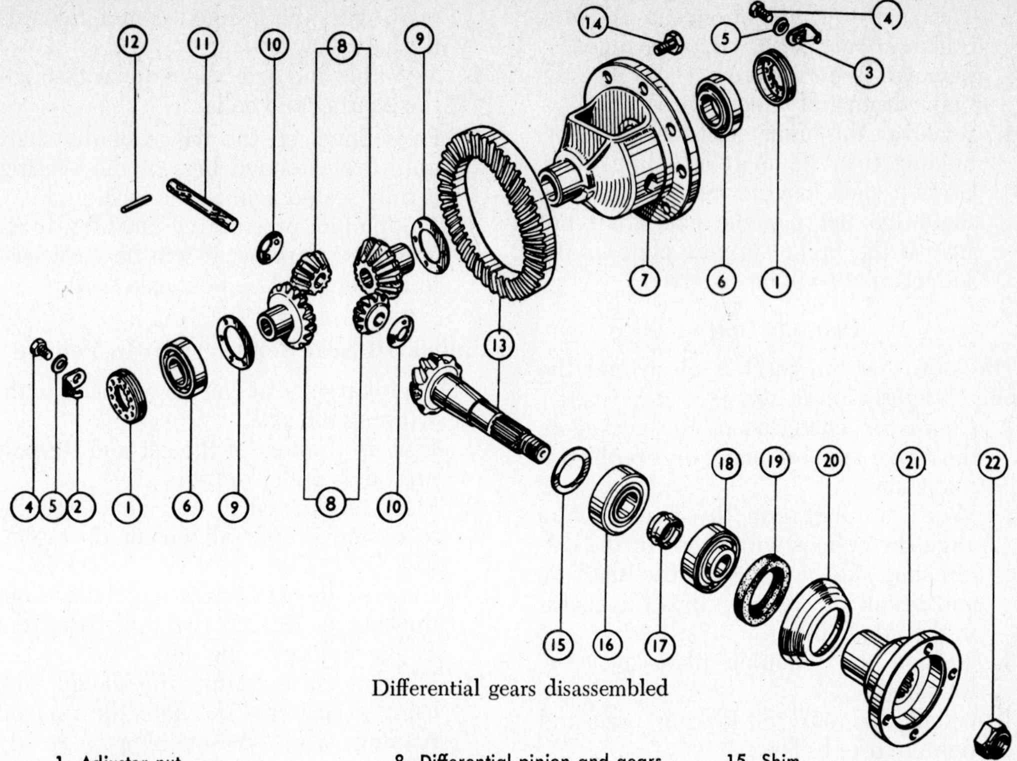

Differential gears disassembled

1. Adjuster nut
2. Locking plate, right
3. Locking plate, left
4. Bolt, locking plate
5. Lock washer
6. Differential bearing
7. Differential case
8. Differential pinion and gears
9. Thrust washer, differential side gear
10. Thrust washer, pinion
11. Cross pin
12. Locking pin
13. Ring gear and pinion
14. Bolt, ring gear
15. Shim
16. Inner bearing, pinion
17. Collapsible spacer
18. Outer bearing, pinion
19. Oil seal
20. Dust cover
21. Flange
22. Nut, flange

just projecting above the upper face of the yoke but with the lower trunnion still engaged with the underside cup assembly. Install the bearing cup assembly complete with seal.

8. Place the yoke on the joint and install the bearing assemblies.
9. Using a soft-faced hammer, lightly tap the forks to relieve bearing pressures.

Drive Axle, Suspension, and Steering

DRIVE AXLE

The drive axle is a semi-floating type using hypoid gear final drive.

The axle housing is of unit construction enclosing a differential carrier and welded axle tubes. The housing assembly also provides four mounting points, with rubber bushings, to which the suspension links are attached. The pinion is carried on two tapered roller bearings adjusted to a preload by a collapsible spacer. A single piece differential case with the hypoid gear assembly is carried in the axle housing on adjustable tapered roller bearings, secured by caps and bolts. Ring gear to pinion mesh is accurately attained by the adjusters which are locked in position by locking plates engaged in the adjuster holes. Steel thrust washers are between the differential gears and the differential case. Each flanged axle shaft is carried on a sealed ball bearing, using a lip type oil seal, which is held by a pressed on ring. No drain plug is provided. If necessary, the oil is drained by removing the rear cover. The breather unit is a plastic assembly located in the top of the axle tube to the right of the differential unit.

Axle Shaft

REMOVAL

1. Jack up the rear of the car and support on stands under the axle.

2. Clean off all dirt from around the brake support plate and axle flange.
3. Remove the setscrew holding the brake drum and remove the drum.
4. Remove the four self-locking nuts holding the axle shaft retaining plate.
5. Using a slide hammer remove the axle shaft. Do not pry the axle shaft out against the brake support plate or the support plate will be distorted.

INSTALLATION

Be sure that the shaft is clean and the spline is lightly lubricated.

1. Check the condition of the gasket on the brake support plate, and replace if necessary.
2. Slide the shaft into the housing and align the splines with those in the differential side gear. Push the shaft in and install the bearing into the recess in the axle housing.
3. Position the retaining plate over the four studs.
4. Install the four self-locking nuts and tighten to 14 ft. lbs.

CAUTION: Do not use the retaining plate to draw the bearing and axle shaft into position. Excessive axle shaft end-play will result.

Axle Shaft Bearing

REMOVAL

1. Position the axle shaft in an arbor press with the flange down.
2. Locate the axle shaft squarely under the press and apply pressure to remove both the collar and the bearing.
3. Discard the collar and bearing.

INSTALLATION

1. Position the retainer plate on the axle shaft with the swaged center towards the axle flange.
2. Assemble the axle shaft down through the bearing and collar.
3. Press down on the flange of the shaft until the extended boss of the bearing is fully seated against the face.
4. A minimum pressure of 3,000 lbs. is required. Otherwise, it will be necessary to install a replacement axle shaft.

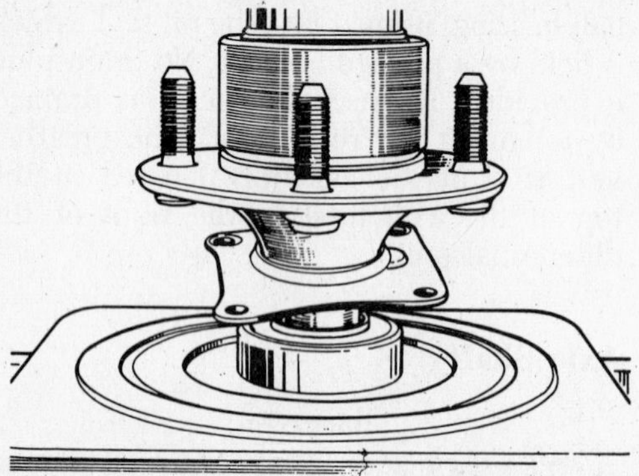

Installing the axle shaft bearing

Pinion Oil Seal Replacement In Vehicle

The pinion oil seal can be replaced without stripping the axle.

1. Jack up the rear of the car and support on stands under the axle.
2. Mark the driveshaft and pinion flanges to ensure proper alignment on assembly.
3. Remove the four nuts and bolts from the flange. Detach the shaft from the flange and tie to one side.
4. Wind a cord around the flange and, using a spring scale, note the preload reading while maintaining a steady pull.
5. Mark the flange and pinion shaft to assist in assembly, and remove the self-locking nut and the flange. Replace the seal.
6. Install the flange, aligning the marks.
7. Install a new pinion nut, being careful not to overtighten at this stage.
8. Tighten the nut until the pinion end play just disappears.
9. Rotate the pinion to seat the bearings.
10. Tighten the nut a very small amount at a time, rotate the pinion and measure the preload. Continue this operation until the previously noted preload has been restored.

The noted preload must not be exceeded. If it is exceeded, it will be necessary to remove the differential assembly to restore the pinion bearing preload using a new collapsible spacer.

Rear Axle

REMOVAL

1. Jack up the car and support on stands forward of the lower links.
2. With the axle supported on a jack, remove the wheels.
3. Mark the driveshaft and pinion flanges to be sure of original alignment on reassembly.

4. Remove the four nuts and bolts from the flange.
5. Detach the shaft from the flange and tie the shaft to one side.
6. Release the handbrake, remove the handbrake cable clevis pin from the rear end, and slide the inner cable back.
7. Detach the rubber boot from the outer cable and the outer cable retainer.
8. Disconnect the brake system at the rear flexible hose connection and seal off.
9. Remove the shock absorber lower mountings. Then, carefully lower the jack and lift out the coil springs.
10. Loosen the upper link front pivot nuts and bolts.
11. Remove the four suspension link to axle pivot nuts and bolts.
12. Lift the upper links off the axle; then, lower the axle unit and draw rearward off the lower links.

Installation

Installation is done by reversing the removal instructions with particular attention to the following items:

1. Install the coil springs.
2. When installing the drive shaft, be sure that it is aligned with the original marks.
3. The pivot nuts and bolts are finally tightened with the car standing on the wheels. Bounce the car a few times to be sure that the bushings are centralized and are not subject to excessive twist.
4. Tighten the pivot nuts and bolts to 14 ft. lbs.
5. Bleed the brake system.
6. Fill the axle to the correct level with multi-purpose gear oil (SAE 90 for above −10°F; SAE 80 for below −10°F).

Disassembly

1. Remove the axle assembly.
2. Place a drip tray under the differential housing and remove the rear cover to drain the oil.
3. Remove both axle shafts.
4. Disconnect and remove the handbrake rod and hydraulic lines to remove the brake support plates.
5. Be sure that the differential bearing caps are suitably identified, as they must be reassembled on their original sides.
6. Remove the locking bolts and plates from the bearing caps.
7. Remove the cap retaining bolts and lift off the caps.
8. Remove the two adjuster nuts, at the same time lifting out the ring gear assembly and bearing outer cones, taking care that the outer cones of the bearings are not interchanged.
9. Mark the flange to pinion shaft location to aid in reassembly and, remove the self-locking nut and the flange.
10. Using a soft mallet, gently tap out the pinion rearward from the housing. The pinion inner bearing and shims will be removed with the pinion.
11. Remove the inner bearing from the pinion.
12. Support the bearing and apply pressure to the threaded end of the pinion. Remove the shims from behind the bearing and save.
13. To remove the pinion shaft oil seal, remove the pinion outer bearing and drive the outer cone out using a soft metal drift.
14. Using suitable tool drive out the inner bearing outer cone.

Pinion Oil Seal

Removal

1. To remove the oil seal, drive one side of the seal inward as far as it will go; this will force the opposite side out of the housing.
2. Using a suitable tool behind the rim of the seal, tap outward to remove. Discard the seal.

Installation

1. Before installing an oil seal, coat the internal flange with grease. Then position in the housing with the flanges inward.
2. Drive the oil seal into position until the tool contacts the face of the housing.

Differential Carrier Bearing

Removal

Bearings are removed from the differential case with a puller.

Bearing Examination

Wash thoroughly and examine the condition of the pinion and differential bearings and the outer cones. Check for any signs of pitting, overheating or any other damage.

If the bearings are satisfactory, re-oil immediately.

If any bearings are damaged or doubtful, the bearings complete with the outer cones must be replaced. Always keep bearings and outer cones together in sets.

Installation

Carefully press the bearing fully into position.

DIFFERENTIAL

Disassembly

1. Remove the ring gear before trying to remove the cross pin, as its removal would be blocked by the teeth of the ring gear.
2. It is unnecessary to remove the differential carrier bearings to disassemble the differential assembly. When the ring gear is to be replaced, mark the ring gear and flange so that it can be replaced in its original position.
3. Remove the eight ring gear bolts and discard.
4. These bolts are of a special design and do not need any extra locking devices. Always use the correct bolts for replacement.
5. Remove the ring gear.
6. Drive out the locking pin holding the cross pin.
7. Push out the cross pin, turn the assembly 90° to bring the pinions opposite the differential case openings, and remove the pinions together with their thrust washers.
8. The side gears and their thrust washers can now be removed.

Inspection

1. Check the gear teeth for pitting, uneven wear or any other damage.
2. Check the fit of the pinions on the cross pin.
3. Check the fit of the axle shaft gears on the shaft splines. These should be a sliding fit with no play.
4. If replacements are to be installed, then the differential gears must be replaced as a complete set including the crosspin and the lockpin.
5. Examine the differential case for wear, scoring or other damage to the thrust faces and side gear bores.

Assembly

1. Install the side gears with the thrust washers in the differential case.
2. Position the pinions and thrust washers at 180° to each other through the openings in the differential case and engage the teeth with those of the side gears.
3. Rotate the complete gear assembly through 90° and line up the pinions and thrust washers with the crosspin holes.
4. Push in the crosspin and line up the lockpin hole.
5. Push the complete gear assembly through 90° and line up the pinions and thrust washers with the crosspin holes.
6. Engage the lockpin to retain the crosspin. Then push the side gear on the cage side (opposite the ring gear) against the pinions. This will fully seat the pinions and the other gear eliminating all end play.
7. Measure the gap between the side gear and the thrust washer, which should not be more than .010″ (0.25mm.).
8. After checking the above clearance, drive in the lockpin and lightly peen over the edge of the hole in the case to hold it.
9. Check that the faces of the ring gear and the case flange are thoroughly clean and smooth.
10. Install the ring gear in the case, with the marks aligned, and install new bolts which must be tightened evenly to 47 ft. lbs.
11. Before installing a new ring gear and pinion, be sure that the gear to pinion ratio is identical to the original gears. Hypoid gears are serviced as a matched pair and must not be replaced individually.

Bevel Pinion Adjustment and Bearing Preload

The bevel pinion must be correctly adjusted in two respects: Position of the pinion relative to the axis of the ring gear, and preload of the bearings.

For an accurate adjustment, it is necessary to use the special differential assembly jig.

To adjust the position of the pinion relative to the ring gear axis, shims are used in position A.

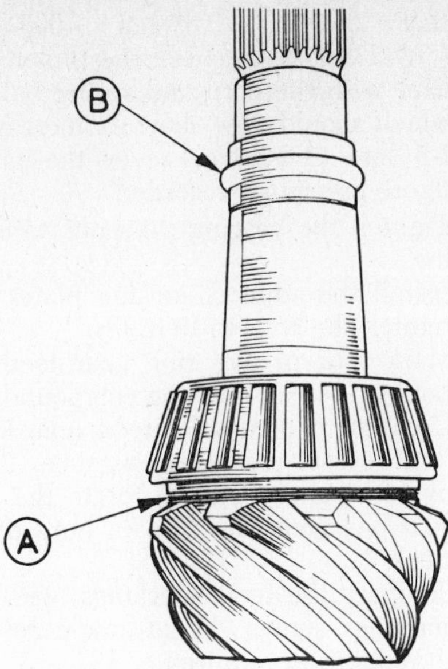

Shims and collapsible spacer in position

Shims of the following thickness are available to provide any adjustment necessary.

.003″ (.08mm.)
.005″ (.13mm.)
.010″ (.25mm.)
.020″ (.50mm.)

1. Assemble the inner pinion bearing lightly oiled to the dummy pinion without shims and insert the assembly into the housing. Install the outer bearing (lightly oiled), spacer and nut. Do not install the oil seal at this time.
2. Hold the pinion head by hand and progressively tighten the nut to absorb all end-play until a slight resistance to turning is felt.
3. Rotate the dummy pinion to seat the bearings. Continue to tighten the nut and rotate the pinion until the nut cannot be tightened by hand any further. A slight drag should now be felt.
4. Place the mandrel in position in the bearing housing.
5. Install the bearing caps and tighten to 15 ft. lbs.
6. Using feeler gauges, carefully measure the gap between the end of the dummy pinion and the mandrel. The measurement obtained is the actual thickness of the shims required between the pinion head and the inner bearing.
7. Select the shims and measure to be sure that the total thickness equals the feeler gauge measurement.
8. Remove the mandel and dummy pinion.
9. Place the shims on the hypoid pinion with any thin shims placed between thick ones.
10. Install assembly jig in press, position bearing with the rollers to the jig, and press the pinion into the bearing. Be sure that the bearing and shims are fully seated.
11. Oil the outer bearing and place in position followed by the oil seal.
12. Oil the inner bearing, place the collapsible spacer in position on the pinion shaft, and insert the pinion into the housing.
13. Install the flange at the position previously marked with a new self-locking nut.
14. Tighten the pinion nut until pinion end play just disappears. Be careful not to overtighten.
15. Rotate the pinion to seat the bearings. Failure to do this could lead to a false pre-load or bearing damage.
16. To measure the preload, wind a cord around the flange and, using a spring scale, note the reading while maintaining a steady running pull.
17. Tightening the nut a very small amount at a time, rotate the pinion and measure the preload until the desired preload is reached:

Original bearings 6-11 lbs. (2.7-5.0kg.)
New bearings 8-15 lbs. (3.6-6.8kg.)

IMPORTANT: Do not back off the nut to lessen the preload. If the correct preload figure is exceeded, a new collapsible spacer must be installed.

18. Make a note of the figure obtained for later calculation.

Differential Backlash Adjustment and Bearing Preload

1. Oil the differential carrier bearings, position the outer cones on their respective bearings and place the assembly into the housing.
2. Place the adjuster nuts in the housing. While maintaining a light downward pressure, screw in each adjuster until it just contacts the bearing. This will ensure that the adjusters are correctly located in the housing threads.

3. Install the bearing caps with the bolts finger-tight.
4. Rotate each adjuster back a turn and then forward again to its original position to be sure it is correctly located in the cap threads.
5. Temporarily tighten the cap bolts to 20 ft. lbs. (2.7kgm.).
6. Carefully screw in both adjusters until the end play is eliminated.
7. Position a dial indicator on the housing and measure the backlash.
8. Turn both adjusters equally to engage the gear deeper into mesh until a backlash reading of .004" (.10mm.) is reached.
9. Mount a dial indicator on the ring gear side bearing cap with the indicator pointer contacting the inner face of the cage side bearing cap.
10. Loosen the cage side adjuster to release any bearing preload which may exist.
11. Set the dial indicator pointer to zero.
12. Tighten the cage side adjuster for a reading of .0015" (.38mm.). This adjustment sets the carrier bearing preload and ring gear to pinion backlash.
13. Mount the dial indicator on the housing and measure the backlash to see that it is between .005-.009" (.13-.23mm.). Recheck the pinion preload with the cord and spring balance which should now show an increase of 4-5 lbs. (1.8-2.3kg.) over the pinion figure previously recorded.
14. Tighten the bearing cap bolts to 36 ft. lbs.
15. Install the adjuster locking plates and tighten the bolts to 16 ft. lbs.
16. Mark four or five ring gear teeth on both sides with marking compound.
17. Use a block of wood forced against the ring gear to create a resistance. Then, by turning the pinion, rotate the ring gear one complete turn in both directions.
18. Compare the teeth markings, with the markings shown. Make any necessary corrections as required.
19. Install the gasket and rear cover with the hydraulic brake line support bracket in position.
20. Position the brake support on the mounting flanges and connect the brake lines and hand brake rod.
21. Install the axle shafts.

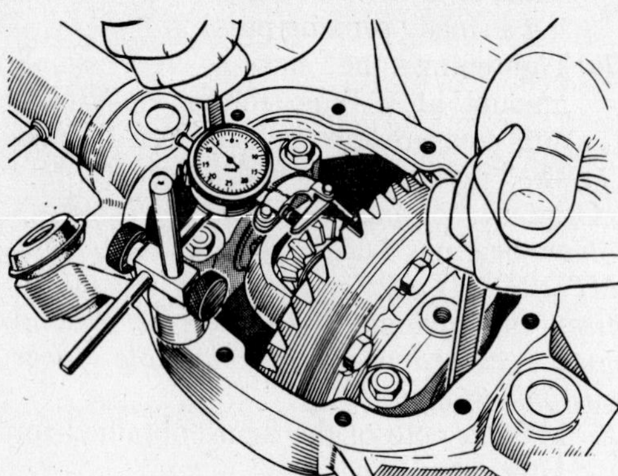
Checking ring gear to pinion backlash

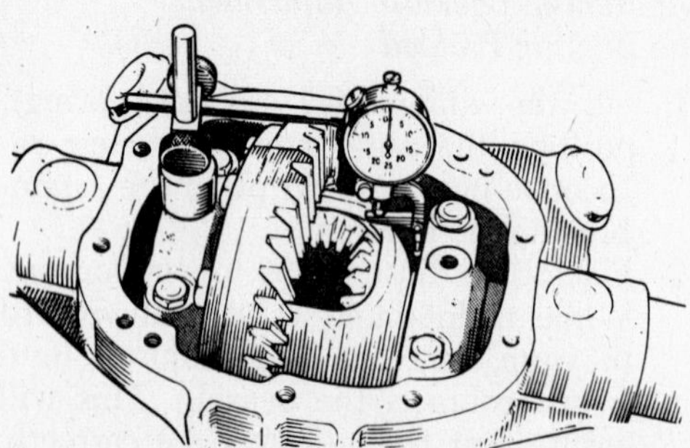
Checking differential carrier bearing preload

Breather

The breather unit is a two piece plastic assembly mounted on the top of the axle tube to the right of the differential unit.

Should the breather become blocked, remove the line and seating cup for cleaning.

Removal

1. Clean off dirt around the breather tube and seat.
2. Pull breather tube upward out of the seating cup.
3. Using a small screwdriver, pry out the seating cup.

Installation

1. Coat the underside of the lip of the seating cup with non-hardening sealing compound.
2. Push the seating cup into the axle housing, followed by the breather tube. The breather tube will expand the seating cup to retain both in the axle tube.

SUSPENSION

Rear Suspension

The rear suspension is a coil spring, four link system that controls both drive and

	TOOTH CONTACT CHART		
	TOOTH CONTACT	CONDITION	REMEDY
A	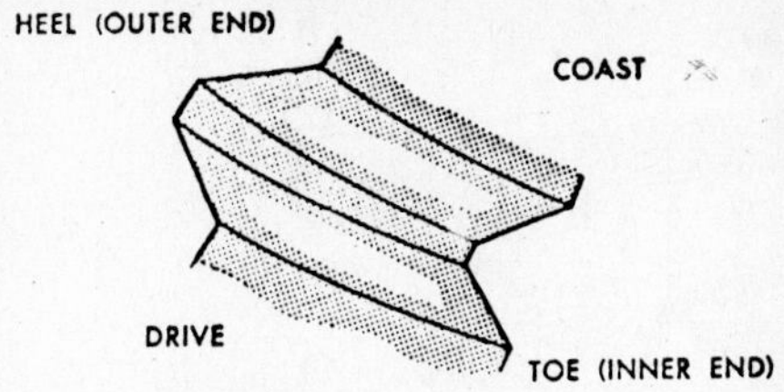 HEEL (OUTER END) COAST DRIVE TOE (INNER END)	IDEAL TOOTH CONTACT EVENLY SPREAD OVER PROFILE, NEARER HEEL THAN TOE.	
B	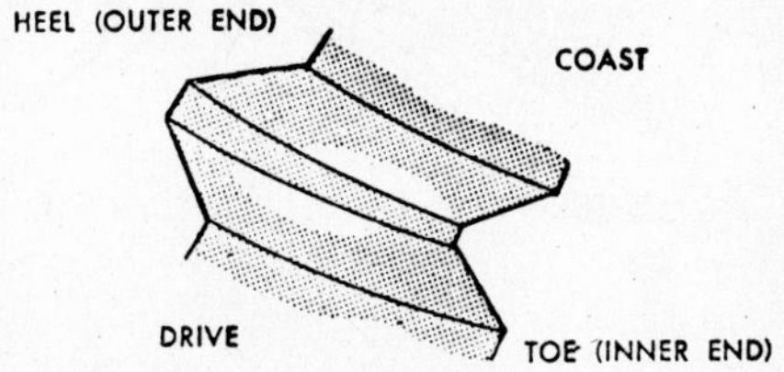 HEEL (OUTER END) COAST DRIVE TOE (INNER END)	HIGH TOOTH CONTACT HEAVY ON THE TOP OF THE DRIVE GEAR TOOTH PROFILE.	MOVE THE DRIVE PINION DEEPER INTO MESH, I.E. INCREASE SHIM THICKNESS.
C	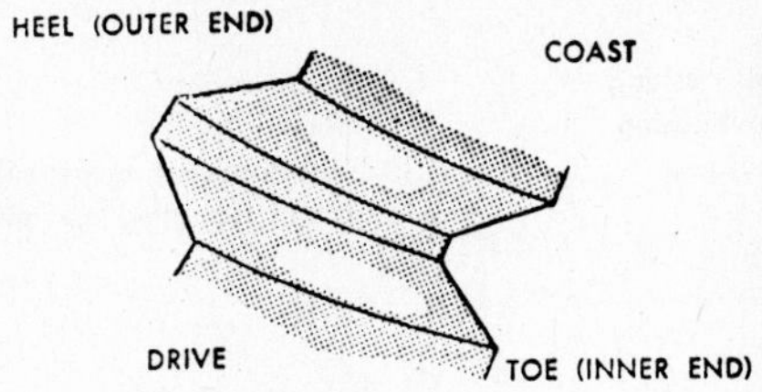 HEEL (OUTER END) COAST DRIVE TOE (INNER END)	LOW TOOTH CONTACT HEAVY IN THE ROOT OF THE DRIVE GEAR TOOTH PROFILE.	MOVE THE DRIVE PINION OUT OF MESH, I.E. DECREASE SHIM THICKNESS.
D	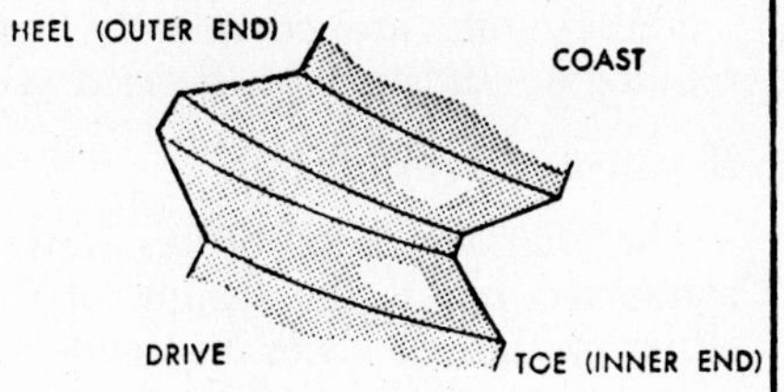 HEEL (OUTER END) COAST DRIVE TOE (INNER END)	TOE CONTACT TIGHT ON THE SMALL END OF THE DRIVE GEAR TOOTH.	MOVE THE DRIVE GEAR OUT OF MESH, I.E. INCREASE BACKLASH BUT DO NOT EXCEED THE MAXIMUM.
E	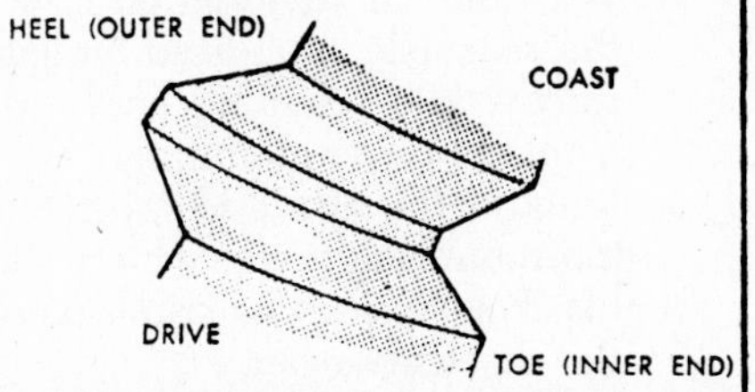 HEEL (OUTER END) COAST DRIVE TOE (INNER END)	HEEL CONTACT TIGHT ON THE LARGE END OF THE DRIVE GEAR TOOTH.	MOVE THE DRIVE GEAR INTO MESH, I.E. DECREASE BACKLASH BUT DO NOT EXCEED THE MINIMUM.

Ring gear contact patterns

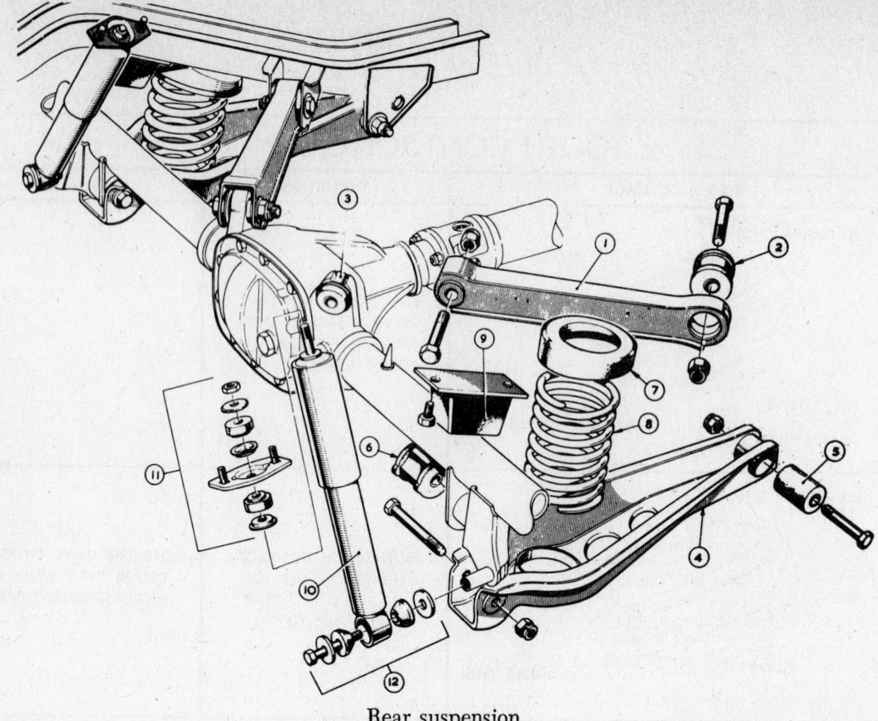

Rear suspension

1. Upper link
2. Upper link front bushing
3. Upper link rear bushing
4. Lower link
5. Lower link front bushing
6. Lower link rear bushing
7. Coil spring insulator
8. Coil spring
9. Bump rubber
10. Shock absorber
11. Upper mounting assembly
12. Lower mounting assembly

brake torque reaction. All four links have rubber bushings at the front, with the rear attached to bushing mounting points on the rear axle housing. Each lower link is mounted at the front to a bracket attached to the body side member and to the underside of the axle at the rear. This controls front and rear movement of the axle. The upper link mounting at the front is similar to the lower link while the rear is mounted on top of the differential housing. This arrangement forms a V which provides lateral location for the axle, and reduces angular variations in the drive line. Each coil spring is mounted at the top in a recessed mount attached to the body side member, with the lower end seated in a housing in the lower link next to the axle. A spring seating rubber is installed between the top of each spring and the recessed mount. Telescopic shock absorbers are mounted at an angle behind the axle.

Rubber bumpers are installed at each side above the axle.

Shock Absorbers

These units are completely sealed. No refilling or adjustment is necessary.

Removal and Installation

The rear shock absorbers must be disconnected unless the weight of the car is either on the wheels or on stands under the rear axle.

1. With the car standing on its wheels, or the rear axle supported on axle stands, remove the retaining bolt and rubbers from the lower mounting.
2. Remove the nuts and washers from the top mounting plate, which are accessible from inside the trunk, and remove the shock absorber.
3. Before installing replacement units, air should be bled from the valves as follows:
4. Test for low fluid level or air trapped in cylinder by holding shock absorber in its normal vertical position and extending and compressing the unit.
5. If air is present, hold shock absorber

in its normal vertical position and fully extend it.

6. Invert unit and compress it. Do not extend unit while inverted.
7. Repeat several times to expel any air trapped in cylinder.
8. If air is still present, replace shock absorber. Repeat the above operations before installing a new shock absorber.
9. Installation is the reverse of removal. Tighten the shock absorber fasteners to 12-13 ft. lbs.

Coil Spring

Removal and Installation

1. Jack up the rear of the car and support the body on a stand positioned under the body side member just forward of the lower link front bracket.
2. With a jack supporting the axle, remove the shock absorber lower mounting and carefully lower the jack until the coil spring can be lifted out.
3. Installation is the reverse of the above procedure.
4. Be sure the coil spring insulator is properly located between the coil spring and the retaining pocket.
5. When installing the coil spring, use a front spring compressor across four of the coils in the middle of the spring. Tighten the compressor just enough to give the spring a slight curve.
6. Place the spring in position with the compressor facing toward the front of the car and the adjuster end through the center hole in the lower link.
7. Raise the axle until the shock absorber, fully extended, can be installed onto its lower mounting.
8. With the top of the spring in contact with the coil spring insulator, release the compressor carefully.

Suspension Links

The following instructions are given to remove any one link at a time but, if necessary to remove all the links, begin by removing the rear axle.

Upper Suspension Links

Removal and Installation

1. The upper links can be removed and installed with the car standing on the wheels if only one link at a time is removed and installed.
2. Remove the pivot nuts and bolts to remove link.
3. Installation is the reverse of removal. It may be necessary to slightly tilt the axle to install the pivot bolts.
4. Final tightening of the pivot bolt nuts must be made with the car standing unloaded on the wheels.
5. Bounce the car a few times before tightening nuts to ensure that the bushings are seated and not twisted.
6. Tighten the pivot bolt nuts to 40 ft. lbs.

FRONT SUSPENSION

The front suspension consists of two vertically mounted strut assemblies, fastened at the top to rubber mounted thrust bearings on the front fender panel. The lower ends are secured to a swivel joint integral with the lower control arms. The strut mounting points determine caster, camber, and steering axis which are non-adjustable. Each strut contains a shock absorber unit within the outer tube, which is also a reservoir for the operating fluid. Coil springs mounted externally on the struts absorb road shocks along with the shock absorber unit, while the riding forces of the vehicle are carried on the upper thrust bearings. A rubber boot centered within the coil spring protects the highly machined surface of the shock absorber rod from road dirt. Rebound is controlled by a stop built into the shock absorber.

Front Hub and Bearings

Removal and Installation

1. Apply the handbrake, jack up the front of the car and support on axle stands.
2. Remove the wheel.
3. Remove the brake caliper with pads.
4. Pry off the hub dust-cap, remove the cotter pin, castellated lock cap, plain nut, and washer.
5. Remove the hub as an assembly, complete with bearings.
6. The larger, inner roller bearing can be removed after removing the grease seal. When new bearings are to be installed, the outer cases must be replaced also.
7. The special spacer for the wiping edge of the grease seal can now be removed from the spindle, if not already removed with the hub assembly.

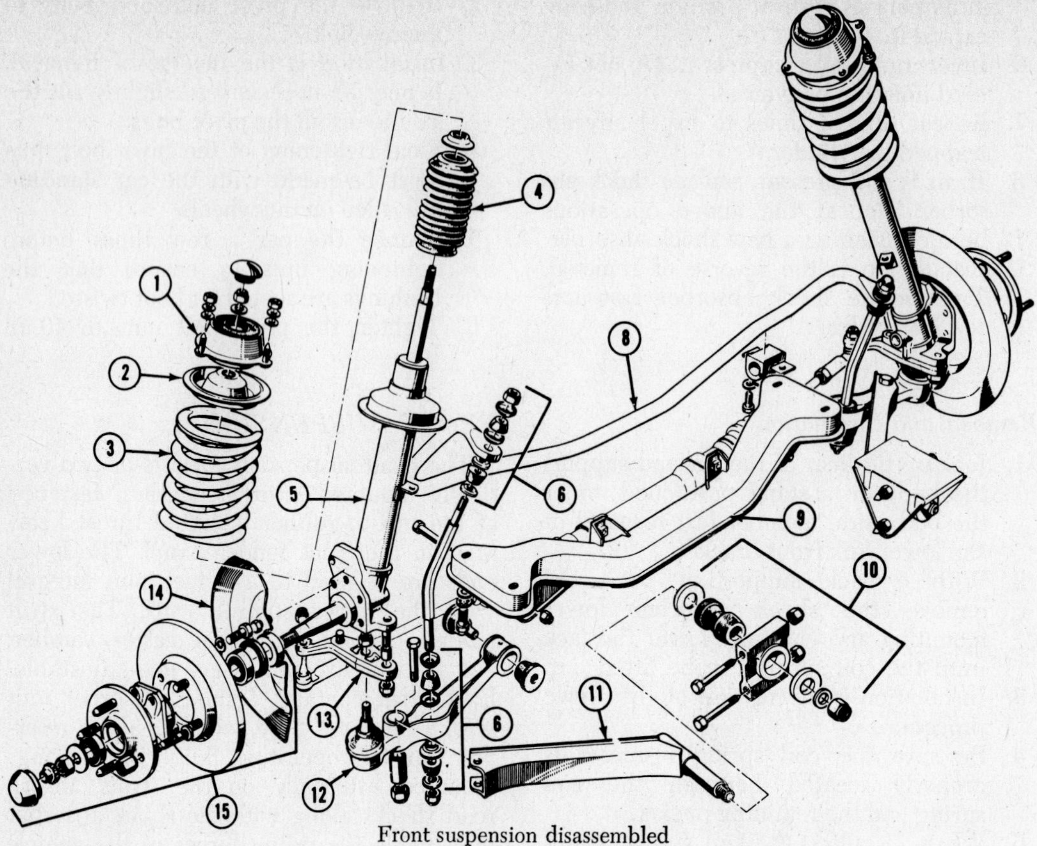

Front suspension disassembled

1. Upper swivel bearing
2. Mounting plate
3. Coil spring
4. Rubber boot
5. Suspension strut
6. Stabilizer bar link end fittings (2)
7. Link
8. Stabilizer bar
9. Cross member
10. Drag strut, front mounting
11. Drag strut
12. Lower control arm
13. Steering arm
14. Shield
15. Hub and brake disc assembly

Assembly and Installation

1. Clean all parts and check the condition of the wheel studs and brake disc. Any loose wheel studs must be replaced.
2. When new bearings are needed, press the outer races into their respective ends of the hub, with the larger internal diameter of both races facing outward.
   All roller and race assemblies must be kept together as units and not changed separately.
3. It is important to pack the hub and roller assemblies with grease. The amount added to the hub must be spread evenly and must not exceed the height of a straight line between the two bearing races.
4. Place the hub on a clean surface with its inner end up and insert the larger

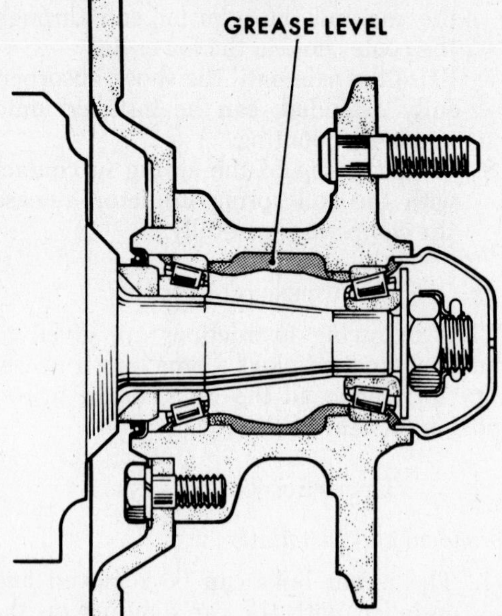

Front hub—sectional view showing correct grease level

inner roller assembly, followed by a new grease seal, lightly greased and with the flange towards the bearing. Press the seal into position, flush with the end of the hub.

5. Press the special spacer, bevelled edge upward, into the center of the grease seal by hand.
6. Install the smaller roller bearing on the outer end of the hub.
7. Position the complete hub on the spindle, carefully holding it in place while fitting the washer and retaining nut.
8. Adjust the wheel bearing.
9. Install the brake caliper.
10. Install the wheel and lower vehicle.

Wheel Bearing Adjustment

The end-play of the front hub bearings must be correct. Otherwise the bearings may become damaged or the brake pads may be knocked back resulting in reduced braking efficiency.

1. Jack up the front of car until the front wheels are clear of the floor. When jacking up the front end of the car, be sure that the jack platform is under the center of the front crossmember.
2. Remove the hub cap from the wheel to be adjusted and pry off the hub dust cap.
3. Remove the cotter pin from the spindle and remove the castellated lock cap.
4. While rotating the wheel and hub, tighten the nut to 15-20 ft. lbs.

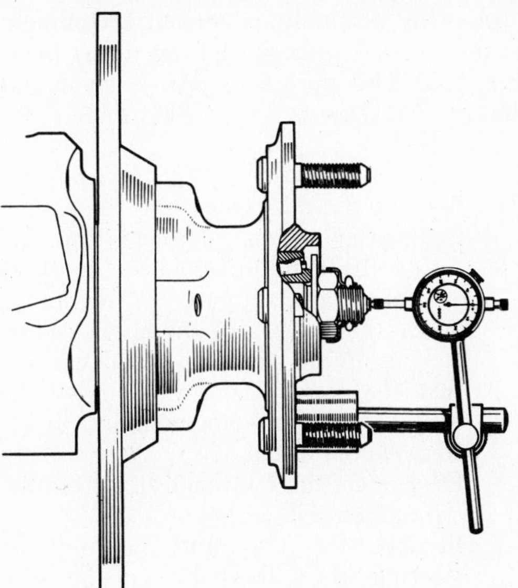

Checking front hub end play with dial indicator

5. Back off the nut 1/6 turn. Rotate the hub, and check the end-play with a dial indicator.
6. When the correct end-play (.002-.004″) is obtained, install the castellated lock cap and a new cotter pin.
7. Install the hub dust cap and hub cap, lower the car, and remove the jack.

NOTE: The hub dust cap must not contain grease when installed.

Stabilizer Bar

The stabilizer bar is located behind the front crossmember, and is held to the body side members by means of rubber insulated brackets.

Removal

1. Leave the weight of the car on the front wheels.
2. Remove the nuts, washers, and rubber bushing securing the lower ends of the links to the lower control arms.
3. Remove the rubber insulated brackets holding the bar to the body side members. Remove the bar as an assembly.
4. If necessary, remove the nuts, washers and rubber bushings from the upper ends of the links.
5. Replace any rubber bushings showing any signs of wear or deterioration.

Installation

Installation is the reverse of the removal procedure with particular attention to the following:

1. The rubber bushings must be compressed into the brackets to ease the installation of the bolts.
2. Be sure that the ends of the bar are forward and angled down when installed to allow free engagement of the links.
3. Install links with the shorter leg facing down.
4. Assemble the washers and rubber bushings in position.
5. Tighten the nuts on each end of the link until the face of the washer at the end of the link is 9/16-5/8″ (14.29 and 15.88mm.) from the end of the link.

Drag Struts

Drag struts are rubber mounted and connected between the forward end of the body underframe and the lower control arm. They stabilize the lower end of the suspension struts.

REMOVAL AND INSTALLATION

Drag struts can be removed with the weight of the car on its wheels.

1. Remove the two nuts and bolts from the mounting bracket on the frame.
2. Remove the nut and bolt from the rear of the lower control arm. It may be necessary to slightly load the front end for the bolt to be removed.
3. Pry the front mounting bracket down and forward and remove the drag strut.
4. Installation is the reverse of the removal procedure.

Drag Strut Mounting Bracket

REMOVAL

1. Remove the drag strut.
2. Remove the front nut and pull the drag strut from the rubber bushing.
3. Remove the rubber bushing by placing the bracket in a vise and inserting a blunt screwdriver behind the thin flange of the bushing, then prying inward. The mounting bracket has an embossed number on one side of the casting.
4. Place the new bushing with the thin flange against the housing. Then, carefully push the flange in with a rounded screwdriver blade and push in the bushing.

INSTALLATION

1. Position the mounting bracket on the drag strut with the embossed number facing forward and toward the center of the car.
2. Install the washer and nut finger tight.
3. Install the strut.

Lower Control Arm

REMOVAL

1. Jack up the car and support on axle stands under the body frame. When jacking up the front end of the car, be sure that the jack platform is under the center of the front crossmember.
2. Remove the nut and disconnect the tie rod from the steering arm.
3. Remove the steering arm to strut nuts.
4. Remove the lower nut, washers, and rubber bushings from the stabilizer bar link.
5. Remove the drag strut.
6. Remove the pivot nut and bolt from lower control arm to crossmember. To remove the bolt from the crossmember, turn the steering to the right stop for the right bolt or to the left stop for left bolt.
7. Remove the lower control arm from the crossmember and remove the rubber bushings from the inner pivot point. The bushings are in two parts and no special tools are needed for their replacement.
8. Remove the nut holding the steering arm to ball joint.
9. Disconnect steering arm from ball joint.

INSTALLATION

Installation is the reverse of the removal instructions with special attention to the following:

1. A new nut must be installed on the ball pin holding the steering arm and tightened to 44 ft. lbs.
2. Be sure that the steering arm fits squarely on the dowels and the faces are fully seated in the strut.
3. The lower control arm to crossmember pivot bolts must be reassembled with the head to the rear. Otherwise damage to the boots on the steering gear may result.
4. Adjust the stabilizer bar link bottom nut for a free play of 9/16-5/8″.

Strut Assembly

A strut assembly is removed complete with hub, coil springs, and top thrust bearing unit. The procedure for removal and installation is the same for either side.

REMOVAL

1. Remove the dust cover and loosen the top bearing nut one complete turn.
2. Apply the handbrake, raise the front of the car and support on axle stands under the body side members. When jacking up the front end of the car, see that the jack platform is under the center of the front crossmember.
3. Remove the wheel.
4. Disconnect the hydraulic line from the strut and install a plug.
5. Remove the two nuts holding the steering arm to the bottom of the strut.
6. Remove the lower nut, rubber bushings, and washers from the stabilizer

bar link, through the lower control arm.

7. Support the strut.
8. Remove the three nuts and washers which hold the upper end of the strut assembly to the inner fender panel. Do not attempt to remove the thrust bearing nut which shows through the hole in the fender panel and which was loosened previously.
9. Remove the complete assembly.

INSTALLATION

Installation of a strut assembly is the reverse of the removal procedure with the following additional requirements:

1. All self-locking nuts should be discarded and replaced by new nuts.
2. All nuts and bolts must be tightened as below. Do not overtighten the rubber mountings on the stabilizer bar link.

Fastener	*Torque (ft. lbs.)*
Strut upper swivel fixing	15
Strut to upper swivel bearing	31
Steering arm to lower strut	58
Drag strut bracket to body	28
Drag strut to bracket	40
Drag strut to lower control arm	36
Stabilizer bar bracket to body	28
Strut nut	48
Lower swivel ball joint to steering arm	44
Lower control arm to crossmember	28
Crossmember to body	54

3. Check the steering alignment on completion of the operation.

Thrust Bearing and Coil Spring

REMOVAL

1. Remove the strut.
2. Mount the complete strut on a wheel and tighten.
3. Place the assembly on a workbench and prevent the strut from moving by placing a wooden wedge between the strut and the tire.
4. Install a coil spring compressor on the coil spring. Observe the following:
   a. The adjuster bolt heads must be facing the bottom of the strut.
   b. The compressing clamps must be opposite each other on the spring.
   c. The claws of the compressing clamps must be placed over the coils of the spring at the extreme ends.
5. Using a socket and ratchet wrench, tighten the spring compressor enough to remove the spring tension from the thrust bearing unit. During the tightening procedure, check that both clamps are equally loaded by giving each adjuster bolt an equal amount of turns.
6. Remove the nut holding the thrust bearing unit to the strut. Remove the locating washer and bearing unit.
7. Lift the coil spring from the assembly and remove the clamps by loosening each adjuster bolt equally a few turns at a time.

CAUTION: The front springs are of unequal length, with the longer one on the right.

INSTALLATION

1. Check the thrust bearing for smooth operation and good condition.
2. Be sure that the rubber boot is correctly positioned on the strut.
3. Install the coil spring compressor on the spring as described above.
4. Place the spring into position on the strut with the adjuster bolt heads towards the bottom of the strut.
5. Place the bearing assembly, locating washer, and nut in place on the strut.
6. Rotate bearing and tighten the nut.

CAUTION: Do not exceed 31 ft.lbs. torque on the thrust bearing securing nut or the thrust bearing will be damaged.

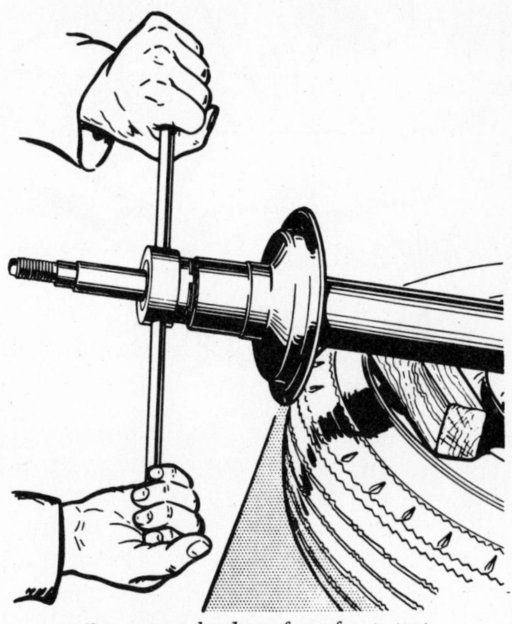

Removing gland nut from front strut

Strut

Disassembly

Remove the thrust bearing and coil spring then proceed as follows:

1. Remove the rubber boot from the shock absorber rod.
2. Push the shock absorber rod fully into the strut until it bottoms.
3. Straighten the staked area which locks the gland nut to the top of the strut.
4. Using a gland nut wrench, remove the nut from the top of the strut.
5. Place an oil tray under the top end of the strut and gently pull the shock absorber rod to dislodge the rubber O-ring, together with the shock absorber rod guide bushing and the shock absorber unit from the strut.
6. Discard remaining oil in the strut.

Assembly

The strut and shock absorber unit must be absolutely clean before assembling.

1. Using a suitable solvent, thoroughly clean the strut inside and outside. Dry with compressed air.
2. Insert the shock absorber unit into the strut.

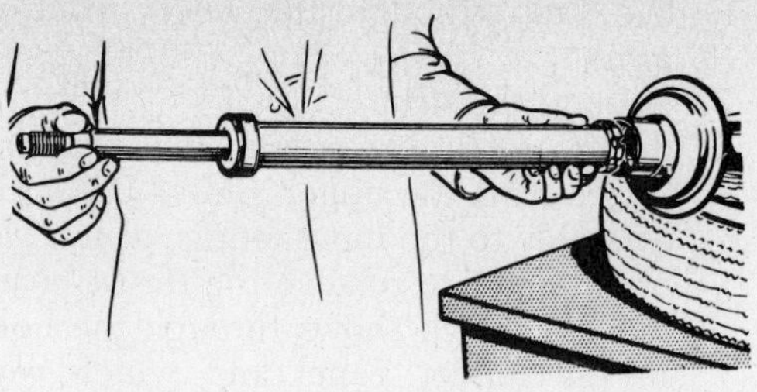

Removing shock absorber from front strut

3. Add clean fresh oil to the assembly, putting equal amounts into the shock absorber unit and strut.
4. Make sure that the shock absorber rod guide bushing and O-ring are installed to the shock absorber in the correct order.
5. Install the gland nut and using a gland nut wrench, together with a torque wrench adapter and a torque wrench, tighten the nut.
6. Prime the shock absorber by moving the shock absorber rod in and out slowly with long strokes until a constant resistance is felt.
7. Stake the top edge of the strut into the slot in the gland nut.

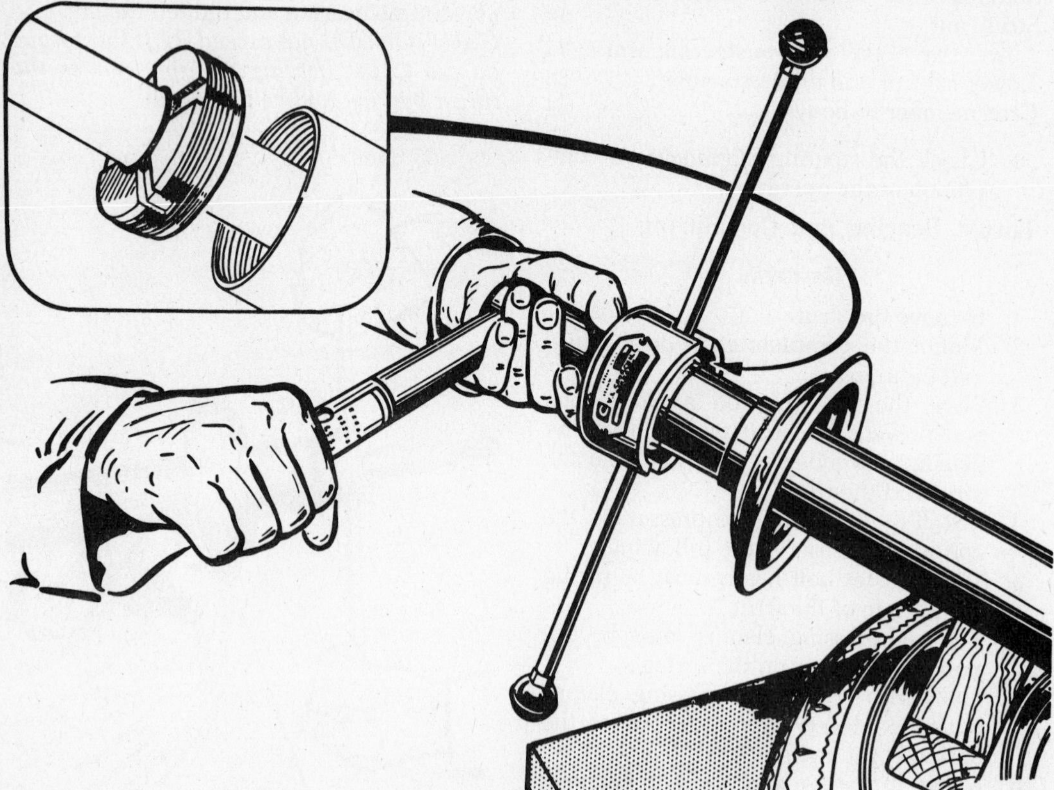

Tightening gland nut to top of strut

8. Install a new rubber boot. Replace the coil spring and thrust bearing.

Front Wheel Alignment

The front wheels must be aligned periodically or when the front suspension or steering linkage has been damaged. The only adjustable alignment angle is toe-in. The other alignment angles are non-adjustable. Refer to the Chassis and Wheel Alignment Specifications Chart for figures. Before beginning alignment, prepare the car as follows:

1. The car must be placed on a level surface and in a position that allows some forward movement, as required by certain types of wheel alignment gauges.
2. The tires must have the same amount of tread on each side and be inflated to the normal running pressures (24 psi front & rear—4 passengers; 30 psi rear—over 4 passengers).
3. Front hub bearings must have the correct end play.
4. The strut swivel bearings and tie rod ball joints must be in good condition.
5. Front wheels must be checked for run-out. Depending on the checking gauge used, the points of maximum run-out may need to be positioned so that they are clear of the contact points of the gauge.

Toe-in

The front wheels toe-in when the distance between the front of the wheels is less than that at the rear of the wheels.

1. Rotate both tie rods an equal amount, until the correct toe-in is obtained.
2. Prepare the car in the manner described above.
3. Set front wheels in the straight ahead position.
4. Check the front wheel alignment with a gauge, following the gauge manufacturer's instructions. Toe-in should be 1/32 to 1/8" or 0°20′ to 0°30′.
5. If the gauge shows the amount of toe-in is incorrect, loosen the ball joint locknuts on both tie rods.
6. Loosen the screws in the rubber boot on the inner ends of the tie rod and check that the boots are free on the tie rods.
7. Tighten the locknuts on the tie rod end joints, taking care not to alter the setting. Center the tie rod positions.
8. Line up the boots on the tie rods, untwisted, and tighten the clamps.

Wheel Angle on Turns

1. Prepare the car in the manner described previously.
2. Check the front wheel alignment (toe-in) and adjust if necessary.
3. Set the front wheels straight ahead.
4. With the front wheels on the turntable gauges, set the gauges to zero.
5. Turn the steering to the right until the left wheel turntable reads 20°. The right turntable should now read 20°.
6. Turn the steering to the left until the right wheel turntable reads 20°. The left turntable should now read 20°.
7. If the angles are unequal, both tie rods should be adjusted.
8. If it cannot be adjusted correctly, the steering linkage is damaged.

Front Wheel Camber Angle

This is the angle of inclination of the front wheels from the vertical when viewed from the front. Inclination outward at the top of the wheel is positive camber, and inclination inward is negative camber. If the wheels are set vertically, the camber will be zero.

1. The angle is non-adjustable, but should be checked in case of accident damage or steering difficulties.
2. Prepare the car in the manner described under Front Wheel Alignment.
3. Install a suitable checking gauge and check according to the manufacturer's instructions. Note the gauge reading. Camber should be +1° to +1°45′.
4. If the camber is incorrect, check the spindle for distortion, the lower swivel bearing and the lower control arm pivot bushing for wear or looseness.

Steering Axis Inclination

Viewed from the front of the vehicle, this is the angle at which the pivoting axis of the front suspension strut assembly is inclined inward from the vertical. The angle is non-adjustable, but should be checked in case of accident damage or steering difficulties.

1. Prepare the car in the manner described earlier.
2. With a suitable gauge check according to the manufacturer's instructions. Note the gauge reading. Steering axis

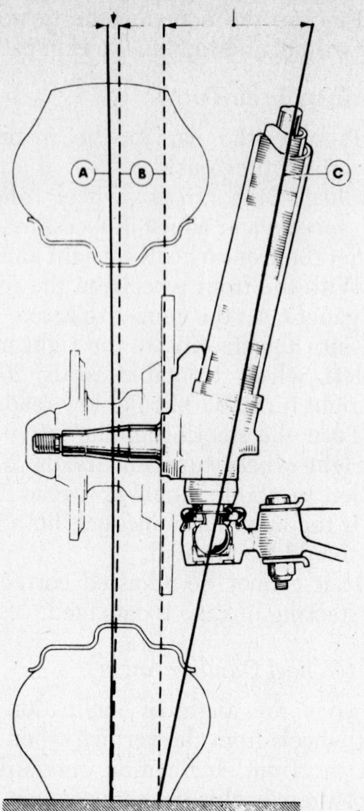

Steering angles. A is wheel angle, B is vertical angle, C is steering axis.

inclination should be 10°30′ to 11°45′ at +1° camber.

3. If the steering axis inclination is incorrect, check the lower control arm pivot bushings and the upper and lower mounting points of the strut assembly for wear and looseness.

Caster Angle

Viewed from the side of the vehicle, caster is the angle at which the front suspension strut is inclined from the vertical. Rearward inclination at the top from the center line is positive while forward inclination is negative caster. If the pivoting axis is vertical, the caster will be zero.

This angle is non-adjustable, but should be checked in case of accident damage or directional instability.

1. Prepare the car in the manner described earlier.
2. Install a suitable gauge and check according to the manufacturer's instructions. Note the gauge reading caster should be +1° to +1°30′.
3. If caster is wrong, check the stabilizer bar, drag strut, lower control arm, and associated parts.

Steering Linkage

A rack and pinion steering gear, with two inline tie rods, connects the steering column and the steering arms. Both tie rods are adjustable and provide a means of adjusting the front wheel alignment.

Aligning the Linkage

For correct wheel angles on turns, and to ensure the correct setting of the steering linkage when new parts have been installed, the following procedure applies:

1. Prepare the car as described earlier.
2. Loosen the locknuts on both tie rods and disconnect the tie rods at their ball joints.
3. Center the steering gear by turning the steering wheel to the mid-position between the stops.
4. Set both front wheels straight ahead and measure the distances from the center of the tire treads to similar positions on each side of the body frame. If these distances are equal, set the scale on the turntable gauges to zero.
5. Adjust both tie rods until their ball joints enter freely into the steering arms without moving the front wheels.
6. Reconnect both tie rods and install new nuts, tightening them to 44 ft. lbs.
7. Check and adjust the front wheel alignment.

Steering Stop Angles

The maximum angles are controlled by the movement of the rack and pinion steering gear and should be 39° (inner wheel) and 37° to 30° (outer wheel).

1. Prepare the car in the manner described earlier.
2. Turn the steering to the right full stop. Read the right turntable scale and compare the reading with that of the left scale.
3. Turn the steering to full left stop. Read the left (inner wheel) turntable scale and compare the reading with that of the right scale.

STEERING

The steering gear is the rack and pinion type; tie rods, operating the steering arms, are attached to each end of the steering

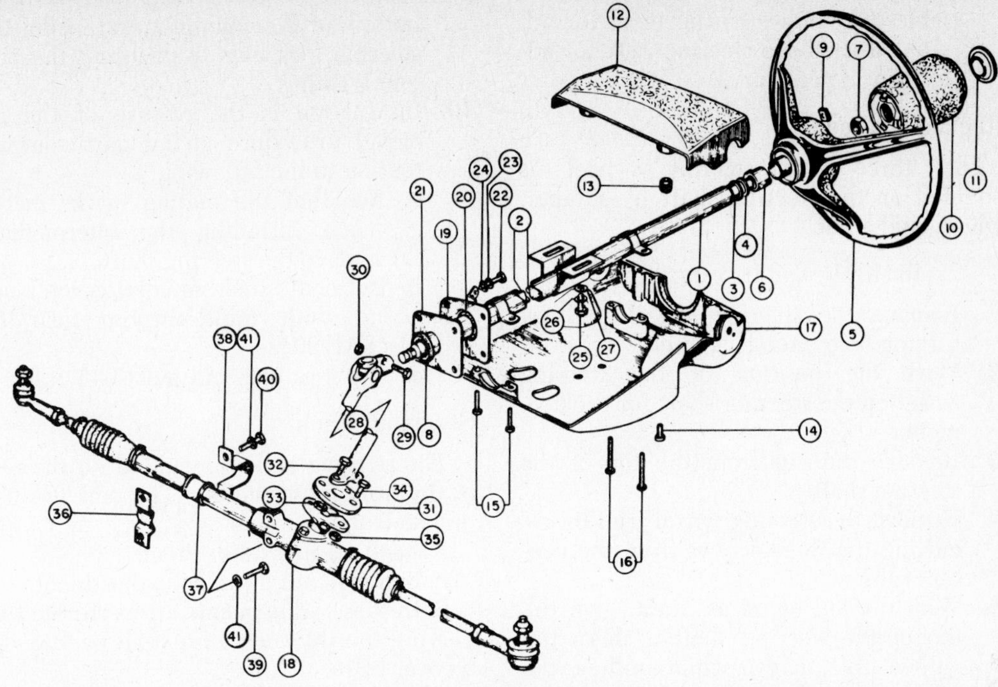

Steering gear disassembled

1. Column jacket
2. Steering shaft
3. Bearing
4. Shim
5. Steering wheel
6. Striker
7. Nut
8. Sprag washer
9. Clip
10. Pad
11. Medallion
12. Column cover (upper)
13. Insert
14. Screw
15. Screw
16. Screw
17. Column cover (lower)
18. Rack
19. Plate
20. Seal
21. Plate
22. Screw
23. Washer
24. Washer
25. Setscrew
26. Washer
27. Washer
28. Shaft (intermediate)
29. Bolt
30. Nut
31. Flexible coupling
32. Bolt
33. Nut
34. Bolt
35. Nut
36. Bracket
37. Insulator
38. Bracket
39. Setscrew
40. Setscrew
41. Washer

rack by tie rod ends enclosed in rubber boots.

Steering wheel movement is transferred by the steering column through an intermediate shaft and a flexible coupling to a helical pinion. Pinion rotation moves the rack laterally and the tie rods, attached to the end of the rack, transfer the movement to the steering arms and causes the wheels to move.

The steering gear assembly is supplied by two different manufacturers, Burman and Cam Gears. The assemblies are interchangeable, but individual components are not interchangeable.

The following checks will show if the linkage or steering gear is worn or damaged:

1. With the front suspension in good condition, maximum free play measured at the rim of the steering wheel should be 3/8″ (9.525mm.).
2. Steering wheel movement while the vehicle is stationary should not make noise. If wear is indicated, proceed as follows:
3. Raise the front of the vehicle, install suitable stands and remove the front wheels.

CAUTION: Do not move the wheels from stop to stop with the front wheels jacked up. This causes pressure to build up, damaging the bellows.

4. Check tie rod ends for looseness and rubber covers for damage. Replace if necessary.
5. Check rubber boots for punctures and oil leaks. Replace if necessary.
6. Check tie rod movement for smooth operation, looseness or end float. Remove steering rack for adjustment if necessary.
7. Observe the pinion input shaft while turning the steering wheel. Any appre-

ciable play indicates the need for adjustment. Remove steering rack for adjustment if necessary.

Steering Wheel

The three-spoke steering wheel is mounted on the steering shaft by a taper, splines, and a nut.

Removal and Installation

1. Remove the steering wheel pad by turning it counterclockwise.
2. Mark the position of the steering wheel on the steering shaft for replacement.
3. Remove the nut from the top of the steering shaft.
4. Remove the steering wheel trim by removing the three screws from the center of the wheel.
5. With the aid of an assistant, give the top of the steering shaft a sharp tap with a soft mallet while pulling the steering wheel up. Do not use heavy blows or pull heavily on the steering wheel as this will disturb the location of the sprag washer at the bottom of the steering shaft, resulting in hard steering.
6. Installation is the reverse of the removal procedure. Make sure that:
   a. Mating marks are aligned.
   b. Steering wheel is correctly aligned with the turn signal striker boss.
   c. Steering wheel locknut is tightened to 32 ft.lbs.

Steering Column

Removal and Installation

1. Disconnect the battery ground cable.
2. Unlock the column.
3. Remove the column cover by removing six screws.
4. Remove the indicator switch from the column by removing two screws.
5. Remove the four screws from the floor opening plate.
6. Remove the two bolts with spacers from the steering support bracket, noting the position of the ground lead.
7. Mark the position of the column in relation to the intermediate shaft.
8. Disconnect the column from the intermediate shaft by removing the bolt and pulling the column from inside the car.
9. Remove the steering shaft from the bottom of the column jacket, using the steering lock boss to push out the bottom bushing.
10. Installation is the reverse of the removal procedure giving particular attention to the following:
   a. See that the mating marks match when installing the intermediate shaft to the steering shaft.
   b. Lubricate steering column top bearing with multi-purpose gear oil (SAE 90).
   c. Tighten bolt and nut to 15 ft.lbs.

Steering Rack

The steering rack is mounted on the rear of the front crossmember. The rack has two adjustments:

1. Rack damper adjustment.
2. Pinion bearing preload adjustment.

Both these adjustments are performed by varying the thickness of a shim pack under a cover plate.

Removal and Installation

1. Jack up the front of the vehicle and place on suitable stands.
2. Remove front wheels.
3. Disconnect the tie rod ends.
4. Disconnect the intermediate shaft from the flexible coupling by removing two nuts and bolts.
5. Remove two bolts from both rack mountings, noting the position of the inner bracket located behind the rubber insulator.
6. Remove steering rack assembly.
7. Installation is the reverse of the removal procedure.
8. Tighten nuts to 18 ft. lbs.

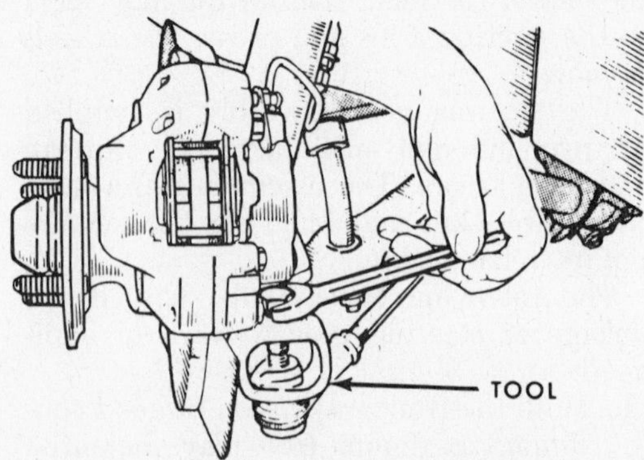

Disconnecting tie rod end

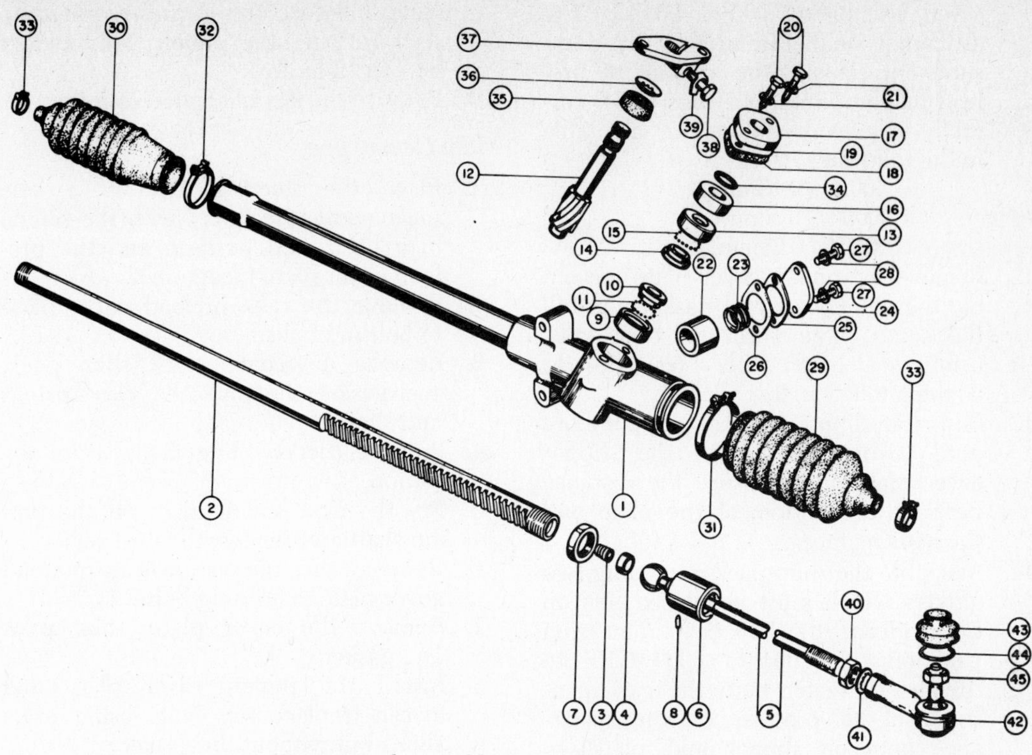

Steering rack assembly (Burman type) disassembled

1. Housing
2. Rack
3. Spring
4. Ball seat
5. Tie Rod
6. Housing
7. Locknut
8. Pin
9. Adjuster
10. Adjuster
11. Bearings
12. Pinion
13. Adjuster
14. Adjuster
15. Bearings
16. Spacer
17. Cover
18. Gasket
19. Shim
20. Setscrew
21. Washer
22. Slipper
23. Spring
24. Cover
25. Gasket
26. Shim
27. Setscrew
28. Washer
29. Boot
30. Boot
31. Clamp
32. Clamp
33. Clamp
34. Seal
35. Seal, dust
36. Retainer, dust seal
37. Flange, pinion
38. Bolt
39. Washer
40. Locknut
41. Washer
42. Tie rod end
43. Seal
44. Retainer
45. Locknut

Adjustment

Burman Type

1. Place the steering rack in a soft jawed vise with the pinion in the horizontal position.
2. Remove the rack preload cover to housing bolts.
3. Remove the cover plate, shim pack, and gasket. Remove the spring and slipper.
4. Remove the coupling flange from the pinion.
5. Pry the pinion dust seal retainer off the pinion shaft and remove the dust seal.
6. Remove the two bolts which secure the piston bearing preload cover plate to the housing.
7. Remove the cover plate shim pack and gasket.
8. Install the pinion cover plate and loosely assemble the bolts without the shims or gasket.

CAUTION: Adding shims increases clearance.

9. Tighten the cover plate bolts evenly until the cover plate barely contacts the pinion bearing.
10. Measure the gap between the cover plate and the steering gear housing with feeler gauges, noting the dimension. Make sure that the cover plate is tightened down evenly by taking feeler gauge measurements next to each bolt.
11. Assemble a shim pack including two gaskets (one on each side of shim pack

when assembled) .002 to .004″ (.05 to .010mm.) smaller than the gap measurement. This is the amount of preload on the pinion bearings when correctly shimmed. Shims are available in the following sizes:

.002″ (0.05mm.)
.005″ (0.13mm.)
.010″ (0.25mm.)

12. Remove the pinion cover plate, assemble the shim pack and gaskets. Install the cover plate with the two bolts, using sealer on the bolt threads. Tighten to 6-8 ft. lbs.
13. Push the slipper into the slipper bore until it bottoms. Install the slipper cover plate and measure the distance between the bottom of the plate and the housing face.
14. Assemble the shim pack, including two gaskets which must be placed one on each side of the shim pack. The shim pack must be .004 to .006″ (.101 to .152mm.) greater than the gap measurement to provide working clearance between slipper and plate, to prevent hard steering.
15. Install the spring into the slipper recess.
16. Install the cover plate and shims with the bolts using sealer on the threads. Tighten to 6-8 ft. lbs.
17. Install the pinion dust seal and retainer.
18. Install the coupling flange to the pinion spline parallel to the center line of the rack, with the rack centered to maintain correct alignment. Use a new tab washer and tighten the bolt to 10-15 ft. lbs.
19. Bolt the flexible flange coupling to the coupling flange and, using a spring scale, measure the torque required to start rotating the pinion. This should be 7 to 12 in. lbs.
20. Remove the flexible flange coupling.

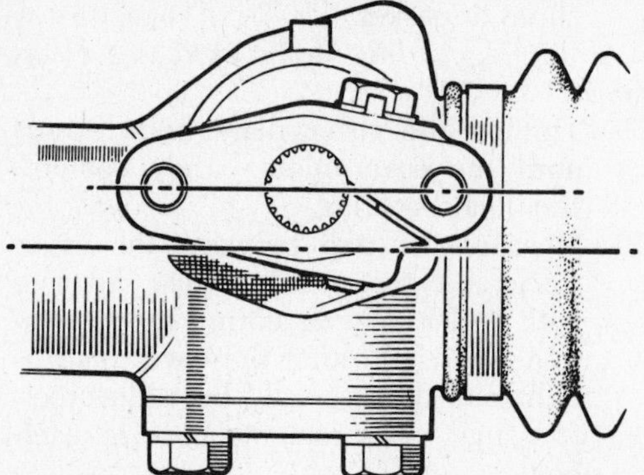

Installing coupling flange to pinion, parallel to rack center line

Cam Gears Type

1. Place the steering rack in a vise (using soft vise jaws) with the pinion in a horizontal position and the preload cover plate facing up.
2. Remove the rack preload cover plate to housing bolts.
3. Remove the cover plate, shim pack, and gasket. Remove the two springs and slipper.
4. Remove the coupling flange from the pinion.
5. Pry the dust seal retainer off the pinion shaft and remove the dust seal.
6. Remove the pinion bearing preload cover plate to housing bolts.
7. Remove the cover plate, shim pack and gasket.
8. Install the pinion cover plate and loosely replace the bolts using extra shims but without the gasket.
9. Tighten the cover plate bolts evenly until the cover plate barely contacts the pinion bearing.

CAUTION: Adding shims decreases clearance.

10. Measure the gap between the cover plate and the steering gear housing with feeler gauges, noting the dimension. Make sure that the cover plate is tightened down evenly by taking feeler gauge measurements next to each bolt.
11. Use a shim pack (including a gasket placed next to the cover plate when assembled) .001 to .003″ (.03 to .07mm.) smaller than the gap measurement; this is the amount of preload on the pinion bearings when correctly shimmed. Shims are available in the following sizes:

.005″ (.13mm.)
.0075″ (.19mm.)
.010″ (.25mm.)

12. Remove the pinion cover plate, assemble the shim pack and gasket. Replace the cover plate and fasten with the two bolts using sealer on the bolt threads. Tighten to 12-15 ft. lbs.
13. Push the slipper into the slipper bore until it bottoms. Measure the distance between the base of the recess in the slipper and the steering gear housing

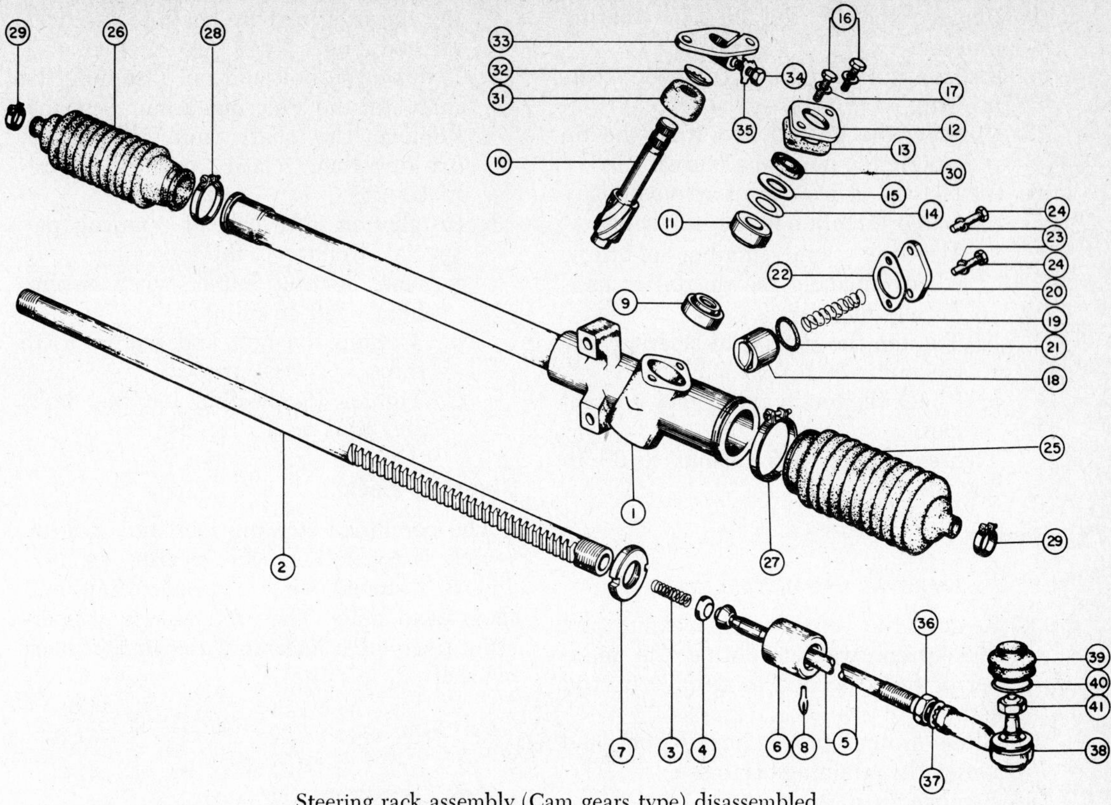

Steering rack assembly (Cam gears type) disassembled

1. Housing
2. Rack
3. Spring
4. Ball seat
5. Tie rod
6. Housing
7. Locknut
8. Pin
9. Bearing
10. Pinion
11. Bearing
12. Cover
13. Gasket
14. Shim
15. Spacer
16. Setscrew
17. Washer
18. Slipper
19. Spring
20. Cover
21. Seal
22. Joint
23. Washer
24. Setscrew
25. Boot
26. Boot
27. Clamp
28. Clamp
29. Clamp
30. Seal
31. Seal, dust
32. Retainer, dust seal
33. Flange, pinion
34. Bolt
35. Washer
36. Locknut
37. Washer
38. Tie rod end
39. Seal
40. Retainer
41. Locknut

face. (The measurement must always be taken from the base of the deeper central recess of the slipper). Note the dimension.

14. To this dimension, add a shim pack and gasket of .002 to .005″ (.050 to .127mm.) thickness.

CAUTION: It is important that this dimension be adjusted accurately as noisy or hard steering may result.

15. Put the spring into the slipper recess.
16. Position the shim pack so that the gasket is next to the cover plate.
17. Install the cover plate, fasten with the two bolts, using sealer on the threads. Tighten to 6-8 ft. lbs.
18. Install the pinion dust seal and retainer.
19. Install the coupling flange to the pinion spline parallel to the center line of the rack, with the rack centered, for correct alignment. Use a new tab washer and tighten the bolt to 10-15 ft. lbs.
20. Bolt the flexible flange coupling to the coupling flange and, using a spring scale, measure the torque required to start rotating the pinion. This should be 7 to 12 in. lbs.

Tie Rod Ends

Removal and Installation

1. Apply the handbrake, jack up the front of the vehicle and place it on stands.
2. Loosen the locknut on the outer end of the tie rod next to the ball joint.

3. Remove the tie rod end to steering arm nut.
4. Remove the tie rod end from the steering arm.
5. Unscrew the tie rod end from the tie rod noting the number of turns.
6. Installation is reverse of removal; pay particular attention to the following:
   a. Use the same number of turns when replacing the tie rod as used during removal.
   b. Tighten the tie rod to steering arm locknut to 32 ft.lbs.
   c. Check the toe-in and wheel stop angles.
7. Tighten the tie rod locknut to 30 ft. lbs.

Boot

REMOVAL AND INSTALLATION

1. Remove the tie rod end, locknut, and shake-proof washer, noting the number of turns needed to remove tie rod end.
2. Clean around the damaged boot and loosen the retaining clamps.
3. Remove the damaged boot.
4. Move the steering wheel slowly to compress the opposite boot and allow oil to drain.
5. Install new boot and clamps and refill with SAE 90 gear oil. Use an oil can having a fine opening in the nozzle.
6. Install the locknut and tie rod end to the tie rod, turning them the same number of turns required to remove them.
7. Check the toe-in and wheel stop angles.
8. Tighten the tie rod locknut to 30 ft. lbs.

Flexible Flange Coupling

REMOVAL AND INSTALLATION

1. Remove the four nuts and bolts fastening the flexible coupling to the pinion shaft flange and intermediate shaft. Remove the flexible coupling.
2. Installation is reverse of the removal procedure.
3. Tighten the attaching bolts to 15 ft. lbs.

Intermediate Shaft

REMOVAL AND INSTALLATION

1. Remove the two nuts and bolts fastening the intermediate shaft to the flexible coupling.
2. Remove the bolt and nut fastening the shaft to the steering column spline. Remove the shaft from the spline, marking their relative position for replacement.
3. Installation is reverse of removal; pay special attention to the following:
   a. Note mating marks when assembling shaft on spline.
   b. Tighten the bolt and nut to 10-15 ft.lbs.
   c. Tighten the flexible coupling bolts and nuts to 15 ft. lbs.

Steering Lock

The combined steering lock and ignition switch is located on the steering column and is fastened by a special clamp and shear-head bolts. The unit has a key operating peg which locks in a slot in the steering shaft.

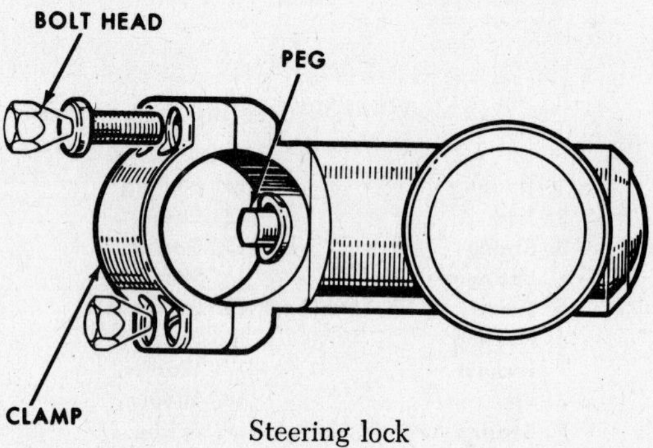

Steering lock

REMOVAL

1. Disconnect the battery ground cable.
2. Remove the cover from the steering column.
3. Disconnect the cables from the ignition switch.
4. Center punch each of the shear-head bolts. If the heads of the bolts appear irregular, they should be flattened before using the center punch.

CAUTION: Do not disturb the slotted screws in the clamp. These must remain firmly in place to permit drilling of the shear-head bolts.

5. Using a ¼" (7mm.) drill, drill a hole ⅛" (3mm.) deep in the bolt heads. The outer portion of the bolt heads will separate from the shank of the bolts if the drill has been correctly centered.

6. Remove the slotted screws from the clamp and withdraw the unit from the steering column. The bolt shanks remaining in the body of the unit can then be removed.

INSTALLATION

1. Place the unit in the Park position with the locking peg disengaged.
2. With the clamp removed, install the unit on the steering column making sure that the peg on the body of the unit seats squarely in the locating hole in the column.
3. Fasten the unit lightly but firmly to the steering column by installing the clamp, screws, and bolts. Apply light torque only, to avoid shearing off the heads of the bolts.
4. Check the operation of the lock. If the lock operates correctly, tighten the screws and apply further torque to shear the heads of the bolts.
5. Connect the cable to the ignition switch.
6. Install the column cover.
7. Reconnect the battery ground cable.

Brakes

Disc brakes are used at the front and drum brakes at the rear. A brake booster unit is used to allow light pedal pressure. The handbrake applies the rear wheel brakes only by a mechanical cable linkage that is independent of the hydraulic brake system.

The front brakes require no adjustment, while the rear brakes are self adjusting. The self adjusting mechanism is actuated by the handbrake mechanism.

The front disc pads should be replaced when the lining thickness is ⅛" (3mm.); the rear brake shoes should be replaced before the lining wears down to the shoe rivet heads.

Correct master cylinder fluid level is ¼" (6mm.) below the filler cap. Use only fluid designated for disc brake systems.

BLEEDING THE BRAKE SYSTEM

1. Be sure that both compartments of the master cylinder are kept filled during bleeding. The rear brakes must be bled first through the bleedscrew located behind the right rear wheel. Then bleed the front brakes, right wheel first.
2. By bleeding the rear brakes first, the front brakes are partly self-bled by the action of the compensating valve. The front brakes are easier to bleed after the rear brakes have been bled.
3. Open the bleedscrew enough to allow fluid to be pumped out (half a turn). Close the bleedscrew immediately after the last stroke of the pedal.
4. Depress the pedal lightly until resistance is felt and allow pedal to return slowly. Repeat until all air has been expelled at each bleedscrew. Do not try the pedal until the bleeding operation is completed as this will cause the piston in the brake warning switch actuator to move thus operating the switch.
5. Should the brake failure warning light light during the bleeding operation, the bleedscrew must be closed and the bleedscrew at the opposite end of the car opened (e.g. if bleeding the front brakes, open the bleedscrew on the rear brakes and vice versa). A steady pressure must then be applied until the light goes out. Release the pressure immediately and close the bleedscrew. Otherwise, the piston will move the opposite direction and need resetting again. When the brake failure warning light goes out, a click will be felt on the pedal as the piston moves back.

MASTER CYLINDER

The braking system uses a direct-acting power-assisted tandem master cylinder with separate outlets to the front and rear brakes.

The master cylinder contains two pistons installed one behind the other. These are supplied with hydraulic fluid from a translucent supply tank which is divided into two compartments by a verticle baffle.

The primary piston is situated at the push rod end of the master cylinder and operates the front brakes, while the secondary piston located at the forward end of the cylinder operates the rear brakes.

Both primary and secondary systems operate through a pressure differential warning actuator (brake warning switch). The actuator is operated by movement of a double ended piston operating between the fluid supply to the front and rear systems.

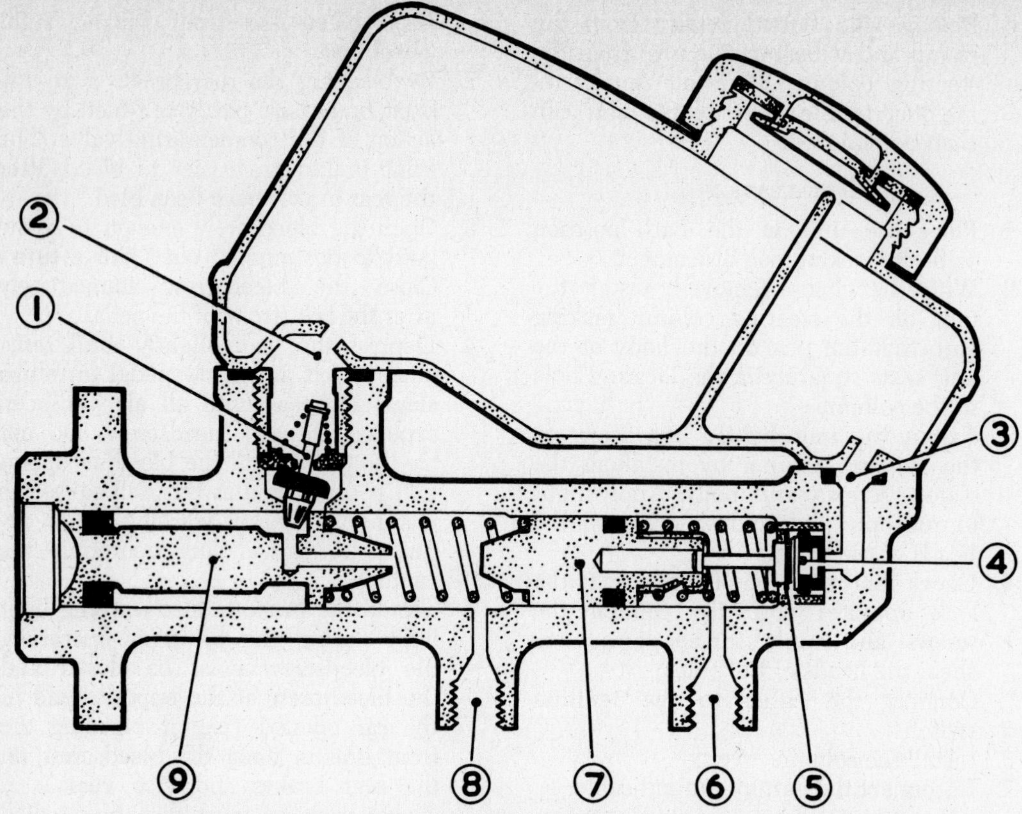

Tandem master cylinder—sectional view

1. Compensating valve
2. Inlet (front brakes)
3. Inlet (rear brakes)
4. Valve stem
5. Washer
6. Outlet (rear brakes)
7. Secondary piston
8. Outlet (front brakes)
9. Primary piston

A pressure failure in either system allows movement of the piston in the direction of the failed system, lighting the actuator and brake warning light.

Removal and Replacement

With Power Assist

1. Disconnect the brake line from the master cylinder.
2. Remove the two nuts and spring washers securing the master cylinder to the front of the power brake unit. Remove the master cylinder.
3. When replacing the master cylinder, bleed the system.

Without Power Assist

1. Disconnect the brake lines from the master cylinder.
2. Detach the pushrod from the foot pedal by removing the cotter pin and withdrawing the clevis pin and washer.
3. Remove the master cylinder by removing the two retaining nuts and washers.
4. Replacing is the reverse of the removal procedure.

Disassembly and Reassembly

1. Clean the cylinder of all road dirt and drain out any surplus fluid.
2. Remove the reservoir by removing the four retaining screws.
3. Unscrew the compensating valve securing nut and remove the seal.
4. Depress the primary plunger and remove the compensating valve. The internal parts can be removed by shaking the cylinder body.
5. Separate the pistons and the intermediate spring.
6. Lift the leaf of the spring retainer and remove the spring and center valve subassembly from the secondary piston. Remove the spring, valve spacer,

and spring washer from the valve stem and the valve from the valve head.

7. Remove the seals from the primary and secondary pistons.
8. Pry out the baffle and remove the cap washer from the filler cap.
9. Replace all seals and parts with those in the service kit. Clean the cylinder and all remaining parts with clean brake fluid. Give special attention to the following points:
10. Examine the cylinder bore and the pistons for visible score marks, ridges, or corrosion. The bore must be smooth. If there is any doubt about its condition, replace the master cylinder.
11. Lubricate all parts immediately before assembly with clean brake fluid.
12. Install the seals on the primary and secondary pistons.
13. Install the valve seal, smallest diameter leading, onto the valve head. Install the spring washer on the valve stem so that it flares away from the valve stem shoulder. Follow with the valve spacer, legs first. Attach the spring retainer to the valve stem, keyhole first. Slide the secondary spring over the spring retainer. Position the subassembly on the secondary piston. The spring must be compressed while the leaf of the spring retainer is pressed down behind the head of the piston. To do this, position the subassembly between the jaws of a bench vise with clean pieces of paper between the subassembly and the vise jaws to avoid contamination. Compress the spring until it is almost collapsed and, using a small screwdriver, press the spring retainer tight back against the secondary piston. Using a pair of pointed-nose pliers, press the spring retainer leaf behind the head of the piston. Be sure that the retainer leaf is straight and firmly located.
14. Install the intermediate spring between the primary and secondary pistons. Liberally lubricate the cylinder bore and the piston seals and insert the piston assembly into the bore, valve end first. Press the primary piston down the bore to install the compensating valve assembly. Install the seal, screw in the compensating valve securing nut, and tighten to 35-40 ft.-lbs.
15. Install the cap washer and baffle to the filler cap. Screw the cap on the reservoir.
16. Position the supply tank on the cylinder and secure with the retaining screws.

BRAKE WARNING SWITCH ACTUATOR

The brake warning switch is two opposed cylinders with a common piston connected between the two hydraulic systems. If both the hydraulic systems operate correctly, the piston will be centered.

The piston is made in two parts, the longest having a radiused groove acting as a ramp for the plunger and ball of an electrical switch assembly which is screwed into the body of the actuator. If the pistons remain balanced, the switch plunger is in the neutral position. If any one system fails, the pistons will be forced from the central position and the switch plunger depressed, lighting the Brake Warning Switch Light.

The warning light will stay lit until the pistons are reset. Movement of the pistons is limited by the adapter and plug which act as stops. Bleed the hydraulic system after correcting the brake problem.

Disassembly and Reassembly

1. Unscrew the end plug, adapter and switch assembly (do not lose the ball).
2. Carefully push out the pistons, taking care not to damage the bore surface and remove the seals.
3. Discard the copper gaskets and piston seals.
4. Clean the remaining parts with brake fluid.
5. Replace the discarded parts.
6. Install the seals to the pistons. Lubricate the pistons, piston seals, and bore with clean brake fluid.
7. Insert the longer piston into the bore (slotted end out,) until the radiused groove is opposite the switch assembly hole.
8. Screw in the assembly and ball and tighten to 20-25 ft. lbs.

NOTE: The pistons must be installed as described. Under no circumstances should the seals pass the central apertures. Otherwise, the seals must be removed and new seals installed.

9. Insert the shorter piston into the bore

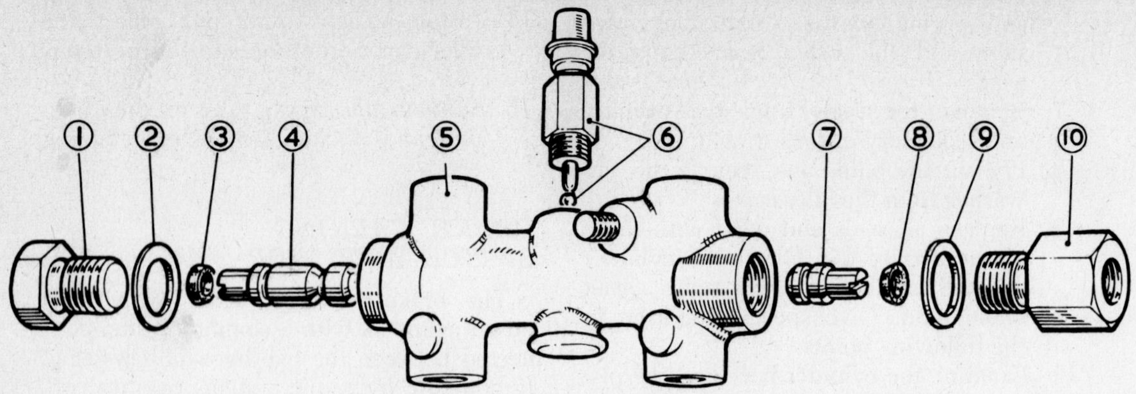

Brake warning switch actuator disassembled

1. Plug
2. Gasket
3. Seal
4. Piston
5. Body
6. Switch assembly and ball
7. Piston
8. Seal
9. Gasket
10. Adapter

(slotted end out) and screw in the plug with the copper gasket.

10. Install the copper gasket to the adapter and screw in the adapter.
11. Tighten the plug and the adapter to 16-20 ft. lbs.

POWER BRAKE

The Supervac power brake unit boosts the effort applied by the driver's foot to the brake pedal. Vacuum in the intake manifold suspends a diaphragm in vacuum and admits atmospheric pressure to one side of

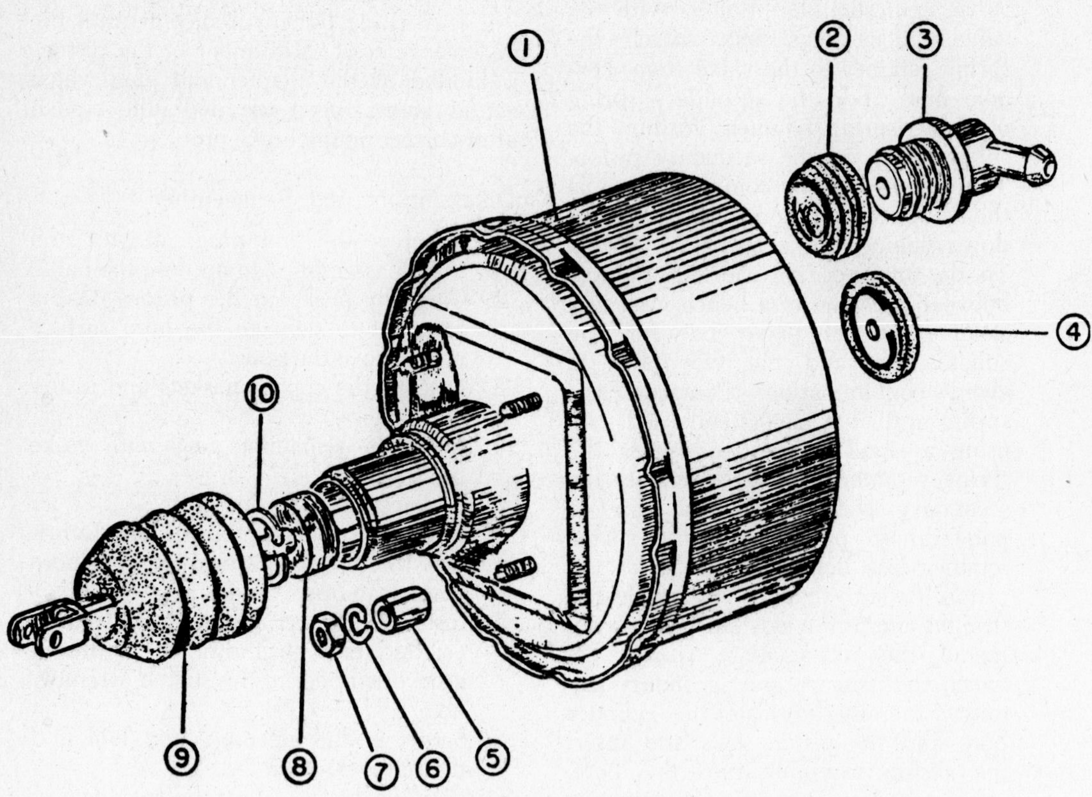

Power brake unit disassembled

1. Servo
2. Grommet
3. Check valve
4. Seal and plate assembly
5. Spacer
6. Washer
7. Nut
8. Filter
9. Dust boot
10. Retainer

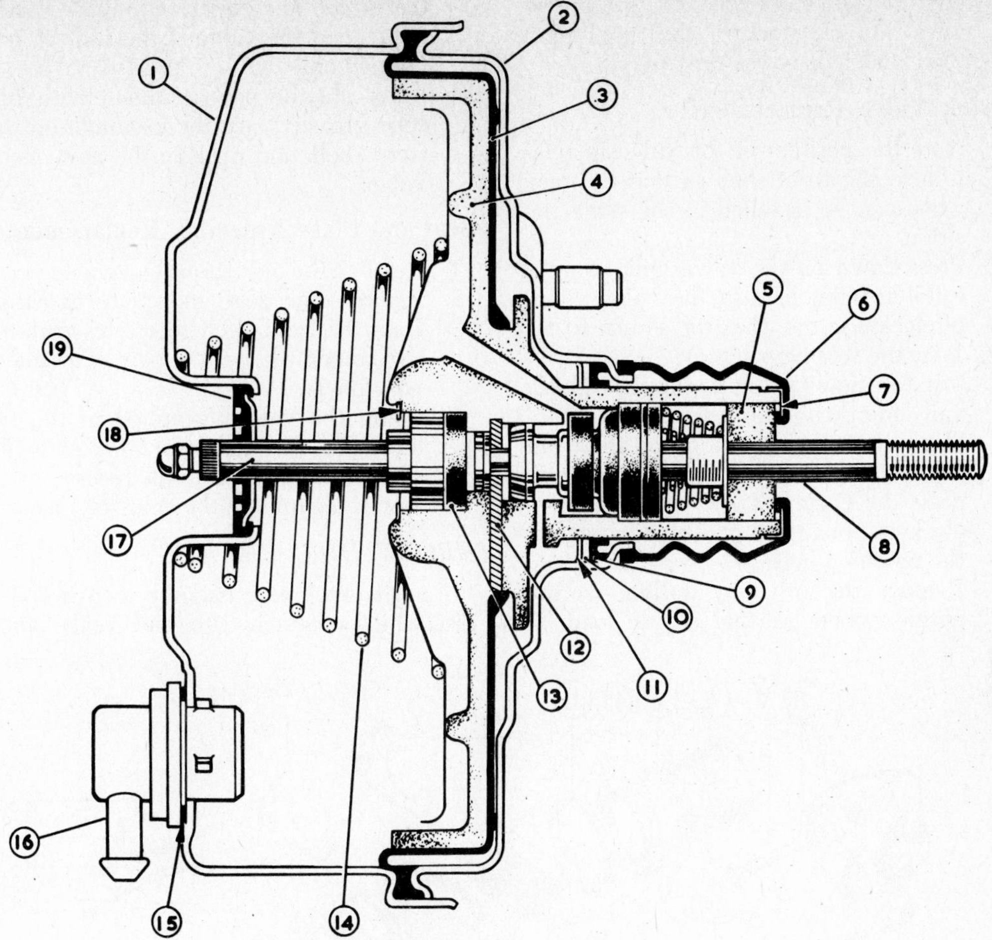

Power brake unit—sectional view

1. Front shell
2. Rear shell
3. Diaphragm
4. Diaphragm plate
5. Filter
6. Dust boot
7. End cap
8. Valve operating rod assembly
9. Seal
10. Bearing
11. Retainer
12. Valve retaining plate
13. Reaction disc
14. Diaphragm return spring
15. O-ring
16. Check valve
17. Hydraulic push rod
18. Sprag washer
19. Seal and plate assembly

the diaphragm, producing the force which aids the driver's pedal. The unit is mounted on the firewall in the engine compartment between the brake pedal and the master cylinder.

NOTE: Servicing of the complete unit is not recommended. Should the unit be suspected when diagnosing any brake fault, it must be replaced.

Filter Replacement

The filter should be replaced every 30,000 miles or 30 months.

1. Disconnect the operating rod from the brake pedal by removing the cotter pin and clevis.
2. Unscrew the four nuts with washers from the unit mounting studs.
3. Detach the four-way connector (brake warning switch) from the inner fender shield by removing one screw and washer. Carefully pull the unit forward enough to reach the filter. Do not lose the spacers behind the unit.
4. Pull back the dust cover and remove the old filter from the diaphragm plate neck. To ease assembly, cut the new filter diagonally from the outer

edge to the center hole. Press the new filter into the neck of the diaphragm plate and replace the dust cover.

Check Valve Replacement

1. Note the position of the valve in relation to the front shell so that the new valve can be installed in the same position.
2. Press down on the valve and, using a suitable wrench, turn the valve counterclockwise one third of a turn to release the retainer rings.
3. Install a new O-ring to the new check valve but do not lubricate.
4. Place the valve in position on the front shell and press on the valve to compress the O-ring. Then, turn the valve clockwise one third of a turn to engage the retaining lugs.
5. Remove the valve by pulling on the nozzle, while exerting a side load. If the nozzle is straight, it may be easier to remove the valve if the hose is left clipped on.
6. Lubricate the new grommet with silicone grease, place the grommet on the front shell, and push in the new check valve.

Seal and Plate Assembly Replacement

1. Remove the unit from the vehicle.
2. Remove the seal and plate assembly from the front shell recess by gripping the center rib with a pair of pointed-nose pliers.
3. Using the grease supplied in the kit, lubricate the new seal and plate assembly and press into the recess.
4. Install the unit on the vehicle.

FRONT DISC BRAKES

Each front brake assembly consists of a disc which is attached to, and rotates with,

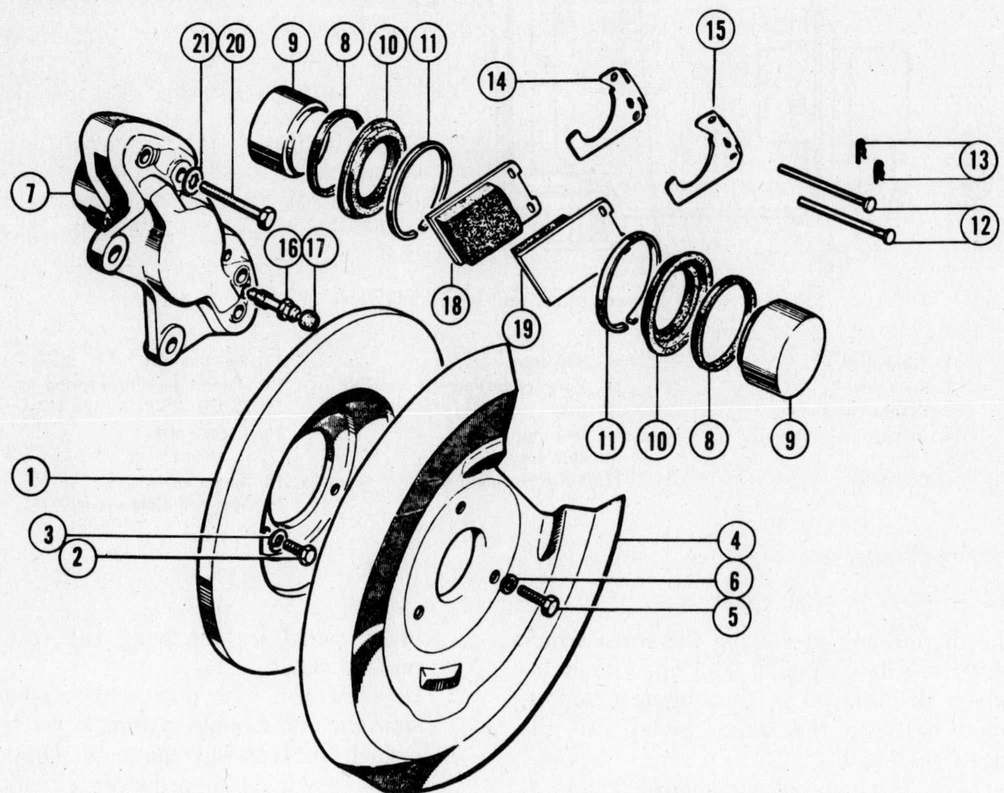

Front disc brake assembly disassembled

1. Disc
2. Bolt
3. Washer
4. Splash shield
5. Bolt
6. Washer
7. Caliper
8. Piston seal
9. Piston
10. Dust boot
11. Ring
12. Pin
13. Clip
14. Damping shim
15. Damping shim
16. Bleed screw
17. Cap
18. Pad
19. Pad
20. Washer
21. Caliper bridge bolt

the wheel hub. A caliper mounted on the stub axle carrier straddles the rotating disc. The cylinder on each side of the caliper contains a piston, protected by a dust cover and a seal positioned in a groove in the cylinder wall. Between the pistons and the disc is a pair of brake pads, retained by pins and spring clips. A metal splash shield on the stub axle carrier, protects the inner face of the disc from road dirt. The outer face is protected by the wheel. On application of the brake pedal, the pistons put equal pressure on each brake pad moving them into contact with the disc.

Piston movement forces out the rectangular sectional seal in the bore as shown in the illustration. When the brake pedal is released, pressure collapses and each rubber seal retracts its piston a slight amount, thus maintaining a constant clearance between the brake pad and the disc when the brakes are released.

Brake Pads

When the lining has worn to about ⅛" (3mm.), the pads must be replaced.

Inspection

1. Apply the handbrake, jack up the front of the car and remove the front wheels.
2. Inspect the thickness of the friction material of the brake pads and renew if necessary.
3. Check the pad retaining pin and the pin retaining clip for wear and replace as necessary.
4. Note the position of the damping shims or anti-rattle shims (if so equipped).

Removal and Replacement

1. Jack up car and remove the wheels. Remove the retaining pins and clips. Remove the pads and damping shims or anti-rattle shims (if so equipped).
2. When installing new pads, open the bleedscrew and push the pistons to the bottom of the bores. Some brake fluid will escape as the pistons are moved.
3. Tighten the bleed screw and clean the pad contact faces of the caliper until all road dirt is removed.
4. Install new pads, with new damping shims. Secure the pads with retaining pins and clips. Bleeding is unnecessary but the foot pedal should be pumped until a solid resistance is felt to position the pads against the disc. Fill the reservoir with the recommended brake fluid. Replace the wheels.

Calipers

Removal

1. Apply the handbrake, jack up the front of the car, and remove the wheel.
2. To remove the caliper, attach one end of a rubber bleed tube to the bleed screw; hang the other end in a container and unscrew one turn. Pump the brake pedal to discharge the fluid. Unscrew the metal brake line from the bracket and detach the caliper by withdrawing the two mounting bolts and washers. Do not unscrew the bolts and separate the two halves of the caliper body.

Disassembly

1. Remove the two brake pads from the caliper.
2. Remove the caliper from the spindle carrier.
3. Clean off all road dirt from the caliper and pistons. Do not split the caliper.
4. Remove the piston dust boots.
5. Pack a clean piece of rag between the pistons, then eject them from the cylinders by applying compressed air to the inlet connection. Pull the piston seal from inside the bore using a plastic or wooden probe to avoid damaging the annular groove. Discard the seal.
6. If necessary, close off the open bore to eject the second piston.

Cleaning

1. Clean all parts with new brake fluid.
2. Examine the cylinder bores and the pistons carefully for signs of damage, abrasion, or corrosion. The pistons may be serviced, but if the cylinder is damaged, install a new caliper.

Reassembly and Installation

1. Lubricate the cylinders with clean brake fluid and install the new piston sealing rings into the grooves.
2. Insert the piston into the cylinder and replace dust boot and retaining ring.
3. To aid assembly, keep the dust boot dry and do not lubricate.
4. Be sure the dust boots are installed correctly and replace the brake pads.
5. Install the caliper on the vehicle

seeing that any shims originally between the mounting faces are correctly positioned.

NOTE: Always service both disc brakes.

6. Reconnect the brake line and bleed the system.

NOTE: Never re-use fluid.

7. Before road testing the car, see that there is enough brake fluid in the reservoir and pump the pedal until a solid resistance is felt to position the pads against the disc.

Disc

The disc should run true to within .004" (.1mm.) between the brake pads. If this tolerance is exceeded, it will cause knock back of the pistons resulting in a pulsating pedal. The disc should be smooth. The scratches and the light scoring which appear after normal use are not harmful, but a heavily scored disc will lessen efficiency and increase pad wear. If there is any doubt about this condition, replace the disc.

When installed, the disc must run equidistant between the caliper cylinders. This should be checked by feeler gauges between the pad faces and the disc face. The gap on opposite sides of the disc may differ by .010" (.25mm.) but the gaps at the two pads on the same side of the disc should be equal. This ensures that the caliper is in line and that the pads and the pistons are square with the discs. Shims should be used at the caliper mounting to correct any discrepancy.

Removal and Replacement

1. Apply the handbrake, jack up the front of the car and remove the front wheel.
2. Remove the caliper from the spindle.
3. Remove the disc and hub assembly from the spindle.
4. Remove the disc from the hub by removing the four bolts and washers.
5. Replacement is the reverse of the removal procedure, giving particular attention to the following:
   a. See that the faces of the hub and disc are free from dirt and burrs. If installing a replacement disc, see that the protective coating is completely washed off and dried.
   b. The bolts are tightened to 33 ft. lbs.
   c. After the disc and hub assembly is replaced, the disc runout should be checked.

Disc Refacing

The refacing of scored or distorted discs by grinding is not recommended and should only be done in extreme circumstances when replacement discs are unavailable. If refacing is essential, the disc must be rotary ground with the vertically mounted grinding wheel crossing the horizontal disc. The disc surface should be flat and parallel with a .001" (0.025mm.) total indicator reading to the mounting face. The surface must be ground to a fine finish. Special care should be taken to remove sharp edges at the inner edge of the inner circumferences of both the ground surfaces. Both sides must be ground equally but the thickness of the disc must not be ground more than .050" (1.2mm.)

The accuracy of this work is extremely important and refacing should be done only if a new disc cannot be obtained.

REAR DRUM BRAKES

The rear drum brake has leading and trailing brake shoes and is operated by a double-acting wheel cylinder. A separate handbrake mechanism is used which automatically adjusts as the linings wear.

The handbrake mechanism consists of a spindle, two levers, a return spring, and a push rod. When the handbrake is applied, the large lever and pushrod expand the shoes against the drum. If the clearance between shoes and drum exceeds a set amount, the smaller lever rotates an adjuster nut on the threaded pushrod, increasing the length of the rod to reduce clearance caused by lining wear. The clearance between shoes and drum is kept to a minimum and no manual adjustment is required.

Brake Shoes

Inspection

1. Block the front wheels, release the handbrake, jack up the rear of the car and remove the rear wheels.
2. Remove the brake drum from the hub by removing the countersunk screw. Clean all dust from the brake drum.
3. Check the brake linings for wear; the linings must not be worn down to the rivets.

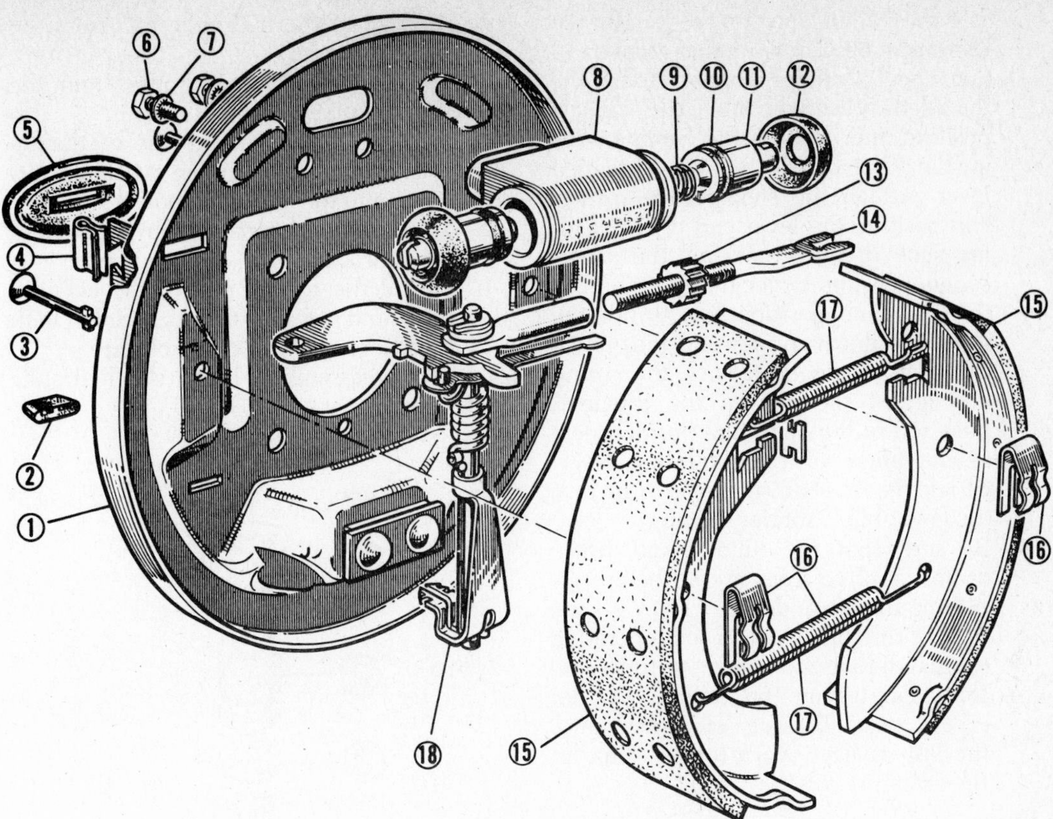

Rear drum brake assembly disassembled

1. Support plate
2. Dirt excluder
3. Pin
4. Lever stop clip
5. Dust cover
6. Bolt
7. Washer
8. Cylinder body
9. Spring
10. Seal
11. Piston
12. Dust cover
13. Adjuster nut
14. Pushrod
15. Shoe
16. Holddown spring
17. Return spring
18. Adjuster assembly

Removal and Repacement

1. Remove the shoe hold down springs and pins, noting the position of the shoes in relation to the wheel cylinder.
2. Pry the leading shoe away from the support plate and remove the trailing shoe from the handbrake lever mechanism. Remove both shoes and springs together with the threaded pushrod.
3. Installation is the reverse of the removal procedure giving special care to the following points:
4. Clean the lever mechanism and support plate, removing any ridges or rust from the six shoe platforms on the support. Check that the pistons are not leaking and move freely.
5. Examine the lever tip which rotates the adjuster nut and the spindle roller which bears against the backplate. If the surface of the roller is worn unevenly, rotate it 90° on the spindle. If the lever tip is worn, a complete new lever mechanism must be installed.
6. Lightly lubricate the moving parts of the lever mechanism (except the lever tip and adjuster nut serrations) with brake grease. Also, lubricate the tips of the replacement shoes, the slots in the wheel cylinder pistons, and the six shoe platforms on the support plate. Take care that brake grease does not touch hydraulic parts or shoe linings.
7. Transfer the lever stop clip from the discarded trailing shoe to the new trailing shoe and install new shoe return springs if necessary.
8. During reassembly, the nut on the threaded pushrod should be screwed down fully toward the fork end. Lo-

cate the trailing shoe on the handbrake lever assembly and in the grooves in the wheel cylinder piston. Insert the threaded pushrod into the female pushrod and position the leading shoe in the forked end of the threaded lever. Attach the shoe return springs and position the lever end of the leading shoe in the groove of the wheel cylinder piston. Lever the other end of the shoe into position and install the shoe hold down springs and pins to secure both shoes. Pull back the spring and adjust the nut on the threaded push rod to the operating position next to the blade of the operating lever. Check the mechanism to be sure that the lower blade rotates the nut.

9. Be sure that the linings and brake drums are free from grease before replacing the brake drum.
10. Adjust the brake shoes by operating the handbrake a number of times before road testing the vehicle. Do not expect peak braking efficiency until the linings have worn to the shape of the drum.

Brake Drum

Removal

If shoe linings are badly neglected and worn down to the rivets, the brake drum will be permanently damaged and removal may be difficult.

1. Disconnect the handbrake cable from the brake adjuster assembly.
2. Remove the clip which acts as a stop for the adjuster lever on the support plate.
3. Pull the lever toward the support plate as far as it will go and remove the drum. If the drum can't be removed using the above method, drill an access hole in the brake drum and proceed as follows:
4. Using the drilled access hole, turn the drum until the adjuster nut and small lever are visible.
5. With the aid of a small screwdriver, turn the adjuster nut to increase the clearance between shoe and drum.

NOTE: Brake drums must be replaced. Refacing the drums is not recommended.

Wheel Cylinders

Removal and Replacement

1. Remove the brake shoes.
2. Disconnect the hydraulic line from the wheel cylinder.
3. Remove the wheel cylinder from the support plate.
4. Replacement is the reverse of the removal procedure, giving particular attention to the following points:

a. Secure the support plate by tightening the four axle flange nuts and bolts.
b. Install the square seal to the cylinder boss and attach the cylinder (with bleedscrew up) to the backplate.
c. After reassembly, bleed the hydraulic system.

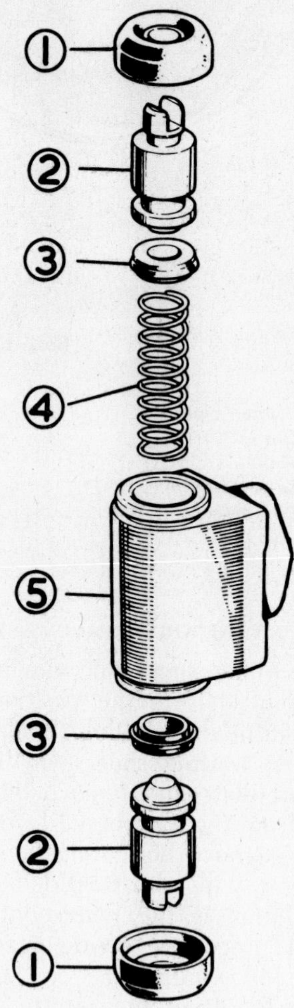

Wheel cylinder disassembled

1. Dust cover
2. Piston
3. Seal
4. Spring
5. Body

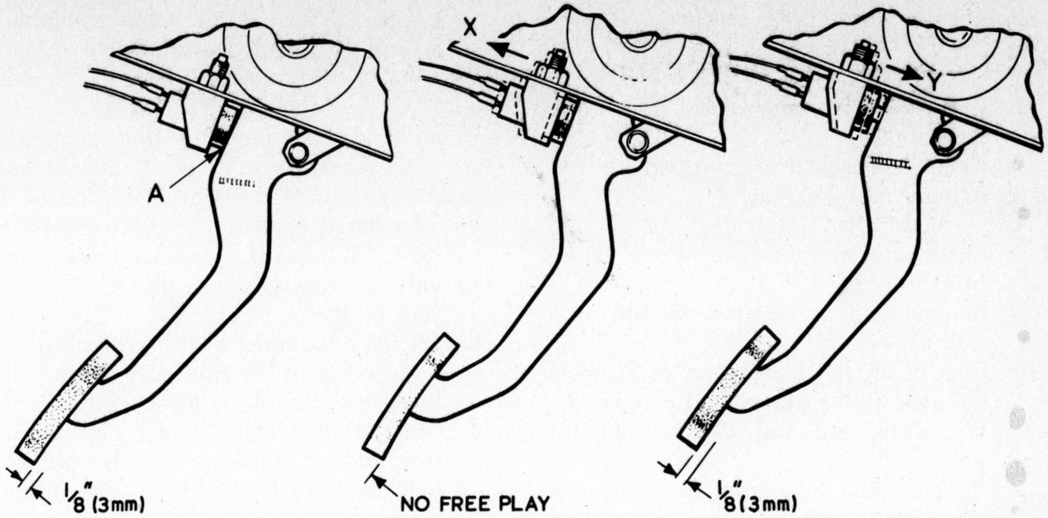

Brake pedal adjustment

Disassembly and Reassembly

1. Clean off dirt and, if working on two wheel cylinders, identify them as left or right.
2. Remove the rubber and pistons complete with rubber seals. The seals can then be removed from their respective pistons.
3 Assembly is the reverse of the disassembly procedure, giving particular attention to the following points:
4. All parts must be very clean and reassembled in equally clean conditions.
5. Dip the pistons and seals in brake fluid to aid assembly in the cylinder. Reassemble the tapered piston seals to the pistons with the wider end of the taper away from the slotted end of the piston. Again dip the pistons and seals in brake fluid and insert the pistons into the housing, seal end first, taking care not to damage the seal. Install the rubber boots in position on the housing and piston.

Backing Plate

Removal and Repacement

1. Remove the wheel cover.
2. Block the front wheels, release the handbrake, jack up the rear of the car, and remove the rear wheel.
3. Remove the brake drum by removing the countersunk screw.
4. Disconnect the handbrake cable or rod.
5. Disconnect hydraulic connections.
6. Remove support plate after removing axle shaft.
7. Replacement is the reverse of the removal procedure, giving particular attention to the following:
   a. Reseal both sealing joints.
   b. Bleed the hydraulic system.
   c. Check rear brake adjustment.

Brake Pedal

Adjustment

The brake pedal adjustment is correct when the pedal rests against the rubber stop and there is at least ⅛" free play at the pedal pad. The pedal position may be adjusted by moving the pedal bracket.
NOTE: After adjustment, check that both brake and clutch pedals are level and that the clutch adjustment (free play) remains correct.

HANDBRAKE

The handbrake operates the rear wheels only. The handbrake lever is located between the front seats and connected to the rear brake drum assemblies by cable and rod linkage.

The rear end of the inner cable is connected to an adjuster lever with the outer casing ending in a bracket mounted to the rear axle housing. The lever attached to the inner cable moves as the handbrake is applied. Then, the opposite adjuster lever attached to the brake rod moves due to the action of the handbrake cable outer casing.

Handbrake Lever and Cable

Removal and Replacement

1. Block the front wheels and release the handbrake.
2. Remove console if so equipped.
3. Remove rear floormat.
4. Unscrew two attaching bolts and remove pin and clevis to release handbrake cable.
5. Remove handbrake lever assembly as a unit.
6. Disconnect the handbrake cable from the rear brake assembly by removing the cotter pin and clevis from the yoke.
7. Unscrew the yoke from the cable adjuster and withdraw the cable from the slot in the mounting bracket.
8. Disconnect the strap on the rear axle housing and pull the cable from the clip on the body.
9. Remove the cable assembly from inside the car.
10. Replacement is the reverse of the removal procedure. After installing handbrake lever and cable assembly, adjust, and check operation.

Adjustment

The handbrake is set during manufacture and should only need adjustment when replacement parts are installed or if the cable has stretched.

With self-adjusting brakes, do not over-adjust the handbrake cable.

1. Jack up the rear of the car.
2. Set the handbrake lever in the off position and then lift the lever one notch.
3. Release the cable adjuster completely.
4. Check that wheel cylinder pistons are free and returning to rest by pulling the lever to feel the brake shoe spring tension.
5. Remove the cable yoke from the lever by removing the cotter pin and clevis.
6. Rotate the sleeve of the cable adjuster clockwise to shorten the cable.
7. Check that both adjuster levers are in the release position. The cable adjustment is correct when the clevis enters freely without tension on the cable.

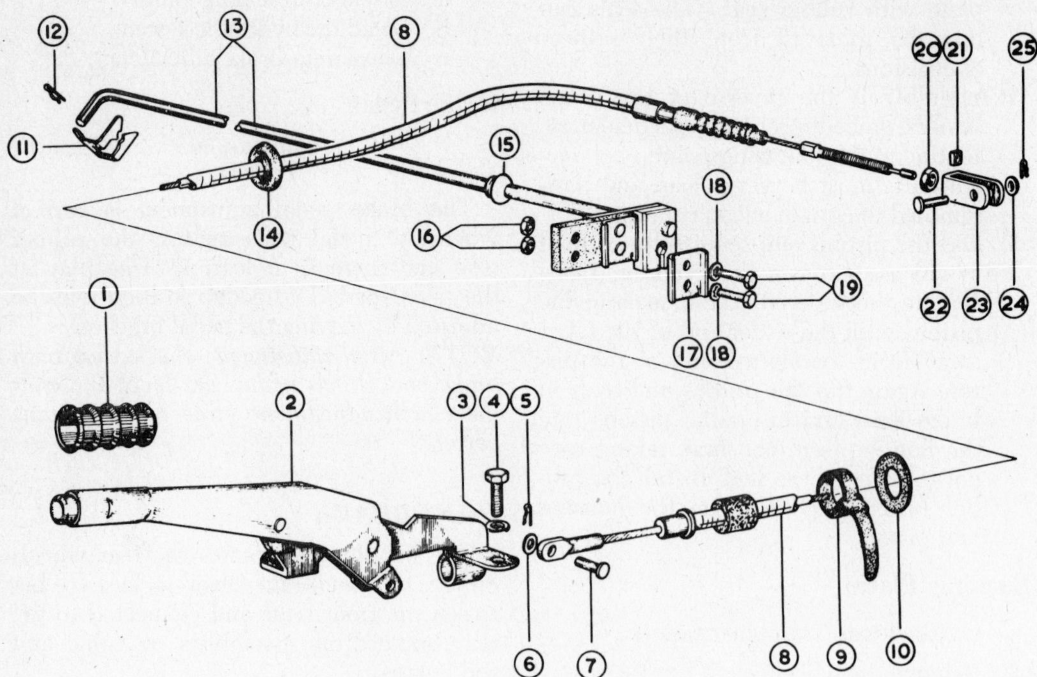

Handbrake assembly disassembled

1. Grip
2. Lever
3. Washer
4. Setscrew
5. Cotter pin
6. Washer
7. Pin
8. Cable
9. Strap
10. Washer
11. Clip
12. Cotter pin
13. Rod
14. Grommet
15. Bearing
16. Nut
17. Stiffener
18. Washer
19. Setscrew
20. Locknut
21. Nut
22. Pin
23. Jaw
24. Washer
25. Cotter pin

8. Install new cotter pin to the clevis pin.
9. Operate the handbrake lever to equalize the linkage, checking that the brakes do not bind and that travel over the ratchet is five notches.
10. When adjustment is correct, apply the handbrake and lower the vehicle.

Accessories

HEATER

The heater system delivers air to the windshield and to the car interior or to both. A flow through ventilation system is built into the body with two outlet vents at the rear roof posts. There are also two upper level air outlets which deliver unheated air at outside temperature only and are unaffected by the heater temperature control. Each upper level outlet has two controls; one directs the air stream while the other regulates the volume of air. The upper level outlets are positioned on each side of the heater controls.

Adjustments

HEAT CONTROL ADJUSTMENT

1. Release spring clip.
2. Move control to blue (cold, to the left).
3. Move lever fully clockwise, install the spring clip to secure the outer cable and check for full movement in each direction.

AIR DISTRIBUTION DOOR ADJUSTMENT

1. Release spring clip.
2. Move control to O (Off, to the left).
3. Move lever fully counterclockwise and install the clip to secure the outer cable. Check for full movement in each direction.

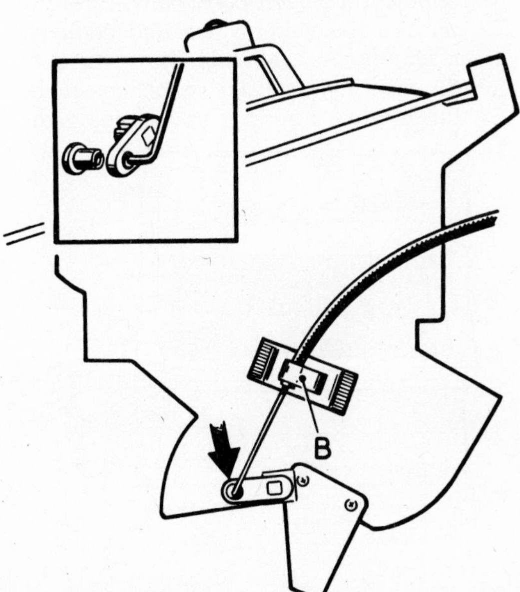

Air distribution door adjustment

Control Unit

REMOVAL AND INSTALLATION

To remove the control assembly with its cables, proceed as follows:

1. Remove the lower instrument panel cover.
2. Using a small probe, compress the spring retainer and remove heater control knob.
3. Remove the upper vent assembly.
4. Remove the control mounting screws.
5. Move the control forward and down.
6. Unclip each cable at the heater end and disconnect.
7. If either cable is to be replaced, unclip from the control and remove the inner cable.
8. Installation is the reverse of removal.

Heater Unit

REMOVAL AND INSTALLATION

1. Remove battery ground cable.
2. Drain radiator, and disconnect each heater hose at firewall.
3. Remove the lower instrument panel cover.
4. Using a small probe, compress the spring retainer and remove heater control knobs. Remove the upper vent and control mounting screws. Remove each defroster duct, move the control forward and down clear of the support rail. Remove the upper vent duct.
5. Remove the two screws securing the heater assembly at the upper mounting points. Move assembly complete with controls to the left, so that the heater pipes clear the firewall opening and the unit front flange, away from the heater support ledge, and remove from the passenger side.
6. Installation is the reverse of the removal procedure.

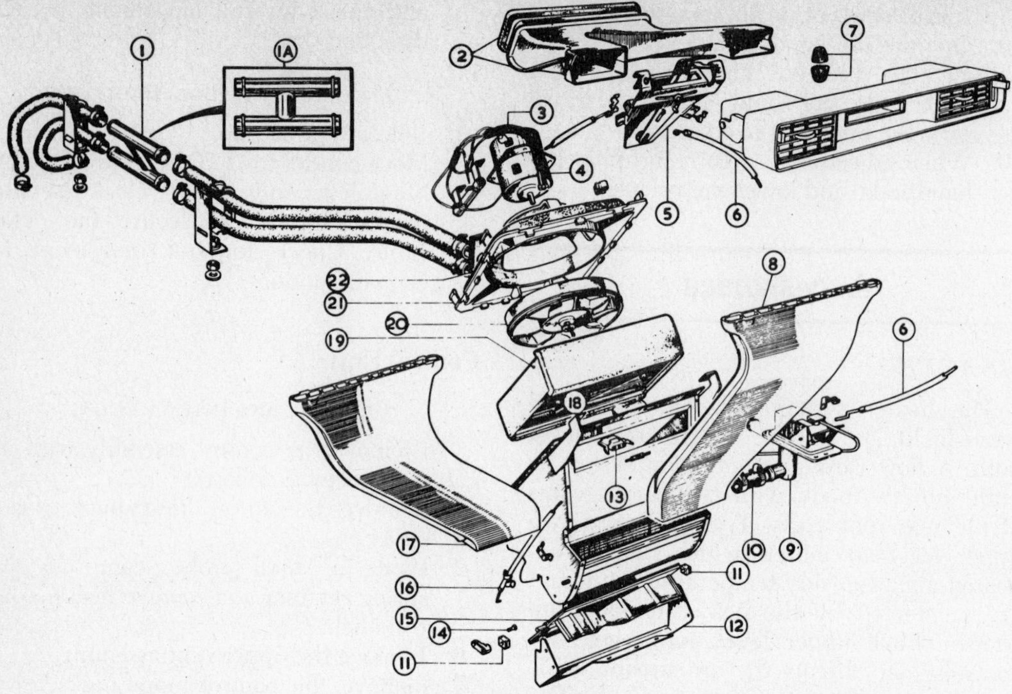

Heater disassembled

1. and 1A. Bypass connector
2. Upper vent duct and seal
3. Blower motor harness
4. Blower motor
5. Control assembly
6. Cable, thermostatic valve
7. Knob, control lever
8. Defroster duct, right
9. Thermostatic water valve and capillary assembly
10. Hose and clamps (valve to core)
11. Bearing, door
12. Deflector plate
13. Socket, blower motor harness
14. Trunnion, cable retaining
15. Door
16. Cable, door
17. Defroster duct, left
18. Clips, capillary
19. Core and seals assembly
20. Fan
21. Fan housing assembly
22. Seal, firewall

Disassembly and Assembly

Whenever a replacement heater core or thermostatic water valve is needed, remove the heater assembly from the car and disassemble it.

1. Disconnect the blower motor harness socket.
2. Remove 8 plastic clips which hold the fan housing assembly.
3. Remove 7 self-tapping screws and remove the deflector plate. Note the position of each door bearing. The wider slot accommodates the thickness of the deflector plate. Set the door in the mid-position, pry out the bearings, and remove the door assembly.
4. Carefully release the capillary from the 4 plastic clips.
5. Remove the water valve to heater core inlet pipe hose clamp and remove the firewall seal.
6. Remove the water valve mounting screws.
7. Turn the heater housing over and remove the heater core. Now, carefully remove the water valve and capillary assembly. Assembly is the reverse of disassembly; special care must be taken when inserting and clipping the

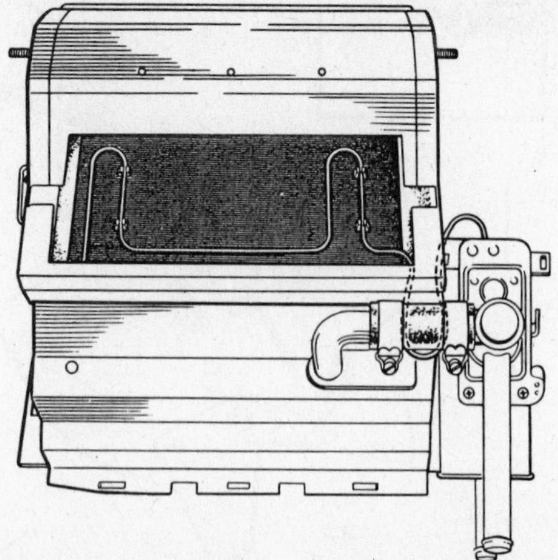

Capillary installed

capillary so that the sensing section is positioned exactly as shown.

CAUTION: When installing a replacement water valve assembly, the capillary should be carefully formed into the correct shape. The original capillary may be used as a template if it has been carefully removed.

Blower Motor

DISASSEMBLY AND ASSEMBLY

1. Remove heater from the car.
2. Remove fan housing assembly.
   To disassemble the fan and blower motor, proceed as follows:
1. Carefully pry off the fan securing clip and remove the fan.
2. Disconnect each motor lead, release the three plastic clips, and remove the motor.
3. To remove the blower motor wiring harness, first remove the connector. Use a small probe to compress the spring tag and remove each lead. Note the position of the color coded leads.
4. Assembly is the reverse of disassembly. Be sure that the harness leads are correctly positioned—green/yellow next to the groove and the black lead in the center, the green/brown lead in the remaining location.

Testing on Vehicle

The test is done by running the wiper motor and measuring running current and wiper speed.

1. Remove the wiper blades and arms.
2. Remove the cartridge fuse (Number 1) from the fuse block and connect an ammeter (0-10 amps.) in its place.
3. Switch off all ignition controlled accessories. Switch on the ignition and check that the ammeter shows no current.
4. Switch on the wipers. Check that the running current shown on the ammeter is 1.5 amp (slow speed)/2.0 amp (high speed) and wiper arm drive shaft cycling is 46-52 rpm (slow speed)/60-70 rpm (high speed).
5. Switch off the wipers and allow them to park before switching off the ignition.
6. Disconnect the ammeter and insert the cartridge fuse.
7. Install the wiper arms and blades in the parked position.

To see if low wiping speed is due to excessive mechanical loading or to poor motor performance, the assembly must be removed from the vehicle and the motor checked with the rotary link disconnected from the bar linkage.

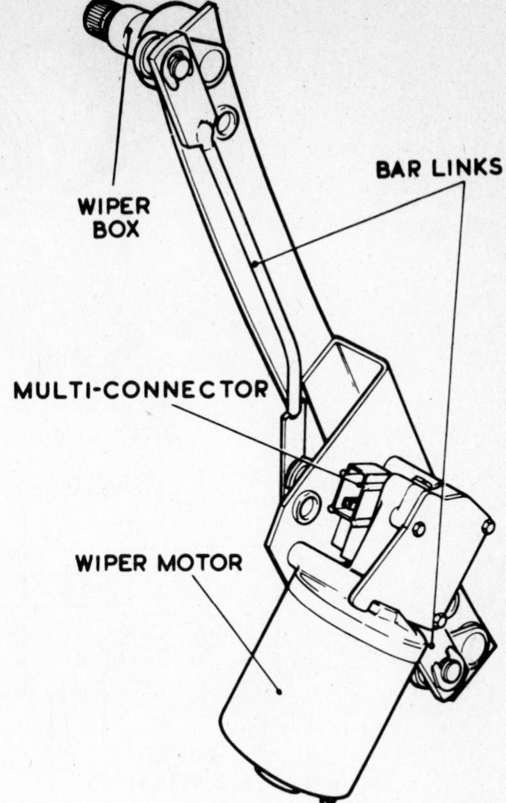

Windshield wiper assembly

Wiper Drive Assembly

REMOVAL AND INSTALLATION

1. Remove the wiper arms and wiper blades. Disconnect electrical wires to motor assembly, carefully marking the wires and their connections for reinstallation. Disconnect the transmission linkage. Remove the washer hoses from the pump assembly. Unscrew the mounting bolts and lift the wiper motor assembly from the car.
2. After repairs, install the motor assembly, transmission linkage, washer hoses, and electrical wires. Install the wiper arms and wiper blades and test the operation of the wipers and the washer pump. Be sure to wet the windshield thoroughly when operating the wipers.

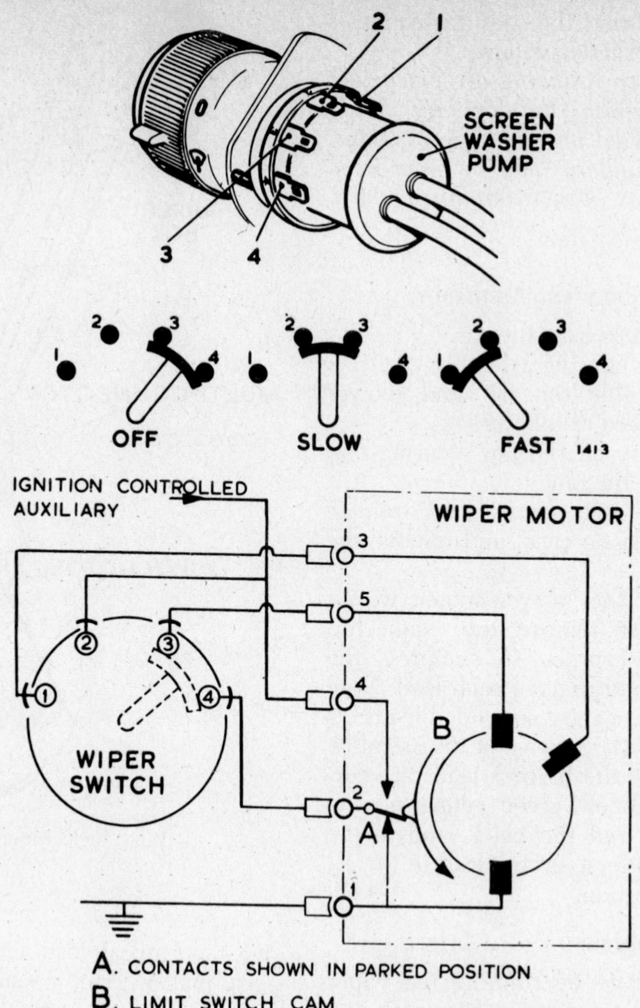

Switch and assembly wiring diagram

Disassembly

1. Remove the wiper assembly.
2. Remove the snap-ring assembly from the pivot on the rotary link.
3. Remove the wiper motor to drive bar assembly, three mounting bolts, and washers. Disengage the motor from the assembly.
4. On the motor, remove the gearbox screws and the cover.
5. Note the position of the rotary link relative to the zero mark on the shaft gear to insure correct positioning on assembly.
6. See that the rotary link does not rotate and damage the gear. Remove the link nut and washer and the link.
7. Remove the shaft and gear complete with dished washer from the gearbox. If it is necessary to separate the shaft from the gear, note the relative positions of the zero mark and gear cam.
8. Remove the yoke bolts. Disengage the yoke and armature from the gearbox.
9. Disengage the armature from the yoke. See that the yoke is isolated from iron shavings which might be attracted to the magnetized pole pieces.
10. Remove both sets of attaching screws and detach the brushgear terminal and switch unit assemblies from the gear box.
11. Loosen the armature end float thrust screw.

Assembly

1. Locate the brushgear, terminal, and switch unit assemblies on the gearbox.

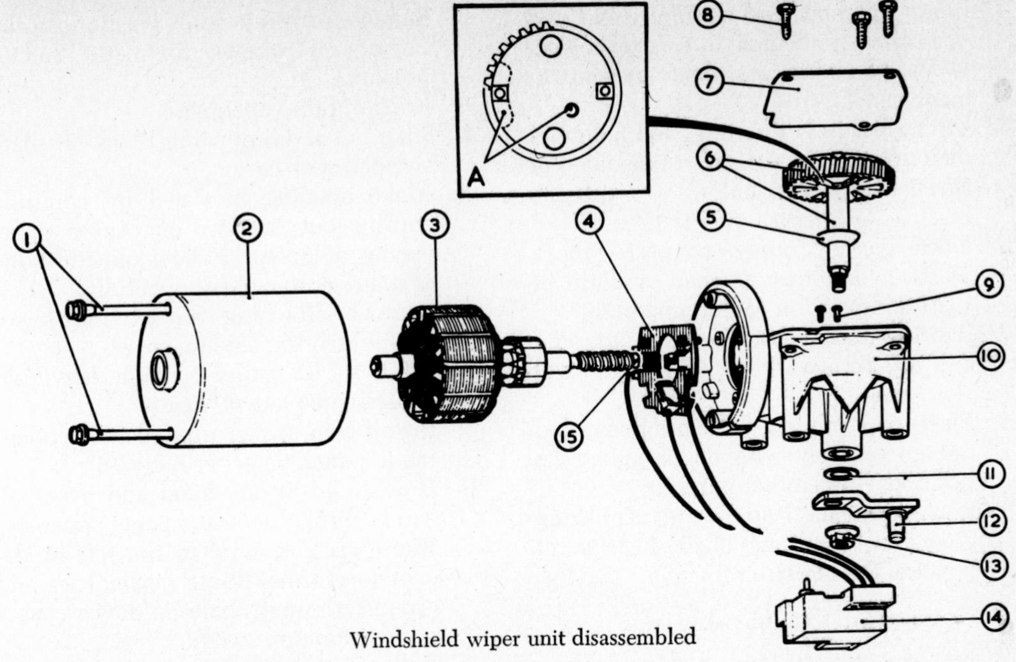

Windshield wiper unit disassembled

1. Yoke through bolt
2. Yoke
3. Armature
4. Brushgear assembly
5. Dished washer
6. Shaft and gear
7. Gearbox cover
8. Cover screws
9. Limit switch attachment screws
10. Gearbox
11. Flat washer
12. Rotary link
13. Link nut
14. Limit switch assembly
15. Nylon thrust pad

Insert and tighten all attaching screws.

2. Apply oil sparingly to the armature shaft bearing surfaces and to the bearing bushings. Soak the felt oiler washer from the yoke end bearing.
3. Insert the worm gear end of the armature shaft into the gearbox bearing bushing, easing the brushes into their boxes and releasing them onto the commutator.
4. See that the thrust disc is in place against the end face of the yoke bearing and insert the soaked felt oiler washer. When replacing the felt oiler washer, see that it has a ⅛″ (3mm.) hole at the center of the felt.
5. Place the yoke over the armature and onto the gearbox. Insert the attaching bolts and tighten to 5 ft. lbs.
6. Set the armature end float as follows:
   a. Tighten the thrust screw until full contact is made.
   b. Unscrew the thrust screw ¼ turn and tighten the locknut.
   c. Install the shaft and gear complete with dished washer in the gearbox. Apply some grease to the gearwheel teeth, gearwheel cam and worm gear.
   d. Install the snap ring assembly to the rotary link pivot.
   e. Install the wiper assembly to the vehicle.
7. Assemble the rotary link to the shaft in the position noted and install the nut and washer. See that the rotary link does not turn and damage the gear. Tighten the link nut.
8. Install the gearbox cover and screws.
9. Engaging the pivot on the rotary link with the drive bar assembly, install and tighten the wiper motor attachment parts.

RADIO & ANTENNA

The radio is a standard AM type with either knob or push button tuning. The ignition switch must be in either Accessory or On position to operate the radio.

Antenna

ORIGINAL INSTALLATION

1. On right cowl, locate and center punch antenna mount hole.
2. Drill 1″ antenna hole.
3. Scrape an area on the underside of cowl 3/8″ completely around hole to bare metal.

4. Route antenna lead through hole and out through opening in side panel between glove compartment and instrument panel.
5. Tip rocker pass through cowl hole and then place it against underside of sheet metal and pull up on antenna mast.
6. Place gasket, upper adapter (black plastic), and trim washer over tip of mast and position on antenna body.
7. Position mast vertically, align adapter, and use trim washer position to cover slot.
8. Place cap nut on antenna body and tighten securely without changing the positions of the other parts.
9. Route antenna lead inside car along groove at lower edge of the instrument panel to the radio.

Removal and Replacement

1. Remove ashtray and plastic ashtray carrier (4 screws).
2. Remove radio mounting screw. Lower rear of radio to ashtray carrier bracket.
3. Remove ashtray carrier bracket (3 screws).
4. Unplug antenna lead from radio and remove from lower instrument panel lip.
5. Remove antenna cap nut, trim washer, upper adapter, and gasket from cowl.
6. Tip antenna rocker to one side and remove antenna assembly.

To install antenna, follow steps 4 through 9 under Original Installation.

Trimming

To trim antenna for best reception:

1. Extend antenna two sections.
2. Turn on radio.
3. Tune radio to a weak station around 1600 khz.
4. Pull right hand (station tuning) knob off shaft.

NOTE: Trimmer hole is round hole directly below tuning shaft. Trimmer Screw is in line with hole and in about 1½". Use small screwdriver to adjust trimmer.

5. Turn trimmer right and left until maximum volume is obtained.
6. Replace tuning knob.

Radio

Original Installation

1. Disconnect battery negative terminal.
2. Remove ashtray and plastic ashtray carrier (4 screws to metal carrier bracket).
3. Prepare radio opening.
   a. Snap out radio opening blank-off plate shipped with car or
   b. Make opening in panel by carefully cutting out section of center panel (using a knife). Follow outside edge of matte chrome bead carefully.
4. Remove attaching screws and lower plastic steering column cover.

CAUTION: This panel contains headlight and wiper switch assemblies.

5. Install trim spacer around radio opening in panel.
6. Hold radio in one hand and insert all wires through radio panel opening. Route speaker wire to the left of the heater controls. Route power lead and ground through hole in lower panel nearest ignition switch.
7. Pull antenna lead through hole and plug into radio antenna jack.
8. Carefully insert radio through opening until spring clips snap into place. Keep radio straight and balance pressure on both sides so clips snap in together.
9. Using screw and lockwasher provided, secure bottom of radio to metal ashtray carrier bracket.
10. Connect bullet lead (white) to terminal on white pigtail from ignition switch.
11. Remove the sheet metal screw that holds the wiper motor to ground and install radio ground wire. Reinstall screw with both ground wires under it. Insure a good ground connection.
12. Reach under panel and loosen nearest wiper motor housing screw two turns and snap other end of wiper motor ground cable under screw and retighten.
13. Reassemble lower steering column cover.
14. Replace ashtray carrier and ashtray.
15. Connect battery negative lead.

Removal

1. Disconnect battery negative lead.
2. Remove ashtray and plastic ashtray carrier (4 screws to metal bracket).
3. Remove radio mounting screw from carrier bracket.
4. Remove speaker.
5. Remove attaching screws and lower

plastic panel from steering column support.

CAUTION: This panel contains headlight and wiper switch column support.

6. Disconnect radio power lead (white) from ignition switch pigtail.
7. Remove screw (right of steering column) and remove radio ground wire.
8. Remove radio knobs (pull straight off).
9. Remove radio control shaft bushing nuts and trim plate.
10. Push radio into panel to release side clips, turn sideways and remove through opening.
11. Disconnect antenna and pull radio leads through opening.

NOTE: To install follow steps 4 through 11 of Original Installation.

Speaker

Original Installation

1. Remove two screws from speaker grille, lift up, and pull out.
2. Install two spring clip nuts on metal edge of speaker opening to align with holes for speaker screws.
3. Apply two foam pads to speaker grille, one at left and one at right about ¾″ in from outer edge.
4. Be sure radio has been installed completely.
5. Connect speaker lead to speaker.
6. Position terminals to the left, slip forward edge under front speaker grille retaining clips. Be sure speaker leads are clear of heater controls.
7. Install speaker mounting screws.
8. Install speaker grille. Check that foam pads close off speaker side opening.

DATSUN SECTION

Index

Introduction

Nissan Motor Company Limited, the producer of Datsun vehicles, was established in 1933. Nissan is Japan's first mass producer and exporter of cars and trucks. The 5,000,000th Nissan-built vehicle was produced in 1969. Small economy sedans, pickup trucks, and sportscars are included in the Datsun line imported to the United States. Datsun was fourth in import sales for 1969, with 58,569 vehicles registered. In 1970, Datsun moved into third place, with 100,541 vehicles registered. Datsun gained international recognition in 1969 by winning the team championship in the East African Safari Rally. The Datsun team took the first six places in its class. Datsun is also a frequent entrant in the grueling Mexican 1000 mile off-road race and has won the 1970 SCCA C–production championship.

Model Identification

Nissan Patrol, four-wheel drive (L60)

RL411 sedan. PL410 and PL411 are similar with slightly different grilles.

SPL310 1,500 cc. sportscar, SPL311 1,600 cc. sportscar, SRL311 2,000 cc. sportscar

L320 1,200 cc. pickup

L520 1,300 cc. pickup

PL521 1,600 cc. pickup

PL510 sedan, 1970 model

LB110 1,200 cc. sedan

KLB110 1,200 cc. coupe

HLS30 (240 Z) coupe

Vehicle and Engine Serial Number Identification

ENGINE NUMBER

The engine number, on the Nissan Patrol engine, is stamped on the lower right front corner of the cylinder block. On all other models, the engine number is stamped on the right side top edge of the cylinder block. The engine serial number is preceded by the engine model code.

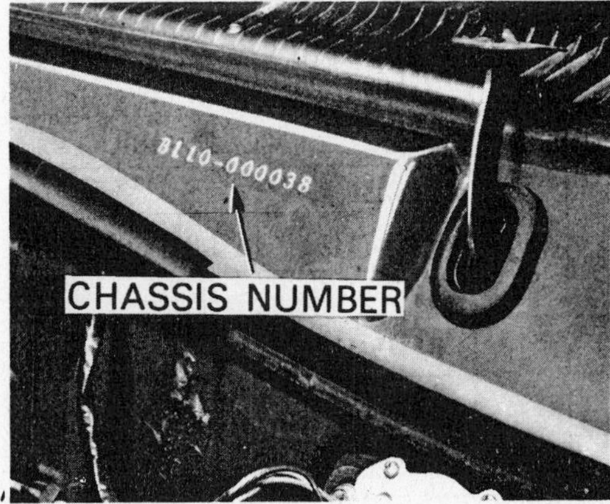

Chassis model and serial number, LB110 1,200 cc. sedan

Engine model and serial number, L24 OHC six

Chassis model and serial number, 240 Z coupe (HL S30)

CHASSIS NUMBER

The Nissan Patrol and L320 pickup

chassis number is located on top of the right frame member, in the engine compartment. On all other models, the chassis number is on the firewall under the hood. Late model vehicles also have the chassis number on a plate attached to the top of the instrument panel on the driver's side. The chassis serial number is preceded by the model designation.

Vehicle Identification Plate

The vehicle identification plate is attached to the hood ledge or the firewall. This plate is mounted on the right front suspension strut housing on the HLS30 (240 Z). The identification plate gives the vehicle model, engine displacement in cc., SAE horsepower rating, wheelbase, engine number, and chassis number.

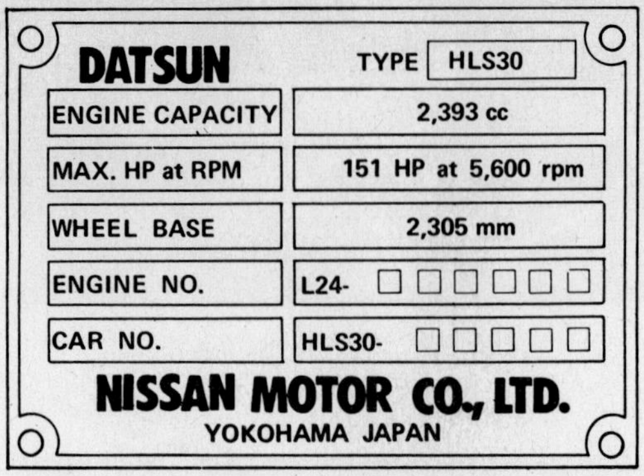

DATSUN TYPE HLS30
ENGINE CAPACITY 2,393 cc
MAX. HP at RPM 151 HP at 5,600 rpm
WHEEL BASE 2,305 mm
ENGINE NO. L24- □□□□□□
CAR NO. HLS30- □□□□□
NISSAN MOTOR CO., LTD.
YOKOHAMA JAPAN

Vehicle identification plate, 240 Z coupe (HLS30)

Engine Identification

Number of Cylinders	*Cu. In. Displacement (cc. Displacement)*	*Type*	*Engine Model Code*
6	241.3 (3,956)	OHV	P
4	72.5 (1,189)	OHV	E1
4	90.6 (1,488)	OHV	G
4	79.0 (1,299)	OHV	J
4	97.3 (1,595)	OHV	R
4	120.9 (1,982)	OHC	U20
4	97.3 (1,595)	OHC	L16
6	146.0 (2,393)	OHC	L24
4	71.5 (1,171)	OHV	A12

Vehicle Identification

Year	Model	Serial Numbers	
1961-1969	L60 Patrol (4 wheel drive)		
To 1966	L320 (1200 Pickup)		
1965	L520 (1300 Pickup)	L520-00001—L520-004603	April 1965—Sept. 1965
1966	L520 (1300 Pickup)	L520-004604—L520-019000	Oct. 1965—Sept. 1966
1967	L520 (1300 Pickup)	L520-019001—L520-160000	Oct. 1966—Sept. 1967
1968	L520 (1300 Pickup)	L520-160001—termination	Oct. 1967—termination
1968	L521 (1300 Pickup)	L521-000001—L521-038554	May 1968—Sept. 1968
1969	L521 (1300 Pickup)	L521-038555—L521-180000	Oct. 1968—June 1969
1970	PL521 (1600 Pickup)	PL521-180071—PL521-255904 PL521-255905—PL521-350000 PL521-350001—	July 1969—Sept. 1969 Oct. 1969—Jan. 1970 Feb. 1970—
1963-1965	PL410 Sedan		
1965-1967	PL411 Sedan	PL411-300000	
1966-1968	RL411 Sedan		
From 1971	LB110 (1200 Sedan)	LB110-00001	
From 1971	KLB110.(1200 Coupe)	LB110-70001	
1968	PL510 (1600 Sedan)	L510-00011—L510-009999 PL510-00011—PL510-040010	Oct. 1967—Sept. 1968
1969	PL510 (1600 Sedan)	L510-010000— PL510-040011—	Oct. 1968—Sept. 1969
1970	PL510 (1600 Sedan)	L510-040000— PL510-095000—	Oct. 1969— July 1969—
1971	PL510 (1600 Sedan)	PL510-200011—	Aug. 1970—
1968	WPL510 (1600 Wagon)	WPL510-800001—WPL510-805000	Oct. 1967—Sept. 1968
1969	WPL510 (1600 Wagon)	WPL510-805001—	Oct. 1968—
1970	WPL510 (1600 Wagon)	WPL510-842001— WPL510-11499—	Oct. 1969— July 1969—
1971	WPL510 (1600 Wagon)	WPL510-883501—	Aug. 1970—
1962-1965	SPL310 (1500 Roadster)		
1965, 1966, 1967	SPL311 (1600 Roadster)	SPL311-10001—SPL311-11000	To engine No. R-40000
Late 1967	SPL311 (1600 Roadster-Metric)	SPL311-11001—SPL311-17000	From engine No. R-40001 —Sept. 1967
1968	SPL311 (1600 Roadster)	SPL311-17001—SPL311-24000	Oct. 1967—Sept. 1968
1969	SPL311 (1600 Roadster)	SPL311-24001—SPL311-27000	Oct. 1968—June 1969
Late 1967	SRL311 (2000 Roadster)	SRL311-00001—SRL311-01000	To Sept. 1967
1968	SRL311 (2000 Roadster)	SRL311-01001—SRL311-03000	Oct. 1967—Sept. 1968
1969	SRL311 (2000 Roadster)	SRL311-07001—SRL311-13000	Oct. 1968—June 1969
From 1971	HLS30 (240 Z Coupe)	HLS30-03013—	

General Engine Specifications

Year	Type (code)	Cu. In. Displacement (cc. Displacement)	Carburetor	Developed Horsepower (SAE) @ rpm	Developed Torque (ft. lbs.) @ rpm	Bore X Stroke inches (mm.)	Compression Ratio	Normal Oil Pressure (psi)
1961-1969 L60 Patrol	OHV 6 (P)	241.3 (3,956)	Single throat downdraft	145 @ 3,600	235 @ 2,000	3.314 X 4.5 (85.7 X 114.3)	7.6:1	50-57
To 1966 L320 1200 Pickup, 1963-1965 PL410 Sedan	OHV 4 (E1)	72.5 (1,189)	Dual throat downdraft	60 @ 5,000	63.7 @ 5,000	2.89 X 2.80 (73 X 71)	8.2:1	54-57
1962-1965 SPL310 1500 Roadster	OHV 4 (G)	90.6 (1,488)	Two SU type side-draft	85 @ 5,600	92 @ 4,400	3.15 X 2.93 (80 X 74)	9.0:1	54-57
1965-1968 L520 1300 Pickup, 1968-1969 L521 1300 Pickup, 1965-1967 PL411 Sedan	OHV 4 (J)	79.0 (1,299)	Dual throat downdraft	67 @ 5,200	77 @ 2,800	2.89 X 3.06 (73 X 77.6)	8.2:1	54-57
1966-1968 RL411 Sedan, 1965-1969 SPL311 1600 Roadster	OHV 4 (R)	97.3 (1,595)	Two SU type side-draft	96 @ 6,000	103 @ 4,000	3.43 X 2.63 (87.2 X 66.8)	9.0:1	54-57
1967-1969 SRL311 2000 Roadster	OHC 4 (U20)	120.9 (1,982)	Two SU type side-draft	135 @ 6,000	132 @ 4,400	3.43 X 3.27 (87.2 X 83)	9.5:1	54-57
1967-1969 SRL311 2000 Roadster	OHC 4 (U20)	120.9 (1,982)	Two Solex type twin-choke sidedraft	150 @ 6,000	138 @ 4,800	3.43 X 3.27 (87.2 X 83)	9.5:1	54-57
From 1968 PL510 1600 Sedan, From 1968 WPL510 1600 Wagon, From 1970 PL521 1600 Pickup	OHC 4 (L16)	97.3 (1,595)	Dual throat downdraft	96 @ 5,600	100 @ 3,600	3.27 X 2.90 (83 X 73.7)	8.5:1	54-57
From 1971 HLS30 240 Z Coupe	OHC 6 (L24)	146.0 (2,393)	Two SU type side-draft	151 @ 5,600	145.7 @ 4,400	3.27 X 2.90 (83 X 73.7)	9.0:1	54-60
From 1971 LB110 1200 Sedan	OHV 4 (A12)	71.5 (1,171)	Dual throat downdraft	69 @ 6,000	70 @ 4,000	2.87 X 2.76 (73 X 70)	9.0:1	54-60

Tune-up Specifications

Year	Model	Spark Plugs Make, Type	Spark Plugs Gap (in.)	Distributor Point Dwell (deg.)	Distributor Point Gap (in.)	Basic Ignition Timing (deg.)	Compression Pressure (psi) @ 350 rpm	Valves Clearance (in.) In.	Valves Clearance (in.) Ex.	Intake Opens (deg.) BTDC	Idle Speed (rpm)	Air:Fuel Ratio (:1) at idle	Percentage of CO at idle
1961-1969	L60	NGK BP-6E	.028-.032	35-45	.018-.022	10 BTDC @ 450	145	.016 Hot	.016 Hot	N.A.	450	N.A.	N.A.
1969	L60 with emission control	NGK BP-6E	.028-.032	35-45	.020	0 TDC @ 700	145	.016 Hot	.016 Hot	N.A.	750	N.A.	N.A.
1963-1965	PL410	NGK BP-6E, Hitachi L45	.028-.032	49-55	.018-.022	15 BTDC @ 600	165	.014 Hot	.014 Hot	14	600	N.A.	N.A.
1962-1965	SPL310	N.A.	.028-.032	49-55	.018-.022	16 BTDC @ 600	182	.017 Hot	.017 Hot	20	600	N.A.	N.A.
1965-1967	PL411	NGK BP-6E	.028-.032	49-55	.018-.022	15 BTDC @ 600	165	.014 Hot	.014 Hot	14	700	N.A.	N.A.
1966-1968	RL411	N.A.	.028-.032	49-55	.018-.022	18 BTDC @ 700	182	.017 Hot	.017 Hot	20	700	N.A.	N.A.
1965-1969	SPL311	NGK BP-6E	.028-.032	49-55	.018-.022	16 BTDC @ 600	181	.017	.017	20	600	N.A.	N.A.
1969	SPL311 with emission control	NGK BP-6E	.032-.036	49-55	.018-.022	0 TDC @ 700	181	.017	.017	20	700	12.0-12.5③	5-7③ 1.8-2.2⑥

Tune-up Specifications

1967-1969	SRL311	NGK BP-6E	.028-.032	49-55	.018-.022	16 BTDC @ 600	166	.008 Hot	.012 Hot	18	600	N.A.	N.A.
1969	SRL311 with emission control	NGK BP-6E	.032-.036	49-55	.018-.022	0 TDC @ 700	166	.008 Hot	.012 Hot	18	700	12.0-12.5③	5-7③ 1.8-2.2⑥
1967-1969	SRL311 with two twin-choke side-draft carburetors	N.A.	.028-.032	51-58	.016-.022	20 BTDC @ 700④	166	.008 Hot	.012 Hot	30	700	N.A.	N.A.
To 1966	L320	NGK BP-6E	.028-.032	49-55	.018-.022	15 BTDC @ 600	163	.014	.014	14	600	N.A.	N.A.
1965-1968	L520	NGK BP-6E	.028-.032	50-55	.018-.022	8 BTDC @ 600⑤	163	.014	.014	14	600	N.A.	N.A.
1969	L520 with emission control, L521	NGK BP-6E	.032-.036	50-55	.018-.022	0 TDC @ 700	163	.014	.014	14	700	13.3-14.5	1-3
1968-1971	PL510, WPL510	NGK BP-6E	.028-.032	49-55	.018-.022	10 BTDC @ idle speed	171	.008 Cold, .010 Hot	.010 Cold, .012 Hot	16 PL510, 12 WPL510	600-700 manual, 575-650 automatic	N.A.	N.A.
1969-1971	PL510, WPL510 with emission control	NGK BP-6E	.032-.036	49-55	.018-.022	5 ATDC @ idle speed	171	.008 Cold, .010 Hot	.010 Cold, .012 Hot	16 PL510, 12 WPL510	700 manual, 600 automatic	12.0-12.5③	1969 2.0-2.4 1970 2-4③
1970-1971	PL521 with emission control	NGK BP-6E	.032-.036	49-55	.018-.022	10 BTDC @ 700	163	.008 Cold, .010 Hot	.010 Cold, .012 Hot	12	700	N.A.	2-4 ③

1971	HLS30 with emission control	NGK BP-6E	N.A.	35-41	.016-.020	5 BTDC @ 750 ⑦	171-185	.008 Cold, .010 Hot	.010 Cold, .012 Hot	16	750 manual, 600 automatic	N.A.	5-7 ⑧
1971	HLS30	NGK BP-6E	.031-.035	35-41	.018-.022	17 BTDC @ 550	171-185	.008 Cold, .010 Hot	.010 Cold, .012 Hot	16	550	N.A.	N.A.
1971-1972	LB110, KLB110 with emission control	NGK BP-6E, Hit-achi L46P	.031-.035	49-55	.018-.022	5 BTDC @ 700	193	.010 Cold, .014 Hot	.010 Cold, .014 Hot	14	700	N.A.	2-3
1972	PL510, WPL510 with emission control	NGK BP-6E	.032-.036-	49-55	.018-.022	7 BTDC@ idle speed	171	.008 Cold, .010 Hot	.010 Cold, .012 Hot	16 PL510, 12 WPL510	700 manual, 600 automatic	12.0-12.5③	2
1972	All other ⑧ models												

①—Torque to 11-15 ft. lbs.
②—NGK BP-6E corresponds to: Autolite AG22
Bosch W175T30.
③—Air pump disconnected
④—Vacuum line disconnected
⑤—Some early models are set at 15 BTDC @ 600.
⑥—Air pump connected
⑦—Automatic with dual point distributor OTDC @ 600 above 40°F, 10BTDC @ 600 below 40°C
⑧—See engine compartment sticker for tune-up specifications.

NOTE: Emission control requires a very precise approach to tune-up. Timing and idle speed are peculiar to the engine and its application, rather than to the engine alone. Data for the particular application will be found on a sticker in the engine compartment on all late models. The results of any adjustments or modifications should be checked with an air-fuel or CO meter.

Firing Order

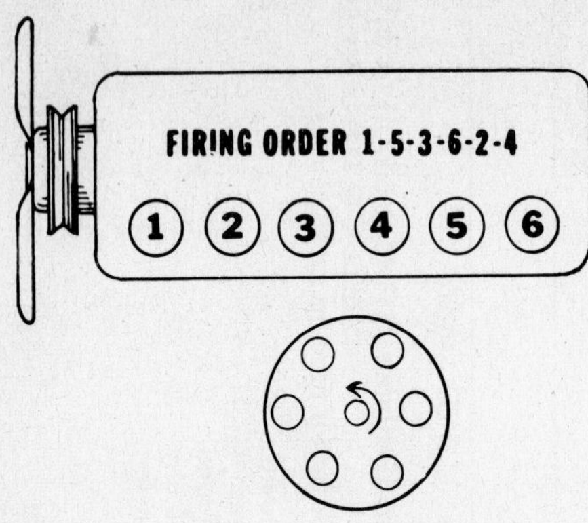

All six cylinder. L24 engine has spark plugs on right side and distributor at front. P engine is as shown.

NOTE: Spark plug wiring arrangements are not shown, except for the L16 engine, as these vary with the placement of the distributor head in the different engine models.

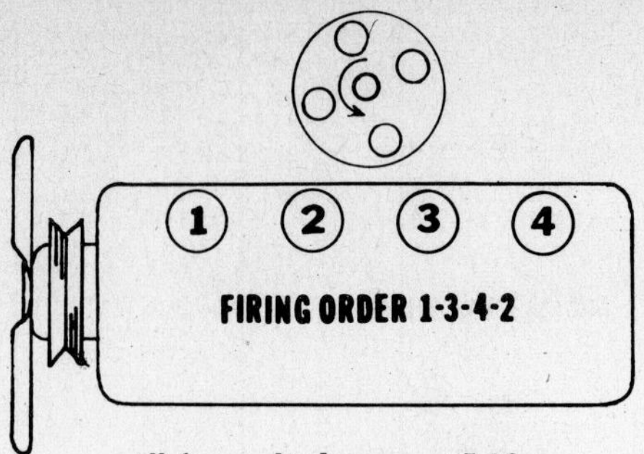

All four cylinder except L16

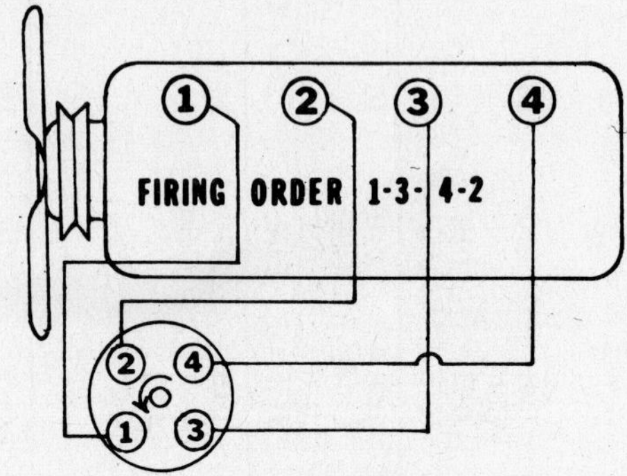

L16 engine

Engine Rebuilding Specifications
Crankshaft

Engine Model	*Main Bearing Journals (in.)*					*Connecting Rod Bearing Journals (in.)*			
	Journal Diameter		*Oil Clearance*	*Shaft End-Play*	*Thrus on No.*	*Journal Diameter*		*Oil Clearance*	*Side-Play*
	New	*Minimum*				*New*	*Minimum*		
P	2.727, 2.685 for No. 1 journal	N.A.	.001-.003 ①	.003-.008 ②	N.A.	2.225	N.A.	N.A.	N.A.
E1	2.000	N.A.	.001-.002 ①	.002-.003 ②	N.A.	1.875	N.A.	N.A.	N.A.
G	2.360	N.A.	.001-.002 ①	.001-.006 ②	N.A.	2.047	N.A.	N.A.	N.A.
J	2.0021-2.0025	N.A.	.001-.002	.002-.003	Center	1.860-1.878	N.A.	N.A.	.008-.012
R	2.3598-2.3602	N.A.	.001-.003	.002-.006	Center	2.0457-2.0463	N.A.	.001-.002	.008-.012
U20	2.4780-2.4785	N.A.	.001-.003 ①	.002-.007 ③	Center	2.0449-2.0454	N.A.	.001-.003	.008-.012
L16	2.1631-2.1636	2.1237-2.1242	.001-.003 ①	.002-.006 ③	3	1.9670-1.9675	1.9276-1.9281	.001-.003	.008-.012
L24	2.1631-2.1636	2.1237-2.1242	.001-.003 ①	.002-.007 ③	Center	1.9670-1.9675	1.9276-1.9281	.001-.002	.008-.012
A12	1.9671-1.9668	1.9272-1.9277	.001-.002 ④	.002-.006 ③	3	1.7701-1.7706	1.7307-1.7313	.001-.002	.008-.012

①—Wear limit—.005
②—Wear limit—.010
③—Wear limit—.012
④—Wear limit—.006

Engine Rebuilding Specifications
Block, Pistons, Rings

Engine Model	Block		Pistons			Rings		Piston to Bore Clearance (in.)
	Bore (in.)		Piston Diameter (in.) •		Wrist Pin Fit	Side Clearance (in.)	End-Gap (in.)	
	New	Maximum Oversize	New	Maximum Oversize				
P	N.A.	N.A.	N.A.	N.A.	push fit	.001-.003 top, .001-.003 2nd, N.A. oil	.010-.016 top, .006-.012 2nd, N.A. oil	N.A.
E1	N.A.	N.A.	N.A.	N.A.	push fit	.001-.003 top, .001-.003 2nd, .002-.003 oil	.008-.013 top, .008-.013 2nd, .008-.013 oil	N.A.
G	N.A.	N.A.	N.A.	N.A.	push fit	.002-.003 top, .001-.003 2nd, .001-.003 oil	.010-.016 top, .006-.012 2nd, .006-.012 oil	N.A.
J	N.A.	N.A.	N.A.	N.A.	push fit	.002-.004 top, .002-.004 2nd, .002-.004 oil	.008-.013 top, .008-.013 2nd, .008-.013 oil	.001-.002
R	3.4281-3.4357	N.A.	N.A.	N.A.	push fit	N.A. top, .001 2nd, .001 oil	.010-.016 top, N.A. 2nd, N.A. oil	.001-.002
U20	3.4331-3.4351	N.A.	3.4323-3.4342	3.4905-3.4925	push fit	.002-.003 top, .001-.003 2nd, .001-.003 oil	.010-.016 top, .006-.012 2nd, .006-.012 oil	.001-.002
L16	3.2677-3.2697	N.A.	3.267-3.269	3.326-3.328	push fit	.002-.003 top, .001-.003 2nd, .001-.003 top,	.009-.015 top, .006-.012 2nd, .006-.012 oil	.001-.002
L24	3.2677-3.2697	N.A.	3.267-3.269	3.326-3.328	push fit	.002-.003 top, .001-.003 2nd, .001-.003 oil	.009-.015 top, .006-.012 2nd, .006-.012 oil	.001-.002
A12	2.8760-2.8740	N.A.	2.8727-2.8747	2.9318-2.9239	push fit	.002-.003 top, .002-.003 2nd, .002-.003 oil	.008-014 top, .008-.014 2nd, .001-.014 oil	.001-.002

Engine Rebuilding Specifications
Valves

Engine Model	Seat Angle (deg.)	Valve Seat Width (in.)	Valve Lift (in.)	Valve Spring Pressure (lbs. @ in.)		Valve Spring Free Length (in.)		Stem to Guide Clearance (in.)		Valve Guide Removable
				Outer	Inner	Outer	Inner	Intake	Exhaust	
P	45	N.A.	.374	132 @ 1.57	None	2.26	None	.002-.003	.002-.003	N.A.
E1	45	N.A.	.323	47 @ 1.13	105 @ 1.21	1.97	2.05	.002-.003	.002-.003	N.A.
G	45	N.A.	.335	47 @ 1.13	134 @ 1.19	1.97	1.93	.001-.002	.002-.003	N.A.
J	45	.064-.065 intake, .064-.065 exhaust	N.A.	N.A.	N.A.	1.97	2.05	.002-.003	.002-.003	Yes
R	45	N.A.	.335	N.A.	N.A.	1.97	1.93	.001-.002	.002-.003	N.A.
U20	45	.055 intake, .069 exhaust	.44②	168 @ 1.17 71 @ 1.62	29 @ 1.54	1.96	1.91	.001-.002	.002-.003	Yes
L16	45	.055-.071 intake, .063-.079 exhaust	.394	105 @ 1.21 64 @ 1.53	56 @ .96 27 @ 1.38	2.05	1.77	.001-.002	.002-.003	Yes
L24	45	.055-.063 intake, .071-.087 exhaust	.413	47 @ 1.57 108 @ 1.16	56 @ .96	1.97	1.76	.001-.002	.002-.003	Yes
A12	45	.051 intake, .071 exhaust	.295	66 @ 1.52 135 @ 1.23	None	1.80	None	.001-.002	.002-.003	Yes

①—Valve angle is 45.5.
②—With two twin-choke sidedraft carburetors—.46

Oil Pump Specifications

Engine	*Pump type*	*Clearance between inner and outer rotor (in.)*	*Tip clearance—gear or rotor to cover (in.)*	*Clearance between outer rotor and body (in.)*	*Gear backlash (in.)*	*Side clearance—gear to body (in.)*	*Maximum oil pressure (psi)*	*Minimum oil pressure (psi) at idle*	*Relief valve spring free length (in.)*	*Relief valve opening pressure (psi)*
P	Gear	—	.006-.009	—	.001-.003	.006-.010	50-57	7-10	1.634	N.A.
E1, J	Rotor	.002-.005	.005-.008	N.A.	—	—	54-57	14-17	N.A.	N.A.
G, R	Gear	—	.002-.004	—	.010-.012	N.A.	54-57	7-10	N.A.	N.A.
U20	Gear	—	.006-.009	—	.012-.016	.002-.004	54-57	7-10	2.453	63.9
L16, L24	Rotor	.002-.005	.005	.006-.008	—	—	54-60	14-17	2.24	54.0-59.7
A12	Rotor	.002-.005	.005	.006-.008	—	—	54-60	13-17	1.71	54.0-59.7

Torque Specifications

Engine Model	*Cylinder Head Bolts (ft. lbs.)*	*Main Bearing Bolts (ft. lbs.)*	*Rod Bearing Bolts (ft. lbs.)*	*Crankshaft Pulley Bolt (ft. lbs.)*	*Flywheel to Crankshaft Bolts (ft. lbs.)*
P	63-65	65	65	N.A.	57
E1	35-45	72-87	20-25	N.A.	35-44
G	50-60	72-87	32-43	N.A.	35-44
J	45	75-80	22-25	N.A.	35-44
R	45-50	71-81	35-45	N.A.	35-44
U20	65	65	65	145	58
L16	40	33-40	20-24	116-130	69-76
L24	47	33-40	20-24	116-130	101
A12	33-35	36-38	25-26	108-116	47-54

Tightening Sequences

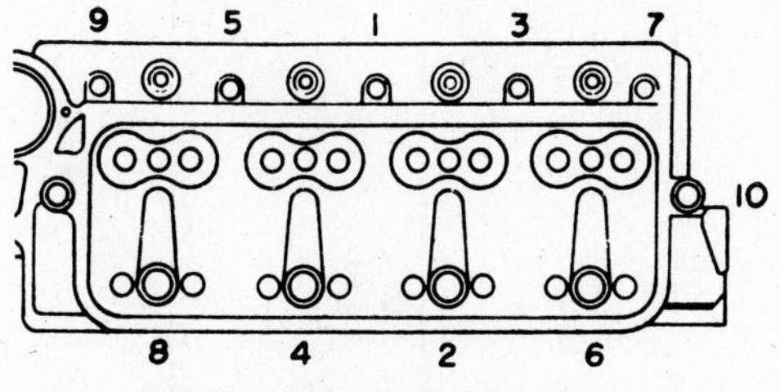

Cylinder head, E1 and J engines

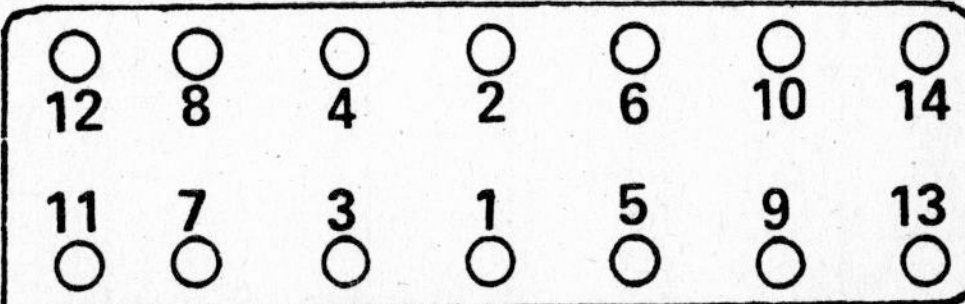

Cylinder head, L24 engine

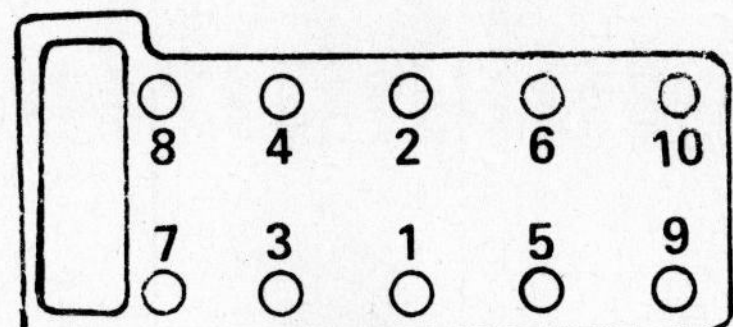

Cylinder head, L16 and U20 engines

Cylinder head, A12, G, and R engines

Carburetor Specifications

Engine Model —Vehicle	Carburetor	Bore Size (in.)	Large Venturi (in.)	Small Venturi (in.)	Main Jet (Number)	Main Air Bleed (Number)	Main Nozzle (in.)	Idle (Slow) Jet (Number)	Idle (Slow) Air Bleed	Bypass Air Bleed (Number)	Power Jet	Accelerator Pump Injector	Fast Idle (deg. of throttle opening at full choke)	Suction Piston Lift (in.)
P—L60	Hitachi VC42-4A	1.42			135	70		25	210					
P with emission control—L60	Rochester 7015013 single throat downdraft													
E1—PL410	Nihonki-kaki 2D30CE dual throat downdraft	1.102, 1.81 sec.	.827, 1.024 sec.		96, 115 sec.	80, 60 sec.		48, 48 sec.	100, 220 2nd, 120 sec.		#55		14	
E1—L320	Nihonki-kaki 2D30C dual throat downdraft	1.102, 1.81 sec.	.827, 1.024 sec.		96, 115 sec.	80, 60 sec.		48, 48 sec.	100, 220 2nd, 120 sec.		55		14	
J—L520	Nihonki-kaki D2630A-5A dual throat downdraft	1.022, 1.180 sec.	.788, 1.06 sec.		90, 145 sec.			48, 48 sec.			#40	#45	14	
J—PL411	Nihonki-kaki D2630A-5A dual throat downdraft	1.022, 1.180 sec.	.788, 1.06 sec.		92, 140 sec.	60, 60 sec.		48, 48 sec.	100, 240 2nd, 120 sec.		#40	.024"	14	

Carburetor Specifications, continued

J with emission control— L520, L521	Hitachi DCA306-4 dual throat downdraft	1.022, 1.180 sec.	.827, 1.01 sec.	.315-.512 prim., .315-.433 sec., .551-.710 2nd	96, 130 sec.	100, 140 sec.	.106/.138 .118/.157 sec.	47, 100 sec.	200, 100 sec.	170	#60		13	
R	Hitachi HJB38W SU type sidedraft	1.495												
R with emission control	Hitachi HJB38W-5 or HJB38W-6 SU type sidedraft	1.495									.092″		6	1.400
U20	Hitachi HJ46W SU type sidedraft	1.81												
U20	Mikuni/ Solex 44PHH twin-choke sidedraft	1.74	.394, 1.456 sec.		180			60				.012″		1.337

Carburetor Specifications, continued

U20 with emission control	Hitachi HJG46W-5 or HJG46W-7 SU type sidedraft	1.805								.100″		4.5
L16—PL510	Hitachi DAF328 dual throat downdraft	1.102, 1.260 sec.	.945, 1.102 sec.	.354	115, 155 sec.	240, 120 sec.		48, 180 sec.	180, 100 sec.			16
L16 with emission control	Hitachi DAF328-8 (auto.), DAF328-6 (std.) DAF328-10 (PL521)	1.101, 1.260 sec.	.906, 1.101 sec.	.355	117 (1969), 115 (1970)	240, 120 sec.	.255/.071 .118 sec.	48, 180 sec.	150, 100 sec.		.020″	16
L24 with emission control—HLS30	Hitachi HJG46W-3A SU type sidedraft	1.811			A							
A12 with emission control—LB110, KLB110	Hitachi DCG306 dual throat downdraft	1.024, 1.181 sec.	.787, 1.024 sec.	.315 prim., .276 sec., .512 2nd	98, 135 sec.	80, 80 sec.	.083, .110 sec.	43, 50 sec.	220, 100 sec.	#60	.020″	17.5

Carburetor Specifications, Continued

Engine Model —Vehicle	Suction Spring (Number)	Metering Needle	Float Chamber Inclination (deg.)	Economizer (in.)	Fuel Level (in.)	Vacuum Jet (Number)
P— L60					.80-.88①	
P with emission control —L60						
E1— PL410				.079	.75①	
E1— L320				#145	.75①	
J— L520					.85①	
J— PL411					.85①	
J with emission control —L520, L521					N.A.	
R					.87-.95①	
R with emission control	23	M-39 with 38W-5, M-70 with 38W-6	0		.87-.95①	
U20 (SU type)					.87-.95①	
U20 (Mikuni/Solex)					See text	
U20 with emission control	32	N-17 with 46W-5, N-25 with 46W-7	8		.87-.95①	
L16— PL510				.071	.87-.95①	
L16 with emission control				.071	.87-.95①	150, 130 sec.
L24 with emission control —HLS30	23	N-27 .079″			.87-.95①	
A12 with emission control —LB110, KLB110					.71-.78①	

①—From float chamber top to fuel level

Brake Specifications

Model	Type		Brake Cylinder Bore (in.)			Brake Drum or Disc Diameter (in.)	
	Front	Rear	Master Cylinder	Wheel Cylinder Front	Wheel Cylinder Rear	Front	Rear
L60	Drum	Drum	1.000	1.000	1.150	11.5	11.5
PL410	Drum	Drum	.875	1.000	.938	N.A.	N.A.
SPL310	Drum	Drum	.875	1.000	.938	N.A.	N.A.
PL411	Drum	Drum	.875	1.000	.938	9.0	9.0
RL411	Disc	Drum	.875	2.000	.938	N.A.	N.A.
SPL311	Disc	Drum	.750	2.125	.813	11.2	9.0
SRL311	Disc	Drum	.750	2.125	.75	11.2	9.0
L320	Drum	Drum	.77	.77	.77	10.0	10.0
L520, L521	Drum	Drum	.750	.750	.750	10.0	10.0
PL510	Disc	Drum	.750	2.000	.813	9.1	9.0
WPL510	Disc	Drum	.750	2.000	.813	9.1	9.0
PL521	Drum	Drum	N.A.	N.A.	N.A.	10.0	10.0
HLS30	Disc	Drum	.875	2.125	.875	10.7	9.0
LB110, KLB110	Disc	Drum	.688	1.894	.688	8.4	8.0

Chassis and Wheel Alignment Specifications

Model	Chassis			Wheel Alignment							
	Wheel-base (in.)	Track (in.)		Caster (deg.)		Camber (deg.)		Toe-In (in.)	Kingpin Inclination (deg.)	Wheel Pivot Ratio (deg.)	
		Front	Rear	Range	Preferred Setting	Range	Preferred Setting			Inner Wheel	Outer Wheel
L60	86.6	54.6	55.3		1°30′		1°30′	.12-.16	6°45′-7°15′	28	25°32′
WL60	98.4	54.6	55.3		1°30′		1°30′	.12-.16	6°45′-7°15′	28	25°32′
PL410	93.8	47.5	47.0		1°30′		1°30′	.06-.13	6°30′	36	28°36′
SPL310	89.8	47.8	47.1		1°30′		1°26′	.06-.13	6°34′	36	28°36′
PL411	93.7	47.5	47.2		0		1°45′	.06-.13	6°15′	36	28°36′
RL411	93.7	47.5	47.2		0		1°45′	.13	6°15′	36	28°36′
SPL311	89.8	50.2	47.2		1°30′		1°25′	.08-.12	6°35′	36°16′	29°20′
SRL311	89.8	50.2	47.2		1°30′		1°25′	.08-.12	6°35′	36°16′	29°20′
L320	97.2	46.1	46.7		3°30′		1°30′	.08-.12	6	34	29°30′
L520	99.6	49.2	49.9		1°50′	50′-1°50′	1°20′	.08-.12	6	34	29°30′
PL510	95.3	50.4	50.4		1°40′		1	.35-.47	8	38-39	22°30′-33°30′
WPL510	95.3	50.2	49.6		2		1°10′	.12-.24	7°50′	38-39	22°30′-33°30′
L521, PL521	99.6	49.2	49.9		3°50′	50′-1°50′	1°20′	.08-.12	6	34	29°30′
HLS30①	90.7	53.3	53.0	2°25′-3°25′	2°55′	20′-1°20′	50′	08-.20	11°40′-12°40′	32-33	31°24′-32°24′
LB110, KLB110	90.6	48.8	49.0	40′-1°40′	1°10′	35′-1°35′	1°05′	.16-.24	7°55′	42-44	35-37

①—Unloaded

Manual Transmission Ratios

Vehicle	*First*	*Second*	*Third*	*Fourth*	*Fifth*	*Reverse*
L60①	2.900	1.562	1.000	None	None	3.015
L320	4.94	3.01	1.73	1.00	None	6.46
L520	3.657	2.177	1.419	1.000	None	3.638
	4.941	3.009	1.726	1.000	None	6.462
PL521	3.657	2.177	1.419	1.000	None	3.638
PL410	3.518	1.725	1.00	None	None	4.125
	3.197	1.725	1.00	None	None	4.125
	3.945	2.94	1.490	1.000	None	5.159
	3.945	2.403	1.490	1.000	None	5.159
PL411	3.197	1.725	1.000	None	None	4.125
	3.94	2.40	1.49	1.00	None	5.159
	3.657	2.177	1.419	1.000	None	3.638
RL411, SPL311, PL510	3.382	2.013	1.312	1.000	None	3.365
SPL310	3.515	2.140	1.328	1.000	None	4.597
SRL311	2.957	1.858	1.311	1.000	.852	2.922
WPL510	3.657	2.177	1.419	1.000	None	3.638
	3.382	2.013	1.312	1.000	None	3.634
	3.382	2.013	1.312	1.000	None	3.634
HLS30	3.549	2.197	1.420	1.000	None	3.164
	2.957	1.857	1.311	1.000	.852	2.922
LB110, KLB110	3.757	2.169	1.404	1.000	None	3.640

① L60 transfer case ratios are 2.264:1 and 1:1.

Clutch Specifications

Vehicle model	*Clutch type*	*Spring tension, free length (lbs. @ in., in.)*	*Release lever or diaphragm distance from flywheel (in.)*	*Facing O.D. X I.D. X thickness (in.)*	*New disc thickness (in.)*	*No. disc springs*	*Minimum allowable depth of rivet head below facing (in.)*	*Maximum allowable disc runout (in.)*	*Pedal height above floor (in.)*	*Pedal free play (in.)*
L60	coil spring	180-190 @ 1.56, N.A.	2.5	10.8 X 6.9 X .14	.47	N.A.	.012	.020	8.1-8.5	1.0-1.5
Early L320	coil spring	132-176 @ 1.41, 1.95	2.26-2.32	7.25 X 5.00 X .14	.346	6	.012	.020	N.A.	.98-1.18
Late L320, PL410, PL411, RL411	coil spring	78-87 @ 1.15, 1.87-1.99	1.98-2.00	7.87 X 5.12 X .14	.338-.358	6	.012	.020	N.A.	1.0-1.5, 1.8-2.0 for PL411 & RL411
SPL310	coil spring	169-178 @ 1.56, 2.17	2.04-2.06	7.87 X 5.76 X .13	.333	6	.012	.020	6.10-6.60	.60-.80
SPL311, SRL311	diaphragm spring	—	N.A.	7.87 X 5.12 X .14	N.A.	N.A.	.012	.020	N.A.	1.9-2.1
PL510 WPL510	coil spring	92.6-101.4 @ 1.15, 2.06	1.97-2.01	7.87 X 5.12 X .14	.339-.354	6	.012	.020	8.15	.98
PL510, WPL510	diaphragm spring	—	1.69-1.77	7.87 X 5.12 X .14	.339-.354	6	.012	.020	8.15	.98
L520, L521, PL521	coil spring	161-179 @ 1.15, 1.87-1.99	1.98-2.01	7.87 X 5.12 X .14	.339-.354	9	.012	.020	5.34, 5.46 without pedal stop	.98
HLS30	diaphragm spring	—	1.69-1.77	8.86 X 5.90 X N.A.	.327-.350	6	.012	.020	8.00	.39-.59
LB110, KLB110	diaphragm spring	—	1.14-1.22	7.09 X 4.92 X N.A.	.299-.315	6	.012	.020	5.57	1.18

Capacities and Pressures

Model	Engine Crankcase Refill after Draining (qts.)		Transmission Refill after Draining (pts.)				Differential (pts.)	Fuel Tank (gals.)	Cooling System (qts.)	Normal Fuel Pressure (psi)	Maximum coolant pressure (psi)
	With Filter	Without Filter	Manual			Auto. (total capacity)					
			3-Speed	4-Speed	5-Speed						
L60	3.6	N.A.	4.2①				2.6 front and rear	19.0	5.2	N.A.	N.A.
PL410	3.3	3.0	3.8				2.0	10.8	5.4	N.A.	6
SPL310	N.A.	4.2		4.6			1.8	11.3	6.9	N.A.	4-6
PL411	N.A.	3.1	3.8	4.7			2.2	11.0	5.7	N.A.	6
RL411	N.A.	3.5		4.3			1.9	11.0	7.1	N.A.	4-6
SPL311	N.A.	4.3		4.6			2.0	11.4	8.4	3.4-4.3	4-6
SRL311	N.A.	4.3			5.4		2.0	11.4	9.0	3.4-4.3	13
SRL311 with two twin-choke carburetors	N.A.	7.5			5.4		2.0	11.4	9.0	3.4-4.3	13
L320	3.8	3.2		4.3			1.8	9.3	5.7	N.A.	N.A.
L520, L521	3.8	3.2		4.2			1.7	10.8	5.9	2.1-2.5	6
PL510	5.2	4.4		6.4		11.4②	1.7	11.9	6.8, 7.2 with heater	2.6-3.4	13
WPL510	5.2	4.4		6.4		11.4②	2.1	11.9	6.8, 7.2 with heater	2.6-3.4	13
PL521	4.4	3.6		4.2			1.7	10.8	6.8, 7.4 with heater	2.6-3.4	13
HLS30	4.7	4.3		3.2	3.2	12.8	2.1	15.9	8.5	3.4-4.3	13
LB110	N.A.	2.9		4.3			1.8	9.3	5.7	N.A.	13

①—4.8 pts.—without power takeoff, 7.8 pts.—transfer case
②—1.5 pts.—oil cooler

Recommended Lubricants (SAE)

Temperature (°F)	Under 10	10-32	32-90	Over 90
Engine Oil API designation: MS, SD, SE	10W-30, 10W, or 5W-20	10W-30, 10W-40, or 10W	10W-30, 10W-40, or 20W	10W-30, 10W-40, 20W-40, or 30W*
Gear Oil API designation: MP, EP, MPS	80	90	90	140

* 40W may be used for high speeds in temperatures over 90.

Electrical Specifications —Battery and Starter

Engine Model	Battery			Starter						
				Lock Test			No Load Test			
	Capacity (Amp. Hrs.)	Volts	Grounded Terminal	Amps	Volts	Torque (ft. lbs.)	Amps	Volts	rpm	Brush Minimum Length (in.)
P	60	12	Neg.	N.A.	N.A.	N.A.	N.A.	N.A.	N.A.	N.A.
E1	50	12	Pos.	<500	8.0	>7.7	60	11	<7,000	N.A.
G	N.A.	12	Pos.	<500	9.5	>7.0	60	11	<7,000	N.A.
J	40,50	12	Neg.	N.A.	N.A.	N.A	60	12	>7,000	.37
R	40,50	12	Neg.	<500	9.5	>6.5	N.A.	N.A.	N.A.	N.A.
U20	50	12	Neg.	<500	6.0	>7.2	60	11	<6,000	.30
L16	50,60 PL510, WPL510; 40,50 L520; 40,50,60 PL521, L521	12	Neg.	<480	6.0	>7.9	60	12	>7,000	.28
L24	N.A.	12	Neg.	<460	6.0	10.1	60	12	>5,000	.49
A12	N.A.	12	Neg.	<420	6.3	>6.5	60	12	>7,000	.37

<—Less than >—More than

Electrical Specifications — AC Regulator

Engine Model	Part Number	Charge Indicator Relay				Voltage Regulator				
		Core Gap (in.)	Back Gap (in.)	Air Gap (in.)	Point Gap (in.)	Core Gap (in.)	Back Gap (in.)	Air Gap (in.)	Point Gap (in.)	Regulated Voltage
G	Mitsubishi RLA-1		.032-.044	.032-.048	.032-.044		.028-.036	.032-.040	.012-.016	N.A.
J	Mitsubishi RL2220B5		.032-.043	.032-.047	.032-.043		.028-.035	.032-.039	.012-.016	14-15
R	Mitsubishi RL-2B		.032-.043	.032-.047	.032-.043		.028-.035	.032-.035	.012-.016	14-15
U20	Mitsubishi RL2220B5		.035-.047	.030-.043	.030-.043		.032-.047	.032-.043	.012-.016	13.5-14.5
L16	Hitachi TL1Z-17		.007	.020-.024	.016-.020		.035-.039	.032-.047	.012-.016	14-15
L24	Hitachi TL1Z-37	.032-.039			.016-.024	.024-.039			.012-.016	14.3-15.3 @ 50F
A12	Hitachi TL1Z-37	.032-.039			.016-.024	.024-.039			.012-.016	14.3-15.3 @ 50F

①—Right unit in regulator case (left unit in TL1Z-17)
②—Left unit in regulator case (right unit in TL1Z-17)

NOTE: Right and left are determined with the regulator terminals or harness plug downward.

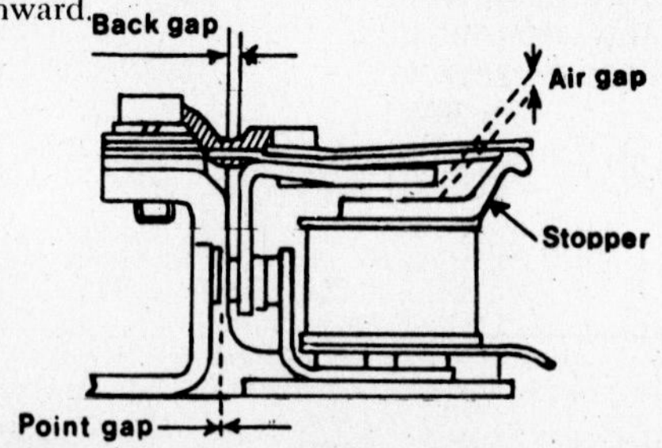

Regulator and charge indicator relay, all except Hitachi TL1Z-37

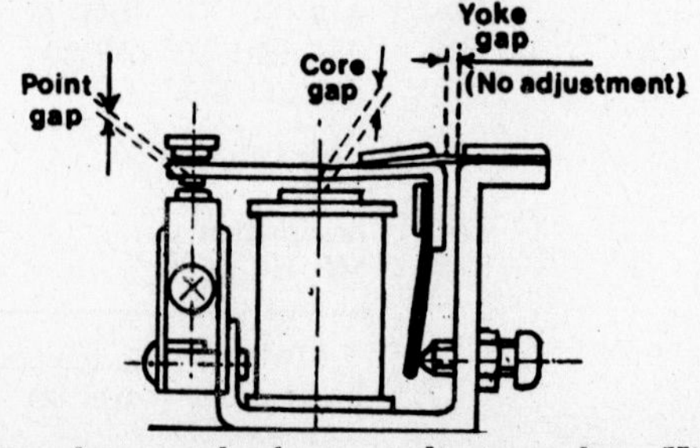

Regulator and charge indicator relay, Hitachi TL1Z-37

Light Bulb Specifications

Model	Usage	Wattage
L60	Headlights	50/42
	Front parking, turn	21/6
	Stop, tail, turn	21/6
	License plate	10
	Instrument panel	8
	Flasher warning light	1.5
PL410	Headlights	37.5/50 37.5
	Parking	8
	Turn	25
	License plate	8
	Interior light	5
	Backup	25
	Warning lights	1.5
	Instrument	5
SPL310	Headlights	50/40
	Front parking, turn	25/5
	Tail, stop	21/6
	License plate	8
	Interior	6
	Instruments, warning	1.5
	Inspection lamp	8
	Radio	1.2
PL411, RL411	Headlights	37.5/50 37.5
	Side markers	8
	Tail	8
	License plate	8
	Stop	25
	Backup	25
	Interior	5
	Fog	35
	Inspection	8
	Parking	8
	Turn	25
	Instrument	3
	Warning	1.5
SPL311, SRL311	Headlight	50/40
	Front turn, parking	25/8
	Stop, tail, turn	25/8
	Backup	15
	License plate	8
	Map	5
	Side marker	8
L520	Headlights	37.5/50 50
	Front parking, turn	25/8
	Tail, stop	25/8
	Rear turn, backup	25
	License plate	8
	Interior	6
L521, PL521	Headlights	37.5/50 37.5
	Front turn, parking	25/8
	Tail, stop	25/8
	Rear turn	25
	Backup	25
	Interior	6
	License plate	8
PL510, WPL510	Headlights	37.5/50 37.5
	Front parking, turn	25/8
	Tail, turn	25/8
	Stop	25
	Backup	25
	License plate	8
	Interior	10
HLS30	Headlights	50/40
	Side marker, turn	23/7
	Side marker, license plate	7.5
	Tail	7
	Stop	23
	Rear turn	23
	Backup	23
	Instrument, warning, glove compartment, clock	3
	Four-way flasher	23
	Inspection	8

Distributor Specifications

Engine Model	Distributor	Centrifugal Advance		Vacuum Advance	
		Start (rpm)	End (deg. @ rpm)	Start (in. Hg.)	End (deg. @ in. Hg.)
J	Hitachi D411-53	450	11-15 @ 2,400	3.9-4.7	6-9 @ 13.4
L16	Hitachi D410-58	450	10 @ 1,500	5.9	9 @ 12.4
L24	Hitachi D606-52	450	6 @ 1,000	3.9	5.5 @ 9.6
A12	Hitachi D412-63	550	12.5 @ 2,100	9.8	6.5 @ 13.8

Electrical Specifications
Alternator

Engine Model	Alternator Part Number	Output @ Generator rpm: rpm	Output @ Generator rpm: Amps (14v.)
J	Mitsubishi AS203A1	2,500	24.5
R	Mitsubishi AC300/12X2R	2,500	24.5, 21.5 @ high temp.
U20	Mitsubishi AS2030A2	2,500	23
L16	Hitachi LT130-41	2,500	22
L24	Hitachi LT145-35	2,500 5,000	>34 >45
A12	Hitachi LT135-05	2,500 5,000	>24 >33

>More than

Fuses and Fusible Links

Model	Fuse Box Location	Fusible Link Location
L320, L520, L521 PL521, PL510, WPL510	Engine compartment, right rear	
L60	Engine compartment, right fender well	
SPL311, SRL311	Inside glove compartment	
LB110 KLB110	Under instrument panel, right of steering column	Between battery and alternator
HLS30	Under ash tray in console	At alternator, at starter

Wiring Diagrams

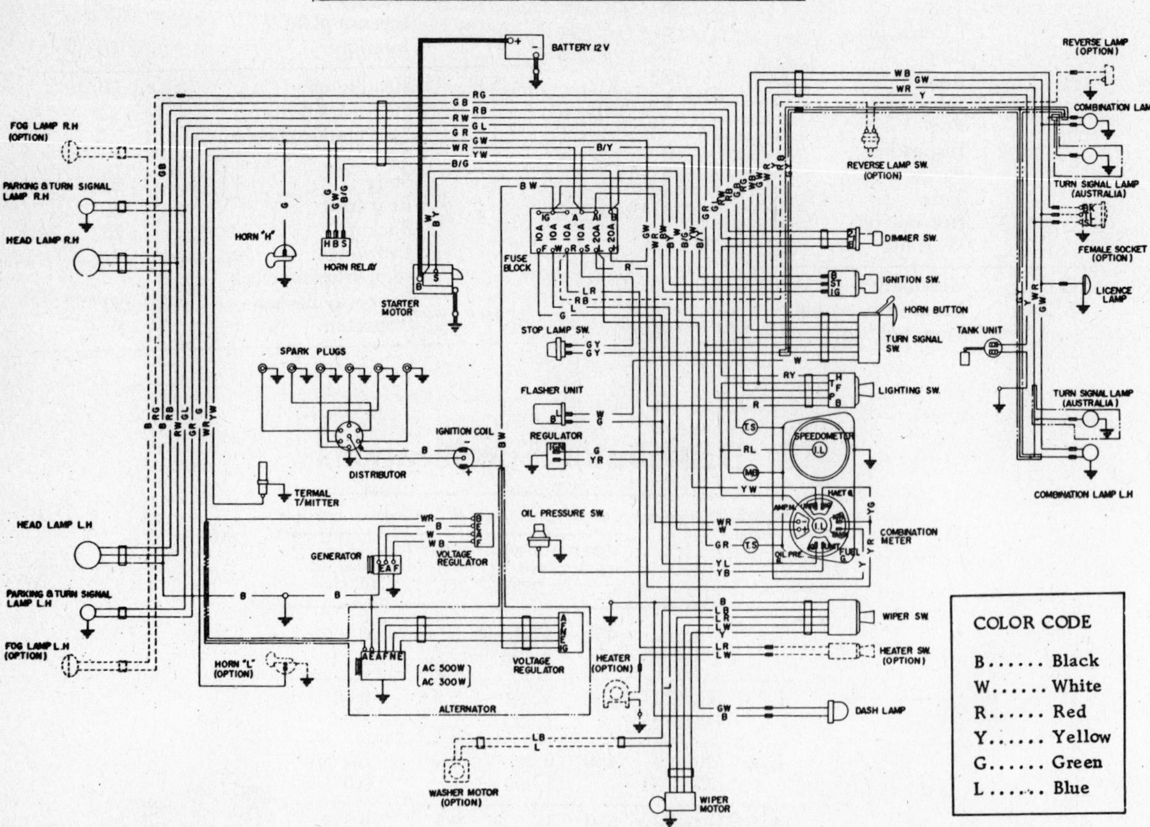

L60

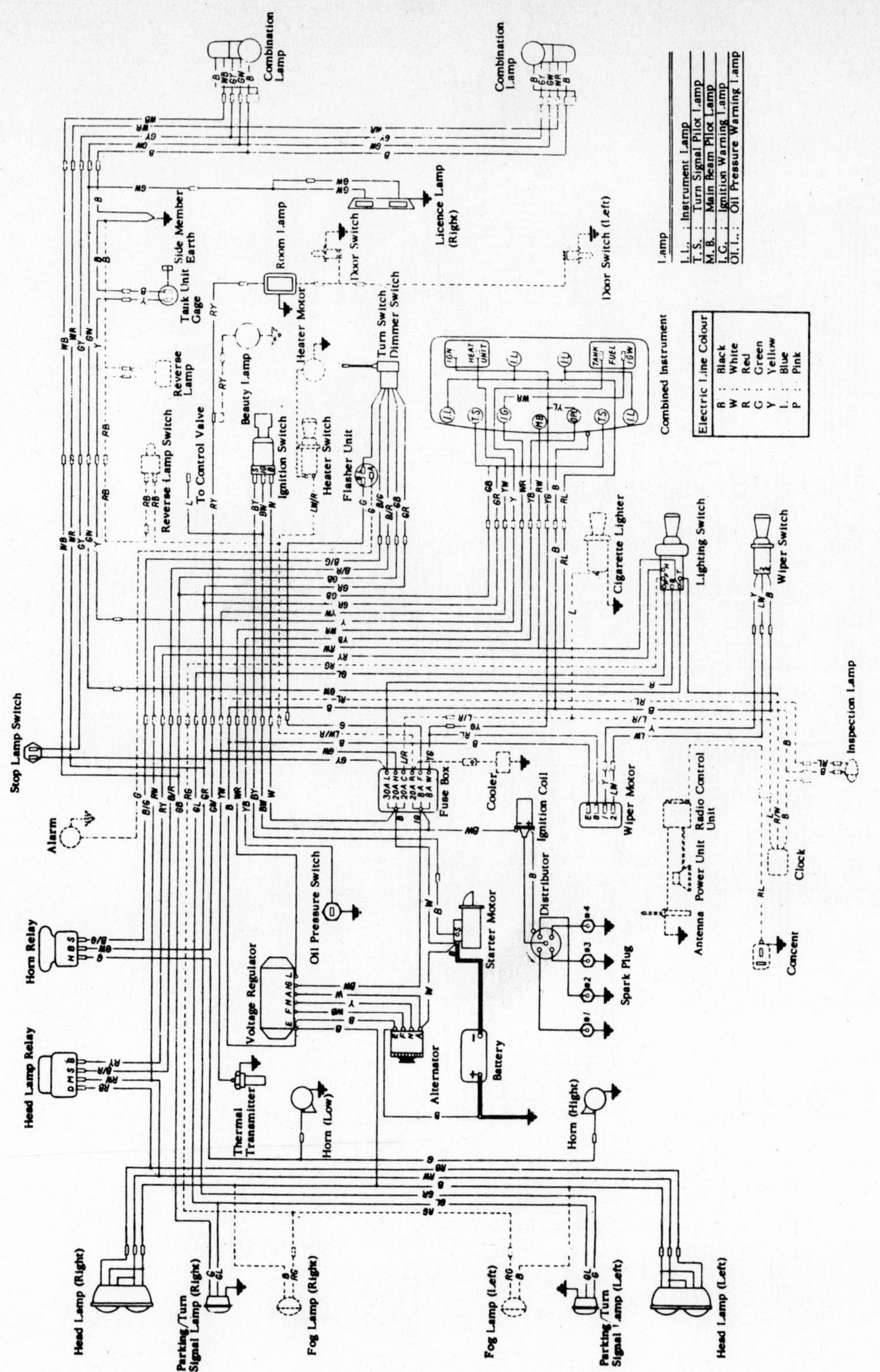
Combination Lamp
Combination Lamp
Side Member Earth
Licence Lamp (Right)
Door Switch
Room Lamp
Door Switch (Left)
Tank Unit Gage
Heater Motor
Turn Switch
Dimmer Switch
Reverse Lamp
Beauty Lamp
Reverse Lamp Switch
To Control Valve
Ignition Switch
Heater Switch
Flasher Unit
Combined Instrument
Lamp
I.L. : Instrument Lamp
T.S. : Turn Signal Pilot Lamp
M.B. : Main Beam Pilot Lamp
I.G. : Ignition Warning Lamp
OI.L. : Oil Pressure Warning Lamp
Electric Line Colour
B : Black
W : White
R : Red
G : Green
Y : Yellow
L : Blue
P : Pink
Cigarette Lighter
Lighting Switch
Wiper Switch
Stop Lamp Switch
Alarm
Fuse Box
Cooler
Ignition Coil
Wiper Motor
Radio Control Unit
Power Unit
Antenna
Clock
Inspection Lamp
Concent
Oil Pressure Switch
Distributor
Spark Plug
Horn Relay
Voltage Regulator
Starter Motor
Head Lamp Relay
Battery
Alternator
Thermal Transmitter
Horn (Low)
Horn (Hight)
Head Lamp (Right)
Parking/Turn Signal Lamp (Right)
Fog Lamp (Right)
Fog Lamp (Left)
Parking/Turn Signal Lamp (Left)
Head Lamp (Left)

PL410

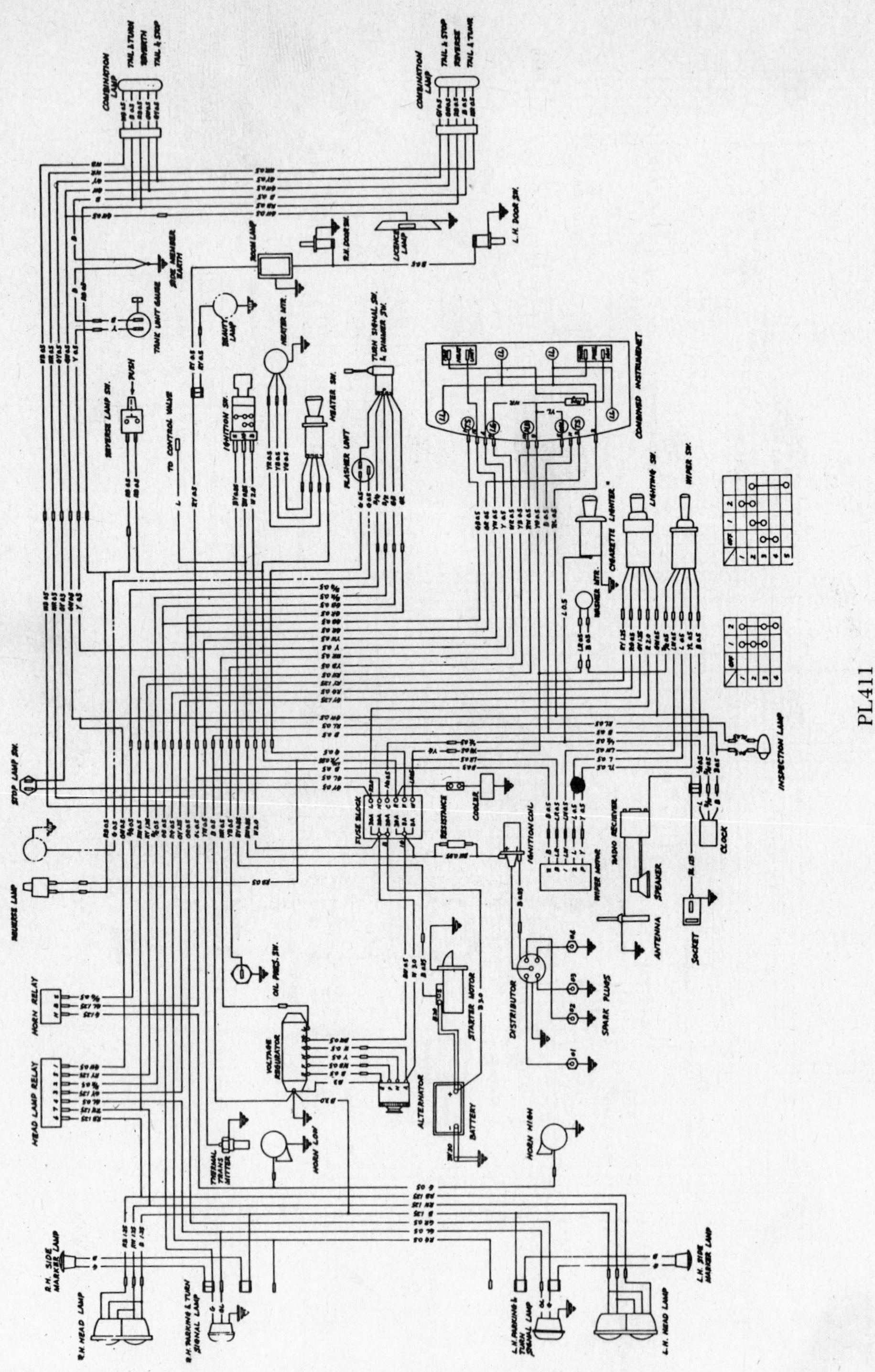
COMBINATION LAMP
TAIL & TURN
REVERSE
TAIL & STOP
LICENCE LAMP
ROOM LAMP
R.H. DOOR SW.
L.H. DOOR SW.
SIDE MEMBER EARTH
TANK UNIT GAUGE
REVERSE LAMP SW.
PUSH
TO CONTROL VALVE
IGNITION SW.
HEATER MTR.
HEATER SW.
FLASHER UNIT
TURN SIGNAL SW. & DIMMER SW.
COMBINED INSTRUMENT
WASHER MTR.
CIGARETTE LIGHTER
LIGHTING SW.
WIPER SW.
INSPECTION LAMP
CLOCK
SOCKET
ANTENNA
SPEAKER
RADIO RECEIVER
WIPER MOTOR
IGNITION COIL
COOLER
RESISTANCE
FUSE BLOCK
DISTRIBUTOR
SPARK PLUGS
STARTER MOTOR
BATTERY
ALTERNATOR
VOLTAGE REGULATOR
OIL PRESS. SW.
STOP LAMP SW.
REVERSE LAMP
HORN RELAY
HEAD LAMP RELAY
THERMAL TRANSMITTER
HORN LOW
HORN HIGH
R.H. SIDE MARKER LAMP
R.H. HEAD LAMP
R.H. PARKING & TURN SIGNAL LAMP
L.H. PARKING & TURN SIGNAL LAMP
L.H. HEAD LAMP
L.H. SIDE MARKER LAMP
PL411

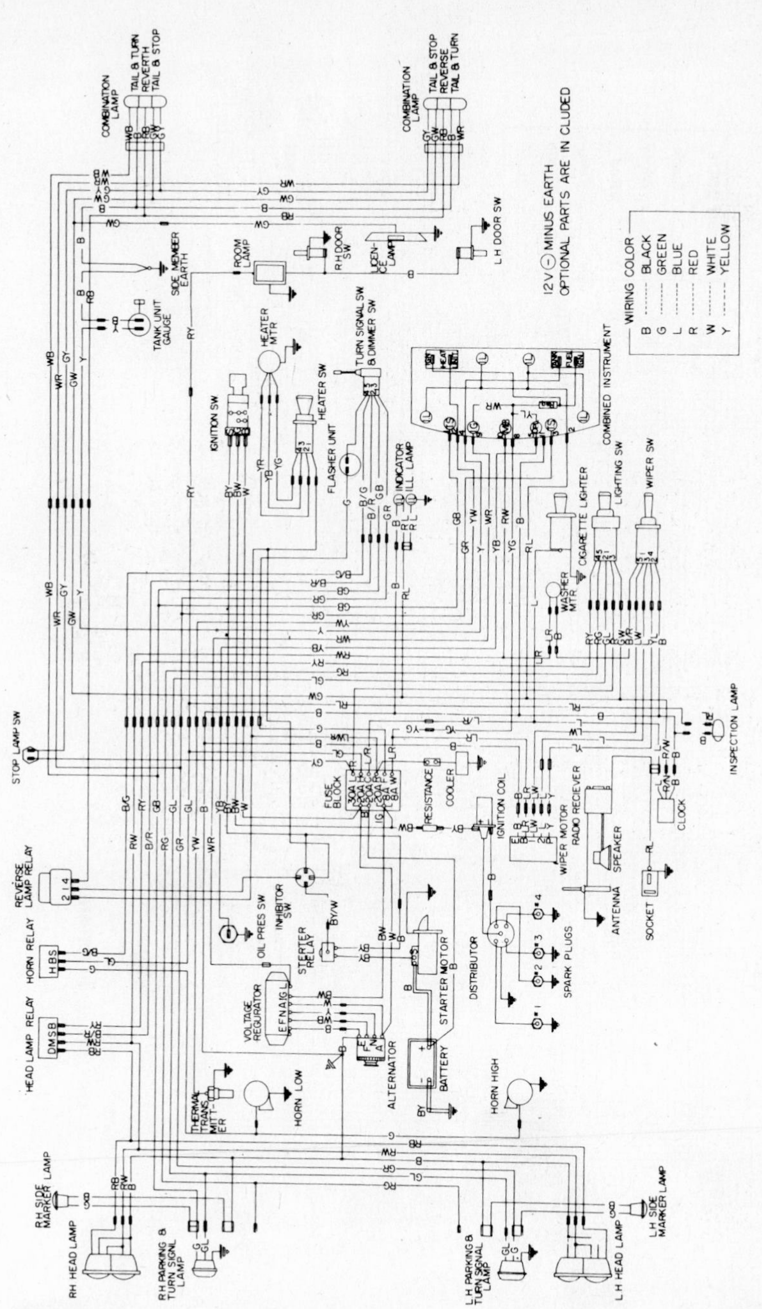
COMBINATION LAMP
TAIL & TURN
REVERTH
TAIL & STOP
COMBINATION LAMP
TAIL & STOP
REVERSE
TAIL & TURN
12V ⊖ MINUS EARTH
OPTIONAL PARTS ARE IN CLUDED
WIRING COLOR
B ...... BLACK
G ...... GREEN
L ...... BLUE
R ...... RED
W ...... WHITE
Y ...... YELLOW
SIDE MEMBER EARTH
ROOM LAMP
R H DOOR SW
LICEN-CE LAMP
L H DOOR SW
TANK UNIT GAUGE
HEATER MTR
TURN SIGNAL SW & DIMMER SW
IGNITION SW
HEATER SW
FLASHER UNIT
INDICATOR ILL LAMP
COMBINED INSTRUMENT
CIGARETTE LIGHTER
LIGHTING SW
WIPER SW
WASHER MTR
STOP LAMP SW
FUSE BLOCK
RESISTANCE
COOLER
IGNITION COIL
WIPER MOTOR
RADIO RECIEVER
SPEAKER
ANTENNA
SOCKET
CLOCK
INSPECTION LAMP
REVERSE LAMP RELAY
HORN RELAY
HEAD LAMP RELAY
OIL PRES SW
INHIBITOR SW
STERTER RELAY
VOLTAGE REGURATOR
STARTER MOTOR
DISTRIBUTOR
SPARK PLUGS
ALTERNATOR
BATTERY
THERMAL TRANS-MITT-ER
HORN LOW
HORN HIGH
RH SIDE MARKER LAMP
RH HEAD LAMP
R H PARKING & TURN SIGNL LAMP
L H PARKING & TURN SIGNAL LAMP
L H HEAD LAMP
LH SIDE MARKER LAMP

RL411

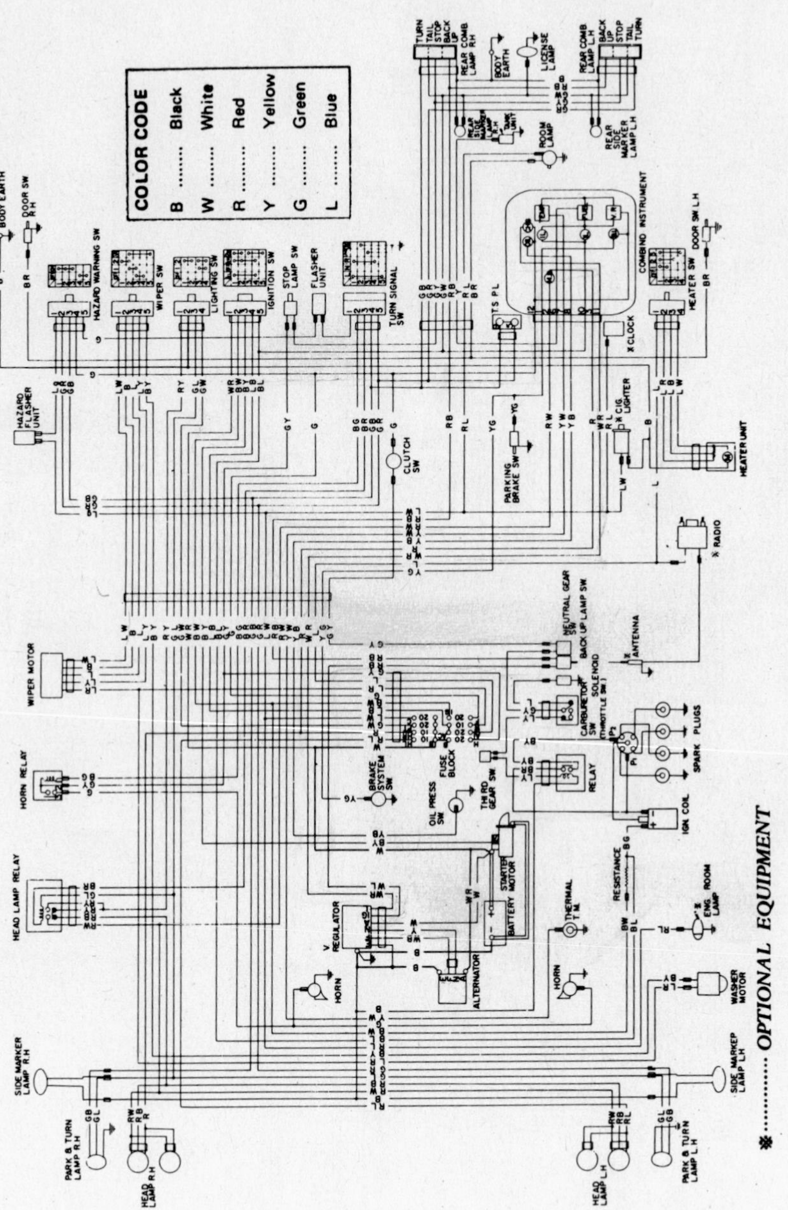

PL510, standard transmission

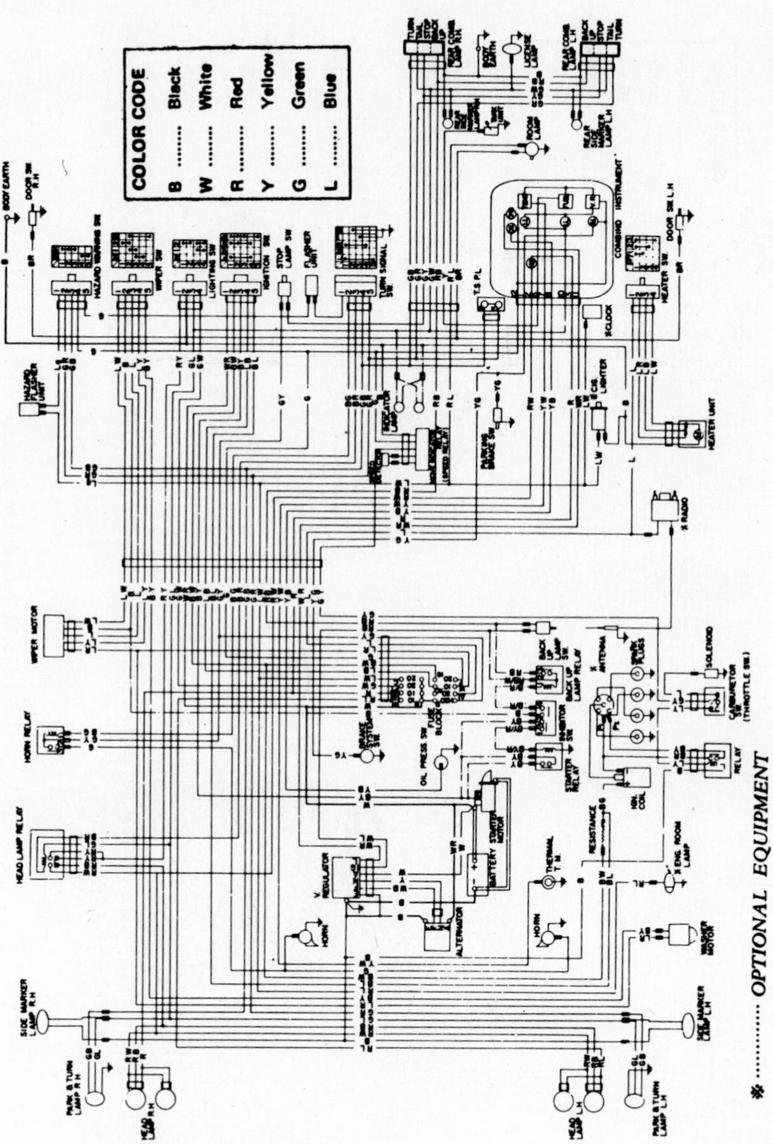

PL510, automatic transmission

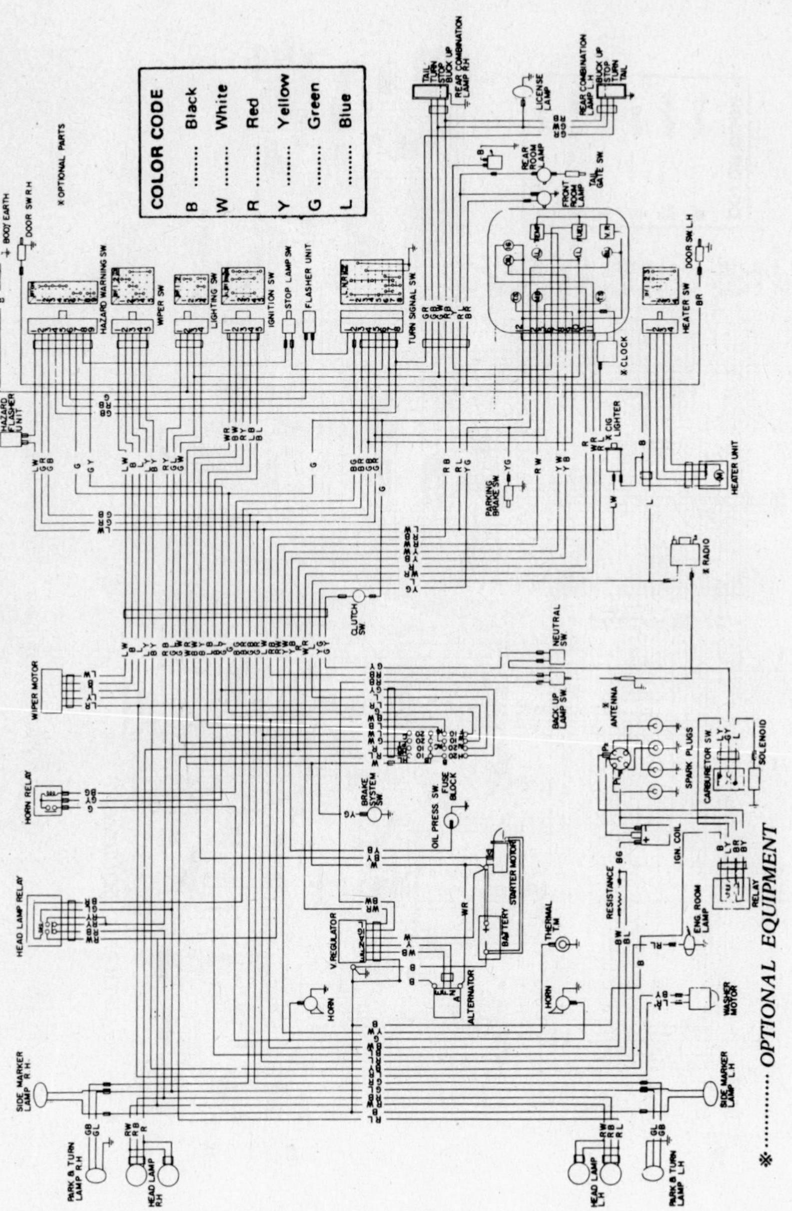

WPL510, standard transmission

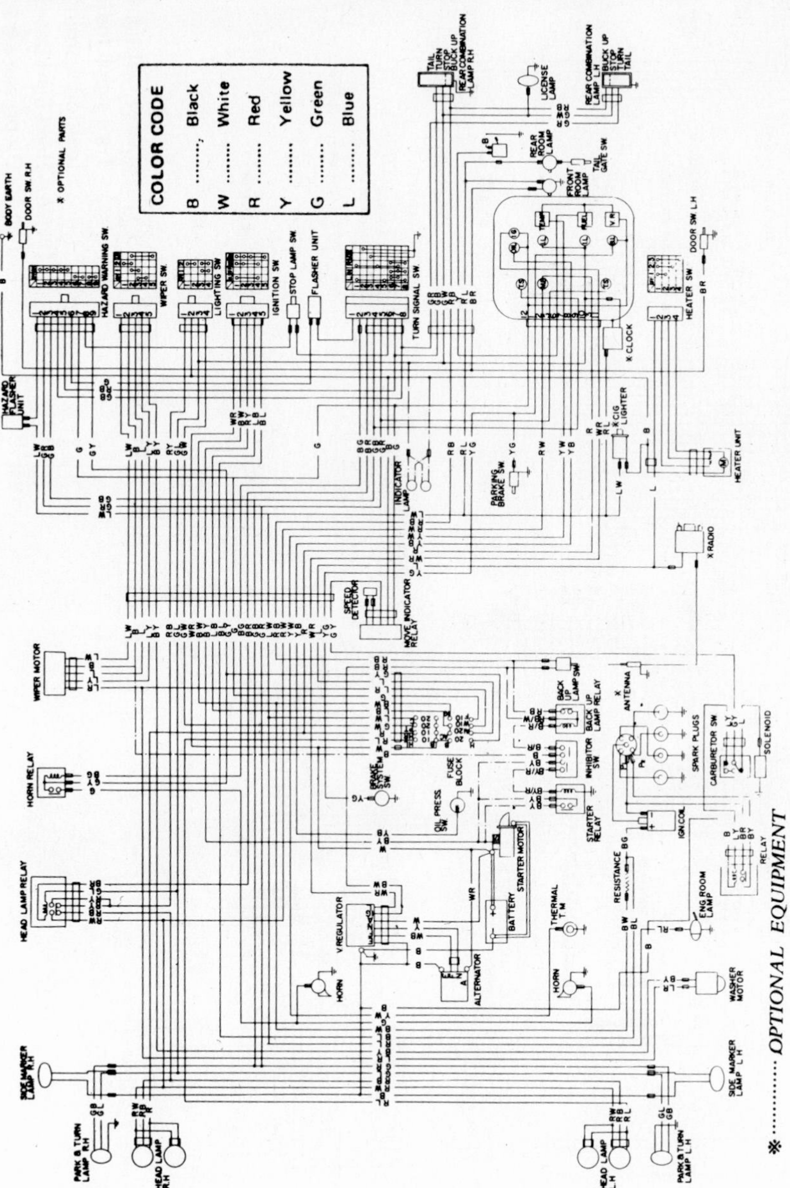

WPL510, automatic transmission

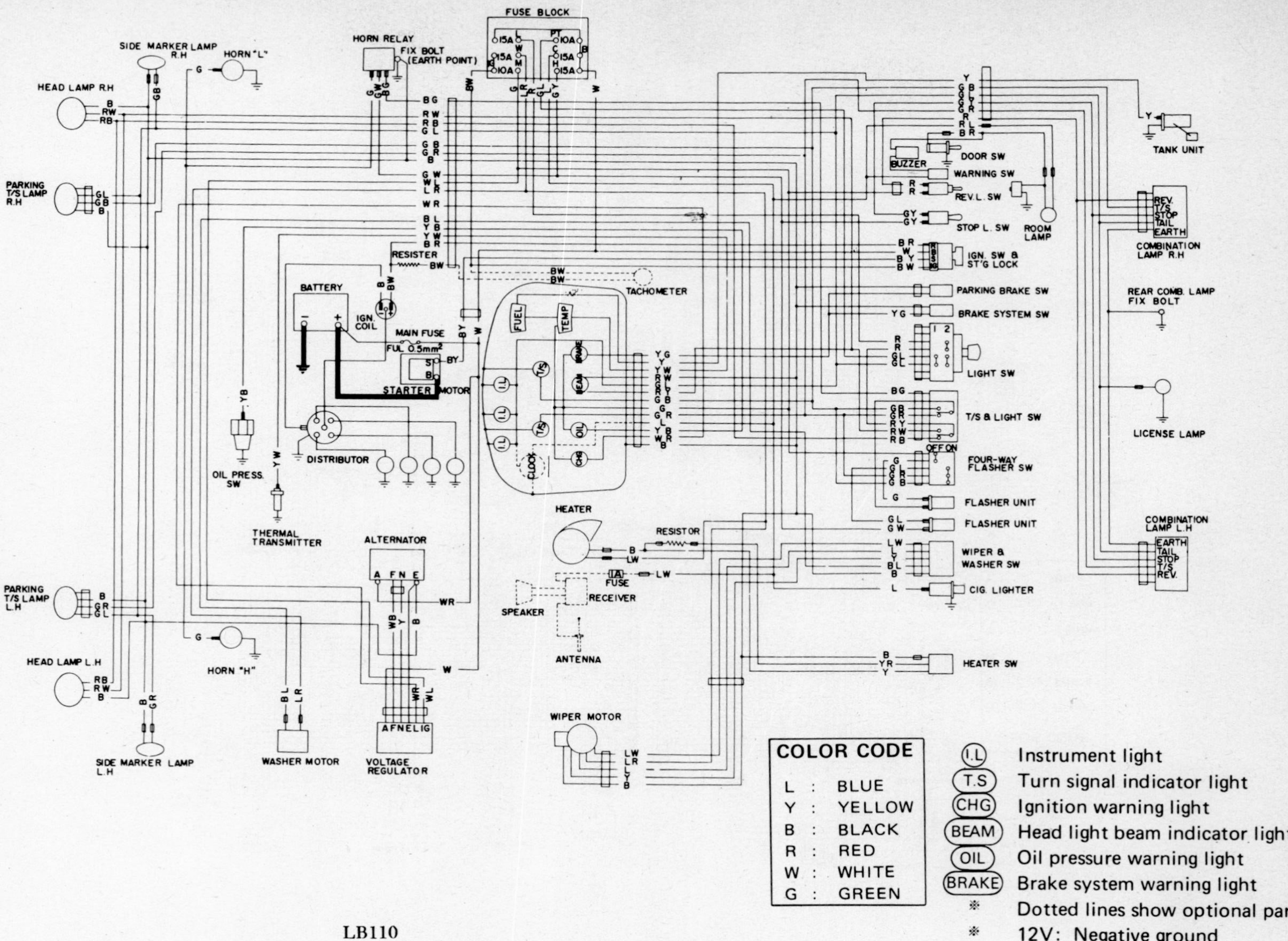
FUSE BLOCK
HORN RELAY
FIX BOLT (EARTH POINT)
SIDE MARKER LAMP R.H
HORN "L"
HEAD LAMP R.H
PARKING T/S LAMP R.H
RESISTER
BATTERY
IGN. COIL
MAIN FUSE
FUL 0.5mm²
STARTER MOTOR
TACHOMETER
FUEL
TEMP
CLOCK
DISTRIBUTOR
OIL PRESS. SW
THERMAL TRANSMITTER
ALTERNATOR
HEATER
RESISTOR
FUSE
SPEAKER
RECEIVER
ANTENNA
PARKING T/S LAMP L.H
HORN "H"
HEAD LAMP L.H
SIDE MARKER LAMP L.H
WASHER MOTOR
VOLTAGE REGULATOR
WIPER MOTOR
TANK UNIT
DOOR SW
BUZZER
WARNING SW
REV.L. SW
STOP L. SW
ROOM LAMP
IGN. SW & ST'G LOCK
COMBINATION LAMP R.H
PARKING BRAKE SW
BRAKE SYSTEM SW
REAR COMB. LAMP FIX BOLT
LIGHT SW
LICENSE LAMP
T/S & LIGHT SW
FOUR-WAY FLASHER SW
FLASHER UNIT
FLASHER UNIT
COMBINATION LAMP L.H
WIPER & WASHER SW
CIG. LIGHTER
HEATER SW
COLOR CODE
L : BLUE
Y : YELLOW
B : BLACK
R : RED
W : WHITE
G : GREEN
I.L Instrument light
T.S Turn signal indicator light
CHG Ignition warning light
BEAM Head light beam indicator light
OIL Oil pressure warning light
BRAKE Brake system warning light
※ Dotted lines show optional parts
※ 12V: Negative ground
LB110

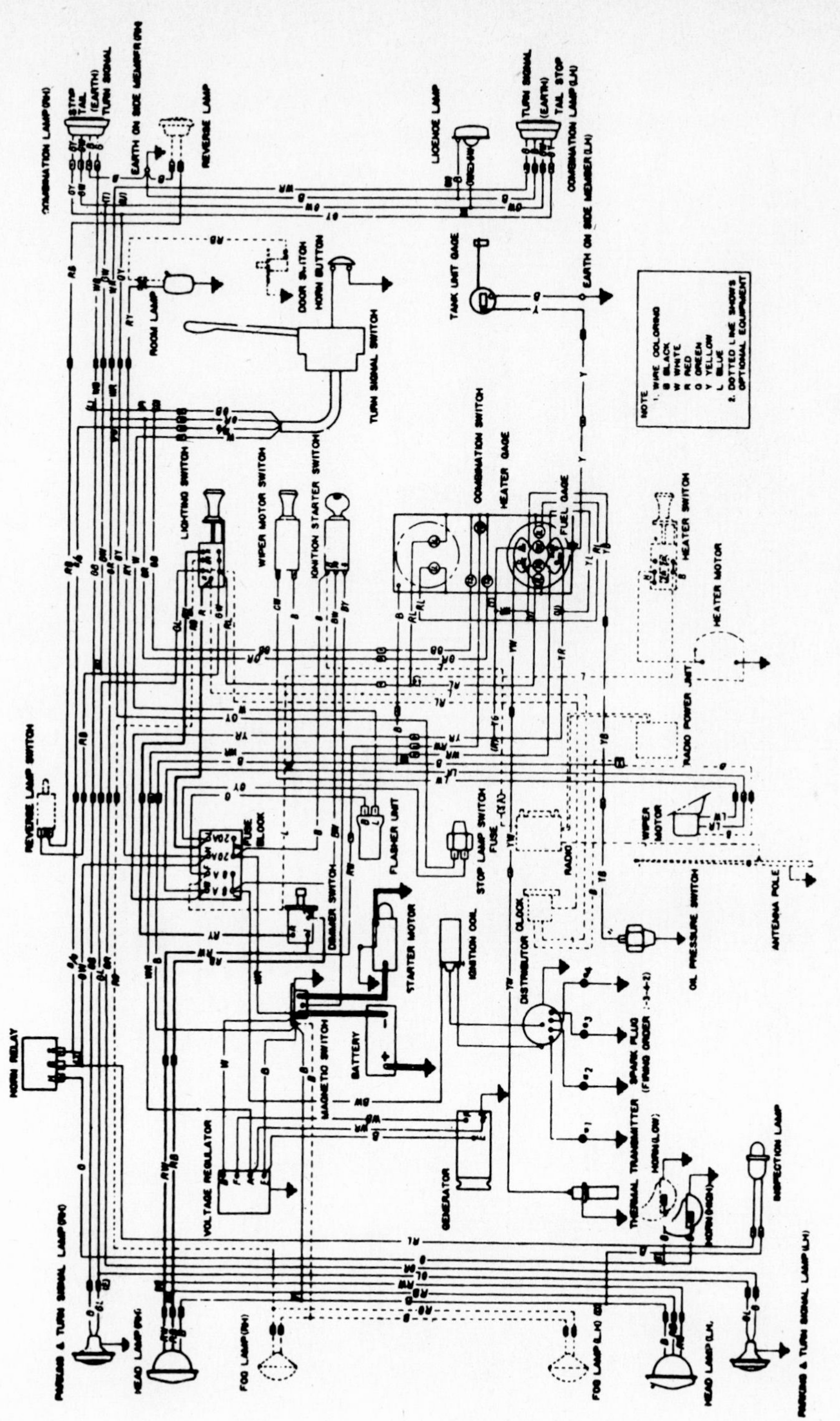

L320

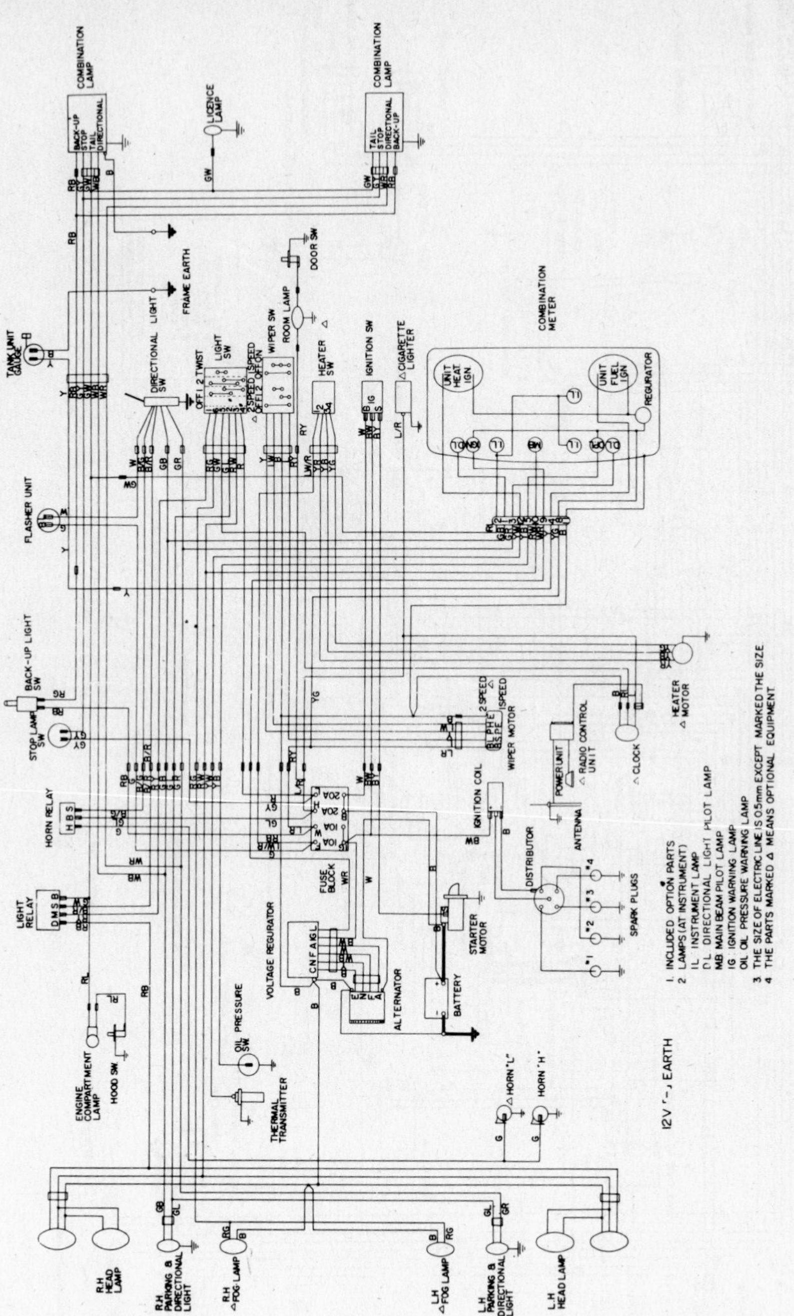

R.H HEAD LAMP
R.H PARKING & DIRECTIONAL LIGHT
R.H △FOG LAMP
L.H △FOG LAMP
L.H PARKING & DIRECTIONAL LIGHT
L.H HEAD LAMP
ENGINE COMPARTMENT LAMP
HOOD SW
LIGHT RELAY
HORN RELAY
STOP LAMP SW
BACK-UP LIGHT SW
FLASHER UNIT
TANK UNIT GAUGE
COMBINATION LAMP
BACK-UP
STOP
TAIL
DIRECTIONAL
DIRECTIONAL LIGHT
FRAME EARTH
DIRECTIONAL SW
LIGHT SW
OFF 1 2 TWIST
WIPER SW
ROOM LAMP
DOOR SW
HEATER SW
IGNITION SW
△CIGARETTE LIGHTER
LICENCE LAMP
COMBINATION METER
UNIT HEAT IGN
UNIT FUEL IGN
REGURATOR
THERMAL TRANSMITTER
OIL PRESSURE SW
VOLTAGE REGURATOR
FUSE BLOCK
ALTERNATOR
BATTERY
STARTER MOTOR
IGNITION COIL
WIPER MOTOR
2 SPEED
1 SPEED
DISTRIBUTOR
ANTENNA
POWER UNIT
△RADIO CONTROL UNIT
△CLOCK
△HEATER MOTOR
△HORN "L"
HORN "H"
SPARK PLUGS
12V (-) EARTH
1. INCLUDED OPTION PARTS
2 LAMPS (AT INSTRUMENT)
IL INSTRUMENT LAMP
DL DIRECTIONAL LIGHT PILOT LAMP
MB MAIN BEAM PILOT LAMP
IG IGNITION WARNING LAMP
OIL OIL PRESSURE WARNING LAMP
3 THE SIZE OF ELECTRIC LINE IS 0.5mm EXCEPT MARKED THE SIZE
4 THE PARTS MARKED △ MEANS OPTIONAL EQUIPMENT

L520

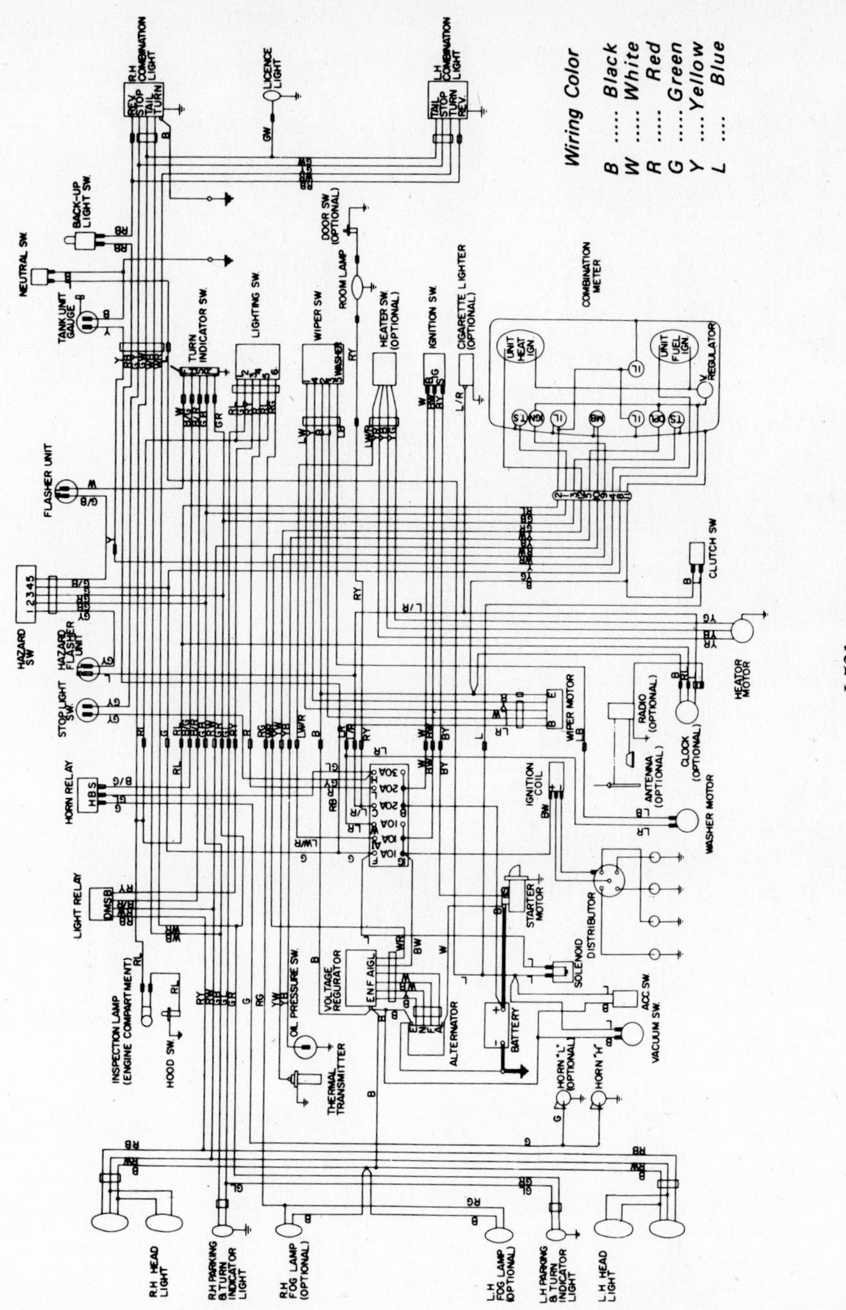
Wiring Color
B .... Black
W .... White
R .... Red
G .... Green
Y .... Yellow
L .... Blue
R.H. COMBINATION LIGHT
LICENCE LIGHT
L.H. COMBINATION LIGHT
BACK-UP LIGHT SW.
NEUTRAL SW.
DOOR SW. (OPTIONAL)
ROOM LAMP
TANK UNIT GAUGE
TURN INDICATOR SW.
LIGHTING SW.
WIPER SW.
HEATER SW. (OPTIONAL)
IGNITION SW.
CIGARETTE LIGHTER (OPTIONAL)
COMBINATION METER
FLASHER UNIT
HAZARD SW.
HAZARD FLASHER UNIT
STOP LIGHT SW.
CLUTCH SW.
HEATER MOTOR
WIPER MOTOR
RADIO (OPTIONAL)
ANTENNA (OPTIONAL)
CLOCK (OPTIONAL)
HORN RELAY
IGNITION COIL
WASHER MOTOR
LIGHT RELAY
DISTRIBUTOR
STARTER MOTOR
SOLENOID
INSPECTION LAMP (ENGINE COMPARTMENT)
HOOD SW.
OIL PRESSURE SW.
VOLTAGE REGURATOR
THERMAL TRANSMITTER
ALTERNATOR
BATTERY
ACC SW.
VACUUM SW.
HORN "L" (OPTIONAL)
HORN "H"
R.H. HEAD LIGHT
R.H PARKING & TURN INDICATOR LIGHT
R.H FOG LAMP (OPTIONAL)
L.H FOG LAMP (OPTIONAL)
L.H PARKING & TURN INDICATOR LIGHT
L.H. HEAD LIGHT

L521

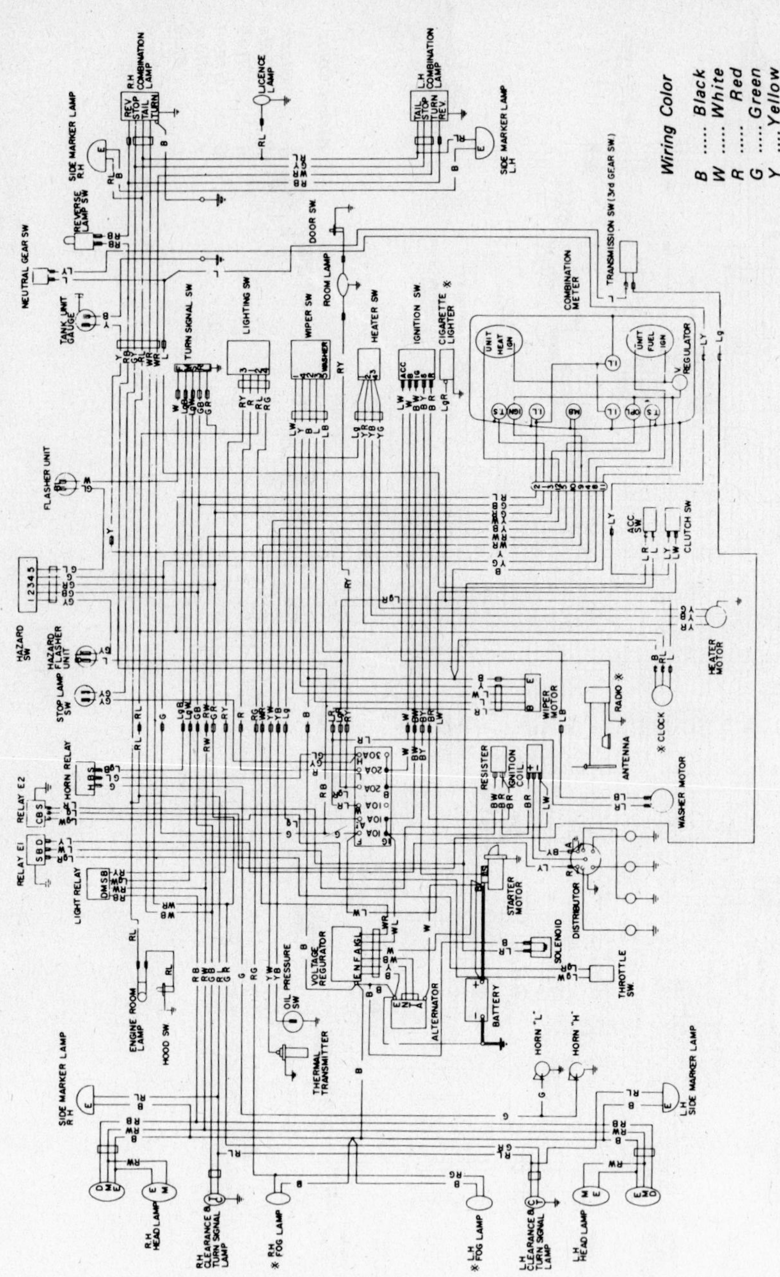

PL521

※........ OPTIONAL EQUIPMENT

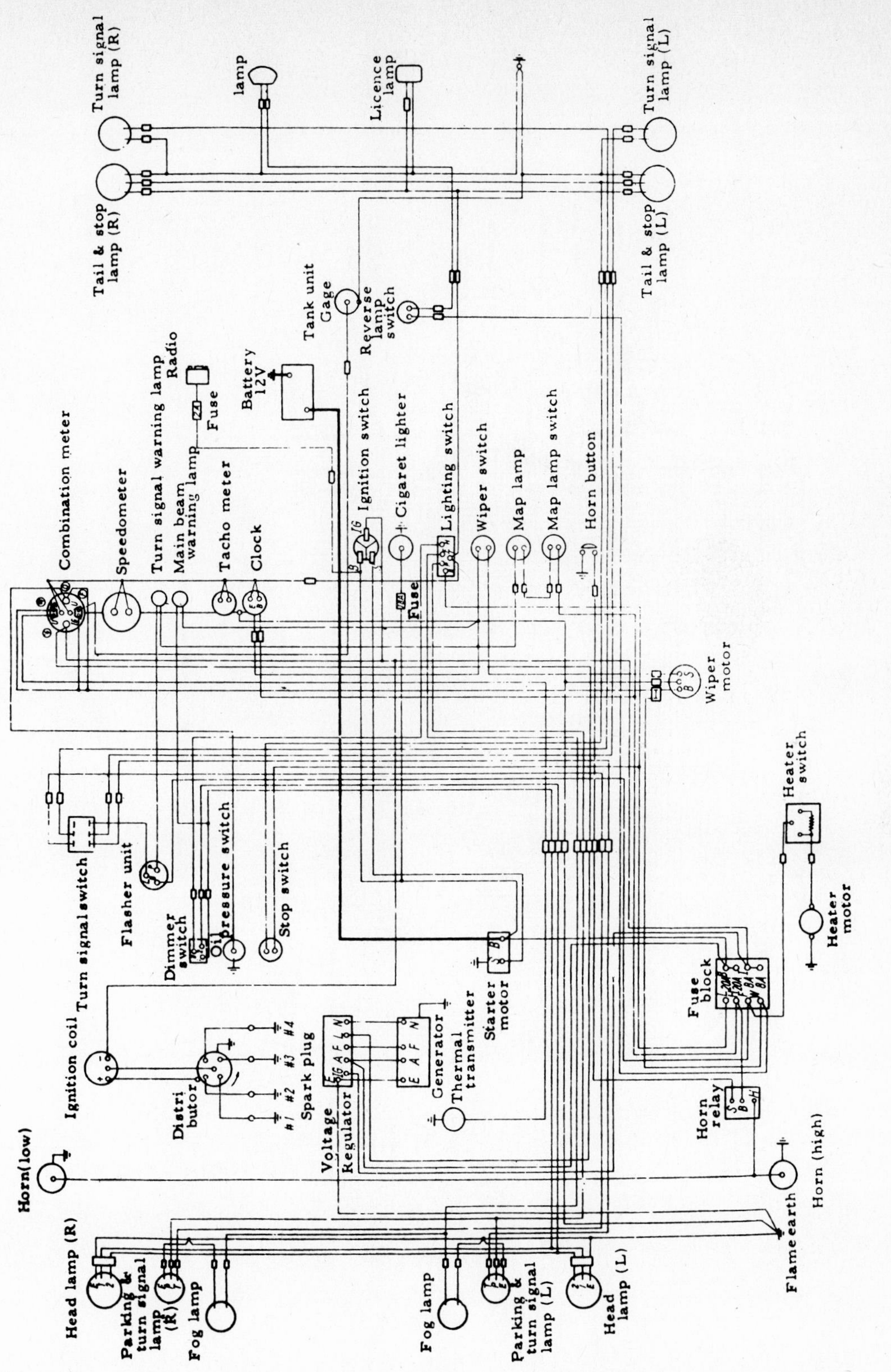
Turn signal lamp (R)
lamp
Licence lamp
Turn signal lamp (L)
Tail & stop lamp (R)
Tail & stop lamp (L)
Tank unit Gage
Reverse lamp switch
Radio
Battery 12V
Fuse
Combination meter
Speedometer
Turn signal warning lamp
Main beam warning lamp
Tacho meter
Clock
Ignition switch
Cigaret lighter
Fuse
Lighting switch
Wiper switch
Map lamp
Map lamp switch
Horn button
Wiper motor
Heater switch
Heater motor
Fuse block
Horn relay
Horn (high)
Flame earth
Starter motor
Generator
Thermal transmitter
Voltage Regulator
Spark plug
Distri butor
Ignition coil
Turn signal switch
Flasher unit
Dimmer switch
Oil pressure switch
Stop switch
Horn(low)
Head lamp (R)
Parking & turn signal lamp (R)
Fog lamp
Fog lamp
Parking & turn signal lamp (L)
Head lamp (L)

SPL310

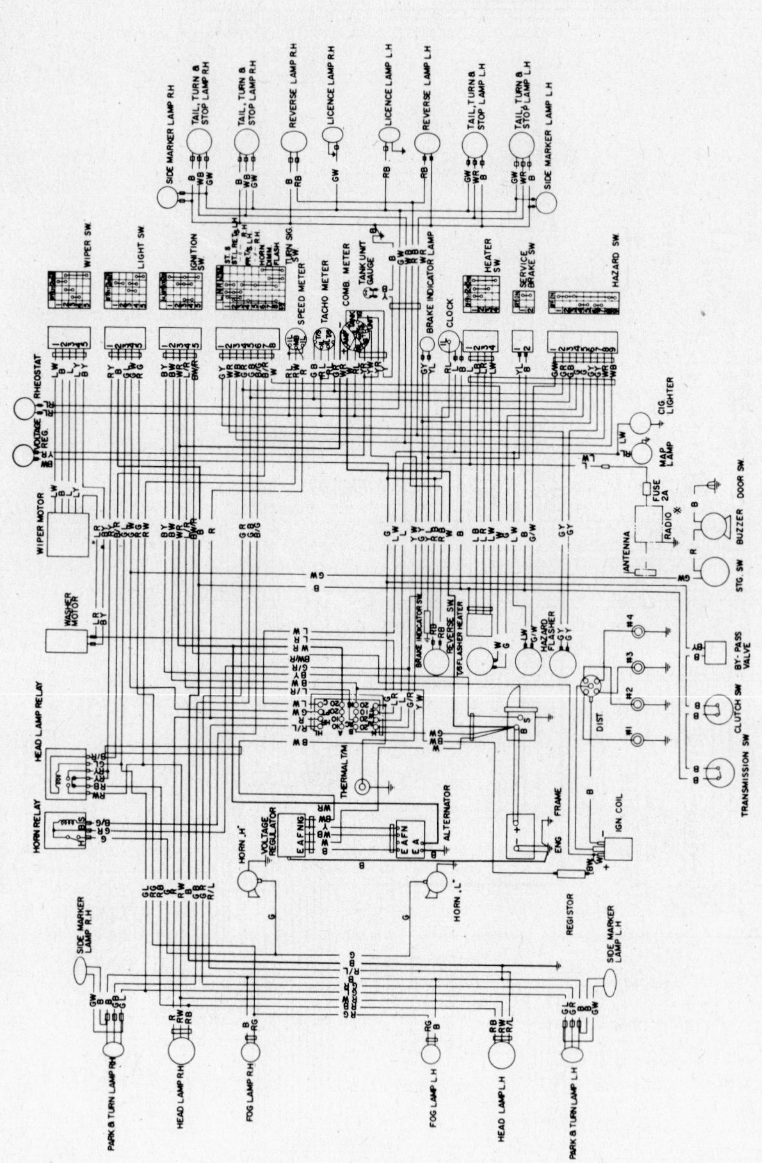
SIDE MARKER LAMP RH
TAIL, TURN & STOP LAMP RH
REVERSE LAMP RH
LICENCE LAMP RH
LICENCE LAMP LH
REVERSE LAMP LH
TAIL, TURN & STOP LAMP LH
SIDE MARKER LAMP LH
WIPER SW
LIGHT SW
IGNITION SW
TURN SIG SW
SPEED METER
TACHO METER
COMB. METER
TANK UNIT GAUGE
BRAKE INDICATOR LAMP
CLOCK
HEATER SW
SERVICE BRAKE SW
HAZARD SW
RHEOSTAT
VOLTAGE REG
WIPER MOTOR
CIG LIGHTER
MAP LAMP
FUSE 2A
RADIO
ANTENNA
BUZZER
DOOR SW
STG. SW
WASHER MOTOR
REVERSE SW
HAZARD FLASHER
HEAD LAMP RELAY
HORN RELAY
BY-PASS VALVE
CLUTCH SW
TRANSMISSION SW
DIST
THERMAL T/M
VOLTAGE REGULATOR
ALTERNATOR
HORN 'H'
HORN 'L'
FRAME
ENG
IGN COIL
REGISTOR
SIDE MARKER LAMP R.H
SIDE MARKER LAMP L.H
PARK & TURN LAMP RH
HEAD LAMP RH
FOG LAMP RH
FOG LAMP LH
HEAD LAMP LH
PARK & TURN LAMP LH

SPL311

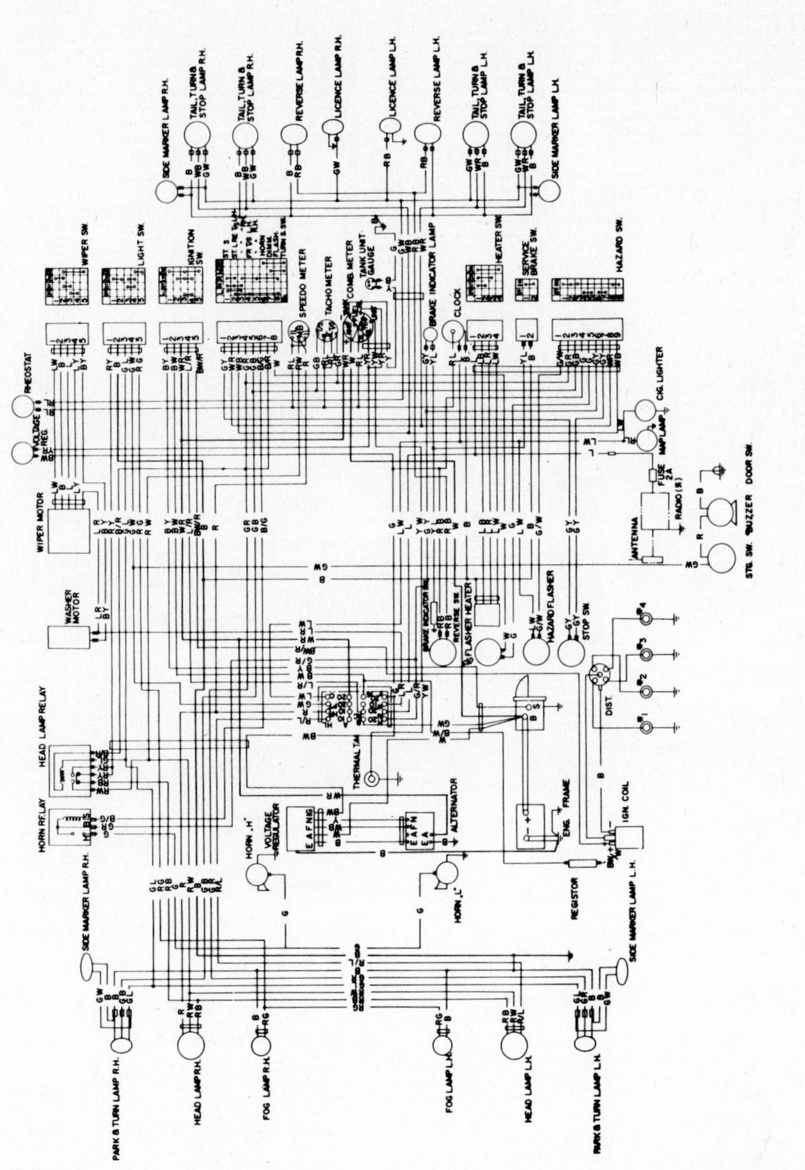
SIDE MARKER LAMP R.H.
TAIL, TURN & STOP LAMP R.H.
REVERSE LAMP R.H.
LICENCE LAMP R.H.
LICENCE LAMP L.H.
REVERSE LAMP L.H.
TAIL, TURN & STOP LAMP L.H.
SIDE MARKER LAMP L.H.
WIPER SW.
LIGHT SW.
IGNITION SW.
SPEEDO METER
TACHOMETER
COMB. METER
TANK UNIT GAUGE
BRAKE INDICATOR LAMP
CLOCK
HEATER SW.
SERVICE BRAKE SW.
HAZARD SW.
RHEOSTAT
VOLTAGE REG.
CIG. LIGHTER
MAP LAMP
FUSE 2A
RADIO
ANTENNA
BUZZER
DOOR SW.
STG. SW.
WIPER MOTOR
WASHER MOTOR
FLASHER
HEATER
HAZARD FLASHER
STOP SW.
DIST.
HEAD LAMP RELAY
HORN RELAY
THERMAL TA
ALTERNATOR
VOLTAGE REGULATOR
FRAME
ENG.
IGN. COIL
HORN "H"
HORN "L"
REGISTOR
SIDE MARKER LAMP R.H.
PARK & TURN LAMP R.H.
HEAD LAMP R.H.
FOG LAMP R.H.
FOG LAMP L.H.
HEAD LAMP L.H.
PARK & TURN LAMP L.H.

SRL311

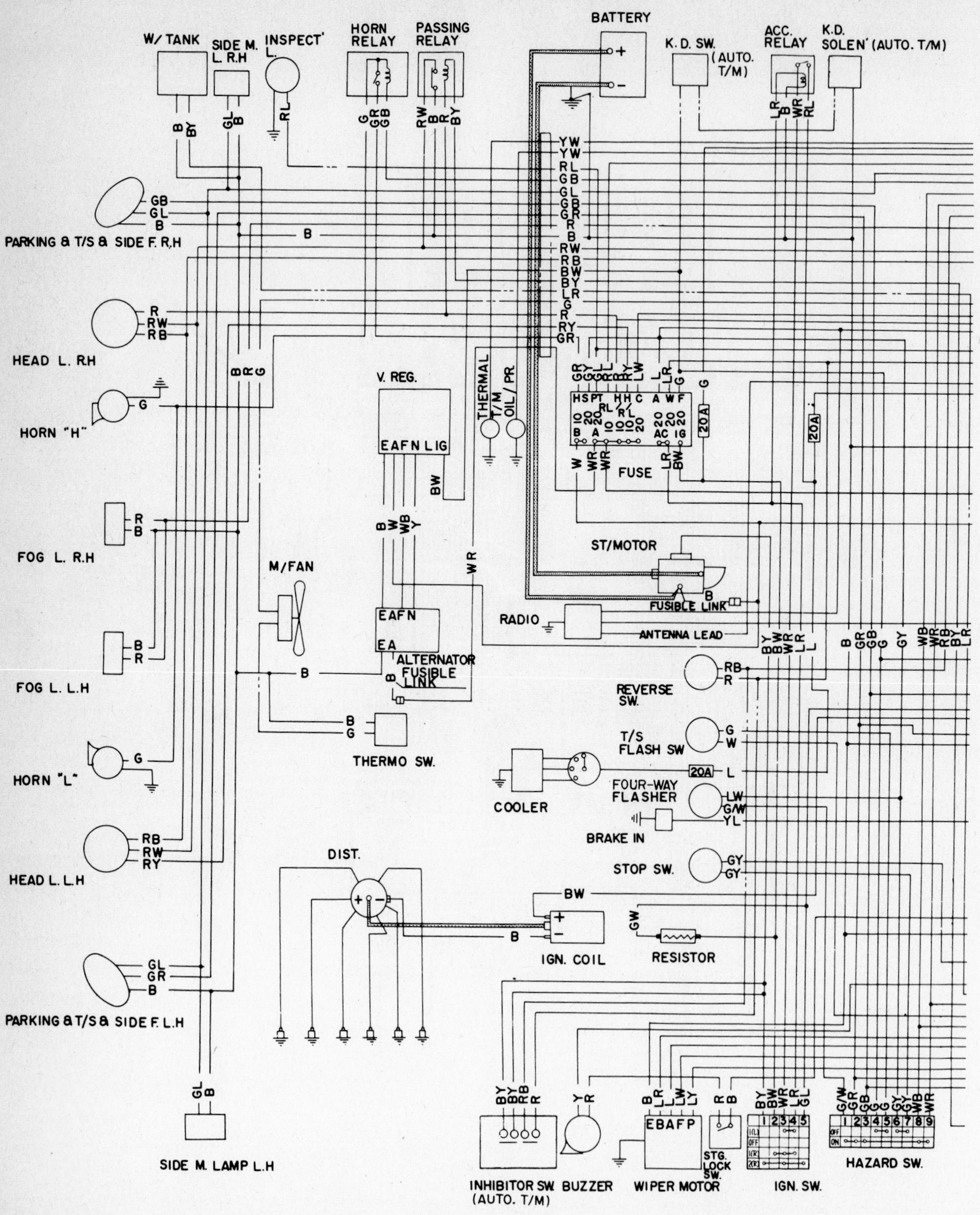

BATTERY
W/TANK
SIDE M. L. R.H
INSPECT' L.
HORN RELAY
PASSING RELAY
K. D. SW. (AUTO. T/M)
ACC. RELAY
K.D. SOLEN' (AUTO. T/M)
PARKING & T/S & SIDE F. R.H
HEAD L. R.H
HORN "H"
V. REG.
THERMAL T/M
OIL/PR
FUSE
FOG L. R.H
ST/MOTOR
M/FAN
RADIO
FUSIBLE LINK
ANTENNA LEAD
FOG L. L.H
ALTERNATOR FUSIBLE LINK
REVERSE SW.
T/S FLASH SW
THERMO SW.
COOLER
HORN "L"
FOUR-WAY FLASHER
BRAKE IN
HEAD L. L.H
DIST.
STOP SW.
IGN. COIL
RESISTOR
PARKING & T/S & SIDE F. L.H
SIDE M. LAMP L.H
INHIBITOR SW. (AUTO. T/M)
BUZZER
WIPER MOTOR
STG. LOCK SW.
IGN. SW.
HAZARD SW.

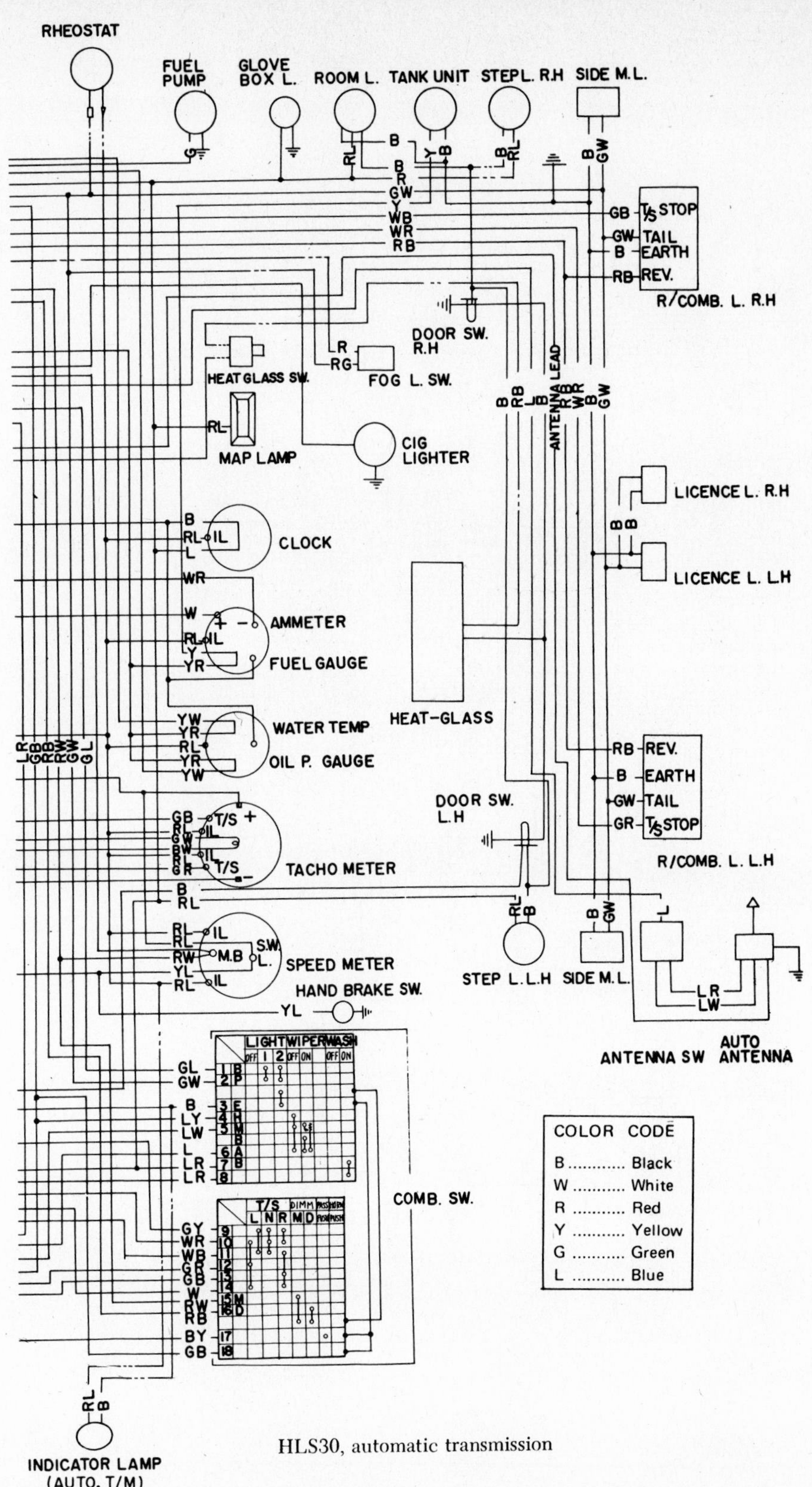

HLS30, automatic transmission

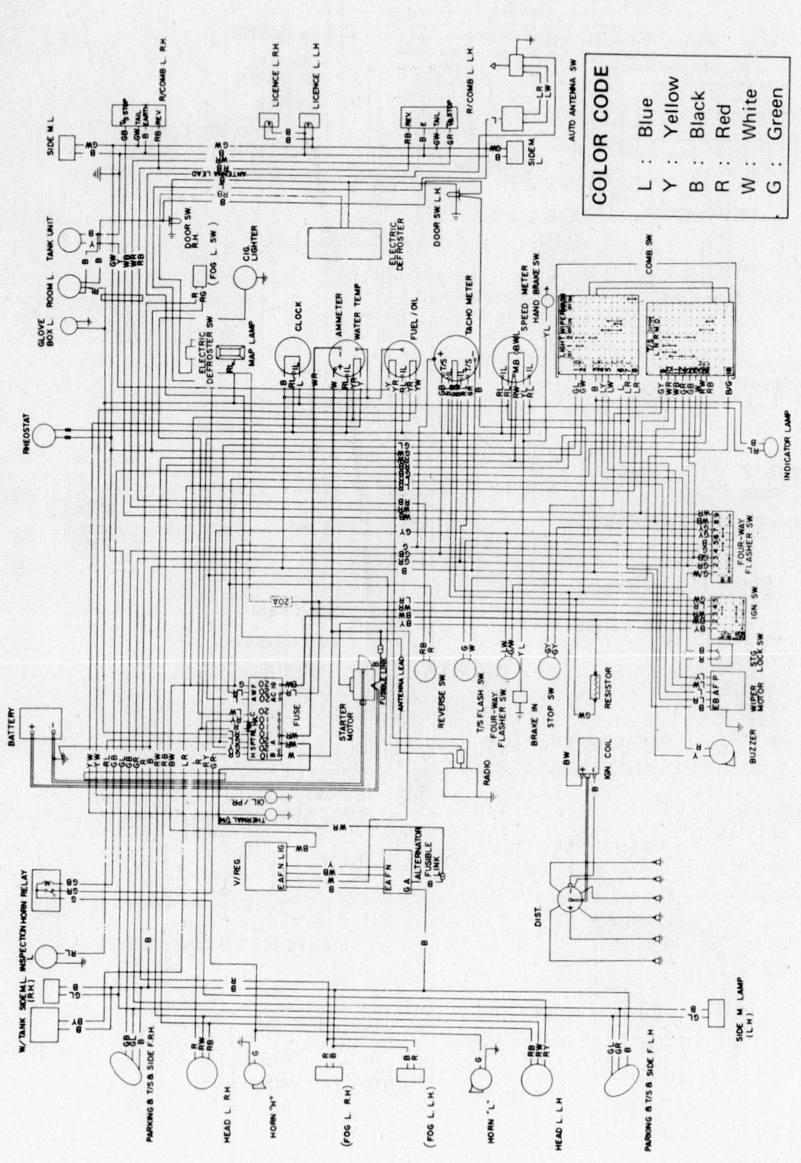

HLS30, standard transmission

Engine Electrical

DISTRIBUTOR

Distributor R&R

When removing the distributor for any reason, note the location of the rotor and mark the relationship of the distributor body to the engine. The distributor can then be replaced precisely in its original location, if the engine has not been turned. If the engine has been turned while the distributor was removed, or the distributor location was not marked, proceed as follows: Find top dead center of the compression stroke of No. 1 cylinder by holding a finger in the spark plug hole and rotating the engine. Compression pressure will force the finger from the hole. The exact location of top dead center can then be found by use of the crankshaft pulley timing marks. In-

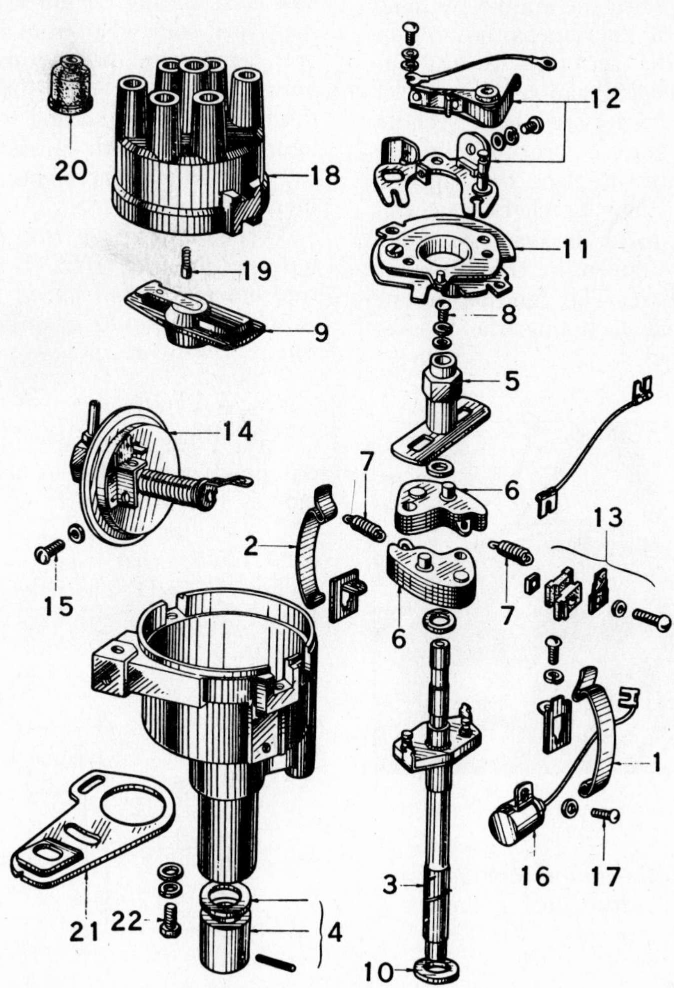

Exploded view of distributor, L16 engine

1. Cap holddown spring
2. Cap holddown spring
3. Shaft
4. Drive pinion
5. Cam
6. Centrifugal advance weights
7. Centrifugal advance springs
8. Screw
9. Rotor
10. Thrust washer
11. Breaker plate
12. Contact set
13. Terminal assembly
14. Vacuum control unit
15. Screw
16. Condenser
17. Screw
18. Cap
19. Carbon brush
20. Rubber boot
21. Holddown plate
22. Bolt

stall the distributor so that the rotor is pointing at the No. 1 spark plug wire and the points are just opening. The ignition wires may now be installed in the distributor cap, following the firing order in the direction of rotation. Set the timing to specifications.

Breaker Point R&R

Release the distributor cap latches and remove the cap and rotor. Check the points for pitting or burning. Use a point file to clean the points. Turn the engine by hand until the distributor cam opens the breaker points. Loosen the setscrew. Adjust the points to the specified gap using a feeler gauge. Tighten the setscrew and recheck the gap. Apply a trace of bearing lubricant to the breaker cam. Replace the cap and rotor. Point dwell may be checked at this point if a dwell meter is available. Point dwell figures are given in the Tune-Up Specifications Chart. The ignition timing should be checked each time the breaker points are adjusted.

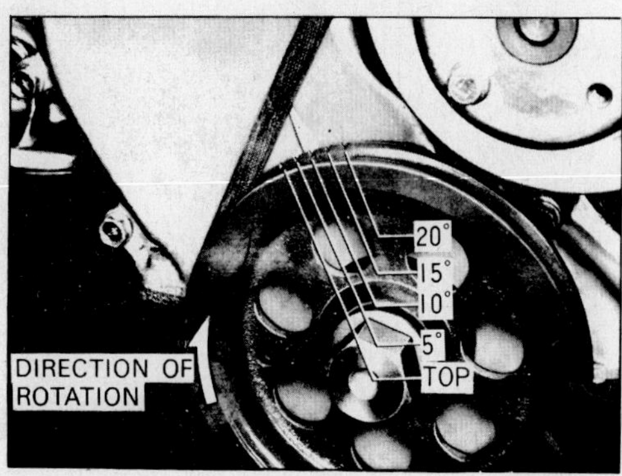

Timing marks, A12 engine

NOTE: Some distributors are equipped with dual points. Adjust both point sets to the specified gap.

Ignition Timing

Ignition timing should be adjusted with the distributor vacuum line disconnected and the engine running at idle speed. A stroboscopic timing light must be used to obtain an accurate setting. The setting is indicated by the pointer on the engine front cover and the markings on the crankshaft pulley. The top dead center, or 0°, mark is located at the extreme left. The next mark may be either 5° or 10° before top dead center, depending on the engine model. The succeeding marks are 5° apart. To set the timing, disconnect the vacuum line and loosen the distributor clamp. Connect the timing light, start the engine, and allow it to idle. Direct the timing light at the pulley markings. Turn the distributor head until the timing pointer and the correct pulley mark are aligned. Some early distributors have a knurled knob for fine adjustments. Tighten the clamp and replace the vacuum line. Timing settings for each model are given in the Tune-Up Specifications Chart. The best setting for an individual engine may vary somewhat from the manufacturer's recommendations and can be found only by a trial and error method. However, the recommended setting is a good general figure. Engines with emission controls must be set exactly to the manufacturer's recommendations.

NOTE: There are two different timing settings for the HLS30 with automatic transmission: an advanced setting for temperatures below 40°F, and a retarded setting for temperatures above 40°F.

GENERATOR

Only L320 and early L60 models are equipped with a DC generator. All other models have the more modern alternator. The generator used on the L320 is the Hitachi G115-53; that used on the L60 is the Hitachi G115-11. The voltage regulator is a Hitachi carbon pile unit.

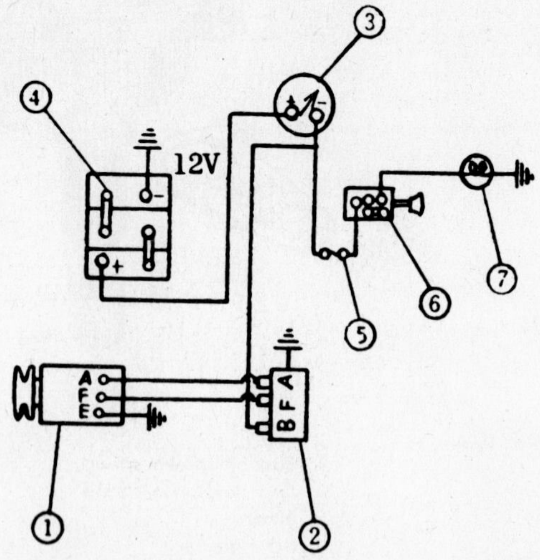

Generating system diagram, models using Hitachi generator

1. Generator
2. Voltage regulator
3. Ammeter
4. Battery
5. Fuse
6. Lighting switch
7. Light (typical electrical load)

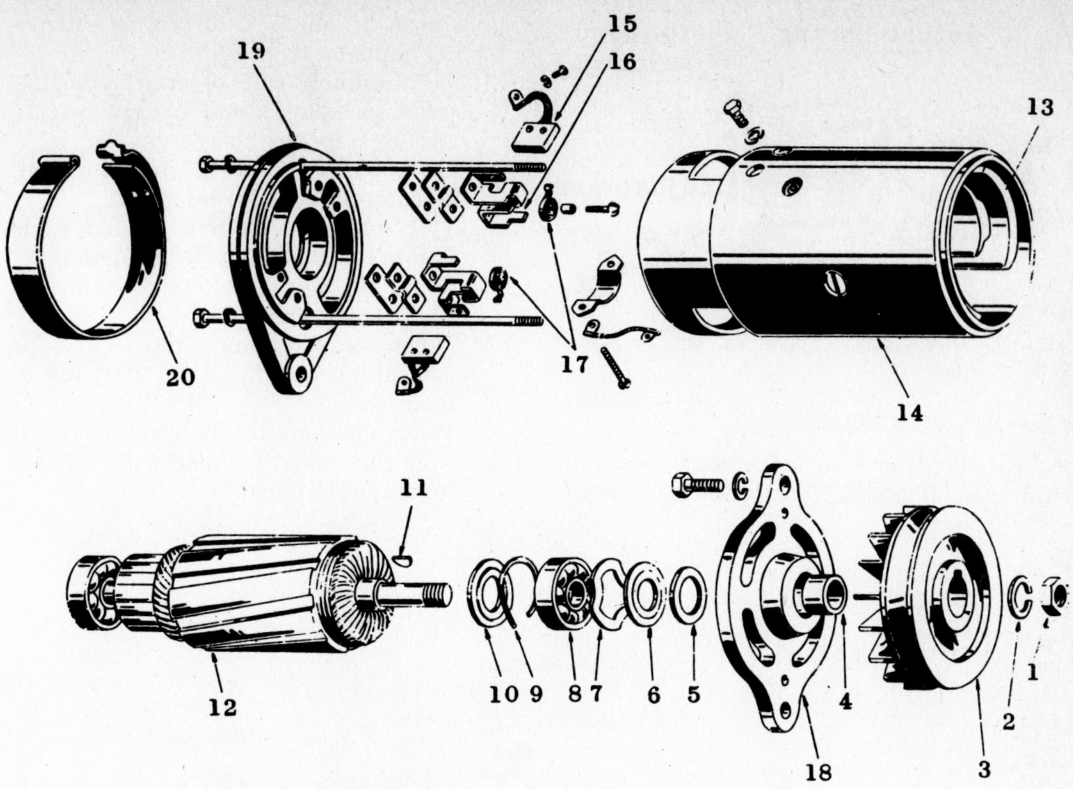

Hitachi generator, L320 and early L60

1. Nut
2. Washer
3. Pulley
4. Spacer
5. Packing
6. Retainer
7. Spring
8. Ball bearing
9. Clip
10. Oil cover
11. Key
12. Armature
13. Field coil
14. Housing
15. Brush
16. Brush holder
17. Brush spring
18. Front cover
19. Rear cover
20. Brush cover

Adjusting Carbon Pile Regulator

The adjustment most often required is that for output voltage. Proceed as follows:

1. Connect a voltmeter to the regulator terminal, A. Connect the other voltmeter lead to ground.
2. Make sure that all electrical loads are switched off. Disconnect the terminal, B.
3. With the engine running at about 1,900 rpm, read the voltage. It should be 15-16 volts.
4. Loosen the pile compression screw lockscrew. To raise voltage, turn the pile compression screw in. To lower voltage, back it out. Tighten the lockscrew after adjustment.

Hitachi carbon pile voltage regulator unit. P-screw is the pile compression screw, used to adjust output voltage. F-screw is flux adjusting screw, used for a preliminary setting when reassembling the unit.

The gaps in the cutout relay should be adjusted and the points dressed, periodically.

Gap	*Opening*
Relay point gap	.036″
Core to arm gap (open)	.028-.031″
Core to arm gap (closed)	.016-.020″

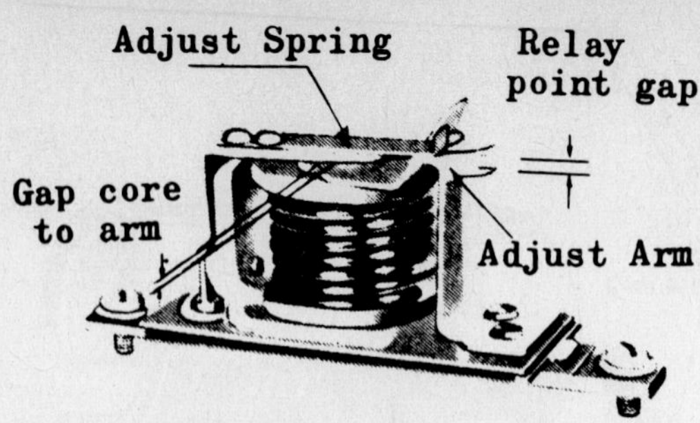

Cutout relay adjusting points for Hitachi carbon pile regulator

AC GENERATOR

An alternator (AC generator) is used on all current models. The following precautions must be observed to prevent alternator and regulator damage:

1. Be absolutely sure of correct polarity when installing a new battery, or connecting a battery charger.
2. Do not short across or ground any alternator or regulator terminals.
3. Disconnect the battery ground cable before replacing any electrical unit.
4. Never operate the alternator with any of the leads disconnected.
5. When steam cleaning the engine, be careful not to subject the alternator to excessive heat.
6. When charging the battery, remove it from the car or disconnect the alternator output terminal.

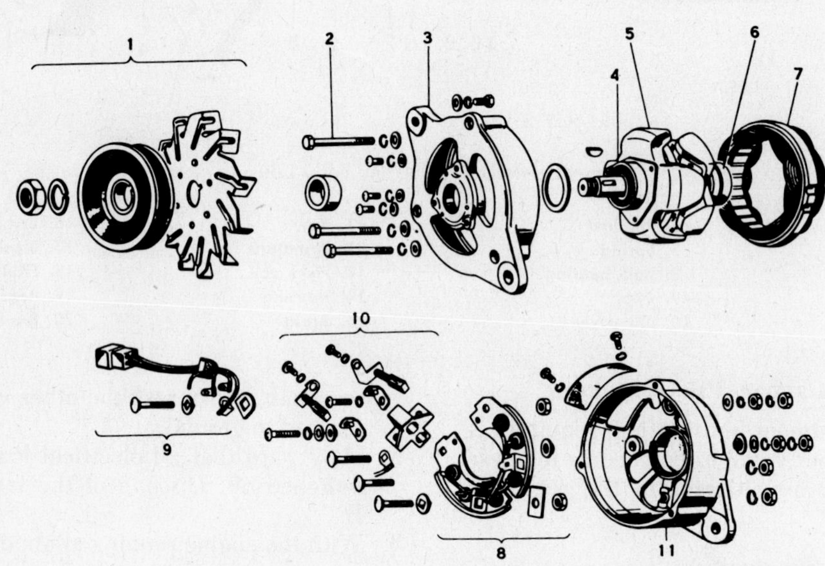

Hitachi alternator

1. Pulley assembly
2. Through bolt
3. Front cover
4. Front bearing
5. Rotor
6. Rear bearing
7. Stator
8. Diode plate assembly
9. Lead wire assembly
10. Brush assembly
11. Rear cover

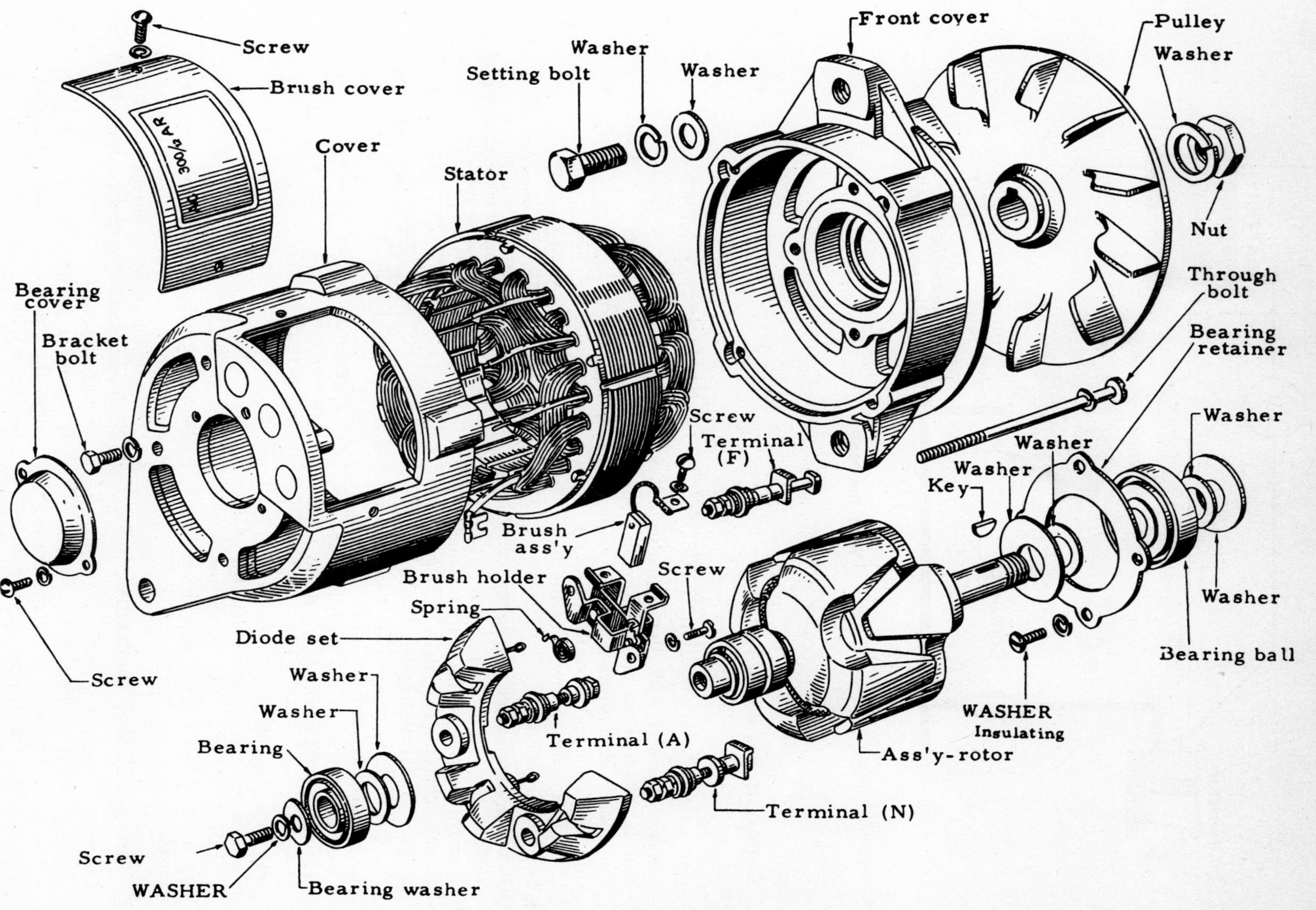

Mitsubishi alternator

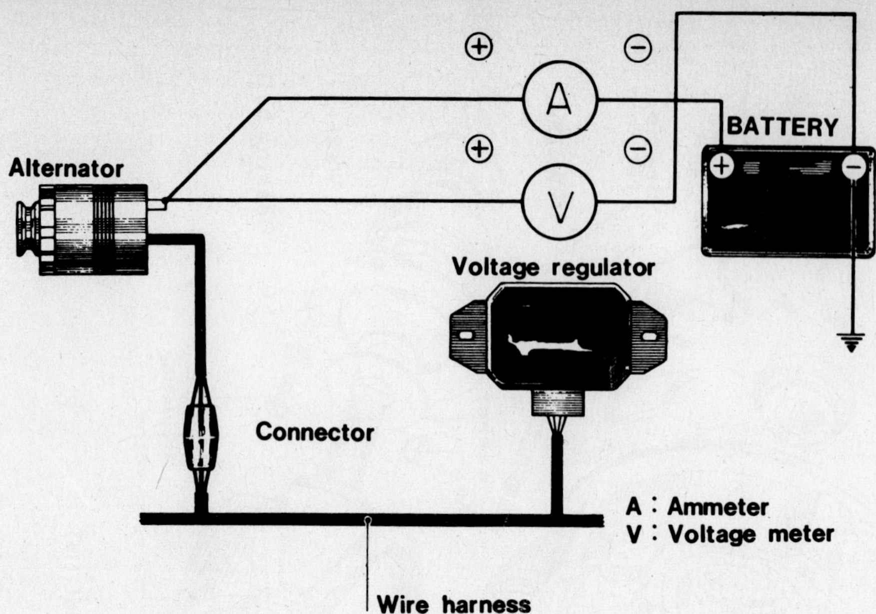

Test setup for AC regulators except Hitachi TL1Z-37

AC Regulator, Regulated Voltage Check

ALL REGULATORS EXCEPT HITACHI TL1Z-37

1. Perform this test with the regulator cool. If voltage is not measured within one minute after starting the engine, stop the engine and allow the regulator to cool. It is imperative that the battery be fully charged.
2. Connect an ammeter and voltmeter as shown.
3. Run the engine at 2,500 rpm. Check that the charging current is less than 5 amps, and that the regulated voltage is as specified in the AC Regulator Electrical Specifications Table. If the charging current is too high, replace the battery with a fully charged one.
4. If voltage is incorrect, set regulator unit gaps to specified clearances.
5. Recheck voltage. If voltage is still incorrect, readjust air gap. Bend stopper up to raise the voltage and down to lower.

HITACHI TL1Z-37 REGULATOR

1. Connect an ammeter, voltmeter, fully charged battery, and resistor as shown.
2. Since this regulator is temperature compensated, the temperature of the regulator cover must be noted. Regulated voltage varies with ambient temperature.

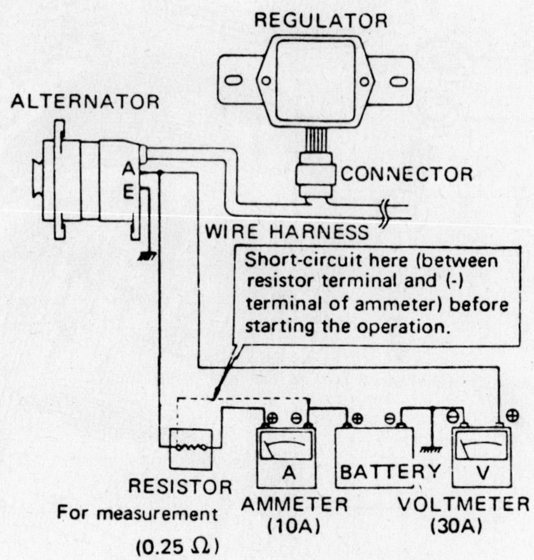

Test setup for Hitachi TL1Z-37 AC regulator

3. Before starting check, bypass ammeter as shown to prevent ammeter damage.
4. Start engine, increase engine speed to 2,500 rpm gradually, and continue for several minutes.
5. If ammeter reading is not below 5 amps, the battery is not fully charged. Replace it with a good one.
6. Return engine to idle speed.
7. Increase engine speed to 2,500 rpm and check voltage.

Ambient temperature (°F)	*Regulated voltage*
14	14.6-15.6
32	14.5-15.5
50	14.3-15.3
68	14.2-15.2
86	14.0-15.0
104	13.9-14.9

8. If voltage is incorrect, set regulator unit gaps to specified figures.
9. Recheck voltage. If voltage is still incorrect, turn in adjusting screw on voltage regulator unit to increase voltage, and turn out to decrease voltage.

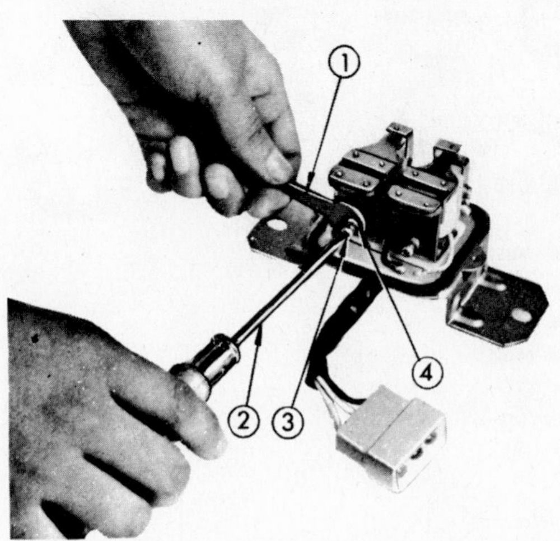

Adjustment of voltage on TL1Z-37 regulator. Wrench, 1, is used to loosen locknut, 4. Screwdriver, 2, is used to turn adjusting screw, 3.

Belt Tension

The correct belt tension for all alternators and generators gives .4-.6″ play on the longest span of the belt. The adjustment is usually made by pivoting the alternator (generator). Overtightening the belt will cause rapid wear to the alternator (generator) and water pump bearings.

BATTERY, STARTER

Battery

All Datsun models are equipped with a 12-volt battery. Vehicles with the El and G engines are unusual in having a positive ground electrical system, rather than the more usual negative ground. The battery is located under the hood in all models except the L60. On the L60, the battery is under the front seat. To gain access to the battery in the HLS30 (240 Z coupe), first open the hood, then the inspection flap in the fender. The inspection flap must be closed before the hood.

Starter

The starter is mounted at the right rear of the engine. The solenoid is mounted on top of the starter and engages the drive pinion through a pivot yoke shift lever.

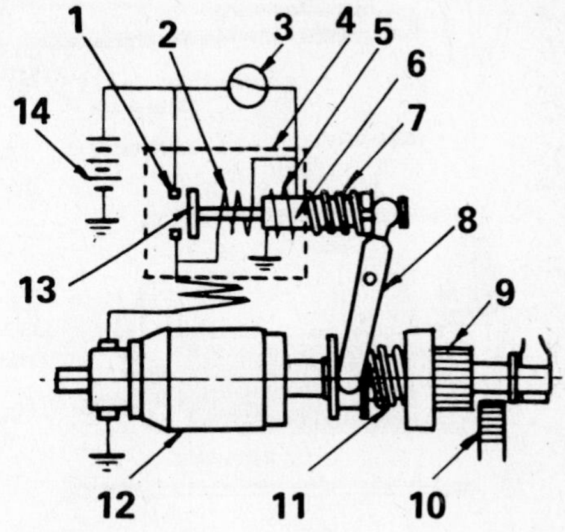

Starter circuit, all vehicles except L320

1. Stationary contact
2. Series coil
3. Ignition switch
4. Solenoid
5. Shunt coil
6. Plunger
7. Return spring
8. Shift lever
9. Drive pinion
10. Ring gear
11. Pinion sleeve spring
12. Armature
13. Moveable contact
14. Battery

One model, the L320 pickup, does not have the solenoid mounted on the starter. This vehicle has a starter motor which uses an inertia drive for engagement.

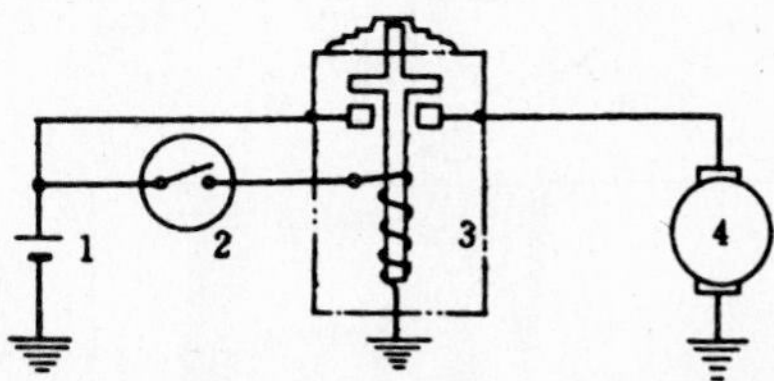

Starter circuit, L320. 1 is battery 2, is starter button, 3 is solenoid, and 4 is starter motor.

Starter R&R, L320 Pickup

1. Disconnect battery ground cable.
2. Disconnect starter power cable. Disconnect starter ground cable, if any.
3. Remove both starter mounting bolts. Pull starter forward and out.
4. Reverse procedure to install.

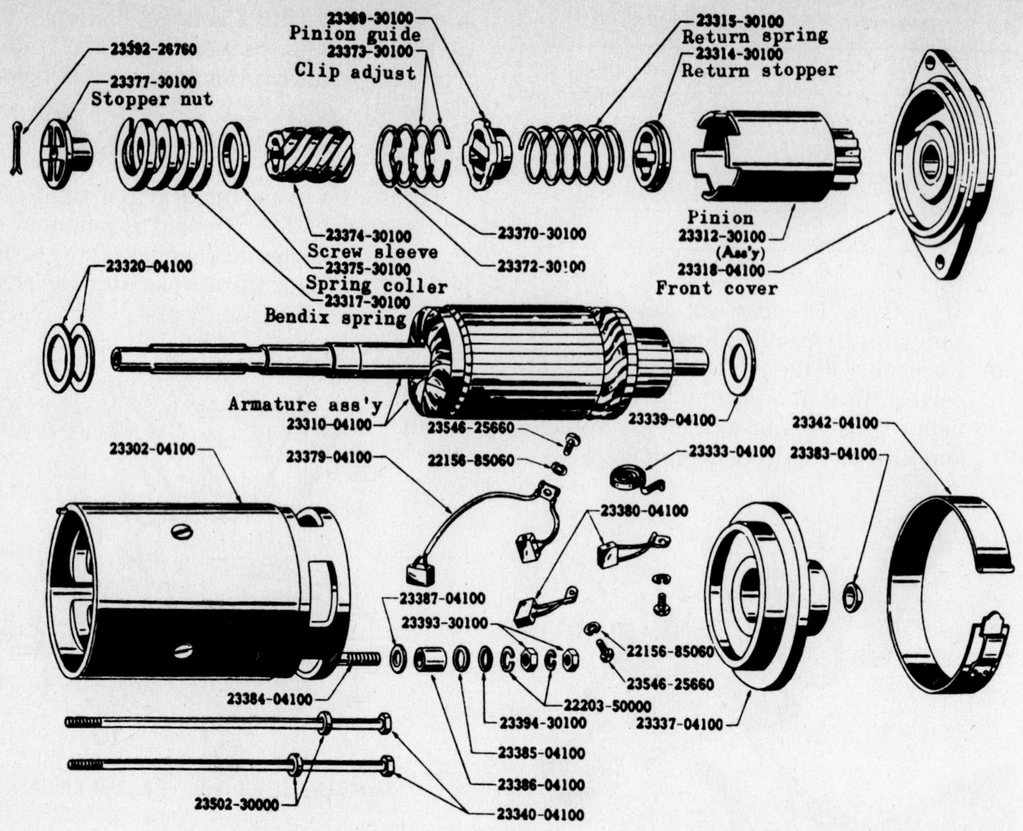

Starter with inertia drive, L320 pickup

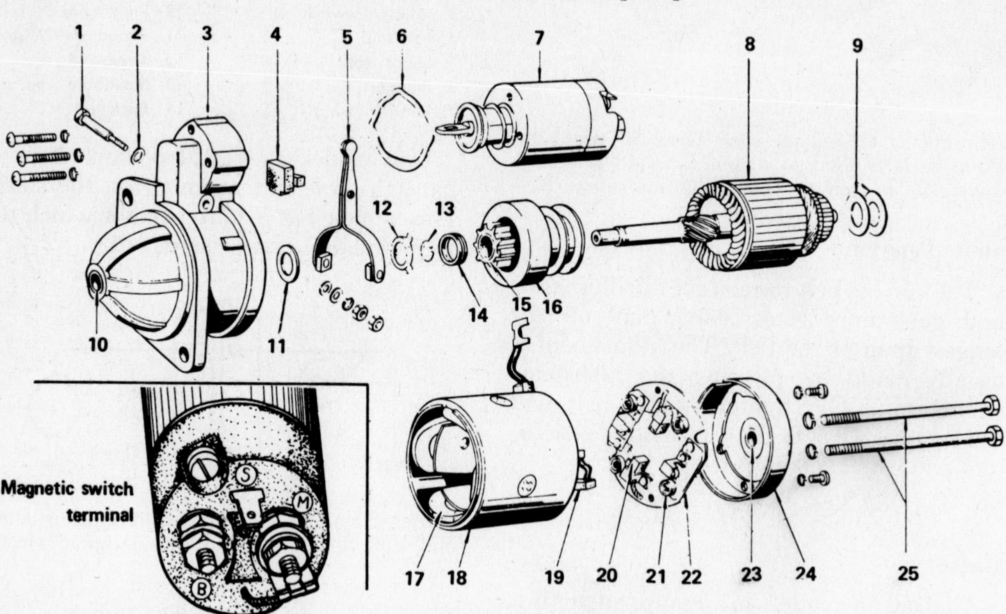

Starter with top-mounted solenoid (magnetic switch), all vehicles but L320. L16 engine starter is shown.

1. Shift lever pin
2. Packing
3. Gear case
4. Dust cover
5. Shift lever
6. Dust cover
7. Solenoid assembly
8. Armature
9. Thrust washer
10. Bushing
11. Thrust washer
12. Stopper washer
13. Stopper clip
14. Pinion stopper
15. Pinion
16. Overrunning clutch
17. Field coil
18. Housing
19. Positive brush
20. Negative brush
21. Brush spring
22. Brush holder assembly
23. Bushing
24. Rear cover
25. Through bolt

STARTER R&R, ALL EXCEPT L320 PICKUP

1. Disconnect battery ground cable.
2. Disconnect switch lead from solenoid switch terminal. This terminal is usually labeled S.
3. Disconnect battery cable from solenoid battery terminal. This terminal is usually labeled B. There is a third solenoid terminal, labeled M, connected to the starter motor.
4. Remove both starter mounting bolts. Pull starter assembly forward and out.
5. Reverse procedure to install.

Fuel System

FUEL FILTER

All engines have a filter in the fuel line. The filter is mounted in the engine compartment. L16, L24, and A12 engines have a nonserviceable cartridge filter. This unit is simply replaced every 24,000 miles. All other models have a glass bowl type filter, with a removeable element. Both types of filter can be visually checked for the presence of excessive sediment or water.

FUEL PUMP

The diaphragm fuel pump is driven from the engine camshaft on all engines except the U20. On the U20 engine, the pump is driven off the engine jackshaft. It is mounted on the side of the engine block on overhead valve engines and the U20 and on the side of the cylinder head on all other overhead camshaft engines. The pump is on the left side of P, El, and J engines and on the right side of all others. The pump on P, El, and J engines has a primer lever which is useful in cold weather and in restarting after running out of fuel.

Fuel Pump R&R

1. Disconnect inlet and outlet lines from pump.
2. Remove mounting bolts.
3. Remove pump and discard gasket.
4. Lubricate the pump rocker arm, rocker arm pin, and lever pin before reinstallation.
5. Bolt the pump into position, using a new gasket.
6. Connect the fuel lines.

CARBURETOR

Two Hitachi sidedraft carburetors are used on G, R, U20, and L24 engines. These carburetors are virtually identical to the British SU carburetors. A few high performance U20 engines are equipped with two twin-choke sidedraft carburetors. These are identical to the German Solex carburetors and are built under license by

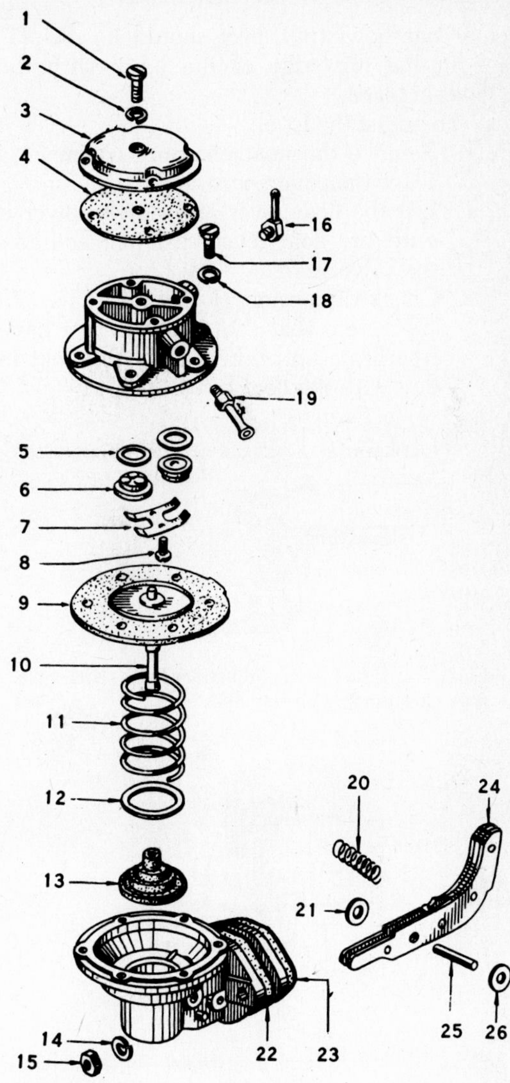

Details of fuel pump, L16 engine pump shown

1. Screw
2. Lockwasher
3. Cover
4. Cover gasket
5. Packing
6. Valve
7. Valve retainer
8. Valve retainer screw
9. Diaphragm
10. Pull rod
11. Spring
12. Seal washer
13. Seal
14. Lockwasher
15. Nut
16. Elbow
17. Screw
18. Lockwasher
19. Connector
20. Spring
21. Rocker arm slide spacer
22. Spacer
23. Gasket
24. Rocker arm
25. Pin
26. Rocker arm slide spacer

Mikuni. All other engines use one downdraft carburetor of various makes and types. For complete details on carburetors see the Carburetor Specifications Chart.

Hitachi/SU Type

Fuel Level Adjustment

Float bowl fuel level should be .87-.95″ from the top edge of the bowl with the float in place.

To adjust the level:

1. Remove the float chamber covers.
2. Place the covers upside down.
3. Lift the float lever and slowly lower it until the float lever seat just contacts the valve stem.
4. Check dimension H. It should be .55-.59″. Note that some carburetors have free floats and others have the float in unit with the float lever.

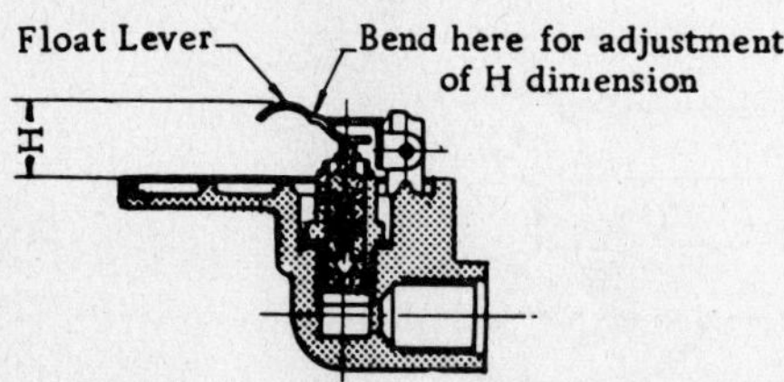

Float bowl fuel level adjustment for Hitachi/SU type carburetor with free float

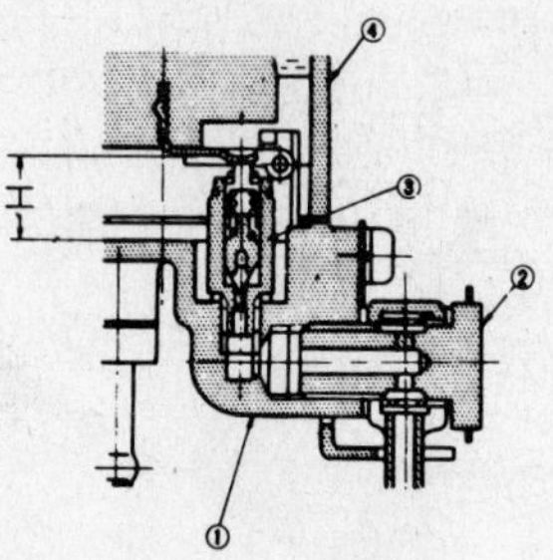

Float bowl fuel level adjustment for Hitachi/SU type carburetor with float in unit with float lever

1. Float chamber cover (unit shown inverted)
2. Filter bolt
3. Needle valve
4. Float chamber

5. Reassemble carburetors. Fuel level should now be correct.

Synchronization and Mixture Adjustment

Two types of dual carburetor linkage have been used. The early type utilizes a flexible cable from the accelerator pedal. The cable turns a cable drum attached to a throttle shaft, which is mounted on the intake manifold. The throttle shaft is connected to each carburetor throttle by a threaded turnbuckle. Each carburetor has an individual throttle adjusting (idle speed) screw. Some models have another idle adjusting screw on the throttle shaft. Synchronization adjustments are made at the turnbuckles. The late type uses a rod linkage from the accelerator pedal to turn an auxiliary throttle shaft. This shaft is connected by a nonadjustable link rod to a throttle shaft linking the carburetor throttles. Each carburetor has an individual throttle adjusting (idle speed) screw. There is also an idle speed adjusting screw on the auxiliary throttle shaft. Synchronizing adjustments are made at a balance screw on the throttle shaft.

Early Hitachi/SU throttle linkage

The engine must be at normal operating temperature to perform carburetor adjustments. Check that the piston damper oil level is correct. If the plunger has one mark, the oil level should be within .2″ of the mark. If the rod has two marks, the oil level should be between the marks. SAE 20 oil should be used in the dampers, except in extremely cold areas where a lighter viscosity may be necessary. To adjust the carburetors:

1. Remove air cleaner.
2. Back out individual carburetor throttle adjusting screws.
3. On early linkage, disconnect front turnbuckle. On late linkage, back out balance screw.
4. On early linkage, adjust rear turnbuckle to standard measurement.

Engine	*Vehicle*	*Std. measurement*
G	SPL310	3.4-3.6″
R	SPL311	2.8″
R	RL411	3.1″
U20	SRL311	2.8″

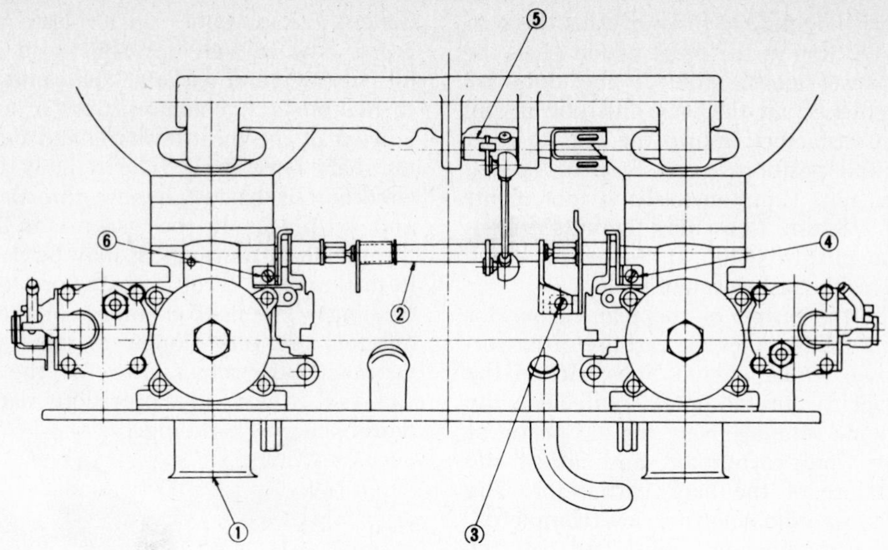

Late Hitachi/SU throttle linkage

1. Air horn
2. Throttle shaft
3. Balance screw
4. Throttle adjusting screw
5. Auxiliary throttle shaft
6. Throttle adjusting screw

5. Tighten both carburetor mixture adjusting nuts fully. Back them off an equal number of turns (2-3) until they reach their stops. Tighten both nuts about 1/2 turn.

Hitachi/SU carburetor mixture adjusting nut

6. Turn in individual carburetor throttle adjusting screws a few turns and start engine. Adjust both screws equally to obtain a reasonable idle speed.
7. Using an air flow meter (Unisyn), measure air flow through each carburetor. Equalize the readings at each carburetor by adjusting the individual throttle adjusting screws. An alternate, and more difficult, method is to equalize air flow by listening to the hiss of each carburetor air intake through a length of rubber hose. The carburetors are now synchronized. This can be checked visually by stopping the engine, raising both carburetor pistons, and observing whether the throttle plates are parallel.
8. Tighten both mixture adjusting nuts simultaneously in increments of 1/8

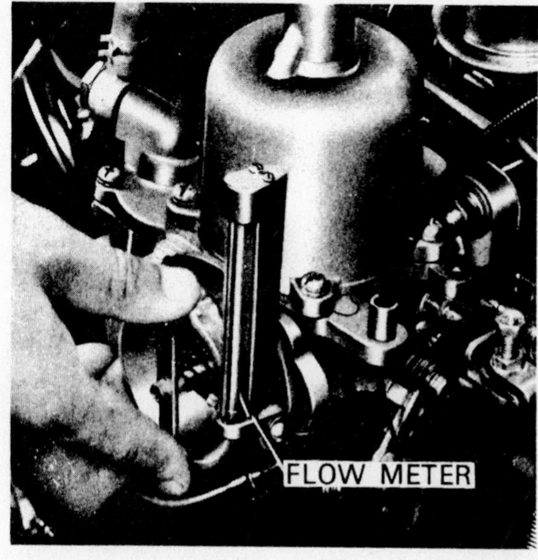

Measuring air flow through Hitachi/SU carburetor

turn. Tightening the nut leans the mixture. Stop at the point which gives the fastest smooth idle. If the nuts are tightened all the way and idle is still unsatisfactory, return the nuts to their initial positions as in Step 5. Loosen the nuts simultaneously in increments of 1/8 turn. Loosening the nuts richens the mixture. Stop at the point which gives the fastest smooth idle.

9. Lift the piston of the rear carburetor 1/2″. This makes the carburetor inoperative. If the engine stalls, richen the front carburetor until it will keep the engine running. Now lift the piston of the front carburetor, and adjust the mixture of the back carburetor. The mixture adjustment is now completed.
10. On early linkage, adjust and connect front turnbuckle. On late linkage, turn in the balance screw to interlock the front and rear throttle shafts.
11. Open throttle suddenly. Engine should accelerate immediately with no hesitation. Both pistons should rise an equal amount. If this is not the case, recheck the synchronization and mixture adjustments.
12. Adjust the idle speed to that specified in the Tune-Up Specifications Chart. If there is a manufacturer's sticker in the engine compartment, it takes precedence.
13. Stop engine and replace air cleaner.

NOTE: On engines with emission control, the mixture adjusting nuts are held by locknuts and are not to be adjusted, except after carburetor overhaul. Adjust the mixture to obtain the air:fuel ratio or percentage of CO at idle speed specified in the Tune-Up Specifications Chart.

Hitachi/SU Overhaul

These carburetors, being precision devices, are capable of being very finely adjusted. For the same reason, they require periodic attention. The factory recommends that they be disassembled and cleaned every six months. The suction piston and chamber often accumulate deposits of grit and varnish. To check for this condition, remove the air cleaner and raise the suction piston about 1/2″ with a finger. Release the piston. It should come down smoothly and evenly. If not, the carburetor must be disassembled and cleaned. If turning the mixture nuts seems to have no effect, the difficulty is probably an air leak at some point. The remedy for this is to replace all packings and gaskets. The same applies to fuel leaks. A common cause of air leaks is wear of the throttle shafts and the throttle shaft bore itself. The remedy for this condition is to install new throttle shafts and bushings. If the carburetor has no throttle shaft bushings, it may be necessary to drill out the throttle shaft bore to install bushings. The float chambers of these carburetors are very similar to those in conventional carburetors. However, the venturi and fuel system are precision made and require careful handling.

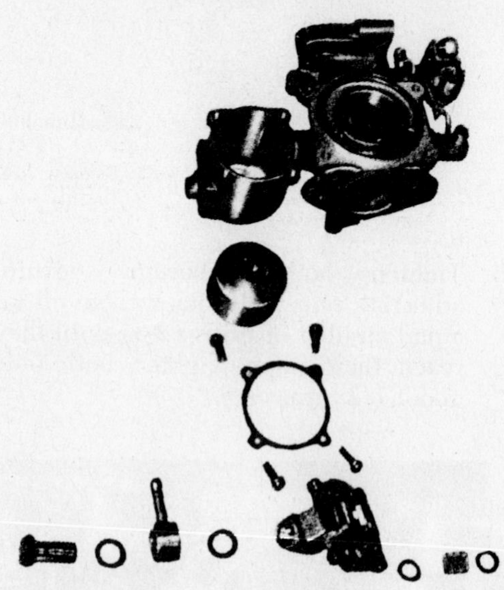

Hitachi/SU float bowl assembly

To disassemble the carburetors:

1. Remove screws and suction chamber.
2. Remove suction spring, nylon packing, and suction piston from chamber. Be extremely careful not to bend the jet needle.
3. Do not remove the jet needle from the suction pistion unless it must be replaced. To remove, loosen jet needle setscrew. Hold the needle with pliers at a point no more than .1″ from the piston. Remove needle by pulling and turning slowly. Replace the needle with the shoulder portion flush with the piston surface. Check this with a straightedge. Tighten the setscrew.
4. Clean all parts of suction chamber assembly with a safe solvent. Reassemble, using all new parts supplied in overhaul kit. Do not lubricate piston.

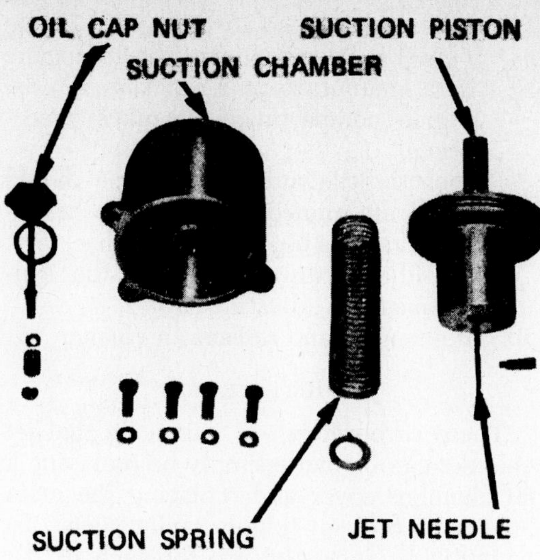

Hitachi/SU suction chamber assembly

5. To dismantle nozzle assembly, remove 4 mm. screw and remove connecting plate from nozzle head by pulling lightly on starter (choke) lever. Remove fuel line and nozzle. Be careful not to bend jet needle if suction chamber assembly is mounted on carburetor. Remove idle (mixture) adjusting nut and spring. Do not remove nozzle sleeve unless absolutely necessary. Special care is required to replace this part. Remove nozzle sleeve setscrew and nozzle sleeve.
6. Clean all parts of nozzle assembly with a safe solvent. Be very careful of nozzle. Do not pass anything through nozzle for cleaning purposes.
7. The jet needle must now be carefully centered in the nozzle, unless the nozzle sleeve and setscrew were not disturbed. Even so, it is a good idea to check this. To center the jet needle, insert nozzle sleeve into carburetor body with setscrew loose. Carefully install the suction piston assembly without the plunger rod. Insert the nozzle without spring and mixture adjusting nut until the nozzle contacts the nozzle sleeve. Position the nozzle sleeve so that the jet needle is centered inside the sleeve and does not contact the sleeve. Test centering by raising and releasing suction piston. It should drop smoothly, making a metallic sound when it hits the stop. Tighten the nozzle sleeve setscrew when the needle is centered.
8. Reassemble nozzle assembly. Replace fuel line. Replace damper plunger rod.
9. Pull starter lever slightly, replace connecting plate and 4 mm. screw.
10. Carburetor synchronization and mix-

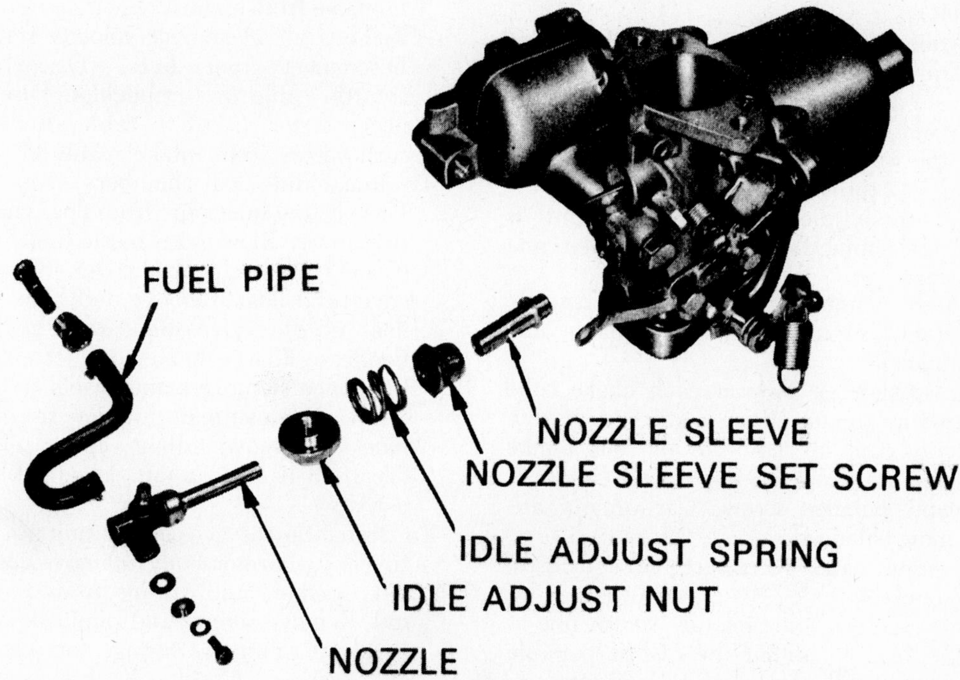

Hitachi/SU nozzle assembly

ture adjustments must be performed after reinstalling carburetors.

Mikuni/Solex Twin-Choke

Fuel Level Adjustment

Float bowl fuel level is controlled by the thickness of the washer under the float needle valve. The standard washer thickness is .04″ (1 mm.). A .02″ (.5 mm.) thick washer is available to raise the fuel level .08″ (2 mm.), and a .06″ (1.5 mm.) washer is available to lower it .08″ (2 mm.). Normal fuel level is .79″ above the center of the main bore. A special fuel level meter is available to measure this. When using the meter, fuel level on the scale should be .67-.75″. The float lever should never be bent to change the fuel level.

Synchronization and Idle Mixture Adjustment

The engine must be at normal operating temperature before making any carburetor adjustments. There is a separate idle mixture adjusting screw for each of the four choke tubes. The relationship between the throttle shafts for the two carburetors is adjusted by a balance screw. A throttle (idle speed) adjusting screw is provided on the linkage between the carburetors. Some installations may also have an individual idle speed adjusting screw for each carburetor.

1. Remove air cleaner, if any. Disconnect turnbuckles from throttle linkage. Back out idle speed adjusting screw(s).
2. Gently screw idle mixture screws in all the way, then back them out about 1-1 1/2 turns.
3. Turn in idle speed screw(s) until it just contacts lever, then tighten one turn.
4. Start engine. Adjust idle speed screw(s) to obtain a reasonable idle speed.
5. Measure air flow at each choke tube with an air flow meter (Unisyn). Equalize air flow in all four choke tubes by use of idle speed screw(s) and balance screw. Carburetors are now balanced.
6. Adjust and reconnect linkage turnbuckles.
7. Adjust each idle mixture screw, one at a time, to obtain the fastest possible smooth idle. Screw in to lean mixture, and out to richen it. Idle mixture is now set.
8. Adjust idle speed to that given in the Tune-Up Specifications Chart. If there is a manufacturer's sticker in the engine compartment, it takes precedence.
9. Open throttle suddenly. Engine should accelerate immediately with no hesitation. If this is not the case, recheck first the idle mixture and then the synchronization adjustments.
10. Stop engine and replace air cleaner.

Jet Replacement

These carburetors are unique in that jet changes can be made simply be removing a jet chamber cover and replacing the main air, main fuel, or idling (pilot) jets. To maintain balance, the jets for each of the choke tubes in both carburetors must all be the same size. This means that four main air or fuel, or pilot jets must be changed together. Jet numbers relate directly to jet drilling diameter, except in the case of main fuel jets which are rated by flow. The larger the main air or pilot jet number, the leaner the mixture. The larger the main fuel jet number, the richer the mixture.

The carburetor venturi tubes can also be replaced readily and are available in a number of sizes.

Mikuni/Solex Overhaul

To remove from engine:

1. Remove air cleaner or velocity stacks. Disconnect fuel lines. Disconnect throttle cable or turnbuckles. Disconnect starter (choke) cable. Remove carburetors from intake manifold.

To disassemble float chamber:

2. Unbolt fuel inlet pipe from float chamber cover. Blow wire mesh fuel filter clean. Unbolt chamber cover. Remove cover and float. Remove and blow out float needle valve. Be careful not to bend the float arm. Remove jet chamber cover. Remove main air jets and jet blocks. Remove main fuel jets from jet blocks. Remove idling (pilot) jets. Clean all parts in a safe solvent. Blow out jets.

To dismantle the accelerator pump:

3. Invert carburetor body. Remove cotter pin, washer, and spring from pump rod. Remove screws and pump bottom cover, diaphragm, spring, top cover, and gasket. Check diaphragm for holes. Shake upper cover; listen for internal check ball. From top of car-

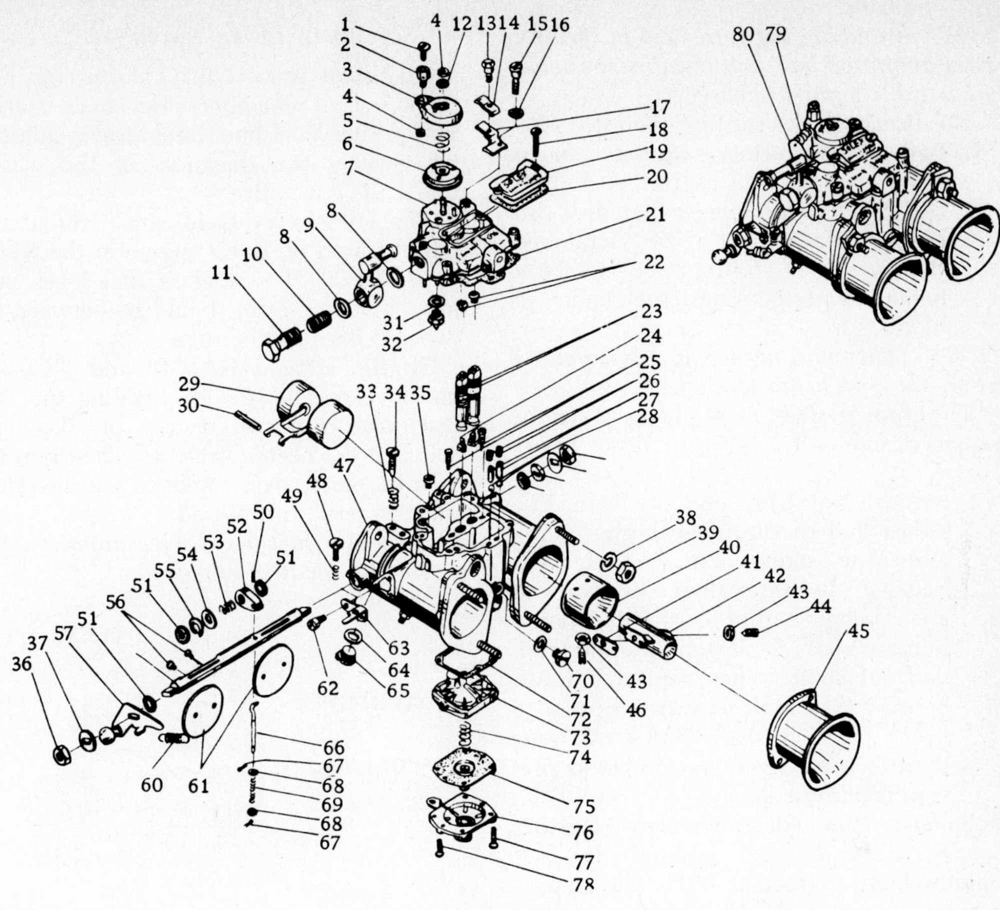

Mikuni/Solex 44PHH carburetor

1. Cable fixing bolt
2. Cable fixing collar
3. Starter cover
4. Snap ring
5. Starter spring
6. Starter disk
7. Float chamber cover
8. Washer
9. Fuel pipe
10. Filter
11. Banjo bolt
12. Washer
13. Spring washer bolt
14. Clip; cable bracket
15. Spring washer screw
16. Washer
17. Starter bracket
18. Fixing screw jet chamber cover
19. Jet chamber cover
20. Gasket; jet chamber cover
21. Gasket; float chamber cover
22. Main air jet
23. Jet block
24. Main jet
25. Pilot jet
26. Plug
27. Pump weight
28. Ball
29. Float
30. Spindle; float
31. Washer
32. Needle valve
33. Volume control screw spring
34. Volume control screw
35. Starter jet
36. Nut
37. Washer
38. Spring washer
39. Nut
40. Outer venturi
41. Gasket-inner venturi
42. Inner venturi
43. Nut
44. Fixing screw
45. Air funnel
46. Fixing screw
47. Main body assembly
48. Slow running adjustment screw
49. Volume control screw spring
50. Stopper pin
51. Dustproof ring
52. Pump intermediate lever
53. Throttle spring
54. Thrust washer
55. Snap ring
56. Fixing screw; throttle
57. Throttle lever
58. Throttle spindle
59. Nut fixing collar
60. Throttle spring
61. Throttle butterfly
62. Spring washer screw
63. Bracket; slow running screw
64. Washer
65. Plug screw
66. Pump control rod
67. Split pin
68. Washer; pump control
69. Spring; pump control
70. Plug screw
71. Washer
72. Gasket; pump cover
73. Pump cover
74. Pump spring
75. Diaphragm assembly
76. Pump cover assembly
77. Fixing screw
78. Fixing screw
79. Starter spring
80. Starter spring bracket

buretor remove plugs, pump weights, and balls.

NOTE: Installing the cotter pin in the end-most pump rod hole will result in the smallest possible pump discharge.

To dismantle the starting pump:

4. Remove snap-ring, washer, starter cover, spring, and starter disk from fuel bowl cover. Check that disk rubbing surfaces are not scratched. Remove the starting jet, centered behind and between the main jet blocks.

NOTE: The starting jet is not effective after the engine has started.

The throttle shaft normally need not be removed, unless it is worn or bent. To remove:

5. Remove nut from end of shaft. File staked end of throttle valve retaining screws so screws can be removed. Remove throttle valves. Be sure to wash filings out of carburetor body. Remove shaft C-clip and stopper pin. Pull out shaft. When replacing shaft, be careful to replace dust seals and to avoid bending shaft. Stake the new throttle valve retaining screws to prevent their loosening.

Remove the idle mixture adjusting screws. Blow out all passages in carburetor body, particularly the idle bypass passages. Reassemble the carburetor, using new gaskets.

Hitachi VC42-4A single throat carburetor

1. Venturi
2. Idle air bleed
3. Idle speed (throttle) adjusting screw
4. Idle mixture adjusting screw
5. Vacuum fitting
6. Idle jet
7. Main air bleed
8. Main jet
9. Power valve
10. Vacuum piston
11. Main nozzle
12. Accelerating pump
13. Accelerating pump nozzle

Downdraft Carburetors

Fuel Level Adjustment

All Nihonkikaki (Nikki) carburetors have a glass float chamber side cover marked with a fuel level line. Fuel level is adjusted by varying the thickness of the washer under the float valve.

The Hitachi VC42-4A single throat carburetor used on the P engine in the Nissan Patrol (L60) has a glass fuel level sight tube. The fuel level should be between the two red lines on the tube.

On the Hitachi DAF328 and DCG306, fuel level is adjusted by bending the float seat tab to obtain a gap of .051-.067″ between the needle valve and float seat tab with the float cover removed and inverted, and the float fully raised.

NOTE: All fuel level measurements are given with the float in place.

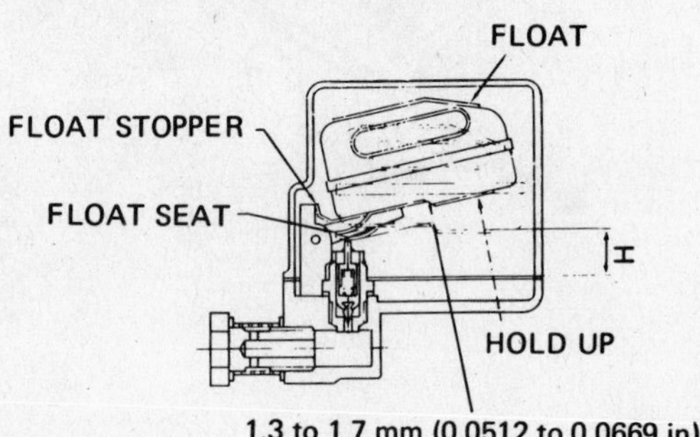

Float adjustment for Hitachi DAF328 and DCG306 carburetors

Idle Mixture Adjustment

Both single and dual throat carburetors have only one idle mixture adjusting screw. Tighten the screw to lean mixture and loosen to richen.

1. For a starting point, gently turn the idle mixture adjusting screw all the way in and back out 2-3 turns.
2. Start the engine and adjust the mixture screw for the fastest smooth idle.
3. Adjust the idle speed screw to obtain the idle speed given in the Tune-Up Specifications Chart.
4. Open the throttle suddenly. The engine should accelerate immediately, without hesitation. If it stumbles or stalls, richen the mixture slightly.
5. On engines with emission control, adjust idle mixture to obtain the air: fuel ratio or percentage CO at idle

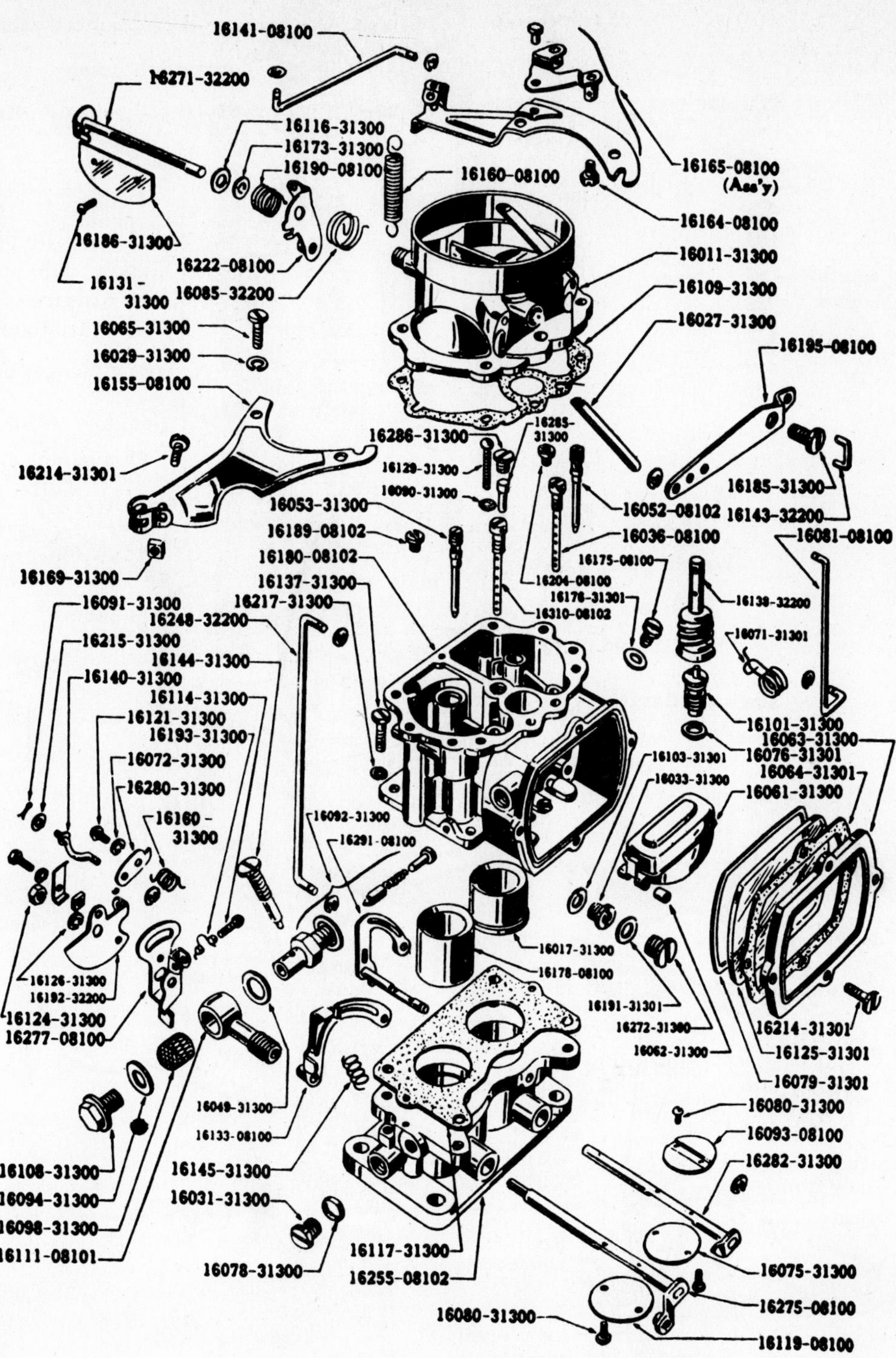

Nihonkikaki 2D30CE dual throat carburetor

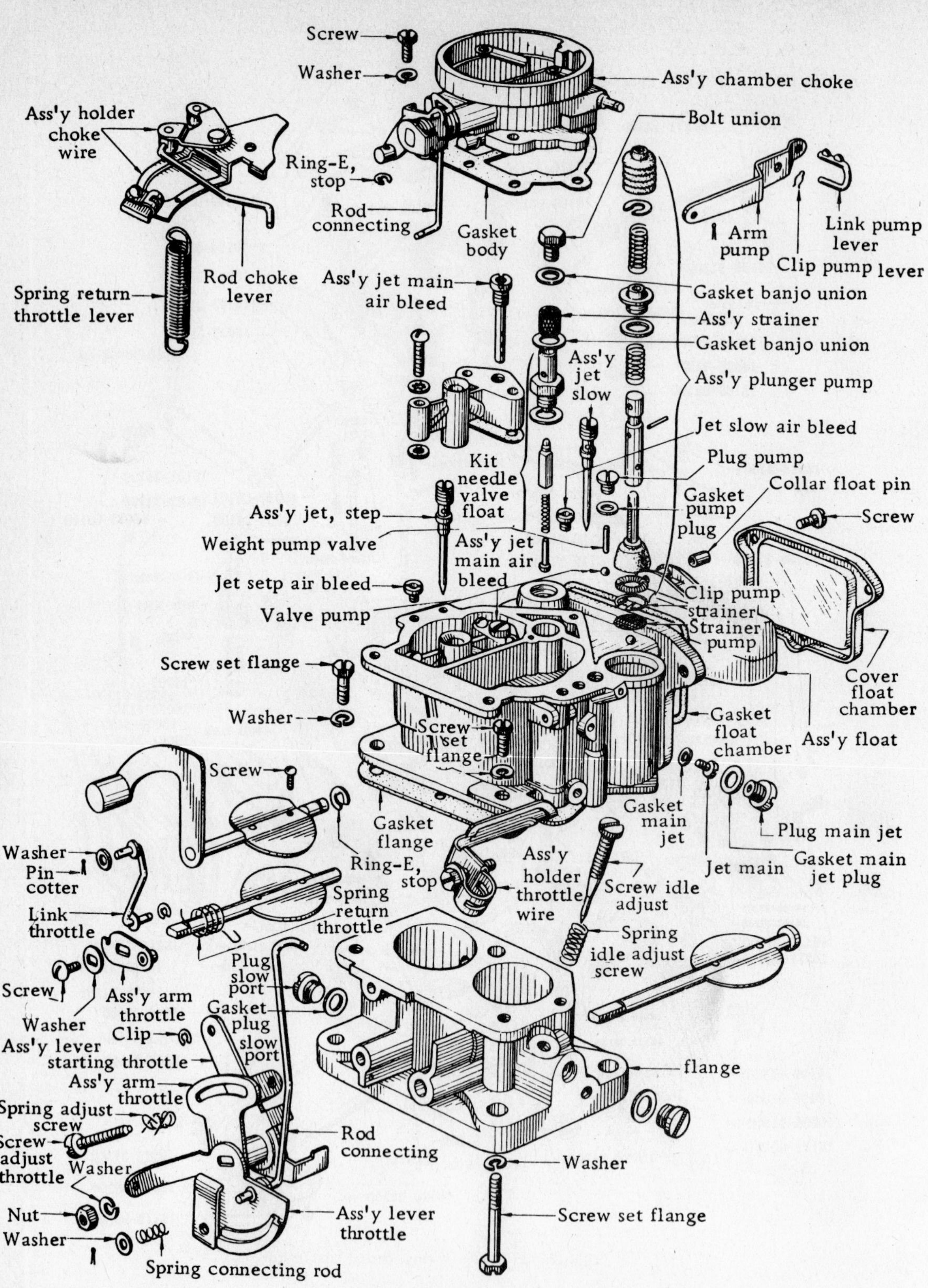
Screw
Washer
Ass'y chamber choke
Ass'y holder choke wire
Bolt union
Ring-E, stop
Rod connecting
Gasket body
Arm pump
Link pump lever
Clip pump lever
Rod choke lever
Spring return throttle lever
Ass'y jet main air bleed
Gasket banjo union
Ass'y strainer
Gasket banjo union
Ass'y jet slow
Ass'y plunger pump
Jet slow air bleed
Kit needle valve float
Plug pump
Collar float pin
Ass'y jet, step
Gasket pump plug
Screw
Weight pump valve
Ass'y jet main air bleed
Jet setp air bleed
Clip pump strainer
Valve pump
Strainer pump
Screw set flange
Cover float chamber
Washer
Gasket float chamber
Ass'y float
Screw set flange
Screw
Gasket flange
Gasket main jet
Plug main jet
Washer
Pin cotter
Ring-E, stop
Ass'y holder throttle wire
Screw idle adjust
Jet main
Gasket main jet plug
Link throttle
Spring return throttle
Spring idle adjust screw
Plug slow port
Screw
Ass'y arm throttle
Gasket plug slow port
Washer
Clip
Ass'y lever starting throttle
flange
Ass'y arm throttle
Spring adjust screw
Rod connecting
Screw adjust throttle
Washer
Washer
Nut
Ass'y lever throttle
Screw set flange
Washer
Spring connecting rod

Nihonkikaki D2630A-5A dual throat carburetor

speed given in the Tune-Up Specifications Chart. Some carburetors have idle mixture limiter caps to prevent unauthorized idle mixture adjustments.

NOTE: If turning the idle mixture screw has no effect, the idling passages are probably clogged.

Throttle Linkage Adjustment

On the PL410 and PL411 sedans, the accelerator linkage must be adjusted to obtain a measurement, D, of 3.4". On all models, check that the throttle is wide open when the accelerator pedal is floored. Some models have an adjustable accelerator pedal stop to prevent strain on the linkage.

Starting Interlock Adjustment

With the choke valve fully closed, the primary throttle valve should be open the angle specified under Fast Idle in the Carburetor Specifications Chart. On the Hitachi DAF328, a throttle valve opening of 16° corresponds to a measurement of .051" between the lower edge of the throttle valve and the inside edge of the primary bore.

Dashpot Adjustment

A dashpot is used on Hitachi DAF328 carburetors with automatic transmission. The dashpot slows the closing of the throttle valve to prevent stalling. The dashpot should be adjusted so that it contacts the

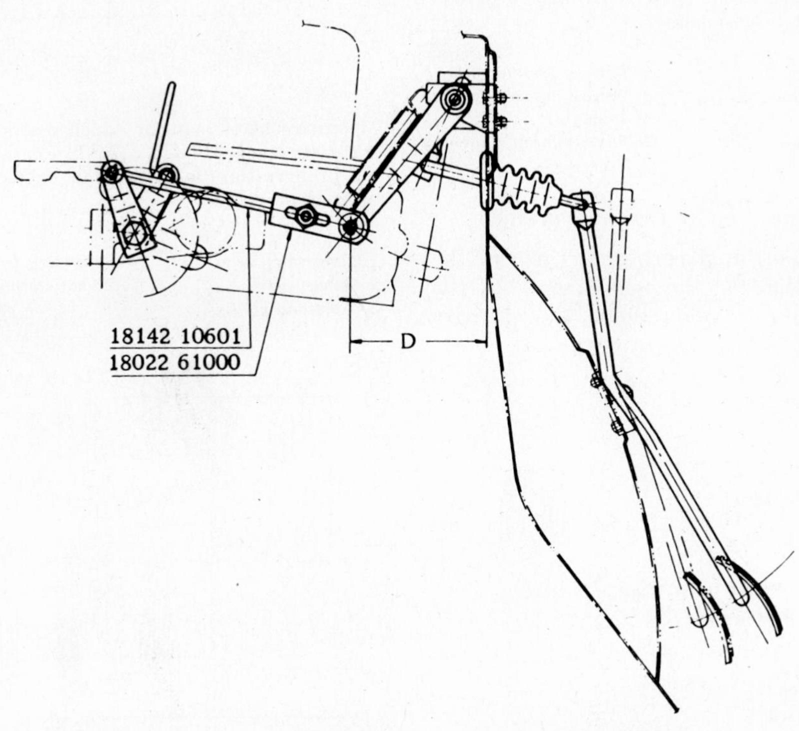

Throttle linkage for PL410 and PL411 sedans. Measurement D should be 3.4".

throttle lever at about 10° of throttle opening on deceleration. 10° corresponds to a measurement of .071″ between the throttle valve and the edge of the primary bore.

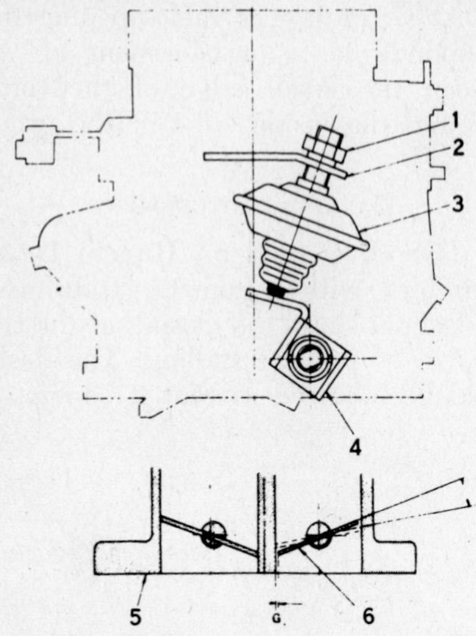

Dashpot installation on Hitachi DAF328 carburetor with automatic transmission

1. Locknut
2. Mounting arm
3. Dashpot
4. Throttle lever
5. Carburetor body
6. Primary throttle valve
α. Primary throttle opening in degrees
G. Primary throttle opening in inches

Secondary Throttle Adjustment

On all two throat carburetors except the Hitachi DAF328, the secondary throttle should begin to open when the primary throttle is open 48°. On the Hitachi DCG306, 48° corresponds to a measurement of .230″ between the lower edge of the primary throttle valve and the inside edge of the primary bore. On the Hitachi DAF328, the secondary throttle begins to open when the primary throttle is open 59° or .358″. Adjust the point of secondary throttle opening by bending the linkage between the two throttles.

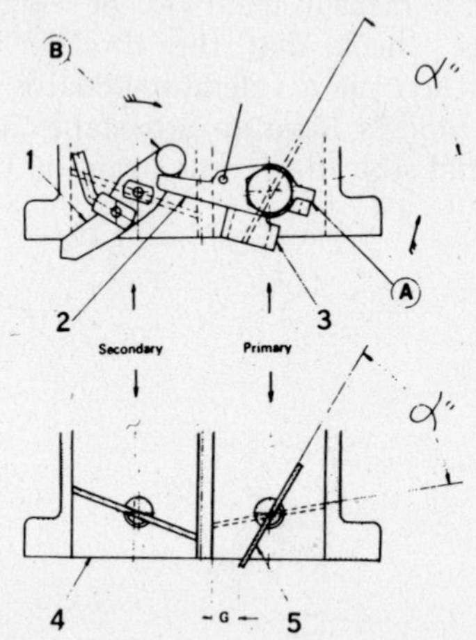

Measurement of point at which secondary throttle starts to open, Hitachi DAF328 carburetor. α is the primary throttle opening in degrees; G is the opening in inches.

1. Connecting lever
2. Return plate
3. Adjusting plate
4. Secondary throttle chamber
5. Primary throttle valve

1. Main nozzle
2. Small venturi
3. Main air bleed
4. Idle jet
5. Idle air bleed
6. Float needle valve
7. Float
8. Emulsion tube
9. Main jet
10. Idle bypass drilling
11. Secondary throttle valve
12. Choke valve
13. Main air bleed
14. Main nozzle
15. Economizer bleed
16. Idle jet
17. Idle economizer
18. Idle air bleed
19. Air vent
20. Side cover
21. Main jet
22. Idle mixture adjusting screw
23. Idle drilling
24. Bypass drilling
25. Primary throttle valve

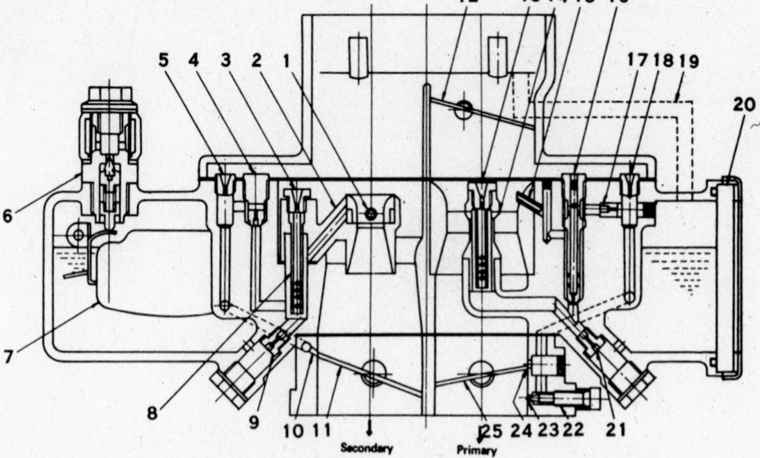

Hitachi DAF328 dual throat carburetor

Downdraft Carburetor Overhaul

Carburetor overhaul involves separating the major components, removing and blowing out all jets, blowing out all passages, washing all parts in a safe solvent, and reassembling with new gaskets. After overhaul, the idle mixture and speed must be adjusted. Carburetor overhaul kits are available, and generally contain complete instructions, a full set of gaskets, and a new float needle valve and accelerator pump parts.

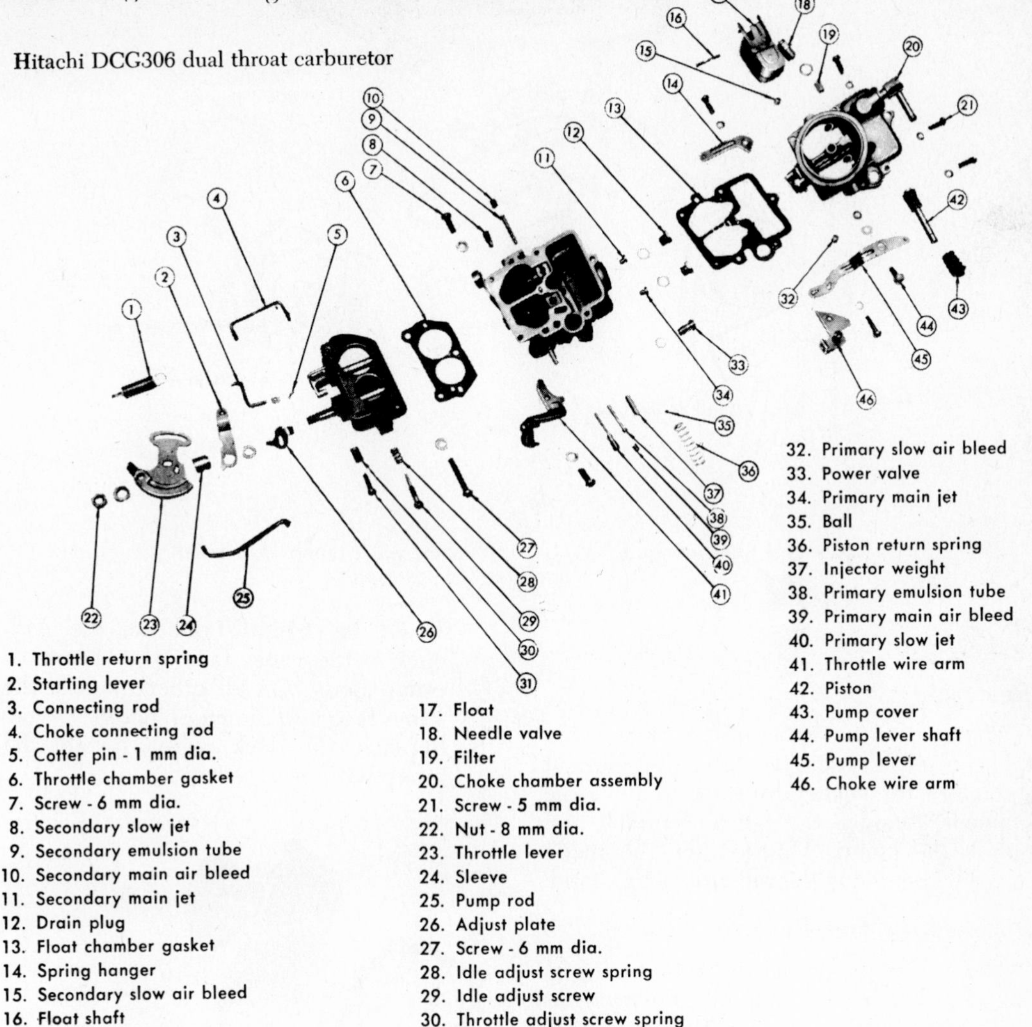

Hitachi DCG306 dual throat carburetor

1. Throttle return spring
2. Starting lever
3. Connecting rod
4. Choke connecting rod
5. Cotter pin - 1 mm dia.
6. Throttle chamber gasket
7. Screw - 6 mm dia.
8. Secondary slow jet
9. Secondary emulsion tube
10. Secondary main air bleed
11. Secondary main jet
12. Drain plug
13. Float chamber gasket
14. Spring hanger
15. Secondary slow air bleed
16. Float shaft
17. Float
18. Needle valve
19. Filter
20. Choke chamber assembly
21. Screw - 5 mm dia.
22. Nut - 8 mm dia.
23. Throttle lever
24. Sleeve
25. Pump rod
26. Adjust plate
27. Screw - 6 mm dia.
28. Idle adjust screw spring
29. Idle adjust screw
30. Throttle adjust screw spring
31. Throttle adjust screw
32. Primary slow air bleed
33. Power valve
34. Primary main jet
35. Ball
36. Piston return spring
37. Injector weight
38. Primary emulsion tube
39. Primary main air bleed
40. Primary slow jet
41. Throttle wire arm
42. Piston
43. Pump cover
44. Pump lever shaft
45. Pump lever
46. Choke wire arm

Cooling System

The coolant level should be checked regularly, at least every two weeks. Loosen the cap a quarter turn to allow the system pressure to escape. On models with an expansion tank, hold the pressure release button on the tank cap. Never remove the cap when the engine is hot or overheated. Scalding from steam may result. When all the pressure has escaped, remove the cap cautiously. The coolant level should be 1/2-1 in. below the filler neck.

Only permanent type antifreeze should be used. Follow the directions on the antifreeze container to determine the quantity necessary for the particular vehicle and the temperature expected. Refer to the Capacities and Pressures Chart for cooling system capacity. The cooling system should be drained and flushed out with clean water once a year. Open both the block and radiator drains. The rust inhibitor in antifreeze gradually loses effectiveness, so it is unwise to reuse antifreeze after flushing the system. In summer weather, a solution of rust inhibitor and water may be used.

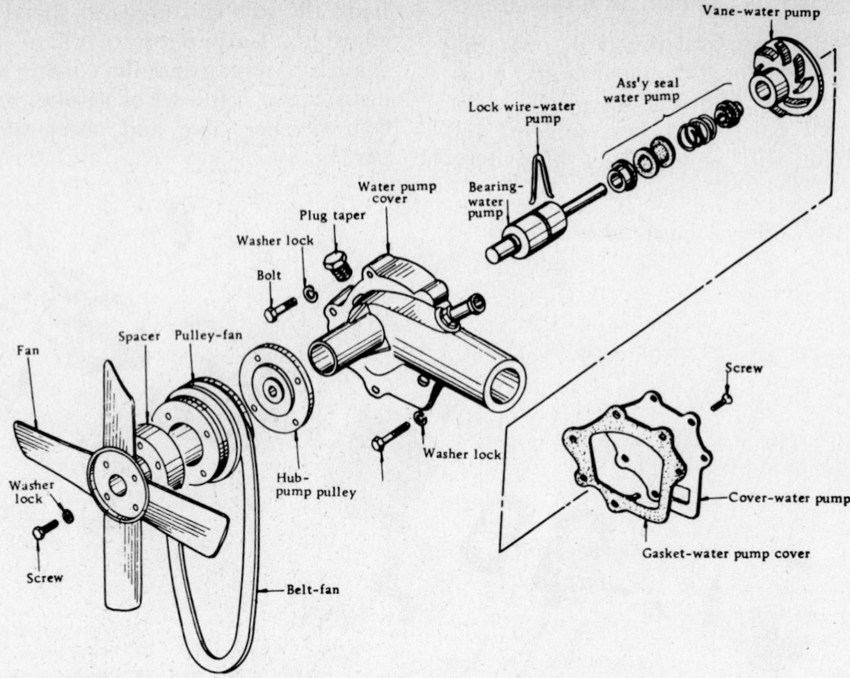

U20 engine water pump. E1, G, J, and R engine water pumps are similar.

WATER PUMP

Removal

To remove the water pump, first drain the coolant. Loosen the adjusting bolt at the alternator (generator) and remove the fan belt. Remove the fan and pulley and unbolt the pump. This job will be made easier by removing the radiator beforehand.

Disassembly and Repair

The water pump on the L16 and L24 engine is made of aluminum and may not be disassembled for repairs. To disassemble and repair the pump on all other engines, proceed as follows:

1. Pull off the pulley hub. Remove the pump rear cover.
2. Remove the lock wire through the opening in the pump body.
3. Press out the shaft from the vanes. The shaft cannot be withdrawn from the hub side.
4. Remove the shaft from the body.
5. Press out the seal. Clean the seal seating surfaces.
6. Apply adhesive to the seal seating edge. Install the new seal.
7. Reassemble the pump. The clearance between the vanes and the pump body should be .016-.020 in. On the A12 engine, the vanes face away from the pump body. On all other models, the vanes face into the pump body.
8. Replace the lock wire. Install the pump with new gaskets.

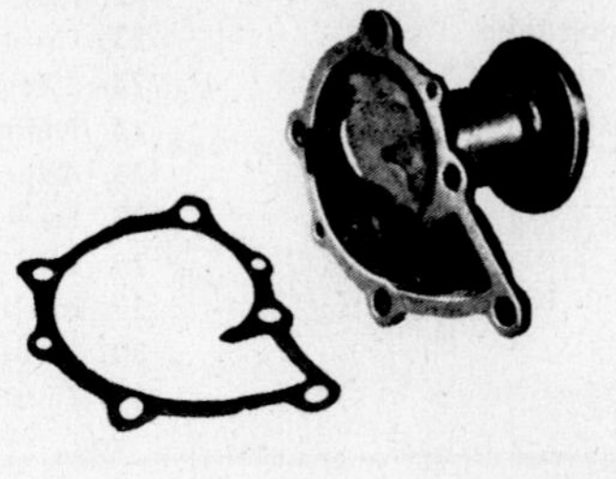

A12 engine water pump and front cover. Note that this pump has no rear cover. The nonrepairable aluminum water pump on the L16 and L24 engines is similar.

THERMOSTAT

The engine thermostat is housed in the water outlet casting on the cylinder head. The thermostat controls the flow of coolant, providing quick engine warmup and regulating coolant temperature. To remove the thermostat, first drain the coolant. Remove the upper radiator hose and unbolt the water outlet elbow. The thermostat may now be removed. To check the thermostat for proper operation, submerge it in a pan of water with a thermometer. The unit should open when the water temperature is the same as that marked on the body of the thermostat. Check that the unit opens fully. Refer to the accompanying chart for data on original equipment thermostats.

Engine	*Opening Temperature of Thermostat (°F)*	*Full Opening of Thermostat (in.)*
P	180	—
E1	164	—
J	170 or 180	—
G,R	176	.374
U20, L16, L24, A12	180	.315 @ 203°F

When heater output is insufficient, the original equipment thermostat may be replaced with one having a higher temperature rating. An engine should never be run without a thermostat, except in an emergency. Reverse the removal procedure to replace a thermostat. When installing a thermostat, be sure that the side with the spring faces into the engine. Always use a new gasket.

Correct thermostat installation

RADIATOR

Radiator R&R

To remove the radiator:

1. Drain coolant.
2. Disconnect upper hose, lower hose, and expansion tank hose.
3. Disconnect automatic transmission oil cooler lines after draining the transmission. Cap the lines to exclude dirt.
4. Remove radiator mounting bolts and radiator. On Nissan Patrol (L60), the grille shell/headlight mounting panel and radiator can be removed as an assembly.
5. Reverse procedure to replace. Fill automatic transmission to proper level.

Engine

Datsun engines are all of the inline type, with either four or six cylinders. Some have overhead valves with a rocker arm arrangement and others have a single overhead camshaft. Engine displacements range from 1,171 to 3,956 cc. Refer to the Engine Identification Chart for identification of engines by model, number of cylinders, displacement, and camshaft location. Engines are referred to by model designation codes throughout this section.

EMISSION CONTROL

Various systems are used to control crankcase vapors, exhaust emissions, and fuel vapors. The accompanying chart shows the systems used with various models and engines.

Year (approximate)	*Model*	*Engine*	*Emission Control Systems*
1969	PL510, WPL510	L16	1,3
1969	SPL311	R	2,3
1969	SRL311	U20	2,3
1969	L520, L521	J	2,4
1969	L60	P	2,4
Starting 1970	PL510, WPL510, PL521	L16	1,3,4,5
Starting 1970	SPL311	R	2,3,4,5
Starting 1970	SRL311	U20	2,3,5

Starting 1971	HLS30	L24	1,3,4,5
Starting 1971	LB110, KLB110	A12	1,4,5

1. Closed crankcase ventilation system
2. Sealed crankcase ventilation system
3. Air pump system
4. Engine modification system
5. Fuel vapor control system

Crankcase Ventilation System

The sealed system consists simply of a tube connecting the valve cover to the carburetor air cleaner. The oil filler cap and the dipstick are sealed. No provision is made for admitting ventilation air into the crankcase. Crankcase vapors are drawn through the carburetor and burned along with the air/fuel mixture.

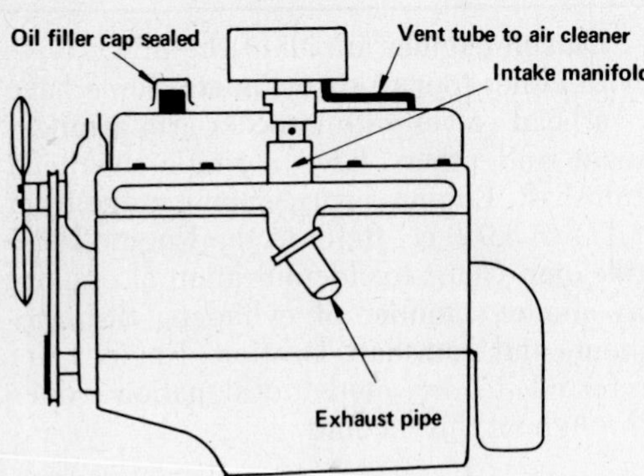

Sealed crankcase ventilation system

The closed system is identical to the sealed system, with the addition of a tube containing a variable orifice valve between the crankcase and the intake manifold. Under high vacuum conditions (idle), vapors are drawn into the intake manifold through the valve. The tube connected to the air cleaner admits ventilation air through the crankcase. Under low vacuum conditions (full-throttle), vapors are drawn through the carburetor as in the sealed system.

The crankcase ventilation system requires no periodic maintenance other than replacement of the variable orifice valve, should it become clogged.

Variable Orifice Valve Test

1. With engine idling, remove hose from valve on intake manifold.
2. A hissing sound should be heard and a vacuum felt at the valve inlet.

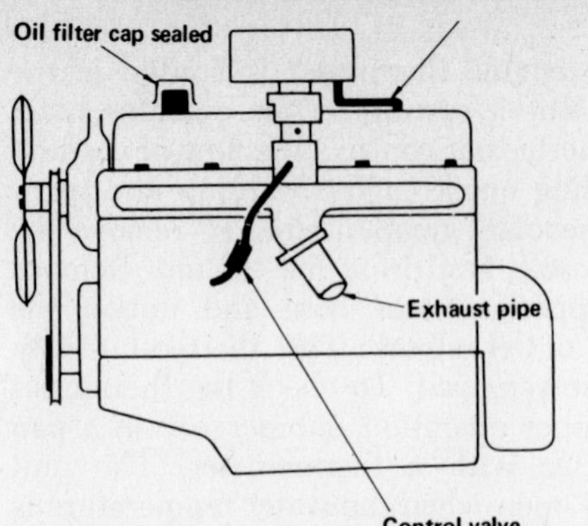

Closed crankcase ventilation system. The control valve is the variable orifice valve referred to in the text.

3. If valve is plugged, replace. Do not clean.

Air Pump System

In this system, an air injection pump, driven by the engine, compresses, distributes, and injects filtered air into the exhaust port of each cylinder. The air combines with unburned hydrocarbons and carbon monoxide to produce harmless compounds. The system includes an air cleaner, the belt driven air pump, a check valve, and an anti-backfire valve.

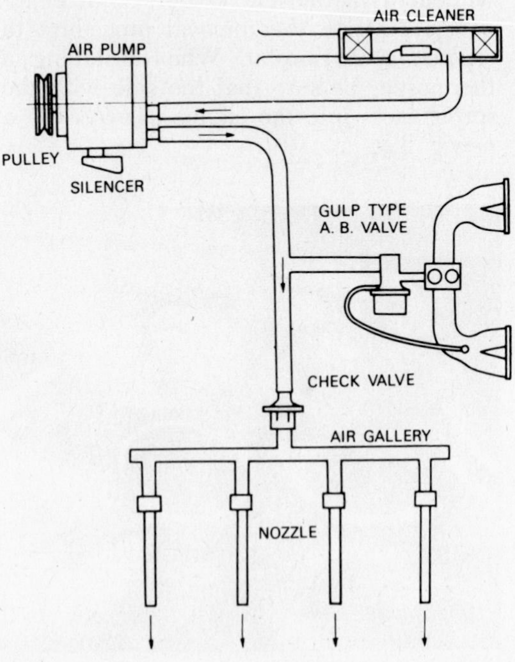

Air pump system

The air pump draws air through a hose connected to the carburetor air cleaner or to a separate air cleaner. The pump is a rotary vane unit with an integral pressure regulating valve. The pump outlet pressure passes through a check valve which prevents exhaust gas from entering the pump in case of insufficient pump outlet pressure. An anti-backfire valve admits air from the air pump into the intake manifold on deceleration to prevent backfiring in the exhaust manifold.

All engines with the air pump system have a series of minor alterations to accommodate the system. These are:

1. Special close-tolerance carburetor. Most engines, except L16, require a slightly rich idle mixture adjustment.
2. Distributor with special advance curve. Ignition timing is retarded about 10° at idle in most cases.
3. Cooling system changes such as larger fan, higher fan speed, and thermostatic fan clutch. This is required to offset the increase in temperature caused by retarded timing at idle. The U20 engine has a thermal modulator valve which gives full distributor vacuum advance at idle if engine temperature becomes excessive.
4. Faster idle speed.
5. Heated air intake on some engines.

The only periodic maintenance required on the air pump system is replacement of the air filter element and adjustment of the drive belt.

Air Pump System Tests and Repairs

Air Pump Test, R&R

To test air pump output pressure:

1. Engine must be at normal operating temperature.
2. Stop engine. Disconnect air supply hose from check valve at exhaust manifold.
3. Start engine. Check pump pressure output at 1,500 rpm. With L16 engine, pressure should be .47″ (12 mm.) Hg or more. With R, U20, or L24 engine, pressure should be .63″ (16 mm.) Hg or more.

To remove and replace air pump:

1. Disconnect hoses from pump.
2. Remove bolt holding pump to belt adjustment arm or adjusting bracket.
3. Unbolt pump from mounting bracket. Remove belt.
4. Remove pump from car.
5. Reverse procedure to install, adjusting the belt to have about 1/2″ play under thumb pressure at the longest span between pulleys.

Check Valve Test, R&R

To test check valve action:

1. Engine must be at normal operating temperature.
2. Stop engine. Disconnect air supply hose from check valve at exhaust manifold.
3. Valve plate inside valve body should be lightly positioned against the valve seat away from the air distributor manifold.
4. Insert a small screwdriver into valve and depress valve plate. Plate should reset freely when released.
5. Start engine. Increase speed to 1,500 rpm and check for exhaust leakage. Valve pulsation or vibration at idle is a normal condition.

To remove and replace check valve:

1. Remove check valve from air gallery pipe, holding the air gallery flange with a wrench.
2. On reinstallation, the proper torque is 65-76 ft. lbs.

Anti-Backfire Valve Test, R&R

To test the anti-backfire valve:

1. Engine must be at normal operating temperature.
2. Disconnect air hose to intake manifold at anti-backfire valve. Plug the hose.
3. Open and close the throttle rapidly. Air flow should be felt at the valve for 1-2 seconds on decleration. If no air flow is felt or flow is felt continuously for more than 2 seconds, replace valve.

To remove anti-backfire valve, simply disconnect the hoses.

Thermal Modulator Test

The thermal modulator is used only on the U20 engine. It provides full vacuum advance at idle if coolant temperature exceeds about 220°F. To test the unit:

1. Remove vacuum tube at distributor.
2. Connect a vacuum gauge to the tube.
3. Run engine until it reaches normal operating temperature.
4. Vacuum should be no more than 4″ (102 mm.) Hg. If it is excessive, the modulator is leaking internally and must be replaced.

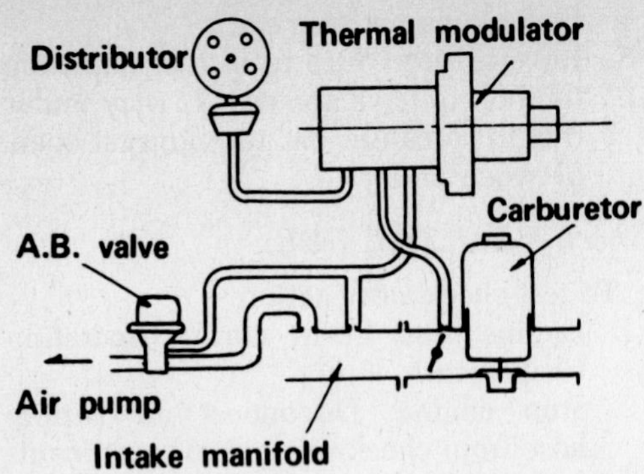

Thermal modulator, U20 engine

Engine Modification System

Engine modifications used on the L520 or L521 pickup with the J engine are:

1. Special carburetor calibrated about three percent leaner than normal for cruise conditions. The idle speed is higher than normal and the extent of idle mixture adjustment is limited. A solenoid valve shuts off the idle fuel system on deceleration. The solenoid valve is regulated by four switches. The throttle valve switch attached to the carburetor is on when the throttle valve is open. The vacuum switch connected to the intake manifold is on when manifold vacuum is less than 22.8″ Hg. The clutch switch on the pedal bracket is on when the pedal is depressed. The neutral switch on the transmission rear extension is on when the transmission is in neutral. If any of these switches are on, the solenoid valve will not shut off the fuel.
2. Heated air intake to prevent icing with the leaner carburetor mixture.
3. Maximum ignition timing retard at low speed and small retard at middle speed ranges. Normal advance is provided at high speeds.

Engine modifications used on the L60 Nissan Patrol with the P engine are:

1. Rochester carburetor with leaner idle and low speed mixture. Faster idle speed.
2. Refined manifold heating for lessened cold starting emissions.
3. Retarded ignition timing at idle and low speed.

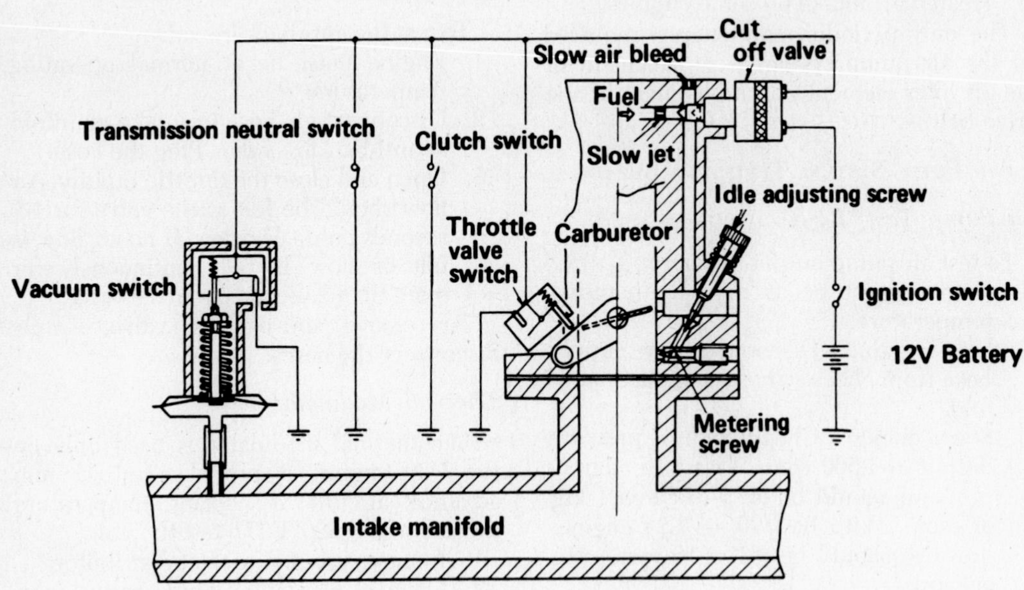

Engine modification system, pickup with J engine

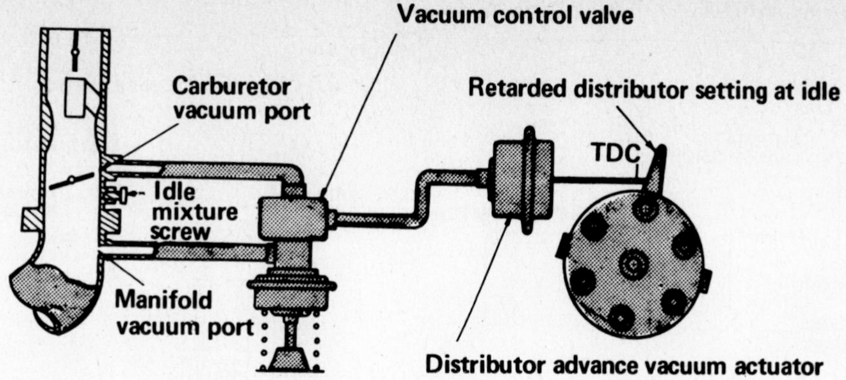

Vacuum control valve which regulates ignition timing, L60 Nissan Patrol with P engine

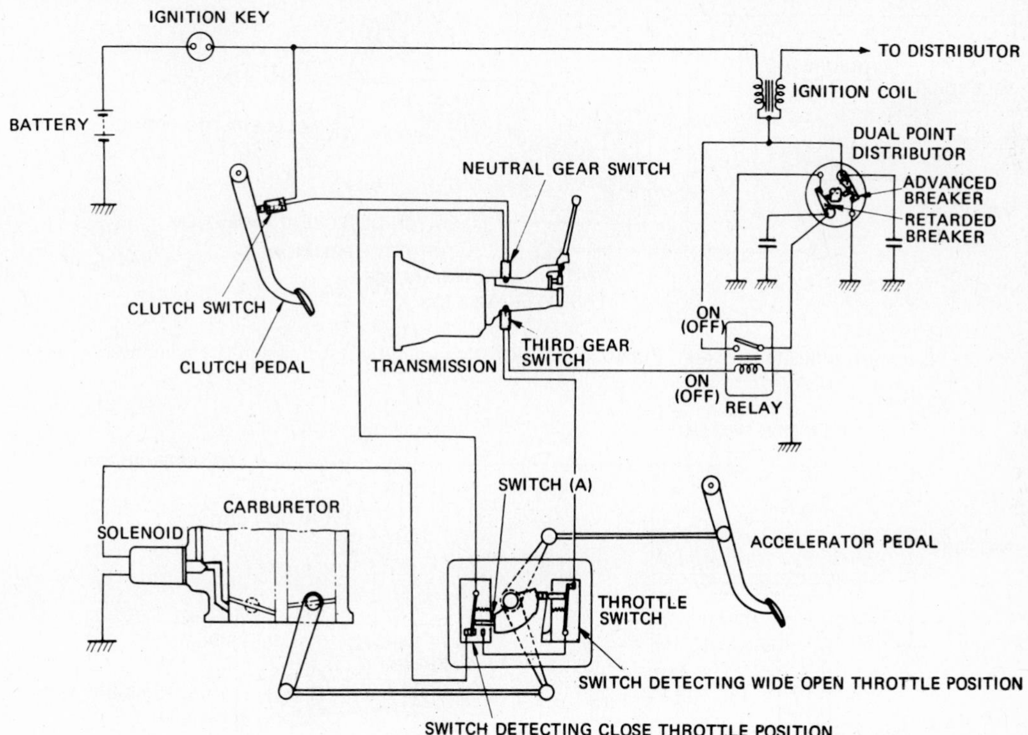

Engine modification system, PL510 and WPL510, manual transmission, L16 engine

4. Vacuum control valve providing advanced ignition timing on deceleration.

Engine modifications used on vehicles with the L16 engine are:

1. Distributor with a secondary set of contact points which are retarded 5°. These secondary points are operational only when cruising or accelerating with a partially open throttle in third gear with manual transmission, or over 13 mph with automatic transmission. A speed sensor is located at the speedometer on automatic transmission models.
2. A solenoid valve in the carburetor opens to supply a lean fuel and air mixture, bypassing the throttle valve, in third gear or over 13 mph as above. The solenoid valve will not open if overridden by a closed throttle switch, a wide open throttle switch, a neutral switch, or a clutch disengaged switch. This arrangement is operational primarily during deceleration, when high intake manifold vacuum is present.

Engine modifications on the SPL311 sports roadster with the R engine consist

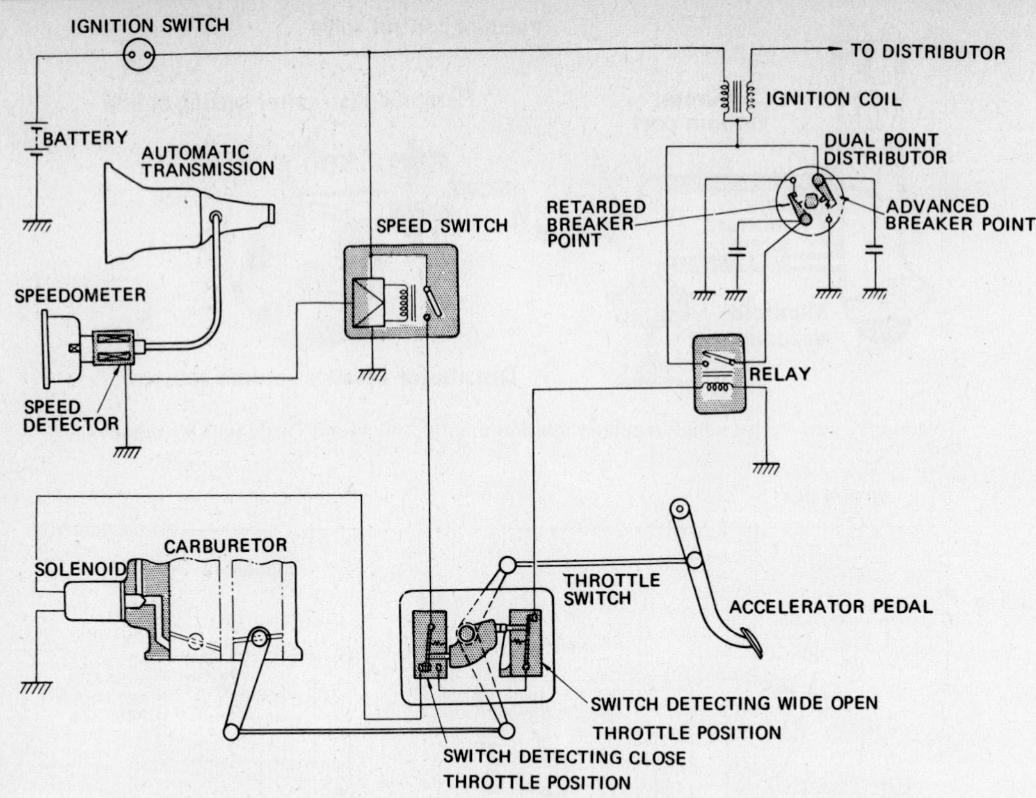

Engine modification system, PL510 and WPL510, automatic transmission, L16 engine

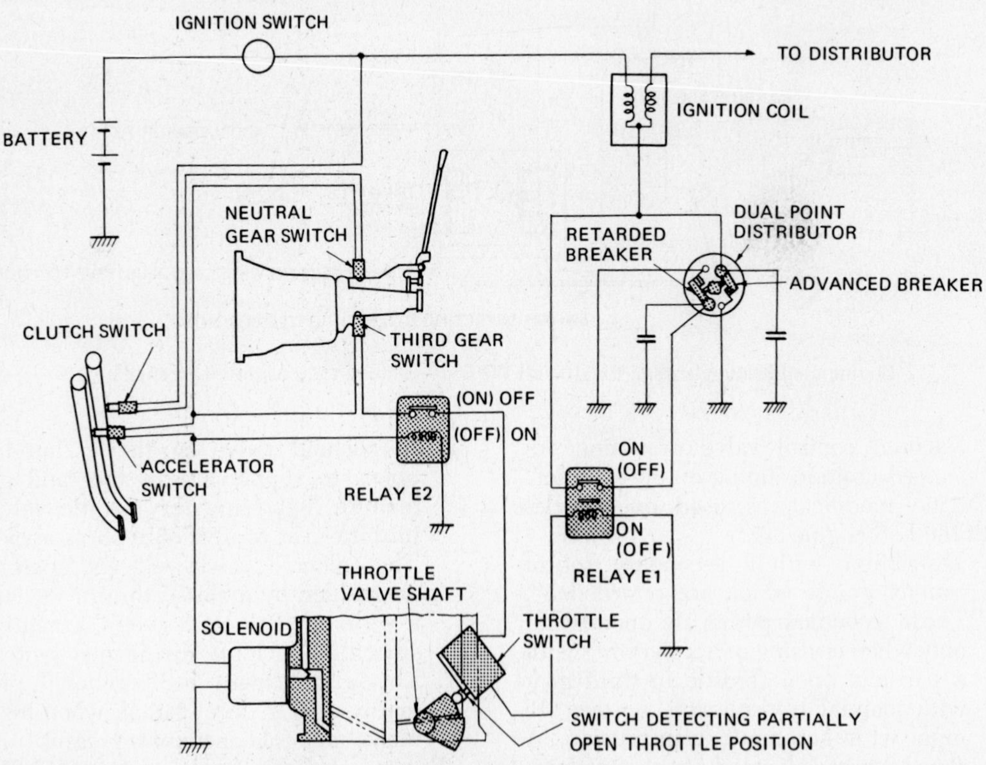

Engine modification system, PL521 pickup, L16 engine

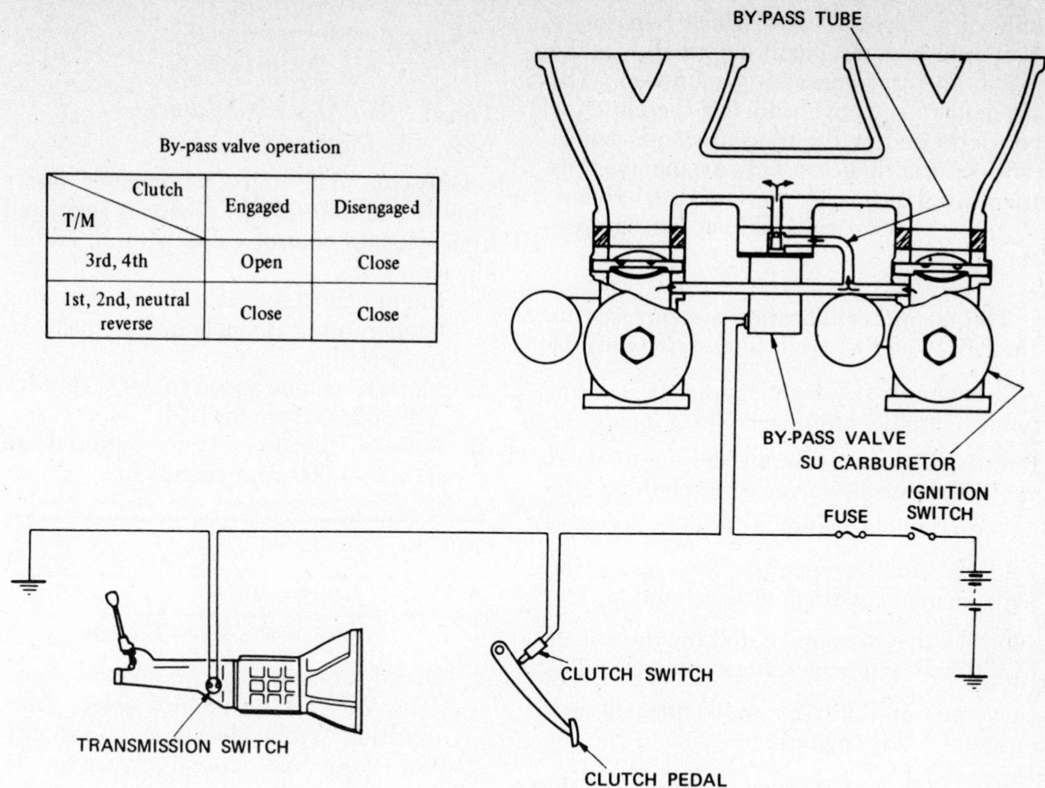

By-pass valve operation

T/M \ Clutch	Engaged	Disengaged
3rd, 4th	Open	Close
1st, 2nd, neutral reverse	Close	Close

Engine modification system, SPL311 sportscar, R engine

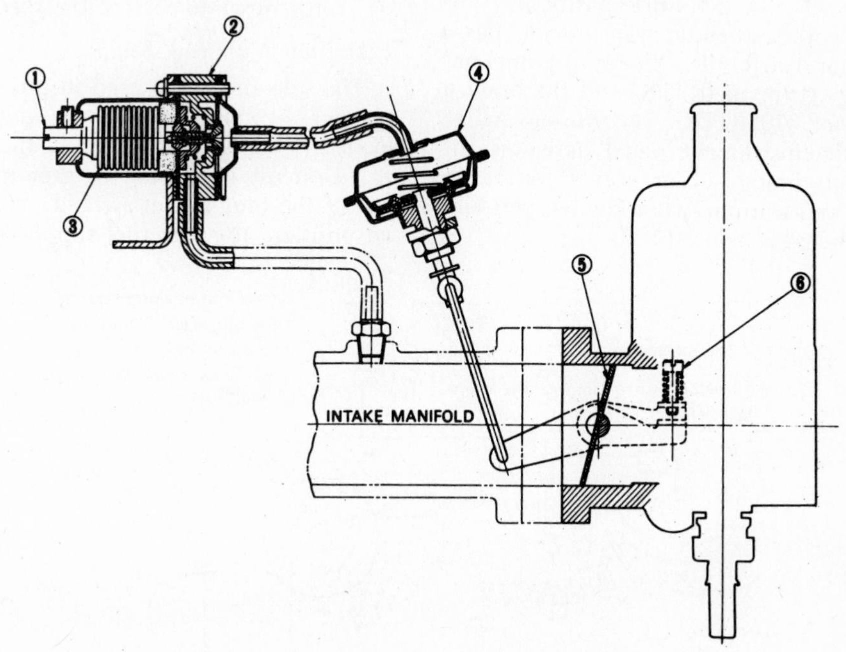

Engine modification system, HLS30 (240 Z) sports coupe, L24 engine

1. Adjusting screw
2. Vacuum control valve
3. Altitude corrector
4. Servo diaphragm
5. Throttle
6. Throttle adjusting screw

only of a solenoid valve which bypasses a lean fuel and air mixture into the intake manifold for improved combustion. The solenoid valve is overridden if the clutch is not depressed or the transmission is not in third or fourth gear. This arrangement is operational primarily during deceleration, when high intake manifold vacuum is present.

The engine modification system used on the LB110 and KLB110 1200 series with the A12 engine is relatively simple. It requires only a throttle positioner which holds the throttle slightly open on deceleration. A vacuum control valve connected to the intake manifold causes a vacuum servo to hold the throttle open slightly during the high vacuum condition of deceleration. The control valve is compensated for the effects of altitude and atmospheric pressure. The carburetor and distributor are specially calibrated for this engine.

The engine modification system for the HLS30 (240 Z) sports coupe with the L24 engine is quite similar to that for the A12 engine, using a vacuum control valve, vacuum servo, and throttle positioner. The HLS30 with automatic transmission has a dual point distributor. One set of points has a timing setting of 0°TDC and the other a setting of 10°BTDC. A thermo-switch under the instrument panel activates the advanced timing set of points for easier starting and warmup when the temperature inside the car is below 40°F.

Engine Modification System Tests, Adjustments

Throttle Positioner Adjustment—L24, A12 Engines

Only the A12 and L24 engines use a throttle positioner. This device is regulated by a vacuum control valve with an adjusting screw.

1. Engine must be at normal operating temperature. A tachometer must be connected.
2. Increase engine speed to 3,000 rpm for A12 or 2,000 rpm for L24.
3. Release throttle. Time required to slow to 1,000 rpm should be:

Engine	*Transmission*	*Time in seconds*
A12	Manual	3.5-4.5
A12	Automatic	2.5-3.5
L24	Manual	3.0

4. To adjust time lag, first loosen lockscrew on vacuum control valve. Turn adjusting screw clockwise to increase time lag, and counterclockwise to decrease.
5. Tighten lockscrew.
6. Repeat Steps 2-5 to check adjustment. If adjustment is correct, engine will settle down to correct idle speed.

Idle Fuel Cutoff—J Engine

The solenoid valve used in this system is opened by electric current and spring-loaded to the closed position. If the solenoid valve circuit is shorted to ground by any one of the four circuit switches being in its on position, the idle fuel supply is cut off.

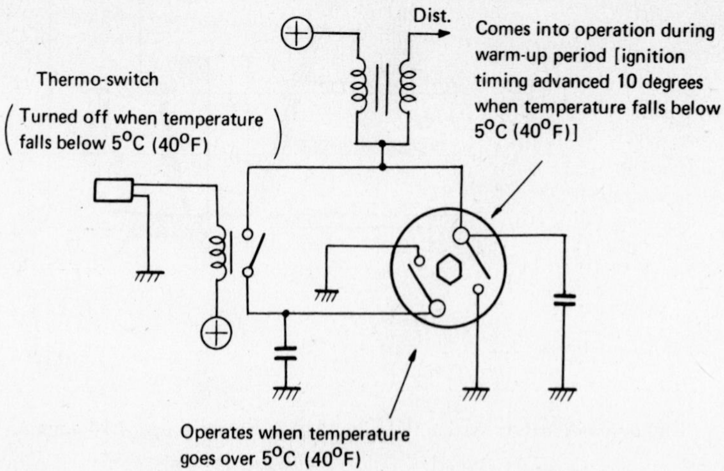

Dual point distributor system, HLS30 automatic

Thus a short circuit or a sticking switch in the circuit will cause the engine to give the symptoms of a clogged idle fuel system. These are stalling, rough idle and low speed operation, but normal operation at higher speeds.

To test the solenoid valve:

1. With the engine running, disconnect the solenoid wires. Valve should cut off fuel and stall engine.
2. Ground one solenoid terminal. Connect battery voltage to the other. Valve should click open.

To test the function of all the system switches, disconnect the wires of the solenoid valve and connect them to a test light. Disconnect the wires of the clutch switch, vacuum switch, and neutral switch.

1. Turn ignition switch on. Do not start engine.
2. Reconnect transmission neutral switch. Check that test light is on with transmission in neutral and off in all other positions. Disconnect transmission neutral switch.
3. Reconnect throttle valve switch. Depress accelerator pedal. Test light should be on. Release accelerator. Light should be off. Disconnect throttle valve switch. Correct adjustment requires that the throttle arm depress the contact arm of the switch about .02″ at rest.
4. Reconnect clutch switch. Check that test light is on when pedal is down and off when pedal is released. Disconnect clutch switch.
5. Reconnect solenoid valve, installing the test lamp in series with the solenoid so that it will indicate when current is supplied. Reconnect transmission neutral switch, throttle valve switch, and vacuum switch but not clutch switch. T-connect a vacuum gauge into the vacuum line between the intake manifold and the vacuum switch. Start and warm up the engine. Depress clutch and shift transmission into gear. Race engine and close throttle rapidly. On deceleration, vacuum should rise and test light should go off. Light should go back on when gauge drops to 20.9-21.6″ Hg.
6. Reconnect all leads.

	IGNITION	ENGINE OR CAR OPERATIONS	Vacuum switch	Throttle valve switch	Clutch switch	Transmission neutral switch	Cut-off valve
PARKING	OFF	None	OFF	OFF	OFF	OFF	OFF
CAR STOPPING	ON	Engine starting & warming up with choke	ON (ON → OFF)	ON	OFF	ON	ON
		Idling	ON	OFF	OFF	ON	ON
		Engine racing	ON → OFF → ON	OFF → ON → OFF	OFF	ON	ON
CRUISING	ON	Car starting & accelerating	ON	ON	OFF → ON → OFF	OFF	ON
		Gear shifting (neutral)	OFF	OFF	ON	ON	ON
		Cruising	ON	ON	OFF	OFF	ON
		Decelerating	OFF	OFF	OFF	OFF	OFF
		Just before car stopping	OFF → ON	OFF	OFF → ON → OFF	ON	ON
REMARK	Electric current	ON	I. manifold V. P.; 20.9 ∿ 21.6 inHg	Throttle valve; opening	Pedal; operating	In neutral	
	Electric current	OFF	I. manifold V. P.; less than 22.8 inHg	Throttle valve; closing	Pedal; not operating	1st, 2nd, 3rd, 4th rev. gear positions	

Switch position chart, pickup, J engine

Distributor Vacuum Control Valve—P Engine

1. The engine must be at normal operating temperature.
2. T-connect a vacuum gauge into the distributor vacuum line.
3. Start engine. Hold speed of 2,000 rpm in neutral for about 5 seconds. Release throttle. When throttle is released, vacuum should increase to above 16" Hg and remain steady for at least 1 second. The vacuum must fall below 4" Hg within 3 seconds after the throttle is released.
4. Turn vacuum control valve adjusting screw counterclockwise to increase the time the vacuum remains above 4" Hg. One turn of the adjusting screw will change the setting by about 1/2" Hg. If adjustment is impossible, replace the valve.

Solenoid Bypass Valve—R Engine

This system uses a solenoid valve which is opened by electric current and spring loaded to the closed position. To test system operation:

1. Switch ignition on.
2. Shift into third or fourth gear.
3. Release clutch pedal slowly. When the clutch switch reaches its closed position, the bypass valve should make an audible click.
4. The operation of the two individual switches can be tested by use of a test light or an ohmmeter. The clutch switch should be closed when the pedal is released. The transmission switch should be closed only in third and fourth gears.

Solenoid Bypass Valve—L16 Engine With Manual Transmission

The solenoid valve is opened by electric current and spring-loaded to the closed position. To test system operation:

1. Disconnect solenoid valve ground lead (black wire). Connect an ammeter between the lead terminal and ground. A test light can also be used; but this only indicates whether current is present or not, while an ammeter measures the amount of current.
2. Switch ignition on.
3. With throttle closed, transmission in gear, and clutch pedal released, ammeter should read about .4 amps. In any other condition, ammeter should read 0 amps.
4. If ammeter reading is not as specified, check each switch and adjust or replace it as necessary. On throttle valve switch, clearance between cam and microswitch body should be .032". Refer to the switch position charts for details.

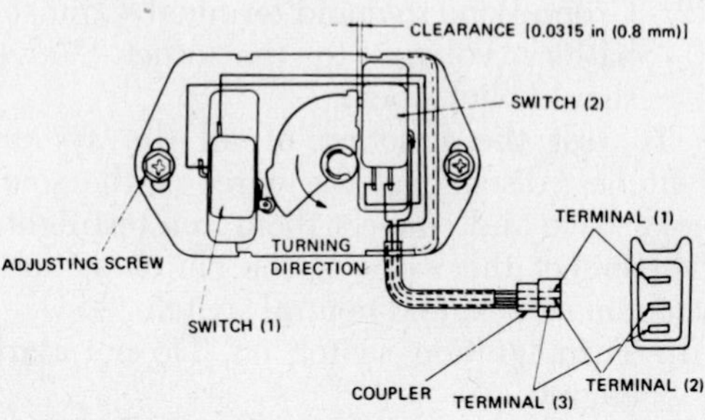

Throttle valve switch, L16 engine, manual transmission

5. Remove ammeter and replace solenoid valve ground lead. Start engine. Connect a jumper wire between the battery output terminal and the solenoid input terminal. The engine speed should rise to about 1,100 rpm.
6. If engine speed does not rise, check solenoid operation.
7. Reconnect leads in their normal locations.

Solenoid Bypass Valve—L16 Engine With Automatic Transmission

1. Disconnect solenoid valve ground lead (black wire). Connect an ammeter between the lead terminal and ground. A test light can also be used; but this only indicates whether current is present or not, while an ammeter measures the amount of current.
2. When speed is over 13 mph with closed throttle, ammeter should read about .4 amps. Below 13 mph or with throttle open, ammeter should read 0 amps.
3. If ammeter reading is not as specified, check each switch and adjust or replace it as necessary. Refer to the switch position charts for details.
4. Remove ammeter and replace solenoid valve ground lead. Start engine. Connect a jumper wire between the battery output terminal and the solenoid

Engine or vehicle operations	Clutch switch	Neutral gear switch	Throttle switch		Third gear switch	Relay	Solenoid valve current	Spark timing	
			Switch detecting close throttle position	Switch detecting wide open throttle position				"Advanced"	"Retarded"
Engine starting & warming up with choke	ON	OFF	OFF	ON	OFF	OFF	OFF	O	——
Engine starting without choke (Hot restarting)	ON	OFF	ON	ON	OFF	OFF	OFF	O	——
Idling	ON	OFF	ON	ON	OFF	OFF	OFF	O	——
Engine racing	ON	OFF	ON →OFF →ON	ON or ON →OFF →ON	OFF	OFF	OFF	O	——
Cruising or accelerating in 3rd gear with partially open throttle	ON	ON	OFF	ON	ON	ON	OFF	——	O
Cruising or accelerating in 1st, 2nd and 4th gear with partially open throttle	ON	ON	OFF	ON	OFF	OFF	OFF	O	——
Cruising or accelerating with wide open throttle	ON	ON	OFF	OFF	ON (3rd) or OFF (1st, 2nd, 4th)	OFF	OFF	O	——
Coasting	ON	ON	ON	ON	ON (3rd) or OFF (1st, 2nd, 4th)	OFF	ON	O	——
Remarks	When the clutch pedal is depressed, this switch is "OFF". And when the pedal is released, the switch is "ON".	When the shift lever is in neutral gear position, this switch is "OFF". And when the lever is in another gear position, the switch is "ON".	When the throttle valve is nearly closed, this switch is "ON". And when the valve is even slightly opened the switch is "OFF".	When the throttle valve is partially opened, this switch is "ON". And when the valve is wide open, the switch is "OFF".	When the shift lever is in 3rd gear, this switch is "ON". And when the lever is in another gear position, the switch is "OFF".	When the relay is "ON", the primary ignition circuit from the ignition coil to "retarded" breaker point is closed, so the "retarded" spark timing is provided.	When the solenoid valve current is "ON", the fuel and air passage is opened and excessive mixture is supplied to reduce HC emission.	When the "retarded" spark timing is provided, HC emission is reduced.	

Switch position chart, PL510 and WPL510, manual transmission, L16 engine

Engine or vehicle operations	Neutral gear switch	Clutch switch	Accelerator switch (Detecting close throttle position)	Relay E_2	Third gear switch	Throttle switch (Detecting wide open throttle position)	Relay E_1	Solenoid valve current	Spark timing	
									"Advanced"	"Retarded"
Engine starting & warming up with choke	OFF	ON	OFF	ON	OFF	ON	OFF	OFF	o	—
Engine starting without choke (Hot restarting)	OFF	ON	ON	ON	OFF	ON	OFF	OFF	o	—
Idling	OFF	ON	ON	ON	OFF	ON	OFF	OFF	o	—
Engine racing	OFF	ON	ON → OFF → ON	ON	OFF	ON or ON → OFF → ON	OFF	OFF	o	—
Cruising or accelerating in 3rd gear with the partially open throttle	ON	ON	OFF	ON	ON	ON	ON	OFF	—	o
Cruising or accelerating in 1st, 2nd and 4th gear with partially open throttle	ON	ON	OFF	ON	OFF	ON	OFF	OFF	o	—
Cruising or accelerating with wide open throttle	ON	ON	OFF	ON	ON (3rd) or OFF (1st, 2nd, 4th)	OFF	OFF	OFF	o	—
Coasting	ON	ON	ON	OFF	ON (3rd) or OFF (1st, 2nd, 4th)	ON	OFF	ON	o	—
Remarks	When the shift lever is in neutral gear position, this switch if "OFF". And when the lever is in ano another gear position, the switch is "ON".	When the clutch pedal is depressed, this switch is "OFF". And when the pedal is released, the switch is "ON".	When the accelerator pedal is "OFF". And when the pedal is released, the switch is "ON".	This relay has the characteristic of "normal close".	When the shift lever is in 3rd gear, this switch is "ON". And when the lever is in another gear position, the switch is "OFF".	When the throttle valve is partially opened, this switch is "ON". And when the valve is wide open, the switch is "OFF".	When the relay E_1 is "ON", the primary ignition circuit from the ignition coil to "retarded" breaker point is closed. So the "retarded" spark timing is provided.	When the solenoid valve current is "ON", the fuel and air passage is opened and excessive mixture is supplied to reduce HC emission.	When the "retarded" spark timing is provided, HC emission is reduced.	

Switch position chart, PL521 pickup, L16 engine

Engine or vehicle operations	Speed switch	Throttle switch		Relay	Solenoid valve current	Spark timing	
		Switch detecting close throttle position	Switch detecting wide open throttle position			"Advanced"	"Retarded"
Engine starting & warming up with choke	OFF	OFF	ON	OFF	OFF	O	——
Engine starting without choke (Hot restarting)	OFF	ON	ON	OFF	OFF	O	——
Idling	OFF	ON	ON	OFF	OFF	O	——
Engine racing	OFF	ON → OFF → ON	ON or ON → OFF → ON	OFF	OFF	O	——
Cruising or accelerating over 13 mph with partially open throttle	ON	OFF	ON	ON	OFF	——	O
Cruising or accelerating under 13 mph with partially open throttle	OFF	OFF	ON	OFF	OFF	O	——
Cruising or accelerating with wide open throttle	ON (over 13 mph) or OFF (under 13 mph)	OFF	OFF	OFF	OFF	O	——
Coasting	ON (over 13 mph) or OFF (under 13 mph)	ON	ON	OFF	ON (over 13 mph) or OFF (under 13 mph)	O	——
Remarks	When the car speed is under 13 mph, this switch is "OFF". And when the speed is over 13 mph, the switch is "ON".	When the throttle valve is nearly closed, this switch is "ON". And when the valve is even slightly opened the switch is "OFF".	When the throttle valve is partially opened, this switch is "ON". And when the valve is widely opened, the switch is "OFF".	When the relay is "ON", the primary ignition circuit from ignition coil to "retarded" breaker point is closed, so the "retarded" spark timing is provided	When the solenoid valve current is "ON", the fuel and air passage is opened and excessive mixture is supplied to reduce HC emission.	When the "retarded" spark timing is provided, HC emission is reduced.	

Switch position chart, PL510 and WP510, automatic transmission, L16 engine

input terminal. The engine speed should rise to about 1,100 rpm.

5. If engine speed does not rise, check solenoid operation.
6. Reconnect leads in their normal locations.

Dual Point Distributor—L16 Engine With Manual Transmission

1. Disconnect lead wires from retarded and advanced terminals on distributor. Connect an ammeter between the lead wire for the retarded points and ground.
2. Switch ignition on.
3. With throttle partially open, shift lever in third gear, and clutch pedal released, ammeter should indicate about 3 amps.
4. With throttle valve wide open or nearly closed, or shift lever in some position other than third, or clutch pedal depressed, ammeter should indicate 0 amps.
5. If ammeter reads 0 amps in Step 3, disconnect terminals of relay (relay E1 on PL521) and measure voltage between terminal with No. 1 punch mark and ground. If voltage is about 12 volts, replace relay. If voltage is 0 volts, check each switch and wiring.
6. If ammeter reads 3 amps in Step 4, check clutch switch, neutral switch, and third gear switch. On PL510 and WPL510, check throttle switch. On PL521, check throttle switch and accelrator switch. Refer to the switch position charts for details.

Dual Point Distributor—L16 Engine With Automatic Transmission

1. Disconnect lead wire of retarded side of distributor. Connect an ammeter between the lead wire and the retarded side terminal.
2. Start engine and drive vehicle.
3. Ammeter should not read 0 amps when

speed is over 13 mph with a partially open throttle. Otherwise, ammeter should read 0 amps.
4. If ammeter reading is not as specified, check speed switch, throttle switch, speed detector, and relay. Refer to the switch position charts for details.

Fuel Vapor Control System

The fuel vapor control system is used on all vehicles sold in the U.S., starting 1970. It has four major components:

1. A sealed gas tank filler cap to prevent vapors from escaping at this point.
2. A vapor separator which returns liquid fuel to the fuel tank, but allows vapors to pass into the system.
3. A vapor vent line connecting the vapor separator to a flow guide valve.
4. A flow guide valve which allows air into the fuel tank and prevents vapors from the crankcase ventilation system from passing into the vapor vent line and fuel tank.

When the engine is not running, fuel vapors accumulate in the fuel tank, vapor separator, and vapor vent line. When the vapor pressure exceeds .4″ (10 mm.) Hg, the flow guide valve opens to allow the vapors to pass into the crankcase ventilation system. Fuel vapors are thus accumulated in the crankcase. When the engine starts, the vapors are disposed of by the crankcase ventilation system. When enough

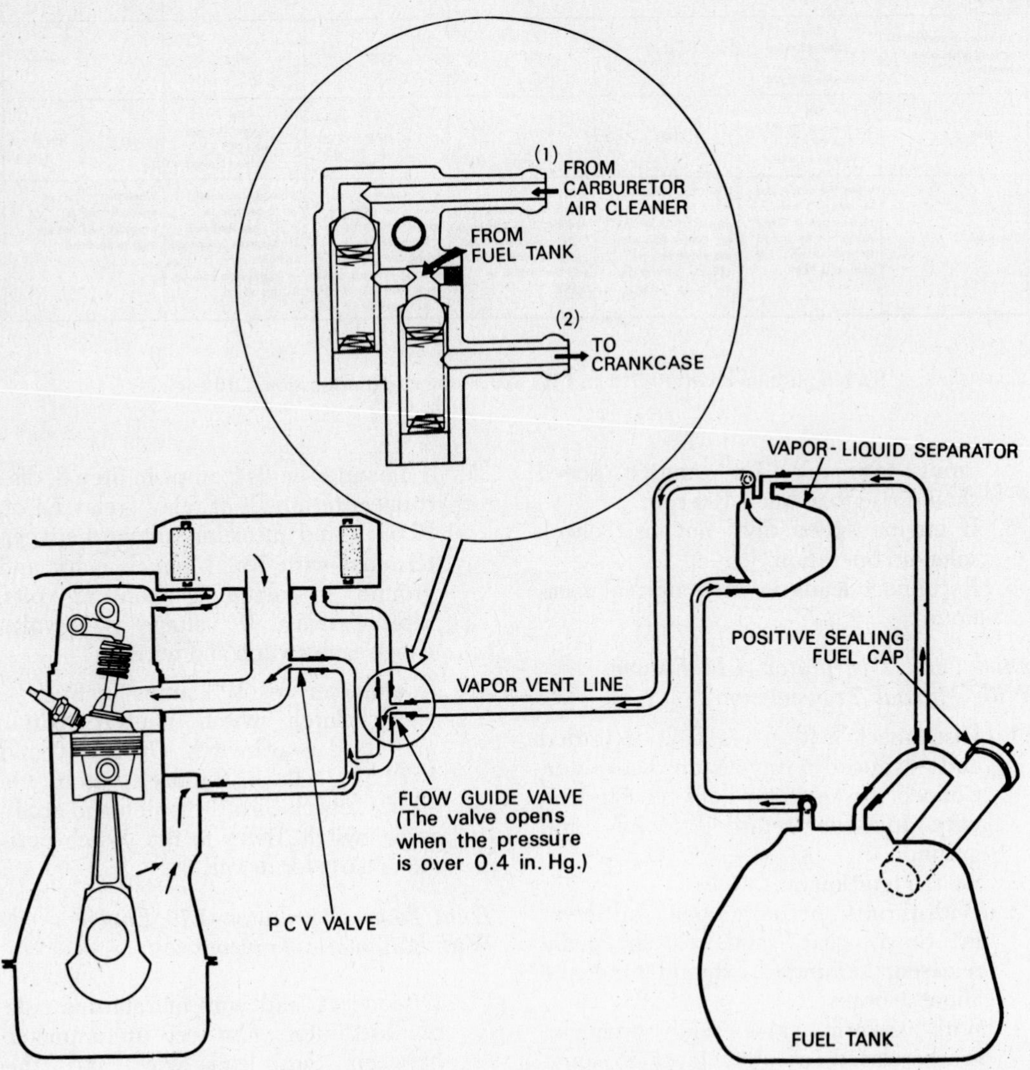

Fuel vapor control system, engines with downdraft carburetor

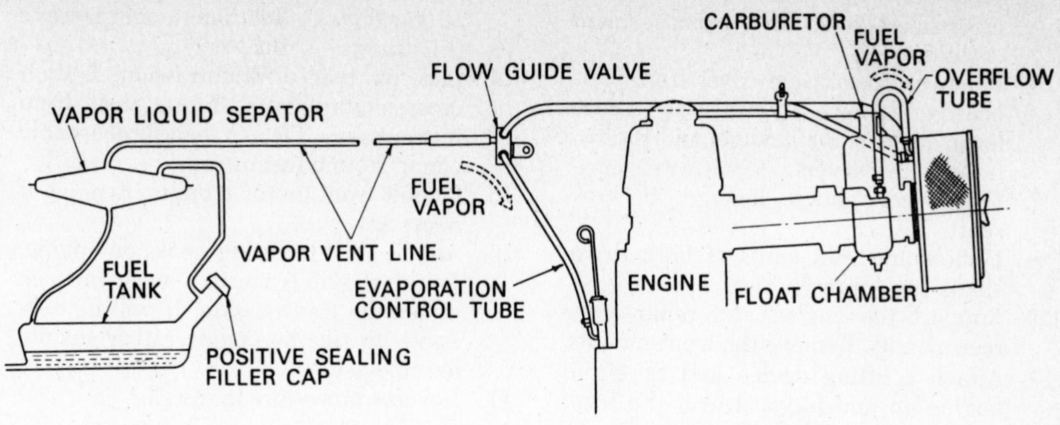

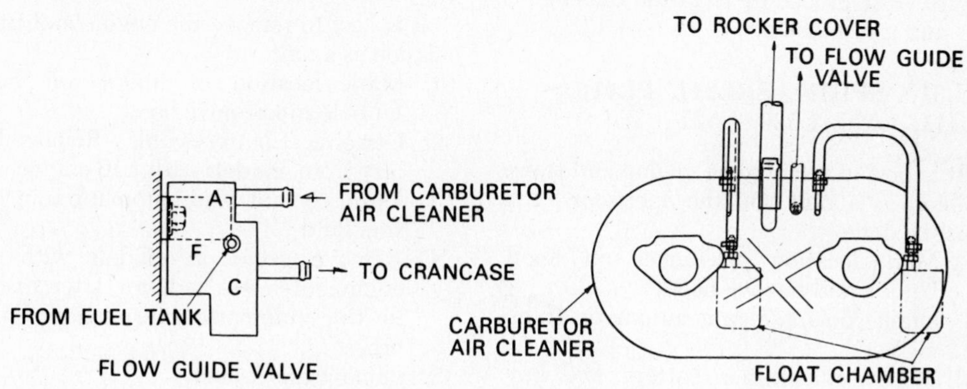

Fuel vapor control system, engines with SU type carburetors

fuel has been used to create a slight vacuum in the fuel tank and fuel vapor control system, the flow guide valve opens to let fresh air from the carburetor air cleaner into the tank.

On engines with SU type carburetors, float bowl vapors are routed through the float bowl overflow tubes to the carburetor air cleaner.

Flow Guide Valve Test

The flow guide valve is mounted in the engine compartment. The valve fittings are marked A, from air cleaner; F, from fuel tank; and C, to crankcase.

1. Blow into the F fitting. Air should come out the C fitting.
2. Blow into the C fitting. Air should not escape.
3. Blow into the A fitting. Air should come out either the F or C fitting, or both.
4. Replace valve if defective.

ENGINE R&R

Nissan Patrol (L60)

The engine, transmission, and transfer case should be removed as a unit.

1. Drain coolant. Open hood fully and rest on windshield.
2. Disconnect front lights at junction block.
3. Disconnect main wiring harness from voltage regulator and junction block on left hood ledge.
4. Disconnect radiator hoses. Unbolt radiator panel and radiator from fenders. Remove radiator and panel as an assembly.
5. Disconnect:
   A. distributor primary wire,
   B. coil high tension wire,
   C. fuel line from fuel pump,
   D. throttle and choke controls from carburetor, and

E. exhaust pipe from exhaust manifold.
6. Remove transmission cover from floorboards. Remove transmission control lever, hand brake linkage, and the two transfer case levers.
7. Disconnect clutch linkage at cross shaft.
8. Unbolt universal joints of both driveshafts from transfer case.
9. Support the engine and remove the rear mounts. Remove the front mounts.
10. Attach a lifting device and raise the engine up and forward over the front crossmember. The chassis may be rolled back to free the engine.
11. Reverse procedure to install the engine and transmission.

SPL310, SPL311, SRL311, PL410, PL411, L320, L520, L521

It is best to remove the engine and transmission as a unit. On the sportscars, this must be done.

1. Mark location of hinges on hood. Unbolt and remove hood.
2. Drain coolant. Drain automatic transmission.
3. Remove air cleaner, battery, and tray.
4. Remove radiator hoses. Remove radiator. On automatic transmission, disconnect oil cooler lines from bottom of radiator, remove oil filler tube and cooler lines from transmission case, and disconnect shift linkage.
5. Disconnect heater hoses.
6. Disconnect fuel line(s) at pump.
7. Disconnect throttle and choke linkage.
8. Remove all electrical connections from ignition coil, distributor, starter, alternator (generator), and oil pressure and water temperature sending units.
9. Remove clutch linkage or slave cylinder. Do not disconnect hydraulic line.
10. Disconnect speedometer cable and reverse switch from transmission. Disconnect neutral start switch on automatic transmission.
11. Remove shift lever from floorshift units. Disconnect column shift linkage.
12. Remove exhaust pipe from manifold. On sportscars, remove manifold from engine first, detach bottom of left rear shock absorber so exhaust system can be pulled to one side, then separate manifold and exhaust pipe.
13. Mark relationship of driveshaft flanges at rear end. Unbolt flanges and remove driveshaft.
14. Jack up rear of transmission. Unbolt crossmember from frame, then from transmission. Detach handbrake cable clamp from transmission.
15. Unbolt front motor mounts. Remove if necessary.
16. Attach hoist to lifting hooks on engine. As the engine is hoisted, lower the jack under the transmission. It will be necessary to tilt the engine rather steeply to remove it.
17. Reverse procedure to install.

PL510, WPL510, PL521, HLS30, LB110, KLB110

It is best to remove the engine and transmission as a unit.

1. Mark location of hinges on hood. Unbolt and remove hood.
2. Disconnect battery cables. Remove battery from models with L16 engine.
3. Drain coolant and automatic transmission fluid.
4. Remove grille on models with L16 engine. Remove radiator after disconnecting automatic transmission coolant tubes.
5. Remove air cleaner.
6. Remove fan and pulley from L16 engine.
7. Disconnect:
   a. water temperature gauge wire,
   b. oil pressure sending unit wire,
   c. ignition distributor primary wire,
   d. starter motor connections,
   e. fuel hose,
   f. alternator leads,
   g. heater hoses, and
   h. throttle and choke connections.
8. Disconnect power brake booster hose from engine.
9. Remove clutch operating cylinder and return spring.
10. Disconnect speedometer cable from transmission. Disconnect backup light switch and any other wiring or attachments to transmission.
11. Disconnect column shift linkage. Remove floorshift lever. On LB110 and KLB110, remove boot, withdraw lock pin, and remove lever from inside car.
12. Detach exhaust pipe from exhaust manifold. Remove front section of exhaust system.
13. Mark relationship of driveshaft flanges and remove driveshaft.

14. Place a jack under the transmission. Remove rear crossmember. On LB110 and KLB110, remove the rear engine mounting nuts.
15. Attach a hoist to the lifting hooks on the engine (at either end of the cylinder head). Support engine.
16. Unbolt front engine mounts. Tilt the engine by lowering the jack under the transmission and raising the hoist.
17. Reverse procedure to install.

CYLINDER HEAD

Cylinder Head R&R

NOTE: To prevent distortion or warping of the cylinder head, allow the engine to cool completely before removing the head bolts.

P, E1, G, J, R, A12 Overhead Valve Engines

To remove the cylinder head on OHV engines:

1. Drain coolant.
2. Disconnect battery ground cable.
3. Remove upper radiator hose. Remove water outlet elbow and thermostat.
4. Remove air cleaner, carburetor, rocker arm cover, and both manifolds.
5. Remove spark plugs.
6. Disconnect temperature gauge connection.
7. On A12, remove head bolts and remove head and rocker arm assembly together. On all other OHV engines, the rocker arm assembly is held down by four of the head bolts and must be removed before the cylinder head. There is a special locking plate under the right rear rocker stud nut. Rap the head with a mallet to loosen it from the block. Remove the head and discard the gasket.
8. Remove the pushrods, keeping them in order.

To replace the cylinder head on OHV engines:

1. Check that head and block surfaces are clean. Check the cylinder head surface with a straightedge and a feeler gauge for flatness. If the head is warped more than .003″, it must be trued. If this is not done, there will probably be a leak. The block surface should also be checked in the same way. If the block is warped more than .003″, it must be trued.

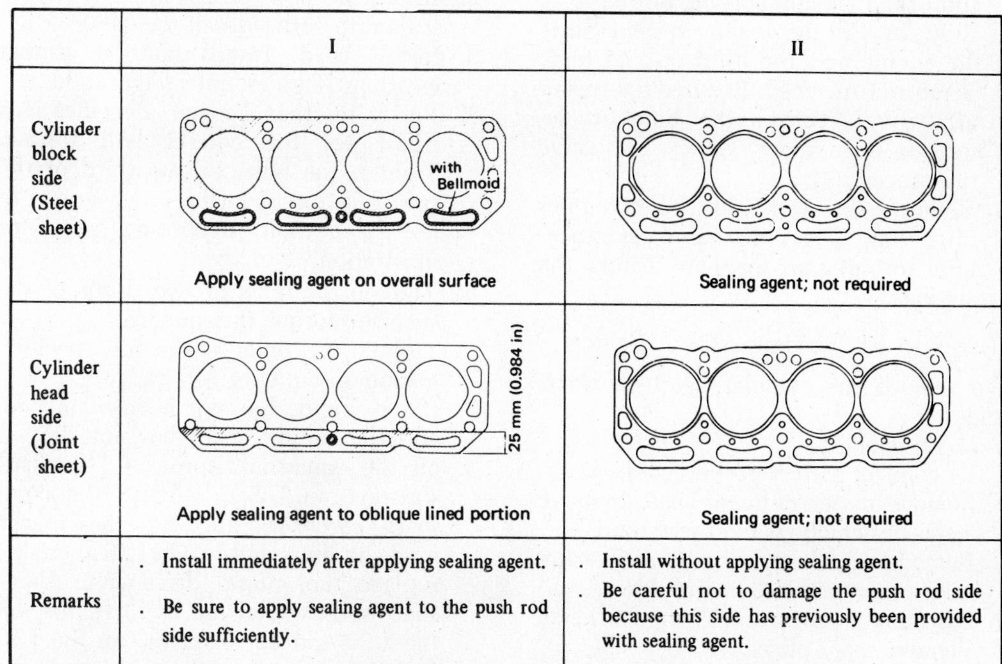

	I	II
Cylinder block side (Steel sheet)	with Bellmoid Apply sealing agent on overall surface	Sealing agent; not required
Cylinder head side (Joint sheet)	25 mm (0.984 in) Apply sealing agent to oblique lined portion	Sealing agent; not required
Remarks	. Install immediately after applying sealing agent. . Be sure to apply sealing agent to the push rod side sufficiently.	. Install without applying sealing agent. . Be careful not to damage the push rod side because this side has previously been provided with sealing agent.

Two types of head gasket which will both fit A12 engine. Note that gasket I requires sealant. Note that gasket II requires no sealant and has two additional triangular cooling passages. Be sure to match the gasket to both the head and the block before installation. If the proper gasket is not installed, leakage or immediate overheating will result.

2. Install a new head gasket. Most gaskets have a TOP marking. Make sure that the proper head gasket is used on the A12 so that no water passages are blocked off.
3. Install the head. Install the pushrods in their original locations. Install the rocker arm assembly. Loosen the rocker arm adjusting screws to prevent bending pushrods when tightening the head bolts. Tighten the head bolts finger tight. On A12, the single bolt marked T must go in the No. 1 position on the center right side of the engine.
4. Refer to the Torque Specifications Chart for the correct head bolt torque. Tighten the bolts to one third of the specified torque in the order shown in the head bolt tightening sequence illustration. On A12, torque the rocker arm mounting bolts to 15-18 ft. lbs.
5. Tighten the bolts to two thirds of the specified torque in sequence.
6. Tighten the bolts to the full specified torque in sequence.
7. Adjust the valves as described under Valve Train. If no cold setting is given, adjust the valves to the normal hot setting.
8. Reassemble the engine. On A12, intake and exhaust manifold bolt torque is 7-10 ft. lbs. Fill the cooling system. Start the engine and run until normal temperature is reached. Remove the rocker arm cover. Torque the bolts in sequence once more. Check the valve clearances.
9. Retorque the head bolts after 600 miles of driving. Check the valve clearances after torquing, as this may disturb the settings.

U20, L16, L24 Overhead Cam Engines

To remove the cylinder head on OHC engines:

1. Drain coolant.
2. Disconnect battery ground cable.
3. Remove upper radiator hose. Remove water outlet elbow and thermostat.
4. Remove air cleaner, carburetor, camshaft cover, and both manifolds.
5. Disconnect temperature gauge at head.
6. Remove spark plugs.
7. Mark the relationship between the camshaft, camshaft sprocket, and timing chain. Remove camshaft sprocket. On L16 and L24, a wooden wedge may be used to prevent the timing chain from slipping off the crankshaft sprocket. If this tool is not available, support the timing chain in some way so that the relationship of the crankshaft sprocket and the timing chain will be unchanged. On U20, unbolt camshaft sprocket, remove cylinder head front cover plate and upper chain tensioner. Support camshaft sprocket to chain guide with a screw. The camshaft sprocket and chain will be left in place when the head is removed.
8. Remove cylinder head front plate and chain tensioner on L16 and L24.
9. Unbolt the cylinder head from the block and the front timing cover. The L16 and L24 use three different size head bolts. Note the original locations of these bolts.

To replace the cylinder head on OHC engines:

1. Check that the head and block surfaces are clean. Check the cylinder head surface for flatness. If the head is warped more than .003″, it must be trued. If this is not done, there will probably be a leak. The block surface should also be checked. If the block is warped more than .003″, it must be trued.
2. Install the new gasket. On L16, apply sealant to both sides of the gasket.
3. Install head. Install bolts in proper locations. Tighten bolts finger tight.
4. Refer to the Torque Specifications Chart for the correct bolt torque. Tighten the bolts to one third of the specified torque in the order shown in the head bolt tightening sequence illustration.
5. Tighten the bolts to two thirds of the specified torque in sequence.
6. Tighten the bolts to the full specified torque in sequence.
7. If the engine has not been disturbed, and the timing chain has not slipped off the crankshaft sprocket (jackshaft sprocket on U20), reinstall the camshaft sprocket, aligning the marks made on disassembly. On L16 and L24, replace fuel pump drive cam. Camshaft sprocket torque is 13 ft. lbs. on the U20 and 36-43 ft. lbs. on the L16 and L24. If the relationship of the crankshaft, camshaft, and timing chain has been disturbed, correct this relationship as described later under Camshaft and Timing Chain.

8. Adjust the valves as described under Valve Train. If no cold setting is given, adjust the valves to the normal hot setting.
9. Reassemble the engine. On U20, intake and exhaust manifold bolt torque is 10-20 ft. lbs. Fill the cooling system. Start the engine and run until normal temperature is reached. Remove the camshaft cover. Torque the bolts in sequence once more. Check the valve clearances.
10. Retorque the head bolts after 600 miles of driving.

VALVE TRAIN

Valve Adjustment

Remove the rocker arm or camshaft cover. Both valves for each cylinder may be adjusted while they are fully closed, on the compression stroke. After the valves have closed, turn the engine another quarter turn to insure that the cam lobes are not exerting pressure on the valves. This can readily be seen on overhead camshaft engines. Loosen the locknuts. Insert the proper size feeler gauge between the valve stem and rocker arm on overhead valve engines, or between the cam lobe and cam follower on overhead cam engines. Valve clearance figures are given in the Tune-Up Specifications Chart. Tighten the adjusting screw until there is a slight drag on the feeler gauge. Tighten the locknut and recheck the clearance. After adjusting the valves for the first cylinder, turn the engine in the normal direction of rotation until the valves for the next cylinder in the firing order close.

Adjusting valve clearances on L24 overhead cam engine

Repeat the adjusting procedure until all valves have been adjusted. Install a new gasket and replace the rocker arm or camshaft cover.

NOTE: Do not run engine with rocker arm or camshaft cover removed. Do not adjust valves with engine running.

Valve Guide Replacement

When replacing cylinder head valve guides, be sure that the guide height above the top of the cylinder head surface is as follows.

Engine	*Guide height*
E1, J	.610-626"
U20	.508-.516"
L16, L24	.409-.417"
A12	.709"
P, G, R	not specified

CAMSHAFT AND TIMING CHAIN

Timing Chain Cover R&R, Oil Seal Replacement

E1, G, J, R, A12 Overhead Valve Engines

1. Remove radiator. Loosen alternator (generator) adjustment and remove belt. Loosen air pump adjustment and remove belt on engines with air pump system.
2. Remove fan and/or water pump. Water pump should be removed from A12 engine.
3. Bend back lock tab from crankshaft pulley nut. Remove nut by affixing a heavy wrench and rapping the wrench with a hammer. The nut must be unscrewed in the opposite direction of normal engine rotation. Pull off pulley.
4. On A12, it is recommended that the oil pan be removed or loosened before the front cover is removed.
5. Unbolt and remove timing chain cover.
6. Replace the crankshaft oil seal in the cover. Most models use a felt seal.
7. Reverse procedure to install, using new gaskets. Apply sealant to both sides of timing cover gasket. On A12 engine, front cover bolt torque is 4 ft. lbs., water pump bolt torque is 7-10 ft. lbs., and oil pan bolt torque is 4 ft. lbs.

U20, L16, L24 Overhead Cam Engines

While it may be possible to perform this operation with the engine in place, Datsun recommends that the engine be removed from the vehicle.

1. Loosen and remove alternator and air pump belts. Remove alternator and air pump.
2. Remove distributor on L16 and L24. Remove cylinder head. This may not be necessary on some engines.
3. Remove fan and pulley.
4. Bend back lock tab from crankshaft pulley nut. Remove nut by affixing a heavy wrench and rapping the wrench with a hammer. The nut must be unscrewed in the opposite direction of normal engine rotation.
5. Remove water pump.
6. Remove oil pan.
7. Remove timing chain cover.
8. Remove old crankshaft oil seal from cover. Press in new seal.
9. Reverse procedure to install, applying sealant to both sides of cover gasket. On L16, check that height difference between cylinder block upper surface and front cover upper surface is less than .006″. Oil pan bolt torque is 4-5 ft. lbs. for all three engines.

Timing Chain and Camshaft R&R

E1, G, J, R, A12 Overhead Valve Engines

It is recommended that this operation be done with the engine removed from the vehicle.

1. Remove timing chain cover.
2. Unbolt and remove chain tensioner.
3. Remove camshaft sprocket retaining bolt.
4. Pull off the camshaft sprocket, easing off the crankshaft sprocket at the same time. Remove both sprockets and chain as an assembly. Be careful not to lose the shims and oil slinger from behind the crankshaft sprocket.
5. Remove distributor, distributor drive spindle, pushrods, and valve lifters.

NOTE: On G, R, and A12, the lifters cannot be removed until the camshaft has been removed.

Remove oil pump and pump driveshaft.

6. Remove engine front mounting plate on El and J.
7. Unbolt and remove camshaft locating plate.
8. Remove camshaft carefully. On G, R, and A12, this will be easier if the block is inverted to prevent the lifters from falling down.
9. Camshaft bearings can be pressed out and replaced. They are available in undersizes, should it be necessary to regrind the camshaft journals.
10. Reinstall camshaft. If locating plate has an oil hole, it should be to the right of the engine. On A12, locating plate is marked with the word LOWER and an arrow. A12 locating plate bolt torque is 3-4 ft. lbs. Be careful to engage drive pin in rear end of camshaft with slot in oil pump driveshaft.
11. Camshaft end-play can be measured after temporarily replacing the camshaft sprocket and securing bolt.

Engine	*Camshaft end-play*
P, E1, J	.003-.007″
G, R	.002-.011″
A12	.001-.003″

If end-play is excessive, replace locating plate. They are available in several sizes.

12. On El and J, replace engine front mounting plate.
13. If crankshaft or camshaft has been replaced, install sprockets temporarily and check that they are parallel. Adjust by shimming under crankshaft sprocket.
14. Assemble sprockets and chain, aligning as illustrated.

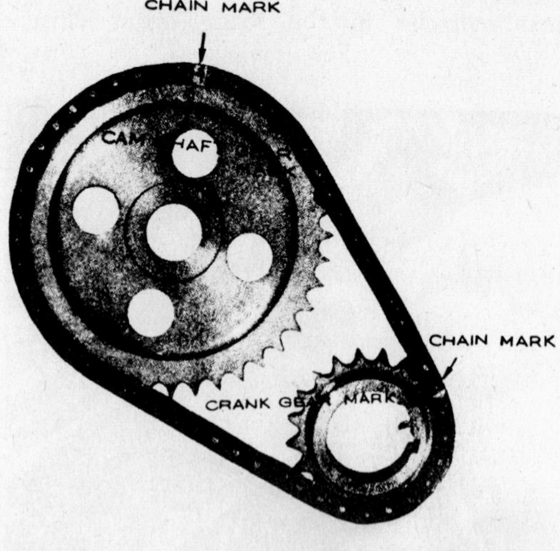

Assembly of sprockets and timing chain, G, J, and R engines

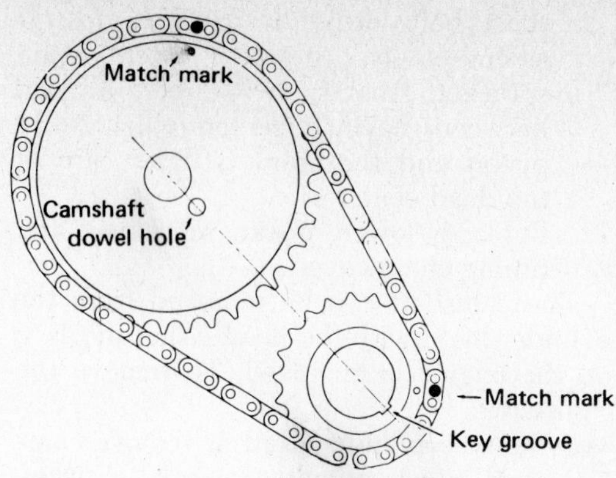

Assembly of sprockets and timing chain, A12 engine

Alignment of timing sprockets with No. 1 cylinder at top dead center, overhead valve (pushrod) engines

Assembly of sprockets and timing chain, E1 engine

15. Turn crankshaft until keyway and No. 1 piston is at top dead center. Install sprockets and chain. Oil slinger behind crankshaft sprocket must be replaced with concave surface to the front. If chain and sprocket installation is correct, sprocket marks must be aligned between the shaft centers when No. 1 piston is at top dead center. A12 camshaft sprocket retaining bolt torque is 33-36 ft. lbs.
16. The rest of the reassembly procedure is the reverse of disassembly. A12 chain tensioner bolt torque is 4-6 ft. lbs.

U20 Overhead Cam Engine

This engine is basically an overhead valve type redesigned to use an overhead camshaft cylinder head. A jackshaft replaces the camshaft in the cylinder block. The overhead camshaft is chain driven from the jackshaft. Thus there are two timing chains. To remove the timing chains:

1. Remove the timing chain cover.
2. Remove the lower chain tensioner.
3. Remove jackshaft outer sprocket retaining bolt.
4. Pull off jackshaft outer sprocket, easing

U20 engine. Note that camshaft sprocket is temporarily supported on the chain guide by a screw.

off crankshaft sprocket at same time. Remove both sprockets and chain as an assembly.

5. Remove screw which was installed during cylinder head removal holding camshaft sprocket to chain guide. If head was not removed, unbolt camshaft sprocket.
6. Remove camshaft chain. Remove jackshaft inner sprocket.
7. Jackshaft may now be removed if necessary.

To replace timing chains:

8. Place camshaft sprocket and jackshaft inner sprocket in camshaft chain, aligning timing marks on sprockets with marks on chain.

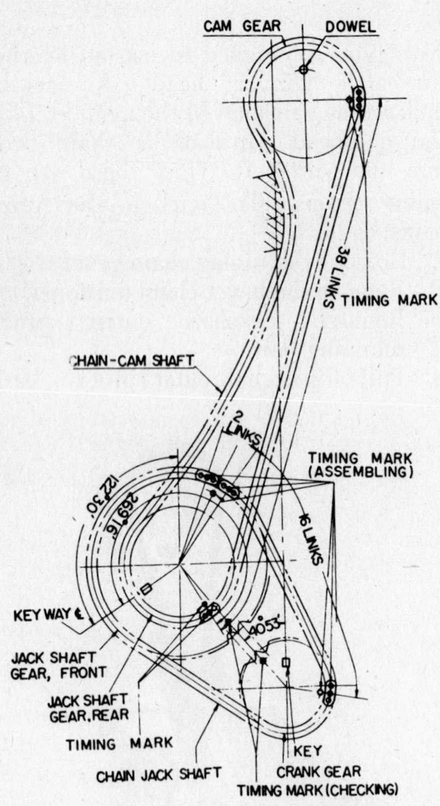

Timing marks for camshaft sprockets and chain, assembling and timing marks for jackshaft sprockets and chain, U20 engine

9. Holding sprockets in position, engage jackshaft inner sprocket keyway with key on jackshaft.
10. Replace screw removed in Step 5.
11. Assemble jackshaft outer sprocket and crankshaft sprocket to chain. Install sprockets and chain on shafts. Jackshaft bolt torque is 33-36 ft. lbs. If assembly is correct, lower chain sprocket marks will be aligned between the shaft centers when No. 1 piston and the crankshaft key are at top dead center.
12. Replace lower chain tensioner and timing chain cover.

The camshaft can be removed from the cylinder head with the head either in place on the engine or removed. To remove the camshaft:

1. Remove cylinder head or remove camshaft cover, unbolt camshaft sprocket, and support sprocket with a screw to chain guide.
2. Unbolt all camshaft bearing caps. Do not remove lower camshaft bearings. If these bearings are removed, an alignment boring procedure will be required to properly realign them.
3. Remove camshaft.

To replace camshaft:

4. Replace camshaft. Torque large bearing cap nuts to 13 ft. lbs. and small nuts to 5 ft. lbs.
5. Check camshaft end-play. It should be .004-.012″.
6. Replace camshaft sprocket, torquing bolts to 13 ft. lbs.
7. Press down valve springs and reinstall rocker arms.
8. Adjust valves.

L16, L24 Overhead Cam Engines

These engines are of true overhead camshaft design, using only a single timing chain. The L16 and L24 are very similar in appearance and construction. To remove the timing chain:

1. Remove timing chain cover. Remove camshaft sprocket if head has not been removed.
2. Remove chain and tensioner.
3. Remove oil slinger and distributor drive gear from crankshaft. Pull off sprocket.

To replace the chain:

4. Install cylinder head (removed during timing chain cover removal).
5. Install crankshaft sprocket, distributor drive gear, and oil slinger with concave side out.
6. Set crankshaft and camshaft keys upward. When turning the shafts, be careful not to force the valves against the pistons.
7. Install sprockets to chain, aligning

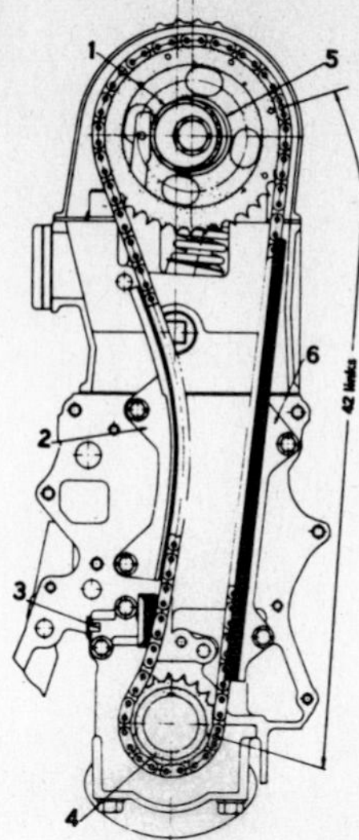

Camshaft chain installation, L16 and L24 engines

1. Fuel pump drive cam
2. Chain guide
3. Chain tensioner
4. Crankshaft sprocket
5. Camshaft sprocket
6. Chain guide

marks on chain with marks on sprockets at left side of engine. There are 42 links between the two chain marks.

8. Install chain and sprockets to engine. Install fuel pump drive cam. Torque camshaft sprocket bolt to 36-43 ft. lbs.
9. Install chain tensioner.
10. Replace timing chain cover.

The camshaft can be removed from the cylinder head with the head either in place on the engine or removed. To remove the camshaft:

1. Remove camshaft cover or cylinder head. Remove fuel pump drive cam and camshaft sprocket. Remove rocker arm springs.
2. Loosen rocker pivot lock nuts and remove rocker arms by pressing down valve springs.
3. Remove camshaft locating plate.
4. Withdraw camshaft carefully. Do not remove camshaft bearings. If these bearings are removed, an alignment boring procedure will be required to properly realign them.

To replace camshaft:

5. Replace camshaft. Install locating plate.
6. Check camshaft end-play. It should be .003-.015″. Adjust by replacing locating plate.
7. Replace sprocket, torquing bolt to 36-43 ft. lbs.
8. Install rocker arms, pressing down valve springs with a screwdriver. Install rocker arm springs.
9. Adjust valves.

ENGINE LUBRICATION

Oil Filter

The oil filter should be replaced every 6,000 miles on all models. Some early engines use a replaceable inner element within a permanent housing. All others use a throw-away cartridge type filter.

Engine	*Filter type*	*Location on engine*
P	Replaceable element	Left side, on bracket
E1, G	Replaceable element	Right side, on bracket
R	Replaceable element or cartridge	Right side, on bracket
J, U20	Cartridge	Right side, on bracket
L16, L24	Cartridge	Right side, screwed into block
A12	Cartridge	Right side, on oil pump

R&R, Replaceable Element Filter

1. Unscrew mounting bolt which passes through housing.
2. Remove housing, element seat, and element. Discard element.
3. Wash out housing in a safe solvent. Dry thoroughly. If bolt is removed from housing, note location of spring, felt washer, and rubber washer.
4. Install new rubber sealing ring into bracket. A tiny bit of grease may help keep the ring in position.
5. Install new element into housing. Replace element seat. Torque bolt to 14-18 ft. lbs.

R&R, Throw-away Cartridge Filter

1. Unscrew cartridge and discard. A strap wrench is a great help in removing these filters. If the cartridge has been overtightened and cannot be unscrewed, drive a long punch through it. Then use the punch as a handle to unscrew the cartridge.

Components of replaceable element oil filter

2. Screw on the new cartridge with a new gasket. Tighten it by hand until it just contacts the block or bracket.
3. Tighten the cartridge 1/2 turn farther by hand. Overtightening these cartridges will cause leaking or extreme difficulty in removing.

Oil Pump R&R

E1, J, G, R, U20

On these engines, the oil pump is mounted inside the oil pan.

1. Drain oil.
2. Remove oil pan and pickup strainer.
3. Unscrew three long bolts holding pump to crankcase.
4. Reverse procedure to install. Torque pump mounting bolts to 6-7 ft. lbs. and oil pan bolts to 4-5 ft. lbs.

A12

The A12 oil pump is mounted on the right side of the engine.

1. Drain oil.
2. Remove front stabilizer.
3. Remove splash shield.
4. Unbolt and withdraw pump from side of engine.
5. Reverse procedure to install. Torque pump mounting bolts to 9-11 ft. lbs.

L16, L24

These oil pumps are mounted at the bottom of the engine front cover.

1. Remove distributor.
2. Drain oil.
3. Remove front stabilizer on L16 models.
4. Remove splash shield.
5. Unbolt and remove oil pump.
6. Before replacing pump, position No. 1 cylinder at top dead center. Install oil pump with spindle punch mark to the front. Torque mounting bolts to 11-15 ft. lbs.
7. Install distributor with rotor pointing to No. 1 spark plug lead in cap.
8. Reverse rest of removal procedure.

Oil Pump Inspection

The pump can readily be disassembled and checked for wear. Refer to the Oil Pump Specifications Chart for clearances. The rotor pump used on E1 and J engines has a chamfered edge on the outer rotor. On reassembly, the chamfer must be toward the base of the pump body.

PISTONS AND CONNECTING RODS

On all engines, it is advisable to mark the connecting rods on removal so that they will be reinstalled in the same cylinder, facing in the same direction. On early engines with a clamp bolt at the top of the connecting rod, the clamp bolt must face toward the camshaft side of the engine. On P, L16, L24, and A12 engines, the oil hole at the bottom of the connecting rod must

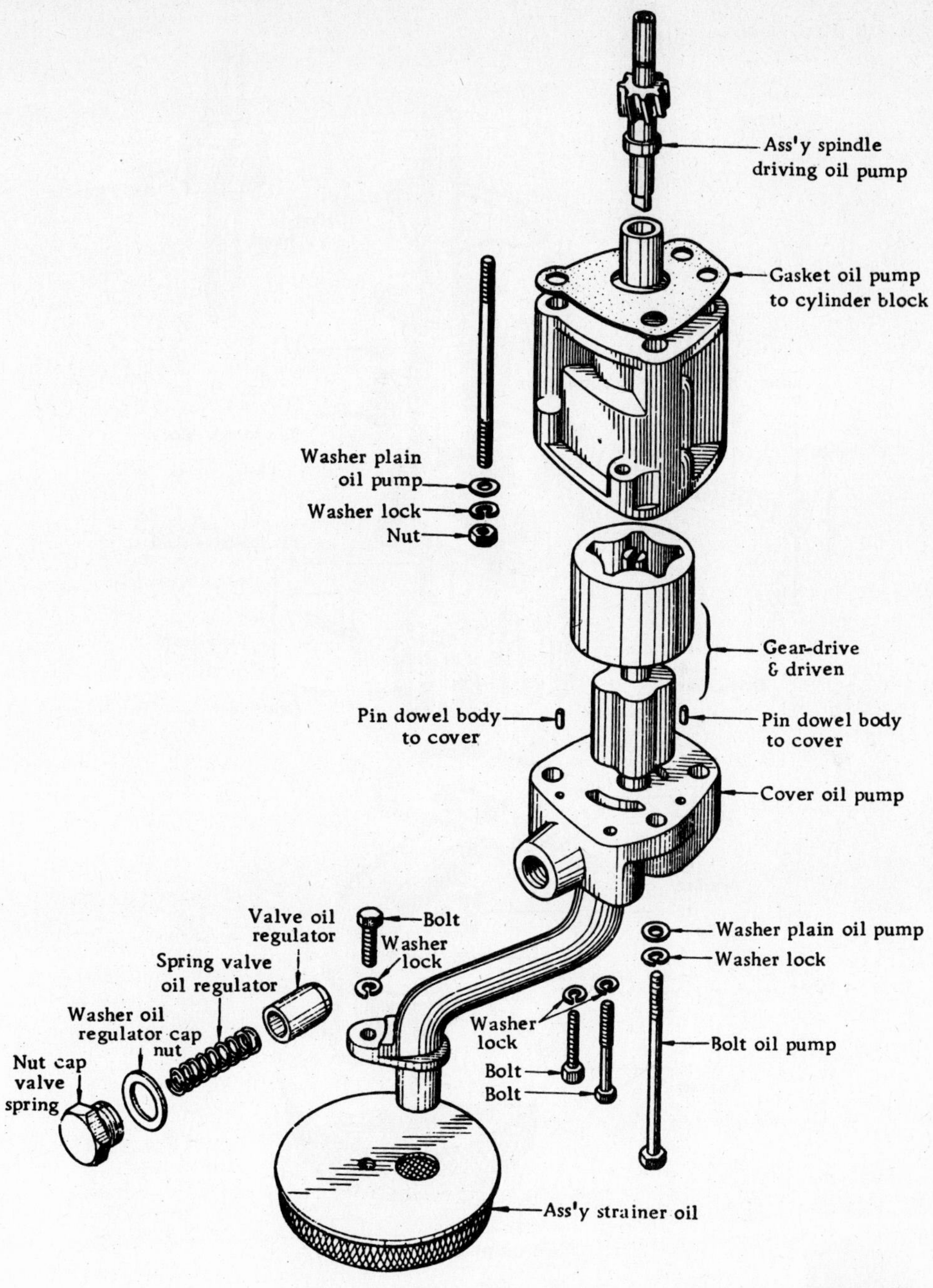
Ass'y spindle driving oil pump
Gasket oil pump to cylinder block
Washer plain oil pump
Washer lock
Nut
Gear-drive & driven
Pin dowel body to cover
Pin dowel body to cover
Cover oil pump
Valve oil regulator
Bolt
Washer lock
Washer plain oil pump
Washer lock
Spring valve oil regulator
Washer oil regulator cap nut
Nut cap valve spring
Washer lock
Bolt
Bolt
Bolt oil pump
Ass'y strainer oil

Rotor oil pump, J engine

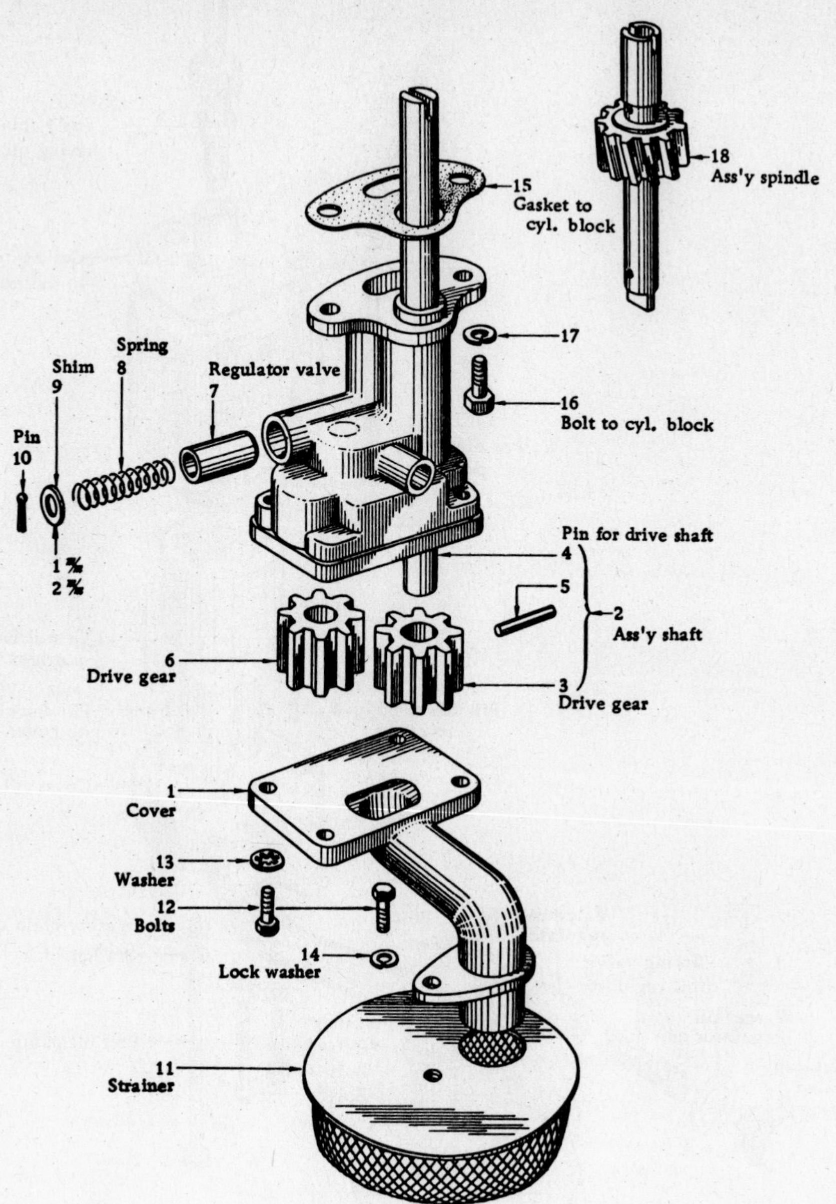

Gear oil pump, R engine

face to the right side. On E1, J, G, and R engines, the split in the piston skirt must face toward the camshaft side of the engine. If the piston has a mark on its top, the mark must be to the front. P, U20, L16, L24, and A12 engines have F marks on the tops of their pistons.

Clutch and Transmission

CLUTCH

R&R

NISSAN PATROL (L60)

1. Remove transfer case and transmission from engine.
2. Remove clutch housing cover, clutch operating lever, shaft, and release bearing.
3. Loosen clutch retaining bolts gradually and in sequence to prevent distortion. Remove bolts.
4. Clutch assembly can be removed through the bottom of the clutch housing.
5. When replacing the clutch assembly, align the disc to the flywheel with a splined dummy shaft. If this is not done, it will be extremely difficult to assemble the transmission to the engine. Tighten bolts alternately and equally to prevent distortion.
6. Replace release bearing, shaft, operating lever, and housing cover.
7. Replace transmission.

MODELS WITH COIL SPRING CLUTCH (EXCEPT L60)

1. Remove transmission from engine.
2. On L16 engine, temporarily lock release lever.
3. Loosen retaining bolts in sequence, a turn at a time. Remove bolts.
4. Remove pressure plate and disc.
5. Replace the disc with the longer chamfered splined end of the hub toward the transmission.
6. Align the disc to the flywheel with a splined dummy shaft.
7. Install the pressure plate. Most models have two pressure plate locating dowels in the flywheel. Tighten the pressure plate bolts in sequence, a turn at a time. Torque to 35 ft. lbs., except on L16 engine. L16 torque is 17-19 ft. lbs.
8. Remove dummy shaft. Unlock release

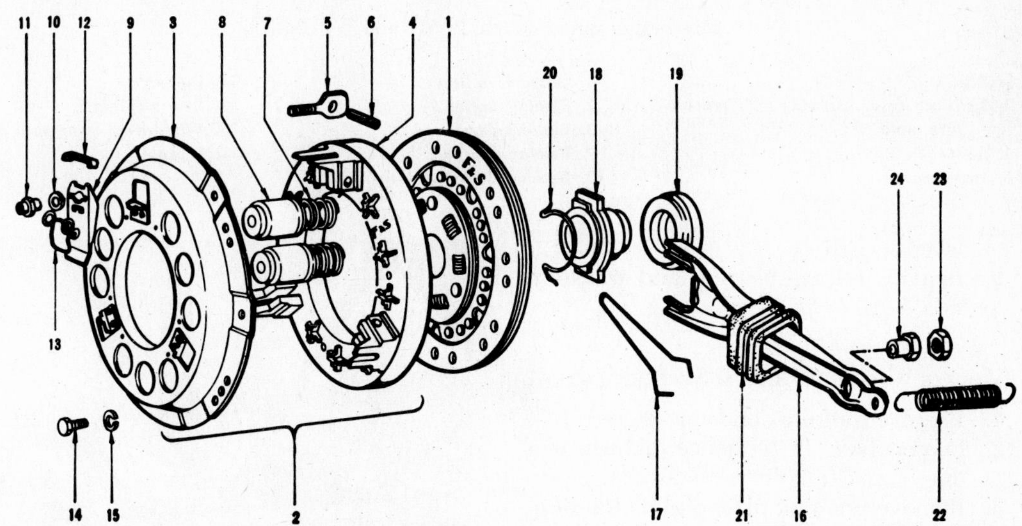

Coil spring clutch, PL510 and WPL510

1. Disc
2. Clutch assembly
3. Clutch cover
4. Pressure plate
5. Pressure plate bolt
6. Eye bolt pin
7. Spring
8. Spring retainer
9. Release lever
10. Release lever seat
11. Locknut
12. Release lever support
13. Retaining spring
14. Bolt
15. Lockwasher
16. Withdrawal lever
17. Retainer spring
18. Bearing sleeve
19. Release bearing
20. Bearing sleeve holder spring
21. Dust cover
22. Return spring
23. Locknut
24. Withdrawal lever push nut

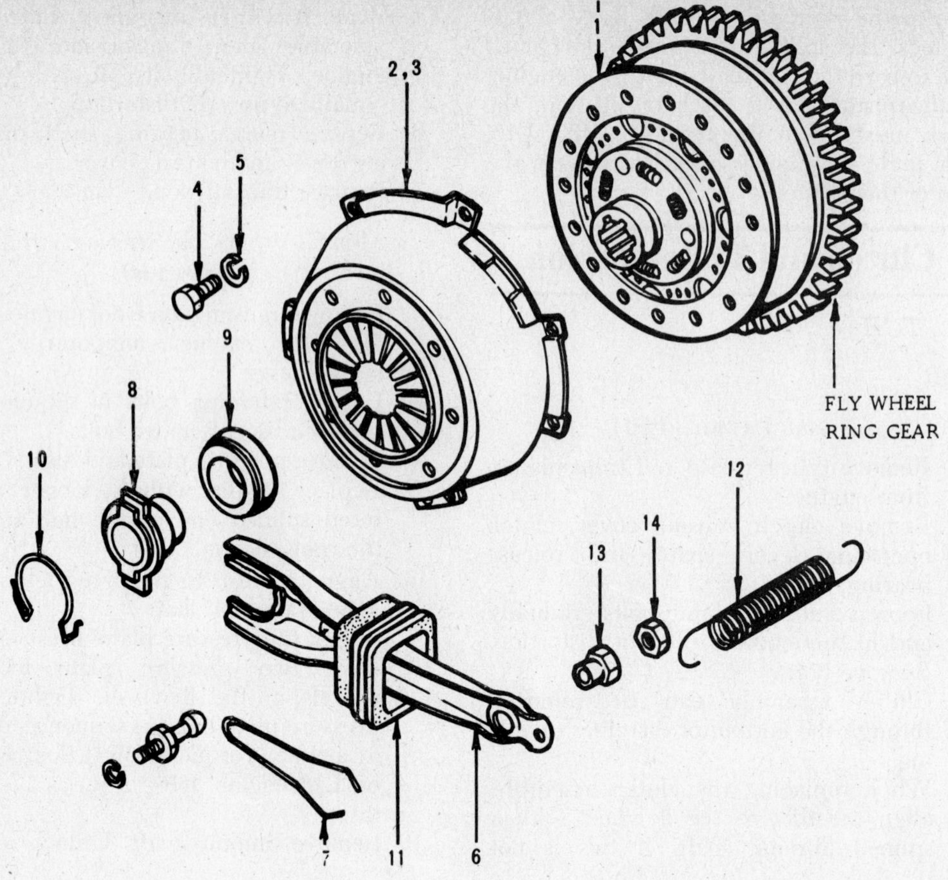

Diaphragm spring clutch, PL510 and WPL510

1. Disc
2, 3. Clutch cover assembly with pressure plate
4. Bolt
5. Lockwasher
6. Withdrawal lever
7. Retainer spring
8. Bearing sleeve
9. Release bearing
10. Bearing sleeve holder spring
11. Dust cover
12. Return spring
13. Withdrawal lever push nut
14. Locknut

lever on L16.

9. Replace release bearing and transmission.

Models With Diaphragm Spring Clutch

1. Remove transmission from engine.
2. Loosen bolts in sequence, a turn at a time. Remove bolts.
3. Remove pressure plate and clutch disc.
4. On A12 and L24 engines, remove release mechanism. Apply multi-purpose grease to bearing sleeve inside groove, contact point of withdrawal lever and bearing sleeve, contact surface of lever ball pin and lever. Replace release mechanism.
5. Install disc, aligning with a splined dummy shaft.
6. Install pressure plate and torque to 17-18 ft. lbs. on L16 and L24, and 11-16 ft. lbs. on A12.

Clutch release mechanism, A12 and L24 engines. 1 is withdrawal lever, 2 is return spring, and 3 is release bearing.

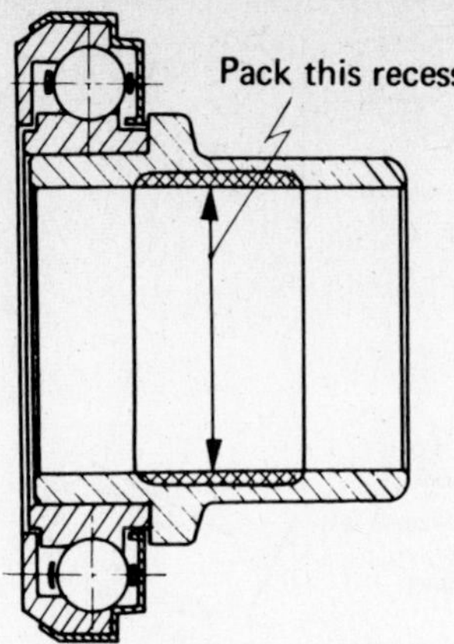

Apply multi-purpose grease where shown on throwout bearing for A12 and L24 engines.

7. Remove dummy shaft.
8. Replace transmission.

Clutch Linkage

Adjustment

Refer to the Clutch Specifications Chart for clutch pedal height above floor and pedal free play.

L60

The early model has a mechanically actuated clutch. Adjust pedal height by changing shim thickness at the pedal stopper. Adjust free play by means of the adjusting nut on the intermediate clutch rod. Tighten the nut to decrease play and loosen to increase.

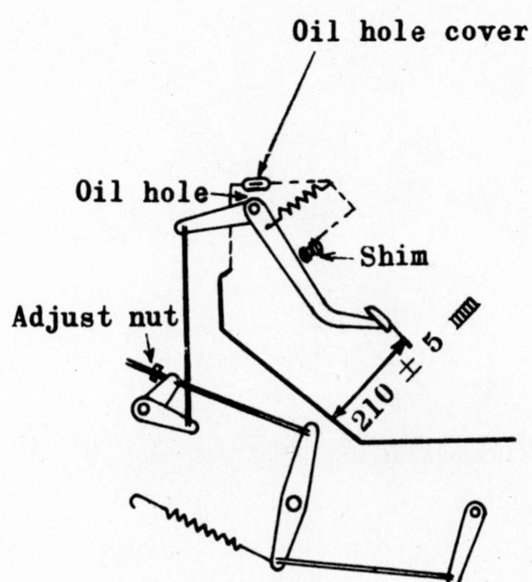

Mechanical clutch linkage, L60

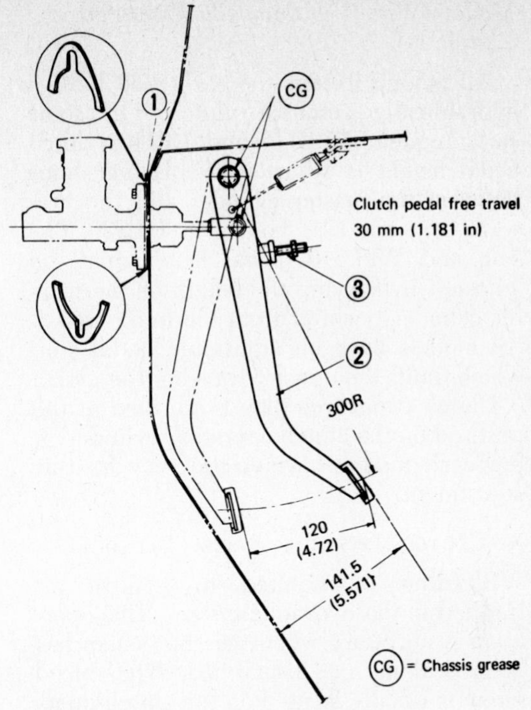

Clutch pedal height adjustment, LB110 and KLB110. A similar method of adjustment is used on all models without an adjustable master cylinder pushrod.

1. Adjusting shims 2. Pedal lever 3. Pedal stopper

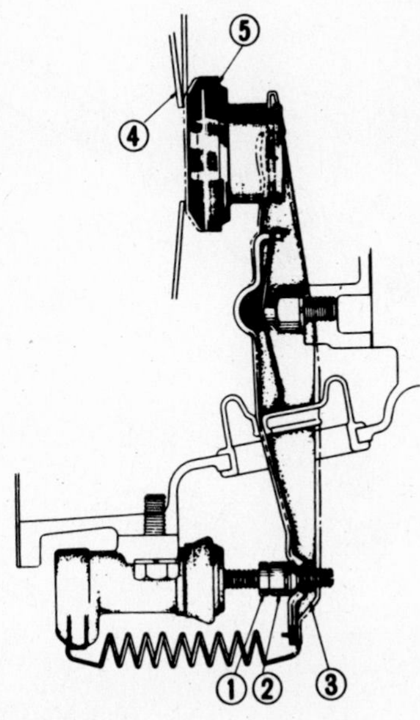

Detail of clutch operating cylinder and withdrawal lever, HLS30. Free play is adjusted at this point on most models with hydraulic clutch.

1. Locknut
2. Adjusting nut
3. Withdrawal lever
4. Diaphragm spring
5. Release bearing

Models With Hydraulically Operated Clutch

All models except the early L60 have a hydraulically actuated clutch. On some early models, KLB110 and LB110, clutch pedal height is adjusted by placing shims between the master cylinder and the firewall. On some late models, as HLS30, PL-510, and WPL510, pedal height may be adjusted by varying the length of the master cylinder pushrod from the brake pedal. All models have an adjustable pedal stop which limits the upward travel of the pedal.

Clutch pedal free play is adjusted at the pushrod on the clutch operating cylinder. A few early models have no provision for this adjustment.

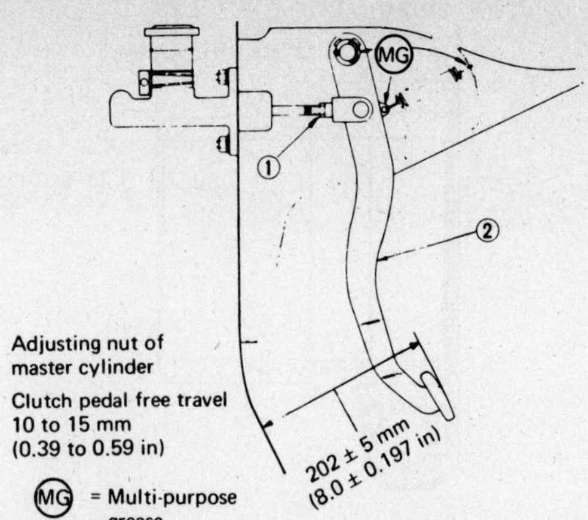

Clutch pedal height adjustment, HLS30. A similar method of adjustment is used on all models with an adjustable master cylinder pushrod.

1. Adjustment locknut
2. Pedal lever

Clutch Hydraulic System Bleeding

Bleeding is required to remove air trapped in the hydraulic system. This operation is necessary whenever the system has been leaking or dismantled. The bleed screw is usually located on the clutch operating (slave) cylinder.

1. Remove bleed screw dust cap.
2. Open bleed screw about ¾ turn.
3. Attach a tube to the bleed screw, immersing the free end in a clean container of brake fluid.
4. Fill master cylinder with fluid.

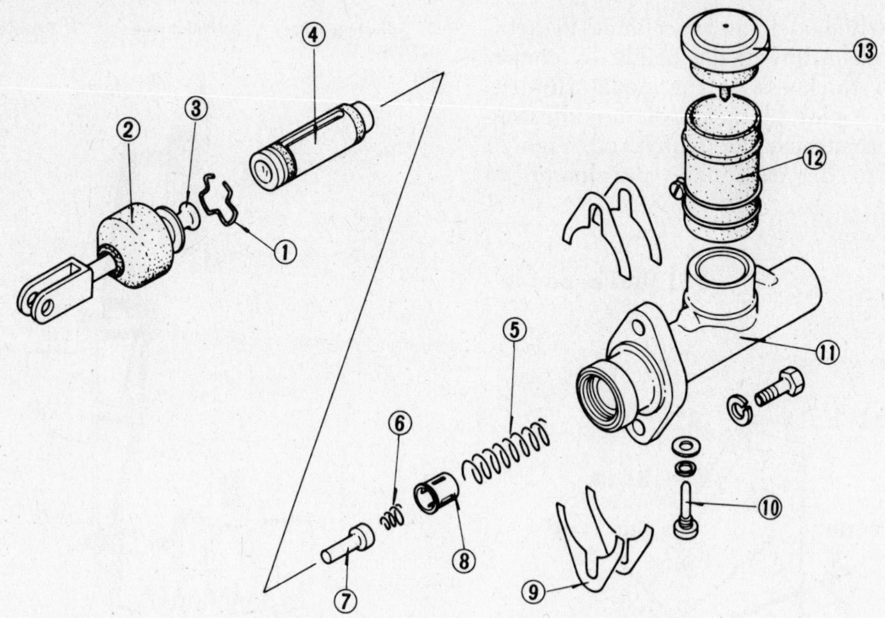

Clutch master cylinder, LB110 and KLB110

1. Snap-ring
2. Dust cover
3. Pushrod
4. Piston
5. Spring
6. Inlet valve spring
7. Inlet valve
8. Spring retainer
9. Shims
10. Inlet valve release pin
11. Housing
12. Fluid reservoir
13. Reservoir cap

5. Depress the clutch pedal quickly. Hold it down. Have an assistant tighten the bleed screw. Allow the pedal to return slowly.
6. Repeat steps 2 and 5 until no more air bubbles are seen in the fluid container.
7. Remove bleed tube. Replace dust cap. Refill master cylinder.

CLUTCH HYDRAULIC SYSTEM REPAIRS

Clutch master and slave cylinders are repaired in much the same way as are brake master and wheel cylinders. Bleeding is required whenever the clutch hydraulic system has been dismantled.

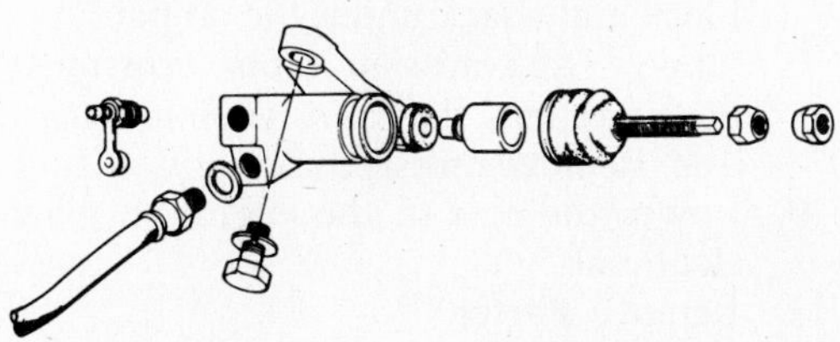

Clutch operating (slave) cylinder, LB110 and KLB110

Removing transfer case rear cover

MANUAL TRANSMISSION

R&R

On SPL310, SPL311, and SRL311 sportscars, the transmission must be removed in unit with the engine; it cannot be removed separately. On all other models, the transmission may be removed separately from under the vehicle. Transmission removal

Main shaft (drive) gear and nut

and replacement procedure for early models is generally similar to that for PL510, WPL510, HLS30, LB110 Manual Transmission.

Nissan Patrol (L60), Separation of Transfer Case and Transmission

1. Drain transmission and transfer case. Disconnect front and rear driveshafts. Disconnect handbrake rod, shifter rods, and speedometer cable.
2. Remove transfer case rear cover.
3. Remove nut and washer securing drive gear to transmission mainshaft.
4. Pull off drive (mainshaft) gear.
5. Remove four capscrews and one nut securing transfer case to transmission.
6. Pull transfer case to rear on a jack.
7. Reverse procedure to reinstall. Adjust handbrake.

LB110 with manual transmission

1. Exhaust pipe
2. Driveshaft
3. Speedometer cable
4. Shift linkage
5. Transmission rear mounting bolts
6. Crossmember mounting bolts

PL510, WPL510, HLS30, LB110, KLB110

1. Raise and support vehicle.
2. On PL510 and WPL510, disconnect handbrake cable at equalizer pivot. Disconnect backup light switch on all models.
3. On PL510 and WPL510, loosen muffler clamps and turn muffler to one side to allow room for driveshaft removal. On HLS30, remove exhaust system. On LB110 and KLB110, disconnect exhaust pipe from manifold.
4. Unbolt driveshaft at rear and remove. Seal the end of the transmission extension housing to prevent leakage.
5. Disconnect speedometer drive cable from transmission.
6. Remove shift lever.
7. Remove clutch operating cylinder from clutch housing.
8. Support the engine with a large wood block and a jack under the oil pan.
9. Unbolt transmission from crossmember. Support the transmission with a jack. Remove crossmember.
10. Lower the rear of the engine to allow clearance.
11. Remove starter.
12. Unbolt transmission. Lower and remove to the rear.
13. Reverse procedure for reinstallation. Check clutch linkage adjustment.

Nissan Patrol (L60) Transmission Overhaul

Disassembly

1. Separate transfer case from transmission.
2. Unbolt and remove gearshift cover.
3. Unbolt and remove bearing retainer and oil seal from front of transmission.
4. Bend back countershaft lockplate and unscrew nut. Drive countergear assembly back about ⅛″. Hook a puller on the bearing snap-ring and pull out the bearing.
5. Drive mainshaft back enough to hook the rear bearing with a puller. Remove the bearing. Slide the rear mainshaft section rearward and upward, out of the top of the case.
6. Remove the front mainshaft bearing snap-ring. Drive the front mainshaft section in, then pull it out of the case. Drive the front bearing out from the inside.
7. Tap the countershaft in from the front and remove it through the top of the case. Remove countershaft front bearing by driving in the outer race.
8. Bend back reverse idler shaft lockplate

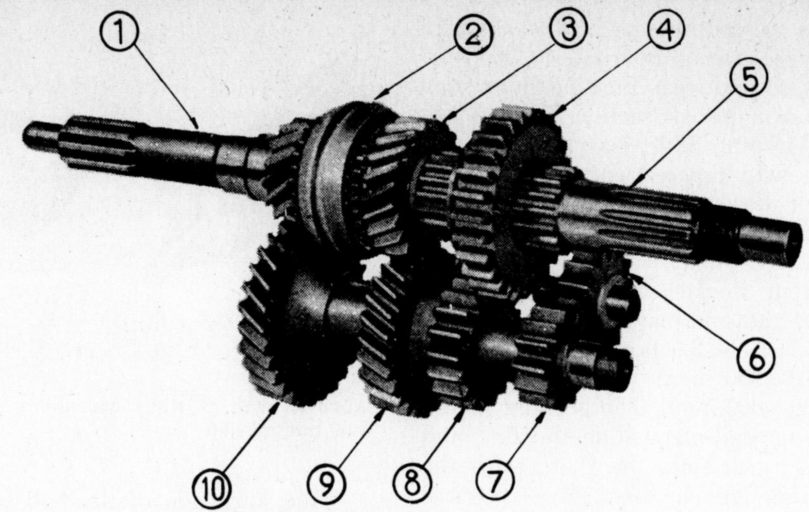

L60 transmission components

1. Front mainshaft section
2. Second and third gear synchronizer unit
3. Second gear
4. Low gear
5. Rear mainshaft section
6. Reverse idler gear
7. Reverse gear
8. Low gear
9. Second gear
10. Drive gear

and remove setscrew. Drive out shaft. Remove idler gear and thrust washer.

Inspection

1. Wash all parts in a safe solvent.
2. Oil the bearings immediately.
3. Slide first and reverse gear into the mainshaft. If play between gear and shaft exceeds .005″ (.125 mm.), replace gear, shaft, or both.
4. The inside diameter of second gear should not exceed 1.503″ (38.175 mm.). The outer diameter of the second gear bushing should not be less than 1.495″ (38 mm.). Replace the gear, bushing, or shaft, if worn. If the pin preventing the bushing from turning is loose, replace bushing and pin. To remove the bushing, remove the snap-ring and thrust washer. Slide off second gear and remove the pin. Drive or press off the bushing. Press on the new bushing.
5. The inside diameter of the idler gear bushing must be no more than .7509″ (19.073 mm.). If the bushing is replaced, ream the new one to fit. Clearance between bushing and shaft should be about .003-.004″.
6. If the idler gear shaft is less than .7432″ (18.879 mm.) in diameter, replace the shaft.
7. Needle bearing rollers must be at least .117″ (2.99 mm.) in diameter.
8. Gear backlash should be .03-.05″ (.075-.125 mm.).
9. Check all parts for excessive wear or damage, replacing as necessary.

Assembly

1. Dip each part in transmission lubricant before assembly.
2. Hold the reverse idler gear in place in the case with the cone end of the hub to the front and thrust washers at each side. Push the idler gear shaft into the case. Align the setscrew hole and insert the setscrew with its lockplate. Tighten the setscrew and bend up the lockplate.

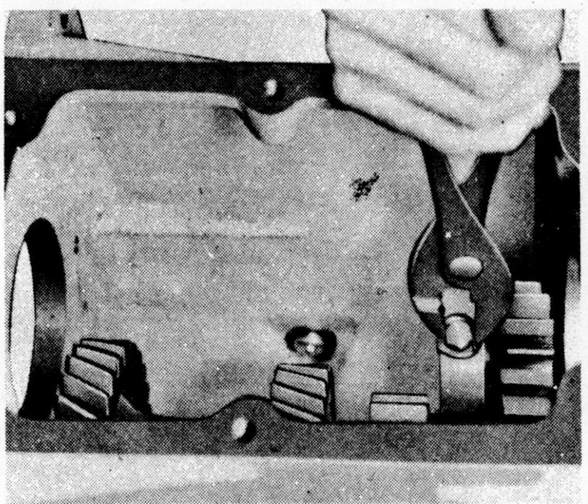

Bending setscrew lockplate, L60 transmission

3. Place the countergear in the case with the large gear to the front.
4. Press second gear bushing onto front of rear mainshaft section. Insert bushing lockpin. Slide second gear onto shaft with tapered end to the front. Install thrust washer and snap-ring. Gear end-play should be .0026-.0050" (.067-.133 mm.). Thrust washers of different thicknesses are available to adjust the end-play. These are .1520-.1535" (3.860-3.900 mm.), .1539-.1555" (3.910-3.950 mm.), and .1559-.1575" (3.960-4.000 mm.). The bushing should have no end-play. Slide the first and reverse gear onto the shaft, with the shift fork groove forward.

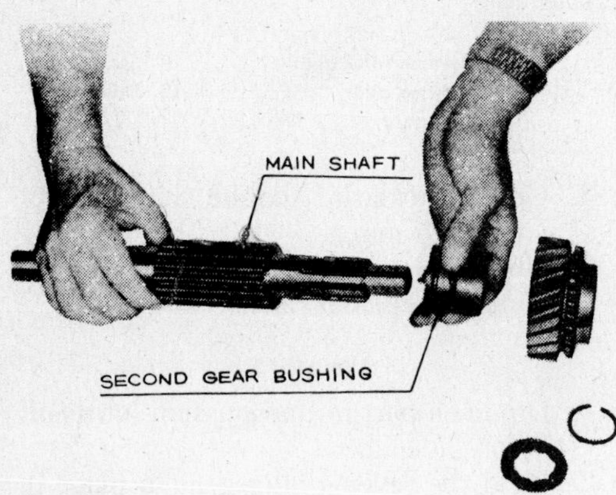

Replacing second gear bushing, L60 transmission

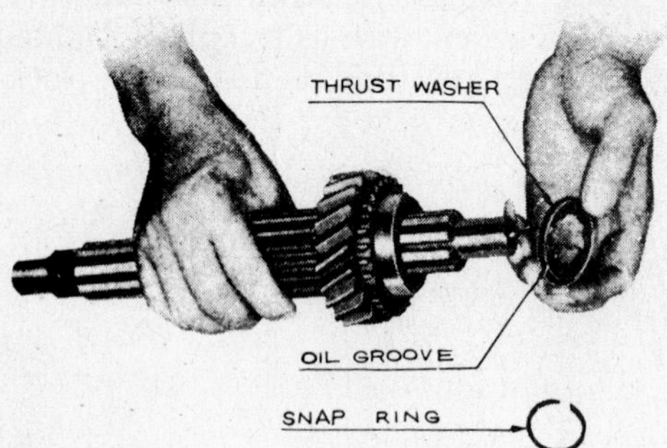

Thrust washer installation, L60 transmission

5. Assemble the synchronizer by installing the balls, springs, locking plates, and sleeve. Install the baulk rings in both sides of the hub. The pointed ends of the ring lugs must face in to the synchronizers. Slide the synchronizer assembly onto the mainshaft with the long side of the hub to the front and the deeper flange to the rear.

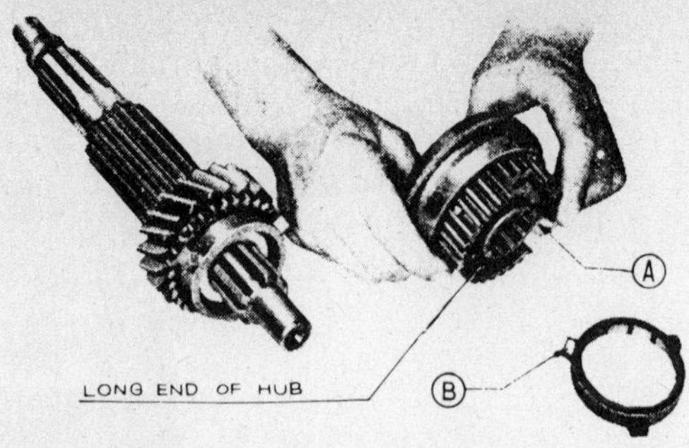

Align A with B when assembling synchronizer, L60 transmission

6. Insert rear mainshaft section into case through the top. Hold the front of the shaft in some way while driving in the rear bearing.

Mainshaft installation (rear section), L60 transmission

7. Drive front mainshaft section and bearing into place.

Installation of mainshaft front section, L60 transmission

8. Insert counter gear assembly through power takeoff cover opening. Insert front washer and drive in roller bearing. Place rear bearing on countershaft and drive into case. Install lockplate and nut at rear. Bend lockplate.
9. Coat front mainshaft section with transmission lubricant where it contacts the front bearing. Install the front bearing retainer.
10. Install cover assembly and gasket, making sure that shifter forks enter their grooves.
11. Refill transmission with recommended gear oil. Note that units with power takeoff have a smaller fluid capacity. See Capacities and Pressures Chart.

Nissan Patrol (L60) Transfer Case Overhaul

Disassembly

1. Separate transfer case from transmission.
2. Remove the brake band assembly. Remove the brake drum. Unbolt and pull off the rear flange.
3. Remove both top covers.
4. Unbolt and pull off the front flange.
5. Unbolt and remove the front bearing retainer.
6. Remove two spring plugs from front cover. Remove two detent springs and balls.
7. Remove the two shift rod eyes from the rods.
8. Unbolt and carefully slide off the front cover, leaving long shift rod in place. Remove the front wheel drive shift rod with fork and sleeve from the front cover. Remove the bearing.

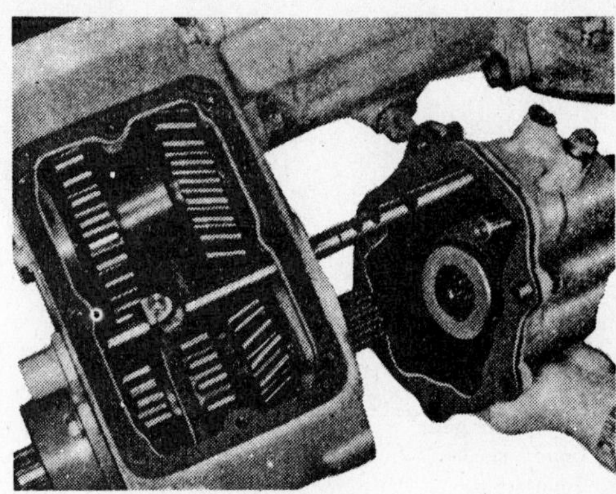

Removing front cover, L60 transfer case

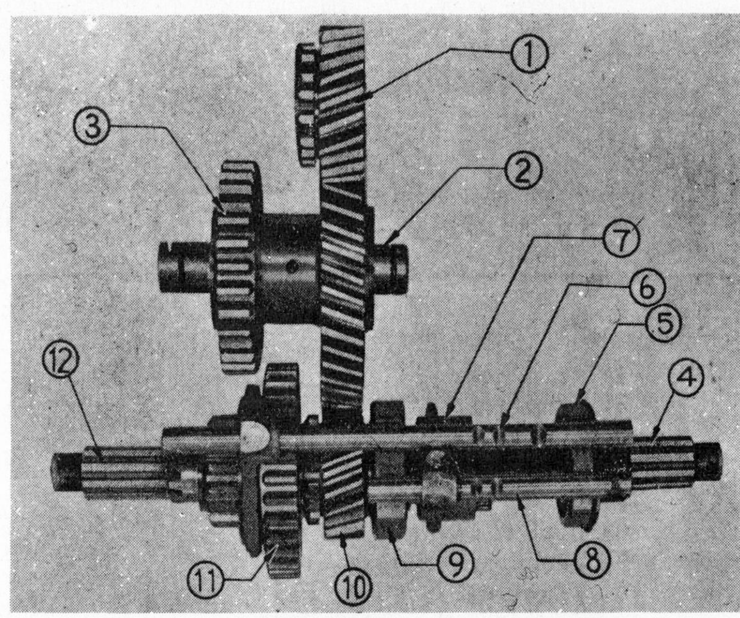

L60 transfer case components

1. Main drive gear
2. Countershaft
3. Countergear
4. Front driveshaft
5. Front bearing
6. High and low range shift rod
7. Front wheel drive sleeve
8. Front wheel drive shift rod
9. Front bearing of rear driveshaft
10. High range gear
11. Low range gear
12. Rear driveshaft

L60 transfer case components

1. Main drive gear
2. Countershaft
3. Countergear
4. Front driveshaft
5. Front bearing
6. High and low range shift rod
7. Front wheel drive sleeve
8. Front wheel drive shift rod
9. Front bearing of rear driveshaft
10. High range gear
11. Low range gear
12. Rear drive shaft

9. Remove the setscrew from the high and low range shift fork (long rod). Slide the shift rod out and remove the fork.
10. Remove the capscrew and countershaft lockplate. Drive the countershaft out with a drift. Remove the countergear and two thrust washers.
11. Remove rear bearing retainer. Remove driveshaft rear bearing with a puller or press driveshaft out to the front. Remove low range gear. If shaft was pressed out, drive rear bearing from case.
12. To disassemble driveshaft, remove snap-ring securing front bearing. Remove spacer washer and pull off bearing. Remove thrust washer and high range gear.

Inspection

1. Wash all parts in a safe solvent. Oil the bearings immediately.
2. Replace the shift rod oil seals.
3. The diameter of the pilot end (rear) of the front driveshaft should be at least .6693″ (17 mm.). If it is less, replace the shaft.
4. The countergear thrust washers must be at least .1311″ (3.33 mm.) thick. If not, replace them. The countershaft must be at least .1249″ (31.73 mm.) in diameter.
5. Drive out and replace the bearing retainer oil seals.
6. The rear driveshaft thrust washer must be at least .142″ (3.6 mm.) thick.
7. Gear backlash should be .004-.006″ (.102-.152 mm.).
8. Check all parts for excessive wear or damage, replacing as necessary.

Assembly

1. To install rear driveshaft, push rear bearing onto driveshaft. Place low range sliding gear into case, channel side to the rear. Insert driveshaft through the gear. Use a dummy bearing at the front to center the shaft. Drive in the rear bearing and driveshaft. Stick the rear bearing retainer gasket to the case with grease. Place the rear driveshaft bearing spacer on the shaft, chamfered side to the bearing. Install the rear bearing retainer and new oil seal. Tighten the bolts

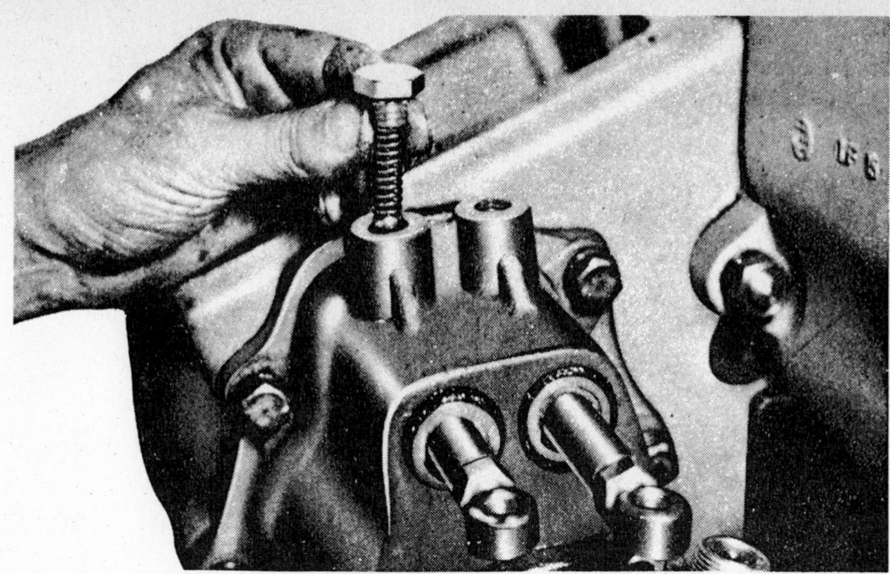

Replacing detent assembly, L60 transfer case

evenly. Coat the oil seal with grease and install the rear flange, using a new cotter pin. Remove the dummy bearing from the front. Slide the high range gear onto the driveshaft, small gear to the rear. Drive in the front bearing. Install the bearing spacer and snap-ring.

2. To install the countershaft, insert the two roller bearings, separated by the spacer, into the gear. Place rear thrust washer in case with the oil grooved side toward the countergear. Use grease to hold the washer in position. Insert a short dummy shaft into the countergear to hold the bearings. Place the rear O-ring onto the countershaft. Place the countergear with the large gear to the front. Insert the front thrust washer and drive the shaft in from the rear. Drive the shaft out to the front enough to install the front O-ring. Position the shaft and install the lockplate.
3. Place high and low range shift fork in case. Insert shaft and fork setscrew. Lockwire setscrew. Attach front wheel drive shift rod to fork. Lockwire setscrew. Place front wheel drive fork on sleeve gear. Insert shift rod into case and place sleeve on driveshaft. Insert needle bearings in driveshaft.
4. Install the front cover with a new gasket, tightening the bolts evenly. Drive in the front driveshaft and bearing assembly.

Flat, ribbed bottom cover of three speed transmission

5. Install the shift rod detent balls, springs, and plugs. Slide the speedometer drive gear onto the shaft. Install the front bearing retainer with a new gasket. Grease the oil seal and install the flange, using a new cotter pin.
6. Replace the case top covers with new gaskets.
7. Replace the brake drum and band assembly. Adjust brake band.
8. Fill case with specified lubricant after reinstalling transfer case to transmission. See Capacities and Pressures Chart.

Three Speed, Bottom Cover Transmission Overhaul—PL410, PL411

This transmission can readily be identi-

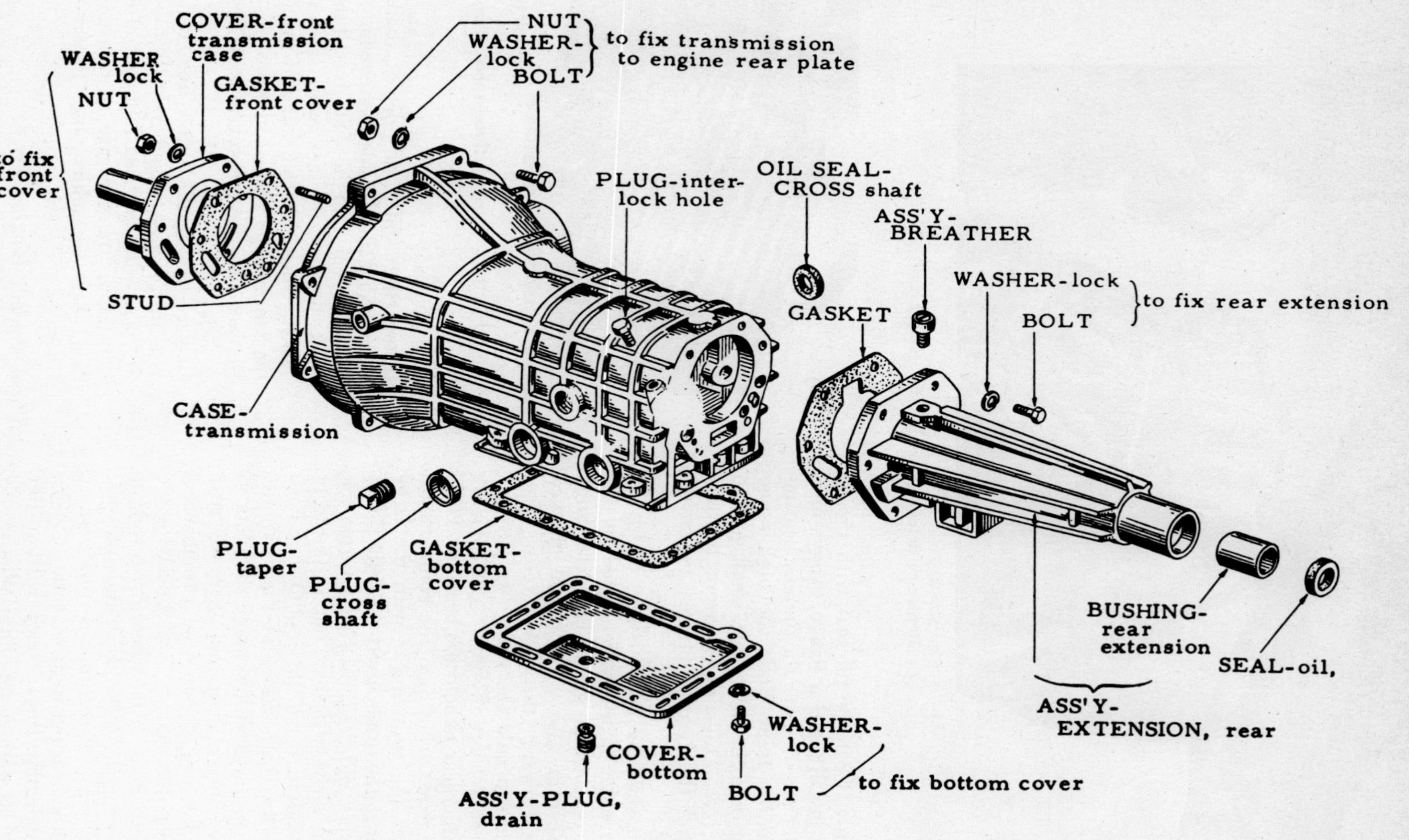

Three speed, bottom cover transmission external components

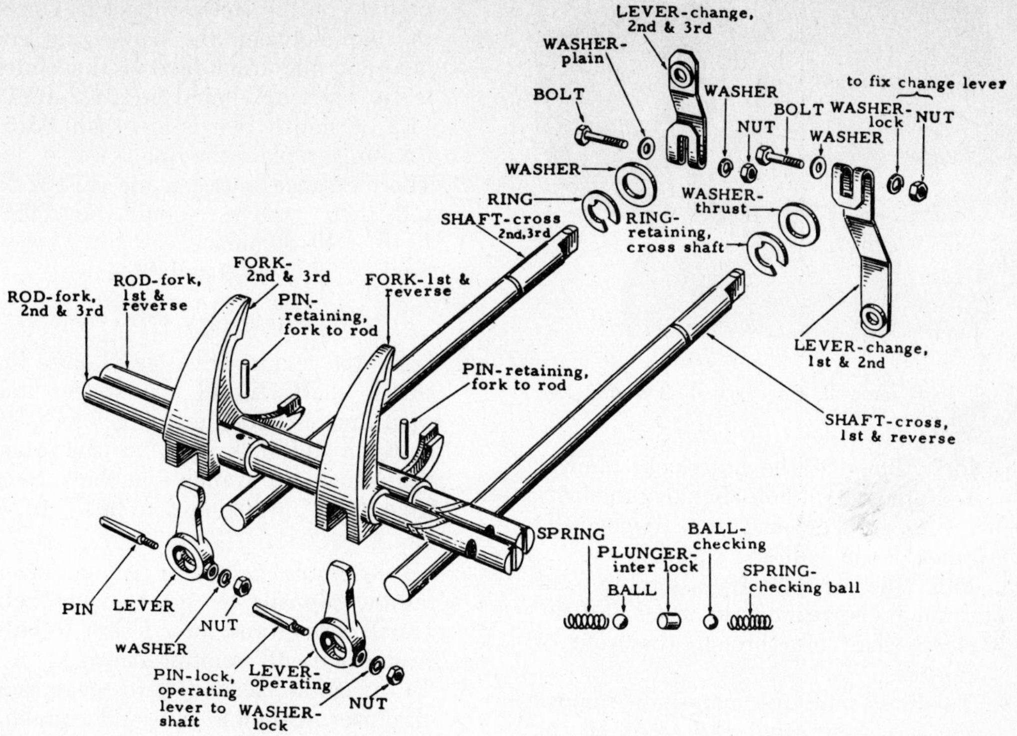

Shifting mechanism for three speed, bottom cover transmission

fied by the flat, ribbed bottom cover. The transmission and clutch housings are a single piece. It was used only with a column shift arrangement.

Disassembly

1. Drain transmission. Remove bottom cover.
2. Remove clutch withdrawal lever and front bearing retainer from clutch housing.
3. Remove speedometer pinion assembly from extension housing. Remove housing.
4. Remove shift shaft locking clips from inside the case. Unscrew the nuts holding the operating lever pins on the shift shafts. Drive out the pins and remove both shift shafts.
5. Remove countershaft and countergear with roller bearings and spacers.
6. Remove reverse idler shaft lockbolt. Remove shaft and gear.
7. Drive out shift fork pins. Unscrew detent plug, spring, and ball from base. Remove the second/third shift rod and

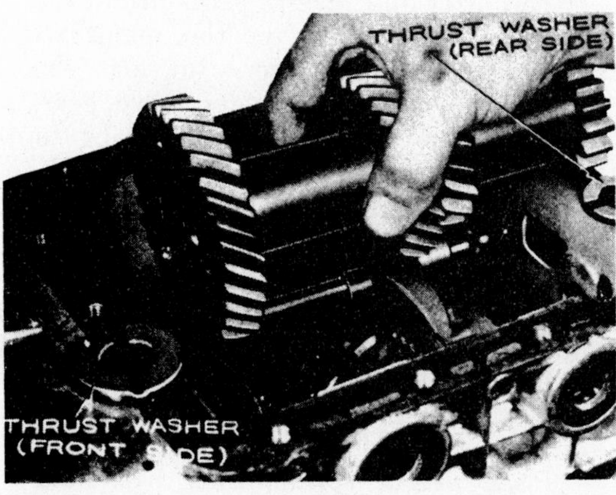

Countergear removal; three speed, bottom cover unit

Mainshaft removal; three speed, bottom cover unit

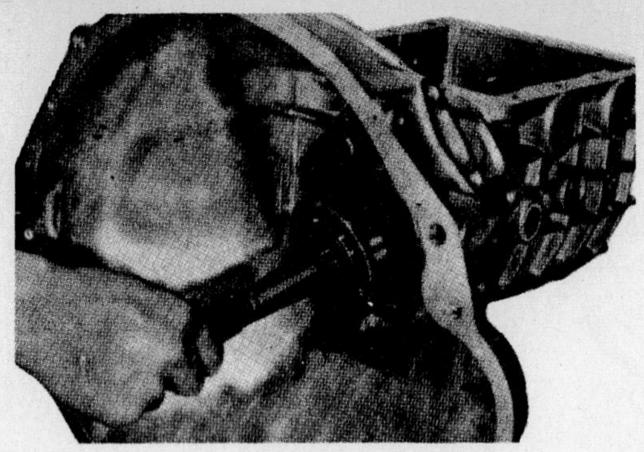

Clutch shaft removal; three speed, bottom cover unit

fork. Remove the interlock plunger from the detent hole. Remove the first/reverse shift rod and fork. Remove the other detent ball and spring.

8. Pull the mainshaft assembly out through the rear of the case. Pull the clutch shaft out through the front of the case.
9. To disassemble the mainshaft, remove the snap-ring from the front of the shaft. Remove second/third synchronizer, hub, and second gear. Remove snap-ring, speedometer drive gear, and spacer with ball. Press off shaft bearing and retainer. Hold reverse gear and strike the end of the mainshaft on a block of wood. Remove reverse and first gears.

Inspection

1. Clean all parts with a safe solvent. Lubricate the bearings with gear oil.
2. Check the mainshaft for straightness. Runout at the rear of the shaft should not exceed .0059″ (.15 mm.). Check that synchronizer hubs slide freely without excessive clearance.
3. Place the synchronizer baulk ring in position on the cone of its gear. Check the gap between the baulk ring end face and the front face of the clutch teeth. The gap should be .0472-.0360″ (1.2-1.6 mm.). If it is less than .0315″ (.8 mm.), replace the ring.

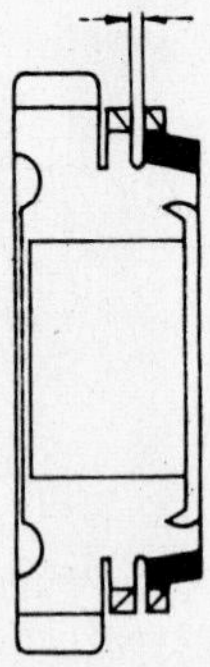

Checking synchronizer baulk ring gap

4. The clearance between the shift forks and their grooves should be .0059-.0118″ (.15-.30 mm.).
5. Replace all O-rings and oil seals.

Assembly

1. Press the main drive gear onto the clutch shaft. Install the spacer and snap-ring. There must be no play between the bearing and snap-ring. Snap-rings are available in thicknesses from .0598″ (1.52 mm.) to 0747″ (1.89 mm.).
2. To assemble first gear synchronizer, install snap-ring on synchronizer hub. Install springs and three inserts to hub. Install hub into coupling sleeve.
3. To assemble second/third gear synchronizer, assemble hub and coupling sleeve. Install three inserts between hub and sleeve. Install a spring ring on each side of the hub.
4. To assemble the mainshaft, slide on second gear with the tapered cone to the front. Install the second gear baulk ring. Install the second/third synchronizer assembly and snap-ring on the front of the shaft. Select a snap-ring which gives an end-play of .0020-.0087″ (.05-.25 mm.). Snap-rings are available in thicknesses from .0630″ (1.60 mm.) to .0709″ (1.80 mm.). Place first gear and its baulk ring on the rear of the shaft with the tapered cone to the rear. Install first gear synchronizer and reverse gear. Install the spacer and press on the mainshaft bearing and retainer. Replace the spacer, ball, speedometer drive gear, and snap-ring. Select a snap-ring to give a first gear end-play of .0020-.0087″ (.05-.22 mm.). Snap-rings are available in thicknesses from .0512″ (1.30 mm.) to .0669″ (1.70 mm.). Second gear end-play should be .0039-.0087″ (.10-.22 mm.).
5. Install clutch shaft and mainshaft into case.
6. Place case with detent hole upward. Place detent spring, then ball, into hole. Install first/reverse shift rod and fork. Insert interlock plunger into hole.

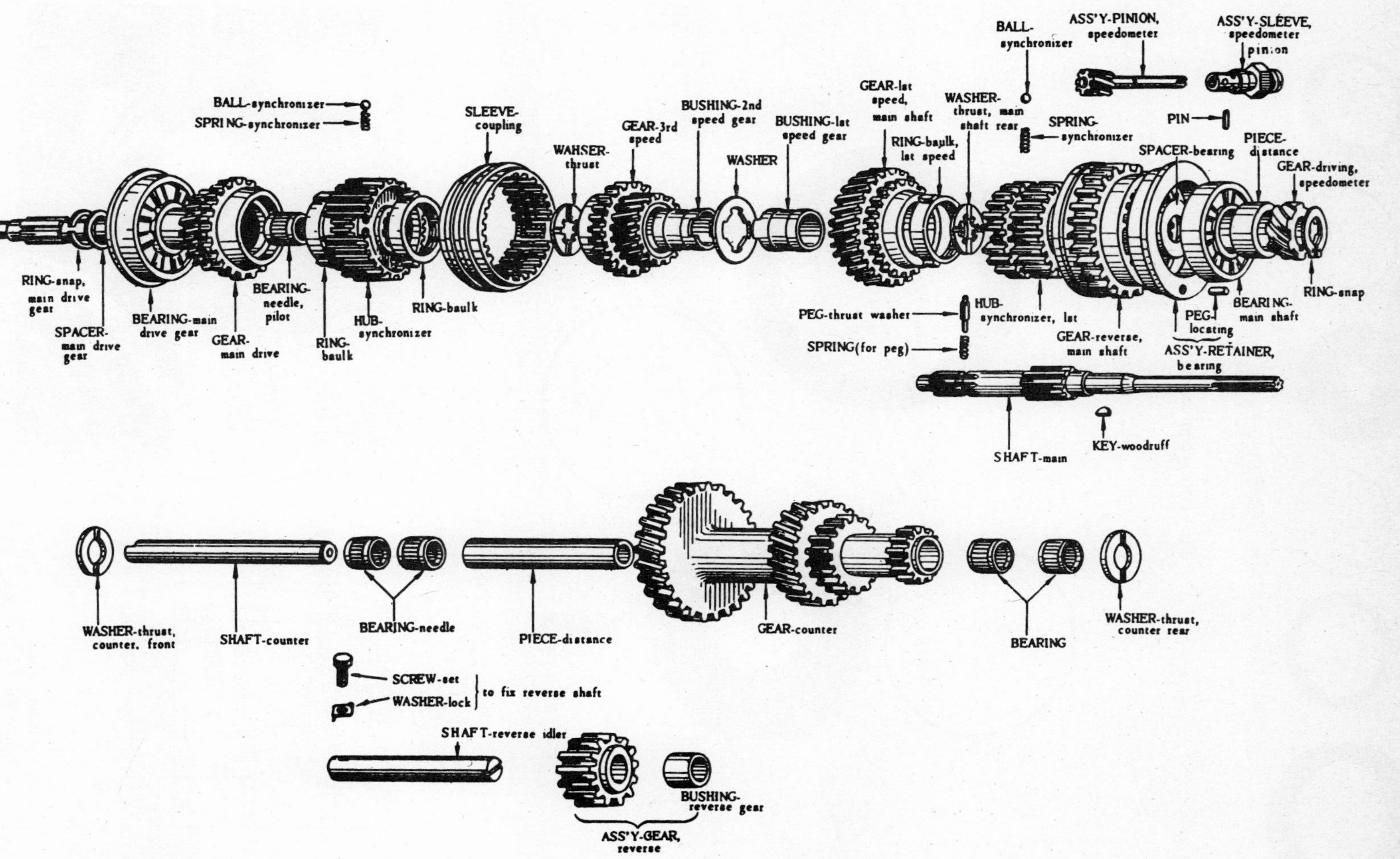
BALL-synchronizer
SPRING-synchronizer
SLEEVE-coupling
WAHSER-thrust
GEAR-3rd speed
BUSHING-2nd speed gear
WASHER
BUSHING-1st speed gear
GEAR-1st speed, main shaft
RING-baulk, 1st speed
WASHER-thrust, main shaft rear
BALL-synchronizer
SPRING-synchronizer
ASS'Y-PINION, speedometer
ASS'Y-SLEEVE, speedometer pinion
PIN
SPACER-bearing
PIECE-distance
GEAR-driving, speedometer
RING-snap, main drive gear
SPACER-main drive gear
BEARING-main drive gear
GEAR-main drive
BEARING-needle, pilot
RING-baulk
HUB-synchronizer
RING-baulk
PEG-thrust washer
SPRING (for peg)
HUB-synchronizer, 1st
GEAR-reverse, main shaft
PEG-locating
ASS'Y-RETAINER, bearing
BEARING-main shaft
RING-snap
SHAFT-main
KEY-woodruff
WASHER-thrust, counter, front
SHAFT-counter
BEARING-needle
PIECE-distance
GEAR-counter
BEARING
WASHER-thrust, counter rear
SCREW-set
WASHER-lock
to fix reverse shaft
SHAFT-reverse idler
BUSHING-reverse gear
ASS'Y-GEAR, reverse

Internal components of three speed, bottom cover transmission

First gear synchronizer

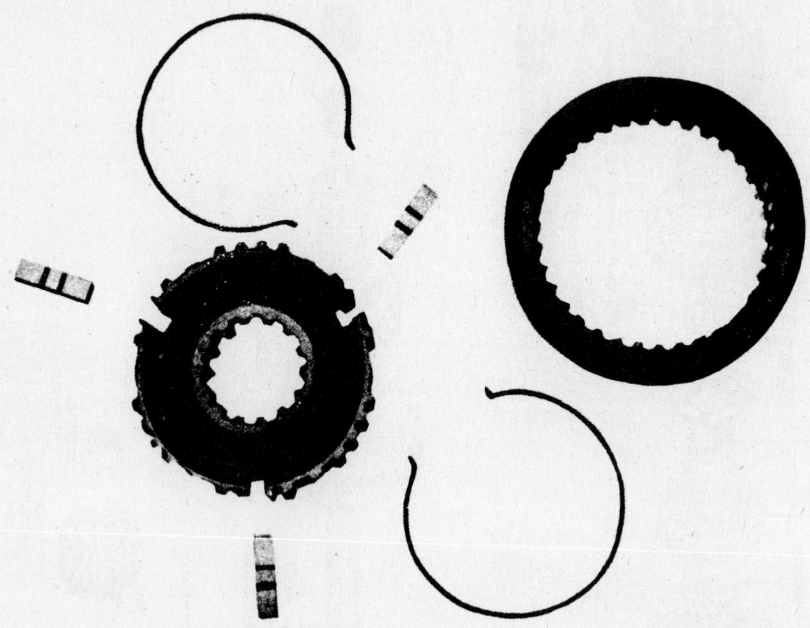

Second gear synchronizer

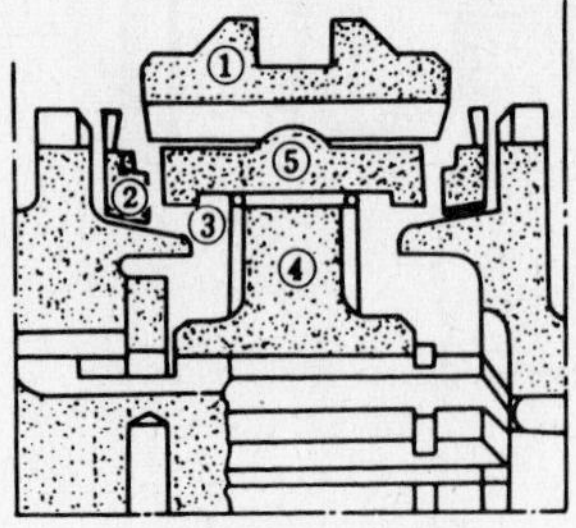

Synchronizer details

1. Synchronizer sleeve
2. Baulk ring
3. Spreader ring
4. Synchronizer hub
5. Insert

Shift rod alignment. Align rods as illustrated for three speed, bottom cover transmission.

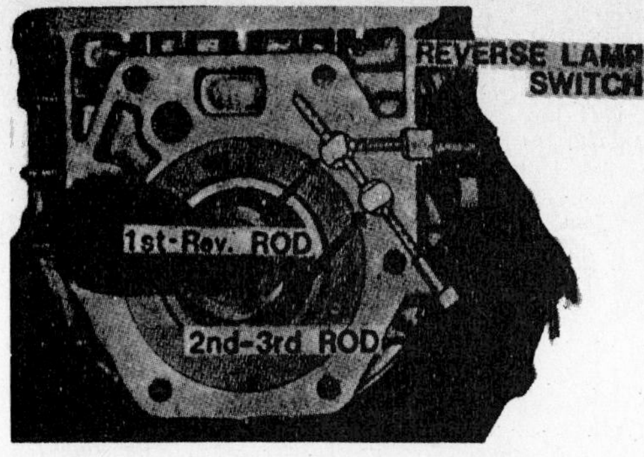

Shift rod interlock details; three speed, bottom cover unit

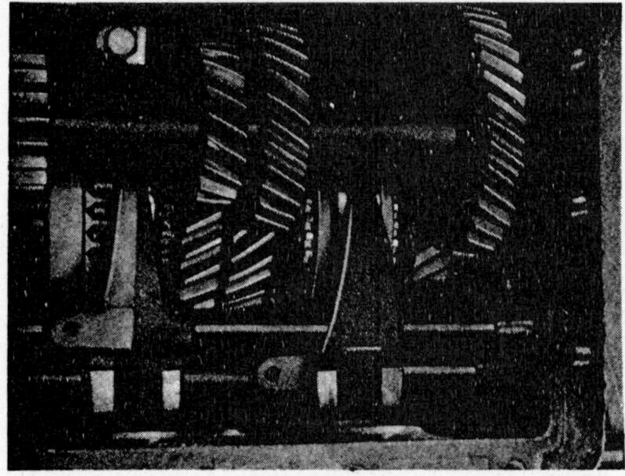

Shift rods and forks installed; three speed, bottom cover unit

Install second/third shift rod and fork. Place the other detent ball, spring, and plug into the detent hole. Use sealant on the plug threads. Fasten the forks to the shift rods with their retaining pins.

7. Install the reverse idler gear and shaft. Install the shaft lockbolt and plate.
8. Replace the countergear and countershaft. Select thrust washers to give a countergear end-play of .0016-.0047″ (.04-.12 mm.). Thrust washers are available in sizes from .151″ (3.83 mm.) to .159″ (4.03 mm.).
9. Install shift shafts with thrust washers, locking clips, and operating levers.
10. Install extension housing to case. Torque bolts to 16-22 ft. lbs.
11. Insert speedometer pinion assembly.
12. Check gear backlash with a dial indicator. It should be .0031-.0051″ (.08-.13 mm.) for all gears.
13. Replace front bearing retainer. Torque bolts to 8-12 ft. lbs. Replace clutch withdrawal lever.
14. Replace bottom cover and torque bolts to 8-12 ft. lbs.
15. See Capacities and Pressures Chart for refill capacity.

Four Speed, Bottom Cover Transmission Overhaul—L520, PL411, RL411, SPL311, PL510, WPL510

This transmission is adapted from and quite similar in appearance to the three speed unit used in the PL410 and PL411. The reverse and reverse idler drive gears are contained in the extension housing to make room for the additional internal gears. On some late units, the cast, ribbed bottom cover is replaced by a stamped steel cover. Virtually all of these transmissions imported to the US have a modified extension housing incorporating a floorshift mechanism. The transmission model number, on the PL510 and WPL510, is F4W(C)63L.

Disassembly

1. Drain transmission.
2. Remove clutch withdrawal lever and release bearing.
3. Remove clevis pin connecting striker rod to shift lever.
4. Remove speedometer drive pinion assembly.
5. Unbolt and remove extension housing, disengaging striker rod from shift rod gates.
6. Remove bottom and front covers.
7. Remove three detent plugs, springs, and balls.
8. Drive out shift fork retaining pins. Remove rods and forks.
9. Move first/second and third/fourth coupling sleeves into gear at the same time to lock the mainshaft.
10. Pull out the countershaft and countergear with the two needle roller bearings and spacers.
11. Remove snap-ring, reverse idler gears, and shaft.
12. Unbolt mainshaft rear bearing retainer.
13. Pull out mainshaft assembly to the rear. Pull out clutch shaft to the front.
14. To disassemble mainshaft, remove snap-ring, third/fourth synchronizer hub and coupling sleeve. Remove third gear, with roller bearing. Remove mainshaft nut, lockplate, speedometer drive gear, and steel ball. Take off reverse gear and hub. Press off bearing

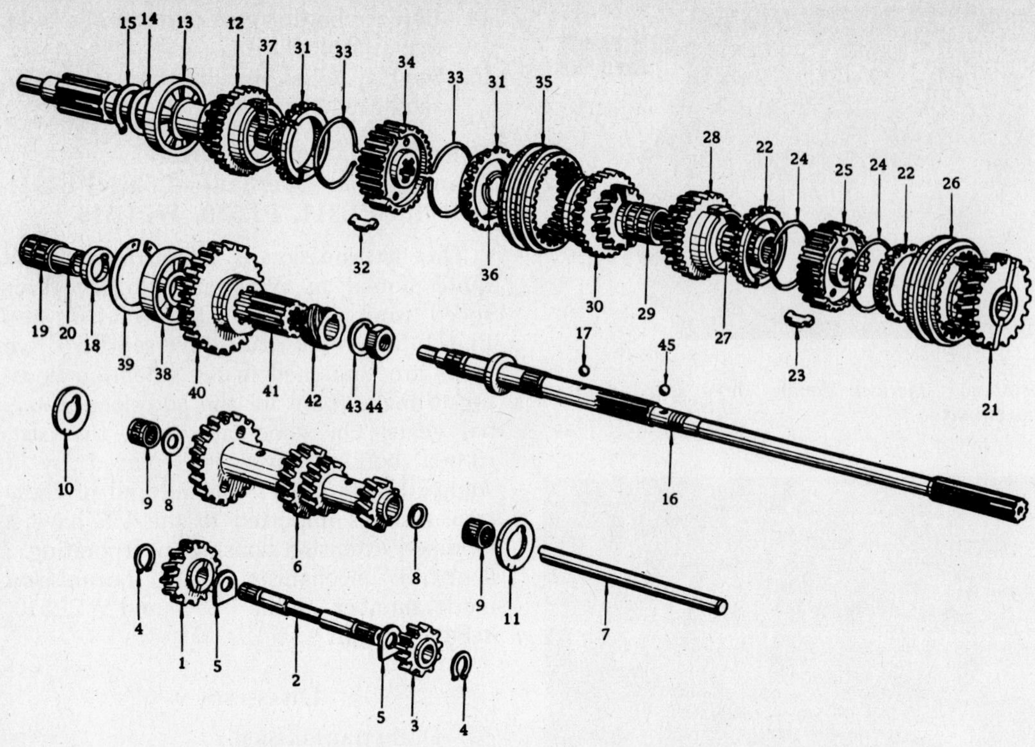

Four speed, bottom cover transmission gear train details

1. Reverse idler gear
2. Reverse idler shaft
3. Main reverse idler gear
4. Snap-ring
5. Thrust washer
6. Countergear
7. Countershaft
8. Spacer
9. Needle bearing
10. Front countershaft thrust washer
11. Rear countershaft thrust washer
12. Main drive gear
13. Main drive gear bearing
14. Washer
15. Snap-ring
16. Mainshaft
17. 5/32″ steel ball
18. Thrust washer
19. Needle bearing
20. First gear bushing
21. First gear
22. Baulk ring
23. Shifting insert
24. Spreader ring
25. First/second synchro hub
26. Coupling sleeve
27. Needle bearing
28. Second gear
29. Needle bearing
30. Third gear
31. Baulk ring
32. Shifting insert
33. Spreader ring
34. Third/fourth synchro hub
35. Coupling sleeve
36. Snap-ring
37. Pilot bearing
38. Bearing
39. Snap-ring
40. Reverse gear
41. Reverse gear hub
42. Speedometer drive gear
43. Lockwasher
44. Nut
45. Steel ball

and retainer. Remove thrust washer and first gear with needle roller bearing and bushing. Be careful not to lose the steel ball which locates the thrust washer. Take off the first/second synchronizer and hub. Remove second gear with needle roller bearing.

Inspection

Inspection procedures are the same as for the three speed transmission used in the PL410 and PL411.

Assembly

Assembly procedures are generally the reverse of disassembly, however the following special instructions are required.

1. On the clutch shaft, there should be no end-play between the bearing and the snap-ring. Snap-rings are available in sizes from .0598″ (1.52 mm.) to .0697″ (1.77 mm.).
2. Some of these transmissions use the same type of synchronizer (Borg Warner) as in the PL410 and PL411 three speed, bottom cover transmission. Others use a servo type synchronizer which utilizes brake bands. To assemble these synchronizers, place each gear on a flat surface. Install the synchronizer ring into the clutch gear. Place the thrust block and anchor block as shown and install the circlip into the groove.
3. Third gear should be adjusted to give an end-play of .0020-.0059″ (.05-.15

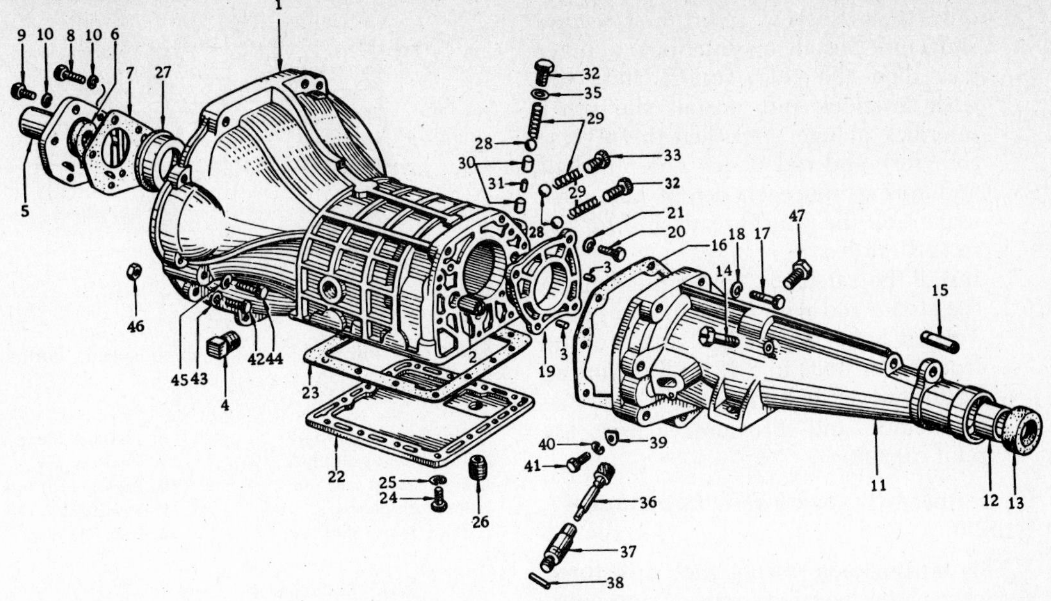

Four speed, bottom cover transmission case details

1. Case
2. Needle bearing
3. Dowel pin
4. Plug
5. Front cover assembly
6. Oil seal
7. Gasket
8. Bolt
9. Bolt
10. Lockwasher
11. Extension housing
12. Bushing
13. Oil seal
14. Breather
15. Striker bushing
16. Gasket
17. Bolt
18. Lockwasher
19. Bearing retainer
20. Bolt
21. Lockwasher
22. Bottom cover
23. Gasket
24. Bolt
25. Lockwasher
26. Drain plug
27. Bearing retainer
28. Detent ball
29. Detent spring
30. Interlock plunger
31. Interlock pin
32. Detent plug
33. Detent plug
34. Not used
35. Washer
36. Speedometer pinion
37. Pinion sleeve
38. Pin
39. Lockplate
40. Lockwasher
41. Bolt
42. Bolt
43. Lockwasher
44. Bolt
45. Lockwasher
46. Nut
47. Plug for backup light switch

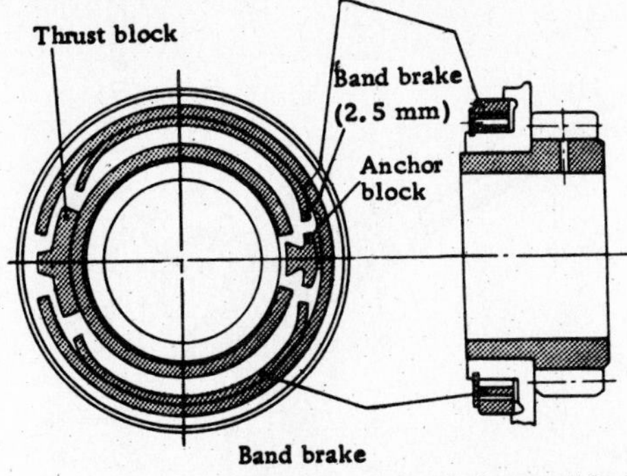

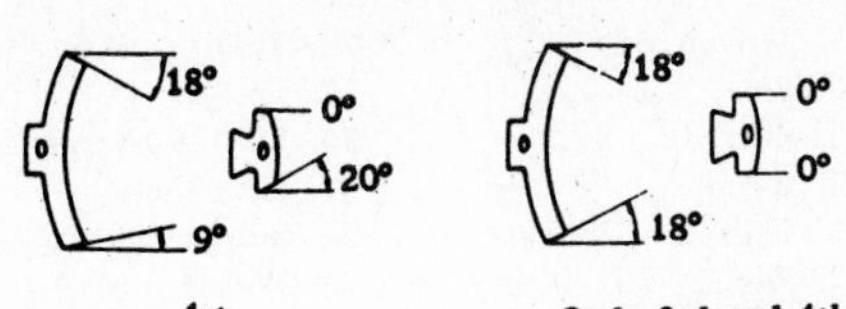

Servo type synchronizer assembly details

mm.). Snap-rings for adjustment are available in sizes from .0551″ (1.40 mm.) to .0630″ (1.60 mm.).

4. Tighten the mainshaft nut to 65-80 ft. lbs.
5. Install the reverse idler driving gear on the reverse shaft and fasten with a snap-ring. Install the shaft and gear into the case, placing a thrust washer between the gear and case. Place a thrust washer, idler gear, and snap-ring on the inside end of the shaft. Idler gear end-play should be .0039-.0118″ (.1-.3 mm.). Snap-rings are available in sizes from .0433″ (1.1 mm.) to .0591″ (1.5 mm.).
6. Countergear end-play should be .0020-.0059″ (.05-.15 mm.). Thrust washers for adjustment are available from .0945″ (2.40 mm.) to .1024″ (2.60 mm.).
7. To assemble shift mechanism, place first/second and third/fourth forks

onto their sleeves. Insert first/second shift rod. Install an interlock plunger and then the third/fourth shift rod with interlock pin. Install the other interlock plunger and then the reverse shift fork and rod. Place a detent ball and spring into each detent hole. Use sealant on the plug threads and torque to 12-15 ft. lbs.

8. Install the extension housing, engaging the striker rod with the shift rod gates. Torque bolts to 16-22 ft. lbs. Torque front cover bolts to 8-12 ft. lbs. Torque bottom cover bolts to 8-12 ft. lbs. See Capacities and Pressures Chart for refill capacity.

Four Speed Transmission Overhaul—HLS30

This transmission is constructed in three sections: clutch housing, transmission housing, and extension housing. There are no case cover plates. There is a cast iron adapter plate between the transmission and extension housings. The transmission model number is F4W71A.

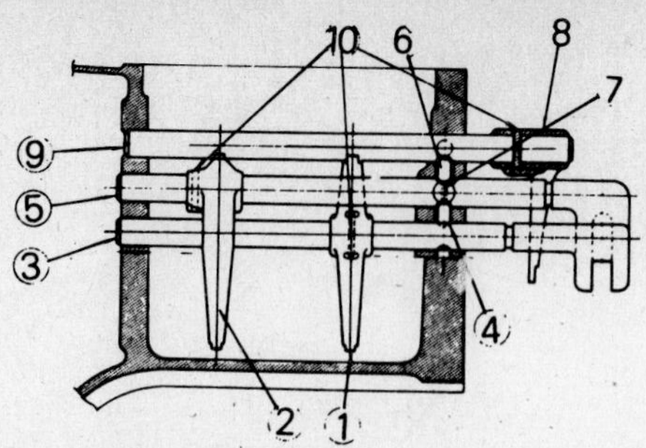

Shift rod and fork details; three speed, bottom cover transmission

1. First/second shift fork
2. Third/fourth shift fork
3. First/second shift rod
4. Interlock plunger
5. Third/fourth shift rod
6. Interlock plunger
7. Interlock pin
8. Reverse shift fork
9. Reverse shift rod
10. Fork retaining pin

Disassembly

1. Remove clutch housing dust cover. Remove retaining spring, release bearing sleeve, and withdrawal lever.

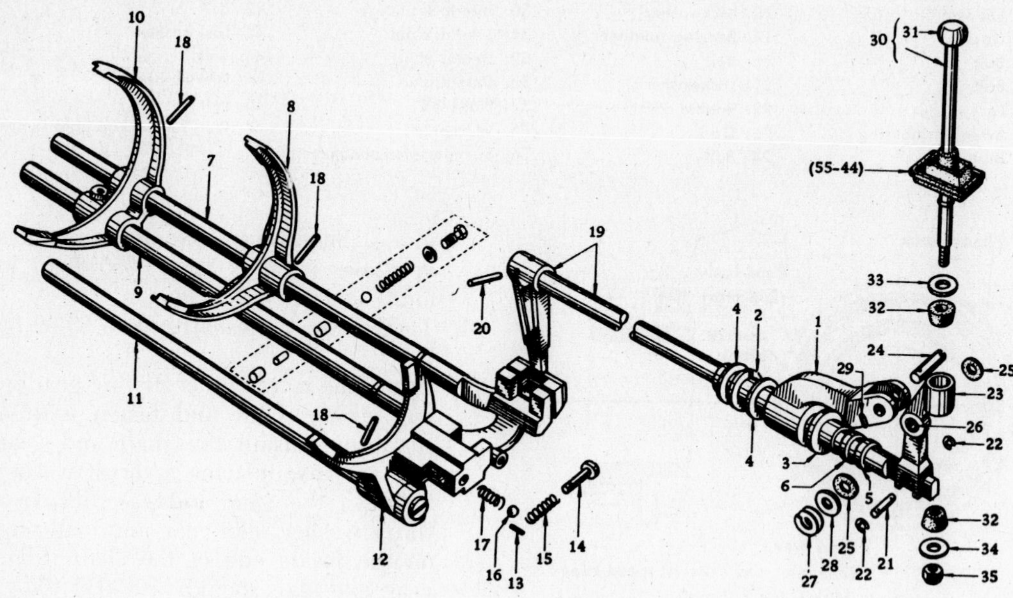

Shifting arrangement for three speed, bottom cover transmission

1. Control arm
2. Striker spring
3. Thrust washer
4. Thrust washer
5. O-ring cap
6. O-ring
7. First/second shift rod
8. First/second shift fork
9. Third/fourth shift rod
10. Third/fourth shift rod
11. Reverse shift rod
12. Reverse shift fork
13. Roll pin
14. Pin
15. Reverse pin return spring
16. Reverse fork check ball
17. Check spring
18. Pin
19. Striker rod
20. Pin
21. Pin
22. C-ring
23. Shift lever bracket
24. Pin
25. Washer
26. Bushing
27. Spring
28. Thrust washer
29. Pin
30. Shift lever assembly
31. Shift knob
32. Rubber bushing
33. Washer
34. Washer
35. Nut
55-44. Rubber boot

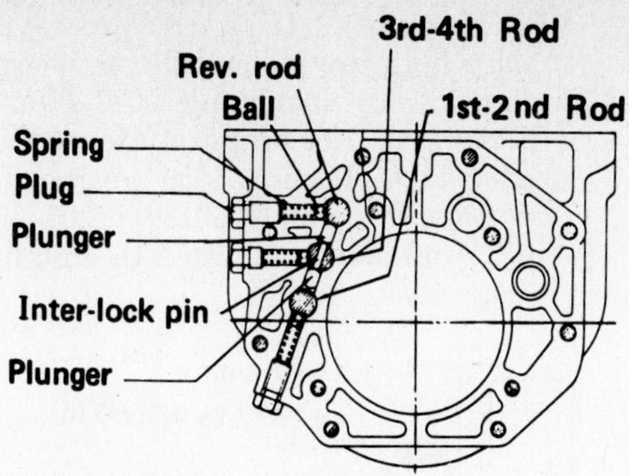

Shift rod interlock details for three speed, bottom cover transmission

2. Remove backup light/neutral safety switch.
3. Unbolt and remove clutch housing, rapping with a soft hammer if necessary. Remove gasket, mainshaft bearing shim, and countershaft bearing shim.
4. Remove speedometer pinion sleeve.
5. Remove striker rod pin from rod. Separate striker rod from shift lever bracket.
6. Unbolt and remove rear extension. It may be necessary to rap the housing with a soft hammer.
7. Remove mainshaft bearing snap-ring.
8. Remove adapter plate and gear assembly from transmission case by rapping with a soft hammer. Hold adapter plate in a vise.
9. Punch out shift fork retaining pins. Remove shift rod snap-rings. Remove detent plugs, springs, and balls from adapter plate. Remove shift rods, being careful not to lose the interlock balls.
10. Remove snap-ring, speedometer drive gear, and locating ball.
11. Bend back mainshaft lock tab. Remove nut, lockwasher. thrust washer, reverse hub, and reverse gear.
12. Remove snap-ring and countershaft reverse gear. Remove snap-ring, reverse idler gear, thrust washer, and needle bearing.
13. Support gear assembly while rapping on the rear of the mainshaft with a soft hammer. An assistant would be helpful to avoid dropping any of the parts. The mainshaft will separate into the forward clutch shaft and the rear mainshaft.
14. Remove setscrew from adapter plate. Remove shaft nut, spring washer, plain washer, and reverse idler shaft.
15. Remove the machine screws holding the bearing retainer with an impact tool. Remove the bearing retainer and the mainshaft rear bushing.
16. To disassemble the mainshaft (rear section), remove the front snap-ring, third/fourth synchronizer assembly, third gear, and needle bearing. From the rear, remove the thrust washer, locating ball, first gear, needle bearing, first gear bushing, first/second synchronizer assembly, second gear, and needle bearing.
17. To disassemble the clutch shaft, remove the snap-ring and bearing spacer. Press off the bearing.

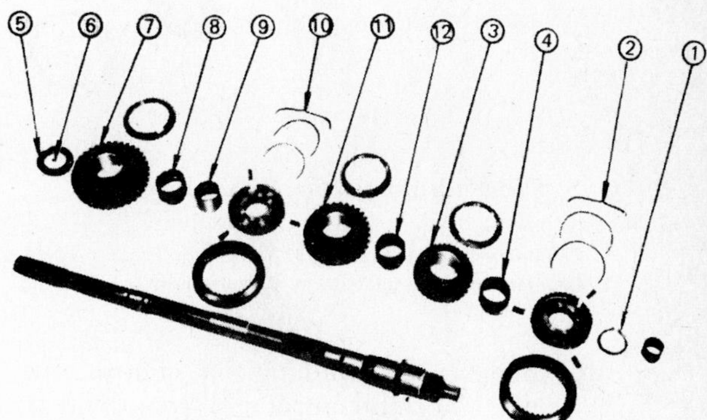

Mainshaft (rear section) assembly, HLS30 four speed

1. Snap-ring
2. Third/fourth synchronizer assembly
3. Third gear
4. Needle bearing
5. Thrust washer
6. Steel locating ball
7. First gear
8. Needle bearing
9. First gear bushing
10. First/second synchronizer assembly
11. Second gear
12. Needle bearing

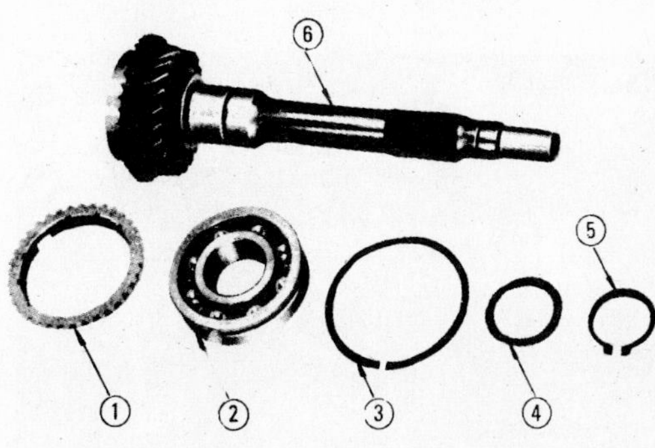

Clutch shaft assembly, HLS30 four speed

1. Baulk ring
2. Main drive bearing (mainshaft front bearing)
3. Bearing ring
4. Bearing spacer
5. Snap-ring
6. Clutch shaft

18. To disassemble the countershaft, press off the front bearing. Press off the rear bearing. Press off the gears and remove the keys.

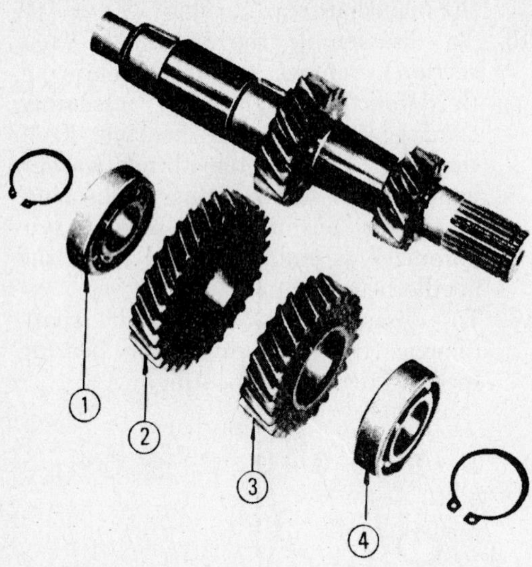

Countershaft assembly, HLS30 four speed

1. Countershaft front bearing
2. Countershaft drive gear
3. Third gear
4. Countershaft rear bearing

19. Remove the retaining pin, control arm pin, and shift control arm from the rear of the extension housing.

Inspection

1. Wash all parts in a safe solvent. Oil bearings immediately. Check all parts for wear or damage. Replace all seals, O-rings, and gaskets.
2. On reassembly, gear backlash between mating gears should be .0020-.0059″ (.05-.15 mm.). If it is excessive, replace both driving and driven gears.
3. Gear end-play should be .0047-.0075″ (.12-.19 mm.) for all gears except the reverse idler. Reverse idler gear end-play should be .0020-.0138″ (.05-.35 mm.). End-play is adjusted by installing snap-rings of different thicknesses.
4. Check the synchronizer baulk ring inside serration for wear. The slot should be .0472-.0550″ (1.2-1.4 mm.) wide.

Checking end-play between second and third gears

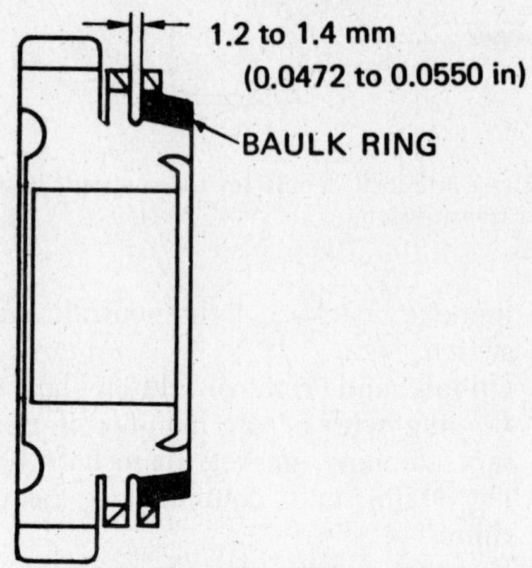

Checking synchronizer baulk ring wear

Assembly

1. Place the O-ring in the front cover. Install the front cover to the clutch housing with a press. Install the front cover oil seal.

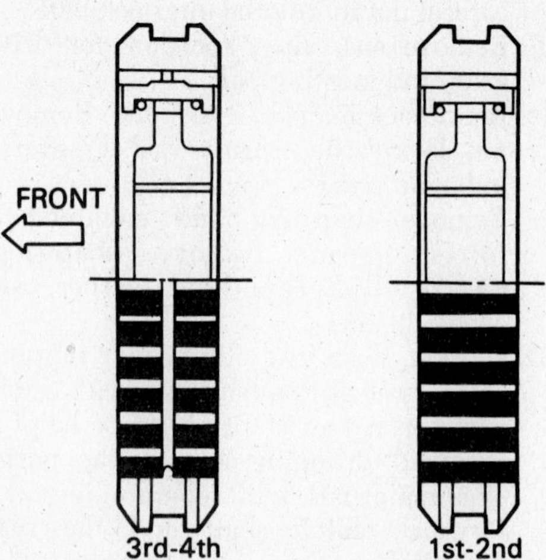

Synchronizer hubs must be installed as shown

2. Install the rear extension oil seal with a drift.
3. Assemble first/second and third/fourth synchronizer assembles. Make sure that the spreader ring gaps are not both on the same side of the unit.
4. On rear end of mainshaft, install needle bearing, second gear, baulk ring, first/second synchronizer assembly, baulk ring, first gear bushing, needle bearing, first gear, locating ball, and thrust washer.
5. Drive or press on mainshaft rear bearing.
6. Install countershaft rear bearing to adapter plate. Drive or press mainshaft rear bearing into adapter plate until bearing snap-ring groove comes through rear side of plate. Install the snap-ring. If it is not tight against the plate, press the bearing back in slightly.
7. Insert the countershaft bearing ring between the countershaft rear bearing and bearing retainer. Install the bearing retainer to the adapter plate, torquing the screws to 9-13 ft. lbs. Stake both ends of the screws with a punch.
8. Insert the reverse idler shaft from the rear of the adapter plate. Torque the setscrew to 9-13 ft. lbs. Install spring washer and plain washer to the idler shaft. Torque the shaft nut to 43-58 ft. lbs.
9. Place the two keys on the countershaft and oil the shaft lightly. Press on third gear and install a snap-ring.

Reverse idler shaft, 2, is located by setscrew, 1.

10. Install the countershaft into its rear bearing.
11. From the front of the mainshaft, install the needle bearing, third gear, baulk ring, third/fourth synchronizer assembly, and snap-ring. Snap-rings are available in thicknesses from .0561″ (1.425 mm.) to .0640″ (1.625 mm.) to adjust gear end-play to the figure specified under Inspection.
12. Press the main drive bearing onto the clutch shaft. Install the main drive gear spacer and a snap-ring. Snap-rings are available in thicknesses from .0710″ (1.80 mm.) to .0820″ (2.08 mm.) to adjust gear end-play to the figure specified under Inspection.
13. Insert a key into the countershaft. Insert the pilot bearing in the clutch shaft assembly. Engage the countershaft drive gear with fourth gear and drive on the countershaft fourth gear with a drift. The rear end of the countershaft should be held steady while driving on the gear, to prevent rear bearing damage.
14. Install the reverse hub, reverse gear, thrust washer, and lock tab on the rear of the mainshaft. Install the shaft nut temporarily.
15. Oil the reverse idler shaft lightly. Install the needle bearing, reverse idler gear, thrust washer, and snap-ring.
16. Place countershaft reverse gear and snap-ring on rear of countershaft. Snap-rings are available in thicknesses from .0433″ (1.1 mm.) to .0590″ (1.5 mm.) to adjust gear end-play to the figure specified under Inspection.
17. Engage both first and second gears to lock the shaft. Torque the mainshaft nut to 130-152 ft. lbs. and bend up the lock tab.
18. On the rear of the mainshaft, install the snap-ring, locating ball, speedometer drive gear, and snap-ring. Snap-rings are available in thicknesses from .0433″ (1.1 mm.) to .0590″ (1.5 mm.).
19. Recheck end-play and backlash of all gears. See Inspection.
20. Place reverse shift fork on reverse gear and install reverse shift rod. Install detent ball, spring, and plug. Install fork retaining pin. Place two interlock balls between reverse shift rod and third/fourth shift rod location. Install third/fourth shift fork and rod. Install detent ball, spring, and plug. This plug

is shorter than the other two. Install fork retaining pin. Place two interlock balls between first/second shift rod location and third/fourth shift rod.

INTER LOCK BALLS AND CHECK BALLS

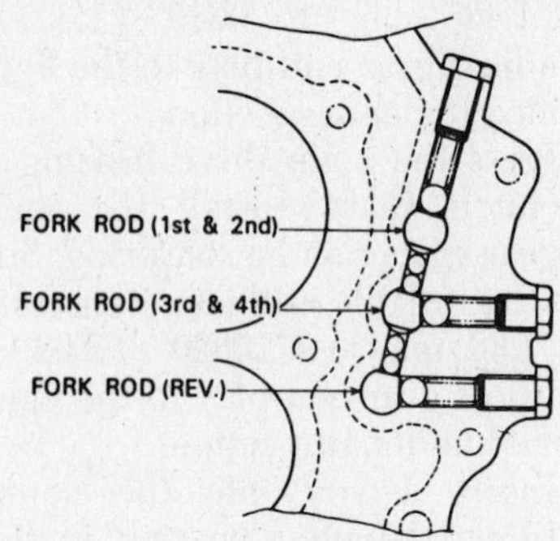

Interlock and detent arrangement, HLS30 four speed

Replacing shift rod snap-ring

Install first/second shift fork and rod. Install detent ball, spring, and plug. Apply locking agent to each detent plug and torque them to 16-22 ft. lbs. Install fork retaining pin.

21. Install shift rod snap-rings.
22. Oil all moving parts and check that all gears can be shifted smoothly.
23. Apply sealant sparingly to the adapter plate and transmission housing. Install the transmission housing to the adapter plate and bolt it down temporarily.
24. Drive in countershaft front bearing with a drift. Place the snap-ring in the

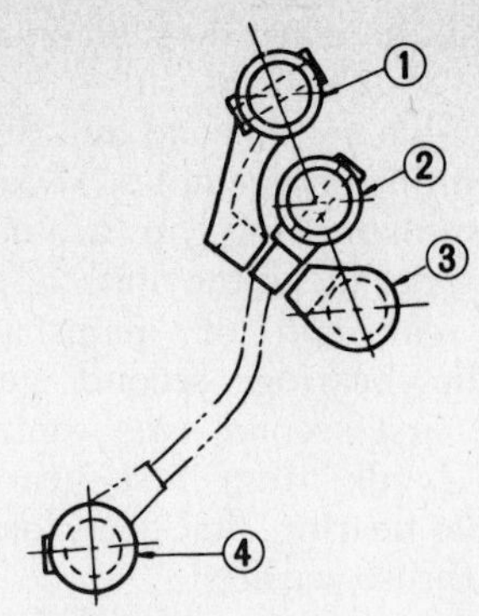

Striker rod and shift fork rod arrangement

1. Reverse shift rod
2. Third/fourth shift rod
3. First/second shift rod
4. Striker rod

mainshaft front bearing.

25. Apply sealant sparingly to adapter plate and extension housing. Align shift rods in neutral positions. Position striker rod to shift rods and bolt down extension housing. Torque to 11-16 ft. lbs. Be careful not to damage the extension housing oil seal in installation.
26. Insert striker rod pin, connect rod to shift lever bracket, and install striker rod pin retaining ring. Replace shift control arm.
27. To select the proper mainshaft bearing shim, first measure the amount the bearing protrudes from the front of the transmission case. This is measurement B. Then measure the depth of the bearing recess in the rear of the clutch housing. This is measurement A.

Measurement A

Required shim thickness is found by subtracting B from A. Shims are available in thicknesses of .0551″ (1.4 mm.) and .0630″ (1.6 mm.).

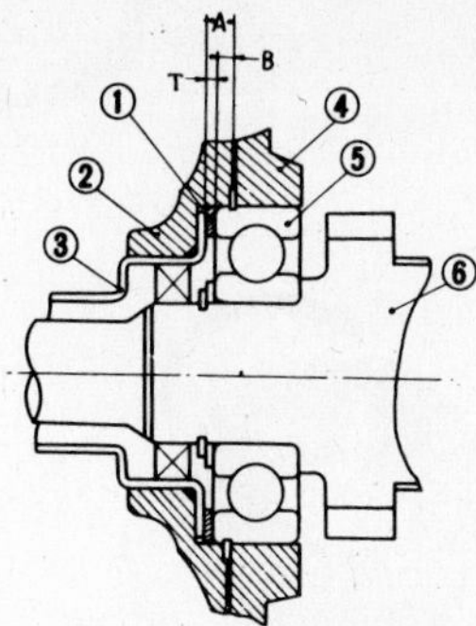

Mainshaft bearing and shim

1. Bearing shim
2. Clutch housing
3. Front cover
4. Transmission case
5. Mainshaft front bearing
6. Clutch shaft

A. Measurement of bearing recess depth in clutch housing
B. Measurement of bearing protrusion from transmission housing
T. Shim thickness

28. To select the proper countershaft front bearing shim, measure the amount that the bearing is recessed into the transmission case. Shim thickness should equal this measurement. Shims are

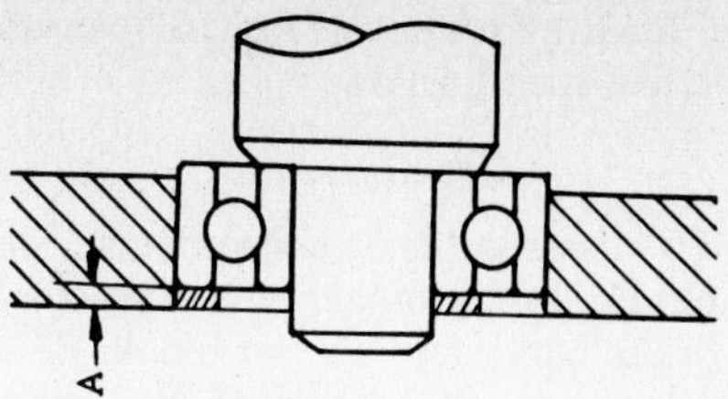

Countershaft bearing and shim, A

available in thicknesses from .0157″ (.4 mm.) to .0394″ (1.0 mm.).

29. Apply sealant sparingly to clutch and transmission housing mating surfaces and torque bolts to 11-16 ft. lbs.
30. Replace clutch operating mechanism.
31. Install shift lever temporarily and check shifting action.
32. Refill transmission. See Capacities and Pressures Chart.

Five Speed Transmission Overhaul—SRL311, HLS30

This transmission is quite similar to the four speed HLS30 unit. The model number is FS5C71A. Servo type synchromesh is used, instead of the Borg Warner type in the four speed. Shift linkage and interlock arrangements are the same, except that the reverse shift rod also operates fifth gear. Most service procedures are identical to

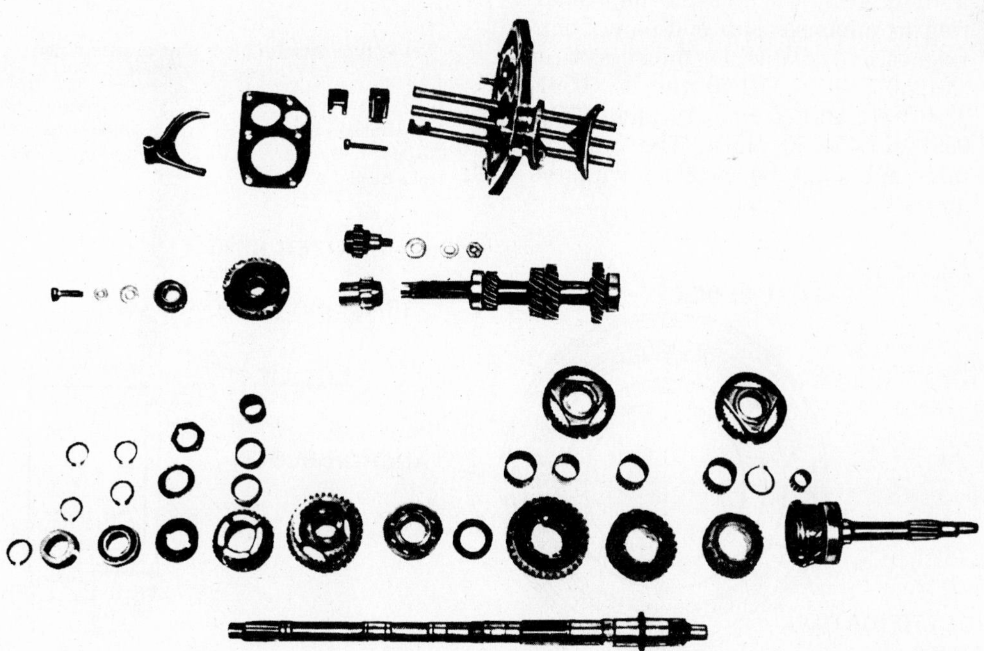

Components of five speed transmission gear train

those for the four speed unit. Those unique to the five speed follow.

Disassembly

1. To disassemble synchronizers, remove circlip, synchronizer ring, thrust block, brake band, and anchor block. Be careful not to mix parts of the different synchronizer assembles.

Inspection

1. Gear backlash should be .0016-.0059" (.04-.15 mm.) for the main drive gear and reverse gear. For first, second, third, and fifth gears it should be .0016-.0079" (.04-.20 mm.).
2. Gear end-play should be:

Gear	*End-Play*
First, Second, Fifth	.0039-.0075" (.12-.19 mm.)
Third	.0039-.0094" (.12-.24 mm.)
Reverse Idler	.0019-.0137" (.05-.35 mm.)

Assembly

1. The synchronizer assemblies for second, third, and fourth are identical. Refer to the illustrations for identification of synchronizer components. When assembling the first gear synchronizer, be sure to install the .0866" (2.2 mm.) thick brake band at the bottom.
2. When assembling the mainshaft, select a third gear synchronizer hub snapring to minimize hub end-play. Snaprings are available in thicknesses of .0610-.0630" (1.55-1.60 mm.), .0591-.0610" (1.50-1.55 mm.), and .0571-0591" (1.45-1.50 mm.). The synchronizer hub must be installed with the longer boss to the rear.

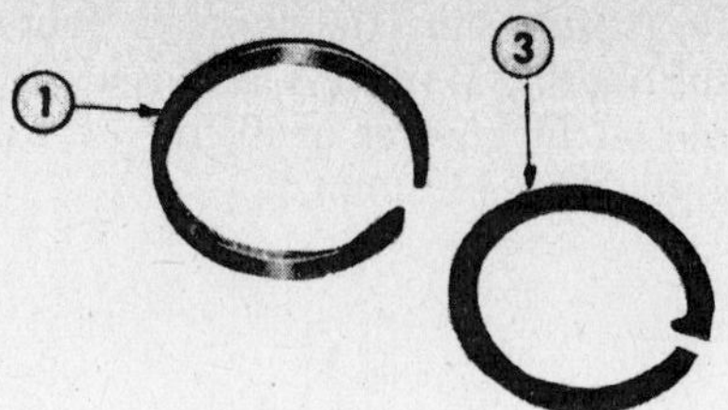

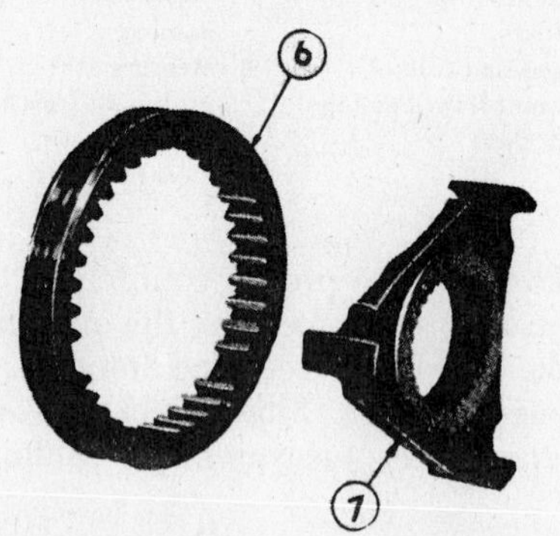

Servo type synchronizer unit disassembled

1. Synchronizer ring
2. Anchor block
3. Circlip
4. Brake band
5. Thrust block
6. Synchronizer sleeve
7. Synchronizer hub

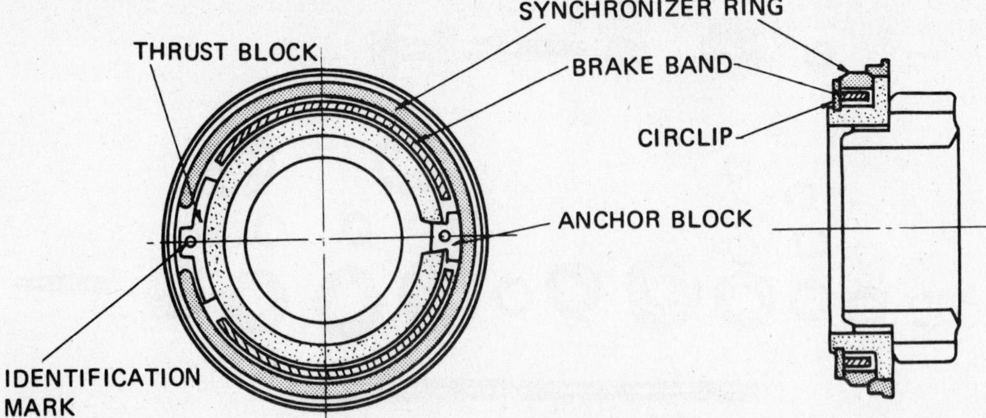

Servo type synchronizer assembled

	4th	3rd	2nd	1st	5th (OD)
Thrust block	(1.24) 31.5; 18°; 8.1 (0.3189)	←	←	(1.24) 31.5; 9°; 8.1 (0.3189)	(1.181) 30; 25°; 8.1 (0.3189)
Anchor block	8.1 (0.3189); 9.7 (0.3819); 15.6 (0. 614)	←	←	(0.3189) 8.1; 9.7 (0.3819); 20°; 15.6 (0.614)	8.1 (0.3189); 9.7 (0.3819); 14.5 (0.571)
Brake band	(1.272) 32.3; 135°; 2.5 (0.0984); 8 (0.3149)	←	←	←	(1.201) 30.5; 139°; 2.2 (0.0866); 8 (0.3149)
Brake band	Same as above	←	←	(1.224) 31.1; 143°; (0.3149) 8; 2.2 (0. 0866)	Same as above
Synchronizer ring	67.7 (2.665); 3.9 (0.1535)	←	←	←	(2.500) 63.5; (0.1377) 3.5
Circlip	56.1 (2.209); 7.8 (0.3071)	←	←	←	52 (2.047); 7.4 (0.2913)

Dimensions of components of servo type synchronizers for five speed transmission. Dimensions are in mm. and (ins.).

3. When reassembling the gear train, install the mainshaft, countershaft, and gears to the adapter plate. To tighten the mainshaft locknuts, tighten the front nut to 15-22 ft. lbs. and the rear nut to 7-15 ft. lbs. Hold the rear nut and force the front nut against it to a torque of 217 ft. lbs. Select a snap-ring to minimize end-play of the fifth gear bearing at the rear of the mainshaft. Snap-rings are available in thicknesses from .0433″ (1.1 mm.) to .0551″ (1.4 mm.).

Mainshaft locknuts, 1 and 2, and snap-ring, 3

Four Speed Transmission Overhaul—LB110, KLB110

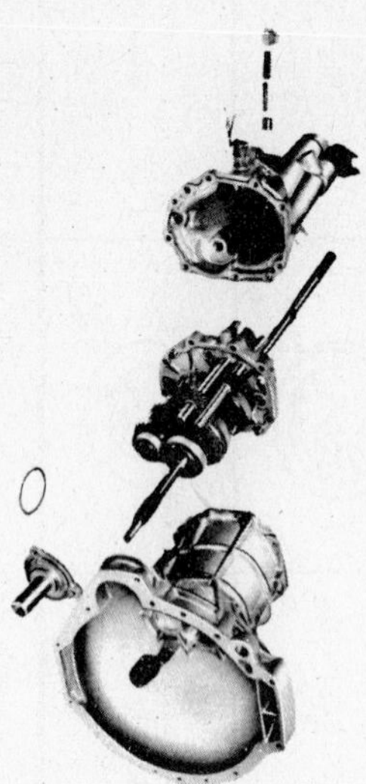
LB110 four speed transmission major assemblies

This transmission is constructed in two sections: a combined clutch and transmission housing. and an extension housing. There is a cast iron adapter plate between the housings. There are no case cover plates. The transmission model number is F4W56.

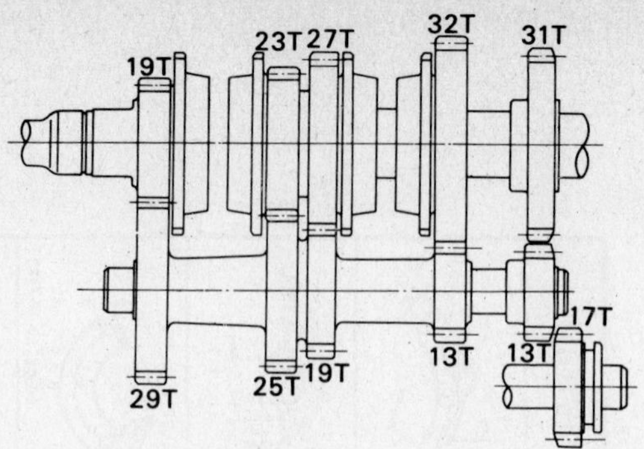

LB110 four speed transmission gear train

Disassembly

1. Drain oil.
2. Remove dust cover, spring, clutch withdrawal lever, and release bearing.
3. Remove front cover from inside clutch housing.
4. From extension housing, remove speedometer drive pinion. Remove striker rod return spring plug, spring, plunger, and bushing. Remove striker rod pin and separate striker rod from shift lever bracket.
5. Unbolt extension housing and remove. Tap it with a soft hammer, if necessary.
6. Separate the adapter plate from the transmission case, being careful not to lose the countershaft bearing washer.

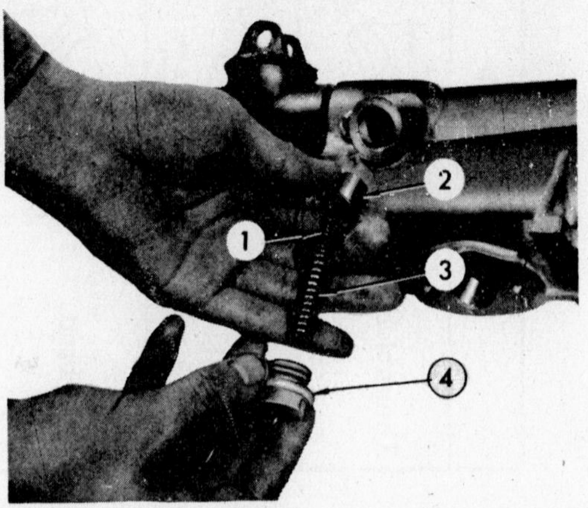

Striker rod return spring parts

1. Plunger
2. Bushing
3. Return spring
4. Plug

7. Clamp the adapter plate in a vise with the reverse idler gear up.
8. Drive out the retaining pin and remove the reverse shift fork and reverse idler gear.
9. Remove the mainshaft rear snap-ring, washer, and reverse gear.
10. Drive out remaining shift fork retaining pins. Remove all three detent plugs, springs, and balls. Remove forks and shift rods. Be careful not to lose the interlock plungers.
11. Tap the rear of the mainshaft with a soft hammer to separate the mainshaft and countershaft from the adapter plate. Be careful not to drop the shafts. Separate clutch shaft from mainshaft.
12. From the front of the mainshaft, remove the needle bearing, synchronizer hub thrust washer, steel locating ball, third/fourth synchronizer, baulk ring, third gear, and needle bearing.

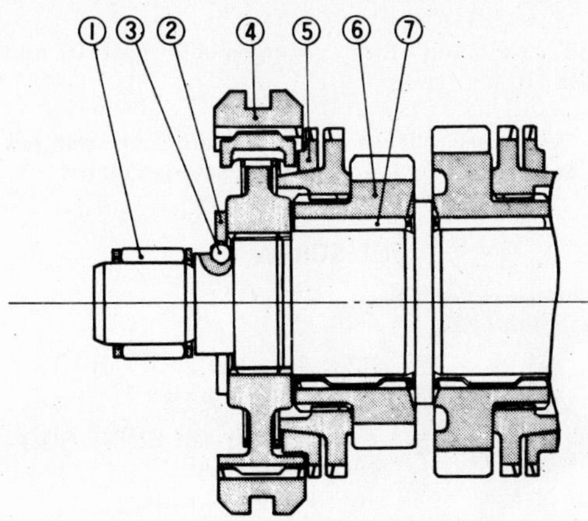

Front of LB110 and KLB110 transmission mainshaft

1. Needle bearing
2. Thrust bearing
3. Steel ball
4. Coupling sleeve
5. Baulk ring
6. Third gear
7. Needle bearing

13. Press off the mainshaft bearing to the rear. Remove the thrust washer, first gear, needle bearing, baulk ring, first/second synchronizer, baulk ring, second gear, and needle bearing.
14. Remove countergear bearing.
15. Remove clutch shaft snap-ring and bearing.

Inspection

1. Clean all parts in a safe solvent. Oil the bearings immediately. Check all

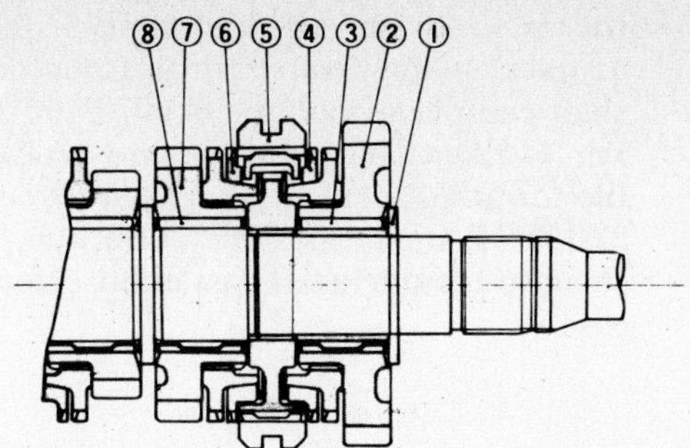

Rear of LB110 and KLB110 transmission mainshaft

1. Thrust washer
2. First gear
3. Needle bearing
4. Baulk ring
5. Coupling sleeve
6. Baulk ring
7. Second gear
8. Needle bearing

parts for wear or damage.

2. Backlash for each pair of gears should be .0031-.0059″ (.08-.15 mm.). If it is excessive, replace both drive and driven gears.
3. Gear end-play is adjusted by using snap-rings of different thicknesses.

Gear	*End-Play*
First, Second	.0059-.0098″ (.15-.25 mm.)
Third	.0059-.0138″ (.15-.35 mm.)

4. Place each baulk ring on the cone of its gear. Check the gap between the baulk ring end face and the clutch teeth front face. The gap should be .0413-.0551″ (1.05-1.40 mm.). If it is less than .0197″ (.5 mm.), replace the bulk ring.

Assembly

1. Press on the countershaft bearings. Install the countershaft assembly into

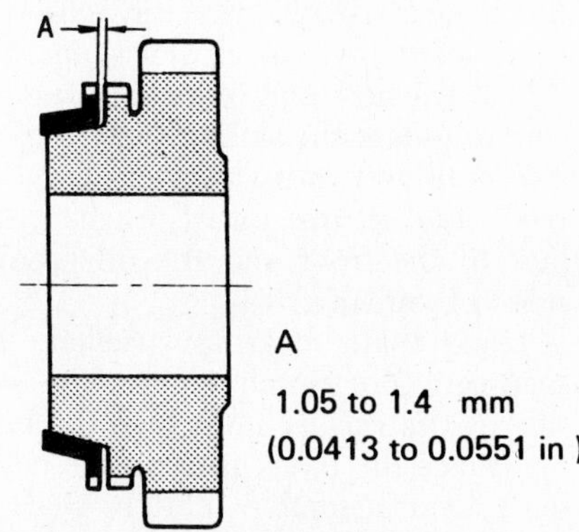

Checking baulk ring gap

the transmission case and replace the adapter plate temporarily. Countershaft end-play should be 0-.0079″ (0-.2 mm.). Front bearing shims are available for adjustment in thicknesses from .0315″ (.8 mm.) to .0512″ (1.3 mm.). Remove countershaft assembly from case.

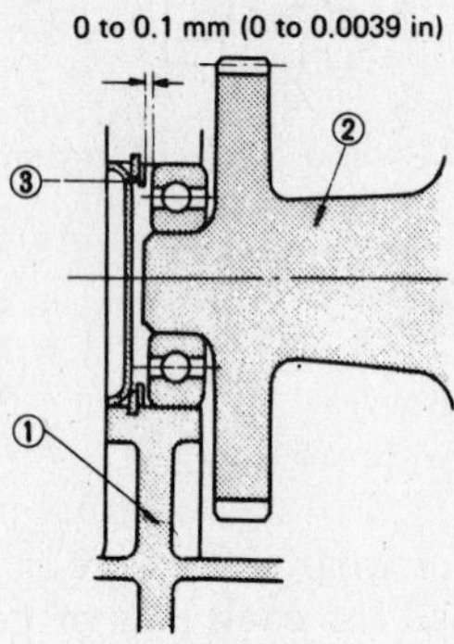

Selecting countershaft front bearing shim

1. Transmission case
2. Countershaft
3. Shim

2. Oil all moving parts on installation.
3. Install coupling sleeve, shifting inserts, and spring on synchronizer hub. Be careful not to hook front and rear ends of spring to same insert. Check that hub and sleeve operate smoothly.
4. Install needle bearing from rear of mainshaft. Install second gear, baulk ring, and synchronizer hub assembly. Align shifting insert to baulk ring groove. Install first gear side needle bearing, baulk ring, and first gear. Install mainshaft thrust washer and press on the rear bearing. On mainshaft front end, replace needle bearing, third gear, baulk ring, synchronizer hub assembly, steel locating ball, thrust washer, and pilot bearing. Be sure to grease the sliding surface of the steel ball and thrust washer. The dimpled side of the thrust washer must face to the front and the oil grooved side to the rear.
5. Replace main bearing, washer, and snap-ring on clutch shaft. The web side of the washer must face the bearing. Place the baulk ring on the clutch shaft and assemble clutch shaft to mainshaft.
6. Align mainshaft assembly with countershaft assembly and install them to the adapter plate by lightly tapping on the clutch shaft with a soft hammer.
7. Place first/second and third/fourth shift forks on shift rods, being careful that forks are not reversed. Install all three shift rods and detent and interlock parts. Apply locking agent to detent plug threads and screw plugs in flush. Make sure that shift forks are in their grooves and drive in the retaining pins.

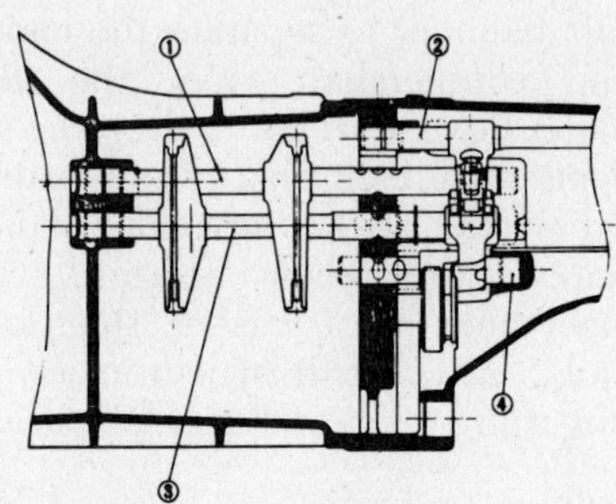

Shift rod and fork arrangement, LB110 and KLB110 four speed

1. First/second shift rod
2. Striker rod
3. Third/fourth shift rod
4. Reverse shift rod

SET SCREW
1st, 2nd SHIFT ROD
PLUNGER
3rd, 4th SHIFT ROD
BALL
SPRING
REVERSE SHIFT ROD

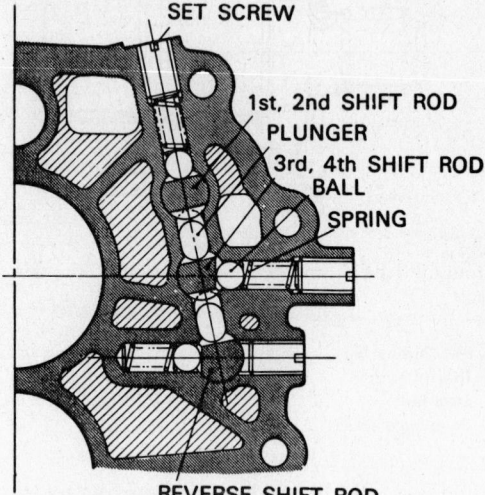

Detent ball and interlock details, LB110 and KLB110 four speed

8. Install mainshaft reverse gear, thrust washer, and snap-ring. Face web side of thrust washer to gear.
9. Replace reverse idler gear and pin on reverse shift fork. Check interlock action by attempting to shift two shift rods at once.

10. Install adapter plate to transmission case. Make sure to install countergear front shim selected in Step 1. Use sealant on the joint and seat the plate by tapping with a soft hammer.
11. Align the striker lever and install the extension housing. Use sealant on the joint. Install bushing, plunger, return spring, and plug. Use sealant on the plug threads. Install striker rod pin and speedometer drive pinion.
12. Select clutch shaft bearing shim(s) by measuring amount bearing outer race is recessed below machined surface for front cover. The depth should be .1969-.2028″ (5.00-5.15 mm.). Shims are available for adjustment in thicknesses of .0039″ (.1 mm.), .0079″ (.2 mm.), and .0197″ (.5 mm.).

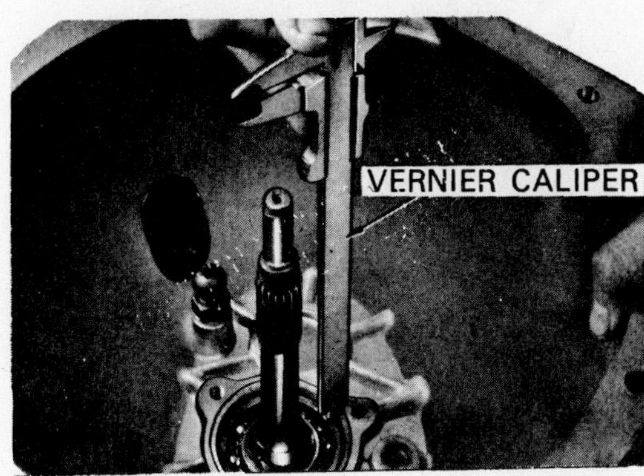

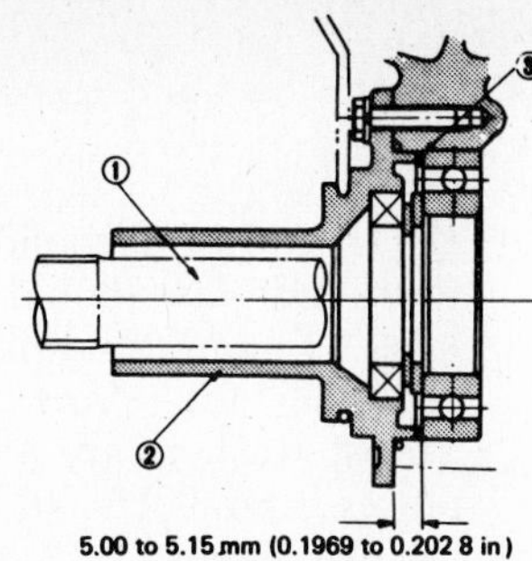

Selecting clutch shaft bearing shims

1. Clutch shaft
2. Front cover
3. Shim for adjusting front cover

13. Place oil seal in front cover, grease the seal lip, and install the cover and O-ring with the shim(s) selected in Step 12.
14. Replace clutch release bearing, return spring, and withdrawal lever.
15. Check shifting action. Rotate clutch shaft slowly in neutral. The rear of the mainshaft should not turn.
16. Refer to the Capacities and Pressures Chart for refill capacity.

Four Speed, Top Cover Transmission Overhaul—PL410, SPL310

This transmission may also be found in some early L520 and PL411 models. The transmission and clutch housings are combined in one piece. The floorshift mechanism is integrated with the top cover. On some models, the shift lever is located further back, above the extension housing.

DISASSEMBLY

1. Drain oil.
2. Remove the clutch withdrawal lever. Remove the transmission top cover.
3. Twist the cap at the base of the shift lever counterclockwise while pressing down.
4. Unbolt and remove top cover.
5. Straighten lock tab, remove setscrew, and tap reverse idler shaft forward. Remove shaft and gear.
6. Drive countershaft forward and out. Remove thrust washers. The countergear cannot be removed yet.
7. Pull the mainshaft out through the rear of the case.
8. Tilt the countergear to clear the clutch shaft gear. Insert a long drift through the mainshaft opening and drive the clutch shaft and bearing forward out of the case.
9. Remove the countergear from the case. To remove the needle roller bearing, break the retaining clips and drive out the bearing.
10. To disassemble the mainshaft, slide off the third/fourth synchronizer from the front. Insert a wire through the hole in the gear cone and depress the spring loaded plunger which locates the splined washer, aligning the washer with the splines. Pull third and second gears, with their bronze sleeves, over the plunger and off the shaft. It may be necessary to immerse the shaft in warm oil to expand the sleeve slightly. Remove the plunger and spring. Remove the splined washer and first gear. At the rear of the shaft, straighten the lock tab, remove the nut, speedometer drive gear, and key. Remove the distance piece (spacer) and bearing.

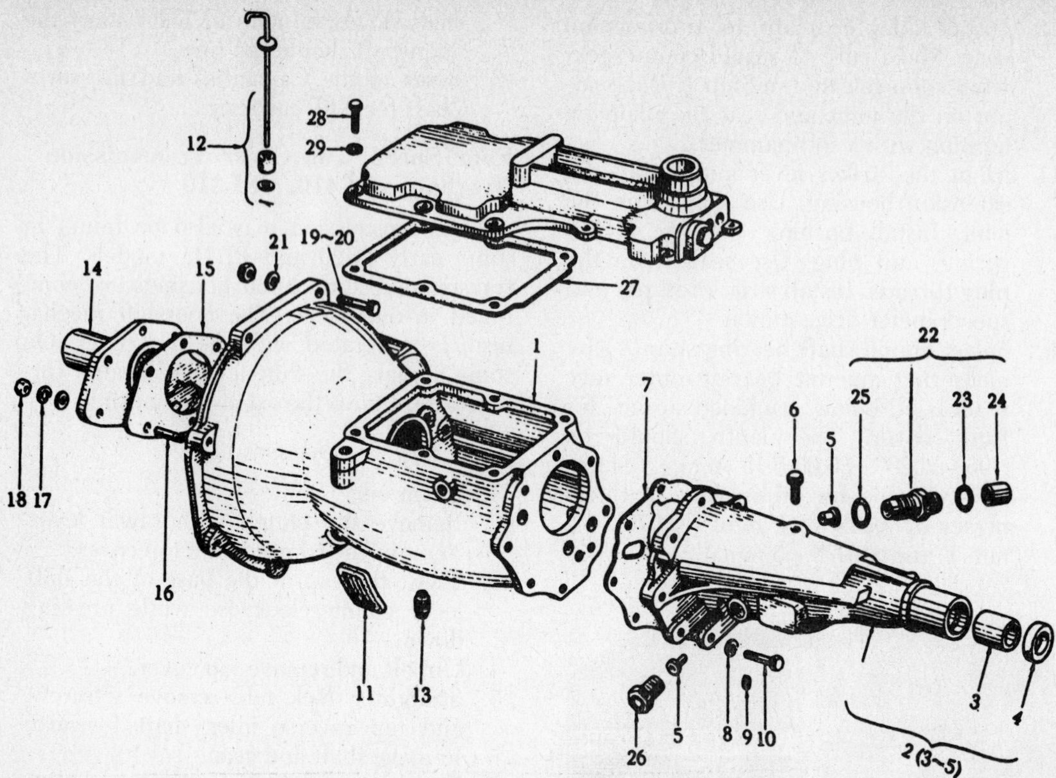

Four speed, top cover transmission case details

1. Case
2. Extension housing
3. Bushing
4. Oil seal
5. Speedometer pinion bushing
6. Breather
7. Gasket
8. Lockwasher
9. Plain washer
10. Bolt
11. Rubber boot
12. Dipstick assembly
13. Drain plug
14. Front cover
15. Gasket
16. Stud
17. Lockwasher
18. Nut
19. Bolt
20. Bolt
21. Lockwasher
22. Speedometer pinion sleeve assembly
23. O-ring
24. O-ring retainer
25. O-ring
26. Speedometer pinion plug
27. Cover gasket
28. Bolt
29. Lockwasher

11. To dismantle the clutch shaft, first remove the needle roller bearings from the rear. Bend back the lock tab, unscrew the left hand threaded nut, and press off the bearing.

Inspection

1. Wash all parts in a safe solvent. Oil bearings immediately.
2. Check all parts for wear or damage.
3. Pry out extension housing oil seal and install a new one.
4. Replace all gaskets.
5. Gear backlash should be .003-.005″ (.075-.125 mm.) between all pairs of gears.

Assembly

1. Install countergear in case with thrust washers. The larger washer must be at the front. Install countershaft. Countergear end-play should be .0015-.0023″ (.04-.06 mm.). End-play is adjusted by changing the rear thrust washer. Thrust washers are available in thicknesses from .0015-.0023″ (.04-.06 mm.) to .154-.156″ (3.91-3.96 mm.). Temporarily replace the countershaft with a smaller diameter rod so that the countergear will not mesh with the mainshaft and clutch shaft gears as they are installed.
2. Press the bearing onto the clutch shaft, replace the washer and nut. Some units may have a snap-ring instead of a nut. Place the 18 needle rollers into the rear of the shaft with a bit of grease. Turn transmission housing so that countergear is out of the way and drive in shaft and bearing from the front.

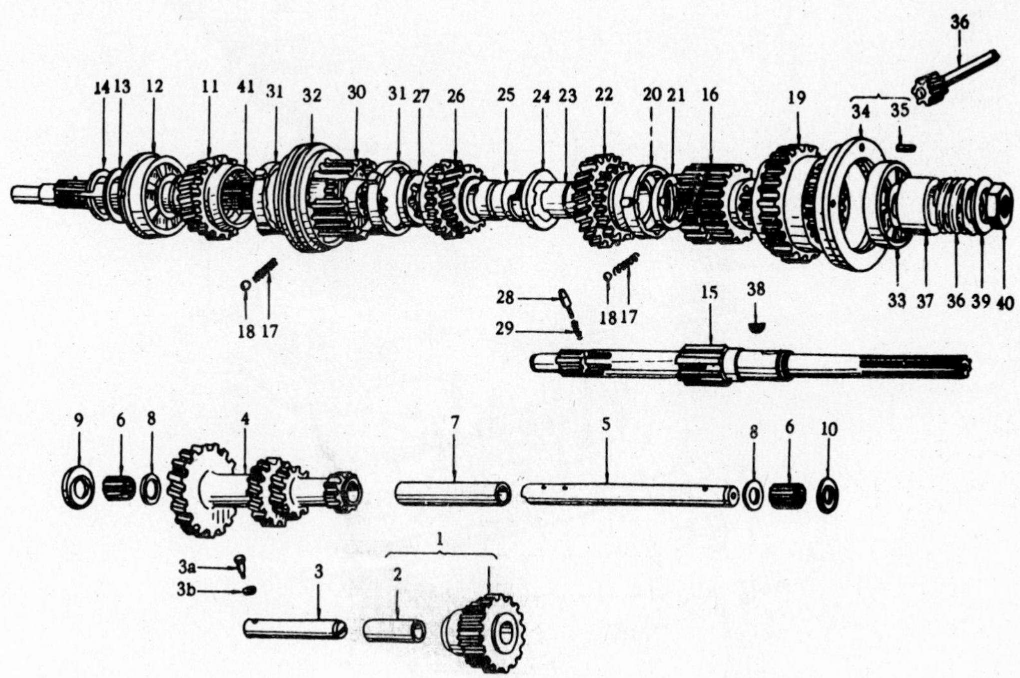

Shaft assemblies, four speed, top cover transmission

1. Reverse idler assembly
2. Bushing
3. Shaft
3a. Setscrew
3b. Lock tab
4. Countergear
5. Countershaft
6. Needle roller
7. Countershaft spacer
8. Needle roller retainer ring
9. Countergear front thrust washer
10. Countergear rear thust washer
11. Main drive (clutch shaft) gear
12. Bearing
13. Bearing spacer
14. Snap-ring
15. Mainshaft
16. Synchronizer hub
17. Synchronizer spring
18. Synchronizer ball
19. Mainshaft gear
20. Second gear baulk ring
21. Mainshaft rear thrust washer
22. Second gear
23. Second gear bushing
24. Thrust washer
25. Third gear bushing
26. Third gear
27. Mainshaft front thrust washer
28. Locking peg
29. Spring
30. Third/fourth synchronizer
31. Third/fourth baulk ring
32. Third/fourth synchronizer sleeve
33. Mainshaft bearing
34. Bearing retainer
35. Locking peg
36. Speedometer drive gears
37. Distance piece
38. Key
39. Lockwasher
40. Mainshaft nut
41. Mainshaft pilot bearing

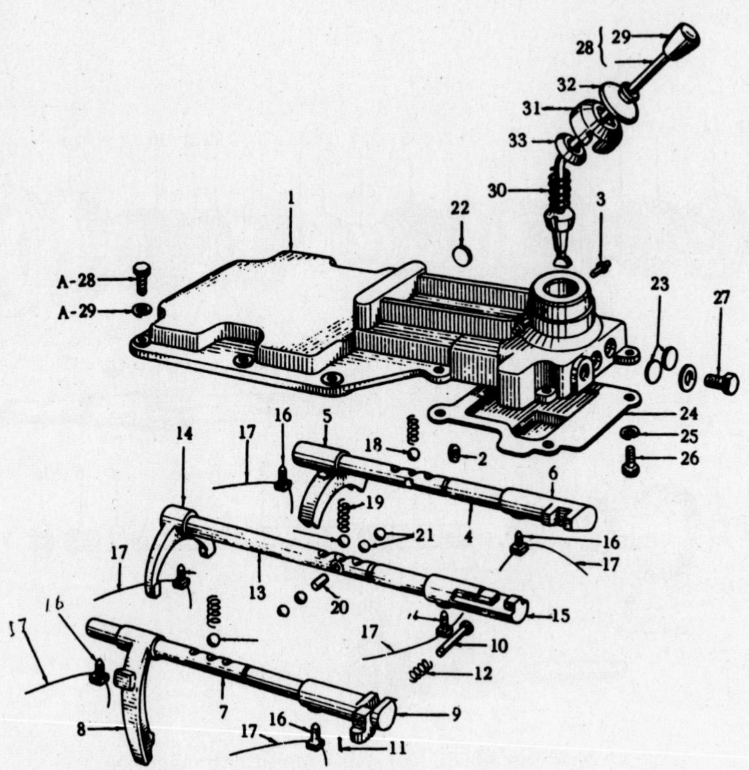

Four speed, top cover transmission top cover and shifting arrangement

1. Top cover
2. Shift rod O-ring
3. Shift lever pivot pin
4. First/second shift rod
5. Shift fork
6. Shift rod bracket
7. Reverse shift rod
8. Shift fork
9. Shift rod bracket
10. Reverse rod pin
11. Cotter pin
12. Spring
13. Third/fourth fork rod
14. Shift fork
15. Shift rod bracket
16. Setscrew
17. Lockwire
18. Detent ball
19. Spring
20. Interlock pin
21. Interlock ball
22. Plug
23. Plug
24. Dust cover
25. Lockwasher
26. Bolt
27. Plug
28. Shift lever
29. Knob
30. Spring
31. Cover cap
32. Rubber boot
33. Spring seat

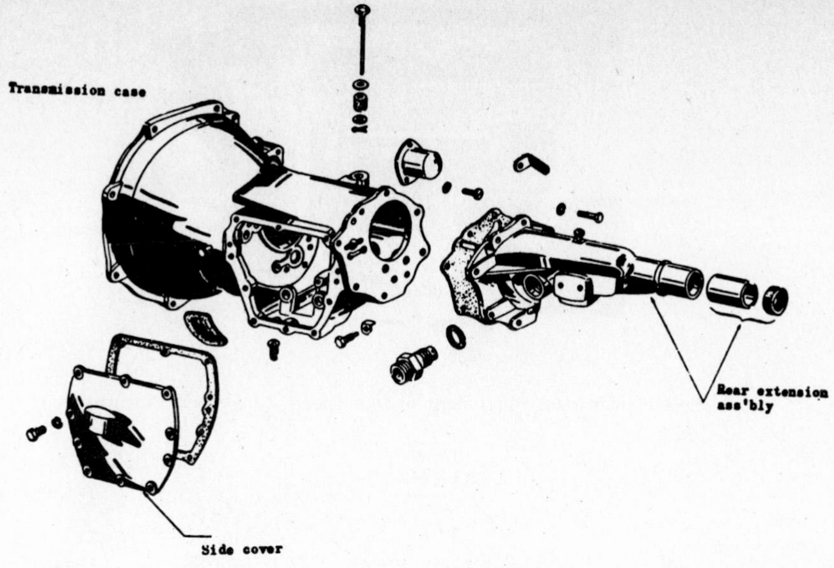

Four speed, side cover transmission case details

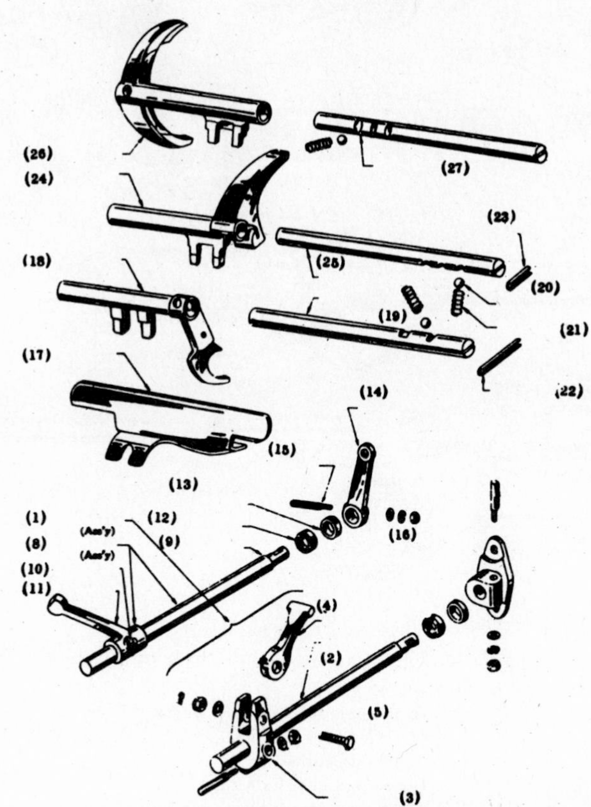

Shift linkage, four speed, side cover transmission

1. Fork assembly
2. Cross shaft
3. Shift fork
4. Operating fork
5. Fulcrum pin
6. Not used
7. Not used
8. Selector cross shaft assembly
9. Selector shaft
10. Taper pin
11. Selector shaft inner lever
12. Oil seal
13. Felt ring
14. Selector cross shaft lever
15. Lock pin
16. Plain washer, lockwasher, nut
17. Shift gate
18. Reverse fork
19. Reverse shift rod
20. Detent ball
21. Detent spring
22. Large shift rod locking strip
23. Small fork rod locking strip
24. First/second shift fork
25. First/second shift rod
26. Third/fourth shift fork
27. Third/fourth shift rod

Details of shifting arrangement of four speed, side cover transmission

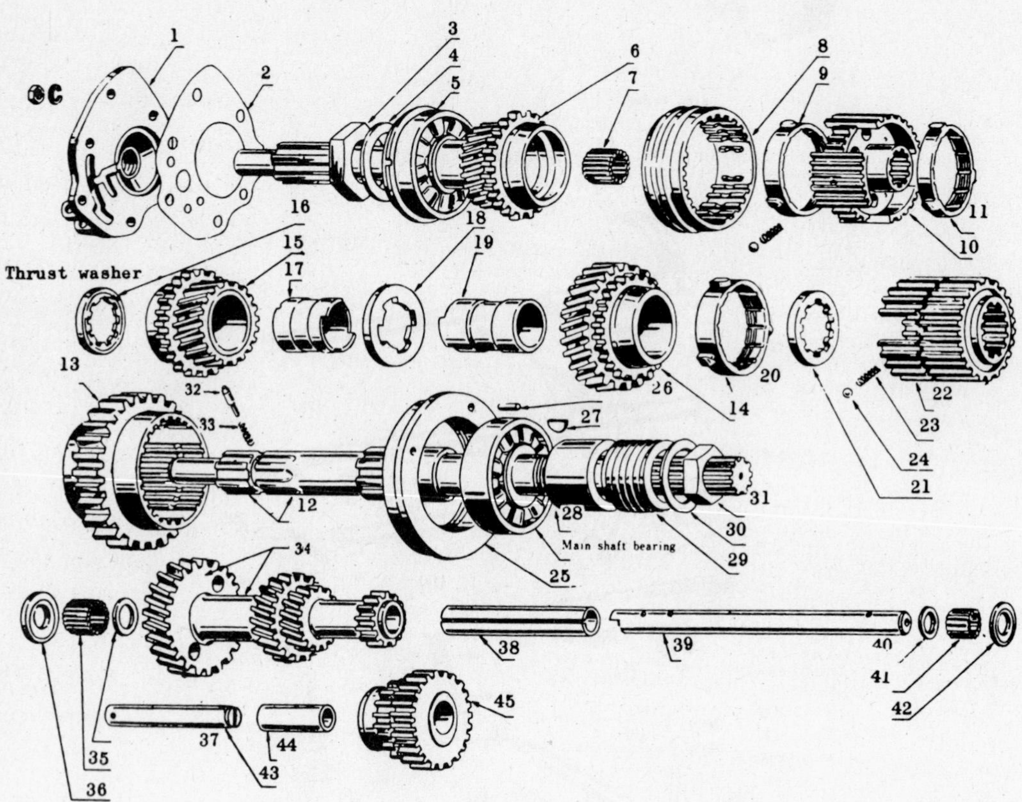

Shaft assemblies, four speed, side cover transmission

1. Front cover
2. Gasket
3. Clutch shaft bearing
4. Lockwasher
5. Clutch shaft gear
6. Clutch shaft gear
7. Mainshaft pilot bearing
8. Third/fourth synchronizer sleeve
9. Synchronizer ring
10. Synchronizer hub
11. Synchronizer ring
12. Mainshaft
13. First gear
14. Second gear
15. Third gear
16. Mainshaft front thrust washer
17. Third gear bushing
18. Thrust washer
19. Second gear bushing
20. Second gear synchronizer ring
21. Mainshaft rear thrust washer
22. Second gear synchronizer hub
23. Synchronizer spring
24. Ball
25. Bearing retainer
26. Bearing retainer locater
27. Key
28. Mainshaft spacer
29. Speedometer drive gear
30. Mainshaft lockwasher
31. Mainshaft nut
32. Locking peg
33. Spring
34. Countergear
35. Countershaft needle rollers
36. Countershaft front thrust washer
37. Snap-ring
38. Spacer
39. Countershaft
40. Snap-ring
41. Needle rollers
42. Thrust washer
43. Reverse idler shaft
44. Bushing
45. Reverse idler gear

3. Press the mainshaft bearing on from the rear. Oil the shaft ahead of the bearing and install first gear with the synchronizer forward. Replace the thrust washer and baulk ring. Expand the second gear sleeve in warm oil and slide it over the shaft. Install second gear, the washer, and the third gear sleeve. The two sleeves are locked together by the washer. Replace third gear. Place spring and plunger into hole in shaft and slide on splined washer. Depress the plunger with a wire through the hole in third gear, and slide the splined washer over the plunger. Turn the washer so that the plunger engages with a groove in the washer. Assemble the two baulk rings to third/fourth synchronizer and coupling sleeve. The large boss of the synchronizer inner splines must face forward. The pointed ends of the baulk ring lugs must face into the synchronizer. Slide third/fourth synchronizer forward slightly to clear countergear and install mainshaft. Second and third gear end-play should be .0048-.0062″ (.12-.16 mm.).
4. Oil and install the countershaft.
5. Replace the reverse idler gear and shaft with setscrew and lock tab. Replace front cover.

Four Speed, Side Cover Transmission Overhaul—L320

This transmission has a two piece case with a side cover. The column shift linkage uses cross shafts with a coupling disc. Overhaul procedures are the same as that for the four speed top cover transmission used on the PL410 and SPL310, after the shift linkage and cross shafts are removed.

AUTOMATIC TRANSMISSION

Only external transmission adjustments and repairs, and transmission removal and replacement, are covered in this book. Automatic transmission internal repairs and overhaul should be left to an authorized repair facility.

The RL411, PL510 up to serial number PL510-117464, and WPL510 up to serial number WPL510-853595 use a British built Borg Warner automatic transmission with a cable operated downshift. Later PL510 and WPL510 models use an American built Borg Warner transmission with vacuum pressure control and a solenoid operated

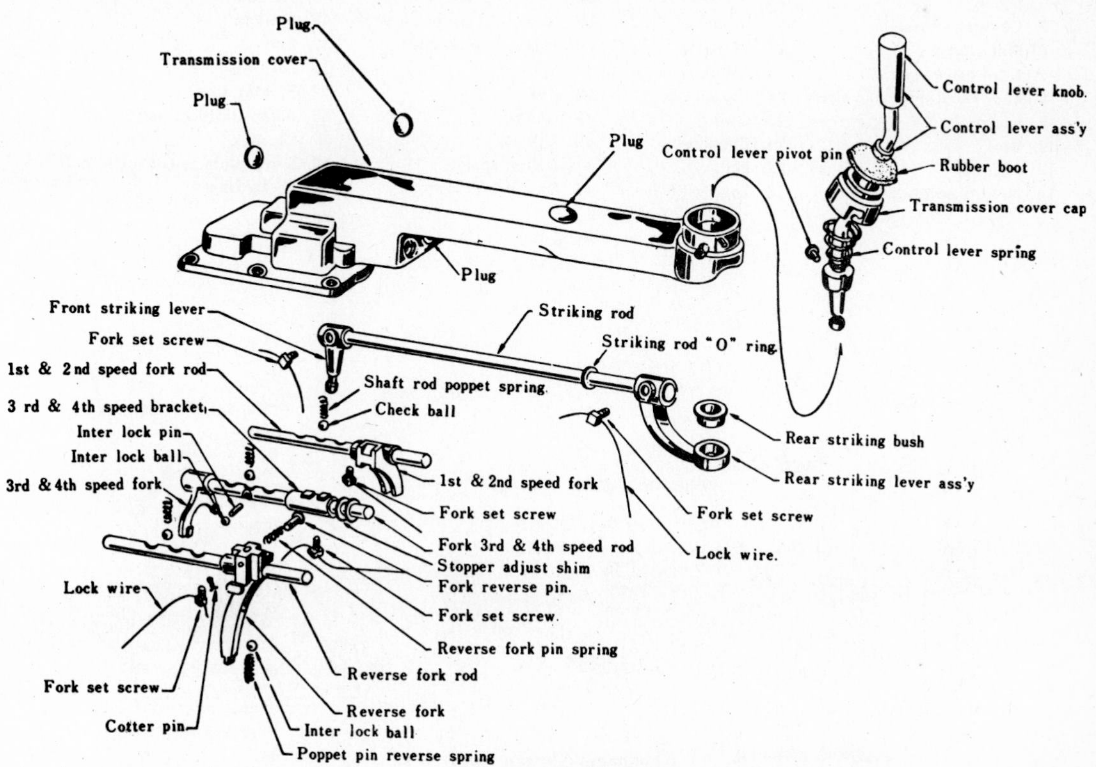

Rear mounted shift lever arrangement for four speed, top cover transmission

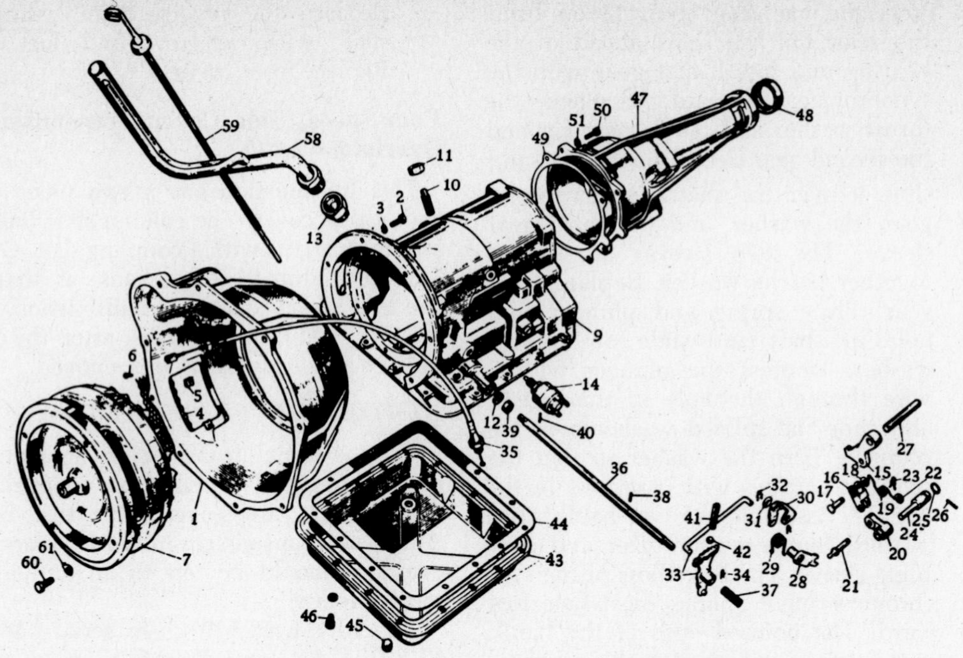

British built Borg Warner automatic transmission

1. Converter housing
2. Housing to case bolt
3. Lockwasher
4. Screen
5. Captive nut
6. Screw
7. Converter assembly
8. Not used
9. Case assembly
10. Rear band adjusting screw
11. Locknut
12. Seal
13. Adapter
14. Neutral safety switch
15. Park pawl
16. Toggle link
17. Toggle link pin
18. Washer
19. Spring
20. Toggle lever
21. Toggle pin
22. Washer
23. Retaining clip
24. Toggle pin
25. O-ring
26. Cotter pin
27. Pin
28. Toggle lift lever
29. Spring
30. Torsion lever
31. Washer
32. Retaining clip
33. Park linkage
34. Retaining clip
35. Downshift cable assembly
36. Manual valve shaft
37. Spring
38. Roll pin
39. Collar
40. Roll pin
41. Detent spring
42. Detent ball
43. Pan
44. Pan gasket
45. Drain plug
46. Bolt
47. Extension housing
48. Oil seal
49. Gasket
50. Bolt
51. Lockwasher

52-57. Not used

58. Filler, dipstick, and breather tube
59. Dipstick
60. Drive plate to converter bolt
61. Lockwasher

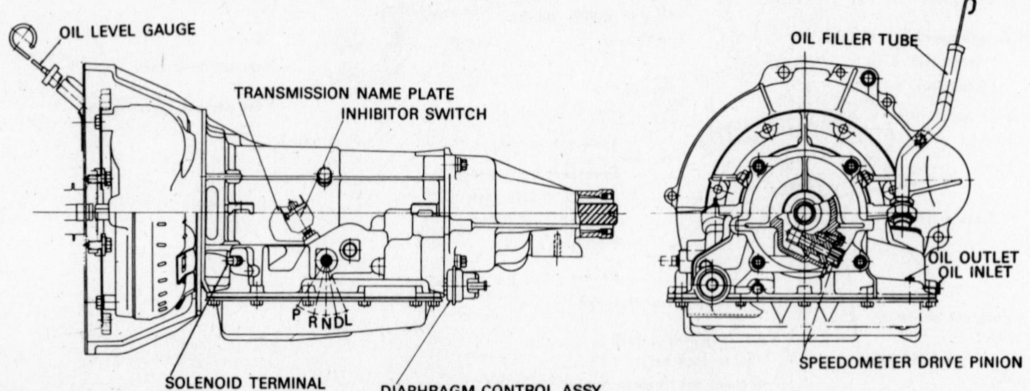

American built Borg Warner automatic transmission

downshift. The HLS30 uses a Nissan unit. There is a model and serial number tag on the left side of the Borg Warner units.

Model no.	*Nissan Part no.*	*Transmission*	*Vehicle*
AS14-35EC	31010-24500	British built BW	RL411, PL510, WPL510
AS2-41	31010A8500	American built BW	PL510, WPL510
3N71A		Nissan	HLS30

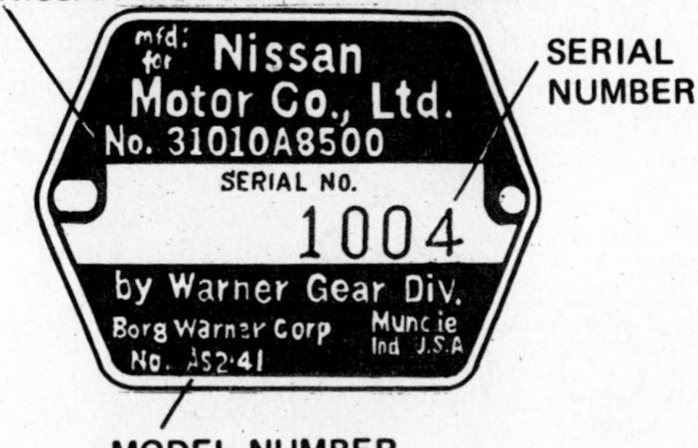

Borg Warner transmission identification tag

Fluid Level Check

The transmission dipstick is at the right rear of the engine. It has a scale on each side, one for COLD and the other for HOT. The transmission is considered hot after 15 miles of highway driving.

1. Park on a level surface with the engine running. If transmission is not hot, shift into Drive, Low, then Neutral. Shift into Neutral (PL510, WPL510) or Park (HLS30). Block the wheels and set the handbrake.

2. Remove, wipe, and replace dipstick. Check fluid level on appropriate scale. The level should be at F.

3. If fluid level is below F, leave the engine running and add fluid through the dipstick tube until the F mark is reached.

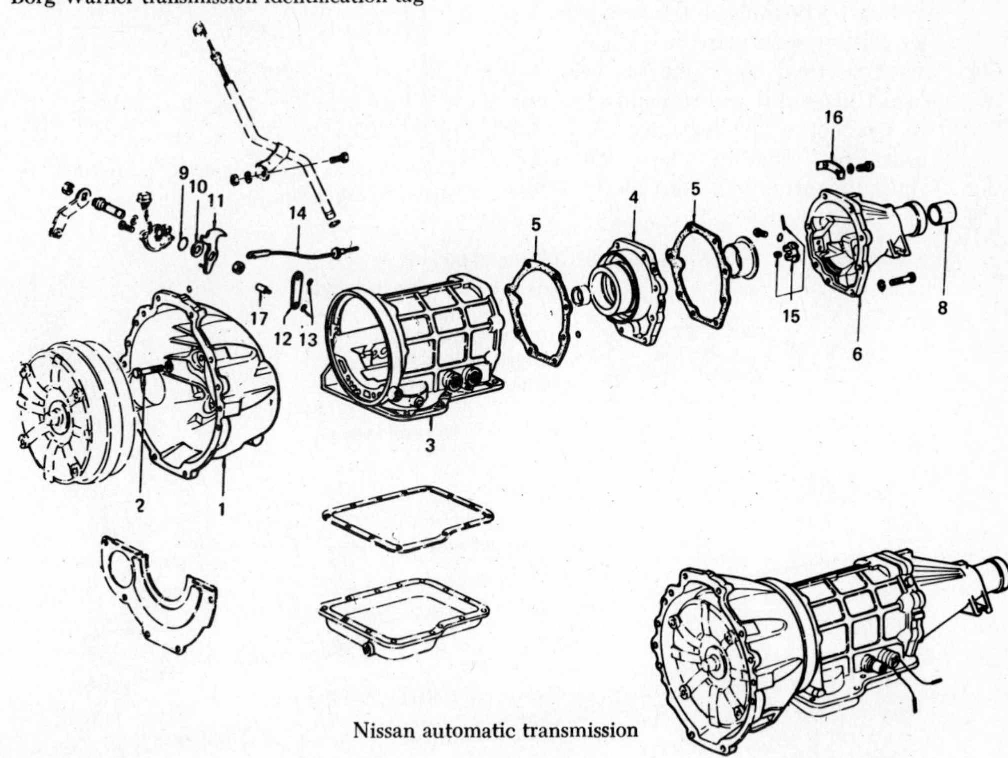

Nissan automatic transmission

1. Converter housing
2. Converter housing to transmission bolt
3. Transmission case
4. Case rear flange
5. Gasket
6. Rear extension housing
7. Not used
8. Bushing
9. O-ring
10. Washer
11. Manual plate
12. Park lever
13. Snap-ring
14. Park rod
15. Park actuator support
16. Breather baffle plate
17. Park lever pin

CAUTION: *Do not overfill, as this may cause transmission malfunction and damage.*

Fluids recommended by the manufacturer are:

British BW Unit	*American BW Unit*	*Nissan Unit*
See owner's manual	Caltex (Texaco) Texamatic Fluid 6673	Caltex (Texaco) Texamatic Fluid
	Shell Automatic Transmission Fluid Dexron	6991 or Texamatic 4571A
	BP Autran DX	Chevron RPM ATF Special
	Mobil ATF 220	Castrol TQF
	Castrol TQ Dexron	BP Autran B
	Union ATF Dexron	Esso (Enco) Glide
	Humble 1956	Mobil ATF 210
		Shell ATF Donax T7

Shift Linkage Adjustment

HLS30 Floorshift

1. Loosen trunnion locknuts at lower end of control lever. Remove selector lever knob and console.
2. Place selector lever in N.
3. Place transmission shift lever in neutral position by pushing it all the way back, then pulling it forward two stops.
4. Check vertical clearance between top of shift lever pin and transmission control bracket. The clearance, A in the illustration, should be .020-.059″. Adjust by turning the nut at the lower end of the selector lever compression rod.
5. Check horizontal clearance, B, of shift lever pin and transmission control bracket. This should be .020″. Adjust with trunnion locknuts.
6. Replace console, making sure that shift pointer is correctly aligned. Install knob.

RL411, PL510, WPL510 Column Shift

1. Loosen trunnion locknuts on upper selector rod. (On the steering column inside the engine compartment).
2. Place selector lever in N. Place transmission shift lever in neutral position, the central of its five positions.

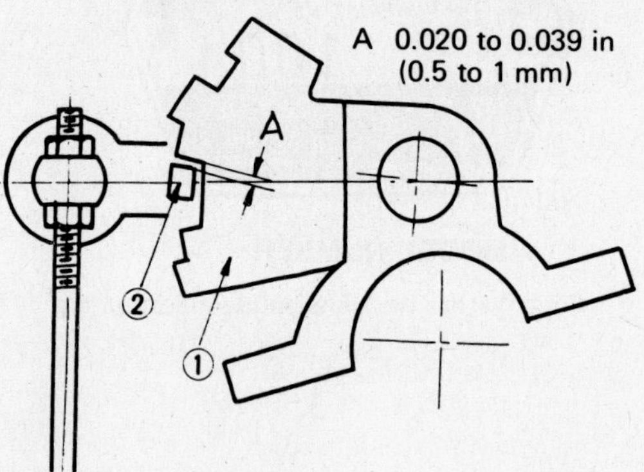

Column shift adjustment. 1 is selector position plate, 2 is stop pin.

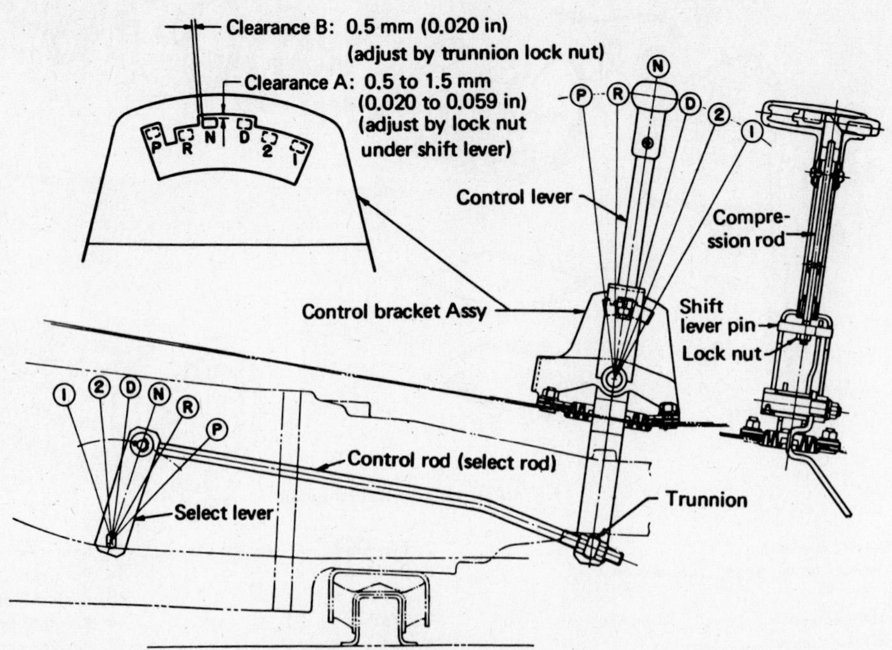

HLS30 floorshift linkage adjustment

3. Adjust locknuts so that the clearance between the stop pin on the lower selector lever and the position plate is .020-.039″.

Downshift Cable Adjustment

RL411, PL510, WPL510

This adjustment is necessary only on early models with the British built Borg Warner transmission. The adjustment is made at the carburetor end of the cable.

1. Check transmission fluid level. Connect a tachometer to the engine.
2. Connect a pressure gauge to the transmission line pressure outlet.

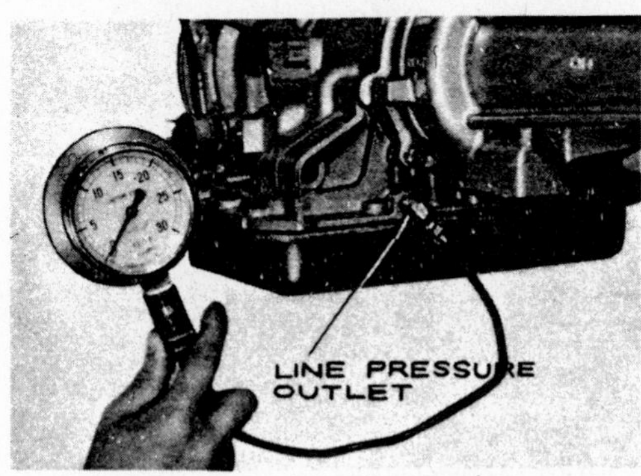

Pressure gauge connected to British BW transmission

3. Start engine and shift into D. The car should be safely blocked and the hand and footbrakes set.
4. Increase engine speed from 500 to 1,000 rpm. The line pressure should rise 15-20 psi.
5. If the pressure rise is less than 15-20 psi, shorten the inner cable with the adjuster.

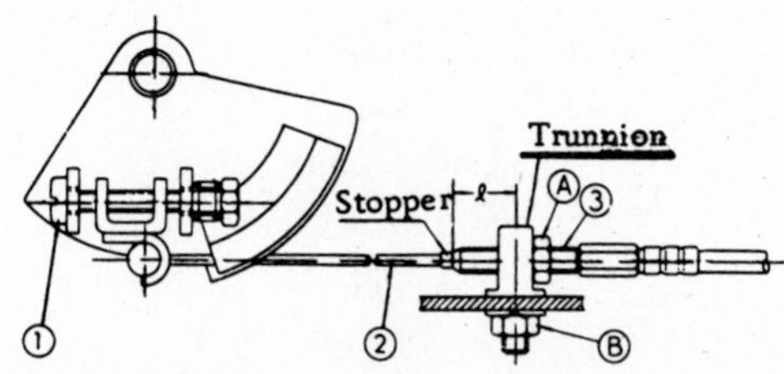

Downshift cable adjuster. 1 is adjuster, 2 is inner cable, 3 is outer cable.

6. If the pressure rise is excessive, lengthen the cable.

NOTE: Do not oil the cable.

Downshift Solenoid Check

PL510, WPL510, HLS30

This solenoid is used on the American Borg Warner and the Nissan transmissions. It is controlled by a downshift switch on the accelerator linkage inside the car. To test switch and solenoid operation:

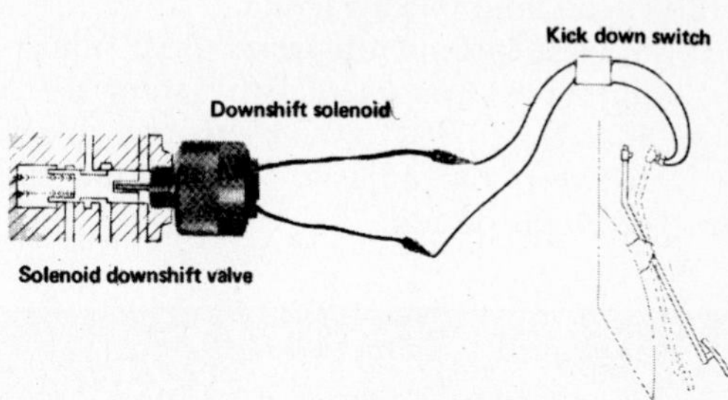

Downshift switch and solenoid, HLS30

1. Turn the ignition on.
2. Push the accelerator all the way down to actuate the switch.
3. The solenoid should click when actuated. Since the solenoid on the Borg Warner transmission is mounted inside the pan, it may be difficult to hear the click. The Nissan transmission solenoid is screwed into the outside of the case. If there is no click, check the switch, wiring, and solenoid.

To remove the solenoid from the Borg Warner transmission, drain and remove the pan. Then push in and turn the solenoid 1/2 turn clockwise to remove.

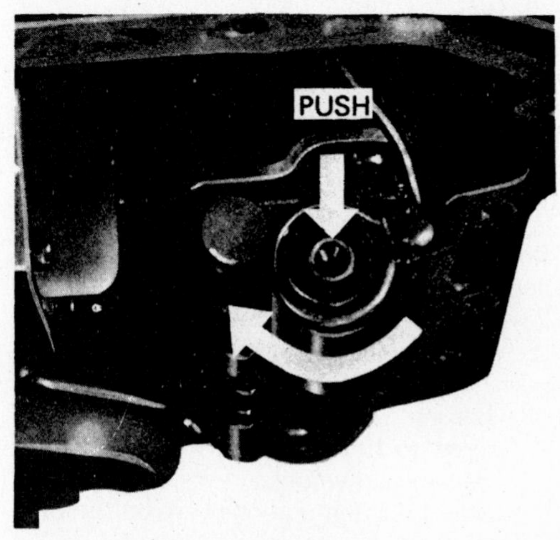

Removal of Borg Warner downshift solenoid

To remove the Nissan solenoid, first drain 2-3 pints of fluid, then unscrew the unit.

Front Band Adjustment

RL411, PL510, WPL510

This adjustment procedure is for the Borg Warner transmissions only.

1. Drain fluid and remove pan.
2. Clean fluid pickup screen.
3. Loosen locknut on front servo adjusting screw. Loosen adjusting screw.
4. Insert a .250″ thick gauge block between the adjusting screw and the servo piston rod.

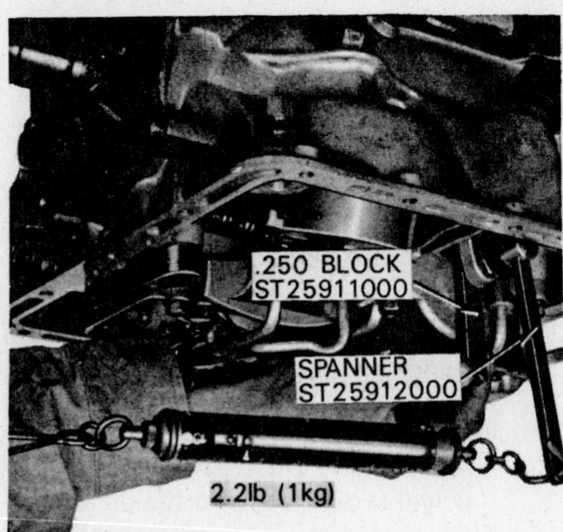

Front band adjustment on Borg Warner transmissions, using a special wrench and a spring scale

5. Tighten adjusting screw to 10 in. lbs. Tighten locknut to 18 ft. lbs.
6. Remove gauge block.
7. Clean and install pan with a new gasket.

Rear Band Adjustment

RL411, PL510, WPL510

This adjustment procedure is for the Borg Warner transmissions only. It may be necessary to unbolt the crossmember and lower the rear of the transmission to get at the adjusting screw on the right side of the case.

1. Loosen locknut. Tighten adjusting screw to 10 ft. lbs.
2. Back off adjusting screw ¾ turn on the American unit and one turn on the British unit.
3. Tighten locknut to 28 ft. lbs.

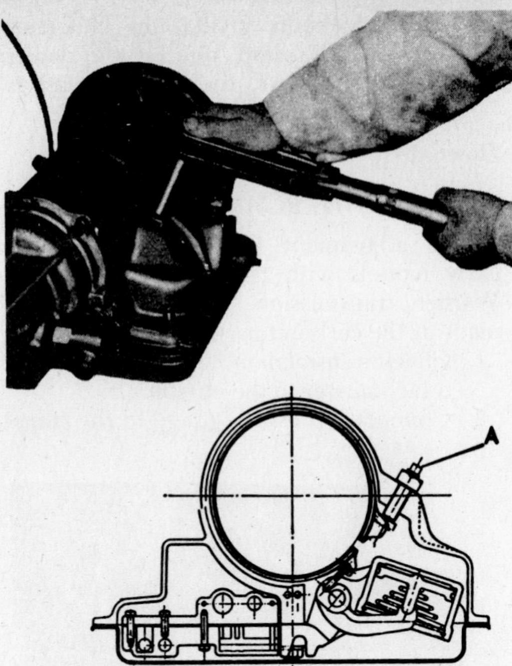

Rear band adjustment on Borg Warner transmissions. A is the adjusting screw.

Neutral Safety and Backup Light Switch Adjustment

RL411, PL510, WPL510

The switch unit is screwed into the left side of the transmission case. The switch terminals marked 1 and 3 are for the neutral safety switch which prevents the engine from being started except in P or N. The terminals 2 and 4 are for the backup light switch.

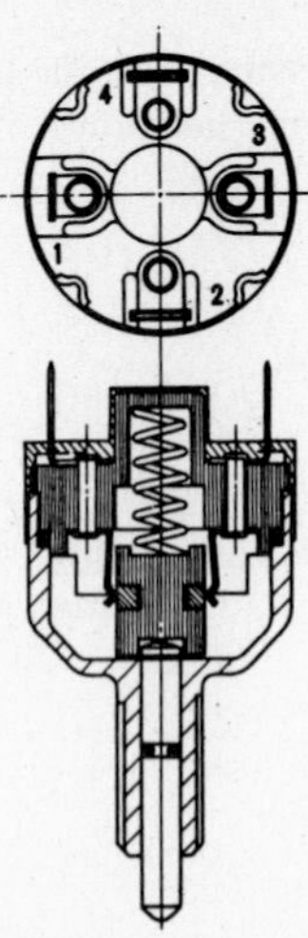

Neutral safety and backup light switch, Borg Warner transmissions

1. Shift into D or L with the engine off. Disconnect switch leads.
2. Connect a test light in series with terminals 1 and 3 and battery current.
3. Loosen the switch locknut. Screw in the switch until the light goes out. The neutral safety switch is now open. Mark the switch position in the case.
4. Connect the test light to terminals 2 and 4. Screw the switch in until the test light goes on. The backup light switch is now closed. Mark the switch position in the case.
5. Screw the switch out to a position midway between the positions marked in Steps 3 and 4. Tighten the locknut to 5 ft. lbs.
6. Check, while holding the brakes on, that the engine will start only in P or N transmission positions. Check that the backup lights go on only in R.

HLS30

The switch unit is bolted to the left side of the transmission case, behind the transmission shift lever. The switch prevents the engine from being started in any transmission position except P or N. It also controls the backup lights.

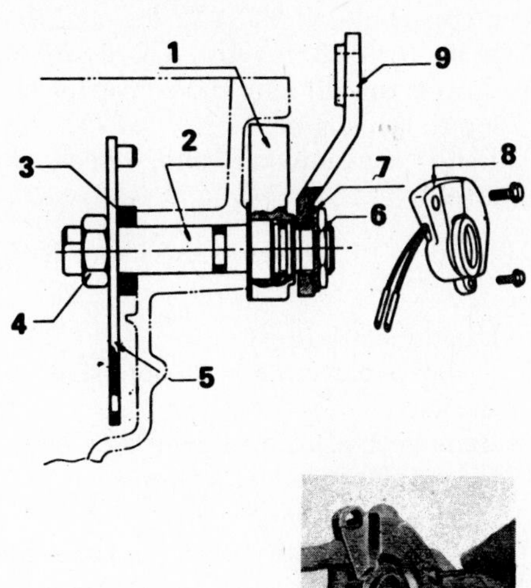

Neutral safety and backup light switch, Nissan transmission

1. **Neutral safety switch**
2. **Manual shaft**
3. **Washer**
4. **Nut**
5. **Manual plate**
6. **Nut**
7. **Washer**
8. **Neutral safety switch**
9. **Transmission shift lever**

1. Remove the transmission shift lever retaining nut and the lever.
2. Remove the switch.
3. Remove the machine screw in the case under the switch.
4. Align the swith to the case by inserting a .059" (1.5 mm.) diameter pin through the hole in the switch into the screw hole. Mark switch location.
5. Remove pin, replace machine screw, install switch as marked, and replace transmission shift lever and retaining nut.
6. Check, while holding the brakes on, that the engine will start only in P or N. Check that the backup lights go on only in R.

Control Pressure Check and Adjustment

PL510, WPL510

This procedure applies only to the American built Borg Warner transmission. Before attempting to adjust transmission shifting control pressure, make sure that the engine vacuum is satisfactory.

1. T-connect a vacuum gauge to the hose at the transmission control unit. The unit is at the left rear of the transmission.
2. Connect a tachometer to the engine.
3. Apply the handbrake, chock the wheels, and set the footbrake.
4. Start the engine and shift into D.
5. Accelerate the engine to 1,200 rpm. Note engine vacuum.

CAUTION: Do not continue this test for more than 10 seconds or transmission overheating and damage will result.

6. The vacuum should be steady and no less than 12.0 in. Hg. (305 mm. Hg.). New engines usually have low and unsteady vacuum for the first 400-500 miles. If the vacuum is too low, correct this condition before any adjustment is made.

To adjust control pressure, proceed as follows:

1. Check transmission fluid level. Remove plug to the right of the transmission control unit at the left rear of the transmission. Connect a pressure gauge.
2. Connect a tachometer to the engine.
3. Apply the handbrake, chock the wheels, and lock the footbrake.
4. Start engine and shift into R. Acceler-

ate engine to 1,200 rpm. See Caution above. Pressure should be 92-98 psi.
5. If pressure is low, remove hose from control unit and turn adjusting screw clockwise. To lower pressure, turn counterclockwise. Turning the screw one complete turn will change the pressure about 10 psi.

Adjusting transmission shifting control pressure on American BW unit

6. The test may be repeated in D and L. The pressure should also be 92-98 psi. The pressure must not be adjusted for D and L.
7. The pressure may also be checked with the engine idling. Idle vacuum must be at least 17.7 in. Hg. (305 mm. Hg.). Transmission pressure in R, D, or L should be 55-68 psi. Idle pressure must not be adjusted.
8. If pressure adjustment is unsuccessful, replacement of the control unit or transmission internal adjustments and repairs may be necessary.

Transmission R&R

RL411, PL510, WPL510 WITH BRITISH BW UNIT

1. Disconnect downshift cable from carburetor.
2. Drain transmission oil pan.
3. Remove driveshaft.
4. Disconnect handbrake mechanism if necessary.
5. Disconnect speedometer cable from transmission. Disconnect neutral safety switch.
6. Disconnect transmission shift linkage. Disconnect oil cooler tubes.
7. Remove filler tube.
8. Unbolt transmission from rear crossmember.
9. Support engine with a jack under the torque converter housing.
10. Remove crossmember. Lower rear of engine slightly.
11. Support transmission with a jack. Place a pan under the torque converter.
12. Remove starter.
13. Remove four bolts retaining torque converter to drive plate. Access is from front through engine mounting plate.
14. Remove converter and transmission assembly to the rear. Be careful not to let converter fall when separating assembly from engine.
15. Reverse procedure to install. Check that drive plate is not warped more than .020″. Plate to crankshaft bolt torque is 40-50 ft. lbs. To ensure correct engagement of front oil pump drive, rotate converter so that drive fingers on hub will be in 9 and 3 o'clock positions. Rotate the slots of the front oil pump driving gear to the same positions. Torque drive plate to torque converter bolts to 25-30 ft. lbs. Torque 3/8″ converter housing to engine bolts to 30-34 ft. lbs. and 5/16″ bolts to 7-10 ft. lbs. There are two dowels for aligning the converter housing to the engine.
16. Refill transmission and check fluid level.

PL510, WPL510 WITH AMERICAN BW UNIT

1. Disconnect battery.
2. Remove carburetor torsion shaft and starter.
3. Remove two torque converter housing to engine capscrews at top.
4. Raise and support car.
5. Disconnect handbrake front cable from center lever.
6. Loosen oil pan bolts and drain transmission.
7. Loosen muffler clamps and turn muffler for clearance. Remove driveshaft after unbolting at rear.
8. Disconnect speedometer cable, vacuum hose, and inhibitor wiring. Disconnect solenoid wire at transmission.
9. Detach oil cooler tubes. Remove filler tube and plug opening.
10. Disconnect lower selector rod and

remove cross shaft assembly.

11. Support the transmission with a suitable jack.
12. Remove rear crossmember. Lower transmission and rear of engine for access to converter to drive plate bolts. Place a pan under the converter.
13. Remove engine rear plate. Mark relationship of converter and drive plate. Remove torque converter to drive plate bolts, screwing bolts out completely one at a time. Remove remaining converter housing to engine capscrews. Pull transmission away from engine.

To replace American built Borg Warner transmission:

14. Check that drive plate is not warped more than .020″. Plate to crankshaft bolt torque is 50 ft. lbs. Place transmission and converter assembly on a jack. Pull transmission forward to start converter hub in crankshaft. Align engine block dowel pin with converter housing aligning hole. Install two lower converter housing attaching bolts and tighten to pull transmission assembly into place. Torque converter housing bolts to 32 ft. lbs. Tighten drive plate to converter bolts to 28 ft. lbs.
15. Install starter motor, shift linkage, speedometer cable, filler tube, and oil cooler tubes.
16. Connect vacuum hose and kickdown solenoid wire.
17. Raise transmission until it contacts floor pan, attach rear crossmember to side rails, lower transmission, and bolt transmission to crossmember.
18. Replace driveshaft, exhaust pipe, and handbrake cable.
19. Lower vehicle, replace battery cable, and carburetor torsion shaft.
20. Pour in 3 quarts of transmission fluid. Set handbrake and start engine. Add 3 more quarts. Move selector lever through all ranges. Add enough fluid to bring level up to F mark.

HLS30

1. Disconnect battery cable.
2. Remove carburetor torsion shaft.
3. Detach transmission control lever.
4. Disconnect inhibitor switch and downshift solenoid wiring.
5. Remove drain plug and drain torque converter.
6. Remove front exhaust pipe.
7. Remove vacuum tube and speedometer cable.
8. Disconnect oil cooler tubes.
9. Remove driveshaft and starter.
10. Support transmission with a jack under the oil pan. Support engine also.
11. Remove rear crossmember.
12. Mark relationship between torque converter and drive plate. Remove four bolts holding converter to drive plate through hole at front, under engine. Unbolt transmission from engine.
13. Reverse procedure for installation. Check that drive plate is warped no more than .020″. Torque drive plate to torque converter and converter housing to engine bolts to 29-36 ft. lbs. Drive plate to crankshaft bolt torque is 8.5 ft. lbs.
14. Refill transmission and check fluid level.

Driveshaft And U-Joints

DRIVESHAFT

R&R

L60

Both front and rear shafts are splined in the center and have a U-joint and flange at each end. There are grease fittings in both U-joints and in the splines. The U-joints also have a pressure relief to prevent over lubrication. To remove either driveshaft, simply unbolt the U-joint flanges at both ends and remove the shaft. The flange bolt torque is 43-51 ft. lbs.

L320, L520, L521, PL521, PL410, PL411, SPL310, SPL311, LB110, KLB110

These driveshafts are all one piece units with a U-joint and flange at the rear, and a U-joint and a splined sleeve yoke which fits into the rear of the transmission, at the front. Early models and trucks generally have U-joints with grease fittings. U-joints without grease fittings must be disassembled for lubrication, usually at 24,000 mile intervals. The splines are lubricated by transmission oil.

1. Be ready to catch oil coming from the rear of the transmission and to plug the extension housing.
2. Unbolt rear flange.
3. Pull driveshaft down and back.
4. Plug the transmission extension housing.

5. Reverse procedure to install, oiling the splines. Flange bolt torque is 15-20 ft. lbs.

PL510, WPL510

These driveshafts are the one piece type with a U-joint and flange at the rear, and a U-joint and a splined sleeve yoke which fits into the rear of the transmission, at the front. The U-joints must be disassembled for lubrication at 24,000 mile intervals. The splines are lubricated by transmission oil.

1. Release handbrake.
2. Loosen PL510 muffler and rotate out of the way.
3. On PL510, remove handbrake rear cable adjusting nut and disconnect left handbrake cable from adjuster.
4. Unbolt rear flange.
5. Pull driveshaft down and back.
6. Plug transmission extension housing.
7. Reverse procedure to install, oiling the splines. Flange bolt torque is 29-62 ft. lbs.

HLS30—Four Speed

This driveshaft is the same type used on the PL510 and WPL510. It is balanced as an assembly.

1. Check that there are spline/flange yoke match marks in two places. If not, mark with chalk.
2. Remove submuffler.
3. Unbolt rear flange.
4. Pull driveshaft down and back.
5. Plug the transmission extension housing.
6. Reverse procedure to install, aligning the match marks and oiling the splines. Flange bolt torque is 18 ft. lbs.

HLS30, SRL311—Five Speed

This driveshaft has a flange at either end and a splined coupling in the center.

1. Carry out Steps 1-3 for HLS30—Four Speed.
2. Unbolt front flange.
3. Remove driveshaft.
4. Reverse procedure to install, aligning match marks. Flange bolt torque is 18 ft. lbs.

U-JOINTS

Disassembly

1. Mark relationship of all components for reassembly.
2. Remove snap-rings. On early units, the snap-rings are seated in the yokes. On later units, the snap-rings seat in the needle bearing races.
3. Tap the yoke with a soft hammer to release one bearing cap. Be careful not to lose the needle rollers.
4. Remove the other bearing caps. Remove the spiders from the yokes.

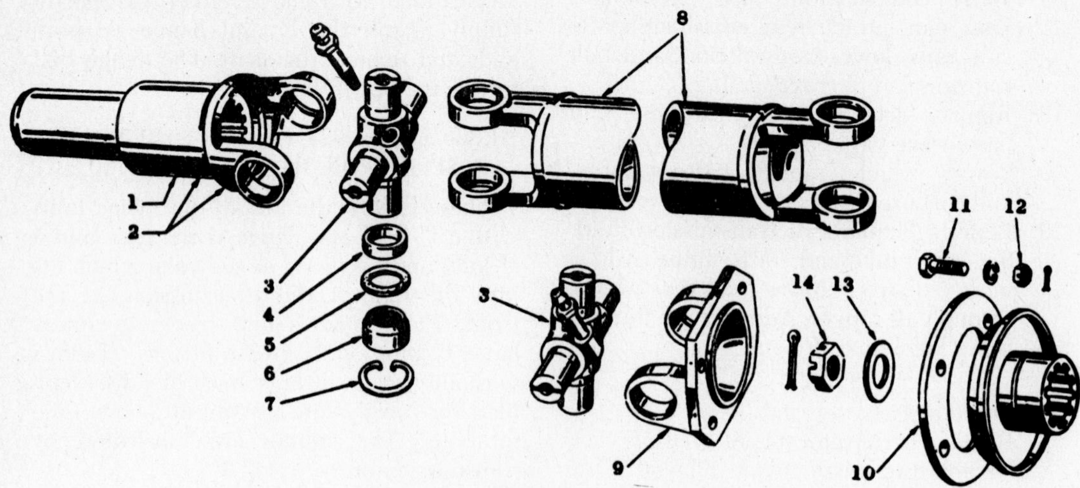

Driveshaft with early type U-joints

1. Dust cover
2. Sleeve yoke
3. Spider with four bearing journals
4. Retainer
5. Oil seal
6. Bearing cap with needle rollers
7. Snap-ring
8. Driveshaft
9. Flange yoke
10. Companion flange
11. Bolt
12. Nut
13. Flat washer
14. Pinion nut

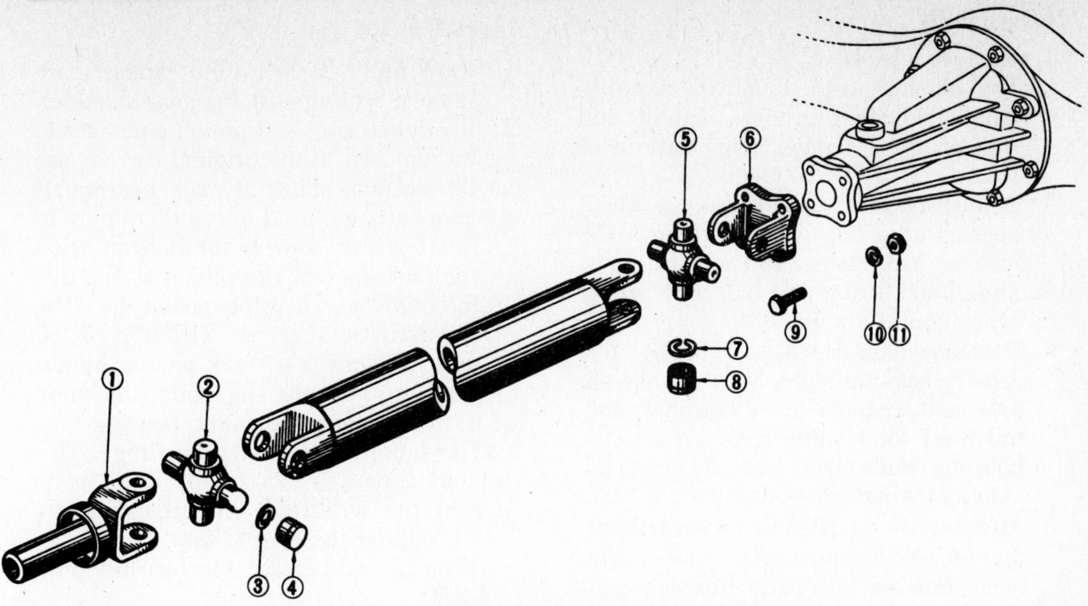

LB110 and KLB110 driveshaft with late type U-joints

1. Sleeve yoke
2. Spider with four bearing journals
3. Bearing race snap-ring
4. Bearing race with needle rollers
5. Spider with four bearing journals
6. Flange yoke
7. Bearing race snap-ring
8. Bearing race with needle rollers
9. Bolt
10. Lockwasher
11. Nut

Inspection

1. Spline backlash should not exceed .0197" (.5 mm.).
2. Driveshaft runout should not exceed .015" (.4 mm.).
3. On late units with snap-rings seated in the needle bearing races, different thicknesses of snap-rings are available for U-joint adjustment. Play should not exceed .0008" (.02 mm.).
4. U-joint spiders must be replaced if their bearing journals are worn more than .0059" (.15 mm.) from their original diameter.

Assembly

1. Place the needle rollers in the races and hold them in place with grease.
2. Put the spider into place in its yokes.
3. Replace all seals.
4. Tap the races into position and secure with the snap-rings.

Drive Axle

All models have solid rear drive axles except the PL510 and HLS30, which have independent rear suspension with the differential carrier solidly mounted. The L60 has solid drive axles front and rear.

NISSAN PATROL (L60) FRONT AXLE

R&R

1. Drain gear oil. Raise vehicle to unload front springs.
2. Disconnect shock absorbers, drag link plug, drag link, stabilizer bar, center brake hose, vertical rebound stop rod, and steering damper.
3. Disconnect front driveshaft. Unbolt axle from springs.
4. Remove front spring shackles and roll axle assembly out.

To replace:

5. Roll axle assembly into place. Secure front spring shackles.
6. Bolt axle to springs with U-bolts and plates. Torque U-bolts to 50-60 ft. lbs.
7. Replace shock absorbers, stabilizer bar, and steering damper.
8. Replace vertical rebound stop rod. The end of the rod should protrude from the locknut .47" (12 mm.). Operating stroke should be 3.34" (85 mm.).
9. Replace driveshaft. Place drag link on steering arm ball and install plug and cotter pin. Connect brake hose.
10. Fill differential. Grease spindle housing and all fittings. Bleed brake system.

Disassembly

1. Remove wheels.
2. Pry off hub cap. Remove snap-ring from axle shaft groove. Unbolt and pull off drive flange, being careful of shims.
3.* Bend back lockwasher. Using a wheel bearing adjusting wrench, remove the locknut, lockwasher, and adjusting nut. Slide brake drum and hub with wheel bearings off the spindle.
4. Disconnect brake hose. Unbolt and remove backing plate. Slide spindle off axle shaft. Remove outer axle shaft and universal joint outer part from axle housing. Pull inner part of universal joint and inner axle shaft out.
5. Remove tie rod. Remove spindle housing upper cap, spring disc, and bearing cone. Remove lower cap. Remove eight capscrews from rear and remove spindle housing.
6. Remove differential cover and gasket. Remove bearing caps, marking their original locations for reassembly. Remove differential assembly, prying cautiously if necessary.
7. Mark differential case halves for reassembly. Remove four nuts and disassemble differential. Release lock plates and remove ring gear. Side bearings must be pulled off.
8. Unbolt and pull off pinion flange. Drive pinion shaft out with a brass drift. Remove pinion shaft shims and spacer, noting shim thickness.

Inspection and Repair

1. Clean all parts in a safe solvent. Oil the bearings immediately.
2. Check inside diameter of bushing inside end of axle housing. If it is more than 1.350″ (35.3 mm.), the bushing must be replaced. A new bushing should be reamed to fit after being pressed in. Be sure that holes in bushing and case are aligned. Replace all axle housing oil seals.
3. When pulling out and replacing the inner and outer pinion bearing cups, be sure that the original shims behind the inner cup are replaced. If new parts are to be used, see Step 2 under Assembly.

The new cups spould be tapped in carefully with a brass drift.

4. The ring and pinion gears must be replaced only as a set.

Assembly

1. Press inner bearing onto pinion shaft. It must seat against the gear shoulder.
2. If original ring and pinion gears are to be replaced in the original carrier, use the original shims at each bearing. If new parts are used, place the pinion in the housing. Check the setting from the back face of the pinion to the differential case bearing centerline. The standard setting is 2.7706″ (70.36 mm.). There is a mark on the pinion head to indicate the shim thickness needed under the inner bearing cup (deviation from standard setting). The mark is read in thousandths of an inch. Add the indicated shim thickness to the standard setting to find the setting distance. Add .002″ for bearing preload.

	Example A	*Example B*
Standard setting	2.7706″	2.7706″
Pinion marking	(+) 2	(−) 2
Add for preload	.002″	.002″
Final setting	2.7746″	2.7706″

3. Replace spacer, original shims, and outer bearing on pinion shaft.
4. Install the pinion flange without the oil seal and torque the nut to 180-215 ft. lbs. The torque required to rotate the pinion shaft should be 9-12 in. lbs., provided that the bearing preload is correct.
5. Remove flange and install a new well-soaked oil seal. Replace flange, retorque nut, and install cotter pin. Recheck pinion setting distance as in Step 2.
6. Assemble side gear and thrust washer to ring gear half of differential case. Lubricate gears and thrust washers. Place spider with gears and thrust washers in case. Install the other thrust washer and side gear. Replace the other case half, aligning the marks made on disassembly. Replace the case bolts, torquing to 50 - 65 ft. lbs. Side gear backlash should be .003-.010″, and can be adjusted by replacing the thrust washers or gears. Lock the nuts with cotter pins. Position the ring gear on the case. Install the lock plates and torque the bolts to 32-42 ft. lbs. Bend up the lock plates.
7. Press the roller bearings on the differential case without shims. Place the

bearing cups on the bearings. Tilt the cups to start the differential assembly into the housing, tapping lightly with a soft hammer until the bearings seat firmly. To determine the thickness of the bearing shims needed, slide the differential assembly from side to side.

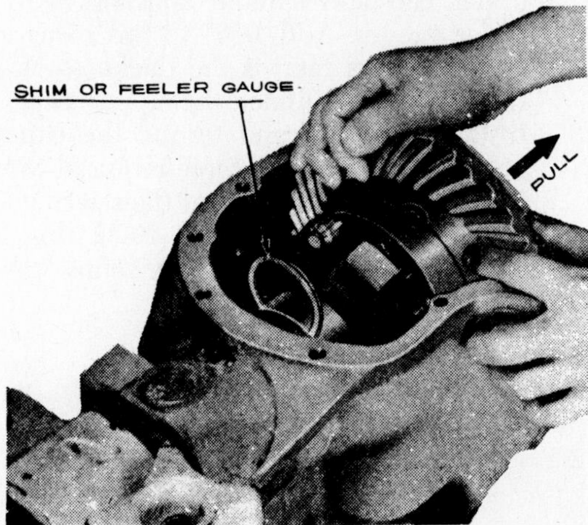

Checking differential side bearing shim thickness needed

Check the clearance between the bearing cup and differential housing with feeler gauges. Add .002″ to the left bearing measurement and .001″ to the right. This gives the proper shim thickness for each side. Now remove the differential assembly, pull off the side bearings, and install the shims. Press the bearings back on and install the differential assembly as above. Replace the bearing caps, aligning the marks made on disassembly. Torque the cap bolts to 62-72 ft. lbs. and lockwire.

8. Mount a dial indicator on the housing with the indicator against a ring gear tooth. Hold the pinion shaft stationary and move the ring gear back and forth to measure backlash. Correct backlash is .005-.007″. To correct backlash, remove differential assembly and move a thickness of shims equal to the backlash error from one side to the other. If backlash is too little, the ring gear must be moved away from the pinion. If it is excessive, the gears must be brought closer together.
9. Check ring gear runout with a dial indicator. If runout exceeds .0025″, remove differential assembly and check bearing seating surfaces for foreign matter. Check the bearings carefully.
10. Check tooth contact pattern with red lead.
11. Replace differential gasket and cover.

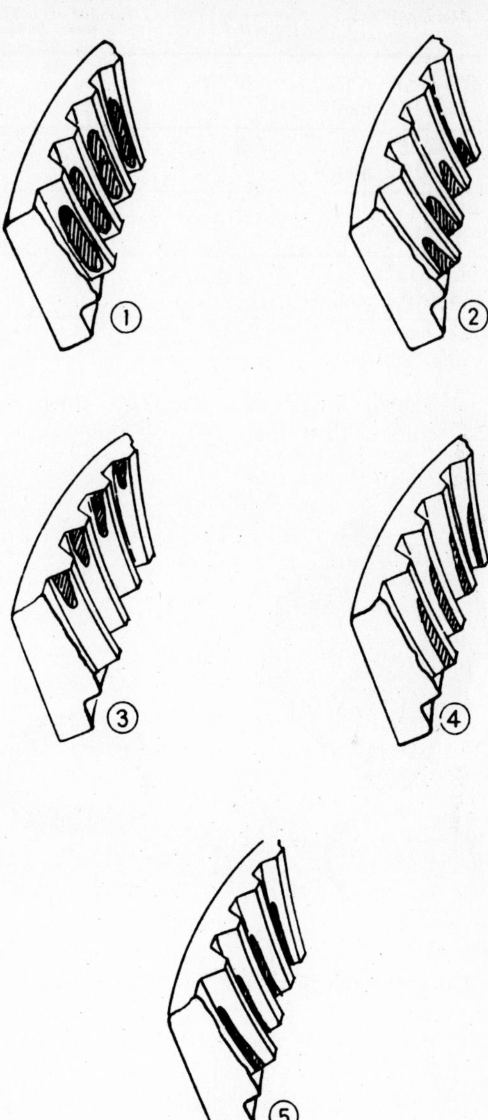

Ring gear tooth contact patterns obtained with red lead

1. Correct tooth contact
2. Short toe contact; move ring gear away from pinion.
3. Short heel contact; move ring gear toward pinion.
4. Contact too high and narrow; pinion should be moved toward center of axle.
5. Contact too low and narrow; pinion should be moved away from center of axle.

12. Grease spindle housing lower cap roller bearing. Install a new O-ring. The number of shims to be used with the lower cap depends upon the bearing width.

Bearing Width	*Number of .005" (.127 mm.) Shims*	*Number of .003" (.075 mm.) Shims*
.630-.634" (16.0-16.1 mm.)	0	0
.634-.638" (16.1-16.2 mm.)	0	1
.638-.643" (16.2-16.3 mm.)	1	1
.643-.646" (16.3-16.4 mm.)	1	2
.646-.650" (16.4-16.5 mm.)	2	2

Install lower cap assembly, torquing nuts to 15 ft. lbs.

Front drive spindle housing lower cap assembly

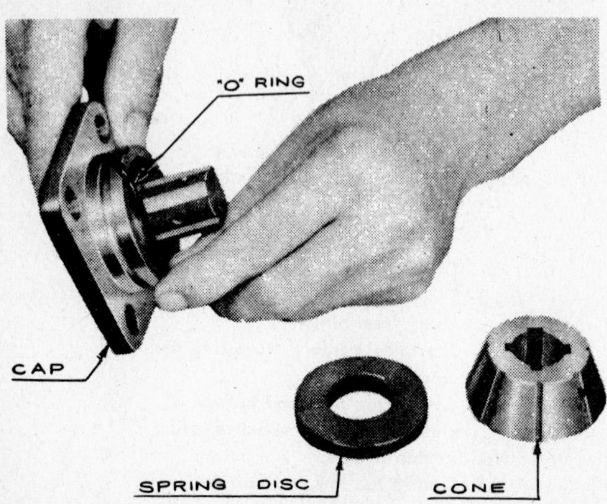

Front drive spindle housing upper cap assembly

13. Place new O-ring, spring disc, and bearing cone on upper cap, aligning grease holes. Insert upper cap assembly to spindle housing without shims. Tighten the four nuts equally until the bearing cone does not turn when the spindle housing is turned back and forth. Check the clearance between the upper cap and spindle housing with feeler gauges. Add .016" to this measurement. This total is the thickness of shims required under the upper cap. Install the shims and torque the cap nuts to 15 ft. lbs. The force required to turn the spindle housing at the steering knuckle arm should be 20-22 lbs. Adjust by adding or removing shims.

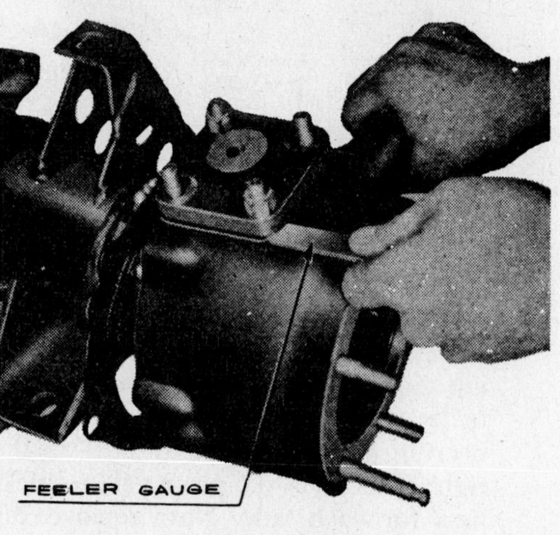

Checking clearance between upper cap and spindle housing

14. Place oil seal on spindle housing flange. Start oil seal retainer bolts. Install oil seal and spring, connecting ends. Bolt down seal retainer.
15. Grease shaft and joint bearing surfaces. Slide in inner axle shaft and inner part of universal joint, aligning axle shaft and differential splines. Slide outer part of universal joint on outer axle shaft. Align universal joint slots and slide outer axle shaft into place.
16. Grease spindle bearing and secure in spindle with lockring. Place spindle on housing. Put backing plate and grease deflector plate on spindle with oil drain hole aligned toward bottom. Bolt in place.
17. Install spindle collar, greasing oil seal contact surface lightly. Pack wheel

bearings. Place inner wheel bearing and oil seal in hub. Assemble hub and brake drum to spindle. Replace outer wheel bearing, thrust washer, and bearing adjusting nut. Tighten adjusting nut until the drum binds when turned, then back off 1/8 turn. Install lockwasher and locknut, bending up lockwasher. Hub turning torque should be 1-3 ft. lbs.

18. Place a straightedge across the spindle and measure between hub and straightedge with feeler gauges to determine the shim thickness required under the drive flange. Replace inner snap-ring, shims, drive flange, lock plates, and nuts. Torque nuts to 25-28 ft. lbs. and bend up lock plates. Replace outer snap-ring on axle shaft groove. Replace hub cap.
19. Reassemble other side in the same way.
20. Install tie rod.

NISSAN PATROL (L60) REAR AXLE

R&R

1. Drain gear oil. Raise vehicle to unload rear springs.
2. Disconnect shock absorbers, stabilizer, and brake hose.
3. Disconnect driveshaft and spring U-bolts. Remove shackles from rear of springs.
4. Roll axle assembly out.

To replace:

5. Roll axle assembly into place. Secure spring shackles.
6. Bolt axle to springs with U-bolts and plates. Torque U-bolts to 50-60 ft. lbs.
7. Replace shock absorbers and stabilizer.
8. Replace driveshaft and brake hose. Fill differential.

Disassembly

1. Unbolt and remove wheels.
2. Remove brake drum retaining screws. Remove brake drum.
3. Unbolt and remove brake backing plate with axle shaft from axle housing.
4. Remove lock plate and bearing locknut. Remove wheel bearing, spacer, backing plate, and bearing cage from axle shaft.
5. Press out four serrated bolts and remove bearing cage from backing plate. Pull outer bearing race and oil seal from bearing cage. Pull inner oil seal from axle housing.
6. The differential is the same as that used in the front axle. Service procedures are the same.
7. Replace all oil seals.

Assembly

1. Press the new oil seal and bearing cup into the bearing cage.
2. Place the bearing cage and brake disc in a press and press the four serrated bolts through both.
3. Put the axle shaft through the backing plate. Put the bearing spacer over the axle shaft into the bearing cage. Put the wheel bearing over the axle shaft and drive the bearing into the bearing cage. Install the lock plate and bearing locknut. Torque the nut to 157 ft. lbs. and bend the lock plate.
4. Place shims .059″ (1.405 mm.) thick between the bearing cage of one rear axle shaft assembly and the axle housing. Fasten the assembly to the housing, torquing the nuts to 21-28 ft. lbs.
5. Install the other axle shaft assembly without any shims and tighten the nuts temporarily. Measure the clearance between the axle housing and the bearing cage with feeler gauges. Subtract .00394″ (.1 mm.) from the measured clearance. The resulting figure is the thickness of shims required at that side. Remove the axle shaft assembly and replace with the shims. Torque the bolts to 21-28 ft. lbs.
6. Measure the end-play of the axle shaft with a dial indicator. It should be .002-.006″ (.05-.15 mm.) If not, install or remove shims to correct. The thickness of the shims on each side must not differ by more than .04″ (1 mm.) from the thickness on the other end of the axle housing. If it does, take some shims from the side with the greater thickness and add them to the other side.

SOLID REAR AXLE—L320, L520, L521, PL521, PL410 PL411, RL411, WPL510, LB110, KLB110, SPL310, SPL311, SRL311

R&R

1. Raise and support rear of vehicle. Remove wheels.

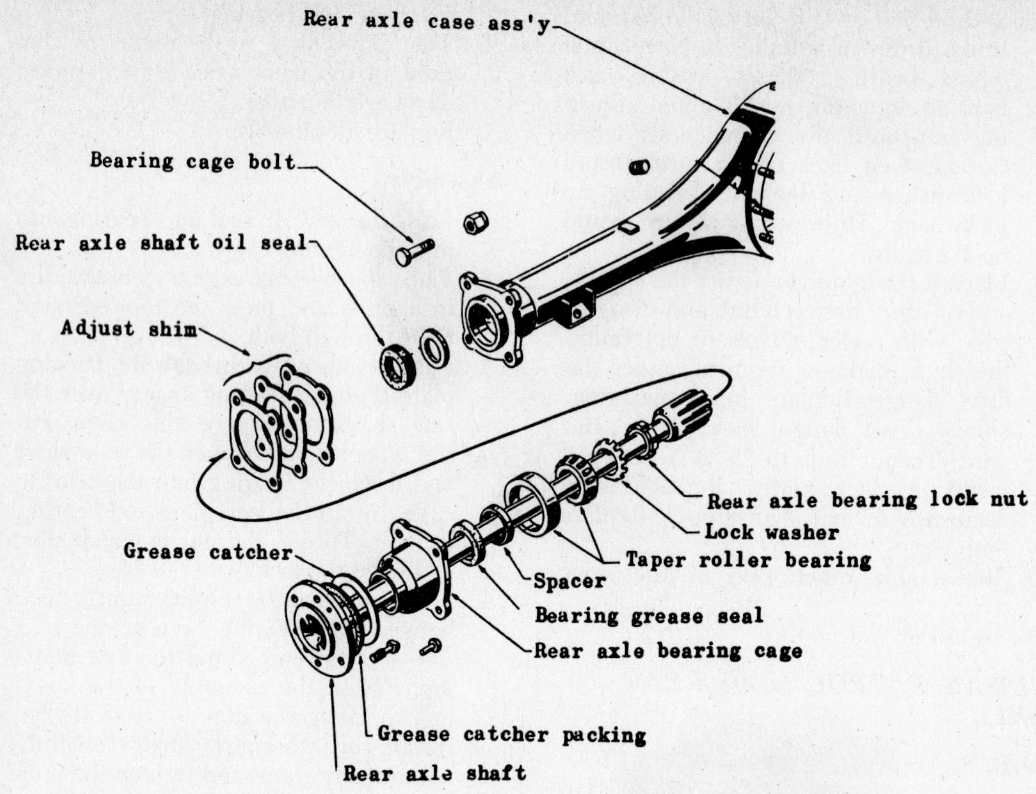

Detail of L320 axle shafts

2. Remove screws and brake drums, backing off brake adjustment if necessary.
3. Disconnect and plug brake hose. Disconnect handbrake cable, driveshaft, and shock absorbers.
4. Support rear axle assembly with a floor jack.
5. Loosen spring U-bolts. Remove rear spring shackles.
6. Remove U-bolts. Lower and remove axle.
7. Reverse procedure to install.

Disassembly

1. Disconnect brake lines at wheel cylinders.
2. Remove handbrake linkage.
3. Drain oil.
4. Unbolt backing plate from axle housing. Pull axle shaft and backing plate out together with a slide hammer.
5. From the rear of the backing plate, press off the bearing collar or cut if off with a cold chisel. The collar should not be reused. Pull out the bearing.

   NOTE: some units use a locknut instead of a bearing collar.
6. Unbolt and pull out the differential carrier from the axle housing.

Assembly

1. Use a new gasket between the axle housing and differential carrier. Torque the bolts to 14-18 ft. lbs. in a diagonal pattern.
2. Install the grease catcher, bearing spacer, bearing packed with grease, and new bearing collar onto the axle shaft. The seal side of the wheel bearing must face the wheel. Coat the oil seal lips with grease. Press on the bearing collar.
3. Adjust the axle end-play by use of shims between the backing plate and axle housing. Specified end-play is .012-.020″ for the WPL510, and .004″ for the LB110 and KLB110. For the L320 and L520, the first axle shaft to be installed should have an end-play of .033-.043″, and the second .004″.

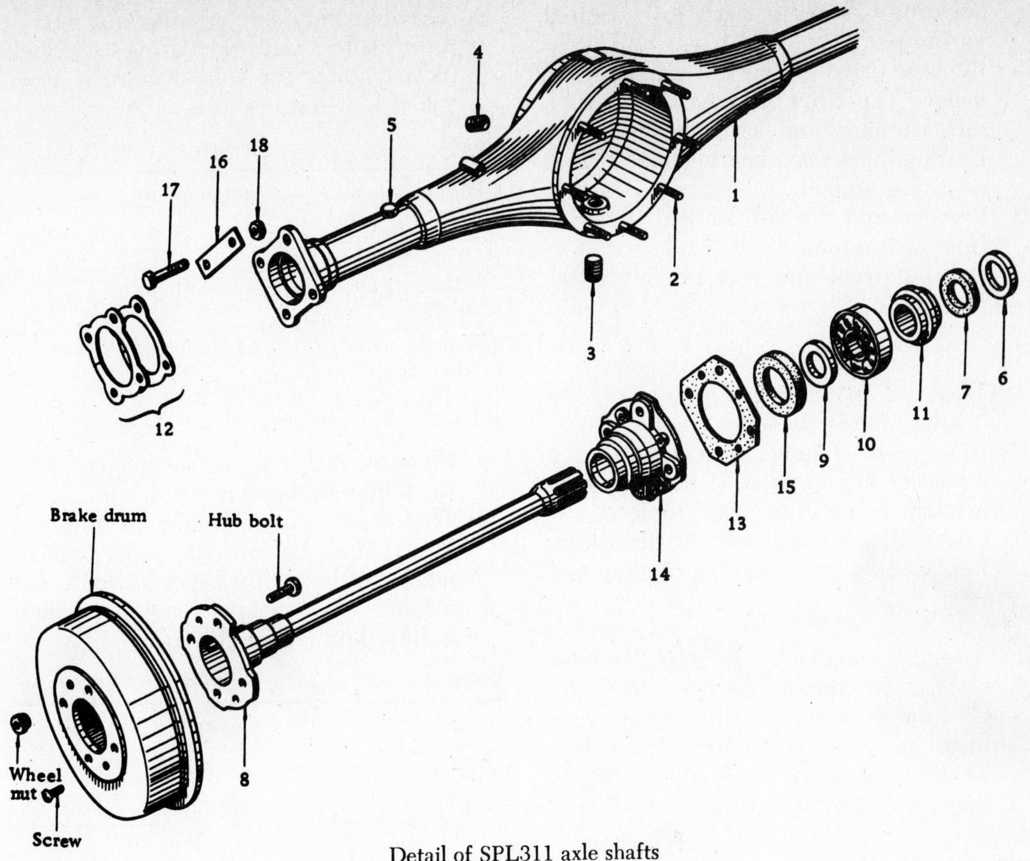

Detail of SPL311 axle shafts

1. Axle housing
2. Stud
3. Drain plug
4. Plug
5. Breather
6. Spacer
7. Oil seal
8. Axle shaft
9. Spacer
10. Bearing
11. Bearing collar
12. Shim
13. Gasket
14. Grease catcher
15. Grease seal
16. Lock plate
17. Bolt
18. Nut

Shims for adjusting axle shaft end-play

4. Specified bolt torque for the brake backing plate is 20-28 ft. lbs. for the WPL510 and 11-15 ft. lbs. for all other models.
5. Refill with oil. See Capacities and Pressures Chart.

Differential Overhaul

Disassembly

1. Remove the side bearing caps, marking their locations for reassembly. Remove the differential assembly from the carrier.
2. Pull off the side bearings. Do not mix left and right side parts.
3. Flatten the lock tabs and unbolt the ring gear, loosening the bolts diagonally.
4. Drive out pinion shaft lock pin from left to right. Remove pinion shaft and pinions, side gears, and thrust washers.

Separate all these parts by original location.

5. Remove drive pinion nut and pull off flange. Tap drive pinion back with a soft hammer and remove with rear bearing inner race, bearing spacer, and adjusting washer.
6. Remove and discard oil seal. Remove front bearing inner race.
7. Pull out front and rear bearing outer races.

Inspection

1. Wash all parts in a safe solvent. Oil bearings immediately.
2. Ring and pinion gears must be replaced only in pairs. If the ring gear is warped more than .002″, replace.
3. Check all parts for wear or distortion. Replace any suspected bearings.

Assembly

1. Assemble pinions, side gears, pinion shaft, and thrust washers in case. Clearance between side gears and thrust washers should be .0020-.0079″. Thrust washers are available in various thicknesses for adjustment.
2. Drive in and peen over the lock pin.
3. Bolt on the ring gear using new lock tabs. Tighten the bolts diagonally. Specified bolt torques are:

Model	*Torque*
L320, L520, WPL510	35-40 ft. lbs.
LB110, KLB110	43-51 ft. lbs.
PL410, PL411, SPL310, SPL311	25-30 ft. lbs.

4. Press the side bearing inner races onto the differential case without shims.
5. The drive pinion height is adjusted with shims behind the rear bearing race. Dealers have special tools for making this measurement. Specified standard pinion heights are:

Model	*Standard Pinion Height*
PL410, PL411, SPL310, SPL311	2.0094″ (51 mm.)

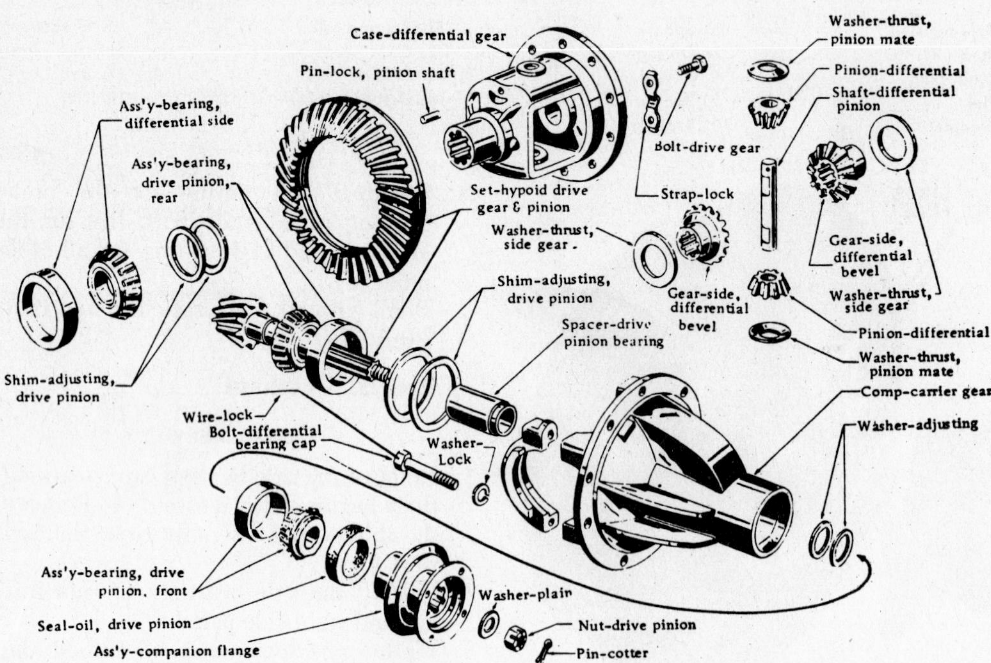

Differential details, WPL510

L320, L520, WPL510	2.4034″ (61 mm.)
LB110, KLB110	1.772″ (45 mm.)

Standard pinion height is measured from the axle centerline to the pinion face. The deviation of the drive pinion from standard size is marked on the pinion face with + for larger and — for smaller. All units except the LB110 and KLB110 are marked in thousandths of an inch. The LB110 and KLB110 pinion is marked in hundredths of a millimeter. If no standard pinion height is specified, the adjustment must be made by use of special tools or by comparing the marks on the old and new drive pinion and adjusting the original shim pack to suit.

Pinion face markings, LB110 and KLB110

6. Press in the drive pinion rear bearing outer race and shims. Press in the front bearing outer race. Press the rear bearing inner race onto the drive pinion.
7. Install the drive pinion into the differential carrier without the bearing washer, spacer, and oil seal. The front bearing inner race and the flange should be installed. Tighten the flange nut until the torque required to turn the shaft (bearing preload) is:

Model	*New Bearing*	*Used Bearing*
LB110, KLB110	5.2-6.9 in. lbs.	2.6-3.5 in. lbs.
WPL510	8.7-11.3 in. lbs.	3.5-4.3 in. lbs.
L320, L520, PL410, PL411, SPL310, SPL311	6.1-8.7 in. lbs.	2.4-3.5 in. lbs.

8. Check the drive pinion height again.
9. Remove drive pinion and replace with bearing spacer. Torque flange nut to specified torque.

Model	*Torque*
WPL510	101-130 ft. lbs.
LB110, KLB110	87-123 ft. lbs.
L320, L520, PL410, PL411, SPL310, SPL311	100-120 ft. lbs.

10. Check that pinion bearing preload is as in Step 7. If it is excessive, a new spacer must be installed.

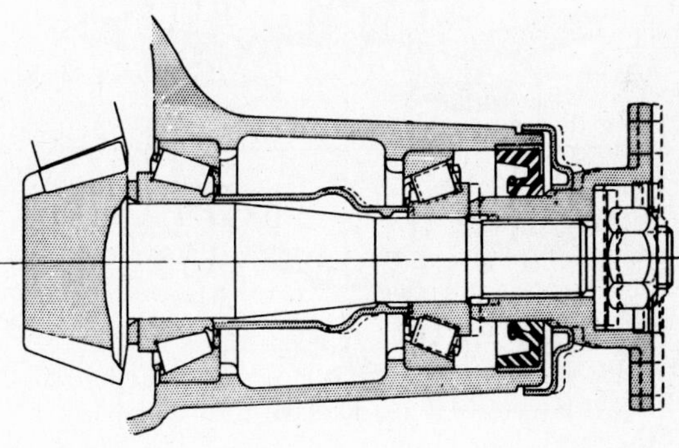

Detail of drive pinion bearing spacer, LB110 and KLB110

11. Remove nut and flange. Press in new oil seal. Pack grease between seal lips. Replace flange and nut, torquing as in Step 9. If cotter pin does not align, file the washer. Do not overtorque.
12. Install differential assembly into carrier, tapping with a soft hammer if necessary. Install side bearing caps in their original locations and torque bolts. Bearing cap bolt torque is 36-43 ft. lbs. for the LB110 and KLB110 and 30-35 ft. lbs. for all others.
13. Side bearing shims are selected by these formulae, for all models except LB110 and KLB110:
    Left side shim thickness=A—C+D+E+.007″
    Right side shim thickness=B—D+F+.006″

Figure	*Location*
A	left bearing housing of gear carrier
B	right bearing housing

C, D	differential case
E	difference from standard size (.7874″) of left bearing
F	difference from standard size of right bearing

All figures are read in thousandths of an inch. If old bearings are being reused, the required shim thickness on each side should be reduced by .001-.003″ to prevent excessive bearing preload.

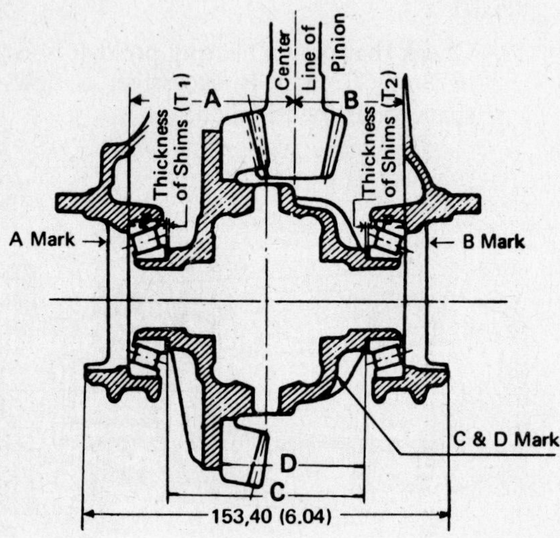

Measurements for selecting side bearing shims, LB110 and KLB110

14. LB110 and KLB110 side bearing shims are selected by these formulae:
    Left side shim thickness=A−C+D+E+.2 mm.
    Right side shim thickness=B−D+F+.2 mm.
    Figures A, B, C, and D are as in Step 13 but are read in hundredths of a millimeter. Figures E and F are the differences of the left and right bearings from standard size (17.5 mm), read in hundredths of a millimeter.
15. Ring and pinion gear backlash should be .0059-.0079″, measured with a dial indicator. If it is excessive, remove some right side shims and place them on the left. If it is too small, change shims from left to right.
16. Make a tooth contact pattern check with red lead. Adjust the drive pinion height and side bearing shims as required.

FINAL DRIVE UNIT—HLS30, PL510

These vehicles have independent rear suspension with the final drive unit mounted solidly. Although the suspension arrangements differ, the final drive units are virtually identical.

R&R

HLS30 (240 Z)

1. Chock the front wheels. Raise and support the rear of the vehicle.
2. Remove the main muffler.
3. Unbolt the driveshaft.
4. Loosen the transverse link spindle inner bolts (on the front of the front differential mounting crossmember) enough to free the crossmember.
5. Unbolt the axle shafts.
6. Support the differential unit with a jack.
7. Remove the two mounting nuts from the rear of the rear differential mounting crossmember.
8. Remove the four nuts from the bottom of the front crossmember.
9. Lower the front crossmember and final drive unit together.
10. Unbolt the front crossmember from the differential unit.
11. Reverse procedure to install. Tighten transverse link spindle inner bolts with vehicle lowered to the ground and with two 150 lb. passengers.

Fastener	*Torque*
Axle shaft bolts	36-43 ft. lbs.
Driveshaft bolts	18 ft. lbs.
Transverse link spindle inner bolts	101-116 ft. lbs.
Differential rear mounting nuts	54-69 ft. lbs.
Differential front mounting and crossmember bolts	23-31 ft. lbs.

PL510

1. Chock the front wheels. Raise and support the rear of the vehicle.
2. Disconnect handbrake rear cable, driveshaft, and axle shafts.
3. Support the differential unit with a jack.
4. Unbolt differential rear mounting crossmember from body.
5. Remove four bolts holding differential to rear suspension crossmember.

6. Remove differential to the rear.
7. Support rear suspension crossmember with stands to prevent damage to the insulators.
8. Unbolt differential rear mounting crossmember from differential.
9. Reverse procedure to install. Pry differential unit into position.

Fastener	*Torque*
Differential mounting cross-member to differential nuts	43-58 ft. lbs.
Differential mounting cross-member to body nuts	62 ft. lbs.
Differential to suspension crossmember nuts	43 ft. lbs.
Driveshaft bolts	29-62 ft. lbs.
Axle shaft bolts	51-58 ft. lbs.

Disassembly

1. Drain oil and remove rear cover.
2. Clamp housing down securely.
3. Check tooth contact pattern with red lead.
4. Check backlash between ring and pinion with a dial indicator. It should be .0039-.0079″.
5. If tooth contact pattern or gear backlash is incorrect, check that runout at the rear of the ring gear does not exceed .0031″.
6. Remove side flange bolts and pull off side flanges with a slide hammer.
7. Unbolt and pull off side retainers. Note original locations of retainers and shims.
8. Remove differential assembly from carrier.
9. Remove bearing outer races from side retainers with an oil seal puller.
10. Hold the drive pinion flange and loosen the nut. Tighten the nut to 123-145 ft. lbs. and check the torque required to turn the drive pinion. It should be 2.6-13 in. lbs. Remove the nut and pull off the flange.
11. Press the drive pinion from the gear carrier with the front and rear bearing inner races, bearing spacers, and adjusting washers. Press out the front pilot bearing.
12. Press the drive pinion from the rear bearing.

NOTE: If the tooth contact pattern and backlash was correct in Steps 3 and 4 and the original ring gear, carrier, drive pinion, rear bearing, and washers are to be reused, it is not necessary to remove the rear bearing.

13. Press the front and rear bearing outer races from the carrier.
14. Pull off the right differential side gear. Spread the lock straps, loosen and remove the ring gear bolts in a diagonal pattern. Remove the ring gear and pull off the left differential side gear. Do not mix right and left side parts.
15. Punch out the pinion shaft lock pin from the ring gear side. Remove the shaft, differential gears, and thrust washers. Note the original location of all parts.
16. To replace the front oil seal, pull off the seal retainer and pull out the seal. Apply grease between the lips of the new oil seal and drive into place. Replace the retainer.

NOTE: The front oil seal can be replaced with the differential mounted on the vehicle, after the driveshaft and flange are removed.

17. To replace the side oil seals, pull out the seal and drive in the new one, applying grease between the seal lips.

NOTE: The side oil seals can be replaced with the differential mounted on the vehicle, after the axle shafts, flanges, and retainers are removed.

Assembly

1. Wash all parts in a safe solvent and oil bearings immediately.
2. Install side and pinion gears into differential case. Replace pinion shaft. Check clearance between side gears and thrust washers. It should be .0039-.0079″ (.1-2 mm). Various thicknesses of thrust washers are available for adjustment.
3. Drive in pinion shaft lock pin. Stake the end of the pin with a punch.
4. Install the ring gear to the differential assembly. Use new lock straps under the bolts. Torque the bolts to 51-58 ft. lbs. in a diagonal pattern, tapping the bolt heads lightly before final torquing.
5. Before pressing on new differential side bearings, check bearing width. Standard width is .787″ (20 mm.).
6. Press front and rear drive pinion bearing outer races into gear carrier.
7. Drive pinion bearing preload turning torque should be 97.2-138.9 in. oz. for new bearings and 41.7-83.3 in. oz. for old bearings, with the pinion flange

1. Oil seal
2. Pinion bearing adjusting washer
3. Pinion bearing adjusting spacer
4. Pinion height adjusting shims
5. Pinion height adjusting washer
6. Lock strap
7. Ring gear retaining bolt
8. Pinion shaft lock pin
9. Side gear thrust washer
10. Side gear
11. Rear cover
12. Ring gear
13. Differential mount
14. Nut
15. Pinion shaft
16. Thrust washer
17. Pinion gear
18. Thrust washer
19. Side gear
20. Side flange bolt
21. Oil seal
22. Side flange
23. Side retainer
24. Bolt
25. O-ring
26. Side bearing
27. Differential gear case
28. Drive pinion rear bearing
29. Drive pinion
30. Pinion bearing preload adjusting spacer and washer
31. Pinion front bearing
32. Front pilot bearing spacer
33. Front pilot bearing
34. Oil seal
35. Drive pinion flange
36. Drive pinion nut

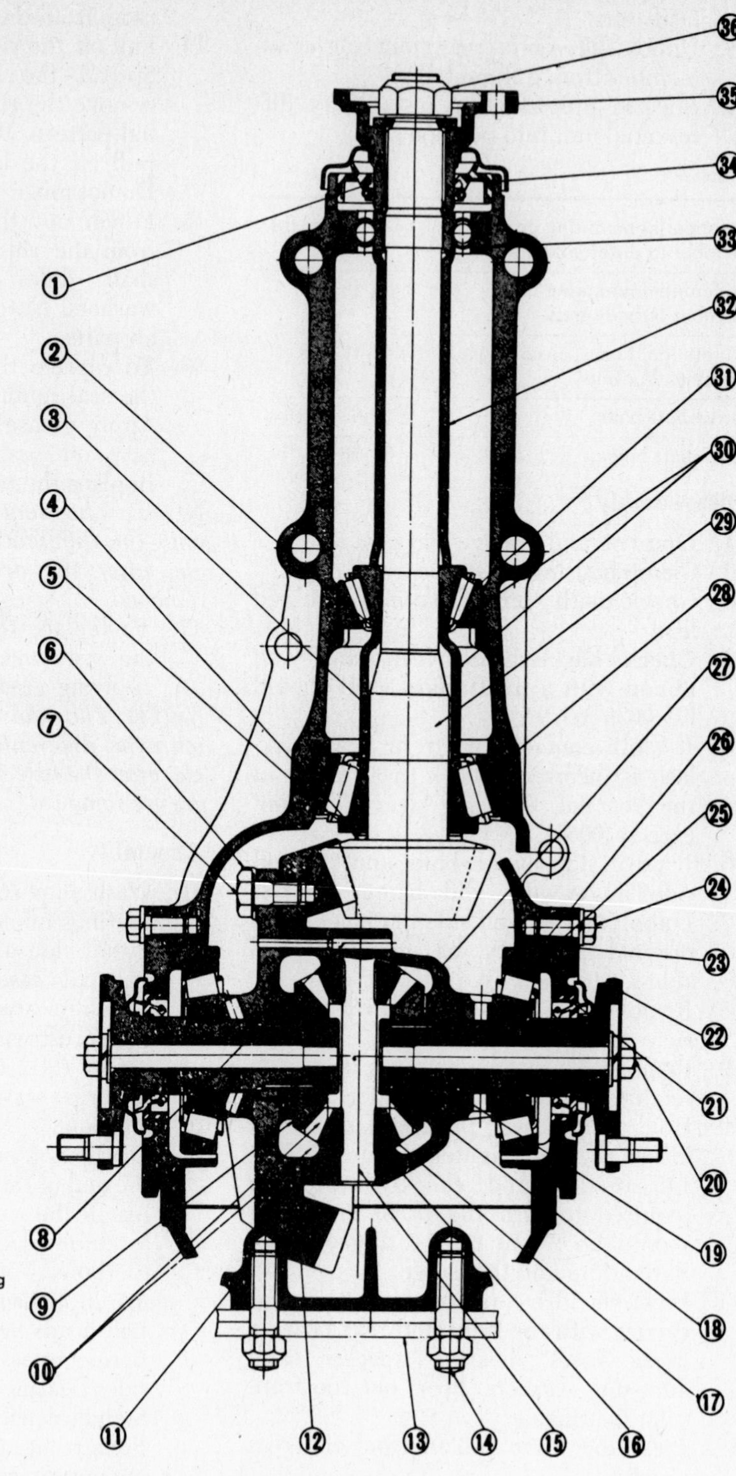

Details of HLS30 and PL510 final drive assembly

nut torqued to 123-145 ft. lbs. and without the oil seal. This is normally checked and adjusted with special tools.

8. Normal drive pinion height is 1.909" (48.5 mm.) from the axle centerline to the pinion face. Special tools are required to make this adjustment. The height is adjusted by a washer and shims between the rear bearing and the drive pinion gear. The deviation of the drive pinion from standard size, in hundredths of a millimeter, is marked on the pinion face with + for larger and — for smaller. If the drive pinion is replaced, compare the old and new marks and adjust the shim pack to suit.

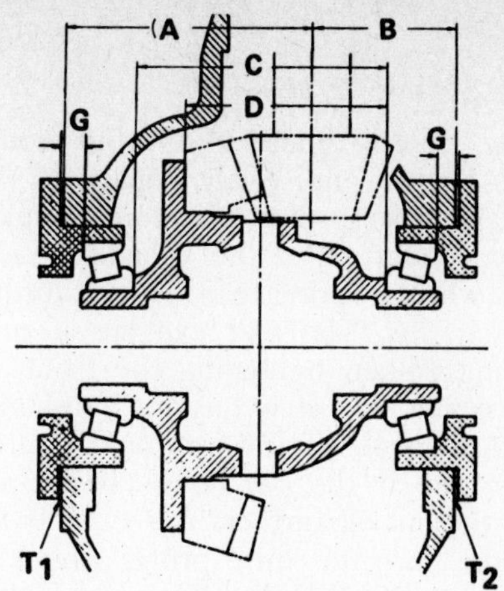

Measurements used in selecting side bearing shims

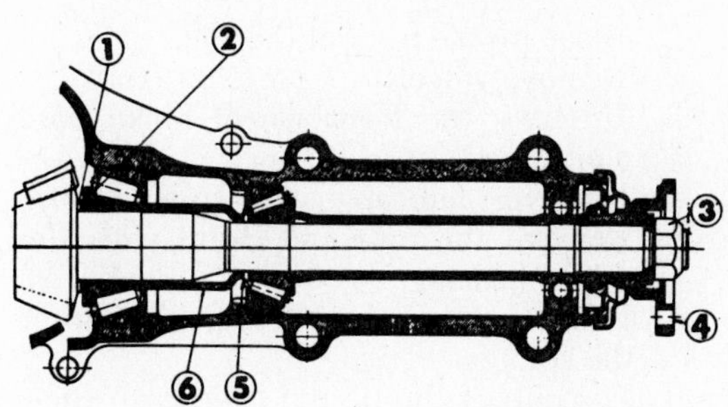

Details of drive pinion installed

1. Pinion bearing adjusting washer
2. Pinion height adjusting shims
3. Pinion nut
4. Pinion flange
5. Pinion bearing adjusting washer
6. Pinion bearing adjusting spacer

9. Install the drive pinion, front pilot bearing, and oil seal. Replace the flange and torque the bolt to 123-145 ft. lbs.
10. Side bearing shims are selected by these formulae:
    Left side shim thickness = A+C+G−D−E+H+.76 mm.
    Right side shim thickness = B+D+G−F−H+.76 mm.

Figure	*Location*
A,B	on gear carrier
C,D	on differential case
F	difference from standard size (20 mm.) of bearing
G	on side retainers
H	on ring gear

All the figures are read in hundredths of a millimeter. If old side bearings are reused, the required shim thickness on each side should be increased by .001-.003" (.03-.07 mm.).

11. Install shims selected in Step 10 and O-rings in side retainers. Install retainers. Bolt torque should be 6.5-8.7 ft. lbs.
12. Check ring and pinion gear backlash. It should be .0039-.0079". If less, move side retainer shims from right to left. If more, move shims from left to right.
13. Check tooth contact pattern with red lead.
14. Replace rear cover and torque bolts to 54-69 ft. lbs. Replace side flanges and torque bolts to 14-19 ft. lbs.
15. Refill differential. See Capacities and Pressures Chart.

Suspension

The L60, Nissan Patrol, is suspended by leaf springs front and rear. The L320, L520, L521, and PL521 pickups have torsion bars in the front and leaf springs in the rear. The PL410, PL411, and RL411 sedans, as well as the SPL310, SPL311, and SRL311 sportscars have front coil and rear leaf springs. The LB110 sedan, KLB110 coupe, and the WPL510 wagon have strut type front suspension with integral coil springs and shock absorbers, and leaf springs in the rear. The PL510 sedan uses struts in the front and coil springs in the rear. The HLS30, 240 Z coupe, has strut type suspension both front and rear. The PL510 and HLS30 have independent rear suspension using axle shafts with U-joints at each end and ball spline joints in the center.

FRONT

Leaf Spring Type—L60

The front suspension on this model is quite simple and easily repaired. When replacing the springs, the bolts should be tightened only after the vehicle is resting on its wheels. Spring rear eye bolt torque is 45-50 ft. lbs. The rear eye has a rubber bushing. When tightening the front shackles, which have steel bushings, tighten the nut fully, back off 1/4 turn, and insert the cotter pin. If the pin holes do not align, back the nut off further. The U-bolts holding the axle to the springs should be torqued to 50-60 ft. lbs. The double-acting shock absorbers are not serviceable. An axle rebound stop bolt connects the front axle to the frame. The bottom end of the bolt should protrude from the locknut .47″ and the operating stroke should be 3.34″. The operating stroke can be adjusted but the bolt should always protrude at least .2″. A rubber axle torque arrester bumper is mounted on the left side of the frame. With springs in good condition, there should be 1.81″ clearance between the bumper and the axle.

Wheel Bearing Adjustment

1. Remove front wheels.
2. Pry off drive flange hub cap.
3. Remove snap-ring from axle shaft groove.
4. Unbolt and pull off drive flange.
5. Bend back lockwasher and remove bearing locknut.
6. Using a bearing adjusting wrench, tighten the adjusting nut until the brake drum binds when turned, then back off 1/8 turn.

NOTE: It is very bad practice to use a hammer and chisel on the adjusting nut.

7. Install lockwasher and locknut, bending back lockwasher.
8. 1-3 ft. lbs. torque should be required to turn the hub. If turning torque is excessive, check the condition of the bearing. The brake drum and hub with wheel bearings can be slid off the spindle after removing the adjusting nut.
9. Replace shims, drive flange, lock plates, and nuts. Torque nuts to 25-28 ft. lbs. and bend up lock plates. Replace snap-ring and hub cap.
10. Replace wheels.

Wheel Alignment

The only alignment adjustment possible on the L60 is toe-in. Toe-in is measured between the wheels, in front of and behind the axle, and is adjusted by changing tie rod length. The specified toe-in is .12-.16″.

Torsion Bar Type—L320, L520, L521, PL521

This independent front suspension uses torsion bar springs, upper and lower links, tubular shock absorbers, and kingpins. The lower suspension links are located fore and aft by tension rods from the front of the frame. The front end height can be adjusted to compensate for normal spring sagging.

Kingpin and Bushing Replacement

1. Block up the front of the truck.
2. Remove wheels.
3. Unscrew the front wheel brake hose connections.
4. Remove hubcap and spindle nut. Remove the hub and drum with the wheel bearing.
5. Remove the brake backing plate from the spindle.
6. Disconnect the tie rod from each spindle.
7. Take out the kingpin lock bolt and remove the upper spindle plug. Drive the kingpin down to remove the bottom plug. Tap out the kingpins.
8. Remove the spindle with the shims and thrust washer.
9. The old bushings should be driven out of the spindle and the new ones driven in. It is advisable to replace the kingpin also. Ream the new bushings to fit the kingpin. The fit should be such that the kingpin, when oiled, can be turned or pushed in or out readily with thumb pressure. Make sure that the bushing holes for the grease fittings are open.
10. On reassembly, use a new spindle thrust washer. Install spindle shims so that the clearance between the upper end of the kingpin boss on the spindle support knuckle and the spindle is .0032-.0051″ (.08-.13 mm.). Use new kingpin expansion plugs. Use a new front hub grease seal. Adjust the front wheel bearing by torquing it to 30 ft. lbs. and backing off ⅛ turn.
11. Grease suspension and bleed brake system.

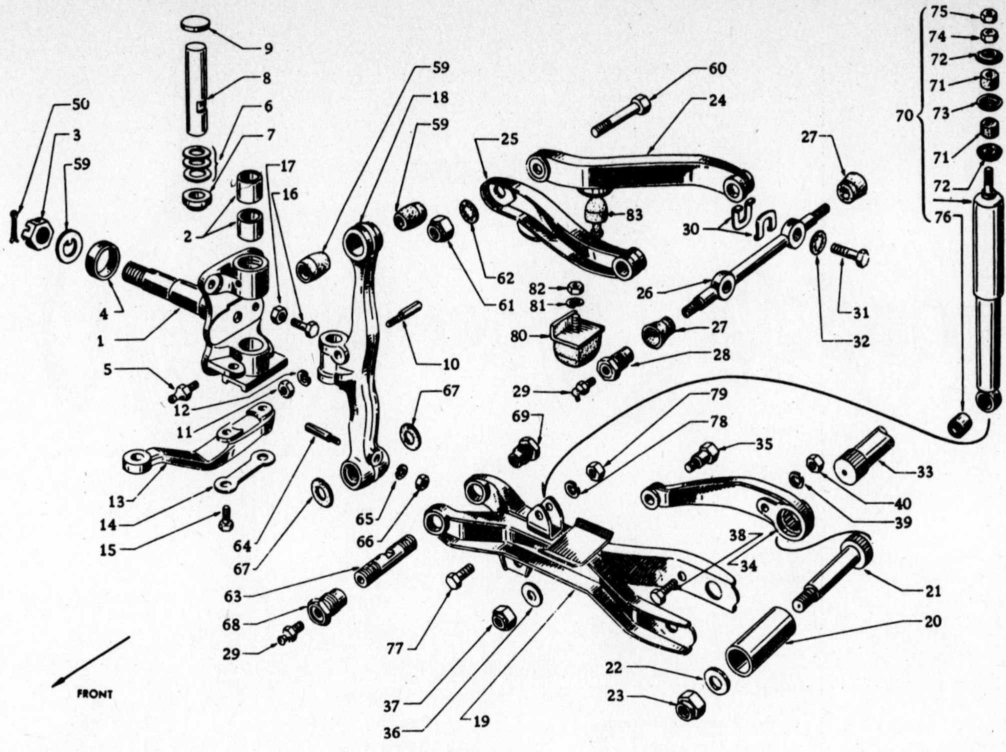

L520 front suspension details

1. Spindle
2. Bushing
3. Spindle nut, used to adjust front wheel bearing
4. Spindle collar
5. Grease nipple
6. Spindle shims
7. Thrust washer
8. Kingpin
9. Plug
10. Lock bolt
11. Nut
12. Lockwasher
13. Steering arm
14. Lockplate
15. Bolt
16. Bolt
17. Nut
18. Spindle support
19. Lower link
20. Lower link bushing
21. Lower link spindle
22. Washer
23. Nut
24. Rear upper link
25. Front upper link
26. Upper link spindle
27. Seal
28. Bushing assembly
29. Grease fitting
30. Camber adjusting shims
31. Spindle upper link bolt
32. Lockwasher
33. Torsion bar
34. Torsion bar front arm
35. Bolt
36. Washer
37. Nut
38. Bolt
39. Lockwasher
40. Nut
41-58. Not used
59. Bushing
60. Fulcrum bolt
61. Nut
62. Lockwasher
63. Fulcrum pin
64. Lock bolt
65. Lockwasher
66. Nut
67. Ring
68. Front bushing assembly
69. Rear bushing assembly
70. Shock absorber assembly
71. Bushing
72. Washer
73. Washer
74. Nut
75. Locknut
76. Bushing
77. Clamp bolt
78. Lockwasher
79. Nut
80. Suspension bound bumper
81. Lockwasher
82. Nut
83. Suspension rebound bumper

Tension Rod Adjustment

There are three adjusting nuts on each tension rod. There is one at the lower suspension link end and two at the frame end. Adjust these nuts until both rubber bushings at the frame end are compressed to .434″ (11 mm.).

Suspension Height Adjustment

1. Jack up the vehicle under the front suspension crossmember to unload the torsion bars.
2. Turn the rear torsion bar anchor bolt right to lower the vehicle and left to raise it.
3. Dimension B in the illustration should be 2.93″ (74.5 mm.) on the L320 and 3.07-3.09″ on the L520, with the vehicle empty and resting on its wheels.

Wheel Alignment

Caster and camber are adjusted by shims placed between the upper suspension link spindle and the crossmember. See the Chassis and Wheel Alignment Specifications Chart for alignment specifications.

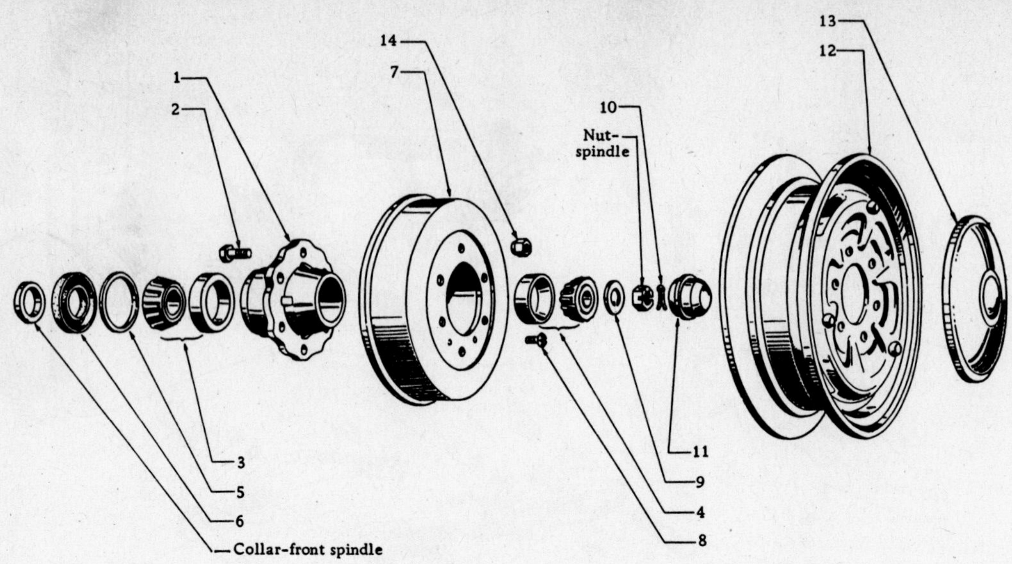

Front hub and drum details, L520

1. Hub
2. Wheel bolt
3. Inner bearing
4. Outer bearing
5. Grease seal spacer
6. Grease seal
7. Brake drum
8. Screw
9. Bearing washer
10. Cotter pin
11. Hubcap
12. Wheel
13. Wheel cover
14. Wheel nut

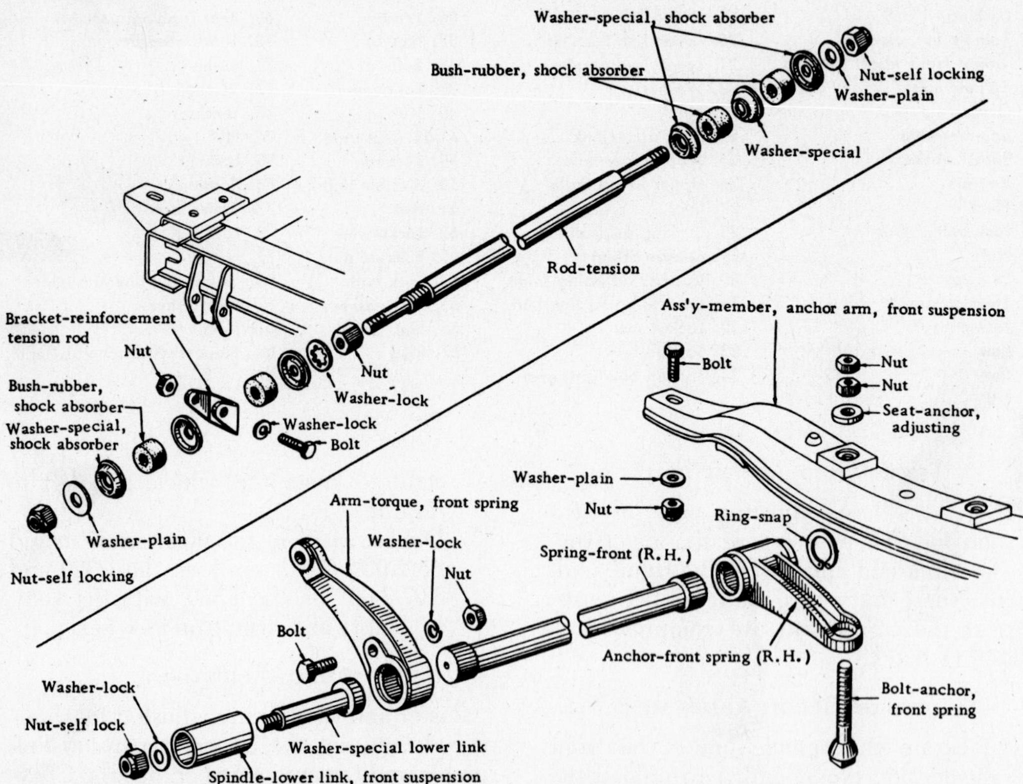

Tension rod assembly, top, and torsion bar assembly, bottom

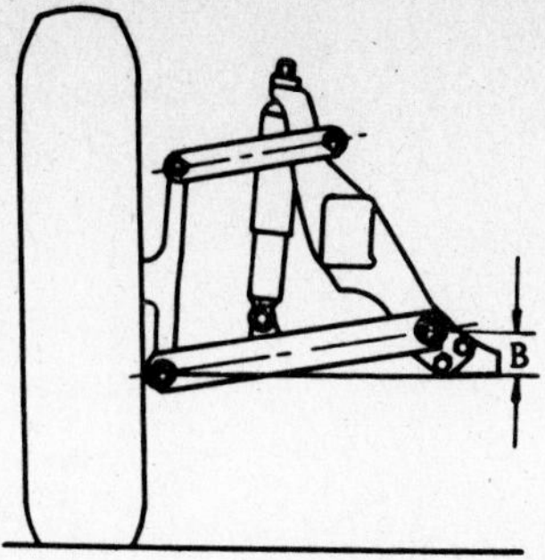

Check measurement B after adjusting front suspension height

Coil Spring Type—PL410, PL411, RL411, SPL310, SPL311, SRL311

This independent front suspension uses coil springs between upper and lower wishbones. The shock absorbers are mounted in the center of each spring. The spindles are connected to the wishbones by ball joints. A cross-chassis stabilizer bar is used.

Wheel Bearing Adjustment

1. Jack up car and remove wheel.
2. Remove hubcap and cotter pin.
3. Torque the spindle nut to 33-36 ft. lbs. for the PL410, and 20-30 ft. lbs. for the PL411 and RL411.
4. Turn the hub a few turns in each direction and retorque the nut.
5. Loosen the nut 40-70°. Insert the cotter pin.
6. Turn the hub a few more turns.
7. Check that the hub turns easily. If not, check wheel bearing condition.
8. Replace hubcap and wheel. Lower car.

Spring R&R

1. Raise and support the front of the car.
2. Unbolt top and bottom mounts and remove shock absorber.
3. Install a coil spring compressor.

NOTE: Be extremely cautious when working with chassis coil springs.

Compress the spring.

4. Unbolt the lower link spindle from the crossmember. An alternate method is to unbolt the lower ball joint. On sportscars, it is also possible to unbolt the lower spring support plate.

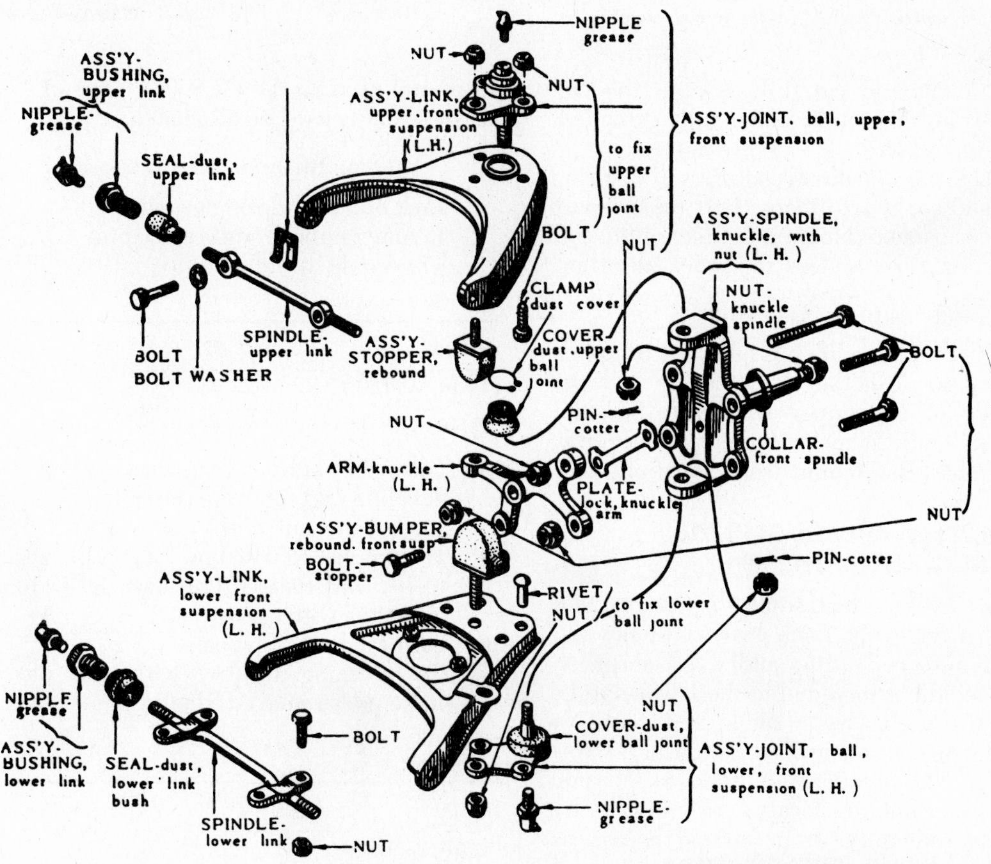

Front suspension details, sedans with coil springs

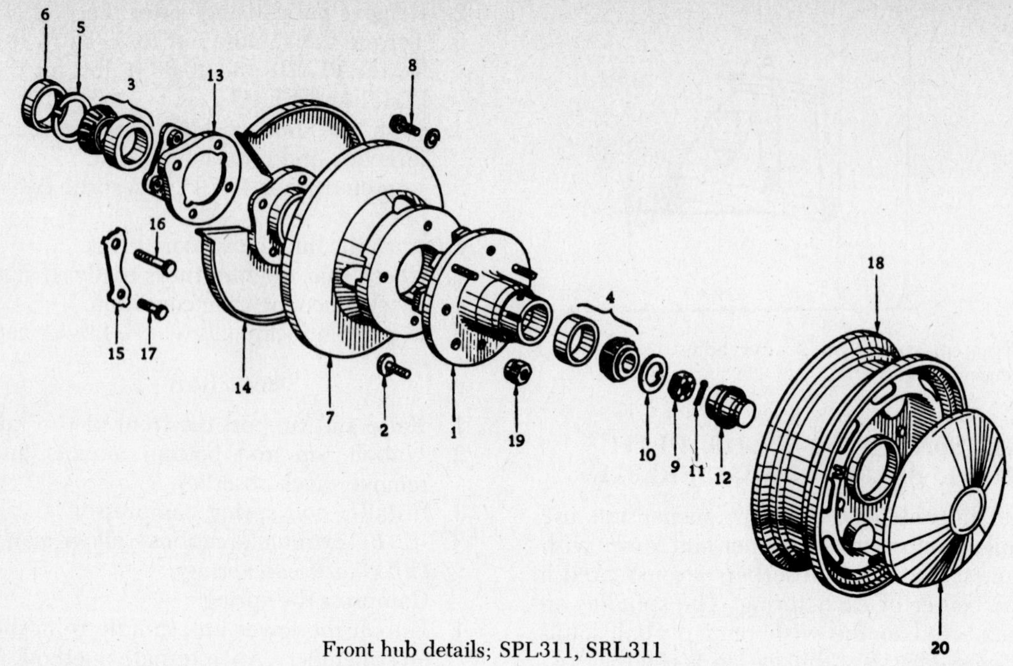

Front hub details; SPL311, SRL311

1. Hub
2. Wheel bolt
3. Inner bearing
4. Outer bearing
5. Oil seal spacer
6. Oil seal
7. Brake rotor (disc)
8. Rotor bolt
9. Spindle nut
10. Bearing washer
11. Cotter pin
12. Hubcap
13. Caliper adapter
14. Not used
15. Lock plate
16. Bolt
17. Bolt
18. Wheel
19. Wheel nut
20. Wheel cover

5. Slowly and carefully release the coil spring. When the coil is fully extended, remove it.
6. On reinstallation, compress the spring and set it into place. Bolt on the part disconnected in Step 4. Release the coil spring and replace the shock absorber.

Wheel Alignment

Caster and camber are adjusted by shims placed between the crossmember and the spindle of the upper wishbone. See the Chassis and Wheel Alignment Specifications Chart for alignment specifications.

Strut Type—PL510, WPL510, LB110, KLB110, HLS30

This independent front suspension uses McPherson struts. Each strut combines the function of coil spring and shock absorber. The spindle is mounted to the lower part of the strut which has a single ball joint. No upper suspension arm is required in this design. The spindle and lower suspension transverse link are located fore and aft by tension rods to the front part of the chassis on the PL510, WPL510, KLB110, and LB110. Compression rods, which run rearward, are used on the HLS30. A cross-chassis sway bar is used on all models.

Wheel Bearing Adjustment

1. Jack up car and remove wheel.
2. Remove hubcap and cotter pin.
3. Torque the spindle nut to:

Model	*Torque (ft. lbs.)*
HLS30	18-22
PL510, WPL510	22-25
LB110, KLB110	16-17

4. Turn the hub a few turns in each direction and retorque the nut.
5. Loosen the nut 60-75° on the HLS30, 90° on the PL510 and WPL510, and 40-70° on the LB110 and KLB110. Insert the cotter pin.
6. Turn the hub a few more turns.
7. Hub turning torque, with the disc brake pads removed, should be:

Model	*Torque (in. lbs.)*	*Pull at hub bolt (lbs.)*
HLS30	3.5-7.4	1.5-3.3
PL510, WPL510 with new bearing and seal	6.1	

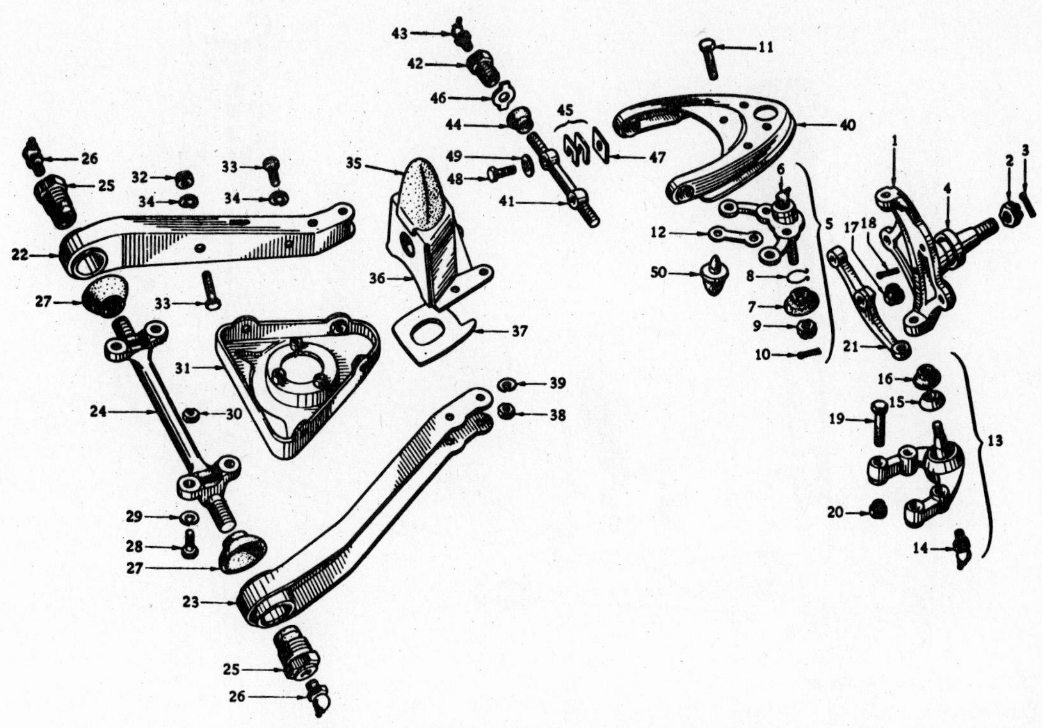

Front suspension details, sportscars with coil springs

1. Spindle assembly
2. Nut
3. Cotter pin
4. Spindle collar
5. Upper ball joint assembly
6. Grease fitting
7. Dust cover
8. Clamp
9. Nut
10. Cotter pin
11. Bolt
12. Lock plate
13. Lower ball joint assembly
14. Grease fitting
15. Inner dust cover
16. Outer rubber dust cover
17. Nut
18. Cotter pin
19. Bolt
20. Nut
21. Steering arm
22. Front lower link
23. Rear lower link
24. Lower link spindle
25. Bushing assembly
26. Grease fitting
27. Dust seal
28. Bolt
29. Lockwasher
30. Nut
31. Lower spring seat
32. Nut
33. Bolt
34. Lockwasher
35. Rebound bumper
36. Bracket
37. Spacer
38. Nut
39. Lockwasher
40. Upper link
41. Upper link spindle
42. Bushing assembly
43. Grease fitting
44. Dust seal
45. Camber shims
46. Lockwasher
47. Caster shim
48. Bolt
49. Lockwasher
50. Rebound bumper

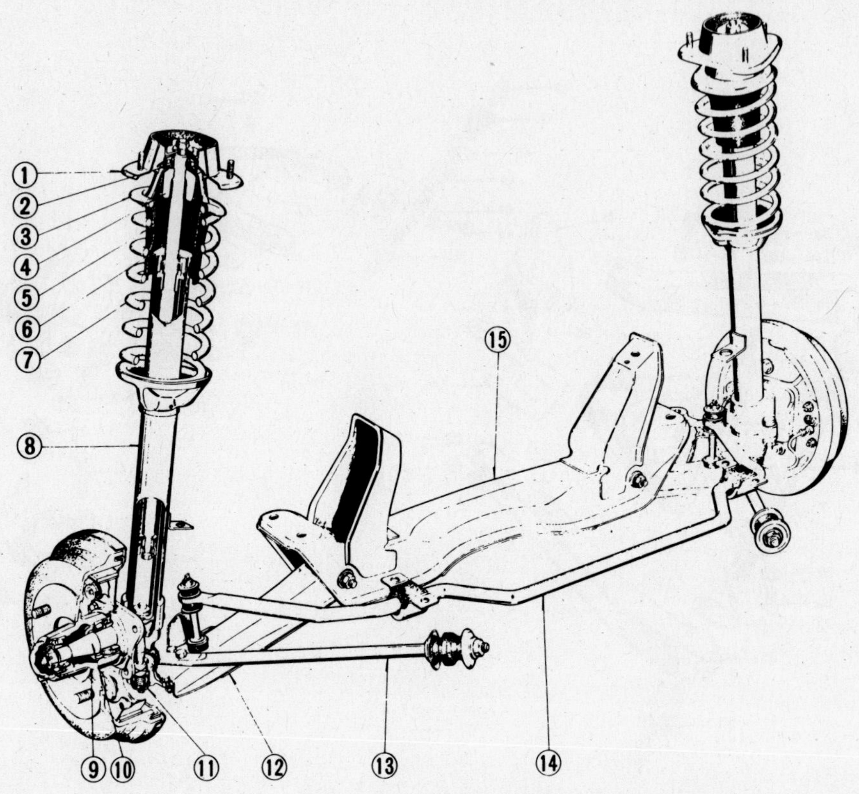

Strut type front suspension, LB110 and KLB110. Other models are quite similar. On HLS30 tension rods are replaced by compression rods which run to the rear.

1. Strut mounting insulator
2. Strut mounting bearing
3. Upper spring seat
4. Bumper rubber
5. Dust cover
6. Piston rod
7. Front spring
8. Strut assembly
9. Hub assembly
10. Spindle
11. Ball joint
12. Transverse link
13. Tension rod
14. Stabilizer
15. Suspension member

PL510, WPL510 with original bearing and seal	3.5	
LB110, KLB110	15.6-20.0	7.1-8.8

If torque is excessive, check wheel bearing condition. There should be no hub end-play.

8. Replace hubcap, brake pads, and wheel. Lower car.

Hub Assembly Repair

1. Jack up vehicle, remove wheel, and disconnect brake hose.
2. Unbolt and remove brake caliper assembly.
3. Remove hubcap, cotter pin, and spindle nut.
4. Remove wheel hub with bearing washer, bearing, and brake rotor.
5. Remove screws and brake splash shield.
6. Disassemble hub. Use a drift in the two grooves inside the hub to drive out the bearing outer race.

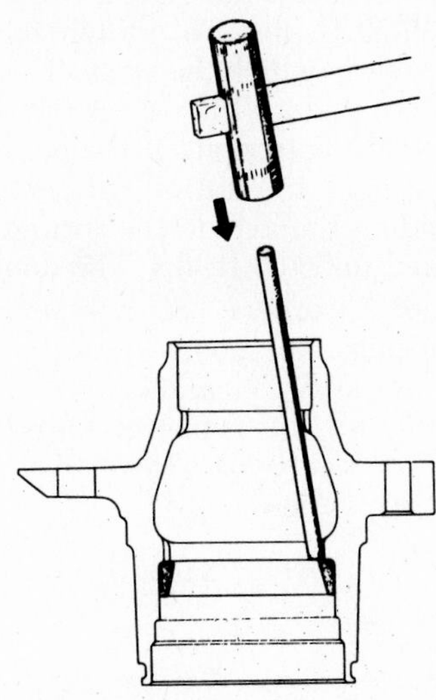

Driving out bearing outer race

7. Drive or press back in the bearing outer race.
8. Pack the bearings, the hub, and the grease seal lip pocket (use a new seal) with grease. Refer to the illustration.
9. Reassemble, and adjust the wheel bearings. Pack some grease into the hubcap and replace it.

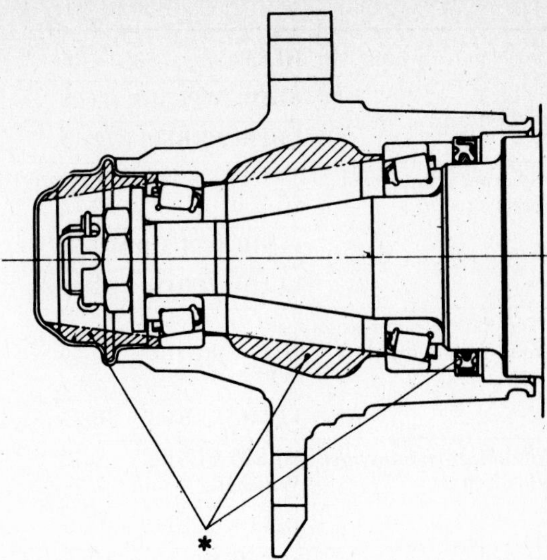

* indicates areas to be filled with grease.

Fastener	*Model*	*Torque (ft. lbs.)*
Splash shield screws	All	2-3
Rotor to hub bolts	PL510, WPL510, HLS30	28-38
	LB110, KLB110	20-27
Caliper bolts	HLS30	11-13
	PL510, WPL510	53-72
	LB110, KLB110	33-44

10. Replace caliper, brake hose, and wheel. Lower vehicle.

Strut R&R

1. Jack up car and support safely. Remove wheel.
2. Disconnect and plug brake hose.
3. Disconnect tension rod (compression rod on HLS30) and stabilizer bar from transverse link.
4. Unbolt the steering arm.
5. Place a jack under the bottom of the strut.
6. Open the hood and remove the nuts holding the top of the strut.
7. Lower the jack slowly and cautiously until the strut assembly can be removed.
8. Reverse the procedure to install. The self locking nuts holding the top of the strut must be replaced.

Fastener	Model	Torque (ft. lbs.)
Strut to body nuts	HLS30	18-25
	PL510, WPL510	28-38
	LB110, KLB110	12-15
Steering arm to strut bolts	HLS30	53-72
	PL510, WPL510	43-58
	LB110, KLB110	33-44
Tension or compression rod to transverse link nut	HLS30, PL510, WPL510	36-46
	LB110, KLB110	16-22
Stabilizer to transverse link bolts	HLS30, PL510, WPL510	9-12
	LB110, KLB110	7-9
Stabilizer to frame bracket bolts	HLS30, PL510, WPL510	14-18
	LB110, KLB110	7-9

NOTE: Special tools are required to disassemble the strut. It is recommended that strut repair be left to an authorized repair facility.

Ball Joint R&R

The lower ball joint should be replaced when up and down (axial) play exceeds the standard play of .0118-.0394″ for the LB110 and KLB110 or .0012-.0136″ for the other models. The ball joint should be greased every 30,000 miles. There is a plugged hole in the bottom of the joint for installation of a grease fitting.

1. Raise and support car so wheels hang free. Remove wheel.
2. Unbolt tension rod (compression rod on HLS30) and stabilizer bar from transverse link.
3. Unbolt strut from steering arm.
4. Remove cotter pin and ball joint stud nut. Separate ball joint and steering arm.
5. Unbolt ball joint from transverse link.
6. Reverse procedure to install new ball joint. Grease the joint after installation.

Fastener	Model	Torque (ft. lbs.)
Ball joint to transverse link bolts	HLS30	36-46
	PL510, WPL510	14-18
	LB110, KLB110	16-22
Ball joint stud nut	All	40-55
Tension rod, compression rod, stabilizer bar, and steering arm	All	See Strut R&R.

Wheel Alignment

Caster and camber angles cannot be adjusted except by replacing worn or bent parts. Suspension height is adjusted by replacing the front springs. Various springs are available for adjustment. Toe-in is adjusted by changing the length of the steering side-rods. The length of these rods should always be equal when measured between their ball joint centers. Steering angles are adjusted by means of a stop bolt on each steering arm. On the LB110 and KLB110 make sure that the clearance between the tire and tension rod is at least 1.181″.

REAR

Leaf Spring Type

L60

When replacing the springs, the bolts should be tightened only after the vehicle is resting on its wheels. The torque for the front spring eye, which has a rubber bushing, is 45-50 ft. lbs. To tighten the spring rear shackles, which have steel bushings, first tighten the nut fully, back off 1/4 turn, and insert the cotter pin. If the pin holes do not align, back the nut off further. The U-bolts holding the axle to the springs should be torqued to 50-60 ft. lbs. The double-acting shock absorbers are not serviceable. With springs in good condition, there should be .515″ clearance between the main leaf and the rubber bumper on the frame. A cross-chassis sway bar is used on the rear suspension.

LB110, KLB110

Spring R&R

1. Raise rear axle until wheels hang free. Support the car on stands. Support the rear axle with a jack.
2. Unbolt bottom end of shock absorber.
3. Unbolt axle from spring leaves. Unbolt and remove front spring bracket. Lower the front of the spring to the floor.
4. Unbolt and remove spring rear shackle.
5. Before reinstallation, coat the front bracket pin, bushing, shackle pin, and shackle bushing with a soap solution.
6. Reverse procedure to install. The front

pin nut and the shock absorber mounting should be tightened before the vehicle is lowered to the floor.

Fastener	*Torque (ft. lbs.)*
Axle U-bolts	23-29
Front spring bracket to body	12-15
Shackle pin nuts	12-15
LB110 Sedan shock absorber upper nuts	26-33
KLB110 Coupe shock absorber upper nuts	7-9
LB110 Sedan shock absorber lower nuts	26-33
KLB110 Coupe shock absorber lower nuts	7-9

Shock Absorber R&R

To remove the rear shock absorbers, simply unbolt the lower and upper ends. The upper nuts are under the rear seat back. The shock absorbers are not serviceable and should be replaced if defective. Mounting bolt torques are given under Spring R & R.

WPL510

Spring R&R

1. Raise rear axle until wheels hang free. Support the car on stands. Support the rear axle with a floor jack.
2. Remove the spare tire.
3. Unbolt bottom end of shock absorber.
4. Unbolt axle from spring leaves.
5. Unbolt front spring bracket from body. Lower spring end and bracket to floor.
6. Unbolt and remove rear shackle.
7. Unbolt bracket from spring.
8. Before reinstallation, coat the front bracket pin and bushing, and the shackle pin and bushing with a soap solution.
9. Reverse procedure to install. The front pin nut and the shock absorber mounting should be tightened after the vehicle is lowered to the floor. Make sure that the elongated flange of the rubber bumper is to the rear.

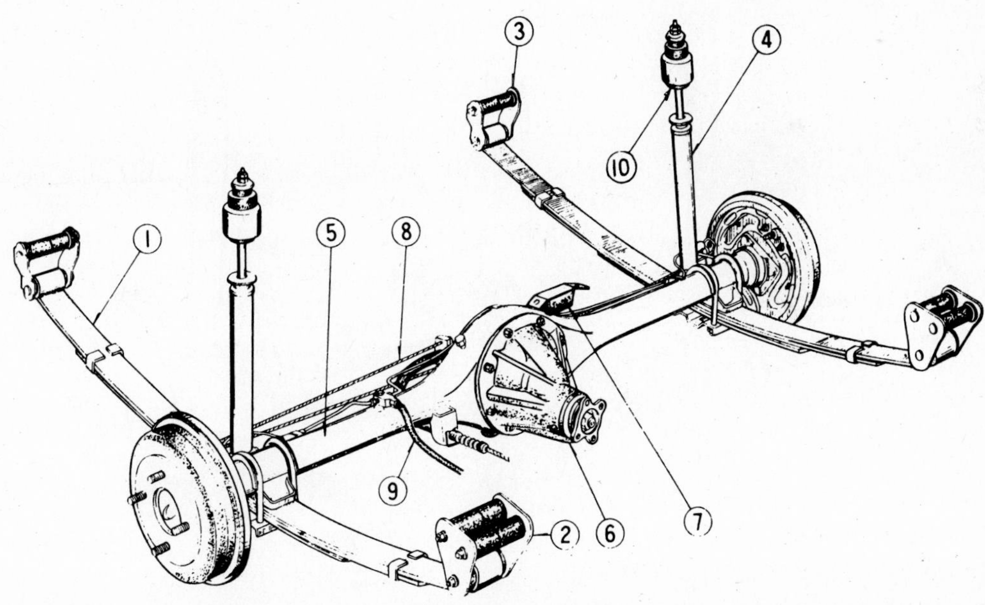

LB110 and KLB110 rear suspension

1. Leaf spring
2. Front mounting
3. Shackle
4. Shock absorber
5. Axle housing
6. Differential carrier
7. Torque arrester
8. Handbrake cable
9. Brake hose
10. Bound bumper

Fastener	Torque (ft. lbs.)
Axle U-bolts	43-47
Shock absorber upper bracket to body	11-18
Shock absorber to upper bracket nuts	12-16
Shock absorber lower nuts	25-33
Spring shackle nuts	33-36
Front pin nuts	33-36
Front bracket to body nuts	13-17

Shock Absorber R&R

When removing the shock absorber, unbolt the upper bracket from the body and remove the shock absorber and bracket as a unit. The shock absorbers are not serviceable and should be replaced if defective. Mounting bolt torques are given under Spring R & R.

Independent Rear Suspension—PL510, HLS30

Coil Spring R&R—PL510

1. Raise rear of vehicle and support on stands.
2. Remove wheels.
3. Disconnect handbrake linkage and return spring.
4. Unbolt axle driveshaft flange at wheel end.
5. Unbolt rubber bumper inside bottom of coil spring.
6. Jack up suspension arm and unbolt shock absorber lower mounting.
7. Lower jack slowly and cautiously. Remove coil spring, spring seat, and rubber bumper.
8. Reverse procedure to install, making sure that the flat face of the spring is at the top.

Fastener	Torque (ft. lbs.)
Axle driveshaft flange nuts	51-58
Rubber bumper nut	15-19
Shock absorber mounting nuts	17

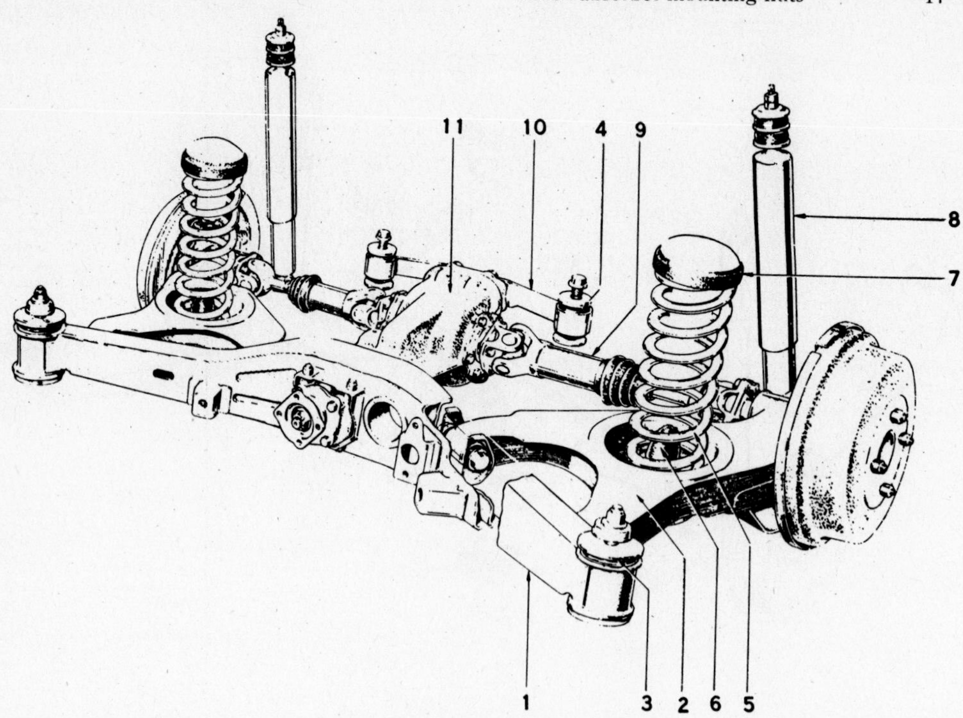

PL510 independent rear suspension

1. Suspension member
2. Suspension arm
3. Member mounting insulator
4. Differential mounting insulator
5. Coil spring
6. Bumper rubber
7. Spring seat
8. Shock absorber
9. Drive shaft
10. Differential mounting member
11. Differential carrier

Strut R&R—HLS30

1. Raise rear of vehicle and support on stands.
2. Remove wheels.
3. Disconnect brake hydraulic line and handbrake cable.
4. Remove nuts from either end of transverse link outer spindle. Remove spindle center locking bolt. Pull out spindle. Separate bottom of strut from transverse link.
5. Unbolt axle driveshaft flange at wheel end.
6. Jack under the lower end of the strut. Remove the strut installation nuts from the tower inside the luggage area. Lower jack and strut gradually.

NOTE: Strut disassembly and repair requires special tools and should be left to an authorized repair facility.

7. Reverse procedure to install. Note that the shorter part of the spindle (measured from the locking bolt notch) should be to the front. Tighten the outer spindle end nuts after the vehicle has been lowered to the floor.

Fastener	*Torque (ft. lbs.)*
Strut installation nut	12-15
Transverse link outer spindle nuts	54-69
Outer spindle locking bolt	7-9
Axle driveshaft flange nuts	36-43

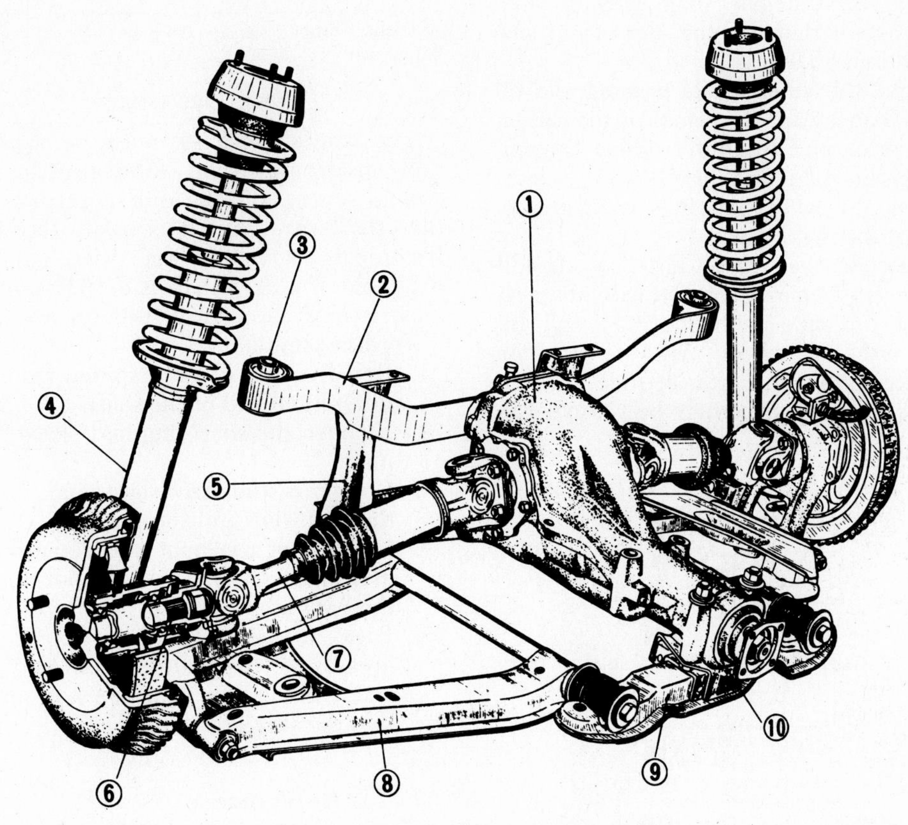

HLS30 independent rear suspension

1. Differential carrier
2. Differential case mount rear member
3. Differential case mount rear insulator
4. Strut assembly
5. Link mount brace
6. Rear axle shaft
7. Drive shaft
8. Transverse link
9. Differential case mount front member
10. Differential case mount front insulator

Shock Absorber R&R—PL510

1. Open the trunk and remove the cover panel.
2. Remove the two nuts holding the top of the shock absorber.
3. The shock absorbers can not be repaired. Replace if defective.
4. Reverse procedure to install. See Coil Spring R&R—PL510 for torque figures.

Wheel Bearing, Seal, and Axle Shaft Service

1. Jack up and support rear of car.
2. Remove wheel and brake drum.
3. Disconnect axle driveshaft from axle shaft at flange.
4. Remove the wheel bearing locknut while holding the axle shaft outer flange from turning.
5. Pull out the axle shaft with a slide hammer. Remove the distance piece and inner flange.
6. Drive the inner wheel bearing and oil seal out toward the center of the car.
7. Press or pull the outer wheel bearing from the axle shaft.
8. Pack the wheel bearings with grease. Coat the seal lip also.
9. Reinstall the wheel bearings. Install the outer bearing on the axle shaft so that the side with the seal will be toward the wheel. Always press or drive on the inner bearing race.
10. The distance piece may be reused if it is not collapsed or deformed. The distance piece must always carry the same mark, A, B, or C, as the bearing housing.
11. Fill the area illustrated with grease.
12. Replace the axle shaft and flange. Tighten the bearing locknut to the specified torque.
13. The torque required to start the axle shaft turning should be 390 in. lbs. or less. This is a 28.7 oz. or less pull at the hub bolt. Axle shaft end-play, checked with a dial indicator, should be 0-0057″.
14. If turning torque or axle shaft play is incorrect, disassemble and install a new distance piece.

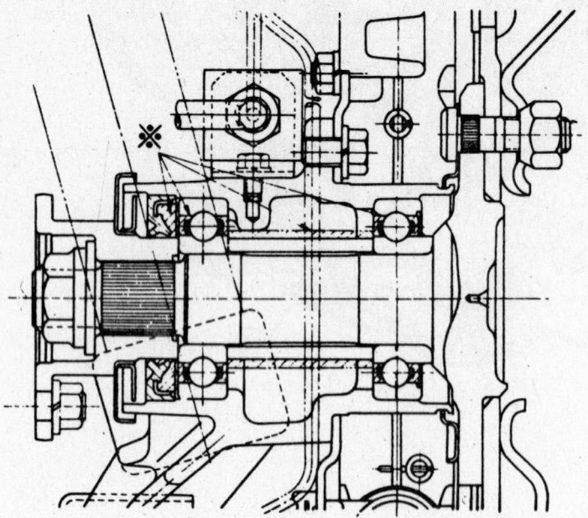

* indicates areas to receive grease

Fastener	*Model*	*Torque (ft. lbs.)*
Wheel nut	All	58-65
Axle driveshaft flange nuts	PL510	51-58
	HLS30	36-43
Bearing locknut	All	181-239
Axle shaft inner flange nut	All	12-17

Axle Driveshaft

The axle driveshafts must be removed and disassembled to lubricate the ball splines every 30,000 miles. Handle the driveshaft carefully; it is easily damaged. No repair parts for the driveshafts are available. If a driveshaft is defective in any way, it must be replaced as an assembly.

To disassemble:

1. Remove the U-joint spider from the differential end of the shaft.
2. Remove the snap-ring and sleeve yoke plug.
3. Compress the driveshaft and remove the snap-ring and stopper.
4. Disconnect the boot and separate the driveshaft carefully so as not to lose the balls and spacer.
5. Pack about 10 grams (.35 oz.) of grease into the ball grooves. Also pack about 35 grams (1.23 oz.) of grease into the area illustrated.

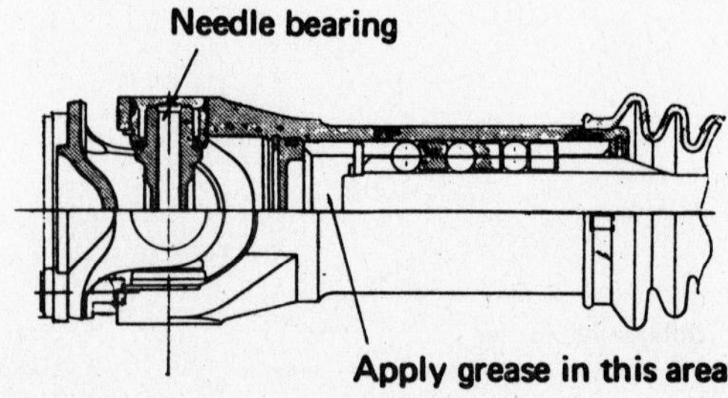

Axle driveshaft cross-section

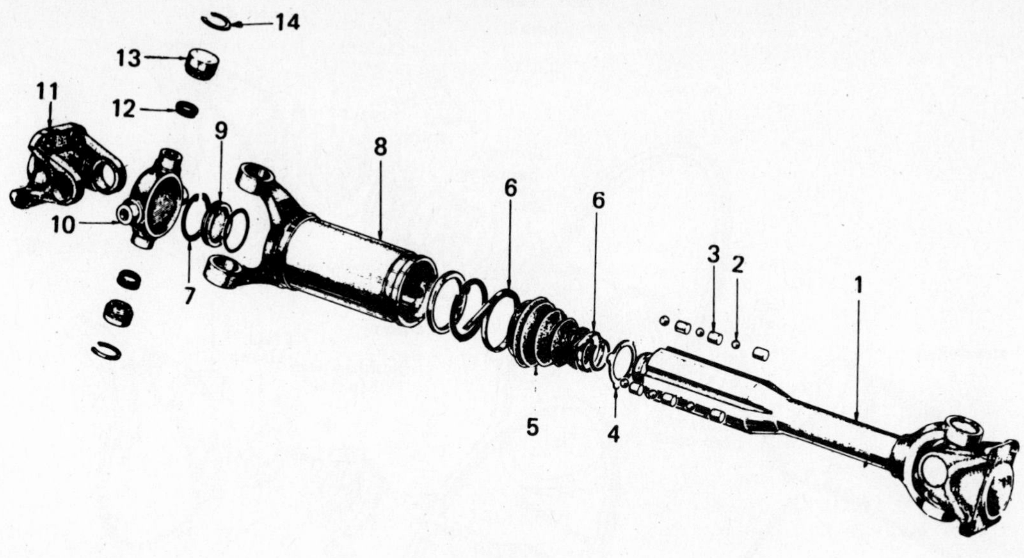

Axle driveshaft for PL510 and HLS30 rear suspension

1. Drive shaft
2. Drive shaft ball
3. Ball spacer
4. Drive shaft stopper
5. Rubber boot
6. Boot band
7. Snap ring
8. Sleeve yoke
9. Sleeve yoke plug
10. Spider journal
11. Flange yoke
12. Oil seal
13. Needle bearing
14. Snap ring

6. Twisting play between the two shaft halves should not exceed .0039″. Check play with the driveshaft completely compressed.
7. While reassembling, adjust U-joint side play to .0008″ or less by selecting suitable snap-rings. Four different thicknesses are available for adjustment. See Wheel Bearing, Seal, and Axle Shaft Service for driveshaft flange nut torque.

Steering

Several types of steering gear are used on Datsun vehicles. These are:

Model	*Type*
L60, L320, L520	Worm and roller
PL410, SPL310, SPL311, SRL311	Cam and lever
PL411, RL411, LB110, KLB110, PL510, WPL510, L521, PL521	Recirculating ball
HLS30	Rack and pinion

PL510, WPL510, SPL311, and SRL311 models starting 1969, and all HLS30, KLB110, and LB110 models, have a steering shaft lock actuated by the ignition lock and a steering column and shaft assembly designed to collapse on impact.

STEERING WHEEL R&R

First remove the horn button or ring. On the L320, L520, and other early models, the horn button assembly is retained by three screws which can be removed from the rear of the wheel. On the PL410, PL411, KLB110 and LB110, the horn ring is

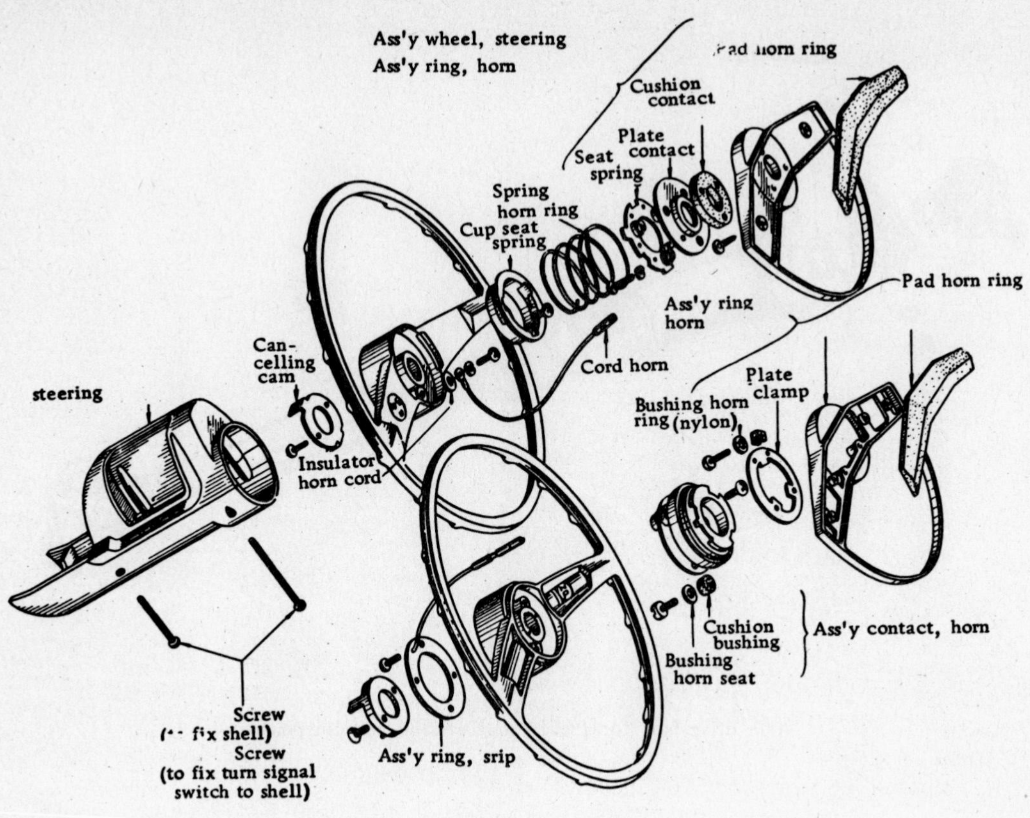

Steering wheel installation, PL410 and PL411

retained by two screws which can be removed from the rear of the wheel spokes. On the SPL310, SPL311, and SRL311, the horn button is retained by a wire snap-ring and can be pried loose. To remove the PL510 and WPL510 horn ring, press in and turn to the left. Pull the HLS30 horn button rearward to remove. Next remove the rest of the horn switching mechanism, noting the relative location of the parts. Hold the steering wheel and remove the nut. Using a puller, remove the steering wheel. Do not attempt to pry or hammer off the wheel. This is particularly important in the case of collapsible steering columns. When replacing the wheel, make sure that it is correctly aligned when the wheels are straight ahead. Do not drive or hammer the wheel into place. Tighten the nut while holding the wheel. Specified wheel nut torque is 22-25 ft. lbs. for the LB110 and KLB110 and 29-36 ft. lbs. for the HLS30. Reinstall the horn button or ring.

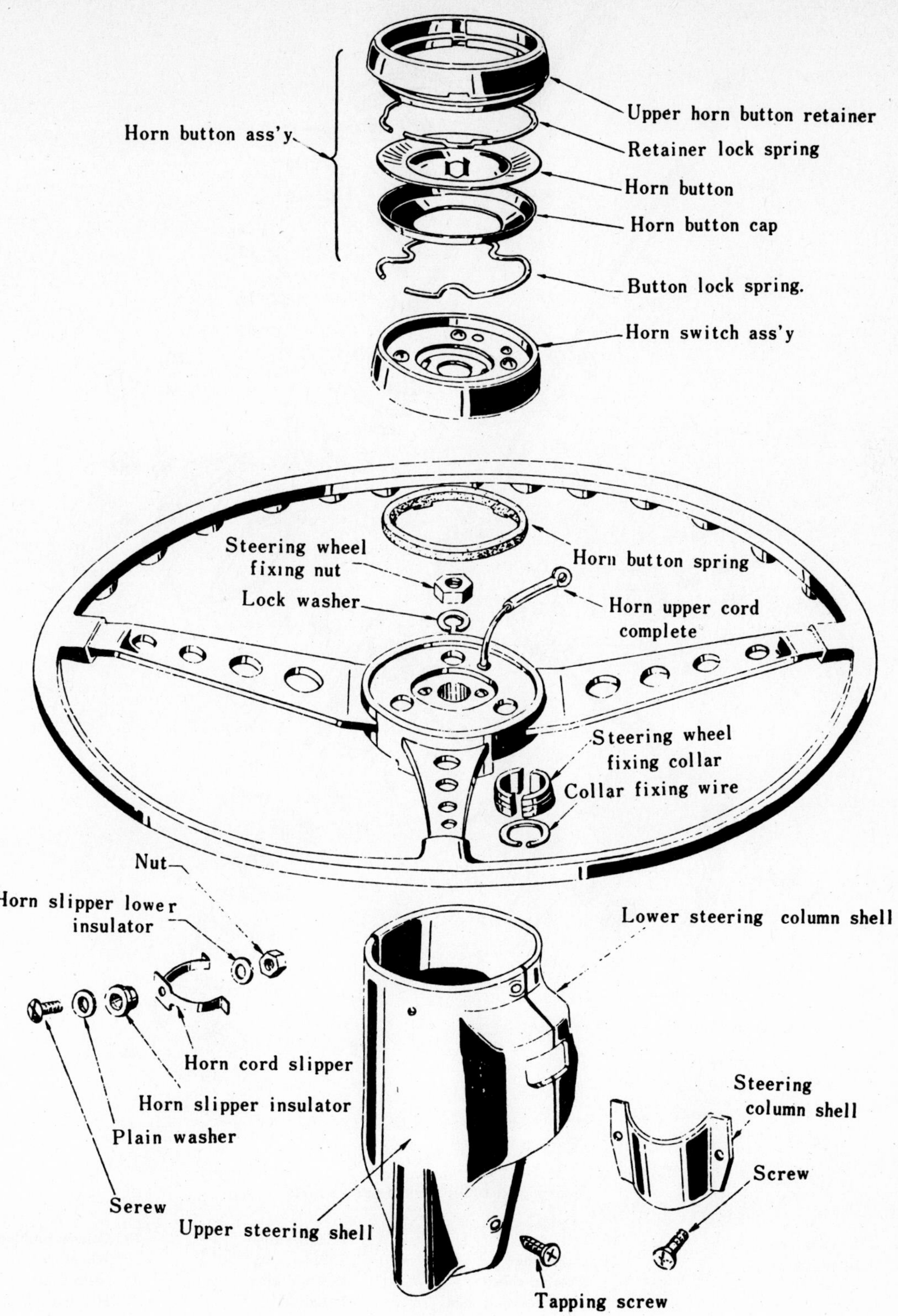

Steering wheel installation; SPL310, SPL311, and SRL311

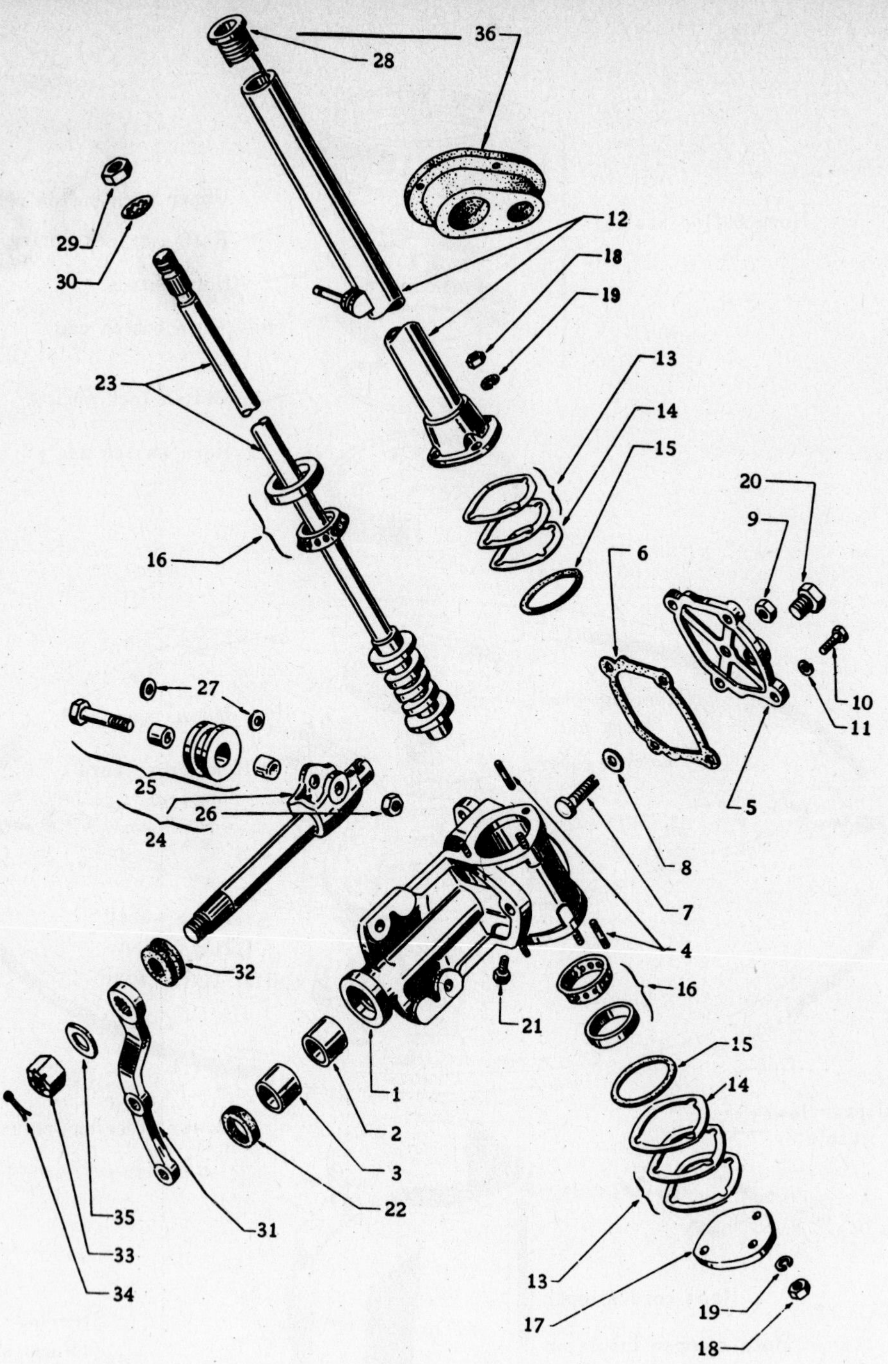

Worm and roller steering gear, L520

1. Steering gear housing
2. Upper bushing
3. Lower bushing
4. Stud
5. Cover
6. Gasket
7. Adjusting screw
8. Adjusting shim
9. Locknut
10. Bolt
11. Lockwasher
12. Steering column
13. Worm bearing shim
14. Shims
15. O-ring
16. Worm bearing
17. Cover
18. Nut
19. Lockwasher
20. Filler plug
21. Drain plug
22. Oil seal
23. Steering shaft
24. Roller shaft
25. Roller and pin
26. Nut
27. Thrust washers
28. Column bushing
29. Wheel nut
30. Lockwasher
31. Steering arm
32. Dust seal
33. Nut
34. Cotter pin
35. Washer
36. Rubber grommet

STEERING GEAR R&R

L60, L320, L520, L521, PL521

1. Remove the steering wheel.
2. Unbolt the steering column from the instrument panel. On models with column shift, unbolt the shift linkage from the column.
3. Disconnect the horn wire.
4. Unscrew the drag link end plug and disconnect the steering arm from the drag link on the L60. On the L320 and L520, disconnect the steering rod from the steering arm.
5. Unbolt the steering gear box from the frame.
6. Pull the box, column, and shaft down and out of the vehicle.
7. Reverse the procedure to install.

PL410, PL411

This procedure is the same as that for L60, L320, L520, L521, PL521 above with the substitution of the following step:

4. Remove the stud nut and pull the steering rod ball joint from the steering arm.

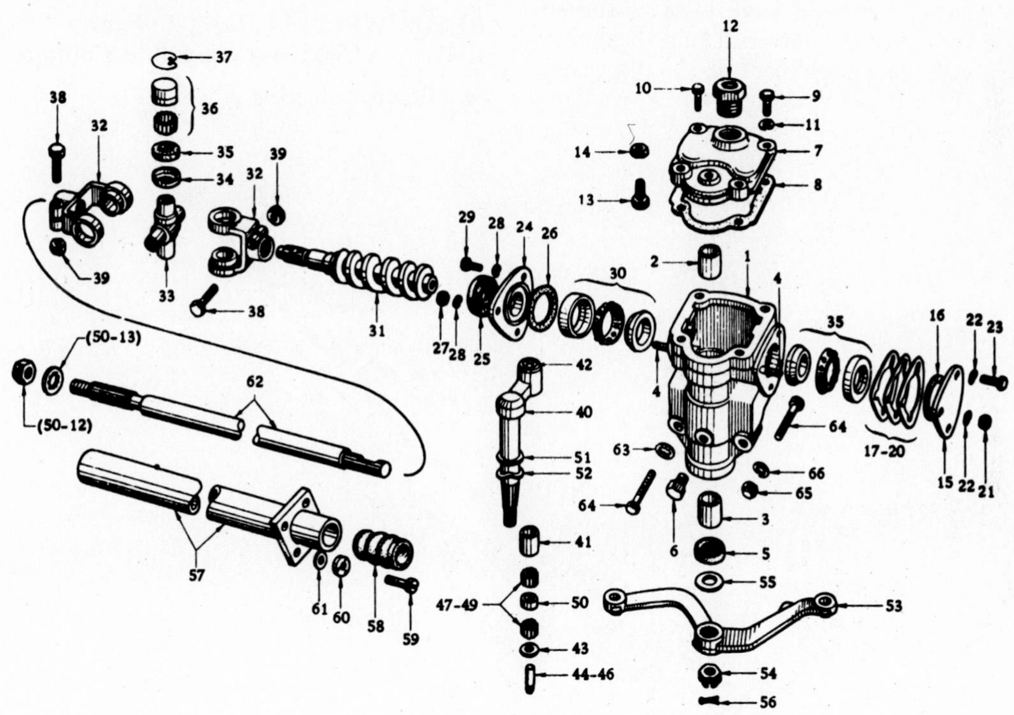

Cam and lever steering gear, SPL311

1. Steering gear housing
2. Bushing
3. Bushing
4. Stud
5. Oil seal
6. Drain plug
7. Cover
8. Gasket
9. Bolt
10. Bolt
11. Lockwasher
12. Filler plug
13. Adjusting screw
14. Locknut
15. Cover
16. O-ring
17-20. Shims
21. Nut
22. Lockwasher
23. Bolt
24. Rear cover
25. Oil seal
26. O-ring
27. Nut
28. Lockwasher
29. Bolt
30. Bearing
31. Worm gear
32. U-joint yoke
33. U-joint spider
34. Oil seal retainer
35. Oil seal
36. Bearing
37. Snap-ring
38. Bolt
39. Nut
40. Rocker shaft (lever)
41. Needle roller race
42. Roller ball plug
43. Needle roller cover
44-46. Roller ball
47-49. Needle rollers
50. Roller spacer
51. Thrust washer
52. Shaft adjusting thrust washer
53. Steering arm
54. Nut
55. Washer
56. Cotter pin
57. Steering column
58. Column bushing
59. Bolt
60. Lockwasher
61. Washer
62. Steering shaft
63. Lockwasher
64. Mounting bolt
65. Nut
66. Lockwasher

SPL310, SPL311, SRL311—Rigid Column
SPL311, SRL311, PL510, WPL510—Collapsible Column

1. Remove the steering shaft U-joint clamp bolt.
2. Remove the stud nut and pull the steering rod ball joint from the steering arm.
3. Unbolt steering gear box from frame and remove. If necessary, remove the horn button and pull the steering wheel and shaft up slightly.
4. Reverse procedure to install. Torque U-joint clamp bolt to 22 ft. lbs. If upper and lower shaft sections of collapsible column have been separated, the slit of the universal joint must align with the punch mark on the upper end of the upper steering shaft.

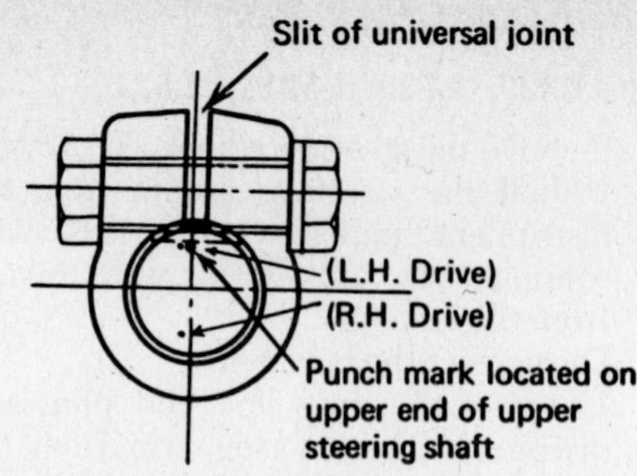

Reassembly details for collapsible column steering shaft

PL510, WPL510—Rigid Column
LB110, KLB110—Collapsible Column

1. Remove steering wheel.

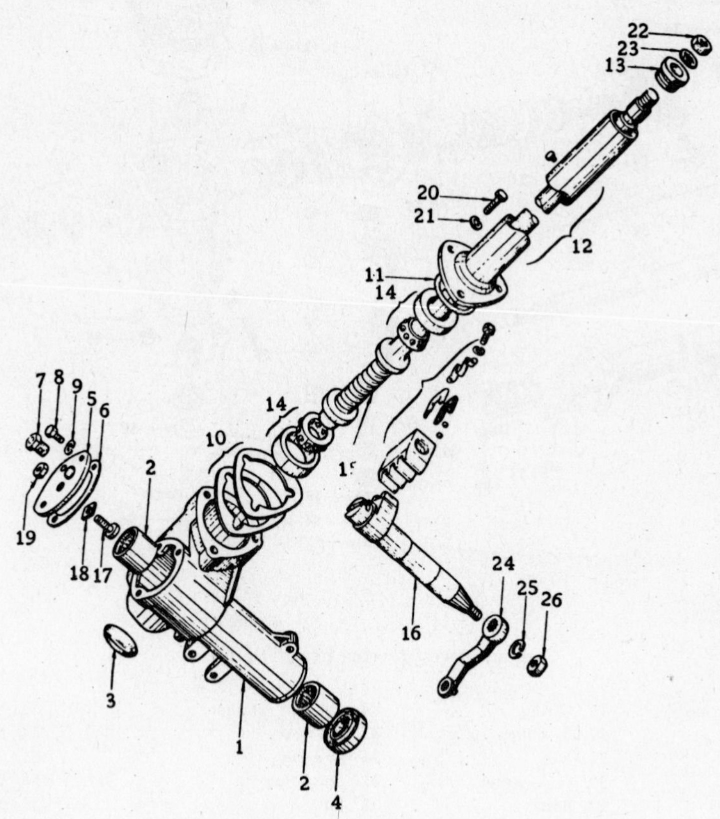

Recirculating ball steering gear, PL411

1. Steering gear housing
2. Needle bearing
3. Plug
4. Oil seal
5. Sector shaft cover
6. Gasket
7. Plug (filler)
8. Bolt
9. Lockwasher
10. Shims for worm bearing
11. O-ring
12. Steering column
13. Bearing
14. Bearing
15. Steering shaft
16. Sector shaft
17. Adjusting screw
18. Adjusting shim
19. Locknut
20. Bolt
21. Lockwasher
22. Nut
23. Washer
24. Steering arm
25. Lockwasher
26. Nut

2. Separate and remove upper steering column shell.
3. Remove turn signal and light switch assembly. Disconnect automatic transmission linkage.
4. Unbolt steering column from instrument panel.
5. Remove steering column hole cover from floorboards.
6. Unbolt steering box from body.
7. Pull assembly out of car toward engine compartment. Be extremely cautious with LB110 and KLB110 collapsible column. Merely dropping or leaning on the assembly could cause enough damage to require replacement.
8. Reverse procedure to install.

Fastener	*Model*	*Torque (ft. lbs.)*
Stud nut	PL510, WPL510	40-55
	LB110, KLB110	22-36
Steering gear box bolts	PL510, WPL510	72
	LB110, KLB110	14-19
Steering column to instrument panel bolts	LB110, KLB110	11-13
Column clamp to column	LB110, KLB110	6-7

HLS30

1. Raise and support front end. Remove front wheels.
2. Loosen clamp bolts at both U-joints. Remove lower joint and shaft assembly from engine compartment.
3. Remove the splash shields.
4. Remove the steering side rod stud nuts and pull the studs from the spindle steering arms.
5. Raise the engine slightly, being careful not to damage the accelerator linkage.
6. Unbolt steering gear housing from suspension crossmember.
7. Remove rack and pinion assembly.
8. Reverse procedure to install. If upper and lower shaft sections of collapsible column have been separated, the slit of the universal joint must align with the punch mark on the upper end of the upper steering shaft.

Fastener	*Torque (ft. lbs.)*
Rubber coupling bolt	11-13
Lower joint bolt	29-36
Side rod stud nut	40-55
Side rod inner socket stopper nut	53-72
Side rod locknut	65

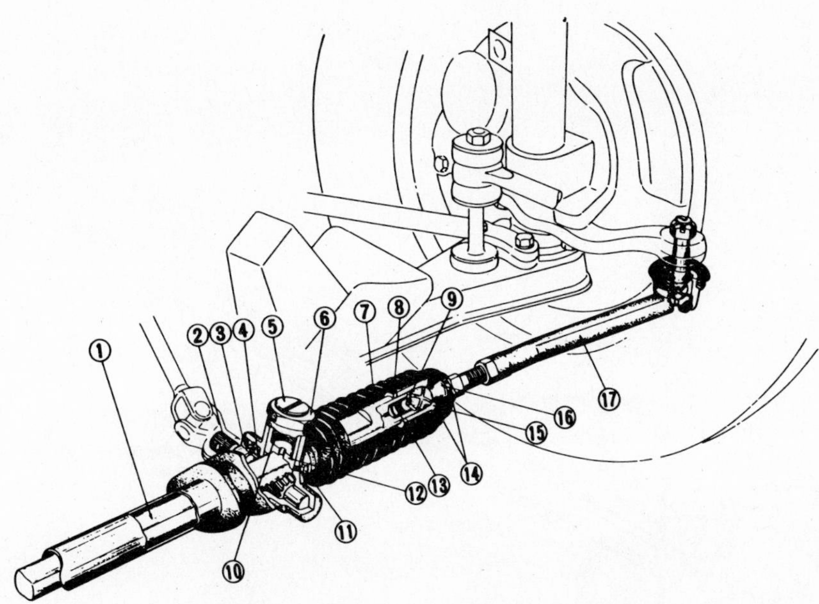

Rack and pinion steering gear, HLS30 (left side shown)

1. Rack
2. Pinion
3. Oil seal
4. Pinion bearing
5. Retainer adjusting screw
6. Locknut
7. Boot
8. Locknut
9. Side rod spring seat
10. Retainer spring
11. Filler plug
12. Retainer
13. Side rod inner spring
14. Dust cover clamp
15. Side rod inner socket
16. Ball stud
17. Side rod

STEERING GEAR ADJUSTMENT

Worm and Roller Adjustment

The backlash adjusting screw is located next to the filler plug on the steering gear box cover.

1. Disconnect the drag link from the steering arm.
2. Loosen the locknut and turn the adjusting screw in clockwise until the mechanism binds.
3. Back off the screw until the unit operates smoothly. Tighten the locknut.
4. Check free play at the end of the steering arm, with the steering gear in the central (straight ahead) position. Free play should be 0-.008″ for the L320 and L520, and 0-.004″ for the L60.
5. Check the force required to turn the steering wheel with a spring scale attached to the wheel rim. It should be .66-1.76 lbs. for the L60, and 1.1-1.5 lbs. for the L320 and L520.
6. Replace the drag link.
7. Maximum permissible play at the steering wheel rim is 1.18″ for the L60, and 1-1.4″ for the other models.

Cam and Lever Adjustment

The adjusting screw is adjacent to the filler plug on the steering gear box cover.

1. Disconnect the steering linkage ball stud from the steering arm.
2. Loosen the locknut and tighten the adjusting screw until there is no steering arm free play in the straight ahead position.
3. Tighten the locknut. Replace the steering linkage.
4. Maximum permissible play at the steering wheel rim is .98-1.38″.

Recirculating Ball Adjustment

The adjusting screw is adjacent to the filler plug on the steering gear box cover.

1. Disconnect steering gear arm from steering linkage.
2. Adjust backlash at steering center point so that play at end of steering gear arm is 0-.004″.
3. Tighten adjusting screw 1/8-1/6 turn more and tighten locknut.
4. Reconnect steering linkage. Specified stud nut torque is 22-36 ft. lbs. for the LB110 and KLB110, and 40-55 ft. lbs. for the PL510 and WPL510.
5. Maximum free play at steering wheel rim should be .79-.98″ for the LB110 and KLB110, .98-1.18″ for the PL510 and WPL510, and 1-1.4″ for all other models.

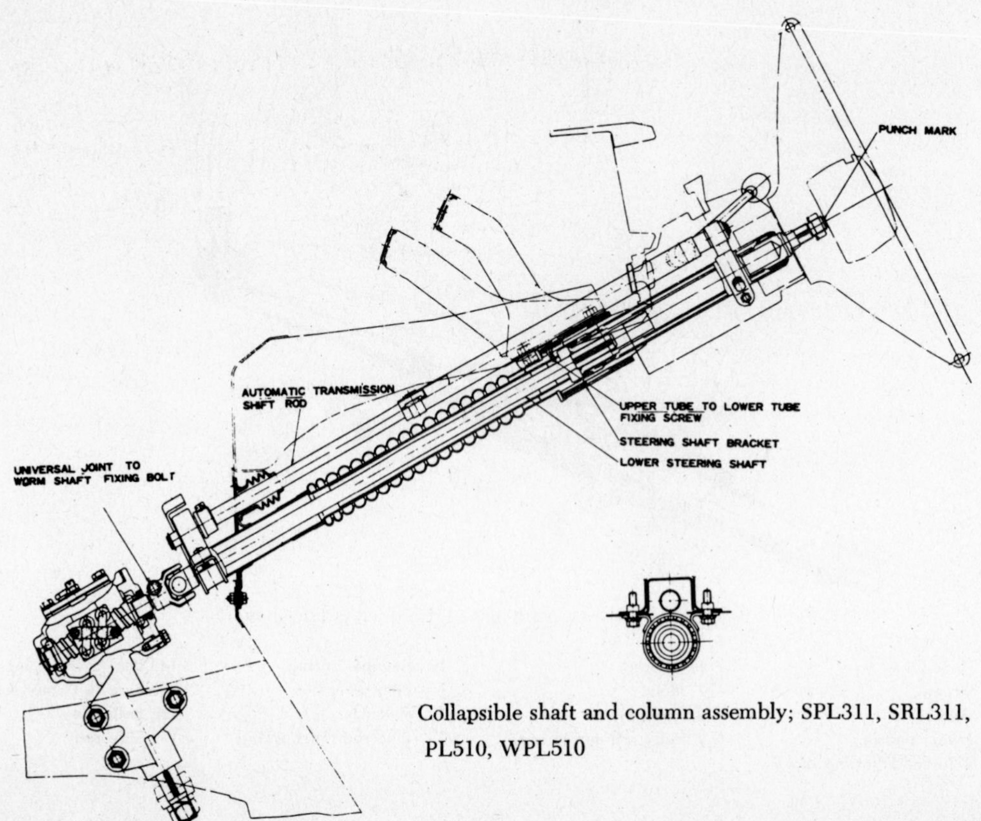

Collapsible shaft and column assembly; SPL311, SRL311, PL510, WPL510

STEERING LOCK

The steering lock/ignition switch/warning buzzer switch assembly is attached to the steering column by special screws whose heads shear off on installation. The screws must be drilled out to remove the assembly. The ignition switch or warning switch can be replaced without removing the assembly. The ignition switch is on the back of the assembly, and the warning switch on the side. The warning buzzer, which sounds when the driver's door is opened with the steering unlocked, is located behind the instrument panel. It is on the left side of the instrument panel on the LB110 and KLB110, and on the steering support on the HLS30.

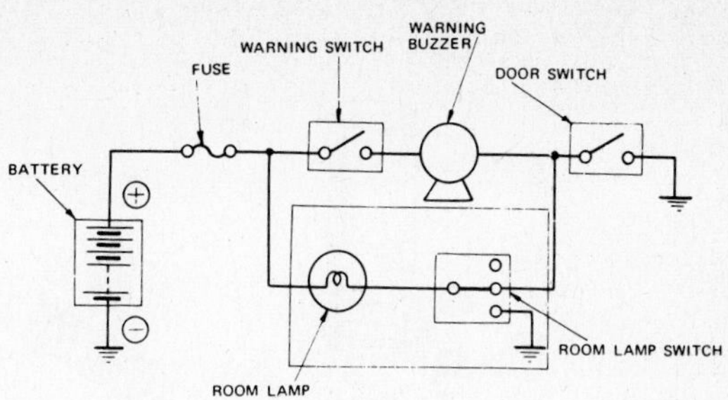

Warning buzzer electrical circuit

Brakes

Front disc brakes are used on all current car models, with drum brakes at the rear. All pickups have a drum brake system front and rear. Starting 1968, all car models are equipped with independent front and rear hydraulic systems with a warning light to indicate loss of pressure in either system. The single circuit master cylinder is retained on pickups. The HLS30 has a vacuum booster system to lessen required pedal pressure. The parking brake, except on the L60, operates the rear brakes through a cable system. On the L60, the handbrake is an external contracting band on the rear output shaft of the transfer case.

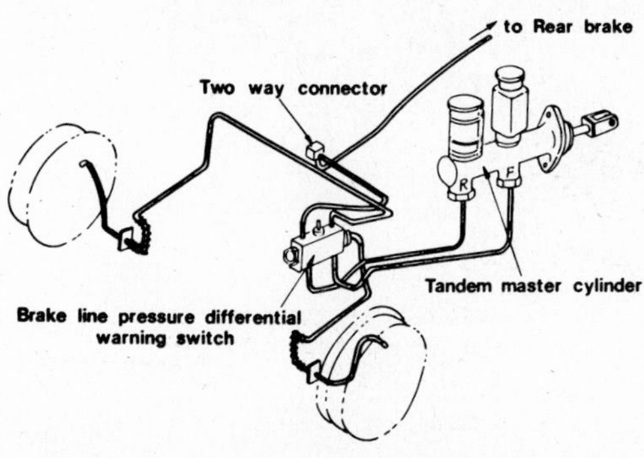

Dual circuit brake system

MASTER CYLINDER

R&R

Clean the outside of the cylinder thoroughly, particularly around the cap and fluid lines. Disconnect the fluid lines and cap them to exclude dirt. Remove the clevis pin connecting the pushrod to the brake pedal arm inside the vehicle. This pin need not be removed on HLS30 models with the vacuum booster. Unbolt the master cylinder from the firewall and remove. If the pushrod is not adjustable, there will be shims between the cylinder and the firewall. These shims, or the adjustable pushrod, are used to adjust brake pedal free play. After installation, bleed the system and check the pedal free play.

NOTE: Ordinary brake fluid will boil and cause brake failure under the high temperatures developed in disc brake systems. Special fluid for disc brake systems must be used.

Pedal Adjustment

Before adjusting the pedal, make sure that the wheelbrakes are correctly adjusted.

Model	*Pedal free play (in.)*	*Pedal pad free height (in.)*
L60	.25-.75	8.1-8.5
L320, L520	.39-.55	
PL410	.50-1.0	
PL411, RL411	.45	
SPL310	.50-1.0	
SPL311, SRL311	.31-.47	
PL510, WPL510		8.15 manual, 7.76 automatic
LB110, KLB110	.24-.59	5.49-5.65
HLS30		7.99

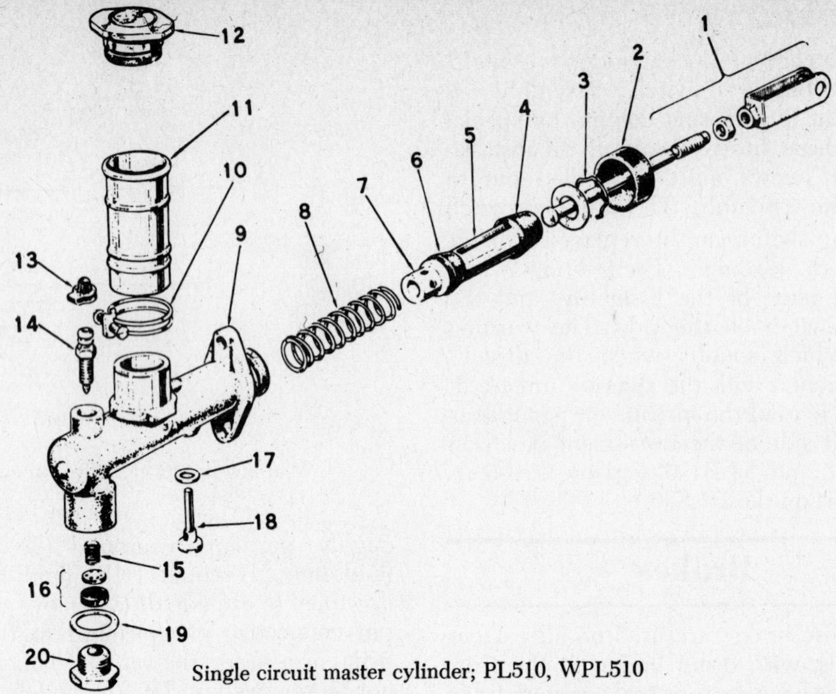

Single circuit master cylinder; PL510, WPL510

1. Pushrod
2. Dust cover
3. Stopper ring
4. Secondary piston cup
5. Master cylinder piston
6. Primary piston cup
7. Inlet valve
8. Piston return spring
9. Master cylinder body
10. Reservoir band
11. Reservoir (available in several sizes and shapes)
12. Reservoir cap
13. Bleeder screw
14. Piston
15. Check valve spring
16. Check valve
17. Packing
18. Piston stopper screw
19. Valve cap gasket
20. Valve cap

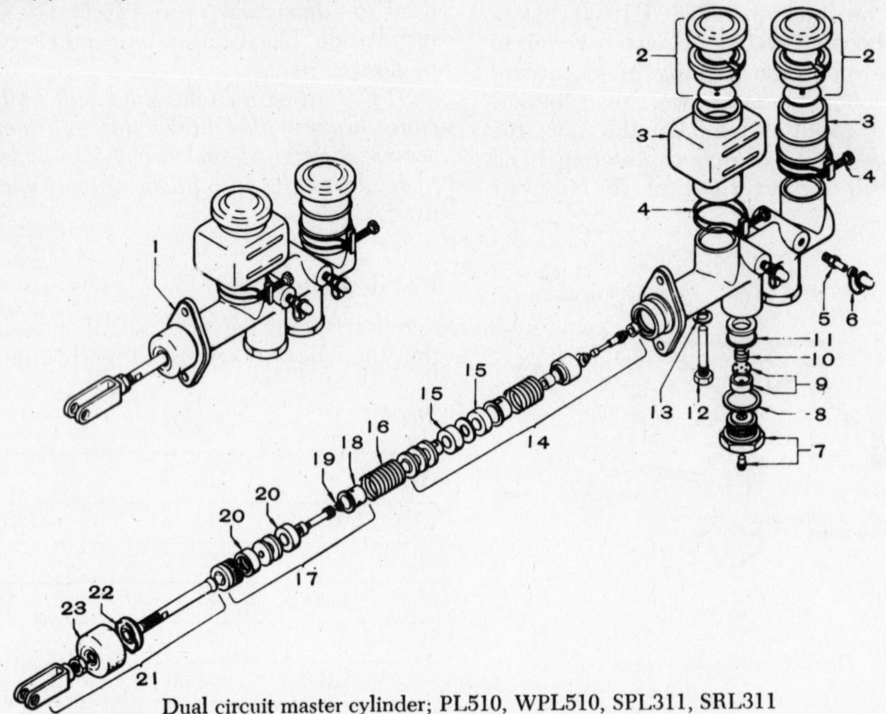

Dual circuit master cylinder; PL510, WPL510, SPL311, SRL311

1. Brake master cylinder
2. Fluid reservoir cap
3. Brake fluid reservoir
4. Reservoir band
5. Bleeder screw
6. Bleeder screw cap
7. Valve cap
8. Gasket
9. Valve
10. Valve spring
11. Valve seat
12. Stopper screw
13. Packing
14. Piston
15. Piston cup
16. Cylinder spring
17. Piston
18. Inlet valve
19. Inlet valve spring
20. Piston cup
21. Pushrod
22. Stopper ring
23. Dust cover

PL510, WPL510, LB110, KLB110, HLS30

1. Loosen the stop pad on the brake pedal so that it does not make contact.
2. Adjust the pushrod length to obtain the specified pedal pad height for the PL510 and WPL510, and a pedal height of 8.11″ for the HLS30. On the LB110 and KLB110, adjust the pedal pad height to 5.65″ by changing the number of shims between the master cylinder and the firewall.
3. Tighten the stop pad until the moveable part of the stoplight switch is completely pushed in on the PL510 and WPL510. On the LB110, KLB110, and HLS30, tighten the pedal stop until the specified pedal pad height is obtained. Make sure that the stoplight screw end surface is flush against the bracket.
4. Check that pedal free play is correct and that the stoplight switch functions properly.

All Other Models

Adjust pedal free play to specified figure by means of adjustable pushrod or shims between master cylinder and firewall.

Overhaul

The master cylinder can be disassembled using the illustrations as a guide. Clean all parts in clean brake fluid. Replace cylinder or piston as necessary if clearance between the two exceeds .006″. Lubricate all parts with clean brake fluid on assembly. Master cylinder rebuilding kits, containing all the wearing parts, are available to simplify overhaul.

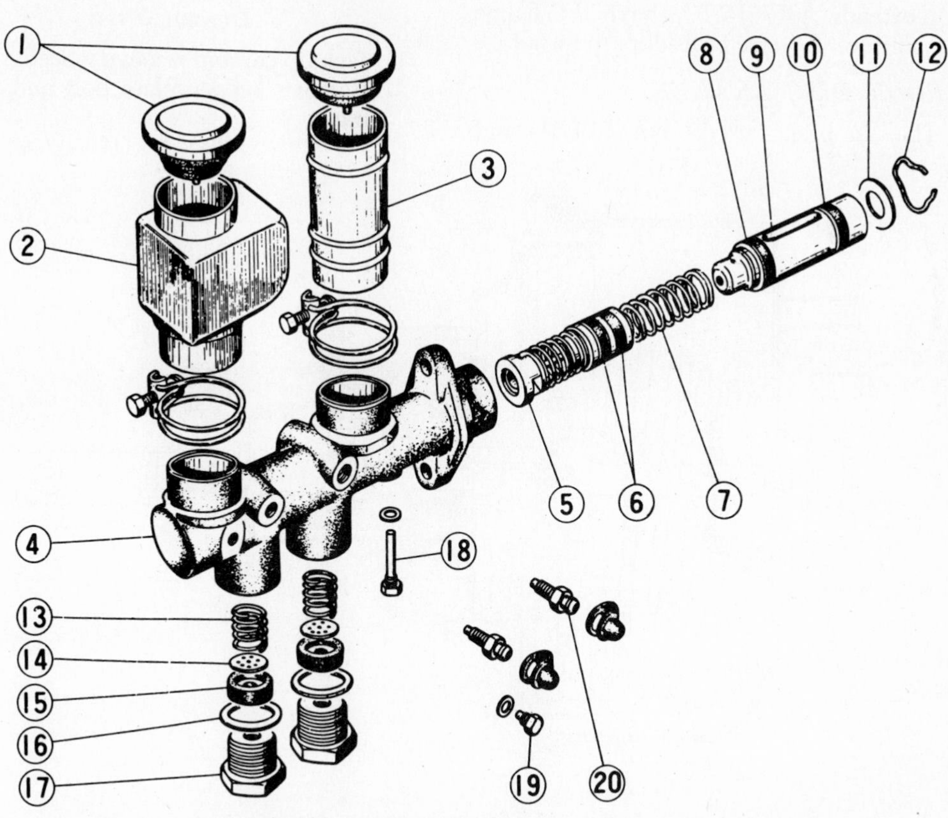

Dual circuit master cylinder, HLS30 with vacuum booster

1. Reservoir cap
2. Brake fluid reservoir
3. Brake fluid reservoir
4. Brake master cylinder
5. Piston assembly
6. Piston cup
7. Cylinder spring
8. Primary piston cup
9. Piston assembly
10. Secondary piston cup
11. Stopper
12. Snap ring
13. Valve spring
14. Check valve assembly
15. Check valve assembly
16. Packing
17. Valve cap screw
18. Stopper bolt
19. Stopper bolt
20. Bleeder

VACUUM BOOSTER

Test

The vacuum booster is located behind the master cylinder on the firewall. To test the unit:

1. T-connect a vacuum gauge into the vacuum line between the check valve and the booster.
2. Start the engine and run until 19.7″ Hg vacuum is read. Stop the engine.
3. Vacuum should not drop more than .98″ Hg per 15 seconds.
4. Check vacuum line and check valve for leakage before replacing booster unit.

R&R

1. Remove brake pedal clevis pin.
2. Remove master cylinder.
3. Unbolt and remove booster from firewall.
4. Adjust pushrod end height so that it extends .1377-.1575″ above the flange surface. Reverse procedure to install.

FRONT DISC BRAKES

The disc brakes used on the SPL311 and SRL311 are the Dunlop type, manufactured under license in Japan. Lockheed type disc brakes are used on the RL411, PL510, and WPL510. Girling type discs are used on the HLS30, KLB110, and LB110.

Minimum safe disc pad thickness (in.)	*Model*	*Type brakes*
.236	SPL311, SRL311	Dunlop (Sumitomo)
.039	RL411, PL510, WPL510	Lockheed (Akebono)
.063	LB110, KLB110	Girling (Tokiko)
.032	HLS30	Girling (Sumitomo)

Brake Pad Replacement

All four front brake pads must always be replaced as a set. Several grades of pads are available for most models for road use, or racing.

DUNLOP TYPE

1. Jack up car and remove wheel.
2. Remove keeper plate bolt and keeper plate.

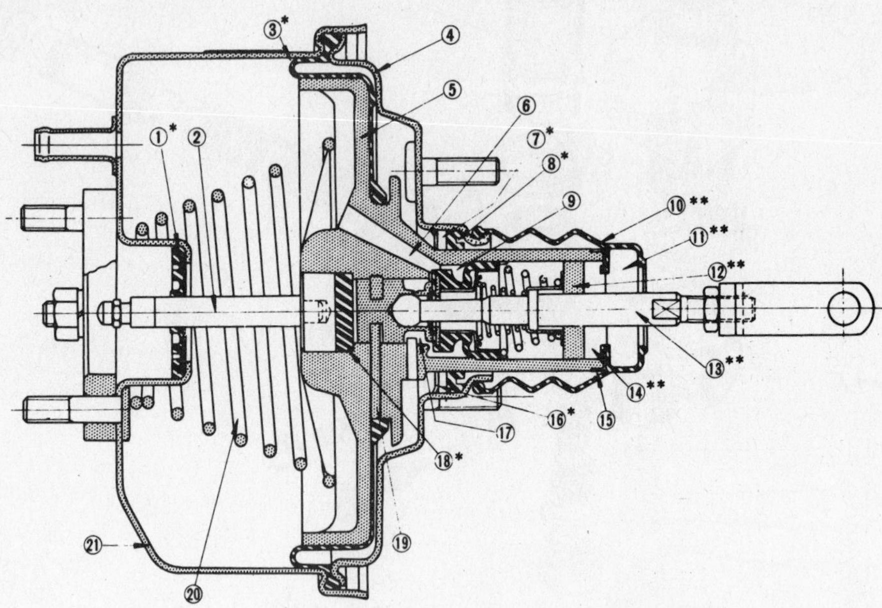

Details of HLS30 brake vacuum booster

1. Plate & seal assembly
2. Push rod
3. Diaphragm
4. Rear shell
5. Power piston (valve body and diaphragm plate)
6. Vacuum route
7. Bearing
8. Seal
9. Vacuum valve
10. Valve body guard
11. Air silencer filter
12. Air silencer filter
13. Valve operating rod assembly
14. Silencer
15. Air silencer retainer
16. Retainer
17. Air valve
18. Reaction disc
19. Stop key
20. Diaphragm return spring
21. Front shell

* Parts in repair Kit A for minor overhaul
** Parts in repair Kit B for major overhaul

3. Pull pads out. A removal tool can easily be made.
4. Thoroughly clean the exposed end of each piston and the caliper assembly. Check rotor (disc) for scoring. If it is badly scored, it must be removed for resurfacing or replacement.
5. Before installing the new pads, the pistons must be pushed back into their cylinders. Be careful not to scratch the pistons or bores.

NOTE: The master cylinder may overflow when the pistons are pushed back. The bleeder screw can be loosened to prevent overflow.

6. Install the new pads. Tighten the bleeder screw if it was loosened.
7. Replace the wheels and pump the brake pedal a few times to seat the pads. This must be done before the car is driven.

Lockheed Type

1. Jack up car and remove wheel.
2. Loosen anti-rattle clip.
3. Loosen bleed screw. Pull caliper plate toward outer end of spindle and push the piston in .118-.157". Be careful not to scratch the pistons or bores.
4. The outer pad can now be pulled out.
5. Pull the caliper plate inward and remove the inner pad.
6. Thoroughly clean the exposed end of each piston and the caliper assembly. Check rotor (disc) for scoring. If it is badly scored, it must be removed for resurfacing or replacement.
7. If the piston has been pushed in far enough, the new pads can be installed.
8. Install the new pads. Tighten the bleeder screw.

Girling Type

1. Jack up car and remove wheel.
2. Remove clip(s), retaining pins, and anti-squeal clips. Remove coil spring on LB110 and KLB110.
3. Using pliers, pull out pads and anti-squeal shims.
4. Thoroughly clean the exposed end of each piston and the caliper assembly. Check rotor (disc) for scoring. If it is badly scored, it must be removed for resurfacing or replacement.
5. Before installing the new pads, the pistons must be pushed back into their cylinders. Be careful not to scratch the pistons or bores.

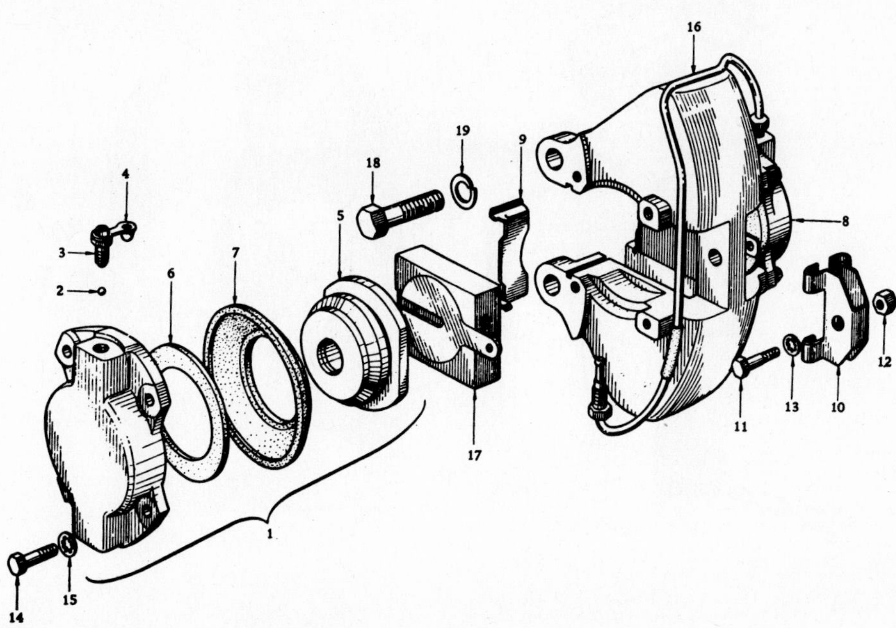

Dunlop type front disc brake; SPL311, SRL311

1. Inner cylinder assembly
2. 13/16" Ball
3. Bleeder screw
4. Bleeder cap
5. Piston
6. Piston packing
7. Dust cover
8. Outer cylinder assembly
9. Support plate
10. Keeper plate
11. Bolt
12. Nut
13. Washer
14. Bolt
15. Washer
16. Bridge tube
17. Pad
18. Bolt
19. Lockwasher

NOTE: The master cylinder may overflow when the pistons are pushed back. The bleeder screw can be loosened to prevent overflow.

Be careful not to push the pistons in too far or the seals will be damaged. The pistons need not be pushed in past a position flush with the edge of the cylinder. Install the new pads and tighten the bleeder screw if it was loosened.

6. Install the anti-squeal shims with the arrow marks pointing in the direction of rotor rotation. On LB110, the coil spring should be installed on the retaining pin furthest from the bleed screw.
7. Replace the wheels and pump the brake pedal a few times to seat the pads. This must be done before the car is driven.

Disc Brake Unit Overhaul

Lockheed Type

1. Jack up and support car. Remove wheel.
2. Disconnect and cap brake hose.
3. Unbolt and remove caliper assembly.
4. Remove spindle nut and rotor with hub.
5. Unbolt and remove rotor from hub.
6. Remove pads. Remove tension springs and pull out cylinder. Apply air or hydraulic pressure to inlet hole to remove piston from cylinder. Remove retainer and seals. The piston seal also serves to retract the piston and should be replaced at every overhaul.
7. If the rotor is scored, it can be machined. Minimum safe rotor thickness is .331″. Rotor runout must not exceed .0024″.

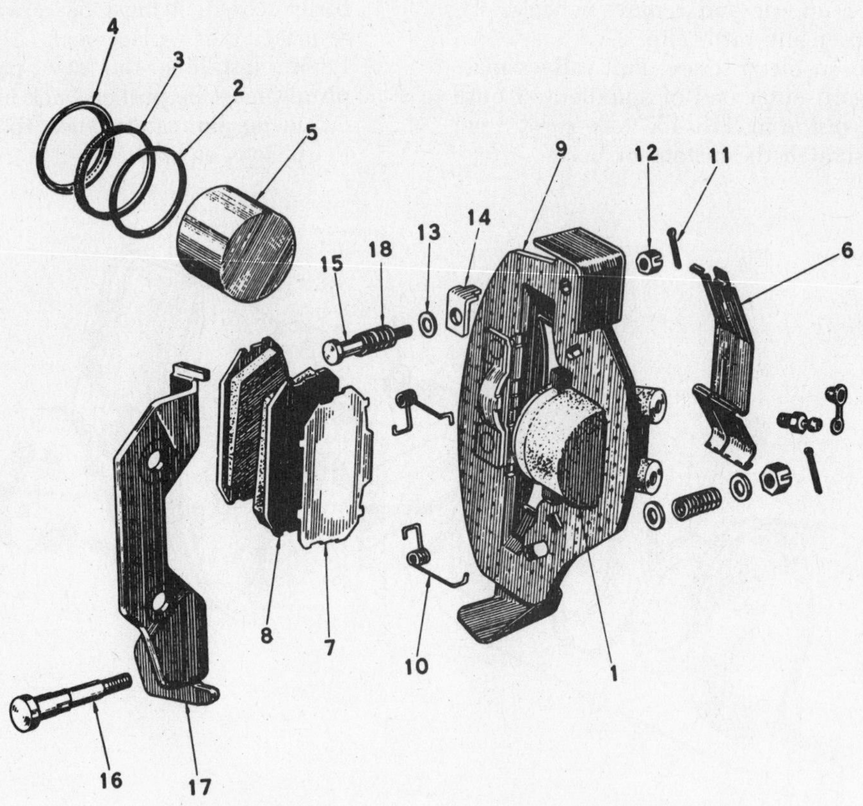

Lockheed type front disc brake; PL510, WPL510

1. Cylinder
2. Piston seal
3. Wiper seal
4. Retainer
5. Piston
6. Clip
7. Shim
8. Pad
9. Caliper plate
10. Tension spring
11. Cotter pin
12. Nut
13. Washer
14. Support bracket
15. Hold down pin
16. Pivot pin
17. Mounting bracket
18. Spring

8. Wash all parts in clean brake fluid. Replace all seals. If cylinder or piston is damaged, replace both.
9. Bolt rotor to hub, torquing bolts to 28-38 ft. lbs. Pack bearings, install hub on spindle, and adjust wheel bearing.
10. Insert new seal in cylinder groove and attach wiper seal. Lubricate cylinder bore with brake fluid. Insert piston cautiously until piston head is almost flush with wiper seal retainer. Relieved part of piston must face pivot pin.
11. Install cylinder into caliper plate and secure with tension springs.
12. Install hold down pin, washer, and nut on support bracket. Install a new cotter pin in the nut.
13. Assemble mounting bracket and caliper plate with pivot pin. Install washer, spring, washer, and nut. Tighten nut completely and lock with a cotter pin.
14. Install caliper assembly to spindle, torquing mounting bolts to 53-65 ft. lbs. Make sure that caliper plate can slide smoothly.
15. Install pads and shims, making sure that they are seated correctly. Seat inner pad first. Make sure anti-rattle clip is positioned correctly.
16. Reconnect brake hose and bleed system.

Girling Type—LB110, KLB110

1. Remove brake pads.
2. Disconnect brake tube.
3. Remove the two bottom strut assembly installation bolts to obtain clearance.
4. Remove caliper assembly mounting bolts.
5. Loosen bleeder screw and press pistons into cylinder.
6. Clamp yoke in a vise and tap yoke head with a hammer to loosen cylinder. Be careful that piston A does not fall out.
7. Remove bias ring from piston A. Remove retaining rings and boots from both pistons. Depress and remove pistons from cylinder. Remove piston seal from the cylinder carefully with the fingers so as not to mar the cylinder wall.
8. Remove yoke springs from yoke.
9. Wash all parts with clean brake fluid.
10. If piston or cylinder is badly worn or

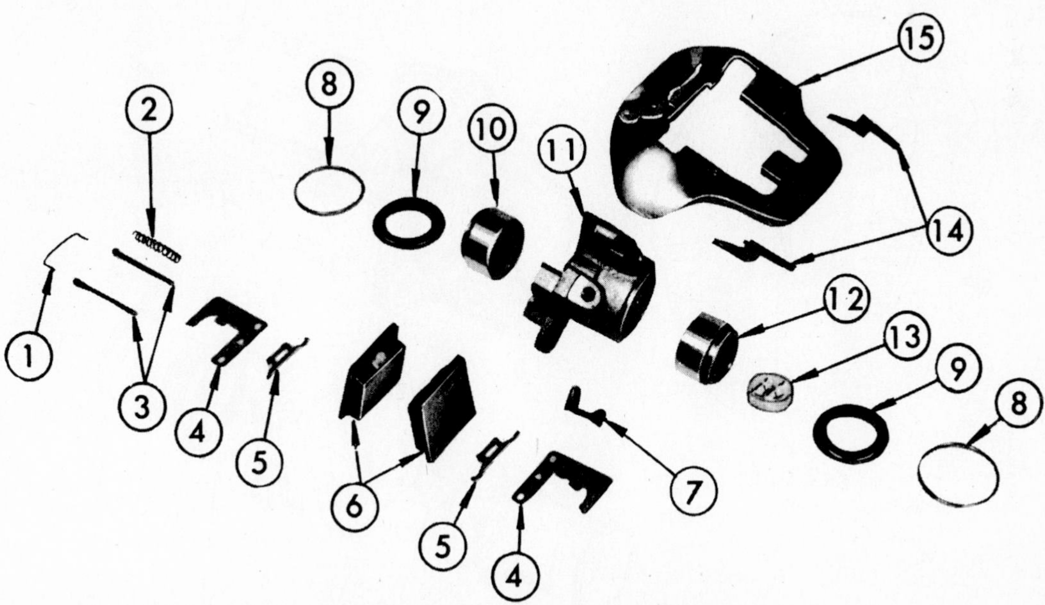

Girling type front disc brake, LB110 and KLB110

1. Clip
2. Spring
3. Pin
4. Shim
5. Hanger spring
6. Brake pad
7. Air bleeder
8. Retaining ring
9. Boot
10. Piston B
11. Cylinder
12. Piston A
13. Bias ring
14. Yoke spring
15. Yoke

scored, replace both. The piston surface is plated and must not be polished with emery paper. Replace all seals. The rotor can be removed and machined if scored, but final thickness must be at least .331". Runout must not exceed .0012".

11. Lubricate cylinder bore with clean brake fluid and install piston seal.
12. Insert bias ring into piston A so that rounded ring portion comes to bottom of piston. Piston A has a small depression inside, while B does not.
13. Lubricate pistons with clean brake fluid and insert into cylinder. Install boot and retaining ring. Yoke groove of bias ring of piston A must align with yoke groove of cylinder.
14. Install yoke springs to yoke so projecting portion faces to disc (rotor).
15. Lubricate sliding portion of cylinder and yoke. Assemble cylinder and yoke by tapping yoke lightly.
16. Replace caliper assembly and pads. Torque mounting bolts to 33-41 ft. lbs. Rotor bolt torque is 20-27 ft. lbs. Strut bolt torque is 33-44 ft. lbs. Bleed the system of air.

Girling Type—HLS30

The caliper halves are not to be separated. If brake fluid leaks from the bridge seal, replace the caliper assembly.

1. Remove pads.
2. Disconnect brake line and caliper mounting bolts.
3. Hold piston in one side and force the other one out with air pressure. Remove the other piston.
4. Remove piston seal from cylinder carefully with the fingers so as not to mar the cylinder wall.
5. Wash all parts with clean brake fluid.
6. If piston or cylinder is badly worn or scored, replace both. The piston surface is plated and must not be polished with emery paper. Replace all seals.
7. With wheel bearing properly adjusted, runout at center of rotor surface should be less then .0059". The rotor can be resurfaced if scored, but must be at least .413" thick after resurfacing.

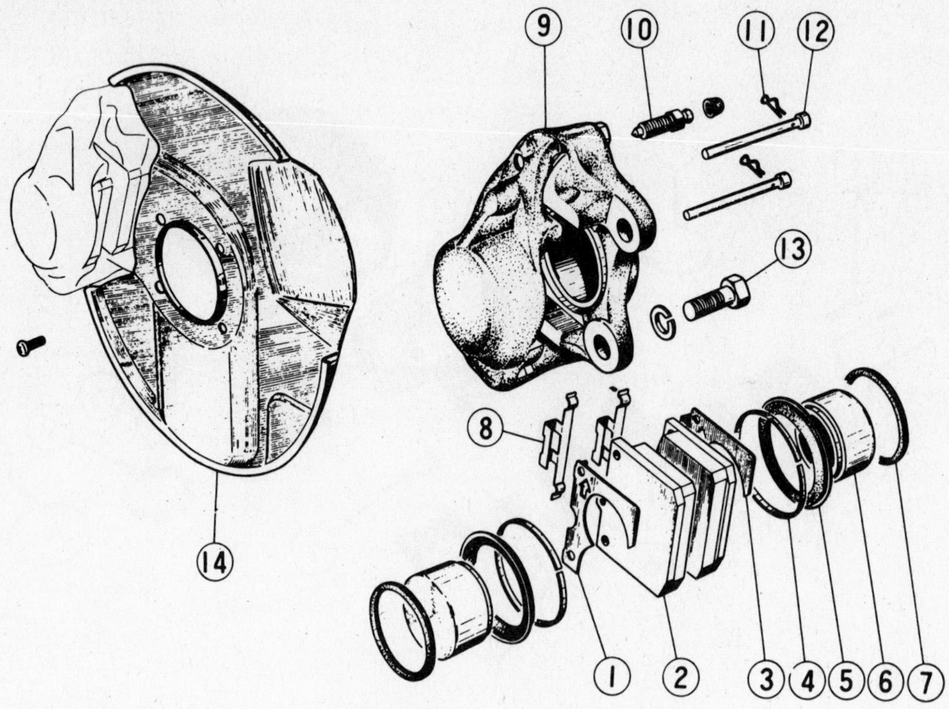

Girling type front disc brake, HLS30

1. Anti-squeal shim, right
2. Pad
3. Anti-squeal shim, left
4. Retaining ring
5. Dust cover
6. Piston
7. Piston seal
8. Anti-squeal spring
9. Caliper assembly
10. Bleeder
11. Clip
12. Retaining pin
13. Caliper fixing bolt
14. Baffle plate

8. Lubricate the piston seal with clean brake fluid and install it.
9. Install dust seals on pistons, lubricate pistons with clean brake fluid, and install pistons into cylinders. Clamp dust seals with retaining rings.
10. Reinstall caliper assembly. Mounting bolt torque is 53-71 ft. lbs. Rotor mounting bolt torque is 28-38 ft. lbs.
11. Replace pads and brake line. Bleed system of air.

Adjustment

Disc brakes are self-adjusting for pad wear and require no periodic adjustment. However, the fluid level in the master cylinder will gradually drop as the pads wear. When filling the master cylinder, use only brake fluid specifically designated for disc brakes. Ordinary brake fluid will boil and cause complete loss of braking power at the high operating temperatures attained in disc brakes.

Proportioning Valve

HLS30

A proportioning valve is installed in the line to the rear brakes on this model to prevent the rear brakes from locking before the front. The valve is operating properly if the front and rear wheels lock simultaneously, or the front wheels lock first. The correct valve is stamped with the part number E4100. Do not use a valve designed for any other vehicle, as the ratio between front and rear pressures will be incorrect. The valve body is marked M on the master cylinder side, and R on the rear brake side. The valve requires no service or adjustment and must be replaced if defective.

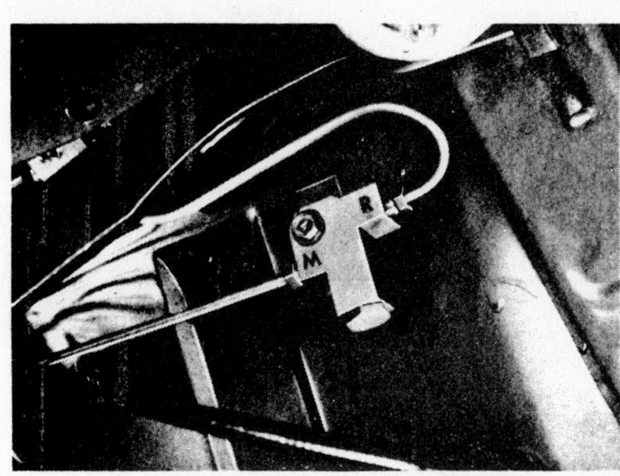

Proportioning valve, HLS30

BRAKE LINE PRESSURE DIFFERENTIAL WARNING LIGHT SWITCH

A pressure sensitive switch in the engine compartment activates a warning light on the instrument panel when a pressure differential of 185-242 psi exists between the front and rear brake systems on models with dual circuit braking systems. Such a large pressure differential indicates a serious problem, such as a fluid leak, in the system affected. The valve requires no service or adjustment and must be replaced if defective.

Brake line pressure differential warning light switch

1. To left front brake
2. From master cylinder (Front)
3. From master cylinder (Rear)
4. To rear brakes
5. To right front brake

DRUM BRAKES

Front drum brakes on all models except the L320 and L520 pickups have two shoes and two hydraulic cylinders at each wheel. These pickups have two shoes and a single hydraulic cylinder at each wheel. The cylinders are bolted to the front brake backing plate. All models have rear drum brakes. Each rear brake assembly has two brake shoes and a single hydraulic cylinder which is free to slide back and forth in a slot in the brake backing plate. On some models the hydraulic cylinder is bolted fast and the adjuster slides.

Lining Replacement

L60 Front

1. Jack up vehicle. Remove front wheels and brake drums. Loosen brake adjust-

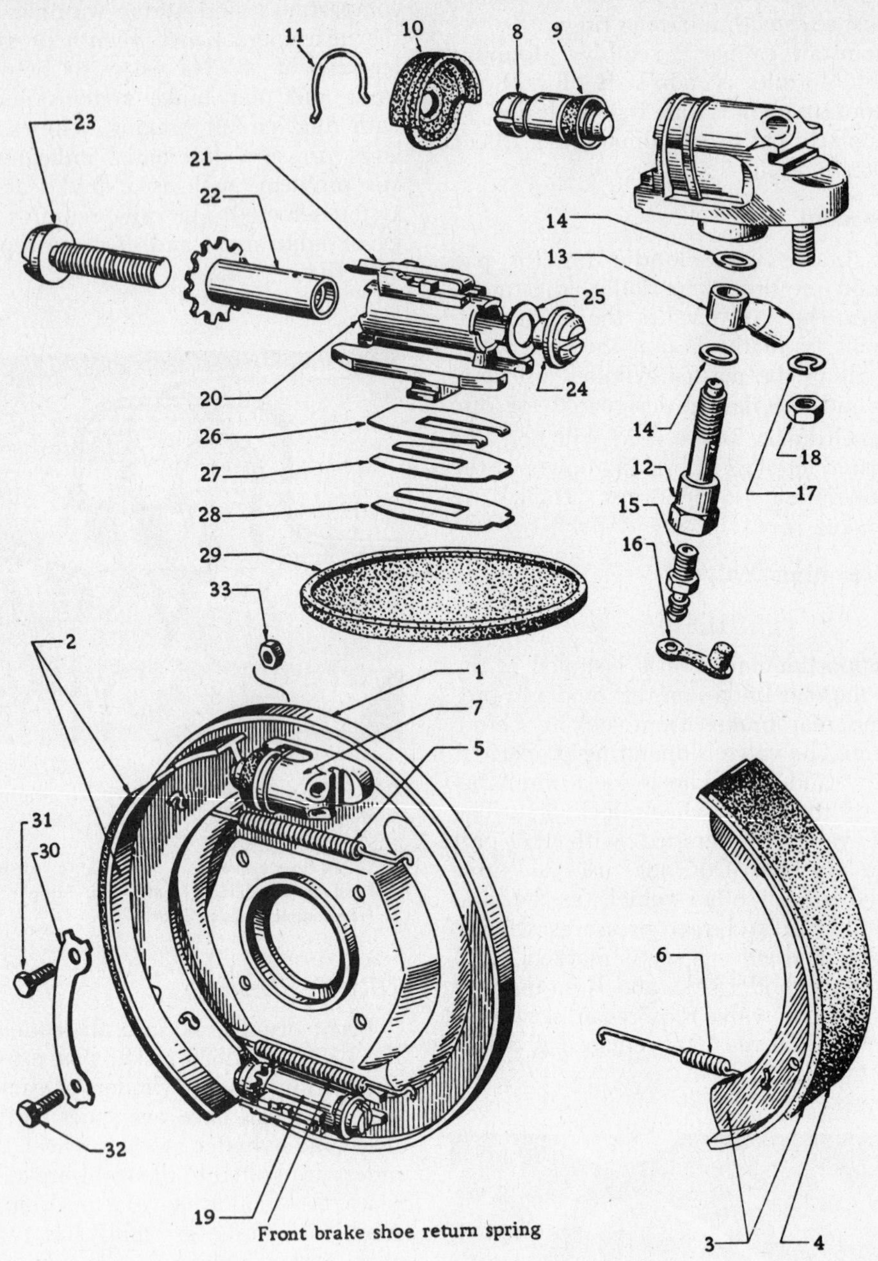

L520 front brake

1. Backing plate
2. Forward shoe
3. Rear shoe
4. Lining
5. Rear shoe return spring
6. Rear shoe return spring
7. Wheel cylinder
8. Piston
9. Piston cup
10. Dust shield
11. Dust shield retainer
12. Connector bolt
13. Connector
14. Washer
15. Bleeder screw
16. Bleeder cap
17. Lockwasher
18. Nut
19. Adjuster
20. Adjuster housing
21. Lock spring
22. Adjuster wheel
23. Adjuster screw
24. Adjuster head
25. Adjuster head shim
26. Adjuster retaining spring
27. Retaining spring lock plate
28. Retaining spring adjusting shim
29. Rubber boot
30. Lock plate
31. Bolt
32. Bolt
33. Nut

ers if drums are difficult to remove.
2. Lift one shoe first from the wheel cylinder slot at one end, and then from the piston slot at the other. Remove the shoe return springs.
3. Remove the second shoe. Place a heavy rubber band around each cylinder to prevent the piston from coming out.
4. Turn adjusters to fully off position.
5. Clean backing plate and inspect cylinder for leaks. The wheel cylinders are attached to the backing plate by three bolts each.
6. Replace upper shoe first. The short end of the return spring should be attached to the shoe and the long end to the bolt on the backing plate. Replace lower shoe. A very thin film of grease may be applied to the pivot points at the ends of the shoes. Be careful not to get grease on the linings or drums.
7. Replace drums and wheels. Adjust brakes. Bleed the hydraulic system of air if the brake lines were disconnected.

L60 Rear

1. Jack up vehicle, remove wheels and brake drums. Back off adjusters if drums are hard to remove.
2. Remove shoes, one at a time. Place a heavy rubber band around the cylinder to prevent the piston from coming out.
3. Turn adjuster to fully off position.
4. Clean backing plate and inspect for leaks. The wheel cylinder is attached to the backing plate by a spring clip and should be free to slide. A very thin film of grease may be applied behind the wheel cylinder. To remove the adjuster, take off the clip and rubber dust cover and remove the two mounting nuts.
5. Hook the return springs into the new shoes. The springs should be between the shoes and the backing plate. A very thin film of grease may be applied to the pivot points at the ends of the brake shoes. Be careful not to get grease on the linings or drums.
6. Place one shoe in the adjuster and piston slots, and pry the other shoe into position.
7. Replace drums and wheels. Adjust brakes. Bleed the hydraulic system of air if the brake lines were disconnected.

PL510, WPL510 Rear

1. Raise vehicle, remove wheels.
2. Release parking brake. Disconnect cross rod from lever of brake cylinder. Remove brake drum. Place a heavy rubber band around the cylinder to prevent the piston from coming out.
3. Remove return springs and shoes.
4. Clean backing plate and check wheel cylinder for leaks. To remove the wheel cylinder, remove brake line, dust cover, plates, and adjusting shims. Clearance between cylinder and piston should not exceed .0059″.
5. The drums must be machined if scored or out of round more than .002″. The drum inside diameter should not be machined beyond 9.04″. Minimum safe lining thickness is .0591″.
6. Hook the return springs into the new shoes. The springs should be between the shoes and the backing plate. The longer return spring must be adjacent to the wheel cylinder. A very thin film of grease may be applied to the pivot points at the ends of the brake shoes. Grease the shoe locating buttons on the backing plate, also. Be careful not to get grease on the linings or drums.
7. Place one shoe in the adjuster and piston slots, and pry the other shoe into position.
8. Replace drums and wheels. Adjust brakes. Bleed the hydraulic system of air if the brake lines were disconnected.
9. Reconnect the handbrake, making sure that it does not cause the shoes to drag when it is released.

LB110, KLB110 Rear

1. Raise vehicle and remove wheels.
2. Loosen handbrake cable, remove clevis pin from wheel cylinder lever, disconnect handbrake cable, and remove return pull spring.
3. Remove brake drum, shoe retainers, return springs, and brake shoes. Loosen brake adjusters if drums are difficult to remove. Place a heavy rubber band around the cylinder to prevent the piston from coming out.
4. Clean backing plate and check wheel cylinder for leaks. To remove the wheel cylinder, remove brake line, dust cover, plates, and adjusting shims. Clearance between cylinder and piston should not exceed .0059″.

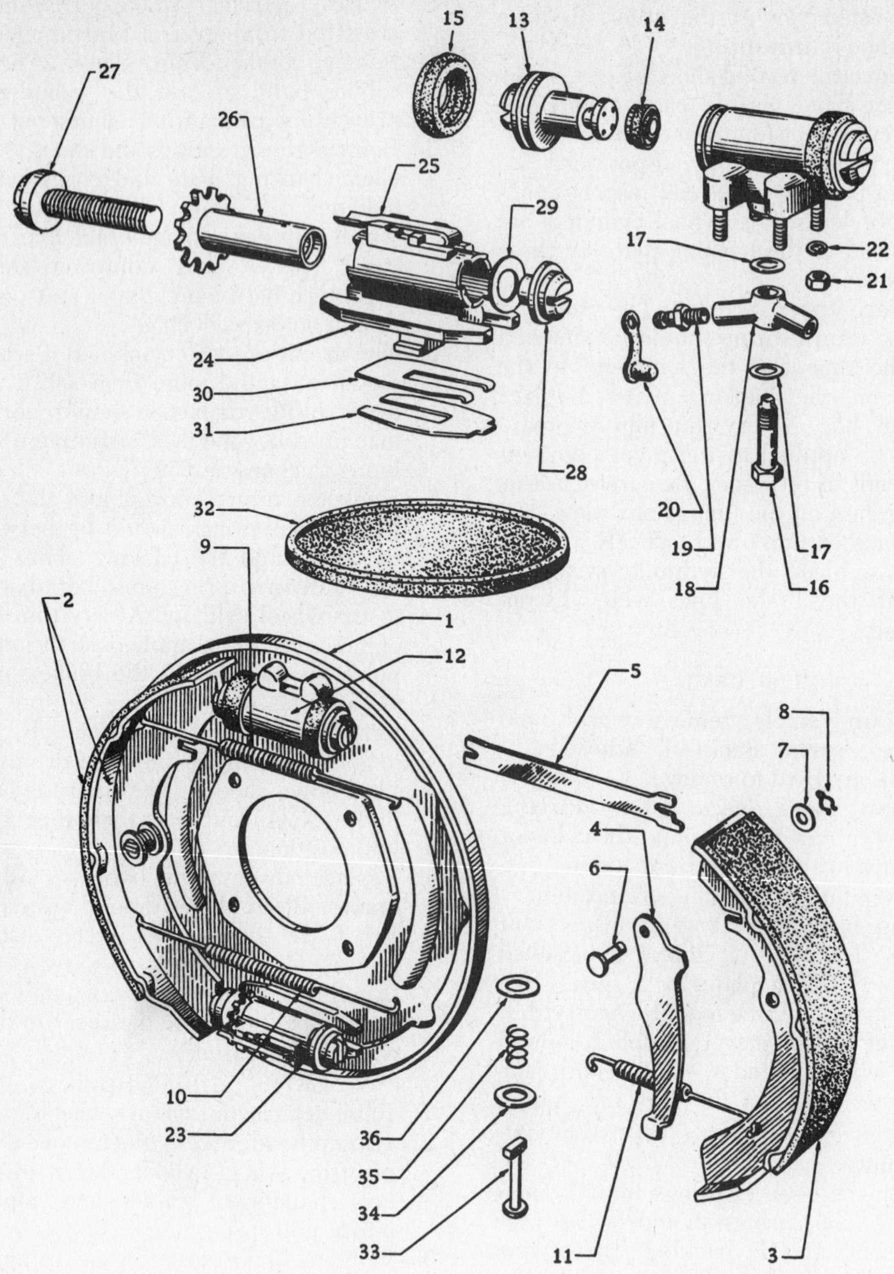

L520 rear brake

1. Backing plate
2. Shoe
3. Lining
4. Handbrake extension link
5. Toggle lever
6. Pin
7. Washer
8. Spring clip
9. Upper return spring
10. Lower return spring
11. Rear shoe return spring
12. Wheel cylinder
13. Piston
14. Piston cup
15. Dust shield
16. Connector bolt
17. Washer
18. Brake line connector
19. Bleeder screw
20. Bleeder cap
21. Nut
22. Lockwasher
23. Adjuster
24. Adjuster housing
25. Lock spring
26. Adjusting wheel
27. Adjuster screw
28. Adjuster head
29. Adjuster head shim
30. Adjuster retaining spring
31. Retaining lock plate
32. Rubber boot
33. Anti-rattle pin
34. Spring seat
35. Anti-rattle spring
36. Retainer

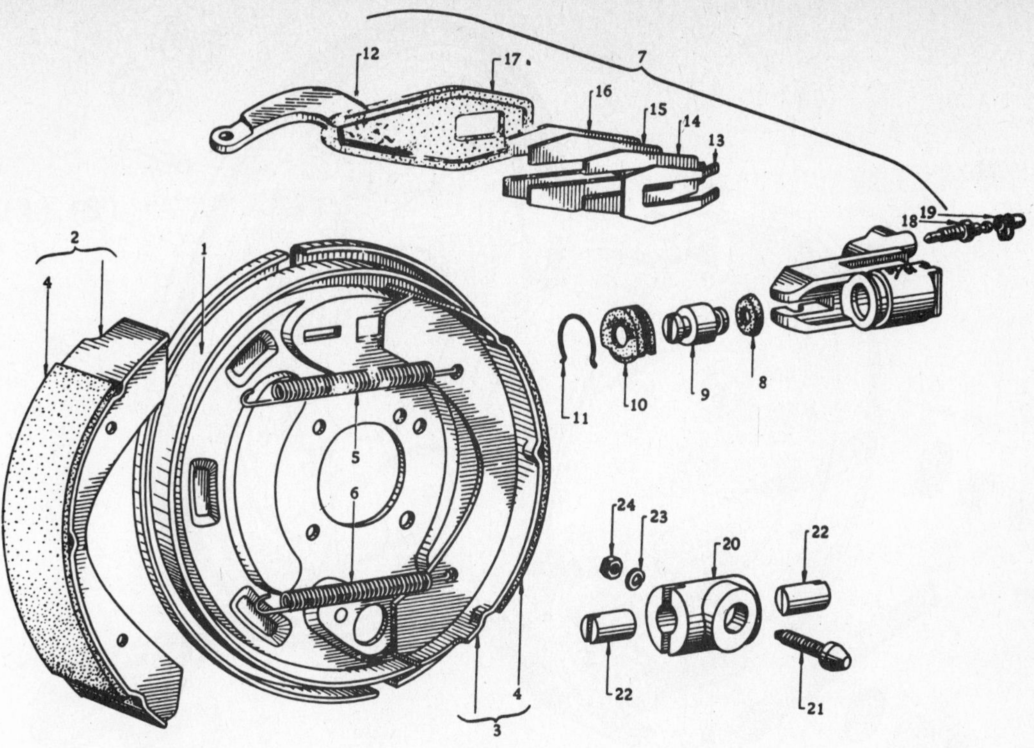

SPL311, SRL311 rear brake

1. Backing plate
2. Forward shoe
3. Rear shoe
4. Brake lining
5. Cylinder side shoe return spring
6. Adjuster side shoe return spring
7. Wheel cylinder assembly
8. Piston cup
9. Cylinder
10. Dust cover
11. Snap-ring
12. Lever
13. Adjusting shim
14. Adjusting shim
15. Plate
16. Plate
17. Dust cover
18. Bleeder screw
19. Bleeder cap
20. Adjuster housing
21. Adjuster wedge
22. Adjuster tappet
23. Lockwasher
24. Nut

5. The drums must be machined if scored or out of round more than .0008″. The drum inside diameter must not be machined beyond 8.04″. Minimum safe lining thickness is .0591″.
6. Follow Steps 6-9 for PL510, WPL510 Rear.

HLS30 Rear

1. Raise and support vehicle. Remove wheel.
2. Remove brake drum. If it is difficult to remove, remove the wheel cylinder lever handbrake clevis pin. Remove the brake drum adjusting hole plug and pry the adjusting lever away from the adjusting wheel with a screwdriver inserted through the adjusting hole. Turn the adjusting wheel down with the screwdriver to loosen the brake shoes. Remove the brake drum.
3. Remove the brake shoe retainers and springs. Remove the shoes and return springs. Place a heavy rubber band around the cylinder to prevent the piston from coming out.
4. Clean backing plate and check for wheel cylinder leaks. To remove the wheel cylinder, detach the brake tube and dust cover, drive the lock plate out toward the front, pull the adjusting plate to the rear, and remove the cylinder. Clearance between cylinder and piston should not exceed .006″.
5. The drums should be machined if scored or out of round more than .002″. The drum inside diameter should not be machined beyond 9.04″. Minimum safe lining thickness is .0591″.
6. On reassembly, apply a very light film of grease to all sliding surfaces. Be careful not to get any on the linings or drums. The wheel cylinder must be free to slide. The longer black return spring must be adjacent to the wheel cylinder.

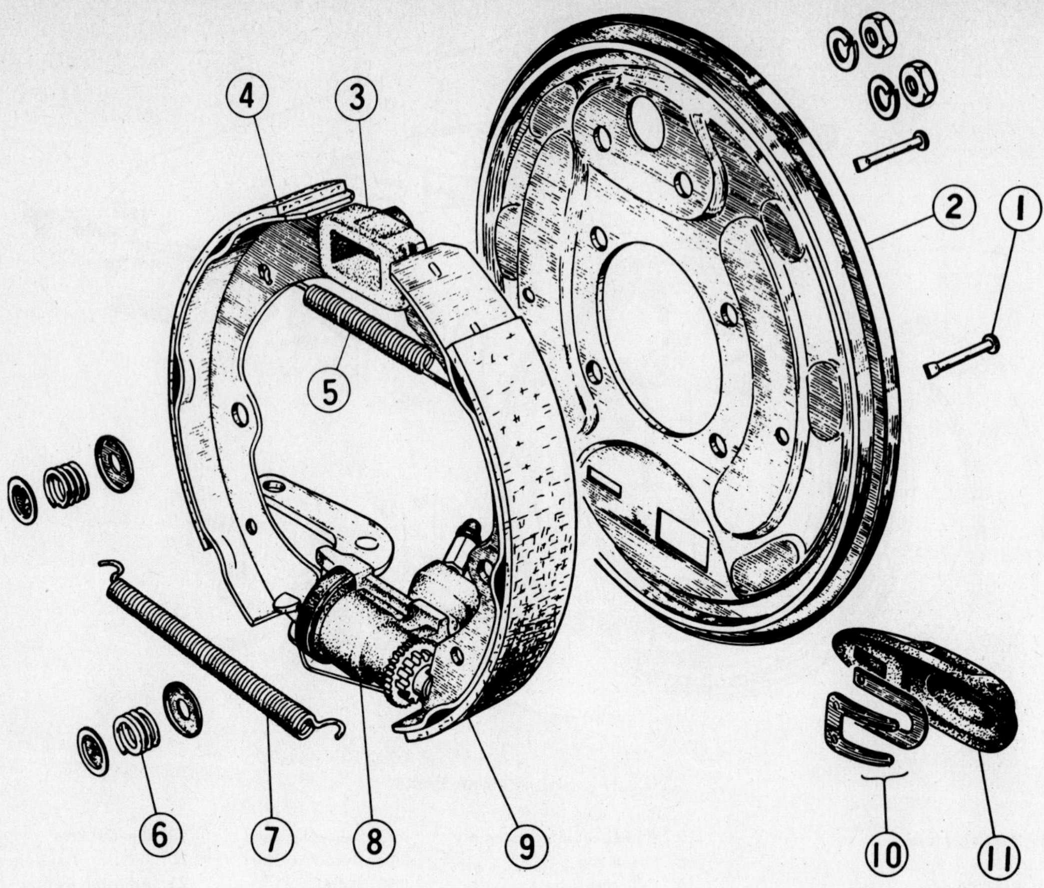

HLS30 rear brake

1. Anti-rattle pin
2. Brake backing plate
3. Anchor block
4. After shoe assembly
5. Return spring
6. Anti-rattle spring
7. Return spring
8. Wheel cylinder
9. Fore shoe assembly
10. Retaining shim
11. Dust cover

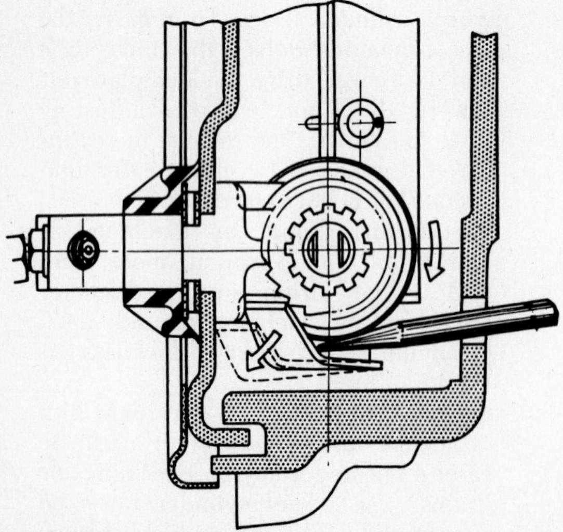

Loosening HLS30 rear brake adjuster

All Other Models

Lining replacement procedures for models not specifically covered above are generally quite similar to the above procedures. Brake drums should not be machined more than .04″ beyond their original inside diameter, and should be machined if scored or out of round more than .002″. Minimum safe lining thickness is .0591″.

Adjustment

There are four basic types of brake adjusting system used.

Adjuster type	*Wheel*	*Model*
Bolt	Front	L60, PL410, PL411, SPL310
	Rear	LB110, KLB110

Bolt with click arrangement	Rear	L60, PL410, PL411, RL411, SPL310, SPL311, SRL311, PL510, WPL510
Star wheel	Front, Rear	L320, L520, L521, PL521
Self adjusting	Rear	HLS30

To adjust brakes, raise wheels, disconnect handbrake linkage from rear wheels, apply brakes hard a few times to center drums, and proceed as follows:

BOLT ADJUSTER

On the front, turn one adjuster bolt on the backing plate until the wheel can no longer be turned, then back off until wheel is free of drag. Repeat the procedure on the other adjuster bolt on the same wheel. On the rear, the adjustment is the same, but one adjuster bolt serves both shoes. The LB110 and KLB110 have two adjusters on each rear wheel.

BOLT ADJUSTER WITH CLICK ARRANGEMENT

This type is used only on rear brakes. The adjuster is located on the backing plate. The adjustment proceeds in clicks or notches. The wheel will often be locked temporarily as the adjuster passes over center for each click. Thus the adjuster is alternately hard and easy to turn. When the wheel is fully locked, back off 1-3 clicks.

STAR WHEEL ADJUSTER

Remove the rubber boot from the backing plate. Insert a screwdriver through the adjusting hole to engage the toothed wheel. Turn the adjuster teeth down until the wheel is locked, then push them up about 12 notches so that the wheel is free of drag.

SELF ADJUSTING

No manual adjustment is required. The self adjusters operate whenever the hand or foot brakes are used.

After Adjustment

After adjusting brakes, reconnect handbrake linkage. Make sure that there is no rear wheel drag with the handbrake released. Loosen the handbrake adjustment if necessary.

HANDBRAKE

Handbrake adjustments are generally not needed, unless the cables have stretched.

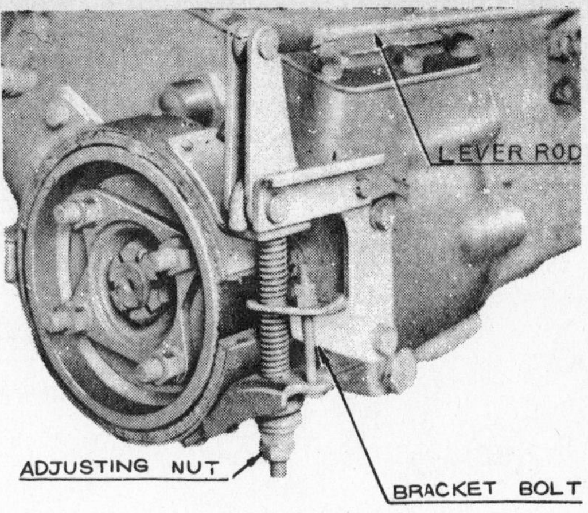

L60 handbrake

Before adjusting the handbrake, except on the L60, adjust the rear brakes. There should be no rear wheel drag when the handbrake is released.

L60

The L60 handbrake is an external contracting band type operating on a drum at the rear of the transfer case. There should be .027-.032″ clearance between the lining and the drum at all points. The upper band is adjusted by an adjusting nut on a large bolt. The lower band is adjusted by a smaller bracket bolt. The length of the rod to the lever can also be adjusted.

All Models except L60 and HLS30

There is an adjusting nut on the cable under the car, usually at the end of the front cable and near the point at which the two cables from the rear wheels come together (the equalizer). The LB110 and KLB110 have a turnbuckle in the cable. LB110 and KLB110 handbrake lever stroke should be 3.09″ or 6 notches. PL510 handle travel should be 3.35-3.74″. WPL510 handle travel should be 4.33-4.72″.

HLS30

The driveshaft must be removed to gain access to the adjusting nut on the front linkage rod.

SYSTEM BLEEDING

Bleeding is required whenever air in the hydraulic fluid causes a spongy feeling pedal and sluggish response. This is almost always the case after some part of the hydraulic system has been repaired or replaced.

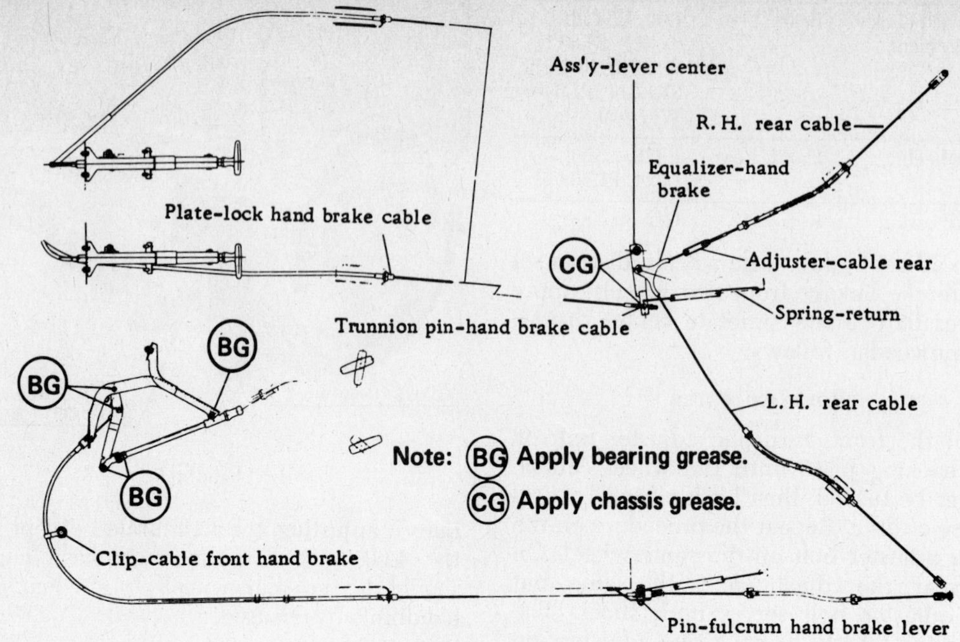

PL510 handbrake linkage

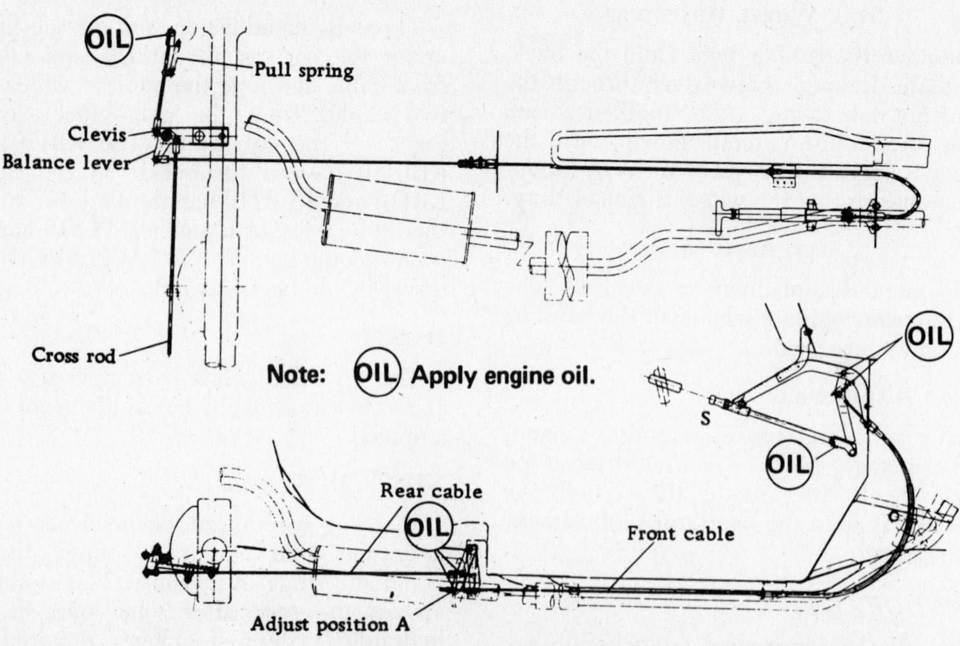

WPL510 handbrake linkage

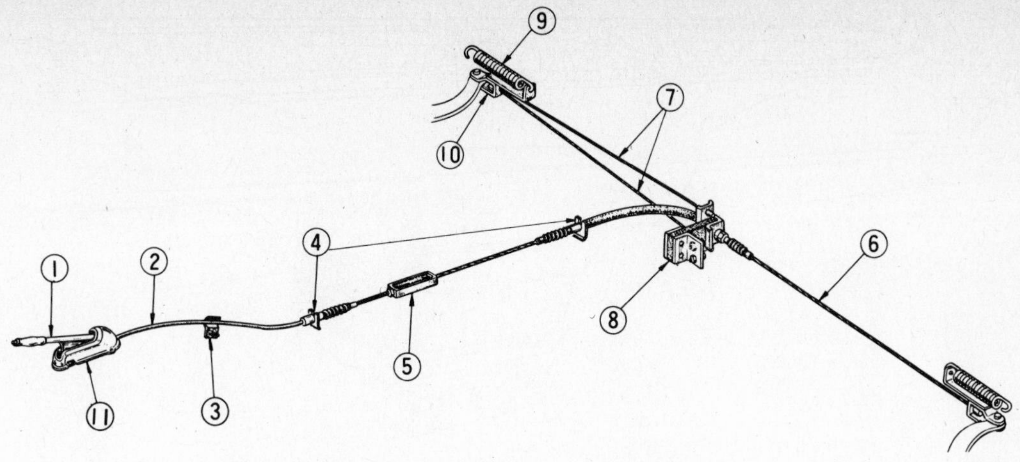

LB110 and KLB110 handbrake linkage

1. Hand brake lever
2. Cable
3. Clip
4. Lock plate
5. Turn-buckle (Hand brake adjuster)
6. Cable
7. Cable
8. Hanger strap
9. Return spring
10. Cable shank
11. Hand brake lever cover

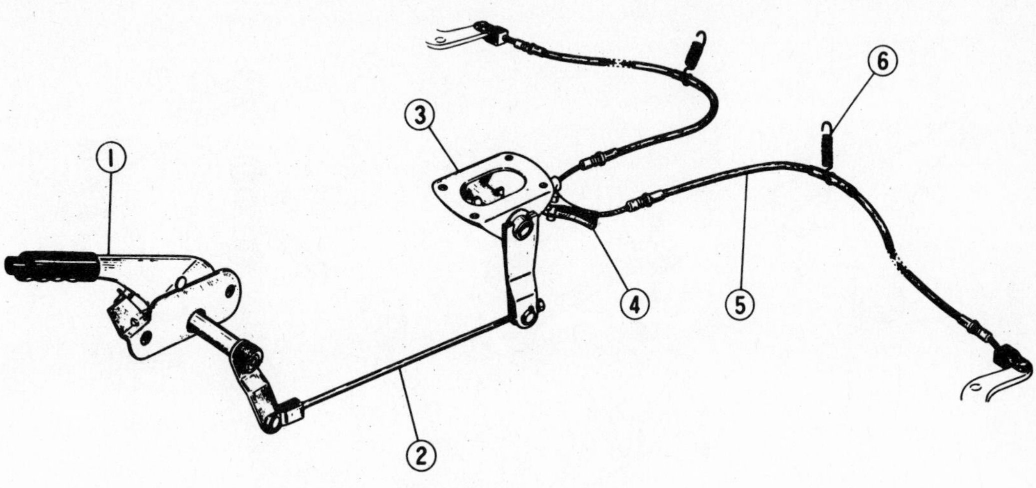

HLS30 handbrake linkage

1. Control lever
2. Front rod
3. Center lever
4. Equalizer
5. Rear cable
6. Hanger spring

1. Fill the master cylinder reservoir with the proper fluid. Special fluid is required for disc brakes.
2. The usual procedure is to bleed at the points furthest from the master cylinder first.
3. Fit a rubber hose over the bleeder screw. Submerge the other end of the hose in clean brake fluid in a clear glass container. Loosen the bleeder screw.
4. Slowly pump the brake pedal several times until fluid free of bubbles is discharged. An assistant is required to pump the pedal.
5. On the last pumping stroke, hold the pedal down and tighten the bleeder screw.
6. Bleed the front brakes in the same way as the rear brakes. Note that some front drum brakes have two hydraulic cylinders and two bleeder screws. Both cylinders must be bled.
7. Check that the brake pedal is now firm. If not, repeat the bleeding operation.

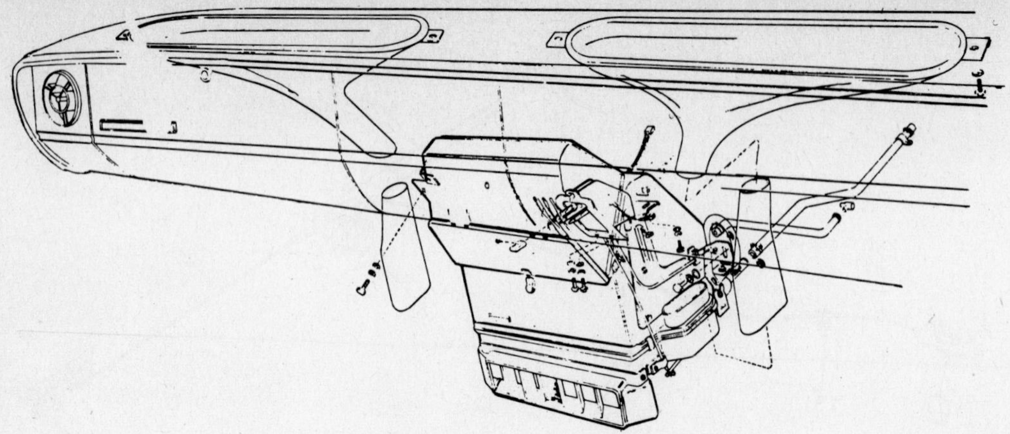

PL510, WPL510 heater unit

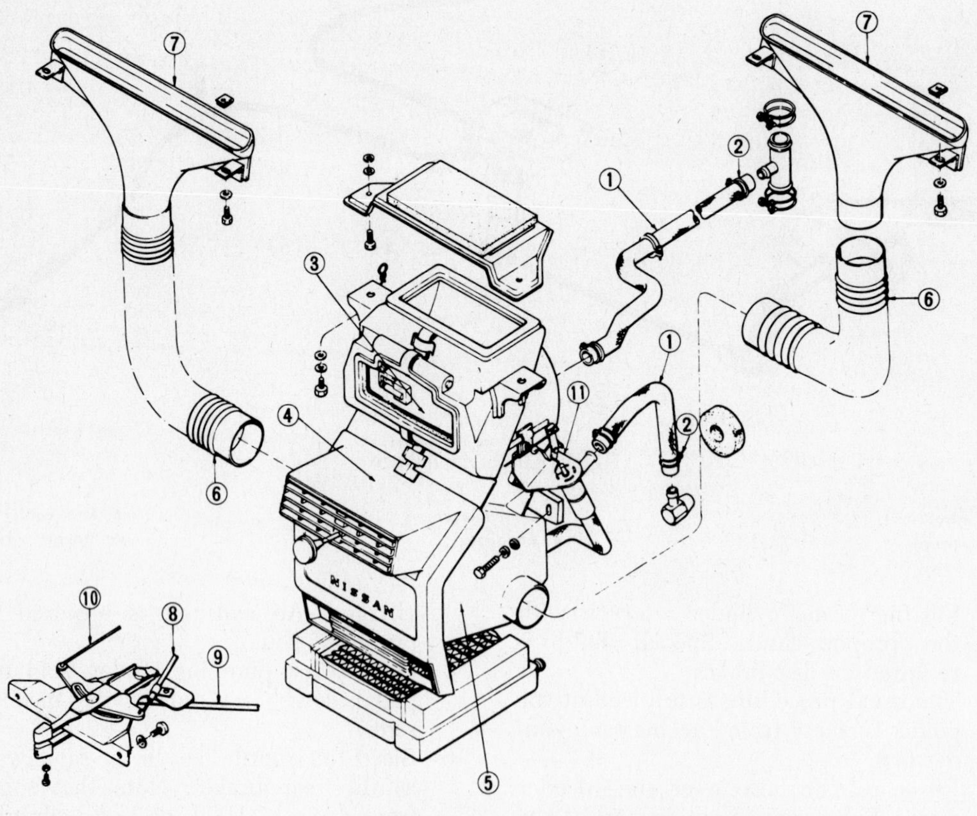

LB110 and KLB110 heater unit

1. Heater hose
2. Clamp
3. Shut valve
4. Vent valve
5. Interior valve
6. Defroster hose
7. Defroster nozzle
8. Control wire
9. Control wire
10. Control rod
11. Water shutoff cock

Heater

HEATER UNIT REMOVAL

PL510, WPL510

1. Drain coolant.
2. Disconnect water pipes to engine.
3. Disconnect blower motor electrical connector.
4. Remove three heater control wires at heater unit.
5. Remove two bolts and ventilator.
6. Remove four bolts and detach heater unit.

LB110, KLB110

1. Remove package tray and ashtray.
2. Disconnect two hoses between heater and engine.
3. Disconnect cables from heater unit and heater controls. Disconnect wiring.
4. Disconnect two control wires from water cock and interior valve, and control rod from shut valve. Set heater control upper lever to DEF and lower lever to OFF.
5. Pull off right and left defroster hoses.
6. Remove four screws holding heater unit to firewall. Remove control knob and remove screws holding control unit to instrument panel. Remove heater unit.

HEATER CORE REMOVAL

PL510, WPL510

1. Remove four clips and separate lower cover.
2. Unbolt and remove heater core.

Headlights

REMOVAL

PL510, WPL510

1. Remove headlight trim.
2. Remove screws and headlight retaining ring.
3. Pull out headlight carefully and pull off wiring plug from rear.

LB110, KLB110

1. On KLB110 coupe, remove screws holding grille to radiator support. On all other models, remove screws and headlight rim.
2. Remove screws and headlight retaining ring.
3. Pull out headlight carefully and pull off wiring plug.

HLS30

To remove the headlight, remove the four retaining screws from inside the wheel opening.

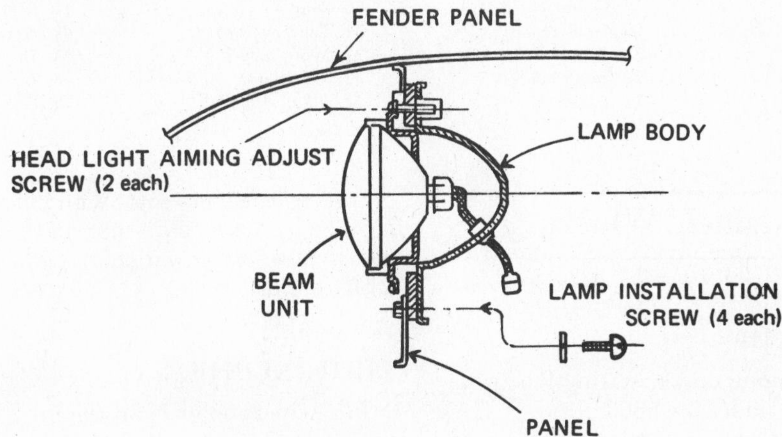

HLS30 headlight assembly details

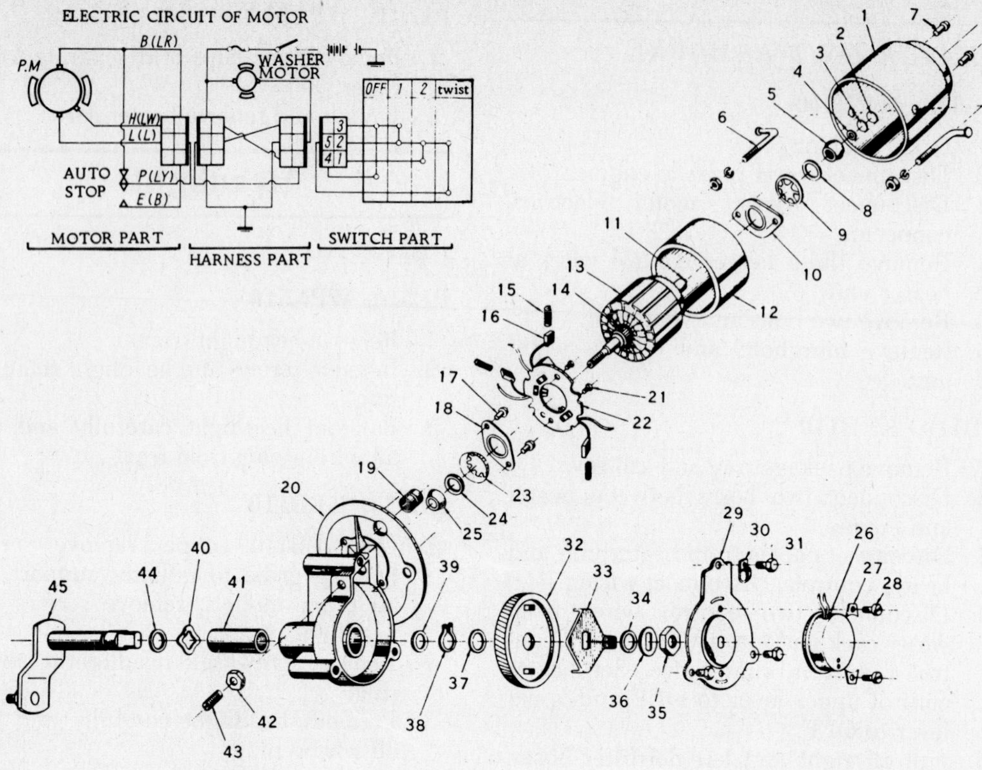

PL510, WPL510 wiper unit

1. Yoke	13. Armature	24. Felt washer	35. Hexagon nut
2. Damper	14. Commutator	25. Bearing	36. Lock washer
3. Armature stopper	15. Brush spring	26. Auto stop cover	37. Plain washer
4. Felt washer	16. Brush	27. Lock plate	38. C type stop ring
5. Bearing	17. Rivet	28. Plain small screw	39. Thrust washer
6. Hook bolt	18. Spring retainer	29. Gear cover	40. Wave washer
7. Rivet	19. Grommet	30. Clip	41. Bearing
8. Felt washer	20. Gear case	31. Tapping screw	42. Hexagon nut
9. Plate spring	21. Tapping screw	32. Worm wheel	43. Thrust screw
10. Spring retainer	22. Brush holder	33. Wheel arm	44. Thrust washer
11. Ball	23. Plate spring	34. Plain washer	45. Gear shaft
12. Magnet ball			

Windshield Wipers

MOTOR REMOVAL

PL510, WPL510

The wiper motor and operating linkage is on the firewall under the hood.

1. Lift wiper arms. Remove securing nuts and detach arms.
2. Remove nuts holding wiper pivots to body.
3. Open hood and unscrew motor from firewall.
4. Disconnect wiring connector and remove wiper motor with linkage.

NOTE: If wipers do not park correctly, adjust position of automatic stop cover on wiper motor.

LB110, KLB110

The wiper motor is on the firewall under the hood. The operating linkage is on the firewall inside the car.

1. Detach motor wiring plug.
2. Inside car, remove nut connecting linkage to wiper shaft.
3. Unbolt and remove wiper motor from firewall.

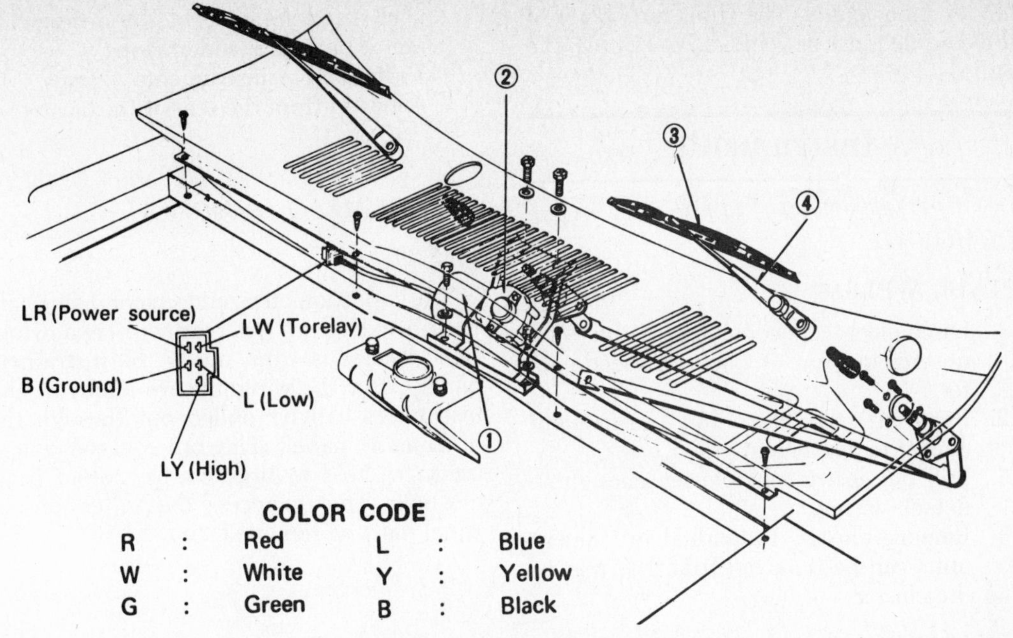

HLS30 wiper installation

1. Wiper motor 2. Auto stop mechanism 3. Wiper blade 4. Wiper arm

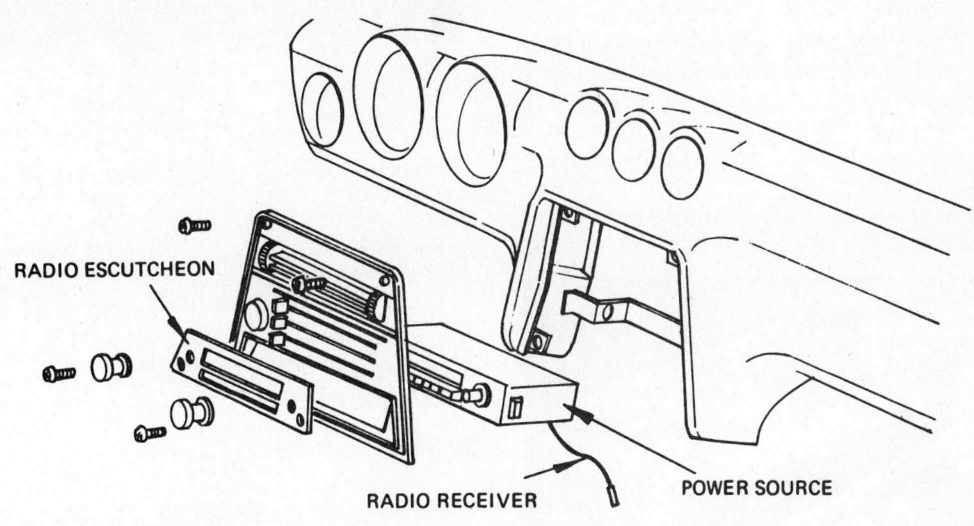

HLS30 radio installation

Radio

REMOVAL

PL510, WPL510

1. Detach all electrical connections.
2. Remove radio knobs and retaining nuts.
3. Remove mounting screws, tip radio down at the rear, and remove.

LB110, KLB110

1. Remove the instrument cluster.
2. Detach all electrical connections.
3. Remove radio knobs and retaining nuts.
4. Remove rear support bracket.
5. Remove radio.

HLS30

The radio is mounted in the center console panel and the speaker in the left fender inner panel. The front face plate of the console must be removed to remove the radio.

Instruments

INSTRUMENT CLUSTER REMOVAL

PL510, WPL510

1. Disconnect speedometer cable by unscrewing nut at back of speedometer.
2. Remove screws holding instrument cluster to instrument panel.
3. Pull out instrument cluster enough to detach wiring.
4. Remove cluster. Individual instrument units can be removed from the rear of the cluster.

LB110, KLB110

1. Disconnect battery negative lead.
2. Depress wiper, light switch, and choke knobs, turning counterclockwise to remove.
3. From the rear, disconnect the lighter wire. Turn and remove lighter outer case.
4. Remove radio and heater knobs.
5. Remove shell cover from steering column.
6. Remove screws holding instrument cluster to instrument panel. Pull out cluster.
7. Disconnect wiring connector. Disconnect speedometer cable by unscrewing nut at back of speedometer.
8. Individual instruments may be removed from the rear of the cluster.

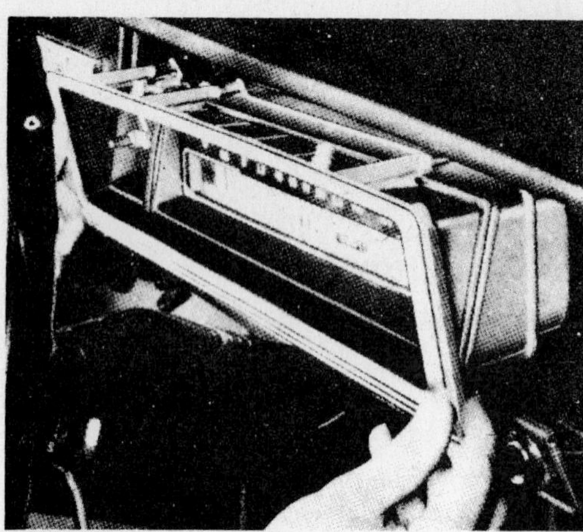

Instrument cluster removal from PL510, WPL510

INSTRUMENT REMOVAL

HLS30

The speedometer and tachometer are both attached at the rear with two wingnuts. Access is from under the instrument panel. After the wingnuts are removed, the instrument can be pulled out through the instrument panel. The other three gauge units are held to brackets by slotted head hex bolts. To gain access, the center console panel must be removed.

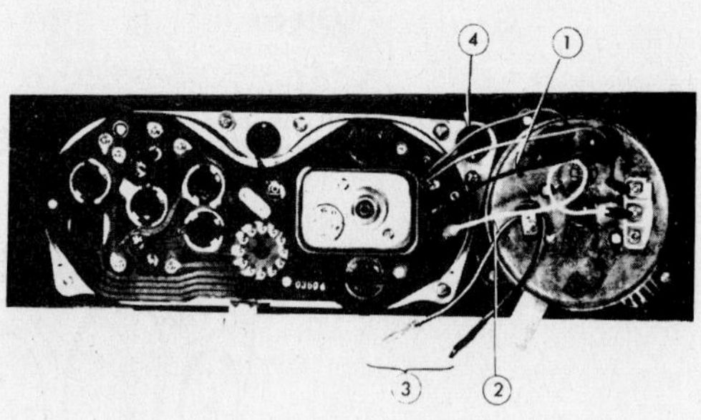

Wiring connections for optional tachometer, LB110 and KLB110

1. Black wire
2. Yellow/red wire
3. Black and white wires
4. Red/green wire

TACHOMETER OR CLOCK INSTALLATION

LB110, KLB110

An optional clock or tachometer can be installed in the space provided to one side of the speedometer.

1. Remove instrument cluster.
2. Remove blank face and install tachometer or clock.
3. Connect wires as shown.
4. On clock, connect blue (or yellow/-red) wire to blue wire in harness along upper edge of instrument panel. On tachometer, connect black and white wires to black/white cable plug in harness.
5. Replace instrument cluster.

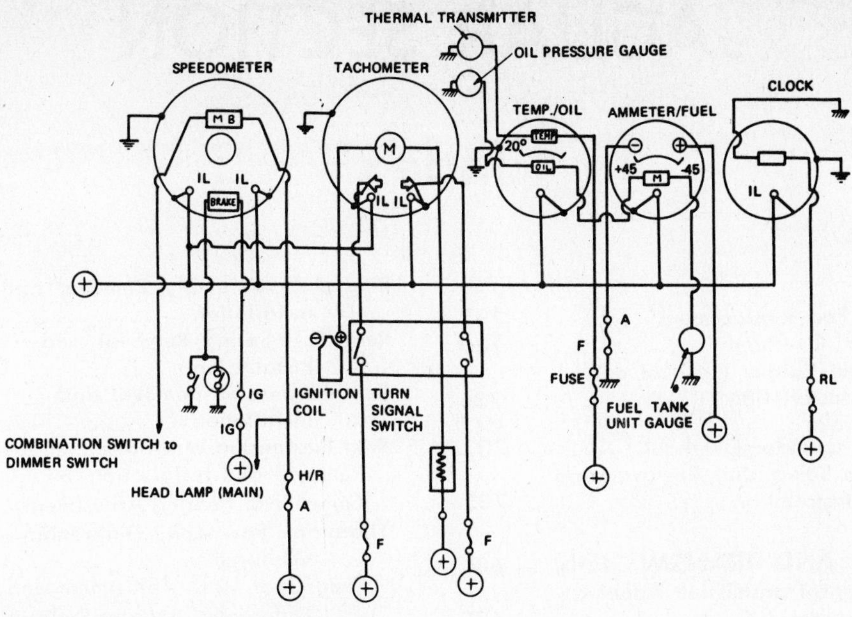

HLS30 instrument wiring diagram

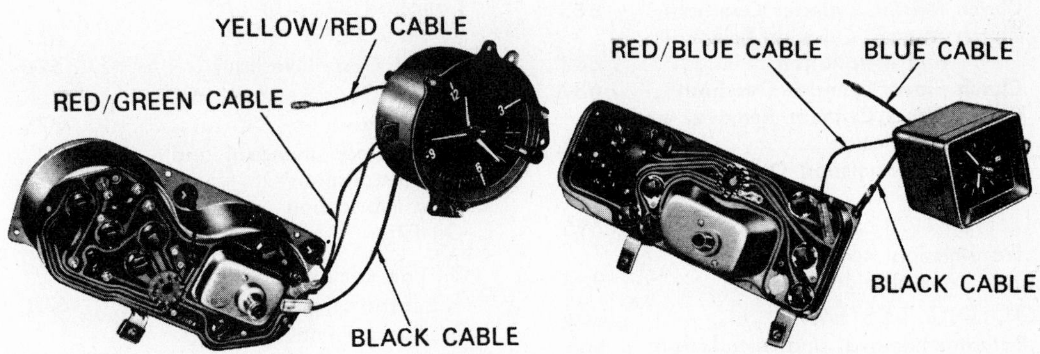

Wiring connections for two optional clocks, LB110 and KLB110

JAGUAR SECTION

Index

Introduction

The Jaguar was first exported to the United States in 1950 as the XK 120 model. It became very popular as one of the first sports cars in this country. The engine, a double-overhead cam inline six (3.4 liter) producing 169 bhp, was originally designed for the Mark VII sedan. The engine performed so well that a sports car body was built for it. This was the XK 120, first sold to the public in 1949, a year before its "predecessor," the Mark VII sedan. The XK 120 and XK 120MC (190 bhp) was produced until 1954 when the larger, more powerful XK 140 (190 bhp) was produced until the arrival of the XK 150 (210 bhp) in 1958. In 1961, the XK 150 was replaced by the all-new XKE. The E Type contained a 3.8 liter (265 bhp) engine until 1965, when it accommodated the larger 4.2 liter (265 bhp) engine coupled to a new all-synchromesh transmission. This car was manufactured in three body styles—a two-seat coupe and a 2+2 (a two-seat coupe with fold-down jump seat accommodations for two more passengers). The 2+2, released late in 1965, was about 9 inches longer than the 1966 coupe, making it possible to install a Borg-Warner three-speed automatic transmission. In 1968, United States and Canadian regulations regarding engine emissions forced Jaguar to modify cars being exported. Modifications included changes in carburetion, ignition, induction, and fuel evaporative systems.

Exterior appearance changes to the basic E type body appeared in 1969. The new U.S. Federal Safety Regulations resulted in the 1969 Series 2 E Type, recognizable by the use of side clearance lights, larger parking lights, tail lights and higher headlights.

In 1970, the two-seat coupe was discontinued but was replaced in America by the XJ6 4.2 liter (210 bhp) model and a 3.8 liter (220 bhp) model. In 1967, the Mark II was renamed the 340 and available only with the 3.4 engine. This car, actually a 3.4 Mark II, was sold in this country for only one year. In 1964, the 3.4S and 3.8S appeared with an all-new independent rear suspension similar to that of the E Type. The 3.4S and 3.8S survived in the United States for three years until 1966. In 1967, the 420 (4.2) became available for only one model year. Power steering, dual master cylinders and limited slip differential were standard on this model. The Mark II, S models, 340 and 420, are sports sedans noticeably smaller than the big sedans such as the Mark IX. The larger Mark X (1962-1964), was replaced by the almost identical 4.2 sedan in 1965 and 1966, and the 420G in 1967. No new Jaguars were produced from 1968-70, when the XJ6 first appeared.

Engine Identification

Number of cylinders	*Cu. In. Displacement (cc's.)*	*Type*
6	210 (3442)	DOHC
6	231 (3781)	DOHC
6	258 (4235)	DOHC

Vehicle Identification

Mark II Sedan (3.4, 3.8)

3.4S or 3.8S Sedan

420 Sedan

XJ6 Sedan

E Type Convertible (1961-1968)—1969-1971 E Type models have side clearance lights and larger tail-lights and parking lights; otherwise they appear the same as the earlier models

E Type Coupe (1961-1968)

E Type 2+2 (1966-68)

E Type Coupe (1969-1970)

Vehicle Number Plate Location

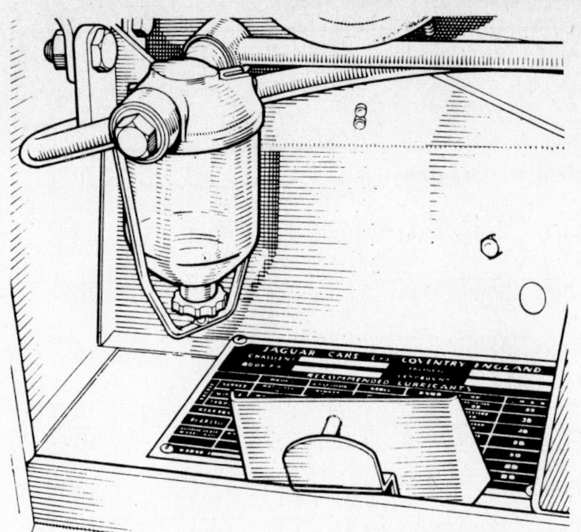

Vehicle number plate location—E Type

Location of vehicle number—Mark II models (340), 3.4S, 3.8S

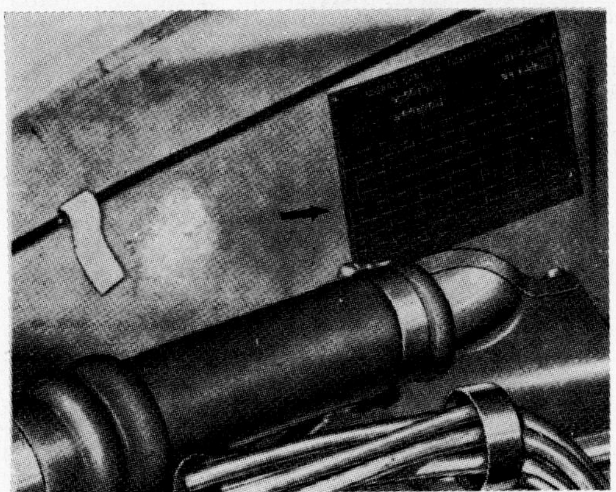

Location of number plate—Mark II models

Engine Number Plate Location

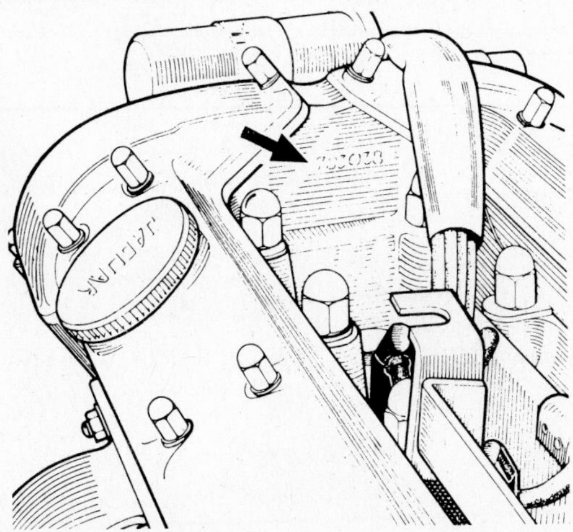

Location of engine number—all models

General Engine Specifications

Year	Type	Cu. In. Displacement (cc)	Carburetor	Developed Horsepower (SAE) @ rpm	Developed Torque (ft. lbs.) @ rpm	Bore and Stroke (in.)	Compression Ratio	Normal Oil Pressure (psi) @ 3000 rpm
1961-64	3.8 E Type	231 (3781)	S.U. (3)	265@5500	260@4000	3.43 x 4.17	9:1	40
1965-67	4.2 E Type	258 (4235)	S.U. (3)	265@5400	275@4000	3.63 x 4.17	9:1	40
1968-71	4.2 E Type	258 (4235)	Stromberg (2)	246@5500	263@3000	3.63 x 4.17	9:1	40
1960-67	3.4 Mark II, 340*	210 (3442)	S.U. (2)	210@5500	215@3000	3.27 x 4.17	9:1	40
1960-66	3.8 Mark II	231 (3781)	S.U. (2)	220@5500	240@3000	3.43 x 4.17	9:1	40
1964-66	3.4S	210 (3442)	S.U. (2)	210@5500	215@3000	3.27 x 4.17	9:1	40
1964-66	3.8S	231 (3781)	S.U. (2)	220@5500	240@3000	3.43 x 4.17	9:1	40
1967*	4.2 420	258 (4235)	S.U. (2)	245@5400	282@4000	3.63 x 4.17	9:1	40
1970-71	4.2 XJ6	258 (4235)	Stromberg (2)	246@5500	263@3000	3.63 x 4.17	9:1	40

* The 340 and 420 models were exported to the United States only in 1967.

Firing Orders

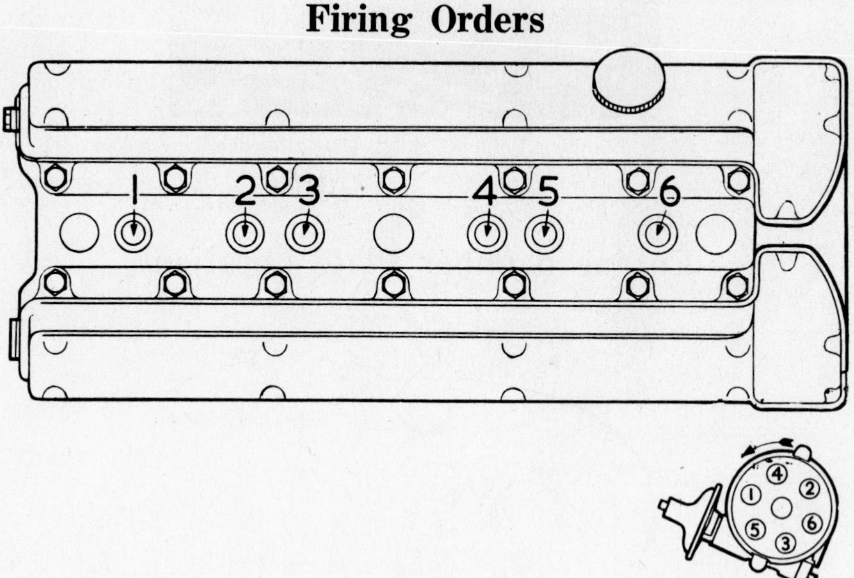

Firing order for all Jaguar DOHC engines (2.4, 2.8, 3.4, 3.8, 4.2)—No. six cylinder is located at front of engine

Tune-up Specifications

Year	Model	Spark plugs Type	Spark plugs Gap (in.)	Distributor Point dwell (deg.)	Distributor Point gap (in.)	Static Ignition Timing (deg.)	Cranking Comp. Pressure (psi)	Valves Clearance (in.) Intake	Valves Clearance (in.) Exhaust	Valves Intake Opens (deg.)	Idle Speed (rpm)
1961-64	3.8 E Type	N11Y	.025	33-37	.014-.016	10B	180	.004	.006	15B①	500
1965-67	4.2 E Type	N5	.025	31-37	.014-.016	10B	180	.004	.006	15B	700⑤
1968-71	4.2 E Type	N11Y	.025	33-37	.014-.016	10B②	150	.012④	.014④	15B	750⑥
1960-67	3.4 Mark II, 340*	UN12Y	.025	33-37	.014-.016	5B③	180	.004	.006	15B①	700⑦
1960-66	3.8 Mark II	UN12Y	.025	33-37	.014-.016	5B③	180	.004	.006	15B①	700⑦
1964-66	3.4S	UN12Y	.025	33-37	.014-.016	5B	180	.004	.006	15B①	700⑧
1964-66	3.8S	UN12Y	.025	33-37	.014-.016	5B	180	.004	.006	15B①	700⑧
1967*	4.2 420	N11Y	.025	31-37	.014-.016	8B	180	.004	.006	15B	700⑤
1970-71	4.2 XJ6	N11Y	.025	33-37	.014-.016	10B②	180	.004	.006	15B	750⑨
1972	All Models	See engine compartment stickers for tune-up specifications.									

* The 340 and 420 models were exported to the United States only in 1967.

① This measurement is made with valve clearances set at .010″.

② 10B is with the vacuum retard line disconnected. Connect the vacuum line and the timing should retard to TDC at idle. In California, strict emission laws require dynamic timing with a strobe light on all vehicles with emission control equipment. 10 BTDC at 1000 rpm is the correct dynamic timing specification for the 4.2 emission control engine.

③ 5 BTDC is the static timing specification for Mark II (3.4, 3.8) models having a paper element air cleaner. A 3.4 liter engine with an oil bath air cleaner requires a static timing of TDC while the 3.8 liter engine with the same type air cleaner (oil) requires a static timing of 10 BTDC.

④ Beginning sometime in 1970, valve clearances for the 4.2 E Type increased to .012″ and .014″. The engine with the larger clearances can be identified by a tag placed on the cam cover or by the presence of a groove situated in the flange at the forward end of the cam.

⑤ 700 rpm for standard transmissions, 500 rpm for automatic transmissions in N.

⑥ 750 rpm for those equipped with standard transmissions, 650 rpm for automatic transmissions in N.

⑦ 700 rpm for those equipped with an all synchromesh transmission, 500 rpm for the automatic (in N) transmission.

⑧ 700 rpm for those equipped with an all synchromesh transmission, 600 rpm for the automatic (in N) transmission and 500 rpm for the non-synchronized low gear transmission.

⑨ 700 rpm for the all synchromesh transmission, 600 rpm for the automatic transmission in N.

B-Before Top Dead Center

Engine Rebuilding Specifications

Crankshaft

	Main Bearing Journals (in.)				Connecting Rod Bearing Journals (in.)			
	Journal diameter 1 through 7	Oil Clearance	Shaft End-Play	Thrust On No.	Journal diameter New	Journal diameter Minimum	Oil Clearance	Side Play
3.8 E Type	2.750-2.7505①	.0025-.0042	.004-.006	4	2.086	2.046	.0015-.0033	.0058-.0087
4.2 E Type	2.750-2.7505	.0025-.0042	.004-.006	4	2.086	2.046	.0015-.0033	.0058-.0087
3.4, 3.8 Mark II	2.750-2.7505①	.0015-.003	.004-.006	4	2.086	2.046	.0023-.0039	.0058-.0087
3.4, 3.8 S Models	2.750-2.7505	.0015-.003	.004-.006	4	2.086	2.046	.0015-.0033	.0058-.0087
420	2.750-2.7505	.0025-.0042	.004-.006	4	2.086	2.046	.0015-.0033	.0058-.0087
XJ6	2.750-2.7505	.0025-.0042	.004-.006	4	2.086	2.046	.0015-.0033	.0058-.0087

① Journals 2, 3, 5, 6—2.7495-2.750.
② 340 model included.

Valves

Model	Seat Angle (deg.)	Valve Lift (in.) Intake	Valve Lift (in.) Exhaust	Valve Spring Pressure Intake and Exhaust (lbs.)	Stem Diameter (in.)	Stem to Guide Clearance (in.) Intake and Exhaust	Valve Guide Removable
3.8 E Type	45	.375	.375	48.4 (outer spring)	5/16	.001-.004	yes
4.2 E Type	45	.375	.375	48.4 (outer spring)	5/16	.001-.004	yes
3.4, 3.8① Mark II	45	.375	.375	48.4 (outer spring)	5/16	.001-.004	yes
3.4, 3.8 S Models	45	.375	.375	48.4 (outer spring)	5/16	.001-.004	yes
4.2 420	45	.375	.375	48.4 (outer spring)	5/16	.001-.004	yes
4.2 XJ6	45	.375	.375	48.4 (outer spring)	5/16	.001-.004	yes

① 340 model included.

Pistons and Rings

Model	Block (in.) Cylinder Bore New	Block (in.) Cylinder Bore Maximum Oversize	Piston diameter New	Piston diameter Maximum Oversize	Pistons (in.) Wrist Pin Diameter (Fit)①	Piston Clearance②	Rings (in.) Side Clearance	Rings (in.) End-Gap
3.8 E Type	3.4252	3.4552	③	.030	.8750-.8752	.0011-.0017	.001-.003	.015-.020 (comp.) .011-.016 (oil)
4.2 E Type	3.625	3.655	③	.030	.8752-.8754	.0007-.0013	.001-.003	.015-.020 (top comp.) .010-.015 (low comp.) .015-.033 (oil)

Engine Rebuilding Specifications
Pistons and Rings

Model	Block (in.)				Pistons (in.)		Rings (in.)	
	Cylinder Bore		Piston diameter		Wrist Pin Diameter (Fit)①	Piston Clearance②	Side Clearance	End-Gap
	New	Maximum Oversize	New	Maximum Oversize				
3.4 Mark II, 340	3.2677	3.2977	③	.030	.8750-.8752	.0011-.0017	.001-.003	.015-.020 (comp.) .011-.016④ (oil)
3.8 Mark II	3.4252	3.4552	③	.030	.8750-.8752	.0011-.0017	.001-.003	.015-.020 (comp.) .011-.016④ (oil)
3.4S	3.2677	3.2977	③	.030	.8750-.8752	.0011-.0017	.001-.003	.015-.020 (comp.) .015-.033 (oil)
3.8S	3.4252	3.4552	③	.030	.8750-.8752	.0011-.0017	.001-.003	.015-.020 (comp.) .015-.033 (oil)
4.2 420	3.625	3.655	③	.030	.8750-.8752	.0011-.0017	.001-.003	.015-.020 (comp.) .015-.033 (oil)
4.2 XJ6	3.625	3.655	③	.030	.8750-.8752	.0007-.0013	.0025 (comp.) .004 (oil)	.015-.020 (comp.) .015-.033 (oil)

① Wrist pins are a push fit into the piston.
② Piston clearance is measured at the bottom of the skirt at 90° to the wrist pin axis.
③ Pistons are a select fit according to cylinder bore size. Each piston is stamped on its crown with a grade identification letter (F, G, H, J, K,) and each cylinder bore has a letter stamped next to the bore. Make sure that the letter on the piston matches the letter next to the bore. The following list gives, according to engine size, the piston identification letter and the cylinder bore size that each piston fits:

	3.4 liter		3.8 liter		4.2 liter
F	3.2673″-3.2676″	F	3.4248″-3.4251″	F	3.6250″-3.6253″
G	3.2677″-3.2680″	G	3.4252″-3.4255″	G	3.6254″-3.6257″
H	3.2681″-3.2684″	H	3.4256″-3.4259″	H	3.6258″-3.6261″
J	3.2685″-3.2688″	J	3.4260″-3.4263″	J	3.6262″-3.6265″
K	3.2689″-3.2692″	K	3.4264″-3.4267″	K	3.6266″-3.6269″

④ Beginning with engine number KH.7999 (3.4) and LC.3703 (3.8), oil ring gap is .015″-.033″.

Distributor Specifications

Year	Model	Distributor Identification	Centrifugal Advance* Start Degrees @ rpm	Centrifugal Advance* Intermediate Degrees @ rpm	Centrifugal Advance* Intermediate Degrees @ rpm	Centrifugal Advance* End Degrees @ rpm	Vacuum Advance* Start Degrees @ ins./Hg	Vacuum Advance* Intermediate Degrees @ ins./Hg	Vacuum Advance* End Deg's. @ ins./Hg
1961-64	3.8 E Type	DMBZ 6A①	0@325	3½-6½@650	9-11@1,300	12@2,000	0@4½	0-3@7½	7-9@20
1965-67	4.2 E Type	22 D6②	0@300	2-4@600	6½-8½@1,250	8½-10½ @2,300	0@4½	0-3@7½	7-9@20
1968-71	4.2 E Type	N.A.	—	7-9@900⑬	9-11@1,500⑬	11½-13½ @2,200⑬	—	—	—
1960-67	3.4, 3.8 Mark II, 340	DMBZ 6A③	0@300	8-10@950	17-19@1,650	24-26@3,500	0@2½	1½-5@6½	10-12@20
		DMBZ 6A④	0@300	8-11@800	14-16@1,700	20-23@3,200	0@1	5½-9@7½	11-13@18
		DMBZ 6A⑤	0@400	7-10@1,100	10-12@1,300	16-18@3,500	0@2½	1½-5@6½	10-12@20
		DMBZ 6A⑥	0@275	7½-10@800	10-12@1,000	17-19@3,200	0@5	3-5@8½	8-10@20
		DMBZ 6A⑦	0@325	0-1½@450	—	12@2,000	0@4½	0-3@7½	7-9@20
		DMBZ 6A⑧	0@250	8-10@1,000	14-16@2,300	19@3,400	0@5	1-4½@10	6-8@25
		DMBZ 6A⑨	0@225	2½-4½@550	8-10@1,100	13@2,000	0@2½	0-3@6	7-9@15
1964-66	3.4 S	22 D6⑩	0@200	8-10@1,000	14-16@2,300	19@3,400	0@5	1-4½@10	6-8@25
	3.8 S	22 D6⑪	0@225	2½-4½@550	8-10@1,100	13@2,000	0@2½	0-3@6	7-9@15
1967	4.2 420	22 D6⑫	0@300	2-4@650	6½-8½@1,250	8½-10½ @2,300	0@4½	0-3@7½	7-9@20
1970-71	4.2 XJ6	N.A.	—	11-13@800⑬	14½-16½ @1,450⑬	16½-18½ @1,850⑬	—	—	—

* Distributor degrees @ distributor rpm—crankshaft values are double distributor values.

① Lucas vacuum number 54410415 and Lucas advance spring number 54410416.

② Lucas vacuum number 54415894 and Lucas advance spring number 55415562.

③ Lucas vacuum number 424374 and Lucas advance spring number 424377.

④ Lucas vacuum number 423461 and Lucas advance spring number 423750.

⑤ Lucas vacuum number 424374 and Lucas advance spring number 425183.

⑥ Lucas vacuum number 421027 and Lucas advance spring number 424950.

⑦ Lucas vacuum number 54410415 and Lucas advance spring number 54410416.

⑧ Lucas vacuum number 54410709 and Lucas advance spring number 425183.

⑨ Lucas vacuum number 421189 and Lucas advance spring number 54411290.

⑩ Lucas vacuum number 54412145 and Lucas advance spring number 5441559.

⑪ Lucas vacuum number 54411969 and Lucas advance spring number 54415560.

⑫ Lucas vacuum number 54415894 and Lucas advance spring number 55415562.

⑬ With vacuum retard connected.

Torque Specifications

Year	Model	Cylinder Head bolts (ft. lbs.)	Main Bearing bolts (ft. lbs.)	Rod Bearing bolts (ft. lbs.)	Crank-shaft Balancer bolt (or nut) (ft. lbs.)	Fly-wheel to Crankshaft bolts (ft. lbs.)	Manifold (ft. lbs.)	
							Intake	Exhaust
1961-64	3.8 E Type	54	83	37	90	67	15	15
1965-67	4.2 E Type	58	83	37	90	67	15	15
1968-71	4.2 E Type	58	83	37	90	67	15	15
1960-67	3.4 Mark II, 340*	54	83	37	90	67	15	15
1960-66	3.8 Mark II	54	83	37	90	67	15	15
1964-66	3.4S	54	83	37	90	67	15	15
1964-66	3.8S	54	83	37	90	67	15	15
1967*	4.2 420	58	83	37	90	67	15	15
1970-71	4.2 XJ6	58	83	37	90	67	15	15

* 340 and 420 models were exported to the United States only in 1967.

Torque Sequences

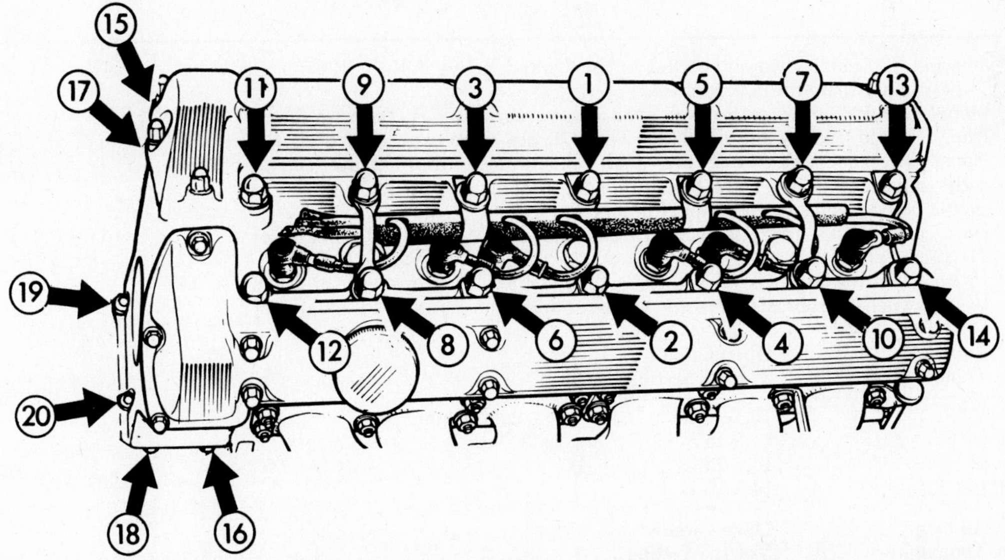

Torque sequence for cylinder head nuts (2.4, 2.8, 3.4, 4.2 liter engines)

Electrical Specifications

Year	Model	Generator				Regulator			
		Model Number	Brush Spring Pressure (oz.)①	Field Resistance (ohms.)	Maximum Output (amps.)	Model Number	Cut-out Relay Volts to Close	Maximum Current (Amps.)	Voltage Regulator Setting
1961-64②	3.8 E Type	C45 PVS-6	28③	6	25	RB 310	12.7-13.3	24-26	⑥
1961-64	3.8 E Type	C42	33④	4.5	30	RB 340	12.6-13.4	29-32	⑦
1960-67	3.4 Mark II, 340*	C45 PVS-6	28③	6	25	RB 310	12.7-13.3	24-26	⑥
1960-66	3.8 Mark II	C45 PVS-6	28③	6	25	RB 310	12.7-13.3	24-26	⑥
1960-67	3.4 Mark II, 340*	C42	33④	6	30	RB 340	12.6-13.4	29-32	⑦
1960-66	3.8 Mark II	C42	33④	6	30	RB 340	12.6-13.4	29-32	⑦
1960-67	3.4 Mark II, 340*	C48	25⑤	6	35	RB 340	12.6-13.4	34-36	⑧
1960-66	3.8 Mark II	C48	25⑤	6	35	RB 340	12.6-13.4	34-36	⑧
1964-66	3.4S	C42	33④	4.5	30	RB 340	12.6-13.4	29-32	⑦
1964-66	3.4S	C48	25⑤	6	35	RB 340	12.6-13.4	34-36	⑧
1964-66	3.8S	C42	33④	4.5	30	RB 340	12.6-13.4	29-32	⑦
1964-66	3.8S	C48	25⑤	6	35	RB 340	12.6-13.4	34-36	⑧

* 340 and 420 models were exported to the United States only in 1967.

① These pressures are for new brushes.

② Model C45 PVS-6 generator was used on the early 3.8 E Type produced from 1961 to 1964 while the later 3.8 E Types were equipped with the model C42 generator during the same time period. Information defining early and later is not available; although, the generators and regulators should be labeled as to their model number.

③ 20 oz. when the brush is worn to the minimum permissible length of 11/32″.

④ 16 oz. when the brush is worn to the minimum permissible length of 1/4″.

⑤ 16 oz. when the brush is worn to the minimum permissible length of 11/32″.

⑥

Ambient Temperature	Open Circuit Voltage Setting	
50°F.	15.1-15.7	@2000 engine rpm
68°F.	14.9-15.5	
86°F.	14.7-15.3	
104°F.	14.5-15.1	

⑦

Ambient Temperature	Open Circuit Voltage Setting	
50°F.	14.9-15.5	@2700 engine rpm
68°F.	14.7-15.3	
86°F.	14.5-15.1	
104°F.	14.3-14.9	

⑧

Ambient Temperature	Open Circuit Voltage Setting	
50°F.	15.0-15.6	@1800 engine rpm
68°F.	14.8-15.4	
86°F.	14.6-15.2	
104°F.	14.4-15.0	

Electrical Specifications—con't

Year	Model	Battery			Starter			
		Capacity (Amp. hours) @ 10 hr. rate	Volts	Grounded Terminal	Lock test			Brush spring tension (oz.)
					Amp.	Volts	Torque (ft. lbs.)	
1961-64	3.8 E Type	55	12	Pos.	430-450	7.4-7.8	22	30-40
1965-71	4.2 E Type	55	12	Neg.	465	7.6	23	52
1960-67	3.4 Mark II, 340*	60	12	Pos.	430-450	7.4-7.8	22	30-40
1960-66	3.8 Mark II	60	12	Pos.	430-450	7.4-7.8	22	30-40
1964-66	3.4S	60	12	Pos.	430-450	7.4-7.8	22	30-40
1964-66	3.8S	60	12	Pos.	430-450	7.4-7.8	22	30-40
1967*	4.2 420	60	12	Neg.	465	7.6	23	52
1970-71	4.2 XJ6	53	12	Neg.	465	7.6	23	52

* 340 and 420 models were exported to the United States only in 1967.

Year	Model	Alternator		
		Model Number	Output @ Alternator rpm (amps.)	Brush Spring Pressure (oz.)
1965-71	4.2 E Type	11AC③	40@4,000	4-5①
1967	4.2 420	11AC	40@4,000	4-5①
1970-71	4.2 XJ6	11AC	40@4,000	4-5①
1970-71	4.2 XJ6	A7④	60@10,000	②

① This pressure is with the spring compressed to a length of 25/32". The pressure changes to 7 1/2-8 1/2 oz. when the spring is compressed to a length of 13/32".

② Replace brushes if worn below the minimum length of .187".

③ Lucas alternator.

④ BUTEC alternator used only in air conditioned models.

Capacities and Pressures

Year	Model	Engine Crankcase Refill after draining (qts.) With Filter	Without Filter	Transmissions (pts.) Refill after draining Manual 3-Speed	Manual 4-Speed	Auto. (Total)	Drive Axle (pts.)	Fuel Tank (gals.)	Cooling System with Heater (qts.)	Normal Fuel Pressure (psi)	Maximum Coolant Pressure (psi)
1961-64	3.8 E Type	9½	9	—	3	—	3¼	16¾	19¼	2	4②
1965-71	4.2 E Type	9½	9	—	3	19	3¼	16¾	19¼	2	7③
1960-67	3.4 Mark II, 340*	7¾	6⅝	N.A.	3①	18	3¼	14½	13¼	2	4
1960-66	3.8 Mark II	7¾	6⅝	N.A.	3①	18	3¼	14½	13¼	2	4
1964-66	3.4S	7¼	7	—	3①	18	3¼	16½	13¼	2	4
1964-66	3.8S	7¼	7	—	3①	18	3¼	16½	13¼	2	4
1967*	4.2 420	7¼	7	—	3①	19	3¼	16½	15¼		4③
1970-71	4.2 XJ6	8¾	8	—	—	19	3¼	29	19¼	2	4③

* 340 and 420 models were exported to the United States only in 1967.
①-4-3/4 pts. if equipped with overdrive.
② 9 psi on those E Types (3.8) equipped with the modified header tank and the header tank to engine hose.
③ 13 psi if equipped with air conditioning.

Brake Specifications

Year	Model	Type Front	Type Rear	Master Cylinder (in.)	Brake Cylinder Bore Caliper Bore Diameter (in.) Front	Rear	Brake Drum or Disc Diameter (in.) Front	Rear
1961-64	3.8 E Type	Disc	Disc	⅝	2⅛	1¾	11	10
1965-71	4.2 E Type	Disc	Disc	⅞	2⅛	1¾	11	10
1960-67	3.4 Mark II, 340*	Disc	Disc	⅞	2⅛	1½	11	11⅜
1960-66	3.8 Mark II	Disc	Disc	⅞	2⅛	1½	11	11⅜
1964-66	3.4S	Disc	Disc	⅞	2⅛	1½	11	10⅜
1964-66	3.8S	Disc	Disc	⅞	2⅛	1½	11	10⅜
1967*	4.2 420	Disc	Disc	⅞	N.A.	N.A.	11	10⅖
1970-71	4.2 XJ6	Disc	Disc	⅞	N.A.	N.A.	11	10⅖

* 340 and 420 models were exported to the United States only in 1967.

Chassis and Wheel Alignment Specifications

Year	Model	Chassis: Wheel-base (in.)	Chassis: Track (ins.) Front	Chassis: Track (ins.) Rear	Wheel Alignment: Caster Range (deg.)	Caster Pref. Setting (deg.)	Camber Range (deg.)	Camber Pref. Setting (deg.)	Toe-In (ins.)	Kingpin Inclination (deg.)	Rear Camber Range (deg.)	Rear Camber Pref. Setting (deg.)
1961-64	3.8 E Type	96	50	50	1½P-2½P	2P	¼N-¾P	¼P	1/16-1/8	4	½N-1N	¾N
1965-71	4.2 E Type	96①	50	50	1½P-2P	1¾P	0-½P	¼P	1/16-1/8	4	½N-1N	¾N
1960-67	3.4 Mark II, 340*	107.4	55②	53.8②	½N-½P	0	0-1P	½P	0-1/16	3½	—	—
1960-66	3.8 Mark II	107.4	55②	53.8②	½N-½P	0	0-1P	½P	0-1/16	3½	—	—
1964-66	3.4S	107.4	55.3③	54.3③	½N-½P	0	0-1P	½P	0-1/8	3½	½N-1N	¾N
1964-66	3.8S	107.4	55.3③	54.3③	½N-½P	0	0-1P	½P	0-1/8	3½	½N-1N	¾N
1967*	4.2 420	107.4	55.3	54.2	½N-½P	0	0-1P	½P	0-1/8	3½	½N-1N	¾N
1970-71	4.2 XJ6	108.9	58.0	58.1	2P-2½P	2¼P	¼P-¾P	½P	1/16-1/8	1½	½N-1N	¾N

* 340 and 420 models were exported to the United States only in 1967.
① 105 inches for the 2+2 coupe.
② If equipped with wire wheels, 55.5 inches for the front and 54.1 for the rear.
③ If equipped with wire wheels, 55.3 inches for the front and 52.9 for the rear.

Fuses and Circuit Breakers

Year	Model	Fuse No.	Circuits	Amps.
1965-71	4.2 E Type	1	Headlights—high beam	35
		2	Headlights—low beam	35
		3	Horns	50
		4	Fuel pump	5
		5	Side, panel, tail and license plate lights	35
		6	Horn relay, windshield washer, radiator fan motor, stop lights	35
		7	Turn signals, heater, wipers, choke, fuel, water, oil gauges	35
		8	Headlight dimmer, interior lights and cigarette lighter	35
		Inline	Electrically heated rear window (optional)	15
		Inline	Radio and optional equipment	5
		Inline	Four-way flashers	35
1960-67	3.4, 3.8 Mark II, 340	—	Interior lights, cigarette lighter and headlight dimmer	35
		—	Heater fan, turn signals, brake lights, gas gauge, overdrive solenoid, back-up light, wipers, overdrive or automatic transmission indicator light, oil pressure gauge, water temperature gauge, windshield washer and horns.	50
1964-66	3.4S, 3.8S	1	Headlights—high beam	35
		2	Headlights—low beam	35
		3	Horn relay, windshield washer, stop lights, turn signals, back-up lights, overdrive solenoid and automatic transmission.	35
		4	Wipers, auxiliary starting carburetor, fuel, oil and water gauges and heater motor.	35
		5	Horns	50
		6	Side, tail, panel and license plate lights	35
		7	Headlight dimmer, interior lights, cigarette lighter	35
		—	Electrically heated rear window (optional)	15
		—	Four-way flashers	35
		—	Overdrive or automatic transmission speed hold	8

Fuses and Circuit Breakers

Year	Model	Fuse No.	Circuits	Amps.
1967	4.2	1	Headlights—high beam	35
	420	2	Headlights—low beam	35
		3	Horn relay, windshield washer, stop lights, turn signals, back-up lights, overdrive solenoid	35
		4	Wipers, auxiliary starting carburetor, fuel, oil and water gauges, heater motor	35
		5	Horns	50
		6	Side, tail, panel and license plate lights	35
		7	Headlight dimmer, interior lights, cigarette lighter	35
		8	Spare fuse	35
		A	Heated rear window (optional)	15
		A	Overdrive solenoid	8
		A	Radio line fuse (when fitted)	8
		A	Four-way flashers	35
		B	Air conditioning equipment (optional)	30
1970-71	4.2 XJ6	1	Windshield washer, instruments, horn relay, tachometer (green wire)	35
		2	Map/interior lights, cigarette lighter, air conditioning relay (opt.) (purple wire)	35
		3	Wipers, turn signals, heater motor, stop lights (green wire)	35
		4	Horns (purple/brown wire)	50
		5	Side and taillights—left-side (red wire)	10
		6	Outer headlight (blue/white)—high beam	35
		7	Inner headlights (blue/slate wire)	35
		8	Outer headlight (blue/purple)—left-side low beam	35
		9	Outer headlight (blue/red)—right-side low beam	35
		10	Side and taillights—right-side (red wire)	10
		—	Four-way flashers	35
		—	Electrically heated rear window	15
		—	Overdrive solenoid/back-up	8

Light Bulb Specifications

Year	Model	Usage	Make	Type	Wattage
1961-71	E Type	Side light	Lucas	989	6
		Front and rear turn signals	Lucas	382	21
		Brake lights and tail lights	Lucas	380	6, 21
		License plate light	Lucas	207	6
		Interior lights (convertible)	Lucas	382	21
		Interior lights (coupe)	Lucas	989	6
		Map light	Lucas	989	6
		Instrument lights, headlight high beam indicator light, ignition warning light, fuel level warning light, handbrake and brake fluid warning light, mixture control warning light	Lucas	987	2.2
		Instrument panel switch lights, turn signal indicator light	Lucas	281	2
1960-67	3.4, 3.8 Mark II 340	Side light, map light, interior light, license plate light, trunk light	Lucas	989	6
		Front and rear turn signals, back-up light	Lucas	382	21
		Taillight and brake lights	Lucas	380	21, 6
		Fog light	Lucas	323	48
		Rear interior light	Lucas	254	6
		Instrument light, high beam indicator light, ignition warning light, fuel warning light, handbrake and brake fluid warning light	Lucas	987	2.2
		Instrument panel switch lights, turn signal indicator lights, overdrive indicator light and automatic trans. indicator light	Lucas	281	1.6

Light Bulb Specifications

Year	Model	Usage	Make	Type	Wattage
1964-66	3.4S, 3.8S	Side light	Lucas	989	6
		Front and rear turn signals	Lucas	382	21
		Tail light and brake lights	Lucas	380	21, 6
		License plate and trunk lights	Lucas	989	6
		Back-up light	Lucas	382	21
		Interior light	Lucas	254	6
		Glovebox light	Lucas	254	6
		Map light	Lucas	989	6
		Headlight high beam indicator light	Lucas	987	2.2
		Ignition warning light	Lucas	987	2.2
		Handbrake and brake fluid warning light	Lucas	987	2.2
		Instrument panel switch light	Lucas	281	2
		Turn signal indicator lights	Lucas	281	2
		Automatic transmission indicator light	Lucas	281	2
		Overdrive light	Lucas	281	2
1967	4.2 420	Outer headlight (main, low beams)	Lucas	410	37.5, 50
		Inner headlight (main beam)	Lucas	410	37.5
		Side light	Lucas	989	6
		Front and rear turn signals	Lucas	382	21
		Tail lights and brake lights	Lucas	380	6, 21
		License plate light	Lucas	989	6
		Back-up lights	Lucas	382	21
		Interior lights	Lucas	254	6
		Glovebox light	Lucas	254	6
		Map light	Lucas	989	6
		Trunk light	Lucas	989	6
		Rear defroster warning light (opt.)	Lucas	987	2.2
		Instrument light, high beam light	Lucas	987	2.2
		Ignition warning light	Lucas	987	2.2
		Handbrake and brake fluid warning light	Lucas	987	2.2
		Four-way flasher lights	Lucas	987	2.2
		Instrument panel switch light	Lucas	281	2
		Turn signal indicator lights	Lucas	281	2
		Overdrive light	Lucas	281	2
		Automatic transmission indicator light	Lucas	281	2
		Heater control panel light	Lucas	286	3
		Fog lamp (opt.)	Phillips	683	48
1970-71	4.2 XJ6	Outer headlight (main, low beams)	Lucas	410	37.5, 50
		Inner headlight (main beam)	Lucas	410	37.5
		Side light	Lucas	989	6
		Front and rear turn signals	Lucas	382	21
		Tail lights and brake lights	Lucas	380	6, 21
		License plate light	Lucas	989	6
		Back-up lights	Lucas	272	10
		Interior lights	Lucas	272	10
		Glovebox light	Lucas	254	6
		Map light	Lucas	989	6
		Trunk light	Lucas	989	6
		Instrument panel, high beam indicator	Lucas	987	2.2
		Instrument panel switch lights	Lucas	281	2
		Turn signal indicator lights	Lucas	281	2
		Automatic transmission indicator light	Lucas	283	3
		Ignition warning light, oil pressure	Lucas	280	1.5
		Four-way flashers	Lucas	280	1.5
		Handbrake and brake fluid warning light	Lucas	280	1.5

Wiring Diagrams

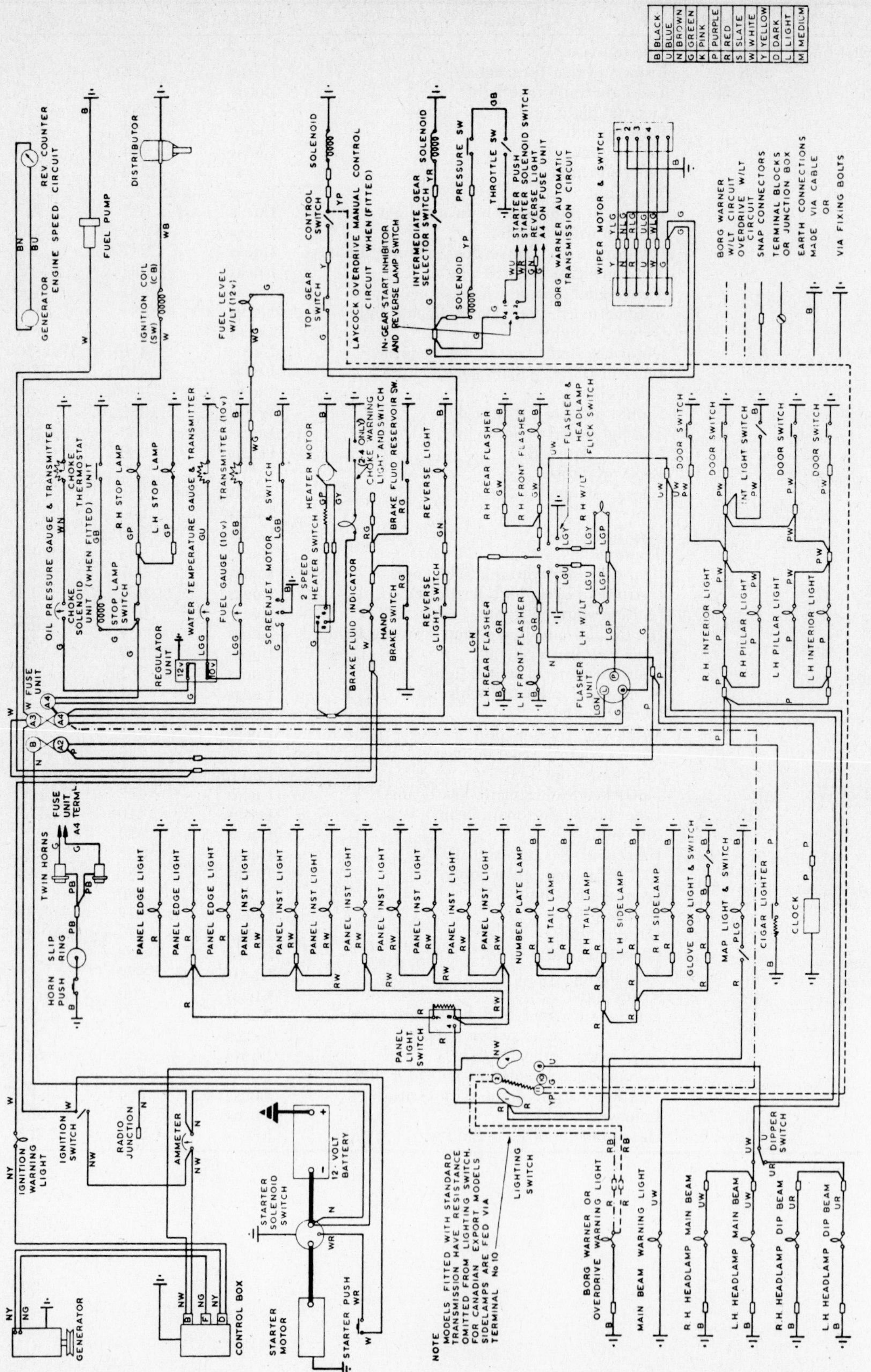

Mark II (3.4, 3.8) and 340 sedans

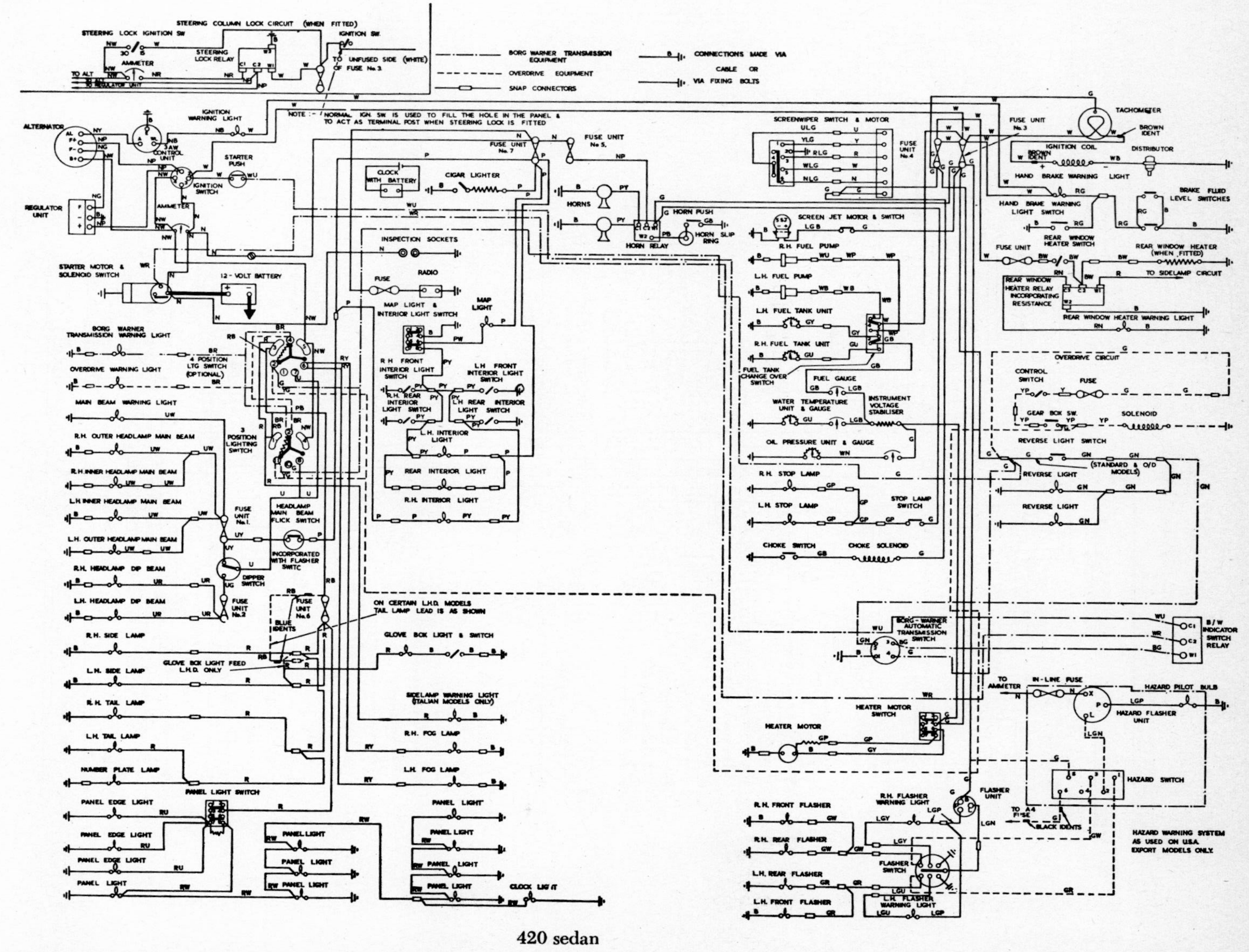
B Black
U Blue
N Brown
G Green
K Pink
P Purple
R Red
S Slate
W White
Y Yellow
D Dark
L Light
M Medium

420 sedan

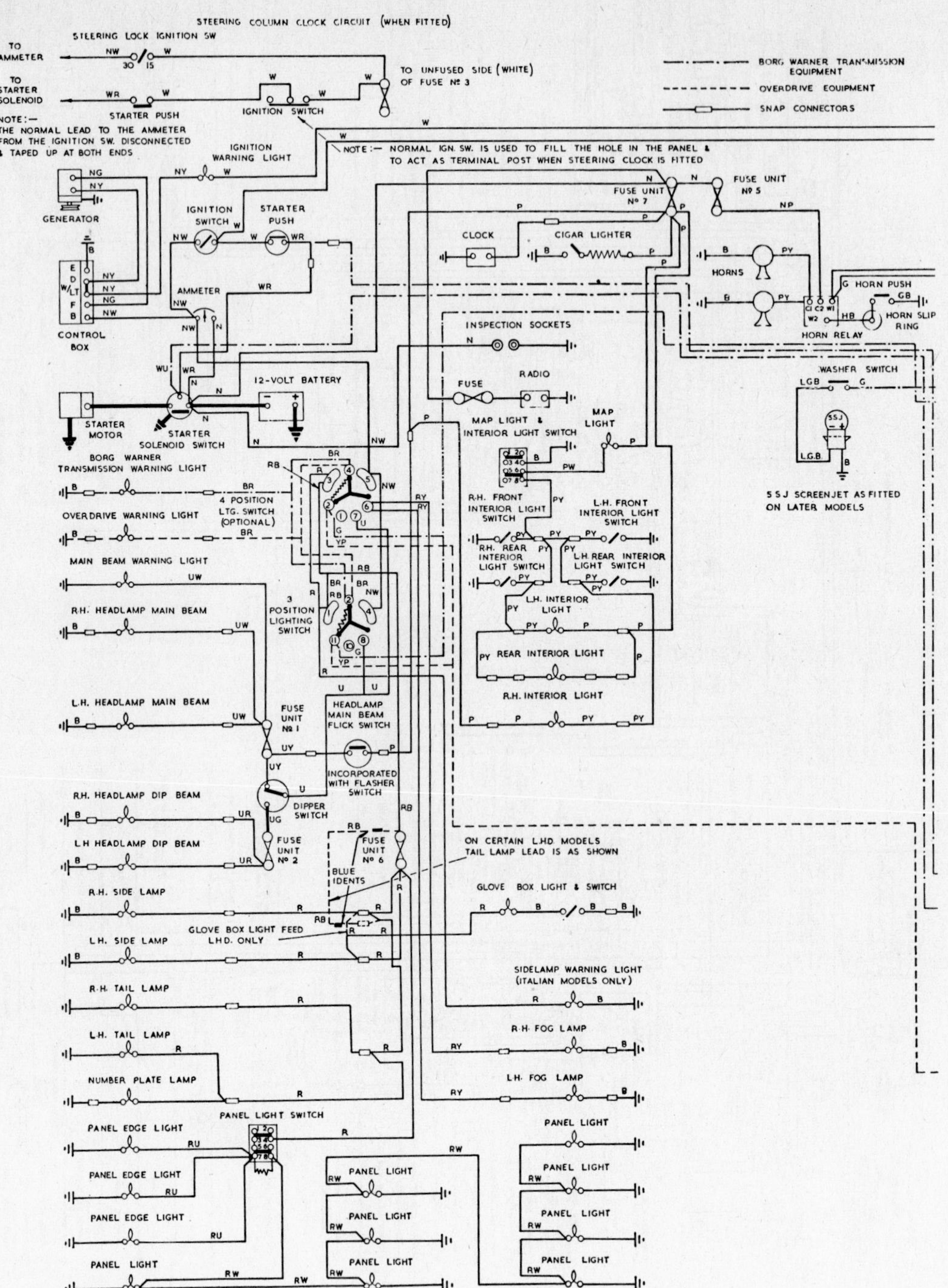

3.4S, 3.8S Sedans

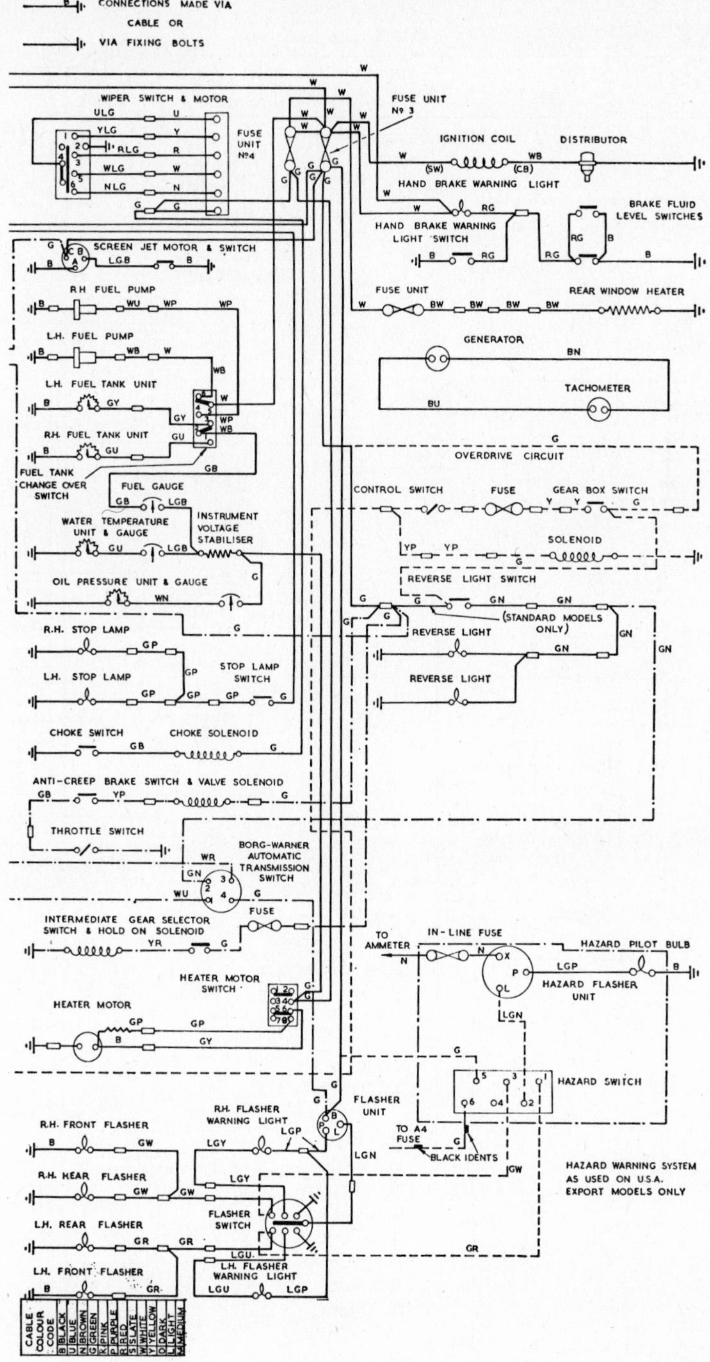
CONNECTIONS MADE VIA CABLE OR VIA FIXING BOLTS
WIPER SWITCH & MOTOR
FUSE UNIT Nº4
FUSE UNIT Nº 3
IGNITION COIL
DISTRIBUTOR
HAND BRAKE WARNING LIGHT
BRAKE FLUID LEVEL SWITCHES
HAND BRAKE WARNING LIGHT SWITCH
SCREEN JET MOTOR & SWITCH
R.H. FUEL PUMP
L.H. FUEL PUMP
FUSE UNIT
REAR WINDOW HEATER
GENERATOR
TACHOMETER
L.H. FUEL TANK UNIT
R.H. FUEL TANK UNIT
FUEL TANK CHANGE OVER SWITCH
FUEL GAUGE
OVERDRIVE CIRCUIT
CONTROL SWITCH
FUSE
GEAR BOX SWITCH
WATER TEMPERATURE UNIT & GAUGE
INSTRUMENT VOLTAGE STABILISER
SOLENOID
OIL PRESSURE UNIT & GAUGE
REVERSE LIGHT SWITCH
(STANDARD MODELS ONLY)
R.H. STOP LAMP
REVERSE LIGHT
L.H. STOP LAMP
STOP LAMP SWITCH
REVERSE LIGHT
CHOKE SWITCH
CHOKE SOLENOID
ANTI-CREEP BRAKE SWITCH & VALVE SOLENOID
THROTTLE SWITCH
BORG-WARNER AUTOMATIC TRANSMISSION SWITCH
INTERMEDIATE GEAR SELECTOR SWITCH & HOLD ON SOLENOID
FUSE
TO AMMETER
IN-LINE FUSE
HAZARD PILOT BULB
HAZARD FLASHER UNIT
HEATER MOTOR SWITCH
HEATER MOTOR
HAZARD SWITCH
R.H. FLASHER WARNING LIGHT
FLASHER UNIT
R.H. FRONT FLASHER
TO A4 FUSE
BLACK IDENTS
R.H. REAR FLASHER
HAZARD WARNING SYSTEM AS USED ON U.S.A. EXPORT MODELS ONLY
FLASHER SWITCH
L.H. REAR FLASHER
L.H. FRONT FLASHER
L.H. FLASHER WARNING LIGHT
CABLE COLOUR CODE
B BLACK
U BLUE
N BROWN
G GREEN
K PINK
P PURPLE
R RED
S SLATE
W WHITE
Y YELLOW
D DARK
L LIGHT
M MEDIUM

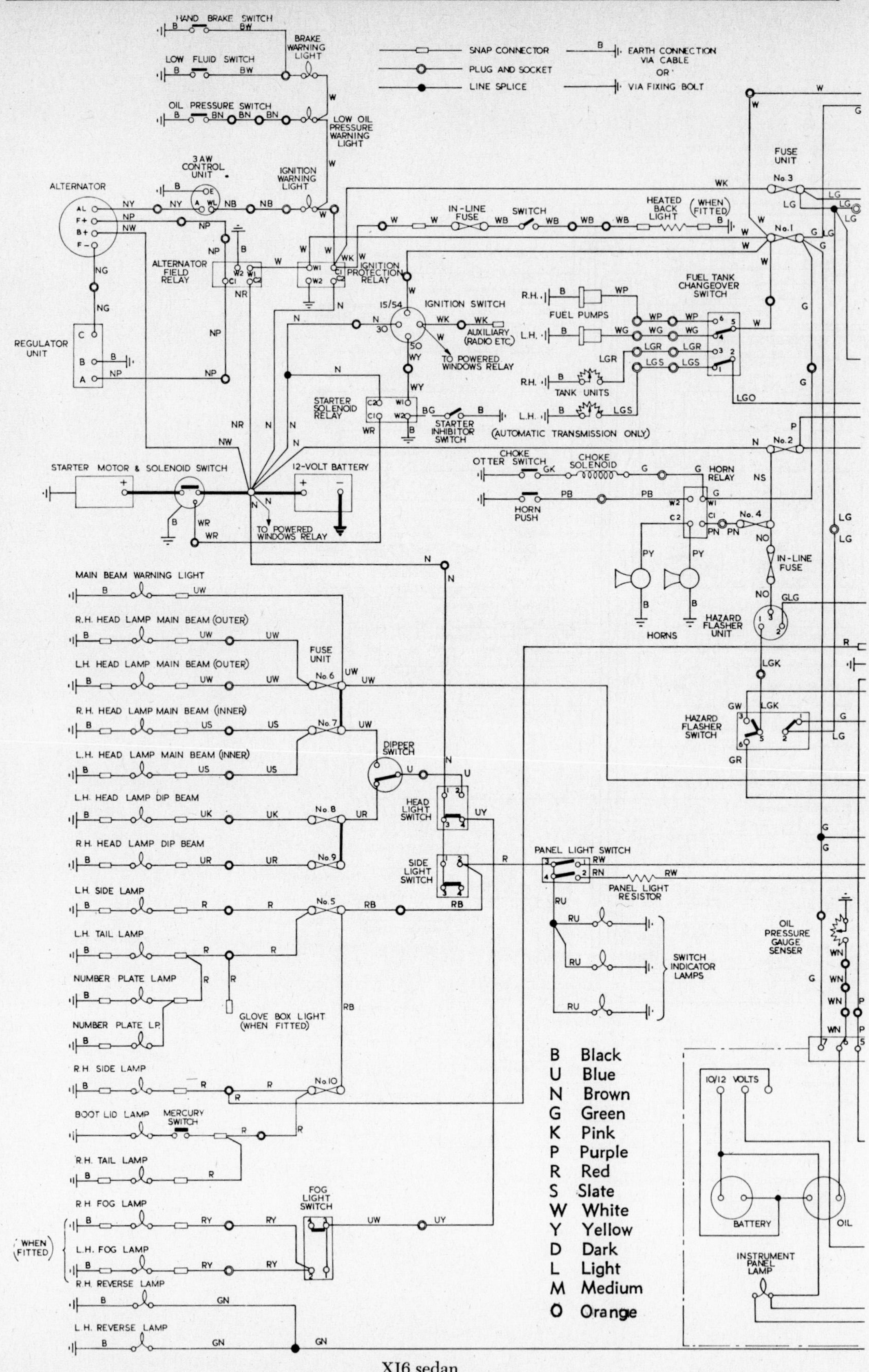
HAND BRAKE SWITCH
BRAKE WARNING LIGHT
LOW FLUID SWITCH
OIL PRESSURE SWITCH
LOW OIL PRESSURE WARNING LIGHT
SNAP CONNECTOR
PLUG AND SOCKET
LINE SPLICE
EARTH CONNECTION VIA CABLE OR
VIA FIXING BOLT
3AW CONTROL UNIT
IGNITION WARNING LIGHT
ALTERNATOR
FUSE UNIT
IN-LINE FUSE
SWITCH
HEATED BACK LIGHT (WHEN FITTED)
ALTERNATOR FIELD RELAY
IGNITION PROTECTION RELAY
REGULATOR UNIT
IGNITION SWITCH
AUXILIARY (RADIO ETC)
TO POWERED WINDOWS RELAY
FUEL PUMPS
FUEL TANK CHANGEOVER SWITCH
TANK UNITS
STARTER SOLENOID RELAY
STARTER INHIBITOR SWITCH
(AUTOMATIC TRANSMISSION ONLY)
STARTER MOTOR & SOLENOID SWITCH
12-VOLT BATTERY
CHOKE OTTER SWITCH
CHOKE SOLENOID
HORN RELAY
HORN PUSH
TO POWERED WINDOWS RELAY
IN-LINE FUSE
HORNS
HAZARD FLASHER UNIT
HAZARD FLASHER SWITCH
MAIN BEAM WARNING LIGHT
R.H. HEAD LAMP MAIN BEAM (OUTER)
L.H. HEAD LAMP MAIN BEAM (OUTER)
R.H. HEAD LAMP MAIN BEAM (INNER)
L.H. HEAD LAMP MAIN BEAM (INNER)
L.H. HEAD LAMP DIP BEAM
R.H. HEAD LAMP DIP BEAM
DIPPER SWITCH
HEAD LIGHT SWITCH
SIDE LIGHT SWITCH
PANEL LIGHT SWITCH
PANEL LIGHT RESISTOR
SWITCH INDICATOR LAMPS
L.H. SIDE LAMP
L.H. TAIL LAMP
NUMBER PLATE LAMP
NUMBER PLATE LP.
GLOVE BOX LIGHT (WHEN FITTED)
OIL PRESSURE GAUGE SENSER
R.H. SIDE LAMP
BOOT LID LAMP
MERCURY SWITCH
R.H. TAIL LAMP
R.H. FOG LAMP
FOG LIGHT SWITCH
(WHEN FITTED)
L.H. FOG LAMP
R.H. REVERSE LAMP
L.H. REVERSE LAMP
10/12 VOLTS
BATTERY
OIL
INSTRUMENT PANEL LAMP
B Black
U Blue
N Brown
G Green
K Pink
P Purple
R Red
S Slate
W White
Y Yellow
D Dark
L Light
M Medium
O Orange

XJ6 sedan

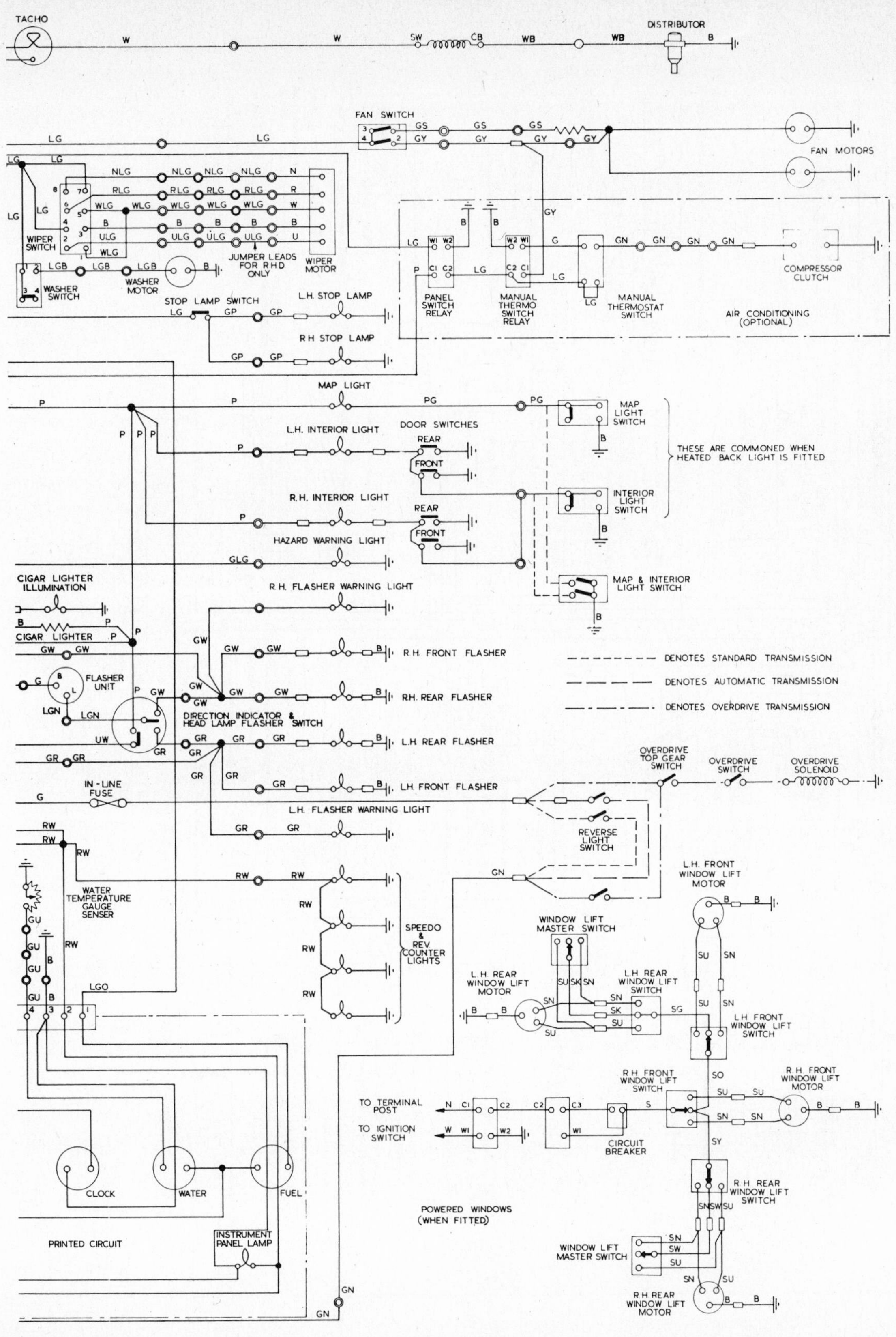
TACHO
DISTRIBUTOR
FAN SWITCH
FAN MOTORS
WIPER SWITCH
JUMPER LEADS FOR RHD ONLY
WIPER MOTOR
WASHER SWITCH
WASHER MOTOR
STOP LAMP SWITCH
L.H. STOP LAMP
R.H. STOP LAMP
PANEL SWITCH RELAY
MANUAL THERMO SWITCH RELAY
MANUAL THERMOSTAT SWITCH
COMPRESSOR CLUTCH
AIR CONDITIONING (OPTIONAL)
MAP LIGHT
MAP LIGHT SWITCH
L.H. INTERIOR LIGHT
DOOR SWITCHES
REAR
FRONT
THESE ARE COMMONED WHEN HEATED BACK LIGHT IS FITTED
R.H. INTERIOR LIGHT
INTERIOR LIGHT SWITCH
HAZARD WARNING LIGHT
MAP & INTERIOR LIGHT SWITCH
CIGAR LIGHTER ILLUMINATION
CIGAR LIGHTER
R.H. FLASHER WARNING LIGHT
R.H. FRONT FLASHER
FLASHER UNIT
R.H. REAR FLASHER
DIRECTION INDICATOR & HEAD LAMP FLASHER SWITCH
L.H. REAR FLASHER
L.H. FRONT FLASHER
DENOTES STANDARD TRANSMISSION
DENOTES AUTOMATIC TRANSMISSION
DENOTES OVERDRIVE TRANSMISSION
OVERDRIVE TOP GEAR SWITCH
OVERDRIVE SWITCH
OVERDRIVE SOLENOID
IN-LINE FUSE
L.H. FLASHER WARNING LIGHT
REVERSE LIGHT SWITCH
WATER TEMPERATURE GAUGE SENSER
SPEEDO & REV. COUNTER LIGHTS
L.H. FRONT WINDOW LIFT MOTOR
WINDOW LIFT MASTER SWITCH
L.H. REAR WINDOW LIFT MOTOR
L.H. REAR WINDOW LIFT SWITCH
L.H. FRONT WINDOW LIFT SWITCH
R.H. FRONT WINDOW LIFT SWITCH
R.H. FRONT WINDOW LIFT MOTOR
TO TERMINAL POST
TO IGNITION SWITCH
CIRCUIT BREAKER
R.H. REAR WINDOW LIFT SWITCH
CLOCK
WATER
FUEL
POWERED WINDOWS (WHEN FITTED)
PRINTED CIRCUIT
INSTRUMENT PANEL LAMP
WINDOW LIFT MASTER SWITCH
R.H. REAR WINDOW LIFT MOTOR

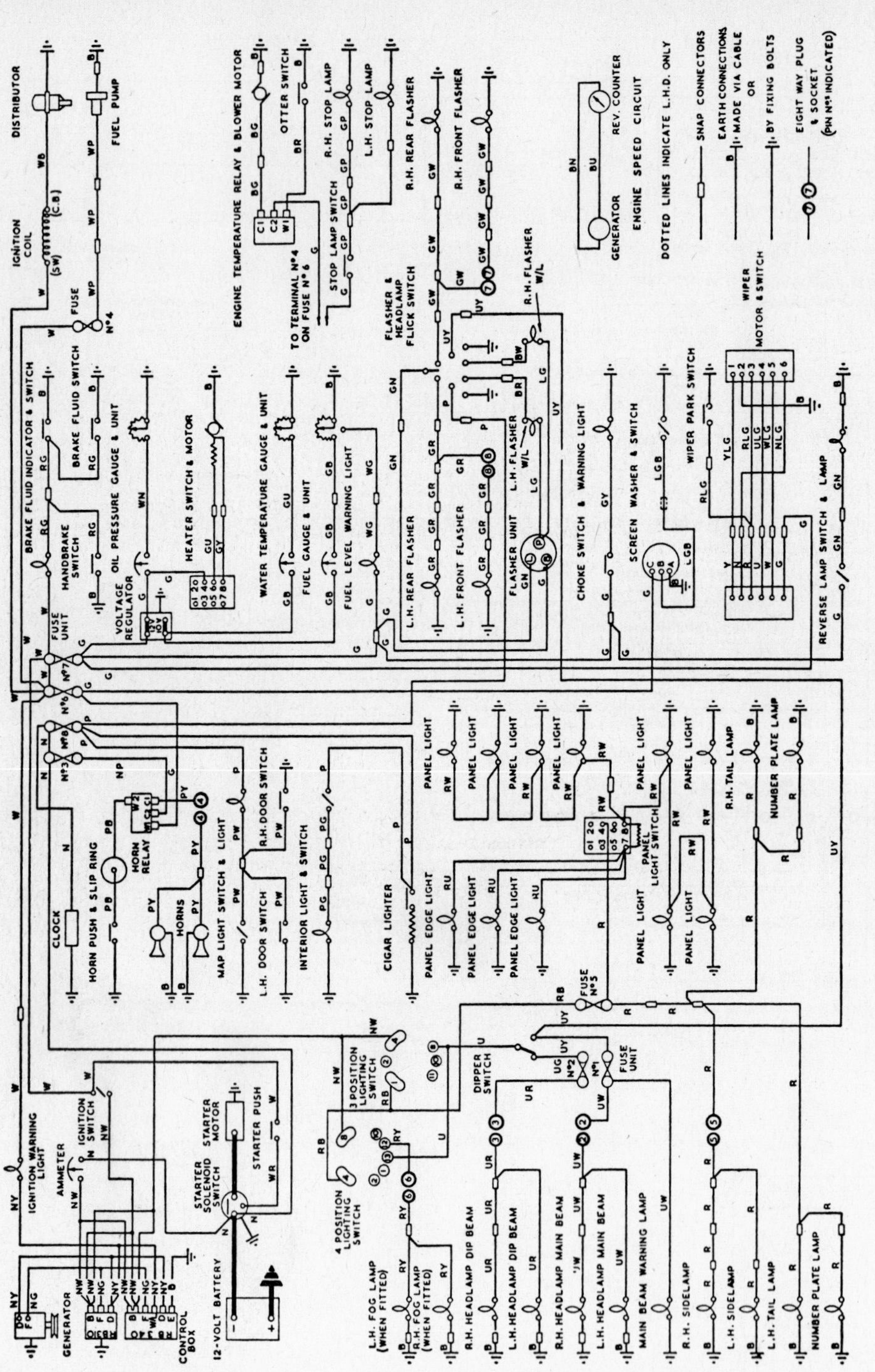

B	BLACK	P	PURPLE	Y	YELLOW
U	BLUE	G	GREEN	D	DARK
N	BROWN	S	SLATE	L	LIGHT
R	RED	W	WHITE	M	MEDIUM

E Type (3.8)

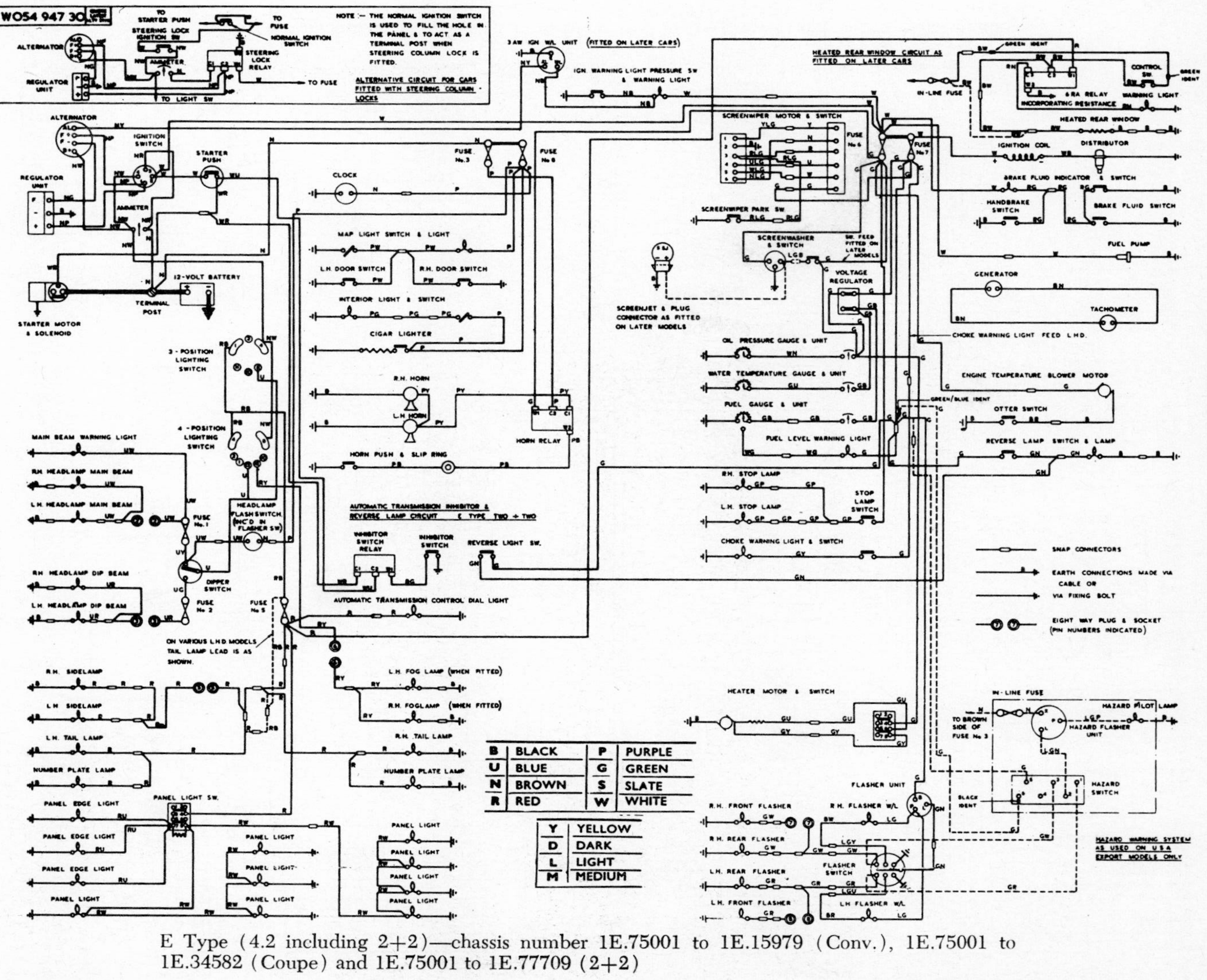

E Type (4.2 including 2+2)—chassis number 1E.75001 to 1E.15979 (Conv.), 1E.75001 to 1E.34582 (Coupe) and 1E.75001 to 1E.77709 (2+2)

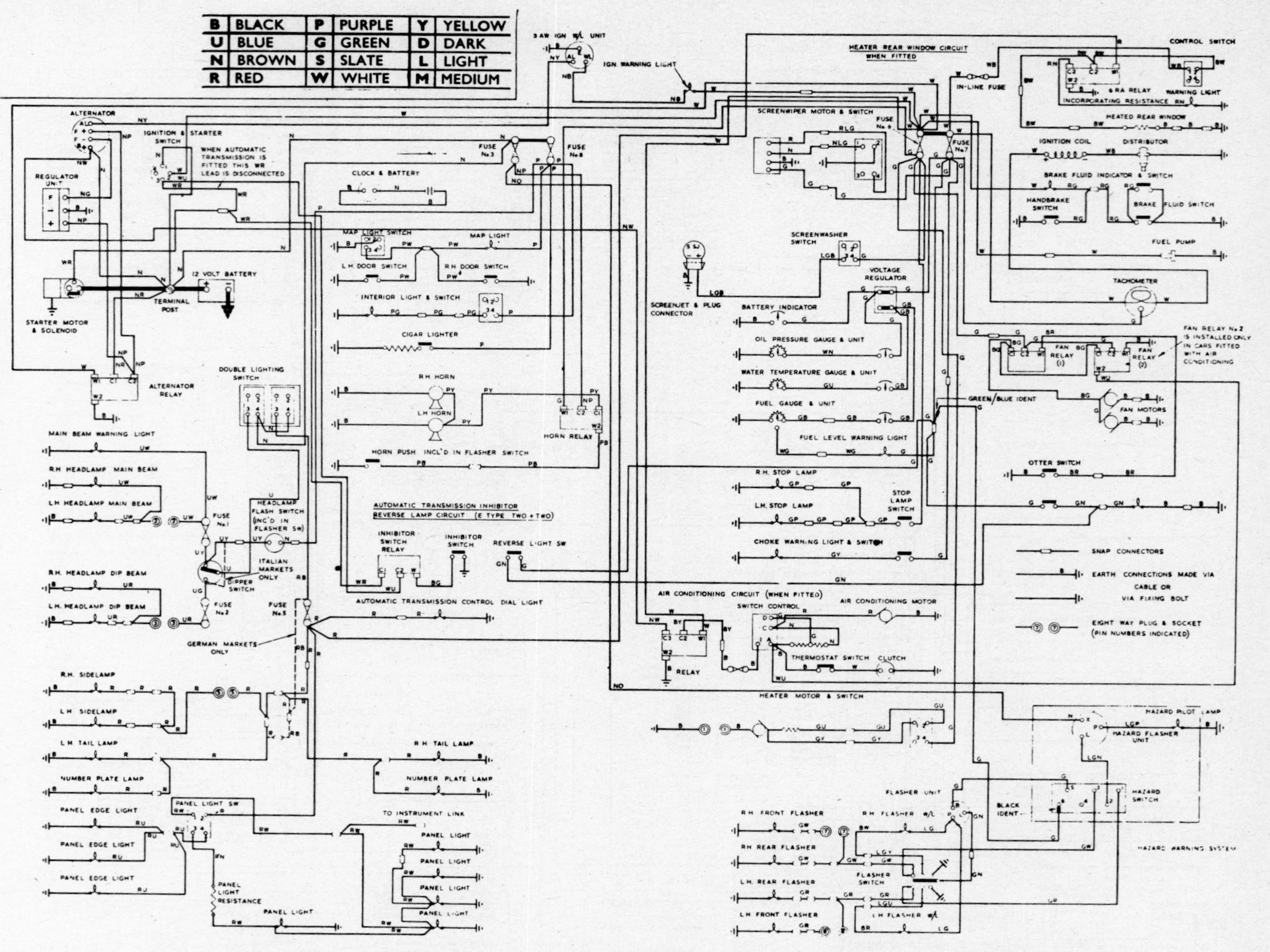

E Type (4.2 including 2+2)—chassis number 1E.15980 (Conv.) and subsequent numbers, 1E.34583 (Coupe) and subsequent numbers and 1E.77710 (2+2) and subsequent numbers

Engine Electrical

DISTRIBUTOR

Removal—Mark II, 3.4S, 3.8S, 420, XJ6, E Type (3.8, 4.2, 2+2)

1. Remove the distributor cap.
2. Remove the low tension wire and vacuum connection.
3. Remove the distributor clamping plate setscrew.

NOTE: If pinch bolt is loosened, it will be necessary to reset the ignition timing.

4. Withdraw the distributor.

Installation

1. To install distributor (if pinch bolt has not been loosened), reverse removal procedures.
2. To insert distributor into block, rotate rotor arm until distributor driving end engages with the distributor driveshaft.
3. Replace and tighten the clamping plate retaining screw.

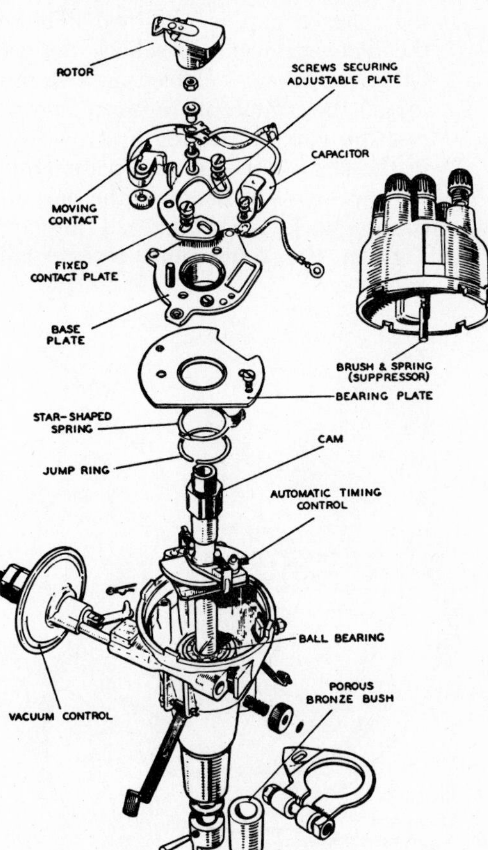

Lucas DMBZ 6A distributor—Mark II (3.4, 3.8), 340, E Type (3.8)

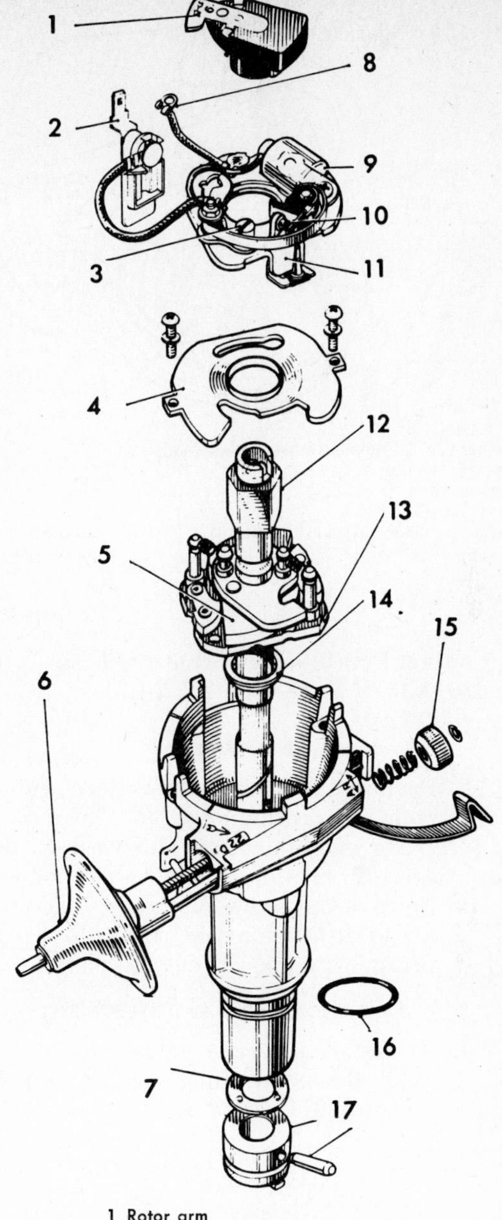

1 Rotor arm
2 Low tension terminal
3 Fixed contact plate securing screw
4 Contact breaker base plate
5 Centrifugal weights
6 Vacuum control unit
7 Thrust washer
8 Contact breaker ground wire
9 Capacitor
10 Contact points
11 Contact breaker moving plate
12 Cam
13 Action plate
14 Spacer
15 Micrometer adjustment nut
16 Oil seal washer
17 Collar and pin

Lucas 22 D6 distributor—3.4S, 3.8S, 420, E Type (1965-67)

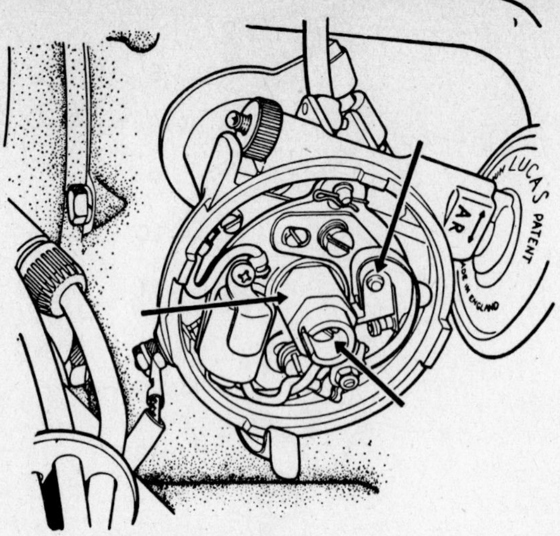

Distributor lubrication points—DMBZ 6A distributor

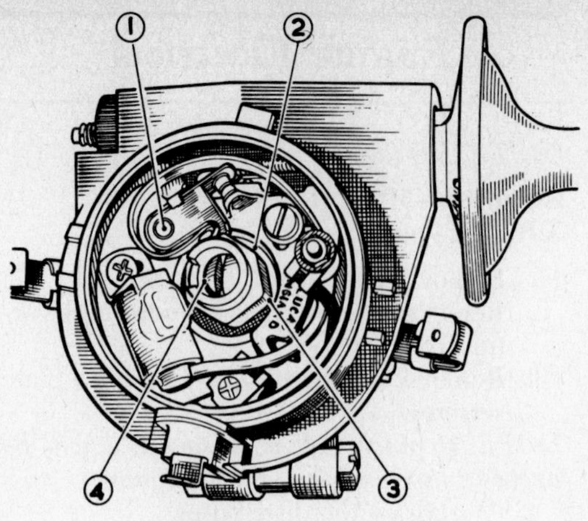

1 Pivot post
2 Contact breaker base plate
3 Cam
4 Rotor arm spindle

Lubrication points on the 22 D6 distributor

Contact Points—Mark II, 3.4S, 3.8S, 420, XJ6, E Type (3.8, 4.2, 2+2)

Removal

1. Remove electrical connections from points to distributor.
2. Being careful not to lose washers or spacers, lift off the movable points.
3. Remove the screw or screws (according to distributor type) from the fixed points plate and lift out the plate.

Installation and Gap Adjustment

1. To install, reverse removal procedure.
2. With the points fully opened, adjust gap to .014″-.016.″
3. On earlier model cars, adjustment is performed by loosening the two contact plate screws and turning the eccentric-headed adjustment screw until the correct gap is obtained. Tighten the plate screws and recheck the gap. On more recent vehicles, just slightly loosen the contact plate screw and adjust the gap by turning a screwdriver in the slot on the contact plate (turning clockwise to decrease the gap and counterclockwise to increase the gap). Tighten the screw and recheck the gap.

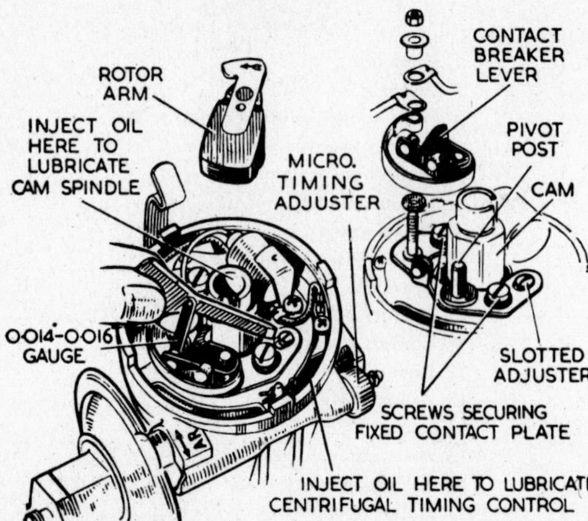

Checking point gap—Mark II (3.4, 3.8), 340, E Type (3.8)

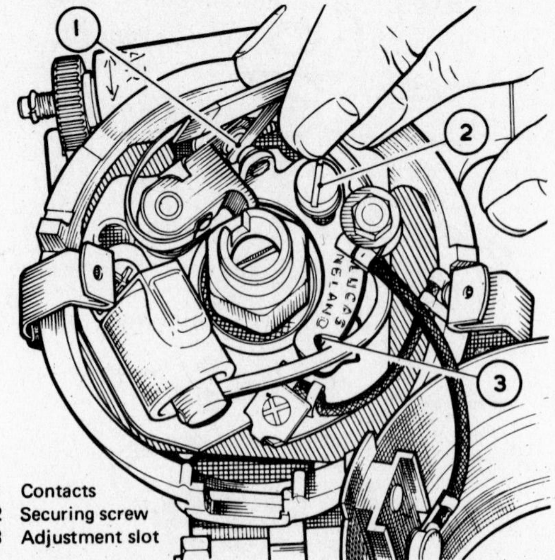

1 Contacts
2 Securing screw
3 Adjustment slot

Checking the point gap on a Lucas 22 D6 distributor—3.4S, 3.8S, 420, E Type (1965-67)

Distributor Installation (After Engine Has Been Disturbed)—Mark II, 3.4S, 3.8S, 420, XJ6, E Type (all)

1. For safety reasons, disconnect coil lead wire.
2. Remove spark plug from number six (front) cylinder and, using a remote starter switch or an assistant, tap starter slowly until compression can be heard or felt escaping from plug hole. At this point, number six cylinder will be on its compression stroke or exhaust stroke. Observe crankshaft damper and continue to tap starter until pointer aligns on TDC mark. This signifies that number six (front) piston is at the top dead center (TDC) of its compression stroke.
3. Insert distributor into block and engage distributor driving end with the driveshaft.
4. Remove distributor cap.
5. Set the micrometer adjustment located on distributor, to the center of the scale.
6. If distributor has been correctly installed and resets flush against block, rotor arm pointer must point to number six (front) cylinder terminal in the cap.
7. Slowly rotate the engine until the specified timing number (see specifications table) on the scale of the crankshaft damper is aligned with the pointer on the oil pan.
8. Connect a 12-volt test light with one wire connected to the distributor terminal and the other to a good ground. Due to the position of the timing pointer, it is suggested that the test lamp method have preference over the timing light.
9. Slowly rotate distributor until test lamp lights.
10. Tighten distributor plate pinch bolt.
11. Recheck timing.
12. Due to differences in fuel octane, it will be necessary to experiment with the various positions of the micrometer adjustment up to six clicks either way. On emission engines (XJ6 and E type), disconnect vacuum retard and, using a strobe light, set timing to 10° B.T.D.C at idle. With retard line connected, timing should retard to T.D.C. at idle. See specifications table.

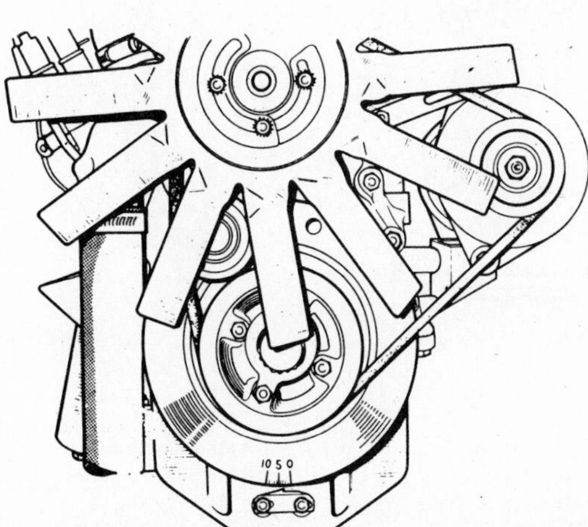

Ignition timing scale with pointer on oil pan—all except XJ6

Ignition timing scale with pointer on block—XJ6

Ignition Timing—Mark II, 3.4S, 3.8S, 420, XJ6, E Type (3.8, 4.2, 2+2)

See Distributor Installation (After Engine Has Been Disturbed), Steps 5-12.

GENERATOR AND ALTERNATOR

CAUTION: If vehicle is equipped with an alternator, observe the following precautions:

1. When checking the car's electrical system, do not use an ohmmeter incorporating a hand driven generator.
2. Do not reverse the battery connections, for this will damage the diode rectifiers of the alternator.
3. Cars equipped with alternators have negative-ground electrical systems.
4. Do not ground the brown-green wire if it has been disconnected from the alternator. It may be wise to cover this wire end with tape if it is to be hanging near a ground.

5. Never ground the alternator main output wire.
6. Diode damage will result if the alternator is run on an open circuit when the field windings are energized.
7. Do not use an elecctric welder on an alternator equipped car without disconnecting the battery, and the wires from the alternator and control unit.
8. Do not attempt to polarize an alternator.

Generator Removal—Includes Models C42, C45 PVS-6, C45 PV-6, C48

On those models equipped with power steering, it will be necessary to disconnect the hoses at the pump assembly (attached to the rear of the generator) and elevate them to prevent oil leakage. When installing the generator, connect the hoses and replace lost fluid. If the car has a windshield washer unit, it may be necessary to remove the bottle and its holder. The following

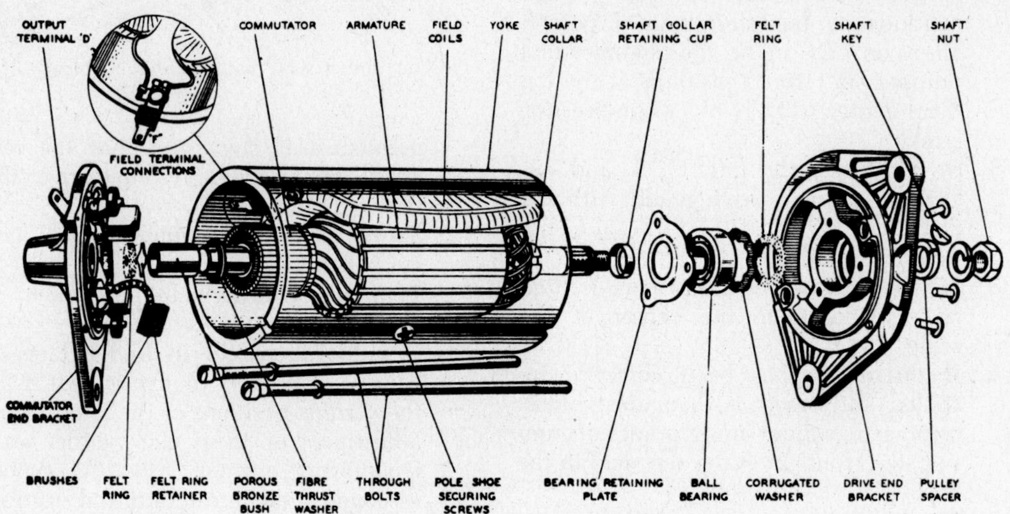

Exploded view of model C42 generator—E Type (3.8), Mark II, 3.4S, 3.8S

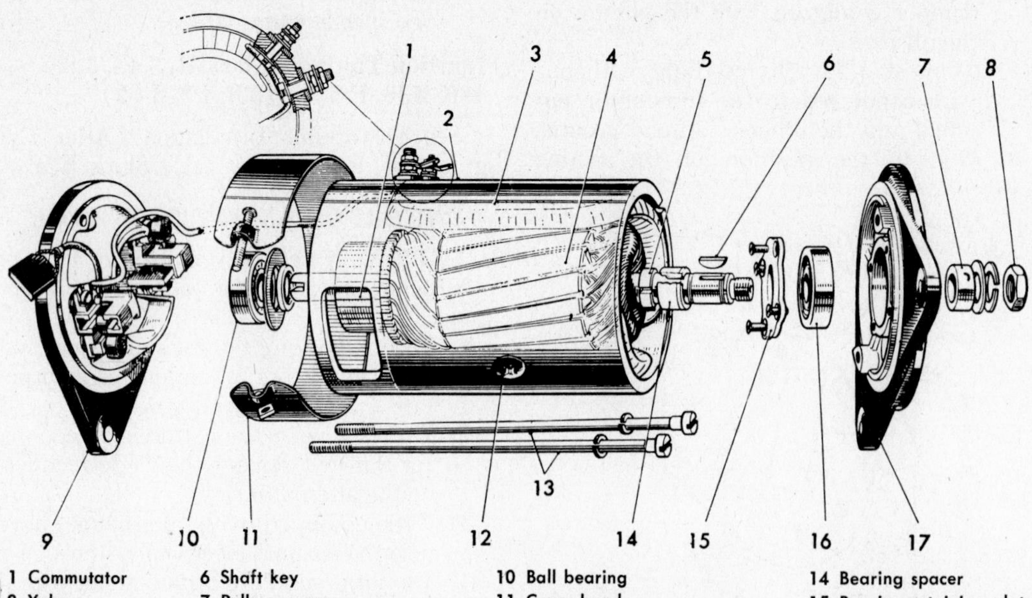

1 Commutator
2 Yoke
3 Field coils
4 Armature
5 Shaft collar
6 Shaft key
7 Pulley spacer
8 Shaft nut
9 Commutator end bracket
10 Ball bearing
11 Cover band
12 Pole shoe securing screws
13 Through-bolts
14 Bearing spacer
15 Bearing retaining plate
16 Ball bearing
17 Drive-end bracket

Exploded view of C48 generator—3.4S, 3.8S, Mark II

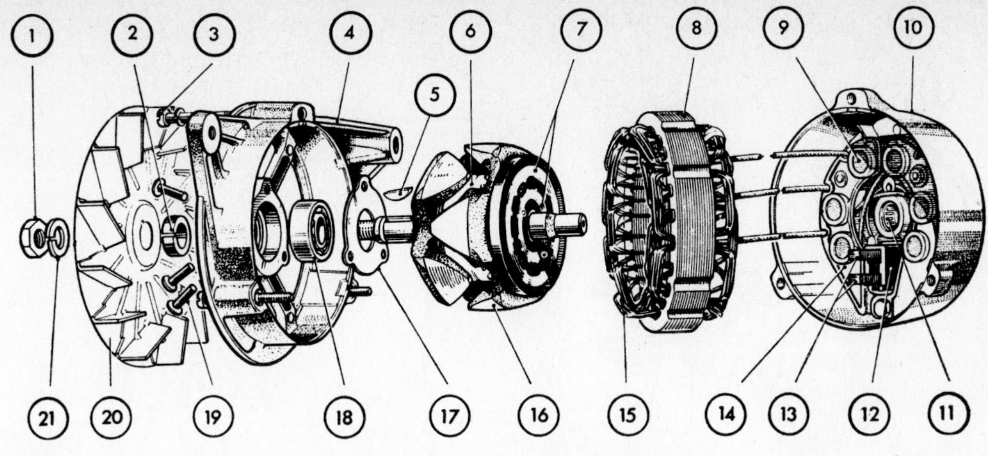

1 Shaft nut
2 Bearing collar
3 Through bolts (3)
4 Drive end-bracket
5 Key
6 Rotor (field) winding
7 Slip-rings
8 Stator laminations
9 Silicon diodes (6)
10 Slip-ring end-bracket
11 Needle roller bearing
12 Brush box moulding
13 Brushes
14 Diode heat sink
15 Stator windings
16 Rotor
17 Bearing retaining plate
18 Ball bearing
19 Bearing retaining plate
20 Fan
21 Spring washer

Exploded view of Lucas 11 A.C. alternator—420, XJ6, E Type (4.2)

generator removal procedure applies to the following models–Mark II (3.4, 3.8), S models (3.4, 3.8), E type (3.8).

1. Disconnect the cables from the rear of the generator, noting that they are of different sizes.
2. Remove the nut and bolt holding the adjusting bracket to the generator.
3. Remove the two mounting bolts and lift out the generator.
4. Remove generator belt.

Generator Installation

1. To install, reverse removal procedure.
2. Install belt and adjust tension to 1/2″ at a point halfway between the water pump and the generator pulleys.

Alternator Removal—Lucas 11 A.C. and Butec

1. Disconnect the cables from the end cover and note the color and location of each so that they can be replaced properly.
2. Remove the mounting bolts and alternator belt.
3. Lift out the alternator.
4. If the car has air-conditioning, it will be necessary to move the compressor in order to gain access to the alternator. Support the compressor in the engine compartment after detaching it.

CAUTION: DO NOT, UNDER ANY CIRCUMSTANCES, LOOSEN OR DISCONNECT THE COMPRESSOR HOSES. REFRIGERANT GAS LEAKAGE MAY CAUSE SERIOUS EYE AND SKIN INJURIES.

Alternator Installation

1. To install, reverse the removal procedure.
2. Install and tighten belt. Belt deflection should be 1/2″ (12 mm.) at a point midway between the two pulleys.

IMPORTANT: When tightening belt tension, apply leverage ONLY to the drive end bracket and not to any other part. In this way, bearing damage can be avoided.

3. If the car is equipped with air-conditioning, replace the compressor and mounting bracket.

VOLTAGE REGULATOR—MARK II, 3.4S, 3.8S, E Type (3.8)

Adjustment—Models RB. 310 and RB. 340

These two regulators are basically the same, each containing three separate units:

a. A single-contact voltage regulator
b. A single-contact current regulator
c. A cut-out relay.

Adjustment procedures for these regulators are basically the same with the exception that the RB 310 uses adjustment screws and the RB 340 uses toothed cams.

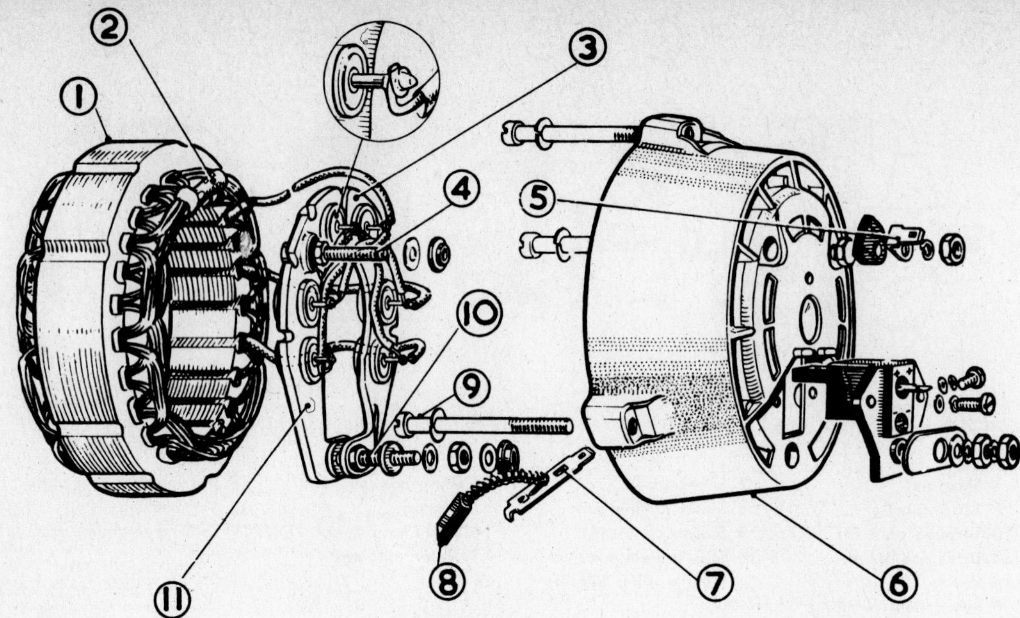

1 Stator
2 Star point
3 Negative heat sink and anode diodes (black)
4 Warning light terminal AL
5 Field terminal
6 Slip-ring end cover
7 Terminal blade retaining tongue
8 Rotor slip-ring brush
9 Through-bolts
10 Output terminals
11 Positive heat sink and cathode base diodes (red)

Exploded view of the slip-ring end cover (11 A.C. alternator)

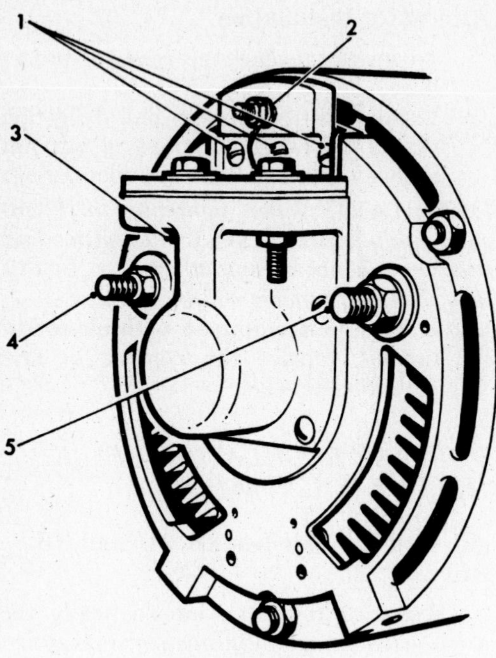

1 A.C. output tappings
2 Sensing diode terminal
3 Field terminal
4 Negative DC terminal
5 Positive DC terminal

BUTEC alternator terminals—XJ6 with air conditioning

Adjustment instructions for each of these units are as follows:

Adjusting the single-contact voltage regulator

1. Adjust this setting if the battery fails to remain charged or if the generator output does not drop when the battery is fully charged.

IMPORTANT: Before touching the regula-

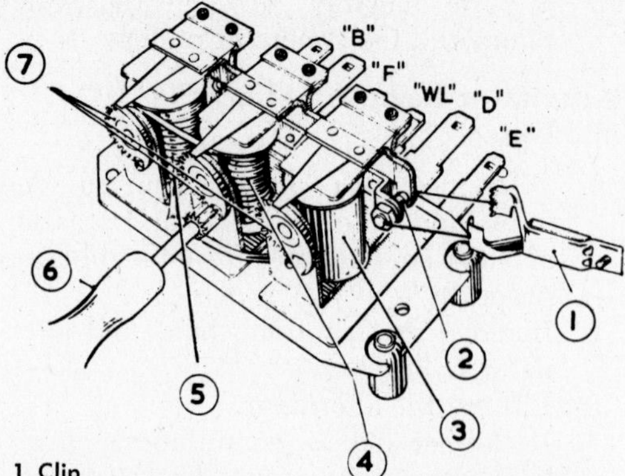

1 Clip
2 Voltage regulator contacts
3 Voltage regulator
4 Current regulator
5 Cut-out relay
6 Setting tool
7 Adjustment cams

Adjuster identification on the RB. 340 regulator showing clip used to close the voltage regulator contacts

tor, make sure that the battery is good and the generator belt is tightened to a deflection of 1/2". Use only a good quality moving coil voltmeter to check the regulator.

2. Disconnect the terminal B wire from the control box.
3. Connect voltmeter leads to terminal D and to a ground.

CAUTION: The voltage regulator adjustment and test should not be carried out for longer than 30 seconds or heating of the shunt coil will result in false readings.

4. Increase engine speed to 2000 rpm (1800 rpm for the C48 generator). This will produce a generator speed of 3000 rpm. At this generator speed, the open circuit voltage reading should be within the following limits:

Charging Circuit	Temperature	Voltage Range
C 45 PV-6 &	50°F.	15.1-15.7
RB 310	68°F.	14.9-15.5
	86°F.	14.7-15.3
	104°F.	14.5-15.1
C 42 &	50°F.	15.0-15.6
RB 340	68°F.	14.8-15.4
	86°F.	14.6-15.2
	104°F.	14.4-15.0
C 48 &	50°F.	15.0-15.6
RB 340	68°F.	14.8-15.4
	86°F.	14.6-15.2
	104°F.	14.4-15.0

5. If the voltmeter reading is not within

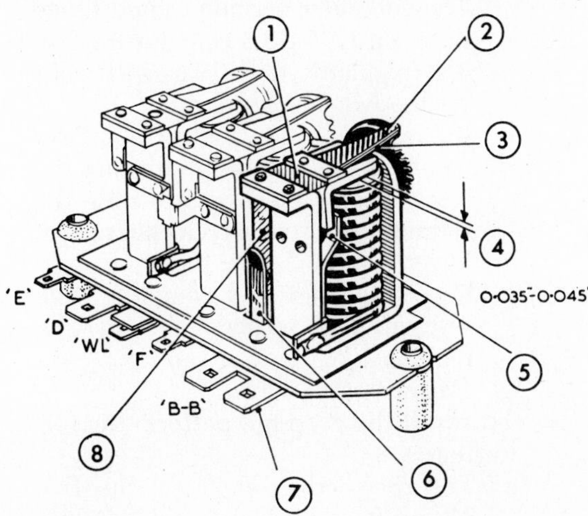

1 Hinge spring
2 Armature
3 Bi-metal backing spring
4 Armature to bobbin core gap
5 Armature back stop
6 Fixed contact bracket
7 B-B terminal plate
8 Moving contact blade

Cut-out air gap setting on the RB. 340 regulator—Mark II (3.4, 3.8), 340, 3.4S, 3.8S, E Type with C42 generator

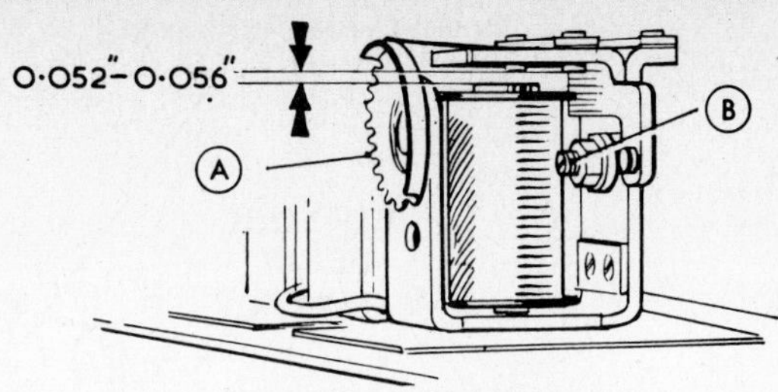

A Turn cam to minimum lift
B Slacken contact screw

Voltage regulator gap setting—RB. 340 regulator

the specified range, adjust as follows:

a. Rotate the voltage adjustment screw or cam clockwise to raise the voltage and counterclockwise to lower it.
b. Turn off engine.
c. Restart engine, raise engine speed to 2000 rpm and make any further adjustments.

Adjusting the single-contact current regulator

1. Short-circuit the voltage regulator contact by placing a clip between the insulated fixed contact bracket and the voltage regulator frame.
2. Disconnect the terminal B wires.
3. Connect an ammeter between the disconnected wires and terminal B.
4. Start engine and run to a speed of 2700 rpm (4000 generator rpm). At this speed, the ammeter should read 24 to 26 amps. (total generator output) for the C45 PV-6 generator and the C45 PVS-6, and 30 amps. for the C42. When testing the C48, run the engine to 1800 rpm (3000 generator rpm). The output for the C48 generator is 35 amps.
5. If the ammeter reading for a particular generator differs greatly from the above specifications, turn the current adjusting screw or cam (the center one) clockwise to raise the setting or counterclockwise to lower it.

CAUTION: This current regulator test should not be carried out longer than 30 seconds or false readings may result.

6. Reconnect all wires.

Adjusting the regulator cut-out relay

If the regulator has been tested and correctly set and the battery still fails to charge, then the cut-out may be set improp-

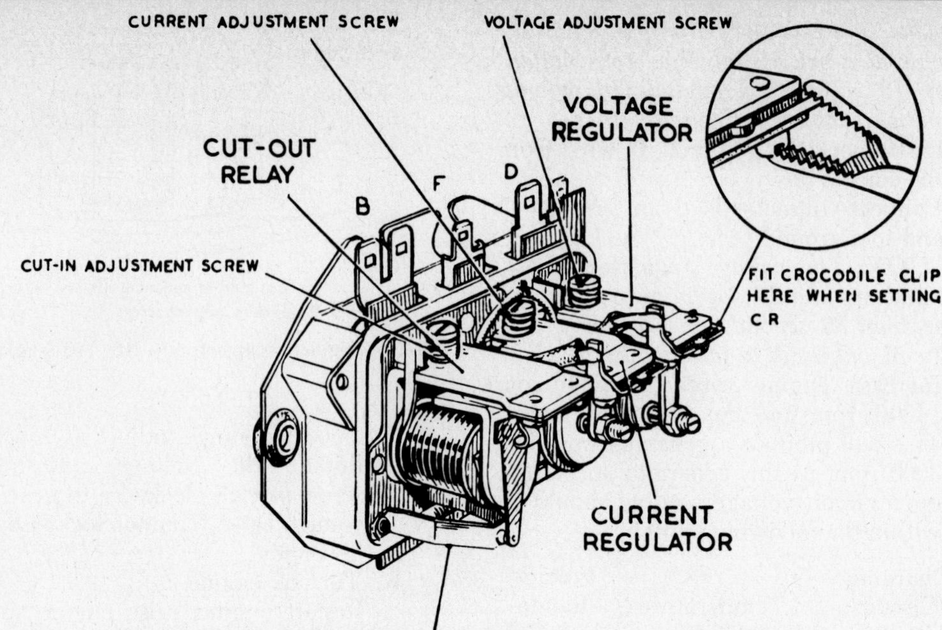

Adjustment screw location on the RB. 310 voltage regulator—early E Type (3.8) with C45 PV-6 generator

erly. There are two adjustments to be made to the cut-out relay: the cut-in adjustment and the drop-off adjustment.

1. To adjust the cut-in, perform the following:
   a. Connect a voltmeter between terminal D and a ground.
   b. Turn on headlamps or other electrical load. It is often difficult to observe contact closing since the cut-in and battery voltages are nearly equal; therefore, if the battery voltage is lowered by the headlamps, the observation is made easier.

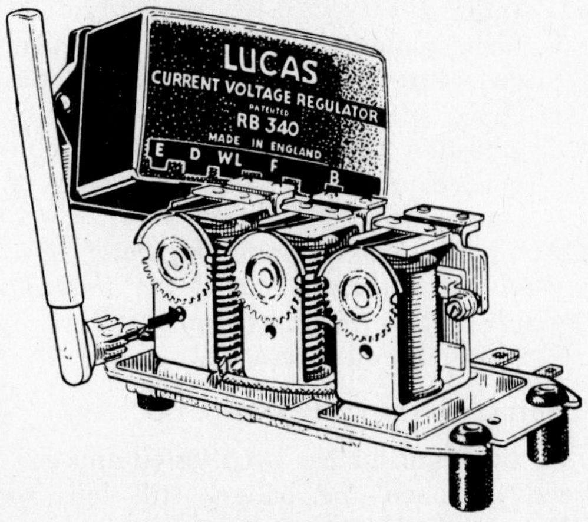

Cut-out adjustment—RB. 340

   c. Start the engine and slowly increase its speed.
   d. Observe the voltmeter. The voltmeter should rise steadily and drop slightly at the moment the contacts close. The cut-in voltage is the voltmeter reading that occurs just before the voltmeter pointer drops. The voltmeter reading should range between 12.7–13.3 volts for the RB. 310 regulator and 12.6–13.4 volts for the RB. 340 regulator.
   e. If the cut-in voltage does not meet specifications, adjust by turning the screw (cam) clockwise to raise the setting or counterclockwise to lower it.
   f. Repeat the test and complete each test within 30 seconds to avoid false readings..
   g. Reconnect all wires.
2. To adjust the drop-off, perform the following:
   a. The specified drop-off for the RB. 310 is 9.5–11.0 volts and 9.3–11.2 volts for the RB. 340.
   b. Remove the wires from the B terminal.
   c. Connect a voltmeter between terminal B and a ground.
   d. Start the engine and increase speed

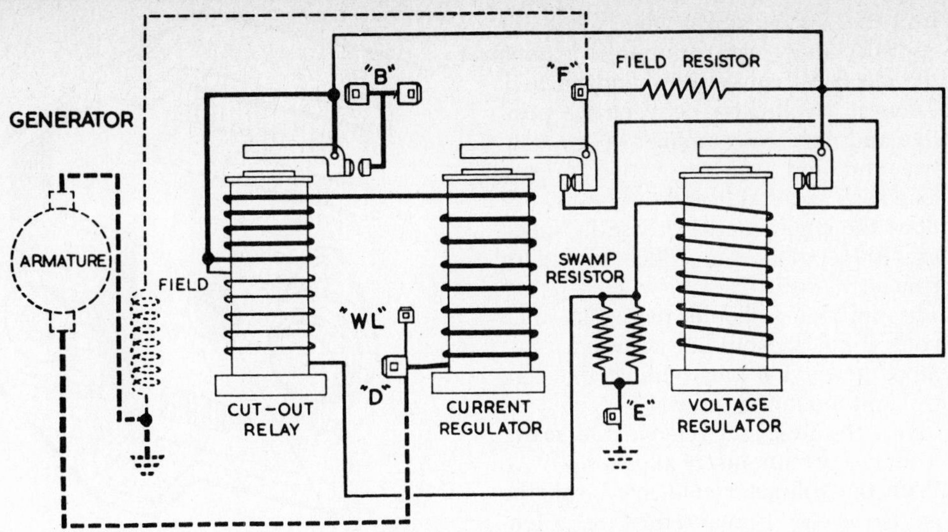

Circuit diagram of the RB. 340 regulator

until the cut-in speed is exceeded (about 1800 engine rpm).

e. Slowly decrease engine speed and observe voltmeter.

f. The contacts should open at the specified voltage (stated in Step a. above) and the voltmeter should suddenly drop to zero.

g. Adjustment is performed by carefully bending the contact bracket Closing the gap will increase the voltage while opening it will decrease it.

Polarization of the DC Regulator—Mark II 3.4S, 3.8S, E Type (3.8)

With the generator and regulator installed in the car, remove the wire from the regulator F (field) terminal and touch it (for just an instant) to the B terminal of the regulator. The generator and regulator are now in the same polarity as the rest of the electrical system.

ALTERNATOR OUTPUT CONTROL UNIT ADJUSTMENT—420, XJ6, E TYPE (4.2)

The 4TR control unit is similar to the vibrating contact voltage regulator except that it operates on transistors rather than vibrating contacts. This unit does not require a cut-out because the alternator diodes prevent reverse current from flowing. The alternator limits the level of current output so a current regulator is not required.

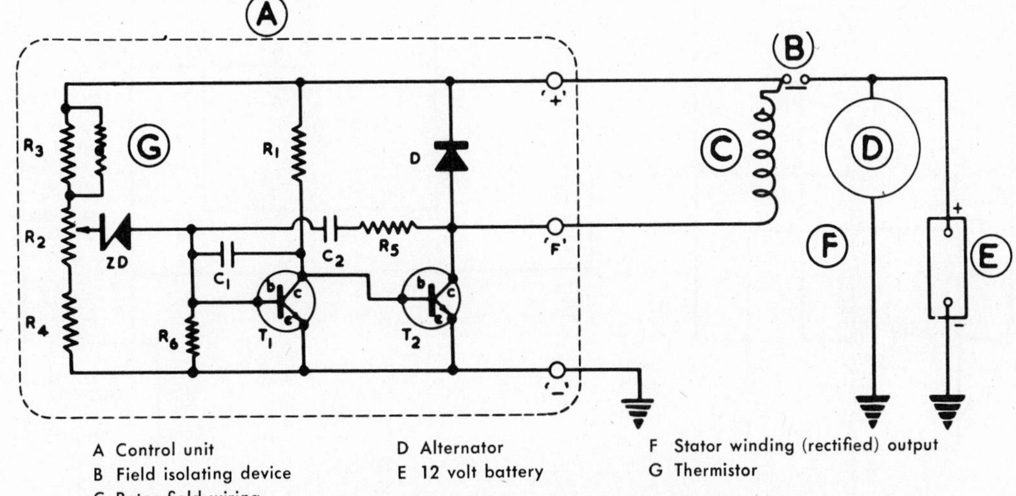

Circuit diagram of the alternator output control unit (Lucas 4TR)—420, XJ6 (without air conditioning), E Type (4.2)

1. Run the engine at charging speed for approximately eight minutes leaving the electrical connections undisturbed.
2. Connect a voltmeter between the positive and negative terminals of the control unit and turn on a two ampere load such as the side and tail lights.
3. Start the engine and increase its speed to 1500 engine rpm (3000 alternator rpm).
4. The voltmeter should read 13.9–14.3 volts; if not, it should be adjusted.
5. Stop the engine and remove the control unit mounting screws.
6. Invert the unit and remove the sealer from the potentiometer adjuster.
7. With the voltmeter connected, run the engine at 1500 rpm and turn the potentiometer adjuster slot clockwise to increase the setting or counterclockwise to decrease it.

CAUTION: Adjustment should be made carefully since only a very small movement of the adjuster causes large voltage changes.

8. Recheck the setting and replace the control unit.
9. If the alternator is functioning properly and the control unit still fails to control voltage to specified limits, re-

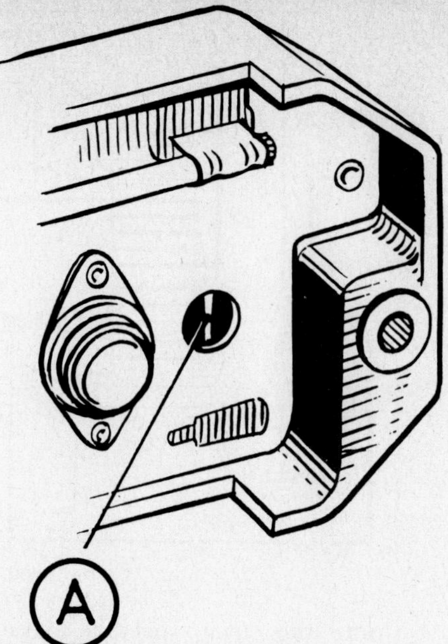

Potentiometer location (A) on the Lucas 4TR control unit—420, XJ6 (without air cond.) and E Type (4.2)

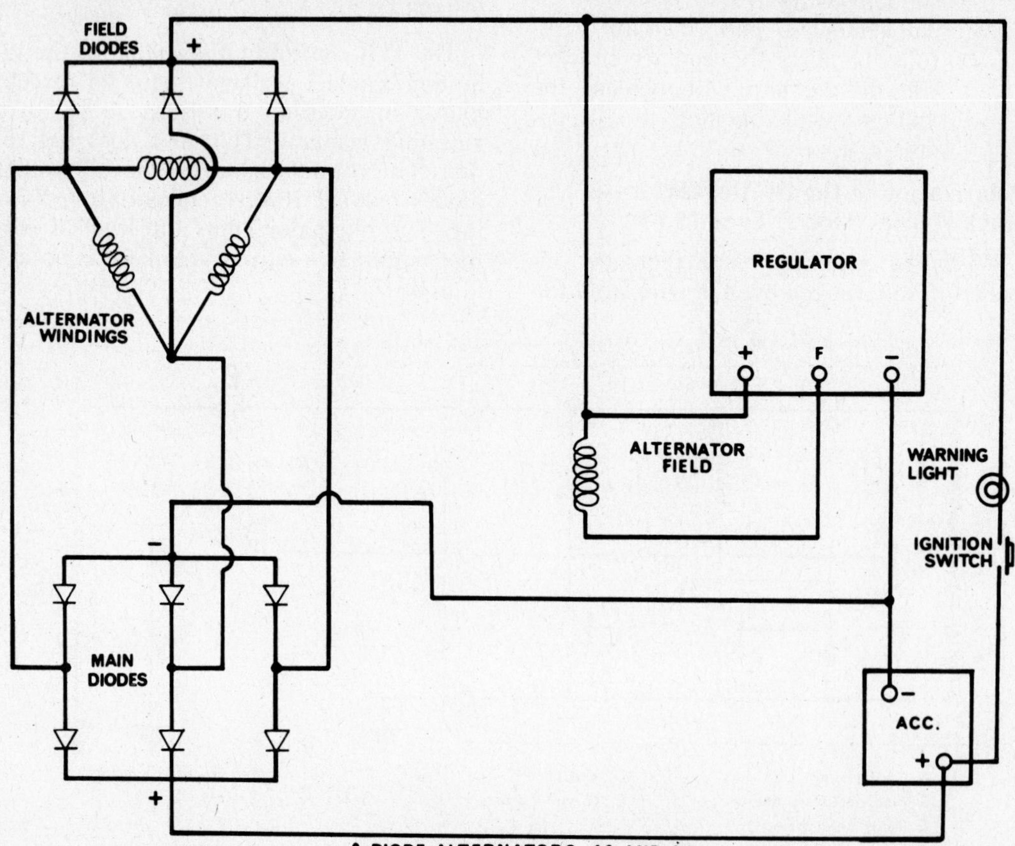

Circuit diagram for the BUTEC alternator—XJ6 with air conditioning

place the unit. Due to its complexity and design, it is not to be disassembled or repaired.

CAUTION: If vehice is equipped with an alternator output control unit, there are certain precautions to be followed. These precautions are listed under the heading "Generator and Alternator".

BATTERY

Maintenance

1. Keep the battery and its connections clean and dry.
2. Check electrolyte level weekly (more frequently in warm weather).
3. When adding water during extremely cold weather, do so just prior to operating the car; in this way, freezing can be prevented.
4. Use only distilled or demineralized water when filling the battery. In an emergency, clean rain water or melted snow can be used but never water containing salt, chemicals, or any impurities.
5. The surface of the electrolyte should be just level with the tops of the separators between the cells.
6. Before installing the cable connectors, clean both the cables and the terminals and coat the terminals with clean petroleum jelly.
7. Keep the vent holes in the filler caps clean.

Service Precautions

1. On some later models, such as the XJ6, a new type of battery is used—the Lucas Model C.A. battery. It is equipped with an air lock device designed to simplify the filling procedure. This device consists of a one-piece vent cover with six (one for each filler hole) perforated tubes attached. The perforations make them functional air valves. Air or water is admitted to the battery only when the tubes are depressed. If the acid level is below the bottom of the tubes, pour distilled water into the trough and allow it to run down until all the tubes are filled. To avoid overfilling, never use a plunger type battery filler because it will depress the sliding tubes. Therefore, always keep the vent cover in position when refilling. This cover contains no rubber sealing plugs so, when removing the battery, extreme caution must be taken to avoid spilling any acid. The C.A. battery has no provision in the cover for the insertion of a heavy discharge tester.
2. *IMPORTANT: Never use an unshielded light when checking a battery, particularly when it is charging. The mixture of hydrogen and oxygen given off by the battery can be very explosive.*
3. All late model Jaguars have a negative ground electrical system but some of the earlier models (Mark II, 340 3.4S, 3.8S, 3.8 E type) had a positive ground system. Before doing any electrical work, be sure you know the grounded side of the electrical system.

Hydrometer Test

1. The specific gravity of the acid in each cell can be measured by the use of a hydrometer. The amount of specific gravity measured determines the condition of the battery.
2. All cells should read approximately the same and the readings adjusted to agree with specific gravity specifications at 60°F.
3. For every 5°F above 60°F add .002 to the hydrometer reading and for every 5°F below, subtract .002 from the reading. This 60°F is electrolyte temperature and should be measured by immersing a thermometer into the electrolyte.
4. To determine battery condition, the specific gravity reading should be compared to the figures in the following table:

State of Battery	*Specific Gravity*
Fully Charged	1.270-1.290
Half Discharged	1.190-1.210
Fully Discharged	1.110-1.130

5. To avoid false readings, do not perform hydrometer test immediately after filling battery.
6. In addition to determining specific gravity of battery acid, the hydrometer test can indicate certain causes for battery failure before it occurs. The readings in each cell should be approximately the same; if not, then an internal fault in the cell is indicated. The appearance of the electrolyte taken into the hydrometer can be an indication of plate condition. If the electro-

lyte is dirty or there are particles in suspension, then the plates may be in bad condition.

Jump Starting Precautions

When jump starting a car, certain precautions should be taken to prevent damage to either car's electrical system:

1. When jump starting a car equipped with an alternator, disconnect the alternator lead before connecting the two batteries. This will prevent the possibility of damage being done to the diodes if the two batteries are incorrectly connected.
2. When linking the two batteries, *make sure* that like terminals are connected —positive to positive, negative to negative—even though one car may be positive ground and the other negative.
3. To avoid sparks, always connect the ground terminals last and disconnect them first.
4. Batteries produce *explosive* hydrogen gas; therefore, be careful not to create sparks around the battery.
5. Make sure that the battery supplying the boost is of the proper voltage and amperage to handle the load. Do not use too much voltage or electrical damage may result.
6. If the engine does not start, do not leave the jumper cables connected unless one engine is running.

STARTER MOTOR

XJ6 (4.2)

This model uses an M45G pre-engaged type starter.

Removal

1. Disconnect the battery.
2. Remove oil gauge sending unit from oil filter body.
3. Disconnect the solenoid and main wires from the starter motor and tag each wire.
4. Remove the setscrews and washers holding the motor to the engine.
5. Remove the starter.

Installation

1. To install, reverse the removal procedure. Since the setscrews are finely threaded, be careful when installing them.

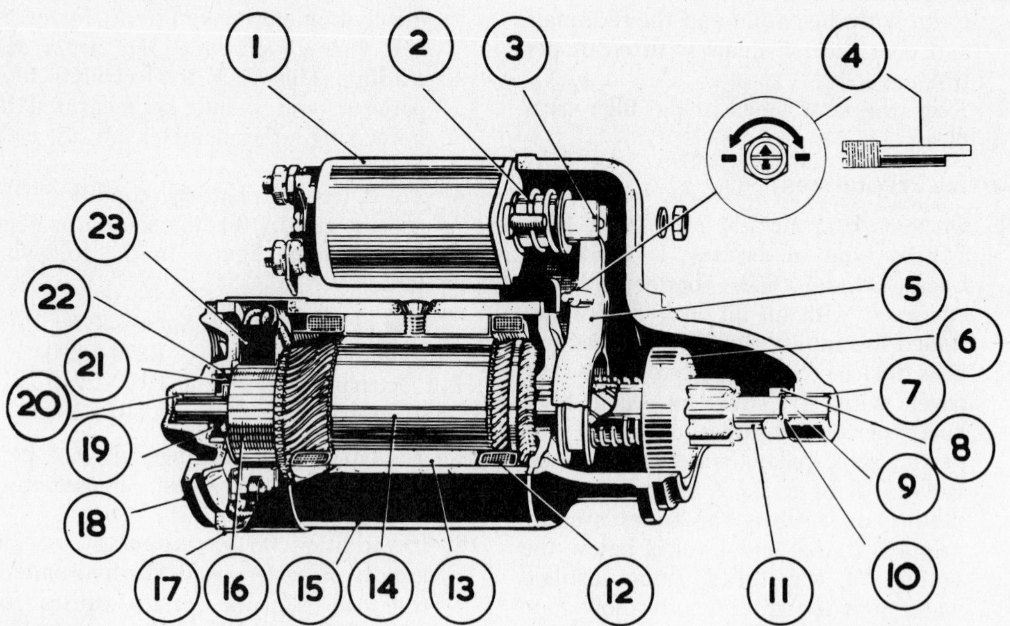

1 Actuating solenoid
2 Return spring
3 Clevis pin
4 Eccentric pivot pin
5 Engaging lever
6 Roller clutch
7 Porous bronze bushing
8 Thrust collar
9 Jump ring
10 Thrust ring
11 Armature shaft extension
12 Field ring
13 Pole shoes
14 Armature
15 Yoke
16 Commutator
17 Band cover
18 Commutator end-bracket
19 Thrust washer
20 Porous bronze bushing
21 Brake shoes and cross peg
22 Brake ring
23 Brushes

Model M45G pre-engaged starter motor—420, XJ6, E Type (4.2)

420

The Jaguar 420 uses a model M45G pre-engaged type starter.

Removal

1. Scribe the position of the hood hinge on the hood.
2. Remove the hood.
3. Remove the battery.
4. Remove the oil filter assembly.
5. Disconnect the wires from the starter and tag them for identification.
6. The motor is secured to its housing by two setscrews and lockwashers. Remove these screws and washers, carefully bend the carburetor drain pipe and remove the starter motor. Difficulty may arise with the bottom setscrew. It must be removed from underneath the car.

Installation

1. To install, reverse the removal procedure.
2. When installing the oil filter unit, replace the joint.

E Type (4.2), 2+2—1965-1971

The E type uses a model M45G pre-engaged type starter.

Removal

1. Disconnect the battery ground.
2. Disconnect the wires from the starter motor and tag them for identification.
3. Remove the distributor.
4. Remove the setscrews and washers holding the motor to the housing.
5. Carefully bend the carburetor drain pipes.
6. Remove the starter motor.

Installation

1. To install, reverse the removal procedure.
2. To prevent cross-threading, carefully install the setscrews.
3. Insert the distributor into the block and turn the rotor until the driving end engages with the distributor driveshaft and drops into place. Secure with the clamping plate. If the pinchbolt has been loosened or removed, the engine will have to be timed. For timing information, see Distributor Installation (After Engine Has Been Disturbed).

E Type (3.8)—1961 through 1964

This E type uses a model M45G inertia drive starter.

Removal

1. Disconnect the battery ground.
2. Detach the wires from the starter motor.
3. Disconnect the rubber hoses from the brake servo vacuum located on the firewall above the starter. Tag or mark these hoses so that they can be replaced to their proper location.
4. Remove the vacuum tank from firewall.
5. Remove starter mounting bolts and lift out starter.

Installation

1. To install, reverse the removal procedure.

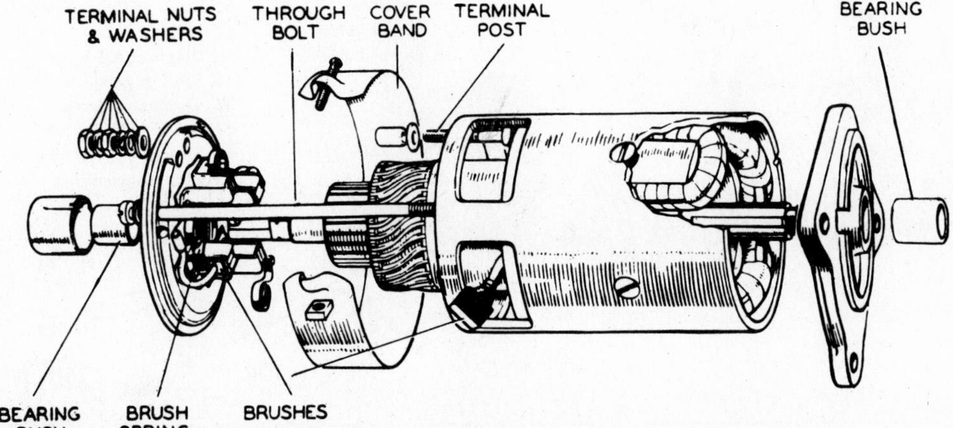

Exploded view of model M45G inertia drive starter—Mark II (3.4, 3.8, 340), 3.4S, 3.8S, E Type (3.8)

3.4S and 3.8S

The 3.4S and the 3.8S models use a model M45G inertia drive starter.

Removal

1. This starter can only be removed from underneath the car.
2. Remove battery ground cable.
3. Disconnect wires from the starter motor.
4. Remove motor securing strap.
5. On those cars having automatic transmissions, disconnect the filler tube extension.
6. Remove starter.

Installation

1. Installation is the reverse of removal.

Mark II Models

The Jaguar Mark II models use either a model M418G or M45G inertia drive starter.

Removal

1. Disconnect battery ground cable.
2. Remove the wires from their starter motor terminals.
3. Remove both seat cushions.
4. Remove gearshift lever knob and panel from between the seats.
5. Remove trim panel from right side of transmission cover.
6. Remove the heater hose from underneath the dash along with the round plate beneath them.
7. Remove the starter motor mounting nuts. The top nut can be reached from inside the car and the bottom nut from under the car.
8. Remove starter mounting bolts and lift out starter.

Installation

1. Installation is the reverse of the removal procedure.

Fuel System

ELECTRIC FUEL PUMP

CAUTION: If the fuel lines (S.U. pumps) need to be cleared by air pressure, be sure to disconnect the outlet line from the

1 Pump body
2 Diaphragm and spindle assembly
3 Armature centralizing roller
4 Impact washer
5 Armature spring
6 Coil housing
7 Screw
8 Ground connector
9 Screw
10 Spring washer
11 Terminal tag
12 Terminal tag
13 Ground tag
14 Rocker pivot pin
15 Rocker mechanism
16 Pedestal
17 Terminal stud
18 Spring washer
19 Lead washer
20 Terminal nut
21 Washer
22 Contact blade
23 Washer
24 Screw
25 Condenser
26 Clip
27 Spring washer
28 Screw
29 End cover
30 Shakeproof washer
31 Lucar connector
32 Nut
33 Insulating sleeve
34 Clamp plate
35 Screw
36 Valve cap
37 Intake valve
38 Outlet valve
39 Sealing washer
40 Filter
41 Diaphragm washer
42 Vent valve
43 Sealing band
44 Intake air bottle cover joint
45 Intake air bottle cover
46 Dished washer
47 Spring washer
48 Screw
49 Outlet connection
50 Fiber washer
51 Cover (delivery flow smoothing device)
52 Screw
53 O-ring
54 Diaphragm barrier
55 Sealing washer
56 Diaphragm plate
57 Rubber diaphragm
58 Spring end cap
59 Diaphragm spring

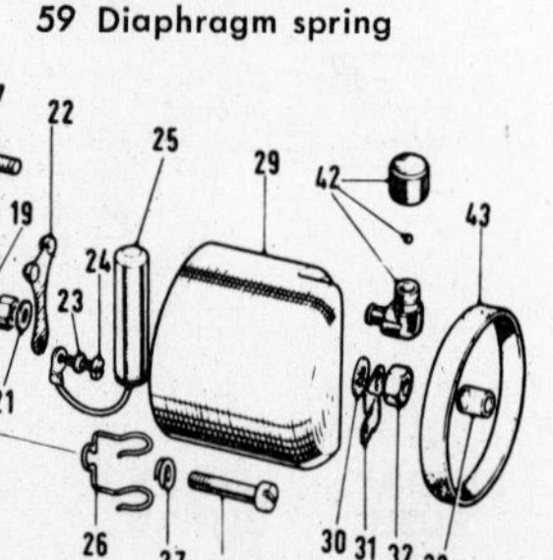

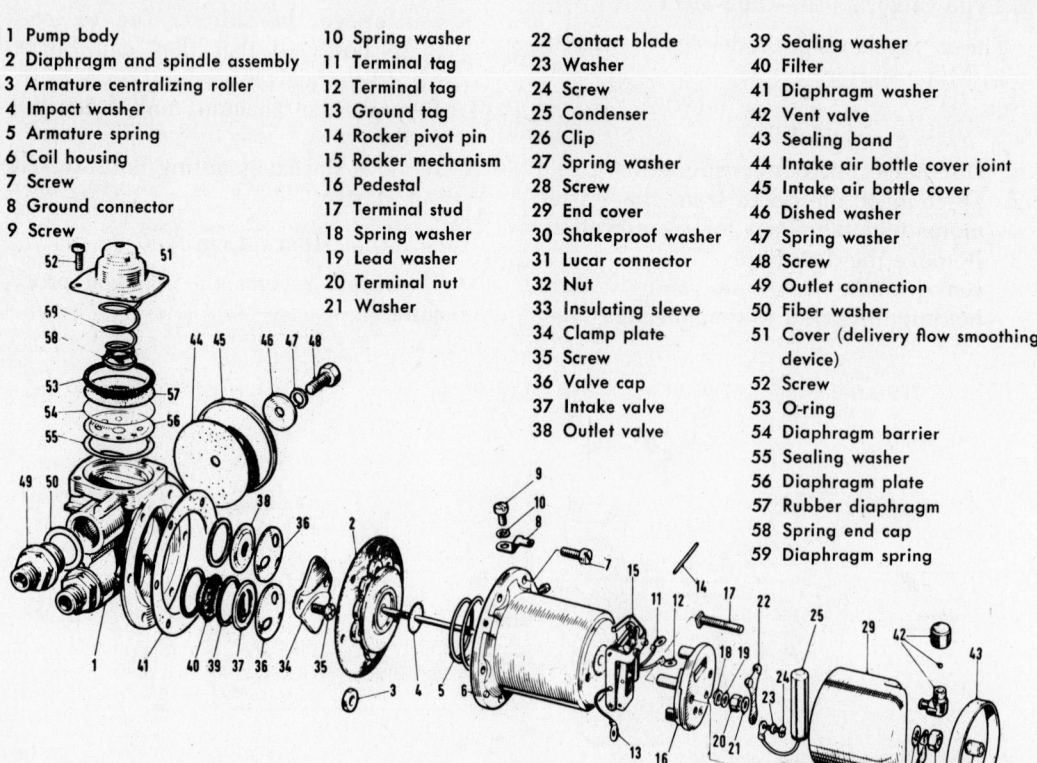

Exploded view of the S.U. AUF. 301 fuel pump—all models exc. early Mark II and 3.8 E Type

pumps. Failure to do this, may damage or displace the Melinex valves.

XJ6

This car uses two S.U. electric fuel pumps mounted in the spare tire well beneath the floor panel in the trunk.

Removal

1. Open trunk, remove floor panel and spare tire.
2. Remove fuel pump cover.
3. Locate the bad pump and drain its connection.
4. Disconnect battery and detach the wires from the bad pump.
5. Remove the pump clamp from the floor panel and lift out the pump.
6. Disconnect the intake and outlet pipes.
7. If deteriorated, replace rubber insulated mounting studs.

Installation

1. To install, reverse removal procedure.

420

This car uses two S.U. (AUF. 301) electric fuel pumps mounted one in each rear wheel well.

Removal

1. Disconnect pump wires.
2. Remove nuts and washers holding the pump clamps to the mounting studs.
3. Remove the pump and disconnect the intake and outlet lines.
4. If deteriorated, replace rubber insulated mounting studs. Deteriorated insulation may cause excessive pump noise.

Installation

1. To install, reverse removal procedures.

E Type (4.2, 2+2)

These models use a single S.U. (AUF. 301) electric fuel pump mounted on the right side of the luggage compartment within the fender panel.

Removal

1. Disconnect intake and outlet lines.
2. Remove the electrical connections from the pump.
3. Remove the nuts securing the pump to the bracket.
4. Lift out the pump.
5. Examine the rubber mounting grommets and replace if deteriorated. Deteriorated grommets can cause excessive pump noise.

Installation

1. To install, reverse removal procedures.

E Type (3.8)—1961-1964

This car uses a Lucas 2FP fuel pump. The unit is fully sealed and mounted inside the fuel tank.

Removal

1. Disconnect the battery.
2. Remove the carpet and floor panels from the luggage compartment.
3. Remove the cover from the electrical junction block located in the spare tire compartment.
4. Disconnect the cables and note that like colors are connected.
5. Remove the fuel line connection from the pump.
6. Drain the fuel tank.
7. Remove the setscrews and lift out the pump and attaching carrier plate.
8. Separate the pump from the carrier plate.

Installation

1. To install, reverse the removal procedure using a new mounting gasket.

IMPORTANT: Located on one of the mounting grommets is a star washer that acts as a ground from the pump to its mounting bracket. Without this washer, electrostatic charges will build up on the pump. Therefore, it is very important that this washer be replaced.

2. When replacing the gas filter, it is advisable that the filter O-ring is lubricated before installation.

3.4S, 3.8S, Mark II—S.U. AUF. 301 (Except early Mark II)

Each of these models is equipped with two S.U. fuel pumps mounted within the rear fender panels. The Mark II uses only one of these pumps. Early Mark II's (see below) used a differently designed S.U. pump.

Removal

For removal and installation procedures, refer to those instructions applicable to the E type (4.2 and 2+2).

Fuel Pump Adjustment

There are two types of S.U. fuel pumps used on Jaguars—the early design (Early Mark 5) having brass disc valves and the later design (S.U. AUF. 301) having Melinex (plastic) valves. The later design was used on those Mark II's (3.4) beginning with chassis No. 179855 and 223683 for those with 3.8 engine. If it becomes necessary to blow out the fuel lines on a car equipped with the later design pump, the outlet lines must be disconnected from the pumps. Failure to disconnect these lines will cause these valves to be damaged or displaced. The early pump has one clearance setting while the current pump has a modified outer rocker with two stop fingers for setting rocker and contact clearances. The S.U. pumps consist of three main assemblies: the main body casting, the diaphragm armature and magnet assembly, and the contact breaker assembly. It operates by a diaphragm pulsated with a solenoid, which is activated by a set of breaker points.

1. Install the contact blade and coil lead to the pedestal.
2. Place the condenser clip under the coil lead clip.
3. Adjust the blade so that the points are slightly above the points of the rocker when the points are closed so that when the points open or close, one pair of points completely covers the other.
4. When pressing the outer rocker onto the coil housing, make sure that the contact blade rests on the small ridge that rises from the pedestal. If it does not, loosen the blade and bend it downward until it rests lightly against

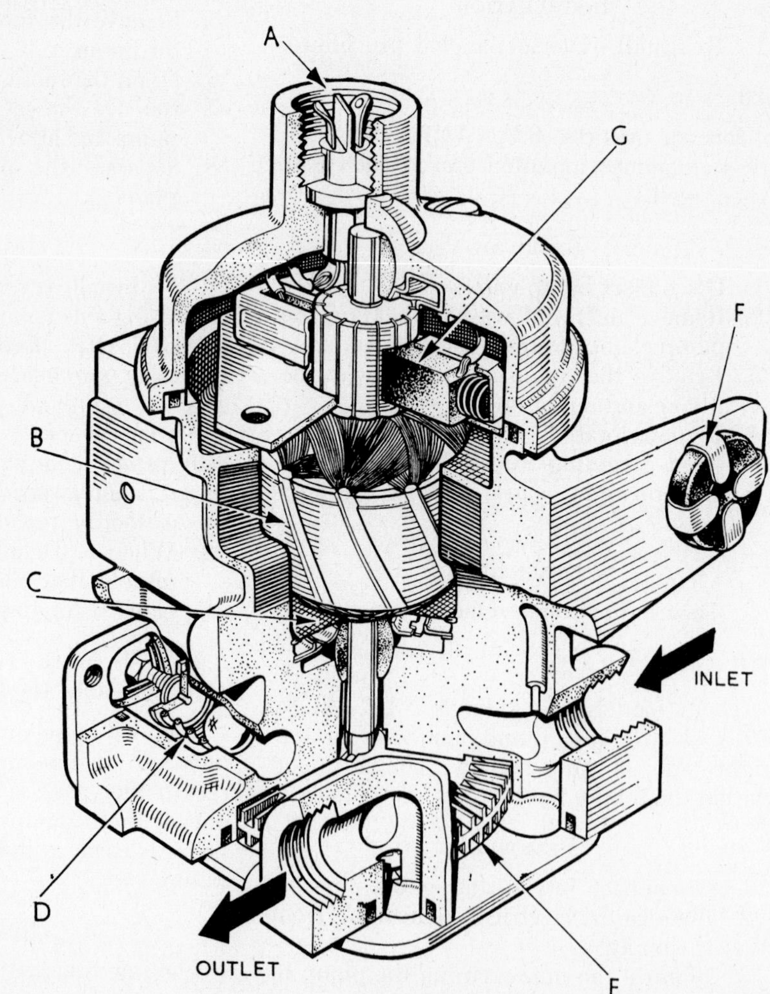

Sectional view of the Lucas 2FP fuel pump—E Type (3.8)

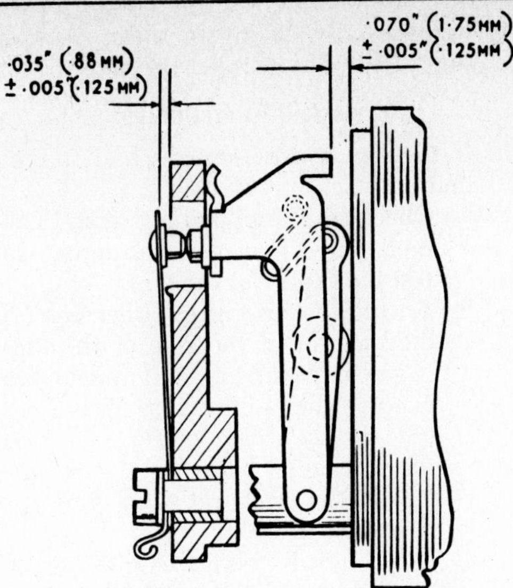

Rocker and contact clearances for the S.U. AUF. 301 fuel pump

the ridge. Bending the blade too much will restrict travel of the rocker mechanism. Correct positioning will produce a gap of .035″ ± .005″ between the pedestal and the tip of the spring blade.

5. Adjust the gap between the rocker finger and coil housing to .070″± .005″ by bending the stop finger.
6. For earlier rocker assemblies (those having a single adjustment), hold the blade against the pedestal ridge, being careful not to press on the overhanging position, and check that the gap between the white fiber rollers and the coil housing is .030″.

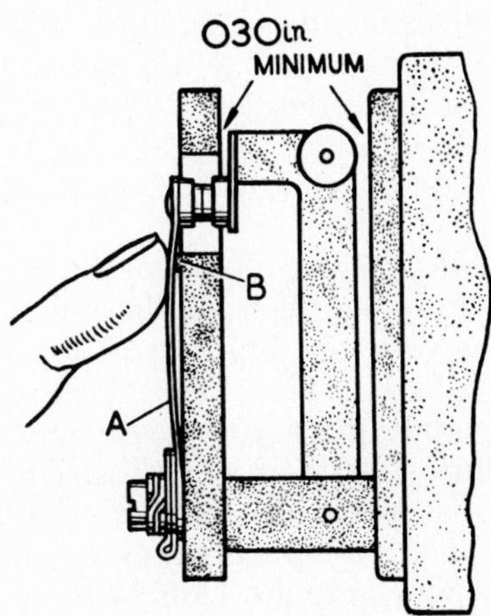

Contact clearance for S.U. fuel pump (early design)—early Mark II. If the contact blade (A) is held against the projection (B), there should be .030″ gap between the white rollers and the pump body. It may be necessary to set the tip of the blade to obtain the correct clearance.

7. To correctly set the diaphragm (on both pump designs), perform the following:
   a. Make the correct contact blade settings (as described above) and remove the contact blade.
   b. With the coil housing assembly in a horizontal position, push the diaphragm spindle in firmly.
   c. Unscrew the diaphragm until the throw-over mechanism just operates.

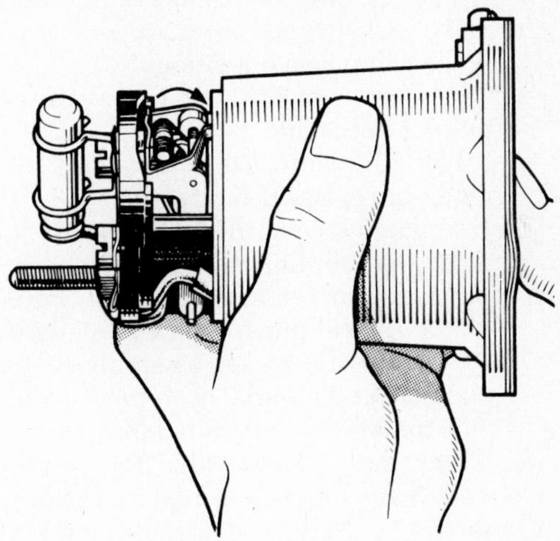
Checking the throw-over of the toggle by pressing slowly and firmly on the diaphragm

Lucas 2FP Fuel Pumps

The Lucas 2FP fuel pump is a sealed unit mounted inside the fuel tank. It consists of a centrifugal pump driven by a permanent field electric motor. A safety fuse (5 amp.) is located in the fuse box.

1. Check fuel pump delivery pressure by attaching a pressure gauge to the fuel line at the carburetor end. If this pressure is higher or lower than 2-2 1/2 psi then the pump will have to be removed and the pressure adjusted.
2. The adjusting screw is located near the bottom of the pump and held in place by a locknut. Turning it counterclockwise reduces the pressure while a clockwise turn increases the delivery pressure.
3. After adjusting the pressure, tighten the locknut and install the unit in the tank.
4. When testing the pump, electricity should be supplied from the battery by connecting the black pump wire to the positive terminal of the battery.

Servicing the Fuel Pumps

S.U. Pumps

1. Clean the pump and check for any cracks, damaged threads or defects. Failure of the pump to clean, may be caused by a varnish-like coating on the components resulting from gum formation in the fuel. If this is the case, a good carburetor cleaner will probably remove the varnish. Small alloy parts should be soaked in methyl alcohol.
2. Check all fittings, connections, lines, seals, gaskets and covers for fuel leaks while pump is in operation.
3. Clean and examine the filter and replace if necessary.
4. Inspect all electrical connections and repair or replace if faulty.
5. Examine the contact breaker points for pitting or burning and, if evident, replace the rocker assembly and spring blade. A steel pin specifically made by S.U. holds the rocker assembly to the pedestal and should be replaced only with an S.U. manufactured pin.
6. Check the pedestal ridge for damage or excessive wear and replace if necessary.

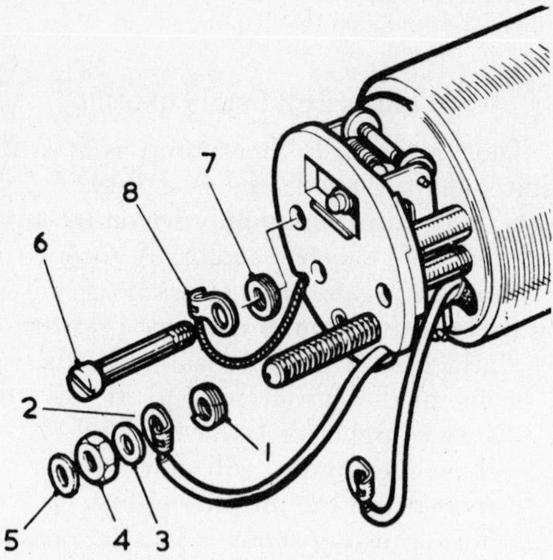

1 Spring washer
2 Terminal tag (2)
3 Lead washer
4 Coned nut
5 End-cover seal washer
6 Pedestal screws
7 Spring washer
8 Ground tag

Installing the pedestal to the coil housing

7. Inspect the end cover vent valve for damage and make sure that the ball valve moves freely.
8. Check the diaphragm for signs of wear and replace if worn.
9. Replace all leaking gaskets, sealing rings, bad bolts or roller bearings.

Lucas 2FP Fuel Pumps

1. If the car is experiencing fuel starvation:
   a. Check the fuel supply first. The fuel gauge may be inaccurate, so test the supply at the tank.
   b. Locate the fuse box (either behind the dash or at the side of the luggage compartment) and replace the 5 amp. fuel pump fuse if burned out. If the fuse is renewed and blows again, check for a short circuit in the electrical connections or in the pump itself.
   c. If the fuse is good, locate the wires connecting the battery to the pump and check the voltage and current at these pump terminals while the ignition switch is on. The voltmeter should read 12 volts and the ammeter reading should not exceed 1.8 amps.
   d. If no voltage is present, the trouble may lie in a broken or bad connection in the switch or wiring.
   e. If the pump is getting no current or more than 1.8 amps., then the pump should be replaced.
2. If the car is experiencing fuel flooding:
   a. Check to see if carburetor needle valves are dirty or worn.
   b. If the needle valves are satisfactory, connect a pressure gauge to the fuel line at the carburetor end. If the pump is receiving 12 volts, then the gauge should read 2-2 1/2 psi of pressure. If the pressure is to be corrected, see Adjustment Procedures, Lucas 2FP Fuel Pumps.

FUEL FILTER

All Jaguars are equipped with an inline gas filter. In addition to this inline type they may have one or more of the following: a carburetor filter for each carburetor, a fuel pump filter and/or a gas tank filter. The inline filter is of the glass bowl type with a flat filter element and should be cleaned with gasoline every 5,000 to 6,000 miles or sooner if the filter bowl contains large amounts of dirt or water. On the XJ6 models, the filter element should be replaced, rather than cleaned, every 12,000 miles or sooner if necessary. The carburetor filter, made of wire mesh, is contained

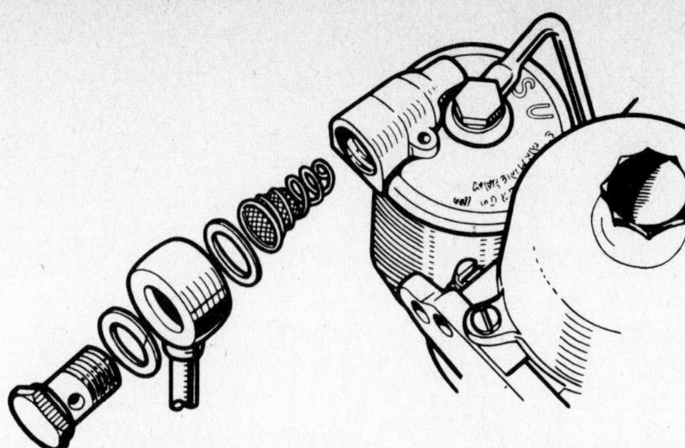

Carburetor filter removal—all S.U. carburetors

within the float chamber housing cap of each carburetor. The filter should be removed and cleaned every 5,000 miles or sooner if necessary. To remove the filter, withdraw the bolt securing the line connection to the chamber. Clean the filter with gasoline but do not use a cloth as it will catch in the wire and leave particles. The filter, when installed, should go in spring first and be followed by a fiber washer, the line connection, the other washer and the bolt. Some early Mark II models used fuel pump filters. To expose the filter, remove the pump base plate and clean the filter with gasoline. This should be done every 10,000 miles or sooner if needed. If car is equipped with a gas tank filter, such as the E type 3.8 and 4.2, it must be cleaned every 10,000 miles. The filter is integrated into the tank drain plug and should be removed and cleaned with gasoline but not exposed to compressed air. Replace cork washer on plug if necessary, lubricate filter O-ring and install plug. Any fuel put back in the tank should be filtered first.

CARBURETOR

S.U. HD 8 (420)

The 420 models use twin S.U. HD. 8 carburetors. Attached to the front carburetor of the S.U. system is an auxiliary carburetor. This is an enrichment device used as an aid to starting.

Removal

1. Remove the air cleaner assembly.
2. Close the valve (if so equipped) on the inline filter and disconnect the line connections from the carburetor float chambers. Do not lose the filters or fiber washers.
3. Completely remove the distributor vacuum advance line.
4. Disconnect the fuel line from the auxiliary carburetor and the overflow lines from their holding clips.
5. Disconnect the wires from the automatic choke solenoid.
6. Disconnect the throttle link rod or cable.
7. On those cars having an automatic transmission, remove the spring clip holding the kick-down link to the rear of the rear carburetor.
8. Disconnect the throttle return springs.
9. Remove the carburetors from the intake manifold.

Installation

1. To install, reverse the removal procedure. Use new carburetor base gaskets, two for each carburetor and place one on each side of the heat spacers.

S.U. HD 6

The Mark II (3.4, 3.8) and the 3.4S and 3.8S models all use twin S.U. HD 6 carburetors.

Removal

1. Remove the air cleaner and air intake pipe.
2. Remove both bolts, line connections, and fiber washers from the float chambers.
3. Detach the two return springs and the vacuum advance lines from the front carburetor.
4. Remove the cover from the solenoid on the auxiliary starting carburetor and remove the attaching wires.
5. Remove overflow line attachments.
6. Detach fitting connecting starting line to auxiliary carburetor.
7. Remove washers from connecting linkage pivot located on the manifold.
8. Disconnect throttle linkage rod.
9. Remove carburetors from manifold.

Installation

1. To install, reverse removal procedure.

S.U. HD 8 (E Type 3.8)

The E type (3.8) is furnished with three S.U. HD 8 carburetors. A manual choke control to operate all three carburetors is provided.

Removal

1. Remove air cleaner assembly.
2. Remove the line connections from the

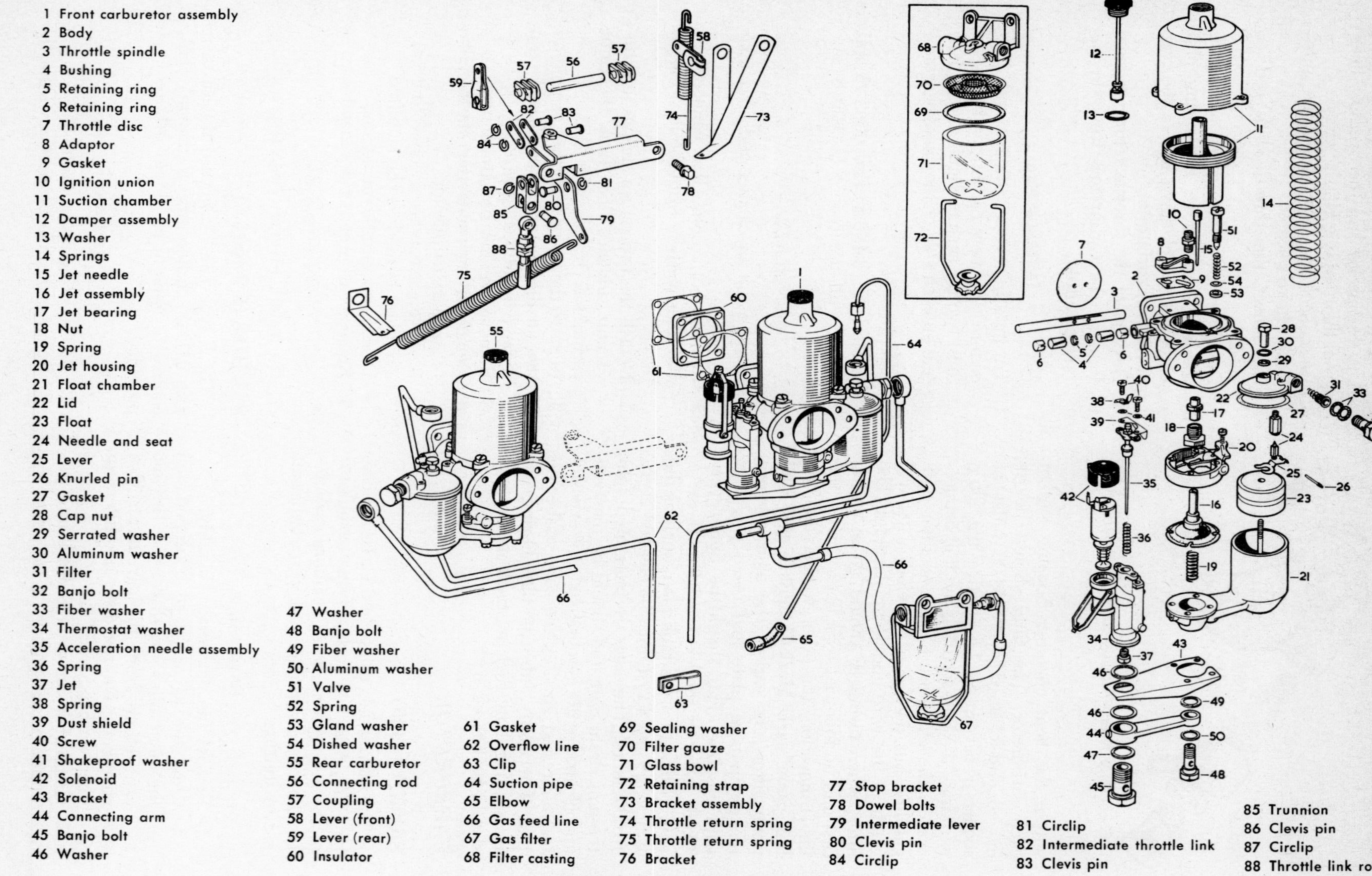

1 Front carburetor assembly
2 Body
3 Throttle spindle
4 Bushing
5 Retaining ring
6 Retaining ring
7 Throttle disc
8 Adaptor
9 Gasket
10 Ignition union
11 Suction chamber
12 Damper assembly
13 Washer
14 Springs
15 Jet needle
16 Jet assembly
17 Jet bearing
18 Nut
19 Spring
20 Jet housing
21 Float chamber
22 Lid
23 Float
24 Needle and seat
25 Lever
26 Knurled pin
27 Gasket
28 Cap nut
29 Serrated washer
30 Aluminum washer
31 Filter
32 Banjo bolt
33 Fiber washer
34 Thermostat washer
35 Acceleration needle assembly
36 Spring
37 Jet
38 Spring
39 Dust shield
40 Screw
41 Shakeproof washer
42 Solenoid
43 Bracket
44 Connecting arm
45 Banjo bolt
46 Washer
47 Washer
48 Banjo bolt
49 Fiber washer
50 Aluminum washer
51 Valve
52 Spring
53 Gland washer
54 Dished washer
55 Rear carburetor
56 Connecting rod
57 Coupling
58 Lever (front)
59 Lever (rear)
60 Insulator
61 Gasket
62 Overflow line
63 Clip
64 Suction pipe
65 Elbow
66 Gas feed line
67 Gas filter
68 Filter casting
69 Sealing washer
70 Filter gauze
71 Glass bowl
72 Retaining strap
73 Bracket assembly
74 Throttle return spring
75 Throttle return spring
76 Bracket
77 Stop bracket
78 Dowel bolts
79 Intermediate lever
80 Clevis pin
84 Circlip
81 Circlip
82 Intermediate throttle link
83 Clevis pin
85 Trunnion
86 Clevis pin
87 Circlip
88 Throttle link rod

Exploded view of the S.U. HD 8 carburetor—420

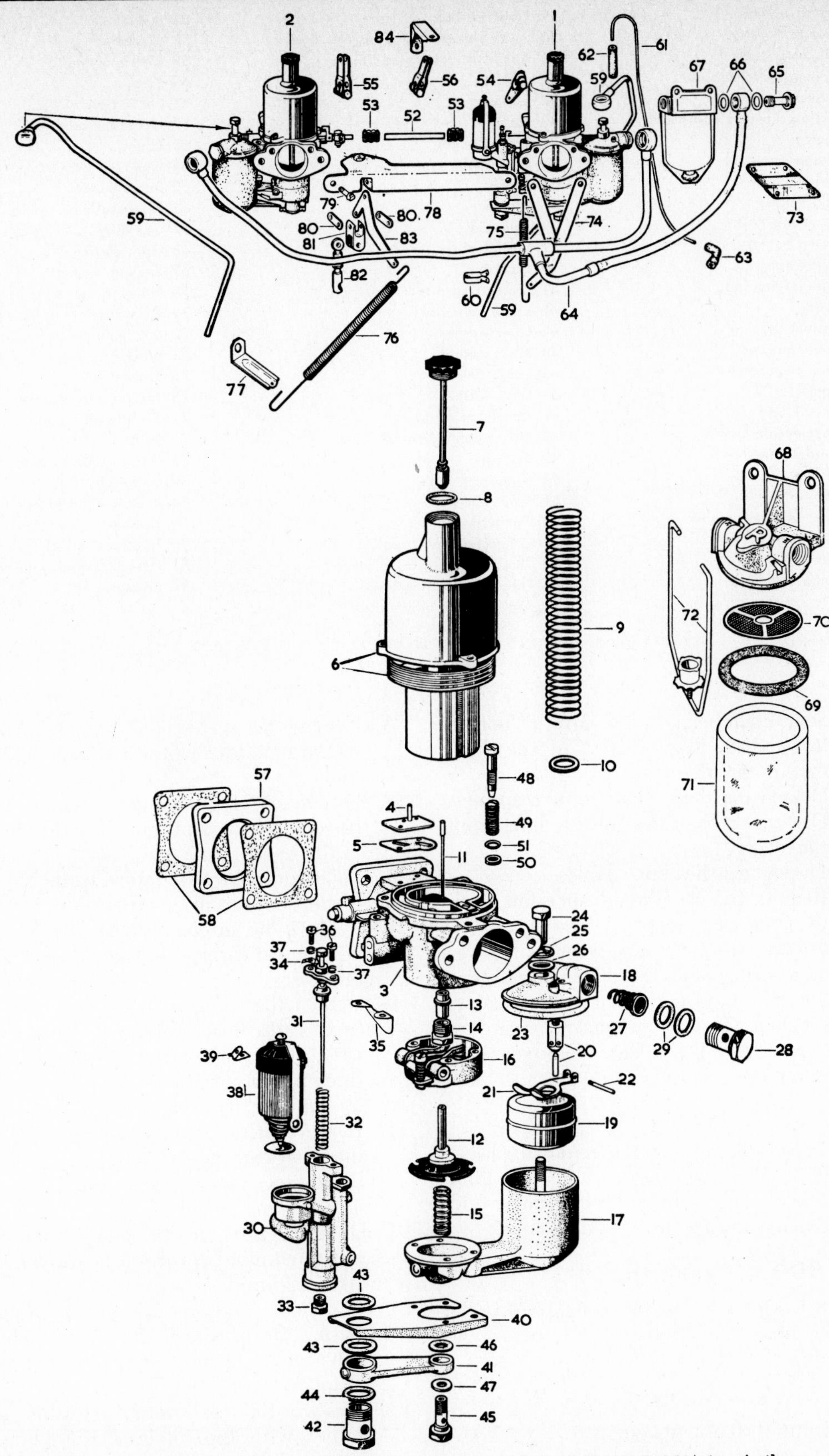

Exploded view of the S.U. HD 6 carburetor—3.4S, 3.8S—Mark II (3.4, 3.8, 340) is similar

1 Front carburetor
2 Rear carburetor
3 Caburetor body
4 Ignition union adaptor
5 Gasket
6 Suction chamber and piston
7 Damper
8 Washer
9 Spring
10 Skid washer
11 Jet needle
12 Jet
13 Jet bearing
14 Nut—jet bearing
15 Spring
16 Jet unit housing
17 Float chamber
18 Float chamber lid
19 Float
20 Needle and seat
21 Float needle lever
22 Knurled pin
23 Gasket
24 Cap nut
25 Fiber serrated washer
26 Aluminum washer
27 Filter
28 Banjo bolt
29 Fiber washer
30 Auxiliary starting carburetor body
31 Auxiliary starting carburetor needle
32 Spring
33 Jet
34 Spring finger
35 Dust shield
36 Screw
37 Washer
38 Solenoid
39 Spring clip
40 Bracket
41 Connecting arm
42 Banjo bolt
43 Fiber washer
44 Fiber washer
45 Banjo bolt
46 Fiber washer
47 Aluminum washer
48 Slow running control valve
49 Spring
50 Neoprene washer
51 Brass washer
52 Connecting rod
53 Connecting rod coupling
54 Throttle return spring lever
55 Throttle operating lever
56 Anti-creep throttle switch
57 Insulator
58 Gasket
59 Overflow line
60 Clip
61 Suction pipe
62 Neoprene tube
63 Elbow
64 Gas feed line
65 Banjo bolt
66 Fiber washer
67 Gas filter
68 Filter casting
69 Sealing washer
70 Filter gauze
71 Glass bowl
72 Retaining strap
73 Bracket
74 Bracket
75 Throttle return spring
76 Throttle return spring
77 Bracket
78 Throttle stop bracket
79 Dowel bolt
80 Intermediate throttle link
81 Trunnion
82 Throttle link rod
83 Intermediate throttle lever
84 Bracket

Exploded view of the S.U. HD 6 carburetor—3.4S, 3.8S

float chambers, being careful not to lose the six fiber washers or the three carburetor filters.

3. Detach the three choke return springs.
4. Disconnect the three throttle links from the levers.
5. Disconnect the choke cables.
6. Remove the vacuum advance line from the front carburetor.
7. Remove the four nuts, washers and return spring bracket from each carburetor and remove the three carburetors together. It may be necessary to remove the choke linkage from each carburetor.

Installation

1. To install, reverse the removal procedure. Use new gaskets, one on either side of each carburetor heat spacer and one to each air cleaner stack flange.

S.U. HD 8 (E Type 4.2)

The E type (4.2) prior to its 1968 emission control carburetion, was equipped with three S.U. HD 8 carburetors.

Removal

1. Drain the cooling system.
2. Disconnect the battery.
3. Remove the water hose going from the intake manifold to the radiator header tank.
4. Disconnect the electrical connections from the thermostat fan control located in the header tank.
5. Remove the throttle return springs.
6. Unclip hose from breather pipe.
7. Remove the air cleaner assembly.
8. Disconnect throttle linkage at rear carburetor.
9. Detach the three fuel line connections from each float chamber. Be careful not to lose the six fiber washers or the three carburetor filters.
10. Disconnect the choke control cables.
11. Remove the vacuum advance line from the front carburetor.
12. Disconnect the wire from the oil pressure sending switch.
13. Disconnect the heater pipes from the water manifold and from below the intake manifold.
14. On those 2+2 models having automatic transmissions, detach the kickdown cable located at the rear of the cylinder head.
15. Remove the carburetor assembly together with the intake manifold and linkage.

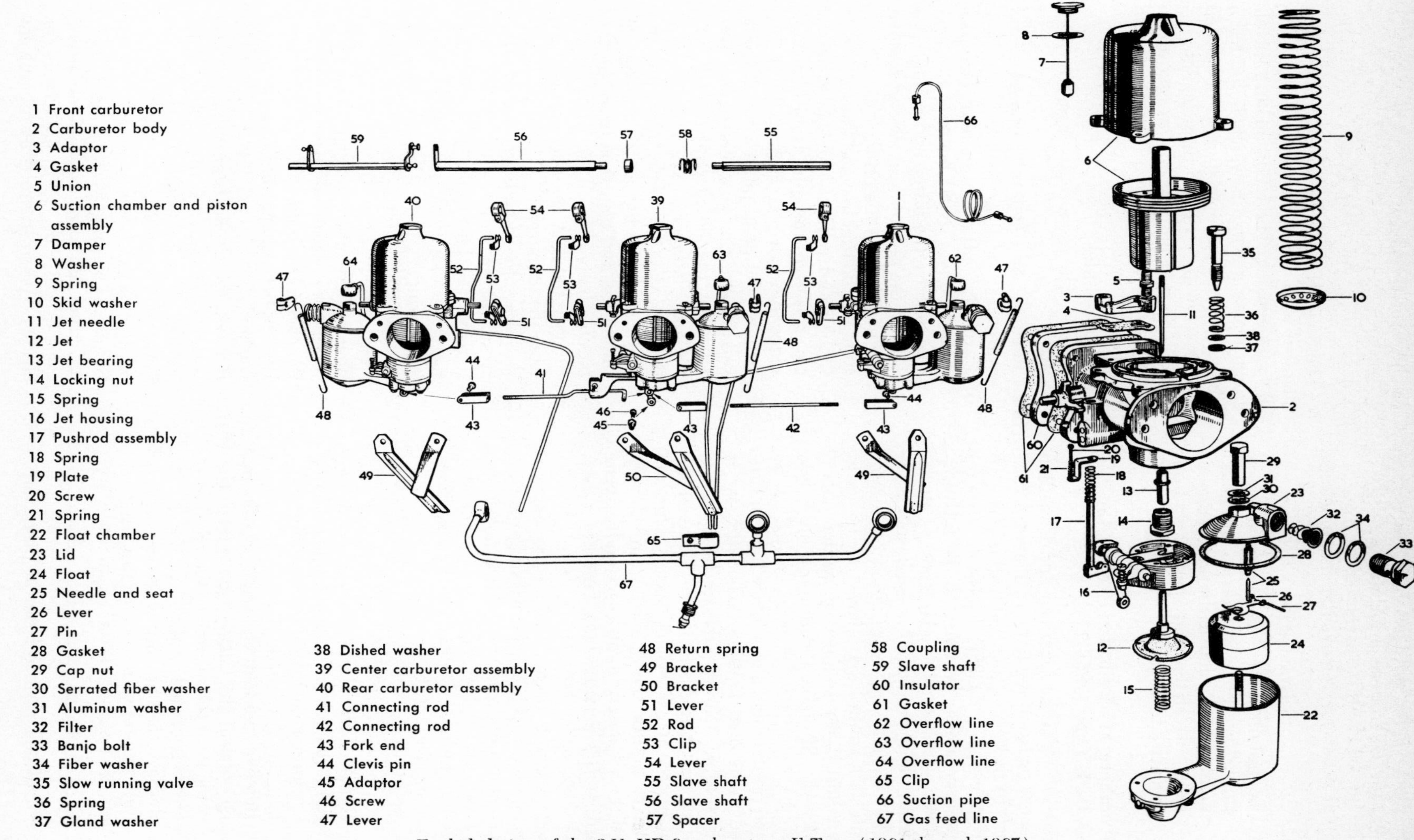

1 Front carburetor
2 Carburetor body
3 Adaptor
4 Gasket
5 Union
6 Suction chamber and piston assembly
7 Damper
8 Washer
9 Spring
10 Skid washer
11 Jet needle
12 Jet
13 Jet bearing
14 Locking nut
15 Spring
16 Jet housing
17 Pushrod assembly
18 Spring
19 Plate
20 Screw
21 Spring
22 Float chamber
23 Lid
24 Float
25 Needle and seat
26 Lever
27 Pin
28 Gasket
29 Cap nut
30 Serrated fiber washer
31 Aluminum washer
32 Filter
33 Banjo bolt
34 Fiber washer
35 Slow running valve
36 Spring
37 Gland washer
38 Dished washer
39 Center carburetor assembly
40 Rear carburetor assembly
41 Connecting rod
42 Connecting rod
43 Fork end
44 Clevis pin
45 Adaptor
46 Screw
47 Lever
48 Return spring
49 Bracket
50 Bracket
51 Lever
52 Rod
53 Clip
54 Lever
55 Slave shaft
56 Slave shaft
57 Spacer
58 Coupling
59 Slave shaft
60 Insulator
61 Gasket
62 Overflow line
63 Overflow line
64 Overflow line
65 Clip
66 Suction pipe
67 Gas feed line

Exploded view of the S.U. HD 8 carburetor—E Type (1961 through 1967)

16. Remove the nuts, washers and spring brackets from each carburetor.
17. Lift off the three carburetors.
18. If necessary, remove the choke linkage.

INSTALLATION

1. To install, reverse the removal procedure. Install new gaskets to the intake manifold, to each carburetor (one on each side of the heat spacer) and one to each air cleaner stack flange.

Stromberg 175 Emission Carburetor —XJ6, E Type (1968-71)

In 1968, due to American and Canadian exhaust emission regulations, Jaguar 4.2 exports to these countries were equipped with Stromberg 175 CD2SE Emission carburetors, very similar in design to the S.U. carburetor. A manual choke and a special starting device mounted to each carburetor make cold starting easier. Each carburetor contains a control that allows the choke to be adjusted for summer or winter operation. The Stromberg carburetor uses two throttles: a primary throttle located in its usual position and a secondary throttle situated in its own housing. When the car is driven at part throttle, the secondary throttle remains closed and intake mixtures are pre-heated by the exhaust gases. After the primary throttle has opened approximately 20°, the secondary throttle gradually opens until, at full throttle, both butterfly valves are wide open and the mixture goes directly through both manifolds to achieve maximum power. The factory suggests that when starting a cold engine, it is not advisable to press down on the accelerator pedal. If the pedal is depressed, a flooding condition may result.

REMOVAL

1. Remove air cleaner assembly. Carefully remove air cleaner stacks from carburetor so that thin mounting gaskets can be re-used.
2. Remove fuel lines from float chambers.
3. Disconnect the linkage going from the primary to the secondary throttles.
4. Disconnect choke cable.
5. Remove the nuts and washers securing the carburetors to the manifold and lift off the two carburetors as an assembly.

INSTALLATION

1. To install, reverse removal procedure.

Carburetor Overhaul

S.U. HD TYPE

The S.U. HD type carburetor uses a float chamber with a cast flange to hold the complete jet housing. The idling mixture travels along a passageway, in which is located a metering screw. The mixture is controlled by this screw instead of a throttle plate. *CAUTION: Do not use compressed air to clean out the float chambers for diaphragm damage will result.*

To disassemble:

1. Remove the carburetors from the vehicle.
2. Remove the hydraulic damper and washer.
3. Carefully, lift the suction chamber straight off to avoid bending the needle. Remove the piston and spring.
4. Loosen the retaining screw and remove the needle from the piston.
5. Remove the fuel line and filter.
6. Unbolt and remove the float chamber cover. Drive the pin from the float hinge to remove the float.
7. Remove the pivot pin, fork and needle valve from the float chamber cover. Unscrew the needle valve seat from the float chamber cover.
8. Remove the top plate and fast idle screw from the top plate. Remove the sliding rod and cam shoe from the carburetor body.
9. Remove the float chamber and jet body from the carburetor.
10. Withdraw the diaphragm and jet and lift off the jet body.
11. Remove the hex head jet screw from the carburetor body and withdraw the jet bearing.
12. Remove the throttle levers from the shafts.
13. Remove the throttle plate from the spindle and withdraw the spindle from the carburetor body.
14. Pry out both gland nuts and the spring washer.
15. Remove the circlip from the piston lift spring and remove the lift pin and spring.
16. Remove the piston guide from the carburetor body.
17. Before assembling, perform the following: soak all carburetor components, except float and seals, in carburetor cleaner. Wash thoroughly in solvent

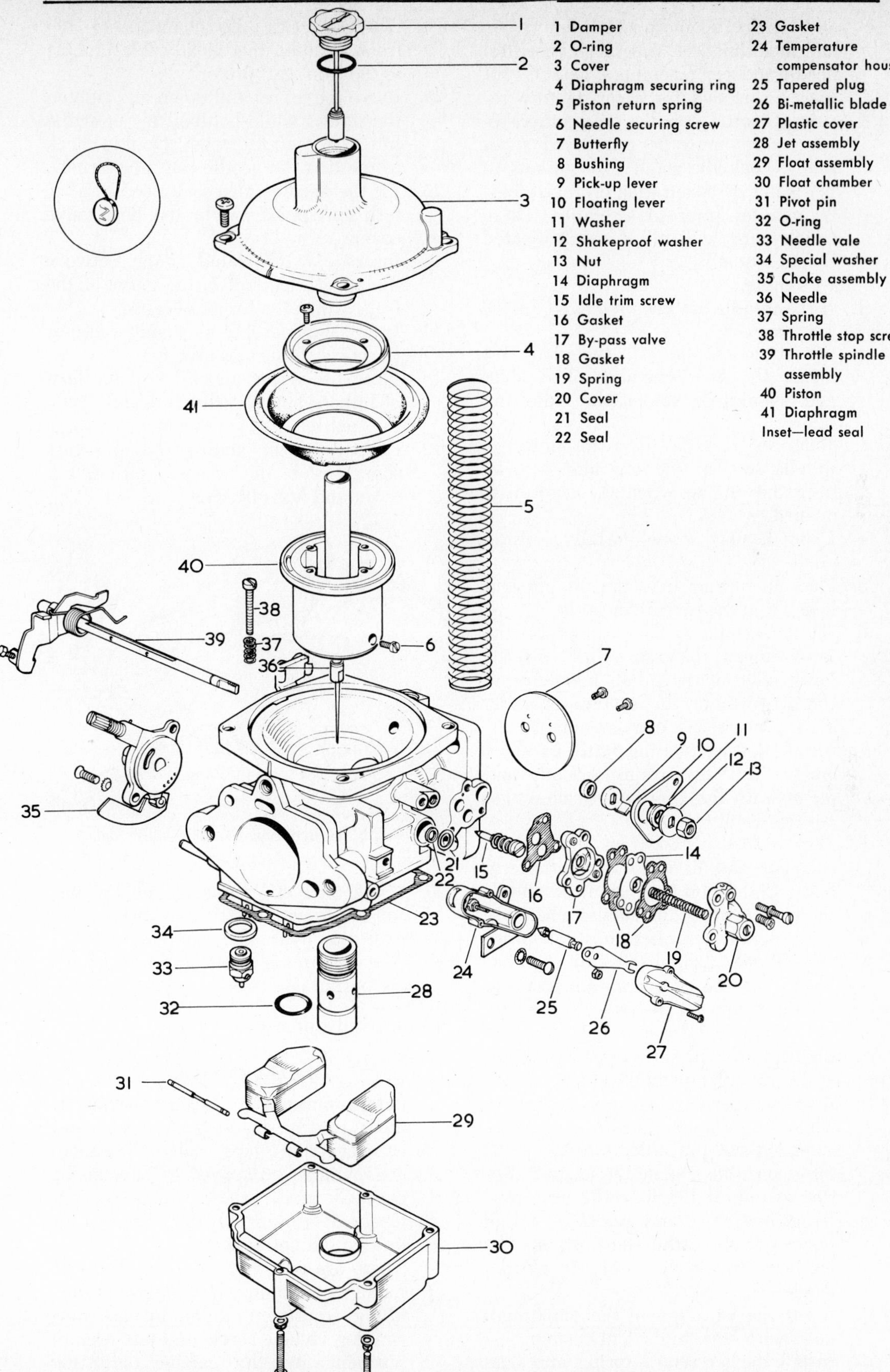

1 Damper
2 O-ring
3 Cover
4 Diaphragm securing ring
5 Piston return spring
6 Needle securing screw
7 Butterfly
8 Bushing
9 Pick-up lever
10 Floating lever
11 Washer
12 Shakeproof washer
13 Nut
14 Diaphragm
15 Idle trim screw
16 Gasket
17 By-pass valve
18 Gasket
19 Spring
20 Cover
21 Seal
22 Seal
23 Gasket
24 Temperature compensator housing
25 Tapered plug
26 Bi-metallic blade
27 Plastic cover
28 Jet assembly
29 Float assembly
30 Float chamber
31 Pivot pin
32 O-ring
33 Needle vale
34 Special washer
35 Choke assembly
36 Needle
37 Spring
38 Throttle stop screw
39 Throttle spindle assembly
40 Piston
41 Diaphragm
Inset—lead seal

Exploded view of the Stromberg (rear) 175 CD2SE carburetor—XJ6, E Type (1968-1971)

and air dry. A good carburetor repair kit, including jet tubes, jet needles, needle and seat assemblies, gaskets and seals, is needed for a satisfactory repair. Throttle spindles and other related parts must be purchased separately. Soak the small cork gaskets in hot water or penetrating oil for at least 30 minutes prior to assembly. These fragile parts will split if not lubricated before assembly.

To assemble:

1. If the spindle has been removed, install new seals.
2. Install the spindle with the plain end facing the float chamber. The lever pad should go under the adjusting screw.
3. Slide the throttle plate through the spindle so that the top moves away from the engine when the throttle is opened.
4. Using a new screw, install a piston guide.
5. Place the spring over the lift pin and install it in the carburetor body.
6. Fit the needle to the piston with the lower edge of the groove flush with the lower edge of the piston body. Install the piston into the suction chamber making sure that it can move freely.
7. Install the jet bearing with its short end toward the carburetor body and secure with the appropriate screw. Do not tighten at this time.
8. Remove the piston from the suction chamber and fit it to the carburetor body. Lightly oil the piston rod and fit the piston spring and suction chamber.
9. The suction chamber must fit properly. Evenly tighten the four chamber nuts. Hold the carburetor upright and lift the piston all the way up. Release the piston and let it fall. If centered properly, the piston should fall freely and land with an audible click.
10. Invert the carburetor and insert the jet while keeping the needle completely extended and protruded into the jet as far as possible. Rotate the jet to center the bearing and tighten the jet screw.
11. Remove the jet and position the jet housing to the carburetor housing. The jet lever should face the air cleaner flange.
12. Insert the jet, aligning the diaphragm holes with holes in the jet housing.
13. Install the jet return spring and float chamber with the chamber to the front. Position the choke cable bracket to the front carburetor.
14. Move the jet up and down and tighten the screws while holding the jet at the full extent of its travel. Double-check to see that the needle can move freely.
15. Fit the needle valve seat, needle valve, fork and pivot pin to the float valve cover.
16. Insert a 7/16" round gauge between the cover face and inside curve of the fork. Adjust the fork if necessary.
17. Install the float into its chamber and fit the cover to the carburetor.
18. Place the spring and filter in the float chamber of each carburetor and attach the fuel lines.
19. Lightly oil the sliding rod and cam shoe. Install the washer, spring, top cover and fast idle screw.

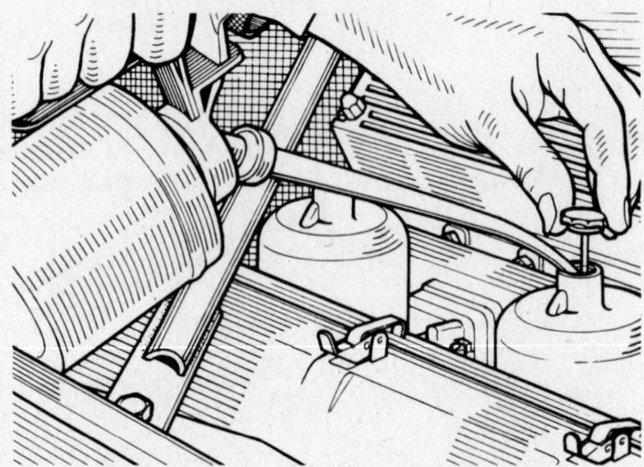

Filling the hydraulic damper—all models

20. Using SAE 20 engine oil, fill the piston rod to within 1/2" from the top. Install the hydraulic damper.
21. The carburetors must now be adjusted for proper operation.

S.U. Carburetor Adjustments

Idle and Mixture

1. Before meaningful carburetor adjustment can be made, spark plug and contact point gaps, valve clearances and cylinder compressions have to be checked and corrected if necessary. Check distributor advance mechanisms and set ignition timing.
2. There are only two adjustments to be made when tuning the S.U. carburetor: idling adjustment made by the slow running volume screw and mixture adjustment by the mixing adjusting

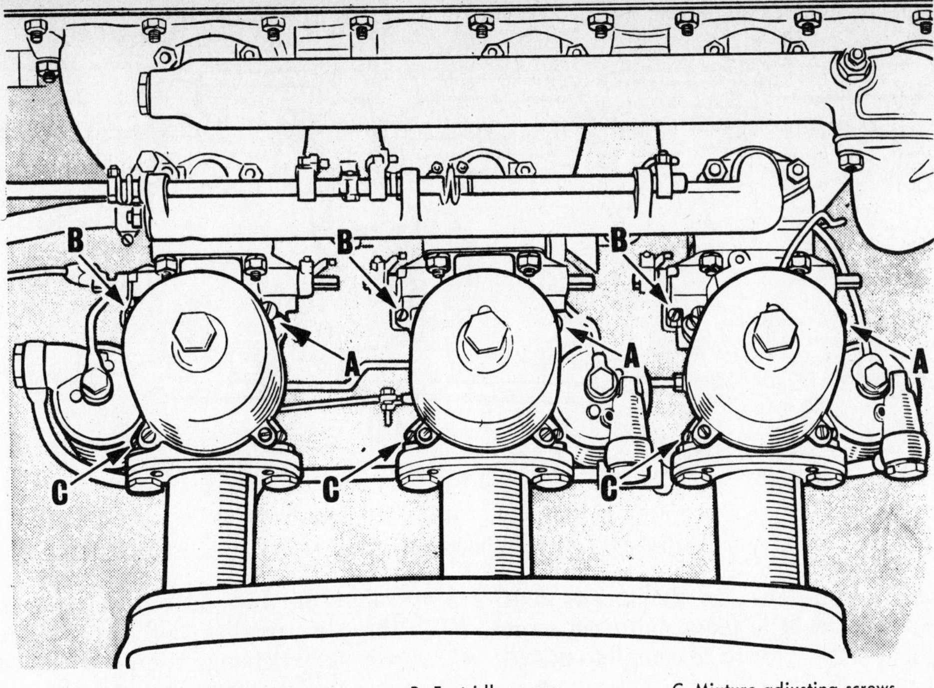

Adjustment screw location—E Type (1961 through 1967)

screws. Correct mixture setting at idle ensures correct mixture at all engine speeds.

3. Make sure that the shoulder of the needles is flush with the base of the pistons, that the pistons move freely in their chambers, that the filters are clean, and that the dampers are filled with the proper oil.
4. Check carburetor mixtures by screwing out the mixture screws until the tops of the jets are flush with the jet bridge in each carburetor. This can be observed after removing the suction chamber

Adjustment screw location—3.4S, 3.8S, 420

A Slow running volume screw B Mixture adjusting screw

Adjustment screw location—Mark II (3.4, 3.8)

and piston. Turn in the screws until the jets begin to move and then screw them in 3-1/2 turns to complete the adjustment.

5. Loosen one clamp bolt on the linkage between the throttle spindles. Make sure that both butterfly valves are completely closed by turning both spindles clockwise (when viewed from the front). Tighten the bolt.
6. Screw in (clockwise) the idling screws until they are fully seated and then back out each screw 2-1/2 turns.
7. Run the engine to normal operating temperature and determine if all the carburetors are drawing equal amounts of air. Using a piece of rubber tubing, place one end to the ear and the other end inside each carburetor intake. Rocarburetors are drawing equal amounts until 500-700 rpm is obtained and the "hissing" of each carburetor is of the same intensity. This method will approximately synchronize the volume of air flowing through the carburetors. A more accurate method of carburetor synchronization can be achieved with a Uni-Syn® carburetor synchronizer. If this gauge shows a difference of more than 1/2" between carburetors, then the carburetors are out of balance and should be placed in proper balance by adjusting the idling screws (slow running volume screw) in the same manner as when using the rubber listening tube.
8. Double-check to see that both butterfly valves are fully closed by turning the throttle spindles and determining if any speed change results. If the valves are closed, there should be no speed change.
9. Readjust the mixture by screwing all the mixture adjustment screws up or down by the same amount until the fastest idle speed is obtained with the engine still running evenly. Adjusting the mixture will probably increase engine speed making it necessary to readjust idling speed.
10. Check the mixture adjustment by lifting the piston of the front carburetor by approximately 1/32".
    a. If the engine speed increases and continues to run faster, the mixture is too rich.
    b. If the engine speed immediately decreases, the mixture is too weak.
    c. If the engine speed increases momentarily and very slightly and returns to the previous level, then the mixture is correct.
11. Perform the same procedure on the other carburetors and, after adjustment, re-check the front carburetor since the carburetors are interdependent.
12. When the mixture is correct, the sound from the tailpipe should be regular and even. A colorless, irregular exhaust with a misfire indicates a mixture that is too lean. If the exhaust sound contains a regular rhythmic misfire and the emission is blackish in color, then the mixture is too rich.

Float Level

It is not advisable to change the float level unless there is a fuel flooding situation. A high float level can cause slow flooding; especially, when the car is on a steep incline. If the float is to be adjusted, perform the following procedure:

1. The float level is correct if a 7/16″ bar will fit snugly between the lid face and the inside curve of the float lever fork when the needle valve is in the closed position. If the clearance is more or

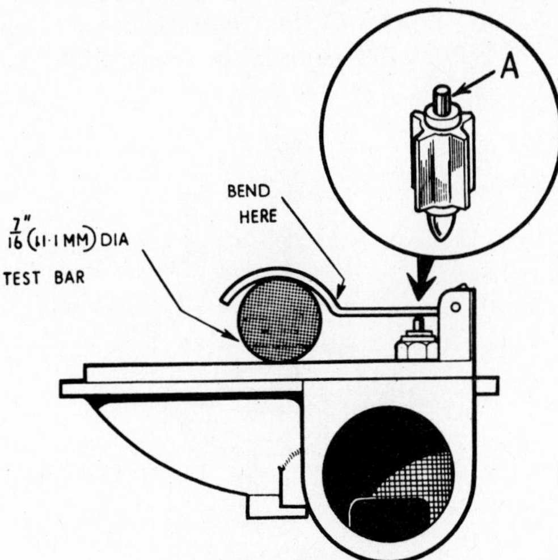

Checking the float level setting—S.U. HD 6, HD 8. Make sure that the spring loaded plunger (A) in the needle is not compressed

less than 7/16″, then the fork lever must be bent in the appropriate direction in order to satisfy this specification. The bend should be made at the intersection of the curved and straight pieces. Both prongs of the fork should be kept level and the straight portion kept perfectly flat.

Centering the Jet

Centering the jet is very important in obtaining proper performance from the S.U. HD type carburetor.

CAUTION: Care should be taken when performing this operation since the needle can be easily bent.

1. Remove the carburetor.
2. Remove the float chamber, jet housing, jet and hydraulic damper.
3. Loosen the jet locking nut about 1/2 turn and replace the jet and diaphragm assembly.
4. When the jet is properly centered, the piston should fall freely and hit the jet

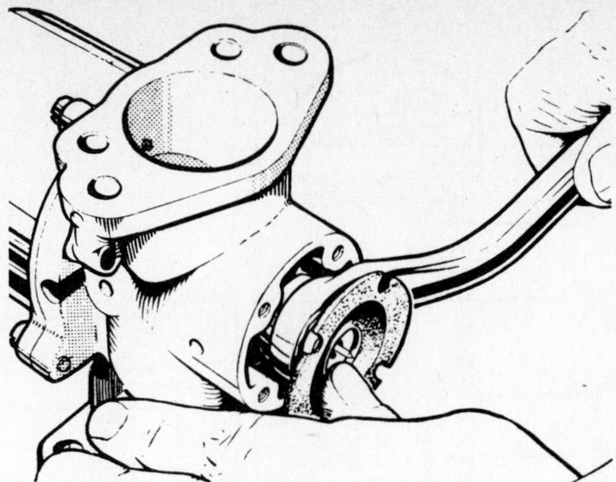

Centering the jet on the S.U. carburetor

bridge with a metallic click.

5. To center the jet, push the jet and diaphragm assembly as high as possible by hand and gently press the piston down on the jet bridge. Tapping on the side of the carburetor will help.
6. With the diaphragm pushed up, and the piston pressed down, tighten the locking nut.
7. Keep the jet and diaphragm assembly in the same position relative to the carburetor body so that the centering adjustment, if correct, will not be lost. It may be helpful to mark one of the jet diaphragm setscrew holes and a corresponding setscrew hole in the carburetor body with a pencil.
8. Check to see if centering is correct by noting the difference in sounds when the piston drops onto the jet when the jet is in its highest position and when the piston is dropped when the jet is in its lowest position. If there is any difference in sound between these conditions, the adjustment process will have to be repeated. Upon completion of the adjustment, adjust the carburetor mixture setting.

Adjusting the Auxiliary Starting Carburetor—Mark II (3.4, 3.8), 3.4S, 3.8S, 420

Some Jaguar models use an enrichment device for starting. This device is actually an auxiliary carburetor that supplies an air-fuel mixture to the engine. A thermostatically operated switch, housed in the water jacket, activates the auxiliary starting carburetor at temperatures below 86-95°F. Variables involved in this unit are: the taper of the needle, the strength of the

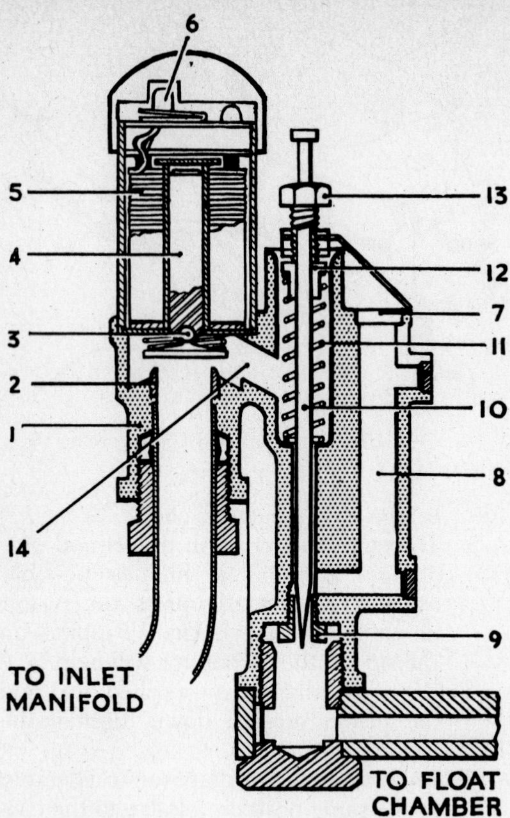

1 Main body
2 Valve seating
3 Valve (ball-jointed disc)
4 Iron core
5 Solenoid
6 Solenoid terminal
7 Air intake
8 Air passage
9 Fuel jet
10 Needle (adjustable)
11 Compression spring
12 Disc (attached to needle)
13 Adjustable stop
14 Mixture passage

Sectional view of the auxiliary starting carburetor —Mark II models, 3.4S, 3.8S, 420

spring, the diameter of the disc and the position of the stop screw, but, adjustment operation is generally limited to the position of the stop screw since the other variables are determined by the manufacturer.

Stop Screw Adjustment

1. Run the engine to normal operating temperature.
2. While the engine is at operating temperature, the solenoid must be activated by using a screwdriver to ground out the terminal of the thermostatic switch. This should cause the auxiliary carburetor to operate and produce a hissing sound. If not, see Step 5.
3. Adjust the stop screw so that the mixture is rich enough to produce a noticeably black exhaust gas but not so rich as to cause the engine to run with obvious irregularity.
4. Turning the screw counterclockwise will raise the needle and enrich the mixture while turning it clockwise will produce a leaner mixture by lowering the needle.
5. If the auxiliary carburetor should fail to function properly, remove and test the thermostatic switch. The switch is secured to the front end of the intake manifold water jacket and can be removed by extracting the three mounting bolts and the electrical connection. The switch should be connected to a 12 volt source and the tip of it immersed into a container of cool water. The water must then be heated from a temperature below 86°F to a temperature above 95°F. If operating properly, the circuit should be closed at temperatures below the 86°F and opened when the temperature climbs above 95°F. If the switch does not satisfy these requirements, then it must be replaced.

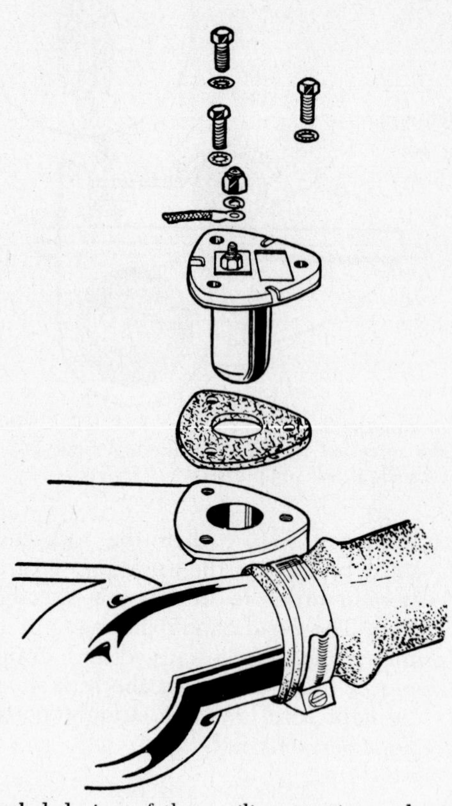

Exploded view of the auxiliary starting carburetor thermostatic switch

THROTTLE LINKAGE ADJUSTMENT PROCEDURES FOR THE S.U. CARBURETOR

1. Loosen clamp bolts and disconnect front carburetor coupling and rear carburetor throttle lever.
2. With both carburetor butterflies fully closed, tighten front coupling.
3. Unscrew intermediate throttle stop and push down on bell crank lever until center A is 1/16″ below a line from center B to the pivot center. When this is accomplished, screw down stop onto intermediate throttle lever and lock it in place. Lock lever to carburetor spindle.
4. It is important that when throttle is closed, the intermediate lever does not contact gas line. Open throttle fully and check that both carburetors are fully opened.

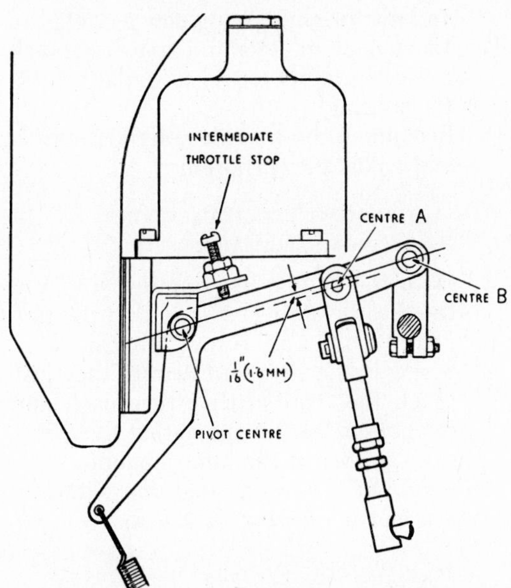

Throttle control linkage setting—S.U. carburetors

Stromberg 175 CD2SE Emission Carburetor

DISASSEMBLY FOR 12,000 MILE SERVICE

Every 12,000 miles, the Stromberg 175 CDSE carburetors should be dismantled and the following parts replaced: the parts contained in Yellow Emission Pack (Part No. 11549) consisting of 2 float chamber gaskets, 2 0-rings for the float chamber plugs and 2 needle valve washers, and 4 manifold/carburetor gaskets and 2 spacers.

1. Remove the carburetors as an assembly. Separate the units and work on one at a time to avoid mixing parts. See carburetor removal procedure.
2. Remove the float chambers and gaskets.
3. Take out the float pivot pin.
4. Make note of the float position so that it can be reassembled correctly.
5. Unscrew the needle valve from the float chamber body.
6. Remove the center plug 0-ring. Thoroughly clean all metal parts in solvent or gasoline using compressed air or lint-free rags to dry them.

ASSEMBLY

1. Place the needle valve, with new washer, into the float chamber body and tighten down.
2. Replace the float assembly and check the float lever as follows: with the carburetor inverted, so that the float assembly closes the needle valve, measure the distance from the face of the carburetor body (with gasket removed) to top of each float. The correct measurement should be 21/32″.
3. Install a new center plug O-ring.
4. Install the float chamber and tighten the screws from the center outward.
5. Replace the carburetors as previously instructed.

DISASSEMBLY FOR 24,000 MILE SERVICE

1. Remove the carburetors as previously described.
2. Disconnect and remove the primary mixture line from the secondary throttle housing and the exhaust mixture housing.
3. Remove the nuts holding the secondary throttle housing to the manifold.
4. Remove the clamp bolt holding the front throttle linkage to the rear throttle linkage.
5. If the car has an automatic transmission, disconnect the linkage between the transmission throttle control shaft and the front throttle operating shaft.
6. Perform the 12,000 mile service on each carburetor and install new needle valve assemblies and washers.
7. Remove the hydraulic damper assembly from the top cover, remove the cover screws and cover.
8. Remove the piston return spring and piston assembly.
9. Drain the oil from the damper and

loosen the needle clamping screw.

10. Carefully withdraw the needle from the piston and set to one side to avoid damage.
11. Remove the diaphragm retaining ring and diaphragm.

ASSEMBLY

1. Install a new diaphragm with its locating tag recessed into the opening provided for it and secure with the retaining ring and four screws.
2. Install the needle into the piston so that the flat part of the needle is in line with the set screw. Use a ruler to position the needle so that its shoulder is aligned with the flat surface of the piston. Tighten the set screw carefully, so as not to overtighten and collapse the base of the needle. The needle is correctly positioned when it is turned slightly toward the throttle and the shoulder of the needle will be flush with the face of the piston.
3. Carefully pass the piston and diaphragm assembly into the main body, guiding the needle into the jet.
4. Locate the outer tag of the diaphragm into the recess provided at the top of the body.
5. Check the assembly by looking down the piston to make sure that the two vacuum transfer holes are toward, and in line with, the throttle spindle and that the needle is turned toward the throttle instead of being vertical.
6. Replace the piston return spring and install the cover while holding the piston against the spring.
7. Install and tighten down the cover with the damper ventilation boss toward the air intake.
8. The piston must travel freely and fall upon the carburetor bridge with an audible metallic click when dropped from its top position.
9. Refill the piston damper, install a new seal and replace the piston damper assembly.
10. Remove the temperature compensator unit.
11. Remove the inner seal from the body and the outer seal from the valve, install new seals and replace the unit, tightening the screws evenly.
12. Take off the compensator cover and check the valve for freedom of movement by lifting it from its seat. When the valve is released it should return freely. Do not apply force to the bi-metal strip or try to change the adjustment. If the valve sticks, remove the nut and screw and lightly clean the bore and valve with gasoline. Replace the bi-metal strip and retension it by tightening the nut only to the point where the valve is just seated.
13. Lift the by-pass valve body from its seat.
14. Install new throttle spindle seals.
15. Install the valve body.
16. Replace the secondary throttle housing and mixture line, using new gaskets.
17. Using new gaskets and spacers, attach the carburetors to the secondary throttle housing.
18. Reconnect the throttle spindle controls and adjust the carburetors.

ADJUSTMENT PROCEDURES FOR THE STROMBERG CARBURETOR

1. With the engine *not* running, unscrew the throttle stop screws so that the primary throttles are completely closed.
2. Screw in the stop screws until they just touch the casting, then turn each one in another 1-1/2 turns so that the throttles are opened the same amount.

IMPORTANT: Be sure that the fast idle screw is not contacting the choke cam, for

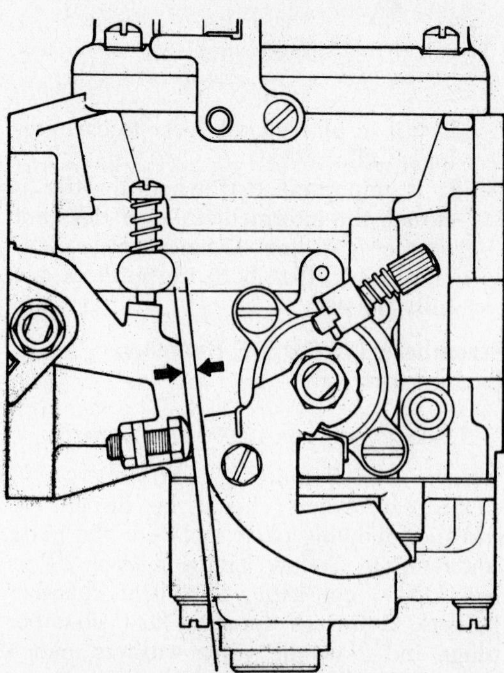

Fast idle screw adjustment—clearance between screw and cam should be .067″

this will cause faulty carburetor synchronization. Both choke cams must be in contact with their stops.

3. With the dashboard choke control fully in, reconnect the choke cables to the cams and check to see that both cams operate at the same time.
4. Start the engine and let it run until operating temperature is reached.
5. Let the engine idle and, using a Unisyn® synchronizer, synchronize the throttles. Tighten the clamping bolts.
6. Turn the throttle stop screws the same amount until an idling speed of 750 rpm (650 rpm in neutral for automatics) is attained.
7. Adjust the choke control cam position by operating the control lever until the cable swivel, the cam securing nut, and the fast idle screw are all in line.
8. Maintaining this alignment, release the locknut and adjust the screw so that a fast idle speed of 1,100 rpm is reached with the engine cold and the surrounding temperature 68°-86°F.
9. Tighten the locknut, replace the vacuum line to the by-pass valve.
10. Replace air cleaner and breather hose.
11. A control in each carburetor allows the choke to be adjusted for summer or winter operation, and is in the form of a spring-loaded plunger which operates against the cam. The position of the stop cross-pin determines the setting. If the pin is lying in the horizontal slot of the casting, the choke is set for winter, and is adjusted for summer by pressing the spring-loaded pin and turning it 90°.
12. The hydraulic piston damper should be filled with SAE 20 oil to within 1/4" from the top of the hollow piston rod. If this is not done, acceleration will suffer due to the pistons being allowed to flutter when the accelerator is rapidly depressed.
13. The idle trim screw provides a slightly leaner mixture. When this screw is fully seated, the maximum enrichment is achieved with emission still being within legal requirements. When tightening the screw, only finger pressure should be used in order to avoid overtightening.

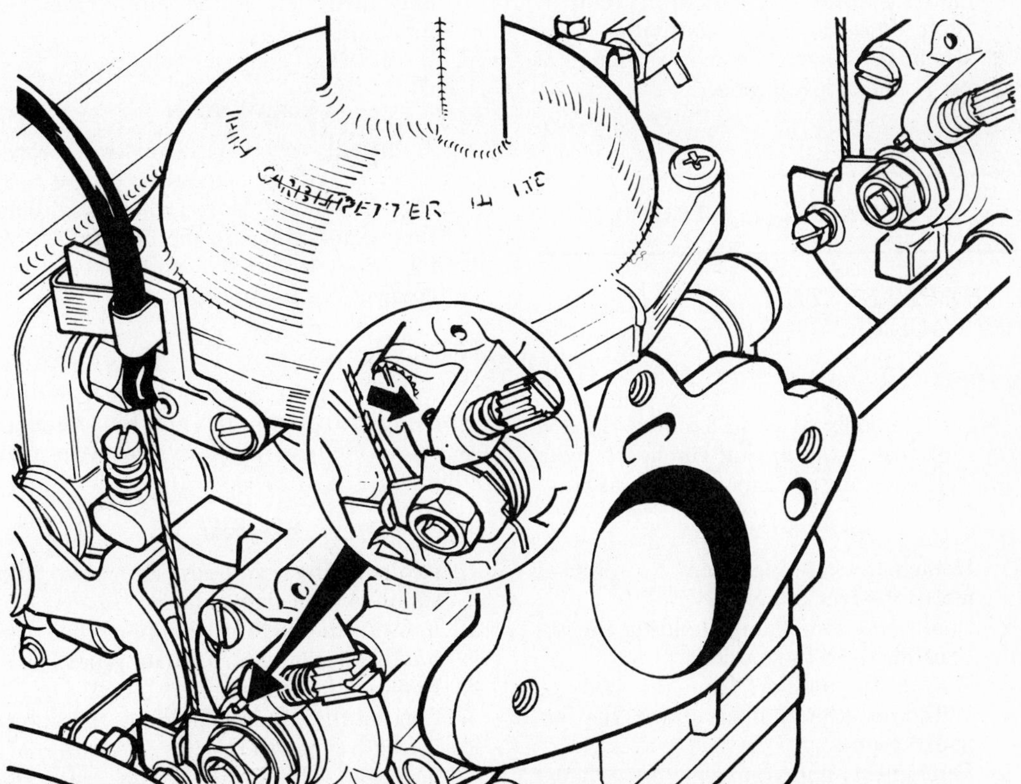

The choke limiting spindle in the Winter setting (inset shows Summer setting)—XJ6, E Type (1968-1971)

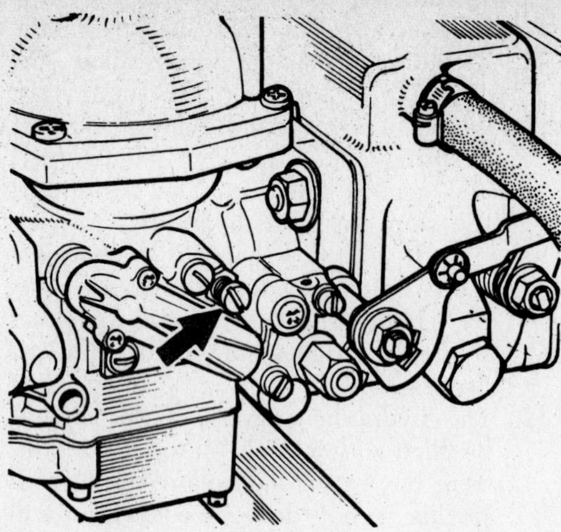

Idle trim screw on Stromberg 175 CD2SE carburetor—XJ6, E Type (1968-1971)

14. Included in this carburetor is a temperature compensator that automatically adjusts for variations in fuel mixture strength caused by heat transfer to the carburetor castings. This compensator is preset at the factory and is not to be adjusted unless the plug is sticking.
15. The Stromberg carburetor also includes a throttle by-pass to prevent the high emissions that normally occur when the engine is over-running, as on a steep downgrade.

Exhaust System

EXHAUST SYSTEM REPLACEMENT

Mark II (3.4 and 3.8)

Mark II models (3.4 and 3.8 liter) have a dual exhaust system that includes twin mufflers joined together into an assembly.

Removal

1. Detach the tailpipes from the bracket under the rear bumper.
2. Loosen the two clamps holding the exhaust pipes to the mufflers.
3. Detach the mufflers from the body.
4. Withdraw the mufflers from the exhaust pipes.
5. Disconnect and remove the exhaust pipes from the exhaust manifold.
6. Remove the two copper sealing rings.

Installation

1. To install, reverse removal procedure. Use new copper sealing rings when connecting exhaust pipes to the manifold.

3.4S, 3.8S and 420

The 3.4S, 3.8S and 420 have a dual exhaust system that includes a front muffler having two inlets and two outlets, two main mufflers and two rear mufflers.

Removal

1. Remove the two tailpipe ring brackets from the body.
2. Loosen the two clamps and remove the tailpipe and rear muffler assemblies.
3. Remove the rubber mounting brackets from the main mufflers.
4. Loosen the two clamps and remove the main mufflers.
5. Remove the intermediate exhaust pipes by loosening the clamps at the front muffler and removing the bolts in the rubber mounting bracket. Loosen the clamps and remove the front muffler.
6. Remove the exhaust pipes from the clamping straps and clutch housing and then detach the pipes from the manifold.
7. Recover the copper sealing rings.

Installation

1. To install, reverse the removal procedure. It will be necessary to use new copper sealing rings when installing the exhaust pipes to the manifold. Run the engine briefly and check the connections for tightness.

XJ6

The XJ6 Jaguar has an exhaust system consisting of two tailpipes and four mufflers (two intermediate mufflers and two rear mufflers).

Removal

1. Remove the tailpipes and save the stainless steel screws for re-use.
2. Loosen the clamps holding the rear mufflers to the intermediate pipes.
3. Remove the rear mufflers.
4. Loosen the clamps holding the intermediate pipes to the intermediate mufflers and release the pipes from the rubber mountings.
5. Loosen the clamps holding the front

mufflers to the front pipes and remove the front mufflers.

6. Remove the right-hand extension pipe and detach the exhaust pipes from the manifold.
7. Remove the sealing rings from the pipe to manifold connections.

INSTALLATION

1. To install, reverse the removal procedure. Use new sealing rings when connecting the pipes to the manifold. Upon completion of installation, run engine briefly and check connections for tightness.

E Type (3.8, 4.2, 2+2)

The E type has a dual exhaust system consisting of two tubular mufflers with connecting tailpipes, a twin muffler assembly and two exhaust pipes.

REMOVAL

1. Loosen the clamps connecting the tailpipes to the muffler assembly.
2. Remove the rear mufflers.
3. Loosen the two clamps holding the front muffler assembly to the two exhaust pipes.
4. Remove the bolts, nuts and washers securing the front muffler assembly to the rubber mounting brackets.
5. Remove the front muffler assembly.
6. Remove the exhaust pipes and their sealing rings from the manifolds.

INSTALLATION

1. Installation is the reverse of removal. When installing the exhaust pipes, it is necessary to use new sealing rings between the pipes and manifold.

Cooling System

RADIATOR

Mark II 3.4S and 3.8S

The Mark II 3.4S and 3.8S models use a film type radiator pressurized by the filler cap which contains a pressure relief valve designed to hold a maximum pressure of 4 psi above the atmospheric pressure in the

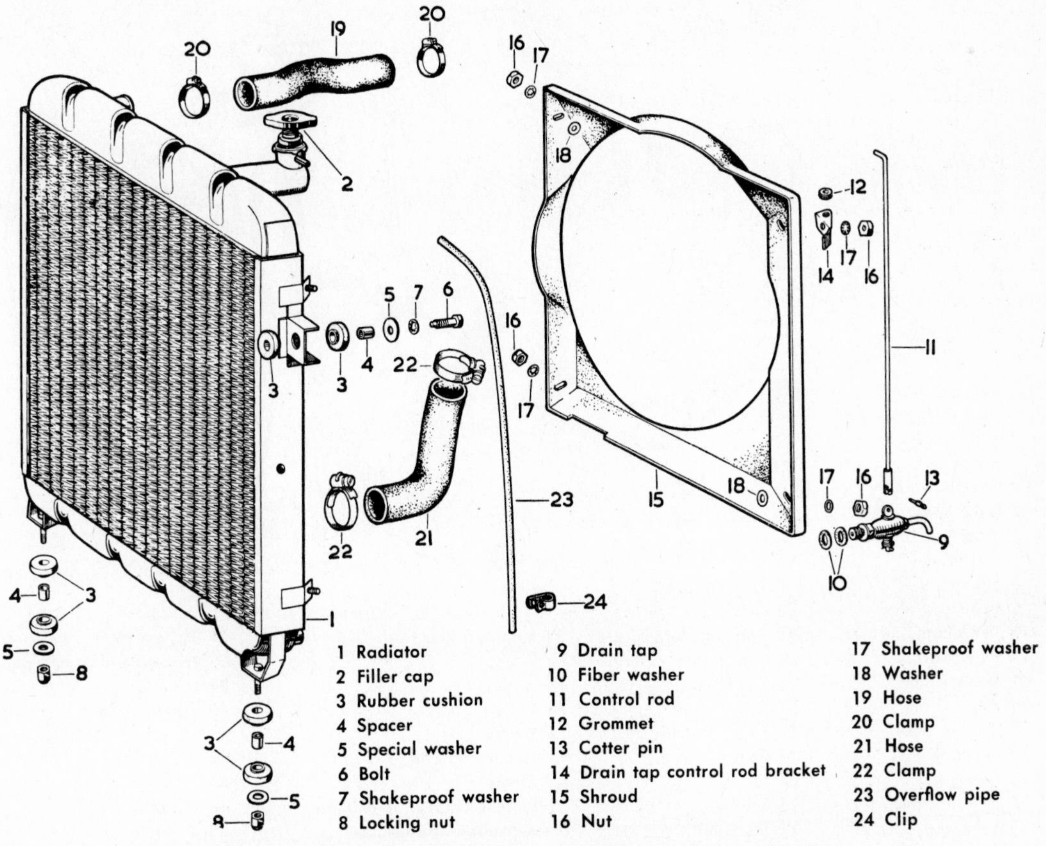

Radiator and related components—Mark II (3.4, 3.8), 3.4S, 3.8S

system. After the valve has opened and the pressure is released, the water cools down and a small valve opens and the atmospheric pressure is restored.

REMOVAL

1. Drain the radiator and disconnect the top and bottom hoses.
2. Detach the radiator shroud and allow it to rest on the water pump housing where it will be out of the way.
3. Remove the control rod from the drain tap and unscrew the drain tap from the radiator block.
4. Remove the mounting screws and nuts and lift out the radiator. If equipped with a shroud, remove it.

CAUTION: The radiator must be kept in an upright position in order to prevent sediment from traveling to the core passages and creating a blockage.

INSTALLATION

1. Installation is the reverse of removal.

420

The 420 model is equipped with a cross-flow type radiator pressurized by a radiator cap rated at 4 psi.

REMOVAL

1. Drain the cooling system and the block. If car has automatic transmission, drain the lower radiator pipe.
2. Remove all radiator hoses.
3. Remove the header tank from the top of the radiator.
4. Separate and remove the split radiator shroud.
5. Remove the fan and Torquatrol unit.
6. Remove the control rod from the drain tap and then remove the tap from the radiator.
7. Detach the front crossmember cover plate from below the radiator grille.
8. Remove the two mounting cushions from beneath the radiator.
9. Disconnect the remaining attachments

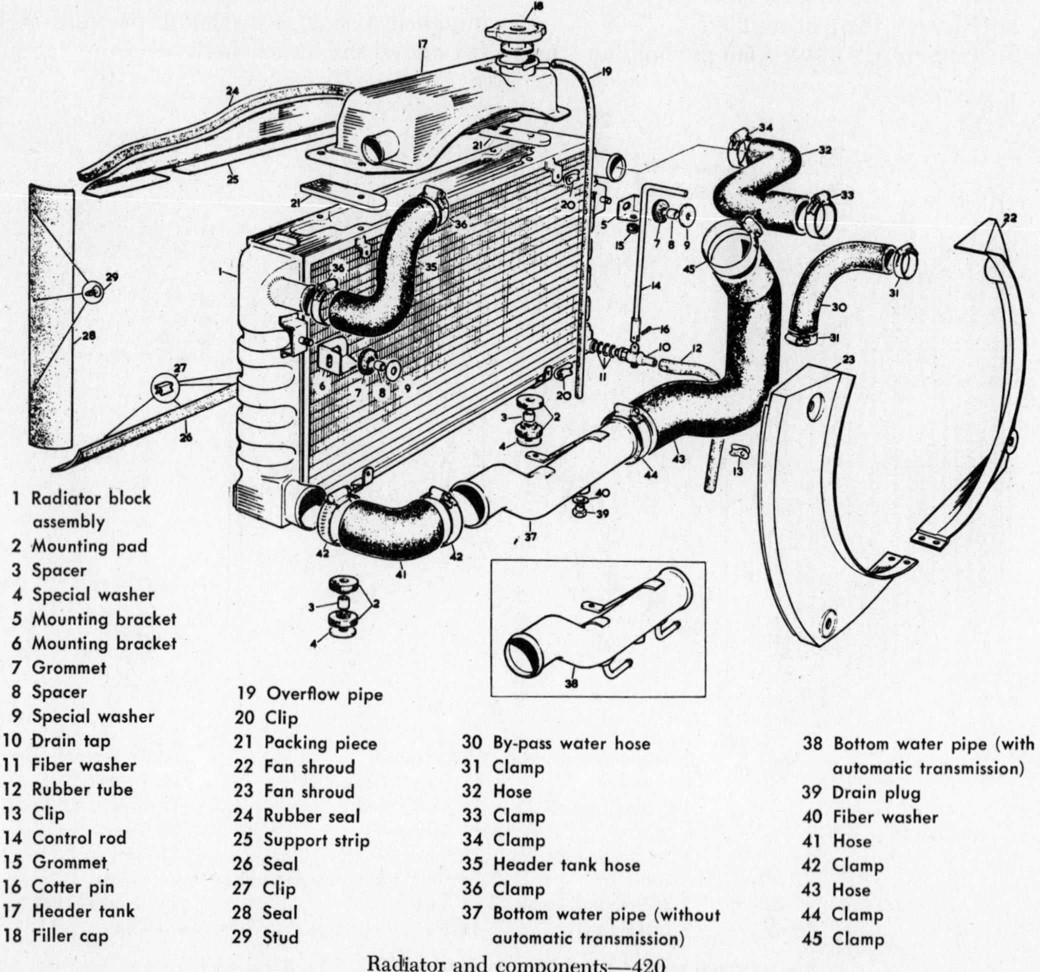

1 Radiator block assembly
2 Mounting pad
3 Spacer
4 Special washer
5 Mounting bracket
6 Mounting bracket
7 Grommet
8 Spacer
9 Special washer
10 Drain tap
11 Fiber washer
12 Rubber tube
13 Clip
14 Control rod
15 Grommet
16 Cotter pin
17 Header tank
18 Filler cap
19 Overflow pipe
20 Clip
21 Packing piece
22 Fan shroud
23 Fan shroud
24 Rubber seal
25 Support strip
26 Seal
27 Clip
28 Seal
29 Stud
30 By-pass water hose
31 Clamp
32 Hose
33 Clamp
34 Clamp
35 Header tank hose
36 Clamp
37 Bottom water pipe (without automatic transmission)
38 Bottom water pipe (with automatic transmission)
39 Drain plug
40 Fiber washer
41 Hose
42 Clamp
43 Hose
44 Clamp
45 Clamp

Radiator and components—420

and carefully remove the radiator from underneath the car.

CAUTION: If car is equipped with air conditioning, the condenser must be removed before it is possible to remove the radiator. This should be attempted ONLY by a qualified air conditioning repairman. Serious injury from refrigeration gas could result if any part of the refrigeration system is disconnected.

Installation

1. To install, reverse removal procedure.

XJ6

The XJ6 has a cross-flow type radiator pressurized by a 4 psi cap on the expansion tank. Air conditioned cars require a 13 psi cap.

Removal

1. Drain the radiator and the block.
2. Drain the bottom water pipe.
3. Disconnect the top and bottom water hoses.
4. Separate the upper from the lower radiator shroud and remove the upper shroud from the car.
5. Remove the crossmember and header tank.
6. Remove the control rod from the drain tap.
7. Remove the lower mounting screws and rubber mounting cushions.
8. Lift out the radiator.
9. If the car has air conditioning, it will be necessary to move the condenser. Detach the condenser from its mounting brackets but *DO NOT, FOR ANY REASON, DISCONNECT ANY OF THE CONDENSER CONNECTIONS —SERIOUS INJURY FROM REFRIGERANT LEAKAGE MAY RESULT. THIS SHOULD BE ATTEMPTED ONLY BY A QUALIFIED REFRIGERATION REPAIRMAN.* To prevent damage, the condenser *MUST* be supported and *MUST* be protected from falling.

Installation

1. To install, reverse the removal procedure.

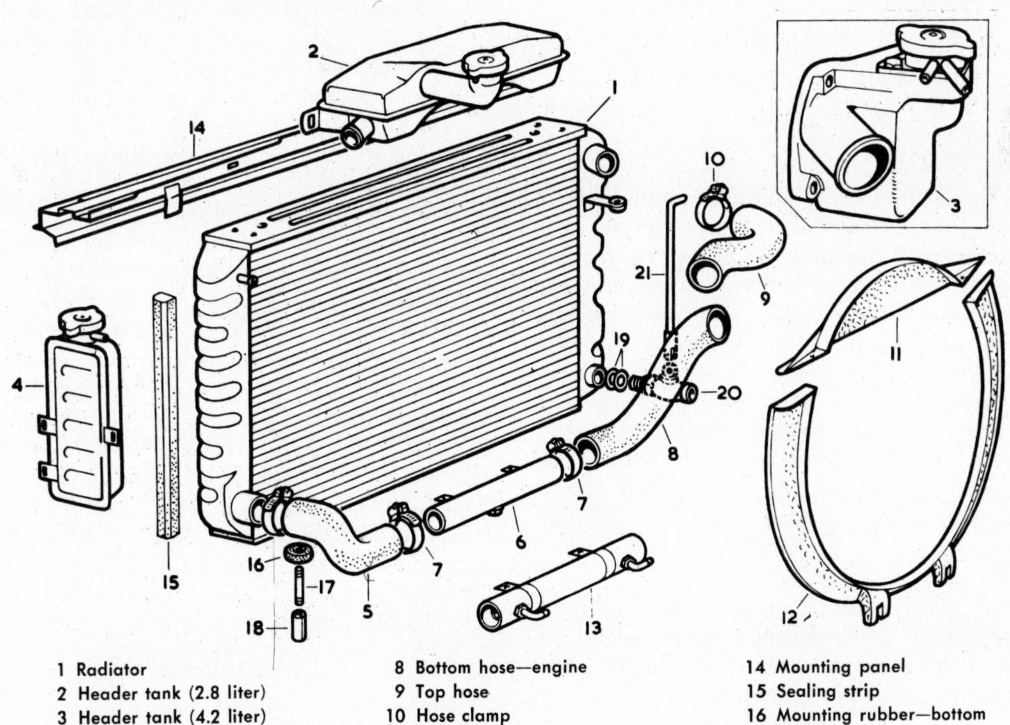

1 Radiator
2 Header tank (2.8 liter)
3 Header tank (4.2 liter)
4 Expansion tank (4.2 liter)
5 Bottom hose—radiator
6 Bottom water pipe—manual transmission
7 Hose clamp
8 Bottom hose—engine
9 Top hose
10 Hose clamp
11 Radiator shroud
12 Radiator shroud
13 Bottom water pipe—automatic transmission
14 Mounting panel
15 Sealing strip
16 Mounting rubber—bottom
17 Mounting stud
18 Spacer
19 Fiber washer
20 Drain tap
21 Drain tap control

Radiator and components—XJ6

E Type (3.8)

The E type (3.8 liter) uses a cross-flow type radiator pressurized by a 4 psi radiator cap mounted on the separate header tank. Later E type (3.8) Jaguars went to a 9 lb. pressure cap in place of the earlier 4 lb. cap. Chassis numbers determine which models used what caps. The following cars use a 9 lb. cap, a modified header tank and an engine to header tank hose: E type coupes, left-hand drive, beginning with chassis number 888241 (right-hand drive, 861091), and convertibles left-hand drive, beginning with chassis number 879044 and on right-hand drive convertibles beginning with number 850657.

Removal

1. Drain the radiator and block.
2. Disconnect all radiator hoses.
3. Remove the bolts attaching the shield on the front sub frame to the radiator mounting brackets.
4. Remove the nuts, washers and mounting cushions from the bottom of the radiator.
5. Carefully remove the radiator.

Installation

1. Installation is the reverse of removal.

E Type (4.2)

The E type (4.2) and 2+2 model use a *cross-flow radiator* pressurized by a 7 psi radiator cap mounted on a separate header tank. Beginning with certain chassis numbers, the E type (4.2) and 2+2 models went to a sealed cooling system with a *vertical flow radiator* and an expansion tank mounted on the firewall. The *pressure cap* is fitted to the *expansion tank* while a *non-pressure cap* is used on the *radiator*. The pressure cap rating is 7 lbs. standard and 13 lbs. for air conditioned cars. The *radiator* should be filled to the *bottom of the filler neck* and the *expansion tank* to the *half-way mark*. The water level must be checked at the *expansion tank* and checked when the system is *cold*. The chassis numbers that apply are as follows:

Model	Chassis Number	
	R.H. Drive	L.H. Drive
Roadster	1E.2051	1E.15980-U.S.A. Only
Coupe	1E.21807	1E.34583-U.S.A. Only
2+2	1E.51213	1E.77709

Removal—Cross-Flow Radiator

1. Drain the radiator.
2. Remove the four hoses—three at top and one on the bottom.
3. On 2+2 models having automatic transmissions, disconnect the oil cooler pipes located at the right side of the radiator block.
4. Remove the two bolts and nuts holding the top support brackets to the header tank mounting. Remove the bottom mounting cushions and nuts.
5. Detach the radiator duct panel from the bottom of the radiator.
6. Carefully remove the radiator from the car.

Installation

1. Installation is the reverse of removal.

Removal—Vertical Flow Radiator

1. Drain the cooling system.
2. Remove the electrical connections from the hood assembly.
3. Remove the hood assembly.
4. Disconnect the top and bottom radiator hoses.
5. Disconnect the oil cooler pipes (2+2 models) if equipped with automatic transmission and block them off.
6. Remove the six setscrews securing the shroud.
7. Disconnect the fan thermostat switch cables.
8. Remove the radiator duct panel.
9. Remove the bottom mounting screws and rubber mounting washers.
10. Lift out the radiator.

CAUTION: If car has air conditioning, leave the condenser in position and remove the radiator carefully so that the condenser is not damaged. DO NOT, UNDER ANY CIRCUMSTANCES DISCONNECT OR LOOSEN ANY OF THE REFRIGERATION HOSES. SERIOUS INJURY FROM REFRIGERANT LEAKAGE MAY RESULT. THIS SHOULD BE ATTEMPTED ONLY BY A QUALIFIED REFRIGERATION REPAIRMAN.

Installation

1. Installation is the reverse of removal.

WATER PUMP

The Jaguar uses a centrifugal vane impeller type water pump. Drilled in the top of the casting is an air vent which goes into a circular depression in the casting. A rubber thrower located on the spindle directs water into this depression and, at this time, the water travels around the depression and empties out through a drain hole and, as a result, prevents the bearing from getting wet.

Mark II and 3.4S and 3.8S Models

Removal

1. Remove the radiator.
2. Loosen the generator bolts and remove the fan belt.
3. Remove the two setscrews. The other four setscrews can be removed when the pulley and damper are removed.
4. Remove the fan and fan pulley being sure to mark the positions of the semicircular balance piece or pieces relative to the fan and fan hub.
5. Disconnect the hoses from the water pump.
6. Remove the water pump.

Installation

1. Reverse the removal procedure and replace the pump to timing cover gasket after coating it lightly with grease.

420 and XJ6

Removal

1. Drain the cooling system and block.
2. Disconnect and remove the header tank.
3. Remove the fan and Torquatrol unit.
4. If so equipped, remove the power steering pump adjusting bolt.
5. If the car has air conditioning, remove the compressor front mounting bracket.
6. Detach the heater hoses.
7. Remove the water pump.

Installation

1. Installation is the reverse of removal.

E Type—All Models

Removal

1. Drain the cooling system.
2. Disconnect the hoses from the header tank.
3. Remove the connections from the thermostatic fan switch and tag to facilitate installation.
4. Remove the nuts and bolts holding the header tank and the right and left radiator brackets.
5. Disconnect the electrical connections from the fan relay and tag them for accurate installation.
6. Remove the header tank support bracket.
7. Disconnect the water pump hoses.
8. Remove the drive belt, pulley and water pump.

Installation

1. To install, reverse the removal procedure. Replace the pump to timing chain cover gasket after lightly coating the gasket with grease.

Engine

EXHAUST EMISSION CONTROL

In 1968, due to American and Canadian exhaust emission regulations, Stromberg 175CD2SE carburetors replaced the traditional S.U. carburetors on Jaguar 4.2 liter cars.

Combined with the two Stromberg carburetors is a Duplex Manifolding System which uses two manifolds. Two throttles are used, connected by linkage so that when the car is driven at part throttle, the secondary throttle remains closed and intake mixtures pass through the primary throttle only.

On 1968 models, exhaust gases heated the fuel mixtures on their way to the combustion chambers. In 1969, a water-heated conditioning chamber was used so that, at part throttle, the fuel mixture would travel through the primary throttle, through the primary mixture pipe (by-passing the secondary) to this chamber where it is heated and then return to the intake manifold just downstream of the closed secondary throttle plate. This system, also used in 1970 and 1971 models (i.e. the water-heated chamber), ensures that the air/fuel mixture remains constant when delivered to the combustion chambers. This makes it possible for a leaner mixture to be used and it prevents the presence of wet fuel in the intake manifold, a major cause of exhaust emissions.

In 1970 and 1971 models, there was included a controlled air temperature system which ensures that the air going to the carburetors is kept at approximately 120°F. A shroud placed over the exhaust manifold

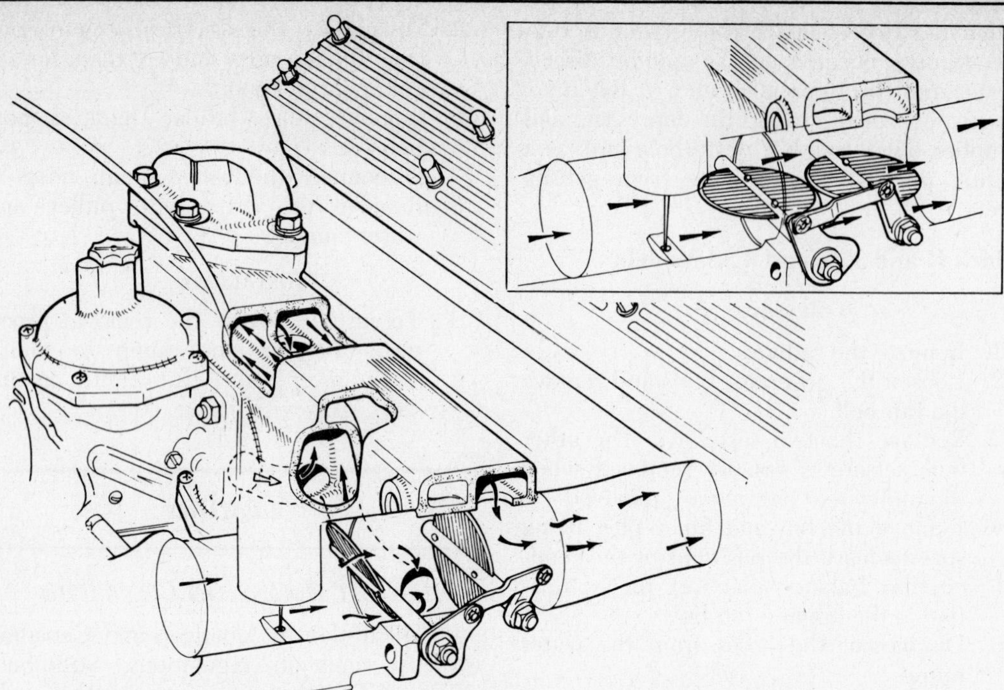

Schematic of carburetors and linkage showing direction of gas flow—XJ6 and E Type (1968-1971)

traps hot air which is then transferred by a duct to a control valve situated in the air cleaner inlet tube. This valve determines the amount of hot air taken from the shroud. A vacuum servo unit controls the position of the valve according to the amount of vacuum coming from the manifold. A thermal sensor, mounted on the air cleaner (clean air side), determines the air temperature entering the carburetors and, by means of a valve in the sensor, regulates the amount of manifold vacuum going to the vacuum servo unit. In this way, the control valve assures that the air temperature around the sensor remains almost constant. When the carburetors reach full throttle, the control valve shuts off the hot air to prevent any performance loss.

Beginning with the 1970 models, Jaguar further reduced emissions with a Fuel Evaporative Control System. This system controls the release of hydrocarbon vapors from the gas tank and carburetor vents. A sealed gas cap forces the gas vapors in the tank to escape through vent lines located at the corner of the tank. These lines carry the vapors into an expansion tank and from there on to the engine compartment where they pass through a canister containing activated charcoal. The charcoal filters out the impurities and the vapors travel on through the engine breather to the carburetors. On XJ6 models, the expansion tank is located within each of the fuel tanks and on the E Type, the tank is a separate unit. Fuel vapors are minimized further by venting the float chambers to the engine side of the air cleaner.

A modified distributor with a redesigned power curve is used with this emission system. Included in the distributor, is a vacuum retard unit that retards the ignition timing by 10° (crankshaft) everytime the throttle is closed. A line connecting the retarding unit to the carburetor picks up manifold vacuum when the throttle is closed. The ignition timing at the crankshaft is 10° BTDC static and TDC at idling speed.

Adjusting the Emission Control System

The only adjustments that can be made to this system are those to the carburetors. See adjustment procedures for the Stromberg carburetor.

ENGINE

Mark II (3.4, 3.8), 3.4S, 3.8S

Removal

1. Mark the hood hinge positions and remove the hood.

2. Remove the air cleaner assembly.
3. Remove the battery and battery tray.
4. Drain the oil pan and take out the dipstick.
5. Drain the radiator and engine block.
6. Detach the engine breather pipe.
7. Remove the washer bottle and the top and bottom water hoses.
8. Remove the generator and note that the brown/yellow wire is connected to the large terminal.
9. Take out the radiator. See the radiator removal section applicable to this model.
10. Disconnect the exhaust system.
11. Remove the heater hoses from the rear of the engine.
12. Disconnect the tachometer leads from the generator.
13. Detach the clutch fluid line from its bracket located at the rear of the cylinder head.
14. Disconnect the oil gauge line from the oil filter.
15. Remove the flexible rubber vacuum hose from the pipe under the intake manifold next to the distributor.
16. Disconnect the starter motor wires.
17. Remove the snap connectors from the transmission harness at the rear of the exhaust manifolds.
18. Disconnect the accelerator linkage.
19. Remove the wire from the temperature gauge sending unit located under or in the side of the water outlet bar.
20. Remove the switch terminal wire from the ignition coil.
21. Remove the locknut and washer from the stabilizer located at the rear of the engine.
22. Remove the carburetors. For instructions, refer to the section on removing the S.U. HD 6 carburetor.
23. Remove the gear shift knob, air distribution pipe cover and rubber grommet.
24. Disconnect the ground strap from the clutch housing bolt.
25. Disconnect the speedometer from the transmission.
26. Remove numbers 3, 6, 8 and 9 cylinder head nuts and attach an engine lifting plate.
27. Remove the front and rear engine mounts and the driveshaft.
28. If the car has an automatic transmission, perform the following:
    a. Remove the transmission mounts.
    b. Disconnect the driveshaft from the transmission and remove the center bearing.
    c. Remove the driveshaft.
    d. Disconnect the control rod from the selector lever.
    e. Remove the selector cable clamp from the reverse servo cylinder located at the front left-side of the transmission.
    f. Disconnect the governor control rod from its lever at the rear of the transmission.
    g. Remove the wires from the anti-creep pressure switch and disconnect the intermediate speed hold solenoid wire.
29. Lift out the engine/transmission assembly.

Installation

1. Installation is the reverse of removal.

420 Models

Removal

1. Mark the positions of the hood hinges and remove the hood.
2. Remove the battery.
3. Drain the oil pan and cooling system.
4. Remove the air cleaner.
5. If car has automatic transmission, remove the oil cooler.
6. Remove the radiator. See radiator removal section applicable to this model before attempting removal and pay special attention to the CAUTION concerning those models equipped with air conditioning.
7. Disconnect and tag (for assembly reference) the wires from the starter motor, coil, alternator, and temperature and oil pressure sending switches.
8. Disconnect the automatic choke cables and the battery ground cable.
9. Remove the fuel line from the carburetor filter bowl.
10. Disconnect the carburetor linkage and, if equipped with automatic transmission, detach the kick-down linkage.
11. Remove the brake vacuum line and the heater vacuum tank hose from under the intake manifold.
12. Detach the heater hoses from the engine.
13. Disconnect and plug the power steering hoses from the pump. Loosen the pump adjusting nuts and push the

pump in toward the engine so that it is out of the way.

14. If car has air conditioning, remove the compressor and its mounting bracket and tie it to the fender out of the way. *DO NOT DISCONNECT OR LOOSEN ANY OF THE HOSES OR CONNECTIONS FROM THE COMPRESSOR.*
15. Disconnect the exhaust pipes from the manifold and the exhaust pipe mounting strap from the bell housing.
16. Detach the speedometer cable.
17. If the car is equipped with automatic transmission, remove the selector cable from its lever on the transmission and the cable clamp from the converter.
18. On those cars having standard transmission and overdrive, remove the gearshift knob and grommet and remove the console. Disconnect the wires from the back-up light switch and overdrive switch and remove the clutch slave cylinder from the bell housing.
19. Remove the rear engine mounting.
20. Disconnect the front of the driveshaft.
21. Lift the engine slightly and remove the front engine mounts and engine stabilizer.
22. Remove the engine.

Installation

1. To install, reverse the removal procedure. When installing the engine, the rear stabilizer should be properly adjusted:
   a. The lower flanged washer should be screwed up the stabilizer pin until the flange hits the bottom of the rubber mounting. The washer can be moved up the pin by inserting a screwdriver in the slot through the center hole of the rubber mounting.
   b. Position the upper flanged washer and tighten down with the nut.

XJ6 Models

Removal

1. Mark the hinge positions and remove the hood.
2. Remove the cross stays from the firewall and fender.
3. Remove the radiator. See the radiator removal section for this model. If car is air conditioned, *DO NOT LOOSEN OR DISCONNECT CONDENSER HOSES*, but refer to *CAUTIONS* in radiator section before attempting to remove condenser.
4. Drain the oil pan and remove the air cleaner.
5. Disconnect the wires from the starter motor and the right-hand engine harness from its connection.
6. Remove and tag (for assembly reference) the coil wires.
7. Disconnect the brake vacuum line from under the intake manifold.
8. Disconnect and cap the power steering hoses.
9. Loosen the adjuster nuts and push the pump in towards the engine so that it is out of the way.
10. Detach the heater hoses from the firewall and the vacuum tank lines from the nonreturn valve.
11. Close the fuel valve and disconnect the carburetor feed line union.
12. Separate the throttle cable from the accelerator and remove the cable through the firewall.
13. Remove the connections from the alternator.
14. Disconnect the exhaust system from the manifold.
15. Remove the air conditioning compressor and bracket and tie to the fender. In so doing, *DO NOT LOOSEN OR DISCONNECT THE COMPRESSOR HOSE CONNECTIONS; REFRIGERANT GAS CAN CAUSE SERIOUS INJURIES.*
16. Remove the ground strap from the bell housing.
17. On those cars with automatic transmissions, disconnect the kick-down cable from the carburetor controls. Remove the selector cable from its lever on the transmission. Detach the cable clamp from the converter.
18. On cars equipped with standard transmission and overdrive, disconnect the overdrive switch and remove the gearshift knob. Remove the transmission harness and detach the clutch slave cylinder from the bell housing. Fabricate a piece of tubing (see illustration) and slip it over the gearshift lever to go through the grommet on the console. Keep the tube in this position to act as a guide when installing the engine.
19. Remove the rear engine mount and disconnect the front of the driveshaft.
20. Remove the front engine mounts.

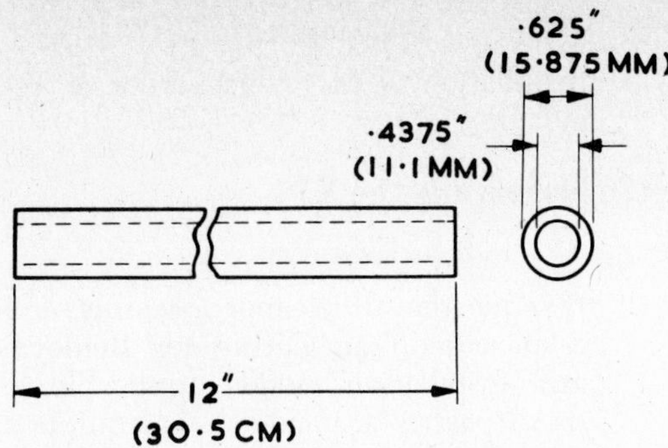

Dimensions for gear shift lever guide tube—XJ6

21. Detach the speedometer cable.
22. Lower the rear of the engine until the gearshift lever has cleared the console grommet.
23. Remove the engine.

INSTALLATION

1. Installation is the reverse of removal.

The E Type (3.8, 4.2, 2+2)

1. Remove the hood.
2. Disconnect the battery.
3. Drain the cooling system.
4. Remove the air cleaner assembly.
5. Disconnect the fuel line from below the center carburetor.
6. Detach the water hoses going to the header tank and loosen the heater hoses going to the manifold.
7. Disconnect the brake vacuum line.
8. Disconnect the two electrical connections from the fan control thermostat located in the header tank.
9. Detach the header tank overflow pipe and remove the header tank and mounting bracket.
10. Disconnect the throttle linkage from the rear carburetor.
11. Remove the wire (green/blue) from the temperature sending unit.
12. Remove the wires from the coil and note their locations for proper reassembly.
13. Disconnect and tag the wires from the starter motor.
14. Remove the oil filter and housing.
15. Remove the lower crankshaft pulley, damper and belt. Detach the timing pointer from the oil pan.

NOTE: Mark the pulley and damper to make installation easier.

16. Remove the upper clamp from the water pump hose.
17. Disconnect the oil pressure sending unit.
18. Remove the tachometer sending unit and wiring.
19. Disconnect and tag (as to location) the generator wires.
20. Remove the exhaust system.
21. Take out the seats, radio and ash tray.
22. Separate the driveshaft tunnel cover from the body.
23. Remove transmission cover assembly and shift lever.
24. Remove the rear engine mount.
25. Separate the driveshaft from the transmission.
26. On cars having automatic transmissions, it will be necessary to:
    a. Remove dipstick assembly from the transmission.
    b. Position the selector lever in L and release the cable from the selector lever and remove the cable clamp from its bracket.
    c. Remove the speedometer cable.
    d. Remove the oil cooler pipes from the transmission and the right side of the radiator.
    e. Disconnect the kickdown cable from the rear of the cylinder head.
    f. Remove the armrest and the cover panel from the transmission tunnel. Disconnect the driveshaft.
27. On all models, including those with automatic transmission, carry out the following instructions:
28. Extract the two lower nuts holding the torsion bar reaction tie plate and tap the bolts back so that they are flush with the face of the tie plate. With the help of an assistant, place a lever between the bolt head and the torsion bar. Apply pressure to the lower bolt head to relieve the tension on the upper bolt. Remove the nut and tap this upper bolt back so that it is flush with the face of the plate. Repeat this for the other side and separate the plate from the bolts.

CAUTION: If the tension is not relieved on the upper bolts, stripped threads will result and the torsion bars will have to be reset.

30. Remove the engine ground strap from light switch situated on the transmission top cover. These wires can be refitted to either terminal.
30. Remove the engine ground strap from the left-hand side member.
31. Disconnect the clutch slave cylinder.

32. Attach the lifting chain to the engine using the lifting straps on the engine or by using a lifting plate. Support the transmission with a jack.
33. Remove the nut and washer from the engine stabilizer.
34. Extract the bolts from the front engine mounts.
35. Remove the speedometer cable.
36. Carefully lift out the engine making sure that nothing is damaged.

Installation

1. To install, reverse the removal procedure. Before replacing the engine, make sure that the brake lines on the crossmembers are not damaged and that the engine does not hit the torsion bar anchor brackets or change the position of the locating bars. Replace the exhaust manifold sealing rings. If any cylinder head nuts have been removed they should be torqued to 54 ft. lbs. on pre-1968 cars and 58 ft. lbs. on the emission controlled models (1968 on). Once the engine and transmission are back in the car, bleed the clutch hydraulic system (see Clutch section) and adjust the engine stabilizer. For stabilizer adjustment procedure, see the engine installation procedure for the 420 models.

INTAKE MANIFOLD

Mark II Models (3.4, 3.8) and the 3.4S and 3.8S

Removal

1. Drain the radiator.
2. Remove the carburetors as instructed in the Carburetor Removal and Installation section for these particular models.
3. Detach the top hose and by-pass hoses from the water outlet pipe.
4. Disconnect the wire from the water temperature sending switch located in the side of the water oulet pipe.
5. Remove the wire from the auxiliary starting carburetor switch.
6. Detach the rubber vacuum hose from the pipe beneath the manifold.
7. Disconnect the heater hose and the accelerator linkage.
8. Remove the nuts and washers and lift off the manifold.

Installation

1. Installation is in reverse order of removal.

420 Models and the XJ6

Removal

1. Remove the air cleaner assembly and carburetors (see Carburetor Removal and Installation section applicable to these particular models). If equipped with emission control, it may be necessary to remove some of this equipment.
2. Remove the distributor cap and tie it up out of the way. Disconnect the lead carrier from the thermostat housing.
3. Drain the radiator and disconnect the hoses from the front of the manifold and the heater hose from the rear.
4. Detach the brake and heater vacuum hoses from beneath the manifold.
5. Disconnect the wires from the carburetor thermostat switch (XJ6) and from temperature sending switch.
6. Remove the manifold.

Installation

1. To install, reverse the removal procedure. When replacing manifold, use new gasket.

E Type (3.8, 4.2, 2+2)

Removal

Unlike the other models which have one piece manifolds, the E type has an intake manifold consisting of three separate aluminum castings with each going to two cylinders.

Beginning with 1968 models, some emission control equipment may have to be removed.

1. Drain the radiator.
2. Remove the carburetors.
3. Disconnect the water hoses from the manifold outlet pipe.
4. Disconnect the wire from the temperature gauge sending unit.
5. Detach the heater hose and servo pipe from the rear of the manifold.
6. Disconnect the accelerator linkage.
7. Remove the intake manifolds, the water manifold and the air balance pipe.

Installation

1. To install, reverse the order of the removal procedure. When replacing the

throttle linkage, note that the backing plate is offset and must be aligned correctly before tightening.

EXHAUST MANIFOLD

Mark II Models, 3.4S, 3.8S, 420, XJ6, E Type (3.8, 4.2, 2+2)

The procedures for removing and installing the exhaust manifold are identical for the above models.

Removal

1. Remove the brass nuts and spring washers holding the pipe flanges to the exhaust manifolds.
2. Remove the 16 nuts and washers and lift off the manifolds.

Installation

1. To install, reverse the removal procedure and replace the gaskets and sealing rings.

CYLINDER HEAD

Mark II (3.4, 3.8), 3.4S and 3.8S, 420, XJ6, E Type (3.8, 4.2, 2+2)

This is an aluminum alloy cylinder head with hemispherical combustion chambers. Cast iron valve seat inserts, tappet bores and valve guides are shrunk into the cylinder head.

Removal

1. Drain the cooling system at the radiator and the block.
2. Mark the hinge positions (to facilitate assembly) and remove the hood (not necessary for the XJ6). On XJ6 models, remove the two fender brace rods.
3. Remove the battery and its tray if necessary.
4. Disconnect the accelerator linkage or cable and remove air cleaner assembly.
5. Detach the vacuum advance line from the front carburetor. On the 420 and XJ6, disconnect the distributor vacuum advance pipe completely.
6. Disconnect the fuel line from the float chamber union or from the filter union.
7. Detach the auxiliary carburetor wires and remove the line between the auxiliary carburetor and the intake manifold.
8. Remove the tachometer lead from the generator if so equipped.
9. Detach the water hoses from the water outlet pipe of the manifold.
10. Remove the wires from the spark plugs and the wire holder from the block.
11. Remove the clutch line bracket from the rear of the head if so equipped.
12. Remove the coil and spark plugs. It may not be necessary to remove the coil on the 420 or XJ6. On the XJ6, remove the coil lead and distributor cap.
13. Disconnect the engine breather pipe and the exhaust manifolds from the engine.
14. Detach the camshaft oil lines from the rear of the head.
15. Separate the heater hose from the rear of the intake manifold.
16. Remove the electrical connector from the water temperature sending unit located in the intake manifold.
17. Separate the vacuum servo line from the rubber hose going to the intake manifold.
18. Lift off the camshaft covers.
19. Remove the breather housing from the front of the head noting the position of the baffle plate with its two vertical holes.
20. Release camshaft tension by loosening the nut on the eccentric idler sprocket shaft, depressing the spring-loaded stop peg and turning the adjuster plate in a clockwise direction. A counterclockwise rotation tightens it.
21. Break the locking wire and remove the setscrews from each camshaft sprocket.

CAUTION: DO NOT rotate the engine or camshafts AFTER disconnecting the sprockets. If it becomes necessary to turn a camshaft once the head has been removed then the other camshaft must be removed or the bearing cap nuts fully loosened to permit the valves to be released.

22. Slide the sprockets up the support brackets and wire them in place so that they are out of the way during head removal.
23. Loosen the 14 head nuts a fraction of a turn each time until they are free. These must be loosened in the proper sequence as shown in the illustration. If the car is equipped with air conditioning, remove the compressor (*without loosening or disconnecting the hoses*) and tie it to the fender so that it is out of the way.

CAUTION: DO NOT, FOR ANY REASON, DISCONNECT ANY OF THE COMPRESSOR HOSE CONNECTIONS, FOR SERIOUS INJURY MAY RESULT.

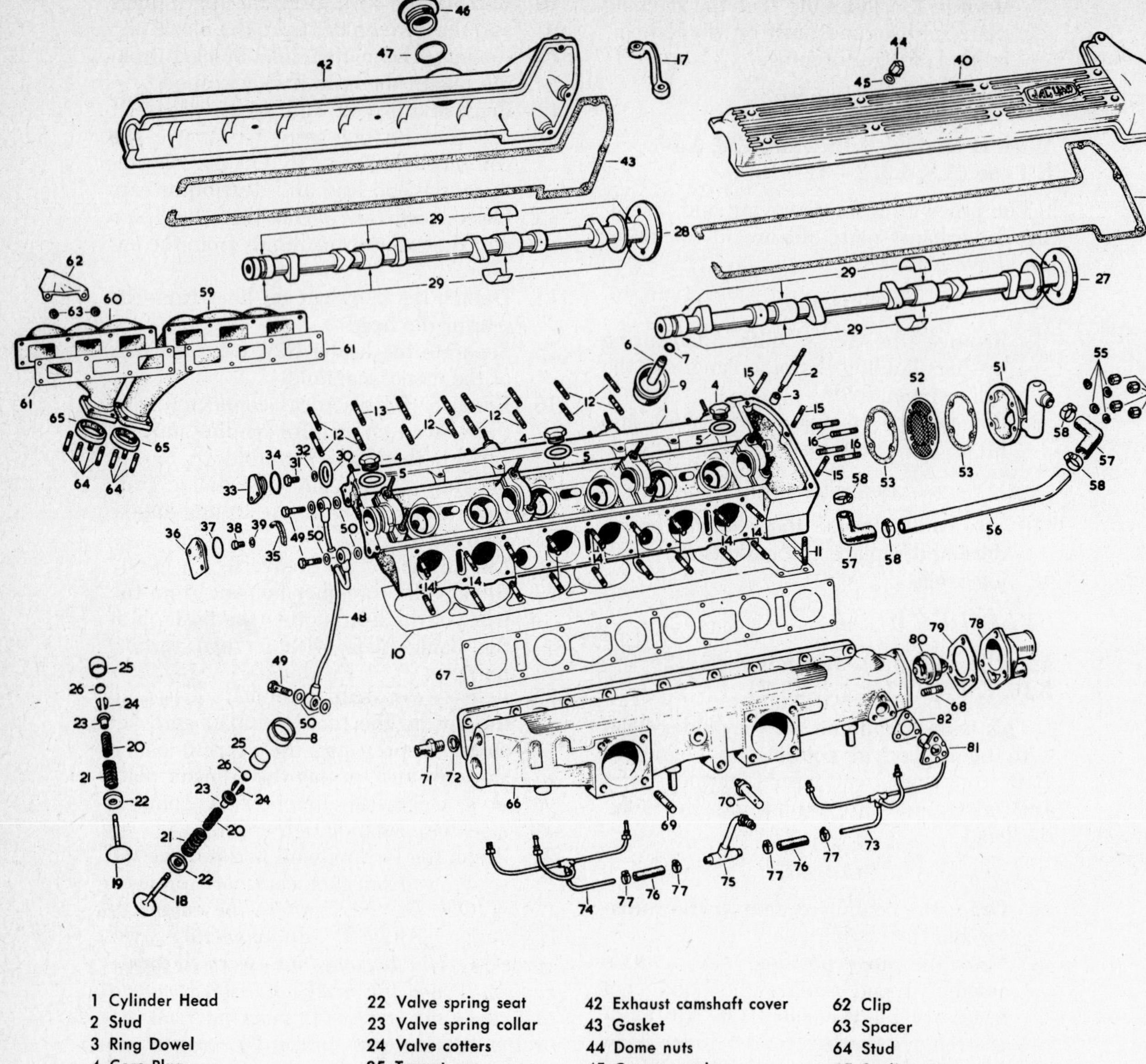

1 Cylinder Head
2 Stud
3 Ring Dowel
4 Core Plug
5 Copper washer
6 Guide
7 Valve guide circlip
8 Valve insert (intake valve)
9 Tappet guide
10 Gasket
11 Stud (short)
12 Stud (exhaust manifold)
13 Stud (exhaust manifold-long)
14 Stud (intake manifold)
15 Stud (camshaft covers)
16 Stud (breather housing)
17 Engine lifting bracket
18 Intake valve
19 Exhaust valve
20 Valve spring (inner)
21 Valve spring (outer)
22 Valve spring seat
23 Valve spring collar
24 Valve cotters
25 Tappet
26 Valve adjusting pad
27 Intake camshaft
28 Exhaust camshaft
29 Bearing (camshaft)
30 Oil thrower
31 Setscrew
32 Copper washer
33 Sealing plug
34 O-ring
35 Seal
36 Sealing plug
37 O-ring
38 Setscrew
39 Copper washer
40 Intake camshaft cover
41 Gasket
42 Exhaust camshaft cover
43 Gasket
44 Dome nuts
45 Copper washer
46 Oil filler cap
47 O-ring
48 Oil pipe
49 Banjo bolt
50 Copper washer
51 Front cover
52 Gauze filter
53 Gasket
54 Dome nuts
55 Spring washer
56 Breather pipe
57 Hose
58 Clip
59 Exhaust manifold-Front
60 Exhaust manifold-Rear
61 Gasket
62 Clip
63 Spacer
64 Stud
65 Sealing ring
66 Intake manifold assembly
67 Gasket
68 Stud
69 Stud
70 Pivot pin
71 Adaptor
72 Washer
73 R.H. Manifold starting pipe
74 L.H. Manifold starting pipe
75 Starting pipe assembly
76 Tube (Neoprene)
77 Clip
78 Pipe—water outlet
79 Gasket
80 Thermostat
81 Thermostat—automatic choke
82 Gasket

Exploded view of cylinder head (420)—with the exception of intake manifold, all models are basically the same

24. Remove the six nuts holding the front of the head and lift off the head complete with the intake manifolds. Remove and discard the head gasket.

CAUTION: Once the head is removed, do not place it face down on a flat surface as the valves protrude below the head and may be damaged. Always support the head on wooden blocks.

Installation

Before replacing the cylinder head, be sure that the camshafts are not out of time, the valves could interfere with the pistons and damage either or both of these.

1. Check that the keyways in the front flanges of the camshafts are at 90° to the camshaft housing face; if not, position it correctly by using a valve timing gauge. If it is necessary to turn a

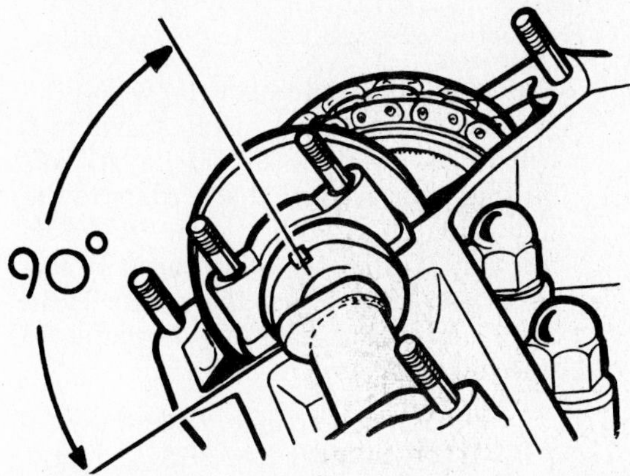

When installing a camshaft, the keyway must be at 90° to the camshaft cover face

camshaft, then the other camshaft must be removed or the bearing cap nuts fully loosened to permit the valves to be released.

CAUTION: DO NOT rotate the engine or camshafts until the camshaft sprockets have been connected to the camshafts. If this advice is not followed, then it will be necessary to retime the camshafts.

2. Place the cylinder head gasket into position, making sure that the side marked Top is, indeed, on top. Install the cylinder head, complete with manifolds, onto the cylinder block.
3. Attach the spark plug wire loom to the third and sixth stud from the front (right-hand side). Place plain washers on these and the two front studs and D washers on the remaining studs. Install the clutch line bracket to the two studs at the rear of the head.
4. Gradually tighten the cylinder head nuts *in the sequence shown* to a torque of 54 ft. lbs.; 58 ft. lbs. for the 420, XJ6 and E Type (4.2, 2+2).
5. Tighten the six nuts that secure the front end of the cylinder head.
6. Check the valve timing as instructed in Valve Adjustment.
7. Using new gaskets, replace the camshaft covers.
8. To install the remaining components, reverse the removal procedure from Step 19.

VALVE TRAIN

Timing the Valves—Mark II, 3.4S, 3.8S, 420, XJ6, E Type (3.8, 4.2, 2+2)

1. Turn the engine so that the number 6 (front) piston is at TDC with the distributor rotor arm pointing to the No. 6 terminal in the distributor cap.
2. Remove the engine breather housing from the front of the head to expose the notched timing chain tension adjusting plate.
3. If applicable, loosen the locknut securing the notched plate.
4. With the camshaft sprocket on the camshaft flanges, tension the chain by pressing the locking plunger in and rotating the adjusting plate counterclockwise. Turn the engine slightly in both directions and recheck the tension. On some models, the adjusting plate can be moved by utilizing the two holes while on others, a special tool must be fabricated (see illustration).

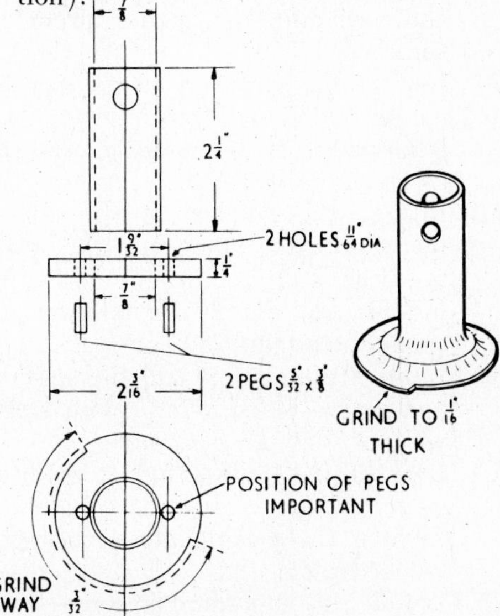

Dimensions for top timing chain adjusting tool

5. When the chain is correctly tensioned, there will be a slight flex on both outer sides below the camshaft sprockets.
6. Release the locking plunger and tighten the locknut.
7. Remove the screws from the camshaft sprockets. If the engine has to be turned to remove them, turn the engine so that No. 6 piston is returned to TDC.
8. Tap the sprockets off the camshaft flanges and accurately position the camshafts with the valve timing gauge making sure that the TDC marks are in exact alignment. The pointer will be aligned with the figure 0.

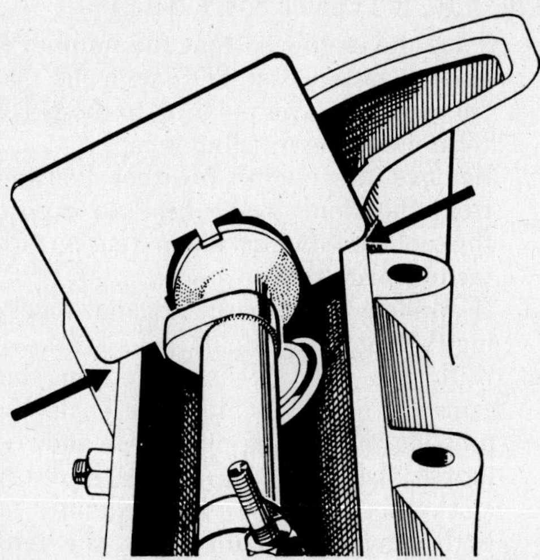

The valve timing gauge must be seated at the points shown by the arrows

9. Remove the circlips holding the adjusting plates to the camshaft sprockets and separate the plates from the sprockets.
10. Replace the sprockets on the camshaft flanges, aligning the adjuster plate holes with those in each camshaft flange.
11. Engage the notches in the adjuster plates with the notches in the sprockets. If difficulty is encountered in aligning the holes exactly, the adjuster plate should be rotated 180°.
12. Replace the circlips and the setscrews and secure the setscrews with locking wire.
13. Recheck the timing chain tension and valve timing.
14. Tighten the locking nut securing the notched plate.
15. Install the breather housing to the head.

Adjusting Valve Clearance—Mark II, 3.4S, 3.8S, 420, XJ6, E Type (all)

1. When the valve clearances are being adjusted, the camshafts should be installed only one at a time in order to avoid interference between the pistons and open valves. While it is possible to check adjustments with both camshafts properly in place, it would be impossible to adjust more than one valve.
2. Measure and record all valve clearances by using a feeler gauge between the heel of each cam and its corresponding tappet. The correct valve clearances are:

Normal Driving
- Intake .... .004″
- Exhaust .... .006″

Racing (E Type–3.8, 4.2, 2+2)
- Intake .... .006″
- Exhaust .... .010″

3. Calculate the difference between the actual clearance of each valve and what the clearance should be. All adjusting pads are coded according to the following chart with a letter etched on the pad. Install the adjusting pad necessary to bring about the proper clearance. Adjusting pads are available in the following sizes:

A	.085 inch	2.16 mm.
B	.086	2.18
C	.087	2.21
D	.088	2.23
E	.089	2.26
F	.090	2.29
G	.091	2.31
H	.092	2.34
I	.093	2.36
J	.094	2.39
K	.095	2.41
L	.096	2.44
M	.097	2.46
N	.098	2.49
O	.099	2.51
P	.100	2.54
Q	.101	2.56
R	.102	2.59
S	.103	2.62
T	.104	2.64
U	.105	2.67
V	.106	2.69
W	.107	2.72
X	.108	2.74
Y	.109	2.77
Z	.110	2.79

4. When installing the camshafts before fitting the head to the engine, make sure that the keyway in the front bearing flange of each camshaft is perpendicular to the camshaft cover face before tightening the camshaft bearing cap nuts to 15 ft. lbs.; 9 ft. lbs. for Mark II models (3.4, 3.8) and XJ6 models.
5. After adjusting all valves, replace the camshafts and cylinder head.

Valve Removal and Installation

See Engine Rebuilding section.

Valve and Valve Seat Resurfacing

See Engine Rebuilding section.

CAMSHAFT AND TIMING CHAIN

Timing Gear Cover and Gear—Mark II Models, 3.4S, 3.8S, 420, XJ6, E Type (All)

The camshafts are driven by two roller chains. The top timing chain is adjusted by means of the idler sprocket, which has an eccentric shaft. The bottom chain is automatically adjusted by a hydraulic tensioner which is bolted to the cylinder block. Nylon or rubber vibration dampers are located at strategic points around both chains.

Removal

1. Remove the cylinder head, radiator, radiator shroud, fan and crankshaft vibration damper.
2. On Mark II models, the 3.4S and 3.8S, remove the front suspension.
3. Remove the split cone from behind the damper.
4. Remove the oil pan.
5. Detach the water pump from the timing cover noting that a gasket is installed between them.
6. Remove the timing cover and seal.
7. Remove the bottom timing chain tensioner by taking out the plug from the end of the tensioner and inserting an Allen wrench into the hole. Turn the wrench clockwise until the cylinder is felt to be fully retracted. This will free the adjuster head from the chain. Detach the tensioner assembly from the block.
8. Remove the screws holding the front and rear mounting brackets and remove the intermediate and bottom vibration dampers.
9. Lift off the timing gear assembly.

Installation

To install the timing gear assembly, reverse the removal procedure. Install the

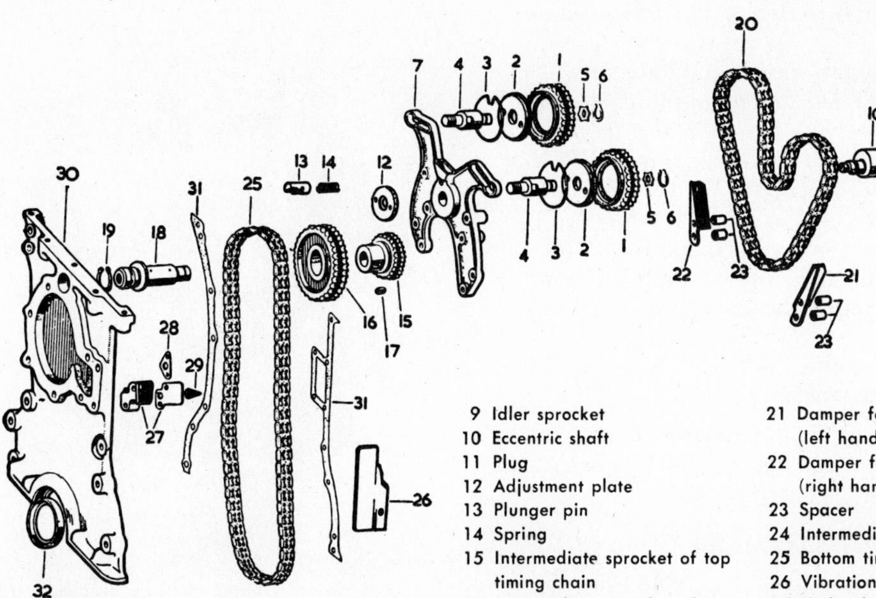

1 Camshaft sprocket
2 Adjusting plate
3 Circlip
4 Guide pin
5 Star washer
6 Circlip
7 Timing gear front mounting bracket
8 Timing gear rear mounting bracket
9 Idler sprocket
10 Eccentric shaft
11 Plug
12 Adjustment plate
13 Plunger pin
14 Spring
15 Intermediate sprocket of top timing chain
16 Intermediate sprocket of lower timing chain
17 Key
18 Shaft
19 Circlip
20 Top timing chain
21 Damper for top timing chain (left hand)
22 Damper for top timing chain (right hand)
23 Spacer
24 Intermediate damper
25 Bottom timing chain
26 Vibration damper
27 Hydraulic chain tensioner
28 Shim
29 Filter gauze
30 Front timing cover
31 Gasket
32 Oil seal

Exploded view of the timing gear

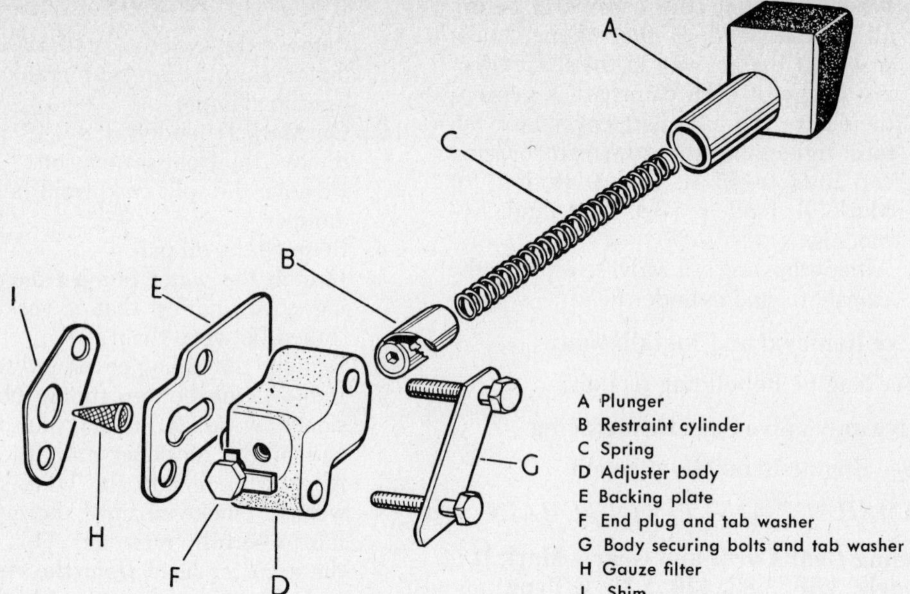

Exploded view of the bottom timing chain tensioner

bottom timing chain tensioner in the following manner:

1. Insert the cone-shaped filter into the oil feed hole in the cylinder block.
2. Install the proper number of shims between the backing plate and the block so that the timing chain will run through the center of the rubber slipper.
3. Install the tab washer and two bolts.

IMPORTANT: Do not attempt to release the locking mechanism until the adjuster has been mounted in the engine WITH THE TIMING CHAIN IN ITS PROPER POSITION.

4. Insert the Allen wrench and turn *clockwise* until the rubber plunger head moves against the chain under spring pressure.
5. Install the plug, and tab washer in the end of the tensioner.

Timing Gear Overhaul—Mark II Models, 3.4S, 3.8S, 420, XJ6, E Type (All)

Disassembly

1. Remove the nut and washer from the front of the idler shaft and detach the plunger and spring.
2. Remove the four nuts holding the front mounting bracket to the rear bracket and withdraw the front bracket from the studs.

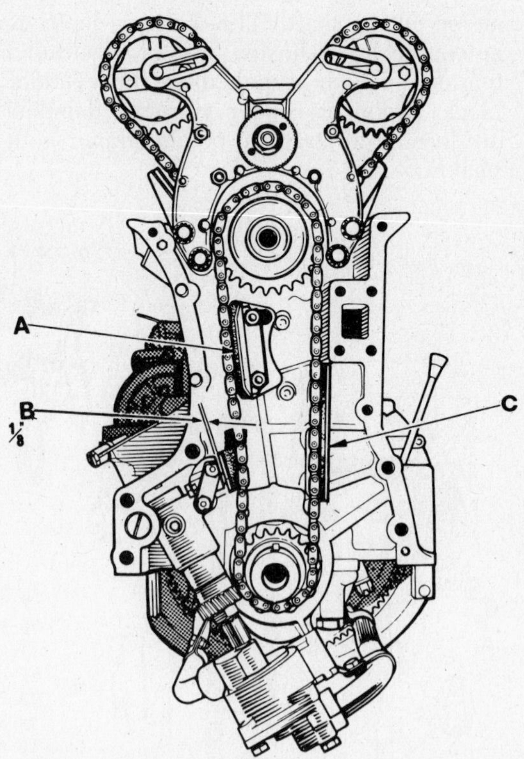

When a new lower timing chain is installed, set the intermediate damper (A) in light contact with the chain when there is 1/8" gap between the rubber slipper and the tensioner body. If the chain is worn, the gap (B) will be increased to prevent interference between the chain and the block. Set the lower damper (C) so that it lightly contacts the chain.

3. Separate the bottom timing chain from the large intermediate sprocket.
4. Remove the intermediate sprockets by detaching the circlip from the end of the shaft and pressing the shaft out of the bracket. The intermediate sprockets on some models are separate and keyed together, although on later models, the intermediate sprocket is made in one piece.

Assembly

1. Replace the eccentric shaft in its hole in the front mounting bracket.
2. Insert the spring and locking plunger (used with the notched adjustment plate) into the hole in the front mounting bracket.
3. Install and tighten the notched adjustment plate.
4. Fit the idler sprocket (21 teeth) on to the eccentric shaft.
5. Place the two intermediate sprockets on their shaft with the larger one in front, then press the shaft through the lower central hole in the rear mounting bracket. Secure in place with the circlip.
6. Replace the top timing chain (the longer chain) on the small intermediate sprocket and the bottom chain on the large intermediate sprocket.
7. Loop the upper chain under the idler sprocket and assemble the two brackets with the dampers between them.
8. Install the intermediate damper to the bottom of the rear mounting bracket.
9. Insert four bolts and lockwashers through the holes in the brackets, dampers and spacers and tighten.

Camshaft

The Jaguar has cast iron camshafts supported by four bearings. Flanges on each side of the front bearing take up the endplay. The camshaft bearings are lubricated by a main gallery pipe going to the rear bearing. Oil then travels through a hole in the camshaft to other holes which lubricate the three remaining bearings. When performing any service to the camshafts, certain precautions must be followed:

a. *DO NOT rotate the engine or camshafts AFTER disconnecting the sprockets. If it becomes necessary to turn a camshaft once the head has been removed, then the other camshaft must be removed or the bearing cap nuts fully loosened to permit the valves to be released.*
b. *Before tightening down the camshaft bearing cap nuts, make sure that the keyway in the front bearing flange of each camshaft is perpendicular (90°) to the camshaft cover face. Using a valve timing gauge to do this will insure accuracy.*

Removal

1. Remove the camshaft covers.
2. Remove the tachometer generator from the right side of the cylinder head and the sealing plug from the left side.
3. Remove the rubber sealing rings.
4. Rotate the engine until No. 6 (front) piston is at TDC on the compression stroke. At this time, the keyway in the front bearing flange of each camshaft should be at 90° to the camshaft cover face.
5. Rotate the engine until the *inaccessible* adjuster plate screws can be removed, and remove them.
6. Return the engine to the point where No. 6 piston is at TDC and remove the remaining adjuster plate screws.
7. Tap the sprockets off their flanges and gradually release the camshaft bearing cap nuts.
8. Remove the bearing cap nuts and note that the caps and cylinder head are marked with corresponding numbers for replacement purposes. It should be observed that the bearing caps are located to the lower bearing housing by hollow dowels.
9. If the same bearing shells are to be reused, they should be tagged as to location and returned to their original positions.
10. Lift out the camshafts from the head.
11. Never scrape or file bearings or bearing caps. Undersize bearings are not supplied by Jaguar, so new parts must replace those that are excessively worn.

Installation

1. Before attempting replacement procedures, it is absolutely necessary that No. 6 piston be at exactly TDC of its compression stroke.
2. Replace the shell bearings in their proper positions.
3. Install each camshaft making sure that the keyways in the front bearing flange

are perpendicular to the camshaft cover face.
4. Install the bearing caps, D washers, spring washers and nuts and gradually tighten the nuts to 15 ft. lbs. On the XJ6 and Mark II models, torque them to 9 ft. lbs.
5. Set the valve timing as described in the Valve Train section.

ENGINE LUBRICATION

Oil Filter

The Jaguar uses a full flow oil filter with a replaceable element. A balance valve, located in the base of the filter, opens at a pressure differential of 10-15 psi (15-20 for the XJ6) in order to provide a safety outlet so that oil will reach the bearings even if the filter element should become completely clogged. It is advisable to change the filter element with every oil change. To replace the element, remove the center bolt, filter body and rubber sealing ring. Clean the inside of the filter body with gasoline, install the element, rubber sealing ring and tighten down. Check for leaks.

Oil Pan—Mark II, 3.4S, 3.8S

The Mark II models have a steel oil pan while the 3.4S and 3.8S have aluminum pans. A rubber hose connects the pan to the oil filter and a gauze bowl type strainer is internally attached and should be cleaned with gasoline at time of pan removal.

Removal

1. Drain the oil pan.
2. Remove the front suspension.
3. Remove the setscrews and nuts and drop the pan.

Installation

1. Clean the pan and scrape the gasket material from the face of the crankcase.
2. Use new gasket and rear oil seal and attach with an adhesive.
3. Fit oil pan and tighten down with the screws and nuts making sure that the short setscrew is installed in the right-hand front corner of the pan.
4. Install front suspension.

Oil Pan—420 and XJ6

Removal

1. Drain the pan.
2. Remove the front suspension and, if necessary, lift the engine with a sling to facilitate removal.
3. Disconnect the oil return hose from the oil filter.
4. On those cars having automatic transmissions, disconnect the oil cooler lines from the radiator and transmission.
5. Unscrew the setscrews and bolts from the pan and remove the pan.
6. Remove the baffle plate and filter basket and wash the basket in gasoline.
7. Detach the oil return pipe flange from the pan and replace the O-ring if necessary.

Installation

1. To install, reverse removal procedure using new gaskets and seals.

Oil Pan—E Type (3.8, 4.2, 2+2)

The E Type has an aluminum oil pan with a rubber hose connecting the pan to the oil filter. A gauze type filter is attached to the pan baffle plate.

Removal

1. Drain the oil pan.
2. Remove the crankshaft damper and oil return hose.
3. It may be necessary to loosen the engine stabilizer and raise the rear of the engine about 1″.
4. Remove the pan and clean thoroughly.

Installation

1. To install, reverse the removal procedure making sure that the short setscrew is fitted to the right-hand front corner of the pan. Use new gaskets and rear oil seal and apply with an adhesive.

Oil Pump—Mark II, 3.4S, 3.8S, 420, XJ6, E Type (All)

The oil pump is an eccentric rotor type and consists of the body, the driving spindle inner rotor, the outer rotor, the cover and the main body.

Removal

1. Remove the oil pan.
2. Detach the suction and delivery lines from the pump.
3. Straighten the tab washers and remove the three bolts holding the pump to the front main bearing cap.
4. Remove the oil pump and the coupling sleeve at the top of the driveshaft.

INSTALLATION

1. Installation is the reverse of removal.

PISTONS AND CONNECTING RODS

Piston and Connecting Rod Removal and Installation

See Engine Rebuilding section.

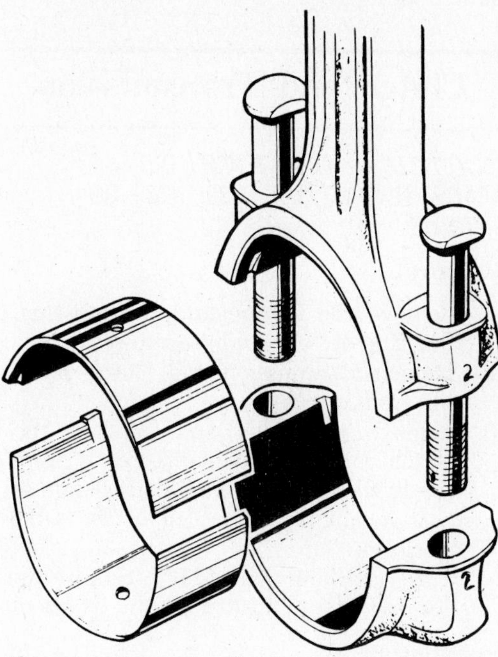

The connecting rod and cap are stamped with the cylinder number from which they came

Piston and Connecting Rod Description and Identification—Mark II, 3.4S, 3.8S, 420, XJ6, E Type (All)

The pistons are made of low-expansion aluminum alloy and are of the semi-split skirt type. Each piston has three rings, two compression and one oil control. The top compression ring is chrome-plated and both the top and second compression rings have a tapered periphery.

All engines have fully floating piston pins held in the piston by a circlip at each end. The pistons or connecting rods in one engine should not vary in weight by more than 3.5 grams.

The pistons will not pass the crankshaft, and therefore have to be removed from the top after the head and oil pan have been removed. Be sure to matchmark the piston and cylinder before removal.

The piston pins and pistons are supplied in selectively assembled sets and are not interchangeable. If the pin is separated from the piston it is important that the pin is returned to this same matching piston. The piston pins are a finger push fit in the piston at a temperature of 68°F. Pistons are available in selective grades according to the engine displacement. These grades are available in standard size pistons only. The grade identification number is stamped on the crown of the piston and on the top face of the cylinder head next to the bores. The piston grades are as follows:

Displacement	Grade	Cylinder Bore Size
3.4 liter	F	3.2673″-3.2676″
	G	3.2677″-3.2680″
	H	3.2681″-3.2684″
	J	3.2685″-3.2688″
	K	3.2689″-3.2692″
3.8 liter	F	3.4248″-3.4251″
	G	3.4252″-3.4255″
	H	3.4256″-3.4259″
	J	3.4260″-3.4263″
	K	3.4264″-3.4267″
4.2 liter	F	3.6250″-3.6253″
	G	3.6254″-3.6257″
	H	3.6258″-3.6261″
	J	3.6262″-3.6265″
	K	3.6266″-3.6269″

In addition, oversize pistons are available in the following sizes: +.010″ o/s, +.020″o/s, and +.030″o/s. As piston grading is strictly for factory production purposes, there are no selective grades in oversize pistons.

Before replacing the pistons, be sure that the rings are properly positioned and have the correct gap and side clearance. Tapered periphery rings should always be fitted with the narrowest part of the ring upward. To help in identifying the narrowest face, a letter T or the word TOP is marked on the proper side. The correct gaps for the 3.4S, 3.8S and 420 engines is .015″–.020″ for the compression rings and .015″–.033″ for the oil control rings. The E Type (3.8) and the Mark II models (3.4, 3.8) have a gap of .015″–.020″ for the compression rings and .011″–.016″ for the oil control rings.

The compression ring setting for the XJ6 (4.2) and the E Type (4.2 and 2+2) is .015″—.020″ for the top ring and .010″—.015″ for the bottom ring while the oil control ring is to be gapped at .015″–.033″. The chrome-plated compression ring must be installed in the top groove of the piston and the side clearance of the rings in the grooves should be .001″–.003″. The expander, installed inside the oil control ring, should be assembled so that the two lugs are positioned in the hole directly above the piston pin hole.

Pistons and connecting rods should be replaced in their respective cylinders, as indicated by the cylinder number with which they are stamped. Remember that number one cylinder is at the rear of the engine. The pistons should be installed with their split on the exhaust side (left side) of the engine. The pistons are marked Front to facilitate proper replacement. A piston ring clamp should be used when installing the rings into the cylinder. Fasten the cap to the connecting rod so that the cylinder numbers stamped on each part are on the same side.

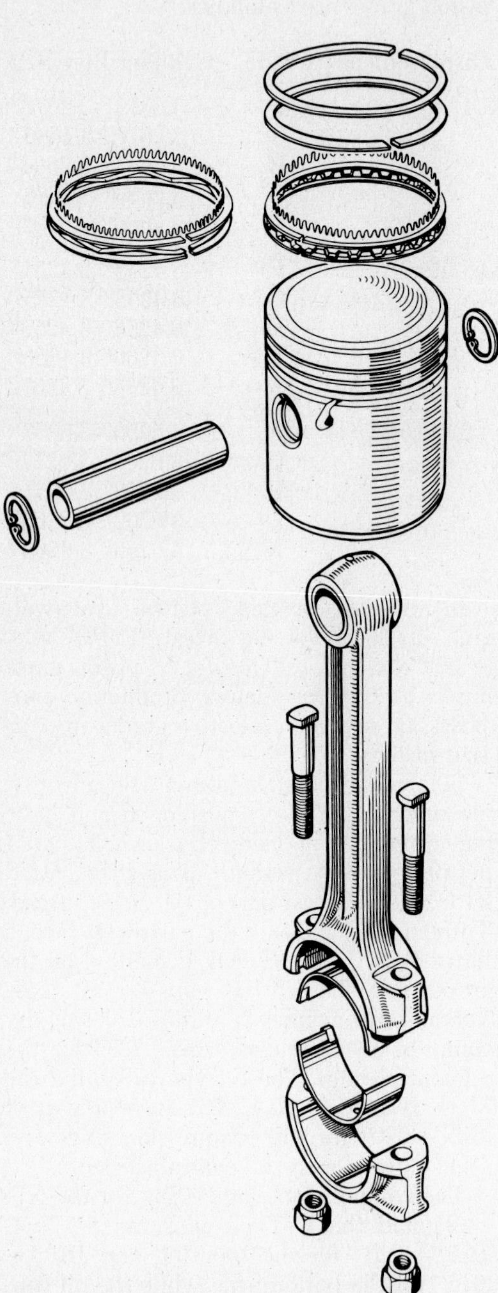

Exploded view of piston and connecting rod showing two types of oil control rings

Clutch and Transmission

CLUTCH AND FLYWHEEL—MARK II, 3.4S, 3.8S, 420, XJ6, E TYPE

Removal

1. Remove the engine and transmission. See Engine Removal procedures.
2. Detach transmission and clutch housing from engine.
3. Remove the bolts and lift out the clutch assembly. Make a mark from the flywheel to the crankshaft flange so that it can be assembled in the same position.
4. Unscrew the flywheel bolts, remove the locking plate and tap off the flywheel.

Installation

1. Place the flywheel on the crankshaft flange so that the balancing mark B is at approximately the BDC position with pistons No. 1 and 6 at the TDC position or merely align the marks made during removal. This will ensure that the balance mark of the flywheel is in line with that of the crankshaft, which is stamped on the crank throw just in front of the rear main journal.
2. Tap the two dowels into position, and replace the locking plate and flywheel bolts. Torque the bolts to 67 ft. lbs. and secure with the locking plate tabs. Assemble the clutch pressure plate to the flywheel, noting that one side of the plate is marked Flywheel Side. Center the pressure plate onto the flywheel by using a dummy shaft—a constant pinion shaft from the transmission will do. To prevent the pressure plate from slipping off center, do not remove the dummy shaft until the cover is in place and the setscrews are tight.

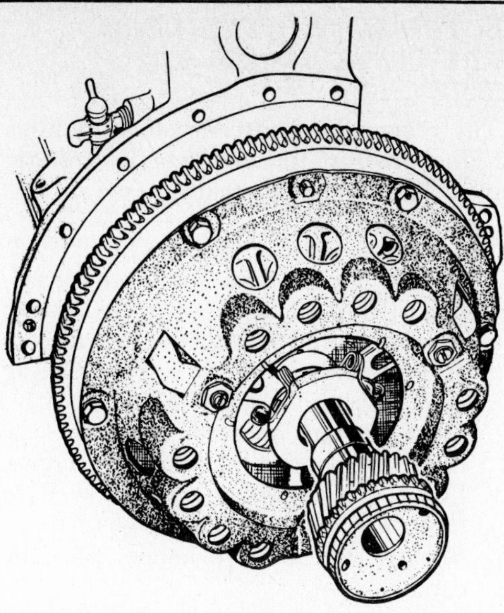

Centering the pressure plate with a dummy shaft

3. Replace the clutch cover assembly so that the B mark on the cover coincides with the B on the flywheel.
4. Secure the cover with the six bolts, and tighten the bolts diagonally a turn at a time. Remove the dummy shaft.

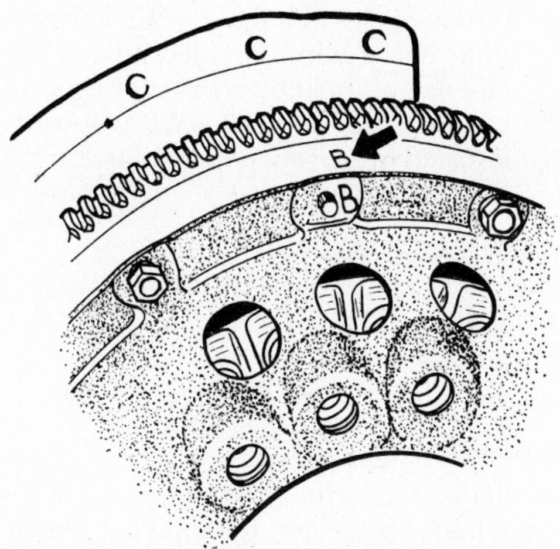

Aligning the balance marks on the flywheel and clutch

Bleeding Procedure for the Clutch System—All Models

If the clutch does not fully disengage and results in shifting problems, then it is quite possible that air has entered the system. Bleed the system in the following manner:

1. Fill the master cylinder with brake fluid, being careful to keep dirt out.
2. Attach a bleeder tube to the nipple tube on the slave cylinder and let the tube hang into a clean glass container partially filled with fluid.
3. Unscrew the bleed nipple one complete turn and have an assistant slowly press the clutch pedal. Tighten the nipple before the pedal reaches the downward limit of its travel and let the pedal return upward by itself.
4. Repeat this operation until the fluid leaving the bleeder tube is free from air bubbles, while making sure that the master cylinder is at least 1/2 full of fluid so that air cannot enter.
5. When the bleeding is completed, fill the master cylinder with *fresh* fluid. Do not re-use the fluid in the jar since it is filled with air.
6. The preceding procedure can be performed without the use of the jar and bleeder tube by merely observing the fluid coming out of the nipple. If the fluid bubbles or squirts out under pressure then it indicates that air is definitely in the system and that it should be bled until the fluid flows out smoothly. The procedure using the jar is a more thorough method since it can be definitely determined that every bit of air is out. It is also a safer procedure since it minimizes the danger of being sprayed in the eyes with fluid.

Clutch Free-play Adjustment—Mark II, 3.4S, 3.8S, 420, XJ6, E Type (All)

The above models are equipped with either a hydrostatic or a non-hydrostatic clutch slave cylinder. The non-hydrostatic cylinders, identified by the *presence* of a clutch return spring, can be adjusted to change clutch free play. To do this, remove the return spring, loosen the locknut and turn the slave cylinder pushrod to change its length. Screwing the rod into the knuckle joint will increase the free travel while screwing it out will decrease the free-play. The proper free-play measurement for those models (except Mark II) having the non-hydrostatic cylinders is 1/16" and is measured on the operating rod between the slave cylinder and the clutch withdrawal lever. To feel this free-play, remove the pedal return spring and move the operating rod to its fullest extent in either direction. The Mark II calls for ¾" free-play measured at the clutch pedal pad inside the

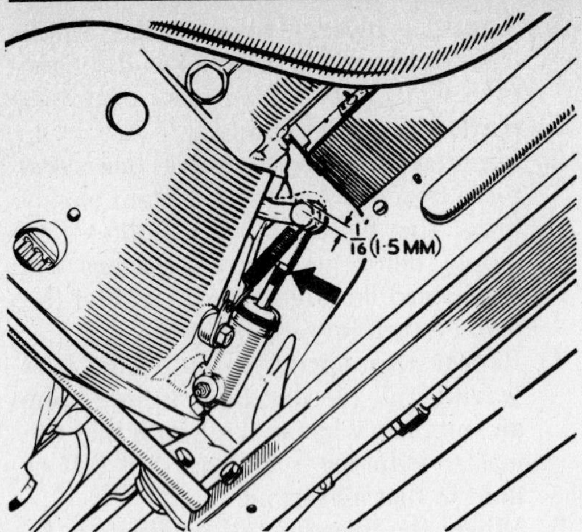

Adjustment of clutch rod free play

car. The hydrostatic slave cylinder, identified by the *absence* of a clutch return spring, automatically compensates for clutch wear and requires no clearance adjustment except when the clutch or slave cylinder is replaced. To adjust the operating rod, proceed as follows:

1. Remove the clevis pin holding the operating rod to the clutch lever.
2. Loosen the fork end locknut.
3. Push the clutch pedal lever away from the slave cylinder until resistance is felt. Keep it in this position.
4. Push the operating rod into the slave cylinder to the limit of its travel and adjust the fork end to the dimension of ¾″ between the center of the fork end

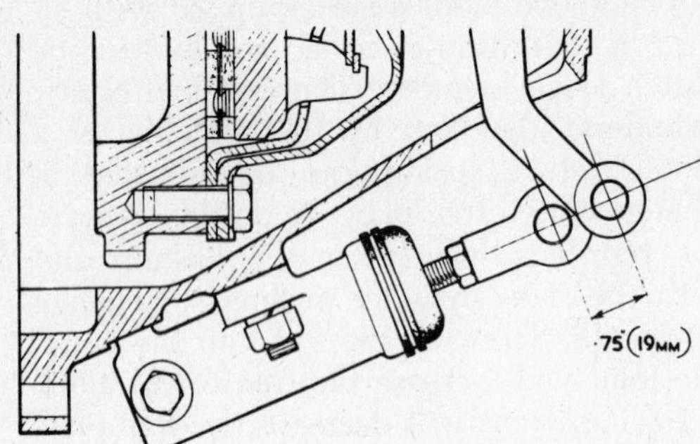

Adjusting the hydrostatic slave cylinder operating rod

and the center of the clutch operating lever. Tighten the locknut.
5. Release the operating rod and connect the fork end to the lever. Install the clevis pin.
6. Bleed the system.

CLUTCH SLAVE CYLINDER—MARK II, 3.4S, 3.8S, 420, XJ6, E TYPE (ALL)

The removal and installation procedures for the hydrostatic and non-hydrostatic slave cylinders are identical.

Removal

1. Disconnect the fluid line from the cylinder. There may be air in the system so care should be taken when disconnecting this line to avoid being sprayed with pressurized fluid.
2. Separate the rubber boot from the body and remove the attaching screws.
3. Leave the operating rod attached to the car.
4. Remove the slave cylinder from the car.

Installation

1. Install the rubber boot onto the operating rod and install the cylinder with the operating rod entering the bore.
2. Secure the cylinder with the attaching screws and install the large end of the boot onto the end of the body.
3. Install the bleeder screw and the fluid line.
4. Bleed the system.
5. If the car is equipped with a hydrostatic slave cylinder (identified by the absence of a clutch return spring), adjust the operating rod according to the instructions given under Clutch Free-Play Adjustment.

OVERHAULING THE CLUTCH SLAVE CYLINDER—MARK II, 3.4S, 3.8S, 420, XJ6, E TYPE (ALL)

The procedure is the same whether the cylinder is hydrostatic or non-hydrostatic.

Disassembly

1. Remove the circlip from the end of the cylinder bore and, by applying *low* air pressure to the fluid line opening, eject the piston and other components.
2. Remove the bleeder screw.

Assembly

1. Before assembling cylinder, coat the internal parts and cylinder bore with rubber grease.
2. Place the spring into the cup filler and insert these parts, spring first, into the cylinder bore. Install the cup (lip side first), piston (flat face innermost) and

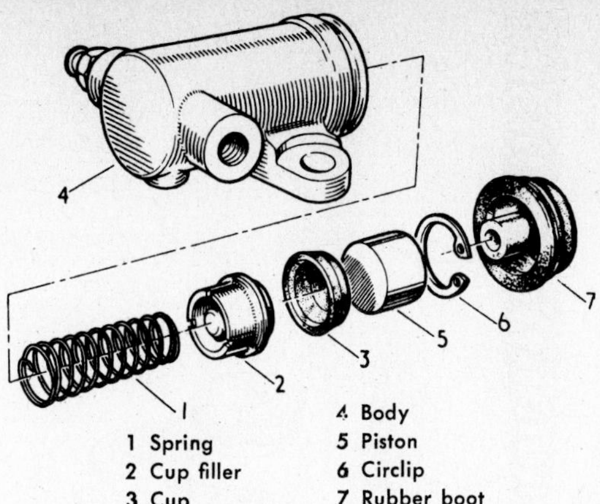

Exploded view of the hydrostatic clutch slave cylinder

circlip. The rubber boot is installed separately onto the operating rod still in the vehicle.

CLUTCH MASTER CYLINDER—MARK II, 3.4S, 3.8S, 420, XJ6, E TYPE (ALL)

The above models except the E Type, 3.4S and 3.8S, use a master cylinder that combines with the fluid reservoir in one case. In the case of the E Type, 3.4S and 3.8S, the fluid reservoir mounted on the firewall is physically separate from the master cylinder. In the combined cylinder-reservoir assembly (as found on the XJ6), there is a small by-pass port located in the cylinder barrel through which excess fluid flows back into the tank thus allowing the operating fork to return to the fully engaged position. This port also compensates for fluid contraction or expansion and permits fluid to enter or escape the system. If this port becomes blocked, the excess fluid would be unable to escape and, as a result, the clutch would slip.

Removal

1. If the car is equipped with a separately, drainable fluid reservoir, drain it.
2. Detach the outlet line from the master cylinder. If the car has the separate fluid reservoir, disconnect the outlet and intake lines.
3. Separate the cylinder from the clutch pedal.
4. Remove the cylinder from the car and drain the fluid.

Installation

1. To install, reverse the removal procedure. Make sure all connections are clean before installing them. Bleed the system.

OVERHAULING THE CLUTCH MASTER CYLINDER

3.4S, 3.8S, E Type (All)

Disassembly

1. Remove the dust cover.
2. Remove the circlip holding the push-rod and a dished washer.
3. Take out the piston and both seals.

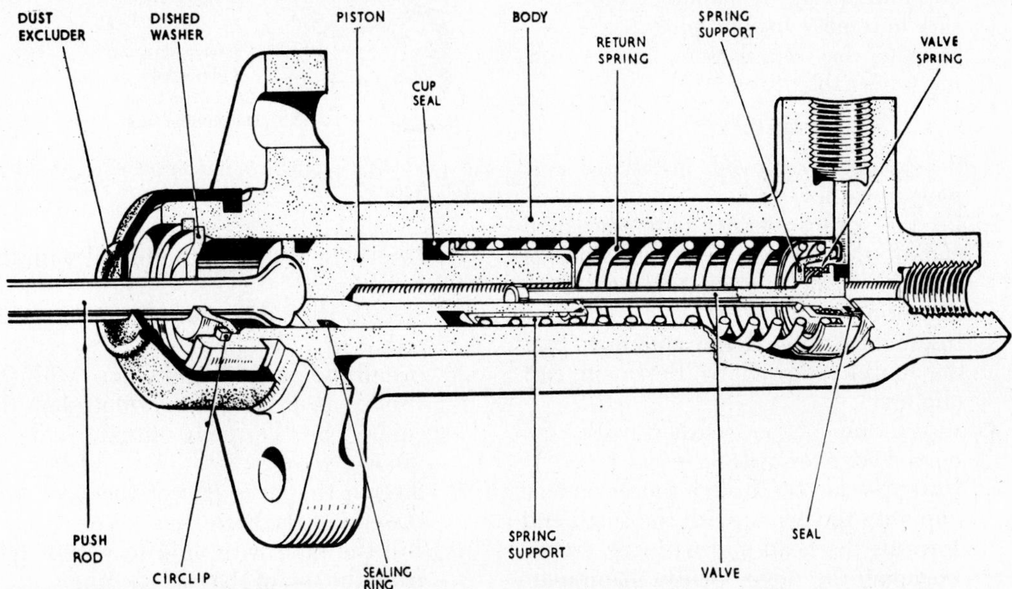

Sectional view of the clutch master cylinder—3.4S, 3.8S, E Type (all)

4. Withdraw the valve assembly, springs and supports.
5. Remove the seal from the end of the valve.

ASSEMBLY

1. Lubricate the new seals and the cylinder bore with brake fluid and install the seal to the end of the valve making sure that the lip of the seal fits snugly in the groove.
2. Install the seals in their grooves around the piston.
3. Insert the piston into the spring support, ensuring that the valve head engages the piston bore.
4. Coat the piston with rubber grease and insert the complete assembly into the cylinder body making sure that the seals do not twist.
5. Install the pushrod and press down on the piston until the dished washer will seat on the shoulder at the head of the cylinder.
6. Replace the circlip and then install the dust cover after filling it with rubber grease.

Mark II, 420, XJ6

DISASSEMBLY

1. Remove the rubber boot from the end of the barrel and move it along the pushrod.
2. Remove the circlip and extract the pushrod, piston, piston washer, main cup and spring. It shouldn't be necessary to remove the end plug.
3. Remove the secondary cup by stretching it over the piston head.

ASSEMBLY

1. If previously removed, install the end plug and a new gasket.
2. Fit the spring retainer onto the small end of the spring. If the retainer is new, bend the tabs over to hold it to the spring.
3. Insert the spring, large end first, into the barrel followed by the main cup (lip first).
4. Insert the piston washer with the curved edge towards the cup.
5. *Using the fingers*, stretch the secondary cup onto the piston with the small end towards the head and with the groove engaging the ridge. Gently manipulate the cup to make sure it seats properly.

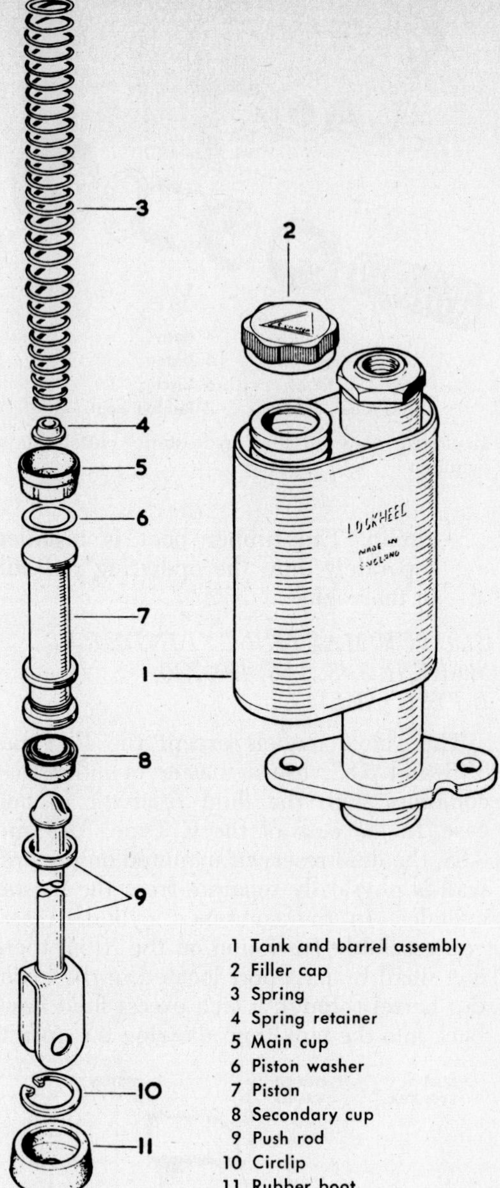

Exploded view of clutch master cylinder—Mark II, 420, XJ6

6. Insert the piston in the barrel with the head up.
7. Stretch the rubber boot onto the pushrod.
8. Install the pushrod and secure with the circlip. It is *very important* that the circlip be correctly fitted into its groove.
9. Stretch the large end of the boot over the end of the barrel.
10. Fill the tank with fluid to within 1/2" from the top of the cap opening.
11. Replace the filler cap, position the cyl-

inder upright and test by pushing the pushrod and piston into the bore and allowing the rod to return unassisted. After doing this once or twice, fluid should flow from the outlet connection.

TRANSMISSION REMOVAL AND INSTALLATION

To remove the transmission, the engine must also be removed. For instructions on transmission removal, see Engine Removal and Installation.

AUTOMATIC TRANSMISSION SHIFT LINKAGE ADJUSTMENT

Borg Warner Transmission

MARK II, 3.4S, 3.8S

This manual selector cable need only be adjusted if it has been removed from the car. To gain access to the selector valve lever it is necessary to remove the exhaust system.

1. Place the selector valve lever in the Drive position (the center position of the five).
2. Position the outer cable in its locating bracket mounted on the transmission. Connect the cable to the selector valve lever making sure that the cable runs in a straight line.
3. Measure the distance between the inner and outer cables at the top end, which should be 3-11/16″.
4. Perform any necessary adjustment on the lower end of the cable. Tighten the collar on the lower ball joint.
5. Place the selector lever in the Drive position. The upper ball joint should now align with the hole in the selector lever control rod.
6. Connect the cable ball joint to the control rod and check the operation of the transmission in all selector positions.

Borg Warner Model 8 Transmission

420 MODELS

1. Place the selector lever in the D2 position and have an assistant hold it in place.
2. From underneath the car, loosen the linkage cable locknut and remove the cable from the selector lever.
3. Place the transmission lever in the D2 detent position by moving it to the Lockup position and then moving it back two detents.
4. Adjust the cable end so that it will easily fit onto the transmission lever.
5. Temporarily connect the cable to the lever.
6. Check the operation of the column lever to see that the indicator points to the right selection.
7. It is important that the gating at L, R, and P positions does not interfere with the transmission lever setting at the detents.
8. When adjustment is correct, make sure that the cable is secured to the lever and that the locknut is tightened.

XJ6

1. Disconnect both ends of the cable.
2. Place the lever in the R position and attach the cable.
3. Adjust the ⅝″ nuts finger tight.
4. Place the lever on the side of the transmission in R position by moving the lever all the way back (P position) and then move forward one detent.
5. Attach and secure the cable. Tighten the ⅝″ locknuts.
6. Check operation of selector lever. The gear selection made by the lever must coincide with the detent position at the transmission. If the selector lever inside the car points to R, then the lever at the transmission must be one detent in front of the P position.
7. Small cable length adjustments should be made with the two locknuts.

E TYPE (2+2)

1. Remove the transmission console assembly and carpeting and remove the screws securing the transmission (left side) cover plate.
2. Remove the linkage cable from the transmission lever.
3. Push the transmission lever fully forward and engage the selector lever into the lockup (low gear) position.
4. Adjust the cable so that it will fit freely onto the transmission lever. Temporarily attach the cable to the lever.
5. Check the operation of the selector lever in all positions making sure that the shift pattern does not interfere with the transmission lever detent positions.
6. The transmission lever must engage the detents positively.
7. Once the adjustment is correct, secure the cable to the lever and tighten.

KICKDOWN CABLE ADJUSTMENT

(Borg Warner Model 8 Transmission)

420, XJ6, E TYPE (2+2)

1. The following tests, made on a flat road, should precede any adjustment attempts:
   a. Place the selector in D1 or D2 and at a minimum throttle opening, the shift from second to third should take place at 1100–1200 rpm. An increase of 200–400 rpm at the shift point indicates *low pressure*.
   b. If at full throttle, the transmission shifts from second to third with a jerk or sharply downshifts from second to first (in D1 when stopping the car) then *high pressure* exists.
   c. Install a pressure gauge to the line pressure point located at the rear face of the transmission (left side) on the 420 or the front on the XJ6.
   d. Start the engine and let it run to normal operating temperature. Place the lever in D1 or D2, firmly set the handbrake and increase the idling speed to 1250 rpm. The pressure gauge should read 72.5±2.5 psi.
2. If the above tests indicate that the 420 cable setting is incorrect, adjustment must be made and made *only* at the fork end. The XJ6 adjustment is made at the link rod.
3. On 420 models, perform the following:
   a. Remove the hood, battery and battery tray.
   b. Place the battery on the floor and reconnect it to the car with a pair of electrical leads.
   c. Loosen the locknut from the fork end, remove the cotter pin and clevis pin.
4. To lower the pressure, turn the fork end clockwise; to raise it, turn counterclockwise. One full turn will change the pressure by approximately 9 psi. Only slight adjustment should be necessary since over-adjustment will result in loss of kickdown or an increase in shift speeds.
5. If removed, install the fork end joint pin and cotter pin and tighten the locknut.
6. Start the engine and check the pressure at 1200 rpm.
7. The carburetor butterfly valves should be closed at idling speed after completing adjustment. If not, they can be adjusted by means of the locknut located on the connecting link between the jackshaft and carburetor spindles.
8. If, after several adjustments, the pressure still fluctuates, check the inner kickdown cable for kinks or bends and replace if necessary.

GOVERNOR LEVER ADJUSTMENT —MARK II, 3.4S, 3.8S

1. Press the accelerator pedal to full throttle. Do not press it so hard as to overcome the "kickdown" overtravel spring in the vertical link located on the left side of the firewall.
2. Turn the governor lever to full throttle position; that is, the point where solid resistance is felt before overcoming the cam detent.
3. With the pedal and the lever in these positions, adjust the length of the governor lever control rod at the large knurled nut. The ball pin should slip easily into the inner hole of the governor lever.
4. Road test and check the kickdown operation.

FRONT BAND ADJUSTMENT

420, E Type (2+2), XJ6 (Borg Warner Model 8 Transmission)

The front band should be adjusted after the first 1,000 miles and at 21,000 mile intervals thereafter.

1. Drain the oil at the oil filter connection and remove the transmission oil pan.
2. Loosen the adjusting screw locknut located on the servo, move the lever and check to see that the screws turn freely in the lever.

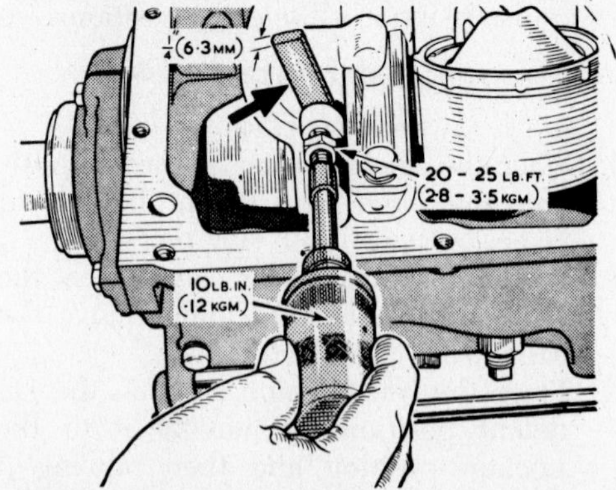

Front band adjustment—Borg Warner Model 8 (420, 2+2, XJ6)

3. Install a 1/4″ gauge between the servo piston pin and the servo adjusting screw, then torque the adjusting screw to 10 in. lbs.
4. Torque the adjusting screw locknut to 20-25 ft. lbs.

REAR BAND ADJUSTMENT

420, E Type (2+2), XJ6 (Borg Warner Model 8 Transmission)

Like the front bands, the rear bands should be adjusted after the first 1,000 miles and at 21,000 mile intervals thereafter.

1. Loosen the adjusting screw locknut (located on the right side of transmission) three or four turns making sure that the adjusting screw works freely in the threads of the case.
2. Torque the adjusting screw to 10 in. lbs.
3. Back off the adjusting screw exactly 1-1/2 turns then torque the locknut to 35–40 ft. lbs.

MANUAL TRANSMISSION

Disassembly—Pre-1965 Transmission

This transmission is synchonized in all gears except first.

1. Drain the transmission.
2. Place the lever in neutral and remove the top cover.

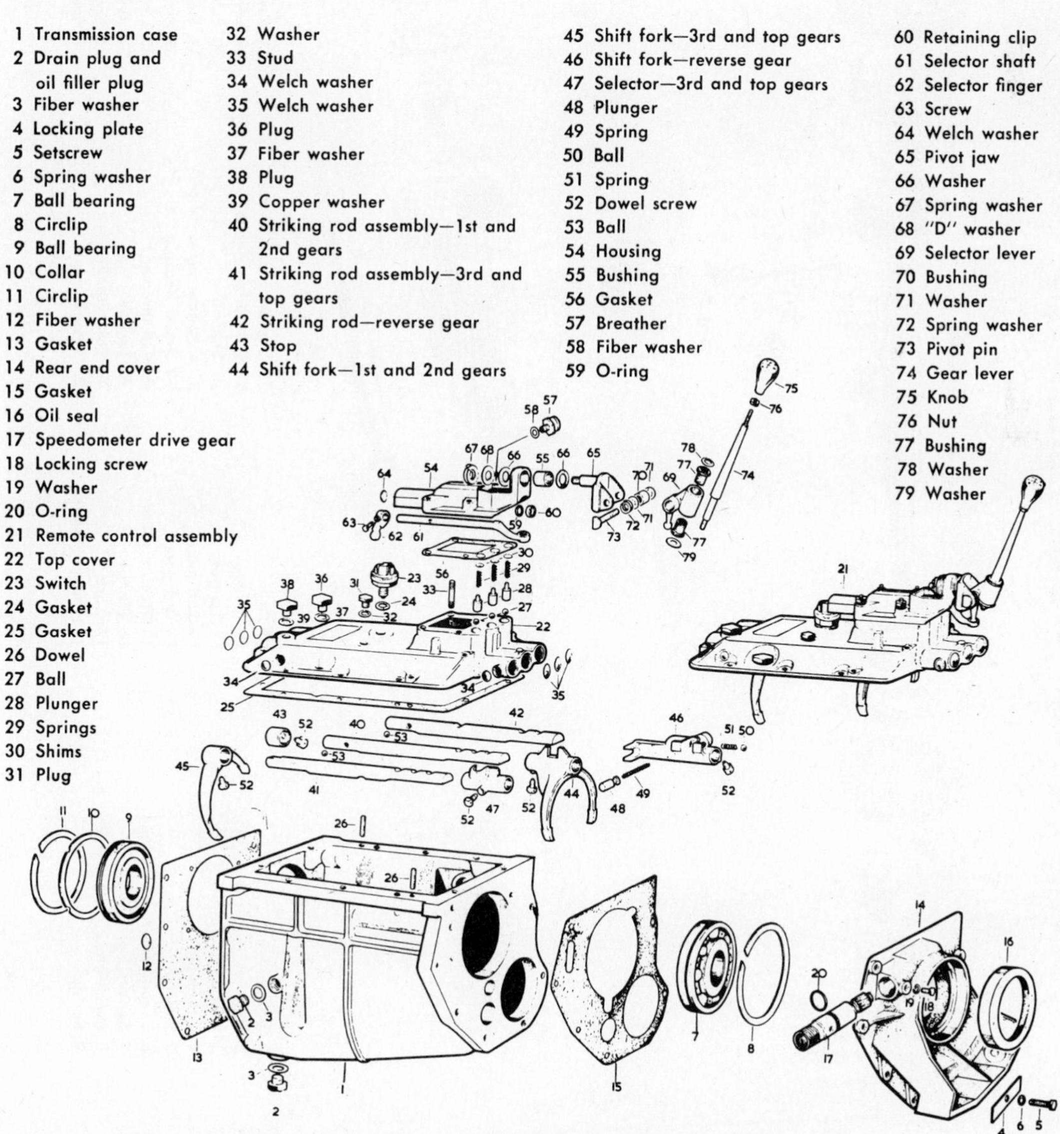

Exploded view of the transmission case and top cover—pre-1965 (non-synchro first)

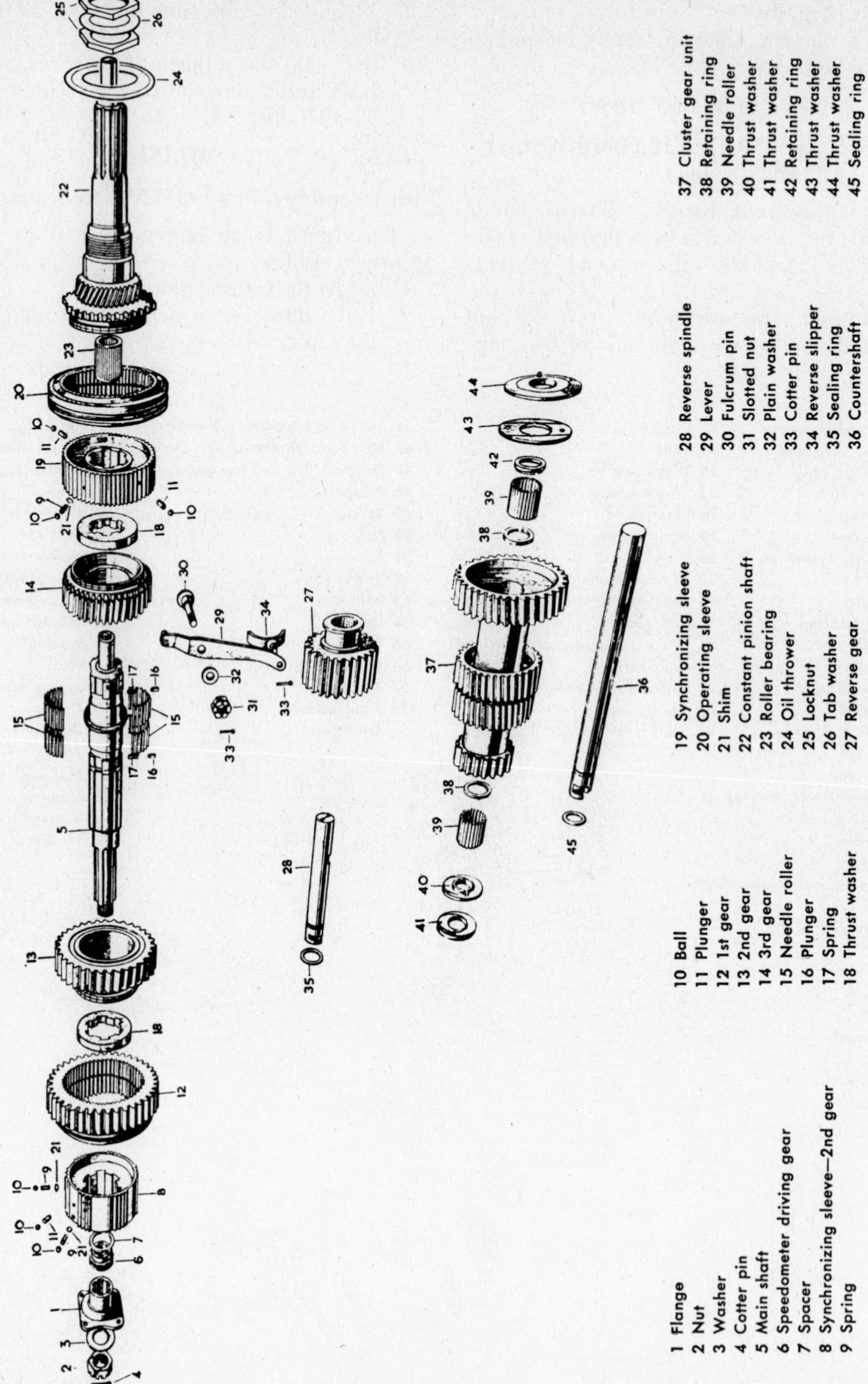
1 Flange
2 Nut
3 Washer
4 Cotter pin
5 Main shaft
6 Speedometer driving gear
7 Spacer
8 Synchronizing sleeve—2nd gear
9 Spring
10 Ball
11 Plunger
12 1st gear
13 2nd gear
14 3rd gear
15 Needle roller
16 Plunger
17 Spring
18 Thrust washer
19 Synchronizing sleeve
20 Operating sleeve
21 Shim
22 Constant pinion shaft
23 Roller bearing
24 Oil thrower
25 Locknut
26 Tab washer
27 Reverse gear
28 Reverse spindle
29 Lever
30 Fulcrum pin
31 Slotted nut
32 Plain washer
33 Cotter pin
34 Reverse slipper
35 Sealing ring
36 Countershaft
37 Cluster gear unit
38 Retaining ring
39 Needle roller
40 Thrust washer
41 Thrust washer
42 Retaining ring
43 Thrust washer
44 Thrust washer
45 Sealing ring

Exploded view of the gears—pre-1965 transmission (non-synchro first)

3. Remove the clutch slave cylinder from the clutch housing.
4. Remove the clutch throwout bearing.
5. Separate the clutch fork from the shaft.
6. Move shaft downward and remove the fork.
7. From inside the clutch housing, remove the locking wire from the two bolts and straighten the tabs of the lockwashers.
8. Remove the clutch housing.
9. Remove the locking screw holding the speedometer driven gear bushing in the extension or end cover (E Type has short mainshaft and therefore uses an end cover instead of a long extension housing) and withdraw the driven gear and bearing.
10. Remove the fiber washer from the front end of the countershaft. On the E Type, engage fourth and first gears. Remove pin, nut and washer and separate the universal joint flange from the mainshaft.
11. On non-overdrive transmissions, remove the seven bolts that hold the rear extension or rear cover to the transmission. Care should be taken not to disturb the countershaft/reverse idler locking plate.
12. Withdraw the extension or rear end cover and shafts while inserting a dummy shaft into the countershaft bore at the front of the transmission case. Keep the dummy shaft in contact with the countershaft until the countershaft is out of the case.

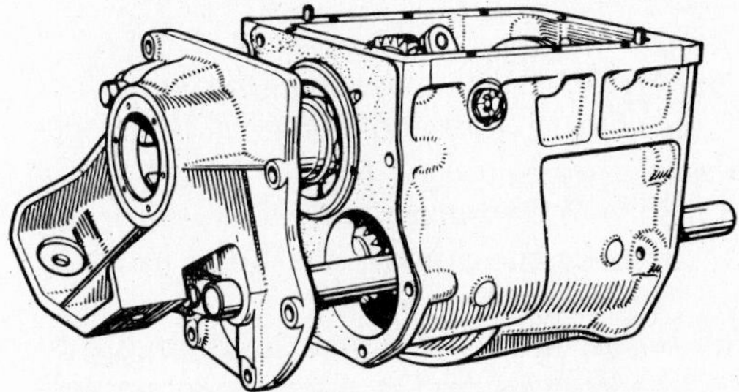

Rear cover removal showing use of dummy shaft

13. Engage fourth and first gears, and on non-overdrive transmissions, straighten the tab washer holding the locknut at the rear of the mainshaft.
14. Unscrew the locknut and withdraw the speedometer drive gear.
15. Remove the woodruff key from the mainshaft.
16. Withdraw the dummy countershaft, allowing the cluster gear to drop into the bottom of the transmission case.
17. On transmissions with overdrive, remove the circlip, plain washer and shims from behind the rear bearing.
18. Rotate the constant pinion shaft until the two cut-away portions of the driving gear are facing the top and bottom of the case.
19. Tap the mainshaft to the front in order to knock the constant pinion shaft and ball bearing forward out of the case. Remove the constant pinion shaft and ball bearing.

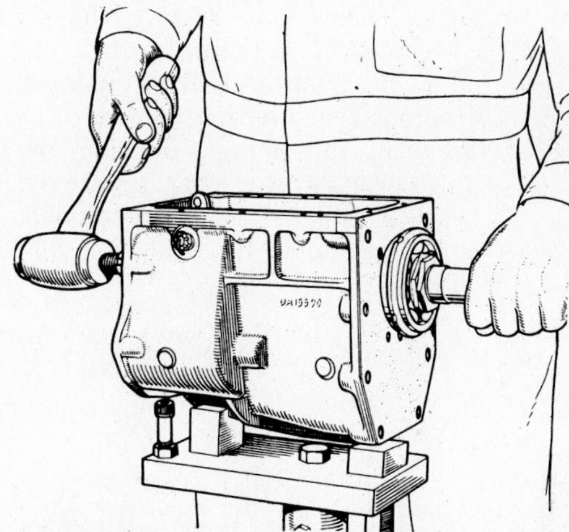

Removing the constant pinion shaft by tapping on the mainshaft

20. Continue to tap the mainshaft forward until it is free of the rear bearing.
21. When the mainshaft has been freed, tap the bearing out of the transmission case.
22. Push the reverse gear forward and out of engagement to clear the mainshaft first gear.
23. Lift the front end of the mainshaft and remove it complete with gears to the front of the case.
24. Move the reverse gear to the rear as far as it will go to clear the countershaft first gear.
25. Lift out the cluster gear unit along with the inner and outer thrust washers at each end.

CAUTION: In removing the cluster gear unit care must be taken not to lose any of the needle bearings.

26. Remove the reverse gear through the top of the case.
27. To disassemble the mainshaft proceed as follows:
    a. Detach the fourth/third gear operating and synchronizing sleeves from the shaft.
    b. Press the operating sleeve from the synchronizing sleeve and remove the six synchronizing balls and springs.
    c. Remove the interlock plungers and balls from the synchronizing sleeve.
    d. Withdraw the second gear synchronizing sleeve complete with first gear to the rear of the shaft.
    e. Press the first gear off the synchronizing sleeve and remove the six synchronizing balls and springs. Remove the interlock ball and plunger from the synchronizing sleeve.
    f. Press in the plunger locking the third gear thrust washer. Rotate the washer until the splines are aligned, and then remove the washer.

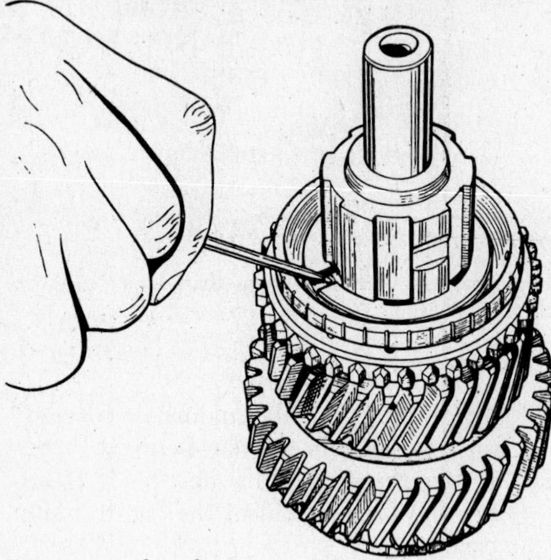

Depressing the plunger in order to remove third speed thrust washer

    g. Remove third gear being careful not to lose any of the needle bearings as the gear is removed.
    h. Remove the spring and plunger.
    i. Press the plunger locking the second gear thrust washer and rotate the washer until the splines align so that the washer can be withdrawn to the rear of the shaft.
    j. Remove the second gear from the rear of the shaft being careful not to lose the needle bearings.
    k. Remove the spring and plunger.
28. To disassemble the constant pinion shaft, proceed as follows:
    a. Straighten the tab washer and remove the locknuts (right-hand thread).
    b. Withdraw the bearing from the shaft and remove the oil thrower.
29. Clean and inspect all parts. Clean bearings with solvent and dry with compressed air.

CAUTION: To prevent bearing damage, do not allow bearings to spin when using compressed air.

Assembly

1. Check the cluster gear end float by inserting a gauge between the bronze thrust washer and the rear of the transmission case. The clearance should be from .002"–.004" and is adjustable by changing the thrust washer to one of the following thicknesses: .152", .156", .159", .162", and .164".

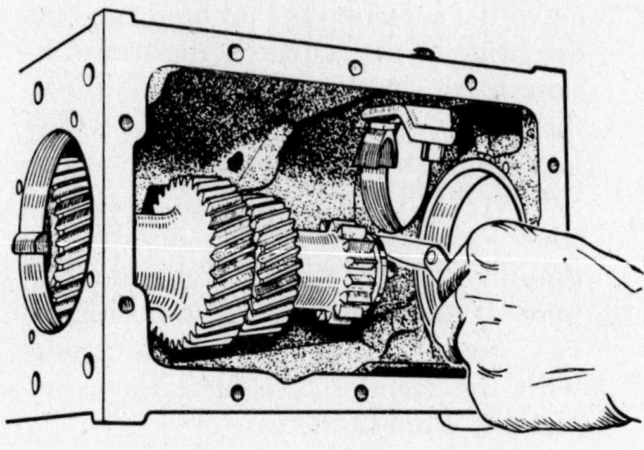

Checking the cluster gear end float

CAUTION: When checking the end float of the cluster gear, do not grip the transmission case in a vice, for this will result in an incorrect measurement.

2. Remove the dummy shaft and insert in its place a thin rod.
3. Install the reverse gear and move it to the rear as far as possible to provide clearance.
4. To assemble the mainshaft, perform the following:
    a. Install the 41 needle bearings behind the shoulder on the mainshaft and slide the second gear onto the rollers with its synchronizing cone to the rear. *NOTE: Holding the bearings in place with grease will make the installation easier.*

b. Install the second gear thrust washer spring and plunger into the plunger hole.

c. Slide the thrust washer up the shaft and over the splines. Align the large hole in the synchronizer cone, then use a steel pin to compress the plunger and rotate the thrust washer into the locked position with the cut-away in line with the plunger.

d. Insert a feeler gauge between the thrust washer and the shoulder on the mainshaft to check the end float of the second gear on the mainshaft. The clearance should be .002″–.004″ and is adjustable by using one of the following thrust washers: .471″/.472″, .473″/.474″, or .475″/.476″.

e. Install the 41 needle bearings in front of the shoulder of the mainshaft and slide the third gear, with synchronizing cone to the front onto the rollers. Greasing the rollers will greatly help assembly.

f. Replace the third gear thrust washer spring and plunger into the plunger hole. Procedures and specifications for installing the third gear are the same as those for second gear installation. Follow steps c and d (above) for third gear installation replacing the word "second" with the word "third".

5. To assemble the second gear synchronizer assembly, perform the following:
   a. Install the springs and balls (and shims, if fitted) to the six blind holes in the synchronizer sleeve.
   b. Assemble the first gear to the second gear synchronizing sleeve so that the relieved tooth of the internal splines in the gear is aligned with the stop pin in the sleeve.
   c. Compress the springs with a hose clamp or by inserting the assembly endwise in a vice and slowly closing the jaws.
   d. Slide the operating sleeve over the synchronizing sleeve until the balls can be heard and felt to engage the neutral position groove.
   e. It should require 62–68 lbs. of force to disengage the synchronizing sleeve from the neutral position in the operating sleeve. This can be done by gripping the operating sleeve in the palms of the hands and pressing the synchronizing sleeve firmly with the fingers until it disengages from the neutral position. Shims are installed underneath the springs to adjust the pressure of the balls against the operating sleeve.

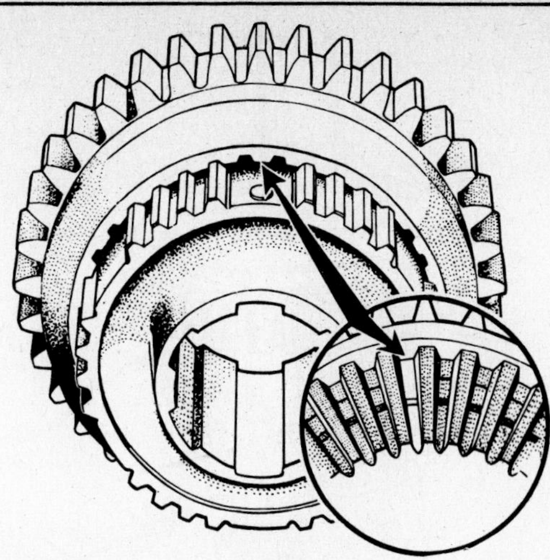

Assemble first gear to the second gear synchronizing sleeve so that the relieved tooth on the inside of the gear is aligned with the stop pin in the sleeve

6. To assemble the second gear assembly to the mainshaft, proceed as follows:
   a. Install the first/second synchronizer assembly to the mainshaft and check to see that the synchronizer sleeve slides freely on the mainshaft when the ball and plunger are not installed. If it does not slide freely, check for freedom on different splines of the mainshaft and check for burrs at the end of the splines.
   b. Remove the synchronizer assembly from the mainshaft, install the ball and plunger, and replace the synchronizer on the mainshaft.
   c. Check the interlock plunger by sliding the outer operating sleeve into the first gear position.
   d. With a slight downward pressure on the synchronizer assembly, second gear should rotate freely without any tendency for the synchronizer cones to rub. If they do rub, a longer plunger should be installed in the synchronizer sleeve. These plungers are available in the fol-

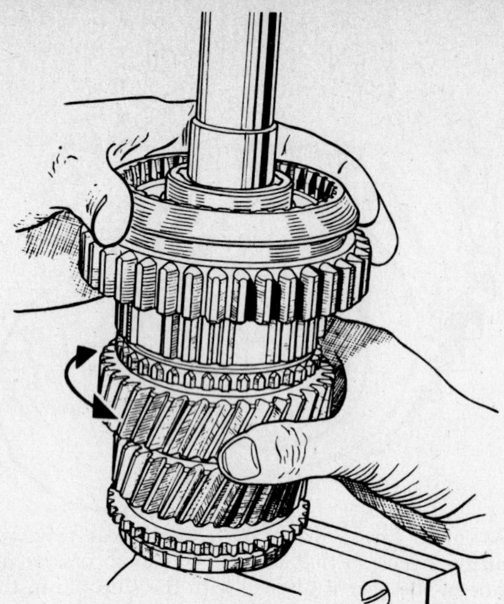

With a slight downward pressure on the synchronizer assembly, second gear should rotate freely without any rubbing of the synchronizer cones

lowing lengths: .490″, .495″, and .500″.

7. To assemble the third/fourth synchronizer assembly, perform the following instructions:
   a. Install the springs and balls and shims (if so fitted) to the six blind holes in the inner synchronizing sleeve with the two relieved teeth in the operating sleeve aligned with the two ball and plunger holes in the synchronizing sleeve.

When assembling the third/fourth synchronizer assembly, the relieved teeth in the operating sleeve must line up with the interlock plunger in the synchronizer sleeve

   b. Compress the springs with the use of a hose clamp or vice and slide the operating sleeve over the synchronizing sleeve until the balls engage the neutral position groove.
   c. About 52 to 58 lbs. of force should be required to disengage the synchronizing sleeve from the neutral position in the operating sleeve. As in the assembly of the second gear synchronizer assembly, the operating sleeve may be gripped in the palms and the synchronizing sleeve pressed with the fingers. The pressure of the balls against the operating sleeve may be adjusted through the use of shims installed underneath the springs and balls.
8. To install the third/fourth synchronizer assembly to the mainshaft, perform the following:
   a. Install the interlock balls and plungers. NOTE: *There are two transverse grooves on the spline of the mainshaft. These take the third/fourth synchronizer assembly, and the relieved tooth at the wide chamfered end of the outer operating sleeve must be in line with the front groove in the mainshaft. If this precaution is not observed, the result will be prevention of full engagement of third and fourth gears due to the locking plungers entering the wrong grooves.*

      The wide chamfered end of the outer operating sleeve must be facing forward; that is, toward the constant pinion shaft end of the transmission.
   b. The inner sleeve should slide freely on the mainshaft when the balls and plungers are not installed. If it does not, check the ends of the splines for burrs.
   c. Install the two balls and plungers in the inner synchronizer sleeve and replace the synchronizer assembly on the mainshaft while paying attention to the information in the preceding NOTE.
   d. Check the interlock plungers by sliding the third/fourth operating sleeve over the third gear dogs.
   e. With third gear engaged, lift and lower the synchronizer assembly. It should be possible to move the as-

sembly about 3/32″ before feeling any drag. If the assembly does not move freely, a shorter third gear plunger should be used in place of the one *not* opposite the relieved tooth in the operating sleeve. Plungers are available in lengths of .490″, .495″, .500″.

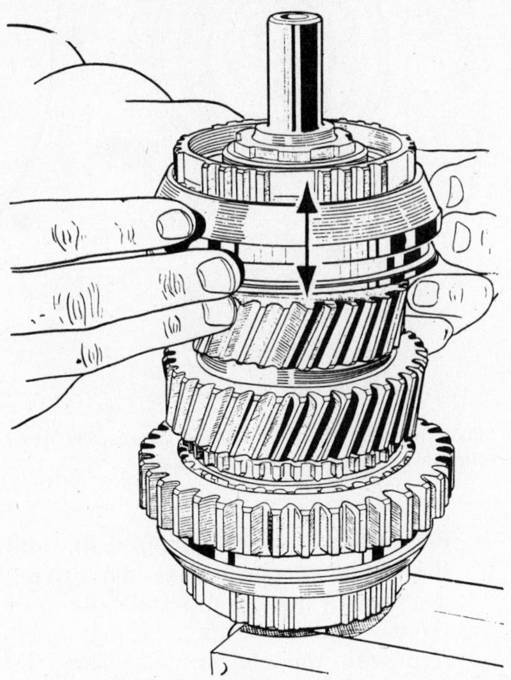

With third gear engaged, lift and lower the synchronizer assembly. It should be possible to move the assembly about 3/32″ before feeling any drag

f. Slide the operating sleeve into the fourth gear position.

g. Lift and lower the synchronizer assembly. It should be possible to move the assembly approximately 3/16″ before feeling any drag. When pressing lightly on the synchronizer assembly, the third gear should be free to rotate with no tendency for the synchronizer cones to rub. If the synchronizer cones do not move freely, a shorter fourth gear plunger is required. If the third gear synchronizer cones are felt to rub, a longer fourth gear plunger should be used. Fourth gear plunger is the one in line with the relieved tooth in the operating sleeve.

9. In assembling the constant pinion shaft, proceed as follows:
   a. Install the oil thrower and ball bearing onto the shaft, followed by the circlip and collar.
   b. Install the nut (right-hand thread), tab washer and locknut.
   c. Place the roller race into the bore of the shaft.

10. To assemble the gears into the transmission case, proceed as follows:
   a. Pass the mainshaft through the top of the case and to the rear through the bearing hole.
   b. Install a new gasket to the front face of the transmission case.
   c. Position the constant pinion shaft at the front of the case with the cutaway portions of the toothed driving member facing the top and bottom of the case. Tap the shaft to the rear until the collar and circlip on the bearing hit against the case.
   d. Holding the constant pinion shaft in position, tap the mainshaft rear bearing into place along with the circlip.
   e. Lift the cluster gear into mesh and insert a dummy countershaft through the countershaft bore in the front of the case.
   f. Engage fourth and first gears, and on non-overdrive transmissions, install the Woodruff key and speedometer drive gear to the mainshaft.
   g. Install the tab washer and locknut and secure. Place the transmission in neutral.
   h. On overdrive transmissions, install the shim or shims, plain washer, and circlip behind the rear bearing.
   i. Install as many shims as necessary to eliminate all end float from the mainshaft.
   j. Install the clutch operating fork and insert the shaft. Replace the locking screw and locknut.
   k. Fit the throwout bearing and the spring clips.
   l. Engage the operating rod of the slave cylinder and slide the cylinder onto the studs.
   m. Place the spring anchor plate on the lower studs and secure. Install the return spring.

11. Install the top cover and new gasket to the transmission, long bolts to the rear,

short to the front. Replace the transmission drain plug and washer.

12. Apply a new gasket to the rear face of the transmission case.
13. Install the extension housing or end cover (E Type) along with the countershaft and reverse shaft.
14. Install a new fiber washer to the front of the countershaft and position the speedometer driven gear and bearing.
15. Apply a new oil seal to the clutch housing with the lip of the seal facing the transmission.
16. Install the clutch housing.

Disassembly—Fully Synchromesh Transmission

In 1965, Jaguar introduced a four-speed transmission with synchromesh on all forward gears.

1. Remove the springs and carbon throwout bearing.
2. Detach the clutch slave cylinder.
3. Remove the Allen screw, pin, and clutch operating fork.
4. Remove the clutch housing from the transmission case.
5. Place the gear shift lever in neutral and remove the transmission top cover.
6. Remove the rear extension as follows:
   a. Lock the transmission by engaging first and reverse gears.
   b. Remove the flange nut and flange.
   c. Remove the rear cover and speedometer pinion and bushing assembly.
   d. Remove the speedometer driving gear from the mainshaft.
   e. Detach the extension and gather the spacer and oil pump driving pin.
7. Remove the oil pump by removing the three countersunk bolts holding the gear housing. Mark the gears so that they can be replaced in the same position.
8. Remove the fiber plug from the front of the countershaft and drive the countershaft out the front of the transmission case.

NOTE: Be sure that the rear washer (pegged to case) drops down in clockwise direction (looking from the rear); otherwise, the washer will be trapped against the reverse gear when the mainshaft is driven forward. The washer can be positioned properly by rocking the transmission case and moving the reverse lever back and forth, or by pushing the washer down with a piece of wire.

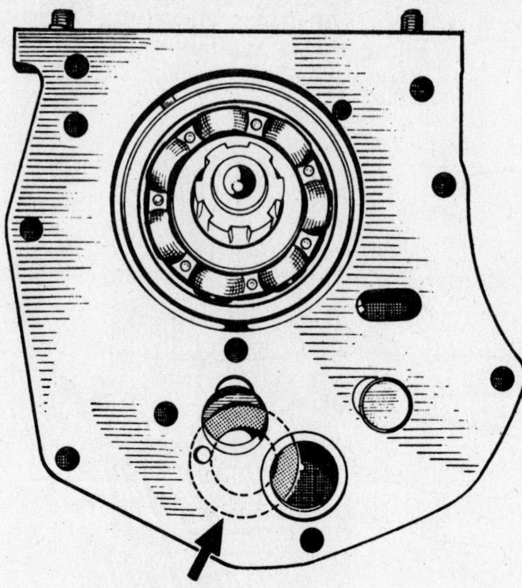

Make sure that the rear washer (pegged to case) drops down in a clockwise direction

9. Rotate the constant pinion shaft until the cut-away portions of the driving gear are facing the top and bottom of the case, otherwise the gear may interfere with the cluster gears. Pry the constant pinion shaft forward from the case.
10. Dismantle the shaft by removing the roller bearing from inside the shaft. Tap back the tab washer and remove the large nut, washer and oil thrower.
11. Rotate the mainshaft until one of the cut-away portions in the third/fourth synchronizer hub is aligned with the countershaft. The mainshaft may now be tapped through the rear bearing while making sure that reverse gear is kept tight against first gear.
12. After removing the rear bearing from the case, place a hose clamp on the mainshaft to prevent the reverse gear from sliding off.
13. Loosen the reverse lever bolt and move the lever to the rear.
14. Lift the mainshaft forward and upward out of the case.
15. Lift out the cluster gear unit and collect the needle bearings.
16. Remove the reverse idler shaft and lift out the gear.

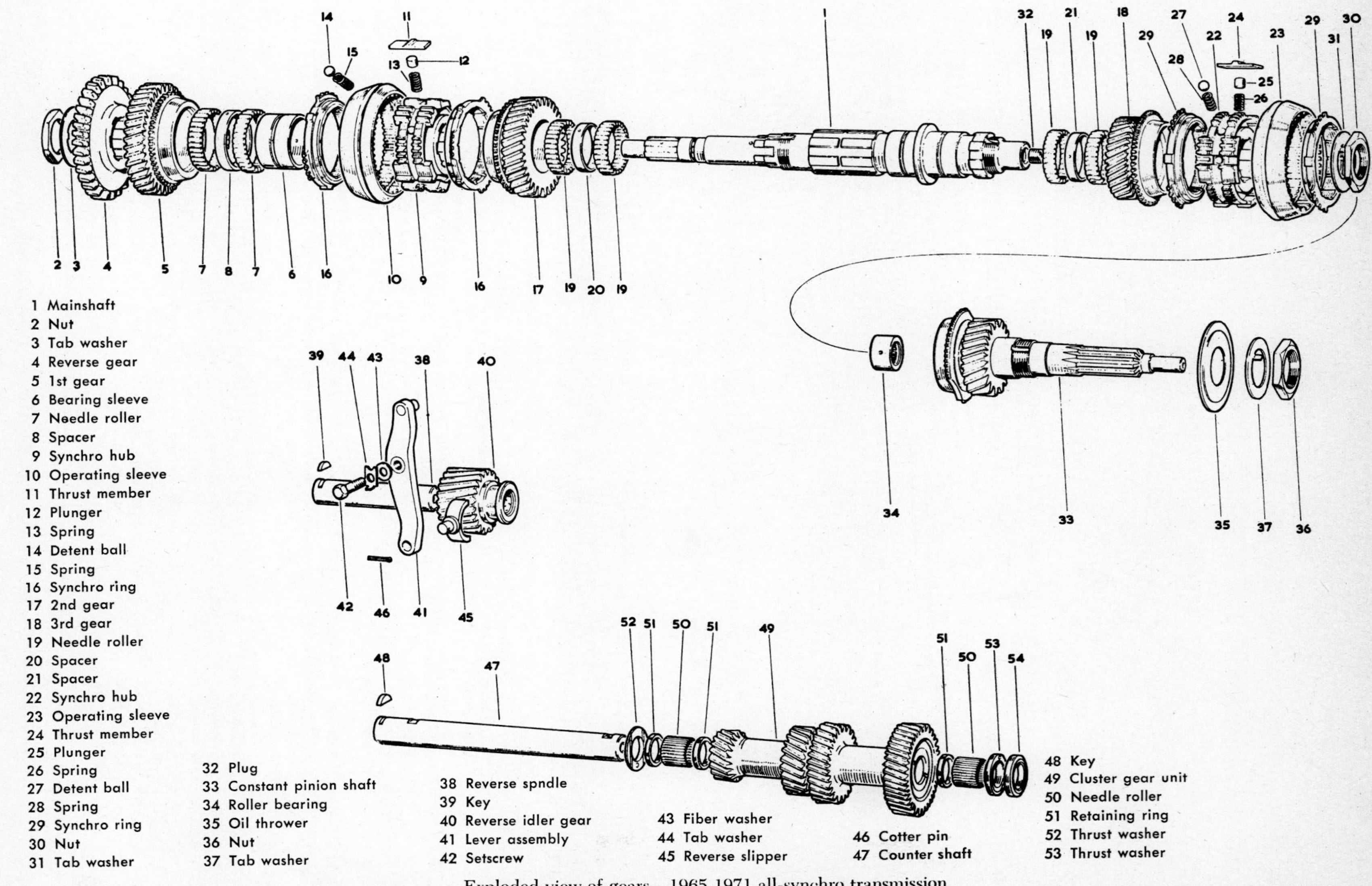
1 Mainshaft
2 Nut
3 Tab washer
4 Reverse gear
5 1st gear
6 Bearing sleeve
7 Needle roller
8 Spacer
9 Synchro hub
10 Operating sleeve
11 Thrust member
12 Plunger
13 Spring
14 Detent ball
15 Spring
16 Synchro ring
17 2nd gear
18 3rd gear
19 Needle roller
20 Spacer
21 Spacer
22 Synchro hub
23 Operating sleeve
24 Thrust member
25 Plunger
26 Spring
27 Detent ball
28 Spring
29 Synchro ring
30 Nut
31 Tab washer
32 Plug
33 Constant pinion shaft
34 Roller bearing
35 Oil thrower
36 Nut
37 Tab washer
38 Reverse spndle
39 Key
40 Reverse idler gear
41 Lever assembly
42 Setscrew
43 Fiber washer
44 Tab washer
45 Reverse slipper
46 Cotter pin
47 Counter shaft
48 Key
49 Cluster gear unit
50 Needle roller
51 Retaining ring
52 Thrust washer
53 Thrust washer

Exploded view of gears—1965-1971 all-synchro transmission

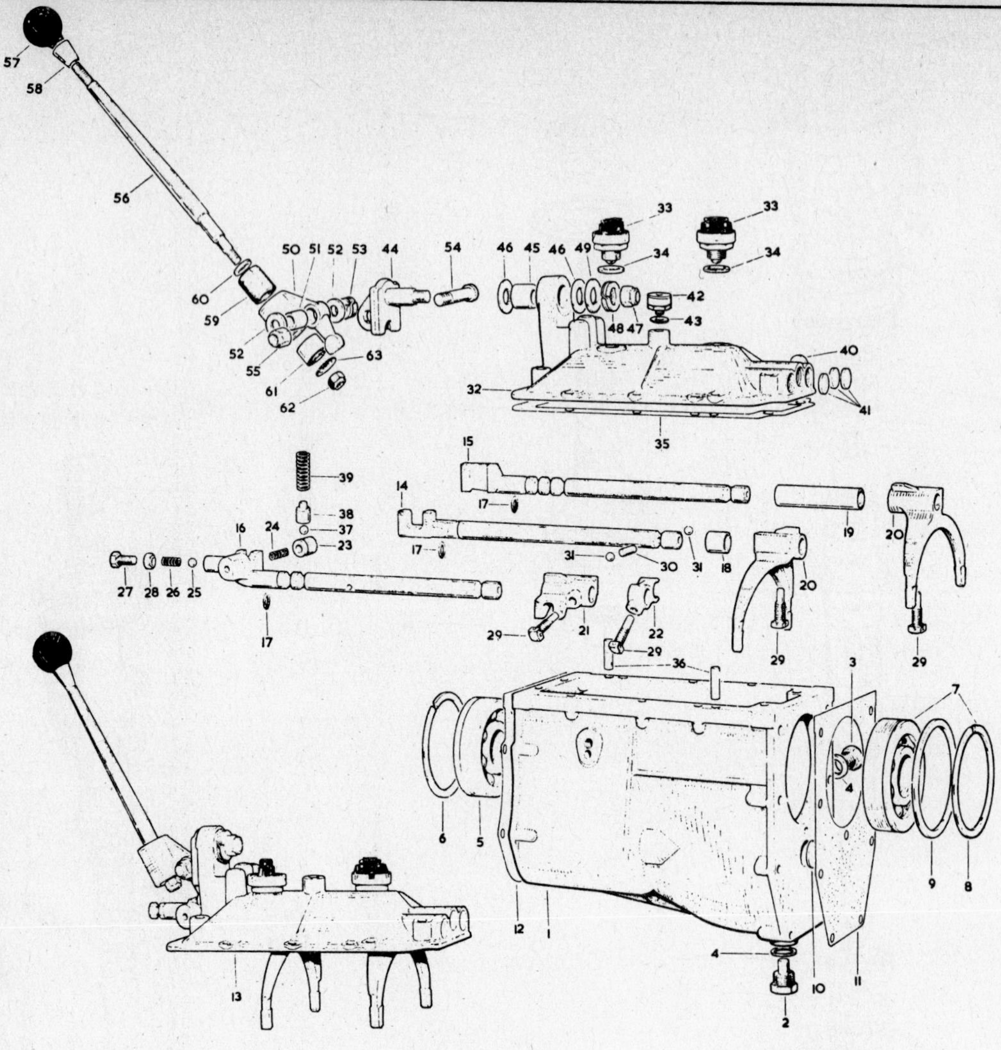

1 Transmission case
2 Oil drain plug
3 Oil filler plug
4 Fiber washer
5 Ball bearing
6 Circlip
7 Ball bearing
8 Circlip
9 Collar
10 Fiber blanking disc
11 Gasket
12 Gasket
13 Remote control assembly
14 Striking rod
15 Striking rod
16 Striking rod
17 O-ring
18 Stop
19 Stop
20 Shift fork
21 Shift fork
22 Locating arm
23 Plunger
24 Spring
25 Ball
26 Spring
27 Screw
28 Nut
29 Dowel screw
30 Roller
31 Ball
32 Top Cover
33 Switch
34 Gasket
35 Gasket
36 Dowel
37 Ball
38 Plunger
39 Spring
40 Welch washer
41 Welch washer
42 Breather
43 Washer
44 Pivot jaw
45 Bushing
46 Washer
47 Nut
48 Washer
49 "D" washer
50 Selector lever
51 Bushing
52 Washer
53 Washer
54 Pivot pin
55 Nut
56 Shift lever
57 Knob
58 Locking cone
59 Upper bushing
60 Washer
61 Lower bushing
62 Nut
63 Washer

Exploded view of the transmission case and top cover—1965-1971 fully synchronized

17. Dismantle the mainshaft as follows:
    a. Remove the hose clamp and withdraw the reverse gear from the mainshaft. *NOTE: The needle bearings are graded by diameter and, as a result, must be kept in sets for their respective positions.*
    b. Withdraw the first gear and 120 needle bearings, spacer and sleeve.
    c. Remove the first/second synchronizer assembly and collect the two loose synchronizer rings.
    d. Remove the second gear and 106 needle bearings, leaving the spacer on the mainshaft.
    e. Straighten the tab washer and remove the large nut holding the third/fourth synchronizer assembly to the mainshaft.
    f. Remove the third/fourth synchronizer assembly from the mainshaft and gather up the two loose synchronizer rings.
    g. Remove the third gear, 106 needle bearings and spacer.
18. Surround the synchronizer assembly with a cloth and push out the synchronizer hub from the operating sleeve. Collect the balls and springs along with the thrust members, plungers and springs.
19. Remove the gear shift lever from the top cover.
20. Remove the third/fourth selector rod and collect the selector, spacing tube and interlock ball.
21. Withdraw the reverse selector rod along with the reverse shift fork, stop spring and detent plunger.
22. Remove the first/second selector rod along with the shift fork and short spacer tube.

Assembly—Fully Synchromesh Transmission

1. Assembly procedures for both synchronizer assemblies (first/second and third/fourth) are the same. The synchronizer hubs appear to be identical but can be distinguished one from the other by the presence of a machined groove on the edge of the third/fourth hub.
2. To assemble the synchronizer assembly, proceed as follows:
    a. Install the synchronizer hub to the operating sleeve making sure that the wide boss of the hub is on the opposite side to the wide chamfer end of the sleeve and that the three balls and springs align with the teeth having the three detent grooves.

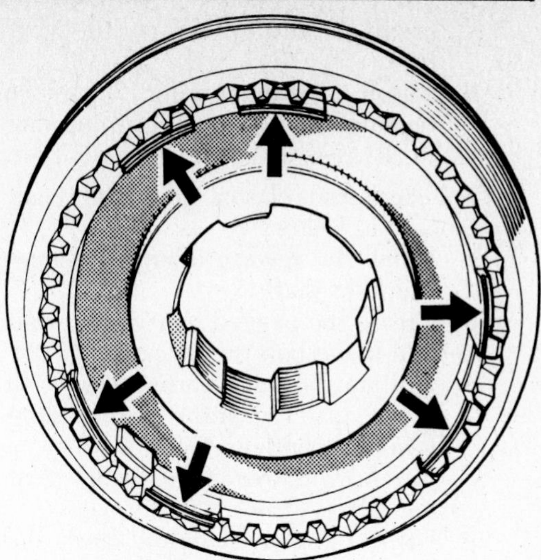

Identifying the third/fourth synchronizer ring

    b. Position the synchronizer hub so that the holes for the ball and springs are exactly level with the top of the operating sleeve.
    c. Install the three springs, plungers and thrust members and hold in place with grease. Press down the thrust members as far as possible, grease the three springs and balls and fit them to the remaining holes.
    d. Using a large hose clamp, compress the springs and carefully lift off the synchronizer assembly from the packing piece.
    e. With the hub slightly depressed, push down on the thrust members with a screwdriver until they engage the neutral groove in the operating sleeve.
    f. Tap the hub down until the balls can be heard and felt to engage the neutral groove.
3. To assemble the cluster gear, perform the following procedure:
    a. Install a retaining ring in the front end of the cluster gear.
    b. Install the 29 needle bearings and hold in place with grease.
    c. Fit the inner thrust washer to the front face of the cluster gear making sure that the peg on the washer

inserts in the groove on the gear face.

d. Install a retaining ring, 29 needle bearings, and another retaining ring to the rear end of the cluster gear.

4. To check the cluster gear and float, proceed as follows:

a. Install the reverse idler gear, lever and idler shaft.

b. Grease the pegged rear washer and fit it to the boss on the casing.

c. Position the outer thrust washer to the front of the cluster gear holding it in place with grease.

d. Carefully lower the cluster gear into place.

e. Insert a dummy shaft and check the clearance between the rear thrust washer and the cluster gear. The clearance should be .004″-.006″ and can be adjusted by changing the thickness of the outer thrust washers. These washers are available in the following thicknesses: .152″, .156″, .159″, .162″, and .164″.

5. To assemble the constant pinion shaft, reverse the disassembly procedure exercising care to seat the bearing squarely on the shaft.

6. To assemble the mainshaft, reverse the disassembly procedure and perform the following instructions:

a. Only the installation of new parts can correct improper mainshaft gear end float. Correct end float on mainshaft gears is .005″-.007″ for first gear and .005″-.008″ for second and third gears.

b. The needle bearings that support the gears on the mainshaft are graded according to diameter and only rollers of one grade should be used with an individual gear. The grade is identified by a 1, 2, or 3 after the part number.

c. The E Type constant pinion, countershaft and third speed gears have a groove running around the periphery of the gear. This groove distinguishes the E Type gear from those found in the same type of transmission on other Jaguar models having different ratios.

d. A hose clamp should be used to prevent the reverse gear from sliding off when the mainshaft is being installed in the transmission case.

7. To install the gears in the transmission case proceed as follows:

a. Remove the dummy shaft from the cluster gear and, *at the same time,* replace it with a thin rod. The rod allows the cluster gear to be lowered into the case so that the mainshaft can be inserted.

b. Install a paper gasket to the front face of the case.

c. Insert the mainshaft through the top of the case and pass the rear of the shaft through the bearing hole.

d. Push the constant pinion shaft through the front of the case with the cutaway portions of the tooth driving member at the top and bottom.

e. Tap the constant pinion shaft into place and enter the front end of the mainshaft into the spigot bearing of the constant pinion shaft.

f. With the constant pinion shaft in position, tap the bearing into place.

g. Using the thin rod as a lever, lift up on the cluster gear and slowly rotate the mainshaft and constant pinion shaft until the cluster gear meshes. Insert the countershaft from the rear and remove the rod. Install the Woodruff key to locate the countershaft to the transmission case.

8. Install the rear extension in the following manner:

a. Coat the oil pump gears and inner pump body with oil and assemble the pump.

b. Secure the pump with the three countersunk screws.

c. Install a paper gasket to the rear face of the transmission case.

d. Install the spacer and driving pin on the oil pump.

e. Bolt the rear extension to the case.

f. Install the speedometer driving gear on the mainshaft.

g. Install the speedometer driven gear and bushing so that the bushing hole is aligned with the hole in the case. Secure with the bolt.

h. Fit a new gasket to the rear cover face. Position a new oil seal (lip facing forward) to the rear cover and install the rear cover.

i. Install the companion flange.

9. To install the overdrive assembly, perform the following:
   a. Fit the adaptor plate with new gasket to the transmission.
   b. Turn the transmission mainshaft so that the cam's highest point will be pointing up. The lower point will now coincide with the overdrive pump rollers. *IMPORTANT: Do not turn the mainshaft again until after the overdrive unit has been fitted.*
   c. Engage first gear.
   d. Fit a new paper gasket to the front of the overdrive unit.
   e. Align the splines of the uni-directional clutch by turning the inner member of the clutch (with a long screwdriver) in a counter-clockwise direction.
   f. Fit the overdrive to the transmission making sure that the pump roller rides on the cam and that the unit pushes up to the adaptor plate (or within 5/8″) with only hand pressure. If it does not, remove the unit and re-align the splines. If it does, tighten the nuts.
10. Assemble the top cover by reversing the disassembly procedure and performing the following instructions:
    a. Make sure that the interlock balls and pin are installed when assembling the selector rods. Use new O-rings on the rods.
    b. Adjust the reverse plunger as follows:
       (1). Install the plunger and spring.
       (2). Install the ball and spring and lightly engage the screw and locknut.
       (3). Press the plunger in all the way and tighten the screw to lock the plunger.
       (4). Slowly loosen the screw until the plunger is just released and the ball engages the circular groove in the plunger.
       (5). Hold the screw in this position and tighten the locknut.
11. To install the top cover, do the following:
    a. Install a new paper gasket.
    b. Shift the transmission and top cover into neutral.
    c. Push the reverse lever to the rear to ensure that the reverse idler gear is not engaged with the reverse gear on the mainshaft.
    d. Engage the selector forks with the grooves on the synchronizer assemblies and tighten down the top cover noting that the nuts and bolts are of different lengths.
12. Replace the clutch housing in the following manner:
    a. Reverse the removal procedure and install a new oil seal with the lip facing the transmission and the metal flange of the seal pressed in fully.
    b. Secure the housing bolts with tab washers except for the two next to the clutch fork trunnions—they are lock wired.
13. The transmission oil pump must be primed as soon as possible by increasing mainshaft speed. This can be done by running the car in fourth gear.

Driveshaft and U-Joints

DRIVESHAFT—MARK II

Mark II models use an open type driveshaft fitted with needle bearing U-joints. The *standard transmission* cars have a driveshaft (fixed length) with a U-joint at each end. Located at the front of the shaft is a splined sleeve which slides on a splined extension of the transmission mainshaft. *Overdrive cars* have a one-piece open driveshaft with a U-joint at each end and a sliding spline at the front. *Automatic transmission* models use a divided driveshaft. The front driveshaft has a U-joint at the front and is supported at the rear by a bearing encased in a rubber mounted plate. The rear driveshaft has a U-joint at each end and a sliding spline to absorb front and rear movement of the rear axle. If the car is equipped with the *fully synchromesh* (all four gears) four speed, the driveshaft used is the same as that used on the overdrive cars.

Standard Transmission Models (Excluding Fully Synchromesh)

Removal

1. Jack up one of the rear wheels so that it clears the ground thus allowing the driveshaft to be rotated.

CAUTION: As a safety measure, block both sides of the other rear wheel.

2. Remove the cotter pins, nuts and washers from the bolts holding the shaft to the rear axle.
3. Separate the two flanges and remove the shaft from the splines at the transmission.

INSTALLATION

1. To install, reverse the removal procedure.

Overdrive and Fully Synchromesh

REMOVAL

1. Raise one rear wheel so that it clears the ground.

CAUTION: Block each side of the other rear wheel.

2. Remove the cotter pins, nuts and washers from the front and rear shaft flanges.
3. Compress the sliding joint and remove the shaft.

INSTALLATION

1. To install the driveshaft, reverse the removal procedure.

Automatic Transmission Models —Divided Driveshaft

REMOVAL—FRONT DRIVESHAFT

1. Remove the ventilated cover from the bottom of the torque converter housing.
2. Place a piece of wood under the torque converter and jack up the engine and transmission.
3. Mark the positions of the center bearing and rear engine mounting brackets in order to facilitate assembly.
4. Remove the bolts from the engine rear support bracket and make note of the number and position of the packing washers located between the bracket and body floor.
5. Separate the engine rear support bracket from the two rubber mounts at the rear of the transmission.
6. Jack up one of the rear wheels and *block the other* as a safety precaution. This will enable the driveshaft to turn.
7. Detach the front and rear of the front driveshaft and support the front end of the rear driveshaft.
8. Remove the bolts and washers holding the driveshaft center bearing bracket to the body and remove the front driveshaft.

INSTALLATION—FRONT DRIVESHAFT

1. Secure the shaft flange to the transmission flange.
2. Bolt the center bearing mounting to the body.
3. Attach the rear of the shaft to the center bearing flange.
4. Install the washers and nuts attaching the rubber mounts on the rear of the transmission to the mounting bracket.
5. Install the engine rear mounting bracket and packing washers.
6. Lower the jack and replace the converter housing cover plate.

REMOVAL—REAR DRIVESHAFT

1. Remove the cotter pins, nuts and washers attaching the front and rear of the shaft.
2. Compress the sliding joint and remove the shaft.

INSTALLATION—REAR DRIVESHAFT

1. To install, reverse the removal procedure.

DRIVESHAFT—3.4S AND 3.8S

The 3.4S and 3.8S are equipped with one of two different driveshaft types—the standard transmission type and that used on overdrive and automatic transmission models. Standard transmission cars have a fixed length shaft with a U- joint at each end and a sliding spline at the front. Overdrive and automatic transmission models are equipped with a driveshaft having a U-joint at each end and a sliding spline (sleeve yoke) enclosed in a rubber boot.

Standard Transmission Models

REMOVAL

1. Jack up one rear wheel and block both sides of the other so that the driveshaft is free to turn.
2. Remove the nuts and washers from the bolts connecting the shaft to the axle flange.
3. Remove the driveshaft from the car.

INSTALLATION

1. To install, reverse the removal procedure.

Overdrive and Automatic Transmission Models

REMOVAL

1. Jack up one rear wheel and block both sides of the other so that the driveshaft is able to turn.
2. Remove the nuts and washers from the front and rear flanges, compress the sliding joint and remove the shaft.

INSTALLATION

1. Installation is the reverse of removal.

DRIVESHAFT—420

All 420's use a fixed length driveshaft with a U-joint at each end and a sliding spline enclosed in a rubber boot at the front end.

REMOVAL

1. Using a jack, compress the spring on the rear engine mount, disassemble the mount and slowly lower the jack to release the spring tension. Remove the mount.
2. Detach the driveshaft from the transmission and rear axle.
3. Compress the sliding spline and remove the driveshaft.

INSTALLATION

1. To install the driveshaft, reverse the above procedure.

DRIVESHAFT—XJ6

The XJ6 is equipped with a divided driveshaft (open type) with the front end of the rear shaft supported in a rubber mounted bearing. The front shaft has a U-joint at each end and a sliding spline protected by a rubber boot.

REMOVAL—FRONT DRIVESHAFT

1. Remove the nuts and bolts from the front and rear flanges.
2. Compress the sliding spline and remove the shaft.

INSTALLATION—FRONT DRIVESHAFT

1. To install, reverse the above procedure.

REMOVAL—REAR DRIVESHAFT

1. Remove the nuts and bolts from the front and rear flanges.
2. To facilitate assembly, mark the location of the center bearing support bracket. Remove the support bracket and note the number of washers between the bracket and the body.
3. Remove the shaft.

INSTALLATION—REAR DRIVESHAFT

1. To install driveshaft, reverse the removal procedure.

DRIVESHAFT—E TYPE (All)

The E Type uses an open driveshaft with a U-joint at each end and a sliding spline at the front.

REMOVAL

1. To remove the driveshaft, it is necessary to remove the engine or rear suspension. It is advisable to choose the latter.
2. Remove the seats.
3. Remove the driveshaft tunnel cover.
4. Detach the transmission cowl from the body.
5. Disconnect and remove the driveshaft.

INSTALLATION

1. To install, reverse the removal procedure.

DIVIDED DRIVESHAFT ALIGNMENT—MARK II AND XJ6

If the engine or rear driveshaft has been removed, it is necessary to align the two driveshafts in order to prevent transmission chatter when starting off from a standing start. Before checking the alignment on the Mark II, disconnect the engine stabilizer located at the rear of the cylinder head. To do this, remove the nut and flanged

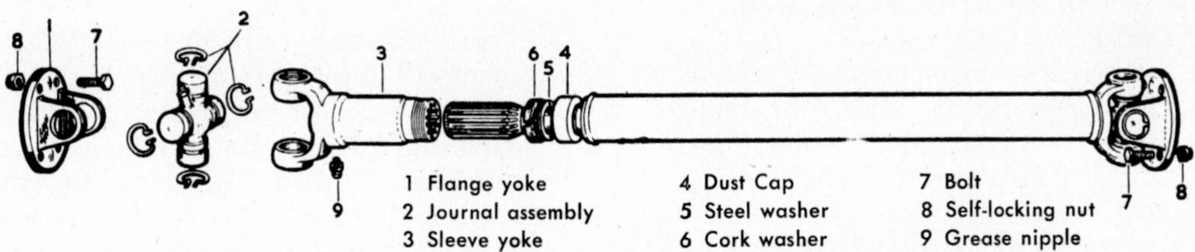

Exploded view of driveshaft—E Type (all)

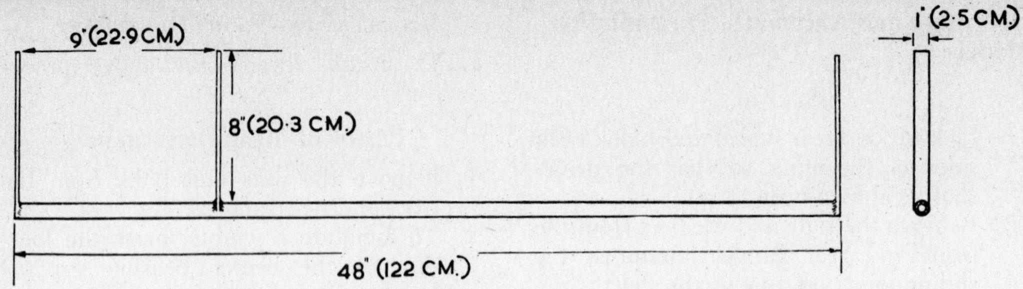

Dimensions for fabricating a driveshaft alignment jig—Mark II

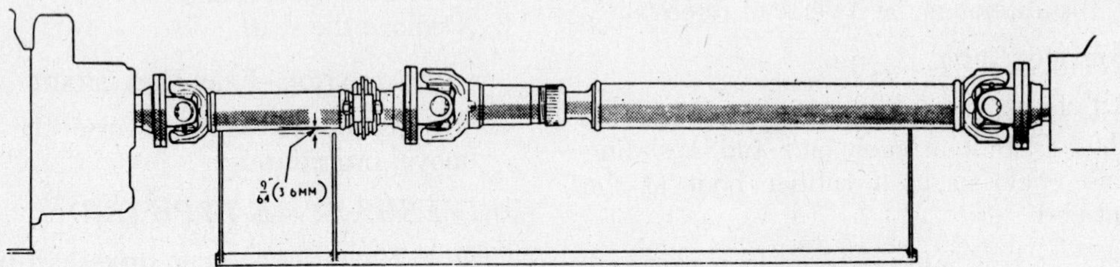
Using fabricated jig for checking height of the front driveshaft —Mark II

washer from the top and screw the lower washer down the center pin by inserting a screwdriver in the washer slot accessible through the hole in the rubber mount. Check the rear engine mounts for distortion.

Mark II

1. Fabricate an alignment jig by welding three pieces of flat bar (8″ x 1″ x 3/16″) exactly in line to a piece of tube measuring 1-1/8″ outside diameter. The three pieces of flat bar should be correctly spaced (see illustration).
2. The two outer legs of the jig should touch the front of the front driveshaft and the rear of the rear driveshaft. The second leg should not touch. There should be a clearance of 9/64″ between the second leg and the rear of the front driveshaft.
3. On those cars having the 3.4 liter engines, the height alignment procedure is the same as the 3.8 except that no clearance should exist, all three legs should touch the shafts at the same time.
4. If height adjustment is necessary, then shims should be added or removed from between the center bearing bracket mounting and the body. Adding shims will lower the bearing while removing them will raise it.
5. Straight line alignment can be determined by using the same jig or three plumb lines. Hold the jig with the three legs touching the front and rear driveshafts. Improper alignment will be obvious.
6. Straight line alignment can be made by enlarging the setscrew holes on the center bearing bracket so that the bracket can be moved to create proper alignment of the shafts.
7. The engine stabilizer will now have to be adjusted.
   a. Raise the lower flanged washer (by inserting a screwdriver in the slot) up the pin until the flange touches the bottom of the rubber mounting.
   b. Install the upper flanged washer and tighten the nut.

XJ6

1. Make up a jig following the dimensions shown in the illustration. Two illustrations are shown; do not confuse the illustration for the XJ6 with the one for the Mark II.
2. For horizontal (straight line) alignment, all three legs of the jig should touch the side of the driveshafts at the same time. If they do not, then adjustment can be made by adding or subtracting shims from between the center bearing bracket and the driveshaft tunnel. Shims should be added to raise the

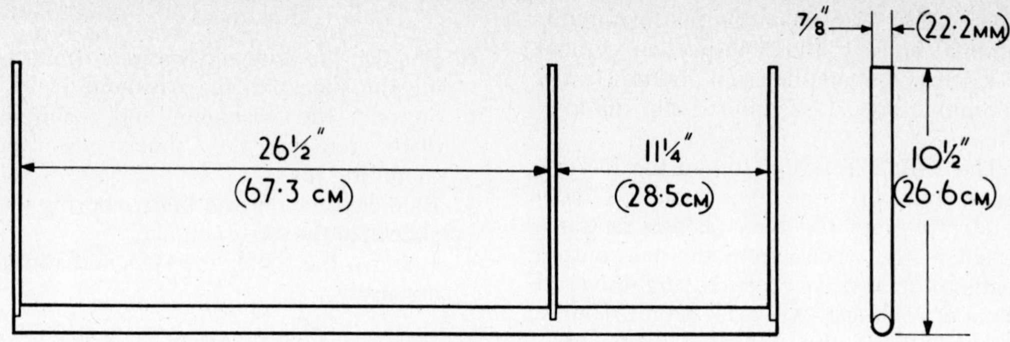

Driveshaft alignment jig—XJ6

center bearing and removed to lower it.

3. For vertical alignment, all three legs of the jig should touch the shafts at the same time. To adjust, loosen the center bearing bracket screws and slide the bracket whichever way necessary to correct shaft alignment.

U-JOINTS—MARK II, 3.4S, 3.8S, 420, XJ6, E TYPE (All)

Check for excessive play of the splined shaft in the splined yoke. Replace the entire driveshaft if circumferential movement, measured on the outside diameter of the spline, exceeds .004".

Removal

1. Remove the rubber boot or unscrew the dust cap and slide the yoke off the splined shaft. Clean thoroughly.
2. Remove the snap-rings from their grooves. It may be necessary to lightly tap the end of the joint to relieve pressure on the ring.
3. Using a soft hammer, tap the yoke lug to loosen the top bearing enough to remove by hand. If this fails to work, it may be driven out from inside with a small drift.
4. Repeat this procedure for the other bearing and remove the yoke.
5. Remove the two remaining bearings by resting the trunnions on a block of wood and tapping on the yoke with a soft hammer.
6. Wash all parts in a safe solvent.

Installation

1. The newer cars have pre-packed universal joints that do not require periodic maintenance. These can be identified by the absence of lubrication nipples. If the U-joint is of this type, then it must be lubricated with the proper grease before assembly. Fill each journal trunnion reservoir with grease and half fill each bearing.
2. If applicable, install the rubber seals to the inner end of each bearing.
3. Insert the journal into the flange yoke.
4. Place one of the bearings into the bore of the yoke and, by using a drift about 1/32" smaller than the bearing, tap the bearing into place.
5. Install the snap-rings and repeat this procedure for the others. The journals should move freely.

IMPORTANT: When replacing the sliding joint, make sure that it is aligned with the fixed yoke at the end of the driveshaft. There are arrows stamped on the two yokes and these arrows should be aligned with one another.

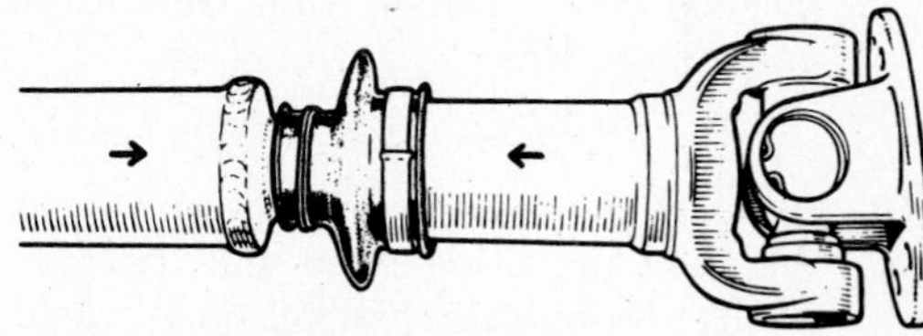

It is important that the sliding joint align with the fixed yoke. Arrows are stamped on these components to facilitate alignment.

Drive Axle and Rear Suspension

The Mark II models use a Salisbury semi-floating type rear axle. The axle shafts are splined to the differential while the outer ends are tapered and keyed to the wheel hubs. A cover on the rear of the differential housing allows inspection without disassembly. Available as an option was the Thornton "Powr-Lok" limited slip differential.

The 3.4S, 3.8S, 420, XJ6 and the E Type use a Salisbury type rear mounted independently from the hubs. Power is transferred to the wheels from the axle output shafts by short drive shafts having universal joints at each end. Available on all models, except XJ6, is the Thornton "Powr-Lok" limited slip differential.

LEAF SPRING REMOVAL AND INSTALLATION

Mark II

The Mark II has a pair of leaf springs mounted with rubber at the front, center and rear. When removing springs, check rubber mounts for deterioration and replace if necessary.

Removal

1. Jack up the car and place on a jackstand.
2. Place a scissors jack under the spring eye and raise the spring enough to relieve the pressure on the center mounting clamp plate.
3. Remove the center mounting clamp plate.
4. Remove the nut and bolt from the spring eye located at the rear of each spring and slowly lower the jack from under the spring.
5. Detach the spring from the front mounting plate.

Installation

1. Connect the front end of the spring to the front mounting plate and the rear of the spring to its bracket on the axle but do not tighten nut.
2. With a jack under the spring eye, raise the spring and install the center mounting clamp plate.
3. Lower the car to the ground and tighten the nut on the spring eye bolt.

REAR COIL SPRING

3.4S, 3.8S, 420, XJ6, E Type (All)

Rear suspension is provided by four coil springs each containing a shock absorber and mounted on either side of the differential housing.

Removal

1. Remove the nuts and washers connecting the shocks to the wishbone.
2. Support the wishbone and, using a drift, remove the shock absorber mounting pin.
3. Remove the nuts and bolts securing the shocks to the crossmember.
4. Remove the shock absorber and spring assembly.

Installation

1. To install, reverse the removal procedure.

AXLE SHAFT

Mark II

Removal

1. Jack up car and remove wheel and fender skirt.
2. Disconnect handbrake cable at the caliper.
3. Disconnect the brake lines and tape the openings to keep out dirt.
4. Remove the brake caliper *being careful not to drop any of the shims since they must be reassembled in the same position; otherwise, the centralization of the caliper would be changed.*
5. Using a puller, remove the hub and disc from the axle shaft.
6. Before continuing, *check the combined end float of the axle shafts.* If it is not .003″ to .005″, then it should be adjusted during assembly by adding or subtracting shims from between the caliper mounting plate and the end of the axle tube.
7. Remove the oil seal retainer and brake caliper mounting plate from the axle tube.
8. Using a suitable puller, remove the axle shaft and bearing.
9. Remove the hub bearing and, if replacement is necessary, take out the inner race. Check the oil seal within the axle tube and replace if necessary.

Installation

To install, reverse the removal procedure, noting the following instructions:

1. Clean the hub bearing so that accurate axle shaft end float can be determined.
2. Install the shaft with the inner race, being careful not to damage the oil seal.

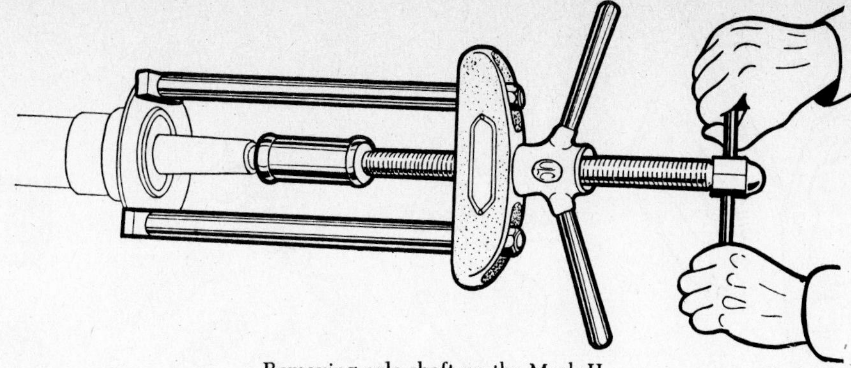

Removing axle shaft on the Mark II

3. Insert the bearing outer race squarely into the housing and replace the hub oil seal if necessary.
4. Using a soft hammer, tap each axle shaft to make sure that the bearing cups are hitting against the caliper mounting plate.
5. With a dial indicator, check the axle shaft end float.

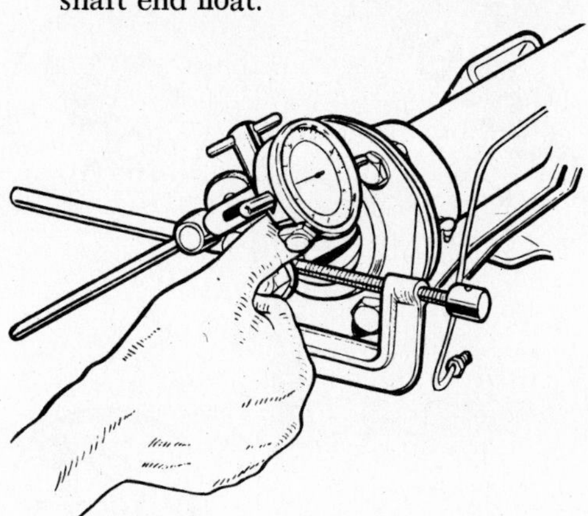

Checking axle shaft end float—Mark II

6. Add or subtract shims to arrive at an axle shaft end float of .003″ to .005″. Adding shims will increase end float while subtracting them will decrease the measurement. Remove or install the same thickness of shims at each end of the axle in order to hold the axle shaft spacer in a central location. These shims are available in .003″, .005″, .010″ and .030″ thicknesses.
7. Install hubs and calipers, brake lines and handbrake cables.
8. Make sure the discs are centered within the calipers and bleed the system.
9. Install the wheels and fender skirts.
10. Grease hub bearings.

REAR SUSPENSION

3.4S, 3.8S, 420, XJ6, E Type (All)

Removal

1. Remove any exhaust pipes or mufflers that may be in the way.
2. If so equipped, remove the radius arm safety strap.
3. Detach the radius arms from the body of the car.
4. Place a piece of hardwood (9″ by 9″ x 1″) between the rear suspension tie plate and a jack. Jack up the car and place two equal size stands under the body in front of the radius arm mounting posts. To prevent body damage, use wood between the jacks and the body.
5. Remove the rear wheels.
6. Remove the anti-sway bar (E Type only).
7. Detach the brake lines from the body.
8. Separate the handbrake cable from the levers mounted on the crossmember.
9. Remove the screw from the handbrake cable adjuster block.
10. Remove the rubber mounts from the crossmember. There may be shims between the mounts and the frame; if so, note the number and location of them.
11. Separate the driveshaft from the differential and *slowly* lower the suspension assembly on the jack while checking for any remaining connections to the car.

Installation

1. To install, reverse the removal procedure. Check all rubber mounts for deterioration before installing them. If the radius arms have been removed, make sure that the rear suspension is at

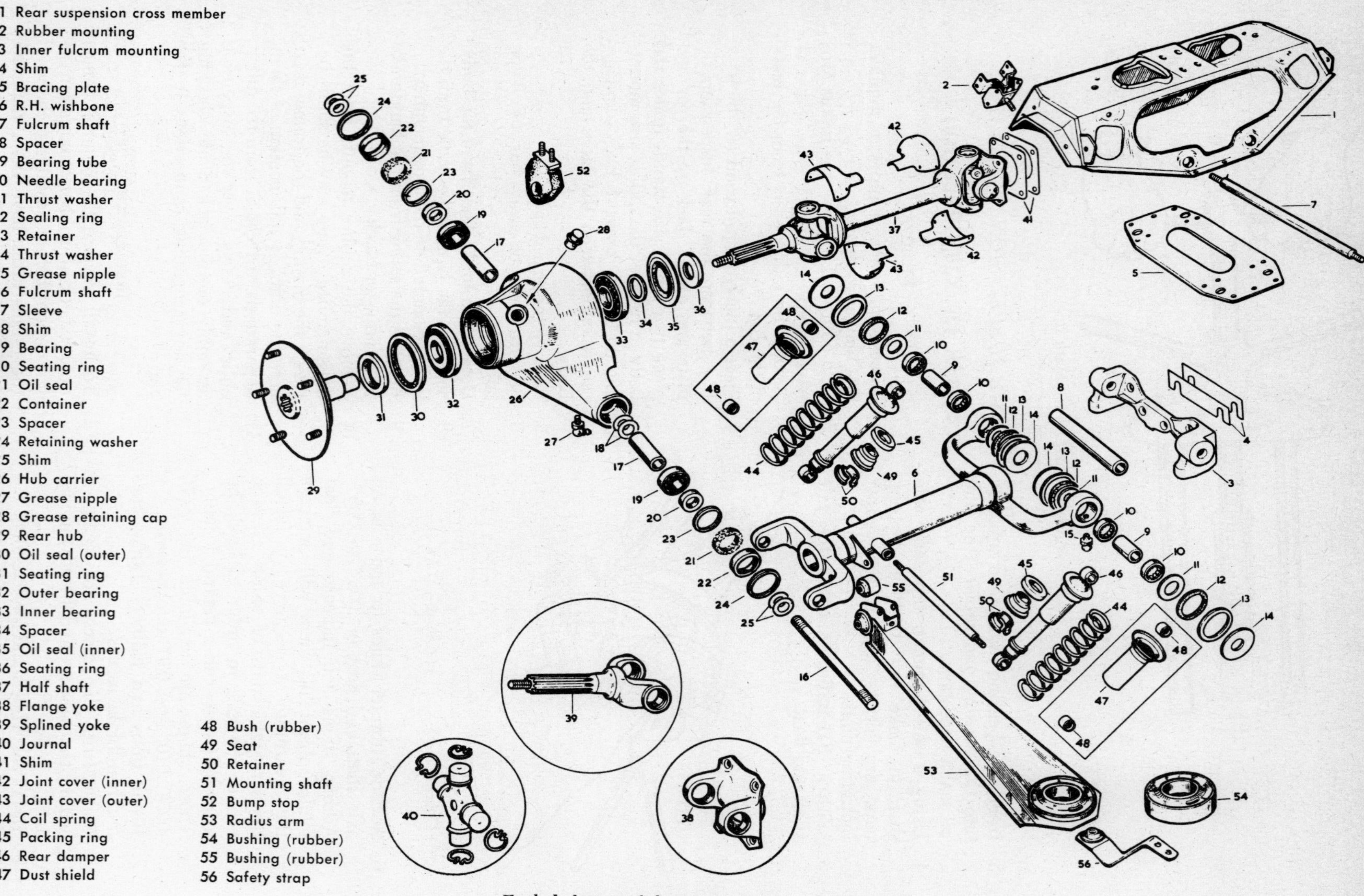

1 Rear suspension cross member
2 Rubber mounting
3 Inner fulcrum mounting
4 Shim
5 Bracing plate
6 R.H. wishbone
7 Fulcrum shaft
8 Spacer
9 Bearing tube
10 Needle bearing
11 Thrust washer
12 Sealing ring
13 Retainer
14 Thrust washer
15 Grease nipple
16 Fulcrum shaft
17 Sleeve
18 Shim
19 Bearing
20 Seating ring
21 Oil seal
22 Container
23 Spacer
24 Retaining washer
25 Shim
26 Hub carrier
27 Grease nipple
28 Grease retaining cap
29 Rear hub
30 Oil seal (outer)
31 Seating ring
32 Outer bearing
33 Inner bearing
34 Spacer
35 Oil seal (inner)
36 Seating ring
37 Half shaft
38 Flange yoke
39 Splined yoke
40 Journal
41 Shim
42 Joint cover (inner)
43 Joint cover (outer)
44 Coil spring
45 Packing ring
46 Rear damper
47 Dust shield
48 Bush (rubber)
49 Seat
50 Retainer
51 Mounting shaft
52 Bump stop
53 Radius arm
54 Bushing (rubber)
55 Bushing (rubber)
56 Safety strap

Exploded view of the rear suspension—420

normal riding height before tightening the radius arms at the wishbone.

HALFSHAFTS, REAR HUBS

3.4S, 3.8S, 420, XJ6, E Type (All)

Unlike the solid axle Mark II models, the above models transfer power from the axle output shafts to the wheels by means of short driveshafts (halfshafts) having U-joints at each end.

Removal

1. Jack up and support the car and remove the wheels.
2. Remove the cotter pin, nut and washer from the halfshaft.
3. Using a suitable puller, remove the hub and hub carrier assembly from the splined end of the halfshaft.
4. Using a drift, remove the lower wishbone outer fulcrum shaft.
5. Remove the hub and hub carrier assembly.
6. Remove the front shock and spring assembly.
7. Remove the four nuts holding the halfshaft inner universal joint to the axle shaft output flange and brake disc. Lift out the halfshaft noting the number of camber shims.
8. To replace U-joints, refer to U-Joints in the Driveshaft and U-Joints section.

Installation

1. Using a solvent, clean the halfshaft and hub splines of all grease.
2. Install the inner oil seal track and end float spacer on the halfshaft.
3. Apply a liquid sealer to the splines and press the hub onto the halfshaft.
4. Fit the washer and nut and torque to 140 ft. lbs. Install the cotter pin.
5. Install the camber shims and position the halfshaft and hub.
6. Install and tighten the four self-locking nuts.
7. Install the front shock and spring assembly and the lower wishbone.
8. If the halfshaft is new, check the rear wheel camber.

REAR SUSPENSION WISHBONE

3.4S, 3.8S, 420, XJ6, E Type (All)

Removal

1. Remove the suspension assembly (see Rear Suspension). Detach the shocks.
2. Loosen the fourteen mounting bolts and remove the tie plate from the bottom of the crossmember that houses the differential assembly.
3. Using a drift, remove the fulcrum shaft holding the hub carrier to the wishbone.
4. Separate the hub carrier from the wishbone and carefully collect the shims (if any are present) noting the number and position so that they may be assembled in the same way.
5. To facilitate assembly, use a rod approximately equal in size to the fulcrum shaft and insert it in the hub carrier so that the internal bearings, seals, washers, etc. will be held in place until it's time to assemble the fulcrum shaft to the carrier.
6. Using a piece of tape, hold the oil seal tracks in place.
7. Separate the radius arm from the wishbone.
8. Remove the fulcrum shaft from the wishbone inner fork and lift out the wishbone assembly. Gather the four outer thrust washers, oil seals and retainers. Check the oil seals for deterioration and replace if necessary.
9. Remove the two bearing tubes.
10. Using a drift, gently tap the needle bearings from the wishbone. Remove the bearing spacer.

Installation

1. If the needle bearings were removed from the inner fork of the wishbone, then press in one roller cage with the engraving on the cage facing outward.
2. Insert the spacing tube and press in the other bearing.
3. Repeat this procedure for the other side of the fork.
4. Insert the bearing tubes and, after coating the washers, seals, and retainers with grease, position them on the wishbone.
5. Align the wishbone to its mounting bracket with the radius arm mounting bracket towards the front of the car. Insert a dummy shaft making sure that it passes through all of the washers, seals, retainers, crossmember and mounting bracket.
6. Coat the fulcrum shaft with grease and tap it into the wishbone assembly thereby displacing the dummy shaft.

As it emerges from the wishbone, hold back the dummy shaft so that it does not exit too quickly thereby causing a washer to drop out of line.

7. Install the tie plate to the crossmember.
8. Install the radius arm and replace the rubber bushings if deteriorated. Fit the large bushing with the two holes in a longitudinal position and, when installing the small bushing, make sure that it is centered in the hole with an equal amount of bushing protruding from each side. Torque the radius arm bolt to 46 ft. lbs.
9. Remove the tape holding the oil seal tracks in position.
10. Align the wishbone with the hub assembly and install a dummy shaft ensuring that the spacers, washers and seals are aligned correctly. Grease the fulcrum shaft and gently tap it into position thereby displacing the dummy shaft. As in Step 6, hold back the dummy shaft as it emerges.
11. Using a feeler gauge, check the clearance between the hub carrier and the wishbone lever and, if necessary, insert shims to center the hub carrier. Torque the fulcrum shaft nuts to 55 ft. lbs.
12. Check the camber.
13. Install the shock absorbers.
14. Install the rear suspension assembly as instructed in the Rear Suspension installation procedure.

Wishbone Outer Pivot Bearing Adjustment—3.4S, 3.8S, 420, XJ6, E Type (All)

1. Remove the hub from the halfshaft.
2. Proper bearing adjustment is .000″ to .002″ and is affected by the shims located between the two fulcrum shaft spacer tubes.
3. Fabricate a jig from a piece of plate steel 7″ x 4″ x 3/8″. Drill a hole in the plate and tap in threads so that the outer fulcrum shaft may be screwed into it. Place the plate in a vice and screw the shaft into the plate and slide an oil seal track onto the shaft. Place the rest of the components (washers, bearings, etc.) minus the oil seals onto the shaft. Include an excessive number of shims between the spacers. Place an inner wishbone fork outer thrust washer onto the shaft so that it contacts the oil seal track. Fill in the remaining space on the shaft with washers, install the nut and torque to 55 ft. lbs.
4. With the plate still in the vice and the hub carrier attached, press the carrier toward the plate while slightly twisting it in order to settle the roller bearings.
5. Exert a steady *pressure against* the hub carrier and, using a feeler gauge, measure the clearance between the large washer and the machined face of the hub carrier.
6. Pull the hub carrier assembly towards the large washer slightly turning the carrier to settle the rollers onto the bearing surface. Apply pressure against the carrier while measuring the clearance between the washer and the machined face of the hub carrier.

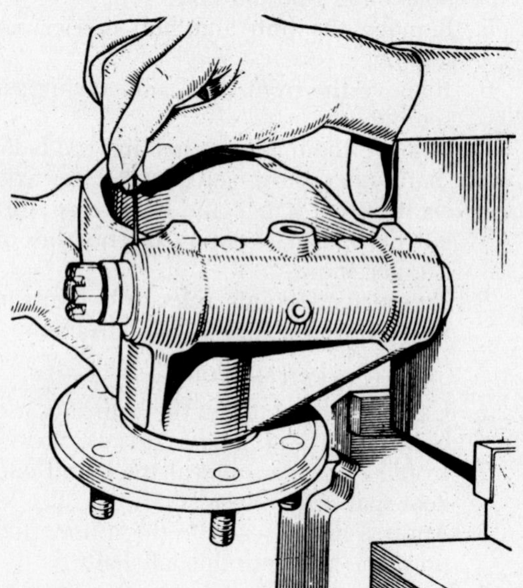

Checking the clearance between the hub carrier and the large washer to determine bearing end-float

7. To arrive at the bearing end float subtract the one measurement from the other. Remove enough shims to create a preload reading of .000″ to .002″.
8. The specified preload is .000″ to .002″ therefore, the average preload would be .001″. For example, if the bearing end float is .010″, add the average preload of .001″ to arrive at .011″. To obtain correct preload, remove .011″ in shims.
9. Install the hub carrier to the halfshaft.
10. Install the new oil seals (lips inward)

and position the fulcrum shaft in the hub carrier.

11. Mount the hub carrier to the wishbone and replace the dummy shaft with the fulcrum shaft.
12. Measure the gap between the hub carrier oil seal tracks (both ends) and the wishbone fork. Shim as necessary until the gap is the same at both ends and therefore, the hub carrier is centered within the wishbone forks. This centering will prevent the fork ends from closing inward. Shims of .004″ thickness with a 1-1/8″ diameter should be used on the 3.4S, 3.8S and the 420. The E Type requires a .004″ shim with a 7/8″ diameter while the XJ6 specifies a shim having a .003″ thickness and a 1-1/8″ diameter.
13. Torque the fulcrum shaft nuts to 55 ft. lbs.

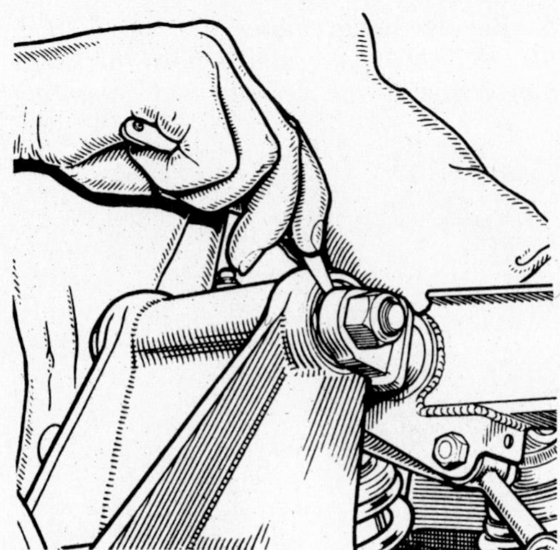

Checking clearance between the hub carrier oil seal tracks and wishbone forks

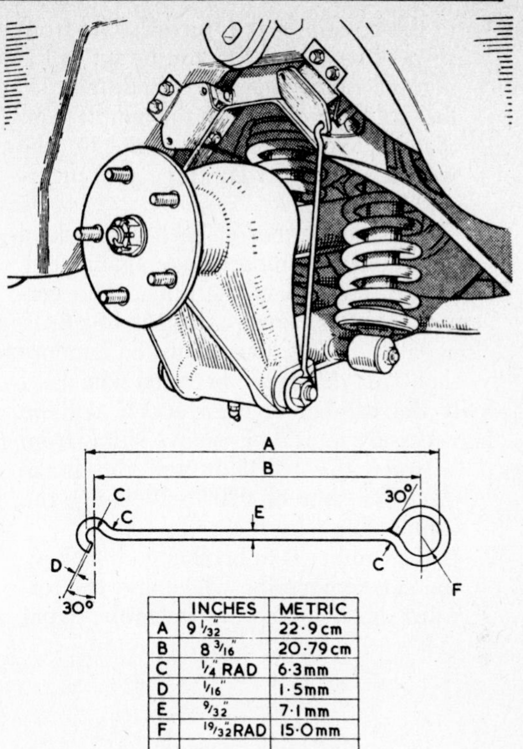

	INCHES	METRIC
A	9 1/32″	22·9 cm
B	8 3/16″	20·79 cm
C	1/4″ RAD	6·3 mm
D	1/16″	1·5 mm
E	9/32″	7·1 mm
F	19/32 RAD	15·0 mm

To check rear camber angle, the suspension must be locked at a specific height by the use of setting links

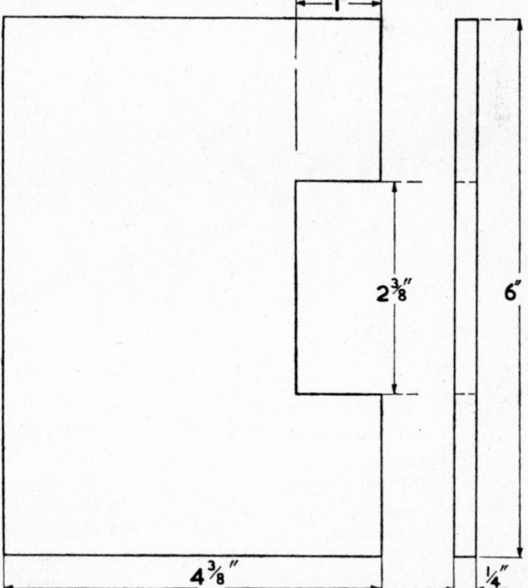

Setting blocks are used on the 420 model to ensure proper vehicle height when making suspension adjustments

ADJUSTING REAR WHEEL CAMBER ANGLE—3.4S, 3.8S, 420, XJ6, E TYPE (All)

1. Position the car on a level surface with the tire pressures set correctly.
2. Camber angles vary with suspension height so it is necessary to lock the rear suspension in the mid-laden position by means of a pair of setting links. Insert one end of the link into the lower hole of the suspension rear mount and push down on the body until the other end of the link can be slipped over the fulcrum shaft nut. Do the same for the other side.
3. On the 420, lock the front suspension by installing setting blocks under the upper wishbone next to the rubber bumper and over the bracket welded

to the bottom of the "turret". The front suspension of the XJ6 can be set to the normal riding height by adding 850 lbs. to the weight of the empty car; that is, roughly equivalent to the weight of the driver, three passengers and full gas tanks.

4. Check the camber of each rear wheel by placing a camber gauge against one rear tire and then the other. The correct camber angle should be 3/4° negative±1/4°. There must be no more than 1/4° difference between wheels.
5. If the camber is incorrect, it will be necessary to add or remove shims from between the halfshaft and the brake disc. One shim of .020″ will change the camber angle by 1/4°.
6. If the camber is to be changed, jack up the car, remove the wheel and the forward shock and spring assembly. Separate the halfshaft from the brake disc and remove or add the necessary number of shims. Install components and repeat for the other side. Recheck camber.

REAR AXLE ASSEMBLY

Mark II

Removal

1. Jack up the car under the rear axle and support with blocks.
2. Remove wheels and release handbrake.
3. Disconnect the handbrake cables at the brake caliper.
4. Disconnect brake lines from calipers and tape over openings to keep out dirt.
5. Remove brake caliper.

IMPORTANT: Carefully remove the shims from between the caliper and mounting

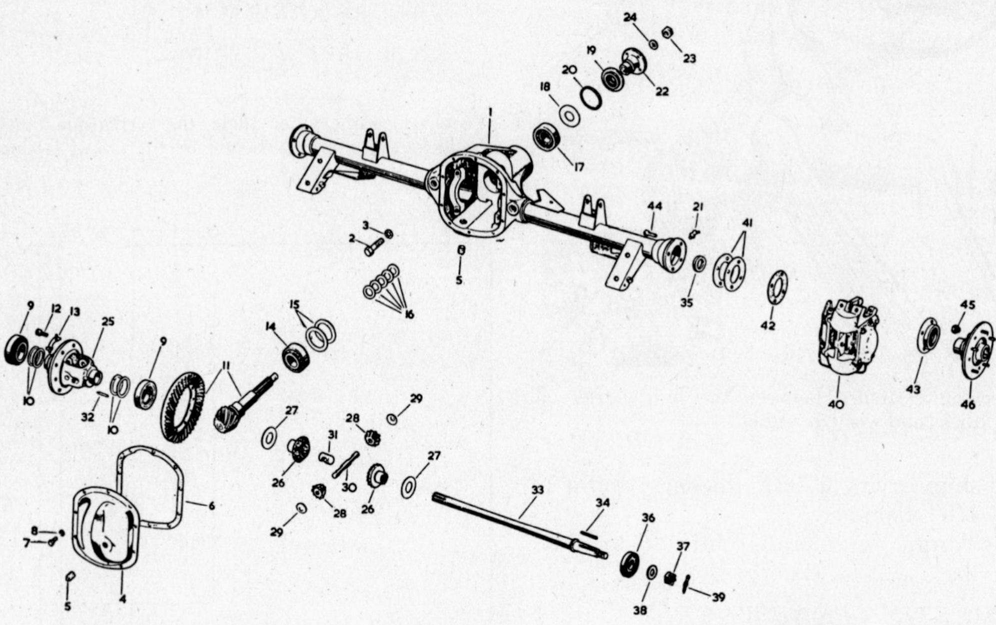

1 Carrier and tube assembly
2 Setscrew
3 Shakeproof washer
4 Rear cover
5 Drain and filler plug
6 Gasket
7 Setscrew
8 Lockwasher
9 Roller bearing
10 Shim
11 Drive gear and pinion
12 Setscrew
13 Lockstrap
14 Roller bearing
15 Shim (inner)
16 Shim (outer)
17 Roller bearing
18 Oil slinger
19 Oil seal
20 Gasket
21 Grease nipple
22 Universal joint flange
23 Nut
24 Washer
25 Differential case
26 Side gear
27 Thrust washer
28 Differential pinion mate gear
29 Thrust washer
30 Pinion mate gear shaft
31 Spacer
32 Pinion mate shaft lock pin
33 Axle shaft
34 Key
35 Oil seal
36 Taper roller bearing
37 Slotted nut
38 Washer
39 Cotter pin
40 Rear brake assembly
41 Shim
42 Gasket
43 Retainer
44 Bolt
45 Self-locking bolt
46 Rear hub

Exploded view of the rear axle—Mark II

plate for they must be returned to their original positions; otherwise, the caliper will be improperly centered.

6. Using a puller, remove hubs.
7. Remove cotter pins and nuts attaching the rear axle companion flange to the driveshaft. Lift out the driveshaft.
8. Detach the brake lines from the rear axle housing and tie them to the frame so that they are out of the way.
9. Remove the handbrake compensator assembly and cables from the rear axle.
10. Detach the shock absorbers from their brackets on the rear axle and compress out of the way.
11. Detach the torque rods from the rear axle and, using a drift, tap out the bolts.
12. Remove the panhard rod along with its rubber bushings and washers.
13. Lower the axle as far as possible on the jack and drift out the bolts from the leaf spring eye.
14. Remove axle assembly from car.

INSTALLATION

1. To install, reverse removal procedure. Bleed the brakes. Adjust the panhard rod as follows:
   a. Place a straight edge along the outside of a rear tire and check the distance from the straight edge to the flange of the chassis side member where the spring center clamping plate is bolted. More specifically, make the measurement to a point between the two bolts that hold the rear spring center clamping plate. Do the same for the other side. The distance must be the same for both sides; if not, turn the panhard rod until they are equal and tighten the connections. *IMPORTANT: The rear tires must be of the same size and pressure before making any adjustments.*

REAR AXLE ASSEMBLY RECONDITIONING

Mark II, XJ6

DISASSEMBLY

NOTE: Due to the complexity of this assembly and the need for special tools, it is suggested that reconditioning be performed only by a properly equipped shop.

1. Remove the axle assembly from the car.
2. Remove the axle shafts as instructed in Axle Shaft—Mark II or Halfshafts, Rear Hubs and U-Joints—XJ6.
3. Drain the lubricant from the carrier housing and remove the cover.
4. Remove the two differential bearing caps.
5. To facilitate differential removal, use a stretching tool. This tool must be used carefully to avoid doing permanent damage to the case by overstretching it. Open the tool with the turn-buckle until it is hand tight and then, using a wrench, *turn it ONLY 1/2 TURN. DO NOT EXCEED 1/2 TURN, even if the differential is still difficult to remove.*
6. Using two levers, pry out the differential. Use padding between the levers and the carrier to prevent any damage. If the stretching tool is not readily available, remove the bearing caps and, using two levers, sloyly pry out the differential being careful not to tilt the unit.
7. Remove the ring gear screws and, using a soft hammer, tap out the ring gear.
8. Punch out the locking pin that holds the pinion mate shaft in place and remove the shaft. The locking pin may be removed in only one direction (see illustration).

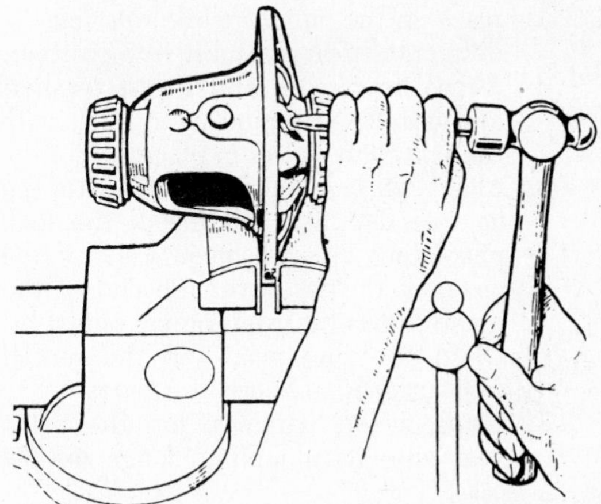

Removing the pinion mate shaft locking pin

9. Remove the axle shaft spacer if so equipped.
10. Turn the side gears until the pinions are opposite the case openings. Remove the gears being careful not to lose the thrust washers behind them.

11. If the ring gear setting is to be changed, then the bearings will have to be removed in order to get at the shims behind them.
12. If the pinion is to be removed, remove the pinion nut and washer and pull off the universal joint companion flange.
13. *PRESS* the pinion out of the outer bearing—driving it out will probably cause damage. Do not mix the shims.
14. Remove the pinion oil seal, slinger and outer bearing cone.
15. If the outer bearing needs replacing, remove the bearing cup with a suitable puller.
16. If the puller is not available, and the old bearing cup is to be discarded, drive out the bearing cup.
17. Using a suitable puller, remove the pinion inner bearing cup being careful not to lose any of the shims located behind the cup. If the inner bearing is to be replaced, the cup may be driven out. If only the pinion setting is to be changed, then the puller should be used to remove the bearing.

Assembly

1. Assemble the side gears and thrust washers.
2. Insert the differential pinions through the case openings and engage them with the side gears.
3. Hold the pinion thrust washers in place on the pinions while rotating the differential gear assembly into position.
4. Align the pinions and thrust washers and install the pinion mate shaft with the axle shaft spacer in place.
5. Align the hole in the shaft with the hole in the case and install the lock pin. Using a punch, peen some of the metal of the case over the end of the pin to prevent it from coming out.
6. Clean the ring gear and differential case surfaces and check for burrs.
7. Using a soft hammer, tap the drive gear onto its mounting flange on the case.
8. Install the ring gear bolts and new locking straps and torque them evenly from 50 to 60 ft. lbs. or 70 to 80 ft. lbs. if equipped with 3/8" diameter bolts. Secure the bolts with the locking tabs.
9. Perform differential bearing adjustment as follows:
   a. Install the differential bearings, without shims, into the differential case. All components must be clean since the presence of dirt might alter the adjustment.
   b. Place the differential assembly, with bearing cups installed, into the gear carrier. At this time, the pinion should not be in the carrier.
   c. Set a dial indicator on the carrier with the button contacting the back face of the ring gear.

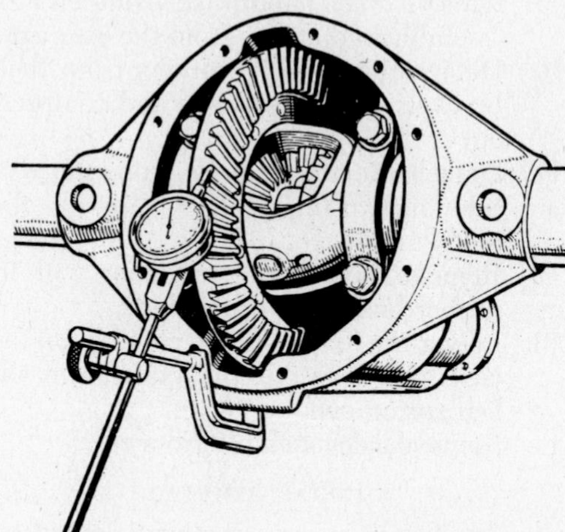

Using a dial indicator to check gear backlash

   d. Insert two levers between the carrier and the bearing cups and move the differential assembly to one side of the carrier.
   e. Set the indicator to zero and move the assembly to the other side of the carrier and note the reading. This is the total clearance between the bearings and the abutment faces of the gear carrier housing. Adding .005" to the total clearance reading will give preload which is also equivalent to the *total* thickness of shims to be used with *both* bearings. These shims must be divided between the two bearings in such a proportion as to create correct backlash and proper gear mesh. In order to determine the correct number of shims to be placed on either side of the case, see step number 5 of Ring Gear Adjustment—Mark II, XJ6.
   f. Remove the differential assembly from the carrier.
10. Adjust the pinion as instructed in Pinion Adjustment—Mark II, XJ6.
11. Adjust the ring gear as described in Ring Gear Adjustment—Mark II, XJ6.

12. Remove the drive pinion nut, washer and companion flange.
13. Install the oil slinger, and pinion oil seal assembly with the dust excluder flange facing up. Some later models had an oil seal gasket which must be installed at this time. Using a piece of pipe or a socket, tap the seal into place.
14. Install the companion flange (U-joint flange), washer and pinion nut and tighten down.
15. Install the rear cover with gasket and attach the ratio tag to one of the bolts.
16. Install the axle shafts and hub bearings.
17. Fill with lubricant.
18. Insert the filler plug and check cover bolts for tightness.
19. Check for oil leaks and grease the hub bearings.

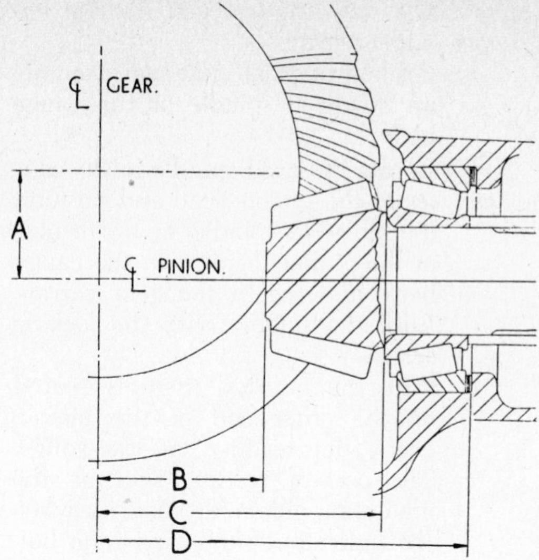

Pinion setting distances—all models

PINION ADJUSTMENT

Mark II, 3.4S, 3.8S, 420, E Type (All)

1. Install the pinion outer bearing cup.
2. Install the pinion bearing inner cup with shims.
3. Press the inner bearing cone on the pinion using a piece of tubing between the press and the cone making certain that only the inner race is contacted and not the roller retainer.
4. The correct pinion setting is etched on the end of the pinion. The pinion and corresponding gear must be replaced as a matched set; therefore, the serial number at the top of the pinion must be the same as that etched on the gear. The number at the left is a production code which is irrevelant to assembly. The letter and number on the right refer to the tolerance on offset or pinion drop dimension also stamped on the cover of the carrier housing. The bottom number gives the cone setting distance of the pinion; that is, the distance from the center of the ring gear to the face of the pinion. A pinion marked zero will be neither too short nor too long but rather, it will perfectly engage with the gear. If the pinion is marked +2, it should be adjusted to the zero cone setting plus .002″, while one etched with –2, is zero minus .002″. The zero cone setting distances for the two axles are below:

		3 HA	4 HA
A.	Pinion Drop	1.375″	1.5″
B.	Zero Cone Setting	2.250″	2.625″
C.	Mounting Distance	3.937″	4.312″
D.	Center Line to Bearing Housing	5.120″ to 5.130″	5.495″ to 5.505″

Therefore, if a pinion is marked–2, the distance from the center of the ring gear to the pinion face should be 2.625″–.002″ or 2.623″ or if the pinion is marked +3, the distance is 2.628″.

5. Once the pinion bearing cups have been installed in the carrier with the original adjusting shims, install the pinion and assembled inner bearing cone.
6. Invert the carrier and support the pinion with a block of wood.
7. If originally fitted, install the pinion bearing spacer.
8. Install the original outer bearing shims on the pinion shank so that they seat on the spacer or the shank shoulder.
9. Install pinion outer bearing cone, companion flange, washer and nut leaving out the oil slinger and oil seal and tighten the nut.
10. Using a dial indicator with adjustable bracket, check the pinion cone setting distance in the following manner:

NOTE: If this type of dial indicator is not available, complete assembly procedures without it and perform "Ring Gear Adjust-

ment". The red lead test will divulge improper pinion setting.

a. Position the dial indicator assembly on the fixed spindle of the gauge body.
b. Locate the fixed spindle in the center of the pinion head and position the movable spindle in the center of the pinion shank with the gauge body underneath the gear carrier. Lock the spindle with the locking screw.
c. With the bracket assembly seated on the other end of the pinion, check the reading on the gauge. The correct reading will be the minimum obtained; that is, when the indicator spindle is at the bottom of the bore. Move the assembly slightly in order to observe the correct reading. The gauge will show the deviation of the pinion setting from the zero cone setting. The direction and magnitude of this deviation must be noted.

11. If the pinion setting is wrong, disassemble the pinion assembly and remove the pinion inner bearing cup. Add or remove shims as necessary from behind the bearing cup and reinstall the shims and cup. Repeat Steps 5 to 10.
12. After achieving correct pinion setting, check the pinion bearing preload. There should be a slight resistance when turning the pinion if there is no pinion end-play. Pinion bearing preload should be 8-12 in. lbs. If the preload must be changed, adjust the number of shims between the outer bearing cone and the pinion shank or spacer. Remove shims to increase preload and add shims to decrease it.

RING GEAR ADJUSTMENT

Mark II, XJ6

1. Place the differential assembly with bearing cups (without shims) in the housing making certain that all components are thoroughly clean.
2. Clamp a dial indicator to the housing with the plunger resting against the back face of the ring gear.
3. Using two levers between the housing and bearing cups, pry the case and ring gear assembly away from the pinion until the opposite bearing cup is seated against the housing.
4. Set the indicator to zero and move the differential assembly toward the pinion until the ring gear is deeply in mesh with the pinion (metal to metal). This indicator reading minus the backlash allowance as etched on the ring gear is equivalent to the thickness of shims to be placed between the differential case and the bearing cone on the ring gear side of the differential.
5. Install these shims to the ring gear side of the differential and the balance of the total shims required to the other side of the case. See Differential Bearing Adjustment. An example of this differential and drive gear adjustment is as follows: Suppose the total indicator reading as described in Differential Bearing Adjustment is .070″. This number plus .005″ for proper preload, results in .075″ which is the total thickness of shims to be used. If the clearance between the drive gear and pinion is .045″ (Steps 1 to 4), subtract the backlash (etched on gear) from this clearance. Assuming that this backlash is .005″, then .045″ —.005″ or .040″ is equal to the thickness of the shims to be placed between the case and bearing cone on the ring gear side of the differential. Subtract this number (.040″) from .075″ to get .035″ which is equal to the thickness of the shims to be placed on the opposite side of the case.
6. Using a stretching fixture, stretch the carrier, *making certain not to exceed 1/2 turn on the turnbuckle* or the casing will be damaged beyond repair.
7. Lower the differential assembly into the case while lightly tapping the bearings into place with a soft hammer. Make sure that the ring gear teeth mesh with the pinion.

CAUTION: At this point, damage to gear teeth can occur easily; therefore, extreme care during installation is essential.

8. If a stretching tool is not available, install the differential assembly by slightly tilting the bearing caps and tapping them lightly with a soft hammer.

IMPORTANT: This method greatly increases the chances of causing bearing and

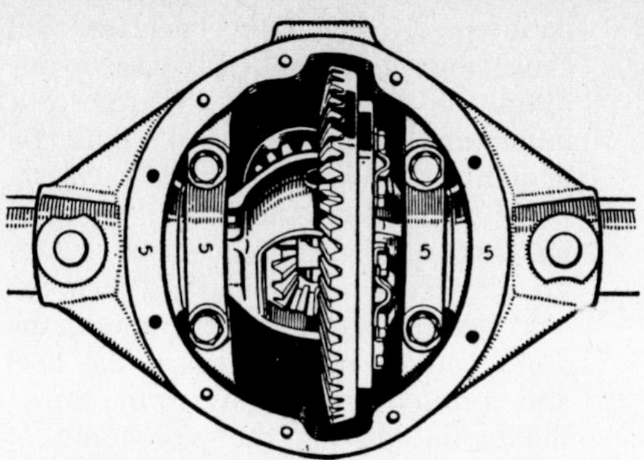

Differential bearing cap markings—all models

gear tooth damage and, as a result, should be used only in an emergency.

9. Install the bearing caps making sure that the number on the cap corresponds with the number on the housing face. Tighten the bolts to 60–65 ft. lbs.
10. Mount a dial indicator on the housing with the plunger against the back face of the ring gear. Turn the pinion and check the runout on the back face which should not exceed .005″. If excessive runout does exist, tear down the assembly and clean the surfaces locating the ring gear making sure to remove all burrs.
11. Remount the dial indicator on the carrier housing with the button against one of the ring gear teeth, as nearly in line with the direction of tooth travel as possible. Move the ring gear by hand and check the backlash reading. It should be the same as that etched on the gear. If it is not the same, transfer shims from one side of the differential case to the other until the correct setting is achieved. To increase backlash, remove shims from the ring gear side of the differential and install them on the opposite side. Backlash is decreased by transferring shims to the ring gear side from the opposite side of the differential case.
12. After setting the backlash, lightly paint a few teeth of the ring gear with red lead. Rotate the ring gear or pinion until a good impression of the tooth contact is made. If everything is in order, the impression should be similar to the ideal tooth contact shown in the illustration and explained under "Tooth Contact."

TOOTH CONTACT—ALL MODELS

To determine if backlash and pinion cone setting are correct, paint the ring gear teeth with oiled red lead and rotate the pinion in the normal direction. Check the tooth impression made on the ring gear and compare it to the illustrations on the tooth contact chart—it will fall into one of five types:

1. Ideal contact—this is the ideal impression formed on the drive (convex) side and coast (concave) side of the gear-teeth. The area of contact is evenly distributed over the working depth of the tooth profile and is situated closer to the toe (small end) than to the heel (large end).
2. High tooth contact—the tooth contact is heavy on the ring gear face; that is, on the upper area of the tooth. This is caused by excessive pinion cone setting distance. To correct this condition, *add* shims between the pinion inner bearing cup and the housing and *adding* the same thickness of preload shims between the pinion bearing spacer, or the shoulder of the pinion shank and outer bearing cone. This will move the tooth bearing *toward* the *toe* on *drive* and to the *heel* on the *coast* side. After doing this, it may be necessary to move the ring gear either into or out of mesh with the pinion as explained in Toe contact or Heel contact below.
3. Low tooth contact—tooth contact is heavy on the lower portion of the ring gear tooth. This is the opposite of high tooth contact and can be corrected in the opposite way. Move the pinion *out* of mesh by increasing the pinion cone setting distance. This can be done by *removing* shims from between the pinion inner bearing cup and housing and *removing* the same thickness of preload shims from between the pinion bearing spacer or the shoulder on the pinion shank and the outer bearing cone. This adjustment will usually move the tooth bearing toward the *heel* on the *drive* side and to the *toe* on the *coast* side. After performing these changes it may be necessary to adjust the ring gear in or out of mesh with the pinion as instructed in Toe contact and Heel contact.
4. Toe contact—occurs when the tooth contact is at the small (toe) end of the ring gear tooth. To correct this condi-

tion, move the drive gear out of mesh (increasing backlash) by moving shims from the ring gear side of the differential to the opposite side.

5. Heel contact—occurs when the tooth contact is concentrated at the large (heel) end of the gear tooth. This can be corrected by moving the ring gear closer into mesh. To do this, reduce backlash by adding shims to the ring gear side of the differential and removing an equal thickness of shims from the opposite side. When correcting the heel bearing, proper backlash must be maintained. Too little backlash will cause noisy gears and early wear in addition to gear scoring. Therefore, a minimum backlash of .004″ must be maintained. When adjusting backlash, move the ring gear instead of the pinion for ring gear movement has a greater effect on backlash. When the *ring gear* is moved out of mesh, the tooth contact moves toward the heel and is raised slightly toward the top of the tooth. Moving the pinion out of mesh raises the tooth contact on the face of the tooth and slightly toward

	TOOTH CONTACT (*DRIVE GEAR*)	CONDITION	REMEDY
A	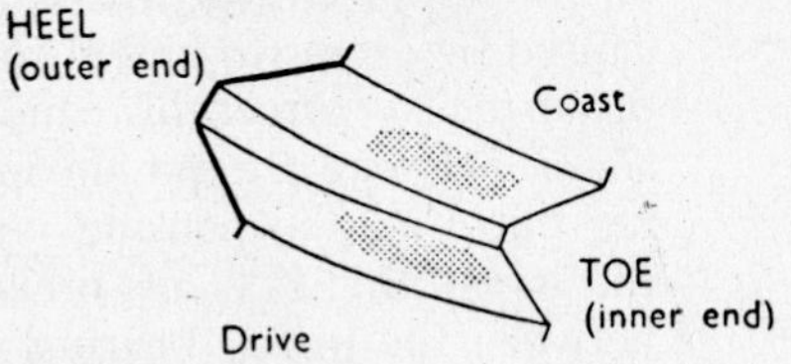 HEEL (outer end) Coast TOE (inner end) Drive	IDEAL TOOTH CONTACT Evenly spread over profile, nearer toe than heel.	o / o
B	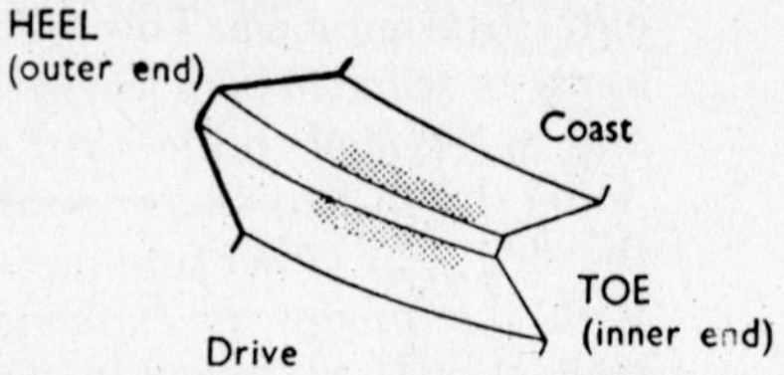 HEEL (outer end) Coast TOE (inner end) Drive	HIGH TOOTH CONTACT Heavy on the top of the drive gear tooth profile.	Move the DRIVE PINION DEEPER INTO MESH. *i.e.*, REDUCE the pinion cone setting.
C	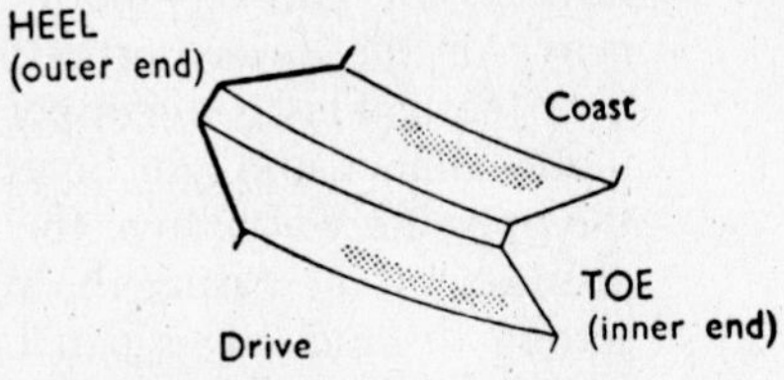 HEEL (outer end) Coast TOE (inner end) Drive	LOW TOOTH CONTACT Heavy in the root of the drive gear tooth profile.	Move the DRIVE PINION OUT OF MESH. *i.e.*, INCREASE the pinion cone setting.
D	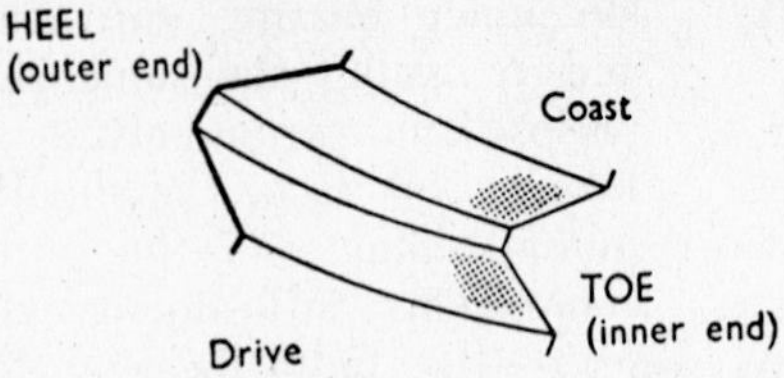 HEEL (outer end) Coast TOE (inner end) Drive	TOE CONTACT Hard on the small end of the drive gear tooth.	Move the DRIVE GEAR OUT OF MESH. *i.e.*, INCREASE backlash.
E	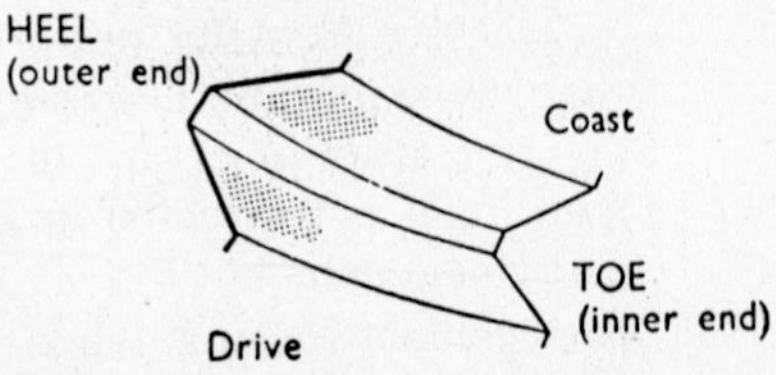 HEEL (outer end) Coast TOE (inner end) Drive	HEEL CONTACT Hard on the large end of the drive gear tooth.	Move the DRIVE GEAR INTO MESH. *i.e.*, DECREASE backlash *but* maintain minimum backlash as given in "Data"

Tooth contact chart

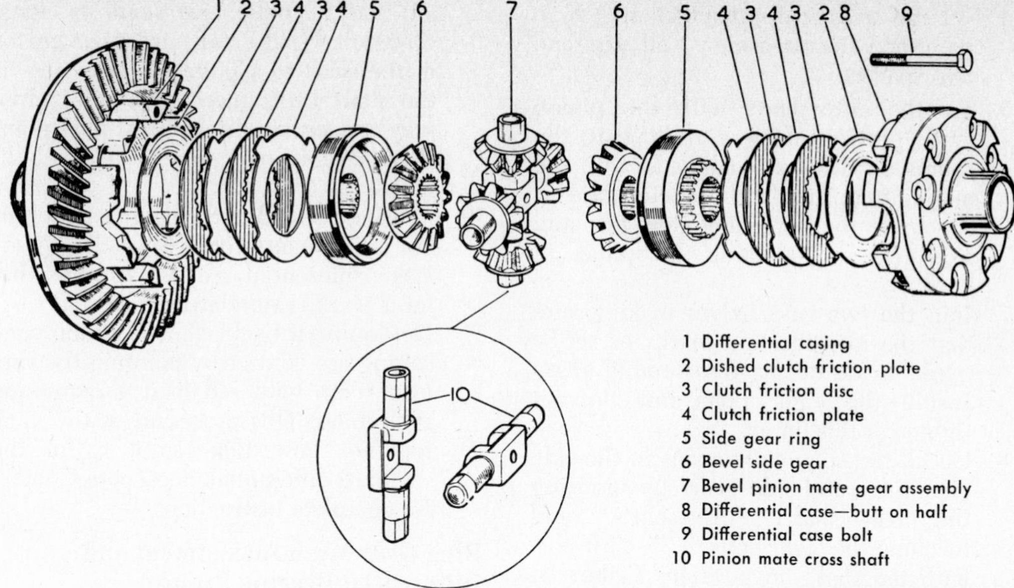

Exploded view of the Thornton Powr-Lok differential—Mark II, 3.4S, 3.8S, 420, E Type (all)

the heel on drive, and toward the toe on coast.

THE THORNTON "POWR-LOK" DIFFERENTIAL

Mark II, 3.4S, 3.8S, 420, E Type (All)

This is a limited slip differential fitted to the above models as standard (optional on Mark II models) equipment. The procedure for removing this differential from the axle housing and removing and installing the pinion is the same as that for a standard differential—see Rear Axle Assembly Reconditioning—Mark II, XJ6. The standard differential drives the wheel which is easiest to turn since the torque is divided equally between the two rear wheels. A limited slip differential directs greater driving force to the wheel with the better traction. Therefore, if a car equipped with a standard differential is stuck in the snow, the wheel with the poorer traction will receive the torque and will spin faster as power is applied. The car with the limited slip differential will transfer the torque through a series of clutches from the spinning wheel to the wheel with the better traction.

CAUTION: When working on a car with a limited slip differential, MAKE SURE BOTH REAR WHEELS ARE JACKED CLEAR OF THE GROUND. If only one wheel is off the ground, DO NOT run the engine with the car in gear; otherwise, the car may drive itself off the jack.

Disassembly

1. Using a soft hammer, remove the ring gear from the differential case.
2. Scribe a line from one case half to the other to ensure that they are properly matched during assembly.
3. Separate the two case halves by removing the eight securing bolts.
4. Remove the clutch discs and plates from one side.
5. Remove the side gear ring.
6. Remove the pinion side gear and the pinion mate cross-shafts with the pinion mate gears.
7. Separate the cross-shafts. On some models these cross-shafts may include two spacers and a roll pin; if so, make sure these pieces are replaced during assembly.
8. Remove the remaining side gear and side gear ring.
9. Take out the remaining clutch discs and plates.

Assembly

1. Install the curved clutch plates with the convex side against each case half. Follow each one with a clutch disc and then another clutch plate.
2. Install the side gear ring so that the serrations on the gear engage with those in the two clutch discs.
3. Place the side gear into the side gear ring so that the splines in both align.

4. Fit the cross-shafts together and, if so equipped, insert a new roll pin and two spacers.
5. Fit the cross-shafts with the pinion mate gears making certain that the ramps on the shafts coincide with the mating ramps in the differential case.
6. Assemble the remaining side gear and side gear ring aligning the splines in both.
7. Join the two case halves making sure that the identification marks or scribe marks made during disassembly align. Install the eight bolts but do not tighten at this time.
8. Check the spline alignment in the side gear rings and side gears by inserting the axle shafts (driveshafts) and torquing the eight bolts to 35–45 ft. lbs. with the shafts in position. Failure to do this will make it nearly impossible to enter the axle shafts after tightening the bolts.
9. Lock one axle shaft and the drive pinion and turn the axle shaft in either direction. Hold a ruler from the center of the shaft to a point 6″ away and if the shaft turns more than 3/4″ (free play) in either direction at this point then excessive component wear is indicated.
10. Bearing preload and ring gear and pinion adjustments for a Mark II "Powr-Lok" differential are the same as that for a Mark II standard differential.
11. Determine if backlash and pinion cone setting are correct by painting the ring gear teeth with red lead and rotating the pinion. This procedure is the same for the "Powr-Lok" as it is for the standard differential. See Tooth Contact for complete instructions.

Ring Gear Mesh Adjustment and Differential Bearing Preload

3.4S, 3.8S, 420, E TYPE

1. Install the pinion without the oil seal and oil thrower and then fit the differ-

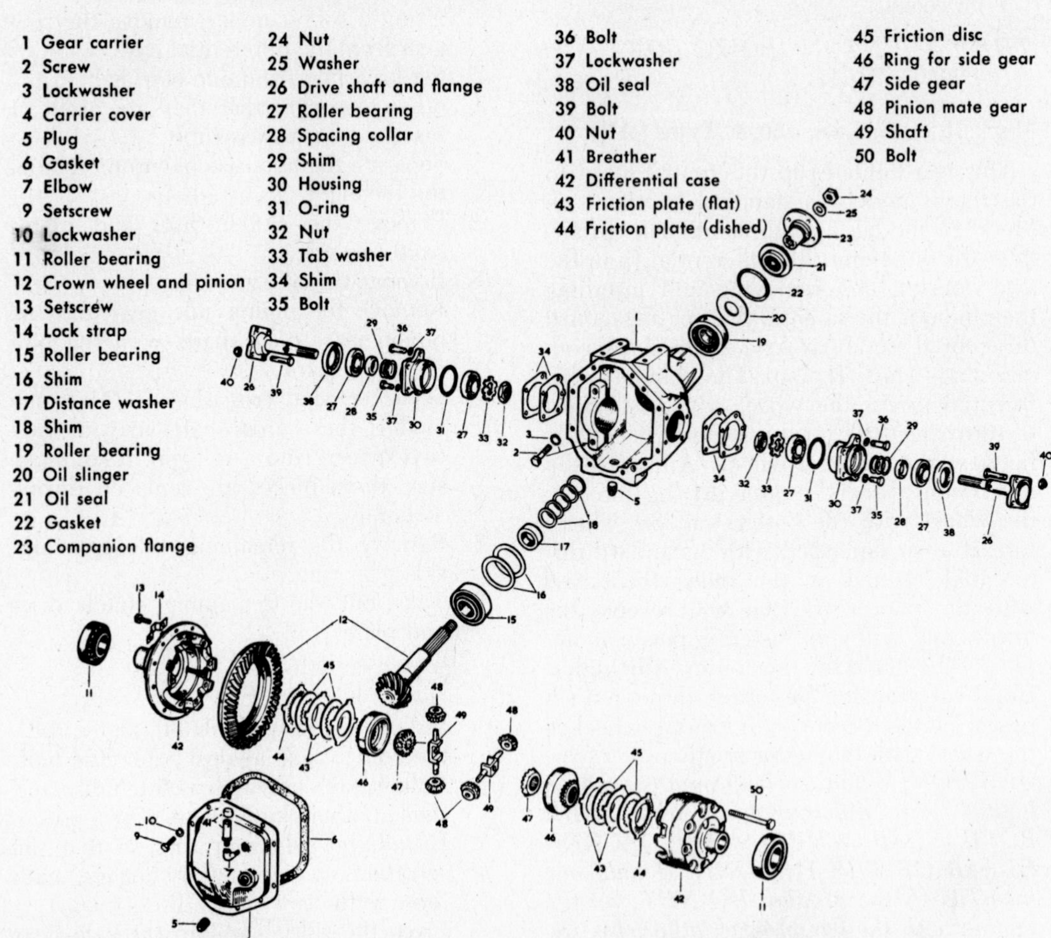

Exploded view of the final drive unit with Powr-Lok—420, 3.4S, 3.8S

ential assembly to the carrier.

2. Install the bearing caps making sure that the numbers on the bearing caps correspond with the numbers on the end cover face. Tighten the bolts to a torque of 60–65 ft. lbs.
3. Mount a dial indicator on the gear carrier with the plunger resting against the back face of the ring gear. Turn the ring gear by hand and check the runout–it should not exceed .005″. If it does exceed this figure, remove the differential assembly from the carrier, detach the ring gear and clean the contacting surfaces of the gear and case and remove all burrs.
4. Reassemble the ring gear to the assembly and install the assembly in the carrier. Recheck the torque on the ring gear bolts (70-80 ft. lbs.), mount the dial indicator and take a runout reading at four points (spaced at 90° intervals) on the back face of the ring gear. If the reading still exceeds .005″, then the ring gear must be replaced. If the runout is correct, proceed to the next step.
5. Install the driveshafts without any shims between the driveshaft bearing housing and the carrier. Check the O-ring on the bearing housing and replace if necessary.
6. Install three bolts (evenly spaced) around each bearing housing.
7. Mount a dial indicator on the carrier with the plunger against one of the ring gear teeth in line with the direction of tooth travel. Move the ring gear by hand to see if the backlash is the same as that etched on the face of the gear. If incorrect, move the ring gear toward or away from the pinion until the backlash is right. To move the ring gear, it is necessary to tighten the bolts in the driveshaft housing on one side of the carrier and loosen the bolts on the other side.
8. When the backlash is correct, measure the gap between the driveshaft bearing housing and the carrier on each side. Check it all the way around to make sure it is even. Make up a shim pack to fill the gap on each side but subtract .003″ from the pack to give the correct preload on the differential bearings. That is, if the backlash etched on the ring gear is .007″, then the gap on one side is .054″ and .046″ for the other. Therefore, the amount of shims necessary will be. 054″—.003″ or .051″ for one side and .046″—.003″ or .043″ for the other.
9. Install the output shafts with shims to the carrier and install and tighten the five bolts to each housing. Check the mesh adjustment by the tooth contact method.

MARK II, 3.4S, 3.8S, 420

The front suspension assembly on the above models consists of a steel crossmember to which are attached the A-arms, stub axle carriers, coil springs, shock absorbers and steering components. Each coil spring is enclosed in a turret and is secured at the bottom to a mounting pan bolted to the lower A-arm. Inside each spring is a shock absorber mounted at the top, to the turret. The upper A-arm is mounted to the fulcrum shaft and cushioned at this point by a rubber bushing. The other end of this A-arm is bolted to the upper ball joint. The inner end of the lower A-arm is mounted on a rubber bushing while the outer end is bolted to the lower ball joint. The ball joints are attached to the stub axle carrier. The wheel hub is supported by two bearings positioned on a shaft located in the stub axle carrier. An anti-sway bar is situated between the two A-arms. The suspension is attached to the frame at four points and cushioned by rubber mounts. When replacing suspension components, premature wear can be prevented by tightening the bolts after the weight of the car is on the ground.

Removal

1. Place a jack under the suspension crossmember and raise the front of the car.
2. Remove the front wheels.
3. Position jack stands (at least 16″ tall) under the chassis side members while leaving the jack under the suspension.
4. Remove the suspension mounting bolts and disconnect the engine stabilizers.
5. Disconnect the anti-sway bar brackets.
6. Detach the brake lines from their brackets.
7. Separate the steering column from the steering box.
8. Lower the suspension assembly from the car.

Installation

1. To install, reverse the removal procedure making sure that the brake discs are positioned straight ahead and that the steering wheel spokes are at three and nine o'clock with the horn ring at the bottom. After installation, bleed the brakes.

XJ6

The front suspension on the XJ6 is very similar to that of the 420 except that the coil springs are mounted in shorter turrets and the shock absorbers are situated outside of the spring.

Removal

1. Disconnect the battery.
2. Place a jack under the front suspension crossmember, raise car and remove front wheels. Support with jack stands but leave jack in position.
3. Using slings, support engine.
4. Disconnect the brake lines from the fender skirts and seal the connections.
5. Disconnect the steering hoses and drain the fluid. Seal the lines to prevent the entry of dirt.
6. Remove the anti-sway bar.
7. Release the shock absorbers from their top mounting points and collect the washers and bushings.
8. Remove the bolt holding the steering column U-joint to the steering box shaft.

IMPORTANT: When separating the lower column universal joint; do not, for any reason, use a hammer, mallet or similar tool to assist in removal. Using force may result in shearing some nylon pegs which will necessitate in replacing the upper column.

Installation

1. To install, reverse the removal procedure. Center the steering wheel and the steering unit before connecting the lower column universal joint. Bleed the steering and brake systems.

E TYPE (All)

The front suspension of the E Type consists of the upper and lower wishbones to which are attached the stub axle carriers, the torsion bars and the shock absorbers. The torsion bars are attached to the lower wishbones at one end and to the frame at the other end. Each torsion bar is controlled by a shock absorber. The top of the shock is attached to a bracket on the frame while the bottom is bolted to the lower wishbone. The inner ends of the upper and lower wishbones are each attached to a fulcrum shaft while the outer ends connect to upper and lower ball joints. An anti-sway bar is situated between the lower wishbones and is secured to the chassis front member. The wheel hubs are each supported by two roller bearings.

The front suspension should not be removed as a unit but rather as separate components.

SHOCK ABSORBERS

Mark II, 3.4S, 3.8S, 420

Before installing the shocks they should be bled of all air that may have accumulated during storage. Hold the shock vertically and make several short strokes followed by two long ones. After the air has been bled, keep the shock in a vertical position until installation. Shock removal can be made easier if the upper and lower wishbones are kept nearly horizontal and parallel to each other by placing a block between the upper wishbone lever and the turret. Make sure that the spacer in the top mounting hole is correctly positioned during installation.

XJ6 and E Type (All)

The top end of the XJ6 shock is mounted to the fender skirt and is accessible from the engine compartment. Prior to installation, check the shocks for air and bleed them if necessary. Bleeding procedure is explained above. Once the full weight of the car is on the suspension, retighten the shock mounting bolts.

IMPORTANT: Before removing the shock from the E Type, support the end of the lower wishbone in order to prevent strain on the upper ball joint.

COIL SPRINGS

Mark II, 3.4S, 3.8S, 420, XJ6

To remove the coil springs, the shocks must be removed and a spring compresser installed in their place. Installation can be made simpler by using 8″ long pilot studs to align the lower wishbone holes with those in the spring seat. On some cars there is a shim located on top of the spring. If this is replaced, do so with one of equal thickness.

TORSION BAR ADJUSTMENT

E Type (All)

Instead of springs, the E Type uses torsion bars. Before performing adjustment, make sure that the car is filled with gas, oil and water. If the tank is not full, the lost weight will have to be compensated for by using some other weight. Remember, a gallon of gas weighs approximately 6-1/2 lbs. Place the car on a pefectly level surface with the wheels straight ahead and the tire pressures set to 23 psi in the front and 25 psi in the rear. Move car forward about three lengths and measure the distance from the ground to the middle of the inner mounting bolt on the lower wishbone lever. This distance, known as standing height, should be 8-3/4″±1/4″ for the 3.8, 3-1/2″ ± 1/4″ for the 4.2 and 3-3/4″±1/4″ for the 2+2. To measure the standing height on the 4.2 models, record the distance from the center of each wheel to the ground (measurement A) and measure from the center line of each inner fulcrum of the lower wishbone assembly to the ground (measurement B). Subtract B from A to get C which should be 3-1/2″±1/4″ for the 4.2 and 3-3/4″±1/4″ for 2+2 cars.

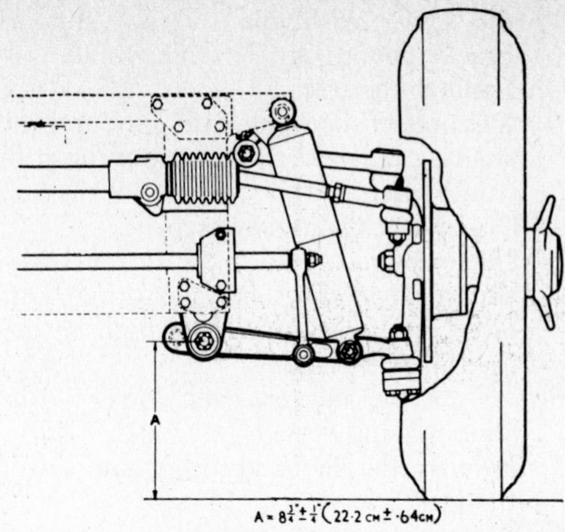

Checking standing height on the 3.8 E Type

1. Jack up the car and place stands under

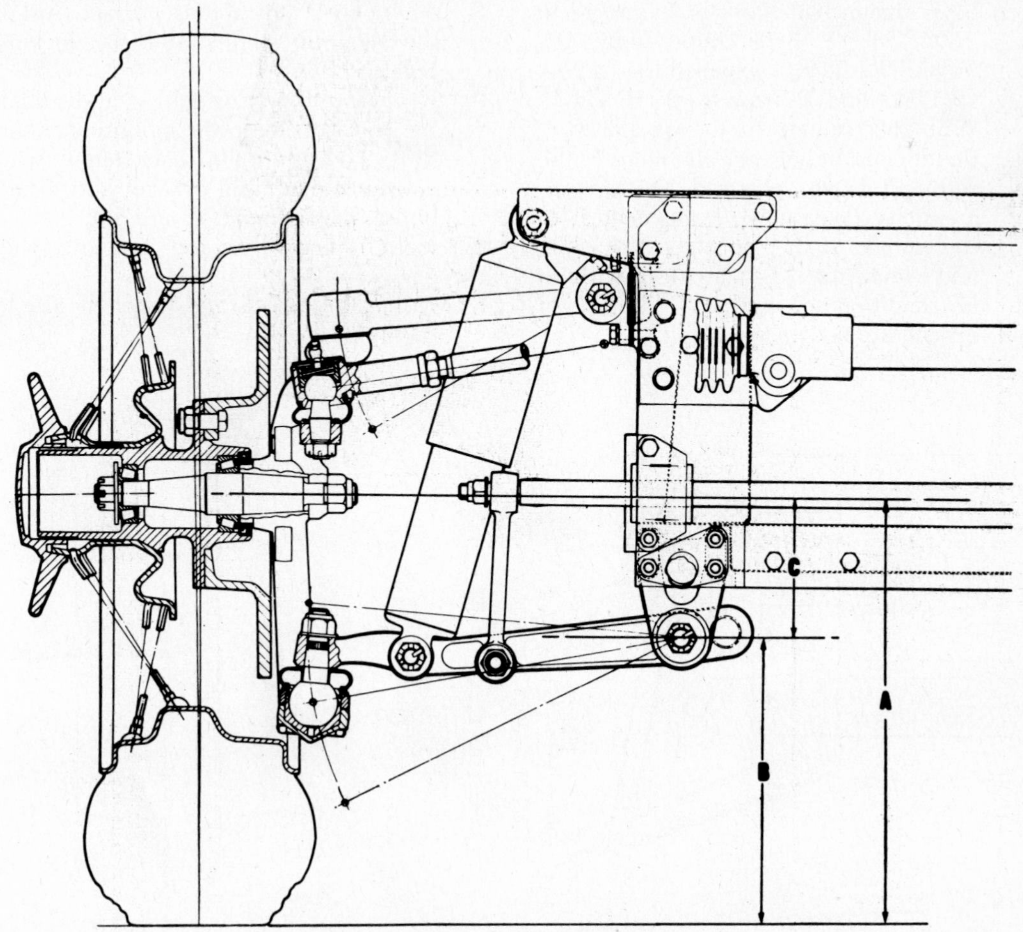

Checking standing height on the E Type (4.2)

the lower wishbone fulcrum support bracket, not under the frame tube.

2. Remove the wheels.
3. Disconnect the upper ball joint and the steering tie rod ball joint from the stub axle carrier.
4. Disconnect the anti-sway bar.
5. Place the jack under the lower wishbone next to the shock mounting bolt. Raise the jack but not enough to lift the car off the stands.
6. Loosen the nut on each lower wishbone mount.
7. Remove the shock absorber and lower the jack.
8. Remove the nuts and bolts from the torsion bar rear adjuster lever. Fabricate and install a setting gauge (see illustration) with holes drilled at 17-13/16" (18 1/4"-2+2,) centers so that it can be fastened to the shock mounting points. The distance between these hole centers changed when larger diameter torsion bars were used. Beginning with the following chassis numbers, torsion bar diameter increased to .780"-.784": E Type coupe (4.2)–1E. 35382, E Type convertible (4.2)–1E.17532 and E Type 2+2–1E.77407. With this change in torsion bar size, the dimension between the holes in the setting links also changed. The new dimensions (measured from center to center) are: 17-3/4" for the coupe (4.2) and convertible (4.2) (with or without air-conditioning) and 18" (18-1/8" if air-conditioned) for the 2+2. The gauge is a rigid bar that approximates the length of the shock with the weight of the car on the ground. Once installed, the gauge should cause the holes in the rear adjuster lever to align with the corresponding holes in the frame. If they do not align, adjustment must be made as follows:
   a. The lever contains splines which engage with splines on the shaft. Decide which direction the lever should be turned in order to align the holes. Mark position of the lever on the shaft, remove it from the shaft, turn it in the direction required and return it to a new position on the shaft. Check again for hole alignment and repeat procedure if not correct. If a finer adjustment is needed, remove the locking bolt and slide the torsion bar out of the front splines. It should be noted that the rear end of the bar has 25 splines while the front end has 24 in order to permit finer adjustment.
9. When lever position is correct, install the mounting bolts and the locking bolt and nut.
10. Remove the setting gauge and attach the shock to its lower mounting point.
11. Raise jack until the shock aligns with its upper mounting bracket and install but do not tighten bolt and nut.
12. Install steering tie rod and anti-sway bar.
13. Install the wheels and lower the car to the ground.

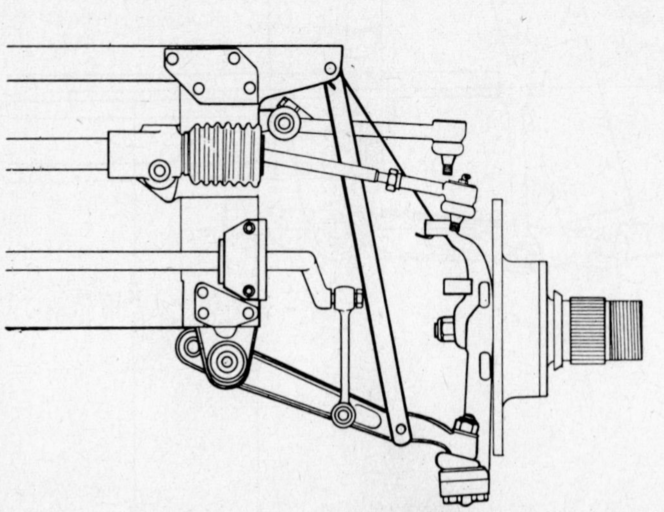

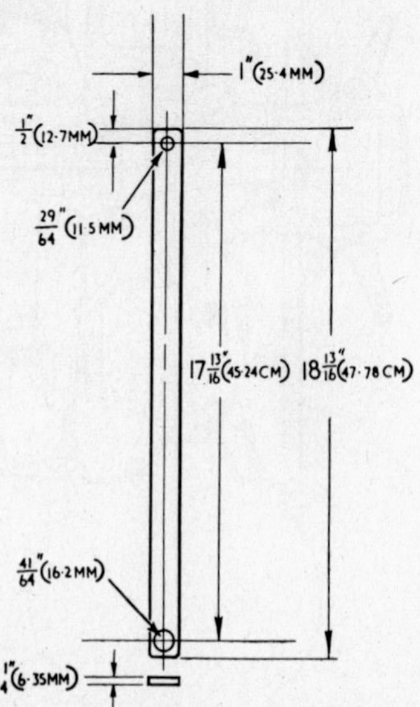

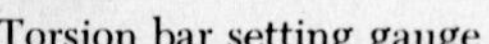
Torsion bar setting gauge

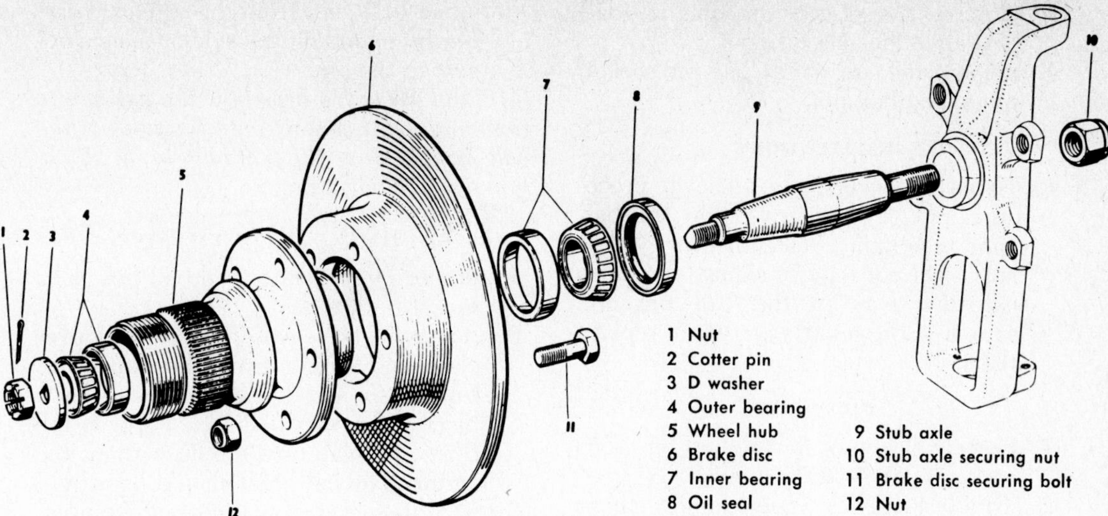

Exploded view of the front hub—E Type (all)

14. Tighten the nuts to the shocks, fulcrum shafts and anti-sway bar and insert cotter pins.
15. Roll car forward a few lengths and check to see that the standing height of the car is at 8-3/4″±1/4″.

ADJUSTING WHEEL BEARING END-PLAY

Mark II, 3.4S, 3.8S, 420, XJ6, E Type (All)

Wheel bearing adjustment should be performed about every 12,000 miles. When the wheel hub is removed make sure the bearings are lubricated and adjusted before the car is returned to service.

1. Correct end-play is .003″–.005″. It is especially important not to exceed .005″ on those cars equipped with disc brakes since brake drag would result.
2. End-play can be measured with a dial indicator—plunger against the hub. If a dial indicator is not available, tighten the hub until there is no end-play and a slight resistance is felt when the hub is rotated.
3. Loosen the hub nut one or two flats and temporarily attach the wheel to see if it spins freely. If it does, install a new cotter pin.

LOWER WISHBONE BALL JOINT

Mark II, 3.4S, 3.8S, 420, XJ6, E Type (All)

Removal

1. Remove the stub axle carrier complete with ball joint.
2. Remove the retaining ring and the rubber gaiter along with the retainer from the top of the ball pin.

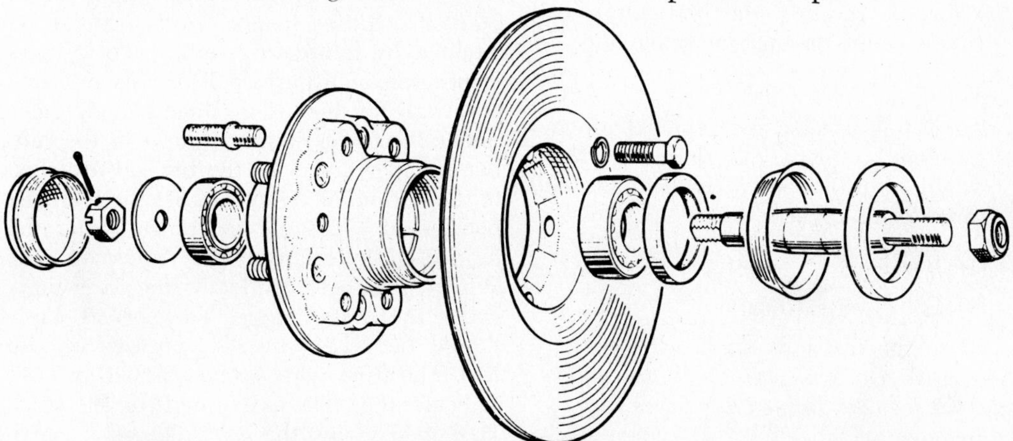

Exploded view of the front hub—Mark II, 3.4S, 3.8S, 420

3. Unscrew the setscrews holding the ball pin cap to the axle carrier.
4. Remove the cap, shims, ball pin socket, spigot and ball pin.

Installation

1. To install, reverse the removal procedure and, if necessary, shim the ball joint to obtain a clearance of .004"–.006". Do not remove shims to take up excessive play in the ball pin and socket. If these parts are worn, replace them.

Adjustment

1. Correct clearance for the ball pin in its socket is .004"–.006"
2. To adjust this clearance, remove shims one at a time until the ball is tight in its socket when the ball cap is tight.
3. Install shims until the clearance is .004"–.006" at which time the shank of the ball pin can be moved by hand.

UPPER WISHBONE BALL JOINT

Mark II, 3.4S, 3.8S, 420, XJ6

Removal

1. Place a jack under the lower wishbone, raise the car and remove the wheel. Unlike the lower ball joint, the upper cannot be disassembled, it must be replaced as a unit.
2. Remove the nuts and bolts holding the ball joint to the upper wishbone lever. Note the number and position of the shims that control caster angle.
3. Remove the nut and washers holding the ball joint to the stub axle carrier. Separate the ball joint from the axle carrier by using a suitable extractor. When performing this procedure be careful not to damage the brake line.

Installation

1. To install, reverse the removal procedure and replace the shims in their original positions in order to retain the same caster angle.

E Type (All)

Removal

1. Raise the car and place on stands.

CAUTION: Do not place jack or stands under the forward frame cross tubes.

2. Remove the wheels.
3. Remove the nut and drift out the upper ball joint from the stub axle carrier by pounding the side of the carrier next to the pin.

IMPORTANT: Do not allow the ball pin to come into hard contact with the sides of the ball socket. Move the ball only in the direction of the elongation.

Adjustment and Installation

1. Proper clearance for the ball pin in its socket is .004".
2. Remove and clean the circlip, cover plate and spring from the ball joint.
3. Insert shims between the cover plate and upper ball socket and install the cover plate and circlip without the spring. The ball joint should be a tight fit in its socket; if not, change the number of shims. Remove shims to the value of .004" and assemble the ball joint *with* the spring. It should now be possible to move the ball pin by hand.
4. Grease the ball joints.
5. If ball pins and sockets are excessively worn, replace them. *Do not attempt to compensate for worn parts by adding shims.*

ADJUSTING FRONT WHEEL CASTER ANGLE

Mark II, 3.4S, 3.8S, 420, XJ6

Prior to checking caster, inspect all bushings for deterioration and excessive wear, check for worn ball joints and inspect the shocks and mounts. Make sure that the car is at its normal riding height. Normal riding height is the height of the car with the driver, three passengers and full gas tanks —approximately 850 lbs. It will help to remember that a gallon of gas weighs about 6-1/2 lbs. Riding height on the 420 can be attained by fabricating setting blocks (see illustration in Adjusting Rear Wheel Camber Angle for dimensions) and placing them under the upper wishbone next to the rubber bumper and over the bracket attached to the bottom of the turret. Set the rear suspension at the same height by using the fabricated links described in Adjusting Rear Wheel Camber Angle. Using a gauge, check the caster angle. The correct angle should be 2-1/4° ± 1/4° positive on the XJ6. The front wheels must be within 1/4° of each other. The caster angle on the Mark II, 3.4S, 3.8S and the 420 is 0° ± 1/2° with the front wheels being no more than 1/2° of each other. Adjustment can be made by moving the shims and/or packing pieces from the rear of the upper ball joint to the front. To decrease negative caster or increase positive caster, move shims from the rear to the front. To increase negative caster or decrease positive caster, move the packing pieces and shims as necessary. To remove slotted shims, it is only necessary to *loosen* the two securing bolts but to remove a packing piece, it is necessary to *remove* the bolts but only after providing a support under the brake disc or lower wishbone. One shim (1/16″) will change the caster angle by 1/4°. If the caster angle is changed the front wheel alignment should be checked and adjusted if necessary. On the XJ6, there must always be four shims between the wishbone levers and the upper ball joint. The other models require a packing piece and 8 shims at this location.

E Type (All)

When adjusting the front caster angle, links must be fabricated and used to hold the suspension at a specific height. The links fit over the top and bottom shock absorber mountings. For details on link dimensions, see Torsion Bar Adjustment. Set the rear suspension at the same height by using similar links—see Adjusting Rear Wheel Camber Angle. Using a gauge, check the caster angle. Proper angle for the E Type must be 2° ± 1/2° positive and should not vary more than 1/2° from wheel to wheel. Adjustment is made by turning the threaded fulcrum shaft on the upper wishbone bracket.

1. Loosen the nuts and the wishbone clamping bolts and turn the shaft with a wrench.
2. Rotate the shaft counterclockwise (as seen from the front of the car) to increase positive caster, clockwise to decrease.
3. After the adjustment, tighten the clamping bolts.
4. Tighten the shaft nuts only after the car is lowered and the full weight of the car has settled on the suspension. This will prevent rubber bushing damage.
5. After completing adjustment, check front wheel alignment and change if necessary.

ADJUSTING FRONT WHEEL CAMBER ANGLE

Mark II, 3.4S, 3.8S, 420

Before checking camber angle, make sure that the car is on a level surface and the tire pressures are correct. The car must be full of oil, water and gas, if not, compensate for it by adding additional weight. If the tank isn't full it will help to remember that a gallon of gas weighs about 6-1/2 lbs. On the 420, lock the front and rear suspensions at a certain height by setting blocks in the front and special links in the rear. For details on these blocks and links, see Adjusting Rear Wheel Camber Angle and Adjusting Front Wheel Caster Angle. Worn suspension components can affect camber angle so it is advisable to check for excessive play in ball joints and worn shocks and rubber bushings before adjusting camber. Proper camber angle for these models is 1/2° ± 1/2° positive with no more than a 1/2° difference between the two wheels. Shims are located at the upper wishbone bracket and since they are slotted they can be removed by merely loosening the two bolts. Inserting shims decreases positive camber while removing them increases positive camber or decreases negative camber. To prevent changing the caster angle, remove or add an equal thickness of shims from behind each bolt; that is, if one 1/16″ shim is removed or inserted from behind one bolt then one of equal thickness will have to be removed or inserted behind the other bolt. A 1/16″ shim will change the camber by approximately 1/4°. Perform the same procedure for the other front wheel and if camber angle is changed for either wheel, wheel alignment should be checked and changed if necessary.

XJ6

Before checking camber angle, make sure that the car is on level surface, that the tires are at the correct pressures and that the suspension components aren't excessively worn. In addition, it is necessary that the car is placed at the proper riding height by being filled with gas, oil and water and the equivalent weight of four persons. The total weight of all these factors approximates 850 lbs. If the gas tanks are not filled, another weight can be substituted for the gas remembering that a gallon of gas weighs approximately 6-1/2 lbs.

1. With the front wheel parallel to the center line of the car, check the camber angle with a proper gauge. Camber angle specified for this car is 1/2° ± 1/4° positive with no more than a 1/4° difference between the front wheels.
2. To change the angle, remove or add shims between the upper wishbone fulcrum lever and the crossmember turret. Since the shims are not slotted, it will be necessary to partially remove the bolts in order to alter the number of shims. Shims must be added to decrease the positive camber and removed to decrease negative camber or increase positive camber. To prevent a caster change, remove or add an equal thickness of shims from each side. A shim of 1/16″ thickness will change the camber by approximately 1/4°.
3. Follow the same procedure for the other wheel. If any camber change is made, check front wheel alignment and set if necessary.

E Type (All)

1. Situate the car on a level surface insuring that the tire pressures are correct.
2. Lock the front and rear suspensions by using special links as described under Adjusting Front Wheel Caster Angle-E Type.
3. Correct camber angle is 1/4° ± 1/2° positive and must not vary more than 1/2° from wheel to wheel.
4. With the front wheel pointing straight ahead, check the camber using a suitable gauge.
5. Adjusting shims are located at the front and rear of the upper wishbone bracket. Add shims to increase positive camber and remove them to increase negative camber or decrease positive camber. Remove or add an equal thickness of shims from each location to avoid changing caster. 1/16″ of shimming will change camber angle by 1/4°.
6. Follow the same procedure for the other wheel. If a camber change is made, check the wheel alignment and set if necessary.

Steering

STEERING WHEEL

Mark II, 3.4S, 3.8S, 420, XJ6, E Type

When installing the steering wheel, position the split cone in the inner column shaft grooves, making sure that the narrow part of the cone is toward the top of the column. Slide the wheel onto the splined shaft so that the two spokes are horizontal when the tires are pointing straight ahead. On the E Type, the center spoke must be in the 6 o'clock position.

CAUTION: If car is equipped with a collapsible column, DO NOT use excessive force when removing or installing the steering wheel as this may collapse the column.

MANUAL STEERING UNIT

The Mark II, 3.4S, 3.8S and the 420 use Burman recirculating ball steering which transmits motion from the inner column worm to the rocker shaft by means of a nut on a series of steel balls. The E Type uses a rack and pinion steering system that transmits motion from the inner column through the pinion to the steering rack.

Mark II

Removal

1. Separate the upper steering column from the lower column by removing the pinch bolt joining the two at the U-joint. Release the column splines from the U-joint by pulling on the steering wheel.
2. Remove the U-joint from the steering box.
3. Remove the nut and washer holding the tie rod end to the Pitman arm. Using a drift, remove the tie rod end.
4. Remove the four bolts and detach the steering unit from the front crossmember.

Installation

1. Attach the steering unit to the front crossmember.
2. Turn the wheels to the straight ahead position and connect the tie rod to the Pitman arm making sure the scribed lines on the shaft and arm align.
3. Connect the lower column to the steering unit.

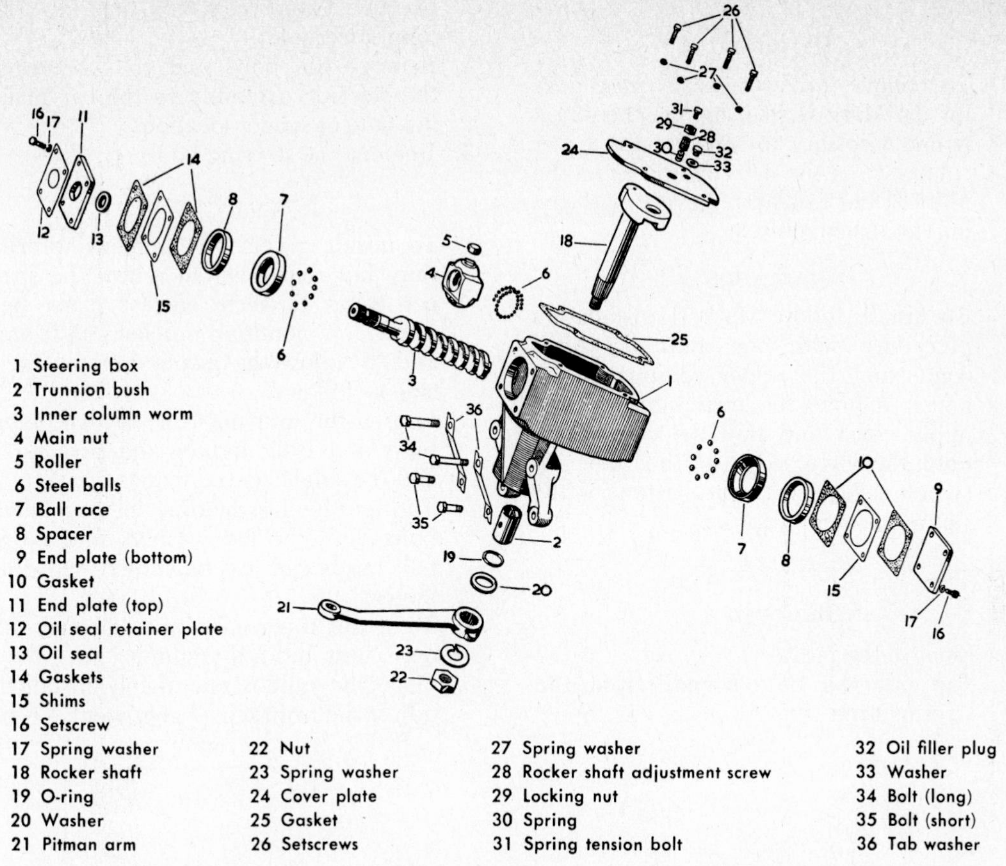

Exploded view of steering gear components—Mark II, 3.4S, 3.8S, 420

4. Install the steering wheel making sure that the wheel spokes are horizontal when the tires are straight ahead.

3.4S, 3.8S

Removal

1. Turn the tires so that they are straight ahead and remember the position of the slot in the top joint of the lower column.
2. From inside the car, remove the clip and retaining ring encircling the outer cover of the steering column. This will expose a slot in the cover through which the plastic thrust bearing can be removed.
3. Separate the upper steering column from the lower by removing the pinch bolt joining the two and pulling up on the steering wheel.
4. Detach the lower column from the steering unit.
5. Remove the nut and washer and drift out the tie rod end from the Pitman arm.
6. Remove the four bolts and detach the steering unit from the front crossmember.

Installation

1. With the tires straight ahead, connect the lower column to the steering unit and fit this assembly to the front crossmember.
2. Connect the Pitman arm to the rocker shaft making sure that the scribed line on the shaft aligns with the correct line on the Pitman arm.
3. Attach the tie rod to the Pitman arm.
4. Install the steering wheel so that its spokes are horizontal when the tires are straight ahead.
5. Connect the lower column to the upper column making sure the slot in the top joint is in the same position as when removed.
6. Depress the upper half of the joint (contained within the upper socket of the lower column) fully and then raise it 1/4″. Tighten the pinch bolt.

420

Removal

1. To remove, follow removal procedure for the Mark II steering. On the 420 it is not necessary to separate the lower column from the steering unit as on the Mark II but instead remove it with the unit as an assembly.

Installation

1. To install, follow Mark II installation procedure with one addition. After connecting the upper column to the lower, remove the turn signal switch upper cover and pull the column up until the lower edge of the indicator switch is level with the bottom of the slot in the nylon trip ring.

E Type

Removal

1. Remove the radiator.
2. Tap out the tie-rod ends from the steering arms.
3. Remove Allen screw from steering column lower joint.
4. Remove the bolts and nuts securing the steering assembly to the car making note of spacer location.
5. Remove the steering housing.

Installation

1. To install, reverse the removal procedure but remember to return the spacer tubes to their correct place between the mounting bracket and frame and to adjust the mounts on the rack side as follows:
2. Loosen the four nuts on the two outer bolts and fully tighten the two inner and the single central fixings.
3. Tighten the nuts holding the two outer bolts until the flat washers under the bolt heads can just be turned with the fingers.
4. Turn the inner lock nuts toward the outer nuts and fully tighten.
5. Once the unit is completely installed, adjust the front wheel alignment.

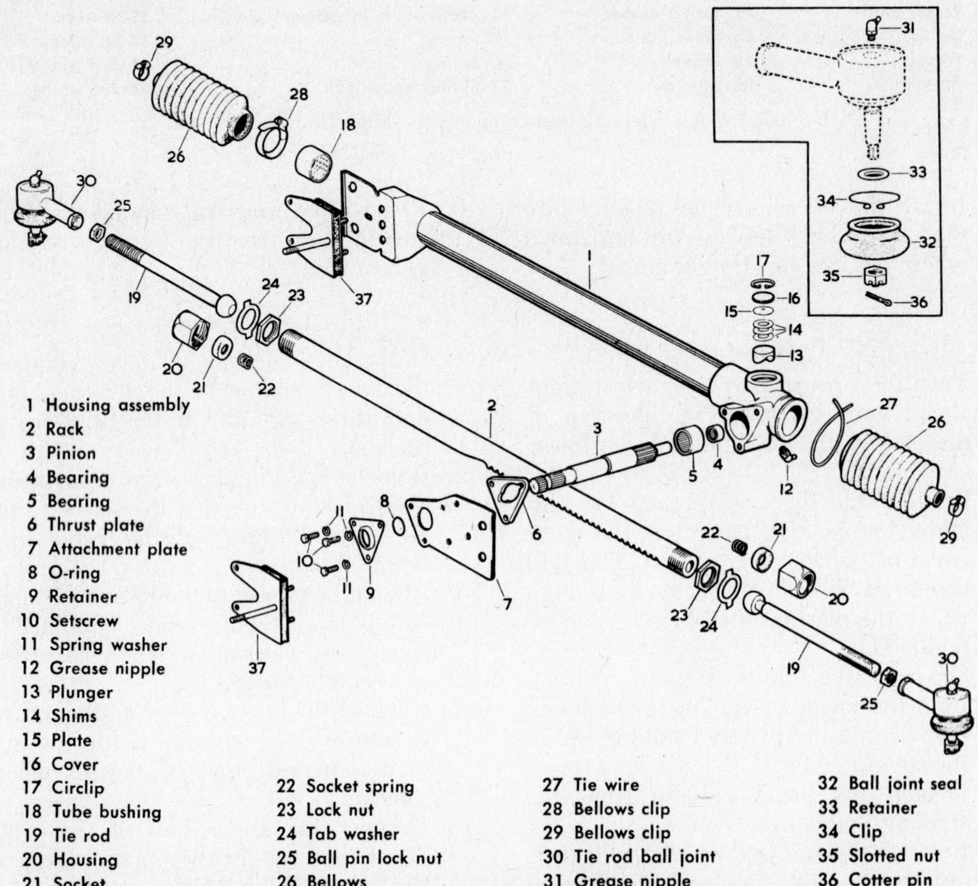

Exploded view of rack and pinion steering unit—E Type (all)

POWER STEERING UNIT

Mark II, 3.4S, 3.8S

These models use a power-assist steering unit consisting of a roller type pump driven off the generator, a fluid reservoir with replaceable filter and a hydraulically assisted recirculating ball type steering box. These components are connected by flexible hoses running from the reservoir to the intake side of the pump and then from the pump outlet to the intake on the steering box and finally returning to the reservoir from the box outlet.

REMOVAL

1. Detach and cover the hoses from the steering box and drain the fluid.
2. For further instructions, refer to Manual Steering Unit—Removal and Installation.

INSTALLATION

1. To install, reverse removal procedure.

420 and Mark II—Adwest Steering

The 420 has a power-assist steering system consisting of the pump and steering box with the fluid reservoir being part of the pump. Fluid flows through hoses from the output side of the pump to the steering box and from the box back to the pump.

REMOVAL

1. To remove the steering box, the car must be on a lift or over a pit.
2. Disconnect the hoses from the steering box and drain the fluid. Tape over the hoses to prevent the entrance of dirt.
3. For further instruction, see Manual Steering Unit—Removal and Installation.

INSTALLATION

1. To install, reverse removal procedure.

XJ6

This is a power-assist steering system consisting of the rack and pinion unit and a

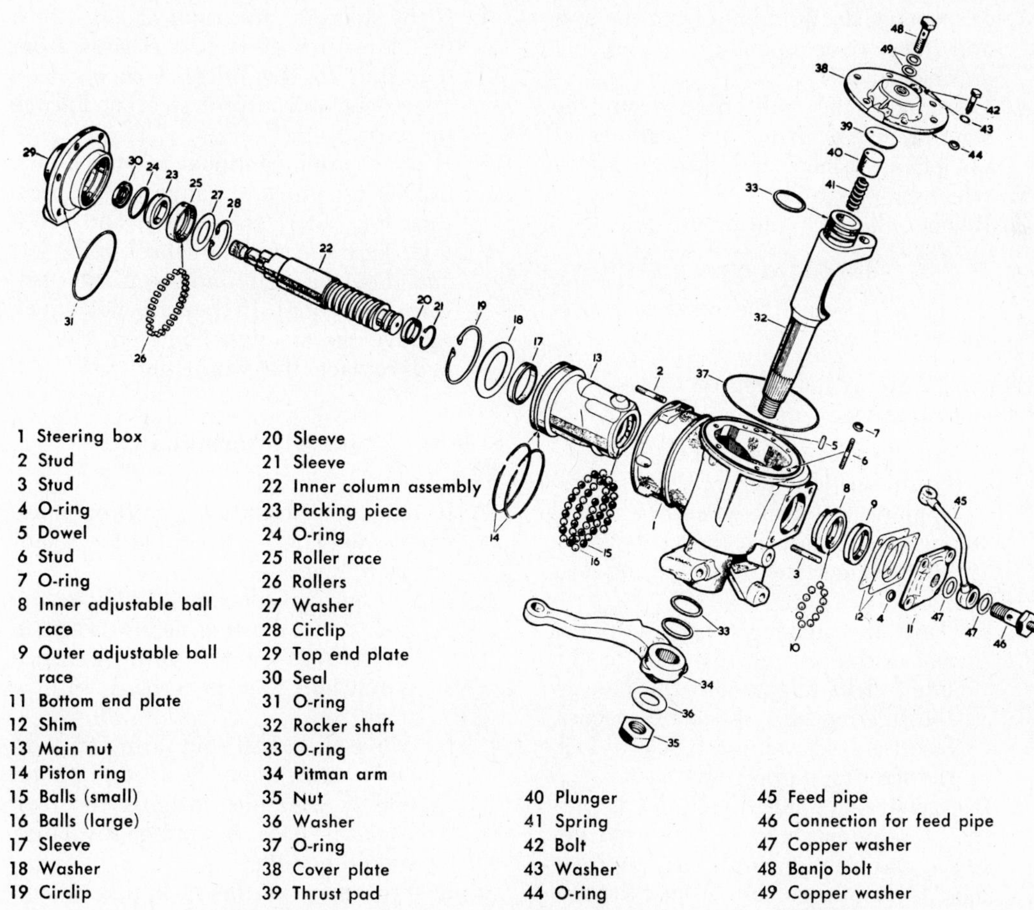

Exploded view of the power assist steering unit—Mark II, 3.4S, 3.8S

pump (integral with the fluid reservoir) with the two connected by flexible hoses. Steering wheel motion is transfered to the wheels by the lower steering column connected to the pinion shaft which in turn engages the rack. The upper and lower columns and mounts are collapsible on impact by means of nylon plugs (upper column) which will shear off under sufficient pressure and by means of a collapsible U-joint situated between the lower column and the pinion shaft.

CAUTION: DO NOT use excessive force to separate the upper universal joint from the steering column as this will shear the nylon plugs contained within the inner column. Likewise, DO NOT use excessive force to remove or install the steering wheel as this may collapse the column.

Removal

1. The rack and pinion unit can only be removed with the car on a lift or over a pit.
2. Remove the upper and lower steering columns.
3. Disconnect the fluid lines from the unit and tape over openings to prevent entrance of dirt.
4. Disconnect the ball joints from the steering levers. Note the positions of the plain washers and thrust washers when disassembling.
5. Remove the rack and pinion assembly.

Installation

1. To install, reverse the removal procedure.

Steering Unit Adjustment on Car—Adwest Steering

1. Center the steering as follows:
   a. Centralization is necessary when aligning the front wheels or checking sector shaft backlash. It is especially important when setting toe-in.
   b. Turn the steering wheel until the slot in the centralizing plate on the input shaft aligns with the hole in the steering box. When this occurs, insert a 1/4″ rod in the hole to lock the steering in this position.
2. If excessive steering wheel play is present, it is probably caused by wear between the cam and roller as found on most high mileage cars. Adjust the sector shaft as follows:
   a. Center the steering. This must be done.
   b. Disconnect the center tie rod from the Pitman arm.
   c. Move the Pitman arm back and forth to feel for excessive backlash.
   d. If this backlash exists, loosen the locknut at the top of the box and screw in the adjuster screw until only slight backlash can be felt.
   e. Tighten the locknut, connect the tie rod to the Pitman arm and road test car.
3. If sector shaft adjustment fails to remove steering wheel play, make the following tests:
   a. With the engine off, manipulate the steering wheel and have an assistant check the input shaft for end-play; that is, it should not move in and out of the housing.
   b. Test drive the car over rough roads and listen for rattles coming from the steering box. Input shaft end-play will cause rattles in addition to steering wheel free play.
4. If the steering pulls right or left, check tire pressures and change tires from one side to the other. Check wheel alignment and inspect steering linkage for wear.
5. If the steering continues to pull, attach a 2000 psi pressure gauge to the pressure line. Start the engine and let it idle. Turn the steering wheel to the left and then the right and see if the pressures are equal. If they are not equal, remove the steering box from the car and replace the worm and valve assembly.

Steering Unit Adjustment on Car—XJ6

1. If the rack produces a rattling noise when traveling on rough surfaces, adjust as follows:
   a. Loosen the locknut holding the rack pad adjusting screw. Turn in on the screw until a firm resistance is felt and then back off 1/16 of a turn.
   b. Move the ball pin arm (tie-rod end) protruding from the pinion end of the tube towards the rack back-up pad. A spring resistance should be felt.
   c. Free play at the rack pad should not exceed .010″. Check this by re-

moving the grease nipple and inserting a dial indicator so that its stem contacts the back of the rack. By pulling the rack against the spring, the total amount of end-play can be determined. If spring resistance is not felt, remove the screw and see if the spring is broken.

   d. Clearance should be minimum to permit smooth operation with no binding at any point.

2. If the steering pulls to the right or left, perform the following checks:
   a. Check tire pressures and tire wear and change the front tires from one side to the other. If the steering now pulls to the other side, the tires are proven to be at fault. If the pull direction remains the same, check front wheel alignment. If alignment fails to help, then the trouble lies in the valve and pinion assembly.
   b. Attach a 100 psi pressure gauge to the pump return line, start the engine and let it idle. The pressure gauge should read approximately 40 psi.
   c. Turn the steering wheel in either direction in a small and equal amount. The pressure should increase an equal amount regardless of which direction the wheel is turned. If the pressure readings are not the same for both directions and the pressure falls slightly before rising then the valve and pinion assembly must be replaced.
   d. If the steering kicks to one side when starting engine, replace the valve and pinion assembly.
   e. The pinion assembly can be removed without removing the rack assembly from the car. Before removing the pinion, back off the rack adjuster pad and readjust to .010″ of end-play when installing. Note the position of the pinch bolt slot in the input shaft so that it is the same when assembling.
3. Ball pin knock occurs when turning and can be eliminated only by replacing a new inner ball pin/tie rod assembly. This can be performed with the rack in place by removing the inner ball joint and tie rod as an assembly. Check the outer ball joint and replace if necessary. Reassemble the new unit to the tie rod and adjust the length between the ball pin centers to 11-3/4.″ Both tie rods must be adjusted to the same length. Apply a large amount of proper grease to the inner ball housing before completing installation. Upon completion of installation, check front wheel alignment.

Power Steering Pump

ROTOR TYPE—MARK II, 3.4S, 3.8S

This pump is an eccentric rotor type using a combined flow and relief valve. The pump is attached to the rear of the generator and operates off the generator shaft.

Removal

1. Disconnect hoses and remove pump from end of generator.

Installation

1. Place flexible coupling on generator shaft and engage slot on pump shaft with tongue on coupling and secure pump to generator.
2. Connect hoses and fittings.

ROLLER TYPE PUMP—MARK II, 3.4S, 3.8S

This roller type pump (Hobourn-Eaton), of a later design than the rotor type, uses a combined flow and relief valve and is attached to the generator.

Removal

1. Disconnect fluid hoses and remove the pump from the rear of the generator.

Installation

1. Attach the pump to the rear of the generator and connect the fluid hoses.

PUMP—420, XJ6

These models use Saginaw pumps mounted on the right front of the engine and driven by a belt from the crankshaft pulley. This is a vane type pump that uses a combined flow and relief valve.

Removal

1. Remove the mounting bracket bolts and the drive belt from the pulley.
2. Disconnect and plug the pressure hoses.
3. Remove the pump from the bracket noting the number and location of the spacers between the pump and the mounting bracket.

Installation

1. To install, reverse the removal procedure.

FRONT WHEEL ALIGNMENT

Mark II, 3.4S, 3.8S, 420 E Type—Manual Steering

1. Make sure that the car is full of gas, water and oil and that the tire pressures are equal and the car is on a level surface.
2. With the wheels straight ahead, check alignment with a proper track setting gauge. Correct alignment should be 0 to 1/8″ total toe-in for the above models with the exception of the E Type. E Type toe-in is 1/16″-1/8″.
3. Push the car forward until the wheels have turned one-half of a revolution and then re-check the alignment.
4. If adjustment is necessary, loosen the bolt at each tie-rod end and turn the rod until the alignment is correct. On the E Type, it is necessary to loosen the bellows clips before turning the tie rods.
5. Tighten the bolts and re-check.

Mark II, 3.4S, 3.8S, 420—Power Steering

1. Set the center tie rod to a length of 16-7/16″. Do *not* use this rod to set toe-in.
2. Make sure the car is on a level surface with the wheels straight ahead. Tire pressures must be equal and as specified.
3. Each wheel must be individually adjusted to one-half the total toe-in of 0 to 1/8″. This can be done by turning each outer tie rod.
4. Centralize the steering as described in Adjusting the Steering Gear while in the Car.
5. Check the panhard setting (Mark II) as described in Rear Axle Assembly—Mark II.
6. If available, use light beam equipment to check toe-in. If not available, place a straightedge between the front and rear wheels (same side) and position it as high as possible on the wheels. The straightedge will not touch the rear wheel due to the wider track at the front. Adjust the track of the front wheel so that the gap between the edge and the front of the rear tire is the same as the gap between the edge and the rear of the rear tire. The front wheel will now be parallel with the rear wheel.
7. Follow the same procedure for the other side of the car.
8. Push the car forward until the wheels have turned one-half of a revolution.

XJ6—Power Steering

1. Place car on level surface and ensure that the tires contain the specified pressures.
2. With the wheels straight ahead, centralize the steering by removing the grease nipple from the rack case and inserting a rod into this hole. Adjust the rack position until the rod engages the locating hole in the rack—the steering is now centralized.
3. Using light beam equipment or a proper track setting gauge, check the alignment. Total toe-in must be 1/16″ —1/8″.
4. If toe-in is incorrect, each wheel must be individually adjusted by turning the tie rods an equal amount until alignment is correct. Before moving the tie rods, loosen the bellows clips so that twisting of the bellows is prevented.
5. Remove the centralizing rod from the rack casing and install the grease nipple.

Brakes

MASTER CYLINDER

Mark II, 3.4S, 3.8S, E Type—Dunlop Type

The master cylinder used on these models is of the single cylinder type mechanically linked to the brake pedal. The E Type is equipped with two identical master cylinders.

Removal

1. Drain the fluid reservoir and disconnect the intake and outlet lines from the master cylinder.
2. Disconnect the cylinder pushrod from the brake pedal and remove the master cylinder from the housing.
3. Replace the master cylinder seals in the following manner:

a. Carefully remove the rubber boot from the end of the cylinder.
b. Remove the circlip and pushrod complete with washer.
c. Remove the piston and both seals.
d. Withdraw the valve assembly with springs and supports and remove the seal from the end of the valve.
e. Lubricate the new seal and the cylinder bore with brake fluid and install the new seal to the end of the valve making sure the lip engages the groove. Install the seals around the piston.
f. Insert the piston into the spring support ensuring that the valve head engages the piston bore.
g. Dip the piston in brake fluid and using a sleeve, insert the assembly into the cylinder being careful not to damage the seals.
h. Install the pushrod and press down on the piston so that the washer will seat on the shoulder of the rod. Install the circlip.
i. Install the rubber boot.

4. Adjust the pushrod free travel (Mark II, 3.4S, 3.8S) in the following manner:
   a. When the brake pedal is in the release position, the cylinder piston must be fully extended to prevent brake drag.
5. To adjust pushrod free travel on the E Type, perform the following:
   a. When the brake pedal is in the release position (not engaged), the cylinder piston must be fully extended to prevent brake drag.
   b. Loosen the locknut at the top master cylinder pushrod and adjust the rod to give 1/16″ free travel. A balance lever will equally distribute this free travel so that each master cylinder will have 1/32″ free travel.
   c. Tighten the locknut at the top master cylinder.
   d. A clearance exists between the pushrod head, the piston and the dished washer to ensure that the piston returns to the fully extended position. This pushrod clearance will produce approximately 1/4″ free play at the pedal.

Installation

1. To install, reverse the removal procedure.

Mark II—Girling Master Cylinder

More recent models used the Girling master cylinders while the earlier models were equipped with cylinders made by Dunlop. Operation, removal and installation procedures for the Dunlop type cylinders apply to the Girling master cylinders.

Disassembly

1. Remove the end cap and the circlip from the cylinder bore.
2. Remove the pushrod, retaining washer and rubber boot as an assembly.
3. Withdraw the piston, valve and spring.
4. Remove the plunger and spring retainer.
5. Remove and discard the non-return valve seal and the piston seal.
6. Clean all parts in brake fluid and inspect cylinder bore for pits.
7. Lubricate (with brake fluid) new seals and install them on the piston and non-return valve.

Assembly

1. To assemble, reverse the disassembly procedure.

420 (Girling), E Type (Dunlop)—Master Cylinder and Reaction Valve

The 420 and E Type have two fluid reservoirs one of which supplies fluid to the pedal connected master cylinder (dual chamber) while the other directs fluid to the dual slave cylinder (dual pistons) attached to the vacuum booster. Attached to the master cylinder is a booster reaction valve consisting of a pair of flow control valves which control air flow to the booster. Acting as a safety feature, is the dual piston slave cylinder; that, is, if one piston fails due to loss of fluid, the other still works. If the front brakes fail, the rear brakes still operate and vice-versa.

Removal and Disassembly

1. Drain fluid from the reservoir.
2. Disconnect the vacuum hoses from the reaction valve and the hydraulic lines from the master cylinder.
3. Separate the cylinder pushrod from the brake pedal.
4. Remove the master cylinder.
5. Obtain a cylinder and valve repair kit.
6. Remove the valve assembly from the outlet port.
7. Remove the rubber boot from the

mouth of the cylinder followed by the circlip, spring retainer and spring.

8. Press down on the piston and remove the circlip from the mouth of the cylinder bore, being careful not to damage the piston.
9. The piston assembly with nylon bearings and rubber seals can now be removed from the cylinder.
10. Remove the plastic bearing, O-ring, secondary cup and other plastic bearing from the piston.
11. Remove the plastic spring retainer from the piston by tapping it with a wrench. Included in the repair kit is a new spring retainer since this part is often damaged during removal. The piston return spring, retainer and lever may now be withdrawn from the cylinder.
12. Remove the filter cover, filter, washer and spring.
13. Remove the valve cover assembly and disassemble by prying off the clip and removing the valve seal.
14. Remove the valve stem and seal from the housing.
15. Separate the diaphragm from its support and remove the housing from the cylinder body.
16. Remove the valve piston assembly by inserting a blunt instrument into the outlet port and pushing the piston out far enough to be removed by hand.

CAUTION: Do not use pliers to remove piston for this will result in damage.

17. Wash parts in denatured alchohol and dry with lint-free cloth or air gun. Inspect all parts for damage or wear.

Assembly and Installation

1. Heavily coat all rubber seals (except the two valve seals) and plastic bearings with brake fluid.
2. Insert the lever (tab first) into the bore making sure the tab engages the recess in the bottom of the bore.
3. Place the piston washer on the piston head (convex side towards the flange) followed by a new main cup and plastic spring retainer.
4. Insert the spring retainer and spring into the cylinder bore checking to see that the tab is still in position.
5. Press the piston assembly into the bore and position the plastic bearing, secondary cup and larger bearing and seal onto the mouth of the cylinder bore.
6. Completely press the assembly down the bore and secure with circlip.
7. Slide the spring and retainer onto the piston and secure with the circlip.
8. Using only the fingers, install a new seal and O-ring onto the valve piston and insert assembly into the cylinder body.
9. Attach the valve housing with new gasket to the cylinder body and torque each screw (with washer) to 160 to 180 in. lbs.
10. Stretch the diaphragm over its support so that it engages the depression in the valve piston.
11. Using fingers only, stretch the valve seal onto the valve stem flange and insert valve stem through the valve cover, place other seal over the stem and secure with snap-on clip.
12. Attach the valve cover assembly to the valve housing.
13. Place the air filter and washer on the valve cover along with the small spring.
14. Install cover onto filter.
15. Install trap valve assembly into outlet port using picture as guide.
16. Install the pushrod and rubber boot.

XJ6

This system is much simpler than that used on the 420 and, as a result, includes fewer components. Absent from the XJ6 is the slave cylinder and the reaction valve used on the 420. The XJ6 uses a dual piston master cylinder attached directly to the vacuum booster unit thus eliminating the need for a separate slave cylinder or a reaction valve to control air flow to the booster. The vacuum booster is mounted in the XJ6 engine compartment and is connected to the brake pedal linkage by the actuating pushrod. The master cylinder houses two pistons each having its own intake and outlet port. The pistons operate independently and if the front brakes should fail, the rear brakes will still work and vice-versa.

Removal and Disassembly

1. Drain fluid from reservoir.
2. Remove the hydraulic lines from the cylinder noting their location in order to facilitate installation.
3. Separate the master cylinder from the vacuum unit.
4. Remove the tipping valve cover and seal.

5. Remove the valve securing nut, press down on the primary plunger and remove the tipping valve.
6. Remove the internal parts and separate the plungers and intermediate spring.
7. Remove the spring and valve sub-assembly from the secondary plunger.
8. Remove the spring, valve spacer and spring washer from the valve stem and detach the seal from the valve head.
9. Inspect all parts for damage or wear and replace if necessary.

Assembly and Installation

1. Lubricate all parts with clean brake fluid.
2. Install the seals to the primary and secondary plungers.
3. Fit the valve seal, small diameter first, onto the valve head.
4. Place the spring washer on the valve stem so that it flares away from the valve stem shoulder. Follow this with the valve spacer, legs first.
5. Attach the spring retainer to the valve stem, keyhole first.
6. Place the secondary spring over the retainer and install on the secondary plunger. Place the spring and retainer in a vice and while the spring is compressed, press the spring retainer back against the secondary plunger. The leaf of the retainer must then be pressed down behind the head of the plunger. Once this is done, clean the spring and retainer assembly with clean brake fluid.
7. Position the intermediate spring between the primary and secondary plungers.
8. Lubricate the cylinder bore and plunger seals with clean brake fluid and carefully insert the plunger assemblies into the bore.
9. Press down on the primary plunger so that it fits the tipping valve.
10. Install the seal and the securing nut and torque to 35–40 ft. lbs. Install the valve cover and new seal.
11. Connect the master cylinder to the booster unit, connect the lines and bleed the brakes.

VACUUM SERVO UNIT

Mark II, 3.4S, 3.8S—Lockheed 6⅞″

Removal

1. Apply the handbrake and remove the right front wheel.
2. Drain the hydraulic system at that caliper.
3. Remove the air cleaner hose from the central port in the servo unit.
4. Disconnect the vacuum hose from the slave cylinder connection.
5. Remove the hydraulic lines from the slave cylinder.
6. Remove the servo unit and support from the car.

Installation

1. To install, reverse the removal procedure making sure that the rubber grommets and spacers are returned to the mounting studs and that the system is bled of all air.

3.4S, 3.8S—Type 8, 8″

Those 3.4S model cars beginning with chassis number 1B 25286 (left-hand drive) and those 3.8S cars beginning with chassis number 1B 76292 (left-hand drive), used the Type 8, 8″ servo unit instead of the 6-7/8″ unit used prior to these numbers. Removal and installation procedures are the same for the Type 8 as the 6-7/8″ unit.

420—Lockheed Type 8 Dual Line

Removal

1. Drain the reservoir going to the slave cylinder.
2. Remove the left front wheel.
3. Remove the fiberglass cover from the servo unit.
4. Disconnect the three flexible hoses and three fittings from the servo unit and slave cylinder and seal to prevent the entrance of dirt.
5. Remove the servo unit and bracket as an assembly.
6. Separate the servo from its bracket.

Installation

1. To install, reverse the removal procedure and bleed the system.

XJ6—Girling Type 100 Supervac

Removal

1. Disconnect the unit from the pedal and the pedal box.
2. Remove the unit from the car.

Installation

1. To install, reverse the removal procedure.

E Type—Bellows Type Vacuum Servo

REMOVAL

1. Detach the vacuum line from the bellows.
2. Disconnect the power lever from the bellows.
3. Remove the bellows from its mounting bracket.

INSTALLATION

1. To install, reverse the removal procedure.

E Type—Remote Servo and Slave Cylinder

REMOVAL

1. Remove the trim from the floor panel on the left side of the car. This will reveal the three nuts holding the unit to the firewall. Remove these nuts.
2. Drain the fluid from the system.
3. Disconnect the fittings and hoses.
4. Remove the battery and carrier.
5. Separate the slave cylinder from its mounting bracket and remove the servo and cylinder as an assembly.

INSTALLATION

1. To install, reverse the removal procedure. Bleed the system.

DISC AND CALIPER

Mark II—Disc Installation

1. Bolt the disc to the hub.
2. Attach the hub to the stub axle or half shaft.
3. Check to see if front and rear wheel bearing end-play measures .003″ to .005″ each—if not, the brakes may drag and/or operate improperly. Front wheel bearings can be adjusted by means of the hub nut at the end of the axle shaft. Rear wheel bearings adjustment is performed by inserting or removing shims located between the axle tube flange and the caliper mounting plate. For further details see front and rear suspension sections.
4. Check the disc for excessive run-out (improper rotation) by clamping a dial indicator to the chassis so that its button rests on the face of the disc. If run-out exceeds .006″, replacement of certain components may be necessary.
5. Install the caliper body with cylinder assemblies using two bolts and lock wire.
6. Check the gap between each side of the caliper and the disc. The gap measurement on each side of the caliper should not vary by more than .010″. If the gap difference is greater than .010″, it will be necessary to use shims to centralize the caliper.
7. Connect the hydraulic lines. When installing the line between the two cylinder housings, it is *important* that the end with the sharpest bend is installed to the inboard cylinder assembly; that is, to the one furthest from the wheel.

3.4S, 3.8S—Installation

1. Using a dial indicator, check front wheel bearing end-play as described in Adjusting Wheel Bearing End-Play. It should not exceed .005″. Check differential output shaft end-play (see appropriate section) and correct if necessary. If either end-play is excessive, brake drag and improper brake function may result.
2. Check disc run-out as described in Step 4 of Mark II—Disc Installation.
3. Install the complete caliper body and check the gap between each side of the caliper and disc. The difference between sides should not exceed .010″—if it does, shims may be used to centralize the caliper.
4. Install the line connecting the two cylinder assemblies and connect the fluid supply line.

420

FRONT DISC REMOVAL

1. Remove the front wheel.
2. Disconnect and tape the hydraulic line.
3. Remove the caliper.
4. Remove the hub as described in the appropriate section.

FRONT DISC INSTALLATION

1. To install, reverse the removal procedure and bleed the system. There are no centralizing shims at the front calipers.

REAR DISC REMOVAL

1. Remove the rear suspension assembly.
2. Remove the two shocks and springs.
3. Remove the four nuts holding the half-shaft inner universal joint and brake

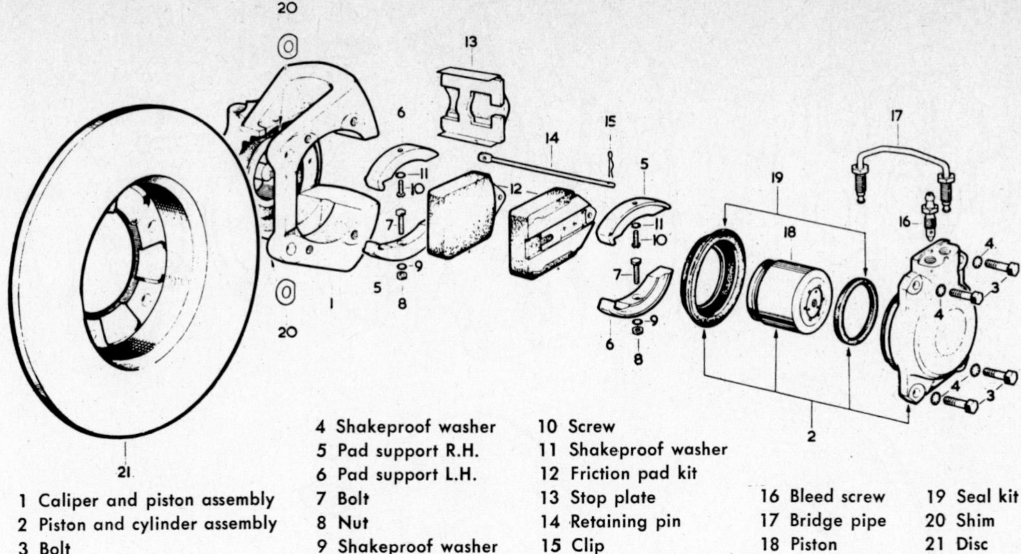

1 Caliper and piston assembly
2 Piston and cylinder assembly
3 Bolt
4 Shakeproof washer
5 Pad support R.H.
6 Pad support L.H.
7 Bolt
8 Nut
9 Shakeproof washer
10 Screw
11 Shakeproof washer
12 Friction pad kit
13 Stop plate
14 Retaining pin
15 Clip
16 Bleed screw
17 Bridge pipe
18 Piston
19 Seal kit
20 Shim
21 Disc

Exploded view of front brake caliper—3.4S, 3.8S

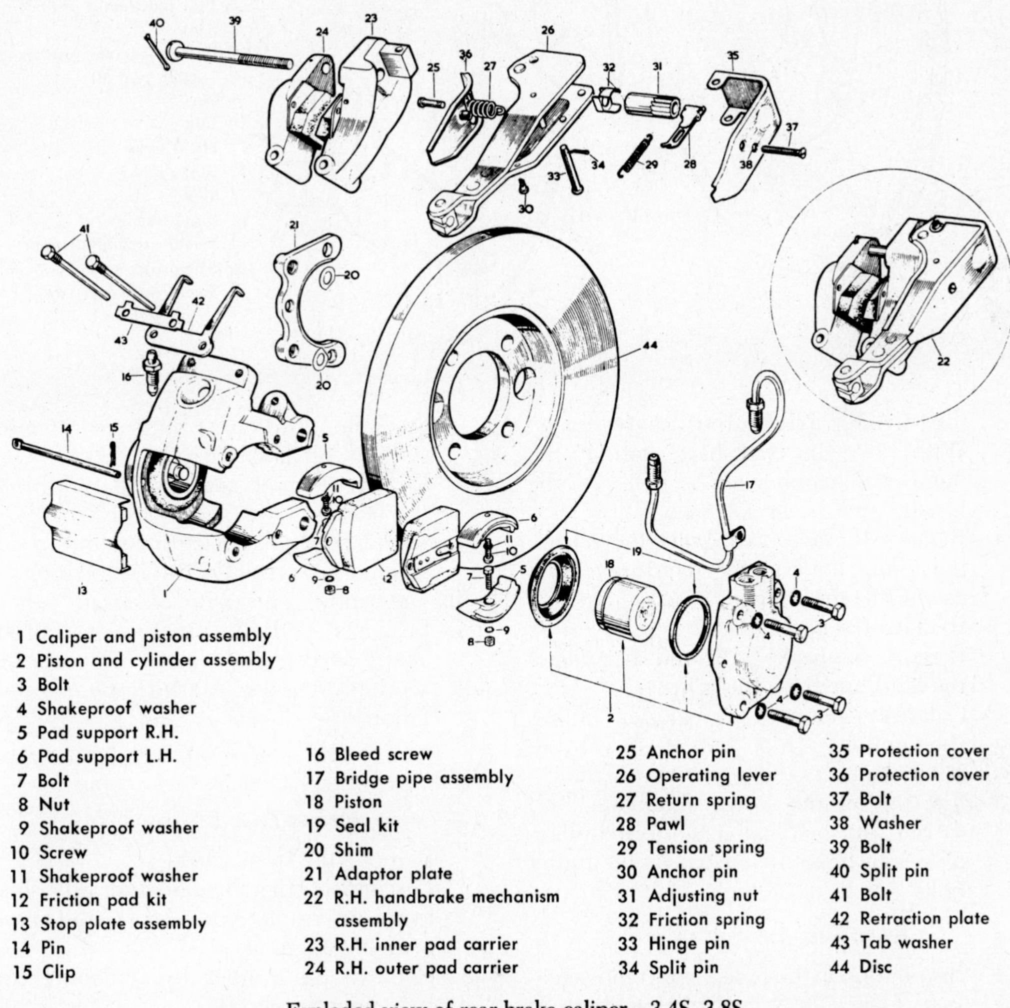

1 Caliper and piston assembly
2 Piston and cylinder assembly
3 Bolt
4 Shakeproof washer
5 Pad support R.H.
6 Pad support L.H.
7 Bolt
8 Nut
9 Shakeproof washer
10 Screw
11 Shakeproof washer
12 Friction pad kit
13 Stop plate assembly
14 Pin
15 Clip
16 Bleed screw
17 Bridge pipe assembly
18 Piston
19 Seal kit
20 Shim
21 Adaptor plate
22 R.H. handbrake mechanism assembly
23 R.H. inner pad carrier
24 R.H. outer pad carrier
25 Anchor pin
26 Operating lever
27 Return spring
28 Pawl
29 Tension spring
30 Anchor pin
31 Adjusting nut
32 Friction spring
33 Hinge pin
34 Split pin
35 Protection cover
36 Protection cover
37 Bolt
38 Washer
39 Bolt
40 Split pin
41 Bolt
42 Retraction plate
43 Tab washer
44 Disc

Exploded view of rear brake caliper—3.4S, 3.8S

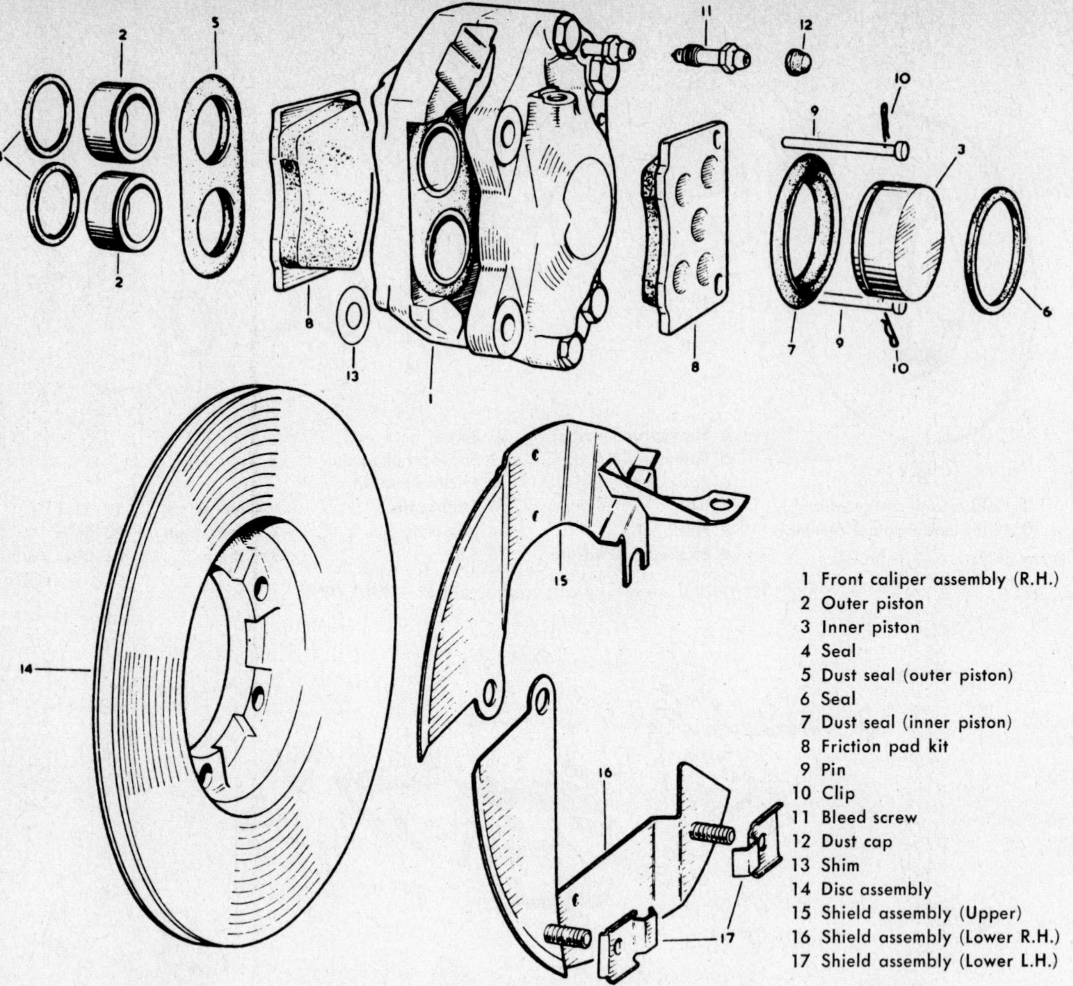

Exploded view of front brake caliper—420

disc to the axle output shaft flange. Withdraw the halfshaft noting the number of camber shims between the U-joint and the brake disc.

4. Remove the two pivot bolts and retraction plate holding the handbrake pad carriers to the caliper.
5. Remove the pad carriers.
6. Remove the brake pads and disconnect the fluid line from the caliper.
7. Carefully remove the caliper noting the number and location of the centralizing shims.
8. Lift up on the lower wishbone, hub carrier and halfshaft assembly and remove the brake disc from its mounting bolts.

Rear Disc Installation

1. Installation is the reverse of removal.
2. Install the caliper centralizing shims in the same position as removed after installing the halfshaft.
3. Install the rear suspension and bleed the brakes.
4. Check the brake disc for run-out as described in Mark II–Disc Installation.
5. Determine end-play of front wheel bearings and the rear axle output shafts as explained in the appropriate section–Step 3 of Mark II–Disc Installation.

XJ6

Front Disc Removal

1. Remove the front wheel.
2. Disconnect the flexible hydraulic line from its frame connection and tape over the opening.
3. Remove the caliper by removing the two mounting bolts.

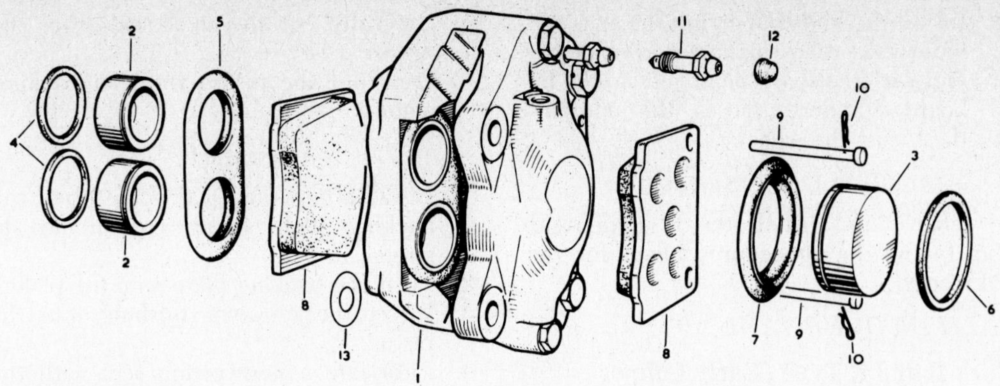

1 Front caliper assembly (R.H.)
2 Outer piston
3 Inner piston
4 Seal
5 Dust seal (outer piston)
6 Seal
7 Dust seal (inner piston)
8 Friction pad kit
9 Pin
10 Clip
11 Bleed screw
12 Dust cap
13 Shim

Exploded view of front brake caliper—XJ6

4. Remove the hub. Separate the disc from the hub.

Front Disc Installation

1. To install, reverse the removal procedure.
2. Check hub bearing end-play and make necessary adjustments.
3. Connect the hydraulic line and bleed the system.

Rear Disc Removal

1. Remove the rear suspension assembly.
2. Remove the brake caliper as follows:
   a. Disconnect the cable from the handbrake linkage and detach the pull-off springs.
   b. Remove the pivot bolts and retraction plate.
   c. Remove the handbrake pad carriers from the caliper.
   d. Remove the hydraulic line from the caliper and plug the opening.
   e. Detach the pads from the caliper.
   f. Remove the caliper.
3. Remove the shock and spring assemblies.
4. Remove the halfshaft noting the number of camber shims located between the U-joint and the brake disc.
5. Lift up on the lower wishbone, hub carrier and halfshaft assembly so that the disc can be removed.

Rear Disc Installation

1. To install, reverse the removal procedure.
2. Make sure that the same number of shims are returned between the halfshaft and the caliper.
3. Install the rear suspension.
4. Bleed the brakes.
5. Check the disc for run-out as detailed in Mark II–Disc Installation.
6. Check front wheel bearing end-play as explained in Step 3 of Mark II–Disc Installation and determine end-play at the rear output shafts as described in the Rear Suspension section.

E Type

Front Disc Removal

1. Remove the front wheel.
2. Disconnect the fluid line from the frame connection and tape over the opening to prevent the entrance of dirt.
3. Carefully remove the caliper noting the number of shims between the caliper and mounting plate.
4. Remove the hub and separate the disc from the hub.

Front Disc Installation

1. Installation is the reverse of removal.
2. Set the front bearing end-play—see Mark II–Disc Installation.
3. Position the caliper and centralize it by adding or removing shims to the area between the caliper and mounting plate. The number of shims is dependent upon the gap between each side of the caliper and the disc—the difference between the gap measurements should not exceed .010″; if it does, make up the difference with shims.

4. Install the line connecting the two cylinder assemblies making sure that the end with the sharp bend goes to the inboard cylinders; that is, the side furthest from the wheel.

Rear Disc Removal

To remove and install the E Type rear disc, follow the procedures given for the 420 model.

CALIPER OVERHAUL

Mark II and E Type (Early Caliper Design)

When replacing the piston seal, replace the dust seal also.

Disassembly

1. Disconnect and seal the hydraulic supply line and remove the line connecting the two cylinder assemblies.
2. Remove the cylinder blocks and thoroughly clean with trichloroethylene. DO NOT use gasoline, kerosene or mineral fluid.
3. Detach the dust seal from the face of the cylinder block.
4. Attach the cylinder block to a fluid line and apply brake pressure to eject the piston assembly. An air hose will do the same job.
5. Remove the plate, seal and bushing from the piston.
6. Carefully cut the dust seal from the piston.
7. Press out the piston from its backing plate.

Assembly

1. Install a new dust seal to the lip of the backing plate being careful not to stretch it.
2. Press the backing plate onto the piston.
3. Insert the retractor bushing into the piston.
4. Lubricate a new piston seal with the brake fluid and install it to the piston face followed by the plate. Peen the screws to the plate.
5. Making sure that the piston and cylinder bore are not damaged and are thoroughly clean (use trichloroethylene). Position the piston assembly on the retractor pin and, using a hand press, press it into the bore.

IMPORTANT: Do not twist or pinch the seal as it enters the cylinder bore.

6. Fit the dust seal to the groove on the cylinder block face.
7. Install the cylinder blocks to the caliper.
8. Install the bridge pipe connecting the two cylinder blocks ensuring that the end with the sharp bend connects to

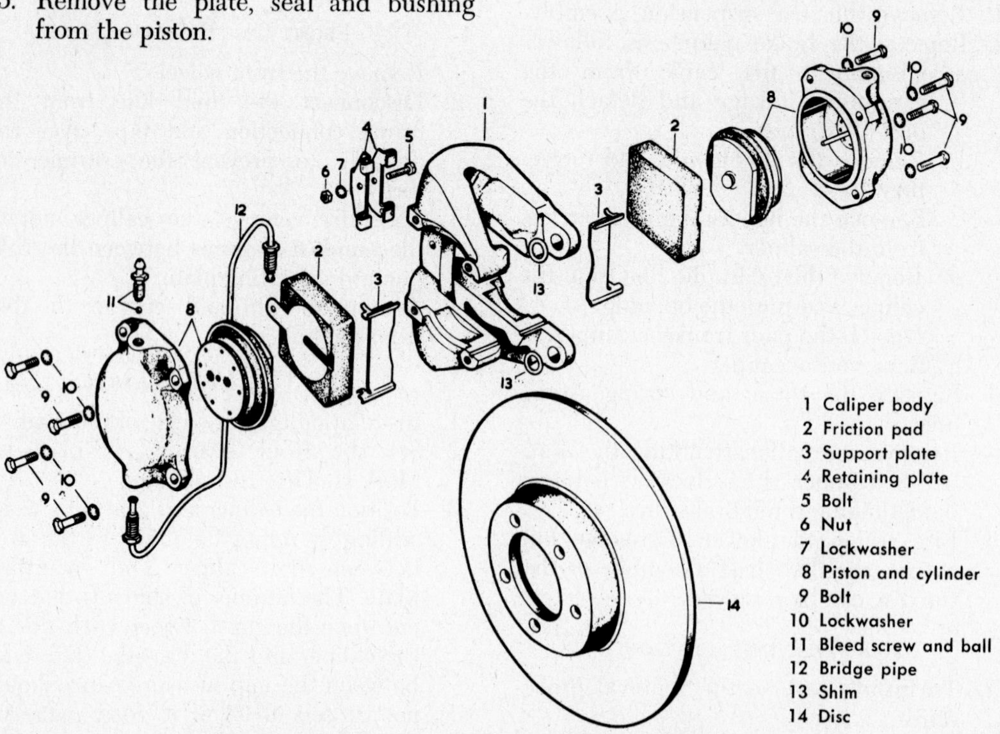

Exploded view of front brake caliper—Mark II and early E Type

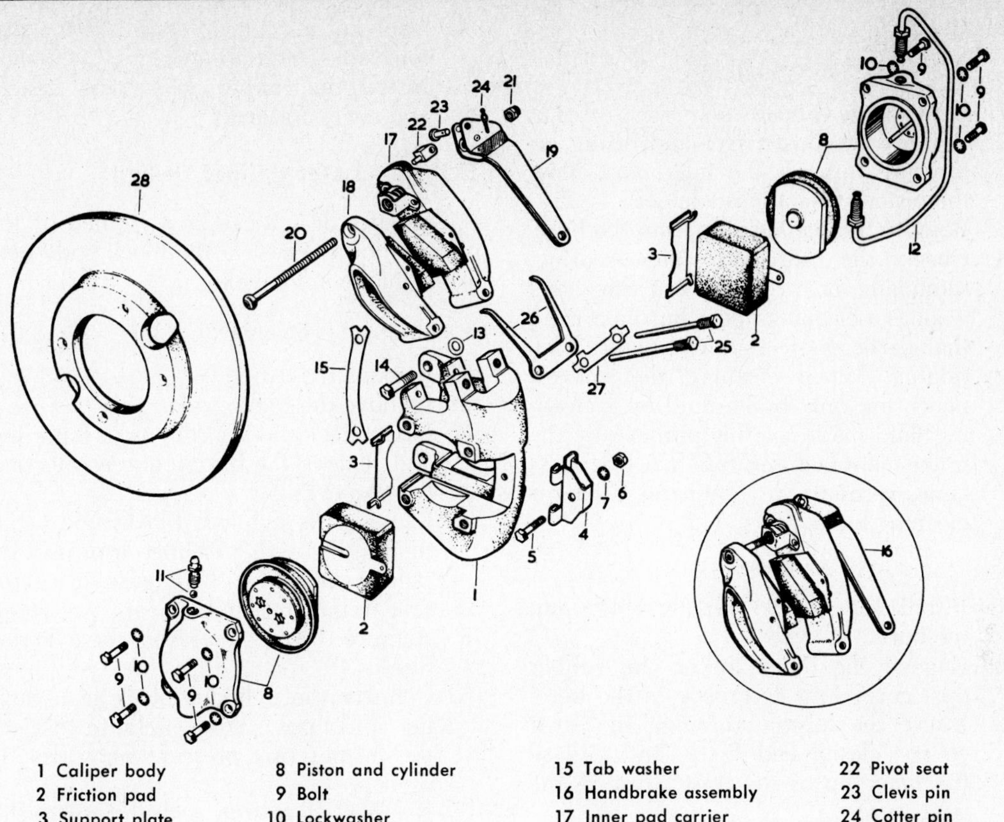

Exploded view of rear brake caliper—Mark II and early E Type

the inboard (furthest from the wheel) cylinder block.

9. Connect the fluid supply line and bleed the system.

3.4S, 3.8S

Disassembly

1. Remove the brake pads.
2. Disconnect and seal the fluid line.
3. Remove the caliper.
4. If only the inboard assembly is defective, it will be necessary to remove the outboard assembly in order to get to it.
5. Thoroughly clean (with brake fluid or a cleaning fluid made by the manufacturer) the assemblies before disassembling further.
6. Remove dust cover from cylinder block face.
7. Eject the piston assembly by connecting the cylinder block to a fluid line or to an air gun.
8. Remove the leaking seal from the cylinder bore, being careful not to scratch the bore.
9. Thoroughly clean the piston and cylinder and check for damage or scoring.
10. Remove any burr or sharp corner from the piston.
11. Soak the seal in brake fluid for a few minutes before inserting in block.

Assembly

1. Position the piston on the retractor pin and, using a hand press, press it into the bore. Apply pressure slowly and evenly ensuring that the piston is going in straight.
2. Install a new dust cover.
3. Install the cylinder assembly to the caliper and assemble the caliper unit to the disc.
4. Connect the main fluid line and install the line going from one cylinder to the other.
5. Install the brake pads, bleed the system and check for leaks.

420 and XJ6

Disassembly

1. Remove the caliper.
2. Remove the dust cover and, using air pressure through the inlet port, blow the pistons from their cylinders.
3. Remove the sealing ring from the bore.
4. Check the bore for any scoring, scratching or rust and use fine steel wool as a cleaning agent but be certain that particles are removed before continuing. When cleaning the components, use only brake fluid or a cleaning fluid made for this purpose by the brake manufacturer. *NEVER USE* gasoline, kerosene, or a mineral fluid for cleaning brake parts.

Assembly

1. Install new rubber sealing rings into the bores.
2. Engage the outer lip of the rubber dust cover into its groove in the bore.
3. Insert the piston through the dust cover (closed end first), and engage the inner lip of the dust cover in the piston groove.
4. Applying an even pressure to the piston, force it into the bore.
5. Install the caliper, bleed the system and check for leaks.

E Type—Later Caliper Design

This later design can be identified by the presence of a C cast in the block body next to the intake union hole.

Disassembly

1. Remove the caliper.
2. Remove the brake pads.
3. Disconnect and seal the main fluid line and remove the bridge line connecting the two cylinders.
4. Remove the cylinder blocks and clean thoroughly with a cleaner approved by Jaguar. DO NOT USE gasoline, kerosene or mineral fluid.
5. Remove the dust seal from the cylinder block.
6. Connect the cylinder block to a fluid line and apply brake pressure to eject the pistons. Air pressure may also be used.
7. Remove the piston seal and dust seal.

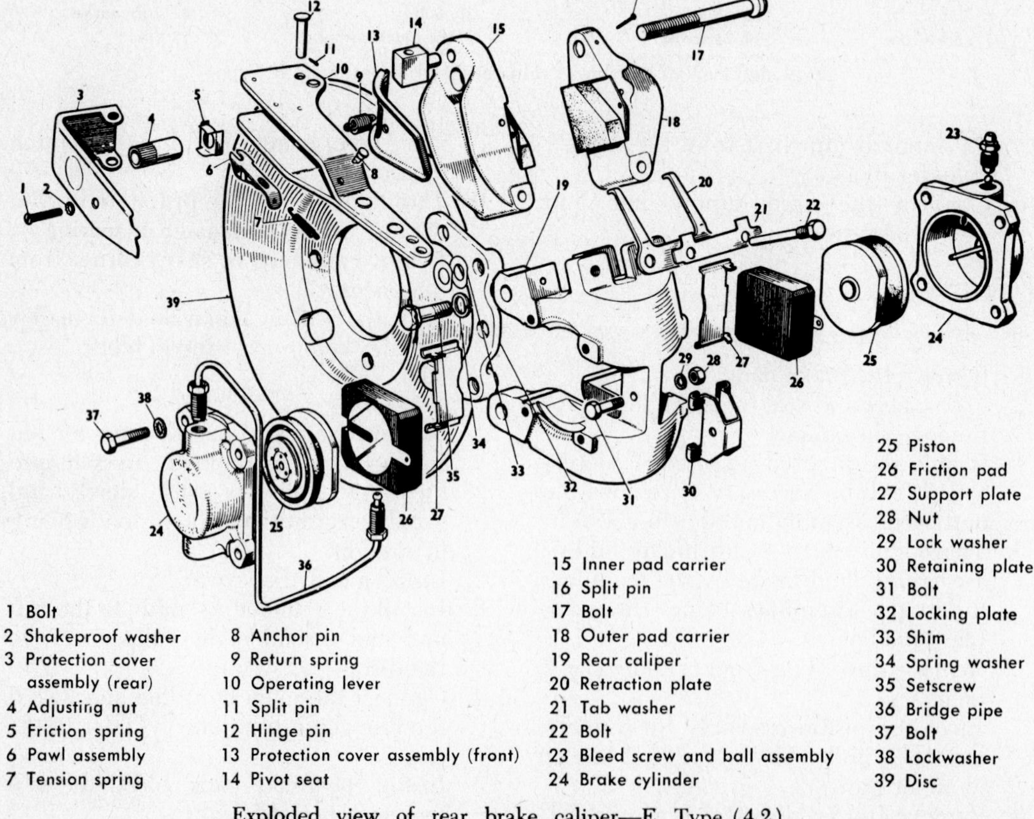

Exploded view of rear brake caliper—E Type (4.2)

Assembly

1. Lubricate the seals with brake fluid and place them on the piston with clean fingers.
2. Position the piston on the retractor pin and evenly press the piston into its bore. Make sure that the piston is going in straight and that the seal is not being twisted or pinched.
3. Fit the outer rim of the dust seal to the groove around the cylinder block face.
4. Position the two support plates.
5. Install the cylinder blocks to the caliper and connect the bridge line making sure that the end with the sharp bend goes to the inboard (furthest from the wheel) cylinder.
6. Bleed the system and check for leaks.

BRAKE PAD REPLACEMENT— ALL MODELS

Brake pads should be checked for wear every 5,000 miles and replaced if less than 1/4" thick at any one point. Fluid level at the reservoir can be noticeably reduced if the pads are excessively worn due to the fact that a greater volume of fluid is necessary to move the piston a greater distance in order to contact a thinner pad. Assemble only one brake at a time since increased fluid pressure would prevent the installation of more than two pads at once.

1. Remove the retaining plate or pins and pull out one of the brake pads. Clean the area around the calipers.

CAUTION: The increased thickness of the new pads will push the pistons into their cylinders thus forcing fluid back through the lines and out of the fluid reservoir. For this reason, it is MOST IMPORTANT that the reservoir be more than half EMPTY before attempting to install new pads. If the reservoir is full during pad installation, fluid will be ejected onto the car body and cause considerable PAINT DAMAGE.

2. Push back the piston and install the new pad. Do the same for the other pad.
3. Install the retaining pins but do not force them into their holes since the pads must be free to move slightly to allow for brake application and automatic adjustment.
4. If so equipped, install retaining plate.
5. Fill the reservoir and bleed system if brakes are spongy or low.

HANDBRAKE

Mark II and E Type—Early Cars

Adjustment

Pad wear will be indicated by excessive lever travel and should be adjusted as follows:

1. Unscrew the adjuster bolt and insert a .004" feeler gauge between one handbrake pad and the disc. Screw in the adjuster bolt until the gauge is just pinched. Remove the gauge and ensure that the disc rotates freely. Do the same for the other wheel.
2. If, after making the above adjustment, the handbrake lever travel is still excessive, adjust the cable as follows:
   a. Screw in the adjustor bolt at each rear brake until the pads are in hard contact with the discs.
   b. Make sure that the handbrake lever is fully released.
   c. Remove the pin holding the fork end to the compensator at the rear end of the main cable. Loosen the locknut and move the fork end so that when it is reconnected to the compensator and the pin is inserted, there is no slack in the main cable and the two cross cables, yet they must not be under tension or they may bind.
   d. Reset the pad clearance (Step 1) using a .004" feeler gauge.

Replacing the Handbrake Pads

1. Block the front wheels, release the handbrake and place transmission in neutral. Remove the rear wheels.
2. Loosen the adjuster bolt located at the top of the outside handbrake pad carrier until its end becomes flush with its nut.
3. Remove the two pads by loosening the nuts and using a hooked tool.
4. To install, insert the two pads into the carriers with the short face up. Locate each pad on the retaining bolt and tighten down.
5. Reset the forked retraction plate by lifting the tabs, loosening and tightening the two pivot bolts and lock the bolt heads with the tabs.

Mark II and E Type—Self-Adjusting Handbrake

This handbrake mechanism compensates for pad wear by automatically providing the proper clearance between the pads and the disc. Operating the handbrake lever in the car pulls an attached cable that is connected to an operating lever located at each rear brake disc. The cable, in turn, pulls this operating lever away from the pad carrier resulting in the pads coming together to contact the disc. When the pads are new, proper clearance exists between the pads and the disc and, when the pads wear, an adjusting mechanism housed within the operating lever works to maintain this proper clearance. As the handbrake is released, a pawl in this adjusting mechanism returns to its normal position and so, too, the pads are returned to their normal position. Although, when clearance between the pad and disc is increased, the pawl will turn the ratchet nut on the end of the adjusting bolt causing the bolt to move inward. This inward movement of the adjusting bolt will pull the pads in closer to the disc and return them to the correct clearance.

Installing the Handbrake Assembly —Mark II and E Type

Removal and disassembly procedures for this assembly are quite obvious. Nevertheless, note should be made during disassembly as to parts location. Installation is rather routine but certain points must be followed:

1. With the assembly out of the car, remove the cotter pin from the slot in the adjusting bolt and screw the bolt in or out until there is a distance of 7/16″ between the pads—this is the thickness of the disc plus 1/16″.
2. Replace the cotter pin and install the caliper on the car.
3. Pull and release the operating lever repeatedly until the ratchet will not operate. This indicates that the correct clearance now exists between the pads and the disc.
4. Connect the two cross cables. Adjust the main cable in the following manner:
   a. Fully release the handbrake lever inside the car.
   b. Loosen the locknut at the rear end of the main cable.
   c. Adjust the cable length by screwing the threaded end into the fork end to a point just short of where the handbrake operating levers (at the calipers) begin to move. Check the adjustment by pressing each operating lever at the same time towards the calipers. While doing this, observe the top of the compensator on the axle—if it moves noticeably, then the cable is too tight. To prevent binding, some slack should be obvious.
5. On certain models, the retraction plates that engage the pad calipers are different, the one for the right brake caliper differs from the one for the left caliper. It is *IMPORTANT* that these are properly positioned. Lay the plates on a table with the prongs and extensions pointing up. One of the plates has a square cut face uppermost—this plate must *ALWAYS* be installed to the *LEFT* caliper.

3.4S, 3.8S, 420, XJ6

These models use a self-adjusting type handbrake assembly that operates in the same manner as the assembly described under Mark II and E Type—Self-Adjusting Handbrake.

Installing the Handbrake Assembly

Removal and disassembly procedures are rather routine but the following instructions should be performed during installation.

1. Install the carrier assembly on each disc making certain that the handbrake pivot bolts are slack.
2. Remove the cotter pin from the head of the adjuster bolt and loosen the bolt until there is about 1/4″ free play between the bolt head and the outer pad carrier.
3. Pull the inner and outer pad carriers away from the disc until there is 1/16″ clearance between each pad and the disc.

IMPORTANT: When performing this step, the brass retraction fingers will bend, but this is nothing to worry about as long as they are not badly distorted. The ends going into the carriers must be fully inserted into the holes to avoid twisting the fingers.

4. Connect the cross cables to the operating levers and adjust the main cable as follows:
   a. Fully release the handbrake cable inside the car.
   b. Loosen the locknut at the end of the cable linkage.
   c. Press the levers toward each caliper (the off position) and adjust the length of the cable to a point just

short of where the levers begin to move. To prevent brake binding, do not place the cable under tension, allow some slack.

REPLACING HANDBRAKE PADS

1. With the carriers out of the car, remove the old pads by loosening the securing nuts and using a hooked tool to pull them out.
2. Install new pads, short face up, making certain that each pad engages the head of the retaining bolt.
3. Install new retraction fingers and assemble the carrier to the caliper allowing the pivot bolts to be slack.
4. Pull and release the operating lever repeatedly until the ratchet stops operating. This indicates that the correct clearance now exists between the pads and the disc. With the handbrake fully applied, tighten pivot bolts.

Heater

HEATER UNIT

Mark II

REMOVAL

1. Drain the water from the radiator and block.
2. Remove the two chrome screws holding the side panels on each side of the heater control panel.
3. Loosen the screws holding the water tap control wire located at the rear of the heater control panel.
4. Unclip the air distribution wire from the lever.
5. Remove the hood from the body of the car.
6. Disconnect a battery terminal.
7. Disconnect the two wires from the blower motor.
8. Remove the air cleaner.
9. Disconnect the water hoses going to the heater.
10. Separate the heater unit from the firewall.

INSTALLATION

1. Apply sealing compound around the mounting holes of the defroster seal.
2. Push the upper lever all the way towards the heater case—this is the hot position.
3. Secure the control wire to the lever.
4. Secure the outer cable in its bracket.
5. Press the lower lever on the side of the heater box into the fully shut position (screen) and place the heater control lever in the screen position.
6. Secure the control wire and the outer cable in their brackets.

E Type (All)

REMOVAL

1. Drain the radiator and block.
2. Disconnect the positive battery terminal.
3. Loosen the clips holding the heater hoses to the heater unit.
4. Loosen the bolt holding the air control cable to the lever.
5. Loosen the bolt holding the conduit casing to the heater and remove the cable.
6. Disconnect the three fan wires.
7. Remove the four bolts and washers securing the heater to the firewall.
8. Detach the bracket and remove the heater.

INSTALLATION

1. To install, reverse the removal procedure but perform the following:
2. Move the heater flap operating lever on the instrument panel to the ON position.
3. Move the heater flap lever fully forward and connect the control cable.

HEATER CORE

3.4S, 3.8S, 420

REMOVAL

1. Drain the radiator and cylinder block.
2. Disconnect the heater hoses.
3. Remove the two-speed unit from the mounting studs.
4. Carefully pry away the plastic covered felt covering the front of the unit.
5. Remove the front cover and take out the cover.

INSTALLATION

1. To install, reverse the removal procedure. Use a rubber cement to fit the plastic-felt covering over the unit.

XJ6

REMOVAL

1. Drain the cooling system.
2. Disconnect the battery.

3. Detach the water hoses.
4. Remove the radio/heater control panel.
5. Disconnect the radio and heater control line connections.
6. Remove the side and center instrument panels.
7. Remove the console.
8. Remove the two struts supporting the dash assembly.
9. Remove the right and left air duct assemblies.
10. Remove the heater assembly from firewall and detach core

INSTALLATION

1. To install, reverse the removal procedure.

HEATER BLOWER MOTOR

Mark II

REMOVAL

1. Remove the heater.
2. Separate the fan from the motor.
3. Remove the motor and ground wire.

INSTALLATION

1. To install blower motor, reverse removal procedure.

3.4S, 3.8S, 420

REMOVAL

1. Disconnect battery ground cable.
2. Disconnect wires at the connectors and detach the ground wire from the firewall.
3. Remove the resistance unit from the mounting studs.
4. Carefully pry off the plastic-felt cover from the front of the unit.
5. Remove the motor complete with fan.
6. Remove the fan from its spindle. Be careful not to disturb the balance weights on the fan.
7. Remove the mounting bracket from the motor noting that a foam joint goes between the bracket and the motor.

INSTALLATION

1. To install, reverse the removal procedure. When assembling the fan to the spindle there must be at least 1/8″ clearance between the fan and mounting bracket and the fan must be straight on the spindle.

XJ6

The XJ6 is equipped with two blower motors attached to the firewall. Attached to each motor is a nylon impeller. Speed changes are controlled by resistance units wired in series.

REMOVAL

1. Disconnect the wires from the resistance units on the firewall.
2. Remove the three screws holding the motor mounting plates to the firewall.

NOTE: These motors rotate in different directions; therefore mark them as to rotation before removing.

3. Remove the motors with plates.
4. Remove the impellers and mounting plates.
5. Faulty units must be replaced since they cannot be repaired.

INSTALLATION

1. To install, reverse removal procedure. Replace any damaged gaskets. Since the two blower motors rotate in different directions, they must be installed in the same location from which they were removed.

E Type

REMOVAL

1. Remove the heater.
2. Remove the motor and fan from the heater case.
3. Separate the fan from the spindle.

INSTALLATION

1. To install, reverse the removal procedure. Remember that a spring clip holds the fan to the spindle.

Windshield Wipers

WIPER MOTOR

Mark II, 3.4S, 3.8S, 420

REMOVAL

1. Remove the wiper arms from the spindles.
2. Disconnect the wires from the motor.
3. Remove the wiper motor from the inner skirt of the right front fender.

Installation

1. To install, reverse the removal procedure.

XJ6

Removal

1. Remove the wiper arms from the spindles.
2. Remove the battery.
3. Disconnect all wires noting their location so that they may be re-connected properly.
4. Remove the motor and drive cable as an assembly.

Installation

1. Installation is the reverse of removal.

E Type—Early Design

Removal

1. Disconnect the battery ground cable.
2. Disconnect the ball joint from the throttle control shaft at the pivot bracket and remove the bracket.
3. Detach the wires from motor.
4. Remove the two screws from the top corners of the instrument panel and lower the panel.
5. At this time, disconnect the ball joint from the center wiper spindle.
6. Remove the motor with attached link rod from the firewall.

Installation

1. To install, reverse the removal procedure. Do not change the length of the link rod since this will upset the timing relation of the wiper arms. It is important that when installing the throttle control pivot bearing bracket, the control rod must be central in its bearing. Adjustment is performed with the two slotted holes in the bracket.

E Type—Later Design

Removal

1. Disconnect the battery.
2. Detach the throttle link rod from the lever and remove rod.
3. Mark the location of the carrier bracket on the firewall and remove the bracket.
4. Tag the wires as to location and disconnect them from the motor.
5. Remove the two top corner screws from the instrument panel and lower the panel.
6. Detach the ball joint from the center spindle bearing.
7. Remove the motor with attached link rod from the firewall.

Installation

1. To install, reverse the removal procedure. Follow installation procedure for E Type–Early Design.

MG SECTION

Index

Introduction

The term "sports car" may possibly have been invented to describe the MG, for it was the MG TC of the late forties and early fifties that kicked off America's fascination with foreign sports and economy cars. The little TC made the reputation that embraces MG even today: it was the embodiment of everything most American cars of the era weren't; it was fun. The latest MGs are somewhat dated technically, but they still provide the sort of excitement that makes driving a pleasure instead of a chore. Today, a good MG TC can command a price far higher than what it originally sold for.

The Evolution of MG Sports Cars of the 1950s

Model/ Year	*Displacement*	*Horsepower*	*Weight*	*0-60 Time*	*Maximum Speed*
MG TC					
1948-50	1,250 cc.	54	1,850	22 sec.	75 mph
MG TD					
1950-53	1,250 cc.	54/57	2,000	20 sec.	80 mph
MG TF					
1954	1,250 cc.	57	2,000	19 sec.	80 mph
1955	1,500 cc.	65	2,000	16 sec.	85 mph
MGA 1500					
1956-59	1,500 cc.	72	2,000	15 sec.	95 mph
MGA Twin Cam					
1958-60	1,600 cc.	108	2,000	10 sec.	115 mph
MGA 1600					
1959-61	1,600 cc.	80	2,000	14 sec.	100 mph
MGA Mk. II					
1961-62	1,600 cc.	93	2,000	12 sec.	105 mph

Model Identification, 1961-71* MG Midget, MGB, MGC, and MG 1100

MG Midget, 1961-70

Roadster version of MGB, 1961-70; MGC, 1968-69

MG Midget, 1971-72

MGB convertible, 1971-72

*—Trim variations from year to year such as the side curtains on the Mk. I Midget, different exterior badge arrangements, etc., are not shown.

GT version of MGB, 1966-70; MGC, 1968-69

MGB GT, 1971-72

MG 1100 sports sedan, 1962-67

Vehicle and Engine Serial Number Identification

VEHICLE NUMBER IDENTIFICATION

The vehicle serial number on all MG models can be found on a stamped plate located in the engine compartment.

Vehicle Identification—Midget

Year	*Model*	*Serial Numbers*
1961-62	Mk. I	G-AN1/*101-16,183
1963-64	Mk. I	G-AN2/*16,184-25,787
1965-66	Mk. II	G-AN3/*25,788-52,389
1967-69	Mk. III	G-AN4/*52,390-74,885
1970-72	Mk. III	G-AN5/*74,886-**

Vehicle Identification—MGB

Year	*Model*	*Serial Numbers*
1961-67	Conv.	G-HN3/*101-138,400
1968-69	Conv.	G-HN4/*138,401-187,210
1970-72	Conv.	G-HN5/*187,211-**
1966-67	GT	G-HD3/*71,933-139,471
1968-69	GT	G-HD4/*139,472-187,840
1970-72	GT	G-HD5/*187,841-**

Vehicle Identification—MGC

Year	*Model*	*Serial Numbers*
1968-69	Conv.	G-CN1/*101-***
1968-69	GT	G-CD1/*101-***

Vehicle Identification—MG 1100

Year	*Model*	*Serial Numbers*
1962-67	2-Door	G-A2S3/*2,094-123,463
1962-67	4-Door	G-AS3/*2,094-123,455

*—An L in the serial number denotes left-hand drive.
**—Series still in production.
***—Finishing serial numbers for North American models not known.

ENGINE NUMBER IDENTIFICATION

The engine serial number on all MG models can be found on a stamped plate riveted to the distributor side of the cylinder block.

Engine Identification—Midget

No. of Cylinders	*Displacement*	*Type*	*Serial Number*
4-inline	948 cc.	OHV	9CG/Da/H 101-36,711
4-inline	1,098 cc.	OHV	10CG/Da/H 101-21,048
4-inline	1,098 cc.	OHV	10CC/Da/H 101-16,300
4-inline	1,275 cc.	OHV	12CC/Da/H 101-16,300
4-inline	1,275 cc.	OHV	12CE/Da/H 101-
4-inline	1,275 cc.	OHV	12CD/Da/H 101-
4-inline	1,275 cc.	OHV	12CJ/Da/H 101-
4-inline	1,275 cc.	OHV	12V/587Z/L 101-

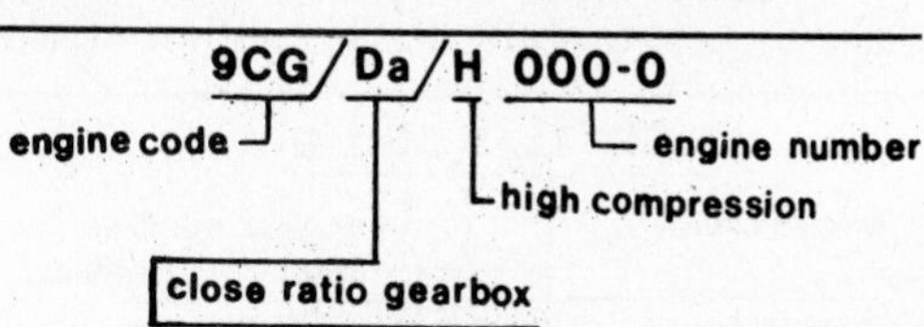

Engine Identification—MGB**

No. of Cylinders	Displacement	Type	Serial Number
4-inline	1,798 cc.	OHV	18G/U/H 101-31,121
4-inline	1,798 cc.	OHV	18GA/U/H 101-17,500
4-inline	1,798 cc.	OHV	18GB/*/H 101-91,200
4-inline	1,798 cc.	OHV	18GF/*/H 101-13,650
4-inline	1,798 cc.	OHV	18GH/*/H 101-
4-inline	1,798 cc.	OHV	18GJ/*/H 101-
4-inline	1,798 cc.	OHV	18GK/*/H 101-
4-inline	1,798 cc.	OHV	18V/584Z/L 101-

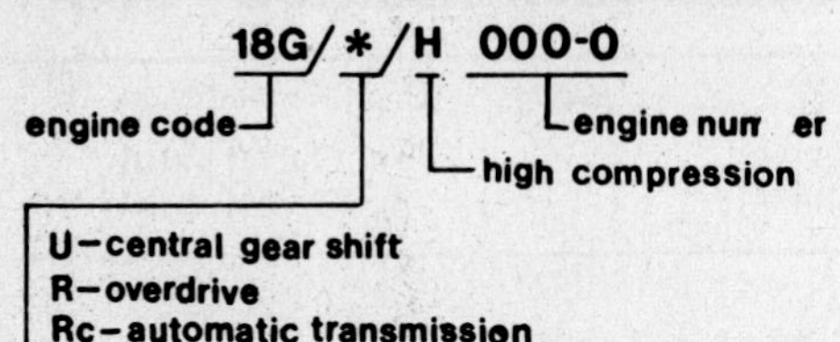

**—In late 1967 and early 1968 a few cars with 18GD or 18GG engines may have been imported. Specifications for these engines are the same as for the 18GF engine except for carburetors, which are the same as those on the 18GB engine.

Engine Identification—MGC

No. of Cylinders	Displacement	Type	Serial Number
6-inline	2,912 cc.	OHV	29GA/*/H 101-

29GA/*/H 000-0
engine code
engine number
high compression
R–overdrive
Rc–automatic transmission
We–fully synchronized 4-speed

Engine Identification—MG 1100

No. of Cylinders	Displacement	Type	Number Serial
4-inline	1,098 cc.	OHV	10GR/Ta/H 101-61,860

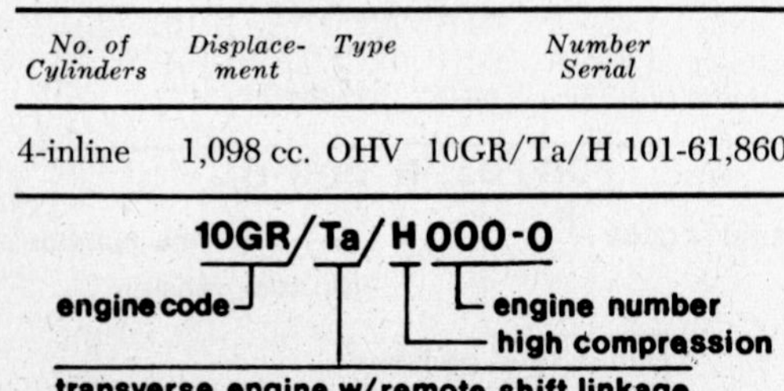

CAUTION: *General adoption of anti-pollution laws has changed the tune-up specifications of almost all engines to reduce crankcase emissions and terminal exhaust products. Timing and idle speed are of particular importance, and the manufacturer's recommendations should be strictly adhered to. This information is clearly displayed in the engine compartment of any car equipped with emission control systems.*

General Engine Specifications

Model/Year	Engine Code	Displacement	Carburetor Type (S.U.)	Advertised Horsepower @RPM	Advertised Torque @RPM	Bore and Stroke (in.)	Comp. Ratio	Oil Pressure
Midget Mk. I								
1961-62	9CG	948 cc.	HS2 (2)	46@5,500	53@3,000	2.478x3.000	8.9:1	30-60
1963-64	10CG	1,098 cc.	HS2 (2)	55@5,500	62@3,250	2.543x3.296	8.9:1	30-60
Midget Mk. II								
1965-66	10CC	1,098 cc.	HS2 (2)	59@5,750	65@3,500	2.543x3.296	8.9:1	30-60
Midget Mk. III								
1967	12CC/12CE	1,275 cc.	HS2 (2)	65@6,000	72@3,000	2.780x3.200	8.8:1	40-70
1968-70	12CD*	1,275 cc.	HS2 (2)	62@6,000	72@3,000	2.780x3.200	8.8:1	40-70
1971	12CJ**	1,275 cc.	HS2 (2)	62@6,000	72@3,000	2.780x3.200	8.8:1	40-70
MGB								
1961-64	18G/18GA	1,798 cc.	HS4 (2)	98@5,400	110@3,000	3.160x3.500	8.8:1	50-80
1965-67	18GB	1,798 cc.	HS4 (2)	98@5,400	110@3,000	3.160x3.500	8.8:1	50-80
1968-69	18GF*	1,798 cc.	HS4 (2)	92@5,200	110@3,000	3.160x3.500	8.8:1	50-80
1970	18GH*	1,798 cc.	HS4 (2)	92@5,200	110@3,000	3.160x3.500	8.8:1	50-80
	18GJ**	1,798 cc.	HS4 (2)	92@5,200	110@3,000	3.160x3.500	8.8:1	50-80
1971	18GK***	1,798 cc.	HS4 (2)	92@5,200	110@3,000	3.160x3.500	8.8:1	50-80
MGC								
1968-69	29GA*	2,912 cc.	HS6 (2)	145@5,250	170@3,500	3.280x3.500	9.0:1	50-70
MG 1100								
1962-67	10GR	1,098 cc.	HS2 (2)	55@5,500	61@2,750	2.543x3.296	8.9:1	50-70

*—Exhaust emission control system fitted.
**—Exhaust emission control and evaporative loss control systems fitted.
***—Exhaust emission control, evaporative loss control, and NOx systems fitted.

Tune-up Specifications

Model/Year	Engine Code	Spark Plugs Champion	Spark Plugs Gap (in.)	Distributor Dwell (deg.)	Distributor Gap (in.)	Timing Static (deg. BTDC)	Compression pressure (psi)	Valves Clearance (in.) Intake	Valves Clearance (in.) Exhaust	Valves Intake Opens (deg.)	Idle Speed (rpm)
Midget Mk. I											
1961-62	9CG	N5	.025	60	.015	4	165	.012C	.012C	5B	1,000
1963-64	10CG	N5	.025	60	.015	5	165	.012C	.012C	5B	1,000
Midget Mk. II											
1965-66	10CC	N5	.025	60	.015	5	165	.012C	.012C	5B	1,000
Midget Mk. III											
1967	12CC/12CE	N9Y	.025	60	.015	7	120	.012C	.012C	5B	700
1968-70	12CD	N9Y	.025	60	.015	4	120	.012C	.012C	5B	1,000
1971	12CJ	N9Y	.025	60	.015	4	120	.012C	.012C	5B	1,000
1972	12V	N9Y	.025	60	.015	N.A.	N.A.	.012H	.012H	N.A.	1,000
MGB											
1961-64	18G/18GA	N9Y	.025	60	.015	10	160	.015C	.015C	16B	500
1965-67	18GB	N9Y	.025	60	.015	10	160	.015C	.015C	16B	500
1968-69	18GF	N9Y	.025	60	.015	10	160	.015C	.015C	16B	900
1970	18GH	N9Y	.025	60	.015	10	160	.015C	.015C	16B	900
	18GJ	N9Y	.025	60	.015	10	160	.015C	.015C	16B	900
1971	18GK	N9Y	.025	60	.015	10	160	.015C	.015C	16B	900
1972	18V	N9Y	.025	60	.015H	N.A.	N.A.	.015H	.015H	N.A.	850
MGC											
1968-69	29GA	N9Y	.025	35	.015	TDC	155	.015C	.015C	16B	850
MG 1100											
1962-67	10GR	N5	.025	60	.015	5	160	.012C	.012C	5B	1,000

B—Before Top Dead Center.
C—Engine cold.
H—Engine hot.
*—See text for dynamic timing specifications.

Firing Order

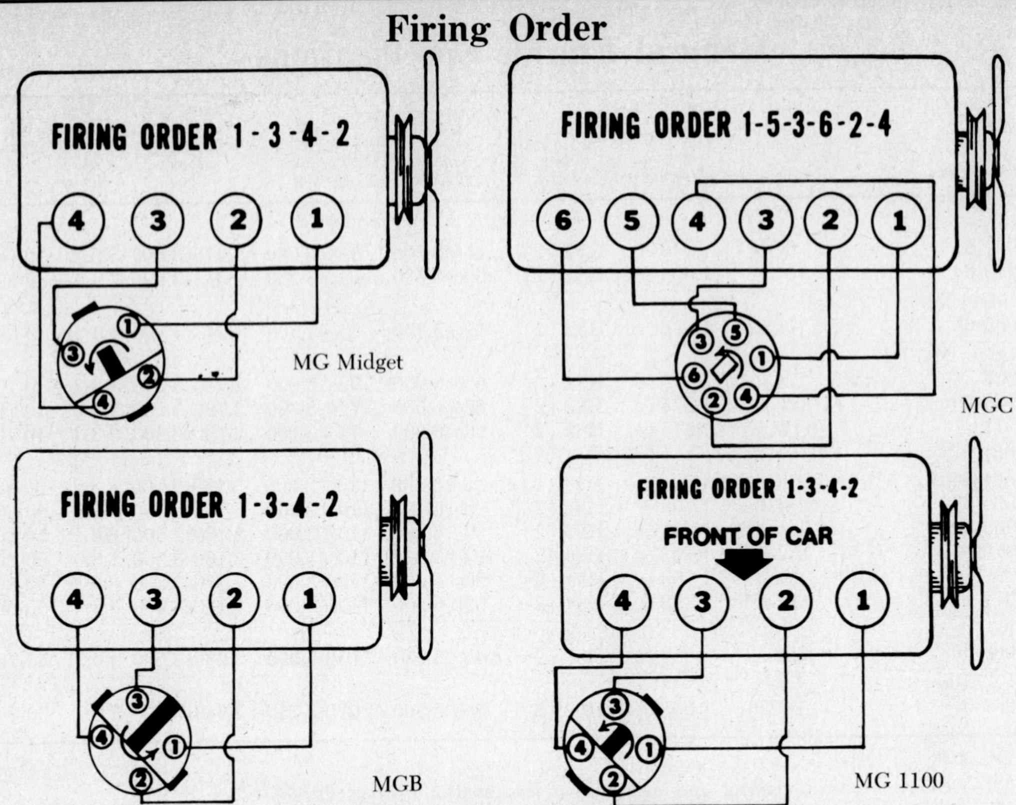

Engine Rebuilding Specifications

Crankshaft Specifications

Model & Engine	Main Bearing Journals (in.) Journal Diameter New	Minimum	Oil Clearance	Shaft End-Play	Thrust On No.	Connecting Rod Bearing Journals (in.) Journal Diameter New	Minimum	Oil Clearance	End-Play
Midget 9CG/10CG	1.7505-1.7510	-.040	.001-.0025	.002-.003	2	1.6254-1.6259	-.040	.001-.0025	.008-.012
10CC	2.0005-2.0010	-.040	.001-.0025	.002-.003	2	1.6254-1.6259	-.040	.001-.0025	.008-.012
12CC/12CE/12CD/12CJ	2.0005-2.0010	-.010*	.001-.0027	.002-.003	2	1.6254-1.6259	-.010*	.001 .0025	.006-.010
MGB 18G/18GA**	2.1262-2.1270	-.040	.001-.0027	.004-.005	2	1.8759-1.8764	-.040	.001-.0027	.008-.012
18GB/18GF/18GH/18GJ/18GK	2.1262-2.1270	-.040	.001-.0027	.004-.005	3	1.8759 1.8764	-.040	.001-.0027	.008-.012
MGC 29GA	2.3742-2.3747	-.020	.0009-.0027	.002-.0036	3	2.0000-2.0005	-.020	.001-.0027	.008-.012
MG 1100 10GR	1.7505-1.7510	-.040	.001-.0027	.002-.003	2	1.6254-1.6259	-.040	.001-.0027	.008-.012

*—Maximum permissible without heat treatment.

**—18G and 18GA engines have 3 main bearings. All later engines have 5 main bearings.

Piston and Ring Specifications

Model & Engine	Piston Specifications (in.)				Ring Specifications (in.)			
	Oversize Maximum	Wrist Pin Diameter	Skirt Clearance		Compression		Oil Control	
			Top	Bottom	End-Gap	Side Clearance	End-Gap	Side Clear-ance
Midget 9CG	+.040	.6244-.6246	.0036-.0042	.0016-.0022	.007-.012	.0015-.0035	.007-.012	.0015-.0035
10CG/10CC	+.020	.6244-.6246	.0021-.0037	.0005-.0011	.007-.012	.002-.004	.012-.028	.0015-.0035
12CC/12CE/12CD/12CJ	+.020	.8123-.8125	.0029-.0037	.0015-.0021	.008-.013*	.0015-.0035	.012-.028	.0015-.0035
MGB 18G/18GA	+.040	.7499-.7501	.0036-.0045	.0018-.0024	.012-.017	.0015-.0035	.012-.017	.0016-.0036
18GB	+.040	.8124-.8127	.0021-.0033	.0006-.0012	.012-.017	.0015-.0035	.012-.017	.0016-.0036
18GF/18GH/18GJ/18GK	+.040	.8125-.8127	.0021-.0033	.0006-.0012	.012-.022	.0015-.0035	.015-.045	.0016-.0036
MGC 29GA	+.040	.8748-.8750	.0028-.0040	.0017-.0023	.012-.016	.0025-.0035	.015-.045	.0016-.0036
MG 1100 10GR	+.020	.6244-.6246	.0021-.0037	.0005-.0011	.007-.012	.002-.004	.012-.028**	.0015-.0035

*—Top compression ring—.011-.016 in.
**—Early models with slotted type rings—.007-.012 in.

Valve Specifications

Model & Engine	Seat Angle (deg.)	Valve Lift (in.)		Valve Head Diameter (in.)		Valve Spring Free Length (in.)		Spring Pressure (lbs.)**		Stem Diameter (in.)		Stem to Guide Clearance (in.)		Guide Height Above Head (in.)
		Intake	Exhaust	Intake	Exhaust	Inner	Outer	Intake	Exhaust	Intake	Exhaust	Intake	Exhaust	
Midget 9CG	45	.312	.312	1.151-1.156	1.000-1.005	1.672	1.750	118	118	.2793-.2798	.2788-.2793	.0015-.0025	.002-.003	19/32
10CG/10CC	45	.312	.312	1.213-1.218	1.000-1.005	1.672	1.750	118	118	.2793-.2798	.2788-.2793	.0015-.0025	.002-.003	19/32
12CC/12CE/ 12CD/12CJ	45	.318	.318	1.307-1.312	1.152-1.156	1.703	1.828	131	131	.2793-.2798	.2788-.2793	.0015-.0025	.0015-.0025	19/32***
MGB All Engine Series	45.5	.3645	.3645	1.562-1.567	1.343-1.348	1.969	2.141	167	167	.3422-.3427	.3417-.3422	.0015-.0025	.002-.003	3/4
MGC 29GA	45	.250	.250	1.745-1.750	1.558-1.563	1.969	2.141	167	167	.3422-.3427	.3422-.3427*	.0016-.0026	.002-.003	5/8
MG 1100 10GR	45	.312	.312	1.213-1.218	1.000-1.005	1.672	1.750	118	118	.2793-.2798	.2788-.2793	.0015-.0025	.002-.003	19/32

*—From engine number 29GA/1401—.3417-.3422 in.

**—Combined pressure of inner and outer valve springs with valve fully open.

***—12CD and 12CJ engines should only use valve guides having an identification groove machined .187 in. from the guide top.

Valve Seat Machining Dimensions

MG MIDGET

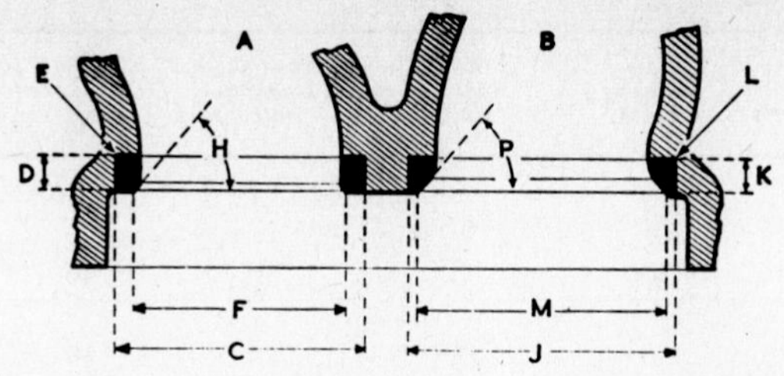

A—EXHAUST (in.)

B—INTAKE (in.)

9CG ENGINE

C. 1.124-1.125
D. 0.186-0.188
E. Max. radius: 0.015
F. 1.0235-1.0435
H. 45 deg.

J. 1.3075-1.3085
K. .0186-.0188
L. Max. radius: 0.015
M. 1.1435-1.1635
P. 45 deg.

10CG/10CC ENGINE

Same as 9CG except:

J. 1.3745-1.3755
M. 1.206-1.226

12CC ENGINE

C. 1.2505-1.2515
D. 0.186-0.188
E. Max. radius: 0.015
F. 1.144-1.164
H. 45 deg.

J. 1.3805-1.3815
K. 0.186-0.188
L. Max. radius: 0.015
M. 1.2995-1.3195
P. 45 deg.

MGB

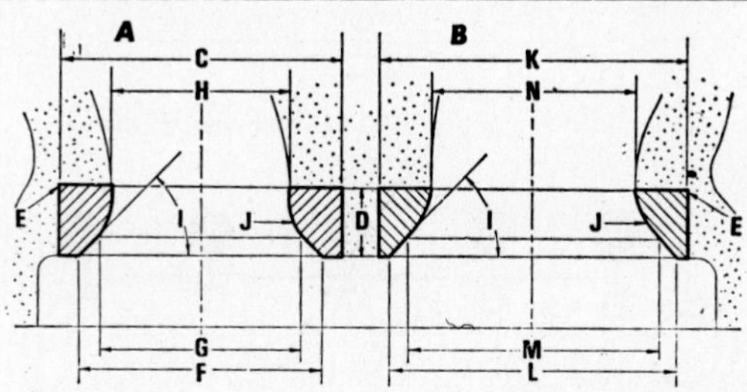

A—EXHAUST (in.)

B—INTAKE (in.)

All Engine Series

C. 1.437-1.438
D. 0.186-0.188
E. Max. radius: 0.015
F. 1.330-1.350
G. 1.218-1.228
H. Port diameter: 1.146-1.166
I. 45 deg.
J. Blend evenly, seat to port.

K. 1.592-1.593
D. 0.186-0.188
E. Max. radius: 0.015
L. 1.552-1.572
M. 1.427-1.447
N. Port diameter: 1.302-1.322
I. 45 deg.
J. Blend evenly, seat to port.

MGC

29GA ENGINE

Valve seat inserts are not available for the MGC; therefore, if the valve seats are too badly burned to be resurfaced the head must be replaced.

MG 1100

10GR ENGINE

Same as Midget with 10CG/10CC engine.

Torque Specifications (ft. lbs.)

Model & Engine	Cylinder Head Bolts	Main Bearing Bolts	Rod Bearing Bolts	Crankshaft Damper* Bolt(s)	Flywheel to Crankshaft Bolt(s)	Manifold Nuts	
						Intake	Ex-haust
Midget 9CG/10CG/ 10CC	40	60	35	70	40	15	15
12CC/12CE/ 12CD/12CJ	42**	60	45***	70	40	15	15
MGB All Engine Series	45-50	70	35-40	70	40	15	15
MGC 29GA	75	75	50	N.A.	50	42	42
MG 1100 10GR	40	60	35	70	110-115	15	15

*—Torque figure given applies to crankshaft pulley on cars not equipped with damper.
**—Studs stamped 22 or with small drill point—50.
***—Nylon-type locknut—32-34.

Tightening Sequences

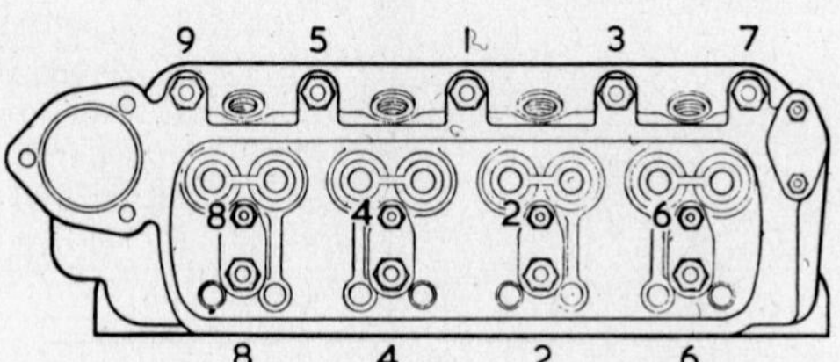

Cylinder head, MG Midget and 1100

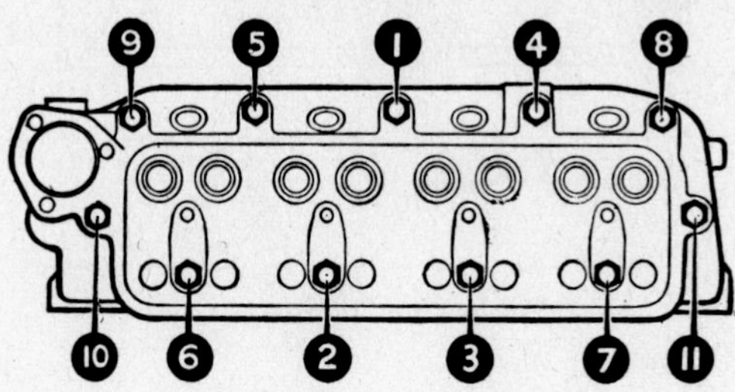

Cylinder head, MGB

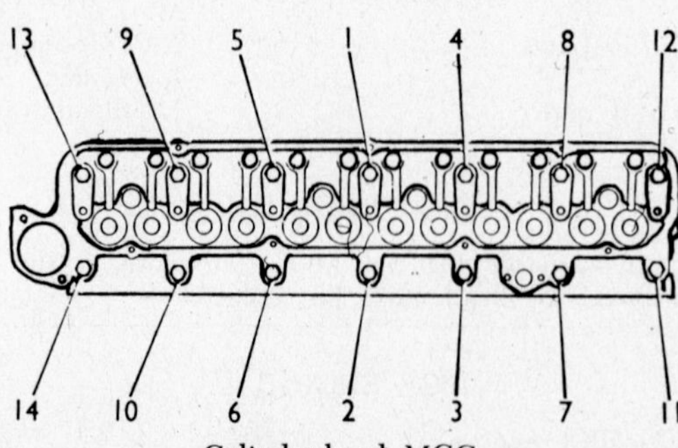

Cylinder head, MGC

Electrical Specifications

Model & Engine	Battery** Capacity (amp. hrs.)	Battery** Volts	Battery** Grounded Terminal	Starter (Lucas) Type	Lock Test Amps	Lock Test Volts	Lock Test Torque (ft. lb.)	No Load Test Amps	No Load Test Volts	No Load Test Rpm	Brush Spring Tension (oz.)
Midget 9CG/10CG/10CC	43	12	Pos.	M35G	250-365	7	6.7	60	11.5	8,000-11,500	25
12CC/12CE/12CD/12CJ	50	12	Neg.*	M35J	250-375	7	7.0	65	11.5	8,000-10,000	28
MGB 18G/18GA/18GB	58	12	Pos.	M418G	450	7	14.5	70	11.5	5,500-8,000	32
18GF/18GH/18GJ/18GK	60	12	Neg.***	M418G	465	7	17.0	70	11.5	5,800-6,500	36
MGC 29GA	64	12	Neg.	M418G	465	7	17.0	70	11.5	5,800-6,500	36
MG 1100 10GR (1962-65)	40	12	Pos.	M35G	250-365	7	6.7	60	11.5	8,000-11,500	25
10GR (1965-67)	50	12	Pos.	M35J	250-375	7	7.0	65	11.5	8,000-10,000	28

*—Positive ground up to car number G-AN4/60,460. Positive ground cars (12CC engine only) use the M35G starter.

**—MGB and MGC equipped with two 6-volt batteries. Specifications apply to the two batteries wired together in series.

***—Positive ground up to car number G-HN4/138,801 (Conv.), and G-HD4/139,824 (GT).

Model & Engine	Generator (Lucas) Type	Output (amps)	Brush Pressure (oz.)	Resistance (ohms)	Regulator (Lucas) Type	Cut-out Relay Points Close (volts)	Cut-out Relay Reverse Current (amps)	Cut-out Relay Points Air Gap (in.)	Maximum Current (amps)	Points Air Gap (in.)
Midget 9CG (1961)	C39	19	18-26	6.0-6.3	RB106	12.7-13.3	5.0	**	19	**
9CG (1962)	C39	19	18-26	6.0-6.3	RB106/2	12.7-13.3	5.0	**	19	**
10CG/10CC	C40/1	22	22-25	6.0	RB106/2	12.7-13.3	5.0	**	19	**
12CC/12CE/12CD/12CJ	C40/1	22	22-25	6.0	RB340*	12.7-13.3	5.0	**	22	**
MGB 18G/18GA/18GB	C40/1	22	22-25	6.0	RB340	12.7-13.3	5.0	**	22	**
MG 1100 10GR	C40/1	22	22-25	6.0	RB340	12.7-13.3	5.0	**	22	**

*—Early cars (12CC engine with positive ground) use the RB106/2 regulator.

**—The settings of the points should never need adjustment. See text for further explanation.

Electrical Specifications (cont'd)

Model & Engine	Alternator (Lucas) Type	Output @ Engine Rpm (amps) 850	Output @ Engine Rpm (amps) 3,300	Field Current Draw (amps @12V)	Brush Tension (oz.)	Regulator (Lucas) Type	Field Relay Air Gap (in.)	Field Relay Point Gap (in.)	Points Close (volts)	Air Gap (in.)	Volts @ 125 deg.
MGB 18GF	16AC	12-15	34	3	7-10	4TR	Transistor type—no adjustment.				14.3-14.7
18GH/18GJ/ 18GK	16ACR	12-15	34	3	7-10	8TR 11TR	Integral with alternator, transistor type—no adjustment.				14.0-14.4 14.0-14.4
MGC 29GA	16AC	12-15	34	3	7-10	4TR	Transistor type—no adjustment.				14.3-14.7

Capacities and Pressures

Model & Engine	Crankcase (qts.) With Filter	Crankcase (qts.) Without Filter	Transmission (pts.) 4-Speed	Transmission (pts.) 4-Speed with O.D.	Transmission (pts.) Auto.	Drive Axle (pts.)	Fuel Tank (gals.)	Coolant w/Heater (qts.)	Fuel Pressure (psi)	Coolant Pressure (max. psi)
Midget 9CG/10CG	4.0	3.5	2.7	—	—	2.1	7.2	6.3	1.5-2.5	7
10CC/12CC/12CE	4.0	3.5	2.7	—	—	2.1	7.2	6.3	2.5-3.0	7
12CD/12CJ	4.0	3.5	2.7	—	—	2.1	7.2*	6.3	2.5-3.0	15
MGB 18G	4.5	4.0	5.6	6.0	—	2.8	10.0	6.0	1.5-2.0	7
18GA	4.5	4.0	5.6	6.0	—	2.8	12.0	6.0	2.5-3.0	7
18GB	4.5	4.0	5.6	6.0	—	2.0	12.0	6.0	2.5-3.0	7
18GF/18GH/ 18GJ/18GK	4.5	4.5	6.0	7.0	12.7	2.0	12.0**	6.0	2.5-3.0	10
MGC 29GA	8.5	8.5	6.3	7.2	17.3	2.0	14.0	11.0	3.5-4.0	14
MG 1100 10GR	5.1	4.6	***	***	***	***	8.0	4.0	2.5-3.0	13

*—12CJ—6.0 gallons.
**—18GJ and 18GK—10.0 gallons.
***—The 4-speed transmission and the differential are incorporated into the crankcase and are lubricated by the engine oil.

Brake Specifications (in.)

Model & Engine	Type (Lockheed) Front	Type (Lockheed) Rear	Brake Cylinder Bore: Master Cylinder	Brake Cylinder Bore: Wheel Cylinder Front	Brake Cylinder Bore: Wheel Cylinder Rear	Disc/Drum Diameter Front	Disc/Drum Diameter Rear
Midget 9CG	drum	drum	7/8	15/16	¾	7.0	7.0
10CG/10CC	disc	drum	3/4	2¼	¾	8¼	7.0
12CC/12CE/ 12CD/12CJ/	disc	drum	1 1/16*	2¼	¾	8¼	7.0
MGB All Engine Series	disc	drum	3/4**	2⅜	¾***	10¾	10.0
MGC 29GA	disc	drum	1.0	N.A.	N.A.	11.0	9.0
MG 1100 10GR	disc	drum	7/10	2¼	¾	8.0	8.0

*—3/4 in. up to vehicle number G-AN4/60,440.
**—1 1/16 in. from vehicle number G-HN4/ 138,401 (Conv.), and G-HD3/138,401 (GT).
***—13/16 in. from vehicle number G-HD3/ 138,401 (GT only).

Chassis and Wheel Alignment Specifications

Model & Engine	Wheelbase (in.)	Track (in.) Front	Track (in.) Rear	Caster (deg.) Range	Caster (deg.) Ideal	Camber (deg.) Range	Camber (deg.) Ideal	Toe-In (in.)	King-Pin Inclination (deg.)	Wheel Pivot Ratio (deg.) Inner	Wheel Pivot Ratio (deg.) Outer
Midget 9CG/10CG/ 10CC	80	45¾	44¾	—	3P	—	¾N	⅛	6¾	20	18½
12CC/12CE/ 12CD/12CJ	80	46 5/16	45¼	—	3P	—	¾N	⅛	6¾	20	19¾
MGB All Engine Series	91	49¼	49¼	5P-7¼P	7P	¼N-1¼P	1P	1/16	8	20	19
MGC 29GA	91	50	49¼	4P-5¼P	5P	1N-⅙P	0	1/16	9	18¾	20
MG 1100 10GR	93½	51½	50⅞	4½P-6½P	5½P	¼N-1¾P	¾P	1/16*	10	21½	20

*—1/16 in. front and rear wheel *toe-out*.

Fuse Specifications

Midget, up to G-AN5 series

1 Regulator
2 35 amp. fuse protecting circuits that operate independently of the ignition switch
3 Fuse block
4 35 amp. fuse protecting circuits that operate only with the ignition switched on
5 Spare fuses

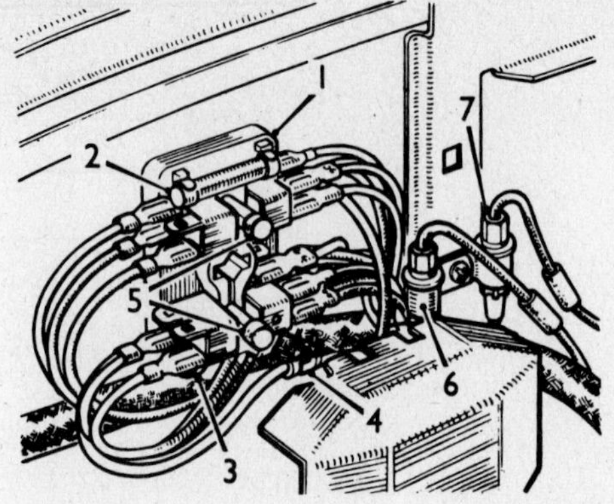

MGB, up to G-HN5 and G-HD5 series; and MGC

1 Fuse block
2 35 amp. fuse protecting circuits that operate independently of the ignition switch
3 35 amp. fuse protecting circuits that operate only with the ignition switched on
4 10 amp. inline fuses protect the windshield wipers and washers, heater blower, emergency flashers, radio, and heated rear window (GT only)
5 Spare fuses
6 10 amp. inline fuse protecting the tail lights
7 10 amp. inline fuse protecting the parking lights

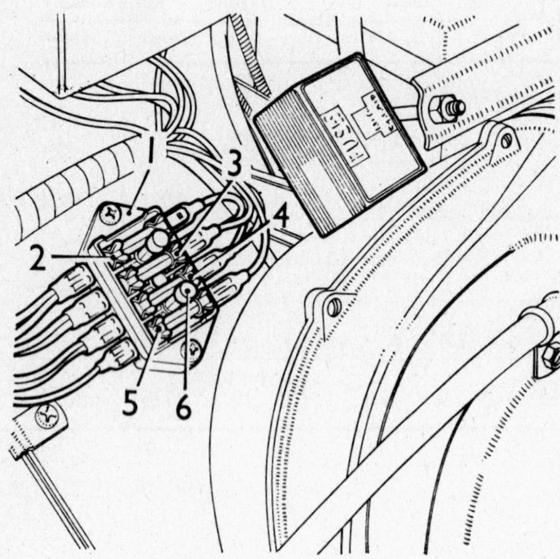

Midget, G-AN5 series

1 Fuse block
2 35 amp. fuse protecting the parking lights
3 35 amp. fuse protecting the tail lights
4 35 amp. fuse protecting circuits that operate only with the ignition switched on
5 35 amp. fuse protecting circuits that operate independently of the ignition switch
6 Spare fuses

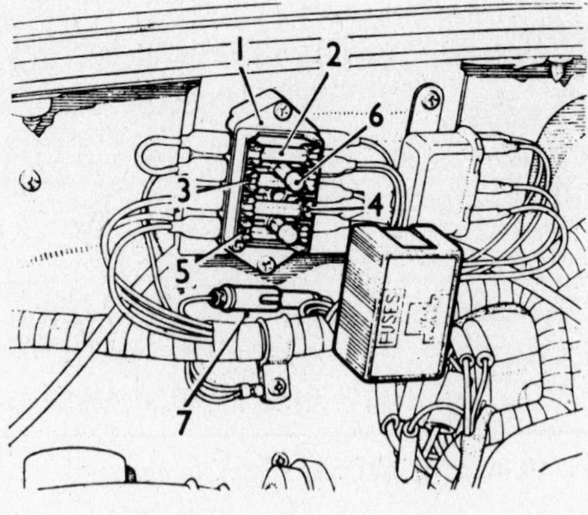

MGB, G-HN5 and G-HD5 series

1 Fuse block
2 35 amp. fuse protecting the parking lights
3 35 amp. fuse protecting the tail lights
4 35 amp. fuse protecting circuits that operate only with the ignition switched on
5 35 amp. fuse protecting circuits that operate independently of the ignition switch
6 Spare fuses
7 10 amp. inline fuses protect the windshield wipers and washers, heater blower, emergency flashers, radio, and heated rear window (GT only)

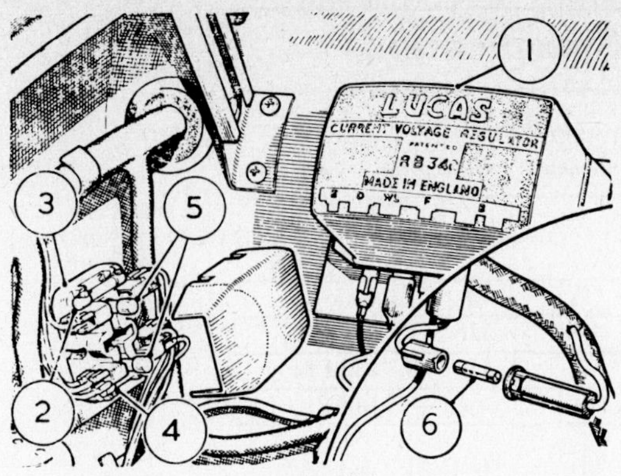

MG 1100

1 Regulator
2 35 amp. fuse protecting circuits that operate independently of the ignition switch
3 Fuse block
4 35 amp. fuse protecting circuits that operate only with the ignition switched on
5 Spare fuses
6 Inline fuse protecting the parking and tail lights

Distributor Specifications

Model & Engine	*Distributor Type (Lucas)*	*Serial Number*	*Centrifugal Advance*			*Vacuum Advance*			*Maximum Distributor Advance (deg. @ rpm)*
			Start (deg. @ rpm)	*Intermediate (deg. @ rpm)*	*Finish (deg. @ rpm)*	*Start (in. Hg.)*	*Finish (in. Hg.)*	*Maximum (deg.)*	
Midget									
9CG	DM2P4	40752**	0-3@750	16@1,800	26@5,000	5	12	12	28@5,000
10CG/10CC	25D4	40919**	0-3@800	16@1,800	32@5,500	4	13	20	32@5,500
12CC/12CE	23D4	40819*	0-3@600	15@2,000	27@6,000	—	—	—	27@6,000
	25D4	41198	1@600	14@2,000	24@5,600	5	8	4-8	24@5,600
12CD/12CJ	25D4	41229	4@600	19@2,500	30@4,300	5	8	4-8	30@4,300
MGB									
18G/18GA/ 18GB/18GF	25D4	40897**	6@600	15@1,600	20@2,200	5	13	20	28@2,200
18GH/18GJ	25D4	41155	10@500	24@1,600	30@3,000	5	13	15	35@3,000
18GK	25D4	41339	10@1,000	24@2,800	30@4,600	7	13	10	30@4,600
MGC									
29GA	25D6	41201	0-6@700	18@2,500	26@5,300	2	6	6	28@5,300
MG 1100									
10GR	25D4	40853**	0-3@700	21@2,800	30@5,000	5	14	7	32@5,000

*—Centrifugal advance only.
**—Distributor advance characteristics should be checked while the distributor is *decelerating* from its maximum speed.

Carburetor Specifications

Model/ Engine	S.U. Type	Throat Diameter (in.)	Main Jet Size (in.)	Jet Needle**** Identification No. Standard	Rich	Lean	Piston Spring Strength (Color identification)
Midget							
9CG	HS2	1.25	.090	V3	V2	GX	light blue
10CG	HS2	1.25	.090	GY	M	GG	blue
10CC	HS2	1.25	.090	AN	H6	GG	blue
12CC/12CE	HS2	1.25	.090	AN	H6	GG	light blue
12CD/12CJ	HS2	1.25	.090	AAC*	—	—	blue
MGB							
18G/18GA	HS4	1.50	.090	MB	6	21	red
18GB	HS4	1.50	.090	FX	6	21	red
18GF/18GH	HS4	1.50	.090	AAL**	—	—	red
18GJ	HS4	1.50	.090	AAE**	—	—	red
18GK	HS4	1.50	.090	AAL	—	—	red
MGC							
29GA	HS6	1.75	.100	BAD***	—	—	yellow
MG 1100							
10GR	HS2	1.25	.090	D3	D6	GV	blue

*—Fixed needle—AN.
**—Fixed needle—FX.
***—Fixed needle—KM.
****—Most emission control engines are fitted with spring-loaded jet needles.

Light Bulb Specifications**

Model/Year	Exterior							Interior		Instrument Panel				
	Front Parking	Front Turn Signal	Stop/Tail	Rear Turn Signal	License	Back-up	Side Marker	Courtesy	Map	Turn Signal Indicator	Engine Warning	Emergency Flashers	Brake Warning	Instrument Illumination
Midget 1961-67	380	382	380	382	989	382	—	—	987	280	987	—	—	987
MGB 1961-67	989	382	380	382	207	382	—	—	987	280	987	—	—	987
MG 1100 1962-67	989	382	380	382	207	—	—	—	281	280	281	—	—	987
Midget 1968-69	380	382	380	382	989	273	—	—	987	987	281	987	280	987
MGB & MGC 1968-69	989	382	380	382	207	273	—	254*	987	987	987	987	280	987
Midget 1970-72	380	382	380	382	989	273	989	—	987	280	281	281	987	987
MGB 1970-72	380	382	380	382	501	273	989	254*	987	987	987	281	987	987

*—GT only.
**—Lucas bulb part numbers.

Wiring Diagrams

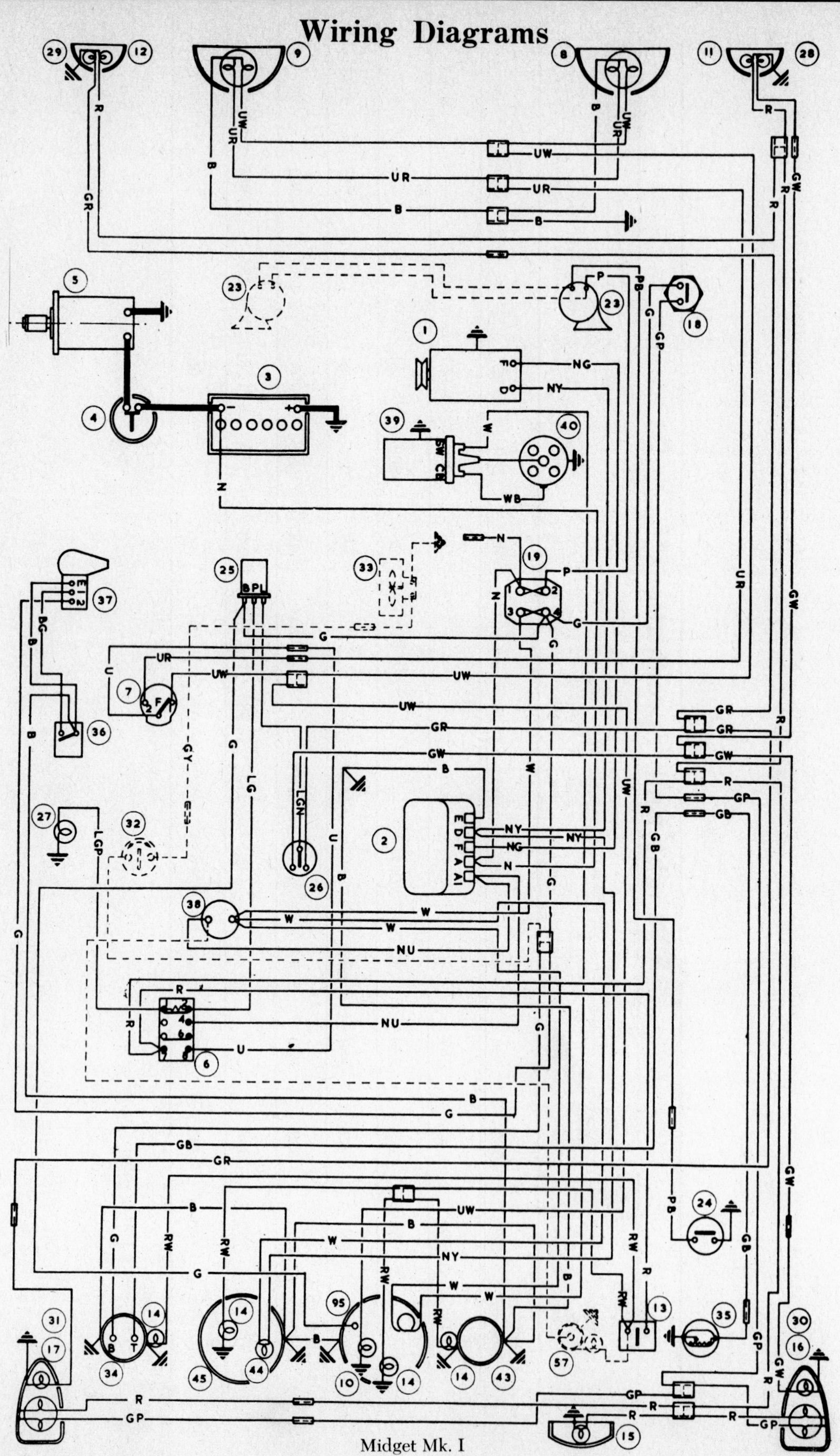

Midget Mk. I

Please see page 767 for wiring diagram key

1 Generator
2 Regulator
3 Battery—12-volt
4 Starter switch
5 Starter motor
6 Lighting switch
7 Headlamp dimmer switch
8 Headlamp—R.H.
9 Headlamp—L.H.
10 High-beam warning lamp
11 R.H. parking lamp
12 L.H. parking lamp
13 Panel lamp switch
14 Panel lamps
15 License lamp
16 Stop and tail lamp—R.H.
17 Stop and tail lamp—L.H.
18 Stop lamp switch
19 Fuse unit
23 Horn (with horns when fitted)
24 Horn-push
25 Flasher unit
26 Turn signal switch
27 Turn signal warning lamp
28 Front turn signal—R.H.
29 Front turn signal—L.H.
30 Rear turn signal—R.H.
31 Rear turn signal—L.H.
32 Heater or fresh-air motor switch (when fitted)
33 Heater or fresh-air motor (when fitted)
34 Fuel gauge
35 Fuel gauge tank unit
36 Windshield wiper switch
37 Windshield wiper motor
38 Ignition switch
39 Ignition coil
40 Distributor
43 Oil pressure gauge
44 Ignition warning lamp
45 Speedometer
57 Cigar-lighter (when fitted)
95 Tachometer (electric) (later cars)

CABLE COLOR CODE

N. Brown.	P. Purple.	W. White.
U. Blue.	G. Green.	Y. Yellow.
R. Red.	LG. Light Green	B. Black.

When a cable has two color code letters the first denotes the main color and the second denotes the tracer color.

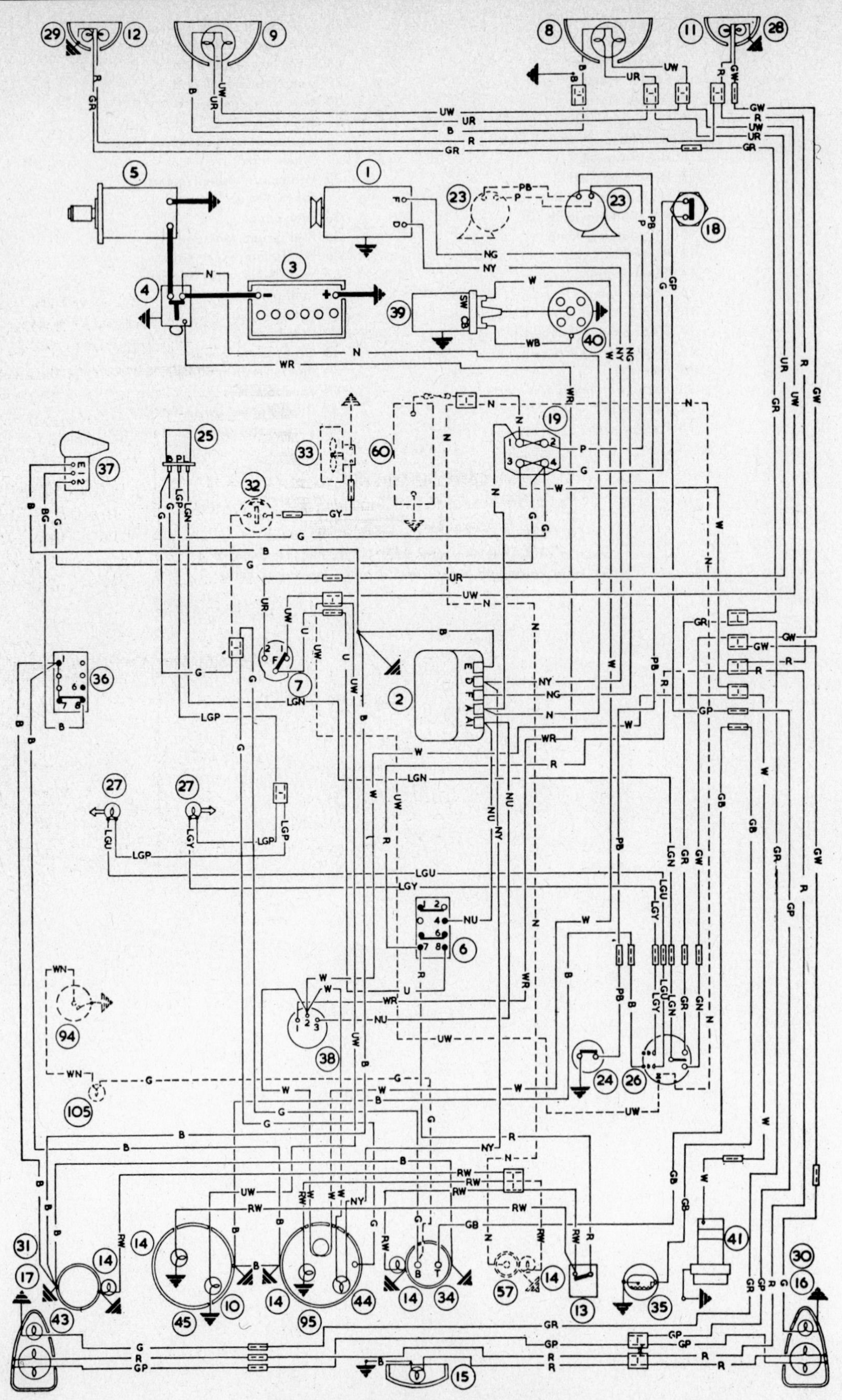

Midget Mk. II & III, positive ground

Please see page 773 for wiring diagram key

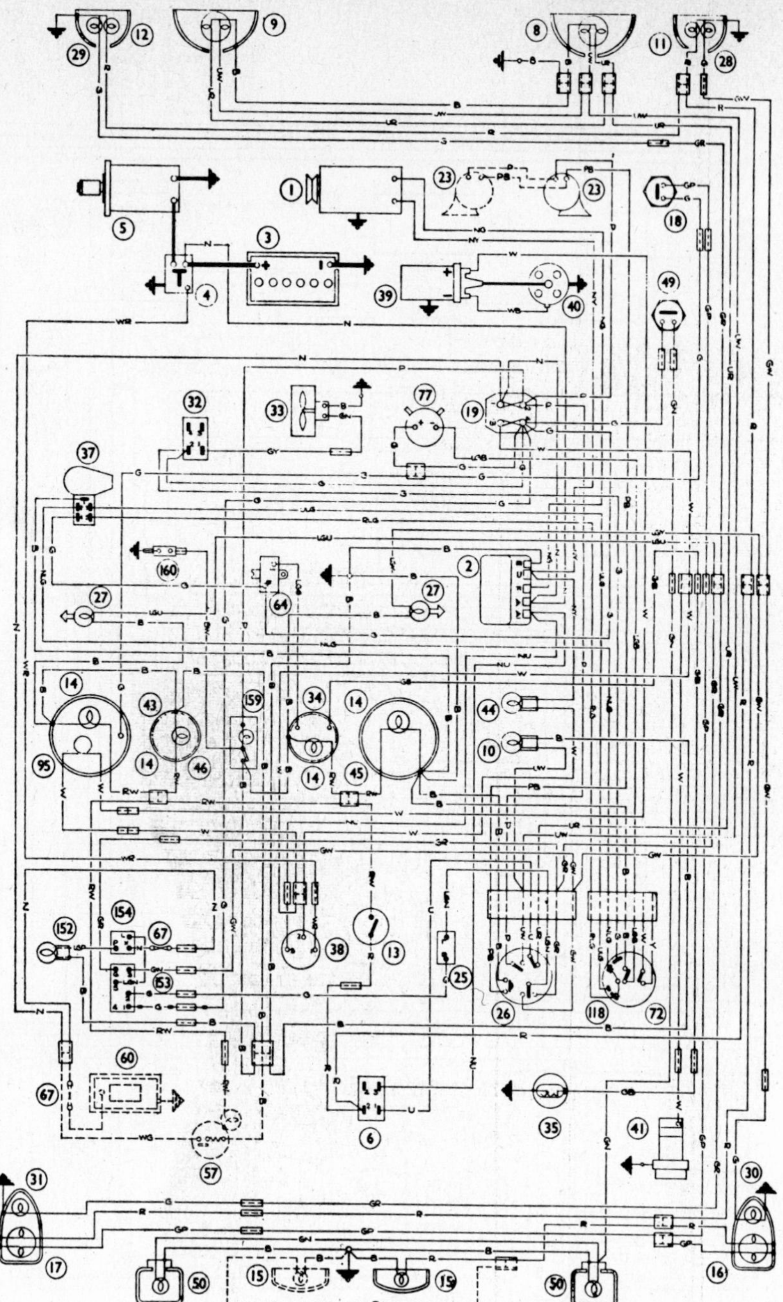

Midget Mk. III from car number G-AN4/60,460, negative ground

Please see page 773 for wiring diagram key

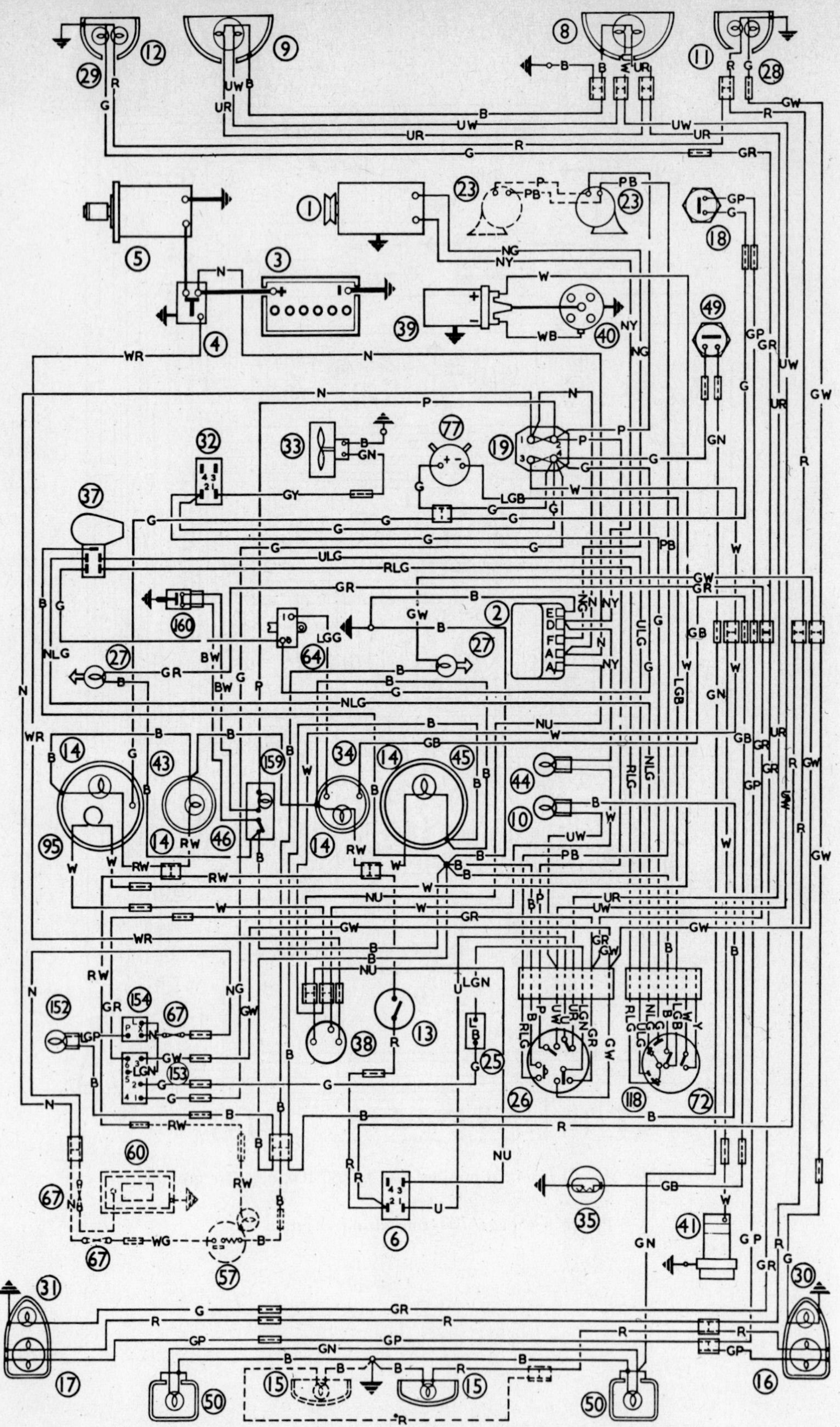

Midget Mk. III from car number G-AN4/66,226, negative ground

Please see page 773 for wiring diagram key

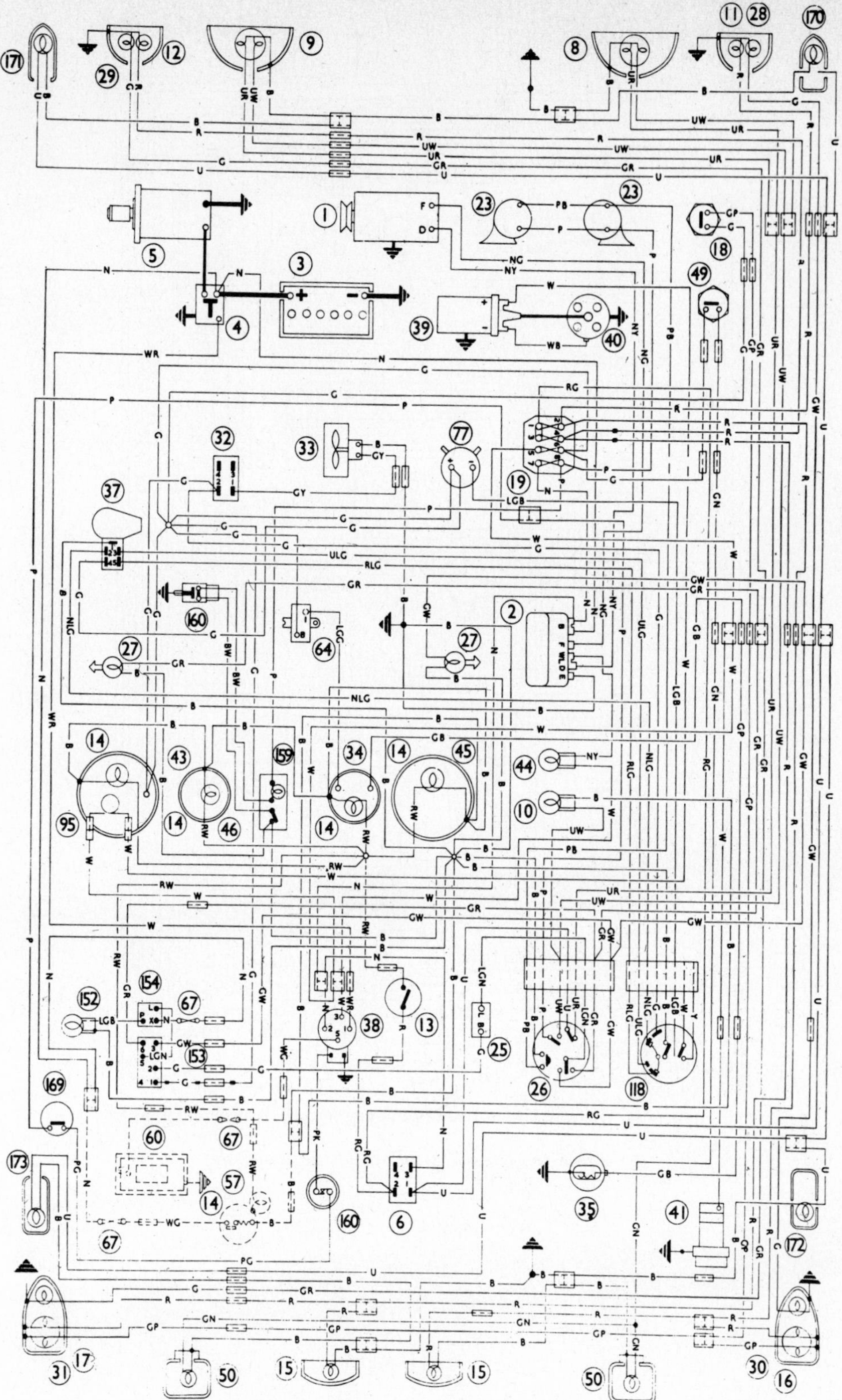

Midget Mk. III from car number G-AN5/74,886, negative ground

Please see page 773 for wiring diagram key

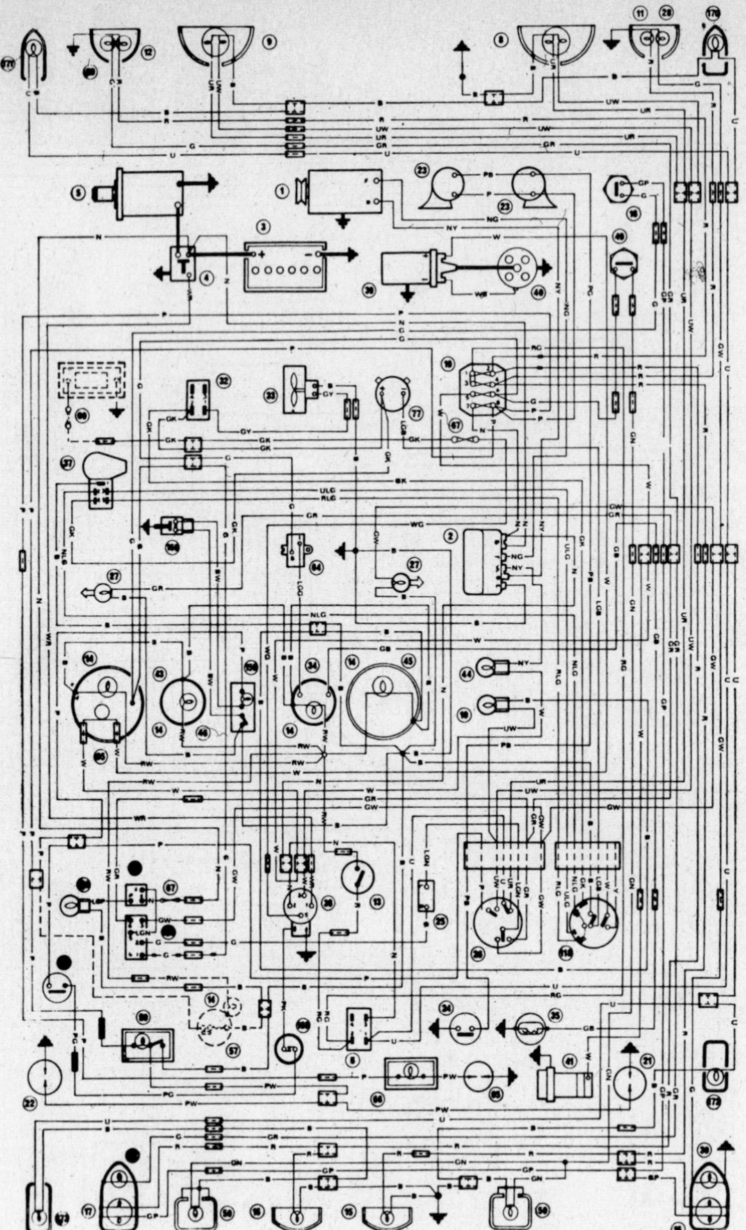

Midget Mk. III from late 1970 (12CJ engine) to 1972, negative ground

Please see page 773 for wiring diagram key

1 Generator
2 Regulator
3 Battery
4 Starter solenoid
5 Starter motor
6 Lighting switch
7 Headlamp dimmer switch
8 R.H. headlamp
9 L.H. headlamp
10 High-beam warning lamp
11 R.H. parking lamp
12 L.H. parking lamp
13 Panel lamp switch
14 Panel lamps
15 License lamp
16 R.H. stop and tail lamp
17 L.H. stop and tail lamp
18 Stop lamp switch
19 Fuse unit
23 Horns
25 Flasher unit
26 Combined direction indicator/headlamp flasher
or
26 Combined direction indicator/headlamp flasher/ high-beam lamp/hornpush switch
27 Turn signal warning lamp
28 R.H. front turn signal
29 L.H. front turn signal
30 R.H. rear turn signal
31 L.H. rear turn signal
32 Heater blower switch
33 Heater blower
34 Fuel gauge
35 Fuel gauge tank unit
37 Windshield wiper motor
38 Ignition/starter switch
39 Ignition coil
40 Distributor
41 Fuel pump
43 Oil pressure gauge
44 Ignition warning lamp
45 Speedometer
46 Radiator temperature gauge
49 Back-up light switch
50 Back-up light
57 Cigar-lighter—illuminated
60 Radio
64 Bi-metal instrument voltage stabilizer
67 Line fuse
77 Windshield washer pump
94 Oil filter switch
95 Tachometer
105 Oil filter warning lamp
118 Combined windshield washer and wiper switch
152 Hazard warning lamp
153 Hazard warning switch
154 Hazard warning flasher unit
159 Brake pressure warning lamp and lamp test push
160 Brake pressure failure switch
168 Ignition key audible warning buzzer
169 Ignition key audible warning door switch
170 R.H. front side marker lamp
171 L.H. front side marker lamp
172 R.H. rear side marker lamp
173 L.H. rear side marker lamp

CABLE COLOR CODE

N. Brown.	P. Purple.	W. White.
U. Blue.	G. Green.	Y. Yellow.
R. Red.	LG. Light Green	B. Black.

When a cable has two color code letters the first denotes the main color and the second denotes the tracer color.

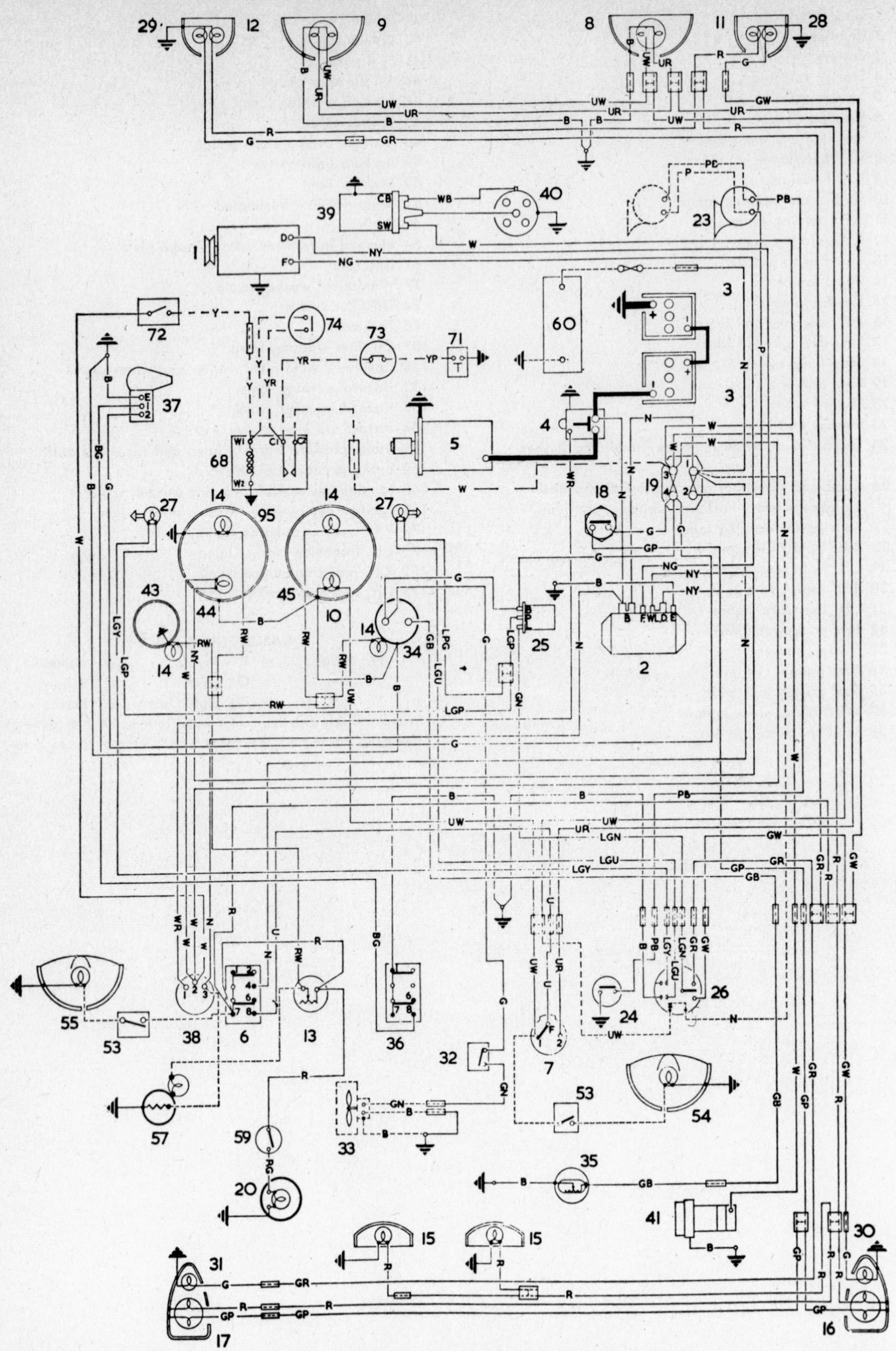

MGB car numbers G-HN3/101-48,765 (Conv.), positive ground

Please see page 780 for wiring diagram key

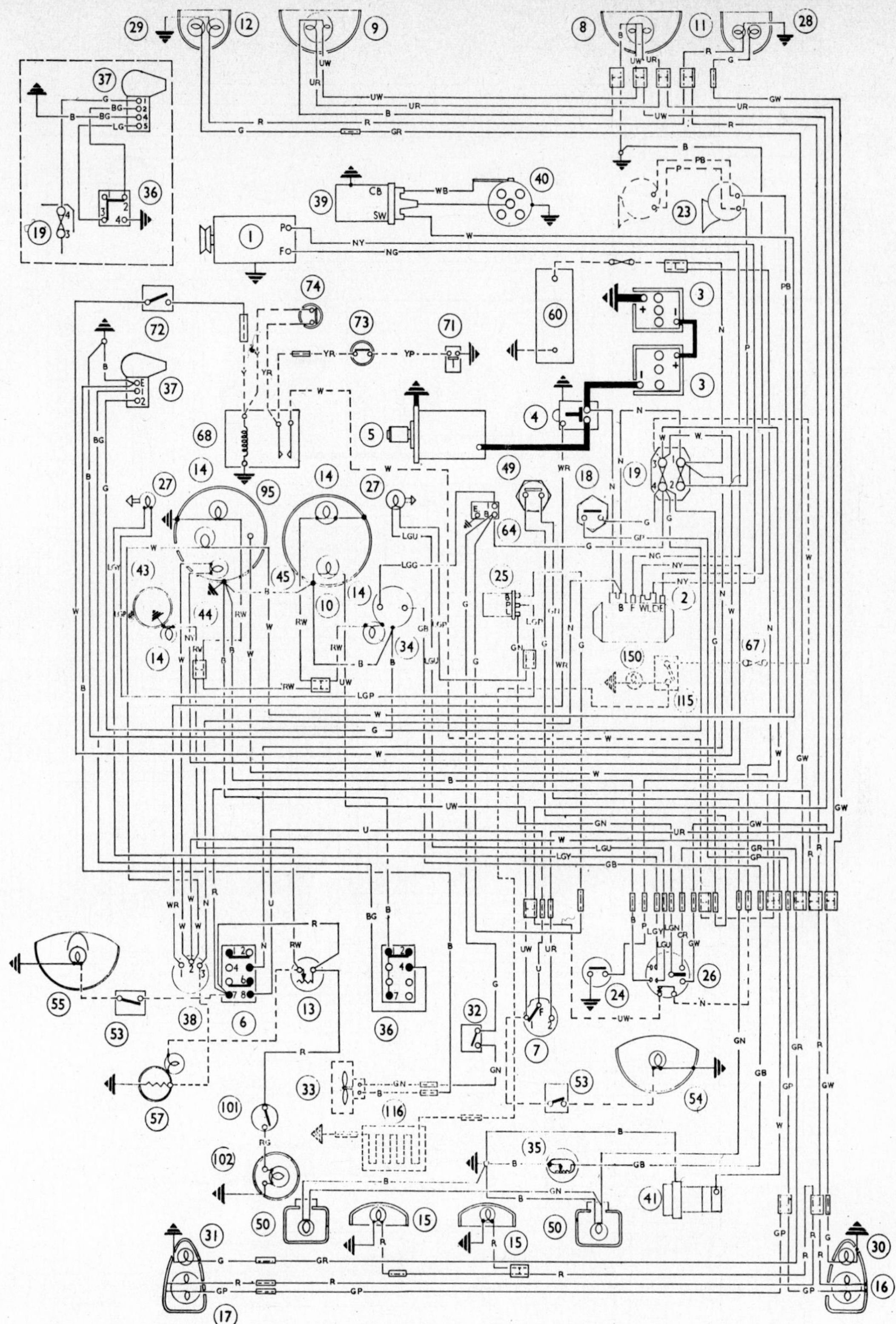

MGB from car number G-HN3/48,766 (Conv.) and G-HD3/71,933 (GT), positive ground

Please see page 780 for wiring diagram key

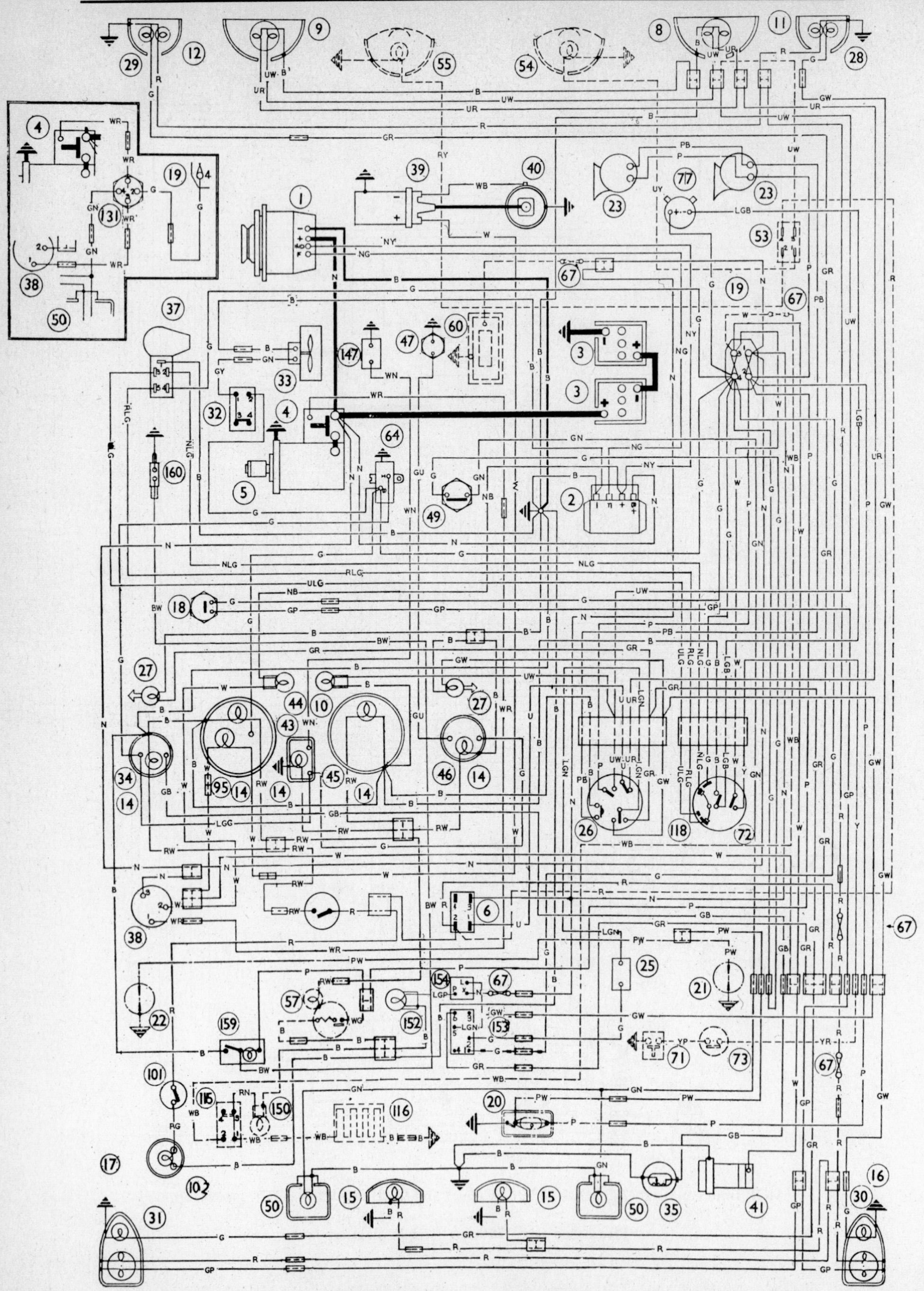

MGB from car number G-HN4/138,401 (Conv.) and G-HD4/139,472 (GT), negative ground

Please see page 780 for wiring diagram key

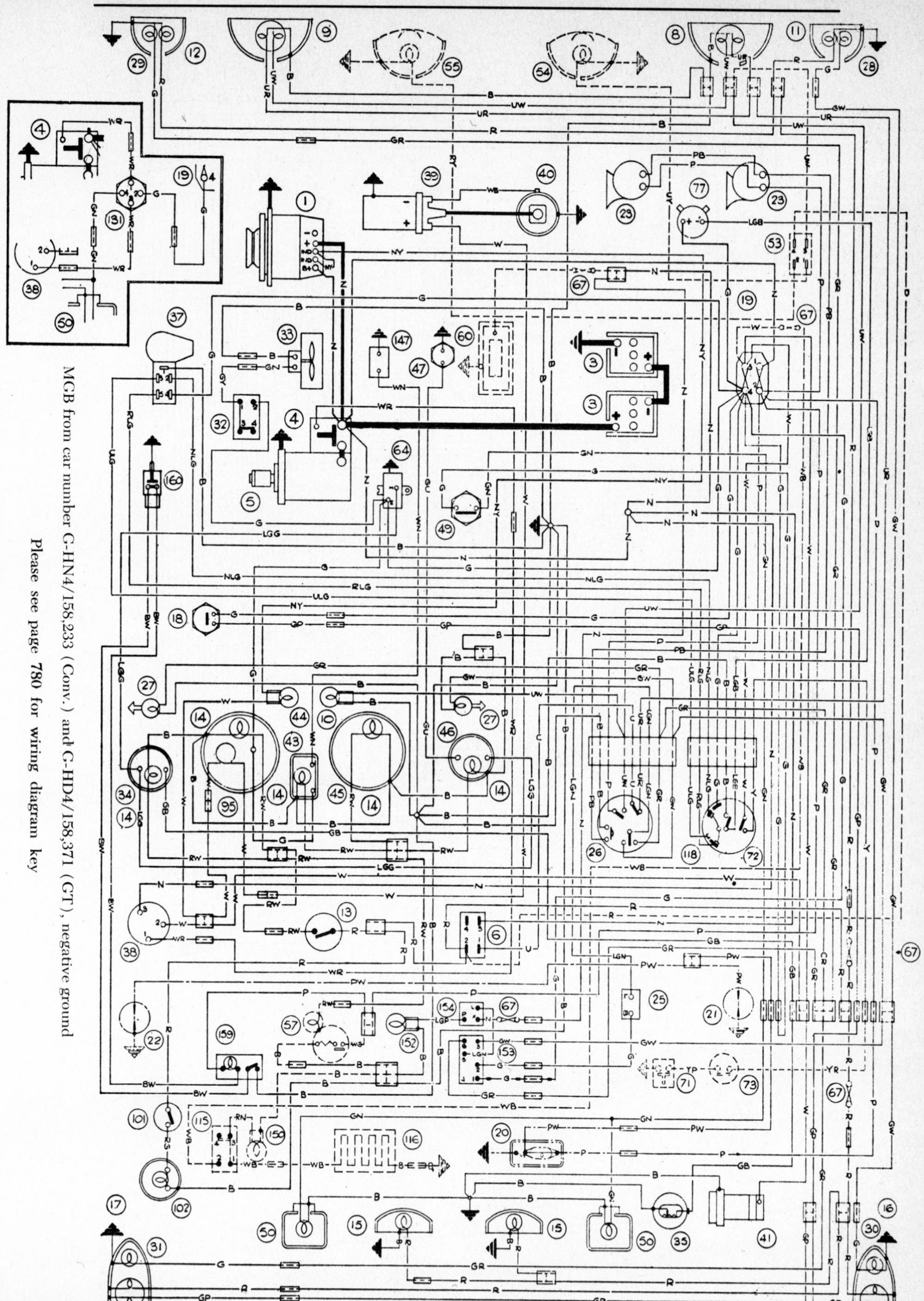

MGB from car number G-HN4/158,233 (Conv.) and G-HD4/158,371 (GT), negative ground

Please see page 780 for wiring diagram key

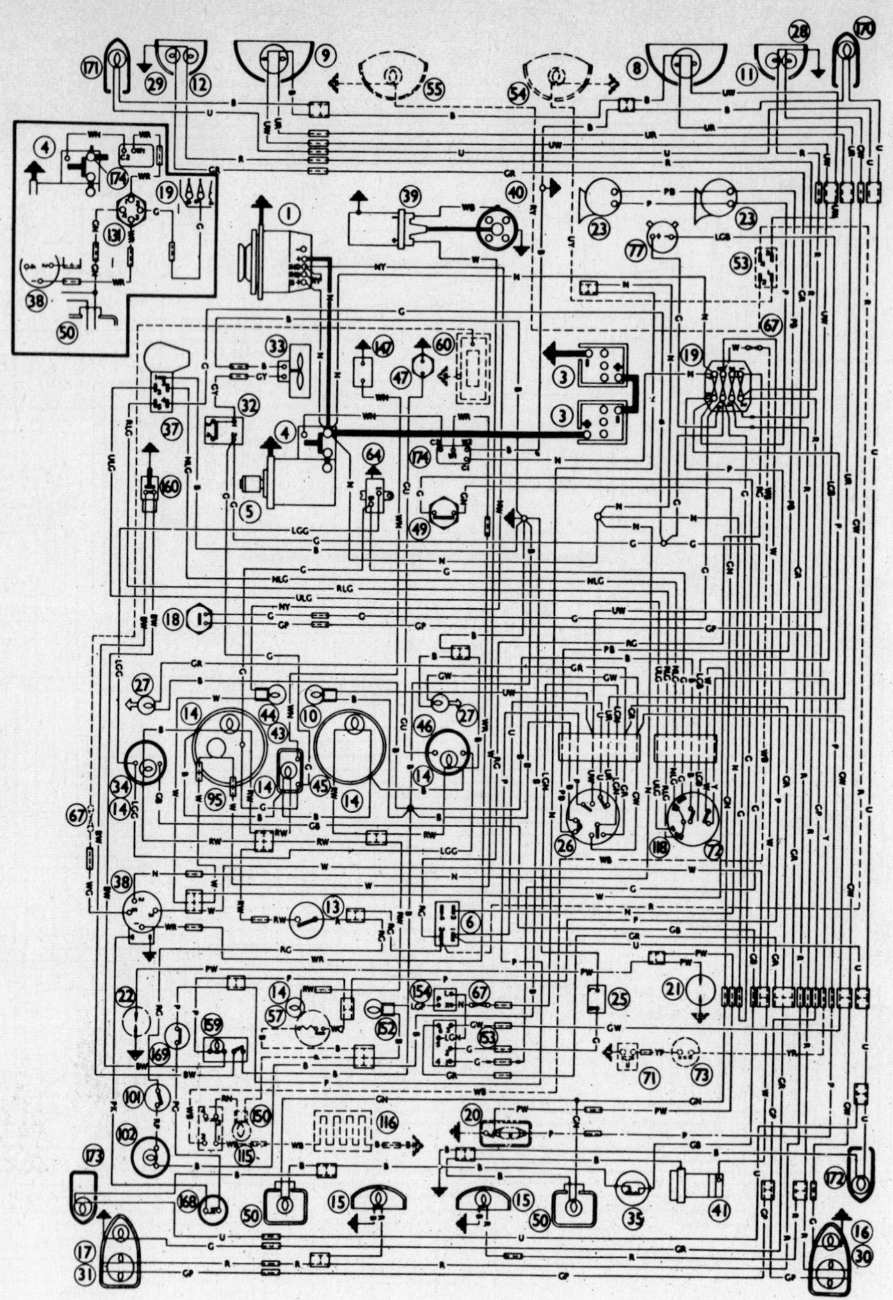

MGB from car number G-HN5/187,170 (Conv.) and G-HD5/187,841 (GT), negative ground

Please see page 780 for wiring diagram key

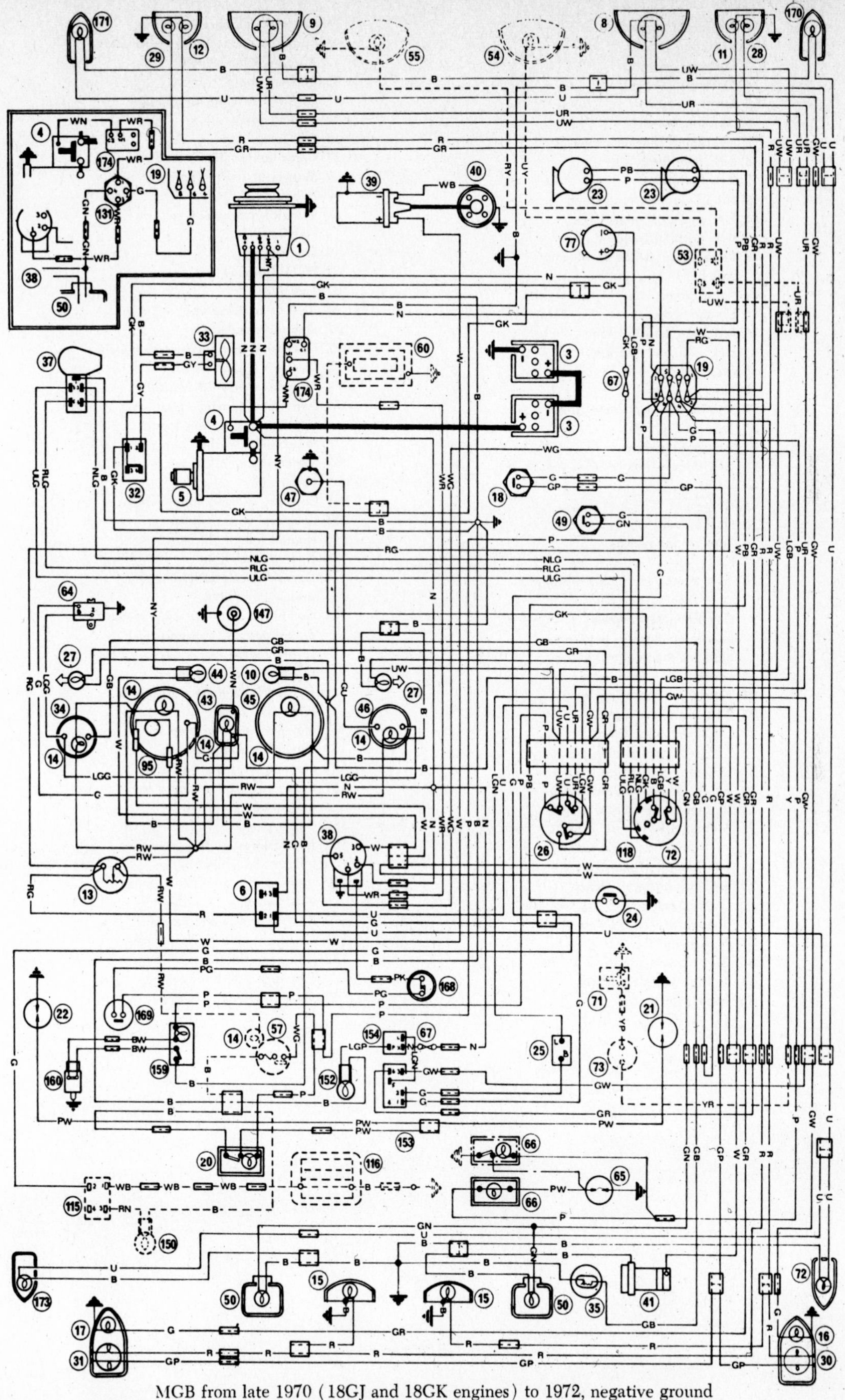

MGB from late 1970 (18GJ and 18GK engines) to 1972, negative ground

Please see page 780 for wiring diagram key

1 Alternator or generator
2 Regulator
3 Batteries—6-volt
4 Starter solenoid
5 Starter motor
6 Lighting switch
7 Headlamp dimmer switch
8 R.H. headlamp
9 L.H. headlamp
10 High-beam warning lamp
11 R.H. parking lamp
12 L.H. parking lamp
13 Panel lamp switch or rheostat switch
14 Panel lamps
15 License lamp
16 R.H. stop and tail lamp
17 L.H. stop and tail lamp
18 Stop lamp switch
19 Fuse unit
20 Interior courtesy lamp or map light (early cars)
21 R.H. door switch
22 L.H. door switch
23 Horns
24 Horn-push
25 Flasher unit
26 Turn signal switch
or
26 Turn signal/headlamp flasher
or
26 Combined turn signal/headlamp flasher/headlamp high-low beam/horn-push switch
27 Turn signal warning lamps
28 R.H. front turn signal
29 L.H. front turn signal
30 R.H. rear turn signal
31 L.H. rear turn signal
32 Heater blower motor switch
33 Heater blower motor
34 Fuel gauge
35 Fuel gauge tank unit
36 Windshield wiper switch
38 Ignition/starter switch
39 Ignition coil
40 Distributor
41 Fuel pump
43 Oil pressure gauge
44 Ignition warning lamp
45 Speedometer
46 Radiator temperature gauge
47 Radiator temperature transmitter
49 Back-up lamp switch
50 Back-up lamp
53 Fog and driving lamp switch
54 Driving lamp
55 Fog lamp
57 Cigar-lighter illuminated
59 Map light switch (early cars)
60 Radio
64 Bi-metal instrument voltage stabilizer
65 Trunk lamp
65 Trunk lamp switch
67 Line fuse
68 Overdrive relay unit
71 Overdrive solenoid
72 Overdrive manual control switch
73 Overdrive gear switch
74 Overdrive throttle switch
76 Automatic gearbox gear selector illumination lamp
77 Windshield washer pump
82 Switch illumination lamp
95 Tachometer
101 Courtesy or map light switch
102 Courtesy or map light
115 Heated back-light switch } GT only
116 Heated back-light } GT only
118 Combined windshield washer and wiper switch
131 Combined back-up lamp switch and automatic transmission safety switch
147 Oil pressure transmitter
150 Heated back-light warning lamp (GT only)
152 Hazard warning lamp
153 Hazard warning switch
154 Hazard warning flasher unit
159 Brake pressure warning lamp and lamp test push
160 Brake pressure failure switch
168 Ignition key audible warning buzzer
169 Ignition key audible warning door switch
170 R.H. front side marker lamp
171 L.H. front side marker lamp
172 R.H. rear side marker lamp
173 L.H. rear side marker lamp
174 Starter solenoid relay

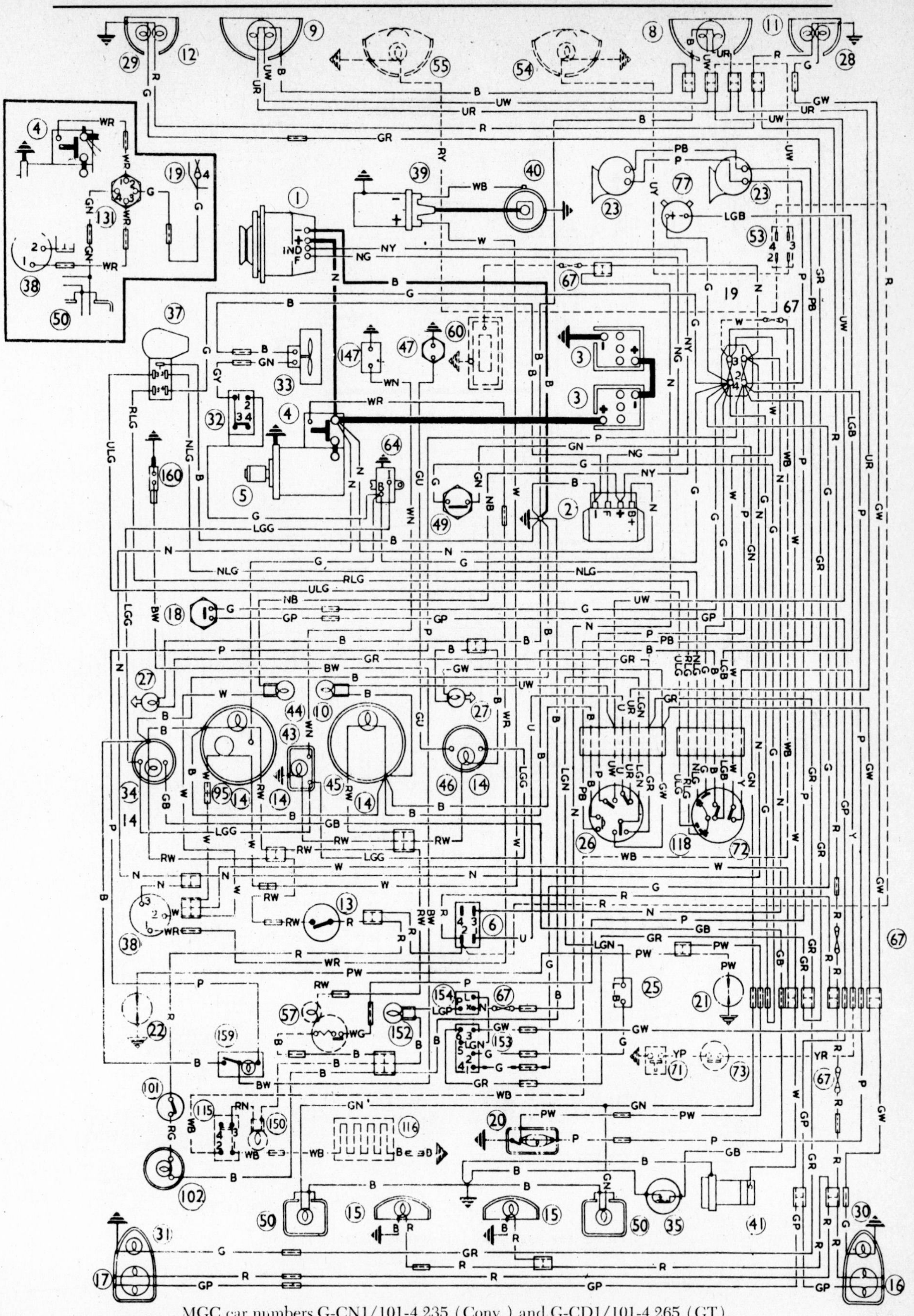

MGC car numbers G-CN1/101-4,235 (Conv.) and G-CD1/101-4,265 (GT)

Please see page 783 for wiring diagram key

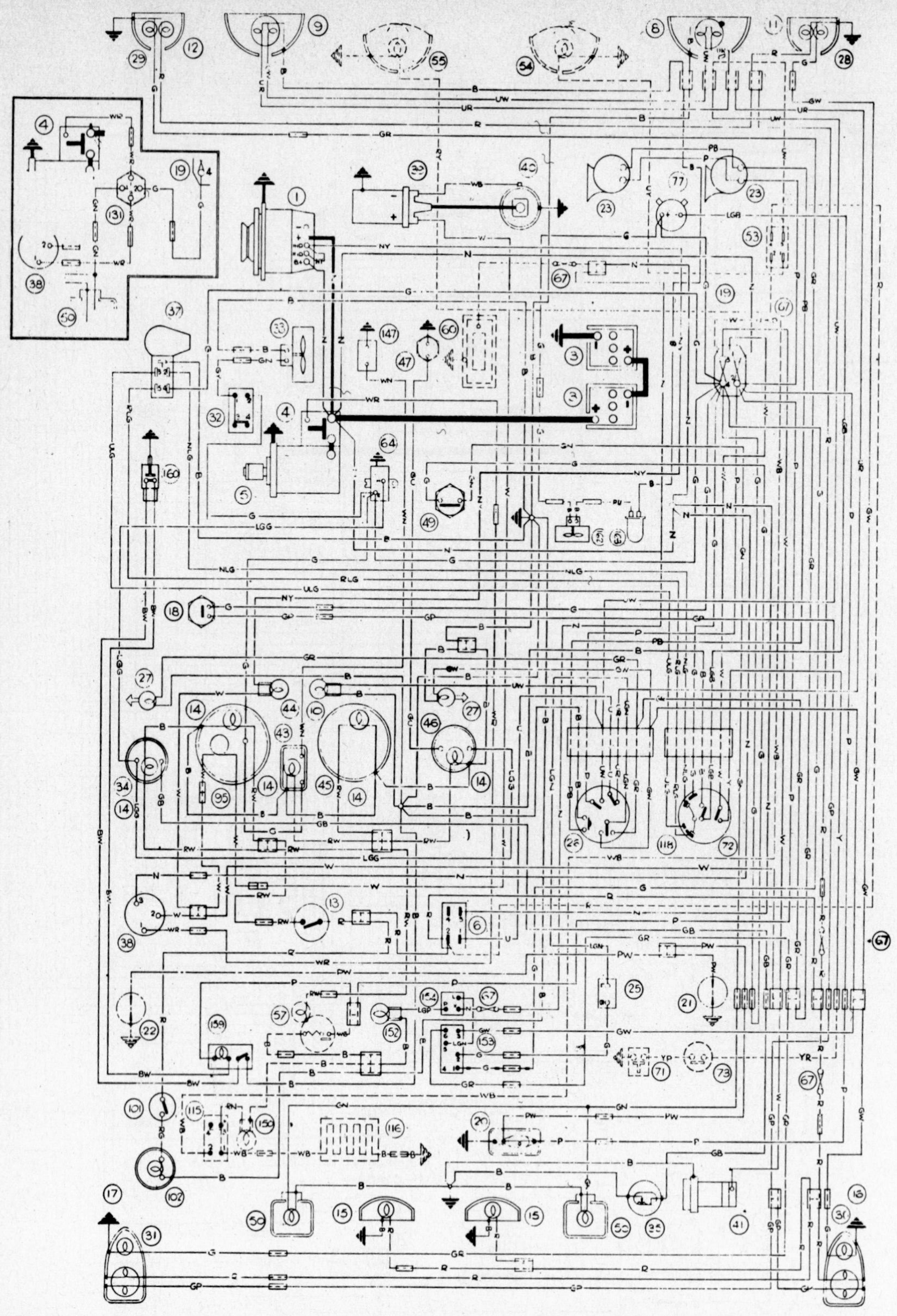

MGC from car number G-CN1/4,236 (Conv.) and G-CD1/4,266 (GT)

Please see page 783 for wiring diagram key

1 Alternator
2 Regulator
3 Battery
4 Starter solenoid
5 Starter motor
6 Lighting switch
7 Headlight dimmer switch
8 RH headlamp
9 LH headlamp
10 High-beam warning lamp
11 RH parking lamp
12 LH parking lamp
13 Panel lamp switch
14 Panel lamps
15 License lamp
16 RH stop and tail lamp
17 LH stop and tail lamp
18 Stop lamp switch
19 Fuse unit
20 Interior lamp } GT only
21 RH door switch } GT only
22 LH door switch } GT only
23 Horns
24 Horn-push
25 Flasher unit
26 Turn signal and headlight flasher switch
27 Turn signal warning lamp
28 RH front turn signal
29 LH front turn signal
30 RH rear turn signal
31 LH rear turn signal
32 Heater blower motor switch
33 Heater blower motor
34 Fuel gauge
35 Fuel gauge tank unit
36 Windshield wiper switch
37 Windshield wiper motor
38 Ignition/starter switch
39 Ignition coil
40 Distributor
41 Fuel pump
43 Oil pressure gauge
44 Ignition warning lamp
45 Speedometer
46 Radiator temperature gauge
47 Radiator temperature transmitter
49 Back-up lamp switch
50 Back-up lamp
53 Fog and driving lamp switch
54 Driving lamp
55 Fog lamp
57 Cigar-lighter—illuminated
60 Radio
64 Bi-metal instrument voltage stabilizer
67 Line fuse (when fitted)
71 Overdrive solenoid
72 Overdrive manual control switch
73 Overdrive gear switch
76 Automatic gearbox gear selector illumination lamp
77 Windshield washer pump
82 Switch illumination lamp
95 Tachometer
101 Map light switch
102 Map light
115 Heated back-light switch } GT only
116 Heated back-light } GT only
131 Combined back-up lamp switch and automatic transmission safety switch
150 Heated back-light warning lamp (GT only)
152 Hazard warning lamp
153 Hazard warning switch
154 Hazard warning flasher unit
159 Brake pressure warning lamp and lamp test push
160 Brake pressure failure switch
162 Blower motor—carburetor
163 Thermostat—blower motor—carburetor

CABLE COLOR CODE

B. Black.	G. Green.	W. White.
U. Blue.	P. Purple.	Y. Yellow.
N. Brown.	R. Red.	LG. Light Green

When a cable has two color code letters the first denotes the main color and the second denotes the tracer color.

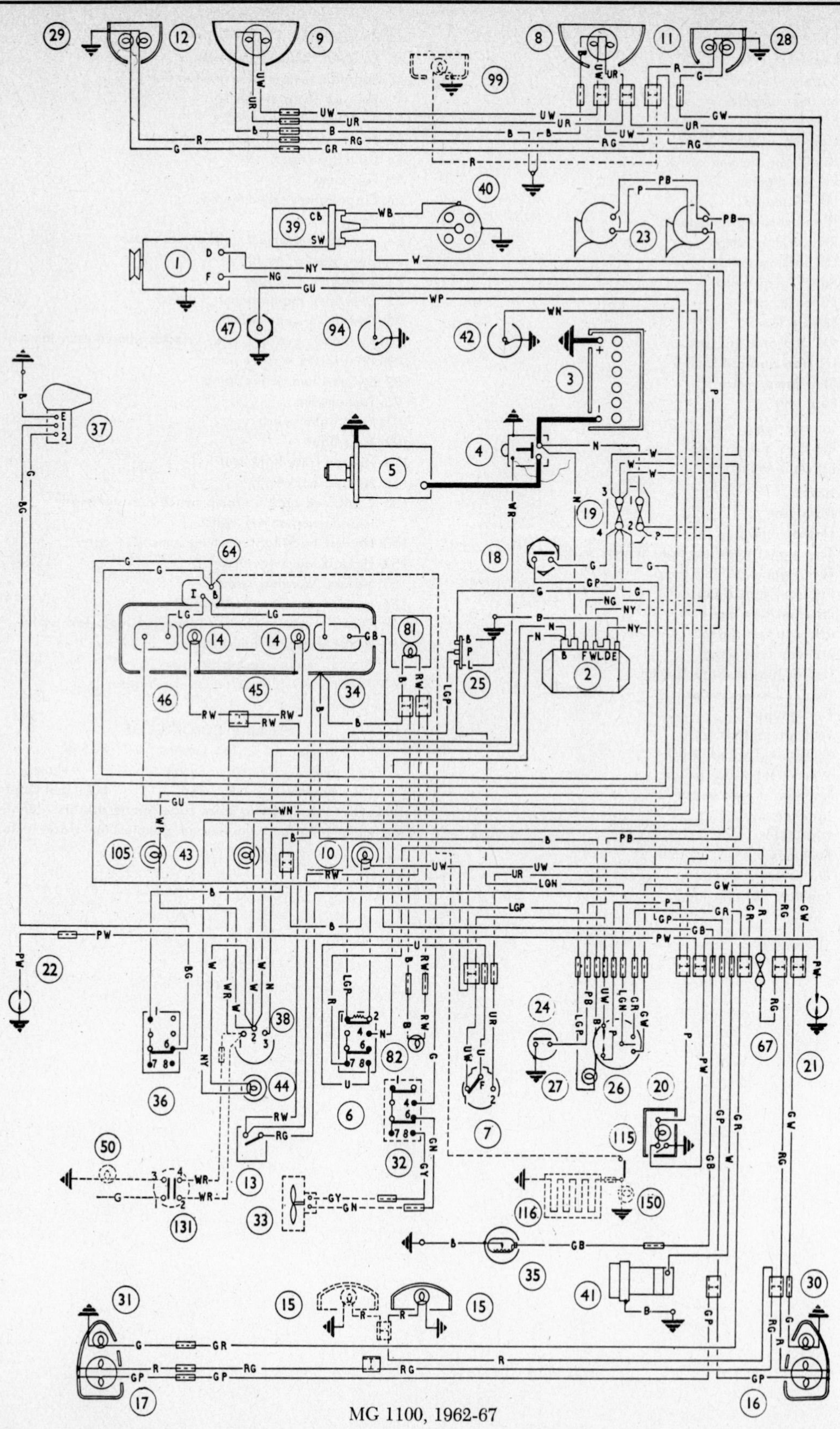

MG 1100, 1962-67

Please see page 785 for wiring diagram key

1 Generator
2 Regulator
3 Battery—12-volt
4 Starter solenoid
5 Starter motor
6 Lighting switch
7 Headlamp dimmer switch
8 Right-hand headlamp
9 Left-hand headlamp
10 High-beam warning lamp
11 Right-hand parking lamp
12 Left-hand parking lamp
13 Panel lamps switch
14 Panel lamps
15 License lamp
16 Right-hand stop and tail lamp
17 Left-hand stop and tail lamp
18 Stop lamp switch
19 Fuse unit (35-amp. 1-2, 34-amp. 3-4)
20 Interior lights
21 Right-hand door switch
22 Left-hand door switch
23 Horn
24 Horn-push
25 Flasher unit
26 Turn signal and headlamp flasher switch
27 Turn signal warning lamp
28 Right-hand front turn signal
29 Left-hand front turn signal
30 Right-hand rear turn signal
31 Left-hand rear turn signal
32 †Heater blower switch
33 †Heater blower
34 Fuel gauge
35 Fuel gauge tank unit
37 Windshield wiper motor
38 Ignition/starter switch
39 Ignition coil
40 Distributor
41 Fuel pump
43 Oil pressure gauge/warning lamp
44 Ignition warning lamp
45 Speedometer
46 Water temperature gauge
47 Water temperature transmitter
48 Ammeter (Princess)
49 †Back-up lamp switch
50 †Back-up lamp
53 Fog lamps switch (Princess)
54 Right-hand fog lamp (Princess)
55 Left-hand fog lamp (Princess)
56 Clock (Princess)
57 Cigar-lighter (Princess)
60 *Radio
64 Bi-metal instrument voltage stabilizer
65 Rear compartment light switch (early Countryman/Traveller)
66 Rear compartment light (early Countryman/Traveller)
67 Line fuse (35-amp.)
77 Electric windshield washer (Princess)
81 Ashtray illumination lamp
82 †Panel lamp-heater switch illumination
83 *Induction heater and thermostat
84 *Suction chamber heater
94 Oil filter switch
95 Tachometer (Riley)
99 Radiator badge lamp (Wolseley)
105 Oil filter warning lamp
115 *Rear window heater switch
116 *Rear window heater unit
118 Combined windshield washer and wiper switch (Princess)
131 Combined back-up light switch/automatic gearbox safety switch (when fitted)
150 *Rear window heater warning light

* Optional extra
† Optional extra/standard some models

CABLE COLOR CODE

N. Brown.	P. Purple.	W. White.
U. Blue.	G. Green.	Y. Yellow.
R. Red.	LG. Light Green	B. Black.

When a cable has two color code letters the first denotes the main color and the second denotes the tracer color.

Engine Electrical

DISTRIBUTOR

Distributor Removal and Installation

The distributor can be removed and replaced without disturbing the ignition timing, provided the pinch-bolt on the clamp that positions the distributor is not loosened.

Remove the distributor cap and disconnect the low tension lead from the terminal on the distributor. Disconnect the vacuum advance line (if applicable) from the diaphragm unit at the distributor.

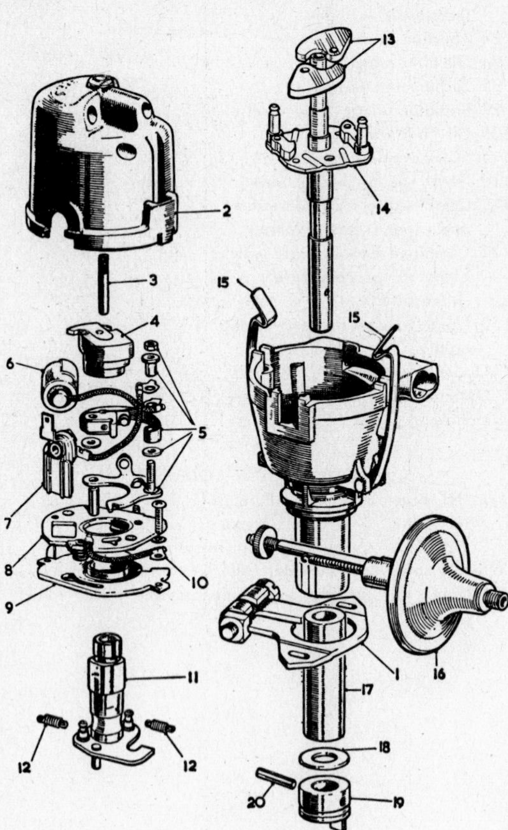

Lucas distributor components

1 Clamp
2 Distributor cap
3 Brush and spring
4 Rotor
5 Breaker points
6 Condenser
7 Low tension connector
8 Moving base plate
9 Stationary base plate
10 Ground wire
11 Cam
12 Centrifugal advance springs
13 Centrifugal advance weights
14 Centrifugal advance plate
15 Cap retaining clips
16 Vacuum advance unit
17 Bushing
18 Thrust washer
19 Driving dog
20 Retaining pin

NOTE: *On Midgets equipped with mechanically driven tachometers it will be necessary to unscrew the tachometer drive from its connection at the rear of the generator.*

Remove the bolts securing the distributor clamp to the cylinder block and lift the distributor out.

To replace the distributor, insert the shaft into the housing until the driving dog rests on the distributor drive shaft. Turn the rotor until the dog is felt to engage in the slot in the drive shaft. Both the driving dog and the slot are offset so that the distributor will not fall into place until it is properly positioned.

Turn the distributor body to align the clamp and housing bolt holes and replace the bolts. Replace the distributor cap, the vacuum advance line, the low tension lead from the coil, and reconnect the tachometer drive to the generator (if applicable).

Breaker Points—Remove and Replace

Remove the distributor. Lift the rotor from the distributor shaft. Make a careful note of the positions of the components so that they may be reassembled correctly.

Unscrew the nut from the moving contact return-spring locating pin and remove the plastic insulating sleeve and the condenser and low tension lead wires.

Remove the screw and washers holding the contact breaker plate and lift out the plate. Remove the condenser screw and lift out the condenser.

Thoroughly clean the distributor body and base plate, making sure that the base

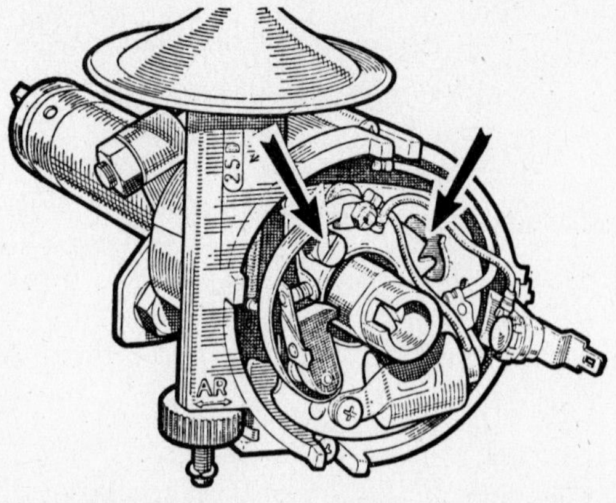

Point gap adjustment is made while the moving contact cam follower is on the high point of one of the cam lobes. Arrows point to the fixed contact securing screw and screwdriver adjustment notches

plate is left without an oily film that could insulate the contact breaker plate from the distributor base plate and prevent the ground circuit from being completed. The vacuum advance diaphragm may be checked by applying a suction where the line connects and watching for movement of the base plate.

Install the contact breaker points and condenser in reverse order of removal. Clean the surfaces of the contact points with a non-oily solvent such as alcohol to remove any preservative coating or dirt, and set the points gap to specification (see TUNE-UP SPECIFICATIONS).

CAUTION: *The order of installation of components on the moving contact return-spring locating pin must be followed exactly or the ignition spark will be short-circuited to ground. The fiber insulating washer must be installed first, followed by the return-spring end loop, the low-tension and condenser lead wires, the insulating sleeve (which slides down between the pin and the return-spring and wire end loops), and the nut.*

Apply one or two drops of engine oil to the felt in the top of the distributor shaft (if applicable). Lightly smear the distributor cam with engine oil or distributor cam lubricant. Replace the rotor.

Replace the distributor. Make sure that the distributor cap is clean and free of cracks and that the contacts and carbon brush are not badly worn. Replace any wiring that is worn, cracked, or stiff with age, and make sure that the high tension wires are securely connected at the distributor cap and the spark plug connectors. Check the ignition timing.

Distributor Installation—When Ignition Timing Has Been Disturbed

Rotate the crankshaft until the notch in the crankshaft pulley aligns with the Top Dead Center (TDC) pointer on the front engine cover (see the appropriate figure under IGNITION TIMING). The MG 1100 timing marks are located on the flywheel (see the following section) and must be aligned with the pointer at the top of the clutch cover inspection hole.

Install the distributor. Tighten the clamp pinch-bolt to align the shaft with the clamp. Install and tighten the clamp hold-down bolts, and loosen the pinch-bolt so that the distributor can be rotated.

Rotate the distributor until it is positioned in relatively the same way as it was before removal (see applicable illustration under FIRING ORDER). The ignition timing can now be set exactly.

Ignition Timing

Static Timing Procedure

Satisfactory results on any MG engine without emission controls can be obtained through static (engine not running) timing if it is done carefully. The only equipment necessary is a test light, which is nothing more than a light bulb (12 volt) with two wires attached so that it will light when connected in parallel with a power source.

Turn the crankshaft in its normal direction of rotation until the notch in the crankshaft pulley aligns with the appropriate pointer on the front engine cover. See TUNE-UP SPECIFICATIONS for correct

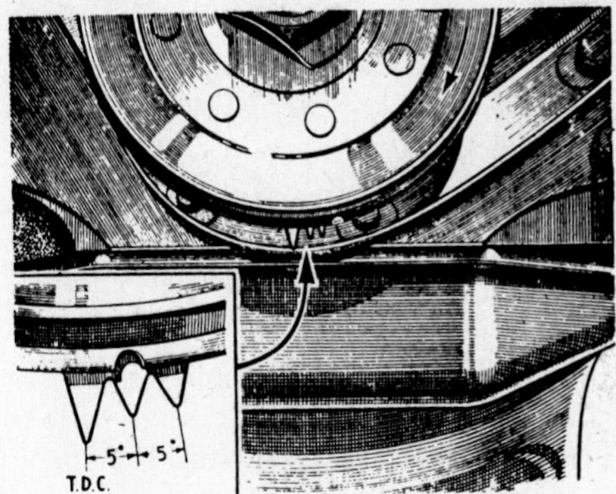

Timing marks, Midget and early MGB

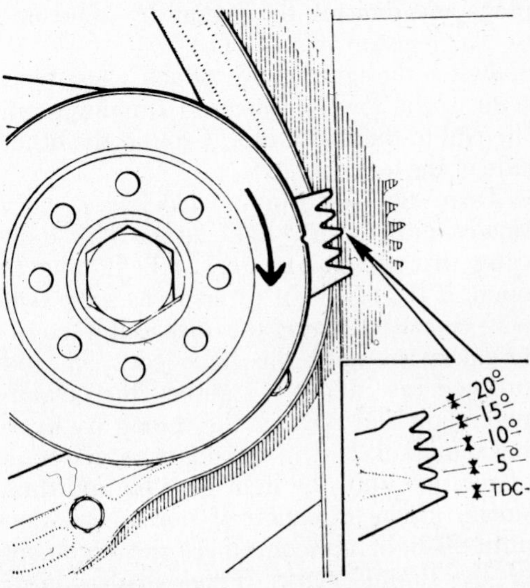

Timing marks, MGB

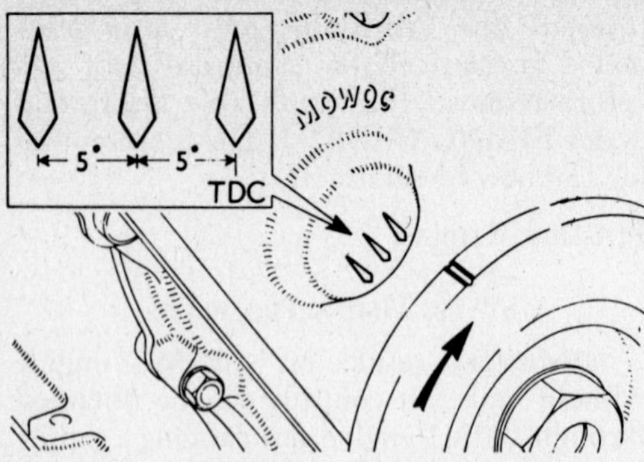

Timing marks, MGC

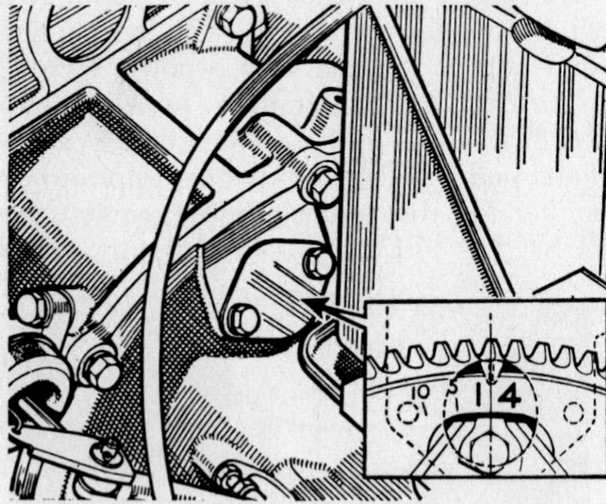
Timing marks, MG 1100

settings. (The MG 1100 timing marks are on the flywheel and may be seen with the aid of a mirror after removing the inspection plate on the clutch cover. TDC is indicated by the mark 1/4 and location of the mark is made easier by removing the spark plugs and rotating the engine by hand until No. 1 piston is at TDC.)

Switch the ignition on. Attach a test light wire to the low tension lead running from the coil to the distributor. Ground the other side of the test light.

Turn the distributor clockwise very slowly until the test light lights. This indicates that the points are just beginning to open. If the test light came on as soon as it was connected, turn the distributor counterclockwise until the light goes off and proceed as above. Tighten the clamp pinch-bolt and recheck the timing by turning the crankshaft in the opposite direction of rotation until the light goes off and then *slowly* in the direction of normal rotation until the light goes on. Check the alignment of the timing marks. Final small adjustments can be made with the vernier adjustment knob on the vacuum advance unit of the distributor. (The space between each mark on the moving barrel equals approximately 5 deg. timing change.)

Dynamic Timing Procedure

Timing Specifications

Model & Engine	*Deg. BTDC @ rpm*
Midget	
12CC/12CE	22@1,000
12CD/12CJ	10@1,000
MGB	
18G/18GA/ 18GB	14@600
18GF/18GH/ 18GJ	20@1,000
18GK	15@1,500
MGC	
29GA	4@1,000

Dynamic (engine running) timing is done with a stroboscopic timing light. Connect the light as per manufacturer's instructions. Mark the notch in the crankshaft pulley with a bright color that will be easily visible (such as yellow crayon). Disconnect and plug the vacuum advance line from the intake manifold.

The engine should be warm and running steadily at the correct rpm when the timing check is made. If the timing is no more than 5 degrees off, correction can usually be made with the vernier adjustment knob on the vacuum advance unit of the distributor. Otherwise, the distributor clamp pinch-bolt will have to be loosened and the distributor rotated to the correct position. Check the timing once again after the pinch-bolt has been tightened, and reconnect the vacuum advance line after final adjustment is made to check operation of the vacuum advance unit.

CHARGING SYSTEM

If a charging system fault is suspected, the first thing to do is visually inspect wires and connections at the battery, generator (or alternator), and regulator. If any defects are found, the generator and regulator units should be tested (after the fault is corrected) to ensure that they have not been damaged by being inadvertently disconnected from the circuit. The battery, if completely discharged, should be at least partially recharged before the generator and regulator tests are made.

If no obvious fault can be found in the charging system circuitry, then the appropriate diagrams and test procedures in the following sections should be referred to. If unsure of which of the individual components a car is equipped with (such as what type of alternator), the ELECTRICAL SPECIFICATIONS charts and the applicable chassis wiring illustration under WIRING DIAGRAMS will prove useful.

Charging System Diagrams

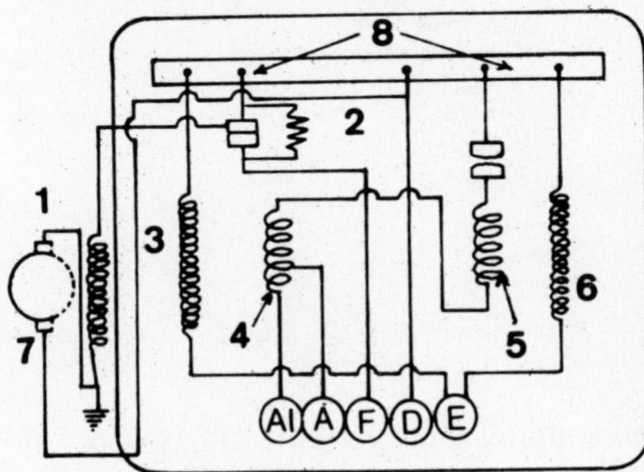

C39 or C40/1 generator with RB106 series regulator

1 Field (internally grounded)
2 Field resistance
3 Shunt coil
4 Tapped series coil (regulator)
5 Series coil (cut-out relay)
6 Shunt coil
7 Armature
8 Regulator and cut-out frame
AI—Battery input
A—Regulated generator output
F—Field
D—Armature (Generator)
E—Ground (Earth)

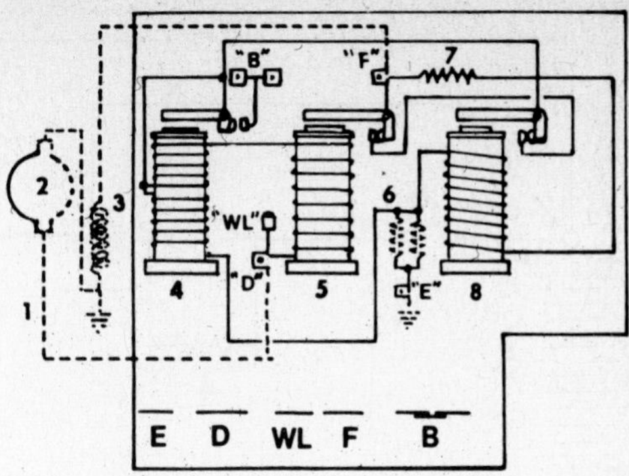

C40/1 generator with RB340 regulator

1 Armature
2 Generator housing
3 Field (internally grounded)
4 Cut-out relay
5 Current regulator
6 Resistor
7 Field resistor
8 Voltage regulator
E—Ground (Earth)
D—Armature (Generator)
WL—Charge Warning Light
F—Field
B—Battery input and regulated generator output

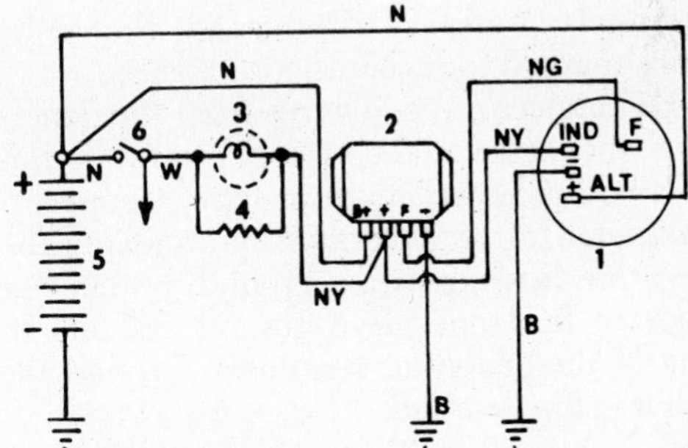

16AC alternator with 4TR regulator

1 Alternator
2 Regulator
3 Warning light
4 Resistor
5 Battery
6 Ignition switch
B+—Battery input
+—Regulated alternator output
F—Field
- —Ground

Cable Color Code
Y—yellow
W—white
G—green
B—black
N—brown

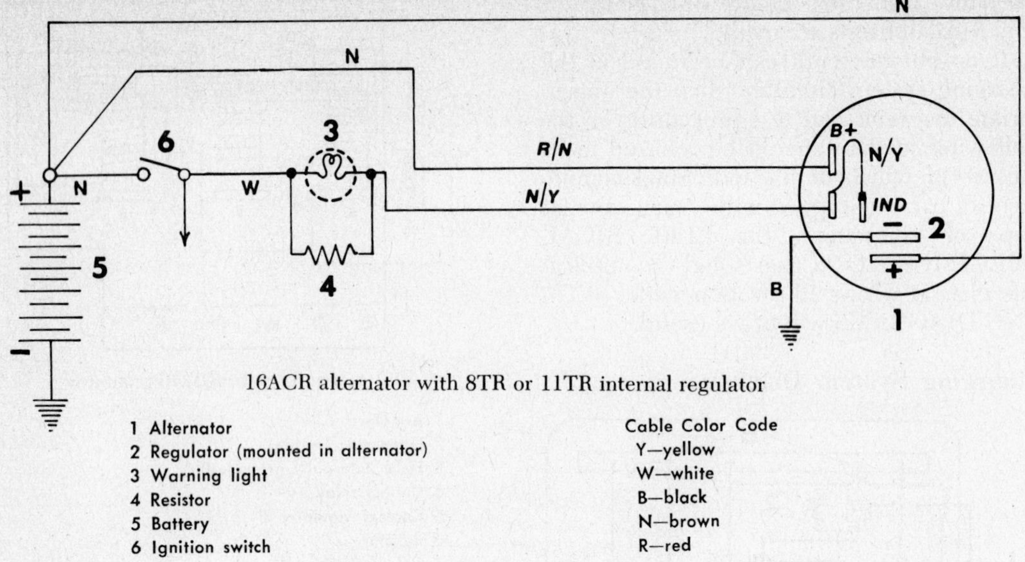

16ACR alternator with 8TR or 11TR internal regulator

1 Alternator
2 Regulator (mounted in alternator)
3 Warning light
4 Resistor
5 Battery
6 Ignition switch

Cable Color Code
Y—yellow
W—white
B—black
N—brown
R—red

Testing the Generator and Generator Regulator

Check the fan belt tension and adjust if necessary. Make sure that generator terminals D and F (armature and field) are in good condition and connect with regulator terminals D and F. The battery should be fully charged for accurate test results.

Disconnect the two wires from the generator and connect the two generator terminals with a short length of wire. Connect a voltmeter to the generator by attaching the negative lead (positive ground system) or positive lead (negative ground system) to one of the generator terminals. Ground the other voltmeter lead.

Start the engine and gradually increase the speed. Voltage should increase rapidly and without fluctuation, and it should not be necessary to run the engine above 2,000 rpm. Do not let the voltmeter reading reach 20 volts.

If there is no voltage at all, check the generator brushes (see GENERATOR SERVICE). Low readings (up to 5 volts) indicate major internal faults and the generator unit should be replaced.

If the voltage readings are good remove the jumper wire from the generator terminals, reconnect the D and F wires, and run the test again. The voltmeter should now read approximately 15 volts at 3,000 rpm. If it does not, the regulator is faulty. If it does, and the battery continues to discharge, the fault will be found in the wiring to the battery (such as a slow voltage leak or a break) or in the battery itself.

If the regulator is suspected as being at fault it is possible that proper adjustment may restore its efficiency (see SERVICING THE GENERATOR AND GENERATOR REGULATOR). However, in most cases it will be found that the unit will have to be replaced.

Servicing the Generator and Generator Regulator

Remove and Replace

The generator may be removed by disconnecting the two wires from the terminals and removing the mounting bolts. When removing the regulator the battery cable leading to the starter should be disconnected at the battery to protect the wiring harness. Disconnect the wires and unscrew the two bolts at the base to remove the regulator. Mark the wires if unsure of their positions on the terminal block.

Both the generator and regulator may be polarized at the same time after they have been installed on the car. Reconnect the battery. Disconnect the wire from regulator terminal F (field) and touch it momentarily to regulator terminal B or AI (battery). Do not hold the wire to the terminal for more than one second. Reconnect the wire to terminal F. The polarity of the generator and regulator will then be in line with the polarity of the vehicle electrical system.

Generator Service

The generator can be lubricated by adding two drops of motor oil at the lubricating hole in the center of the rear end bearing plate.

The only service that can be performed on the generator in the event of failure (without special tools) is polishing the commutator and replacing the brushes. The brushes and commutator are accessible after the commutator end-bracket is removed. The generator will have to be removed and the two long through-bolts withdrawn to accomplish this.

To replace the brushes, lift the brush

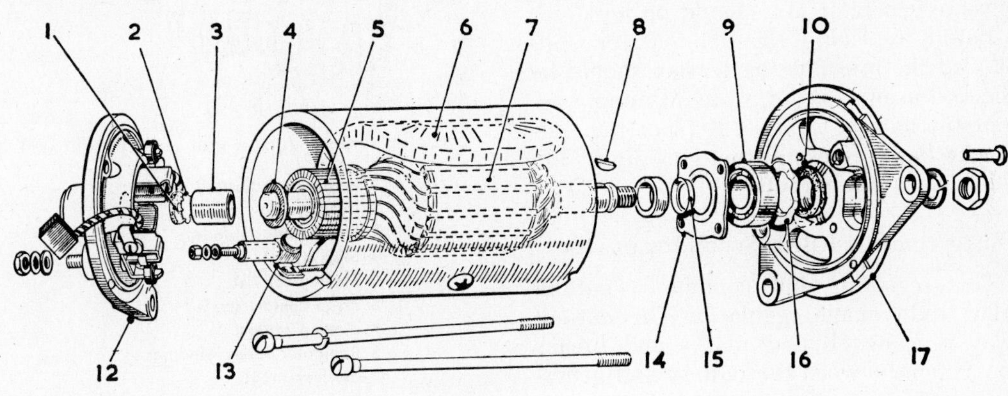

C39 generator

1 Felt pad
2 Aluminum disc
3 Bronze bushing
4 Fiber washer
5 Commutator
6 Field coils
7 Armature
8 Woodruff key
9 Bearing
10 Felt washer
11 Brush
12 Commutator end bracket
13 Field terminal post
14 Bearing retaining plate
15 Cup washer
16 Corrugated washer
17 Driving end-bracket

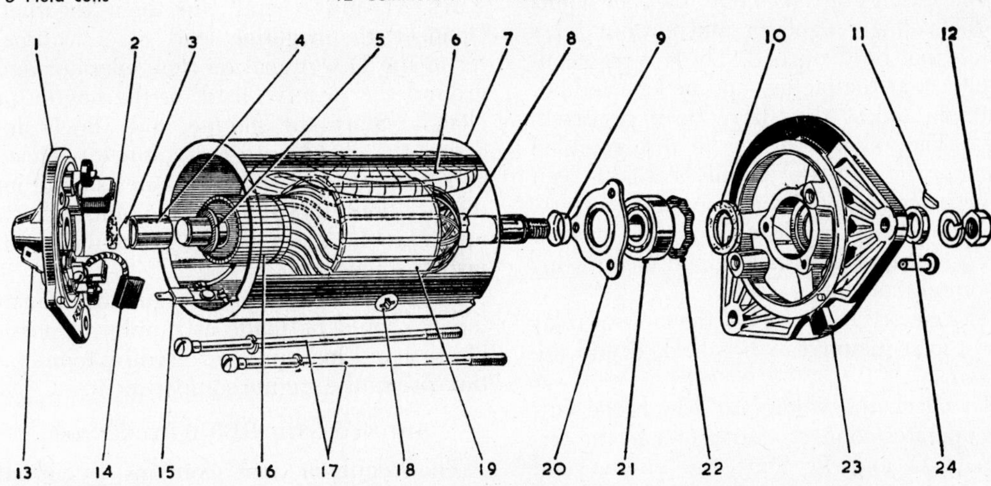

C40/1 generator

1 Commutator end bracket
2 Felt ring
3 Felt ring retainer
4 Bronze bushing
5 Thrust washer
6 Field coils
7 Yoke
8 Shaft collar
9 Shaft collar retaining cup
10 Felt ring
11 Woodruff key
12 Shaft nut
13 Amature terminal D
14 Brushes
15 Field terminal F
16 Commutator
17 Through-bolts
18 Shoe securing screws
19 Armature
20 Bearing retaining plate
21 Ball bearing
22 Corrugated washer
23 Driving end-bracket
24 Pulley spacer

springs out of the way and withdraw the brushes from their holders. Unscrew the brush wire ends and install the new ones. Make sure that the brushes move freely in the holders. If they have a tendency to stick, their sides should be smoothed with a light file.

The commutator should be smooth and free from pits or burned spots. It may be polished using fine emery or sandpaper while rotating the armature. If the commutator segments are badly burned or other internal faults are suspected through testing, the generator unit should be replaced.

Before replacing the commutator end-bracket the brush spring tension should be checked using a spring scale. Minimum acceptable tension is 15 oz. Replace the end-bracket and reinstall the generator. Recheck generator output.

Adjusting the RB106 Series Regulator

This regulator unit contains a cut-out relay and voltage regulator. The cut-out relay is a switch that makes and breaks connection between the battery and generator to prevent the battery from discharging through the generator when the engine is stopped or running slowly. The voltage regulator controls generator output in accordance with battery draw and its state of charge.

The settings of the contact breaker points of the voltage regulator and cut-out relay should not be disturbed. These were accurately set at the factory and never need adjustment unless they have been disassembled. They should never be disassembled because the regulator is only available as a unit; parts are not available. If necessary, the points may be cleaned using a strip of fine sandpaper and then wiped clean using a non-oily solvent.

The electrical settings of the cut-out relay and the regulator can be checked and adjusted.

To check the voltage at which the cut-out operates connect a voltmeter to the terminals D and E. Start the engine and slowly increase its speed until the cut-out points close. At the point just before the needle drops back the voltmeter should read between 12.7 and 13.3 volts. If the reading is not within these limits adjustment can be made at the cut-out adjusting screw. Recheck voltage after adjustment is made.

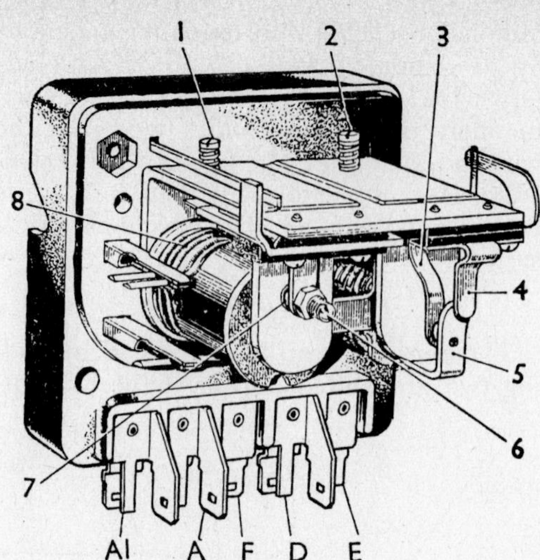

RB106 series regulator unit (cover removed)

1 Regulator adjusting screw
2 Cut-out relay adjusting screw
3 Fixed contact blade
4 Stop arm
5 Moving contact
6 Fixed contact screw
7 Moving contact
8 Regulator series windings
AI—Battery input
A—Regulated generator output
F—Field
D—Armature (Generator)
E—Ground (Earth)

To check the regulator setting disconnect wires AI and A and clip them together. Connect the negative lead of a voltmeter to the D terminal on the generator and ground the positive lead on the engine or chassis. Start the engine and slowly increase the speed until the voltmeter "flicks" and then steadies. The voltmeter should indicate about 16 volts at this point. Adjustment can be made with the regulator adjusting screw.

Both the cut-out and regulator adjustments should be made as rapidly as possible to avoid inaccuracy caused by temperature rise in the engine compartment.

Adjusting the RB340 Regulator

The regulator unit contains a cut-out relay, voltage regulator, and current regulator. Its functions are the same as the RB106 regulator except that the RB340 has the addition of the current (amperage) regulator to further monitor generator output.

As with the RB106 regulator, the settings of the contact breaker points in the RB340 unit should not be altered. (see ADJUST-

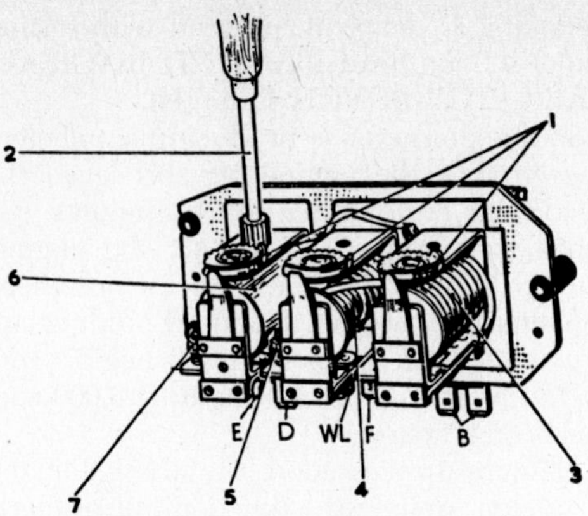

RB340 regulator unit (cover removed)

1 Adjusting cams
2 Lucas adjusting tool (not essential)
3 Cut-out relay
4 Current regulator
5 Current regulator points
6 Voltage regulator
7 Voltage regulator points
E—Ground (Earth)
D—Armature (Generator)
WL—Charge Warning Light
F—Field
B—Battery input and regulated generator output

ING THE RB106 SERIES REGULATOR)

The electrical settings of the cut-out relay and the two regulators can be checked and adjusted.

To check the voltage at which the cut-out operates connect a voltmeter between the regulator terminal D and ground. Start the engine, switch on the headlights, and slowly increase engine speed until the cut-out points close. At the point just before the needle drops back (points close) the voltmeter should read between 12.7 and 13.3 volts. If the reading is not within these limits adjustment can be made by turning the toothed adjustment cam on the cut-out relay. Recheck voltage after adjustment is made.

To check the voltage regulator setting disconnect the two wires from the B terminals and clip the wires together. Connect a voltmeter between terminal D and ground. Start the engine and run it to about 2,000 rpm, at which point the voltmeter should read approximately 15 volts. The reading may be slightly higher on a cold day or lower on a hot day (±1 volt). Adjustment can be made by rotating the adjustment cam on the voltage regulator.

To check the current regulator setting short out the *voltage* regulator points by clipping them together. Disconnect the two wires from the B terminals and clip them together. Connect an ammeter between those wires and one of the B terminals. Start the engine, switch on all lights and accessories, and run the engine up to about 2,000 rpm, at which point the ammeter should indicate a steady current of 19-22 amps. Adjustment can be made at the current regulator adjustment cam.

All adjustments should be made as quickly as possible to avoid inaccuracy caused by temperature rise in the engine compartment.

Unsteady readings obtained on any of the checks may be due to dirt or oil on the contact points.

Testing the Alternator

Precautions

1. Do not run the engine with the batteries out of the circuit or any of the charging circuits wires disconnected (except as given in test procedures).
2. All charging circuit electrical connections must be clean and tight, and the drive belt properly adjusted.
3. Correct battery and alternator polarity (negative ground) must be maintained or the alternator will be destroyed.
4. If arc welding equipment is used on the car the alternator and regulator leads must be disconnected.

16AC Type, On-Vehicle Testing

Disconnect the plug-in connector block from the regulator. Connect the (+) and (−) terminals at the connector block with a jumper wire. Switch on the ignition. The ignition warning light should glow. If it does not, check the warning light bulb and the continuity of the wires between the ignition switch and the regulator. Make sure that the (−) wire leading from the regulator connector block makes a good ground connection. Correct any of the above (if faulty) before proceeding with the testing.

Leave the one end of the jumper wire connected to the (−) terminal and connect the other end to the F terminal. Connect an ammeter between (+) terminal at the connector block and the starter solenoid. Switch on the headlights and accessories to load the battery, and start the engine. The ammeter should show a charge of approximately 15 amps at 1,000 engine rpm and 30 amps at 2,000 engine rpm. *Do not run the engine above 2,000 rpm with the regulator out of the charging circuit.*

If the ammeter reading indicates that the alternator is deficient, proceed with testing under section head 16AC AND 16ACR ALTERNATOR BENCH TESTING.

If the alternator is producing a sufficient charge shut the engine off and leave the headlights on for three to five minutes. Remove the jumper wire and plug the connector block back into the regulator (leaving the ammeter connected). Start the engine, and, with lights on and accessories on, check the alternator output. It should produce approximately 15 amps at 1,000 rpm and at least 25 amps by the time 3,000 rpm has been reached.

If the output is good, the alternator and regulator units are functioning properly and any fault existing in the charging system will be found in the wiring to the battery (such as a slow voltage leak) or in the battery itself.

If the output is insufficient, replace the regulator unit and run the final test again as a check.

16ACR Type, On-Vehicle Testing

Disconnect the wires from the alternator and remove the plastic end cover. Turn the ignition on and ground the wire that connects to terminal F on the alternator (the brown/yellow wire). The ignition warning light should be on. If it is not, check the warning light bulb and the continuity of the wires between the ignition switch and the alternator. Correct any faults before proceeding with the testing.

Reconnect the wires to the alternator as originally found. If the wires are not connected to the terminals correctly the alternator will be destroyed. Refer to CHARGING SYSTEM DIAGRAMS if unsure of the connections.

Connect one end of a jumper wire to terminal F on the alternator and ground the other end. Connect an ammeter between the (+) terminal at the alternator and the starter solenoid. Start the engine and switch on the headlights and accessories to load the battery. The ammeter should show a charge of approximately 15 amps at 1,000 engine rpm and 30 amps at 2,000 engine rpm. *Do not run the engine above 2,000 rpm with the regulator out of the charging circuit.*

If the ammeter reading indicates that the alternator is deficient, proceed with testing under section head 16AC AND 16ACR ALTERNATOR BENCH TESTING.

If the alternator is producing a sufficient charge shut the engine off and leave the headlights on for three to five minutes. Remove the jumper wire. Start the engine, and, with lights and accessories on, check the alternator output. It should produce approximately 15 amps at 1,000 engine rpm and at least 25 amps by the time 3,000 rpm has been reached.

If the output is good, the alternator and regulator units are functioning properly and any fault in the charging system will be found in the wiring to the battery (such as a slow voltage leak) or in the battery itself.

If the output is insufficient, replace the regulator and run the final test again as a check.

16AC and 16ACR Alternator Bench Testing

Remove the alternator from the car (see ALTERNATOR AND REGULATOR—REMOVE AND REPLACE). Remove the plastic end cover. Unsolder the three wires from the rectifier pack, noting their positions.

CAUTION: *When soldering or unsoldering the connections a pair of long-nose pliers must be used as a heat-sink on the diode pins or the diodes will be destroyed. Use care not to bend the pins with the pliers.*

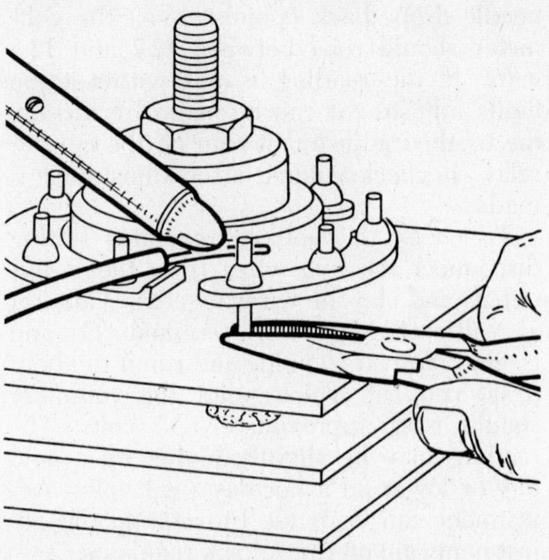

Use pliers as a heat-sink when soldering rectifier connections

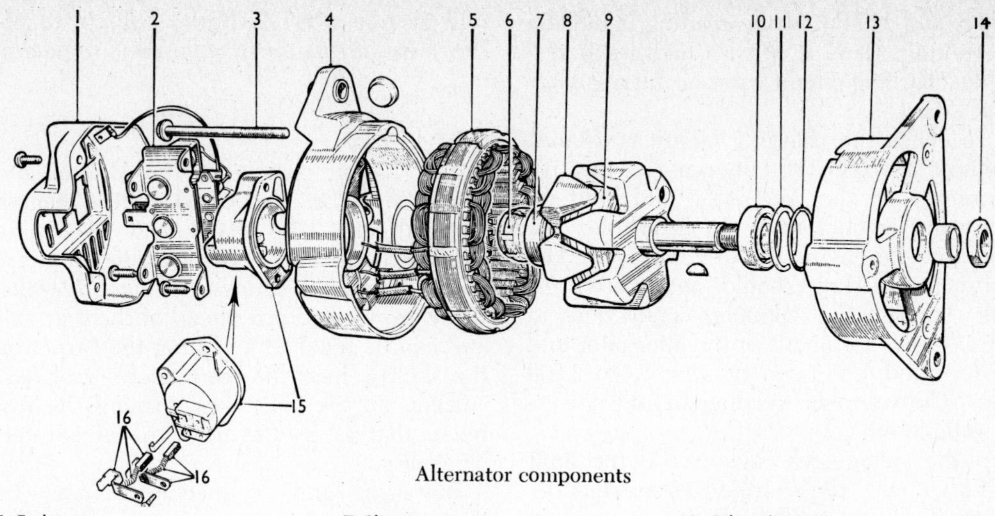

Alternator components

1 End cover
2 Rectifier pack
3 Through-bolt
4 End bracket
5 Stator
6 Slip-rings
7 Slip-ring bearing
8 Rotor
9 Field windings
10 Drive end bearing
11 Circlip
12 Oil sealing ring
13 Drive end-bracket
14 Shaft nut
15 Brush holder box
16 Brush assembly

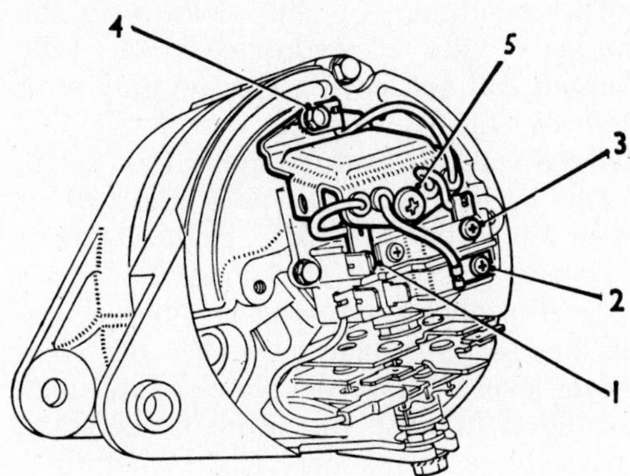

Regulator connections in the 16ACR alternator

1 Battery input (B+)
2 Alternator output (+)
3 Field (F)
4 Ground (—)
5 Mounting screw

Remove the brush holder box retaining screws. Disconnect the regulator ground wire (ACR type only). Loosen the rectifier pack retaining nuts and remove the rectifier pack and brush holder box (and ACR regulator).

The rectifier pack may be tested by connecting a 12-volt battery and a test light in turn to each of the nine diode pins and its corresponding heat-sink, then reversing the connections. The lamp should light with the current flowing in one direction only.

If the lamp lights in both directions or fails to light in either for any one of the diodes, the rectifier pack must be replaced and the alternator installed on the car and retested.

If the rectifier pack test indicates that it is functioning properly, the alternator brushes should then be checked. The brushes should protrude at least 0.20 in. from the holder, and spring pressure should be a minimum of 7 oz. Replace the brush assemblies if necessary and install and retest the alternator.

If both the rectifier pack and the brush assemblies appear to be in good condition, a major internal fault in the alternator is indicated and the unit should be replaced.

Testing the Alternator Regulator

Types 4TR, 8TR, and 11TR, On-Vehicle Testing

Connect an ammeter between the (+) main output terminal on the alternator and the starter solenoid. Connect a voltmeter across the battery terminals. Start the engine and run it at 2,000 rpm. If the ammeter reads zero, the regulator must be replaced.

If the ammeter registers a current flow, adjust the engine speed until the ammeter reads approximately 5 amps. The voltmeter reading should then be between 14.3 and 14.7 volts (4TR), or 14.0 and 14.4 volts

(8TR and 11TR). If the reading is outside these limits there is either a high resistance in the charging circuit wires or the regulator unit is bad.

To check the charging circuit resistance connect a voltmeter between the positive terminals of the alternator and battery. Start the engine, turn the headlights on, and run the engine up to 2,000 rpm. The voltmeter reading should not exceed 0.5 volt. Transfer the voltmeter connections to the negative terminals of the alternator and battery and again run the engine to 2,000 rpm. The voltmeter reading should not exceed 0.25 volt.

If the voltage readings exceed the limit in either case, the charging circuit has developed an area of high resistance that must be traced and eliminated.

If charging circuit resistance is normal, the regulator unit must be replaced and alternator output checked. (see TESTING THE ALTERNATOR).

Alternator and Regulator—Remove and Replace

16AC and 16ACR Alternators

To remove the alternator disconnect the hoses from the air pump outlets. Loosen the air pump mounting bolt. Remove the bolt from the air pump adjusting strut. Slip the belt off of the air pump pulley and raise the pump. Disconnect the wires from the alternator (do not let the wire that connects to the B+ terminal on the alternator touch ground). Remove the alternator mounting bolts, slip the belt from the pulley, and remove the alternator. Installation is in reverse order of removal.

4TR, 8TR, and 11TR Regulators

The 4TR regulator is used only with the 16AC alternator and is conventionally mounted in the engine compartment. To remove this unit, simply pull the plug-in connector block from the base and remove the mounting screws.

The 8TR and 11TR regulators are used interchangeably with the 16ACR alternator. The regulator unit is located *inside the alternator.* To replace it the alternator must be removed from the car. When the plastic alternator end-cover is removed the regulator is accessible. Note the positions of the regulator leads and remove them. Remove the lower mounting screw and the regulator will be free. NOTE: *Never attempt to polarize an alternator or alternator regulator.*

BATTERY

The 12-volt battery in the Midget and the 1100 sedan is located in the engine compartment. The MGB and MGC are equipped with two 6-volt batteries that are wired together in series to produce 12-volts. They are located just ahead of the rear axle and can be reached by lifting the carpet on the shelf behind the front seats (rear seat cushion on the GT), and turning the fasteners that secure the access panel counterclockwise.

Batteries and connections may be cleaned with a baking soda and water solution. Care should be taken not to allow any of the solution to enter the cells. After cleaning, the battery cable ends and terminals should be coated with grease or paint to retard corrosion.

The condition of the cells may be checked with a hydrometer. A fully charged cell will have a specific gravity of at least 1.270, while a completely discharged cell will read no higher than 1.130.

The battery may be quick charged at 30-40 amps, but a trickle charge at about 5 amps is less likely to damage the plates and will probably last longer. When charging the battery make sure that the electrolyte level is above the plates. Water may be added to raise the level if necessary. Leave the cell caps loose while charging is taking place to avoid a pressure buildup, and disconnect one side of the battery if it is to be charged on the car.

CAUTION: *Always connect the positive battery charger lead to the positive battery terminal and the negative lead to the negative terminal. If connected in reverse the battery may explode, and on alternator-equipped cars the alternator and regulator units may be damaged. Correct battery polarity must be maintained and the engine must not be run with the battery disconnected or the alternator on cars so equipped will be destroyed.*

NOTE: *On alternator-equipped cars, whenever the battery is disconnected it should not be reconnected unless it is fully charged, as the alternator will recharge it to a level no higher than its state of charge when connection to the vehicle electrical system is made.*

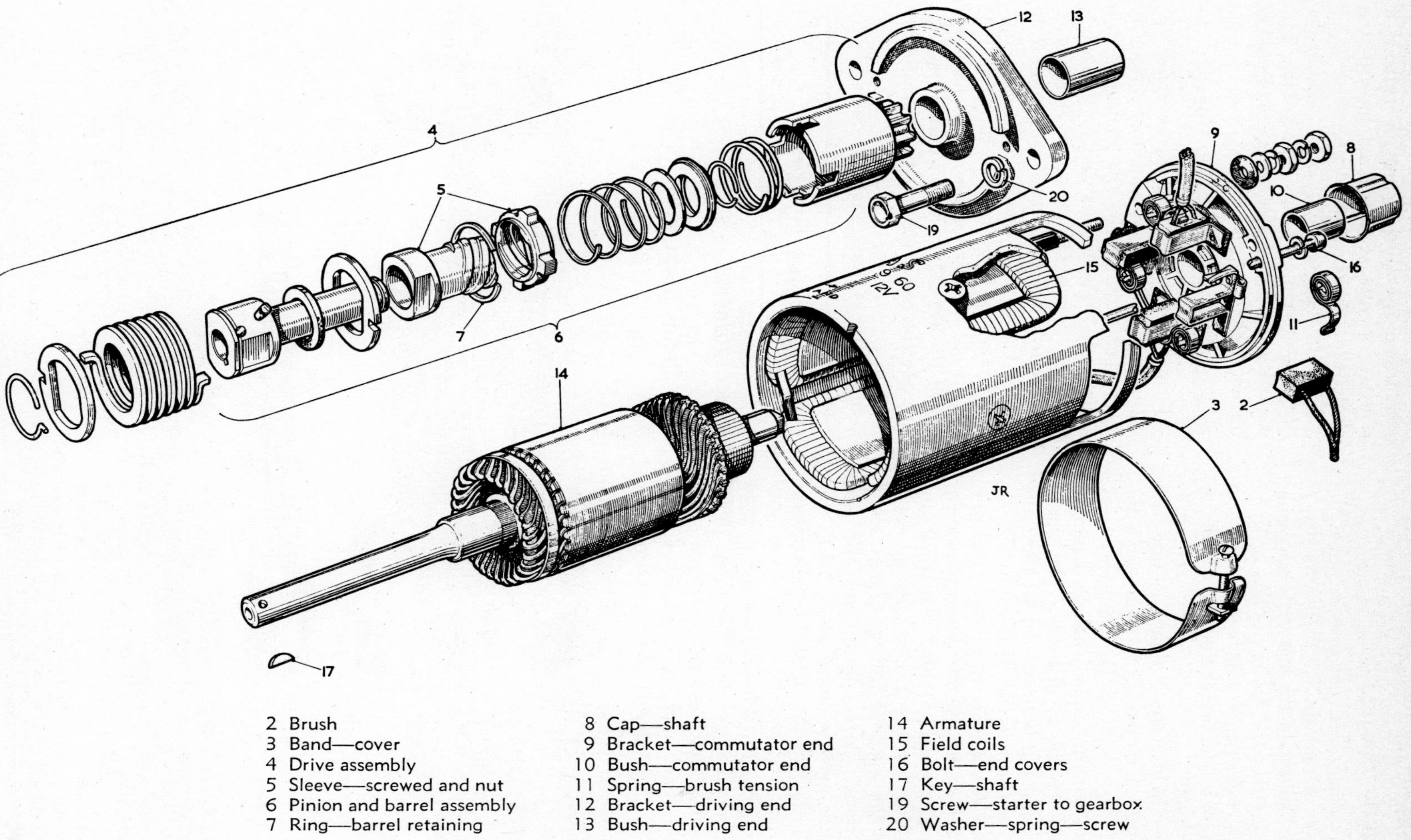

2 Brush	8 Cap—shaft	14 Armature
3 Band—cover	9 Bracket—commutator end	15 Field coils
4 Drive assembly	10 Bush—commutator end	16 Bolt—end covers
5 Sleeve—screwed and nut	11 Spring—brush tension	17 Key—shaft
6 Pinion and barrel assembly	12 Bracket—driving end	19 Screw—starter to gearbox
7 Ring—barrel retaining	13 Bush—driving end	20 Washer—spring—screw

Type M418 starter components

STARTER

Testing the Starter

If the starter will not operate, turn the headlights on and observe their intensity. If they are dim when the starter is not being operated, either the battery is low or there is a high resistance in the battery cables in the form of a bad connection or an aging or corroded wire.

If the lights are bright, operate the starter switch momentarily and watch the lights.

If they remain bright, connect a jumper wire between the small wire on the starter solenoid and the battery lead on the large terminal of the solenoid. If the starter operates when the connection is made, the ignition switch or the wires between the switch and the solenoid are faulty. (On 1970 and later MGBs there is also a solenoid relay between the solenoid and ignition switch.) If the starter does not operate and the lights dim when connection is made, replace the starter; or, if the lights remain bright, replace the solenoid.

If the lights dim when the starter control is operated, check to see if the starter drive is jammed by putting the car in gear and rocking it back and forth gently. If the starter then operates, remove it and replace the drive assembly, and examine the flywheel gear for worn or broken teeth. If it will not operate after rocking the car, the starter unit must be replaced.

Refer to the Troubleshooting section for further starter motor tests. The vehicle wiring diagrams may also prove helpful in tracing faults.

Remove and Replace—All Models

Disconnect the battery. Remove the distributor (MGB and Midget only). Remove the splash-pan under the starter (1100 sedan only). Disconnect and tag the wires from the starter. On the MGC it is necessary to disconnect the steering column from the universal joint near the steering box, unbolt the steering box, and turn the front wheels out so that the box can be lowered out of the way. The starter mounting bolts can now be removed and the starter withdrawn.

Installation is the reverse of removal.

Fuel System

FUEL PUMP

Fuel Pump Location

The Midget Mk. I uses a conventional

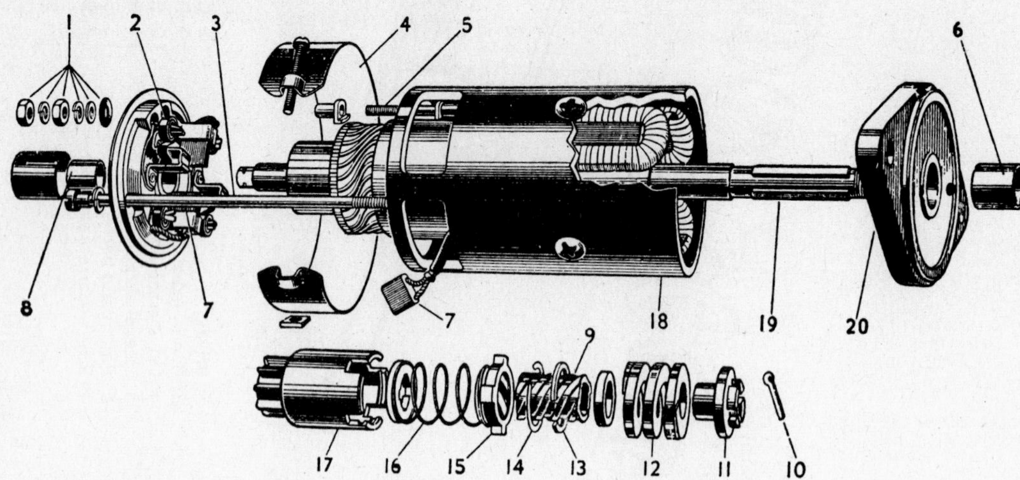

1 Terminal nuts and washers
2 Brush spring
3 Through-bolt
4 Band cover
5 Terminal post
6 Bearing bush
7 Brushes
8 Bearing bush
9 Sleeve
10 Split pin
11 Shaft nut
12 Main spring
13 Retaining ring
14 Washer
15 Control nut
16 Restraining spring
17 Pinion and barrel
18 Yoke
19 Armature shaft
20 Driving end bracket

Type M35 starter components

AC mechanical fuel pump that is bolted to the side of the cylinder block.

All MG models except the Midget Mk. I use an S.U. electrical fuel pump that is located at the rear of the car. On the Midget, MGB, and MGC it is underneath the car on the right-hand side. On very early 1100 sedans the pump is underneath the trunk, while on later cars it is located in the trunk next to the spare tire.

Fuel Pump—Remove and Replace

AC Mechanical Pump

Disconnect and cap the fuel lines at the pump. Remove the two bolts holding the pump to the engine and lift the pump away.

When replacing the pump, make sure that the gasket between the pump and the engine is serviceable. Always start the fuel line connections into the pump by hand to avoid cross-threading the fittings.

S.U. Electric Pump

Disconnect the electrical supply and ground wires from the pump, and insulate the supply wire against grounding. Disconnect the fuel lines and the breather pipe (later cars) from the pump and cap the fuel lines. Remove the pump bracket bolts and remove the pump.

When installing the pump, make sure that the ground wire makes a good connection and that the breather pipe is correctly routed.

Testing the Fuel Pump on the Vehicle

AC Mechanical Pump

The fuel pump pressure can be checked by disconnecting the pump output line at the carburetors and attaching a pressure gauge to it. Cranking the engine for a few seconds will show whether or not the pressure is within specification (see CAPACITIES AND PRESSURES). If pressure is low, disconnect the fuel pump intake line and check for fuel flow from the tank. If the line is not blocked, see SERVICING THE FUEL PUMP.

S.U. Electric Pump

S.U. electric fuel pumps maintain a low, constant pressure, thus making fuel delivery more even and easing the load on the tempermental carburetor needle and seat

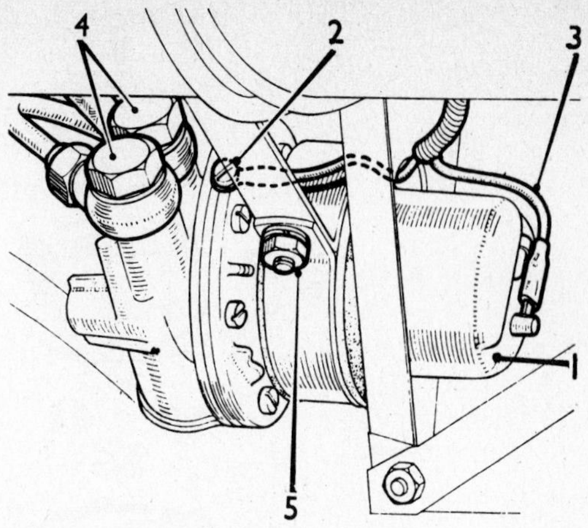

Typical S.U. fuel pump installed on the vehicle

1 End-cover
2 Ground wire connection
3 Supply (battery) wire
4 Fuel line intake and outlet fittings
5 Mounting bracket bolt and nut

units. When fuel pressure drops below a predetermined level the pump will operate (audible as a series of clicks), and when pressure is built up again it will shut itself off.

To check pump operation, disconnect the fuel line at the carburetors and switch the ignition on. The pump should be heard to operate and fuel should flow readily from the line.

If it does not, disconnect the output line at the pump and switch the ignition on again. If the pump now operates, the fuel line to the carburetors is blocked and should be cleared with compressed air. If the pump does not operate, disconnect the fuel intake line from the pump and check for a free flow of gasoline from the tank. The line may be cleared, if necessary, with compressed air by pressurizing the gas tank through the tank filler tube.

CAUTION: *Never blow compressed air through the fuel pump, and on vehicles equipped with Evaporative Loss Control systems the fuel lines must never be pressurized unless the absorption canister is disconnected.*

If the fuel lines are clear and the pump will not operate, the electrical connections at the pump should be checked. Switch on the ignition and connect a test light between the supply (battery) wire and ground. If it does not light, the pump is not being supplied with electricity. If it does

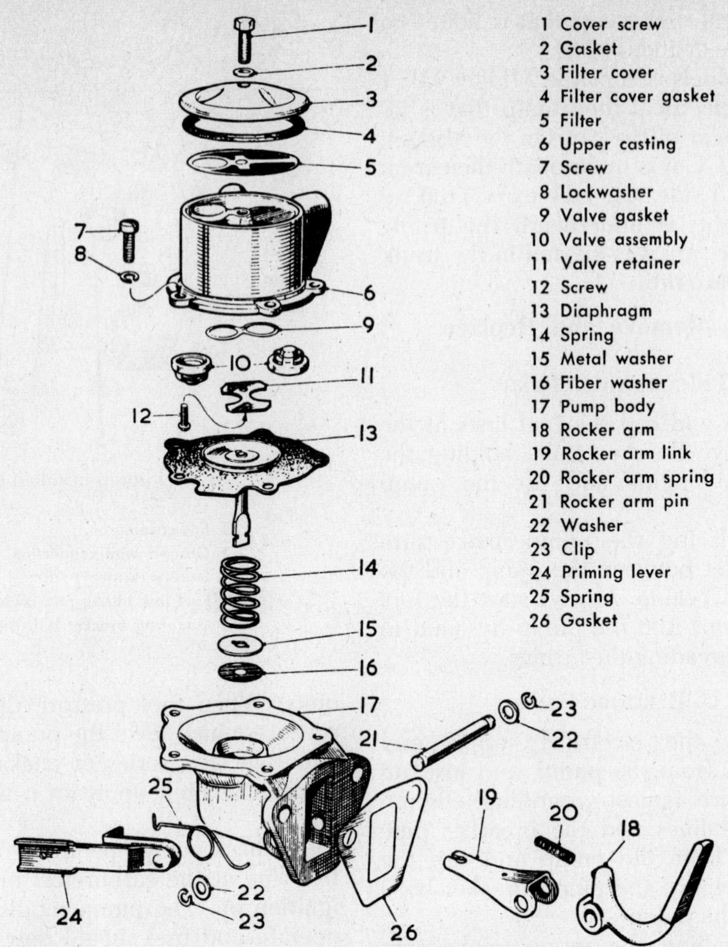

A.C. mechanical fuel pump components

light, check the ground wire continuity by connecting a jumper wire between the ground terminal on the pump and a good chassis ground.

If the pump still does not operate, the fault lies in the pump unit itself. Refer to the following section.

Servicing the Fuel Pump

AC Mechanical Pump

If the pump is not operating correctly, unscrew the top cover securing bolt and remove the cover and the thin disc-type filter. If the filter has obviously been restricting fuel flow, cleaning it may restore the efficiency of the pump. If the filter is not clogged or if pump pressure is still not acceptable after a dirty filter has been cleared, remove the upper casting screws, remove the casting, and inspect the diaphragm for cracks, holes, and rotting. The diaphragm may be removed by rotating it one-quarter turn in either direction.

The fuel pump unit should be replaced if the diaphragm appears to be in good condition or if pump pressure is still low when a new diaphragm has been installed.

S.U. Electric Pump

If the pump unit is not operating correctly, remove it from the vehicle. Remove the intake and outlet line fittings from the pump body and remove the small fuel filter (if fitted). Examine the ports for any foreign matter that may be lodged inside. Clean the ports, if necessary, and clean and replace the filter and line fittings.

Remove the plastic end cover by removing the electrical terminal retaining nut and the rubber or tape joint seal. Examine the contact points for burning, and check the contact rotor assembly movement. If the end-cover was not sealed properly, the con-

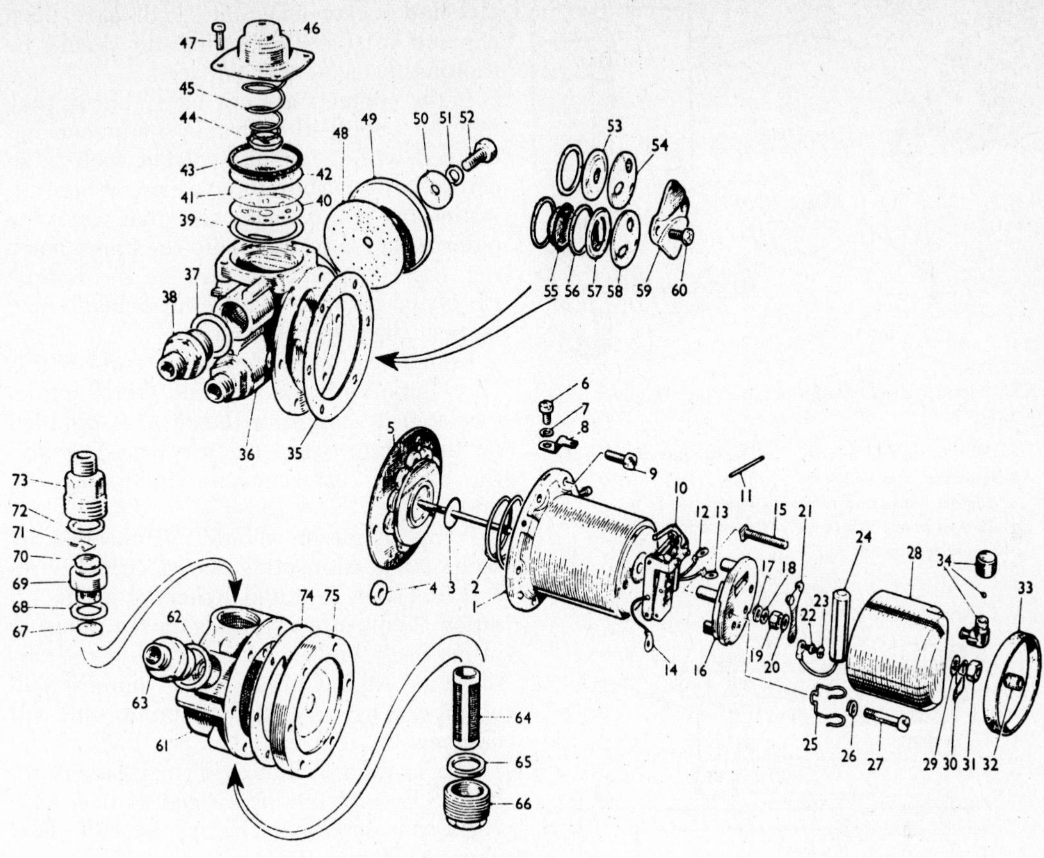

1 Coil housing
2 Armature spring
3 Impact washer
4 Armature centralizing roller
5 Diaphragm and spindle assembly
6 Set screw
7 Spring washer
8 Ground connector
9 Set screw
10 Rocker mechanism
11 Rocker pivot pin
12 Terminal tag
13 Terminal tag
14 Ground tag
15 Terminal stud
16 Pedestal
17 Spring washer
18 Lead washer
19 Terminal nut
20 End cover seal washer
21 Contact blade
22 Washer
23 Contact blade screw
24 Condenser
25 Condenser clip
26 Spring washer
27 Pedestal screw
28 End cover
29 Shakeproof washer
30 Lucar connector
31 Nut
32 Insulating sleeve
33 Sealing band
34 Vent valve

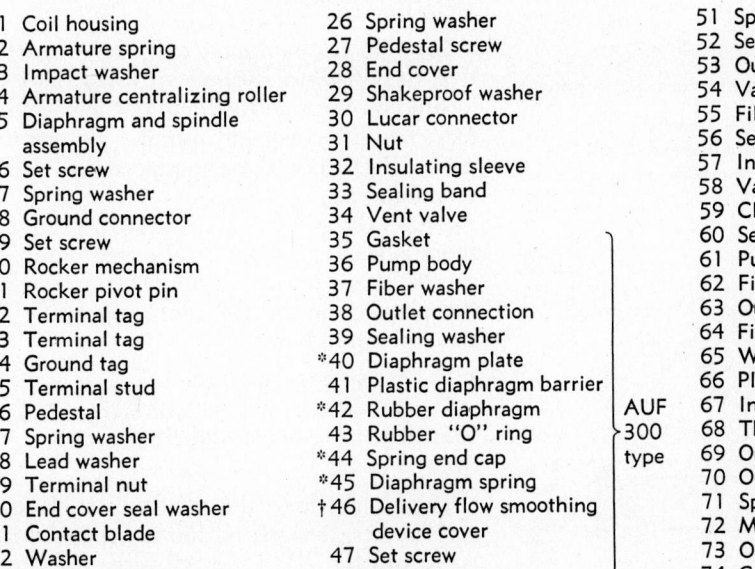

AUF 300 type:
35 Gasket
36 Pump body
37 Fiber washer
38 Outlet connection
39 Sealing washer
*40 Diaphragm plate
41 Plastic diaphragm barrier
*42 Rubber diaphragm
43 Rubber "O" ring
*44 Spring end cap
*45 Diaphragm spring
†46 Delivery flow smoothing device cover
47 Set screw
48 Gasket
49 Inlet air bottle cover
50 Dished washer

AUF 300 type:
51 Spring washer
52 Set screw
53 Outlet valve
54 Valve cap
55 Filter
56 Sealing washer
57 Inlet valve
58 Valve cap
59 Clamp plate
60 Set screw

HP type:
61 Pump body
62 Fiber washer
63 Outlet connection
64 Filter
65 Washer
66 Plug
67 Inlet valve
68 Thin fiber washer
69 Outlet valve cage
70 Outlet valve
71 Spring clip
72 Medium fiber washer
73 Outlet connection
74 Gasket
75 Sandwich plate

* Early pumps
† Delivery air bottle (later pumps)

Exploded view of the AUF300 and HP fuel pump components.

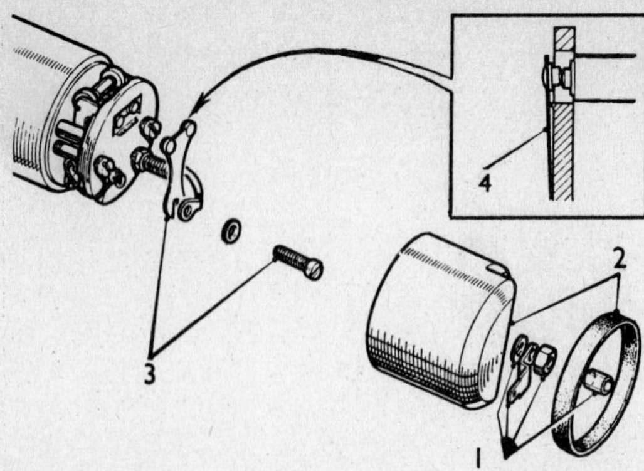

S.U. electric fuel pump contact points cover and contact blade

1 Insulator sleeve, retaining nut, connector and washer
2 Joint seal and end-cover
3 Contact blade and retaining screw
4 Contact points should be centered and blade should rest on rib

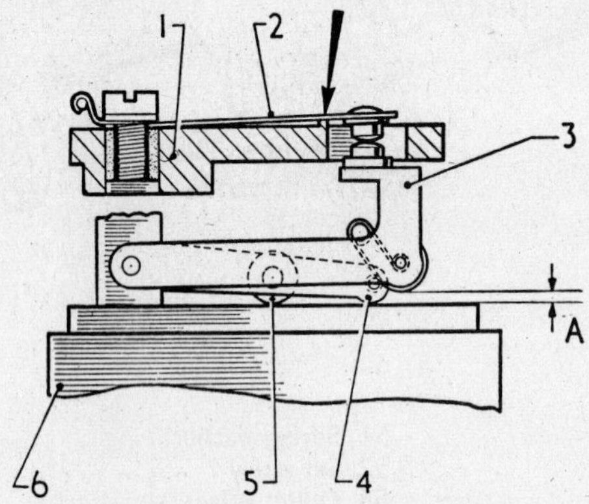

Early S.U. contact points and rocker assembly

1 Pedestal
2 Contact blade
3 Outer rocker
4 Inner rocker
5 Trunnion
6 Housing
A—0.030 in.

Later type S.U. contact points and rocker assembly

1 Pedestal
2 Contact blade
3 Outer rocker
4 Inner rocker
5 Trunnion
6 Housing
A—0.035 in.
B—0.070 in.

tact and rocker assemblies will have been exposed to water and dirt and should be thoroughly cleaned or replaced.

If the contacts are not badly burnt, they may be smoothed with fine sandpaper and cleaned with a non-oily solvent such as an aerosol-type carburetor cleaner.. When adjusting the points, make sure that when the outer rocker is pressed onto the pump housing, the contact blade rests on the narrow rib of the pedestal. The contact blade may be bent slightly if necessary.

Proper sealing of the plastic end-cover is very important. Check that there are no cracks in it, and, after the cover is installed on the pump, wrap electrical tape around the mating surface of the pump housing and cover.

Pump operation should be checked by temporarily connecting the electrical wires and fuel lines to it and switching on the ignition. Allow a few seconds for the pump to prime itself, and check fuel flow at the carburetors. At this point, if the pump is still not operating correctly, the pump unit will have to be replaced. Do not discard the pump, as most MG dealers carry factory rebuilt S.U. fuel pumps instead of new ones (at a considerable savings), and will allow about $3.00 on the old unit.

FUEL FILTER

On vehicles equipped with the Evaporative Loss Control system an inline filter is located on the fuel feed line to the carburetors. The filter element requires no maintenance, but should be replaced at 12,000 mile intervals.

On early MGBs with the 18G engine there is a filter located in the fuel pump. It can be removed for cleaning by unscrewing the plug, opposing the fuel output line, in the fuel pump body.

S.U. CARBURETORS

Identification of Model Type and Size

There are three different types of S.U. carburetors, designated the H type, the HS type, and the HD type. All three are quite similar in operation, the main difference being in fuel feed from the float bowl, and in main jet adjustment.

The HS type, which is the most widely used, incorporates a flexible tube from the bottom of the float bowl to the main jet tube to feed the jet. The jet is adjusted

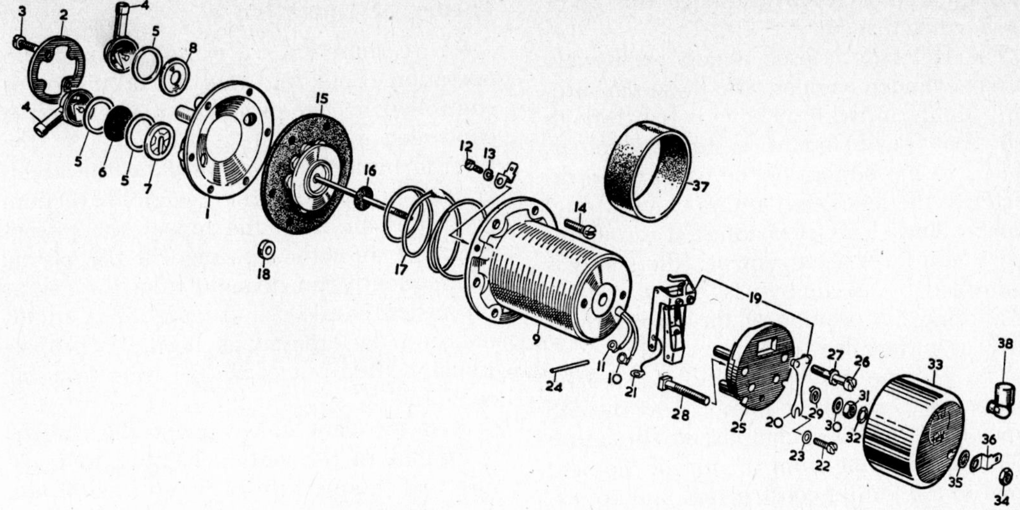

1 Body
2 Spring clamp plate
3 Screw
4 Nozzle—inlet/outlet
5 Sealing washer
6 Filter
7 Valve—inlet
8 Valve—outlet
9 Housing—oil
10 Tag—5 B.A. terminal
11 Tag—2 B.A. terminal
12 Screw—ground
13 Washer—spring
14 Screw—housing to body
15 Diaphragm assembly
16 Impact washer
17 Spring
18 Roller
19 Rocker and blade
20 Blade
21 Tag—2 B.A. terminal
22 Screw for blade
23 Washer—dished
24 Spindle for contact breaker
25 Pedestal
26 Screw—pedestal to housing
27 Washer—spring
28 Screw for terminal
29 Washer—spring
30 Washer—lead—for screw
31 Nut for screw
32 Spacer—nut to cover
33 Cover—end
34 Nut for cover
35 Washer—shakeproof
36 Connector—Lucar
37 Packing sleeve
38 Non-return valve

Exploded view of the AUF200 electric fuel pump used in later model MG Midgets and the MG 1100.

Inline fuel filter on cars with Evaporative Loss Control system

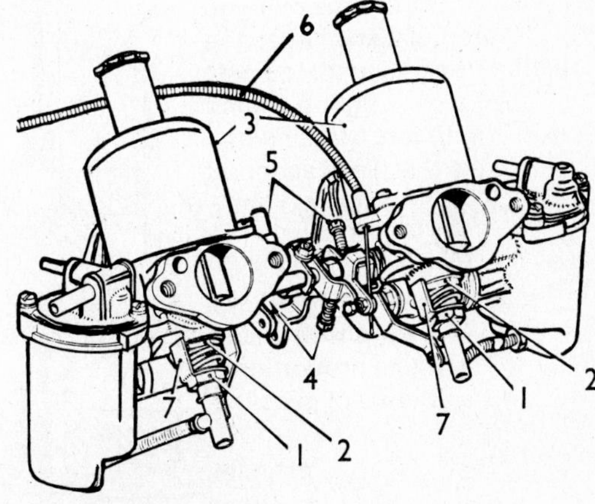

Twin HS type carburetor installation

1 Jet adjusting nuts
2 Jet assembly locknuts
3 Piston-chambers
4 Fast idle adjusting screws
5 Throttle adjusting screws
6 Choke cable
7 Jet adjusting nut restrictors (Emission Control only)

Fuel filter and plug, early MGBs, located in fuel filter body

through a nut that moves the jet tube up or down when turned.

The HD type is used almost exclusively on six-cylinder engines. On these carburetors, fuel from the float bowl is fed through the float bowl mount casting which is bolted to the bottom of the carburetor, directly to the jet. There are no external fuel transfer lines. The jet is adjusted through a screw and lever arrangement. Idle speed is controlled by an air by-pass screw instead of altering the position of the throttle butterfly as in the other types.

The H type, which is obsolete and no longer used, is almost identical to the HS type. Fuel feed is accomplished through a metal line leading from the top of the float bowl to the jet. Jet construction and adjustment is the same as the HS type. This carburetor is found on most MGs built before 1960.

Size of the carburetor throttle bore, or throat, can be determined by the model number on all three types. The number following the carburetor type identification letters indicates throat size in eighths of an inch over one inch. Thus, an HS4 carburetor has a 1 1/2 inch throat, an H2 carburetor has a 1 1/4 inch throat, and an HD8 carburetor has a 2 inch throat.

Theory of Operation

S.U. carburetors are extremely simple in operation. Both fuel and air admission is controlled by the piston position, which is controlled by manifold vacuum. As the throttle butterfly (controlled by the accelerator) is opened, the manifold vacuum evacuates air from the top of the piston-chamber through a passage in the piston. Consequently, on demand from the engine the piston is raised and more air is admitted, and the tapered jet needle is proportionally lifted out of the jet tube to admit more fuel.

A spring (not shown in the illustration) is located in the piston-chamber to make sure that the piston is fully returned at idle and to control piston response to a given amount of vacuum. Stronger and weaker springs are available to adapt the carburetors to engine modifications. Jet needles of different diameter and taper are also available to facilitate fine tuning.

The piston damper, also known as the dashpot, controls the rate of piston rise so that the engine will not hesitate under sudden acceleration due to an excessive volume of fuel/air mixture.

S.U. carburetors are sometimes referred to as the constant velocity or, constant vac-

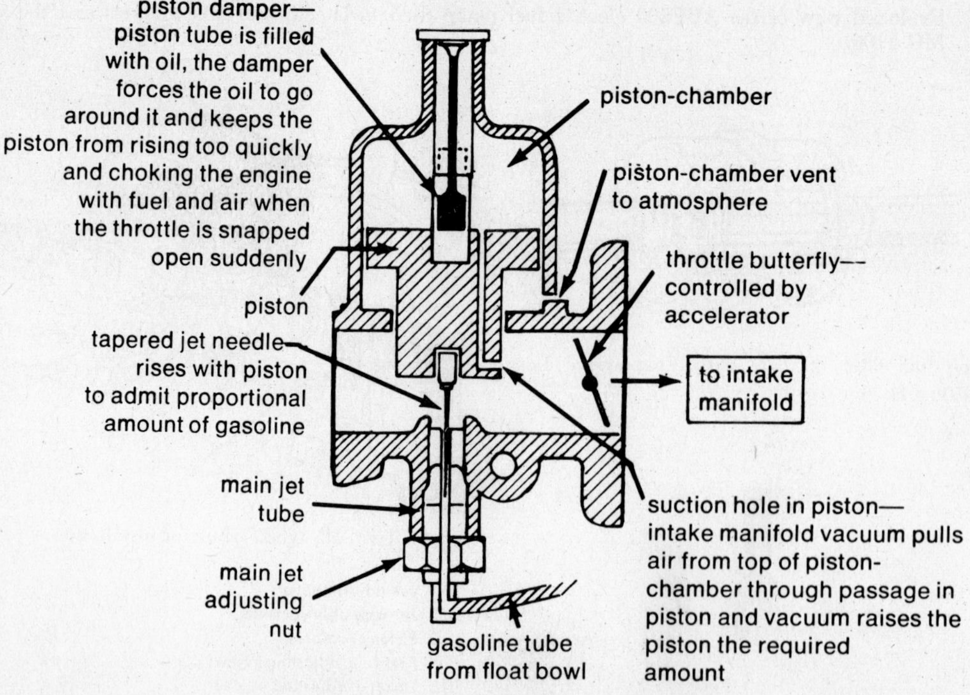

S.U. carburetor cross-section—theory of operation

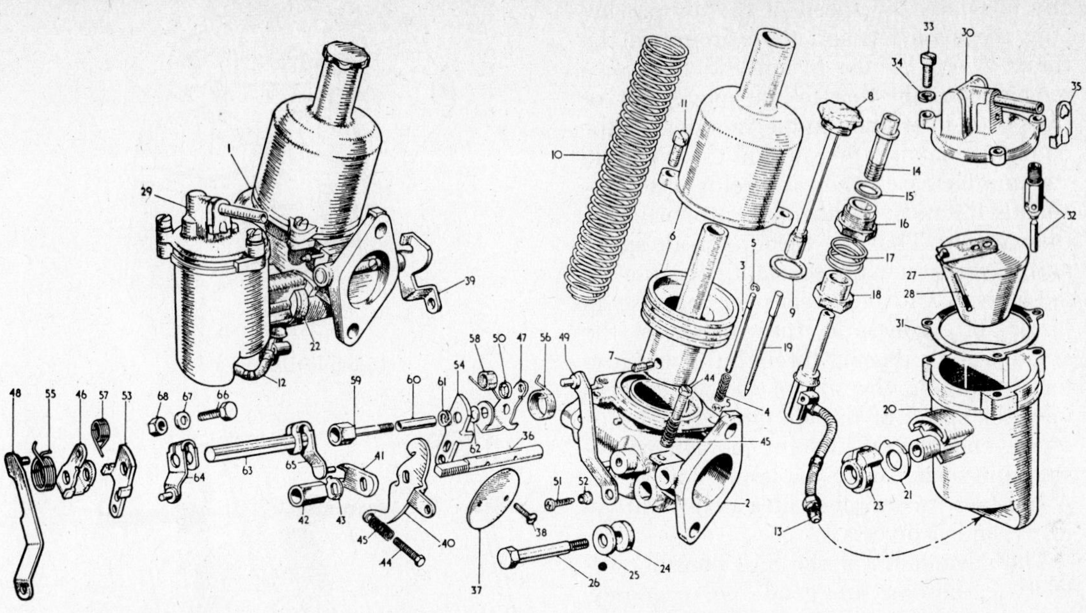

1 Carburetor body (left)
2 Carburetor body (right)
3 Piston lifting pin
4 Spring
5 Circlip
6 Piston chamber assembly
7 Screw
8 Cap and damper assembly
9 Fibre washer
10 Piston spring
11 Screw
12 Jet assembly (left carburetor)
13 Jet assembly (right carburetor)
14 Bearing
15 Washer
16 Screw
17 Spring
18 Screw
19 Needle
20 Float-chamber
21 Support washer
22 Rubber grommet (left carburetor)
23 Rubber grommet (right carburetor)
24 Washer (rubber)
25 Washer (steel)
26 Bolt
27 Float assembly
28 Lever pin
29 Float-chamber lid (left carburetor)
30 Float-chamber lid (right carburetor)
31 Washer
32 Needle and seat assembly
33 Screw
34 Spring washer
35 Baffle plate
36 Throttle spindle
37 Throttle disc
38 Screw
39 Throttle return lever (left carburetor)
40 Throttle return lever (right carburetor)
41 Lost motion lever
42 Nut
43 Tab washer
44 Throttle screw stop
45 Spring
46 Pick-up lever (left carburetor)
47 Pick-up lever (right carburetor)
48 Link (left carburetor)
49 Link (right carburetor)
50 Washer
51 Screw
52 Bush
53 Cam lever (left carburetor)
54 Cam lever (right carburetor)
55 Pick-up lever spring (left carburetor)
56 Pick-up lever spring (right carburetor)
57 Cam lever spring (left carburetor)
58 Cam lever spring (right carburetor)
59 Bolt
60 Tube
61 Spring washer
62 Distance piece
63 Jet rod
64 Lever and pin assembly (left carburetor)
65 Lever and pin assembly (right carburetor)
66 Bolt
67 Washer
68 Nut

A typical MG dual carburetor setup, exploded view.

uum type. A constant velocity carburetor is one in which the speed of the air passing over the main jet, and the vacuum in the throat (between the piston and butterfly) remain constant due to the movement of the piston in relation to the vacuum. As the engine demands more air and the manifold vacuum increases, the carburetor piston responds instantly by lifting in proportion to the vacuum. Thus the carburetor air speed and vacuum remain constant, because an increase in vacuum means an increase in piston lift, which in turn increases the amount of air passing through the carburetor by altering the size of the air passage (not the speed of the air through the passage), and neutralizing the momentary increase in suction with the larger flow of air. A constant vacuum indicates a constant velocity, and vice-versa.

The advantages of the S.U. constant velocity carburetor are good fuel economy, smooth throttle response, and steady performance throughout the entire rpm range.

Adjusting and Maintaining Twin HS Type Carburetor Installations

Since 1930, when Morris Garages purchased the firm, MGs have been equipped with S.U. (Skinners Union) carburetors. All MG models covered in this book have twin HS type S.U. carburetors, while most earlier models have two H type carburetors. The maintenance and tuning procedures for HS carburetors are applicable to the H type as well.

Before the carburetors are adjusted, there are several preliminary checks that should be made. Start the engine and spray a solvent such as an aerosol-type carburetor cleaner on the carburetor bodies where the throttle spindles pivot. If the engine speed varies, there is an indication of an air leak at those points and adjustment of the carburetors will prove to be futile. The carburetors should be rebuilt and the throttle spindles and bushings replaced if the carburetors are expected to respond to adjustment.

Check the carburetor pistons for sticking by lifting them all the way and letting them fall. Their descent should be steady, and a metallic click should be heard when they hit bottom. If there is evidence of sticking, remove and clean the pistons in solvent. Do not lubricate any part of the piston except the rod. Check that the piston damper

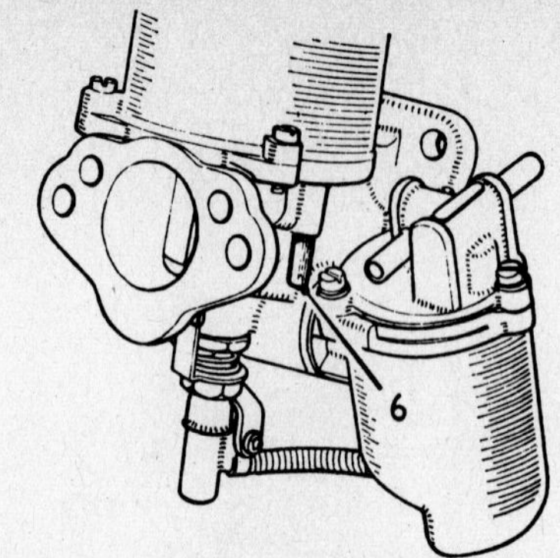

Piston lifting pin (6)

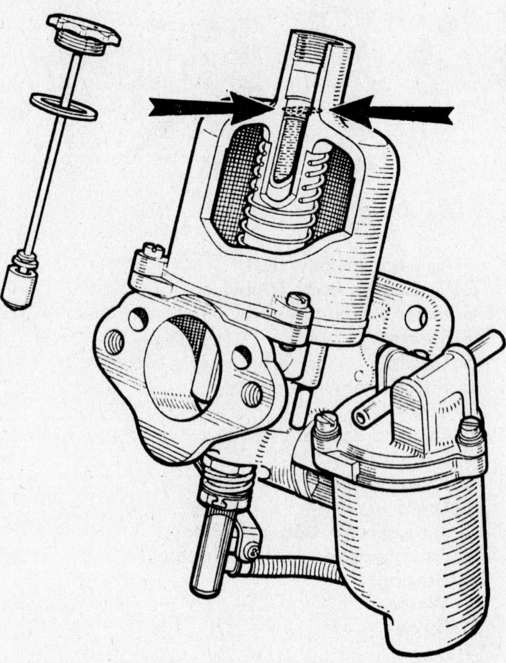

Piston damper chamber should be topped up with light engine oil to a level ½ in. above the piston tube. Dust-proofed carburetors (no vent hole in the damper cap) should have the oil level maintained at ½ in. below the tube

chambers have the proper amount of oil. On carburetors with vented damper caps the level should be 1/2 in. above the piston rod, and with non-vented caps the level should be 1/2 in. below the rod.

A dirty air filter will affect the carburetors quite noticeably. If carburetor adjustment is carried out with air filters off, the engine will run badly when they are replaced unless they are clean. MG uses replaceable paper filter elements.

The carburetor bodies and throttle linkage should be cleaned before adjustments are made. Check the manifold and carburetor nuts for looseness which could cause an air leak.

Start the engine and warm it to normal operating temperature. Loosen the throttle linkage interconnection clamps so that the carburetor throttles may be synchronized. Loosen the choke (jet control) linkage interconnection clamps. Run the engine at about 3,000 rpm for a few seconds to clear it out, and let it drop back to idle. Using a Unisyn or other carburetor balance meter, adjust the idle (see TUNE-UP SPECIFICATIONS) via the throttle adjusting screws so that when correct speed is ob-

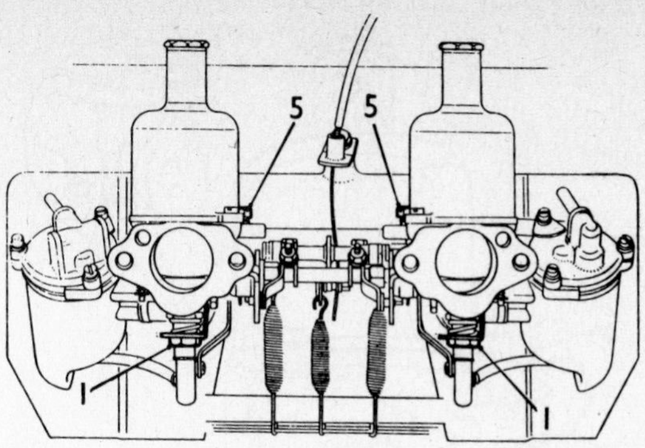

Idle adjusting screws (5), and jet adjusting nuts (1)

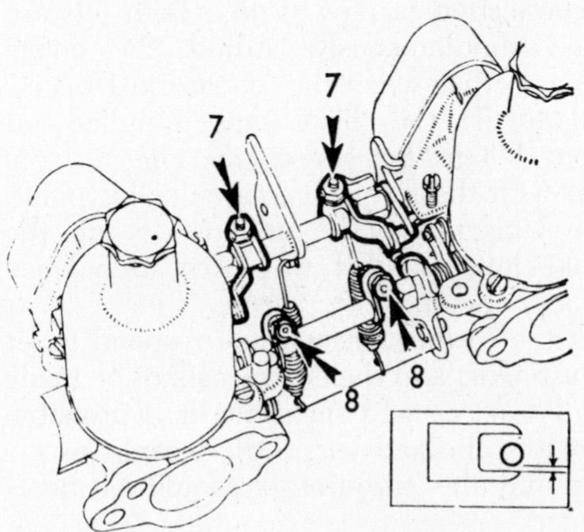

Throttle interconnection clamping levers (7) and jet interconnection clamp bolts (8). Inset shows clearance between the link pin and the lower edge of the fork.

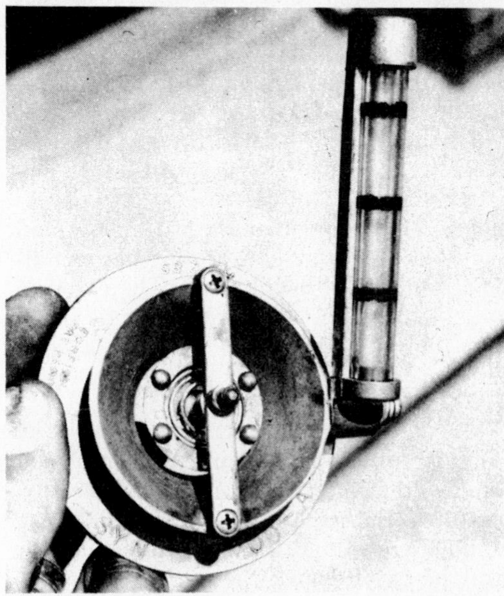

The Unisyn—a balance meter used to synchronize carburetors

tained both carburetors register the same draw on the Unisyn.

The carburetors are now synchronized at idle, and must be set also for off-idle operation. Set the throttle interconnection clamps so that the link pin is 0.012 in. away from the lower edge of the fork (see illustration), and tighten the clamps. Open the throttles by pulling on the accelerator cable until the engine is just above idle speed, and check carburetor balance at this point with the Unisyn. If there is a balance difference of more than 1/2 in. on the meter, loosen one of the interconnection clamps and position it so that the carburetor drawing less in the meter will open slightly sooner than the other one. Tighten the clamp and recheck balance. Repeat the operation, if necessary, until balance is satisfactory.

Carburetor mixture strength is adjusted by turning the jet adjusting nut up to lean the mixture and down to richen it. Mixture strength is checked for the individual carburetors by lifting the piston very slightly (about 1/32 in.) and listening for a change in engine speed. If the engine slows down and remains at the lowered speed, the mixture is too lean. If the engine speeds up slightly and then returns to its original idle, the mixture is correct. If the engine speeds up and remains at the higher speed, the mixture is too rich. If jet adjustment is necessary, turn the adjusting nut one flat at a time and pause to check for any change in engine response.

On Emission Control System carburetors with jet adjusting nut restrictors, it will not be possible to adjust the mixture in the preceding manner because of the limited range of adjustment. Turn the jet adjusting nut on both carburetors over the full range of ad-

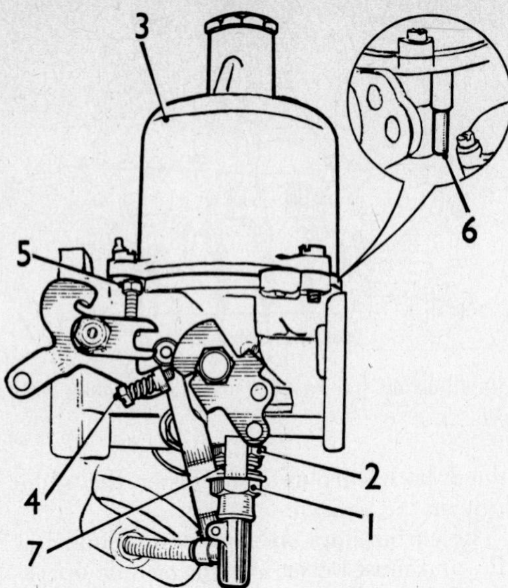

Emission control carburetor adjustment points

1 Jet adjusting nut
2 Jet assembly locknut
3 Piston-chamber
4 Fast idle adjusting screw (actuated by the choke)
5 Throttle (idle) adjusting screw
6 Piston lifting pin
7 Jet adjustment restrictor
(Emission Control System only)

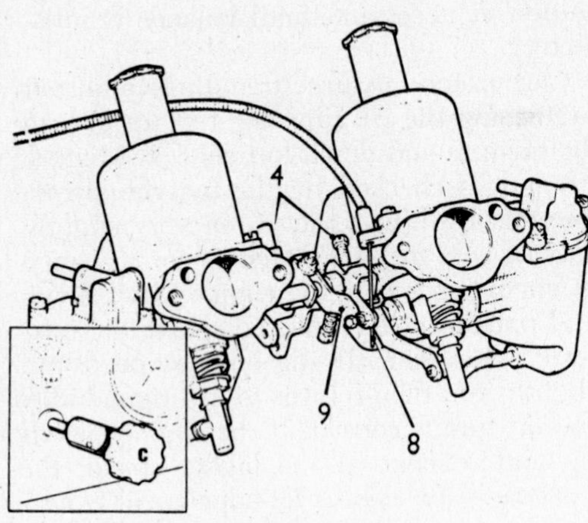

Idle adjustment points

4 Idle adjustment screws
8 Choke cable
9 Choke linkage and fast idle screw
Inset—The fast idle screws should be adjusted to raise the engine speed to 1,200 rpm with the choke knob ¼ in. from the dashboard, at which point the jet tubes have just begun to be lifted by the choke arms.

justment, selecting the setting where maximum idle speed is consistent with smoothness. Do not remove or reposition the jet adjusting nut restrictors, as the adjusting range permitted is in the range of minimum exhaust emissions.

Altering the mixture strength will have altered the engine speed in either case, and the idle will have to be reset. Both of the throttle screws should be turned an equal amount so that carburetor synchronization will not be upset.

With throttle synchronization and mixture strength set, the choke (jet lifting) linkage can be adjusted. Set the linkage interconnection clamps so that both jets are lifted simultaneously. Adjust the choke cable so that when the jets are just beginning to lift, the choke knob is pulled out about 1/4 in. Set the engine idle at 1,200 rpm with the fast idle screws at this point. The Unisyn may be used to set up the choke linkage as it was used to balance throttle openings.

If the carburetors will not respond to jet adjustments and the engine cannot be made to idle or respond smoothly, it is probable that jet tube and jet needle wear is excessive and the carburetors should be overhauled.

Carburetor Removal and Installation

Remove the air filters. Disconnect the fuel lines and remove the overflow tubes from the float chamber. Disconnect the accelerator and choke cables. Disconnect the vacuum advance line and remove the throttle return springs. Unbolt the carburetor retaining nuts and remove the carburetors, being careful not to bend the throttle linkage.

Installation is in reverse order of removal. Make sure that the carburetor and manifold spacer gaskets are in good condition or an air leak will result. The carburetors and linkages will have to be adjusted after reinstallation.

Rebuilding HS Type Carburetors

Remove the carburetors from the vehicle. If the throttle spindles are to be replaced remove the throttle levers and butterfly, and slide the spindle out. Remove the retaining screws and lift the piston-chamber straight off. Remove the spring and carefully lift the piston out. Unscrew the piston damper from the top of the piston-chamber.

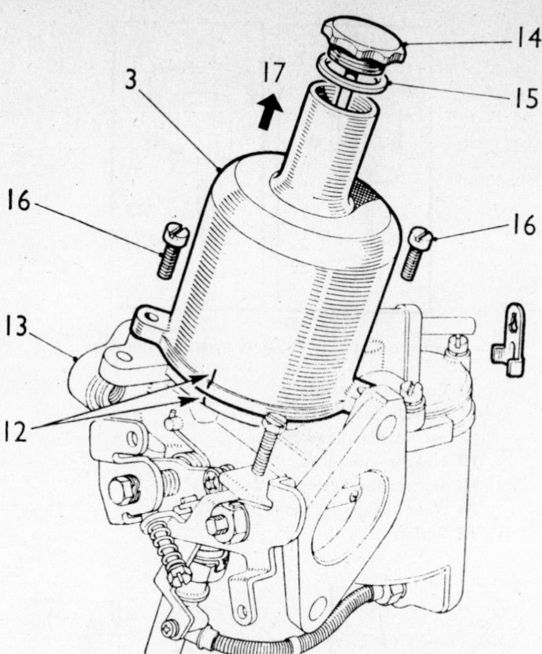

Piston chamber and damper

3 Piston chamber
12 Alignment marks—to be scratched in before removal of chamber
13 Carburetor body
14 Piston damper cap
15 Washer
16 Piston chamber retaining screws
17 Lift chamber straight off when removing

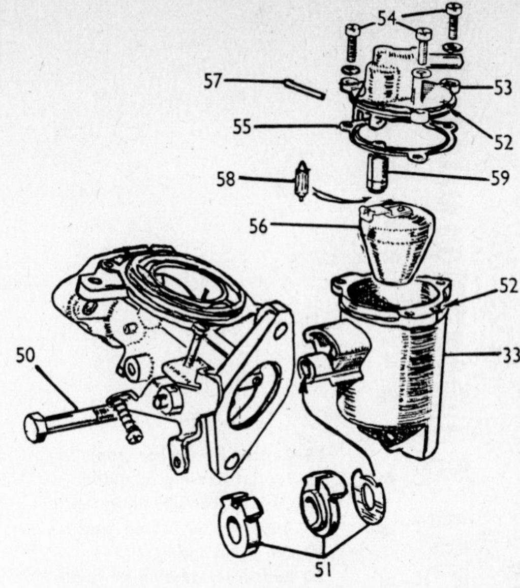

Float bowl components

33 Float bowl
50 Mounting bolt
51 Mounting washers
52 Alignment marks—to be scribed in upon removal
53 Float bowl cover
54 Retaining screws
55 Gasket
56 Float
57 Float hinge pin
58 & 59 Needle and seat assembly

Unscrew the fuel transfer line from the bottom of the float chamber. Unbolt and remove the float chamber from the carburetor body. Remove the float cover and remove the float by pressing out the hinge pin with an ice pick or small drift. Unscrew the needle and seat from the cover.

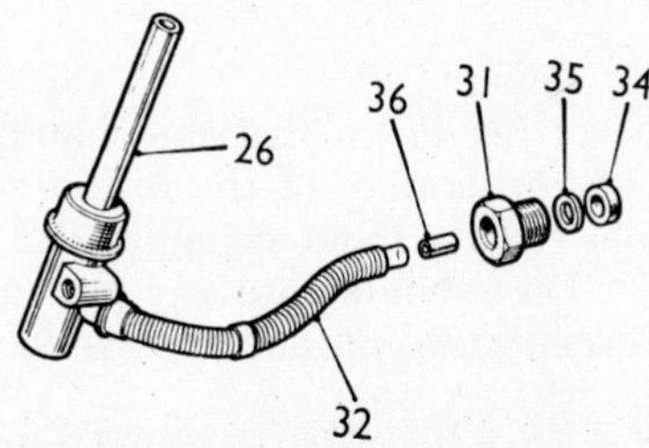

Jet tube and fuel transfer line

26 Jet tube
31 Fuel transfer line retaining nut
32 Fuel transfer line
34 Gasket (gland washer)
35 Washer
36 Ferrule

Remove the pivot pin from the jet lifting (choke) arm at the bottom of the jet assembly. Unscrew the jet assembly locknut and withdraw the jet assembly. Pull the jet tube out and lift the top jet bearing off. The small spring, washers, and gaskets can now be removed. Unscrew the jet adjusting nut from the bottom jet bearing and remove the gaskets, the spring, and the washer.

All carburetor components except the float and seals should be soaked in acid-type carburetor cleaner for about an hour, then washed thoroughly with solvent and air dried. Components included in good carburetor rebuilding kits should include jet tubes, jet needles, needle and seat assemblies, and all gaskets and seals. If throttle spindles or bushings or any other carburetor parts are needed they will have to be purchased separately. The small cork gaskets (jet gland washers) should be soaked in hot water or penetrating oil for at least half an hour before they are assembled onto the jet, or they will invariably split.

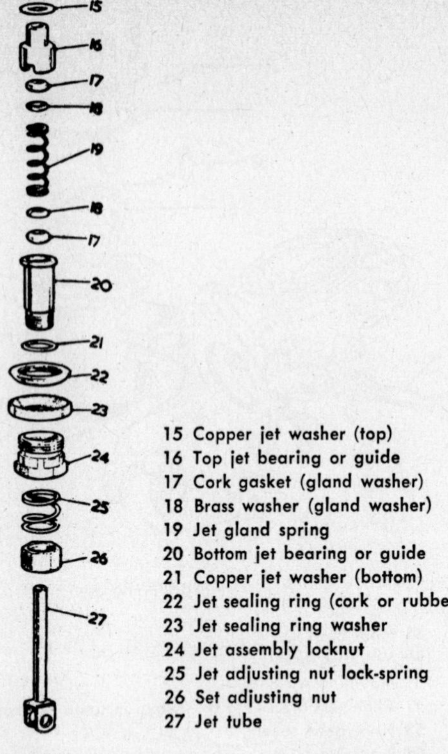

15 Copper jet washer (top)
16 Top jet bearing or guide
17 Cork gasket (gland washer)
18 Brass washer (gland washer)
19 Jet gland spring
20 Bottom jet bearing or guide
21 Copper jet washer (bottom)
22 Jet sealing ring (cork or rubber)
23 Jet sealing ring washer
24 Jet assembly locknut
25 Jet adjusting nut lock-spring
26 Set adjusting nut
27 Jet tube

Correct order of assembly of the main jet, including washers and gaskets

Assembly is in reverse order of disassembly. When the jet is fully assembled the jet tube should be a close fit without any lateral play, but it should be free to move smoothly up and down in the jet assembly. A few drops of oil or polishing the tube lightly may be necessary to achieve this. If the jet sealing ring washer is made of cork, it should be soaked in hot water for a minute or two before installation. Float height should be adjusted (see illustration). In-

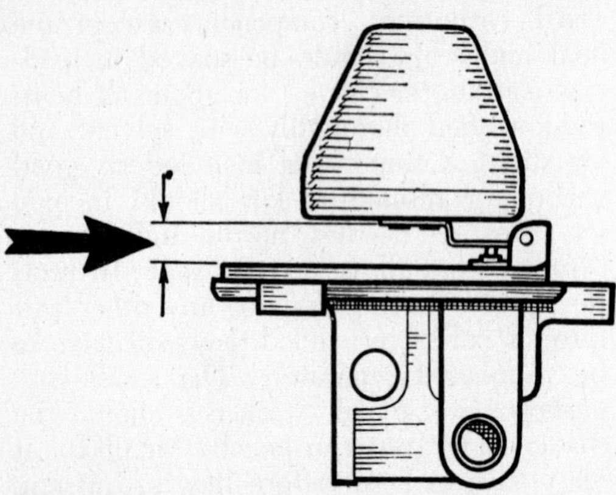

Float height, as illustrated, should be ⅛ in. for all models

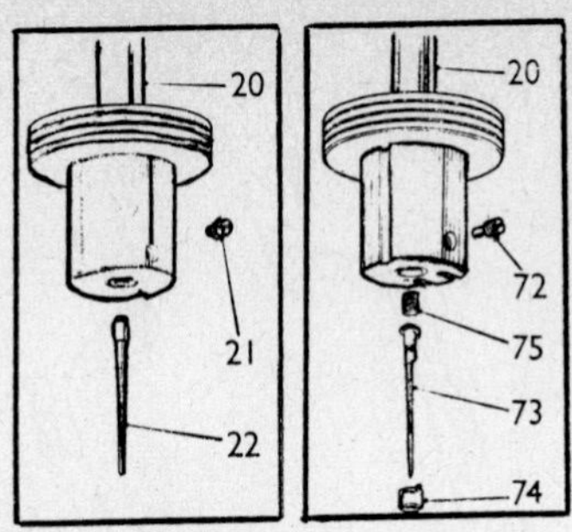

Fixed and spring-loaded type jet needles

20 Carburetor piston
21 Needle lock-screw
22 Jet needle (fixed type)
72 Needle lock-screw
73 Jet needle (spring-loaded type)
74 Needle support guide
75 Spring

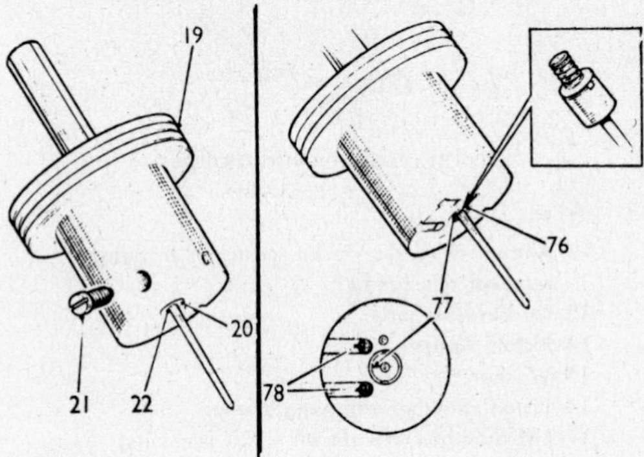

Installation of fixed and spring-loaded type jet needles

19 Piston
20 Needle
21 Needle retaining screw
22 The square shoulder or small taper on the needle shank should be flush with the bottom of the piston
76 Lower guide edge should be flush with the bottom of the piston
77 Needle alignment mark
78 Piston alignment marks

stall the jet needle so that the shoulder is even with the bottom of the piston(see illustrations for fixed and spring-loaded type needles). Do not lubricate any part of the piston except the surface of the damper tube.

After the jet assembly is fitted into the carburetor body and before it is fully tightened, the jet will have to be centered so that the needle will fit into it evenly and without binding. With the piston removed, look down into the bore and center the top of the jet in the hole by moving the bottom of the jet assembly. Partially tighten the jet assembly locknut. Insert the piston, with the needle installed, into the bore. Push the jet tube all the way up in the jet assembly. Temporarily install the piston-chamber over the piston. Lift the piston all the way and let it fall. It should fall smoothly and seat with a distinct click. If the jet is not centered properly the needle will hang up in the jet tube and the piston will not fall all the way. Several tries will probably be needed before the piston falls freely. Be sure to check it once more after the jet assembly locknut is fully tightened.

The jet restrictor on Emission Control System carburetors cannot be accurately repositioned without the aid of an exhaust gas analyzer. If an analyzer is available, lock the restrictor in the range where carbon dioxide emissions from the engine are just inside the maximum allowable level. If an analyzer is not available, adjust the jet as for an earlier engine without emission controls and have the emissions level checked at the earliest possible date.

Carburetor synchronization and jet adjustment should be carefully performed when the units have been rebuilt. Refer to the preceding section.

Exhaust System

The exhaust systems used on MGs are generally of a straightforward design, using, in most cases, straight-through mufflers and rubber-insulated hangers. However, new cars are equipped with exhaust systems that are welded into a solid unit, and when a muffler or other component requires replacement the defective part must be cut off. Except in the case of some Midget models, the exhaust system can be purchased in individual component pieces and does not have to be replaced as a complete unit. Welding may be necessary when only part of the original exhaust system, such as an intermediate pipe, is replaced on the MGB or MGC. Welding can be avoided by replacing the original exhaust system completely with component parts on those models. Normal U-clamps can then be used to fasten the parts together.

The 1100 sedan and the Midget up to 1968 do not use any gasket between the front pipe and the exhaust manifold. A pinch-type clamp is used to join the pipe and manifold flanges together directly. It is important that a quantity of muffler sealer and a new clamp are used at this connection whenever the pipe has been removed. If the pipe flange is damaged or bent in any way the pipe should be replaced, because the connection will inevitably leak or come apart.

In all cases, muffler sealer should be used at any joint in the exhaust system where gasket is not used. U-clamps used at the joints should not be fully tightened until all components are in place, so that the entire system can be lined up with the hangers and prevented from making contact with the frame or underpan. When muffler sealer has been used, allow it to set for about two hours before driving the car.

An exhaust leak is a dangerous defect, because the effects of carbon monoxide poisoning are virtually undetectable until damage has been done. Check the exhaust system at least twice a year, and correct any leaks as soon as possible.

Cooling System

RADIATOR REMOVAL AND INSTALLATION

MG Midget

1. Drain the cooling system by opening the radiator tap
2. Disconnect the upper and lower hoses from the radiator.
3. Disconnect the fresh air induction pipe from the front shroud.
4. Remove the temperature sending unit from the right side of the radiator (early models only).
5. Disconnect the oil cooler lines on cars so equipped.
6. Remove the radiator retaining bolts and lift the radiator out (complete with shroud, Mk. III).
7. Installation is in reverse order of removal.

MGB

1. Open the radiator tap and drain the coolant.
2. Disconnect the upper and lower radiator hoses.
3. If the car is not equipped with an oil cooler, remove the shroud bolts and remove the radiator and shroud as an assembly.

4. If the car has an oil cooler, loosen the shroud mounting bolts, remove the overflow hose clamp, and remove the radiator to shroud bolts. Withdraw the radiator from the shroud.
5. Installation is in reverse order of removal.

MGC

1. Open the radiator tap and drain the coolant.
2. Remove the washer bottle from the radiator shroud.
3. Disconnect the upper and lower hoses from the radiator.
4. Remove the expansion tank hose clamp from the radiator shroud.
5. Remove the bolt and remove the top radiator-to-shroud bridge piece.
6. Remove the radiator mounting screws, push the shroud over the fan, and lift the radiator out.
7. Installation is in reverse order of removal.

MG 1100

1. Open the radiator tap and drain the coolant.
2. Remove the upper shroud support bracket.
3. Remove the bolt holding the lower support bracket to the transmission case.
4. Disconnect the upper and lower radiator hoses.
5. Disconnect the expansion tank hose from the radiator (if applicable).
6. Remove the bolts holding the radiator to the shroud, remove the top of the shroud, and lift the radiator out.
7. Installation is in reverse order of removal.

WATER PUMP REMOVAL AND INSTALLATION

MG Midget—Removal

1. Remove the radiator.
2. Remove the fan retaining bolts and remove the fan.
3. Loosen the air pump mounting bolts, remove the adjusting strut bolt, remove the belt and swivel and pump up out of the way (Emission Control models only).
4. Loosen the generator mounting bolts, remove the belt, remove the top mounting bolts and lower the generator out of the way.
5. Disconnect the by-pass hose and lower radiator from the water pump.
6. Remove the water pump mounting bolts and remove the pump.

MGB—Removal

1. Remove the radiator.
2. Remove the generator or alternator.
3. Remove the fan and pulley retaining bolts and remove the fan.
4. Remove the water pump mounting bolts and remove the pump.

MGC—Removal

1. Remove the radiator.
2. Loosen the alternator mounting bolts and remove the fan belt.
3. Unbolt the fan and allow it to rest on the bottom radiator shroud.
4. Remove the fan-to-pulley spacer and remove the pulley.
5. Disconnect the hoses from the pump, unscrew the mounting bolts, and remove the water pump.

MG 1100—Removal

1. Remove the radiator.
2. Remove the hoses from the water pump.
3. Remove the generator and belt.
4. Unbolt and remove the fan blades and water pump pulley.
5. Unbolt and remove the water pump.

All Models—Installation

Installation in all cases is a reversal of removal procedures. Make sure that the mating surface of the cylinder block is cleaned of pieces of the old gasket that may remain. Always use a new gasket, and torque the mounting bolts evenly.

Thermostat

The thermostat on all MGs is located in the aluminum housing, bolted to the cylinder head, that connects to the upper radiator hose. Replacement involves simply unbolting the housing and lifting out the thermostat. Before unbolting the housing, drain (and save) about half of the coolant from the radiator to prevent loss when the housing is removed. Thermostats of three different opening temperatures are available: 160° F., 180° F., and 190° F. The 180° thermostat is suitable for all around use in most climates, while the 160° and 190°

thermostats can be used in very hot or cold weather, respectively.

The thermostat should always be installed with the bellows or spring facing downwards towards the block. Use a new gasket between the thermostat housing and the cylinder head. If the gasket is made of cork, as some replacements are, be careful not to overtighten the housing nuts or the cork will be completely crushed out and will not seal.

NOTE: *Never remove the thermostat in an attempt to cure overheating, as this may cause a blown head gasket, burnt valves, etc. due to localized overheating. Instead, install a restricting washer or a gutted thermostat body.*

Engine

EXHAUST EMISSION CONTROL

Emission Control Applications

Model/ Year	*Engine Code*	*Emission Control System Type*
Midget		
1963-67	10CG/10CC/ 12CC/12CE	PCV
1968-70	12CD	PCV/EAI
1971	12CJ*	EAI/ELC
MGB		
1963-67	18GA/18GB	PCV
1968-69	18GF	PCV/EAI
1970	18GH** 18GJ	PCV/EAI EAI/ELC
1971	18GK	EAI/ELC/NOx
MGC		
1968-69	29GA	PCV/EAI
MG 1100		
1962-67	10GR	PCV

PCV—Positive Crankcase Ventilation.
EAI—Exhaust Air Injection.
ELC—Evaporative Loss Control.
NOx—Nitrogen Oxide control.
*—Some 12CJ engines also incorporate the NOx modifications.
**—18GH engines have no PCV valve. Crankcase fumes are drawn through the oil separator to the intake manifold by carburetor vacuum. Service by simply replacing the oil filler cap at 12,000 mile intervals.

NOTE: *Models equipped with the Evaporative Loss Control system are provided with a crankcase ventilation system integral with the ELC. The only service required is to replace the oil filler cap at 12,000 mile intervals.*

Positive Crankcase Ventilation

The PCV system prevents crankcase fumes from venting to the atmosphere by routing them back to the intake manifold and reburning them in the combustion chambers. A non-operational PCV system can cause sludge formations and overheating. The only components in the system are the PCV valve and one-way breather type oil filler cap. To test the efficiency of the valve, remove the oil filler cap while the engine is idling. If the engine speed does not rise slightly (about 200 rpm), the valve is not operating properly and should be replaced. Valve components should be cleaned and inspected at 6,000 mile intervals, and the oil filler cap replaced every 12,000 miles.

Exhaust Air Injection

OPERATION

The EAI system consists of a belt driven air pump that forces air into the exhaust port of each cylinder, causing a reburning of exhaust gases in order to reduce the number of harmful emissions.

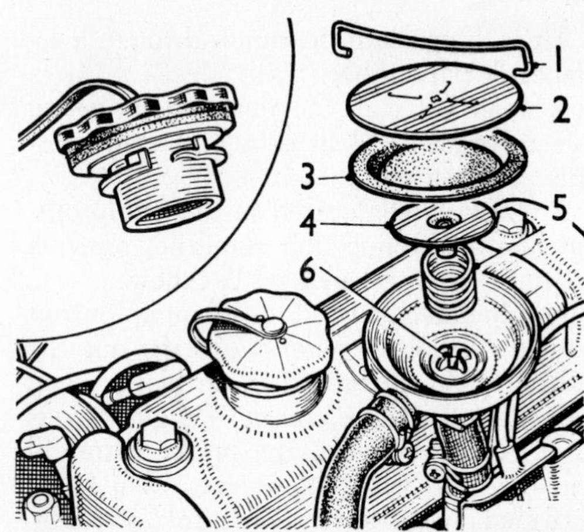

PCV valve components. Test the PCV valve by removing the oil filler cap with the engine idling —if the engine does not speed up, service or replace the valve

1 Retaining clip
2 Cover
3 Diaphragm
4 Metering valve
5 Spring
6 Guides (later type valves)

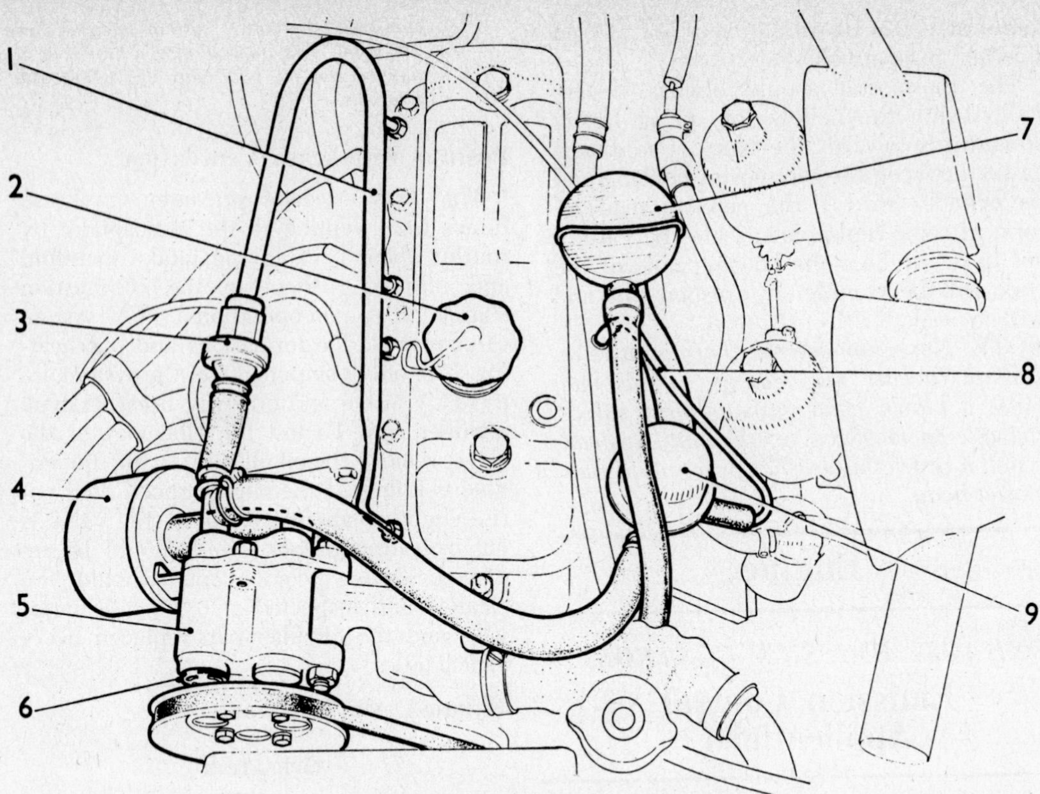

Components of the Exhaust Air Injection system

1 Air manifold
2 Oil filler cap
3 Check valve
4 Air pump air filter
5 Air pump
6 Relief valve
7 PCV valve
8 Vacuum sensing line
9 Gulp valve

Air is drawn into the pump through a replaceable paper filter.

A relief valve in the pump vents excessive air pressure, created by high rpm operation, to the atmosphere.

A check valve, located in the pump output line to the injection manifold, protects the pump from exhaust gas backflow.

A gulp valve, located in the pump output line to the intake manifold, leans out the rich fuel/air mixture that develops when the engine is decelerating (engine overrun). A line between the intake manifold and the gulp valve allows the valve to be activated by changes in manifold vacuum. On some engines a restrictor is located in the output line between the pump and valve to prevent engine surge when the valve is operating.

In addition to the air pump and its attendant equipment, all vehicles with emission control systems are equipped with the distributor and carburetors modified to meet emission standards. These units are covered separately in the ENGINE ELECTRICAL and FUEL SYSTEM sections, as well as in the SPECIFICATIONS section.

The efficient and trouble-free operation of the emission control system depends to a large extent upon the engine being correctly tuned. Proper tuning specifications given for a particular engine should be strictly adhered to (see TUNE-UP SPECIFICATIONS).

Maintenance

At the time of an engine tune-up (6,000 miles recommended), the entire exhaust air injection system should be inspected. Clean or replace the air pump air filter element. Check the air hoses and connections for any evidence of leaking. (This is very important, because an air leak can cause overheating, resulting in burnt valves, a blown head gasket, etc.) Check the air pump drive belt tension and adjust it if necessary. Properly adjusted, the belt should have a total defection of 1/2 inch midway between

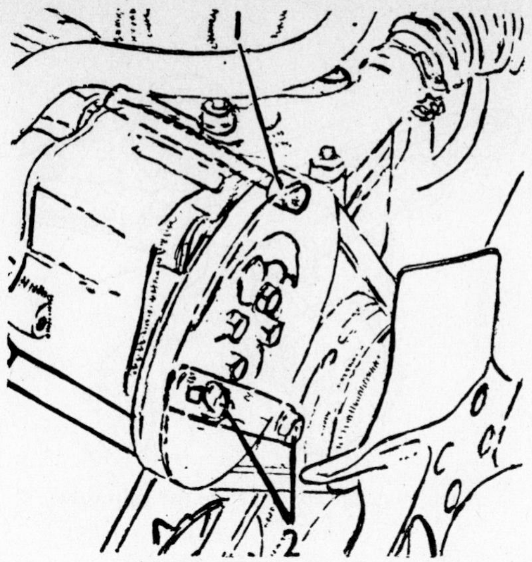

Air pump mounting bolt (1) and adjusting strut bolts (2), MGB and Midget

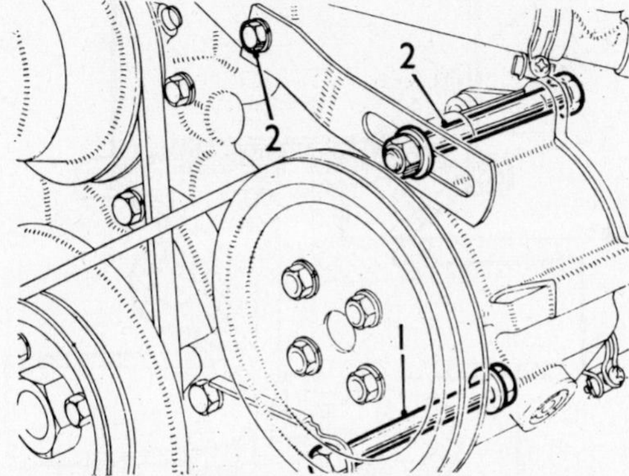

Air pump mounting bolt (1) and adjusting strut bolts (2), MGC

the pulleys. Adjustment is made by loosening the mounting bolt and adjusting strut bolts, in the same manner as generator adjustment.

Component Testing

To check the air pump and relief valve, first make sure that the pump drive belt is properly adjusted and that the air filter is clean. Disconnect and plug the air supply hose to the gulp valve. Disconnect the injection manifold air hose at the check valve, and connect a pressure gauge to the hose. At an engine speed of 1,000 rpm (Midget–1,200 rpm), the pressure gauge should not read less than 2.75 lb./sq. in. If a lower reading is obtained, tape the relief

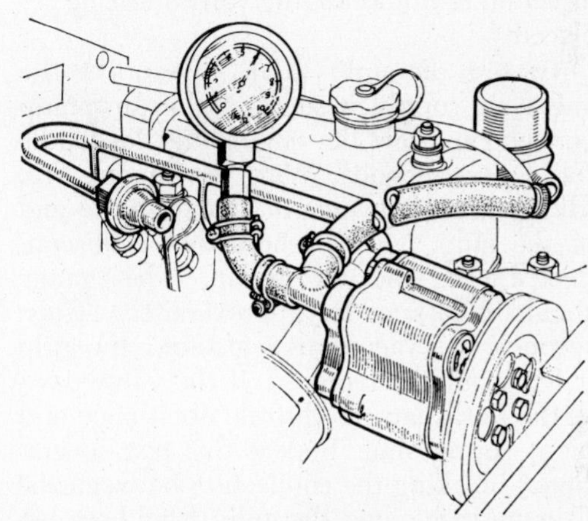

Air pump pressure check

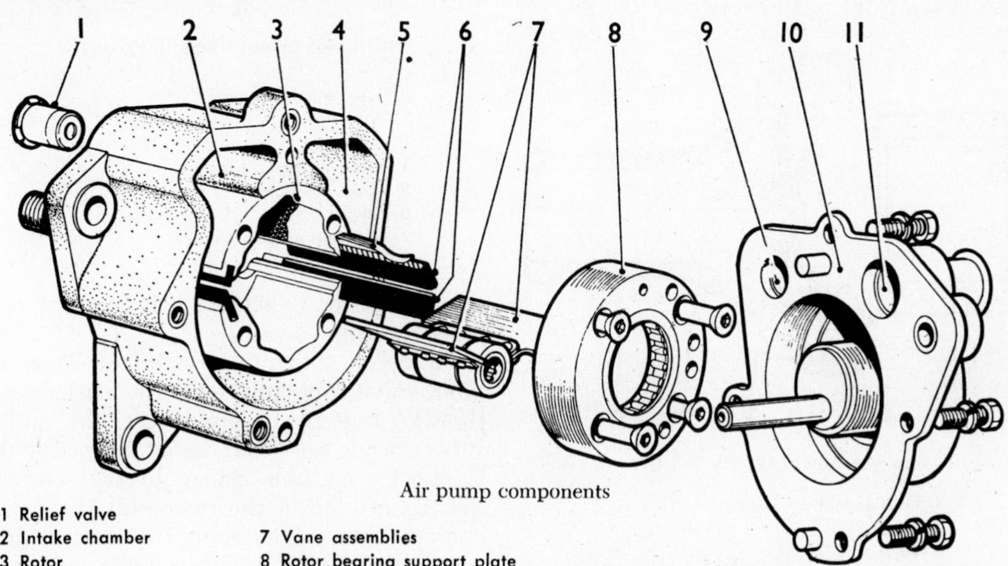

Air pump components

1 Relief valve
2 Intake chamber
3 Rotor
4 Output chamber
5 Spring
6 Carbons
7 Vane assemblies
8 Rotor bearing support plate
9 Output port
10 End-cover
11 Intake port

valve shut and repeat the test. If the reading is now satisfactory, replace the relief valve (it can be removed by prying with a screwdriver or with a gear puller). If the reading is still low, replace or overhaul the air pump unit.

NOTE: *If the pump is removed for service, do not hold it in a vise. Even a small amount of pressure will distort the pump body.*

To test the check valve, disconnect the air supply hose from the valve and unscrew it from the injection manifold. Blow through the valve at each connection (do not use compressed air). Air should pass through the valve only from the air supply side (from the air pump) to the manifold connection. If air passes in the opposite direction or not at all, the valve must be replaced.

To test the gulp valve, disconnect the valve air supply hose from the air pump connection. Start the engine and let it idle for a few seconds. With the engine still idling, connect a vacuum gauge to the end of the gulp valve air hose that is disconnected from the air pump. The gauge should read zero for approximately fifteen seconds. If a vacuum is registered, the gulp valve should be replaced. If the valve passes the test, snap the throttle open once and let it spring shut. Repeat this test several times, breaking the connection between the vacuum gauge and the gulp valve hose before each operation of the throttle to return the gauge to zero. In every case the gauge should register a vacuum. If it does not, replace the gulp valve.

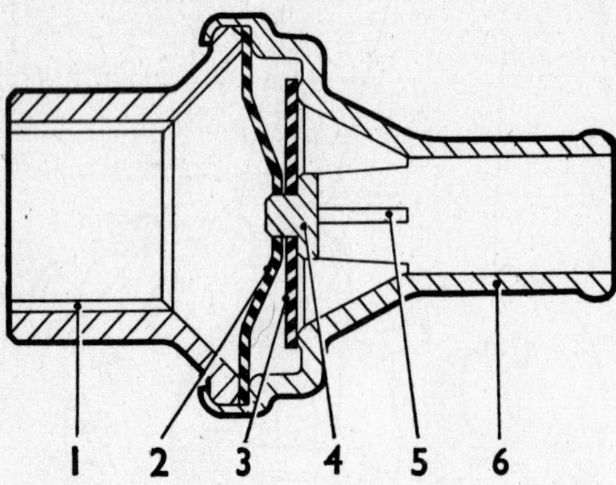

Cross-section of the check valve

1 Air manifold connection
2 Diaphragm
3 Valve
4 Valve pilot
5 Guides
6 Air supply connection

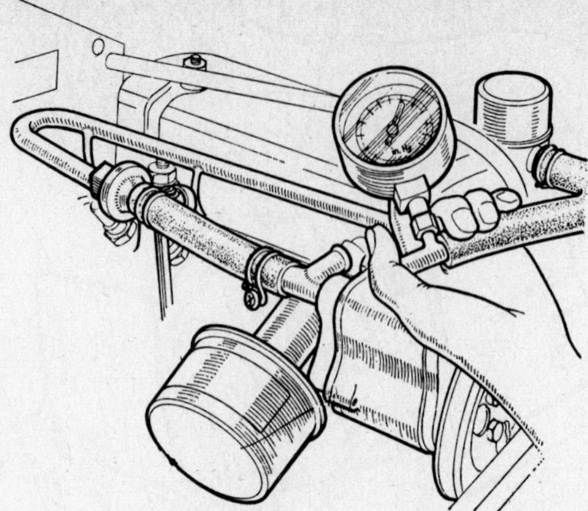

Vacuum gauge connected to the gulp valve

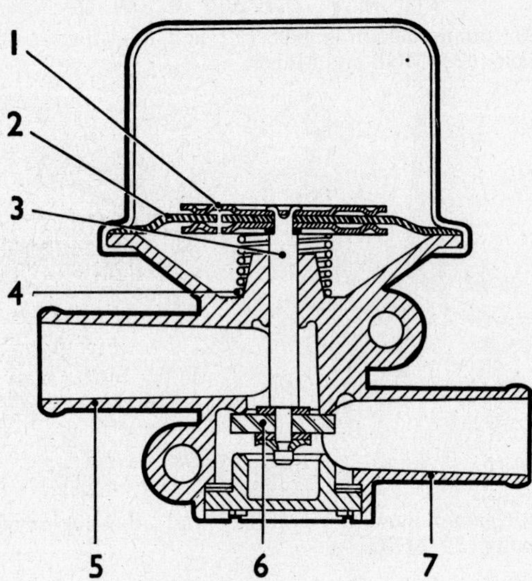

Cross-section of the gulp valve

1 Pressure balance hole
2 Diaphragm
3 Valve stem
4 Return spring
5 Intake manifold hose connection
6 Valve
7 Air pump hose connection

To check the intake manifold vacuum limit valve (integral with the carburetor throttle butterfly), disconnect the gulp valve sensing line from the intake manifold. Connect a vacuum gauge to the sensing line connection at the manifold. With the engine at normal operating temperature, increase the engine speed to 3,000 rpm and let the throttle snap shut. The vacuum gauge reading should immediately rise to

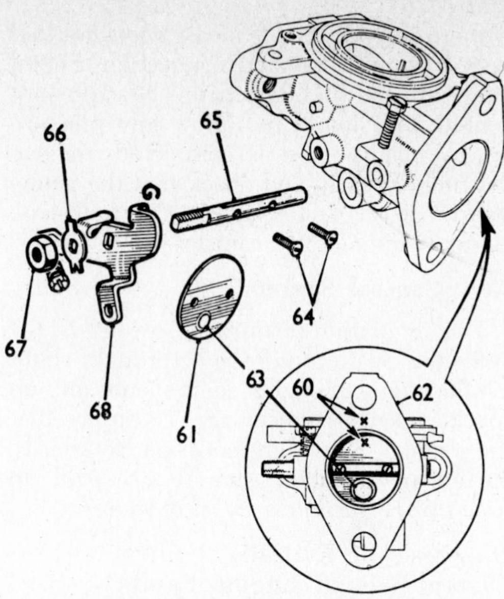

Throttle butterfly and vacuum limit valve

60 Alignment marks (scribed in)
61 Throttle butterfly
62 Carburetor body
63 Intake manifold vacuum limit valve
64 Butterfly retaining screws
65 Throttle shaft
66 Locktab
67 Spindle nut
68 Throttle lever

between 20.5 and 22.0 in. vacuum. If the reading is outside these limits, the carburetors must be removed and the throttle butterflies replaced. Make sure, in each carburetor, that the butterfly is centered in the bore before the securing screws are tightened. Carburetor removal and tuning procedures can be found in the FUEL SYSTEM section.

Evaporative Loss Control System

The system is designed to collect fuel vapor from the fuel tank and carburetor float chambers. The vapor is stored in the adsorption canister while the engine is stopped, and when the engine is restarted it passes through the crankcase ventilation system and into the combustion chambers. Vapors are drawn into the engine directly when the engine is running. An air bleed chamber is located in the fuel tank to prevent overfilling, and a small separation tank, between the fuel tank and adsorption canister, prevents liquid fuel from being drawn into the canister.

The only component of the system that needs servicing is the adsorption canister. The filter pad should be replaced at 12,000 mile intervals, and the canister unit should be replaced at 50,000 miles. If the canister becomes saturated with fuel, it must be replaced sooner. Do not attempt to clear the

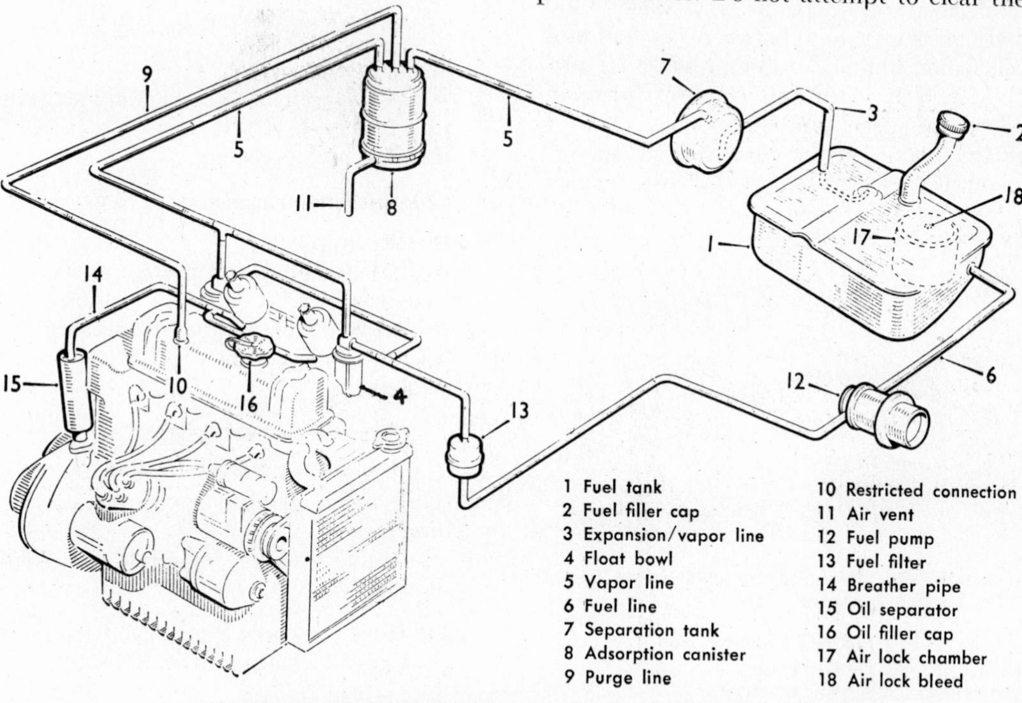

1 Fuel tank
2 Fuel filler cap
3 Expansion/vapor line
4 Float bowl
5 Vapor line
6 Fuel line
7 Separation tank
8 Adsorption canister
9 Purge line
10 Restricted connection
11 Air vent
12 Fuel pump
13 Fuel filter
14 Breather pipe
15 Oil separator
16 Oil filler cap
17 Air lock chamber
18 Air lock bleed

Components of the Evaporative Loss Control system, MGB and Midget

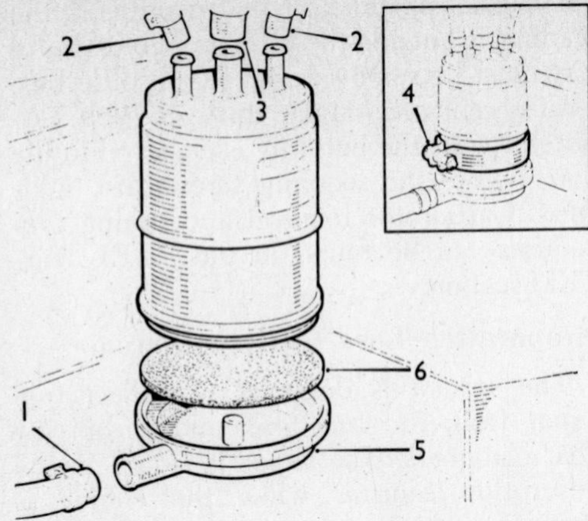

Adsorption canister filter pad replacement

1 Air vent tube
2 Vapor lines
3 Purge pipe
4 Canister clamp
5 End cap
6 Filter pad

canister with compressed air. To remove the canister, disconnect the lines and loosen the clamp screw, and lift it out. To replace the filter pad, unscrew the lower end cap of the canister. Remove the filter, clean the cap, install a new filter, and replace the end cap.

To pressure check the fuel system for leaks, first make sure that there is fuel in the tank and that the fuel system is primed. Disconnect the fuel tank ventilation line from the adsorption canister. Connect a low scale pressure gauge between the fuel tank ventilation line and a low pressure air supply (such as a tire pump). Pressurize the system to 1 psi. *Do not exceed this pressure at any time.* The pressure should not fall below 1/2 psi over a period of ten seconds.

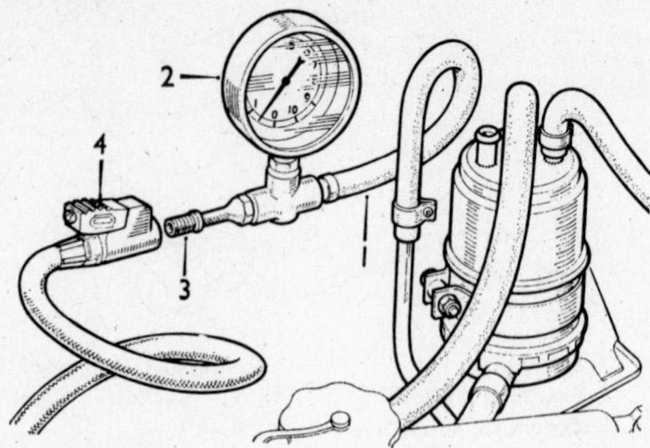

Air supply and pressure gauge connections to test the fuel system for leaks

1 Fuel tank ventilation pipe
2 Pressure gauge
3 Air hose connector
4 Low pressure air supply

If there is evidence of a leak, check all fuel system components and connections beginning with the fuel filler cap. The cap is not vented and should not allow any pressure loss. When the test is completed, remove the fuel filler cap and check that the gauge returns to zero. Reconnect the fuel tank ventilation line to the canister.

NO_X Control System

The regulation of nitrogen oxide (NO_X) emissions is accomplished through slight modifications to engine components, and no special service is necessary. To ensure that the engine is within emission standards, particular attention should be paid to tune-up specifications and procedures.

Diagnosis of Emission Control System-Related Engine Faults

BACKFIRE IN EXHAUST SYSTEM

1. Leak in intake system
2. Leak in exhaust system
3. Defective gulp valve
4. Gulp valve air hose or vacuum sensing line leak
5. Defective intake manifold vacuum limit valve
6. Incorrect ignition timing
7. Distributor vacuum advance not operating correctly

POOR THROTTLE RESPONSE

1. Faulty gulp valve
2. Gulp valve air hose or vacuum sensing line leak
3. Leak in intake system

ENGINE SURGE AT CRUISING SPEEDS

1. Faulty gulp valve
2. Gulp valve air hose or vacuum sensing line leak
3. Restricted air supply to adsorption canister (Evaporative Loss Control system)

ERRATIC IDLING OR STALLING

1. Faulty gulp valve
2. Gulp valve air hose or vacuum sensing line leak
3. Defective intake manifold vacuum limit valve

AIR HOSE BETWEEN PUMP AND CHECK VALVE OVERHEATED OR BURNT

1. Faulty check valve
2. Air pump not pumping

Noisy Air Pump

1. Incorrect belt tension
2. Belt pulleys damaged, loose, or misaligned
3. Pump seizing or failing

Engine Overheating

1. Incorrect ignition timing
2. Air injector missing from manifold
3. Faulty relief valve in pump
4. Choke linkage sticking or cable not fully returned

Engine Overheating Due to Sudden Over-Lean Mixture

1. Air leak in intake system
2. Air leak into crankcase
3. Faulty PCV valve diaphragm (early cars)
4. Crankcase breather hose to carburetor leak (later cars)

Fuel Starvation on Evaporative Loss Control Equipped Cars

1. Air supply to adsorption canister restricted
2. Vapor line between fuel tank and adsorption canister blocked

ENGINE REMOVAL AND INSTALLATION

MG Midget

The engine of the Midget can be removed with or without the transmission. Either way, the preliminary steps are:

1. Drain the crankcase.
2. Disconnect the battery.
3. Remove the hood.
4. Disconnect the radiator and heater hoses and oil cooler lines (late models only), and remove the radiator.
5. Disconnect the choke and throttle cables and tachometer cable (Mk. I only).
6. Disconnect the oil pressure gauge pipe from the engine.
7. Disconnect and tag all electrical connections to the engine.
8. Disconnect the high tension wires from the coil and spark plugs, and remove the distributor cap.
9. Unbolt the exhaust header pipe from the manifold and tie the pipe out of the way.
10. Remove the air cleaners and disconnect the fuel line.

At this point, the engine can be removed either with or without the transmission. If it is desired to remove only the engine:

1. Remove the starter motor.
2. Remove the fuel filter bowl (Mk. I only).
3. Support the transmission with a jack, and remove the bell housing bolts.
4. Connect a hoist to the engine and unbolt the right-side engine mount from the chassis bracket.
5. Disconnect the left-side engine mount from the front engine plate and lift the engine from the vehicle, taking care not to damage the transmission mainshaft.

If it is desired to remove the engine and the transmission as a unit:

1. Drain the transmission oil and disconnect the back-up light switch lead (later models only).
2. Remove the gearshift lever cover, and remove the spring cap, spring, and plunger.
3. Unbolt the shift lever retaining plate and lift out the lever.
4. With the carpet turned back, remove the rear transmission mount bolts.
5. From underneath the car, unscrew the speedometer cable from the transmission housing and release the cable support bracket from the bell housing.
6. Unbolt the clutch slave cylinder from the bell housing.
7. Unbolt the driveshaft from the differential flange and slide it out. Be sure to mark the flanges so that the driveshaft can be reinstalled correctly.
8. Connect a hoist to the engine and remove the remaining transmission mounting bolts.
9. Unbolt the right-side engine mount from the chassis bracket and disconnect the left-side mount from the front engine plate.
10. Lift the engine/transmission unit from the vehicle.

Installation of the engine or engine/transmission unit is in reverse order of removal. Be sure to refill the engine, transmission, and radiator.

MGB

The engine of the MGB can be removed with or without the transmission. Either way, the preliminary steps are:

1. Drain the crankcase.
2. Disconnect the batteries.

3. Remove the hood.
4. Disconnect the oil cooler and pressure gauge lines from the engine.
5. Disconnect the heater and radiator hoses, and unbolt and remove the radiator, radiator shroud, and oil cooler as a unit.
6. Disconnect and mark all electrical connections to the engine.
7. Disconnect the high tension leads from the coil and spark plugs, and remove the distributor cap.
8. Disconnect the choke and throttle cables and the tachometer cable (early models only).
9. Unbolt the exhaust header pipe from the manifold, and disconnect the bell housing bracket.
10. Remove the air cleaners and disconnect the fuel line.

At this point, the engine can be removed either with or without the transmission. If it is desired to remove only the engine:

1. Support the transmission with a jack, and remove the bell housing bolts.
2. Remove the bolts holding the front engine mounts to the frame.
3. Connect a hoist to the engine and lift it from the chassis, taking care not to damage the transmission mainshaft or the oil pan.

If it is desired to remove the engine and transmission as a unit:

1. Drain the transmission oil and disconnect the back-up light switch lead (later models only).
2. Disconnect the overdrive solenoid wire or the automatic transmission starter inhibitor wire, where applicable.
3. Unbolt the clutch slave cylinder from the bell housing.
4. Disconnect the speedometer cable from the transmission.
5. Unbolt the driveshaft from the differential flange and slide it out. Be sure to mark the flanges so that the driveshaft can be reinstalled in its original position.
6. Lift the gearshift boot, unbolt the lever retaining screws, and remove shift lever (manual transmission).
7. Disconnect the gearshift lever from the transmission shaft, and disconnect the downshift cable from the carburetors (automatic transmission).
8. Connect a hoist to the engine and remove the rear crossmember and the transmission mounts, along with the transmission stabilizer rod or bracket.
9. Remove the bolts securing the front engine mounts to the frame.
10. Lift the engine/transmission unit from the vehicle.

Installation of the engine or engine/transmission unit is in reverse order of removal. Be sure to refill the engine, transmission, and radiator.

MGC

The engine and transmission of the MGC are removed as a unit. Removal is accomplished in the following manner:

1. Disconnect the batteries and remove the hood.
2. Drain the crankcase and the transmission.
3. Drain the radiator, disconnect the radiator and heater hoses and remove the radiator (see RADIATOR REMOVAL AND INSTALLATION).
4. Disconnect and mark all electrical connections to the engine.
5. Disconnect the wires from the coil to the distributor.
6. Remove the air cleaners and disconnect the fuel line.
7. Disconnect the choke and throttle cables, and the throttle relay linkage (overdrive and automatic transmissions).
8. Disconnect the brake booster vacuum line from the intake manifold.
9. Disconnect the engine oil cooler and automatic transmission oil cooler lines (if applicable).
10. Disconnect the water temperature and oil pressure gauge lines from the engine.
11. Lift the gearshift boot, remove the lever retaining bolts, and remove the shift lever (manual transmission).
12. Disconnect the manual control rod from the shift lever, underneath the car (automatic transmission).
13. Disconnect the speedometer cable from the gearbox.
14. Unbolt the clutch slave cylinder from the bell housing.
15. Mark the flanges for replacement and disconnect the driveshaft.
16. Support the rear of the engine and disconnect the rear crossmember from the body.
17. Unbolt the exhaust header pipes from

the manifold and tie them out of the way.
18. Attach a hoist to the engine and unbolt the engine mounts from the frame.
19. Raise the engine just enough to gain access to the transmission wires, and mark and disconnect the wires. Be sure to disconnect the harness clips from the transmission case.
20. Lift the engine/transmission unit from the vehicle.

Installation is in reverse order of removal. Be sure to refill the engine, transmission, and radiator when they have been reinstalled.

MG 1100

The engine and transmission of the 1100 sedan are removed together, as the transmission is located in the engine crankcase. Removal is accomplished in the following manner:

1. Disconnect the battery and remove the hood.
2. Drain the crankcase.
3. Disconnect the ground lead from the clutch housing.
4. Tag and disconnect the electrical leads from the distributor, coil, and generator.
5. Remove the starter motor.
6. Remove the air cleaner and carburetors.
7. Drain the radiator and disconnect the heater control valve cable and heater hoses. The radiator is lifted out with the engine unit.
8. Disconnect the radiator overflow hose from the expansion tank.
9. Disconnect the speedometer cable at the transmission (early cars) or cable coupling (late cars).
10. Lift the gearshift boot, unbolt the lever retaining plate and remove the lever. Remove the two bolts securing shift linkage housing to the floor tunnel.
11. Remove the clutch lever spring. Unbolt the slave cylinder and tie it out of the way.
12. Jack up the front end and place stands beneath the frame side-members.
13. Unbolt the exhaust pipe from the manifold and disconnect the pipe support from the transmission housing.
14. Remove the four set-screws securing the shift linkage housing to the transmission and remove the housing.
15. Remove the U-bolts from the inner axle shaft joints and push the shafts into the outer joint to remove the rubber couplings.
16. Remove the two left-side engine mount nuts that secure the mount to the bracket.
17. Attach a hoist to the engine.
18. Unbolt the right engine mount bracket.
19. Remove the bolts securing the rear engine mount bracket to the sub-frame.
20. Lift the power unit from the car, making certain that all cables and lines are clear of the engine.

Installation is in reverse order of removal. Be sure to refill the crankcase and radiator when the unit has been reinstalled.

INTAKE/EXHAUST MANIFOLD REMOVAL AND INSTALLATION

MG Midget—Removal

1. Remove the carburetors and air cleaners (see CARBURETOR REMOVAL AND INSTALLATION).
2. Unbolt the exhaust pipe from the exhaust manifold.
3. Unbolt the heater pipe clamps from the intake manifold.
4. Unscrew the PCV valve hose from the manifold connection (if applicable).
5. Disconnect the vacuum advance and gulp valve lines from the intake manifold (if applicable).
6. Unbolt and remove the manifolds.

MGB—Removal

1. Remove the carburetors and air cleaners (see CARBURETOR REMOVAL AND INSTALLATION).
2. Disconnect the distributor vacuum advance line and the gulp valve line (if applicable).
3. Unscrew the PCV valve hose from the intake manifold connection (if applicable).
4. Unbolt the heater pipe clamps from the intake manifold (early models only).
5. Unbolt the exhaust header pipes from the exhaust manifold.
6. Unbolt and remove the manifolds.

MGC—Removal

1. Remove the carburetors and air cleaners (see CARBURETOR REMOVAL AND INSTALLATION).
2. Disconnect the brake booster vacuum line from the intake manifold.

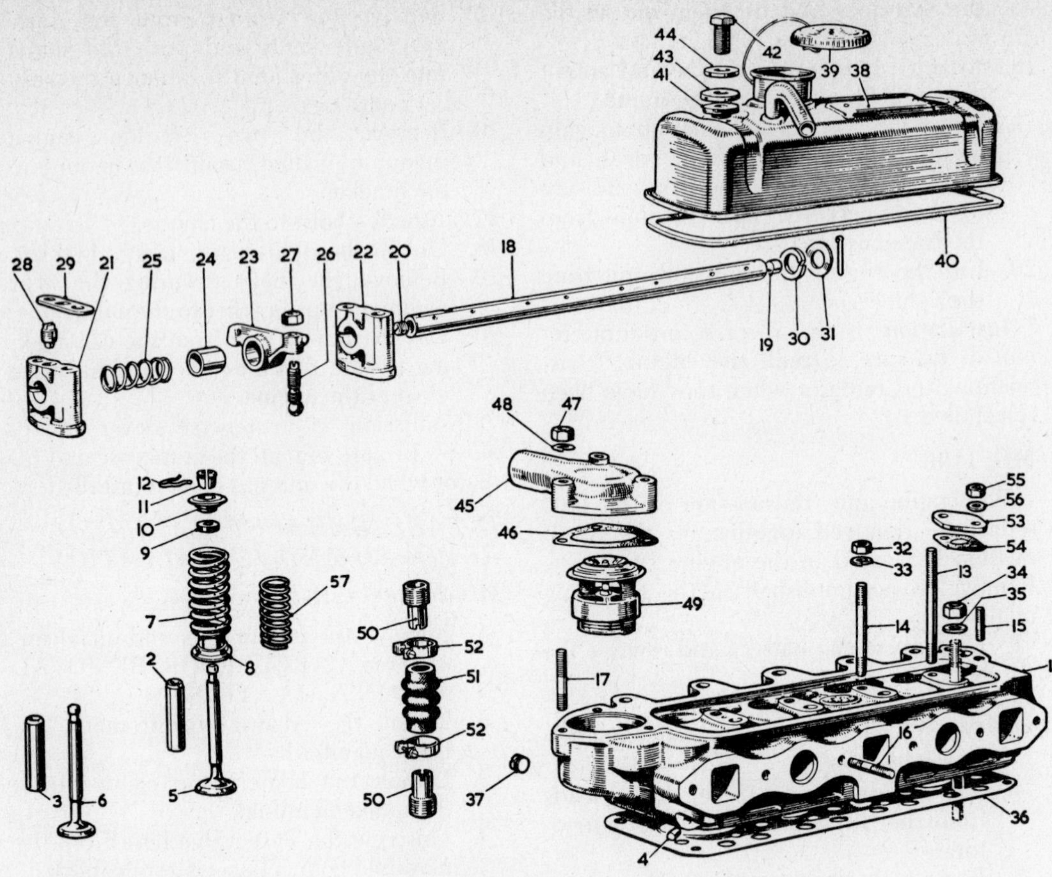

1 Cylinder head with valve guides
2 Inlet valve guide
3 Exhaust valve guide
4 Oil hole plug
5 Inlet valve
6 Exhaust valve
7 Outer valve spring
8 Shroud for valve guide
9 Valve packing ring
10 Valve spring cup
11 Valve cotter
12 Valve cotter circlip
13 Rocker bracket stud (long)
14 Rocker bracket stud (short)
15 Cover-plate stud
16 Manifold stud
17 Water outlet elbow stud
18 Valve rocker shaft (plugged)
19 Rocker shaft plug (plain)
20 Rocker shaft plug (screwed)
21 Rocker shaft bracket (tapped)
22 Rocker shaft bracket (plain)
23 Rocker (bushed)
24 Rocker bush
25 Rocker spacing spring
26 Tappet adjusting screw
27 Locknut
28 Rocker shaft locating screw
29 Rocker shaft bracket plate
30 Spring washer
31 Washer
32 Nut
33 Spring washer
34 Cylinder head nut
35 Washer
36 Cylinder head gasket
37 Thermal indicator boss screwed plug
38 Valve rocker cover
39 Oil filler cap
40 Cover joint
41 Cover bush
42 Nut
43 Distance piece
44 Cup washer
45 Water outlet elbow
46 Joint
47 Nut
48 Spring washer
49 Thermostat
50 By-pass adaptor
51 By-pass connector (rubber)
52 By-pass clip
53 Cover-plate
54 Joint (plate to cylinder head)
55 Cover nut
56 Spring washer
57 Inner valve spring

MG Midget cylinder head components, typical of all models with minor variations

3. Disconnect the PCV valve hose, gulp valve line, and distributor vacuum advance line from the intake manifold.
4. Disconnect and temporarily relocate the throttle relay bracket assembly.
5. Disconnect the two fuel overflow pipes from the intake manifold.
6. Unbolt the exhaust header pipes from the exhaust manifold.
7. If the manifolds are to be separated, unbolt the intake manifold support brackets from the exhaust manifold.
8. Unbolt and remove the manifolds.

MG 1100—Removal

1. Remove the carburetors and air cleaner (see CARBURETOR REMOVAL AND INSTALLATION).
2. Unbolt the exhaust pipe from the exhaust manifold.
3. Disconnect the PCV valve and distributor vacuum advance line from the intake manifold.
4. Unbolt and remove the manifolds.

Installation—All Models

Manifold installation in all cases is in reverse order of removal. Thoroughly clean the mating surfaces and use new gaskets. The perforated metal face of the gasket should face the manifold. New exhaust header ring gaskets should be used on the MGB, MGC, and late Midget models. It may be necessary to use a new exhaust pipe clamp on the MG 1100 and early Midget. Be sure to tighten the manifold studs evenly (see TORQUE SPECIFICATIONS).

CYLINDER HEAD REMOVAL AND INSTALLATION

Removal—All Models

All MGs, with the exception of the MGA Twin-Cam which is not covered in this book, have water-cooled, inline, pushrod operated overhead valve engines with four or six cylinders. As such, cylinder head operations on the different models are closely related and some generalities can be assumed.

The cylinder head nuts should be loosened, gradually, in the same order as they are tightened, to prevent the head from warping (see TIGHTENING SEQUENCES). For the same reason, the head should be removed only when the engine is cold. When the cylinder head nuts and all accessories have been unbolted from the head, it may be necessary to tap each side of the head with a rubber mallet to break the head gasket seal. When the head is free, lift it evenly over the studs. If any water has found its way into the cylinders it should be immediately removed and the cylinder walls coated with oil. If the head is not to be reinstalled for a day or more, it is a good idea to stuff towels into the cylinders to protect them.

The cylinder head removal procedure for all models is as follows:

1. Drain the radiator.
2. Disconnect the radiator and heater hoses from the cylinder head.
3. Remove the heater control valve and unbolt the top radiator bracket (1100 sedan only).
4. Remove the carburetors and air cleaners, and unbolt the manifolds and pull them back out of the way.
5. Remove the rocker cover and remove the cylinder head nuts in the proper order (see TIGHTENING SEQUENCES).
6. Lift the rocker shaft assembly off (applying inward pressure at the ends on the MGC) and remove the pushrods, keeping them in order.
7. Remove the spark plugs and disconnect the water temperature sending unit from the head.
8. Disconnect the air supply hose from the check valve (Emission Control models only).
9. Unbolt the air pump from its mounting point on the head (four-cylinder Emission Control models only).
10. Lift the head from the cylinder block.

Installation—All Models

Installation is in reverse order of removal. Thoroughly clean the mating surfaces of the cylinder block and head, and always use a new gasket. The gasket is marked Top and Front to facilitate correct installation. Gasket sealing compound is not necessary, but may be used. Cylinder head nuts should be tightened gradually, in the correct sequence (see TIGHTENING SEQUENCES), and to the proper torque value (see TORQUE SPECIFICATIONS). When the head has been tightened the valves must be adjusted (see VALVE ADJUSTMENT). After running the engine for between 200 and 500 miles the head should be retorqued and the valves readjusted.

Valves No. 4 and 7 open, valves No. 5 and 2 correctly positioned for adjustment

When retorquing the head, simply back off each nut slightly and retighten to specification, one at a time and in the proper sequence.

VALVE TRAIN

Valve Adjustment

Valve clearances for the different MG models can be found in TUNE-UP SPECIFICATIONS. Adjustment procedures for all models are the same. Valve adjustment should be carried out at every engine tune-up or whenever excessive valve train noise is noticed. Loose valve clearance will generally only cause a metallic thrashing sound, while over-tight adjustment can cause rough running and burnt valves.

To adjust the valves, remove the rocker cover and provide a means of turning the engine over slowly. Although the engine may be turned over by hand or with the ignition switch, the best methods are by manually operating the starter solenoid (early models only) or connecting an auxiliary starter wire to the solenoid. To operate the solenoid by hand on early models, simply push in the small shaft or rubber cover at the rear of switch or pull the actuation cable (Midget Mk. I only). An auxiliary starter wire can be either a two-position switch with one lead connected to the battery cable terminal at the solenoid and the other lead connected to the small gauge wire at the separate solenoid terminal, or

Valve Open	Adjust this Valve: Six Cylinder	Adjust this Valve: Four Cylinder
1	12	8
2	11	7
3	10	6
4	9	5
5	8	4
6	7	3
7	6	2
8	5	1
9	4	
10	3	
11	2	
12	1	

Valve rocker clearance adjusting sequence for four and six cylinder engines.

Using a feeler gauge to measure valve clearance. The arrow points to the adjusting screw and locknut

simply a short length of wire connected momentarily in the above manner to turn the engine over.

CAUTION: Make sure that the transmission is in neutral before turning the engine over while outside the vehicle.

In order to adjust an individual valve, it must be in a certain relationship to the camshaft; i.e., it must be on the low side of the camshaft lobe. Because the relationship of one valve to the action of another is known (through camshaft configuration), it is possible to position one of the valves in its fully opened position (valve spring compressed) and thus know that another valve is correctly positioned for adjustment. If a line is drawn at the midpoint of the head separating the valves into two equal groups, then this relationship is symmetrical. In other words, if one of the end valves is open, then the valve at the opposite end can be adjusted; if the second valve in from one end is open, the second valve in from the other end can be adjusted, etc.

When a valve is correctly positioned for adjustment, check the clearance between the valve stem and the rocker arm. If clearance is incorrect, loosen the adjusting screw locknut and turn the screw (clockwise to decrease clearance, counterclockwise to increase clearance) until the feeler gauge blade slides in and out with some resistance. To double check adjustment, try inserting the next size thinner and next size thicker feeler blade. If, for example, desired clearance is .010 in., the .009 in. blade should fit quite easily, while the .011 or .012 in. blade should be too thick to fit. When correct clearance has been obtained, hold the adjusting screw from turning and tighten the locknut. Recheck clearance in case the adjustment screw turned slightly when the locknut was tightened.

When all valves have been adjusted, reinstall the rocker cover. Make sure that the cover gasket is in good condition or an oil leak will develop. Breather hose connections at the rocker cover (if any) should be tight.

Valve Removal and Installation

See ENGINE REBUILDING.

Valve Guide Removal and Installation

See the ENGINE REBUILDING and VALVE SPECIFICATIONS.

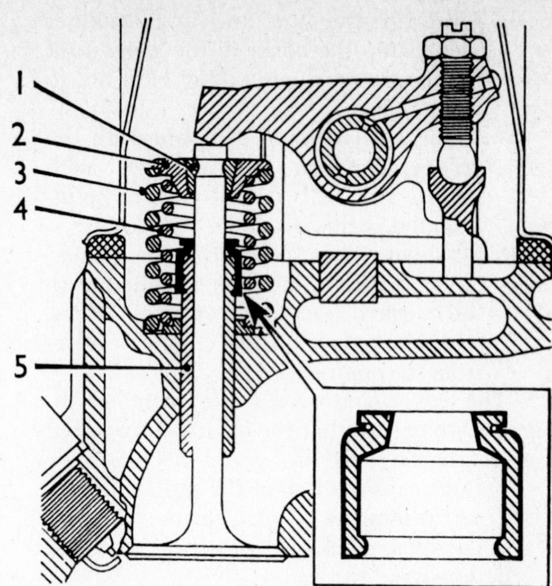

The valve components assembled, typical of all models

1 Cotter pins
2 Retainer cup
3 Outer spring
4 Inner spring
5 Valve guide
Insert: valve stem oil seal

Valve and Valve Seat Resurfacing

See ENGINE REBUILDING and VALVE SPECIFICATIONS.

CAMSHAFT AND TIMING CHAIN

Timing Gear Cover Removal and Installation and Oil Seal Replacement

MG MIDGET

To remove the timing gear cover:

1. Remove the radiator.
2. Loosen the generator adjustment bolts and remove the fan belt.

NOTE: On 1968 and later Midgets it is necessary to unbolt the engine mounts and exhaust pipe in order to raise the front of the engine to provide clearance for removal of the pulley.

3. Bend the locktab back and unscrew the crankshaft pulley nut.
4. Carefully pry the pulley from the crankshaft.
5. Unbolt and remove the timing gear cover.

To replace the timing gear cover oil seal:

1. Pry the old seal out of the cover.

2. Lubricate the new seal and install it evenly into the cover in the same position as the old one, taking care not to damage it.
3. If the seal is made of rubber, fill the groove between the seal lips with grease. Felt seals do not need to be lubricated in this manner.
4. Make sure that the oil thrower behind the crankshaft pulley is installed with the concave side (early engines) or the face marked F (later engines) away from the engine.

The cover and pulley are installed together to ensure that the oil seal is centered correctly. To reinstall:

1. Lubricate the hub of the pulley and insert it into the oil seal, turning the pulley in a clockwise direction to avoid damaging the seal.
2. Align the pulley keyway with the crankshaft key and push the pulley (with the cover and cover gasket) onto the crankshaft.
3. Replace the cover bolts and tighten them evenly.
4. Tighten and lock the crankshaft pulley nut.
5. Reinstall the fan belt, and replace and fill the radiator.

MGB

Timing gear cover removal and installation and oil seal replacement procedures for the MGB are the same as for the Midget, with one exception: on 18GB and later engines, the steering rack must be unbolted from the body and moved forward to provide clearance for removal of the crankshaft pulley. It is not necessary to raise the front of the engine to remove the pulley on the MGB.

MGC

To remove the timing gear cover:

1. Remove the radiator.
2. Drain the crankcase.
3. Remove the transmission stone guard.
4. Unbolt and lower the oil pan, allowing it to rest in the front crossmember.
5. Unbolt the alternator adjustment strut and loosen the adjustment (pivot) bolt.
6. Remove the fan belt and unbolt and remove the fan.
7. Remove the spacer and the water pump pulley.
8. Bend the locktab back and unscrew the crankshaft nut.
9. Remove the crankshaft pulley/damper unit.
10. Unbolt and remove the timing gear cover.

To replace the timing gear cover oil seal:

1. Pry the old seal out of the cover.
2. Lubricate the new seal and install it evenly into the cover in the same position as the old one.

Installation of the cover is in reverse order of removal. Always use a new gasket between the cover and cylinder block. Torque the oil pan bolts to 6 ft. lb., and the cover bolts to 25 ft. lb. Do not forget to refill the crankcase with fresh oil.

MG 1100

Timing gear cover removal and installation and oil seal replacement procedures for the 1100 sedan are the same as for the Midget.

Timing Gear and Chain—Removal and Installation, All Models

The camshafts in all MG engines are driven by a chain from the crankshaft. The MG 1100 and Midget models have an endless, single-row timing chain without a tensioner, while the MGB and MGC have an endless, duplex chain and a chain tensioner. Chain tensioner removal and service procedures can be found under TIMING CHAIN TENSIONER SERVICE–MGB and MGC.

The crankshaft and camshaft timing gears and the timing chain usually do not require service or replacement unless, due to high mileage or improper lubrication, gear tooth wear is noticeable. If wear is evident, replace all three components. Worn gears or chain stretch as isolated problems almost never occur.

To remove the chain and gears, first remove the timing gear cover (see preceding section). On the MGB and MGC, remove the chain tensioner or retract and lock the rubbing block by removing the plug from the tensioner body and turning the adjusting bolt clockwise (see following section). Bend the locktab back and remove the camshaft timing gear nut. The camshaft and crankshaft timing gears may now be removed together with the chain by easing the gears off of the shafts simultaneously, using a puller or suitable levers.

When replacing the timing chain and gears, set the crankshaft with its keyway at twelve o'clock and the camshaft with its

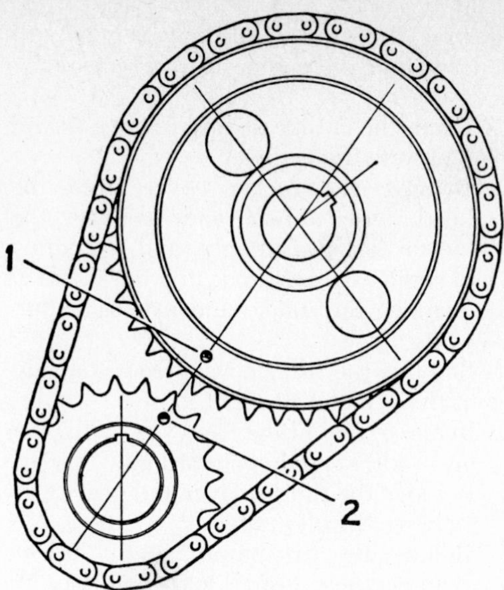

Timing gear marks—Midget, MGB, and 1100 sedan

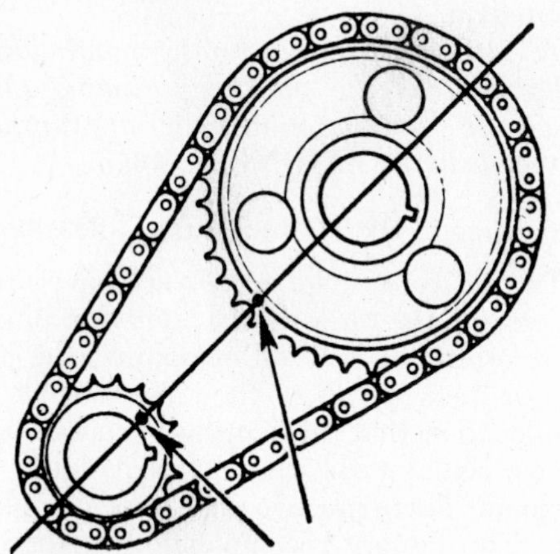

Timing gear marks—MGC

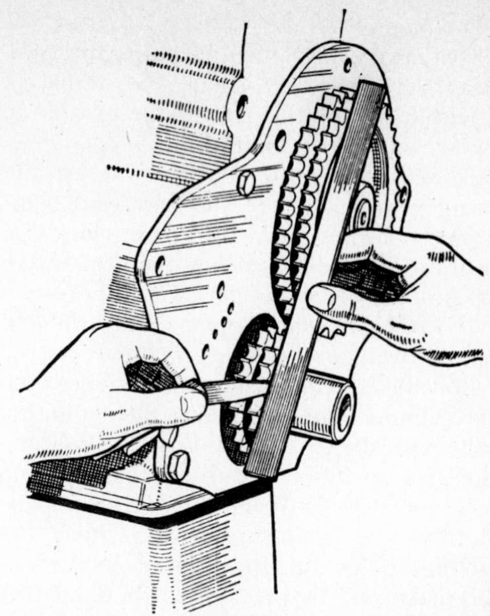

Gear alignment can be checked using a straightedge and feeler gauge

keyway at one o'clock as seen from the front (see illustration). The washers behind the crankshaft gear are spacers to align the two gears properly. When reassembling, the same number of washers should be installed as were removed *unless* any of the following components have been replaced: crankshaft, crankshaft main bearings and thrust washers, crankshaft timing gear, camshaft, camshaft timing gear, or camshaft locating plate. If any of the above components have been replaced, timing gear alignment can be checked and adjusted by placing a straightedge across the gear sides and adding or subtracting washers to eliminate any gaps between the gear side surfaces and the straightedge (after the gears have been installed). To install the timing gears and chain, assemble the chain onto the gears with the gear marks facing each other so that a line drawn through them would pass through the camshaft and crankshaft axes (see illustration). Keeping the gears in this position, start the crankshaft gear onto the crankshaft (with the gear keyway and crankshaft key aligned). Install the camshaft gear onto the camshaft, turning the camshaft to align the key with the keyway if necessary. Make a final check of alignment of the timing gears and gear marks, and install the camshaft gear lockwasher and nut. Replace the timing cover.

Timing Chain Tensioner Service —MGB and MGC

To remove the tensioner (after the timing gear cover has been removed), first unscrew the plug from the tensioner body. Using a ⅛ in. Allen wrench, turn the tension adjusting bolt clockwise until the rubbing block is fully retracted and locked behind the limit peg. Unbolt and remove the tensioner and its backing plate.

Withdraw the rubbing block and plunger from the tensioner body, and turn the tension adjusting bolt clockwise until the piston and spring are released. Clean the components in solvent and blow out the oil passages with compressed air. Check the bore of the tensioner body for ovality. If the diameter of the bore at or near the mouth varies more than 0.003 in., the complete tensioner unit should be replaced. If within the limit given, it is acceptable to replace just the rubbing block.

To reassemble the tensioner, insert the spring and piston into the bore and compress the spring. Turn the piston clockwise until the inner end is below the peg. Install the rubbing block plunger into the bore. CAUTION: *Do not attempt to turn the tension adjusting bolt counterclockwise.*

Bolt the backing plate and tensioner onto the cylinder block and lock the mounting bolts with the locktab. Release the rubbing block for operation by turning the adjusting bolt clockwise until the block contacts the chain under spring pressure. Check the rubbing block for freedom of movement and make sure that it does not bind against the backing plate. Replace and lock the plug in the tensioner body.

Camshaft Removal and Installation

MG Midget Mk. I and II (948 and 1,098 cc.)—Removal

Removal of the camshaft from Mk. I and II Midgets can be accomplished without removing the engine from the chassis. The following procedure can, however, be utilized whether the engine is in or out of the car.

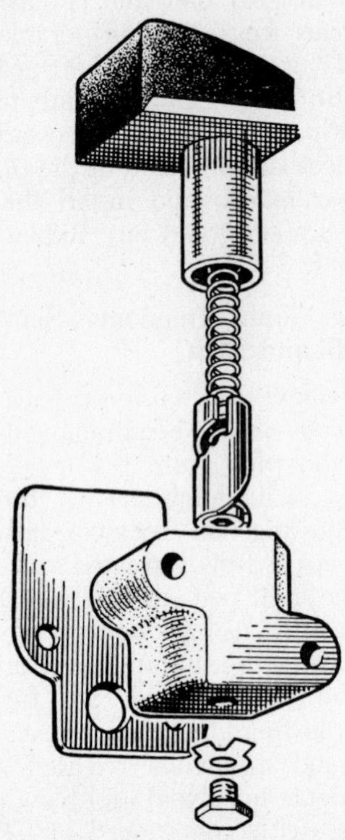

Timing chain tensioner components

1. Drain the crankcase and remove the oil pan from the engine.
2. Remove the rocker cover from the head and unbolt and remove the rocker shaft assembly and pushrods (keeping the pushrods in order).
3. Remove the intake and exhaust manifolds.
4. Remove the lifter covers from the side of the cylinder block.
5. Remove the lifters, and, as with the pushrods, keep them in order.
6. Remove the timing cover and gears.
7. Remove the oil pump.
8. Remove the distributor.
9. Remove the camshaft locating plate.
10. Pull the camshaft from the front of the engine, rotating it slowly to assist removal.

NOTE: *Removal procedures for individual units such as the oil pump, timing gear cover, etc., can be found under appropriate subheads in the ENGINE section.*

MG Midget Mk. III (1,275 cc.)—Removal

The 1,275 cc. engine does not have lifter covers on the side of the cylinder block; therefore, some method of holding the lifters all the way up in their bores must be employed so that the camshaft can be withdrawn without the cam lobes hanging up on them. There are two ways to accomplish this. The factory recommended method is to:

1. Drain the crankcase and remove the engine.
2. Remove the rocker cover and unbolt and remove the rocker shaft assembly and pushrods (keeping the pushrods in order).
3. Remove the timing cover and gears.
4. Remove the oil pan.
5. Remove the distributor.
6. Remove the camshaft locating plate.
7. Invert the engine to allow the lifters to fall into their bores.
8. Withdraw the camshaft, rotating it slowly to assist removal. If the oil pump drive flange comes away with the camshaft, replace it on the pump driveshaft with the drive lug towards the pump.

The alternative method of removing the camshaft does not require removal of the engine, but does necessitate a technique of retaining the lifters that is not factory approved. However, as with any repair procedure, if care and common sense are exercised, wasted time and effort can be avoided. The procedure is as follows:

1. Drain the crankcase and remove the oil pan.
2. Remove the rocker cover, rocker shaft assembly, and pushrods. (Keep the pushrods in order.)
3. Remove the timing cover and camshaft gear.
4. Remove the distributor.
5. Remove the camshaft locating plate.
6. From underneath the car, coat the lifters with a thick lubricant such as a petroleum base grease and push them up into their bores. They should remain in this position long enough to remove and replace the camshaft.
7. Withdraw the camshaft while rotating it slowly. If the oil pump drive flange comes out with the cam, replace it on the pump driveshaft with the drive lug towards the pump.

NOTE: *Removal procedures for individual units such as the timing gear cover can be found under appropriate subheads in the ENGINE section.*

MGB—Removal

Camshaft removal procedures for the MGB are the same as for the Midget Mk. I and II, with one exception: if the car is equipped with a mechanically driven tachometer, disconnect the cable and unbolt and remove the drive gear.

MGC—Removal

Removal of the camshaft from the MGC can be accomplished without removing the engine from the chassis. The procedure is as follows:

1. Remove the radiator grille.
2. Remove the timing cover and gears.
3. Remove the rocker cover and unbolt and remove the rocker shaft assembly and pushrods (keeping the pushrods in order).
4. Remove the alternator and unbolt and remove the three lifter covers from the side of the cylinder block. Withdraw the lifters, keeping them in order.
5. Remove the distributor and lift out the distributor drive gear. The gear may be removed by screwing a 7/16 in. SAE bolt into the drive to provide a lifting point.
6. Remove the lines from the oil cooler and unbolt and remove the cooler.
7. Unbolt the camshaft locating plate.
8. Withdraw the camshaft gently from the engine.

NOTE: *Removal procedures for individual units such as the timing gear cover can be found under appropriate subheads in the ENGINE section.*

MG 1100—Removal

Camshaft removal procedures for the MG 1100 are the same as for the Midget Mk I and II, with these exceptions:

1. The engine/transmission unit must be removed from the vehicle.
2. Step No. 1 and 7 are not applicable to the 1100 sedan and can be eliminated from the procedure for that vehicle.

Installation—All Models

Camshaft installation in all cases is in reverse order of removal. Camshaft bearings, except in cases of insufficient lubrication, almost never need replacement. Clearance can be checked with a feeler gauge. Replacement of bearings requires special pullers and machine tools (for align-boring) and should be left to a machine shop.

Camshaft end-float can be checked before installation by assembling the locating plate and timing gear onto the camshaft and measuring fore and aft play. If it exceeds specification, the locating plate should be replaced.

Camshaft Specifications (in.)

Model	*End Float*	*Oil Clearance*
Midget	.003-.007	.001-.002
MGB	.003-.007	.001-.002
MGC	.003-.006	.001-.002
MG 1100	.003-.007	.001-.002

NOTE: *Valve lift for the different engine models can be found under VALVE SPECIFICATIONS. Intake valve opening timing (deg. BTDC) can be found under TUNE-UP SPECIFICATIONS.*

After the camshaft has been installed, it is very important that the distributor drive gear be repositioned so that the ignition timing is in proper relationship to the valve timing. Refer to the following section.

Distributor Drive Gear Installation—4 Cylinder Models

It is important that the distributor drive gear is positioned correctly with respect to the camshaft. In order to facilitate lifting the gear out of mesh with the camshaft gear so that it can be rotated, it is possible to screw a 5/16 in. SAE bolt into the center of the gear to provide a lifting point.

Rotate the crankshaft until No. 1 piston is at TDC on the compression stroke. In this position both valves on No. 1 cylinder will be closed, while both valves on No. 4 cylinder will be partially open. Also, the timing gear marks (crankshaft and camshaft timing gears) should be facing each other in a straight line through the shaft centers at this point.

Hold the drive gear with the large offset uppermost and the slot just below horizontal, and drop the gear into engagement. As the gear engages with the camshaft the slot will turn counterclockwise until it is in the "twenty-of-two" position (see illustration). Remove the bolt from the gear and install the distributor.

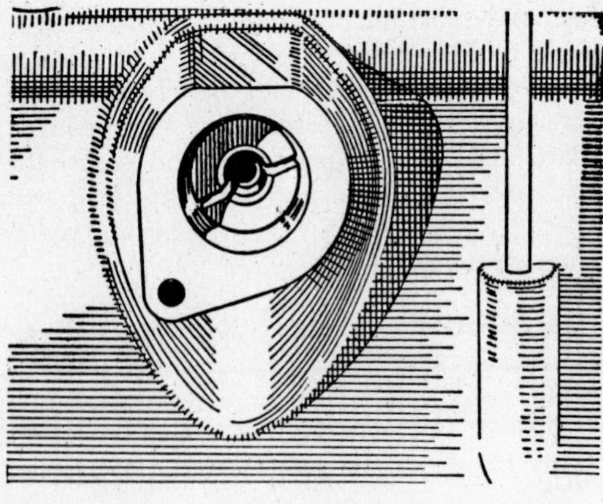

Four cylinder models—correct postioning of the distributor drive gear, with No. 1 piston at TDC of its compression stroke

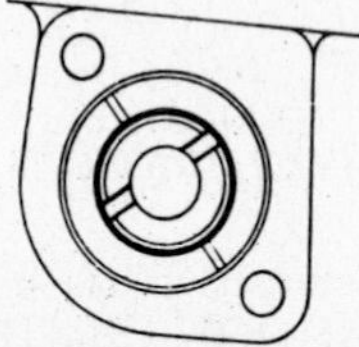

MGC—correct positioning of the distributor drive gear, with No. 6 piston at approximately 8° BTDC on its compression stroke

Distributor Drive Gear Installation—MGC

Turn the crankshaft until No. 6 piston is approximately 8° BTDC on its compression stroke. In this position both valves on No. 6 cylinder will be closed, while both valves on No. 1 cylinder will be partially open.

Hold the drive gear with the small offset uppermost (large offset away from the engine) and the slot just below horizontal, and drop the gear into engagement. As the gear engages with the camshaft the slot will turn counterclockwise until it is in the "twenty-of-two" position (see illustration). Remove the bolt from the gear and install the distributor.

ENGINE LUBRICATION

System Type

All MG engines are completely pressure lubricated. The engine/transmission unit of the MG 1100 is lubricated by a common oil supply, and it is particularly important with this model to use the best oil available and to change the filter (as well as the oil) regularly. All engines are equipped with a full-flow oil filter, a wire mesh filter at the oil pump pickup, and an oil pressure relief valve. In addition, some engines are equipped with an oil cooler.

Engine Oil Characteristics

In a normal automobile, engine oil is subjected to many extreme conditions, and it must not only perform the job of lubrication, but it must also cool the internal engine components. Ambient temperatures, cold starting, and high and low rpm operation all represent severe conditions under which the oil must perform well. In addition, chemical by-products from combustion will contaminate and cripple the efficiency of oil if it is not changed often enough.

When gasoline is burned in an engine, the following products are formed in addition to the exhaust gases themselves: water, unburned gasoline, soot, resins and varnishes, nitrogen and sulfuric acids, insoluble lead salts, and hydrochloric and hydrobromic acids.

When the engine is warmed up to normal operating temperature, almost all of these products of combustion are either blown out of the exhaust or treated by the anti-pollution components of the engine. However, when the engine is cold, as occurs in

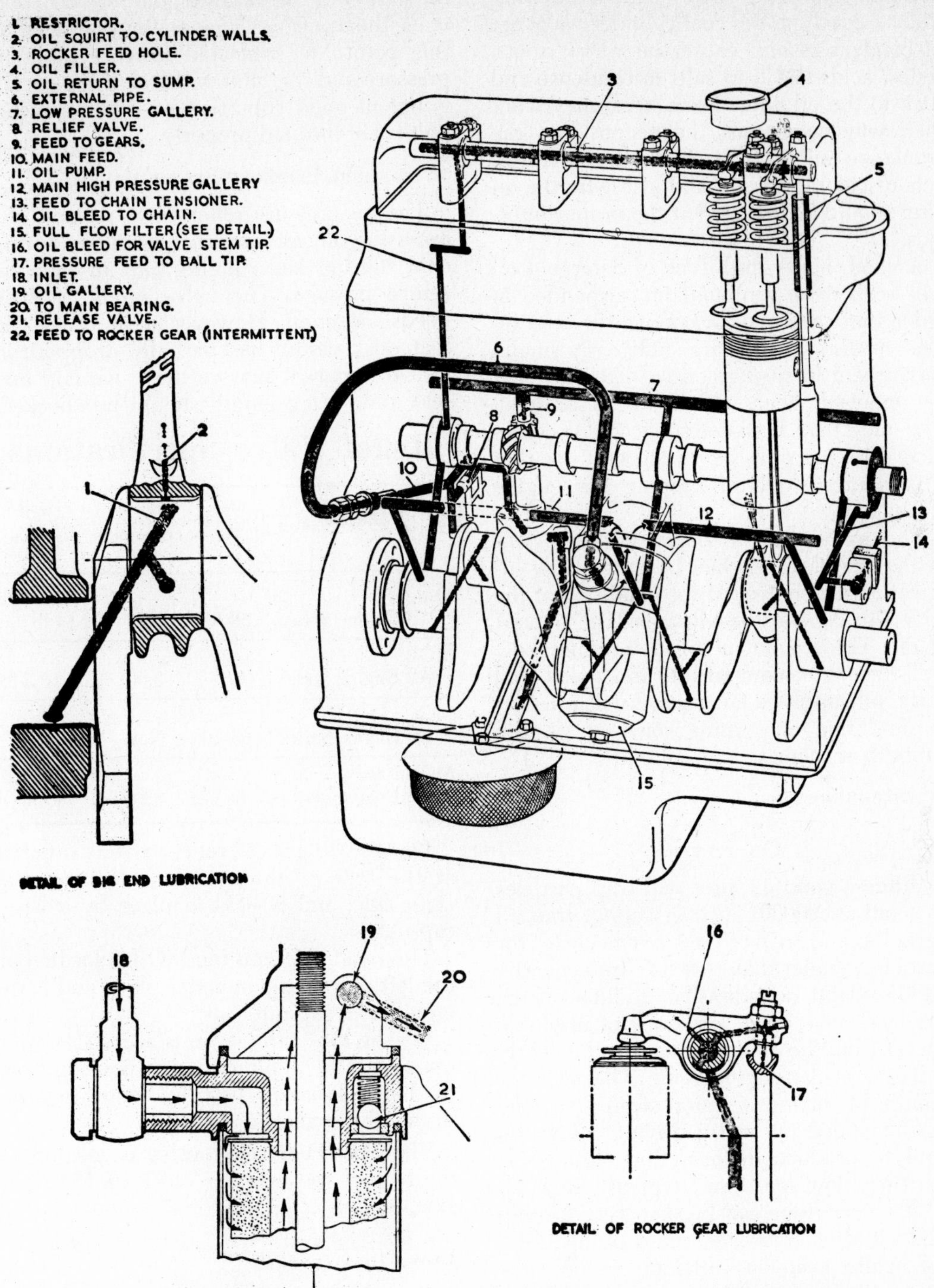
1. RESTRICTOR.
2. OIL SQUIRT TO CYLINDER WALLS.
3. ROCKER FEED HOLE.
4. OIL FILLER.
5. OIL RETURN TO SUMP.
6. EXTERNAL PIPE.
7. LOW PRESSURE GALLERY.
8. RELIEF VALVE.
9. FEED TO GEARS.
10. MAIN FEED.
11. OIL PUMP.
12. MAIN HIGH PRESSURE GALLERY
13. FEED TO CHAIN TENSIONER.
14. OIL BLEED TO CHAIN.
15. FULL FLOW FILTER (SEE DETAIL)
16. OIL BLEED FOR VALVE STEM TIP.
17. PRESSURE FEED TO BALL TIP.
18. INLET.
19. OIL GALLERY.
20. TO MAIN BEARING.
21. RELEASE VALVE.
22. FEED TO ROCKER GEAR (INTERMITTENT)
DETAIL OF BIG END LUBRICATION
DETAIL FULL FLOW FILTER
DETAIL OF ROCKER GEAR LUBRICATION

Engine lubrication system

stop-and-go driving with frequent stopping and/or standing, the cool cylinder walls act as condensers and cause the water, soots, resins, acids and lead salts to condense and stick to the oil films. From here, they work their way down past the pistons into the crankcase oil. This is the reason why oil gets discolored in use, and also why the oil filter should be changed at the proper intervals.

A good, heavy-duty type of detergent oil will keep these contaminants suspended in order that they can be removed by the oil filter or else (if they are sufficiently small) carry them in suspension so that they will be removed whenever the oil is drained. The fact that high-detergent oil becomes dirty with use only serves to point out that it is doing its job of keeping the engine clean.

The quantity of oil, too, is very important to the life of an engine, because while lubrication depends upon the condition of the oil it also depends heavily upon the amount of oil. The amount of oil determines how well the engine components are cooled, and if the oil supply is low the oil will run hotter and thin out, losing some of its film strength or "cling".

Maintenance

Oil Filter

While a good oil filter will trap particles as small as .000001 inch, it cannot trap all particles, and in fact does not need to, for particles smaller than this size are generally harmless and non-abrasive. A filter which would remove every last trace of insoluble matter from the oil would have to be nearly as large as the engine itself. The oil filter should be changed more often than the recommended interval if driving conditions tend to produce deposits and sludge—i.e. short-trip, low speed, or frequent idling. An oil filter cartridge can become very heavily sludged after only 2,000 miles of city driving, while a similar cartridge in the same car might be in perfect working condition after a cross-country trip of 5,000 miles. How long a filter will last—how soon it plugs up—depends almost entirely upon the operating conditions of the engine. High speeds can't hurt a good engine, but dirt and sludge and acids definitely can.

When replacing the element in the canister-type oil filter, *always* check or replace the gasket in the oil filter adapter body that seals the canister. The sealing surfaces at this point are subjected to very high oil pressure and the filter will leak if the gasket is not in good condition or if the canister bolt is not torqued properly.

Oil Pressure Relief Valve

The oil pressure relief valve releases the excessive oil pressure that develops during cold starting and running into an extra oil return passage. The valve rarely, if ever, needs attention. However, if it is noticed that oil pressure has partially dropped off for no apparent reason, the valve cup and seat and spring length should be checked.

Relief Valve Specifications

Model & Engine	*Valve Opens (lb./sq. in.)*	*Spring Free Length (in.)*	*Spring Load Installed*
Midget			
All Engine Series	50-60	2.86	13-14 lb.
MGB			
All Engine Series	70	3.00	15.5-16.5 lb.
MGC			
All Engine Series	65-70	N.A.	N.A.
MG 1100			
All Engine Series	60	2.86	13-14 lb.

On the Midget the relief valve is situated at the rear of the cylinder block on the right side, and is held in place by a large cap-nut.

The relief valve on the MGB is located at the left rear of the cylinder block and is retained by a cap-nut.

On the MGC the valve is accessible after removing the oil filter adapter housing from the block. Press on the valve center to withdraw the valve assembly.

The MG 1100 relief valve is located at the rear of the cylinder block on the right side, under a cap-nut.

Low Oil Pressure

If a drop in engine oil pressure is noticed, the following possibilities should be investigated:

1. Insufficient supply of oil.
2. Incorrect grade of oil.
3. Dirty oil filter.
4. Restricted oil cooler passages.
5. Wire mesh filter at oil pump pickup clogged.

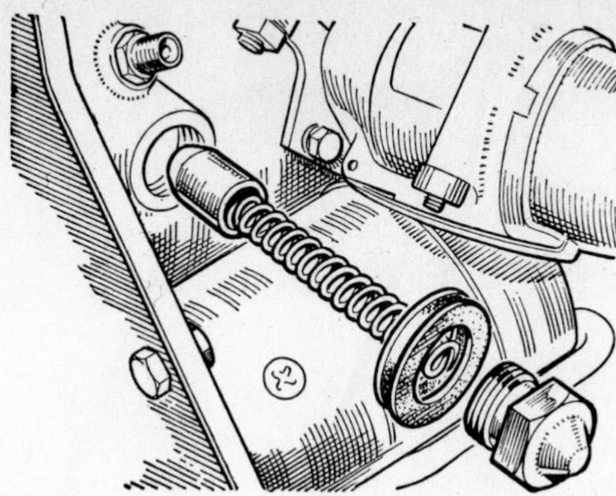

Oil pressure relief valve—Midget. The valve differs only in location on the other models

6. Oil pump failure or pickup connection leakage.
7. Relief valve failure.
8. Oil diluted with gasoline or water.
9. Oil filter, cooler, or pressure gauge line leakage.
10. Worn main or connecting rod bearings.

Oil Pan Removal and Installation

MG Midget

Drain the oil and unbolt and lower the oil pan. Always replace the two pan gaskets and the two main bearing cork seals when the pan has been removed. It may be necessary to soak the cork seals in hot water to keep them from breaking when installing them.

MGB

Drain the oil. Drain the radiator and disconnect the hoses. Unbolt the engine mounts and lift the front of the engine enough to gain access to the front oil pan bolts. Unbolt and lower the pan. Clean the cylinder block and oil pan mating surfaces and replace the pan gasket to preclude the possibility of an oil leak.

MGC

Manual transmission models:

Remove the timing gear cover. Unbolt the oil pan and let it rest on the crossmember. Unbolt the engine mounts, lift the front of the engine, and slide the oil pan out. Be sure to use a new pan gasket.

Automatic transmission models:

On MGCs equipped with automatic transmission the engine must be removed to provide clearance for removal of the oil pan. Once the engine is out of the car, the pan can simply be unbolted and removed. Be *sure* to use a new gasket.

MG 1100

The transmission is located inside the engine crankcase on the 1100 sedan, and there is no oil pan as such. To gain access to internal engine components the engine/transmission unit must be removed from the car separated. See TRANSMISSION REMOVAL AND INSTALLATION.

Oil Cooler Removal and Installation

On all models equipped with oil coolers, disconnect the lines from the cooler and unbolt and remove the cooler unit. When replacing, start the line fittings onto the connections by hand to avoid crossing the threads. Tighten the fittings, check the engine oil, and start the engine. Let the engine idle until oil pressure is developed, and check the oil lines for leaks. Shut the engine off and recheck the oil level.

Oil Pump Removal and Installation

MG Midget

1. Remove the engine from the car.
2. Unbolt the clutch assembly from the flywheel.
3. Bend back the locktabs and unbolt the flywheel.
4. Unbolt and remove the rear engine plate.
5. Remove the three bolts and withdraw the oil pump assembly.

Installation is in reverse order of removal. Be careful, when installing the paper gasket, that the intake and delivery ports are not obstructed. Use a new gasket if the old one is damaged in any way, and use new locktabs.

MGB

1. Remove the oil pan.
2. Remove the three nuts that secure the pump to the crankcase and withdraw the pump assembly.

Installation is in reverse order of removal. Use a new gasket when the pump is reinstalled.

MGC

1. Remove the oil pan.
2. Unbolt and withdraw the oil pump assembly from the crankcase.
3. Installation is in reverse order of removal.

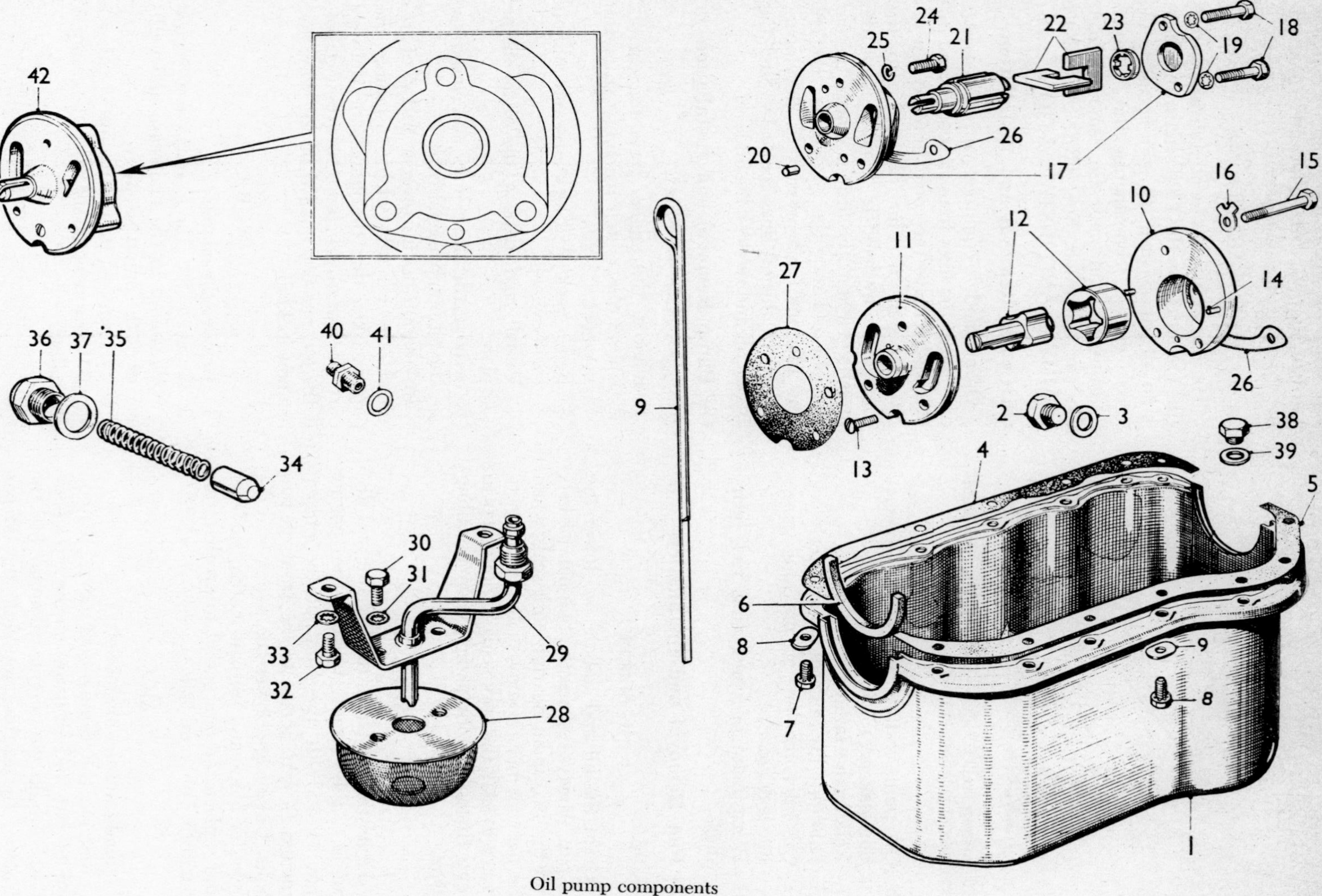

Oil pump components

1 Oil pan
2 Drain plug
3 Washer
4 Oil pan gasket
5 Oil pan gasket
6 Main bearing cork seal
7 Oil pan bolt
8 Washer
9 Dip stick
10 Oil pump body
11 Cover
12 Inner and outer rotors
13 Cover screws
14 Dowel
15 Pump mounting bolt
16 Lockwasher
(11–16: Hobourn-Eaton pump)
17 Body and cover assembly
18 Screw
19 Lockwasher
20 Dowel
21 Rotor
22 Vane
23 Sleeve
24 Pump mountnig bolt
(17–24: Burman pump)
25 Lockwasher
26 Lockplate (all pumps)
27 Gasket
28 Wire mesh filter
29 Oil pickup pipe
30 Screw
31 Lockwasher
32 Screw
33 Lockwasher
34 Oil relief valve
35 Spring
36 Cap-nut
37 Washer
38 Oil priming plug
39 Copper washer
40 Oil pressure feed connection
41 Fiber washer
42 Pump assembly—Concentric Engineering type

MG 1100

1. Remove the engine/transmission unit from the chassis.
2. Unbolt and remove the flywheel and clutch assembly.
3. Remove the flywheel housing from the engine unit.
4. Bend back the locktabs and unbolt the oil pump from the crankcase.
5. Withdraw the pump assembly, noting the position of the slot in the drive shaft in order to assist replacement.

Installation is in reverse order of removal. Be careful, when installing the paper gasket, that the intake and delivery ports are not obstructed. Use new locktabs, and use a new gasket if the old one is damaged in any way.

Oil Pump Service

MG Midget

Concentric Engineering pump:

The Concentric pump is replaceable as a unit only; parts are not available.

Burman pump:

Remove the pump cover and withdraw the rotor and vane assembly. Remove the sleeve from the end of the rotor and remove the vanes. Replace any worn or galled parts. Coat all parts with motor oil before assembly.

Hobourn-Eaton pump:

Remove the pump cover and lift out the inner and outer rotors. Check clearance between the outer rotor and the pump body. If the clearance exceeds 0.010 in., the complete pump assembly should be renewed.

Check clearance between the rotor lobes (see illustration). Replace the rotors if clearance exceeds 0.006 in.

Check the rotor end float (see illustration). If the clearance exceeds 0.005 in., remove the dowels from the pump body mating surface and mill or lap the surface until clearance is within specification.

Coat all parts with fresh motor oil before assembling. Install the outer rotor in the

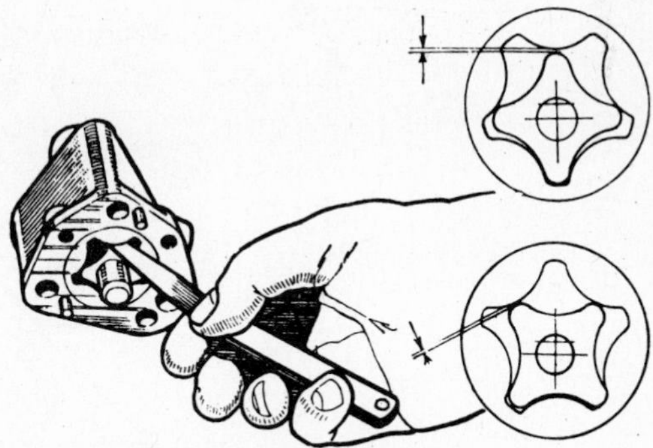

Oil pump rotor position while checking lobe clearances

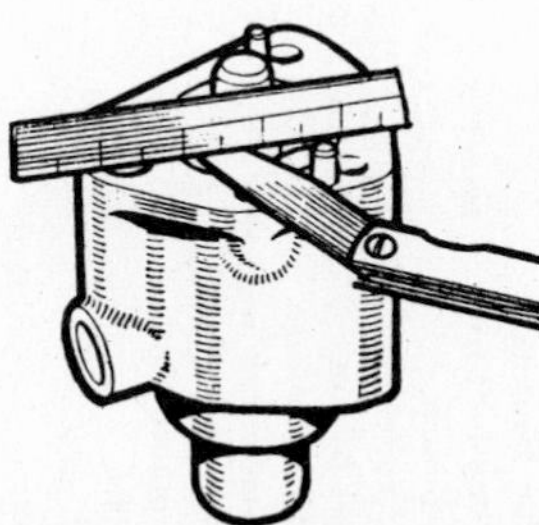

Use a straightedge and feeler gauge to check rotor end-play

Identification and Component Illustrations

MG Midget

1 Connecting rod cap
2 Rod bolt
3 Locktab
4 Clamp bolt
5 Spring washer
6 Main bearing
7 Crankshaft with oil restrictors and bush
8 Oil restrictor
9 Pilot bushing
10 Main bearing
11 Upper thrust washer
12 Lower thrust washer
13 Crankshaft gear
14 Shim
15 Oil thrower
16 Gear and crankshaft key
17 Camshaft with oil pump driving pin
18 Oil pump driving pin
19 Locating plate
20 Plate to crankcase bolt
21 Lockwasher
22 Camshaft gear with tensioner rings
23 Tensioner ring
24 Gear key
25 Gear nut
26 Locktab
27 Camshaft driving chain
38 Crankshaft pulley
29 Pulley retaining bolt
31 Flywheel with starter ring and dowels
32 Starter ring
33 Dowel
34 Flywheel to crankshaft screw
35 Locktab
36 Lifter
37 Pushrod
38 Distributor housing
39 Screw
40 Lockwasher
41 Distributor drive gear

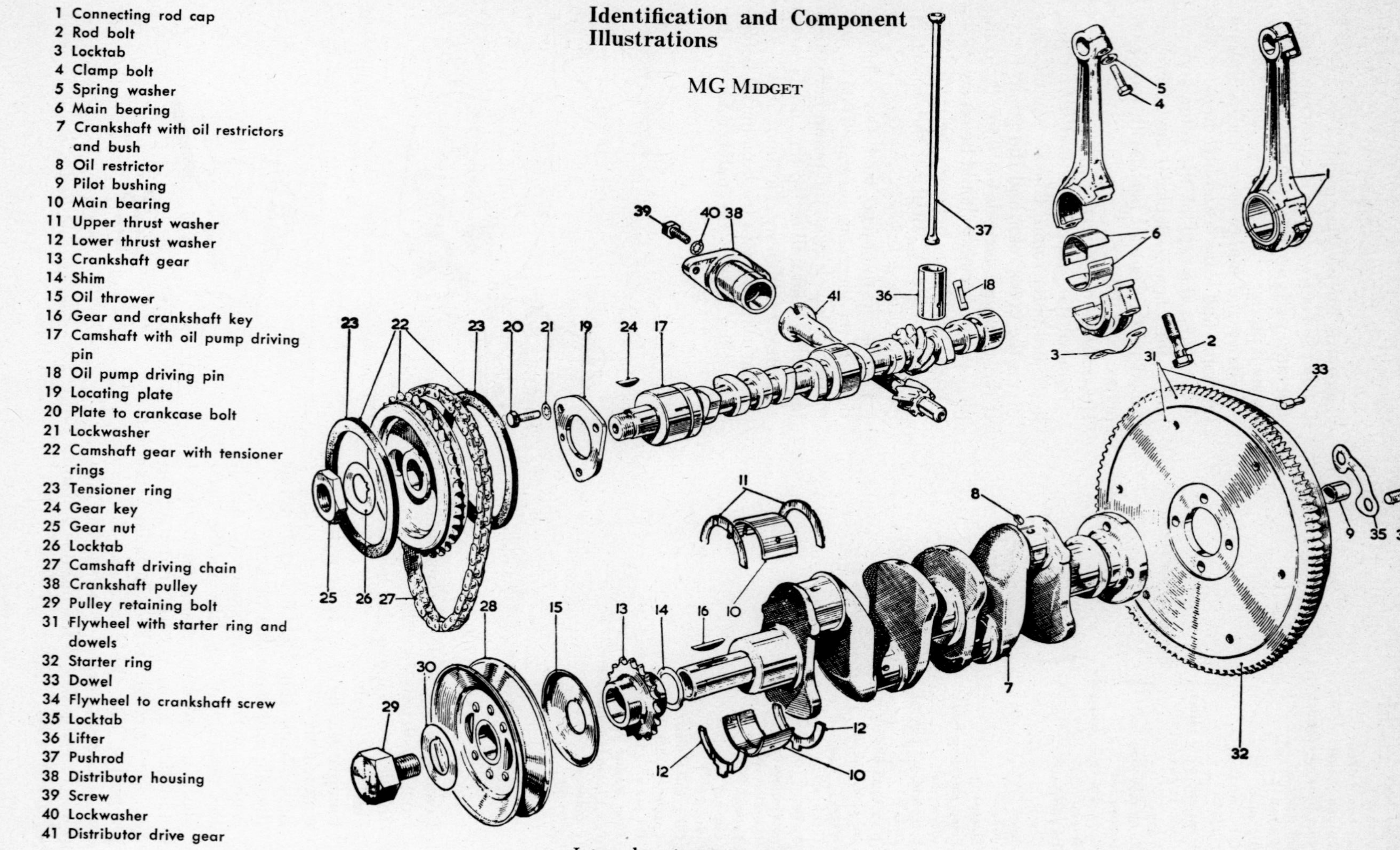

Internal engine components

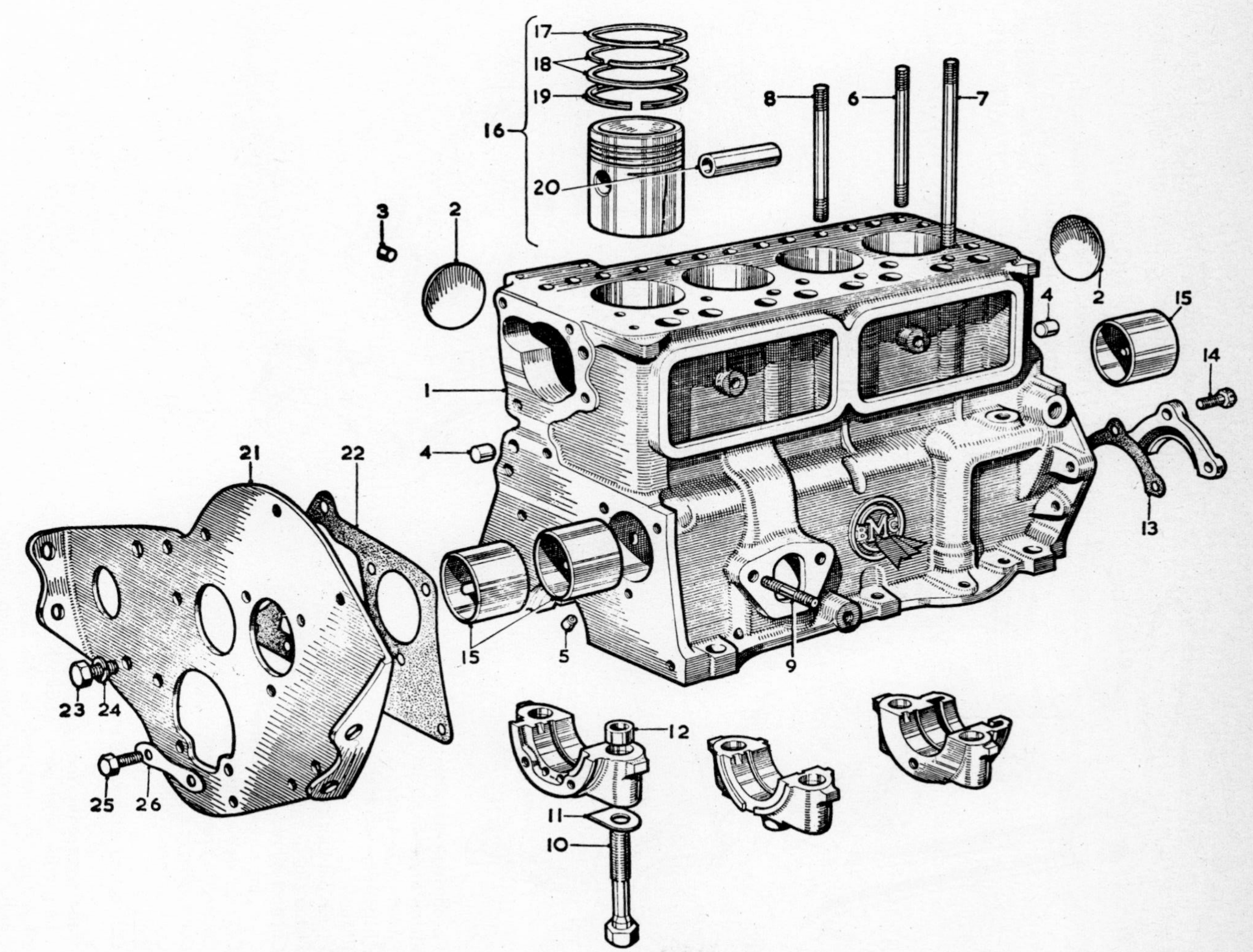

1 Block assembly
2 Freeze plug
3 Oil pressure relief valve passage plug
4 Oil gallery plug
5 Camshaft bearing oil feed restrictor
6 Cylinder head stud
7 Cylinder head stud (long)
8 Cylinder head stud (short)
9 Fuel pump stud
10 Main bearing bolt
11 Locktab
12 Main bearing cap dowel
13 Rear cover gasket
14 Rear cover bolt
15 Camshaft bearing liners
16 Piston assembly
17 Compression ring (plain)
18 Compression ring (taper)
19 Oil ring
20 Wrist pin
21 Engine mounting plate (front)
22 Mounting plate gasket
23 Mounting plate bolt
24 Washer
25 Mounting plate to bearing bolt
26 Locktab

Cylinder block components

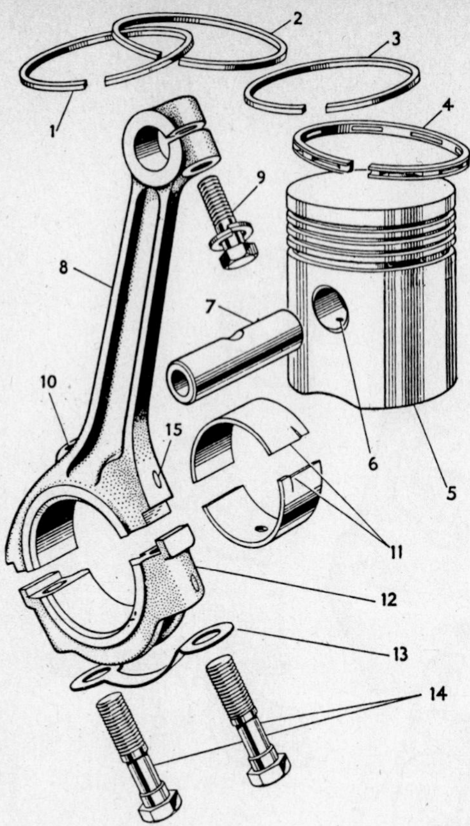

1 Piston ring—parallel
2 Piston ring—taper
3 Piston ring—taper
4 Piston ring—scraper
5 Piston
6 Piston pin lubricating hole
7 Piston pin
8 Connecting rod
9 Clamping screw and washer
10 Cylinder wall lubricating jet
11 Connecting rod bearings
12 Connecting rod cap
13 Lock washer
14 Bolts
15 Connecting rod and cap marking

Piston and connecting rod components, early cars with clamp-type wrist pins. Mark the pistons so that they may be installed in the same bore, facing in the same direction. Oversize pistons have their oversize dimension stamped on the piston crown

pump body with the beveled end at the drive end of the pump body. Check the pump for freedom of movement after assembly.

MGB

MGB oil pump service procedures are identical to those of the Hobourn-Eaton pump on the Midget.

MGC

The oil pump on the MGC is replaceable as a unit only; parts are not available.

MG 1100

The 1100 sedan is equipped with either the Concentric Engineering or Hobourn-Eaton oil pump, as used on the Midget. (See OIL PUMP SERVICE/MG MIDGET.)

CRANKSHAFT, CONNECTING RODS, PISTONS AND RINGS

Removal and Installation

See ENGINE REBUILDING.

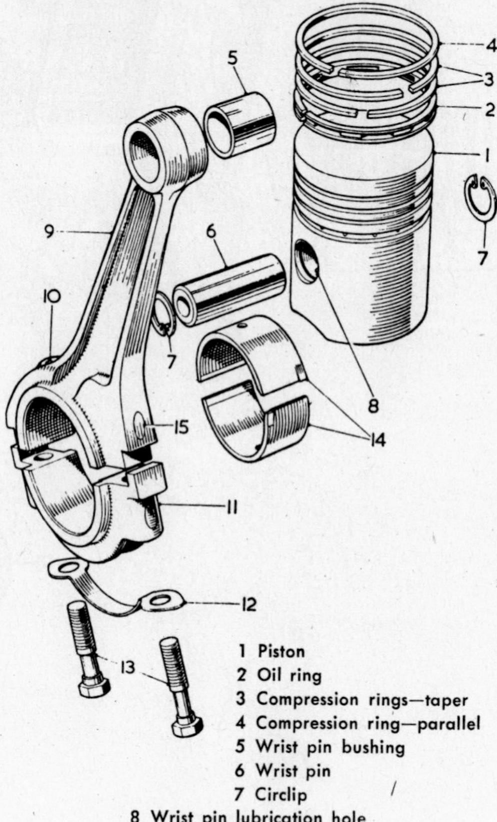

1 Piston
2 Oil ring
3 Compression rings—taper
4 Compression ring—parallel
5 Wrist pin bushing
6 Wrist pin
7 Circlip
8 Wrist pin lubrication hole
9 Connecting rod
10 Cylinder wall lubrication jet
11 Connecting rod bearing cap
12 Locktab
13 Rod bolts
14 Rod bearings
15 Connecting rod and cap assembly marks

Piston and connecting rod components, engines with floating wrist pins. Mark the pistons so that they may be installed in the same bore, facing in the same direction. Oversize pistons have their oversize dimension stamped on the piston crown. Late engines have straight (no offset) rods with press-fit wrist pins

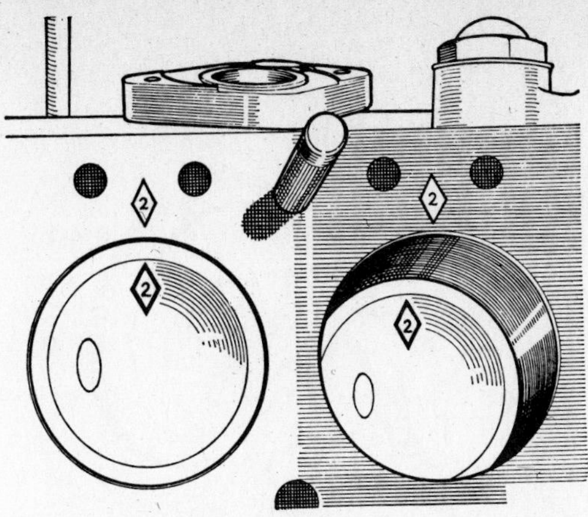

On engines with floating or press-fit type wrist pins the pistons are select-fitted to the bores, and the piston crowns and cylinders are marked with identifying numbers enclosed in a diamond. Oversize dimensions (if any) are enclosed in an ellipse.

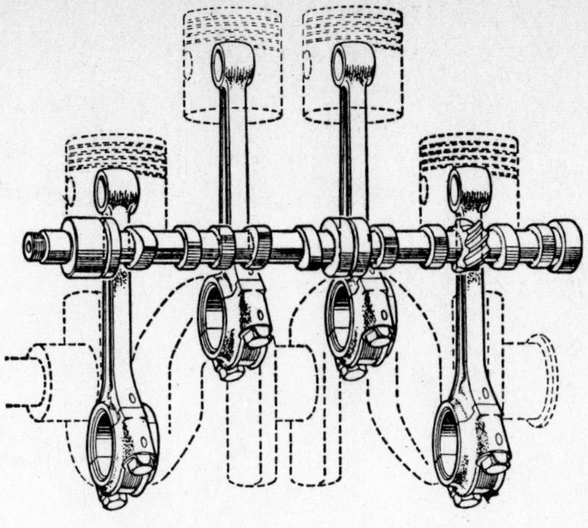

Correct relationship of rods to crankshaft, engines with floating wrist pins

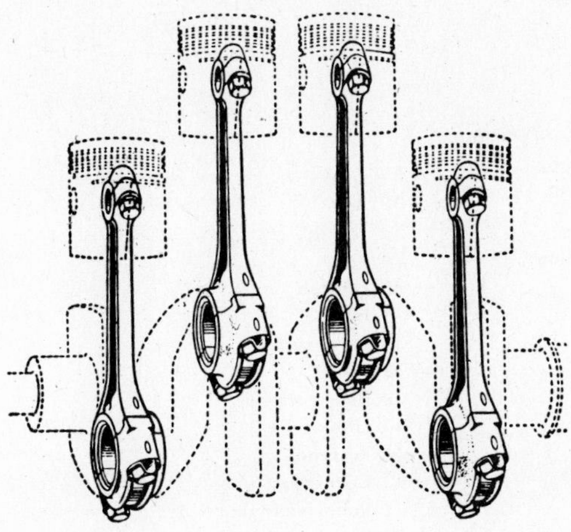

Correct relationship of rods to crankshaft, engines with clamp type wrist pins

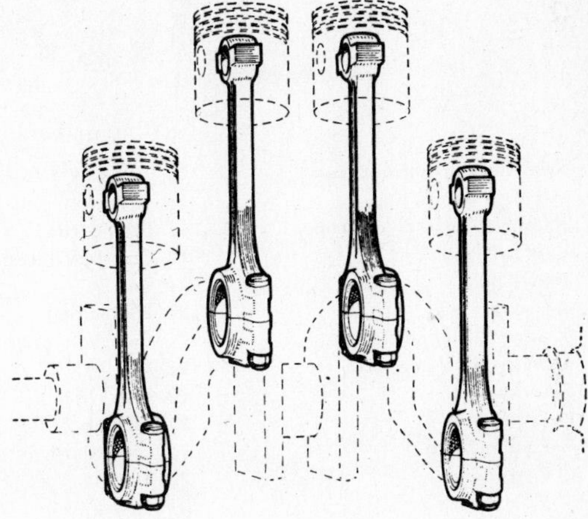

Correct relationship of rods to crankshaft, 1,275 cc. engines

MGB

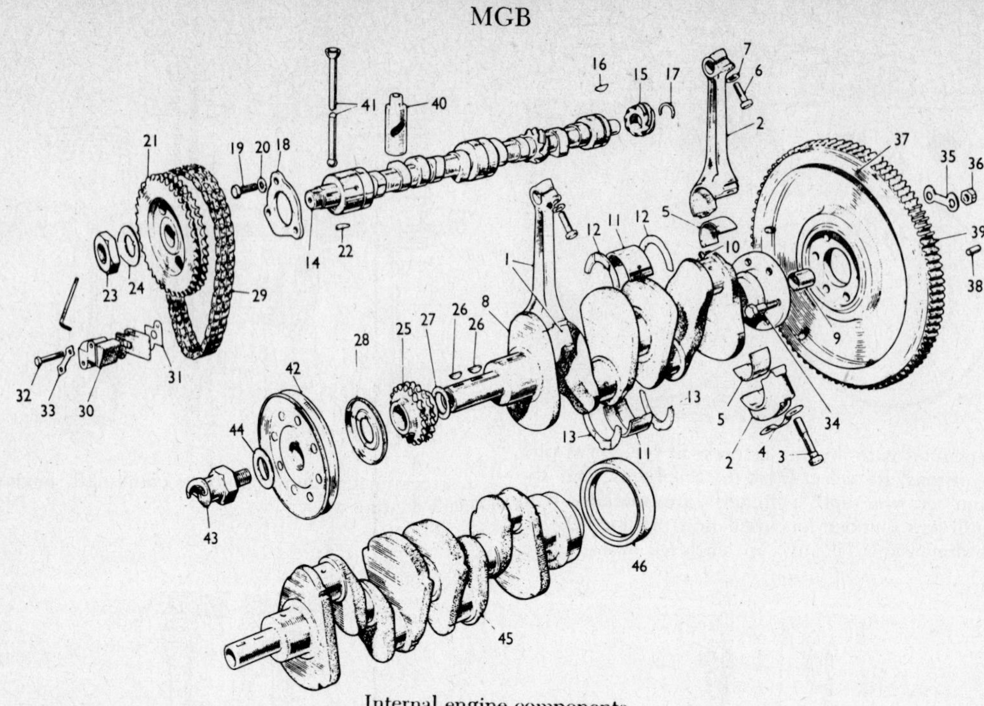

Internal engine components

1 Connecting rod and cap (No. 1 and 3)
2 Connecting rod and cap (No. 2 and 4)
3 Rod bolt
4 Locktab
5 Connecting rod bearing
6 Wrist pin clamp bolt
7 Lockwasher
8 Crankshaft
9 Pilot bushing
10 Plug
11 Main bearing
12 Upper thrust washer
13 Lower thrust washer
14 Camshaft
15 Tachometer drive gear
16 Tachometer gear key
17 Spring clip
18 Camshaft locating plate
19 Bolt
20 Lockwasher
21 Camshaft gear
22 Key
23 Nut
24 Locktab
25 Crankshaft gear
26 Key
27 Shim
28 Oil thrower
29 Timing chain
30 Chain tensioner
31 Gasket
32 Bolt
33 Locktab
34 Bolt
35 Locktab
36 Nut
37 Flywheel
38 Dowel
39 Ring gear
40 Lifter
41 Pushrod
42 Crankshaft pulley
43 Pulley retaining nut
44 Lockwasher
45 Crankshaft
46 Oil seal

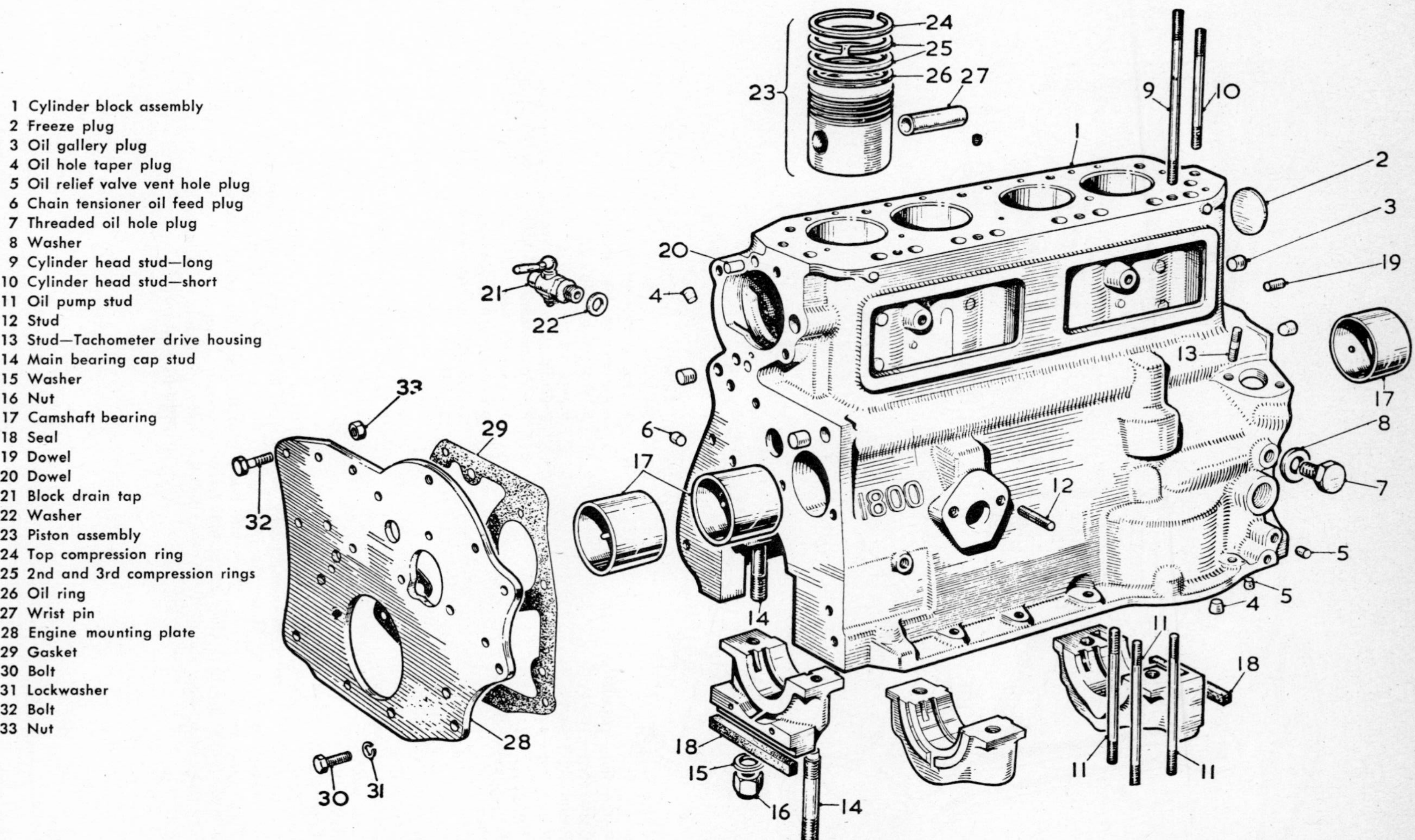

Cylinder block components

1 Cylinder block assembly
2 Freeze plug
3 Oil gallery plug
4 Oil hole taper plug
5 Oil relief valve vent hole plug
6 Chain tensioner oil feed plug
7 Threaded oil hole plug
8 Washer
9 Cylinder head stud—long
10 Cylinder head stud—short
11 Oil pump stud
12 Stud
13 Stud—Tachometer drive housing
14 Main bearing cap stud
15 Washer
16 Nut
17 Camshaft bearing
18 Seal
19 Dowel
20 Dowel
21 Block drain tap
22 Washer
23 Piston assembly
24 Top compression ring
25 2nd and 3rd compression rings
26 Oil ring
27 Wrist pin
28 Engine mounting plate
29 Gasket
30 Bolt
31 Lockwasher
32 Bolt
33 Nut

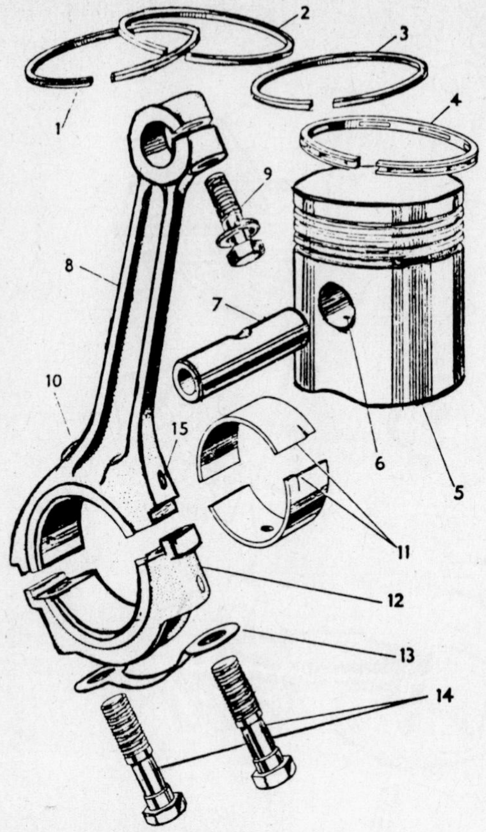

1 Piston ring—parallel
2 Piston ring—taper
3 Piston ring—taper
4 Piston ring—scraper
5 Piston
6 Piston pin lubricating hole
7 Piston pin
8 Connecting rod
9 Clamping screw and washer
10 Cylinder wall lubricating jet
11 Connecting rod bearings
12 Connecting rod cap
13 Lock washer
14 Bolts
15 Connecting rod and cap marking

Piston and connecting rod components, early cars with clamp-type wrist pins. Mark the pistons so that they may be installed in the same bore, facing in the same direction. Oversize pistons have their oversize dimension stamped on the piston crown

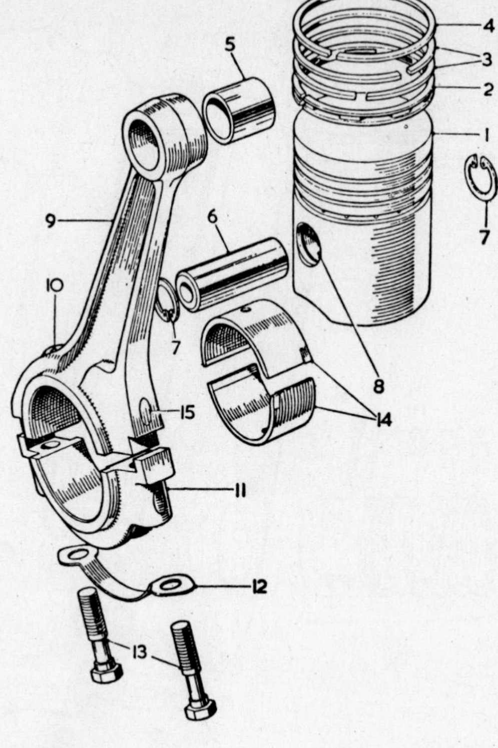

1 Piston
2 Oil ring
3 Compression rings—taper
4 Compression ring—parallel
5 Wrist pin bushing
6 Wrist pin
7 Circlip
8 Wrist pin lubrication hole
9 Connecting rod
10 Cylinder wall lubrication jet
11 Connecting rod bearing cap
12 Locktab
13 Rod bolts
14 Rod bearings
15 Connecting rod and cap assembly marks

Piston and connecting rod components, engines with floating wrist pins. Mark the pistons so that they may be installed in the same bore, facing in the same direction. Oversize pistons have their oversize dimension stamped on the piston crown. Late engines have straight (no offset) rods with press-fit wrist pins

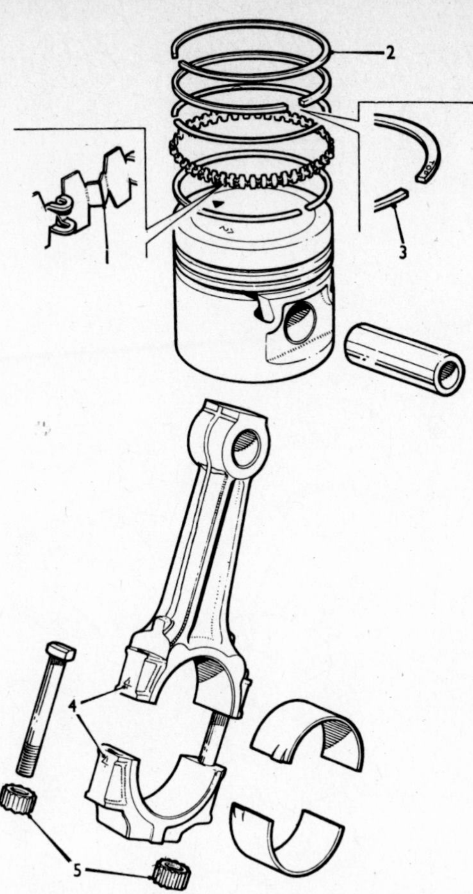

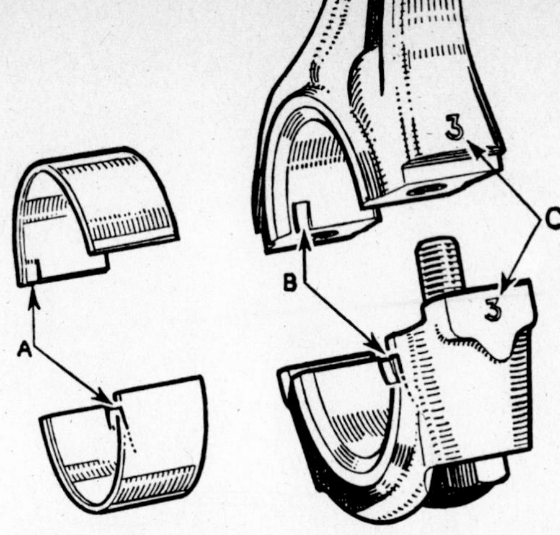

The rod and cap should be assembled as shown. The numbers C indicate the cylinder from which the rod and cap were removed. A and B point to the rod bearing locating grooves and tags

Piston and connecting rod components, with press-fit wrist pins (18GF and later engines). The rods and caps are marked with the number of the cylinder (1, 2, 3, or 4) that they belong to. The Front or ▲ mark on the piston crown should be toward the front of the engine. If the pistons are removed from the rods, mark them so that they may be installed in the same cylinder

1 Oil ring expander ends must meet
2 Top compression ring
3 Second compression ring
4 Connecting rod and cap identification
5 Spline-type rod nut

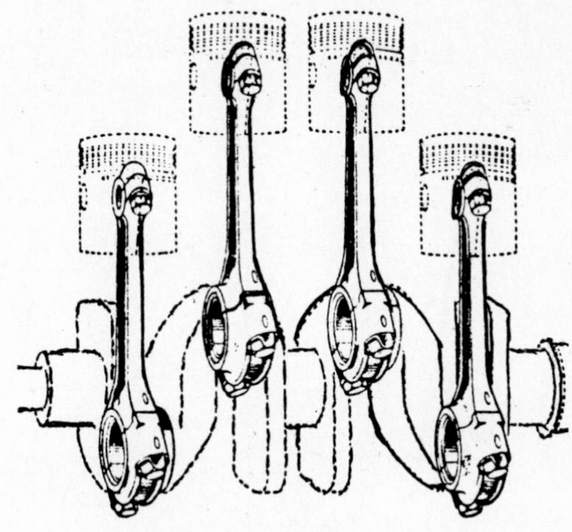

Correct relationship of rods to crankshaft, engines with clamp type wrist pins

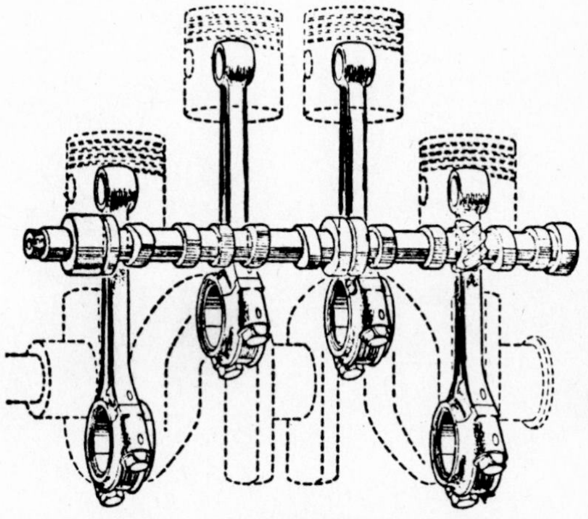

Correct relationship of rods to crankshaft, engines with floating wrist pins

MGC

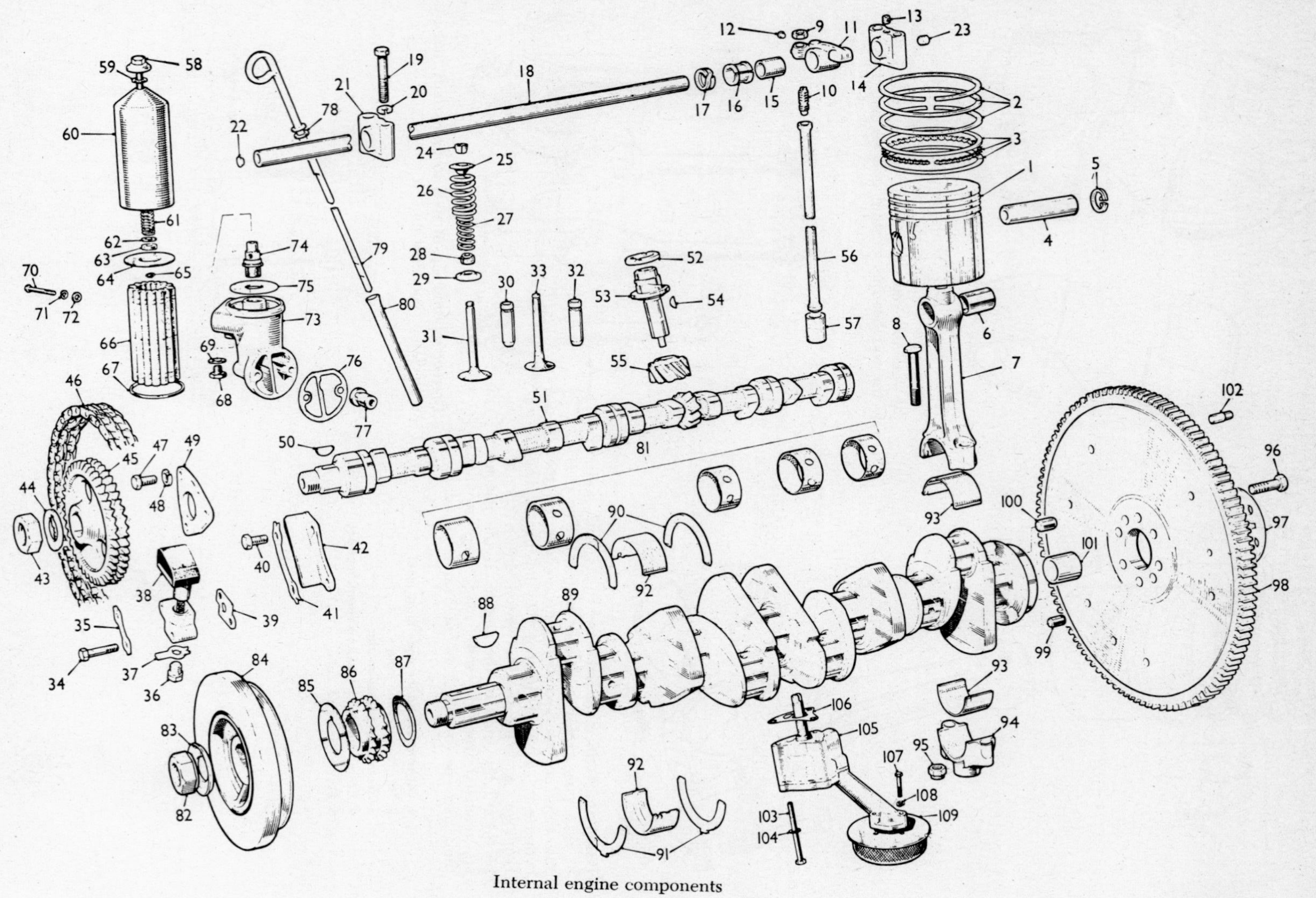

Internal engine components

1 Piston
2 Piston rings—compression
3 Piston ring—oil control
4 Wrist pin
5 Circlip
6 Wrist pin bushing
7 Connecting rod
8 Rod bolt
9 Locknut
10 Valve adjusting screw
11 Valve rocker
12 Rivet
13 Locating screw for rocker shaft
14 Support bracket (tapped) for rocker shaft
15 A Rocker arm bushing
16 Spacer
17 Spring washer
18 Valve rocker shaft
19 Bolt
20 Spring washer
21 Support bracket (plain) for rocker shaft
22 Plug
23 Screw plug
24 Valve cotters
25 Cup for valve springs
26 Outer valve spring
27 Inner valve spring
28 Sealing ring for valve stem
29 Collar for valve spring
30 Guide for intake valve
31 Intake valve
32 Guide for exhaust valve
33 Exhaust valve
34 Set screw for tensioner
35 Locktab
36 Plug
37 Locktab
38 Timing chain tensioner
39 Gasket for timing chain tensioner
40 Bolt
41 Locktab
42 Damper for timing chain
43 Nut for camshaft
44 Lockwasher
45 Chain wheel for camshaft
46 Timing chain
47 Locating plate bolt
48 Spring washer
49 Locating plate
50 Key for camshaft gear
51 Camshaft
52 Thrust washer
53 Shaft for distributor gear
54 Key for distributor gear
55 Distributor drive gear
56 Pushrod
57 Lifter
58 Bolt
59 Sealing washer
60 Container for oil filter
61 Pressure plate spring
62 Washer
63 Felt washer
64 Pressure plaie
65 Circlip
66 Filter
67 Sealing ring
68 Drain plug
69 Washer (copper)
70 Filter head bolt
71 Spring washer
72 Plain washer
73 Filter head
74 Anchor insert
75 Pressure plate
76 Gasket for filter head
77 Oil pressure release valve
78 Washer for dipstick
79 Dipstick
80 Guide tube for dipstick
81 Camshaft bearing
82 Crankshaft nut
83 Lockwasher for crankshaft nut
84 Crankshaft pulley
85 Oil thrower
86 Chain wheel
87 Shim for chain wheel
88 Key for chain wheel
89 Crankshaft
90 Thrust washers—upper
91 Thrust washers—lower
92 Main bearing
93 Connecting rod bearing
94 Connecting rod cap
95 Nut
96 Flywheel bolt
97 Lockwasher
98 Flywheel
99 Dowel—small
100 Dowel—large
101 Pilot bushing
102 Dowel—clutch to flywheel
103 Oil pump bolt
104 Spring washer
105 Oil pump
106 Oil pump gasket
107 Screw
108 Spring washer
109 Oil pump strainer

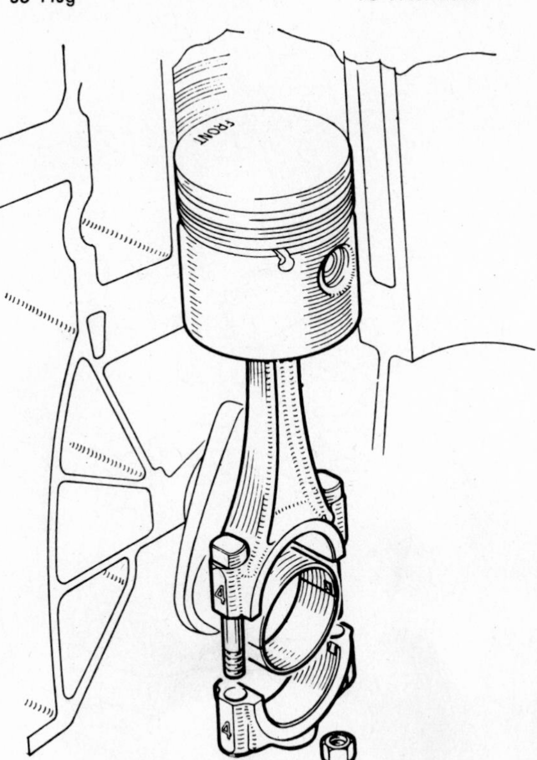

Correct installation of rod and piston assembly. The cylinder number is stamped on the rod and cap, and should be facing away from the camshaft. The piston crown is marked Front to facilitate installation

MG 1100

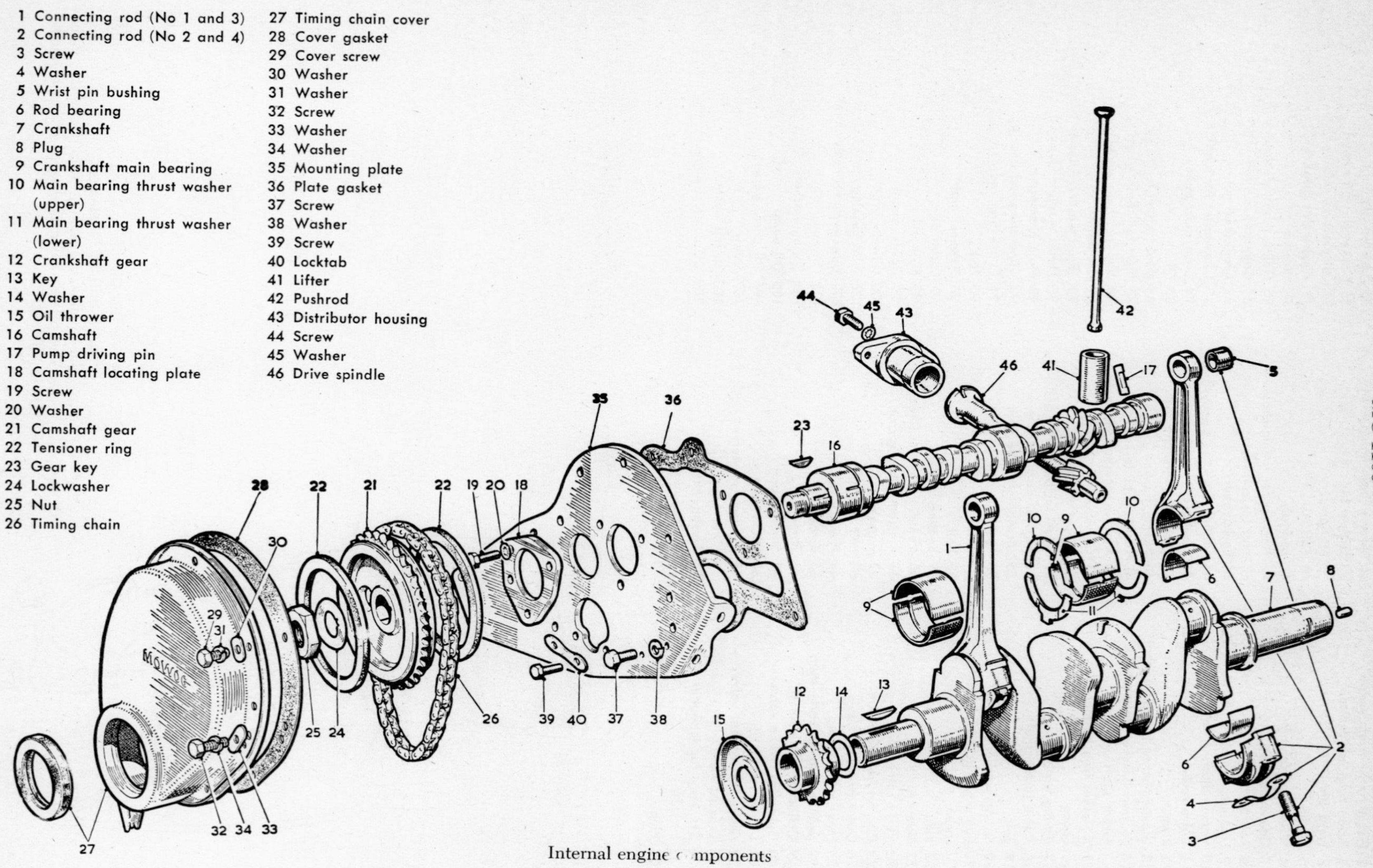
1 Connecting rod (No 1 and 3)
2 Connecting rod (No 2 and 4)
3 Screw
4 Washer
5 Wrist pin bushing
6 Rod bearing
7 Crankshaft
8 Plug
9 Crankshaft main bearing
10 Main bearing thrust washer (upper)
11 Main bearing thrust washer (lower)
12 Crankshaft gear
13 Key
14 Washer
15 Oil thrower
16 Camshaft
17 Pump driving pin
18 Camshaft locating plate
19 Screw
20 Washer
21 Camshaft gear
22 Tensioner ring
23 Gear key
24 Lockwasher
25 Nut
26 Timing chain
27 Timing chain cover
28 Cover gasket
29 Cover screw
30 Washer
31 Washer
32 Screw
33 Washer
34 Washer
35 Mounting plate
36 Plate gasket
37 Screw
38 Washer
39 Screw
40 Locktab
41 Lifter
42 Pushrod
43 Distributor housing
44 Screw
45 Washer
46 Drive spindle

Internal engine components

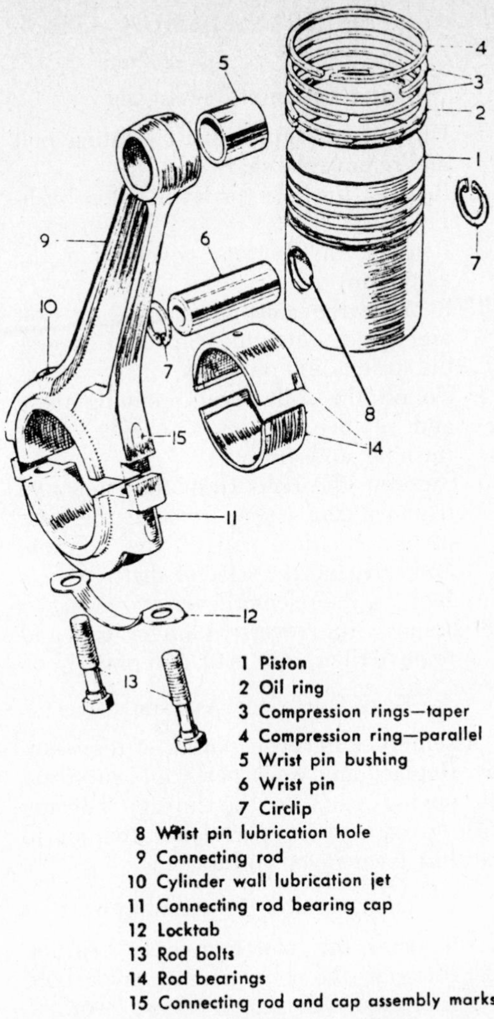

Piston and connecting rod components, engines with floating wrist pins. Mark the pistons so that they may be installed in the same bore, facing in the same direction. Oversize pistons have their oversize dimension stamped on the piston crown. Late engines have straight (no offset) rods with press-fit wrist pins

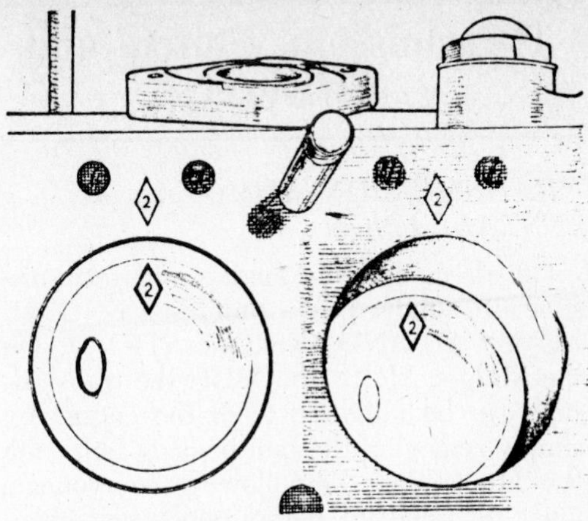

On engines with floating or press-fit type wrist pins the pistons are select-fitted to the bores, and the piston crowns and cylinders are marked with identifying numbers enclosed in a diamond. Oversize dimensions (if any) are enclosed in an ellipse.

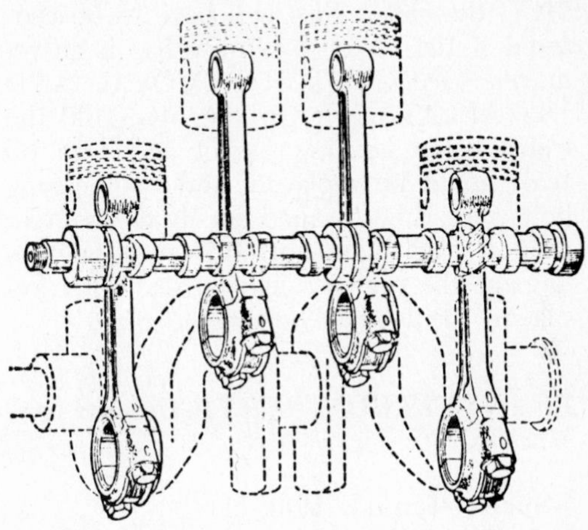

Correct relationship of rods to crankshaft, engines with floating wrist pins

Transmission, Clutch, and Flywheel

TRANSMISSION REMOVAL AND INSTALLATION

On all models the engine and transmission are removed as a unit (see ENGINE REMOVAL AND INSTALLATION). On the Midget, MGB, and MGC the transmission can be unbolted from the engine by simply removing the bell housing bolts. On the 1100 sedan the following components must be removed before the transmission housing can be unbolted from the cylinder block: clutch cover housing, flywheel, clutch assembly, starter motor, and flywheel housing.

Installation in all cases is in reverse order of removal. On the Midget, MGB, and MGC the clutch disc will have to be centered if the clutch assembly has been removed (see CLUTCH REMOVAL AND INSTALLATION). On the MG 1100 the transmission housing gasket and cork oil seal should be replaced, and the housing bolts should be torqued evenly to maintain proper gear alignment. Be careful not to damage the primary gear oil seal when replacing the flywheel housing.

TRANSMISSION SERVICE—MG MIDGET

4-Speed Manual, 1961-71, Rebuilding Procedures

After the transmission is removed from the vehicle and separated from the engine, disassembly begins with:

Rear Extension Removal and Installation

1. Unbolt and remove the speedometer drive from the extension.
2. Unbolt and remove the shift linkage housing.
3. Unbolt the extension and remove it by pulling back slightly and turning it counterclockwise so that the selector lever will clear the selector forks.

At this point, if it is desired to rebuild the shift linkage, the extension components can be disassembled.

Installation of the extension is a reversal of removal procedures. To determine shim thickness, see TRANSMISSION ASSEMBLY.

Rear Extension Disassembly

1. Unscrew the guide shaft locating bolt and remove the shaft.
2. Remove the selector lever nylon bushing.
3. Remove the bottom cover from the extension.
4. Remove the shift lever locating bolt and spring retaining cap, and remove the springs and plungers.
5. Unbolt the shift lever retaining plate and remove the lever, O-ring, pivot bushing, and spring.
6. Unscrew the bolts from the front and rear selector levers, remove the core plugs at either end of the housing, and drive out the selector shaft.
7. Remove the selector levers.
8. Remove the reverse plunger cap and remove the spring, ball, and pin.

Rear Extension Assembly

Assembly is in reverse order of disassembly. Replace any worn parts, and lubricate all moving parts in the linkage housing with grease (paying particular attention to the shift lever pivot bushing).

Transmission Disassembly

1. Remove the clutch release bearing.
2. Unscrew the locknut and pivot bolt, and remove the clutch release lever.
3. Unbolt and remove the front cover, and remove the gasket and shim.
4. Remove the side cover and gasket.
5. Remove the two springs from the front edge of the cover mating surface, and tilt the transmission to remove the two plungers.
6. Remove the two plugs from the side cover side of the transmission case and remove the reverse plunger and springs and the selector interlock ball and spring.
7. Put the transmission into neutral, and, working through the drain plug hole, remove the three selector fork lockbolts.
8. Tap the selector rods out through the back of the transmission. As the rods are being drawn out take care to remove the two interlock balls from the front of the transmission case.
9. Tap the countershaft out of the front of the case with a soft-metal drift.

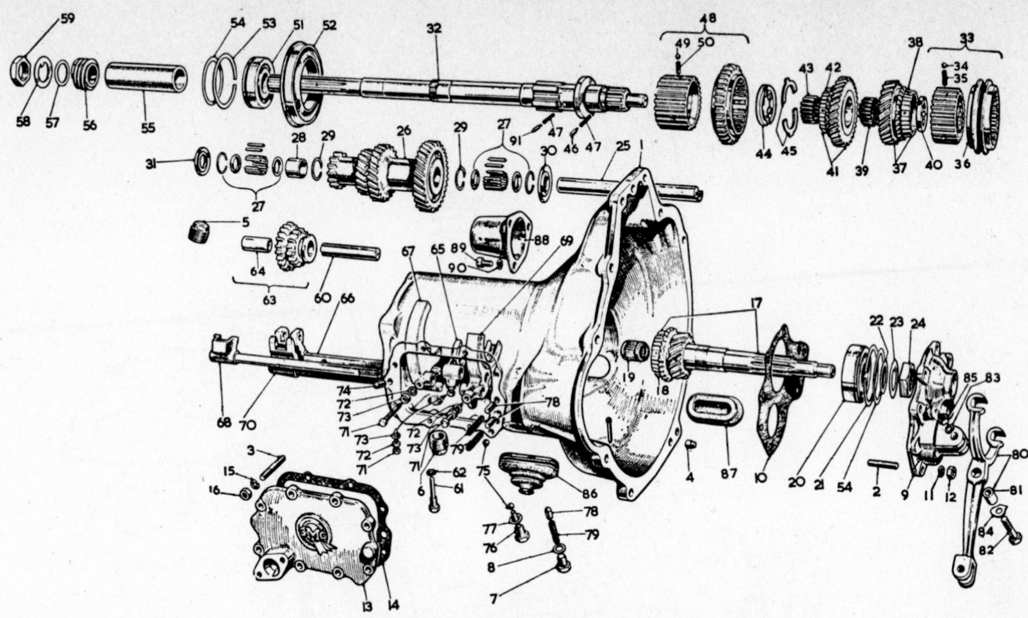

MG Midget transmission components

1 Case assembly
2 Stud
3 Stud
4 Dowel
5 Filler plug
6 Drain plug
7 Plug for reverse plunger spring
8 Washer
9 Front cover
10 Front cover gasket
11 Lockwasher
12 Nut
13 Side cover
14 Side cover gasket
15 Lockwasher
16 Nut
17 Input shaft with cone
18 Synchronizer
19 Needle-roller bearing
20 Ball bearing
21 Snapring
22 Washer
23 Lockwasher
24 Nut
25 Countershaft
26 Clustergear
27 Needle-roller bearing with snapring
28 Spacer
29 Snapring
30 Thrust washer (front)
31 Thrust washer (rear)
32 Mainshaft
33 Third and fourth gear synchronizer
34 Ball
35 Spring
36 Sleeve
37 Third gear with cone
38 Synchronizer
39 Needle roller
40 Third gear collar
41 Second gear with cone
42 Synchronizer
43 Needle roller
44 Second gear collar
45 Washer
46 Peg
47 Peg spring
48 First gear assembly
49 Ball
50 Ball spring
51 Ball bearing
52 Bearing housing
53 Snapring
54 Bearing shim
55 Spacer
56 Speedometer gear
57 Washer
58 Lockwasher
59 Nut
60 Reverse shaft
61 Screw
62 Lockwasher
63 Reverse gear and bushing
64 Bushing
65 Reverse fork
66 Reverse fork rod
67 First and second fork
68 First and second fork rod
69 Third and fourth fork
70 Third and fourth fork rod
71 Fork lockbolt
72 Lockwasher
73 Nut
74 Interlock plunger
75 Interlock ball
76 Plug
77 Washer
78 Fork rod plunger
79 Spring
80 Clutch release lever with bushing
81 Bushing
82 Bolt
83 Lockwasher
84 Locktab
85 Nut
86 Dust cover
87 Dust cover
88 Starter pinion cover
89 Screw
90 Washer
91 Peg

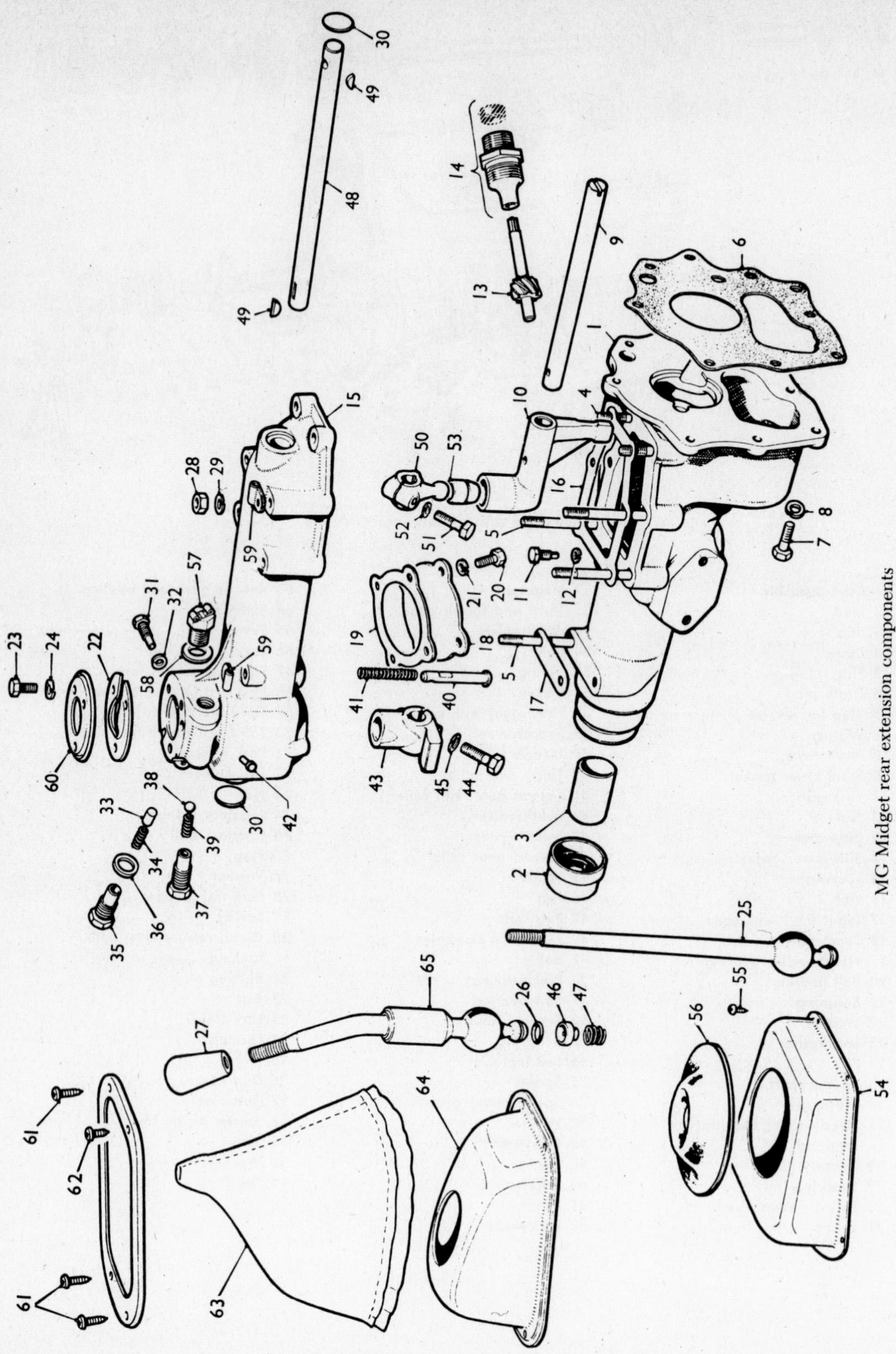

MG Midget rear extension components

1 Rear extension
2 Oil seal
3 Bushing
4 Extension short stud
5 Extension long stud
6 Gasket
7 Screw
8 Lockwasher
9 Guide shaft
10 Selector lever
11 Selector lever locating peg
12 Lockwasher
13 Speedometer pinion
14 Speedometer pinion oil seal assembly
15 Shift linkage housing
17 Gasket
18 Gasket cover
19 Gasket
20 Bolt
21 Lockwasher
22 Lever seat cover
23 Bolt
24 Lockwasher
25 Shift lever
26 O-ring
27 Knob
28 Stud nut
29 Lockwasher
30 Core plug
31 Lever locating bolt
32 Lockwasher
33 Plunger
34 Spring
35 Spring retaining cap
36 Washer
37 Reverse selector detent plug
38 Ball
39 Spring
40 Reverse selector plunger
41 Spring
42 Reverse selector plunger locating pin
43 Rear selector lever
44 Bolt
45 Lockwasher
46 Bushing
47 Spring
48 Selector shaft
49 Key
50 Front selector lever
51 Bolt
52 Lockwasher
53 Front selector lever bushing
54 Cover
55 Bolt
56 Grommet
57 Back-up light switch
58 Washer
59 Clip
60 Retaining plate
61 Self-tapping screw (long)
62 Self-tapping screw (short)
63 Boot
64 Boot support
65 Shift lever

10. Withdraw the mainshaft from the rear of the case.
11. Drive the input shaft out of the front of the case with a soft-metal drift.
12. Lift out the clustergear and thrust washers.
13. Remove the reverse shaft locating bolt. Place a screwdriver on the slotted end of the shaft and push it into the transmission with a twisting motion.
14. Remove the reverse gear and shaft.

Transmission Assembly

Assembly is the reverse of disassembly. The following points should be noted:

1. Clustergear end-float should be 0.001-0.003 in. (Mk. I and II) or 0.003-0.005 in. (Mk. III). If end-float exceeds these limits, the thrust washers should be replaced. Several thicknesses are available.
2. Determine shim thickness for the front and rear covers when any mainshaft or input shaft components have been replaced as follows: Measure the depth of the cover recess and the amount by which the bearing outer race protrudes from the case. Install and tighten the cover with the gasket in place to allow it to be compressed. Take off the cover and measure the gasket thickness. Add this measurement to the depth of the cover recess and subtract the amount by which the bearing protrudes. The result gives the thickness of shims to be used.

Gear Train Component Replacement

When rebuilding a transmission, all bearings should be replaced as a matter of course. Gear and synchronizer assemblies, if worn or broken, should be replaced as assembly units.

When disassembling the mainshaft components, do not disassemble the third and fourth gear synchronizer assembly or first gear assembly. A special tool is needed to install the spring-loaded balls that are released from the hub when the unit is taken apart. British Leyland can supply the tool (part number 18G 144), or a piece of pipe with an inside diameter slightly larger than the hub diameter can be used. A hole must be drilled in the pipe through which the springs and balls can be loaded.

When assembling components onto the countershaft on early models, the uncaged needle bearings can be held in place with grease.

On later models, make sure that the first and second gear assembly is correctly positioned on the mainshaft. The plunger in the hub must align with the cut-away tooth in the gear, and the cone end of the hub and tapered side of the gear teeth must be on opposite sides of the assembly. If the gears are not assembled in this manner it will be impossible to engage second gear.

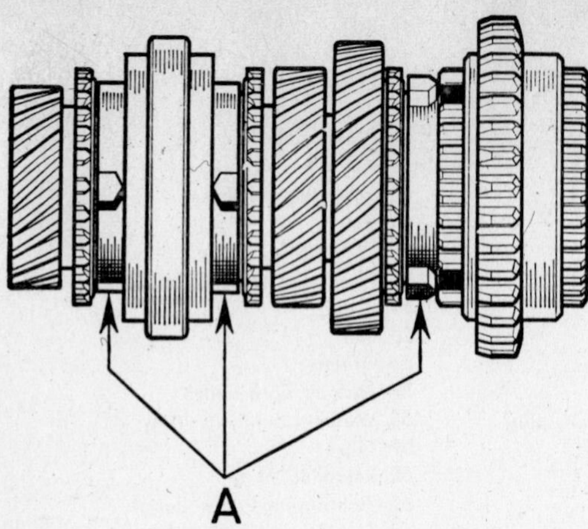

Mainshaft gear assembly, showing the synchronizer rings (A), later cars

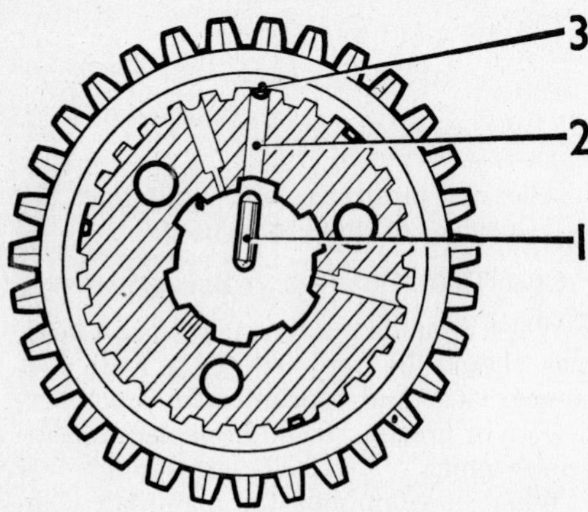

First and second gear assembly. The plunger (1) must align (2) with the cut-away tooth (3) in the gear. If the gear is incorrectly assembled on the hub it will be impossible to engage second gear

TRANSMISSION SERVICE—MGB AND MGC

MGB 4-Speed Manual, 1961-67 (non-synchro first gear), Rebuilding Procedures

After the transmission is removed from the vehicle and separated from the engine, disassembly begins with:

Rear Extension Removal and Installation

1. Remove the dipstick, drain plug, and speedometer drive.
2. Remove the driveshaft flange.
3. Unbolt and remove the shift lever tower.
4. Remove the extension side cover.
5. Remove the interlock plate and bracket.
6. Loosen the clamp bolt on the front gear selector lever, and unbolt and remove the rear extension.

At this point, if it is desired to rebuild the shift linkage, the extension components can be disassembled. Installation of the extension is in reverse order of removal.

Rear Extension Disassembly

1. Withdraw the rear selector lever and the selector shaft from the extension.
2. Remove the circlip from the spring cover at the base of the shift lever and remove the two lever locating bolts. Remove the lever.
3. Unscrew the reverse plunger detent bolt from the rear of the shift lever tower and remove the spring and ball.
4. From the side of the tower remove the reverse plunger locating pin and remove the plunger and spring (released from inside the tower).
5. Remove the oil seal and bearing if they are to be replaced.

Rear Extension Assembly

Assembly is in reverse order of disassembly. Replace worn parts, and lubricate the shift lever pivot bushing (nylon) with motor oil.

Transmission Disassembly

1. Remove the side cover and gasket.
2. Cut the lockwire, unscrew the three selector lever bolts, and remove the levers.
3. Unbolt and remove the selector rod locating block, and remove the three balls and springs that are released when the block is withdrawn.
4. Loosen the shift fork locknuts and bolts, slide the selector rods out, and remove the forks. The selector rods may be tapped out, if necessary, using a soft-metal drift.
5. Unbolt and remove the front cover, the gasket, and the input shaft bearing shims.
6. Remove the cover oil seal if it is to be replaced.
7. Unscrew the reverse shaft locating bolt and remove the shaft and gear.
8. Using a soft-metal drift, drive the countershaft out towards the front of

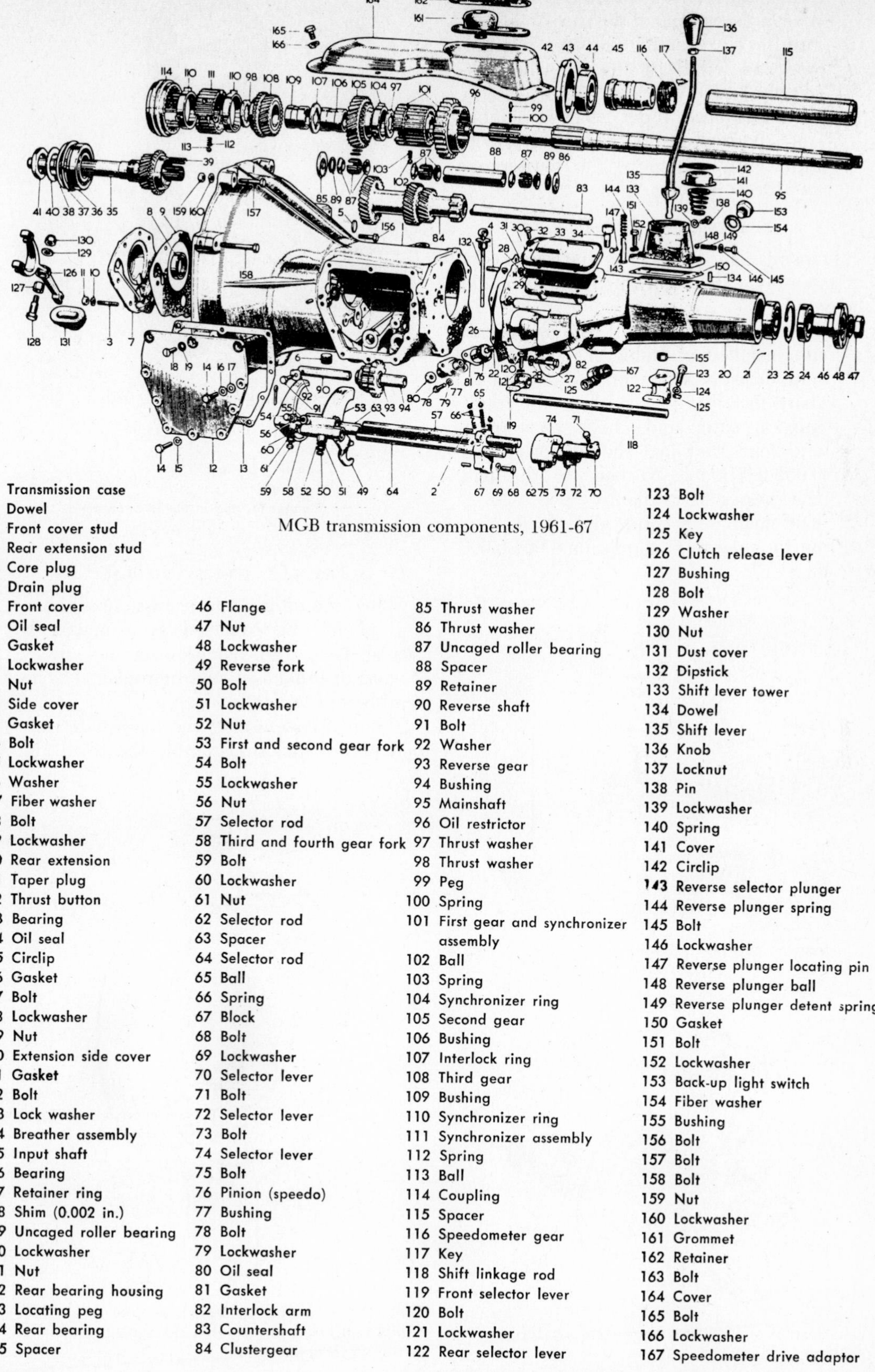

MGB transmission components, 1961-67

1 Transmission case
2 Dowel
3 Front cover stud
4 Rear extension stud
5 Core plug
6 Drain plug
7 Front cover
8 Oil seal
9 Gasket
10 Lockwasher
11 Nut
12 Side cover
13 Gasket
14 Bolt
15 Lockwasher
16 Washer
17 Fiber washer
18 Bolt
19 Lockwasher
20 Rear extension
21 Taper plug
22 Thrust button
23 Bearing
24 Oil seal
25 Circlip
26 Gasket
27 Bolt
28 Lockwasher
29 Nut
30 Extension side cover
31 Gasket
32 Bolt
33 Lock washer
34 Breather assembly
35 Input shaft
36 Bearing
37 Retainer ring
38 Shim (0.002 in.)
39 Uncaged roller bearing
40 Lockwasher
41 Nut
42 Rear bearing housing
43 Locating peg
44 Rear bearing
45 Spacer
46 Flange
47 Nut
48 Lockwasher
49 Reverse fork
50 Bolt
51 Lockwasher
52 Nut
53 First and second gear fork
54 Bolt
55 Lockwasher
56 Nut
57 Selector rod
58 Third and fourth gear fork
59 Bolt
60 Lockwasher
61 Nut
62 Selector rod
63 Spacer
64 Selector rod
65 Ball
66 Spring
67 Block
68 Bolt
69 Lockwasher
70 Selector lever
71 Bolt
72 Selector lever
73 Bolt
74 Selector lever
75 Bolt
76 Pinion (speedo)
77 Bushing
78 Bolt
79 Lockwasher
80 Oil seal
81 Gasket
82 Interlock arm
83 Countershaft
84 Clustergear
85 Thrust washer
86 Thrust washer
87 Uncaged roller bearing
88 Spacer
89 Retainer
90 Reverse shaft
91 Bolt
92 Washer
93 Reverse gear
94 Bushing
95 Mainshaft
96 Oil restrictor
97 Thrust washer
98 Thrust washer
99 Peg
100 Spring
101 First gear and synchronizer assembly
102 Ball
103 Spring
104 Synchronizer ring
105 Second gear
106 Bushing
107 Interlock ring
108 Third gear
109 Bushing
110 Synchronizer ring
111 Synchronizer assembly
112 Spring
113 Ball
114 Coupling
115 Spacer
116 Speedometer gear
117 Key
118 Shift linkage rod
119 Front selector lever
120 Bolt
121 Lockwasher
122 Rear selector lever
123 Bolt
124 Lockwasher
125 Key
126 Clutch release lever
127 Bushing
128 Bolt
129 Washer
130 Nut
131 Dust cover
132 Dipstick
133 Shift lever tower
134 Dowel
135 Shift lever
136 Knob
137 Locknut
138 Pin
139 Lockwasher
140 Spring
141 Cover
142 Circlip
143 Reverse selector plunger
144 Reverse plunger spring
145 Bolt
146 Lockwasher
147 Reverse plunger locating pin
148 Reverse plunger ball
149 Reverse plunger detent spring
150 Gasket
151 Bolt
152 Lockwasher
153 Back-up light switch
154 Fiber washer
155 Bushing
156 Bolt
157 Bolt
158 Bolt
159 Nut
160 Lockwasher
161 Grommet
162 Retainer
163 Bolt
164 Cover
165 Bolt
166 Lockwasher
167 Speedometer drive adaptor

the transmission and leave the clustergear in the bottom of the case.

9. Pull the rear bearing housing from the case and withdraw the mainshaft assembly.
10. Withdraw the input shaft assembly from the front of the case, using a drift if necessary. Remove the clustergear and thrust washers.

Transmission Assembly

Transmission assembly is the reverse of disassembly. The following points should be noted:

1. Before the input shaft and mainshaft are installed assemble the clustergear and thrust washers onto the countershaft, install the assembly in the transmission case, and check clustergear end-float. End-float should not exceed 0.002-0.003 in. Washers of different thicknesses are available.
2. End-float of second and third gear on the mainshaft should be 0.004-0.006 in.

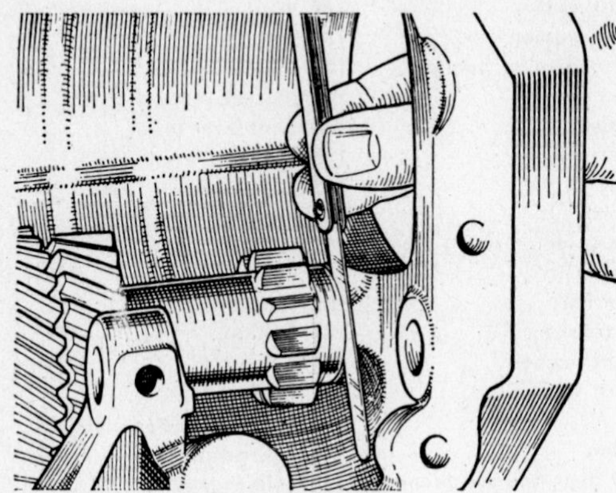

Clustergear end-play should not exceed 0.002-0.003 in.

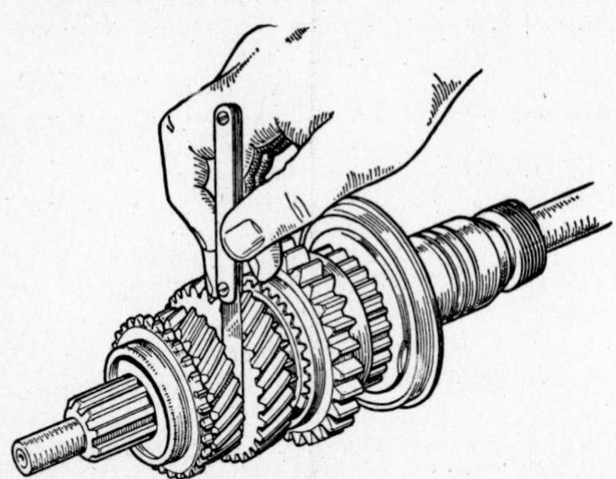

End-float of second and third gear on the mainshaft should be 0.004-0.006 in.

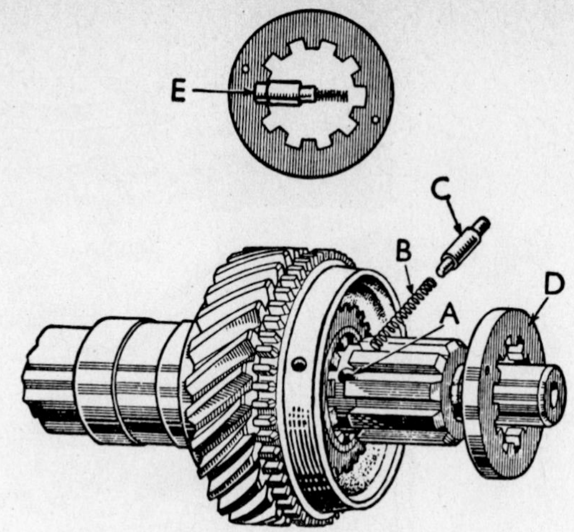

Positioning the mainshaft gears

A Hole for spring and plunger
B Spring
C Locating plunger
D Lockwasher
E Plunger located in the lockwasher

Gear Train Component Replacement

When rebuilding a transmission, all bearings should be replaced as a matter of course. Gear and synchronizer assemblies, if worn or broken, should be replaced as assembly units.

When disassembling the mainshaft components, do not disassemble the third and

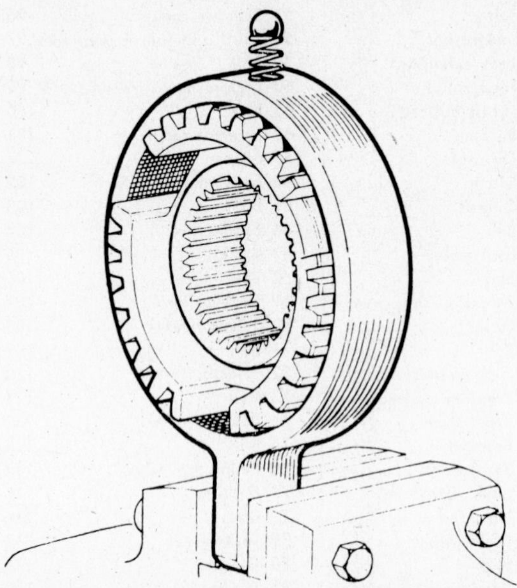

Tool 18G 222 (up to 1968) or tool 18G 1026 (1968 on), used to assemble the springs and balls in the synchronizers

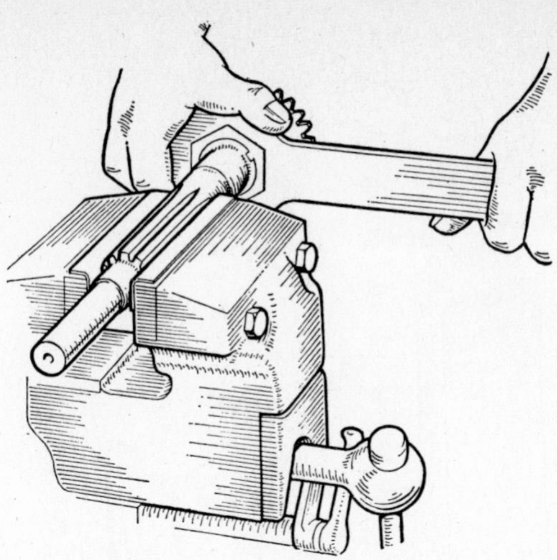

The input shaft locknut has a left-hand thread

fourth gear synchronizer assembly or first gear assembly. A special tool is needed to install the spring-loaded balls that are released from the hub when the unit is taken apart. British Leyland can supply the tool (part number 18G 222), or a piece of pipe with an inside diameter slightly larger than the hub diameter can be used. A hole must be drilled in the pipe through which the springs and balls can be loaded.

The uncaged roller bearings used in early transmissions can be held in position during assembly using grease.

To disassemble the input shaft assembly the large locknut must be removed. *This locknut has a left-hand thread.*

MGB/MGC 4-Speed Manual (fully synchronized), 1968-71

After the transmission is removed from the vehicle and separated from the engine, disassembly begins with:

Rear Extension Removal and Installation

1. Remove the driveshaft flange.
2. Unbolt and remove the shift linkage housing.
3. Withdraw the selector interlock arm and plate assembly.
4. Unbolt and remove the extension and mainshaft shims.

At this point, if it is desired to rebuild the shift linkage, the extension components can be disassembled.

Installation of the extension is in reverse order of removal. To determine shim thickness, see TRANSMISSION ASSEMBLY.

Rear Extension Disassembly

1. Remove the snap-ring and oil seal from the rear of the extension and press the bearing out if it is to be replaced.
2. Remove the shift lever locating bolt from the shift linkage housing.
3. Remove the retaining cap and remove the damper and spring at the base of the shift lever.
4. Unbolt the shift lever retaining plate and remove the lever.
5. Loosen the clamp bolt at the selector lever and withdraw the linkage shaft.

Rear Extension Assembly

Assembly is in reverse order of disassembly. The nylon shift lever pivot bushing should be replaced and lubricated with motor oil.

Transmission Disassembly

1. Remove the clutch release bearing and release lever.
2. Unbolt and remove the front cover and bearing shims.
3. Unbolt and remove the side cover.
4. Remove the selector detent plunger plugs and springs.
5. Remove the selector fork and selector lever retaining bolts.
6. Withdraw the selector rods and remove the selector forks.
7. Bend back the locktab on the reverse shaft retaining bolt and remove the bolt. Remove the shaft and withdraw the gear.
8. Carefully drive the countershaft out of the transmission case.
9. Drive the input shaft assembly forward out of the case, making sure it is clear of the clustergear.
10. Remove the spacer and shims from the mainshaft.
11. Remove the rear extension mounting studs from the rear of the transmission case.
12. Check that the mainshaft components are clear of the clustergear teeth, and press the mainshaft assembly out the back of the transmission. Remove the clustergear.

Transmission Assembly

Transmission assembly is in reverse order of disassembly. The following points should be noted:

1. When the rear extension housing or

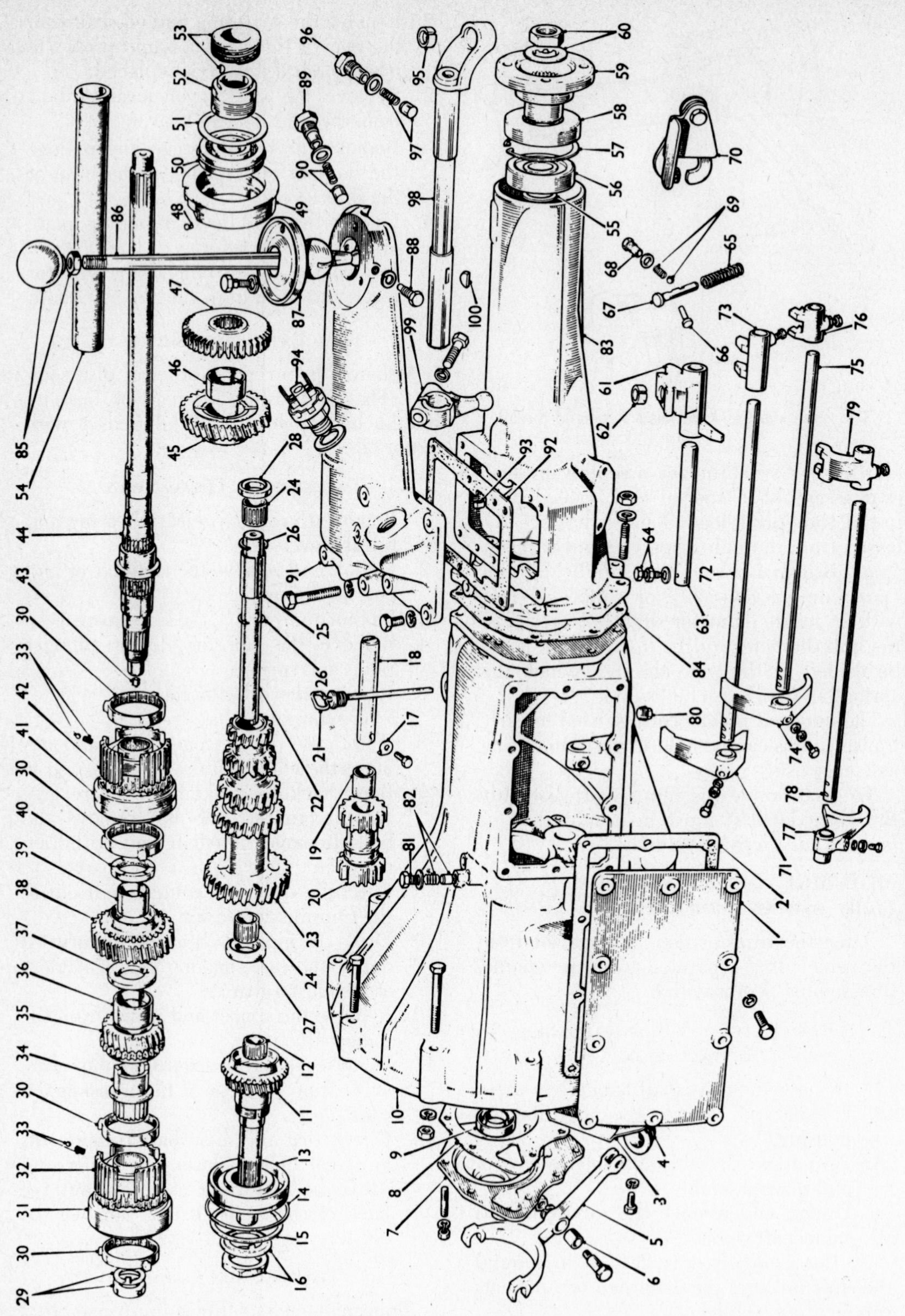

MGB/MGC transmission components, from 1968

1 Side cover
2 Gasket for side cover
3 Stone guard
4 Dust cover
5 Clutch release lever
6 Bushing
7 Front cover
8 Gasket for front cover
9 Oil seal
10 Gearbox main casing
11 Input shaft
12 Needle roller bearing
13 Bearing
14 Snapring
15 Shim
16 Lockwasher and nut
17 Screw and lockwasher
18 Reverse idler shaft
19 Bushing
20 Reverse idler gear
21 Oil level indicator
22 Countershaft
23 Clustergear
24 Needle roller bearing
25 Spacer
26 Snapring
27 Front thrust washer
28 Rear thrust washer
29 Nut and lockwasher
30 Synchronizer ring
31 Sliding coupling for first and second gear
32 Synchronizer
33 Ball and spring
34 Sleeve
35 Third gear
36 Bushing
87 Interlocking thrust washer
38 Second gear
39 Bushing
40 Thrust washer
41 Sliding coupling for third and fourth gear
42 Synchronizer
43 Oil restrictor
44 Mainshaft
45 First gear
46 Bushing
47 Reverse gear
48 Locating peg
49 Bearing housing
50 Bearing
51 Shim
52 Spacer
53 Speedometer gear and driving gear
54 Spacer
55 Shim
56 Bearing
57 Circlip
58 Oil seal
59 Driving flange
60 Nut and lockwasher
61 Selector
62 Bushing
63 Selector levershaft
64 Locating bolt and locknut for selector shaft
65 Spring for reverse plunger
66 Locating pin for reverse plunger
67 Reverse plunger
68 Plug
69 Detent plunger and spring
70 Interlock arm
71 First and second selector fork
72 First and second selector rod
73 First and second selector
74 Third and fourth selector fork
75 Third and fourth selector rod
76 Third and fourth selector
77 Reverse selector fork
78 Reverse selector rod
79 Reverse selector
80 Drain plug
81 Plug
82 Detent spring and plunger
83 Rear extension
84 Gasket for rear extension
85 Knob
86 Shift lever
87 Retainer plate
88 Locating pin
89 Plunger retaining cap
90 Plunger and spring
91 Shift linkage housing
92 Gasket for remote control housing
93 Dowel
94 Back-up light switch
95 Bushing
96 Damper retaining cap
97 Damper and spring
98 Linkage shaft
99 Selector lever
100 Key for selector lever

any mainshaft components have been replaced, the shim thickness for the rear extension must be checked. Temporarily install the extension with the gasket, to allow the gasket to be compressed. Remove the extension and measure the amount the bearing is recessed from the transmission case mating surface, and add to this the thickness from the extension bearing surface to the extension mating surface. Use the number of shims required to make the second distance equal to or 0.001 in. less than the first distance.

2. If the front cover or any of the input shaft components have been replaced, the shim thickness for the front cover must be checked. Temporarily install the cover with the gasket, to allow the gasket to be compressed. Measure the amount that the bearing protrudes from the transmission case. Measure the distance from the cover mating surface to the face of the cover bearing surface and add to this the thickness of the gasket. Use the number of shims required to make the second distance equal to or 0.001 in. less than the first distance.

Gear Train Component Replacement

Gear train replacement notes for the earlier non-synchromesh first gear transmission are applicable to the later type. See the preceding section.

MGB/MGC Automatic, 1968-71

Gear Selector Adjustment

1. Set the lever to the N position on the selector quadrant.
2. Disconnect the linkage rod from the linkage lever on the transmission. It may be necessary to temporarily remove the lever retaining nut to provide clearance for pulling the rod away from the lever.
3. Move the lever to the neutral position by moving it back (counterclockwise) as far as it will go and then forward two clicks.
4. Loosen the locknuts on the rod adjuster and turn the adjuster in the required direction until the linkage rod fits easily into the linkage lever.
5. Reconnect the rod and lever and tighten the adjuster locknuts.

Throttle Down-Shift Cable Adjustment

A high-pressure test gauge is required to test and adjust the down-shift mechanism. If a gauge is available, proceed as follows:

1. With the engine at normal running temperature and at the proper idle speed, check that the crimped stop on the down-shift valve inner cable just contacts the outer cable.
2. Remove the pressure take-off plug at the rear of the transmission just above the oil pan, and connect the gauge.
3. With the transmission in neutral and the engine at the correct idle speed, pressure should be 55-65 psi.
4. With the transmission in drive and the engine at 1,000 rpm (vehicle stationary), pressure should be 90-100 psi.
5. Pressures can be changed, if necessary, by resetting the cable adjuster.

TRANSMISSION SERVICE—MG 1100

4-Speed Manual, 1962-67, Rebuilding Procedures

After the power unit is removed from the vehicle and the transmission is separated from the engine, disassembly begins with:

Differential Removal

1. Remove the idler gear with its thrust washers.
2. Unbolt and remove the shift linkage housing from the transmission case.
3. Release the shift linkage.
4. Unbolt and remove the driveshaft flanges. Do not use the transmission case as a leverage point when removing the flanges, as serious damage to the case can result.
5. Unbolt and remove the final drive end covers.
6. Remove the differential housing stud nuts, and withdraw the housing and differential assembly.

Differential Disassembly and Assembly

1. Withdraw the two differential bearings.
2. Bend back the locktabs and remove the six bolts securing the drive gear to the hub.
3. Mark the relative position of the gear and hub for installation, and separate them.

SHIFT SPEEDS										
	Up-shifts				Down-shifts					
Driving conditions	1–2		2–3		3–2		3–1		2–1	
	m.p.h.	km.p.h.	m.p.h.	km.p.h.	m.p.h.	km.p.h.	m.p.h.	km.p.h.	m.p.h.	km.p.h.
'D' Selected										
Minimum throttle	9–14	14–22	14–18							
Full throttle	28–34	45–55	45–54							
Forced throttle (kick-down)	35–42	56–67	63–69		54–60	86–96	22–29	35–46	22–29	35–46
'L2' Selected										
Minimum throttle	9–14	14–22							2–5	3–8
Full throttle	28–34	45–55								
Forced throttle (kick-down)	35–42	56–67							22–29	35–46
'L1' Selected										
Minimum throttle									10–15	16–24

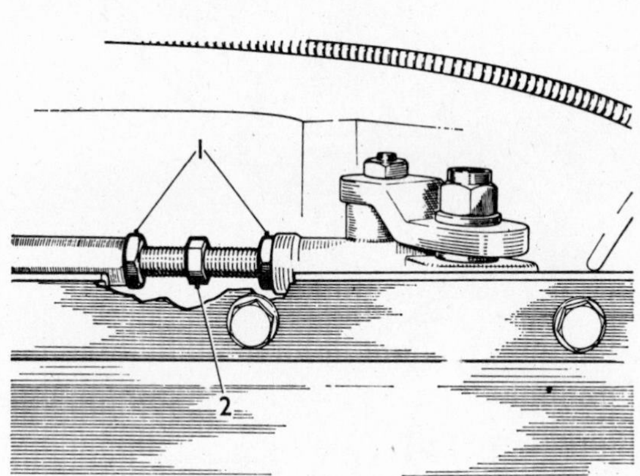

Linkage rod adjuster, showing the locknuts (1) and the adjuster (2)

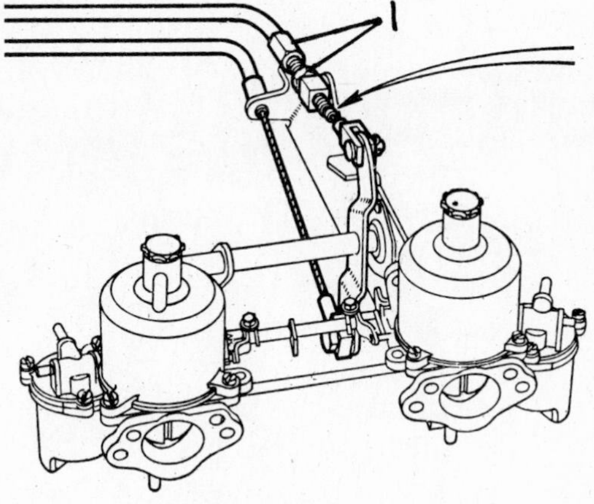

Throttle down-shift cable, showing the cable stop (arrow) and the locknut and adjuster (1)

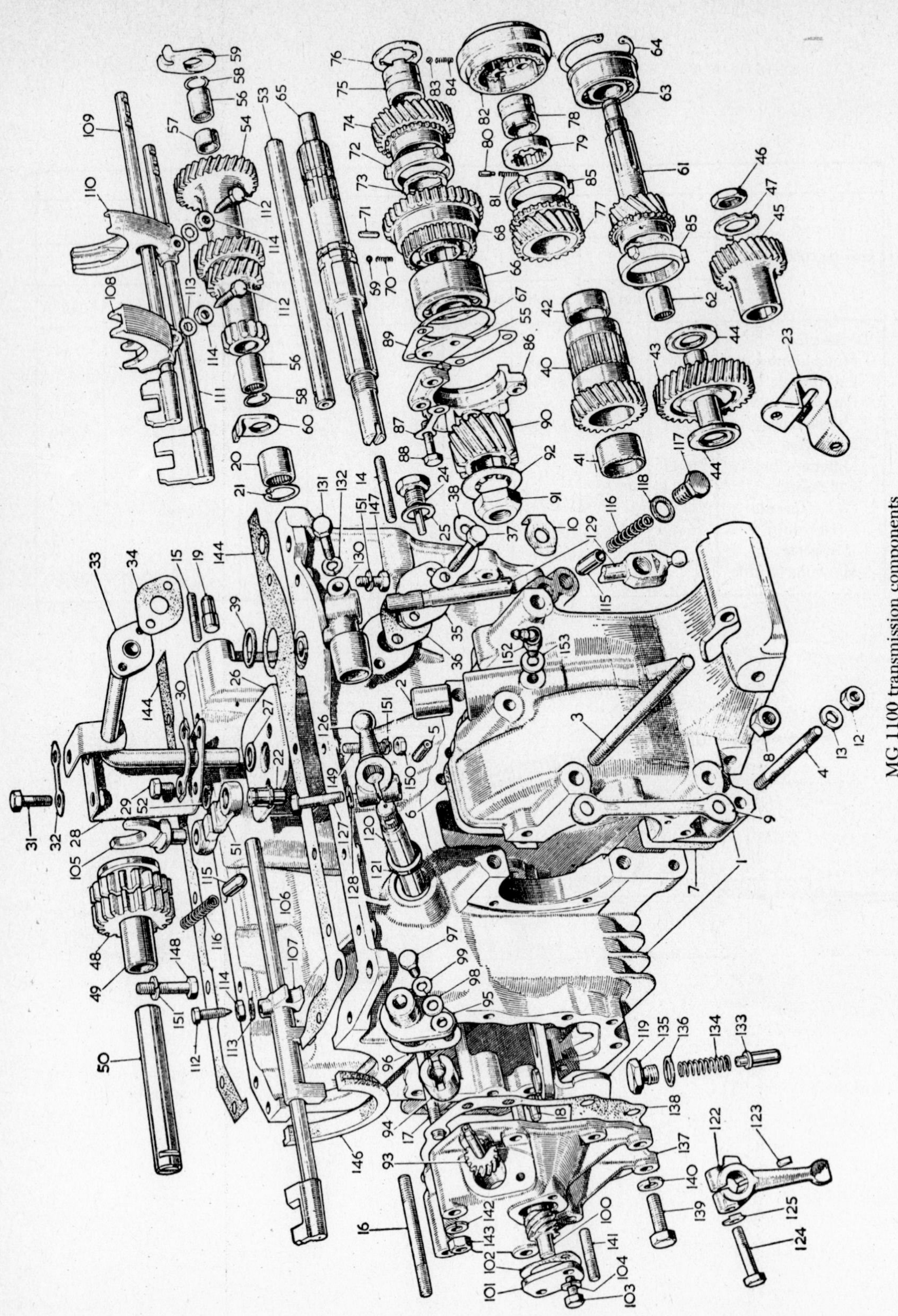

MG 1100 transmission components

1 Transmission case
2 Bushing
3 Differential cover stud
4 Differential cover stud
5 Differential cover dowel
6 Differential cover gasket
7 Differential cover gasket
8 Differential cover stud nut
9 Washer
10 Washer
12 Differential cover stud nut
13 Washer
14 Flywheel housing stud
15 Flywheel housing stud
16 Front cover stud (long)
17 Front cover stud (short)
18 Front cover dowel
19 Flywheel housing dowel
20 Idler gear bearing
21 Bearing circlip
22 Operating lever pin
23 Exhaust pipe bracket
24 Drain plug
25 Plug washer
26 Oil strainer
27 Sealing ring
28 Strainer bracket
29 Bolt
30 Washer
31 Bolt
32 Washer
33 Oil pickup pipe
34 Gasket
35 Pipe flange
36 Gasket
37 Pipe bolt
38 Washer
39 O-ring
40 Primary gear
41 Bushing
42 Bushing
43 Idler gear
44 Idler gear thrust washer
45 Input shaft gear
46 Nut
47 Locktab
48 Reverse gear
49 Bushing
50 Reverse shaft
51 Reverse operating lever
52 Pivot pin circlip
53 Countershaft
54 Clustergear
55 Lockplate
56 Bearing
57 Spacer
58 Retaining ring
59 Thrust washer (rear)
60 Thrust washer (front)
61 Input shaft
62 Input shaft roller bearing
63 Ball bearing
64 Circlip
65 Mainshaft
66 Mainshaft bearing
67 Circlip
68 First gear
69 Synchronizer ball
70 Spring
71 Second gear synchronizer plunger
72 Synchronizer ring
73 Second gear thrust washer
74 Second gear
75 Bushing
76 Interlock ring
77 Third gear
78 Bushing
79 Thrust washer
80 Thrust washer peg
81 Spring
82 Third/top synchronizer
83 Ball
84 Spring
85 Synchronizer ring
86 Bearing retainer
87 Locktab
88 Screw
89 Bearing shim
90 Final drive pinion
91 Nut
92 Washer
93 Speedometer pinion
94 Bushing
95 Bushing assembly
96 Gasket
97 Bush screw
98 Washer
99 Washer
100 Speedometer spindle and gear
101 End plate
102 Gasket
103 Bolt
104 Washer
105 Reverse fork
106 Reverse fork rod
107 Fork rod selector
108. First and second fork
109 First and second fork rod
110 Third and fourth fork
111 Third and fourth fork rod
112 Selector bolt
113 Washer
114 Locknut
115 Plunger fork end
116 Plunger spring
117 Plug
118 Plug washer
119 Shift gate
120 Gear linkage shaft
121 Oil seal
122 Operating lever
123 Key
124 Lever screw
125 Washer
126 Linkage lever
127 Lever bolt
128 Washer
129 Linkage control shaft
130 Shaft lever
131 Bolt
132 Washer
133 Reverse detent plunger
134 Plunger spring
135 Spring plug
136 Plug washer
137 Front cover
138 Gasket
139 Cover bolt
140 Washer
141 Mounting adaptor stud
142 Washer
143 Nut
144 Gasket
145 Gasket
146 Bearing cap oil seal
147 Transmission to crankcase bolt
148 Transmission to crankcase bolt (long)
149 Transmission to crankcase stud
150 Nut
151 Washer
152 lubricator differential cover
153 Lubricator differential cover washer

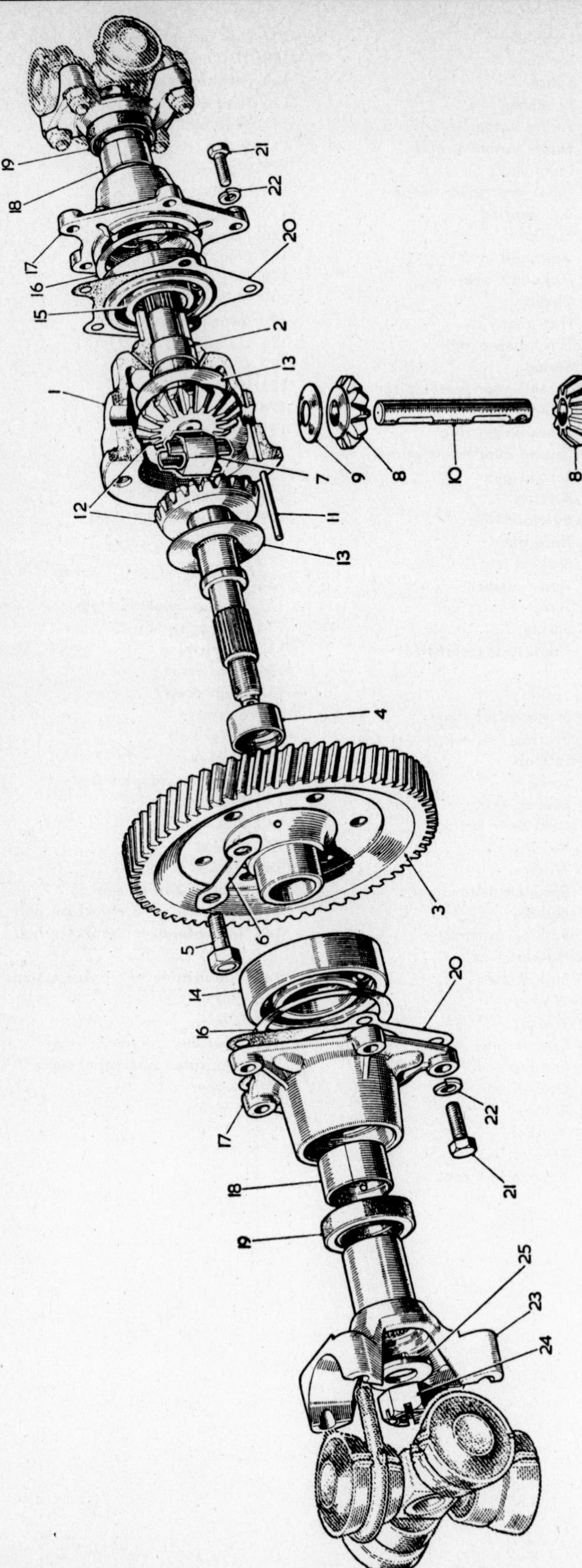

MG 1100 differential components

1 Differential case
2 Case bushing
3 Drive gear
4 Gear bushing
5 Gear bolt
6 Locktab
7 Thrust block
8 Differential pinion
9 Pinion thrust washer
10 Center pin
11 Pin peg
12 Differential gear
13 Gear thrust washer
14 Drive gear bearing
15 Case bearing
16 Bearing shim
17 End-cover
18 Cover bushing
19 Oil seal
20 Gasket
21 End cover screw
22 Washer
23 Driveshaft flange
24 Flange nut
25 Washer

4. Tap out the taper pin to release the pinion center pin, thrust block, and pinion assembly.

Assembly is in reverse order of disassembly. Be sure that the thrust washers are replaced with their chamfered bores against the machined face of the gears.

Differential Installation

1. Place the differential assembly in the transmission case, with a slight bias towards the flywheel side. Install the housing and tighten the nuts sufficiently to hold the bearings, but loose enough to allow the assembly to be moved sideways.
2. Install the right-side end cover and tighten the nuts evenly, to pull the differential away from the flywheel and ensure full contact between the bearing and bearing register.
3. Install the left-side end cover without the gasket and tighten the bolts evenly until the cover register contacts the bearing outer race. Measure the gap between the cover and the case in several places. Remove the cover and install it with the gasket and enough shims so that the above gap would have measured between 0.008-0.009 in. For example, if the gap measured 0.005 in., a 0.003 in. shim or combination of shims should be used.

NOTE: Later assemblies are fitted with larger bearings, which must be installed with the word Thrust facing the end cover. Since pre-load is increased with these bearings, adjust the gap with shims so that it would be 0.011 in. before the gasket is installed.

4. Tighten the differential housing nuts.
5. Install the driveshaft flanges. Make sure that both flanges are equally free to rotate.
6. Align and install the shift linkage rod, and install the linkage housing.

Transmission Disassembly

1. Remove the reverse detent plug, and remove the plunger and spring.
2. Remove the clamp and key from the inner end of the gear selector shaft and pull the shaft out.
3. Remove the speedometer drive assembly.
4. Unbolt and remove the front cover.

A

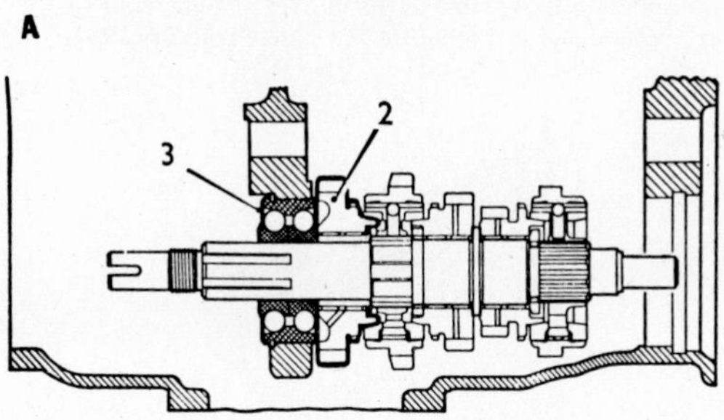

B

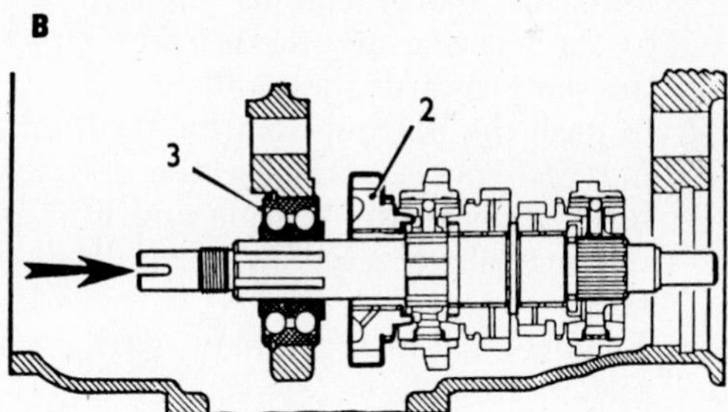

C

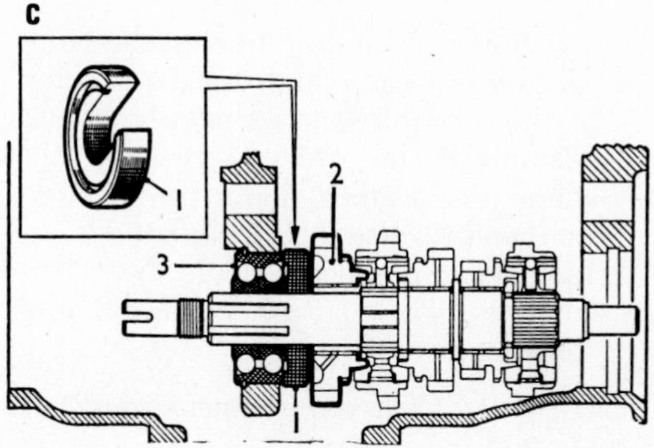

D

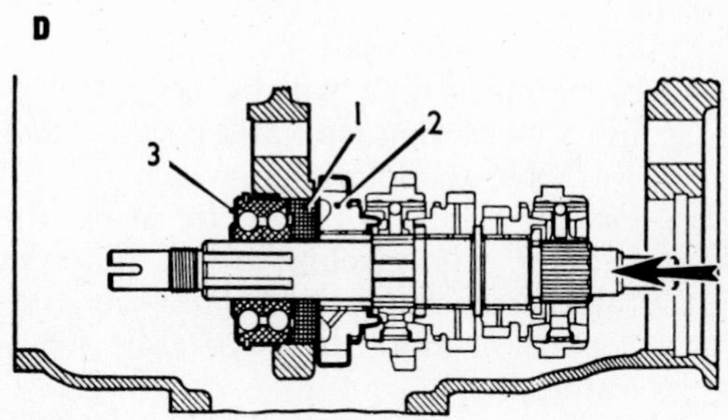

Using the special spacer to remove the mainshaft assembly

1 Spacer, MG part number 18G 613
2 First gear assembly
3 Mainshaft bearing

5. Remove the selector interlock arm.
6. Disconnect and remove the oil pickup pipe.
7. Remove the circlip and remove the input shaft roller bearing.
8. Lock first and third gears together, using the selector shafts.
9. Bend the locktab back and remove the input shaft nut. Remove the final drive gear nut and remove the input gear and final drive gear.
10. Bend the locktabs back and unbolt and remove the mainshaft bearing retainer and shims.
11. Remove the countershaft and reverse shaft lockplate, and remove the clustergear and thrust washers.
12. Unscrew the plugs from the outside of the case and remove the selector rod interlock plungers and springs.
13. Remove the circlip from the input shaft and withdraw the shaft with the bearing from the case.
14. To remove the mainshaft assembly it is necessary to remove the mainshaft bearing using a special spacer, MG part number 18G 613. Drive the mainshaft towards the outside of the case until the spacer can be inserted between first gear and the bearing. Drive the shaft towards the center of the case to push the bearing from the web, taking care not to damage the selector forks. Remove the bearing and lift out the mainshaft assembly. See illustration.
15. Remove the reverse shaft, gear, and selector fork.

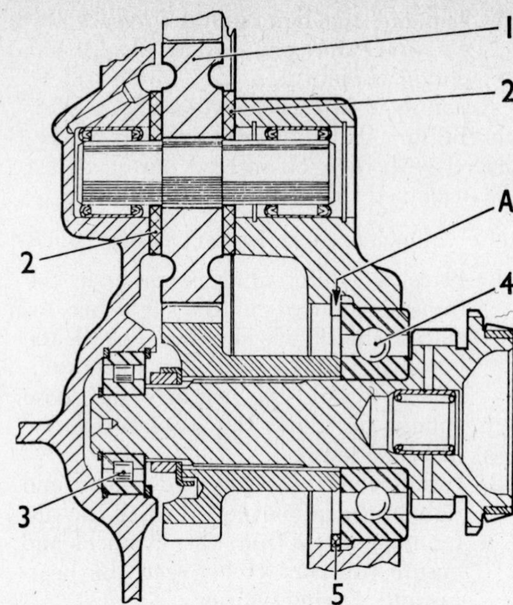

A section through the input shaft and idler gear. Measure the gap (A) with tool 18G 569, and use the appropriate circlip

1 Idler gear
2 Thrust washers
3 Input shaft roller bearing
4 Input shaft ball bearing
5 Circlip

When gap is 0.096-0.098 in., use circlip 2A 3710
When gap is 0.098-0.100 in., use circlip 2A 3711

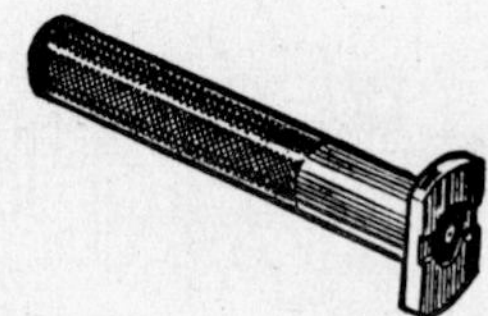

Tool 18G 569, available from MG dealers

Transmission Assembly

Transmission assembly is in reverse order of disassembly. The following points should be noted:

1. If any input shaft components have been replaced, it will be necessary to use a measuring tool, MG part number 18G 569, to determine which of two circlips should be used to retain the bearing. The circlips are of different thicknesses, and determine the end-float of the input shaft assembly. See illustration.
2. Clustergear end-float should be 0.002-0.006 in. Thrust washers of different thicknesses are available.
3. To adjust mainshaft end-float, install the mainshaft bearing retainer without any shims and lightly tighten the bolts. Measure the gap, and use the number of shims required to reduce the gap to 0.000-0.001 in. Make sure that the shims are installed under the countershaft and reverse shaft lockplate.
4. Idler gear end-float should be 0.003-0.008 in. Thrust washers of different thicknesses are available.

Gear Train Component Replacement

When rebuilding a transmission, all bearings should be replaced as a matter of course. Gear and synchronizer assemblies, if worn or broken, should be replaced as assembly units.

When disassembling the mainshaft components, do not disassemble the third and fourth gear synchronizer assembly or first gear assembly. A special tool is needed to install the spring-loaded balls that are released from the hub when the unit is taken apart. British Leyland can supply the tool (part number 18G 572), or a piece of pipe with an inside diameter slightly larger than the hub diameter can be used. A hole must be drilled in the pipe through which the springs and balls can be loaded.

The uncaged countershaft roller bearings can be replaced by the caged roller bearings used in later (fully synchronized) transmissions.

If the second and third gear bushing were removed from the mainshaft, new ones must be used to obtain the required interference fit. Heat the new bushings to 350-400° F. before installing.

The end-float for second gear and third gear on the mainshaft should be 0.0035-0.0055 in.

Make sure that the first and second gear assembly is correctly positioned on the mainshaft. The plunger in the hub must align with the cut-away tooth in the gear, and the cone end of the hub and tapered side of the gear teeth must be on opposite sides of the assembly. If the gears are not assembled in this manner it will be impossible to engage second gear.

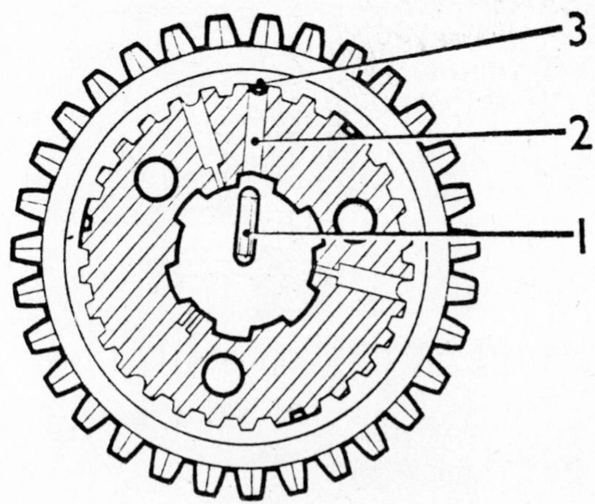

First and second gear assembly. The plunger (1) must align (2) with the cut-away tooth (3) in the gear. If the gear is incorrectly assembled on the hub it will be impossible to engage second gear

OVERDRIVE SERVICE—MGB AND MGC

Description

The MGB and MGC use an electrically operated Laycock de Normanville overdrive unit that is bolted to the rear of the transmission. The MGB up to 1968 uses the type D overdrive, while the 1968 and later MGB and MGC use the type LH overdrive. Both types are similar in operation principle, differing only in detail design. The overdrive unit operates in both third and fourth gears.

The overdrive gearset and clutch is hydraulically operated. The hydraulic system, in turn, is actuated by the electric control system, which consists of:

A). The cockpit toggle switch, that controls overdrive operation.

B). The solenoid, actuated by the toggle switch, that opens the hydraulic control valve.

C). The gear switch, which allows the overdrive to operate only in the top two gears.

D). The throttle switch, vacuum controlled, that overrides the toggle switch under closed throttle conditions and allows the overdrive to operate only when the throttle is open.

E). The relay, an electro-magnetic switch used with the throttle switch as a safeguard against changing out of overdrive with the throttle closed.

On the type D overdrive, the setting of the hydraulic valve operating lever can be checked and adjusted after the small cover-plate is removed from the right side of the unit. The lever is correctly set when a 3/16 in. rod can be passed through the hole in the lever into the hole in the case with the solenoid energized, i.e., with the ignition and overdrive switches on and the transmission in third or fourth gear. To adjust the lever, screw the adjusting nut on the solenoid plunger in the required direction, holding the plunger against rotation, until the rod can be inserted. The rod fork should just contact the nut with the rod in position. Operate the toggle switch several times and check that the rod can still be inserted. Solenoid current should not exceed 2 amps. A current reading of 17 amps. indicates that the plunger is not moving far enough to switch from the operating to the holding coil, and the plunger should be readjusted.

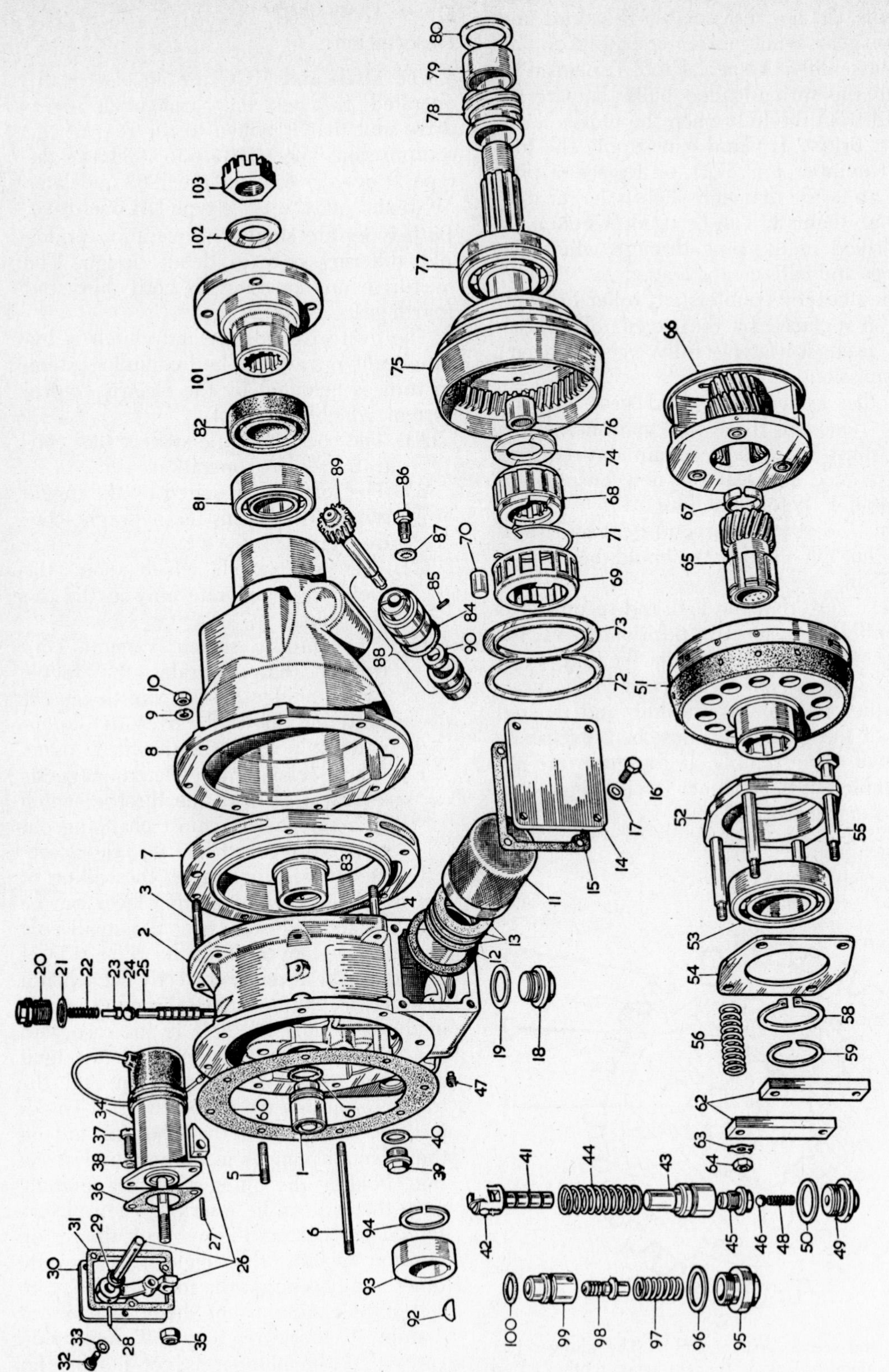

Type D overdrive components, MGB 1961-67

1 Operating piston
2 Main casing assembly
3 Stud—main casing to rear casing
4 Stud—main casing to rear casing
5 Stud—main casing to gearbox adaptor
6 Stud—main casing to gearbox adaptor
7 Brake ring
8 Intermediate casing
9 Lockwasher
10 Nut
11 Filter
12 Sealing plate
13 Magnetic rings
14 Side cover-plate
15 Gasket
16 Bolt
17 Lockwasher
18 Drain plug
19 Washer
20 Plug for operating valve
21 Washer
22 Spring—operating valve
23 Plunger—operating valve
24 Steel ball
25 Operating valve
26 Operating valve lever assembly
27 Pin
28 Pin
29 O-ring
30 Cover—solenoid
31 Gasket
32 Bolt
33 Lockwasher
34 Solenoid
35 Locknut
36 Gasket
37 Bolt
38 Lockwasher
39 Plug
40 Washer
41 Pump plunger
42 Pin
43 Pump body
44 Pump plunger spring
45 Non-return valve body
46 Steel ball
47 Bolt
48 Spring—non-return valve
49 Plug non-return valve
50 Washer
51 Clutch assembly
52 Bearing housing
53 Thrust bearing
54 Retainer plate
55 Bolt
56 Spring—clutch return
58 Circlip
59 Snapring
60 Gasket
61 O-ring
62 Spacer
63 Locktab
64 Nut
65 Sun wheel assembly
66 Planet carrier
67 Locating ring
68 Inner member—uni-directional clutch
69 Cage
70 Roller
71 Spring
72 Snapring
73 Oil thrower
74 Thrust bearing
75 Annulus assembly
76 Bearing—needle-roller
77 Bearing—inner
78 Speedometer gear
79 Bushing
80 Thrust washer
81 Bearing
82 Oil seal
83 Mainshaft bushing
84 O-ring
85 Pin
86 Lockbolt
87 Washer
88 Speedometer drive bearing assembly
89 Speedometer gear
90 Oil seal--speedometer bearing
92 Key
93 Cam
94 Snapring
95 Plug—relief valve
96 Washer
97 Spring
98 Plunger
99 Relief valve body
100 O-ring
101 Flange
102 Washer
103 Nut

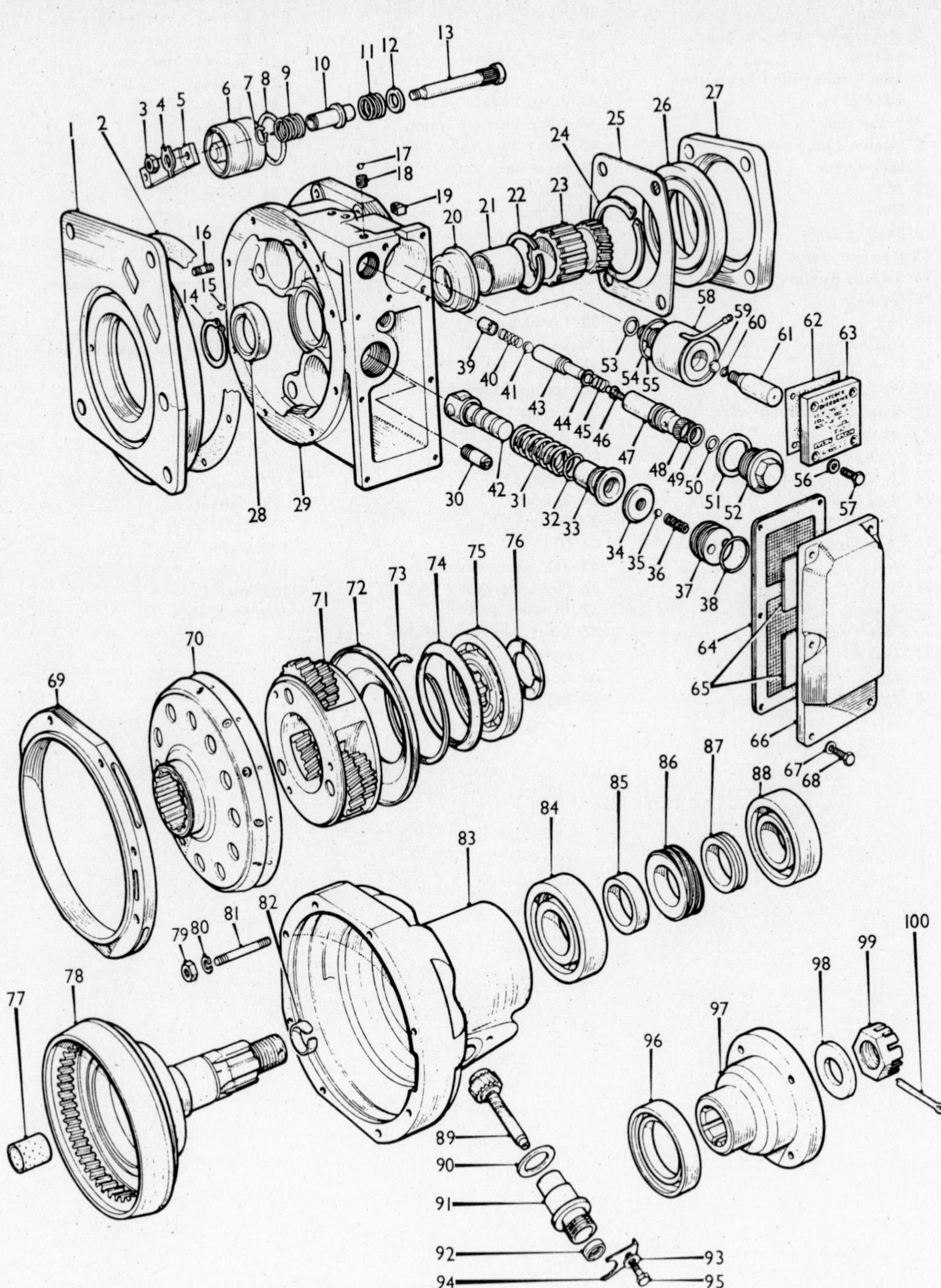

Type LH overdrive components, MGB/MGC 1968 on

1 Adaptor plate
2 Gasket
3 Nut
4 Locktab
5 Spacer
6 Operating piston
7 Circlip
8 O-ring
9 Spring
10 Thrust rod
11 Spring
12 Washer
13 Thrust housing pin
14 Circlip
15 Key
16 Stud
17 Steel ball
18 Plug
19 Grommet
20 Sun wheel thrust bushing
21 Sun wheel bushing
22 Circlip
23 Sun wheel
24 Circlip
25 Retaining plate
26 Thrust ball-race
27 Thrust ring
28 Pump cam
29 Main casing
30 Pump suction tube
31 Spring
32 O-ring
33 Pump body
34 Non-return valve seat
35 Valve ball
36 Valve spring
37 Pump plug
38 O ring
39 Low pressure valve plug
40 Valve spring
41 Valve ball
42 Pump plunger
43 Low pressure valve body
44 Washer
45 Relief valve spring
46 Valve plunger
47 Valve body
48 Filter
49 O-ring
50 O-ring
51 Washer
52 Plug
53 O-ring
54 Solenoid valve body
55 O-ring
56 Washer
57 Bolt
58 Solenoid coil
59 Valve ball
60 O-ring
61 Solenoid plunger
62 Gasket
63 Solenoid cover
64 Sump filter and gasket
65 Filter magnets
66 Sump
67 Washer
68 Bolt
69 Brake-ring
70 Clutch sliding member
71 Planet carrier assembly
72 Oil catcher
73 Circlip
74 Oil thrower
75 Uni-directional clutch
76 Thrust washer
77 Bus
78 Annulus
79 Nut
80 Washer
81 Stud
82 Spring ring
83 Rear casing
84 Annulus front bearing
85 Spacer
86 Speedometer drive gear
87 Selective spacer
88 Annulus rear bearing
89 Speedometer driven gear
90 Sealing washer
91 Speedometer bearing
92 Oil seal
93 Retaining clip
94 Washer
95 Bolt
96 Oil seal
97 Drive flange
98 Washer
99 Nut
100 Cotter pin

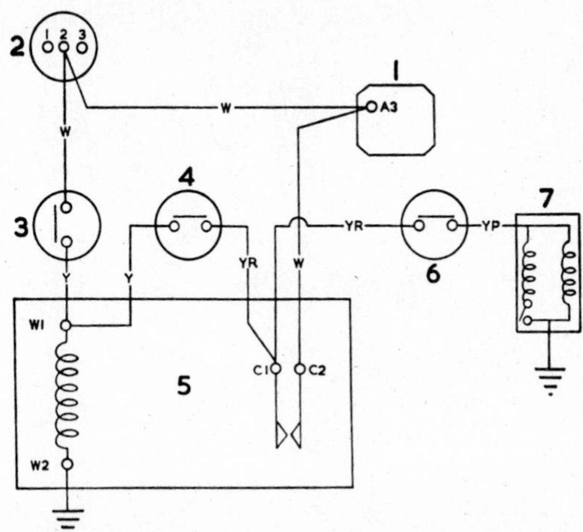

Overdrive electrical circuit wiring diagram

1 Fuse block
2 Ignition switch
3 Toggle (operating) switch
4 Throttle switch
5 Relay
6 Gear switch
7 Solenoid

Cable Color Code
P—purple
R—red
W—white
Y—yellow

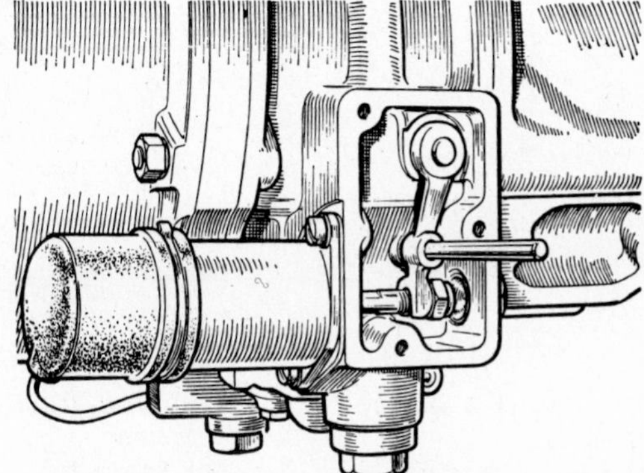

Type D overdrive, checking the setting of the valve lever using a 3/16 in. diameter rod

Lubrication

The overdrive shares a common oil supply with the transmission. Therefore, when the transmission is drained and refilled or checked, the overdrive oil is automatically taken care of.

CAUTION: Do not use any anti-friction additive in a transmission that is equipped with overdrive, as it will cause the overdrive clutch to slip.

CLUTCH REMOVAL AND INSTALLATION

MG Midget, MGB, and MGC

Remove the engine from the car, and, if the engine and transmission are removed as a unit, separate them. Loosen the clutch pressure plate bolts gradually until the spring pressure is released, and remove the pressure plate and disc from the flywheel.

Examine the flywheel surface for scoring and signs of overheating. If scored at all, the flywheel should be turned down on a lathe or replaced. If it appears to have been overheated (blue discoloration), the surface should be checked for warpage and turned down if necessary. If disc wear is evident, the pressure plate and release bearing, as well as the disc, should be replaced. The pilot bushing in the end of the crankshaft should be checked for wear and replaced if galled or elongated. Lubricate the bushing with a graphite base grease or white grease such as *Molykote*.

Upon reinstallation of the disc and pressure plate the disc must be centered so that the transmission mainshaft will engage the pilot bushing as well as the disc splines. To accomplish this, install the disc and pressure plate on the flywheel with the bolts only finger tight so that the disc can be moved. At this point a dummy transmission mainshaft or clutch aligning tool (available from most tool manufacturers and from MG dealers) should be inserted through the disc hub and into the pilot bushing to hold the disc in position while the pressure plate bolts are tightened. Tighten the bolts gradually and evenly, and remove the centering tool. If a new coil spring type pres-

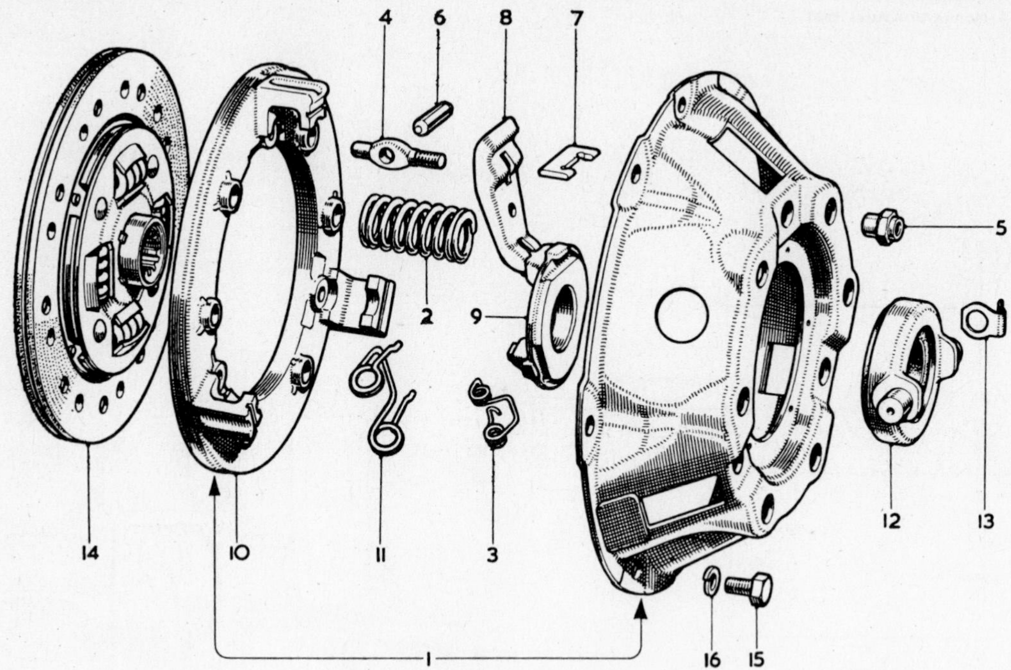

MG Midget clutch components

1 Pressure plate assembly
2 Spring
3 Release fork retainer
4 Eyebolt
5 Eyebolt nut
6 Release fork pin
7 Strut
8 Release fork
9 Thrust plate
10 Pressure plate
11 Anti-rattle spring
12 Release bearing
13 Retainer
14 Disc
15 Pressure plate mounting bolt
16 Lockwasher

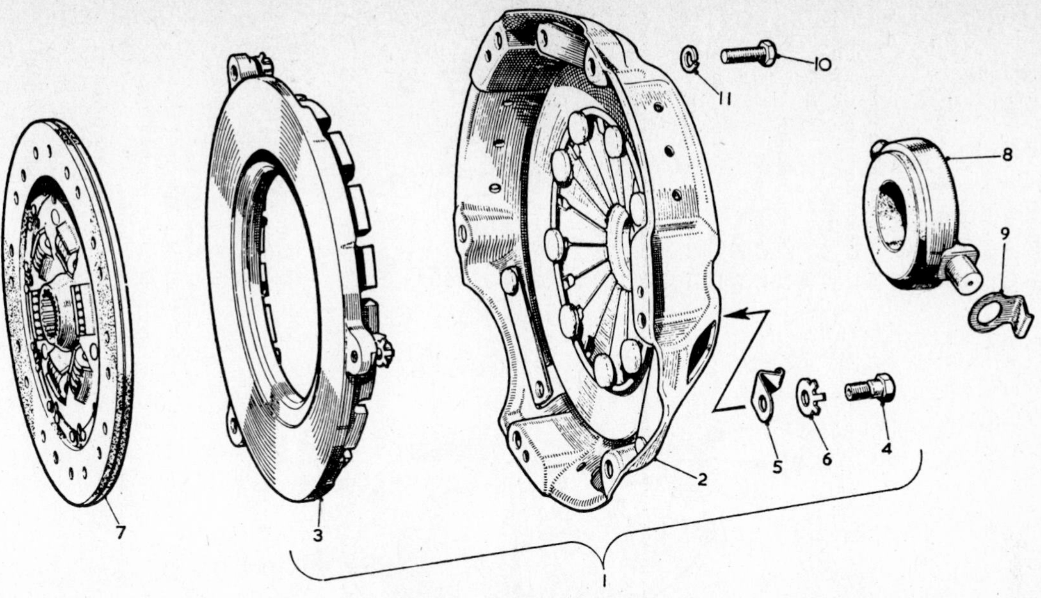

MGB/MGC clutch components

1 Pressure plate assembly
2 Cover with driving struts and springs
3 Pressure plate
4 Strut bolt
5 Clip
6 Locktab
7 Disc
8 Release bearing
9 Bearing retainer clip
10 Pressure plate mounting bolt
11 Lockwasher

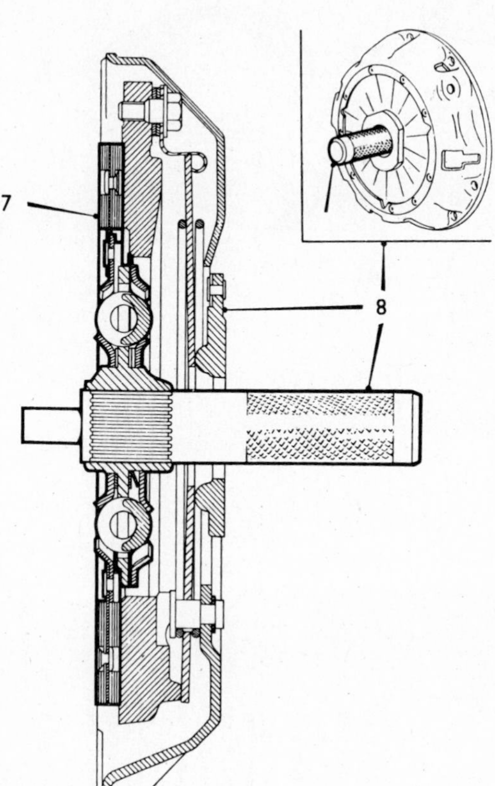

Clutch aligning tool (8) used to center the disc (7)

sure plate is used, be sure to remove the small U-shaped tabs that keep the springs slightly compressed. The tabs are used to prevent distortion of the plate, due to its unloaded condition, during storage and shipping. Bolt the transmission back onto the engine if they were removed as a unit, and reinstall the engine in the chassis.

NOTE: *If a clutch centering tool is not available it is possible to center the disc by eye, if it is done very carefully. If trouble is experienced in mating the engine and transmission, the indication is that the disc is not centered properly and it should be rechecked.*

MG 1100

The clutch and flywheel on the 1100 sedan can be replaced without removing the engine/transmission unit from the car. The procedure is as follows:

1. Remove the battery and battery holder.
2. Remove the starter.
3. Remove the spark plugs so that the engine may be more easily turned over by hand.
4. Remove the clevis pin from the clutch release lever pivot and remove the spring.

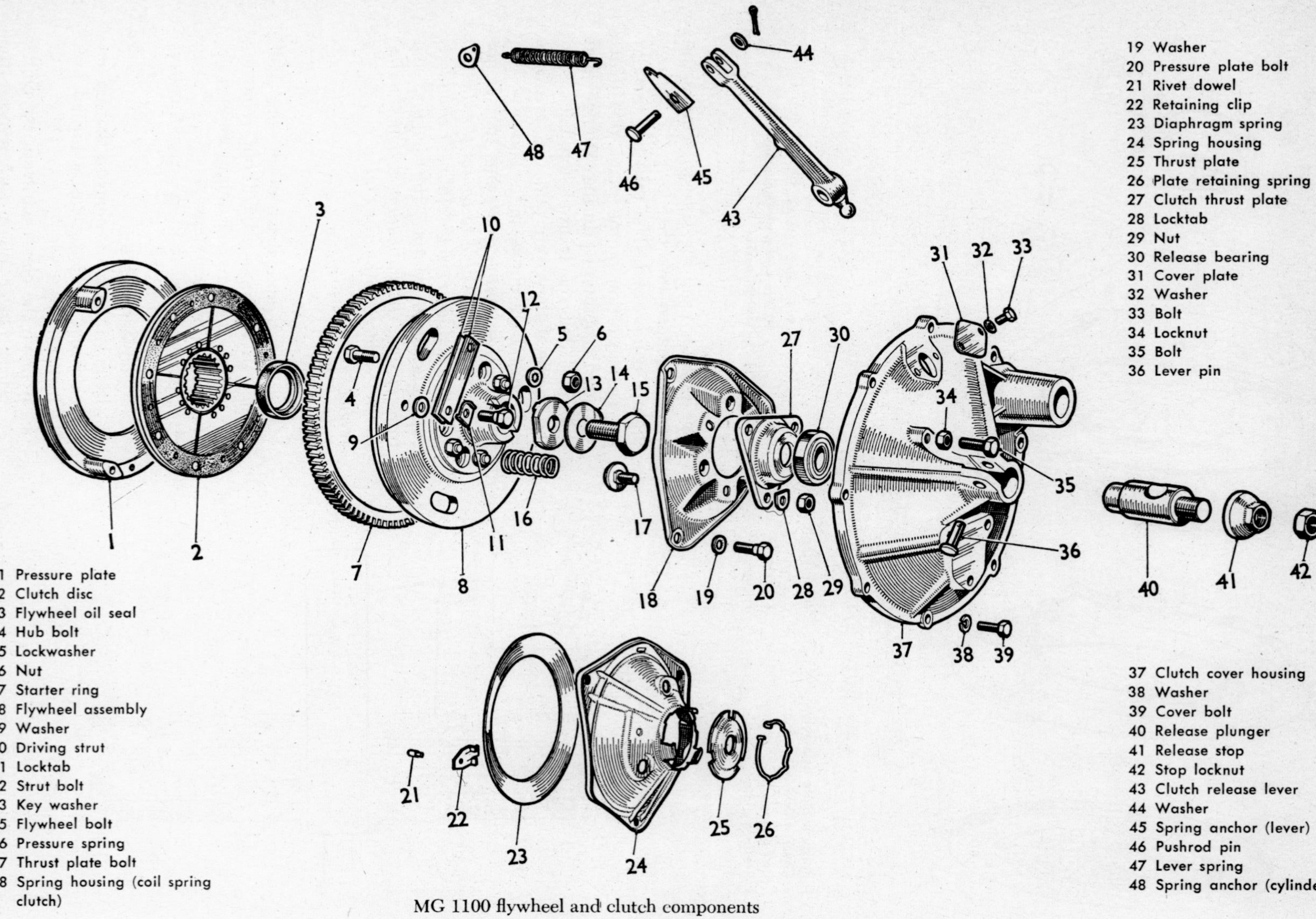

1 Pressure plate
2 Clutch disc
3 Flywheel oil seal
4 Hub bolt
5 Lockwasher
6 Nut
7 Starter ring
8 Flywheel assembly
9 Washer
10 Driving strut
11 Locktab
12 Strut bolt
13 Key washer
15 Flywheel bolt
16 Pressure spring
17 Thrust plate bolt
18 Spring housing (coil spring clutch)
19 Washer
20 Pressure plate bolt
21 Rivet dowel
22 Retaining clip
23 Diaphragm spring
24 Spring housing
25 Thrust plate
26 Plate retaining spring
27 Clutch thrust plate
28 Locktab
29 Nut
30 Release bearing
31 Cover plate
32 Washer
33 Bolt
34 Locknut
35 Bolt
36 Lever pin
37 Clutch cover housing
38 Washer
39 Cover bolt
40 Release plunger
41 Release stop
42 Stop locknut
43 Clutch release lever
44 Washer
45 Spring anchor (lever)
46 Pushrod pin
47 Lever spring
48 Spring anchor (cylinder)

MG 1100 flywheel and clutch components

5. Unbolt the slave cylinder from the flywheel housing and position it out of the way.
6. Unbolt the top radiator support bracket from the cylinder head.
7. Unbolt the rear (passenger side) engine mount from the chassis sub-frame and raise the engine enough to permit the cover to be removed. Watch that the fan blades do not contact and damage the radiator.
8. Unbolt and remove the clutch cover housing.
9. If the clutch is the coil spring type, unbolt the thrust plate from the spring housing.
10. Bend back the flywheel bolt locktab and remove the bolt, locktab, and washer.

The flywheel and clutch assembly can now be removed. The flywheel hub and crankshaft end are tapered, making the flywheel very difficult to remove in most cases. A special service tool is available from British Leyland to accomplish this, but if it is not available, care, patience, and a large hammer will usually suffice. Use a relatively soft piece of metal such as a brass drift or lead block to take the impact of the hammer so that the flywheel will not be damaged, and be careful not to strike against the pressure plate or starter gear. Turn the flywheel a few degrees now and then to distribute the impact force all around the hub. A torch may be used to heat the flywheel hub as a last resort. Do not apply an excessive amount of heat or the flywheel oil seal may be damaged. Replacement of the seal requires removal of the flywheel housing.

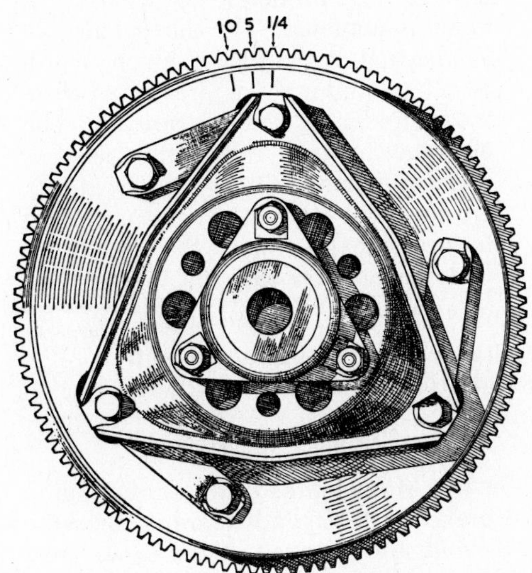

MG 1100 flywheel and spring cover assembly, showing the flywheel ignition timing marks

When the flywheel gives an indication of breaking loose, turn it until the 1/4 mark is at twelve o'clock (No. 1 position at TDC) to prevent the primary gear C-washer from dropping down behind the flywheel oil seal. Keep the flywheel in a vertical position as it is pulled from the crankshaft to prevent oil that is drawn past the seal when the assembly is removed from wetting the clutch disc. A slight amount of oil leakage during removal is normal.

Remove the three pressure plate bolts and separate the pressure plate, disc, flywheel, and spring cover. The disc should be replaced as a matter of course, and the pressure plate and flywheel should be examined for scoring and overheating (blue discoloration). If either condition exists, the pressure plate should be replaced and the flywheel turned down on a lathe or replaced. A coil spring type spring housing assembly should normally be replaced at this time. A diaphragm type spring will not need replacement unless it is broken or the flywheel has been overheated (which may have weakened the spring). With either type of clutch the old pressure plate bolts should not be reused; however, substitute bolts *must not* be used. Replacements must be purchased from an MG dealer, as the bolts are a special type. If the release bearing is noisy or sloppy it should be removed with a gear puller and a replacement pressed onto the shaft.

Installation is in reverse order of removal. Lubricate the oil seal and wipe the crankshaft and flywheel tapers clean before installing. The flywheel bolt should be tightened to 110-115 ft. lbs.

Adjustments

When the clutch has been replaced, it will be necessary to adjust the release lever stop and the release bearing stop. The lever stop should be adjusted first, and the procedure is as follows:

1. Pull the release lever outwards until all free movement is taken up.
2. Using a feeler gauge, check the gap between the lever and the head of the adjustment bolt. The gap should be 0.020 in.

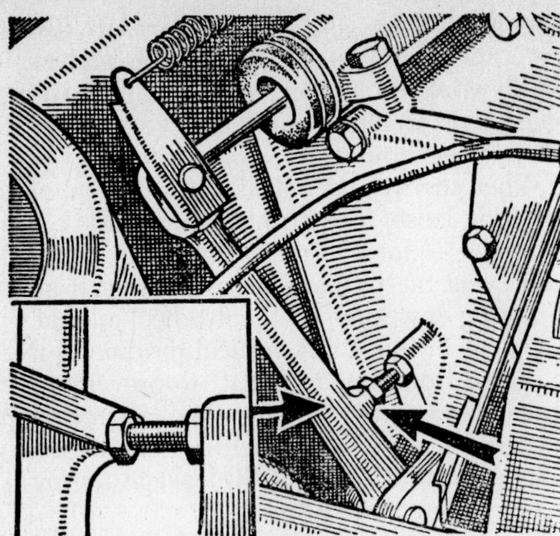

Clutch release lever clearance adjustment. A gap of 0.020 in. should exist between the lever and adjustment bolt

3. If adjustment is necessary, loosen the locknut and turn the adjustment bolt in the required direction until the proper clearance is obtained. Tighten the locknut.

Periodic adjustment of the release lever may be necessary as wear occurs; however, the release bearing stop should need adjustment only when the clutch is replaced. To adjust the bearing stop:

1. Screw the stop and locknut away from the clutch cover housing to the limit of travel.

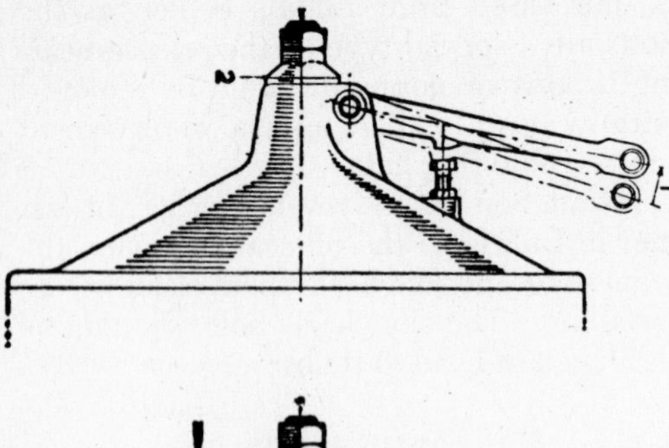

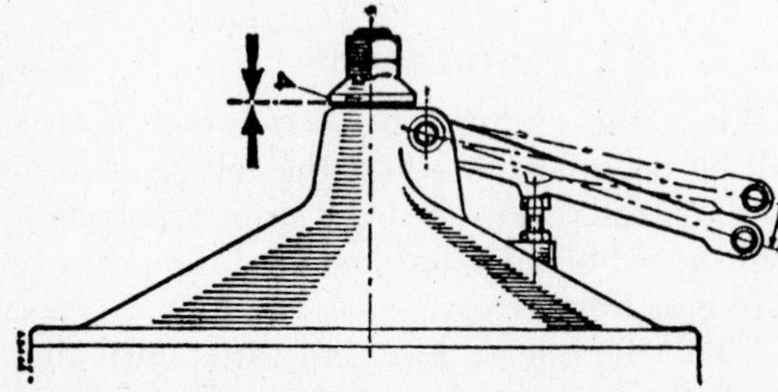

Clutch release bearing stop adjustment. Clutch pedal depressed (1), with the bearing stop (2) turned in to contact the cover. Clutch pedal released (3), and the stop (4) turned in a further 0.002-0.005 in.

2. Have a helper fully depress and hold the clutch pedal. Screw the stop in until it contacts the housing.
3. Release the clutch pedal, and turn the stop in a further 0.002-0.005 in. (approximately 30° rotation).
4. Tighten the locknut, and recheck the release lever stop clearance.

CLUTCH HYDRAULIC SYSTEM

Description

The clutch hydraulic system consists of a master cylinder and reservoir mounted on the firewall, a slave cylinder bolted to the fluid bell housing, and a hydraulic line connecting them. When the clutch pedal is depressed, fluid pressure is transmitted through the master cylinder to the slave cylinder, moving the clutch release lever.

Fluid Recommendation

Heavy-duty brake fluid is recommended for use in the clutch hydraulic system. Only brake fluid conforming to SAE specification J1703 should be used.

Adjustments

No adjustments to the master or slave cylinder should be attempted, with the following exceptions:

1. On the Mk. I and II Midget, the freeplay of the master cylinder pushrod may require adjustment if the master cylinder has been rebuilt. The pushrod should have a minimum free movement of 1/32 in. before the master cylinder is actuated. The movement can be checked at the pedal, which should travel a minimum of 3/16 in. before the cylinder is felt to operate. The clearance can be felt if the pedal is pushed by hand.
2. On the 1100 sedan it may be necessary to occasionally adjust the clutch release lever stop. See CLUTCH REMOVAL AND INSTALLATION.

Master Cylinder—Removal and Installation

MG Midget Mk. I and II

On the Midget Mk. I and II the clutch and brake master cylinders are in the same body, and are removed at the same time. To remove the master cylinder, first disconnect the pushrods from the pedals. Disconnect the hydraulic lines from the cylinder body and cap them. Remove the two cylinder mounting bolts and lift the cylinder body out.

Installation is in reverse order of removal. When the lines have been reconnected, the brakes, as well as the clutch, should be bled.

MG Midget Mk. III, MGB, MGC, and MG 1100

To remove the clutch master cylinder, remove the screws securing the mounting bracket cover plate and lift the cover off (all except the MG 1100). Disconnect the pushrod from the clutch pedal. Disconnect the hydraulic line from the clutch master cylinder and cap it. Remove the cylinder mounting bolts and lift the cylinder out.

Installation is in reverse order of removal. When the hydraulic line has been reconnected the clutch hydraulic system must be bled.

Slave Cylinder—Removal and Installation

On all models, to remove the slave cylinder simply disconnect and cap the hydraulic line, disconnect the pushrod from the clutch release lever, and unbolt and remove the cylinder.

Installation is in reverse order of removal. When the hydraulic line has been reconnected, the clutch hydraulic system must be bled.

Master and Slave Cylinder Rebuilding

The accompanying illustrations clearly show the order of disassembly and assembly for the various hydraulic cylinders. Rebuilding kits are available, and usually contain the rubber seals and metal washers. Pistons and springs are available as individual pieces.

When the piston assembly has been removed from the cylinder, examine the bore. If it is pitted or scored the entire cylinder assembly should be replaced. If bore damage is light it may be honed, but in most cases the repair will not be lasting and the cylinder may begin to leak again after a short time. When honing a cylinder, occa-

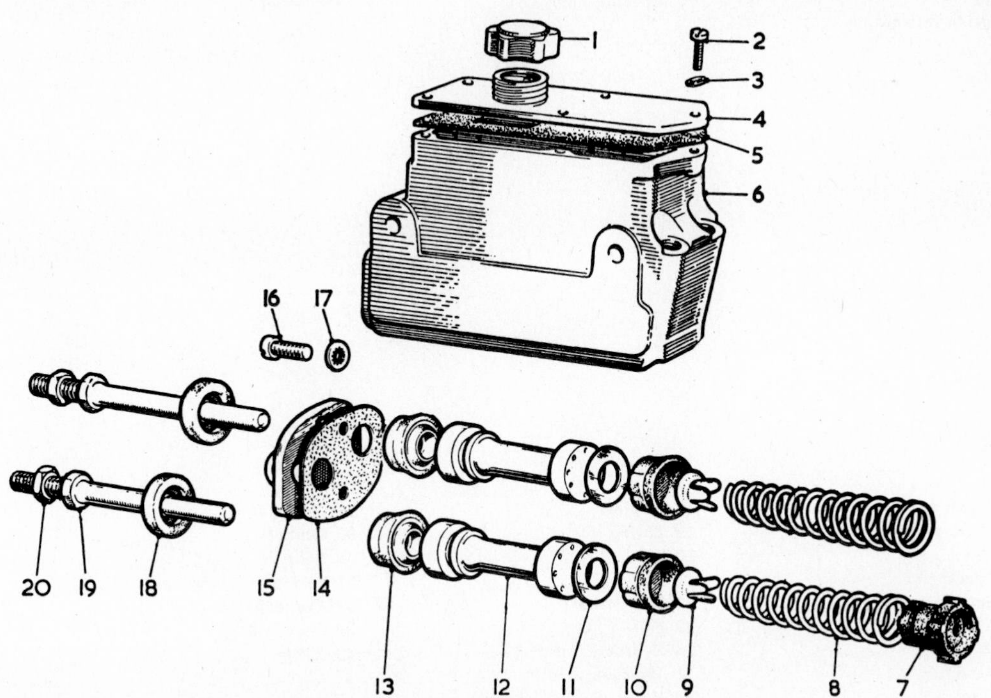

Midget Mk. I and II, clutch and brake master cylinder components

1 Filler cap
2 Screw
3 Washer
4 Tank cover
5 Gasket
6 Cylinder body
7 Check valve (brake only)
8 Return spring
9 Spring retainer
10 Main cup
11 Piston washer
12 Piston
13 Secondary cup
14 Gasket
15 Retaining plate
16 Screw
17 Lockwasher
18 Rubber boot
19 Pushrod
20 Pushrod adjuster

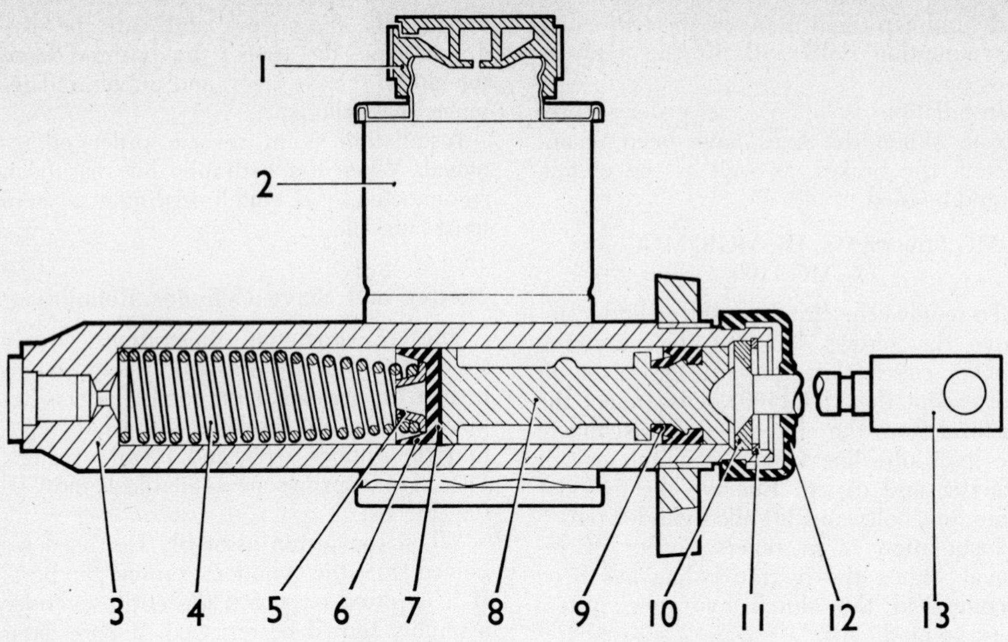

Midget Mk. III clutch master cylinder components

1 Filler cap
2 Reservoir
3 Body
4 Spring
5 Spring retainer
6 Main cup
7 Piston washer
8 Piston
9 Secondary cup
10 Dished washer
11 Circlip
12 Rubber boot
13 Pushrod

1 Clutch pedal
2 Bushing
3 Pedal pad
4 Spacer
5 Spring
6 Clevis pin
7 Washer
8 Reservoir
9 Cap
10 Gasket
11 Boot
12 Circlip
13 Pushrod
14 Secondary cup
15 Piston
16 Piston washer
17 Main cup
18 Retainer
19 Spring
20 Bolt
21 Bolt
22 Lockwasher
23 Nut
24 Hydraulic line
25 Hydraulic line
26 Hydraulic line (rubber)
27 Locknut
28 Lockwasher
29 Gasket
30 Clip
31 Clip
32 Banjo connection
33 Banjo bolt
34 Gasket
35 Gasket
36 Body
37 Spring
38 Cup expander
39 Seal (cup)
40 Piston
41 Clip
42 Boot
43 Clip
44 Pushrod
45 Bolt
46 Lockwasher
47 Clevis pin
48 Washer
49 Bleed screw

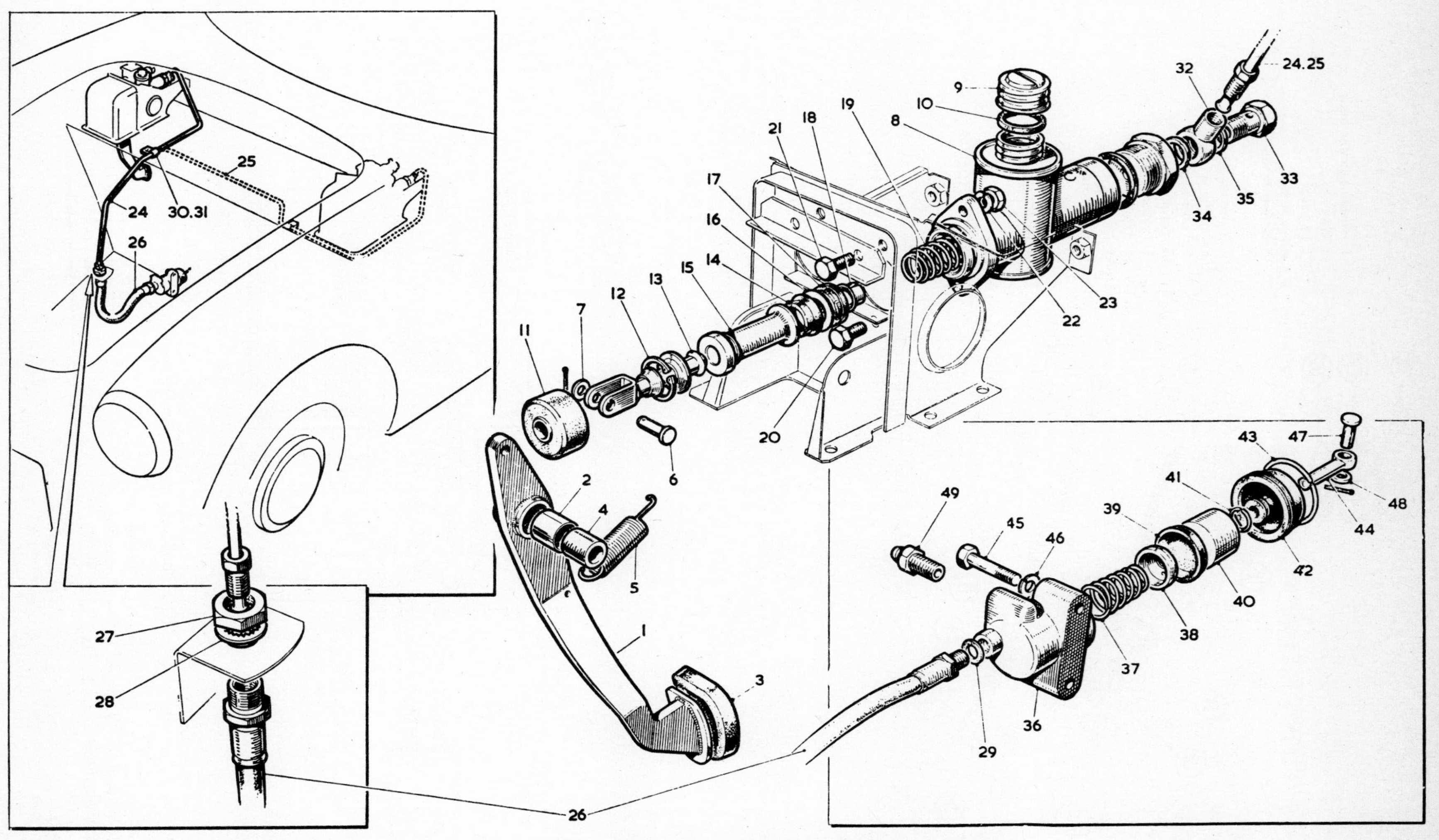

MGB clutch hydraulic system components

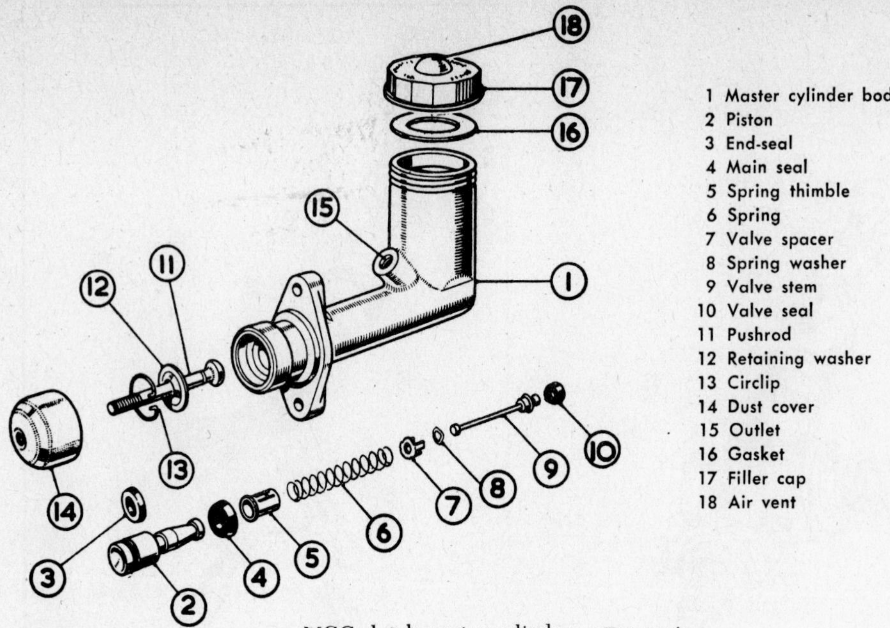

MGC clutch master cylinder components

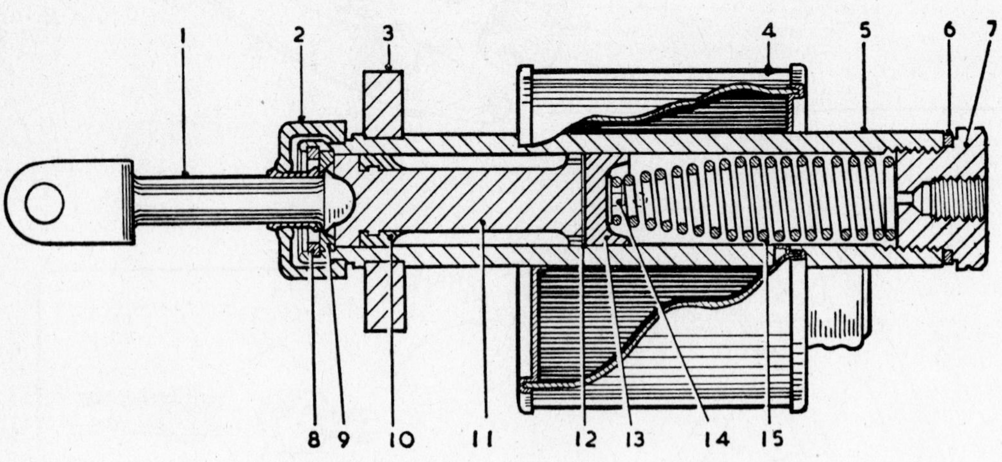

MG 1100 clutch master cylinder, sectional view

1 Pushrod
2 Rubber boot
3 Mounting flange
4 Reservoir
5 Body
6 Washer
7 End plug
8 Circlip
9 Stop-washer
10 Secondary cup
11 Piston
12 Piston washer
13 Main cup
14 Spring retainer
15 Return spring

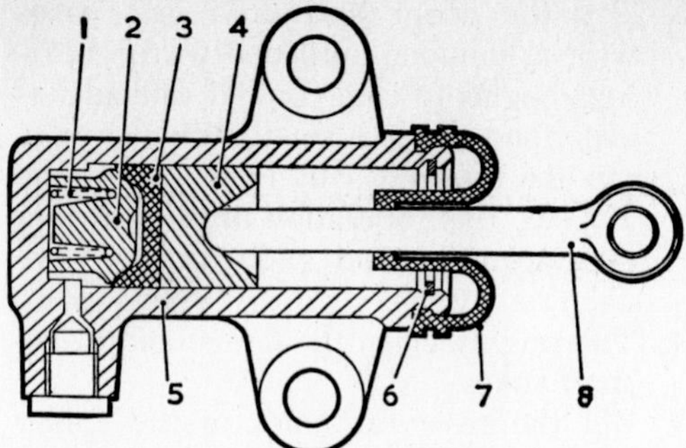

Clutch slave cylinder, sectional view

1 Spring
2 Cup expander
3 Cup
4 Piston
5 Body
6 Circlip
7 Rubber boot
8 Pushrod

sionally dip the hone in clean brake fluid for lubrication.

Whenever a cylinder is disassembled for inspection or rebuilding the rubber seals should be replaced as a matter of course. Before installing the seals lubricate them thoroughly with brake fluid or the special lubricant that is included in some rebuilding kits. All internal components of the cylinder, especially the bore, must be completely free of dirt and grit or the cylinder may leak or fail to operate properly. When installing the piston and seals into the bore make sure that the seal lips are not turned back as they enter the cylinder. Once the cylinder has been installed on the car the clutch hydraulic system must be bled.

Bleeding the Clutch Hydraulic System

The purpose of bleeding the hydraulic system is to expel air that is trapped in the cylinders and lines. Air in the system is what gives the pedal a spongy feel, because air can be compressed while a liquid, for all practical purposes, cannot be. Bleeding is accomplished in the following manner:

1. Fill the master cylinder with brake fluid. (Recheck the fluid level often during bleeding.)
2. Attach a rubber tube to the slave cylinder bleed valve and immerse the other end of the tube in a jar or can containing a small amount of clean brake fluid.
3. With a helper in the car pump the clutch pedal several times until some resistance can be felt, hold the pedal down, and open the bleed valve about 1/2 turn.

Bleeding the clutch hydraulic system at the slave cylinder

4. With the bleed valve still open, pump the pedal slowly through its full travel several times. Close the bleed valve and check the pedal for firmness and proper free-play (about 0.5-1.0 in. free-play before the release bearing contacts the pressure plate).
5. If sponginess or excessive free-play indicates that some air is still in the system, it may be necessary to repeat step 3 until the fluid running from the bleed valve is clear and free of air bubbles.

FLYWHEEL REMOVAL AND INSTALLATION

On the Midget, MGB, and MGC the flywheel can be unbolted after the clutch assembly has been removed and the flywheel bolt locktabs have been bent back. On some engines there is a crankshaft mark that should be aligned with the corresponding flywheel mark when installing the flywheel. On engines without alignment marks the flywheel position relative to the crankshaft should be noted or marked before removal. Flywheel bolts should not be reused, because they are shear bolts. When a shear bolt has been stressed in one plane, as a flywheel bolt is, and is reinstalled, it will be loaded in a different plane. The resultant strain on the bolt will sometimes be enough to break it apart along the original stress lines.

Flywheel removal and installation procedures for the MG 1100 can be found in the preceding section.

Driveshaft and U-Joints

Driveshaft Specifications

Model	*Type*	*Diameter (in.)*	*Length (in.)*
Midget	Tubular, rev. spline	1.75	26.25*
MGB	Tubular, spline	2.00	25.35**
MGC	Tubular, spline	N.A.	N.A.
MG 1100	Solid, spline	N.A.	N.A.

*—Length between U-joint centers.
**—Length of shaft assembly. With overdrive, length is 26.47 in.

DRIVESHAFT REMOVAL AND INSTALLATION

To remove the driveshaft on the Midget, MGB, and MGC mark the U-joint flanges and the transmission and differential flanges (for assembly purposes). Remove the nuts and bolts from the flanges and lower the driveshaft assembly. When reinstalling the driveshaft make sure that the alignment marks on the flanges are positioned correctly.

Removal of either or both of the MG 1100 driveshafts requires special equipment to depressurize the hydrolastic (air/water) suspension. Such specialized work should be referred to an MG dealer, who has the tools and experience to perform it.

U-JOINT REMOVAL AND INSTALLATION

MG Midget, MGB and MGC

NOTE: If only the rear U-joint is to be replaced, unbolt the differential flange from the driveshaft flange and pull the driveshaft out towards the rear of the car to separate the driveshaft at the spline. On the MGC the spline cover (rubber boot) must be loosened before separation.

After the driveshaft has been removed and the outside surfaces of the U-joints have been cleaned:

1. Remove all four snap-rings retaining the bearing cups. If the ring does not come out, tap the bearing cup lightly to relieve pressure on the ring.
2. Tap the flange and driveshaft yokes with a hammer until one of the bearings begins to come out. If difficulty is experienced, use a small screwdriver to tap the bearings out from the inside. Repeat this operation until all four bearing cups and their rollers have been removed.
3. Thoroughly clean the flange and driveshaft yokes.
4. Fill the reservoir holes in the spider journals with grease (sealed joints without grease fittings).
5. Fill the bearing cups to a depth of 1/8 in. with grease and install the needle rollers in the cups.
6. Install the seals on the spider journals (sealed joints).
7. Position the spider inside the flange yoke and install the bearings and snap-rings. Place the spider inside the driveshaft yoke and install the remaining two bearings and snap-rings.

NOTE: Make sure that the grease fittings on joints so equipped face away from the flanges, towards the center of the driveshaft.

8. Lubricate the joint with a grease gun (early type with grease fitting).
9. Check the joint for freedom of movement. If it binds tap it lightly with a soft-metal or wooden hammer to relieve pressure from the bearing cups on the ends of the journals.
10. Remove any surplus grease from the joint and replace the driveshaft.

MG 1100

Inboard Joints

The rubber couplings at the inboard ends of the driveshafts should be replaced when, under hard acceleration, a lurching or shuddering is noticed in the drive train. If the car is driven far under this condition the metal spider that is encased by the rubber will begin to protrude from the ends of the coupling. When this happens the spider will begin to rub on the transmission case and, if uncorrected, it will wear right through the case.

Damage can be circumvented by replacing both couplings as soon as necessary. To remove a coupling, unbolt and remove the four U-bolts that retain the coupling. Push the axle shaft into the outboard joint to gain enough clearance to remove the coupling. It may be necessary to disconnect the

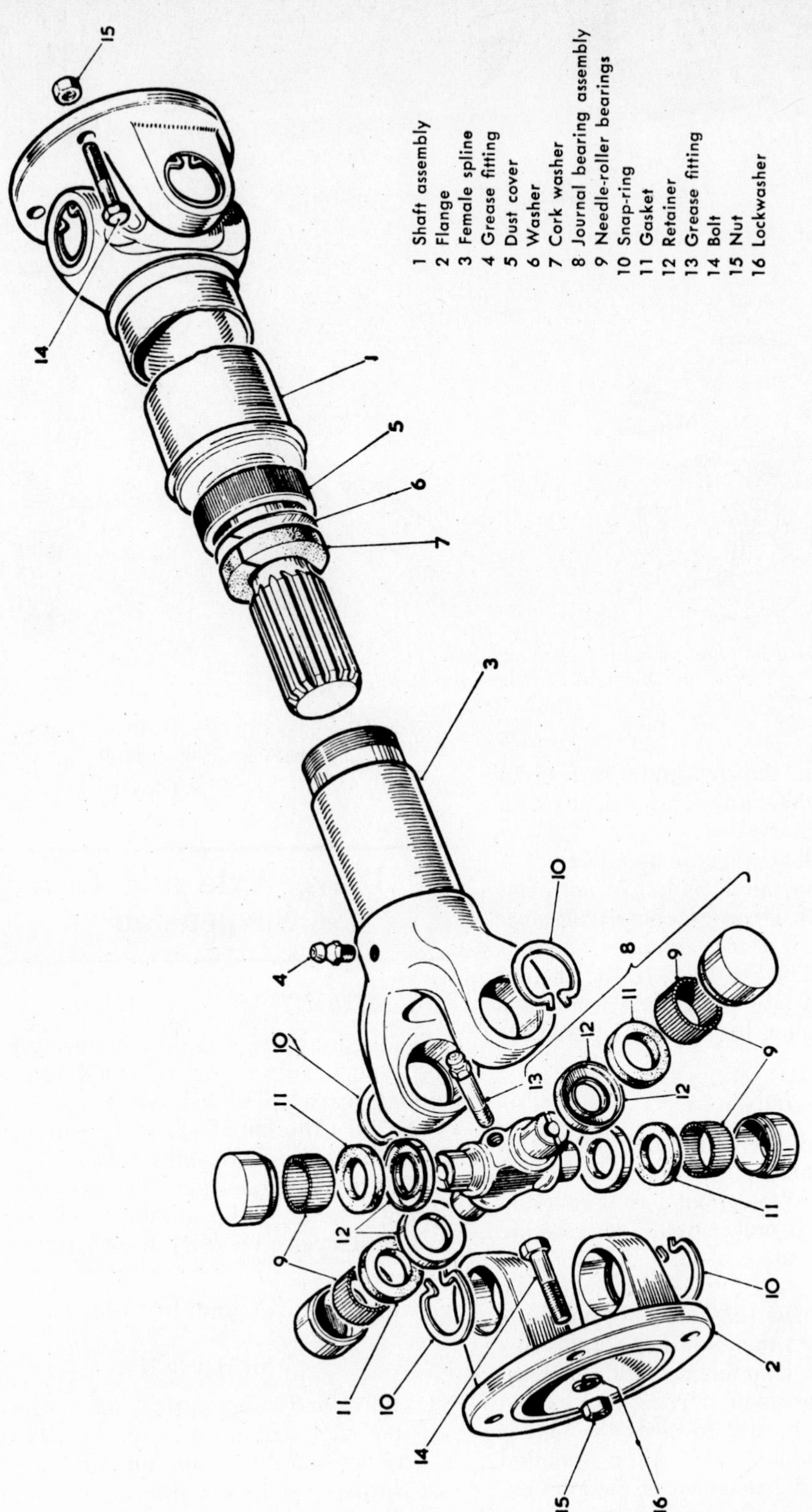

MGB driveshaft components

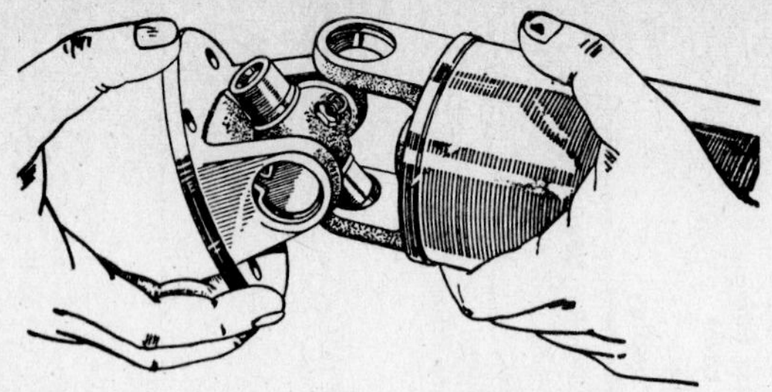

Separate the joint after two of the bearings have been removed

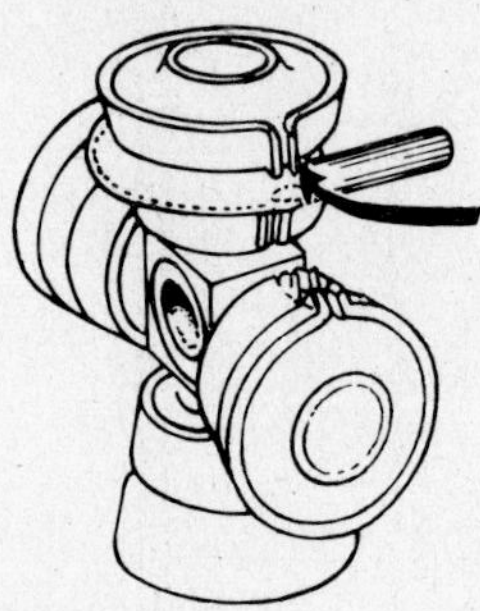

The MG 1100 inboard U-joint, or rubber coupling, showing one of the U-bolts and the tabs referred to in the text (arrow)

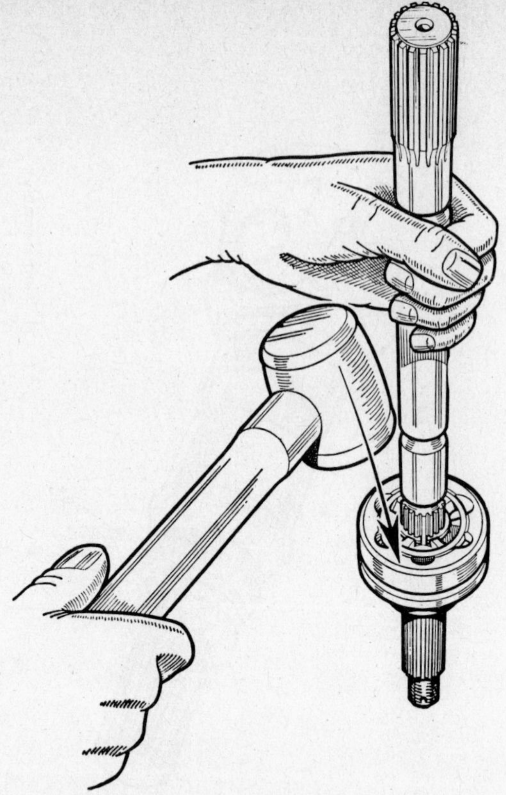

Bell joint used on 1100

tie-rod end from the steering arm in order to swivel the wheel a few extra degrees for more clearance.

When installing a coupling always use new locknuts on the U-bolts. *Do not overtighten the nuts. Overtightening will cause premature failure of the coupling.* The nuts should be tightened to 10-12 ft. lb., or until the small metal tabs protruding from each end of the coupling have closed up and are touching.

Outboard Joints

The outboard joints are of the constant-velocity type known as bell joints. Unless the protective rubber boot has been damaged, these joints will normally last the life of the car. Indicative of joint deterioration is a sound like machine-gun fire when the wheels are turned full-lock and power is being applied. As the joint deteriorates further the noise will commence with decreasingly fewer degrees of steering lock necessary to induce it, and towards the end it will machine-gun even when pointed straight ahead. Replacement of the joint entails depressurizing the hydrolastic suspension system, and should be left to an MG dealer.

Drive Axle and Rear Suspension

MG MIDGET

The rear axle is of the three-quarter floating type incorporating a hypoid ring and pinion gearset. The axle shafts, pinion oil seal, and differential assembly can be removed with the drive axle in place.

The rear suspension consists of leaf springs, serving also to locate the drive axle, and lever-type shock absorbers.

Spring Removal and Installation

Mk. I and II

1. Raise and support the rear of the car on the chassis, and place the jack under the axle to support it. The springs must be in the unloaded position.
2. Remove the forward spring mounting bolts.

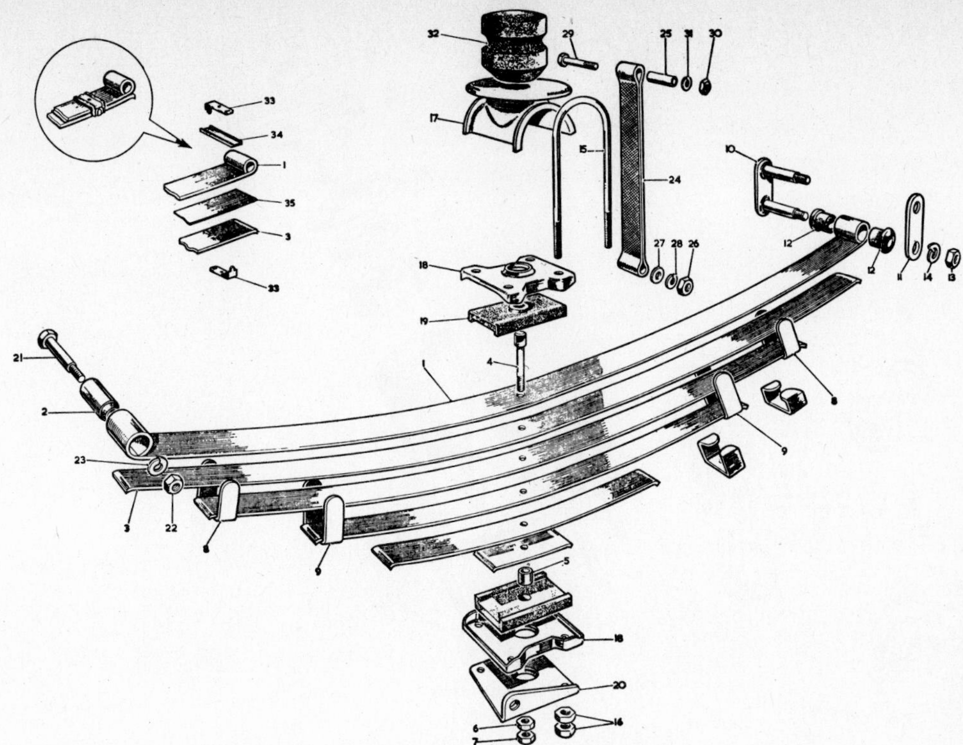

Rear suspension components, MGB and MGC. Applicable also the Midget, with slight variations

1 Leaf assembly
2 Bushing
3 Leaf
4 Bolt
5 Spacer
6 Nut
7 Locknut
8 Clip
9 Clip
10 Shackle pins
11 Shackle plate
12 Bushing
13 Nut
14 Lockwasher
15 U-bolt
16 Nut
17 Pedestal
18 Plate
19 Pad
20 Bracket—shock absorber to spring
21 Front mounting bolt
22 Nut
23 Washer
24 Limit strap
25 Spacer
26 Nut
27 Washer
28 Lockwasher
29 Bolt
30 Nut
31 Lockwasher
32 Bump rubber
33 Clip
34 Pad
35 Insulating strip later type only.

1 Case assembly
2 Gear carrier stud
3 Bearing retaining nut
4 Gear carrier to axle case nut
5 Lockwasher
6 Washer
7 Breather assembly
8 Drain plug
9 Gasket
10 Carrier assembly
11 Bearing cap stud
12 Washer
13 Lockwasher
14 Nut
15 Filler plug
16 Differential bearing
17 Shim
18 Differential cage
19 Spidergear
20 Thrust washer
21 Differential pinion
22 Thrust washer
23 Pinion pin
24 Pinion peg
25 Ring and pinion gearset
26 Bolt
27 Locktab
28 Pinion thrust washer
29 Inner pinion bearing
30 Bearing spacer
31 Pinion outer bearing
32 Oil seal
33 Dust cover
34 Differential drive flange
35 Pinion nut
36 Lockwasher
37 Hub assembly
38 Wheel stud
39 Nut
40 Oil seal
41 Hub bearing
42 Oil seal ring
43 Gasket
44 Axle shaft
45 Screw
46 Rubber block
47 Axle shaft
48 Hub assembly
49 Wheel stud
50 Hub extension
51 Core plug

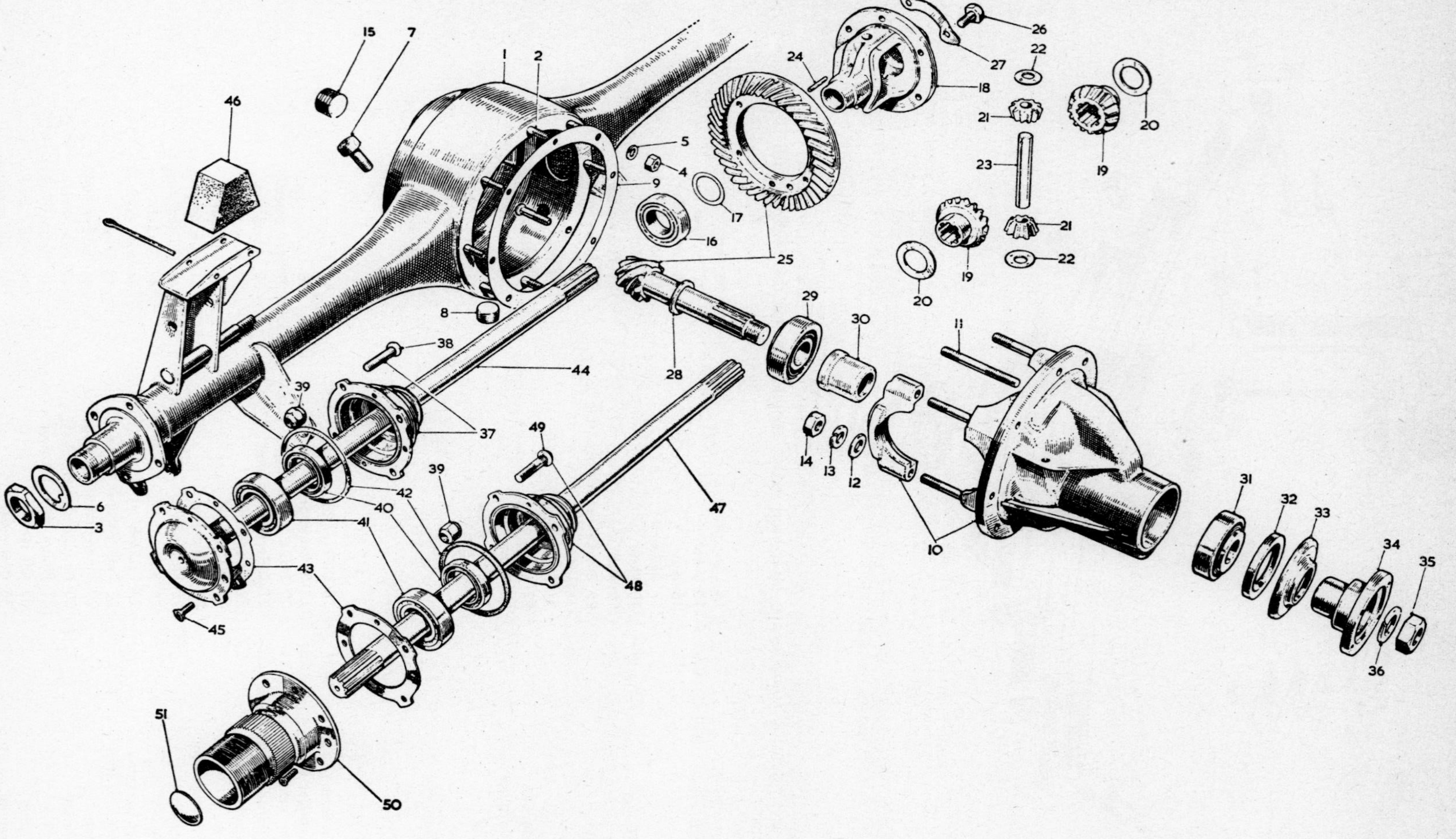

MG Midget drive axle components

3. Remove the U-bolt securing the spring to the axle and pull the spring out of its mounting.
4. Installation is in reverse order of removal.

Mk. III

1. Raise and support the car as above.
2. Remove the wheels.
3. From inside the car remove the bolts securing the spring anchor bracket to the body.
4. From beneath the car remove the two front bracket bolts.
5. Remove the four U-bolt nuts and the shock absorber anchor plate.
6. Remove the rear shackle nuts, pins, and plates, and remove the spring.
7. Installation is in reverse order of removal. The axle limit strap may be removed to facilitate U-bolt installation. Tighten the spring bolt fully after the car is lowered and the spring is loaded.

Shock Absorber Removal and Installation

To remove a rear shock absorber simply disconnect the connecting link arm from the shock lever and unbolt the unit. Shock absorbers should be replaced in axle sets (pairs). If a new shock absorber appears to operate erratically, allow the hydraulic fluid a few minutes to become de-aerated.

Shock Absorber Maintenance

The shock absorbers require no periodic maintenance. If a shock unit is not working well the fluid level may be topped up. Use hydraulic jack oil, available at hardware and auto parts stores. Fill the shock up to the level of the plug.
CAUTION: If any dirt or grit is allowed to enter the shock absorber the internal damper unit will be destroyed.
If it does not work after filling it must be replaced. Examine the condition of the link arm pivots at this time and replace if necessary.

Axle Shaft Removal and Installation

1. Raise the rear of the vehicle and support it under the springs.
2. Release the parking brake and back off

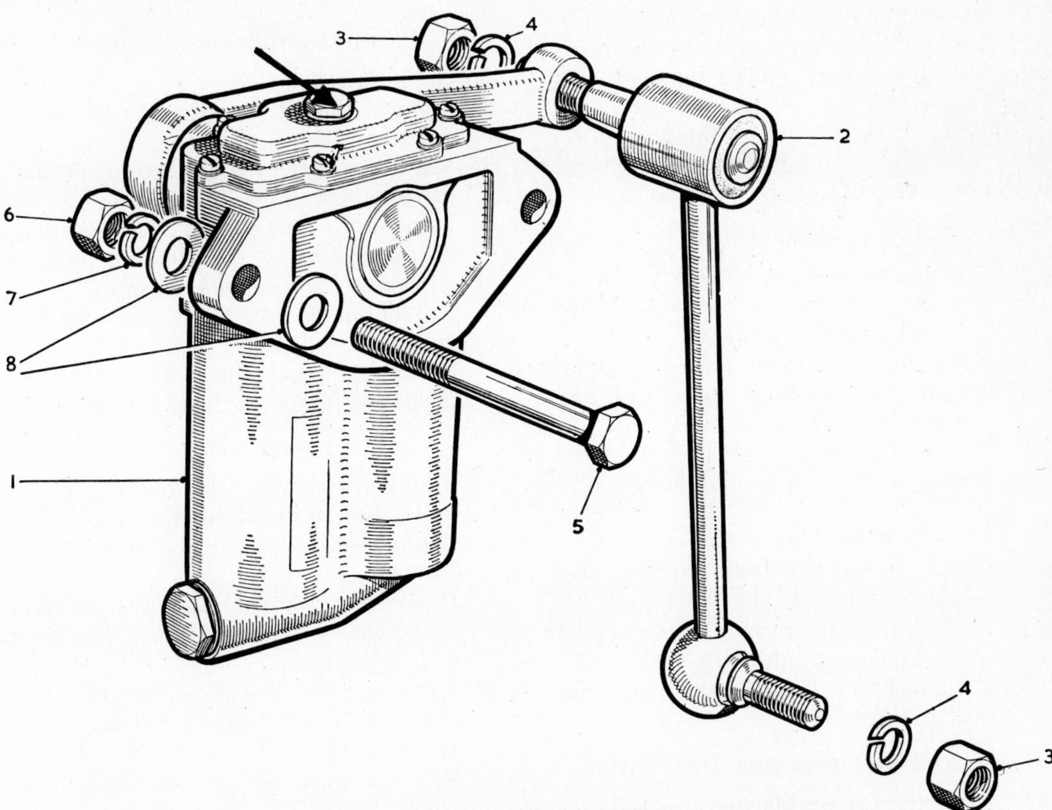

Lever-type rear shock absorber—Midget, MGB, and MGC

the brake adjusters if the wheel does not spin freely.

3. Remove the brake drum retaining screws and remove the drum.

WIRE WHEELS:

4. Remove the nuts securing the axle hub to the splined wheel hub.
5. Remove the splined wheel hub, and withdraw the axle shaft, gasket, and O-ring.

DISC WHEELS:

4. Remove the axle shaft retaining screws and withdraw the axle and gasket.
5. Installation is in reverse order of removal. Always use a new gasket and O-ring (wire wheels). Adjust the brakes if necessary after the wheels have been installed.

Axle Hub Removal and Installation

1. Remove the brake drum and axle shaft as described above.
2. Remove the large hub retaining nut and lockwasher.
3. Remove the hub complete with bearing and seal. To accomplish this, a slide hammer may be used, in lieu of service tool 18G 304.

Before installing the hub pack the bearing with grease and replace the seal. If a hand-made hub flange gasket is to be used it must be at least 0.010 in. thick or an oil leak will result. Installation is in reverse order of removal.

Pinion Oil Seal Replacement

The pinion oil seal can be replaced without removing or disassembling the drive axle. The procedure is as follows:

1. Mark the driveshaft and differential flanges (to facilitate assembly) and disconnect the driveshaft.
2. Remove the nut and washer from the center of the differential flange, and withdraw the flange and end-cover from the pinion shaft.
3. Extract the oil seal from the case, and lubricate and install the new seal.
4. Replace the end cover and flange, and tighten the nut to 140 ft. lb.
5. Reconnect the driveshaft, taking care to align the marks.

Drive Axle Removal and Installation

1. Raise the car by placing a jack under the axle. Place jack stands under the chassis, but leave the jack in position to support the axle.
2. Remove the exhaust system.
3. Mark the flanges and disconnect the driveshaft from the differential flange.
4. Release the axle limit straps (be sure the jack is supporting the axle).
5. Disconnect the shock absorber lever from the link arm.
6. Disconnect the parking brake cable at the cable adjustment.
7. Disconnect the hydraulic brake line at the main junction just forward of the differential housing.
8. Remove the U-bolt nuts (Mk. III only).
9. Unscrew and remove the rear shackle pins.
10. Lower and remove the axle assembly.
11. Installation is in reverse order of removal. On the Mk. III the spring bolts should not be tightened until the car has been lowered (springs loaded). Failure to take this precaution will lead to early deterioration of the rubber spring bushings.

Differential Service

Removal and Installation

1. Drain the drive axle.
2. Remove the axle shafts as previously described.
3. Mark the flanges and disconnect the driveshaft from the differential.
4. Remove the nuts securing the differential assembly to the drive axle and withdraw the complete assembly.
5. Installation is in reverse order of removal. Always use a new gasket, and make sure that the differential and drive axle mating surfaces are clean.

Disassembly

1. Mark and remove the housing caps, and withdraw the differential cage.
2. Remove the bearings and shims from the cage.
3. Bend back the locktabs, remove the ring gear bolts, and remove the ring gear.
4. Drive out the dowel pin locating the pinion shaft. The pin is 1/8 in. in diameter, and it must be driven out from the ring gear side of the differential cage.
5. Remove the pinions and thrust wash-

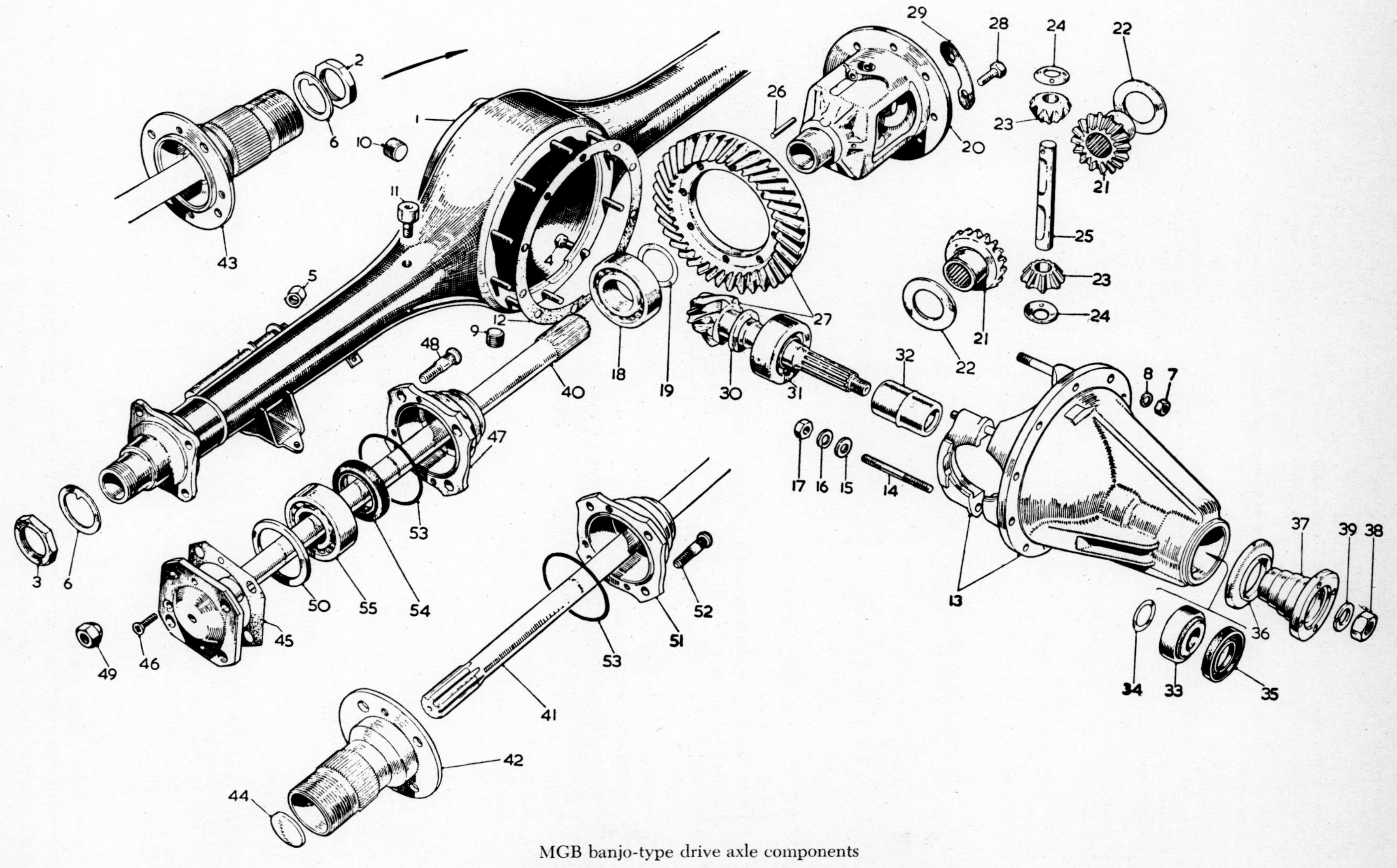

MGB banjo-type drive axle components

1 Case assembly
2 Nut
3 Nut
4 Gear carrier stud
5 Nut
6 Washer
7 Nut
8 Lockwasher
9 Drain plug
10 Filler plug
11 Breather
12 Gasket
13 Carrier assembly
14 Bearing cap stud
15 Washer
16 Lockwasher
17 Nut
18 Differential bearing
19 Shim
20 Differential cage
21 Spider gear
22 Thrust washer
23 Pinion
24 Thrust washer
25 Pinion shaft
26 Pinion shaft locating pin
27 Ring and pinion gearset
28 Bolt
29 Locktab
30 Thrust washer
31 Inner pinion bearing
32 Spacer
33 Outer pinion bearing
34 Shim
35 Oil seal
36 Dust cover
37 Differential drive flange
38 Nut
39 Lockwasher
40 Axle shaft (disc wheels)
41 Axle shaft
42 Wheel hub—RH
43 Wheel hub- LH
44 Core plug
45 Gasket
46 Screw
47 Axle hub
48 Wheel stud
49 Stud nut
50 Spacer
51 Axle hub
52 Wheel stud
53 O-ring
54 Oil seal
55 Hub bearing
wire wheels
disc wheels
wire wheels

ers. Remove the pinion nut, drive flange, and end-cover.

6. Drive the pinion shaft towards the rear through the carrier. It will carry with it the inner race and rollers of the rear bearing.
7. Remove the inner race of the front bearing and the oil seal.
8. Remove the bearing outer races using a puller.
9. Slide off the pinion sleeve and shims.
10. Remove the rear bearing inner race, the spacer, and the bearing outer race.

Assembly

If no components other than the oil seal have been replaced, assembly is in reverse order of disassembly. Note that the thrust face of the differential bearings are marked with the word Thrust.

If any gears or bearings have been replaced, see DIFFERENTIAL GEAR ADJUSTMENT.

MGB, BANJO-TYPE AXLE

The banjo axle was installed in MGB convertibles with engines 18G, 18GA, and 18GB. However, some cars with the 18GB engine were fitted with the tubed-type axle, as were all of the GTs. The only sure way to tell which axle is installed in a convertible with the 18GB engine is to look. The axle housing shapes are quite different.

The banjo axle is of the three-quarter floating type incorporating a hypoid ring and pinion gearset. The axle shafts, pinion oil seal, and differential assembly can be removed with the drive axle in place.

The rear suspension consists of leaf springs, serving also to locate the drive axle, and lever-type shock absorbers.

Spring Removal and Installation

1. Remove the wheel adjacent to the spring.
2. Raise and support the rear of the car on the chassis, and place the jack under the axle to support it. The springs must be in the unloaded position.
3. Disconnect the shock absorber lever from the connecting link, and disconnect the axle limit strap.
4. Unbolt the shackle plates and drive out the shackle pins.
5. Remove the spring front mounting bolt.
6. Unbolt and remove the two U-bolts, and remove the shock absorber bracket, plate, and pad which are freed when the U-bolts are removed.
7. Remove the spring and upper spring mount.
8. Installation is in reverse order of removal.

Shock Absorber Removal and Installation

Refer to the preceding section on the MG Midget. Procedures are the same for the MGB.

Shock Absorber Maintenance

Refer to the preceding section on the MG Midget. Procedures are the same. To gain access to the shock absorber fill plug on the MGB, remove the rubber plug from the rear floor panel.

Axle Shaft Removal and Installation

See the preceding section on the MG Midget. Procedures are the same for the MGB.

Axle Hub Removal and Installation

See the preceding section on the MG Midget. Procedures are the same for the MGB, except that the bearing spacer in the MGB hub assembly must protrude 0.001-0.004 in. beyond the outer face of the hub when the bearing is pressed into position.

Pinion Oil Seal Replacement

See the preceding section on the MG Midget. Procedures, including the torque value given for the Midget, are applicable to the MGB.

Drive Axle Removal and Installation

1. Raise the car by placing a jack under the axle. Place jack stands under the chassis, but leave the jack in position to support the axle.
2. Mark the flanges and disconnect the driveshaft from the differential flange.
3. Remove the exhaust system from the resonator on back.
4. Disconnect the axle limit straps (be sure the jack is supporting the axle).
5. Disconnect the shock absorber lever from the link.
6. Disconnect the parking brake pivot from the axle, release the retaining clamp, and disconnect the cables at each brake.
7. Disconnect the hydraulic brake line at the main junction near the axle and release the line retaining clamp at the battery box bracket.
8. Remove the spring front mounting bolts.
9. Remove the U-bolts and upper and lower mounts.
10. Lower and remove the axle assembly.
11. Installation is in reverse order of removal.

Differential Service

Removal and Installation

See the preceding section on the MG Midget. Procedures are the same for the MGB.

Disassembly

See the preceding section on the MG Midget. Procedures are the same for the MGB, except that the dowel pin locating the pinion shaft is 3/16 in. in diameter.

Assembly

See the preceding section on the MG Midget.

MGB, TUBED-TYPE AXLE

The tubed-type axle has been used on the MGB/GT since the introduction of that model, and has been used on the convertible beginning with the 18GB engine series. However, some convertibles with the 18GB engine (early in the series) had the banjo axle, which was fitted to earlier models. The only way to tell which axle is installed in a convertible with the 18GB engine is by visual inspection. The axle housing shapes are quite different.

The tubed-type axle is semi-floating, with a hypoid ring and pinion gearset. The axle shafts and the pinion oil seal can be removed with the drive axle in place. The drive axle must be removed to remove the differential assembly.

The rear suspension is identical to the suspension on cars with the banjo axle, and all service procedures are the same. Refer to the preceding section for information on rear springs and shock absorbers.

NOTE: The GT uses stronger springs which should not be used on the convertible except in axle sets (pairs).

Axle Shaft and Axle Hub Removal and Installation

The axle shaft and hub are removed together on cars with the tubed-type axle. The procedure is as follows:

1. Raise the rear of the car and remove the wheel.
2. Back off the brake adjuster if the brake

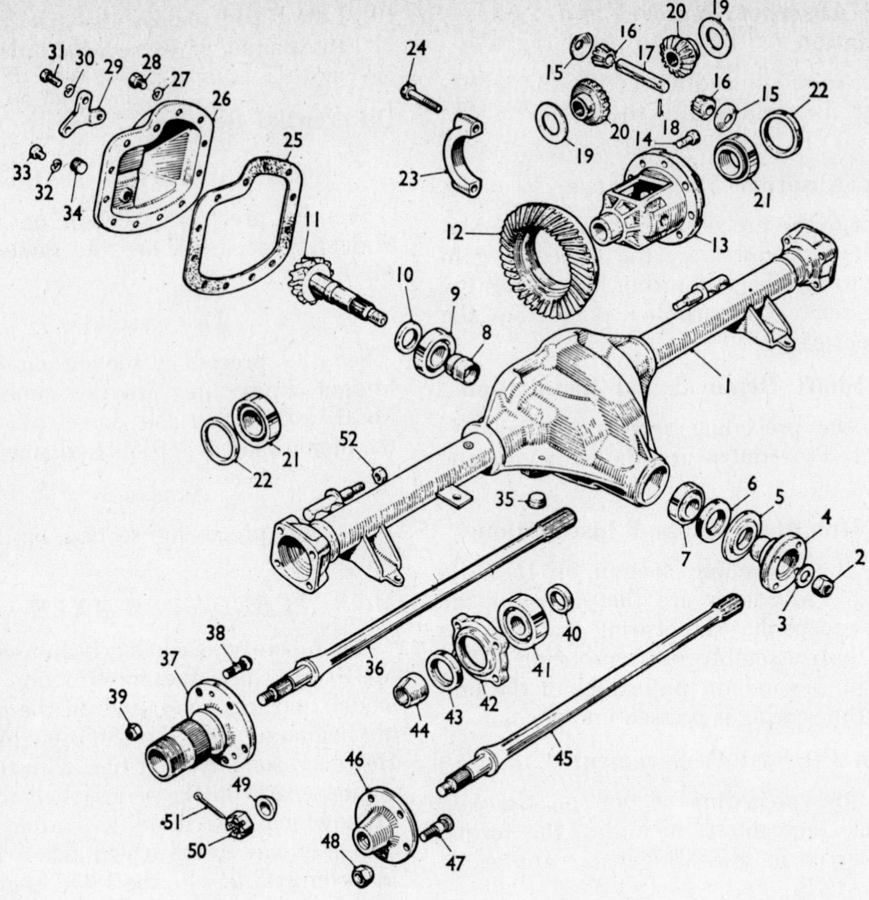

MGB/MGC tubed-type drive axle components

1 Case assembly	18 Pinion shaft locating pin	35 Drain plug
2 Nut	19 Thrust washer	36 Axle shaft (Wire wheels)
3 Washer	20 Spider gears	37 Wheel hub (Wire wheels)
4 Differential drive flange	21 Differential bearing	38 Stud (Wire wheels)
5 Dust cover	22 Spacers	39 Nut (Wire wheels)
6 Oil seal	23 Bearing cap	40 Bearing spacer
7 Outer pinion bearing	24 Bolt	41 Bearing
8 Bearing spacer	25 Gasket	42 Bearing cap
9 Inner pinion bearing	26 Axle case cover	43 Oil seal
10 Pinion thrust washer	27 Lockwasher	44 Oil seal collar
11 Pinion	28 Bolts	45 Axle shaft (Disc wheels)
12 Ring gear	29 Parking brake bracket	46 Wheel hub (Disc wheels)
13 Differential cage	30 Lockwasher	47 Wheel stud (Disc wheels)
14 Bolt	31 Bolt	48 Wheel nut (Disc wheels)
15 Thrust washer	32 Lockwasher	49 Axle shaft collar
16 Differential pinions	33 Bolt	50 Axle shaft nut
17 Pinion shaft	34 Filler and level plug	51 Cotter pin

drum will not spin freely, and remove the drum.

3. Remove the cotter pin and unscrew the axle shaft nut. Withdraw the wheel hub.
4. Disconnect the parking brake cable and hydraulic line, and remove the backing plate.
5. Remove the oil seal collar, bearing cap, and oil seal from the axle shaft.
6. Attach a slide hammer to the hub and remove it, and withdraw the axle shaft.

Installation is in reverse order of removal. The oil seal should be replaced at this time. Bleed and adjust the brakes after the drums have been installed.

Pinion Oil Seal Replacement

1. Raise the car and drain the drive axle.
2. Mark the flanges (to facilitate correct assembly) and disconnect the driveshaft from the differential flange.
3. Using a torque wrench measure and record the amount of torque required to rotate the pinion.
4. Remove the flange retaining nut, remove the flange, and extract the oil seal.
5. Lubricate and install the new oil seal, and install the flange, washer, and nut. Tighten the nut *gradually* until resistance is felt.
6. Rotate the pinion to settle the bearings and measure the torque required to rotate the pinion. If the reading is less than the reading obtained in step 3, tighten the nut *a very small amount*, resettle the bearings and recheck the torque reading. Repeat until the reading is equal to the reading in step 3, but *not less than 4-6 in. lb*.

CAUTION: Preload buildup is rapid, tighten the nut with extreme care. If an original torque reading in excess of 6 in. lb. is obtained, the axle must be disassembled and a new collapsible spacer installed.

7. Reconnect the driveshaft and fill the axle with hypoid gear oil.

Drive Axle Removal and Installation

See the preceding section on the MGB with banjo-type axle. Procedures are the same for both axle types.

Differential Service

Removal and Installation

Not only does removal of the differential unit require a special tool to stretch the axle case, but it is very easy to permanently damage the case while using the special tool. For these reasons removal and installation of the differential should be left to an MG dealer.

Disassembly

1. Bend back the locktabs and unbolt and remove the ring gear.
2. Drive out the pinion shaft locating pin and turn the spider gears until the pinions are opposite the openings in the differential cage. Remove the pinions and thrust washers.
3. Remove the spider gears and thrust washers.
4. If necessary, the inner bearing races may be removed with a puller.

Assembly

If no components other than the oil seal or collapsible spacer have been replaced, assembly is in reverse order of disassembly.

If any gears or bearings have been replaced, see DIFFERENTIAL GEAR ADJUSTMENT.

MGC

See the preceding section on the MGB with tubed-type axle. The MGC drive axle and rear suspension assembly is virtually identical, and procedures are the same.

MG 1100

The 1100 sedan has no drive axle as such, being front wheel drive. Removal and procedures for the differential can be found under TRANSMISSION SERVICE—MG 1100. Both the transmission and differential are located in the engine crankcase, and are lubricated by the engine oil. Halfshaft or axle shaft and U-joint service procedures can be found under DRIVESHAFT AND U-JOINTS. For a description of the hydrolastic suspension system on the 1100, see FRONT SUSPENSION.

DIFFERENTIAL GEAR ADJUSTMENT

Pinion Depth Adjustment

Pinion depth adjustment is an adjustment of the pinion mounting distance D (see illustration). In the absence of special factory tools for measuring this distance the pinion can be accurately positioned by taking note of the markings on the original

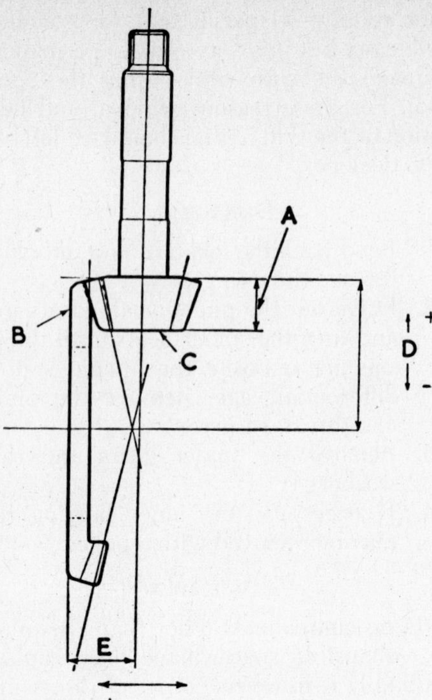

Ring and pinion gearset positioning

A Pinion thickness
B Ring gear backlash specification figure marked at this point
C Pinion thickness (deviation from normal) marked at this point
D Pinion mounting distance (pinion depth)
E Ring gear mounting distance (mesh adjustment)

and replacement pinions and using suitable shims behind the pinion head. A number with a plus or minus sign is etched into the pinion head C, which is the deviation (in thousandths of an inch) of pinion head thickness from nominal. If there is not an etched number on the pinion head the pinion is of nominal thickness. If, for example, the old pinion s marked −2 and the new pinion is marked −2, the same shims may be used behind the pinion head. If, however, the new pinion is marked −5 a shim or combination of shims 0.003 in. thick must be added as compensation. Therefore, if the new pinion is undersize as compared to the old one shims must be added, and if the new pinion is oversize shim thickness must be decreased proportionately.

Pinion Bearing Preload

Preload adjustment is automatically made by the collapsible spacer when the differential drive flange nut is tightened. *It is of extreme importance that the nut is not overtightened.* See PINION OIL SEAL REPLACEMENT under the applicable model section for tightening procedures and torque values. The collapsible spacer should be replaced whenever the differential is disassembled.

Differential Bearing Preload and Ring Gear Mesh Adjustment

Bearing preload and mesh adjustment can be made simultaneously by first measuring total differential end-play using a dial indicator to determine shim thickness needed. Either the ring or pinion must be removed to accurately measure end-play. To this measurement must be added 0.004 in., which is the amount of pinch needed to properly preload the bearings (all models). With both gears in position, shift the differential assembly to one side so that the gap at Y is reduced to zero, and measure ring gear backlash with a dial indicator. From the measurement obtained subtract the correct backlash figure, which is etched into the rear face of the ring gear. This will give the shim thickness required at Y. Subtract this figure from A + 0.004 in., and the remainder will be shim thickness required.

Example:

End-float A 0.060
Plus 0.004 in. preload 0.004
Total shim thickness required 0.064
Shim thickness at Y:
Backlash with zero gap at Y 0.020
Subtract specified backlash* 0.005
*(Marked on ring gear.)
Shim thickness needed 0.015
Shim thickness at X:
Total shim thickness 0.064
Subtract shims needed at Y 0.015
Shim thickness needed 0.049

If the above calculations have been done correctly, backlash should be within specification and the ring gear should be meshing properly with the pinion gear. Gear mesh can be checked by painting the ring gear teeth with red lead or machinist's blue dye and rotating the gear to obtain a mesh pattern (see illustration). If correction is necessary do not alter the total number of shims (total thickness), but increase or decrease thickness as needed.

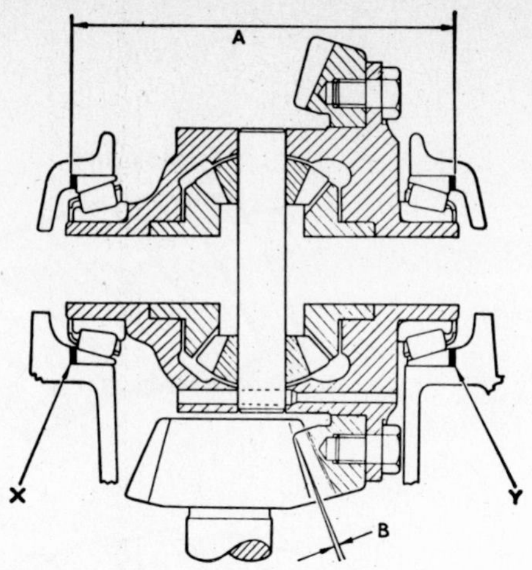

Differential bearing preload and ring gear mesh adjustment (see text)

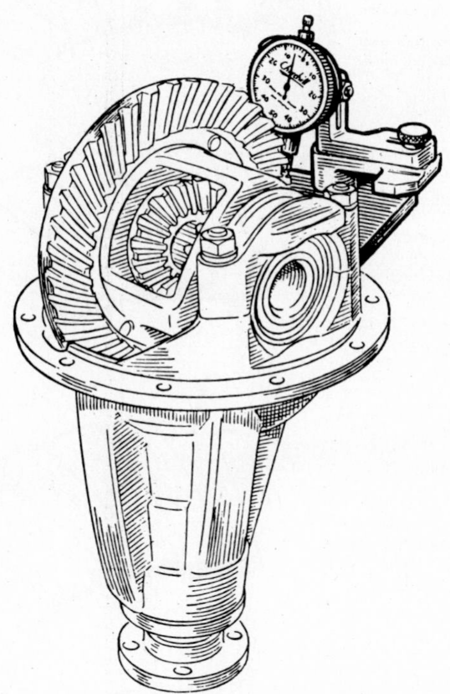

Checking ring gear backlash, Midget and MGB (banjo axle)

Checking ring gear backlash, MGB and MGC (tubed-type axle)

Front Suspension

SUSPENSION TYPE

MG Midget, MGB, and MGC

The MG Midget and MGB independent front suspensions utilize lever-type shock absorbers and coil springs. The shock absorber lever acts as the upper wishbone, while the lower wishbone is a conventional pressed steel A-frame. Kingpins are used, rather than ball joints, to locate the front hubs and allow them to swivel. An anti-roll bar is installed as an option on some models. The MGC suspension is quite similar, except that it uses pressed steel upper wishbones along with telescopic shock absorbers and torsion bars in place of coil springs. Caster, camber, and kingpin inclination angles are non-adjustable with one exception: camber is adjustable on the MGC via shims under the upper wishbone pivot bracket. Front wheel toe-in settings can be found under CHASSIS AND WHEEL ALIGNMENT SPECIFICATIONS.

MG 1100

The suspension used on the MG 1100 is known as the "hydrolastic" suspension. Its purpose is to reduce pitching and rolling, and to give a smooth, flat ride with the best possible handling characteristics. This suspension design has no springs and consists of two front and two rear displacer units which are intercoupled longitudinally. Each displacer unit is made of steel and rubber and consists of a piston, a diaphragm, a lower and upper chamber hous-

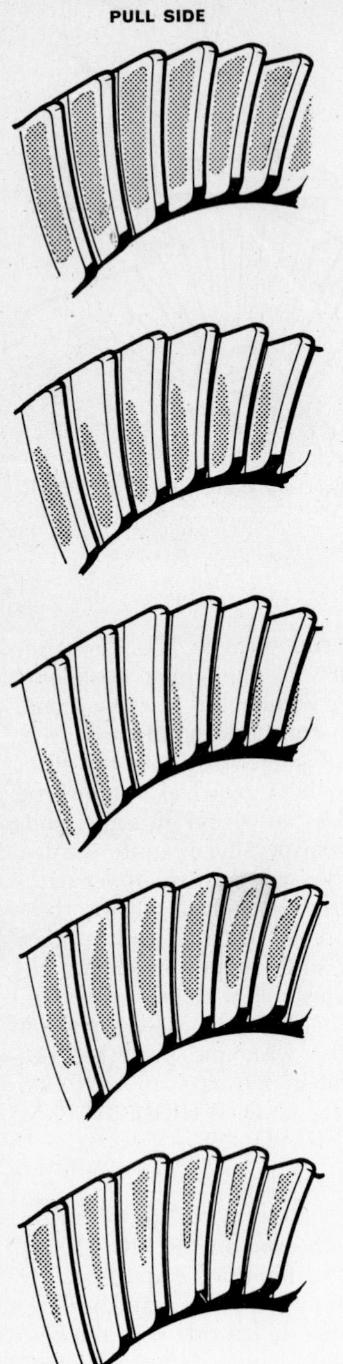

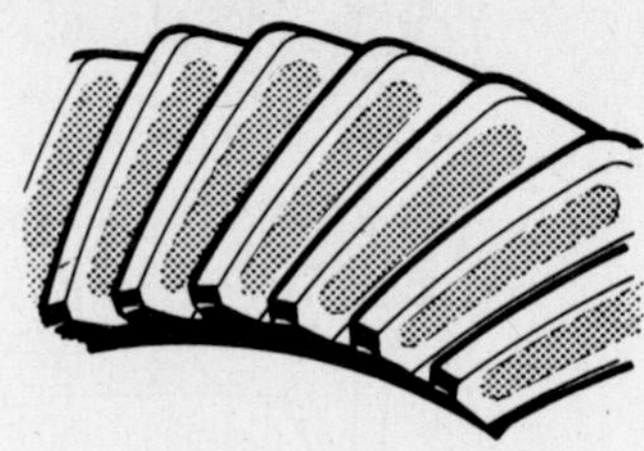

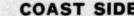

Correct tooth contact.

Contact pattern should be evenly spread over ring gear teeth, on both pull and coast sides.

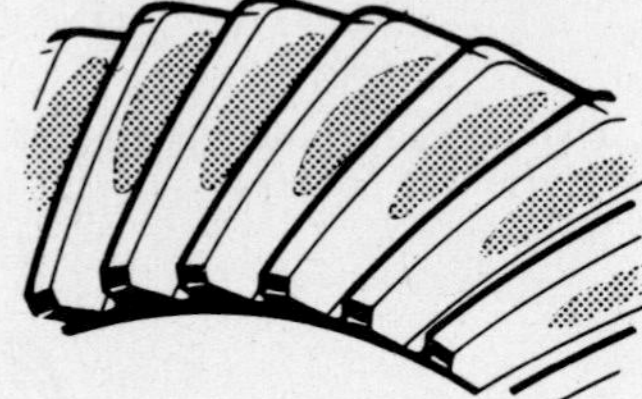

Incorrect contact.

Pull side: heavy contact at tooth toe, toward the center.

Coast side: heavy contact at tooth heel, toward the center.

Move pinion away from ring gear by reducing thrust washer thickness.

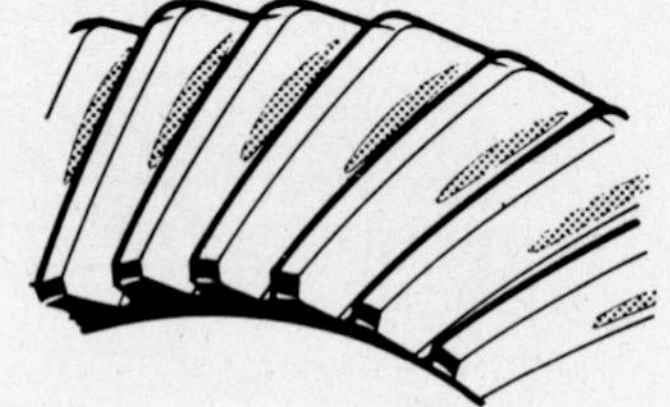

Incorrect contact.

Pull side: heavy contact on toe, at tooth flank bottom.

Coast side: heavy contact on heel, at tooth flank bottom.

Move pinion away from ring gear by reducing thrust washer thickness.

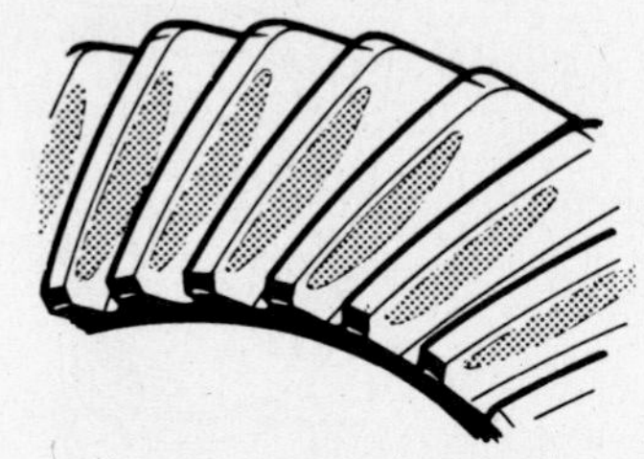

Incorrect contact.

Pull side: heavy contact at tooth heel and toward the center.

Coast side: heavy contact at tooth toe and toward the center.

Move the pinion toward ring gear by increasing thrust washer thickness.

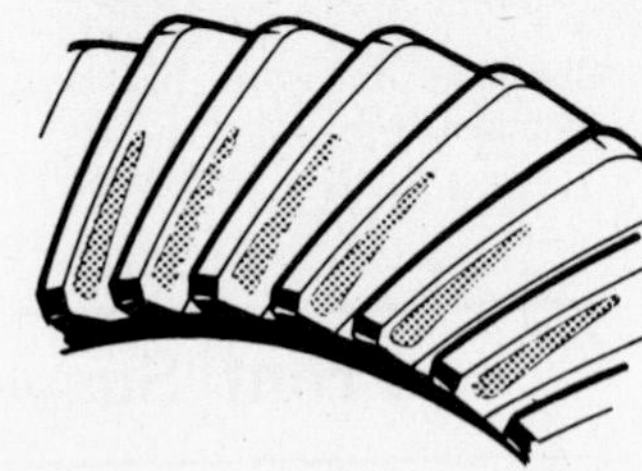

Incorrect contact.

Pull side: heavy contact on heel, at tooth face.

Coast side: heavy contact on toe, at tooth face.

Move the pinion toward ring gear by increasing thrust washer thickness.

Ring gear tooth contact patterns and adjustments.

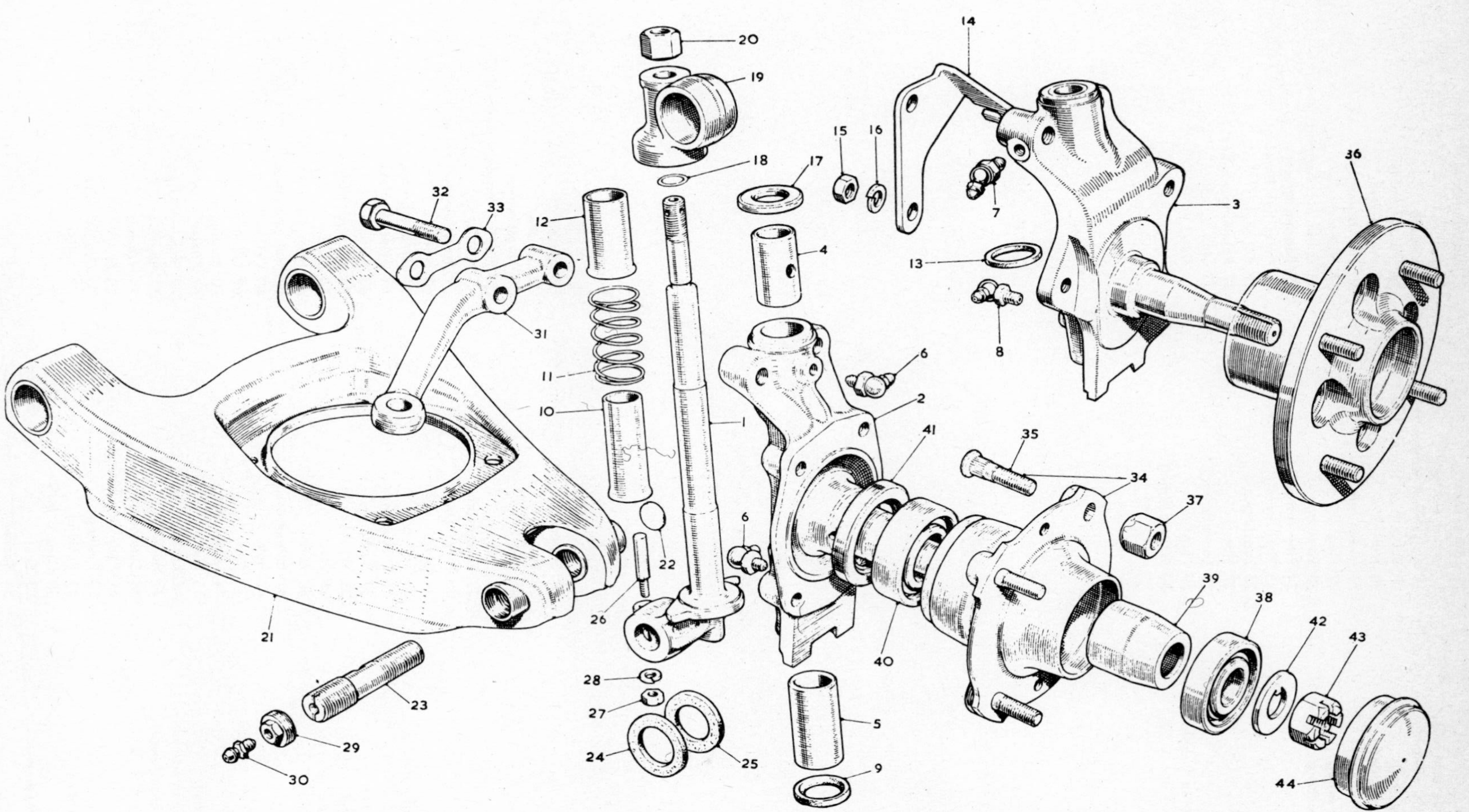

MG Midget front suspension components

1 Kingpin
2 Stub axle assembly
3 Stub axle assembly
4 Bushing (top)
5 Bushing (bottom)
6 Grease fitting
7 Grease fitting
8 Grease fitting
9 Seal
10 Spacer
11 Spring
12 Spacer
13 Seal
14 Brake hose lockplate
15 Nut
16 Lockwasher
17 Thrust washer
18 Adjustment washer
19 Suspension trunnion link
20 Nut
21 Lower link
22 Plug
23 Pivot bolt
24 Ring (large)
25 Ring (small)
26 Locating pin
27 Nut
28 Lockwasher
29 Plug
30 Grease fitting
31 Steering arm
32 Bolt
33 Locktab
34 Hub assembly
35 Wheel stud
36 Hub assembly
37 Nut
38 Outer hub bearing
39 Bearing spacer
40 Inner hub bearing
41 Oil seal
42 Retaining washer
43 Nut
44 Cap

1 Crossmember
2 Bolt
3 Pad
4 Pad
5 Plate
6 Nut
7 Washer
8 Shock absorber
9 Bolt
10 Lockwasher
11 Pivot bolt
12 Bushing
13 Nut
14 Spring
15 Plate
16 Bolt
17 Nut
18 Lockwasher
19 Spring pan assembly
20 Wishbone assembly
21 Bolt
22 Bolt
23 Nut
24 Lockwasher
25 Spacer
26 Thrust washer
27 Seal
28 Support
29 Nut
30 Bolt
31 Nut
32 Lockwasher
33 Pivot bracket
34 Bolt
35 Nut
36 Lockwasher
37 Bushing
38 Washer
39 Nut
40 Buffer
41 Spacer
42 Bolt
43 Bolt
44 Lockwasher
45 Nut
46 Kingpin
47 Bushing
48 Setscrew
49 Stub axle assembly
50 Bushing
51 Bushing
52 Grease fitting
53 Seal
54 Spacer
55 Spring
56 Spacer
57 Thrust washer
58 Floating thrust washer—.052 to .057 in.
59 Trunnion—suspension link.
60 Nut
61 Grease fitting
62 Steering arm
63 Bolt
64 Hub assembly
65 Stud
66 Nut
67 Hub assembly
68 Collar
69 Oil seal
70 Bearing
71 Spacer
72 Shim—.003 in.
73 Bearing
74 Washer
75 Nut
76 Grease cap
77 Collar

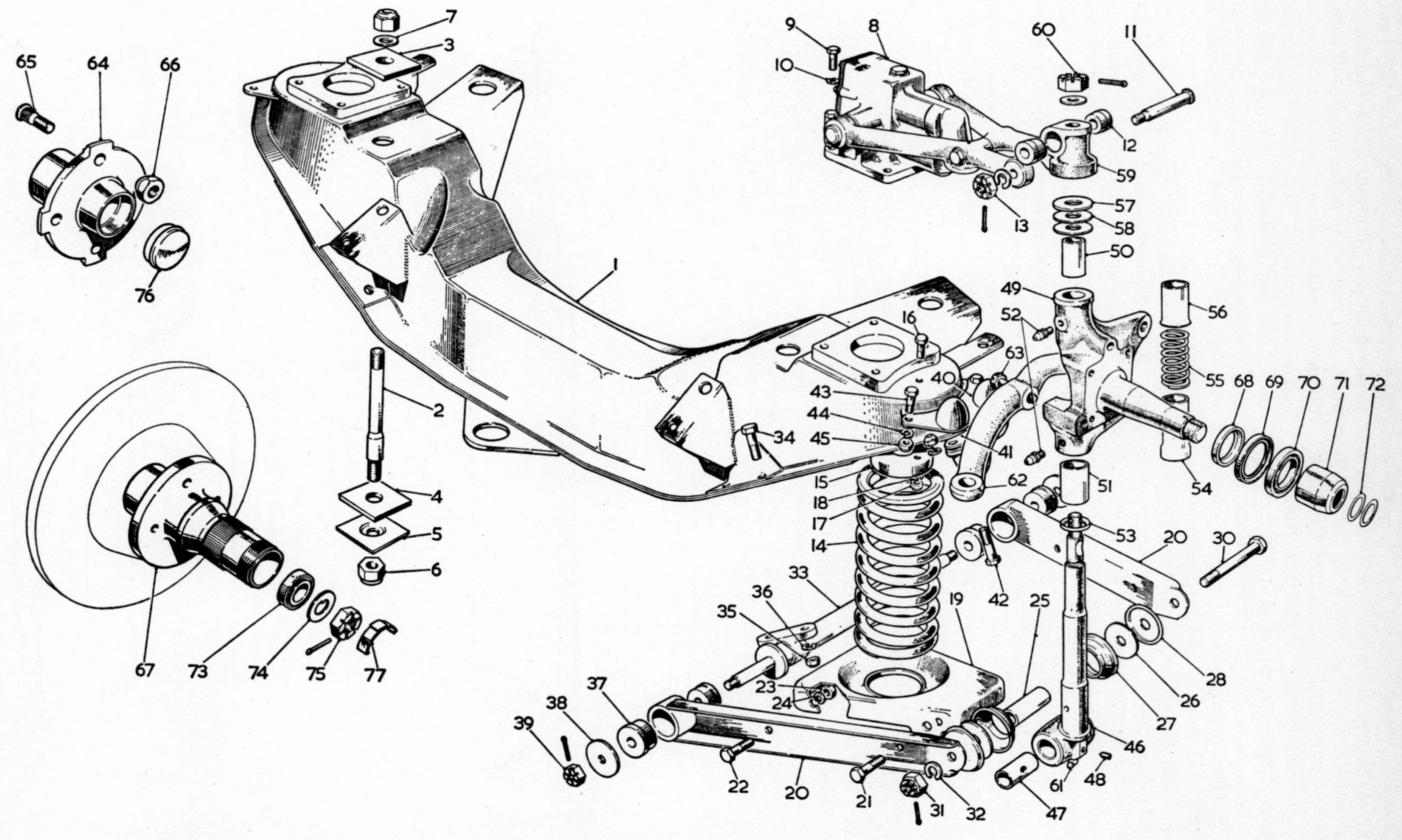

MGB front suspension components

ing, and a conical spring of compressed rubber. Whenever the front wheels meet a road irregularity, the piston is forced to push the diaphragm upward, and increased pressure causes some of the fluid from the bottom chamber to move to the top chamber. Because of the pressure increase and the fluid displacement, the rubber springs deflect, and fluid is discharged from the front displacer unit through the interconnecting pipe into the rear displacer unit. The fluid entering the rear displacer unit forces the diaphragm to react against the piston, which causes the car height at the rear to be raised. The action previously described is virtually simultaneous, and the car thereby rides level and without a pitching motion of the body. The suspension action is the same whenever the rear wheels meet an irregularity in the road.

The fluid used in the suspension system of the MG 1100 is a mixture of water and alcohol and also contains an anticorrosive agent. The front suspension of the MG 1100 is made up of upper and lower arms of unequal length which are located in the side members of the front sub-frame with the outer ends attached by means of ball joints to the hubs. In addition to the hydrolastic units, the rear suspension consists of independent trailing arms, auxiliary springs, and an anti-roll bar. The caster and camber angles are non-adjustable, having been determined during manufacture. The front *and rear* wheels should have a *toe-out* of 1/16 inch.

Before carrying out any major work on the MG 1100 suspension, it is first necessary that the system be completely depressurized, and in some cases evacuated. When the component overhaul has been completed, the system has to be repressurized to the recommended pressure. For these operations special service equipment is obviously necessary; therefore, it is advisable to trust suspension work on the MG 1100 to your authorized MG dealer.

WHEEL BEARING REMOVAL AND INSTALLATION—ALL MODELS

The front wheel bearings are of the taper-roller type. The inner end of the hub is fitted with an oil seal, and a spacer and

The MG 1100 suspension in action. Top picture shows the rear rising in response to the upward motion of the front wheels. Bottom picture shows the front rising in response to the rear wheels hitting a bump. Note that car remains level.

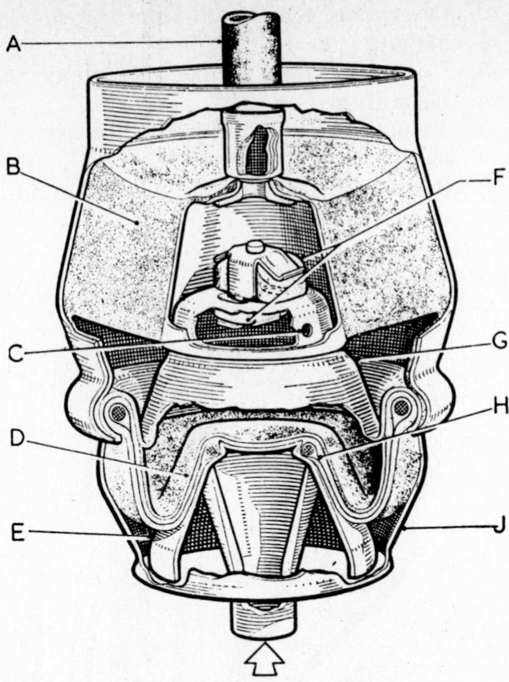

A Interconnecting pipe
B Rubber spring
C Damper bleed
D Butyl liner
E Tapered piston
F Damper valves
G Fluid-separating member
H Rubber diaphragm (nylon-reinforced)
J Tapered cylinder

Cross-sectional view of a MG 1100 hydrolastic unit.

shims are interposed between the inner and outer bearing. The hub assembly is held to the stub axle by means of a washer, nut and cotter pin. The outer end of the hub is closed by a grease-retaining cap.

In order to remove the front hub, the front of the car should be jacked up and the wheel removed. Remove the studs holding the brake caliper to the stub axle, and support the caliper. Remove the grease retainer and the cotter pin from the stub axle nut, and unscrew the nut. Withdraw the hub and disc assembly. Withdraw the bearing retaining washer, the outer bearing, shims, spacer, inner bearing, oil seal collar and oil seal. The outer races should be left in the hub unless they are to be replaced. The bearings should be washed in solvent and then dried thoroughly with compressed air or with a lint free cloth. Rollers should be examined for chips, pitting, or other damage. The inner and outer races should be inspected. Damaged or suspect bearings should be replaced. Rollers and races should be replaced only as a complete set. After they have been examined, the bearings should be submerged in clean motor oil.

In reinstalling the hub, if the bearing outer races have been removed the new ones should be refitted by pressing them into the hub. Each bearing should be filled with grease. The cavity between the bearing and the oil seal should also be filled with grease and the spacer lightly smeared. Do not fill the cavity between the bearings or the grease retaining cap with grease. With the inner bearing fitted to its race, and the collar and seal fitted to the hub, the spacer and outer bearings should be positioned and the hub assembled to the axle. The hub bearings should then be adjusted in order to obtain an end-float of between 0.002 and 0.004 in. Shims of different thicknesses are available, but should not be necessary in most cases. The nut should be tightened to 50-70 ft. lb. (150 ft. lb. minimum on the MG 1100). The broad tightening torque range is given so that the cotter pin slot can be lined up. Fit a new cotter pin and install the grease cap.

SHOCK ABSORBER REMOVAL AND INSTALLATION

MG Midget and MGB

1. Place a jack under the lower wishbone and raise the wheel.
2. Remove the top kingpin pivot bolt and swing the wheel down, taking care not to strain the brake line.

NOTE: The clamp bolt must be removed before the pivot bolt can be withdrawn.

3. Unbolt and remove the shock absorber unit.
4. Installation is in reverse order of removal.

MGC

1. Place a jack under the lower wishbone and raise and remove the wheel.
2. Remove the air filters (when working on the left side).
3. Remove the top locknut, securing nut, washer, and rubber bushing from the shock absorber.
4. Remove the lower mounting bolt and withdraw the shock absorber.
5. Installation is in reverse order of removal. The rubber bushings should be replaced as a matter of course along with a new shock absorber unit.

SHOCK ABSORBER MAINTENANCE

MG Midget and MGB

See the shock absorber maintenance section for the Midget under DRIVE AXLE AND REAR SUSPENSION.

MGC

The telescopic front shock absorbers require no maintenance and must be replaced when defective. It is not possible to fill or adjust them.

ANTI-ROLL BAR

On cars equipped with an anti-roll bar the rubber bushings should be inspected and lubricated periodically. Do not use motor oil or any other type of oil that attacks rubber on the bushings. Thicker competition anti-roll bars are available from British Leyland.

KINGPIN REPLACEMENT—MG MIDGET, MGB, AND MGC

1. Place a jack under the lower wishbone and raise and remove the wheel.
2. Disconnect the tie-rod from the steering arm.
3. Unbolt the brake caliper and support it clear of the hub.
4. Remove the hub and brake disc assembly.
5. Remove the top kingpin pivot bolt and swing the stub axle down.

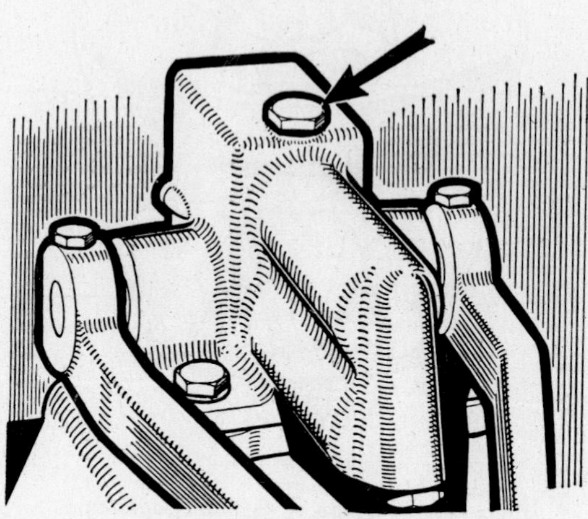

Front shock absorber fill plug, Midget and MGB

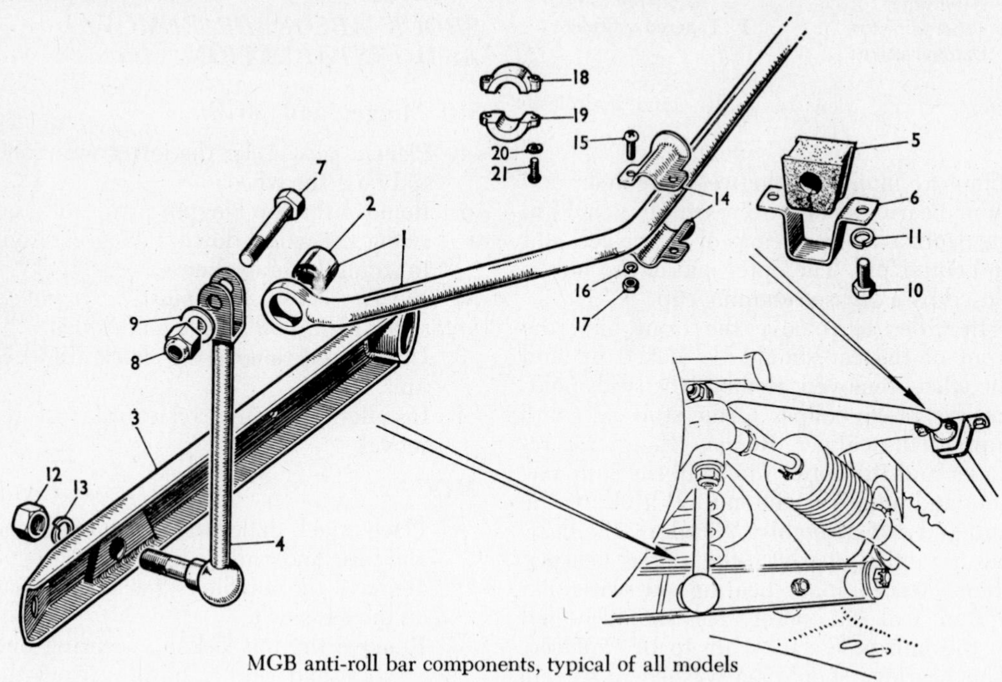

MGB anti-roll bar components, typical of all models

1 Anti-roll bar assembly
2 Bushing
3 Bottom wishbone arm
4 Anti-roll bar link
5 Anti-roll bar bushing
6 Bushing strap
7 Bolt
8 Nut
9 Plain washer
10 Bolt
11 Lockwasher
12 Nut
13 Lockwasher
14 Stop clamp
15 Screw
16 Lockwasher
17 Nut
18 Upper clamp half
19 Lower clamp half
20 Lockwasher
21 Screw
GT only.

6. On the Midget, remove the nut from the lower pivot locating pin and drive the pin completely out. Unscrew the pivot end plug (core plug on later models) and unscrew the pivot using a screwdriver.
7. On the MGB and MGC, unscrew the nut from the lower pivot bolt and remove the bolt.
8. Withdraw the stub axle and kingpin assembly from the lower control arm.
9. Unscrew the nut from the top of the stub axle and kingpin assembly and remove the kingpin, washers, and seals.
10. Press the bushings out from the bottom of the axle.
11. Install the new bushings, taking care that the open end of the oil groove enters first and that the hole in the bushing is in line with the lubrication channel in the axle.
12. On the MGB and MGC the bushings must be line-bored after installation. (Most machine shops can perform this operation.)
    The bushings should be machined to these dimensions:
    MGB—top bushing: 0.7815-0.7820 in.
    bottom bushing: 0.9075-0.9080 in.
    MGC—top bushing: 0.8125-0.8130 in.
    bottom bushing: 0.9375-0.9380 in.
13. On the Midget the kingpin bushings do not require reaming. However, the kingpin should be lubricated and installed to check the fit. If it takes excessive effort to rotate the kingpin, the bushing surfaces may be refinished using a brake cylinder hone.
14. Install the kingpin in the axle body along with the washers and seals, as removed, and tighten the nut.
15. Lubricate the bushings via the grease fittings using a high pressure grease gun, and check the resistance of the kingpin to rotation. If it is excessively stiff, remove the nut and substitute a thinner floating thrust washer (MGB and MGC) or a thicker adjustment washer (Midget).

From this point on, installation is in reverse order of removal.

SPRING REMOVAL AND INSTALLATION—MG MIDGET AND MGB

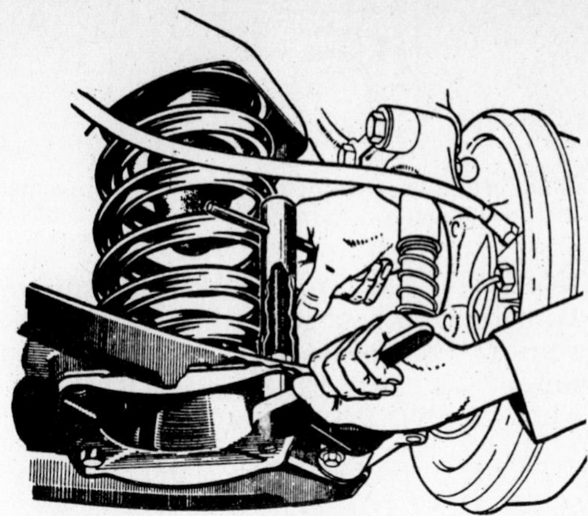

The spring can be removed from the Midget by using two long slave bolts, diagonally mounted, to slowly release spring tension

Removal of a front spring requires a spring compressor. Once the spring is slightly compressed the spring seat can be unbolted and the spring withdrawn. If a spring compressor is not available, remove two of the spring seat mounting bolts as shown and substitute two long slave bolts that will allow the spring to expand slowly when unbolted evenly (Midget only).

Installation is in reverse order of removal.

TORSION BAR ADJUSTMENT —MGC

Torsion bar adjustment is made by turning the vernier lever adjustment bolt at the rear of the torsion bar. Turn the adjustment bolt in the required direction until

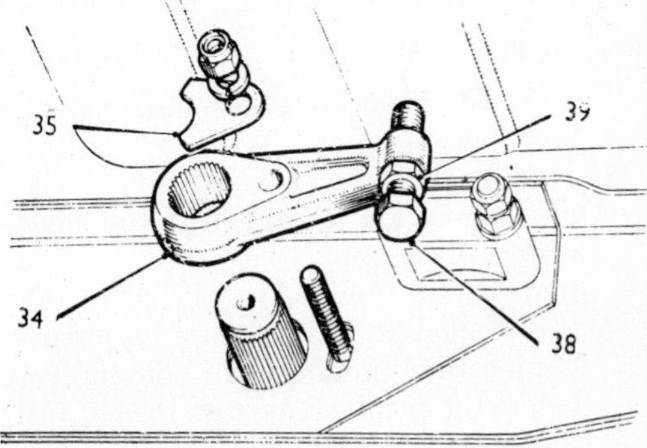

Torsion bar vernier lever and adjustment bolt, MGC

34. Vernier lever
35. Torsion bar retaining plate
38. Adjustment bolt
39. Locknut

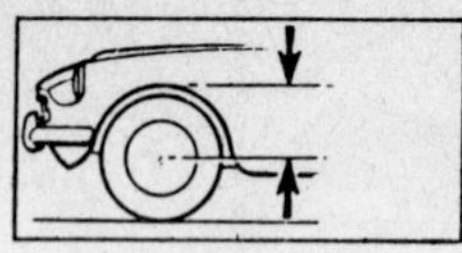

Ride height is measured between wheel center and fender arch, shown by arrows

ride height is 13 7/8 ± 1/4 in. Be sure to tighten the locknut when the adjustment is correct. For torsion bar removal procedures, see LOWER WISHBONE REMOVAL AND INSTALLATION.

UPPER WISHBONE REMOVAL AND INSTALLATION

MG Midget and MGB

The upper wishbone is formed by the shock absorber lever. See SHOCK ABSORBER REMOVAL AND INSTALLATION.

MGC

1. Remove the shock absorber.
2. Disconnect the anti-roll bar strut.
3. Remove the top kingpin pivot bolt.
4. Unbolt the wishbone pivot bracket and remove the wishbone, taking care to note the number of shims used behind the bracket. Note also that the pivot bracket lockwashers are behind the locktabs.
5. Installation is in reverse order of removal. Check the condition of the bushings before replacing the wishbone.

LOWER WISHBONE REMOVAL AND INSTALLATION

MG Midget and MGB

1. Raise the front of the car and remove the wheel.
2. Remove the spring.
3. Disconnect the tie rod from the steering arm.
4. Remove the lower kingpin pivot. On the Midget it is necessary to remove the locating pin and pivot bolt end cap before the pivot can be unscrewed.
5. Swivel the stub axle and hub assembly up slightly and support it.
6. Unbolt the wishbone pivot bracket and remove the wishbone.

MGC

Removal of a lower wishbone requires unloading and removal of the torsion bar. The procedure is as follows:

1. Place a jack under the wishbone and raise and remove the wheel.
2. Disconnect the tie-rod from the steering arm.
3. Remove the shock absorber.
4. Remove the lower kingpin pivot bolt.
5. Place a jackstand under the chassis and lower the jack.
6. Remove the wishbone inner pivot nut and unbolt and remove the front half of the wishbone.
7. At the rear of the torsion bar remove the nut and small retaining plate from the vernier lever. Remove the lever and pull the bar out about two inches.

CAUTION: Do not scratch or center-punch the torsion bar or exchange the bars from right to left (when both are removed at the same time).

8. Remove the rear half of the wishbone.
9. Installation is in reverse order of removal. The following points should be noted:

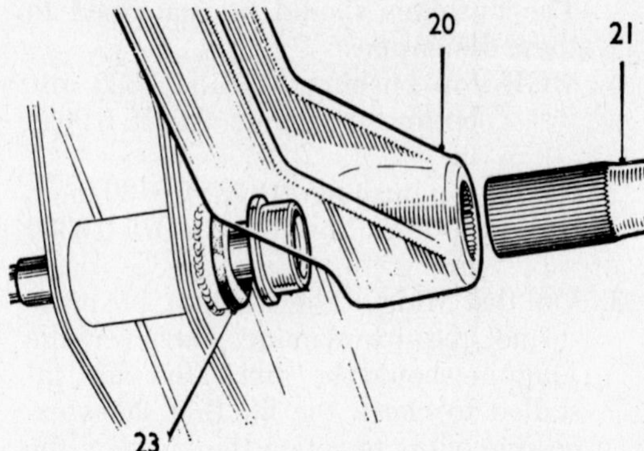

Assemble the rear half of the wishbone (20) and torsion bar (21), and install in the pivot with the bushing (23) in place

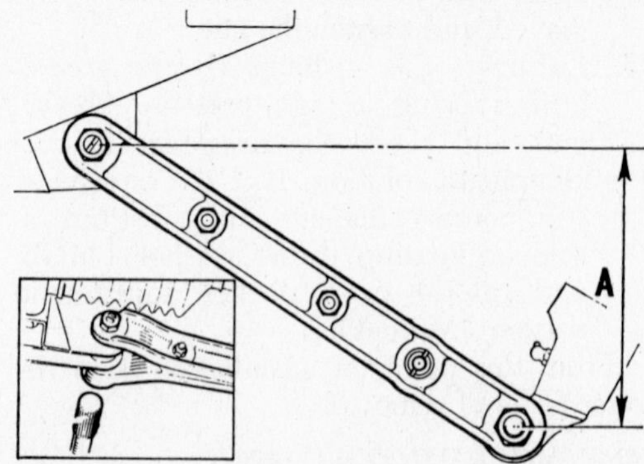

To position the torsion bar correctly the lower wishbone pivot must be 6½ in. (A) below the upper pivot

A). Check the condition of the pivot bushings.

B). The torsion bar position must be set while the rear half of the wishbone is installed. Position the stud that locates the vernier lever retaining plate at the midpoint of its total travel. Install the rear half of the wishbone on the torsion bar and push the bar all the way into the wishbone pivot. Position the rear half of the wishbone so that the horizontal centerline of the outer pivot is 6 1/2 in. below the horizontal centerline of the inner pivot. Install the vernier lever and retaining plate. When wishbone installation is complete and the wheel(s) have been reinstalled the torsion bar setting must be precisely adjusted. See TORSION BAR ADJUSTMENT —MGC.

Steering

STEERING WHEEL REMOVAL AND INSTALLATION—ALL MODELS

Cars With Plastic Steering Wheel Rims

1. Pry off the steering wheel hub emblem housing. On some models the hornbutton is released after three small setscrews in the steering wheel hub are loosened.
2. Remove the wheel retaining nut.
3. Mark the steering shaft and hub to facilitate correct installation and remove the wheel. It may be necessary to use a puller if the wheel does not come off easily.
4. Installation is in reverse order of removal. Make sure that the steering wheel is centered when the front wheels are straight ahead. The steering wheel nut in all cases should be tightened to 40 ft. lbs.

Cars With Leather Covered or Wood Steering Wheel Rims

1. Pry off the steering wheel hub emblem housing.
2. Bend back the locktabs, remove the wheel retaining bolts, and remove the wheel.
3. Installation is in reverse order of removal. The retaining bolts should be tightened to 12-17 ft. lb.

STEERING GEAR REMOVAL AND INSTALLATION

1967 and Earlier Cars

MG MIDGET

1. Remove the clamp bolt at the splined lower end of the steering column and disengage the column from the splines.
2. Disconnect the tie-rods from the steering arms.
3. Unbolt the steering rack brackets from the crossmember and remove the rack complete with tie-rods and brackets.

Installation is in reverse order of removal. The following point should be noted. To ensure correct pinion alignment, do not tighten the bolts securing the rack to the brackets until the rack has been attached to the steering column and the brackets attached to the crossmember.

MGB

1. Disconnect the tie-rods from the steering arms.
2. Turn the steering wheel to full right lock and remove the clamp bolt at the lower end of the steering column.
3. Unbolt the rack from the crossmember, noting the number of shims (if any) between the rack and the bracket.
4. Remove the rack complete with tie-rods.
5. Installation is in reverse order of removal. To ensure correct steering column alignment the following procedure should be noted:
6. Set the steering in the straight-ahead position and check that that the turn signal cancellation stud at the top of the column is positioned correctly.
7. Make sure that the column U-joint has complete freedom of movement before the rack mounting bolts are tightened. The joint should not be offset at all during installation or the steering will be stiff and the pinion upper bearing will wear prematurely.
8. If it is necessary for correct alignment the steering column support bracket and plate may be shifted, and shims added or removed between the steering rack and crossmember.

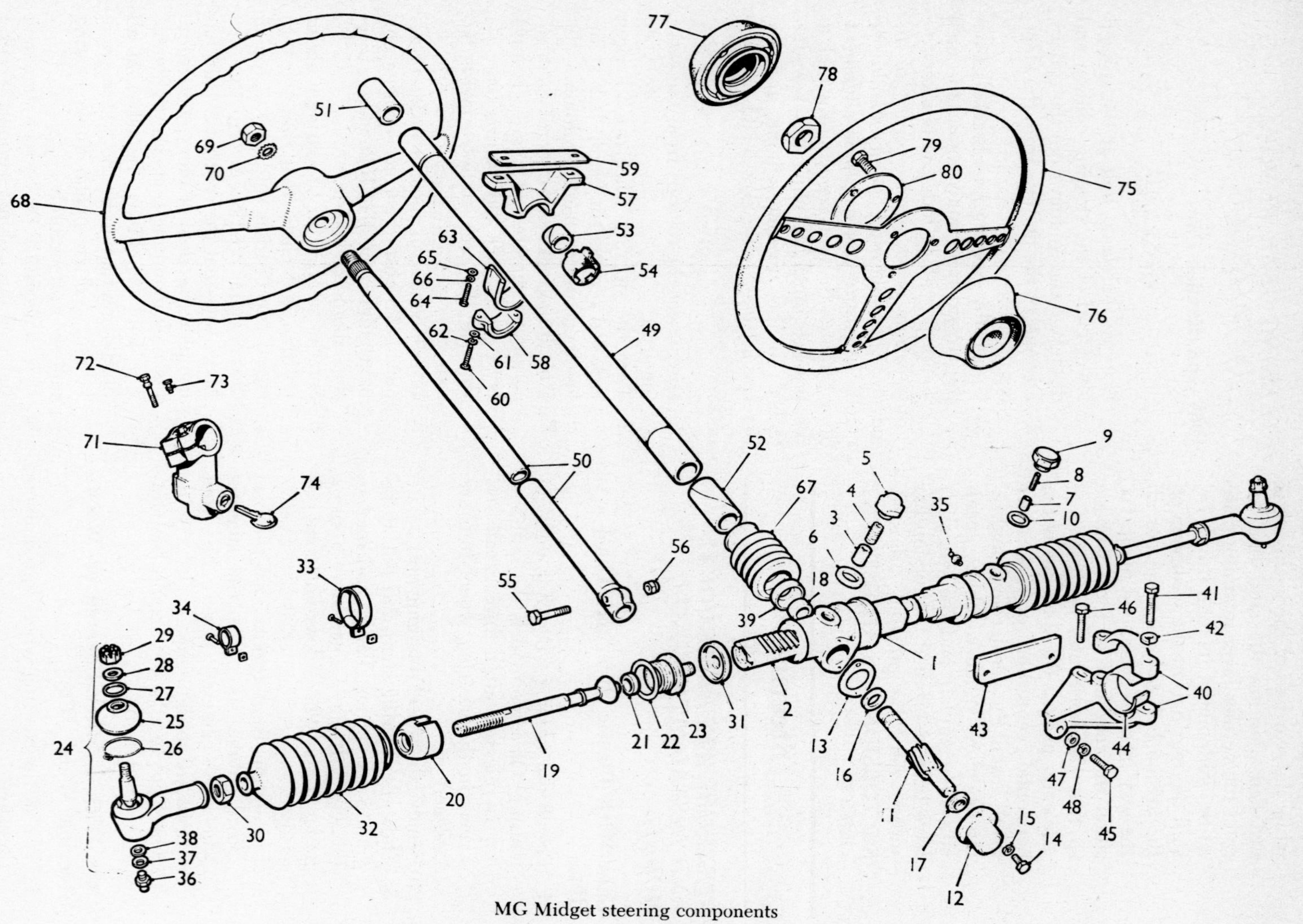

MG Midget steering components

1 Rack housing
2 Rack
3 Damper
4 Damper spring
5 Damper housing
6 Shim
7 Secondary damper pad
8 Secondary damper spring
9 Secondary damper housing
10 Housing washer
11 Pinion
12 Pinion tail bearing
13 Shim
14 Bolt
15 Lockwasher
16 Pinion thrust washer (top)
17 Pinion thrust washer (bottom)
18 Pinion seal
19 Tie-rod
20 Ball housing (female)
21 Ball seat
22 Shim
23 Ball housing (male)
24 Ball socket assembly
25 Boot
26 Clip
27 Ring
28 Plain washer
29 Nut
30 Locknut
31 Lockwasher
32 Seal
33 Clip (inner)
34 Clip (outer)
35 Grease fitting
36 Grease fitting
37 Dished washer
38 Fiber washer
39 Retainer
40 Bracket and cap assembly
41 Bolt
42 Lockwasher
43 Seating
44 Gasket
45 Bolt
46 Bolt
47 Plain washer
48 Lockwasher
49 Outer column
50 Inner column tube
51 Felt bushing (top)
52 Felt bushing (bottom)
53 Felt bushing (bottom)
54 Clip
55 Bolt
56 Nut
57 Bracket
58 Bracket cap
59 Shim
60 Bolt
61 Plain washer
62 Lockwasher
63 Gasket
64 Bolt
65 Plain washer
66 Lockwasher
67 Boot
68 Steering wheel
69 Nut
70 Lockwasher
71 Steering column lock
72 Shear bolt
73 Locating screw
74 Lock key
75 Steering wheel
76 Steering wheel nut
77 Emblem housing
78 Nut
79 Bolt
80 Ring
Midget Mk. III

1 Housing assembly
2 Bushing
3 Seal
4 Rack
5 Yoke
6 Damper
7 Spring
8 Shim
9 Gasket
10 Cover plate
11 Bolt
12 Lockwasher
13 Pinion
14 Grease fitting
15 Pinion bearing
16 Nut
17 Lockwasher
18 End cover
19 Gasket
20 Bolt
21 Lockwasher
22 Tie-rod
23 Ball seat
24 Thrust spring
25 Housing
26 Locknut
27 Seal
28 Clip
29 Clip
30 Socket assembly
31 Boot
32 Retainer
33 Spring
34 Washer
35 Nut
36 Locknut
37 Bolt
38 Nut
39 Lockwasher
40 Steering column U-joint
41 Yoke
42 Journal assembly
43 Seal
44 Retainer
45 Circlip
46 Bolt
47 Nut
48 Lockwasher
49 Column assembly—inner
50 Column assembly—inner—R.H.D.
51 Column tube
52 Column tube—R.H.D.
53 Bearing
54 Bearing
55 Bushing (felt)
56 Clip
57 Steering wheel
58 Nut
59 Clamp
60 Spacer
61 Bolt
62 Washer
63 Lockwasher
64 Nut
65 Bracket
66 Plate
67 Nut
68 Lockwasher
69. Boot
70 Lock assembly—steering and ignition
71 Key
72 Shim
73 Rivet
74 Bushing locating screw
75 Bushing
76 Wheel hub
77 Steering wheel
78 Ring
79 Bolt
80 Nut
81 Emblem housing
82 Wheel hub
83 Steering wheel
84 Ring
85 Bolt
86 Horn push contact
87 Horn push
When steering lock is fitted.
1970 and later cars.

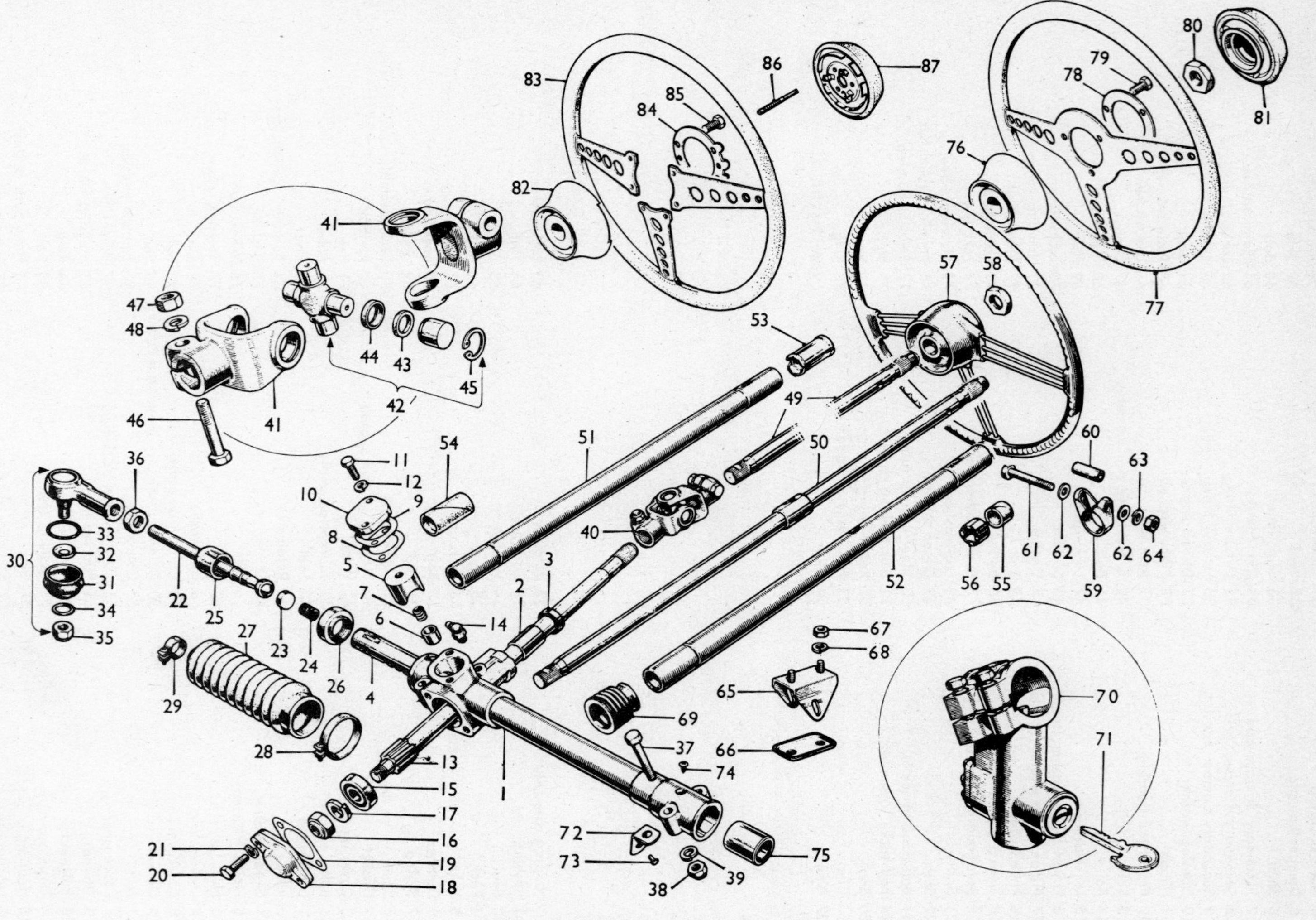

MGB and MGC steering components

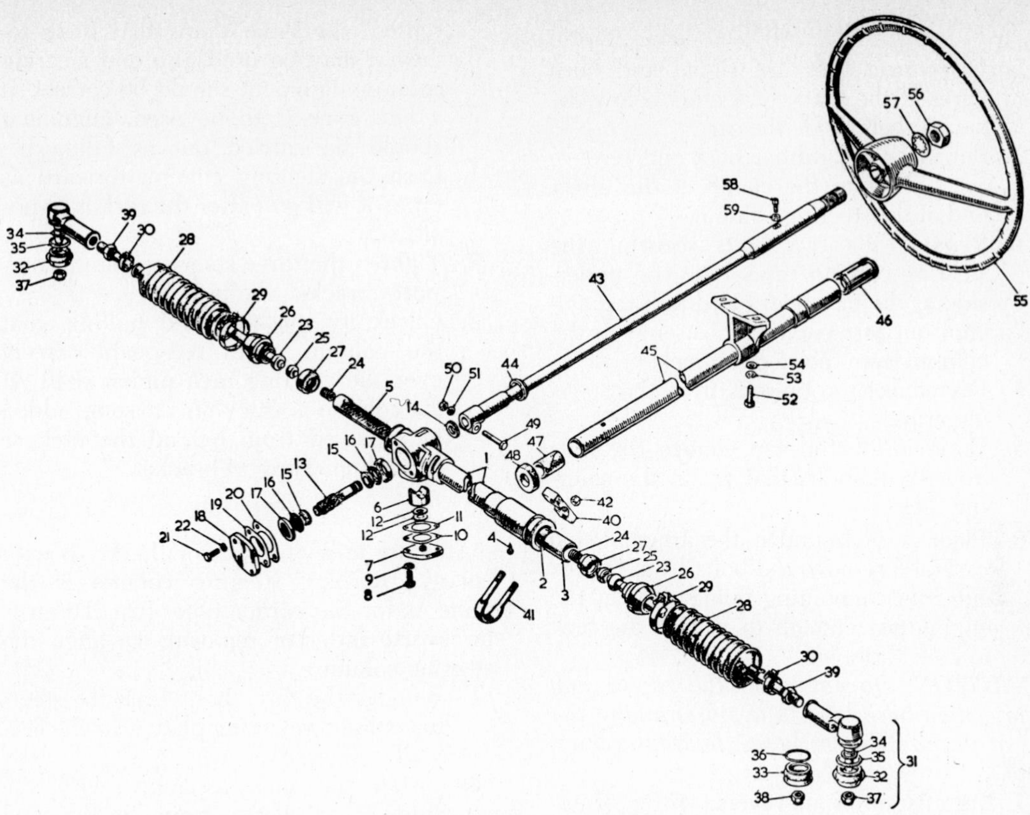

MG 1100 steering components

1 Rack housing
2 Felt bushing
3 Bushing housing
4 Housing screws
5 Rack
6 Damper yoke
7 Damper cover
8 Cover bolt
9 Lockwasher
10 Shim
11 Gasket
12 Disc spring
13 Pinion
14 Oil seal
15 Ball cone
16 Ball cage
17 Ball cup
18 End cover
19 Shim
20 Gasket
21 Cover bolt
22 Lockwasher
23 Tie-rod
24 Thrust spring
25 Ball seat
26 Ball housing
27 Locknut
28 Rubber boot
29 Seal clip (inner)
30 Seal clip (outer)
31 Ball socket assembly
32 Rubber boot
33 Rubber boot
34 Boot washer
35 Circlip
36 Circlip
37 Nut
38 Nut
39 Locknut
40 Clamp base
41 U-bolt
42 Nut
43 Column assembly
44 Washer
45 Column tube
46 Column bearing (upper)
47 Column bearirg (lower)
48 Sealing washer
49 Pinion clamp bolt
50 Nut
51 Washer
52 Column screw
53 Lockwasher
54 Washer
55 Steering wheel
56 Steering wheel nut
57 Washer
58 Stud
59 Locknut

MG 1100

1. Disconnect the turn signal and horn wires at the snap connectors below the parcel shelf inside the car.
2. Pull back the rubber boot and remove the bolt from the clamp at the lower end of the steering column.
3. Remove the two bolts securing the steering column support to the underside of the dashboard and pull the column out just enough to disengage the column from the steering rack.
4. Disconnect the tie-rods from the steering arms.
5. From inside the car remove the nuts from the U-bolts that retain the steering rack.
6. Place a jack under the transmission case and remove the bolts from the six sub-frame mounting points. Lower the engine just enough to permit the rack to be withdrawn.

CAUTION: Do not lower the engine any more than necessary to avoid straining the suspension displacer hoses, hydraulic lines, etc.

7. Installation is in reverse order of removal. Do not tighten the steering column support bolts or rack U-bolt nuts fully until the column lower clamp bolt has been tightened. This will ensure correct alignment of the column.

1968 and Later Cars (energy-absorbing steering column)

MG MIDGET

1. Remove the radiator.
2. Disconnect the tie-rods from the steering arms.
3. Remove the bolt from the clamp at the lower end of the steering column.
4. Unbolt the rack from the crossmember and move it forward as far as possible. Note the number of shims used under the rack.
5. Remove the three bolts from the steering column retaining plate near the firewall.
6. Loosen the three steering column support bracket bolts from inside the car and pull the column back far enough to disengage it from the rack.
7. Remove the right front wheel and withdraw the rack assembly.
8. Installation is in reverse order of removal. If the original rack is to be reused, the same shims that were removed may be used also and steering column alignment should be correct. If a new rack is to be used, alignment should be carried out as follows:
   1. Push the steering column forward as far as it will go (after the rack is in position).
   2. Tighten the three steering column support bracket bolts.
   3. Check, by pushing and pulling, that the column slides reasonably freely over the steering rack pinion shaft. If the column is stiff shims may be added or removed from behind the rack or the column support bracket.

MGB

Steering rack removal for the MGB with energy-absorbing steering column is the same as for the earlier type. Installation is in reverse order of removal. To align the steering column:

1. Remove the three bolts from the steering column retaining plate near the firewall.
2. Install the rack assembly with the shims that were originally removed and check, by pushing and pulling, that the column slides reaonably freely over the steering rack pinion shaft. If the column is stiff shims may be added or removed from behind the rack or the steering column support bracket.

MGC

1. Raise the front of the car and support it under the lower wishbones.
2. Disconnect the tie-rods from the steering arms.
3. Remove the bolt from the clamp at the lower end of the steering column.
4. Unbolt and remove the rack assembly, noting the number of shims used (if any).
5. Installation is in reverse order of removal. To align the steering column follow steps 1 and 2 for the MGB, above.

STEERING GEAR SERVICE

The rack and pinion steering used on MGs should never need reconditioning or adjustment if it is properly lubricated. If it becomes necessary to replace any components in the steering rack the following points should be noted:

MG Midget

1. The ball joints at the inner ends of the tie-rods should be a tight sliding fit without play. Adjustment may be made by substituting washers of different thickness at the ball joint seat.
2. The center tooth on the rack must be in line with the mark on the pinion shaft.
3. Pinion shaft end-float should be 0.002-0.005 in. Shims of different thicknesses are available.

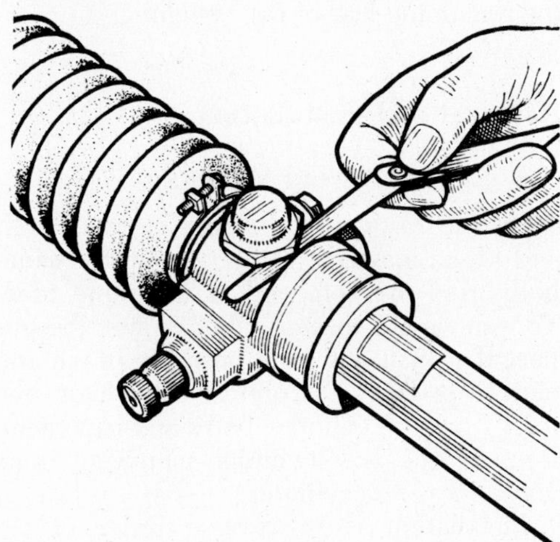

Using a feeler gauge to measure clearance between the damper cap and rack housing

4. Measure the clearance between the damper cap and the rack housing without shims installed (see illustration). To this measurement add 0.002-0.005 in. The figure obtained will give the correct thickness of shims to be used under the cap. Use gasket sealer on the mating surfaces.
5. When the pinion oil seal has been replaced pump approximately 10 fl. oz. of SAE 90 hypoid gear oil into the housing through the fitting.

MGB and MGC

1. When installed, the tie-rods should be held firmly without free-play. The ball joint lockring should be tightened to 33-37 ft. lbs.
2. Measure the clearance between the damper cover and the housing (without the spring or shims installed) after the cover is tightened to where it is just possible to rotate the pinion by pulling the rack through the housing. To this measurement add 0.0005-0.003 in. to arrive at the correct thickness of shims to be used under the cover. Use gasket sealer on the mating surfaces.
3. When the rubber boots have been installed pour or pump into the housing 1/2 pt. of SAE 90 hypoid gear oil.

MG 1100

1. Install the pinion bearings, the pinion, and the rack. Install the pinion end cover without the shims and measure the clearance between the cover and the housing. Remove and reinstall the cover with shims to the value of the measurement obtained minus 0.001-0.003 in. Use gasket sealer on the mating surfaces.
2. Make sure that the tie-rod inner ball joints are firmly held in place but free to slide in any direction. The lockrings should be tightened to 33-37 ft. lb.
3. Damper adjustment, early type:
   Install the yoke and spring and install the cover. Tighten the cover bolts until it is just possible to rotate the pinion by sliding the rack through the housing. Measure the clearance between the plate and the housing and use shims to the value of the measurement minus 0.001-0.003 in. Use gasket sealer on the mating surfaces.
   Damper adjustment, later type:
   Install the yoke and cover without the spring or shims. Tighten the cover bolts until it is just possible to rotate the pinion by sliding the rack through the housing. Measure the clearance between the cover and housing and use shims to the value of the measurement plus 0.002-0.005 in. Use gasket sealer on the mating surfaces.
4. When the rubber boots have been installed pour 1/2 pt. of SAE 140 EP oil into the housing.

STEERING/IGNITION LOCK SWITCH—1968 AND LATER CARS

Removal and Installation—All Models

1. Disconnect the battery(s).
2. Mark and disconnect the wires from the ignition switch.
3. Insert the key and unlock the steering.
4. Unbolt the lock bracket through the

access hole in the upper surface. On some models it will be necessary to use an *easy-out* to remove the bolts.

5. Loosen the steering column support bracket to aid in removal, and withdraw the lock/switch assembly.
6. Installation is in reverse order of removal.

Brakes

All models except for the Midget Mk. I have disc brakes in the front and drum brakes in the rear, with a mechanically actuated parking brake operating on both rear brakes. The Midget Mk. I uses drum brakes all around. The disc brakes, as is usual, are automatically self-adjusting. The drum brakes must be manually adjusted. The MGC and some MGBs are equipped with a vacuum operated brake booster. All 1968 and later models are equipped with a dual braking system incorporating a dual master cylinder, pressure differential warning switch, and brake failure warning light. British Leyland recommends that *Castrol Girling Amber* or *Lockheed Super Heavy Duty* brake fluid be used in the hydraulic system; however, any brake fluid conforming to SAE specification J1703 may be used. Flush the hydraulic system at the manufacturer's recommended intervals.

MASTER CYLINDER

On all models built prior to 1968 a conventional Lockheed single master cylinder is used. Since 1968 a dual master cylinder has been used in compliance with federal law. The dual master cylinder is actually two master cylinders operating in the same bore, designed so that the front and rear brakes have separate hydraulic systems. Malfunction in either system has no effect on the other system but is immediately evident to the driver because of the additional pedal travel and effort required to operate the remaining half of the system.

Removal and Installation

MG MIDGET MK. I AND II

On the Midget Mk. I and II the clutch and brake master cylinders are in the same body, and are removed at the same time. To remove the master cylinder, first disconnect the pushrods from both the brake and clutch pedals. Disconnect the hydraulic lines from the cylinder body and cap them. Remove the two cylinder mounting bolts and remove the cylinder.

Installation is in reverse order of removal. When the lines have been reconnected, the clutch, as well as the brakes, should be bled.

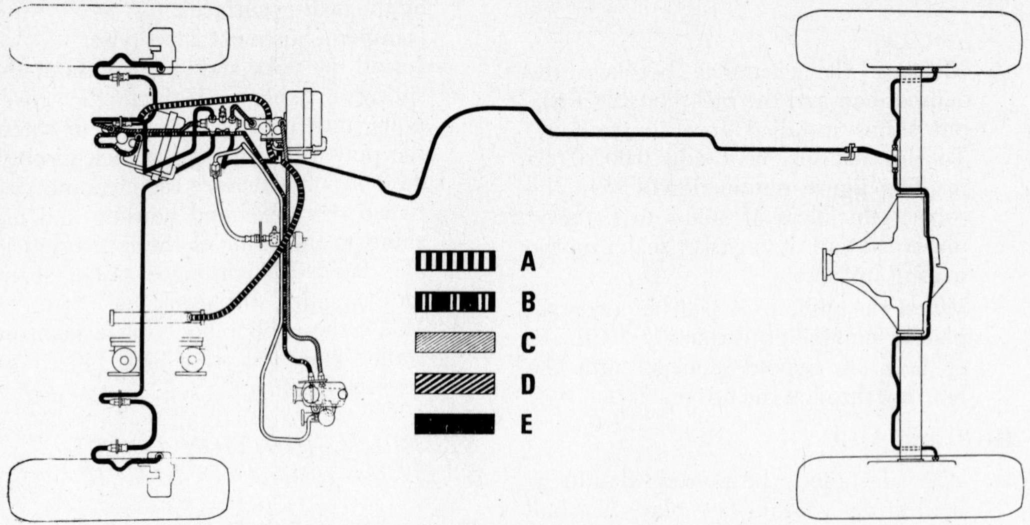

Hydraulic brake system, with dual master cylinder and power booster

A—Booster vacuum line
B—Master cylinder to front servo
C—Master cylinder to rear servo
D—Sevo to pressure differential warning switch
E—Pressure differential warning switch to brakes

MG Midget Mk. III, MGB, MGC, and MG 1100

To remove the brake master cylinder, remove the screws securing the mounting bracket cover plate and lift the cover off (all except MG 1100). Disconnect and cap the hydraulic line(s) from the cylinder. Remove the mounting bolts and lift the cylinder out.

Installation is in reverse order of removal. When the hydraulic lines have been reconnected the brakes must be bled.

Master Cylinder Rebuilding

The accompanying illustrations show the order of disassembly and assembly for the various cylinders. Rebuilding kits are available, and usually contain the check valve, rubber seals, and metal washers. Pistons and springs are available as individual pieces.

When the piston assembly has been removed from the cylinder, examine the bore. If it is pitted or scored the entire cylinder assembly should be replaced. If bore damage is light it may be honed, but in most cases the repair will not be lasting and the cylinder may begin to leak again after a short time. When honing a cylinder, occasionally dip the hone in clean brake fluid for lubrication.

Whenever a cylinder is disassembled for inspection or rebuilding the rubber seals should be replaced as a matter of course. Before installing the seals lubricate them thoroughly with brake fluid or the special lubricant that is included in some rebuilding kits. All internal components of the cylinder, especially the bore, must be completely free of dirt and grit or the cylinder may leak or fail to operate properly. When installing the piston and seals into the bore make sure that the seal lips are not turned back as they enter the cylinder. Once the cylinder has been installed on the car the brakes must be bled.

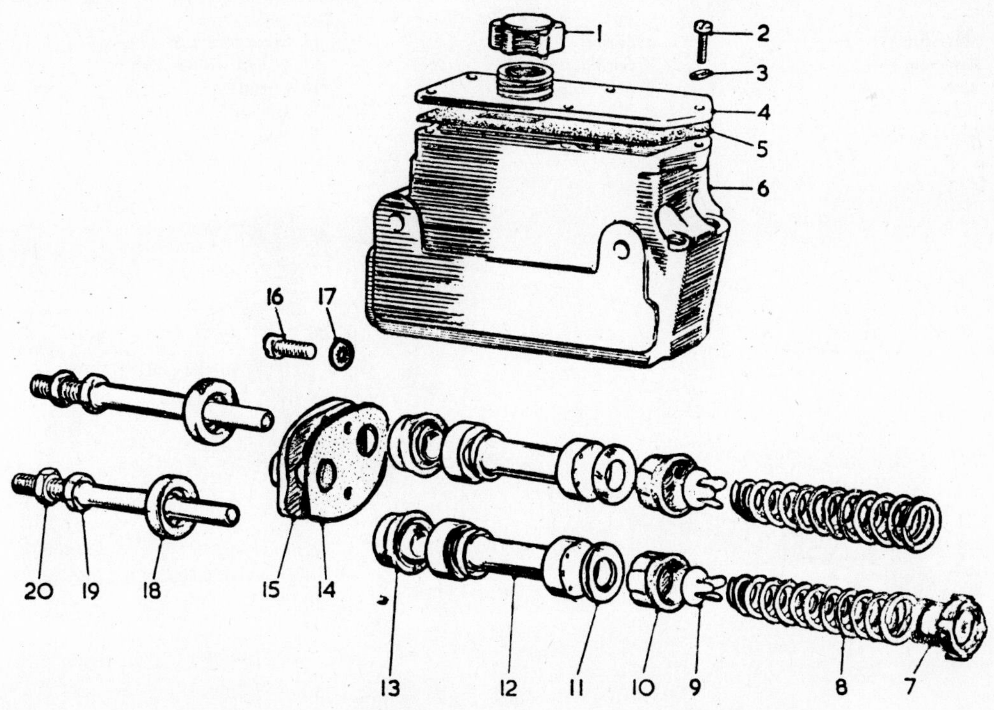

Midget Mk. I and II, clutch and brake master cylinder components

1 Filler cap
2 Screw
3 Washer
4 Tank cover
5 Gasket
6 Cylinder body
7 Check valve (brake only)
8 Return spring
9 Spring retainer
10 Main cup
11 Piston washer
12 Piston
13 Secondary cup
14 Gasket
15 Retaining plate
16 Screw
17 Lockwasher
18 Rubber boot
19 Pushrod
20 Pushrod adjuster

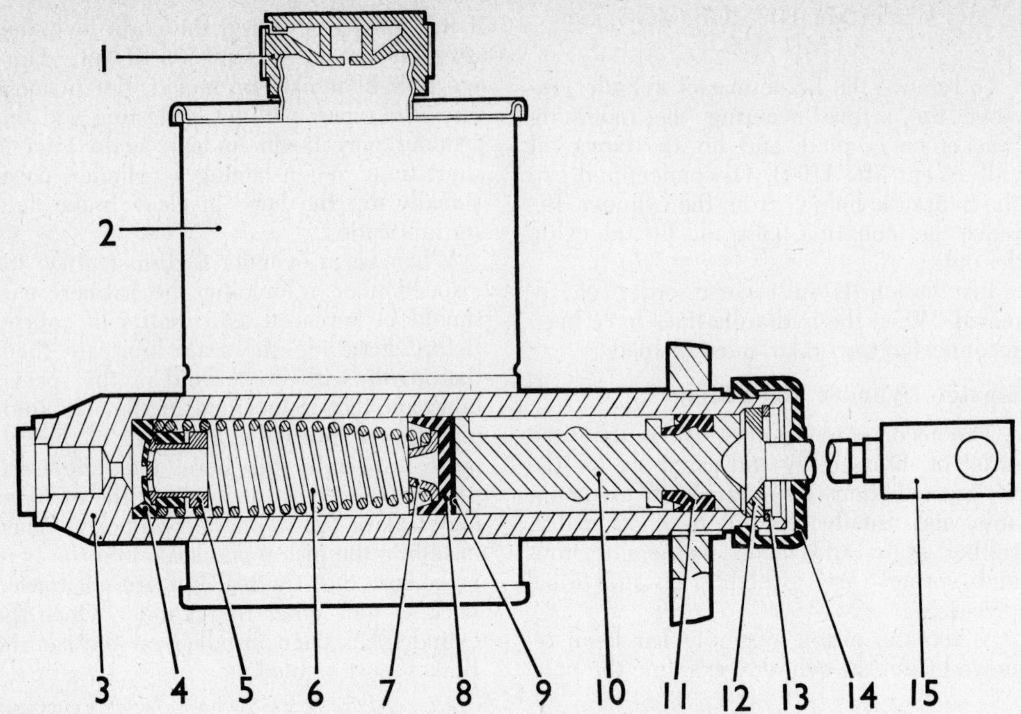

Cross-section of the Midget Mk. III single master cylinder

1 Filler cap
2 Reservoir
3 Body
4 Valve
5 Valve seat
6 Spring
7 Spring retainer
8 Main cup
9 Piston wash
10 Piston
11 Secondary cup
12 Dished washer
13 Circlip
14 Rubber boot
15 Pushrod

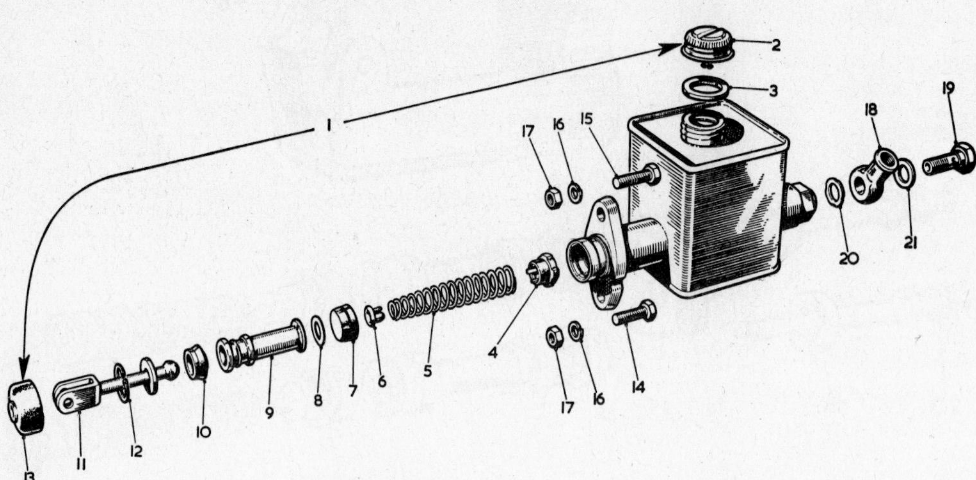

MGB single master cylinder components

1 Cylinder and supply tank assembly
2 Filler cap
3 Seal
4 Valve assembly
5 Spring
6 Spring retainer
7 Main cup
8 Washer
9 Piston
10 Secondary cup
11 Pushrod
12 Circlip
13 Boot
14 Mounting bolt
15 Mounting bolt
16 Lockwasher
17 Nut
18 Banjo
19 Bolt
20 Gasket
21 Gasket

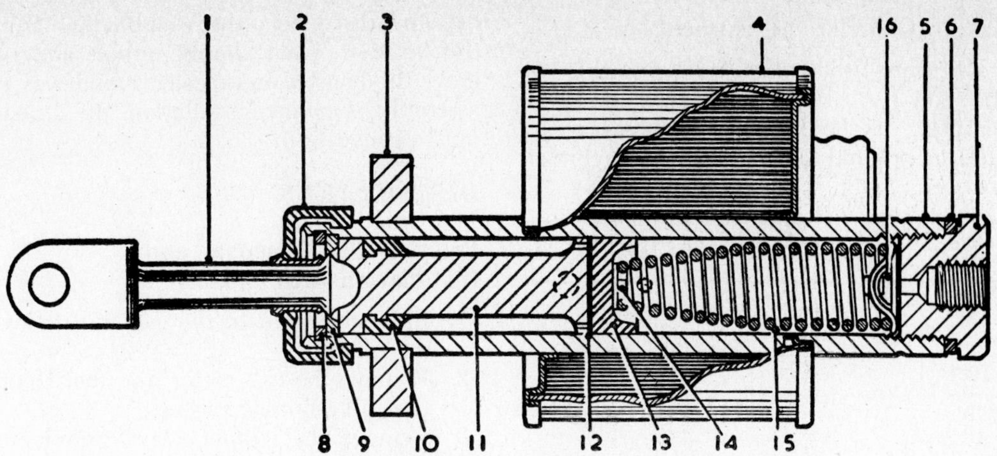

MG 1100 master cylinder in cross-section

1 Pushrod
2 Rubber boot
3 Mounting flange
4 Supply tank
5 Cylinder body
6 Washer
7 End plug
8 Circlip
9 Stop-washer
10 Secondary cup
11 Piston
12 Piston washer
13 Main cup
14 Spring retainer
15 Return spring
16 Check valve

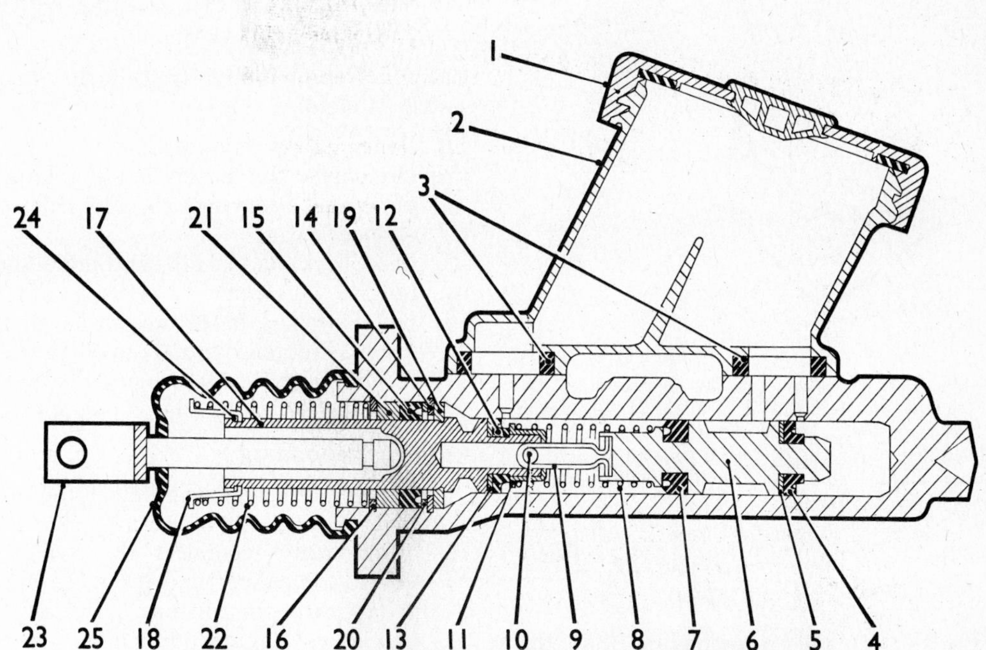

Cross-section of the dual master cylinder used on all models since 1968

1 Filler cap
2 Plastic reservoir
3 Reservoir seals
4 Main cup
5 Piston washer
6 Piston
7 Main cup
8 Spring
9 Piston link
10 Pin
11 Pin retainer
12 Main cup
13 Pinion washer
14 Circlip
15 Cup
16 Circlip
17 Piston
18 Spring retainer
19 Stop washer
20 Washer
21 Spacer
22 Spring
23 Pushrod
24 Retainer ring

Master Cylinder Adjustment

The only adjustment it is possible to make on the master cylinder is pushrod free-play. It should not be necessary to alter the original setting unless the cylinder has been rebuilt.

Model	Free-Play at Push-Rod (in.)	Free-Play at Pedal (in.)
Midget		
1961-67	1/32	3/16
1968-71	N.A.	1/8
MGB		
All Series	N.A.	1/8
MGC		
1968-69	N.A.	1/8
MG 1100		
1962-67	Non-adjustable	

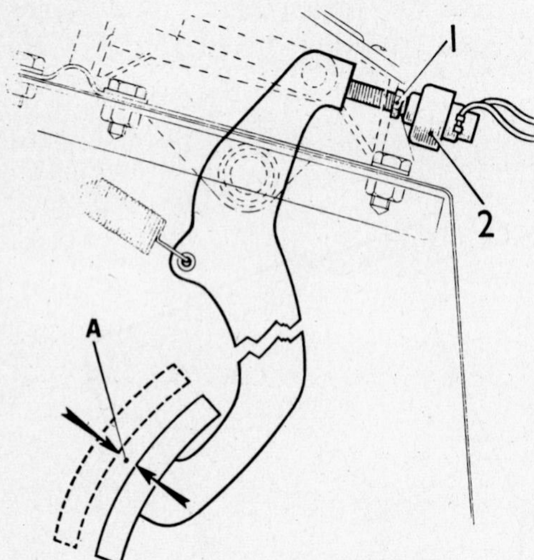

Brake pedal free-play (A) is measured at the pedal pad, and adjustment is made at the master cylinder pushrod. Brake light switch (2) and adjustment nut (1), as used on later cars, is shown. Earlier cars use a hydraulically actuated brake light switch

POWER BRAKES

British Leyland recommends that the brake booster be replaced as a unit if trouble is experienced. A Lockheed Type 6 booster is used on the MGB, and a Girling Mk. 2B is used on the MGC. Exploded views of both units are shown.

Removal and Installation

To remove the booster, first disconnect the hydraulic line(s) from the master cylinder and disconnect the vacuum line from the booster. Then simply unbolt and remove the booster and master cylinder as an assembly. Upon reinstallation the brakes must be bled.

DISC BRAKES

Friction Pad Removal and Installation—All Models

1. Raise the front of the car and remove the wheel.
2. Remove the two cotter pins that locate the pad retaining spring(s).
3. Remove the retaining spring and pull the pads and anti-squeal shims from the caliper.
4. Installation is in reverse order of removal. It may be necessary to push the pistons back into the caliper so that the new pads will fit. Be careful not to mar the disc in doing so. Install the anti-squeal shims in their original positions or they will not function properly. Pads should never be allowed to wear to a thickness of less than 1/16 in. Replace pads in axle sets (two pair).

Caliper Removal and Installation —All Models

1. Remove the friction pads.
2. Disconnect the hydraulic line retaining plate and disconnect the line from the caliper.
3. Bend back the locktabs and unbolt and remove the caliper.
4. Installation is in reverse order of removal. Tighten the bolts to 40-45 ft. lb. It will be necessary to bleed the brakes after the hydraulic line is reconnected.

Caliper Rebuilding

1. Remove the caliper and clean the exterior.
2. Temporarily reconnect the hydraulic line to the caliper and press the brake pedal until the pistons protrude far enough to be removed by hand.
3. Remove the dust seals and retainers, taking care not to damage the piston bores.
4. Remove the seals from the pistons using a non-metallic instrument.

NOTE: It is not normally necessary to separate the caliper halves. If the separation is necessary the fluid transfer hole seal, bridge bolts, and bolt locktabs must *be re-*

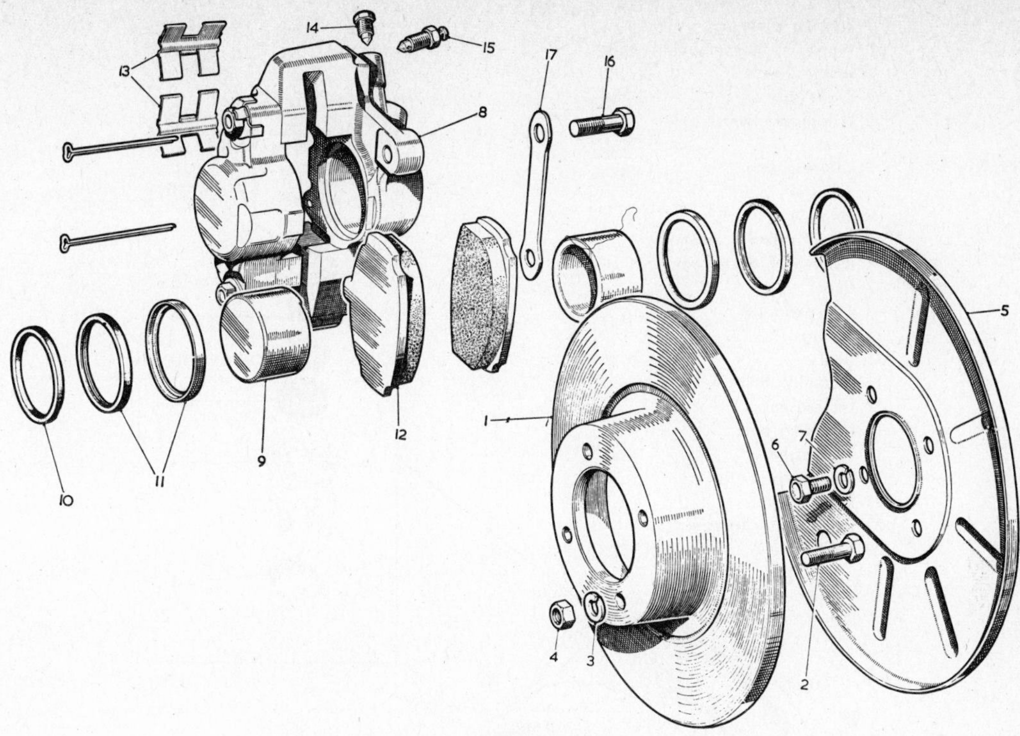

MGB disc brake components, typical of all models

1 Disc
2 Bolt
3 Lockwasher
4 Nut
5 Dust cover
6 Bolt
7 Lockwasher
8 Caliper
9 Piston
10 Piston seal
11 Dust seal and retainer
12 Pad
13 Retaining springs
14 Plug
15 Bleed valve
16 Bolt
17 Locktab

placed with new parts. Only use bolts obtained from an MG dealer that are supplied for this special application. Torque the bolts to 34-37 ft. lb.

5. Clean all components in solvent and dry thoroughly with compressed air.
6. Examine the pistons and bores for wear or damage. Damaged pistons should be replaced. Slight bore roughness can be removed with crocus cloth or a brake cylinder hone. Remove all traces of grit from the bore after refinishing. Badly pitted or damaged bores cannot be refinished; the caliper must be replaced.
7. Coat the pistons and piston seals with brake fluid and install the seals on the pistons.
8. Loosen the bleed valve one turn and install the pistons in the bores with the piston cut-away facing inwards. Press the piston in until approximately 3/8 in. of the piston is protruding from the bore.
9. Install the dust seals on the pistons.
10. Install the caliper(s) and bleed the brakes.

Disc Removal and Installation—All Models

1. Remove the caliper.
2. Remove the grease cap and cotter pin, and remove the hub retaining nut. Withdraw the hub assembly.
3. Unbolt and remove the disc from the hub.
4. Installation is in reverse order of removal.

Disc Resurfacing

Model	*Original Thickness*	*Permissible Regrind*	*Maximum Runout*	*Parallel Variation*	*Surface Finish (max. micro in.)*
Midget	N.A.	none	0.006	N.A.	—
MGB	.340-.350	-0.040	0.003	0.001	63
MGC	N.A.	none	0.003	N.A.	—
MG 1100	N.A.	none	0.006	N.A.	—

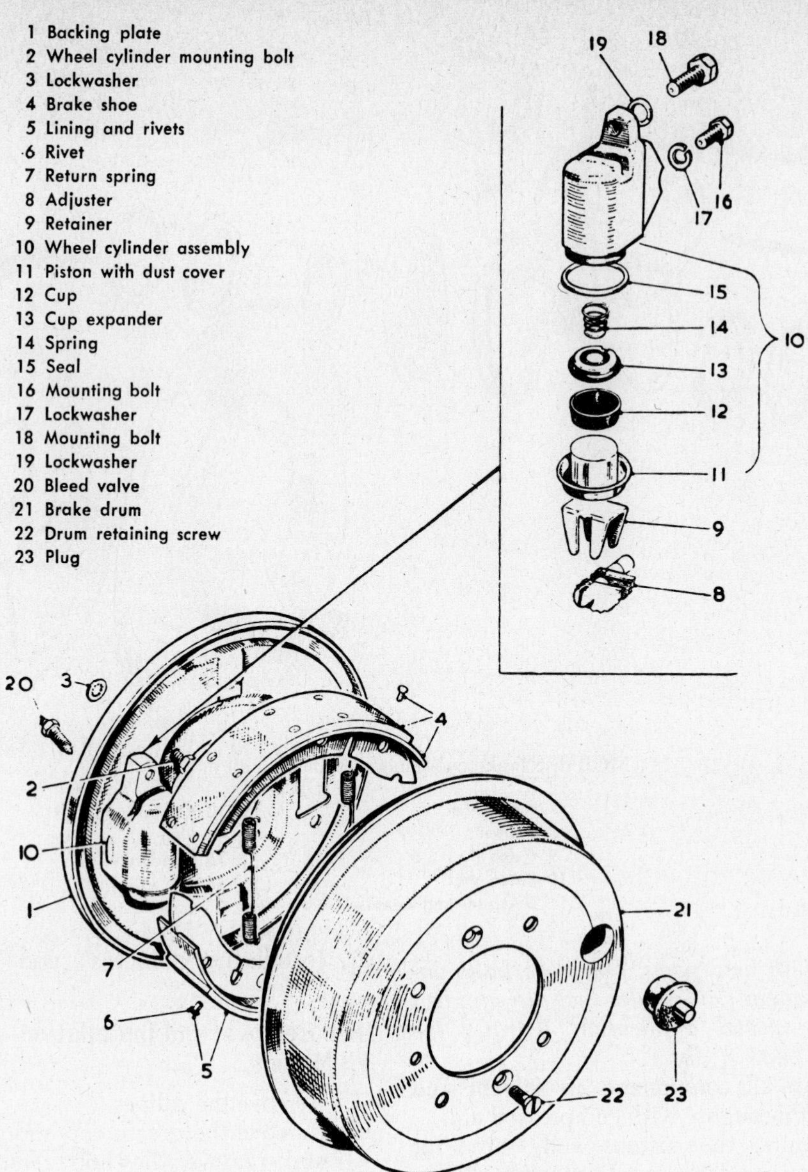

Midget Mk. I front and rear brake components

Any disc that is badly scored should be replaced. Light scoring is not detrimental to the operation of the brakes, but friction pad life will be reduced. Runout is measured at the outer edge of the disc friction surface with a dial indicator or runout gauge. Parallelism refers to variations in the thickness of the disc. The disc should be measured for parallelism at four equally spaced points around the friction surface.

DRUM BRAKES

Adjustment—MG Midget Mk. I and MGC

1. Raise the car and remove the wheel.
2. Remove the rubber plug in the drum access hole.
3. Rotate the drum until one of the adjusters is accessible through the hole.
4. Using a screwdriver, turn the adjuster

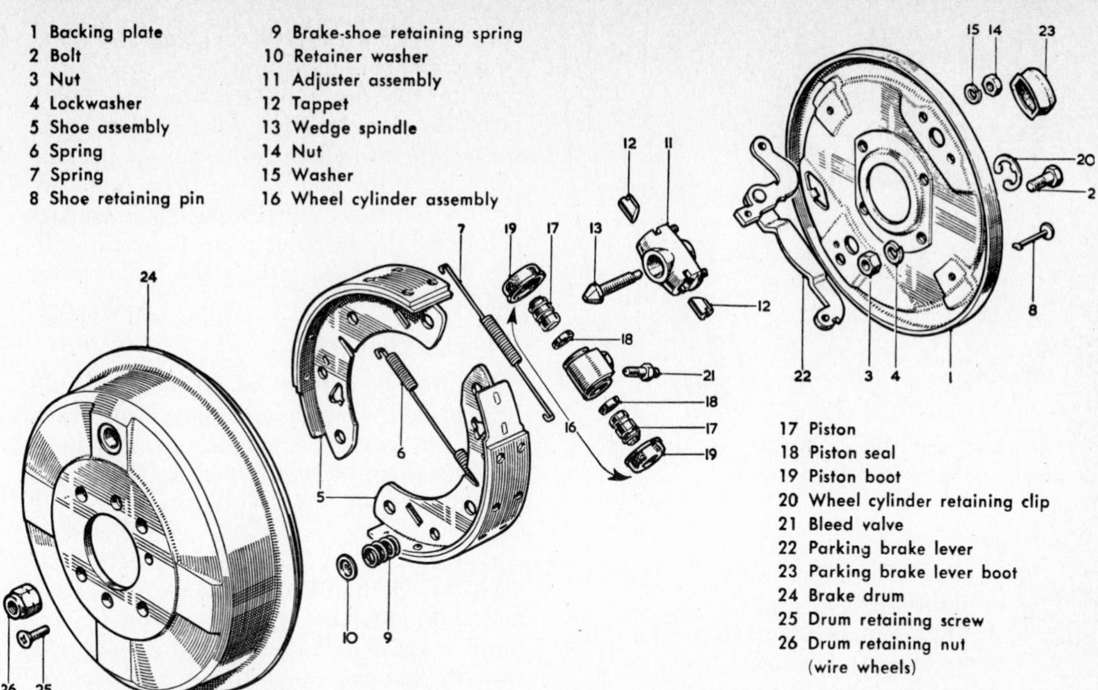

Midget Mk. II and III, MGB, MGC ,and MG 1100 rear brake components. Adjuster configurations and shoe retaining springs vary between the different models. The brake drum shown does not apply to the MG 1100, as its brake drum is integral with the hub

clockwise until the brake shoe contacts the drum.

5. Turn the adjuster back one or two notches until the drum can rotate freely.
6. Turn the drum until the other adjuster is accessible and repeat steps 4 and 5.

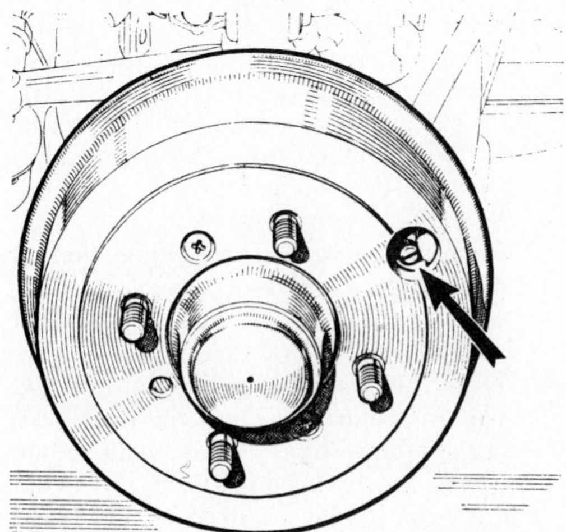

Midget Mk. I brake adjuster. The adjuster head is slotted and is turned with a screwdriver

7. Apply the brakes hard to set the shoes and recheck adjustment.
8. Adjust the other brakes in the same manner.

Adjustment—All Models Except Midget Mk. I and MGC

1. Raise the car.
2. Using a suitable tool, turn the square-headed adjuster bolt (located on the backing plate) clockwise until the wheel is nearly locked.

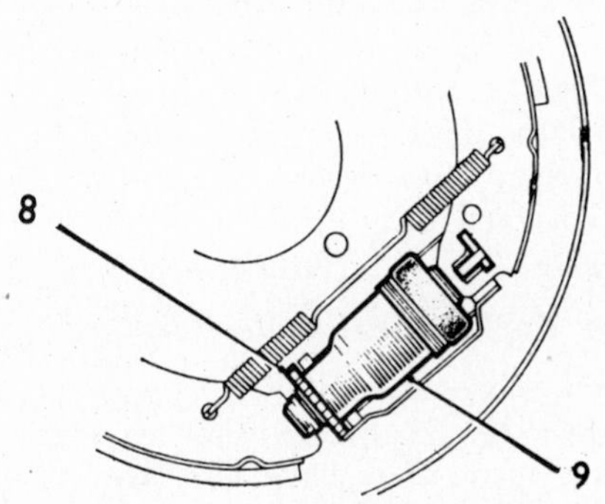

MGC brake adjuster (8) at the end of the wheel cylinder (9). Turn the adjuster clockwise (down) to tighten the brakes, and counterclockwise (up) to loosen the brakes

Adjuster bolt. Turn clockwise to tighten the brakes, counterclockwise to loosen

3. Back off the adjuster one or two flats until the wheel can spin freely.
4. Apply the brakes hard to set the shoes and recheck adjustment.
5. Adjust the other rear brake in the same manner.

Drum Removal and Installation—All Models

1. Raise the car and remove the wheel.
2. Back off the brake adjuster if the drum will not spin freely.
3. Remove the drum retaining screws or nuts and pull the drum off of the hub. On the MG 1100 it is necessary to remove the grease cap and wheel bearing nut, and use a puller or slide hammer to remove the drum.
4. Installation is in reverse order of removal. Adjust the brakes when the drum has been replaced on the hub.

Drum Refinishing

If a drum is badly scored or warped it should be replaced. Light scoring or distortion can be corrected by turning the drum on a lathe. It is generally accepted that no more than 0.015 in. of metal should be removed (increasing drum diameter by 0.030 in.).

Shoe Replacement

Brake shoes should always be replaced in axle sets. Replace riveted shoe assemblies or linings when they have less than 40% of original thickness left at the thinnest point, and bonded shoe assemblies or linings when they have less than 25% of original thickness left at the thinnest point. Examine the linings for signs of cracking and oil or brake fluid contamination.

With the drum off examine the wheel cylinders for leakage. Check the brake springs for stretching and clean the backing plate after the shoes have been removed. Lightly lubricate the brake shoe contact points on the backing plate before installing the new shoes. Adjust the brakes after installation.

Wheel Cylinders

Ideally, wheel cylinder assemblies should be replaced when they begin to leak. However, seal kits are available and a rebuilt cylinder should function well if it has been rebuilt carefully. Use the illustrations at the beginning of the brake section for disassembly and assembly, and refer to MASTER CYLINDER REBUILDING for inspection and rebuilding notes. It is possible to rebuild a wheel cylinder without removing it from the backing plate. In any case, cleanliness is of extreme importance. Adjust and bleed the brakes after the drum has been reinstalled.

PRESSURE DIFFERENTIAL WARNING SWITCH—1968 AND LATER CARS

The pressure differential warning switch, used in conjunction with the dual master cylinder, is nothing more than an electrical switch connected to a hydraulic cylinder that reacts to a drop in pressure from either of the braking systems. When this happens the switch is tripped and the dashboard warning light is activated, indicating a failure of one of the brake systems. To centralize the valve and turn off the warning light after the brake fault has been repaired it is usually only necessary to bleed the brakes. If the light remains on after the brakes have been bled:

1. Switch the ignition on.
2. Loosen the brake line connection at the pressure differential switch opposite the side of the brake system that was repaired.
3. Press the brake pedal slowly until the valve is centralized and the light goes out. Tighten the brake line connection. Check the brake fluid level and pedal firmness. It may be necessary to bleed the brakes again.

The electrical switch is replaceable separately from the hydraulic cylinder assem-

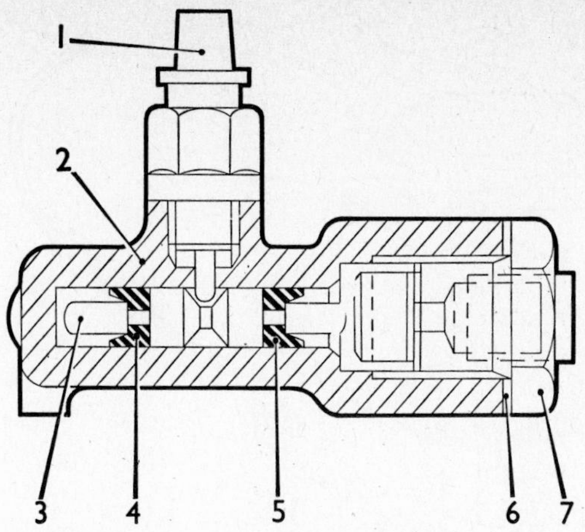

Cross-section of the pressure differential warning switch

1 Electrical switch
2 Valve body
3 Shuttle valve piston
4 Piston seal
5 Piston seal
6 Copper washer
7 End plug

bly. If the hydraulic valve is faulty it may be rebuilt in the same manner as a brake master cylinder. Replacement seals are available.

PRESSURE REGULATING VALVE —MG 1100

A pressure regulating valve is installed on the hydraulic line to the rear brakes to prevent them from locking under hard braking. Unequal brake proportioning, resulting in premature front or rear wheel lockup, is indicative of a faulty regulating valve. Do not attempt to adjust or rebuild the valve, as it *must* function exactly as designed in order for the car to stop quickly. Replace the valve if it is suspected that it is not operating properly.

BRAKE BLEEDING

The purpose of bleeding the brakes is to expel air trapped in the hydraulic system. There are two methods of accomplishing this. The quickest and easiest of the two is pressure bleeding, but special pressure equipment is needed to externally pressurize the hydraulic system. The other, more commonly used method is gravity bleeding. *NOTE: Only brake fluid conforming to SAE specification J1703 should be used.*

Gravity Bleeding Procedure

1. Clean the bleed valve at each wheel.
2. Attach a small rubber hose to the bleed valve on one of the rear wheel cylinders and place the other end in a container of brake fluid.
3. Top up the master cylinder with brake fluid (check often during bleeding).
4. Open the bleed valve about one-quarter turn, press the brake pedal to the floor and slowly release it. Continue until no more air bubbles are forced from the cylinder on application of the brake pedal.
5. Repeat for each of the remaining wheel cylinders, beginning with the other rear wheel.

PARKING BRAKE ADJUSTMENT —ALL MODELS

Adjustment can be made at the brake balance lever where the main parking brake cable splits into separate cables for each rear wheel, underneath the car near the axle. Adjust the cable so that the brake is fully applied when the lever is pulled up four or five notches. Some cars have grease fittings on the cables and balance lever pivot. and these points must be lubricated regularly to prevent brake drag.

Windshield Wipers—All Models

The wiper motor and transmission on all models is mounted on a bracket underneath the dashboard. Drive is transmitted from the motor to the wiper arm gearboxes via a spiral cable known as the cross-head and rack. Except for a motor failure, which is rare, the only component that may require replacement is the cross-head and rack. To replace the cross-head and rack it is necessary to remove the motor and wiper arm gearboxes. The procedure is as follows:

1. Disconnect the electrical wires from the wiper motor.
2. Remove the wiper arms and wiper arm pivot nuts.
3. Unbolt the motor and withdraw the motor complete with drive cables and wiper arm pivots and gearboxes.
4. Loosen the cover screws in each wiper arm gearbox and remove the rack housings.

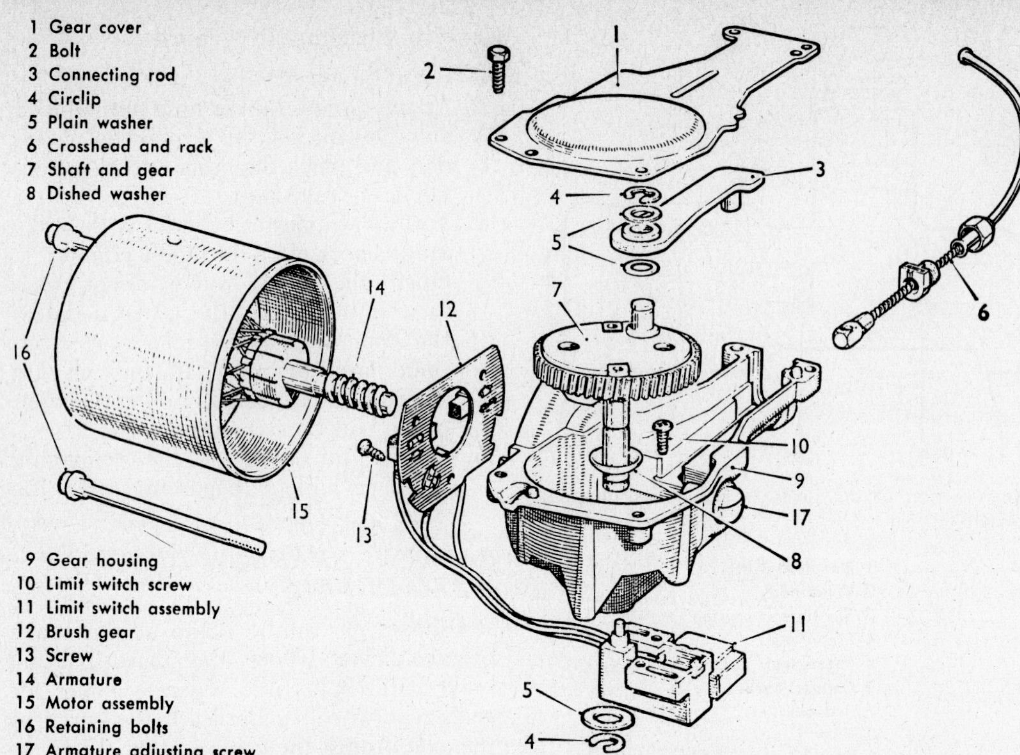

Windshield wiper motor and transmission components

5. Remove the wiper motor gearbox cover and disconnect the cross-head and rack from the motor.

Installation is in reverse order of removal. Do not kink or bind the drive cable in any way, and make sure that the wiper arm gearboxes are lined up correctly.

Competition Modification

Many competition parts are available for almost any MG model. Write to:

Special Tuning Department
Abingdon-on-Thames
Berkshire, England
also
British Leyland
Competition Department
P.O. Box 1957
Gardence, California 92040

Full details of various stages of modification are given in the following booklets, available from MG dealers:

MG Midget: Part no. C-AKD 5098, Tuning booklet.

MGB: Part no. C-AKD 4034G, Tuning booklet.

(Other models are available.)

A partial listing of some of the competition parts available:

Engine: camshaft, timing gears, bearings, hardened crankshaft, cylinder head, valves, valve gear, valve springs, pistons, lightened flywheel, large capacity oil pan, oil cooler, larger S.U. carburetors, Weber carburetors, Distributor, exhaust system

Transmission: close ratio gears, competition clutch

Drive axle: many final drive ratios, limited slip

Suspension: anti-roll bars, shock absorbers, springs, wide wheels

Brakes: competition pads and linings

PEUGEOT SECTION

Index

Introduction

Peugeot history began in 1889, when Armand Peugeot built his first automobile. During the period between 1913 and 1919, Peugeot dominated the Indianapolis racing scene. The most successful Peugeot year in racing was 1916, when the French car took Indianapolis, the American Grand Prix, and the Vanderbilt Cup. In more contemporary competition Peugeot has come in first overall in the East African Safari for 1963, '66, '67 and '68.

Peugeot was first imported into the United States in 1958. The 404 sedan became available in 1961 and complemented the Peugeot line with a somewhat higher priced model. The 404 included in its option list an automatic transmission, which had previously been unavailable on the 403. In 1964, the 404 engine was improved with five main bearings instead of the previous three. The year 1966 saw the 403 phased out. The unique worm and roller torque tube rear axle configuration of the 404 was changed to a more conventional hypoid type in 1967. The 504 model was introduced in 1968 and imported to the United States in late 1969. Its engine is similar in design to the 404, but is slightly larger at 110 cubic inches.

The 504 suspension is fully independent. Braking is handled by four wheel disc brakes. Two transmissions are available on the 504, a column shift four-speed manual and a floor selector ZF three-speed automatic. For 1971, the 504 engine has been enlarged to 120 cu. in. and power has increased from 87 to 98 horsepower.

The latest addition to the Peugeot cars is the 304 sedan and station wagon. The 304 departs from the past Peugeot practice of a front mounted engine driving the rear wheels, by having a transversely mounted engine driving the front wheels. The gearbox and differential are located directly beneath the engine block, making for a compact power unit. The 304 is stopped by combination of front discs and rear drums.

Year and Model Identification

403

404

504

304

Vehicle and Engine Serial Number Identification

Vehicle number identification

The vehicle number combines the model identification with the engine number, and is stamped on a plate above or below the manufacturer's plate located on the right fender-wall. On post 1968 models, the vehicle number may also be found on the top left of the dashboard.

Vehicle serial number location

504 engine production number (top) and engine serial number (bottom)

Engine number identification

The engine serial number of the 403 and 404 models may be found on the lower left side of the block.

The engine serial number for the 504 model is located stamped on a pad above

403 and 404 engine number location

the left motor mount. The engine production number is located above the serial number about midway between the fuel pump and the oil filler tube.

The engine serial number for the 304 model is located on a plate on the front face of the block to the left of the exhaust manifold. The engine production number is located on the rear face of the block about midway between the starter and the fuel pump.

304 engine number location

304 engine serial number location

Vehicle Identification

Year	*Model*	*Starting Serial Number*
1960	403 Sedan	2357801
1961	404 Sedan	4005100
1961	403 Sedan	2377070
1962	403 Sedan	2489000
1962	404 Sedan	4102900
1963	403 Sedan	2554224
1963	404 Sedan	4223805
1964	403 Sedan	2582323
1964	404 Sedan	4403001
1965	403 Sedan	2651489
1965	404 Sedan	5029151
1965	404 Wagon	1923370
1965	404 Convertible	4498001
1966	403 Sedan	2664234
1966	404 Sedan	5183338
1966	404 Wagon	1925732
1966	404 Convertible	4498275
1967	404 Sedan	5311001
1967	404 Wagon	1928101
1967	404 Convertible	4498801
1968	404 Sedan	8325001
1968	404 Wagon	1932385
1968	404 Convertible	0000000
1969	404 Sedan	8327278
1969	404 Sedan/Automatic	8352502
1969	404 Wagon	1934164
1969	404 Wagon/Automatic	7100888
1969	504 Sedan	1065501
1970	504 Sedan	1078611
1970	504 Sedan/Automatic	1120401
1971	504 Sedan	1180001
1971	304 Sedan	302001

Engine Identification

Number of Cylinders	Cu. In. (cc) Displacement	Type	Serial Number or Code (Model)
4	89.6 (1486)	OHV	TN3 (403)
4	98.7 (1618)	OHV	XC (404)
4	98.7 (1618)	OHV	XC5 (404)
4	98.7 (1618)	OHV	XC6 (404)
4	110 (1796)	OHV	XM (504)
4	78.5 (1288)	OHC	XL3 (304)
4	120.23 (1971)	OHV	XM (504)

General Engine Specifications

Year	Model	Cu. In. (cc) Displacement	Carburetor	Developed Horsepower SAE @rpm	Developed Torque (ft. lbs. @rpm)	Bore x Stroke (in.)	Compression Ratio	Normal Oil Pressure (psi)
1960-65	403	89.6 (1486)	Solex 32PBIC①	58@ 4900	74.5@ 2500	3.15 x 2.87	7:1	40
1961-64	404	98.7 (1618)	Solex 34PBICA2	75@ 5400	94@ 2250	3.31 x 2.87	7.4:1	40
1965-66	404	98.7 (1618)	Solex 34PBICA3	76@ 5500	96.2@ 2500	3.31 x 2.87	7.6:1	40
1967	404	98.7 (1618)	Solex 34PBICA3	80@ 5600	97.5@ 2500	3.31 x 2.87	8.3:1	40
1968-69	404	98.7 (1618)	Solex 34PBICA4②	80@ 5600	97.5@ 2500	3.31 x 2.87	8.3:1	40
1969-70	504	110 (1796)	Solex 32 & 34③ PBICA	87@ 5500	108@ 3000	3.31 x 3.19	8.35:1	45
1970-71	504	120 (1971)	Solex 32.35④ SEIEA	98@ 5500	124@ 3000	3.46 x 3.19	8.35:1	45
1971	304	78.5 (1288)	Solex 34 PBISA4	70@ 6000	73.7@ 3750	2.99 x 2.80	8.8:1	40

①—Some models used a Zenith 34 WI downdraft carburetor.
②—All carburetors from this model on include an Econostat device for mixture control at slow and fast idle.
③—Twin carburetors.
④—Two barrel carburetor with two different size throttle bores.

Tune-up Specifications

Year	Model	Spark Plugs Make Type	Spark Plugs Gap (in.)	Distributor Point Dwell (deg)	Distributor Point Gap (in.)	Ignition Timing (deg)	Cranking Compression (psi)	Valves Clearance (in.) Intake	Valves Clearance (in.) Exhaust	Valves Intake Opens (deg)	Idle Speed rpm
1960-65	TN3 (403)	AC 45F CH L8	.025	57	.016	9.5 BTDC	N.A.	.004	.010	TDC	500
1961-64	XC (404)	AC 44F AU AE6 CH L8, L10	.025	57	.020	11 BTDC	N.A.	.004	.010	N.A.	620
1965-66	XC5 (404)	AC C44XL AU AG4 CH N5	.025	57	.020	11 BTDC	N.A.	.004	.010	N.A.	620

Tune-up Specifications

Year	Model	Spark Plugs Make Type	Spark Plugs Gap (in.)	Distributor Point Dwell (deg)	Distributor Point Gap (in.)	Ignition Timing (deg)	Cranking Compression (psi)	Valves Clearance (in.) Intake	Valves Clearance (in.) Exhaust	Valves Intake Opens (deg)	Idle Speed rpm
1967	XC6 (404)	AC C44XL AU AG4 CH N5	.025	57	.020	11 BTDC	N.A.	.004	.010	N.A.	620
1968-69	XC6 (404)	AC C44XL AU AG4 CH N5	.025	57	.020	11 BTDC	N.A.	.004	.010	N.A.	750
1969-70	XM (504)	AC 44XL CH N7Y	.024	57	.016	TDC	156	.004	.010	TDC	820
1971	XL3 (304)	AC 42XL CH N7Y	.024	57	.014	5 BTDC	N.A.	.004	.010	N.A.	800
1971	XM (504)	AC 44XL CH N7Y	.024	57	.014	TDC	N.A.	.004	.010	N.A.	800
1972	All Models	See engine compartment stickers for tune-up specifications.									

CAUTION: *The advent of air pollution control standards has affected tune-up procedures. Idle speeds, engine timing, and other specified engine settings should be adhered to strictly. If discrepancies exist between the specifications above and those listed on the tune-up sticker in the engine compartment, the specifications on the tune-up sticker should be considered valid.*

Firing Order

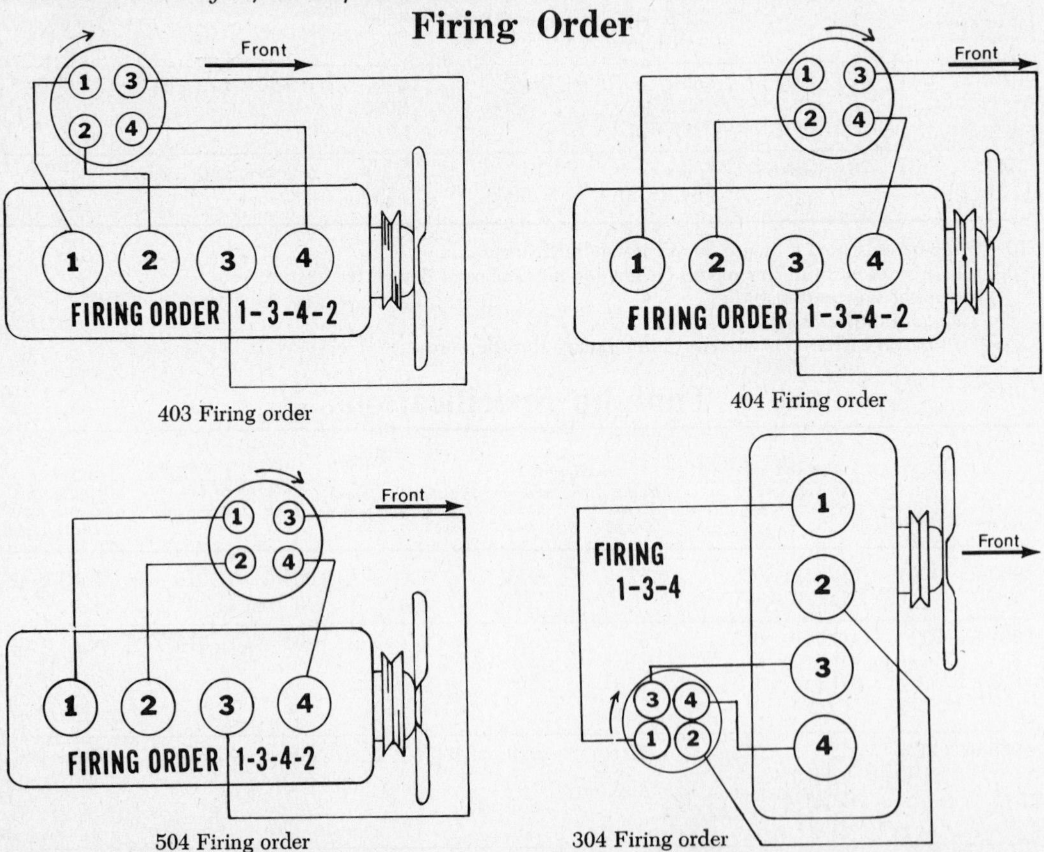

403 Firing order

404 Firing order

504 Firing order

304 Firing order

Engine Rebuilding Specifications

	Crankshaft				
	Main Bearing Journals (in.)				
	Journal Diameter				
Model	New	Minimum	Oil Clearance	Shaft End-Play	Thrust On Number
TN3	1 1.77	1.738	.002-.003	.006-.009	3
	2 2.01	1.978	.002-.003		
	3 1.97	1.938	.002-.003		
XC	1 2.34	2.308	.002-.003	.003-.008	3
	2 2.31	2.278	.002-.003		
	3 2.01	1.978	.002-.003		
XC5	1 2.34	2.308	.002-.003	.003-.008	5
	2 2.31	2.278	.002-.003		
	3 2.25	2.218	.002-.003		
	4 2.21	2.178	.002-.003		
	5 2.01	1.978	.002-.003		
XC6	1 2.34	2.308	.002-.003	.003-.008	5
	2 2.31	2.278	.002-.003		
	3 2.25	2.218	.002-.003		
	4 2.21	2.178	.002-.003		
	5 2.01	1.978	.002-.003		
XM	1 2.34	2.308	.002-.003	.003-.008	5
	2 2.31	2.278	.002-.003		
	3 2.25	2.218	.002-.003		
	4 2.21	2.178	.002-.003		
	5 2.01	1.978	.002-.003		
XL3	1 1.85	N.A.	N.A.	.003-.009	2
	2 1.85	N.A.	N.A.		
	3 1.85	N.A.	N.A.		
	4 1.85	N.A.	N.A.		
	5 1.85	N.A.	N.A.		

	Crankshaft			
	Connecting Rod Bearing Journals (in.)			
	Journal Diameter			
Model	New	Minimum	Oil Clearance	End-Play
TN3	1.77	1.73	.001-.002	.003-.006
XC	1.97	1.94	.001-.002	.003-.006
XC5	1.97	1.94	.001-.002	.003-.006
XC6	1.97	1.94	.001-.002	.003-.006
XM	1.97	1.94	.001-.002	.003-.006
XL3	1.77	N.A.	N.A.	N.A.

Engine Rebuilding Specifications

Model	Cylinder Liner (in.)	Pistons (in.) Diameter		Pistons (in.) Wrist Pin Diameter (fit)	Rings (in.) End Gap	Rings (in.) Piston Clearance
TN3 I	3.1496-3.1500①	3.1472-3.1476②	A	.8658	.016-.020	.0019-.0028
II	3.1501-3.1505	3.1477-3.1481	B	(inf)	.016-.020	.0019-.0028
III	3.1505-3.1509	3.1481-3.1485	C	.8663	.016-.020	.0019-.0028
IV	3.1509-3.1513	3.1485-3.1489	D	(free)	.016-.020	.0019-.0028
XC I	3.3070-3.3075	3.3047-3.3051	A	.8658	.016-.020	.0019-.0028
II	3.3075-3.3079	3.3051-3.3056	B	(inf)	.016-.020	.0019-.0028
III	3.3079-3.3083	3.3056-3.3060	C	.8663	.016-.020	.0019-.0028
IV	3.3083-3.3088	3.3060-3.3064	D	(free)	.016-.020	.0019-.0028
XC5 I	3.3070-3.3075	3.3047-3.3051	A	.8658	.016-.020	.0019-.0028
II	3.3075-3.3079	3.3051-3.3056	B	(inf)	.016-.020	.0019-.0028
III	3.3079-3.3083	3.3056-3.3060	C	.8663	.016-.020	.0019-.0028
IV	3.3083-3.3088	3.3060-3.3064	D	(free)	.016-.020	.0019-.0028
XC6 I	3.3070-3.3075	3.3047-3.3051	A	.8658	.016-.020	.0019-.0028
II	3.3075-3.3079	3.3051-3.3056	B	(inf)	.016-.020	.0019-.0028
III	3.3079-3.3083	3.3056-3.3060	C	.8663	.016-.020	.0019-.0028
IV	3.3083-3.3088	3.3060-3.3064	D	(free)	.016-.020	.0019-.0028

Model	Cylinder Liner (in.)	Pistons (in.) Diameter	Pistons (in.) Wrist Pin Diameter (fit)	Rings (in.) End Gap	Rings (in.) Piston Clearance
XM I (Early)	3.3070-3.3075	3.3047-3.3051 A	.8658 (inf)	.016-.020	.0019-.0028
II	3.3075-3.3079	3.3051-3.3056 B		.016-.020	.0019-.0028
III	3.3079-3.3083	3.3056-3.3060 C	.8663 (free)	.016-.020	.0019-.0028
IV	3.3083-3.3088	3.3060-3.3064 D		.016-.020	.0019-.0028
XM (Late)	3.4570-3.4575	3.4547-3.4551	.9055	.016-.020	.0019-.0028
XL3	2.960	2.940	.8071		

①—Identifying mark or marks are located on edge of cylinder liner in the form of one to four grooves.

②—Identifying letter is located on top of piston. An "A" piston corresponds to a "I" liner, a "B" piston to a "II" liner, etc.

Model	Valves: Seat Angle (deg.) Intake	Seat Angle (deg.) Exhaust	Valve Spring Pressure (lbs.) Inner	Valve Spring Pressure (lbs.) Outer	Valve Spring Free Length (in.) Inner	Valve Spring Free Length (in.) Outer	Stem Diameter (in.) Intake	Stem Diameter (in.) Exhaust	Valve Stem Clearance (in.) Intake	Valve Stem Clearance (in.) Exhaust	Valve Guide Removable
TN3	30	45	35	78	1.60	1.84	.3354	.3346	.008	.008	yes
XC	30	45	50	80	1.68	1.85	.3354	.3346	.008	.008	yes
XC5 (early)	30	45	50	80	1.68	1.85	.3354	.3346	.008	.008	yes
XC5 (late)	30	45	50	80	1.68	1.85	.3158	.3150	.008	.008	yes
XC6	30	45	50	80	1.68	1.85	.3158	.3150	.008	.008	yes
XM	30	45	50	80	1.68	1.85	.3158	.3150	.008	.008	yes
XL3	30	45	N.A.	N.A.	1.69	1.89	.3158	.3150	N.A.	N.A.	yes

Engine Tightening Specifications

Model	Cylinder Head Bolts (ft. lbs.) Initial	Cylinder Head Bolts (ft. lbs.) Final	Main Bearing Bolts (ft. lbs.)	Rod Bearing Bolts (ft. lbs.)	Crankshaft Balancer Bolt (ft. lbs.)	Flywheel to Crankshaft Bolts (ft. lbs.)	Cam Gear (ft. lbs.)
403	35	55	55	30-35	75	45	15
404	35	55	55	30-35	75	45	15
504	43.5	60.2	54	29	123	49	12.4
304	29	40	38	29	47	65①	15

①—Pinion to crankshaft attaching nut.

Tightening Sequences

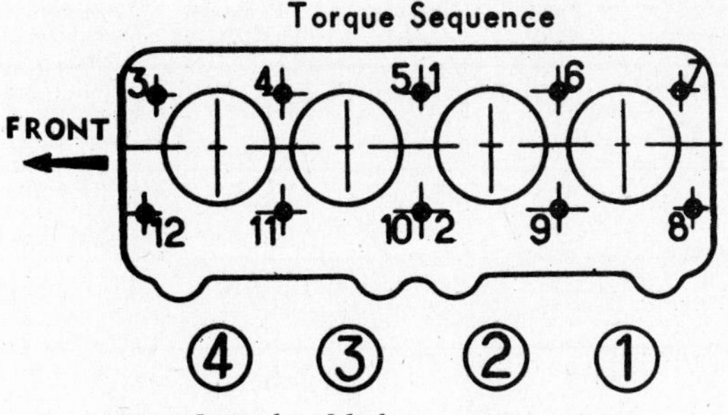

403 and 404 head bolt torque sequence

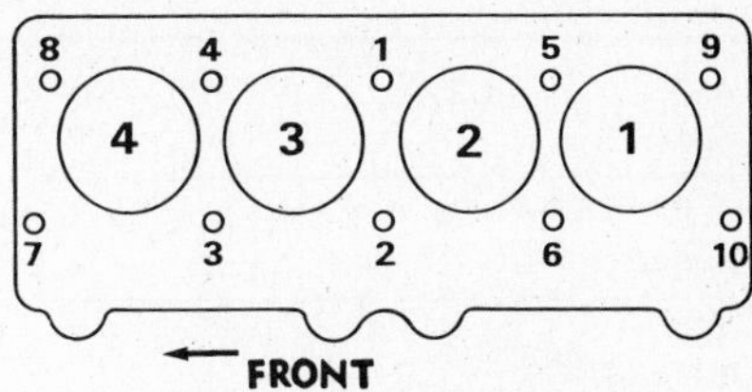

504 head bolt torque sequence

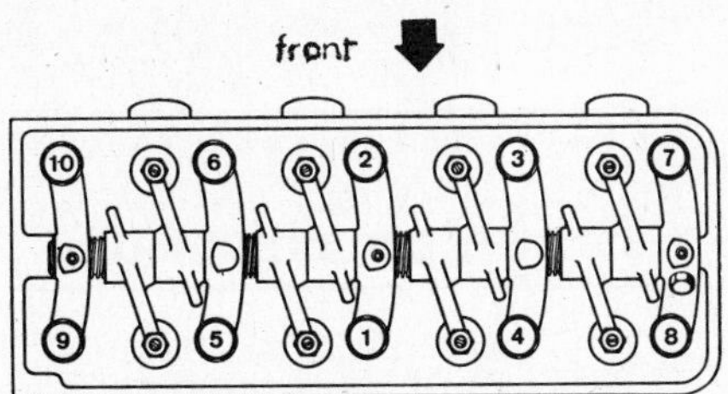

304 head bolt torque sequence

Electrical Specifications

Model	Battery Capacity (amp. hr.)	Battery Volts	Grounded Terminal	Starter Lock Test Amps	Starter Lock Test Volts	Starter Lock Test Torque (ft. lbs.)	Starter No Load Test Amps	Starter No Load Test Volts	Starter No Load Test rpm
403	58	12	Negative	260	7.2	9.7	240	11.5	7500
404	55	12	Negative	260	7.2	9.7	240	11.5	7500
504	65	12	Negative	N.A.	N.A.	N.A.	N.A.	N.A.	N.A.
304	45	12	Negative	400	N.A.	7.2	240	N.A.	N.A.

Electrical Specifications

Model	Generator Part Number	Generator Field Resistance (ohms)	Regulator Part Number	Regulator Cut-out Relay Volts to Close	Regulator Max Current (amps)
403	Ducellier 265C	N.A.	1341	N.A.	18
404	Ducellier 7210a or 7210g	6.5-7.5	8198A	N.A.	18
404	Paris-Rhone G11	N.A.	YD21	12-13.2	23

Model	Alternator Part Number	Alternator Output @1500 rpm
404	Sev/ Motorola A12/30	30 amperes
	Paris-Rhone A13Rr15	30 amperes
504	Ducellier 7529A	N.A.
304	Sev/ Motorola 5701.61	35 amperes

Capacities and Pressures

Model	Engine Crankcase (qts.)	Transmission Manual (pts.)	Transmission Automatic (pts.)	Drive Axle (pts.)	Fuel Tank (gal.)	Cooling System (qts.)	Normal Fuel Pressure (psi)	Max Coolant Pressure (psi)
403 Sedan	4.25	3.25		3.5	13.25	9.5	1.3-1.9	4
404 Sedan	4.25	3	11	3	14.5	8.5	1.3-1.9	4
404 Wagon	4.25	3	11	3	13.25	8.5	1.3-1.9	4
504 Sedan	4.25	2.5	10.9	2.5	14.8	8.5	N.A.	N.A.
304 Sedan	3.5①	—	—	—	11	5.6	N.A.	N.A.
304 Wagon	3.5①	—	—	—	9.18	5.6	N.A.	N.A.

①—Engine, transmission, and drive axle are lubricated by the one oil sump.

Brake Specifications

Model and Year	Front	Rear	Brake Cylinder Bore (in.) Master Cylinder	Wheel Cylinder (in.) Front	Wheel Cylinder (in.) Rear	Brake Drum or Disc Diameter (in.) Front	Brake Drum or Disc Diameter (in.) Rear
1960-65 403	Drum	Drum	.866	1.125	1	10	10
1961-64 404	Drum	Drum	.866	1.125	1	10	10
1965-67 404	Drum	Drum	.866	1.375	.76	11.2	11.2
1968-69 404	Disc	Drum	.75	1.36① 1.92	.81	10.9	10
1969-71 504	Disc	Disc	.75	2.126	1.693	10.75	10.75
1971 304	Disc	Drum	.75	1.89	.75	10	9

①—Three pistons on each front brake, two 1.36″ dia. and one 1.92″ dia.

Chassis and Wheel Alignment Specifications

Model	Chassis			Wheel Alignment			
	Wheelbase (in.)	Track (in.) Front	Track (in.) Rear	Caster (deg.)	Camber (deg.)	Toe-in (in.)	Kingpin Inclination (deg.)
403 Sedan	105	52.8	52	2° ± 1°	0°10′ ± 45′	.08 ± .04	10°
404 Sedan	104.3	53.3	49.3	2° ± 1°	½° ± ¾°	.062 ± .015	9°50′ ± 10′
404 Wagon	111.8	52.8	51.2	2° ± 1°	½° ± ¾°	.062 ± .015	9°50′ ± 10′
504 Sedan	108	52.8	53.5	2°40′ ± 30′	0°38′ ± 30′	.130 ± .039	8°54′ ± 30′
304 Sedan	101.9	52	50	0°30′ ± 30′	0°30′ ± 45′	.079 ± .039	9°30′ ± 30′
304 Wagon	101.9	52	50	0°30′ ± 30′	0°30′ ± 45′	.079 ± .039	9°30′ ± 30′

NOTE: *Toe-in is the only specification which may be adjusted. Any differences from specifications require a complete check of the suspension to pinpoint the cause. Always replace faulty parts and never attempt to correct deviations by bending components.*

Fuses

Year	Model	Circuit	Amperage
1960-65	403	Left to right: 1. Front and rear lights.	10
		2. Dome light and horns	18
		3. Turn signals, stop lights, and fan.	10
		4. Heater and windshield wiper motor.	10
1961-66	404	Bottom to top: 1. Front and rear lights.	10
		2. Dome light and horns.	18
		3. Turn signals, stop lights, fan.	10
		4. Heater and windshield wiper motor.	10
1967	404	1. Left park and tail lights, dash lights, and license light (wagon).	15
		2. Horns, lighter, glovebox light, dome light, and trunk light.	15
		3. Turn signals, warning lights, stop lights, and fan.	8
		4. Heater, windshield wiper motor, fuel, oil, and temperature gauges, and power brake vacuum choke.	15
		5. Right park and tail light and license light (sedan).	15
1968-69	404	1. Instrument lights, front and rear lights, trunk and dome lights.	15
		2. Horns, glovebox light, lighter, turn signals, flashers, and clock.	15
		3. Backup and stop lights, and fan.	8
		4. Oil, brake, temperature, and fuel gauge lights, and heater.	15
		5. Wiper motor.	15
1969-71	504	1. Side and fender lights, license light, instrument lights, heater light.	5
		2. Lighter, horns, interior lights, trunk light, clock, flashers, rear window heater.	10
		3. Back-up lights, stop lights, fan, electro-valve control.	10
		4. Turn signals, gauges and warning lights.	10
		5. Wiper motor, heater, and heater relay.	10
1971	304	1. Front and rear lights, license light, instrument lights, and clock light.	5
		2. Ceiling light, clock, and trunk light.	10
		3. Stop lights, fan, and back-up lights.	10
		4. Blower, wiper motor, warning lights, turn signals, and flasher.	10

Distributor Specifications①

Model	Distributor Identification	Centrifugal Advance (deg @ rpm)			Vacuum Advance		
		Start	Intermediate	Maximum	Start (in./Hg)	Maximum (in./Hg)	Maximum (deg.)
403	Ducellier M12	1000	5@1500	14@2000	6	11.8	8
403	Ducellier M3	900	5@1500	12@2050	6	11.8	5
404	Ducellier XC	500	9@1500	17@2100	4.5	16.5	8.5
504	Ducellier M48	500	9@1500	14@2500	5	11.8	5
304	Ducellier M43	500	8@1200	13@2650	4	8.6	6

①—Specifications are given in distributor degrees @ distributor rpm. To obtain crankshaft values, multiply each specification (degrees and rpm) by 2.

Light Bulb Specifications

Model	Usage	Type	Wattage
403-404	Headlights	12 Volt	
	Front parking and turn signals	1073	24
	Rear turn signals	1073	24
	Stop lights	1073	24
	Tail lights	89	6
	Trunk light	67	3
	Instrument lights	1816	3
	License light (1967 up)	89	6
504	Headlights	12 Volt	
	Front and rear side lights	67	3
	Front and rear turn signals, stop and back-up lights	1073	24
	License light, trunk light, and glovebox light	67	3
	Interior lights		7
	Warning lights and heater		7
	Instrument lights and flasher		4

Model	Usage	Type	Wattage
304	Headlights	12 Volt	40/45
	Front and rear turn signals and stop lights		21
	Front and rear side lights, license light, and trunk light		5
	Instrument lights and flasher		3
	Dome light		7
	Clock light	51	1.5

Carburetor Specifications

Carburetor	Throttle Bore (mm)	Main Jet	Air Metering Jet	Idle Jet	Needle Valve	Float Weight (gr)
Zenith 34WI	34	120	N.A.	N.A.	N.A.	12
Solex 32PBIC	32	120	170	45	1.5	5.7
Solex 32PBICA	32	130	160/170	55/50	1.7	5.7
Solex 34PBICA3/4	34	135/137.5	160	45	1.7	5.7
Solex 32 & 34						
32PBICA.8	32	120	195	55	1.5	5.7
34PBICA.8	34	130	200	50	1.5	5.7
Solex 34PBISA4	34	132.5	150	55	1.5	5.7

Wiring Diagrams

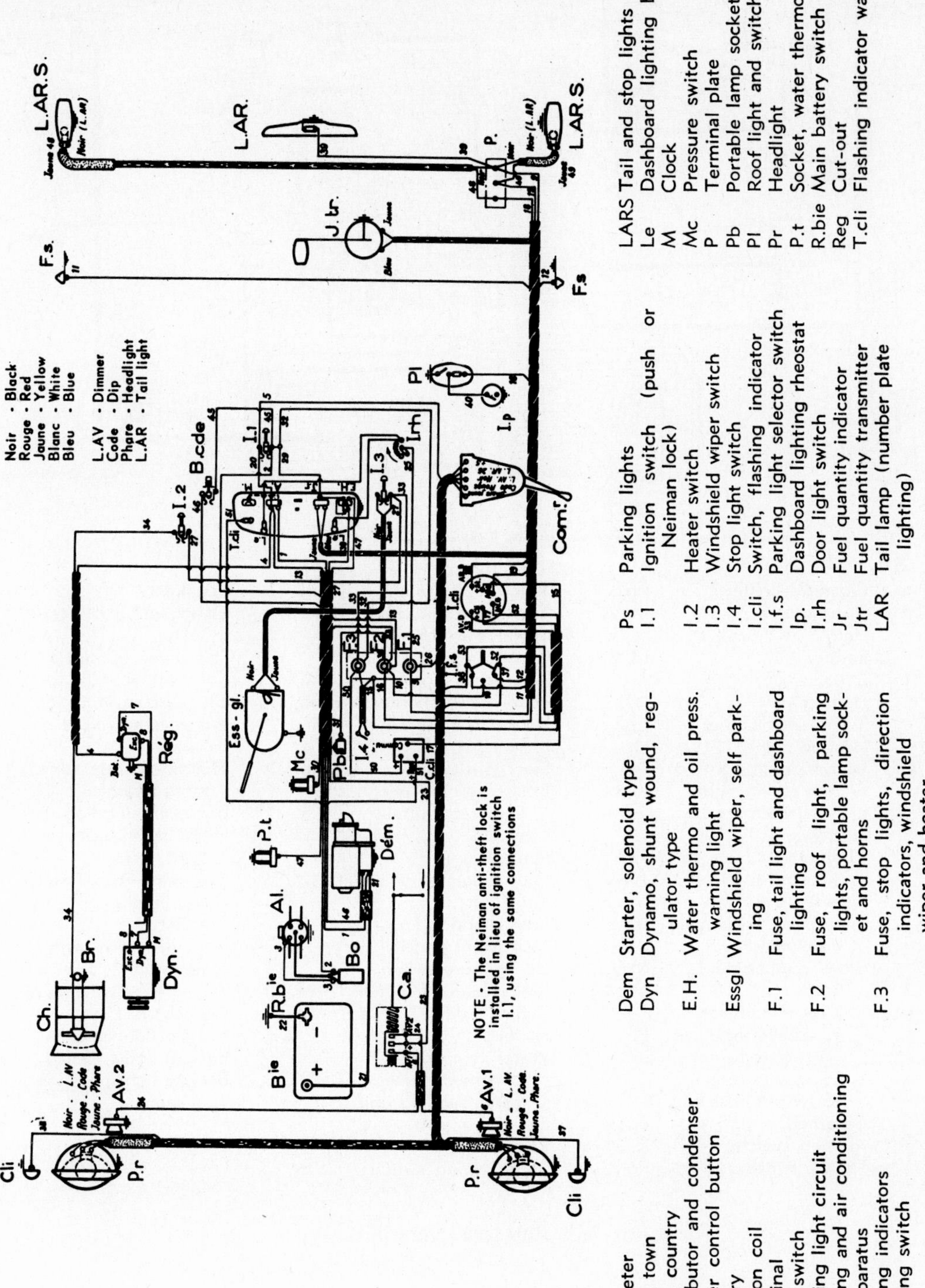

A	Ammeter	Dem	Starter, solenoid type
AV1	Horn, town	Dyn	Dynamo, shunt wound, regulator type
AV2	Horn, country	E.H.	Water thermo and oil press. warning light
Al	Distributor and condenser	Essgl	Windshield wiper, self parking
Bcde	Starter control button	F.1	Fuse, tail light and dashboard lighting
Bie	Battery	F.2	Fuse, roof light, parking lights, portable lamp socket and horns
Bo	Ignition coil	F.3	Fuse, stop lights, direction indicators, windshield wiper and heater
Br	Terminal		
Ca	Horn switch		
C.cli.	Flashing light circuit		
Ch	Heating and air conditioning apparatus		
Cli.	Flashing indicators		
Com	Lighting switch		

Ps	Parking lights	LARS	Tail and stop lights
I.1	Ignition switch (push or Neiman lock)	Le	Dashboard lighting bulb
I.2	Heater switch	M	Clock
I.3	Windshield wiper switch	Mc	Pressure switch
I.4	Stop light switch	P	Terminal plate
I.cli	Switch, flashing indicator	Pb	Portable lamp socket
I.f.s	Parking light selector switch	Pl	Roof light and switch
Ip.	Dashboard lighting rheostat	Pr	Headlight
I.rh	Door light switch	P.t	Socket, water thermo
Jr	Fuel quantity indicator	R.bie	Main battery switch
Jtr	Fuel quantity transmitter	Reg	Cut-out
LAR	Tail lamp (number plate lighting)	T.cli	Flashing indicator warning

Wiring diagram for 403.

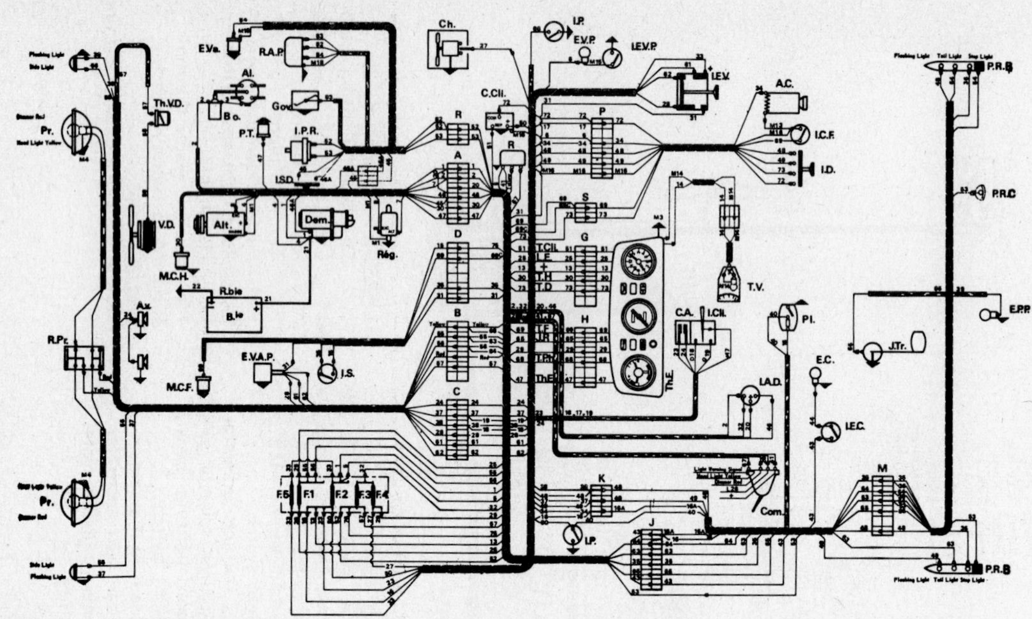

------ Spécial équipement for 404 fitted with automatic transmission ZF

A.C.	Cigarette lighter
AL	Distributor
AV.	Horn
Bie	Battery
Bo.	Coil
C.A.	Horn control
C.Cli.	Turn signal flasher
Ch.	Heating
Cli.AR	Rear flashing light
Cli.AV.	Front flashing light
Com.	Lighting switch
Dem.	Starter
Alt.	Alternator
E.C.	Trunk light
E.pp	License plate light
E.V.A.P.	Two-speed windshield wiper motor
E.V.P.	Glove compartment, light
F1	15 ampere fuse
F2	15 ampere fuse
F3	8 ampere fuse
F4	15 ampere fuse
F5	15 ampere fuse
Gov.	Governor
I.A.D.	Ignition switch
I.Cli.	Flasher switch
I.e.c.	Trunk light switch
I.E.V.	Two-speed windshield wiper switch
I.E.v.p.	Glove compartment light switch
I.d.	Four-way flasher switch
I.p.r.	Door (courtesy light) switch
I.s.	Stop light switch
I.c.f.	Brake warning pilot light test button switch
J.r.	Fuel gauge
J.Tr.	Fuel gauge sending unit
L.A.R.	Tail light
L.AV.	Front parking light
L.e.	Instrument panel light
M.ch.	Oil pressure switch
M.c.f.	Brake warning switch
Pl.	Ceiling (dome) light
Pr.	Headlights
Pt.	Water temperature (thermometer) gauge sending unit
E.v.a.	Electro-vacuum valve
R.	Relay
Rbie.	Battery wing switch
Reg.	Regulator
RA.p.	Antipollution device relay
S.	Stop light terminals
T.Cli.	Turn signal indicator
T.h.	Oil pressure indicator
Th.e.	Water temperature gauge
Th.V.D.	Thermo-contact controlled fan
T.F.	Brake warning light
T.Ph.	High beam indicator light
T.D.	Four-way flasher warning light
V.D.	Fan clutch
+ AC	+ live with ignition on
+ P	+ live always
A.toR.	Connectors
I.P.R.	Backup light switch
P.R.B.	Backup lights, Sedan
P.R.C.	Backup lights, Station Wagon

Wiring diagram for 404 sedan and station wagon.

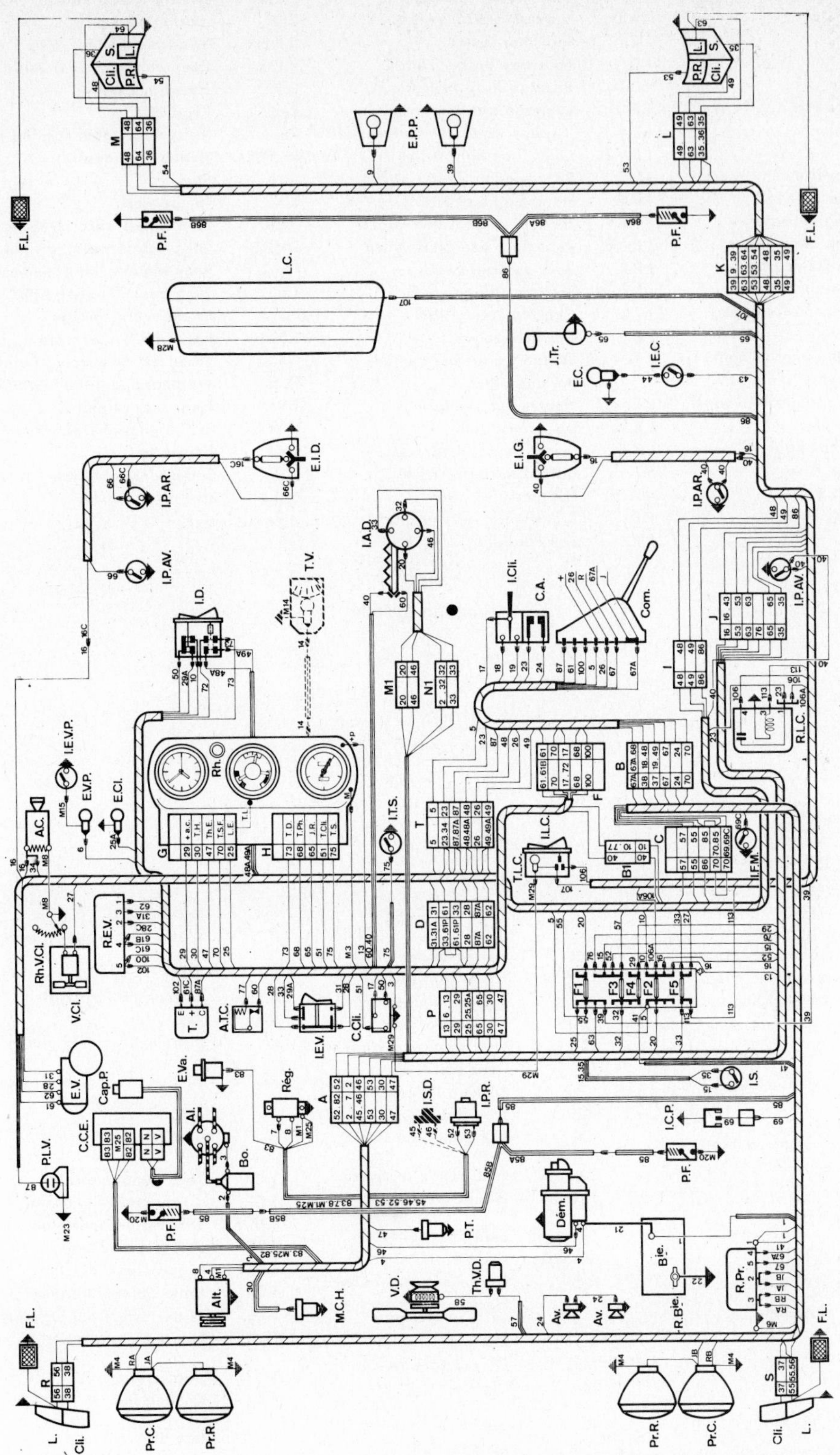

Wiring diagram for 504

A to T Connectors
A.C. Cigarette lighter
Al. Distributor with condenser
Alt. Alternator
A.T.C. Buzzer
Av. Horns
Bie. Battery
Bo. Ignition coil
Cap.P. Governor
C.A. Horn
C.C.E. Electrovalve control box
C.Cli. Flasher unit
Cli. Flashing indicator
Com. Lighting commutator
Dem. Starter (solenoid type)
E.C. Luggage boot light
E.Cl. Heater control lighting
E.I.D. Right-hand interior light
E.I.G. Left-hand interior light
E.P.P. Registration plate light
E.V. 2 speed windscreen wiper
E.Va Electrovalve
E.V.P. Glove box light
F.1. 5 amp. Fuse
F.2. 10 amp. Fuse
F.3. 10 amp. Fuse
F.4. 10 amp. Fuse
F.5. 10 amp. Fuse
F.L. Side marker lights
I.A.D. Ignition/starter switch
I.Cli. Indicator switch
I.D. Four-way flasher switch
I.C.P. Pressure drop indicator
I.E.C. Luggage trunk light switch
I.E.V. 2 speed windscreen wiper switch
I.E.V.P. Glove box light switch
I.L.C. Rear window heater switch
I.F.M. Hand brake switch
I.P.AV. Front door operated switch
I.P.AR. Rear door operated switch
I.P.R. Back-up light switch
I.S.D. Starting safety switch
I.T.S. Choke warning light
J.R. Gauge receiver
J.Tr. Gauge transmitter
L. Parking lights
L.C. Heater rear window
L.E. Dashboard lights
L.V.E. Electric windshield washer
M. Instrument panel earth
M.C.H. Oil pressure switch
P.F. Brake wear warning pad
P.R. Reverse light
Pr. Headlamp
P.T. Temperature gauge transmitter
R.Bie. Battery master switch
R.D. Starter relay
R.F.E.V. Windshield wiper relay
R.L.C. Rear window heater relay
R.Pr. Headlamp relay
Reg. Regulator
Rh. Instrument panel lighting rheostat
Rh.V.C. Heater fan rheostat
S. Stop
T. Temporisor
T.Cli. Turn signal warning light
T.H. Oil pressure warning light
T.L.C. Rear window heater indicator
T.ph. High beam warning light
T.S. Choke warning light
T.S.D. Four-way flasher warning light
T.S.F. Brake safety warning light
Th.E Water temperature warning light
T.V. Gear shift pattern
Th.V.D. Self-disengaging fan thermo-switch
V.Cl. Heater fan
V.D. Self-disengaging fan
+a.c. Live after contact
+P. Live

Wiring diagram for 504

A to Z Connectors
A.C. Cigarette lighter
Al Distributor with condensor
Alt. Alternator
A.T.C. Ignition key warning buzzer
Av. Horns
Bie Battery
Bo. Ignition coil
Cap. P. Sensing head
C.C.E. Electrovalve control box
C.Cli. Flasher unit
Cli. Flasher
Com. Light switch
Dem. Starter (solenoid)
E.C. Trunk light
E.P.P. License plate light
E.V. Windshield wiper
E.Va. Electrovalve
F.1-F.4 Fuses
F.L. Side marker lights
I.A.D. Antitheft lock-ignition starter switch
I.Cli. Turn signal switch
I.C.P. Pressure drop indicator
I.D. 4 way flasher switch
I.E.C. Trunk light switch
I.E.V. 2 speed windshield wiper
I.F.M. Handbrake switch
I.L.R.Ch. Rear window heater switch
I.P. Door switch
I.P.R. Back-up light switch
I.S. Stop light switch
I.V. Tail gate light switch
J.R. Fuel gauge receiver
J. Tr. Gauge transmitter
L. Side light
L.A.R.Ch. Heated rear window
L.E. Instrument panel light
L.V.E. Electric windscreen washer
M. Ground
M.C.H. Oil pressure switch
Mo. Clock
Pl. Ceiling light and switch
P.R. Back-up light
P.R. Headlamps
P.T. Water temperature gauge pick up
R. Relay
R.Bie Battery master switch
Reg. Regulator
Rh. Instrument panel lighting control
RhV.Cl. Heater fan control switch
R.Ph. Headlamps relay
S. Stop lights
T.Cli. Turn signal indicator
T.D. 4 way flasher indicator
T.H. Oil pressure indicator
T.L. Side light indicator
T.Ph. High beam indicator
T.S.F. Brake safety indicator
Th.E. Water temperature gauge
Th.V.D. Fan thermostat switch
V.Cl. Heater fan
V.D. Cooling fan
+ a.c. Live after contact.

Wiring diagram for 304 sedan and station wagon—NOTE: Dotted line indicates use with station wagon models.

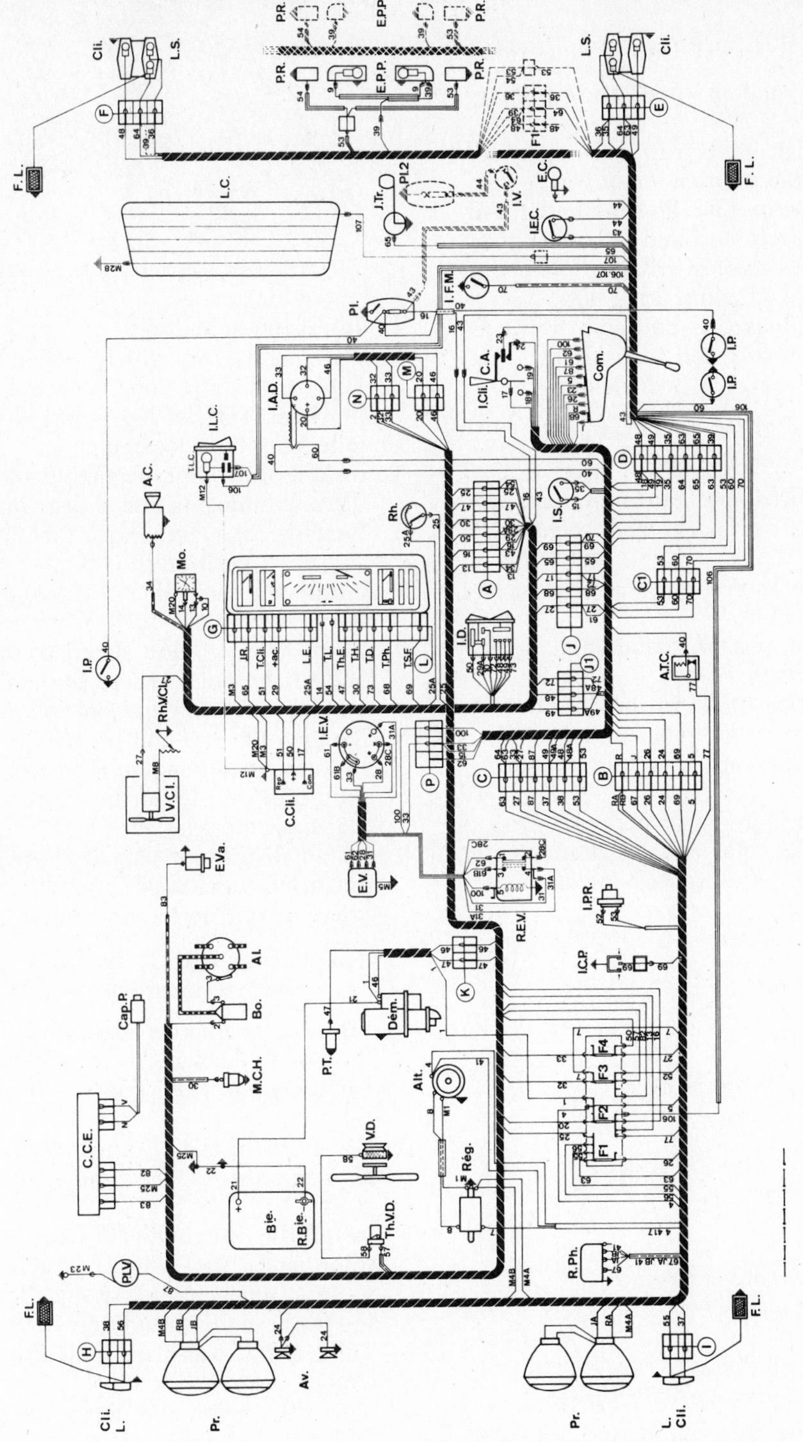

Wiring diagram for 304 sedan and station wagon—NOTE: Dotted line indicates use with station wagon models.

Engine Electrical

Distributor

Distributor Removal and Installation

1. Remove vacuum line and primary wire.
2. Remove distributor cap with wires still installed and position out of way.
3. Loosen nut on the adjusting collar and pull distributor up and out of engine.
4. To replace, insert distributor into collar and engage oil pump drive slot.
5. Vacuum advance should point towards the rear on 403 and towards the carburetor on 404, 504, and 304 models.

Breaker Points—Removal and Replacement

1. Remove distributor cap and rotor.
2. Disconnect primary and condenser wires.
3. Remove lockscrew and eccentric screw.
4. Remove points.
5. To replace, position points and lightly tighten screws.
6. Turn engine over to bring rubbing block of points on tip of cam lobe.
7. Adjust point gap to proper specifications.
8. Connect primary and condenser wires.
9. Replace the rotor and distributor cap.
10. Start engine and check dwell angle with a meter.

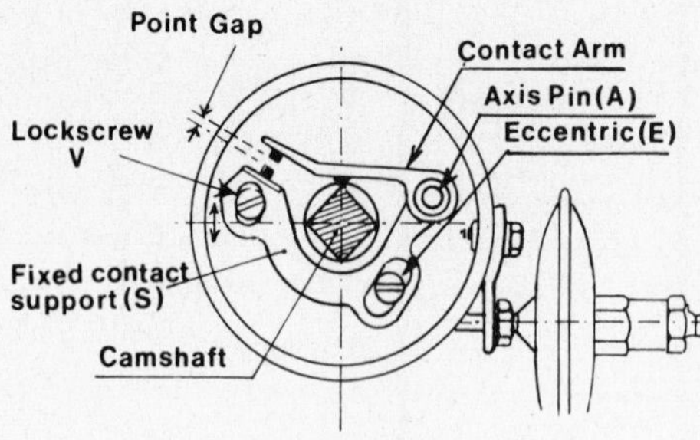

Distributor points

Distributor Installation—With engine disturbed 403 and 404

These models have no timing mark. A hole in the right side of the clutch housing allows a 5/16″ rod (Phillips screw-driver will suffice) to be inserted for TDC determination.

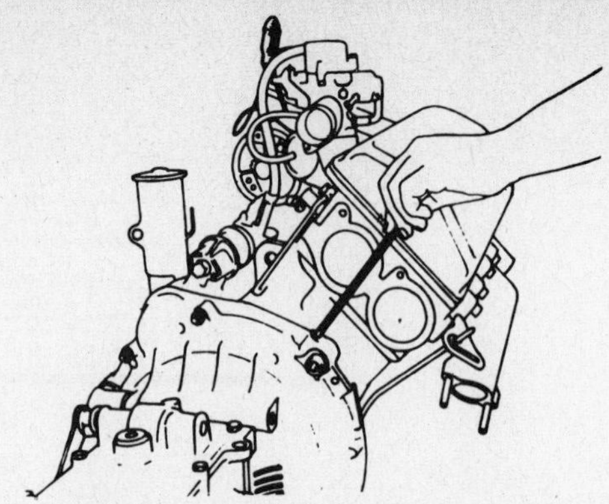

TDC determination for 403 and 404

1. Insert rod in housing.
2. Turn engine over slowly by hand.
3. When rod drops into slot machined in flywheel, TDC of No. 1 and No. 4 cylinders has been located.
4. Install distributor, engaging oil pump drive with dog on end of distributor.
5. Replace rotor and check that it points to correct position in cap.
6. Install one lead of a test lamp to the primary wire and one lead to ground.
7. Turn the distributor slowly to the right and at the point where the lamp goes on, tighten the adjustment collar.
8. Remove the rod and check the setting by turning the engine. The rod should drop into the slot at the exact moment that the lamp goes on.
9. Install distributor cap and wires. Any fine adjustment may be made with the knurled knob on the distributor base.

Distributor Installation—With engine disturbed 504 and 304

1. Turn the engine over by hand to align the timing mark on the crankshaft pulley with the TDC line on the timing tab.
2. Determine if the piston is at TDC end of compression, beginning of firing stroke.
3. Install the distributor, turning it so the rotor is in No. 1 firing position. The vacuum advance unit should be pointing towards the carburetor.
4. Tighten the collar nut and install the cap.
5. Start the engine and check the timing with a timing light.

Ignition Timing—403 and 404

1. Set point gap or dwell to correct specification.

2. Proceed as in distributor installation section.

IGNITION TIMING—504 AND 304

1. Set point gap or dwell to the correct specification.
2. Connect a timing light to No. 1 spark plug and spark plug wire.
3. Disconnect and plug the vacuum advance unit.
4. Mark the scribed line on the crankshaft pulley with chalk for visibility.
5. Start the engine and observe the timing mark on the pulley.
6. Loosen the locknut on the distributor and turn the distributor as necessary to obtain the correct timing.

Timing mark and plate on 504

Generator and Regulator—403 and 404

These models are equipped with either Paris-Rhone or Ducellier DC generators and regulators. Specifications being scarce for these units, it is recommended that any extensive service be performed by a dealer. The regulator is a sealed unit, in case of malfunction it should be replaced.

Alternator and AC Regulator—404, 504, and 304

404 models beginning with numbers 5311001, 8251301, and 1928101, and all 504 and 304 models are equipped with alternators. As with the DC generator, any major service is best left to the dealer.

CAUTION: *Never disconnect the alternator/battery lead when the engine is running. When charging the battery, disconnect both positive and negative leads. Never ground the regulator/alternator wire.*

Battery terminal protectors and master switch

Battery

All Peugeots are equipped with a 12 volt negative ground battery. A battery master switch, used as a main cut-out, is located on the negative terminal. Loosening the switch two full turns disconnects the battery. The battery is removed by unscrewing the protective terminals and loosening the battery clamp. On 403 and 404 models, periodically place one or two drops of SAE 50 oil in the terminal protectors. On 504 and 304 models, smear grease on the lower half of the terminal before installing the protectors.

Starter Removal and Installation

1. Disconnect the battery.
2. Disconnect wires from terminals at starter.
3. Remove bolts in clutch housing and engine block.
4. Lift out starter.
5. Reverse procedure to install.

Fuel System

Fuel Pump

Fuel pumps on 403, 404 and 504 models are actuated directly by an eccentric on the camshaft. The 304 fuel pump is driven by a pushrod off the oil pump drive. Fuel pumps are of the mechanical AC type. To remove a fuel pump, disconnect fuel lines, two bolts, and remove the pump. The stroke can be adjusted by adding or removing gaskets at the flange. 403 and 404 fuel pumps may be disassembled for repairs. 504 and 304 fuel pumps are sealed. To reinstall, fit the gasket(s), insert the lever (engaging pushrod on 304), tighten bolts, and reconnect fuel lines.

Fuel Filter

The fuel filter is located in the carburetor, behind or under the fuel intake fitting. To replace, remove the bolt or fitting and insert new filter.

Carburetor Removal

1. Remove air cleaner, linkage, vacuum line, and water hoses.
2. Remove carburetor retaining nuts and remove carburetor.
3. Reverse procedure to install.

Carburetor Overhaul

The exploded drawing shown is for the 32 PBICA Solex carburetor. Different model Solex carburetors vary only in minor details. Disassembly proceeds as follows:

1. Remove float chamber cover by removing three screws.
2. Remove float from cover by releasing needle valve lock clip and sliding float arm off pivot pin.
3. Remove needle valve assembly from cover.
4. Remove pump injector tube with a screwdriver.
5. Remove correction jet and main vent tube.
6. Remove enricher jet and idle jet.
7. Remove main metering jet carrier and jet.
8. Remove pump jet aand pump ball check valve.
9. Remove enricher air jet and volume control screw.
10. Remove choke control cover (choke lever is identified by No. 3).
11. Remove accelerator pump housing with a screwdriver.
12. Remove control rod cotter pin.
13. Immerse metal parts in carburetor solvent.
14. Using a rebuilding kit, reassemble carburetor with new gaskets and parts in a reverse order.

Carburetor Adjustment

Float level is adjusted by installing a thicker or thinner gasket under the needle valve. Thin gaskets raise the fuel level; thick gaskets lower it. A further adjustment is possible by bending the float arm. With the engine idling and the car level, the needle valve should be partially closed and near height indicated in specifications. After shutting the engine off, the needle valve should close completely.

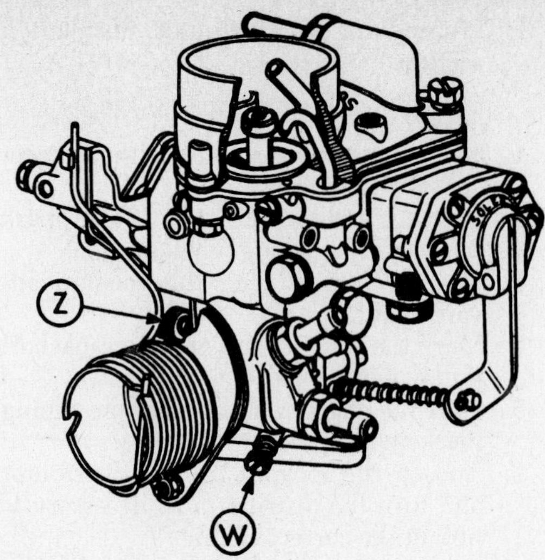

Z Throttle stop screw
W Volume control screw

Solex 32 PBICA idle adjustments.

Idle adjustment is made with the engine at operating temperature and fan engaged. Slightly tighten throttle stop screw to increase the speed of the engine. Loosen volume control screw until engine begins to idle roughly. Then tighten screw slowly until engine idles smoothly. Slowly loosen stop screw to adjust to specification. Never completely tighten volume control screw.

Idle adjustment on the Solex 32 & 34 compound carburetor used on early 504 models is as follows:

1. Normalize engine and check that fan is engaged. Disconnect the regulator feed to the alternator.
2. Set normal idle by turning screw Z to obtain 860 rpm and adjust screw W for maximum idle speed.
3. Using screw Z bring idle speed back up to 860 rpm, and use W to again find maximum idle speed.
4. Repeat above until the maximum speed obtainable using the mixture screw is 860 rpm, then screw in W to bring the idling speed up to 800 rpm.
5. Fast idle is adjusted by disconnecting the 3 pin connector from the electronic control box to obtain fast idle.
6. Remove the domed nut and slacken the locknut.
7. Adjust the stop screw to obtain 1500 rpm (using a 3mm (3/25″) Allen wrench).
8. Tighten the locknut No. 2 and refit the

1 Body with throttle spindle, butterfly, screws and dust proof rings
2 Throttle butterfly
3 Throttle spindle
4 Throttle butterfly, fixing screw
5 Throttle spindle abutment plate only
8 Slow running adjustment screw
9 Slow running adjustment screw spring
13 Throttle spindle washer (for throttle butterfly)
15 Volume control screw
9 Volume control screw spring
23 Starter valve complete
36 Starter spindle end nut
36 Throttle spindle end nut
43 Starter air jet
45 Starter cover
46 Starter cover fixing screw
47 Starter lever with cable swivel
50 Starter cable swivel screw
50a. Starter cable locking screw
62 Float
65 Float chamber gasket
70 Main metering jet
71 Main jet carrier
72 Main jet carrier washer
73 Correction jet
74 Idle jet
75 Starter petrol jet
76 Gp, Gs and pump inlet valve washer
86 Main vent tube
101 Choke tube
102 Choke tube fixing screw
103 Float chamber cover
110 Float toggle spindle
115 Needle valve washer
116 Needle valve complete with washer
126 Float chamber assembly screw
127 Spring washer for same
136 Flange washer
158 Pump intermediate actuating lever
160 Pump control rod
165 Accelerating pump
166 Pump assembly fixing screw
167 Pump body gasket
217 Filter
336 Pump control rod adjustment nut
337 Adjustment nut counternut
338 Pump injector assembly
339 Pump injector support fixing screw
340 Pump injector support gasket
342 Pump control rod spring
343 Control rod retaining washer
349 Pump inlet valve
350 Pump jet
353 Pump filter gauze
354 Dust seal
395 Throttle control
396 Throttle control return spring
397 Cable fixing screw for throttle control
398 Nut for cable fixing screw
399 Spring washer for cable fixing screw
459 Fuel inlet
496 Washer fuel inlet

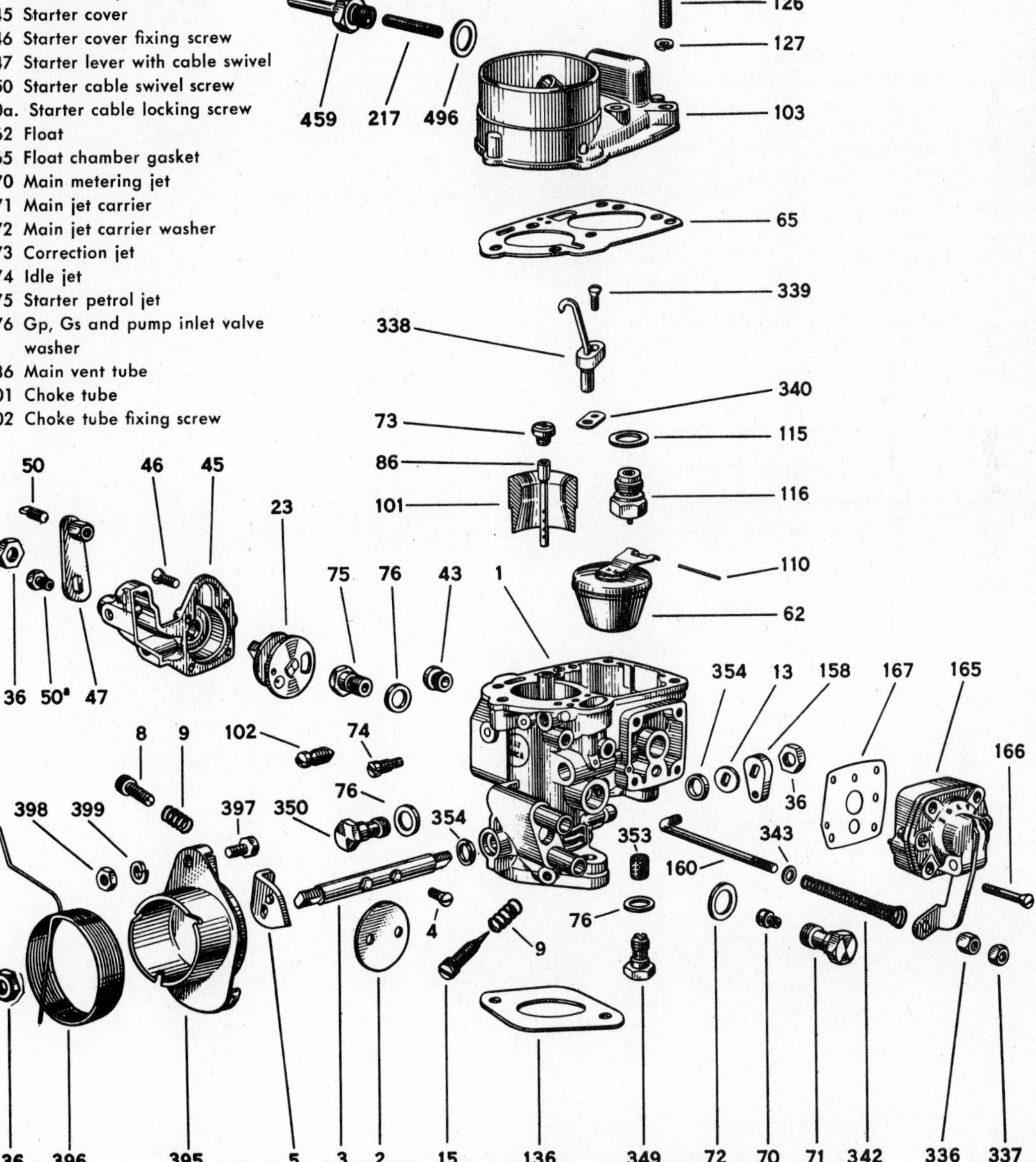

Solex 32 PBICA carburetor

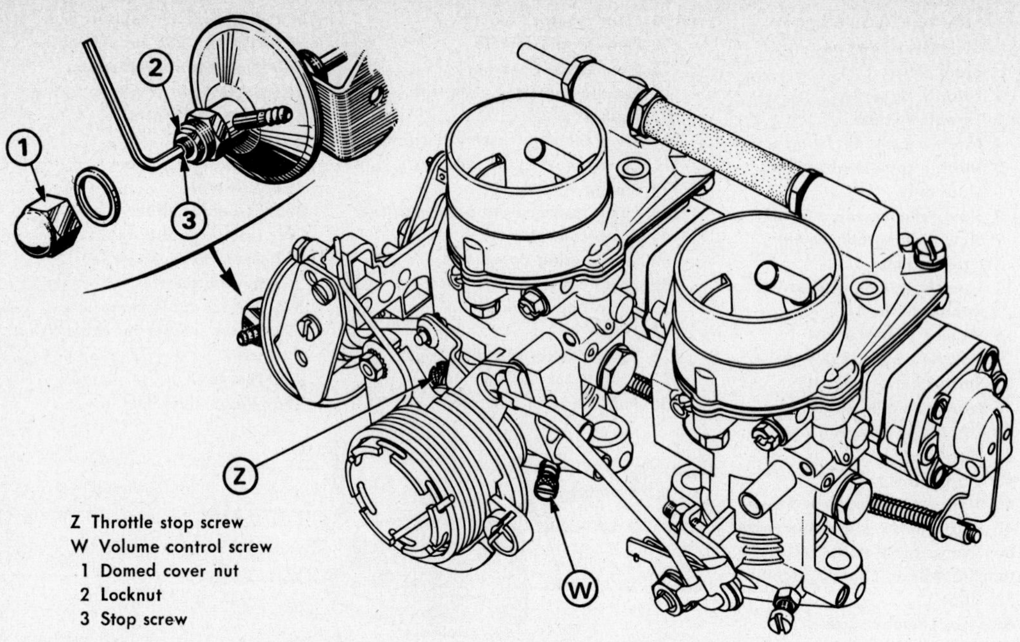

Solex 32 and 34 compound carburetor adjustments

3 pin connector. After a few moments the idle should drop to 800 rpm.

9. Connect the regulator lead.

NOTE: Never alter setting of the screw under the mixture screw. No adjustment should be made on the second carburetor.

Exhaust System

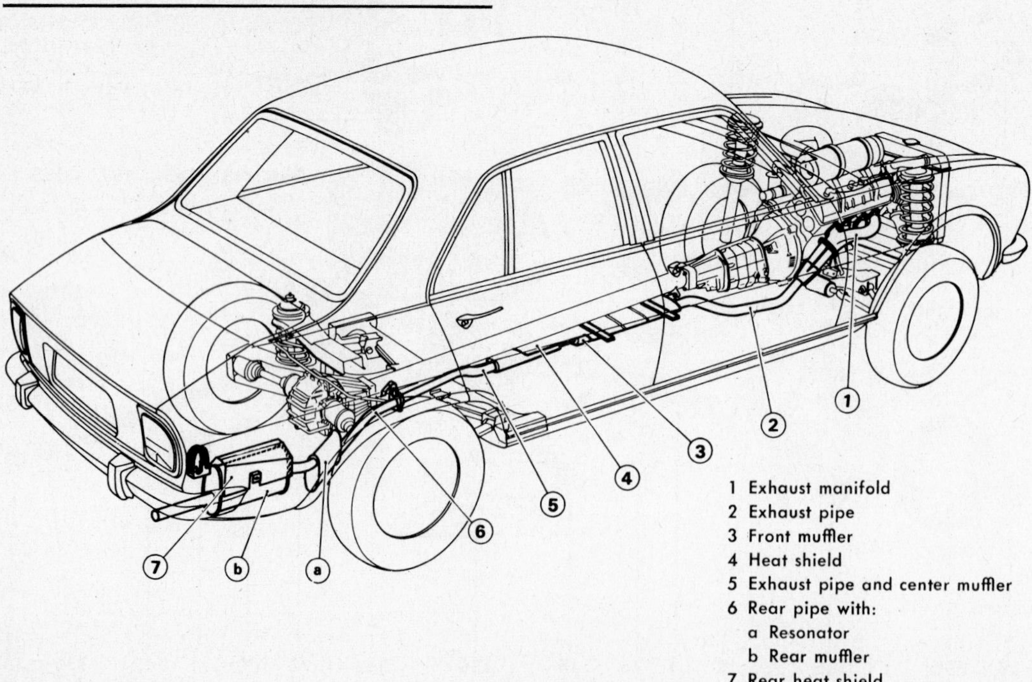

504 exhaust system

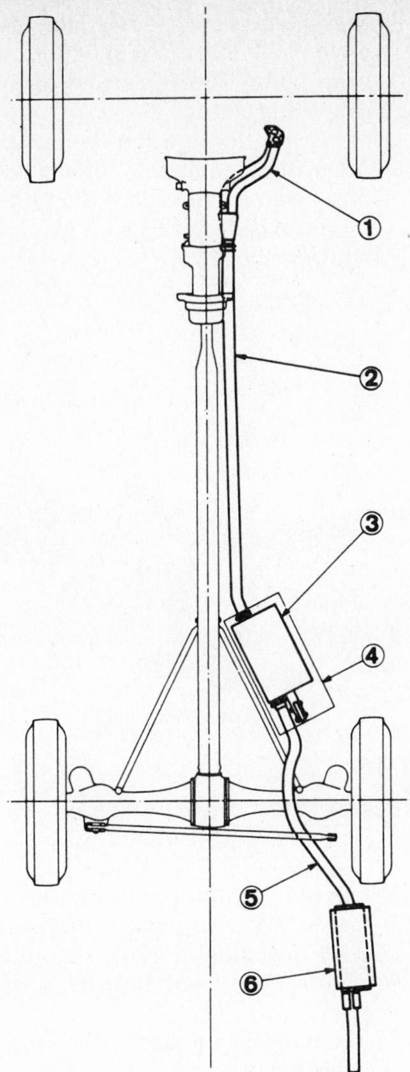

Exhaust system of the 404 XC6 engine.

Cooling System

Radiator

403 and 404 models have a drain control rod on the engine block, which must be opened before the cooling system can be drained. Cooling systems are then drained by opening the petcock at the bottom of the radiator (heater petcock on 403 also). The heater controls in all models must be on maximum heat to drain the complete system. To remove the radiator, drain the system, remove hoses, and remove the support bolts.

Water Pump

Removal and Installation—403

1. Drain system and remove hoses.
2. Withdraw pump pulley after removing nut and washer.
3. Remove key. Remove castellated nut together with felt seal and washer.
4. Drive pin out towards the rear, using a mallet if necessary.
5. Drive grooved pin out of pump turbine, remove turbine and withdraw seal. Remove front bearing by driving pin forward using an aluminum drift.
6. Remove spacer bushing and front bearing retaining ring and rear bearing.
7. Remove oil nipple.
8. Drive water pump shaft out towards the front. The washer and felt seal will come out also.
9. To install, put bearing retaining ring in pump shaft groove.
10. Install rear felt seal (coat with grease). Install backing washer inside pump body.
11. Engage shaft by its smooth end.
12. Install seal ring, turbine, and grooved pin at end of shaft.
13. Peen metal slightly around edge of pin hole.
14. Install rear bushing, spacer bushing, front bearing retaining ring, front bearing, front backing washer, and seal (coated with grease).
15. Install castellated nut and pulley. Tighten nut to 15-20 ft. lbs.
16. Install oil nipple.

Removal—404

1. Drain cooling system.
2. Remove hoses and fan belt.
3. Disconnect contact wire No. 57 on the brush holder.
4. Remove five mounting screws and remove water pump.

Removal—504

1. Drain radiator.
2. Remove hoses, fan belt, and then radiator.
3. Disconnect water pump heater joint.
4. Disconnect self-disengaging fan brush holder.
5. Remove four attaching bolts and remove pump.

Installation—404 and 504

1. Clean mating surfaces of pump and cylinder head.
2. Apply Permatex No. 2 on both sides of new gasket and install pump in reverse order of removal.
3. Adjust fan belt, install radiator (504), connect hoses, and refill cooling system.

Remove and Install—304

1. Drain cooling system.
2. Remove water pump hose and fan belt.
3. Remove four retaining bolts and remove water pump.
4. When installing, place a new O-ring in the block and tighten retaining bolts.
5. Install hose.
6. When installing fan belt, follow procedure outlined below and never fit the belt by passing it over the pulleys.
7. Fit the belt on crankshaft and water pump pulleys, taking care not to twist it more than 90°.
8. Engage the tensioner pulley on the fan belt and bolt tensioner to block.
9. Making use of the adjuster, tighten the fan belt until the distance between the two reference marks increases from 3.94″ to 4.02″. Tighten the tensioner pivot nut to 29 ft. lbs. and the support bolts to 13 ft. lbs.
10. Tighten the tensioner pulley nut.

Water Pump Overhaul—404 and 504

1. Overhaul requires a small gear puller, vise, improvised pulley holders, and the use of a drill press.

Center nut removal

2. Pulley holders may be fashioned from wood to look like those in figure.
3. Clamp pump in vise as shown and remove center nut.
4. Hold the pulley and tap the end of the shaft with a mallet to disengage the pump body; do not place the pulley on the bronze collector ring.
5. Withdraw the key.

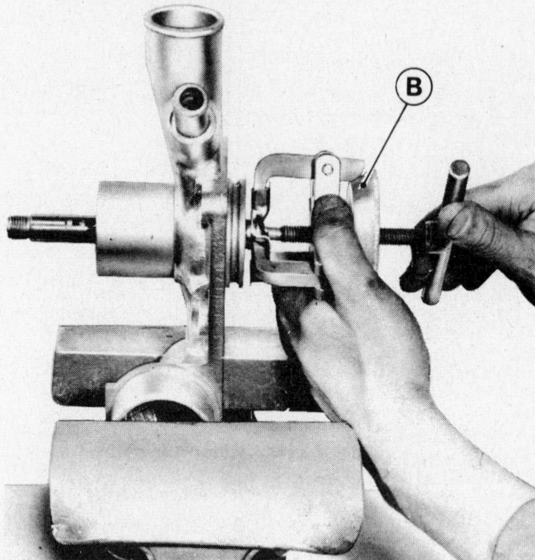

Impeller removal

6. While holding the pump in a vise, use the gear puller to remove the impeller and seal assembly.
7. Withdraw the front bearing retaining clip.
8. Place pump in boiling water for about one minute.
9. Remove the shaft and its bearings on a press.
10. If necessary, withdraw the front and rear bearings.
11. Check the condition of the bearings, seal, and bearing surfaces in the pump body.
12. Check the electromagnet with an ammeter and a 12 volt battery. Connect one lead to the collector ring and one to the pulley.
13. This check can also be made with an ohmmeter which should indicate 20 ohms. Normal reading is .8 ohms; if the reading is less than .8 ohms, the winding is broken and if more than .8 ohms, the winding is grounded.
14. To assemble, coat bearings with a multipurpose grease and install them on shaft with their open sides facing each other.

15. Place the pump body in boiling water, then install the shaft with a press or a drift.

CAUTION: *Be careful not to cock the shaft in the housing while starting to seat the bearings.*

16. Position the bearing snap-ring.
17. Lubricate the rear end of the shaft and install a new seal.
18. Engage the impeller into the driving fingers of the seal and over the splines on the shaft.
19. Press the impeller on gently with a bushing (I.D. .50″, O.D. .875″).
20. Check and reset, if necessary, the position of the impeller. The impeller should rotate without runout, with a maximum clearance of .040″ between impeller blades and pump collar.
21. At the front of the shaft, install the key, electromagnet pulley, and fan. Torque center nut to 25 ft. lbs. and lock it.
22. Check gap between fan and magnet. Clearance at all points around the hub should be set at .015″ by turning the three adjustment screws. Lock screws.

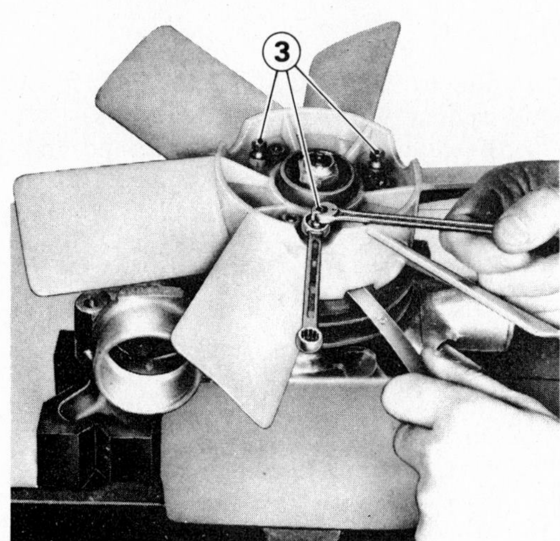

Fan and magnet clearance adjustment screws (3)

23. Test fan clutch by connecting the positive terminal of a battery to the brush wire and the negative to the pump body.
24. Start engine and allow to reach 183°F. At this point the fan should be engaged, and should disengage when temperature drops to 167°F.
25. If fan clutch does not operate, check the fuse. If the fuse is not burned out, make the following test.
26. Short circuit thermocontact terminals, if fan engages replace thermocontact. If fan engages or disengages outside of the specified limit, replace the thermocontact.

Thermostat

On the 403, 404, and 504 models the thermostat is located in the outlet hose. Most models are equipped with a 162° thermostat, but for operation in colder weather a 190° thermostat is available. To remove thermostat (all except 304), remove hose and withdraw thermostat. To install, insert thermostat and install hose. The thermostat on the 304 is located in the alternator sup-

304 thermostat removal

port on the cylinder head. To remove: drain radiator, disconnect battery, and remove alternator by removing belt tensioner, belt, and wiring. Remove five bolts and then remove support. Remove thermostat. To replace, reverse procedures using a new gasket.

Engine

Air Emission Controls

Positive Crankcase Ventilation

Late model 404's, and all 504 and 304 models are equipped with a PCV system. At each tune-up the valve and/or metering orifice should be cleaned. A clogged or defective valve should be replaced and all ventilation hoses checked for condition.

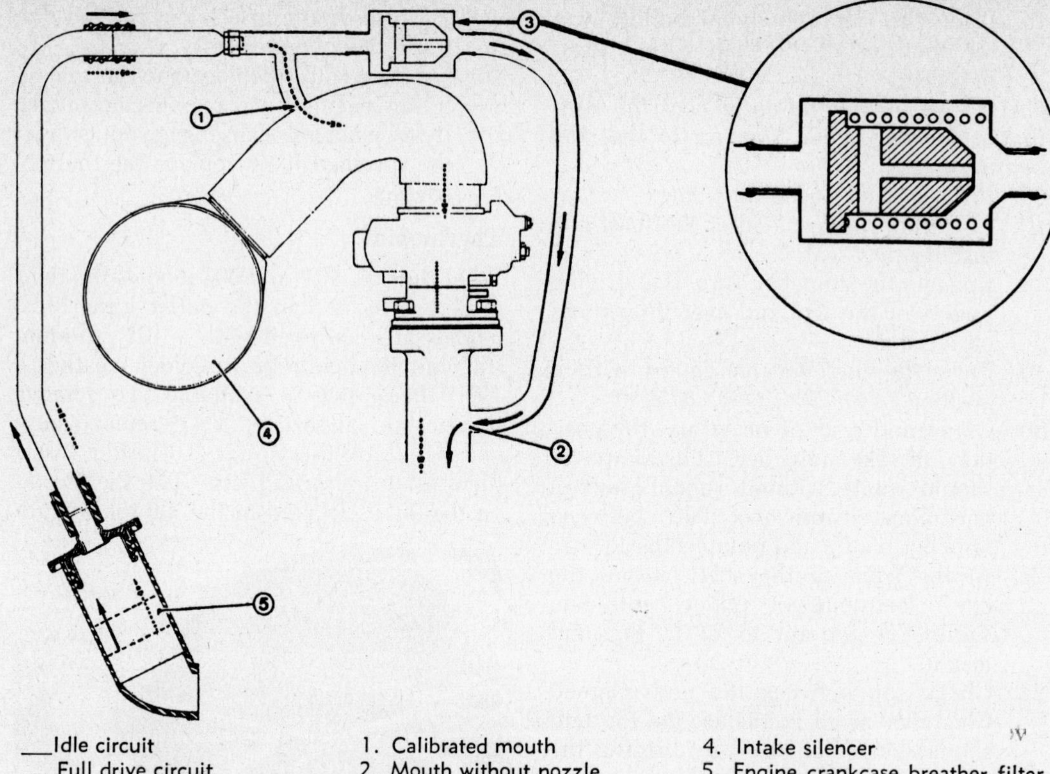

Positive crankcase ventilation (PCV) system.

"Coppolair" Anti-Pollution Device

Introduced on later model 404's and found on all 504 and 304 models, this device controls the mixture during acceleration and limits the amount of vacuum in the intake manifold on deceleration. The "Econostat" (Coppolair adjustment screw) is factory calibrated and this adjustment should not be changed.

Fuel Tank Anti-evaporation Device

The fuel tanks of 504 and 304 models are fitted with an anti-evaporation device to prevent gasoline vapor from escaping into the atmosphere.

Engine

Engine Removal and Installation—403

1. The engine may be removed with or without the transmission attached. The following procedure is for removal of engine only.
2. Raise vehicle and support with jackstands.
3. Remove hood, drain cooling system, and crankcase.
4. Remove radiator, battery, and air cleaner.
5. Disconnect generator leads and linkages.
6. Disconnect front exhaust pipe.
7. Disconnect heater pipe at cylinder head.
8. Disconnect fuel line at pump, remove starter, and unbolt exhaust pipe at clutch housing.
9. Remove clutch linkage and install jack under clutch housing.
10. Unbolt clutch housing and remove deflector plates.
11. Unbolt engine at front and install hoist.
12. Tilt engine towards back and pull engine out, clearing front crossmember with a minimum of space.
13. If engine and transmission are to be removed as a unit, do not install support jack or unbolt clutch housing.
14. After installing chain hoist by passing the chain under the clutch housing, disconnect the rear rubber mounting ring.
15. Remove the rear mount support and

let the torque tube rest on the brake equalizer.

16. Raise engine and transmission while tilting the transmission to clear the front crossmember.
17. To reinstall, reverse above procedure making sure engine to transmission alignment is correct (if engine was removed without transmission) as engine is lowered onto mounts.

ENGINE REMOVAL AND INSTALLATION—404

1. Disconnect and remove battery.
2. Drain cooling system and crankcase.
3. Remove hood, windshield washers, and jar.
4. Remove air cleaner and hoses, ignition coil and horn.
5. Disconnect alternator, temperature gauge, fan thermal contact, and oil pressure contact wires.
6. Disconnect radiator, heater hoses, and carburetor hoses.
7. Remove radiator with return heater hose.
8. Disconnect accelerator cable and choke cable.
9. Remove fuel line from the oil breather.
10. Remove baffles from clutch housing, two bolts holding exhaust pipe to manifold, and the bolt holding the exhaust pipe clamp on the transmission housing.
11. Support clutch housing with a jack and remove three bolts holding it to engine.
12. Attach chain hooks to lifting eyes on engine block.
13. Remove nuts from front mounts and free engine by pulling to the front.
14. When engine is free, turn it towards the right to remove from car.
15. To install, sit engine into bay turned to the right.
16. Place transmission in fourth gear and align transmission and engine.
17. Replace baffle plates and lower engine onto front mount. Install radiator.
18. Connect all hoses and wiring. Refill with oil and water.
19. Install starter and battery.

ENGINE REMOVAL AND INSTALLATION—504

1. Drain cooling system and crankcase.
2. Disconnect and remove battery and its mounting.
3. Remove the hood, radiator hoses, and radiator.
4. Remove heater hoses from engine and carburetor heater pipe from three way joint.
5. Remove fuel line, vacuum line, and wires from alternator.
6. Disconnect oil pressure switch, coil, thermostatic connector, starter switch, and fan switch.
7. Disconnect choke and accelerator linkage.
8. Remove the coil, starter, and flywheel plates.
9. Remove two Allen screws securing steering rack housing to the front crossmember. Turn steering wheel to the left and lower the housing.
10. Remove three nuts securing exhaust pipe to the manifold.
11. Remove the nut securing the damper to torque tube and disengage the lug.
12. Remove three clutch housing screws and install lifting hooks into holes provided in block.
13. Raise engine slightly and remove four bolts holding engine supports to crossmember.
14. Tie right brake line out of way.
15. Raise engine until transmission touches driveshaft tunnel.
16. Position a jack under transmission to hold it against tunnel.
17. Separate engine from transmission by jerking it slightly, without altering the position of the chain.
18. Pull engine up and out of compartment.
19. To install, lower engine into compartment. Put transmission into gear.
20. While turning the crankshaft by hand, couple the engine and transmission.
21. Check engine-transmission alignment and do not force them together or clutch plate distortion will result.
22. Reverse removal procedures. Refill with oil and coolant.

ENGINE REMOVAL AND INSTALLATION—304

1. Remove hood, battery, and radiator.
2. Disconnect heater hoses and fan thermoswitch.
3. Disconnect alternator, regulator ground, and starter.
4. Disconnect cylinder head thermoswitch, distributor, and oil pressure switch.
5. Remove air filter and accelerator and choke controls.
6. Remove the clutch slave cylinder with-

out disconnecting it and place it on the master cylinder.

7. Remove shift linkage from cover and disconnect the speedometer cable.
8. Separate the exhaust pipe from the manifold and remove the bolt securing the pipe collar to the gearbox.
9. Remove the stabilizer link nuts.
10. Disconnect the lower arms and recover the cups and rubber bushings.

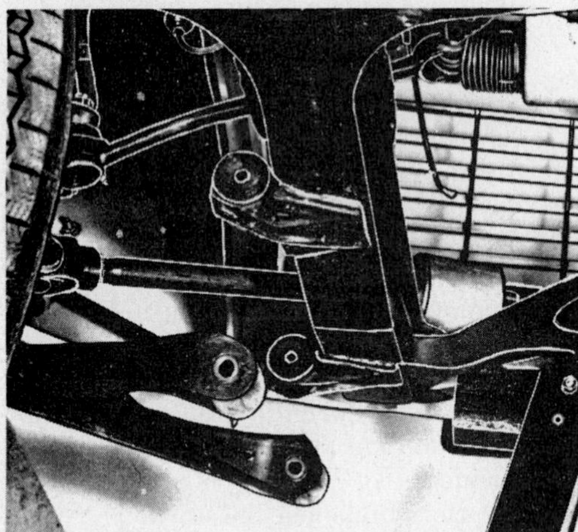

Lower arm disconnected

11. Raise the front of the car by the upper frame crossmember and chock car under lower crossmember.
12. Remove the pivots from the two front lower arms.
13. Disengage the driveshafts by spreading the left and right suspension units and then secure the shafts in this position using clamps.

CAUTION: *Avoid striking the oil bearing seal faces.*

14. Remove the two nuts holding lower left and right hand rubber blocks.
15. Remove bolts securing the steering box to the cradle.
16. Connect hoist to brackets provided on block and raise engine slightly to free blocks.
17. Unbolt engine mounts. Raise and withdraw engine unit, rocking it slightly to avoid the steering box.

CAUTION: *Any moving of the car, with engine removed, must be done with a jack or dollies, in order not to damage the driveshafts.*

18. Before installation of engine; check and if necessary, replace the driveshaft oil seals in the differential housing.
19. Smear grease on oil seal lips.

304 engine removal

20. Position the power unit on its support in the car.
21. Remove hoist. Tighten upper and lower rubber mount nuts to 24 ft. lbs, after refitting heat plate between engine right side.
22. Tighten steering box bolts to 22 ft. lbs.
23. Insert the driveshafts in the differential after removing clamps and cleaning the oil seal bearing faces.
24. Position the lower arms for assembly, fit new washers between the rubber bushings and lower arm yokes.
25. Grease and insert the pivots. Fit new nuts, but do not tighten them.
26. Reconnect the stabilizer bar links to the lower arms.
27. Fit the cups and the spacer as shown in figure. Do not tighten the nuts.

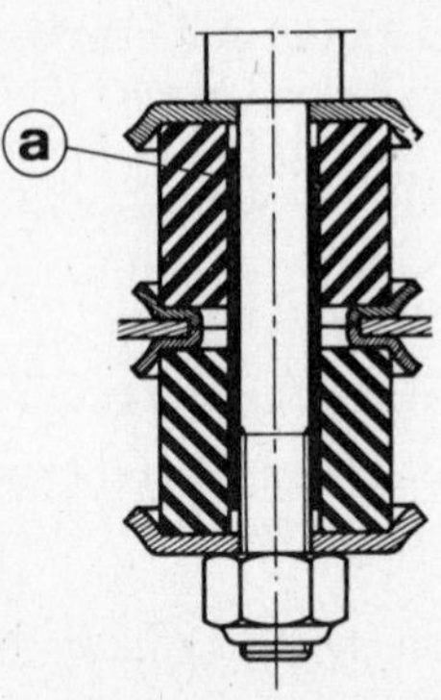

Stabilizer bushings (2)

28. Move car to obtain correct riding position.
29. Tighten the nuts on the lower arm pivots to 25 ft. lbs. Tighten the stabilizer link nuts to 13 ft. lbs.

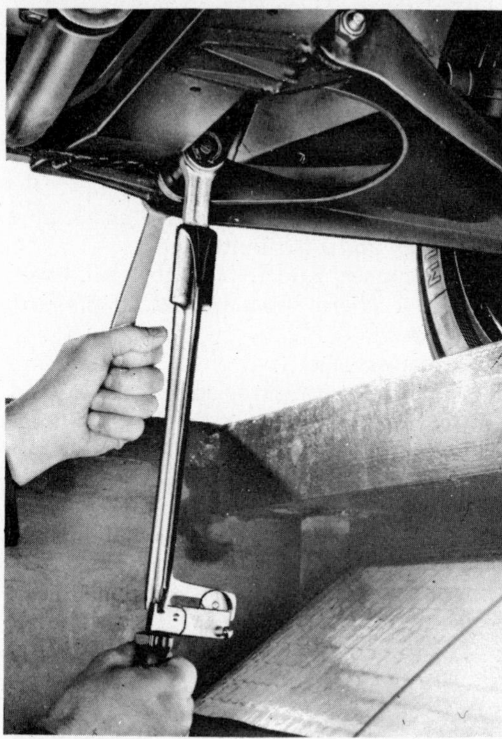

Tightening lower arm pivot bolts

30. Reinstall radiator, battery, starter, distributor, and alternator.
31. Reconnect all hoses and wiring in reverse order of removal.

Carburetor seal

Manifolds

Intake Manifold Removal and Installation—403, 404 and 504

The intake manifold on these models is of the short, single runner type. To remove, disconnect fuel line, vacuum hose, heater hoses, and air cleaner. Disconnect the accelerator linkage from the carburetor. Carburetor and manifold may be removed as a unit by leaving carburetor bolted to manifold and just removing manifold bolts. To install, insert new seal and insert diffuser (if so equipped) small diameter down. Complete installation by reversing removal procedure.

Intake Manifold Removal and Installation—304

The 304 intake manifold is the four runner type, with the carburetor centrally mounted. To remove, take off air cleaner, disconnect vacuum line, fuel line, and water inlet-outlet hoses. Disconnect accelerator linkage from carburetor. Carburetor and manifold may be removed as a unit by unbolting eight manifold bolts. Reverse procedure to install.

Exhaust Manifold Removal and Installation

Remove nuts and clamp retaining exhaust pipe to manifold and pull out of way. Remove eight bolts and remove manifold. Reverse procedure to install.

Cylinder Head

Cylinder Head Removal and Installation—403, 404, and 504

1. Disconnect the battery and drain the cooling system. Only remove head when engine is cold.
2. Remove the distributor cap and wires, spark plugs, radiator upper hose, fan belt, and generator/alternator mount from head.
3. Disconnect radiator bottom hose and the heater hoses.
4. Remove fuel line, vacuum line, PCV line, carburetor inlet and outlet hoses, carburetor heat tube, and linkage at carburetor.
5. Disconnect thermostatic switch lead and brush holder for self-disengaging fan (if so equipped).
6. Remove the air filter, carburetor and intake manifold, and rocker cover.

7. Disconnect exhaust pipe bracket from under the car.
8. Remove the cylinder head bolts and rocker arm shaft nuts alternately.
9. Remove spark plug tube cups and seals.
10. Disengage the rocker shaft.
11. Remove pushrods, marking them for return to proper location.

NOTE: Long pushrods are for the exhaust and the short for the intake.

12. Remove cylinder head by lifting straight up holding spark plug tubes.
13. Lock the cylinder liners with two retainers, which can be improvised from two bolts (same thread size, but shorter in length than head bolts) and flat washers of sufficient diameter to cover liner edges.

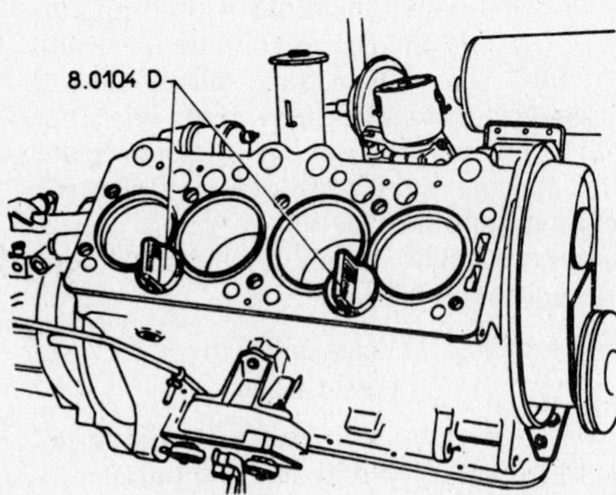

Cylinder sleeve holders in position

14. To replace head, remove cylinder liner retainers.
15. Place a greased head gasket (with the word "Dessus" facing up) on the block.
16. Use of two guides (long Phillips screwdrivers or lengths of tubing) will facilitate gasket positioning.
17. Position cylinder head and refit rocker shaft assembly.
18. Replace the pushrods in their original holes, with their ball ends down.
19. Install the bolts, oiled and with flat washers, into the head and block.
20. Engage the exhaust manifold onto the bracket, using a new gasket.
21. Tighten bolts according to specifications, using the proper sequence.
22. Adjust the rocker arms: intake .006″ and exhaust .012″. After 600 miles, readjust to normal clearance and torque cylinder head bolts again.
23. Replace accessories, hoses, and wiring removed. Refill cooling system.

Cylinder Head Removal and Installation—304

To prevent distortion of the cylinder head, only remove it when engine is cold.

1. Drain the coolant and oil.
2. Remove the battery and unclip the starter cable.
3. Remove the air filter and rocker arm cover.
4. Disconnect the ground cable from the cylinder head and remove spark plug wires and distributor cap.
5. Disconnect and remove the coil, alternator, thermo-switch, and oil pressure switch.
6. Remove the fuel lines from pump, heater hoses from head, carburetor and intake manifold, and choke and accelerator cables.
7. Separate the upper radiator mounting lug and remove the top hose.
8. Separate the exhaust pipe and remove the damper.

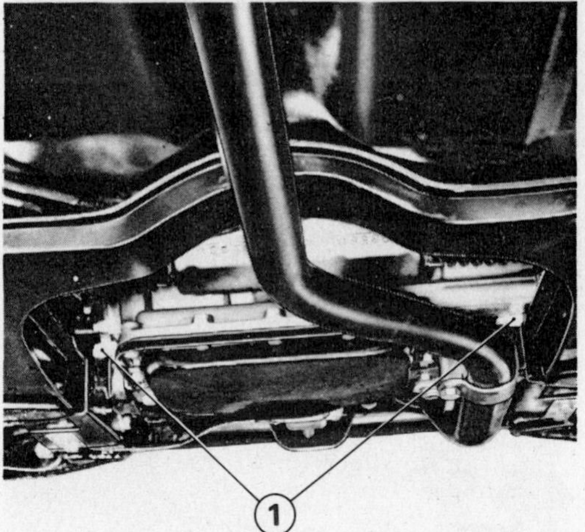

Support block (1) positioning

9. Place two blocks (2/5″ x 1″ x 3″) between the gearbox and the frame. Position a block (8 3/4″ x 1 3/5″ x 3/5″) between the cylinder block and the frame.
10. Remove the two upper rubber blocks from mounts and upper left intermediate support.
11. Remove the timing gear housing.
12. Unload the chain tensioner, remove camshaft gear, and timing chain.
13. Remove cylinder head bolts and recover nuts.

Support block positioning

CAUTION: *Hold nuts 4 and 8 in place in order to prevent them from falling behind the water pump.*

14. Remove the rocker shaft, cylinder head, and head gasket. Cylinder head must be pivoted on the centering pin on the left rear corner of the block without raising it, in order not to "free" the cylinder liners.

Cylinder liner retainers (8.011BC)

15. Secure cylinder liners with improvised metal straps bolted to block as in figure.

CAUTION: *The cylinder head surface should not be machined.*

16. When installing head, position the reference mark on the crankshaft gear horizontally to avoid contact between the valves and pistons.
17. Clean cylinder head and block surfaces. Remove retaining clamps.
18. Place gasket on block and fit head on. A rod placed in the bolt hole opposite the centering pin will facilitate placement.
19. Fit the rocker shaft in the end supports, engaging the centering pins in the head.
20. Fit the timing cover temporarily without the gasket using two bolts to aid in positioning the head gasket.
21. Oil and install the head bolts. Pretighten them to 29 ft. lbs.
22. Remove the timing gear cover.
23. Remove guide and install corresponding head bolt. Tighten bolts to final torque of 40 ft. lbs.
24. Set timing and install timing gear cover.
25. Install upper left intermediate support and tighten bolt on alternator support to 15 ft. lbs. and bolts on head and block to 24 ft. lbs.
26. Reinstall two rubber block supports and tighten the support on inner fender to 15 ft. lbs. and rubber block nut to 24 ft. lbs.
27. Adjust valve clearances to .004″ intake and .010″ exhaust.
28. Install rocker cover, starter, alternator, and connect all wiring.
29. Install and adjust fan belt.
30. Install battery, carburetor and intake manifold, and distributor.
31. Connect accelerator and choke cables.
32. Refit hoses in reverse order of removal and refill radiator and crankcase.

Valve Train

Valve Adjustment

Valve to rocker arm clearance is adjusted only when engine is cold. The clearances for all models are: .004″ on intake and .010″ on exhaust. Rocker arms are adjusted by the following pattern:

Valve Open	*Adjust*
Exhaust 1	Intake 3 Exhaust 4
Exhaust 3	Intake 4 Exhaust 2
Exhaust 4	Intake 2 Exhaust 1
Exhaust 2	Intake 1 Exhaust 3

Valve Removal and Installation

See Engine Rebuilding Section.

Valve and Valve Seat Resurfacing

Oversize valve seats are available from Peugeot in sizes of .008″(.20 mm) and

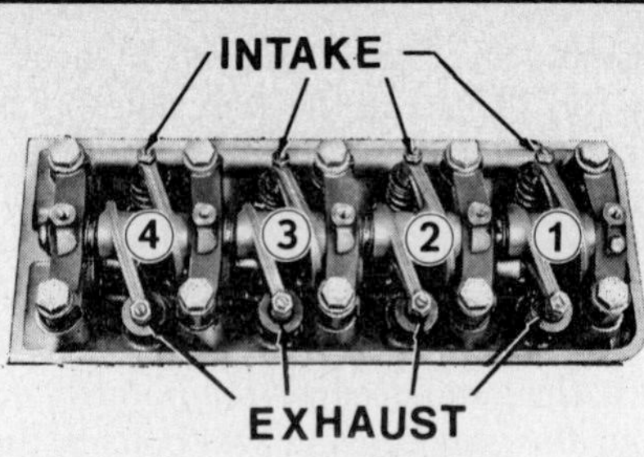

Rocker arm adjusters

.020″(.50 mm). Oversize valve guides are available in two oversizes. See Engine Rebuilding section for valve servicing procedures.

Camshaft and Timing Chain

Timing Gear Cover Removal and Installation—403, 404, and 504

Remove fan belt. Remove large nut on crankshaft. Remove pulley and key. Remove timing cover retaining bolts. Remove oil slinger. Install in reverse order of removal. Tighten crank nut to 75 ft. lbs. on 403 and 404 models, and 123 ft. lbs. on the 504.

Timing Gear Cover Removal and Installation—304

1. Disconnect and remove the battery.
2. Drain the oil.
3. Remove rocker arm cover, coil, and distributor.
4. Disconnect oil pressure switch and fuel lines from the pump.
5. Place a block (2/5″ x 1″ x 3″) between the gearbox and the lower engine support.

Timing cover removal

6. Remove the upper right-hand mounting block.
7. Remove the timing gear cover bolts and the ground cable. Remove cover.
8. To install, clean mating surfaces of cover and block.
9. Turn engine to bring No. 4 piston to TDC, end of exhaust, beginning of intake in order to obtain correct distributor driveshaft positioning.
10. Install a new gasket and oil passage O-ring.
11. Position the distributor driveshaft with smaller side towards the mating face and groove parallel with mating face.
12. Install the timing gear housing on cylinder block. Driveshaft will rotate one tooth clockwise.

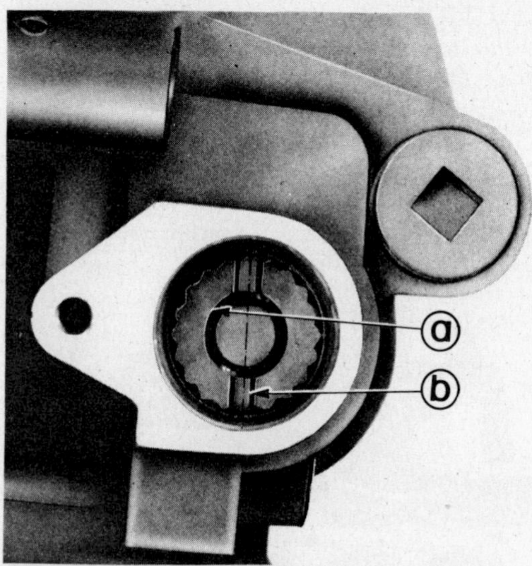

Distributor drive positioning—a is smaller side and b centerline

Camshaft positioning, 304

13. Refit the seventeen bolts and ground strap stud. Tighten bolts to 11 ft. lbs.
14. Cut timing gear gasket flush with upper mating face.
15. Connect ground strap, coil, fuel lines, and oil pressure switch.
16. Install upper right mount. Tighten support on inner fender to 14 ft. lbs. and rubber block securing nut to 24 ft. lbs.
17. Remove block from under gearbox. Refit air cleaner and refill engine with oil.

Camshaft Removal and Installation —403, 404, and 504

1. Remove cylinder head and timing chain cover as previously outlined.
2. Remove valve lifters and mark for assembly.
3. Remove distributor and oil pump drive.
4. It is not necessary to remove the chain tensioner on the 403, but is necessary on the 404 and 504.
5. To remove tensioner, screw out stopper screw and insert a 3 mm Allen wrench. Turn to right and release the pad from the spring action.
6. Remove the tensioner and filter.
7. On all models, remove camshaft gear, timing chain, timing gear support plate, and gasket.
8. Remove the camshaft front plate and withdraw camshaft carefully to avoid scoring bearings.
9. To install, lubricate camshaft lobes and journals and insert into block.
10. Camshaft timing in the 403 is performed with the gauge and special tools shown in the figure.
11. Install gear and chain. Install timing cover, pulley, and cylinder head.
12. 404 and 504 models are timed by positioning the timing chain on the crank and camshaft gears as shown in the figure.
13. Install camshaft gear and turn crank gear so scribed mark points down and camshaft gear mark points up.
14. Install timing chain and position it so that the two copper or cadmium plated links are centered on cam gear mark and the single plated link is centered on the crank gear mark.
15. Install timing cover, pulley, and cylinder head using a reversed removal procedure.

404 and 504 timing chain positioning

Camshaft Removal and Installation—304

1. Remove cylinder head as previously outlined (unless engine is out of car, in which case it is only necessary to remove timing gear cover).
2. Remove camshaft retainer and back off rocker arm adjusters.
3. Carefully extract camshaft without scoring bearings.
4. To install, lubricate camshaft lobes and bearing journals.
5. Turn camshaft to obtain positioning shown in figure.
6. Install timing chain and position so copper plated links are on either side of mark on cam gear. Install chain on crank gear so that single plated link is bisected by mark on gear.
7. Load the tensioner by turning Allen key clockwise.
8. Fit and lock tensioner sealing bolt by bending tab over it.

Timing Chain Tensioner Adjustment—403

1. Timing chain tensioner adjustment on the 403 is accomplished by use of a 14 mm (.56″) open end wrench to adjust an eccentric bearing.
2. To adjust, remove timing cover and loosen locknut. Turn eccentric counterclockwise to its extreme position, then allow it to return slightly to prevent excessive tension.

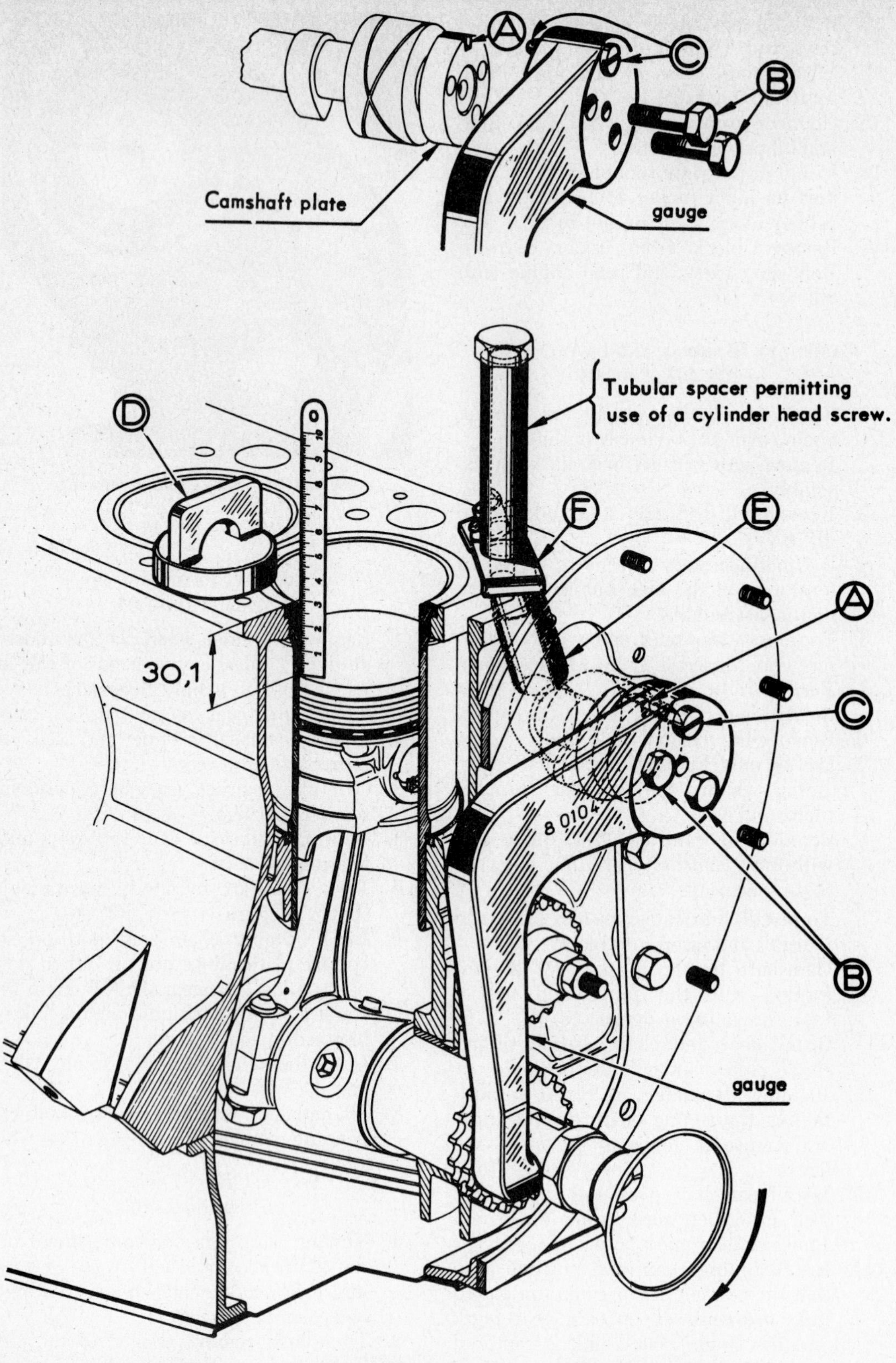

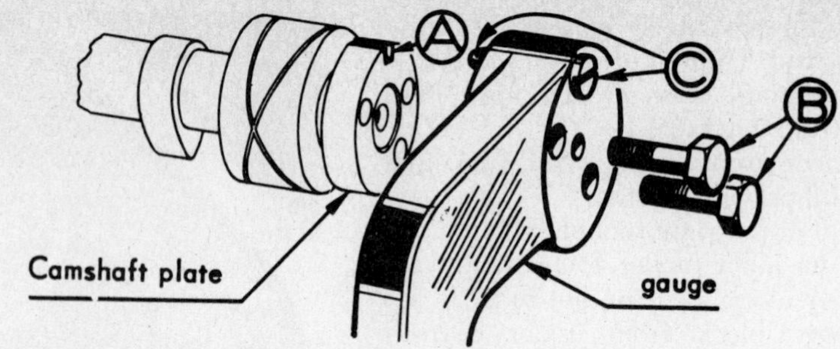

A
C
B
Camshaft plate
gauge
D
Tubular spacer permitting
use of a cylinder head screw.
F
E
A
30,1
C
8 0104
B
gauge

A Notch
B Camshaft bolts
C Set screw
D Cylinder liner retainers
E Dummy valve lifter
F Clamp

403 timing procedure with gauge

3. Tighten locknut and install timing cover.
4. Correct tension gives a deflection of .26″.

Timing Chain Tensioner Adjustment—404, 504, and 304

No adjustment, other than initial loading after removal or replacement, is necessary on these models. The tension of the spring is regulated for maximum life of the shoe and silence of operation.

Timing Chain Tensioner Removal and Installation—403

To remove tensioner on 403, remove nut and eccentric. To install, press eccentric on shaft and adjust.

Timing Chain Tensioner Removal and Installation—404, 504, and 304

Relieve tensioner by turning the piston to the right with an Allen wrench, after removing screw. Remove two bolts and remove tensioner. To install, be sure tensioner is flush with block and torque the two mounting bolts to 5 ft. lbs. Load the tensioner by turning the Allen screw slowly to the right until you hear the piston release under spring tension. Install and lock the cover screw.

Engine Lubrication

Peugeots employ a full pressure lubricating system driven by gear type oil pump. All models utilize a filter in their oiling system.

Oil Filter

The 403 and early 404 models use a permanent wire mesh filter, which may be replaced with the disposable cartridge used on the later 404. From 1968 on, all 404, 504 and 304 models use a spin-off type oil filter. A new filter should be installed at every other oil change.

The replaceable cartridge for 403 and 404 models is a Purflux L105C, AC 65, or Fram CH-915PL. The spin-off filter for late 404's and all 504's is a Purflux LS152 or a Fram PH 2846. The spin-off filter for the 304 is a Purflux LS152A.

Oil Pump

The oil pump on the three main bearing engines (403 and 404) is removed after the pan has been dropped (be sure to drain the oil). Remove the blind nut on the side of the block and unscrew the pointed bolt. The oil pump may now be removed. To remove the oil pump on five main bearing engines (404 and 504), drain the oil, remove the oil pan, the three bolts on the pump, and the pump itself. To install either pump, position the pump on the centering pins and install mounting bolts. Make sure that the drive blade is correctly in place. Tighten the three bolts to 7 ft. lbs. The 304 oil pump is located on the bottom left of the engine in the end cover casting. Access to the oil pump gears is obtained by removing the pump cover.

If the oil pump driveshaft (on 403, 404, and 504 models) is removed during engine servicing, it must be properly repositioned or ignition timing will be incorrect. On the 403, with No. 1 cylinder in firing position, pump gear must be in position shown.

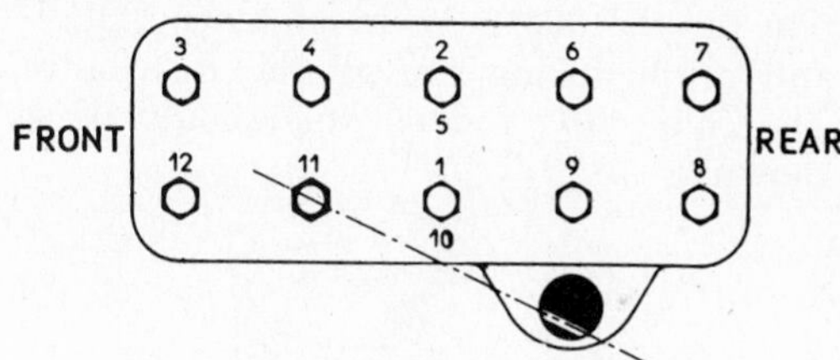

403 oil pump driveshaft position

On 404 and 504, insert shaft so that small side of slot faces toward rear and the slot is at a 70° angle with the longitudinal axis of the engine. Engaging shaft 2nd gear teeth will cause rotation of shaft. Slot should now line up with pushrod and bolt holes as shown.

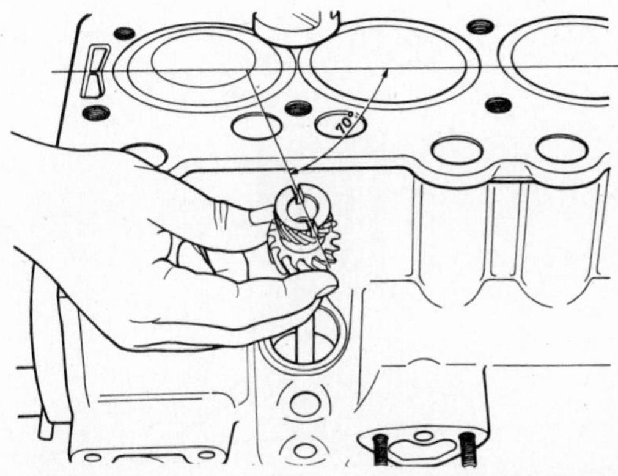

404 and 504 initial oil pump driveshaft position

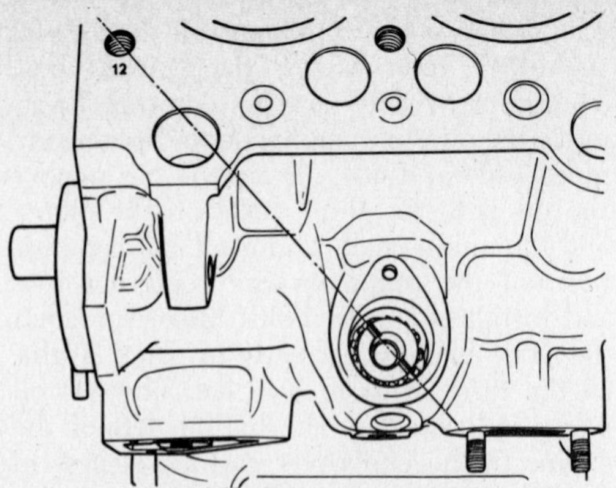

404 and 504 final oil pump driveshaft position

Piston and Connecting Rods

Correct piston positioning for 403, 404, and 504 is with "AV" mark facing toward front of block and slot in skirt facing the camshaft. The reference mark "AV" is located on skirt of 403 pistons, and on top of 404 and 504 pistons. Correct piston position for the 304 is with reference "DIST" and arrow facing toward the distributor. The connecting rod oil hole should be as shown.

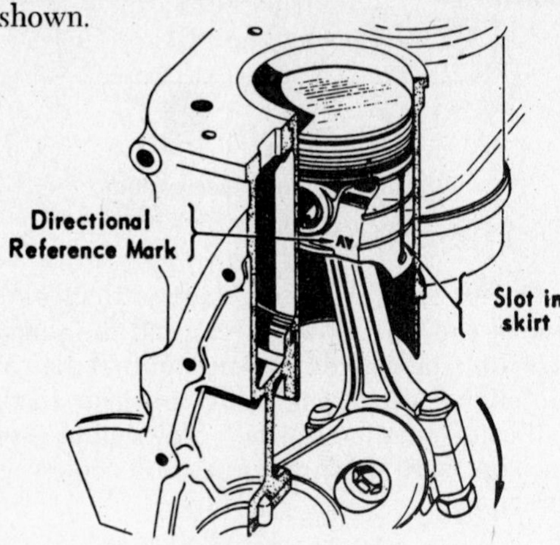

403 piston marking

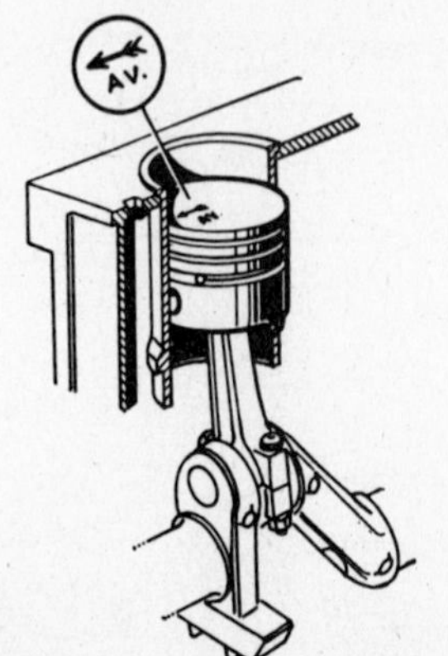

404 and 504 piston marking

304 piston marking

Pistons are matched to cylinder liners. Four sizes of piston-cylinder liner combinations are available. Pistons are identified A,B,C,D and cylinders I,II,III,IV. Cylinder liners are not overbored, and oversize pistons are not available. Connecting rods are numbered 1 through 6, which denote different weights. If it is necessary to replace a connecting rod, be sure to replace it with a connecting rod having the same identification number.

The wet cylinder sleeves of all Peugeot models are removable. A sleeve may be removed after the cylinder head and piston and rod assembly is removed. Liners are positioned at the lower end by a machined bore in the block and at the upper end by a shoulder in the cylinder head mating surface. Installed liners should extend above the cylinder head: .005″(.12mm) on 403 and 404 models, from 0″ to .003″ (.07mm) on 504's, and between .008″(.19 mm) and .012″(.26 mm) on 304's. Different size seals are available should an adjustment be necessary to bring the liner protrusion within specifications.

Piston and Connecting Rod Removal and Installation

See Engine Rebuilding Section.

Clutch and Transmission

Clutch and Transmission Removal and Installation—403 and 404

It is necessary to detach and pull the rear axle backward for clearance when removing the transmission and/or clutch.

1. Disconnect the battery and gear linkage.
2. Support the rear of the engine with a jack.
3. Disconnect and remove the starter.
4. Disconnect the speedometer cable.
5. Remove the bellhousing baffle plates.
6. Remove the two exhaust pipe to exhaust manifold nuts and exhaust pipe to housing clamp nut.
7. Remove the throwout bearing lubrication line (404).
8. Remove clutch shaft bearing cap and the return spring.
9. Disconnect handbrake cables from the floorboard and support plate.
10. Disconnect the flexible brake hose clamp and remove fuel and brake line clamp.
11. Remove the bolt and two nuts holding the rear mount.
12. Remove the four Allen bolts from the torque tube front cover (body must be jacked up to gain access for top two bolts).
13. Disconnect the stabilizer bar and rear shock absorbers from the rear axle housing.
14. Jack the rear of the body up and remove the rear springs.
15. Pull the rear axle assembly towards the rear.
16. Remove the engine/transmission rear mount.
17. Jack the transmission slightly to clear the steering column.
18. Remove the three Allen bolts holding the bellhousing to the engine.
19. Remove the transmission.
20. If removing clutch also, mark the pressure plate cover and flywheel for assembly.
21. Remove Allen bolts and clutch assembly.
22. When installing, lubricate the pilot bearing in the crankshaft and the splines of the input shaft.
23. Assemble the clutch assembly to the flywheel in the same position as when removed.
24. Use a clutch pilot tool or old input shaft to center the clutch plate while torquing the pressure plate bolts to 14 ft. lbs.
25. Install the transmission using the reverse of the removal procedure.

Clutch Removal and Installation—504

1. If the clutch is to be removed, the engine must be removed first. See Engine Removal.
2. With engine removed, mark flywheel to pressure plate relationship.
3. Remove the six Allen bolts and remove the pressure plate and clutch disc.
4. When assembling, position the clutch disc with a pilot tool or an old mainshaft.
5. Install the pressure plate and position on flywheel according to previously made marks.
6. Tighten bolts to 11 ft. lbs.
7. Check thrust ball bearing for condition and replace if necessary.
8. Pack splines and front of shaft with grease, also lubricate the thrust bearing guide sleeve.
9. Install the engine as described in that section.

Transmission Removal and Installation—504

1. Disconnect the battery and drain the transmission oil.
2. Remove the coil, radiator upper mount, and both radiator lower mounting bolts on the front crossmember.
3. Remove starter bolts and free from the flywheel without disconnecting the wires.
4. Remove the air cleaner.
5. Remove the three nuts holding the exhaust pipe to the manifold, and the nut holding the front muffler.
6. Remove the upper attaching nut of the rear pipe hanger and the rear hanger on the body.
7. Turn the steering wheel clockwise to disengage the front pipe and let it rest on the rear crossmember.
8. Remove the muffler heat shield.
9. Install a jack under the bellhousing.
10. Remove the torque tube to transmission attaching bolts.
11. Remove the Allen bolts holding the

differential under the suspension crossmember.
12. Separate the torque tube from the transmission by about 3/4″.
13. Insert a plate to the end of the torque tube to hold the inner driveshaft (similar to the one illustrated) and attach it to the outer tube by the lower two bolt holes.

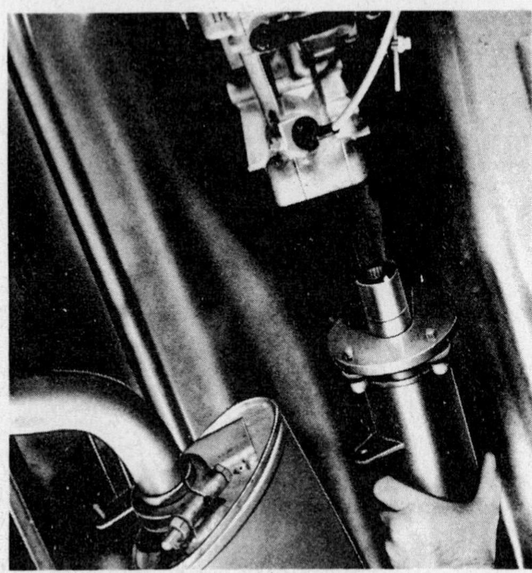

Torque tube removal

14. Pull the driveshaft out completely from the transmission.
15. Release the clutch slave cylinder without disconnecting it.
16. Remove the shift levers from the transmission and column link.
17. Disconnect the back-up light switch, ground wire, and speedometer cable.
18. Remove the steering damper bolt and steering gear housing bolts.
19. Remove the jack from under the bellhousing.
20. Remove the three Allen bolts holding the transmission to the engine.
21. Attach a hoist to the front engine lift bracket and raise and rotate the engine on its mounts as far as possible to disengage the transmission under the tunnel.
22. Place a wooden block under the radiator to prevent its weight from damaging the hoses.
23. Turn the transmission 1/4 turn counterclockwise to clear the starter and remove.
24. Remove the clutch throwout bearing.
25. When installing, lubricate the front

504 transmission removal

shaft and throwout bearing.
26. Engage the throwout bearing with the release fork by rotating the bearing clockwise.
27. Position the transmission, carefully engaging the input shaft in the clutch plate.
28. Install the three Allen bolts with new washers and tighten to 40 ft. lbs.
29. Remove the block placed under the radiator.
30. Lower the engine and remove the hoist.
31. Align engine-transmission with the torque tube using a jack.
32. Lubricate the driveshaft splines with grease and engage the driveshaft in the transmission.
33. Remove the inner driveshaft holding plate and completely engage the torque tube with the transmission.
34. Install the four Allen bolts and tighten to 44 ft. lbs.
35. Install the ground, back-up switch, and speedometer cable on the transmission. CAUTION: *Drive gear should just be engaged on the pinion, only the locknut should be tightened.*
36. Install the column shift lever, control rods, and transmission drain plug with a new seal (tighten to 20 ft. lbs.).
37. Install the bellhousing plates, clutch slave cylinder, and steering gear housing.
38. Install radiator on front crossmember and tighten bolts to 7 ft. lbs.
39. Install the muffler heat shield and ex-

haust pipe assembly, using a new gasket.

40. Install the two differential bolts with new washers and tighten to 27 ft. lbs.
41. Install upper radiator mounts, upper clutch housing plate, and starter. Tighten starter bolts to 14.5 ft. lbs.
42. Install and connect the remaining components using a reverse procedure of removal.
43. Fill the transmission with 20/40 weight oil and check the clutch and gear shift adjustments.

Clutch Removal and Installation—304

1. The clutch may be removed without removing the engine. Disconnect the battery, drain the cooling system, and remove the radiator.
2. Remove the fan belt and move the belt tensioner aside.
3. Remove the alternator and regulator after disconnecting the battery wire.
4. Disconnect the clutch return spring.
5. Loosen, but do not remove, the two left front tie rod studs.
6. Remove the two bolts attaching the left front tie rod fork to the alternator support.
7. Position the tie rod and fork assembly to one side.
8. Disconnect the heater hose from the water pump.
9. Rotate the engine until the tab lock for the pulley attachment screw faces downward.
10. Loosen the pulley screw using the special tool illustrated or a large offset screwdriver.
11. Remove the air cleaner.

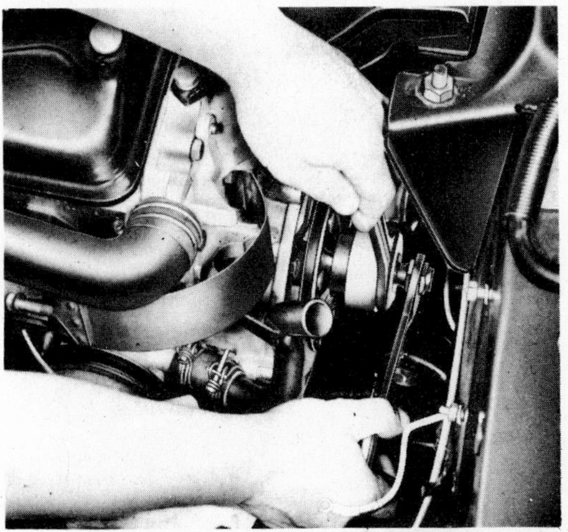

Loosening pulley screw —304

12. While holding the crankshaft pulley, loosen the attaching bolt further.
13. Remove the crankshaft pulley and backing spring, if so equipped.
14. Remove the clutch housing cover and throwout bearing.
15. Align the pressure plate notch with the 8 mm pin hole in the clutch housing.

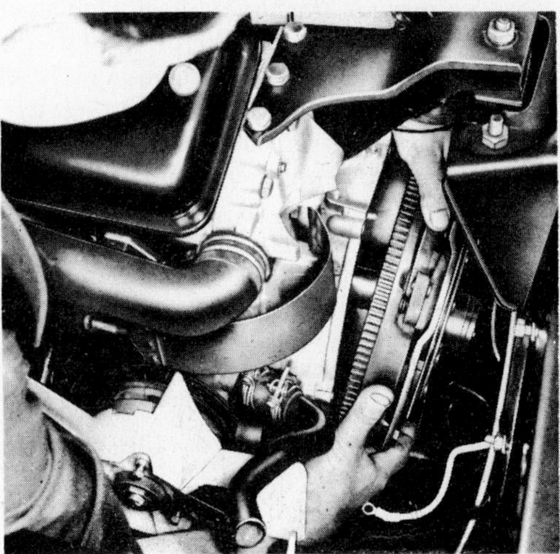

Clutch removal—304

16. Remove the clutch using a puller.
17. Before installation, clean the shaft and splined drive gear and lubricate with a moly spray. CAUTION: *Do not spray lubricant on the drive gear oil seal surface.*
18. Make sure that the crankshaft reference hole is aligned with the top of the cylinder.

Clutch alignment—304

19. Position the clutch assembly on the crankshaft so that the notch on the clutch cover aligns with the hole in the clutch housing.
20. Rotate the clutch back and forth so as to engage the clutch disc over the gear. NOTE: *The six clutch assembly bolts must not be tightened in order to allow centering of the clutch disc.*
21. Temporarily install the crankshaft pulley and tighten the attachment screw slightly to fully engage the clutch.
22. Tighten the six clutch assembly bolts to 18 ft. lbs. and then remove the crank pulley.
23. Pack the clutch hub groove with grease.
24. Install the throwout bearing and, if so equipped, the thrust bearing.
25. Install the clutch housing cover, making sure that the flat side of the clutch fork is facing towards the throwout bearing.
26. Tighten the clutch housing cover bolts to 7 ft. lbs. and refit the crankshaft pulley, making sure that it engages the locking ball on the clutch hub.
27. Install the attaching bolt with a new tab and tighten to 47 ft. lbs. while holding the pulley. Bend the tab and lock after tightening.
28. Install components in reverse order of removal and adjust fan belt and clutch free travel (described in clutch adjustment section).

Transmission Removal and Installation—304

The transmission is bolted to the bottom of the engine crankcase, therefore removal requires removing the entire unit from the car. Separation of the transmission from the engine is described in the transmission repair section. See Engine Removal section for power unit removal procedure.

Clutch Linkage

Clutch linkage is mechanically operated on 403 and 404 models to 1968. Starting in 1968, the 404 was equipped with a hydraulically actuated clutch. All 504 and 304 models use hydraulic clutch linkage.

Clutch Linkage Adjustment—403 and 404

Clutch pedal free play may require adjustment on 403 models and 404s up until 1968 cars which require no free play adjustment. Free play is measured from the resting position of the clutch pedal to the point where disengagement begins. The free play for 403 and early 404 models is .75″ (19 mm). Free play for 404 models from Serial No. 4218973 to Serial No. 8325001 should be 1.5″ (38 mm).

Adjustment is made by turning a nut on the end of the clutch pedal withdrawal rod located under the hood behind the brake fluid reservoir. To reduce the travel, turn the nut clockwise, and to increase travel, turn it counterclockwise. Make the free play check by hand rather than by foot for a more accurate feel of the travel.

Clutch pedal adjustment for 403.

Clutch Linkage Adjustment—1968, 1969 404 and 504

No adjustment is necessary on these models.

Clutch Linkage Adjustment—304

Free pedal travel should be between 1.2″ and 1.4″. The free travel of the adjustment screw should be 0.10″. If unable to obtain the correct free travel after adjusting the screw to the above specifications; check, and if necessary, bleed the hydraulic system.

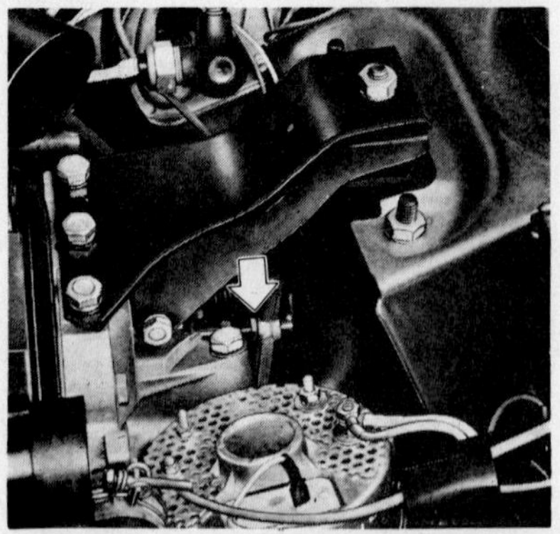

304 clutch adjustment screw

Shift Linkage

Shift Linkage—403 and Early 404 (Manual)

Place shift lever in second gear. Loosen the securing nut of the shift control rod (arrow). Center the rod in free play and tighten the nut.

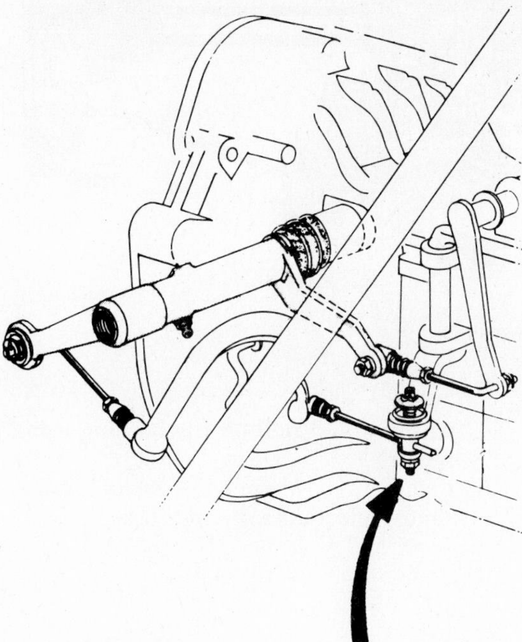

403 and early 404 shift linkage adjustment—manual transmission

Shift Linkage Adjustment—404 (Automatic)

The only adjustments required on the ZF automatic transmission are the selector and accelerator pedal linkages on the outside of the transmission, and these are made by adjusting the lengths of the control rods.

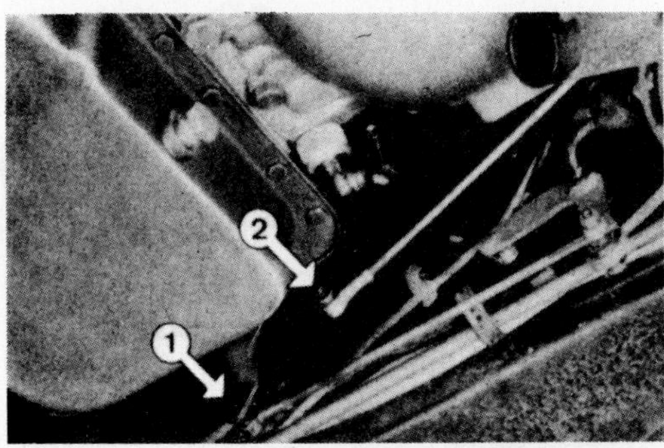

Adjustment of selector rod (1) and accelerator rod (2) on ZF automatic transmission

Selector adjustment

There are positioning ball checks in the case. With lever at the third ball check, the selector dial should be at N position.

Accelerator pedal adjustment

The "full throttle" carburetor position should occure at full throttle position of the transmission control. To obtain this:

1. Place selector on position N and apply parking brake.
2. Disconnect rod on transmission case.
3. Start engine and allow it to idle.
4. Move accelerator load adjustment lever forward by hand on transmission case, starting from its resting position.
5. Note sudden stiffness opposing further motion. This resistance to lever rotation indicates the full throttle position. Keep lever in this position.
6. Stop engine.
7. Open carburetor to full throttle (maximum opening of throttle).
8. Adjust length of accelerator rod accordingly. Connect rod.

Manual Transmission

Peugeot manual transmissions are synchronized in all four forward speeds. 403 models produced prior to mid-1960 used the C2 transmission with an overdrive fourth gear. 403 models produced after mid-1960 and 404 models up to 1968 are equipped with the C3 transmission. 404 models starting in 1968 and all 504 models use the BA7 transmission. The BA7 transmission used in the 504 is basically the same as that used in the 404 except for larger diameter mainshaft bearings, helically cut reverse gear, different speedometer drive, and different shift linkage. The 304 uses the BB6 transmission, which is bolted directly to the bottom of the engine block. Transmission overhaul is sometimes illustrated using special Peugeot tools, however, these are not absolutely necessary and suitable replacement tools are commercially available or can be improvised.

Transmission Disassembly—C2

1. Remove the two plugs and drain the transmission. Support transmission in a cradle or fixture and clean housing.
2. Remove clutch and housing and gearbox cover.
3. Engage 2nd and reverse gears.
4. Remove Allen screw from universal and remove universal.

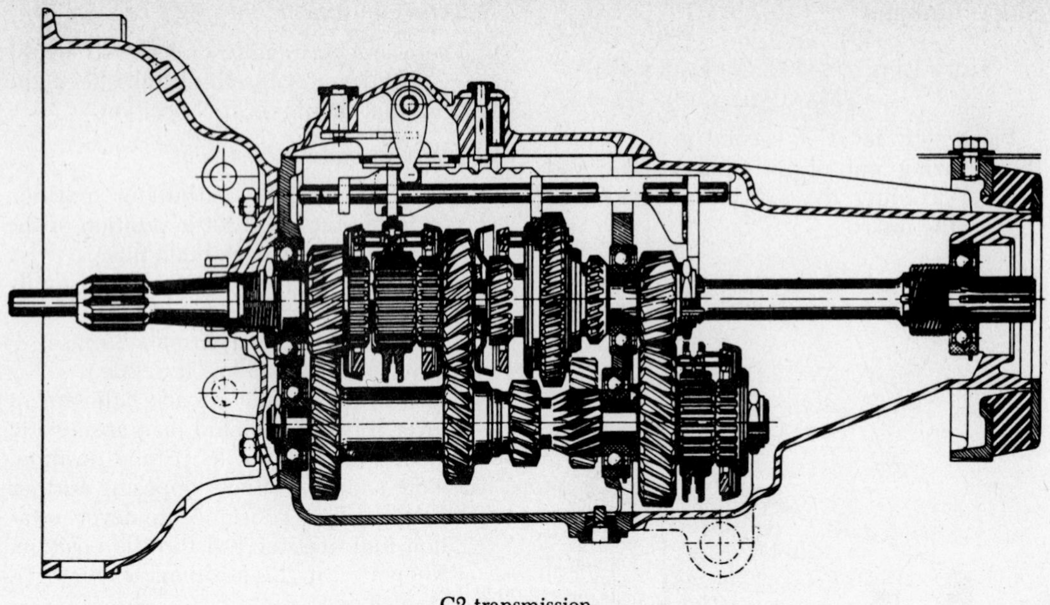

C2 transmission.

5. Remove speedometer control socket assembly using puller.
6. Remove six overdrive housing nuts and washers, and pull off the housing using puller.
7. Remove speedometer control screw, shims, selector shafts and forks.

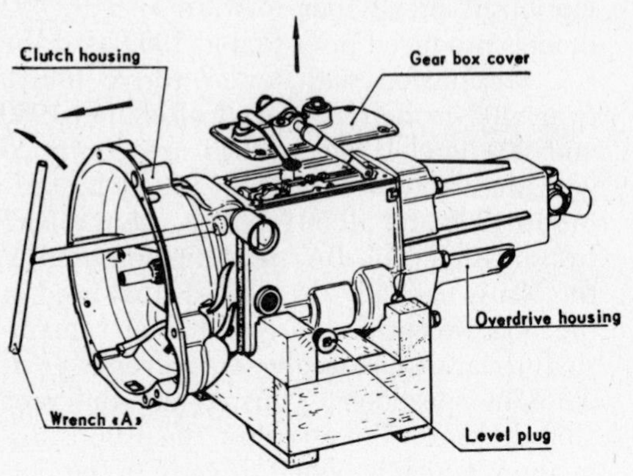

C2 disassembly (Steps 1, 2).

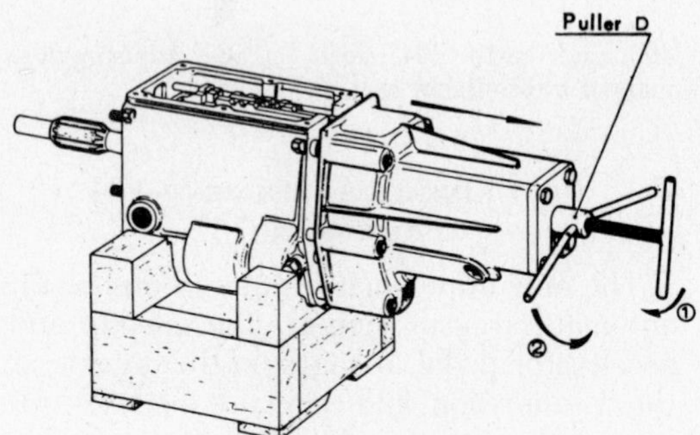

C2 disassembly (Step 6).

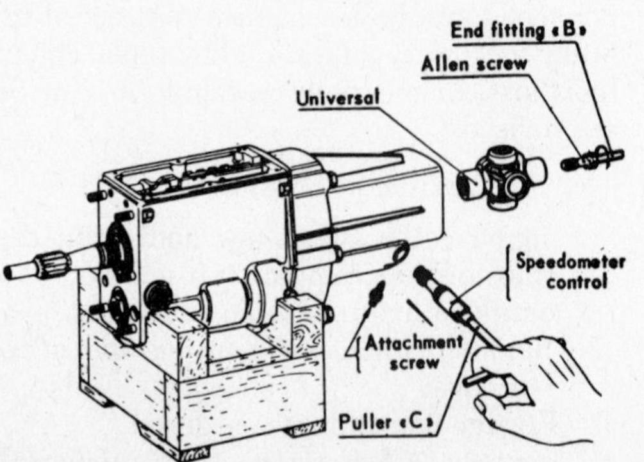

C2 disassembly (Steps 3, 4, 5).

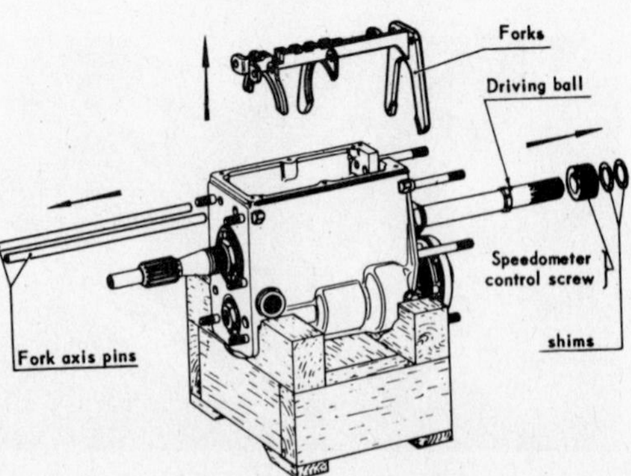

C2 disassembly (Step 7).

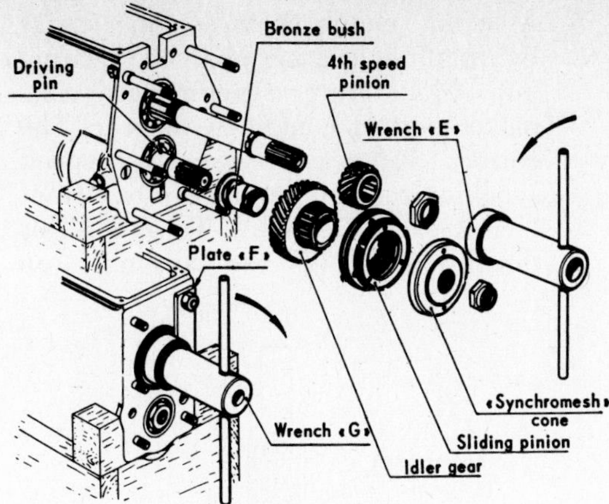

C2 disassembly (Steps 8–12).

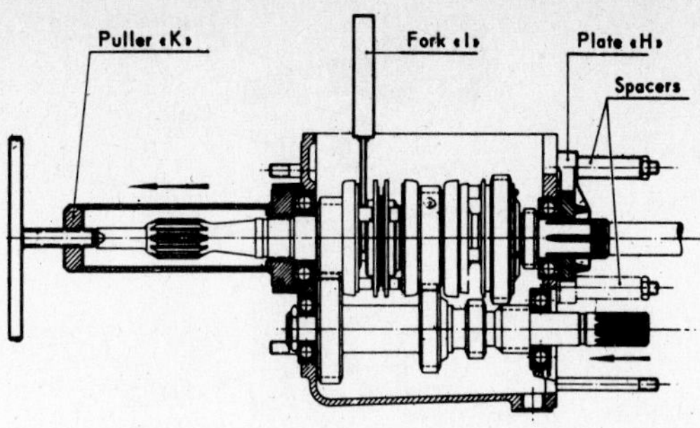

C2 disassembly (Steps 13, 14, 15).

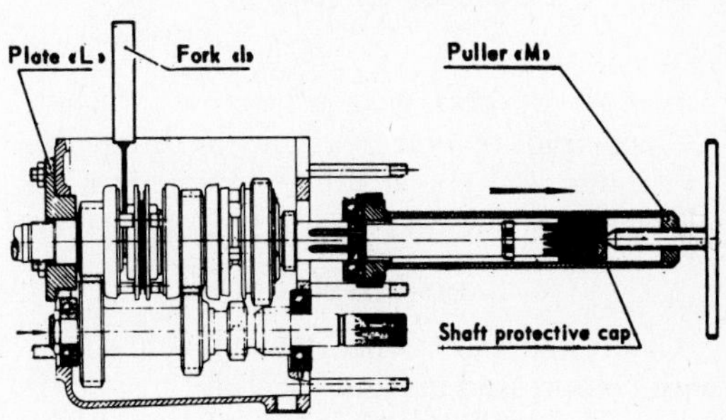

C2 disassembly (Steps 16–18).

8. Unlock the 4th speed gear and idler pinion nuts.
9. Remove the 4th speed gear idler pinion locking nut and idler assembly.
10. Remove bronze bushing and driving pin.
11. Remove 4th speed gear nut and pull the gear.
12. Install plate, then unlock and remove the left-hand thread clutch shaft lock-nut. Remove plate.
13. Install fork being careful not to force it into position which will distort the synchronizer bars.
14. Install plate. Remove intermediate shaft rear bearing snap-ring. Using a wooden mallet, tap intermediate shaft rear end gently to free clutch shaft retainer.
15. Remove retainer and pull clutch shaft bearing. Remove plate.
16. Install plate. Remove rear bearing snap-ring from intermediate shaft. Using a wooden mallet, tap intermediate shaft front end gently to free center bearing groove from main input shaft.
17. Install protective cap on the end of the input shaft and pull bearing.
18. Remove fork and plate; then remove deflector ring and shims.
19. Disconnect mainshaft (input) from clutch shaft (engine shaft), then remove the mainshaft and clutch shaft from the inside. CAUTION: *Avoid forcing clutch shaft cone while removing mainshaft.*
20. Install spacer at end of intermediate shaft. Then pull rear bearing.
21. Remove intermediate shaft through inside with front bearing in place. Re-

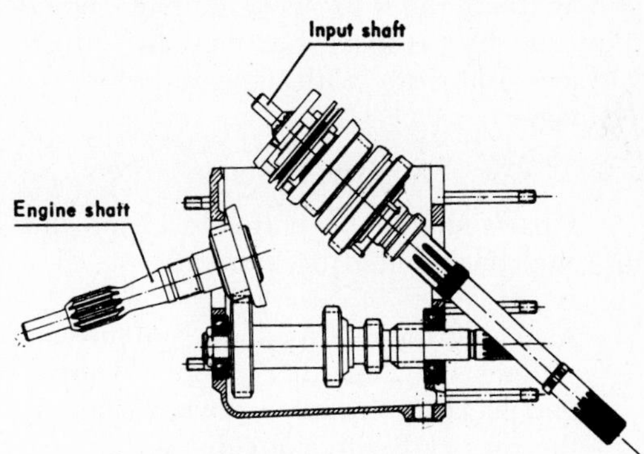

C2 disassembly (Step 19).

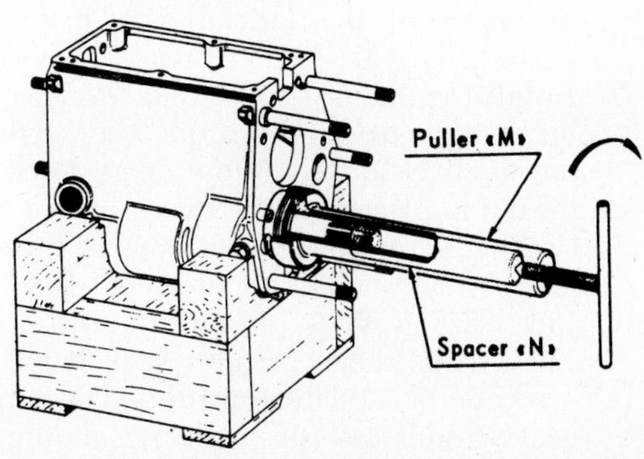

C2 disassembly (Step 20).

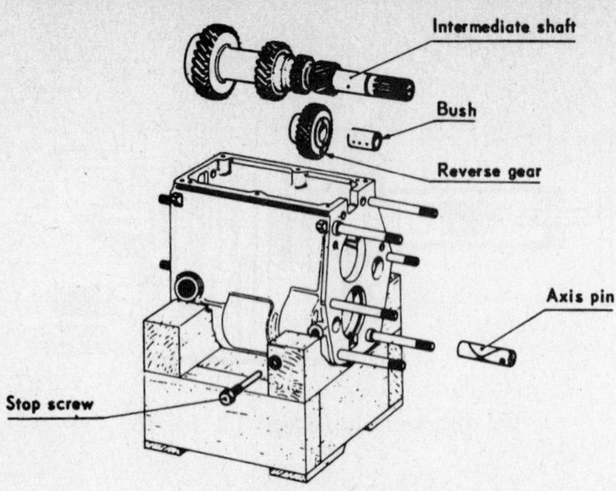

C2 disassembly (Step 21).

move reverse gear stopscrew, washer, axis pin, reverse gear and bushing. Remove 2nd speed idler pinion after removing nut and bearing, if necessary.

Parts Inspection

Clean the case with solvent, blow dry with compressed air and carefully inspect it for cracks or burrs. Smooth off any burrs with a fine file. Check gears and bushings and replace worn or damaged ones. Wash bearings in clean solvent and hold bearings still in their races to avoid damage while blowing dry. Inspect bearings for rough surfaces. Lubricate with light oil before replacing.

Assembly—C2

All parts should be perfectly clean and dry, and they should be lubricated as they are assembled.

1. Assemble the intermediate shaft by installing the 2nd idler pinion, bearing and locknut. Install a new washer at the rear end with the convex side out.
2. Assemble the main shaft by installing 1st speed synchronizer cone, drive pin, 2nd speed gear bronze bushing, 2nd speed gear and synchronizer cone, making sure the latter bears firmly against the gear.
3. Install the 2nd-3rd speed synchronizer hub with a new nut. Torque the locknut to 36-44 ft. lbs. (5 to 6 mkg). Lock the nut in place in the groove.
4. Check 2nd speed gear for correct side play which should be between .014" and .022" (.35 to .55 mm). Install 2nd-3rd speed synchronizer with index marks on bars facing toward 2nd speed gear. Install 1st speed-reverse sliding gear.
5. Assemble clutch shaft (engine shaft) by installing locating plate and bearing nut. Make sure synchronizer cone makes perfect contact with gear. The correct distance between 3rd speed synchronizer cone and gear box front face is 1.9" (47.5 mm). To obtain this dimension, place the assembly on

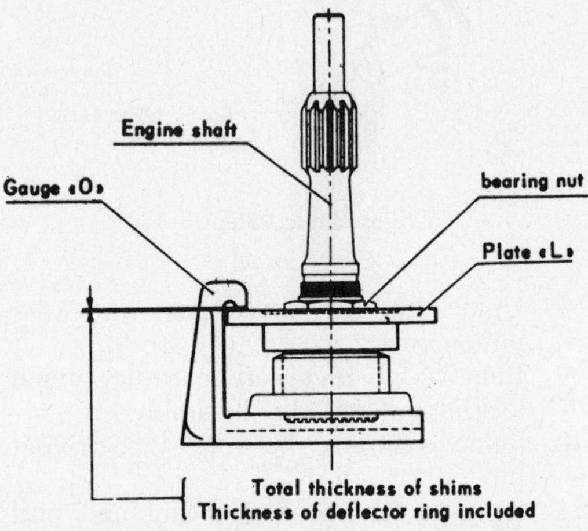

Use of gauges to obtain correct distance between third gear synchronizer cone and gear box front face.

gauge 0 and determine the total thickness of the shims to be added. This measurement should include the thickness of the deflector ring.

6. Install reverse gear together with its bushing. Engage axis pin. CAUTION: *The lubrication hole should always be facing toward the exterior of the housing.*
7. Install reverse gear retaining screw.
8. Observe direction of installation for the intermediate shaft rear bearing snap ring. Insert intermediate shaft into position through the inside, while engaging front bearing into its housing. Remove snap-ring and install rear bearing in position using body of puller. (The bearing groove should be facing toward the exterior.)
9. Insert clutch shaft (engine shaft) and input shaft through the inside. Engage input shaft front end into the Nadella socket on the clutch shaft.
10. Install locating plate. Install fork between 3rd speed gear and 2nd-3rd speed hub. Install center bearing using body of puller (the bearing groove should be facing toward the exterior).

11. Remove locating plate. Install center bearing backing plate with its spacers. Install shims and deflector ring on clutch shaft. Install clutch shaft bearing segment into its groove.
12. Install bearing, using body of puller and a wooden mallet. Engage two speeds (2nd-reverse) using wrench. Install a new clutch shaft bearing nut. Torque nut, and lock with punch mark in groove. Remove fork and plate.
13. Install 4th speed gear using a new nut. On cars after Serial No. 2035930, it will be necessary to heat the 4th speed gear in an oil bath at 100° C. to facilitate assembly. Tighten, using wrench and locknut into two grooves.
14. Install bronze bushing and its retaining pin. Install 4th speed idler pinion assembly with a new nut. Torque to 36-44 ft. lbs. (5 to 6 mkg) on shafts without milled grooves; 15-22 ft. lbs. (2 to 3 mkg) on shafts with milled grooves. Lock nut in grooves. Install clutch housing with paper gasket. Install speedometer control screw.

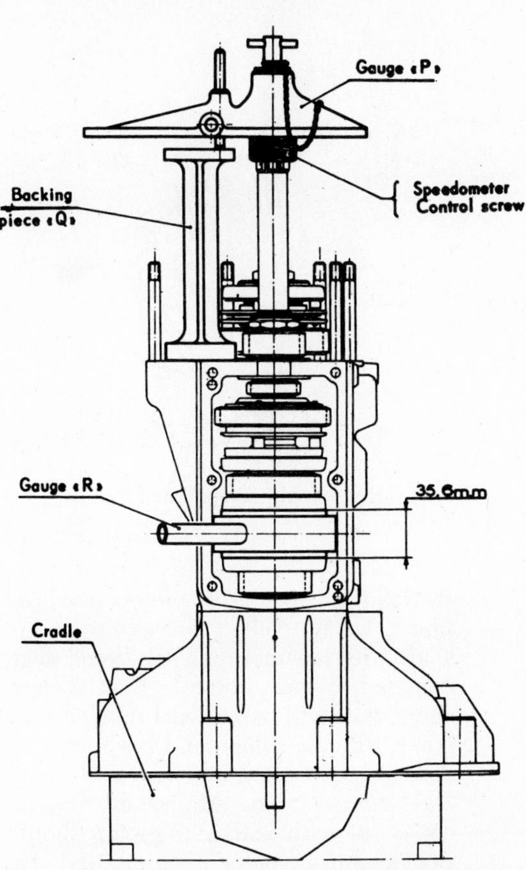

Measurements on synchronizer assembly.

15. Determine thickness of shims necessary to obtain 1.4″ (35.6 mm) between the 2nd and 3rd speed synchronizer cones by using gauge and backing piece. Install gauge on the 2nd and 3rd speed synchronizers.

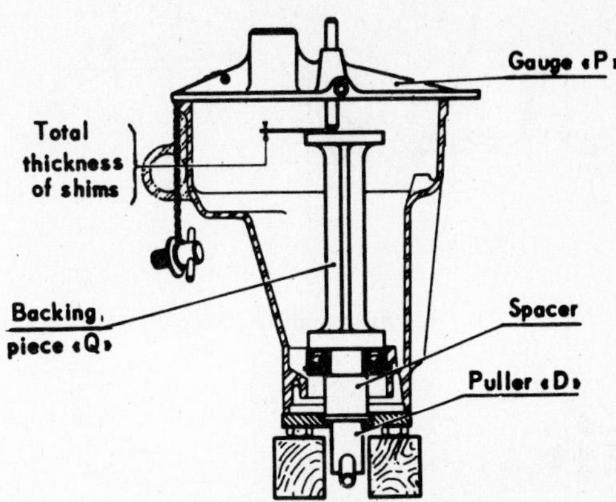

Measurements on overdrive housing.

16. Then install gauge on the overdrive housing and measure the total thickness of shims required.
17. Remove gauges and install required shims on mainshaft. Install selector forks and insert fork axis pins. Make sure locating bushings are in place in gearbox rear face.
18. Install overdrive housing using Permatex for a good seal. Install and tighten overdrive housing nuts. Shift gears to neutral and install speedometer control with its attachment screw. Tighten screw slightly to clear puller. Install the universal and locknut. Install cover gasket using Permatex. Operate all gears in succession to be sure they engage freely before installing transmission. Fill with SAE 40 motor oil.

Transmission Disassembly—C3

1. Remove oil level and drain plugs and drain completely. Install assembly on cradle or fixture and clean housing. Remove clutch housing using wrench. Remove transmission cover.
2. Engage gears 4th and reverse. Remove Allen screw from universal joint and remove universal joint. Remove speedometer drive sleeve lockscrew and take out speedometer driven gear using puller.
3. Remove six screws and washers from rear housing and pull housing. Save

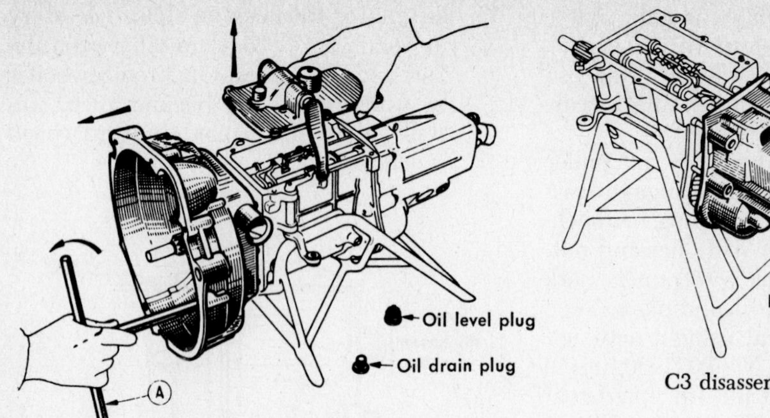

C3 disassembly (Step 1).

C3 disassembly (Steps 3 and 4).

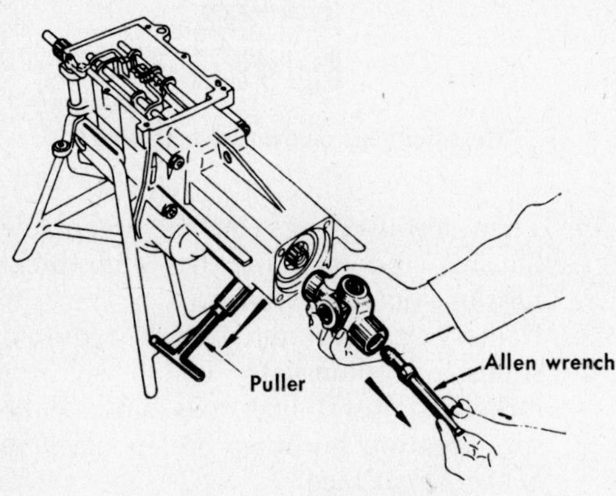

C3 disassembly (Step 2).

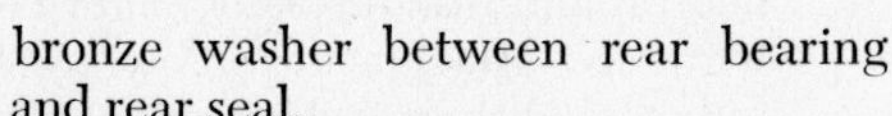

bronze washer between rear bearing and rear seal.

4. Remove adjustment shims and speedometer drive screw from mainshaft. Remove reverse idler pinion shaft lockscrew, then remove shaft, reverse idler pinion and its washers. Remove selector fork axis pins and selector forks.
5. Install clamp to keep 1st gear engaged. Make sure 4th also remains engaged. Using puller, pull out mainshaft assembly complete with bearing, protecting washer, lockring and nut. Remove puller.
6. Install plate fitted with wrench, while maintaining 4th speed dog engaged. At the same time engage 2nd speed. Loosen pinion locknut on mainshaft. Unlock and remove 1st gear pinion locknut from intermediate shaft. Remove plate, wrench and locknut from the mainshaft, and then remove clamp.

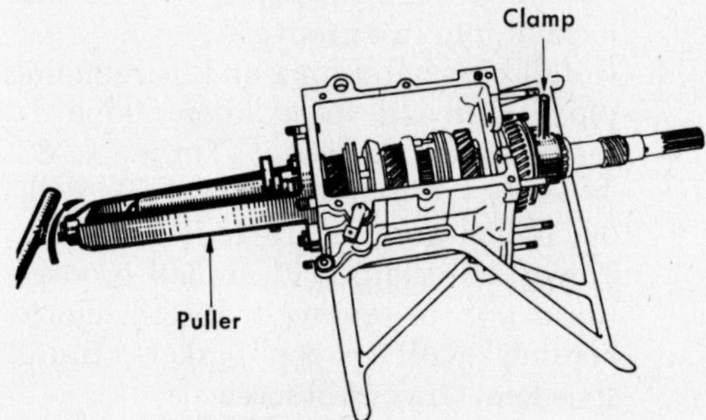

C3 disassembly (Step 5).

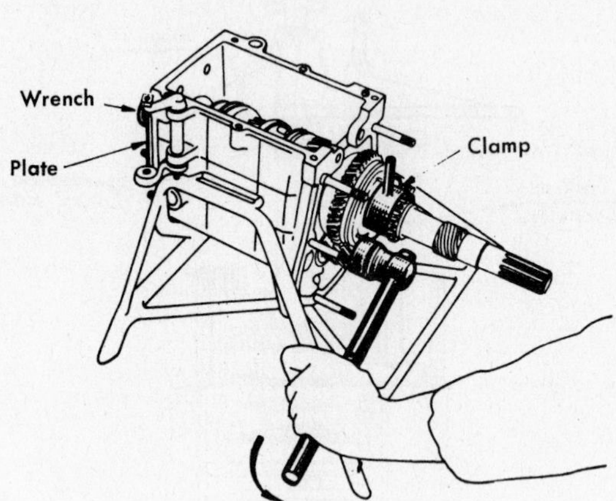

C3 disassembly (Steps 6 and 7).

7. Remove 1st gear drive pinion synchronizer. Using mallet, drive out mainshaft while maintaining 4th speed gear engaged. Remove the following as they come out: 4th gear synchronizer and cone, 3rd gear pinion and bushing, 2nd and 3rd gear synchronizer and hub, 2nd gear pinion. Mainshaft should come out with 2nd gear pinion shoulder bushing, center bearing and 1st speed gear synchronizer cone in place.

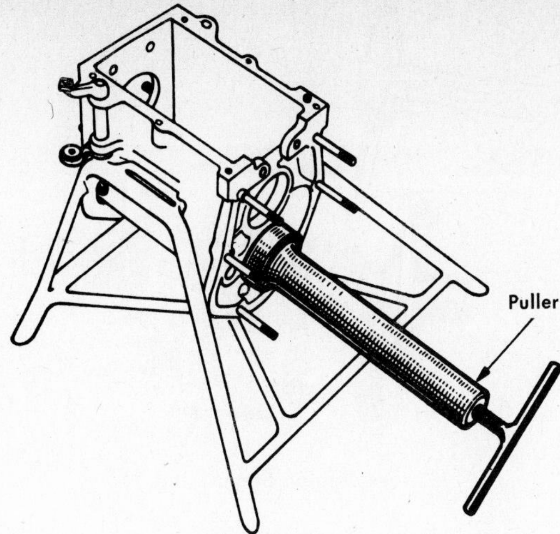

C3 disassembly (Step 8).

8. Using pliers, disengage bearing snapring from intermediate shaft. Push intermediate shaft toward the rear until clear from bearing groove. Using puller and spacer, pull rear bearing. Push front bearing toward rear and free it from its housing. Take out intermediate shaft through inside of housing.
9. Whenever the gear-shift lever is removed it becomes necessary to mark the lower lever for correct position after removing the securing nut. Incorrect positioning of this lever will cause trouble in shifting. The angle formed by the upper and lower levers should be 59°.
10. Clean the case with solvent, blow dry with compressed air and carefully inspect it for cracks or burrs. Smooth off any burrs with a fine file. Check gears and bushings and replace worn or damaged ones. Wash bearings in clean solvent and hold bearings still in their races to avoid damage while blowing dry. Inspect bearings for rough surfaces. Lubricate with light oil before replacing.

Rear Bearing Replacement

The bearing in the rear housing is replaced by removing the oil seal, bearing snapring, adjustment shim and old bearing (use a drift to remove bearing), and determining the thickness of the shim required to hold the new bearing in its housing without any side play.

The shim is to be inserted between the bearing and lockring. Three different thicknesses are available .074″, .078″ and .082″ (1.89, 1.99, and 2.01 mm). To select the correct one, proceed as follows:

1. Install new bearing without shim, but with lockring.

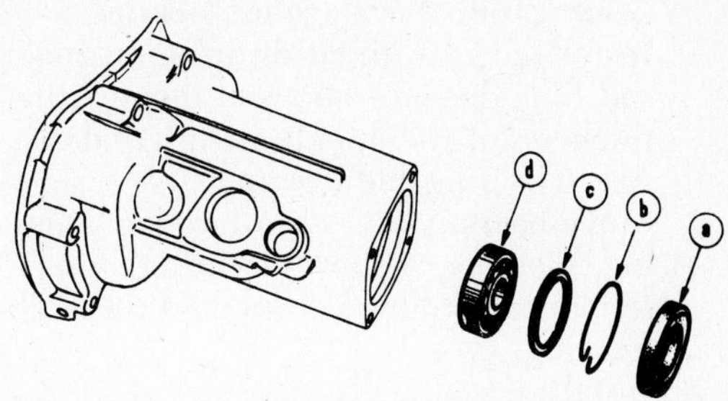

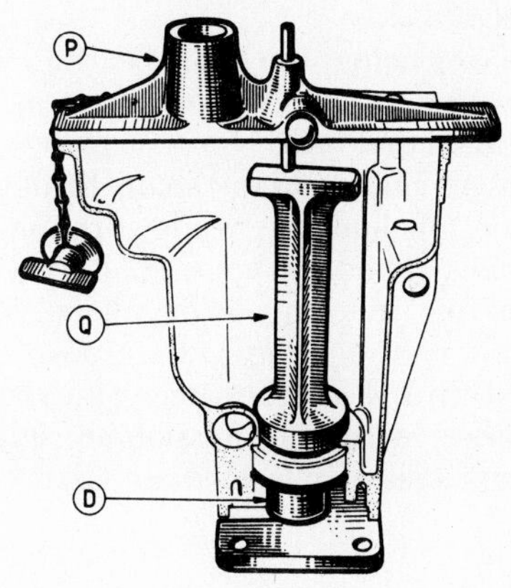

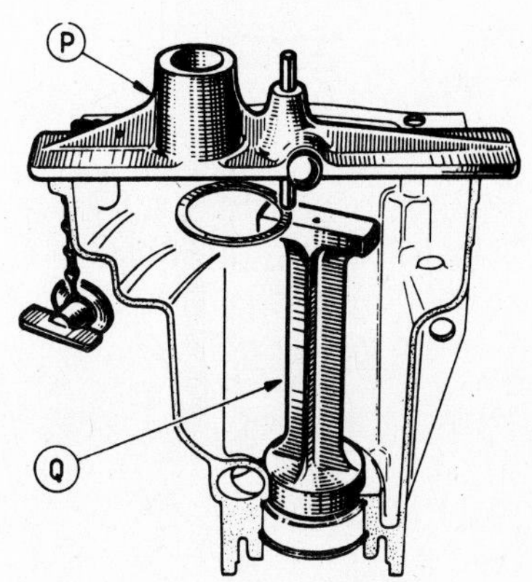

a Oil seal
b Snap-ring
c Adjustment shim
d Bearing
D Puller
P Gauge
Q Gauge

Replacing rear bearing.

2. Install puller and its spacer in order to hold bearing against housing shoulder.
3. Place a gauge on bearing and gauge on housing upper face. Bring rod into contact with block and lock it into position (uppermost position of bearing).
4. Remove the gauges and then remove puller and spacer. Using a drift, bring bearing fully down against lockring.
5. Install gauge without disturbing gauge rod. The distance between them is the thickness of the shim to be inserted between bearing and lockring.
6. Move bearing back onto bearing housing shoulder, remove lockring, insert shim as determined above and reinstall lockring.
7. Install oil seal.

Assembly—C3

All parts should be perfectly clean and dry, and they should be lubricated as they are assembled:

1. In replacing the rear bearing, install bearing, shim, lockring and new oil seal, in that order.
2. Insert intermediate shaft through inside of housing while driving front bearing into its housing. Remove rear bearing snapring using pliers, and install rear bearing with groove facing outward. Push bearing using body of puller, with transmission upright and front end of intermediate shaft resting on a wooden block. Make sure snapring is correctly engaged in bearing groove.
3. Install 1st gear pinion on intermediate shaft splines. Hold in position by means of a new nut temporarily screwed in hand tight. Bring mainshaft into position, rear end first. Install the following in this order: 2nd gear pinion (a) 2nd/3rd gear synchronizer and hub (b), 3rd gear pinion and bushing (c), 4th gear pinion (d) and its synchronizer (e).
4. Engage shaft until center bearing has fully entered housing. Hold assembly using a new nut temporarily screwed in hand tight on main shaft.
5. Install plate and wrench. Install 1st reverse sliding gear. Install clamp to keep 1st gear engaged. Engage 2nd and 1st gear. Torque 1st gear pinion to intermediate shaft at 50 ft. lbs. Stake

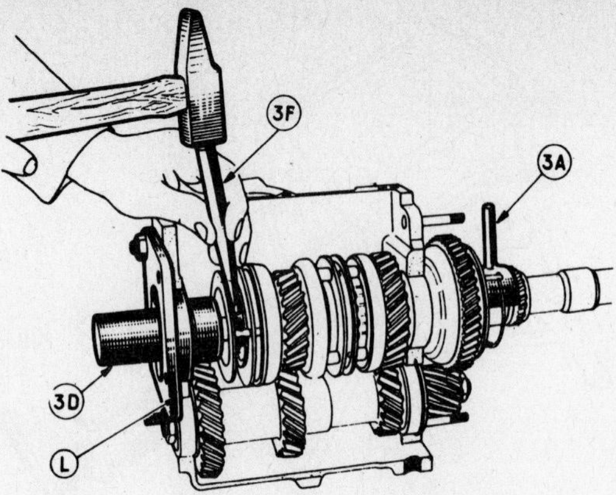

C3 reassembly (Steps 3 and 4).

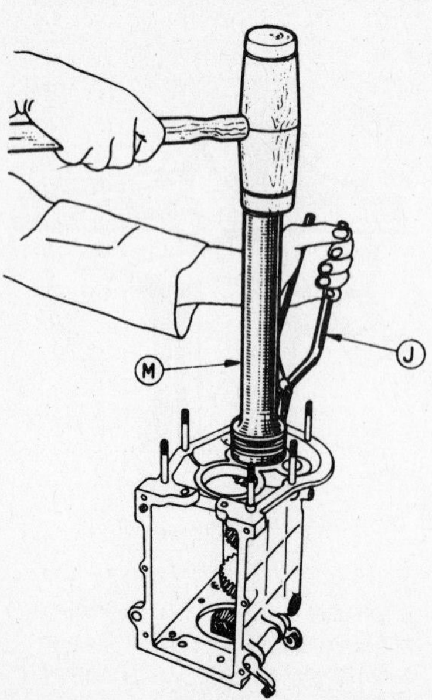

C3 reassembly (Steps 1 and 2).

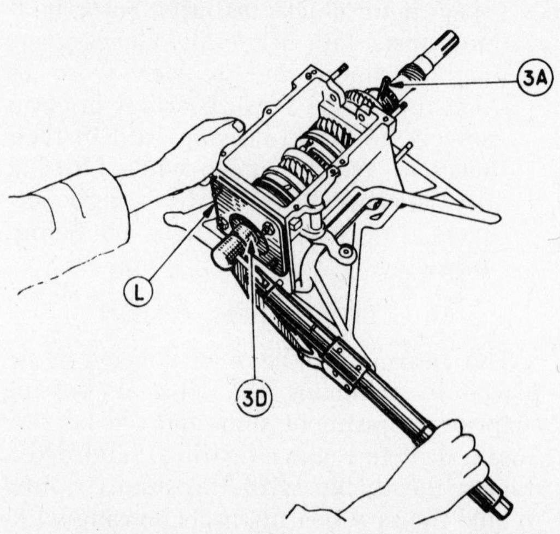

C3 reassembly (Step 5).

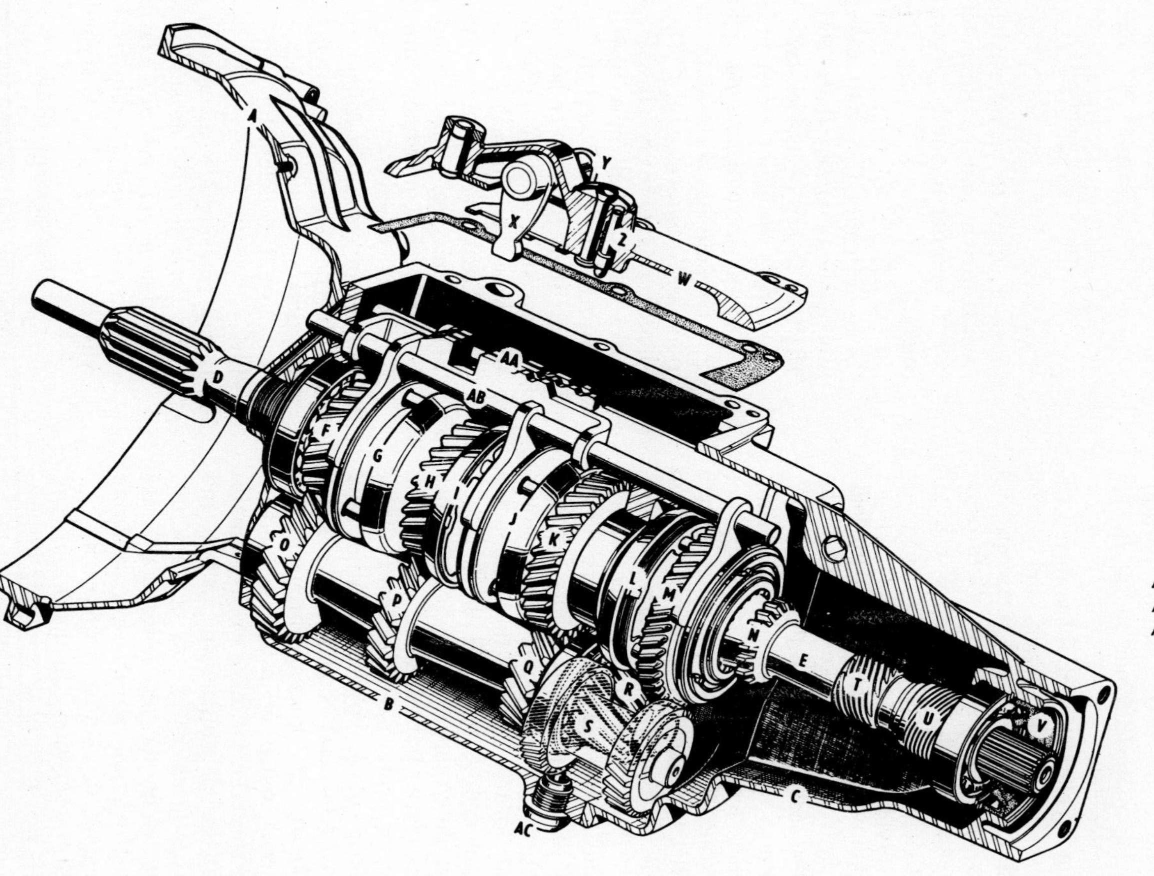

A. Bell housing
B. Transmission case
C. 1st reverse gear extension housing
D. Input shaft
E. Output shaft
F. Constant mesh 4th gear
G. 4th gear (direct drive) synchromesh
H. 3rd gear pinion
I. 3rd gear synchromesh
J. 2nd gear synchromesh
K. 2nd gear pinion
L. 1st gear synchromesh
M. 1st—reverse sliding gear
N. Reverse gear dog clutches
O. Constant mesh pinion
P. Constant mesh 3rd gear pinion
Q. Constant mesh 2nd gear pinion
R. 1st—Reverse idler pinion
S. Reverse gear pinion
T. Governor driving gear (JAEGER Automatic clutch only)
U. Speedometer driving gear
V. Seal
W. Transmission gear shift cover
X. Forks shifting lever
Y. Gearshift lever
Z. Fork shafts lock pin
AA. Forks
AB. Fork shafts
AC. Drain plug (magnetic)

Type C3 transmission.

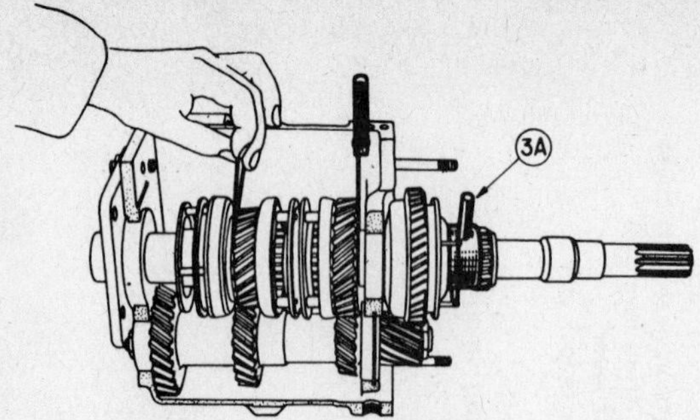

C3 reassembly (Step 6–8).

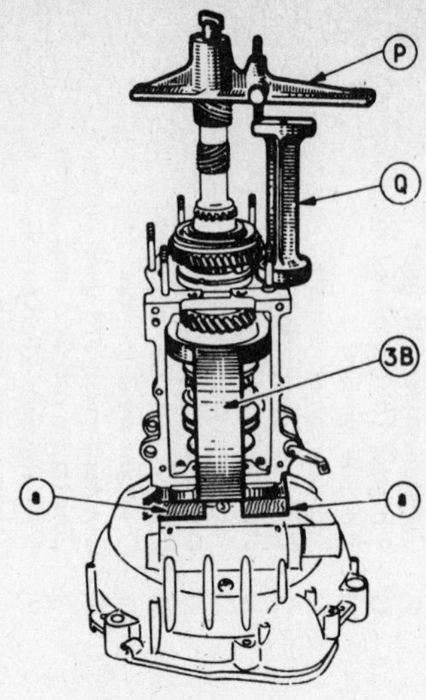

C3 reassembly (Steps 9–14).

carefully to both milled portions. Torque mainshaft nut to 20 ft. lbs. using wrench.

6. Using feelers, check clearances between 2nd gear pinion and pinion bushing shoulder and between 3rd gear pinion and 4th gear. Both clearances should be .012″ to .024″ (.3 to .5 mm).
7. If proper clearances are obtained, withdraw wrench until mainshaft locknut is freed, and stake locknut to the milled grooves using a punch.
8. Remove plate, wrench and clamp. Install mainshaft with bearing and lockring fitted. Tap lockring with a mallet to make sure it is firmly seated in its recess. Install gauge and attach it to transmission front face by means of two nuts. With gears in neutral, the gauge should fit into synchronizer, and 2nd gear pinion cone should come to rest against the fork when transmission is held vertically.
9. Lay clutch housing down on bench and place transmission upright on housing using a .75″ (19 mm) thick wooden block between gearbox and housing on each side of drive shaft. Make sure 2nd gear synchronizer cone is firmly seated against gauge, and install speedometer drive worm on mainshaft. Install gauge P in position and hold it firmly by means of its screw. Bring gauge Q into position on rear face of transmission housing and bring gauge rod into contact with block.
10. With transmission rear housing resting on its rear end, place gauge Q in position on bearing and gauge P on upper bearing surface. The distance between rod and gauge determines the thickness of shims to be inserted between rear bearing and speedometer drive worm in order to obtain proper adjustment.
11. Install adjustment shims as determined by use of gauge Q. Install reverse idler pinion, washers and shaft, and secure shaft by means of its lockscrew. Check protecting washers for correct installation, with oil cavities facing pinion.
12. Lay transmission horizontally on a support and remove gauge 3B. Shafts should rotate freely. Install selector forks and fork axis pins. Install clutch housing with paper gasket. Check locating rings for correct positioning on rear face of transmission housing.
13. Install rear housing, using Permatex for a good seal. Torque nuts to 15 ft. lbs. Install universal joint, including the bronze washer, and make sure it is lubricated. Engage two gears, and torque universal joint Allen screw to 50 ft. lbs. Loosen and re-torque to 10 ft. lbs. Stake carefully. With gears in neutral, install speedometer drive assembly.
14. Install transmission cover with gasket using Permatex. Before installation of transmission on vehicle, engage all speeds. All should operate freely. Fill with 1 1/2 quarts of SAE 40 motor oil.

Disassembly—BA7

1. Support the transmission in a cradle or fixture and clean outside surfaces.
2. Remove the clutch release fork, clutch

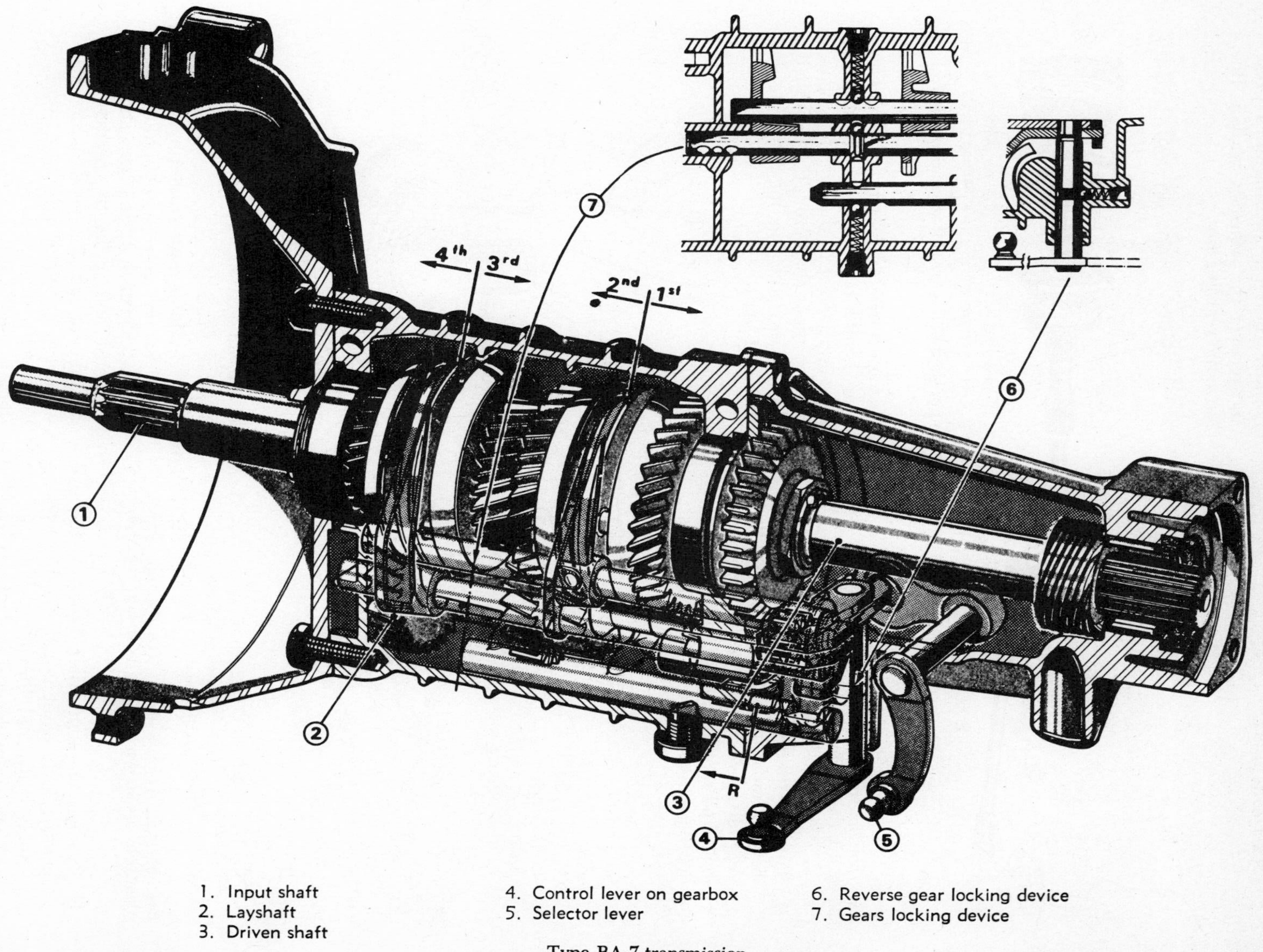

1. Input shaft
2. Layshaft
3. Driven shaft
4. Control lever on gearbox
5. Selector lever
6. Reverse gear locking device
7. Gears locking device

Type BA-7 transmission.

housing, and back-up light switch.

3. Remove the speedometer drive stop screw and remove speedometer drive socket with pliers.

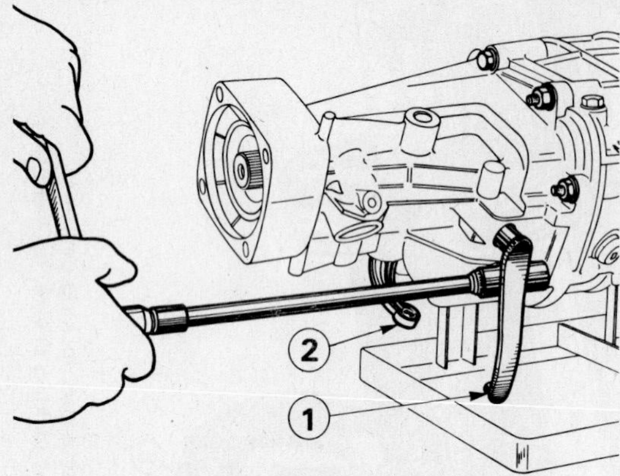

Rear housing removal—BA7. The shiftlever is shown at 1, the selector lever at 2.

4. Turn the transmission over, set lever to neutral and pull selector lever to the rear. Remove the seven rear housing bolts and remove the rear housing (tap with rubber mallet to free, if necessary).

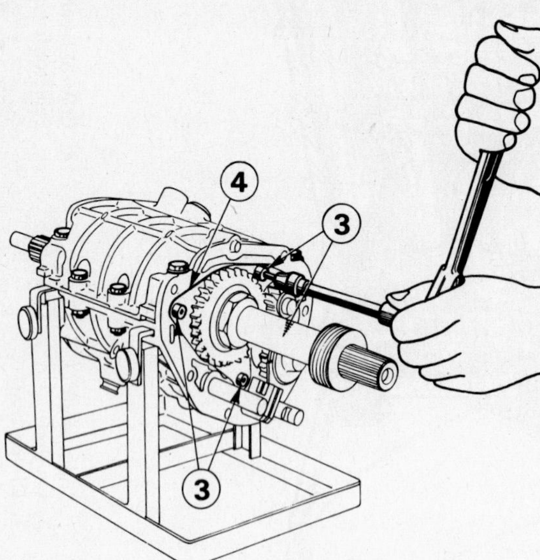

Bearing lock removal—BA7. The bearing lock Allen bolts are shown at 3, the beaming lock at 4.

5. Remove the four Allen bolts on the bearing lock, eight upper housing assembly bolts, and the upper housing. Lift out complete gear and pinion assembly.
6. From the intermediate shaft remove: snap-ring from the intermediate shaft reverse gear, spring washer, intermediate shaft reverse gear, and the bearing outer race.
7. Remove the front bearing on a press and recover the adjusting washer. Remove the rear bearing.

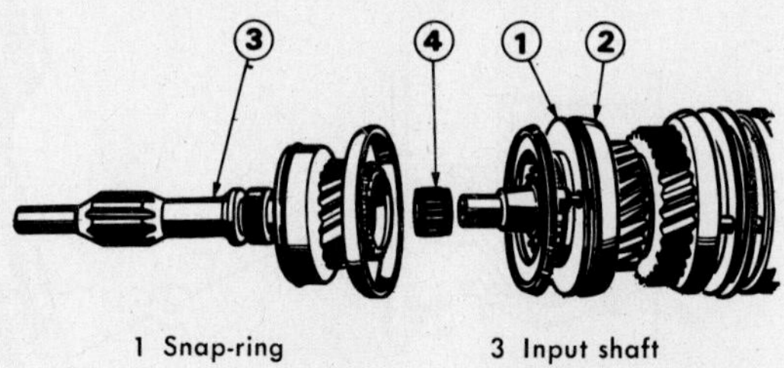

Input shaft and mainshaft separation—BA7

8. Engage third and fourth speed sliding gear 1 into third speed synchronizer cone and hold it in this position. Separate the input shaft from the mainshaft and remove the bearing from inside the input shaft.

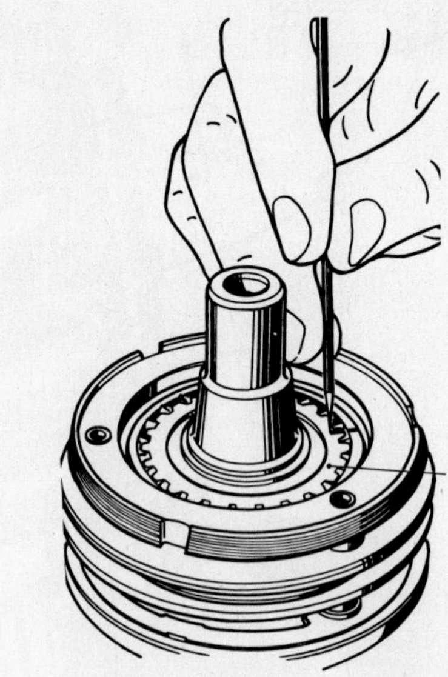

Scribing 3rd/4th speed sliding gear and hub—BA7

9. Remove the grease from the 3rd/4th speed synchronizer without disengaging the dog gear. Install the mainshaft in a vise and scribe the position and direction of 3rd/4th speed sliding gear with respect to the hub.
10. Remove the sliding gear.
11. Remove snap-ring and spring washer from 3rd/4th speed synchronizer. Completely unscrew nut while holding the mainshaft reverse gear.

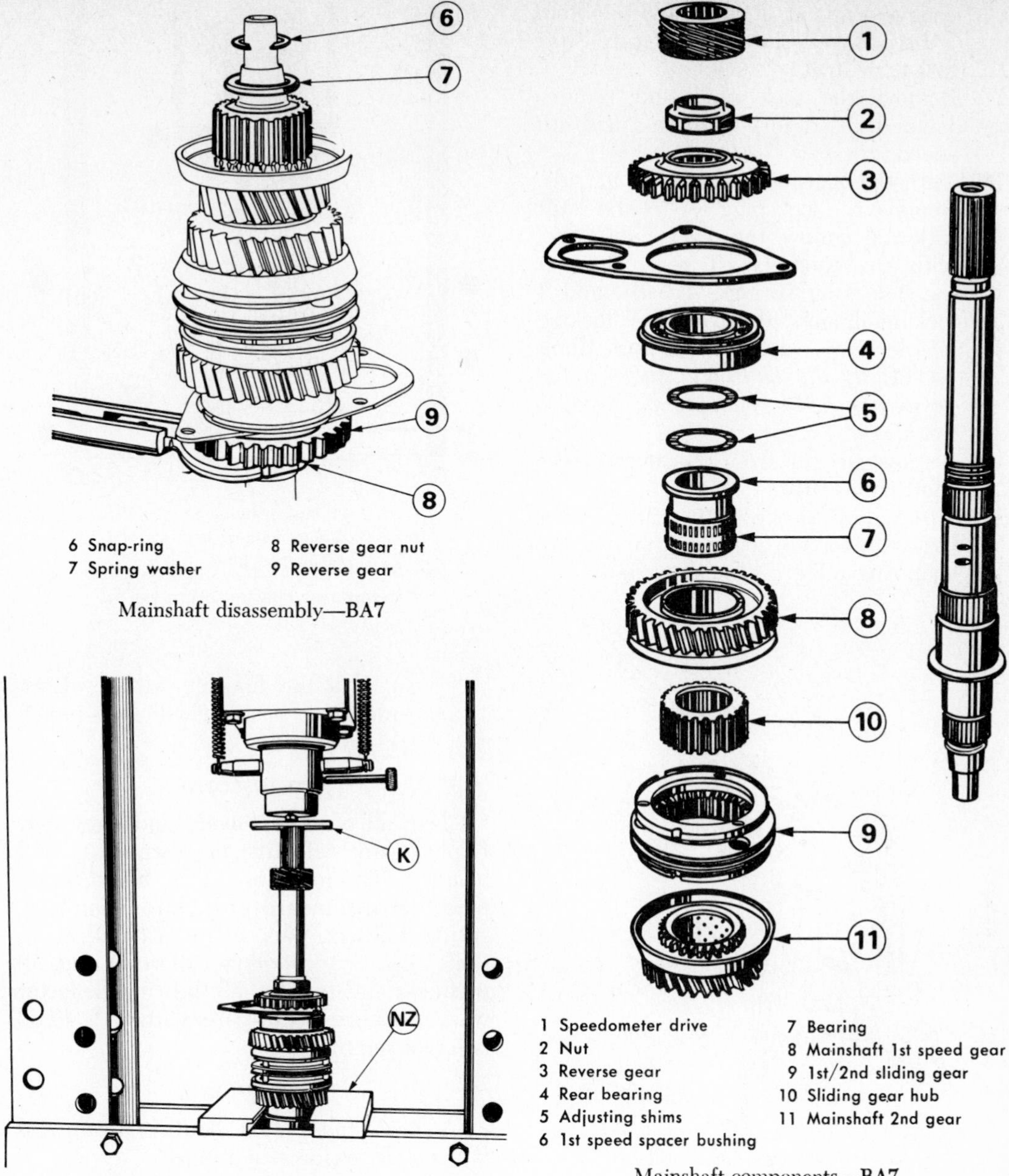

Mainshaft disassembly—BA7

Pressing rear bearing off the mainshaft—BA7

Mainshaft components—BA7

12. Press off the synchronizer hub and 3rd speed mainshaft.
13. Install the mainshaft on a press using a plate. Using a plate held by one of the rear housing bolts (tightened to 7 ft. lbs.), press the mainshaft downwards to free the rear bearing. Continue to press the mainshaft down and free the speedometer drive.
14. Remove the plate and then remove: speedometer drive, nut, reverse gear, rear bearing backing plate, rear bearing, adjusting shims, first speed spacer bushing, bearing, 1st speed gear, 1st/2nd speed synchronizer (without removing sliding gear from hub), and mainshaft 2nd speed. Remove grease from parts and mark their positions.
15. On the input shaft, remove the snap-ring and spring washer. Press off the bearing and recover it, the deflector washer, and adjusting shims.
16. Engage 2nd gear and remove the pin from 1st/2nd speed shift fork with a drift. Return shift fork to neutral and

engage 4th gear. Remove the pin from 3rd/4th speed shift fork. Return shift fork to neutral.

17. Remove the lock plug and remove 1st/2nd speed fork shaft and 3rd/4th speed fork shaft.
18. Turn the transmission case on its side. Remove the lock plug for reverse shift fork and remove the reverse shift fork with the countershaft gear. Recover the 3 locking springs, 4 balls, and 1 locking finger. Recover the locking needle from 3rd/4th speed fork shaft. NOTE: *If the balls are stuck in the passage, a 1/4″ rod may be used to free them.*
19. Remove the pin from the reverse gear shaft with a drift.
20. If the guide sleeve in the clutch housing requires replacement, remove the snap-ring and press the sleeve out.

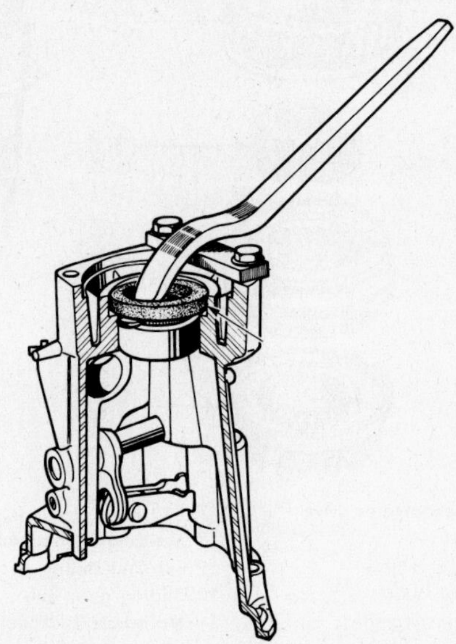

Rear housing bearing seal removal—BA7

21. The rear housing bearing should be replaced during overhaul. Remove the rear oil seal as shown. Install a plate on the housing K to prevent damaging the surface and pry the seal out.
22. Using a pipe or bushing of suitable size, press the bearing out. If the rear housing gear controls are defective, the unit must be replaced. CAUTION: *Cover supporting plate Z with cardboard to prevent damaging the surface of the housing.*
23. Remove the neutral ball lock plug. Clean the ball and its recess. Coat the plug with sealer and tighten until it is

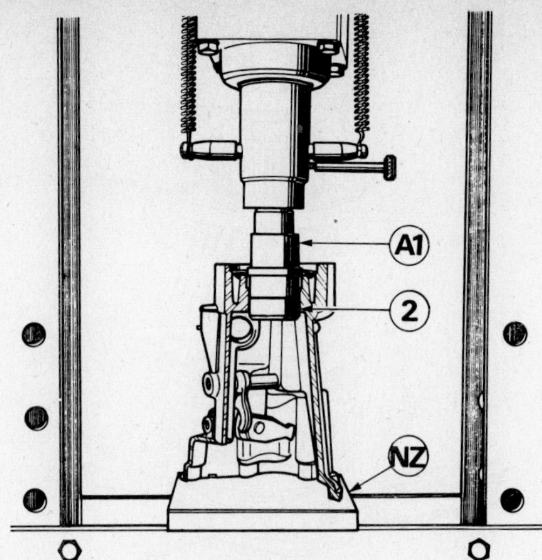

A1 Pipe or bushing
2 Rear housing bearing
NZ Support plate

Pressing rear housing bearing—BA7

flush with the housing surface. Lock the plug into position with two punch marks.

Parts Inspection

Clean all parts in solvent and blow dry. Replace any defective or worn gears and bearings. The following parts should be replaced as a standard procedure: snap-ring, spring washers, pins, mainshaft nut, mainshaft oil seal, speedometer drive O-ring, all washers, and input shaft bearing deflector washer. Lubricate all parts with SAE 40 oil before assembly.

Assembly

1. Check the clutch housing front and rear faces for straightness.
2. If the clutch housing guide sleeve was removed, install a new sleeve with a mallet and a new snap-ring.
3. Press the bearing in the rear housing as shown and press the oil seal into position until it bottoms.
4. Check for positive action of the neutral ball lock by moving the selector lever in both directions. Check that plug is flush with the housing surface. If the ball lock is malfunctioning, remove the plug and check spring and ball condition. Replace any defective parts.
5. On the left side housing, install reverse gear shaft with a mallet. Make sure that the pin holes align. Install a new

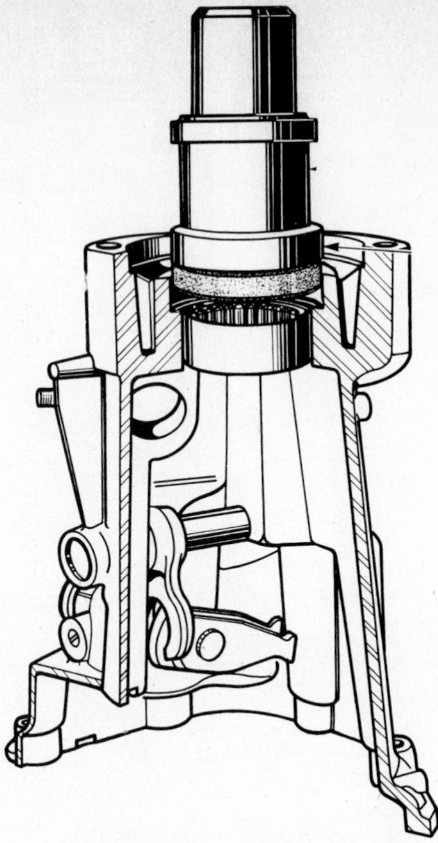

Rear housing bearing installation—BA7

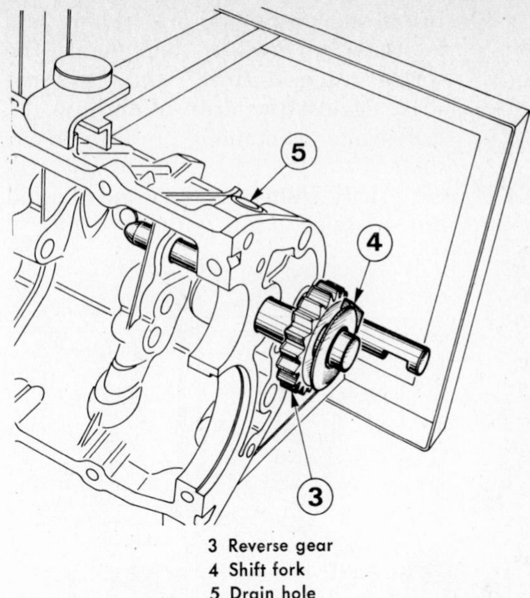

3 Reverse gear
4 Shift fork
5 Drain hole

Reverse gear and shift fork installation—BA7

pin, coated with grease, by tapping in with a drift.

6. Turn the transmission half so that drain hole is up. Install reverse gear pinion together with shift fork.

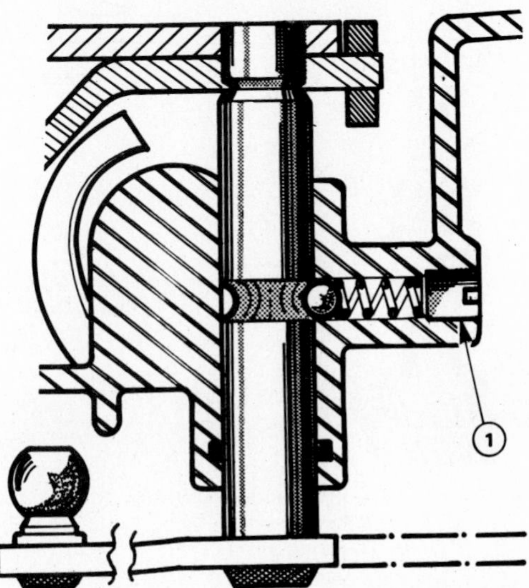

Neutral ball lock—BA7. One indicates the neutral ball lock plug.

7. Insert the ball and spring into the locking passage. Coat the threads of plug with sealer and tighten to 7 ft. lbs. Move reverse shift fork into neutral.
8. Position the housing so that the locking passage is up and install 3rd/4th and reverse locking finger. Grease the locking needle and insert it into its housing in 3rd/4th gear selector fork shaft.

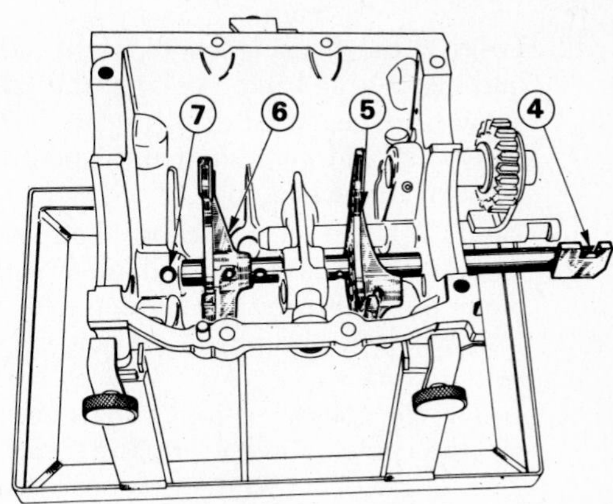

4 Fork shaft
5 1st/2nd gear selector fork
6 3rd/4th gear selector fork
7 Locking ball hole

Selector fork installation—BA7

9. Turn transmission half as shown. Install the 1st/2nd selector fork (larger of two) and 3rd/4th selector fork. Insert fork shaft until it is flush with ball lock hole.

10. Insert one spring and one locking ball into passage. Press the ball against the spring using a drift, while pushing shaft against the drift. Withdraw the drift while maintaining pressure on the shaft.
11. Set shaft into neutral and install 3rd/4th selector fork with a new pin.

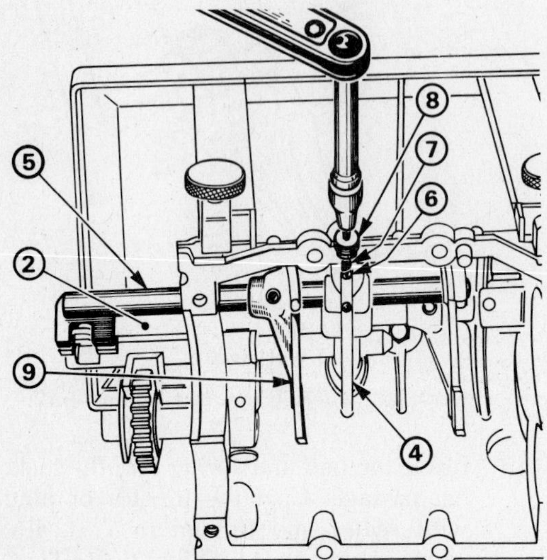

2 3rd/4th gear shaft
4 Locking ball passage
5 1st/2nd gear shaft
6 1st/2nd gear locking ball
7 Spring
8 Plug
9 1st/2nd selector fork

Locking ball installation—BA7

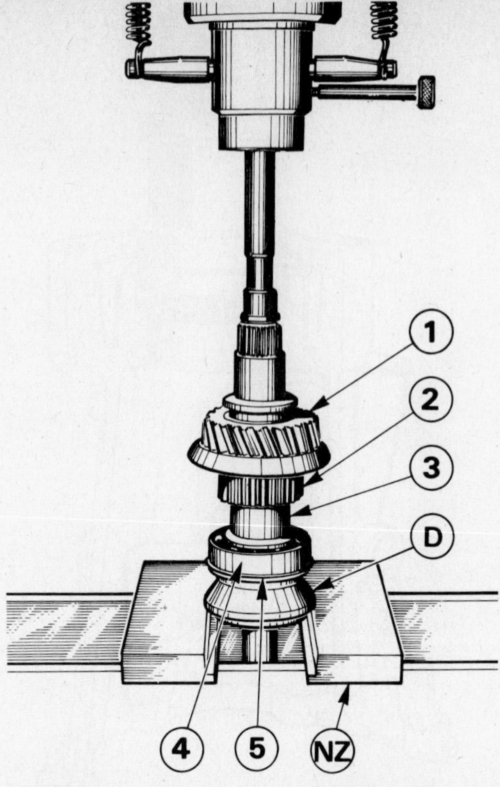

1 2nd gear
2 1st/2nd gear synchronizer hub
3 1st gear spacer
4 Bearing
5 Snap-ring
NZ Plate
D Installation ring

Mainshaft Assembly—BA7

12. Position the housing on its right side and insert a ball into passage, the ball should rest against 3rd/4th gear shaft. Insert 1st/2nd gear shaft until neutral position is reached.
13. Insert 1st/2nd gear locking ball and spring into passage. Install plug with sealer on its threads and tighten to 7 ft. lbs. Install a new pin in 1st/2nd gear selector fork.
14. Install the following input shaft parts on the press surface: spacer, drive gear, one bearing with a new snap-ring on upper surface, and ring. Press the bearing onto the shaft until it bottoms.
15. Install the following parts on the mainshaft: mainshaft 2nd gear pinion, 1st/2nd gear synchronizer hub, 1st gear spacer, bearing with new snap-ring on bottom face. Press the bearing into place.
16. On the mainshaft, install a new nut and tighten to 40 ft. lbs.
17. Install the front and rear bearings on

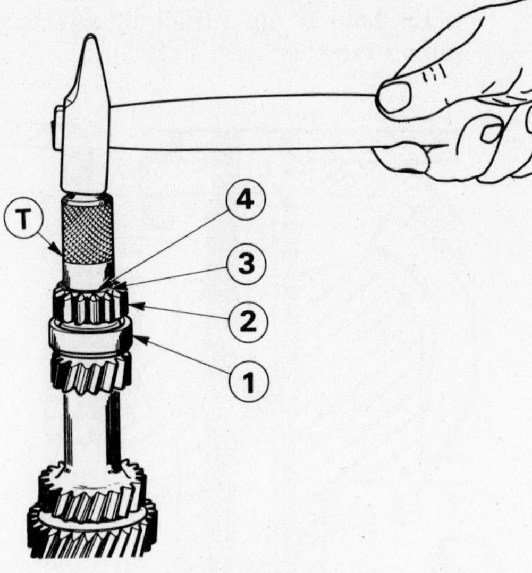

1 Rear bearing outer race
2 Reverse gear
3 Spring washer
4 Snap-ring
T Driver

Intermediate shaft bearing installation—BA7

the intermediate shaft. Position the rear bearing outer race, reverse gear pinion, a new spring washer, and a new snap-ring on the intermediate shaft. Engage the snap-ring in the mounting groove using a driver.

18. Install the parts on the mainshaft in the following order, making sure to align the reference marks made during disassembly: 2nd gear pinion, synchronizer hub along with sliding gear, 1st gear pinion, cage bearing, spacer bushing, adjustment shims, and rear bearing with snap-ring facing the rear. Bearing is pressed on. NOTE: *Adjustment shims are available in thicknesses of* .006″ (0.15 mm), .008″ (0.20 mm), .010″ (0.25 mm), and .020″ (0.50 mm).
19. Install the mainshaft assembly in the larger hole of the backing plate. The machined surface of this must contact bearing. Engage the reverse gear with chamfered edge of teeth towards the rear. Install a new nut and tighten to 40 ft. lbs.

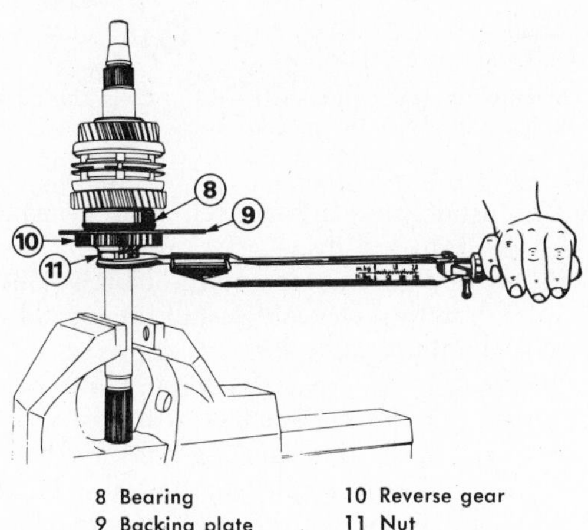

8 Bearing
9 Backing plate
10 Reverse gear
11 Nut

Installing the mainshaft in the backing plate—BA7

20. Press the speedometer drive gear on the mainshaft.
21. Install the 3rd gear mainshaft pinion and 3rd/4th gear synchronizer hub. Install a new spring washer and snap-ring.
22. Install the 3rd/4th gear sliding gear, making sure the reference marks are in correct position. Engage third gear.
23. Install components on the input shaft in the following order: adjustment shims, deflector washer, bearing, spring washers, and snap-ring.
24. Position the input shaft assembly on the press as shown, resting on a spacer. Slide a pipe or drift over the input shaft and exert slight pressure to compress the spring washer and align the snap-ring with its groove. Using pliers, squeeze the snap-ring until its outside diameter is the same as that of the drift.
25. Install the bearing in the drive gear. Assemble the input shaft and mainshaft. Move 3rd/4th speed sliding gear back to the neutral position. Install the

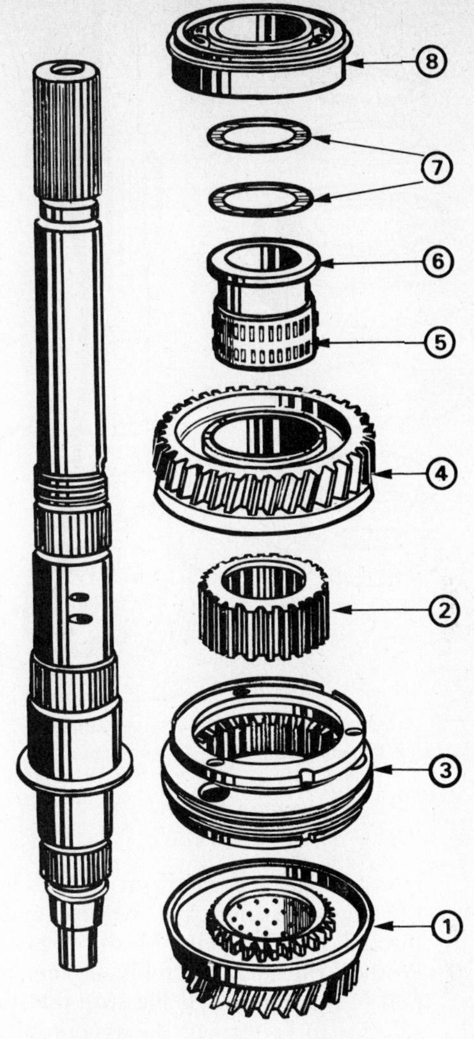

1 2nd gear
2 Synchronizer hub
3 Sliding gear
4 1st gear
5 Bearing
6 Spacer bushing
7 Shims
8 Rear bearing

Mainshaft assembly—BA7

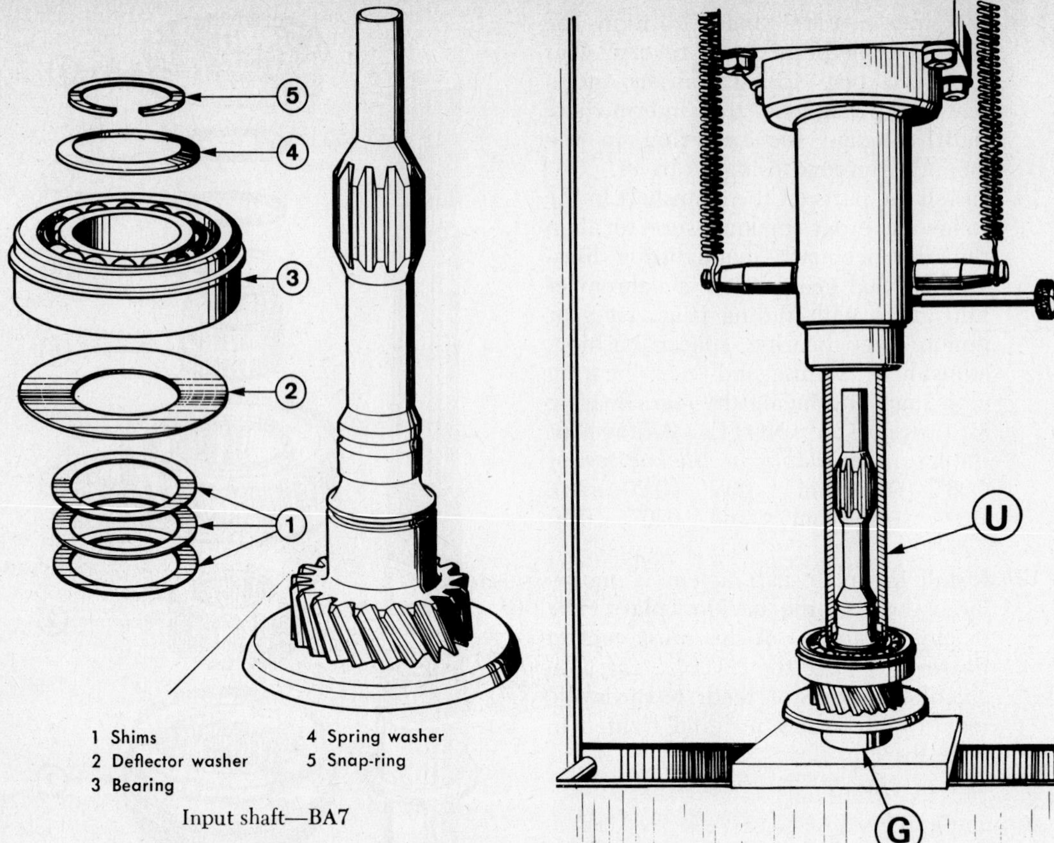

Input shaft—BA7

Assembling the input shaft—BA7. U is the pipe or bushing and G the spacer.

intermediate gear shaft on this assembly by passing the reverse gear through backing plate. Mesh the gears.

26. Position the gear assembly in the left half of the housing, being sure that the selector forks engage the synchronizer rings correctly. Install the intermediate gear shaft front bearing outer race. Coat the mating surfaces with sealer and install the right half of the housing.

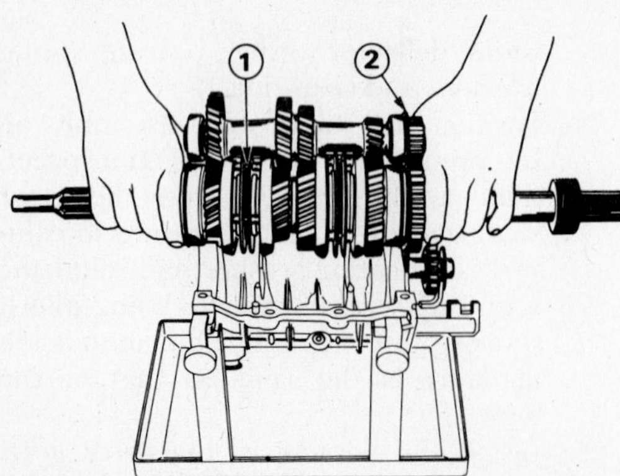

Gear assembly installation into half housing—BA7. The 3rd/4th sliding gear is at 1, the backing plate at 2.

27. Install and tighten the four housing bolts to 4 ft. lbs.
28. Coat the rear face of the clutch housing with sealer and install the six bolts. Tighten to 20 ft. lbs.
29. Install the rear backing plate and tighten the Allen bolts to 7 ft. lbs.
30. Loosen the four housing bolts and heat the housing while rotating the input shaft. Retighten the four bolts to 11 ft. lbs.
31. Install the four half housing assembly bolts and nuts and tighten to 7 ft. lbs. Coat the rear housing mating faces with sealer and install with the studs and four bolts.
32. Pull selector lever completely back. Tighten the seven rear housing bolts and studs to 11 ft. lbs. Oil the rear housing bearing.
33. Install the speedometer drive with a new O-ring, coated with grease. Rotate into position by turning with pliers. Install the stop screw and locknut.
34. On the inside of the clutch housing, in-

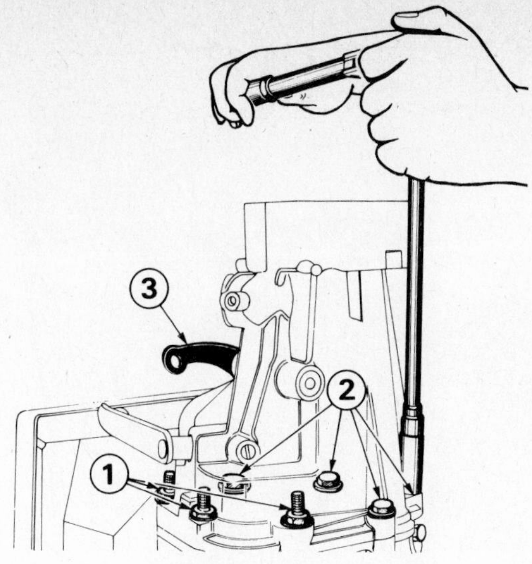

1 Studs
2 Attaching bolts
3 Selector lever

Rear housing installation—BA7

sert the rubber cup in the groove behind the ball and fill with grease. Lightly coat the guide sleeve with grease.

35. Slide the clutch fork from the inside towards the outside of the housing. Using a screwdriver to raise the fork backing spring, engage the fork on the ball with the spring pressing on the rubber cup.

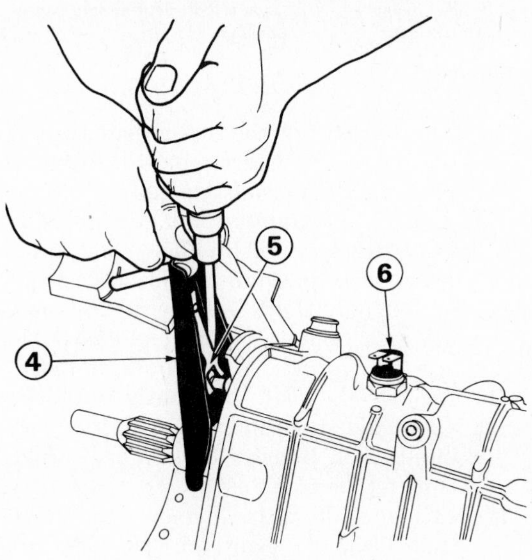

4 Clutch fork
5 Fork spring
6 Back-up switch

Clutch fork installation—BA7

36. Install the back-up light switch with a new seal. NOTE: *Copper switches are tightened to 9 ft. lbs. and steel switches to 20 ft. lbs.*
37. Before installation into the car, engage all gears to make sure that they operate freely. Fill the transmission with SAE 20/40 motor oil.

Disassembly—BB6

1. Engine should be removed from the car as previously outlined. Remove the clutch housing, clutch assembly, and timing gear cover as outlined in those sections.
2. Separate the transmission case from the engine block by removing the fourteen attaching bolts.
3. Turn the transmission over and remove the oil pan and oil pump strainer. CAUTION: *The spacer for the right side drain plug is installed at the factory with hard setting Loctite and should not be removed.*
4. Remove the bolts holding the left and right covers of the differential housing, and remove the differential assembly.
5. If repairs are to be performed on the differential, proceed as follows. If differential repair is not necessary, skip to step 9.
6. Remove the six bolts which retain the differential ring gear. Remove the left half casing, differential side gear, and the thrust washer.
7. Using a mallet, drive the ring gear off the casing. Remove the differential pinion shaft, the two thrust washers, the second differential side gear, and thrust washer.
8. To remove the differential bearings, use a bearing extractor and thrust pad.
9. Remove the external oil pipe and two fitting bolts.
10. Remove the gear selector cover and gasket. Remove the locking springs and balls.
11. Engage reverse and remove the pin from the reverse gear fork. Recover the ball and spring from the reverse gear selector by pivoting it upwards.
12. Remove the pin from the reverse gear selector and recover the reverse gear fork, shaft, and the reverse gear selector.
13. Remove the countershaft bearing retaining plate. Remove the snap-ring and spring washer.

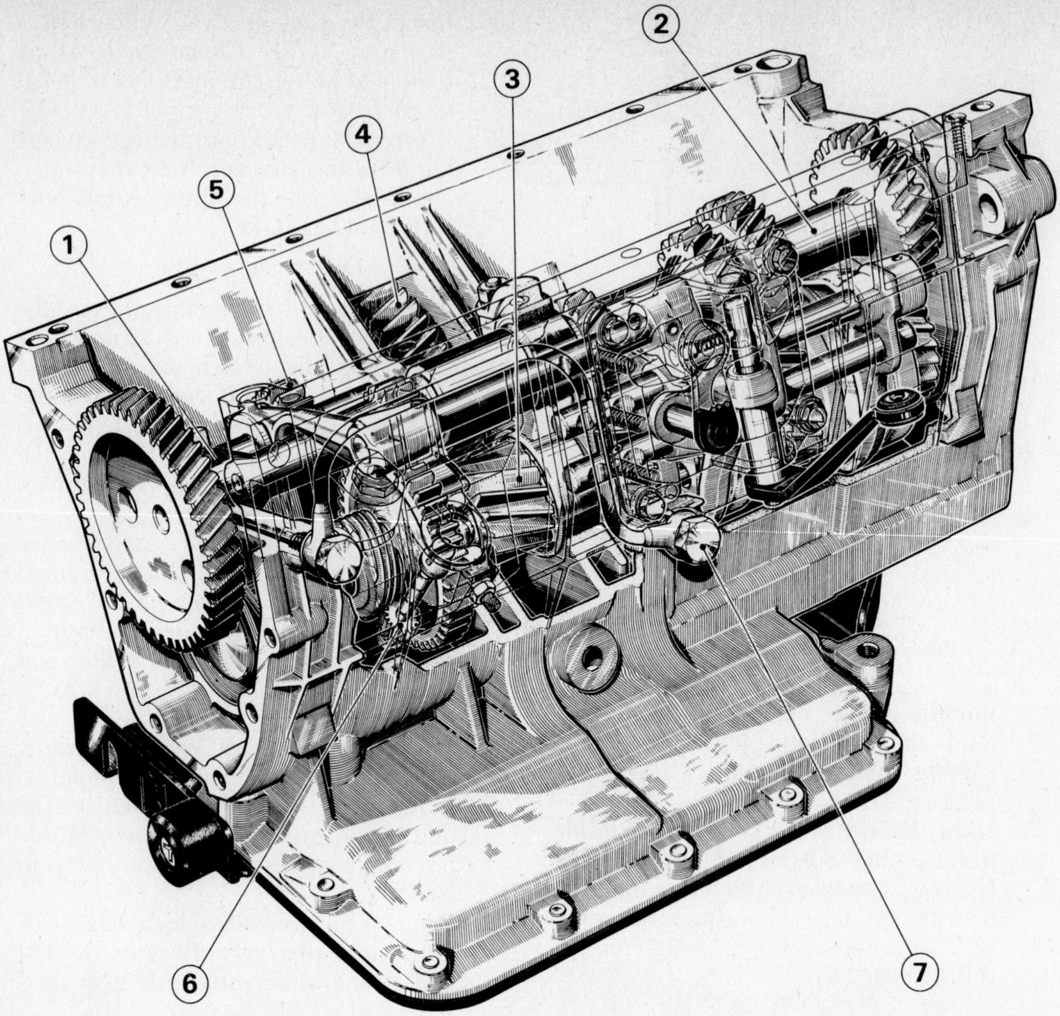

1 Input shaft
2 Countershaft
3 Differential drive gear
4 Differential ring gear
5 Reverse gear idler pinion
6 Speedometer drive gear
7 Countershaft bearing lubrication passage

304 BB6 transmission

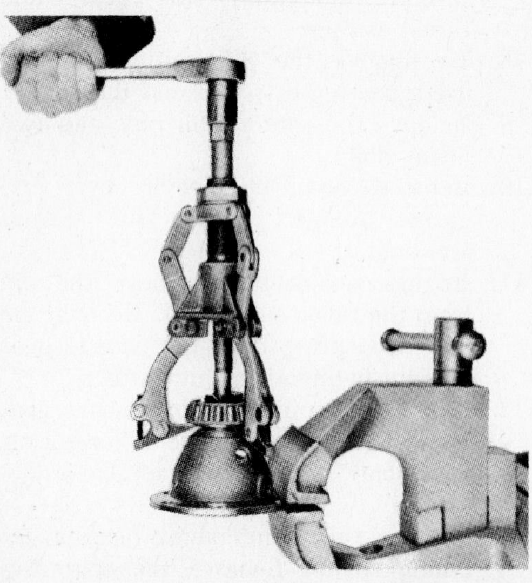

Differential bearing removal—BB6

14. Tap the end of the input shaft to free the bearing and ease removal. Install a plate on the transmission end.
15. Remove the countershaft bearing with an extractor. CAUTION: *Snap-ring must be in position in the input shaft and countershaft, otherwise 2nd and 4th gear pinions will contact and damage their respective synchronizer cones.*
16. Remove the plate previously installed. Close the snap-ring and withdraw the input shaft. Remove the center bearing cap and the countershaft.
17. Engage 4th gear. Remove the pins from 3rd/4th gear selector, 3rd/4th gear selector fork, and reverse sliding gear shaft.
18. Remove the reverse gear shaft and the sliding gear.

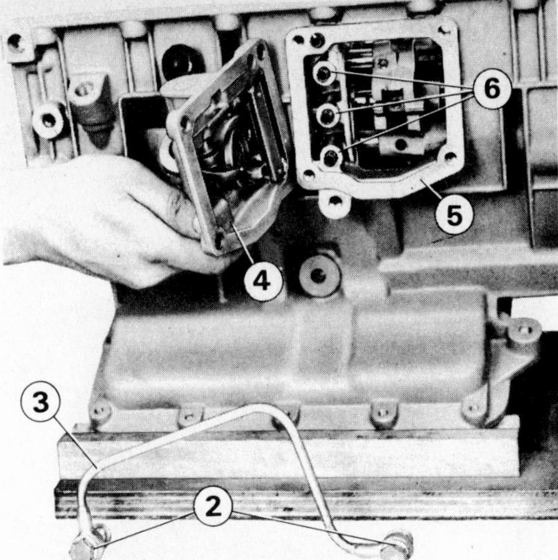

2 Union bolts
3 Oil pipe
4 Selector cover
5 Gasket
6 Locking springs and balls

Selector cover removal—BB6

Countershaft bearing removal—BB6, HIZ is the plate, G the bearing extractors

19. Remove the 3rd/4th gear selector fork shaft after rotating it 1/4 turn to prevent the locking finger from falling out. Remove the 3rd/4th gear selector.
20. Engage 2nd gear and remove the pin from the 1st/2nd gear selector fork. Remove the 1st/2nd selector fork shaft and the forks.
21. Recover the two locking fingers from the gear selector fork shaft.
22. Remove the speedometer drive lock-screw and remove the driving bushing by turning 1/2 turn clockwise.
23. Remove the mainshaft snap-rings and spring washers from both ends.
24. Remove the speedometer drive and the reverse gear.
25. Attach the plate used for removing the countershaft bearing to the end of the transmission case. Install the housing in the press, resting it on the plate.

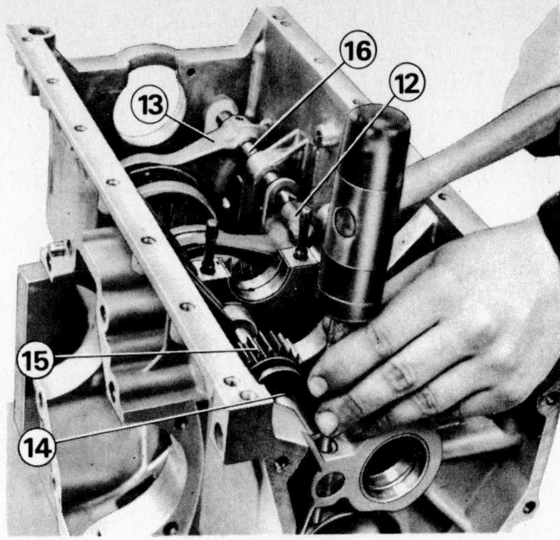

12 3rd/4th gear selector
13 3rd/4th gear selector fork
14 Reverse sliding gear shaft
15 Reverse sliding gear
16 3rd/4th gear selector fork shaft

3rd/4th gear selector fork and reverse sliding gear shaft removal—BB6

18 Bearing inner race
19 4th gear spacer
20 4th gear and bushing

Bearing and race removal—BB6

Spread the mainshaft snap-ring and drive out the shaft until the housing plug is pushed out by the shaft. Use a rod with a maximum diameter of .787″.

26. Remove the needle bearing inner race, 4th gear spacer, and 4th gear pinion and bushing.

27. Install a thrust pad on the bearing outer race and press out.
28. With the housing on the worktable, remove the mainshaft with its two bearings, 3rd/4th gear synchronizers, 3rd gear pinion and bushing, spacer, 2nd gear pinion and bushing, 1st/2nd gear synchronizer, 1st gear pinion and bushing, and shims. NOTE: *Do not separate synchronizers and hubs. Mark them as to relative position in the transmission.*
29. Remove the ball and roller bearings from the mainshaft.

Parts Inspection

Clean the transmission parts in solvent. Clean transmission mating faces with a cloth soaked in solvent, do not scrape them or use abrasives. Check the condition of the oil passages and countershaft and input shaft bearings. The transmission housing, differential housing, and countershaft bearing cap are machined after assembly and therefore never replaced separately. If replacement of the input pinion bushing is necessary, the bushing must be reamed to between 1.47650″ (37.505mm) and 1.47657″ (37.533mm). This machining should be done by a machine shop equipped to align bore main bearings, as all three bearings must be perfectly aligned. Replace washers throughout the transmission. Lubricate all parts with SAE 20/40 motor oil as they are assembled.

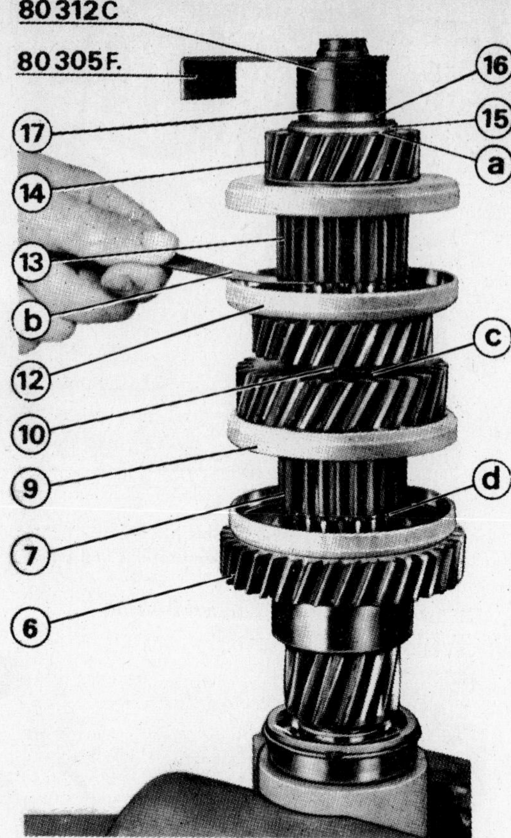

6 1st gear bushing and pinions
7 Synchronizer hub
9 2nd gear bushing and pinion
10 Spacer
12 3rd gear bushing and pinion
13 Synchronizer hub
14 4th gear
15 4th gear bushing
17 Shims, Fork, Spacer

Mainshaft assembly—BB6

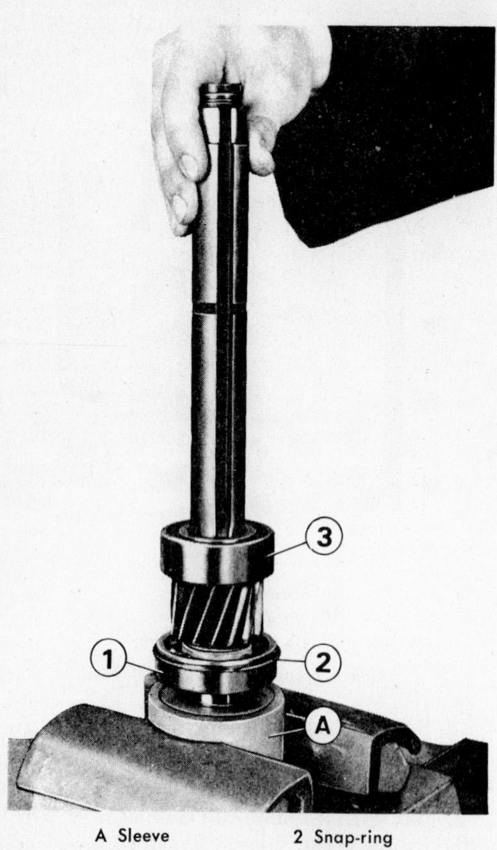

A Sleeve
1 Bearing
2 Snap-ring
3 Bearing

Mainshaft bearing installation—BB6

Assembly—BB6

1. Install the bearing with the groove towards the gear. Install a new snap-ring in the groove. Install bearing.
2. Assemble the following parts on the mainshaft: 1st gear bushing and pinion, synchronizer hub, 2nd gear bushing and pinion, spacer, 3rd gear bushing and pinion, synchronizer hub, 4th gear pinion and bushing, and spacer.
3. Install a piece of tubing the same

length as the distance between a fork in the snap-ring groove and spacer. Fork may be made from flat stock. Determine the number of shims to be installed under the fork to obtain a tight fit with the fork inserted in the snap-ring groove.

4. Permissible play at points a, b, c, and d should be between .008″ (.20mm) and .014″ (.35mm). Pinion bushings should be replaced if play exceeds these limits.
5. Spacer 16 is available in sizes from .126″(3.2mm) to 190″(4.8mm) in .016″(.4mm) increments. Shims 17 are .006″(.15mm). Spacer 10, between 2nd gear bushing and 3rd gear bushing, is available in increments of .002″ (.05mm) from .79″(2mm) to .114″ (2.9mm). Shims between the bearing and 1st gear bushing are available in sizes of .006″(.15mm), .008″(.20mm), .010″(25mm), and .020″(.50mm).
6. After determining correct spacer and shim sizes, disassemble the mainshaft assembly.

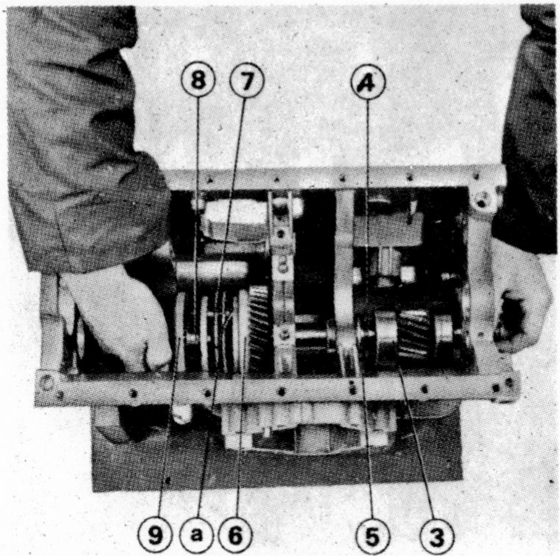

3 Bearing
4 Shims
5 1st gear bushing
6 1st gear
7 1st/2nd gear synchronizer
8 2nd gear bushing
9 2nd gear pinion
a Reference groove

Mainshaft installation—BB6

7. Place shim(s) between the bearing and the 1st gear bushing. Install the snap-ring in its groove in the housing.
8. Partially engage the mainshaft in the housing and install the following: 1st gear pinion, the 1st/2nd gear synchronizer and hub (with groove reference mark on the 1st gear side, the hub synchronizer reference marks in line), the 2nd gear bushing, and the 2nd gear pinion.

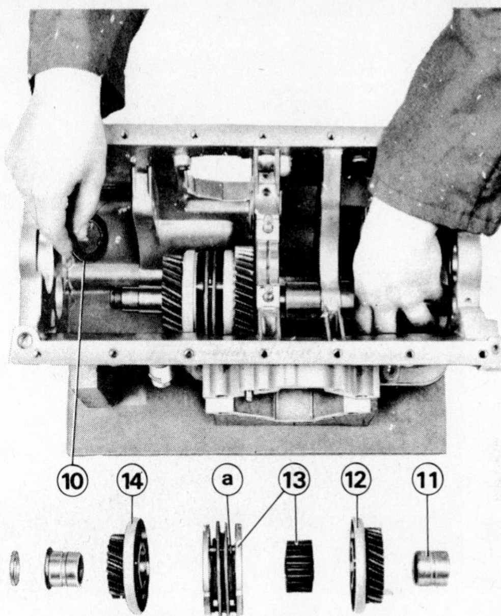

11 3rd gear bushing
12 3rd gear pinion
13 Hub
14 4th gear
a 3rd/4th synchronizer

Mainshaft assembly—BB6

9. Install: spacer, 3rd gear bushing and pinion, hub, and 3rd/4th gear synchronizer (with groove reference marks in line).
10. Slightly raise the mainshaft and fit the 4th gear pinion.
11. Hold the bearing snap-ring and engage the mainshaft using a mallet and driver. Continue until the snap-ring engages in the bearing groove.
12. Engage the 4th gear bushing through the bearing hole. Install the reverse gear pinion with the small shoulder against the bearing. Install the speedometer drive gear.
13. Check the side play at the speedometer gear. If excessive, place shims between reverse gear and the speedometer gear. Shims available are: .006″(.15 mm) and .020″(.50 mm). Install a new spring and snap-ring.
14. Install the plate, previously used, and position a spacer between the mainshaft end and the plate. Position the spacer, shims (if required), and the roller bearing (with inscription up) on the end of the shaft.

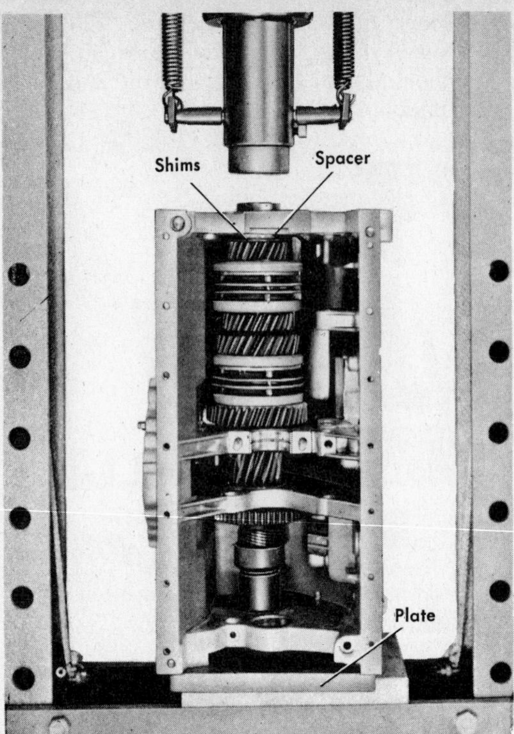

Mainshaft bearing installation—BB6

15. Using a ring, insert the bearing until it bottoms. Place a new washer and snap-ring on the end of the shaft. Engage the snap-ring in the groove.
16. Remove the ring and check snap-ring fit with a pair of pliers. Measure the outer diameter of the snap-ring, which should not exceed .89″ (22.6 mm).
17. Remove the plate and the spacer.
18. Install a new end plug coated with sealer by tapping it in with a drift.
19. Install the speedometer drive bushing, with a new seal, by turning it 1/2 turn.
20. Position the 1st/2nd and 3rd/4th gear selector forks in their respective synchronizers. Engage 1st/2nd selector fork shaft from the right, make sure that the locking notch is on the same axis as the vertical hole. Insert a locking finger.
21. After making sure that the locking finger is in place and does not protrude into the 3rd/4th gear selector shaft hole, place the 3rd/4th selector shaft in position.
22. Position it with the two flats facing upwards and insert the locking finger, after greasing it.
23. Insert the shaft in this position. Install the selector control from the right with the ramp up, until it is in line with the 1st/2nd gear shaft.

3rd/4th gear selector shaft installation—BB6

24. Turn the 3rd/4th gear shaft 1/4 turn towards the selector cover opening. Using new pins, secure the shafts, forks, and selector controls.
25. Insert the reverse sliding gear shaft in the housing and install the gear with the groove facing out.
26. Install the center bearing cap and tighten the nuts to 16 ft. lbs.
27. Install a new snap-ring in the groove on the end of the input shaft and engage the input shaft into the countershaft.
28. Compress the snap-ring and push the

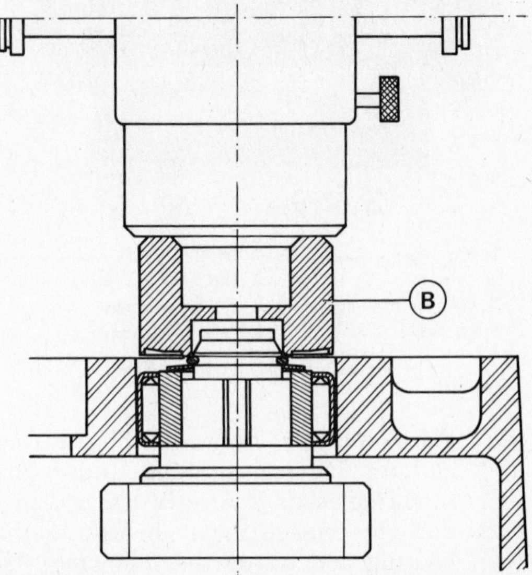

Mainshaft bearing installation using positioning ring B—BB6

input shaft in until the snap-ring engages in the countershaft groove.

29. Install plate and a spacer between the input pinion and the plate. Place the transmission upright and rest it on the plate. Install the bearing (groove facing out).
30. Install a new cup washer and snap-ring. Outer diameter of the snap-ring should not be more than .89″(22.6 mm).
31. Remove the plate and fit the triangular bearing retaining plate. Tighten the three bolts to 7 ft. lbs. NOTE: *Make sure that the countershaft turns freely. If it does not, loosen the bearing cap nuts and tap the shaft until it can be turned freely.*
32. Position the 2nd locking finger and install the reverse gear selector fork.
33. Engage the shaft from the right. The locking notches must face the rear of the housing. Install a new pin in the selector control.

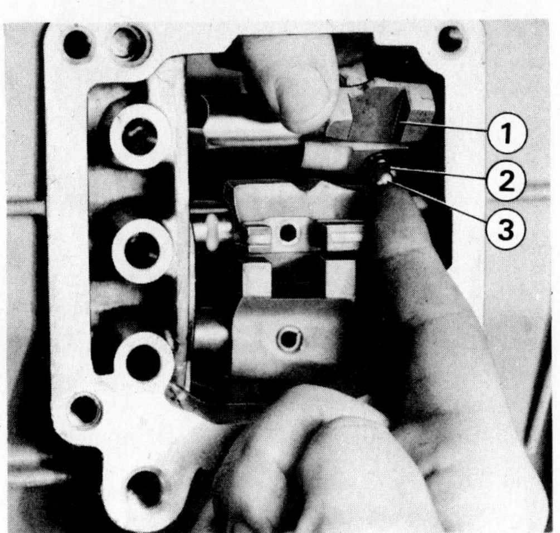

1 Selector
2 Spring
3 Ball

Selector spring and ball installation—BB6

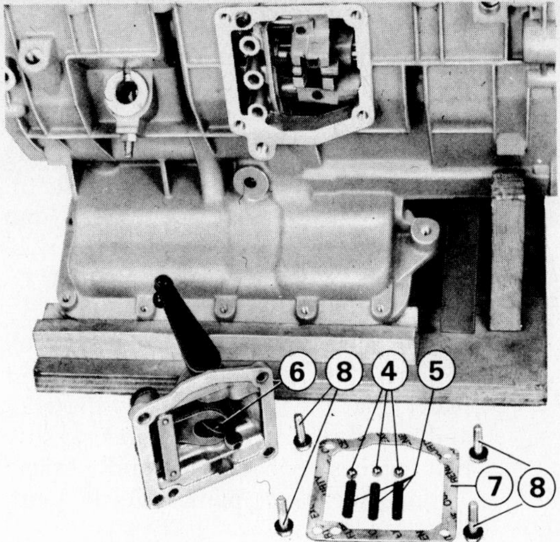

4 Balls
5 Springs
6 Selector cover
7 Gasket
8 Attaching bolts

Selector cover installation—BB6

34. Push the selector to the right and pivot it upwards. Install the spring (free height 1.03″) and the ball into the selector.
35. Compress the spring while lowering the selector and return to neutral. Pin the reverse gear fork to its shaft with a new pin.
36. Install locking balls and springs into position (free height of springs: 1.16″). Install the selector cover with a new gasket. Install the bolts with new washers and torque to 7 ft. lbs.
37. Install the thrust washer, differential side gear, differential pinion gears and their thrust washers into the differential casing. Install the differential pinion shaft.
38. Install the thrust washer and differential side gear into the differential casing. Assemble the differential.

1 Differential case
2 Thrust washer
3 Side gear
4 Pinion gear
5 Thrust washer
6 Pinion shaft
7 Differential case
8 Thrust washer
9 Side gear

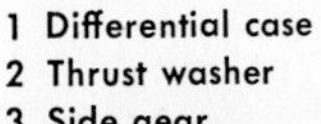
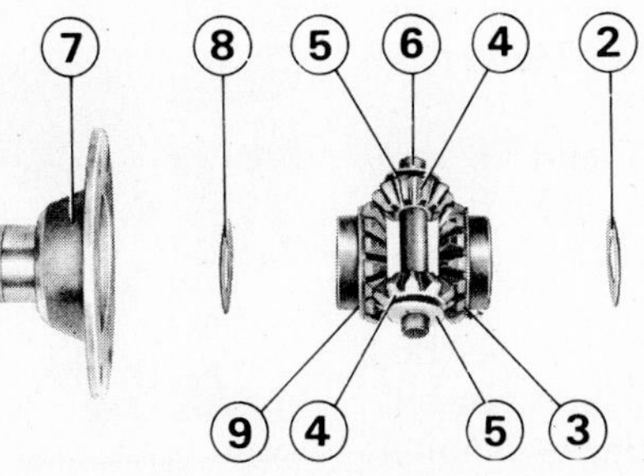

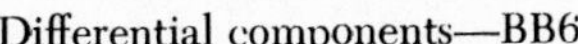

Differential components—BB6

39. Install the ring gear using new bolts and washers. Tighten to 42 ft. lbs.
40. Press differential bearings on, using a thrust pad.
41. Coat the differential housing mating faces with sealer. Install the differential and cover using the four 8 mm bolts with new washers and four 10 mm bolts with new washers and O-rings. Do not tighten.
42. Install a new, greased O-ring and oil seal on the right differential cover plate. Coat the bearing face with sealer and install the cover plate making sure that notches are horizontal and vertical. Tighten the cover plate bolts to 14 ft. lbs.
43. Install a clamp on the left side of the differential and gently bring the outer bearing race into contact with the bearing without forcing. Using a depth gauge, determine the distance from the outer race to the cover surface.
44. Determine the number of shims (.004"-0.1 mm) necessary by comparing the gauge reading to the left-hand plate.
45. Remove the clamp from the left side of the differential. Loosen the right side cover bolts and tighten the housing bolts: 8 mm bolts to 14 ft. lbs. and 10 mm bolts to 29 ft. lbs.
46. Install a new greased O-ring and a seal ring on the left-hand plate. Coat the mating faces with sealer. Install the left-hand cover (same positioning as right) and insert the shims at the same time. Tighten the bolts to 14 ft. lbs.
47. Install the oil pump strainer and tighten the three bolts to 4 ft. lbs. Install the pan with a new gasket.
48. Install the eight 7 mm bolts with their thrust plates, two 8 mm bolts with centering pin cover plates, and three 8 mm bolts. Tighten 7 mm bolts to 7 ft. lbs. and 8 mm bolts to 13 ft. lbs.
49. Install the limiting stops on the side supports of the pan plate. Tighten to 24 ft. lbs.
50. Install a new lockwasher and 36 mm nut on the spacer. Tighten to 25 ft. lbs. and bend the lockwasher up and around the nut.
51. Check the condition of the oil line. Replace the four copper washers. Install the oil line and torque the two union bolts to 13 ft. lbs.

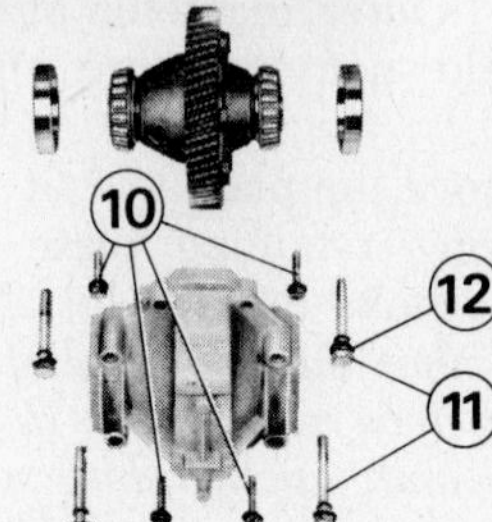

10 8 mm cover bolts
11 10 mm cover bolts
12 O-rings

Assembling the differential—BB6

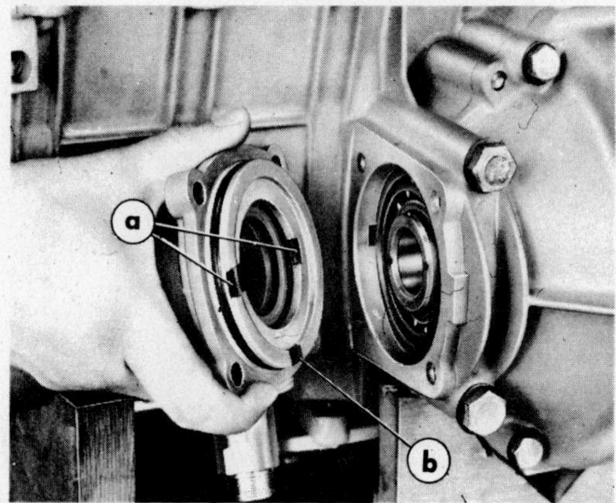

Differential cover plate—BB6. The notches are at a, the groove at b.

Depth measurement from outer race to differential cover—BB6. M is the clamp, N the depth gauge.

52. Before installing the transmission to the engine, check for free engagement of all gears. Fill the engine-transmission with SAE 20/40 motor oil after installation.

Driveshaft

Driveshaft

403, 404, and 504 models use a torque tube driveshaft. This type of driveshaft consists of an outer tube which takes the thrust of the rear wheels which are in turn driven by an inner shaft. The inner shaft is statically and dynamically balanced, and is supported in the torque tube by a center bearing mounted on rubber rings within the tube. The 403 and 404 torque tube is 68.96″ long, the inner shaft is 66.4″ long and 1.46″ in diameter. The 504 torque tube is 66.53″ long and the inner driveshaft has a diameter of 1.65″. The 403 and 404 inner shaft is joined to the transmission by a universal joint. The 504 driveshaft is splined directly to the transmission and differential. The 304 front wheels are driven by two slip-jointed axle driveshafts.

Driveshaft Removal and Installation—403 and 404

See Rear Axle and Differential Removal Section.

Driveshaft Removal and Installation—504

1. Drain the differential and remove the brake compensator lever pivot from the body, letting it hang by its spring.
2. Remove the four torque tube to differential housing nuts. Remove the two Allen bolts which hold the differential housing to the crossmember.
3. Pull the differential back from the torque tube and support it with a wooden block. Remove the spring from within the torque tube. NOTE: *The differential can be bolted to the crossmember with two bolts to allow the car to be moved.*
4. Remove the four Allen bolts holding the tube to the transmission and pull it back about 3/4″.
5. Insert a plate on the torque tube end to support the inner shaft. Install two bolts through the plate to hold it to the tube.

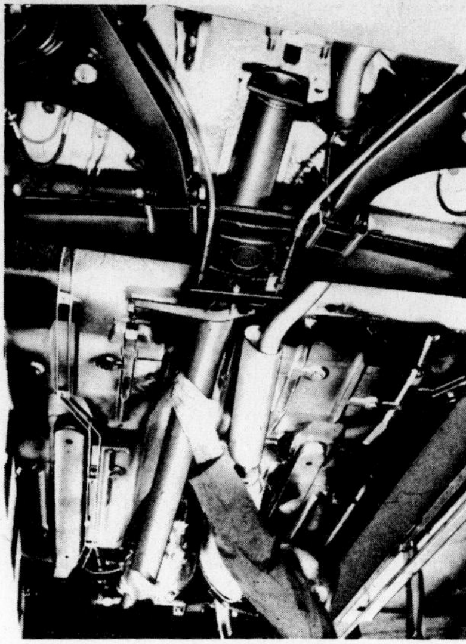

Torque tube removal—504

6. Lower the exhaust pipe at the front.
7. Pull the inner shaft from the transmission and remove the assembly by pulling it down and towards the front.
8. When installing, coat the inner shaft splines with grease and engage the transmission output shaft.
9. Remove the inner shaft holding plate and install the four transmission to torque tube bolts. Tighten to 44 ft. lbs.
10. Coat the rear inner shaft splines with grease. Install the spring inside the tube.
11. Install the torque tube to the differential and tighten the four nuts to 44 ft. lbs.
12. Install the differential onto the crossmember and tighten the two bolts to 27 ft. lbs.
13. Install the brake compensator lever.
14. Fill the differential with GP 90 gear lube.

Driveshaft Removal and Installation—304

1. Drain the oil pan.
2. Jack the car up and install stands under the rear part of the engine cradle.
3. Remove the wheel and clean the axle cover and steering knuckle.
4. Loosen and remove the hub, holding it as shown.
5. Disconnect the stabilizer link from the suspension arm.
6. Remove the suspension arm attaching bolts, pull the hub assembly towards

1 Supporting point
2 Stabilizer link

Hub nut removal—304

you, and separate the driveshaft from the hub.

7. Remove the driveshaft, being careful not to damage the seal ring lips. NOTE: *Each time a driveshaft is removed, the differential bearing cover seal must be replaced.*
8. Grease the space between the axle ring lips and the knuckle.
9. Carefully install the shaft on the axle. Coat the shaft grooves on the hub side with grease.
10. Pull the suspension assembly towards you and install the shaft in the hub. Install the stabilizer link in the suspension arm.
11. Position the suspension arm on the engine cradle. Insert the bolts and nuts, tighten them hand-tight.
12. Install the hub nut and washer. Tighten to 180 ft. lbs. while holding the hub. Lock the hub with the grooves provided.
13. Install the wheel(s) and tighten the lug nuts to 43 ft. lbs.
14. Make sure that the stabilizer link is positioned correctly and install the nut hand-tight.
15. Move the car a few feet, then tighten the suspension spindle nuts to 20 ft. lbs. and the stabilizer link nut to 9 ft. lbs.
16. Fill the engine-transmission with SAE 20/40 motor oil.

Driveshaft separation—304. The seal ring mating surface is at 3.

Driveshaft Center Bearing Removal and Installation—403, 404, and 504

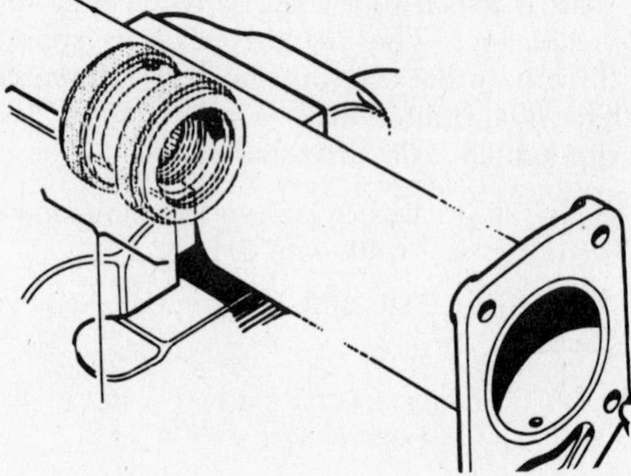

Torque tube center bearing—404

1. With the inner shaft removed from the torque tube, install the tube in a vise and remove the center bearing grease nipple.
2. Lubricate the inside rear part of the torque tube to allow the center bearing assembly to slide out freely.
3. Install a bearing puller of sufficient length to reach the bearing. Tighten the puller and slide the bearing out.
4. Clean and inspect the parts.
5. Before installing the bearing, lubricate the inner surface of the tube and dip the bearing in oil.
6. Insert the bearing into the tube. Using a slide hammer, tap the bearing into position.
7. Install the bearing grease nipple.

304 driveshaft joints. The wheel side joint is at 1, differential side joint at 2.

The 304 axle driveshafts are roller jointed on the wheel side and equipped with a sliding roller (tulip) joint on the axle side. The outer joint cannot be repaired, the shaft must be replaced if the joint is defective. The protective covers on both joints may be replaced, however changing the cover at the wheel side involves changing the inside cover also. To disassemble:

1. With axle driveshaft out of car, install the driveshaft in a vise. Tape the ends of the seal ring mating faces with masking tape and moderately tighten the vise on the inner joint.
2. Carefully remove the steel cap by tapping with a mallet and chisel.
3. Move the driveshaft up in the vise and clamp the vise on the shaft itself (using soft jaws or rags to protect the shaft).

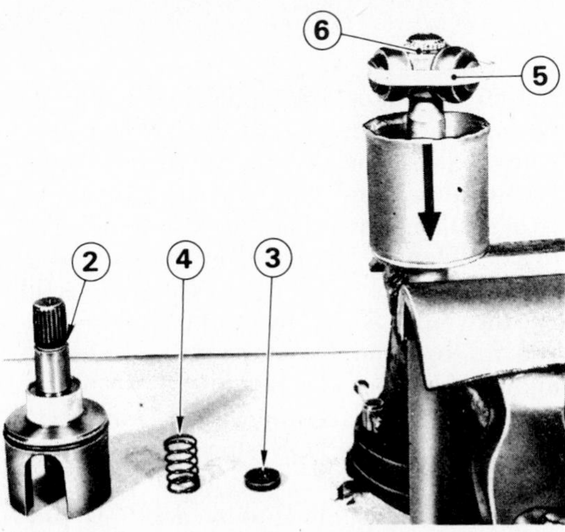

2 Splined sleeve
3 Thrust cup
4 Spring
5 Joint roller
6 Snap-ring

Inner joint disassembly

4. Pull the steel cap downward, and remove the sleeve, thrust cup, and spring. Tape the rollers on the shaft and remove the snap-ring.
5. Mark one of the driveshaft grooves and the tulip joint for later positioning. Remove the tulip joint and thrust ring.
6. Remove the rubber cover assembly and holding ring.
7. Install the opposite (wheel side) end of the shaft in the vise and remove the steel cap in the same manner as the inner end.

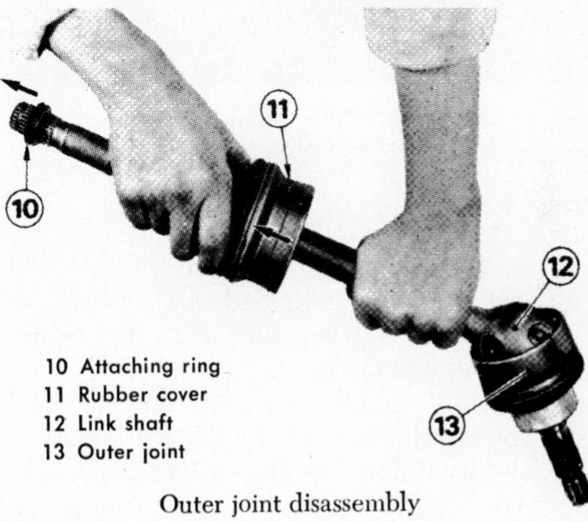

10 Attaching ring
11 Rubber cover
12 Link shaft
13 Outer joint

Outer joint disassembly

8. Remove the rubber cover assembly and holding ring from the free end of the shaft. CAUTION: *Do not separate the link shaft from the outer joint.*
9. Clean all parts and replace defective parts.
10. Install a new outer joint cover assembly on the free end of the shaft. Make sure that the rubber cover lips fit into the grooves on the shaft.
11. Install a new O-ring in its groove and fill the cap with grease (approx. 8.5 oz.).
12. Install the outer joint until it is 3/4″ below the top of the cap, tapping with a mallet if necessary.
13. Tap around the outside edge to bottom the cap. Be careful not to strike the seal ring mating surface. Check the outside diameter of the cap, which should not exceed 3.5″ at the O-ring level.
14. Pry the edge of the cover up and squeeze any excess air out. Install the rubber cover holding ring.

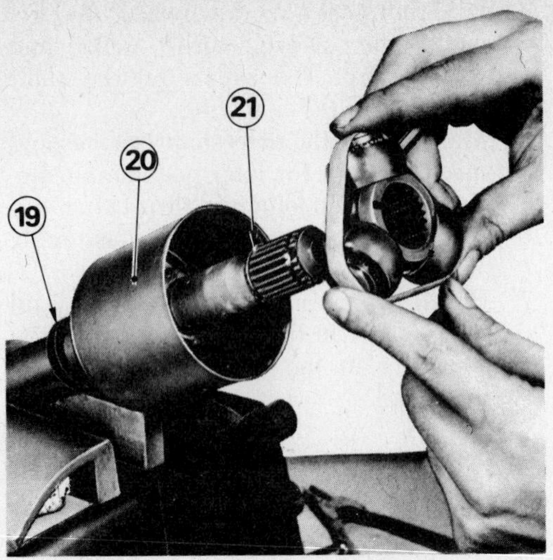

19 Attaching ring
20 Cover assembly
21 Stop-ring

Inner joint assembly

15. At the inner joint end of the shaft, install the rubber ring and the rubber cover assembly.
16. Install a new stop-ring on the shaft below the splines. Install the old tulip joint, lining up the reference marks, and mark the new joint so that it will be in the same position.
17. Install the new joint, positioning exactly the same as the old one.
18. Install a new snap-ring and fill the sleeve with grease (approx. 4 oz.). Install a new O-ring on the sleeve. Install the cup, spring, and the sleeve.
19. Seal the cap in the same manner as the outer joint.
20. Install the driveshaft(s).

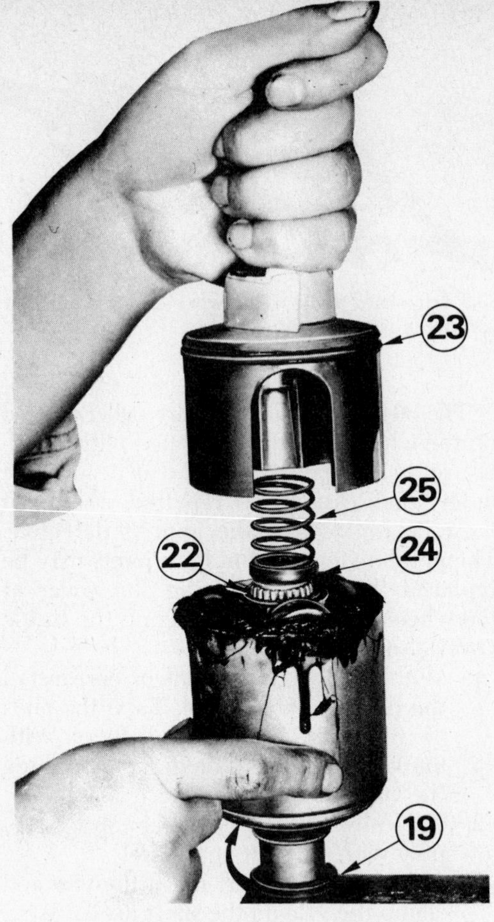

19 Attaching ring
22 Snap-ring
23 O-ring
24 Cup
25 Spring

Outer joint assembly

Drive Axle

Rear Axle and Differential—403 and 404

The 403 and 404 are front engine-rear wheel drive cars. All 403 and 404 models until 1967 were equipped with a worm drive differential in an aluminum rear axle. This consisted of left and right housings, and a center casting for the differential. The differential utilized a bronze ring gear and a steel worm. This unusual worm drive rear axle had the design goal of allowing a lower center of gravity for the vehicle.

1967 and later 404 models are equipped with a more conventional hypoid rear axle. The housing for the hypoid rear is reinforced aluminum alloy and is made up of two sections assembled by 10 bolts. The drive pinion is supported in the front section by two roller bearings. These are held on the input shaft by a nut torqued to 200 ft. lbs., and by a spacer and ring to allow preload of the bearings. The adjusting ring is available in widths from .241″ to .293″ (6.04 to 7.33 mm) in increments of .001″ (.03 mm).

Adjustment of the pinion depth is provided by a washer, available in five thicknesses from .002″ to .02″ (.05 to .5mm), situated between the outer race of the rear bearing and its seat in the housing.

The ring gear also forms the left shell of the differential. The right shell of the

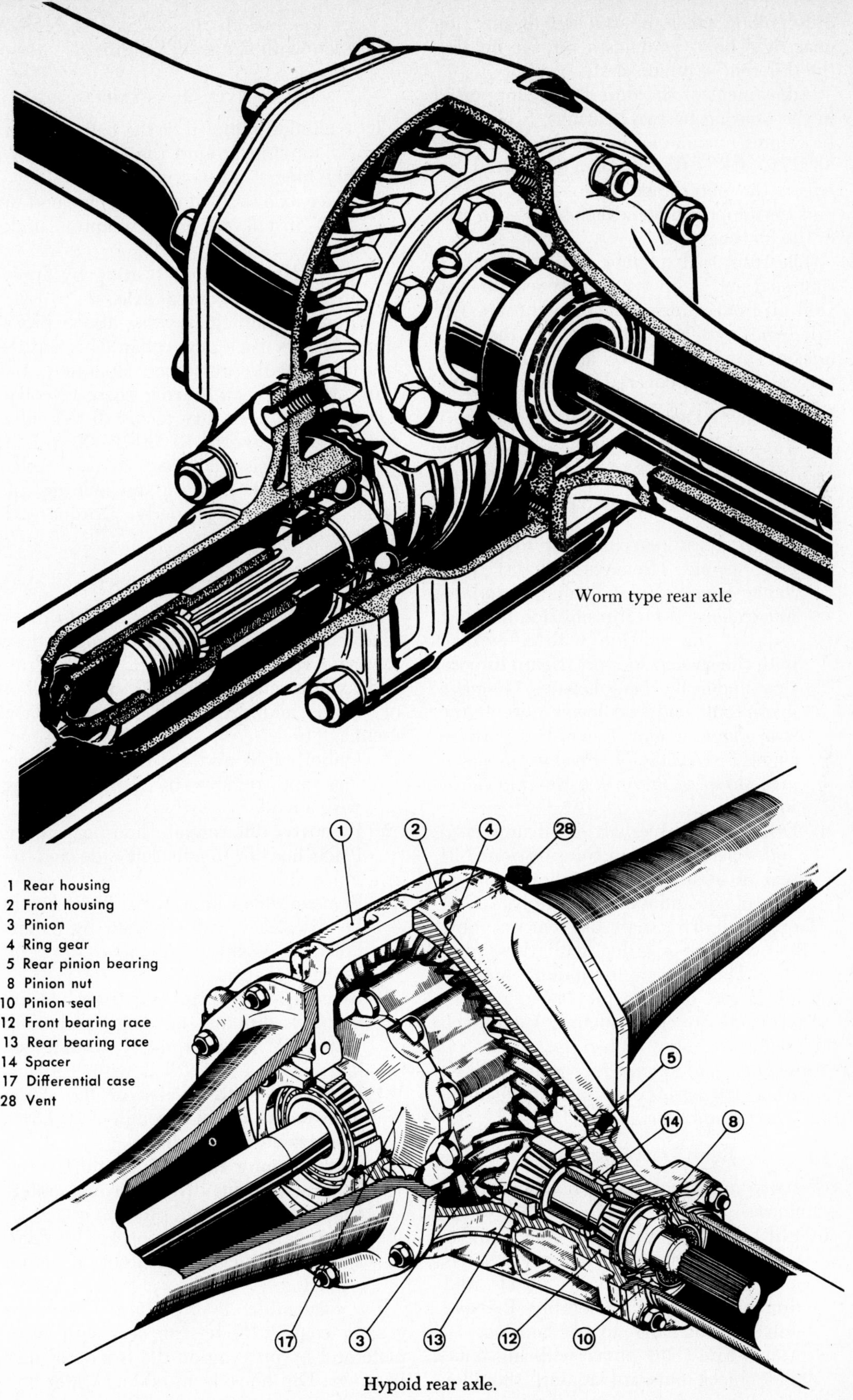

Worm type rear axle

Hypoid rear axle.

differential, which is attached to the ring gear by 8 bolts, contains a pin for holding the differential pinion shaft.

Adjustment of the differential, supported in the housing by two bearings, is obtained by shims, available in thicknesses from .002″ to .04″ (.05 to 1 mm), inserted between the outer race of the side bearing and the support plate attached to each side of the housing.

The front seal retainer consists of an O-ring seal and a lip type inner seal to prevent oil from entering the torque tube. The axle housings are attached to the rear housing by 8 bolts. The left housing contains a vent tube covered with a plastic lid.

Removal of Driveshaft and Rear Axle

1. Disconnect shock absorbers, stabilizing bar, parking brake cables and hydraulic brake hose (plug end of brake line).
2. Lift body at rear in order to remove coil springs. Remove exhaust pipe flange from exhaust manifold, and remove clamp from transmission housing.
3. Support transmission with a jack or with the special support stirrup in position under flywheel housing. Remove upper bolt and two lower nuts of the rear engine mount. Lower transmission slightly. CAUTION: *do not allow engine sump to lie on the steering housing.*
4. Disconnect driveshaft front universal and separate it from transmission. Lift rear of body enough to allow removal of rear axle and wheel assembly.

To reinstall drive shaft and rear assembly proceed in reverse order, with these precautions: The rear engine mount must be free of grease, oil or paint. Never use trichlorethylene to clean mount. Coat each side with Permatex. When installing coil springs, first coil should face rear. NOTE: *Right and left springs are interchangeable. Bleed brakes after connecting line.*

Rear Axle Removal

Remove and disassemble rear axle shaft as follows:

1. Lift car at rear and place stands under axle shaft housings. Remove wheels and brake drum. Mark wheels and drums for proper reassembly. Remove nuts securing flange to axle housing.
2. Attach axle shaft puller with lug nuts. Slide block outward against shoulder of the tool to release axle shaft complete with flange and bearing.

Rear Axle Disassembly

1. Facilitate removal of the collar by gently tapping around the outside with a hammer.
2. Place axle shaft in a vise, spline end up, and install a press adaptor under flange.
3. Press off collar and bearing by applying pressure to end of axle.

When assembling, reverse above procedure. Always use a new collar. This and the bearing must be pressed on separately. Use bushing to press on bearing, then the collar. The pressure necessary to install the collar should be between 13,000-16,000 psi. If less pressure is required, a new collar should be used. Be sure the bearing and collar are seated properly. Torque axle shaft nuts to 10 ft. lbs.

Servicing the Differential

The following sequence is used to disassemble the differential after having drained rear axle, removed driveshaft, wheels, drum and axle assemblies. Always mark position of wheels and drums for proper replacement.

1. Unbolt right and left-hand axle housings and remove by gently tapping with a mallet.
2. Remove differential housing cover. Place housing on its left side and remove differential.
3. Remove differential bolts. These are to be discarded and replaced by 6 new bolts at assembly. Remove front oil seal and spacer.
4. Remove steel worm gear from housing by first dipping housing in boiling water. When adequately heated, set housing in a vise fitted with lead jaw faces and with splines of the worm gear facing down through vise. Drive worm gear, using a drift.
5. Remove outer races of the differential bearings using drift. Do not interchange outer races.
6. Clean parts, blow dry, inspect for damage and lubricate with light oil before replacing.

To reassemble, first prepare the worm gear by coating the bearing seat with lubriplate and by pressing on the front and rear bearings. Dip housing in boiling water and install worm gear in housing as follows:

1. Position housing vertically with filling plug facing downward in a vise fitted with lead jaws. Place worm gear in housing and while holding worm gear, install front spacer without its rubber ring and hold in place by means of the cast iron plate. Carefully tighten plate by means of the two diagonally opposed nuts.
2. Turn housing upside down, and using an appropriate drift, gently tap bearing outer race toward the front to assure correct positioning.
3. Install outer races of the side bearings, one in the housing and one in the cover, approximately .040″ (1 mm) from the outer face. Install each in the side from which it was removed.

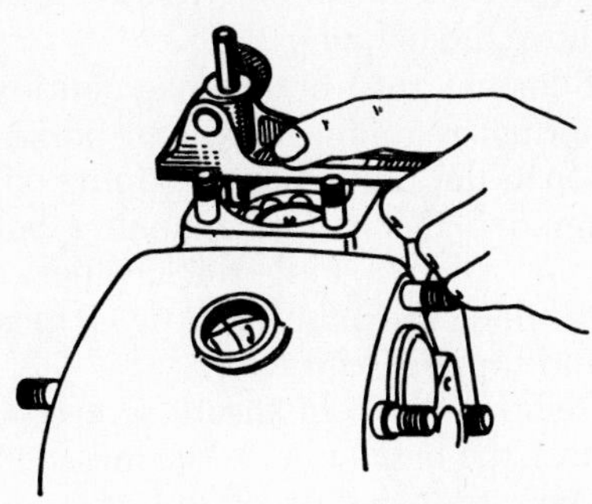

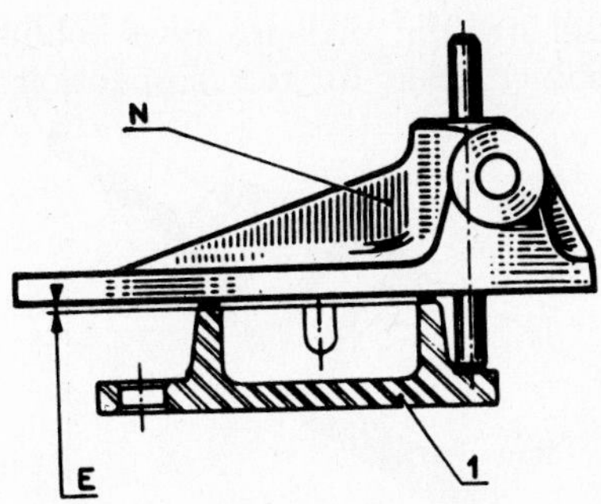

Measuring required thickness of shims E.

4. Allow housing to cool, and make sure worm gear rotates freely but without play. Using depth gauge, determine thickness of shims. (Place gauge across machine surface directly behind worm gear and push plunger to touch the outer race of rear bearing. Lock the plunger.)
5. Apply depth gauge on the rear cap (1) of the worm gear to determine the thickness of shims accurately. Install shims, then worm gear rear cap, setting the groove to face either side. Coat mating surfaces with Permatex.
6. Remove cast iron plate. Install oil seal at front of worm gear and rubber ring on front spacer, setting groove to face either side.

Assemble differential as follows:

1. Install differential pinion gears with blocks and shaft.
2. Install side gears in differential side plates with new composition thrust washers.

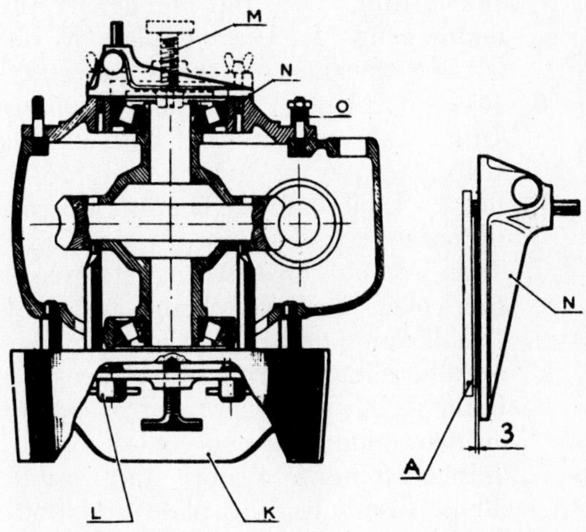

Measuring thickness of required shims for universal.

3. Mount side plates onto bronze gear with the .312″ (7.8 mm) holes aligned with the ends of the pinion gear shaft.
4. Assemble parts with 6 new bolts, .398″ (10 mm) diameter for models up to Serial No. 4071371 and .437″ (11 mm) thereafter. The heads of the bolts must be on the same side as the marks on the bronze gear.
5. Torque bolts to 50 ft. lbs. Differential should turn freely. Stake bolts by punching metal into one castellation of each nut.

Install and adjust differential as follows:

1. Place differential in housing with marked side of bronze gear facing up. The differential is properly seated in the lower side bearing if it turns freely by rotating the worm gear shaft.
2. Install cover on the differential housing using paper gasket coated with Permatex. Make sure locating boss is next to the drain plug. To assure positive tightening, it is necessary to install spacers. Turn assembly over to rest on the cover side.

3. Align the two .312″ (7.8 mm) holes in the differential side plate with the two holes in the differential housing. Install tool in position with both fingers fitted through the two holes.
4. Secure clamp to press tool onto differential housing. Turn assembly over using press tool as a support.
5. Install clamp and apply slight pressure on the outer race of the differential bearing. Hold depth gauge against housing side, push the plunger to touch the outer race of the differential bearing. Lock the plunger. Apply depth gauge on bearing plate to determine thickness of shims necessary.
6. Remove clamp and install shims. Install bearing plate and both locking strips. Torque the four bolts to 25 ft. lbs. Lock the bolts by bending up corners of the strips.
7. Turn assembly over so that it rests on the cover. Remove clamp and tool. Install clamp and apply slight pressure on differential bearing outer race.
8. Using depth gauge proceed as before to determine thickness of shims required. Remove clamp and install shims. Install bearing plate and both locking strips. Torque the four bolts to 25 ft. lbs. Lock bolts by bending up the corners of the strips. The rear axle is now correctly adjusted.
9. Remove spacers to install righthand axle housing.
10. Reinstall differential in car and fill with GP90 gear oil.

Rear Axle and Differential—504

The 504 uses a front engine to drive the rear wheels. The differential is mounted on a frame crossmember and each wheel is driven by its own slip-jointed driveshaft. The differential is the conventional hypoid type.

Removal and Installation of Differential and Driveshafts

1. Jack up the rear and install stands under the suspension arms.
2. Remove the left and/or right wheel, depending on which axle shafts are being pulled.
3. Install a hub holding device and loosen the hub nut without removing it. Remove the holder.
4. Remove the brake pad anti-squeak spring, retaining fork, and brake pads.
5. Open the brake hose retaining clip and remove the caliper retaining bolts (8 mm Allen). Pull the caliper away, bending the hose as little as possible, and support with wire.
6. Remove the crosshead screws which hold the brake disc to the hub.
7. Mark the position of the screw on the disc and remove the disc.
8. Remove the 4 Allen screws holding the hub carrier to the suspension arm.

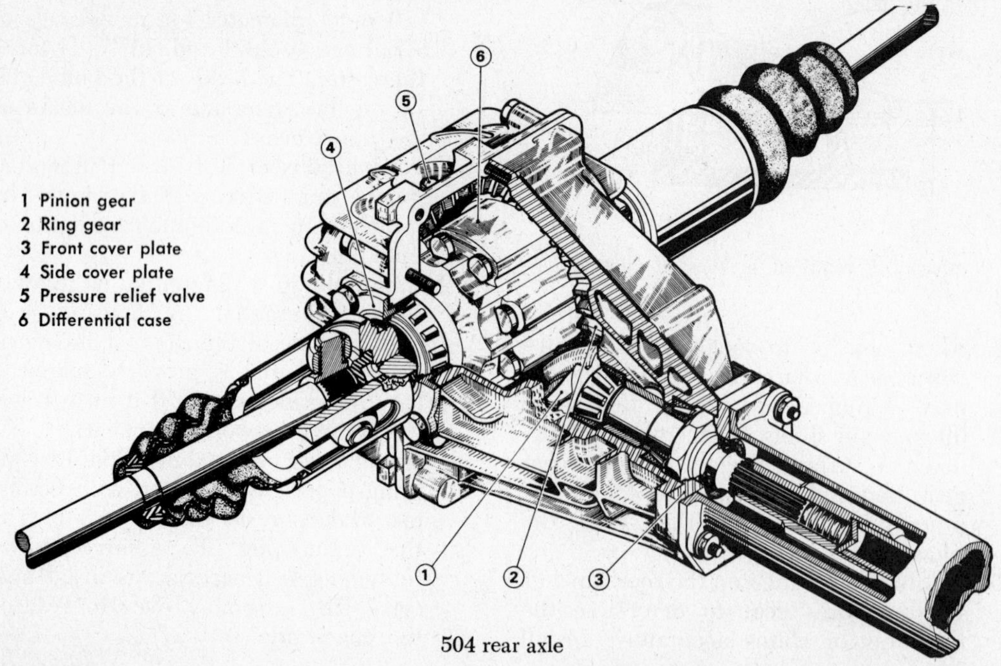

504 rear axle

Brake removal—504. The anti-squeal spring is at 1, the retaining fork at 2, and the pads at 3.

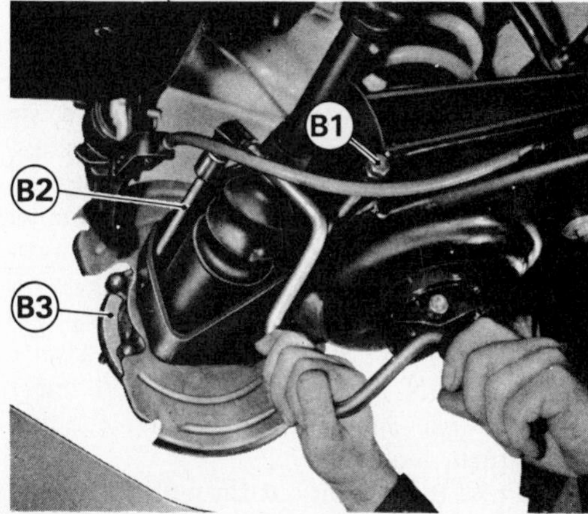

Hub removal—504 B1, B2 are the bolts, B3 the plate.

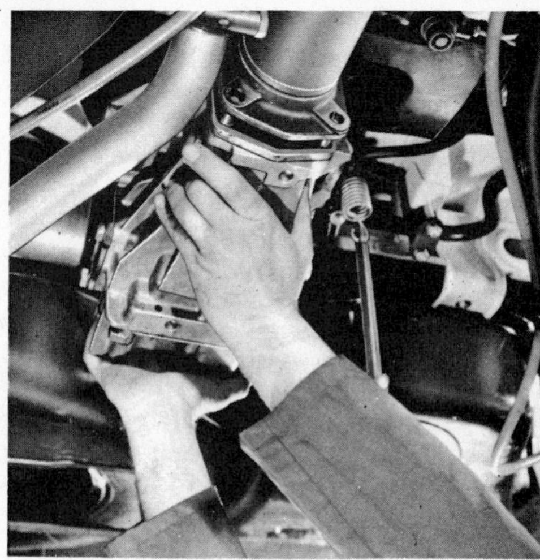
Differential removal—504.

NOTE: *A hole is provided in the hub for wrench access.*

9. Remove the hub carrier-axle shaft assembly, using long bolts positioned diagonally and a plate installed on the hub. Tighten the bolts alternately and the carrier will pull away from the arm.
10. If the axle shaft is being replaced, remove the nut and press the shaft out of the hub. Leave the hub and shaft assembled if the shaft is not being replaced. See the axle shaft section for service procedures.
11. Drain the differential and remove the brake compensator lever pivot, letting it hang by its spring.
12. Remove the four nuts holding the torque tube to the differential to the crossmember.
13. Pull the differential housing to the rear and then left, this will disengage it. Recover the spring from within the torque tube.
14. Before installing, check the condition of the differential housing oil seals.
15. Coat the space between the two lips of each seal with bearing grease. Grease the axle shaft splines.
16. Insert the spring into the torque tube and install the differential housing, first to the right axle shaft and then to the torque tube.
17. Install the four torque tube nuts with new washers and tighten to 44 ft. lbs.
18. Install the two differential to crossmember bolts with new washers and tighten to 27 ft. lbs.
19. Mount the hub carrier-axle shaft in its housing on the rear arm. Carefully install the splined end of the axle shaft into the differential. Install the four Allen screws in the hub and tighten to 29 ft. lbs.
20. Install the brake disc in the position marked during removal. Install the caliper using new washers and tighten to 31 ft. lbs.
21. Install the brake pads and retaining fork and tighten to 13 ft. lbs. Reinstall the anti-squeak spring (arrow points in direction of disc rotation).
22. Install the brake line on the suspension arm clip.
23. Install the holding tool on the hub and tighten the axle shaft nut to 189 ft. lbs. Punch the grooves on the nut to secure to hub.

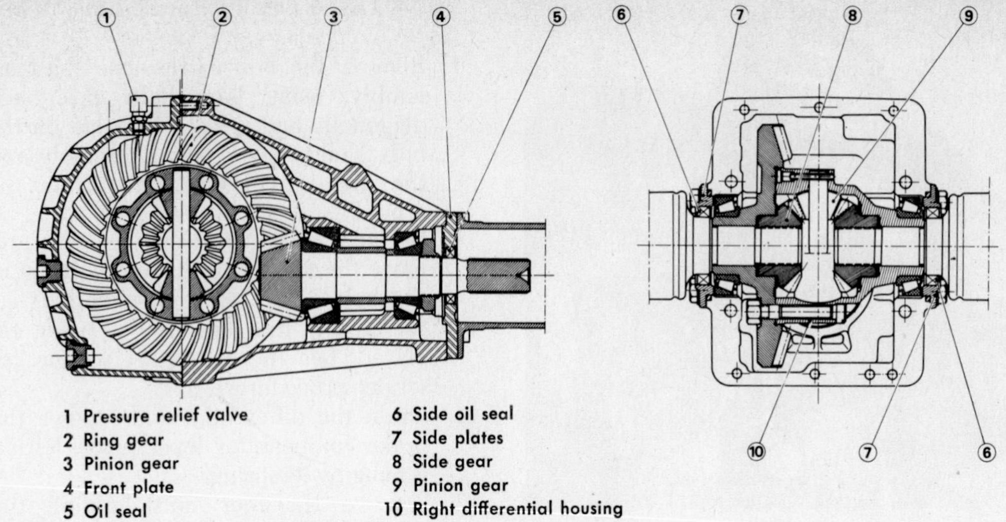

504 differential

24. Install the wheel or wheels and tighten the lugs to 44 ft. lbs. Fill differential with GP 90 gear oil. Tighten the drain plugs to 20 ft. lbs.

Servicing the Differential

1. Clean the housing and remove the drive oil seal support plate.
2. Fasten a flat plate to the front of the housing to allow it to be clamped in a vise.

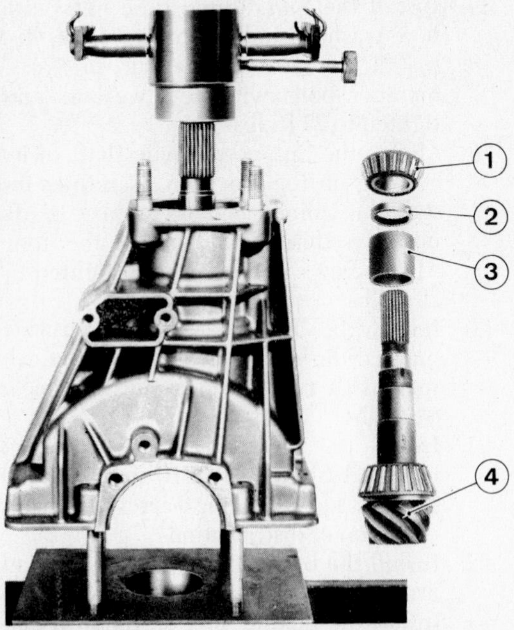

Pinion disassembly—504

3. Loosen all bolts and assembly nuts of the two half casings.
4. Remove the front attachment bolts of the differential bearing side plates, six assembly bolts of the half housings, and four nuts on the rear housing.
5. Remove the rear housing. A mallet may be needed to separate the housings.
6. Clamp the front housing in a vise and loosen the drive pinion nut. Use a socket N held by the stud and nut 1 and use socket M to loosen the nut (turn clockwise).
7. Press the pinion out through the inside of the housing and remove the front bearing, adjustment spacer, spacer, and the pinion with the rear bearing.
8. Remove the pinion bearing races with an extractor and recover the adjustment shims and thrust washer.
9. Press the rear bearing off the pinion.
10. Remove the eight differential bolts and remove the differential from the ring gear. Recover the left side gear and thrust washer.
11. Press the ring gear from the bearing. Press the right side bearing from the differential case.
12. Remove the pinion shaft lock pin (use a 1/5″ drift), pinion shaft, pinion gear, washers, right side gear, and thrust washer.
13. When assembling, clean all parts in solvent and blow dry. Spray moly lubricant into the pinion bearing housings.

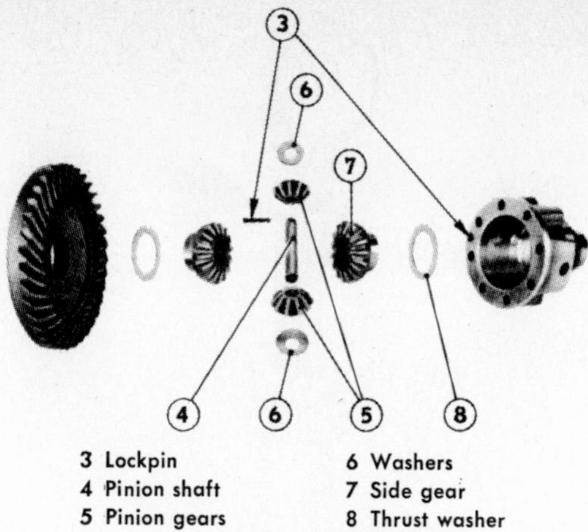

3 Lockpin
4 Pinion shaft
5 Pinion gears
6 Washers
7 Side gear
8 Thrust washer

Differential components—504

14. The following parts should be replaced: differential bearings, pinion bearings, washers, pinion nut, differential assembly bolts, pinion oil seal, differential bearing thrust plate O-rings, and oil seals.
15. Make sure that the front bearing slides freely on the pinion shaft. Polish the shaft with crocus cloth until the bearing just slides on as free fit. Smooth any burrs on the front pinion end with a fine stone.
16. Press the rear bearing onto the pinion shaft.
17. With the housing in a vise, install the thrust washer and outer bearing races back to back using a bolt, plate, and nut. Torque the nut to 101 ft. lbs. Oil the bearings with SAE 20/40 motor oil.
18. Install dial indicator support on the housing and secure with a clamp. Install a feeler rod into the support and bring it into contact with the rear face of the pinion. Position the dial indicator feeler so that it rests on the upper surface of rod. Set the dial indicator on 4, for example, and move it so that the feeler contacts the machined edge. The displacement shown will indicate the depth of rod. Record the number.

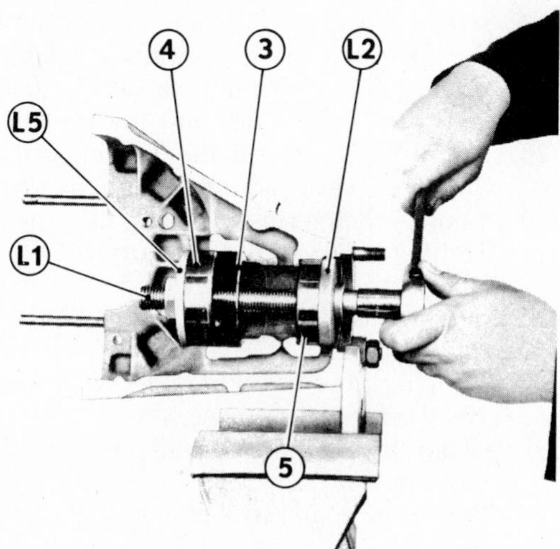

L1, L2, L5 Bearing installer
3 Thrust washer
4, 5 Front bearing races

Rear bearing installation—504

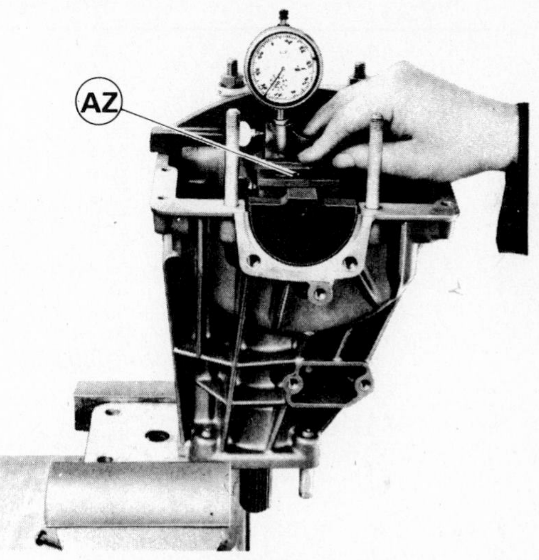

Measuring mesh distance—504

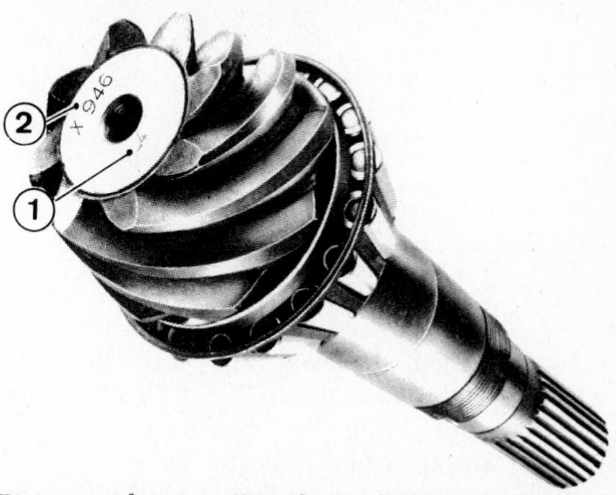

Pinion numbering—504. The mesh distance is at 1, the gear set number at 2.

19. Two reference numbers are scribed on the pinion rear face. Number one is the meshing distance, and is run from zero to twenty and from zero to minus ten. The other number is preceded by a letter and is the gear set number; the

same number will appear on the ring gear.

20. Using the table, find the corresponding guide number for the reference number marked on the pinion. The difference between the dial indicator reading and the guide number gives the thickness of the shim to be installed between the rear bearing outer race and the thrust washer (to the nearest 0.05 mm).

NOTE: *If using a dial indicator calibrated in inches, multiply the reading by* 0.0394.

Reference Number	*Corresponding Guide Number*
-10	20
- 9	21
- 8	22
- 7	23
- 6	24
- 5	25
- 4	26
- 3	27
- 2	28
- 1	29
0	30
1	31
2	32
3	33
4	34
5	35
6	36
7	37
8	38
9	39
10	40
11	41
12	42
13	43
14	44
15	45
16	46
17	47
18	48
19	49
20	50

21. Place the pinion shaft in a vise and install the long spacer, front bearing (installed backwards), and the nut. Tighten the nut to 203 ft. lbs. Paint one pinion spline for reference.
22. Install a dial indicator as shown, with extension facing the painted spline. Set the dial on 1, for example, and remove it without changing the reading.
23. Remove the rear bearing outer race with an extractor. Install the thrust washer and the adjustment shims previously determined into the bottom of the bearing housing.
24. Remove the nut and the front bearing from the pinion shaft, and reinstall in the housing with the long spacer, front bearing, and the nut. Tighten to 7 ft. lbs. and rotate the pinion ten times in each direction. Repeat the tightening and turning until the nut can no longer be tightened under 7 ft. lbs.

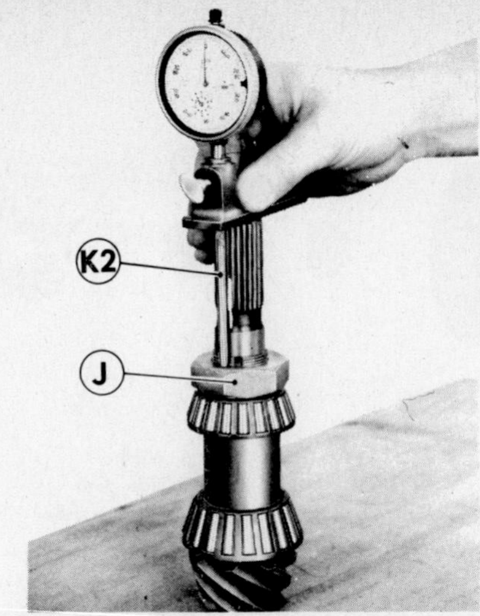

Measuring for shim determination—504. J indicates the pinion nut, K2 the dial indicator feeler.

25. Using the same painted spline, take another reading between the end of the pinion shaft and the nut with the dial preset to 1. Make a note of the reading on the dial and find the difference between the two figures. Subtract .003″ (.06 mm). The number obtained gives the thickness of the shim to be installed between the front bearing and the long spacer. Shims are available from .238″ (6.04 mm) to .289″ (7.33 mm) in .0015″ (.03 mm) increments.
26. Install the pinion in the housing with the long spacer, adjustment shims previously determined, and the nut. Tighten to 203 ft. lbs. and turn the pinion several times to check for proper bearing installation.
27. Install the rear axle vertically in a vise and check the travel of feeler as in step 10. This measurement should correspond to the guide number ±.002″ (.05 mm).
28. Punch the four castellations on the nut to lock it.
29. Clean the front oil seal housing and pry the oil seal out with a tire iron, being careful not to damage the inset deflector. NOTE: *If the deflector is*

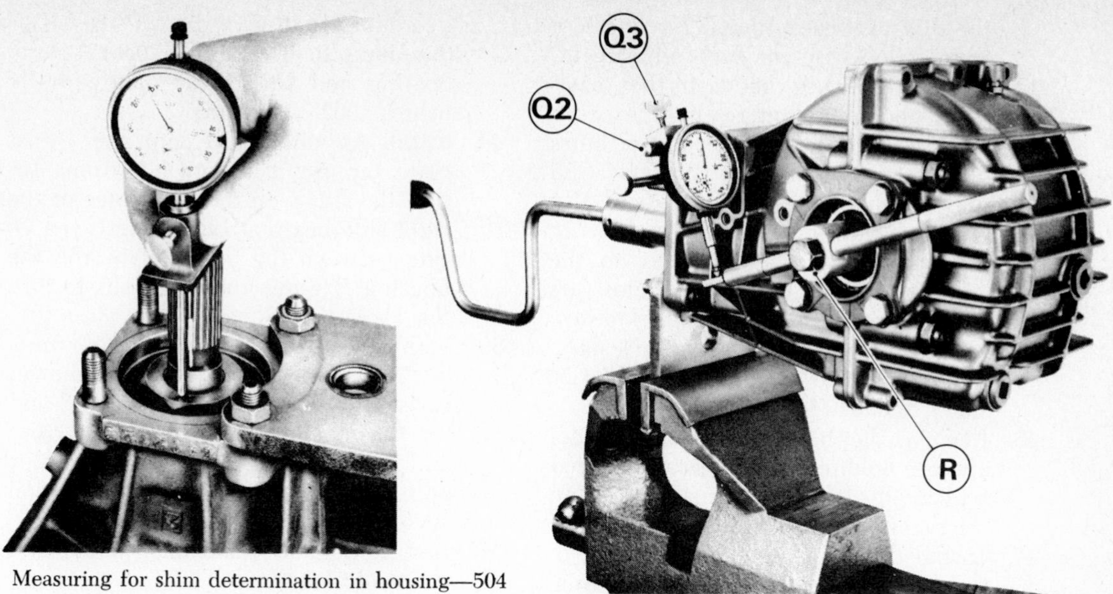

Measuring for shim determination in housing—504

Measuring gear backlash—504

damaged, the complete oil seal housing should be replaced.

30. Dip the new seal in oil and tap into the housing until it bottoms.
31. Coat the front face of the differential housing with sealer and install the oil seal housing. Tighten the four nuts to 7 ft. lbs.
32. Oil all the differential parts before assembly. Install a new dimpled washer (with dimples out) into the differential gear housing. Install the right side gear, pinion gears with washers, pinion gear shaft with pin holes aligned, and a new pin flush with the differential gear housing surface.
33. Lay the ring gear on a flat surface and install the dimpled washer, side gear, assembled differential gear housing, and the eight assembly bolts and nuts (handtight).
34. Clamp the differential assembly in a vise and crosstighten the eight nuts to 51 ft. lbs.
35. Press the oil seals from the two differential side plates.
36. Clean new bearings and press them onto the differential assembly. Oil bearings with SAE 20/40 motor oil.
37. Install the housing vertically in a vise. Coat the mating surfaces with sealer and oil the housing bearing recesses. Install the ring gear and differential assembly. Install the rear cover with the four nuts tightened to 6 ft. lbs.
38. Install the bearing side plate (left) without shims. Install four bolts and tighten to 6 ft. lbs. Loosen nuts and hand tighten.
39. Clamp the differential in a vise with the right side up. Install a clamp and hand tighten with the screw to bring the differential down as far as possible.
40. Rotate the differential five times in each direction. Tap on the housing with a mallet for proper assembly. Check tightness of the clamp. Tighten the rear cover nuts to 6 ft. lbs.
41. Install the differential in the vise in a horizontal position. Install backlash measuring tool, making sure that one of the radial grooves is in line with the arrow on the tool. Lock the center bolt.
42. Install support rod in the front upper housing. Mount the dial indicator with holder so that the feeler is between the two marks on the tool and so that the feeler and tool are at a right angle to each other.
43. Carefully turn the drive pinion counterclockwise to set the dial indicator on 0. Press the lever down gently. The dial will indicate the backlash between the ring gear and the pinion. Note the reading.
44. Repeat the above operation at three more points, using the other three gaps in tool lined up with the groove in the ring gear used for the first reading. Make a note of each reading and reset

the dial to 0 each time. Turn the tool counterclockwise for each adjustment.

45. If the difference between the maximum and minimum readings exceeds .004″ (.10 mm), check for dirt or burrs on the gear teeth. Subtract .006″ (.15 mm) from the lowest figure and this will give the thickness of the shims to be installed on the left side, to the nearest .002″ (.05 mm). Shims are available in the following thicknesses: .002″ (.05 mm), .004″ (.10 mm), .008″ (.20 mm), .016″ (.40 mm), .020″ (.50 mm), and .040″ (1 mm).
46. Remove the backlash measuring tool and the holding clamp. Install an oiled seal in the left side thrust plate. Tap the seal in until it bottoms.
47. Install the shims on the outer race of the left bearing. Install a new O-ring, coated with grease, between the thrust plate and the housing. Tighten the four bolts to 6 ft. lbs.
48. Install the housing horizontally in a vise with the right side up. Measure the depth of the bearing in the housing and measure the distance from the inner plate surface to the top of the inner ring. The difference between the two figures will give the thicknesses of the shims to be installed between the bearing and the thrust plate, to the nearest .002″ (.05 mm).
49. Install an oiled seal into the thrust plate, tapping it in until it bottoms. Install the shims on the outer race of the right side bearing. Install a greased O-ring between the thrust plate and the housing. Tighten the four bolts to 6 ft. lbs.
50. Tighten the eight bolts and four nuts to 25 ft. lbs. in the sequence shown. Loosen the four nuts 5, 6, 7, and 8 and tap the rear housing to mate the front and rear housings. Tighten the four nuts to 40 ft. lbs. and turn the pinion several times in both directions.
51. Install the six assembly bolts and tighten to 7 ft. lbs.
52. Install the differential and fill with GP 90 gear oil.

Servicing the Axle Driveshafts

The procedure described may be used on either the wheel or differential ends of the driveshaft. The differential end has the shorter of the two covers.

1. Clamp the driveshaft vertically in a

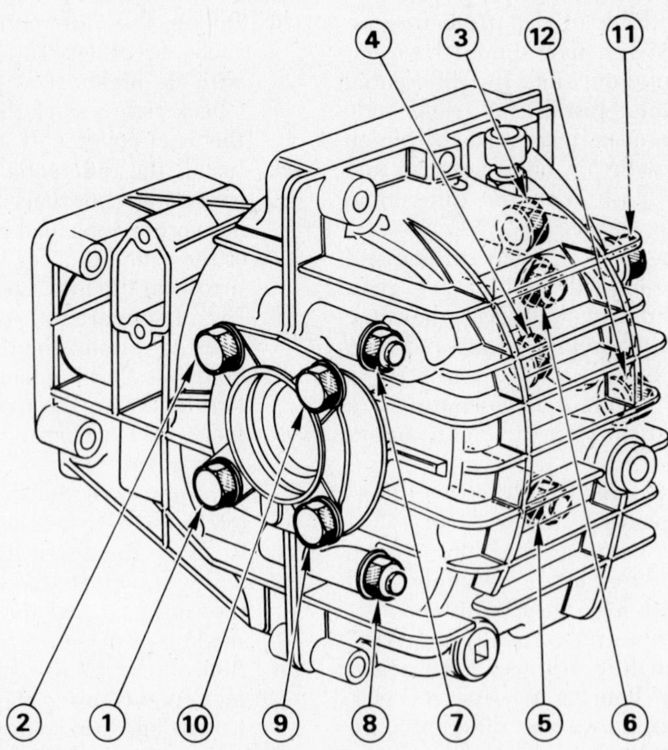

Axle housing tightening sequence—504

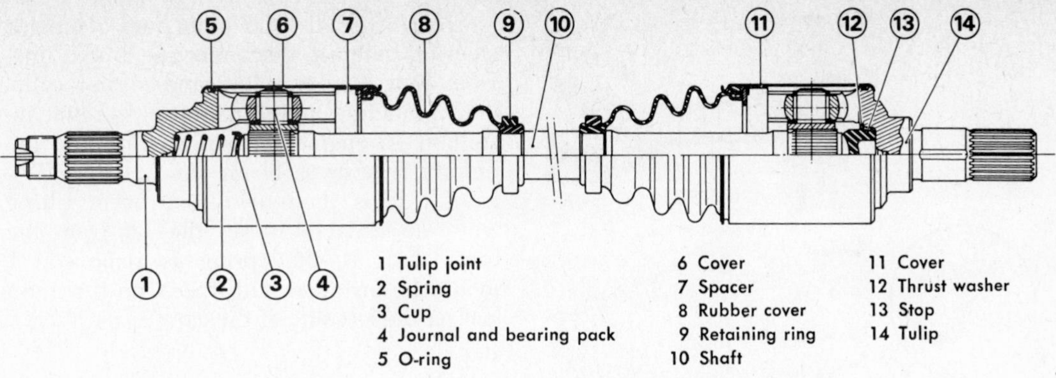

504 axle driveshaft joints

504 axle driveshaft

vise with soft jaws or wrap the shaft with a rag. Protect the oil seal bearing face with masking tape.

2. Using end cutters, carefully bend the cover back. Loosen the cover by tapping on it lightly with a mallet.
3. Remove the splined shaft by pulling it up and off. On the wheel side, recover the spring and thrust cup. Lower the rubber cover as far as possible on the shaft.

Joint cover removal

4. Wrap the tulip joint with masking tape. Clean as much old grease from the assembly as possible. Do not use a degreasing solvent.
5. The tulip joints must be pressed off the shaft.
6. Remove the retaining ring and slide the cover assembly off the shaft. Removal procedure is the same for either end.
7. Check the condition of the nylon stop ring inside the cupped end of the splined shaft. If it is worn or damaged, it can be removed by chiseling it out carefully. Tap a new stop in with a drift.

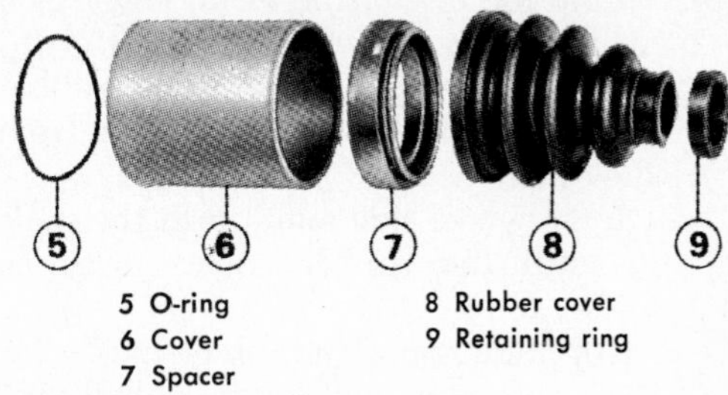

Cover assembly

8. When reassembling, remember that the shorter cover is used on the differential side. Assemble the rubber cover and spacer and insert into the cover after greasing it. Push the spacer in until it bottoms.
9. Install the shaft vertically in a vise. Slide the retaining ring and assembled cover over the shaft.
10. Install the tulip joint on the shaft. Using a hammer and drift, tap the joint down until it bottoms. Make sure that

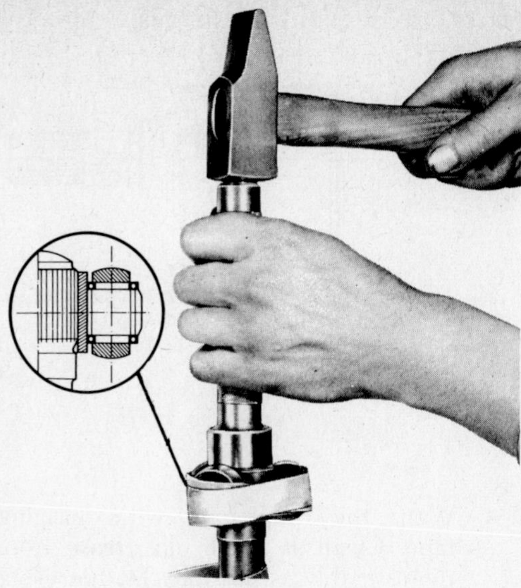

Bearing installation

the lower part of the bearing pack is flush with the groove at the bottom of the shaft.

11. Punch the splines on the shaft towards the hub of the joint. Make the punch marks at three equi-distant points.
12. Grease the joint and the inside of the cover (approx. 3.6 oz.).
13. Remove the masking tape from the joint. On the wheel side, replace the thrust cup and spring. Install a new O-ring on the splined shaft.
14. Crimp the end of the metal cover over while pressing down on the shaft.
15. Install the retaining ring on the rubber cover and squeeze any excess air from the cover.
16. On the wheel side joint, push the shaft in until the rubber cover measures 3.5″.
17. At the differential side joint, push the shaft into the joint until it bottoms. Check the free sliding action of the joints by moving them manually.

Suspension

Front Suspension—403

The front suspension of the 403 consists of a nine leaf transverse spring with lever type hydraulic shock absorbers at the top.

Suspension Service

Servicing of the 403 front end is accomplished by lifting the body above the suspension after disconnecting and removing steering column, disconnecting brake lines from four way coupling and master cylinder, removing engine mounting screws, installing an engine support stirrup, and unbolting rear cross beam from chassis. The front axle is then held to prevent tilting while an assistant raises the car from the front end. If the spring is removed, it should be installed with the X on the main leaf on the left side of the car.

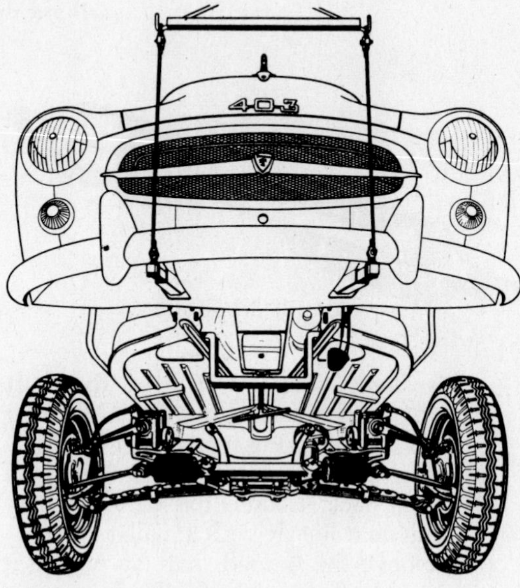

Front end of 403 is serviced by lifting body of vehicle.

Rear Suspension—403

The 403 employs coil springs at the rear to support a live axle. Dampening is accomplished through the use of two telescopic shock absorbers. The rear axle is located longitudinally by diagonal radius rods and laterally by a Panhard rod attached to the axle and body.

Front Suspension—404

The 404 utilizes a MacPherson strut suspension at the front, which consists of telescopic shock absorbers with concentric coil springs. The strut is attached at the top to the inner fender and at the bottom is located by an arm. After 1964, the 404 front suspension also included a stabilizer bar.

Front Suspension Removal

With the front of the vehicle on stands at the crossmembers, and wheels hanging, proceed as follows to remove front suspension:

1. Remove wheels, marking their position on the wheel and hub, remove hub and brake backing plate. The brake line need not be disconnected unless other work is to be done at the time.
2. Disconnect tie rod and ball joint by removing cotter pin and nut, and tapping end of steering arm gently with a hammer.
3. Remove the pin bolts of the two lower arms.
4. Remove the three upper mounting bolts of the assembly (accessible from under the hood, on the inner fender panel).
5. Remove suspension assembly from vehicle. Recover the rubber washer from the front arm mount.

FRONT SUSPENSION INSTALLATION

1. Position assembly under the inner fender panel and support in place with a chock or horse under the balljoint. Check that the water drain hole faces

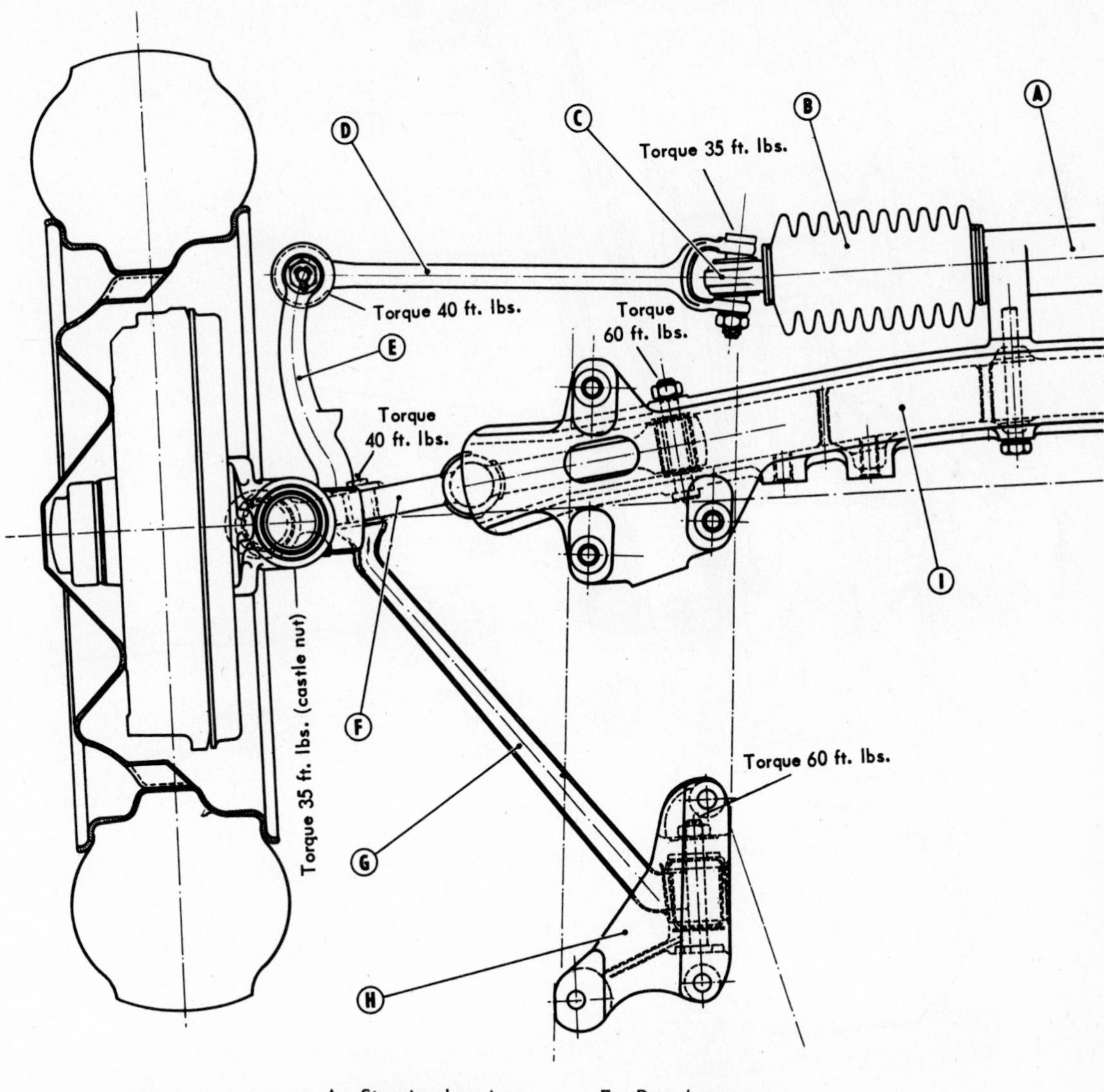

A. Steering housing
B. Steering bellows
C. Steering rack connection
D. Tie rod
E. Steering arm
F. Rear lower arm
G. Front lower arm
H. Front lower arm support
I. Front crossmember

Front axle assembly of the 404.

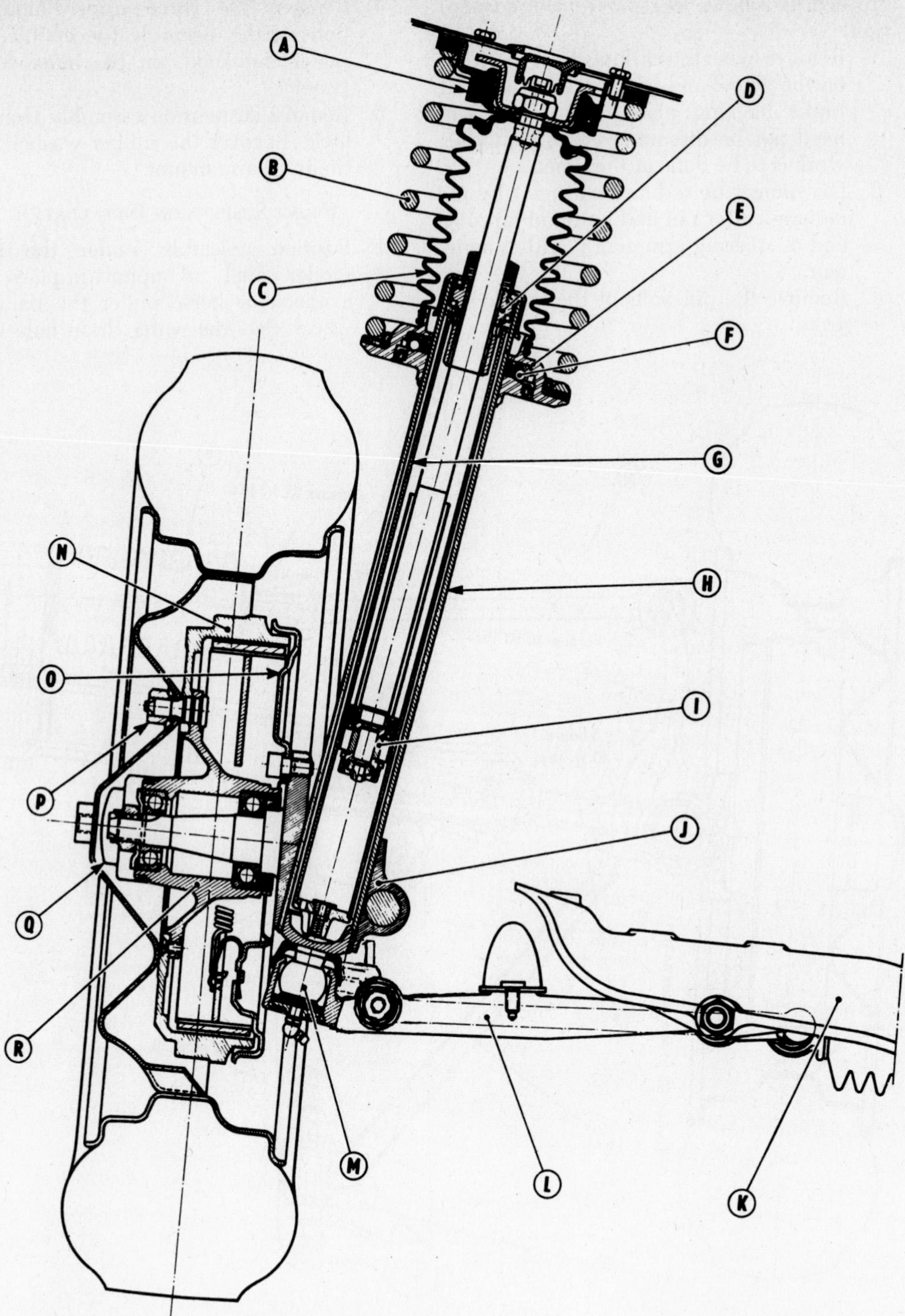

A. Shock absorber upper mount
B. Coil spring
C. Rubber bellows
D. Shock absorber cover nut
E. Coil spring lower seat
F. Ball bearing
G. Shock absorber body
H. Shock absorber housing
I. Piston
J. Spindle assembly
K. Front crossmember
L. Lower arms assembly
M. Lower arms ball joint
N. Brake drum
O. Brake backing plate
P. Wheel lug nut (45 ft lbs)
Q. Wheel bearing grease cap
R. Hub

Front suspension of 404.

the interior of the vehicle.

2. Torque the three bolts to 10 ft. lbs. and insert the cap into the center hole.
3. Position the rear lower arm in the crossmember and insert the pin bolt with the head toward the front, only as far as the splines.

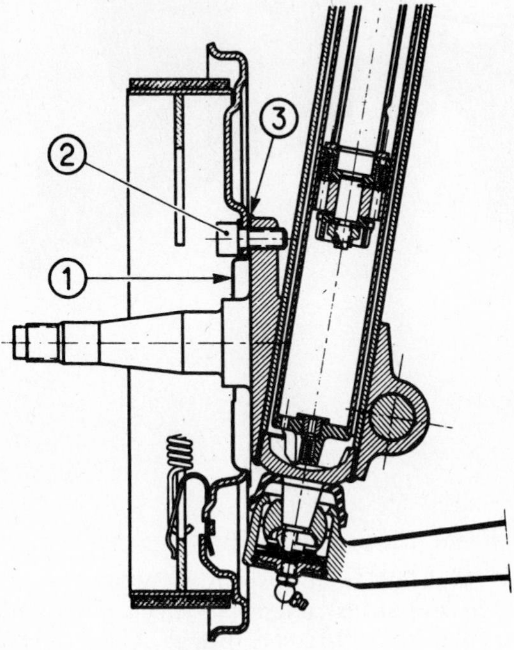

1 Seal
2 Hub bolt
3 Spindle sealing surface

Front suspension installation.

4. Position the front arm in its mounting shackle. Install the pin bolt without engaging the splines.
5. Install brake backing plate and grease retainer. Check that the upper bolt does not touch the shock absorber body, and torque to 45 ft. lbs. Lock threads with a center punch.
6. To seal the openings around the spindle body, apply Permatex around the outside of the intersection.
7. Install the hub with the brake drum. Use new nut and torque to 21 ft. lbs. Loosen nut then torque to 7 ft. lbs. Lock the nut carefully with a punch. Check to be sure drum turns freely.
8. Install grease cap with at least one-half ounce of multipurpose grease in cap. Mount wheel in the same position that it was removed.
9. Torque wheel nuts to 45 ft. lbs. Lower vehicle to floor.
10. Place a .75″ (19 mm) wooden block between the rubber bumper and the front axle. Load front of vehicle until front axle contacts the wooden block. At this point the rubber bushings are in neutral position. Drive in the pin bolts and torque to 60 ft. lbs. Install cotter pins.
11. Torque the connecting nut of the arms to 30 ft. lbs. Lock the nut in the two milled grooves with a punch.
12. Reconnect the tie rod end, and torque the nut to 40 ft. lbs. Install cotter pins. If the brake line was disconnected, reconnect and bleed the system.
13. Check and adjust the toe-in to .062″ (1.55 mm.)

Wheel Bearing Replacement

Jack front of vehicle from under crossmember. Remove front wheel and brake drum after having marked their positions. Then remove grease cap and hub.

Remove outer bearing inner race. Support hub, and using an outer bearing remover lightly tap out outer race.

Remove inner bearing and seal by inserting inner bearing remover into hub and lightly tapping out outer race and seal.

Clean all parts with solvent and dry. Check the spacing of the balls on the tracks of the races, and check for rough or chipped surfaces on balls. Replace worn or defective bearings.

Before installing new bearings, coat the bearings and the inside of the hub with multipurpose grease.

Install the outer bearing complete, then remove the inner race. Install inner bearing and check that bearings seat properly against shoulders. Install seal against the inner bearing, then replace inner race of outer bearing.

Use a new nut and torque to 21 ft. lbs. Loosen nut slightly. Torque to 7 ft. lbs. and carefully lock nut by turning two sides into the milled groove with a punch. Add one-half ounce of grease to cap and install.

Mount brake drum and wheel in their original position. Torque wheel lugs to 45 ft. lbs.

Rear Suspension—404

The rear suspension on the 404 consists of a live axle with coil springs. The rear axle is located longitudinally by two diagonal radius arms and laterally by a Panhard rod. Dampening is provided by two tele-

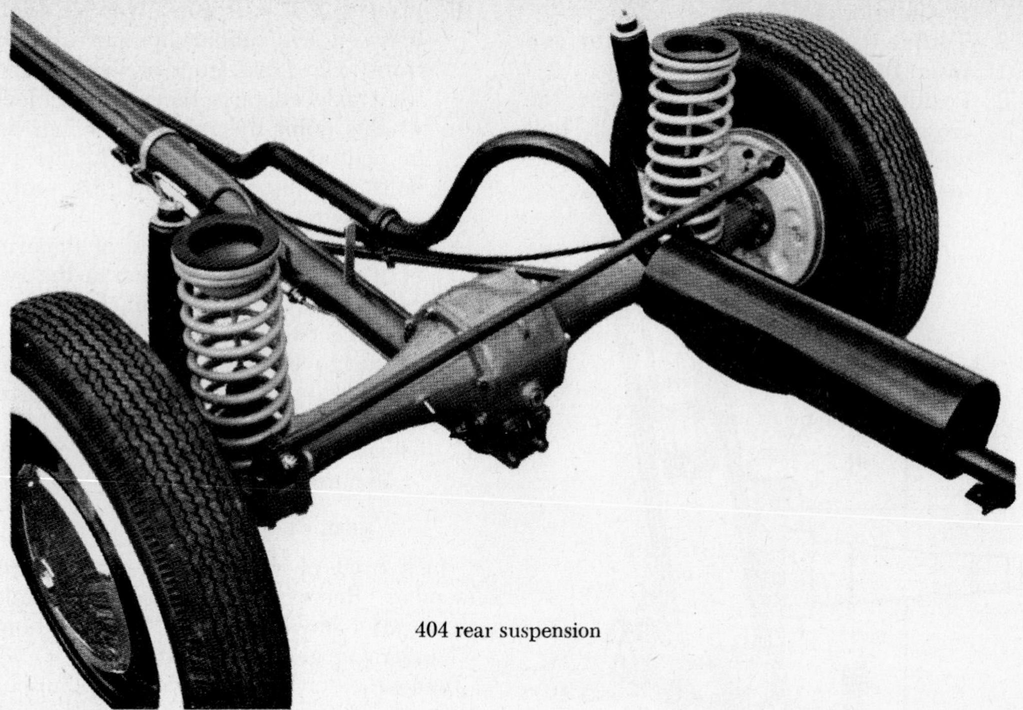

404 rear suspension

scopic shock absorbers. The body must be raised at the rear to remove the coil springs. When installing the springs, the end of the bottom coil should be pointing rearward.

Front Suspension—504

The 504 front suspension utilizes MacPherson struts, telescopic shock absorbers contained within coil springs. The suspension assembly is attached to the inner fender at the top and located by a triangular arm at the bottom. A one inch stabilizer bar is used to control body roll.

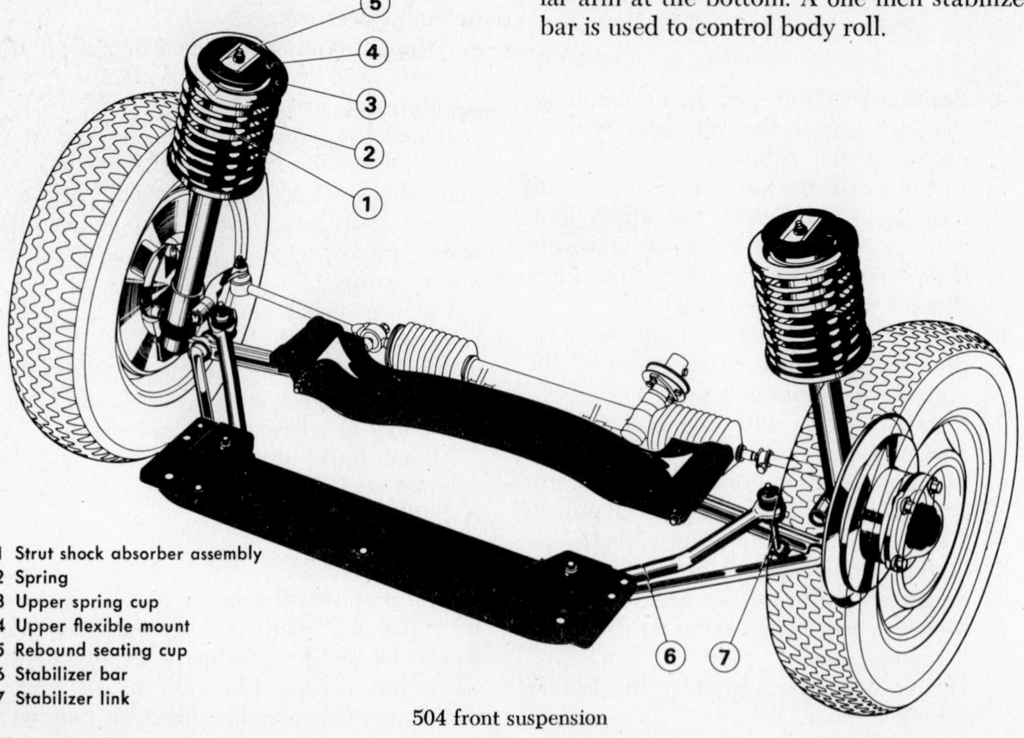

504 front suspension

STRUT REMOVAL AND REPLACEMENT

1. Jack the car up in front, using the crossmember as a jacking point. Place stands under the front crossmember and remove the wheel(s).
2. Remove the brake caliper and hang it from the body without disconnecting the hose.

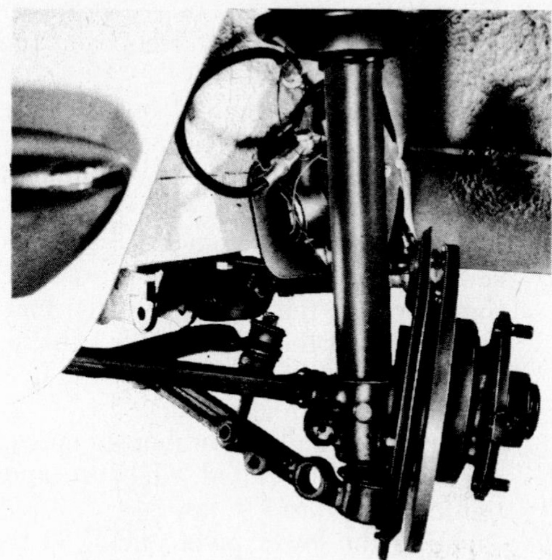

Tie-rod and stabilizer link removal

3. Disconnect the tie-rod end and the stabilizer link from the lower arm.
4. Tap the rear arm pivot to disengage the splined part. Remove the nut holding the front arm to the rear arm.
5. Install a floor jack under the wheel hub. Remove the bolts securing the upper spring holder to the inner fender.
6. Holding the spring by one of its coils, lower the jack and remove the strut assembly.
7. When installing, position the upper holder so that the cup is parallel with the axis of the car.
8. Position the strut assembly under the fender with a jack supporting it. Raise the strut and align the bolt holes. Install and tighten the bolts to 7 ft. lbs.
9. Install the following parts on the front arm: thrust washers, cup, and half bushing.
10. Install the front arm in the rear arm eye and mount the second half bushing and a new nut.
11. Engage the rear arm pivot with the head pointing rearward and flush with the splines. Install a new nut, but do not tighten.

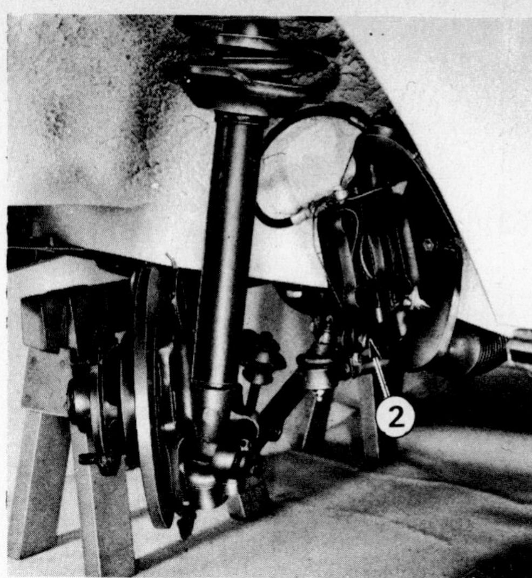

Arm assembly. The pivot is at 2.

12. Install the stabilizer connecting link on the rear arm, by engaging the pivot with the top facing rearward. Install a new nut and washer.
13. Install the tie-rod end in the arm, making sure the cotter pin hole is at a right angle to the rod. Tighten the nut to 33 ft. lbs. and install a cotter pin.
14. Reinstall the brake caliper and tighten the bolts to 51 ft. lbs.
15. Reinstall the wheel and tighten the lug nuts to 44 ft. lbs.
16. Lower the car.
17. From underneath, with the car on a lift, install the rear arm pivot.
18. Tighten the pivot nut, bushing nut, and stabilizer link nut to 33 ft. lbs. Install a PAL lock nut on the link nut.

HUB REMOVAL AND INSTALLATION

1. Jack the front of the car up and support with stands under the crossmember. Remove the wheel.
2. Remove the brake caliper and hang it from the body, without removing the brake hose.
3. Remove the hub nut cap and the nut.
4. Pull the hub assembly off.
5. Install the hub on the spindle with the inner race flush with the spindle shoulder.
6. Install the inner shoulder against the inner race of the bearing.
7. Install a new nut and temporarily tighten to 22 ft. lbs. Loosen and finally tighten to 8 ft. lbs. Lock the nut by punching the two grooves provided.

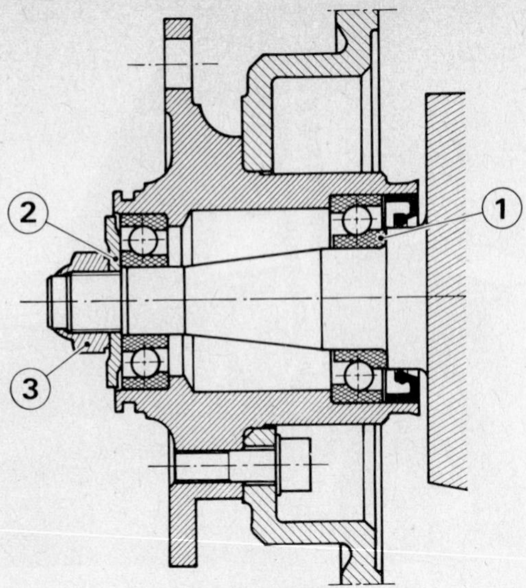

1 Inner bearing race
2 Inner shoulder
3 Hub nut

Hub assembly

8. Install the hub cap with a small amount of grease inside.
9. Clean the brake disc with solvent and reinstall the caliper. Tighten the bolts to 51 ft. lbs.
10. Install the wheel and tighten the lugs to 44 ft. lbs.

Rear Suspension—504

The 504 rear suspension consists of semi-trailing arms, independently coil sprung wheels, and a telescopic shock within each spring. A .71″ stabilizer bar controls body roll.

Shock Absorber Removal and Installation

1. From inside the trunk, remove the shock absorber nut while holding the flat on the absorber body with a 5 mm open end wrench.
2. Remove the upper metal cup and the rubber washer.
3. Remove the lower nut holding the shock absorber to the rear arm.
4. Remove the shock absorber through the hole in the rear arm.
5. Use new rubber grommets when reinstalling the shock absorbers. Install the shock up into the arm so that the hole lines up with the one provided in the rear arm. Install the lower pivot bolt and nut without tightening.
6. At the top, install the rubber grommet, upper cup with raised edge up, and tighten the nut to 7 ft. lbs.
7. Tightern the lower pivot nut to 33 ft. lbs.

Spring Removal and Installation

1. Jack the rear of the car up and support with stands.
2. Remove the clamp holding the exhaust pipe to the body.
3. Remove the two stabilizer clamps and disengage the stabilizer bar clamps

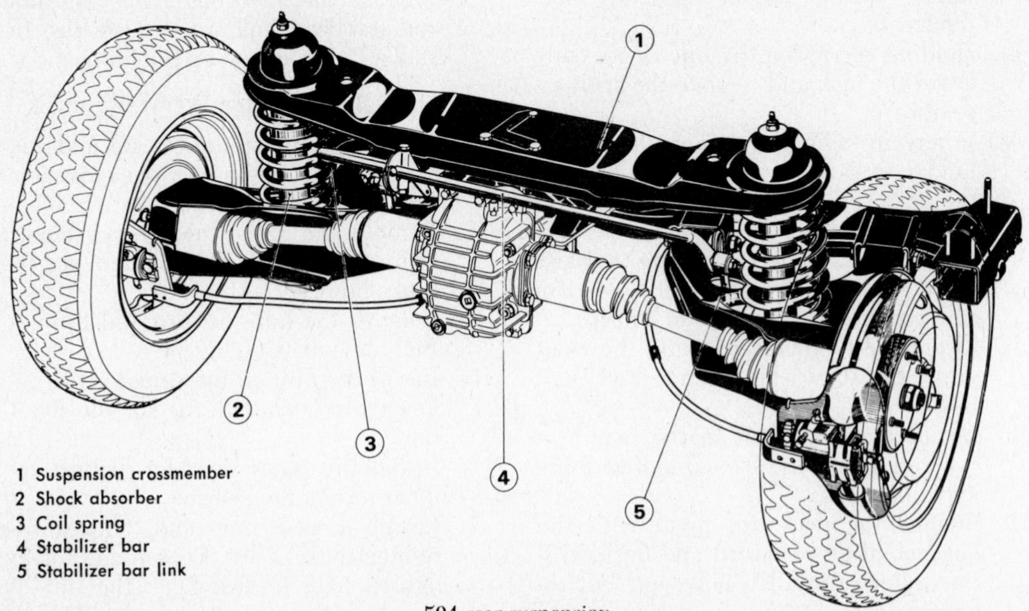

1 Suspension crossmember
2 Shock absorber
3 Coil spring
4 Stabilizer bar
5 Stabilizer bar link

504 rear suspension

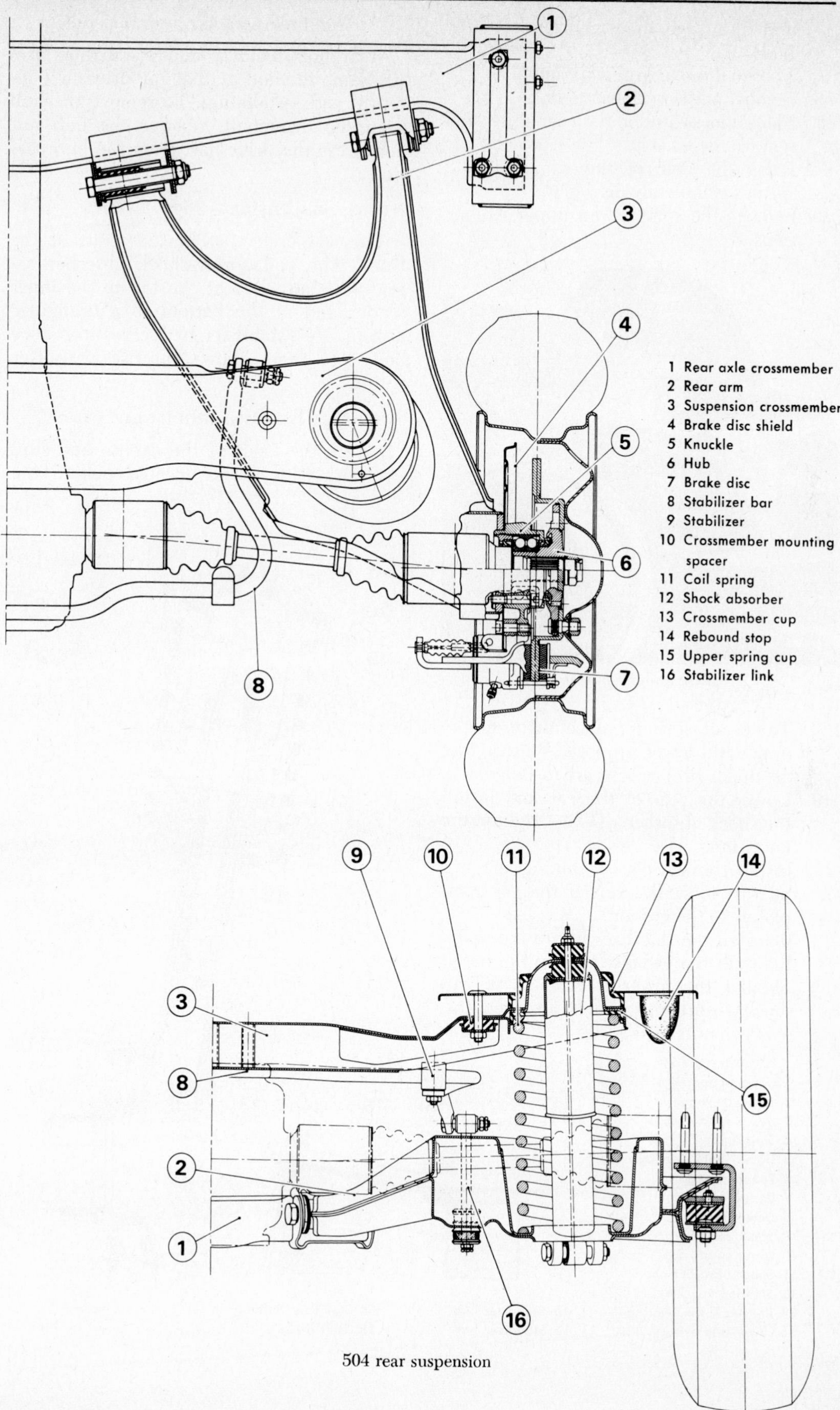
1
2
3
4
5
6
7
8
1 Rear axle crossmember
2 Rear arm
3 Suspension crossmember
4 Brake disc shield
5 Knuckle
6 Hub
7 Brake disc
8 Stabilizer bar
9 Stabilizer
10 Crossmember mounting spacer
11 Coil spring
12 Shock absorber
13 Crossmember cup
14 Rebound stop
15 Upper spring cup
16 Stabilizer link
9
10
11
12
13
14
3
8
15
2
1
16

504 rear suspension

and disengage the stabilizer from the body.

4. Loosen the rear arm pivot nuts.
5. Remove the shock absorbers.
6. Place blocks under the rear arms and remove the wheels.
7. Raise the rear of the car until the springs completely disengage.
8. Remove the springs and upper rubber cups.

Rear spring removal

9. To install springs, place them in the upper and lower supports. Be sure that the upper rubber cups are installed.
10. Lower the rear of the car and install the shock absorbers. Do not tighten the lower nuts.
11. Install the wheels, tightening the lug nuts to 43 ft. lbs. Lower the car completely to the ground.
12. Reinstall the stabilizer bar to the body. Reinstall the exhaust pipe to the body.
13. Tighten the lower pivot nuts of the shock absorbers to 33 ft. lbs. and the rear arm nuts to 47 ft. lbs.

Hub Removal and Installation

Rear hub removal and installation uses the same method as that for driveshaft removal and installation. To remove the hub from the driveshaft, remove the hub nut and press the driveshaft from the hub carrier.

Front Suspension—304

The 304 uses MacPherson struts at the front. The coil spring-shock absorber assembly is attached at the top to the inner fender and at the bottom to a triangular arm. A 3/4″ stabilizer bar serves to reduce body roll and allow the use of softer springs.

Strut Removal and Installation

1. Jack the front of the car up and support with stands located behind the

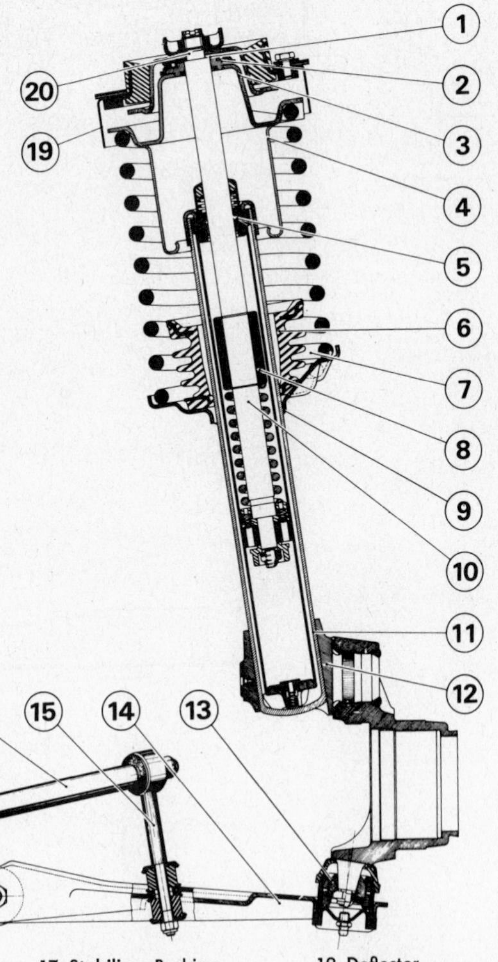

1 Upper support
2 Thrust bearing
3 Upper spring cup
4 Stop cup
5 Upper shock bearing
6 Rebound stop
7 Spring
8 Detent stop
9 Shock absorber rod
10 Lower spring cup
11 Shock absorber body
12 Steering knuckle
13 Knuckle lower bearing
14 Lower arm
15 Stabilizer link
16 Stabilizer bar
17 Stabilizer Bushing
18 Stub frame
19 Deflector
20 Thrust washer

304 front suspension

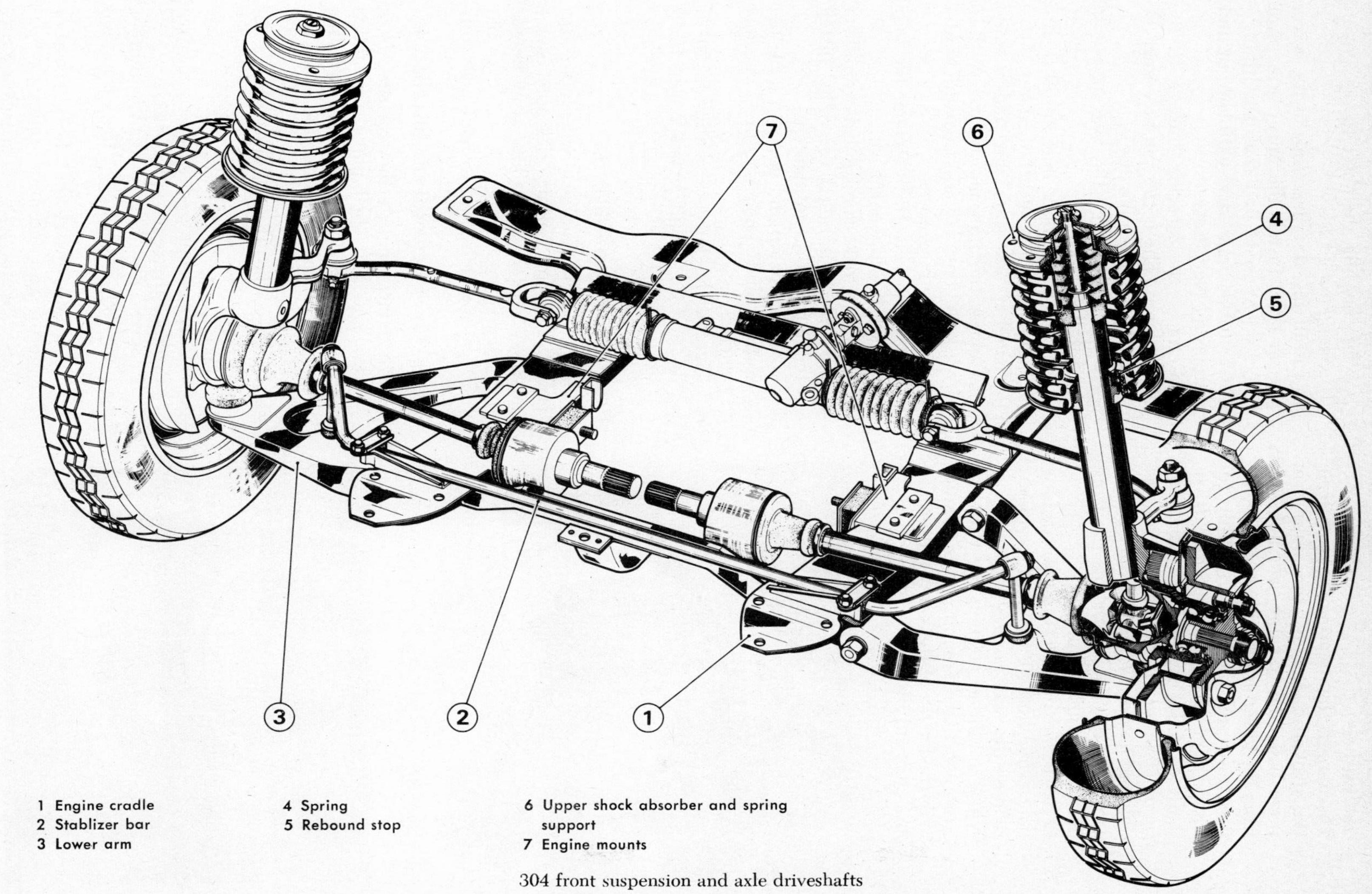

1 Engine cradle
2 Stablizer bar
3 Lower arm
4 Spring
5 Rebound stop
6 Upper shock absorber and spring support
7 Engine mounts

304 front suspension and axle driveshafts

wheelwell. Remove the wheels.
2. While holding the hub, remove the nut and washer.
3. Disconnect the steering linkage from the strut arm. Remove the lower arm pivot bolts and the stabilizer link bolt from the lower arm.
4. Carefully pull the strut assembly towards you, while holding the driveshaft. CAUTION: *If the driveshaft should fall out, damage to the oil seal ring and loss of engine oil could result.*
5. Move the driveshaft towards the front onto the stabilizer bar.
6. Remove the upper support attaching bolts while holding the strut assembly. Remove the strut assembly.
7. When installing, position the strut assembly so that the limit cup is parallel with the length of the car. Tighten the three bolts to 7 ft. lbs.

Strut assembly removal. The splined hub is at 6.

Limit cup positioning. The limit cup is at 2.

8. Grease the splined end of the driveshaft and engage the hub carefully, while holding the shaft to prevent its coming out.
9. Install the stabilizer link in the lower arm hole. Install the lower arm pivot bolts (greased) and nuts handtight.
10. Clean the brake disc with solvent and reinstall the caliper.
11. Connect the steering linkage to the strut arm. The cotter pin hole must be parallel to the brake disc.
12. Install and tighten the bearing nut to 31 ft. lbs.
13. Tighten the caliper bolts to 36 ft. lbs. Tighten the hose attachment nut.
14. Install a new hub nut and washer. Tighten the hub nut to 180 ft. lbs., while holding the hub. Lock the nut by punching the grooves.
15. Install the wheels, tightening the lugs to 44 ft. lbs. Lower the car.
16. Check to make sure that the stabilizer bar link is installed correctly. Install the nuts, but do not tighten.
17. Push the car up and down to settle the springs and bushings to a normal height.
18. Tighten the lower arm nuts to 20 ft. lbs. and the stabilizer link nut to 13 ft. lbs.

Rear Suspension—304

The 304's undriven rear wheels are suspended by coil spring-telescopic shock units and located by trailing arms hinged on a lateral crossmember. A stabilizer bar of .59″ diameter is used to limit body roll.

Spring-Shock Removal and Installation

1. On sedans, remove the rear seat, back rest, and rear shelf panel. On station wagons, strip the upholstery from the upper attaching point of the shock absorber.
2. Remove the three upper shock absorber nuts.
3. Raise the rear of the car.
4. Install jackstands under the rear crossmember and remove the wheels.
5. Remove the lower shock absorber pivot bolt and remove the suspension unit.
6. To install, insert the shock absorber onto the arm and install the pivot bolt.
7. Raise the arm with a floor jack to bring the suspension assembly into the upper

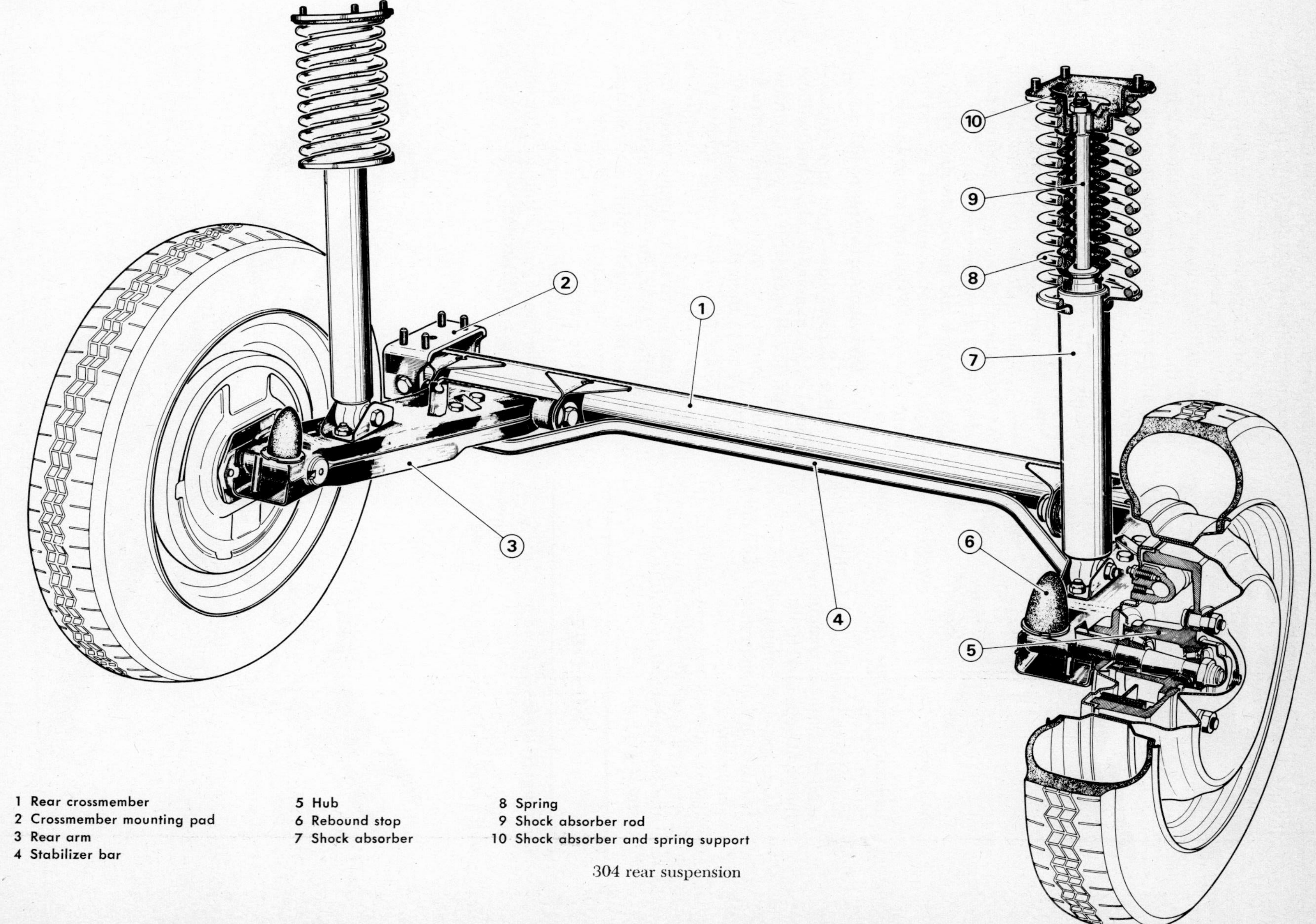

1 Rear crossmember
2 Crossmember mounting pad
3 Rear arm
4 Stabilizer bar
5 Hub
6 Rebound stop
7 Shock absorber
8 Spring
9 Shock absorber rod
10 Shock absorber and spring support

304 rear suspension

Shock absorber-spring assembly installation

mounting position. Tighten the three nuts to 7 ft. lbs.

8. Continue to raise the arm with the jack until the spring is compressed. Tighten the pivot bolts to 40 ft. lbs.
9. Raise the arm completely to the rebound stop and then install the wheels and lower.
10. Install the back rest, seat cushion, and rear shelf panel on sedans and recover the shock absorber mounting plate on station wagons.

Steering

Steering Systems

Peugeot 403 and 404 cars are equipped with a rack and pinion type of steering gear incorporating an automatic play takeup device employing two spring loaded plungers. One plunger located on the pinion side takes up steering wheel angular play, while the one on the rack side acts as a steering damper and takes up axial play. The left tie rod of the 404 is secured to the rack by a ball joint providing, through fractions of a turn, a very accurate adjustment of the toe-in; i.e., one turn equalling .125″ (on wheels). The steering ratio of the 404 is 18.6 to 1. For the 403, it is 16.5 to 1.

The 504 uses a rack and pinion steering system which is similar to the one used on the 404, except for the overall steering ratio which is 22:1 instead of 18.6:1. The 304 also uses rack and pinion steering which is controlled through a universal jointed column. The overall steering ratio is 18.6:1.

Steering Adjustment—403

After all parts have been inspected and found to be thoroughly clean and without defects, install rack with its yoke in transversal position so that its end protrudes 2.8″ (71 mm) from the steering gear housing. Engage pinion and upper rubber seal in position so that axis of holes provided in yoke is parallel to rack. Torque pinion nut to 9 ft. lbs. Lubricate. Then install horn control switch support plate and plunger spring retaining plates using Permatex cement and no gasket.

Make a preliminary adjustment by turning threaded rack end fitting to protrude .64″ (16 mm), as illustrated.

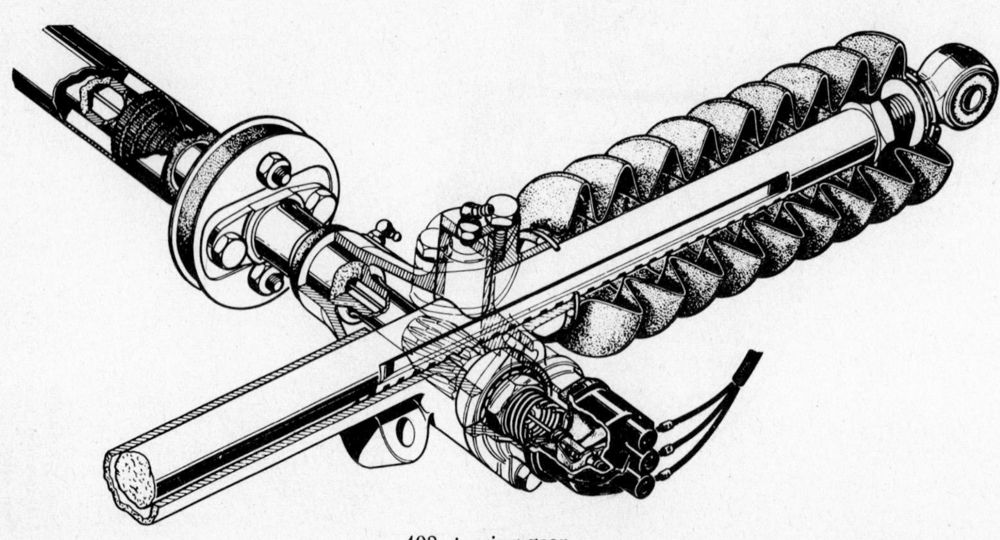

403 steering gear

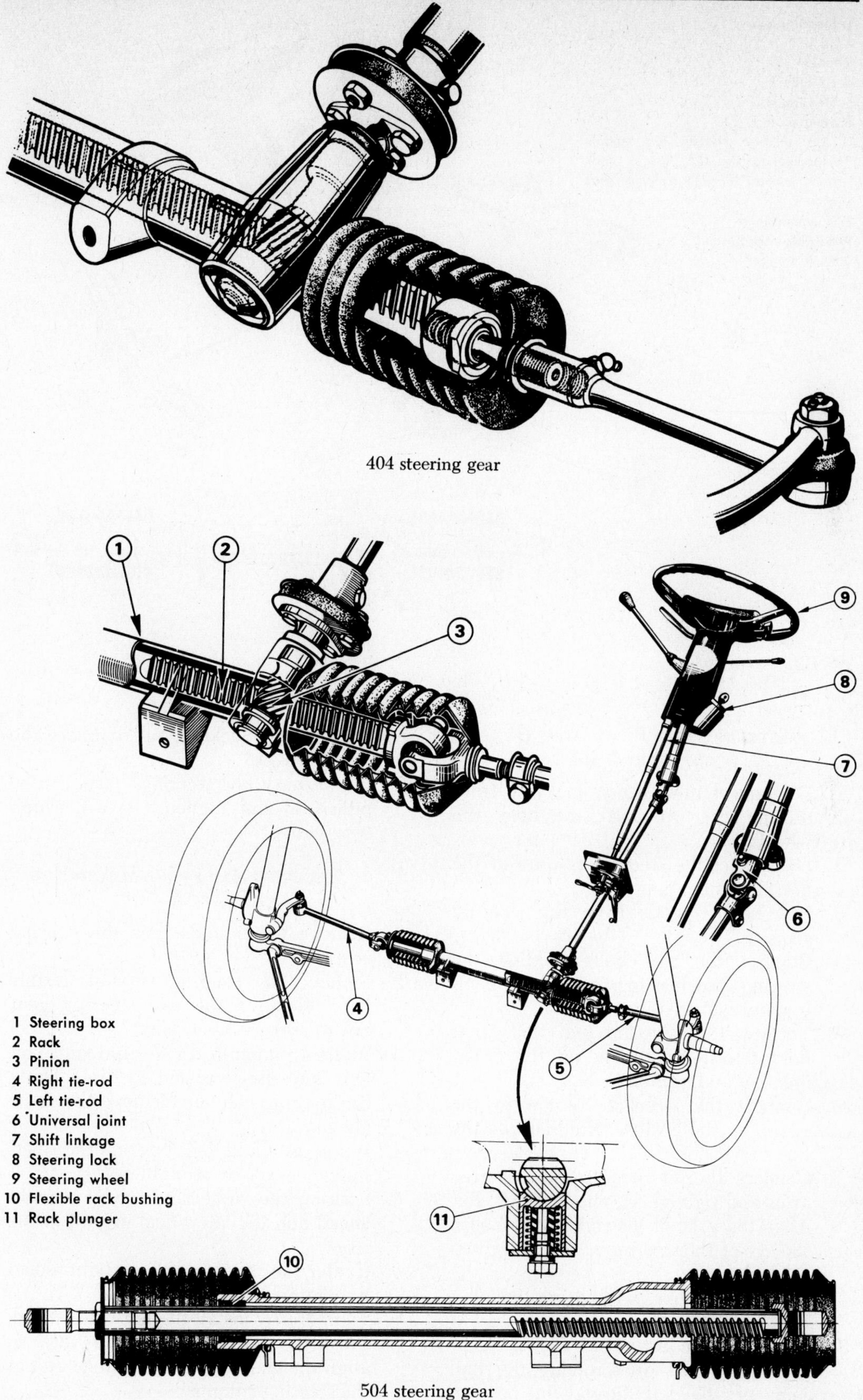

404 steering gear

504 steering gear

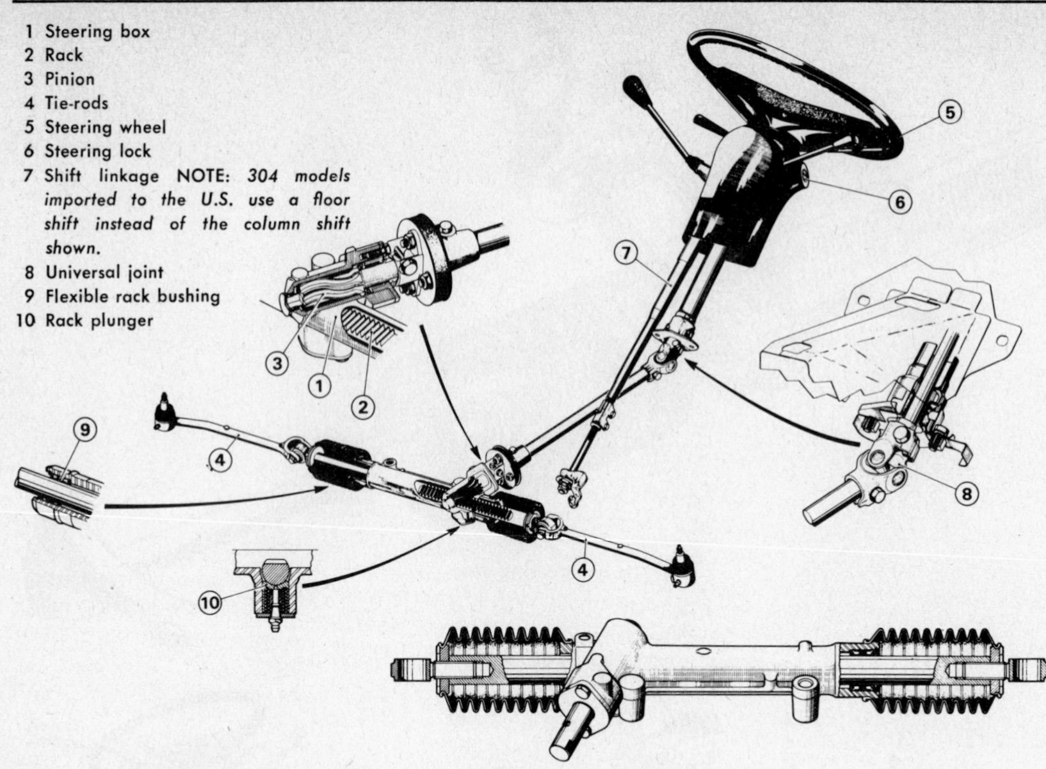

Steering Gear Removal and Installation—404

1. Disconnect the battery. Jack the front of the car up and straighten the wheels.
2. Disconnect the steering column at the flexible rubber joint.
3. Pull both tie-rods from the steering arms.
4. Remove the two bolts holding the steering gear housing to the crossmember and remove the assembly.
5. To install, insert the two bolts that hold the steering gear on the crossmember and tighten to 30 ft. lbs.
6. Connect the steering column to the clamp on the flexible joint. Torque the bolt to 7 ft. lbs.
7. Connect the tie-rods to the steering arms and tighten the nuts to 35 ft. lbs.
8. Align the yoke of the right tie-rod with the eye of the steering rack and tighten the locknut.
9. Tighten the yoke pin bolt and install a cotter pin.
10. Adjust the toe-in to .062″ (1.5 mm) ± .015 (.37 mm) by screwing the ball joint of the left tie-rod in or out. Tighten the locknut and connect the rubber cover.
11. If necessary, the steering wheel can be pulled off and aligned. Use a C clamp type puller.

Steering Gear Removal and Installation—504

1. Remove the tie-rods from the steering arms.
2. Remove the steering column flexible joint. Remove the two steering gear box to crossmember bolts.
3. Insert a punch in the flexible joint bolt hole and use it to aid in disengaging the steering column. Remove the steering gear.
4. When installing, first position the steering wheel spokes straight up.
5. Position the right-hand wheel straight ahead and the left wheel inward at the front.
6. Center the steering rack straight ahead in relation to the steering box.
7. Temporarily install the left side tie-rod. Turn the steering joint 1/4 turn to align the clamp with the splined end of the steering column.

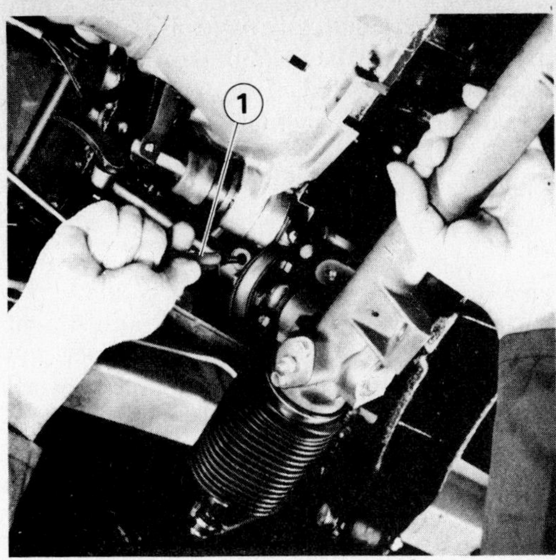

Steering gear removal. The drift is indicated by 1.

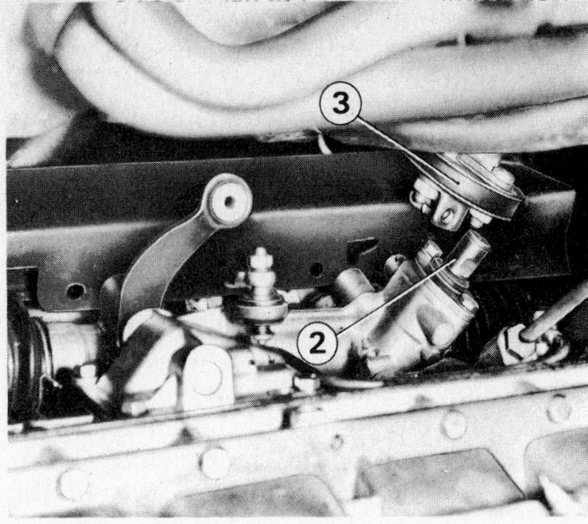

Disconnecting steering column—304. The pinion is at 2, the bushing at 3.

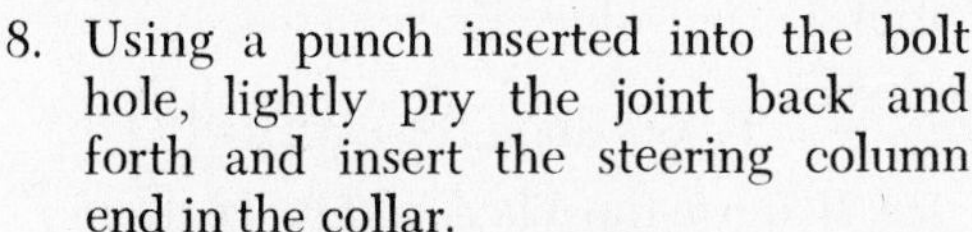

8. Using a punch inserted into the bolt hole, lightly pry the joint back and forth and insert the steering column end in the collar.
9. Tighten the two steering gear to cross-member bolts to 24 ft. lbs. Tighten the flexible joint nut to 7 ft. lbs.
10. Install the tie-rod on the left side and check the alignment of the two flats on the ball joint and connecting yoke.
11. Position the cotter pin holes at a right angle to the tie-rod. Install new washers and nuts. Tighten to 31 ft. lbs. and install cotter pins.
12. Set the toe-in.

Steering Gear Removal and Installation—304

1. Remove the tie-rod ends from the steering arms.
2. Disconnect the bolt holding the steering column to the steering box at the flexible joint.
3. Remove the two steering box to engine cradle bolts. Turn the left front wheel inward as far as possible.
4. Disconnect the steering column from the steering box. Check the condition of the rubber joint and replace it if necessary.
5. To reinstall, engage the steering box from the left side. Connect it to the column at the flexible joint.
6. Install the flexible joint bolt and the two mounting bolts without tightening.
7. While holding the column upwards toward the steering wheel, tighten the flexible joint bolts to 7 ft. lbs.
8. Position the steering rack in the center position and move the tie-rod ends so that the cotter pin holes are pointing straight ahead.
9. Connect the tie-rods to the steering arms and install the nuts without tightening.
10. Tighten the two steering box bolts to 25 ft. lbs. and the two tie-rod nuts to 31 ft. lbs. Cotter pin the tie-rod ends.
11. Straighten the wheels and steering wheel. Adjust the toe-in to specifications. Adjustment is made at the tie-rod eyes.

Steering Wheel Removal—304

1. Remove the steering wheel padding, which is attached at the back of the wheel by two screws.

304 steering wheel removal

2. Loosen the steering wheel nut until its shoulder is flush with the end of the steering column.
3. Tap the column with a mallet while pulling the wheel up until it comes free. Mark the column and wheel for installation.
4. When installing the same wheel, align the reference marks. If the wheel is new, position it so that the spokes are horizontal.
5. Install a flat washer and a new nut. Adjust the position of the wheel, if necessary, and tighten the nut to 33 ft. lbs. Lock the nut by distorting it in the grooves provided. Install the padding.

Brakes

Service Brakes—403 and 404 (up to 1968)

The 403 and early 404 models used 10″ drum brakes front and rear. These Lockheed brakes use two single piston wheel cylinders at each front wheel and one double piston wheel cylinder at the rear. The drums are cast iron and secured to the hub with three bolts. Drums more than .004″ out of round should be turned down. Drums should not be turned down more than .040″. Beginning in 1966, the 404 was equipped with larger 11.2″ drums and larger linings. Braking assistance was provided by a Hydrovac power unit, which uses manifold vacuum to lessen the necessary pedal pressure. A rear brake compensator was also added in 1966. The compensator automatically controls the pressure transmitted to the rear brake cylinders according to the load of the vehicle. Parking brakes are cable actuated and utilize the rear brakes. Adjustment is made at the cable equalizing yoke.

Brake Adjustment

Adjustment of the brakes is made by means of two square-headed adjustment cams on each plate. Jack front wheel and turn one of the adjustment squares forward until jaw locks drum. Then slightly rotate square in opposite direction until wheel turns freely. Use same procedure for other adjustment square. Repeat for both front wheels. The front brakes are then properly adjusted. Rotate adjustment squares on rear wheels in opposite direction from those of front. Do not adjust brake pedal.

Brake Shoe Replacement

1. Remove the wheel and brake drum.
2. Remove the outer springs with pliers.
3. Remove both inner springs by placing the blade of a screwdriver on the end of the spring hook, and tapping the screwdriver handle.
4. Remove the lateral springs and brake shoes.
5. Engage a rod under the spring wire and pry gently in the direction of the arrow.
6. The spring hook will then disengage from the anchor pin. While holding the tool in position, insert a screwdriver between the spring hook and the anchor pin, and remove the spring.

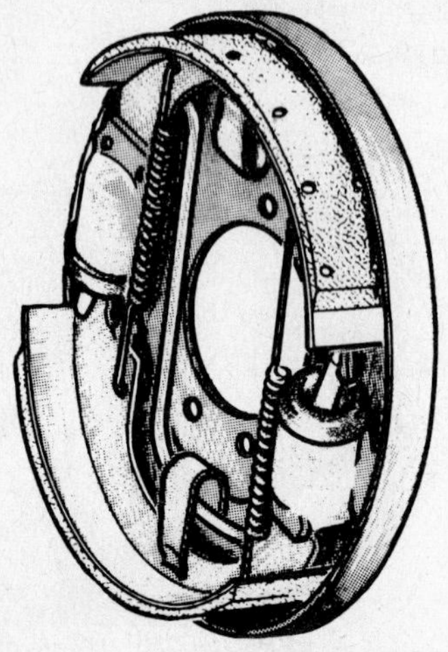

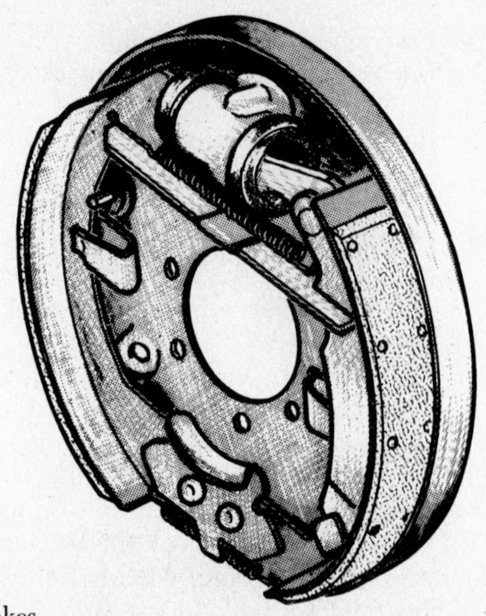

403 and early 404 brakes

Use of tool in removing inner springs.

7. Install the brake shoes against the backing plate and secure with lateral springs.
8. Install both inner springs, closing the larger hooks slightly if necessary.
9. Install both outer springs.
10. Install drum and wheel and adjust brakes.

Service Brakes—404 (1968 and 1969)

The late model 404's, excepting station wagons, use 10.9″ Girling disc brakes at the front and 10″ drums at the rear. Station wagons continue to use four wheel drums, so service procedures for them are the same as the earlier 404 model. Power assist is provided by a Hydrovac unit. Parking brakes utilize the rear drums and are actuated by cables. Adjustment is made at the rear equalizing yoke.

Brake Adjustment

The front disc brakes are self-compensating for wear, and only the rear brakes require adjustment.

1. Raise the rear of the car.
2. Turn the front adjustment cam in the forward direction, until it can no longer be turned.
3. Turn the adjuster in the opposite direction while revolving the wheel. Stop turning the adjuster when no more friction can be felt on the wheel.
4. Use the same procedure on the rear adjuster, but turn it towards the rear.

Brake Service

Front disc brake pad replacement uses the same procedure as outlined for the 504. Rear brake shoe replacement is similar to that described for the four wheel drum brake cars.

Service Brakes—504

The 504 is equipped with 10.75″ Girling disc brakes on all four wheels. Power braking assistance is standard equipment and is provided by a Mastervac unit. A rear brake compensator senses changes in weight and deceleration and equalizes front and rear braking forces. The parking brakes are cable actuated, and use the rear discs. Parking brake adjustment is made at the rear equalizing yoke.

Pad Replacement

The brake pads incorporate wear warning indicators. Pads should be replaced whenever these become visible. To replace pads, proceed as follows:

1. Jack the car up and remove the wheels.
2. Brush or blow any accumulated dirt from the caliper and brake assembly. Be careful not to damage the rubber dust covers.
3. Connect a bleed tube to the bleed screw, and to a jar containing brake fluid.
4. Remove the pad pressure spring and then remove the securing fork.
5. Open the bleed screw. Using pliers, press on the caliper edge and the inner pad to push the inboard piston into its recess.
6. Proceeding in the same way, push the outboard piston into its recess. Brake fluid will squirt into the jar.
7. Close the bleed screw and remove the tube.
8. Remove the worn pads.
9. Check the wheel cylinders for indications of leaks. Make sure the brake disc is free from any deep grooves, as this will cause premature pad wear.
10. Clean the brake disc with a solvent; trichlorethylene is a suitable cleaner.
11. Install new pads (with anti-squeal plates, if so equipped), being careful to position them properly.
12. Insert the pad securing fork and install the pad pressure spring.
13. Proceed in the same manner at the other wheels.
14. When the pads have been replaced, check that the bleed screws are all closed.
15. Step on the brake pedal several times, until you feel a strong resistance. At this point, the pistons have seated correctly on the disc.

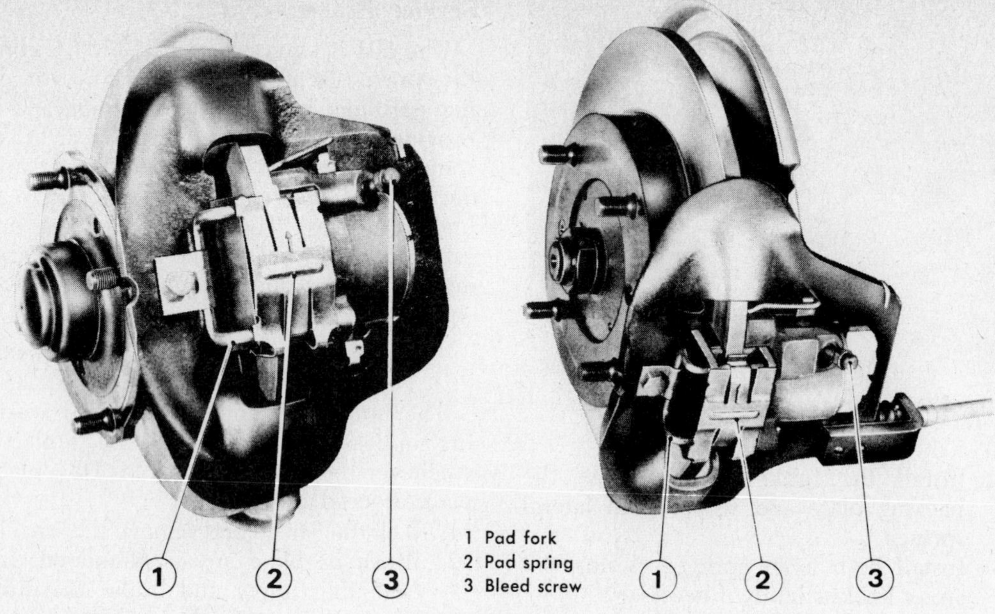

504 brakes

16. Fill the master cylinder to the proper level.

Service Brakes—304

The 304 is equipped with Girling 10″ disc brakes on the front wheels and HCSF 9″ drum brakes on the rear. The braking system includes a Mastervac power booster and a rear brake compensator. The parking brake uses cables to activate the rear drums. Adjustment is made at the rear equalizing yoke.

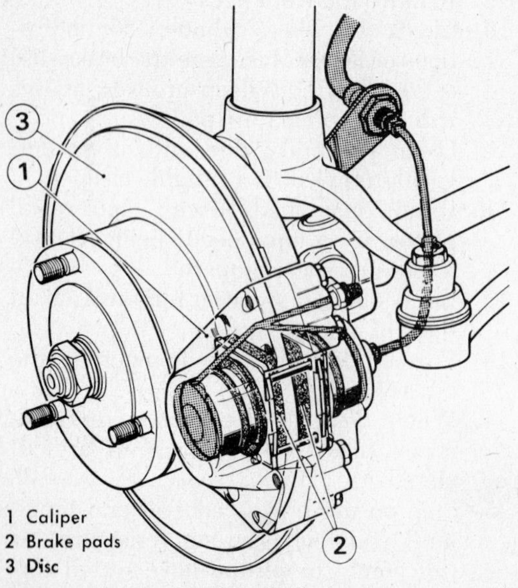

304 front brakes

Front Pad Replacement

Front brake pads should be replaced as soon as their thickness approaches .079″ (2 mm).

1. Jack up the front of the car and install jackstands.
2. Remove the wheels and blow off any accumulated dirt from the brake assembly. Be careful not to damage or move the piston rubber dust covers.
3. Install a bleed tube on the caliper bleed screw and run it into a jar containing brake fluid.
4. Remove the pad retaining pin clips and work the retaining pins out. Open the bleed screws one turn.
5. Using pliers, press the inside piston into its recess.
6. Repeat this procedure for the outside piston.
7. Some fluid will be forced into the jar. Close the bleed screw and remove the tube.
8. Remove the old brake pads.
9. Check for wheel cylinder leaks, grooves in the brake disc, and check the disc for warpage.
10. Clean the brake disc with a greaseless solvent.
11. Install new pads along with antisqueak shim plates. The arrow should point in the direction of forward disc rotation.
12. Install the two pad retaining clips,

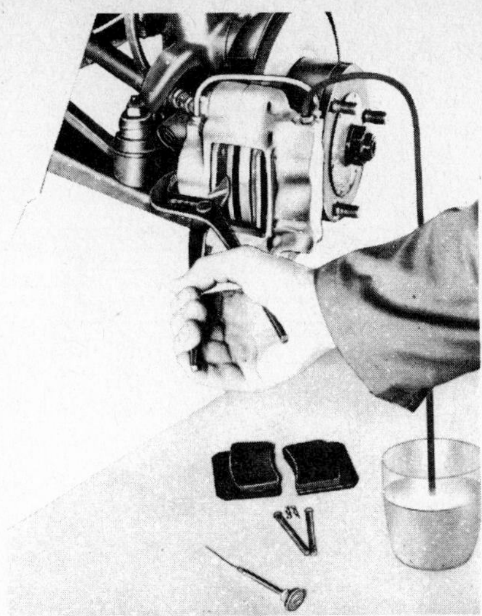

Pad removal

working from the inside out. Insert the retaining pin clips, being careful not to damage the inner cylinder dust cover.

13. Tighten the bleed screws after all four pads have been installed.
14. Depress the brake pedal several times, until you feel a strong resistance. At this point, the pistons are bearing properly on the pads, and the pads bearing properly on the disc.
15. Fill the master cylinder with fluid.

Rear Brake Service and Adjustment

The rear drum brakes on the 304 are replaced in the same manner as the 404 drum brakes. They are adjusted as follows:

1. Raise the rear wheels.
2. Turn the front adjustment cam in a forward direction until the wheel locks up.
3. Turn in the opposite direction until it will rotate freely.
4. Adjust the other cam as above, but turn it in the opposite direction.

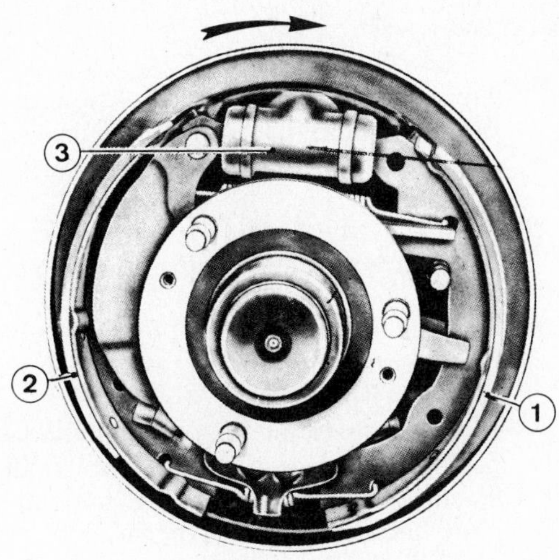

1 Leading shoe
2 Trailing shoe
3 Wheel cylinder

304 rear brakes

Master Cylinder and Hydraulic System

403 and 404 models up to 1966 used glass reservoir master cylinder with no power assist in the circuit. The master cylinder is located on the firewall on all Peugeot cars. Drum brake cars have two single piston wheel cylinders on each front brake and a double piston cylinder for each rear wheel. Hydrovac power assist was added to the 404 in 1966, along with a brake compensator. The Hydrovac consists of a vacuum cylinder, control valve, hydraulic servo cylinder, and vacuum check valve. The rear brake compensator automatically controls the pressure transmitted to the rear brake cylinders according to the vehicle load.

Beginning in 1968, 404 models were equipped with dual circuit hydraulic systems in order to comply with Federal safety regulations. This system employs tandem master cylinders and is divided so that one circuit operates the front brakes and the other operates the rear wheels.

The 504 uses two pistons for each disc. The master cylinder is the clutch and brake fluid reservoir. Power assistance is provided by a Mastervac unit. The 304 uses double pistons at each front wheel and one double piston wheel cylinder for each rear wheel. The 304 also uses a Mastervac to reduce required pedal pressure. Late model 404's, and all 504 and 304 cars have a brake warning light which advises of any hydraulic system trouble.

Bleeding the Hydraulic System—403, 404, and 504

On non-power assisted brakes, proceed as follows:

1. Remove the master cylinder filler cap.
2. Remove the rubber cap from the bleeder valve and install a hose with one end in a jar containing brake fluid.
3. Open the bleeder at the wheel cylinder.
4. Depress the pedal by hand, allowing it to return slowly. Continue until no more bubbles come out of the hose.

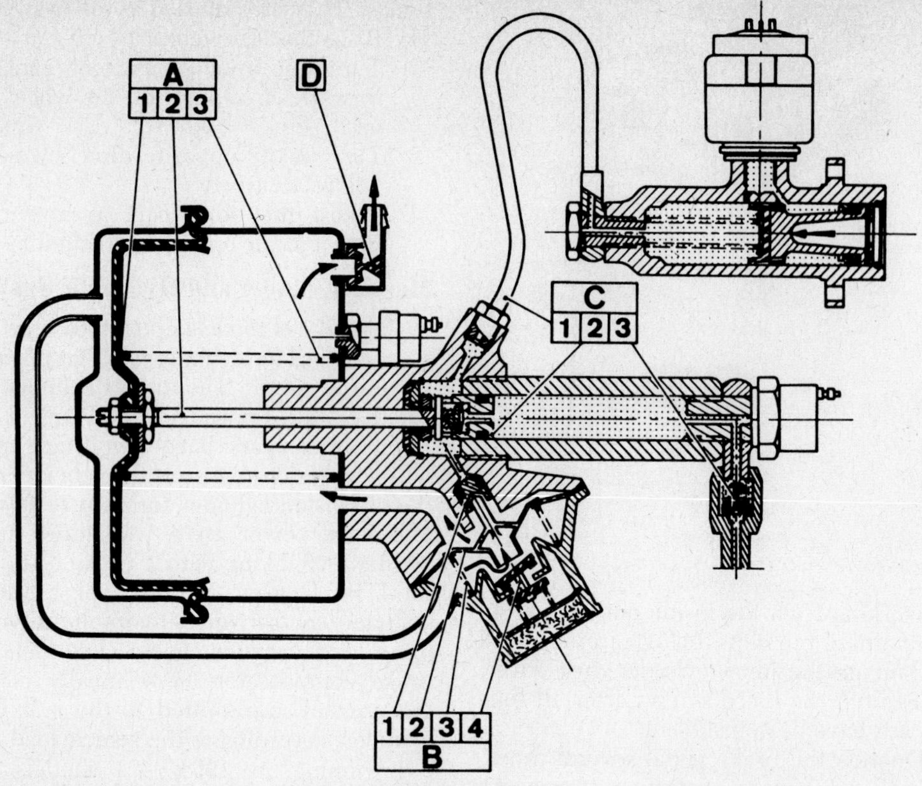

Vacuum cylinder (A):
Vacuum reservoir connected to intake manifold.
Piston (1)
Push rod (2)
Vacuum piston spring (3)

Control valve (B):
Operates by master cylinder pressure, controls movement of vacuum cylinder piston.
Piston (1)
Control valve (2)
Control valve spring (3)
Double valve (4)

Hydraulic servo cylinder (C):
Transmits effort exerted by vacuum cylinder piston to the brake circuit.
Pressure line from master cylinder (1)
Servo piston (2)
Residual check valve (3)

Vacuum check valve (D):
Holds vacuum in cylinder when engine is stopped to allow temporary reserve of power assistance.

Major components of Hydrovac power brake system on 404's.

5. Close the bleeder and replace the rubber cap.
6. Proceed from the longest brake line to shortest, using the above procedure.
7. Refill the master cylinder.

On Mastervac equipped cars, use the same procedure, except that the engine should be running at an idle.

Bleeding the Hydraulic System—304

1. Raise the car and block the wheels.
2. Remove the front wheels and release the handbrake.
3. Turn the rear brake adjuster upwards until it locks and note the position of the adjusting wrench with reference to the wheel.
4. Turn the adjusters in the opposite direction until the wheels are locked and again note the wrench to wheel relationship.
5. Turn the adjuster to the center of the two extremes and apply the handbrake.
6. Connect a bleeder tube to the right front screw and dip the end in a jar containing brake fluid.
7. Have an assistant step on the brake pedal and loosen the right front bleeder. Continue bleeding until no more bubbles appear in the jar.
8. Refill the master cylinder.
9. Tighten the right front bleeder, and repeat the bleeding procedure on the left front.

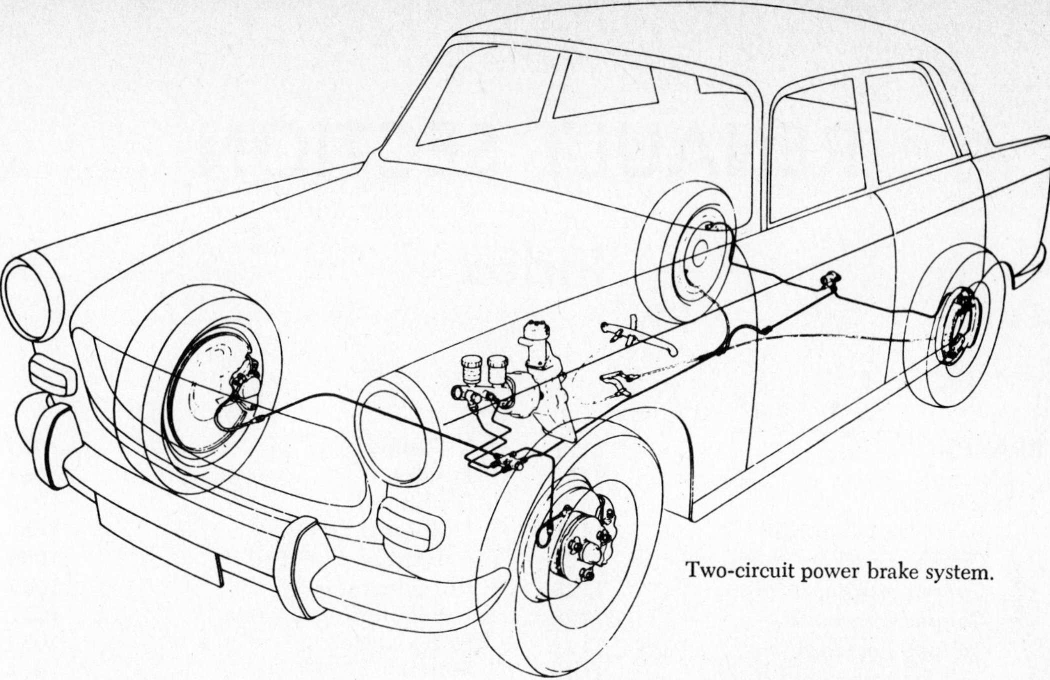

Two-circuit power brake system.

10. Bleed the rear brakes in the conventional manner.

11. Adjust the rear brakes by turning the front adjuster down until the wheel locks. Depress the brake pedal once or twice so that the brake shoe is positioned correctly.

12. Turn the adjuster in the opposite direction until the brake drum barely contacts the shoe and the wheel turns freely.

13. Adjust the rear adjuster in the same manner, and then adjust the other rear wheel brake similarly.

304 rear brake adjustment

Windshield Wipers

Windshield Wipers—404

The wiper system incorporates rigid linkage to operate the wiper transmissions and arms in parallel. Linkages and transmissions are secured on a frame support and can be removed as a complete unit. The parking switch, which leaves the blades in a horizontal position when turned off, is mounted on the wiper motor transmission.

An automatic brake is incorporated in the wiper motor located in the engine compartment to prevent the motor from spinning after the wipers are in their parking position. If this brake is out of adjustment, it may cause any of these conditions: sluggish operation of wipers, motor will not start or may run for a few minutes then stop, blow fuses.

The adjustment is easily accomplished as follows:

1. Remove the motor cover.

The windshield wiper motor drain is 2.5 A.

2. Remove the two screws holding the brush support. This allows the brake shoe pivot to realign itself in the slot.
3. Tighten the two screws, check fuse and test the motor for free operation by switching on motor. If motor does not run freely, repeat Step 2.
4. Replace cover.

RENAULT SECTION

Index

Introduction

Covered in this section are all Renault models imported into this country from 1964-1971. They are the Dauphine from 1964 to the end of its production in 1967, the Renault 8 in the same model years, and the Caravelle sports model, last produced in 1967. The Renault 10 replaced the 8 in 1967, and is covered in all American versions. The front wheel drive Renault 16, a spacious, economical family sedan, well suited to American motoring needs, was introduced in late 1968. Its larger displacement engine and superior handling traits have been included in the new Renault 12, a trim and lively front wheel drive model, offered in sedan and wagon bodies.

Renault Dauphine, 1964-67

Year and Model Identification

Renault 10, 1964-71

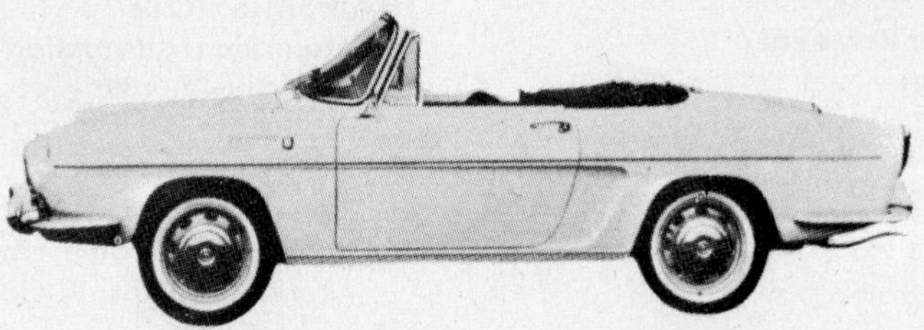

Renault Caravelle, 1964-67

Renault 8, 1964-67

Renault 16, 1969-71

Renault 12, 1971

Vehicle and Engine Serial Number Identification

SERIAL NUMBER LOCATION

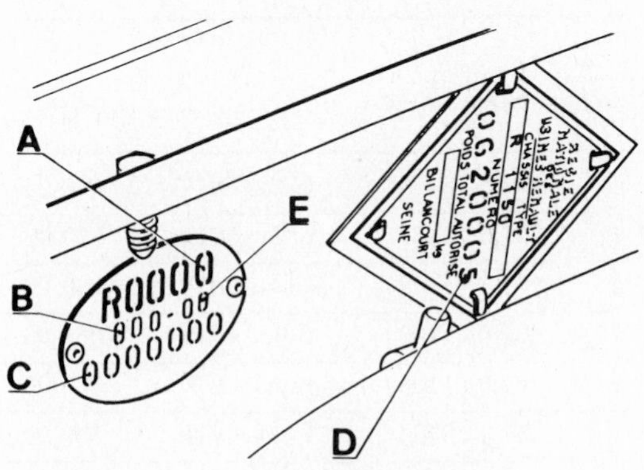

Serial number identification plate

Vehicle identification number: on diamond-shaped and oval plates in front compartment.

Engine number identification: stamped on rectangular plate on side of engine block.

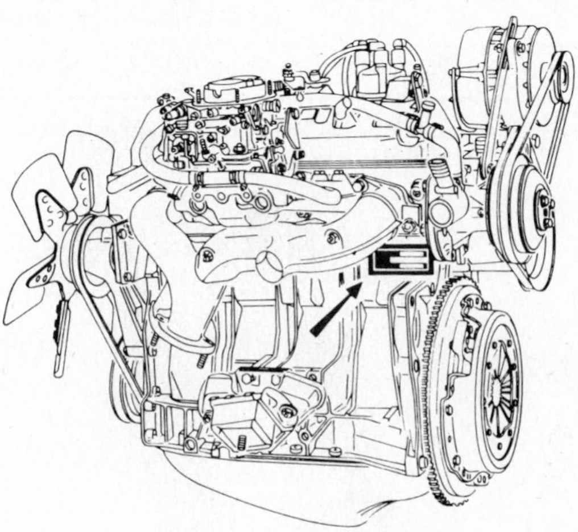

Engine identification plate

Vehicle Identification

Year	*Model*	*Starting Serial Number*
1964	Dauphine	R10940600001, R10950050001
	Renault 8	R11302906685, R11323450001
	Caravelle	R11330190001, R1131 (Coupe)
1965	Dauphine	R10940603835, R10950053201
	Renault 8	R11302908000, R11323450001
	Caravelle	R11310090927, R11330190001
1966	Dauphine	R10940603835, R10950053201
	Renault 8	R11302909000, R1132345001
	Caravelle	R11330190001
	Gordini	R1134
1967	Dauphine	R10950055009, R1094
	Renault 8	R1130, R1132
	Renault 10	R119006488785, R119206488785
	Caravelle	R1133191638
1968	Renault 10	R1190
1969	Renault 10	R1190
	Renault 16	R1152
1970	Renault 10 (A.T.)	R1190
	Renault 10 (M.T.)	R1192
	Renault 16 (M.T.)	R1152
	Renault 16 (A.T.)	R1153

Vehicle Identification

Year	Model	Starting Serial Number
1971	Renault 10 (A.T.)	R1190
	Renault 10 (M.T.)	R1192
	Renault 12 (Sedan)	R1172
	Renault 12 (Station Wagon)	R1331
	Renault 16 (M.T.)	R1152
	Renault 16 (A.T.)	R1153
1972	Renault 12 (Sedan)	R1172
	Renault 12 (Station Wagon)	R1331
	Renault 12 (Sedan)	R1178 (California)
	Renault 12 (Station Wagon)	R1332 (California)
	Renault 16 (M.T.)	R1152
	Renault 16 (A.T.)	R1153
	Renault 16 (A.T.)	R1155 (California)

NOTE: *Some Renault serial numbers run sequentially only within model years. Therefore, in these series vehicle serial numbers are not an indication of model year.*

TRANSMISSION IDENTIFICATION

The manual transmission may be identified by a plate attached to the left front top of the transmission case. The top number indicates the transmission type, the bottom is the fabrication number.

On automatic transmissions, this plate is affixed at the top of the converter housing.

INTERPRETING VEHICLE IDENTIFICATION PLATES

The diamond shaped plate (D) carries the vehicle chassis number. The oval plate contains the following information and is read as follows:

Position A: Vehicle type
B: Vehicle equipment (All U.S. models are Renault normal road types).
C. Fabrication number
E. Version number.

Engine Identification

Number of cylinders	Cu. In. Displacement (cc's.)	Type	Code (1)
4	51.5 (845)	Inline OHV	670-05
4	51.5 (845)	Inline OHV	670-06
4	67.6 (1108)	Inline OHV	688-02
4	67.6 (1108)	Inline OHV	688-03
4	67.6 (1108)	Inline OHV	688-06
4	58.4 (956)	Inline OHV	689-01
4	58.4 (956)	Inline OHV	689-02
4	58.4 (956)	Inline OHV	689-03
4	78.7 (1289)	Inline OHV	810-04
4	95.5 (1565)	Inline OHV	821-02
4	95.5 (1565)	Inline OHV	821-04
4	95.5 (1565)	Inline OHV	821-10
4	95.5 (1565)	Inline OHV	821-11
4	100.5 (1647)	Inline OHV	841-04
4	100.5 (1647)	Inline OHV	841-11

① This number is located on a plate attached to side of cylinder block.

General Engine Specifications

Year	Type	Cu. In. Displacement (cc's.)	Carburetor (Solex unless noted)	Developed Horsepower SAE @ rpm	Developed Torque (ft. lbs.) @ rpm	Bore and Stroke (in.)	Compression Ratio (To 1)	Normal Oil Pressure (p.s.i.)
1964-67	670-05	51.5 (845)	32 PIBT	40@5,000	50@3,300	2.284x 3.150	8.0	20-35
1964-67	670-06	51.5 (845)	Zenith 28 IFT	32@4,500	50@2,000	2.284x 3.150	8.0	20-35
1964-68	688-02	67.6 (1108)	32 DISTA	46@4,600	60@3,000	2.756x 2.835	8.5	10-50
1969	688-02	67.6 (1108)	26/32 DIDSA-4	46@4,600	57@3,000	2.756x 2.835	8.5	10-50
1964-65 1966-67	688-03	67.6 (1108)	32 DITA-3 Weber 32 DIR	55@4,600 58@5,400	60@3,000	2.756x 2.835	8.5	10-50
1968	688-06	67.6 (1108)	26/32 DIDTA-5	48@4,600	60@3,000	2.756x 2.835	8.5	10-50
1969	688-06	67.6 (1108)	26/32 DIDTA-5	48@4,600	57@3,000	2.756x 2.835	8.5	10-50
1970	688-06	67.6 (1108)	26/32 SDIDA-2	48@4,600	57@3,000	2.756x 2.835	8.5	10-50
1971	688-06	67.6 (1108)	26/32 DIDSA-8	48@4,600	57@3,000	2.756x 2.835	8.5	10-50
1964-67	689-01 689-02 689-03	58.4 (956)	32 PDIST (to Sept 66) Weber 32 DIR (Oct 66)	48@5,000	55@2,500	2.559x 2.835	8.5	10-50
1970	810-04	78.7 (1289)	26/32 SDIDA-2 26/32 DIDTA-5 26/32 DIDSA-10	56@4,600	70@2,300	2.874x 3.031	8.0	10-50
1971	810-04	78.7 (1289)	26/32 DIDSA-10	56@4,600	70@2,300	2.874x 3.031	8.0	10-50
1969	821-02	95.5 (1565)	26/32 DIDSA-3	70@5,200	85@2,500	3.032x 3.307	8.5	30-80
1970	821-02	95.5 (1565)	26/32 DIDSA-8	70@5,200	85@2,500	3.032x 3.307	8.5	30-80
1971	821-04	95.5 (1565)	26/32 DIDSA-8	70@5,200	86@2,500	3.032x 3.307	8.5	30-80
1971	821-10	95.5 (1565)	32/32 SEIEMA	73@5,000	88@3,000	3.032x 3.307	8.5	30-80
1972	821-10	95.5 (1565)	26/32 DIDSA-8	70@5,200	N.A.	3.032x 3.307	8.6	30-80
1972	821-11	95.5 (1565)	26/32 DIDSA-8	73@5,000	N.A.	3.032x 3.307	8.6	30-80
1972	841-04	100.5 (1647)	32/32 SEIEMA	73@5,000	N.A.	3.107x 3.307	7.5	30-80
1972	841-11	100.5 (1647)	32/32 SEIEMA	73@5,000	N.A.	3.107x 3.307	7.5	30-80

Distributor Specifications

Distributor Identification	*Centrifugal Advance*[2]				*Vacuum Advance*[2]		
1	*Start Degrees @ rpm*	*Intermediate Degrees @ rpm*	*Intermediate Degrees @ rpm*	*End Degrees @ rpm*	*Start Degrees @ in./Hg*	*Inter-mediate Degrees @ in./Hg*	*End Deg's. @ in./Hg*
S.E.V. XCXD	.5@750	5@1200	8.5@1500	10.5@1950	1@6.3	5.5@10	13@16
Ducellier WWRO	.5@600	2.5@1000	7@2000	9@2500	.5@6.1	5.5@10	11@14.4
SEV A65 C33	1@750	13.5@1275	15.5@1750	17.5@2250	1@4.8	7@9	10@12.8
SEV A96 C33	.5@700	5.5@1000	15@2000	16.5@2300	.3@3.6	6.7@8.7	10@12.8
Ducellier R259 C33	1@800	13@1400	16@2000	19@2500	1@4.5	7@8	10@12.8
Ducellier, SEV R242 C34	1@600	8.7@1000	16.9@2000	21@2500	1@4	3.4@8	5.5@13.5
Ducellier R241 D60	1@600	6@1000	10@1500	16@2250	1@3.2	6.6@8	9.3@14
Ducellier R246 D59	1@650	10@1000	13.6@1500	19@2350	1.5@4	4.6@8	7@14
Ducellier, SEV A67 C34	1@525	10@1000	12@1500	14@2250	1@4	3.4@8	5.5@13.5
Ducellier, SEV A94 C34	1@525	10@1000	12@1500	19@2500	1@4	3.4@8	5.5@13.5
Ducellier, SEV R236 C34	1@400	11@1000	14@2000	16@2750	1@4	3.4@8	5.5@13.5
Ducellier R258 D60	1@650	5@950	8@1500	13@2450	1@3.2	6.6@8	9.3@14

① Distributor identification codes are stamped on a metal tag on the distributor housing. They identify the advance characteristics and not the actual part number of the distributor. Renault distributors of different manufacture are built with a given advance curve for a given powertrain combination; hence, the letter code identifies the proper distributor regardless of maker. To meet emission control standards, many new advance curves have been added; however, they are not available at press time.

② Distributor degrees at distributor rpm.

Tune-Up Specifications

Year	Model	Spark plugs Make Type	Spark plugs Gap (in.)	Distributor Point dwell (deg.)	Distributor Point Gap (in.)	Basic Ignition Timing (deg.)	Cranking Comp. Pressure (p.s.i.)	Valves Clearance (in.) Intake	Valves Clearance (in.) Exhaust	Idle Speed (rpm)
1964-65	Dauphine	AC 44F	.025	57	.016-.020	TDC	①	.007	.010	650
1964-66	Renault 8	AC 43FS	.025	57	.016-.020	TDC	①	.006	.008	650
1964-66	Caravelle	AC 44F	.025	57	.016-.020	TDC	①	.006	.008	650
1966	Dauphine	AC 44F	.025	57	.016-.020	TDC	①	.006	.008	650
1967	Dauphine	AC 44F	.025	57	.016-.020	TDC	①	.007	.010	700
1967	Renault 8	AC 43FS	.028	57	.016-.020	TDC	①	.007	.010	700
1967	Renault 10	AC 43FS	.028	57	.016-.020	TDC	①	.007	.010	700
1967	Caravelle	AC 44F	.028	57	.016-.020	TDC	①	.007	.010	700
1968-69	Renault 10	Champ. L87Y	.028	57	.016-.020	TDC	①	.006	.008	700
1969	Renault 16	AC 44XL	.024	57	.016-.020	TDC	①	.008	.016	700
1970-71	Renault 10	Champ. L87Y	.028	57	.016-.020	TDC②	①	.008	.010	700
1970-72	Renault 16	AC 44XL	.024	57	.016-.020	TDC	①	.008	.010	700
1971-72	Renault 12	AC 44XL	.024	57	.016-.020	TDC	①	.008	.010	700

① All cylinders within 10% of highest.
NOTE: Since 1968 car manufacturers supply tune-up data on a sticker in the engine compartment. Should conflict exist between above data and sticker data, sticker data should be regarded as correct.
② 1971 timing is 3° ATDC.

Engine Rebuilding Specifications

Year	Model	Crankshaft							
		Main Bearing Journals (in.)					Connecting Rod Bearing Journals (in.)		
		Journal diameter		Oil Clear-ance	Shaft End-Play	Thrust On No.	Journal diameter		Oil Clearance
		New	Minimum				New	Minimum	
1964-67	Dauphine	1.575	1.535	①	.002-.010	2	1.496	1.476	①
1964-67	Renault 8	1.811	1.7914	①	.002-.008	3	1.731	1.7114	①
1964-67	Caravelle	1.811	1.7914	①	.002-.008	3	1.731	1.7114	①
1967-71	Renault 10	1.811	1.8014	①	.002-.008	3	1.731	1.7114	①
1969-71	Renault 16	2.158	2.148	①	.002-.009	3	1.890	1.880	①
1971	Renault 12	2.158	2.148	①	.002-.009	3	1.890	1.880	①

① Renault does not publish bearing oil clearances.

Firing Order

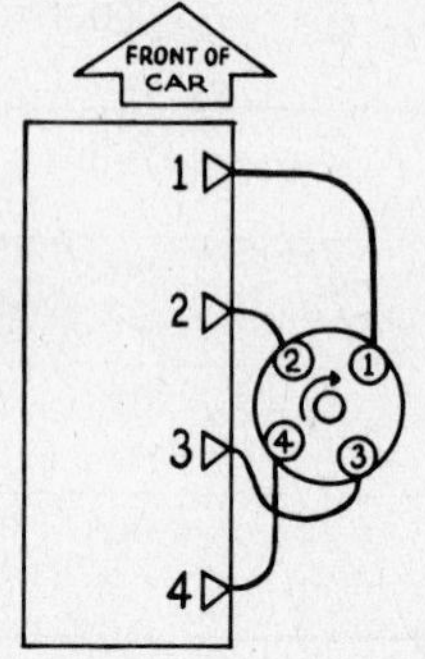

Ignition wiring and firing order, all Renaults.

Engine Rebuilding Specifications

Engine	Cylinder Block		Pistons			
	Bore (in.)		Piston diameter		Rings	
cu. in. (cc's)	New 1	Maxi-mum Over-size	New (in.)	Maxi-mum Over-size (in.)	End Gap	Side Clear-ance
51.5 (845)	2.284	②	①	②	③	③
58.4 (956)	2.559	②	①	②	③	③
67.6 (1108)	2.756	②	①	②	③	③
78.7 (1289)	2.874	②	①	②	③	③
95.5 (1565)	3.032	②	①	②	③	③
100.5 (1647)	3.107	②	①	②	③	③

① All dimensions are nominal. Renault engines are wet-sleeve type, with liners and piston assemblies (including rings and pins) clearanced at the factory.

② No reboring of original cylinders is permitted, nor are oversize pistons available. Replace worn parts with new, standard size piston and liner assemblies.

③ All piston rings are properly gapped and clearanced at time of manufacture. No adjustment is needed.

Engine Rebuilding Specifications
Valves

Engine Cu. in. (cc's)	Seat Width (in.)③		Valve Lift (in.)		Valve Spring Pressure (lbs.) Int./Exh.	Stem Diameter (in.)	Stem to Guide Clearance		Valve Guide Re-movable?
	Int.	Exh.	Int.	Exh.			Int.	Exh.	
51.5 (845)	.059	.071	N.A.	N.A.	45@15/16 in.①	.276	N.A.	N.A.	Yes
58.4 (956)	.055	.067	N.A.	N.A.	30@1 1/4 in.①	.276	N.A.	N.A.	Yes
67.6 (1108)	.050	.065	N.A.	N.A.	30@1 9/32 in.①	.276	N.A.	N.A.	Yes
78.7 (1289)	.050	.065	N.A.	N.A.	80@63/64 in.①	.276	N.A.	N.A.	Yes
95.5 (1565)	.060	.070	.319	.295	99@1 9/64 in.②	.315	.002	.0025	Yes
100.5 (1647)	.060	.070	.319	.295	99@1 9/64 in.②	.315	.002	.0025	Yes

① Test pressure at test length
② Outer spring test pressure only. Inner springs 20 lbs. @3/4 in.
③ All engines valve at angle is 45°.

Torque Specifications

Engine Cu. in. (cc's)	Cylinder Head bolts (ft. lbs.)	Main Bearing bolts (ft. lbs.)	Rod Bearing bolts (ft. lbs.)	Flywheel to Crankshaft bolts (ft. lbs.)	Manifold (ft. lbs.)	
					Intake	Exhaust
51.5 (845)	45	45	25	N.A.	N.A.	N.A.
58.4 (956)	45	45	25	35	N.A.	N.A.
67.6 (1108)	45	45	25	35	N.A.	N.A.
78.7 (1289)	45	45	35	35	N.A.	N.A.
95.5 (1565)	55	45	30	40	10-20	10-20
100.5 (1647)	55	45	30	40	10-20	10-20

Starter Specifications

Year	Model	Lock test Amp.	Volts	Torque (ft. lbs.)	Brush Spring Length (in.)
1964-67	Dauphine	320	12	6	5/16 (minimum)
1964-67	Renault 8	320	12	6	19/32-19/64 (new)
1964-67	Caravelle	320	12	6	19/32-19/64 (new)
1967	Renault 10	320	12	6	19/32-19/64 (new)
1968	Renault 10	330	12	6.5	19/32-19/64 (new)
1969-71	Renault 10	330	12	7	19/32-19/64 (new)
1971	Renault 12	375	12	9	N.A.
1969-71	Renault 16	400	12	13	7/16 (Minimum)

Tightening Sequences

NOTE: When installing main bearing caps, tighten thrust bearing cap first.

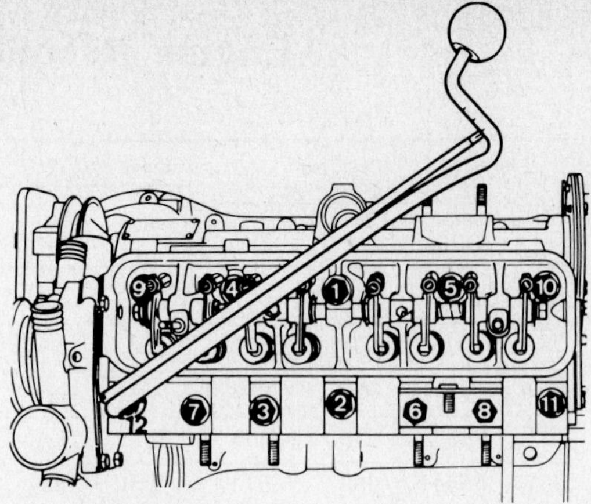

Dauphine cylinder head bolt tightening sequence

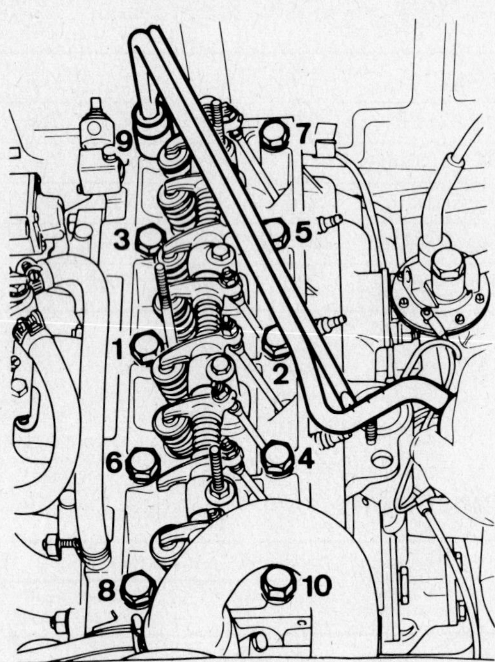

Renault 8, 10, and Caravelle cylinder head bolt tightening sequence

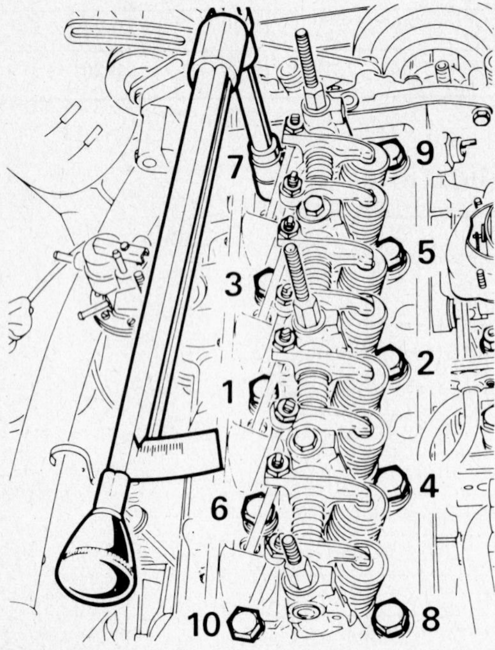

Renault 12 and 16 head bolt tightening sequence

Battery Specifications

Year	Model	Battery		
		Capacity (Amp. hours)	Volts	Grounded Terminal
1964-66	Dauphine	40/50	12	Negative
1967	Dauphine	40	12	Negative
1964-67	Renault 8	45	12	Negative
1964-67	Caravelle	40	12	Negative
1967	Renault 10	40	12	Negative
1968-71	Renault 10	45	12	Negative
1971	Renault 12	45	12	Negative
1969-71	Renault 16	45	12	Negative

Alternator Specifications

Year-Model	Part Number	Field Coil Resistance (Ohms)	Output@ Engine rpm (Amps)
1969-71 Renault 12 Renault 16	Sev A14/30	5.2	30@3000

Generator/Regulator Specifications

Year-Model	Generator: Part Number	Brush Length (in.) New	Output (watts)	Regulator: Cut-out Relay Volts to Close	No-load voltage@ rpm
Dauphine 1964-67	Bosch LJ/GG/240/12/2400/AR14	1.00②	240	12.5-13.2	13.9-14.9 @N.A.
Renault 8 1964-67	Bosch LJ/GG/240/12/2400/AR21	29/32	240	9.6	14.6-15.2 @3000
Caravelle③	Paris-Rhone G10-C14	19/32③	290	10	N.A.
1964-67	Ducellier 7267G	.866①	290	9.6	14.4-15.2 @3000
Renault 10 1967	Ducellier 7267G	.866①	290	9.6	14.4-15.2 @3000
Renault 10 1968	Bosch LJ/GG/240/12/2400/AR21	29/32	240	9.6	14.6-15.2 @4500
Renault 10 1969	Ducellier 7348	.866①	290	9.6	14.4-15.4 @4500
Renault 10 1970-71	Bosch LJ/GG/240/12/2400/AR21	1.00	240	9.6	14.4-15.4 @4500

① .433 in. minimum length
② .55 in. minimum length; 16-21 oz. tension
③ 5/16″ minimum length

Capacities and Pressures

Year-Model	Engine Crankcase capacity (qts.) With Filter	Transaxle Capacities (pts.) Manual 3-Speed	Manual 4-Speed	Auto.	Fuel Tank (gals.)	Cooling System with Heater (qts.)
1964-67 Dauphine	2.75	3.5	3.5	3.5	8	5.25
1964-67 Renault 8	2.75	3.5	4	3.5	10	8
1964-67 Caravelle	2.75	—	4	3.5	10	8
1967-69 Renault 10	2.75	—	4	3.5	10	7.5
1970 Renault 10 Automatic trans.	2.75	—	—	4	10	7.5
1970 Renault 10 Manual trans.	3.12	—	4	—	10	7.5
1971 Renault 10	3.5	—	4	4	10	7.5
1969-72 Renault 16	4.5	—	3.5	13	13.2	7
1971-72 Renault 12	4.5	—	4	13	13.2	9.5

Carburetor Specifications

Type (Solex except where noted)	*Venturi Size (mm)*	*Main Jet (mm)*	*Air Correct. Jet (mm)*	*Needle Valve (mm)*	*Float Weight (grams)*	*Power Jet (mm)*	*Accel. Pump Jet (mm)*	*Idle Jet (mm)*
32 PIBT	22	110	195	1.5	5.7	110	40	45
28 IFT Zenith	20.5	98	70	1.5	N.A.	90	—	40
32 DISTA	23	120	140	1.5	5.7	120	40	45
32 DISTA①	23	117	130	1.5	5.7	120	40	45
32 DITA-3②	23	122.5	130	1.5	5.7	85	—	45
26/32 DIDTA-5								
Primary	20.5	115	115	1.5	7.3	—	—	60
Secondary	22	125	160	N.A.	N.A.	N.A.	N.A.	—
26/32 DIDSA-4								
Primary	20.5	117.5	70	1.5	5.7	—	—	60
Secondary	22	117.5	150	N.A.	N.A.	N.A.	N.A.	42.5
26/32 DIDSA-3								
Primary	23.5	125	115	1.5	7.3	—	—	60
Secondary	26	140	140	N.A.	N.A.	N.A.	N.A.	50
26/32 DIDSA-8								
Primary	23.5	120	110	1.7	7.3	—	35	65
Secondary	26	165	85	N.A.	N.A.	N.A.	N.A.	80
26/32 DIDSA-10								
Primary	23.5	120	120	1.7	7.3	—	40	65
Secondary	26	155	100	N.A.	N.A.	N.A.	N.A.	95
26/32 SDIDA-2								
Primary	22	120	100	1.7	7.3	—	—	65
Secondary	26	117.5	110	N.A.	N.A.	N.A.	N.A.	75
32/32 SEIEMA (MK .522)								
Primary	23	117	140	1.7	N.A.	—	45	50
Secondary	24	155	130	N.A.	N.A.	N.A.	N.A.	80
32/32 SEIEMA (MK.506)								
Primary	23	115	140	1.7	N.A.	—	45	52.5
Secondary	24	167.5	130	N.A.	N.A.	N.A.	N.A.	80
32 PDIST②	26	125	100	1.5	5.7	85	40	45
32 DIR Weber								
Primary	23	125	160	1.75	11	—	—	50
Secondary	24	125	150	N.A.		N.A.	N.A.	60
26/32 DIDTA-5								
Primary	—	115	115	1.5	7.3	—	—	60
Secondary	—	125	160	N.A.	N.A.	—	—	42.5

① From Chassis #321-574 onward.

② Some 32 DITA carburetors may utilize different main and air correction jets to compensate for altitude.

Brake Specifications

Year/Model	Type Front	Type Rear	Brake Master Cylinder (in.)	Piston Cylinder Bore (in.) Front	Piston Cylinder Bore (in.) Rear	Brake Drum or Disc Diameter (in.) Front	Brake Drum or Disc Diameter (in.) Rear
1964-67 Dauphine	Disc	Disc	.867	1.496	1.259	10.25	10.25
1964-67 Renault 8	Disc	Disc	.867	1.496	1.259	10.25	10.25
1964-67 Caravelle	Disc	Disc	.867	1.496	1.259	10.25	10.25
1967-71 Renault 10	Disc	Disc	.758	1.516	1.259	10.25	10.25
1969-72 Renault 16	Disc	Drum	.749	1.889	.866①	10.00	9.00
1971-72 Renault 12	Disc	Drum	.748	1.889	.867①	9.00	7.08②

① Wheel cylinder bore
② 9.00 in. on station wagon

Chassis and Wheel Alignment Specifications

Year/Model	Chassis: Wheel-base	Chassis: Track (in.) Front	Chassis: Track (in.) Rear	Wheel Alignment: Caster Range	Caster Pref.	Camber Range	Camber Pref.	Toe-in (in.)	King pin Inclination (deg.)
1964-67 Dauphine	89.37	49.19	48.12	—	9°②	—	1°40′②	1/8-3/16	11.5
1964-67 Renault 8	89.37	49.22	48.03	7°-11°	9°	—	1°40′①	5/64	9.5
1964-67 Caravelle	89.37	49.5	48.25	7°-11°	9°	—	1°40′①	5/64	9.5
1967-71 Renault 10	89.37	49.25	48.25	7°-11°	9°	—	1°40′①	5/64	9.5
1969-72 Renault 16	104.31	52.87	50.87	2°-3°30′	3°	15′-1°	0°15′	1/16	14
1971-72 Renault 12	96	51.62	51.62	N.A.	4°	1°-2°①	1°30′	0-1/8	13-15

① Camber is not adjustable.
② Caster and camber are not adjustable.

Fuses

Model	Circuit	Amperage
Dauphine	A.T. Decelerator	5
	A.T. Electromagnet	5
	A.T. Motor	10
	A.T. Main circuit	25
	Ignition Switch	25
	Instrument panel	25
Renault 8	Ignition switch	25
	Main circuit	25
	A.T. Main circuit	25
Caravelle	Ignition switch	25
	Main circuit	25

NOTE: *A.T.=automatic transmission*

Model	Circuit	Amperage
Renault 10	Main circuit	25
	Flasher unit	25
	Anti-pollution system	25
Renault 16	Ignition switch	25
	Main circuit	25
Renault 12	Interior, parking, trunk, lights	8
	Lighter and windshield wipers	8
	Stoplights, instruments, heater, rear window defroster	8
	Flashers and A.T. circuit	5

Wiring Diagrams

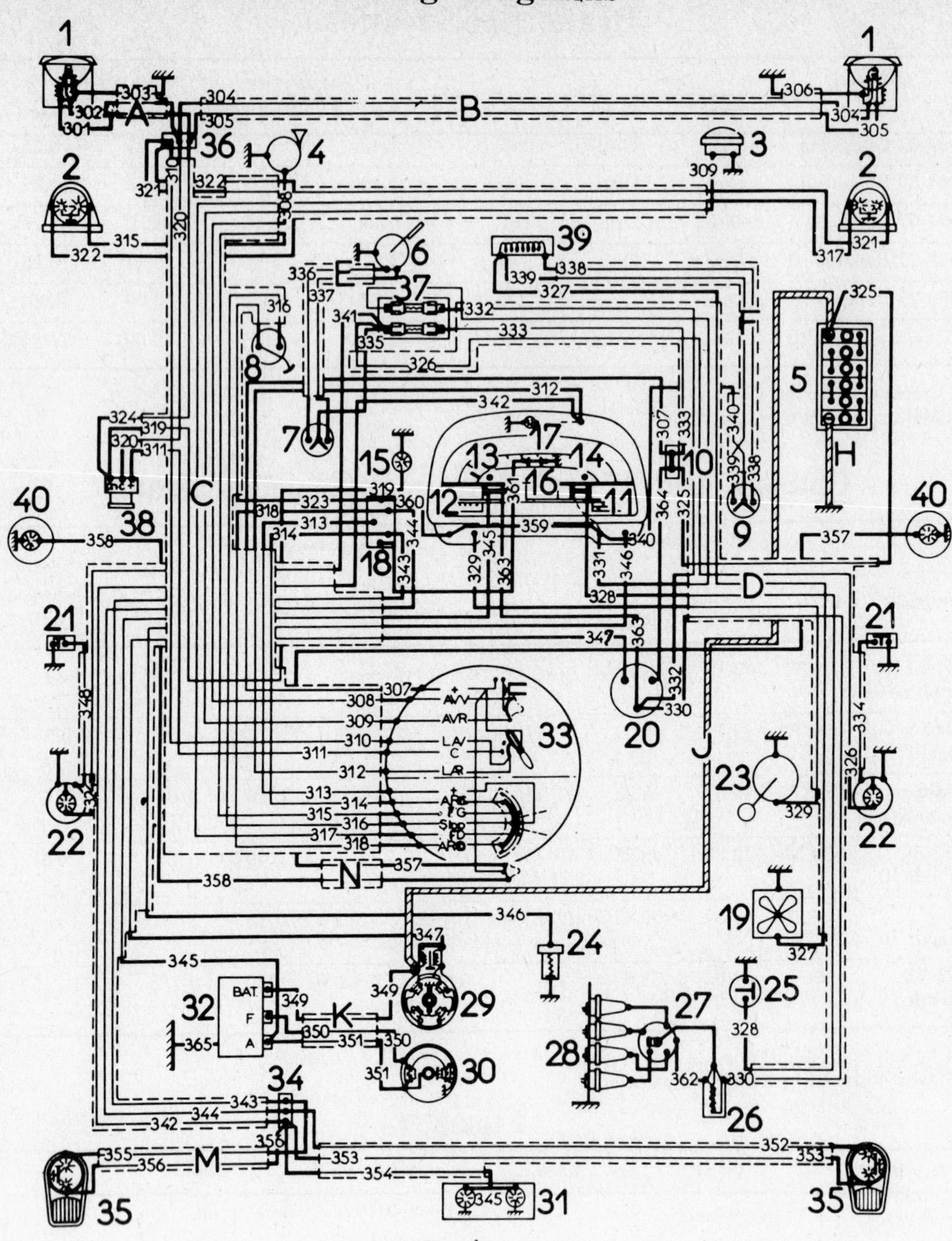

Dauphine

1 Right and left-hand headlights
2 Side and direction indicator lights
3 Road horn
4 Town horn
5 Battery
6 Windshield wipers
7 Windshield wiper switch
8 Stop switch
9 Heater switch
10 Connection plate behind instrument panel (2 terminals)
11 Water temperature indicator
12 Fuel gauge
13 Charge-discharge gauge
14 Oil pressure warning light
15 Headlight Hi Beam indicator
16 Turn signal
17 Instrument panel light
18 Flasher unit
19 Heater
20 Ignition switch
21 Right and left-hand door switches
22 Right and left-hand interior lights
23 Fuel gauge
24 Temperature switch
25 Oil pressure switch
26 Ignition coil
27 Distributor
28 Spark plugs
29 Starter
30 Generator
31 License plate lights
32 Voltage regulator (3 unit)
33 Horn lighting and direction indicator switch
34 Rear connection plate (3 terminals)
35 Rear right and left-hand tail, stop and direction indicator lights
36 Front connection plate (3 terminals)
37 Fuse box
38 Foot operated dipswitch
39 Heater resistor
40 Right and left-hand parking lights

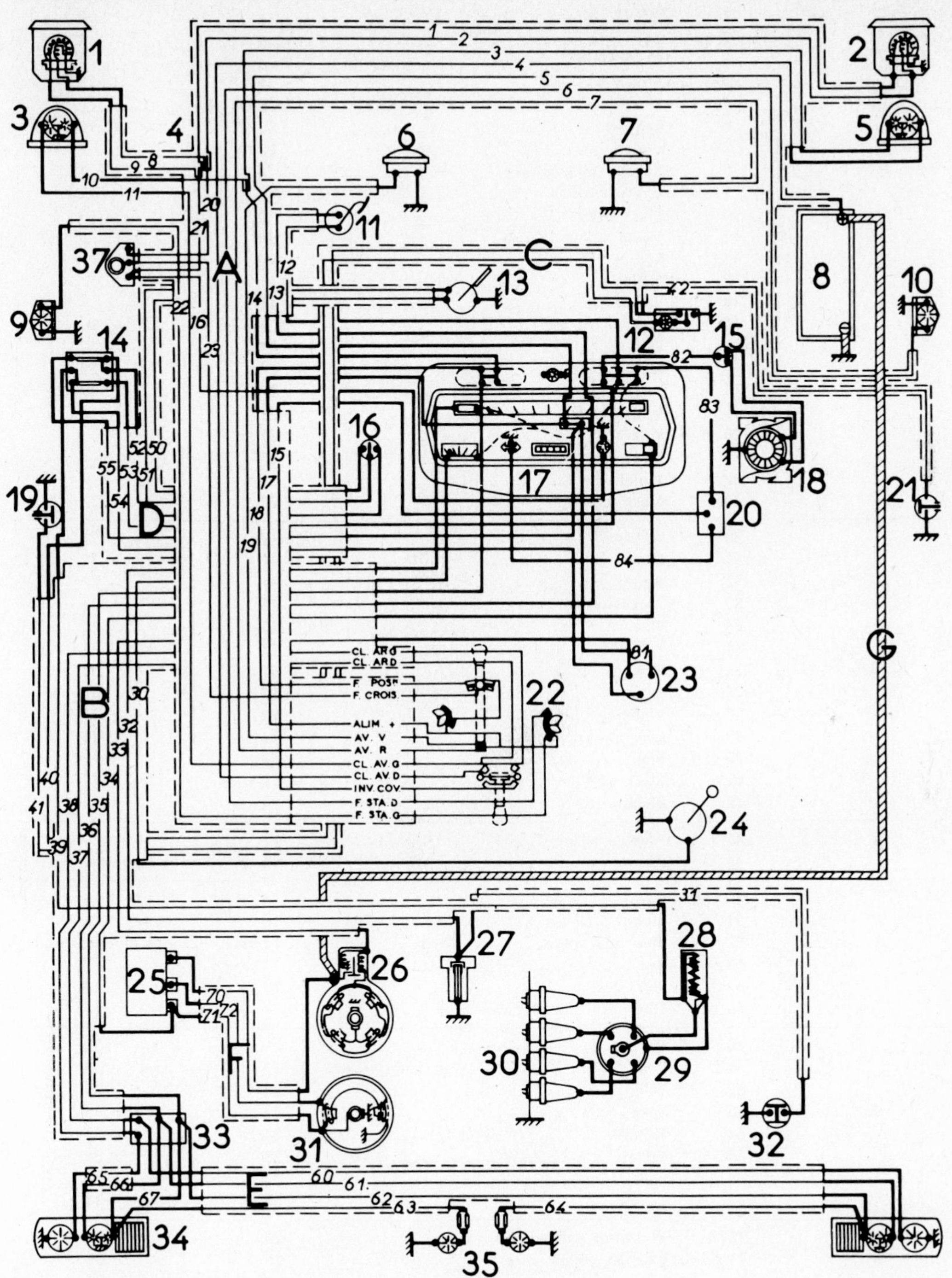
A
B
C
D
E
G
CL. ARG
CL. ARD
F. POSR
F. CROIS.
ALIM. +
AV. V
AV. R
CL. AV. G
CL. AV. D
INV. COV.
F. STA. D
F. STA. G

Renault 8

Reference		Sleeve and wire color	Wire connected	
Harness	Wire		From	To
	1	Green wire	4	2
	2	Salmon pink wire	4	2
	3	Black wire	4	2
	4	Brown	22	5
	5	Blue	8	17
	6	Red wire	22	10
	7	Violet	22	7
	8	Salmon pink wire	4	1
	9	Green wire	4	1
	10	Black wire	4	3
A	11	Violet	22	3
	12	Red	17	11
	13	Pink	11	17
	14	Yellow	17	4
	15	Blue	22	20
	16	Blue	17	37
	17	Blue	17	22
	18	Yellow	22	17
	19	White	22	6
	20	Pink	37	4
	21	Blue wire	37	4
	22	Violet	22	9
	23	Black	22	37
	30	Yellow	17	24
	31	Black	17	32
	32	Brown	17	27
	33	Aluminium	23	26
	34	Blue	17	25
	35	Yellow	17	33
B	36	Pink	17	33
	37	Brown	22	33
	38	Violet	22	33
	39	Red	14	28
	40	Blue	14	12
	41	Black wire	19	12
	42	Black wire	21	12
C	45	Aluminium wire	12	connecting
	46	Aluminium wire	12	to harness B
	50	Green	16	13
	51	Blue	16	13
D	52	Blue and white	14 Blue	16 Blue and white
	53	Red	14	17
	54	Red	23	14
	55	Blue	17	14
	60	Brown	33	36
	61	Pink	33	36
	62	Yellow	33	36
E	63	Yellow	34	35
	64	Yellow	36	35
	65	Violet	33	34
	66	Pink	33	34
	67	Yellow	33	34
	70	White on yellow wire	25	26
F	71	Blue on yellow wire	25	31
	72	Green	25	31
G	80		8	26
	81	Blue-White	17 Blue	23 (White)
	82	Red	17	15
Single	83	Red	17	20
wires	84	Black wire	17	20

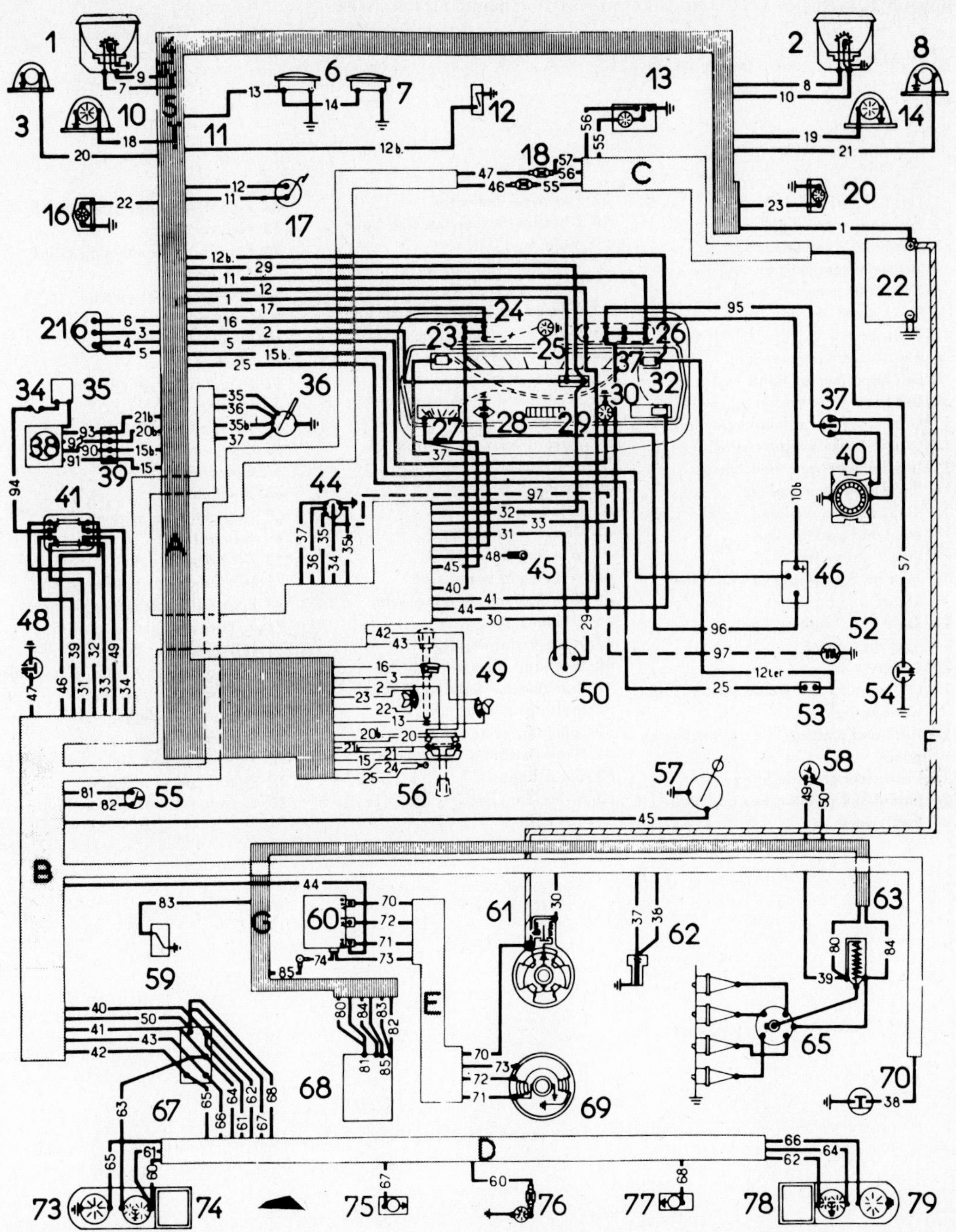

Renault 10, vehicles 347174-477141 manual transmission

Renault 10, vehicles 347174-477141 manual transmission

Renault 10, vehicles 477142 to end of importation manual transmission

Renault 10, automatic transmission

1 Left-hand headlight
2 Right-hand headlight
3 Left-hand front sidelight
4 Dipped beam junction
5 Headlight junction
6 Road horn
7 Town horn
8 Right-hand front sidelight
9 Left-hand marker lights
10 Left-hand front flasher
11 Left-hand front sidelight junction
12 Loss of brake pressure switch
13 Interior light rear view mirror
14 Right-hand front flasher
15 Right-hand illuminated marker lights
16 Left-hand parking light
17 Stop light switch
18 Interior light wiring junction box
19 Right-hand front sidelight junction
20 Right-hand parking light
21 Foot dipswitch
22 Battery
23 Oil pressure and water temperature warning light
24 Left-hand junction box on instrument panel
25 Instrument panel lighting
26 Right-hand junction box on instrument panel
27 Fuel level indicator
28 Direction flasher warning light
29 Main feed
30 Headlight high beam warning
31 Brake pressure warning light
32 Charge-discharge warning light
33 Hazard warning switch (1970)
34 Flasher unit fuse
35 Flasher unit
36 Windshield wiper motor
37 Heater switch
38 Hazard warning light switch
39 Junction box
40 Heater
41 Fuse box
42 Choke warning light
43 Warning light (1970)
44 Windshield wiper switch
45 Rear harness coupling point
46 Flasher unit
47 Hazard warning light
48 Left-hand door pillar switch
49 Combination lighting direction indicator switch
50 Ignition-starter switch
51 Choke warning light switch
52 Cigar lighter
53 Switch for checking brake pressure loss bulb
54 Right-hand door pillar switch
55 Neutral switch
56 Front harness coupling point
57 Fuel gauge
58 Reversing light switch
59 Solenoid flap valve
60 Regulator
61 Starter
62 Temperature sender switch
63 Ignition coil
64 Anti-pollution fuse box (1970)
65 Distributor
66 Governor
67 Junction box
68 Anti-pollution system relay
69 Generator
70 Oil pressure switch
71 Left-hand rear marker lights
72 Rear light assemblies junction
72bis Back-up light junction
73 Left-hand rear flasher
74 Left-hand rear light and stop light
75 Left-hand back-up light
76 License plate light
77 Right-hand back-up light
78 Right-hand rear light and stoplight
79 Right-hand rear flasher
80 Right-hand rear marker lights

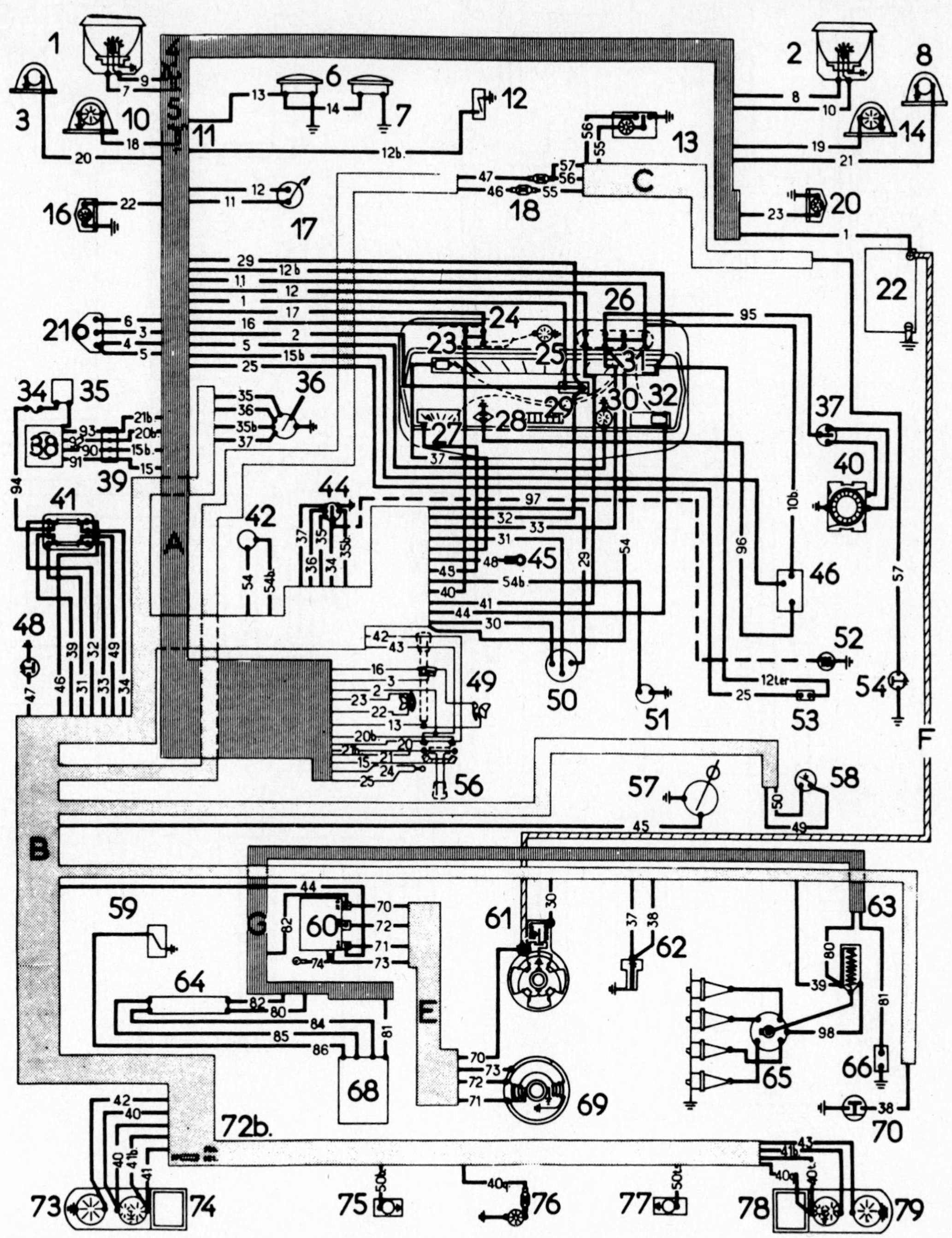

Renault 10, vehicles 477142 to end of importation, manual transmission

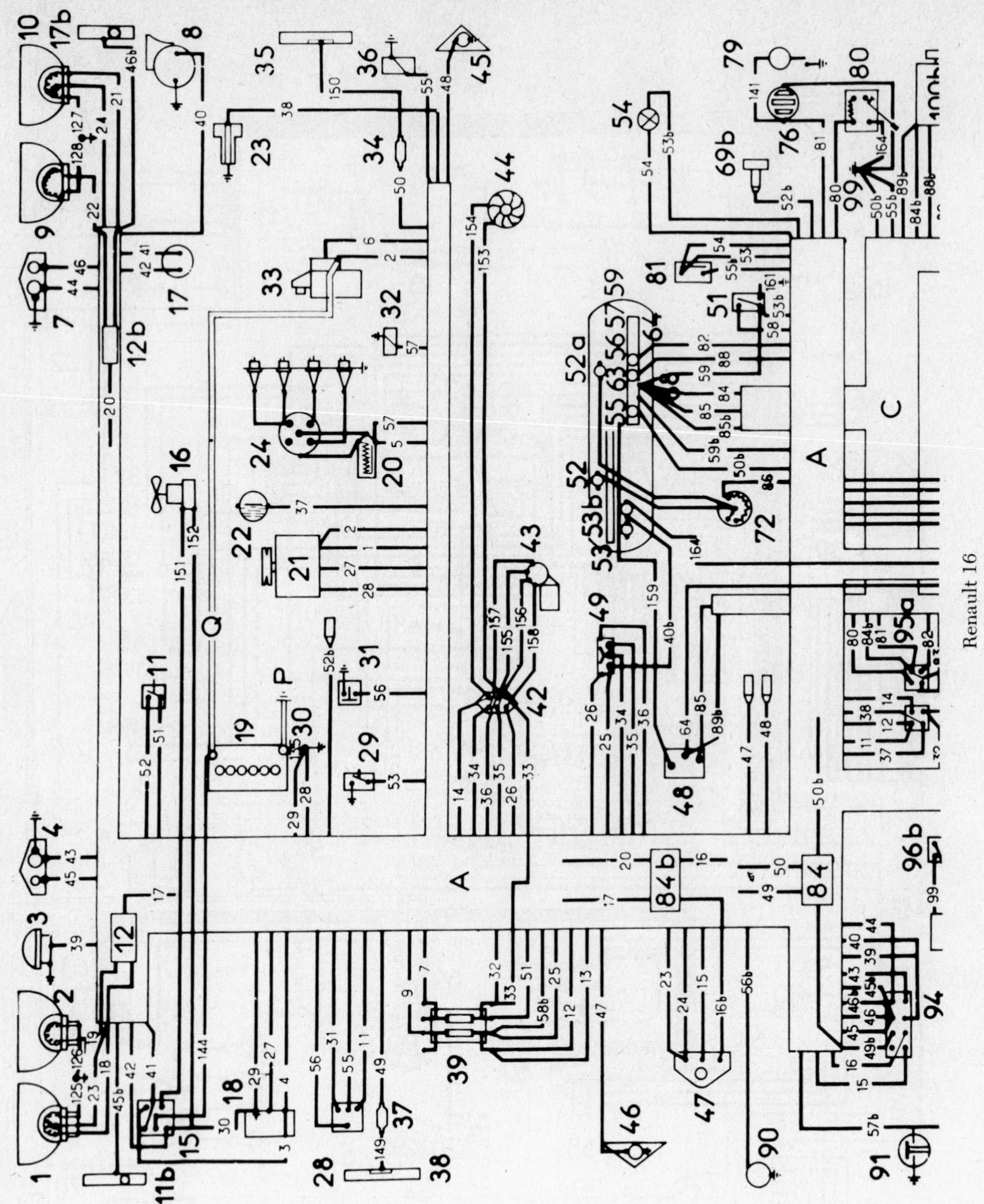

Renault 16

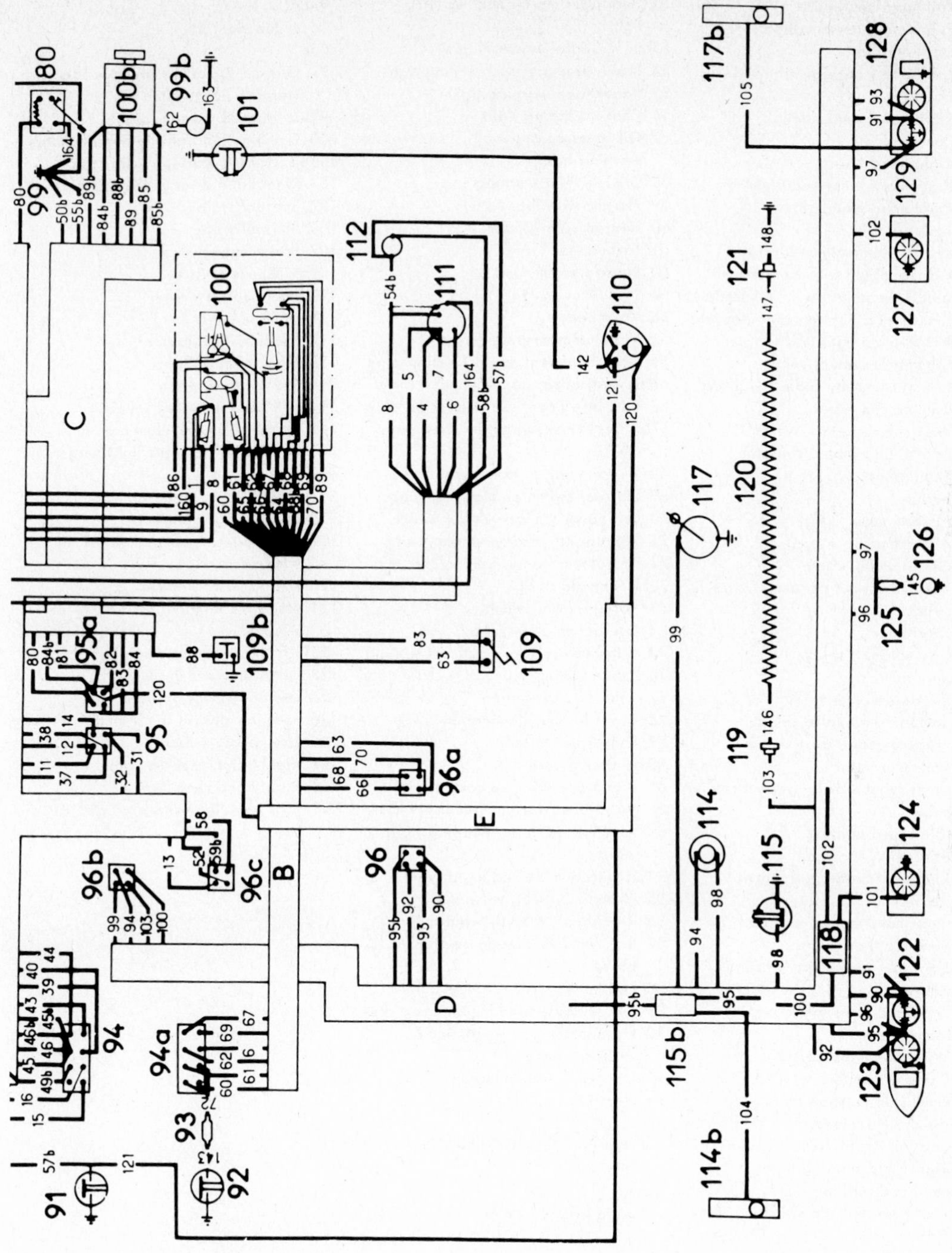
80
99
99b
100b
101
100
112
111
110
117b
128
129
127
121
117
120
126
125
119
114
115
124
118
122
123
114b
115b
95a
109b
109
95
96a
96b
96c
96
94
94a
93
91
92
B
C
D
E

Renault 16

1 Left-hand headlight
2 Left-hand inner headlight
3 Left-hand horn
4 Left-hand front sidelight and flasher
7 Right-hand front sidelight and flasher
8 Right-hand horn
9 Right-hand inner headlight
10 Right-hand headlight
11 Back-up light switch
11bis L.H. illuminated reflector
12 L.H. headlight wire connection
12bis R.H. headlight wire connection
13 L.H. driving light junction sleeve
14 R.H. driving light junction sleeve
15 Cooling fan motor relay
15bis Front junction plate (+ direct)
16 Cooling fan motor
17 Water temperature switch
17bis R.H. illuminated reflector
18 Regulator
19 Battery
20 Ignition coil
21 Alternator
22 Oil pressure switch
23 Thermal cut-out or temperature switch
24 Distributor
25 Driving lights relay
26 Sunroof relay
27 Window winder relay
28 Solenoid flap valve relay
29 Brake pressure drop switch
30 Battery ground
31 Centrifugal switch on speedometer cable
32 Idle speed damper
33 Starter
34 R.H. front brake pad junction sleeve
35 Right hand front brake pad
36 Solenoid flap valve
37 L.H. front brake pad junction sleeve
38 Left hand front brake pad
39 Main fusebox
40 Window winder fusebox
41 Sunroof fusebox
42 Cowl side junction plate
43 Windshield wiper
44 Heating-Ventilation
45 Right-hand parking light
46 Left-hand parking light
47 Foot operated dip switch
48 Flasher unit
49 Windshield wiper switch
50 Driving light switch
51 Heated rear window switch
52 (
Instrument panel lighting
52a (

53 Headlight main beam warning light
53bis Ignition key warning
54 Brake pressure loss warning light
55 Handbrake warning light
56 Choke warning light
57 Oil pressure and water temperature warning light
58 Driving light warning
59 Flasher warning
60 Heated rear window light
61 Tachometer
62 Speedometer
63 Fuel level gauge
64 Voltmeter
65 Water temperature gauge
66 L.H. instrument panel junction plug
66bis Instrument panel junction plate
67 R.H. instrument panel junction plug
67bis Instrument panel junction plate (+ direct)
68 + terminal on instrument panel
69 Sunroof switch or blanking plug
70 Left-hand window winder switch
71 Right-hand window winder switch
72 Instrument panel lighting rheostat
72bis Electric clock
73 Parking light switch
74 Sunroof thermal cut-out
75 Instrument panel & sunroof ground
76 Cigar lighter
77 Ashtray illumination
78 Cigar lighter illumination
79 Glove pocket light
80 Heater rheostat
81 Brake pressure loss control switch
82 Windshield washer pedal switch
84 Junction on brake warning light wires
84bis Junction on headlight wires
85 Ground for R.H. w. winder
86 Right-hand window winder
87 R.H. window winder junction plate
88 Left-hand window winder
89 L.H. window winder junction plate
90 Ground for L.H. w. winder & front crossmember
91 Left-hand door pillar switch
92 Handbrake switch

93 Junction sleeves for handbrake wires
94 (
Junction block
94a (
95 (
Junction block
95a (
96 (
Junction block
96a (

96b (
Junction block
96c (
99 Ground for brake pressure loss warning light switch (R. 1152)
99bis Hazard warning light
100 Combination lighting-flasher switch
100bis Hazard warning light switch
101 Right-hand door pillar switch
107 Sunroof motor
108 Sunroof track
109 Brake light switch
109bis Choke switch
110 Roof courtesy light
111 Interior light
112 Ignition illumination
113 Map reading light
114 Trunk illumination
114bis L.H. illuminated reflector
115 Switch for trunk illumination
115bis Junction for rear light wires
117 Fuel gauge
117bis R.H. illuminated reflector
118 Back-up light junction
119 Positive terminal for heated rear window
120 Heated rear window
121 Negative terminal for heated rear window
122 L.H. rear light and stoplight
123 Left-hand rear flasher
124 Left-hand back-up light
125 Junction sleeves for rear light wires
126 License plate light
127 Right-hand back-up light
128 Right-hand rear flasher
129 R.H. rear light and stoplight

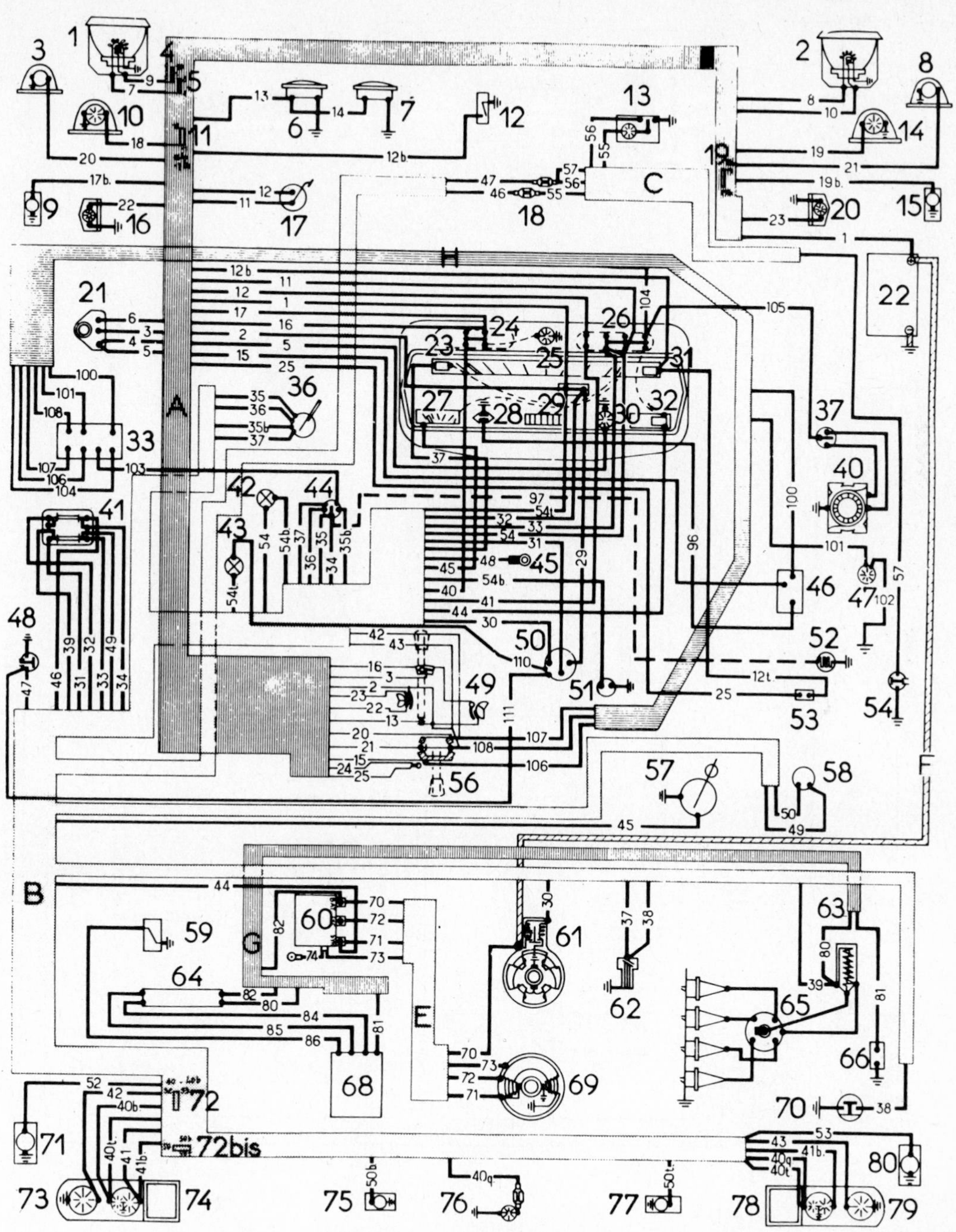

Renault 10, automatic transmission

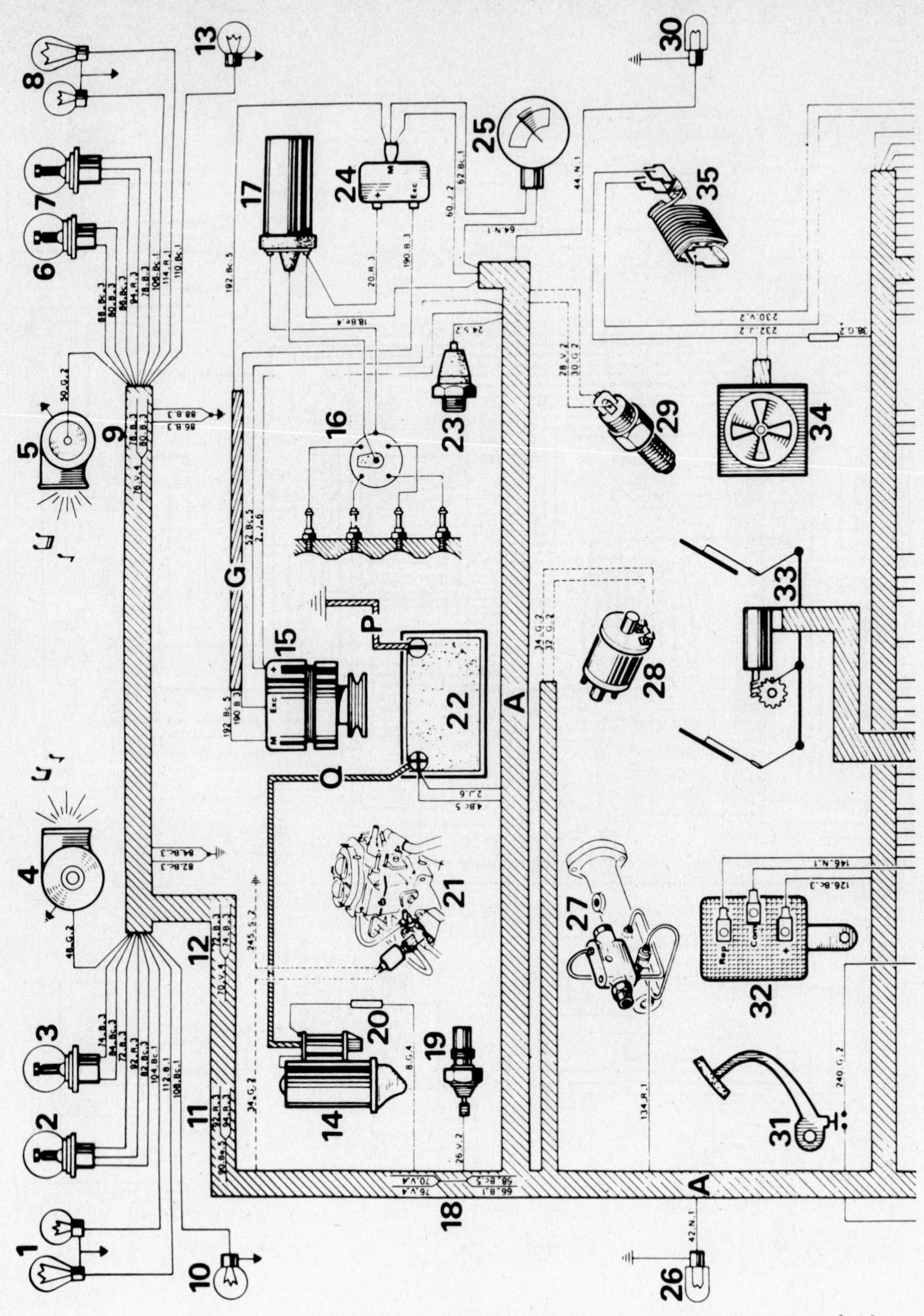

Renault 12

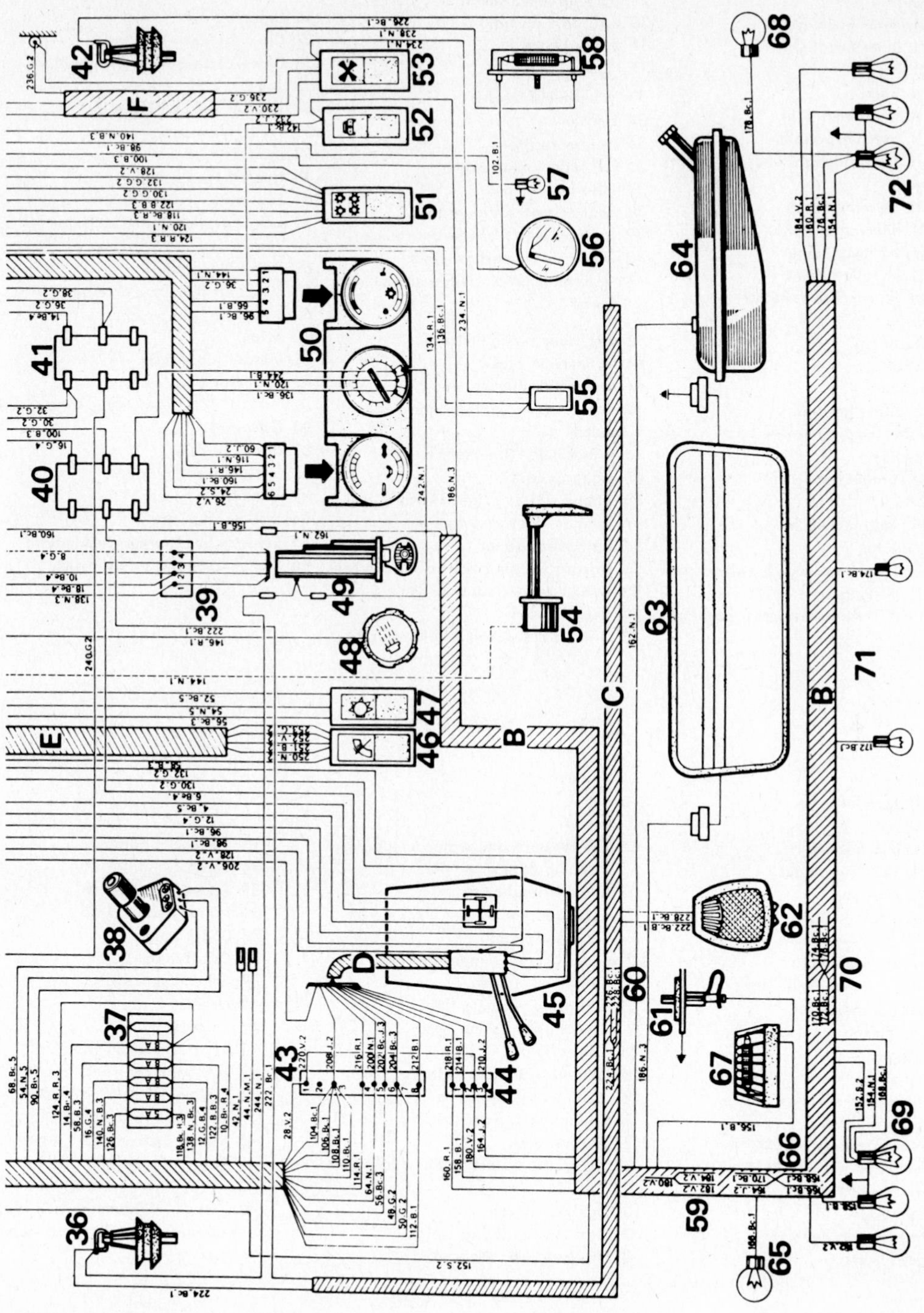
36
37
38
39
40
41
42
43
44
45
46
47
48
49
50
51
52
53
54
55
56
57
58
59
60
61
62
63
64
65
66
67
68
69
70
71
72
B
C
D
E
F

Renault 12

1 L.H. front sidelight and directional signal
2 L.H. outer headlight
3 L.H. inner headlight
4 L.H. horn
5 R.H. horn
6 R.H. inner headlight
7 R.H. outer headlight
8 R.H. front sidelight and directional signal
9 R.H. headlight joint
10 L.H. illuminated reflector
11 Dipped beam joint
12 L.H. headlight joint
13 R.H. illuminated reflector
14 Starter
15 Alternator
16 Distributor
17 Ignition coil
18 Headlight junction
19 Water temperature switch
20 Junction
21 Carburetor decelerator
22 Battery
23 Oil pressure switch
24 Regulator
25 Windshield washer electric pump
26 L.H. parking light
27 Brake line pressure drop warning light
28 Governor
29 Back-up lamp switch
30 R.H. parking light
31 Brake switch
32 Flasher unit
33 Windshield washer
34 Heater
35 Heater resistor
36 L.H. door pillar switch
37 Fuse box
38 Foot operated dipswitch
39 Ignition switch connection block
40 Direct + connection block
41 + after ignition switch connection block
42 R.H. door pillar switch
43 Connection block
44 Connection block
45 Combination lighting—turn signal switch
46 Windshield wiper switch
47 Lighting switch
48 Choke warning light switch
49 Ignition—starter switch
50 Instrument panel
51 Hazard warning light system switch
52 Heater rear window switch
52 Heater switch
54 Handbrake warning light switch
55 Brake line pressure drop warning light
56 Cigar lighter
57 Cigar lighter illumination
58 Glove compartment illumination
59 Joint
60 Interior light wiring joint
61 Trunk illumination switch
62 Interior light
63 Heated rear window
64 Fuel tank
65 L.H. rear illuminated reflector
66 Jack
67 Trunk illumination
68 R.H. rear illuminated reflector
69 L.H. rear light assembly
70 Joint
71 License plate light
72 R.H. rear light assembly

Automatic transmission

80 Governor
81 Computer unit
82 Sealed junction box
83 Connection block
84 Kick-down switch
85 Selector line marker illumination
86 Starter solenoid safety switch

Caravelle, 1964-65

1 Left-hand headlight
2 Right-hand headlight
3 Road horn
4 Road horn
5 Front left-hand side light and direction indicator
6 Front right-hand side light and direction indicator
7 Town horn
8 Battery
9 Stop switch
10 Windscreen wipers
11 Interior light
12 Left-hand parking light
13 Right-hand parking light
14 Heater switch
15 Fuel gauge
16 Speedometer light
17 Speedometer
18 Oil pressure and water temperature warning light
19 Direction indicator
21 Left-hand connection block on instrument panel
21a Right-hand connection block on instrument panel
22 Charging warning light
23 Headlight warning light
24 Cigar lighter
25 Windshield wiper switch
26 Left-hand door switch
26a Right-hand door switch
27 Flasher unit
28 Connection block under dashboard
29 Fuses
30 Ignition switch
31 Horn and lighting switch
32 Fuel contents rheostat
33 Voltage regulator
34 Starter
35 Temperature switch
36 Ignition coil
37 Spark plugs
38 Distributor
39 Oil pressure switch
40 Heater
41 Generator
42 Rear connection block
43 Left-hand rear and stoplight
44 Right-hand rear and stoplight
45 Left-hand rear turn signal
46 Right-hand rear turn signal
47 License plate light
48a Lower front connection block
48b Upper front connection block
49 Connection under dashboard

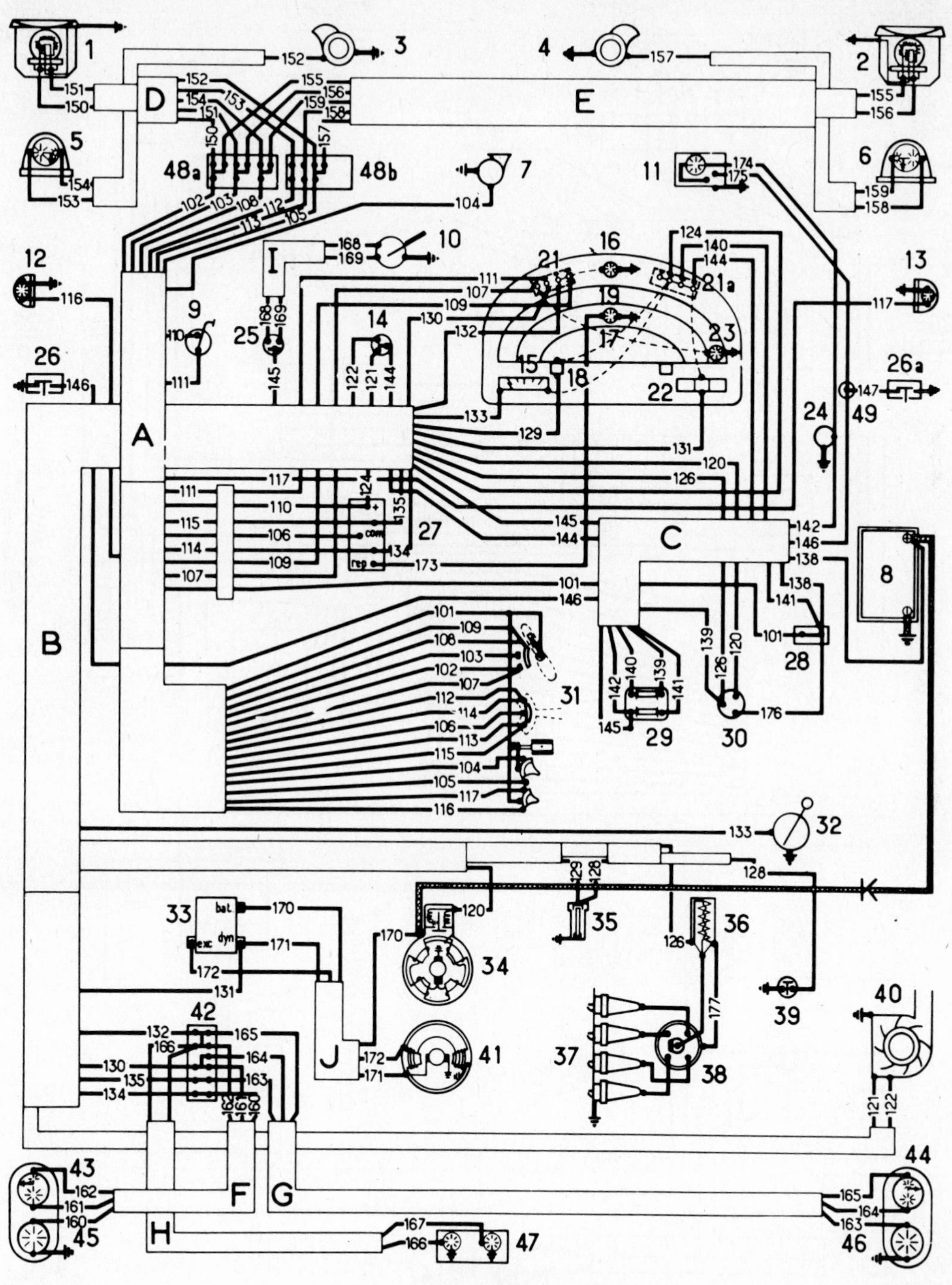

Caravelle, 1964-65

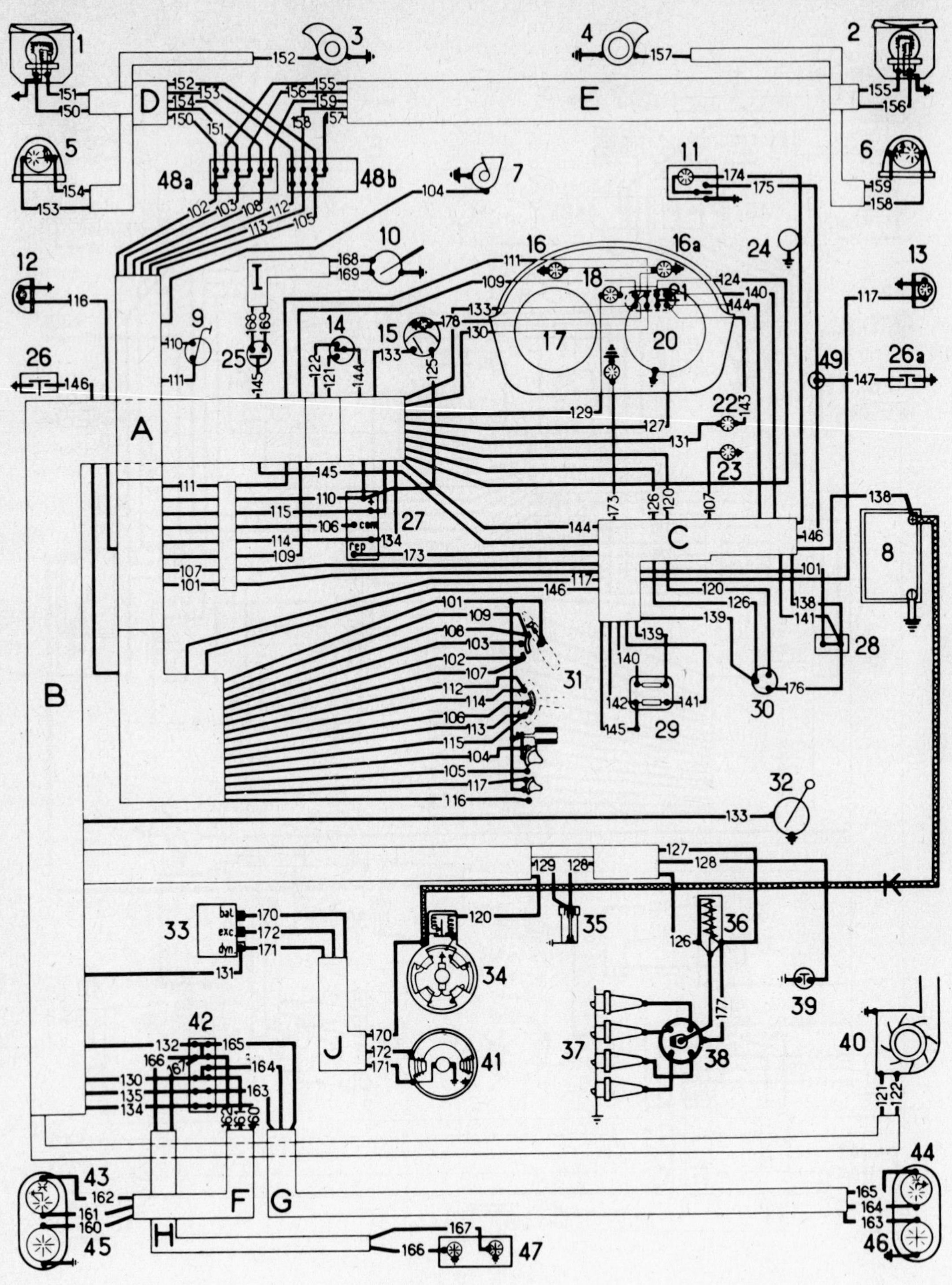

Caravelle, 1966-67

Caravelle, 1966-67

1 Left-hand headlight
2 Right-hand headlight
3 Road horn
4 Road horn
5 Left-hand side light and front direction indicator
6 Right-hand side light and front direction indicator
7 Town horn
8 Battery
9 Stop switch
10 Windshield wiper
11 Interior light
12 Left-hand parking light
13 Right-hand parking light
14 Heater switch
15 Fuel contents indicator
16 Speedometer light
16a Tachometer light
17 Speedometer
18 Oil pressure and water temperature warning light
19 Flasher
20 Tachometer
21 Instrument panel connection block
22 Charge-discharge indicator
23 Headlight warning light
24 Cigar lighter
25 Windshield wiper switch
26 Left-hand door light
26a Right-hand door light
27 Flasher unit
28 Connection plate under dashboard
29 Fuses
30 Ignition switch
31 Horn and lighting switch
32 Fuel contents rheostat
33 Voltage regulator
34 Starter
35 Temperature switch
36 Ignition coil
37 Spark plugs
38 Distributor
39 Pressure switch
40 Heater
41 Generator
42 Rear connection block
43 Left-hand rear and stoplight
44 Right-hand rear and stoplight
45 Rear left-hand direction indicator
46 Rear right-hand direction indicator
47 Number plate light
48a Front lower connection block
48b Front upper connection block
49 Connection under dashboard

Engine Electrical

DISTRIBUTOR REMOVAL AND REPLACEMENT

All Models

1. Remove the distributor cap.
2. Rotate No. 1 cylinder to TDC.
3. Disconnect all lines and wiring at distributor.
4. Mark position of rotor on distributor case.
5. Loosen retaining screw, remove clamp, and lift distributor from block.
6. Installation is the reverse of removal. Be sure to install distributor with the rotor and scribed mark aligned.

DISTRIBUTOR INSTALLATION —ENGINE DISTURBED

ALL MODELS EXCEPT 12 (ALL) AND 16 WITH AUTOMATIC TRANSMISSION

1. Rotate engine to align timing mark with zero line on the flywheel.
2. Connect test lamp circuit between distributor and ground. Turn ignition on.
3. Rotate distributor counterclockwise until light goes on. Tighten distributor bolt.
4. Finalize ignition timing with timing light.

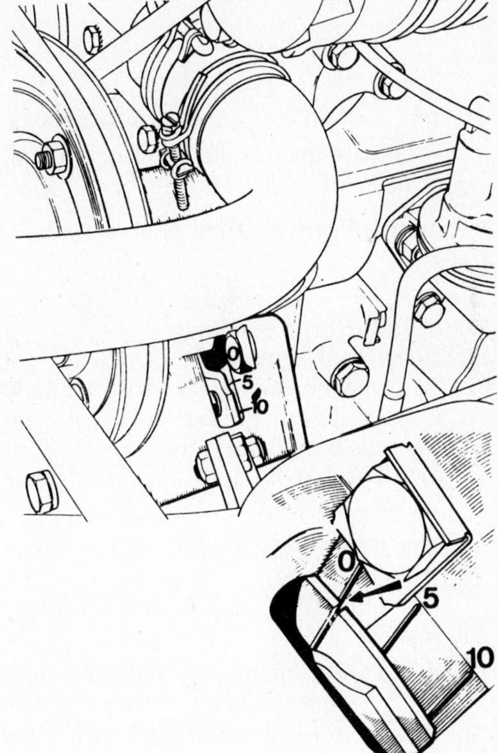

Flywheel timing mark and zero line—all models except 12 (all) and 16 with automatic transmission

Renault 12, Manual Transmission

1. On this vehicle, flywheel has two timing marks. Mark one is TDC, mark two is 3° BTDC. Align timing mark two

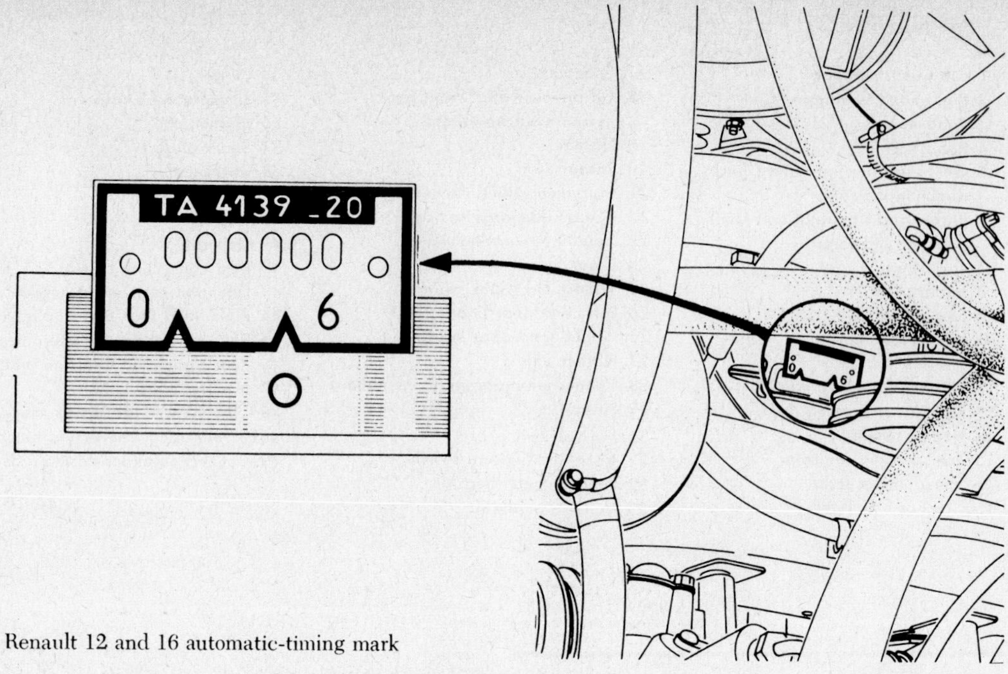

Renault 12 and 16 automatic-timing mark

with small 0. Proceed using steps 3, 4 in Distributor Installation, Engine Disturbed.

Automatic Transmission, Renault 12 and 16

1. TDC is indicated by a small hole drilled in converter housing.
2. Remove all spark plugs.
3. Turn engine counterclockwise till hole is aligned with graduation 6 mark on transmission identification plate. Proceed using steps 2, 3, 4 of Distributor Installation, Engine Disturbed.

BREAKER POINT REMOVAL AND INSTALLATION

All Models

1. Remove distributor cap and rotor with No. 1 cylinder at TDC.
2. Remove breaker points, and with clean rag, wipe old cam grease from distributor cam.
3. Install new points with rubbing block on highest point of cam lobe. *Note: Apply fresh cam lube very sparingly.* Make the preliminary point gap setting with the aid of a feeler gauge. Lock point plate screws.
4. Start engine and finalize adjustment with dwell meter.

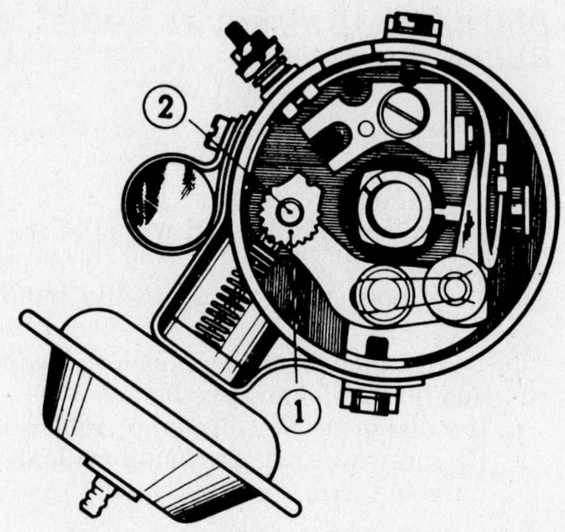

1 Outer vacuum advance cam
2 Inner vacuum advance cam

Distributor vacuum advance adjusting cam

NOTE: On some engines, it may be necessary to check the vacuum unit. The operation of the vacuum unit must not change the point setting. Using the finger, plug the hole on the vacuum capsule and operate the rod which is secured to the diaphragm. Check that the point gap is the same in two extreme positions, with no vacuum and with maximum vacuum. If variation exists, turn the eccentric cam inside the toothed

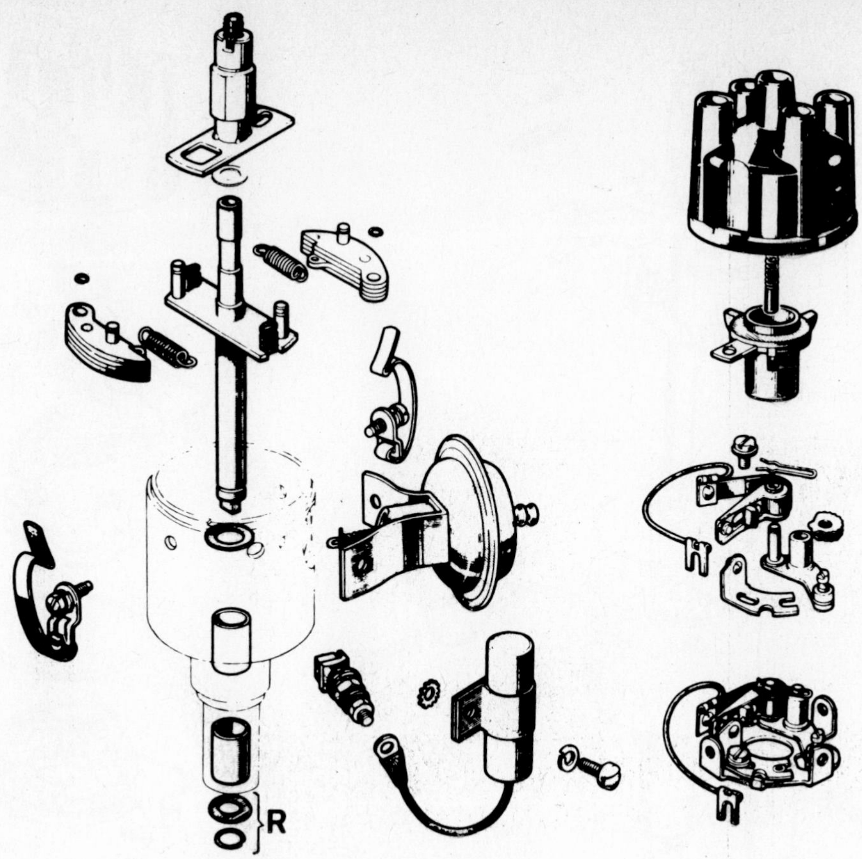

Ducellier distributor

wheel to obtain the correct gap in both positions.

DC GENERATOR AND REGULATOR

DC Generator

The DC generator has its armature supported at each end of the shaft by ball bearings. Some models are lubricated with heat resistant grease and require no attention under normal conditions. Others must be oiled every few thousand miles. If bearings are lubricated during an overhaul of the generator, never use chassis grease.

Two carbon brushes are held by spring pressure against the commutator. These brushes should be inspected every 6,000 miles and replaced if worn badly to prevent damage to the commutator. *Never oil brushes.*

The commutator consists of copper sections which are insulated from each other and from the armature shaft. The sections receive electrical current from an armature coil (winding) and pass the current to the brushes. Occasionally, the insulation between the commutator sections must be trimmed back below the commutator surface.

When checking brushes and commutator, examine brushes for wear and ensure that brushes move freely in their guides. Oil-soaked brushes must be replaced by new ones of the same type. Adjust the contact face of the new brushes to the curvature of the commutator by placing a strip of very fine sand paper (not emery cloth) between the brush and commutator. Work tip of carbon brush until full contact is made, remove the sand paper, and blow out the carbon dust. A dirty or oily commutator can be cleaned with a lint free cloth soaked in clean solvent. Take care to prevent dirt from seeping into bearing. To prevent fire, wipe off all solvent and allow parts to dry completely before operating the generator.

DC Regulator

Since generator voltage is determined by the speed of the armature and the exciting

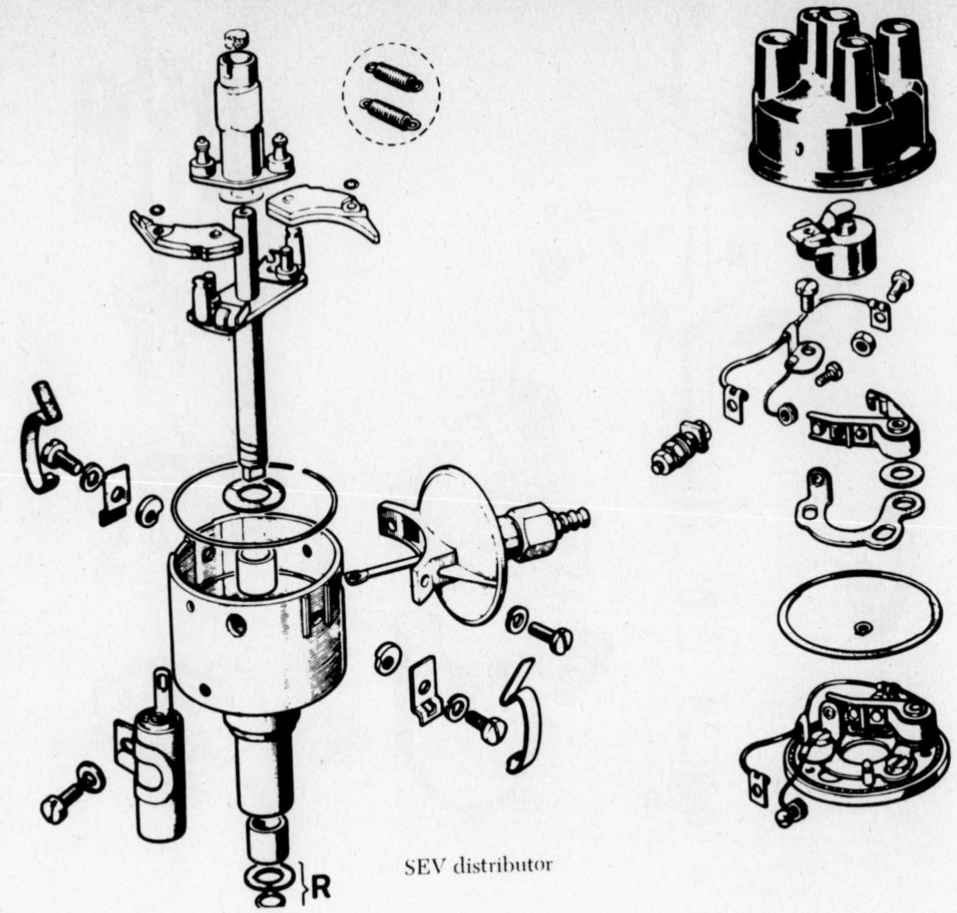

SEV distributor

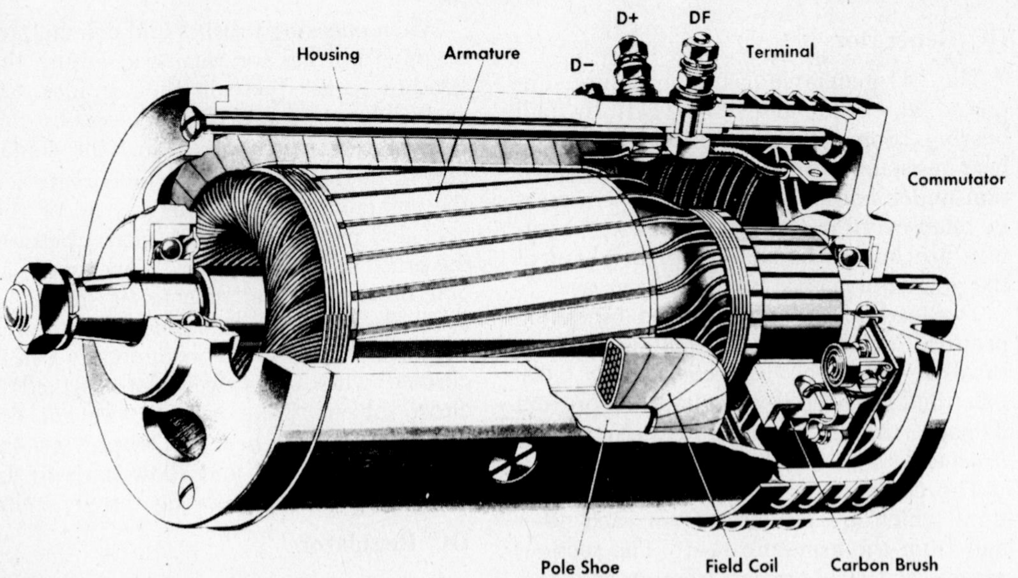

Bosch DC generator in cutaway view. Models vary in shaft dimensions.

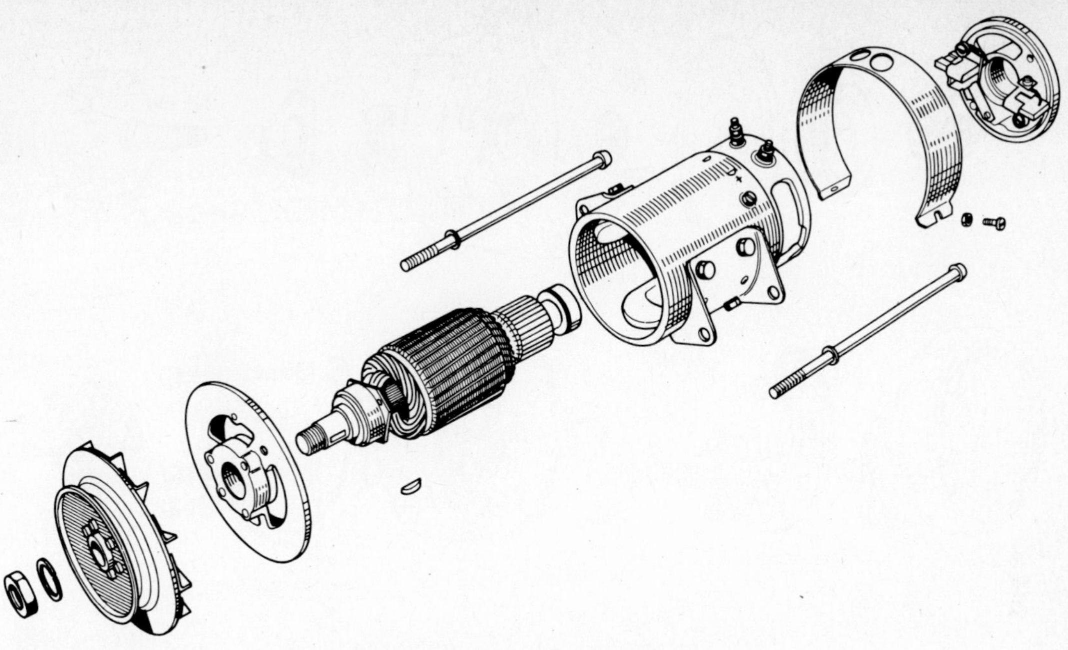

Bosch DC generator in exploded view.

current in the magnetic field, a constant voltage output can be maintained theoretically by controlling the exciting current or the armature speed. However, armature speed is based on engine rpm and is, therefore, not independently controllable. So the regulator maintains a constant voltage output by interrupting the exciting current.

When replacing a regulator, first check that the field coils of the generator are not grounded. Polarize DC generator to prevent damaging the regulator and to ensure proper charging.

Cutout Relay Closing Voltage

Connect voltmeter positive lead to regular 61 D+ terminal. Attach negative lead to ground. Connect ammeter in series with B+ terminal and the disconnected wire, placing positive ammeter lead on B+ terminal and negative lead on battery wire. Increase engine speed and observe voltage increase and then drop slightly (when cutout relay points close) as circuit is completed to battery. The highest voltmeter reading before the drop is the closing voltage. If closing voltage is not within limits, adjust closing voltage by bending cutout relay spring support. Increase spring tension to increase closing voltage; decrease spring tension to decrease closing voltage. Sealed regulators cannot be adjusted.

ALTERNATOR AND REGULATOR

The AC generator-alternator has the field windings carried in a rotor that is mounted at both ends in ball bearings. Lubrication is maintained by sealed-in grease.

Alternator

The alternator is a continuous output (even at idle) diode-rectified generator. It has three-phase stator windings assembled on the inside of the housing. Rectifier diodes are connected to the windings (three diodes to each phase) which change AC voltage into direct current (DC). The diodes only allow current to flow in one direction, from the generator to the battery. Battery current cannot discharge through the generator and, therefore, a current breaker is not needed in the regulator.

Testing Alternator

The capability of the alternator to produce substantial current at idle speed presents a potential danger when testing. One precaution is to use a rheostat in the field circuit when bypassing the regulator in a test. The rheostat permits positive control of the amount of current allowed through the field circuit and also prevents high current from ruining the alternator while testing.

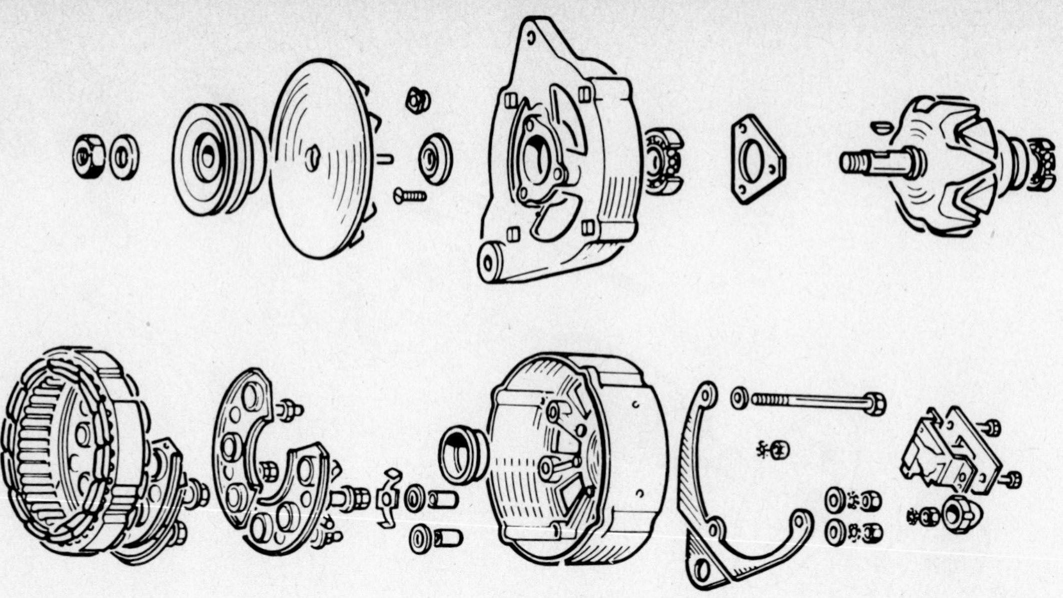

SEV alternator as used on Renault 12 and 16

WARNING: Keep battery ground cable disconnected while changing wires on alternator and regulator.

To pinpoint charging failure to either the regulator or alternator, disconnect alternator field lead from the regulator and attach this lead (or use jumper wire) to output (Bat) terminal on alternator. Have engine started and fast idle at 1500 rpm only 10 to 15 seconds for test. A longer test will overheat alternator. If the alternator charges with field and output terminals joined, the regulator is faulty. If alternator does not charge, it is defective.

To test amperage output of alternator, connect an ammeter between the output terminal of the alternator and its wire leading to the regulator. Connect a voltmeter from the same output terminal to ground (use ground strap on alternator). Again take the alternator field lead from the regulator and attach it to the output terminal of alternator. Test only up to 15 seconds while engine idles—enough time for the ammeter reading to rise equally with voltmeter to 30 amps/30 volts.

Remove field jump wire from output terminal and reconnect wire to field terminal of regulator. Start engine and run until hot. Set idle speed so ammeter reads 10 amperes. Turn on high beam headlights, which should draw 8 to 10 amps. Alternator output should increase by the same amount, raising the ammeter reading to 18-20 amps. A defective regulator on a new car must be returned sealed for the warranty to be valid.

To prevent damage to electrical components and to assure reliable test results, observe the suggestions below.

1. Check tension of alternator drive belt.
2. Disconnect battery cables, clean them and test condition and charge of battery. Battery must be more than half charged.
3. Be absolutely sure of polarity before connecting battery in the test circuit. Reversed polarity will ruin the alternator diodes.
4. Disconnect both battery cables when making a battery charger hook-up. Never use a battery charger to start engine. Be sure of polarity hook-up when using a booster battery for starting.
5. Never ground the alternator output or the battery terminal.
6. Never ground the field circuit between alternator and regulator.
7. Never run any alternator on an open circuit with the field energized.
8. Never try to polarize an alternator.
9. Do not test alternator by attempting to run it like a motor.
10. The regulator cover must be in place when making test readings because the

regulator parts are temperature sensitive.

11. The ignition switch must be off when removing or installing the regulator cover.
12. Use only insulated tools to make adjustments to the regulator.
13. When adjusting engine idle speed, put an electrical load on the engine by turning on the lights, heater, and other accessories.

BATTERY

Batteries should be checked periodically for proper output and good connections. A weak power supply lowers the efficiency of the engine as well as placing a greater drag on the generator.

Battery terminals must be kept clean of corrosion. A stiff wire brush and a solution of baking soda and water make an effective cleaning combination.

Be sure not to allow baking soda to contaminate battery. After terminals are cleaned, coat them with vaseline to prevent further deterioration.

Inspect the battery case for cracks and weakness. Check the density (specific gravity) of the battery electrolyte with a hydrometer. Readings from a fully charged battery will depend on the make but will fall in the range of 1.260 to 1.310 times as heavy as pure water at 80°F. *NOTE: All cells should produce nearly equal readings.* If one or two cell readings are sharply lower, those cells are defective. The average test voltage of each cell is 2 volts. It increases to about 2.5 to 2.7 volts while the battery is being charged and decreases to between 2.1 and 2.0 volts soon after the charging current has been cut off. The battery is discharged when the cell voltage has dropped to approximately 1.8 volts under no-load test condition.

As a battery releases its charge, sulphate ions in the electrolyte become attached to the battery plates, reducing the density of the fluid. The specific gravity of the electrolyte varies not only with the percentage of acid in the liquid, but also with temperature. As temperature increases, the electrolyte expands so that specific gravity is reduced in this second way. As temperature drops, the electrolyte contracts and gravity increases. To correct readings for temperature variation, add .004 to the hydrometer reading for every 10°F that the electrolyte is above 80°F and subtract .004 for every 10°F that the electrolyte is below 80°F.

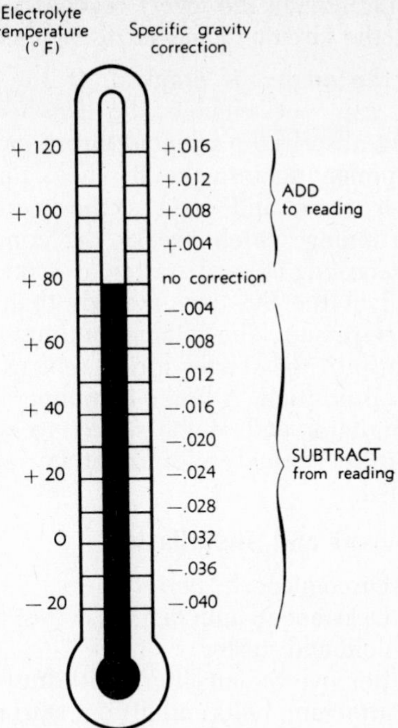

Temperature affects the specific gravity readings of batteries.

Hydrometer readings	*Condition*
1.260-1.310	Fully charged
1.230-1.250	3/4 charged
1.200-1.220	1/2 charged
1.170-1.190	1/4 charged
1.140-1.160	Almost discharged
1.110-1.130	Fully discharged

Charging a weak battery is best done by a slow-charge method. If quick charging is attempted, check the cell voltages and the color of the electrolyte a few minutes after charge is started. If cell voltages are not uniform or if electrolyte is discolored with brown sediment, quick charging should be stopped in favor of a slow charge. In either case, do not let electrolyte temperature exceed 120°F.

STARTER

The starter is a brush-type, series-wound motor operated by a solenoid. The armature shaft, supported in two bushings which are permanently packed with lubricant, has a spline which carries an overrunning clutch and a pinion assembly.

When the starter is switched on, the solenoid throws the pinion gear into mesh with the flywheel by means of the actuating lever and guide ring. When the solenoid (while moving the lever) reaches a contact disc, the circuit to the starter is completed and the engine is cranked. If the pinion gear can not engage the flywheel, the spring absorbs the solenoid thrust and holds the pinion against the flywheel until the starter turns and meshes the teeth. The overrunning clutch breaks the connection between engine and starter as soon as the speed of the flywheel exceeds that of the starter pinion. The pinion continues in full mesh until the starter spring returns it to a neutral position. A brake is mounted at the commutator end of the starter to stop the armature quickly for another start if needed.

Removal and Installation

1. Disconnect the battery.
2. Disconnect and tag all wires to solenoid and starter.
3. Remove the air filter. Withdraw starter attaching bolts and lift out starter.
4. Installation is reverse of removal.

Checking Brushes and Commutator

Remove starter end cap to inspect brushes for wear and free movement in their guides. Replace brushes which are excessively worn, oil saturated, or have loose connectors. Install brushes with the flexible connectors positioned so they will not hinder brush movement. Use a complete set even if only one brush is needed. Check tension of brush springs, replacing weak ones.

Clean the commutator with a lint-free cloth wrapped around a piece of wood and dampened in trichloroethylene.

Fuel System

FUEL PUMP AND FILTER

The mechanical fuel pump, powered at

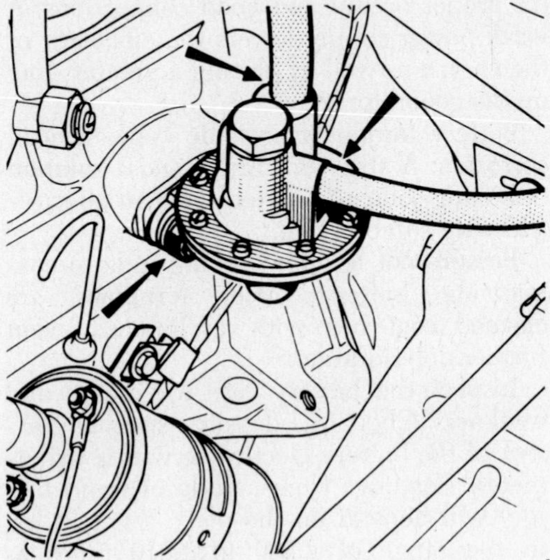

Fuel pump location—Arrows denote fittings and bolts to be removed when servicing is necessary.

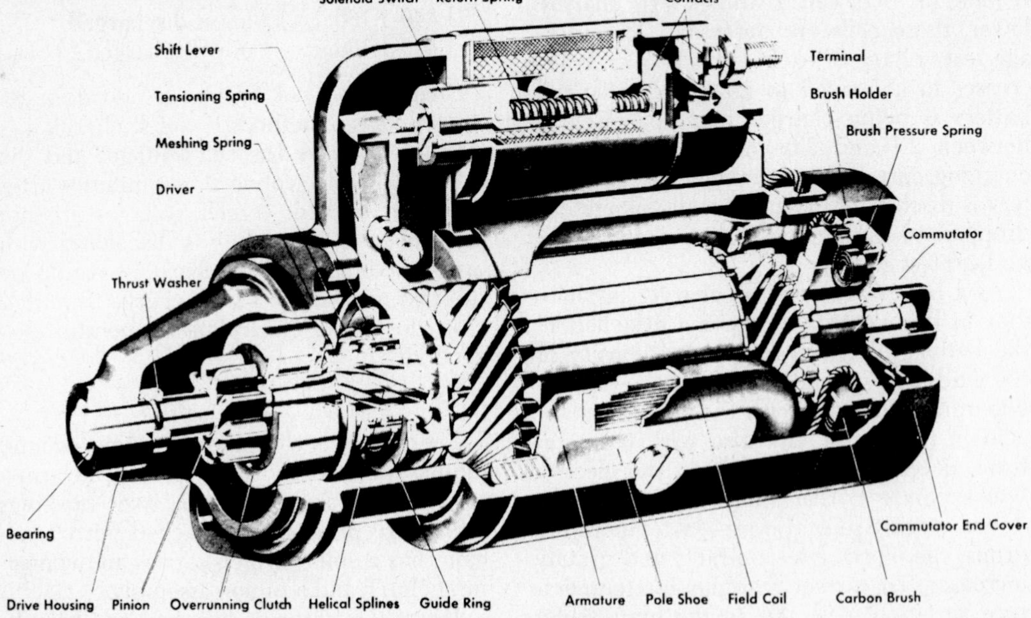

Cross section of Bosch starter.

camshaft speed by a cam, is simply constructed and easily checked for malfunction. Some Renault fuel pumps have a fuel filter screen located in the top of the pump. These can be quickly opened and cleaned. When installing cover, check fit of gasket.

Fuel Pressure and Capacity

Fuel pressure is determined by the action of the diaphragm spring in the fuel pump. A weak spring lowers fuel pressure which causes a lean combustion mixture. Extreme spring tension creates full pressures that are too high, causing carburetor flooding.

To check fuel-pump pressure, insert a T joint in the fuel line at the pump outlet to the carburetor and connect a pressure gauge to it.

The pumping capacity of the fuel pump varies with the length of stroke of the pump diaphragm. The stroke is affected by wearing of the diaphragm linkage and the camlobe.

The length of stroke amounts to only a few tenths of a millimeter in normal operation but this must be precise to ensure peak fuel pump performance. Stroke is altered by adding or removing gaskets at the flange. But, too many or too few gaskets will damage the diaphragm or linkage.

Reconditioning the Fuel Pump

Remove fuel lines carefully to prevent rupturing them, plug the ends of the pipes, and remove pump from engine housing. Scratch a mark across the diaphragm flanges to simplify later reassembly. This prevents accidental changing of the lead-in-angle of the fuel lines which might occur if the top section is put back on facing a different direction.

Remove screws from the diaphragm flanges and separate the two sections of the pump. Press down on diaphragm to release rocker arm link. Remove retainer clips from rocker arm pin and punch out pin. Take out link, rocker arm, and rocker arm spring.

Disassemble the top section by removing hex retaining screw, cover, and screen. Carefully remove valve covers so that parts don't fly out. Illustration has numbered steps for disassembling pump.

Wash parts in solvent and dry with air. Replace worn parts. Replacement part kits are available.

Metal parts coated with white oxide have been water damaged and should be replaced to prevent fouling of carburetor jets.

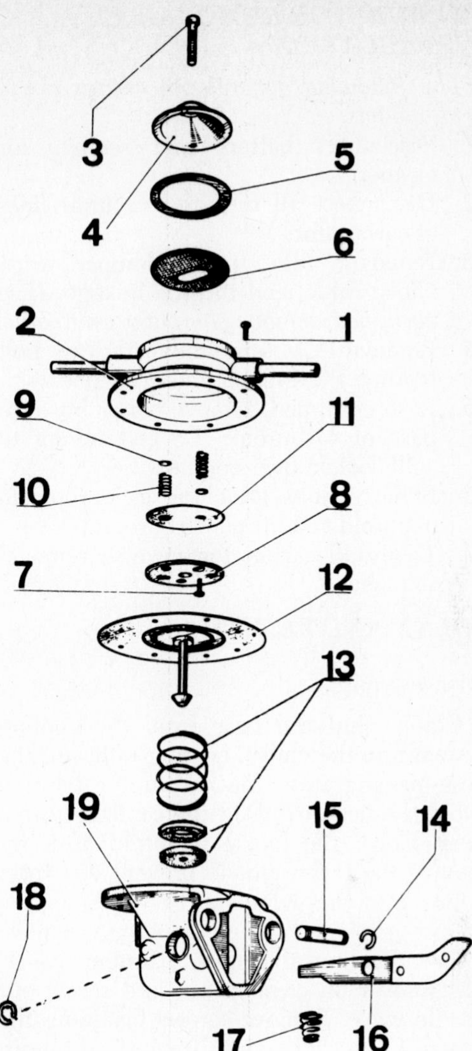

Follow numbered steps to disassemble the fuel pump. Wash parts in solvent and dry with air.

Reassembly of the fuel pump is the reverse of disassembly. Assemble the rocker arm and link and hold them together with thin rod or metal inserted through pivot pin holes. Install diaphragm spring and diaphragm. Then turn over pump so rocker link drops toward diaphragm connection. Press diaphragm in and hook it onto link. Insert rocker pivot pin and secure it.

Press in rocker arm linkage enough to make diaphragm stay flat between the flanges while turning in flange screws until screwheads touch lock washers. At this point, push rocker linkage in as far as possible to stretch diaphragm and tighten down flange screws. Premature diaphragm wear is avoided by pre-stretching the diaphragm in this way.

CARBURETOR REMOVAL AND INSTALLATION

The following general procedures apply to all models.

1. Disconnect battery and remove air cleaner.
2. Disconnect all fuel and vacuum lines at carburetor.
3. Remove: idle speed damper wire, choke cable, and throttle linkage. *If so equipped, remove computer unit cable.*
4. Remove PCV hose and withdraw bolt holding PCV valve. Remove valve.
5. If so equipped, remove water hoses at base of carburetor. Be certain not to spill coolant over engine.
6. Remove bolts attaching carburetor to manifold and lift off carburetor.
7. To install carburetor, reverse removal sequence.

SOLEX AND ZENITH

Disassembly

Clamp shut the hose from the cooling system into the choke, heating unit and the hose passing from the carburetor base to avoid the need to bleed the cooling system later. Cover the intake manifold after removing the carburetor to prevent dirt from falling into the cylinders. Referring to the proper exploded view drawing, remove screws holding the float chamber cover. Place cover on clean paper and screw out needle valve. Remove screws fastening the cover of the choke and dismantle the unit. On carburetors with a disc-valve starter, take off the assembly, and then remove starter fuel jet located to left of cover. Remove starter air jet.

When removing all assemblies, note all jet sizes. On double barrel carburetors keep twin components separated to prevent accidental interchanges when reassembling carburetor.

Remove air correction jet (high speed air bleed) from emulsion (main vent) assembly in throat, extract the emulsion tube from inside, and take out the emulsion tube holder. Remove the accelerator pump injector screw and the injection assembly.

From the float chamber, lift out the float toggle (float arm), its spindle (pin), and float.

Disconnect the accelerator pump lever from its pump control rod and then usscrew the four corner fixing screws to remove pump assembly. Remove the pump inlet valve, strainer, and washer. Unscrew the accelerator pump jet from the housing. Take out the main (metering) jet carrier and jet from the carburetor housing

Remove the idle volume control screw (idle mixture adjustment) from throat below throttle butterfly. Remove idle (pilot) jet and idle (pilot) air bleed. The venturi (choke tube) is removable by loosening a set screw.

Solex 32 DITA 3 is a downdraft carburetor with a choke operated by a thermostatic spring which is expanded by hot water from the cooling system. The base of the carburetor is also water heated. The choke water casing cannot be repaired. When reassembling, place the mark on the casing in line with that on the float chamber cover.

The carburetor reference number is marked on a plate which is screwed to the float chamber cover.

Solex 32 PDIST is a downdraft carburetor with a choke operated by thermostatic spring which is expanded by heat from the exhaust manifold. The base of the carburetor is water heated.

When refitting the casing with the thermostatic spring, turn it in a clockwise direction in order to place the punch mark in line with that in the housing.

The carburetor reference number is on a plate attached to the float cover.

Solex 32 PIBT and Zenith 28 IFT are downdraft carburetors. The Solex has a starter disc-valve operated by a thermostatic spring which is expanded by heat from the exhaust manifold.

The carburetor reference number is on a plate attached to the float cover.

Solex DIDSA 3 is a downdraft double barrel carburetor with a vacuum controlled progressive throttle linkage and a special device that maintains a partial opening of the first barrel throttle plate when decelerating.

Meeting federal exhaust emission requirements, the Renault double-carburetion system (DCS) includes special engine pistons with reduced clearance at the top, an intake manifold and a cylinder head with separate ports, and an ignition distributor with centrifugal advance and vacuum advance devices.

The following four operations are the only ones possible on the DCS that will not alter factory emission control settings:

1. Removing and installing the carburetor cover for replacement of gasket, jets, float, needle valve, accelerating pump nozzle and check valve; 2. Replacing the vacuum-diaphragm (lung) unit; 3. Replacing the choke linkage; and 4. Replacing the idle jet fuel shut-off solenoid valve.

Cleaning Carburetor Parts

Carburetor part replacement kits are recommended for each overhaul. Kits contain a complete set of gaskets and new parts to replace those that generally deteriorate most rapidly. Not substituting all of the new parts supplied in the kits usually results in poor performance later.

Wash carburetor parts—except for diaphragm—in a carburetor cleaner, rinse in solvent, and blow dry with compressed air.

Carburetors have numerous small passages that can be fouled by carbon and gummy deposits. Soak metal parts in carburetor solvent until thoroughly clean. However, the solvent will weaken or destroy cork, plastic and leather components. These parts should be wiped clean with a lint free cloth. Clean the diaphragms only in a safe solvent to prevent deterioration. Clean each jet and valve separately to avoid interchanges during reassembly.

Check the shaft of the throttle valve for too much play that allows air leakage (affecting starting and idling). Inspect float spindle and other moving parts for wear. Replace float if gasoline has leaked into it. The accelerator pump check valve (no return ball valve) should pass air one way but not the other. Test for proper valve seating by blowing and sucking on valve, and replace if necessary. Wash it again to remove breath moisture. Carefully clean all fuel channels in the float bowl and cover. Blow out these channels in both directions so that ball valves and seats are clean and action is free.

Replace the accelerator pump diaphragm because it loses properties when exposed to air. Replace the carburetor flange gasket.

While the carburetor is disassembled, check the bowl cover with a straight edge for warped surfaces. Also check the manifold flange for straightness; a warped flange leaks air that causes hard starting.

Take care not to tighten needle valves into seats. Uneven jetting will result. Inspect valves and seats closely for wear and damage.

Assembly—All Models, Solex and Zenith

Referring to exploded view diagrams, and using new gasketing and other soft parts where needed, place the washer, spring and pump cover arm over the pump control rod and secure them with cotter pin or locking nut provided.

If accelerator pump was taken apart, reassemble it by placing the spring in the pump body lower section, the diaphragm assembly in the pump cover, and fastening both groups together with the short, center pump cover screws. Hold pump arm steady while tightening screws to keep diaphragm from distorting. In assembling carburetor parts, tighten all screws gradually (one and then another) as though using torque procedures.

Replace emulsion tubes (with open ends up), jets and carriers, pump check valve, and idle adjusting screw. Install choke unit. In many cases the starter jet has the same thread size as the correction jets. Check stamped jet sizes against specifications.

Screw in idle adjustment until it gently touches seat and then back off one and one-half turns for the basic setting.

NOTE: The adjustments of screws numbered 1, 2 and 3 in the illustration are factory set with precision equipment.

Use a *new* needle valve and seat. Install float assembly and put on float chamber cover with new gasket.

When the choke is completely closed, the throttle valve should be slightly open. Check the initial opening with a rod gauge of diameter meeting specifications listed. Adjust initial opening for each model as follows.

Solex PDIST

With lever on highest part of cam, loosen screw and slide rod in the sleeve. Tighten screw at initial opening of 0.85±0.10 mm (.033±.004 in.).

Solex PBIT

Turn the adjustment screw in or out when it is on the highest part of the notched cam. Initial opening must be 0.55 mm (.022 in.).

Solex DITA

When cold, the throttle initial opening is determined by the thrust rod attached to the lever in which the idling speed adjusting screw rests. Set engine idling speed

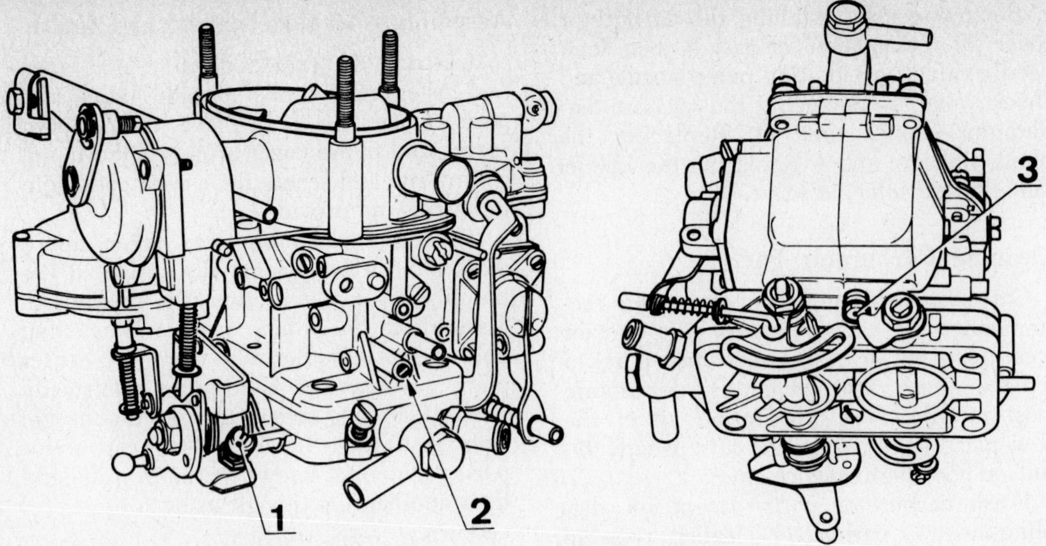

Solex carburetor DIDSA. Factory-set screws are numbered.

accurately to 600-650 rpm to obtain correct initial opening.

CARBURETOR ADJUSTMENTS —ALL EXCEPT WEBER 32 DIR

With clean carburetor installed and proper fuel pump pressure feeding the float chamber, several basic tune-up adjustments can be made to the carburetor.

Float Level

With the car sitting level and the engine idling, the needle valve on the carburetor should be partially closed. Shut off the engine and the needle valve should close completely.

Float level is adjusted by installing a thicker or thinner gasket under the needle valve. Thin gaskets raise the fuel level. Thick gaskets lower it. Further adjustment is possible by bending the float arm. The proper level is most easily determined with a glass gauge that fits into the main-jet carrier.

Accelerator Pump

The amount of fuel discharged by the accelerator pump is adjustable on some carburetor models by changing the location of the accelerator pump arm on the connecting rod.

The pump jet size determines the *dura-*

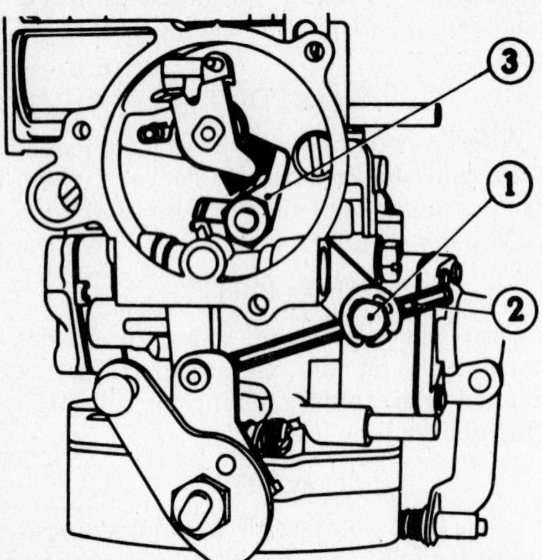

Adjusting throttle-valve opening on Solex PDIST.

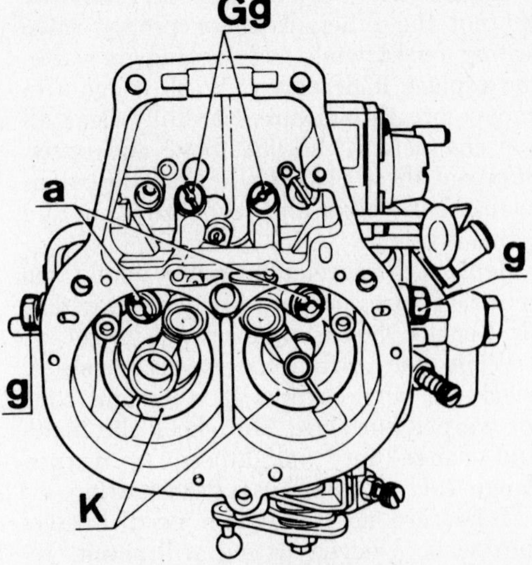

Jet arrangement on Solex double-barrel carburetors; DIDSA model is shown.

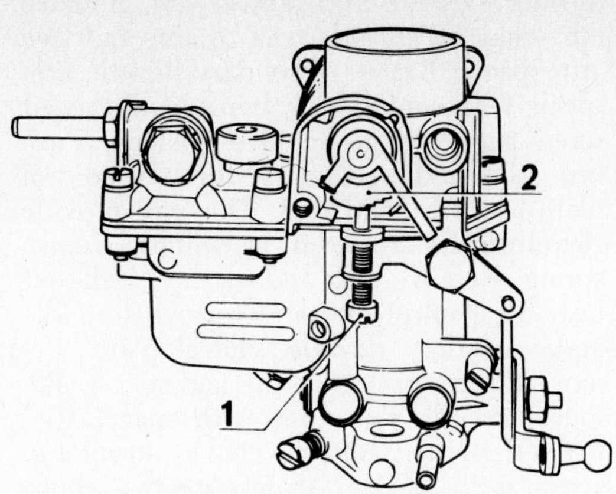

Adjusting throttle-valve opening on Solex PIBT.

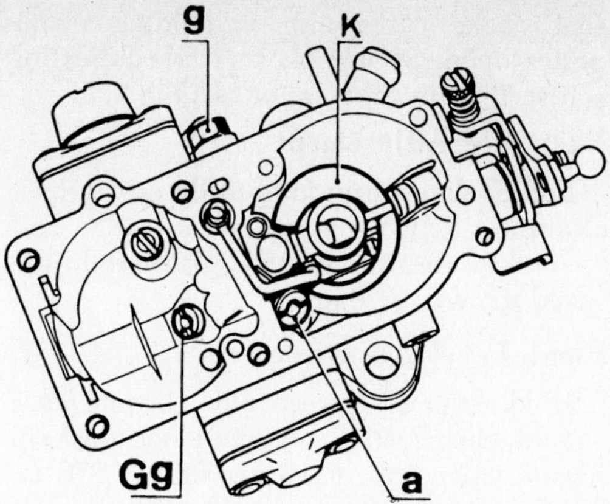

Jet arrangement on Solex DITA and PDIST carburetors.

tion of each ejection, *not* the quantity injected.

Throttle Linkage

Check adjustment of the throttle linkage. The throttle valves must open and close with free travel from idle to full power.

1. Lubricate all moving joints with one or two drops of engine oil while moving throttle control.
2. Lubricate accelerator pump rod and linkage.
3. Disconnect all ball joints and sockets, partly fill cups with high temperature grease, and reconnect.
4. Move linkage back and forth to check for free movement. Linkage for automatic transmission must not have any play in it, but must return to idle position freely and completely.

Idle—Single Barrel Carburetors

The single-barrel carburetor can only be adjusted satisfactorily when the engine is in good mechanical condition and the timing is perfect. Remove idle mixture screw and inspect needle tip for burrs, grooves, and other deformities. Make basic adjustment on screw by gently closing jet into seat and then reopening it one and one-half turns.

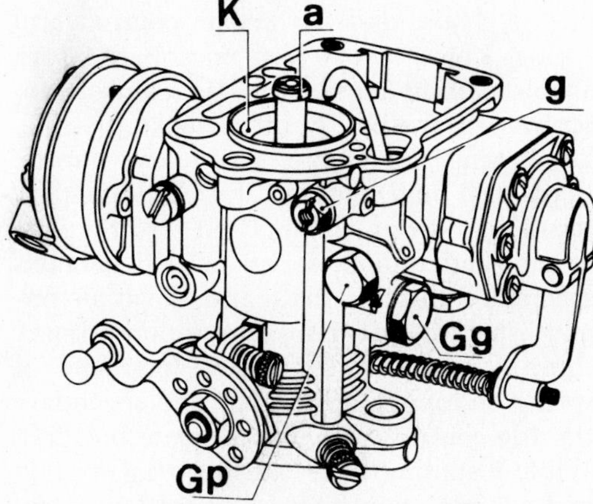

Jet arrangement on Solex PIBT carburetor. Jet Ga is on the opposite side near the choke.

Warm engine to operating temperature, remove air cleaner, disconnect throttle linkage at ball joints, turn idle speed stop screw to a normal idling speed. Readjust idle mixture screw for fine tuning. And again, set the idle speed stop screw. Install air cleaner. The engine should not die by quick shutting of the throttle or release of the clutch pedal in neutral.

Adjust carubretor rod so that it connects with the linkage without pushing or pulling the throttle valve.

WEBER 32 DIR ADJUSTMENTS

Idle Speed

With engine at operating temperature and choke control off, attach a tachometer to engine. Turn idle speed adjusting screw to obtain proper speed.

Idle Mixture Adjustment

Engine must be at operating temperature with choke control off. Turn idle mixture screw till engine begins to stutter. Back screw off till engine smooths out. It may be necessary to perform the idle speed adjustment again.

Adjusting Choke Cable and Housing

Fully insert choke cable housing in accelerator pump cover housing. Tighten choke cable housing screw. Insert choke cable in choke cable adjuster. Push choke control knob fully in, then back out 1/16 in. Check that choke cable arm is holding choke plates open. Secure choke cable adjusting screw. Be sure cable is not binding.

Fast Idle Adjustment

Pull choke control knob fully out. Adjust clearance between stop on fast idle and secondary throttle control plate and idle speed screw to .070 in.

Float Level Adjustment

Hold cover body vertically. Be sure float weight closes valve but does not push in needle valve ball. Float should be .276 in. from cover gasket when held against cover body. To obtain this value, bend float level tab. Be certain tab surface is perpendicular to needle valve axis. Measure float travel. It should be .354 in. With cover body vertical, lift float to highest position. Measurement should be .591 in. frim float to cover gasket. Bend float drop tab to obtain this.

Check that needle valve spring hook does not bind; be certain that float does not rub bowl walls.

Weber 32 DIR Disassembly

Extract hairpin clip from lower choke shaft link. Remove all cover body screws and lift off cover. Do not damage gasket or float. Using a drift, remove float pin. Remove float and needle valve with cover gasket. Lift out the needle valve seat and seal. Remove intake screen plug with screen. Remove upper hairpin clip from choke shaft link. Remove link and dust cover. Choke plate screws are peened to prevent loosening. If they are to be renewed, new ones must be available. After removal, lift out choke plate and shaft with link end first. Remove: accelerator pump nozzle screw, nozzle, and seal. Take out the primary and secondary correction jet. Invert main body and take out air/fuel mixture tubes. Remove idle jet screws and primary and secondary idle jet. Lift out primary and secondary main jets. Remove accelerator pump cover screws and cover.

NOTE: Diaphragm beneath cover is under spring tension.

Remove choke cable housing screw. Lift out the accelerator pump diaphragm assembly with its spring. Remove idle mixture screw with its spring. Take out accelerator pump metering screw. Remove choke cable link and hairpin clip. Take out choke cable link. Remove: choke cable arm screw, arm, and adjusting screw. Straighten primary throttle lock tab and remove nut. Remove tab. Take off throttle control arm and free arm spacer. Extract secondary throttle arm spring with control arm. Remove idle speed screw and spring. Remove bushing. Push fast idle and secondary throttle control plate towards shaft end. This will provide clearance for removal of throttle return spring. Remove clip and washer. Take off fast idle control link and remove fast idle and secondary throttle control plate. Remove throttle return spring and spacer. Remove throttle shaft nut with spacer. Remove shaft arm. Remove choke control arm screw with washer. Slowly remove choke control arm; relieve tension on arm spring slowly. Do not stretch choke plate relief spring. Take out spring. Turn fast idle control link and align keyway. Remove link and arm spring. Remove choke shaft free arm link with its screw. Throttle plate screws have been peened. If they must be removed, new ones must be available. Mark throttle plates, and primary and secondary throttle shafts in relation to each other. Remove throttle plate screws and slide plate from shaft. Take out secondary throttle adjustment screw.

Assembly

Slide the primary and secondary throttle shafts in position. Place throttle plates in position in reference to mating marks. Place new throttle plate screws in position. Tap throttle plate while inserting screws to assure proper alignment. Peen screws with caution. Install choke shaft link arm with shoulder screw. Place choke control arm spring in main body. Be sure straight end is in body recess. Insert keyed end of fast idle control link in tab hole of cable arm. Place tab in hook end of choke control arm spring. Rotate choke arm one quarter turn against spring tension. Install control arm screw with washer. Position choke plate relief spring. Assemble secondary throttle shaft arm and washer. Install secondary throttle adjusting screw. Hold throttle plate closed, and tighten screw until it contacts secondary throttle shaft arm. Position primary shaft spacer. Loosely position primary throttle return spring. Place loop end of spring on tongue of fast idle and secondary throttle control plate. Install plate on shaft. While installing plate, place spring straight end against main body. Be sure lower end of fast idle control link is in groove. Install secondary throttle bushing, and arm with pin, in groove of secondary throttle shaft arm. Install free arm spacer throttle control arm, and nut with lock tab. Tighten nut. Be sure linkage operates properly and bend tab to secure nut.

Assemble fast idle control washer with hairpin clip in bottom of fast idle control link. Next, install the secondary throttle spring. Insert the idle speed adjusting screw with its spring. Turn one revolution more than where screw begins operation of throttle plate. Install choke cable adjusting screw, arm, and shoulder screw. Assemble choke cable link, clip, and hairpin clip. Assemble idle mixture screw and spring. Seat needle lightly against seat. Back off two turns. Install accelerator pump spring in proper recess. Position accelerator pump diaphragm so that screw holes are aligned. Install pump cover and screws. Align roller arm with cam on primary throttle shaft. Install choke cable housing screw. Install primary and secondary main jet. Install idle jet screws, and primary and secondary idle jet. Install air/fuel mixture screws with primary and secondary correction jet. Assemble accelerator pump nozzle seal, nozzle, and screw. Position the accelerator pump metering screw. Place choke plate shaft into cover body. Insert choke plates and four new screws. Peen screw heads. Place dust cover in body. Insert choke shaft link through dust cover, position in choke plate shaft arm, and secure with clip. Install intake screen and plug. Install needle valve seat and seal. Install gasket to cover body. Install needle valve on float and install assembly on cover body with float pin. Install cover on main body and secure with screws and washers. Install bottom of choke shaft link and secure with hairpin clip.

Idle—Engines with DCS

Perform the following steps to adjust the idle speed of all emission carburetors. DCS carburetors have an adjustable idle air bypass system, with an air passage entrance above the throttle valve, a passage exit below the throttle valve, and an air (speed) adjusting screw in between. Idle speed adjustment is made only with the by pass air adjusting screw, not by changing the throttle stop screw position. However, if the stop screw setting has been disturbed accidentally, adjust it first with air cleaner installed, choke valve open, and engine temperature at normal. Follow the throttle stop screw adjustment procedures below.

1. With engine idling, fully close idle air adjustment screw (uppermost screw).
2. Adjust idle mixture screw to achieve the highest possible idle speed.
3. Adjust *throttle stop screw* as required to obtain idle speed of 600 to 650 rpm. The throttle valve is now properly reset.

Continue with the air and mixture adjustments until engine idles perfectly (taking care not to disturb the throttle stop screw).

1. With air cleaner installed, choke valve open and engine temperature at normal, adjust idle speed with *air adjusting screw* (uppermost screw) to 700 rpm.
2. Adjust *idle mixture needle* until the highest possible rpm is achieved.
3. If idle speed is now higher, readjust idle air screw to 715 rpm.
4. Repeat steps 2 and 3 until the maximum speed possible by turning the mixture screw to 700 rpm.
5. Last, lower engine speed to 675 rpm by turning the lower screw (mixture) clockwise. Whenever idle speed is changed, always make a careful mixture needle adjustment last. This reduces the carbon monoxide emission by leaning out the idle.

Accelerated Idle

The throttle plate is kept partially open when the engine decelerates by the operation of a vacuum diaphragm unit. This reduces the greatest part of exhaust pollutants. Do not confuse *accelerated idle* with *fast idle* which results from the operation of the choke when the engine is cold. Follow the accelerated idle adjustment steps below.

1. Attach an electronic tachometer and disconnect the wire which feeds the solenoid valve.
2. Hold nut E (see illustration) with a 16 mm wrench; loosen nut D with a 10 mm wrench; and turn set screw C with a 3 mm wrench until the accelerated idle speed of 1300-1400 rpm is obtained.
3. Tighten locknuts carefully and accelerate the engine quickly and briefly a few times to check the setting.
4. Connect the wire to the solenoid valve.

The centrifugal switch that sends the electrical impulse to the solenoid operates

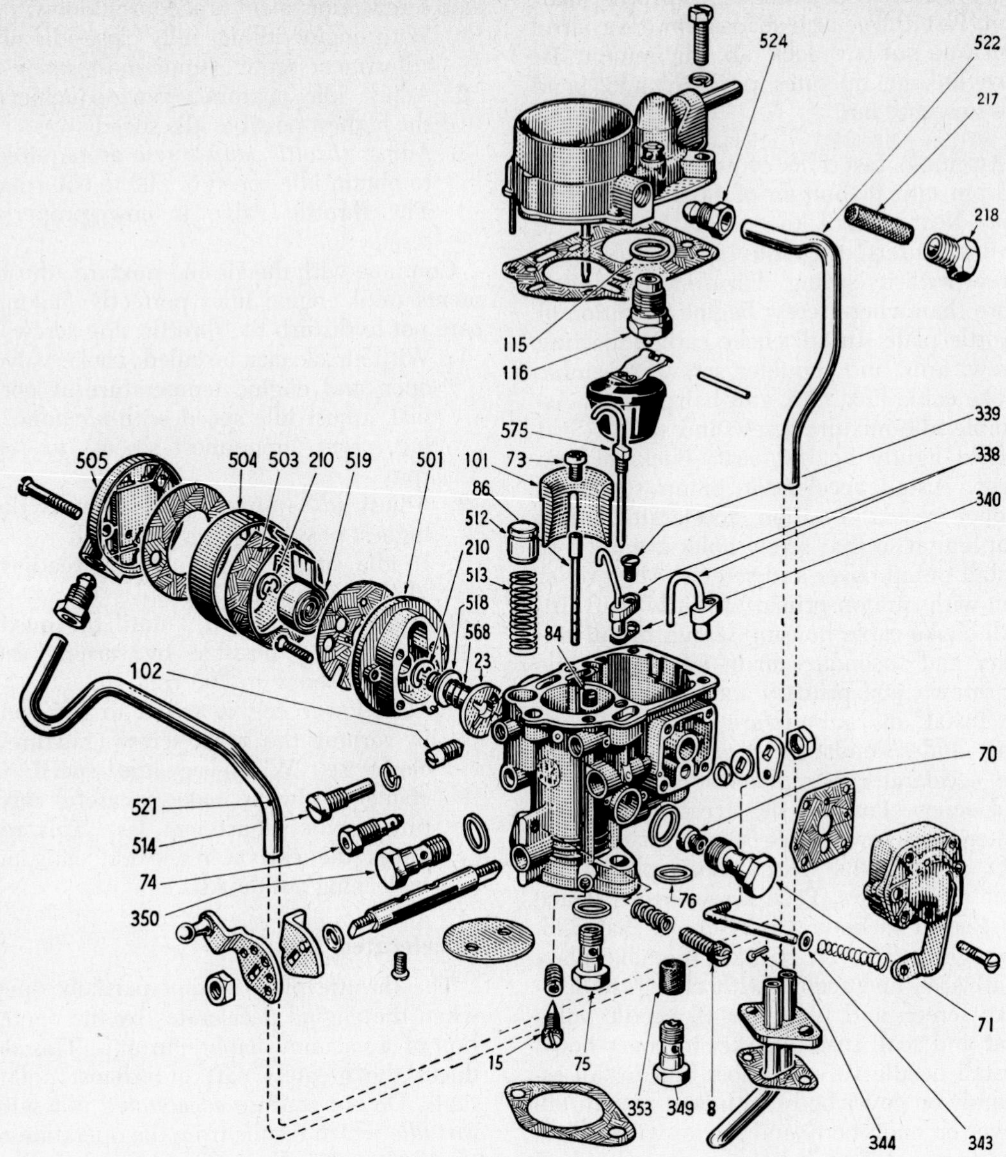

Solex 32 PIBT, with automatic disc-valve starter

8. Idle speed adjustment screw
15. Volume control screw
23. Starter valve
70. Main jet (Gg)
71. Main jet carrier
72. Main jet carrier washer
73. Correction jet (a)
74. Idle jet (g)
75. Starter fuel jet (Gs)
76. Pump valve washer
84. Idling air bleed (u)
86. Emulsion tube (s)
101. Venturi
102. Venturi set screw
115. Needle valve washer
116. Needle valve (P)
210. Circlips
217. Fuel filter screen
218. Filter plug
338. Pump injector (high or low)
339. Pump injector fixing screw
340. Injector washer
343. Spring retaining washer
344. Control rod split pin
349. Pump inlet valve
350. Pump jet (Gp)
353. Pump filter screen
501. Starter valve housing
503. Insulating strip for bi-metal casing
504. Bi-metal casing
505. Cover for bi-metal casing
512. Auto starter piston
513. Spring for piston
514. Piston stop screw
518. Retaining washer
519. Bi-metal coil
521. Pipe for heat
522. Cold air intake tube
524. Union for intake tube
568. Starter valve spring
575. Econostat

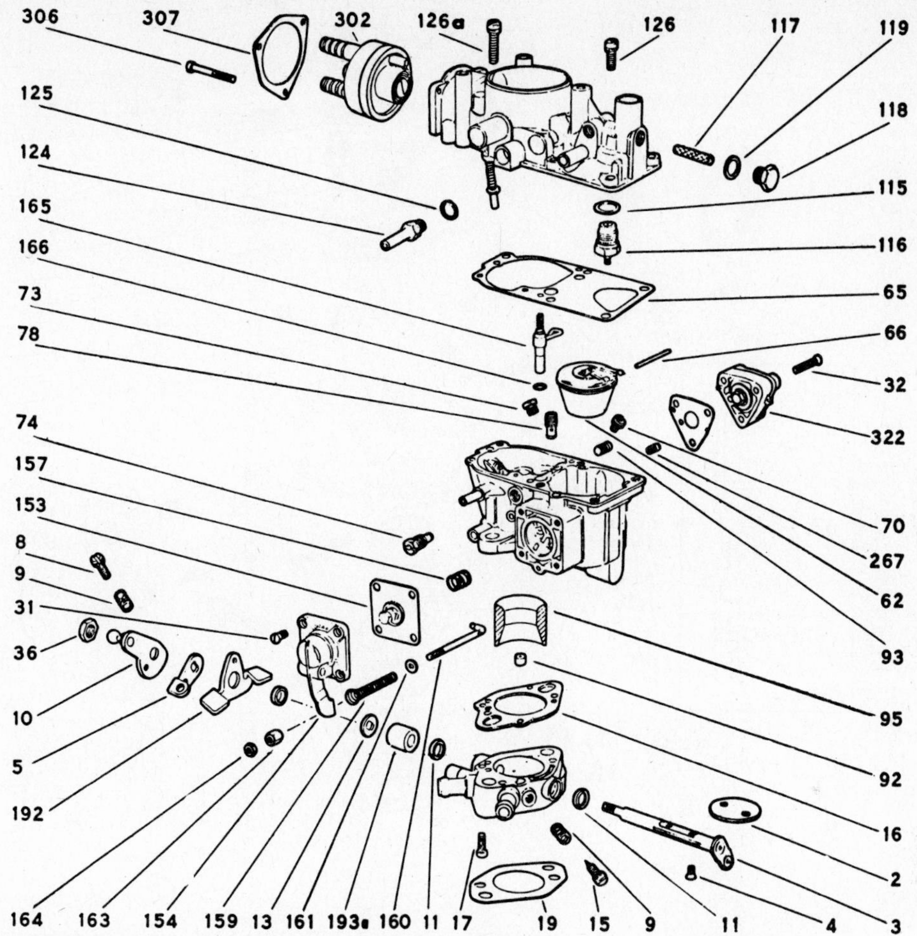

2. Throttle valve
3. Throttle spindle
4. Throttle-fixing screw
5. Idle-stop plate
8. Idle-adjustment screw
9. Spring
10. Throttle lever
11. Dust-proof ring
13. Spindle washer
15. Volume-control screw
17. Throttle-body fixing screw
19. Flange gasket
36. Spindle end nut
192. Intermediate lever
193a. Spacer
16. Gasket
62. Float (F)
66. Float-toggle spindle
70. Main jet (Gg)
73. Correction jet (a)
74. Pilot jet (g)
78. Pump inlet valve
92. Venturi-locating plug
93. Venturi-fixing screw
95. Venturi (K)
165. Accelerator-pump injector
166. Washer
267. Enrichment jet
32. Enrichment-valve cover screw
322. Enrichment-valve housing
65. Float-chamber gasket
115. Needle-valve washer
116. Needle valve
117. Fuel screen
118. Filter plug
119. Plug washer
124. Fuel line union
125. Union washer
126. Float-chamber screw
302. Automatic choke
306. Collar screw
307. Retaining collar
31. Accelerator-pump fixing screw
153. Pump diaphragm
154. Accelerator-pump cover
157. Diaphragm spring
159. Control rod spring
160. Pump control rod
161. Retaining washer
163. Adjustment nut
164. Locknut

Solex 32 DITA-3 carburetor.

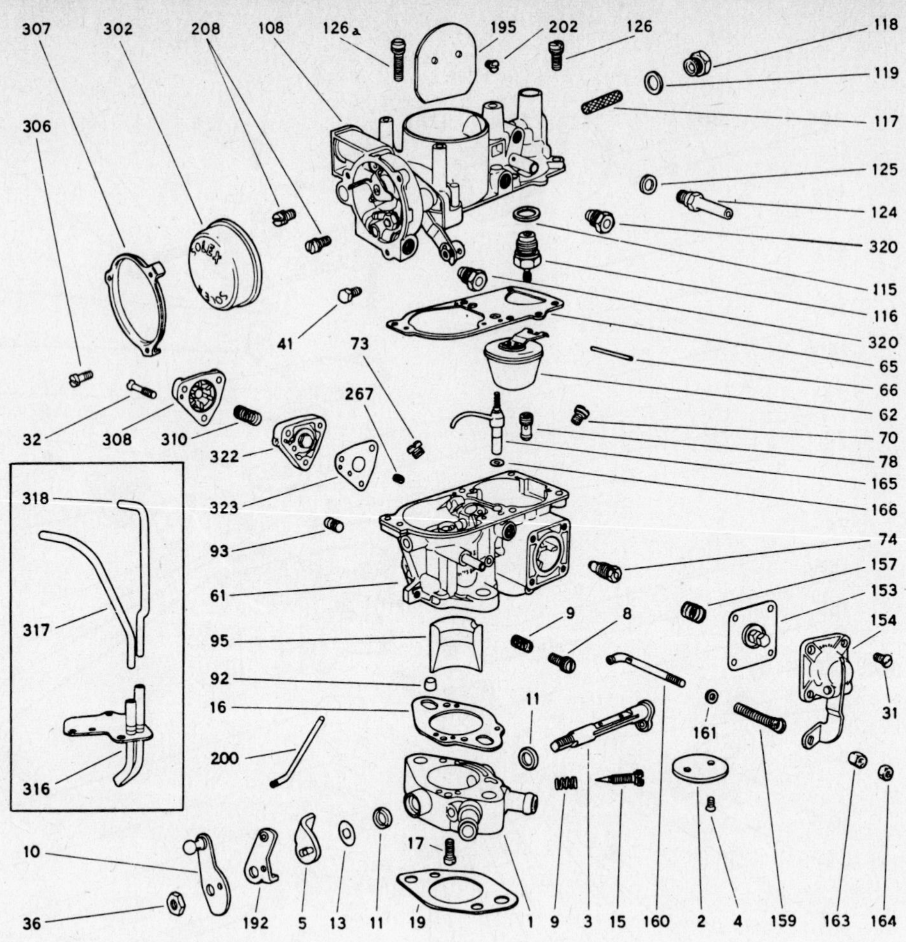

Solex 32 DISTA and Solex 32 PDIST carburetors. The PDIST has a pre-atomizer and set screw not shown.

within a specified mph speed range. It cannot be adjusted. However, it should be checked.

1. At the solenoid valve, pull back the clear plastic sleeve to bare a portion of the feed wire.

   Connect the alligator clip of the test lamp to the bare portion of the wire. Be very careful to keep the clip away from the solenoid valve body to prevent grounding which would damage the centrifugal switch when the ignition is turned on. Ground the other lead of the test lamp.
2. Secure the test lamp in a location where it can be seen easily from inside the car.
3. Start the engine and let it run until it reaches normal operating temperature. Check that the normal idle is within the specified range: 650 to 700 rpm.
4. Drive the car in second gear until it reaches approximately 25 mph. Remove your foot from the accelerator pedal and let the car decelerate. The test lamp should light up.
5. If the test lamp does not light up, accelerate to approximately 40 mph. Remove your foot from the accelerator pedal and apply the brakes very lightly to slow the engine down progressively until the test lamp lights up, and read the speed from the speedometer.

Fast Idle Adjustment

NOTE: A CO meter must be used to perform this adjustment.

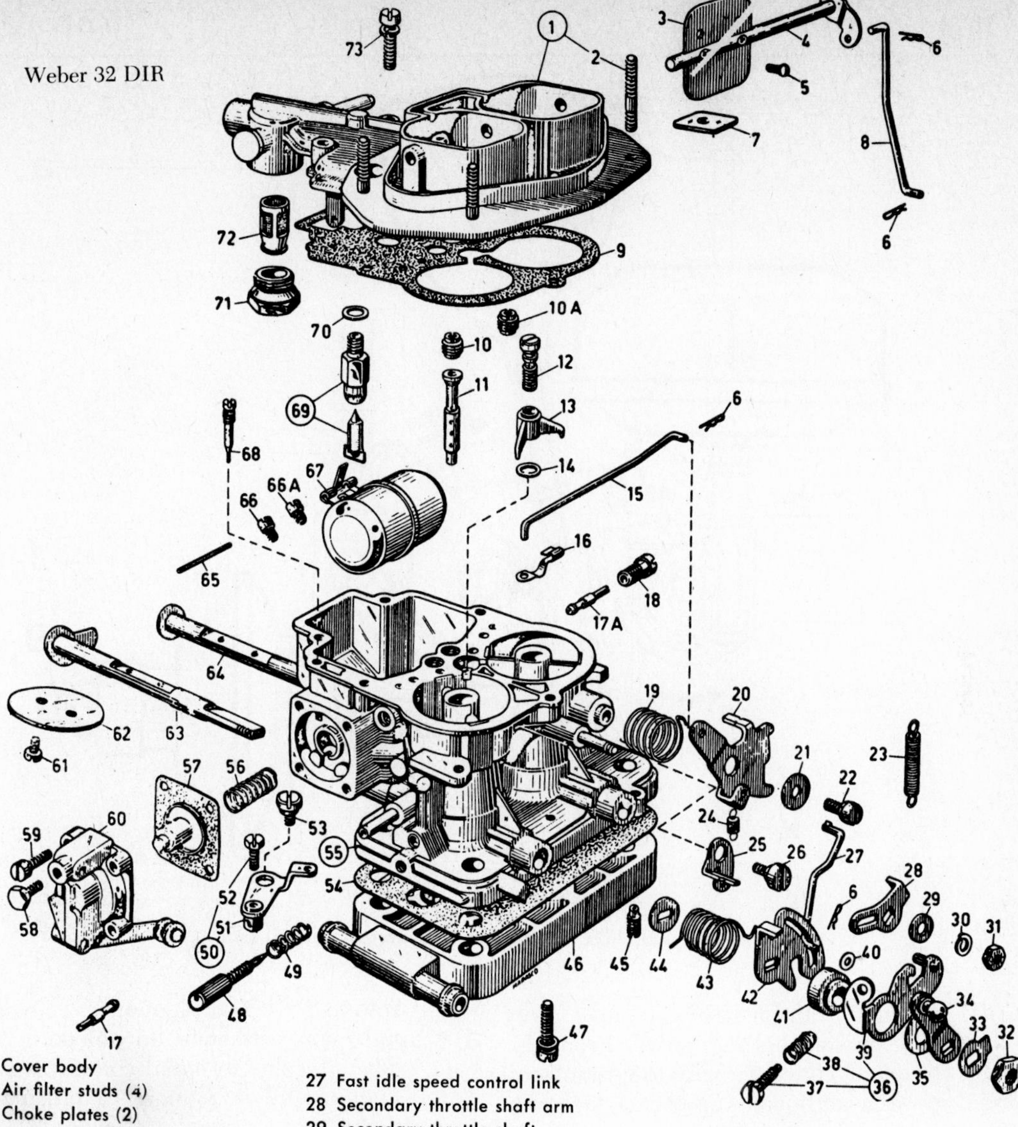

1 Cover body
2 Air filter studs (4)
3 Choke plates (2)
4 Choke plate shaft
5 Choke plate screws (4)
6 Hairpin clips (4)
7 Dust cover
8 Choke shaft link
9 Cover gasket
10 Primary correction jet
10a Secondary correction jet
11 Air/fuel mixture tube (2)
12 Accelerating pump nozzle screw
13 Accelerating pump nozzle
14 Accelerating pump nozzle seal
15 Choke cable link
16 Choke cable link clip
17 Primary idle jet
17a Secondary idle jet
18 Idle jet screw (2)
19 Choke control arm spring
20 Choke control arm
21 Choke control arm washer
22 Choke control arm screw
23 Secondary throttle control arm spring
24 Choke plate relief spring
25 Choke shaft link free arm
26 Choke shaft link free arm shoulder screw
27 Fast idle speed control link
28 Secondary throttle shaft arm
29 Secondary throttle shaft washer
30 Secondary throttle shaft lockwasher
31 Secondary throttle shaft nut
32 Primary throttle shaft nut
33 Primary throttle shaft locktab
34 Throttle control arm
35 Free arm spacer
36 Idle speed adjustment
37 Idle speed adjustment screw
38 Idle speed adjustment spring
39 Secondary throttle control arm
40 Fast idle speed control link washer
41 Secondary throttle control arm bushing
42 Fast idle and secondary throttle control plate
43 Primary throttle return spring
44 Primary throttle shaft spacer
45 Secondary throttle adjustment screw
46 Coolant circulation body
47 Coolant circulation body screws (2)
48 Idle mixture adjustment screw
49 Idle mixture adjustment spring
50 Choke cable arm
51 Choke cable adjustment
52 Choke cable adjustment screw
53 Choke cable arm shoulder screw
54 Main body gasket
55 Main body
56 Accelerating pump spring
57 Accelerating pump diaphragm assembly
58 Choke cable housing set screw
59 Accelerating pump cover screws (4)
60 Accelerating pump cover
61 Throttle plate screws (4)
62 Throttle plates (2)
63 Primary throttle shaft
64 Secondary throttle shaft
65 Float pin
66 Primary main jet
66A Secondary Main Jet
67 Float
68 Accelerating pump discharge metering screw
69 Needle valve assembly
70 Needle valve assembly seal
71 Inlet screen plug
72 Inlet screen
73 Cover body screws (5)

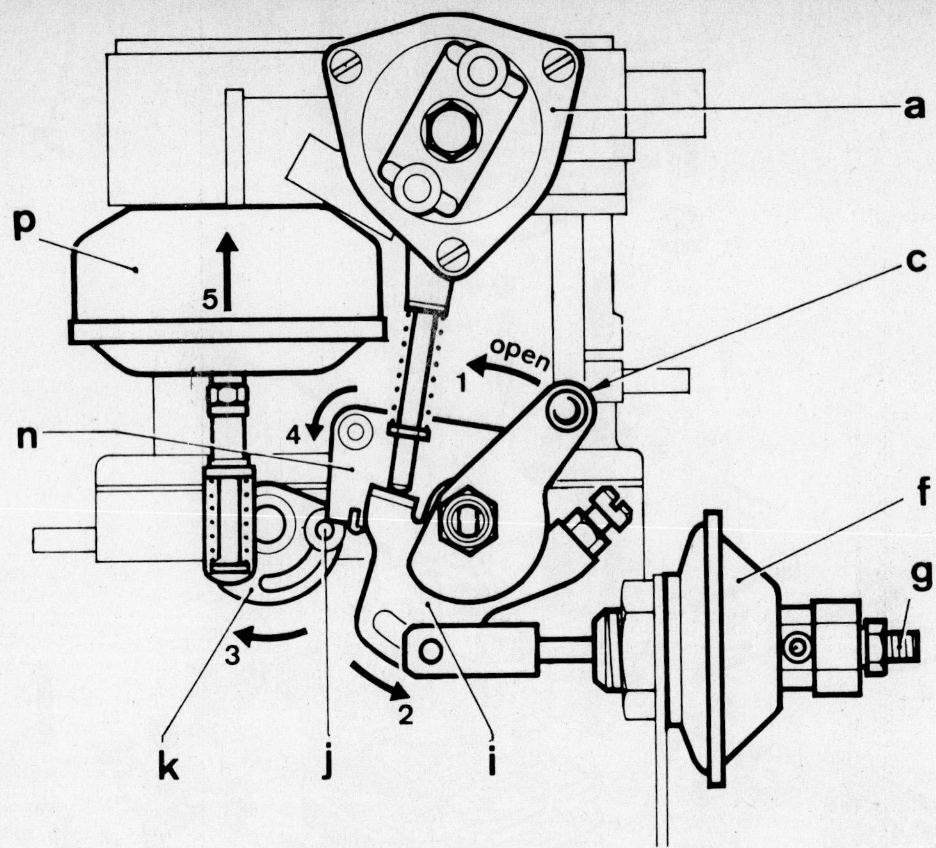

Accelerated idle system on carburetors since 1968.

1. Manual transmission: Remove grey wire on solenoid flap valve. From this terminal, connect a wire to ignition coil positive terminal. Connect a tachometer and refer to instructions below.

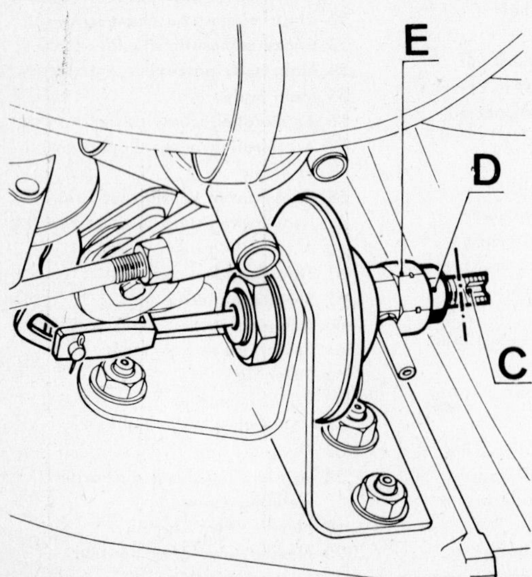

Adjust accelerated idle on DCS solenoid valve.

Automatic Transmissions: Remove pink wire attached to solenoid flap valve. To this terminal connect a wire and ground it. Connect a tachometer and refer to instructions below.

All Transmissions

2. Adjust screw C to give 1400-1500 rpm.
3. Check CO percentage. It may be ad-

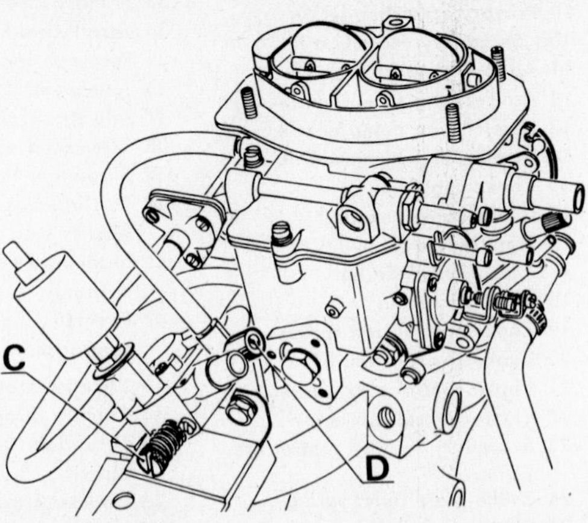

Adjusting fast idle, DCS equipped vehicles.

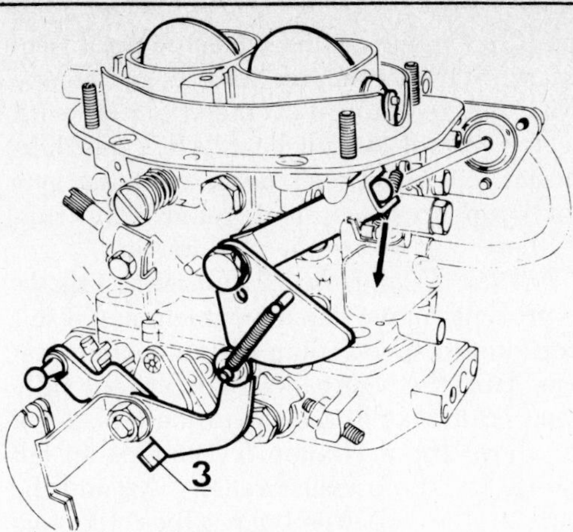

Adjusting initial throttle opening by moving lug (3)

justed to 2% or less by turning screw D.

4. After adjustment is complete, return appropriate wire to original position.

Initial Throttle Opening

Close choke flap. Place a #57 drill (.043″ diameter) between throttle and carburetor body bore. Adjust to drill size by moving lug.

Troubleshooting the Accelerated Idle System

Standard Transmission

If engine remains at accelerated idle when it should be at normal idle, connect a test lamp between the solenoid valve and ground.

1. *If test lamp does not light when transaxle is in neutral*, check the circuit through the neutral switch and correct the problem.
2. *If test lamp does not light when a gear is engaged*, check the circuit through the rpm switch and correct the problem.
3. *If test lamp lights*, disconnect vacuum line from the diaphragm and crimp the end of the line to prevent air from entering. If normal idle speed is restored, replace the solenoid valve. If normal idle speed *is not restored*, check the free play between the diaphragm rod and the throttle lever. Correct the free play to 1/16 in. by adjusting position of diaphragm bracket. Check the throttle cable, throttle linkage, and the accelerated idle linkage for binding.

If engine remains at normal idle when it should be at accelerated idle, engage a gear and disconnect the gray wire at the solenoid valve feed terminal.

1. *If accelerated idle is obtained*, reconnect the gray wire and disconnect one of the wires from the neutral switch. If accelerated idle is obtained, replace the neutral switch; if accelerated idle is not obtained, replace the rpm switch.
2. *If accelerated idle is not obtained*, connect the diaphragm unit directly with the intake manifold using a length of tubing that's in good condition. If accelerated idle is obtained, replace the vacuum hoses. If installation of new hoses does not restore accelerated idle, replace the solenoid valve. If accelerated idle is still not obtained, loosen the adjustment screw of the vacuum diaphragm unit. If this does not restore the accelerated idle, replace the diaphragm unit.

Automatic Transmission

If engine remains at accelerated idle when it should be at normal idle, shift transmission into neutral and connect a test lamp between the solenoid valve and ground.

1. *If test lamp does not light up*, check the continuity of the circuit controlled by the governor.
2. *If test lamp lights up*, complete the steps under 3 in the first part of the guide for a standard transmission.

If engine remains at normal idle when it should be at accelerated idle, raise the rear end of the car so the rear wheels clear the ground, secure the car in position, start the engine, press the city switch, push shift button No. 2, and have an assistant watch the vacuum diaphragm unit. Accelerate slowly until the speedometer indicates an approximate speed of 35 mph.

If the diaphragm rod does not come into play with the idle linkage, disconnect the gray wire from the solenoid valve feed terminal. If accelerated idle is obtained, replace the governor. If accelerated idle is not obtained, complete the steps under 2 in the second part of the guide for a standard transmission.

Cooling System

DRAINING AND FILLING

Due to the Renault cooling system being sealed, the following procedures must be followed. The Dauphine and Caravelle system can be easily drained if on a level surface by removing the radiator fill cap, the bleed (top) and drain (bottom) screws on the right side of the heater, the radiator drain tap at the bottom on the left side, and the engine block drain plug next to the pulley end of the generator.

When refilling the cooling system, leave the heater bleed screw open to avoid trapping pockets of air. Close the bleed screw when water comes out. Run the engine a few minutes to open the thermostat—the radiator will burp out air—and then top up the radiator. Drain the 8, the 10, the 12 and the 16 in the following manner. Leaving the radiator cap sealed, remove the *expansion chamber valve* and then the radiator *drain plug*. The fluid will run out slowly at first while the expansion chamber is draining. When the drain reaches a full flow the chamber is empty. Unseal and remove the radiator fill cap. Open the heater control lever on the dash to full heat and then open the bleed valve on the heater unit. The 16 heater bleed is on the firewall. Remove the engine drain plug. In addition, *on the 12 and 16 only*, open the carburetor bleed screw that is on the choke casing.

Fill the 8 system with all drain plugs tightened. First pour 1 1/2 quarts of coolant into the expansion chamber through the pressure valve opening. Screw in this valve. Next fill the radiator. If there is no bleed screw on the water pump, the upper radiator hose at the water pump can be removed to let trapped air escape. Start the engine and open the heater unit bleed screw (with heater control on full heat) until the air has escaped. Let the engine run until the thermostat opens (the radiator water will become turbulent and the upper hose will get warm). Top up the radiator and secure the cap. Stop the engine and seal the radiator cap.

To fill the 10 system, first fill the expansion chamber to the maximum level mark. Fit the valve to the chamber (air leakage will switch on the red warning light) and tighten the cap. Fill the radiator, removing the bleed screw on the water pump if necessary. Start the engine and let air escape from the radiator unit bleed screw with heater control on full heat. After the thermostat opens (upper radiator hose gets hot), top up the system, remove the funnel-hose, and secure the radiator cap.

Fill the 16 and the 12 system as follows to prevent engine damage which may result from improper bleeding of the cooling system. Turn the heat control knob to the fully open position. Fill the expansion tank 1 1/4 in. above the maximum level mark. Install the gasket, the pressure relief valve and the cap on the expansion jar. Open the two bleed screws and fill the radiator. When the radiator is full, clamp the two hoses as close as possible to the water pump. Run the engine at fast idle (1500 rpm) and add coolant mixture as necessary to keep the radiator full. When the coolant runs through the bleeder screws in a continuous stream free from air, close the bleeder screws. From then on, do not open them. Remove the hose clamps, fill the radiator, and install the radiator cap. When the radiator fan starts running, stop the engine. When the engine has cooled down, check the coolant level in the expansion jar.

RADIATOR REMOVAL

Disconnect battery and drain cooling system. To remove the radiator, the metal panel that supports it must be removed. Disconnect the air filter intake hose, and lower radiator hose at the tail light wires from the terminal block. Remove the bolts and screws along both sides and across the bottom of the panel, tilt the panel toward the rear and lift it out. On the 12 and 16, remove the spare tire. Disconnect all radiator hoses. Disconnect the fan motor and temperature switch wires. Extract the radiator bolts and remove radiator. The radiator is easily unbolted from the panel. Remove the radiator from the panel with the hose and valve of the expansion chamber (10). The 8 expansion chamber can be unbolted or its hose can be removed from the radiator.

The expansion chamber can be removed from the car without draining the cooling system. Pinch flat the hose leading to the chamber. Then unscrew the cap (10) or the hose at the chamber (8). Unbolt and remove the chamber. When refitting the chamber, tighten the bolts until the spring becomes coil-bound (10 only), then loosen it by one turn. Fill the expansion chamber up to the maximum level mark. The 8 chamber requires 1 1/2 quarts. Fit the valve and tighten the cap. On the 8, attach hose. On other models, unpinch the hose from the radiator.

WATER PUMP REMOVAL

The water pump opens into two housings, the pump body and the cover assembly. The cover assembly was separately replaceable for the 8, but now, for all models, the entire pump is replaced. Before fitting a new gasket between the housings, carefully clean the gasket flanges. In order to remove the water pump, disconnect the battery and drain cooling system. The radiator panel must be tilted back out of the way. Use the steps in the previous section. In addition, disconnect the water hose to the carburetor at the pump, and the two heater hoses at the pump. If necessary, remove the alternator belt. Remove the fan belt tensioner from the water pump, the fan, the pulley, and the belt. Remove the bolts securing the water pump and jar it loose with a plastic or rubber mallet.

To replace pump, reverse removal procedure.

Water Pump Overhaul

To dismantle the water pump, remove the plate, unlock and unscrew the shaft nut, remove the pulley and take out the key, and push out the shaft on a press. Remove the bearing circlip. Apply pressure to the bearing at the pulley end. Remove the spacer and the second circlip. Press out the bearing at the impeller end and put aside the shaft retaining snap-ring. Push out the sealing ring. Clean and check all parts. A repair kit is available.

When assembling pump follow the numbered steps shown, fill the body with grease and tighten the shaft nut to 15 ft. lbs.

Fan Belt Tensioner

To disassemble the fan belt tensioner, remove the circlip and take off the pulley. Remove the circlip at the end of the shaft. Push off the bearings with a small press or puller. Clean and inspect all parts. When assembling tensioner, follow the numbered

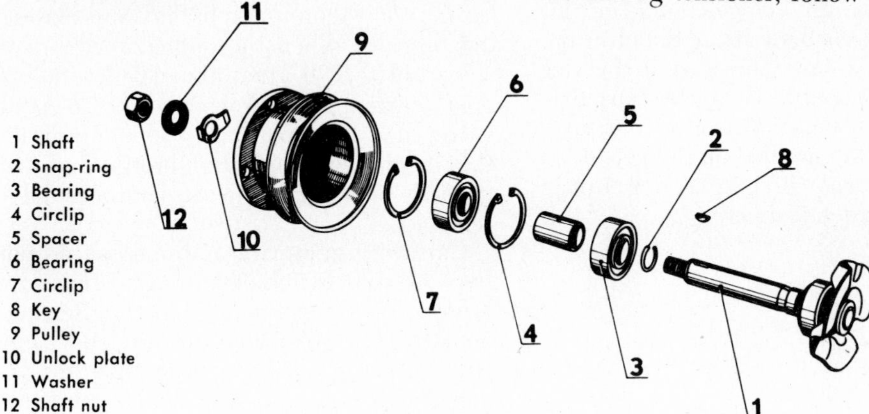

Dauphine water pump.

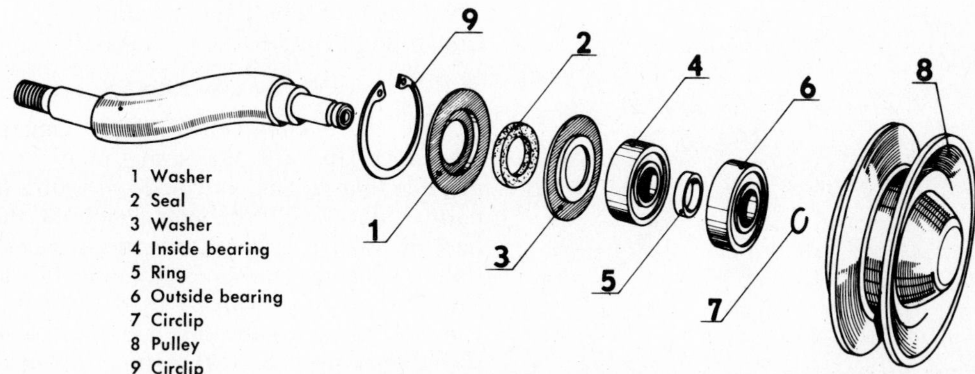

Dauphine fan-belt tensioner.

steps down, fitting the inside bearing with the seal towards the felt and the outside bearing with the seal towards the pulley. Place grease between the bearings.

Proper belt tension is just enough to keep belt snug without slippage, or 1/2″ maximum deflection.

Thermostat

The thermostat is positioned on the water pump. When tightening the radiator hose over the thermostat, screw ends of wire clamp to within 1/4 inch of each other.

The thermostat opening temperature can be checked by placing the thermostat in a pan of water with a thermometer having a high range. Slowly heat the water while checking the thermostat valve movement.

Engine

EMISSION CONTROL SYSTEM (DCS)

Since 1968, Renault, in compliance with Federal law, has installed an exhaust emission system on all vehicles sold in this country. These changes are outlined in detail in this section and necessary carburetor adjustments are outlined in the Fuel System section. All emission control measures listed may not be installed on the vehicle in question; however, 1971-72 models utilize all components detailed here.

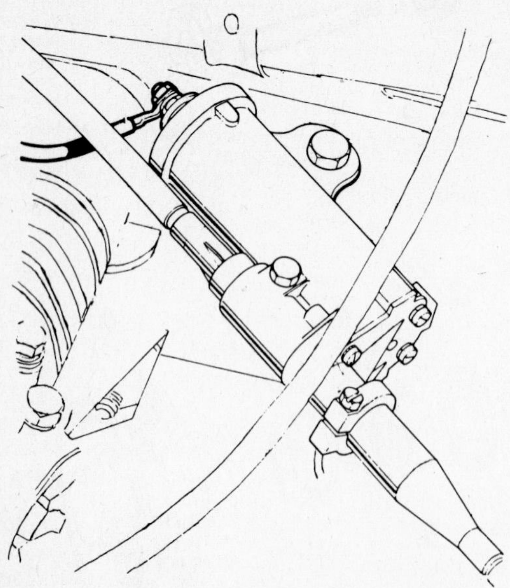

Centrifugal (RPM) switch

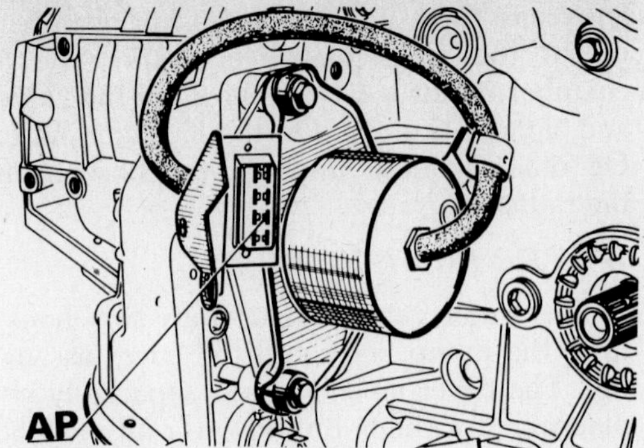

The computer unit (AP), or transmission governor switch

The Centrifugal (rpm) Switch and the Computer Unit

The rpm switch (on manual transmission), located on the back panel to the left of the radiator, is basically a small electronic tachometer which reads the engine rpm and closes and opens a set of contact points according to engine rpm. The contact points close when the engine slows down to 1500-1400 rpm. When the points are closed, current flows to the solenoid valve, thereby shutting off the vacuum, releasing the vacuum diaphragm, and closing the throttle. When the engine speed rises above 1450-1530 rpm, the contact points open, current stops flowing to the solenoid valve, the valve opens, the vacuum pulls on the diaphragm, and the throttle remains partially open when the accelerator pedal is released.

Cars with automatic transmission do not have an rpm switch. The transmission governor, called a *computer unit* by Renault, actuates the solenoid valve in the same way. However, the governor operates according to road speed, which requires actual movement of the wheels when checking the solenoid.

The Neutral Switch and Vacuum Controlled Progressive Linkage

Neutral Switch

Since the opening range of the contact points overlaps with the closing range, it is possible that an engine would not return to normal idle. To prevent this condition, the neutral switch is fitted to the standard transmission (not needed on automatic) to keep the solenoid valve closed when the transaxle is in neutral. When the driver shifts to neutral the carburetor is freed to return to normal idle.

Vacuum Controlled Progressive Linkage

The secondary barrel of the carburetor is actuated by another vacuum diaphragm unit; the vacuum which moves the lung is taken from the venturis of the two barrels. As rpm increases, the greater vacuum smoothly opens the second barrel.

The amount the secondary barrel opens is determined by how far the throttle lever, bearing against the intermediate plate, releases the stop pin on the secondary throttle lever. When the 1st throttle is wide open, the second throttle can be fully opened by the vacuum lung.

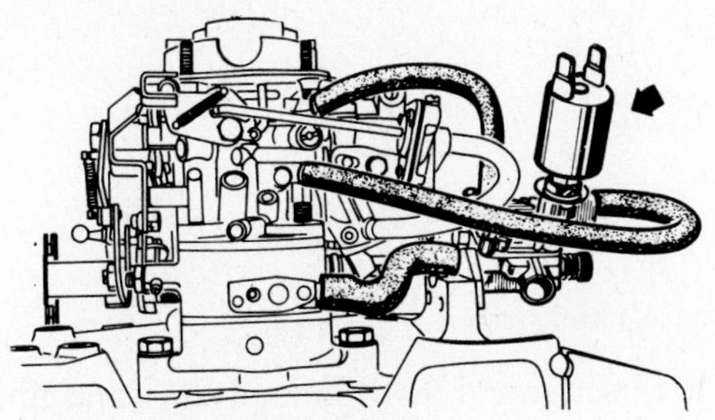

The decelerator (arrow)

The Decelerator

Located on the intake manifold and connected to the carburetor, the decelerator supplies additional air/fuel to the engine when the throttle is closed. It is operated by a solenoid flap valve. When vacuum in the manifold becomes strong enough to move a small integral diaphragm, the solenoid flap valve is opened. When the decelerator obtains air/fuel mixture, it is sucked into the throttle butterfly underside by intake manifold vacuum. This produces a condition of fast idling.

When vehicle speed reaches 15-16 mph, the rpm switch contacts open. No vacuum is then supplied to the decelerator diaphragm. Springs return all components to the normally closed position and the engine returns to a standard idle condition.

Fuel Vapor Recirculation System

Basically, this circuit is a sealed fuel system. It allows no fuel vapor to escape into the atmosphere. It consists of an air tight fuel filler cap, an expansion reservoir, an activated charcoal accumulator, and the necessary connective piping.

In operation, fuel (either liquid or vapor) stored either in the accumulator or expansion chamber is vented to the carburetor instead of the outside. It is controlled by a valve on the carburetor float chamber top.

Air Intake Preheating System

This system allows both fresh and heated air to flow into the carburetor. It is controlled by a lever located on the filter front. In temperatures consistently above 50°, move the lever to high position to allow outside air to enter the air cleaner. When temperatures are below 50°, do the opposite to allow preheated air from the exhaust manifold area to flow into the carburetor.

This adjustment lessens emissions by supplying air to the engine at a more or less even temperature. This, in turn, allows the

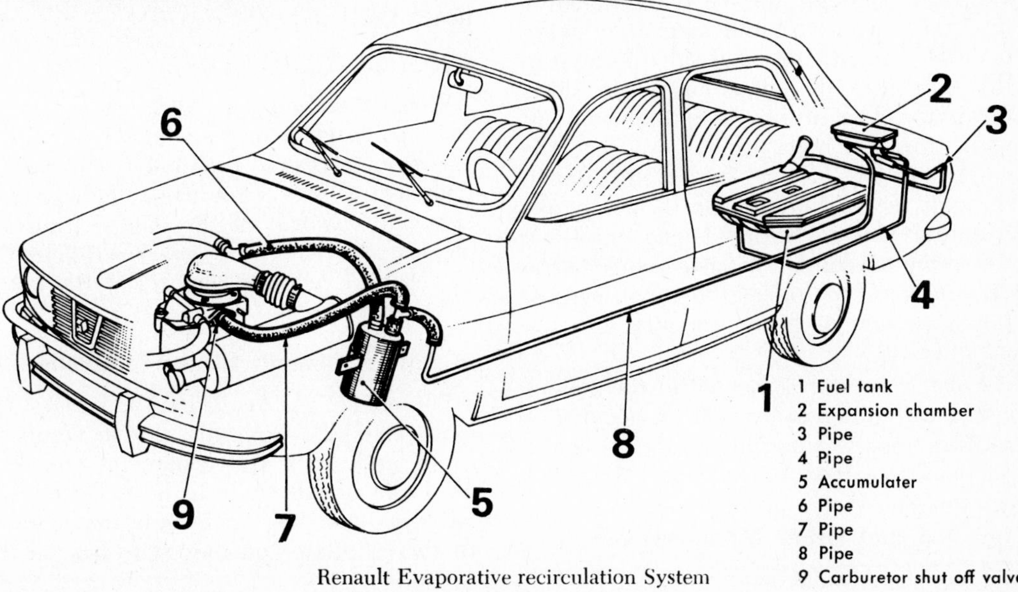

Renault Evaporative recirculation System

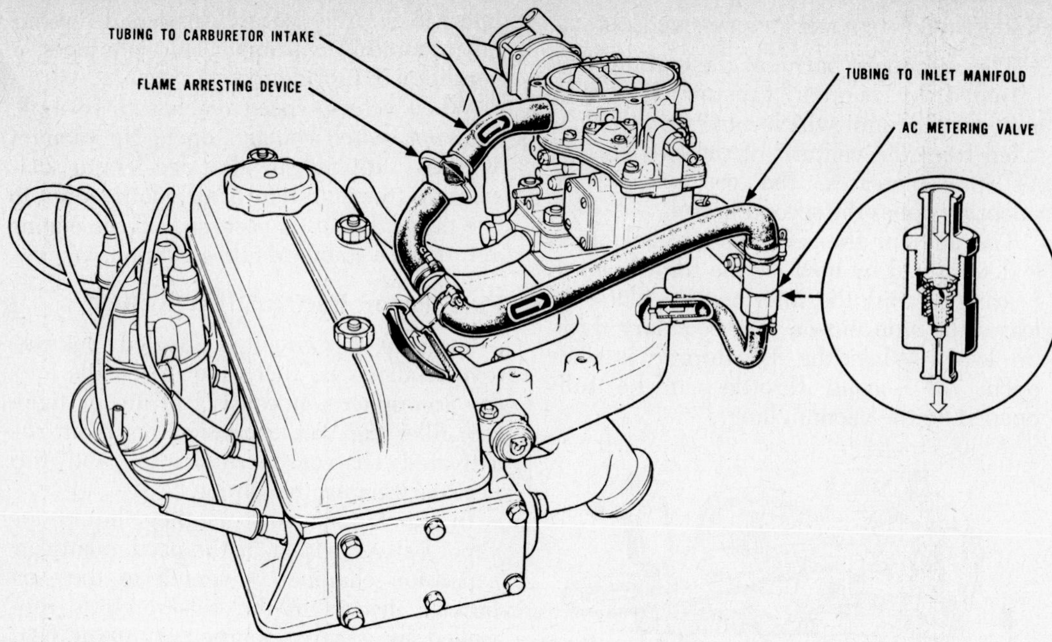

Crankcase (PCV) emission control system

carburetor to be set leaner. Heated air mixes with fuel in a more even manner; thereby improving combustion efficiency.

Because of the above modifications, there exists the possibility of the engine running on, or dieseling, after the ignition is switched off. To prevent this, a vacuum reservoir is fitted between the vacuum diaphragm (refer to decelerator) and the solenoid flap valve. This chokes the engine air supply when the ignition is turned off.

PCV Valve

Crankcase fumes are drawn from the crankcase through the rocker arm cover into the carburetor and into the intake manifold. An AC metering valve located in the tubing to the intake manifold slows down the flow of fumes to the manifold while there is high vacuum, so that the major portion of the fumes are drawn through the carburetor. But when intake manifold vacuum drops (open throttle), the spring tension in the valve overrides the vacuum and fully opens the valve, permitting full flow of fumes directly into the manifold.

A flame arrestor is located in the tubing to the carburetor to prevent an accidental backfire from flashing through the tubing to the crankcase. The AC valve and the flame arrestor must be cleaned periodically.

Ignition and Other Modifications

Since the introduction of emission laws, it has been found that spark advance and timing has a large effect on exhaust emissions. Consequently, timing has been retarded and the spark advance curve comes in more slowly and peaks later. While this helps emissions, it causes some power loss.

In many cases, the pistons and intake manifold have been redesigned for smoother flow and burning of the air/fuel mixture. Along with this, Renault uses a 2 barrel carburetor with small primaries and large secondaries. This allows the engine to run leaner mixtures in the lower speed ranges while retaining the second barrel for heavy loads and higher speeds.

ENGINE REMOVAL

Renault engines can be serviced, for the most part, while in place in the car body. However, access to the clutch requires detachment of the engine from the transmission and removal of the engine from the chassis. Servicing the gearbox-differential (transaxle) requires removal of the entire powerplant.

Renault 8, Renault 10, and Caravelle

Disconnect one lead from the battery, remove the jack from the engine compartment, and drain the cooling system. Remove the air filter with its hose. Detach the lower radiator hose and the heater hoses at the water pump and the upper hose at the radiator.

The radiator supporting panel must be removed. Mark the position of the electrical leads into and out of the connection block on the panel and remove these leads. Unscrew the panel along both sides and across the bottom. Remove it.

On the right side of the engine, disconnect the fuel line at the pump, the oil pressure switch lead at the sensor near the timing chain cover, and the battery input lead at the ignition coil. Loosen the heater hose retaining clips and slip out the hoses. A lifting frame is made to bolt to opposite ends of the cylinder head. If this or a similar attachment is to be used, remove the rocker arm cover.

On the left side of the engine, disconnect the temperature switch lead from the end of the block, the throttle cable at the cotter pin, the starter and solenoid leads, and the generator leads. If the transmission is automatic, remove the governor linkage from the carburetor and the decelerator lead from its solenoid and retaining clips.

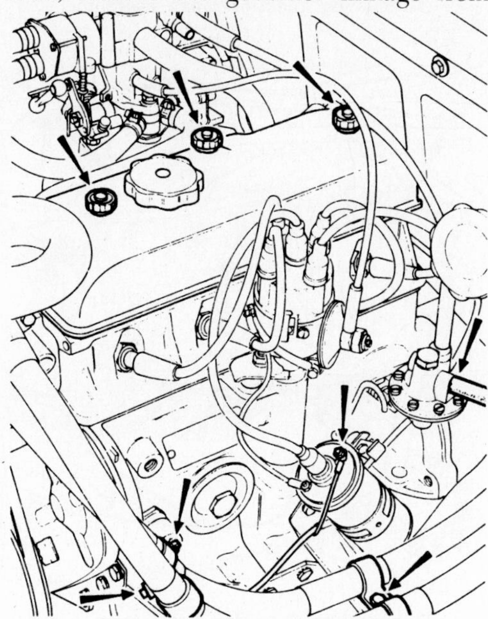

Right side of engine, R-8 and R-10.

Unbolt the exhaust pipe at the manifold and remove the muffler from the engine and chassis. Disconnect the splash pans from the chassis. The two bolts at each side that also attach the bumper support need only to be loosened so that the splash pans can be lifted over and out. Removal of the four bolts holding the pans to the one rigid support across the back may not be necessary.

To separate the engine from the bell housing, remove the three starter bolts; unlock and remove the nuts and bolts which secure the engine to the clutch housing (the upper bolts cannot fully come out because of the firewall); and remove the clutch protection plate and stiffening bar from underneath.

If either of the engine studs comes out as the nut is being unscrewed, be sure to remove the nut from the stud and tighten the stud into the engine housing (both studs have protective sleeves that fit across the joint) before reassembling the two parts.

Carefully secure a sling around the engine (do not press against the manifold) and take the weight off the mounts with a hoist. Remove the four bolts securing the engine crossmember. Free the engine toward the rear and remove it through the top or bottom.

To remove the complete powerplant (not loosening the starter or engine from the bell housing) follow the steps below.

Loosen the rear wheel nuts, then jack up the car and set it on trestles, and remove the loosened wheels. Disconnect the handbrake cable, the control bar to the chassis, and the clutch cable at the clutch fork. Free the clutch adjustment fitting from the protective rubber tube on gearbox type 330. On gearboxes 318 and 325, there is a hollow screw and collar.

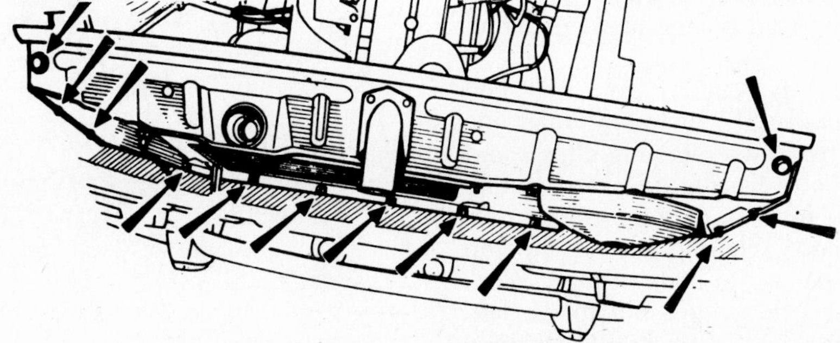

Attachment points of radiator-supporting panel.

If removing powerplant with automatic transmission, unfasten and unplug the control harnesses from the actuator and solenoid (detach the harnesses from their securing bracket), unscrew the large bolt on the brush holder of the magnetic coupler (inside the coupler bottom shield), and pull the holder out.

Disconnect the gear shift link, the speedometer drive cable, and the input line of brake pressure distributor. Free the accelerator cable from its bracket on the differential and detach the transmission ground strap.

Support the engine, transmission and axles. Remove the axle override pads and the bolts next to those that hold the rear end crossmember to the chassis rails. Unbolt the engine crossmember from its mounts. Lower the powerplant. Separate the engine from the transaxle assembly.

Dauphine

Disconnect one lead from the battery, remove the jack from the engine compartment, and drain the cooling system. Remove the air filter with its hose. Unbolt the exhaust pipe at the manifold. Disconnect the accelerator cable and unhook the return spring. Remove the generator leads, the temperature switch lead, and the upper water hose at the water pump (not necessary if removing entire powerplant). If the transmission is automatic, remove the governor linkage from the carburetor and the decelerator lead from its solenoid and retaining clips. Unbolt the muffler from the engine and chassis. Disconnect the starter cables. Detach the heater leads and the two heater hoses at the water pump. Remove the heater assembly from the body where held by three nuts. Remove the radiator cardboard and the engine splash pans.

Disconnect the oil pressure switch lead and the ignition coil input lead (do not ground ignition lead if transmission is automatic).

To separate the engine from the bell housing, disconnect the fuel pump inlet line (extract line from two retaining clips), and the lower radiator hose at the water pump.

Remove the lower radiator securing nuts and the radiator securing bar at the top (1965 model secures to body at top). Work radiator around the engine out to the left. Unlock and remove the four nuts attaching the engine to the bell housing. Unscrew the

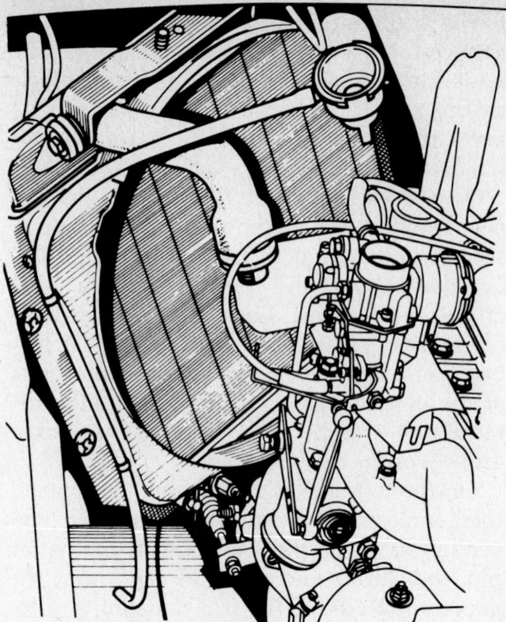

Removing radiator from Dauphine.

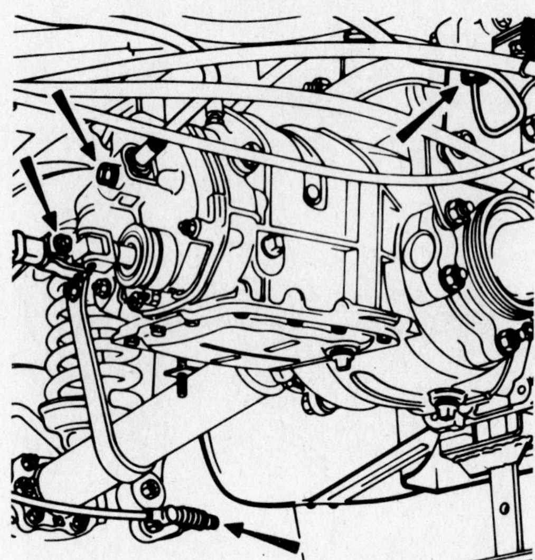

Detaching Dauphine trans-axle from chassis.

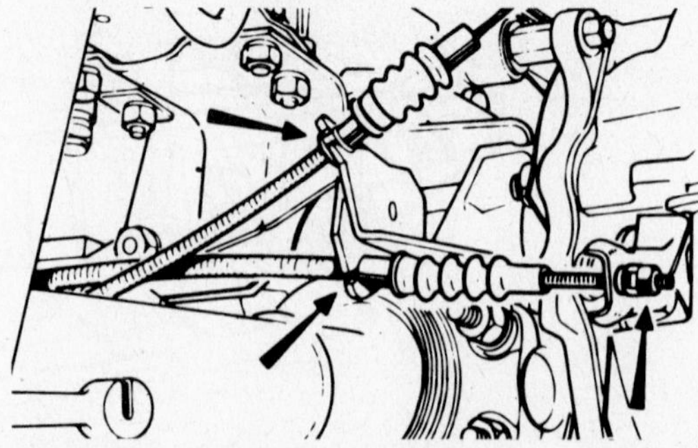

Detaching Dauphine clutch and accelerator cables.

three bolts which secure the oil pan to the gearbox, removing the stiffener plate.

Attach a hoist to the block and take the engine weight off of the mounts. Unbolt the engine crossmember from the chassis. Carefully pull the engine toward the rear to free it from the transmission, and lift it out.

To remove the complete powerplant, make the disconnection steps up through the ignition coil input lead, except for the upper radiator hose which is not removed. In addition, remove the two securing bolts to the gas tank fill pipe.

Disconnect the handbrake cables (at the wheels), the gearshift link, the input line from the brake pressure limiting valve, and the clutch cable at the withdrawal fork. Push out the clutch and accelerator cables from their brackets.

If removing powerplant with automatic transmission, unfasten and unplug the control harnesses from the actuator and solenoid (detach the harnesses from their securing bracket), unscrew the large bolt on the brush holder of the magnetic coupler (inside the coupler bottom shield), pull the holder down and out of the coupler.

Position a jack under the powerplant. Unbolt the rear suspension crossmember from the chassis rails. Unbolt the engine crossmember at the chassis mounts. Lower the powerplant carefully.

Renault 12

The engine may be removed without the transmission. Remove the hood and disconnect the battery. Lift off the air cleaner and drain the cooling system. Remove the radiator, starter, and camshaft pulley drive belt. Remove the fan belt. Remove top bolt (only) holding engine/transmission assembly together. While pushing engine backward with a breaker bar, remove the fan and pulley. Disconnect the exhaust pipe at the exhaust manifold and at the transmission rear crossmember. Remove clutch shield. Fit hoist to engine and take weight off mounting bolts. On the engine right-side, remove side mounting pad bolts and three bolts on side member. Perform a similar operation on the left side. Slightly raise engine and remove bolts from the right and left mounting brackets. Raise engine until transmission top touches underside of steering crossmember. At this time, firmly support transmission with appropriate tool. Remove the engine/transmission holding bolts. Pull engine forward and remove from vehicle.

To install engine, reverse removal procedure. Lubricate clutch splines with grease and use Loctite on crankshaft pulley retaining bolt.

Renault 16

The engine and gearbox must be removed together. Disconnect the battery. Remove the spare wheel. Drain the cooling system and gearbox. Remove the front hood retaining cable so the hood can be raised to its maximum.

Remove the fan and its casing, the air filter and the spare wheel support. Disconnect the alternator leads, the fuel inlet line at the pump, the fuel return pipe to the tank, the electrical input lead at the ignition coil, and the accelerator spring and link. Remove the accelerator cable idle lever. Disconnect the heater radiator hoses at the water pump, the lead from the temperature switch on the cylinder head, and the starter leads. Remove the exhaust pipe clamp and the upper bolt on the starter.

Turn the steering wheel to the right and disconnect the right-hand link from the adjustable end fitting. Next turn the wheel to the left to disconnect the left link. Remove the two bolts which secure the steering flexible coupling to the steering column. Remove the battery ground strap from the engine. Disconnect the oil pressure switch lead. Unbolt the steering crossmember. Remove the steering assembly by turning the steering to lock at the right. Free the left-hand end of the assembly toward the front.

Disconnect the speedometer drive cable and the link at the gearshift lever. Remove the two bolts that secure the gearshift to the gearbox and pull back the control. Hook it to the battery support.

Remove the front gearbox rubber mount and its bracket. Push out the roll pins in the axle shafts (next to the gearbox housing) with a drift. Fit an axle shaft retaining tool to prevent damaging the joint. Place a jack between the gearbox and the left-hand side chassis member. Jack the axle shaft free from the pinion. Disconnect the clutch cable, free the bellows and push out the end of the cable from the end stop.

Place the jack on the right-hand side. Again push the gearbox over to free the axle shaft from the pinion.

After taking the weight of the powerplant by a sling, remove the engine side mounting bolts. Sling the transmission, too, and lift the powerplant from the body.

Do not place lifting load on the engine manifold or on the cylinder head bolts. Sling can be bolted to engine at bell housing above the starter on one side and where the ground cable attaches to the cylinder block on the distributor side. The gearbox can be hooked or bolted through the hole provided on the top.

Install the powerplant in the body in reverse order to removal, but noting the following: lightly grease the clutch shaft splines; grease the pinion splines and align the pin hole in one of the splines in the axle shaft with that on the top of one of the splines of the pinion.

INTAKE/EXHAUST MANIFOLD REMOVAL

Non–Emission Controlled Vehicles

Be sure engine is totally cold before proceeding.

1. Disconnect battery.
2. Disconnect accelerator linkage and spring.
3. Remove air cleaner and carburetor.
4. Disconnect the exhaust pipe and clamp.
5. Remove manifold nuts and lift off manifold.
6. To install manifold, reverse removal procedures. Start engine and raise to operating temperature. Shut off and allow to cool for 50 minutes. Check nut torque.

Emission Controlled Vehicles

Be sure engine is totally cold before proceeding.

1. Disconnect battery.
2. Remove air filter and accelerator linkage.
3. Clamp manifold water hoses and remove. Be sure not to spill coolant over engine.
4. Disconnect PCV, fuel, vacuum, and emission control hoses.
5. Disconnect choke control, decelerator, and computer unit cables.
6. Disconnect exhaust pipe from manifold.
7. Remove warm air breathing system.
8. Remove timing cover bracket (if so equipped).
9. Remove manifold bolts and lift off manifold.
10. To install manifold, reverse removal procedure.

CYLINDER HEAD REMOVAL

Renault 8, Dauphine, Caravelle, and Renault 10 (To Engine No. 323 500)

Disconnect battery; drain cooling system; remove air filter and intake hose; unbolt the exhaust pipe at the manifold; disconnect the accelerator cable and temperature switch lead; detach lower radiator hose at water pump and upper hose at radiator; unfasten both heater hoses at pump. On 8 or 10, unbolt radiator panel and pull it rearward. Remove the fan belt tensioner and the belt.

Remove the fuel and vacuum pipes from the carburetor, the coil and spark plug leads, and the distributor input lead. Take off the distributor and the rocker cover. Remove the intake/exhaust manifold.

Unscrew the cylinder head bolts, slightly lift the head (except 10 since 1968) and remove the pushrods. Keep them in order. Lift off the head and take out the gasket. Clean the gasket face on the cylinder block and screw bolts with large washers into the block to hold the cylinder sleeves in place.

On Dauphine, disconnect the radiator support. Removal of the radiator is not necessary.

Renault 10 (from Engine No. 323 500), Renault 12 and Renault 16

To remove the 16 head, disconnect the battery, remove the spare wheel, drain the cooling system, and remove the air filter, distributor and alternator. Disconnect the heater hoses and radiator hoses at the water pump. Remove the outer flange on the camshaft pulley. Take off the drive belts to the pump and alternator. Remove the crankcase emission valve and hose, the fuel and vacuum pipes at the carburetor. Disconnect the temperature switch lead, the accelerator link, the coil input wire. Remove the exhaust pipe from the manifold, the rocker cover, the rocker assembly, and the pushrods (keep them in order). On the 12, remove the side crossmember to allow the exhaust pipe to drop as far down as possible.

For both the 16 and 10, the head gasket sticks to all parts it touches—*do not lift the cylinder head.* Instead, remove all of the head bolts except for the center bolt on the distributor side. Leave this in place as a pivot and to prevent the head from rising. Tap the ends of the head with a plastic mallet to move it off the cylinder block as shown. Remove the center bolt and gently lift the head, removing the tappets in order. Do not scrape the gasket faces; use a trichlorethylene solvent to remove the remaining gasket material.

CYLINDER HEAD INSTALLATION

Dauphine, R-8, and Caravelle

Remove the bolts that retain the cylinder sleeves. Fit the head gasket dry with the crimped edges towards the block. Fit the head and install the pushrods in the proper position. Tighten the head bolts in the correct order to the specified torque. Adjust the valve clearance as specified. Install the remaining parts in the reverse order of disassembly. After 600 miles, check cylinder head torque. Cylinder head bolts are to be loosened by a quarter turn before being finally torqued.

R-10 and R-16

To install the R-10 and R-16 cylinder head, two special tools or suitable substitutes are required. Two dowels that are the size of a bolt but without a head are needed to position the gasket and head. A second U type positioning tool attaches to the front side of the cylinder block.

Fit the head gasket with sealer over the two special dowels positioned on the block as shown. Once it touches the block it cannot be moved; discard an incorrectly positioned gasket. Fit the tappet compartment rubber gasket, avoiding any overlap with the head gasket at the ends. Place the tappets in the head and tap them lightly into position. Check the distributor drive pinion for correct position. Position the cylinder head, lowering it slowly to the block. Before it touches the gasket, place the manifold face against the two lugs of the U type

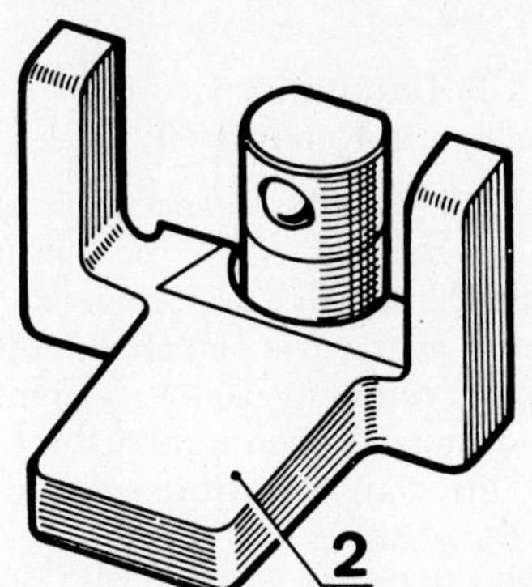

Renault 10 and Renault 16 head U tool positioner

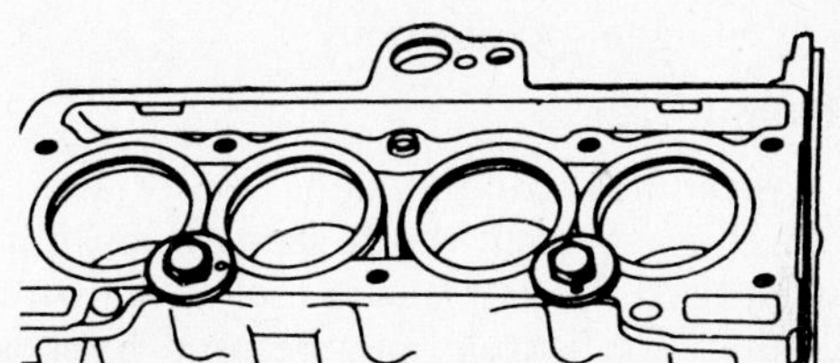

Hold cylinder sleeves in place by screwing bolts with large washers into the head.

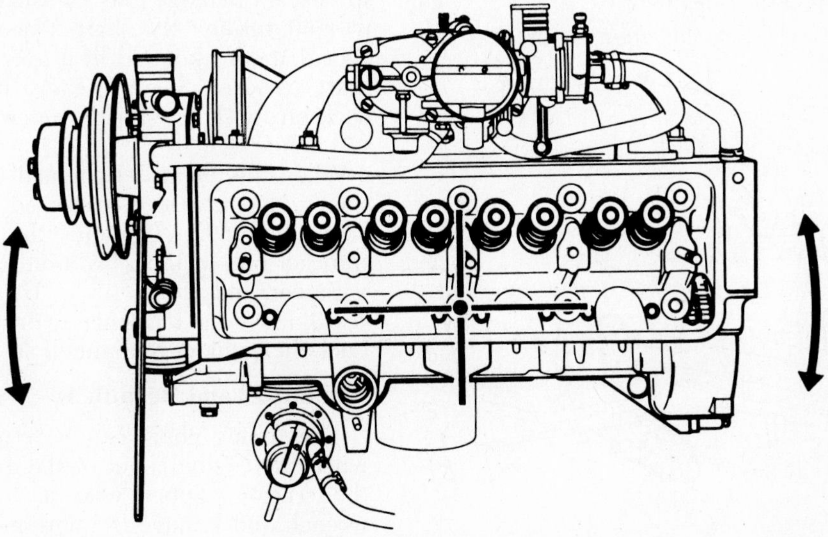

Break gasket seal on R-10 and R-16 cylinder heads by rotating head so the cylinder sleeves are not dislodged.

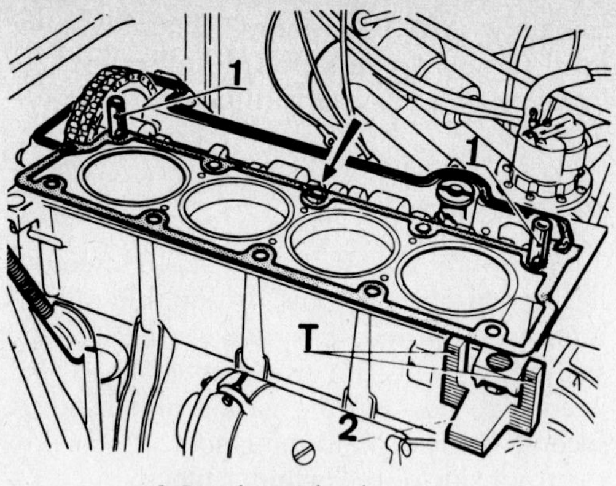

Renault 10 and Renault 16 special tool positioning

tool installed as shown. Seat the head. Remove both special tools. Screw the lightly oiled head bolts in evenly. Torque bolts in two stages to 55 ft. lbs. Adjust valves to specified lash. Bring engine to operating temperature and allow to cool for 50 minutes. Loosen head bolts one quarter turn and torque as specified. Again check valve lash. After 300 miles, check head bolt torque by loosening one quarter turn and tightening to specifications.

Renault 12

Procedures are the same as for the 10 and 16 except that the U-shaped positioner is not used. In its place, a tool as shown or a suitable substitute may be used for positioning purposes. The head gasket is fitted dry.

VALVE ADJUSTMENT

Adjust valves cold, after engine has not been run a few hours. Move engine by hand to open each of the exhaust valves in turn.

Open valve	*Adjust*
Exhaust 1	I-3, E-4
Exhaust 3	I-4, E-2
Exhaust 4	I-2, E-1
Exhaust 2	I-1, E-3

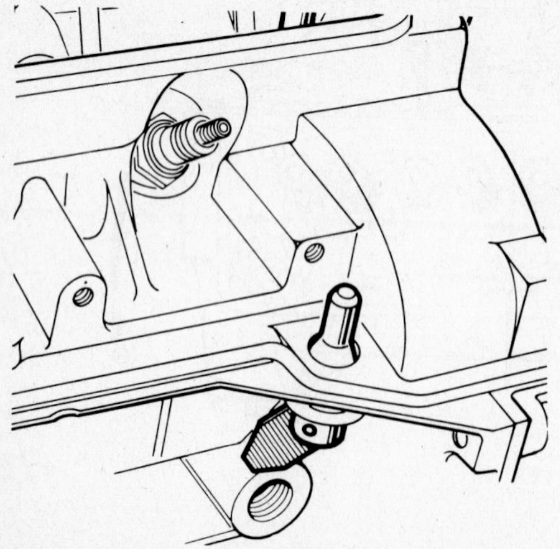

Renault 12 installation special tool location

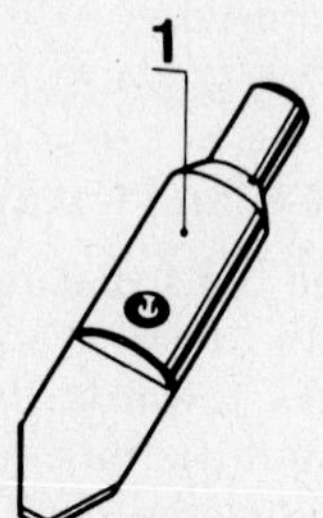

Renault 12 head installation positioning tool

TIMING CHAIN AND TIMING GEARS

Renault 8, Dauphine, Caravelle, and Renault 10

The timing chain is accessible with the engine in the car after the oil pan and the crankshaft pulley are removed. Remove the timing gear cover. Unlock and unscrew the slipper retaining screw (3 mm Allen) in the tensioner. Then unbolt the tensioner. Unbolt the camshaft sprocket and remove it with the chain.

Install the timing chain with the two reference marks towards each other and along a line passing through the centers of both sprockets. Remove the camshaft sprocket without turning the shaft. Place the chain over that sprocket and fit it over the crankshaft sprocket. Slip the camshaft sprocket back on its shaft with the reference marks still in line.

When the chain is tightened by the tensioner, the reference marks no longer appear aligned. Tighten the camshaft sprocket bolt to 15 ft. lbs. Bolt on the chain tensioner and thrust plate. Use the Allen key to move the tensioner against the chain. Lock the cylinder retaining bolt.

Renault 12 and Renault 16

The timing chain can be removed only when the engine is out of the car. Back off the tension slipper with a 3 mm Allen wrench and remove the tensioner. Remove the crankshaft sprocket bolt and the chain guide lugs. Unscrew the two bolts securing

Unlocking timing-chain tensioner with Allen wrench.

the camshaft flange. Pull off the crankshaft sprocket (with puller) while pulling back the camshaft. With the chain off, remove the camshaft.

When assembling chain, oil the camshaft bearing areas and insert the shaft most of the way in. Place the chain on the cam sprocket and position the stamp mark directly toward the camshaft. Turn the crankshaft to bring the key upright and position the sprocket with the stamp mark facing the camshaft centerline. With marks centered, slip off the sprocket, engage the chain on it, and fit the sprocket back onto the crankshaft. After the chain is tensioned, the reference marks will not line up. Tighten the crankshaft bolt to 45 ft. lbs. When aligning the chain guide, allow clearance to the chain of 0.8 mm (.032 in.) when the chain is tensioned.

TIMING GEAR COVER —ALL MODELS

The timing gear cover has a seal that can only be pressed out of the casing. Use the proper tools to change the seal so that the cover is not distorted. Smear the cover gasket with joint compound, position the cover on the engine block with an aligning tool, and tighten down evenly. Fit the crankshaft pulley and tighten down the cranking dog.

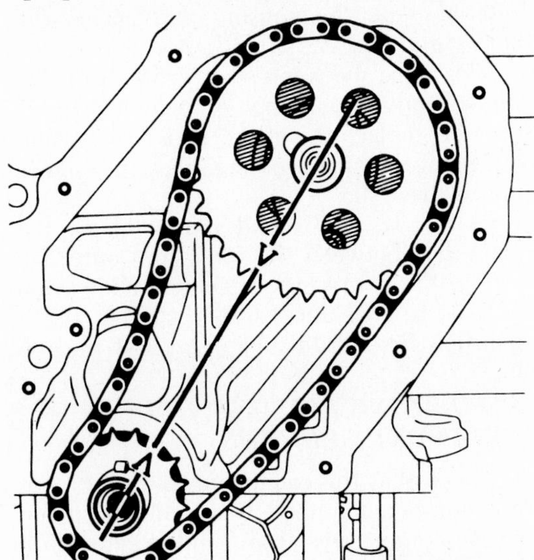

Aligning timing chain sprockets.

TIMING GEARS

Dauphine

With timing gear cover off, remove the cotter pin and nut (left hand thread) from the idle wheel in the center. Remove the two camshaft flange securing bolts to pull out the camshaft (top gear). The idle wheel shaft and back plate of the timing gear case are now accessible.

Assemble timing gears in reverse order, noting alignment of reference marks on the gears.

CAMSHAFT AND CHAIN TENSIONER REMOVAL AND INSTALLATION

NOTE: The following general procedures apply to all engines.

1. Remove engine from vehicle.
2. Remove cylinder head, rocker arms, and pushrods. Be sure to keep them in the order of their respective cylinders.
3. Remove cylinder liner clamps. Remove oil pump and distributor drive gear.
4. Remove three cam front bearing bolts and remove bearings.
5. Remove chain tensioner by loosening retaining cylinder screws and turning cylinder clockwise with an Allen wrench.
6. Remove crank sprocket retaining bolt with chain guide shoes. Remove the camshaft flange securing bolts.
7. Remove as one assembly the crank sprocket and chain. Camshaft should be eased out with the above assembly.

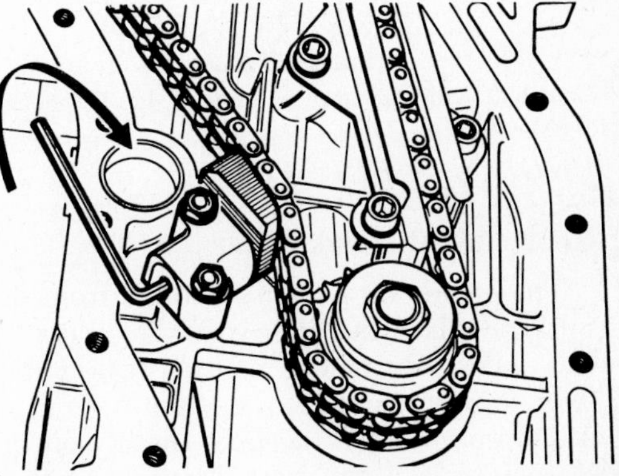

Chain tensioner removal

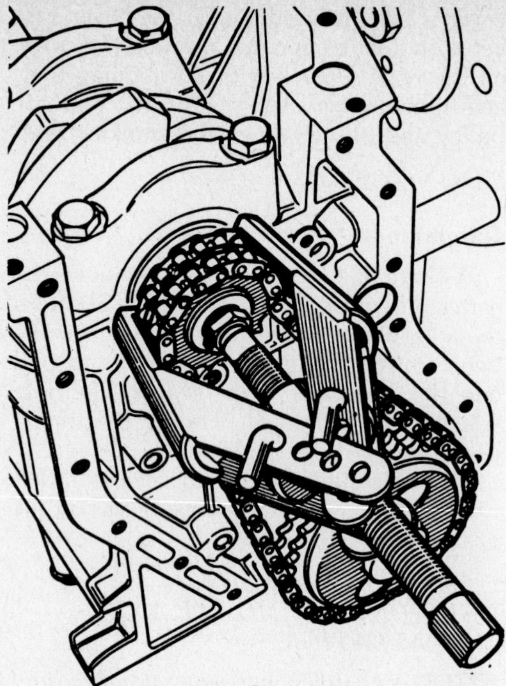

Crank sprocket, chain, and camshaft removal

8. To install chain tensioner and cam, reverse removal procedure. Chain is properly tensioned when all slack is removed. Be sure not to over tighten.

NOTE: On the 12 and 16, the camshaft sprocket must be changed whenever the engine is dismantled. Camshaft flange clearance for all engines is .002-.0045 in.

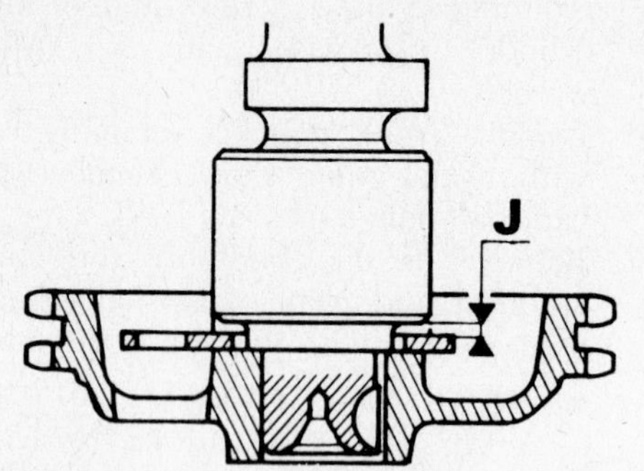

Camshaft flange clearance, Renault 12. Dimension J:.002-.0045″

ENGINE LUBRICATION

Replacing Oil and Filter

The engine oil is easily drained from the sump. Replace the filter cartridge every 6,000 miles. On some models, turn entire filter to unscrew it from engine. A strap or chain tool might be needed. Lightly oil the seal and clean the base before installing filter. Retighten the cartridge after warming up the engine. Add an additional 1/2 pint of oil to the engine.

Removing Oil Pan

Remove the oil pan with car raised. Drain the engine oil, unbolt the two bolts which secure the bell housing stiffening bar, and remove the oil pan bolts. Clean the flanges of the cork and rubber gaskets.

To refit the oil pan position the rubber gaskets and hold them in place with a little joint compound. Smear the side gaskets with compound, position them so that they overlap the ends of the bearing gaskets. The cork gaskets can be held in place with dowels set in some of the bolt holes. Fit the oil pan and tighten the bolts. Install the stiffening plate. Replace the oil.

Measuring Oil Pressure

On the 8, 10 and Caravelle, oil pressure should read at least 10 psi at 600 rpm and 50 psi at 4000 rpm. The Dauphine engine oil pressures are minimum 17 psi at 500 rpm and 34 psi at 4000 rpm. R-12 pressure should be 30 psi at idle and 60-70 psi at 4,000 rpm. R-16 oil pressure should be 30 psi at idle and 60-80 psi at 4,000 rpm. Unscrew the oil pressure switch (on the distributor side) and connect an oil pressure gauge in its place.

Oil Pump Overhaul

With the oil pan off, unscrew the bolts securing the oil pump. The pump housing unbolts into two halves. Open it with care to prevent loss of the seat to the pressure relief ball. *The Dauphine pump has a separate plug on the housing that covers the spring and ball.*

Clearance between the gears and the pump body should not exceed .008 in. If greater, replace the gears. Polish the gasket flanges if they are scored. Check the splines on the drive shaft.

In the 12 and 16 oil pump, check the clearance between the inner and outer rotors in the two positions shown. Dimension A: 0.04 to 0.29 mm (.002 in.-.012 in.). Dimension B: 0.02 to 0.14 mm (.001 in.-.006 in.).

REPLACING PISTONS, RODS, CYLINDER SLEEVES

Check that the connecting rods and caps are numbered, unbolt them, and push out pistons and rods from underneath. Bolt each bearing shell and cap back on its rod to avoid interchanging the parts.

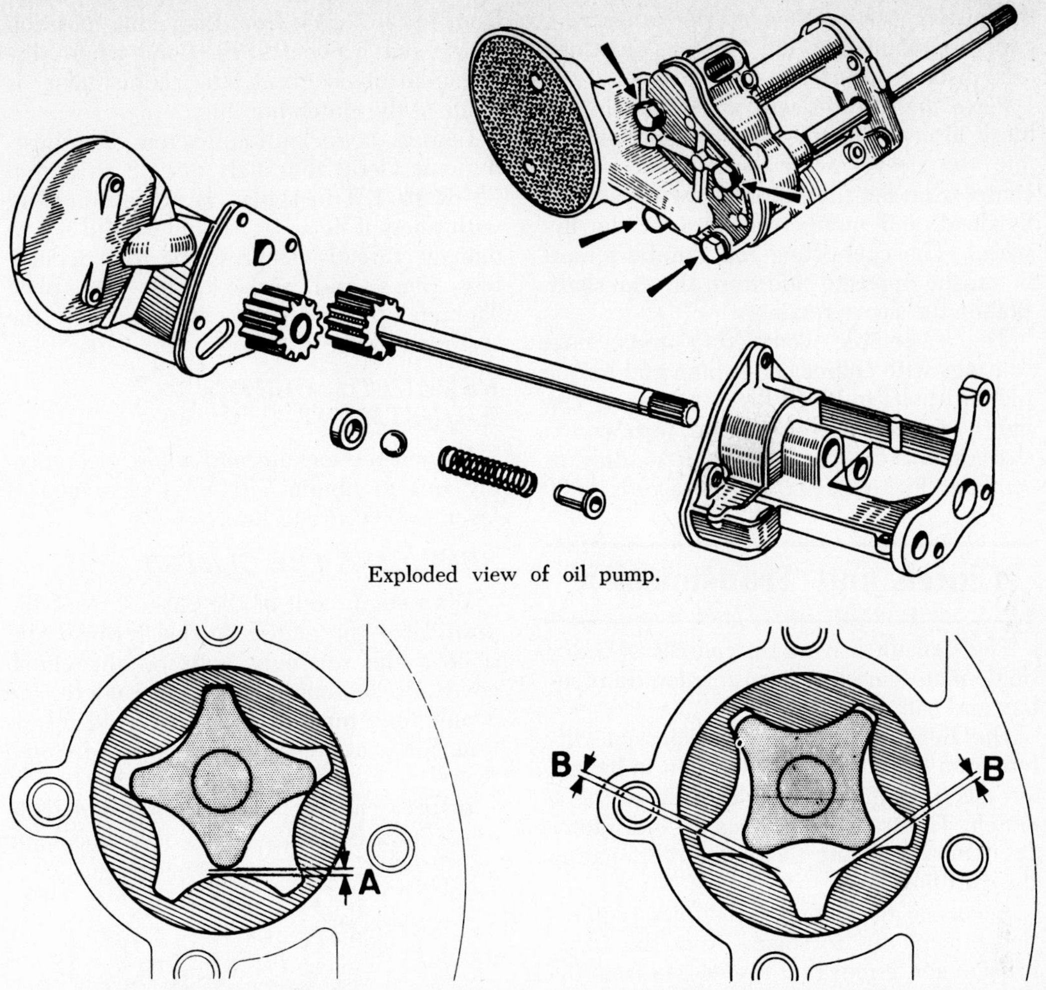

Exploded view of oil pump.

Oil pump on Renault 16. Check clearance between inner and outer rotors in positions shown.

Use a ring expander to remove piston rings, expanding rings as little as possible to avoid breaking or bending them.

Inspect cylinder sleeves for scoring, roughness, or other excessive wear. Use a cylinder gauge to check for cylinder taper and out-of-round at top, middle, and bottom of bore.

If a piston or cylinder sleeve is damaged or worn excessively, it is best to replace the complete sleeve set so that weight balance and compression are maintained.

Fit the lower seal to each cylinder sleeve with a thin blade having smooth, round edges. Place the sleeves into the block, pressing on them with hand to ensure firm seating. Check the sleeve projection above block.

Sleeve Protrusion

12 engine = .15 to .20 mm (.006-.008 in.)

Seal sizes = .003 mm blue; .10 mm, red; .12 mm, green (.003 in. blue, .004 in. red, .005 in. green)

16 engine = 0.14 to 0.19 mm (.0055 in.-.0075 in.)

Seal sizes = 0.07 mm, blue; 0.1 mm, red; 0.13 mm. green. (.0028 in.; .004 in.; .005 in.)

Caravelle, 10 and 8 engines = 0.05 to 0.12 mm (.002 in.-.005 in.)

Seal sizes are same as for R-16

Dauphine engines = 0.08 to 0.15 mm (.003 in.-.006 in.)

Seal sizes = 0.9 mm; 0.95 mm; 1.0 mm. (.035 in.; .037 in.; .040 in.)

Piston Rings

Remove rings from piston with ring expander to prevent deforming ring. Check piston rings for good condition.

Install piston rings (lightly oiled) with an expander. The gap on the U-flex oil ring should be in line with the unpierced part of the piston groove. Stagger the other ring gaps approximately 120° apart (one-third total distance around).

Place the piston-sleeve assemblies in the block after fitting the lightly oiled pistons into the sleeves with the help of a ring compressor. Set the piston arrow to face the flywheel, and numbers from 1 at the flywheel. The connecting rod numbers must be on the opposite side from the camshaft. Bolt on the sleeve retainers.

To reassemble connecting rods, coat bearings with engine oil, tighten and torque rod cap bolts to 25 ft. lbs, tap bearing cap lightly to assure seating, and turn crankshaft to make sure there is no binding or scuffing. Tighten R-12 and R-16 rods to 30 ft. lbs.

Clutch and Transmission

The Renault drive train consists of a dry single-plate clutch, a transmission-differential, and half axles.

The Renault automatic transmission differs from the standard drive train in having an electromagnetic coupler instead of a clutch. The transmission has a servo motor (actuator) to shift the gears, eliminating the shift linkage.

Access to the clutch or coupler requires detachment of the engine from the transmission and removal of the engine from the chassis.

Servicing the transmission-differential (transaxle) requires removal of the entire powerplant.

CLUTCH ADJUSTMENT (EXCEPT RENAULT 12)

Clutch pedal free play should measure from 3/4 to 1 inch from the resting position of the clutch pedal to the point where disengagement begins. The adjustment is made at the clutch housing.

Loosen the locknut and screw the adjusting nut along the shaft until 2 to 3 mm (5/64 to 1/8 in.) play is achieved. Hold with pliers if necessary being careful not to damage threads. Depress the foot pedal a few times and recheck the free play. Tighten the locknut and grease the threaded rod.

RENAULT 12 CLUTCH ADJUSTMENT

Loosen the locknut and adjust clearanceing nut to obtain 7/64-9/64 clearance at lever end. Secure locknut.

SERVICING THE CLUTCH

With engine out of the chassis, mark the position of the clutch on the flywheel and remove the retaining bolts on the clutch cover by loosening them alternately and evenly, one turn at a time to avoid distortion. Remove the pressure plate and clutch disc.

Inspect clutch parts for wear and damage. Check friction surfaces of flywheel and

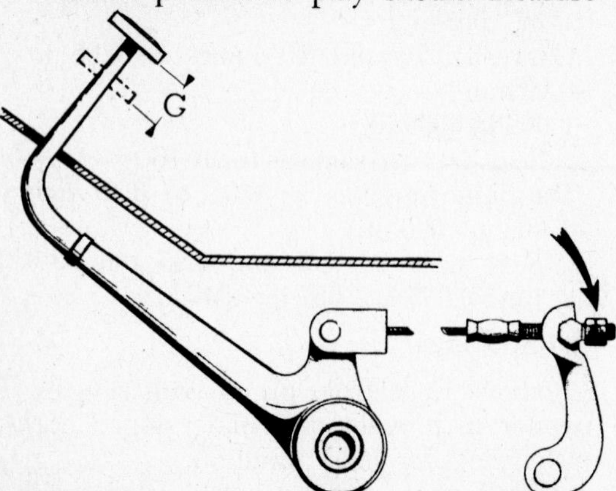

Clutch pedal free-play is ¾ in. at G, adjusted a clutch housing (2 to 3 mm).

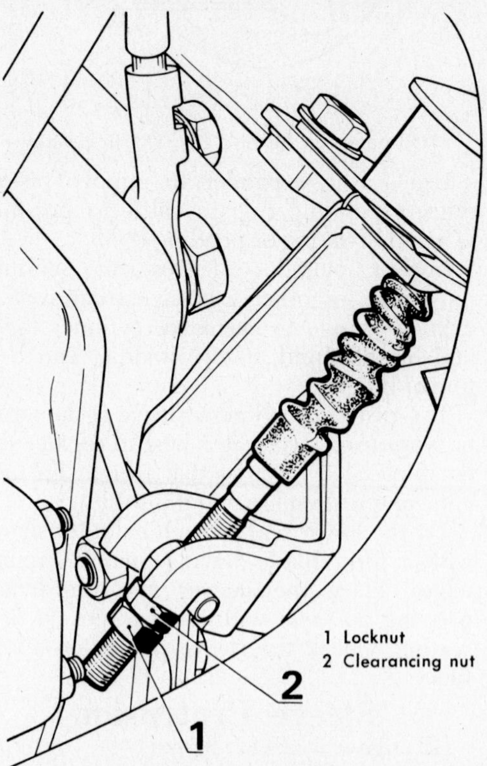

Renault 12 clutch adjustment

pressure plate for scoring, ends of release fingers for wear, and clutch facings for wear or oil saturation. On the 12 and 16, the clutch assembly cannot be serviced. It must be replaced.

A flywheel that is scored or discolored can be polished or lightly machined. Push out the locating dowels and machine faces A and B by same amount in order to maintain dimension d = 0.5 ± 0.1 mm (.016 to .024 in.). However dimension c must not be reduced below 27 mm (1.059 to 1.067 in.).

Fit new locating dowels, keeping their projection (e) at 7 ± 0.25 mm (.226 to .286 in.) measured from flywheel face A. Fit the flywheel with new lock bolts tightened to 40 ft. lbs. Inspect clutch disc for distortion. Lateral runout should not exceed 0.6 mm (.023 in.) at the outer diameter. The thickness of a new disc is 7.4 mm (.292 in.). Test out the disc hub on the shaft drive splines for easy slip fit, without side play.

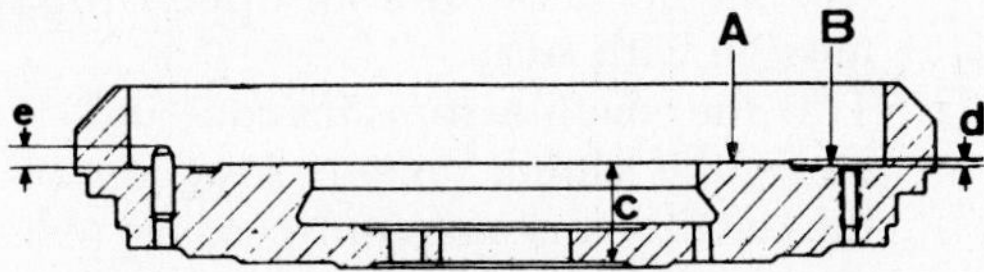

Check flywheel for wear and damage.

Check the release bearing for wear, binding, or roughness. Free the spring from the release bearing trunnions. Lift the tabs and free the withdrawal fork from the bearing. Grease the trunnion and the release fork pivot point on the clutch housing with Molykote BR. 2 grease or equivalent. Fit the release bearing to the withdrawal fork. Slowly push down the tab on the fork ensuring that the bearing turns freely. Do not distort the trunnion. Hook the spring in place. Tighten the tubular screw and fold down the locking tab. *NOTE: Do not clean disc or release bearing in solvent.* Inspect surface on drive spline and check bushing in flywheel.

When assembling clutch, ensure that the clutch face on the flywheel is perfectly clean. Fit clutch disc to the flywheel (with the offset on the hub towards the gearbox) with a drift or a cut-off clutch sliding shaft so that it is exactly centered in the flywheel. Align the marks. Tighten bolts evenly, only one or two turns at a time, to prevent distortion of the cover.

To remove the clutch control cable, detach the body undertrays. Disconnect the link from the clutch pedal. Push out the cable cover end stop from its lug on the crossmember. Disconnect the cable from the withdrawal fork, freeing it from the hollow screw, the rubber tube and the clip.

To remove the clutch pedal, lift the mat inside the car and remove the pedal assembly cover plate. Remove the front chassis undertray, unhook the return spring, disconnect the link at the pedal, remove the shaft retaining bolt, and pull the shaft to remove the pedal from inside the car. Don't lose the spacing washers.

TRANSAXLE REMOVAL & INSTALLATION

Renault 8, Renault 10, and Caravelle

Disconnect the battery. Remove the air filter. Disconnect the accelerator cable. Remove the muffler. Disconnect the starter leads. Remove the left-hand engine tray. Remove the starter. Loosen the rear wheels. Place the car on stands. Remove the wheels. Drain the gearbox.

On each side, disconnect the tie bar at the wheel end; disconnect the handbrake cable; remove the brake caliper without disconnecting the hose; put aside the brake pads.

Compress the spring. Disconnect the shock absorber at the top, one end of the strap, and the shock absorber at its lower attachment point. Take out the shock absorber followed by the spring.

Free the starter cable from its clip on the crossmember and the accelerator cable from its support (left-hand side). Remove the side pad securing bolts and remove the pad together with the accelerator cable support on the left-hand side. Mark the half shells with reference to the differential carrier and the housing.

Remove the half shell securing nuts and pull back the half shells. Remove the half shaft. Hold the differential carrier in place by means of two nuts.

Remove the clutch bottom tray and stiffening bar. Disconnect the clutch cable from the withdrawal fork. Free the adjustable end fitting from the protecting rubber. Disconnect the gearshift link and the speedometer drive cable.

Place a jack under the engine sump. Remove the bolt which secures the gearbox to the suspension crossmember. Lower the jack in order to free the rubber pad from the crossmember. Remove the nuts and bolts which secure the clutch housing to the engine. Remove the gearbox-clutch housing assembly. Raise the engine with the jack in order to return it to its normal position.

When refitting the gearbox, carry out the removing operations in reverse paying attention to the following points:

a. Lightly grease the end of the clutch shaft.
b. Smear the thrust face of the half shells with jointing compound and fit them while paying attention to the position marks made during dismantling.
c. Place the plain washers on the half shells at the side mounting pad points and the accelerator cable support point.
d. Fill the gearbox with oil.

Dauphine

Drain the gearbox and remove the power plant. Remove the radiator. Disconnect the brake pipes from each hose. Remove the hose retaining clips. Compress the springs. Remove the shock absorber at upper securing points. Disconnect one end of each of the straps. Remove the bolts that secure the side mounting pads to the crossmember. Remove the crossmember center securing bolt. Remove the crossmember and take out the springs.

Mark the positions of the carrier half shells with respect to the differential carriers and the housing. Remove the half shell securing nuts and pull back the shells. Remove the half shafts and take out the universal joints. Hold the differential carriers in place by means of two nuts.

Unlock and remove the nuts and bolts which secure the gearbox to the engine. Separate the gearbox from the engine.

Refit the gearbox by carrying out the removing operations in reverse, paying attention to the following points:

a. Lightly grease the end of the clutch shaft.
b. Smear the half shell joint faces with jointing compound and fit them by following the reference marks made during dismantling.
c. Fit the plain washers to the half shells at the mounting pad and accelerator-cable clamp securing points.
d. Top up the unit with oil after refitting the power unit assembly to the car.

Renault 12 (Type 352-10)

1. Remove the battery, air cleaner and starter.
2. Disconnect clutch cable and remove the clutch cable bracket.
3. Remove both water pump and cam pulley.
4. Tilt alternator towards the vehicle center and secure in this position.
5. Jack front of vehicle and drain transmission.
6. Using a drift, remove driveshaft rollpin.
7. On both sides of vehicle, remove the steering and upper suspension ball joints.
8. Tilt the stub axle and remove from the transaxle.
9. Remove the speedometer cable, the gearshft control, and the back-up light wires.
10. Remove the tubular crossmember, the exhaust pipe, and the transmission crossmember. Be sure to support transmission with jack.
11. Tilt the engine/transmission and remove the clutch shield. Also, remove the engine/transmission securing bolts.
12. To install transmission, reverse removal procedure. When installing, lubricate clutch shaft splines with appropriate grease.
13. Be sure to line up the rollpin hole at pinion shaft spline bottom with pinion gear spline. When replacing rollpins, use sealer.
14. When gear lever is installed, place in fourth gear. Leave lever loose and tighten gear shift control arm bolt.
15. When installing transmission, do not forget to adjust clutch.

Renault 12 (Type 352-10) and Renault 16 (Type 336) Adjustments and Torque Specifications

Ring gear backlash: .005-.010 in.
Ring gear preload, used bearing: none
Ring gear preload, new bearing: 2-7 lbs.
Ring gear preload, new bearing: 2-7 ft. lbs.
Case bolt torque: 7 mm-15 ft. lbs., 8 mm-2-7 ft. lbs.
Cover bolts: 10 ft. lbs.
Differential carrier lock bolts: 15 ft. lbs.
Clutch case bolts: 8 mm-15 ft. lbs.: 10 mm-30 ft. lbs.

Reverse gear shaft: 20 ft. lbs.
Ring gear bolts: 65-80 ft. lbs.
Speedometer drive nut, secondary shaft: 75-85 ft. lbs.

Renault 16 (Type 336)

1. Disconnect the battery, remove the spare tire, and drain the transmission.
2. Remove the clutch shield. Remove the fan and shroud.
3. Disconnect the battery clamp from its attachment to the steering box.
4. If so equipped, remove spare tire cross-member.
5. Pinch shut the hose from the radiator to the expansion chamber. Take off expansion chamber cap.
6. Unbolt radiator, and without removing hoses, swing it over the engine.
7. Remove the speedometer drive cable at the centrifugal switch. Remove switch bolt and move switch out of way.
8. Move steering wheel to extreme left and disconnect right steering arm at end fitting. Perform the same operations to the left steering arm.
9. Remove bolts securing steering cross-member to cowl. Pull steering to full right, and pull out towards left front.
10. Remove the clamp shaft pulley outer flange, the adjusting shims, drive belt, and pulley. Remove bolts holding steering damper to column.
11. Disconnect the speedometer cable, back-up light wires, and shift linkage. Remove bolts holding gear lever and move to one side.
12. Remove bolts holding front transmission mounting pad and remove with bracket.
13. Using a drift, remove rollpins from yoke.
14. Place retaining clips on yoke to prevent separation.
15. Position jack between gearbox and left side member. Raise gearbox and remove yoke and drive gear.
16. Disconnect clutch cable. Remove cable stop bracket.
17. Remove two left-hand engine/transmission securing bolts.
18. On right side, repeat steps 15 to 17.
19. Remove starter.
20. Move transmission fully forward. Raise gearbox front and lift out in a straight up position. Be sure not to damage radiator.
21. To install transaxle, reverse removal procedure.
22. Be sure to use a new clutch shield. Grease clutch shaft splines, with a small amount of grease.
23. When securing starter, do not tighten till all operations are performed.
24. Grease drive gear splines before replacing.
25. Be sure to align rollpin holes in yoke splines with drive gear splines. Use sealer on these holes.
26. When fitting water pump belt, slowly tighten outer flange nuts while turning engine. Do not use cam pulley nut to rotate engine. It must be accomplished with car in fourth gear and by rotation of wheels.
27. Adjust belt deflection to 3/32-5/32″. Be sure to adjust clutch and refill gearbox with EP 80 lubricant.

TRANSAXLE OVERHAUL

Type 330 (4 Speed Synchromesh)

Disassembly

Support the gearbox on a stand or bench. Remove the clutch housing. Take off the front cover (speedometer housing) by removing the securing bolts, pulling back the cover until it makes contact with the control shaft lug, pushing out the rollpin from the shift lever using a drift, and removing the control shaft, the control lever and the cover. Remove the spacer and adjusting shims from the primary shaft bearings. Unbolt the two halves of the gearbox housing.

Remove the secondary shaft and the stud which retains the outer track ring on the double tapered roller bearings. Remove the primary shaft. Remove the differential. Remove differential carriers from each half-housing.

Gearshift Control on First Model

Push out the roll pin from the fork with a drift. Remove the 3rd-4th shaft and its end fitting, and the fork (put aside the locking ball and the spring). Remove the locking disc from between the shafts.

Pull the reverse shaft out as far as it will go from the control end. Push out the roll pin from the 1st-2nd shift fork by means of a drift. Remove the fork. Push out the roll pin from the reverse shaft end fitting with a drift. Remove the end fitting. Remove the 1st-2nd shaft (put aside the locking ball and spring).

Unscrew the reverse swivel lever shaft and remove the swivel lever. Using a drift push out the roll pin from the reverse shaft positioning fork (the pin makes contact with the housing; turn the shaft and extract the pin with a pair of pliers). Remove the reverse shaft and the shift fork.

Second Model Gearshift Control

Push out the roll pin from the shift fork, using a drift. Remove the shaft and the fork (put aside the locking ball and spring). Remove the locking disc from between the shafts.

Remove the reverse shaft as far as it will go from the control end. Push out the roll pin from the pin. Remove the fork and the shaft.

Remove the reverse swivel shaft and put aside the swivel lever. Push out the roll pin from the reverse shaft positioning fork. The pin will make contact with the housing. Turn the shaft and extract the pin with a pair of pliers. Remove the reverse shaft and the fork.

Detach the gearwheel retaining circlip from the pinion and remove the shaft, the gearwheel, the friction washer and the guide. Put aside the locking ball and the spring.

Remove the bearing track rings and the adjusting washers. Separate the clutch shaft from the primary shaft by pushing out the roll pin, using drift. Extract the bearings at the differential end. *NOTE: Any operation carried out on the synchronizer hub of the 1st-2nd gear will involve using an electric oven with temperatures to 485° for reassembling.*

Grip the first speed gear in a vise. Engage first speed. Loosen the speedometer

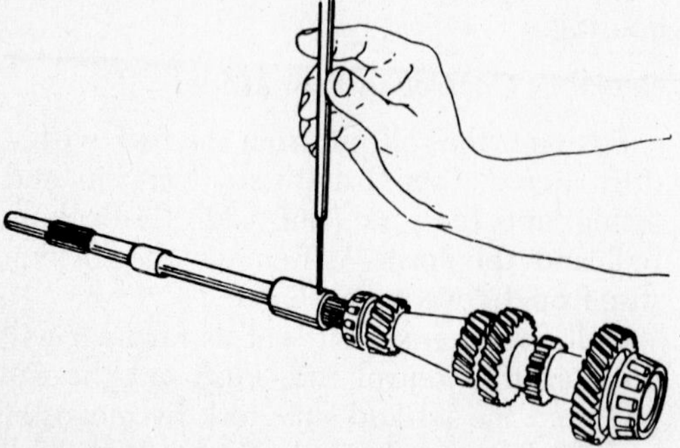

Separating clutch shaft from primary shaft.

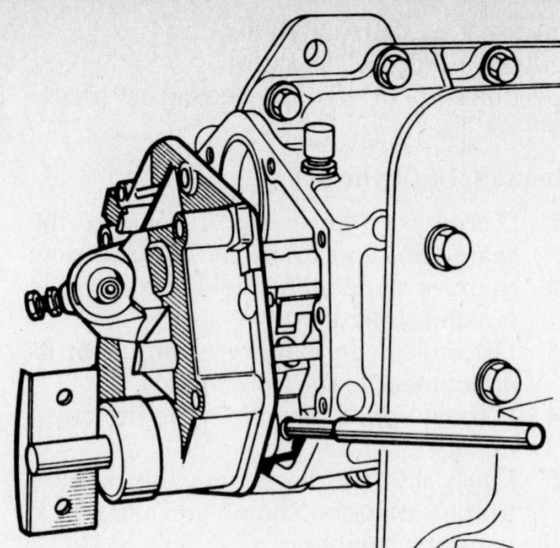

Removing transmission front cover. Push roll pin out with drift.

drive worm and unscrew it with a spanner. Remove the double tapered roller bearing, the pinion adjusting washer, the fourth speed gearwheel and its ring, and the synchronizer sliding gearwheel from the 3rd-4th synchronizer and the keys (mark position of the sliding gearwheel with the reference to the hub). Extract the 3rd-4th speed synchronizer hub. Remove the retaining key, the stop-washer, the third speed gearwheel and its ring, the second speed gearwheel stop-washer, the gearwheel and its ring. Remove the 1st-2nd speed synchronizer sliding gear (mark its position with reference to the hub) and the synchronizer hub stop-washer.

Extract the 1st-2nd speed synchronizer hub. Remove the first speed synchronizer ring, stop-washer, and gear.
NOTE: The bearing cannot be removed. Extract the bearing on the ring gear side. Extract the bearing on the differential housing side. Remove and throw away the eight bolts that secure the ring gear to the differential housing. Push out with a drift the roll pin which retains the side gear shaft. Separate the various parts.

Extract the bearing track rings, the adjusting shims, and the seals, taking the load on these last components.

Remove the gearwheel, the guide and the O ring seal. Clean and inspect all parts. The seals, self-locking bolts, and rollpins must be replaced by new ones.

Assembly

The final drive pinion and ring gear are lapped together in manufacture and are

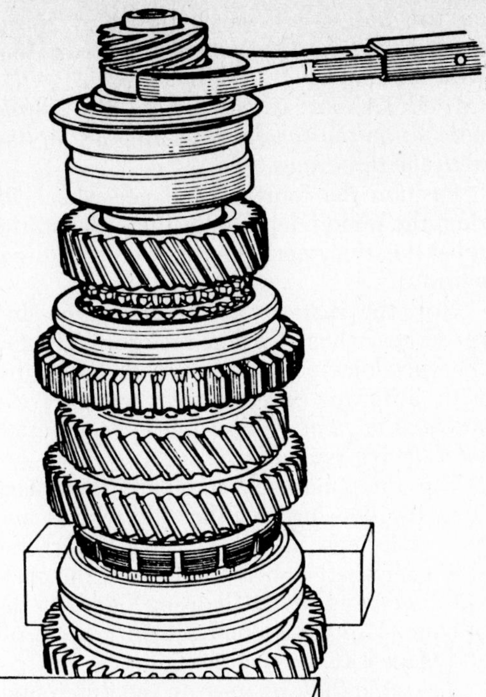

Assembled secondary shaft.

therefore inseparable. Replacing one of these parts requires replacing the other. A common reference number is shown on both.

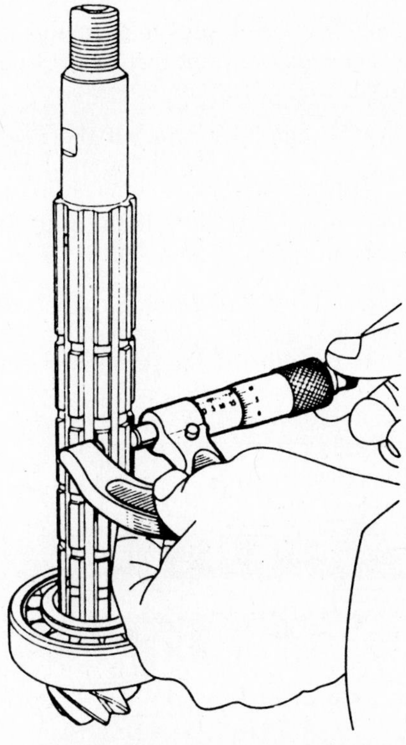

Measure drive pinion size across two splines.

The synchronizer hubs are matched with the final drive pinion. If the final drive pinion, the ring gear or the roller bearing is damaged, replace the ring gear and pinion set.

IMPORTANT: On some transmissions the roller bearing is retained by a circlip on the outer track ring which requires a groove in the gearbox housing. The bearing without a circlip can be fitted in a housing which has a groove in it. However, the bearing with a circlip cannot be fitted to a housing which has no groove. Synchronizers may be installed again unless damaged.

If replacement of the synchronizer hub or final drive pinion is necessary, measure the damaged final drive pinion so that the replacement size matches.

Measure the final drive pinion across two splines with a micrometer. Make measurements at various points on the synchronizer and across several different splines in order to obtain an average.

Final drive pinion size
Type 330

Transmission	*Color code*
16.55 to 16.57 mm (.6516 to .6523 in.)	White
16.58 to 16.60 mm (.6527 to.6535 in.)	Red
16.61 to 16.63 mm (.6539 to .6547 in.)	Blue
16.64 to 16.66 mm (.6551 to .6559 in.)	Yellow
16.67 to 16.69 mm (.6563 to .6571 in.)	Green

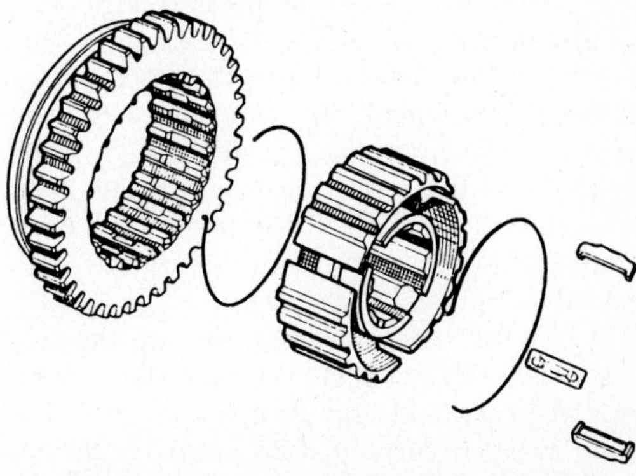

Third and fourth synchronizer of 330 gearbox.

Fit the synchronizer hubs to the final drive pinion on a press. Heat 1st-2nd speed hub to 485°F. Keep 3rd-4th hub cold.

The sliding gearwheel and the hub are matched, so they should both be marked before taken apart. Place reference marks on the second speed gearwheel side (on the same side as the chamfer on the sliding gearwheel so that it is visible after the hub has been fitted). Place the hub in an electric oven and heat it to 250°C (482°F). Always heat hub (485°F) before reassembling the secondary cluster.

If the 3rd-4th synchronizer has been dismantled and can be used again, assemble as follows: Place on the hub the three keys, the two springs (engage one end of each spring in the same key with the free ends on either side), and the sliding gearwheel. The groove on the sliding gearwheel should be on the opposite side of the two notches in the hub. Align the mark on the sliding gearwheel with that on the hub.

Place the spring on the first speed gearwheel so that it covers three of the notches. Place the 1st speed gearwheel and its ring on the final drive pinion (together with its bearing). Put on the stop washer, retaining it by means of a dummy key (such as a key which has had the horn removed). Place the dummy key in one of the keyways having a lubrication hole.

Heat the 1st-2nd speed hub and place it on the final drive pinion in the correct position. One of the unsplined areas is to be opposite the dummy key.

Press the hub on until it makes contact with the stop ring. Hold the synchronizer ring in the central position with the lugs below the level of the stop ring so as not to damage the spring. Retain the pressure for a short time until the hub cools down (it can be cooled with compressed air). Release the spring. Remove the dummy key.

Place the 1st-2nd speed synchronizer sliding gearwheel in position with the chamfer towards the second speed gearwheel and the reference mark in line with the one on the hub. Position the hub stop washer, turning it to align the splines with those on the final drive pinion.

Place the synchronizer spring on the second speed gearwheel. Position the second speed gearwheel and its ring. Position the stop washer, turning it to align its splines with those of the final drive pinion tailshaft.

Position the third speed gearwheel with its ring. Position the stop washer, and the retaining key (in a keyway having a lubrication hole).

Press on the 3rd-4th speed synchronizer until it makes contact with the stop washer of the third speed gearwheel. The notches on the hub are towards the third speed gearwheel side. One notch is to be in line with the stop key.

IMPORTANT: Check that the three notches on the synchronizer ring are in line with the three keys.

Position the fourth speed gearwheel, its ring, the pinion depth adjusting washer, the roller bearing, and the speedometer drive worm.

Grip the shaft in a vise across the first speed gearwheel. Engage first gear. Tighten the speedometer drive worm to 85 ft. lbs. with a torque wrench. *Do not lock the worm; the pinion depth must be adjusted later during assembly.*

Dip one pinion gear in oil and then place it in the housing. Set the side wheels and their bearings in the housing. Insert the side gear shaft (align the hole in the shaft with the hole in the housing) and fit the roll pin. Dip the second pinion gear in oil and place it in the ring gear.

Assemble the ring gear on the differential housing using *new* self-locking bolts. Tighten the 10 mm bolts to 45 ft. lbs., the 11 mm bolts to 60-70 ft. lbs. Fit the two bearings with a press.

ADJUSTMENTS—TYPE 330

Pinion Depth

The final drive pinion is in the correct position when its front face is at distance A from the ring gear.

A = 50.50 mm (1.988 in.) if the ring gear is secured to the differential housing with 10 mm bolts.

A = 51 mm (2.008 in.) if the ring gear is secured by 11 mm bolts.

Place a washer of a suitable thickness between the double tapered roller bearing and the shoulder of the secondary shaft. In

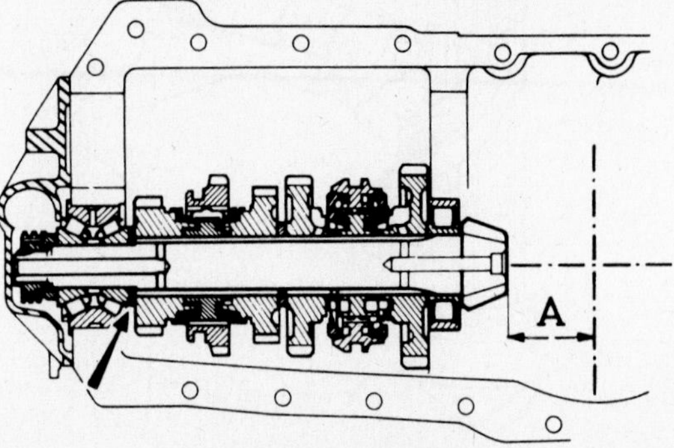

Measure pinion depth from ring gear

some instances the pinion depth is greater than dimension A. *The difference between the actual dimension (X) and dimension A is then marked on the front face of the pinion,* beside the matching reference. It is given in hundredths of a millimeter.

Mount the left half housing on a support. Fit the secondary shaft. Fit the right half housing and secure it in place by a few bolts (do not tighten them). Temporarily fit the speedometer drive housing to hold the roller bearing track ring in place. Tighten the half housing securing bolts. Fit gauge, with graduated rule against the front face of the pinion and the plate with the O reference pressed against the right half housing.

If the dimension is less than the correct pinion depth replace the pinion depth adjusting washer by a *thinner one*.

If the dimension is greater than the correct pinion depth replace the pinion depth adjusting washer by a *thicker* one.

Washers are available in thicknesses from 3.50 to 4.10 mm (.138 to .162 in.) varying with increments of 5/100 of a millimeter (.002 in.). When the final adjustment has been obtained remove the gauge, the speedometer drive housing, and the right half housing. Remove the secondary shaft assembly and lock the speedometer drive worm.

Ring Gear and Pinion Backlash

Place the plug in the position normally occupied by the oil seal. Position the bearing track ring (*push it fully down on the press*). Fit each differential carrier to the corresponding half housing (reference marks made during dismantling), using the paper gaskets. Fit in place in the differential carrier. Secure the differential carrier by a mimimum of four nuts, but do not fully tighten them. Fit the differential together with its bearings. Fit the secondary shaft assembly. Fit the right half housing and secure it by a few bolts (do not fully tighten them). Temporarily fit the speedometer drive housing and then tighten the half housing bolts. Tighten the differential carrier securing nuts to 35 ft. lbs.

Adjust the plugs against the track rings without forcing them. Check that the plugs turn freely until they make contact. On each side, measure the clearance between each crossbar and its plug.

On the right hand side: 0.80 mm (.032 in.).
On the left hand side: 0.95mm (.037 in.)

This measurement is necessary in order to be able to adjust the bearings.

When the ring gear and pinion backlash approaches the correct figure, mount a dial indicator on the housing and set the indica-

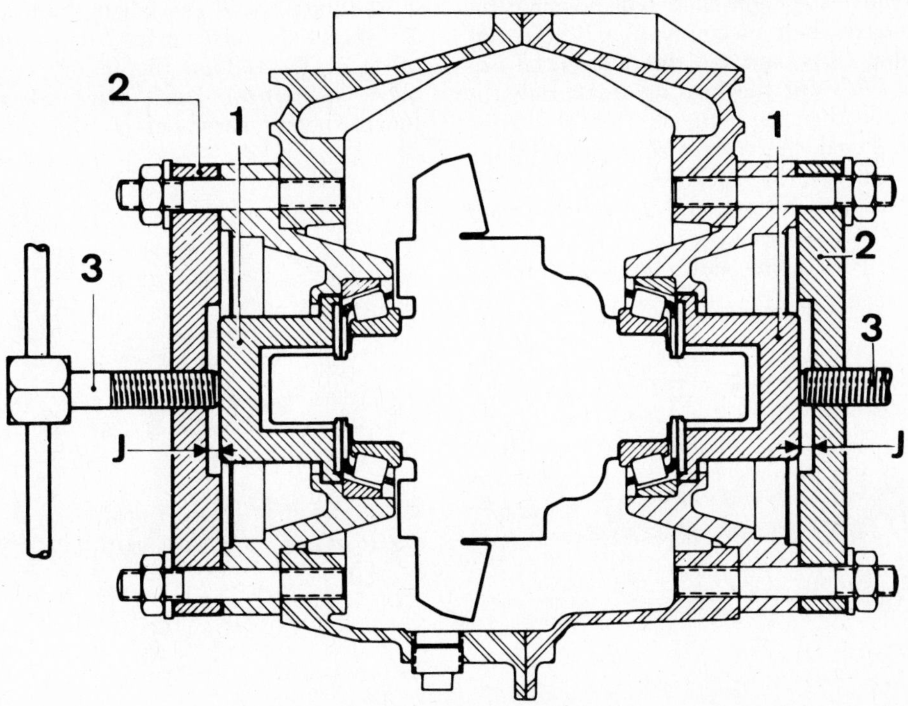

Measure clearance J with a feeler gauge

tor plunger in contact with one of the ring gear teeth. Adjust until a backlash of between 0.12 and 0.24 mm (.005 to .010 in.) is obtained. Repeat the backlash measurement on several of the ring gear teeth and calculate the average. When the adjustment is made, remove the dial indicator and its bracket.

Shim the Differential Bearings

The bearings are adjusted by placing a shim pack under the bearing track rings under the differential carrier. Measure the clearance between tool cross bar and the bearing placed without a shim. This measurement is to be carried out at the same point as that of clearance. For example:

Right-hand side: 2.30 mm (.091 in.)
Left-hand side: 2.50 mm (.085 in.)

The shim pack which is to be placed under each differential carrier must be equal to K-J. For example:

Right-hand side: 2.30 – .80 = 1.50 mm (.091 –.032 = .059 in.)
Left-hand side: 2.15 – .95 = 1.20 mm (.085 – .037 = .048 in.)

The shim pack to be used in this manner provides no play in the bearings—the correct setting for the original bearings.

Remove the right-hand half housing, the secondary shaft assembly, the differential, the tool cross bars and the differential carriers. Push out the bearing track rings by taking load on the plungers. In each carrier, place a seal, the correct shim pack (shims are available in thicknesses of: 0.1, 0.2, 0.25, 0.5, and 1 mm), and the bearing track rings (with a press).

When installing new bearings preload must be applied. The differential must rotate under resistance. *A thickness of shims equal to 0.15 mm (.006 in.) must be added to each differential carrier* shim size calculated above. Use a minimum of shims.

Bearing Preload

With the differential carriers mounted and the housing bolts tightened to 35 ft. lbs., turn the differential through a number of turns to centralize the bearings. Wrap a string around the differential carrier. Attach a spring balance to the string. The differential should rotate under a load of from 2 to 7 lbs. This is the load necessary to cause the differential to rotate. If the adjustment is incorrect, increase or reduce the thickness of the shim pack by the same amount at each differential carrier.

When the adjustment is complete, separate the half housings, remove the differential and differential carriers.

Primary Shaft

On the primary shaft, place the bearing track rings and the adjusting washer removed during dismantling. To correctly position the primary shaft, fit the primary shaft and the secondary shaft assembly to the left half housing. Face A of the third speed gearwheel on the primary shaft should be offset with reference to Face C on the third speed gearwheel of the secondary shaft. The offset A-to-C must equal the offset of Face B on the fourth-speed primary gearwheel from Face D of the fourth-speed gearwheel on the secondary

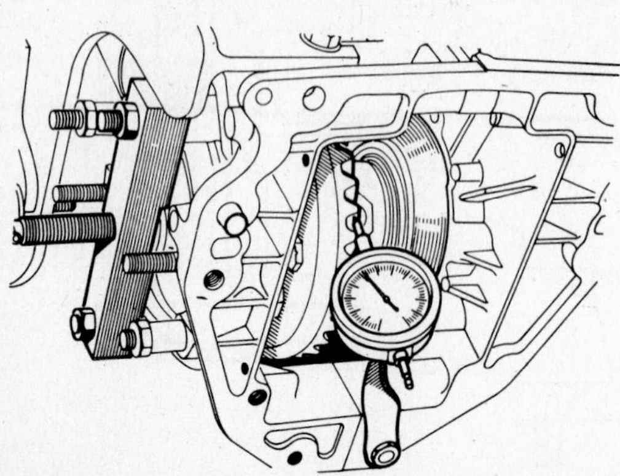

Measuring pinion backlash with dial gauge.

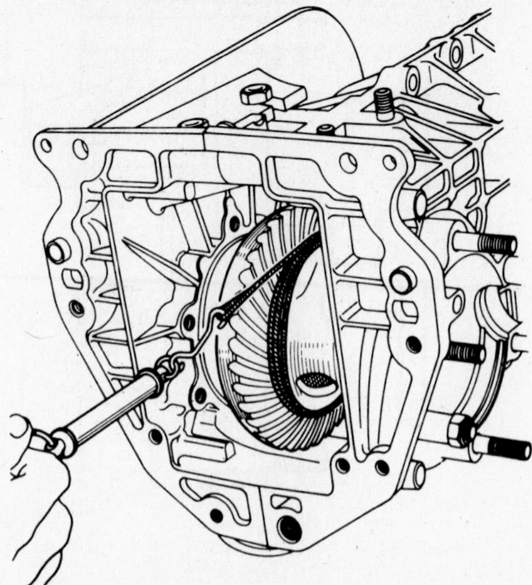

Measuring differential pre-load.

shaft. This adjustment is obtained with adjusting washers in thicknesses 2, 2.25, 2.5, 2.75, 3, 3.25, 3.5, 3.75, and 4 mm. When the adjustment has been completed remove the secondary shaft assembly.

Primary Shaft Bearing Adjustment

With the primary shaft in position, fit the right hand housing without bolting it in place. Fit the shim packs (C) and spacer. *The shaft should turn freely but without play and the spacer should project past the housing face by 0.2 mm (.008 in.)*, which is the thickness of the front housing paper gasket. Place a rule against the spacer and measure the space between the rule and the housing with a set of feeler gauges. If the adjustment is incorrect, change the thickness of shim packs. When the adjustment has been completed remove the right hand housing and the primary shaft. Assemble the clutch shaft to the primary shaft by fitting a roll pin to it.

Gearshaft Control Assembly

Insert the reverse shaft and place the positioning fork (through the hub on the differential side). Pin it by means of drift. Fit the reverse shaft swivel lever, inserting its end into the slot in the reverse shaft. Tighten its pivot pin to 20 ft. lbs. using torque wrench. Fit the 1st-2nd speed shaft locking ball and spring. Insert the shaft. Position the reverse shaft end fitting and pin it in place. Fit the 1st-2nd speed shaft fork (with the hubs toward the control end) and pin it in place. Place the locking disc between the shafts. Insert the 3rd-4th shaft locking ball and spring. Engage the shaft and fit the fork (with the hub towards the differential end) and pin it in place.

Insert the reverse shaft and fit the positioning fork (with the hub towards the differential end). Split pin it with a drift. Fit the reverse swivel lever, inserting its end into slot in the reverse shaft. Tighten the pivot pin to 20 ft. lbs. using torque wrench.

Fit the 1st-2nd shaft locking ball and spring. Insert the shaft. Fit the 1st-2nd speed shift fork (with the hub toward the control end) and pin it in place. Fit the locking disc between the shafts. Fit the 3rd-4th speed shaft locking ball and spring. Insert the shaft and fit the fork (with the hub toward the differential end) and pin it in place.

Place the locking ball and spring in the right hand housing. Insert the shaft and fit the gearwheel (with the hub towards the differential end) followed by the friction washer (with the bronze face against the gearwheel). Fit the guide from inside the bore and push the shaft fully in. Fit the gearwheel retaining circlip. In the left hand housing fit the differential, the primary shaft, and the secondary assembly. Smear the flanges of the half housings with sealing compound. Fit the right hand housing; take care that the end of the reverse idle lever enters the slot in the reverse gearwheel

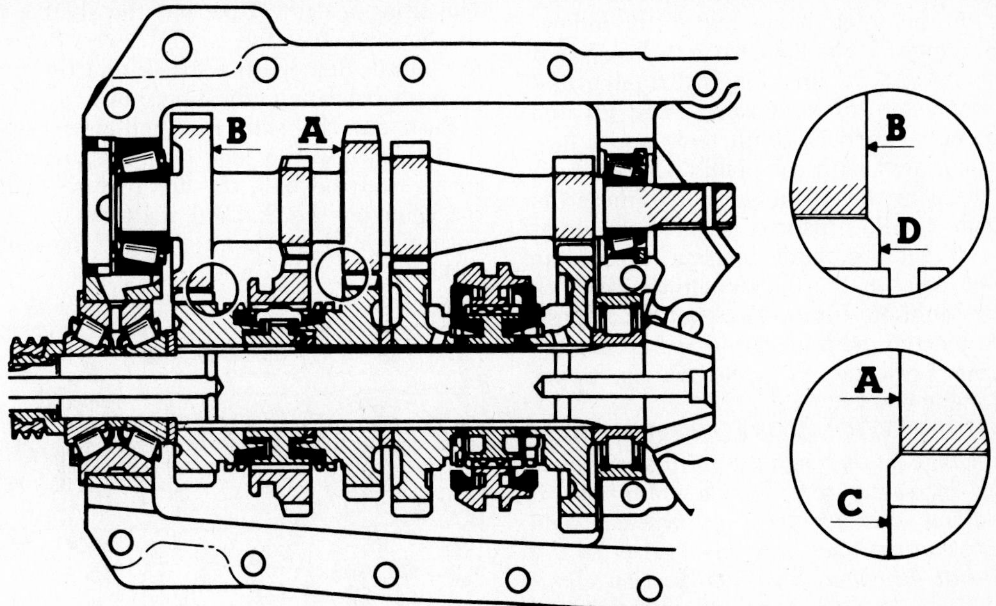

Offset of primary- and secondary-shaft gearwheels.

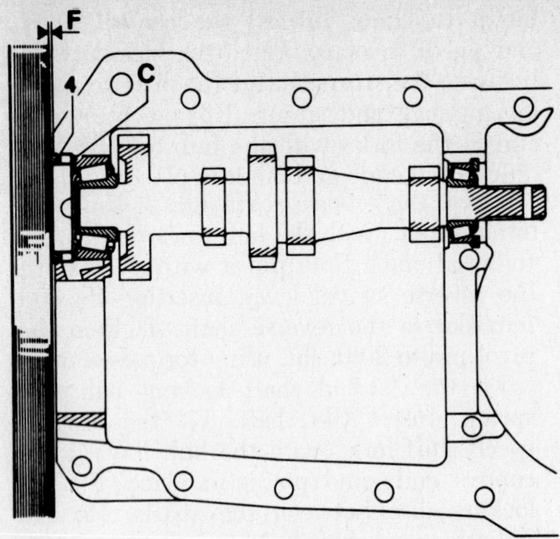

Adjusting primary-shaft bearings.

shaft. Bolt the housing together. *Do not fully tighten the nuts.* The nuts are on the right-hand side with the exception of the three bolts under the axle which are fitted in the opposite direction to permit the clutch control to clear. Fit the adjusting shims and the spacer for the primary shaft bearing. Fit the control lever to the shift fork shaft. Fit the speedometer drive housing (with its paper gasket smeared with sealer) while engaging the shaft in the control lever. Pin the lever to its shaft. Secure the speedometer drive housing without fully tightening the nuts. Fully tighten the nuts which connect the two half housings in the order shown, and to the following torques: 7 mm bolts to 15 ft. lbs.; 8 mm bolts to 20 ft. lbs. Finally, tighten the speedometer drive housing nuts. Fit the differential carriers (with their paper gaskets smeared with compound). Hold them in place by means of two nuts. Smear the clutch housing paper gasket with compound. Fit the clutch housing. Smear the pivot boss on the clutch withdrawal fork with Molykote BR 2. Place the fork in position together with its spring and secure the spring. Lock the tab washer. Fit the upper retaining bracket.

MODIFICATION NOTE: The thickness of the flange on the engine front crossmember was increased to 1.8 mm, requiring a modified gearbox securing bracket. The pad securing holes have been offset in the upward direction. This modification eliminated the shims between the bracket and the box and modified the mounting studs on the box itself. The unthreaded length is now 3 mm.

Fitting a new box with an old type bracket involves fitting the old type studs and also fitting the spacers between the bracket and the gearbox.

Fitting the new bracket to an old type box (with an old type crossmember) involves fitting the new studs and removing the shims.

Fitting a new rear crossmember involves fitting a new bracket, fitting the new studs, and removing the shims.

Fill the gearbox with oil after it is refitted to the vehicle.

Type 325 (Automatic)

Disassembly

Support the gearbox on a stand or bench. Remove the damping weights.

Remove the clutch-release fork, the clutch housing, the universal joints, and the differential carriers. Pull the two ends of the clutch shaft pin retaining spring together and slide it along the shaft. Push out the pin.

Take out the differential by placing one of the cut-outs in the housing opposite a boss on the casing in order to be able to free the ring gear.

Remove the lower cover plate and the speedometer drive housing. First, engage first gear and pull back the cover housing until it makes contact with the lug on the control shaft. Push out the control lever roll pin, using a drift. Take out the shaft and the housing; free the control lever. Return to neutral. Remove the spacer and the primary shaft bearing adjusting shims.

Push out the shift fork roll pins using drift. Unscrew the lock stop. Remove the spring and the ball, the first-reverse shaft, the plunger, the 2nd-3rd shaft (take care with the ball and spring), and the shift forks.

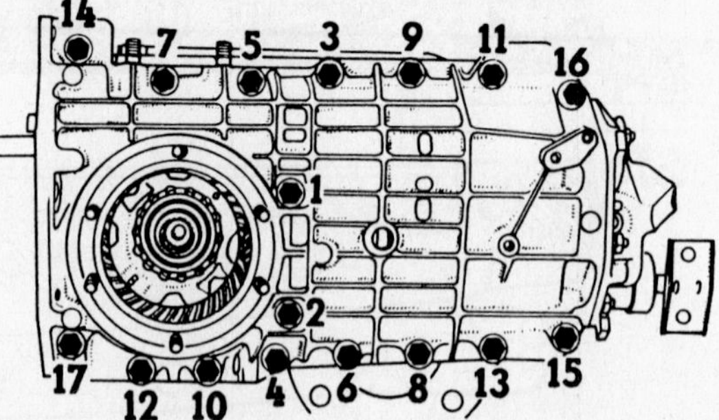

Tightening sequence for transaxle

NOTE: To remove the first-reverse shift fork, engage reverse, free the fork from the sliding gearwheel, then turn it through a quarter of a turn.

Hold the secondary shaft by engaging two gears simultaneously. Unlock and unscrew the nut which acts as the speedometer drive worm. Return to the neutral position.

Remove the double taper roller bearing, the pinion depth adjusting washer, and the locking key of the gearwheel stop washer.

Remove the primary shaft bearing and reverse-shaft retaining plate. Remove the reverse shaft and its ring to allow the reverse gearwheel to drop into the housing.

Gently knock the secondary shaft toward the differential end. Bring the third gearwheel against the housing. When the stop washer is accessible, turn it and slide it along the shaft.

Bring the assembly (the 2nd-3rd synchronizer and the second speed gearwheel) against the third speed gearwheel. When the stop washer is accessible, turn it and slide it along the shaft.

Slowly pull out the shaft while removing the gearwheels. Pull out the reverse gearwheel and the stop washer. Push out the primary shaft towards the differential end and put aside the bearing track ring. Remove the bearing at the differential end. The shaft is now free and can be removed from the housing without first removing the second bearing.

Push out the bearing track ring at the speedometer drive end. Extract the primary shaft bearing. Extract the secondary shaft bearing. Remove the differential bearings with the extractor.

Remove and throw away the six bolts which hold the ring gear to the housing

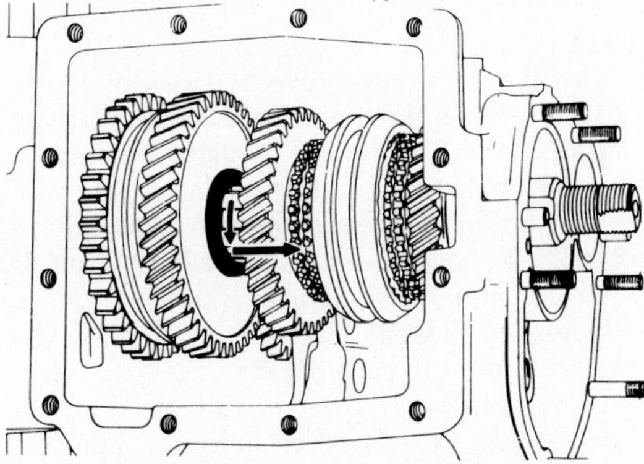

Disassembling the secondary shaft.

after first having broken the welded tracks. Separate the various parts.

Using a press, remove the bearing track rings, the adjusting shims, and the oil seals from carriers.

Remove the speedometer drive pinion and the nylon bushing from the speedometer drive housing.

Assembly

Dip one pinion gear in oil and place it in the housing. Set the side gears and their friction washers in the housing (align the hole in the shaft with that in the housing) and fit the roll-pin. Dip the second pinion gear in oil and place it in the ring gear. Secure the ring gear to the housing with *new* self-locking bolts (permanently lock them with an electrically brazed tack). Tighten bolts to 45 ft. lbs.

Before reassembling the rest of the unit, adjust the pinion depth, the ring gear and pinion backlash, and the differential bearing preload.

The drive pinion and the ring gear are lapped together during manufacture. Replacing one requires replacement of the other. A common reference number is inscribed on the ring gear and the pinion.

NOTE: A groove has been machined at the double bearing locating point on the pinion of the strengthened ring gear and pinion fitted to the Renault 1130 in order to identify them.

The pinion is in the correct position when its front face is a distance of A = 48.5 mm (1.910 in.) from the ring gear center line. Adjust this position by placing a washer of a suitable thickness between the double taper roller bearing and the shoulder on the secondary shaft.

In some instances dimension A is not the pinion depth. The difference between the true pinion depth and dimension A is then marked on the front face of the pinion beside the matching reference numbers. It is given in hundredths of a millimeter. The pinion depth is then equal to A plus the difference noted.

Check the pinion depth by securing the housing to a support. Press the bearing on to the secondary shaft. Set the shaft into the housing. Fit the pinion depth adjusting washer. Fit the roller bearing and the speedometer drive worm.

NOTE: The roller bearing is adjusted by the manufacturer and should not be dismantled. When fitting a new bearing a re-

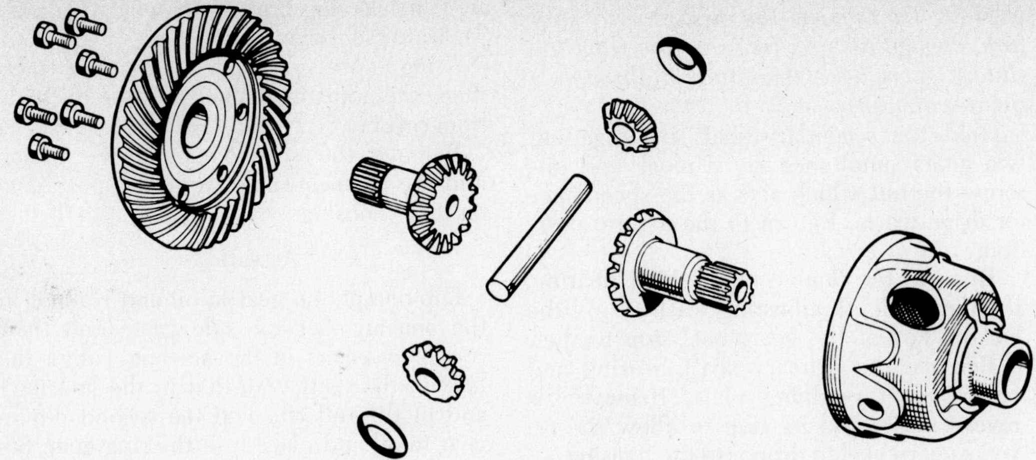

New type differential for 325 gearbox.

sistance to rotation is felt in the secondary shaft. This resistance is quite normal. If the original bearing is refitted ensure that there is no play.

Tighten the speedometer drive worm to 85 ft. lbs. Temporarily fit the speedometer-drive housing to hold the bearing track ring in place. Fit tool with the graduated rule against the front face of the pinion and the plate with the mark C pressed against the housing. *The dimension opposite the O mark should equal the pinion depth. If the dimension reading is less,* replace the adjusting washer with a *thinner one.*

To adjust ring gear and pinion backlash, place the differential in the housing. Place adjusting mandrel tool on the differential. Place the differential carriers (fitted with paper gaskets) on the housing. Fit the corresponding half shells and tighten them to 35 ft. lbs.

Mount a dial indicator on the housing placing its plunger in contact with one tooth of the ring gear. Tighten the screw on the special tool at the ring gear side until a backlash of between .12 mm and .25 mm (from .005 to .010 in.), is obtained. Tighten the screw on the other side, ensuring that the backlash does not change. Remove the half shells, the differential carriers, the tool and the baffle washers. Remove the differential from the housing. Remove the speedometer drive housing and the secondary shaft.

The adjustment is made by placing shims under the bearing track rings, inside the differential carriers. The thickness of the shim pack (C) to be placed in the carrier is determined by taking the difference between the thickness (C1) of the adjusting mandrel tool and thickness (C2) of the bearing. C = C1 — C2

Measure the thickness C1 of the adjusting tool with a micrometer.

Place the bearing and its track ring on tool and tighten down the assembly. Measure the thickness of the bearing and the fixture C3, by means of a micrometer. The thickness of the bearing is therefore: C2 = C3 — 10 mm (— .394 in.) (the thickness of the fixture). *The shim pack must make the differential rotate without play.*

If new bearings are fitted the differential should turn with a resistance of between 7 to 16 in.-lbs. The adjustment obtained by the method already described provided a rotation of the differential without any play. Add a shim 0.1 mm (.004 in.) thick to each differential carrier. Fit the oil seals, adjusting shims, and bearing track rings (pressed on) in the differential carriers. Press the bearings on the differential. Place the differential in the housing. Fit the differential carriers and the half shells; tighten the nuts to a torque of 35 ft. lbs. Turn the differential several turns, by hand, to centralize the bearings. Wrap a string around the differential housing. Attach a spring balance to the string and pull evenly. *The differential should turn under a load of between 3 lbs 12 ozs to 8 lbs 1 oz.* If the adjustment is incorrect increase or reduce the thickness of the shim pack by the same amount in each carrier.

Press on the bearing at the speedometer drive end. Set the shaft into the housing. Press on the bearing at the differential end. Fit the track ring over the bearing at the

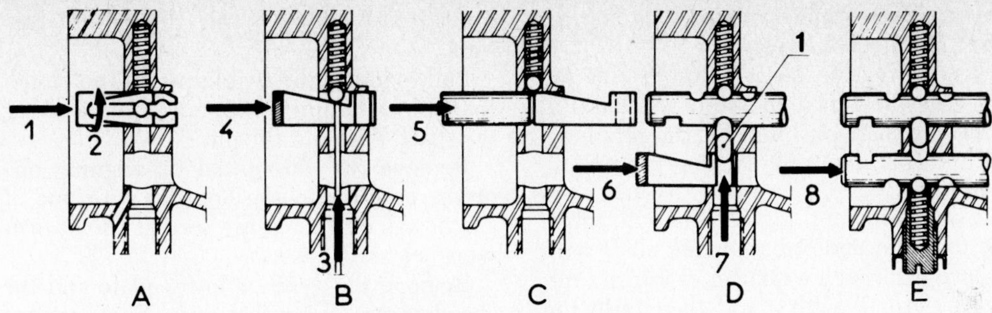

Transmission-locking system.

differential end. *The track ring should be flush with the edge of the housing.* Temporarily fit the retaining plate to the bearing at the differential end. Fit the track ring of the bearing at the speedometer drive end.

Push in the track ring of the bearing at the speedometer drive end until *the shaft turns freely without any play.* Place adjusting shims behind the track ring followed by the spacer. The spacer should be flush with the edge of the housing. Temporarily fit the speedometer drive housing together with its paper gasket. Strike the differential end of the shaft in order to bed down the adjusting shims. Check the rotation of the shaft.

Remove the bearing retaining plate, the speedometer drive housing, the spacer and the adjusting shims.

Stick the stop washer in its location with grease (bronze face towards the gearwheel). Fit the double gearwheel with the spur gear at the differential end.

First speed synchronizer. Place spring on the first speed gearwheel so that it covers the three slots. Fit the sliding gearwheel to the hub with the teeth on the opposite side to the counterbore on the hub. Place the synchronizer cone on the sliding gearwheel. Fit the first speed gearwheel. Hold the parts in place by means of two sheet steel clips.

NOTE: The sliding gearwheel and the hub are matched.

Fit the three keys and two springs in place on hub. Engage one end of each of the springs in the same key with the free ends on opposite sides of the key. Engage the hub into the sliding ring.

NOTE: The sliding ring and hub are matched.

Gradually introduce the secondary shaft fitted with its bearing into the housing fitting the following parts to it.

a. First speed synchronizer (with teeth towards the differential)
b. Splined washer
c. Second speed gearwheel and the dog ring
d. 2nd-3rd speed synchronizer with its unsplined portion in line with the keyway (a) in the secondary shaft
e. Splined washer
f. Dog ring and the third speed gearwheel

Push the first speed synchronizer toward the differential. Fit the splined washer.

Push the 2nd-3rd speed gearwheel synchronizer assembly against the first-speed synchronizer. Fit the splined washer.

Introduce the key into its keyway to lock the two washers. Remove the two clips in order to free the first-gear synchronizer. Push the secondary shaft fully home while turning the gearwheels in order to avoid damaging their teeth. Fit the pinion-depth adjusting washer. Fit the roller bearing. Engage two gears simultaneously and tighten

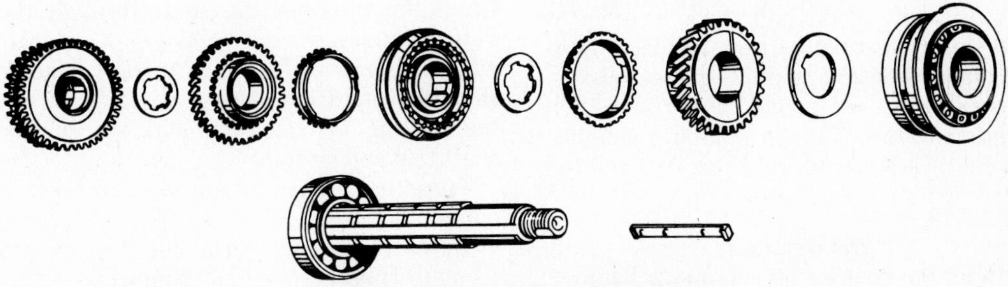
Parts of secondary shaft in 325 gearbox.

down the speedometer worm to a torque of 85 ft. lbs. Lock it in place.

Pass the reverse shaft through the reverse gearwheel and the stop washer. Fit the reverse shaft bushing. Fit the retaining plate and fold down the locking tab with a pair of pliers.

Fit the spring and replace the ball. Introduce tool into 2nd-3rd shift fork shaft bore and turn it through a quarter of a turn (A).

Push the ball with a rod then push the tool towards the inside of the housing (B).

Fit the shift fork shaft (C) and the shift fork. Pin it in place with a drift.

Introduce plunger using an appropriate tool. Fit the first-reverse shift fork, engaging reverse. Engage the fork in the housing and turn it through a quarter of a turn. Place it in the sliding gearwheel groove and return to the neutral position.

Fit the first-reverse shift fork shaft and pin the fork in place. Place the ball and spring in position, screw in and tighten down the lock stop after smearing its screw thread with locking compound.

NOTE: The first-reverse and 2nd-3rd locking springs are identical.

Fit the seal, the speedometer drive wheel and its nylon bushing (align its groove with the set bolt hole) into the speedometer drive housing. Engage first gear. Fit the control lever. Position the speedometer drive housing, together with its paper gasket smeared with sealing compound, against the housing. Fit the control lever shaft and pin the lever in place. Return to neutral and secure the cover housing. Fit the lower cover plate with its gasket smeared with compound.

Place the differential in the housing. Refit the clutch shaft together with its pin retaining spring. Fit the pin and hold it in place with the spring. Refit the differential carriers with their paper gaskets smeared with compound (follow the reference marks made during dismantling). Fit the universal joints.

Temporarily fit the half shells in order to hold the differential carriers in place. Refit the clutch housing with its paper gaskets smeared with compound. Fit the clutch withdrawal fork. Fit the damping weights. Fill the gearbox with oil after it is refitted to the car.

Type 318

Disassembly

Mount the gearbox on a support. Remove the end plate together with the clutch withdrawal fork. Remove the differential carriers.

Pull together the two horns on the clutch shaft pin retaining spring and slide it along the shaft. Push out the pin.

Remove the differential by aligning one of the cut-outs in the housing with one of the bosses on the casing so that the crownwheel clears.

Remove the gearbox lower plate and the speedometer drive housing. First engage third gear then pull back the housing until it makes contact with the control shaft clevis. Push out the control-lever roll pin, using a drift. Remove the shaft and the housing; free the control lever. Return the box to the neutral position. Remove the primary shaft bearing spacer and adjusting shims.

Push out the roll pins from the 1st-2nd and 3rd-4th shift forks, using a drift.

Unscrew the locking system plug after first loosening the locknut. Remove the spring and the ball. Remove the 1st-2nd shift fork shaft (the fork is not removed), the locking plunger, the 3rd-4th shift-fork shaft and the fork.

Don't lose the locking ball and spring.

Lock the secondary shaft by simultaneously engaging two gears. Unlock and unscrew the nut which serves as the speedometer drive worm. Return the box to the neutral position.

Remove the double taper roller bearing, and pinion-depth adjusting washer, and the gearbox stop washer locating key.

Tap the secondary shaft toward the differential end. Pull the fourth speed gearwheel against the housing. The stop washer is then accessible.

First turn it then slide it along the shaft. Bring the third-speed synchronizer-gearwheel assembly against the fourth-speed gearwheel. The second stop washer is then accessible.

Turn it then slide it along the shaft. Gradually pull out the shaft through the differential end and remove the gearwheels. Remove the primary shaft bearing stop plate and the reverse shaft. Take out the locking system stop, and the reverse shaft ball and spring.

Turn the shaft until the control lever is completely freed from the reverse sleeve. Remove the sleeve. Push out the roll pin using drift and remove the control lever.

Remove the reverse gearwheel retaining

circlip from its groove. Take out the reverse shaft, the gearwheel, the washer and the circlip. Remove the reverse shaft locking plungers Nos. 2 and 3 after first unscrewing their plugs.

Push the primary shaft toward the differential and put aside the bearing track ring. Extract the bearing from the differential end. The shaft is now free and can be removed from the housing without taking off the second bearing.

Push out the bearing track ring from the speedometer drive end. Extract the bearing from the primary shaft. Remove the secondary shaft bearing with a press.

Since manufacturing number 32 461 gearbox type 318 ring gear has been fitted with the same ring gear and pinion, and the same differential as those fitted to the gearboxes of R 1130 vehicles.

Old Type

Remove the bearing on the differential housing side using extractor and press. Unlock and unscrew the five ring gear bolts. Separate the ring gear from the housing and remove the pinion gear. Extract the bearing. Remove the side gear shaft retaining pin. Separate the various parts.

New Type

Remove the bearing from the house end using extractor. Remove and throw away the six ring gear securing bolts. Separate the ring gear from the housing and take out the pinion gear. Remove the bearing with extractor. Push out the roll pin which retains the shaft. Separate the various parts.

Using a press, remove the bearing track rings, the adjusting shims, and the seals from the differential carriers.

Remove the nylon bushing and the speedometer drive pinion.

Locking plates, washers, roll pins and seals should be replaced by new parts.

Assembly

Old Type Differential

Place pinion gear (dipped in oil), side gears, and their bushings in the housing. Insert the side gear shaft (align the shaft hole with that in the housing) and fit the pin. Dip the second pinion gear in oil and place it in the ring gear. Fit the ring gear to the housing (with the tab on the locking plate covering the shear pin). Torque bolts to 35 ft lbs.

New Type Differential

See instructions under section for type 325 gearbox.

Adjust the pinion depth, the ring gear to pinion backlash, and the differential bearings before completing assembly of the gearbox. The adjustment instructions are the same for type 318 as for type 325. *See the adjustment steps for the 325, but use only the specifications listed for the type 318*

Assemble the primary shaft and adjust the bearing end play as described for type 325.

Insert the reverse shaft from the differential end. Slide the gearwheel (with the teeth on the differential side), the stop washer (with the bronze face towards the gearwheel) and the circlip onto the shaft. Insert plunger into its bore. Place the control lever on the reverse shaft and pin it in place.

Insert the reverse sleeve. Swing the shaft and place the control lever in the cut-out in the sleeve. Secure the primary and reverse shaft bearing retaining plate in position and fold down the locking plate. Insert locking plunger No. 2 into its location. Screw in the plunger bore plugs after smearing the thread with sealing compound. Lock them by means of a punch mark.

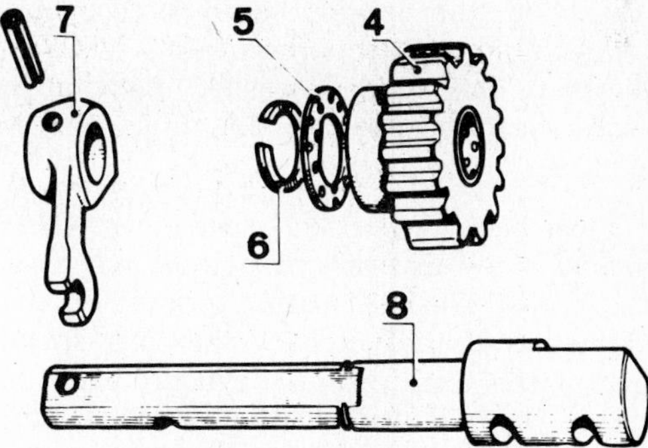

Parts of reverse shaft, 318 gearbox.

Set the locking system as shown for type 325.

Assemble the secondary shaft and second speed synchronizer. Fit the key retaining ring, the two springs and the three keys on the hub. Engage one end of each of the springs in the same key, with the two other ends on the opposite sides of the key.

Engage the hub into the sliding gearwheel with the groove at the toothed end. The sliding gearwheel and the hub are matched.

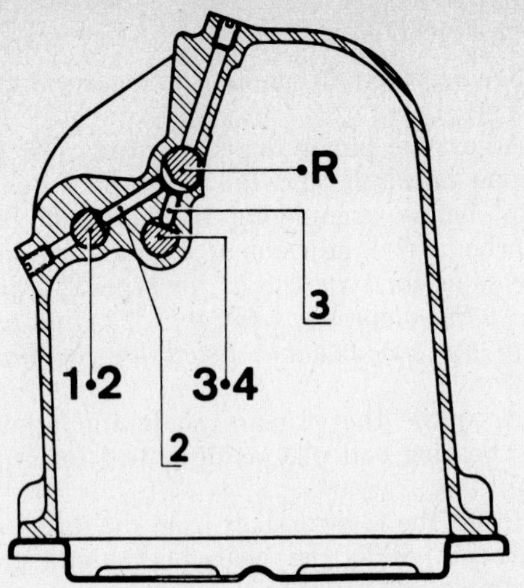

Reverse-shaft locking plungers Nos. 2 and 3.

Place the three keys and the two springs on the hub. Engage one end of each of the springs into the same key with the other ends on the opposite sides of the key. Insert the hub into sliding sleeve. The sliding sleeve and the hub are matched.

Place the 1st-2nd sliding gearwheel on its shift fork (with the teeth towards the speedometer drive end). Progressively insert the shaft into the housing fitting the following parts in the order given: the 2nd speed gearwheel, the dog ring, the splined washer, the third-speed gearwheel, and the dog ring, the 3rd-4th speed synchronizer with the unsplined portion in line with the keyway, the splined washer, the fourth-speed gearwheel and the dog ring.

Push back the 1st-2nd speed gearwheel assembly towards the differential and clear the splined washer locating groove. Fit the splined washer. Pull back the third-speed gearwheel and 3rd-4th synchronizer to clear the splined washer groove. Fit washer. Push key fully into its keyway. Fit the pinion-depth adjusting washer. Fit the double roller bearing. Engage two gears simultaneously and tighten down the speedometer drive worm (85 ft lbs). Lock the worm.

Pull back the 3rd-4th shift fork and fit the fork. Pin it in place. Fit the ball and the spring. Screw down and tighten the locking system stop after first smearing its thread with sealing compound. Insert the reverse shaft ball and spring. Screw down the locking plug after smearing its thread with compound. Tighten the locknut by turning it through a quarter of a turn after it has made contact with the housing.

Fit the seal, the speedometer drive pinion and its nylon bushing (align its slot with the set bolt hole into the speedometer drive housing).

Engage second gear. Fit the shift fork shaft control lever. Fit the housing with its paper gasket smeared with jointing compound.

Fit the control lever shaft, and pin the lever in place. Return to the neutral position and secure the cover housing in place. Fit the lower cover plate with its paper gasket smeared with jointing compound.

Place the differential in the housing. Refit the clutch shaft together with its pin-retaining spring. Fit the pin and lock it by means of the spring.

Refit the differential carriers together with their paper gaskets, smeared with jointing compound (*follow the reference marks made during dismantling*).

Fit the universal joints. Temporarily fit the differential carrier half shells to hold the carriers in place. Refit the end plate with its paper gasket smeared with jointing compound.

NOTE: Fill the gearbox with oil after it is installed in the car.

Remove and refit the speedometer drive housing as described for gearbox type 330.

Renault 12 and Renault 16 Transaxle

Disassembly

1. Remove clutch housing bolts and remove clutch. Remove front housing bolts and lift off housing. Set spacer and shaft bearing assembly aside for future reference.
2. Remove differential lockwasher. Remove half housing bolts and separate housing.
3. Pull out secondary gear train with stop peg.
4. Pull out primary shaft and differential.
5. Using a drift, remove roll pin at third and fourth shift fork. Remove fork with shaft. Do not lose ball and spring. Remove the locking disc between the shafts.
6. Locate the first gear. Pull reverse gear shaft fully back. Using a drift, remove first and second gear rollpin. Remove shaft and fork. Retain ball and spring for future use. Loosen and remove first gear swivel pin.
7. Remove reverse gear shaft positioning

roll pin. Remove shaft with fork.

8. Remove reverse gear wheel circlip with all small parts. Place in order for easy assembly.

Half Housing Disassembly

Mark position of side cover with respect to half housing. Remove side cover.

1. Press bearing cages from case.
2. Primary shaft.

Remove bearing cages with washer. Remove clutch shaft from primary shaft by extracting roll pin. Remove all bearings from differential side.

Secondary Shaft

Unscrew all parts. Start at speedometer drive worm end. When removing third and fourth sliding gears, mark position with reference to hub. Pull off with appropriate tool. Also, mark position of first and second sliding gear. When all gears are removed, place retaining clip on shaft to prevent roller bearings from being lost. Be sure to keep all gears in order for easy assembly.

Differential

1. Using puller, pull off bearings. Ring gear bolts may first have to be removed.

NOTE: These bolts must not be used again.

Using a drift, punch out roll pins holding side gears in position.

2. Remove the speedometer drive gear, O ring seal, circlip (it so equipped), thrust washer and bellows, and all remaining small parts.
3. Punch out with drift the selector fork control lever pin. Also, remove the external control lever pin.

Assembly

All rollpins, seals, and self-locking bolts must be replaced. Two types of ring gears and pinions were used. One has a circlip on the final drive bearing, the other does not. If it has a circlip, it can only be fitted in a housing with a groove. Ring gears and pinions are matched; they are stamped with identical numbers. When replacing one, the other must also be replaced. If synchros are worn, they must be replaced and matched with the final drive pinion. To do this, measure along two splines on final drive pinion shaft. Do this at three points and take the average reading. If measurement is .6539-.6547", order a blue synchro hub. If measurement is .6651-.6559", order a yellow synchro hub. The first-second synchro hubs must be press fitted on drive pinion shaft while hot. They must be heated to 482°F.

1. Place synchro spring on first gear wheel. Be sure it covers three notches. Assemble first gear wheel and stop washer on final drive pinion. Turn it and fit temporarily with a dummy key (made by removing the curved end of a washer retaining key). Place key on spline oil hole.
2. Place first-second gear hub in oven. When heated to 482°, fit drive pinion shaft with splined section opposite dummy key. Be sure chamfer on splines faces first gear wheel side. With the aid of a press, fit wheel on until it contacts stop washer. Be sure synchro ring is level. Keep pressure on until hub cools considerably. Then remove both press and dummy key.
3. Assemble first-second synchro with the chamfer towards the second gear wheel. Assemble stop washer with splines opposite final drive pinion.
4. Place synchronizer spring on second gear wheel. Fit gear to shaft with stop washer splines aligned with those on final drive pinion.
5. Fit the third gear wheel in the same manner as outlined above. Be sure retaining key is fitted in keyway with an oil hole. Fit third-fourth synchro. Be sure notches on synchro ring are in line with notches on retaining key.
6. Place fourth gear wheel and synchro ring on shaft. Fit pinion adjusting washer with tapered roller bearing and speedometer drive gear.
7. Tighten assembled shaft in vice. Torque to 75-85 ft. lbs. Do not lock. Pinion protrusion adjustment must be performed later.
8. Check play between third and fourth speed gear synchro ring and hub. It should be .008" minimum. Be sure all other gears are tightly packed.

Differential

NOTE: Many special tools are needed to perform the following operations. They should not be attempted unless they are readily available.

1. Place bakelite washer with oil groove on pinion side in differential housing. Use spacer .077-.079 in. (normal) or .080-.082 in. (excessive wear).

2. Assemble ring and pinion gear with washers in housing. Be sure locking peg is in housing hole.
3. Secure gear in housing with roll pins. Lubricate pinion and fit to ring gear. With self locking bolts, fasten ring gear to housing. Torque to 70 ft. lbs. for .394" bolts, and 60-80 ft. lbs. for .434" bolts.
4. Fit O ring seal to pinion. After assembly, differential may be difficult to turn. To test, lock one pinion and check torque required to rotate other. It should be 10 in. lbs. maximum for sleeved differential, 15 in. lbs. for an unsleeved one.

Pinion Protrusion Adjustment

NOTE: Before proceeding further, the following adjustments must be made.

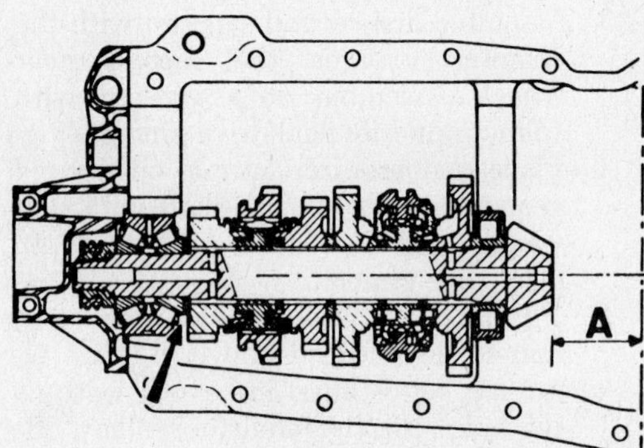

Pinion protrusion checking

This distance (dimension A, see illustration) is from drive pinion front to ring gear center line. It is obtained by a shim between tapered roller bearing and secondary shaft shoulder. Three different differential types, needing different shim thicknesses, are used.

#1 Pinion gear bolts .394 in., final drive pinion bearing .827 in. Nominal pinion depth: 2.032 in.

#2 Pinion bolts are .434 in., final drive pinion width is .748 in. Nominal pinion depth is 2.087 in.

#3 Two types are used. A flat face pinion, with nominal pinion depth of 2.087 in., and a shoulder face pinion, with a nominal pinion depth of 2.032 in.

NOTE: In most cases, dimension A may not be the correct depth. This is caused by the fitting of a pinion which may differ from nominal dimensions. If this is the case, this variation will be stamped in millimeters on pinion front face. In any case, pinion protrusion must be checked.

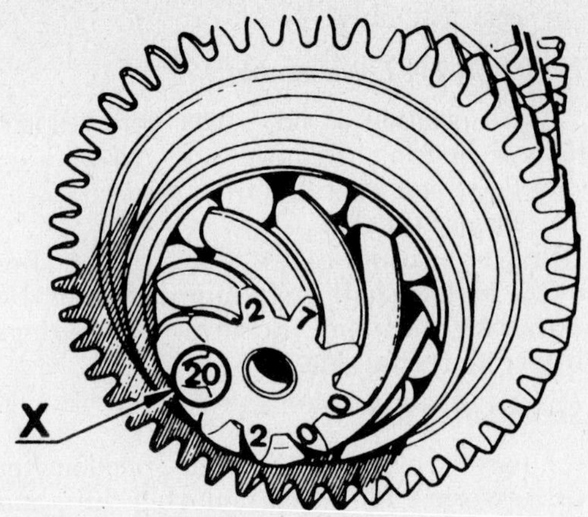

Pinion variation marking

Checking 2.087 in. pinion (nominal)

Add the height of the spacer (1.575 in.) to the radius of the shaft on plug mandrel (.394 in.). Subtract this total from the desired pinion depth (2.087 in.). Resulting number (dimension X) is the required shim thickness for a ring and pinion of nominal dimensions.

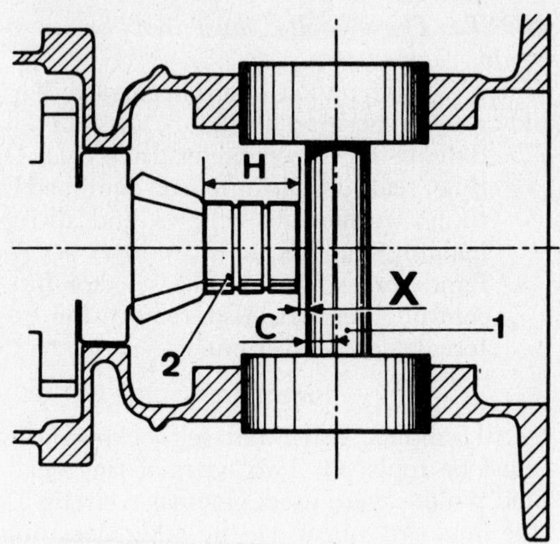

Establishing pinion depth

Checking 2.032 in. pinion (nominal)

Add the height of the spacer (1.614 in.) to the radius of the shaft on plug mandrel (.394 in.). Subtract this total from desired pinion depth (2.032 in.). Resulting number (dimension X) is the required shim thickness for a ring and pinion of nominal dimensions.

Checking 2.087 in. pinion (flat and shoulder face)

Add the height of the spacer (1.673 in.) to the radius of the shaft on plug mandrel (.394 in.). Subtract this total from the desired pinion depth (2.087 in.). Resulting number (dimension X) is the required shim thickness for a ring and pinion of nominal dimensions.

Fasten housings together and fit secondary shaft. Temporarily replace front housing. Tighten bolts. Measure with a feeler gauge the actual dimension X between spacer and mandrel. If the dimension is less than nominal, use a thinner washer. If it is more, use a thicker one. Washer sizes available are from .138 in.-.162 in. When this step is completed, remove all tools, and pull apart all housings. Remove secondary shaft and lock speedometer worm in position.

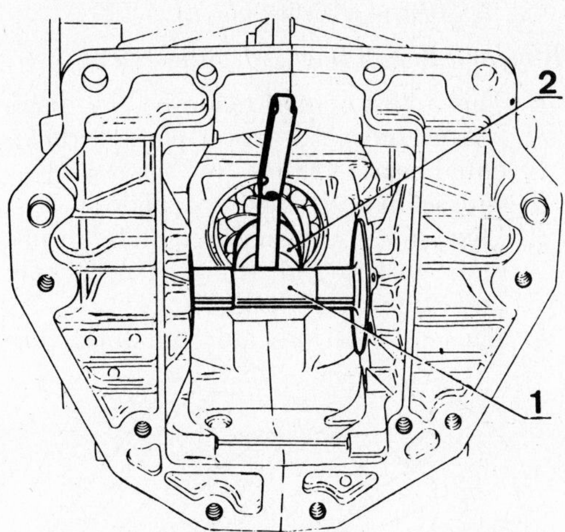

1 Ring gear center line positioner 2 Spacer

Use a feeler gauge to establish depth of protrusion

Differential Bearing Adjustment

1. Place bearing track ring in proper place in left half housing. Do not press fully in.
2. Fit original adjusting shims, paper gasket, and side cover plate to housing. Torque side cover bolts to 15 ft. lbs.
3. Place differential and bearings into half housing. Fit right and left housing halfs together. Torque .276 in. bolts to 15 ft. lbs., and .315 in. bolts to 20 ft. lbs. Place bearing track ring in right half housing. Do not fully seat.
4. When original wheel bearings are to be reused, the differential must rotate without play. Position original shims under right hand half housing track. Fit gasket and side cover. Slowly tighten cover plate to close space between track and bearing. If differential becomes difficult to rotate before cover plate bolts are fully tightened, remove shims. If differential has no resistance to rotation after bolts are finally tightened, add shims. Side cover bolt torque is 15 ft. lbs.

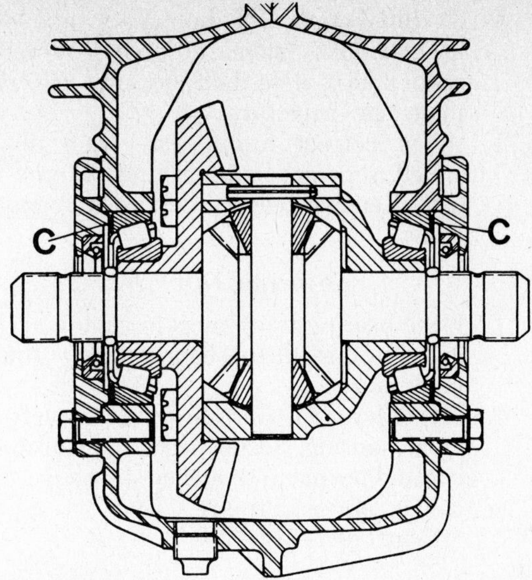

Differential bearing adjustment and placement of shims (c)

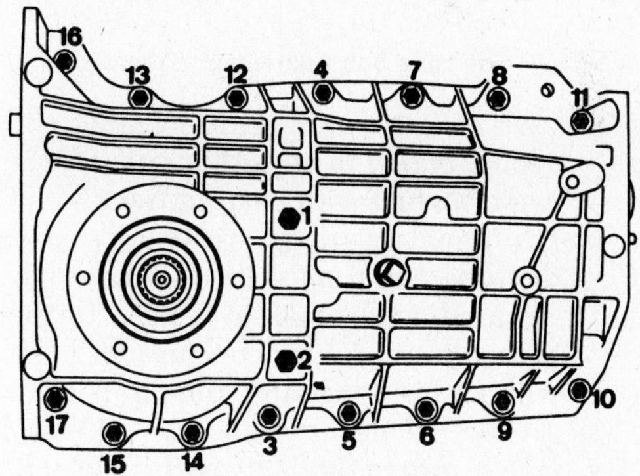

Side cover plate tightening sequence

5. New wheel bearings. Fit original shims to right-hand half housing. Position gasket and side plate. Slowly tighten plate bolts to close track bearing gap. Tighten plate cover bolts to 15 ft. lbs.

Bearing Preload

1. Rotate differential 15 times to properly seat bearings.
2. Attach an in. lbs. torque wrench to the differential housing. The differential should rotate with 2-7 in. lbs. of turning torque.

3. If differential will not meet above specifications, increase/decrease shim pack under right half housing cover plate as necessary.
4. When correct torque has been obtained, separate housings and differential. Remove cover side plate and shims.

Adjusting Nut

1. Place bearing track rings in each housing. Position them slightly below the inner face.
2. Fit differential and bearings in left-hand housing. Secure right housing to left and torque in sequence shown.
   .276 in. bolts—15 ft. lbs.
   .315 in. bolts—20 ft. lbs.

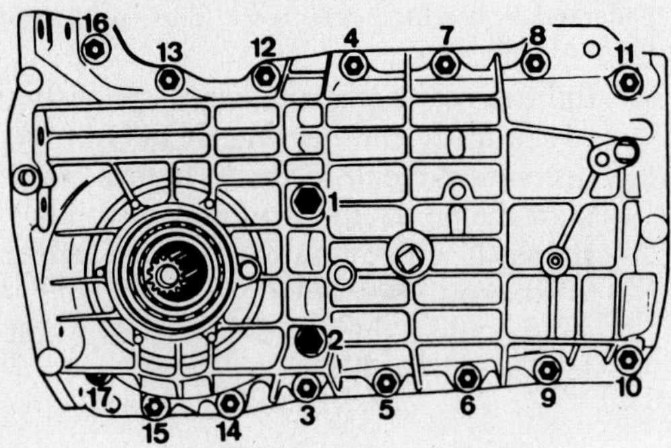

Housing bolt tightening sequence

3. Coat nut threads with locking compound. Screw in adjusting nuts till they make contact with bearing track.
4. If original bearings are being reused, the differential must turn without play. Turn adjusting nuts in a little further. Screw in nut 1 further than nut 2. This will ensure ring and pinion backlash greater than is necessary. *NOTE: When differential can be turned without play, stop adjusting.* Mark nut position with reference to housing. Remove right housing and differential.

5. If using new bearings, they must have a preload. Differential should rotate with a resistance of 6-18 ozs., measured with a spring scale. Continue to screw in nuts. Screw nut one in further than the other. This will ensure adequate gear backlash. When differential becomes hard to rotate, check preload as previously described. Mark nuts with respect to housing. Remove right half housing and differential.

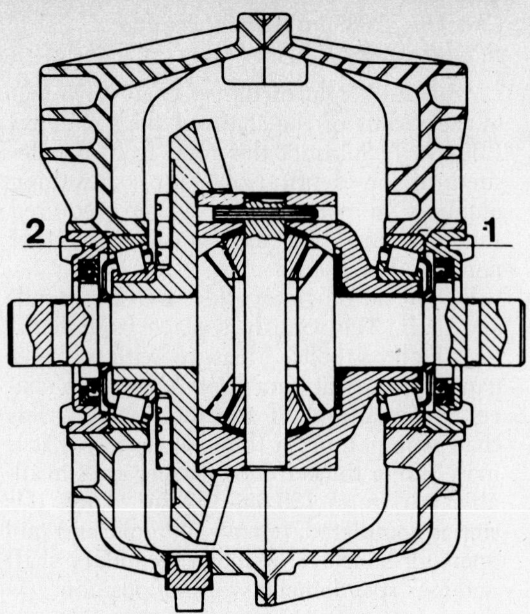

Location of adjusting nuts (1 and 2)

Ring and Pinion Backlash Adjustment

1. This adjustment is made by the distribution under side cover plate of differential bearing shims.
2. Fit seal in both side cover plates.
3. Place side cover on differential housing with gasket and shims. Insert bolts and torque to 15 ft. lbs.
4. Place a dial indicator on differential

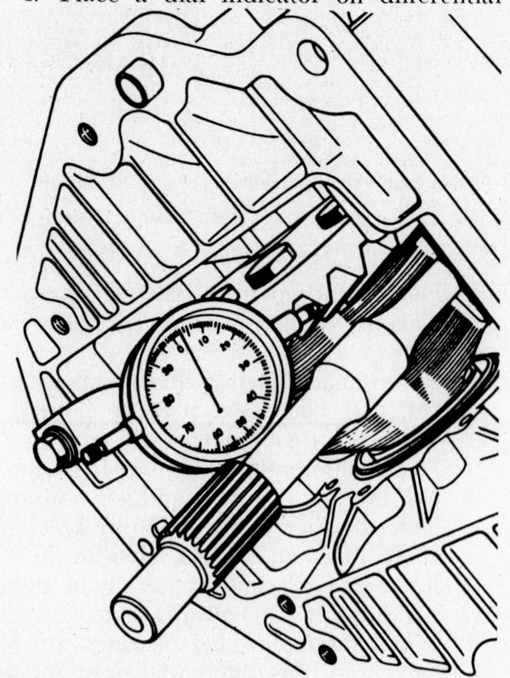

Checking ring and pinion backlash

housing. Place plunger on tooth. Be sure it is at a right angle to case flank and at case extreme outer edge.

5. Fit side cover plate and shims to ring gear end. Tighten bolts and check rotation. Backlash: .005-.010."
6. If correct backlash is noted before bolts are fully tightened, shim thickness at cover plate is excessive. Remove shims and fit under opposite cover plate.
7. If correct backlash is still not obtained after tightening bolts, again remove shims and fit under cover on ring gear side.
8. After correct backlash is obtained, remove side cover and use sealant on gaskets. Fit side cover and torque to 15 ft. lbs.

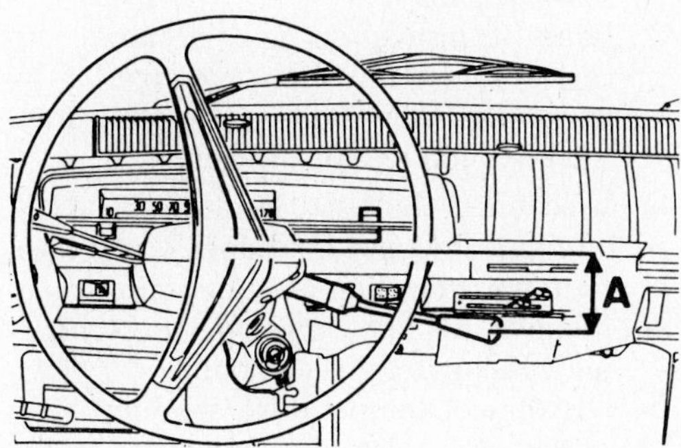

Position gear lever so end is 1 13/16±25/64" below a horizontal line passing through steering wheel center.

Renault 12 and 16 Gear Linkage/Lever Adjustment

1. Place car in fourth gear. Loosen screws holding steering column tube together. They are located in the engine compartment.
2. Move gear lever to free column. Be sure gear lever is still in fourth gear.
3. Position gear lever vertically so end is 1 13/16±25/64" below a horizontal line passing through steering wheel center.
4. Position lever with steering column so tube hole is opposite roll pin. With hand, hold lever in this position.
5. Tighten bolts. Check gearbox operation.

PRIMARY SHAFT POSITIONING AND BEARING ADJUSTMENT

For these adjustments, refer to Type 330 gearbox and perform adjustments in identical manner.

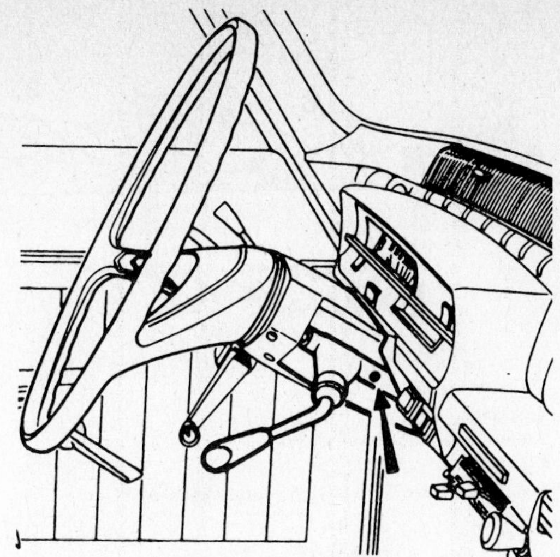

Tube hole/rollpin location

Gearshift Control Assembly

1. Follow Type 330 gearbox assembly procedures as they apply to the gear shift control and the reverse gear shaft.
2. Using a drift, pin external control to shaft. Be sure rollpin slot is at a right angle to the external shaft. Place second rollpin inside first; be sure its slot is at a right angle to outer rollpin. Place rubber bellows on shaft.
3. Fit first spring, washer, second spring, and internal control lever in housing. Place shaft through all above components. Using drift, pin internal control lever to shaft with pin slot at a right angle to shaft. Insert second rollpin, with slot at right angle to outer pin slot.
4. Fit on shaft: thrust washers, springs, circlips, protective bellows. Assemble breather and speedometer drive gear onto shaft. Be sure speedometer sleeve is fitted with proper O-ring.
5. Position the differential, primary shaft, and secondary shaft assembly with lock peg in left-hand housing. Use sealant on housing assembly ends.
6. Fit housing halves together. Be sure reverse swivel lever end fits in reverse gear wheel shaft slot. Insert housing bolts; do not tighten.
7. Insert primary shaft shims, spacer, and gasket. Use appropriate sealer. Fit front housing. Be sure internal control lever engages selector shaft slots. Insert, but do not tighten, front housing bolts.

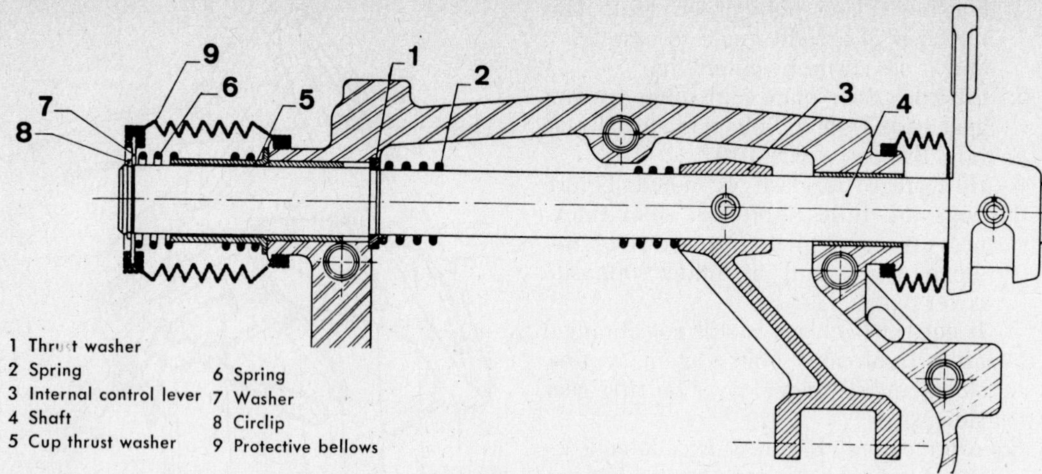

Primary shaft assembly

8. Tighten half housing bolts in proper sequence.

Torque
.276 in. bolts–15 ft. lbs.
.315 in. bolts–20 ft. lbs.

AUTOMATIC TRANSMISSION

The Renault automatic transmission, still basically the same design as when introduced in 1963, consists of a three-speed fully synchronized transmission, with an electric servo actuating motor for shifting, an electromagnetic clutch, a decelerator solenoid to cut engine speed for shifts, a control governor, and a sealed relay unit that initiates and synchronizes the shifting action.

Removal

NOTE: The following general procedures apply to all models.

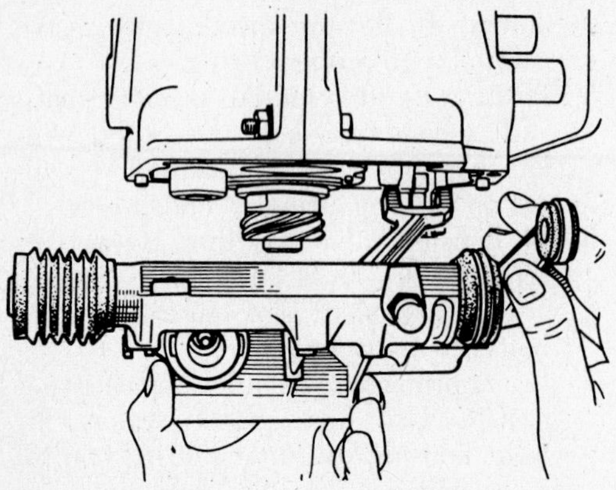

Installing front housing

1. Jack the front of the vehicle and remove wheels.
2. Drain transmission and remove converter cover. Disconnect converter by removing four bolts between crossmember and engine oil pan.
3. Disconnect battery. Remove hood retaining cable and hold open with strap. Remove expansion chamber clip.
4. Remove tie bar between wheel housings. Remove camshaft pulley.
5. Disconnect temperature sending wires at radiator. Also, disconnect fan wires.
6. Remove radiator bolts and place expansion chamber on wheel housing. Swing radiator out of way and place on engine top.
7. Disconnect spark plugs, speedometer cable, governor cable, and gear change control arm.
8. Remove computer unit (if so equipped). Disconnect transmission ground wire and harness. Disconnect transmission vacuum line.
9. Turn steering wheel fully left and remove right steering arm. Perform same operation to left steering arm.
10. Remove bolts holding round coupling on steering column. Remove steering gear crossmember and related parts.
11. Using drift, punch out transmission yoke rollpins at rubber bellows.
12. Using a clamp, fasten transmission yoke together.
13. Remove brake calipers and upper ball joints.
14. Remove transmission yoke from pinion and place protection over exposed pinion end.

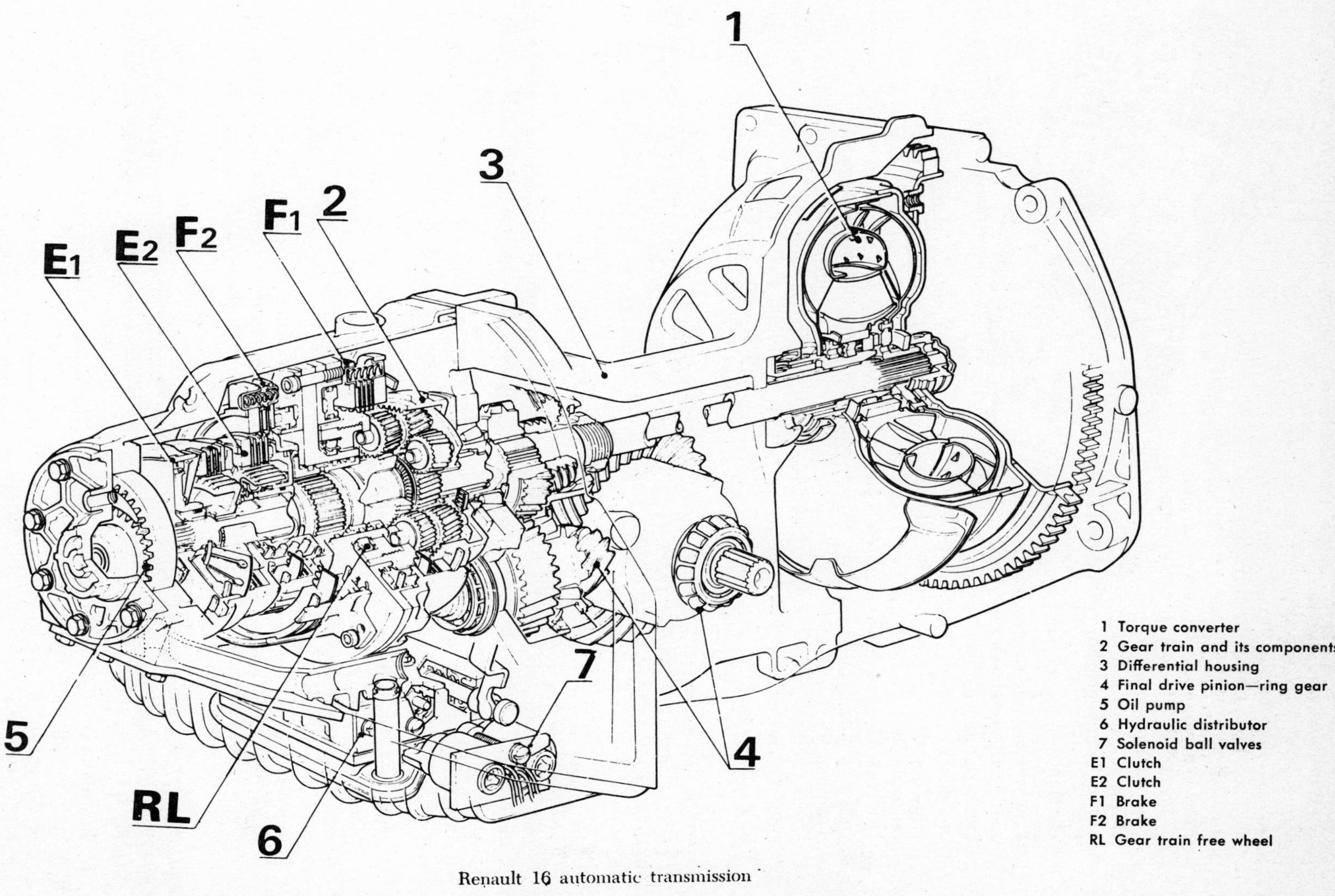

Renault 16 automatic transmission

15. Remove nuts holding transmission to front mountings. Remove bolts securing transmission to engine.
16. Using hoist bar and hoist, lift transmission slightly and break from front support. Lower gearbox on front crossmember.
17. After separation, use a retaining plate or other suitable tool to avoid dislocation of torque converter.
18. Hoist gearbox from vehicle. Be sure not to damage gearbox central ball.

Installation

1. Lower gearbox into engine bay. Remove torque converter retainer.
2. Converter drive plate has white mark on flange. Torque converter has a matching mark. They must be aligned on assembly.
3. Use new lockwashers. Tighten converter bolts in rotation in three stages. Torque to 18 ft. lbs.
4. Grease pinion splines before installation. Be sure O-ring seal is in acceptable condition.
5. To proceed, reverse removal procedure.

DAUPHINE GOVERNOR AND THROTTLE LINKAGE ADJUSTMENT

1. Refer to R-8 Governor/Throttle Adjustment and perform steps one and two.
2. Screw end of U link as required to make lamp circuit shut off when tip of link is centered between prongs. Lamp should light for rest of throttle linkage travel.
3. Open throttle fully by pulling cable. Check gap between governor arm and stop. It should be 1/16″. To widen gap, bend S curve of U link towards bracket. To decrease, reverse procedure. After obtaining proper clearance, again perform Step 2. Adjust as necessary.

RENAULT 8 AND RENAULT 10 GOVERNOR AND THROTTLE LINKAGE ADJUSTMENT

1. To perform this adjustment, a test lamp circuit must be used. To do this, secure a wire to the transmission governor. Connect test lamp to battery positive terminal at regulator; connect other lead to blue wire. Be sure to use a test lamp of .12 watts or less. Ground transmission governor wire.

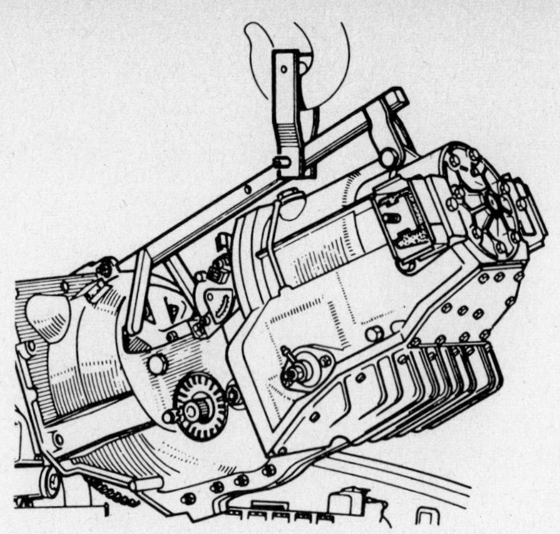

Removing automatic transmission

2. Bring engine to operating temperature. Adjust idle mixture and speed. Check fast idle cam. It should be free, and idle speed screw should be resting against stop.
3. Loosen locknut. Turn adjusting nut to make test light shut off when stud is at center point of circle. Test circuit should light again for rest of throttle linkage travel.
4. Be sure upper stud behind sector does not contact stop when throttle is fully opened. Stud and stop should have a 1/16 in. gap. When this is accomplished, tighten locknut.

RENAULT 12 AND 16 AUTOMATIC TRANSMISSION ADJUSTMENTS

NOTE: After performing this adjustment, kick-down switch must also be adjusted.

Governor Cable

1. Adjust sleeve stop to middle position. Place control cable into slot in control quadrant.
2. Attach cable opposite end to cam at carburetor. Push accelerator fully down. Tension cable by moving sleeve stop. Cable must have no play.
3. Clearance between quadrant and index should be .012-.020″.

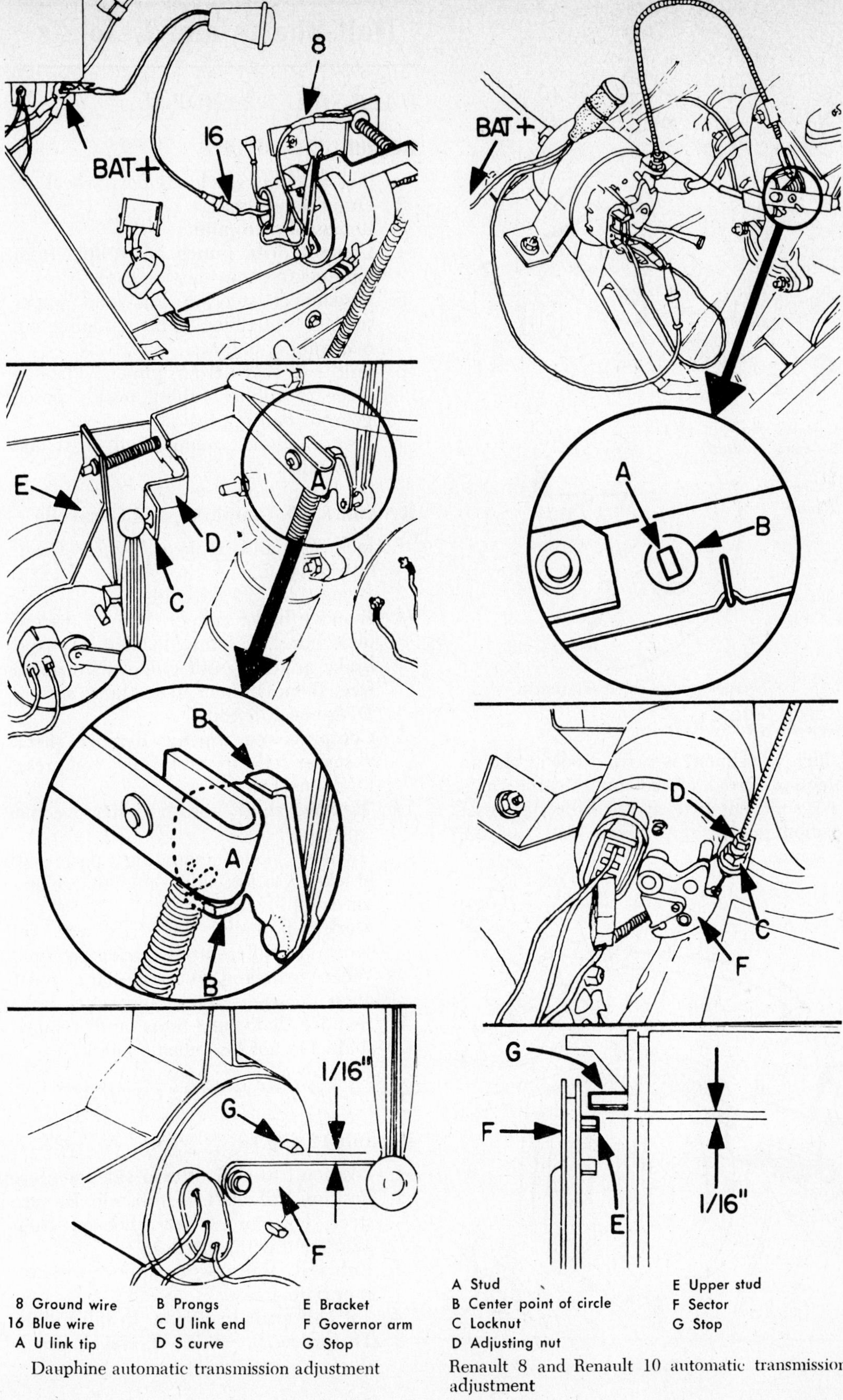

8 Ground wire
16 Blue wire
A U link tip
B Prongs
C U link end
D S curve
E Bracket
F Governor arm
G Stop

Dauphine automatic transmission adjustment

A Stud
B Center point of circle
C Locknut
D Adjusting nut
E Upper stud
F Sector
G Stop

Renault 8 and Renault 10 automatic transmission adjustment

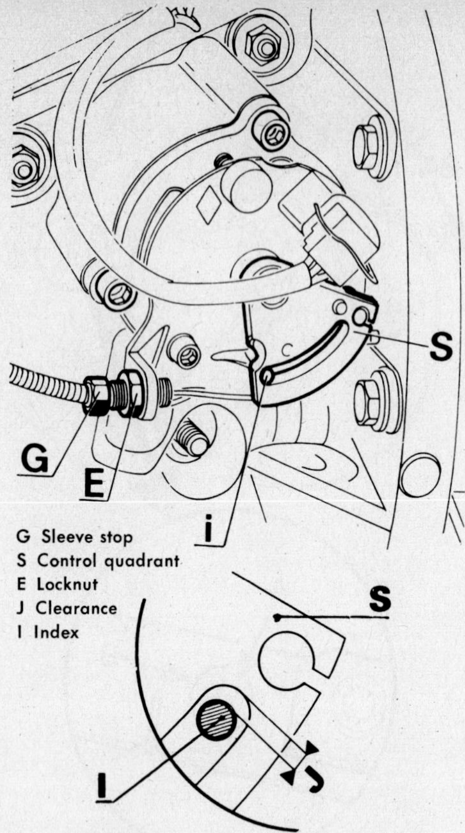

Governor control cable adjustment

Kick-down Switch

This adjustment is carried out at the accelerator pedal. Accelerator cable must have sufficient play at the fully depressed position so that stop sleeve has 1/8-5/32" clearance.

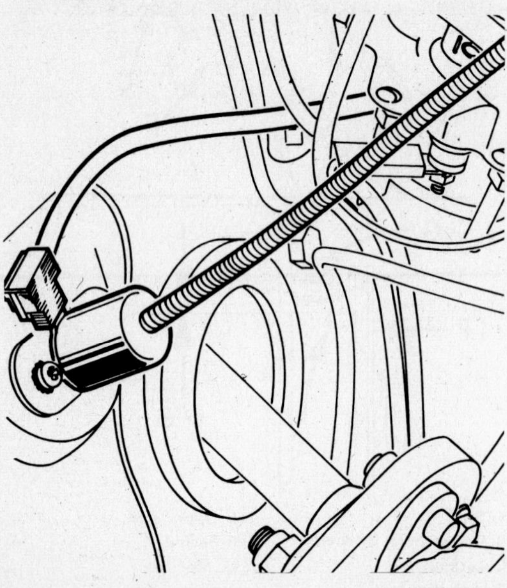

Automatic transmission kick-down switch

Half-Shafts and U-Joints

HALF-SHAFT REMOVAL

Renault 12 and 16

1. Jack front of vehicle. Remove wheel.
2. Drain transmission.
3. Remove brake caliper.
4. Using a drift, punch out rollpin from joint nearest transmission case.
5. Disconnect steering link and upper suspension ball joints. Fit retaining tool over rubber bellows.
6. Pull half-shaft from pinion. Place a piece of rubber tubing over exposed gearbox housing seal.
7. Using a puller, remove half-shaft and stub axle.

Renault 8, 10, Dauphine, and Caravelle

1. Jack car and remove wheel. Drain transmission.
2. Remove handbrake cable.
3. Remove brake caliper. Do not disconnect hose. Unscrew locknut of hand brake adjuster until guide plate pin is free. Remove inner plate thrust spring.
4. Disconnect tie rod.
5. Compress rear spring. Remove shock absorber at top and fully compress. Disconnect strap.
6. Remove shock absorber. Remove rear spring.
7. Remove side mounting pad with bracket. On left side, remove accelerator cable.
8. Mark differential half-shaft with respect to differential carrier position. When installing, mating marks must align.
9. Remove half-shaft nuts and remove shaft. Do not lose needle bearings.

HALF-SHAFT INSTALLATION

Renault 12 and 16

1. Position half-shaft in rear side member.
2. Position half-shaft in stub axle. Be sure steel deflector is not knocked from alignment with stub axle.
3. Lubricate transmission splines with appropriate grease.
4. Fit half shaft to pinion. Install rollpin.
5. To proceed, reverse removal procedure.

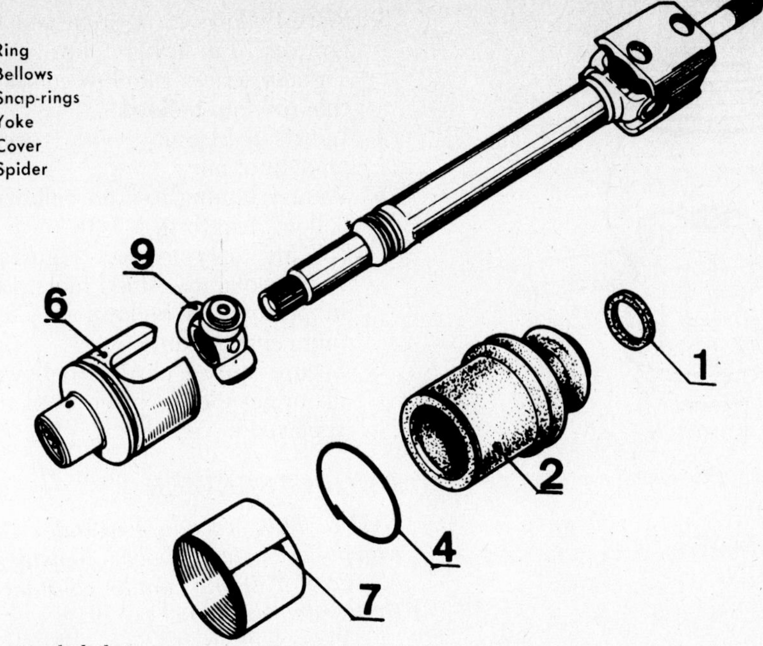

Half-shaft—exploded view

Torque Specifications

Upper suspension and steering ball joints: 25 ft. lbs.
Hub nut: 90 ft. lbs.

Renault 8, 10, Dauphine and Caravelle

1. Lubricate half-shafts with joining compound.
2. To replace half-shafts, reverse removal procedure. Torque nuts to 35 ft. lbs.
3. Do not forget to adjust handbrake. Car must have rear wheels on ground. Also, pedal must be held down while tightening locknut.

NOTE: Starting in April, 1971, new type half-shafts were installed. A new type lower control arm has also been put into service. Old type control arms may not be used with new type half-shafts. In addition, new and old type control arms and shafts may not be mixed on the same vehicle. However, old type shafts can be used with new type control arms if both half-shafts are replaced.

U-JOINT REMOVAL

Renault 8, 10, Dauphine, Caravelle

On these models, U-joints cannot be repaired. Servicing is by replacement only. Removal consists of removing the half-shafts and pulling out the joint. Installation is the reverse of the above. Be sure to properly lubricate joint before replacing.

RUBBER BELLOWS REMOVAL

All Models

NOTE: Two types are used. Procedures, except for length specifications, are identical.

1. Remove clips from bellows. Using a suitable tool, mark position of yokes in relation to each other.

2. Note position of balls in yoke. They should be replaced in the same position.

3. Cut rubber bellows from shaft.

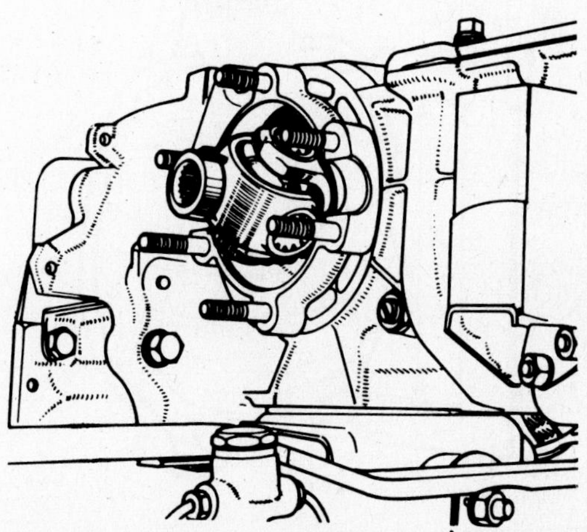

On Renault 8, 10, and Dauphine, U joints must be replaced in their entirety

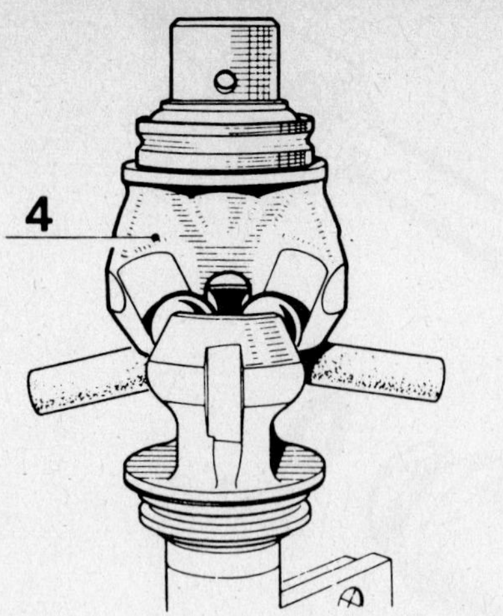

Fitting rubber yoke (4) while removing rubber tubing

RUBBER BELLOWS INSTALLATION

All Models

1. Place shaft in vise. Be sure jaws are as close to joint as possible.
2. Place a small piece of rubber tube (1.393" diameter) in yoke jaws. Place four balls opposite ramps. Place upper yoke in position. Slowly withdraw rubber tube.

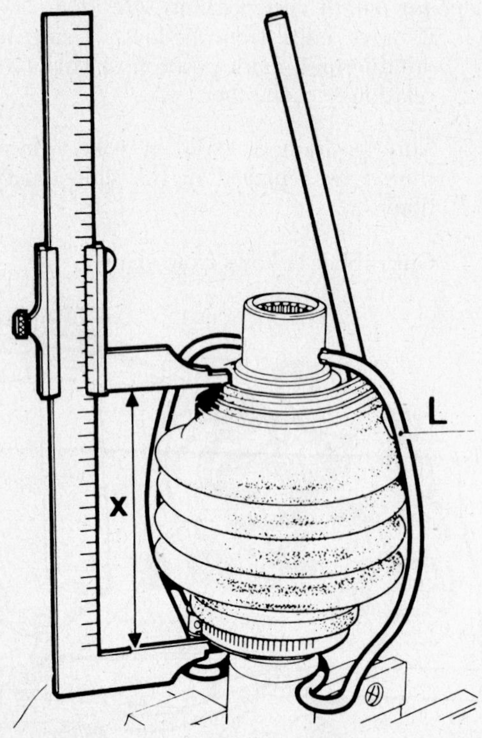

Adjusting bellows length to the proper dimension

3. Place bellows in position and locate in grooves. Fit lower clips and rings. Tighten screws till clips contract. Place thin rod into bellows.
4. Lubricate joint with appropriate amount of oil.
5. Place retaining tool on bellows. Adjust bellows length to 4 7/16" or 5 3/4" according to type used. Figures are between yoke machined faces. Leave rod in position in bellows to allow minimum entry of air.
6. Secure upper clip to bellows. Leave clamping tool in place until bellows is replaced in vehicle.

U-JOINT SERVICE

NOTE: This procedure includes all models except as noted above. Renault u-joints consist of a sliding contact constant velocity three sided trunnion.

1. Place half-shaft in vise. Slowly remove springs and circlip without damage.
2. Remove yoke from trunnion. Immediately upon removing yoke, place a rubber band or other suitable holding device around trunnion. This is necessary to prevent loss of needle bearings.
3. Using press, remove joint from shaft.
4. Replace joint on shaft with chamfer towards tube. With a mallet, drive into position until chamfer touches tube shoulder.

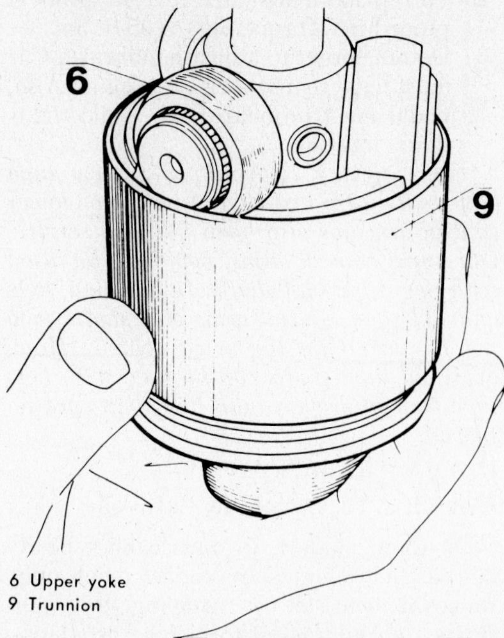

6 Upper yoke
9 Trunnion

Removing upper yoke

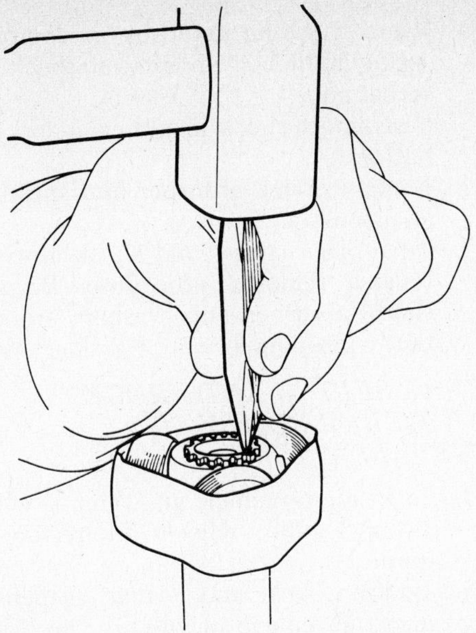
Stake splined metal at 120° intervals to lock joint to shaft

5. Using a pin punch, deform splined metal at 120° intervals to lock joint to shaft.
6. Assemble in reverse order of disassembly.

Suspension

RENAULT 16

This vehicle utilizes torsion bars at all four wheels and anti-roll bars at the front and rear.

Stub Axle Carrier

Removal

1. Jack vehicle and remove wheels.
2. Without removing hose, remove brake caliper. In addition, remove the differential plate and caliper bracket.
3. Using a puller, remove hub and disc assembly.
4. Remove upper, lower, and steering ball joints.
5. Pull out stub axle with half shaft.

Installation

1. Position stub axle and hub/disc assembly in vehicle. Place lower ball joint in position first.
2. Using appropriate tool, insert half shaft.
3. Tighten ball joint securing nuts and torque stub axle retaining nut to 115 ft. lbs.
4. Replace caliper bracket (be sure it is properly shimmed), deflector, and brake caliper.
5. Check wheel alignment.

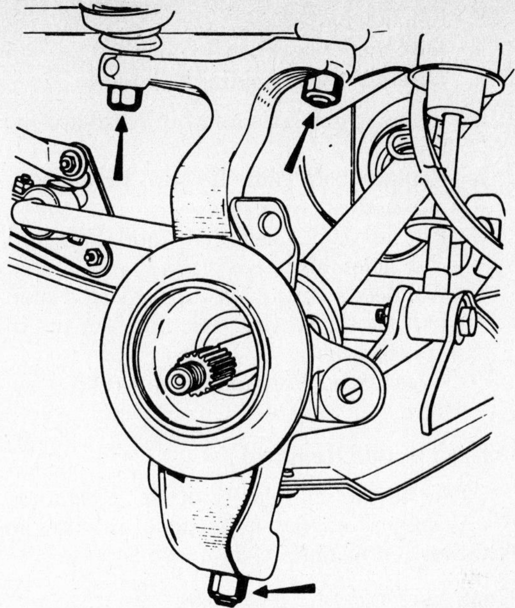
Stub axle removal

Upper Ball Joint Replacement

1. Jack vehicle and remove wheels. Disconnect upper ball joint and steering ball joint.
2. Drill rivet heads and remove ball joint. Be sure to fit thrust plate inside suspension arm.
3. Replace rivets with bolts. Be sure bolt heads are on dust cover side.
4. Connect upper ball joint and steering ball joint. Be sure to check wheel alignment.

Torque Specifications

Lower ball joint nut: 35 ft. lbs.
Upper ball joint nut: 25 ft. lbs.
Upper/Lower suspension arm bolts: 30 ft. lbs.
Steering arm pin: 25 ft. lbs.

Lower Ball Joint Replacement

1. Jack car and remove wheels. Drain transmission.
2. Remove brake calipers. Disconnect steering arm and upper ball joints. Do not fully remove fastenings.

3. Remove half-shafts.
4. Disconnect lower ball joints.
5. Drill out rivets holding ball joints.
6. Remove stub axle and hub/disc assembly.
7. Replace ball joint; be sure bolt heads are on dust cover side.
8. Fit stub axle, half-shaft, and hub and disc assembly.
9. Connect steering and upper suspension ball joints. Fit stub axle nut. Torque to specifications.
10. Check wheel alignment and refill gearbox.

Torsion Bar Removal

Due to the complexity of this operation, it is suggested that it be done only by an authorized dealer.

RENAULT 12

This vehicle uses coil springs at both front and rear. In addition, front and rear anti-roll bars are utilized.

Ball Joint and Stub Axle Service

To service these items, refer to and following procedures for the R-16.

Front Spring and Shock Absorber Removal and Installation

1. Jack vehicle and remove wheels.
2. Using a spring compressor, compress spring until bottom lifts off shock absorber cup.
3. Disconnect shock absorber at top and bottom.
4. Remove shock absorber and spring as an assembly.
5. To replace spring and shock absorber reverse removal procedure. Be sure shock absorber cup washers are correctly positioned.

REAR SPRING AND SHOCK ABSORBER REMOVAL & INSTALLATION

1. Jack side of vehicle and remove wheel. Be sure other wheels are resting on ground.
2. Position jack under rear suspension arm and remove spring.

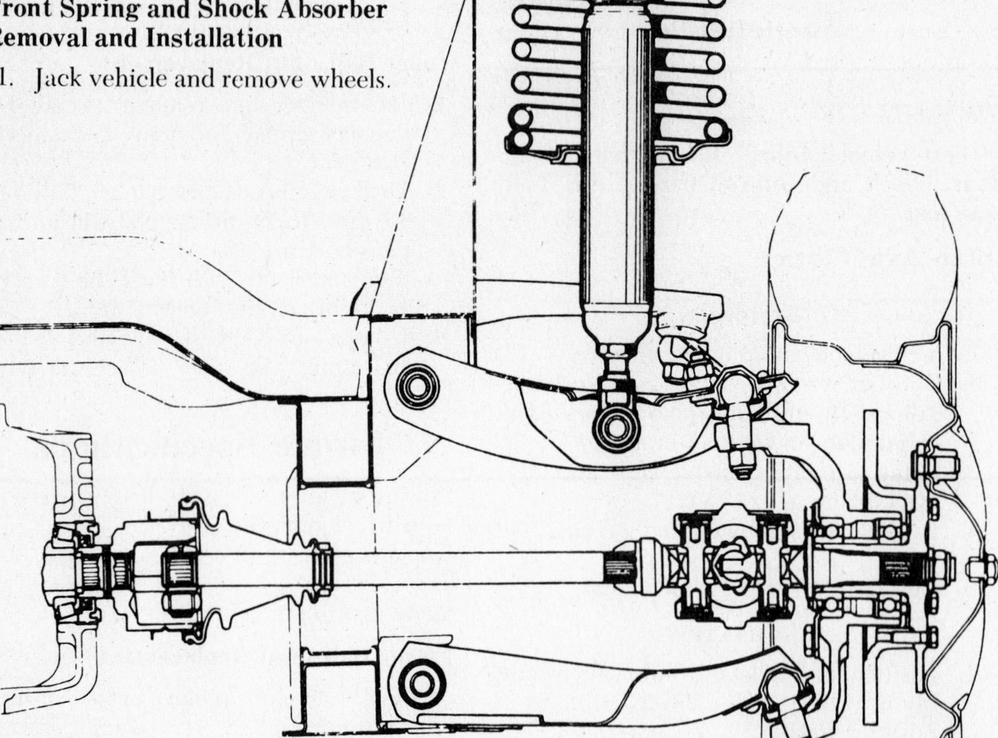

Renault 12 front suspension

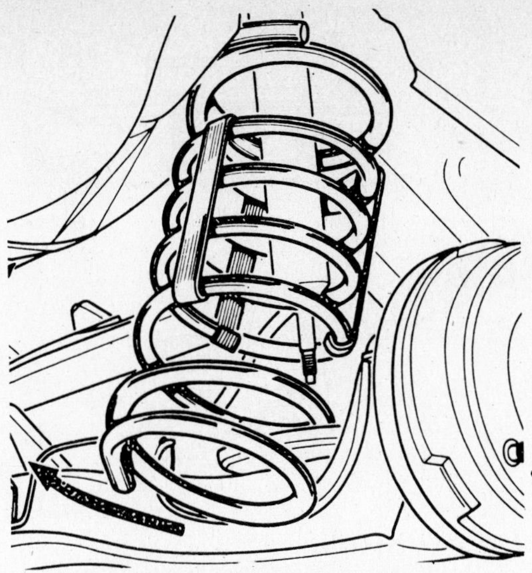

Rear spring and shock removal

3. *CAUTION: Using appropriate tool, clamp four middle spring coils in compressed position. Clamp at three points 120° apart. Slowly remove jack.*
4. Disconnect shock absorber at bottom. Remove spring.
5. To install spring and shock absorber, reverse removal procedure.

RENAULT 10

This vehicle utilizes the same suspension system as the Renault 12. All suspension service is identical, except as noted below.

Torque Specifications

Lower suspension arm hinge pin nut: 60-70 ft. lbs.
Upper suspension arm hinge pin nut: 40-55 ft. lbs.
Steering link pin: 20-30 ft. lbs.
Shock absorber lower attaching point: 10-20 ft. lbs.
Front stub axle ball joint nut: 45-50 ft. lbs.
Brake hose to caliper: 15 ft. lbs.

RENAULT 8, DAUPHINE, AND CARAVELLE

These vehicles, except for utilizing a front roll bar only, use the same suspension as the Renault 12.

Torque Specifications

Lower suspension arm: 60-75 ft. lbs.
Upper suspension arm: 40-55 ft. lbs.
Suspension ball joints: 60-75 ft. lbs.
Steering ball joints: 25-30 ft. lbs.
Shock absorber bolts: 25 ft. lbs.
Deflector to stub axle fastenings: 25-40 ft. lbs.
Ball joint to suspension arm: 5 ft. lbs.

Steering

All models use two basic types of steering gear. The early type may be serviced; the later may not. They may be told apart by the lack of removable fittings on the non-serviceable type. All models utilize rack and pinion steering.

STEERING UNIT REMOVAL

All Models

Disconnect battery. On some models, it may be necessary to remove the battery box. Remove the front wheel and spare tire. Disconnect the two steering links (tie rods) at the ball joints. Unpin and remove the two securing nuts on the steering column flexible coupling. Remove the brake hose. Unpin and remove the two nuts which secure the steering box to the front cross-member (or the NYLSTOP nuts depending on which are used). Turn wheels to full right lock. Remove the steering assembly by taking it out through one side of the vehicle.

To refit the steering assembly, carry out the removing operations in reverse taking care to split pin the two nuts which secure the steering box to the brackets. If NYLSTOP nuts are used they are to be tightened to a torque of 15 ft. lbs. The heads of the bolts should be on the bracket side.

Pin the two nuts that connect the flexible coupling to the flange, tightening nuts to 5 to 10 ft. lbs. The heads of the bolts should be on the coupling side.

When using a new steering box on the 16, use height adjusting shims totaling .079". On other vehicles and when replacing original gear box, use the original shims. Be sure to check the steering wheel alignment and toe in.

Brake System

Two basic types of brake systems have been utilized on these vehicles. The Dauphine, 8, Caravelle, and Renault 10 have

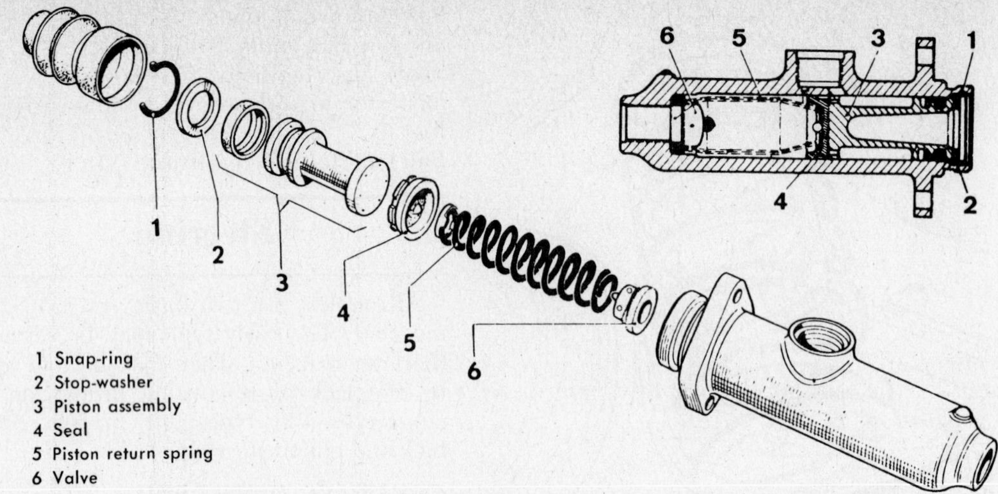

Dauphine and Renault 8 master cylinder

used disc brakes at both the front and rear wheels. The Renault 12 and 16 use a front disc/rear drum combination.

MASTER CYLINDER

Early models utilize a single line type master cylinder. To comply with safety regulations, later models employed a tandem type unit.

Single Master Cylinder Service

The following general procedures apply to all models equipped with a single type master cylinder.

Disconnect battery. Remove the spare wheel and front undertray. Disconnect the stop switch leads. Block the pipe to the master cylinder at its outlet in the reservoir bottle. Unscrew the stop switch. Remove the two cylinder securing bolts, free the master cylinder and remove the hose to the reservoir.

Disassemble the cylinder by removing the rubber bellows, the snap ring, the stop washer, the entire piston, the seal, the piston return spring, and the entire valve.

NOTE: The valve has four holes in it to prevent residual pressure in the braking system. Keep these holes clean.

All the parts are cleaned with denatured alcohol. Inspect parts and replace defective ones. Dip the parts in the type of brake fluid indicated on the reservoir bottle.

From Renault 10 vehicle no. 87 349 a master cylinder with a double sealing secondary cup is used. This type is supplied as a spare part for R-10's and requires replacement of the eye-ended rod, thrust rod, and thrust rod nut. To assemble master cylinder, reverse disassembly procedures.

Adjust brake pedal free play (master cylinder clearance) after installing master cylinder.

Adjust master cylinder clearance by screwing thrust rod in or out. Disconnect return spring from brake pedal. Loosen locknut on the thrust rod. Screw the rod in or out to obtain clearance at the brake pedal of approximately 13/64". Tighten locknut and connect the spring. Bleed brake system.

Tandem Master Cylinder Service

The dual (tandem) master cylinder has two compensator reservoirs, two piston assemblies, and a pressure drop indicator. The dual cylinder operates in the same way as the single cylinder, except that braking is still possible after one circuit has failed.

The brake pressure indicator detects a difference in hydraulic pressure in the two brake circuits. Balance between the two circuits can be destroyed by air in the hydraulic lines, fluid leakage, or an operating defect in the master cylinder. Removal procedures are the same as for single type cylinders. To disassemble, place master cylinder in vise fitted with soft padding. Remove fluid bottles. Utilizing a small piece of wood, press both pistons down. Remove the stop screw, plug, and copper washers. Remove the secondary piston, spring, and primary piston. Avoid scratching bore. Next, lift out spring ring and stop washer. Loosen and remove fitting for the residual pressure valve. Follow same cleaning procedures as for single type master cylinders. To assem-

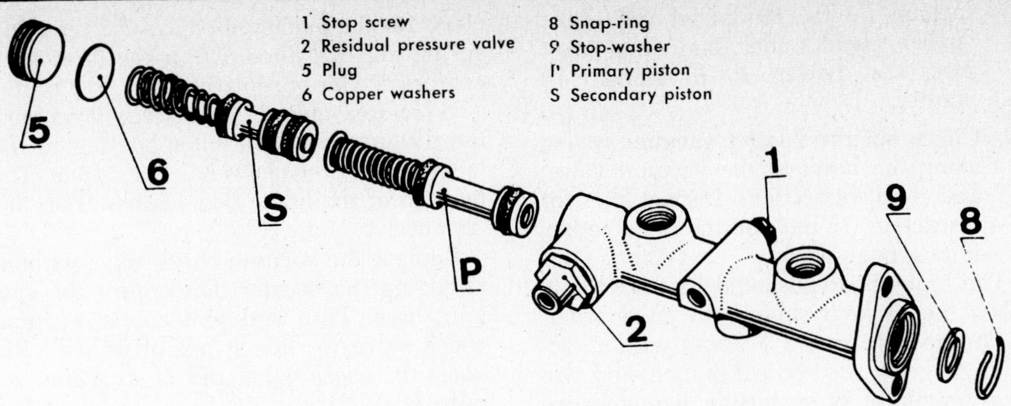

Renault 16 tandem (dual) type master cylinder

ble, lubricate all parts with brake fluid. Replace stop washer, snap-ring, and the primary and secondary piston. Replace new copper washer and plug. Torque plug to 75 ft. lbs. Press pistons down into bore 3/16″. Fit stop-screw with appropriate copper washer. Replace the pressure valve and install fluid reservoir with new seals. Adjust master cylinder clearance free play in same manner as for single type cylinders. On the 16, pushrod clearance should be 1/64″; on all other vehicles equipped with a dual master cylinder, 13/64″. If car is equipped with power brakes, adjust clearance on power brake unit. Do not forget to bleed braking system.

VACUUM BRAKE BOOSTER

The Master-Vac brake booster is a vacuum power unit that reduces the amount of foot pressure required for braking. The booster is mechanically controlled by the foot pedal and conveys this pressure along with an engine vacuum assistance to the master cylinder. A vacuum control valve prevents air from flowing back into booster when engine is not running.

Checking Brake Booster Operation

The operation of the brake booster can be quickly checked with these steps.

1. With engine off, use up all vacuum by depressing brake pedal several times.
2. Hold pedal down and start engine. As

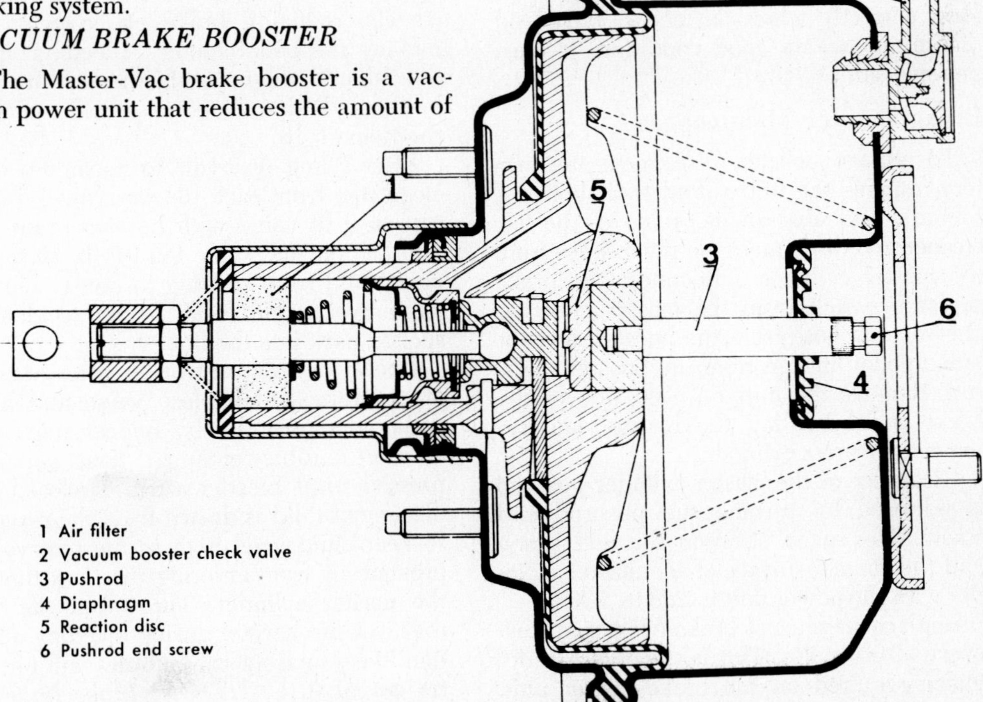

Vacuum-brake booster unit.

vacuum builds, the pedal will move farther (held under same foot pressure) as power is developed by booster.

3. Check out the booster vacuum system along the hose, at the vacuum valve, and at all connections. Inspect filter for restriction. If the booster is defective, it must be replaced.

The brake booster should be tested only when the brake system is in good order. Make the test using a T fitting with a vacuum gauge on the vertical branch, and two short lengths of 3/8 in. outside diameter copper tubing on the horizontal branches. Connect a shut off valve to the left branch (with gauge facing you). Fit the right branch with a short length of 3/8 in. outside diameter flexible hose.

Disconnect the vacuum hose from the booster and connect it to the left branch of the gauge assembly. Connect the right branch to the booster. Open the shut off valve. Start the engine and let it idle for one minute. Close the shut off valve, read the gauge and stop the engine. Check the vacuum gauge again. If the vacuum drops more than one inch of mercury in 15 seconds, the booster check valve or the diaphragm is defective. These are the only two parts, other than the air filter, which can be replaced. If the power unit does not perform correctly when the check valve and diaphragm are in good condition, it must be replaced.

Brake Booster Maintenance

To remove booster, disconnect the battery, remove the brake fluid from both reservoirs and discard it, remove the air cleaner and disconnect the brake lines from the master cylinder. Disconnect the brake pressure switch from the master cylinder, the vacuum hose from the booster, and the brake pedal linkage from the booster pushrod. Remove the nuts on each side of the brake pedal holding the booster and remove the master cylinder.

Clearance of the master cylinder pushrod is adjusted by turning the pushrod end screw. The space between the end screw and the contact surface of the master cylinder with the power unit is .228 to .236 in.

Replace air filter of brake booster at least every 12,000 miles. This is the only maintenance required on the brake power unit. Disconnect the linkage from the brake pedal; loosen the locknut; and unscrew the clevis for the linkage. Remove the retaining spring and air filter. Clean the filter with compressed air or replace it.

When assembling clevis, screw it on until the distance from the filter housing to the inner edge of the clevis hole is 1-5/8 in. The position of the brake pedal is based on this distance.

Replace the vacuum check valve without removing the booster. Disconnect the vacuum hose. Turn and pull on the vacuum check valve to slide it out of its seal. Replace the check valve and/or its seal as required.

If replacing the power unit pushrod, do not pull out the pushrod. This might cause the reaction disc to fall inside the power unit housing. Remove the flange-adaptor plate and tape the end-splines of the pushrod to prevent damage to the new seal. Remove the old seal and lubricate the pushrod. Slide the new seal over the pushrod and using a length of 1-1/2 in. outside diamater pipe, drive the seal gently into place. Position the adaptor plate on the booster housing so it does not interfere with the check valve. Center the plate and tighten the nuts.

Bleeding the Brake System

Air, being compressible, cushions fluid movement from the brake pedal to the wheels, reducing brake effectiveness and making the pedal spongy. Bleeding operation should begin at farthest point from master cylinder. Bleed disc brakes first on the Renault 16.

After filling reservoir to maximum level, clean dirt from each bleeder valve, remove cap, and fit valve with hose to drain fluid into jar that has some fluid in it. Hose prevents fluid from seeping to lining. Fluid in jar prevents air from being accidentally sucked back into the line.

Open valve almost three-quarter turn, depress brake pedal, close valve and allow pedal to return slowly. Repeat steps until no more bubbles enter jar. Keep pedal depressed until bleeder valve is closed. Replacement fluid is drawn from the reservoir so keep fluid level high in the reservoir to prevent air from entering the lines through the master cylinder. Throw out the fluid that was discharged during bleeding operation because all of the bubbles will not settle out of it. *CAUTION: Brake fluid will destroy paint.*

Complete flushing of brake system is sug-

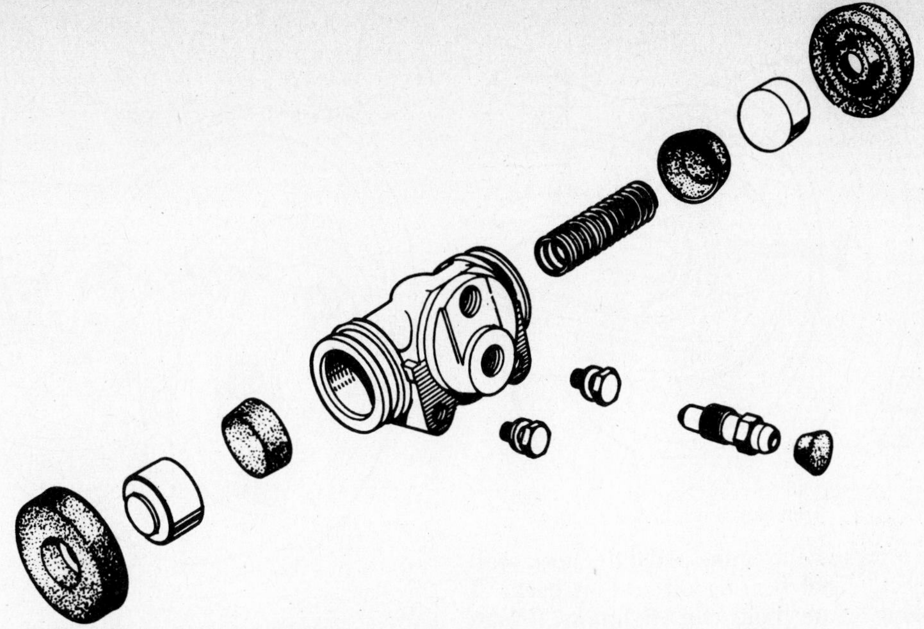

Wheel cylinder for drum brakes.

gested whenever new brake system parts are installed. Fluid with any trace of mineral oil should not be used to flush system.

DRUM BRAKE SERVICE

Brake Shoe Replacement

Remove drum assembly for access to brake shoes. Remove return springs, spring retainers, dowel pins, and springs on shoes. Place clamps on brake cylinder plungers. Disconnect handbrake cable. Brake shoes are specially bonded—replace shoes and linings as unit. If brakes are replaced on one side, do same for other side so that braking effectiveness is equal. Keep hands clean while handling new linings. Coat brake shoe retaining clips on the brake anchor plate side with sealing compound.

Wheel Cylinder Inspection and Overhaul

Carefully pull lower edges of wheel cylinder boots away from cylinders and note if interior is wet—an indication of brake fluid seepage past the piston cup. If so, cylinder overhaul is required.

Clean dirt from all surrounding surfaces and then loosen connecting line and unscrew wheel brake cylinder. Seal off brake line.

Dismantle boots, pistons, cups, and spring from cylinder. Unscrew bleeder valve. Replace boots and cups if possible; clean other parts with fresh brake fluid. Use no fluid containing even a trace of mineral oil.

Light scratches and corrosion can be polished from pistons and bore with fine emery cloth or steel wool. Dip all parts in brake fluid and reassemble.

Install the wheel-brake cylinders in reverse order to disassembly. Check oil seal and bearings for condition. Clean brake-drum hub and bearing and repack with grease. Adjust, bleed, and road test the brakes for performance.

Brake Drum Conditioning

Thoroughly clean and inspect brake drums for cracks, scoring and out-of-round. Polish out slight scores with emery cloth. Shallow grooves can be removed by boring if oversized linings are obtainable. Out of round drums cause excessive wear on other brake parts as well as on tires. Drums should not be worn down or machined to .08 in. beyond their original size. Keep runout less than .004 in. Measure for runout by checking along open and closed edges of machined surface and at right angles. Keep diameter variations of brake drums on opposite sides less than .008 in. for equal braking.

To regain center contact with brake shoes, grind linings to .020 in. under drum diameter.

When reinstalling brake drum, inspect all brake pipe and hose connections for fluid leaks. Tighten these connections and apply

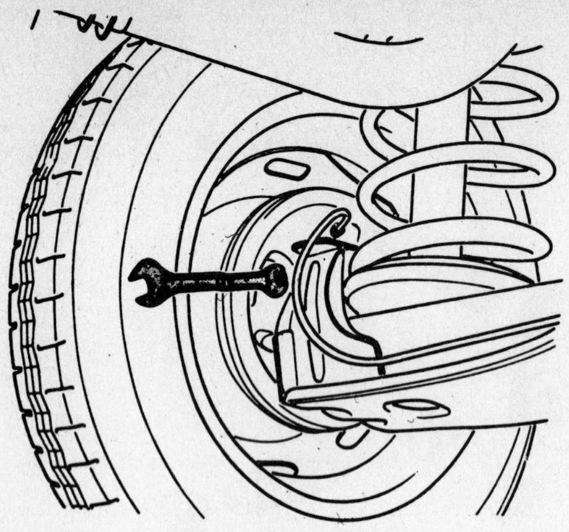

Adjusting drum brakes

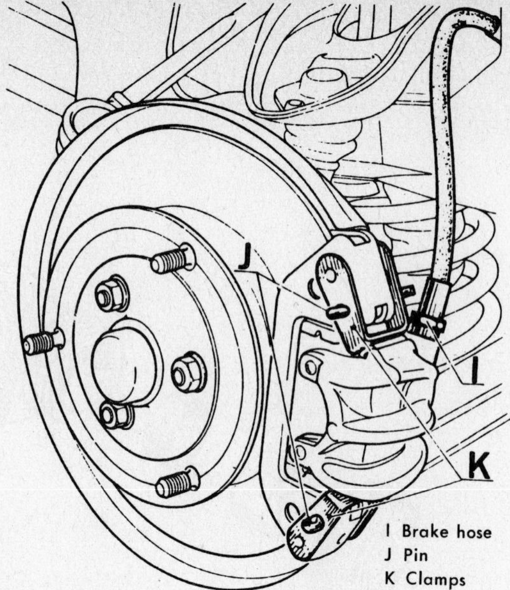

Removing caliper of disc brake.

heavy pressure to brake pedal to check seal. Inspect wheel bearing oil seals. Check all backing plate bolts for tightness. Clean away all dirt from assemblies and repack wheel bearings.

Adjusting Drum Brakes

Always adjust leading shoe first. This is accomplished by turning adjustment eccentrics on wheel backing plate. Turn clockwise to bring linings closer to drum, turn counterclockwise to move them away.

DISC BRAKE SERVICE

Brake Caliper Removal

Plug the brake reservoir outlet. Unscrew the pipe union and remove its clip. At the front wheel, loosen the brake hose; remove pins; swing back the clamps; and remove the caliper. At the rear wheel—loosen hose; unscrew large nut against the guide plate; remove guide plate; and disconnect the handbrake cable by removing pin. Remove the cable from the handbrake lever; remove pins; pull back swing clamps; remove the caliper.

To install caliper, carry out the removing operations in reverse, replacing the seal between the hose and the caliper. Bleed the braking system. Adjust the handbrake.

Caliper Overhaul

Remove cap. Unscrew nut holding the end of pin with screwdriver. Lightly tap out the piston, using a bronze drift against the pin where it projects from the caliper. Remove the seal from its groove with a plastic pin to prevent scratching the metal. *Do not dismantle the assembly inside the piston.*

Clean piston and caliper in trichlorethylene. Brush the outside of the caliper with small stiff bristled brush, then clean the inside around the groove. The groove must be completely grease free. Brush the groove a second time in fresh trichlorethylene. The caliper-piston assembly must be carefully cleaned in denatured alcohol to remove all traces of the trichlorethylene.

Inspect the piston and caliper for any scoring, corrosion traces, or rough areas. Replace worn assembly. Lubricate the bore and groove in the caliper with brake fluid and fit a new seal, also to be lubricated.

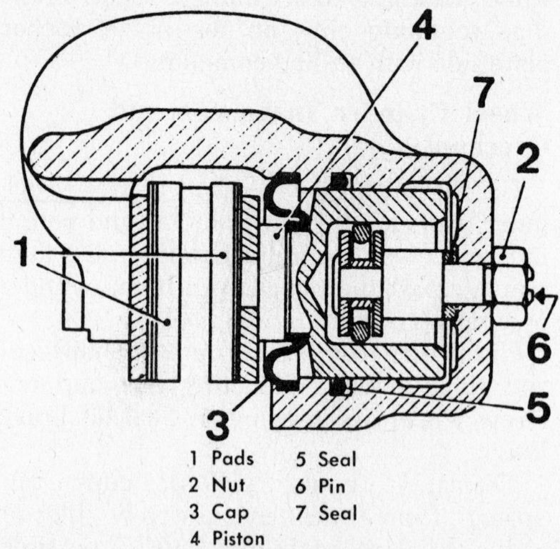

Cross section of caliper.

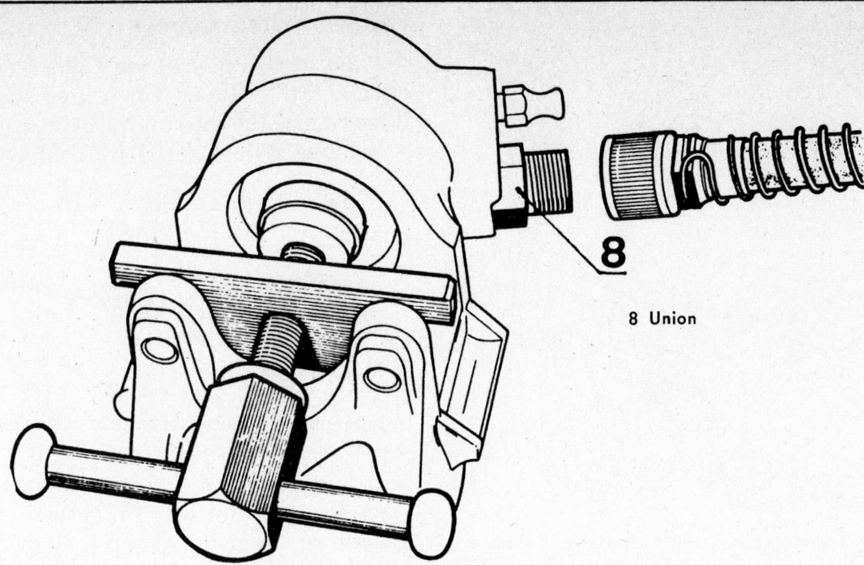

Brake piston clamped for testing caliper.

Fit the piston into the bore of the caliper by hand only, without tapping or forcing it which will damage the seal. First hold the piston with seal in the vertical position with the thread of pin upwards. Next, align piston and bore perfectly and slowly push the piston in with the thumbs. Guide the pin through its hole with a small screwdriver. Bring the reference mark on the piston to the same side as the bleed screw. Tighten nut on pin to 10 ft. lbs.

Testing Caliper

The caliper seal must be seated to prevent brake fluid leakage after the brake is assembled. Position the seal and test for leaks as follows. Place a compressing tool against the piston as shown. Leave off the dust cap. Screw a union into the caliper and attach a compressed air line with a shut-off valve.

Immerse the caliper in a tank of denatured alcohol. Raise the air pressure to 5 psi and then close off valve again. Screw tool in and out between a quarter and a half turn to slightly move the piston. Move piston 10 to 20 times in order to bleed out any air trapped in the caliper seal groove. Repeat operation at pressures of 10 psi, 15 psi, 20 psi, and 30 psi. Leakage can be detected by bubbles rising through the denatured alcohol.

If leaks occur when the piston is the original one, replace the piston. If the piston is new, replace the caliper. If both caliper and piston are in good condition, smear the periphery of the piston and the cavity between piston and caliper bore with grease. Fit a new dust cap.

IMPORTANT: To make subsequent bleeding operations easier, fill the caliper with brake fluid through the air hose union. Remove the bleed screw and tilt the caliper from side to side while filling. Then refit the bleed screw.

Brake Pads

Remove pins, tilt back the swing clamps, and remove the caliper without disconnecting the hose. At the rear wheel, also unscrew the large nut holding the guide plate and free the plate.

Remove the dust cap and clean the end of the piston with denatured alcohol. Set a tool against the piston to prevent it from

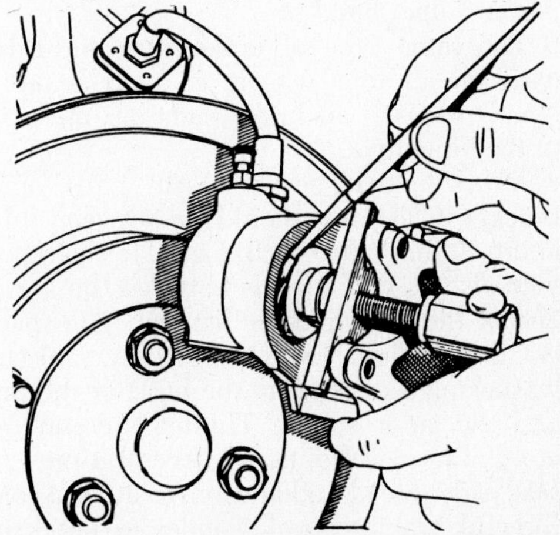

Grease exposed edge of brake piston.

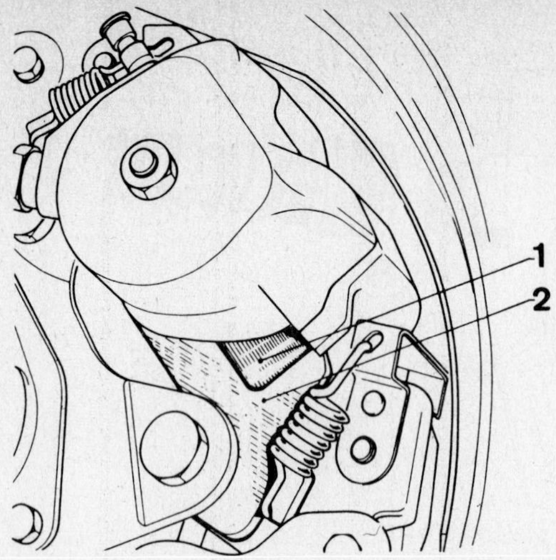

Checking brake-pad thickness of R-16. Measure distance that brake pad (1) on piston side is from caliper bracket (2)—not to exceed 5 mm (13/64 in.).

coming out of position and then operate the brake pedal to push the piston out about one millimeter. Grease the exposed circumference of the piston, using an artist paint brush. Then push the piston to the brake of its cylinder and refit the dust cap after having cleaned it with denatured alcohol.

If either pad is worn down to a thickness of .08 in., both brake friction pads must be replaced so that braking is always equal. Oily, cracked, or defaced pads need replacement. Remove high spots on friction pads with cut stone file before installing.

Install brake pads by carrying out removal operations in reverse and replacing split pins and anti-rattle rubbers.

NOTE: Front brake pads have either one or two flanges. Pads with single flange are positioned with the flange towards the top of the caliper bracket.

The same type of brake pads must be used on all four wheels to keep braking equal. Replace all brake pads on one axle at the same time.

Adjust clearance between pads and bracket. Clearance should be between 0.15 and 0.30 mm (.006 to .012 in.). If clearance exceeds this add spacers between the lower end of the pads and the bracket. The spacers are secured by a pin with a rubber washer placed between the head of the pin and the outer spacer. Tighten nut moderately. Press brake pedal several times to seat pads. Bleed and add brake fluid. Avoid forceful braking for 125 miles to break in pads.

Caliper Swing Clamps

The swing clamps must line up when closed on the caliper. Check and straighten, if necessary, the tabs on the clamps.

Remove swing clamp by drilling off the

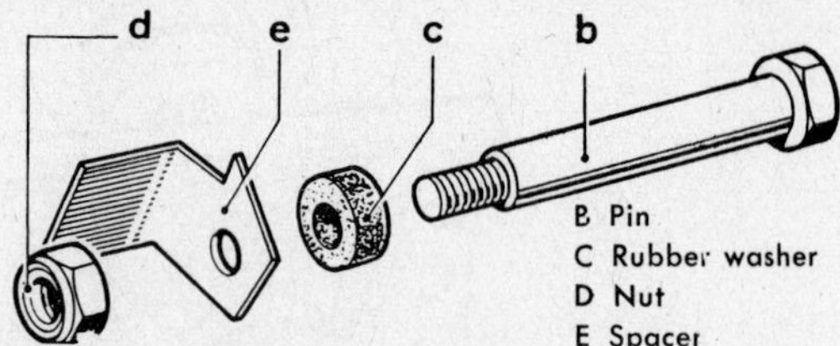

Adjust pad-to-bracket clearance with spacer (e) on pin (b).

securing pin with a 6 mm diameter drill. Tap the pin inward. Fit a new pin and peen it so the swing clamp is slightly stiff to move. Check the position of the tabs.

Caliper Bracket Clearance

Clearances (a) and (b) between each face of the disc and folded edges of the bracket should be 2.5 mm ± 0.5 (3/32 in. ± 1/64 in.). Make this measurement with a set of feeler gauges at the point where the brake pads make contact with the horizontal folded edge of the caliper bracket. If the caliper bracket is offset so that it is outside this tolerance, adjust its position with shim D for front brake bracket, or shim E for rear brake bracket. Insert D-type shims

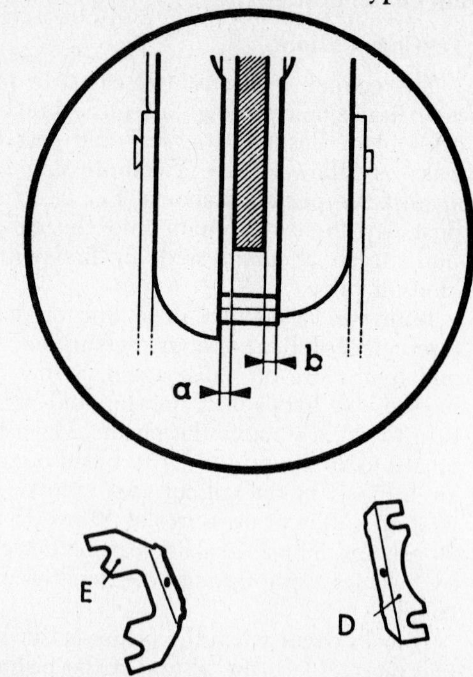

Adjust caliper bracket-to-disc clearance with shims (E and D).

on front wheel between the stub axle carrier and the caliper bracket. Tighten the securing nuts to 15 ft. lbs. Insert E-type shims on rear wheel between the caliper bracket and the half shaft tube. Tighten nuts to 15 ft. lbs.

Removing Brake Disc or Bracket

At front wheel, remove the caliper and hub grease cap. Unpin and remove the hub nut and its thrust washer from the outer bearing. Remove the nuts which secure the caliper bracket to the stub axle carrier. Pull off entire assembly with puller. Brake discs cannot be refaced; replace a damaged disc.

Tighten the hub nut to 20 ft. lbs., then

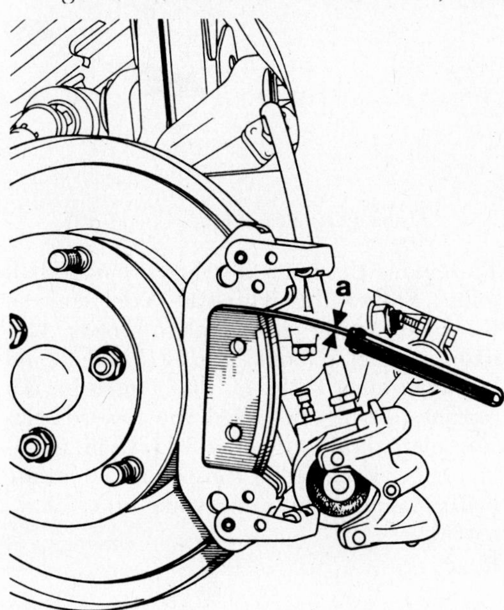

Brake pad clearance at caliper bracket: .006-.012″

loosen it by one-half to one and one-half notches and split pin it. Knock the end of the stub axle with a mallet to position the inner bearing. Maximum play = 0.35 mm (.014 in.) measured at 200 mm (7-7/8 in.) from the wheel center.

Tighten hub nut to 145 ft. lbs.; caliper bracket securing nuts to 15 ft. lbs.; bearing flange securing nuts to 35 ft. lbs.; tie bar securing nut to 70 ft. lbs.

Each time the caliper bracket is removed, check its shimming with reference to the disc.

HANDBRAKE (PARKING) ADJUSTMENT ALL EXCEPT MODELS RENAULT 12 AND RENAULT 16

Adjust parking brake with lever com-

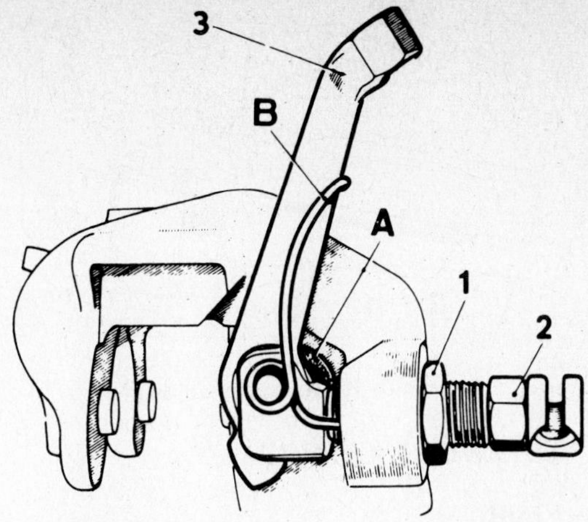

1. Lock nut
2. Adjusting screw
3. Handbrake lever (clevis)

A. Rubber disc
B. Spring

Handbrake adjustment assembly.

pletely released. Lift rear of vehicle. Test for cable free movement and equal tightening action at both brakes. Loosen the large handbrake lock nut. Tighten screw while turning the wheel until the disc is lightly gripped by the brake; then back off screw by one-quarter to one half turn until the wheel turns freely. Apply the hand brake. Tighten the lock nut.

Renault 12

Jack vehicle rear and release handbrake. Loosen locknut on handbrake rod. Tighten adjusting nut till linings just contact brake drum. Secure locknuts.

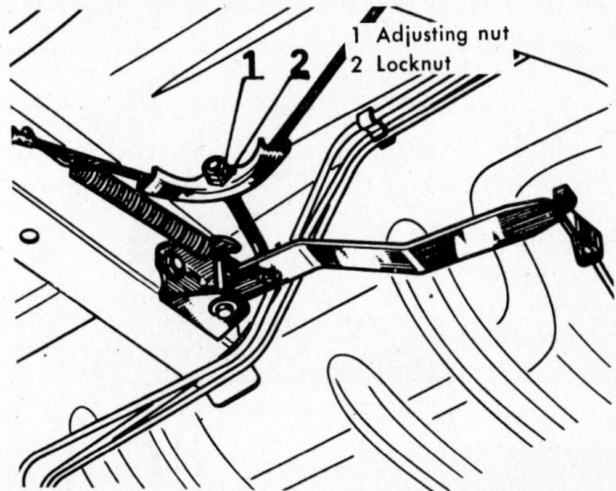

Renault 12 handbrake adjustment

Renault 16

Jack vehicle and release handbrake. Loosen locknuts and turn sleeve till linings just contact brake drum. Secure locknuts.

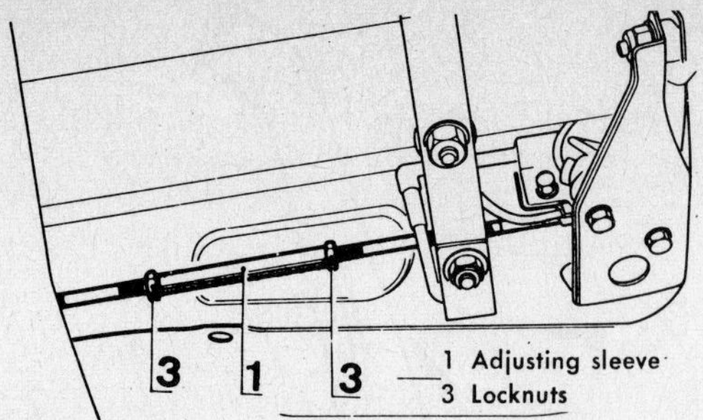

Renault 16 handbrake adjustment

WHEEL BEARINGS

Front

RENAULT 8, RENAULT 10, DAUPHINE, CARAVELLE

Remove hub/disc assembly. Extract bearing from the stub axle with a puller tool. The new bearing and its seal can be pressed on by tightening the wheel nut against a heavy spacer that is resting against the bearing.

Adjust the bearing play after ensuring that the bearings are properly installed. Tighten the hub nut to 20 ft. lbs. while turning the wheel. Loosen the nut one-half to one and one-half notches and split pin it. Then strike the hub to bed down the outer bearing and then fit the cap three-quarters full of grease.

Maximum permissible play is 0.35 mm (.014″) measured on a dial indicator in contact with the wheel 7-7/8 in. from the axle center.

RENAULT 12, RENAULT 16

Outer bearing may be removed in the same manner as the R-8, 10, and Dauphine.

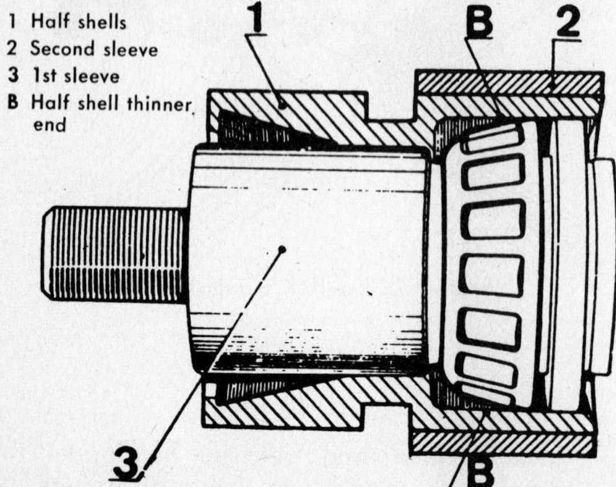

Renault 12 and 16 inner bearing removal

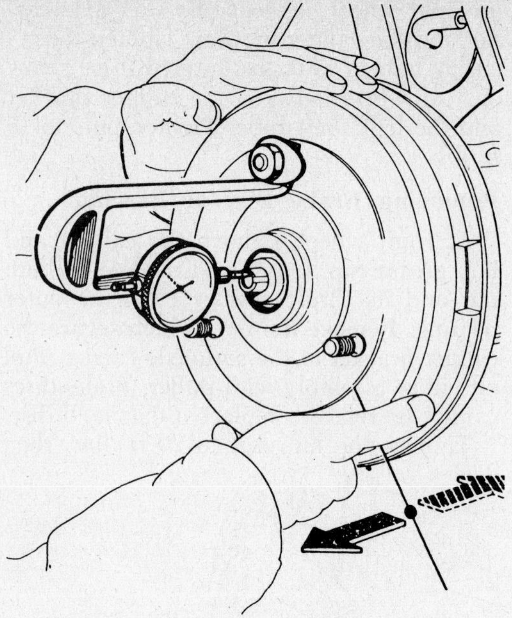

Using dial indicator to check end-play

To remove the inner bearings, remove ball joints. Follow this with stub axle removal. Remove bearing closure plate screws. Utilizing a press, remove bearing. Load should be taken on 3 15/32 in. diameter tube. To replace bearing, fit sealed end towards closure plate. Position with a 2 11/16 in. diameter tube. Use sealing compound on closure plate. Assemble hub in reverse order of removal.

Rear

RENAULT 8, RENAULT 10, DAUPHINE AND CARAVELLE

Remove hub/disc assembly and stub axle. Remove bearing with puller.

Replace rear bearing and seal on a press. The bearing with a nylon cage is to be fitted with the balls visible from the screwed end of the half shaft so that the disc on the nylon cage faces towards the universal joint end. The seal is fitted to the flange on the press with the lip on the seal towards the bearing. Tighten nuts through flange of the half shaft to 35 ft. lbs.

RENAULT 12 AND 16

Remove outer bearing hub/drum assembly and removing bearing with puller. Replace outer bearing by reversing removal procedure.

To remove inner bearing with thrust washer, remove hub/drum assembly. Fit sleeve tool (or bushing) and half shells with thinner end around washer. Hold assembly together with second sleeve. Place protective cup on stub axle end. Remove entire assembly with puller. To replace inner bearing, heat washer and position on stub shaft. Replace bearing track rings with mandrel. Position new seal and pack with grease. Replace stub axle outer bearing and thrust washer. To adjust bearing play, torque hub nut to 25 ft. lbs. Turn drum while tightening. Loosen nut 1/4 turn. Tighten screw to remove bearing end-play. Fit dial indicator to hub; install bracket to any wheel stud and secure with nut. Adjust end-play to .002-.004 in. Fit lockplate and cotter pin. Pack with grease and adjust brakes.

Heater

REMOVAL

Dauphine and Caravelle

1. Disconnect battery and drain cooling system. Disconnect input and ground leads. Remove heater ducts and all securing bolts. Remove heater.
2. To install heater assembly, reverse removal procedure.

Renault 8 and Renault 10

1. Disconnect battery and drain cooling system.
2. Remove screws holding heater controls to glove compartment panel.
3. Remove trunk lid latch cable bracket.
4. Remove glove compartment and lower tray panel. Remove wiper arm protective casing from upper right attachment point.
5. Remove all dashboard securing screws; do not disconnect dashboard electrical connections or remove dashboard.
6. Remove water valve control cable and cable cover stops.
7. Disconnect heater motor wire at control casing.
8. Remove heater bolts; lift dashboard slightly and remove heater.
9. To install heater assembly, reverse removal procedure.

RENAULT 8 HEATER MOTOR/ RADIATOR REMOVAL

Remove heater from vehicle. Remove nuts securing back plate to casing. Remove fan by removing central Allen key. Disconnect all leads and unbolt motor from attachment. *CAUTION: Do not lose motor washers.* To remove heater radiator, drain cooling system and remove all heater hoses and bolts. Lift our radiator.

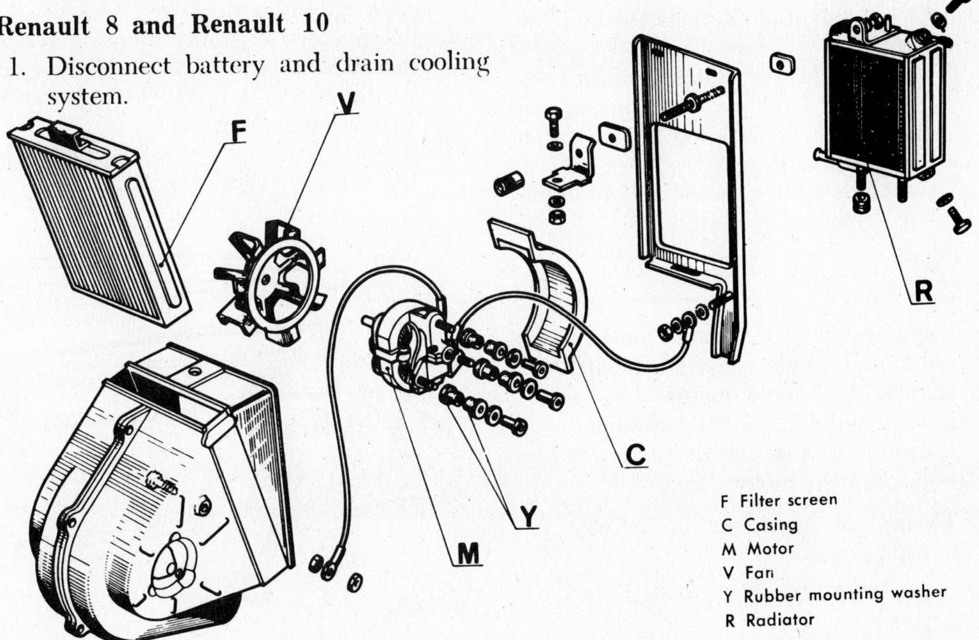

Dauphine heater assembly

RENAULT 8 HEATER MOTOR/ RADIATOR INSTALLATION

Assemble heater motor washers in order shown in illustration. Place first washer inside casing, other washers outside casing. Fit screw and spacer and secure. To re-

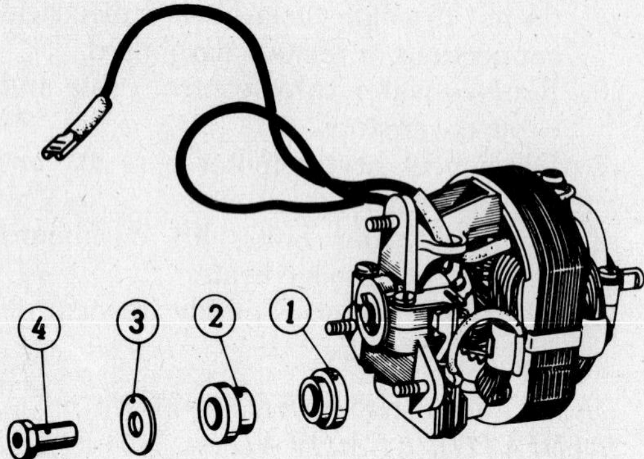

Renault 8 heater motor—assemble washers in order shown.

place motor and radiator, reverse removal procedure.

RENAULT 10 AND DAUPHINE HEATER MOTOR AND RADIATOR REMOVAL/INSTALLATION

1. Remove heater from vehicle.
2. Remove filter screen and casing.
3. Lift out fan unit. Pull motor and fan apart.
4. To remove heater radiator, drain cooling system. Disconnect all hoses and remove all bolts holding heater radiator in position. Remove radiator.
5. To replace heater motor and radiator, reverse removal procedure.

RENAULT 12 HEATER MOTOR REMOVAL

1. Motor housing is located under dash left side. Pull glove box cardboard tray slightly to reveal motor. Disconnect battery and drain cooling system.
2. Disconnect wire leads and remove bolts. Remove motor.
3. To replace heater motor, reverse removal procedure.

RENAULT 12 HEATER RADIATOR REMOVAL

1. Remove grill panel at windshield base. Disconnect battery and drain cooling system. Disconnect hoses.

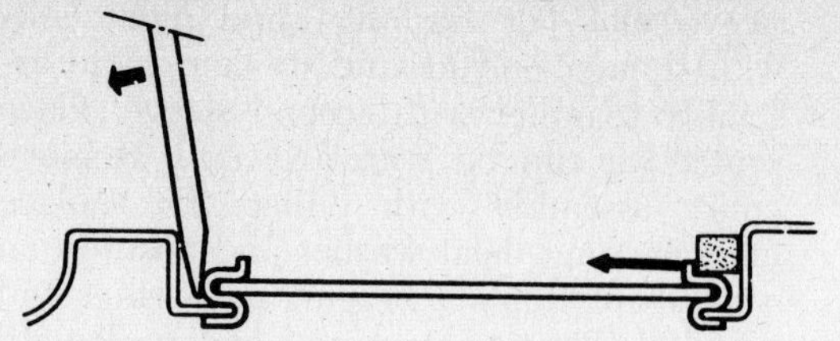

Removing S securing pieces,.Renault 16

2. Cut radiator hook retaining wires.
3. Lift hooks and disconnect heater valve. Inside vehicle, remove heater valve securing nuts.
4. Remove radiator towards vehicle front.
5. To replace, reverse removal procedure.

RENAULT 16 HEATER MOTOR REMOVAL/INSTALLATION

1. Disconnect battery and drain cooling system. Remove ventilation grill at engine compartment rear. To do this, free reverse S securing pieces with screwdriver.
2. The top rear crossmember, located at the back of the engine compartment, immediately below the windshield, must be removed. To do this, remove securing clips by pushing. Remove circlips and disconnect eye.
3. Remove crossmember securing screws. In addition, remove plate securing nuts located under windshield wiper arms. Lift out crossmember.
4. Remove leads and screws at fan motor. Lift out fan motor.

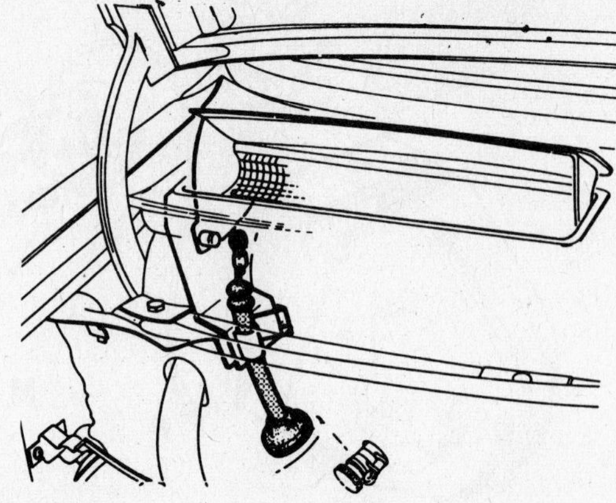

Securing clip and eye removal, Renault 16

5. To replace motor, reverse removal procedure. When properly installed, fan motor should revolve counter clockwise.

RENAULT 16 HEATER RADIATOR REMOVAL

1. Disconnect battery and drain cooling system.
2. Remove the crossmember as detailed in Renault 16 Heater Motor Removal, Steps 1-3.
3. Remove radiator securing clips and lift out radiator.
4. To replace radiator, reverse removal procedures.

Windshield Wipers

MOTOR REMOVAL

Dauphine and Caravelle

1. Disconnect battery. Remove glove box on driver's side.
2. Lift off wiper arms. Disconnect wiper motor electrical leads.
3. Unscrew wiper motor nuts and remove wiring retaining clips. Be certain not to lose any small parts.
4. Remove wiper assembly.
5. To replace assembly, reverse removal procedure.

Dauphine and Caravelle Wiper Adjustment

1. Wet windshield. Start wiper and stop after three cycles.
2. Wiper should stop 3/4″ from windshield frame in park position. If wiper arm is out of adjustment, remove arm by lifting from splined cylinder.
3. Replace wiper arm at proper adjustment position. Adjustment procedure is now complete.

Renault 8 Wiper Motor Removal

1. Disconnect battery.
2. Remove tray under dashboard (inside vehicle). Remove windshield wiper protective cover. Disconnect wiper motor at drive link.
3. In engine bay, disconnect motor leads. Remove bolts securing motor to backing plate and lift out motor.
4. To replace motor, reverse removal procedure.

Renault 8 Windshield Wiper Adjustment

Follow adjustment procedures for the Dauphine. Wiper stop adjustment is 2-3/8″ from windshield frame.

Renault 16 Wiper Motor and Plate Removal

1. To remove wiper motor, the crossmember must first be removed. These procedures are outlined in Renault 16 Heater Removal Steps 1-3.
2. After removing crossmember, disconnect wiper leads and remove back plate securing screws with back plate.
3. Remove motor. To install motor, reverse removal procedure.

Renault 16 Wiper Motor Adjustment

Place wiper blades in park position. Align links A and B as shown in illustration.

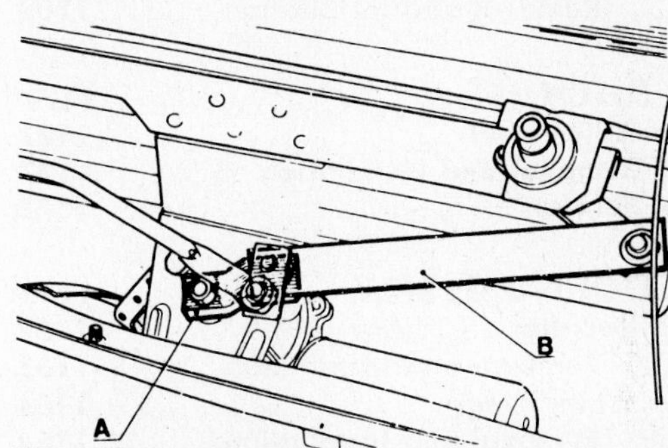

Renault 16 wiper motor adjustment

Renault 12 Wiper Motor Removal

1. Remove wiper arms and outer securing nuts.
2. Inside vehicle, remove heater control panel.
3. Remove rubber air flap.
4. In engine compartment, unscrew wiper motor plate screws.
5. Remove plate with attached motor at ends by lifting towards steering column right side.
6. When installing, be sure arms A and B are aligned as in illustration.

SUBARU SECTION

Index

Introduction

The Subaru was first introduced in America on a limited basis, in the form of very light (360 cc.) trucks, in 1964. The Model 360 Sedan, a competitor in Japan's popular 360 cc. class, was the first Subaru imported to the United States in quantity; however, this model was ill suited for American traffic, with limited size and power. In 1970, the Star (FF-1), a larger more powerful sedan with an 1100 cc. engine was introduced. Displacement was increased to 1300 cc. (Model G) in 1971. The Star is available in both sedan and station wagon versions.

Year and Model Identification

360 Sedan

360 Custom

360 Truck

360 Van

FF-1 Sedan

FF-1 Station Wagon

FF-1 Model G Sedan

Vehicle and Engine Serial Numbers

360 Sedan and Custom

The Vehicle Identification Plate is located in the upper right corner of the trunk. The engine number is stamped on the crankcase, below and to the right of the intake manifold.

360 Truck and Van

The Vehicle Identification Plate is located under the floor mat, immediately in front of the driver's seat. The engine number is stamped on the crankcase, below and to the right of the intake manifold.

FF-1

The Vehicle Identification Number is stamped on a tab located on the top of the dashboard on the driver's side, visible through the windshield. The Vehicle Identification Plate is on the bulkhead in the engine compartment, behind the windshield washer reservoir. The engine number is stamped on the crankcase, behind the distributor. The 1100 cc. engine code is EA61. The 1300 cc. (Model G) engine code is EA62.

FF-1 engine number location

Vehicle Identification

Year	Model	Body Style	Code
1968-70	360	Sedan, Custom Truck Van	K111L K153L K163L
1970-71	FF-1	Sedan Station Wagon	A14L A43L
1971-72	FF-1 (Model G)	Sedan Station Wagon	A15L A44L

General Engine Specifications

Year	Type	Cu. In. Displacement (cc.)	Carburetor	Advertized Horsepower @ rpm (SAE)	Advertized Torque @ rpm (ft. lbs.)	Bore and Stroke (in.)	Comp. Ratio	Normal Oil Pressure (psi)
1968-70	2 cylinder, 2 stroke, air cooled	22.2 (356)	1 bbl.	25 @ 5500	25.3 @ 4600	2.42 x 2.36	6.7:1	—
1970-71	4 cylinder, horizontally opposed	66.4 (1088)	2 bbl.	62 @ 6000	62.9 @ 3200	2.99 x 2.36	9.0:1	42-57
1971-72	4 cylinder, horizontally opposed	77.3 (1267)	2 bbl.	80 @ 6400	73.1 @ 4000	3.23 x 2.36	9.0:1	42-57

Tune-up Specifications

Year	Model	Spark Plugs: Make (Type)	Spark Plugs: Gap	Distributor: Point Dwell (deg.)	Distributor: Point Gap (in.)	Basic Ignition Timing (deg.) @ rpm	Cranking Compression Pressure (psi)	Valves: Clearance (in.) Intake	Valves: Clearance (in.) Exhaust	Valves: Intake Opens (deg.)	Idle Speed (rpm)
1968-70	360	NGK (B7H)	.028	① 48-53 ② 47	.020 .018	11B @ 2000	129	③	③	③	700
1970-71	FF-1	NGK (B6E)	.030	49-55	.020	TDC @ 850	178	.008-.009 (cold)	.010-.011 (cold)	20B	850
1971-72	FF-1 (G)	NGK (B6E)	.030	49-55	.020	TDC @ 750	178	.011-.013 (cold)	.011-.013 (cold)	24B	750

B—Before Top Dead Center
TDC—Top Dead Center
①—Hitachi Distributor
②—Nippon Denso Distributor

③—Port timing for the two cycle engine:
Intake opens—53° Before top dead center
Intake closes—53° After top dead center
Exhaust opens—68° Before bottom dead center
Exhaust closes—68° After bottom dead center

Firing Order

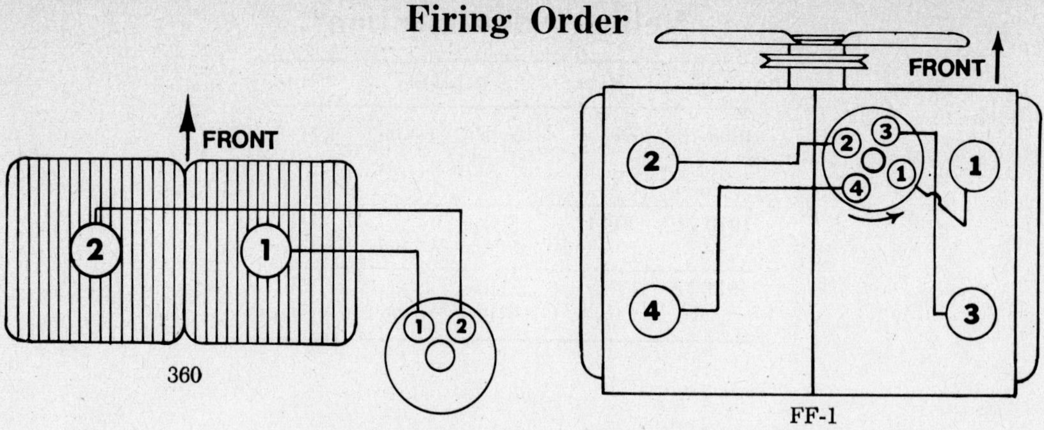

Engine Rebuilding Specifications

Year	Model *	Crankshaft: Main Bearing Journals (in.): Journal Diameter: New	Minimum	Oil Clearance	Shaft End-Play	Thrust On No.	Connecting Rod Bearing Journals (in.): Journal Diameter: New	Minimum	Oil Clearance	Side Play
1970-72	FF-1	1.9665-1.9669	1.9468	.0012-.0026	.0016-.0049	2	1.7712-1.7719	1.7515	.C012-.0026	.0039-.0073

*—The Model 360 utilizes a roller crankshaft, which may only be serviced as an assembly. The crankshaft and connecting rod assembly must be replaced if the following tolerances are exceeded:

Connecting rod side clearance (in.)	.0394
Ball bearing side clearance (in.)	.0118
Connecting rod radial play (in.) (bearing clearance)	.0236
Ball bearing radial play (in.) (bearing clearance)	.0039

Year	Model	Seat Angle (deg.)	Minimum Valve Seat Width (in.)	Valve Lift (in.) Intake	Valve Lift (in.) Exhaust	Spring Pressure (lbs.) Intake	Spring Pressure (lbs.) Exhaust	Spring Installed Height (in.)	Stem Diameter (in.) Intake	Stem Diameter (in.) Exhaust	Stem to Guide Clearance (in.) Intake	Stem to Guide Clearance (in.) Exhaust	Valve Guides Removable
1970-71	FF-1	45	3/64	N.A.	N.A.	① 96-111	96-111	① 1.10	.3134-.3140	.3125-.3134	.0010-.0022	.0016-.0030	yes
						② 42-49	42-49	② 1.02					
1971-72	FF-1 (G)	45	3/64	N.A.	N.A.	① 101-116	101-111	① 1.22	.3134-.3140	.3128-.3134	.0010-.0022	.0016-.0028	yes
						② 40-47	40-47	② 1.14					

①—Outer spring ②—Inner spring

Engine Rebuilding Specifications

		Pistons (in.)					Rings (in.)		
		Cylinder Bore		Piston Diameter					
Year	Model	New	Maximum	New	Maximum Oversize	Wrist Pin Diameter (Fit)	Ring No.	Side clearance	End-Gap
1968-69	360	2.4218-2.4220	2.4715	2.4190-2.4192	2.4685	.7078-.7082 *	Top	.0032-.0047	.0039-.0118
							Middle	.0016-.0027	.0039-.0118
							Lower	.0016-.0027	.0039-.0118
1970-71	FF-1	①	3.0153	(A) 2.9933-2.9938 (B) 2.9929-2.9935 (C) 2.9926-2.9932	3.0135	.7477-.7480 **	Top	.0014-.0029	.0079-.0157
							Middle	.0010-.0025	.0079-.0157
							Oil	0	.0118-.0354
1971-72	FF-1 (G)	②	3.2491	(A) 3.2270-3.2275 (B) 3.2266-3.2274 (C) 3.2263-3.2269	3.2472	.7870-.7874 **	Top	.0014-.0029	.0079-.0196
							Middle	.0010-.0025	.0079-.0196
							Oil	0	.0118-.0354

①—Honed .0006-.0018 over piston diameter.
②—Honed .0008-.0019 over piston diameter.
*—Light press fit after heating the piston in warm oil.
**—Thumb press fit.

Torque Specifications

Year	Model	Cylinder Head Bolts (ft. lbs.)	Crankcase Halves (ft. lbs.)	Rod Bearing Caps (ft. lbs.)	Crankshaft Pulley (ft. lbs.)	Flywheel to Crankshaft Bolts (ft. lbs.)	Intake Manifold (ft. lbs.)	Exhaust Manifold (ft. lbs.)
1968-70	360	35-38	15-18	—	① 42-44	② 41-45	N.A.	N.A.
1970-71	FF-1	30-35	③ 26-31 ④ 17-20 ⑤ 3-4	35-38	39-42	30-33	13-16	7-9
1971-72	FF-1 (G)	37-42	③ 26-31 ④ 17-20 ⑤ 3-4	35-38	39-42	30-33	13-16	7-9

①—Cooling fan to crankshaft nut
②—Clutch to crankshaft bolt
③—10 mm. nuts and bolts
④—8 mm. nuts and bolts
⑤—6 mm. nuts and bolts

Torque Sequences

360 cylinder head

360 crankcase

FF-1 cylinder head

Electrical Specifications

Year	Model	Battery Capacity (amp hrs.)	Battery Volts	Battery Grounded Terminal	Starter Lock Test Amps	Lock Test Volts	Lock Test Torque (ft. lbs.)	No Load Test Amps	No Load Test Volts	No Load Test RPM	Brush Spring Tension (oz.)
1968-70	360	26	12	Negative	240	12	2.9	40	12	10000	26.4
1970-71	FF-1	32	12	Negative	430	8.5	8.0	55	11	3500	35-54
1971-72	FF-1 (G)	35	12	Negative	470	9.5	9.4	50	11	5000	35-54

Year	Model	Generator Part Number	Brush Spring Pressure (oz.)	Field Resistance (ohms)	Generator Output (amps)	Regulator Part Number	Volts to Close Cut-out Relay	Reverse Current (amps)	Voltage Regulator Setting (volts w/ no load)
1968-70	360	27000-116	32	N.A.	22.5	26000-125	12.5-13.5	1-8	15-16

Electrical Specifications

Year	Model	*Alternator* Part Number	*Alternator* Output (amps) @ Alternator rpm	*Alternator* Brush Spring Pressure (oz.)	*Regulator* Part Number	*Regulator* Charge Relay Air Gap (in.)	*Regulator* Charge Relay Point Gap (in.)	*Regulator* Voltage Regulator Volts to Close	*Regulator* Voltage Regulator Air Gap (in.)	*Regulator* Voltage Regulator Point Gap (in.)
1970-71	FF-1	LT 130-59A	30 @ 5000	11-13.5	TL1Z-27	.032-.039	.016-.024	14-15	.024-.039	.012-.016
1971-72	FF-1 (G)	LT 170-75	30 @ 5000	11-13.5	TL1Z-54	.032-.039	.016-.024	14-15	.024-.039	.012-.016

Distributor Specifications

Year	Model	Distributor Identification	*Centrifugal Advance* Start (rpm)	*Centrifugal Advance* Intermediate*	*Centrifugal Advance* End*	*Vacuum Advance* Start (in. Hg.)	*Vacuum Advance* End**
1968-70	360	① 29100-136-0 ② D203-31	2000	N.A.	7 @ 4000	—	—
1970-72	FF-1	D414-51	475-625	15 @ 1900	34 @ 4800	3.1	18 @ 17.9

*—Crankshaft degrees @ crankshaft rpm
**—Crankshaft degrees @ in. Hg.
①—Nippon Denso distributor
②—Hitachi distributor

Capacities and Pressures

Year	Model	*Engine Crankcase Refill After Draining (qts.)* With Filter	*Engine Crankcase Refill After Draining (qts.)* Without Filter	Transmission Refill After Draining (pts.)	Drive Axle (pts.)	Fuel Tank (gals.)	Cooling System With Heater (qts.)	Normal Fuel Pressure (psi)	Maximum Coolant Pressure (psi)
968-70	360	—	① 2.6	⑤ 3.4	—	② 6.6 ③ 5.3 ④ 8.0	—	2.5-4.5	—
1970-71	FF-1	3	2.75	⑤ 5.2	—	② 11.9 ⑥ 9.5	6.21	3.1	14.2
1971-72	FF-1 (G)	3	2.75	⑤ 5.2	—	② 11.9 ⑥ 9.5	6.21	3.1	14.2

①—Oil reservoir capacity
②—Sedan
③—Custom
④—Truck and Van
⑤—Common sump
⑥—Station wagon

Chassis and Wheel Alignment Specifications

		Chassis			Wheel Alignment							
			Track (in.)		Caster		Camber				Wheel Pivot Ratio	
Year	Model	Wheelbase (in.)	Front	Rear	Range	Preferred Setting	Range	Preferred Setting	Toe-in (in.)	King-Pin Inclination	Inner Wheel	Outer Wheel
1968-69	360 Sedan & Custom	70.9	44.9	42.1	①	13°17′	1°30′-2°	2°	.47-.63	7°	N.A.	N.A.
1968-70	360 Truck & Van	68.9	44.1	42.5	①	13°10′	1°30′-2°30′	2°	.47-.67	7°	N.A.	N.A.
1970-71	FF-1	95.3	48.2	47.4	1°30′-2°	2°	1°20′-1°50′	1°50′	.2	2°20′	36°20′	34°20′
1971-72	FF-1 (G)	95.3	48.2	② 47.4 ③ 48.6	1°30′-2°	2°	1°20′-1°50′	1°50′	.2	2°20′	36°20′	34°20′

①—Due to the single trailing arm suspension used on the Model 360, caster is determined by the position of the suspension relative to the body. In order to maintain the proper caster setting, ride height must adhere to specifications. Those specifications are as follows, measured vertically from the center of the front and rear torsion bars to a level surface:

Model	Front (in.) *	Rear (in.) *
Sedan	12.40-12.78	9.40-9.84
Custom	12.40-12.78	9.81-10.15
Truck and Van	10.6-11.0	10.0-10.2

*—Unloaded vehicle with properly inflated tires
②—Sedan
③—Station wagon

Brake Specifications

		Type		Brake Cylinder Bore (in.)			Brake Drum Diameter (in.)		Maximum Drum Diameter (in.)	
					Wheel Cylinder					
Year	Model	Front	Rear	Master Cylinder	Front	Rear	Front	Rear	Front	Rear
1968-70	360	Drum	Drum	.750	.8125	.6875	6.69	6.69	6.71	6.71
1970-72	FF-1	Drum	Drum	.7489-.7501	.9374-.9394	① .6248-.6265 ② .6874-.6891	① 8.01 ② 9.01	7.09	① 8.08 ② 9.04	7.17

①—Sedan ②—Station wagon

Fuses and Circuit Breakers

Year	Model	Circuit	Type	Amperage
1968-69	360 Sedan & Custom	Headlights, parking lights, license plate light, high beam indicator, instrument light, interior light, horn, windshield wipers.	Fuse	20
		Stop lights, turn signals, back-up lights, instruments, charge indicator, oil level indicator	Fuse	15
		Ignition	Fuse	25
1968-70	360 Truck & Van	Battery	Fuse①	25
		Headlights, parking lights, tail lights, license plate light, side marker lights, hazard flashers, high beam indicator, interior light, windshield wiper	Fuse	20
		Turn signals, charge indicator, oil level indicator, instruments	Fuse	5
		Ignition, back-up lights, stop lights, horn	Fuse	15
1970-72	FF-1	Ignition, horn, key warning buzzer	Fuse	25
		Headlights, parking lights, instrument lights, windshield washers	Fuse	25
		Lighter, radio, interior light, wiper	Fuse	20
		Back-up light, turn signals, stop lights, charge indicator, oil pressure indicator, instruments, brake warning light, fuel pump, blower motor	Fuse	10
		Side marker lights, tail lights, license plate lights, instrument lights, map light	Fuse	10

①—In the wire between the battery and the ignition switch.

Light Bulb Specifications

Year	Model	Usage	Type	Wattage
1968-70	360	*Headlight*	Sealed beam (two stage)	50/40
		Front turn signal and parking light, rear turn signal and stop light	Dual filament	23/7
		Tail light, license plate light, interior light	Single filament	8
		Instrument light, charge indicator, oil level indicator	Single filament	3
		Side marker light	Single filament	6
1970-72	FF-1	Headlight	Sealed beam (two stage)	50/40
		Front turn signal and parking light	Dual filament (amber)	23/8
		Rear turn signal, stop and parking light	Dual filament (red)	23/8
		Back-up light①	Single filament	23
		License plate light	Single filament	8
		Front side marker light	Single filament (amber)	6
		Rear side marker light	Single filament (red)	6
		Instrument light, map light	Single filament	3
		Charge, turn signal, high beam, and oil pressure indicators, brake warning light	Single filament (red)	3
		Interior light	Single filament	8

①—2 used on Sedan, 1 on Station Wagon

Wiring Diagrams

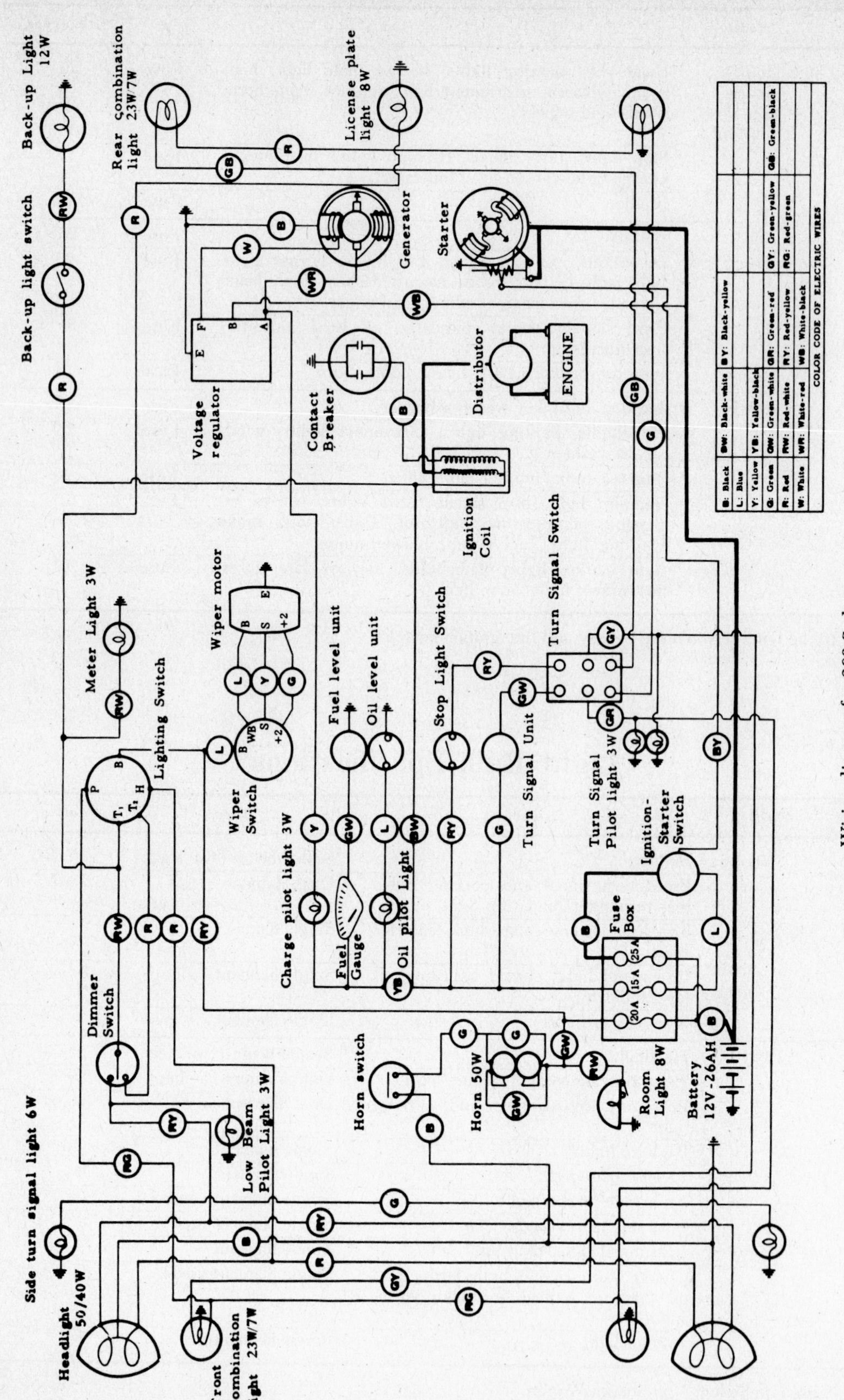

Wiring diagram for 360 Sedan

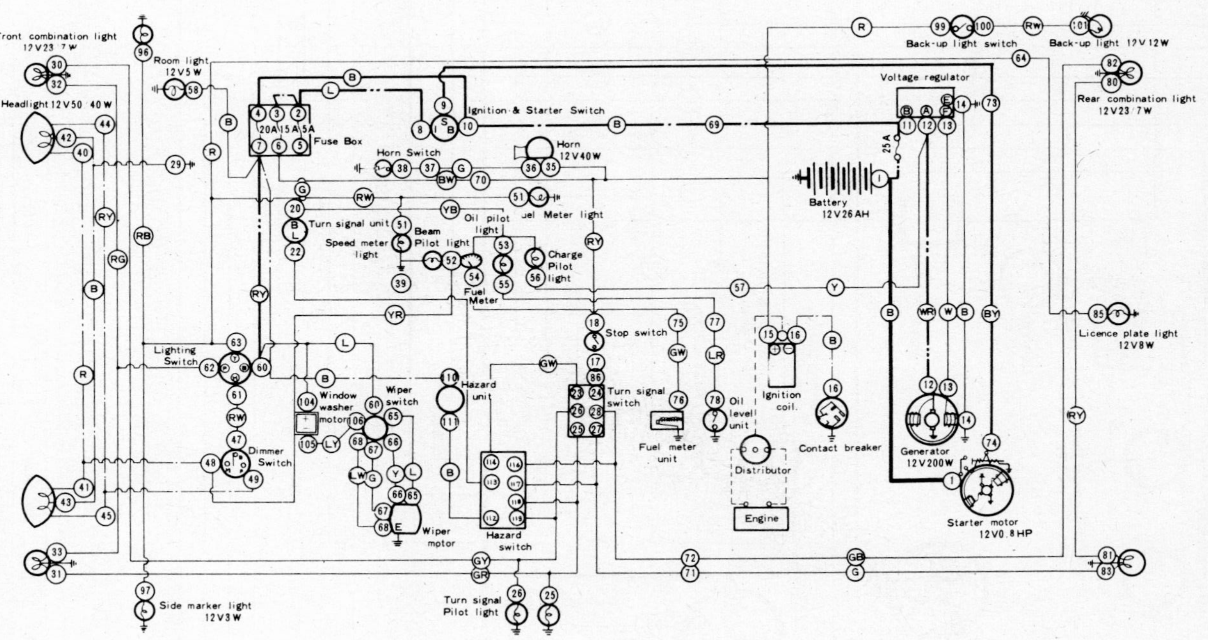

Circuit	Mark	Cdor	Mark	Color	Mark	Color	Mark	Color	Mark	Color
Ground	B	Black								
Others	L	Blue	LW	Blue/White	LR	Blue/Red				
Meters	Y	Yellow	YG	Yellow/Green	YR	Yellow/Red	YW	Yellow/White	YB	Yellow/Black
Signals	G	Green	GR	Green/Red	GY	Green/Yellow	GW	Green/White	GB	Green/Black
Illumination	R	Red	RG	Red/Green	RY	Red/Yellow	RW	Red/White		
Charging	W	White	WR	White/Red						
Starting	B	Black	BW	Black/Yellow	BY	Black/Yellow				

Wiring diagram for 360 Truck and Van

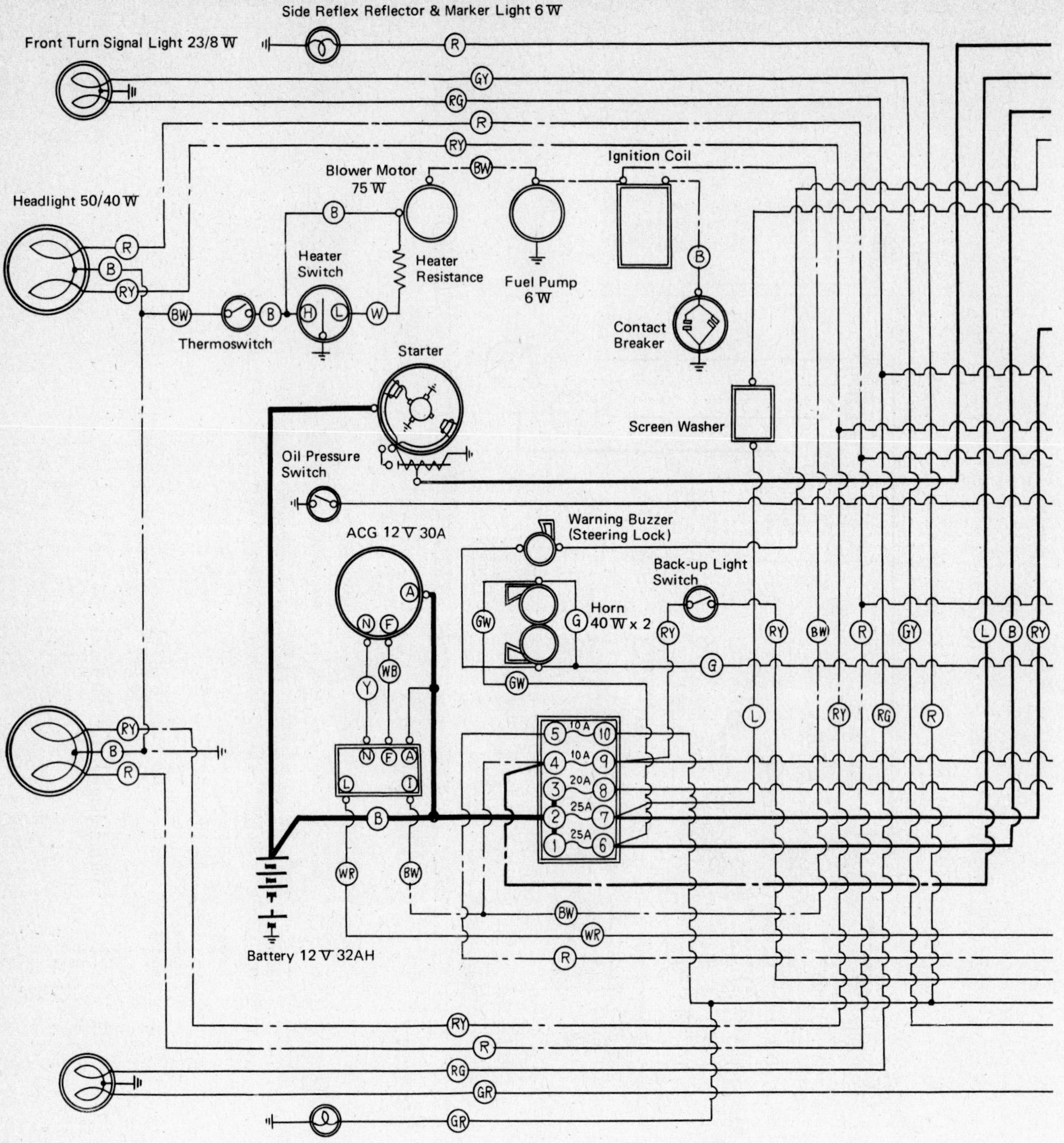

L	Blue	**LW**	Blue-white	**LR**	Blue-red				
R	Red	**RW**	Red-white	**RG**	Red-green	**RY**	Red-yellow	**RB**	Red-black
G	Green	**GW**	Green-white	**GR**	Green-red	**GY**	Green-yellow		
Y	Yellow	**YR**	Yellow-red	**YG**	Yellow-green				
W	White	**WB**	White-black	**WR**	White-red				
B	Black	**BW**	Black-white	**BY**	Black-yellow				

Color Code of Electric Wires

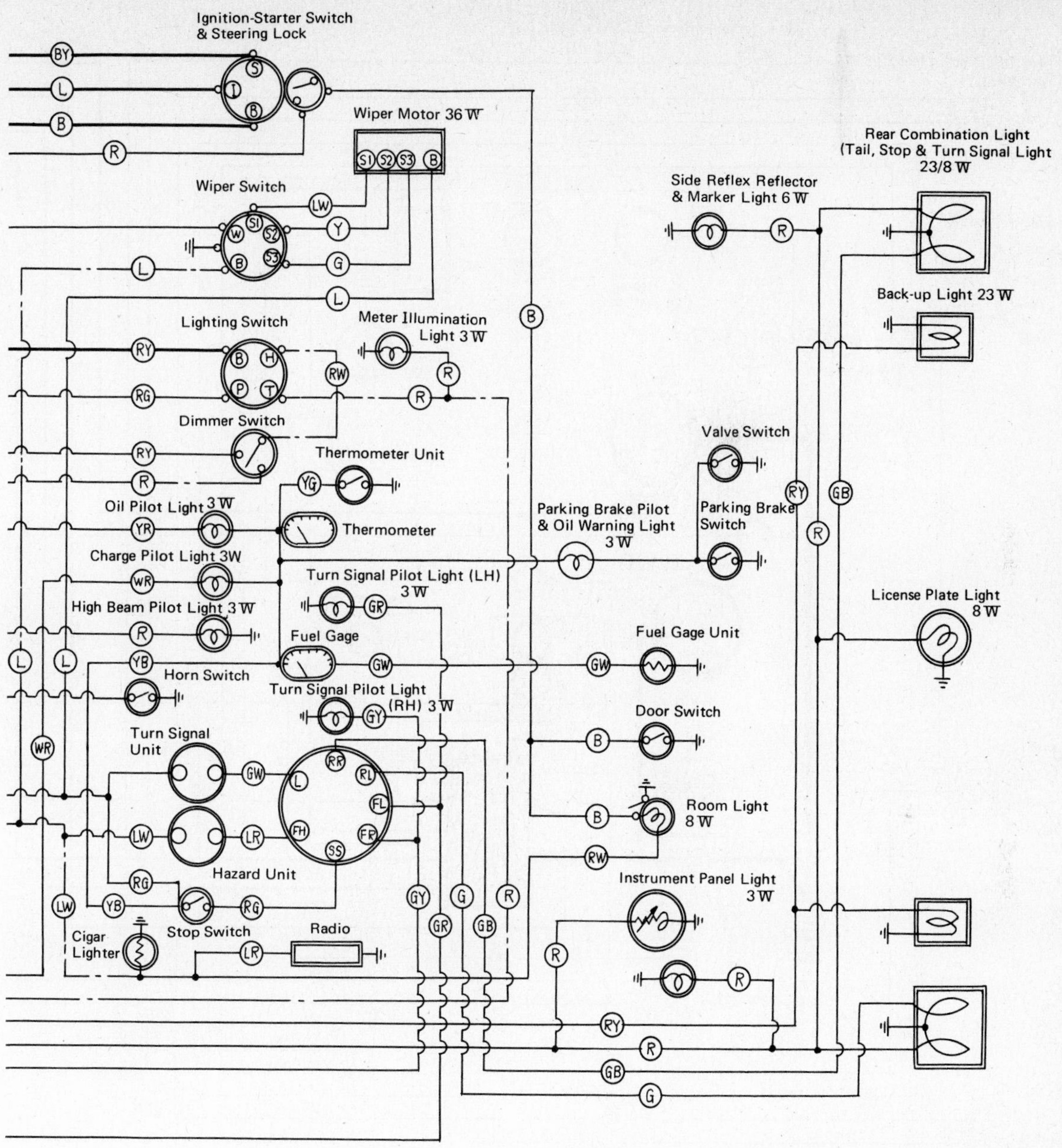

Wiring diagram for FF-1 Sedan

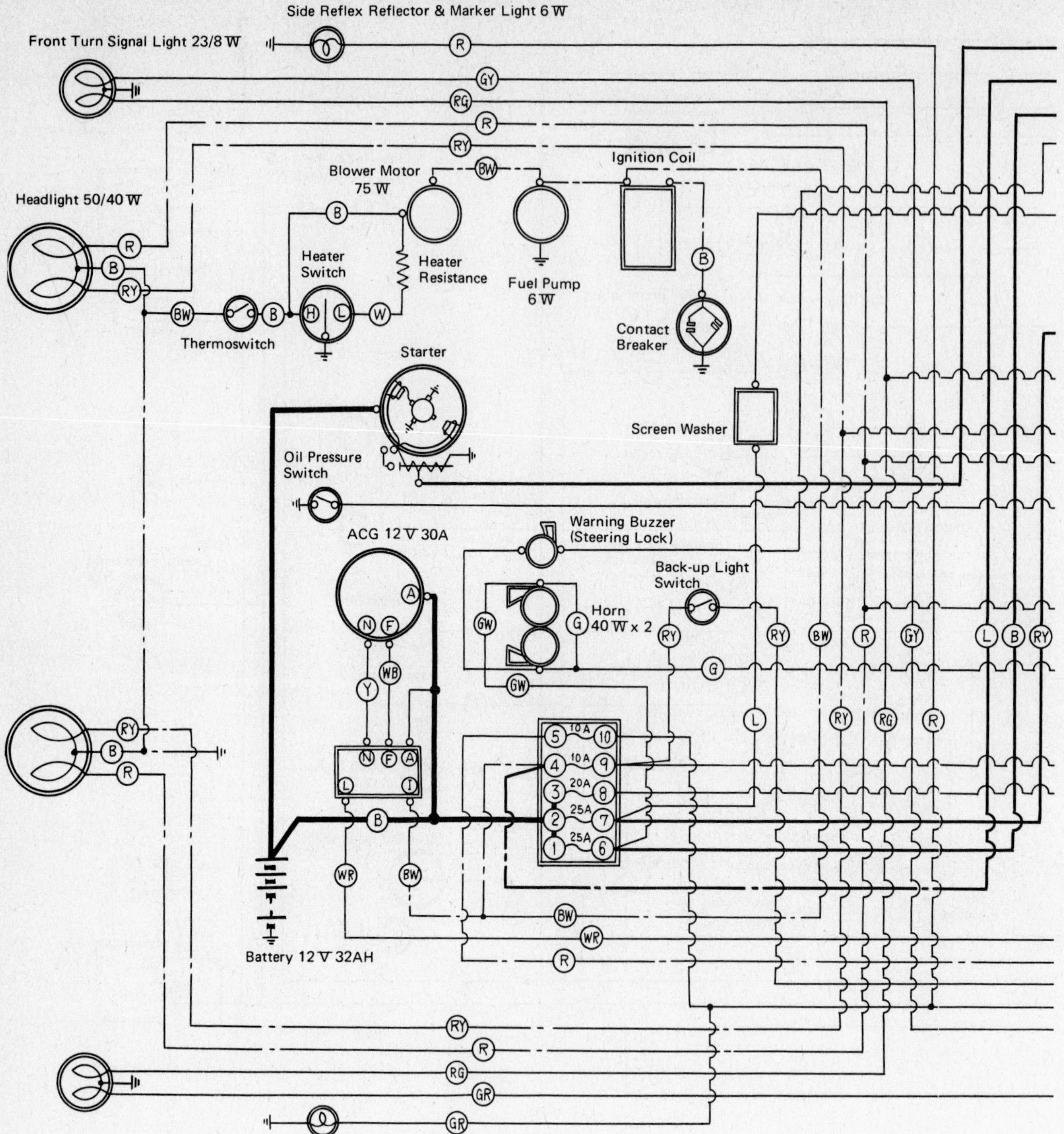

L	Blue	LW	Blue-white	LR	Blue-red				
R	Red	RW	Red-white	RG	Red-green	RY	Red-yellow	RB	Red-black
G	Green	GW	Green-white	GR	Green-red	GY	Green-yellow		
Y	Yellow	YR	Yellow-red	YG	Yellow-green				
W	White	WB	White-black	WR	White-red				
B	Black	BW	Black-white	BY	Black-yellow				

Color Code of Electric Wires

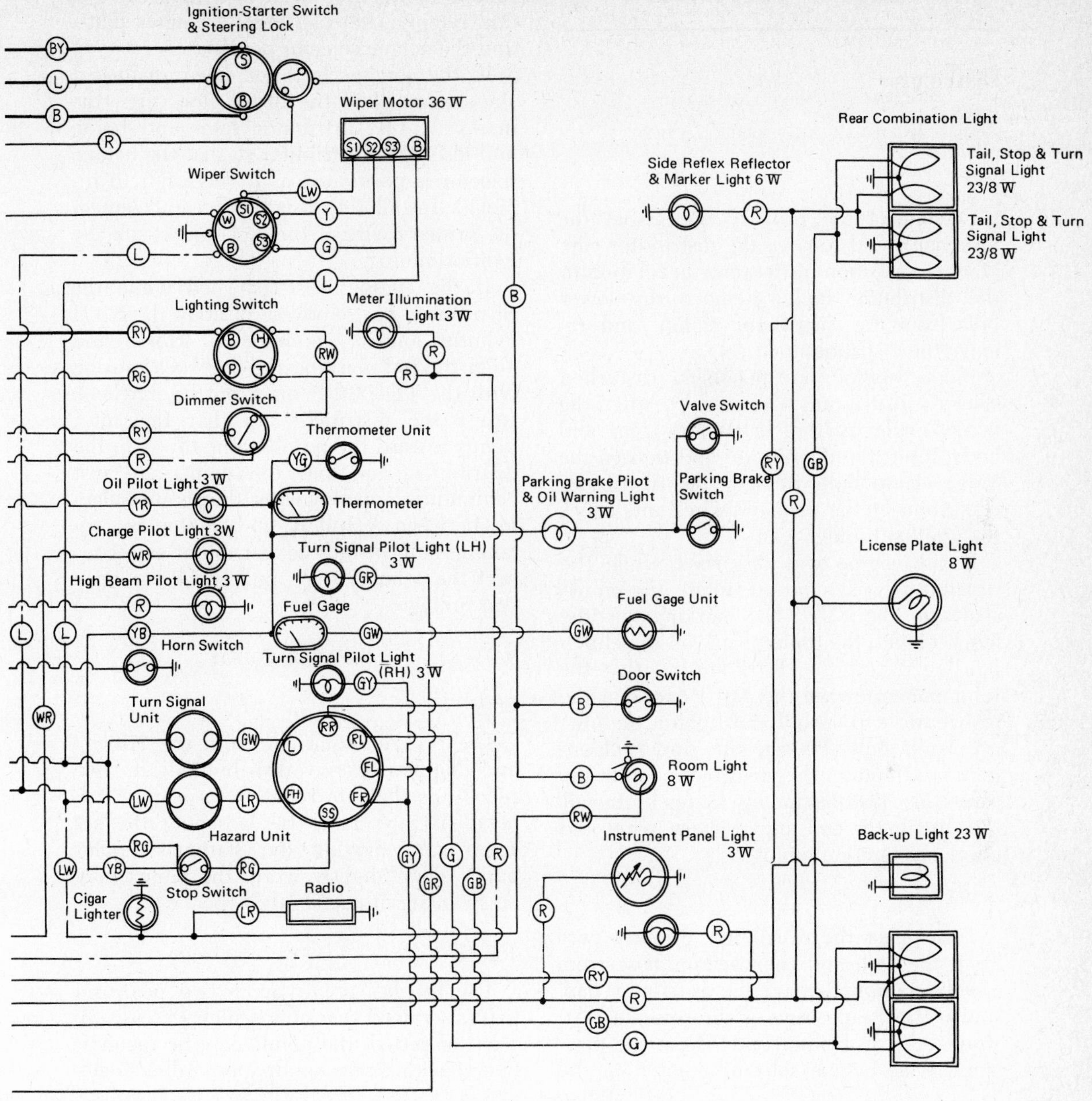

Wiring diagram for FF-1 Station Wagon

Engine Electrical

Distributor

Removal and Installation

360

Disconnect the primary wire from the distributor and remove the distributor cap. Mark the position of the rotor in relation to the distributor body. Remove the lower bolt from the distributor clamp, and remove the distributor.

If the engine has not been disturbed since the distributor was removed, align the marks made on the distributor rotor and body, insert the distributor, and tighten the lower clamp bolt. Replace the distributor cap, connect the primary wire, and check the ignition timing.

If the engine was disturbed while the distributor was removed, rotate the crankshaft to align the 11° marking on the flywheel with the timing mark on the clutch housing. Insert the distributor so that the rotor points toward the No. 1 tower in the distributor cap, install and tighten the lower clamp bolt. Loosen the upper clamp bolt, and rotate the distributor until the points are just beginning to open. Install the distributor cap and primary wire, and check the ignition timing.

FF-1

Disconnect the distributor primary wire from the coil, and the vacuum hose from the distributor. Remove the distributor cap, and mark the position of the rotor in relation to the distributor body. Note the position of the octane selector pointer on the octane selector scale. Remove the bolt retaining the distributor at the octane selector and remove the distributor, retainer plate, and the octane selector pointer.

If the engine has not been disturbed since removal of the distributor, align the marks on the distributor rotor and body, and insert the distributor so that the octane selector is positioned as it was prior to removal. Install the distributor cap, connect the primary wire at the coil, and check the ignition timing.

If the engine was disturbed while the distributor was removed, position the No. 1 cylinder on its compression stroke, and align the red mark on the flywheel housing with the TDC (0°) mark on the flywheel. Insert the distributor so that the rotor points toward the number one tower in the distributor cap, and the points are just beginning to open. Center the octane selector between A and R, and tighten the retaining bolt. Install the distributor cap, connect the primary wire, and check the ignition timing.

Breaker Points

360

The breaker points on both the Hitachi and Nippon Denso distributors are two piece sets that are replaced as a unit. Adjustments are made by loosening the set screw and moving the stationary point base. When slightly worn, the points may be cleaned with #00 sandpaper.

FF-1

The breaker points are a two piece set that is serviced as a unit. Unless excessively worn or pitted, the points may be reconditioned with #500 sandpaper. Adjustments

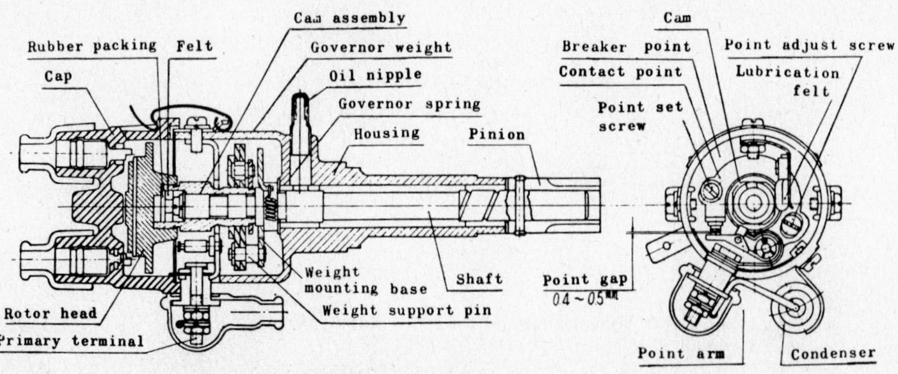

360 distributor—cross-section

are made by turning an eccentric screw in a slot in the stationary point base.

Ignition Timing

360

The ignition timing marks are located on the edge of the flywheel, graduated in 1° increments from 10° to 15°. The marks are visible through a port in the clutch housing, behind the generator, adjacent to the distributor. Ignition timing is adjusted by loosening the upper distributor clamp bolt and rotating the distributor counter-clockwise to advance timing, or clockwise to retard timing.

FF-1

The ignition timing marks are located on the edge of the flywheel, graduated in 2° increments from 0° to 16°. The marks are visible through a port in the flywheel housing, immediately behind the dipstick. The

360 timing marks

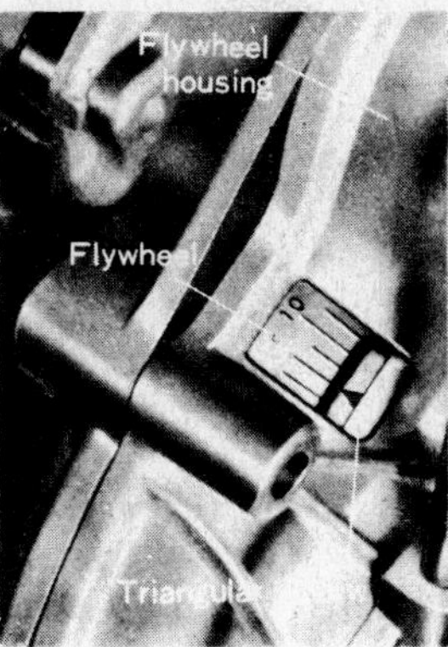

FF-1 timing marks

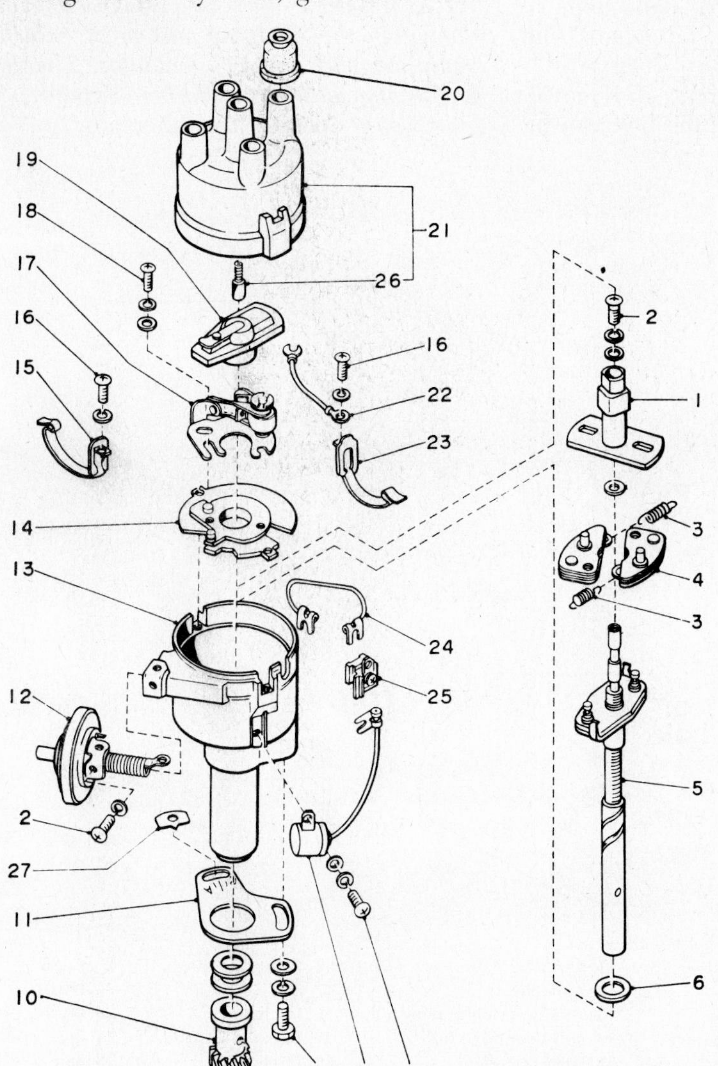

1 Cam
2 Screw
3 Governor spring
4 Governor weight
5 Shaft
6 Washer
7 Screw
8 Condenser
9 Bolt
10 Gear
11 Plate
12 Vacuum unit
13 Housing
14 Breaker plate
15 Clamp
16 Screw
17 Breaker points
18 Breaker point set screw
19 Rotor
20 Boot
21 Cap
22 Ground wire
23 Clamp
24 Lead wire
25 Terminal
26 Carbon brush
27 Pointer

FF-1 distributor—exploded view

ignition timing is adjusted by loosening the bolt opposite the octane selector on the retaining plate, and rotating the distributor clockwise to advance timing, or counterclockwise to retard timing. After adjusting the timing, adjust the octane selector so that the engine knocks slightly under sudden acceleration from low speeds in fourth gear.

Generator

Removal and Installation

360

The 360 utilizes a DC generator. Remove and code the three leads from the generator terminals. Loosen the generator mounting bolts, and the lower bolt of the adjusting arm, and remove the drive belt. Remove the three mounting bolts, and remove the generator.

Install in the reverse order of removal. Adjust belt tension so that the belt can be depressed 5/8″ to 3/4″ when pressed at its center. NOTE: *When the generator is removed from a DC charging circuit, the system must be polarized upon installation. Momentarily connect a jumper between the battery (B or 51) and armature (A or D+) terminals of the regulator to ensure proper polarity.*

FF-1

The FF-1 utilizes an AC generator (alternator). To remove, remove the air cleaner assembly, unplug the electrical connector, and remove the three retaining bolts. The air cleaner bracket will remain suspended on the spark plug wires.

Install in the reverse order of removal. Adjust fan belt tension so that the belt may be depressed .4″ at its center.

CAUTION: *Care must be taken to avoid damaging the charging system of vehicles equipped with an AC generator. The following precautions should be observed:*

1. Never operate the alternator on an

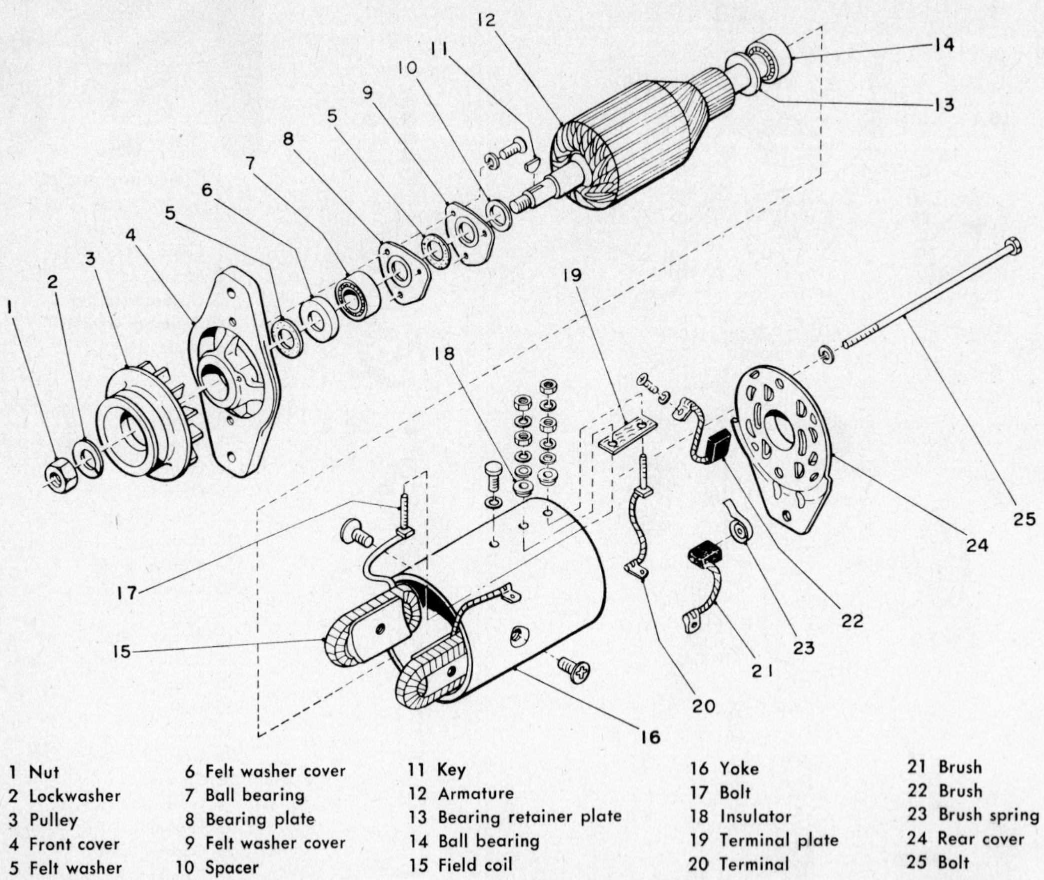

1 Nut	6 Felt washer cover	11 Key	16 Yoke	21 Brush
2 Lockwasher	7 Ball bearing	12 Armature	17 Bolt	22 Brush
3 Pulley	8 Bearing plate	13 Bearing retainer plate	18 Insulator	23 Brush spring
4 Front cover	9 Felt washer cover	14 Ball bearing	19 Terminal plate	24 Rear cover
5 Felt washer	10 Spacer	15 Field coil	20 Terminal	25 Bolt

360 generator—exploded view

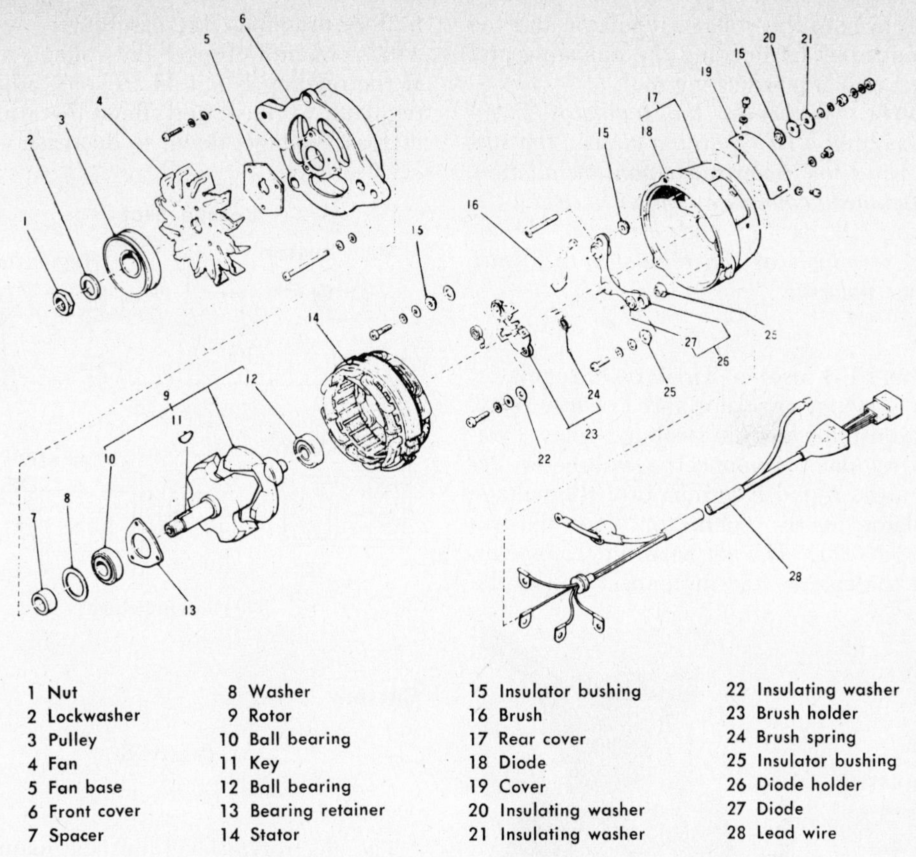

FF-1 alternator—exploded view

open circuit (battery disconnected).

2. When installing the battery, connect the ground terminal (negative) before connecting the positive terminal.
3. When arc welding anywhere on the vehicle, always disconnect the alternator.

Regulator

Adjustments

360

The 360 uses a Bosch type regulator, with voltage regulator and cut-out relay. Most difficulties with this regulator can be solved by cleaning the points with fine emery cloth followed by rinsing with trichloroethylene. The no-load voltage is adjusted by disconnecting the lead from the B (or 51) terminal of the regulator, and connecting a voltmeter between this terminal and ground. Start the engine and adjust the regulator to specifications at 2000 rpm. Lower engine speed to idle following each adjustment, to avoid the effect of magnetic retention causing inaccurate readings.

The cut-in voltage of the cut-out relay is adjusted by attaching a voltmeter between the A (or D+) terminals of the generator and regulator (the lead is removed from the circuit), and slowly increasing engine speed until the voltage drops abruptly. The voltage reading just prior to the drop is the cut-in voltage of the relay. Adjustments are

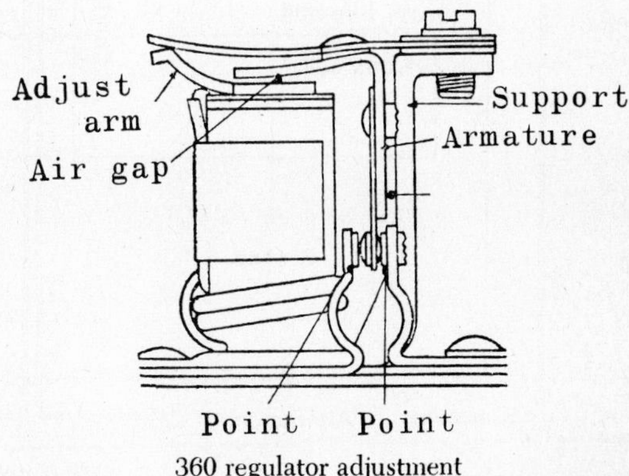

360 regulator adjustment

made to both the voltage regulator and the cut-out relay by bending the adjusting arm with a regulator adjusting tool.

NOTE: *Whenever the regulator is removed from a DC charging circuit, the system must be polarized upon installation. Momentarily connect a jumper between the battery (B or 51) and armature (A or D+) terminals of the regulator to ensure proper polarity.*

FF-1

The FF-1 uses a Tirril type regulator, with a voltage regulator and a charge relay. To adjust the constant-voltage relay (voltage regulator), connect a voltmeter between the A and E terminals of the voltage regulator at the connector (see illustration). NOTE: *Do not separate connector.* Start the engine, and disconnect one of the battery terminals. Increase engine speed to 1560 rpm, and observe the voltage reading. If the reading is not 14-15 volts, adjust the regulator as illustrated. Bend the arm up to increase voltage, down to decrease voltage.

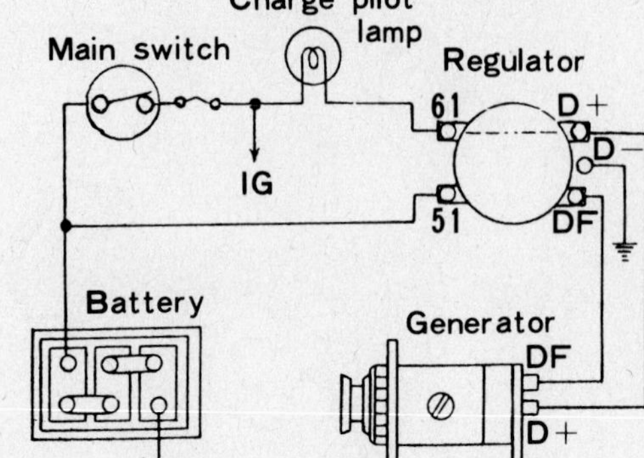

360 charging circuit

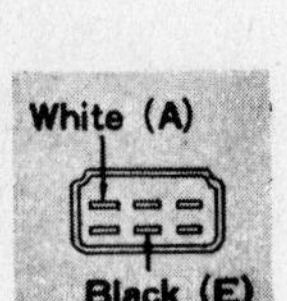

FF-1 regulator connector

FF-1 voltage regulator adjustment

Battery

MAINTENANCE

360, FF-1

The electrolyte level must be maintained (distilled water is recommended), and the terminals must be kept clean and free from corrosion. The specific gravity of the electrolyte should not fall below 1.196 at 68° F. Should it drop below this point, the battery

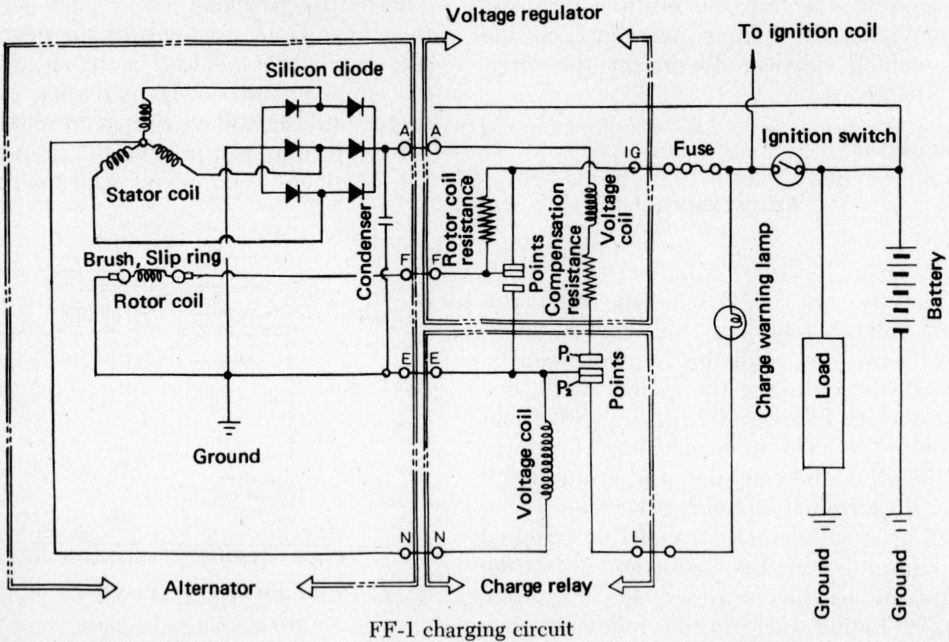

FF-1 charging circuit

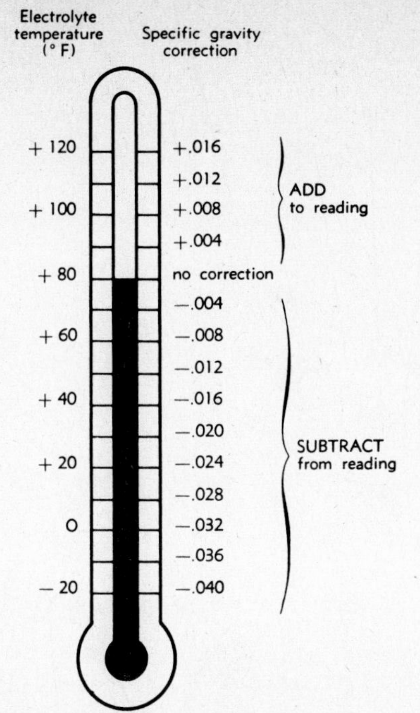

The effect of temperature on the specific gravity of battery electrolyte

should be charged. If the battery takes the charge, and the specific gravity drops repeatedly, the charging system should be investigated.

CAUTION: *When jump starting a vehicle equipped with an AC generator, ensure that proper polarity is observed, and that the cables are removed as soon after starting as possible, in order to avoid damaging the charging system.*

Starter

Removal and Installation

360

Remove the rear underpan from the vehicle. Code for identification and remove all leads from the starter. Back out the bolt opposite the starter on the clutch housing, and remove the nut from the starter mount. Remove the starter from the underside of the vehicle.

Install in the reverse order of removal.

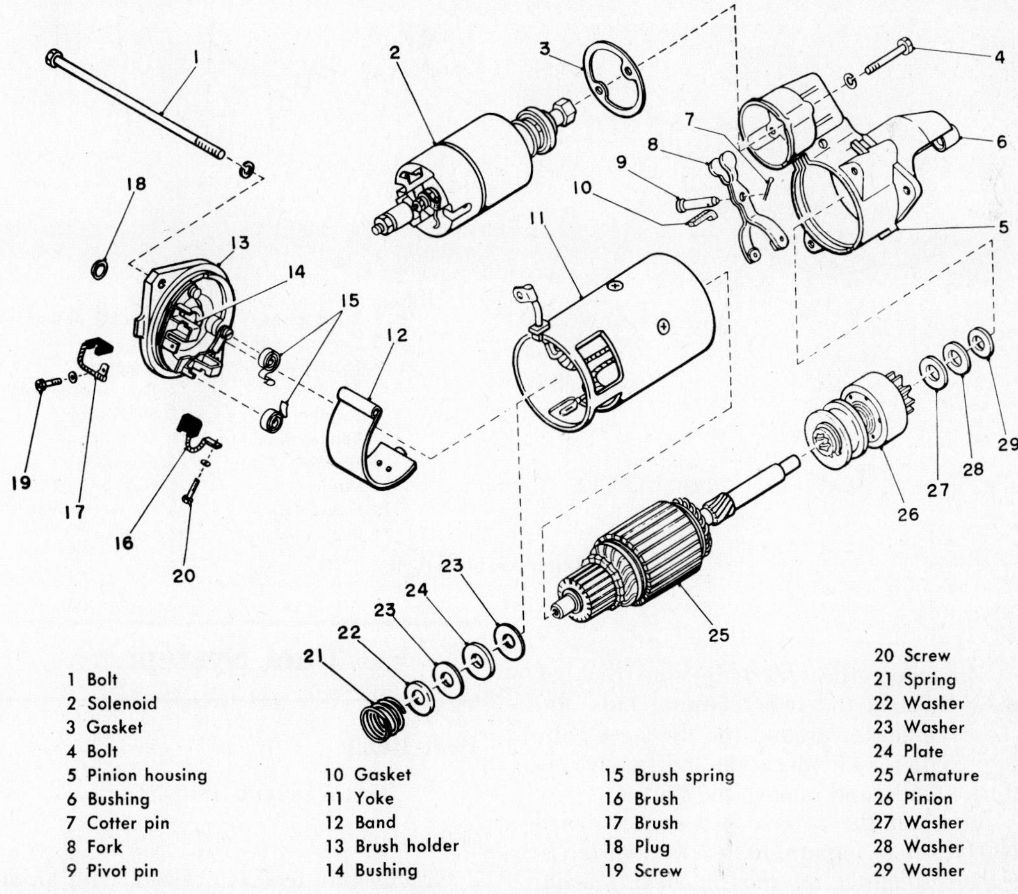

360 starter—exploded view

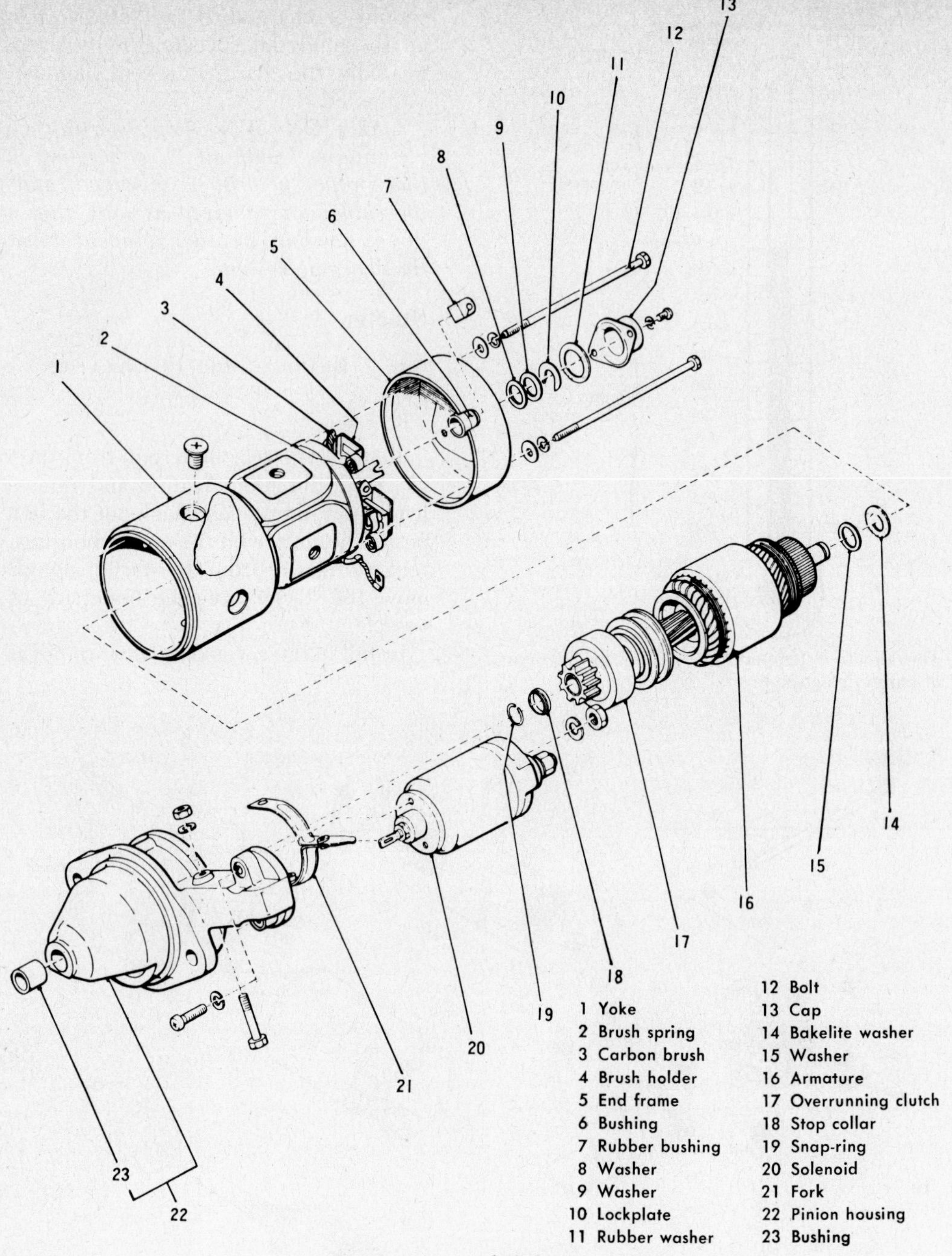

FF-1 starter—exploded view

FF-1

Disconnect the terminals from the battery. Remove the two retaining nuts, and slide the starter around the flywheel housing. Code for identification and remove the starter leads, and remove the starter.

Install in the reverse order of removal. NOTE: *It is important that the starter be seated squarely on the flywheel housing mating surface when installed.*

Fuel System

Fuel Pump

REMOVAL AND INSTALLATION

360 Sedan

Gravity fuel feed is utilized, with an automatic vacuum operated shut-off valve lo-

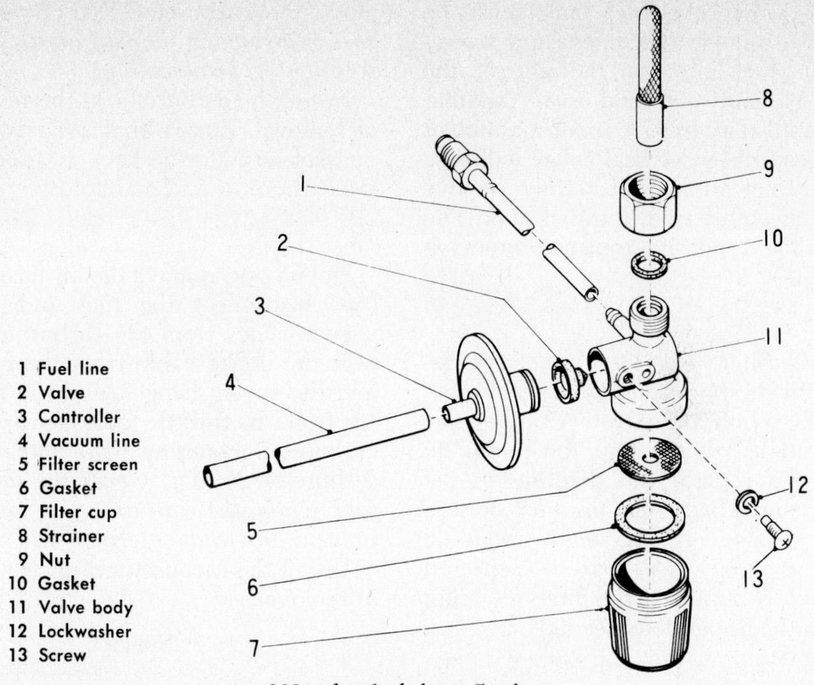

360 sedan fuel shut-off valve

cated on the bottom of the fuel tank. Prior to removal of the valve, the fuel tank must be drained. Remove the fuel line from the carburetor, place it in a suitable container, and apply suction to the control hose. If the valve is not functioning properly, and suction fails to open the valve, loosen the screw on the side of the valve body and slowly pull and turn the diaphragm case until fuel begins to flow. Unclip the fuel and control hoses from the fan housing, remove the retaining nut, and remove the valve.

Install in the reverse order of removal.

360 Custom, Truck, and Van

A fuel pump actuated by crankcase pressure differential is used. It is mounted on the crankcase, below and to the left of the intake manifold. To remove, detach and plug the input fuel line (left side), remove the two retaining nuts, and remove the pump. Disconnect the output fuel line from the pump.

Install in the reverse order of removal.

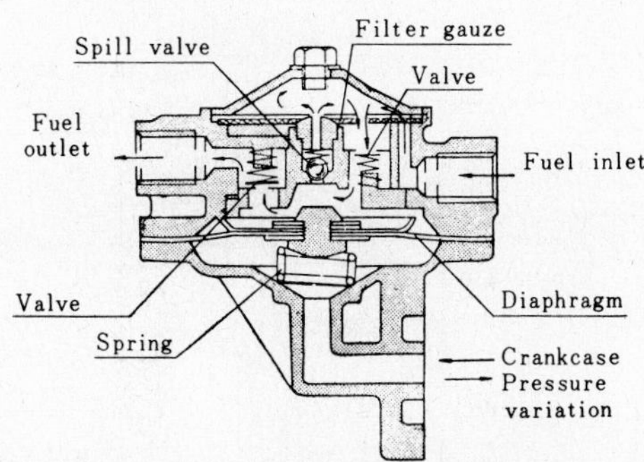

360 Custom, truck and van fuel pump

FF-1

An electric fuel pump is utilized. The pump is located directly below the spare tire, in the rear of the engine compartment. To remove the pump, remove the spare tire, disconnect the fuel lines, and remove the two retaining bolts.

Install in the reverse order of removal.

NOTE: *The pump ground wire must be connected to one of the retaining bolts.*

SERVICE

360 Sedan

All service operations other than cleaning the fuel strainer may be performed with the valve assembly installed on the car. To clean or replace the filter, ensure that the valve is closed, remove the filter cup and gasket, and remove the filter by tapping the valve body lightly on the side. When installing the filter, tighten the filter cup approximately 1/10 turn after it contacts the gasket surface. To replace the diaphragm or needle valve, the fuel tank must be drained. To remove the diaphragm assembly, loosen the screw on the side of the valve body, and pull and turn the diaphragm until it is free. A small amount of oil on the needle valve seal collar will ease assembly. To clean the fuel strainer, remove the valve assembly from the fuel tank. The strainer should not be replaced unless it is damaged.

360 Custom, Truck, and Van

The fuel filter may be cleaned or replaced with the pump installed, by removing the cover bolt and cover. All other service operations require that the pump be removed. To replace the diaphragm, the upper and lower body sections must be separated, by removing the eight retaining screws. The pump valves may be inspected or removed by removing the three retaining bolts from the upper body section.

FF-1

The pump is of the sealed type, and service is limited to cleaning the plunger (in gasoline), and cleaning or replacement of the fuel filter element. Access to these parts is obtained by removing the spring clip from the end housing of the pump.

Carburetor

Removal and Installation

360

Disconnect the throttle, choke, and oil pump control cables from the throttle and choke levers by removing the retaining nuts. Remove the choke and throttle cables from the mounting brackets. Remove the fresh air duct hose from the carburetor inlet, the fuel inlet hose from the float bowl, and the two carburetor retaining nuts. Remove the carburetor. NOTE: *It is often easier to remove the carburetor and intake manifold as an assembly.*

Install the carburetor in the reverse order of removal. Ensure that a sandwich gasket (gasket-insulator-gasket) is used between the carburetor and manifold.

FF-1

Unbolt and remove the air cleaner assembly. Disconnect the fuel and distributor vacuum lines from the carburetor. Disconnect the choke cable from the choke lever and the spring hanger, and the throttle cable from the throttle lever. Remove the four carburetor mounting bolts and remove the carburetor. NOTE: *Cover the intake manifold while the carburetor is removed, to prevent dirt from entering.*

Install the carburetor in the reverse order of removal.

Service

360

A one barrel side-draft carburetor, adjustable through the use of various size jets is used. The slow and main air bleed jets are located under a cover plate on top of the carburetor. The main jet is in a retainer threaded into the base of the carburetor. All jets are threaded, and are accessible with the carburetor installed on the vehicle. No provision for float adjustment is made, but the float chamber should be flushed periodically, by removing the float cover and main jet retainer, and pouring gasoline through the chamber.

Adjust idle as follows: Back out the idle mixture screw 2 full turns from the fully closed position, start the engine, and allow it to idle until it reaches operating temperature. Back out the idle speed screw until the point at which the engine idles

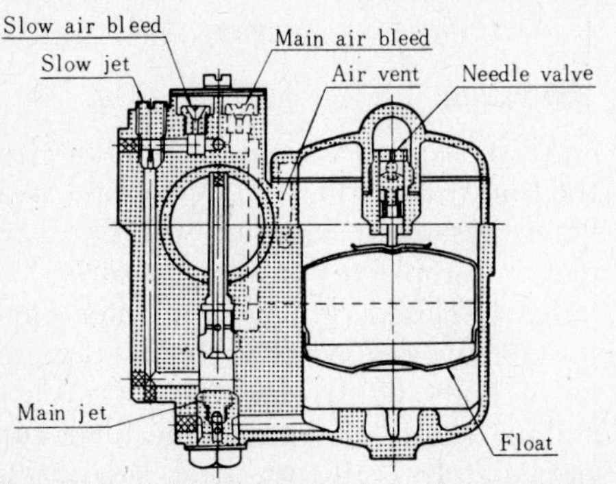

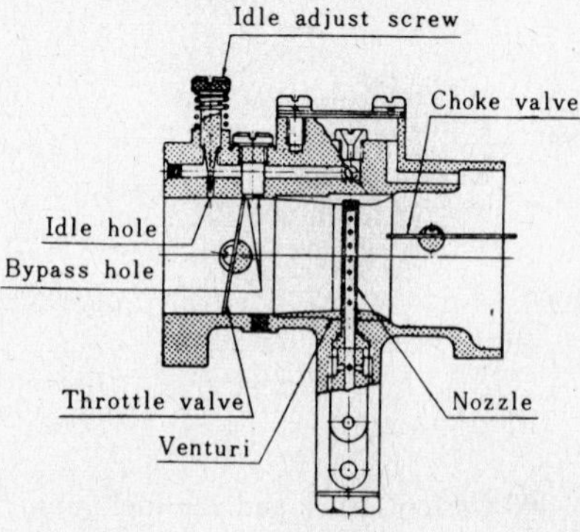

360 carburetor

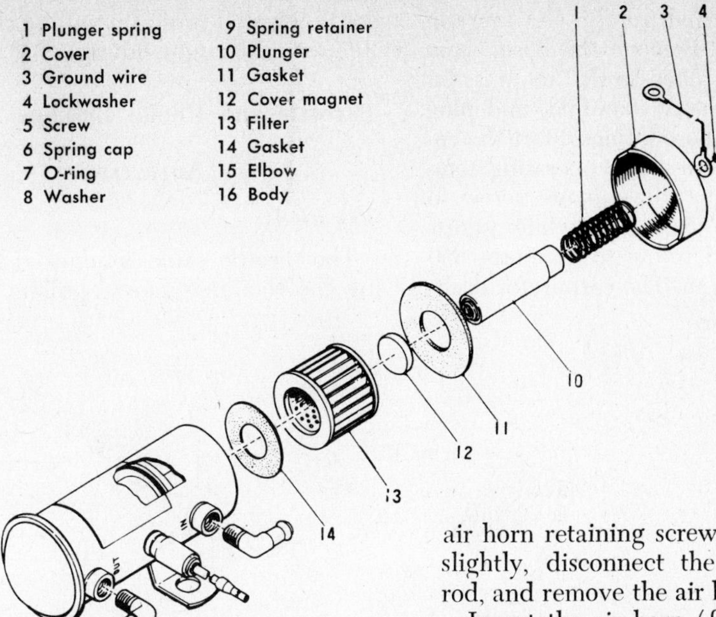

FF-1 electric fuel pump

roughly and rpm drops off. Turn the idle mixture screw in until the idle smoothes and the rpm stabilizes. Stop turning the screw when maximum rpm is achieved. Adjust the idle to the correct rpm with the idle speed screw.

FF-1

A two barrel carburetor with progressive secondary linkage is used. The progressive linkage is adjusted with the carburetor removed from the vehicle. It is adjusted so that when the connecting rod contacts the end of the groove in the secondary actuating lever, the primary throttle is open approximately 1/4″ (this may be measured with the shaft of a drill bit). Adjust by bending the secondary connecting rod. The fast idle is adjusted by bending the choke connecting rod so that the throttle plate is open approximately .035″ in fast idle position.

The float level may be adjusted with the carburetor installed on the engine, by removing the air horn as follows: Disconnect the accelerator pump actuating rod from the pump lever. Remove the throttle return spring. Disconnect the choke cable from the choke lever, and remove it from the spring hanger. Remove the spring hanger, the choke bellcrank, and the remaining air horn retaining screws. Lift the air horn slightly, disconnect the choke connecting rod, and remove the air horn.

Invert the air horn (float up), and measure the distance between the surface of the air horn and the float. Bend the float arm until the clearance is approximately .41″. Invert the air horn to its installed position, and measure the distance between the float arm and the needle valve stem. This dimension should be .050-.065″, and is adjusted by bending the float stops.

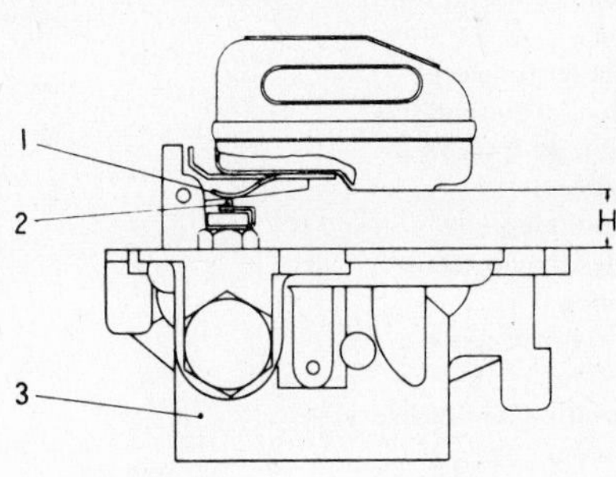

FF-1 float level adjustment

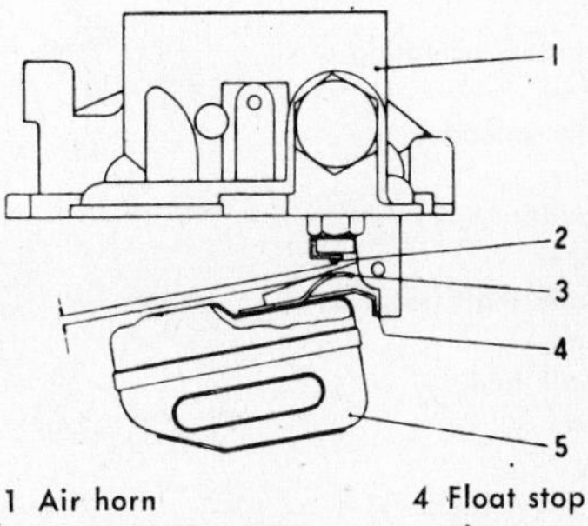

FF-1 float drop adjustment

The idle is adjusted using a CO (carbon monoxide) meter. Remove the hoses from the air distributor tubes, so that no air is injected into the exhaust manifold, and plug the air distributor hose fittings. Start the engine and allow it to reach operating temperature. Adjust the idle mixture screw to 9.5% (Model G–7.5%) CO, while adjusting the idle speed screw to maintain 850 (Model G–750) rpm. The carburetor dashpot is adjusted so that it will be compressed .16″ with the engine idling.

Throttle and Choke Linkage

Adjustment

360, FF-1

The throttle cable is adjusted by loosening the retaining screw, pulling the cable

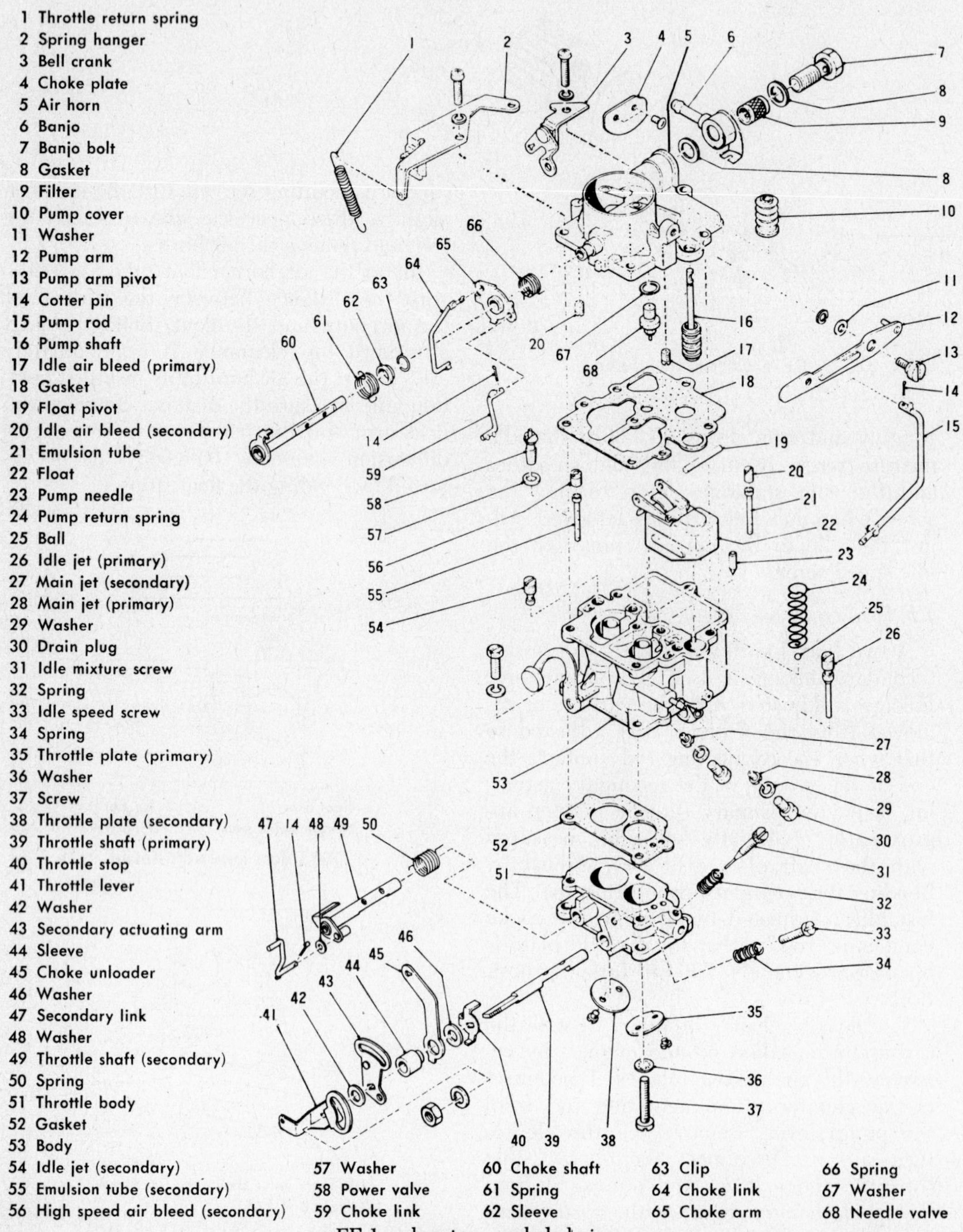

FF-1 carburetor—exploded view

lightly to remove slack, and tightening the screw. The choke cable is adjusted in a similar manner, however, a retaining nut is used rather than a screw. NOTE: *When adjusting, ensure that both the choke plate and the choke control are in the full open position, and that the accelerator and throttle plate are fully closed.*

Exhaust System

Exhaust Pipe

REMOVAL AND INSTALLATION

360

A resonator is used as the exhaust pipe on the 360. It is removed by removing the trap door (Sedan—vertical, behind the rear seat back; Custom—horizontal, on the rear shelf; Truck and Van—vertical, on the engine cover in the bed), and separating the split clamps at the muffler and the exhaust manifold.

Install in the reverse order of removal.

FF-1

Disconnect the exhaust pipe from the right and left-hand exhaust manifolds, and from the muffler extension pipe (adjacent to the rear crossmember), and unbolt the hanger at the rear crossmember. Remove the front mounting bracket from the bottom of the transaxle, and lower the exhaust pipe away.

Install in the reverse order of removal.

Muffler and Tail Pipe

REMOVAL AND INSTALLATION

360

Separate the split clamp that attaches the exhaust pipe to the muffler. The muffler and tail pipe assembly is removed from the underside of the vehicle, by removing four mounting bolts.

To install, mount the muffler, but do not tighten the mounting bolts. Attach and tighten the split clamp to the muffler-exhaust pipe joint, then tighten the four mounting bolts.

FF-1

Disconnect the muffler from the exhaust pipe, unbolt the tail pipe hanger bracket, and remove the muffler and tailpipe assembly.

To install, support the muffler by loosely attaching the muffler hanger, and attach the exhaust pipe to the muffler. Position the tailpipe hanger and bracket so that the rubber support is not stressed front to rear or twisted, and tighten the bolts. If the rubber support block is stretched excessively, insert spacers between the mounting bracket and underpan. NOTE: *Check to ensure that no part of the exhaust system contacts the underpan, to avoid excessive noise or vibration.*

Cooling System

Radiator

REMOVAL AND INSTALLATION

FF-1

A main radiator, sub-radiator, and reservoir tank are utilized. They can be removed individually or as an assembly. To remove as an assembly proceed as follows:

1. Remove the grill.
2. Remove the drain plug, and drain the coolant.
3. Disconnect the radiator hoses from the top of the main and sub-radiators, and from the bottom of the main radiator (water pump side).

When removing the engine:

4. Disconnect the heater control cable, by removing the circlip which retains the

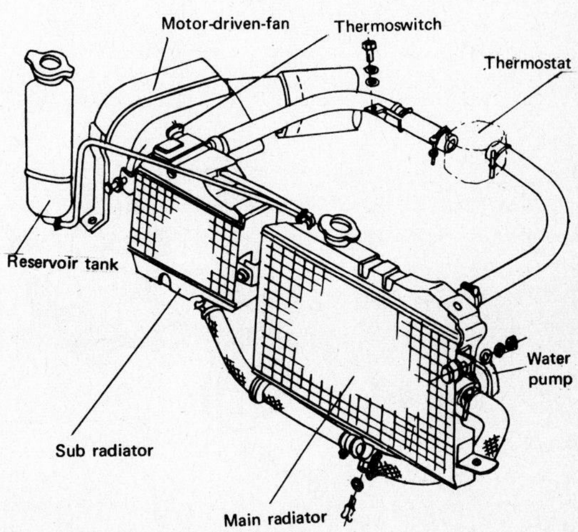

FF-1 cooling system

FF-1 radiator assembly removal

inner cable, and the nut which retains the sheath to the bracket. Loosen the clamp that retains the heater duct to the blower casing, and remove the blower casing mounting bolts.

When not removing the engine:

4. Remove the bolts that retain the sub-radiator shroud to the blower casing.
5. Remove the four screws and two bolts that retain the radiator bracket, and remove the radiator assembly.

NOTE: *Do not remove the bolt between the radiators.*

To remove only the main radiator proceed as follows:

1. Remove the grill.
2. Remove the drain plug and drain the coolant.
3. Disconnect all hoses from the main radiator.
4. Remove the center and right-hand radiator mounting bolts, and the four screws retaining the radiator bracket.
5. Remove the main radiator and bracket, leaving the sub-radiator suspended on the left-hand mounting bolt and the blower motor casing.

To remove only the sub-radiator:

1. Remove the grill.
2. Remove the drain plug and drain the coolant.
3. Disconnect the radiator snroud from the blower casing.
4. Remove the center and left-hand radiator retaining bolts, and remove the sub-radiator.

Install in the reverse order of removal.

Water Pump

Removal and Installation

FF-1

A centrifugal water pump, mounted on the front of the engine, is utilized. To remove, drain the coolant, and remove the radiator hose from the pump. Remove the drive belt, unbolt and lift out the pump.

Install in the reverse order of removal.

Service

FF-1

Service of the water pump is limited to replacement of the carbon seal, replacement of the rear cover gasket, and inspection of tolerances. The pump is serviced as follows:

1. Remove the rear cover plate and gasket.
2. Remove the pulley from the pump with a puller.

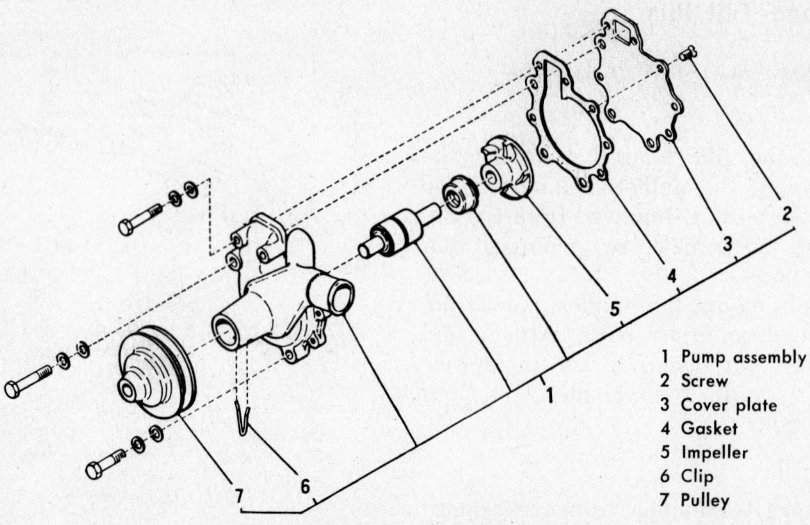

FF-1 water pump—exploded view

3. Extract the shaft retaining clip, and press or tap the shaft from the pump body.
4. Tap the impeller from the shaft with a hammer and a brass drift.
5. Inspect the seal and spring, and replace if necessary.

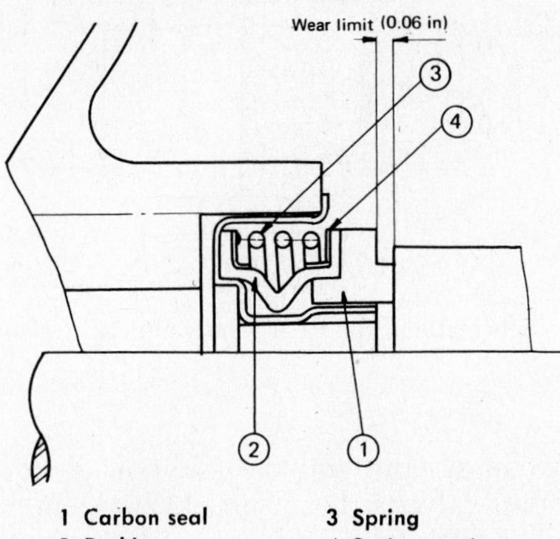

Water pump seal inspection

6. Press the shaft into the pump body and install the retaining clip.
7. Press or tap the seal and impeller onto the shaft, so that the clearance between the impeller vanes and the pump body is .020″-.026″.

Checking impeller vane to pump body clearance

8. Press on the pulley, so that the clearance between the center of the pulley groove and the rear of the pump body is 2.60″.
9. Coat the rear cover gasket with gasket cement on both sides and install the rear cover.

Thermostat

Removal and Installation

FF-1

A wax pellet type thermostat, which opens fully by 203° F. is used. It is removed by removing the air cleaner assembly and the thermostat cover, which is adjacent to the carburetor.

Install in the reverse order of removal.

NOTE: *It is essential to the proper operation of the cooling system that the thermostat be installed in the proper direction.*

Engine

Emission Control

360

The 360 uses no emission controls, since it is below the minimum displacement requiring Federal emission controls.

FF-1

The FF-1 utilizes positive crankcase ventilation, exhaust air injection, and carburetor and distributor modifications to meet emission standards. The positive crankcase ventilation system draws vapor through a vent in the air cleaner from a vent in the top of the right-hand valve cover. An oil separator is used to remove any liquid that may be drawn through the system. The system requires no service or maintenance oth-

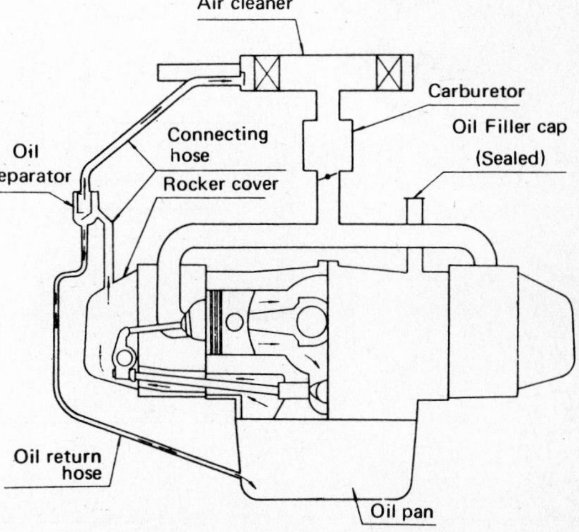

Schematic of the FF-1 PCV system

er than an occasional check to ensure that the hoses are intact and not clogged.

The air injection system draws air from the air cleaner (inside the element) through a pump, which distributes air at approximately 1.4 psi to the exhaust manifolds. A check valve is used to prevent backup of exhaust gases into the pump should exhaust manifold pressure exceed pump output pressure. A relief valve is included in the pump to prevent pressure buildup should pump pressure become excessive, or the check valve be closed. The pump should be checked periodically with a pressure gauge to ensure that it and the relief valve are functioning properly. Test the check valve by applying low pressure air to the exhaust manifold side of the valve. If the valve permits any passage of air it must be replaced. An anti-afterburn valve, which prevents backfiring by limiting the amount of air injected into the exhaust manifold on sudden deceleration, is used. To test the anti-afterburn valve, remove the hose from the end of the valve, accelerate the engine and release the throttle. Suction should be present at the hose fitting for 1-5 seconds after the throttle is closed. If suction is not present, replace the valve.

FF-1 (Model G)

The Model G emission control system is basically the same as the above, with modifications to the positive crankcase ventilation system, and the addition of an air bypass valve to the air injection system.

The positive crankcase ventilation system adds a second hose, from the left-hand valve cover to the air cleaner, and integrates the oil separator into the air cleaner assembly. The air bypass valve is a cable operated valve, which opens as the choke plate closes. This valve diverts a portion of the air that would normally be injected into the exhaust manifold to the air cleaner, preventing excessive combustion in the exhaust manifold during choke operation.

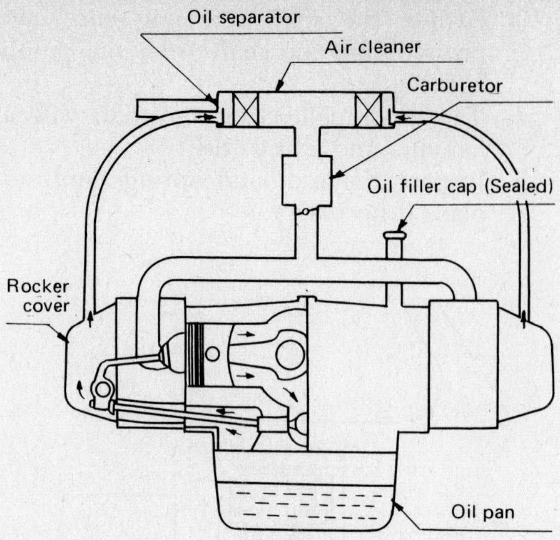

Schematic of the FF-1 Model G PCV system

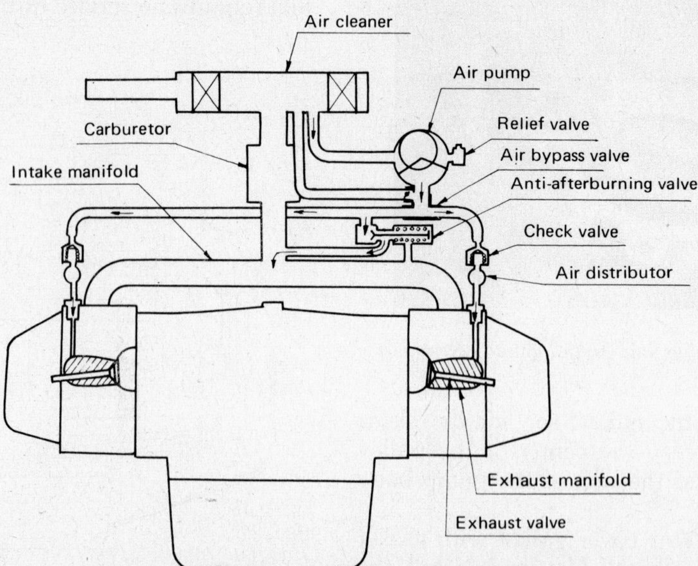

Schematic of the FF-1 Model G air injection system

Removal and Installation

Model 360

Prior to removal of the engine from the 360, the vehicle must be supported firmly, with the rear wheels suspended. The trap doors must also be removed (Sedan—behind the rear seat; Custom—on the rear shelf; Truck and Van—at the rear of the bed). The power train is removed as a unit.

1. Remove the ground strap from the battery.
2. Remove the rear underpan and disconnect the diagonal brace from the crossmember. Loosen the mounting bolt at the opposite end of the brace, and position it so as not to interfere with removal of the engine.
3. Remove the two drain plugs and drain the fluid from the transmission.
4. Loosen the retaining bracket bolt, remove the adjusting nut, and disconnect the clutch cable. Remove the clutch clevis pin from the clutch lever (if loose).
5. Disconnect all air ducts from, and remove the air cleaner.
6. Clamp and disconnect the fuel line from the fuel tank to the carburetor (Sedan) or the fuel pump (Custom, Truck, and Van), and remove the fuel control valve vacuum line.
7. Clamp and remove the oil line from the oil pump.
8. Disconnect the throttle and choke control cables from the carburetor.
9. Remove the hood (Custom, Truck, and Van), or the hood lock and cable support bracket (Sedan).
10. Remove the rear bumper.
11. Remove the rear skirt (Sedan and Custom).
12. Code and remove the wires from the starter and generator, remove the coil high tension lead, and disconnect the distributor primary wire. Separate the back-up light connectors (adjacent to the heater duct).
13. Remove the cooling fan fresh air hose from the fan shroud, and the heater hose from the exhaust manifold shroud.
14. Loosen the clip-rings and slide the axle boots outward on the axle. Cut the safety wire, remove the axle-U-joint bolts, and move the axles away from the transaxle.
15. Remove the retaining bolt, and separate the shift rod from the shifter shaft.
16. Support the engine on a stand or dolly that will permit the engine to be pulled rearward from the vehicle.
17. Remove the retaining nuts, and carefully push the bolts from the engine front mounting bracket.
18. Remove the nuts from the rear crossmember retaining bolts, and pull the bolts out only far enough to permit removal of the crossmember. The bolts should remain installed on the vehicle.

The drive train may now be removed by pulling rearward, exercising care that no wires or hoses are caught during removal.

Install the drive train in the reverse order of removal. When installing the axles, torque bolts to 22-24 ft. lbs., and safety wire.

FF-1

The FF-1 engine may be removed individually (late models only) or as a part of the power train assembly. To remove only the engine, proceed as follows:

1. Disconnect the battery positive terminal.
2. Separate the horn wire connectors and the hood stay lower retaining nut. Remove the hood hinge to body mounting bolts, leaving the hinges mounted on the hood, and lift off the hood.
3. Remove the grill, the front bumper, and the front skirt.
4. Detach the hood lock mechanism from the radiator bracket. NOTE: *Do not separate the cables from the lock mechanism.*
5. Disconnect the ground cables from the cylinder head and engine compartment bulkhead.
6. Remove the drain plug from the main

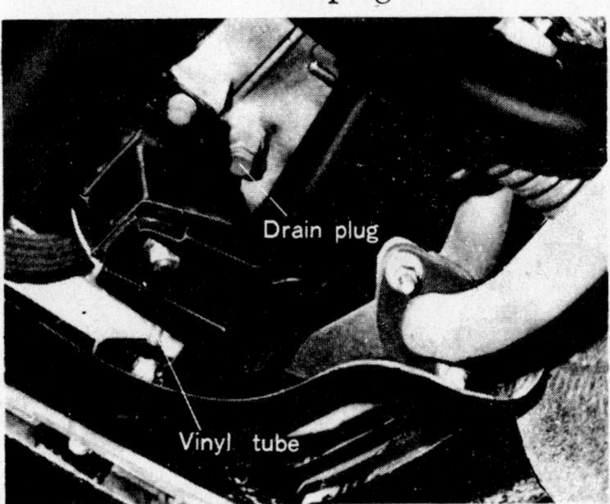

FF-1 cylinder head drain plug

radiator and loosen the drain fittings on the cylinder heads (adjacent to the engine mounts) to drain the coolant. Drain the engine oil.

7. Remove the air cleaner and detach the fuel line from the carburetor. Disconnect the throttle and choke cable from the carburetor.
8. Disconnect the following electrical connections:
   a. high tension and primary lead from the distributor,
   b. alternator connector from regulator connector,
   c. three connectors from the blower motor casing,
   d. connectors from the oil pressure and thermostat switch,
   e. two wires from the thermoswitch on the sub radiator.
9. Remove the radiator assembly including the blower casing.
10. Disconnect the right and left-hand exhaust pipe from the exhaust manifolds.
11. Unbolt the right and left-hand engine mounts, leaving the rubber mounting pads bolted to the engine, and support the engine with a chain hoist by the front and rear hangers.
12. Separate the engine from the transaxle by removing the four mounting bolts, and slide the engine forward until the clutch shaft and starter housing are clear, at which time the engine can be lifted and removed from the vehicle.

To remove the entire power train, the following additional procedures must be performed:

After step 9:

a. Disconnect the brake pipe from the brake hose (have a container available to prevent fluid spillage) and plug both fittings.
b. Remove the clutch return spring and pedal control rod, and dismount the clutch cross-shaft bracket on the body side. Remove the transmission side ball stud using an adjustable wrench.
c. Lock the handbrake, and separate the double-offset joints from the brake drums by removing the three retaining bolts. Lower the joints away by turning the steering wheel to full lock.
d. Release the handbrake, and disconnect the cable so that it may be withdrawn with the power train.

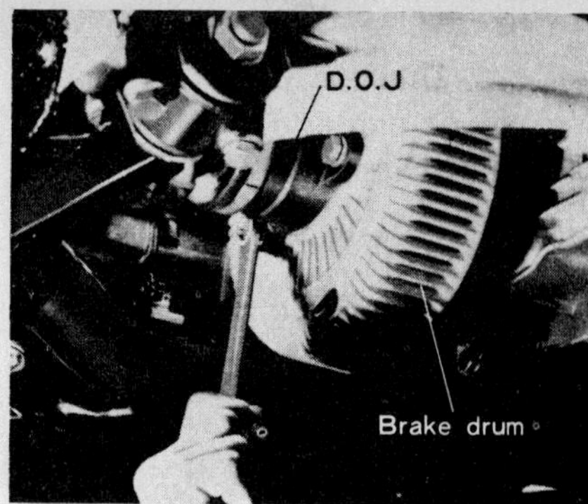

Unbolting the double-offset joint

e. Remove the carpeting and cover plate from the front floorboard center hump. Loosen the clamp, and slide the shift rod cover tube rearward. Separate the shifter shaft from the shift rod by tapping the roll pin out of the shaft.
f. Detach the speedometer cable from the speedometer and pull it into the engine compartment, to be removed with the power train.
g. Remove the starter motor.

After step 10:

a. Detach the exhaust pipe from its mount on the bottom of the transaxle.
b. Unbolt the right and left-hand engine mounts, leaving the rubber mounting pads bolted to the engine. Unbolt the transaxle rear mount. Support the power train with a chain hoist attached to the front and rear hangers.
c. Slowly lift the engine, until clearance exists for the brake drums to clear the crossmember, and pull the power train forward and out of the vehicle.

FF-1 engine removal

Install in the reverse order of removal. When mounting the engine, ensure that the locator dimples on the front crossmember enter the holes on the mounting pads. Torque the front mounts 15-21 ft. lbs., the large rear mount bolt 33-40 ft. lbs., and the small rear mount bolts 18-25 ft. lbs.

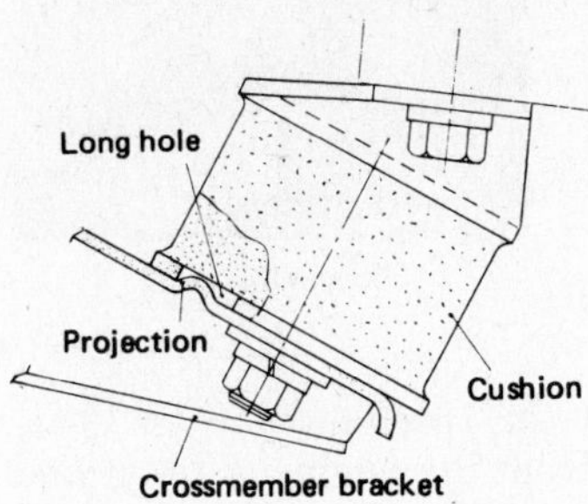

FF-1 engine mount alignment

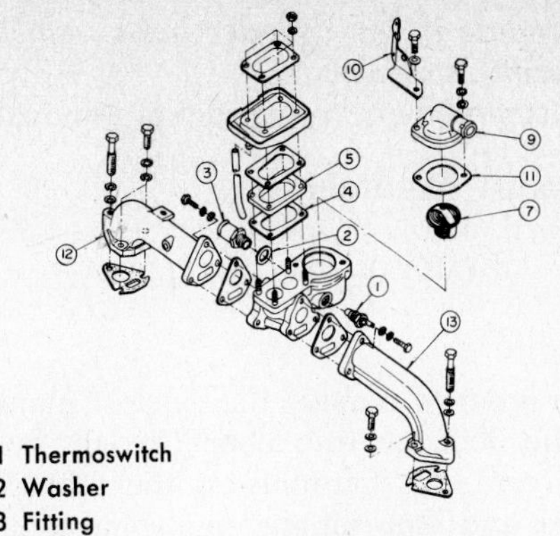

FF-1 intake manifold—exploded view

Intake Manifold

Removal and Installation

360

The intake manifold is removed with the carburetor attached. Prior to the removal of the manifold, the throttle, choke and oil pump cables must be disconnected from the carburetor. Remove the fuel line from the carburetor, and the vacuum line from the intake manifold (Sedan). Unbolt the four retaining nuts, and remove the carburetor and manifold assembly.

Install in the reverse order of removal.

FF-1

The intake manifold may be removed with or without the carburetor. If the carburetor is to remain on the manifold, the throttle and choke cables and brackets must be disconnected, and the fuel line detached. Detach all coolant hoses from the thermostat case and cover, and disconnect the wiring connector from the thermoswitch. Remove all lines from the anti-afterburn valve (leave the valve mounted on the manifold). Unbolt the air injection distributor mounting brackets from the manifold, and remove the air bypass valve (if so equipped). Unbolt the intake manifold from the cylinder heads, and remove the manifold assembly. The intake manifold (not Model G) may be disassembled further by unbolting the manifold halves from the thermostat case. NOTE: *Cover the in-*

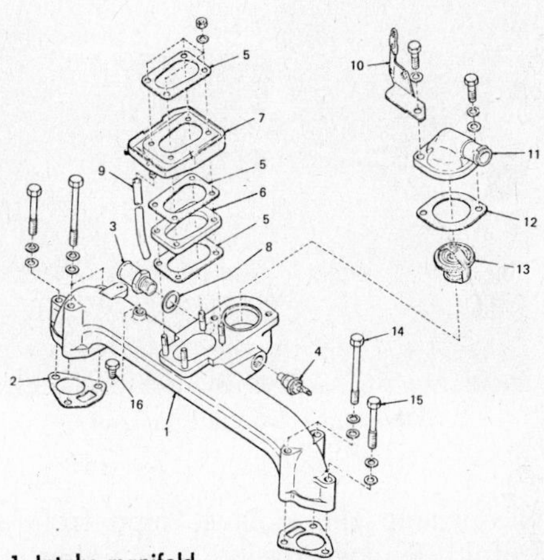

FF-1 Model G intake manifold—exploded view

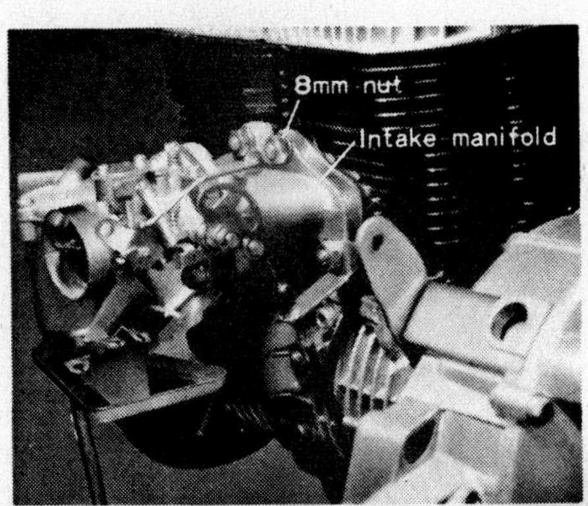

360 intake manifold

take ports in the cylinder heads while the manifold is removed.

Install in the reverse order of removal.

Exhaust Manifold

Removal and Installation

360

In order to remove the exhaust manifold of the 360, the trap door (Sedan—behind the rear seat; Custom—on the rear shelf; Truck and Van—on ahe engine cover in the bed) must be removed. Unclamp and remove the heater duct from the manifold. Remove the shroud above the manifold,

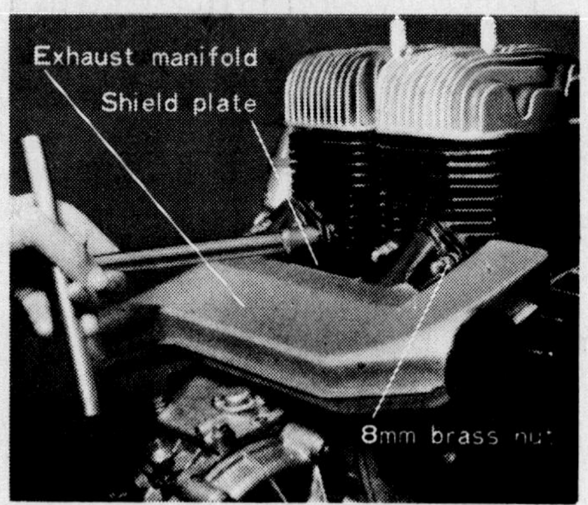

360 exhaust manifold removal

and unclamp the exhaust pipe from the manifold. Remove the brass retaining nuts, and remove the manifold.

Install in the reverse order of removal.

FF-1

Disconnect the left and right-hand exhaust pipes from the manifolds. Loosen (do not remove) the brass exhaust manifold retaining nuts, and swing the manifolds around until the slots in the flanges permit removal.

Install in the reverse order of removal. NOTE: *When attaching the manifolds to the exhaust pipes, be sure to install insulator washers, to prevent seizure of the bolts.*

Cylinder Head

Removal and Installation

360

The cylinder head must be removed with the engine cold, to prevent warpage. Remove the spark plug leads and spark plugs.

360 engine cowl

Unbolt the cowl and the air duct, and remove from the engine. Unbolt and remove the cylinder heads.

Install the cylinder heads in the reverse order of removal. The cylinder head gasket must be installed with the proper side facing the cylinder (see illustration). Torque the heads in the proper sequence, in stages, until the specified torque is reached.

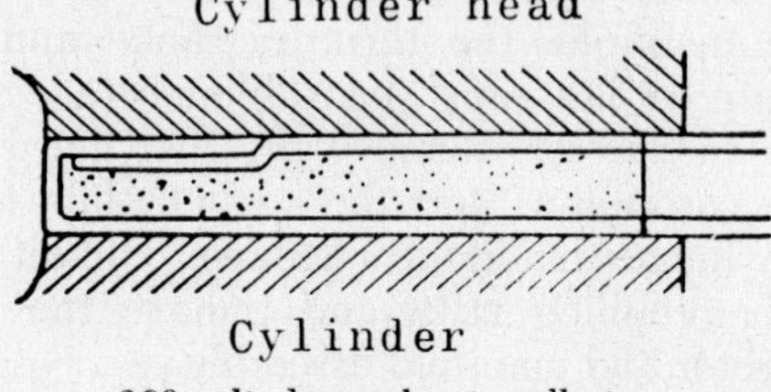

360 cylinder gasket installation

FF-1

The engine must be removed from the vehicle to remove the cylinder heads. Although it is physically possible (on some models) to remove the cylinder heads with the engine installed, head gasket failure will result upon installation, due to misalignment of the cylinders. The cylinder heads should be removed with the engine cold to prevent warpage.

Remove the engine from the vehicle and mount it on a work stand. Unbolt and remove the intake and exhaust manifolds. Remove the spark plugs. Disconnect the crankcase ventilation hose(s) and remove the valve covers. Loosen the alternator adjusting bolts, and unbolt the alternator bracket from the cylinder head. Remove the air injection distributor tubes from the cylinder heads by unscrewing the fittings. NOTE: *Do not distort the injection tubes.* Gradually loosen the head bolts in the reverse of the tightening sequence, and remove the cylinder heads and pushrods.

The cylinder heads must be installed with the cylinders vertical, to avoid misalignment, and to permit the head gasket to crush evenly around the cylinder. Prior to installation of the heads, cylinder liner projection must be checked (see below). Install the heads in the reverse order of removal. Torque in the specified sequence, in stages, using a spacer (see illustration) in

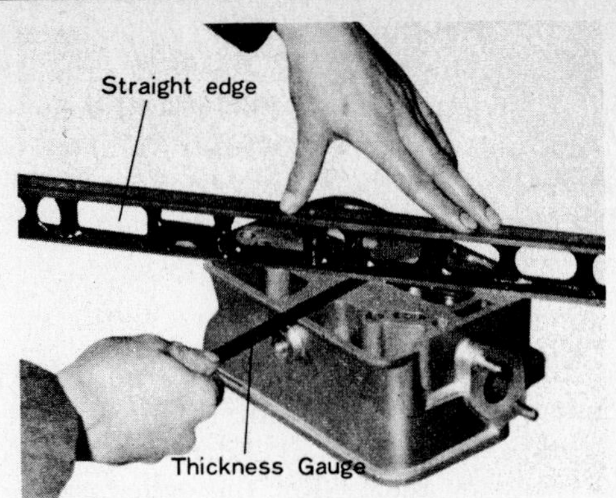

Checking FF-1 cylinder head for warpage

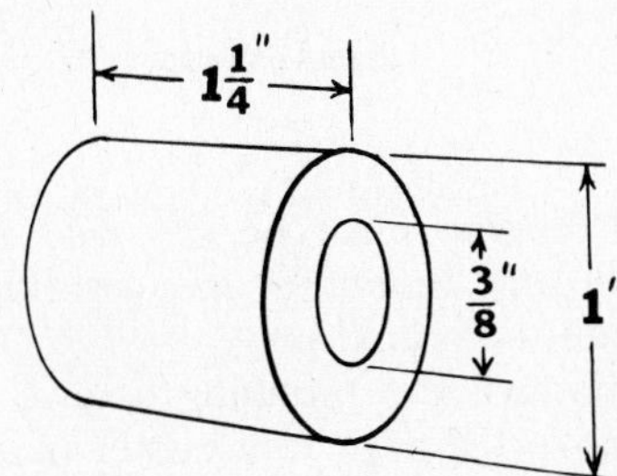

FF-1 cylinder head installation spacer

place of the rocker shaft support. After the head is torqued to specifications, remove the rocker shaft bolts (or nuts) and the spacers, and install the rocker shafts.

Service

360

Carbon can be removed from the cylinder head using a hardwood chisel, or a wire brush in an electric drill. Check the cylinder heads for warpage on a surface plate. Should warpage exceed .008″, the cylinder heads must be resurfaced or replaced.

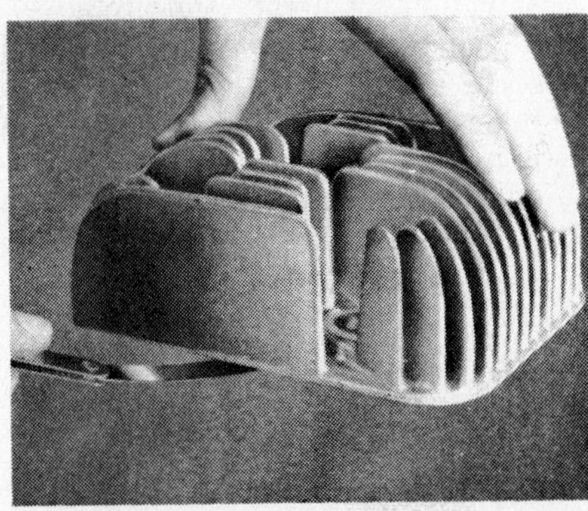
Checking 360 cylinder head for warpage

FF-1

Check the cylinder heads for warpage using a straight edge. Should warpage exceed .002″, the cylinder head must be resurfaced (grinding limit .0197″). The valve seats must be replaced should valve sink exceed approximately .040″. Valve guides are pressed in, and should be replaced if clearance exceeds .0022″ (intake) or .003″ (exhaust). The intake valve guide should extend .59″ (Model G—.71″) and the exhaust .79″ (Model G—.91″) from the spring seat.

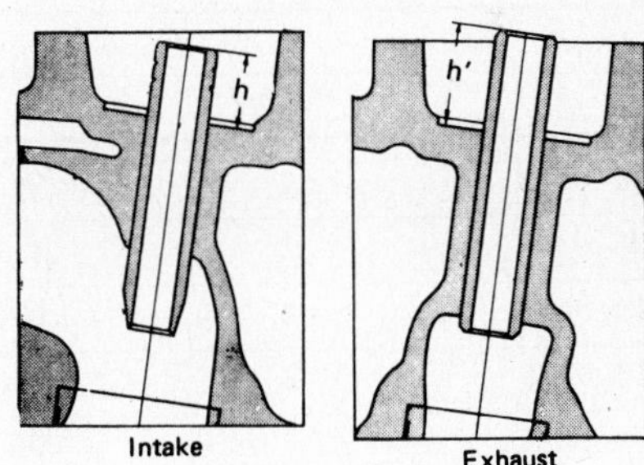

Valve guide installed height

Cylinders

Removal and Installation

360

Individual finned cylinders are used. Following the removal of the intake and exhaust manifolds, and the cylinder heads, remove the retaining nuts from the base of the cylinders. Tap the cylinders lightly to unseat the gaskets, and pull the cylinders up and off.

With the pistons installed on the engine, compress the rings and guide the cylinders over the pistons. Align the cylinders with the mounting studs, and loosely install the retaining nuts. Attach the exhaust manifold, and rotate the crankshaft several revolutions. Tighten the retaining nuts to 18-20 ft. lbs., and install the cylinder heads and intake manifold.

FF-1

Slip-in, wet cylinder liners are used. The liners are removed with the engine on a workbench and the cylinders vertical. Following the removal of the cylinder heads, position each piston at bottom dead center, and remove the cylinders and gaskets as a set.

Prior to installation of the cylinder liners, liner protection above the cylinder head mating surface must be checked, and the proper gasket selected. Measure the height of the cylinder liner (dimension A). Measure the distance from the cylinder liner seat in the case to the cylinder head mating surface (dimension B). Cylinder liner projection should be .007-.009″ (dimension C). Use the equation (B + C) − A = Gasket thickness to determine the correct gasket thickness, and select a gasket from the following chart.

Thickness (in.)	*Stripes*	
	Number	*Color*
.0404-.0408	2	White
.0408-.0412	2	Yellow
.0412-.0416	2	Green
.0416-.0420	2	Red
.0420-.0424	2	Black
.0424-.0427	1	Blue
.0427-.0431	1	Yellow
.0431-.0435	1	White

A second method may be employed to determine cylinder liner projection. Install each cylinder liner and its gasket (without piston) into the case. Using a straight edge and feeler gauges, determine cylinder liner projection for each cylinder. Compare this measurement to specifications (.007-.009″) to determine whether projection must be increased or decreased. Remove each cylinder, and measure its gasket with a micrometer. Add or subtract the necessary amount (to increase or decrease projection) to the measured gasket thickness, and obtain a gasket of the correct thickness (see above).

Following selection of the gaskets, install the new gaskets onto the liners, and using a ring compressor, insert the pistons into the bottom of the cylinders, leaving the piston pin bore exposed. Position the piston and liner assemblies over the connecting rods, insert the piston pins and lockrings, and press the liners into the case. Install the cylinder heads, and check cranking compression to determine that the gaskets have seated.

Crankcase

Separation

360

The engine must be removed from the vehicle and mounted on a workbench to separate the crankcase.

1. Remove the retaining screws, and remove the cap from center of the cooling fan. Remove the large nut securing the fan to the crankshaft, and pull off the fan.
2. Remove all air ducting other than the fan shroud from the engine.
3. Unbolt the six retaining bolts, and lift off the fan shroud.
4. Detach all cables, and remove the intake manifold and carburetor. Unbolt and remove the exhaust manifold.
5. Unbolt and remove the starter and generator.
6. Disconnect the oil pump hose from the crankcase. Position the No. 1 cylinder at top dead center (according to the marks on the flywheel), and mark the position of the generator drive pulley on the clutch housing cover, to avoid having to time the ignition during installation. Unbolt and remove the clutch housing cover and clutch assembly.
7. Remove the clutch housing retaining bolts and nuts. Wrap the clutch splines with paper to protect the clutch housing seal, and slide off the clutch housing by tapping it lightly around its edge with a rubber mallet.
8. Tap the Woodruff key out of the crankshaft nose, and remove the primary reduction gear.
9. Unbolt and remove the cylinder heads and the cylinders.

10. Remove the four retaining bolts, and pull the crankcase end cover off.
11. Remove all bolts and nuts from the crankcase, and by tapping alternately from side-to-side of the crankcase, separate the crankcase halves.

Assemble in the reverse order of disassembly. Prior to joining the crankcase halves, thoroughly clean the mating surfaces, and coat with sealer (as shown). When installing the crankcase end cover, position the identification mark upward.

360 crankcase separation

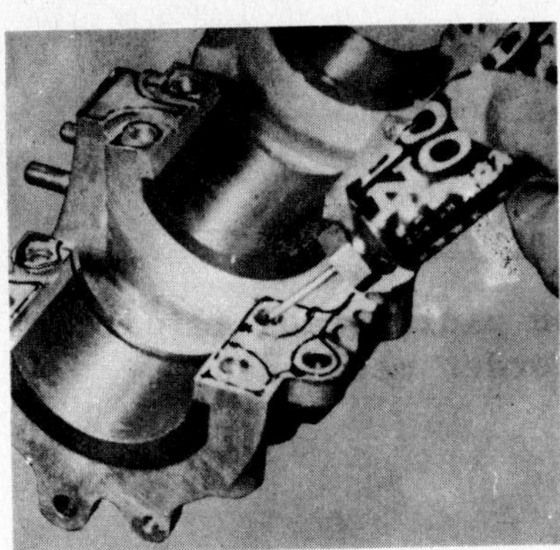
360 crankcase sealing

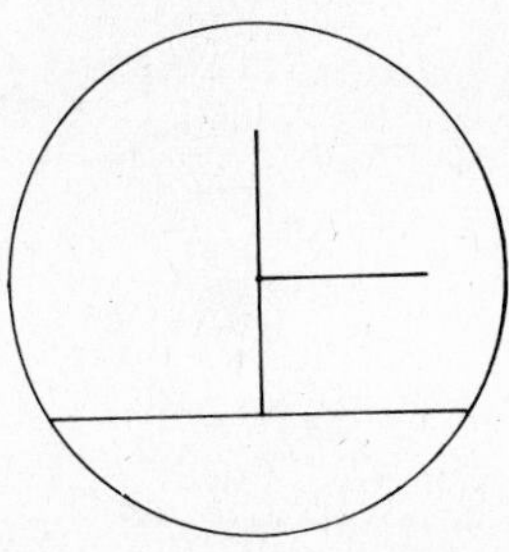
360 crankcase end cover identification mark

FF-1

Prior to separating the crankcase, the engine must be removed from the vehicle and positioned on a workbench. All ancillaries, and the intake and exhaust manifolds must be removed. The case is separated as follows:

1. Remove the clutch pressure plate and disc, by gradually backing the six mounting bolts out one turn at a time, until clutch pressure is released.
2. Unbolt and remove the flywheel and the flywheel housing.
3. Remove the dipstick and the oil breather tube.
4. Lift out the distributor, and unbolt and remove the water pump.
5. Remove the cast water pipes and the water hose from the engine as a unit.

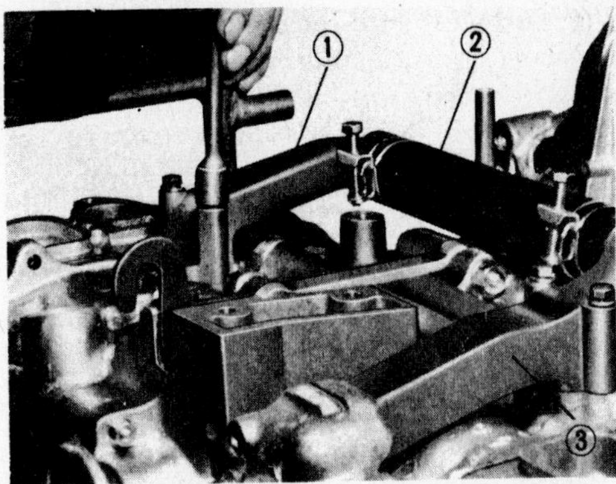

Removing the cast water pipes (1 and 3) and hose (3)

6. Using a puller, remove the crankshaft pulley.
7. Unbolt the oil pump, and remove the pump and filter as a unit.

Removing the FF-1 oil pickup (1)

8. Invert the engine and remove the oil pan and pickup.
9. Remove the cylinder heads. Using a hex key, remove the four access plugs from the sides of the crankcase.
10. Pull the cylinder liners out of the case, and remove the pistons, by removing the circlips and pushing the piston pins out through the access holes in the case.
11. Position the slot in the camshaft gear over the thrust plate retaining bolts, flatten the lock tabs, and remove the bolts.
12. Remove the nuts and bolt, and separate the case halves.

Assemble in the reverse order of disassembly. When installing the crankshaft and camshaft, ensure that the timing marks are aligned (as shown). Prior to joining the crankcase halves, thoroughly clean the mating surfaces, and coat with sealer. The flywheel match marks must be aligned (as shown) prior to installation of the flywheel.

FF-1 camshaft timing marks

FF-1 Model G camshaft timing marks

Valve Train

Adjustments

FF-1

Prior to adjusting the valves, ensure that the cylinder head bolts are torqued to specifications. The adjusting sequence is the same as the firing order (1-3-2-4). Posi-

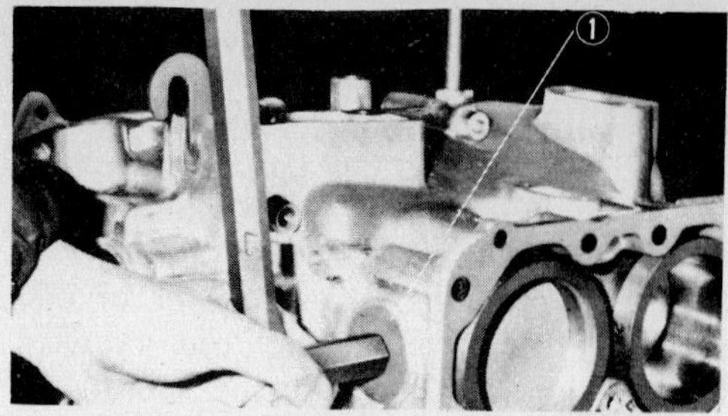

Removing the crankcase access plugs

1 Camshaft gear
2 Locktab
3 Retainer bolt

Removing the camshaft gear

FF-1 flywheel alignment marks

FF-1 Model G flywheel alignment marks

tion No. 1 cylinder at top dead center of its compression stroke, and adjust its valves. Rotate the crankshaft 180° (indicated on the flywheel) for each valve thereafter. The valves are adjusted with the engine cold, using a feeler gauge between the rocker arm and the valve stem, by loosening the locknut and turning the adjusting bolt.

Camshaft

Removal and Installation

FF-1

The camshaft turns on journals machined directly into the crankcase. To remove the camshaft, the engine must be removed from the vehicle, and the crankcase separated (see above).

Install the camshaft in the reverse order of removal. When installing the camshaft, ensure that the timing marks are aligned as shown). Prior to installation of the camshaft, end-play should be checked using a feeler gauge. Should end-play exceed .012″,

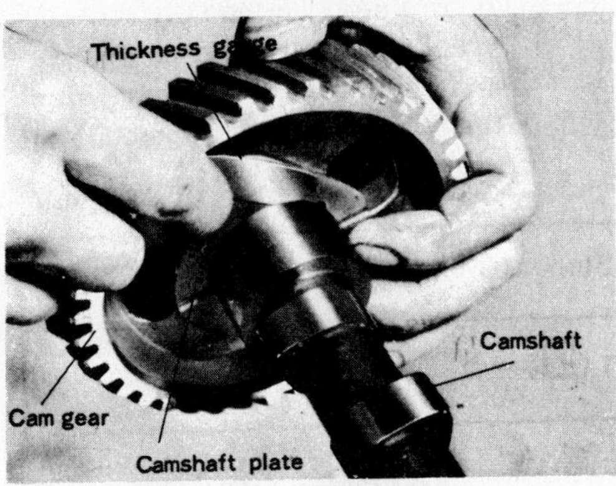

Checking camshaft end-play

the camshaft gear must be pressed from the camshaft, and the thrust plate replaced. Gear backlash should be checked upon installation into the case. If backlash exceeds .006″, the camshaft gear should be replaced. When pressing the camshaft gear on, support the camshaft behind the gear boss.

Engine Lubrication

360

A forced lubrication system, based on a controlled flow plunger pump, is utilized. Oil flow is metered dependent on engine speed and throttle position.

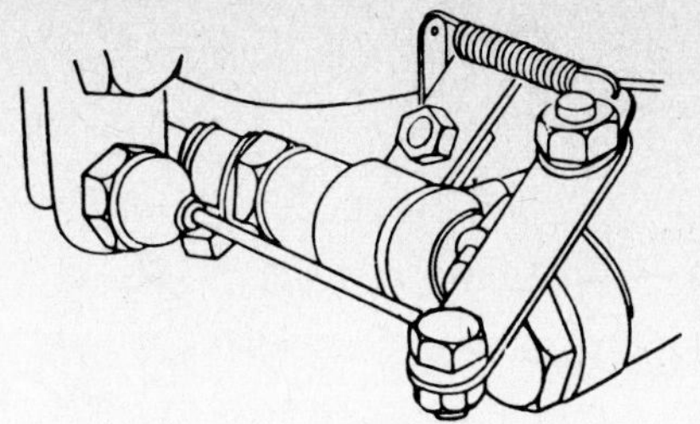
360 oil pump adjustment

The control cable is adjusted as follows: Back out the carburetor throttle stop screw fully, and remove the cable attaching bolt at the pump. Move the pump lever to the right until it contacts its stop, and insert the attaching bolt. Test the adjustment to ensure that the pump lever moves as soon as the throttle is opened, and adjust the idle to specifications.

FF-1

The system consists of a trochoid pump driven by the camshaft, and a full flow oil filter. A relief valve controls pressure build-up, to prevent excessive pressure in the system. Should the filter become clogged. or its flow capacity be exceeded, a bypass valve prevents backup. For any service other than replacing the filter, the pump assembly must be removed.

The pump may be reconditioned as follows: Remove the filter canister, and separate the halves of the pump body. Remove and clean the bypass and relief valves. Take out the inner and outer rotors and check the passages in the pump body for clogging. Check the inner rotor shaft and bushings for wear, and replace if excessively worn.

Install the rotors, and check the outer rotor to body clearance. If clearance exceeds

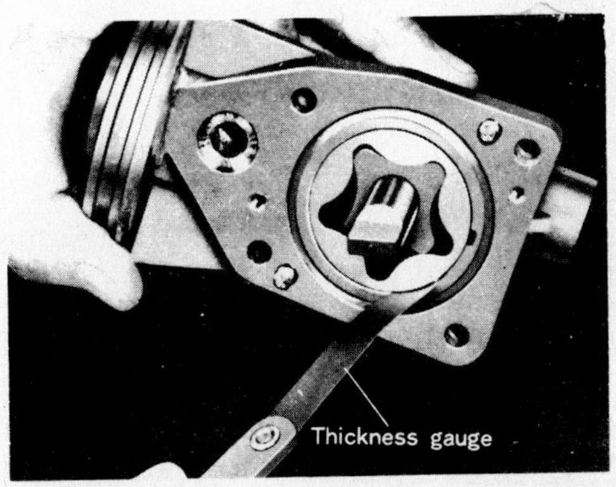

Checking rotor to body clearance

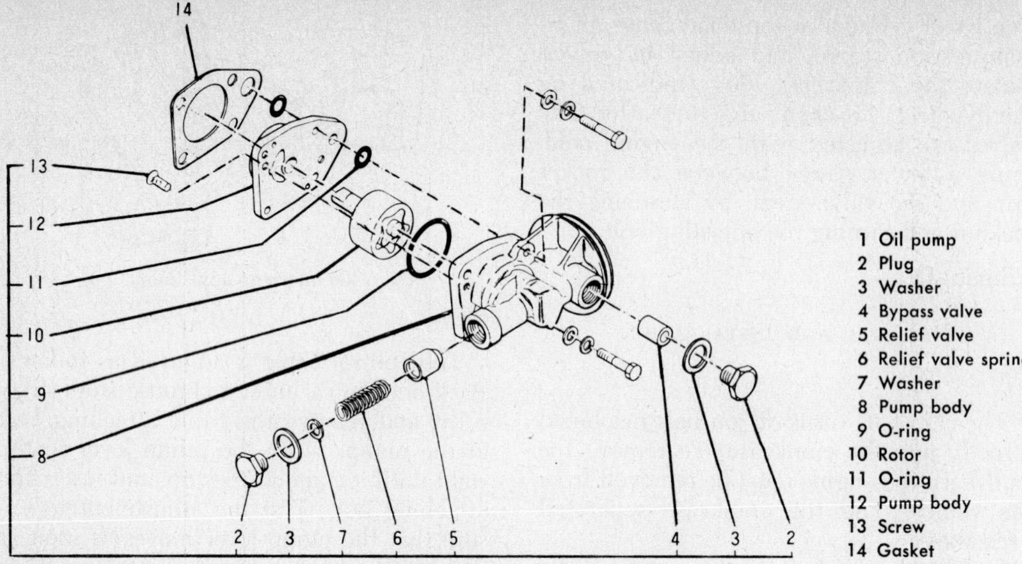

FF-1 oil pump—exploded view

.010″, the rotor must be replaced. Replace either or both rotors if end clearance exceeds .008″. Check the relief valve spring pressure at its installed length (1.32″). If spring pressure is below 7 lbs., replace the spring. Assemble the pump using new O-rings.

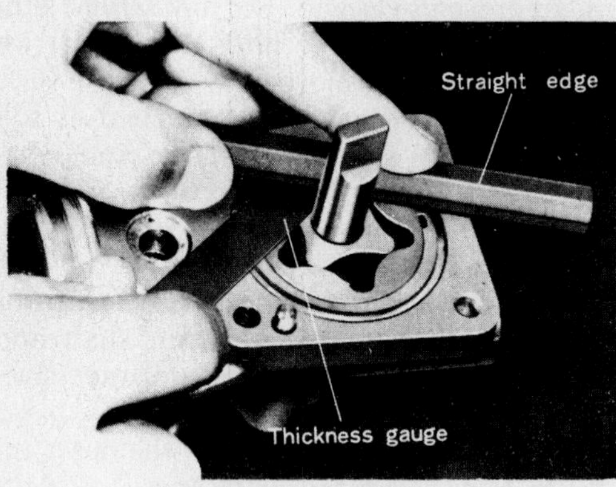

Checking rotor end clearance

Pistons and Connecting Rods

Orientation

360

Install the pistons so that the arrow points toward the intake manifold side of the engine. To ensure proper operation, pistons must be installed in the cylinder from which they were removed. If pistons are reversed, the engine will run poorly. The connecting rods are not removable from the crankshaft.

FF-1

The pistons are installed in the liners with arrow on the inside of the piston dome aligned with the mark on the upper lip of the cylinder liner. The piston and liner assembly is installed in the case with this mark pointing toward the front of the engine. The connecting rods are installed with the name mark toward the front of the engine, and the caps are installed on the rods with the projecting ribs forward.

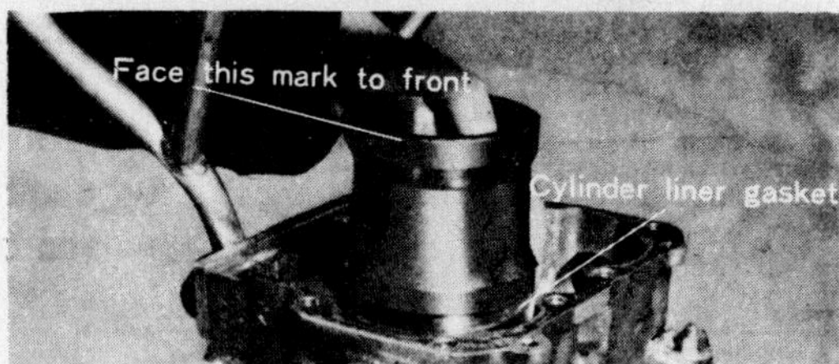

FF-1 cylinder liner and piston installation

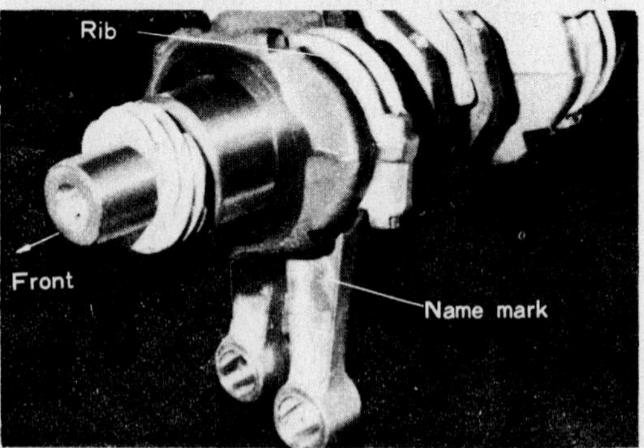

FF-1 connecting rod and cap installation

Clutch and Transmission

Clutch

Adjustments

360

The clutch is adjusted by means of a wing nut at the clutch lever, under the rear of the car. Turn this nut so that there is approximately 1″ free play at the clutch pedal.

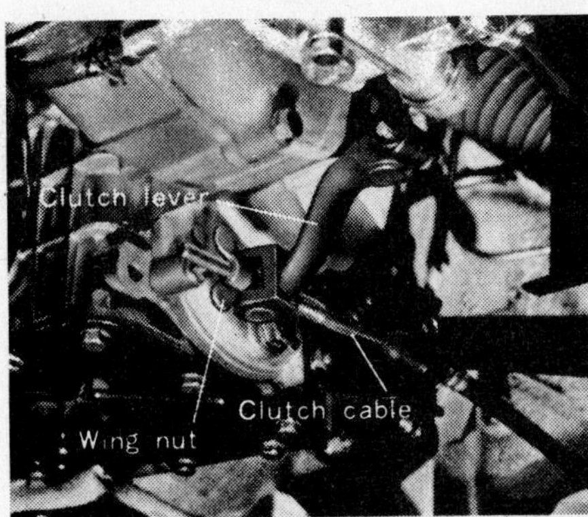

360 clutch adjusting nut

FF-1 clutch pedal return stop

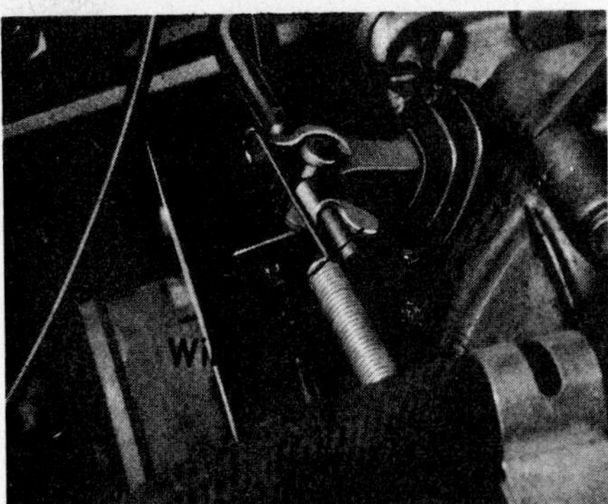
FF-1 clutch adjusting nut

FF-1

Adjust the clutch pedal return stop-bolt (on the pedal mount bracket) so that the clutch pedal travel is 4.9-5.1″. Following this adjustment, turn the wing nut at the clutch lever (under the hood) to adjust pedal free play to .4-.6″.

Removal and Installation

360

The clutch may be removed with the power train installed in the vehicle. In order to remove the clutch, the clutch cover must be removed as follows. Disconnect the ground strap from the battery. Remove the underpan, and disconnect the clutch cable from the clutch lever by removing the wing nut. Loosen and remove the V-belt and the generator. Disconnect the primary wire from the distributor and remove the distributor cap. Rotate the crankshaft to position the No. 1 cylinder at top dead center, and mark the position of the pulley relative to the clutch cover, to avoid having to time the ignition when the cover is installed. Remove the retaining bolts (including the starter through bolt), and tapping lightly with a rubber mallet around its edge, remove the clutch cover. Unbolt and remove the spline coupling from the clutch assembly. Slightly loosen the clutch retaining bolt, and separate the clutch assembly from the crankshaft taper using a puller. Remove the retaining bolt and clutch assembly.

Prior to installation of the clutch assembly, primary reduction gear clearance must be checked (see below). Thoroughly clean the crankshaft taper, and install the clutch assembly, aligning the matching marks. Install and tighten the retaining bolt to 41-45 ft. lbs. Match the marks on the clutch as-

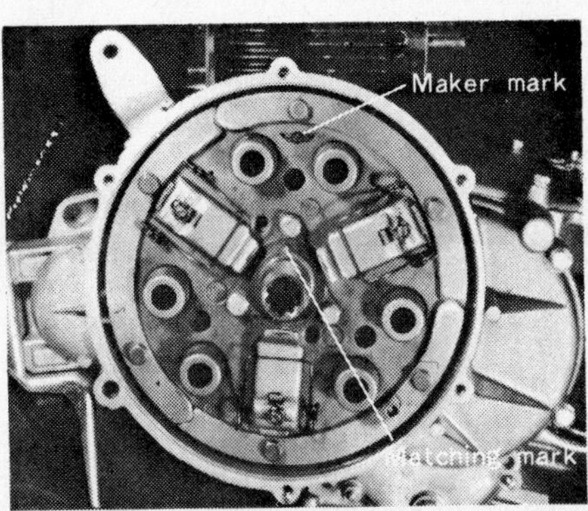

Spline coupling alignment

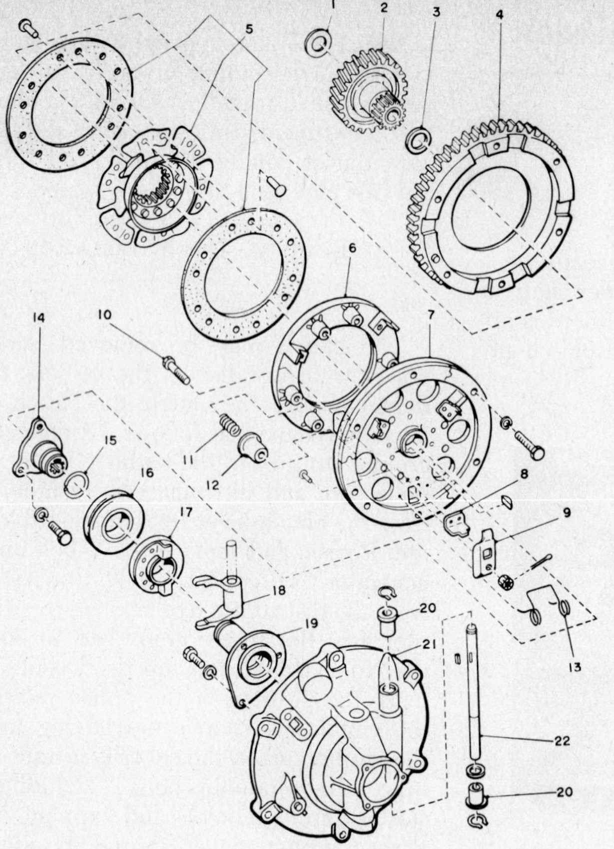

1 Spacer
2 Primary reduction gear
3 Shim
4 Flywheel
5 Disc
6 Pressure plate
7 Cover
8 Pivot
9 Release finger
10 Bolt
11 Spring
12 Cap
13 Spring
14 Spline coupling
15 Snap-ring
16 Release bearing
17 Thrust plate
18 Fork
19 Guide
20 Bushing
21 Clutch housing cover
22 Release fork shaft

360 clutch assembly—exploded view

sembly and the spline coupling (as shown), and install the coupling. Lightly lubricate the coupling spline with grease. Continue assembly in the reverse order of disassembly.

FF-1

In order to remove the clutch, the engine must be removed from the vehicle. Gradually back out the six retaining bolts, one turn at a time, and remove the clutch plate and disc.

When installing the clutch, use a pilot to ensure proper disc alignment, and gradually tighten the cover bolts to 7-9 ft. lbs.
NOTE: *When installing the clutch cover, ensure that the marks on the flywheel and the clutch are at least 120° apart.*

Service

360

The clutch assembly is separated by loosening the six retaining bolts, one turn at a time, until spring pressure is released, and removing the bolts. Inspect the disc, and replace if the surface of the friction material is worn beyond .012″ above the rivets. While the clutch is disassembled, primary reduction gear side clearance is checked. Install only the clutch pressure plate on the

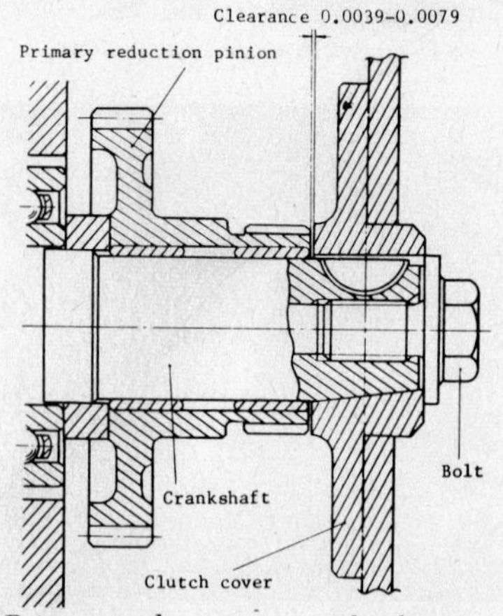

Primary reduction gear side clearance

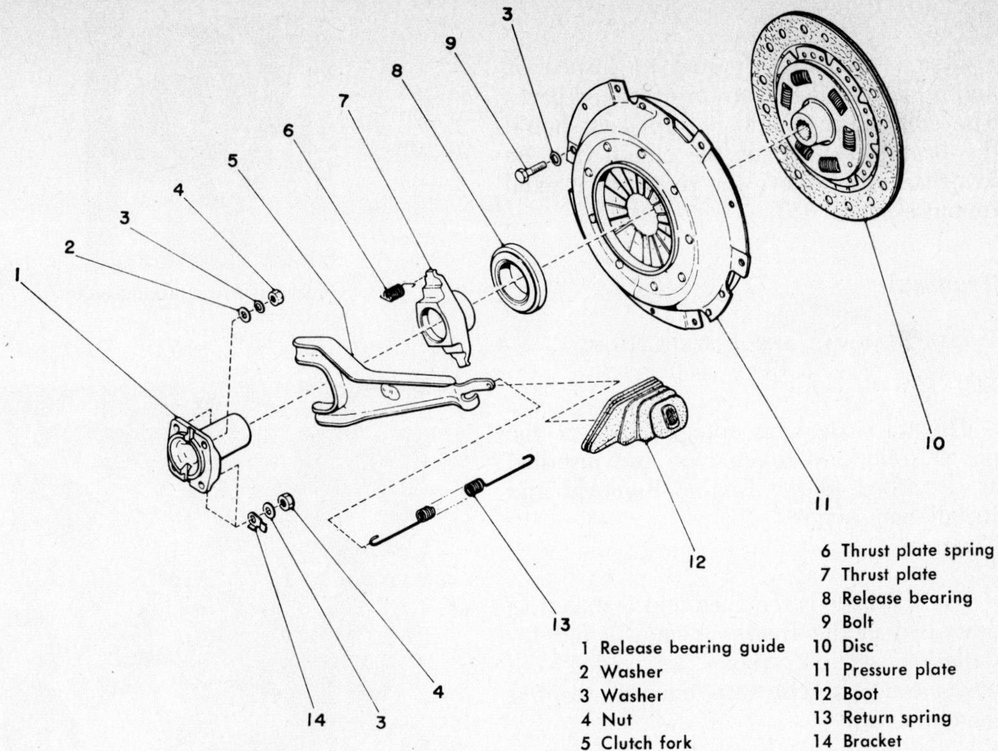

FF-1 clutch assembly—exploded view

crankshaft taper, and torque the retaining bolt to specifications. Measure primary reduction gear side clearance using feeler gauges, and adjust to .0039-.0079″ using shim washers.

To assemble the clutch, approximately center the disc on the flywheel, align the index pin and install the clutch plate, and finger tighten the retaining bolts. Position the clutch assembly in the clutch housing so that the clutch disc engages the primary reduction gear, and the clutch plate seats on the crankshaft taper. Tighten the six retaining bolts, and remove the clutch assembly from the clutch housing.

Following clutch service, clutch finger height must be adjusted. A template must be fabricated according to the illustration. Remove the cotter pins from the three castellated nuts on the release fingers. Position the template as illustrated, and turn the bolts with a screwdriver while holding the castellated nuts to adjust height.

360 clutch release finger adjustment

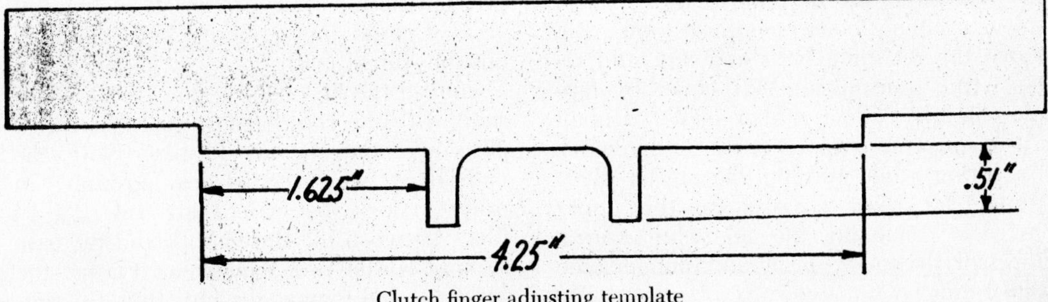

Clutch finger adjusting template

FF-1

Clutch service is limited to inspection and replacement of worn or damaged parts. The clutch disc should be replaced should the friction surface of the clutch disc be less than .012″ above the rivets, or if axial runout exceeds .020″.

Transaxle

Removal and Installation

360

The transaxle is an integral part of the power train, and is removed and installed as described in the Engine Removal and Installation section.

FF-1

The transaxle is removed and installed as described in the Engine Removal and Installation section. When separating the power train, exercise care to avoid warping the clutch disc.

Reconditioning

360

Prior to reconditioning the power train should be mounted on a workbench, and the gear oil drained (2 plugs). Remove all ducts and shrouds, the exhaust manifold, and the cooling fan. Unbolt and remove the generator and starter, and the clutch housing cover. Remove the clutch assembly and the clutch housing. NOTE: *Cover the primary reduction gear splines with paper to protect the clutch housing seal during removal.* Tap out the Woodruff key, and remove the primary reduction gear.

Flatten the lock tabs on the primary drive gear retaining nut, and remove the nut. Using a puller, remove the main drive gear. Remove the retaining bolts, and pull off the crankcase end cover. Insert two 8 mm. bolts into each U-joint yoke, and wedge with a pry bar in order to remove the oil seal sleeve retaining bolts (see illustration). Remove the retaining bolts and nut, and remove the transmission side cover by tapping lightly with a rubber mallet. Unbolt the transmission upper cover, and remove by lifting while turning the shifter shaft counterclockwise. Disassemble the upper cover by removing the side plug, spring and ball, the cover, spring and plunger (see illustration).

Oil seal sleeve retaining bolts

Transmission upper cover removal

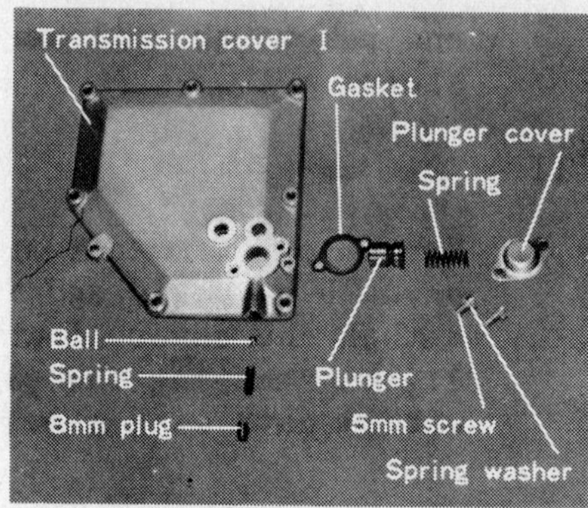

Disassembled transmission upper cover

Shift the transmission into neutral, and pull out both shifter arm shafts and shifter arms. Loosen the retaining bolt, and pull out the shifter shaft.

Engage the first driven gear on the main shaft with the countershaft gear (first gear position), and the synchronizer with the main drive gear (second gear position), in order to lock the main shaft. Insert a 1″ block between the shifter fork and the case to limit shifter fork movement. Flatten the locktabs, and remove the nuts from the syn-

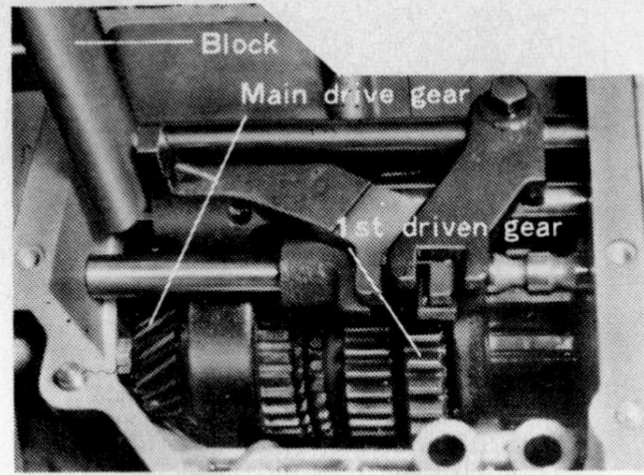

Block used to limit shifter fork movement

chronizer hub and drive gear. Unbolt the bearing retainer plate and the oil gutter from the opposite side of the case. Tap the shift fork rail out of the shift fork, and remove the shift fork, synchronizer assembly, driven gear, needle bearing, and washer. Remove the drive gear and final reduction pinion. Remove the bolt which retains the shifter arm on the shifter rail. Remove the retaining nuts, and pull the transmission case away from the housing. Disassemble the transmission case by removing the locknut and pulling out the shift lever, and by removing the plug and pulling out the shifter fork rail, spring, and ball.

Drive gear and final reduction pinion removal

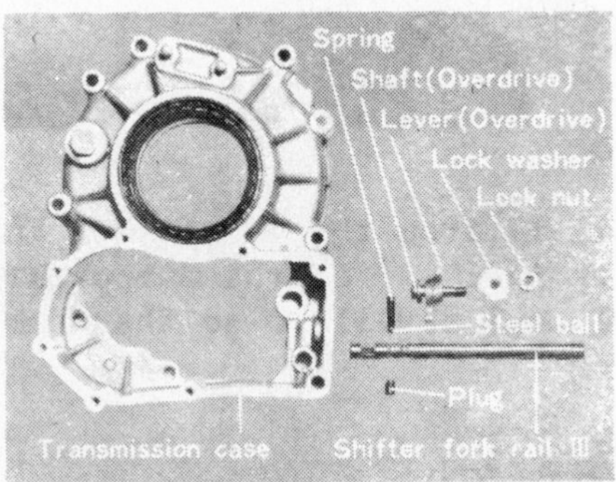

Disassembled transmission case

Remove the differential assembly from the housing by tapping around the edge of the gear. Note the number of shims between the differential and bearing.

Using a puller, remove the counter shaft bearings from the housing. Pull the shifter fork rails out of the housing and remove the shifter forks. Shifter fork rail I (nearest crankshaft) is removed from the output side of the housing, and shifter fork rail II from the input side. Exercise care to avoid having the detent ball and spring pop out while removing the shaft.

Unbolt the mainshaft bearing retainer plate inside the transmission. Using a puller, extract the main drive gear and ball bearing together. Remove the bearing retainer plate from the output side of the housing, and tap the input end of the mainshaft to free the bearing. Remove the snap-ring from the mainshaft, hold the gear cluster together, and pull the mainshaft out of the housing. Remove the gear cluster from the housing and wire together. Unbolt and remove the lower transmission cover, and lift out the countershaft. Tap the reverse idler gear shaft out of the housing and remove the reverse idler gear.

Removing mainshaft snap-ring

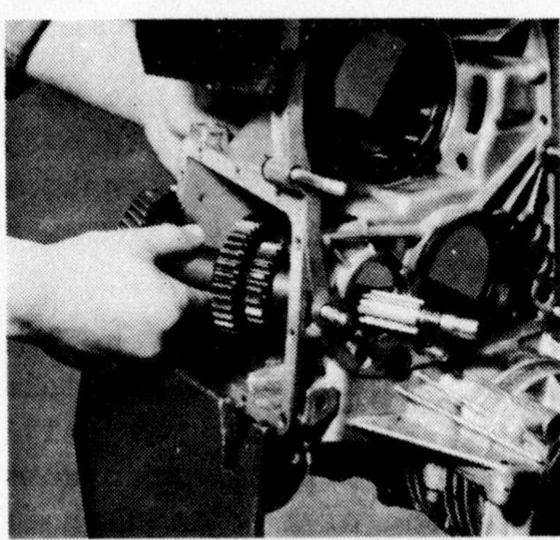
Countershaft removal and installation

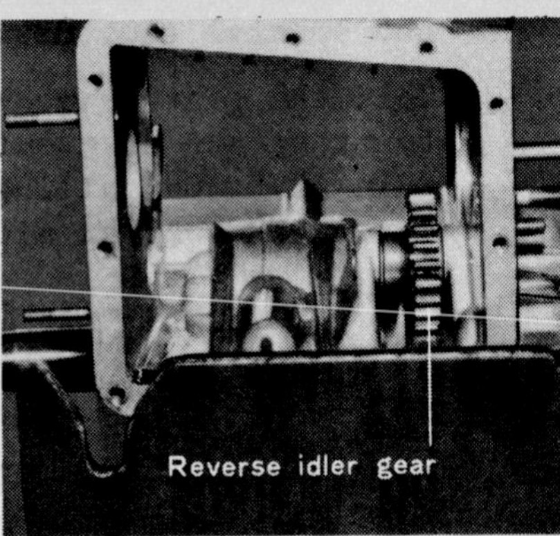

Reverse idler gear

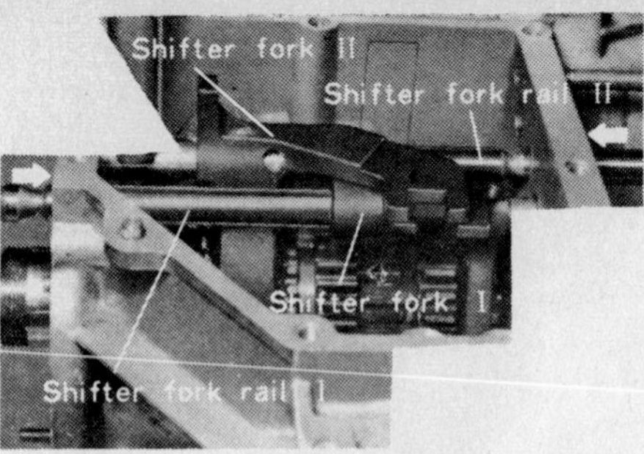

Shifter forks and rails

Inspect all parts for excessive wear or damage. Replace all ball bearings that will not rotate smoothly, or have excessive radial or axial play. Main drive gear needle bearings should be replaced if radial play exceeds .006″. When clearance between a synchronizer ring and the gear, with the cones fully engaged, is less than .012″, replace the ring.

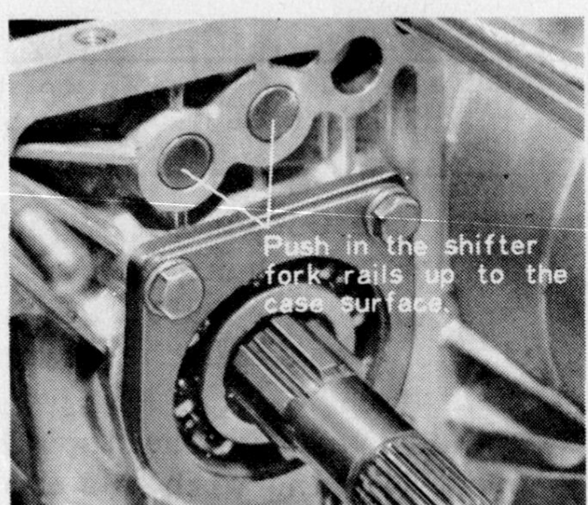

Shifter fork and rail installation

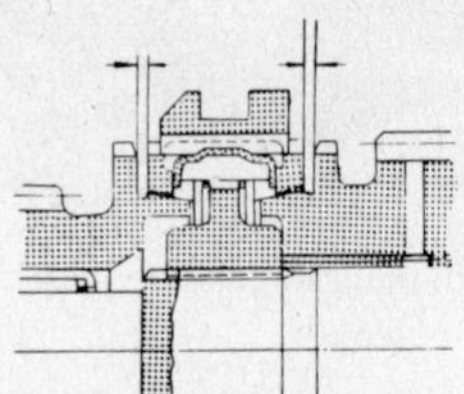

Synchronizer ring clearance

Position a washer on each side of the reverse idler gear, and install the gear in the housing. Tap the reverse idler gear shaft into position. Install the countershaft, and the lower transmission cover.

Insert the mainshaft from the output side of the housing, and assemble the gear cluster on the shaft in the order in which it was removed. Install the mainshaft snap-ring. Using a piece of thickwall tubing as a drift, install the output side mainshaft bearing (marked side facing outward) so that it seats in its retainer. In the same manner, install the main drive gear and bearing, and both countershaft bearings flush with the housing outer surface. Install both mainshaft bearing retainer plates.

Hold the detent ball in shifter fork I, and insert shifter fork rail I from the input side of the housing. Install shifter fork and rail II in a similar manner, from the output side of the housing. Position the rail ends flush with the housing (as illustrated), and insert a 1″ block, as used during disassembly, to limit shifter fork movement. Install the large bearing retainer plate and the oil gutter on the input side of the housing.

Position the shims removed during disassembly, and tap the differential into position. Reassemble the transmission case in the reverse order of disassembly. Insert the shifter fork rail into the housing, and install the shifter fork on the rail. Guide the transmission case into position, and torque the retaining nuts to 14.5 ft. lbs. Install and

Installing the differential assembly

tighten the shifter arm retaining bolt. Install the drive gear and final reduction pinion in the transmission case.

Position the washer, needle bearing, driven gear, synchronizer assembly and shift fork on the end of the mainshaft, and engage the shift lever in the shift fork. Install and tighten the locknut on the countershaft to 43 ft. lbs., and the locknut on the mainshaft to 33 ft. lbs., and bend up the locktabs to secure the nuts. Install the transmission side cover.

Fill the grooves of the differential case seals with grease, and install the oil seal sleeves in the reverse order of removal. Assemble the transmission upper cover in the reverse order of disassembly. Coat the side plug with sealer, and adjust so that the plug extends .040″ above the surface of the cover (see illustration). Position selector arm II and shifter arm I in the case, and install the shifter arm shafts. Engage selector arm I in shifter arm I and selector arm II, and insert the shifter shaft through the case into selector arm I. Install the shifter shaft retaining bolt. Install the transmission upper cover, and check to ensure that the shift mechanism is operating properly.

Install the primary drive gear, and tighten the nut to 41-46 ft. lbs. Bend up the locktabs, and continue assembly in the reverse order of disassembly.

FF-1

A split case transaxle is utilized. Due to this, and the fact that components are pressed onto the transmission shafts, a considerable number of special factory tools are required for reconditioning. For this reason, it is suggested that transaxle reconditioning be referred to a Subaru dealer.

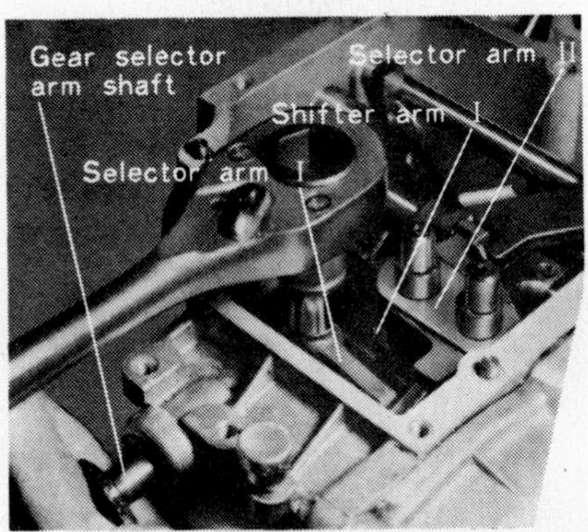

Shift mechanism assembly

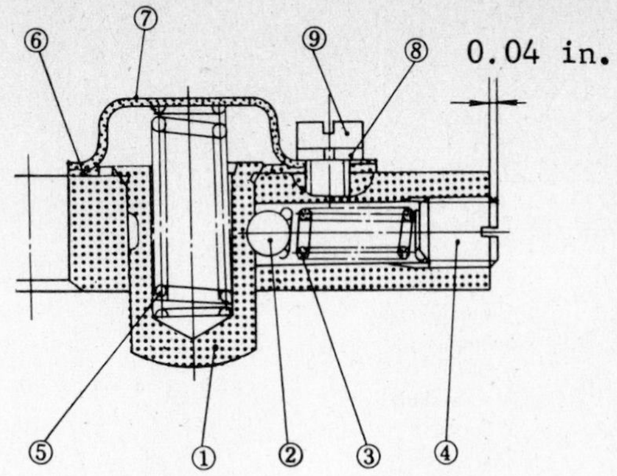

1 Plunger
2 Steel ball
3 Spring
4 Plug
5 Spring
6 Gasket
7 Plunger cover
8 Washer
9 Screw

Transmission upper cover—cross-section

Shifter operation

Drive Axle and U-joints

Removal and Installation

360

Swing axles are used, mounted inboard on U-joints which are an integral part of the differential assembly, and outboard on hubs that bolt to trailing arms.

To remove the axles proceed as follows. Remove the clips from the boot on the inner end of the axle shaft, and slide the boot to the outer end of the axle. Cut the safety wire retaining the axle-to-U-joint bolts, and remove the bolts. Unbolt and remove the wheel and tire. Extract the cotter pin, and remove the brake drum retaining nut. Using a puller, remove the brake drum from

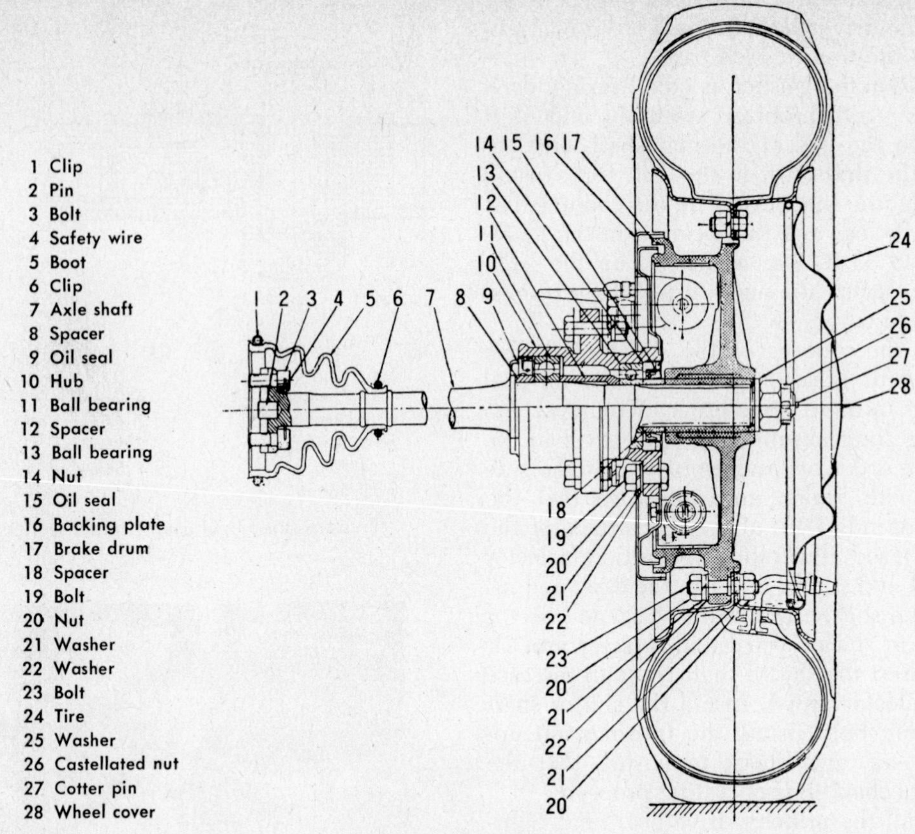

360 drive axle—cross-section

the axle shaft. NOTE: *Apply even pressure to the circumference of the brake drum to avoid distortion.* Support the hub on a jackstand, and unbolt the shock absorber lower mount. Adjust the bolt at the center arm of the torsion bar to relax the bar (see below). Remove the jackstand, and unbolt the brake backing plate from the hub. Support the backing plate in an out of the way position, so as not to stress the brake hose. Unbolt the hub from the trailing arm, and remove the axle.

Install the axle in the reverse order of removal. Torque the axle-to-U-joint bolts to 20-30 ft. lbs., and safety wire in place.

In order to remove the U-joints, it is necessary to disassemble the transaxle up to and including differential removal (see above). Install in the reverse order of removal.

FF-1

The drive axle consists of a double-offset joint, an axle shaft, a constant velocity joint, and a stub axle. To remove the drive axle proceed as follows: Engage the parking brake and remove the wheel and tire. Flatten the lockplate, and remove the hub nut. Remove the retaining bolts, and separate the double-offset joint from the brake drum. Detach the inner panel from the wheel well. Turn the steering knuckle to full lock, and pull the stub shaft out of the hub. Slide the axle shaft out of the wheel well.

Install in the reverse order of removal.

FF-1 drive axle removal

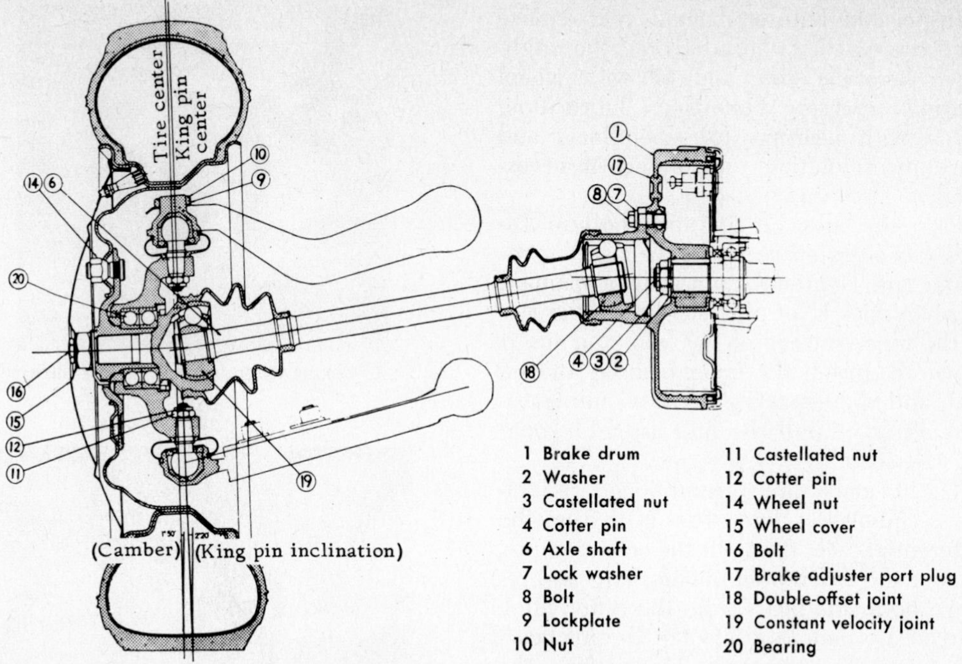

FF-1 drive axle—cross-section

Tighten the hub nut to 87-101 ft. lbs., and bend the locktab. NOTE: *Excessive torque will cause bearing damage.*

RECONDITIONING

360

Extract the axle shaft from the hub assembly using a puller. Inspect the shaft, and replace if worn or damaged. Remove spacers A and C (see illustration) from the hub assembly. Using a spanner, remove the retaining nut from the outside of the hub. Push the outer and inner bearings from the hub (as illustrated), using a puller.

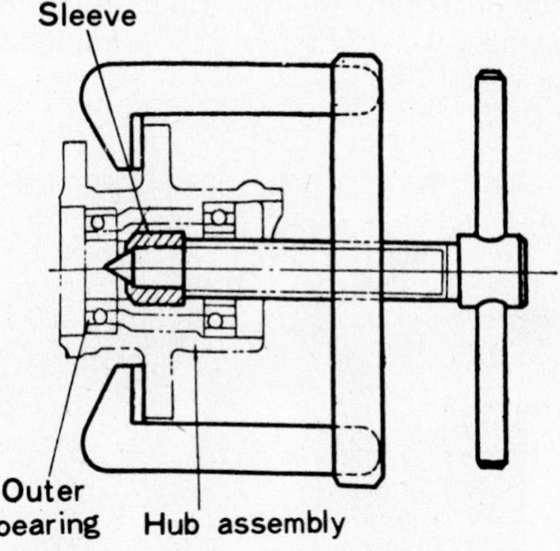

Removing the 360 rear hub outer bearing

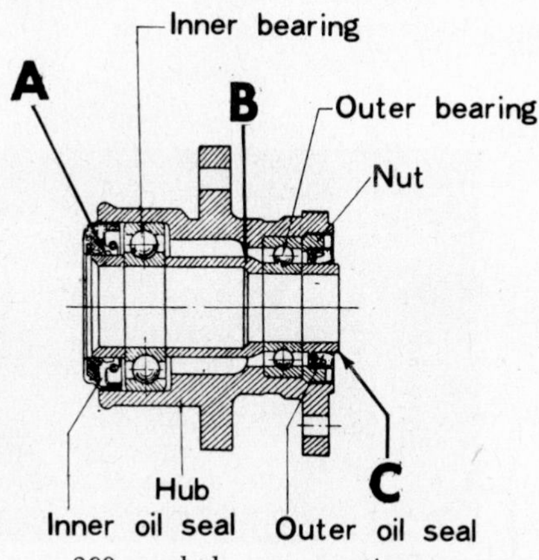

360 rear hub—cross-section

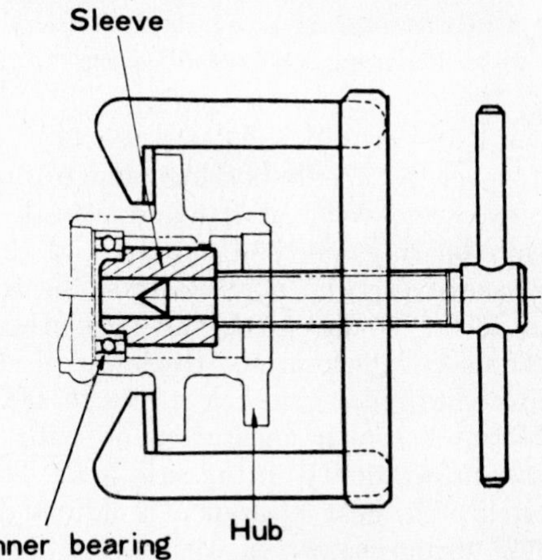

Removing the 360 rear hub inner bearing

Inspect the hub for damage, and replace if necessary. Clean both bearings thoroughly in kerosene, dry, and fill with wheel bearing grease. Following lubrication, check both bearings for smoothness and freedom of rotation, and replace if necessary.

Press the outer bearing into the hub. Install the outer oil seal and the bearing retainer nut. Tighten the nut using a spanner. Apply a thick layer of wheel bearing grease to the inner surface of the hub, and insert spacer B. Install the inner bearing and oil seal, and slide spacers A and C into position. Press or pull the hub assembly onto the axle shaft.

The U-joints are reconditioned as follows. Unbolt the differential gear from the differential case. Push out the retaining pin, remove the differential pinion shaft, and remove both side gears from the differential. Thread a 6 mm. bolt into the U-joint bearing caps, and separate the U-joint from the side gear. NOTE: *Exercise care to avoid losing the bearing needles.* In a similar manner, remove one bearing cap from the U-joint yoke, and remove the trunnion from the yoke.

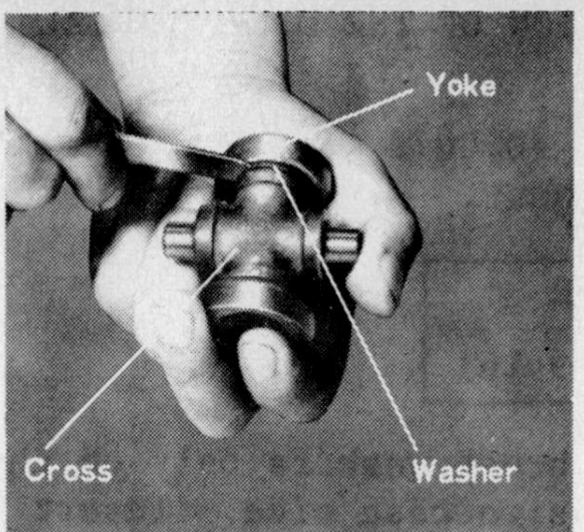

Checking trunnion-to-yoke clearance

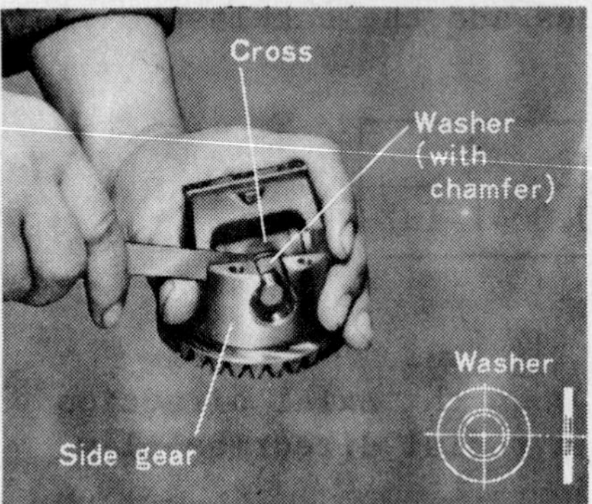

Checking trunnion-to-side gear clearance

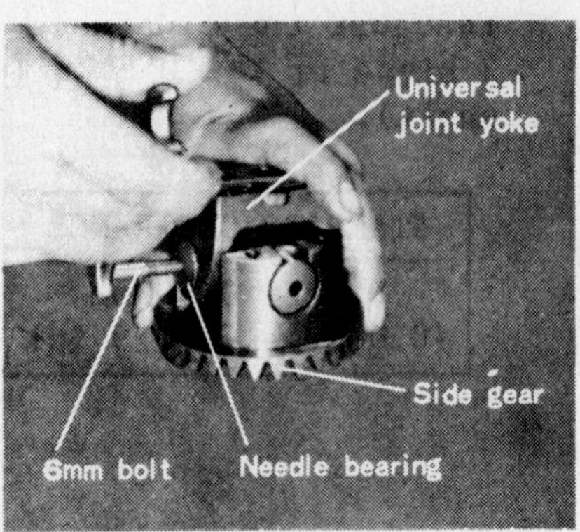

Removing 360 U-joint bearings

Inspect the needle bearings and trunnion for excessive wear or damage. Install the needle bearings on the trunnion, and check for excessive radial play. Position the trunnion in the U-joint yoke, and measure side clearance. Determine the thickness of shim required to reduce side clearance to .0002″. Perform a similar measurement with the trunnion positioned in the side gear. Trunnion to side gear clearance is adjusted to .0002″ using chamfered washers of the appropriate thickness.

Assemble the trunnion to the U-joint yoke and side gear using shims (as determined above). Grease the needle bearings, and press the bearings in using a vise, so that the inner surface of the bearings is flush with the inner surface of the yoke and side gear. Assemble the differential in the reverse order of disassembly. Measure clearance between the side gears and the pinion shaft block using feeler gauges. Should clearance exceed .008″, correct using a larger pinion shaft block.

Differential side gear axial clearance

FF-1

Remove the bands from the boots at both the constant velocity and double-offset joints, and slide the boots away from the joints. Pry the circlip out of the double-offset joint, and slide the outer race of the joint off of the shaft. Remove the balls from

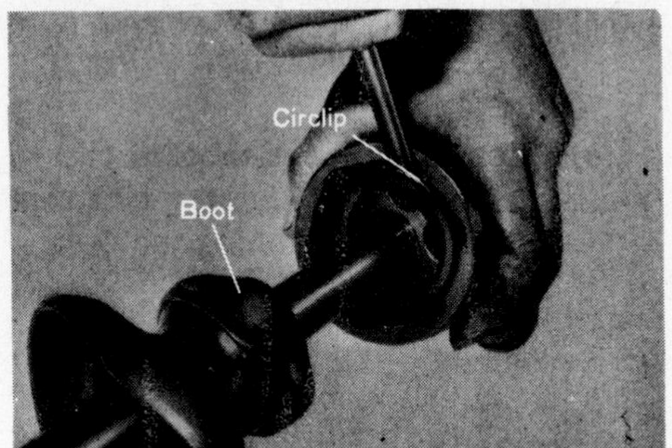

Removing the double-offset joint circlip

the cage, rotate the cage slightly, and slide the cage inward on the axle shaft. Using snap-ring pliers, remove the outer snap-ring retaining the inner race to the shaft. Slide the inner race, cage, and boot off of the axle shaft. NOTE: *Exercise care to avoid damaging the boot on the inner snap-ring.* Pull back the constant velocity joint boot and pivot the stub axle around the joint far enough to expose a ball. Remove the exposed ball, and continue this procedure until all balls are removed, at which time the outer race (stub axle) may be removed from the axle shaft. Remove the retaining snap-ring, and slide the inner race off of the shaft.

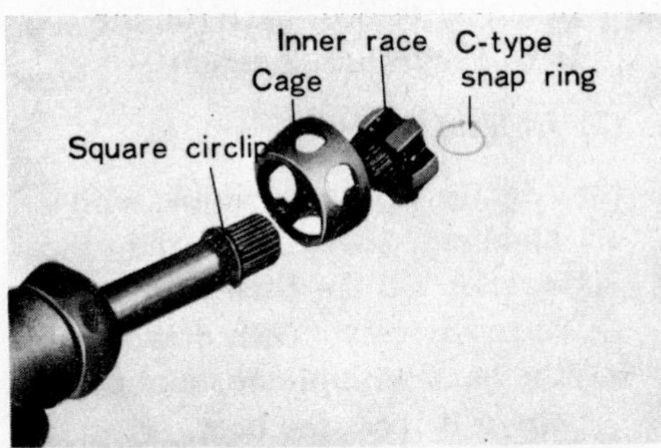

Disassembled double-offset joint

Inspect the parts of both joints for wear, damage, or corrosion, and replace if necessary. Examine the axle shaft for bending or distortion, and replace if evident. Should the boots be dried out, cracked, or distorted they must be replaced.

Install the constant velocity joint inner race on the axle shaft, and retain with a snap-ring. Assemble the joint in the opposite order of disassembly. Slide the double-offset joint cage onto the shaft, with the counterbore toward the end of the shaft. Install the inner race on the shaft, and install the retaining snap-ring. Position the cage over the inner race, and fill the cage pockets with grease. Insert the balls into the cage. Fill the well in the outer race with approximately 1 oz. grease, and slide the outer race onto the axle shaft. Install the retaining circlip, and add 1 oz. more grease to the interior of the joint. Fill the boot with approximately 1 oz. grease, and slide it into position over the double-offset joint. Fill the constant velocity joint boot with 3 oz. grease, and install the boot over the joint. Band the boots on both joints tightly enough that they cannot be turned by hand. NOTE: *Use only grease specified for use in constant velocity joints.*

Suspension

Front

360

The front suspension consists of single trailing arms, pivoted on ball studs which are mounted directly on the body structure. Kingpins are pivoted in brackets welded to the end of the trailing arms. Torsion bars, coaxial with the pivot of the trailing arms, act on a center arm, which in turn acts on a center spring (see illustration). Shock absorbers are mounted to studs at approximately the center of the trailing arms.

Caster is a function of ride height, and therefore is not adjustable by means other than adjusting ride height. Camber is not normally adjusted; however, should camber be outside specifications, it may be altered by loosening the ball stud retaining nut, and inserting shims between the ball stud and body. Toe-in is adjusted by turning the adjusting sleeves on the tie-rods.

FF-1

Unequal length upper and lower control arms are utilized. The lower arm is wishbone type, and the upper single link type.

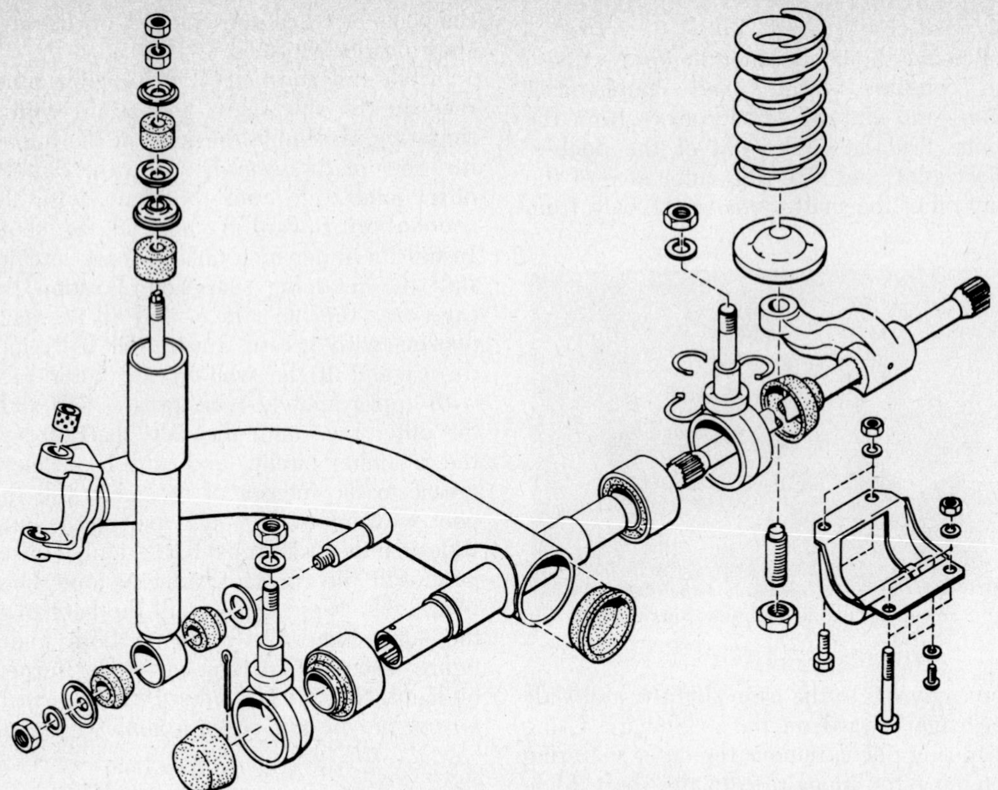

360 front suspension—exploded view

The torsion bar and shock absorber both mount to the upper arm, and the steering knuckle is mounted to both arms with ball joints. Unsprung weight is greatly reduced, and center-point steering (centerline of the ball joint pivots on the tire centerline) is facilitated by the use of inboard brakes.

Caster and camber are controlled by hex-

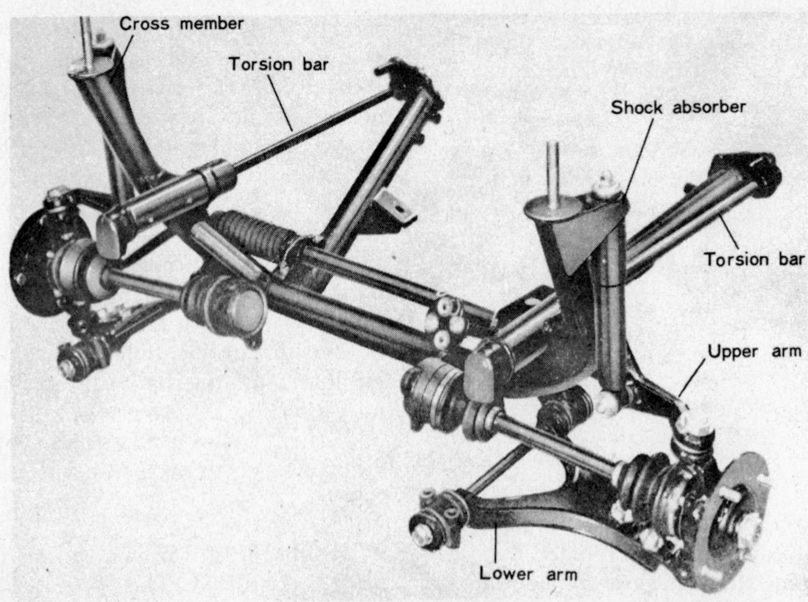

FF-1 front suspension

agonal cams which control the position of the lower ball joint on the control arm. Rotating the inner (caster) or outer (camber) cam 2 flats changes caster or camber 1°. Toe-in is adjusted by loosening the locknuts, and turning the tie-rods.

Torsion Bars

360

The torsion bars are removed and installed as follows: Raise the front of the car, and turn the ride height adjustment bolt counterclockwise to relax the torsion bars and center spring. Remove the shock absorber upper nuts. Pull off the cap from the end of the trailing arm pivot tube, and extract the cotter pin from the tube. Slide the torsion bar(s) out.

Install in the reverse order of removal. Each torsion bar is marked R or L, on the center arm end, to indicate on which side the bar is installed. CAUTION: *Installation on the incorrect side will result in premature failure of the bar.* During installation, index the missing tooth on the torsion bar splines to the double teeth in the center arm. Following installation, adjust ride height.

FF-1

Torsion bar removal and installation is performed as follows: Raise the vehicle, and loosen the ride height adjusting cam retainer. Remove the shock absorber upper retaining nuts. Flatten the locktab, and remove the upper ball joint upper nut. Remove both torsion bar lock bolts and nuts, at the adjuster arm and the upper control arm. Rotate the upper control arm away from the ball point, and then down, to fully relax the torsion bar. Remove the adjuster arm, and slide the torsion bar out.

Install in the reverse order of removal. CAUTION: *Do not interchange torsion bars side-to-side.* Index the missing tooth on the torsion bar splines with the double tooth on the anchor arm. Following installation, adjust ride height.

Ride Height Adjustment

360

Ride height is adjusted by turning the center bolt (bolts—Truck and Van) clockwise to raise, and counterclockwise to lower the vehicle.

360 sedan and Custom front ride height adjusting bolt

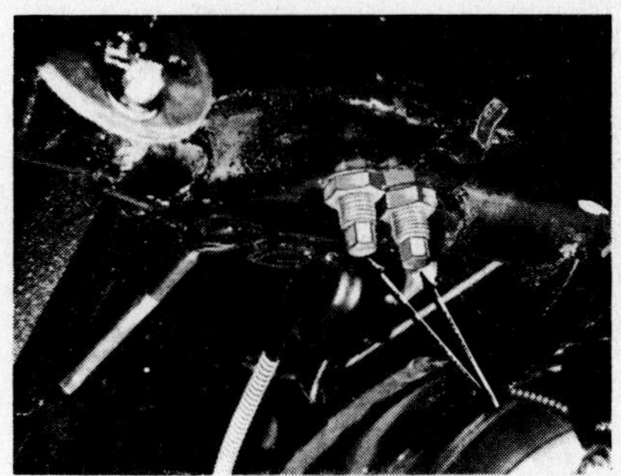

360 truck and van front ride height adjusting bolts

FF-1

Ride height is adjusted by turning an adjusting cam at the front of each torsion bar. Turning the cam clockwise raises, and counterclockwise lowers vehicle height. Access to the cam is obtained through the slot below the front bumper.

Wheel Bearings

360

Tapered roller bearings are utilized. The bearings are serviced as follows: Raise the vehicle, remove the wheel, and unbolt the grease cap. Flatten the locktab, and remove the brake drum retaining nut. Using a puller, remove the brake drum. NOTE: *Apply uniform pressure to the circumference of the brake drum to avoid distortion.* Lift out the bearing inner races and the inner seal. Using a thin drift, tap out the bearing outer races. CAUTION: *Exercise care to avoid damaging bearing inner races or seats.*

Lubricate with wheel bearing grease, and install the wheel bearings in the reverse order of removal. Adjust the wheel bearing play by tightening the retaining nut fully, back off the nut 1/6-1/8 turn, and install the locktab.

FF-1

Twin, axial thrust ball bearings are used. In order to service the bearings, the steering knuckle-hub assembly must be removed from the vehicle. Raise the vehicle, actuate the parking brake, and remove the wheel. Flatten the lockplate, and remove the hub retaining nut. Remove the cotter pin and nut, and separate the tie-rod end from the steering knuckle using a puller. Note the position of the caster and camber adjusting cams on the lower control arm (see illustration), and unbolt the lower ball joint from the control arm. Flatten the lockplate, and remove the nut retaining the upper ball joint to the upper control arm. Slide the axle shaft out of the hub, and remove the hub knuckle assembly from the vehicle. Support the knuckle with three pins inserted through the three holes in the hub, and using a piece of tubing approximately 1.3″

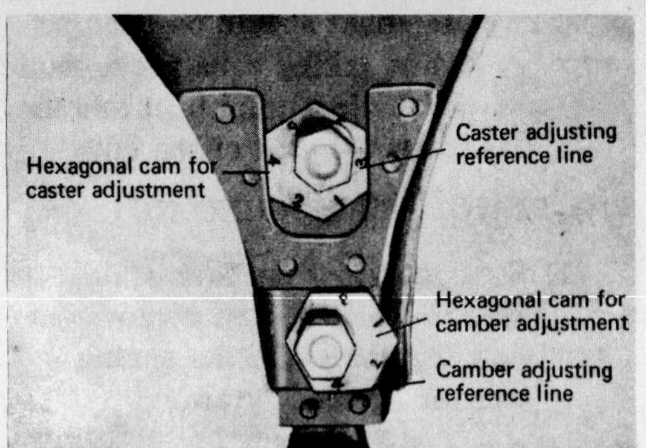

FF-1 caster and camber adjusting cams

diameter as a drift, tap the hub out of the knuckle assembly. Straighten the lockplate, and remove the lockplate retaining bolts. Remove the inner seal, and back out the bearing retainer nut using spanner. Remove the outer oil seal, and tap the bearings out of the knuckle using a large drift.

NOTE: *Front wheel bearings are replaced as a set. Do not replace bearings individually.* Fill the wheel bearings with grease, and install the knuckle (as illustrat-

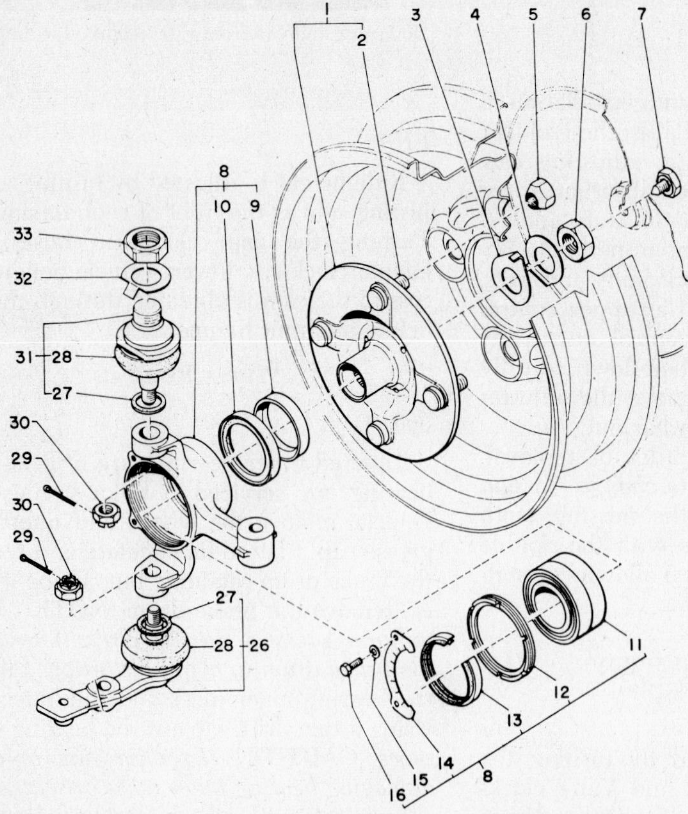

FF-1 front hub—exploded view

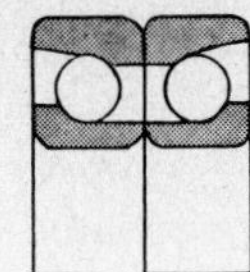

Cross-sectional view of FF-1 front wheel bearing installation showing correct position of races

ed) using a drift. Press the outer seal into the knuckle, so that it extends approximately .040" beyond the lip of the knuckle, and insert the hub spacer. Tighten the bearing retainer nut to 115-133 ft. lbs., using a spanner. Install the lockplate, and bend a tab down to engage the bearing retainer nut. Press in the inner seal carefully, to avoid damaging the seal lip. Grease the seal lips, and tap the hub into the knuckle assembly. Continue assembly in the reverse order of disassembly. Torque the hub nut to 86-101 ft. lbs.

Kingpins

360

In order to service the kingpins, it is necessary to remove the trailing arms. Remove the torsion bars as described above. Remove the cotter pin and castellated nut, and separate the tie-rod end from the steering knuckle using a puller. Loosen the retaining bolt, and pull the speedometer cable out of the steering knuckle using pliers

Removing the 360 speedometer cable from the spindle

(left side only). Unbolt and remove the dust cap, and remove the brake drum retaining nut. Using a puller, remove the brake drum. NOTE: *Apply uniform pressure to the circumference of the drum, to prevent distortion.* Unbolt the brake backing plate from the steering knuckle, and support it in an out of the way position so as not to stress the brake hose. Remove the inner and outer ball stud retaining nuts, and remove the trailing arm from the vehicle.

Clamp the trailing arm in a vise, and tap the kingpin retaining pin out of the steering knuckle. Unscrew the grease fitting from

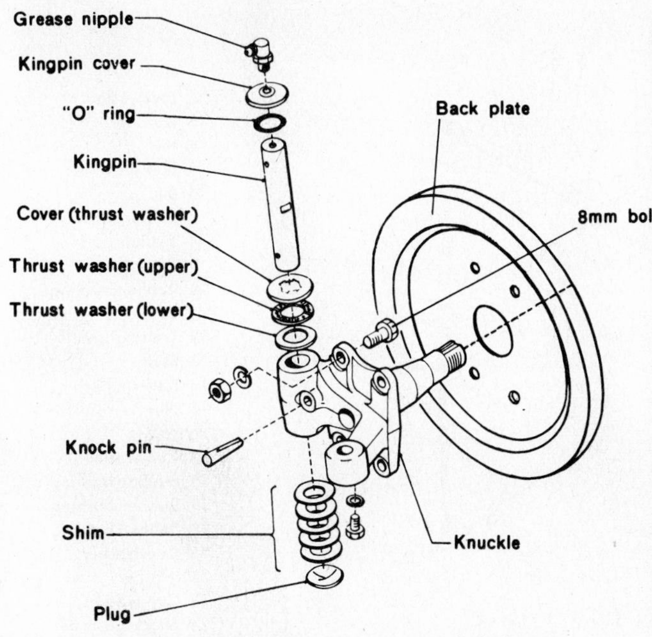

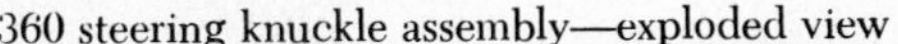

360 steering knuckle assembly—exploded view

Removing the kingpin retaining pin

the end of the kingpin, and remove the fitting, cover, and O-ring. Using a drift, tap the kingpin out of the steering knuckle, and separate the knuckle from the trailing arm.

Inspect the trailing arm yoke bushings for excessive wear or damage. Replace the bushings if necessary, by tapping the bushings out and in with a drift or piece of pipe of the approximate O.D. of the bushing. CAUTION: *The oil grooves in the bushings must be positioned as they were prior to removal, in order to ensure proper lubrication.* Insert the bushings so that they are flush with the inside of the trailing arm yoke.

Trail fit the steering knuckle and thrust washers to the trailing arm yoke, to determine the shims required. Shims are available in thicknesses ranging from .004-.016″. Assemble the training arm, knuckle, thrust washers and shims, and insert the kingpin. Tap the expansion plug in place in the trailing arm yoke, and stake in position. Install the O-ring, cover, and grease fitting, and lubricate the kingpin. Install the trailing arm in the vehicle in the reverse order of removal.

Ball Joints

FF-1

In order to service ball joints, it is necessary to remove the steering knuckle-hub assembly from the vehicle, as described above under Wheel Bearings. Following removal, the ball joints may be separated from the steering knuckle by removing the cotter pin and castellated nut, and extracting the ball joint stud using a puller.

Install ball joints in the reverse order of removal. Torque ball joint studs to 43-65 ft. lbs.

Rear

360

Full trailing arms, mounted directly to transverse torsion bars, are utilized. The trailing arms are bolted to the rear hubs, to which the shock absorbers mount.

FF-1

Early sedans and all station wagons utilize full trailing arms, mounted to transverse torsion bars, with an auxiliary center spring. Shock absorbers mount to the trailing arm, close to the stub axle.

Late sedans and Model G sedans use semi-trailing arms mounted to torque tubes, which act on an internal torsion bar. shock absorbers are mounted to the trailing arm, close to the stub axle.

Torsion Bars

360

The torsion bars are removed and installed as follows: Raise the rear of the ve-

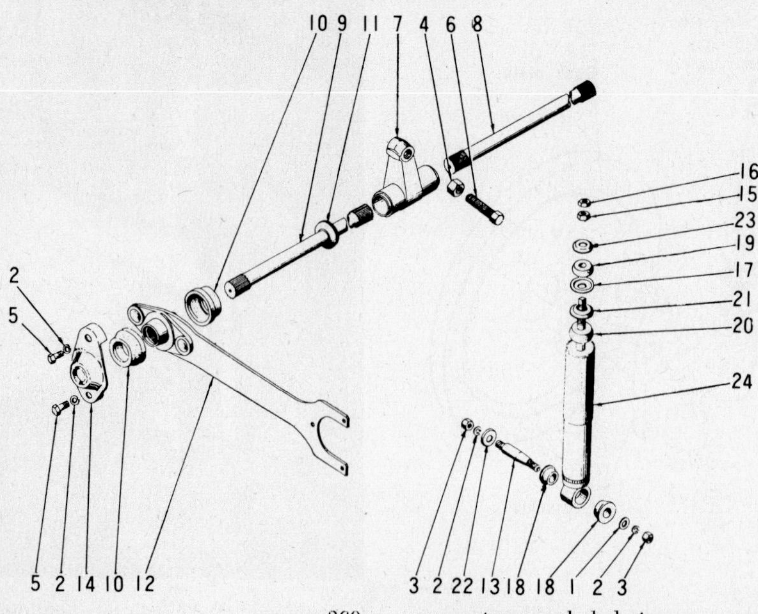

1 Washer
2 Lockwasher
3 Nut
4 Nut
5 Bolt
6 Bolt
7 Center arm
8 Torsion bar
9 Torsion bar
10 Rubber bushing
11 Boot
12 Trailing arm
13 Stud
14 Cover
15 Nut
16 Nut
17 Cup washer
18 Rubber bushing
19 Rubber bushing
20 Rubber bushing
21 Cup washer
22 Washer
23 Cup washer
24 Shock absorber

360 rear suspension—exploded view

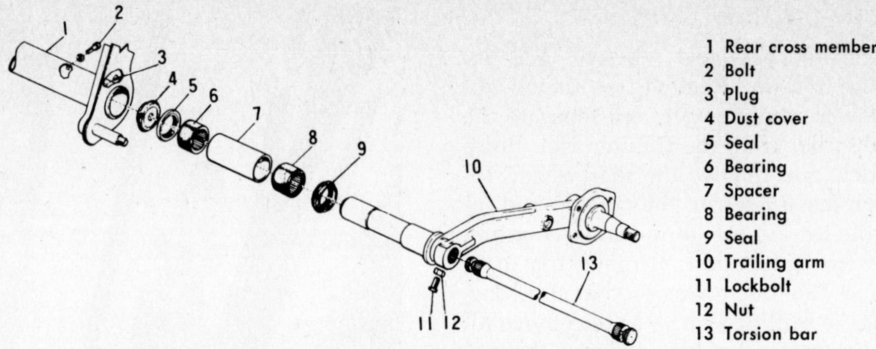

FF-1 (early sedan and all station wagons) rear suspension—exploded view

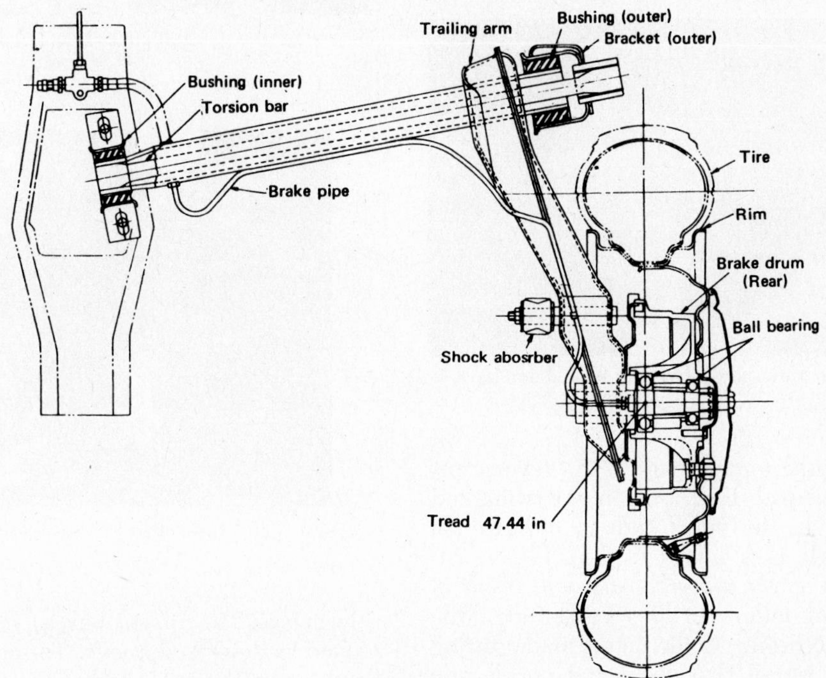

FF-1 (late sedan and Model G sedan) rear suspension—exploded view

hicle and remove the wheel. Loosen the center arm adjusting bolt (see below) to relax the torsion bars. Unbolt and remove the torsion bar cover, and slide the trailing arm off of the torsion bar. Swing the trailing arm out of the way, and slide the torsion bar out of the vehicle.

During installation, ensure that the missing tooth on the torsion bar ends engages the double teeth in the center arm and trailing arm. Each torsion bar is marked R or L, on the center arm end, to indicate on which side the bar is installed. CAUTION: *Installation on the incorrect side will result in premature failure of the bar.* Install the torsion bars in the reverse order of removal, and adjust ride height.

FF-1 (Early Sedans and all Station Wagons)

The torsion bars are removed and installed as follows: Raise the rear of the vehicle and remove the wheel. Using a hex key (8 mm.), loosen the center arm and spring to relax the torsion bars. Remove the nut and retaining plate from the crossmember mounting bracket. Back out the lock bolts at each end of the torsion bar to be removed, thread a bolt into the bar, and pull it out of the crossmember.

Torsion bars are marked R or L, and must be installed on the correct side. CAUTION: *Installation on the incorrect side will result in premature failure of the bars.* Install in the reverse order of removal, and adjust ride height (see below).

FF-1 (Late and Model G Sedans)

The torsion bars are removed and installed as follows: Remove the shock absorber lower retaining nut, and separate the shock absorber from the trailing arm. Raise the vehicle and remove the rear wheel. Index mark the splines on the outside and inside of the torsion bar, to indicate mounting position for installation. Remove the lockbolt from the outer torsion bar bushing. Position the trailing arm so as to remove all load from the torsion bar, and tap the torsion bar out.

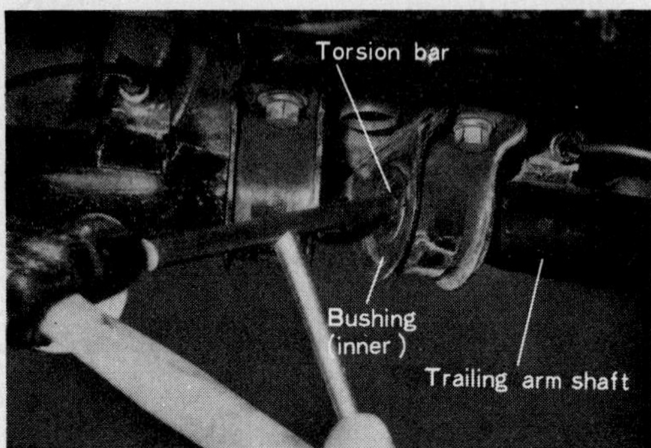

FF-1 (late sedan and Model G sedan) torsion bar removal

Install the torsion bars in the reverse order of removal. Each torsion bar is marked R or L, on the outer end, to indicate on which side it is installed. CAUTION: *Installation on the incorrect side will result in premature failure of the bars.* Index the splines according to the marks made during removal, install the wheel and check ride height. If necessary, adjust ride height as indicated below. Remount the shock absorber after the vehicle has been lowered.

Ride Height Adjustment

360

Rear ride height is adjusted by turning the center arm bolt clockwise to raise and counterclockwise to lower the vehicle.

FF-1 (Early Sedans and all Station Wagons)

Adjust rear ride height by turning a socket head bolt (8 mm.), clockwise to raise, and counterclockwise to lower the vehicle. The bolt is accessible through a port in the trunk.

FF-1 (Late Sedans and Model G Sedans)

No routine ride height adjustment is provided. Should it be necessary to adjust

360 sedan and Custom rear ride height adjusting bolt

360 truck and van rear ride height adjusting bolt

ride height, the torsion bar(s) must be removed as described above. To increase ride height, turn the outer end of the torsion bar in the direction of the arrow (on the end of the bar), and the inner end in the opposite direction an equal number of teeth. Decrease ride height by reversing the above. Shifting the torsion bar one tooth will alter ride height approximately .2".

Wheel Bearings

360

Rear wheel bearing service is described above under Drive Axle and U-Joint Reconditioning.

FF-1 (Early Sedans and all Station Wagons)

Raise the rear of the vehicle and remove the wheel. Unbolt and remove the grease cap. Flatten the lockplate, and remove the hub nut. Pull off the brake drum, and remove the inner bearing inner race using a

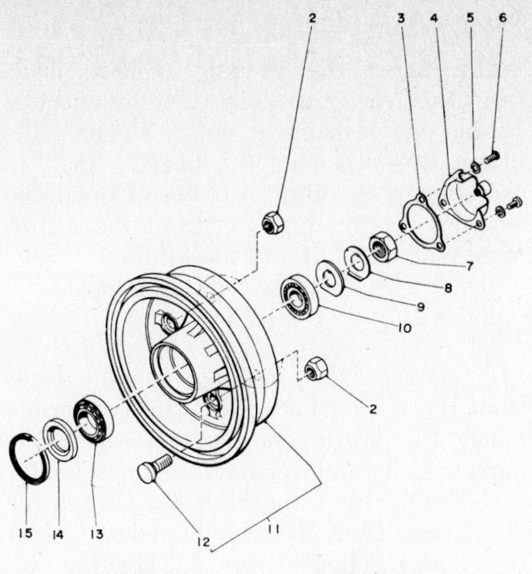

2 Wheel nut	9 Washer
3 Gasket	10 Roller bearing
4 Grease cap	11 Brake drum
5 Lockwasher	12 Wheel stud
6 Screw	13 Roller bearing
7 Nut	14 Spacer
8 Lockplate	15 Seal

FF-1 (early sedan and all station wagons) rear wheel bearings

Lubricate all parts with wheel bearing grease, and install in the reverse order of removal. To adjust wheel bearing play, tighten the retaining nut fully, and back off 1/10-1/8 turn.

FF-1 (Late Sedans and Model G Sedans)

Raise the rear of the vehicle and remove the wheel. Unbolt and remove the grease cap. Extract the cotter pin, and remove the castellated nut. Using a puller, remove the brake drum. NOTE: *Apply uniform pressure to the circumference of the brake drum to avoid distortion.*

Using a piece of pipe approximately the I.D. of the inner bearing, press out the outer bearing and spacer (as illustrated). Press out the outer bearing using a larger piece of pipe. Press in the outer bearing puller (if necessary). Tap the outer bearing outer race, and the inner bearing outer race and seal out of the brake drum using a thin drift. NOTE: *Exercise care to avoid damaging the bearing races or seats.*

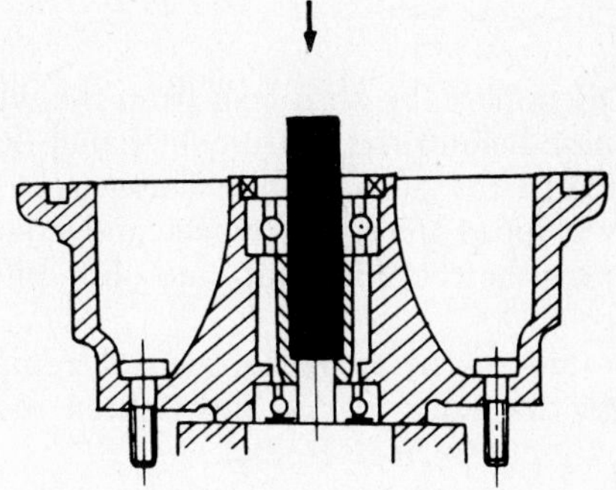

Removing the outer bearing and spacer

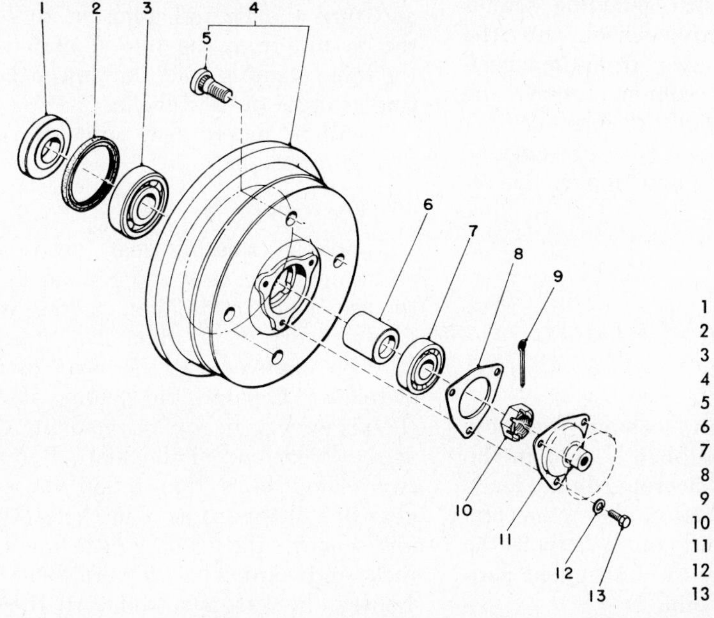

1 Spacer
2 Seal
3 Ball bearing
4 Brake drum
5 Wheel stud
6 Bearing spacer
7 Ball bearing
8 Bearing retainer
9 Cotter pin
10 Castellated nut
11 Grease cap
12 Lockwasher
13 Bolt

FF-1 (late sedan and Model G sedan) rear wheel bearings

(press outer race), sealed side outward. Coat the inside of the hub with a thick layer of wheel bearing grease, and press in the spacer and inner bearing (press both races). Press in the oil seal, flush with the end of the hub. Clean the spindle, and install the spacer and the drum assembly. Tighten the retaining nut to 80-145 ft. lbs., and install the cotter pin and grease cap.

Steering

Steering Wheel

Removal and Installation

360

Disconnect the horn lead from the wiring harness behind the instrument panel. Press, and turn the horn button clockwise to remove. Index mark the wheel and column, remove the retaining nut, and slide off the wheel.

Install in the reverse order of removal. Align the index marks, and tighten the retaining nut to 29-33 ft. lbs.

FF-1

Disconnect the horn lead from the wiring harness below the instrument panel. Remove the two horn bar retaining screws from behind the steering wheel, press the bar down, and slide it away from the wheel. Index the wheel and column, remove the retaining nut, and pull off the wheel.

Install in the reverse order of removal. Align the index marks, and tighten the retaining nut to 20-29 ft. lbs.

Steering Column

Removal and Installation

360 Sedan and Custom

Separate the steering column from the steering gear at the rubber U-joint in the trunk. Disconnect the steering column leads from the wiring harness at the connectors behind the instrument panel. Unbolt the support bracket below the instrument panel, and lift out the column.

Install in the reverse order of removal.

360 Truck and Van

Disconnect the steering column leads from the wiring harness at the connectors behind the instrument panel. Remove the clamp bolt attaching the steering shaft to the primary steering gear box. Unbolt the steering column brackets from the instrument panel, and lift out the column.

Install in the reverse order of removal.

FF-1

Disconnect the steering column leads from the wiring harness at the connectors below the instrument panel. Remove the parcel shelf, and separate the accelerator pedal and cable from the lever. Detach the clutch rod from the clutch pedal. Unbolt the master cylinder from the steering column. Separate the steering shaft from the steering gear at the rubber U-joint adjacent to the double-offset joint. Unbolt the steering column support bracket below the instrument panel, and remove the steering column.

Install in the reverse order of removal.

Steering Gear

Removal and Installation

360 Sedan and Custom

Separate the steering shaft from the steering gear at the rubber U-joint in the trunk. Unclamp the speedometer cable from the left tie-rod. Loosen the locknut, and turn the tie rod adjuster, to separate the tie-rod from the tie-rod end. Remove the four retaining bolts, and lower the steerring gear out of the vehicle.

Install in the reverse order of removal, and adjust toe-in.

360 Truck and Van

A primary steering gear box is used in addition to the rack and pinion, to permit the use of rack and pinion steering with the cab-over driver position. The gear boxes may be removed together or individually, as follows: Separate the steering shaft from the primary gear box by removing the bolt at the lower end of the shaft. Remove the two clamp bolts that retain the primary gear box to the frame. Cut the safety wire, and separate the primary gear box from the rack and pinion at the rubber U-joint. Loosen the locknuts, and turn the tie-rod adjusters, to separate the tie-rods from the tie-rod ends. Remove the four retaining bolts, and lower the steering gear out of the vehicle.

Install in the reverse order of removal, and adjust toe-in if necessary. When installing only the rack and pinion, align the shaft with the primary gear box shaft, so that the units turn freely. When installing the primary gear box, do not tighten the retaining bolts until the unit is aligned so that it turns freely.

FF-1

Raise the vehicle and remove the front wheels. Remove the cotter pins and castellated nuts, and separate the tie-rod ends from the steering knuckles using a puller. Unbolt the steering shaft from the rack and pinion at the rubber U-joint adjacent to the double-offset joint. Cut the safety wire, and remove the four bolts retaining the steering gear to the crossmember. Slide the steering gear out of the vehicle.

Install in the reverse order of removal.

Reconditioning

360 Sedan and Custom

Remove the boots from both ends of the housing. Pull the cotter pin out of the rack, and remove the cap with a screwdriver. Remove the spacer, spring, and ball seat from the end of the rack. Remove the snap-rings retaining the boots on the tie-rods, and remove the boots. Lift out the tie-rods, and slide off the slide cover. Flatten the locktab, and remove the retaining nut and stop plate from the pinion end of the rack. Extract the rack from the housing. Thread out the eccentric rack bushing (pinion end) using a spanner. Remove the pinion end cover, remove the retainer washer from the pinion shaft, and remove the pinion from the housing.

Inspect all parts, and repair or replace if necessary. Should the pinion bushings or oil seal need replacement, they must be driven out and in using an appropriate drift (18 mm.) The rack bushing remaining in the

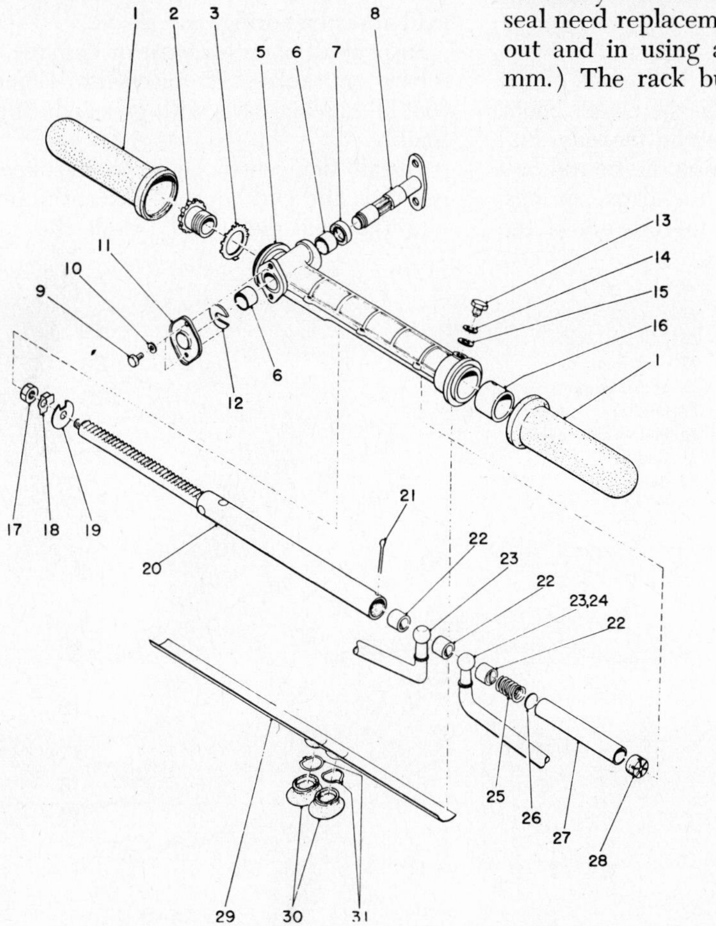

360 sedan and Custom steering gear—exploded view

housing may be removed and replaced by loosening the lock bolt. Liberally grease all moving parts during assembly.

Insert a new lockplate in the pinion end of the housing, and thread in the eccentric bushing (do not engage the locktabs). Apply a thick layer of grease to the housing, and insert the pinion. Install the pinion thrust washer and end cover. Insert the rack into the housing. Mount a dial indicator with its stem on the axis of the rack, hold the pinion from turning, and adjust rack backlash to zero by rotating the eccentric bushing. Following the adjustment, engage the locktabs into the eccentric bushing slots. Install the stop-plate, lockplate, and retaining nut, and engage the lockplate securely with the nut and rack. Assemble the parts in the tie-rod end of the rack in the reverse order of removal. Tighten the cap in the end of the rack until the spring is fully compressed, and back off to the first position where it is possible to install the cotter pin. Install the boots on the ends of the housing.

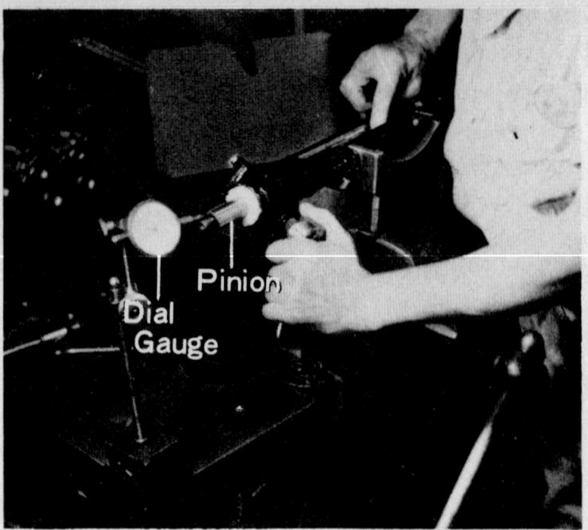

360 sedan and Custom rack end-play adjustment

360 Truck and Van

Remove the boots from both ends of the housing, the tube between the center boots, and the dust boots from the tie-rods. Pull out the cotter pins retaining the tie-rod ball seat caps, and remove the caps, springs, and ball seats. Slide the tie-rods out of the rack. Remove the three bolts retaining the steering gear box end housing, and slide the rack and end housing away from the steering gear box. Unbolt the pinion end cover, remove the thrust washer from the pinion, and pull the pinion out of the gear box. Loosen the locknut, and remove the preload adjuster, spring, and sleeve.

Inspect all parts for wear or damage, and repair or replace if necessary. Liberally coat all moving parts with grease during assembly.

Install the center boots to the steering gear box and end housing. Insert the pinion into the gear box, and install the thrust

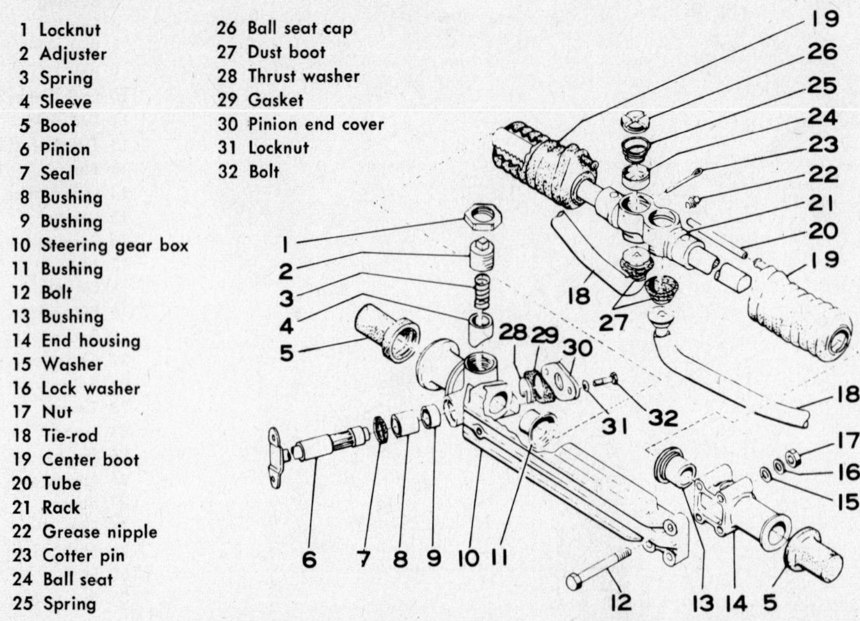

360 truck and van steering gear—exploded view

washer and end cover. Apply a thick layer of grease on the rack, and assemble the end housing, rack, and steering gear box. Tighten the end housing bolts finger tight. Install the preload adjuster in the reverse order of removal. Tighten the adjuster fully, back off 15-30° to obtain the proper preload, and tighten the locknut. Tighten the end housing bolts fully (8-14 ft. lbs.). Fill the tie-rod ball seats with grease, and assemble in the reverse order of disassembly. Tighten the ball seat caps fully, and back off until it is possible to insert the cotter pins. Position the center boots on the rack, and install the center tube. Fill with grease through the grease nipple in the rack.

No provision for maintenance or service is made on the primary steering gear box. Should a malfunction occur, the unit must be replaced.

FF-1

Flatten the lockplates, loosen the locknuts, and unscrew the tie-rods from the steering gear. Flatten the lockplates and remove the ball joints from the ends of the

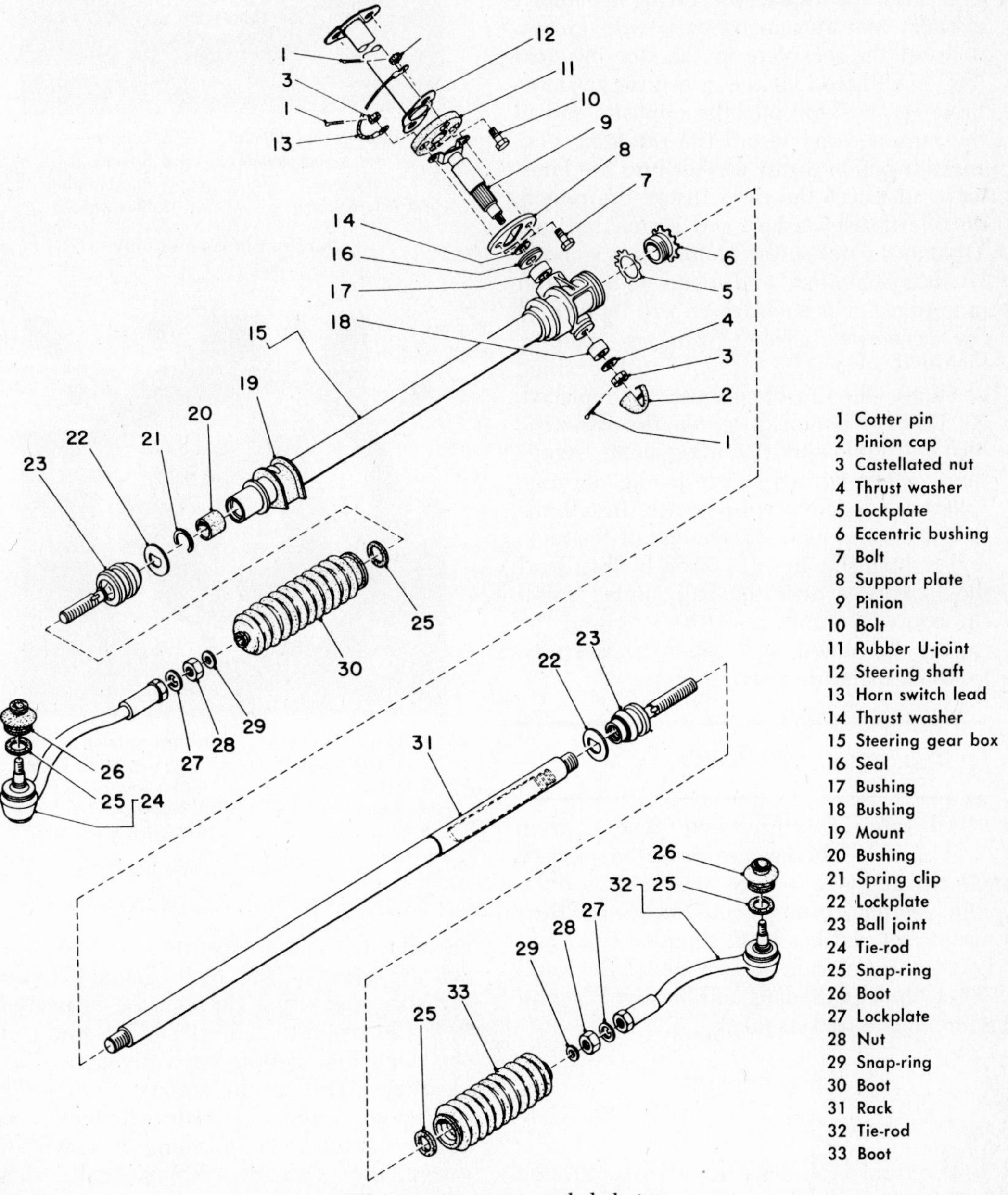

FF-1 steering gear—exploded view

rack. Remove the boots from the ends of the rack, and the cap from the end of the pinion. Extract the cotter pin, unthread the retaining nut, and pull the pinion out of the steering gear box. Following removal of the pinion, remove the rack from the housing. Flatten the locktab, and remove the eccentric bushing using a spanner. In order to remove the bushing from the opposite end of the housing, the spring clip retainer must be removed.

Inspect all parts for excessive wear or damage, and replace if necessary. If chatter marks are evident on the ball joint(s), the joint must be replaced. During assembly, liberally coat all moving parts with grease.

Insert the lockplate in the steering gear box, and thread in the eccentric bushing. Press the bushing into the opposite end of the housing, and install the retaining clip. Insert a pinion thrust washer into the housing, and install the rack. Install the pinion, outside thrust washer, and castellated nut. Tighten the nut so the pinion turns smoothly without binding, and retain with a cotter pin. Adjust gear backlash to zero by turning the eccentric bushing using a spanner. Should backlash be present in all bushing positions, the bushing must be replaced. NOTE: *Do not over-tighten the eccentric bushing.* Following the adjustment, engage the locktabs with the slots in the bushing. Fill the ball joints with grease, install the lockplates and joints on the end of the rack, and tighten the joints to 50-58 ft. lbs. Bend the lockplates over the ball joints. Install the boots on the ends of the rack and the cap on the pinion, and install the locknuts, lockplates, and tie-rods.

1 Upper wheel cylinder
2 Lower wheel cylinder
3 Brake shoe
4 Return spring
5 Retainer
6 Spindle
7 Backing plate
8 Star wheel

360 front brake assembly

1 Wheel cylinder
2 Parking brake lever
3 Spring
4 Retainer
5 Brake shoe
6 Return spring
7 Parking brake cable
8 Star wheel
9 Star wheel
10 Parking brake lever

360 rear brake assembly

Brakes

All models utilize four wheel drum brakes. Front brakes are mounted inboard on the FF-1 to reduce unsprung weight, and permit center-point steering. Rear drum material has been changed from aluminum to cast iron on late model FF-1 and FF-1 Model G Sedans and Station Wagons, to eliminate brake squeal.

Adjustments

360

The front brakes are adjusted by turning a star wheel at each wheel cylinder. Align the adjuster holes in the drum with the star wheels. Insert a .004″ feeler gauge between the shoe and drum through the inspection hole (90° from the adjuster hole), and turn the star wheel with a screwdriver to adjust clearance. Pulling the screwdriver handle up reduces upper wheel cylinder brake shoe clearance, and pushing it down reduces lower wheel cylinder brake shoe clearance.

Checking 360 brake adjustment

The rear brakes are adjusted in a similar manner, using feeler gauges, by turning two star wheels mounted in an anchor block at the bottom of the brake assembly. Pushing the screwdriver handle downward reduces brake shoe clearance in both cases.

The parking brake is adjusted by loosening the locknut(s), and turning the turnbuckle located below the interior compartment. Adjust so that the parking brake is fully engaged when the lever is pulled 4 or 5 notches. Ensure that the parking brake releases fully when the lever is lowered. NOTE: *It is necessary that the rear service brakes be adjusted prior to adjusting the parking brake.*

FF-1

The front brakes are self-adjusting, and seldom if ever require manual adjustment. For this reason, prior to manual adjustment, ensure that the self-adjuster is functioning, and that brake linings are not excessively worn. To adjust the front brakes,

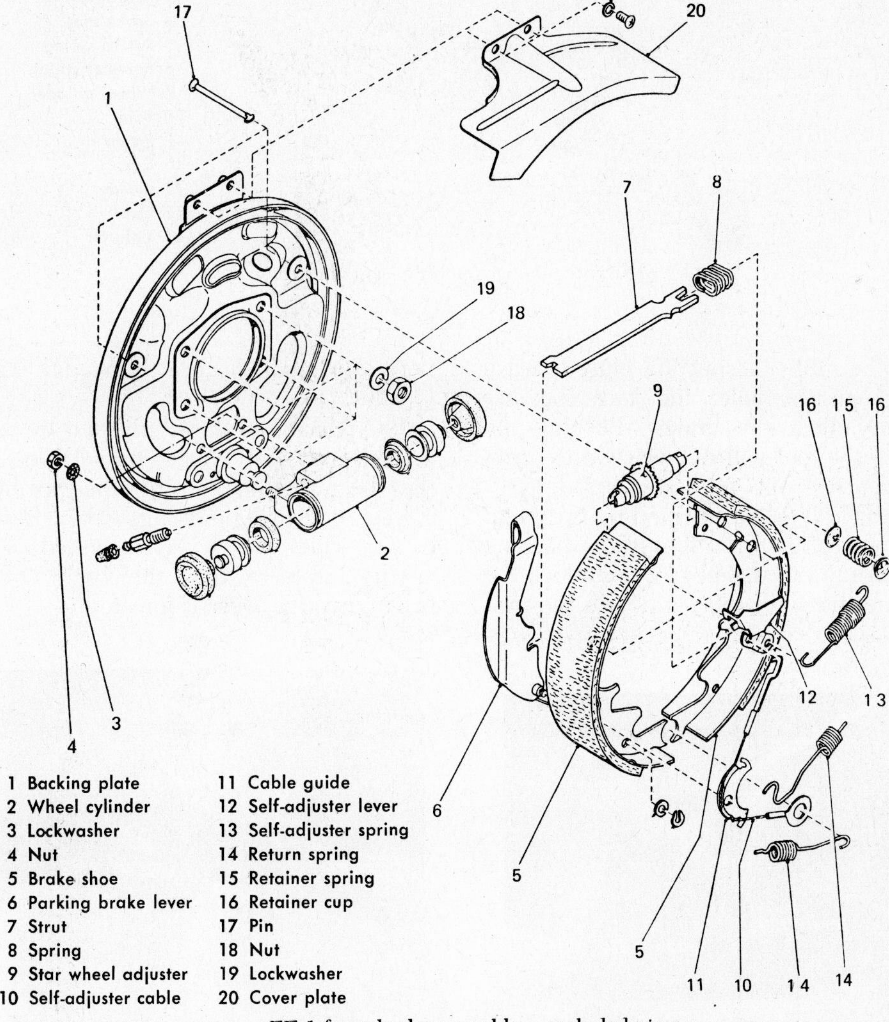

FF-1 front brake assembly—exploded view

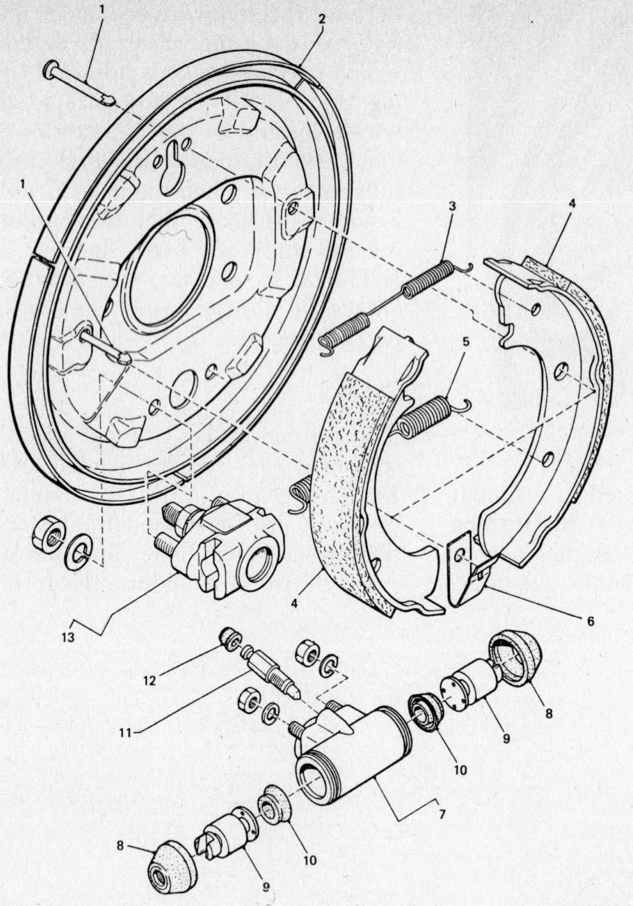

FF-1 rear brake assembly—exploded view

remove the rubber inspection plug, insert a tool through the hole, and turn the star wheel to adjust the brakes. Pushing the handle of the tool will reduce shoe to drum clearance.

The rear brakes are adjusted by turning a wedge located at the bottom of the backing plate. Turn the wedge clockwise to lock the brake, and back off 180° to obtain the proper adjustment. Secure the wedge with its locknut.

The parking brake is adjusted by removing the shift shaft cover (tunnel), loosening the locknut, and turning the turnbuckle. Adjust so that the parking brake is fully engaged when the lever is pulled 7 or 8 notches. Ensure that the brake releases fully when the lever is lowered.

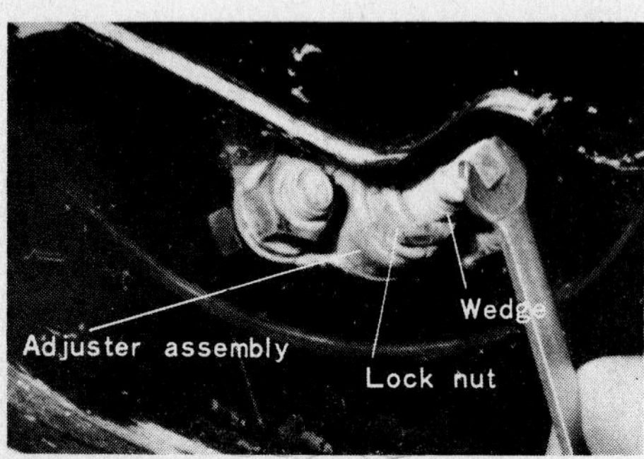

Adjusting FF-1 rear brakes

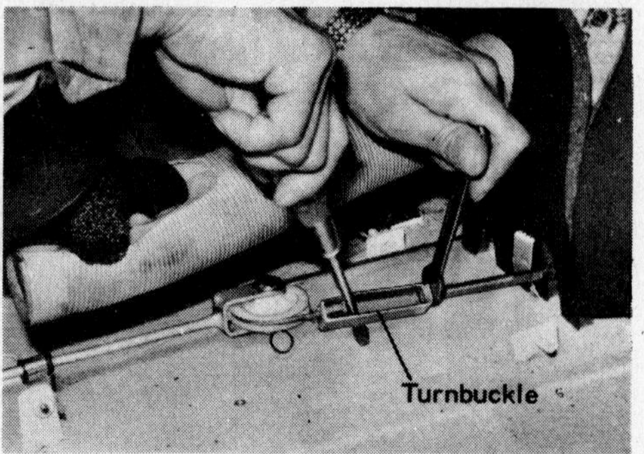

Adjusting FF-1 parking brake

Master Cylinder

Removal and Installation

360 Sedan and Custom

Disconnect the battery ground terminal, and remove the floor mat from the driver's side. Loosen the retaining screws, and remove the floorboard. Disconnect the stop light switch lead, and separate the switch from the master cylinder. Clamp the vinyl tube from the reservoir to the master cylinder at the master cylinder, and remove it from the master cylinder fitting. Disconnect the brake line from the master cylinder output fitting. Unbolt and remove the master cylinder by pulling upward.

Install in the reverse order of removal. Following installation, bleed the brakes and adjust pedal free play. Pedal play is adjusted by loosening the pushrod nuts at the brake pedal clevis, and adjusting pushrod to piston clearance so that pedal free play is .8-1″.

360 Truck and Van

Remove the pedal covers from the brake and clutch pedals. Unbolt and remove the steering column. Remove the driver's side underpan, and detach the accelerator cable from the pedal linkage. Unscrew and remove the driver's side floorboard. Clamp the vinyl tube from the reservoir to the master cylinder at the master cylinder, and remove it from the master cylinder fitting. Disconnect the brake line from the master cylinder output fitting. Unbolt and remove the master cylinder.

Install in the reverse order of removal. Following installation, bleed the brakes and adjust the pedal free play. Pedal play is adjusted in the same manner as the Sedan and Custom (above).

FF-1

Position a container below the master cylinder, and cover the driver's side floorboard for protection. Clamp the vinyl tubes from the master cylinder to the reservoirs at the master cylinder end, and remove them from the master cylinder fittings. NOTE: *Exercise care to avoid spilling brake fluid.* Remove the cotter pin retaining the pushrod clevis pin, and push out the pin. Disconnect the brake lines from the master cylinder output fittings, unbolt and remove the master cylinder.

Install in the reverse order of removal. Following installation bleed the brakes.

Reconditioning

360

Remove the boot from the end of the master cylinder, and unscrew the reservoir fitting. Using a drift, press the piston into the cylinder, and pry out the snap-ring retaining the stop-washer. Slowly release spring pressure, and remove all parts from the master cylinder bore.

Inspect all parts for excessive wear or damage. If the cylinder bore is excessively worn or scored, replace the entire assembly. Lubricate all parts with brake fluid during assembly.

Insert the valve seat, check valve and spring into the cylinder. Press the cup, piston, and stop-washer into the cylinder using a drift, and install the retaining snap-ring. Screw the fitting into position, and install the boot.

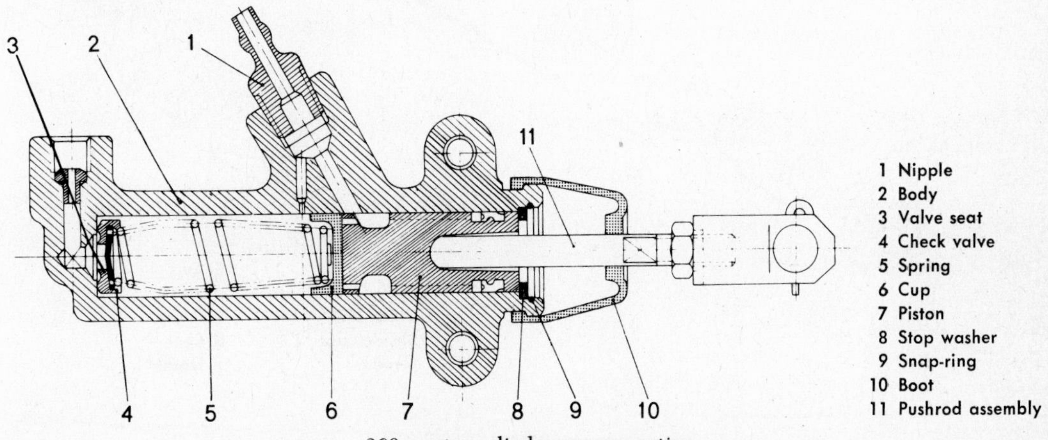

360 master cylinder—cross-section

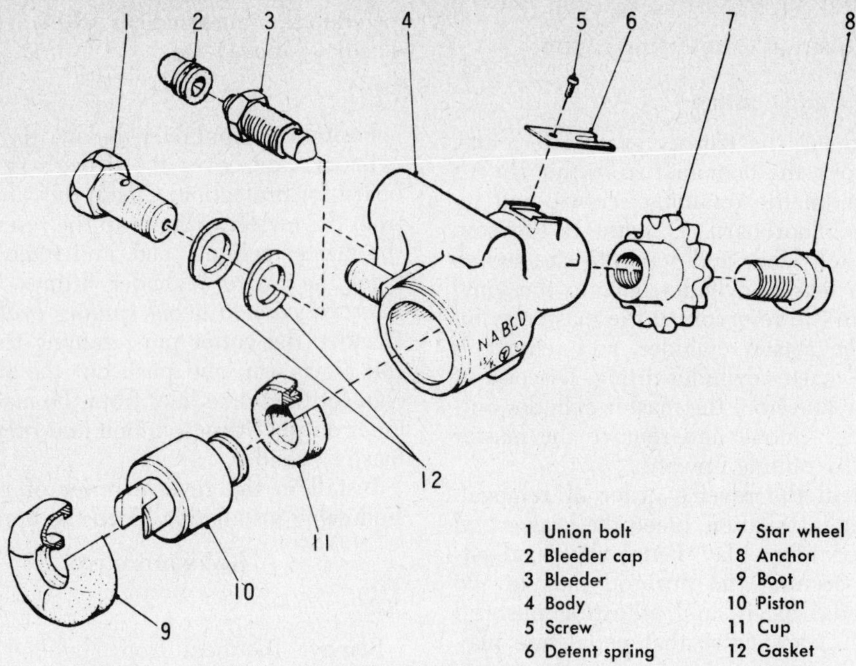

360 front wheel cylinder—exploded view

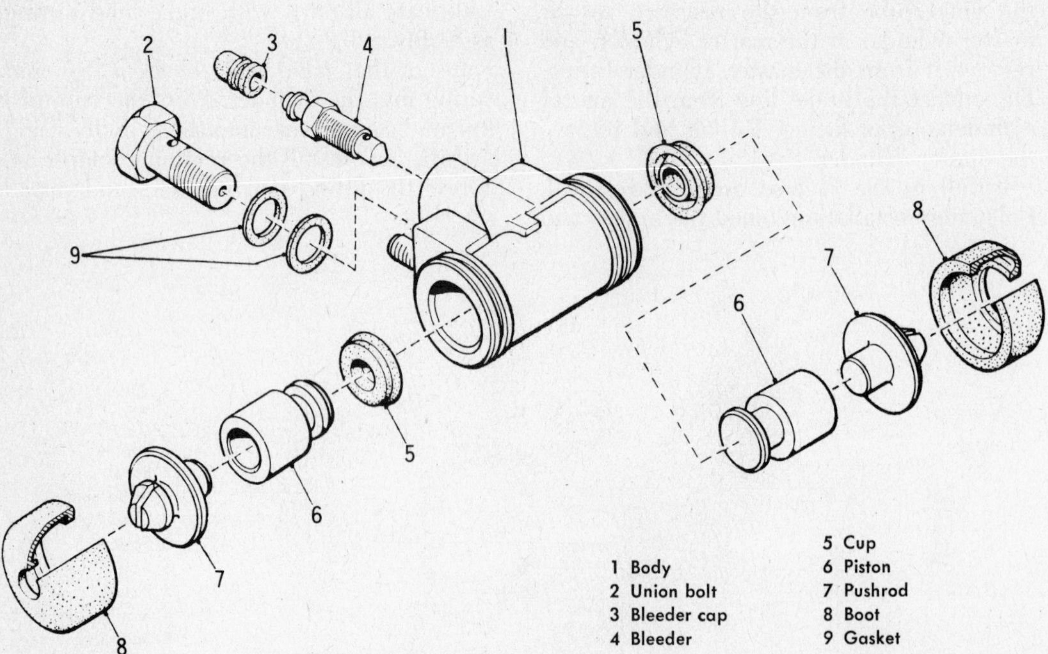

360 rear wheel cylinder—exploded view

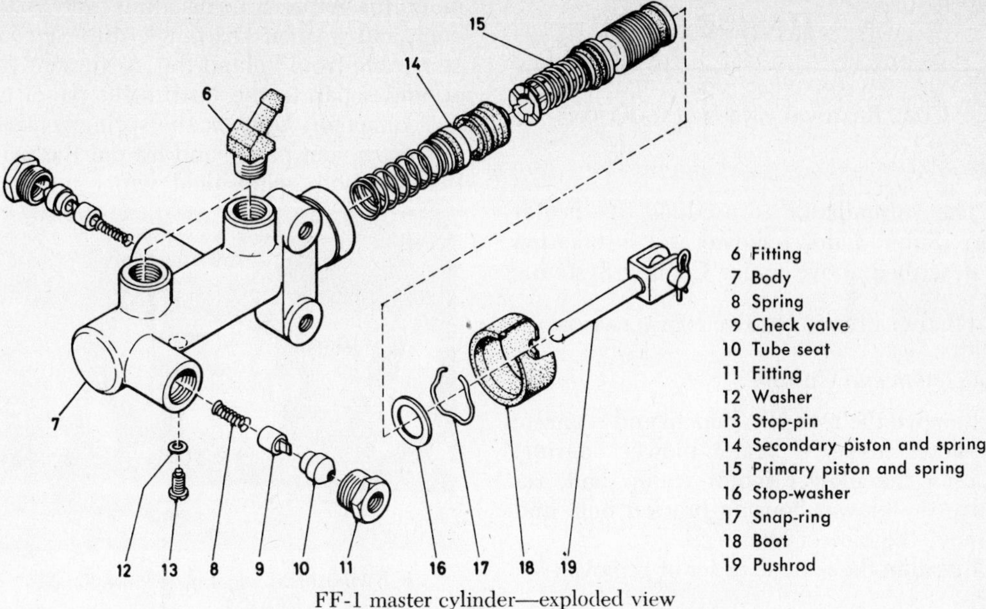

FF-1 master cylinder—exploded view

FF-1

Remove the boot from the end of the master cylinder. Unscrew and remove all fittings from the cylinder body. Remove the stop-pin from the lower portion of the body. Press the pushrod into the cylinder, and pry out the snap-ring retaining the stop washer. Slowly release spring pressure, and remove all parts from the master cylinder bore.

Inspect all parts for excessive wear or damage. If the cylinder bore is excessively worn or scored, replace the entire assembly. Lubricate all parts with brake fluid during assembly.

Insert the check valves and springs into the master cylinder, and screw in the brake line fittings. Insert the springs and pistons into the cylinder bore in the reverse order of removal. Place the stop-washer in position, press the pistons into the bore using the pushrod, and install the retaining snap-ring over the stop washer. Install the stop pin in the lower portion of the body. Screw the reservoir fittings into the body, in the same position as they were previously installed. Snap the boot into position, and insert the pushrod.

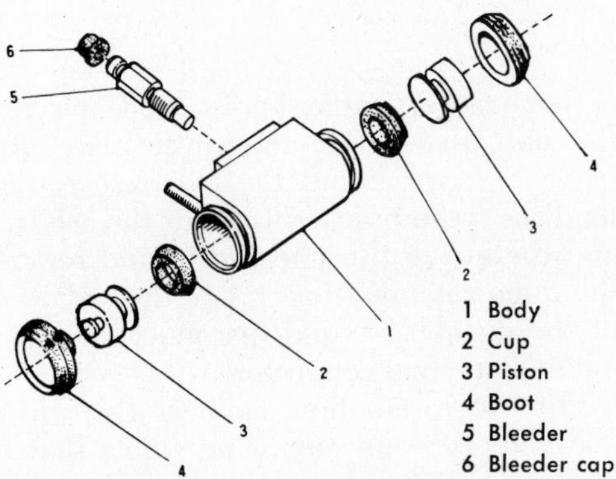

FF-1 front wheel cylinder—exploded view

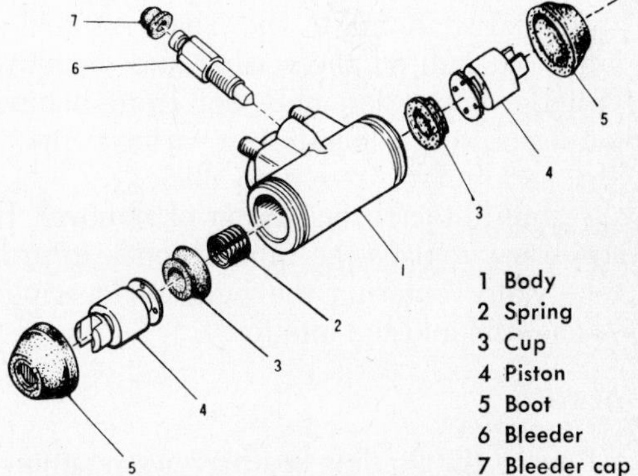

FF-1 rear wheel cylinder—exploded view

Heater

Core Removal and Installation

FF-1

The sub-radiator is used as the heater core. Sub-radiator removal and installation is described above under Cooling System.

Blower Removal and Installation

360 Sedan and Custom

Remove the rear seat bench, and separate all hoses from the heater blower housing. Loosen the blower motor clamp bolt, remove the blower housing bracket bolt, and remove the blower housing.

Install in the reverse order of removal.

FF-1

Disconnect the heater control cable at the blower housing, by removing the circlip which retains the cable, and the nut that retains the sheath to the bracket. Separate the blower motor wiring connectors at the motor, unclamp and remove the heater duct from the blower housing. Unbolt the sub-radiator shroud from the housing, remove the housing mounting bolts, and lift out of the vehicle.

Install in the reverse order of removal.

Windshield Wipers

Motor Removal and Installation

360

Disconnect the ground cable from the battery. Remove the windshield wiper arms, and the rubber boots over the wiper arm shafts. Remove the shaft retaining nuts, and pull off the washer and bushing. Pull the wiper assembly out from behind the dashboard, separate the wiring connectors, and remove from the vehicle.

Install in the reverse order of removal. If necessary, replace the rubber boots, to prevent water entering the windshield wiper mechanism and the interior.

FF-1

Loosen the Phillips head screws retaining the wiper arms, and remove the arms. Remove the wiper arm installing nut, rubber boot, and washer. Disconnect the speedometer cable from behind the instrument panel, and separate the instrument panel wiring connector. Unhook the spring retaining the instrument panel, and lift out the panel. Remove both windshield wiper motor re-

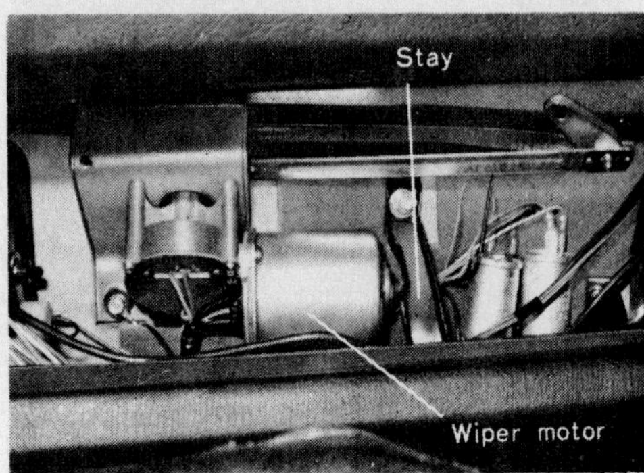

FF-1 windshield wiper motor installation

taining bolts, and slide the wiper assembly from behind the dashboard.

Install in the reverse order of removal.

Radio

Removal and Installation

360

Disconnect the wiring connectors and antenna lead from the radio, below the dashboard. Remove the retaining bolts from both sides of the radio, and slide it out of the dashboard.

Install in the reverse order of removal. Following installation, extend the antenna fully, and adjust the antenna trimmer as follows: Adjust the tuner to a station in the area of 1400 kc. Turn the antenna trimmer screw until optimum reception is achieved. Should there be no station in the area of 1400 kc, adjust the trimmer until static is loudest.

FF-1

Remove the radio knobs, and unscrew the nuts that retain the cover plate. Remove the cover, and the two screws that hold the radio bracket. Lift out the ash tray and the heater duct behind it, and remove the radio retaining bolt. Slide the radio out of the dashboard, and disconnect the wiring and antenna connectors.

Prior to installation, connect the wiring and antenna connectors, and adjust the antenna trimmer as described above. Install in the reverse order of removal.

TOYOTA SECTION

Index

Introduction

The Toyota Motor Sales Co., Ltd., has been producing automobiles since 1935. The Toyota line imported into the United States currently includes the Corolla, Corona, Corona Mk. II, Crown, Celica sports coupe, four wheel drive Land Cruiser, and the Hi-Lux pickup truck.

Toyota is now second in the sales of imported cars in the U.S. A. reputation for quality, reliability, and economy, originally established by the RT43 and RT52 series Coronas in the mid 1960's, has made Toyota a major force in the imported car marketplace. During the past years Toyota has greatly enlarged its potential with an expanded line of models for the United States market.

Every vehicle in Toyota's lineup is a conventional, but well-executed design. All are front engine, rear wheel drive designs with four or six cylinder inline, water cooled engines. All are equipped with four-speed or optional automatic transmissions, coupled to a live axle at the rear. All of the passenger cars are equipped with disc brakes at the front. Many features are included as standard equipment, such as reclining bucket seats, carpeting, and tinted windows.

Model Identification

Corolla sedan, KE10

Corolla Sprinter, KE15

Corolla wagon, KE16

Corolla sedan, KE20, TE21

Corolla coupe KE25, TE27

Corolla wagon, KE26, TE28

Corona sedan, RT43

Corona coupe, RT52

Corona sedan, RT83

Corona Mark II coupe, RT72

Corona coupe, RT93

Corona Mark II sedan, RT62

Corona Mark II wagon, RT78

Crown sedan, MS45

Lite Stout, RK series

Crown wagon, MS47

HiLux, RN series

Crown sedan, MS55

Land Cruiser, FJ40

Crown wagon, MS53

Land Cruiser wagon, FJ55

Vehicle and Engine Identification

Model/Year	*Series Identification Number*	*Engine Identification Code*
Corolla 1968-70		
Sedan	KE10	K-C, 3K-C
Sprinter	KE15	K-C, 3K-C
Station Wagon	KE16	K-C, 3K-C
Corolla 1971-72		
Sedan	KE20	3K-C
	TE21	2T-C
Coupe	KE25	3K-C
	TE27	2T-C
Station Wagon	KE26	3K-C
	TE28	2T-C
Corona 1965-69		
Sedan	RT43	3R-B, 3R-C
Coupe (from 1967)	RT52	3R-C
Corona 1970-72		
Sedan	RT83	8R-C
Coupe (from 1971)	RT93	8R-C
Corona Mark II 1969-72		
Sedan	RT62	8R-C
Coupe	RT72	8R-C
Station Wagon	RT78	8R-C
Celica ST 1971-72		
Coupe	RA20	8R-C
Crown 1966-68		
Sedan	MS45	2M
Station Wagon	MS47	2M
Crown 1969-71		
Sedan	MS55	2M
Station Wagon	MS53	2M
Crown 1972		
Sedan	MS63	4M
Coupe	MS65	4M
Station Wagon	MS75	4M
Lite Stout		
½ ton Pickup	RK41, RK43	3R
Hi-Lux 1969-72		
½ ton Pickup	RN11, RN12	8R-C
Land Cruiser 1965-68		
Soft Top/Hard Top	FJ40	F
Soft Top	FJ42	F
Soft Top	FJ43	F
Utility Wagon	FJ45	F
Land Cruiser 1969-72		
Soft Top/Hard Top	FJ40	FA
Station Wagon	FJ55	FA

Engine Identification

Engine Code	Cu. In. Displacement (cc)	Number of Cylinders	Type
K-C	65.7 (1,077)	4	ohv
3K-C	71.1 (1,166)	4	ohv
2T-C	96.9 (1,588)	4	ohv
8R-C	113.4 (1,858)	4	ohc
3-R, 3R-B, 3R-C	115.8 (1,897)	4	ohv
2M	137.5 (2,253)	6	ohc
4M	158.6 (2,600)	6	ohc
F, FA	236.7 (3,878)	6	ohv

Vehicle and Engine Serial Number Identification

The vehicle identification plate is located in the engine compartment, usually on the inner right front fender well. In addition, the chassis number is stamped on the cowl (unit construction bodies), or frame rail (vehicles with separate frames).

Engine Number Identification

The engine identification plate is located on the right side of the cylinder block, below No. 1 spark plug or directly below the oil filter (Crown only).

Engine serial number—except Crown

Engine serial number—Crown

General Engine Specifications

Engine	Cu. In. Displacement (cc)	Carburetion	Developed Horsepower SAE @ rpm	Developed Torque (ft. lbs.) @ rpm	Bore x Stroke (in.)	Compression Ratio	Normal Oil Pressure (psi)
K-C	65.7 (1,077)	2 bbl.	60@6,000	61.5@3,800	2.95 x 2.40	9.0:1	51-63
3K-C	71.1 (1,166)	2 bbl.	73@6,000	74.2@3,800	2.95 x 2.60	9.0:1	51-63
2T-C	96.9 (1,588)	2 bbl.	102@6,000	101@3,800	3.35 x 2.76	8.5:1	N.A.
8R-C	113.4 (1,858)	2 bbl.	108@5,500	117@3,600	3.39 x 3.15	9.0:1	57-71
3-R	115.8 (1,897)	2 bbl.	95@5,000	110@3,400	3.46 x 3.07	8.0:1	53-61
3R-B, 3R-C	115.8 (1,897)	2 bbl.	90@4,600	110@2,600	3.46 x 3.07	8.0:1	53-61
2M	137.5 (2,253)	2 bbl.	115@5,200	127@3,600	2.95 x 3.35	8.8:1	57-71
4M	158.6 (2,600)	2 bbl.	140@5,200	N.A.	N.A.	8.0:1	N.A.
F	236.7 (3,878)	1 bbl.	145@4,000	217@2,000	3.54 x 4.00	7.8:1	44-50
FA	236.7 (3,878)	2 bbl.	155@4,000	230@2,000	3.54 x 4.00	7.8:1	44-50

Tune-up Specifications

Engine Code	Spark Plugs Type	Spark Plugs Gap (in.)	Distributor Point dwell (deg. ±2)	Distributor Point gap (in.)	Basic Ignition Timing (deg.)*	Cranking Comp. Pressure (psi)	Valves Clearance (in.)-Hot Intake	Valves Clearance (in.)-Hot Exhaust	Valves Intake Opens (deg.)	Idle Speed (rpm) Standard	Idle Speed (rpm) Auto.
K-C	W200T30	.030	52	.016-.020	5A	171	.008	.014	16B	650	650
3K-C	W200T30	.030	52	.031	5A	170	.008	.012	N.A.	650	650
2T-C	W200T30	.030	52	.016-.020	5B	160	.007	.013	16B	750	650
8R-C	W200T30	.030	52	.016-.020	TDC	164	.008	.014	15B	650	650
3-R	W200T30	.030	52	.016-.020	12B	156	.008	.014	18B	550	550
3R-B	W200T30	.030	52	.016-.020	12B	156	.008	.014	23B	550	550
3R-C	W200T30	.030	52	.016-.020	TDC①	156	.008	.014	10B	750	650
2M	W200T30	.030	41	.016-.020	TDC	156	.007	.010	16B	650	650
F, FA	②	.035	41	.016-.020	7B	145	.008	.014	17B	600	—

*—With engine idle set to specified speed
①—With automatic transmission, 5B
②—1967 and prior (up to engine no. 243297) use W175T6 (3/8 in. reach)
1968 and later (after engine no. 243298) use W175T30 (3/4 in. reach)
A—After top dead center
B—Before top dead center
TDC—Top dead center

CAUTION: General adoption of anti-pollution laws has changed the design of almost all car engine production to effectively reduce crankcase emission and terminal exhaust products. It has been necessary to adopt stricter tune-up rules, especially timing and idle speed procedures. Both of these values are peculiar to the engine and to its application, rather than to the engine alone. With this in mind, car manufacturers supply idle speed data for the engine and application involved. This information is clearly displayed in the engine compartment of each vehicle.

Firing Order

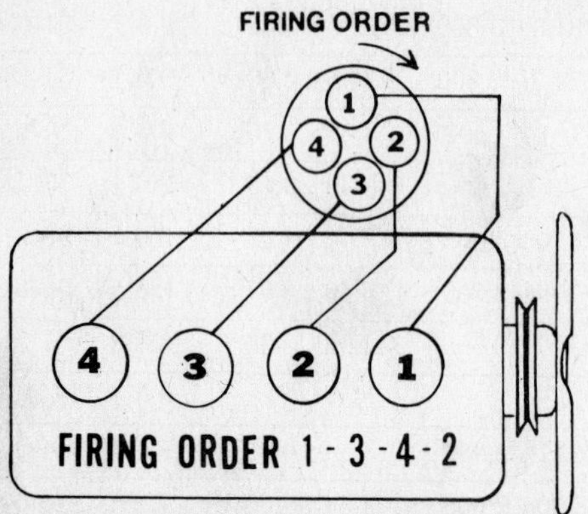

All four-cylinder engines

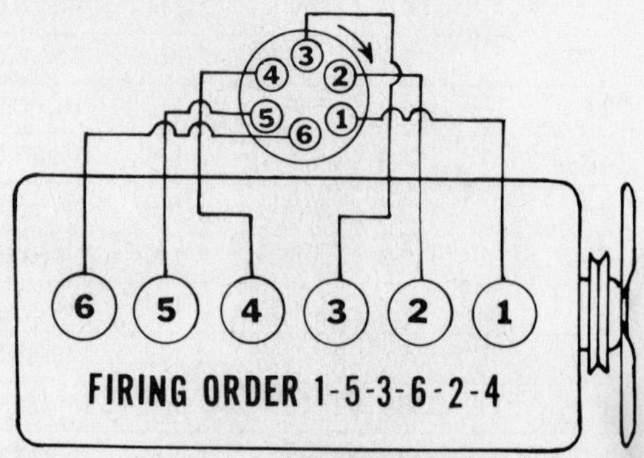

All six-cylinder engines

Engine Rebuilding Specifications

Engine Model	Main Bearing Journal Dia. (in.)	Con Rod Bearing Journal Dia. (in.)	Camshaft Journal Dia. (in.)	Cylinder Bore Dia. (in.)	Piston Ring Side Clearance (in.)	Piston Ring End-Gap (in.)	Main Bearing oil Clearance (in.)	Rod Bearing oil Clearance (in.)	Crankshaft End-play (in.)	Maximum Runout of Flywheel (in.)	Piston to Bore Clearance (in.)	Con Rod to Crankpin Side-play (in.)
K-C	1.9585-1.9685	1.6526-1.6535	1.7011-1.7018/1st 1.6913-1.6920/2nd 1.6814-1.6823/3rd 1.6716-1.6722/4th	2.955-2.957	.001-.003/1st .0008-.002/2nd .0006-.002/3rd	.006-.014	.0006-.0016 Limit .004	.0006-.0016 Limit .004	.0016-.0087 Limit .0118	.008	.001-.002	.004-.008
3K-C	1.9675-1.9685	1.6525-1.6535	1.7010-1.7020/1st 1.6910-1.6920/2nd 1.6810-1.6820/3rd 1.6710-1.6720/4th	2.952-2.955	.0011-.0027/1st .0007-.0023/2nd .0006-.0023/3rd	.006-.014	.0005-.0015 Limit .004	.0006-.0015 Limit .004	N.A.	.008	.001-.002	.004-.008
2T-C	2.2829-2.2834	1.8890-1.8900	N.A.	3.346-3.348	.0008-.0024	.004-.012	.0012-.0024	.0008 .0020	.003-.007	N.A.	.0024-.0031	.0063-.0102
8R-C	2.3613-2.3622	2.0857-2.0866	1.3768-1.3778	3.3857-3.3861 ③	.001-.003/1st .001-.003/2nd .001-.003/3rd	.004-.012	.0008-.0020 Limit .003	.0008-.0020 Limit .003	.002-.010 Limit .012	.008	.001-.002	.0043-.0097
3R 3R-B 3R-C	2.3634-2.3640	2.1648-2.1654	1.8291-1.8297/1st 1.8192-1.8198/2nd 1.8094-1.8100/3rd 1.7996-1.8002/4th 1.7898-1.7904/5th	3.4645-3.4651	.0012-.0027/1st .0012-.0027/2nd .0010-.0027/3rd	.0078-.0158/1st .0059-.0137/2nd .0059-.0137/3rd	.0008-.0022	.0010-.0024	.002-.009	.008	.0012-.0020	.0067-.0110
2M	2.3616-2.3622	2.0466-2.0472	1.3771-1.3778	2.9527-2.9535 ①	.0012-.0028/1st .0008-.0024/2nd oil ring-O	compression rings .006-.014 oil rings .008-.020	.0007-.0017 Limit .003	.0006-.002 Limit .003	.0020-.0100	.008	.0012-.0020	.0043-.0097
F, FA	2.6366-2.6378/1 2.6957-2.6969/2 2.7547-2.7559/3 2.8138-2.8150/4	2.1252-2.1260	1.8880-1.8888/1st 1.8289-1.8297/2nd 1.7699-1.7707/3rd 1.7108-1.7116/4th	3.5415-3.5435 ②	.0016-.0031/1st .0016-.0031/2nd .0016-.0031/3rd .0016-.0033/4th	.0059-.0177/1st .0059-.0157/2nd .0059-.0177/3rd .0059-.0157/4th	.0012-.0018 Limit .004	.0008-.0024 Limit .004	.0012-.0051	.008	.0012-.0020	.004-.009

①—Bore diameter covers total range of No. 1 and No. 2 sizes.

②—Bores marked "O." Other sizes:

Mark	*Size*
1	3.5515-3.5535
2	3.5615-3.5635
3	3.5715-3.5735
4	3.5815-3.5835

③—For 85.965 mm. pistons.

Valves

Engine Code	Valve Seat Angle (deg.)	Valve Stem Diameter (in.)		Valve Seat Width (in.)		Valve Face Width (in.)		Valve Springs										*Stem to Guide Clearance (in.)
								Free Lgth. (in.)		Installed Lgth. (in.)				Installed Press. (lbs.)				
										Intake		Exhaust		Intake		Exhaust		
		Intake	Exhaust	Intake	Exhaust	Intake	Exhaust	Inner	Outer	Inner	Outer	Inner	Outer	Inner	Outer	Inner	Outer	
K-C	45	.313	.313	.055	.059	.031	.035	—	1.76	—	1.51	—	1.51	—	70.1	—	70.1	.0030 .0010-
3K-C	45	.3139- .3143	.3134- .3145	.056	.059	.031	.035	—	1.83	—	1.52	—	1.52	—	N.A.	—	N.A.	.0010- .0020
2T-C	45	.3138- .3142	.3138- .3142	.055	.055	.020	.028	—	1.66	—	1.48	—	1.48	—	58.4	—	58.4	.0012- .0028
8R-C	45	N.A.	N.A.	.055	.055	.028	.028	1.74	1.83	1.49	1.65	1.47	1.61	12.1	46.5	15.6	.0014-46.5 .0030	
3R 3R-B 3R-C	45	.354	.354	.055	.055	.030	.040	1.78	2.16	1.56	1.87	1.56	1.88	14.7	53.9	14.0	53.0	.0016- .0028
2M	45	.3140- .3143	.3120- .3140	.055	.055	.031	.039	1.79	2.06	1.54	1.65	1.54	1.66	11.9	67.8	11.4	66.5	.0014- .0027
F FA	45	.3138- .3144	.3134- .3140	.055	.055	.031	.039	1.79	2.08	1.59	1.71	1.60	1.72	7.9	45.0	7.5	44.0	.0014- .0028

*—All models are equipped with removable valve guides

Carburetor Specifications

Engine Code	Float Level (in.)	Throttle Bore Diameter (in.)		Main Jet Diameter (in.)		Primary Venturi inner diameter (in.)		Secondary Venturi inner diameter (in.)		Power Valve operating vacuum (in. Hg.)	Throttle Valve fully closed angle (deg.)		Choke Valve fully closed angle (deg.)	Power Jet diameter (in.)	Pump Jet diameter (in.)
		Primary	Secondary	Primary	Secondary	Main	Secondary	Main	Secondary		Primary	Secondary			
K-C	.256	1.102	1.102	.0425	.0689	.827	.945	.276	.315	3.15-3.94	N.A.	N.A.	N.A.	.0276	N.A.
2T-C*	.138	1.18	1.33	.0425	N.A.	N.A.	N.A.	N.A.	N.A.	N.A.	N.A.	N.A.	N.A.	N.A.	N.A.
8R-C	.037	1.34	1.42	.016	.053	.98	.35	1.02	.28	3.54-3.94	9	20	20	.032	.020
3R	N.A.	1.260	1.378	.045	.067	1.945	1.102	N.A.	N.A.	N.A.	N.A.	N.A.	N.A.	.031	.021
3R-B 3R-C	.867	1.261	1.379	.043	.057	.946	.394	1.103	.394	3.15-3.94	7	20	10	.24	.020
2M	.374	1.38	1.38	.04	.067	.98	1.18	.575	.614	3.1-3.9	N.A.	N.A.	N.A.	.036	.012
F, FA	.315	1.574	1.574	.059	.106	1.220	1.378	.344	.394	3.15	N.A.	N.A.	N.A.	.087	.024

*—2T-C Idle screw adjustment: 2 ⅝ turns

Distributor Specifications

Engine Code	Centrifugal Advance: Start Degrees @ rpm	Centrifugal Advance: Intermediate Degrees @ rpm	Centrifugal Advance: End Degrees @ rpm	Vacuum Advance: Start Degrees @ ins. Hg.	Vacuum Advance: Intermediate Degrees @ ins. Hg.	Vacuum Advance: End Degrees @ ins. Hg.
K-C	0 @ 500	11-13 @ 1,650	13-15 @ 3,000	0 @ 4.34	2.5-5.5 @ 5.91	6.5-9.5 @ 10.65
3K-C	0 @ 500	11-13 @ 1,650	13-15 @ 3,000	0 @ 4.52	2.5-5.5 @ 5.91	6.5-9.5 @ 10.62
2T-C	0 @ 500	8.5 @ 1,000	16.5 @ 2,300	0 @3.15	4 @ 4.72	9 @ 6.10
8R-C	0 @ 600	12.5-14.5 @ 1,100	19-21 @ 2,300	0 @ 3.94	5-7 @ 9.84	6-8 @ 12.60
3R	0 @ 480	8.5-10.5 @ 1,200	13-15 @ 2,500	0 @ 2.36	7.7-9.7 @ 7.09	10-12 @ 9.84
3R-B	0 @ 480	6-8 @ 1,000	13-15 @ 2,500	0 @ 2.36	5-7 @ 4.73	10-12 @ 9.84
3R-C	0 @ 480	8.7-10.7 @ 1,000	16.5-18.5 @ 2,500	0 @ 2.36	5-7 @ 4.73	10-14 @ 9.84
2M	0 @ 480	5.5-7.5 @ 900	9-11 @ 2,200	0 @ 3.70	7-9 @ 9.8	9-11 @ 13.4
F FA	0 @ 500	5.5-7.5 @ 1,000	14-16 @ 2,200	0 @ 4.1	5.2-7.2 @ 7.8	7.5-9.5 @ 11.8

Torque Specifications*

Engine Code	Cylinder Head bolts	Main Bearing bolts	Rod Bearing bolts	Flywheel bolts	Intake Manifold bolts	Exhaust Manifold bolts	Rocker Arm bolts	Camshaft Bearing Caps
K-C	36-48	39-47	29-37	39-48	14-22	14-22	13-16	—
3K-C	39-48	39-48	29-38	39-48	14-22	14-22	13-16	—
2T-C	52-64	52-64	30-36	42-48	7-12	7-12	N.A.	—
8R-C	75-85	72-80	42-48	43-48	20-25	20-25	12-17	—
3R 3R-B 3R-C	80-85	75-80	43-51	43-49	18-30	14-22	15-15	—
2M	①	71-78	30-35	41-45	22-29	10-14	22-32	12-16
F FA	83-98	②	35-55	43-51	14-22	14-22	③	—

*—All values given in ft. lbs.
①—8mm bolts 11-15; 13mm bolts 54-61
②—No. 1,2 and 3 bearings 90-108; No. 4 bearing 76-94
③—8mm bolts 14-21; 10mm bolts 25-30

Tightening Sequences

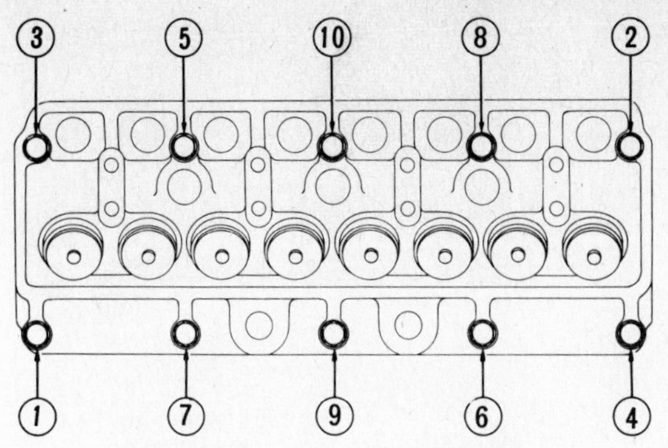

K-C, 3K-C cylinder head bolt removal

2M cylinder head bolt removal

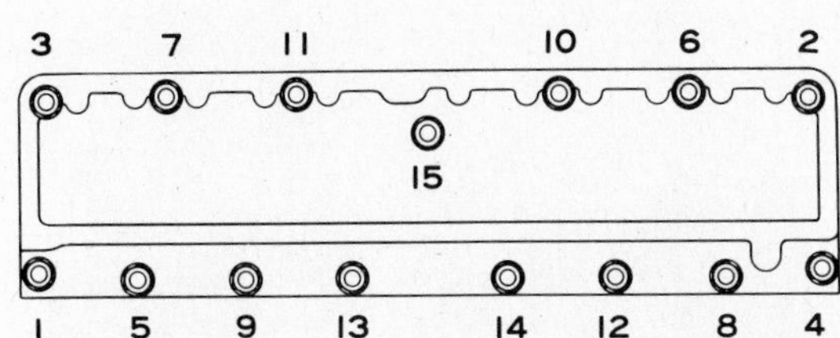

F, FA cylinder head bolt removal

2M cylinder head bolt tightening

8R-C cylinder head bolt removal

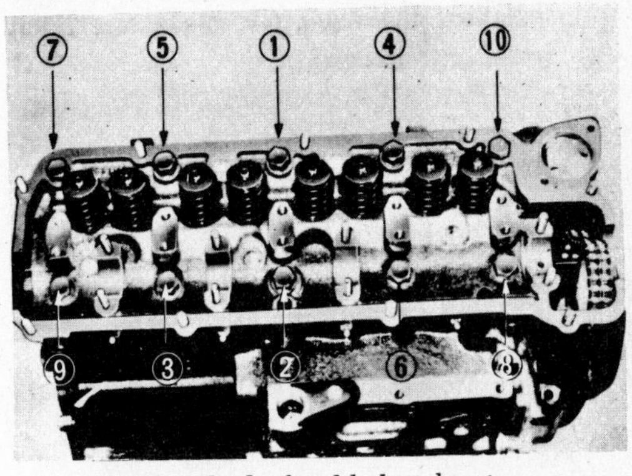

8R-C cylinder head bolt tightening

3R, 3R-B, 3R-C cylinder head bolt removal

3R, 3R-B, 3R-C cylinder head bolt tightening

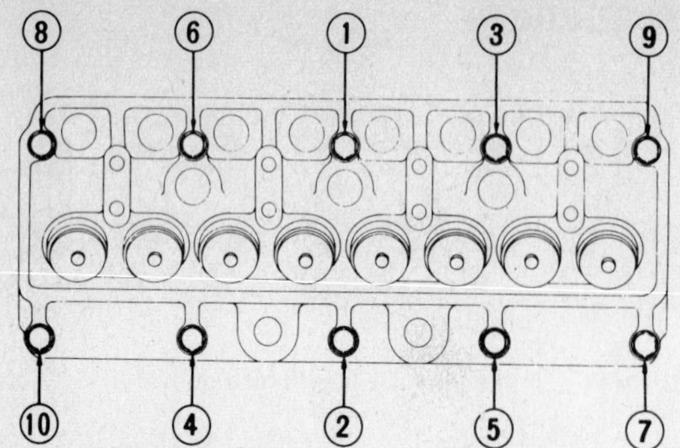

K-C, 3K-C cylinder head bolt tightening

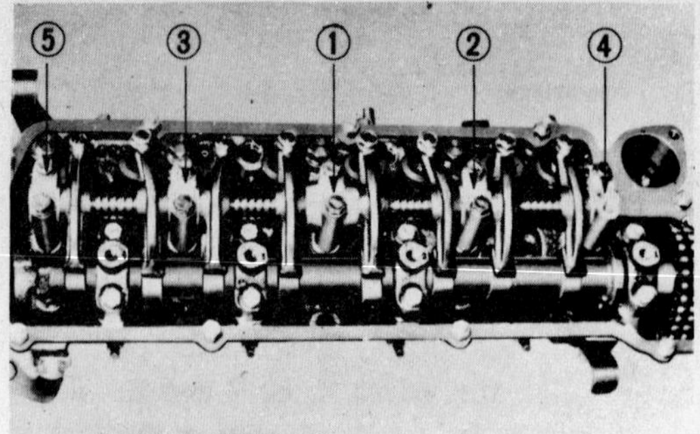

8R-C valve rocker support tightening

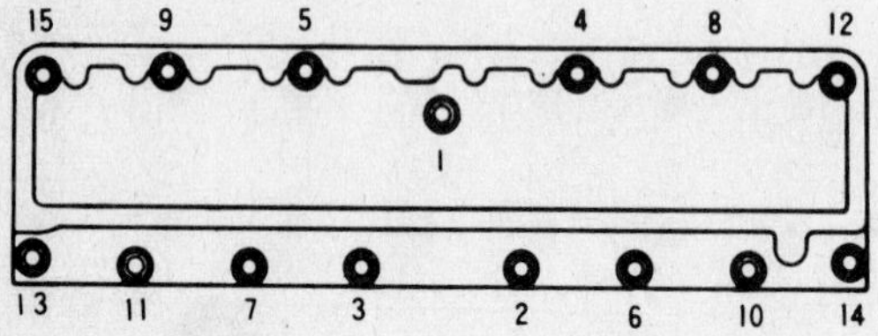

F, FA engine cylinder head bolt tightening

2M rocker shaft bolt removal

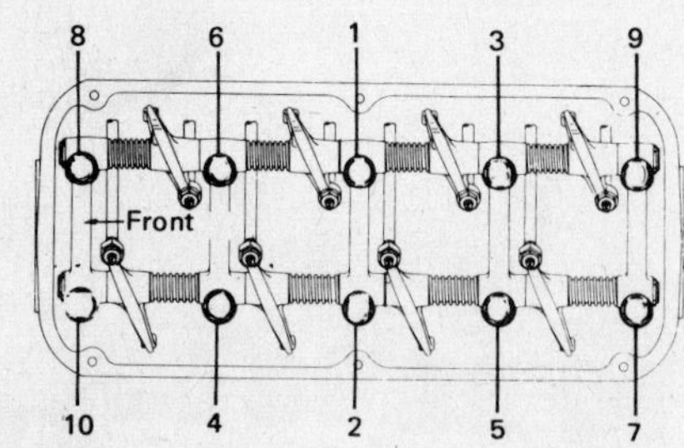

2T-C cylinder head bolt tightening

2M main cap tightening

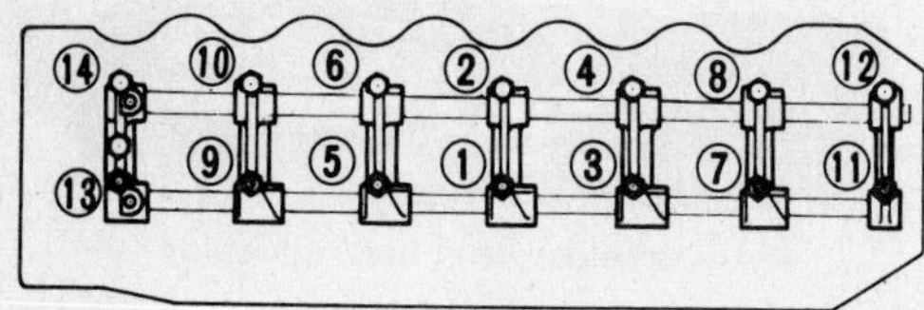

TORQUE: 3~4.5m-kg
(22~32 ft-lb)

2M engine cylinder head bolt tightening

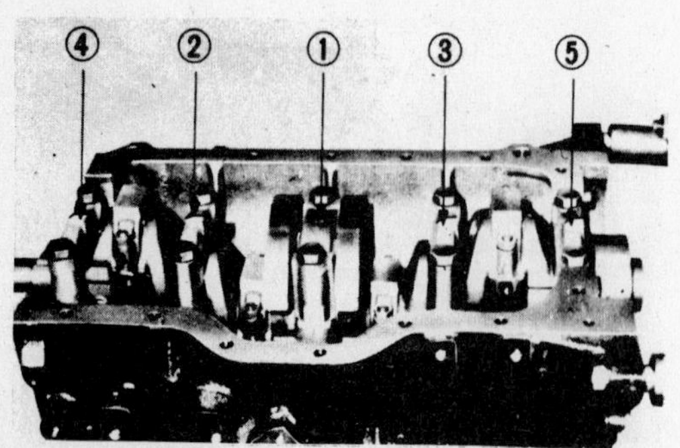

8R-C bearing cap tightening

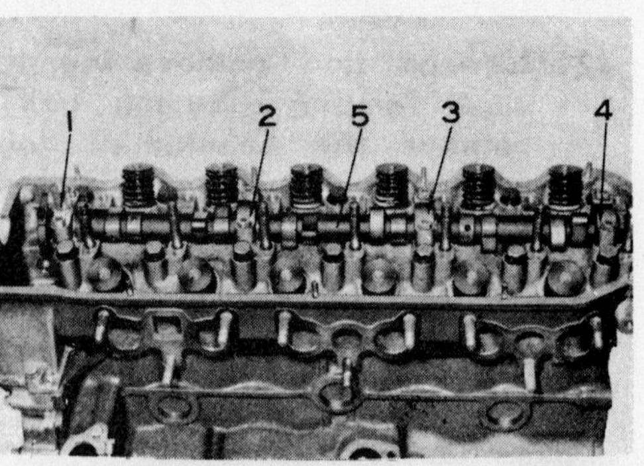

2M, 8R-C cam bearing removal

8R-C rocker shaft removal

Electrical Specifications

Engine Code	Battery: Capacity (Amp. hours)	Battery: Volts	Battery: Grounded Terminal	Starter Lock Test: Amp.	Starter Lock Test: Volts	Starter Lock Test: Torque (ft. lbs.)	Starter No Load Test: Amp.	Starter No Load Test: Volts	Starter No Load Test: RPM	Brush Spring Tension (oz.)
K-C	32	12	Negative	450	8.5	8.0	55	11	3,500	36.8-48.0
2T-C	35	12	Negative	470	7.7	9.5	50	11	5,000	21.0-47.0
8R-C	40①	12	Negative	550	7.0	10.0	45	11	6,000	36.8-48.0
3R 3R-B 3R-C	50	12	Negative	550	7.0	10.1	45	11	6,000	36.8-48.0
2M	40	12	Negative	380	7.7	7.2	50	11	3,000	41.0-46.0
F FA	50	12	Negative	430	7.3	10.5	45	11	3,500	36.0-38.0

①—60 amp. hour battery optional

Engine Code	Alternator Number	Output @ Alternator rpm	Field Relay: Point Gap (in.)	Field Relay: Spring Deflection (in.)	AC Regulator: Point Gap (in.)	AC Regulator: Armature Gap (in.)	AC Regulator: Volts to Close	AC Regulator: Volts @ 125°
K-C	N.A. ①	40 @ 3,500	.016-.047	.008-.018	.010-.012	.024-.032	4.5-5.8	13.5-14.5
	N.A. ②	25 @ 3,000	N.A.	.008-.024	.012-.018	.012	N.A.	N.A.
2T-C	N.A.	30 @ 1,100	N.A.	N.A.	.012-.018	N.A.	4.5-5.8	13.8-14.8
8R-C	N.A.	40 @ 3,500	.016-.047	.008-.018	.010-.018	.024-.031	4.5-5.8	13.8-14.8
3R 3R-B	27020-21011	40 @ 3,500	.016-.047	.008-.018	.010-.018	.024-.034	4.5-5.8	13.8-14.8
3R-C	27020-22010	25 @ 3,500	.016-.047	.008-.018	.010-.018	.024-.034	4.5-5.8	13.8-14.8
2M	N.A.	40 @ 3,500	.016-.047	.008-.024	.012-.018	.012	4.5-5.8	13.8-14.8
F FA	N.A.	40 @ 3,500	N.A.	N.A.	.010-.018	N.A.	N.A.	13.6-14.6

①—Early production
②—Late production

Capacities and Pressures

Model	Engine Model	Engine Crankcase Refill after Draining (qts.)		Transmission (qts.)		Transfer Case (qts.)	Drive Axle (pts.)	Fuel Tank (gals.)	Cooling System with Heater (qts.)	Normal Fuel Pressure (psi)	Maximum Coolant Pressure (psi)
		With Filter	Without Filter	4-Speed Manual	Automatic						
Crown	2M	5.6	4.8	2.1	6.7	—	2.6	17.2①	10.8②	3.6-5.0	11-15
	5R	5.1	4.2	2.1	6.7	—	2.6	17.2①	7.2	2.8-4.3	7
Land Cruiser	F, FA	9.0	7.4	3.3	—	1.8	2.6③	18.5④	17.7⑤	3.4-4.8	4⑩
Corona Mark II	8R-C	5.3	4.3	2.1	7.4	—	2.1	13.7	7.8⑥	2.8-4.3	11-15
Corolla	K-C	N.A.	2.9	N.A.	N.A.	—	N.A.	9.5	5.0	3.0-4.5	7.1
	3K-C	3.5	2.9	1.8	5.0	—	2.0	12.0⑦	5.6	N.A.	7
	2T-C	3.9	3.0	1.6	5.0	—	2.0	12.0⑦	6.8	N.A.	N.A.
Hi-Lux Pickup	8R-C	5.3	N.A.	1.8	—	—	2.2	12.1	8.8	N.A.	N.A.
Corona	3R-B	5.1	N.A.	2.1	N.A.	—	2.2	11.9⑧	N.A.	2.8-4.3	7
	3R-C	5.1	N.A.	2.1	N.A.	—	2.2	11.0⑨	9.0	2.8-4.3	7
	8R-C	5.6	4.6	2.1	7.4	—	2.2	13.2	8.4	2.8-4.3	11-15

①—Sedan, hardtop, wagon, and pickup 15.9 gals.
②—With reserve tank. Without reserve tank capacity is 9.6 qts.
③—Front and rear drive axles
④—Wagon 23.7 gals.
⑤—With front and rear heaters. Without heater capacity is 16 qts.
⑥—Without heater
⑦—Wagon capacity is 11.0 gals.
⑧—Four-door sedan. Hardtop holds 11.0 gals.
⑨—Hardtop
⑩—Pressure for FJ55 is 7 psi

Brake Specifications

Model	Brake Drum Diameter (in.)	Brake Disc Diameter (in.)	Master Cylinder Bore (in.)	Wheel Cylinder Bore (in.)	
				Front	Rear
Corona RT40	9.0	—	0.750	0.813-0.815	0.625-0.628
RT80	9.0	N.A.	0.751-0.753	0.876-① 0.878	0.625-0.627
RT83	9.0	N.A.	0.876-0.878	0.876-① 0.878	0.813-0.815
RT86	9.0	N.A.	0.751-0.753	0.876-① 0.878	0.688-0.690
Corona Mark II	9.0	9.5	0.875-0.877	0.875-0.877	0.688-0.689
Corolla	7.9	7.9	0.626	0.750②	0.687
Crown (Post 1967)	9.1	10.5	0.750-0.752	1.124-1.127	0.750-0.752
Land Cruiser	11.4	—	1.000-1.002	1.122-1.124	N.A.
Stout	11.4③	—	1.000-1.002	N.A.	N.A.
Hi-Lux	9.1	—	1.000-1.002	1.250-1.252	0.813-0.815

①—Disc cylinder bore is 2.002-2.004 in.
②—Disc cylinder bore is 1.75 in.
③—9.0 in. for rear brakes

Chassis and Wheel Alignment Specifications

Model	Chassis			Wheel Alignment			
	Wheel-base (ins.)	Track (ins.) Front	Track (ins.) Rear	Caster (degrees)	Camber (degrees)	Toe-in (ins.)	King-pin inclination (degrees)
Corona	95.7	51.2	50.4	20′	1°20′	0.16-0.24	6°55′
Corona Mark II	98.8	52.2	52.0	10+45′−15′	1°15′±30′	0.24-0.31	6°45′
Corolla	91.9	49.4	49.0	2 sedan and coupe, 1°40′ wagon	50′	0.12	7°55′
Crown	105.9	53.5①	54.3	−30′±30′②	25′±30′	0.16±0.04	7°20′
Land Cruiser	90.0③	55.3	55.1	1	1°	0.12-0.20	9°30′
Stout	110.2	54.7	53.2	1°30′	2°	0.12-0.16	7°
Hi-Lux	99.8	50.8	50.8	−20′	1°	0.24	7°15′

①—With disc brake front track is 53.9 in.
②—For MS53 series caster is −40′±30′. For MS57 series caster is −50′±30′.
③—For FJ43 wheelbase is 95.7 in. For FJ45 wheelbase is 116.1 in.

Fuses

Model	Circuit	Amps.
Corolla		
	1. Headlight high beam (R)	10
	2. Headlight high beam (L) and high beam indicator light	10
	3. Headlight low beam (R)	10
	4. Headlight low beam (L)	10
	5. Tail, parking, license plate, meter pilot, heater control, side marker lights	10
	6. Horns, stop light, and lock warning buzzer	20
	7. Cigarette lighter, interior light, and clock	20
	8. Heater, gauges, backup lights, and brake warning light	20
	9. Wiper and washer motors	15
	10. Turn signal lights	15
Corona		
	1. Headlight high beam (R) and high beam indicator light	10
	2. Headlight high beam (L)	10
	3. Headlight low beam (R)	10
	4. Headlight low beam (L)	10
	5. Tail, parking, license plate, and meter pilot lights	10
	6. Horns and stop lights	20
	7. Cigarette lighter, interior light, and clock	20
	8. Heater, gauge, and backup light	20
	9. Wiper and washer motors	15
	10. Turn signal lights	15
Corona Mark II		
	1. Headlight high beam (R)	10
	2. Headlight high beam (L)	10
	3. Headlight low beam (R)	10
	4. Headlight low beam (L)	10
	5. Parking, tail, and license plate lights	10
	6. Horn and stop light	20
	7. Cigarette lighter, clock, interior light, and meter pilot light	20
	8. Heater, backup light and gauges	20
	9. Wiper and washer motor	15
	10. Turn signal lights	15
Crown		
	1. Headlight low beam (L)	10
	2. Headlight low beam (R)	10
	3. Tail, license plate, and glove compartment lights	10
	4. Front parking lights	5
	5. Headlight high beam (L)	10
	6. Headlight high beam (R) and high beam indicator light	10
	7. Power window	30
	8. Meter pilot light	5
	9. Radio	5
	10. Cigarette lighter, clock, inspection light socket, horn, stop lights, interior lights and courtesy lights	20
	11. Heater	20
	12. Gauges and backup lights	5
	13. Turn signal lights and voltage regulator	10
	14. Wiper and washer motors	15
Land Cruiser		
	1. Headlights, combination meter light, interior light	20
	2. Horn, cigarette lighter, stop light	20
	3. Spare	20
	4. Fuel, temperature, oil pressure gauges	5
	5. Heater, wiper, and washer motors	15
	6. Turn signal lights, charging circuit	15
Hi-Lux		
	1. Headlights, parking lights, interior lights	20
	2. Horn, stop light, cigarette lighter	20
	3. Hazard warning lights	20
	4. Charge warning and oil pressure indicator lights, water temperature and fuel gauges and backup lights	5
	5. Wiper motor and heater	15
	6. Turn signal lights	15

Light Bulb Specifications

Model	*Usage*	*Wattage*
Corolla	Headlights	50/40
	Front turn signal	23/8
	License plate	7.5
	Backup	23
	Side turn signal	7.5
	Stop and tail	23/8
	Dome	4
	Front parking	3.4
	Rear parking	3.4
	Heater control indicator	3
Crown	Front turn signal	23/8
	Parking	7.5
	Tail and stop	23/8
	Back up	23
	Rear turn signal	23
	License plate	7.5
	Interior	6
	Trunk	10
	Engine	10
	Door	10
Hi-Lux	Headlight, outer	37.5/50
	Headlight, inner	37.5
	Parking	25/8
	Turn signal	25/8
	Rear combination	25/8
	Backup	25
	License plate	8
	Interior	10
Corona	Front turn signal and parking	23/8
	Front/rear side marker lights	8
	Stop, tail, rear turn signal	23/8
	Backup	23
	License plate	7.5
	Dome	10
Corona Mark II	Headlight, inner	37.5/50
	Headlight, outer	37.5/50
	Front/rear turn signal, backup	25
	Parking, side marker, tail	8
Land Cruiser	Headlight	50/40
	Parking	8
	Front turn signal	25/8
	Tail, stop	25/8
	License plate	10
	Backup	25

Wiring Diagrams

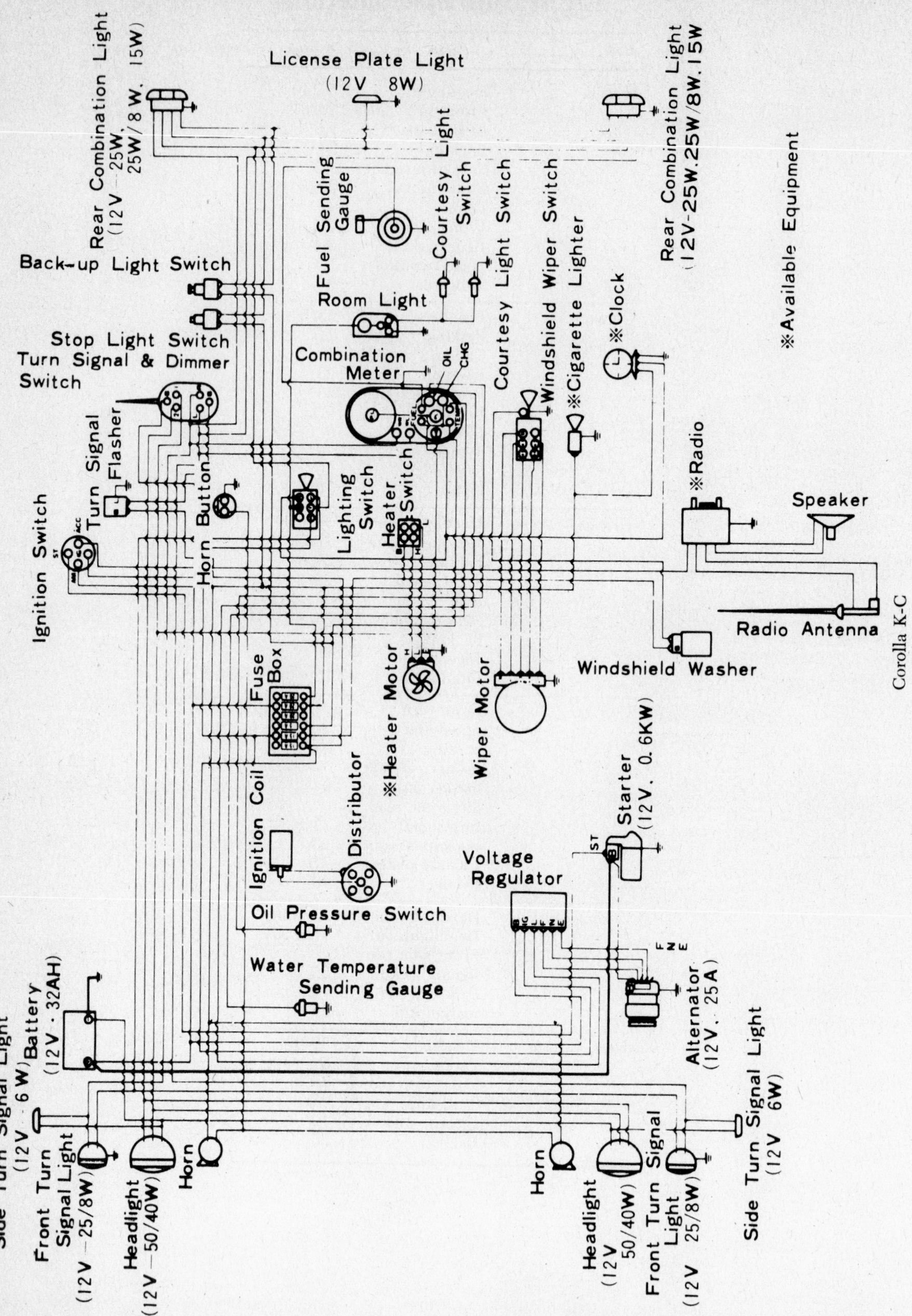

Corolla K-C

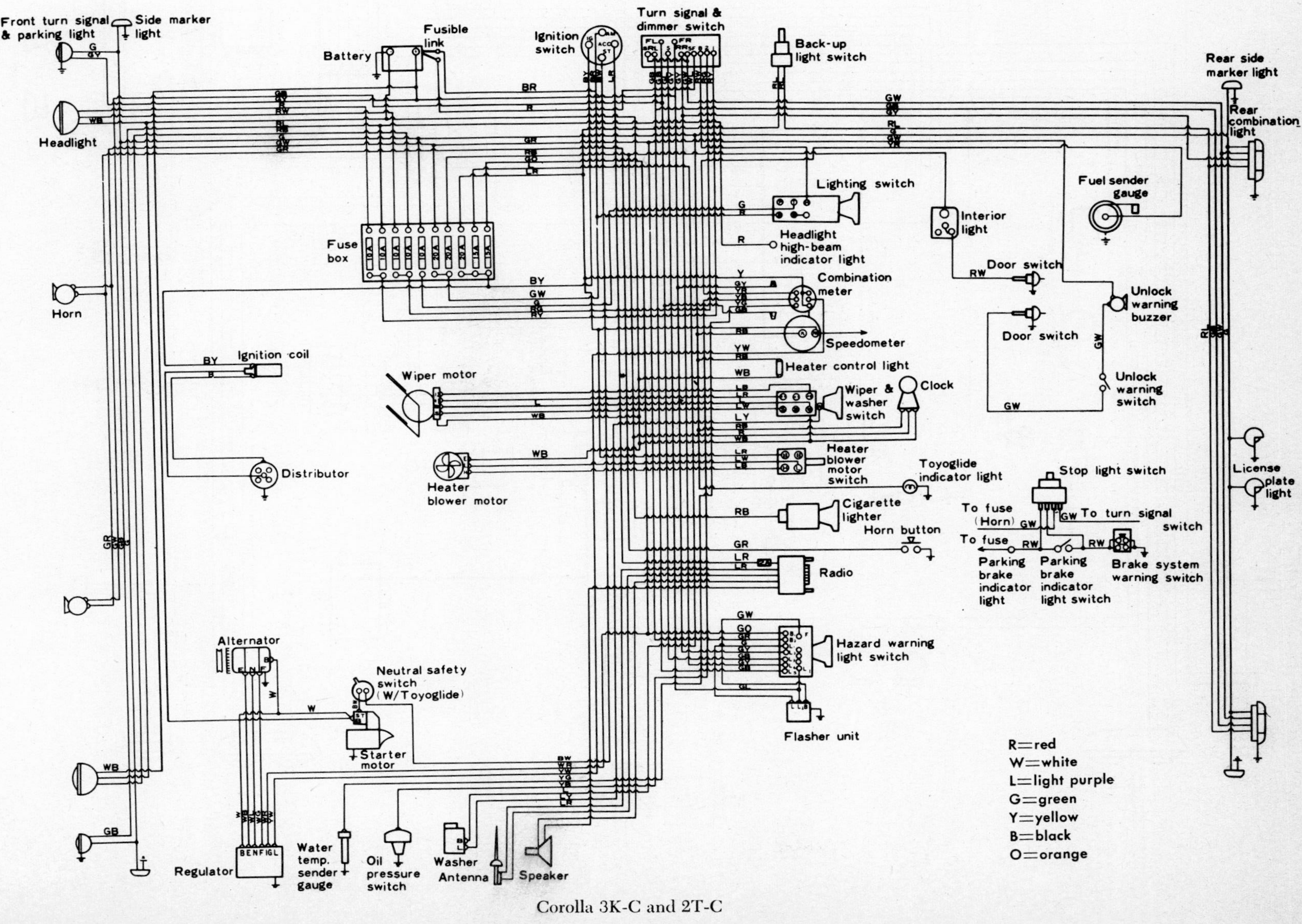

Corolla 3K-C and 2T-C

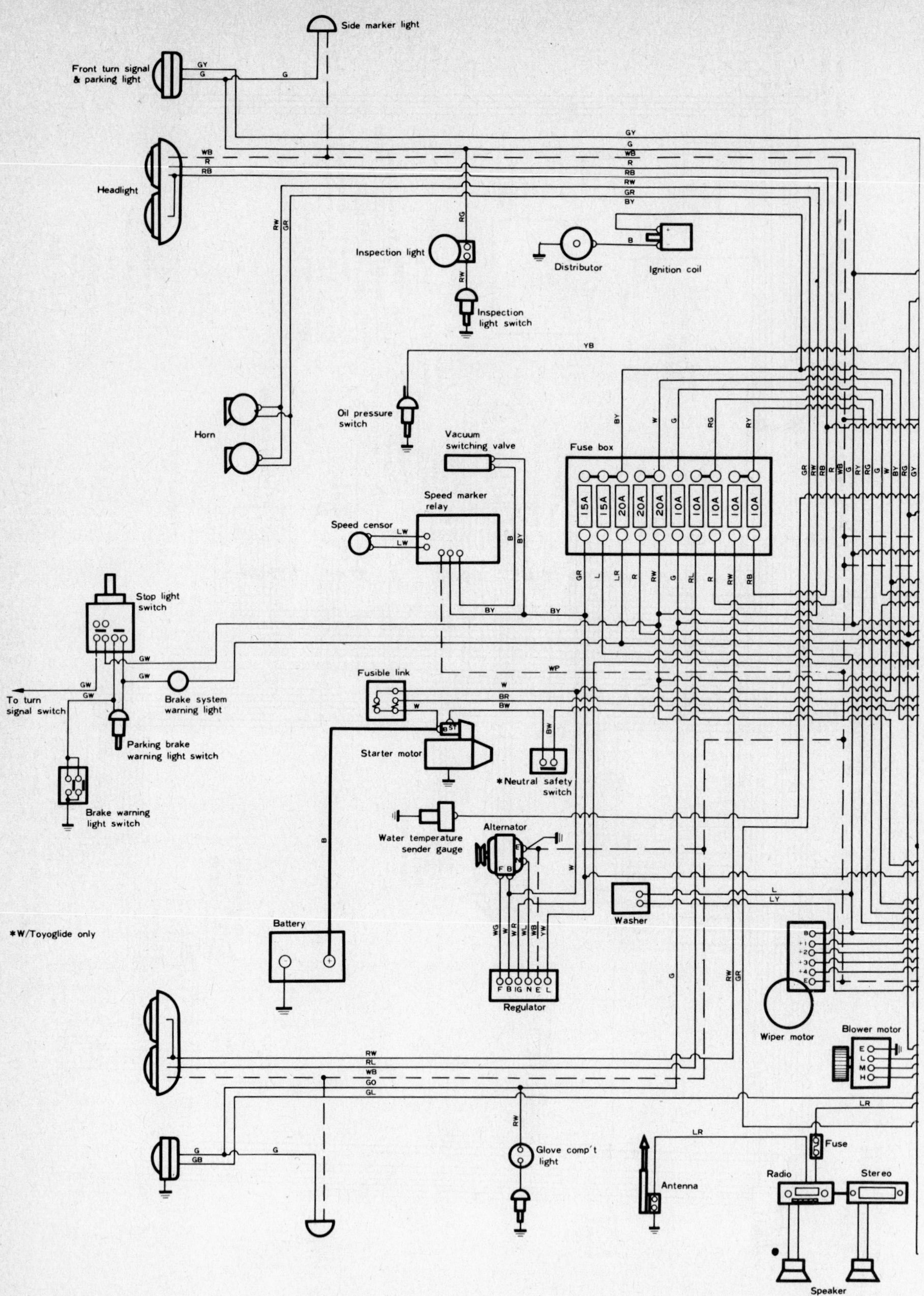
Side marker light
Front turn signal & parking light
Headlight
Inspection light
Distributor
Ignition coil
Inspection light switch
Oil pressure switch
Horn
Vacuum switching valve
Fuse box
Speed marker relay
Speed censor
Stop light switch
To turn signal switch
Brake system warning light
Parking brake warning light switch
Brake warning light switch
Fusible link
Starter motor
*Neutral safety switch
Water temperature sender gauge
Alternator
Washer
Battery
Regulator
Wiper motor
Blower motor
*W/Toyoglide only
Glove comp't light
Antenna
Fuse
Radio
Stereo
Speaker

Corona 8R-C

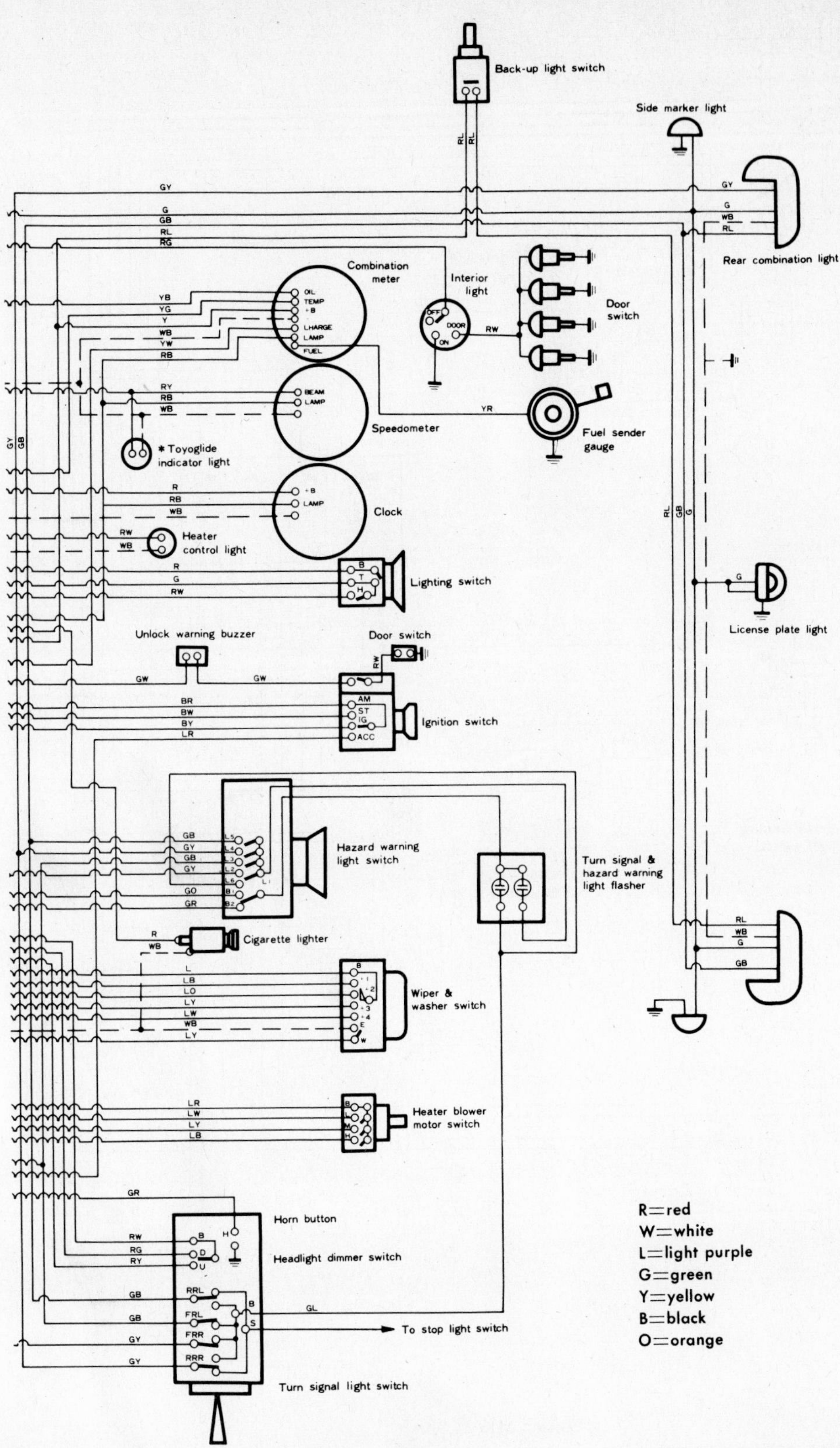
Back-up light switch
Side marker light
Rear combination light
Combination meter
Interior light
Door switch
Speedometer
Fuel sender gauge
* Toyoglide indicator light
Clock
Heater control light
Lighting switch
License plate light
Unlock warning buzzer
Door switch
Ignition switch
Hazard warning light switch
Turn signal & hazard warning light flasher
Cigarette lighter
Wiper & washer switch
Heater blower motor switch
Horn button
Headlight dimmer switch
To stop light switch
Turn signal light switch
R=red
W=white
L=light purple
G=green
Y=yellow
B=black
O=orange

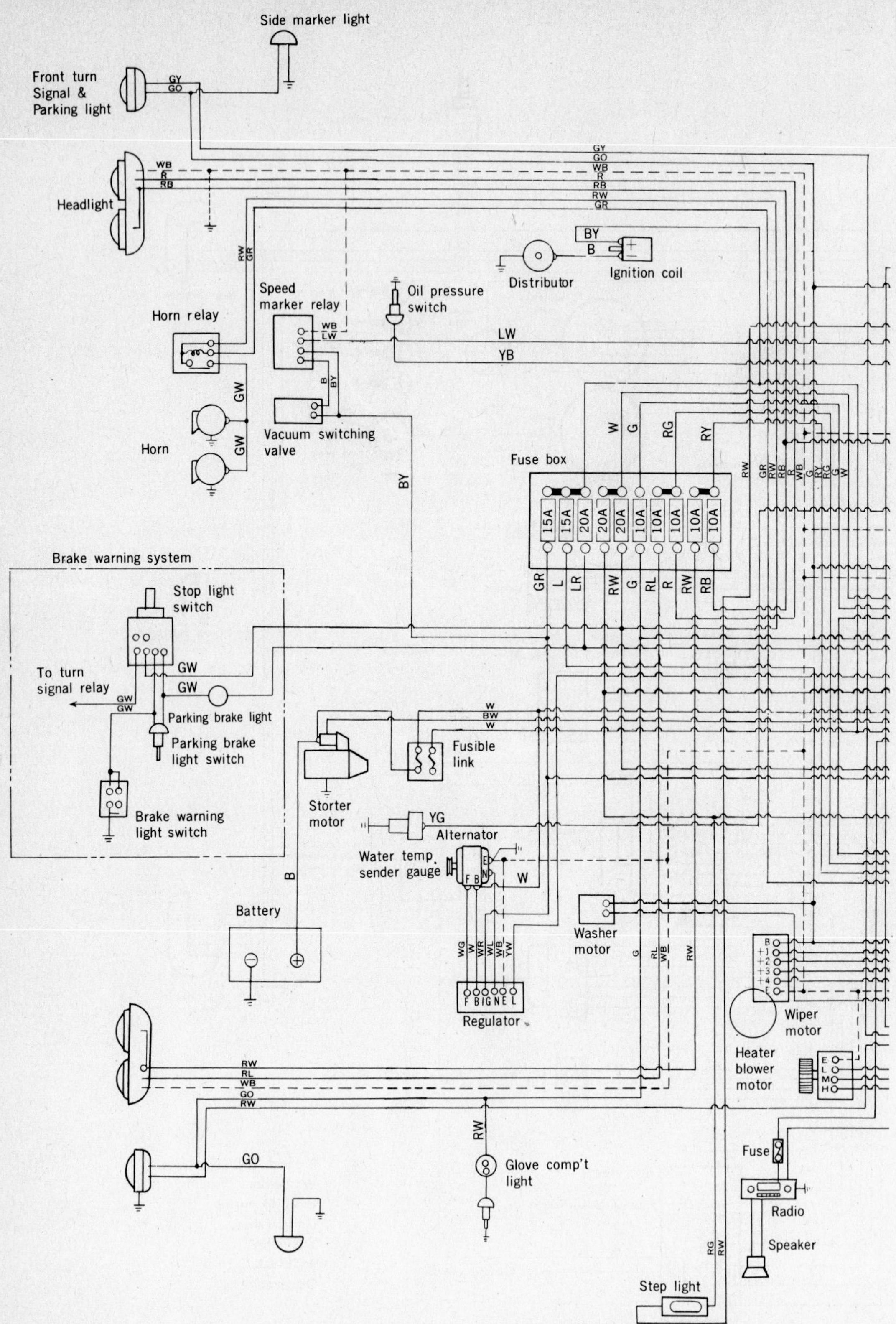

Corona MK. II 8R-C

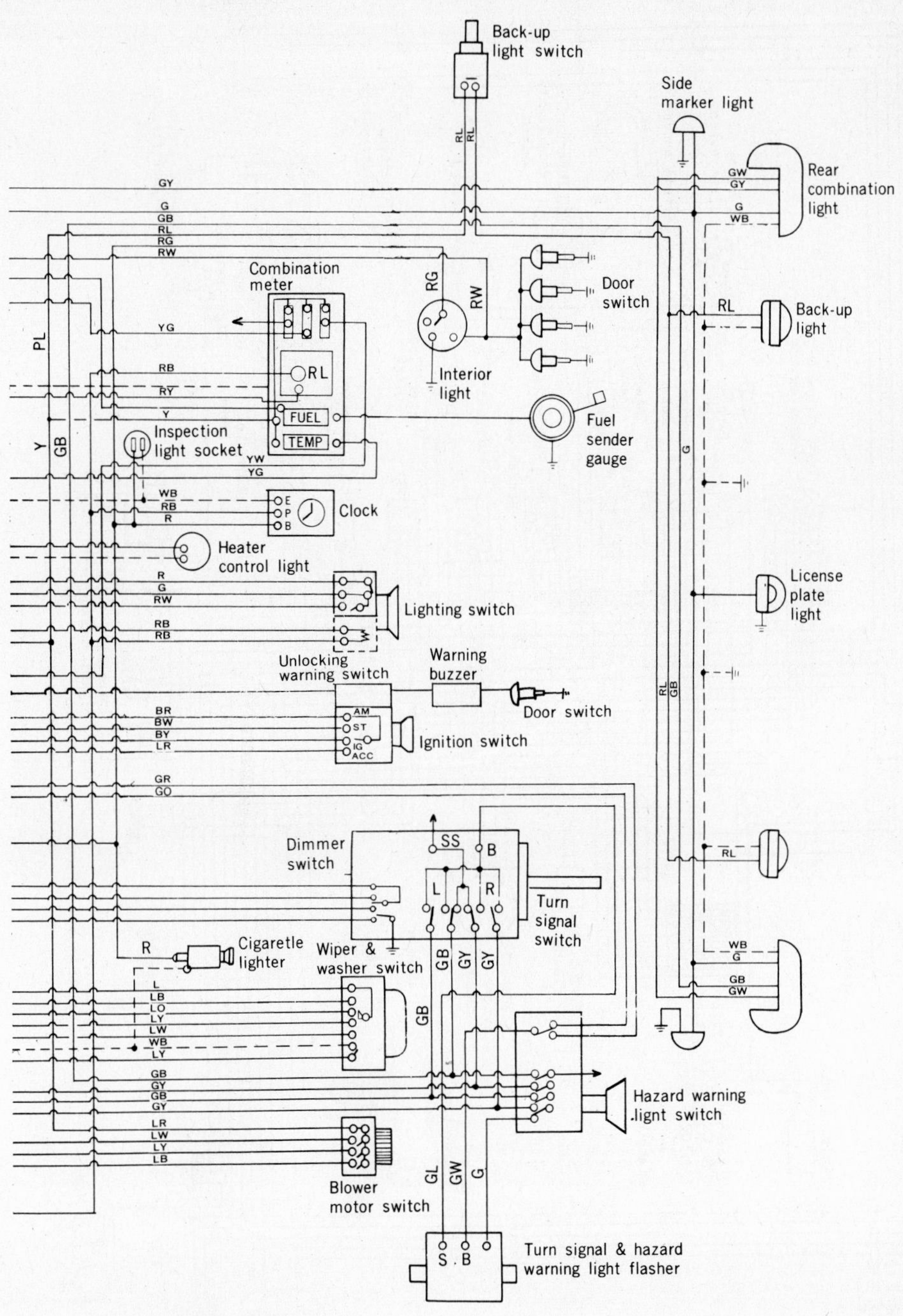

R=red
W=white
L=light purple
G=green
Y=yellow
B=black
O=orange

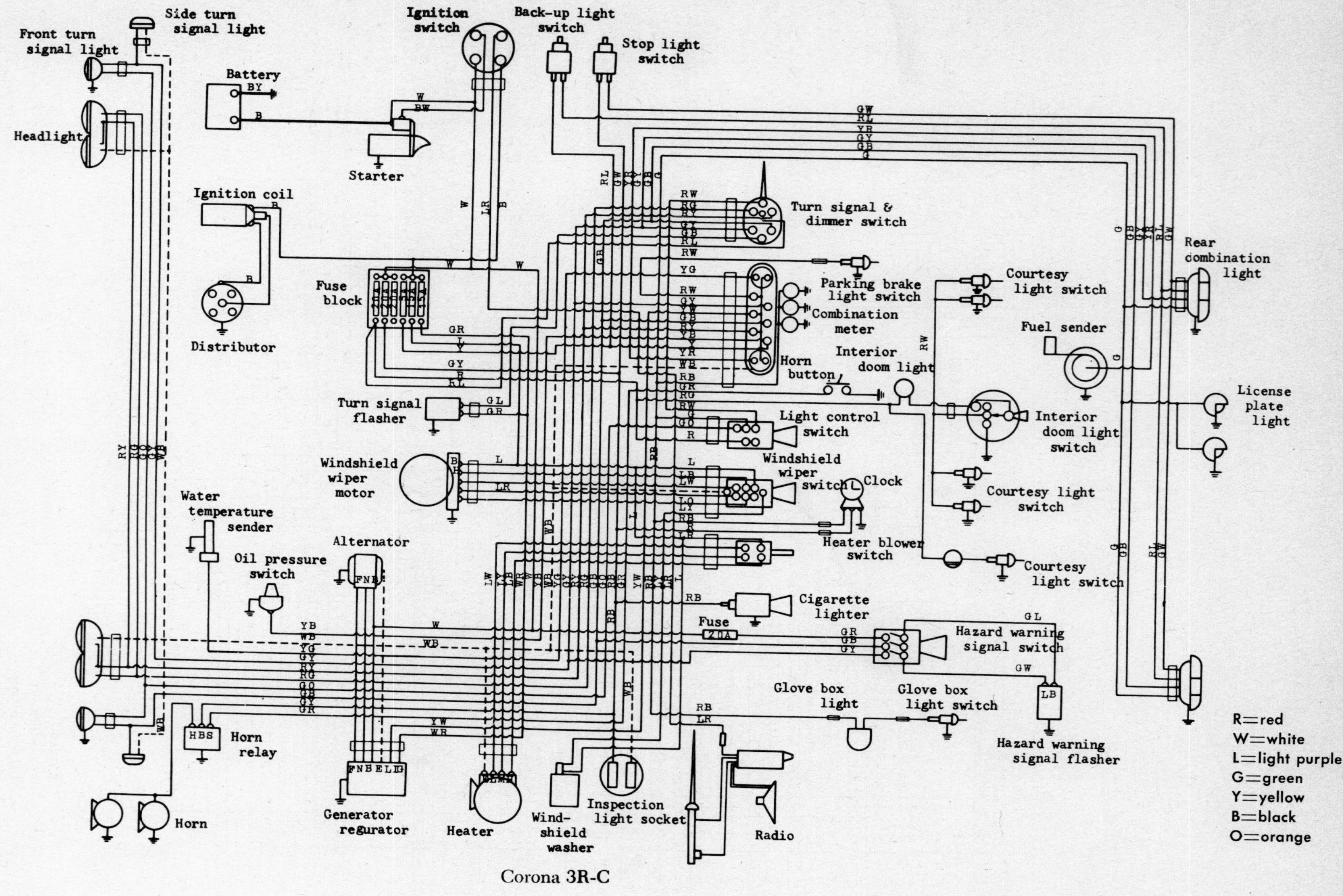
Front turn signal light
Side turn signal light
Headlight
Battery
Starter
Ignition switch
Back-up light switch
Stop light switch
Ignition coil
Distributor
Fuse block
Turn signal & dimmer switch
Parking brake light switch
Combination meter
Interior doom light
Horn button
Turn signal flasher
Light control switch
Windshield wiper motor
Windshield wiper switch
Clock
Water temperature sender
Oil pressure switch
Alternator
Heater blower switch
Cigarette lighter
Fuse
Hazard warning signal switch
Glove box light
Glove box light switch
Hazard warning signal flasher
Horn relay
Horn
Generator regurator
Heater
Wind-shield washer
Inspection light socket
Radio
Courtesy light switch
Fuel sender
Interior doom light switch
Courtesy light switch
Courtesy light switch
Rear combination light
License plate light
R=red
W=white
L=light purple
G=green
Y=yellow
B=black
O=orange

Corona 3R-C

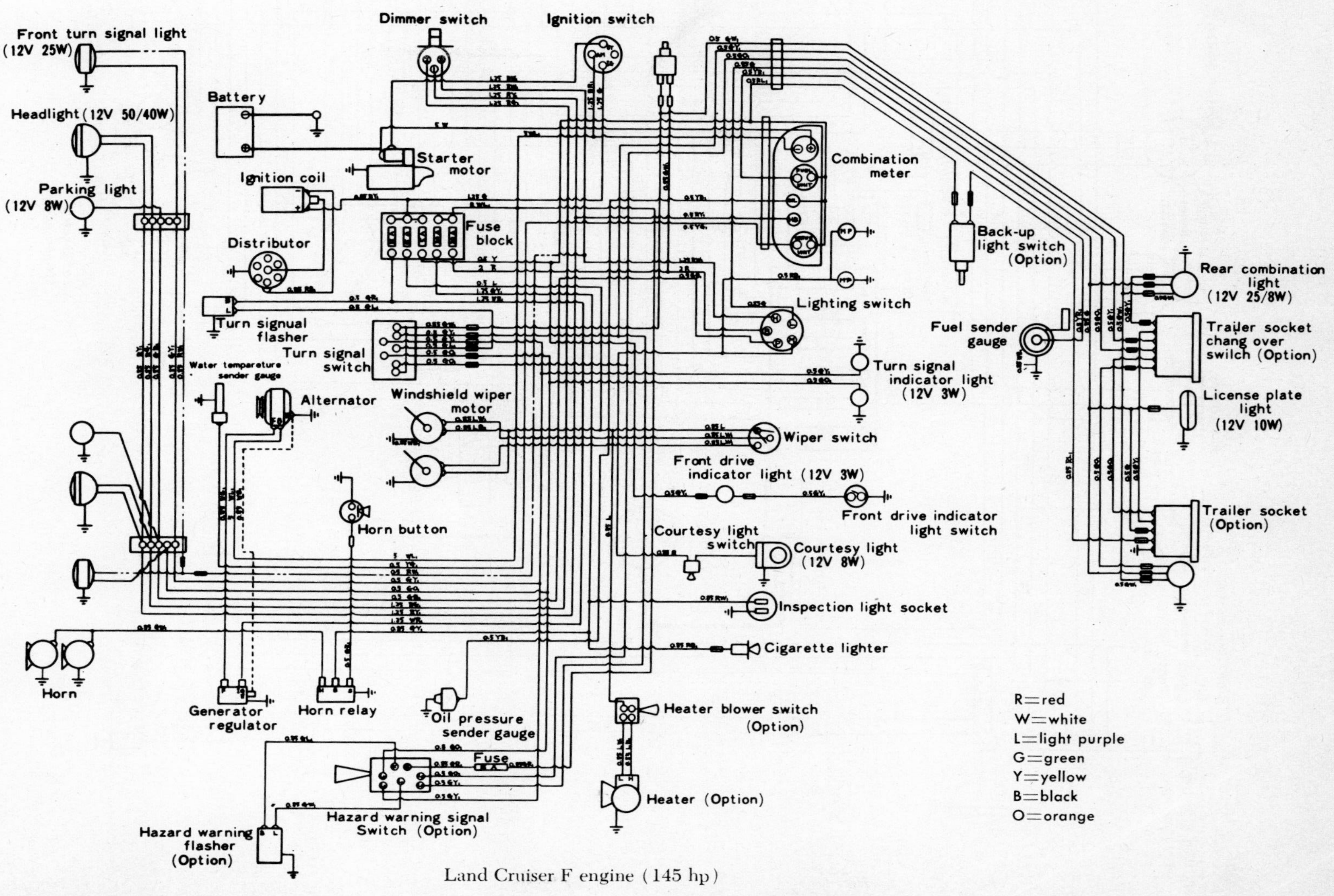

Land Cruiser F engine (145 hp)

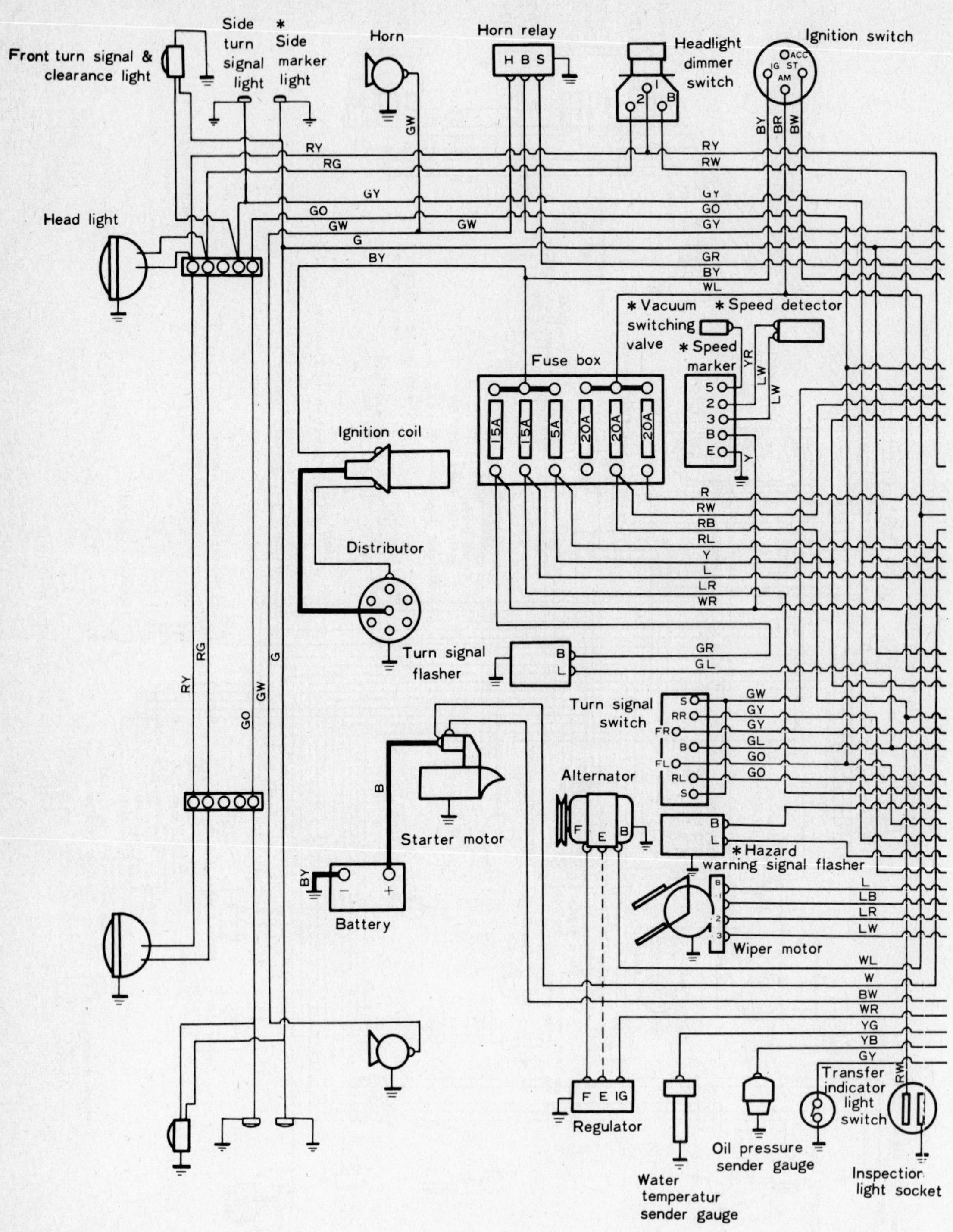
Front turn signal & clearance light
Side turn signal light
* Side marker light
Horn
Horn relay
H B S
Headlight dimmer switch
Ignition switch
ACC
IG
ST
AM
Head light
* Vacuum switching valve
* Speed detector
* Speed marker
Fuse box
15A
15A
5A
20A
20A
20A
Ignition coil
Distributor
Turn signal flasher
Turn signal switch
Alternator
Starter motor
Battery
* Hazard warning signal flasher
Wiper motor
Regulator
F E IG
Water temperatur sender gauge
Oil pressure sender gauge
Transfer indicator light switch
Inspection light socket

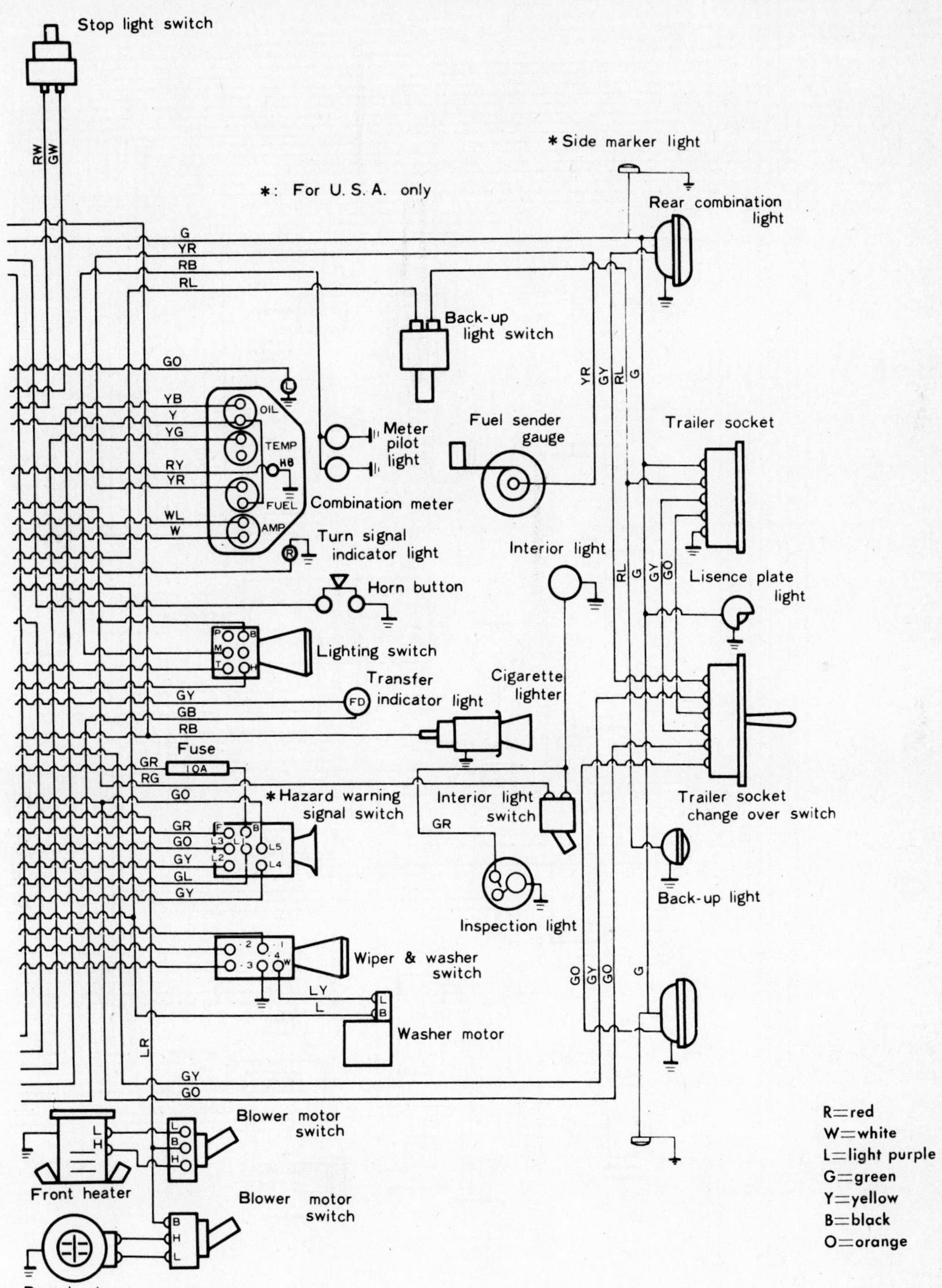

Land Cruiser FA engine (155 hp)

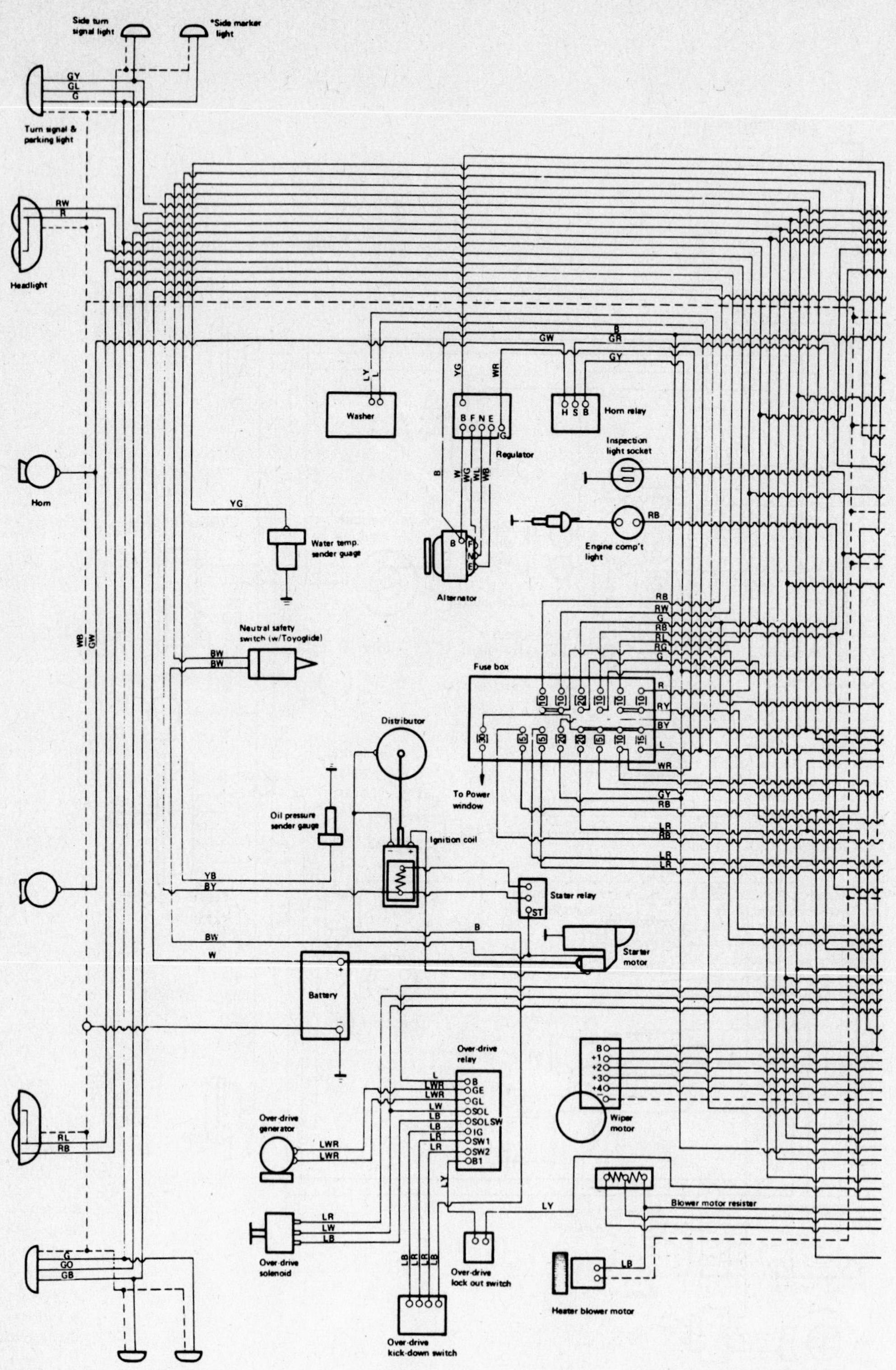
Side turn signal light
*Side marker light
Turn signal & parking light
Headlight
Horn
Washer
Regulator
Horn relay
Inspection light socket
Engine comp't light
Water temp. sender guage
Alternator
Neutral safety switch (w/Toyoglide)
Fuse box
To Power window
Distributor
Oil pressure sender gauge
Ignition coil
Stater relay
Starter motor
Battery
Over-drive relay
Over-drive generator
Over-drive solenoid
Over-drive lock out switch
Over-drive kick-down switch
Wiper motor
Blower motor resister
Heater blower motor

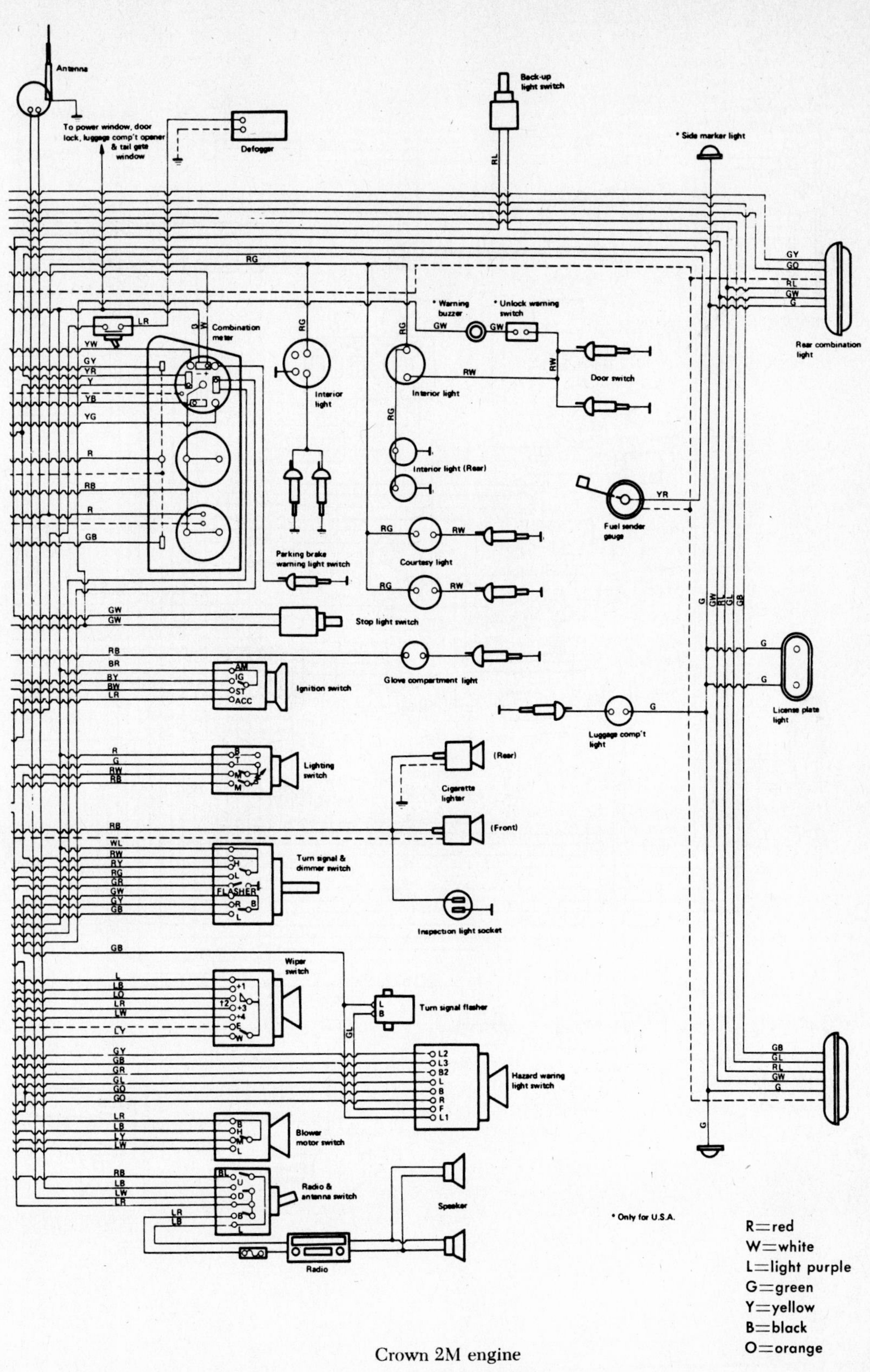

Crown 2M engine

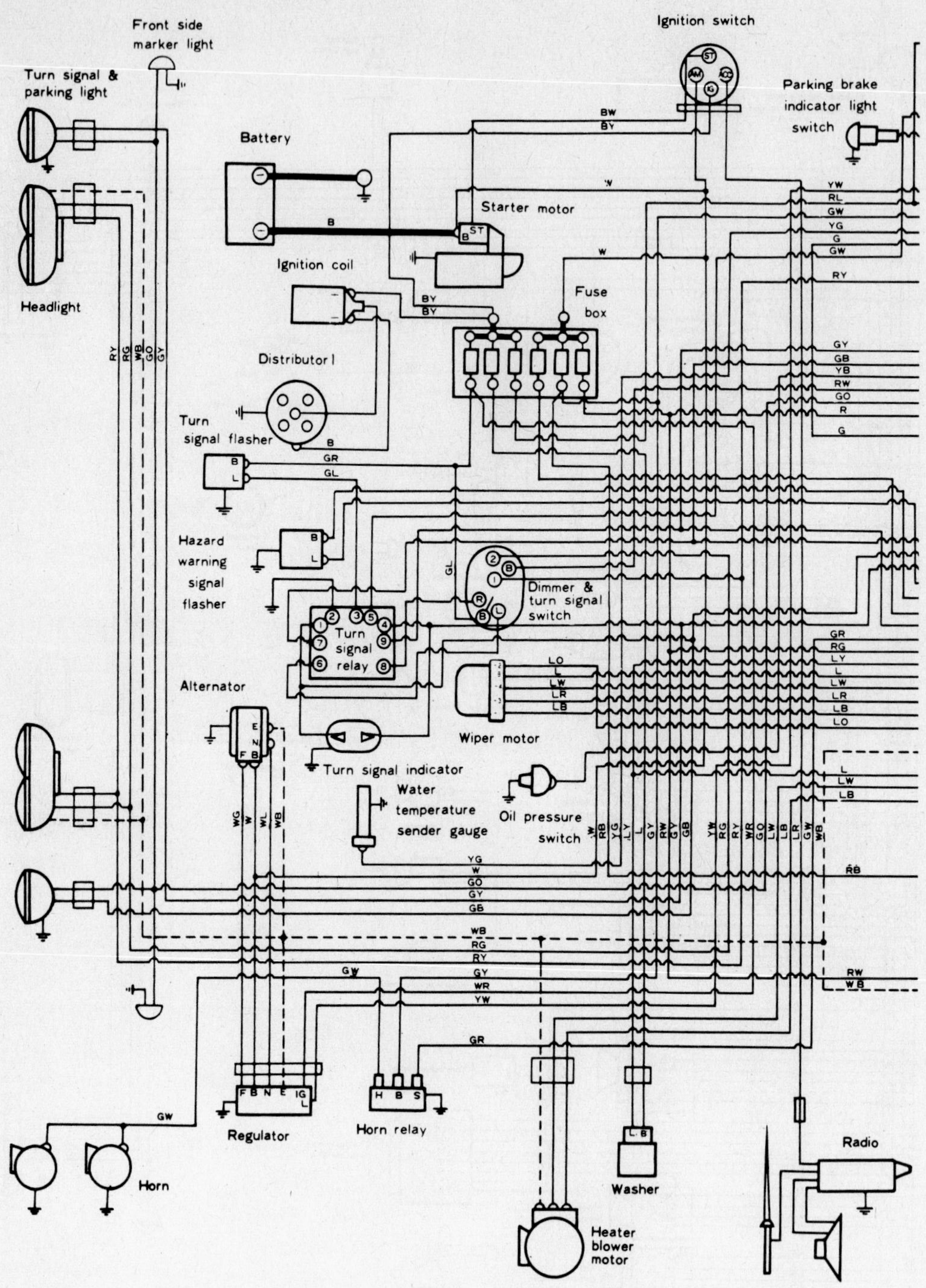
Front side marker light
Turn signal & parking light
Headlight
Battery
Starter motor
Ignition coil
Ignition switch
Parking brake indicator light switch
Fuse box
Distributor
Turn signal flasher
Hazard warning signal flasher
Dimmer & turn signal switch
Turn signal relay
Wiper motor
Alternator
Turn signal indicator
Water temperature sender gauge
Oil pressure switch
Regulator
Horn relay
Horn
Washer
Heater blower motor
Radio

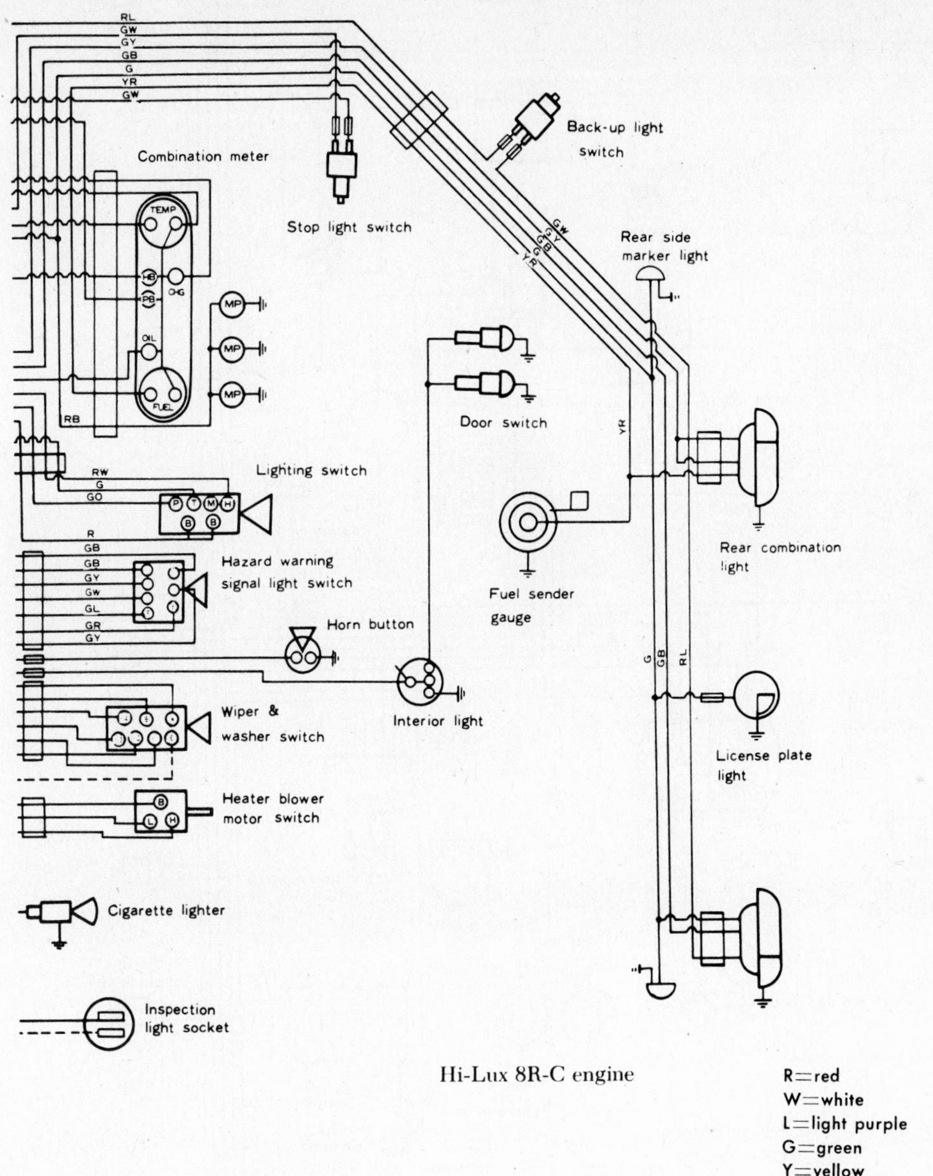

Hi-Lux 8R-C engine

R=red
W=white
L=light purple
G=green
Y=yellow
B=black
O=orange

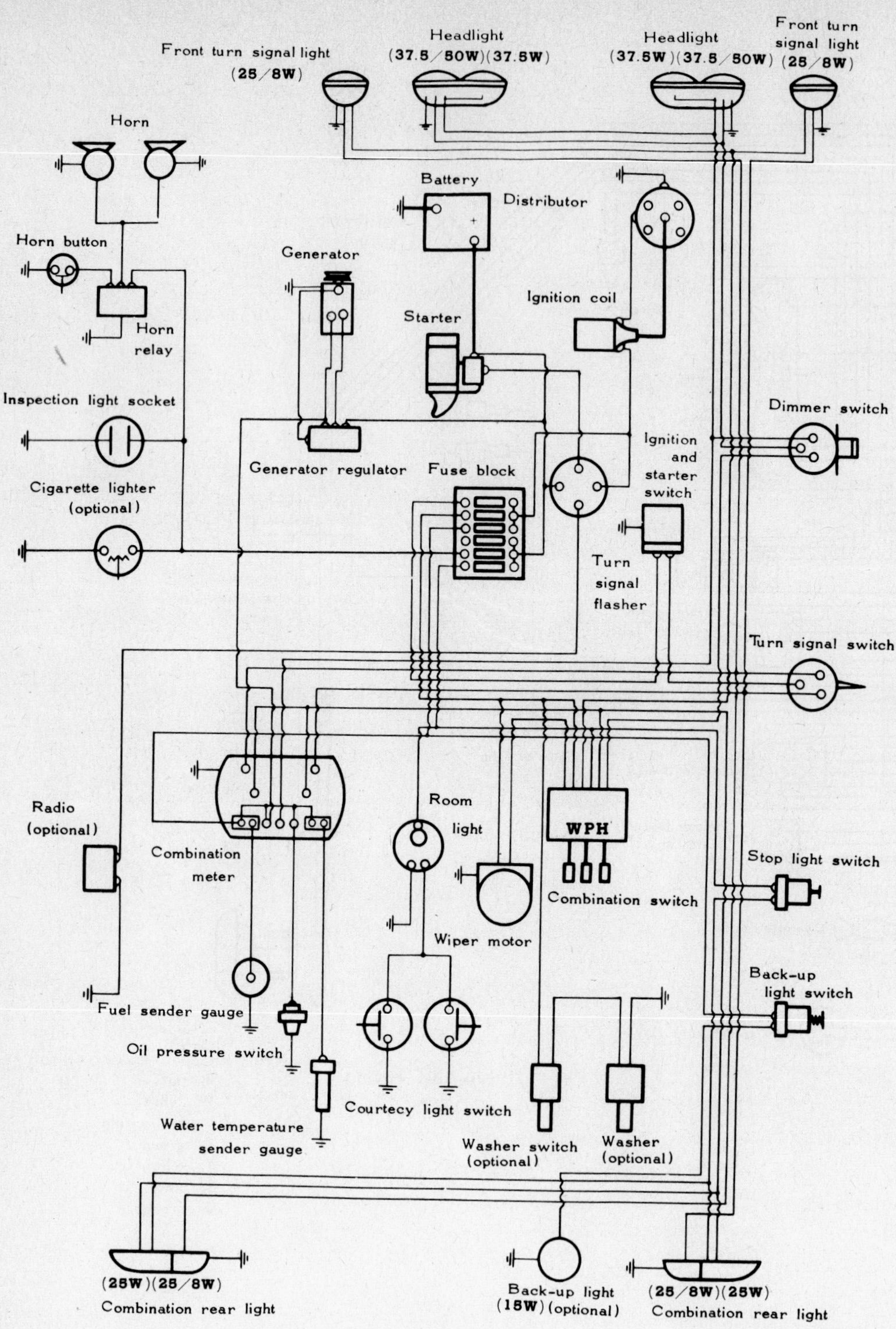

Lite Stout

R=red
W=white
L=light purple
G=green
Y=yellow
B=black
O=orange

Engine Electrical

DISTRIBUTOR

Removal and Installation

Release distributor cap clips and remove cap. Rotate engine until the distributor rotor is in the 12 o'clock position in relation to nearest engine side. This will allow spiral drive gear to be easily repositioned.

Mark the distributor body and engine block so that the distributor may be installed in the same relative position. Disconnect the coil primary wire at the distributor. Remove vacuum lines. Loosen base clamp pinch bolt and lift out distributor.

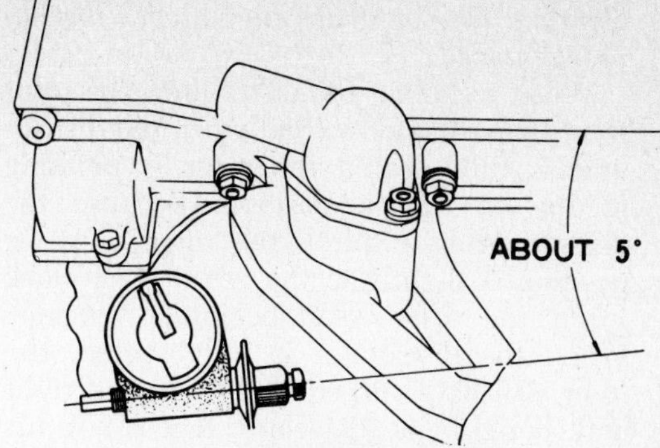

Distributor installation position.

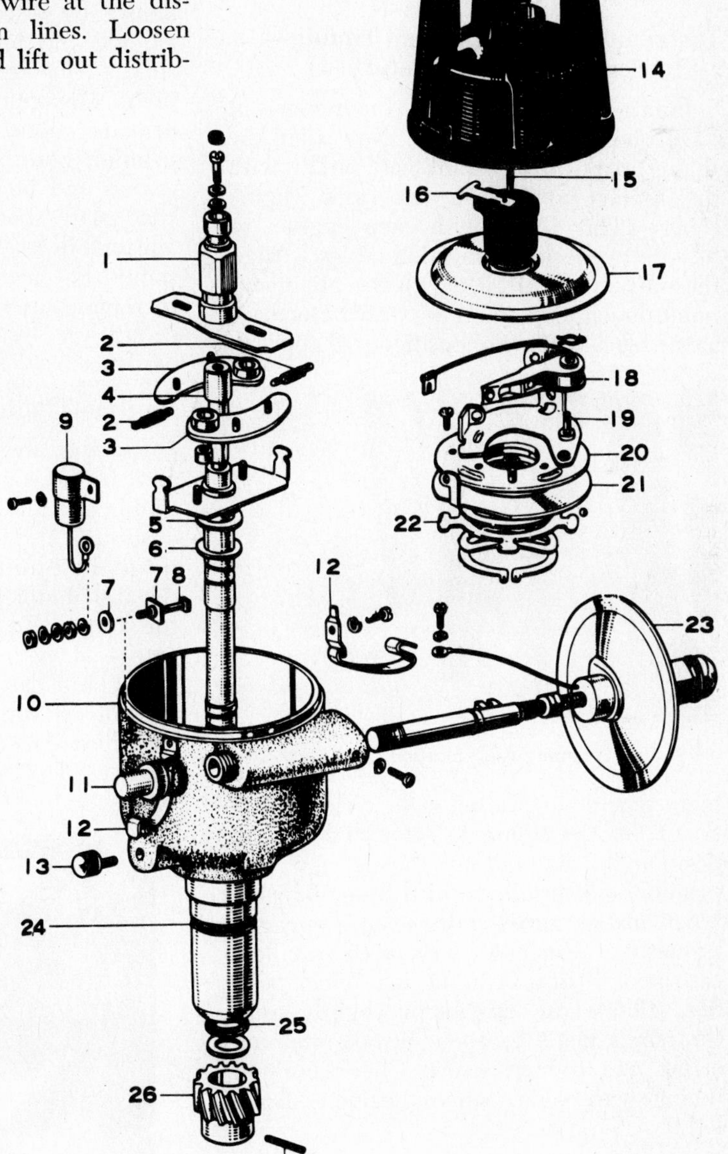

1 Distributor cam
2 Governor spring
3 Governor weight
4 Governor shaft and plate
5 Steel washer
6 Bakelite washer
7 Terminal insulator
8 Terminal bolt
9 Condenser
10 Distributor housing
11 Adjuster cover
12 Housing cap spring
13 Oil cup
14 Distributor cap
15 Carbon center piece
16 Rotor
17 Dust proof cover
18 Breaker
19 Contact point
20 Breaker plate
21 Stationary plate
22 Spring set
23 Vacuum advance unit
24 O-ring
25 Washer
26 Spiral gear
27 Pin

Typical distributor

Caution: Do not rotate engine with distributor removed.

When installing the distributor, the rotor must be positioned so that when the distributor is fully seated the rotor is pointing at the 12 o'clock position. Because the drive gear is a spiral, the rotor must be positioned slightly to the left of 12 o'clock when the drive gear begins to engage. When the distributor is fully seated, the rotor will have turned slightly to the right and should be at 12 o'clock. If it is not, lift the distributor until the gear is disengaged. Turn the rotor as needed and reseat distributor. After rotor is correctly positioned, ignition timing must be reset.

Distributor Installation and Timing—(After engine has been disturbed)

Rotate engine so that No. 1 cylinder is at TDC on compression stroke. Now align the timing mark on the crankshaft pulley with the timing pointer on the front engine cover. (This varies with each engine, so be sure to check specification tables.) Align the oil pump shaft slot with the alignment point punch marked on the distributor base at the block. (The slot position will approximate ten minutes after eight o'clock position.) Set the octane selector dial at zero position, the distributor at the eleven o'clock position and install the distributor into the block, making sure the drive slot is engaged properly. If distributor is correctly installed, the rotor will now be in the one o'clock position. Rotate the distributor slightly until the points begin to open. Install retaining clamp and tighten screw. Check ignition timing, with engine running, using a strobe light.

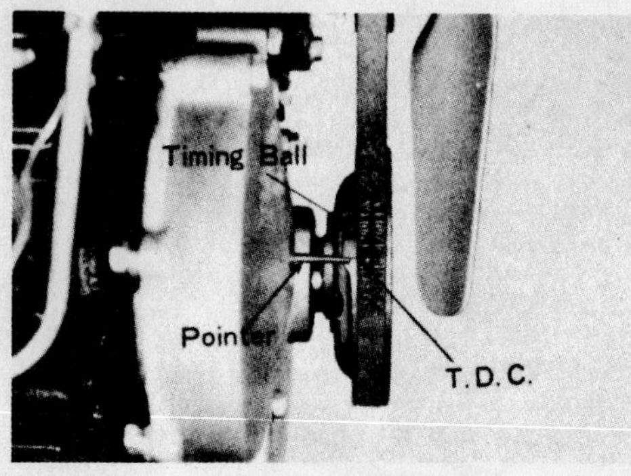

Timing mark location.

Point Removal and Replacement

Remove the distributor cap, rotor, and dust cover (if fitted). Extract the condenser by disconnecting the wire and removing the retaining screw. Pull off retaining clip from top of moving contact pivot. Disconnect the point wire from the primary connector on the side of the distributor body. Remove point base plate screws and lift points out. The distributor base plate should be wiped clean of dirt and oil. Before installing new points, they should be cleaned with a non oily solvent to remove preservative. Replacement procedure is by reversal of the removal sequence.

Adjusting distributor contact point gap.

Ignition Timing

Use a timing light to set ignition timing, as it is more accurate method than static timing and allows distributor advance to be observed throughout the engine speed range. Be sure to set the octane selector on the distributor to *zero* (center marks) before timing. To facilitate reading the timing marks, it is best to clean off the crank pulley and dab a spot of white paint onto the correct timing mark. The timing may be adjusted according to the type of gasoline used. The best proof of a correctly

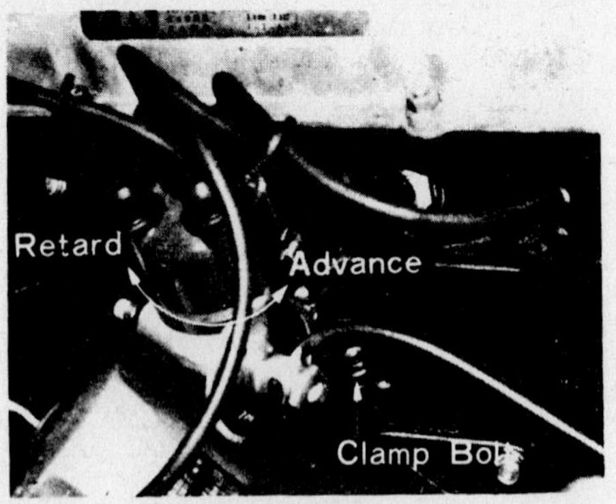

Ignition timing adjustment

timed engine is a road test; run the car at about 20 mph and depress the accelerator quickly. If the timing is correct, no pinging will be heard. If there is pinging, turn the octane selector knob toward R. One 360° turn of the selector knob is equal to 5°. *NOTE: Any change from the manufacturer's specified ignition timing will affect exhaust emission levels.*

ALTERNATOR

The alternator (alternating current generator) is totally different in all major aspects from the DC generator (direct current) in spite of certain physical similarities. The alternator has a rotating field coil and a stationary armature. Brushes are used to carry current into the unit rather than out. Two continuous slip rings are used instead of a segmented commutator and three pairs of silicon diodes (rectifiers) convert the alternating current into direct current. The familiar test methods used for DC generators are no longer valid, and the following precautions must be observed if damage to the alternator system is to be avoided.

1. The wire at the alternator "B" terminal is always hot and is connected directly to the battery.
2. Current to the alternator "F" terminal is controlled by the ignition switch.
3. Do not run engine for any length of time with the "B" terminal disconnected, as the alternator will overheat and the voltage relay coil will burn out. If, for some reason, the engine must be run with the "B" terminal disconnected, also disconnect the "F" terminal.
4. Do not connect any condenser or noise suppressor to the "F" terminal.
5. When quick charging, always disconnect the battery ground cable. Also disconnect the cable whenever any arc (electric) welding is to be done on the car.
6. Beware of reversing polarity when *jump starting* the car, especially when using a battery of uncertain polarity. Disconnect ground cable to prevent damage to the system through reversed polarity.
7. Remember that it is possible for a car to run with a battery incorrectly installed. Of course, the diodes will be damaged, the ignition points rapidly burned out and the signal flasher may catch fire. All Toyota models officially imported to the USA have a negative-ground system.

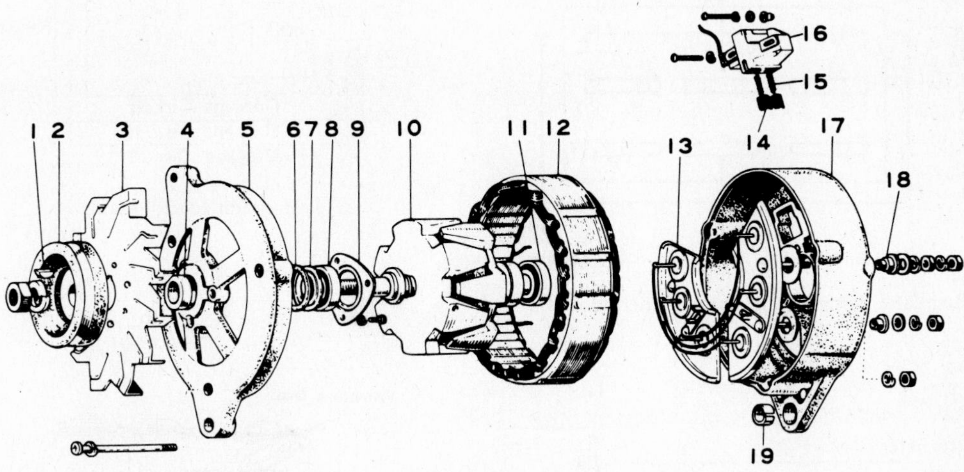

Alternator components.

1. Key
2. Alternator pulley
3. Alternator fan
4. Space collar
5. Drive end frame
6. Felt ring
7. Felt ring cover
8. Bearing
9. Bearing retainer plate
10. Rotor
11. Bearing
12. Stator
13. Rectifier holder
14. Brush
15. Brush spring
16. Brush holder
17. Rectifier end frame
18. "B" terminal insulator
19. Bushing

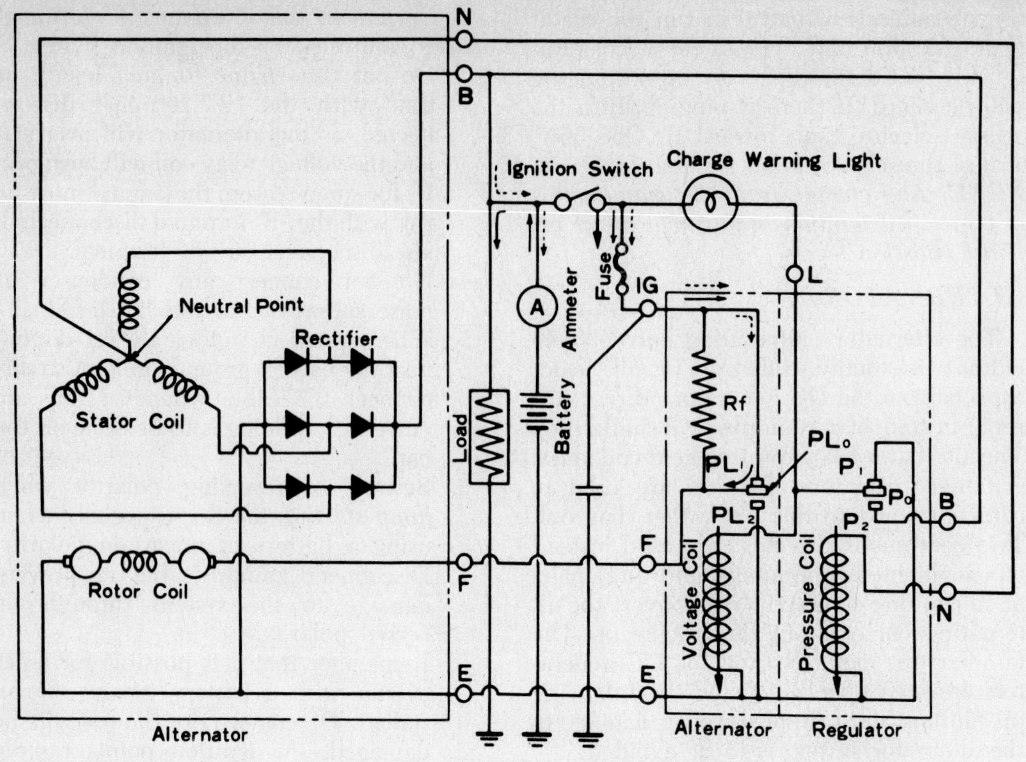

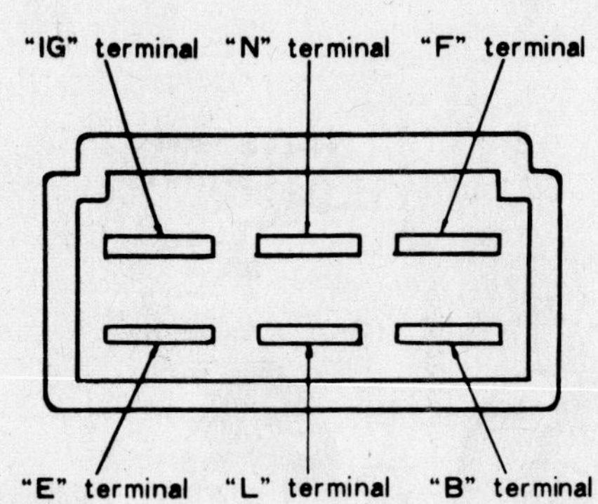

Regulator harness plug terminal identification.

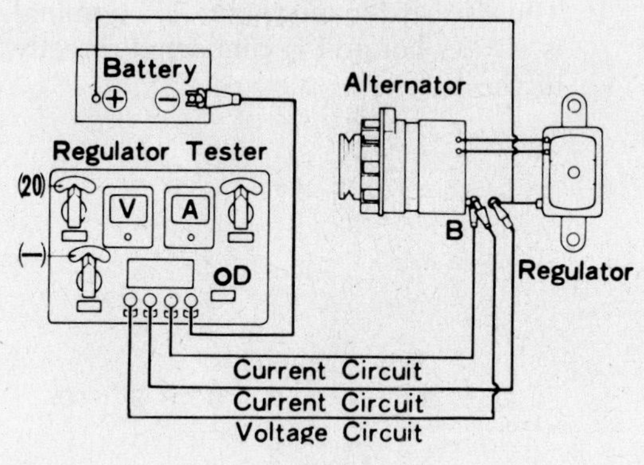

Test circuit for alternator.

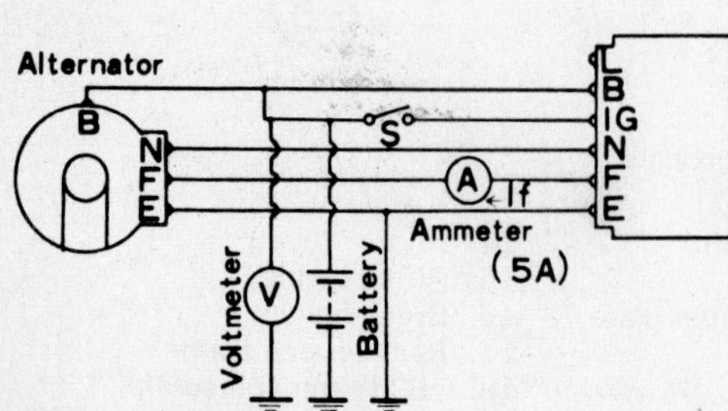

Voltage regulator test circuit.

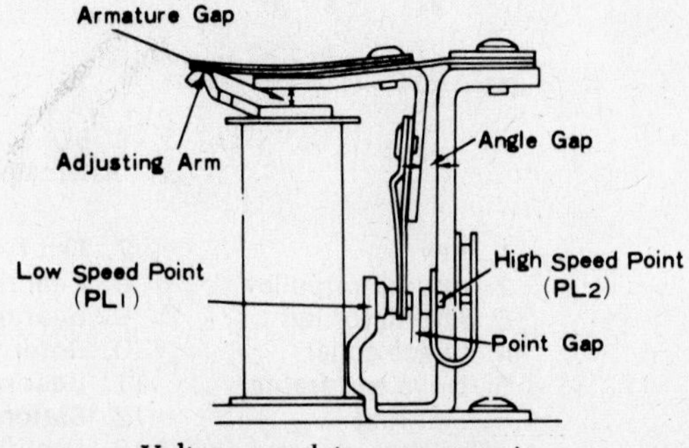

Voltage regulator components.

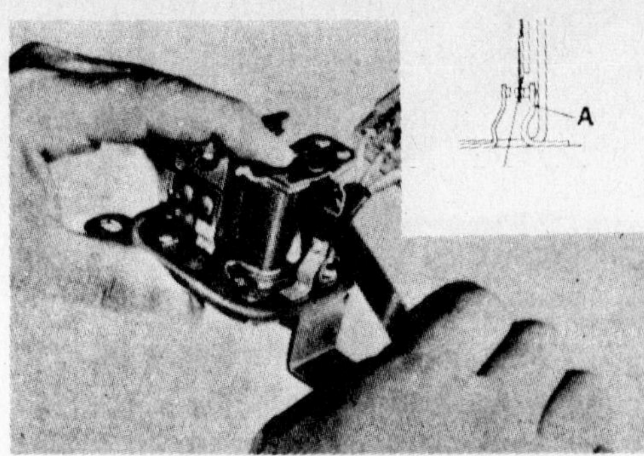

Checking voltage relay spring deflection.

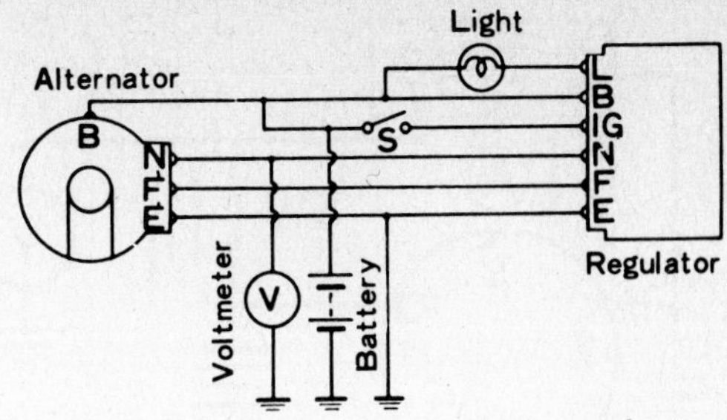

Voltage relay (warning lamp) test circuit.

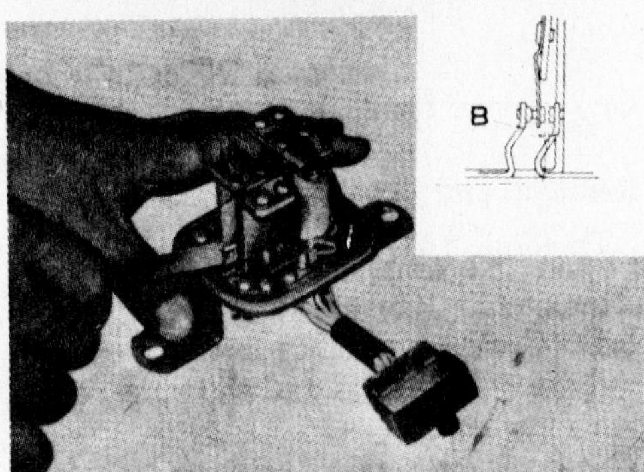

Checking point gap.

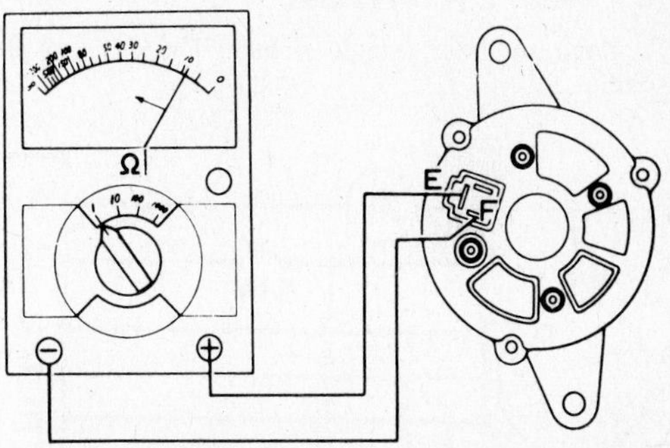

Checking resistance between F and E terminals.

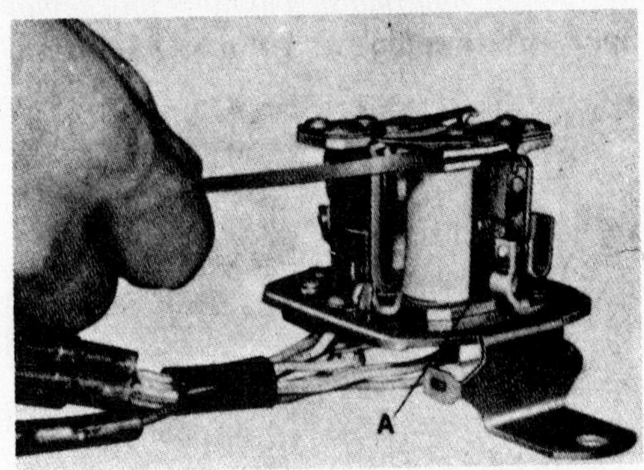

Checking armature gap.

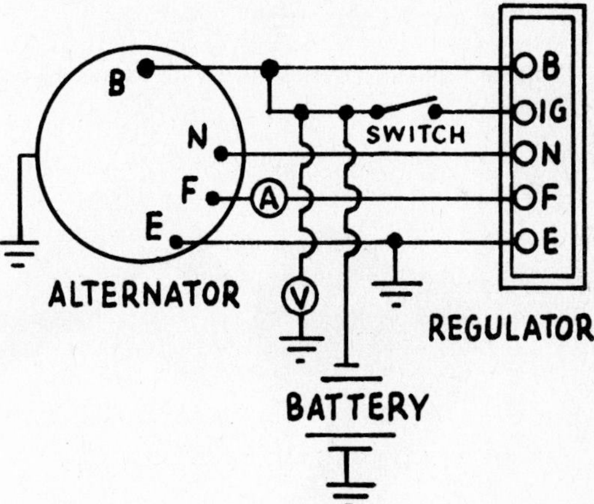

Voltage regulator (two-element with ammeter) test circuit.

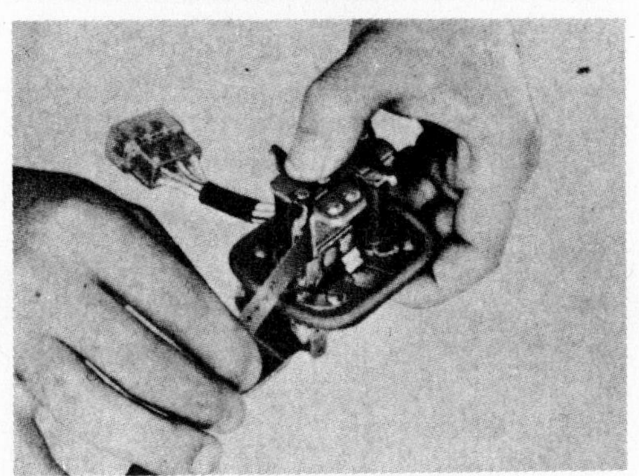
Checking angle gap—0.008″.

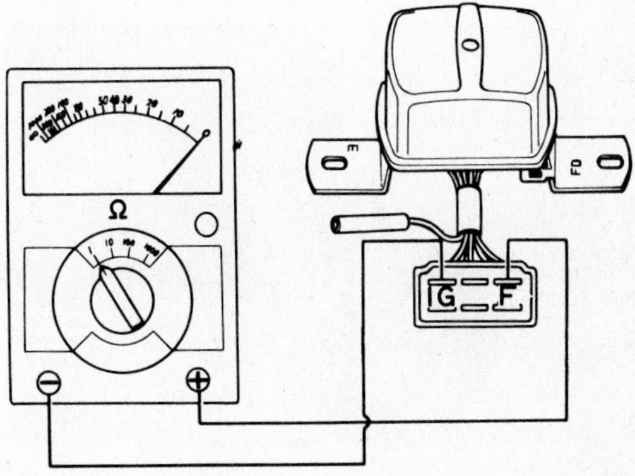

Checking resistance between IG and F terminals.

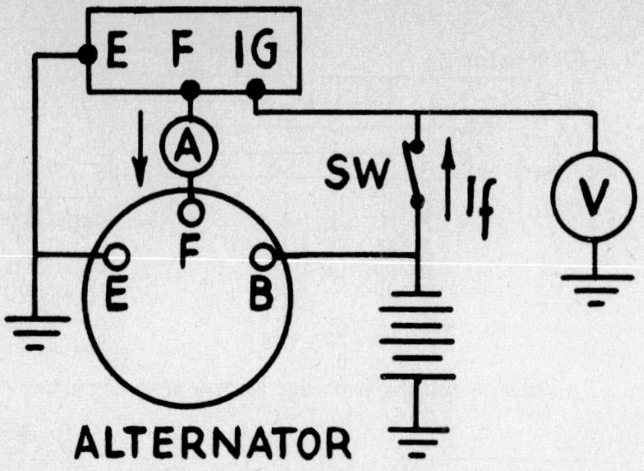

Voltage regulator (single element F-type) test circuit.

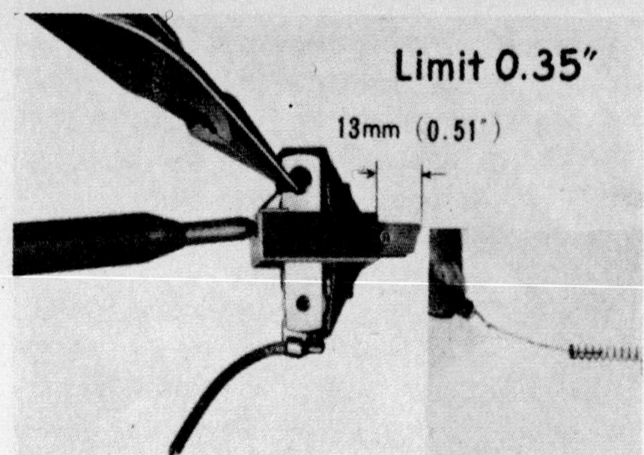

Replacing alternator brush.

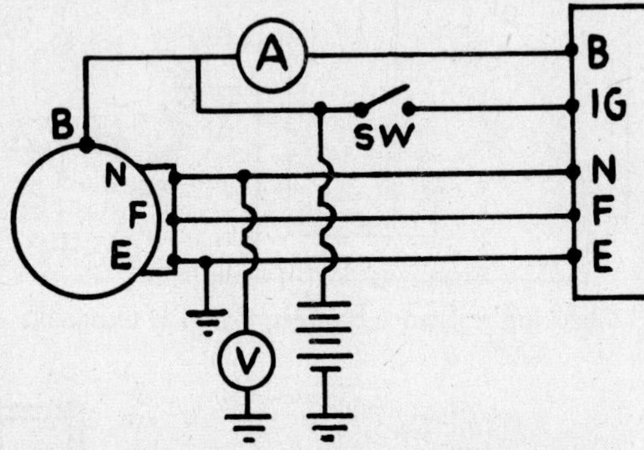

Voltage regulator (two-element with ammeter) test circuit.

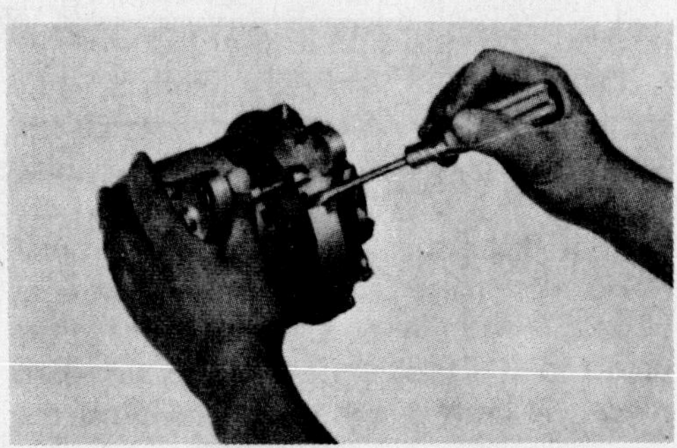

Removing alternator drive end frame.

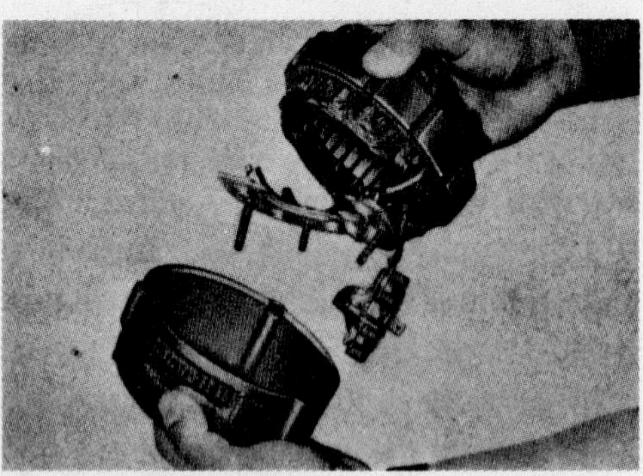

Removing alternator stator and rectifier holder.

STARTER MOTOR

Removal and Replacement

Disconnect the battery-to-starter cable at the battery. Disconnect wires at starter relay, remove retaining nuts and pull out starter. *NOTE: On K-series cars it is necessary to remove the air cleaner, disconnect the choke and accelerator cables at the carburetor, disconnect the front exhaust pipe flange at the exhaust manifold and remove the entire manifold assembly before removing the starter motor; or remove from underneath.*

To replace starter, reverse removal procedure.

Solenoid Test

Adjust the free length of the plunger to 1.340″ as illustrated. Late Corona models have a special relay in the starter circuit to overcome certain cold weather starting conditions. Full 12-volt battery current is fed to the coil (bypassing the resistance) to produce the hottest possible spark when cranking the engine.

Fuel System

FUEL PUMP

A diaphragm-type pump is used on all models. It consists of a lower body containing a rocker arm and spring, diaphragm and pull rod. The upper body contains two valves and inlet and outlet fittings, as well as the top cover.

Removal

It is best to first disconnect the battery to prevent accidental cranking of the en-

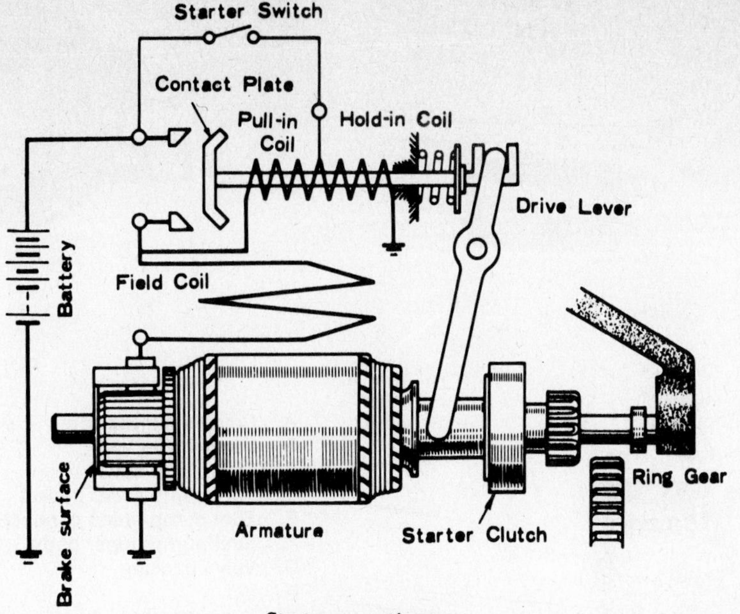

Starter operation.

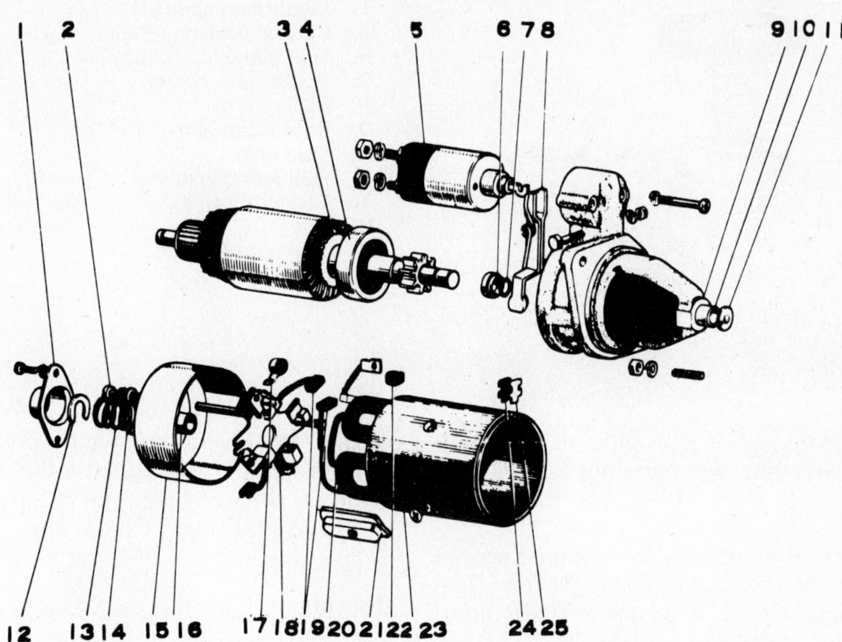

Starter motor components.

1 End frame cover
2 Through bolt
3 Armature
4 Starter clutch
5 Solenoid
6 Pinion stop collar
7 Snap-ring
8 Drive lever w/spring
9 Starter drive housing
10 Housing bushing
11 Bushing cover
12 Lockwasher
13 Brake spring
14 Rubber ring
15 Commutator end frame
16 End frame bushing
17 Brush spring
18 Brush holder
19 Brush
20 Field coil
21 Pole core
22 Insulator
23 Yoke
24 Rubber plate
25 Plate

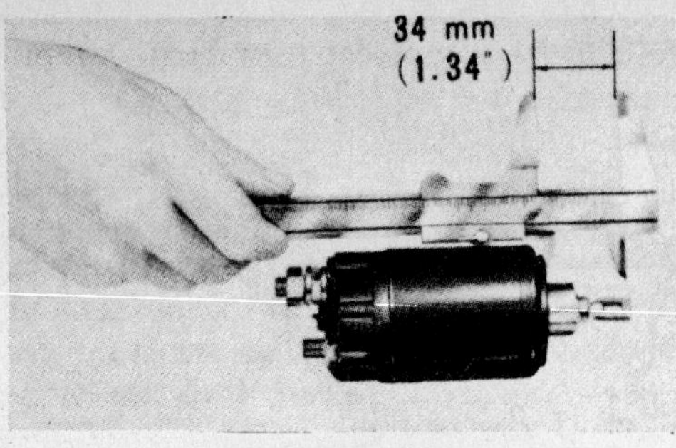

Solenoid testing

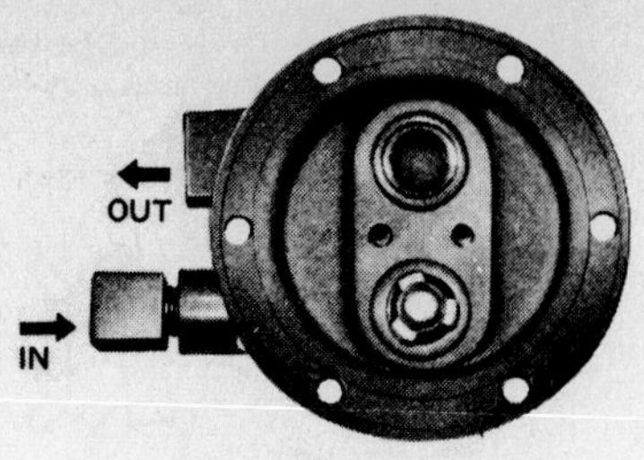

Fuel pump valve assembly

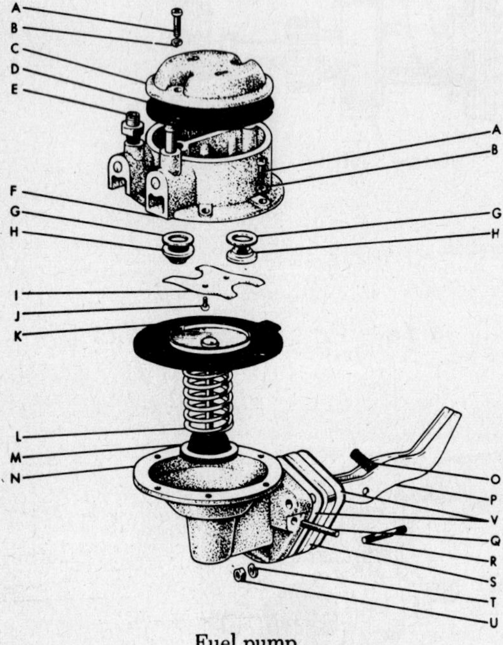

Fuel pump.

gine. Disconnect the two pipes at the pump and remove the two mounting bolts.

Disassembly

Remove the upper body retaining screws and lift off the upper body. *NOTE: The diaphragm may stick to one or both sides.* From the underside, remove the valve retaining screws and the retainer, valves and gaskets. Press down on the diaphragm and unhook the pull rod from the diaphragm stem, then remove the diaphragm. Drive out the rocker arm pin (towards the knurled end) using a drift and remove rocker arm and spring.

Inspection

Wash all parts in clean solvent and dry off with compressed air. Check the cover for cracks or distortion. Also check both bodies for cracks and worn pin holes or crossed screw threads. Check the diaphragm for tears or stretching, and the pull rod for a distorted eyelet. Check the valves for proper seating.

Testing

Pressure Test

Remove the fuel outlet line at the pump and connect a pressure gauge to the pump side. Start engine and run for a few seconds —if pressure is not within specifications, replace the diaphragm spring.

Volume Test

Disconnect fuel line at carburetor and connect a gravity feed fuel supply to the carburetor fuel inlet. Connect the fuel pump output line in such a way that the pump output can be collected in a measured container. Start engine and run at specified speed for one minute. If discharge quantity is less than specified, check fuel filter visually for obstructions and perform vacuum test before replacing pump.

Vacuum Test

Reconnect all fuel lines at pump and carburetor. Disconnect fuel inlet line at filter and connect vacuum gauge to filter inlet side. If vacuum is much higher than specified, the filter is clogged and should be replaced. Low vacuum usually indicates a weak diaphragm spring. If engine is fitted with a felt element, cleaning is best done by blowing out with compressed air from the inside. If the felt is oil soaked or very dirty, it may be washed in clean gasoline and then dried. It is not recommended that felt-type filters be cleaned more than three times.

Fuel Pump Specifications

Model	*Volume/Min. @ RPM (pts.)*	*Pressure (psi)*	*Vacuum (in. Hg.)*
F, FA	4.4 @ 1,000	3.4-4.8	19.7
K-C	1.8 @ 2,900	3.0-4.5	15.7
3R, 3R-B, 3R-C, 8R-C	3.4 @ 2,500	2.8-4.3	15.7
2M	3.8 @ 1,500	3.60-5.00	15.7
2T-C	N.A.	2.8-3.2	N.A.

Assembly

Reverse order of disassembly. A quick way to check the valves for proper installation is to make sure the inlet valve bulges towards the diaphragm and the outlet valve away from it. (*In* and *out* are marked on the body.)

Installation

Always use a fresh gasket when installing the pump. Be careful not to cross-thread the pipe fittings; use no wrench until at least two turns are threaded fully. Tighten the mounting bolts again after running the engine, then check fuel pump delivery pressure with gauge.

AIR FILTER

Most models are equipped with an air filter having a replaceable paper element. Change element every 12,000 miles, or sooner if the engine is operated under severe dirt and dust conditions. A simple test to determine the degree of filter clogging can be made by holding a 50-Watt light bulb inside the filter element. If the light can be seen through the element, element is still usable.

GLASS BOWL FUEL FILTER

This unit consists of the filter housing or body, a glass bowl and gasket and the replaceable filter element. A filter in normal

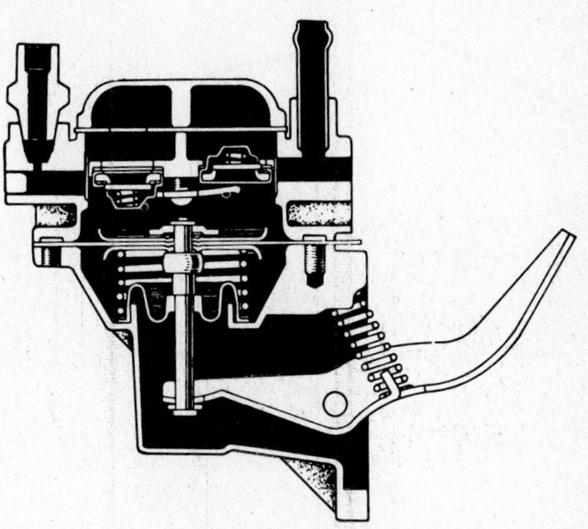

Fuel pump cross-section.

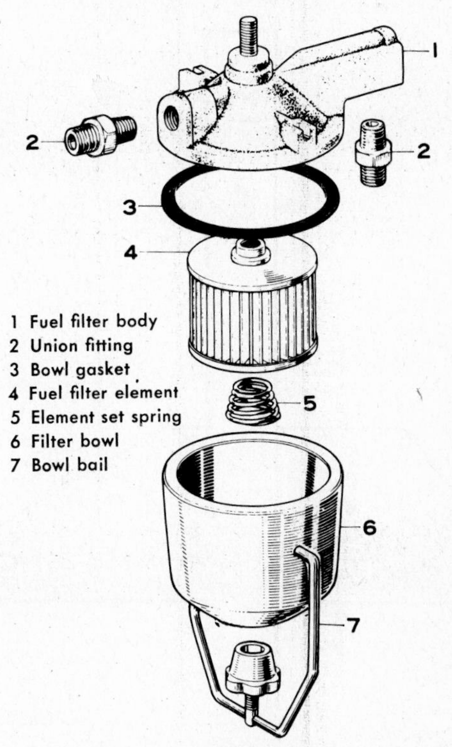

Fuel filter

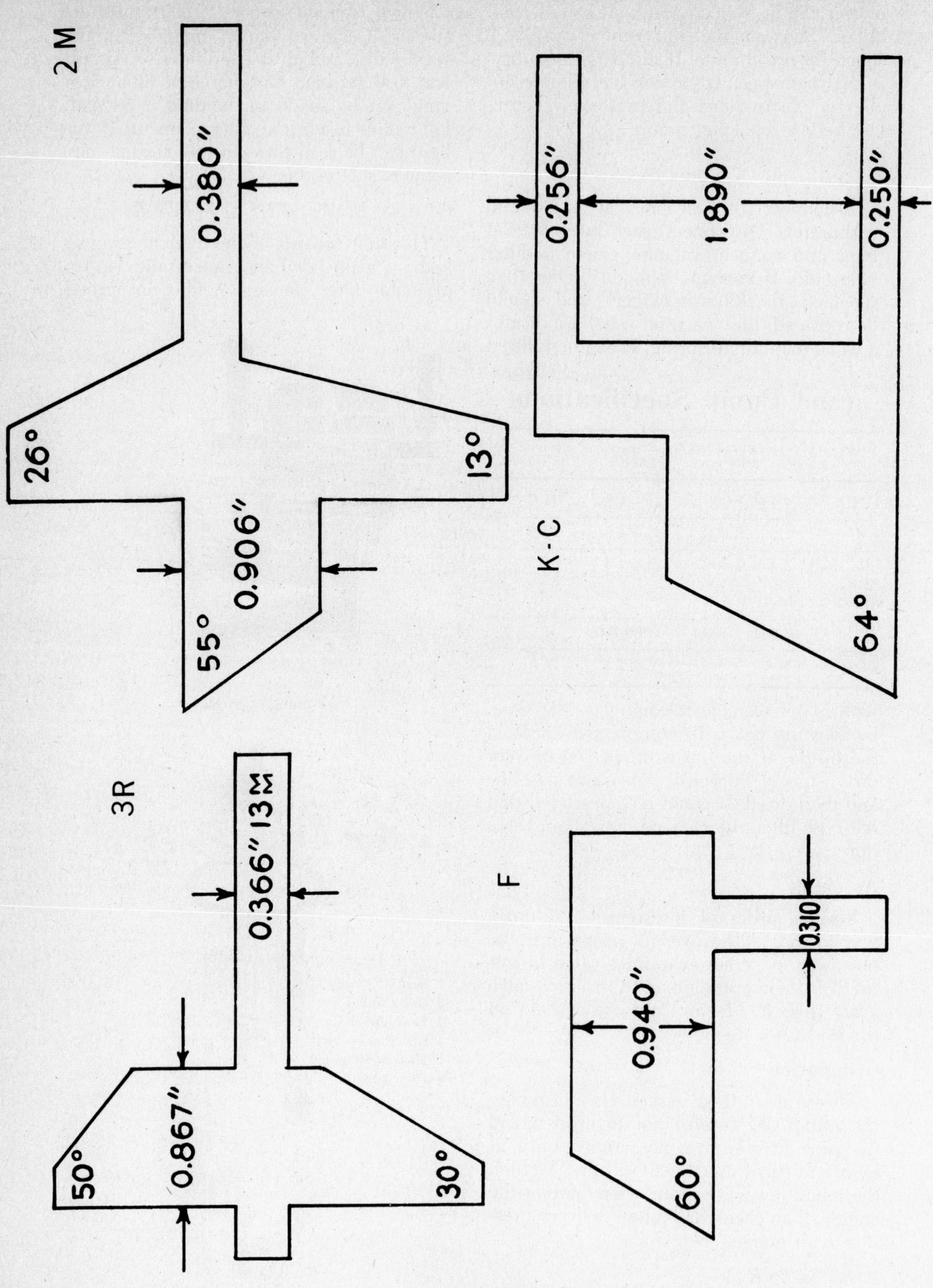

Carburetor gauges.

operation is never more than one-half full of fuel; more than that indicates that the element is clogged and should be cleaned or replaced. Cleaning is done by washing the element in clean fuel and blowing it out with compressed air. Replace the element every 12,000 miles, or sooner if dirty, waterlogged or clogged. When installing the bowl, make sure the bowl gasket is properly seated in the body or the pump will not be able to draw fuel from the tank. An old gasket can be reused(if no other is available) by reversing it so that it presents a fairly flat surface to the bowl side.

CARBURETORS

The carburetors used on Toyota models are conventional two-barrel, downdraft types similar to domestic carburetors. The main circuits are: *primary*, for normal operational requirements; *secondary*, to supply high speed fuel needs; *float*, to supply fuel to the primary and secondary circuits; *accelerator*, to supply fuel for quick and safe

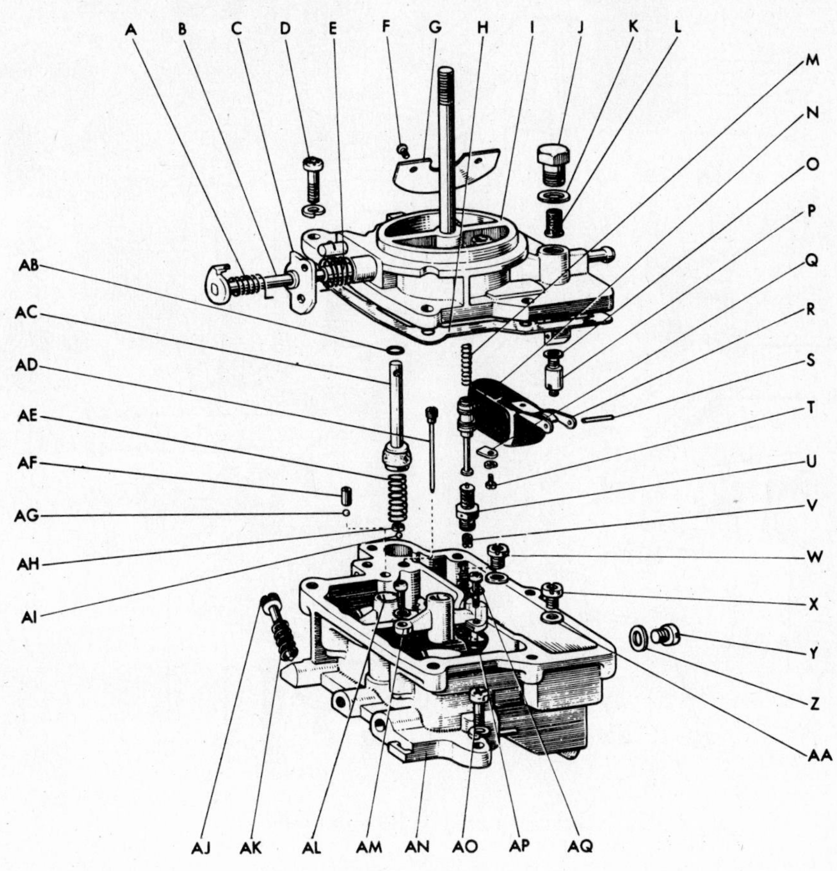

K-C carburetor

A. Choke valve relief spring
B. Choke shaft
C. Choke lever
D. Screw
E. Choke return spring
F. Screw
G. Choke valve
H. Air horn gasket
I. Air horn
J. Main passage plug
K. Inlet strainer gasket
L. Strainer
M. Power piston spring
N. Power piston
O. Needle valve seat gasket
P. Needle valve
Q. Power piston stopper
R. Float
S. Float lever pin
T. Screw
U. Power valve
V. Power jet
W. Primary main jet
X. Secondary main jet
Y. Drain plug
Z. Gasket
AA. Main jet gasket
AB. O-ring
AC. Pump plunger
AD. Slow jet
AE. Pump damping spring
AF. Pump discharge weight
AG. Check ball
AH. Check ball retainer
AI. Check ball
AJ. Throttle adjusting screw
AK. Spring
AL. Primary small venturi
AM. Secondary small venturi
AN. Main body
AO. Screw
AP. Venturi No. 1 gasket
AQ. Screw

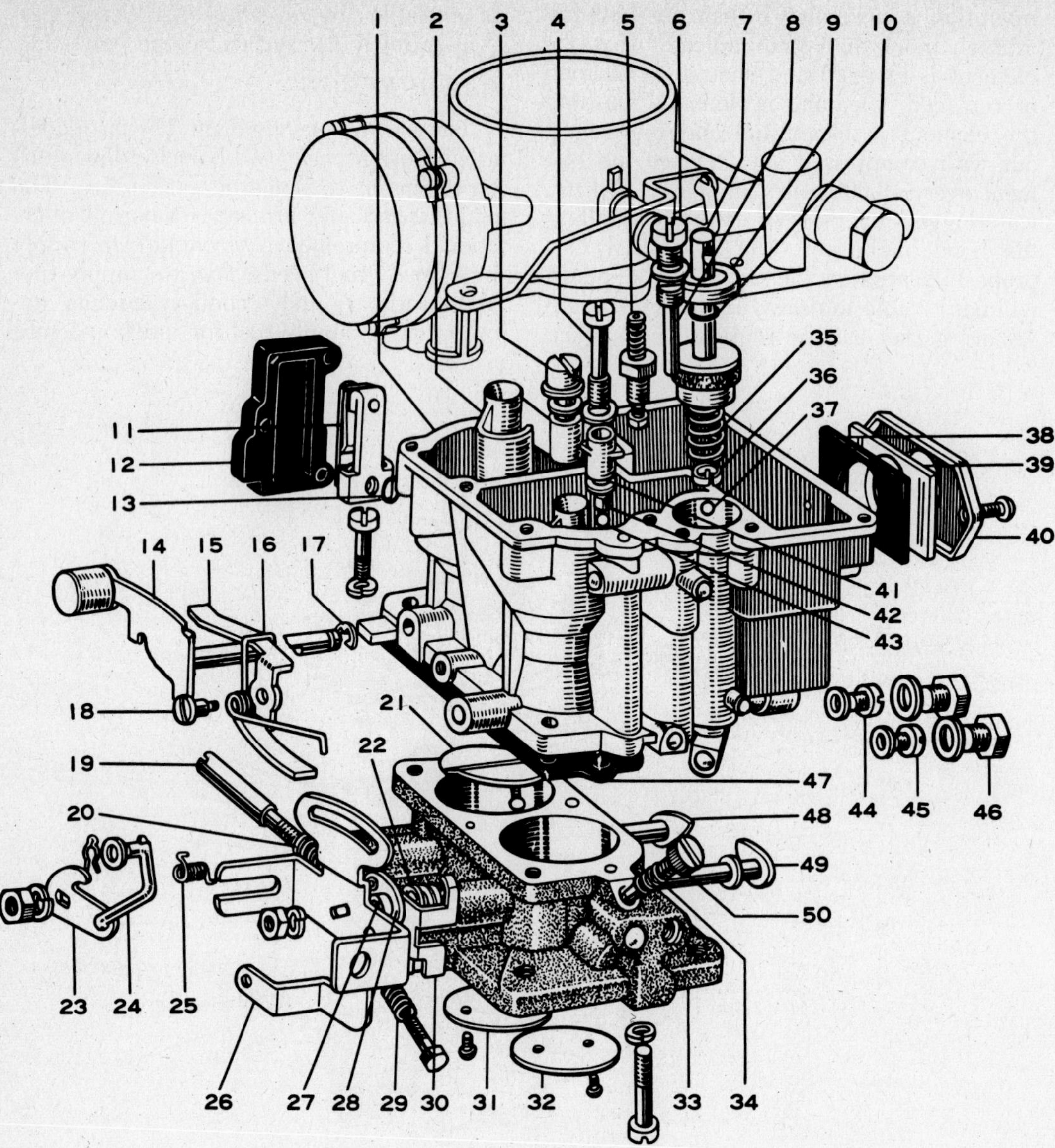

Carburetor used on RS series vehicles.

1. Body
2. Secondary small venturi
3. Primary main air bleed
4. Pump jet screw
5. Power valve
6. Slow passage plug
7. Pump plunger
8. Slow jet
9. Plunger guide
10. O-ring
11. Thermostatic valve
12. Thermostatic valve cover
13. O-ring
14. High speed valve shaft
15. High speed valve stopper lever
16. High speed valve stopper lever spring
17. E-ring
18. Stopper lever securing screw
19. Throttle adjusting screw
20. Throttle adjusting spring
21. High speed valve
22. Retainer ring
23. Secondary throttle lever
24. Throttle shaft link
25. Secondary throttle return spring
26. Primary throttle shaft arm
27. Throttle lever collar
28. Fast idle lever
29. Fast idle adjusting spring
30. Fast idle adjusting lever
31. Secondary throttle valve
32. Primary throttle valve
33. Flange
34. Idle adjusting screw spring
35. Pump damping spring
36. Discharge check valve retainer
37. Steel ball
38. Level gauge gasket
39. Level gauge glass
40. Level gauge clamp
41. Pump jet
42. Pump discharge weight
43. Steel ball
44. Secondary main jet
45. Primary main jet
46. Main passage plug
47. Body flange gasket
48. Secondary throttle shaft
49. Primary throttle shaft
50. Idle adjusting screw

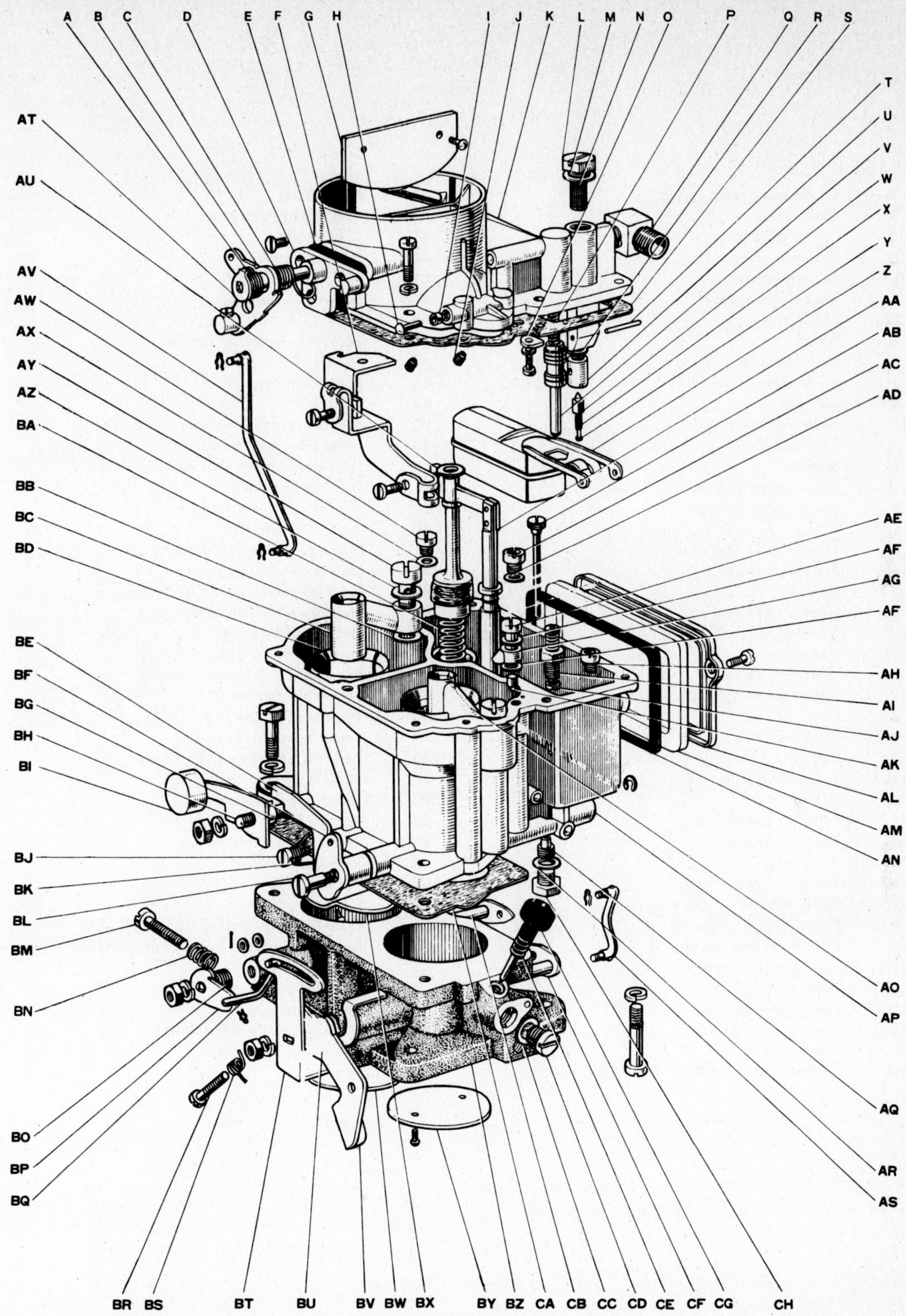

F, FA carburetor

F, FA carburetor

A	Choke valve relief spring	AR	Plug gasket
B	Choke lever	AS	Pump connecting link
C	Choke valve spring	AT	Choke shaft
D	Choke lever adapter	AU	Plunger washer
E	Adapter gasket	AV	Fast idle connector
F	Choke wire support	AW	Secondary main jet
G	Choke valve	AX	Gasket
H	Plug	AY	Secondary main air bleeder
I	Economizer jet	AZ	Gasket
J	Air bleeder	BA	Pump damping spring
K	Air horn	BB	Gasket
L	Main passage plug	BC	Secondary small venturi
M	Plug gasket	BD	Secondary main venturi
N	Strainer	BE	High speed valve stop lever
O	Power piston stopper	BF	Fast idle cam
P	Power piston spring	BG	High speed valve stopper
Q	Fitting	BH	High speed shaft
R	Needle valve seat gasket	BI	High speed valve shaft lever
S	Air horn gasket	BJ	Stop lever attaching screw
T	Float pin	BK	High speed valve stop lever spring
U	Needle valve seat	BL	Fast idle attaching screw
V	Power piston	BM	Throttle adjusting screw
W	Needle valve	BN	Throttle adjusting screw spring
X	Needle valve spring	BO	Secondary throttle back spring
Y	Needle valve push pin	BP	Secondary throttle lever
Z	Float	BQ	Throttle shaft link
AA	Lifter rod	BR	Fast idle adjusting screw
AB	Slow jet	BS	Fast idle adjusting screw spring
AC	Primary main jet	BT	Primary throttle shaft arm
AD	Gasket	BU	Throttle lever collar
AE	Pump jet screw	BV	Throttle lever
AF	Pump jet gasket	BW	Secondary throttle valve
AG	Pump jet	BX	High speed valve
AH	Spare jet	BY	Primary throttle valve
AI	Power valve	BZ	Flange
AJ	Power jet	CA	Body to flange gasket
AK	Pump discharge weight	CB	Secondary throttle valve shaft
AL	Level gauge retainer	CC	Gasket
AM	Level gauge glass	CD	Idle port plug
AN	Level gauge gasket	CE	Idle adjusting screw spring
AO	Primary small venturi	CF	Primary throttle valve shaft
AP	Main body	CG	Idle adjusting screw
AQ	Discharge check valve	CH	Plug

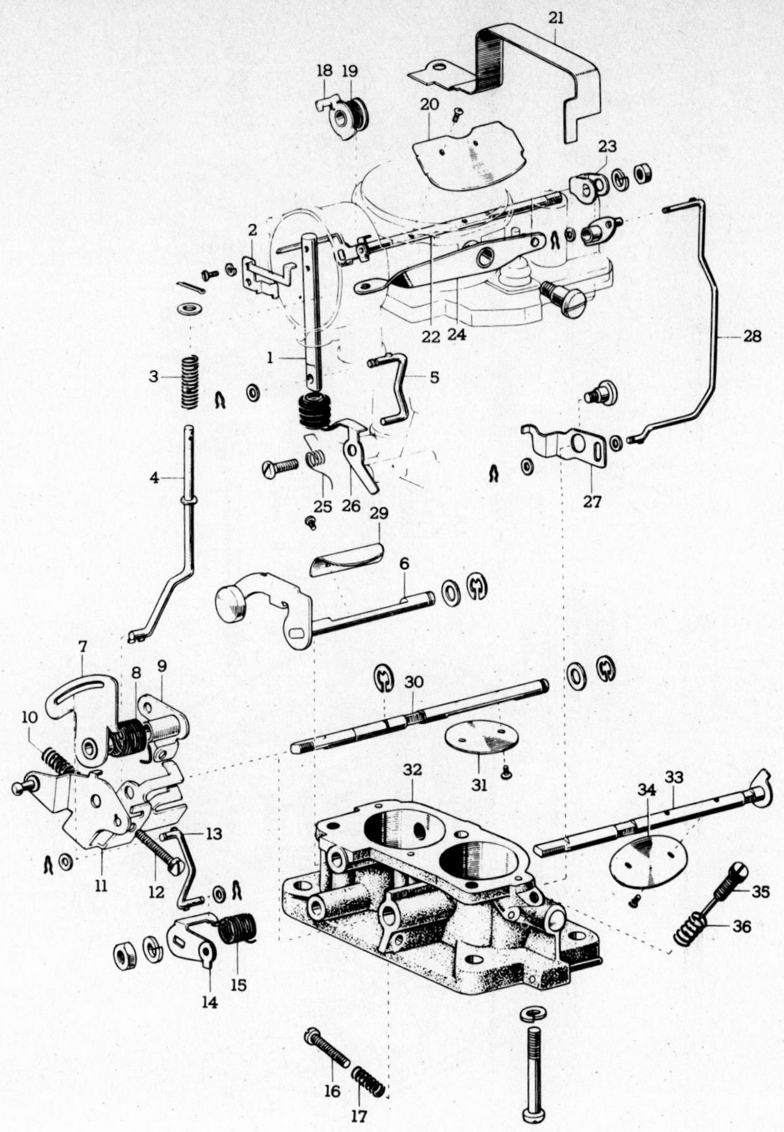

8R-C carburetor

1 Sliding rod
2 Fast idle cam follower
3 Pump spring
4 Pump connecting link
5 Connecting link
6 High speed valve shaft
7 Connecting arm
8 Return spring
9 Fast idle adjusting lever
10 Fast idle screw spring
11 Primary throttle shaft arm
12 Fast idle adjusting screw
13 Throttle shaft link
14 Secondary throttle lever
15 Secondary throttle return spring
16 Speed adjusting screw
17 Speed adjusting screw spring
18 Fast idle cam
19 Fast idle cam spring
20 Choke valve
21 Reloader cover
22 Choke shaft
23 Choke lever
24 Pump lever
25 Stopper lever spring
26 High speed valve stopper lever
27 Reloader lever
28 Reloader connecting link
29 High speed valve
30 Primary throttle valve shaft
31 Primary throttle valve
32 Flange
33 Secondary throttle valve shaft
34 Secondary throttle valve
35 Mixture adjusting screw
36 Mixture adjusting screw spring

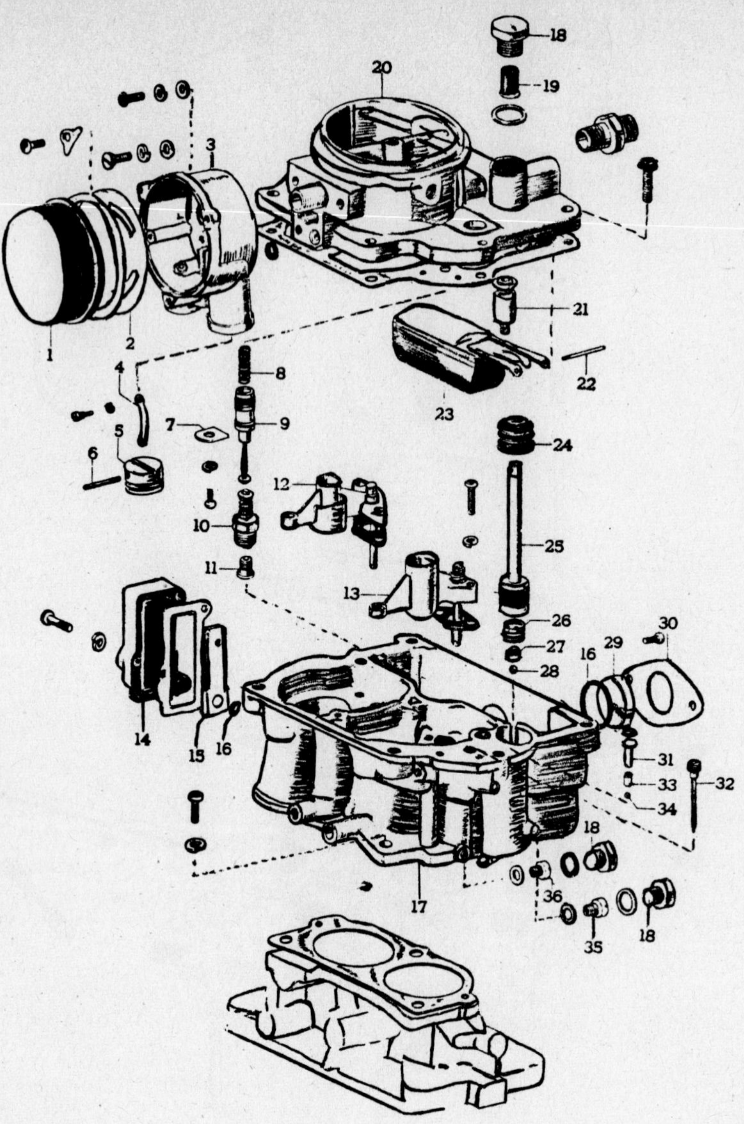

8R-C carburetor

1 Coil housing
2 Coil housing plate
3 Thermostat case
4 Piston connector
5 Vacuum piston
6 Piston pin
7 Power piston stopper
8 Power piston spring
9 Power piston
10 Power valve
11 Power jet
12 Secondary small venturi
13 Primary small venturi
14 Cover
15 Thermostatic valve
16 O-ring
17 Main body
18 Main passage plug
19 Strainer
20 Air horn
21 Needle valve sub-assembly
22 Float lever pin
23 Float
24 Boot
25 Pump plunger
26 Plunger spring
27 Check ball retainer
28 Check ball
29 Level gauge glass
30 Level gauge glass clamp
31 Stopper
32 Slow jet
33 Pump discharge weight
34 Check ball
35 Primary main jet
36 Secondary main jet

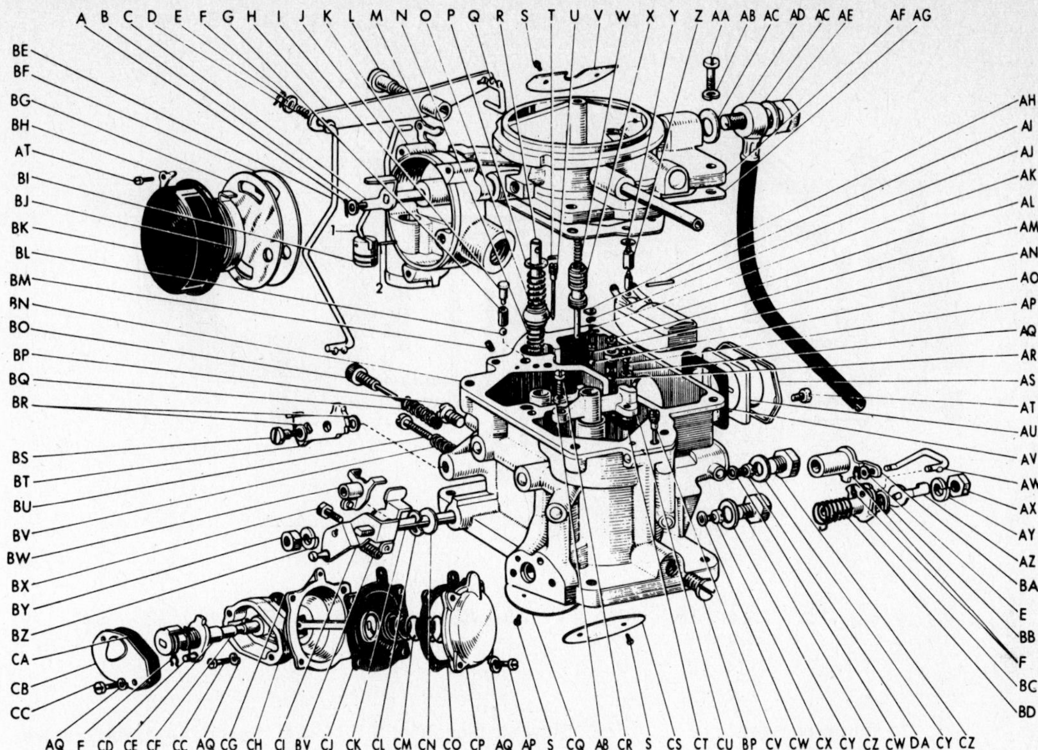

Typical carburetor, showing all components.

A. Cotter pin
B. Plain washer
C. Choke shaft
D. Pump arm pushing spring
E. Pushing spring retainer
F. Snap-ring
G. Pump discharge weight
H. Pump lever
I. Discharge weight stopper
J. Choke lever link
K. Thermostat case
L. Pump lever attaching screw
M. Fast idle cam lever (for choke link)
N. Pump damper spring
O. Pump spring
P. Pump spring retainer
Q. Pump connecting link
R. Pump plunger
S. Valve attaching screw
T. Pin
U. Primary slow jet
V. Choke valve
W. Power piston spring
X. Power piston
Y. Needle valve seat gasket
Z. Needle valve
AA. Screw
AB. Lockwasher
AC. Union fitting gasket
AD. Fuel hose
AE. Strainer
AF. Air horn
AG. Air horn gasket
AH. Power piston stopper
AI. Float lever pin
AJ. Lockwasher
AK. Stopper retaining screw
AL. Float
AM. Power valve
AN. Plug
AO. Steel ball
AP. Screw
AQ. Lockwasher
AR. Power jet
AS. Level gauge glass retainer
AT. Screw
AU. Level gauge glass
AV. Level gauge glass gasket
AW. Connecting link
AX. Throttle lever retaining nut
AY. Lockwasher
AZ. Secondary link arm
BA. Primary link lever
BB. Retainer ring
BC. Secondary link lever
BD. Secondary throttle return spring
BE. Pump connecting link
BF. Coil housing plate
BG. Coil housing gasket
BH. Coil housing retainer
BI. Vacuum piston
BJ. Thermostat bi-metal
BK. Coil housing
BL. Steel ball
BM. Slow passage plug
BN. Body
BO. Idle adjusting screw
BP. Plug
BQ. Idle adjusting screw spring
BR. Spacer
BS. Fast idle cam retaining screw
BT. Fast idle cam
BU. Throttle adjusting screw
BV. Fast idle adjusting spring
BW. Fast idle lever
BX. Fast idle adjusting screw
BY. Nut
BZ. Lockwasher
CA. Gasket
CB. Diaphragm housing cover
CC. Screw
CD. Diaphragm relief lever
CE. Collar
CF. Secondary throttle shaft
CG. Diaphragm housing gasket
CH. Diaphragm housing
CI. Primary throttle lever
CJ. Diaphragm rod
CK. Primary throttle shaft
CL. Retainer ring
CM. Diaphragm spring
CN. Primary throttle shaft shim
CO. Diaphragm gasket
CP. Diaphragm housing cap
CQ. Primary throttle valve
CR. Retaining screw
CS. Secondary throttle valve
CT. Venturi gasket
CU. Secondary small venturi
CV. Secondary slow jet
CW. Main jet gasket
CX. Secondary main jet
CY. Main passage plug gasket
CZ. Main passage plug
DA. Primary main jet
1. Piston connector
2. Piston pin

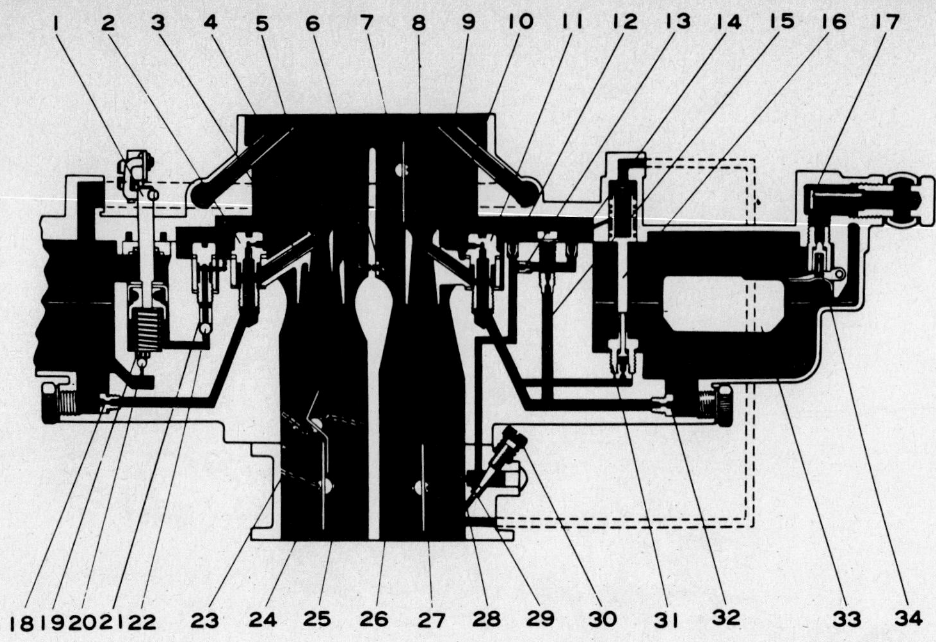

3R-C carburetor

1. Pump plunger
2. Secondary main air bleed
3. Secondary main nozzle
4. Air vent
5. Secondary small venturi
6. Pump jet
7. Choke valve
8. Primary small venturi
9. Air vent
10. Primary main nozzle
11. Primary main air bleed
12. Slow air bleed No. 2
13. Economizer jet
14. Slow air bleed No. 1
15. Slow jet
16. Power piston
17. Strainer
18. Secondary main jet
19. Check ball retainer
20. Steel ball (inlet)
21. Pump discharge weight
22. Steel ball (outlet)
23. High speed valve
24. Secondary throttle valve
25. Secondary bore
26. Primary bore
27. Primary throttle valve
28. Idle port
29. Slow port
30. Idle adjusting screw
31. Power valve
32. Primary main jet
33. Float
34. Needle valve

acceleration; *choke*, for reliable starting in cold weather; and *power valve*, for fuel economy. Although slight differences in appearance may be noted, these carburetors are basically alike. Of course, different jets and settings are demanded by the different engines to which they are fitted.

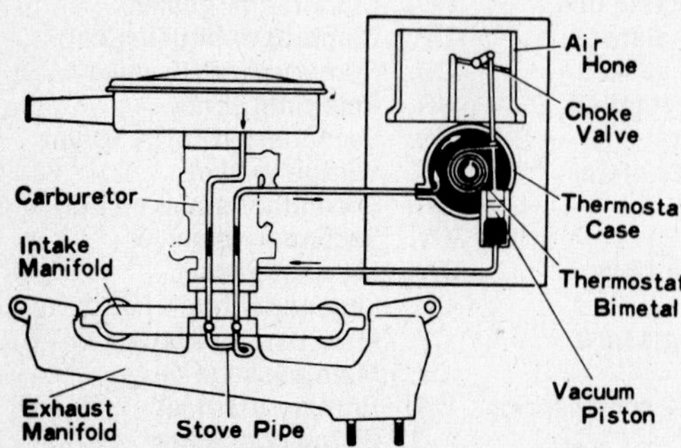

Automatic choke system.

Removal

Remove air filter housing, disconnect all air hoses from filter base and disconnect battery ground cable. Disconnect fuel line, choke pipe and distributor vacuum line. Remove accelerator linkage (with automatic transmission, also remove throttle rod to transmission). Remove the four nuts that secure the carburetor to manifold and lift off carburetor and gasket. Cover the open manifold with a clean rag to prevent small objects from dropping into the engine.

Adjustment

Float level Set by bending the tabs. If the correct level gauge is unavailable, use a ⅜″ drill bit under the float, holding the air horn upside down.

Secondary throttle valve opening Hold the primary valve at a 30° angle before the fully open position and observe whether

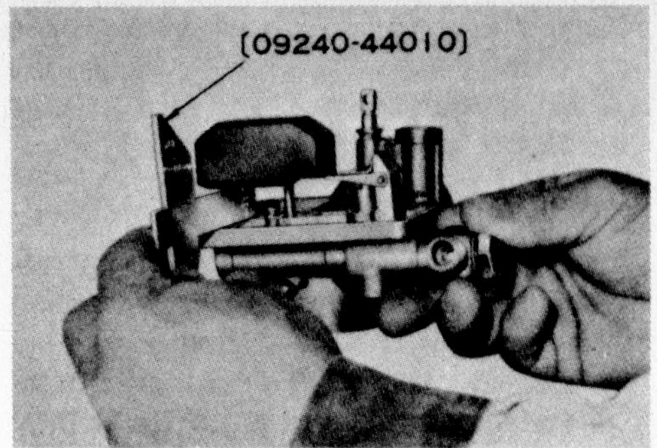

Checking float level.

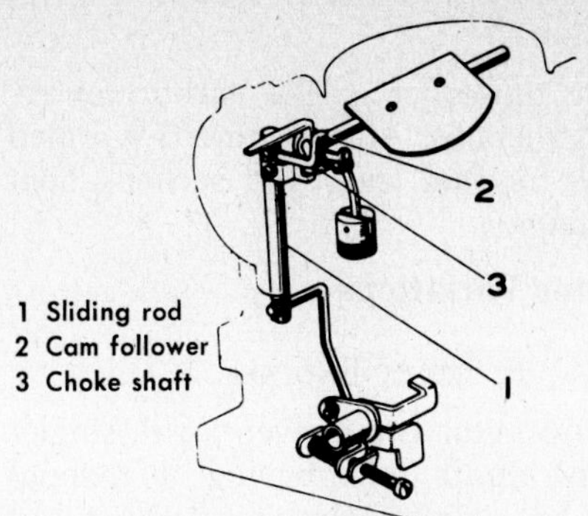

Unloader.

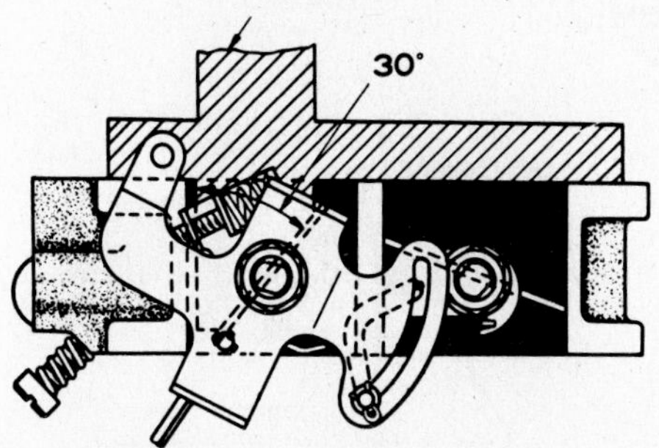

Adjusting secondary throttle valve

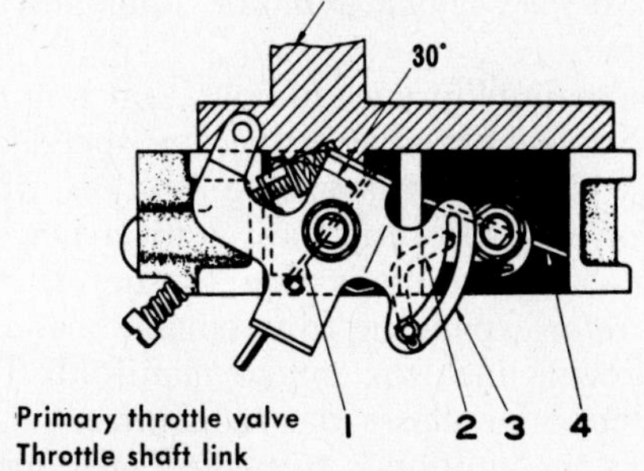

Initial opening angle

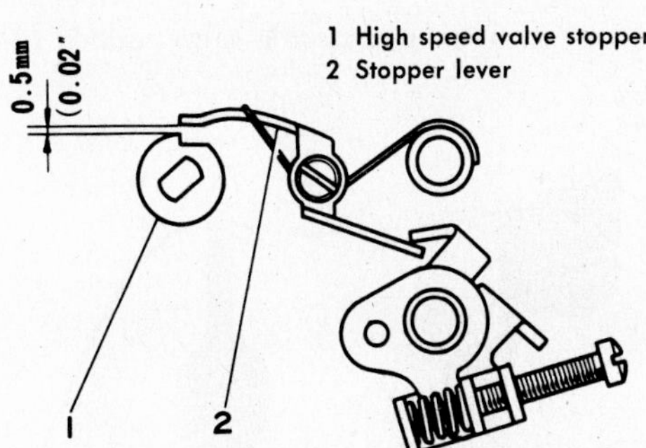

Adjusting high speed stopper lever

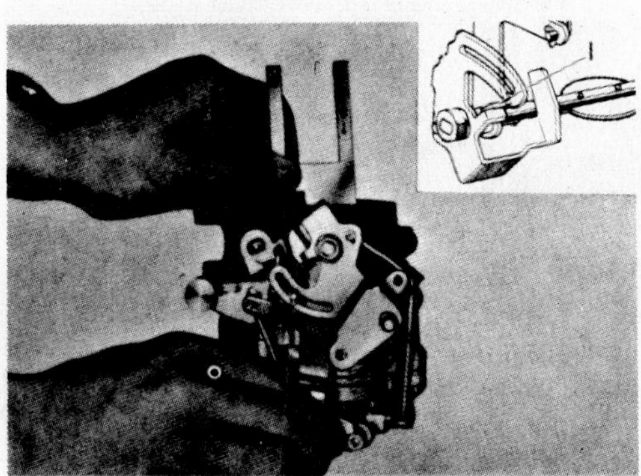

Adjusting fast idle.

the throttle shaft link touches the end of the groove in the throttle shaft arm. If necessary, bend the arm until contact is made without opening the secondary valve, then check for smooth operation.

High speed stop lever Check the clearance between the stop and the lever at the point where the secondary valve begins opening; it should be 0.020″. To adjust, bend the stop lever slightly.

Fast idle speed With the choke fully closed, adjust the fast idle screw to give 0.040″ clearance between the primary throttle valve and the carburetor bore.

Unloader Fit a 50° gauge into the throttle opening and bend the fast idle cam follower so that the choke begins to open at the 50° throttle plate opening position.

Choke This should be adjusted with the carburetor installed on a running engine. The choke should be fully closed with a cold engine; fully open after the engine comes to proper operating temperature. Adjust by loosening the three choke housing screws and turning the housing clockwise to lean the mixture (make choke open sooner) and counterclockwise to richen the mixture (make choke open later). One mark on the housing equals about 7° F.

Installation

Reverse the order of the carburetor removal instructions. After engine is warmed up, check for fuel leaks and recheck float level settings.

Carburetor Variations

F Series Engines

This carburetor is a conventional, single-barrel downdraft unit having a manual choke. It has six main circuits: 1) float and vent; 2) low speed; 3) high speed; 4) accelerator; 5) choke and fast idle; and 6) power.

The main difference in operation is in the added solenoid valve in the low speed circuit, which prevents engine "run-on" after ignition shut-off (especially with a hot engine). This run-on is due to fuel in the carburetor expanding from engine heat and overflowing into the intake manifold. The solenoid valve closes the economizer jet as soon as the ignition is turned off and opens it as soon as the ignition is turned on again.

K-C Series Engines

A conventional two-barrel carburetor with manual choke is used. An "Auxiliary Slow System" has been incorporated to prevent excessive discharge of unburnt gases during deceleration. High manifold vacuum acts on a diaphragm (through the vacuum sensing line), opening the spring-loaded valve and allowing both fuel and air to enter the intake manifold. The proper air-fuel ratio needed for proper combustion, within the limits of emission control standards, is thus maintained.

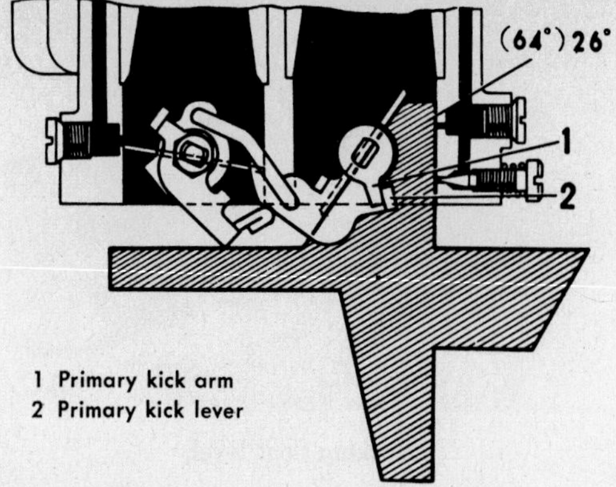

Adjusting start of secondary throttle valve opening (2M).

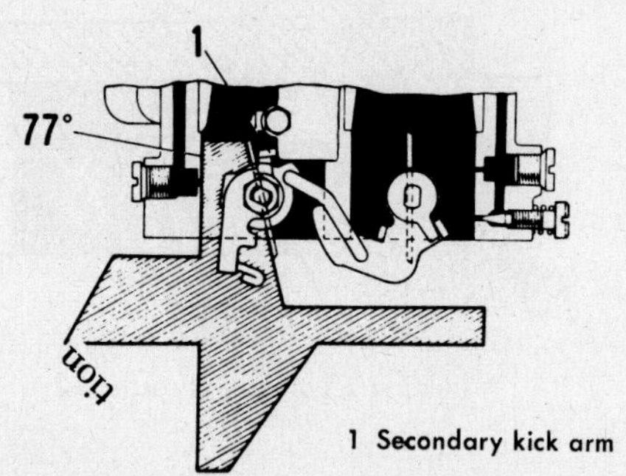

Adjusting fully open throttle valve position (2M).

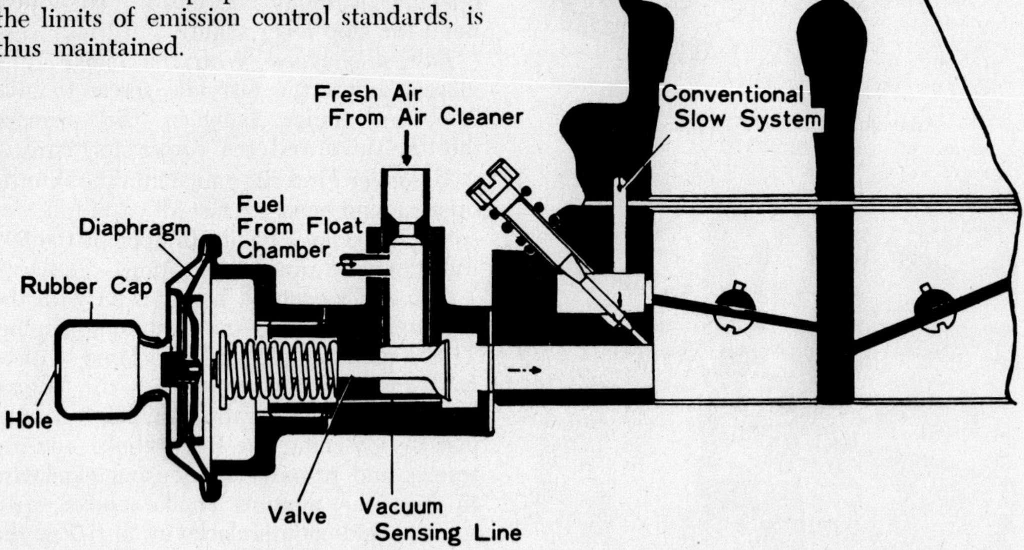

Auxiliary Slow System-Corolla K-C

Inspecting the A.S. system

Remove the rubber cap and check for air (suction) leaks due to a defective diaphragm. Close off the air hose from the air cleaner and, if there is a change in engine speed, replace the diaphragm. Disconnect the air hose from the air cleaner and rev up the engine. If no air is drawn in during deceleration, the diaphragm is defective.

Check the fuel line from float chamber to A.S. valve for obstructions. Sometimes the engine will "hunt" or surge at low and medium speeds. This is due to insufficient pressure on the diaphragm spring and the problem can be cured by a simple modification. Remove the valve from the carburetor and unscrew the valve bodies. Depress the brass plate on top of the diaphragm and insert a small C-washer of about 0.025″ thickness under the valve stem head so as to increase the spring pressure. This will serve to keep the valve fully seated regardless of slight variations in manifold vacuum at low and medium engine speeds. *NOTE: If the outside of the diaphragm is wet, replace valve assembly.*

8R-C Series Engines

A *reloader* has been added to prevent the throttle valve from opening during automatic choke operation on 8R-C engines. The following settings are different for these carburetors:

Fast Idle Primary throttle valve opens 11° when choke is fully closed.

Unloader Choke valve should open 19° when throttle is fully opened.

Reloader Unit should drop freely (of its own weight) when the choke valve is opened by hand.

NOTE: The reloader lever should disengage smoothly from the stop when the choke valve plate is opened manually (50° from fully closed position).

2M Series Engines

A conventional two-barrel carburetor is used. The secondary throttle plate is controlled by a vacuum diaphragm and the jets are larger than those on other carburetors. Settings are as follows:

Fast idle With choke valve closed, the upper part of the idle cam should touch the fast idle lever. If not, bend the link. Now, adjust fast idle screw so that the primary throttle valve is opened 11°, giving a clearance with the carburetor body of 0.050″.

Cooling System

RADIATOR

Removal

Drain all coolant, disconnect and remove all radiator hoses and disconnect the two oil cooler lines, if fitted. Remove upper shroud section (where fitted) and take off fan blade. Remove bolts that secure the radiator to support and carefully lift out the radiator.

Reverse removal procedure to install. Tighten hose clamps securely and remember to retighten them after a few hours of engine operation.

WATER PUMP

Removal

First drain the cooling system at the radiator drain plug at the bottom of the lower tank—no petcocks are used. Discon-

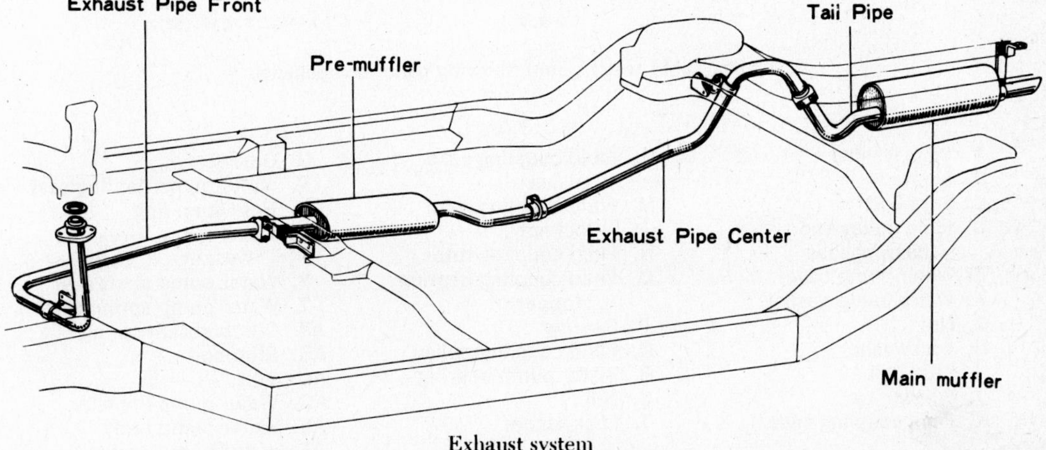

Exhaust system

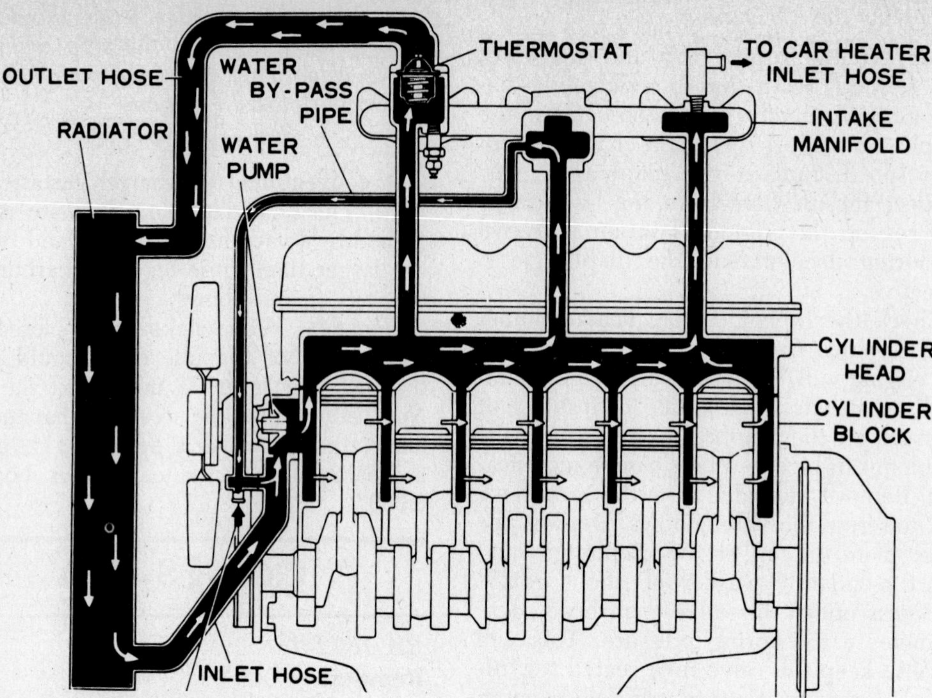

Typical cooling system schematic—2M engine illustrated.

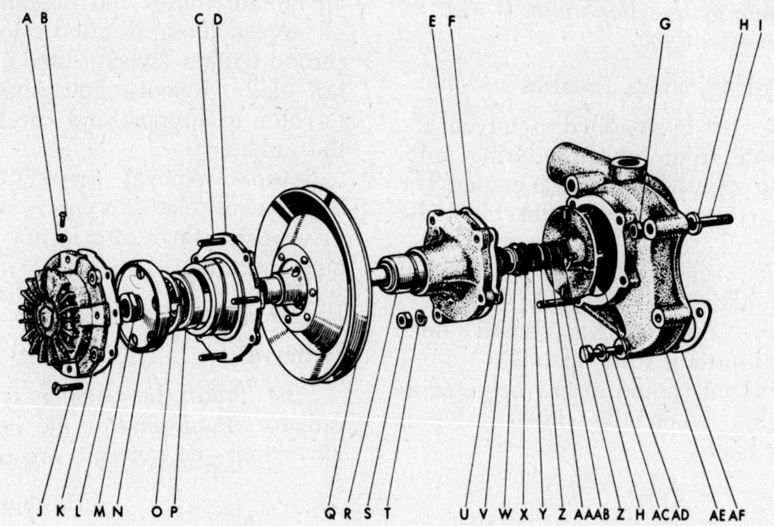

Crown (2M) water pump, showing major components.

A. Plain washer
B. Screw
C. Stud bolt
D. Fluid pulley and bearing case
E. Water pump cover
F. Water pump gasket
G. Nut
H. Lockwasher
I. Stud bolt
J. Screw
K. Fluid coupling case
L. Fluid coupling case gasket
M. Fluid coupling rotor locknut
N. Fluid coupling rotor
O. Fluid coupling bearing stopper
P. Bearing
Q. Fluid coupling pulley
R. Water pump bearing
S. Nut
T. Lockwasher
U. Gasket
V. Water pump floating seat
W. Hole snap-ring
X. Water pump thrust washer
Y. Water pump shaft seal
Z. Water pump spring seat
AA. Compression spring
AB. Stud bolt
AC. Bolt
AD. Water pump impeller
AE. Water pump body
AF. Water pump gasket

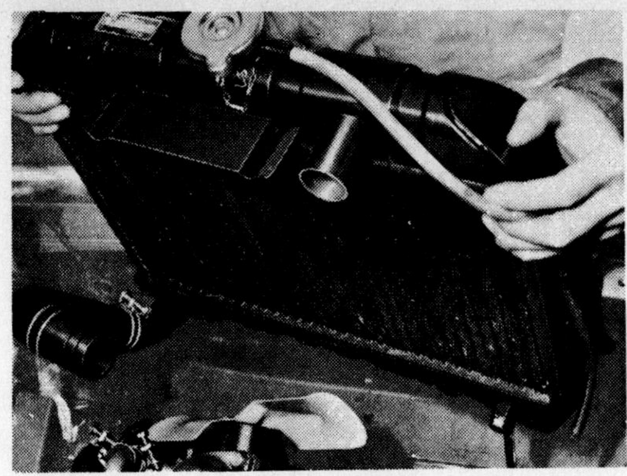

Radiator removal

nect the radiator and heater hoses, then remove the upper fan shroud, fan blade and V-belt. Remove the air pump belt (where fitted) and the bolts that hold the water pump to the engine. Carefully remove the pump, being careful not to damage the radiator core in the process.

Disassembly

Remove pump cover assembly from housing, then remove fluid coupling case from coupling bearing housing. Where no fluid coupling is fitted, simply remove fan pulley hub with a suitable puller. Place fluid coupling pulley in vise, avoiding damage to pulley, and remove fluid coupling.

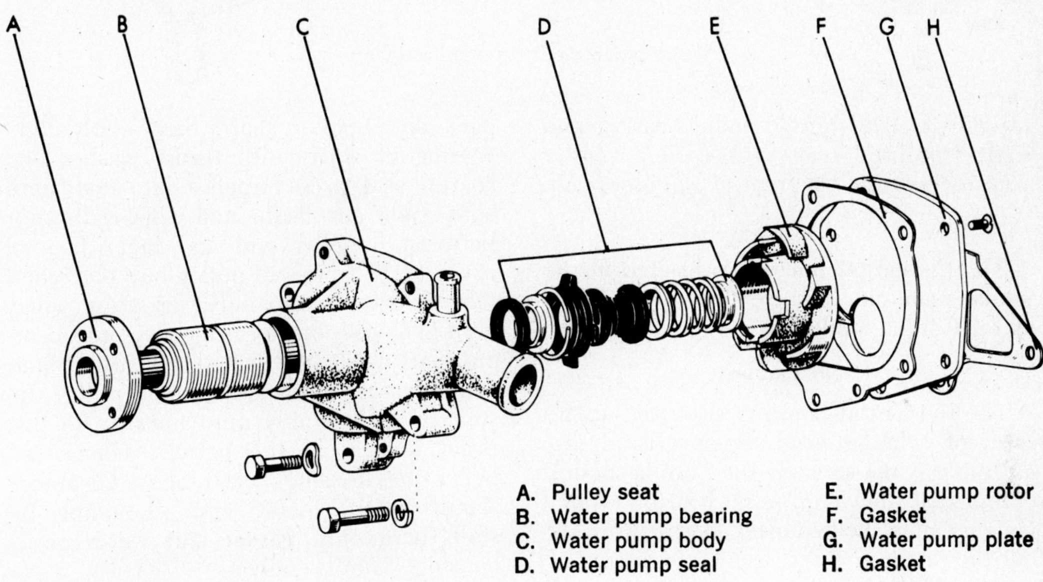

A. Pulley seat
B. Water pump bearing
C. Water pump body
D. Water pump seal
E. Water pump rotor
F. Gasket
G. Water pump plate
H. Gasket

Corolla water pump, showing major components.

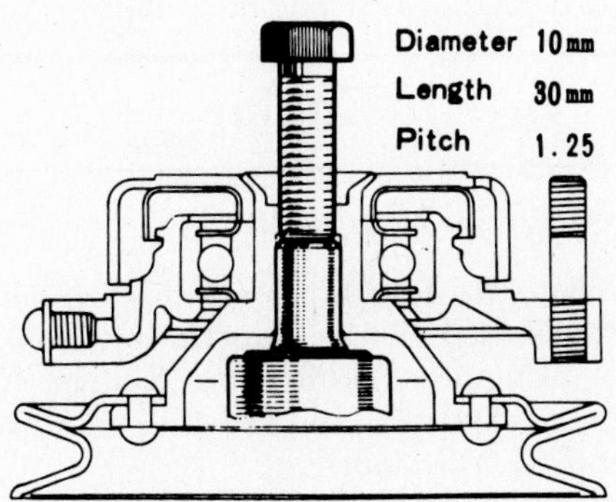

Fluid coupling removal.

Remove thermostat housing and gasket, then press the impeller from the shaft. Remove snap-ring from impeller and take off the seal pack. *NOTE: In order to press the bearing and shaft out of the water pump housing, first heat the housing to about 185° F. DO NOT REMOVE THE BEARING AND SHAFT UNLESS DAMAGED OR DEFECTIVE.* Remove the floating seal and gasket from housing.

COROLLA

Remove pulley hub with suitable puller, then remove plate and gasket from rear of pump. Remove impeller assembly from rear with a suitable puller, heat pump housing

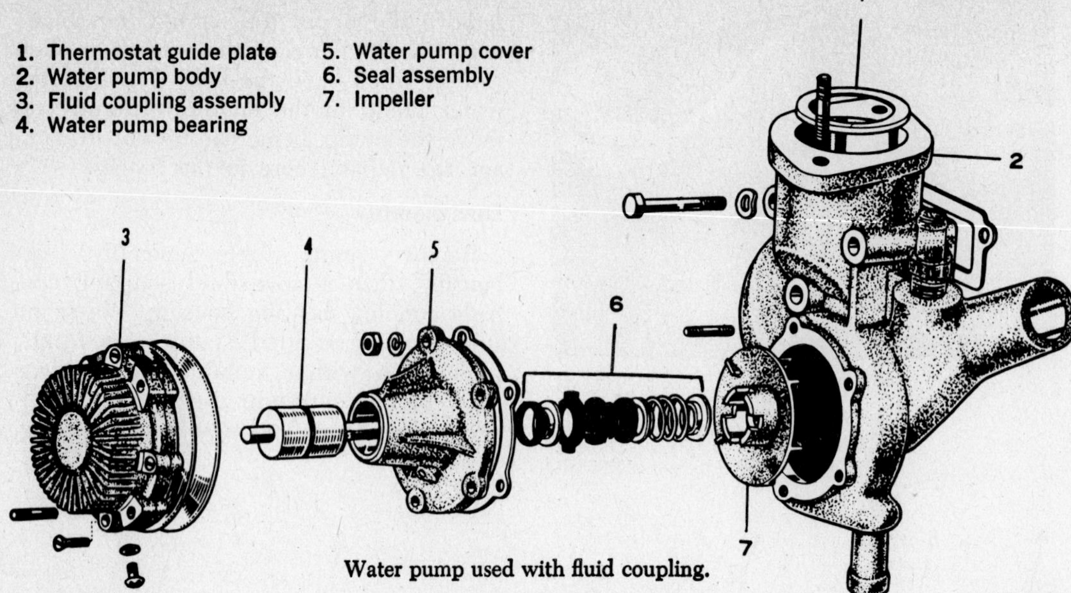

Water pump used with fluid coupling.

to 185° F. and press out the bearing and shaft from the rear. *NOTE: Thermostat housing is located at front of cylinder head.*

CROWN

The thermostat housing is located at the intake manifold. Disassembly is the same as for Corona models.

LAND CRUISER

The thermostat housing is located at the front of cylinder head. Removal and disassembly is the same as for Corolla model, except that the water pump bearing retaining clip must be removed before pressing out the bearing.

Inspection

Extra care should be exercised when handling the fluid coupling, as it must be replaced if damaged. Wash all parts thoroughly using no solvents. Check water pump housings for cracks, distortion and wear. Check impeller, snap-ring groove, thrust washer and seal surface for wear. Replace all worn components with those from impeller repair kit. Check water pump cover for distortion, cracks and wear at floating seal surface and check bearing for play, noise or wear.

Assembly

Install new gasket and floating seal into cover, heat cover to 185° F. and press in bearing assembly until end of bearing is seated flush with face of cover. Mount seal pack on impeller shaft, then apply light coating of silicone to thrust washer and floating seal, press impeller onto shaft until both ends are flush, and check distance between impeller end and inner face of cover (1.12″). Install pulley hub onto shaft (direct drive pump only) or press pulley with fluid coupling bearing case onto bearing shaft until fully seated and install fluid coupling case, with gasket, onto pulley. Install cover assembly onto housing so that drain hole is at the bottom. Check impeller-to-housing clearance. Clearance should be 0.012-0.028″ for all pumps. Install thermostat, gasket and water outlet housing (Corona only).

Installation

Bolt pump to engine using new gasket and Permatex, then tighten bolts to 7-12 ft. lbs. Adjust fan belt tension, start engine and test for leaks or noise. Refill radiator with coolant with engine running.

Engine

EMISSION CONTROL

There are four types of emission control systems used. These are: Air Injection System, Engine Modification System, Case Storage System, and Positive Crankcase Ventilation System.

Emission controlled cars have *either* the Air Injection System or the Engine Modi-

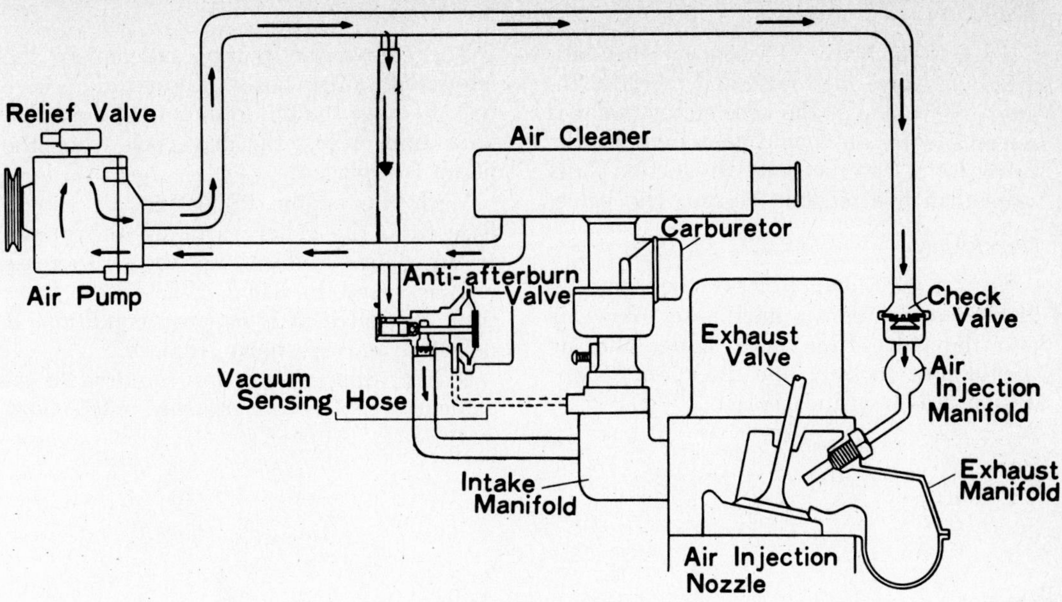

Air Injection System

fication System. Beginning 1971, all models are equipped with the Case Storage System. Those 1970 models sold in California are also equipped with the Case Storage System. Some 1967 through 1969 models are equipped with the Air Injection System. All current models are equipped with the Positive Crankcase Ventilation System (PCV).

Identification

The Air Injection System is identified by the air pump mounted at the front of the engine. The Engine Modification System (also called the Improved Combustion System) can be identified by the vacuum switching valve mounted on the left firewall. The Case Storage System can be identified by the sealed gasoline filler cap. The Positive Crankcase Ventilation System can be identified by the closed oil filler cap.

Air Injection System

The Air Injection System controls exhaust emissions by burning hydrocarbons and carbon monoxide in the exhaust ports of the cylinder head. Air is injected into the exhaust ports near each exhaust valve. The oxygen in the air and the heat of the exhaust gas induces combustion during the exhaust stroke, reducing the hydrocarbons and carbon monoxide to harmless gases. These gases flow from the exhaust system to the atmosphere.

The Air Injection System consists of an air pump, an anti-afterburn valve, a check valve, an air manifold for the cylinder head, an air injection nozzle for the exhaust port of each cylinder, and connecting air supply hoses and a vacuum sensing line. The 3K-C and 3R-C engines have an air control valve included in the system. An Auxiliary Slow (carburetor modifications) System is used on 3K-C and 2M engines.

Maintenance

Drive Belt

The drive belt deflection should be as follows when about 22 lbs. of pressure is applied to the middle of the belt between the air pump pulley and the crankshaft pulley. Adjust the deflection if necessary.

Engine	*Belt Deflection*
3K-C	0.5-0.7″
3R-C	0.6-0.8″
2M	0.4-0.6″

To adjust belt tension for a 3R-C engine, first loosen the idler pulley attaching bolt, and turn the idler pulley adjusting bolt; *clockwise* to increase the tension, *counterclockwise* to decrease the tension. After adjusting, tighten the attaching bolt to 8.7-13.7 ft. lbs. For a 2M or 3K-C engine, loosen the adjusting arm bolt to move the air pump until proper belt tension is obtained.

Anti-Afterburn Valve

To test the valve: Disconnect the anti-afterburn valve inlet hose and race the engine. The moment the accelerator pedal is released, some air should be drawn into the valve for a few seconds. If suction lasts more than five seconds, replace the valve.

Check Valve

To test the valve: Remove the valve by disconnecting the air inlet hose. Blow air into the valve from both sides. The air should flow in only one direction. If defective, unscrew and replace.

Air Pump

To remove the pump: Disconnect the inlet and outlet hoses. Loosen the drive belt. Remove the pump mounting bolts and the pump. Adjust the drive belt when the pump is replaced.

With the engine idling, no air should flow from the relief valve on the pump. If air flows, replace the valve. Increase engine speed to 3,000 rpm. If air flows from the valve, it is in good condition. If defective or very noisy, replace.

NOTE: Special tools are required to remove and replace the pressure relief valve.

1. Housing cover
2. Rear bearing
3. Rotor ring
4. Shoe spring
5. Carbon shoe
6. Vane
7. Rotor housing
8. Housing cover attaching bolt
9. Rotor ring screw
10. Rear seal
11. Pulley plate
12. Pulley
13. Key
14. Lockwasher
15. Locknut
16. Knock pin

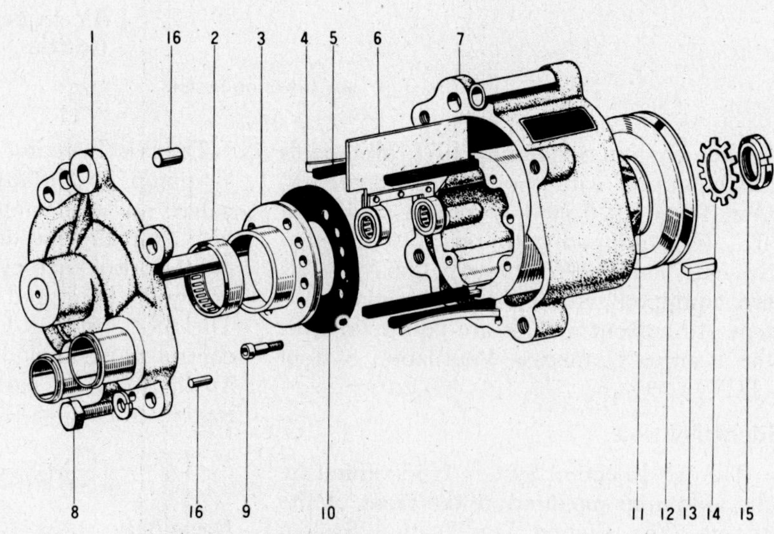

Air pump disassembled.

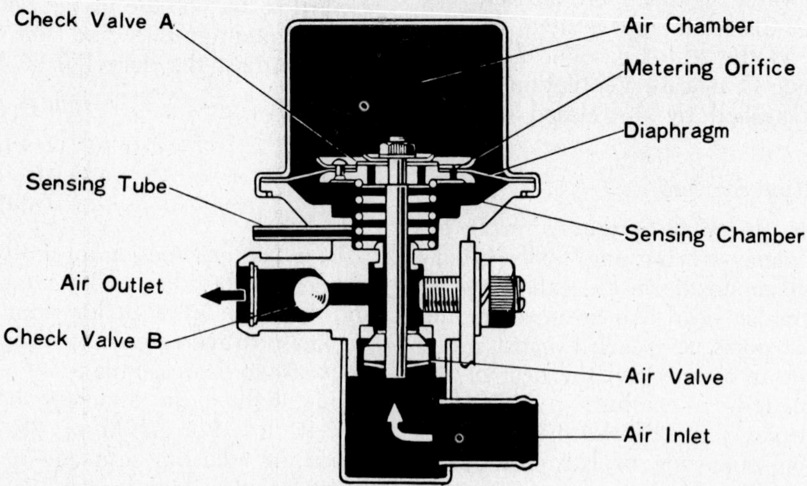

Anti-afterburn valve.

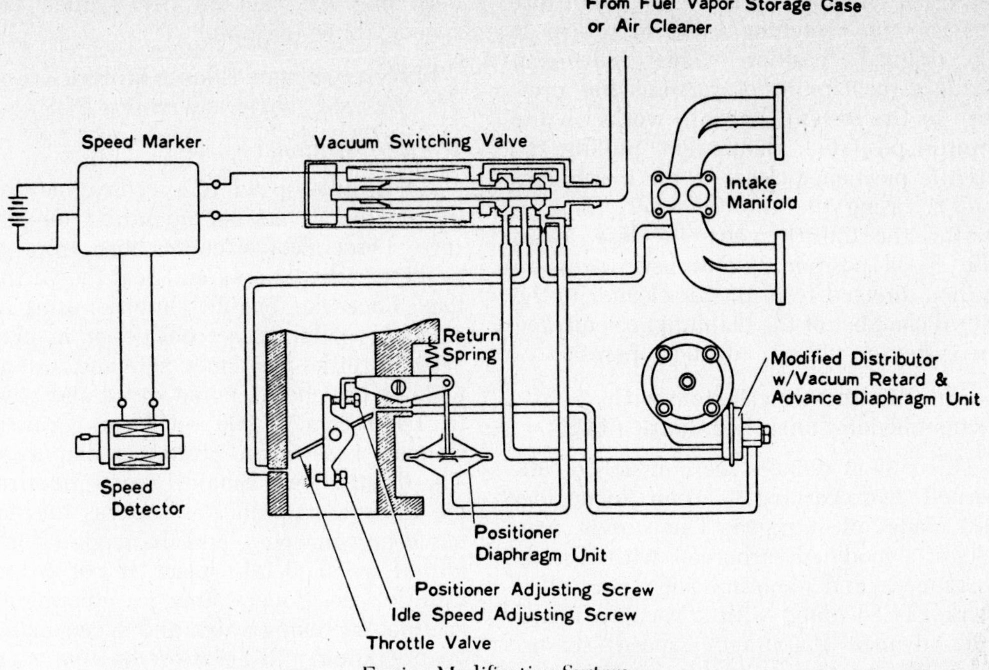

Engine Modification System

Air Injection Manifold

To remove the manifold: Remove the check valve. Remove the nuts holding the manifold to the cylinder head; remove the manifold. For 2M engines, remove the exhaust manifold before removing the air injection manifold. Install manifold by reversing the removal procedure.

Air Injection Nozzles

To replace the nozzles: Remove the air injection manifold. Remove the cylinder head and tap the nozzles (not used on 3K-C engine) out lightly with a plastic hammer. Replace the cylinder head. Position a new air injection nozzle on the cylinder head and install the air injection manifold by tightening the securing nuts.

Auxiliary Slow System

Remove the rubber cap from the valve on the carburetor. Check for air suction at idle speed. If there is no air suction the diaphragm is defective. Close the air inlet hose leading from the air cleaner to the Auxiliary Slow System at idle speed, and check that there is no change in engine operation.

Race the engine. Check that air is drawn in by the Auxiliary Slow System at deceleration. If any of the above checks indicate a defective Auxiliary Slow System, replace the valve assembly.

Engine Modification System without Transmission Controlled Spark (TCS)

This system reduces emission of unburned hydrocarbons and carbon monoxide. It consists of a modified carburetor with a throttle positioner, a modified distributor with a vacuum retard and advance diaphragm, a speed detector, a speed marker, and a vacuum switching valve.

The modified carburetor includes many improvements to help promote combustion of the air-fuel mixture in the combustion chambers, and the engine is therefore able to run smoothly with a lean mixture, with reduced emission of unburned hydrocarbons and carbon monoxide.

A throttle positioner on the carburetor in the throttle linkage keeps the throttle valve slightly open during deceleration. This reduces the vacuum underneath the throttle valve, which in turn retards the ignition timing to compensate for the loss of the engine braking caused by the open throttle valve. When the opening angle of the throttle valve exceeds the angle set by the throttle valve positioner, the engine resumes operation at the designed ignition timing for normal driving. During deceleration, throttle positioner prevents the throttle valve from returning completely and intake manifold vacuum is directed to the retard chamber of the distributor diaphragm. Further deceleration to below 11 mph (8R-C) or 14 mph (F) will cause the vacuum switching valve to return to its original position. This movement changes the circuits of vacuum and pressure in the system. Vacuum works on the throttle positioner diaphragm, pulling the throttle positioner closer to the diaphragm and releasing the throttle lever, thus allowing the throttle valve to close to an idle speed position. Atmospheric pressure is then directed from the air cleaner to the retard chamber of the diaphragm, returning the system to normal advance operation.

Engine Modification System with Transmission Controlled Spark (TCS)

This system reduces the emission of unburned hydrocarbons, carbon monoxide, and oxides of nitrogen. The system consists of a modified carburetor with throttle positioner and transmission controlled spark (TCS) along with a vacuum retard and advance diaphragm, speed sensor, speed marker, thermo-senser, spark control computer, vacuum switching valve, and modified distributor. (A shift point senser is used on manual transmission 8R-C engines.) The modified carburetor results in a lean mixture, with reduced emission of hydrocarbons and carbon monoxide. The throttle positioner is similar to the throttle positioner described for the Engine Modification System without TCS.

Transmission Controlled Spark (TCS) delays the ignition timing under certain running conditions to control the emission of oxides of nitrogen (NO_X). The required running conditions are (1) coolant temperature between 140° to 230° F, (2) vehicle speed below 35 mph (except for 8R-C with manual transmission, which must have transmission in 1st, 2nd, or 3rd gear). When decelerating from speeds above 35 mph, TCS will not operate until the speed decreases to 13 mph (8R-C with automatic transmission) or 30 mph (2T-C). In the 8R-C engine, the vacuum at the carburetor advance port acts on the distributor diaphragm on the retard side and delays the ignition timing if TCS is operating. In the 2T-C, the vacuum at the carburetor advancer port is shut off when TCS is operating. When TCS is off, the vehicle operates normally. The vacuum at the carburetor advancer port acts on the distributor diaphragm advancer side to permit spark advance. The mixture control valve on the 2T-C engine prevents the mixture from becoming too rich on deceleration from speeds above 35 mph.

Maintenance of Engine Modification System (with or without TCS)

Throttle Positioner

Adjust idle speed to specifications with the engine at normal operating temperature. Disconnect vacuum hose from the positioner diaphragm, and seal the vacuum line. Race the engine slightly, using accelerator pedal, to set positioner in place. With throttle positioner set, and using a tachometer, check engine speed and adjust to 1,400 rpm (1,000 on Land Cruiser). Connect hose to the positioner diaphragm. The throttle lever should become free from the throttle positioner as soon as the hose has been connected, and the engine should idle at specified idle speed. If not, inspect throttle positioner linkage, diaphragm, vacuum switching valve and speed marker for operation, and hoses for leakage.

Vacuum Retard and Advance Diaphragm Unit

Warm up engine, connect a tachometer and adjust idle speed to specifications. Disconnect hose leading from vacuum switching valve to adapter on intake manifold and seal it. Disconnect hose which connects vacuum switching valve with retard chamber of distributor retard and advance diaphragm at the switching valve, and connect it with intake manifold adapter. Note that engine speed decreases when the hose is connected to the intake manifold. If no change in engine speed occurs, replace distributor vacuum assembly.

Speed Detector (F engines, 1970 8R-C engines)

To test the unit: Check that wires are properly connected. Inspect speed detector for generating voltage by using an AC voltmeter connected between the output wires. The voltage should be 6.1 volts (F) or 10.2 volts (8R-C) at 37.5 mph. If the voltage is lower than 4.1 volts (F) or 7.1 volts (8R-C), replace the speed detector. Make certain that the speedometer registers correctly before inspecting the speed detector.

Speed Sensor (1971 8R-C, 2T-C engines)

To test the unit: With the car standing still, disconnect the speedometer cable from the transmission. Using a circuit tester, check that there are 6 on-off pulses for each cable rotation on the 8R-C (4 for 2T-C). When driving at 10 mph, use an oscilloscope to check the number of pulses. The 8R-C should have 900-1,150 pulses per minute. The 2T-C should have 600-766 pulses per minute. If the measured values fail to confirm the specified values, replace the speedometer assembly.

Speed Marker (1970—all engines)

Check wires for proper connections. Check that the vacuum switching valve operates when the speedometer indicates over 10.5 to 15 mph. If the vacuum switching valve does not operate, check for defects, and replace if necessary. Inspect the speed marker for output and determine whether it is at fault by checking the whole system.

Speed Marker (1971 8R-C engines)

To check the throttle positioner circuit, disconnect the speed marker socket. Drive the vehicle with a voltage tester connected. When accelerating, the voltage should drop from 12 volts to 0 volt when speed reaches 25 mph. When decelerating, voltage should rise from 0 volt to 12 volts when speed reaches 11 mph.

To inspect the Transmission Controlled Spark circuit on automatic transmission vehicles, disconnect the speed marker socket. Drive the vehicle with a voltage tester connected. When accelerating, the voltage should drop from 7 volts to 0 volts when speed reaches 35 mph. When decelerating, the voltage must reach 7 volts (from 0 volts) when the speed drops below 13 mph. Replace the speed marker if it fails to function as specified.

Speed Marker (1971 F engines)

Check the wires for proper connections, and correct if necessary. Check that the

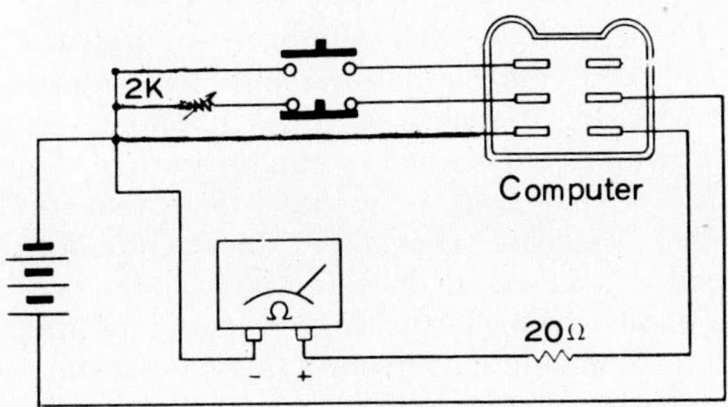

Testing T.C.S. system

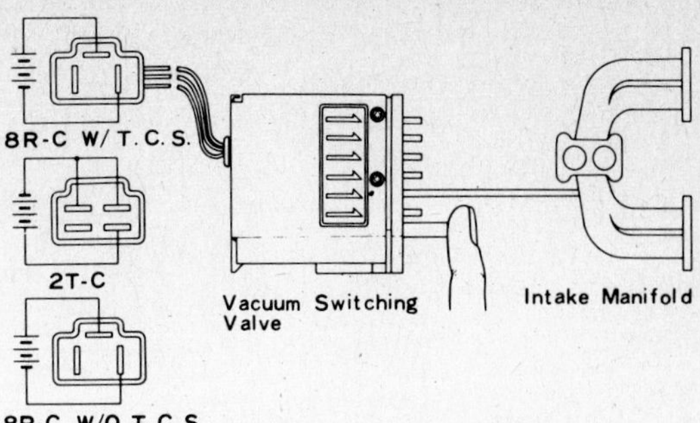

Inspecting the vacuum switching valve

vacuum switching valve operates when the speedometer indicates over 14 mph. If the vacuum switching valve does not operate, check for defects, and replace if necessary. Inspect the speed marker for operation and determine whether it is at fault by checking the whole system.

Vacuum Switching Valve (1971 8R-C engines, with TCS)

To test the unit: Measure the resistance of the magnetic coil. Disconnect the vacuum switching valve connector and measure the resistances as shown. The resistances should be: between (+) and TCS: 28 ohms; between (+) and TP: 18.7 ohms. Inspect the air passages. Disconnect the wiring, and remove the vacuum switching valve from the vehicle. Connect a fully charged battery. Blow air into each passage, and inspect the operation of each valve. If the vacuum switching valve does not operate check for defects in the wiring. Replace the vacuum switching valve if there is no defect in the wiring.

Vacuum Switching Valve (1971 8R-C engines, without TCS)

To test the unit: Measure the resistance of the magnetic coil. Disconnect the vacuum switching valve connectors and measure the resistance as shown. The resistance should be 18.7 ohms. The vacuum switching valve may be tested as described for the 1971 8R-C without TCS.

Vacuum Switching Valve (2T-C engines)

To test the unit: Measure the continuous resistance of the magnetic coil. Disconnect the vacuum switching valve connectors and measure the resistance as shown. The resistances should be: between (+) and TP: 28 ohms; between (+) and MC: 56 ohms; between (+) and TCS 56 ohms. Test the valve as for the 1971 8R-C without TCS.

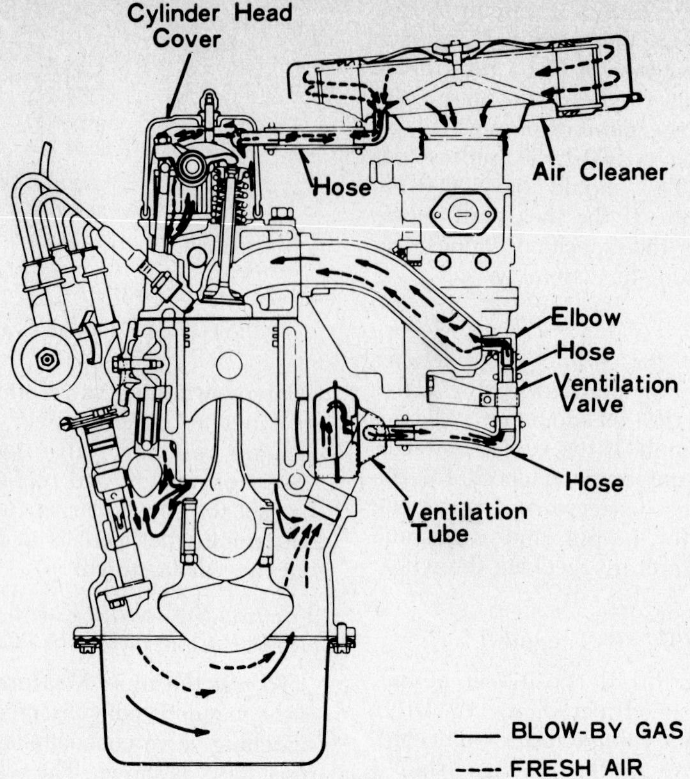

Corona (3RC) PCV system.

Case Storage System

This system reduces hydrocarbon emissions from the fuel system. There are two versions; that used on engines with the Engine Modification System incorporates the vacuum switching valve, while that on engines with the Air Injection System has a purge control valve.

Maintenance

Purge Control Valve (with Air Injection System)

Disconnect the hose from the fuel tank. Increase the engine speed slowly to 2,500 rpm. Check for suction. If there is no suction, replace the valve.

Vacuum Switching Valve (with Engine Modification System)

Check the vacuum switching valve as described above. Connect a fully charged battery to the vacuum switching valve. Then, with the vacuum switching valve actuated, disconnect the hose from the vapor line. Start the engine, and check to see if there is suction. If there is no suction, replace the vacuum switching valve.

Positive Crankcase Ventilation (PCV) System

The PCV system controls crankcase blow-by gases. It consists of a ventilation valve and hoses leading from the crankcase to the intake manifold. This system returns blow-by gases to the combustion chambers where they are reburned. Ventilating air from the air cleaner enters the engine through the cylinder head cover or the ventilation tube. The air, laden with crankcase vapors, passes through the ventilation tube into the ventilation valve which regulates the amount of air flow to meet changing conditions. Air is then drawn into the intake manifold through the connecting hose. The ventilation valve is operated by the difference in pressure between the crankcase and the intake manifold. When there is no difference in pressure (engine off) or the pressure of the intake manifold is greater than that of the crankcase (backfire), the ventilation valve is closed. If there is a large difference (engine idling), the high vacuum of the intake manifold overcomes the valve spring, and the valve is pulled toward the intake manifold side. The air passes through the restricted passage between the valve and the housing. When the difference is small (normal operation), the valve remains in a position where spring pressure and intake manifold vacuum balance.

ENGINE REMOVAL AND REPLACEMENT

Removal

It is advisable to remove both engine and transmission together, unless special transmission supports are available. *NOTE: The following steps are common to all engines. Special operations for specific models are indicated separately.*

Remove hood, radiator grille and radiator support, then remove battery from car (for protection) and disconnect all electrical wiring. To save assembly time, mark each disconnected wire and terminal with a small tag. Now, drain coolant and engine oil. Disconnect radiator and heater hoses and remove radiator. Disconnect and remove, as necessary, all fuel lines, choke and accelerator control cables and wires. Disconnect rear transmission mounts and remove drive shaft, then remove fan. Disconnect exhaust pipe(s). Install lifting hooks or eyebolts. *NOTE: Since the engine must be sharply tilted in order to clear the firewall, it will be necessary to jack up the car and support it on jack stands.*

F, FA SERIES

Remove engine crankcase stone guards. Remove gearshift linkage, transfer control intermediate rod from control shaft, and engine ground strap. Disconnect front motor mounts and rear engine supports, then remove passenger seat and gasoline tank assembly. Remove transmission cover and parking brake lock plate from firewall; disconnect speedometer cable. Unhook clutch release spring and remove clutch release cylinder. Remove crossmember.

Replacement

Installation of engine is done by reversing removal order. Before connecting hoist, bolt clutch, or converter, and transmission to the engine. Install oil cooler lines and brackets and bolt clutch release cylinder to clutch fork. Fill transmission with proper quantity and grade of lubricant before installation.

CYLINDER HEAD REMOVAL AND REPLACEMENT (OVERHEAD VALVE ENGINES)

1. Disconnect battery. Drain cooling system and remove air cleaner.
2. Remove the accelerator cable and the carburetor throttle arm. Disconnect the carburetor choke wire.
3. If so equipped, disconnect water hose retainer from cylinder head cover.
4. Remove water pump and water valve hoses (if so equipped).
5. Remove heater control cable from water valve (if installed).
6. Disconnect cylinder head PCV hose.
7. Remove valve cover.
8. Remove rocker arm bolts and lift off rocker arms.
9. Remove push rods.
10. Disconnect upper radiator hose at water outlet.
11. Remove primary wires from spark plugs.
12. Remove windshield washer assembly.

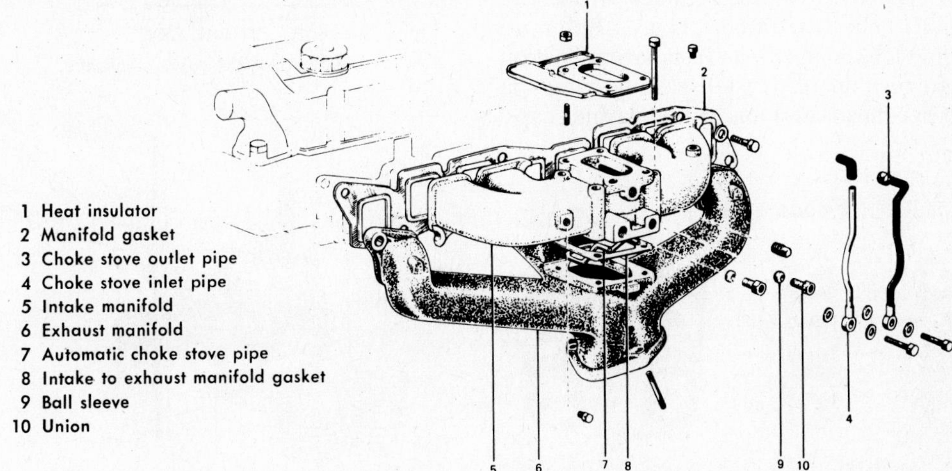

Intake/exhaust manifold assembly

13. Disconnect exhaust pipe flange from exhaust manifold.
14. Using proper sequence, loosen cylinder head bolts in three stages. *Caution: To prevent cylinder head warpage, engine must be totally cold when performing above operations. In addition, some engines utilize dowel pins to aid in cylinder head alignment. Therefore, lift head vertically from block. Do not slide.*

To replace cylinder head, reverse removal procedure. Be sure to utilize proper head bolt torque and tightening sequence. Proper head bolt torque should be reached in four stages. When installing new gasket, be sure to use appropriate sealer.

CYLINDER HEAD AND CAMSHAFT REMOVAL AND REPLACEMENT (OVERHEAD CAM ENGINES)

2M and 8R-C Engines

Note: Camshaft may be removed with cylinder head still attached to block.

Remove valve cover. Extract union bolts and union. On 8R-C engines, remove the oil delivery lines. Drain coolant. Using proper removal sequence, loosen rocker shaft bolts in three stages and remove rocker arms. Check valve timing and remove chain tensioner. Remove timing gear. Using proper sequence, remove camshaft bearing caps and bearings. Remove camshaft.

Note: Camshaft caps and bearings are matched. Be sure to replace bearings in original caps.

Remove cylinder head bolts and cylinder head.

To replace: Install cylinder head and torque bolts in three stages. Refer to Timing Chain and Gear Installation Section for further details. Install cam bearings on cylinder head and on cam bearing caps. Place camshaft in position. Install cam bearing caps and torque to specifications. Cam bearing caps should be installed with prominent face towards front of engine. Caps are numbered; be sure to install caps in proper order.

Camshaft oil clearance: .001-.002″
Camshaft thrust clearance: .0017-.0066″

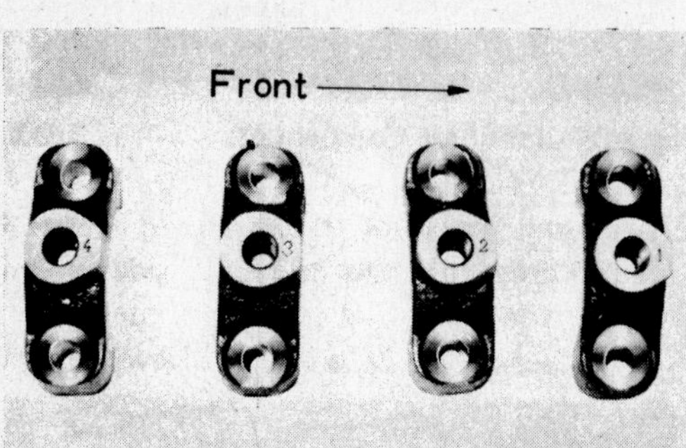

Cam bearing caps

VALVES

Adjusting Valve Clearance

Note: The procedure for adjusting valves on overhead valve engines with the engine running as given here is the method recommended by Toyota. It is also possible to adjust the valves with the engine off.

2M Engine

First, align the indent hole on the front side of the camshaft No. 1 bearing cap with the timing line on the camshaft gear flange. At this point, the groove on the crankshaft damper and the "zero" mark on the timing chain cover also should be in alignment. With the marks lined up, No. 1 piston will be at TDC and the intake valves (1), (2) and (4) in the illustration can now be adjusted to 0.004″ and the exhaust valves (1), (3) and (5) can be adjusted to 0.007″. Rotate the crankshaft one full revolution (in the normal direction of rota-

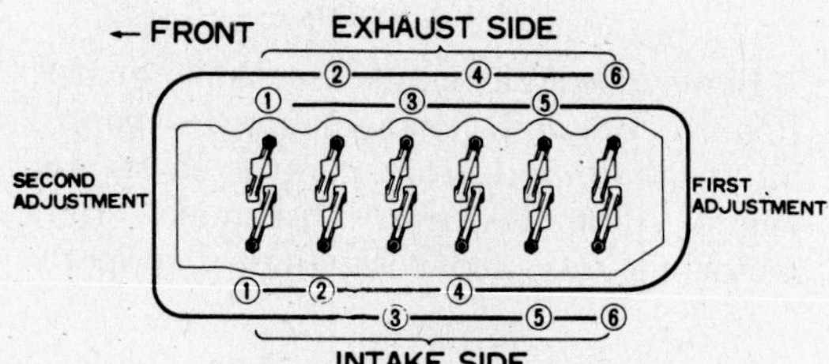

Adjusting 2M valve clearance.

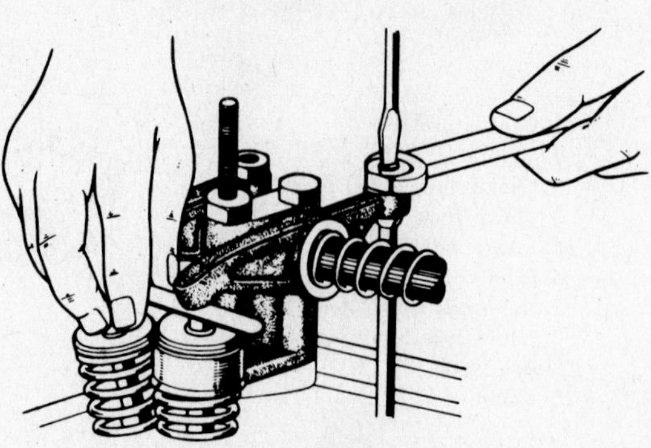

Adjusting the valves

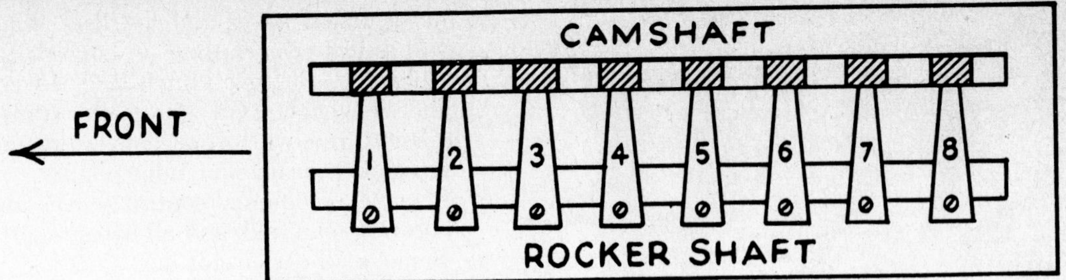

8R-C engine valve adjustment sequence

tion) and again line up the marks on the crankshaft damper and timing chain cover. The intake valves (3), (5) and (6) and the exhaust valves (2), (4) and (6) can now be adjusted. After adjustment is completed, tighten the locknuts to 12-16 ft. lbs.

F, FA Engine

The engine must be at normal operating temperature (170-185°F.) and the cylinder head bolts and manifold bolts must be tightened to specifications before adjusting valves. Start the engine and set idle speed to 500 rpm, then check the clearance on the running engine by sliding a feeler gauge between the rocker arm and valve stem. The feeler gauge should be able to be pulled out with slight resistance. If not, adjust by loosening locknut and turning adjusting screw until proper clearance is attained.

K-C, 3R-B, 3R-C Engine

Set engine idle speed to 550 rpm. Refer to F, FA engine valve adjustment procedures and proceed in identical manner.

8R-C Engine

Turn piston to TDC (No. 1 cylinder) on compression stroke, then adjust rocker arms (1), (2), (3) and (5); turn crankshaft one complete revolution in the normal direction of rotation, then adjust rocker arms (4), (6), (7) and (8).

3K-C, 2T-C Engine

Set engine idle speed to specified normal rpm for this engine. Refer to F, FA engine procedures above and adjust in identical manner.

TIMING CHAIN AND COVER REMOVAL (OVERHEAD CAM ENGINES)

8R-C Engine

Note: This operation requires engine to be removed from vehicle.

Remove camshaft from head. Using proper sequence, remove cylinder head bolts in three stages and remove cylinder head. If engine is still in vehicle, remove at this point. Once accomplished, remove crank pulley bolt and crank pulley. Invert engine so oil pan is at top. Remove oil pan. Remove timing chain cover. Remove the secondary timing chain, camshaft drive gear, the 2nd chain tensioner, and first chain tensioner. Remove crankshaft timing gear, drive shaft gear, and the primary timing chain. Next, remove the vibration damper. Be sure to separate chains to avoid confusion when reinstalling.

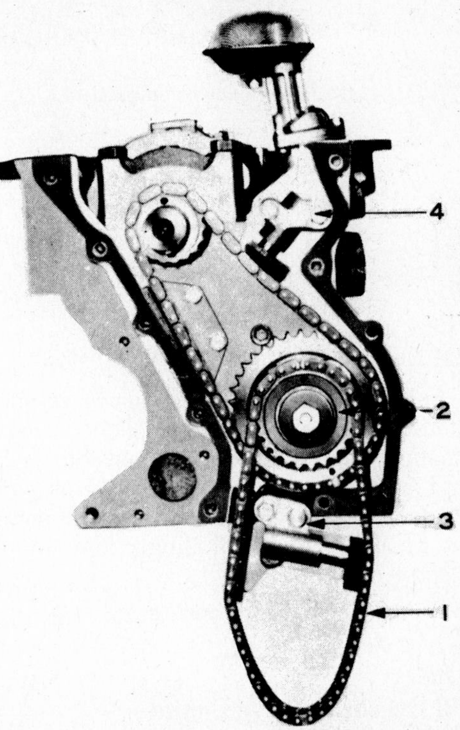

Secondary timing chain removal

1 Secondary timing chain
2 Camshaft drive gear
3 2nd chain tensioner
4 1st chain tensioner

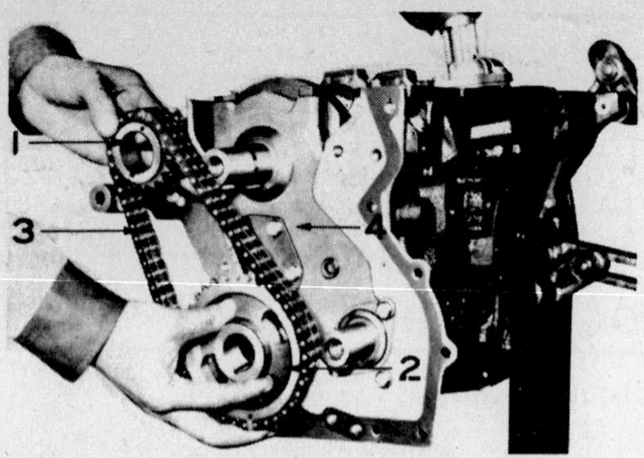

Primary timing chain removal

1 Crankshaft timing gear
2 Driveshaft gear
3 Primary timing chain
4 Vibration damper

2M engine timing chain removal

1 Tensioner gear
2 Tensioner arm
3 Vibration damper
4 Vibration guide
5 Secondary vibration damper
6 Oil slinger

2M Engine

Follow 8R-C removal sequence to completion of engine removal. Then remove timing chain cover. Remove tensioner gear and arm. Remove vibration damper and guide. Remove secondary vibration damper. Finally, remove oil slinger and lift out chain.

CAMSHAFT AND TIMING CHAIN REMOVAL

All Overhead Valve Engines

The following general instructions apply to all overhead valve engines.

1. Remove engine and transmission from vehicle. On cars with automatic transmission, remove all lines and hoses. Remove starter motor and alternator.
2. Mark clutch cover and flywheel. This will aid in reassembling in correct relationship. Remove clutch disc, cover, and flywheel. (On automatic transmission, remove torque converter and separate transmission from engine.)
3. Remove air pump, control valve, air injection manifold, and all hoses.
4. Remove all carburetor lines.
5. Remove distributor, fuel pump, and oil filter.
6. Remove water pump and outlet flange.
7. Remove carburetor and manifold.
8. Remove temperature and oil pressure sending units.
9. Remove cylinder head assembly. Be sure to follow proper removal sequence.
10. Remove push rods and valve lifters.
11. Invert engine and remove oil pan.
12. Remove oil pump assembly.
13. Remove crankshaft pulley nut and pulley.
14. Unbolt timing gear cover and remove oil nozzle.
15. Remove crankshaft thrust plate. Remove cam and timing gear. Be sure not to damage camshaft bearings.

CAMSHAFT AND TIMING CHAIN INSTALLATION

All Overhead Valve Engines

Install camshaft assembly and align the timing gears as marked. Tighten thrust plate to 14.5 ft. lbs. and recheck the backlash. Install timing gear oil nozzle into cylinder block and align discharge hole towards the timing gears. Stake in place with a centerpunch. Install timing gear cover and crankshaft pulley, using a new oil seal. Tighten pulley nut. Install oil pump assembly and outlet pipe, then install oil pan and gasket.

Camshaft timing marks

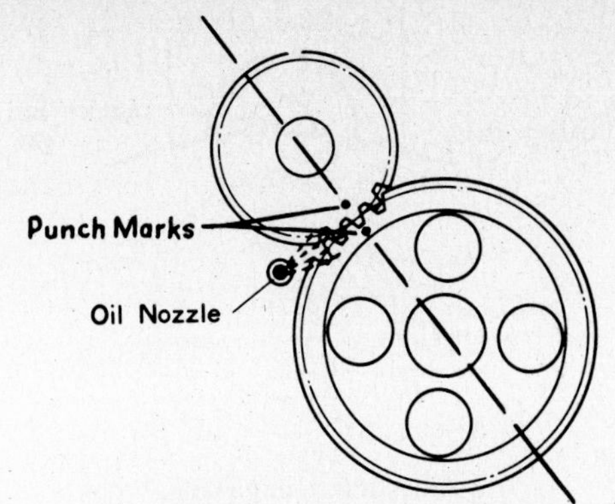

Timing gears and oil nozzle position.

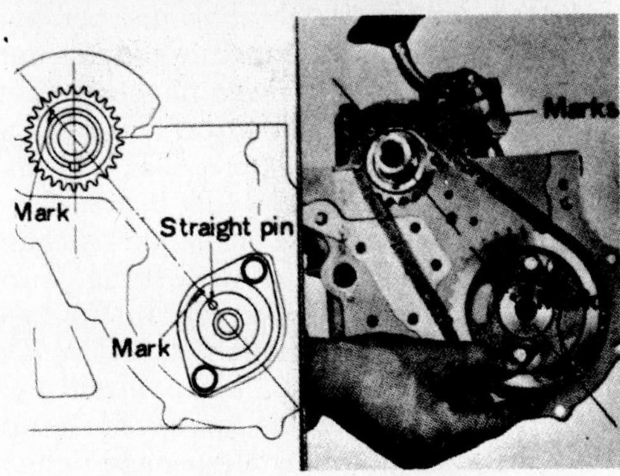

Installing timing chain, Corolla.

Install cylinder head and gasket and tighten, in correct sequence, to specified torque. Install valve lifters, pushrods and rocker shaft assembly, followed by pushrod covers, oil pressure sending unit, temperature sending unit, engine draincock vent tube and dipstick tube. Tighten manifolds and gaskets from center outwards, then install carburetor, covering it with a clean cloth to prevent entry of dirt or small objects.

Install choke stove pipes into manifold. Next install (not necessarily in order mentioned) oil filter, alternator, engine mounts, water pump and thermostat housing, fanbelt, air injection pump and belt, air injection manifolds and valves, heater pipes, distributor, fuel pump, spark plugs, and any other parts or accessories that were removed, such as flywheel, converter and starter motor. *Do not install valve cover prior to engine installation.*

TIMING CHAIN AND GEAR INSTALLATION

2M Engine

When installing the timing gears, the punch marks on the gear faces must face front (out). Check camshaft end-play between the front support and camshaft gear flange. If the clearance exceeds 0.012″, replace the No. 2 bearing. Normal play is 0.002-0.006″. Inspect the cam lobes for wear. Small irregularities may be honed out with a smooth oilstone.

Use micrometer to measure the cam lobe wear. Limits are 1.535″ intake and 1.496″ exhaust. Check camshaft bearings in their caps with PLASTIGAGE.

Remove chain tensioner snap-ring from front of unit and take out components in order shown. Test the spring—if installed pressure is less than 8.5 lbs., replace spring. If body-to-plunger clearance is more than 0.005″, replace the defective part/s.

Tensioner Specifications

Body inner diameter	0.590 -0.592″
Plunger diameter	0.588 -0.589″
Spring free length	4.331″
Spring installed length	2.476″
Spring installed pressure	9.5 lbs.

Chain tensioner (1) and timing gear bolt (2).

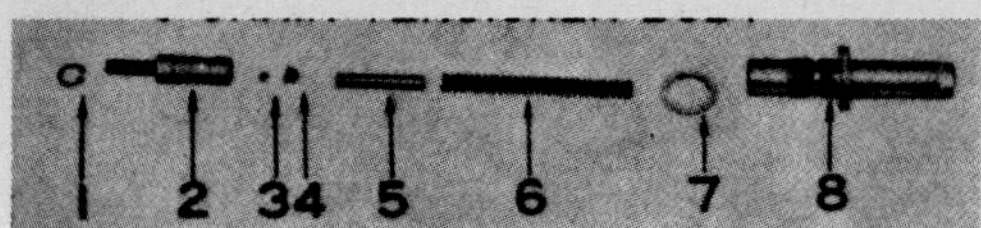

Chain tensioner components.

1. Hole snap ring
2. Chain tension plunger
3. Ball
4. Check ball retainer
5. Chain tensioner bar
6. Compression spring
7. Gasket
8. Chain tensioner body

Camshaft bearing cap
Indent hole (2)
Timing mark (1)
No. 1 HOLE
No. 2 HOLE
STRAIGHT PIN
No. 3 HOLE

Adjusting timing chain.

Check the rubbing pads of the timing chain vibration dampers for wear and cracks and replace units if necessary. A loose timing chain can cause late (retarded) valve timing and, thus, poor engine performance.

Before installing the timing chain and testing chain tension, make sure cylinder head is properly tightened and that the chain is tight against the tension pads. Next align the V-notch on the crankshaft pulley with the timing marks on the timing gear cover. Check that the timing mark (notch) in the camshaft flange is visible through the indent hole in the camshaft front bearing cap. It is necessary to look straight through the hole (0.160″ diameter).

If the timing notch is off the mark in a counterclockwise direction, adjust the chain by removing the chain sprocket and rotating it clockwise until the timing mark lines up with the indent hole. There are three indent holes spaced 6° apart. If the timing chain cannot be lined up with the third hole, it is stretched beyond adjustment and must be replaced.

Check the tension gear teeth, shaft and bushing for wear. Measure shaft and bushing—shaft diameter is 0.786″. bushing diameter is 0.787-0.788″, end-play is 0.002-0.026″.

Install the oil pump shaft assembly into the block and tighten the thrust plate lock bolt. Position No. 1 cylinder at TDC. At this point, the trademark on the crankshaft gear must face, and be in line with, the trademark on the pump drive gear. *NOTE: The timing mark on the crankshaft gear is a plain 0 (not the Japanese Toyota symbol), and in the No. 1 TDC position it will face straight up (12 O'clock).* Next, put the tension gear onto its pin at the upper part of the block. Fit the chain loosely around the gears already installed. *NOTE: The timing chain has no marked links.*

Install the chain vibration damper and damper guide, then secure the guide mounting bolts. Place oil slinger on crankshaft, then install timing chain cover and gaskets. *NOTE: 8mm. bolts equals 7-12 ft. lbs. and 10mm. bolts equals 14-22 ft. lbs.* Now, pull the slack out of the chain and tie chain to the vibration damper with string. Turn the engine over and cover the timing case opening with a clean cloth. *CAUTION: Do not rotate engine until chain installation and timing adjustment is completed.* Install the crankshaft vibration damper and tighten

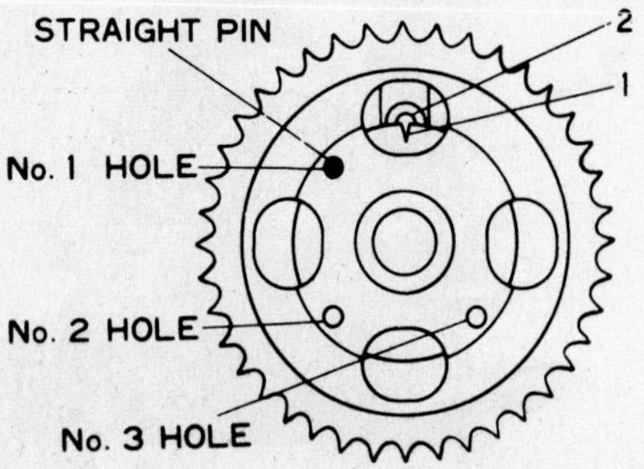

Aligning holes in timing gear.

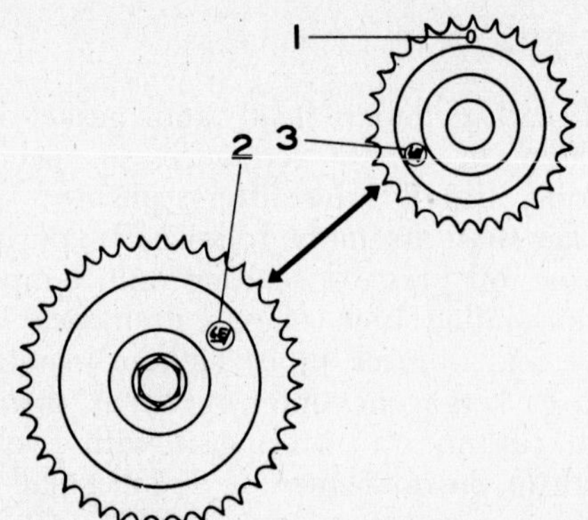

Aligning timing marks; Toyota symbols at (2) and (3), zero mark at (1).

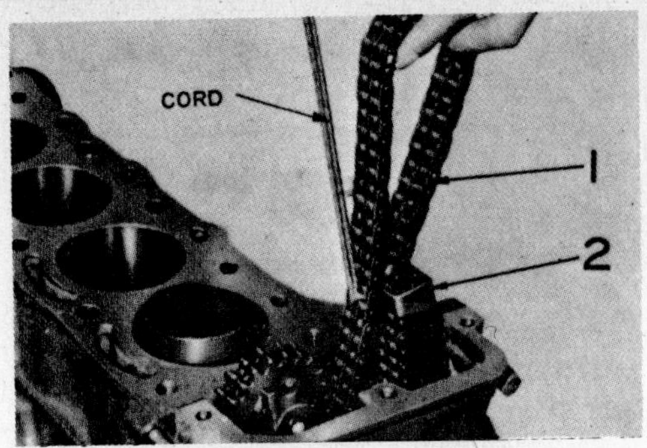

Installing timing chain.

Timing gear installation

the locking bolt to 43-50 ft. lbs. Reset the timing mark on the crankshaft pulley with the O mark on the cover.

To install the timing chain and gear to camshaft, align the indent hole on the camshaft front bearing cap with the timing notch on the camshaft flange. Recheck the position of the crankshaft timing mark on the pulley. Secure camshaft to prevent movement (which could result in jumped timing), then align the dowel pin on the camshaft flange with the No. 2 hole of the timing gear, release the chain and insert the timing gear into the chain loop so that there is equal tension on both sides of the chain. The gear should seat on the camshaft flange without excessive jiggling which, again, could result in jumped timing. Install and tighten the left-hand thread gear retaining bolt (torque to 47-54 ft. lbs.). Bend the lock tab to secure the bolt and remove the covering rag from the timing cover.

Install the chain tensioner, using a new gasket, and torque to 21-29 ft. lbs. Check that the plunger is free to move back at least 0.200" in its housing. If not, adjust by adding gaskets between the housing and the block.

8R-C Engine

Note: Engine must be in an inverted position to perform this operation.

1. Rotate No. 1 piston to TDC. Rotate oil pump driveshaft to a perpendicular position. Align crank timing gear mark and oil pump driveshaft gear with timing chain marks. Install primary timing chain, oil pump driveshaft gear, and crankshaft timing gear.
2. Install chain vibration damper.
3. Place timing chain cover gasket in position. Install primary and secondary chain tensioners. Chain tensioner bolt torque is 18 ft. lbs.
4. Place camshaft drive gear on oil pump drive shaft and torque retaining nut to 50-73 ft. lbs.
5. Place secondary timing chain on camshaft drive gear and align marks. Tension chain by securing with cord. This will prevent chain from dropping from position.
6. Place timing chain cover in position. Torque to 11-15 ft. lbs. Turn entire engine to normal position.
7. Replace head on engine and install camshaft.
8. Align timing chain marks with cam timing gear dowel pin hole. Install timing gear on cam. Match marks should be in an upright position. Install rocker arms and torque to specifications in four stages. Connect oil lines and union bolts. Torque to 11-16 ft. lbs.

LUBRICATING SYSTEM

Two types of filters are used: disposable (cartridge) filters on all Corolla and Crown models, and paper replaceable elements on the Corona and Land Cruiser models. Lubrication of the internal engine parts is full flow (see table footnote) with a trochoid oil pump supplying the pressure. Oil pressure relief valves are situated in the pump body and an additional bypass valve is incorporated with the filter to avoid oil starvation if the element becomes clogged.

Removing Oil Pump

On K series cars, the engine must be removed; on F series cars, the engine skid plates, flywheel side and bottom covers and the front drive shaft. All other models require that the motor mounts be disconnected and the engine jacked up far enough to remove the oil pan.

1. Plane washer
2. Oil pump body
3. Oil pump cover gasket
4. Oil pump shaft
5. Oil pump drive rotor
6. Oil pump drive rotor pin
7. Oil pump driven rotor
8. Oil pump cover
9. Oil strainer
10. Relief valve plug
11. Relief valve gasket
12. Relief valve spring
13. Relief valve
14. Union
15. Ball sleeve
16. Union nut
17. Oil pump outlet pipe

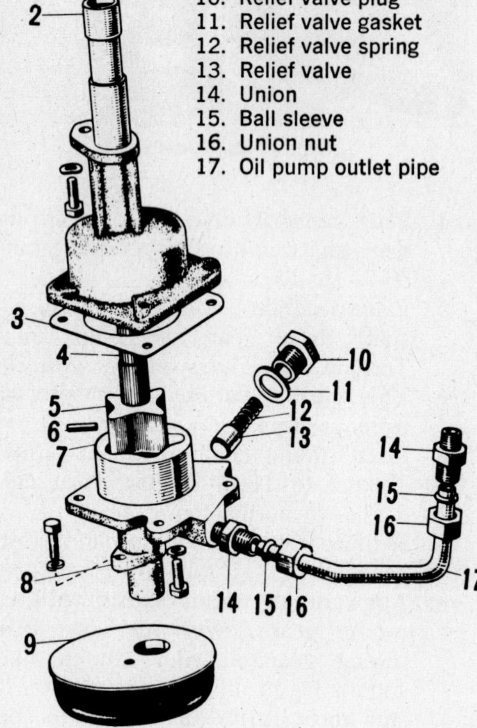

Corona oil pump

Oil pump removal is simply a matter of taking out all bolts and disconnecting the oil pipes and screens. The drive gear on the 2M type is secured to the shaft with a snap-ring.

Inspecting oil pump

Wash the pump thoroughly and allow to air dry. Check for shiny spots which indicate wear and scuffing. Check backlash of gears and measure free length of relief valve spring, then check play between gears and housing, gears and pump cover and between gears themselves. See specification chart for tolerances.

Installing Oil Pump

Always use new gaskets during assembly. Oil all moving parts before installation

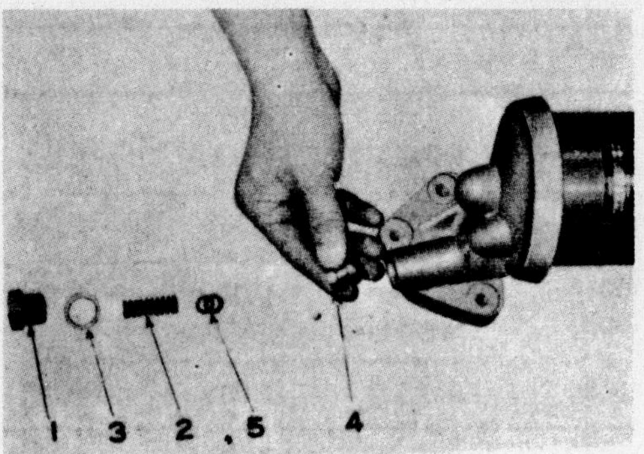

Removing oil bypass valve from filter housing.

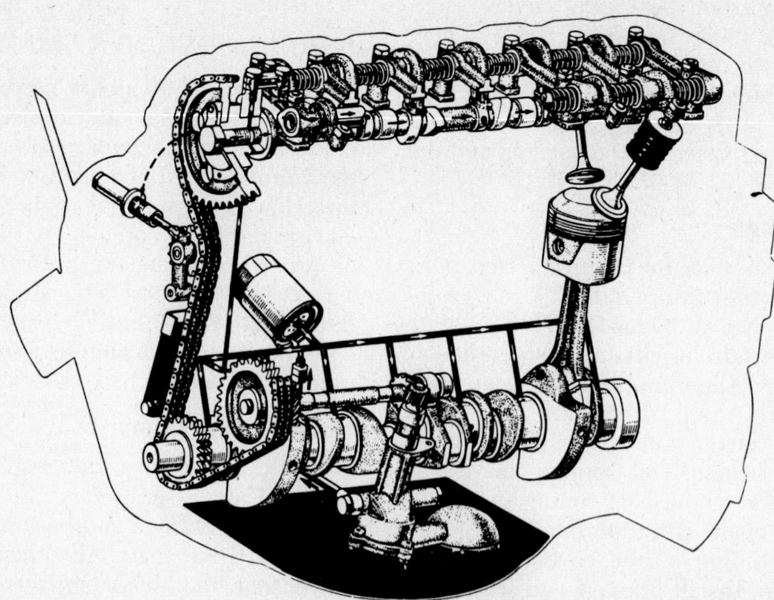

Crown (2M) engine lubricating system, showing direction of oil circulation.

Oil Pump Specifications

	Engine Type				
	8R-C	*K-C, 3K-C*	*3R, 3R-B, 3R-C*	*2M*	*F, FA*
Pump type	Rotor	Rotor	Rotor	Rotor	Rotor
Gear to housing (in.)	0.004-0.006	0.004-0.006	0.004-0.006	0.004-0.006	0.001-0.004
Limit: (in.)	0.008	0.008	0.008	0.008	0.008
Gear to gear (in.)	0.004-0.006	.002-.006	.003-.005	0.004-0.006	0.018-0.026
Limit: (in.)	0.008	0.008	0.008	0.008	0.037
Gear to cover (in.)	0.001-0.003	0.001-0.003	0.001-0.003	0.001-0.003	0.001-0.003
Limit (in.)	0.006	0.006	0.006	0.006	0.006
Relief valve spring free length	1.850	—	1.850	2.173	Adjust 44-50 psi
Relief valve opens at psi:	57-71	51-63	53-61	57-71	44-50

Note: F series—bypass type with twin gear pump and external, adjustable relief valve.

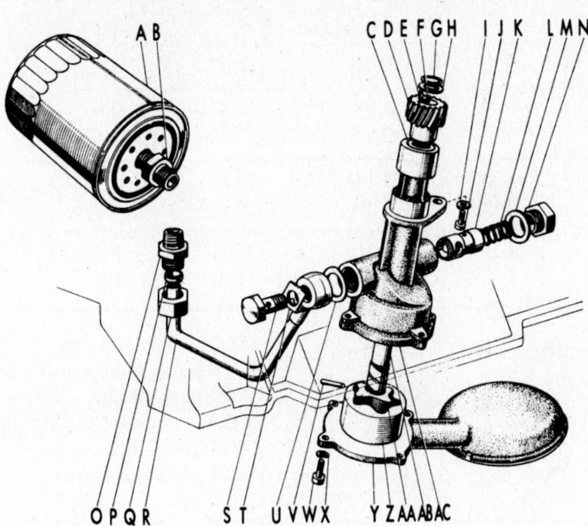

2M engine oil pump

A Oil filter
B Union fitting
C Plain washer
D Oil pump driveshaft gear
E Key
F Plug
G Snap-ring
H Spacer
I Lock washer
J Bolt
K Oil pump relief valve
L Relief valve spring
M Relief valve gasket
N Relief valve plug
O Olive straight connector
P Olive (oil seal)
Q Olive E nut
R Oil pump outlet pipe
S Union bolt
T Lock washer
U Gasket
V Oil pump drive rotor pin
W Bolt
X Lock washer
Y Oil pump cover
Z Oil pump driven rotor
AA Oil pump drive rotor
AB Oil pump shaft
AC Oil pump body

and prime the oil pump with fresh oil before installing oil pan. Check the pump output before starting the engine by first removing the high tension coil wire, then the oil pressure sending unit. Crank engine with starter. Oil should flow from the opening if the pump is working.

PISTONS

All pistons are available in oversizes from .010″-.060″. If cylinder block requires a larger oversize than .060″, block must be sleeved to accept .060″ maximum oversize pistons. All pistons are marked on top surface with piston diameter, pin size, and front marks. When connecting rods are assembled to pistons, piston front mark and connecting rod front mark must be facing in same direction.

Clutch and Transmission

CLUTCH

The clutch is a single-plate, dry-disc type. Some early models, and all F series, use a coil-spring pressure plate. Later models use a diaphragm-spring pressure plate. Clutch release bearings are sealed ball bearing units which need no lubrication and should never be washed in any kind of solvent. All clutches except those on the Corolla KE series are hydraulically operated.

Clutch Specifications

Series Identification	Disc diameter (in.)	Master cylinder diameter (in.)	Slave cylinder diameter (in.)	Full pedal travel (in.)	Free play at pedal (in.)	Free play at fork (in.)	Cover to plate torque (ft. lbs.)	Cover to flywheel torque (ft. lbs.)
KE①	7.09	none	none	5.5-5.9	0.6-0.8	N.A.	3-5	7-11
KE②	N.A.	none	none	5.5-5.9	0.8-1.4	N.A.	13.7-22.4	10.9-15.9
RT	7.78	0.62	0.59	6.0-6.2	0.8-1.6	0.08-0.14	N.A.	7.2-11.6
MS	7.87	0.75	0.75	5.5-5.9	1.4-2.0	0.08-0.14	N.A.	6-9.5
FJ	10.8	0.75	0.75	6.7	1.4	0.21	22-32	11-16
RN	8.8	0.62	0.59	6.7	1.2	0.14	3-5	7-11
RK	9	N.A.	0.59	7.3	N.A.	0.15	N.A.	5.8-9.4
RS	8.82	0.75	0.75	5.5-5.9	1.4-2.0	0.14-0.20	N.A.	6-9.5
TE	N.A.	N.A.	N.A.	6.4-6.8	1.0-1.8	0.10-0.14	10.9-15.9	11-14

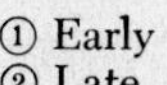
① Early
② Late

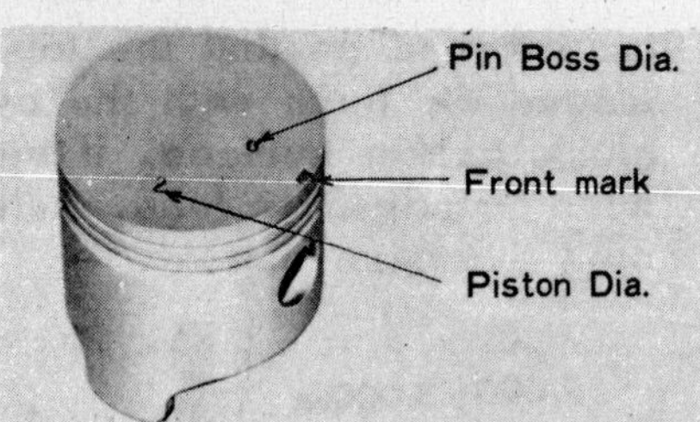

Piston markings

Piston and connecting rod assembly showing mating marks

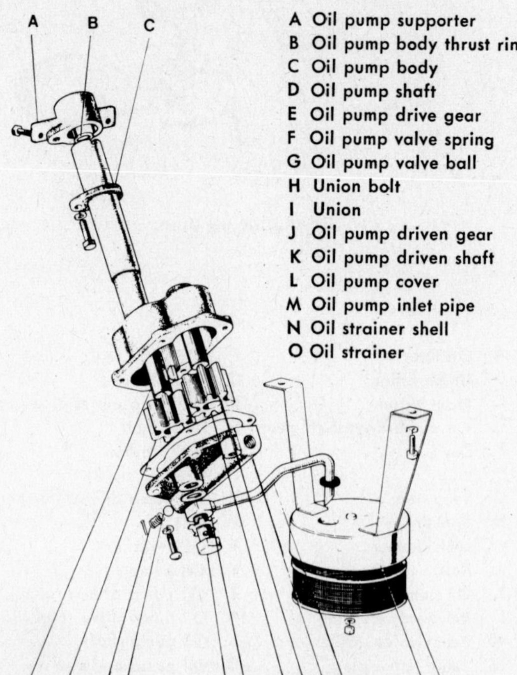

F engine oil pump

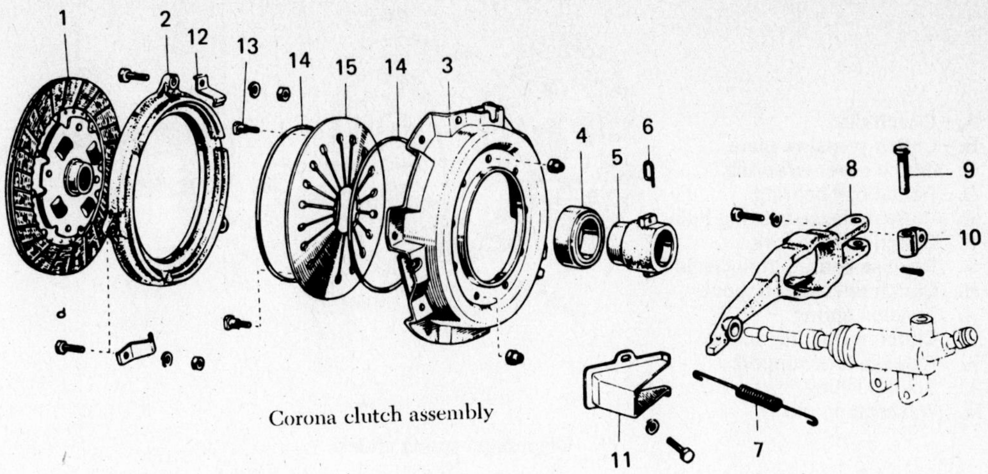

Corona clutch assembly

1 Disc assembly, clutch
2 Plate, clutch pressure
3 Cover, clutch
4 Bearing, radial belt
5 Hub, clutch release bearing
6 Clip, release bearing
7 Spring, tension
8 Fork, clutch release
9 Pin, w/serration
10 Support, release fork
11 Seal, dust
12 Spring, clutch retacting
13 Bolt, diaphragm spring set
14 Ring, clutch pivot
15 Spring, clutch diaphragm

A. Clutch disc assembly
B. Clutch pressure plate subassembly
C. Round rivet
D. Clutch cover subassembly
E. Tension spring
F. Clutch pressure lever
G. Plate washer
H. Nut
I. Radial ball bearing
J. Clutch release bearing hub
K. Release bearing hub clip
L. Bolt
M. Spring washer
N. Clutch release fork assembly
O. W/knurling pin
P. Solid bushing
Q. Release fork support subassembly
R. Cotter pin
S. Clutch pressure plate bolt
T. Compression spring
U. Spring washer
V. Bolt
W. Clutch release fork dust shield
X. Plate washer
Y. Spring washer
Z. Bolt

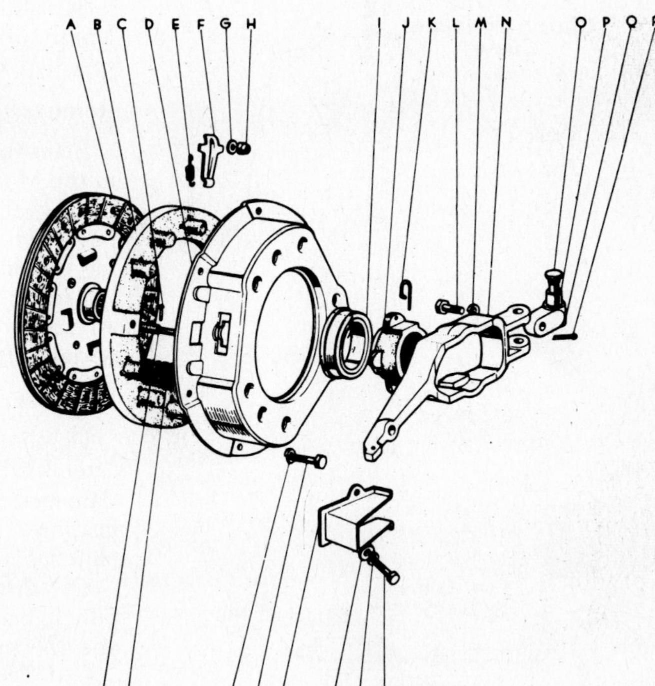

Coil spring clutch.

A. Clutch disc
B. Clutch pressure plate
C. Clutch cover w/spring
D. Radial ball bearing
E. Clutch release bearing hub
F. Clutch release fork
G. Release bearing hub clevis
H. Clutch release fork boot
I. Tension spring
J. Clutch retracting spring
K. Release fork support
L. Solid bushing
M. W/serration pin

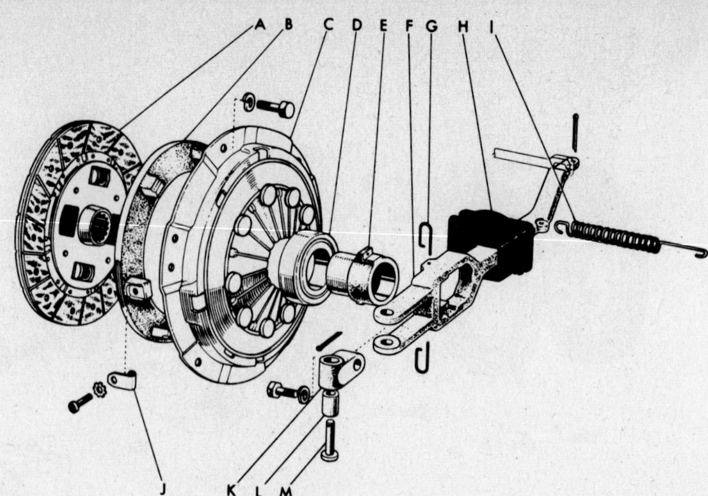

Diaphragm spring clutch.

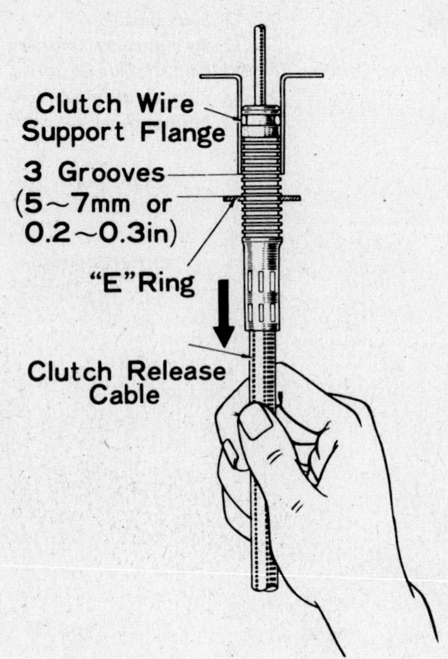

Adjusting pedal free-play

Adjustment

Adjust the clutch pedal with the pedal stopper bolt to the full pedal travel specified in the Clutch Specifications Chart. The height is measured from the floor board to the top center of the pedal pad. Adjust the clutch pedal free play by loosening the locknut and turning the pushrod. Then tighten the locknut. This adjustment should be made with the tension spring in place. To adjust the play of the clutch release fork, loosen the locknut, then adjust the length of the rod, until the play is as specified in the chart.

Removal

Remove the transmission, as described in the Manual Transmission Section. Stamp mating marks on the clutch cover and the flywheel to maintain balance positioning. Remove the clutch cover bolts by first loosening them evenly, one turn at a time, all around to prevent warping the clutch cover. Lift off the cover and disc.

Disassembly

Diaphragm clutches should not be disassembled unless the diaphragm spring is damaged or its pressure is below specifications. Replace defective diaphragm clutches as a unit.

To disassemble coil spring clutches, punch mating marks on the clutch cover and the pressure plate.

CAUTION: The following procedure is dangerous unless the proper equipment is used. The spring pressure can exert enough

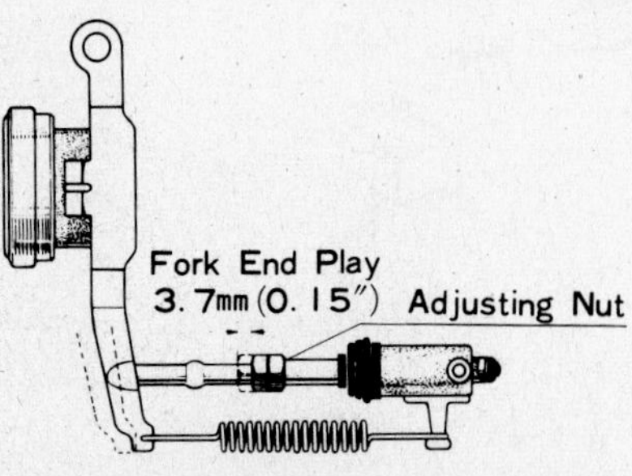

Clutch release fork adjustment

Clutch cover removal showing mating marks

force to cause injury and may damage the cover. Place a piece of wood on the top of the clutch cover. With a press, compress the clutch cover slightly, so that the clutch release lever set nuts can be removed. After removing the nuts, slowly release the pressure and remove the cover assembly. Take out the pressure springs, pull the cotter pins from the release lever pins and remove the pins. Separate the clutch cover, clutch springs, clutch release levers and the clutch pressure plate.

Inspection

Do not wash the clutch disc or release bearing. Check the disc for lining wear and broken rivets or springs. If there is less than 0.012″ of lining showing above the rivet heads, replace the disc. Check the runout of the disc. The runout limit is 0.020″. Check the splines and free-travel on the gear shaft, then check torsion rubbers for distortion or wear. Wash off all cover parts and check lever tips for wear, distortion or cracks. Test all springs for load and squareness. If the pressure plate bearing surface is blue or shows tiny crack marks, reface or replace the pressure plate assembly. Limit for refacing is 0.030″.

Check the clutch release bearing; if it feels rough or is noisy, replace it. Replace clutch parts after 50,000 miles, as metal components are usually fatigued by that time and may fail in service. Also, inspect the clutch fork fingers for wear, the fork pivot ball and spring for looseness and the pilot bearing in the crankshaft for wear.

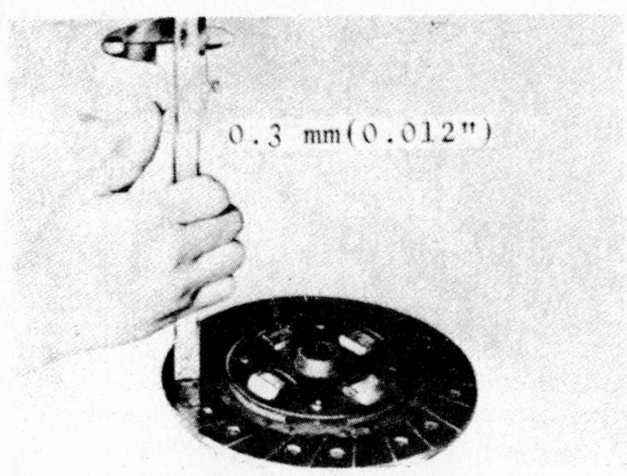

Checking clutch lining wear.

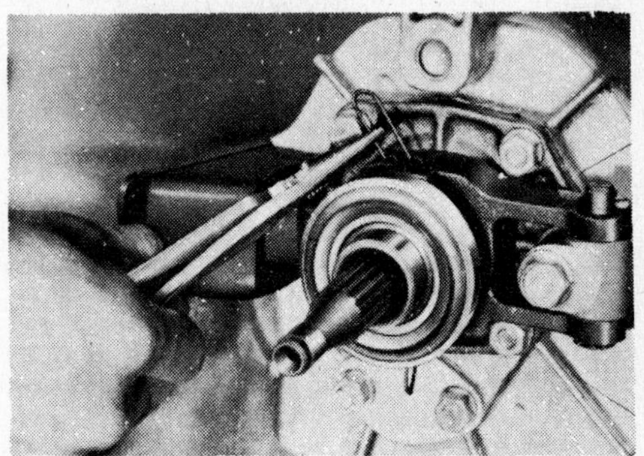

Release fork installation

Adjusting clutch lever height using special gauge.

Assembly

Apply a light coat of silicone lubricant to all moving parts of the clutch prior to installation. Install the lever pins into the release lever pin holes, then fit the release levers and pressure plate pins. Lock the assembly with cotter pins. Install the release lever yokes onto the levers, then place the pressure plate face down and install the springs onto their seats. Place the clutch cover carefully over the pressure plate, aligning the punch marks. Place a wooden block on the cover and press down until the locking nuts can be assembled and tightened equally all around to prevent warping the cover. Secure the yoke bolts to the cover and torque to 22-32 ft. lbs. Mount the disc and clutch assembly onto the flywheel. Center the disc using a clutch pilot tool, or the transmission input shaft itself if no tool is available. This must be done carefully or the transmission will not line up with the clutch disc splines. Now, adjust the release lever height. The difference between fingers must not exceed 0.002″. Install the release fork into transmission case and connect the spring clips to the bearing, making sure the bearing moves freely on the shaft. *NOTE: Install the disc with flat surface towards the flywheel.*

Hydraulic Clutch

The clutch master cylinder is serviced and bled in the same manner as the brake master cylinder.

To remove and replace the slave cylinder, first unhook the release fork spring, then screw in the pushrod until it can be disengaged from the fork; disconnect the flexible hose and remove the mounting bolts and spring bracket. Remove the boot and pushrods, then remove the release piston with its mounted cup. Pull off the cup if necessary.

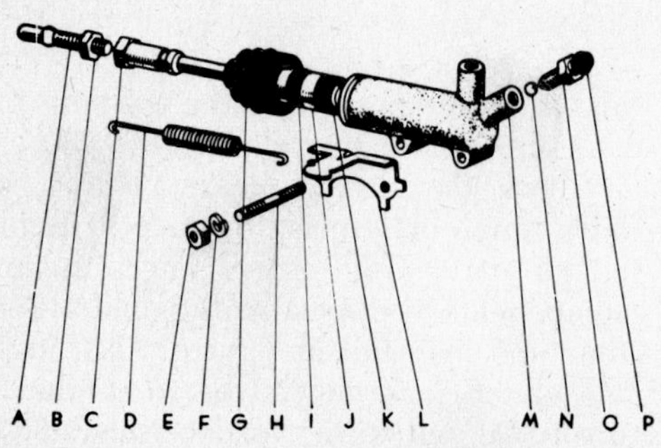

Clutch slave cylinder.

A. Release cylinder pushrod No. 2
B. Nut
C. Release cylinder pushrod No. 1
D. Tension spring
E. Nut
F. Spring washer
G. Release cylinder boot
H. Stud bolt
I. Cylinder cup
J. Release cylinder piston
K. Cylinder cup
L. Release fork retracting spring hanger
M. Clutch release cylinder assembly
N. Ball

Wash all parts thoroughly in clean brake fluid or alcohol. *Do not use any other solvents.* Inspect all parts for signs of wear, scuffing or scoring. Inside of cylinder may be honed out, if necessary, but the honing limit is 0.004″. Always use a new cup.

Assemble all parts after coating with fresh brake fluid. Mount cup on piston and insert assembly into cylinder, then place boot on rods and fit to cylinder. Install slave cylinder onto transmission housing and engage clutch release fork. Adjust play between fork and rod per specification, then bleed the clutch hydraulic system.

MANUAL TRANSMISSION

Removal

Corolla

Remove floormat and shift lever boot, then press shift lever cap down and turn it counterclockwise to release. Cover the opening with a clean rag to prevent entry of dirt, then disconnect back up switch and positive battery cable. Remove radiator inlet hose and turn fan blade to horizontal position. Jack up car and place stands under

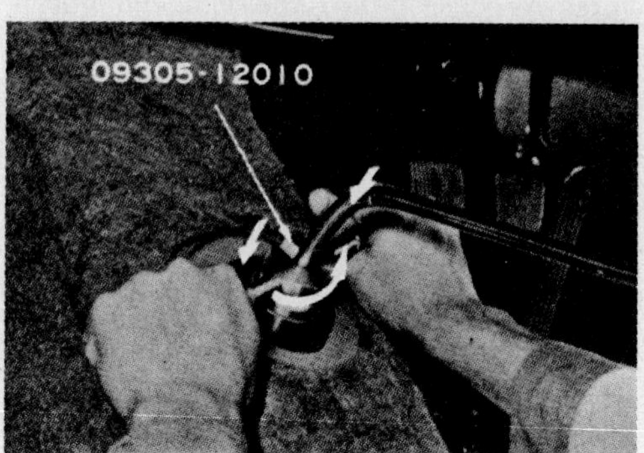

Removing shift lever collar.

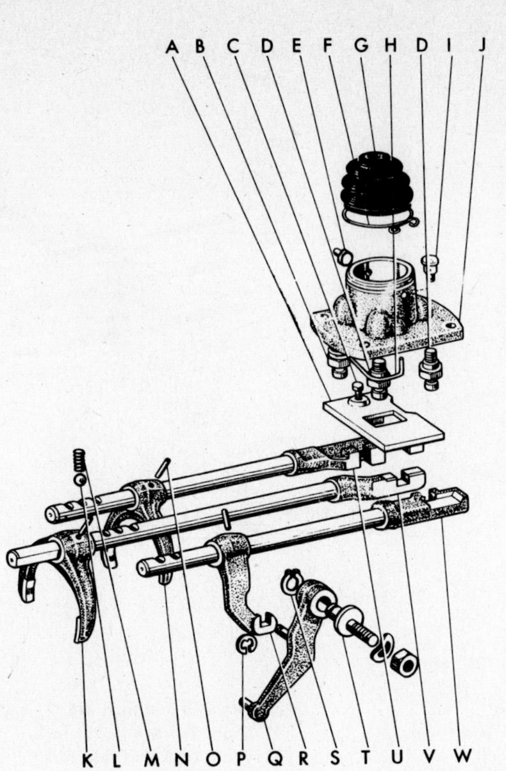

Corolla shift linkage

A	Shift interlock plate
B	Shift interlock plate set bolt No. 2
C	Hexagon bolt
D	Shift interlock plate set bolt No. 1
E	Control lever cap pin
F	Clip
G	Shift lever cap boot
H	Torsion spring
I	Breather plug
J	Control shift lever retainer
K	Third & fourth shift fork
L	Detent ball
M	Detent ball spring
N	First & second shift fork
O	Slotted spring pin
P	E ring
Q	Reverse shift arm
R	Reverse shift fork
S	Snap-ring
T	Shift arm pivot
U	First and second shift fork shaft
V	Third & fourth shift fork shaft
W	Reverse shift fork shaft
X	Shift lever
Y	Compression spring
Z	Shift lever spring seat
AA	Shift lever cap
AB	Hexagon bolt
AC	Shift lever knob

frame, then disconnect exhaust flange. Disconnect and remove drive shaft; plug hole to prevent oil loss. Disconnect speedometer cable and exhaust pipe hanger from extension housing. Place jack under front of transmission and remove two bolts (only) from rear mount. Remove rear transmission support (crossmember) and remove the jack.

Remove starter motor and the two bolts that hold the stiffener plate to the transmission case. Disconnect and remove clutch cable, then remove the two lower and the four upper bolts that hold the transmission to the engine block. *NOTE: Upper bolts are best removed using a 17mm. socket and a 20″ extension on ratchet.* Remove transmission to the rear, pulling straight back until free of the clutch and flywheel housing.

Corona

Corona transmission removal is similar to Corolla. Remove gear lever knob and boot, then remove shift lever bracket from extension housing; lever and the small bushing from bracket. Disconnect clutch cylinder from housing, but do not disconnect hydraulic hose. Remove handbrake equalizer bracket and cables.

On Corona models having remote control linkage, first jack up car and support it on axle stands. Disconnect battery ground wire, exhaust flange and pipe clamp. Remove parking brake equalizer bracket; disconnect speedometer cable and remove flywheel housing cover. Remove clutch release cylinder and pushrod (do not disconnect the hydraulic line or depress the clutch pedal), then disconnect the shift rods from the shift levers and remove the cross shaft

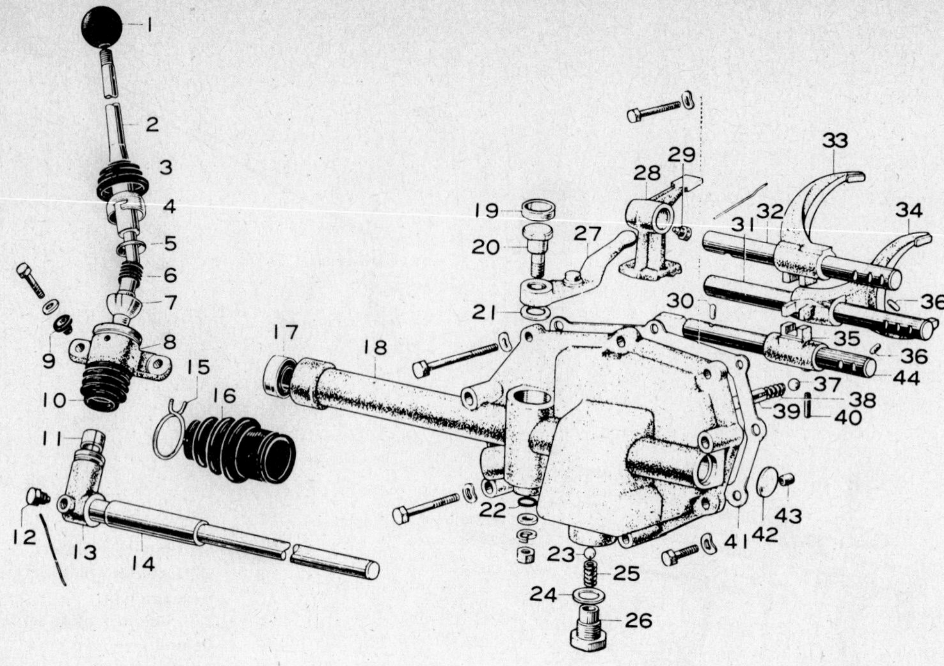

Corona shift linkage

1 Knob sub assembly, shift lever
2 Lever, shift, No. 2
3 Boot, shaft & select lever, No. 3
4 Cap, shift lever
5 Seat, shift lever spring
6 Spring, compression
7 Lever, shift, No. 1
8 Retainer sub assembly, control shift lever
9 Bushing, control shift lever retainer
10 Boot, shift & select lever, No. 2
11 Bushing, shift lever
12 Bolt (for shift lever lock)
13 Housing, shift lever
14 Shaft, shift & select lever
15 Clip
16 Boot, shift & select lever, No. 1
17 Seal, type T oil
18 Cover, transmission case
19 Plug, tight
20 Pivot, shift arm
21 Washer, plate
22 O-ring
23 Ball, gear shift fork lock
24 Gasket (for ball holder)
25 Spring, compression
26 Holder, reverse restrict ball
27 Arm, reverse shift
28 Lever, shift & select
29 Bolt (for shift lever lock)
30 Pin, shift interlock, No. 2
31 Shaft, 3rd & 4th shift fork
32 Shaft, 1st & 2nd shift fork
33 Fork, 1st & 2nd shift
34 Fork, 3rd & 4th shift
35 Head, reverse shift
36 Pin, shift interlock, No. 1
37 Ball, gear shift fork lock
38 Spring, compression
39 Seat, shift detent ball spring, No. 1
40 Pin, slotted spring
41 Gasket, transmission case cover
42 Plug, expansion
43 Plug, ring
44 Shaft, reverse shift fork

and its support knob. Disconnect the drive shaft and plug the hole to prevent oil leaks. Jack up rear of engine (use a piece of wood to protect oil pan) and remove the rear support member. Remove all bolts and slide transmission to rear until clear of clutch, then lower to floor.

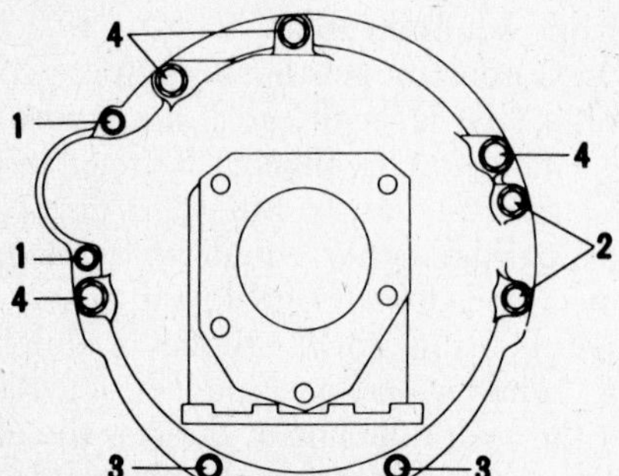

Transmission hold-down bolts.

Mark II

Disconnect the battery and starter cable. Disconnect the exhaust pipe flange and clamp. Remove the equalizer support bracket. Disconnect the speedometer cable. Disconnect the shift linkage and shift lever retainer. Unbolt the clutch slave cylinder, but do not disconnect the hydraulic line. Remove the driveshaft and plug the transmission flange to prevent oil leakage. Support the transmission with a jack and remove the rear crossmember. Lower the jack, unbolt the bell housing from the engine, and withdraw the transmission towards the rear. Be careful not to damage the mainshaft.

Crown

Removal is the same as for Corona models, including the procedures concerning remote control linkage, with the following exceptions: the starter motor, torque rod support and torque rod must be removed.

LAND CRUISER

Remove skid plate and disconnect front and rear drive shafts. Drain the oil, remove the transmission cover, and disconnect all shift levers and links. Disconnect parking brake cable from lever, remove speedometer cable and disconnect wires from front wheel drive indicator switch. Remove all vacuum hoses, remove flywheel housing cover and loosen all bolts that hold transmission to clutch housing. Slide transmission to rear until it clears the clutch housing. *NOTE: The combined weight of transmission and transfer case makes it advisable to use a transmission jack for this operation.*

HI-LUX

Remove or disconnect the following parts; battery cable, starter bolt and nut, shift lever assembly, parking brake cable, speedometer cable, wiring for backup light switch, and exhaust pipe clamp. Drain the transmission. Remove the release cylinder assembly with the flexible hose attached. Remove the driveshaft, and install a spare universal joint on the transmission (to prevent transmission oil from leaking.)

Support the transmission with a jack, and remove the engine rear support member. Lower the jack, disconnect the clutch housing from the cylinder block, and remove the transmission to the rear.

Installation, All Models

To replace manual transmissions, reverse removal procedures. Be sure to fill transmission with proper quantity and type of lubricant.

Overhaul, Corolla

DISASSEMBLY

Remove back up switch and wiring, speedometer pinion and sleeve and clutch fork and bearing with sleeve. Remove transmission oil pan and thoroughly wash inside of gearbox and dry off with air. *NOTE: A number of measurements must be taken before the transmission is disassembled.* Remove shift lever retaining cover from extension housing, then remove extension housing. Remove countershaft cover and front bearing retainer, along with oil seal. First loosen, then remove, all five nuts that hold the transmission case cover. Remove cover slowly or the shift rail detent balls will fly out. Remove lock bolt and reverse idler shaft, along with gear and spacer.

Now, using a dial indicator, measure the gear backlash and end-play. Write these measurements down for later reference during assembly. Drive out countergear shaft, using a brass punch, towards rear of case; remove the two thrust washers and the four needle roller bearings.

With a small punch (3/16″ dia.) drive the roll pins from the shift forks.

Remove, in order, reverse shift rail, first-second shift rail and third-fourth shift rail. Remove the three detent balls and the shift forks.

Remove output shaft, together with bearing retainer, then remove needle bearing and synchronizer ring from input shaft (main drive gear) and remove shaft from front of case.

Before disassembling: measure end-play of first, second, and third gears on mainshaft, then remove snap-ring at front of shaft and pull off third-fourth synchronizer hub, spacer and synchronizer ring. *CAUTION: Synchronizer rings must not be mixed; tag each ring as it is removed.*

Remove snap-ring and speedometer drive gear, along with Woodruff key. Straighten lock tab and remove locknut from mainshaft (rear). Mark and save all shims.

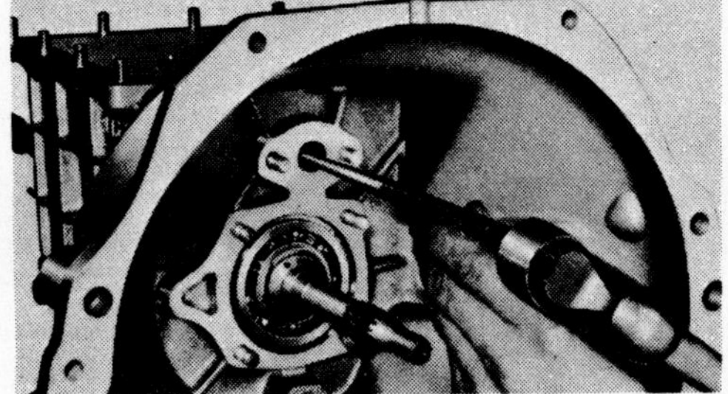

Removing countershaft.

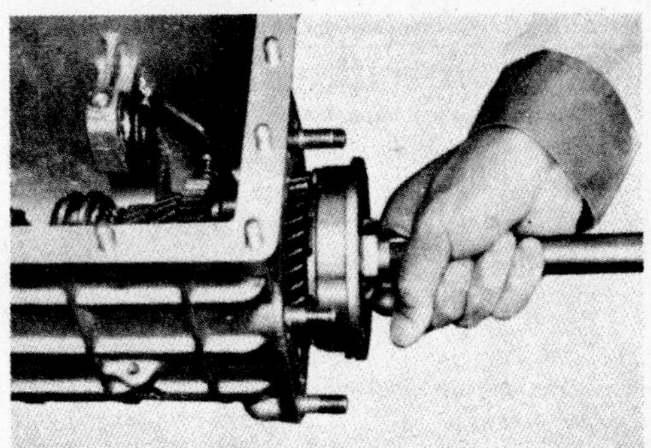

Removing output shaft.

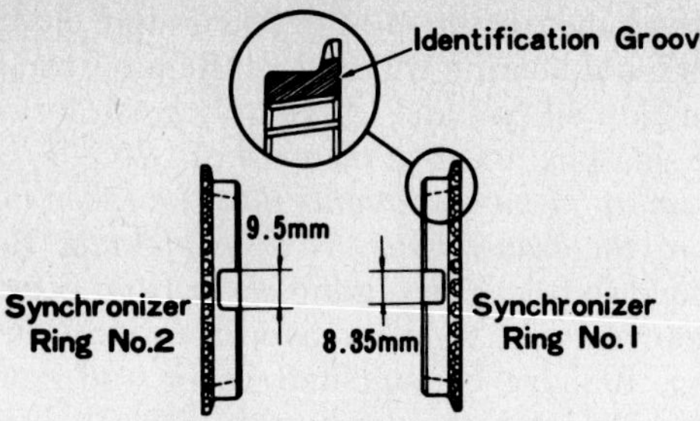

Synchronizer ring differences.

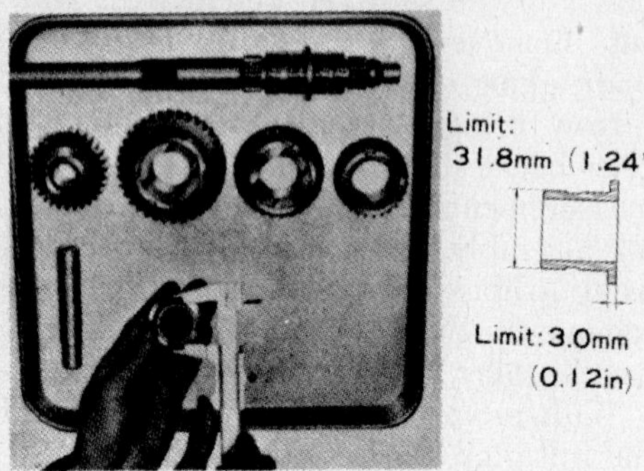

Checking first gear bushing.

Remove rear bearing retainer, first gear and bushing with ball, first-second synchronizer mechanism, synchronizer rings and second gear, then disassemble all synchronizer mechanisms.

Inspection

Wash all parts and blow off with compressed air, then check for chipped, broken or bent parts.

If there was excessive end-play when it was checked during disassembly, select the proper thrust washers to obtain correct end-play of gears, then check transmission case for wear.

Specifications

Gear	*Normal*	*Limit*
Backlash between gears and countergear		
Input (main drive)	0.004″	0.008″
3rd gear	0.004″	0.008″
2nd gear	0.004″	0.008″
1st gear	0.004″	0.008″
Reverse gear	0.006″	0.012″
Reverse idler	0.007″	0.012″
End-play of gears (thrust clearance)		
Countergear	.002-.020″	0.020″
1st gear	.004-.012″	0.020″
2nd gear	.006-.012″	0.020″
3rd gear	.004-.010″	0.020″

Output shaft (mainshaft) dimensions
Flange wear limit—0.140″
Bearing seat limit—1.240″ diameter
Runout limit—0.001″

Countergear
Thrust washer limit—0.067″
Note: Input shaft bearing snap-rings are available in two sizes to allow proper seating of shaft.

Synchronizer hub groove width
Shift fork seat limit—0.300″

Shift fork to hub clearance
Wear limit—0.030″

Synchronizer ring test
Clearance between ring and gear—must be greater than 0.016″
Note: Light hand pressure seating only.

Reverse idler gear
Shaft wear limit—0.700″

Clutch release bearing retainer
Outer diameter limit—1.090″ (replace if scored)

Rear extension housing bushing
New bushing reaming limits—1.260-1.261″
Clearance between drive shaft flange and bushing—0.0004-0.0024″
Note: Old bushing must be removed by heating housing in boiling water. Slot of new bushing faces upwards.

Assembly

Always use new oil seals and gaskets. Apply thin coats of Permatex to all gaskets and mating surfaces and lightly oil all gears, bearings and bushings before installation. Grease or oil all oil seal contact surfaces.

1. Place synchronizer hub into sleeve, fit the three shift keys (open end facing inwards) into the slots in the sleeve and install shift key retaining springs with open ends 120° apart. *NOTE: The third-fourth synchronizer hub is fitted with the wide shoulder facing forwards. The first-second synchronizer rings are different from each other and from the third-fourth rings.*
2. Assemble first-second synchronizer mechanism, as above, and fit into reverse gear from the rear.
3. Install second gear and synchronizer ring onto output shaft from rear.
4. Install first-second synchronizer ring onto output shaft, carefully aligning the grooves in the rings with the shaft keys. Check width of grooves before installation. *Do not use force during this installation step.*
5. Install first gear synchronizer ring, first

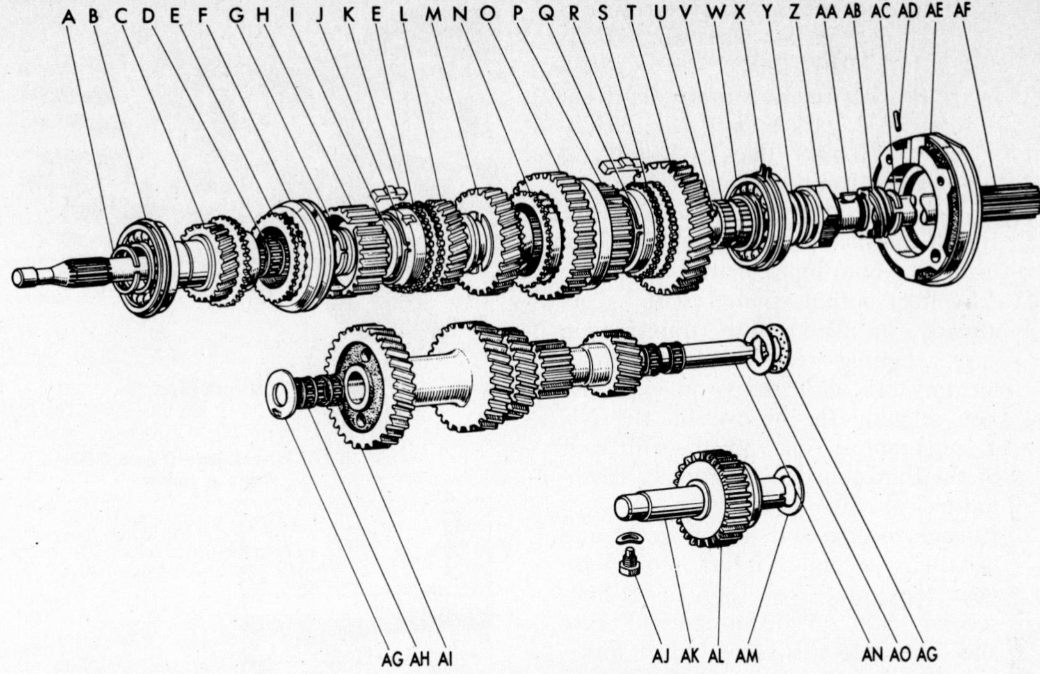

Transmission components.

A. Shaft snap-ring
B. Bearing (transmission front)
C. Input shaft
D. Needle roller bearing
E. Synchronizer ring No. 3
F. Transmission hub sleeve
G. Shaft snap-ring
H. Transmission clutch hub No. 2
I. Clutch hub spacer
J. Synchromesh shifting key spring No. 2
K. Synchromesh shifting key No. 2
L. Side gear
M. Second gear
N. Synchronizer ring No. 2
O. Reverse gear
P. Transmission clutch hub No. 1
Q. Synchromesh shifting key spring No. 1
R. Synchromesh shifting key No. 1
S. Synchronizer ring No. 1
T. First gear
U. Ball
V. First gear bushing
W. Bearing (transmission rear)
X. Shaft snap-ring.
Y. Shim
Z. Nut
AA. Woodruff key
AB. Speedometer drive gear
AC. Shaft snap-ring
AD. Slotted split pin
AE. Output shaft rear retainer
AF. Output shaft
AG. Countergear case side thrust washer
AH. Needle roller bearing
AI. Countergear
AJ. Shaft retaining bolt
AK. Reverse idler gear shaft
AL. Reverse idler gear
AM. Spacer
AN. Counter shaft
AO. Countergear side thrust washer No. 1

gear and bushing with ball onto output shaft.

6. Assemble rear bearing with retainer, shims and locknut, with lock tab to rear of output shaft. Change size of shim pack in order to avoid using the same portion of the lock tab again. Tighten locknut to 60-80 ft. lbs.
7. Assemble third gear, synchronizer ring, synchronizer hub and spacer, third-fourth synchronizer mechanism onto output shaft from the front (wide shoulder of hub faces forward).
8. Select the proper snap-ring to obtain correct end-play and install onto output shaft. Snap-rings come in three sizes: 0.079″, 0.083″ and 0.087″.
9. Fit snap-rings and speedometer drive gear (with Woodruff key) onto rear part of output shaft.
10. Check all gears for excessive end-play.
11. Install input shaft into transmission case.
12. Select front bearing retainer gasket as follows:

a. If bearing retainer is recessed into case, use gasket part No. 33133-12010 (0.010" thick).

b. If bearing retainer protrudes from case, use gasket part No. 33133-22010 (0.030" thick). Install oil seal into front bearing retainer and tighten retainer bolts to 7-12 ft. lbs.

13. Install needle bearing and synchronizer ring onto input shaft.
14. Assemble output shaft (with gears already installed) into transmission case, aligning rear bearing retainer locating pin with groove in case and also aligning the grooves in the No. 4. synchronizer ring with the shift keys of the third-fourth synchronizer mechanism.
15. Engage reverse and second gears and install first-second shift fork into reverse gear, then rotate fork 180°. Insert first-second shift rail from rear of case and slide into first-second shift fork.
16. Install third-fourth shift fork onto third-fourth synchronizer sleeve and rotate fork 180°. Insert third-fourth shift rail into case through shift fork.
17. Install the reverse shaft shift fork into case by engaging the center of the reverse shift arm. Install the reverse shift fork shaft into case and the reverse shift fork.
18. Secure all shift forks to shift rails with the three roll pins, using a 3/16" punch to seat them.
19. Install countergear with needle bearings and thrust washers; check end-play. Washers come in four sizes to allow proper clearance adjustment. Insert countershaft from rear, slotted end of shaft faces rear and lines up horizontally with the case. Install cover and gasket, then tighten bolts to 7-12 ft. lbs.

Checking thrust clearance between each gear.

Installing shift fork pins.

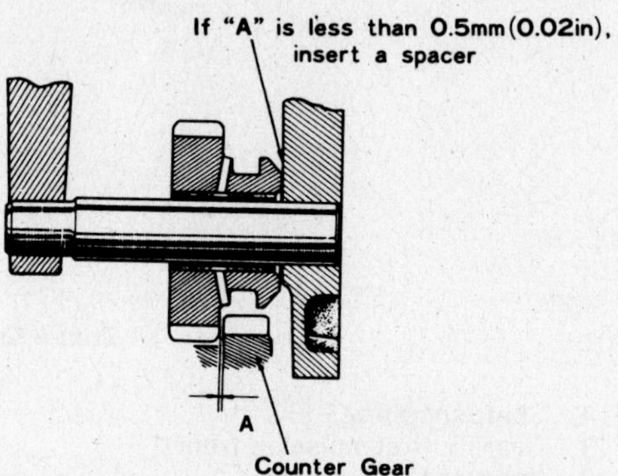
If "A" is less than 0.5mm(0.02in), insert a spacer
A
Counter Gear

Checking reverse idler gear position.

20. Engage groove of reverse idler gear with pin of reverse shift arm, then insert reverse idler shaft so that the hole in the shaft lines up with the hole in the front support boss.
21. Check end-clearance between reverse idler gear and countergear. Install shims, as needed, to correct fit. Tighten reverse idler shaft retaining screw to 10-13 ft. lbs.
22. Install the three detent balls and springs and tighten cover bolts to 3-7 ft. lbs.
23. Loosen locknut and unscrew reverse shift arm pivot bolt. Adjust clearance between reverse idler gear teeth and teeth of countergear so that there is 0.060" clearance in neutral. Tighten locknut.
24. Check clearance between bottom of reverse idler gear groove and top of reverse shift arm. Correct clearance is 0.020-0.060"; adjustable at the pivot. Check that reverse gear does not touch reverse idler gear when first gear is engaged.
25. Install extension housing (with bush-

ing and seal) and tighten bolts to 15-20 ft. lbs.

26. Install speedometer pinion and sleeve (pre-oiled).
27. Grease (or oil) the interlock plate and install onto gear lever retainer plate.
28. Position shift rails in neutral, then bolt gear lever retainer plate to case.
29. Check all clearances and check for smooth gear operation before tightening the cover bolts. Maximum torque on these bolts is 5.0 ft. lbs.
30. Apply light coat of Lubriplate to clutch release bearing sleeve and fork. Install and tighten clutch fork bolt to 14-22 ft. lbs.
31. Test and install back up switch and wires.

Torque Specifications

Case to engine	36-50 ft. lbs.
Case to stiffener plate	11-16 ft. lbs.
Case to starter motor	25-32 ft. lbs.
Extension housing to rear mount	15-22 ft. lbs.
Rear mount to crossmember	22-32 ft. lbs.
Crossmember to body (chassis)	25-40 ft. lbs.

Overhaul, Land Cruiser Three-Speed

Disassembly

First, remove the clutch release fork, then the front bearing retainer and case cover. Remove the cotter pin from the straight screw plug, then remove the plug, lock ball and compression spring. Loosen and remove the fork shaft screw plug, then place a brass drift on one end of the fork shaft and drive the shaft out of the case (to the rear). Remove the shift forks and the extension housing. (It helps to move the hub sleeve to the third gear position.) Remove the synchronizer ring from the input shaft, place a brass drift on the front of the countershaft, and drive the shaft out (to the rear). Remove the input shaft, thrust washers and countergear (it fell to the bottom of the case), then, using the brass drift, drive the reverse idler gear shaft out (to the rear).

Remove the outer shift lever lock pin, shift levers, cotter pin and interlock support shaft. Unscrew the four shift shaft housing bolts and remove the housing from the case. To remove the 12 rollers in the input shaft, first remove the snap-ring. Using snap-ring pliers, unhook the output shaft snap-ring and pull all components from the shaft. Now, remove the speedometer driven gear from the extension housing, expand the output shaft snap-ring and drive the shaft forward and out of the housing. Clamp the shaft in a vise, remove the snap-ring that holds the speedometer drive gear and remove the gear and oil baffle.

The rear bearing is secured with a snap-ring. Although it is recommended that the bearing be pressed off the shaft with an arbor press, striking one end of the shaft sharply on a hardwood block often is sufficient.

Inspection and Assembly

After disassembly, wash all parts thoroughly and inspect the front and rear bearings for roughness. Wash the bearings thoroughly, then apply a few drops of light oil and spin by hand. Any scoring or roughness of the balls indicates an unusable bearing. The front bearing is replaced in the same manner as the rear; remove the snap-ring and press or pull the bearing from the shaft. Check the gears for tooth wear or chipping, then check the synchronizer ring cone for burrs or scoring. The synchronizer teeth are especially susceptible to wear, the result of which is grinding during shifting. Place the ring on its cone and check the clearance between the gear and ring; it should be greater than 0.040″. Check all bushings for abnormal wear and/or scoring, then examine the countershaft and input shaft rollers for pits or roughness. If the rollers are badly scored it is almost impossible to effect a lasting repair without replacing the roller bearing surfaces—the shafts themselves in this case.

To assemble, install the shifting key retainer and the rear bearing onto the output shaft, then select a snap-ring thick enough to reduce the longitudinal play of the rear bearing to the smallest possible value. Assemble the oil baffle, then install snap-ring, speedometer drive gear and its snap-ring. Install the output shaft assembly into the extension housing, securing it with a thick enough snap-ring that play in the housing is kept to a minimum. Now, install the speedometer driven gear and the shaft sleeve.

Install the shifting keys and the first and

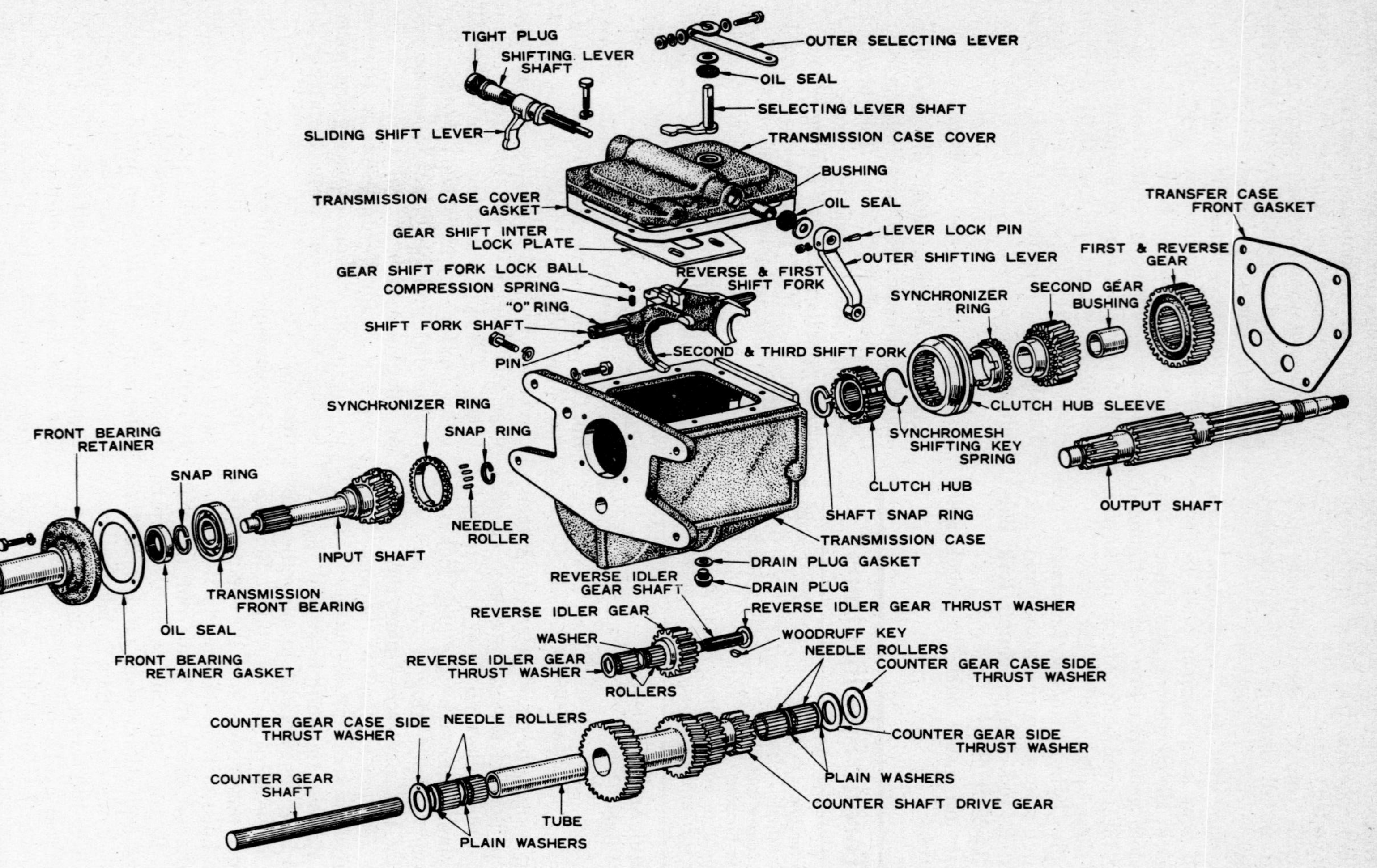

Land Cruiser three speed transmission

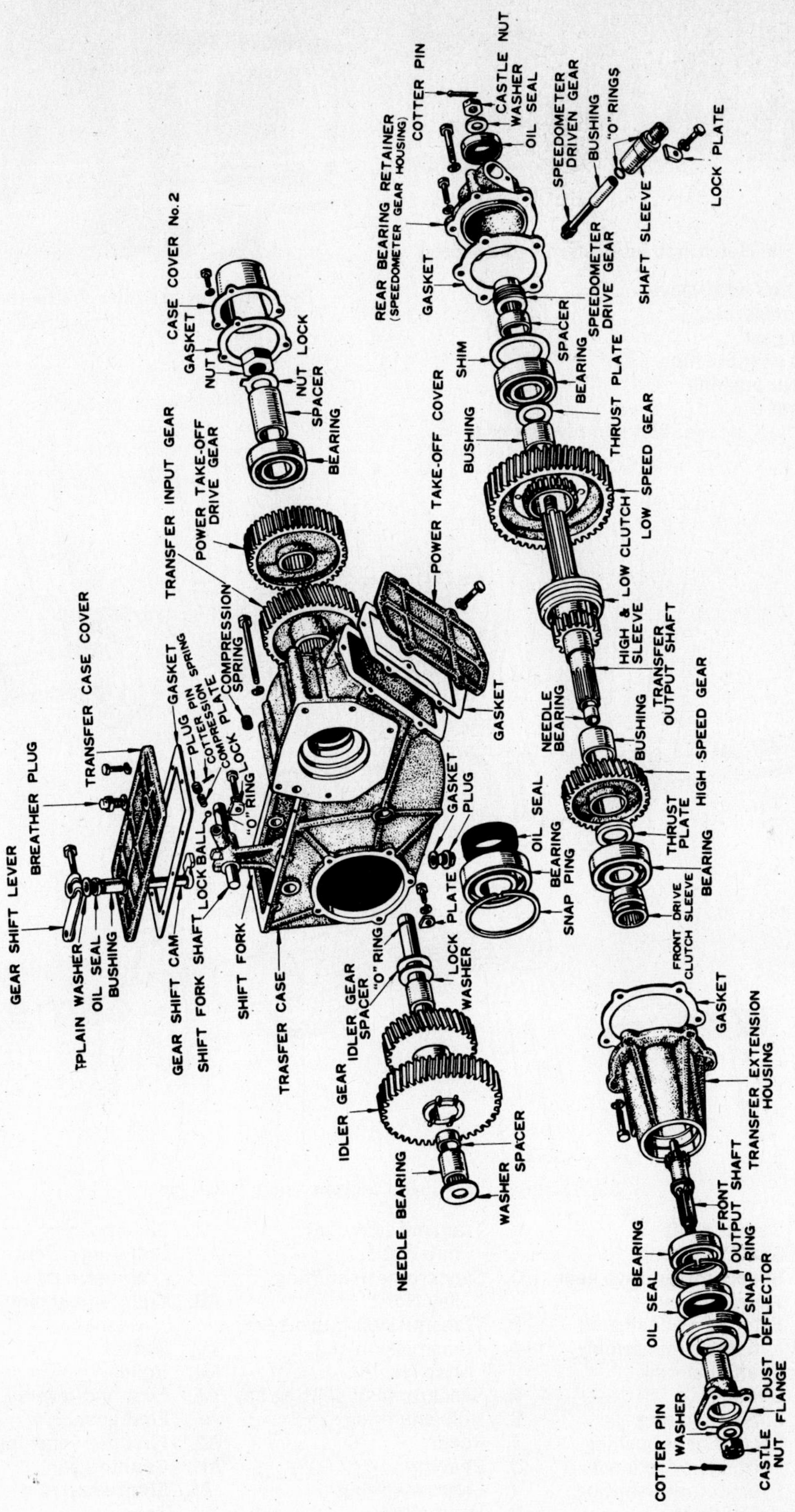

Land Cruiser four-wheel drive transfer case.

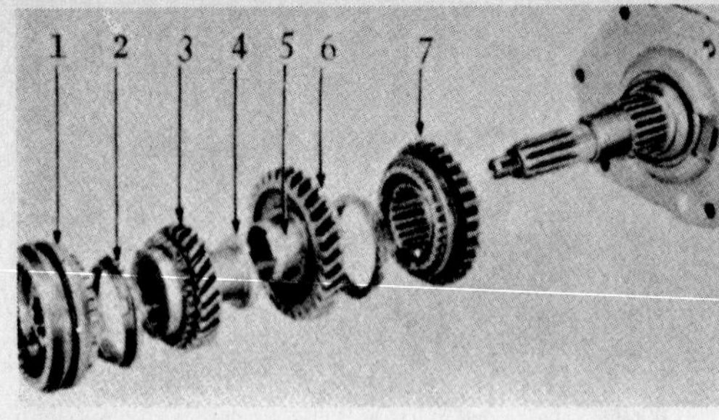

Removing the clutch hub and sleeve—three-speed.

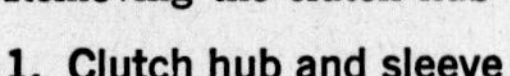

1. Clutch hub and sleeve
2. Synchronizer ring
3. Second gear
4. Second gear bushing
5. First gear bushing
6. First gear
7. Clutch hub, sleeve, first and reverse gear

Removing reverse idler shaft—three-speed.

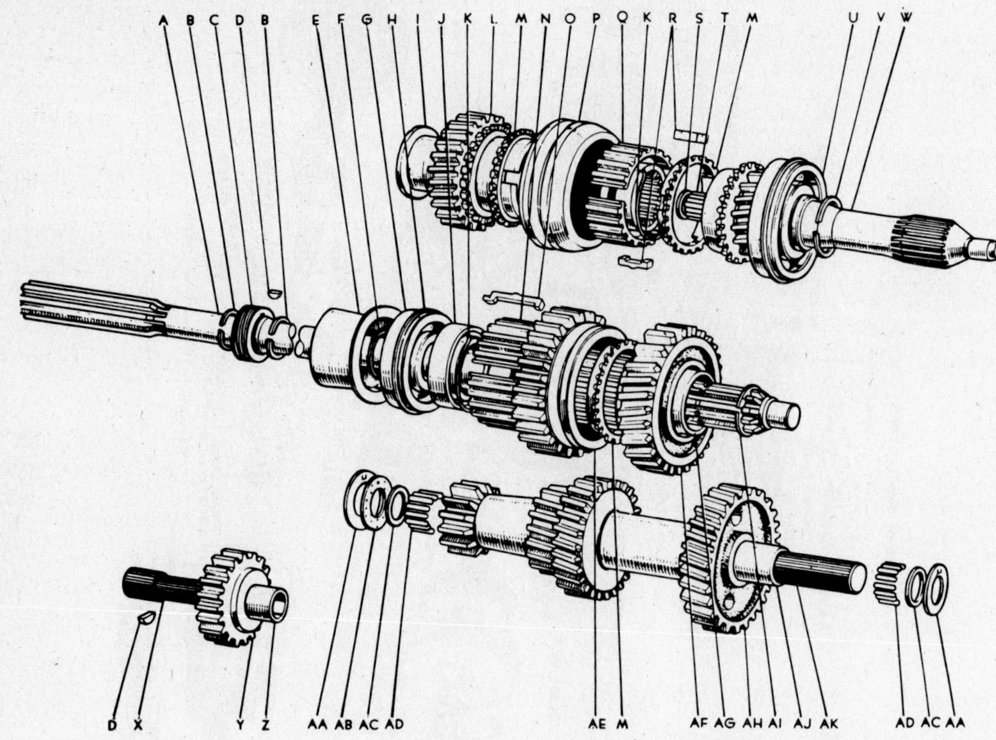

Land Cruiser three speed transmission internal parts

A. Output shaft
B. Shaft snap-ring
C. Speedometer drive gear
D. Woodruff key
E. Extension housing oil baffle subassembly
F. Shaft snap-ring
G. Bearing
H. Shaft snap-ring
I. Second gear bushing
J. Shifting key retainer
K. Synchromesh shifting key spring
L. Second gear
M. Synchronizer ring No. 2
N. Transmission clutch hub No. 1
O. Synchromesh shifting key No. 1
P. Transmission hub sleeve
Q. Transmission clutch hub No. 2
R. Synchromesh shifting key
S. Hole snap-ring
T. Roller
U. Bearing
V. Shaft snap-ring
W. Input shaft
X. Reverse idler gear shaft
Y. Reverse idler gear subassembly
Z. Solid bushing
AA. Countergear case side thrust washer
AB. Countergear side thrust washer
AC. Spacer
AD. Roller
AE. First and reverse gear
AF. First gear
AG. First gear bushing
AH. Countergear
AI. Shaft snap-ring
AJ. Tube
AK. Countershaft

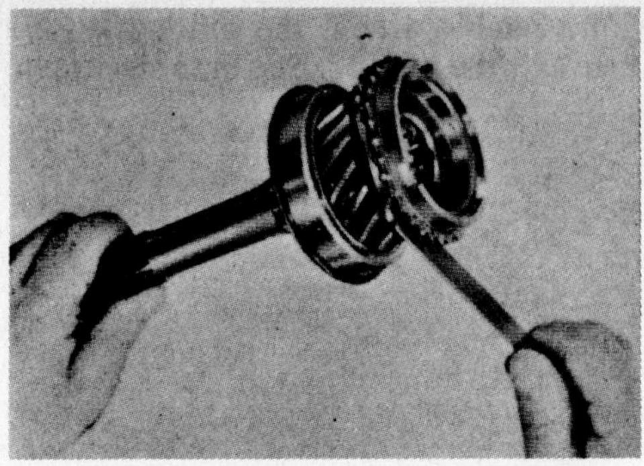

Inspecting synchronizer ring—three-speed.

Assembling clutch hub—three-speed.

Assembling clutch hub—three-speed.

1. Locking rings
2. Shift keys
3. Clutch hub
4. First and reverse gear

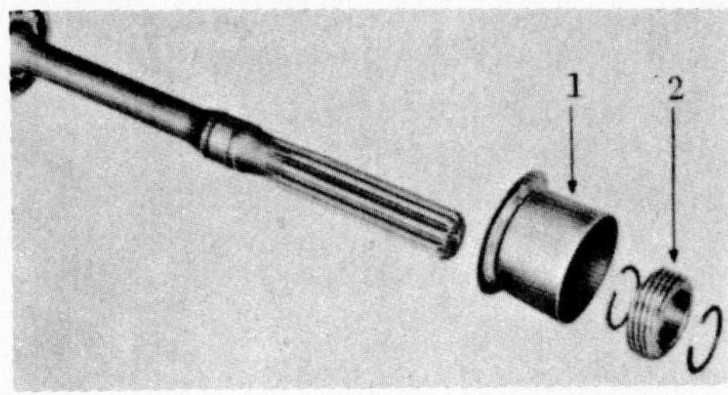

Assembling speedometer drive gear—three-speed.

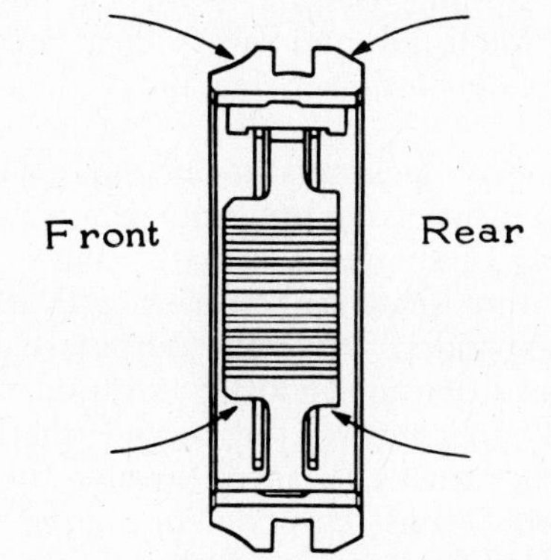

Clutch hub correctly installed—three speed.

reverse gear into the clutch hub, with the flat sides of the keys facing the groove in the first and reverse gear. Install the key lock rings with their ends 120° apart (to keep tension equal), then install the completed assembly onto the output shaft, fitting the shifting keys into their retainer in the process. Slide the first gear bushing onto the output shaft; assemble the synchronizer ring and first gear and slide them on next. Slide the second gear bushing onto the shaft, aligning the notches with the first gear bushing; slide second gear onto shaft.

Assemble the three shifting keys and the other clutch hub sleeve and install into clutch hub, installing the key lock rings 120° apart as before, then slide the assembled unit onto the output shaft. Select and install a snap-ring having enough thickness to result in 0.004-0.010″ second gear thrust gap, then pack the input shaft with wheel bearing grease and insert the twelve bearing rollers and snap-ring. Assemble the gearshift lever mechanism and install into transmission case (from the inside), then hook up shift levers. Install the reverse idler gear and shaft (embossed side facing front) and lock the shaft using a Woodruff key. Assemble the countergear and its rollers (23 per end), spacer tubes and thrust washers, holding the assembly together with a dummy shaft. Lay the assembly in the bottom, of the transmission case, press the front bearing onto the input shaft (using a snap-ring of proper thickness to keep play to a minimum) and install the input shaft into the transmission case. Bolt the front bearing retainer and paper gasket to the front of the case, install Woodruff key into the countergear cut-out, then push countergear shaft through the case and gear, thus displacing the dummy shaft. *NOTE: Make sure the Woodruff key is lined up properly.*

With the countergear installed, measure its thrust play using a feeler gauge. Specified clearance is 0.002-0.010″, which can be corrected using different thrust washers. Install the third speed synchronizer ring onto the input shaft gear, then install the extension housing, lining up all notches and keys. *NOTE: Before installing, position hub sleeve in third gear position.* Check the clearance between the clutch hub sleeve, third gear and second gear; the sum of these clearances must be greater than 0.40″. This clearance can be corrected using different gaskets, plus liquid sealer.

Install first and reverse shift fork and second and third shift fork onto first and reverse gear and hub sleeve, respectively. Now, insert the shift fork shaft from the rear, the even grooves toward the front of the transmission. Lock the shaft in place with the screw plug, then insert the lock balls and springs into the forks and screw the plugs in so that only one thread shows above the fork surface. Secure using cotter pins. Install the case cover, after first making sure the transmission gears move without binding and the shift levers select the proper gears.

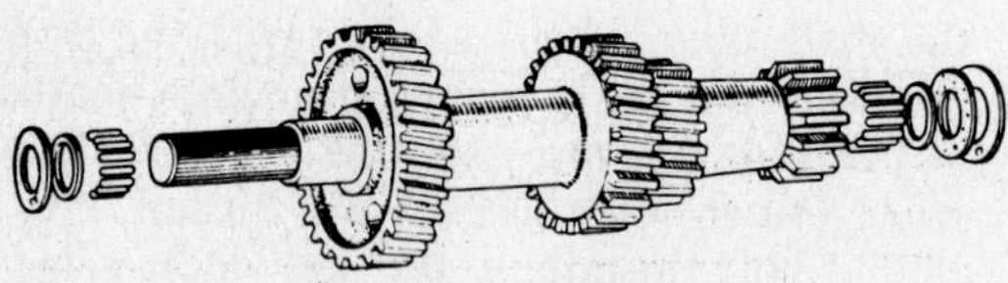

Countergear and shaft components—three-speed.

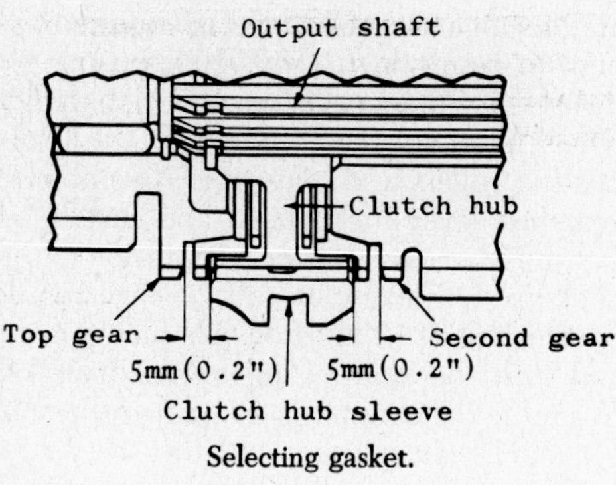

Selecting gasket.

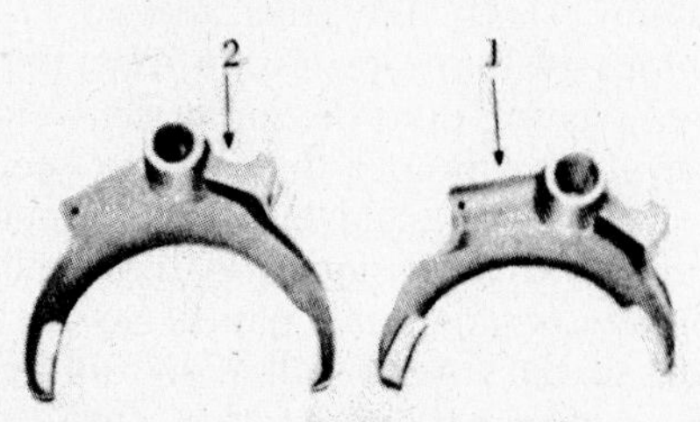

Gearshift forks; (1) is first and reverse, (2) is second and third.

Overhaul; Corona, Mark II, Hi-Lux

Disassembly

Remove the clutch release fork and the release bearing hub assembly. Remove the clutch housing from the gear case. Remove the front bearing retainer and transmission case cover assembly. Before removing the internal parts, check the countergear thrust clearance with a feeler gauge, record the reading, then pick the proper adjusting gear side thrust washer to obtain the specified clearance of .002-.006″.

Remove the bolts retaining the extension housing to the transmission case. Turn and align the cut portion of the extension housing with the countershaft. Use a dummy shaft and drive out the countershaft and the Woodruff key to the rear. Remove the extension housing and the output shaft and gear assembly.

Remove the input shaft with the bearing.

Take the countergear assembly and the thrust washers out of the transmission case. Remove the dummy shaft, roller bearings, and the spacer from the countergear.

Using a brass rod, gently tap the reverse idler gear shaft toward the rear and remove it. Remove the reverse idler gear. Check and record the following clearances; first gear thrust clearance, third gear thrust clearance, second gear thrust clearance, and clearance between snap-ring and clutch hub.

Remove the shaft snap-ring at the front end of the output shaft. Slide the synchronizer unit, synchronizer ring, third gear, third gear bushing, thrust washer, second gear bushing, second gear, synchronizer ring, clutch hub and reverse gear assembly and the synchronizer ring, out of the output shaft.

Remove lock plate and speedometer driven gear assembly from the extension housing. Expand the shaft snap-ring on the output shaft rear bearing with a snapring expander. Drive the output shaft out of the extension housing with a mallet. Check and record the output shaft rear bearing thrust clearance. Remove the shaft snap-ring and speedometer drive gear, Woodruff key, and oil baffle.

Remove the shaft snap-rings. Place the

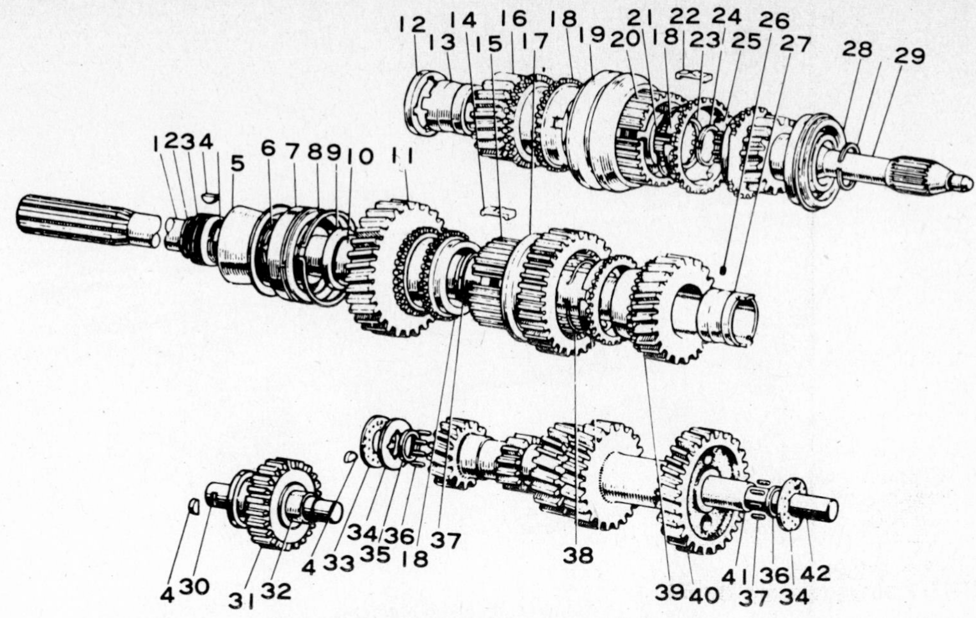

Corona and Hi-Lux transmission gear cluster

1 Output shaft
2 Shaft snap-ring
3 Speedometer drive gear
4 Woodruff key
5 Extension housing baffle
6 Shaft snap-ring
7 Radial ball bearing
8 Shaft snap-ring
9 Spacer
10 Bi-metal formed bushing
11 First gear
12 Second & third gear thrust washer
13 Third gear bushing
14 Synchromesh shifting key No. 1
15 Transmission clutch hub No. 1
16 Third gear
17 Reverse gear
18 Synchronizer ring
19 Transmission sleeve
20 Transmission clutch hub No. 2
21 Synchromesh shifting key spring
22 Synchromesh shifting key No. 2
23 Shaft snap-ring
24 Hole snap-ring
25 Roller
26 Straight pin
27 Second gear bushing
28 Bearing
29 Input shaft
30 Reverse idler gear shaft
31 Reverse idler gear
32 Bi-metal formed bushing
33 Counter gear case side thrust washer
34 Counter gear side thrust washer
35 Spacer
36 Roller
37 Shaft snap-ring
38 Synchromesh shifting key spring
39 Second gear
40 Counter gear
41 Tube
42 Countershaft

first gear on vise anvils, and press out first gear, spacer, and the bearing from the output shaft.

Transmission Case Cover Disassembly

Loosen and remove the backup light switch. Move the third and fourth shift fork into the fourth speed position (to the front). Using a long drift punch, drive out the slotted spring pin which connects the shift fork to the shift fork shaft. Slide the shift fork shaft out of the rear of the case cover gradually, preventing the lock ball from popping out under spring tension. Remove the lock ball, spring and the two interlock pins from the case cover.

Drive the slotted spring pin out of the first and second shift fork and the shift fork shaft in the same manner. Remove the shift fork shaft and the shift fork, then remove the lock ball and the spring from the case cover. Remove shift arm pivot locknut. Remove the shift arm from the case cover. Drive out the slotted spring pin, and remove the reverse shift head and the shift fork shaft. Remove the lock ball and the spring. Remove the selector outer lever and the selector lever shaft. Remove the shift lever shaft lockbolt, slide out the shift lever shaft from the case cover. Be careful to prevent the lock ball from popping out under spring tension. Remove the sliding shift lever, lock ball and the spring. Remove the wire and shift lever lockbolt. Remove the shift and selector lever shaft towards the rear side of the case.

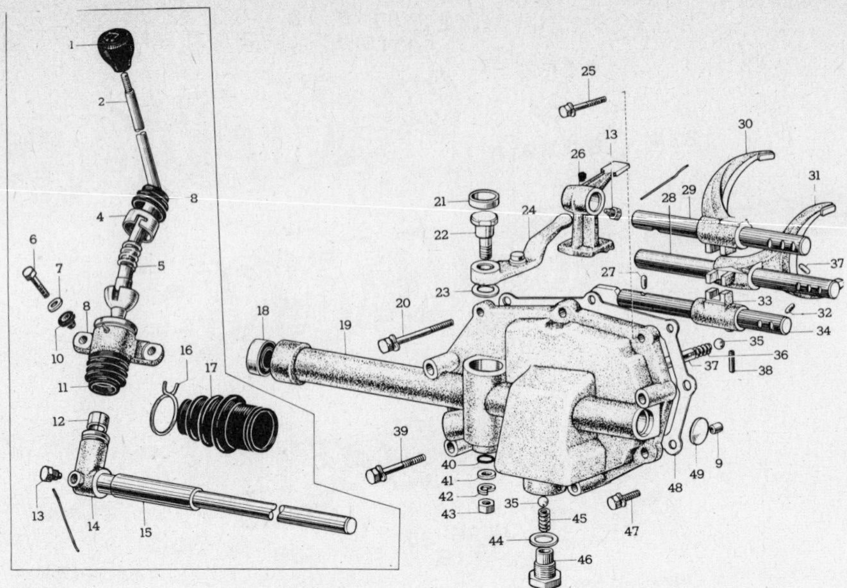

Shift linkage components

1 Shift lever knob
2 Shift lever
3 Shift & select lever boot No. 3
4 Shift lever cap
5 Compression spring
6 Bolt
7 Plate washer
8 Control shift lever retainer
9 Ring pin
10 Control shift lever retainer bush
11 Shift & select lever boot No. 2
12 Shift lever bushing
13 Shift fork lock bolt
14 Shift lever housing
15 Shift & select lever shaft
16 Clip
17 Shift & select lever boot No. 1
18 Oil seal
19 Transmission case cover
20 Bolt w/washer
21 Tight plug
22 Shift arm pivot
23 Plate washer
24 Reverse shift arm
25 Bolt w/washer
26 Shift & select lever
27 Shift interlock pin No. 2
28 3rd & 2nd shift fork shaft
29 1st & 2nd shift fork shaft
30 1st & 2nd shift fork
31 3rd & 4th shift fork
32 Shift interlock pin No. 1
33 Reverse shift head
34 Reverse shift fork shaft
35 Gear shift fork lock ball
36 Compression spring
37 Shift detent ball spring seat
38 Slotted spring pin
39 Bolt w/washer
40 O ring
41 Plate washer
42 Spring washer
43 Nut
44 Drain plug gasket
45 Compression spring
46 Reverse restrict ball holder
47 Bolt w/washer
48 Transmission case cover gasket
49 Expansion plug

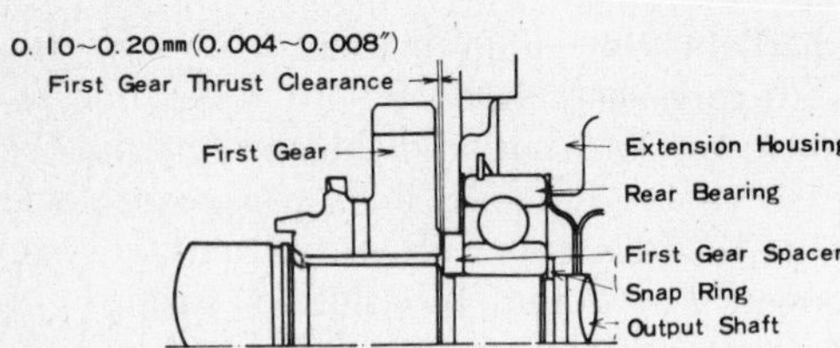

Me. suring first gear thrust clearance

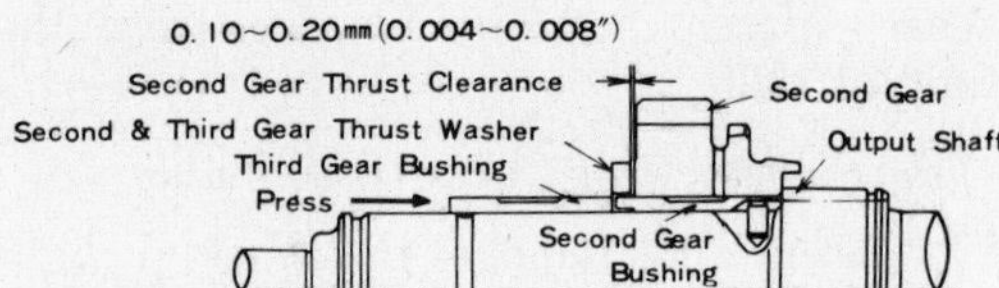

Measuring second gear thrust clearance

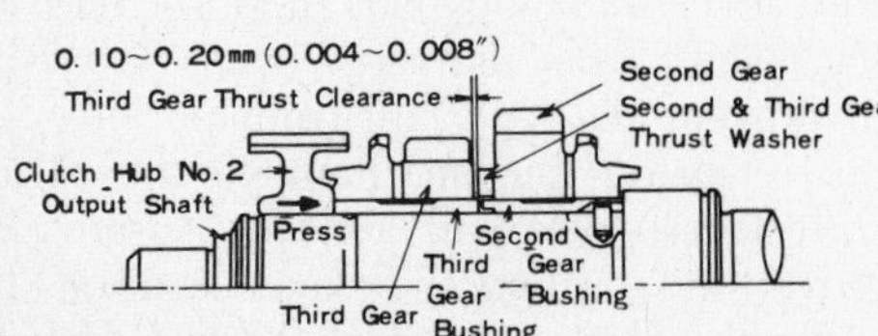

Measuring third gear thrust clearance

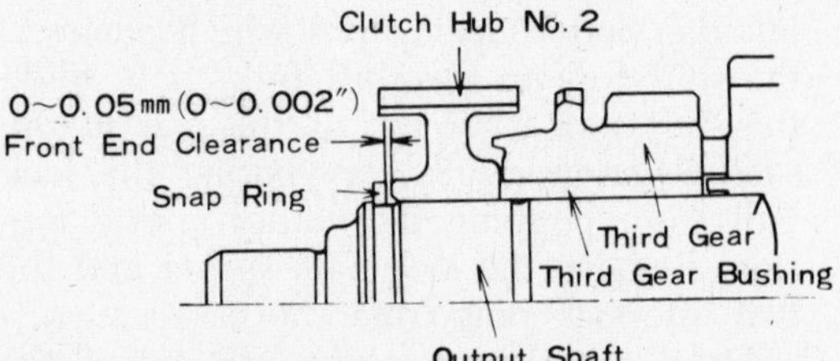

Snap-ring to clutch hub clearance

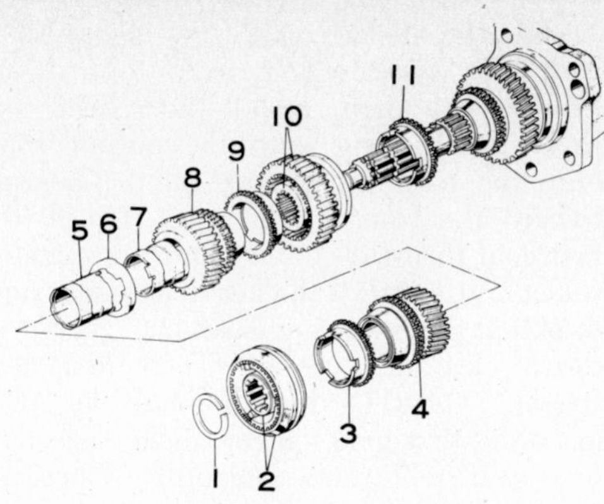

Output shaft components

1 Snap-ring
2 Synchronizer unit
3 Synchronizer ring
4 Third gear
5 Third gear bushing
6 Thrust washer
7 Second gear bushing
8 Second gear
9 Synchronizer ring
10 Clutch hub and reverse gear assembly
11 Synchronizer ring

Inspection

Case, Case Cover, and Extension Housing

Wash all disassembled parts thoroughly. Check the transmission case, case cover and the extension housing for cracks; check the bearing fitting portions and gasket surfaces for burrs and nicks.

Gears

Check the gears for tooth wear or damage. Also check the tooth contact condition (which may cause noise). Check the synchronizer ring contacting surface of the gear cone for uneven wear or roughness.

Check the shaft bores of the gears for wear and roughness, and check the bearing roller contact surface for scores or damage.

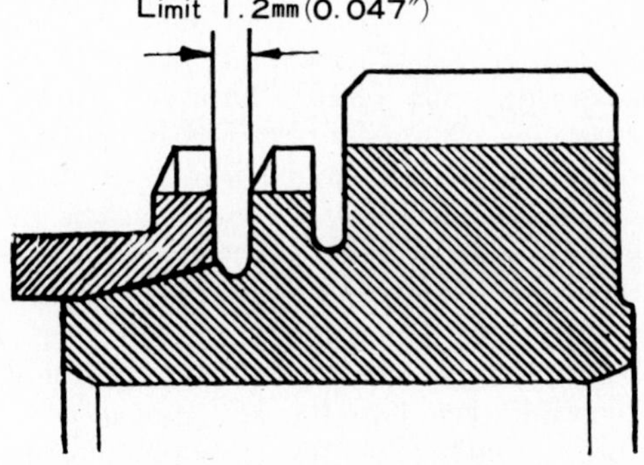

Synchronizer ring inspection

Specified gear backlash

Input shaft gear to countergear: .004"
Third gear to countergear: .004"
Second gear to countergear: .004"
First gear to countergear: .004"
Reverse idler gear to countergear: .005"
Reverse idler gear to reverse gear: .005"

Synchronizer Rings

Check the synchronizer rings for tooth wear or damage. Place the synchronizer ring on the respective gear cone, and check the clearance between the synchronizer gear and the synchronizer ring. If the clearance is less than .047" replace the synchronizer ring or the gear.

Synchronizer

Check the shifting keys for abnormal wear or warpage. Replace if defective. Check the shifting key springs for weakness or bent condition. Check the splines of the clutch hub and hub sleeves for wear or damage. The hub and hub sleeve must be replaced as a set if either is defective.

Output Shaft

Check the output shaft splines, snap-ring grooves, bearing contact surfaces, bearing fitting portions and oil seal lip contact surface for wear, scores, or damage. Check output shaft for runout. If the runout exceeds 0.0012", replace shaft. To measure runout, place a dial indicator on the center point of the shaft and rotate the shaft slowly to read the maximum and minimum values. The runout equals the maximum value minus the minimum value divided by two.

Bearings and Bushings

Check the bearings for roughness and wear. Check for noise or damage by rotating the bearing after applying a few drops of oil. To remove the input shaft bearing, remove the shaft snap-ring with a snap-ring expander, then remove the bearing from the input shaft with a puller. Check the bushings and the bearing rollers for abnormal wear. If the wear is excessive, replace the bushing/s or the bearing rollers.

Gearshift Mechanism

Inspect the shift forks and the sliding shift lever contact surfaces for wear and distortion. Check the clearance between each shift fork and relative hub sleeve, and if the clearance exceeds the service limit, replace the shift fork(s), hub sleeve or gear(s). The clearance limit for the shift fork to hub sleeve and gears is .04″. The clearance limit for sliding shift lever to shift forks and shift head is .04″.

Check each shift fork and the shift fork shaft for smooth movement and for damage or distortion. Check the shift lever shaft splines for wear, and check the sliding shift lever for smooth movement. Check the detents of the shift fork shafts for wear or damage. Check the shift fork lock ball for wear or cracks, and check the lock ball springs for excessive weakness.

Speedometer Gear and Oil Seal

Check the speedometer drive and driven gears for scoring and wear. Replace all oil seals and O-rings. Remove the oil seal in the rear end of the extension housing using a puller.

Extension Housing Bushing

Inspect the extension housing bushing for wear or scoring. To replace the bushing, press the bushing out of the extension housing to the front side. To install, align the oil grooves of the bushing and the extension housing, and press the bushing into the housing. After installing the bushing, ream the bushing to fit the outer diameter of the universal joint sleeve yoke.

Assembly

Always install new gaskets, apply liquid sealer or gasket cement when assembling. Apply a thin coating of transmission lubricant on all parts before installation. Thrust clearances of gears and bearings are important factors for smooth gear shifting. Therefore, select and assemble thrust washers, snap-rings and spacers of proper thickness.

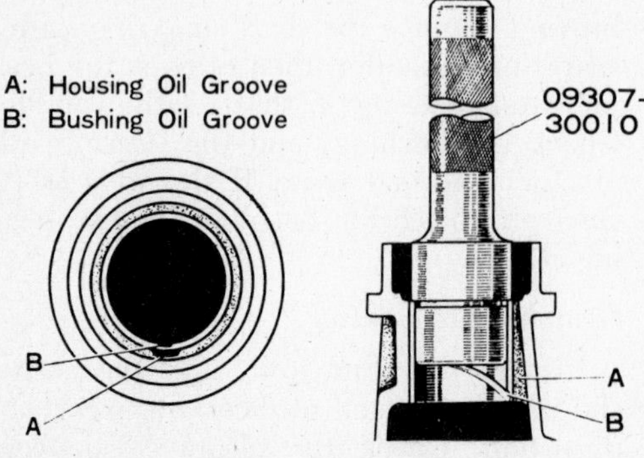

Bushing installation

Slide the first gear onto the output shaft with the synchronizer gear toward the front of the shaft. Install the spacer, and press the bearing onto the output shaft with the snap-ring groove on the bearing toward the front of the shaft. Check the first gear thrust clearance, and if necessary, select and install a thicker first gear spacer to obtain the following clearance. First gear thrust clearance: .004-.008″. A first gear spacer, .209-.211″ thick is available. After installing first gear spacer, make sure that first gear will rotate smoothly. Checking the first gear thrust clearance must be performed with the rear bearing snap-ring installed.

Check the clearance between the rear bearing and the snap-ring, and if necessary select and install a thicker snap-ring to obtain an output shaft rear bearing thrust clearance of 0-.002″. Six thicknesses of rear bearing snap-rings are available. Check the clearance between the second gear and second and third gear thrust washer while pressing the third gear bushing against the second gear, and if necessary, file off the rear end of the second gear bushing with sand paper on the surface plate to obtain a second gear thrust clearance of .004-.008″. Five thicknesses of second and third gear thrust washers are available. A second gear bushing 1.264-1.265″ long is available.

Check the clearance between the third gear and second and third gear thrust washer while pressing the clutch hub against the third gear, and if necessary, file off the front end of the third gear bushing as well as the second gear bushing to obtain .004-.008″ third gear thrust clearance. A third gear bushing 1.382-1.384″ long is available. Make sure that gears rotate smoothly while pressing the clutch hub against third gear.

Check the clearance between the front end snap-ring and clutch hub. If necessary, use a thicker front end snap-ring to obtain 0-.002″ clearance between the snap-ring and clutch hub. If specified clearance cannot be obtained by installing snap-ring, select and install a thicker second and third gear thrust washer, then install a front end snap-ring of proper thickness. Front end snap-rings are available in ten thicknesses. Install the oil baffle and the shaft snap-ring. Install the Woodruff key into the key groove of the output shaft. Slide the speedometer drive gear onto the output shaft, then install the

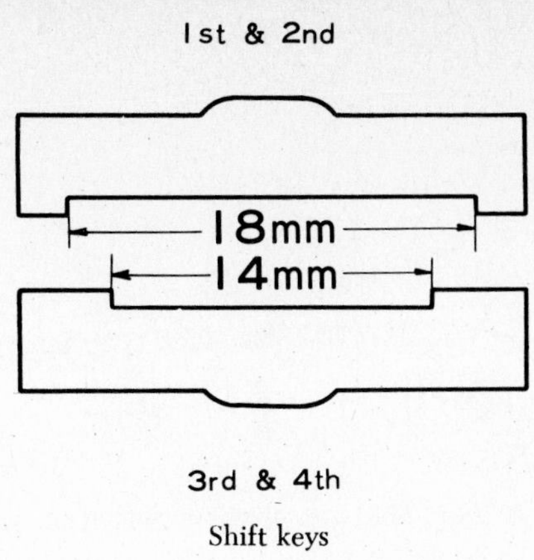

Shift keys

shaft snap-ring and secure the gear. Install the shaft snap-ring into the groove of the extension housing front end. Expand the shaft snap-ring with a snap-ring expander, then assemble the output shaft into the extension housing. When assembling the output shaft, install the universal joint sleeve yoke temporarily onto the output shaft rear end to prevent damaging the extension housing bushing and the oil seal, and to properly center the output shaft.

Assemble the synchronizer unit by installing the two shifting springs onto the clutch hub with open ends of the springs 120° apart, so that the spring tension on each shifting key will be uniform. Place the three shifting keys into the clutch hub key slots and onto the shifting springs.

CAUTION: There are two kinds of shifting keys in this transmission. The keys with the shorter straddle length should be installed on the third and fourth synchronizer unit.

Next, slide the hub sleeve onto the clutch hub. The clutch hubs and the hub sleeve or the reverse gear are matched, and should be kept together as an assembly for smooth operation. Assemble the first and second synchronizer unit in the same manner as described. Install the synchronizer ring, reverse gear, and synchronizer ring onto the output shaft. Align the cut portions of the synchronizer rings with the shifting keys on the clutch hub. Slide the second gear bushing onto the output shaft, and align the bushing groove with the straight pin on the output shaft. Install the second gear onto the bushing of the output shaft. Install the second and third gear thrust washer, and align the indents of the thrust washer and the claws of the bushing. Install the third gear bushing, third gear, synchronizer ring and the third and fourth synchronizer unit onto the output shaft. Install the shaft snap-ring onto the output shaft. Check the first gear, second gear and the third gear on the output shaft for smooth rotation, and also check the synchronizer units for smooth movement.

Press the bearing onto the input shaft with the snap-ring on the bearing toward the front. Select and install the proper shaft snap-ring to obtain minimum thrust play on the input shaft. Shaft snap-rings are available in two sizes; No. 1 is .096-.102″ thick, No. 2 is .091-.095″ thick.

Coat the bearing rollers with grease, and coat the bore of the input shaft gear. Install the bearing rollers into the bore, then install the hole snap-ring. Position the reverse idler gear into the transmission case with the shift fork groove toward the rear. Align the key groove of the reverse idler gear shaft and the cut portion of the transmission case, and drive the shaft through the gear and into the transmission case. Secure the shaft by installing the Woodruff key. Install the collar into the countergear, then install the two needle roller bearings into both sides of the countergear. Insert the dummy shaft into the countergear. Position the countergear assembly, case side thrust washers and the proper adjusting gear side thrust washer which was determined when disassembling the transmission, onto the bottom of the transmission case. Countergear thrust clearance is .002-.006″. Side thrust washers are available in fourteen sizes. After installing the side thrust washer, make sure that the countergear rotates smoothly. Install the input shaft assembly onto the transmission case. Install the output shaft and gears, and the extension housing assembly with the gasket onto the transmission case. Turn and align the cut portion of the extension housing with the countershaft bore of the transmission. Next, align the bores of the transmission case and the countergear. Install the countershaft from the rear of the transmission case. Secure the countershaft by installing the Wood-

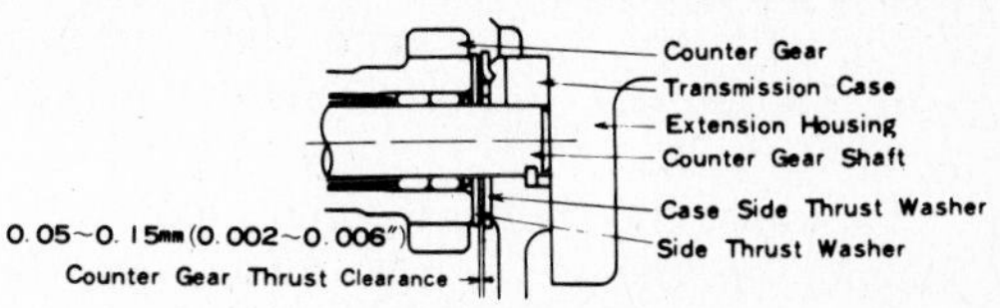

Countergear thrust clearance

ruff key onto the end of the shaft. Tighten the extension housing retaining bolts to 22-33 ft. lbs. Install the speedometer driven gear into the extension housing, and secure the driven gear sleeve with the lock plate. Install the front bearing retainer with the gasket. Apply liquid sealer on the threads of the bolts, and torque the front bearing retainer attaching bolts to 3-5 ft. lbs. Install the clutch housing onto the transmission case. Lubricate the clutch release bearing hub bore with multipurpose grease, and install the clutch release fork and hub assembly onto the transmission case.

To assemble the transmission case cover, install the shift arm pivot onto the reverse shift arm, and insert into the case. Assemble the shift and selector lever shaft together with the shift and selector lever, and secure the bolt with a wire. Insert the reverse shift fork shaft compression spring and lock ball into the case, and insert the fork shaft from the rear side, then secure the shift head with a new slotted spring pin. Align the fork shaft positioning groove with the shift interlock pin groove. Align the reverse shift arm knob with the reverse shift fork shaft, and install the O-ring, washer and the nut onto the shift arm pivot. Insert the shift interlock pin into the rear side of the case cover and the compression spring and lock ball into the front side, and assemble the shift fork together with the first and second shift fork shaft. Secure the shift fork with a new slotted spring pin. Align the shift fork shaft positioning groove with the shift interlock pin groove. Insert the two shift interlock pins into the front side of the case cover. Insert the compression spring and the lock ball, and assemble the shift fork together with the third and fourth shift fork shaft, then secure the shift fork with a new slotted spring pin. Install the lock ball, compression spring and the reverse restricting ball holder.

Check all shift forks for smooth movement. Install the back-up light switch on the case cover. Align each shift fork and the reverse shift arm with the respective gears, and install the transmission case cover with the gasket onto the transmission. Torque the case cover retaining bolts to 11-16 ft. lbs.

To adjust the shift arm pivot, loosen the locknut on the shift arm pivot, turn the shift arm pivot clockwise until friction is

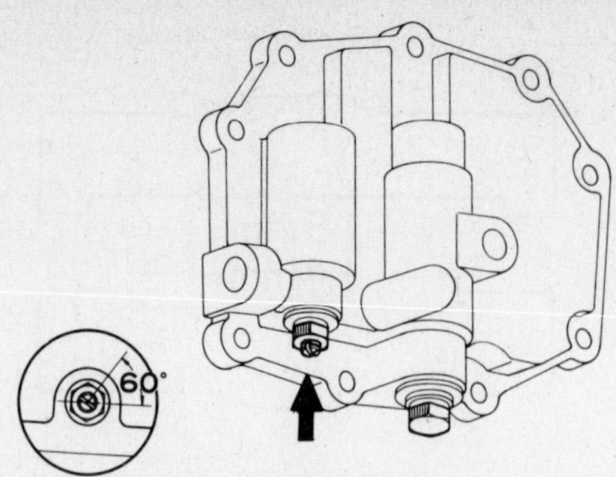

Shift arm pivot adjustment

felt, when the reverse idler gear contacts with the first gear and/or the countergear. Next, from this position, turn the shift arm pivot counterclockwise approximately 90 degrees. Tighten the pivot locknut securely. With the input shaft rotating, make sure that there is no noise and that the reverse idler gear does not contact other gears in the transmission. If no friction is felt when the shift arm pivot is turned clockwise, set the pivot line mark at 60 degrees rearward from its horizontal position to the case cover surface. If necessary, replace the oil seal in the extension housing after assembling the transmission using the oil seal puller, and pull out the oil seal together with the dust seal.

Installation

Follow the removal procedures in the reverse order. When assembling the oil seal and the dust seal, coat the lip of the oil seal with multipurpose grease, and apply gear lubricant on the dust seal.

CAUTION: Apply multipurpose grease onto the input shaft splines and the release bearing contact surface with the clutch release levers. When installing the transmission assembly onto the cylinder block, do not forget to install the clamp of the clutch pipe. Install the clamps of the wiring and the fuel tube on the engine mounting rear brackets when tightening the bracket bolts. Fill the transmission with gear lubricant up to the filler hole. The lubricant should be 2 quarts of SAE 90. Adjust the clutch release fork free play to .145".

AUTOMATIC TRANSMISSION

Two- and three-speed transmissions are currently in use. All late model Crown and all Mark II models use the three-speed transmission, while the Corona and the early Crown use the two-speed transmission.

The new Corolla two-speed unit is slightly different from the early type, having only one band and two clutches, whereas the early type has only one clutch and uses two bands. All (except early series) have floorshift controls. The two-speed types are of a design similar to the domestic Powerglide and the three-speed is similar to the Borg Warner transmission.

Coded serial numbers are stamped in the left rear side of the transmission case.
Example of code: 9B-1097
9=1969 B=2nd month (February)

All two speed automatics use Type A fluid; all three speed automatics use Type F.

Removal

Two-Speed Transmission

Disconnect battery. Drain all coolant from engine and disconnect radiator inlet hose. Disconnect throttle link from carburetor bell-crank (remove air filter if necessary). Remove exhaust pipe flange nuts, then jack up car and support on stands. Drain transmission oil, remove drive shaft and remove exhaust pipe bracket from transmission case. Disconnect exhaust pipe and transmission shift rod from control shaft. Disconnect throttle link rod from throttle valve lever, then disconnect speedometer drive cable. Remove the four bolts from the rear support and take off the crossmember. (Support the transmission with a suitable jack.) Remove the clamp from the two oil cooler lines and disconnect both lines, then remove the seven bolts that hold the transmission case to the bellhousing. Withdraw the transmission slowly so as not to damage the oil seal. *CAUTION: There will be some oil in the converter, so be prepared with a drain pan.*

Torque Converter

Loosen and remove the six bolts that hold the converter to the drive plate. Access is through the special hole provided in the lower bellhousing plate. Rotate the converter by turning the crank pulley.

Converter Drive Plate and Ring Gear

Remove the ten transmission housing bolts from the bellhousing and remove the housing. Remove the six bolts that attach the ring gear and drive plate to the crankshaft. It is best to mark both the converter and the drive plate so that they can be installed in their original positions.

Three-Speed Transmission

Disconnect battery. Remove air cleaner and disconnect accelerator torque link (early models) or cable (late models), disconnect throttle link rod at carburetor side, then disconnect back-up light wiring at firewall (on early models). Jack up car and support on stands, then drain transmission oil. (Use a clean receptacle so that the oil can be checked for color, smell and foreign matter.) Disconnect all shift linkage. On early models, remove the cross shaft from the frame. Disconnect throttle link rod at transmission side and remove speedometer cable, oil cooler lines and parking brake equalizer bracket. Loosen the exhaust flange nuts and remove the exhaust pipe clamp and bracket. Remove drive shaft and rear mounting bracket, then lower the rear end of the transmission carefully. Support engine with a suitable jack stand and remove the seven bolts that hold the transmission to the engine.

Installation

Two-Speed Transmission

Reverse the order of the removal procedures, with the following precautions. Do not extend the crankshaft locating dowel more than .315″ from the end. Tighten the drive plate to 45-47 ft. lbs. When installing the torque converter position the drive plate as it was during removal. Tighten the drive plate to pump impeller front disc to 7.5-9.5 ft. lbs. First tighten the eight bolts finger tight, then to the specified torque.

When installing the transmission, align the pump drive keys of the pump impeller with the key holes of the pump drive gear. After installing the transmission, adjust the throttle link connecting rod, and the selector lever (see Adjustments).

Fill the transmission with 3.2 quarts of automatic transmission fluid (Type A, Suffix A only), and then start the engine. Run the engine at idle speed, with the selector lever at N. Add fluid gradually up to the F line of the level gauge. After warming the engine, fill the transmission with automatic transmission fluid. The capacity is 4.8 quarts. Adjust the engine idle to 600 rpm, with the selector at N.

Pump drive key alignment

Road test the vehicle. With the selector lever at D, check the point at which the transmission shifts. Check for shock, noise and slippage, with the selector lever in all positions. Check for leakage from the transmission.

TORQUE SPECIFICATIONS

Drive plate to crankshaft: 33-39 ft. lbs.
Drive plate to torque converter: 8-11 ft. lbs.
Transmission housing to engine: 37-50 ft. lbs.
Transmission housing to case: 14-22 ft. lbs.

THREE-SPEED TRANSMISSION

Reverse the order of the removal procedures with the following precautions. Install the drive plate and ring gear, tighten the attaching bolts to 37-43 ft. lbs. After assembling the torque converter to the transmission, the clearance should be about .59". Before installing the transmission, install the oil pump locator pin on the torque converter to facilitate installation.

While rotating the crankshaft, tighten the converter attaching bolts a little at a time. After installing the throttle connecting second rod, make sure the throttle valve lever indicator aligns with the mark on the transmission with the carburetor throttle valve fully opened. If required, adjust the rod.

To install the transmission control rod correctly, move the transmission lever to N, and the selector lever to N. Fill the transmission with 1.3 gals. of automatic transmission fluid (Type F only), then start the engine. Run the engine at idle speed and apply the brakes while moving the selector lever through all positions, then return it to N.

After warming the engine, move the selector lever through all positions, then back to N, and check the fluid level. Fill as necessary. Capacity is 1.85 gals.

Adjust the engine idle to 550-650 rpm with the selector lever at D. Road test the vehicle. With the selector lever at 2 or D, check the point at which the transmission shifts. Check for shock, noise and slipping with the selector lever in all positions. Check for leaks from the transmission.

Adjustments

THREE-SPEED TRANSMISSION

Floorshift Lever

When the transmission gears are in neutral, the selector lever should indicate N.

Unless the selector lever knob button is pushed, the transmission cannot be shifted to L, R or P. In P, the vehicle should be locked. The selector lever should move smoothly and be fully in the detent in all gears.

To adjust the connecting rod swivel position, first check all bushings for wear.

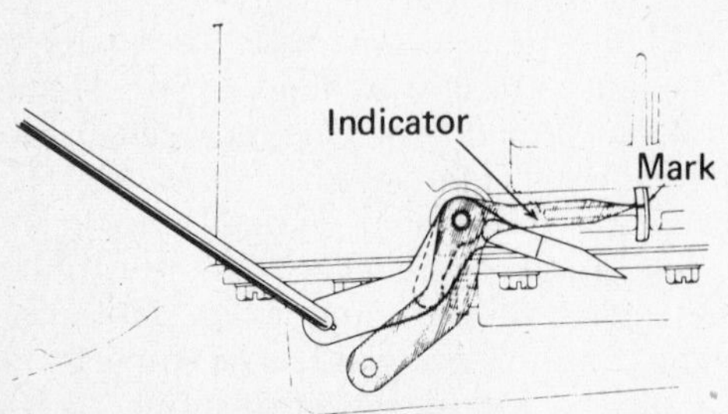

Throttle rod adjustment

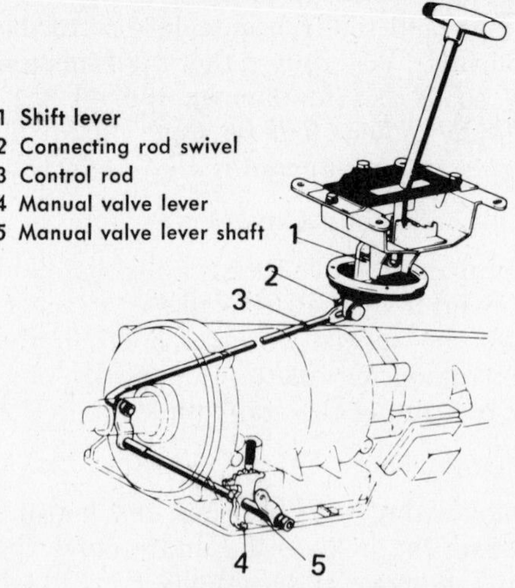

Selector lever assembly

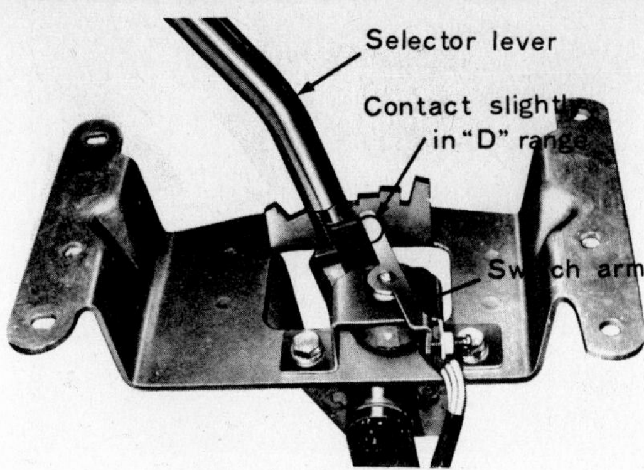

Switch installation position

Loosen the connecting rod swivel locknut, then move the manual valve lever on the transmission to N. Move the selector lever to N. Lock the connecting rod swivel with the locknut. Adjust the length of the parking lockrod by loosening the parking lock swivel locknuts. Check all bushings for wear. Move the selector lever to P. Move the parking lock shaft to the locking position. Lock the parking lockrod swivel with the locknuts.

Neutral Safety and Backup Switch

The engine should start with the selector lever in N or P only. If necessary, remove the selector lever assembly and adjust the switch. Loosen the switch retaining bolt, and install the switch so that the switch arm slightly contacts the selector lever when the selector lever is in D. Check the switch with a tester. After installation check the switch for operation. Make sure the backup light glows only with the selector lever in R.

Throttle Link Connecting Rod

With the carburetor throttle valve fully opened, the indicator on the throttle valve lever should align with the mark on the transmission. If necessary, adjust the length of the connecting rod. Loosen the locknuts on each end of the turnbuckle. Disconnect the connecting rod from the carburetor. Adjust the length of the connecting rod with the turnbuckle so that the throttle link connecting rod end aligns with the attaching portion on the carburetor when the throttle valve lever indicator aligns with the mark on the case and the carburetor throttle valve is fully open. After locking the turnbuckle and connecting the rod to the carburetor, check that the throttle valve lever indicator aligns with the mark on the transmission, with the carburetor throttle valve fully open. Road test the vehicle and adjust if necessary.

TWO-SPEED TRANSMISSION (OLD TYPE)

Control Rod

When the selector lever is at N, the transmission gears should also be in neutral. If necessary, adjust as follows. Set the transmission side control intermediate shaft lever to neutral. To position the control indicator at N, loosen the locknut on the connecting rod swivel, and adjust to change the length of the control rod. Make sure the transmission goes all the way into L and N.

Neutral Safety Switch

The engine should start with the selector lever in N or P only. If necessary, adjust the safety switch.

To adjust the starter safety switch, use a circuit tester. To stop the lever at 6 ±1° (2.2″ at lever end), adjust with the small screw and then secure with the nut.

CAUTION: The set position will not change, as it is locked with the screw. It will only change from wear of the screw contact end point or by bending the arm.

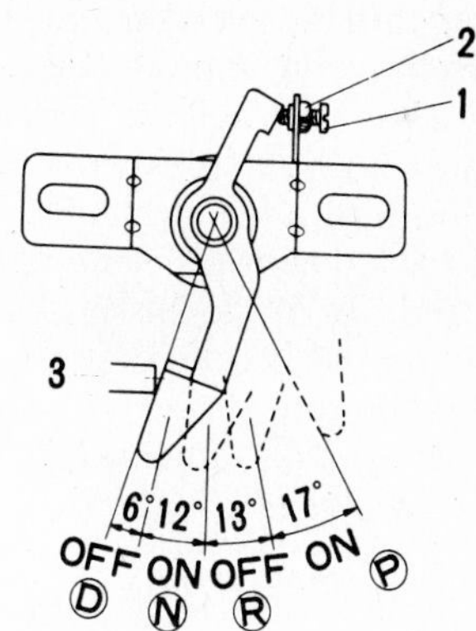

Starter safety switch adjustment

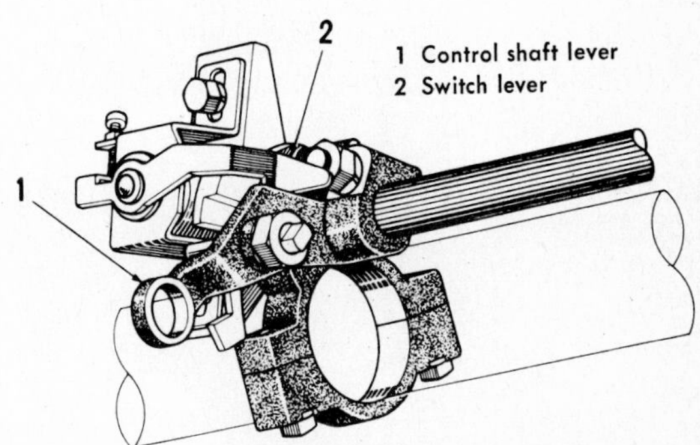

Adjustment location

Set the selector lever at D and adjust the contacting position of the control shaft lever and the switch lever by moving the set plate, and then secure the switch. After the adjustment, check that the starter works at N and P, and doesn't work at D, L, and R.

Throttle Link Connecting Rod

Remove the air cleaner. Disconnect the throttle link connecting rod from the accelerator bellcrank. Loosen the upper and lower locknuts on the turnbuckle to free it. Fully open the carburetor throttle valve, and adjust the rod length so that the connecting rod ball joint and the carburetor bellcrank ball can be connected without any stress when the stamped marks on the throttle valve outer lever and the transmission housing side cover are aligned. Next, firmly secure the rod.

CAUTION: *The alignment of the marks will change whenever the transmission side cover, throttle lever outer lever, throttle valve lever or the downshift plug is replaced or when it is overhauled. Therefore, after the above adjustment, further check by performing the following procedures during road test, and adjust if necessary.*

Depress the accelerator pedal halfway (the throttle valve should reach 1/2 of its opening angle). When the speed reaches 28-31 mph, fully depress the accelerator pedal. The transmission should downshift. If it does not downshift, lengthen the connecting rod. If it downshifts before the accelerator pedal is fully depressed, shorten the connecting rod.

CAUTION: *The downshift mechanism will not work above 36 mph.*

Brake Band (for low servo)

Raise the front of the car, support with

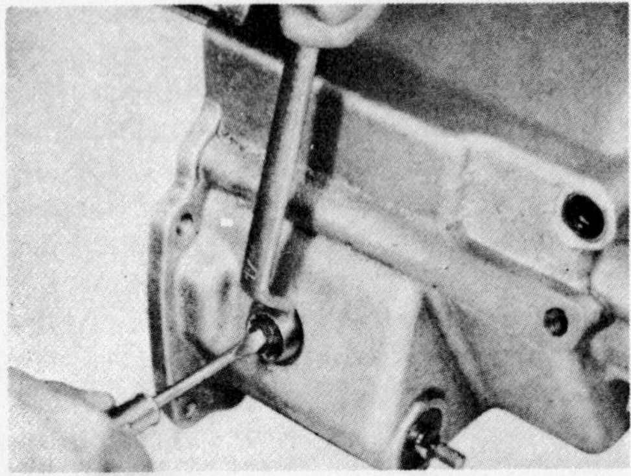

Adjusting low brake band.

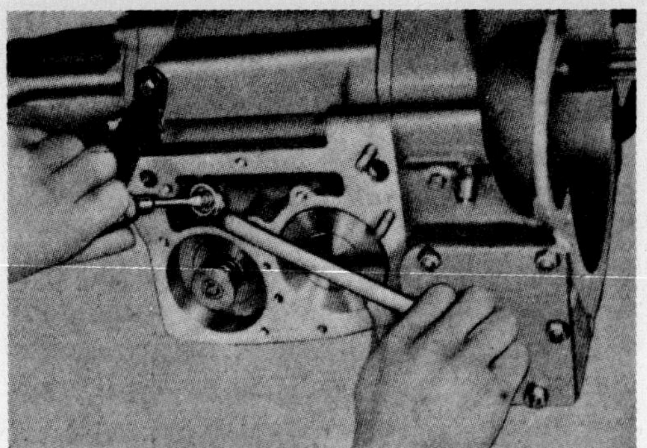

Adjusting reverse brake band.

jackstands. Remove the brake band anchor bolt cap from the transmission case, and loosen the nut locking the anchor bolt. Fully tighten the anchor bolt, then loosen it 3 turns. Secure it in this position using a screwdriver, and tighten the nut. Install the anchor bolt cap. CAUTION: *Apply packing sealer onto the cap. Remove the stands and lower the car.*

Brake Band (for reverse servo)

Raise the car and support with jackstands. Remove the control rod from the intermediate shaft. Wash and clean the case side cover. Remove the transmission drain plug and drain transmission. Remove the union nut on the oil cooler tube coupling and the clamp. When removing the side cover, bend the oil cooler tube to ease removal. Remove the pressure regulator valve seat and spring. Remove the case side cover, and remove the reverse servo piston compression spring. Loosen the anchor bolt locknut, and fully tighten the anchor bolt. Then loosen 4 3/4 turns from this position. Tighten the nut with a screwdriver.

CAUTION: *The tightening torque of the anchor bolt is 2.8-3.6 ft. lbs., but fully tightening with a 10″ screwdriver will be satisfactory.* After the adjustment, assemble the components. Refill the transmission with fluid. After starting the engine, inspect for oil leaks.

Two-Speed Transmission (new type)

Selector Lever

Move the selector lever to N. Loosen the locknut on the control rod swivel, and move the manual valve to N. Adjust the length of the control rod, so that the transmission will be fully in neutral when the selector lever is at N. As a final check, operate the shift

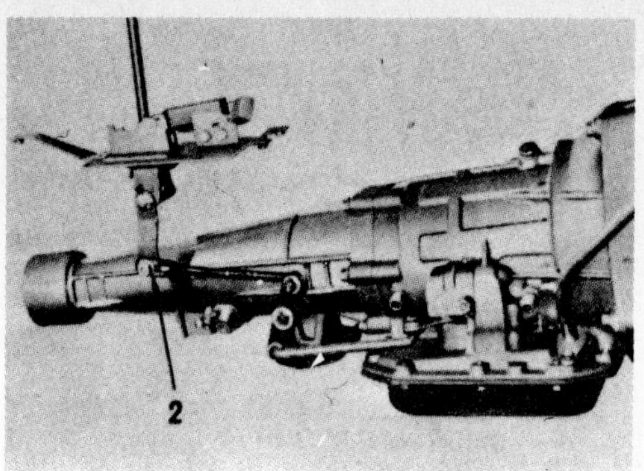
2

Adjusting shift lever.

lever in all positions to make sure that the manual lever on the transmission is fully in the detent in all gears. Adjust the manual shift rod if required.

Neutral Safety Switch

Check the operation of the switch. The engine should start with the selector lever in N or P only. To adjust the switch, install so that the shaft of the switch slightly contacts the push plate of the shift lever when the selector lever is in D. Check that the backup light glows only when the selector lever is in R. Using a tester, check the switch for proper contact.

Throttle Link Connecting Rod

Fully open the carburetor throttle valve. Loosen the locknuts on each end of the turnbuckle. Adjust the length of the connecting rod with the turnbuckle so that the throttle link indicator aligns with the mark on the transmission case. After locking the turnbuckle, confirm that the throttle link indicator aligns with the mark on the transmission with the carburetor throttle valve fully open. Road test the vehicle.

Tighten securely
and loosen 3½ turns

Adjusting low brake band.

Low Servo Brake Band

Lower the rear of the transmission. Tighten the anchor bolt securely, and loosen it exactly 3 1/2 turns. Secure the anchor bolt by tightening the locknut to 17-22 ft. lbs.

Driveshaft and U-Joints

The most common problems with driveshafts concern the universal joints. Seldom do drive shafts need to be replaced (other than in collision cases) and balancing a driveshaft is rarely necessary (other than for competition).

REMOVAL

Jack up rear end of car and support on stands. Remove the four bolts from the rear yoke and slide the driveshaft out of the transmission. Plug hole with a clean rag to prevent oil leakage.

DISASSEMBLY

Punch mark both yokes and driveshaft for correct reassembly. Remove the snap-ring from inside the yoke, then, with the help of two sockets (9/16" and 1 1/4") press out the bearing cups, one at a time.

INSPECTION

Inspect the cup bores for out-of-round (wear) condition. Inspect front yoke and splines for wear and rust, then check that welded balance weights are still in place. Inspect needle rollers and spider (cross) for signs of wear. Replace all worn parts.

ASSEMBLY

Install the grease seals on the spider (soft side UP). Pack cup and needle rollers with grease and install seal into cup, then fit snap-ring into groove on cup and install assembly on spider. Place spider into yoke bore from inside, and press into place in vise. Repeat on other cups.

Select snap-rings so that there is less than 0.002" play. Snap-rings come in four sizes; always use the same size snap-ring for both sides.

INSTALLATION

Lightly oil the splines of the front yoke and carefully insert into transmission so as not to damage the oil seal. Connect the rear yoke flange to the yoke and tighten the four bolts.

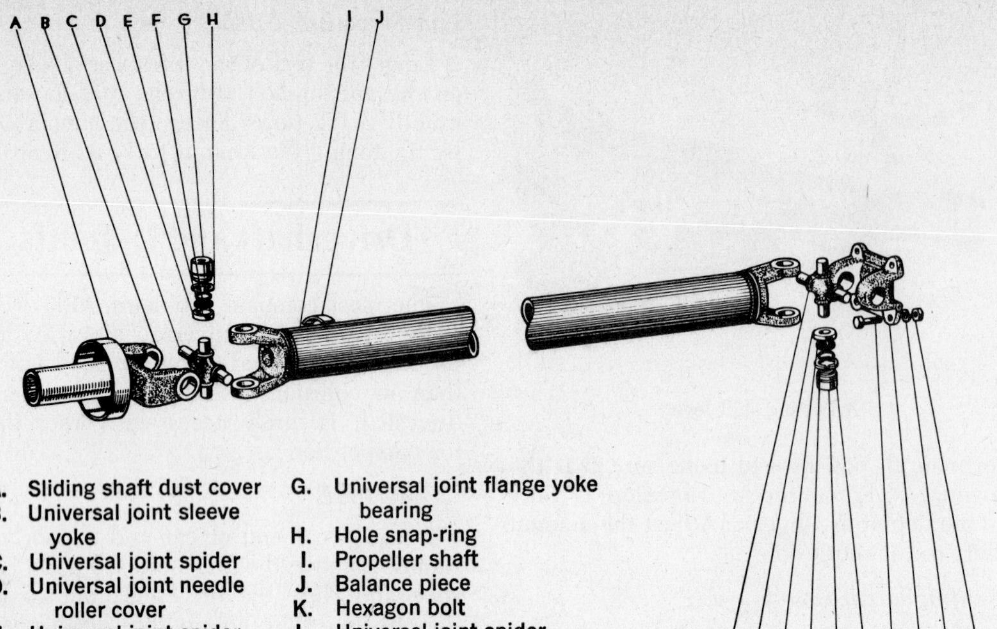

A. Sliding shaft dust cover
B. Universal joint sleeve yoke
C. Universal joint spider
D. Universal joint needle roller cover
E. Universal joint spider bearing seal
F. O-ring
G. Universal joint flange yoke bearing
H. Hole snap-ring
I. Propeller shaft
J. Balance piece
K. Hexagon bolt
L. Universal joint spider
M. Lockwasher
N. Nut

Driveshaft and U-joint exploded view

Installing yoke.

Drive Axle

NOTE: *Rear axle servicing is a complex operation. Repair should not be attempted unless the special tools and knowledge required are readily available.*

DIFFERENTIAL CARRIER

Removal

Jack the car and remove the rear wheels, drain the oil and remove the brake drums. Remove the four nuts that hold the backing plate (access is through the service hole in the axle flange), then remove the axle shaft with an impact puller (the backing plate comes off with the axle). Remove the other axle shaft in the same manner, then disconnect the driveshaft at the pinion yoke. Remove the differential carrier nuts and remove the carrier assembly from the housing, then install the drain plug.

Disassembly

Thoroughly wash and rinse the carrier—blow dry with compressed air. Securely clamp the carrier in a vise or suitable stand. Apply a light coating of mechanic's blue (or lipstick) to the teeth of the ring gear as explained later. Applying a slight drag on the ring gear to avoid backlash, rotate the pinion in a smooth and continuous manner to obtain a good tooth pattern on the ring gear. Next, attach a dial indicator gauge to the carrier base and check the ring gear backlash, as explained later. Also check ring gear runout at this time. If the tooth pattern obtained is correct, and the backlash and runout are within limits, any gear noise must come from the spider or side gears.

With the dial indicator gauge set up on the carrier, check the backlash between spider gears and side gears. Excessive backlash usually is due to either worn thrust washers or a worn spider shaft. Check side gear thrust clearance with a feeler gauge.

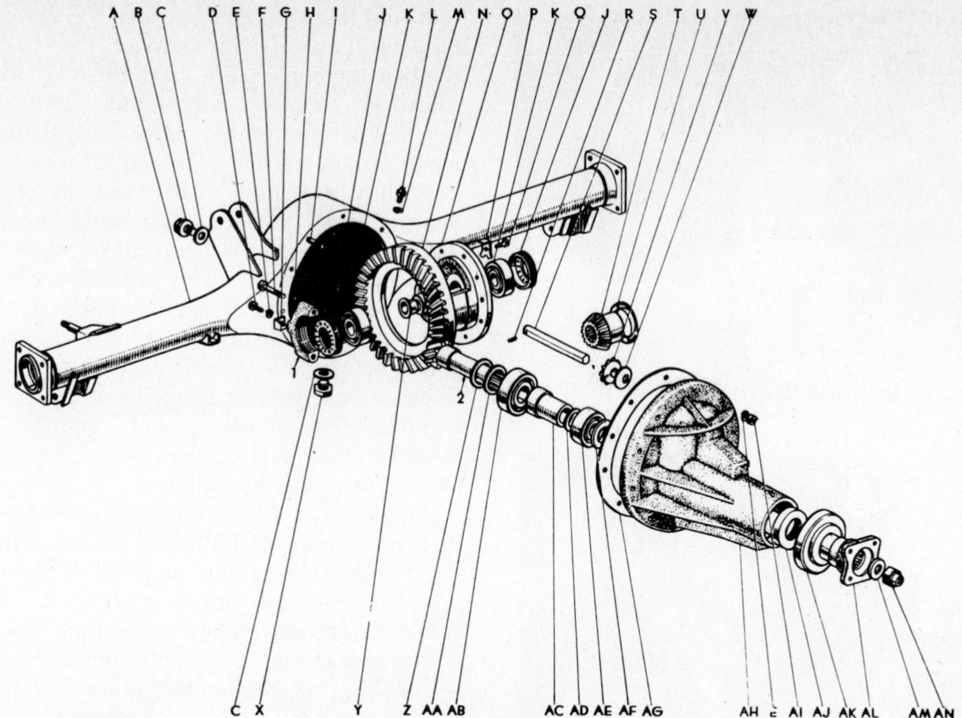

Differential components.

A. Housing assy
B. Filler plug
C. Gasket
D. Bolt
E. Lock washer
F. Hexagon bolt
G. Bearing adjusting nut lock
H. Lock washer
I. Stud
J. Bearing adjusting nut
K. Bearing
L. Breather plug
M. Lock washer
N. Ring gear and drive pinion 1 and 2
O. Case
P. Lock plate
Q. Bolt
R. Lock pin
S. Pinion shaft
T. Side gear
U. Thrust washer
V. Pinion
W. Thrust washer
X. Drain plug
Y. Oil reservoir
Z. Spacer
AA. Shim
AB. Bearing
AC. Spacer
AD. Shim
AE. Bearing
AF. Oil slinger
AG. Gasket
AH. Carrier
AI. Nut
AJ. Oil seal
AK. Dust deflector
AL. Universal joint flange
AM. Flat washer
AN. Nut

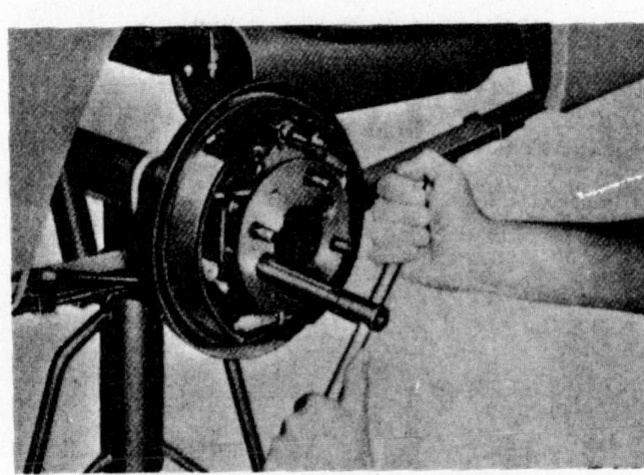

Removing backing plate nuts.

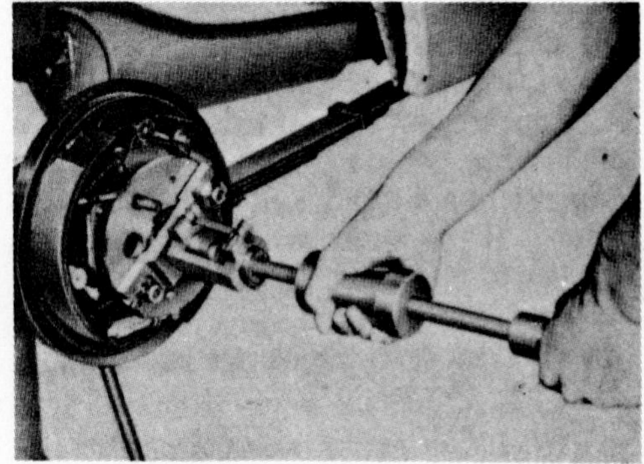

Removing rear axle shaft.

Removing differential carrier.

Applying red lead to gear teeth

Checking ring gear runout.

If everything checks out within specifications, test the preload on the differential drive pinion nut. Punch mark both pinion and nut in their original positions, then LOOSEN the pinion nut about 1/2 turn and torque to specifications. If the punch marks line up again (within 60°) the pinion preload was correct.

Punch mark both the carrier and the side bearing caps for identification, remove locknuts and take off caps. Remove the differential case assembly from carrier. Do not mix the bearing cups; paint mark them for identification. Remove differential pinion nut (do not let the pinion drop out), then remove pinion spacer, yoke and oil seal.

With a brass punch, drive out the pinion bearing cups. *NOTE: This should be done only when the bearings are to be replaced.* Press or pull off the drive pinion rear bearing. Avoid damaging the flat spacer behind the bearing. Measure the spacer thickness and note the measurement for future use. Remove both side bearings from the differential case and mark them "L" and "R" for identification. *NOTE: Remove side bearings only if they must be replaced.*

Punch mark differential case and cover, then remove cover bolts and cover (where fitted). Remove spider shaft and pinions, side gears and all thrust washers. *NOTE: Some differential types have four spider pinion gears; punch mark the gears before removal so they can be correctly reinstalled.*

Inspection

Check all bearing cones and cups for wear. Inspect tooth surfaces of all gears carefully and inspect all thrust washers for wear and signs of slipping in their seats. Check all gear shafts for scoring, wear or distortion. Finally, inspect the case and carrier housing for cracks or other damage. Also check case for signs of wear at the side gear bores, bearing cap and mounting hubs.

Assembly

Wash and clean all parts before installation. Lightly oil all bearings and gear shafts, except ring gear and drive pinion teeth. Place the side gears and the spider gears, with their thrust washers, into the differential case. Insert the spider shaft and align the lock pin holes in case and shaft. Fit the case cover in place and install lock pin (bolt) and tighten cover bolts to specification; check play. If the side bearings were removed, install them now. If the ring gear was removed, install it now. Tighten bolts in symmetrical sequence to avoid distortion and runout.

Install drive pinion bearing cups into carrier housing, using a suitable installing tool. Make sure cups are seated solidly. Assemble drive pinion rear bearing to drive pinion and insert into carrier housing. Install spacer and front bearing to drive pinion; install yoke and tighten nut to specifications.

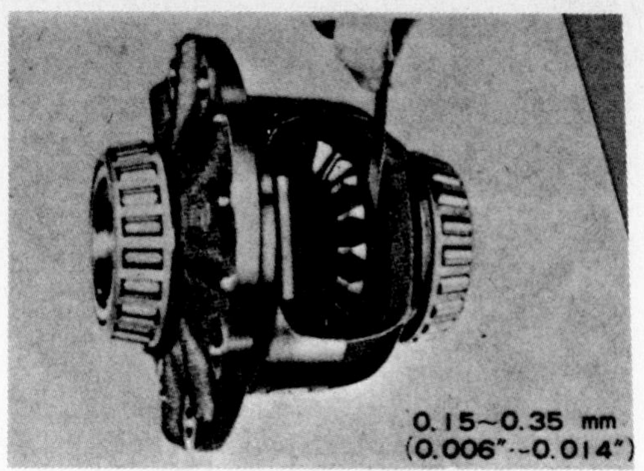

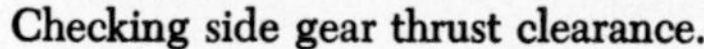
Checking side gear thrust clearance.

Checking side play.

Rear Axle Specifications

Model		*K*	*RT*	*MS*	*FJ*	*KE*	*TE*	*RK*	*RN*
BACKLASH (in.)									
Ring gear and pinion		.004-.006	.005-.007	.005-.007	.006-.008	.004-.006	.004-.006	.005-.007	.006-.008
Side gears, spider gears		.001-.006	.002-.008	N.A.	N.A.	.0008-.0060	.0008-.0060	.004	.002-.008
Side gear to case		N.A.	N.A.	.006-.014	.006-.014	.0008-.0060	.0008-.0060	.006-.014	.002-.008
Axle shaft end-play		.002-.014	.002-.014	N.A.	.002-.018	N.A.	N.A.	N.A.	N.A.
RUNOUT (in.)									
Ring gear		.0016	.0016	.0020	.0040	.0016	.0016	N.A.	.004
Differential case		.0016	.0016	.0020	.0040	N.A.	N.A.	.05	N.A.
Axle shaft (center)		.0015	.0015	.0020	.0025	.008	.008	N.A.	N.A.
TORQUE (ft. lbs.)									
Ring gear to case		45-55	50-60	50-70	72-87	66.5-76.1	66.5-76.1	50-65	53-64
Side bearing cap		40-47	37-52	50-70	65-80	39.8-47.0	39.8-47.0	52-63	51-65
Carrier to housing		15-22	20-25	20-25	30-40	15-22	15-22	14.5-21.7	14-22
Case cover to case		N.A.	18-26	18-26	N.A.	N.A.	N.A.	N.A.	N.A.
Spider shaft lock bolt		N.A.	11-16	11-16	N.A.	11-16	11-16	N.A.	N.A.
Differential pinion nut		95-110	125-130	115-145	145-175	123-145	123-145	123-145	120-152
PRELOAD (in. lbs.)									
Pinion bearings	New*	2.8-4.8	7.0-9.2	7.0-9.2	12-15	2.6-4.9	4.4-7	10-11	8-11
	Old*	1.0-2.8	4.8-7.0	4.8-7.0	4.8-8.2	2.9	2.9	N.A.	N.A.

* Without oil seal and differential gears installed.

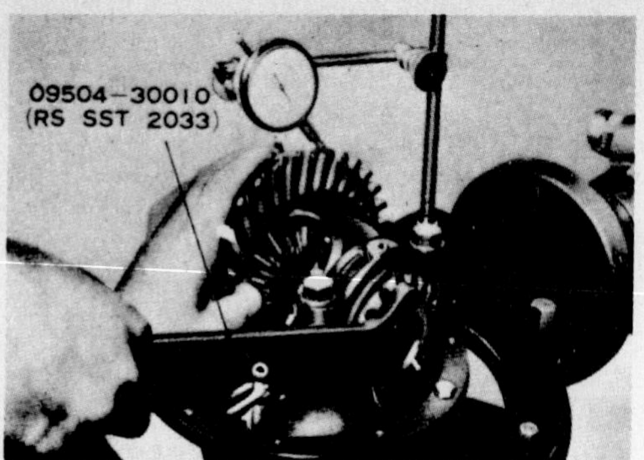

Adjusting backlash.

(Drive pinion oil seal is NOT installed at this point.) The drive pinion preload is measured in in. lbs. (not ft. lbs.). Adjust preload by changing the length of the bearing spacer (between front and rear bearings) until the required preload is obtained.

Place the previously assembled differential case into position in the bearing hubs and put the caps into position as marked (L and R). Set the case so that there will be the least amount of backlash between ring gear and pinion (in order to save time adjusting). Install the adjusting nuts (also marked L and R) and take care not to cross-thread them. Finger-tighten the bearing caps until the threads are lined up correctly, then tighten slowly.

Differential Side Bearing Preload Adjustment

Back off the right-hand adjusting nut (ring gear teeth side) and screw in the other nut until almost no backlash is felt. Attach a dial indicator gauge so that it reads at right angles to the back of the ring gear, then screw in the right-hand adjusting nut until the gauge indicates that all side play has been eliminated. Tighten the adjusting nut another one or one and one-half notches (depending on the fit of the lock tabs). Recheck the preload on the drive pinion as before; this time the specifications are different (see table). If too loose, readjust side bearing preload; if too tight, adjust the ring gear backlash.

Ring Gear and Pinion Backlash Adjustment

Install dial indicator gauge so that it contacts the ring gear teeth at right angles. Adjust the backlash to specifications. If too great, adjust by loosening the bearing cap bolts slightly and screwing the right-hand adjusting nut (ring gear teeth side) OUT about two notches. Tighten the left-hand adjusting nut the same amount. *NOTE: One notch of the adjusting nut equals about 0.002″ of backlash.* Recheck the backlash, then tighten the bearing cap nuts.

Ring Gear and Pinion Tooth Pattern Test

Using a dial indicator gauge, recheck all runout dimensions (ring gear back, ring gear outer circumference and differential case). Apply a thin coat of mechanic's blue, red

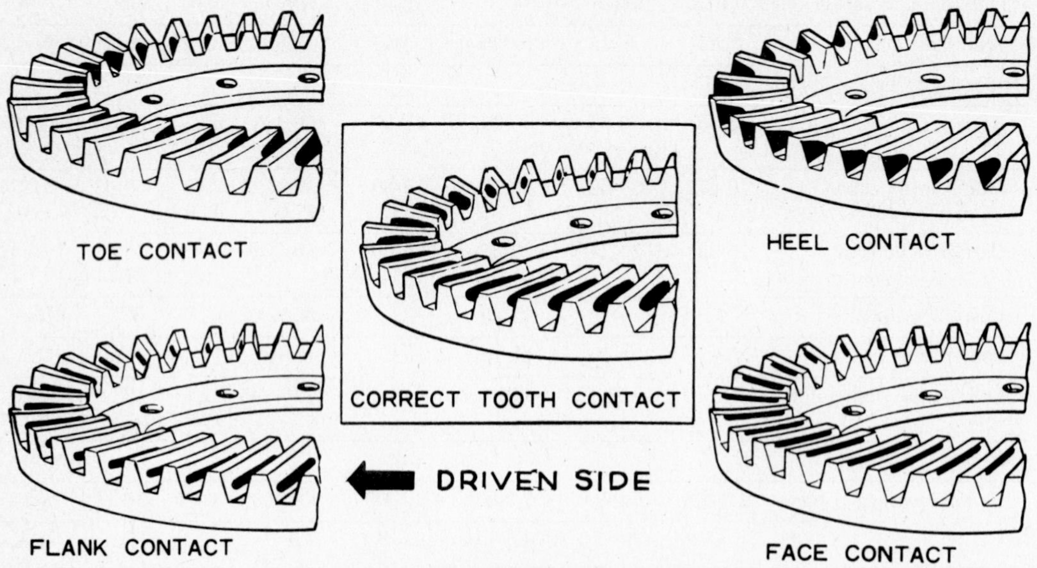

Ring gear tooth pattern.

lead or even lipstick to the ring gear teeth. Rotate the gear several times, applying a light drag to the ring gear. Rotate gear in both directions. Inspect tooth pattern. There are four basic tooth patterns: heel, toe, flank and face. Most often the tooth pattern obtained will be a combination of two of these patterns and the adjustments must be made accordingly.

Heel contact Move the drive pinion IN by increasing the thickness of the spacer (between pinion head and rear bearing). Readjust backlash by moving ring gear away from pinion.

Face contact Adjust same as above.

Toe contact Adjust by moving the drive pinion OUT by reducing the thickness of the spacer. Readjust backlash.

Flank contact Adjust same as toe contact.

Continue assembling as follows:

Remove drive pinion nut and install seal into differential carrier housing, then install oil slinger, dust shield and yoke and retorque the pinion nut as specified. Install the differential carrier assembly into the axle housing. Apply Permatex to the new gasket and tighten to specifications. Connect the universal joint flange to the yoke and tighten securely, then insert the two axle shafts and secure backing plates. Refill with proper grade oil and secure filler and drain plugs. Slide front yoke of drive shaft into transmission and secure rear universal to rear flange, then remove jack stands.

AXLE SHAFTS

Rear Axle Shaft

Disassembly

Remove axle shaft as previously described in the Differential Carrier Removal Section. Using a cold chisel, split the axle bearing retainer (or grind it off) and pull off the bearing, oil seal and grease catcher. The hub bolts then can be pressed out. Install nut to prevent thread damage. *NOTE: The axle inner oil seal should be replaced only if it leaks.*

Assembly

Press in the new hub bolts, then assemble the outer retainer, spacer and bearing to the shaft by pressing them into place. The inner retainer must be preheated to about 300° F. and quickly installed so that it will seat properly.

Measure the thickness of the backing plate and select gasket to match as follows: the combined thicknesses of gasket and plate should total 0.120″ ± 0.003″. Apply Permatex to both sides of bearing retainer gasket and rear axle end gasket and install both onto the axle shaft, then place the axle shaft into the axle housing without damaging the oil seal. Whenever possible, use NEW nuts to secure the backing plate to the axle housing; tighten to specifications. *CAUTION: Do not mistake the top for the bottom of backing plate end and retainer*

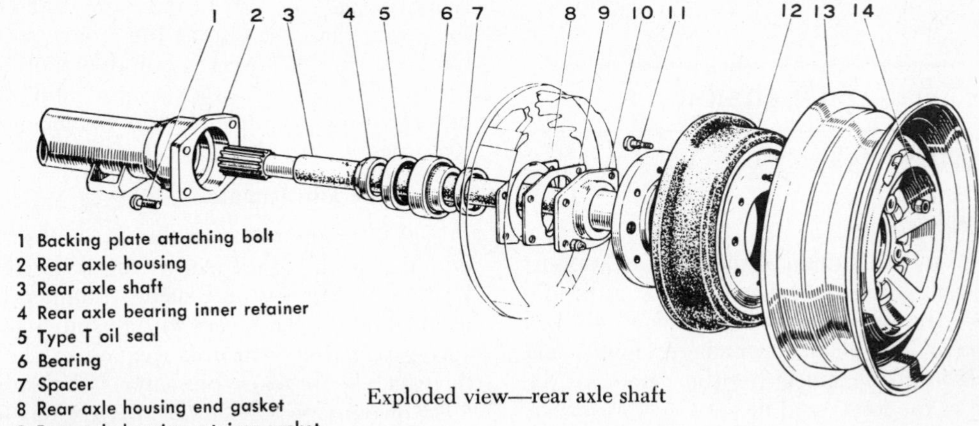

Exploded view—rear axle shaft

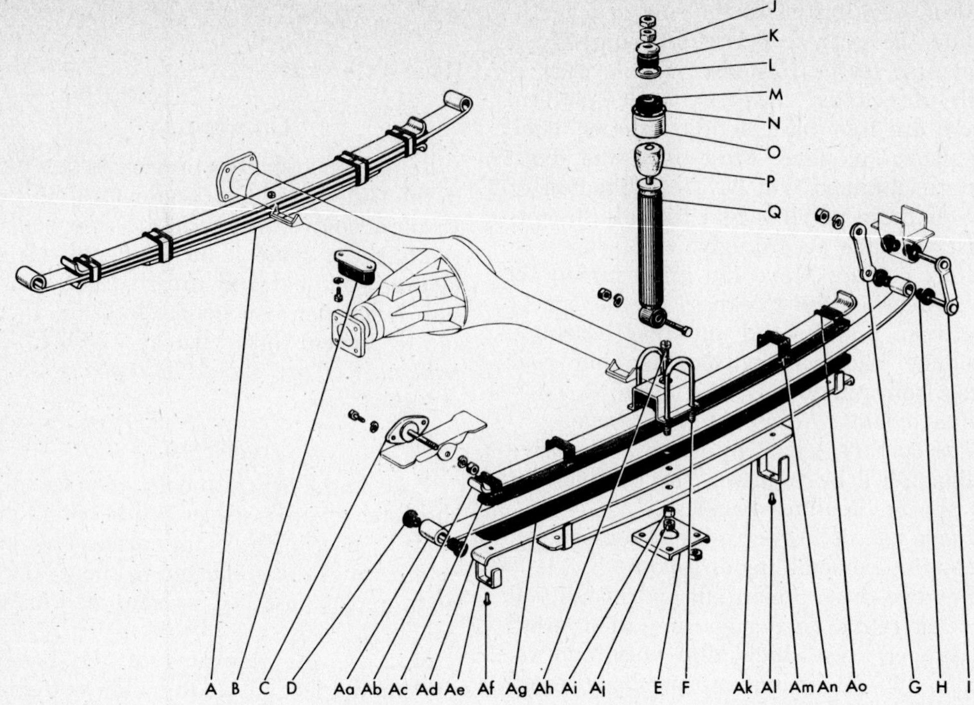

Exploded view—rear suspension

A	Rear spring assembly	L	Shock absorber cushion retainer	AF	Round head rivet
B	Differential carrier bumper	M	Shock absorber cushion	AG	Rear spring interleaf
C	Spring bracket pin	N	Cushion retainer	AH	Rear spring center bolt
D	Bushing	O	Rear bumper cover	AI	Spacer
E	Rear spring U-bolt seat	P	Rear spring bumper	AJ	Nut
F	U-bolt	Q	Rear shock absorber	AK	Rear leaf spring with clip
G	Spring shackle outer plate	AA	Rear leaf spring	AL	Round head rivet
H	Bushing	AB	Rear leaf spring tension	AM	Rear spring clip
I	Spring shackle	AC	Rear spring interleaf	AN	Rear spring clip spacer
J	Shock absorber cushion retainer	AD	Rear leaf spring with clip	AO	Rear spring clip spacer
K	Shock absorber cushion	AE	Rear spring clip		

gaskets. Bleed brakes and reconnect parking brake. Check oil level; use hypoid SAE 90.

Suspension

REAR SUSPENSION

Removal

Raise the rear end of the car, and support the rear axle housing with jackstands. Remove the rear wheels. Open the trunk, and remove the nuts, cushion retainer, and cushion of the shock absorber. Remove the bolt at the lower end of the shock absorber, then remove the shock absorber. Remove the U-bolt attaching nuts, the U-bolt seat, and the under spring pad. Remove the shackle attaching nuts, and the shackle plate from the rear end of the spring.

Pry the shackle with a suitable bar, remove the shackle and the four bushings. Remove the two bolts, and nut attaching the spring bracket pin, at the front end of the rear spring. Insert a suitable tool between the spring bracket pin and the bracket, and pry them apart. Remove the rear spring with the bracket pin.

Inspection and Repair

Check the operation of the shock absorbers and check for oil leaks. Check the rod, bushing, cushions, and spring bumper for wear and defects. Check the bushings and spring pads for wear and weakness. Check the shackle, bracket pin, and U-bolts for wear or damage. Check the rear springs for breakage, cracks or weak leaves.

Installation

Install the rubber bushings into the front end of the spring, and connect the front end

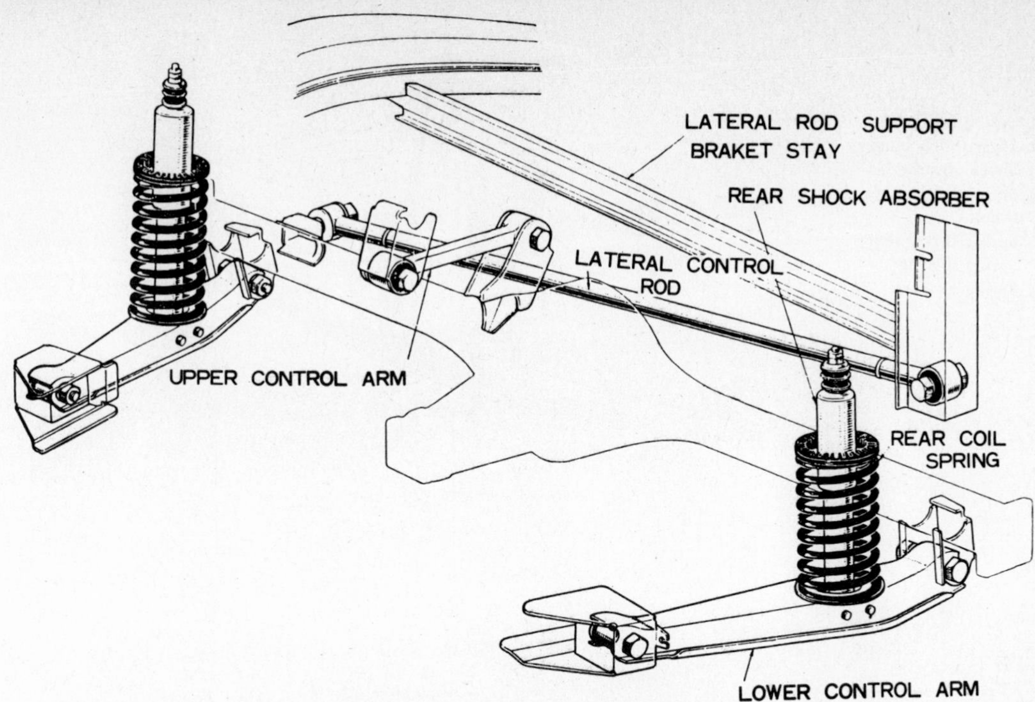

Exploded view of Crown rear suspension

of the spring to the front bracket of the body by installing the bracket pin. Next, tighten the two bolts, and one nut onto the bracket pin finger tight. Install the rubber bushings into the rear end of the spring and rear bracket of the body by installing the shackle, then install the shackle plate and washers. Tighten the attaching nuts finger tight. Install the upper pad and pad retainer between the rear spring and the rear axle housing seat, then install the U-bolts, lower pad, and U-bolt seat, and tighten the U-bolt attaching nuts to 22-32 ft. lbs. Change the supporting positions from the jack up plate of the body to the rear axle housing. Tighten the two bolts attaching bracket pin to 7-12 ft. lbs. and tighten the nut to 15-22 ft. lbs. Tighten the shackle attaching nuts to 15-22 ft. lbs. Install the rear spring bumper, bumper cover, cushion retainer, and the cushion onto the rod of the shock absorber, and install the rod of the shock absorber onto the bracket of the body. Next, install the cushion retainer, cushion, cushion retainer, and the nut, then tighten the nut until the top end of the shock absorber rod protrudes .47-.51″. Tighten the other nut to 14-22 ft. lbs. Install the lower end of the shock absorber onto the rear axle housing, and tighten the attaching nut to 25-40 ft. lbs. Install the wheels, and tighten the wheel nuts to 65-90 ft. lbs.

FRONT SUSPENSION

Suspension is of conventional design with unequal wishbones and coil springs. A transverse leaf spring arrangement is used on early Corollas. Land Cruiser models have regular semi-elliptic springs supporting the front drive axle. On Corona and Crown models, the entire front suspension unit can be dismounted by removing four rubber-insulated bolts and disconnecting brake lines, steering linkage and sway bar.

Coil Spring Suspension Removal (One Side)

Jack up car and place on stands. Remove wheel and upper shock absorber nut, then remove lower shock absorber bracket and withdraw shock absorber. Disconnect stabilizer bar and steering linkage at lower arm only and place jack under lower arm so that the bolts can be removed from the lower ball joint. Slowly lower jack until coil spring can be removed safely. If spring need not be removed, leave it in place and proceed

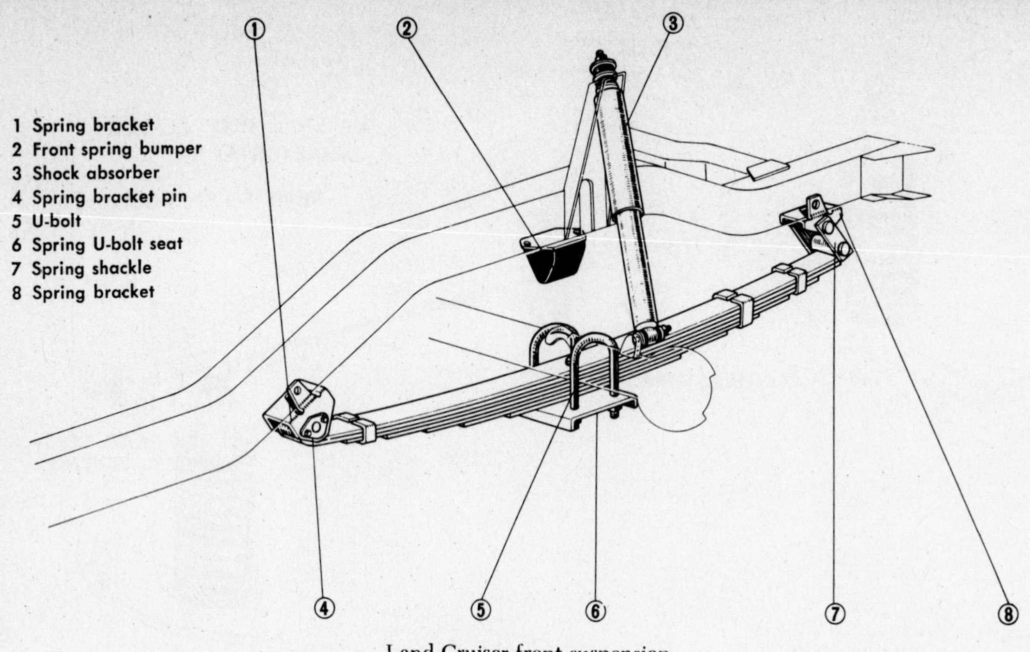

Land Cruiser front suspension

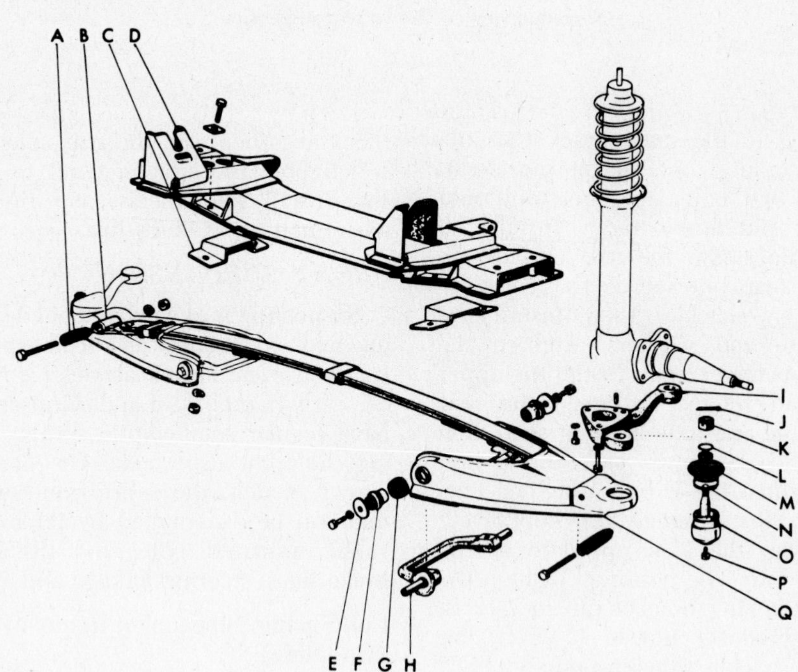

Early Corolla front suspension

A. Front spring bushing
B. Front spring leaf
C. Front spring seat
D. Front suspension crossmember
E. Plate washer
F. Lower arm bushing
G. Lower arm strut bushing
H. Lower arm shaft
I. Steering knuckle arm
J. Cotter pin
K. Castle nut
L. Ring
M. Lower ball joint dust cover
N. Set ring
O. Lower ball joint
P. W/head tapered screw plug
Q. Suspension lower arm

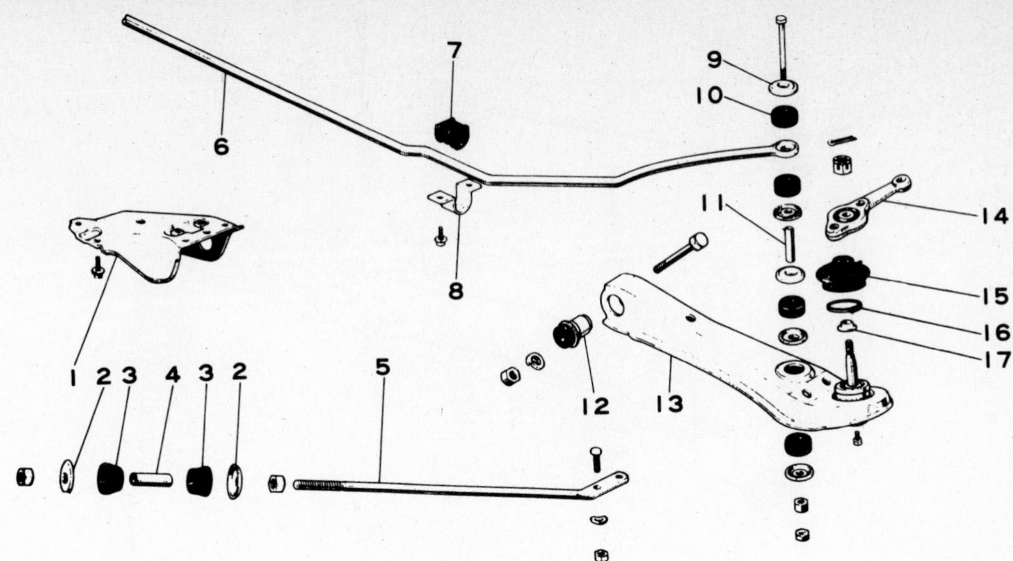

Late Corolla front suspension

1 Strut bar bracket left
2 Strut bar cushion retainer
3 Strut bar cushion
4 Collar
5 Strut bar
6 Stabilizer bar
7 Stabilizer bushing
8 Stabilizer bracket
9 Cushion retainer
10 Stabilizer cushion
11 Collar
12 Suspension lower arm bushing
13 Suspension lower arm
14 Steering knuckle arm
15 Lower ball joint dust cover
16 Set ring
17 Lower ball joint dust plate

as follows: remove upper ball joint nut and remove steering knuckle from upper control arm. Do not disconnect brake hose unless necessary. To remove upper and lower control arms from chassis, simply remove the mounting bolts from each, taking care to keep the adjusting shims marked for later assembly and alignment.

Coil Spring Front Suspension Inspection (One Side)

Check shock absorber for leaks. Replace shock if there is more than 1″ slack in either direction, or if the outer case is dented or bent. Check control arm pivot bushings and replace bushings if necessary. Also check control arms for damaged or worn threads. Check coil spring for distortion and cracks, compare to spring specifications. Check spring insulator and replace if cracked or deformed.

Coil Spring Front Suspension Installation (One Side)

Assemble the upper and lower control arms and pivot bushings, turning each pivot bushing an equal amount. Assemble upper ball joint to arm. Insert spring into seat and, using a pry bar, work spring into the lower arm. Place jack under lower arm and slowly raise until spring is compressed enough to allow the lower ball joint to be connected and tightened. Make sure spring is seated properly at both ends. *NOTE: It may be necessary to remove the spring rebound damper to facilitate installation.* Now, insert the shock absorber and tighten at both ends.

Ball Joint Inspection Without Removal

Upper ball joint

Disconnect from steering knuckle and check free-play by hand. Replace if ball joint is noticeably loose.

Lower ball joint

Jack up car under lower control arm, then check play of wheel. Replace ball joint if play at wheel rim exceeds 0.1″ vertical motion or 0.25″ horizontal motion. Make sure dust covers are securely glued to ball joints.

Ball Joint Removal and Installation

Corolla

Removal

1. Remove wheel, brake drum, and backing plate.
2. Disconnect lower arm assembly. Re-

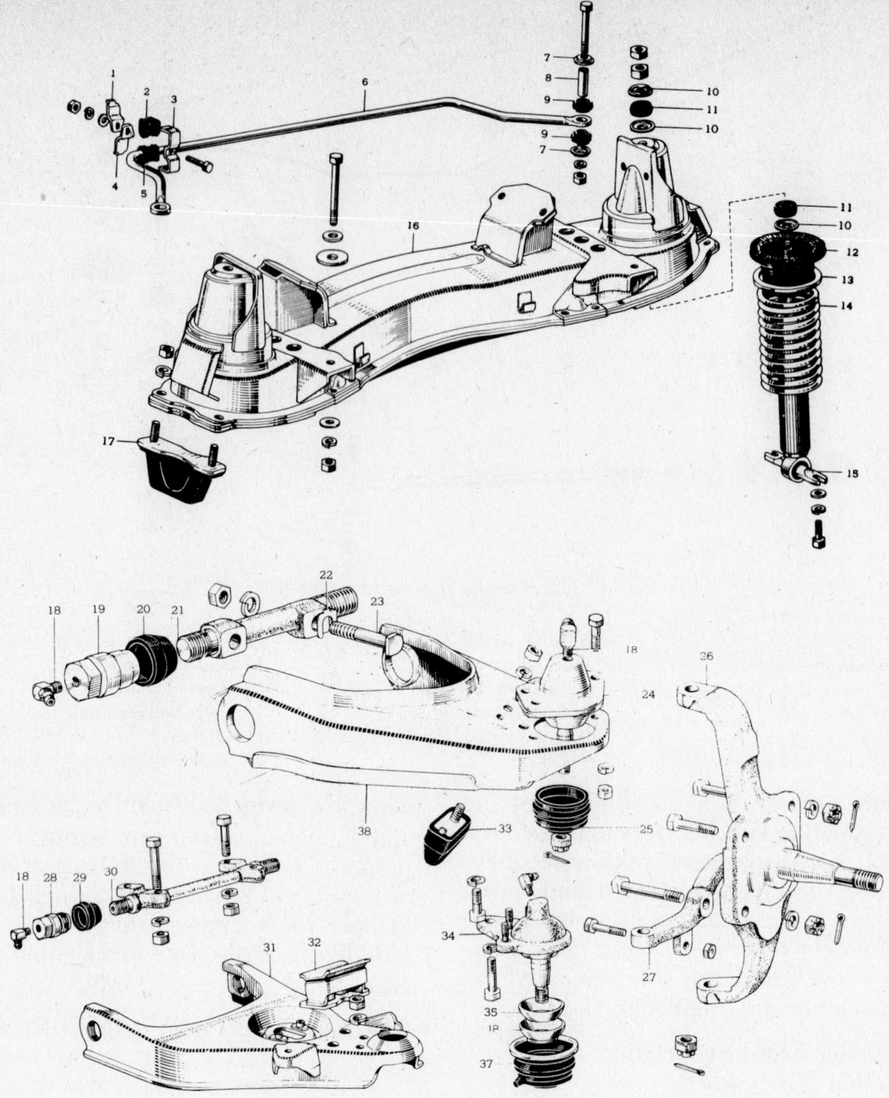

Hi-Lux front suspension

1 Stabilizer link cover
2 Stabilizer bushing
3 Stabilizer link
4 Stabilizer link cover
5 Stabilizer bushing
6 Stabilizer bar
7 Cushion retainer
8 Collar
9 Stabilizer cushion
10 Cushion retainer
11 Shock absorber cushion
12 Front oil insulator
13 Front coil spring spacer
14 Front coil spring
15 Front shock absorber
16 Front suspension cross-member
17 Front spring bumper
18 Grease fitting
19 Arm pivot bushing
20 Arm pivot dust seal
21 Upper suspension inner shaft
22 Camber adjusting shim
23 Upper shaft set bolt
24 Upper ball joint
25 Dust cover
26 Steering knuckle
27 Steering knuckle arm
28 Arm pivot bushing
29 Arm pivot dust seal
30 Lower suspension inner shaft
31 Lower suspension arm
32 Lower arm bumper stopper plate
33 Front spring bumper
34 Lower ball joint
35 Lower ball joint dust seal inner plate
36 Lower ball joint dust seal outer plate
37 Lower ball joint dust cover
38 Upper suspension arm

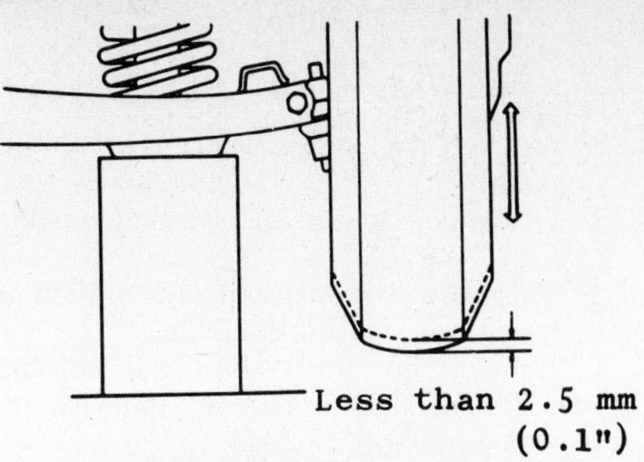

Checking ball joint vertical play.

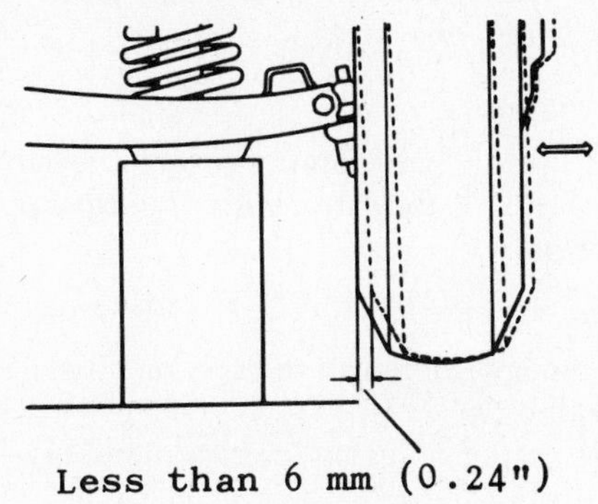

Checking ball joint side play.

move cotter pin and nut from ball joint stud.

3. Using appropriate tool, remove knuckle arm from ball joint. Pry off ball joint dust cover.
4. With the aid of a press, remove ball joint from suspension arm.

Installation

To install ball joints, reverse removal procedures. Be sure to lubricate ball joint with a molybdenum disulphide lithium base grease. Do not use any other type.

TORQUE SPECIFICATIONS

Knuckle arm to ball joint: 36-53 ft. lbs.
Crossmember to frame: 30-40 ft. lbs.
Lower arm bushing: 30-40 ft. lbs.
Lower arm shaft to front crossmember: 50-60 ft. lbs.
Front spring bushing to suspension arm: 11-16 ft. lbs.
Knuckle arm to shock absorber: 15-22 ft. lbs.
Tierod end to steering knuckle: 22-32 ft. lbs. lbs.
Hub nut: 65-85 ft. lbs.

CORONA (ALL) AND MARK II

Removal

1. Remove wheel. Support lower arm with jack. Disconnect upper and lower ball joints and remove steering knuckle.
2. Pry off dust cover and dust cover plate. Remove ball joint.

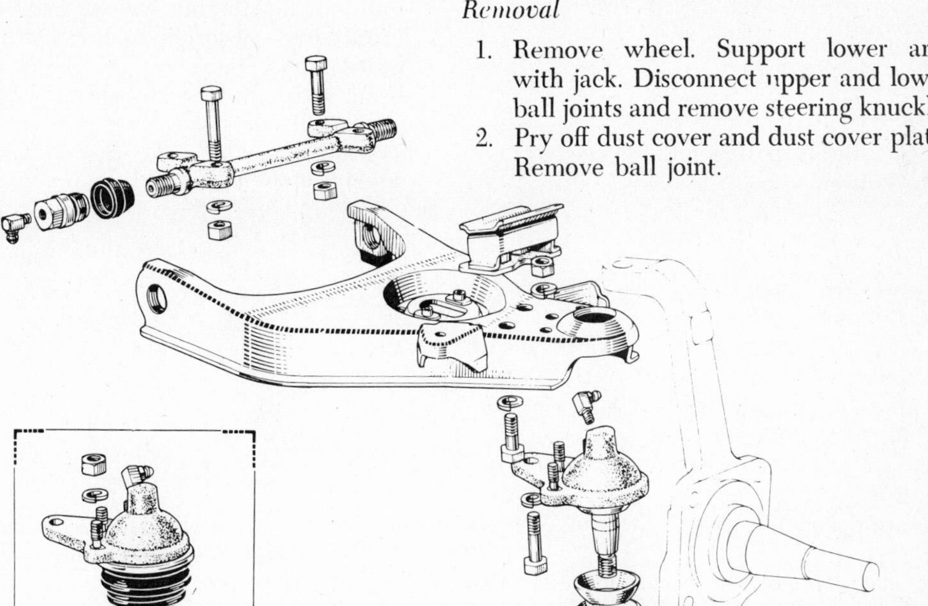

Lower suspension arm with ball joint insert

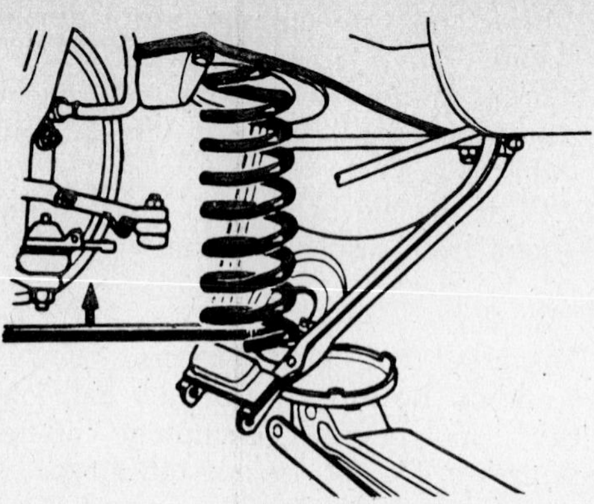

Lowering A-frame and coil spring.

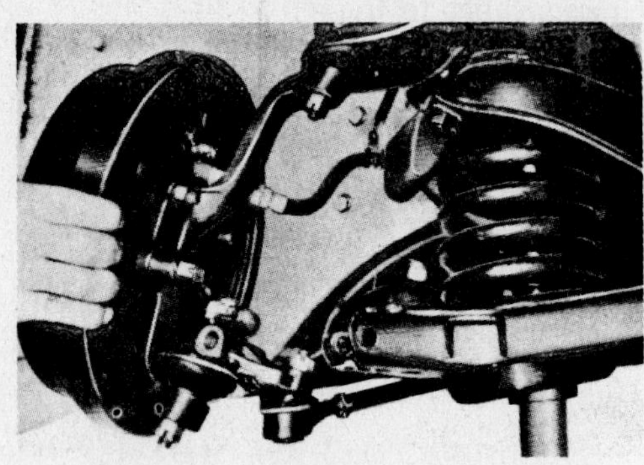

Disconnecting steering knuckle.

Installation

To install ball joint, reverse removal procedure.

Torque Specifications

Upper arm shaft to suspension member: 36-47 ft. lbs.
Lower arm to suspension member: 51-65 ft. lbs.
Upper ball joint to steering knuckle: 40-51 ft. lbs.
Lower ball joint to steering knuckle: 51-65 ft. lbs.
Steering knuckle arm to steering knuckle: 40-50 ft. lbs.
Steering knuckle to backing plate: 40-50 ft. lbs.
Lower arm to strut bar: 40-50 ft. lbs.
Strut bar to frame: 55-80 ft. lbs.
Shock absorber upper mount to suspension member: 14-22 ft. lbs.
Shock absorber lower mount to suspension arm: 11-16 ft. lbs.
Wheel nut to front wheel hub: 65-87 ft. lbs.

Hi-Lux

Removal

1. Jack vehicle and support front cross-member.
2. Disconnect tie rod and steering knuckle arm.
3. Raise lower suspension arm until it is free from steering knuckle.
4. Remove nut and cotter pin holding ball joint stud to steering knuckle. Remove steering knuckle.
5. Remove ball joint grease fitting. Remove retaining nut and ball joint.

Note: When removing both ball joints, remove lower one first.

Installation

To install ball joints, reverse removal procedure. Lubricate with multipurpose grease only.

Torque Specifications

Upper suspension arm to cross member: 95-153 ft. lbs.
Lower suspension arm to cross member: 51-65 ft. lbs.
Front shock absorber to frame: 14-22 ft. lbs.
Ball joint to steering knuckle: 65-94 ft. lbs.
Front shock absorber to lower arm: 11-16 ft. lbs.
Front shock absorber to spring U bolt seat: 25-40 ft. lbs.
Steering knuckle to steering knuckle arm: 49-60 ft. lbs.

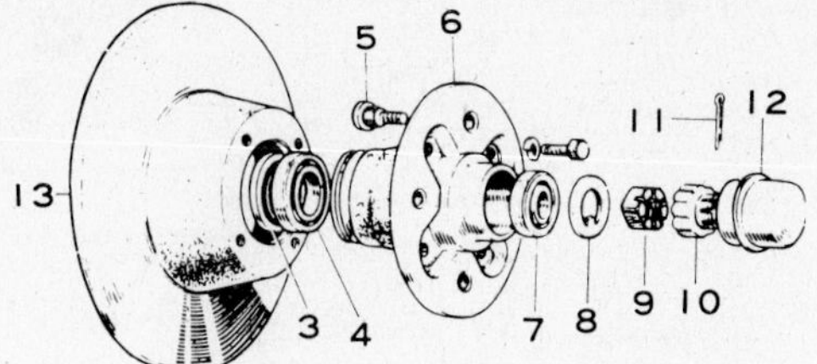

Exploded view—front axle hub

1 Gasket, knuckle grease retainer cap
2 Cap, knuckle grease retainer
3 Seal, type V oil
4 Bearing, tapered roller
5 Bolt, hub
6 Hub, front axle
7 Bearing, tapered roller
8 Washer, lock
9 Nut
10 Cap, front wheel adjusting
11 Pin, cotter
12 Cap, front hub grease
13 Disc, front

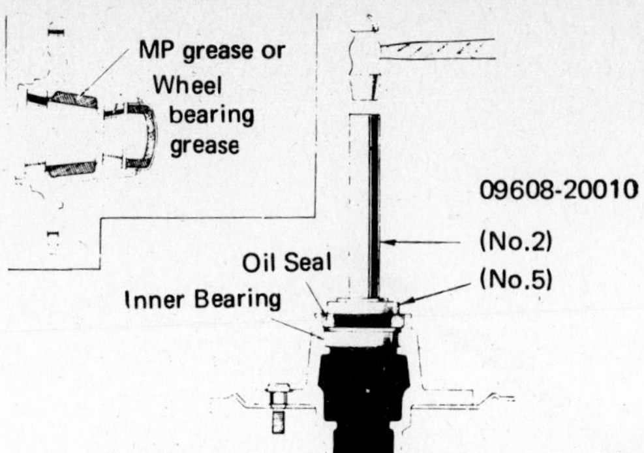

Front wheel bearing installation

Front wheel bearing preload measurement

Wheel Bearing Replacement—Corolla, Corona, Mark II, Hi-Lux

Removal

1. Jack car and remove wheel with brake assembly.
2. Drive out inner and outer bearing cup with oil seal.
3. Lubricate bearing rollers and axle hub.
4. Place inner bearing cone into axle hub and press oil seal into place.

Installation and Adjustment

1. Replace front hub and brake assembly.
2. Tighten castle nut to 1.9-2.3 ft. lbs. Rotate drum to be certain bearings are properly seated.
3. Loosen castle nut to finger tightness. Again torque to above specifications.
4. To check bearing preload, measurement should be taken at uppermost wheel stud. Preload should be 1.5-3.5 ft. lbs.
5. Replace adjusting cap and position grooves so cotter pin may be inserted. Fit cotter pin and press on grease cap.

Steering

Corona steering is of the recirculating ball type having needle bearings on the sector shaft. Steering ratio is 20.8:1; Mark II has a variable ratio of 19.5-21.5:1. Crown models have a variable ratio of 20.5-23.6:1. Land Cruisers use a sector roller and worm with a 21:1 ratio, Corollas use sector roller and worm with an 18.1:1 ratio. All use two sintered bushings on the sector shaft except Corolla.

STEERING WHEEL

Removal

Disconnect horn and turn signal wires under dash panel. Depress horn ring and remove by twisting counterclockwise. Remove spring, take off steering column nut and lift off horn contact seat. Punch mark steering wheel position on shaft and remove wheel using a puller. (This should be done carefully, especially on late models with the collapsible steering column.) Remove screws and turn signal switch assembly from housing. Remove upper (remote shift) shaft E-washer and ring. Remove contact (horn) ring housing and pull off the upper column bearing.

On Crown models having remote shift and automatic transmission, the shift indicator is connected to the shift lever by a small wire attached to a plastic bushing. Use extra care during removal, as this bushing is very fragile. To remove wheel, turn signal lever must be turned to the left.

Installation

Proceed in reverse order of disassembly. Torque wheel housing nuts to 3-5 ft. lbs.; steering wheel nut to 15-22 ft. lbs.

STEERING GEAR BOX

Removal

Corona (all) and Mark II

1. Remove pitman arm.
2. Extract bolts holding flexible coupling to worm shaft.
3. Remove bolts holding housing and remove steering gear box.

Hi-Lux

1. Remove steering wheel and steering column cover.

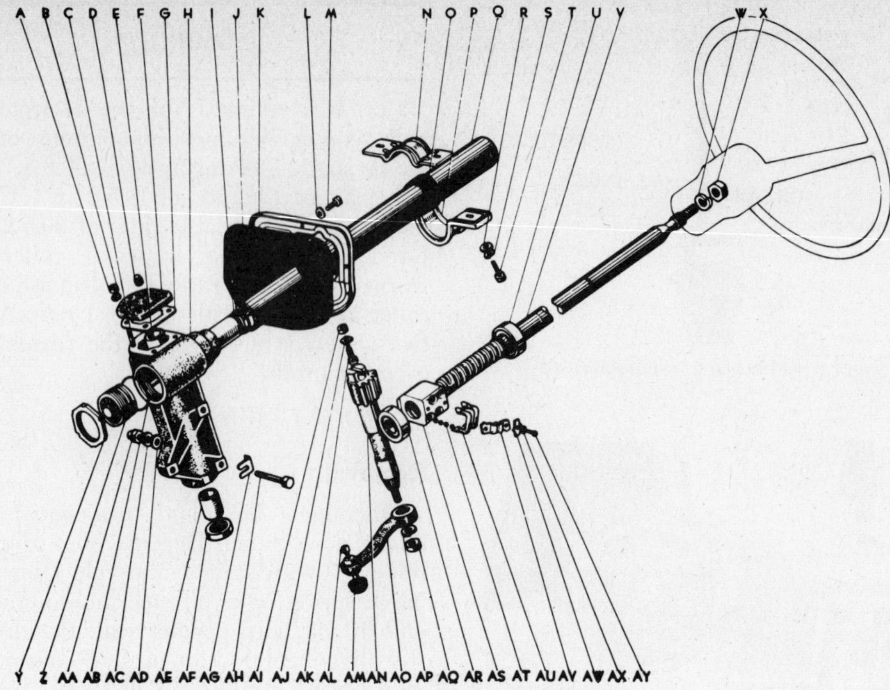

Corona steering assembly.

A. Nut
B. Spring washer
C. Stud bolt
D. Breather plug
E. Bimetal formed bushing
F. Sector shaft end cover
G. Sector shaft end gasket
H. Steering gear housing
I. O-ring
J. Steering column hole seal
K. Steering column hole cover
L. Plate washer
M. Bolt
N. Steering column upper clamp
O. Steering column clamp grommet
P. Steering column lower clamp
Q. Steering column tube
R. Plate washer
S. Spring washer
T. Bolt
U. Bearing
V. Steering mainshaft
W. Spring washer
X. Nut
Y. Worm bearing adjusting screw locknut
Z. Worm bearing adjusting screw
AA. Nut
AB. O-ring
AC. Wave washer
AD. Plate washer
AE. Bimetal formed bushing or needle roller bearing
AF. Type "S" oil seal
AG. Steering post adjusting shim
AH. Bolt
AI. Nut
AJ. Sector shaft thrust washer
AK. Sector shaft adjusting screw
AL. Grease fitting
AM. Steering link joint dust seal
AN. Steering sector shaft
AO. Pitman arm
AP. Spring washer
AQ. Nut
AR. Bearing
AS. Mainshaft ball nut
AT. Ball
AU. Mainshaft ball guide
AV. Mainshaft ball guide clamp
AW. Ball guide clamp screw lock plate
AX. Spring washer
AY. Pan screw

2. Remove bolt holding flexible covering to worm shaft. Remove carpeting in steering shaft-firewall area.
3. Extract steering column bolt holding inside firewall cover plate to firewall.
4. Remove steering column bracket and pull column inside vehicle.
5. Jack front of vehicle and support on front suspension crossmember. Remove left front wheel.
6. Disconnect pitman arm from sector shaft by removing nut and lock washer.
7. Extract steering gear housing bolts and remove by pulling toward car interior.

Corolla

It is necessary first to remove the entire manifold section and also to loosen the

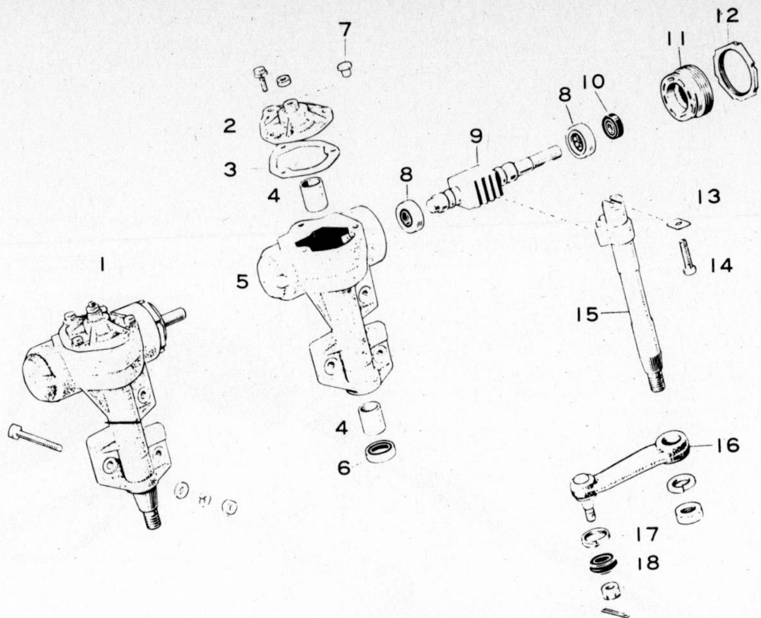

Hi-Lux steering gear box

1 Housing assembly, steering gear
2 Cover, sector shaft end
3 Gasket, end cover
4 Bush, bimetal formed
5 Housing, steering gear
6 Seal, type S oil
7 Plug, breather
8 Bearing
9 Worm assembly, steering
10 Seal, type T oil
11 Screw, worm bearing adjusting
12 Nut, screw lock
13 Washer, sector shaft thrust
14 Screw, sector shaft adjusting
15 Shaft, steering sector
16 Arm sub assembly, pitman
17 Ring, set
18 Seat, dust

front exhaust pipe hanger. Disconnect the wiring harness at the steering column, then remove horn button by lifting it straight up. Remove contact spring and punch mark steering column and nut. Remove wheel nut and pull wheel off using a puller, then position turn signal lever to right and remove the switch retaining screws and switch. Loosen the steering column attaching screws under the turn signal switch and remove the switch assembly from the housing. Remove the steering housing clamp from the column tube, without completely dismantling it. *NOTE: At this point it will be possible to drive off the upper collar and bushing with a suitable punch.* Remove package tray, steering column clamp bolts and clamp. Under the hood, disconnect wires from temperature and oil pressure sending switches; also disconnect speedometer cable from steering gear box. Jack up car and place stands under front jacking points.

Punch mark sector shaft and pitman arm and remove arm with puller, then remove the splash shield from underside of the engine. Remove the three bolts that hold the steering box to frame, then remove entire steering assembly by pulling it out from under the car (towards the front).

Land Cruiser

1. Jack up front of vehicle and remove wheels.
2. Remove steering worm yoke bolts and steering worm. Remove main and intermediate shafts.
3. Remove pitman arm nut from sector shaft. Punch mating marks on pitman and sector shaft arms. Disconnect sector shaft and pitman arm.
4. Remove bolts holding steering gear housing to bracket. Remove steering gear box.

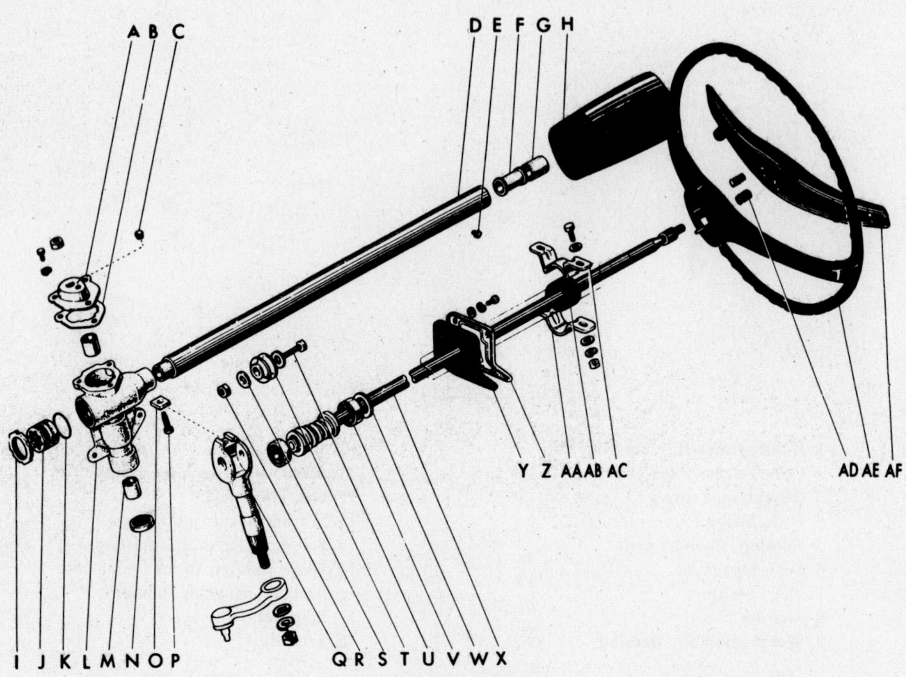

Corolla steering assembly.

A. Sector shaft end cover
B. Sector shaft end cover gasket
C. Steering gear housing oil plug
D. Steering column tube
E. Steering housing clamp
F. Bushing
G. Collar
H. Steering housing
I. Worm bearing adjusting lock nut
J. Worm bearing adjusting screw
K. O-ring
L. Steering gear housing
M. Bi-metal formed bushing
N. "S" type oil seal
O. Sector shaft thrust washer
P. Sector shaft adjusting screw
Q. Steering sector shaft
R. Hexagon nut
S. Shim
T. Steering sector roller
U. Steering sector roller shaft
V. Radial ball bearing
W. Shim
X. Steering main shaft
Y. Steering column weather seal
Z. Steering column opening cover plate
AA. Steering column lower clamp
AB. Grommet
AC. Steering column upper clamp
AD. Compression spring
AE. Steering wheel
AF. Horn button

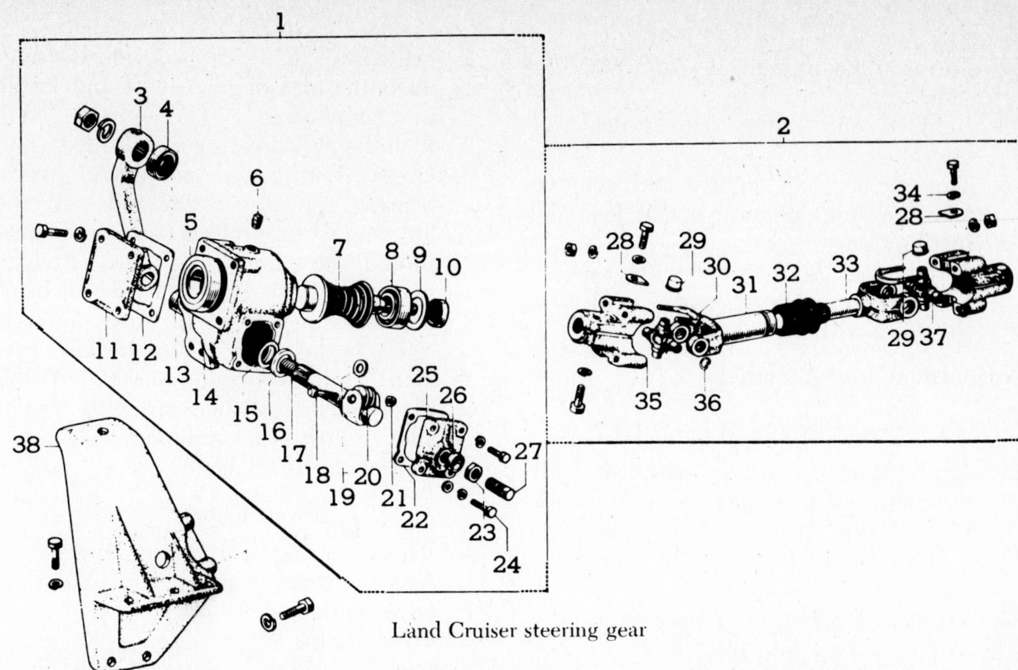

Land Cruiser steering gear

1 Steering gear housing assembly
2 Steering intermediate shaft assembly
3 Pitman arm
4 Oil seal
5 Steering worm front bearing
6 Plug
7 Steering worm
8 Steering worm rear bearing
9 Adjusting shim
10 Oil seal
11 Gear housing end cover
12 Gasket
13 Sector shaft bushing
14 Steering gear housing
15 Adjusting shim
16 Adjusting plate
17 Steering sector shaft
18 Sector roller shaft
19 Shim
20 Sector roller
21 Nut
22 Gasket
23 Lock nut
24 Bolt
25 Sector shaft end cover
26 Bushing
27 Set bolt
28 Cup stopper plate No. 1
29 Spider bearing
30 U bolt
31 Steering sliding yoke
32 Dust cover
33 Steering sliding shaft
34 Lock washer
35 Steering worm yoke
36 Hole snap-ring
37 Universal joint spider
38 Steering gear housing bracket

Disassembly

Corona (all), Mark II, and Hi-Lux

1. Loosen locknut on sector shaft bolt. Remove bolt and pull out end cover and sector shaft. Note position of adjusting screw and shims.
2. Remove worm bearing adjusting screw and locknut.

Sector shaft removal

3. Take the worm gear assembly and bearing from gear housing.

Caution: Ball nut must not be removed from worm assembly. If defective, replace entire assembly.

Corolla

1. Place housing in vise. Remove bolts holding end cover to gear housing. Loosen sector shaft adjusting screw. Remove end cover. Screw in sector shaft adjusting screw.
2. Remove sector shaft.
3. Extract worm bearing adjusting screw and locknut.
4. Remove O-ring between adjusting screw race and bearing.
5. Place a nut on top end of mainshaft. Tap lightly and remove bearings with mainshaft from housing. Be sure to keep all parts separated.
6. Remove all remaining bushings and races.

LAND CRUISER

1. Drain lubricant from box and place in vise.
2. Remove end cover with bolts and gasket.
3. Tap sector shaft lightly and remove from housing. Be sure not to lose adjusting shims.
4. Lift out gear housing end with gasket.
5. Lightly tap steering worm end and drive out with bearings.

Adjustment and Assembly

CORONA (ALL), MARK II, AND HI-LUX

1. Apply lubricant to oil seal lip and all bearings and moving parts.
2. Place worm gear into housing. Install worm adjusting screw and locknut.
3. To obtain worm shaft preload, adjust worm bearing adjusting screw to obtain a preload (turning torque) of 9-13 ft. lbs. Tighten locknut to 58-73 ft. lbs.

Measuring worm shaft preload

4. Place adjusting screw and shim on sector shaft. Thrust clearance should be .0035″ maximum. (Various shims are available.)
5. Install end cover with gasket and sector shaft assembly into gear housing. Completely loosen adjusting screw. Be sure ball nut and sector shaft gear are at center position. If necessary, position with fingers.
6. Adjust sector shaft adjusting screw to obtain a preload (turning torque) of 18-24 ft. lbs. Be sure worm and sector gear are at center position.
7. Sector shaft must have no backlash within 5° right or left of center. To check, install pitman arm and measure at arm end. Torque nut to 14-23 ft. lbs.

COROLLA

1. Lubricate all bearings. Place bearings on both sides of mainshaft and install in gear housing.
2. Install lower bearing outer race.
3. Grease O-ring and install with worm bearing adjusting screw and locknut.
4. Steering worm preload (turning torque) should be 2.6-3.7 ft. lbs. Preload may be adjusted with the worm bearing adjusting screw. Be sure adjusting screw is stationary when checking preload. Tighten locknut to 60-70 ft. lbs.
5. Place thrust washer on sector shaft and adjust to minimum clearance (shims are available).

LAND CRUISER

1. Place steering worm into housing.
2. Install front bearing cup and end cover with gasket. Torque end cover to 11-14 ft. lbs.
3. Install original sector shaft with shims and end plate. Position sector shaft end toward steering worm. While holding sector shaft in position, check steering worm and sector roller backlash. Adjust to zero with adjusting shims.

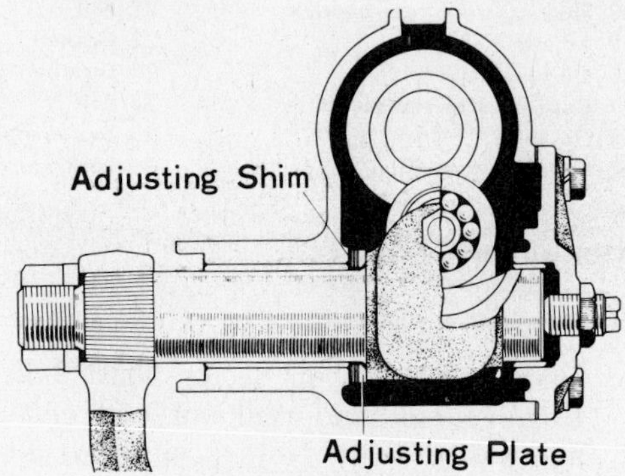

Adjusting backlash

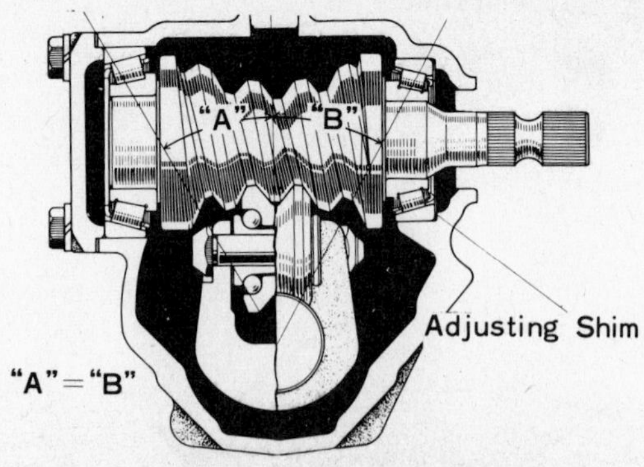

Steering worm gear centering

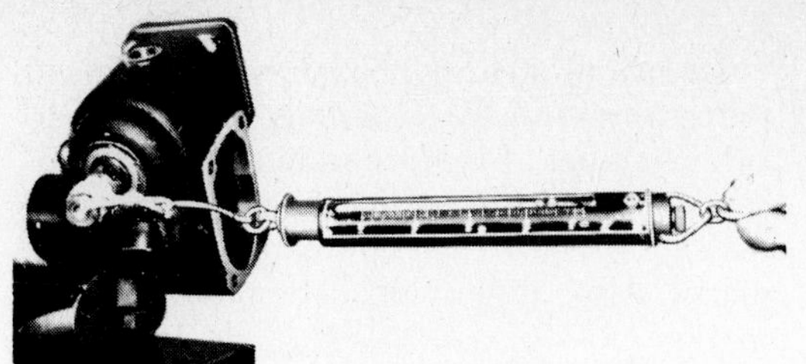
Worm bearing preload checking

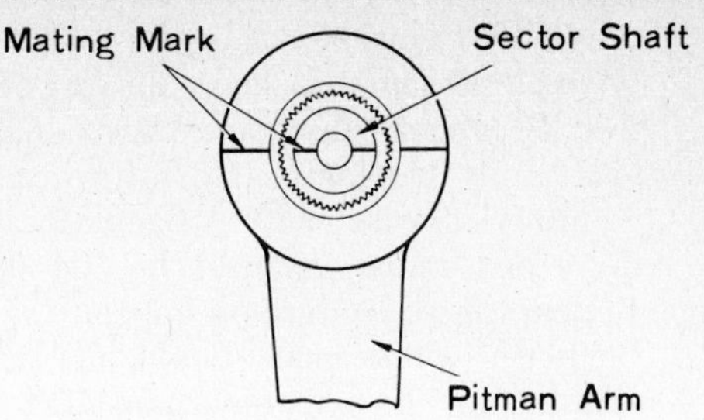

Pitman arm/sector shaft alignment

4. Install sector shaft cover with gasket and set bolt.
5. Position pitman arm in sector shaft. Set backlash to zero by means of set bolt. Backlash must be set at center position. This is one half of total number of turns from extreme right to left.
6. Turn steering worm fully clockwise. Attach dial gauge to pitman arm and check end-play. Record this figure. Turn steering worm fully counter clockwise. End-play should be identical. If this requires adjustment, accomplish this with steering worm adjusting shims. Install behind worm rear bearing cup. Increase shim height if play decreases clockwise. To increase, reverse this procedure.
7. After performing the above, remove sector shaft with end cover.
8. Before steering worm is assembled, lubricate bearings. Preload must be checked without worm oil seal assembled.
9. Place worm assembly into gear housing. Install end cover with gasket. Torque cover to 11-14 ft. lbs.
10. Check worm shaft preload (turning torque). This should be 9-14 in. lbs. Adjust by changing to end cover gasket of proper height. Many sizes are available.
11. Position sector shaft plate with tapered face towards shaft flange. Place shims on shaft.
12. Place shaft into housing with end cover and gasket. Torque to 11-14 ft. lbs. Adjust set bolt to reduce end-play to zero. Do not overtighten. Backlash should be set at worm gear center point. To locate, turn worm gear from one extreme to the other while counting number of turns. Turn back exactly half way. Center point is now located.
13. Again check sector roller backlash.

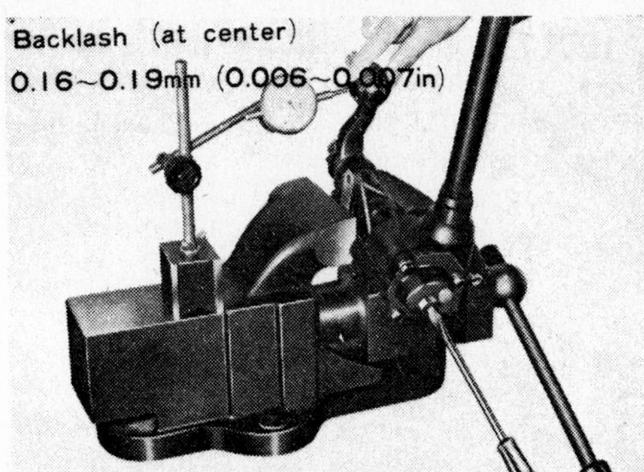

Adjusting worm and sector backlash

Reduce to zero as described above. Tighten set bolt.
14. Install sector shaft andworm oil seals.
15. Fill steering box with lubricant.

Installation

Corona (all), Mark II, and Hi-Lux

1. Install gear housing in position by reversing removal procedure and torqueing to 25-36 ft. lbs.
2. Install pitman arm into sector shaft and align mating marks. Secure with nut torqued to 80-90 ft. lbs.
3. Fill gearbox with lubricant.
4. Position steering column assembly while aligning coupling yoke. Install clamp in position.
5. Install steering wheel and firewall cover.
6. Lubricate shaft end and S type oil seal. Install shaft with adjusting bolt and washer.
7. Install end cover gasket and end cover. Screw in adjusting bolt.
8. Install bolts and clamp on end cover. Torque to 11-16 ft. lbs.
9. Without tightening locknut, attach pitman arm to sector shaft. Be sure sector shaft is at worm gear center and adjust backlash to .006-.007″ at pitman

arm end (Turn sector shaft screw to adjust.) Tighten locknut to 18-29 ft. lbs. To check the above, turn mainshaft fully clockwise. Now turn shaft counterclockwise 180°. Backlash, as described above, should be .04-.06″. Repeat this procedure on opposite side. Backlash difference between sides should not be greater than .03″. If clockwise backlash is more than counterclockwise, increase shim thickness between gear housing and upper bearing outer race. If situation is the opposite, decrease shim thickness. After performing the above, again adjust worm bearing preload.

10. Lubricate bushings and install with collar into column tube.

Corolla

To install steering box, reverse removal procedure. When installing gear box to side member, place column tube into instrument panel to aid in alignment. Be sure to align sector shaft-pitman arm mating marks. Also, align mainshaft-steering wheel marks.

Steering box to turn signal switch: .016″
Turn signal switch to steering wheel: .12″

Land Cruiser

1. Mount gear housing into housing bracket.
2. Align mating marks on pitman arm and sector shaft. Torque pitman arm to 119-141 ft. lbs.
3. Set wheels to straight ahead position. Install intermediate shaft assembly.
4. Tighten steering worm yoke bolts.

Brakes

All models are equipped with four-wheel hydraulic brakes and mechanically operated parking brakes acting on rear wheels only.

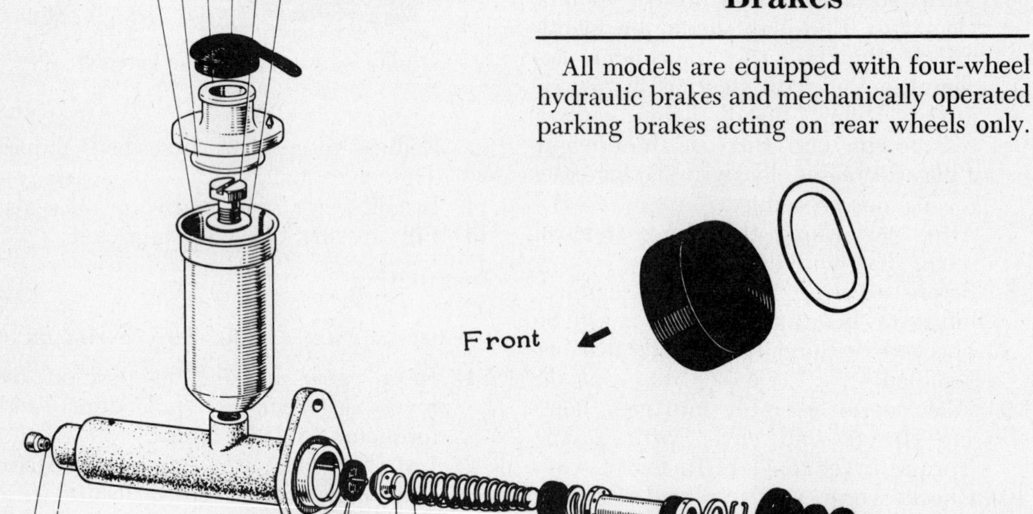

Single circuit master cylinder components.

A. Master cylinder reservoir
B. Master cylinder reservoir float
C. Reservoir cap
D. Reservoir filler cap
E. Master cylinder reservoir set bolt
F. Reservoir set bolt washer
G. Union seat
H. Master cylinder body
I. Bolt
J. Outlet check valve seat gasket
K. Spring washer
L. Nut
M. Outlet check valve
N. Piston return spring
O. Cylinder cup
P. Piston cup spacer
Q. Cylinder cup
R. Master cylinder piston
S. Plate washer
T. Hole snap-ring
U. Master cylinder boot
V. Master cylinder pushrod
W. Nut
X. Cylinder pushrod clevis

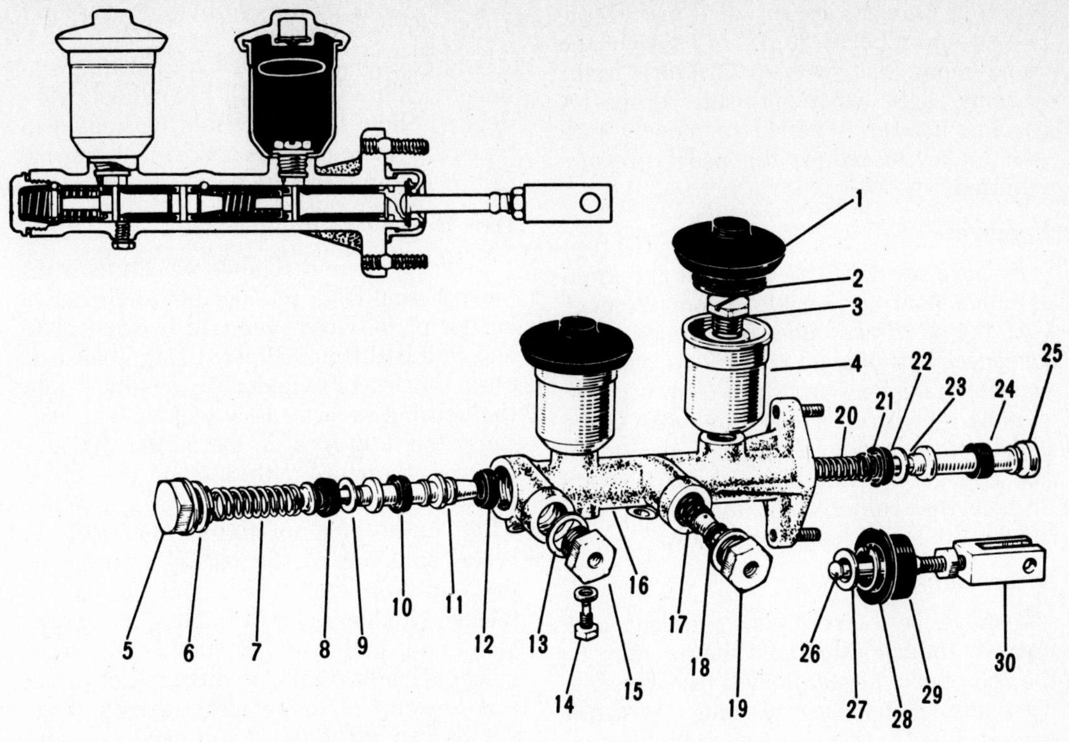

Dual circuit master cylinder components.

1. Reservoir filler cap
2. Reservoir float
3. Reservoir set bolt
4. Master cylinder reservoir
5. Master cylinder plug
6. Gasket
7. Compression spring
8. Cylinder cup
9. Piston cup spacer
10. Cylinder cup
11. Master cylinder piston No. 2
12. Cylinder cup
13. Gasket
14. Piston stop bolt
15. Valve plug
16. Tandem master cylinder body
17. Compression spring
18. Master cylinder outlet check valve
19. Valve plug
20. Compression
21. Piston return spring retainer
22. Cylinder cup
23. Master cylinder piston cup spacer
24. Cylinder cup
25. Master cylinder piston No. 1
26. Master cylinder pushrod
27. Master cylinder piston stop plate
28. Hole snap-ring
29. Master cylinder boot
30. Master cylinder pushrod clevis

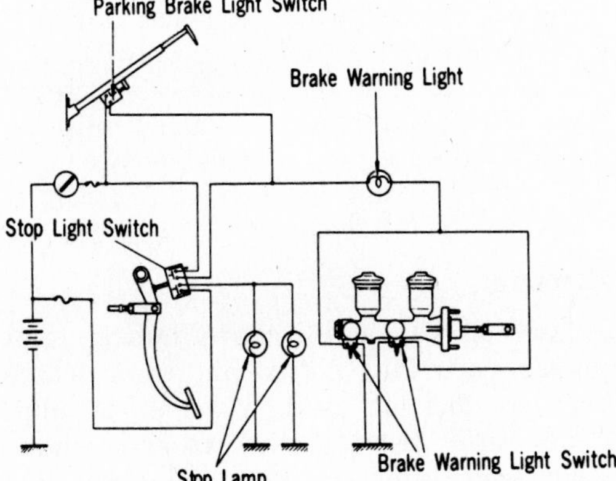

Brake warning light circuit.

All late models are equipped with dual (tandem) master cylinders, in accordance with federal standards, and Corona and Crown are additionally equipped with a brake pressure control valve. Some models have power assisted front disc brakes. A common warning light is connected to both parking brake lever and hydraulic system pressure switch.

MASTER CYLINDER

Early models use single cylinder type master cylinders. Later models use dual (tandem) type master cylinders, with a separate system for front and rear brakes.

Warning switches are installed to indicate pressure drop below 80 psi. in either of the two systems. The switches turn on a brake warning light when pressure drops. A vacuum booster is added to models with disc brakes to reduce the pedal pressure required.

Removal

Remove reservoir cap and float and drain as much fluid as possible before removal. *CAUTION: Brake fluid will cause paint damage if not immediately rinsed off.* Disconnect brake lines and wires from warning switches (where fitted), unhook brake pedal return spring, disconnect clevis pin and disengage pushrod from pedal. Remove all bolts that hold cylinder to firewall, then lift out the master cylinder.

Disassembly

Remove the reservoir caps and floats and unscrew the bolts that hold the reservoir to the main body. (Later models have integral reservoirs.) Remove warning switches (where fitted), then remove from rear of cylinder, in order, boot and snap-ring, stop plate (washer), piston No. 1 with spacer, cylinder cup, spring retainer and spring. Remove end plug and gasket from front of cylinder, then remove the front piston stop bolt from underneath, pull out the spring and its retainer, piston No. 2, spacer and cylinder cup. Remove the two outlet fittings, washers, check valves and springs. Remove the piston cups from their seats on the pistons only if they are to be replaced.

Inspection

After washing all parts in brake fluid, dry with compressed air. Inspect cylinder bore for wear, scuff marks or nicks. Cylinders may be honed slightly, but limit is 0.006″. In view of the importance of the master cylinder, it is recommended that it be replaced rather than overhauled.

Assembly

Reverse the sequence of disassembly. Absolute cleanliness is important, and all parts must be coated with clean brake fluid. Bleed the master cylinder and make sure all lines are tightened correctly and do not leak. Use fluid that meets specifications (for standard brakes) and use the special disc brake fluid for disc brake equipped cars.

DISC BRAKES

These units are of the self-adjusting, stationary caliper type with two wheel cylinders per side. Repairs should be limited to replacing brake pads, as overhaul of internal caliper components requires special tools.

Disc Brake Pad Replacement

Jack up car and remove wheel, then remove E-ring from retainer pin and remove keeper plate. Hook onto pad backing plate and pull pad from caliper. Using a flat bar, push the wheel cylinder pistons back into the housing as far as they will go. This will cause the fluid level in the master cylinder to rise; therefore either open the bleed screw at each side of the wheel cylinder while pushing in on the piston or drain brake fluid out of the master cylinder to prevent overflow. Thoroughly clean all wheel cylinders before installing new pads. Slide new pad onto pin protruding from wheel cylinder piston, so that the slot in the pad backing plate is fully engaged. Pads are marked #1 and #2 and have an arrow pointing in the direction of forward rotation of the wheel. Install plate, retainer pin and E-ring, then refill master cylinder to correct level and adjust brakes by repeated application of the pedal until a firm and high pedal is obtained. *CAUTION: Do not drive the car before the pads are fully seated.* Disc brakes are bled in the same manner as drum brakes.

Thickness limit: .035″
Runout: .006″

Brake Pressure Control Valve

To prevent rear wheel lock-up during panic stops, a control valve has been incorporated into the brake system. Its function is to reduce brake pressure to the rear wheel cylinders, in proportion to pedal pressure, in a fixed ratio. A defective valve causes partial or total brake failure (in case of leaks or ruptured lines). Valves must be replaced as an assembly if defective.

DRUM BRAKES

Removal

Jack up car and remove hubcap and grease cap. Pull cotter pin from wheel bearing locknut and remove locknut. Temporarily install grease cap and remove wheel and drum as a unit. (This prevents bearings from dropping onto the floor.)

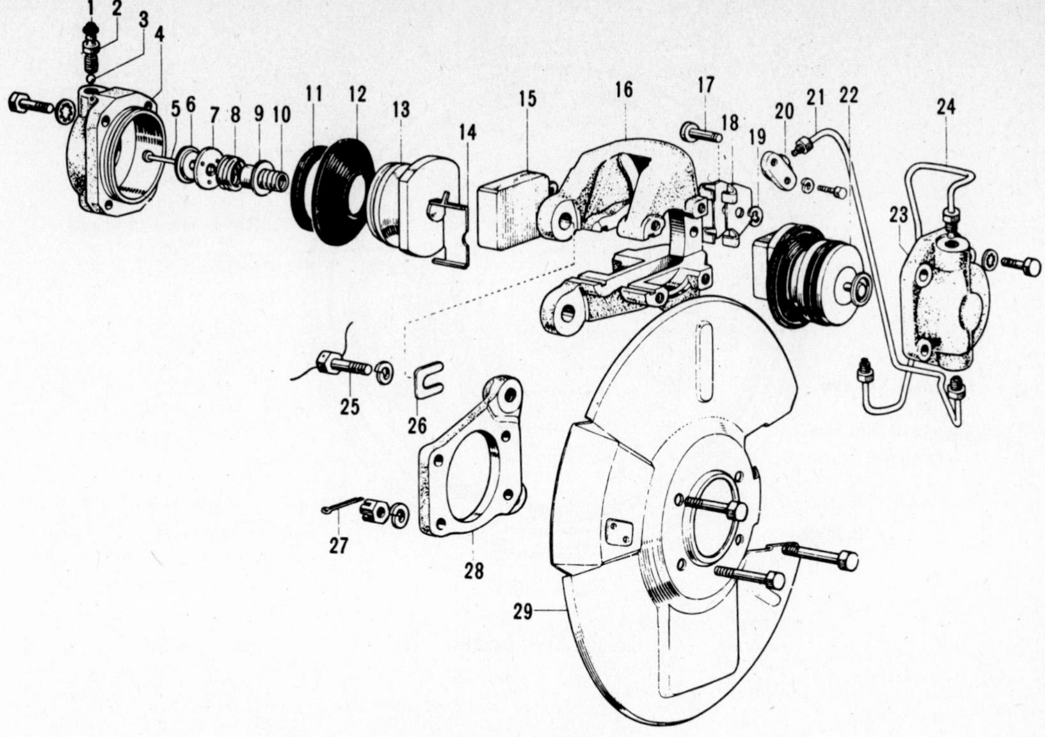

Disc brake components.

1. Bleed plug cap
2. Bleed plug
3. Ball
4. Disc brake cylinder No. 2
5. Pin
6. Retract pin cap
7. Spring retaining plate
8. Compression spring
9. Bushing housing
10. Retract bushing
11. Piston seal
12. Cylinder boot
13. Disc brake piston
14. Pad support plate
15. Disc brake pad
16. Disc brake caliper
17. Pin
18. Keep plate
19. E-ring
20. Two-way connector
21. Wheel cylinder front tube
22. Disc brake piston
23. Disc brake cylinder No. 1
24. Cylinder bridge tube
25. Head with hexagon bolt
26. Caliper support shim
27. Cotter pin
28. Caliper support bracket
29. Disc brake front dust cover

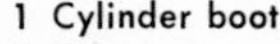

1 Cylinder boot
2 Piston
3 Ring
4 Disc brake cylinder body
5 Breather plug cap
6 Breather plug
7 Union seat

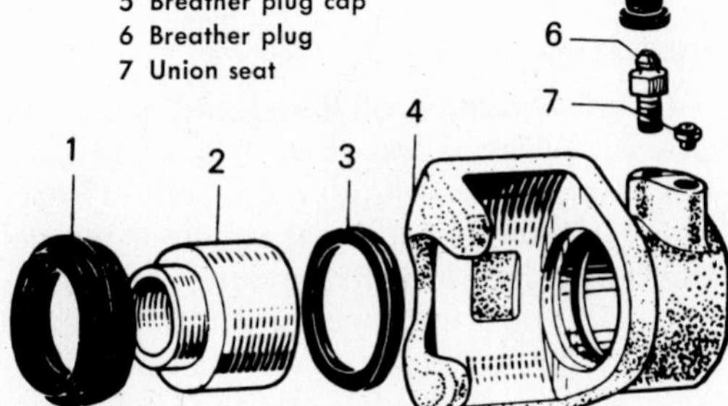

Exploded view of wheel cylinder

Inspecting disc runout

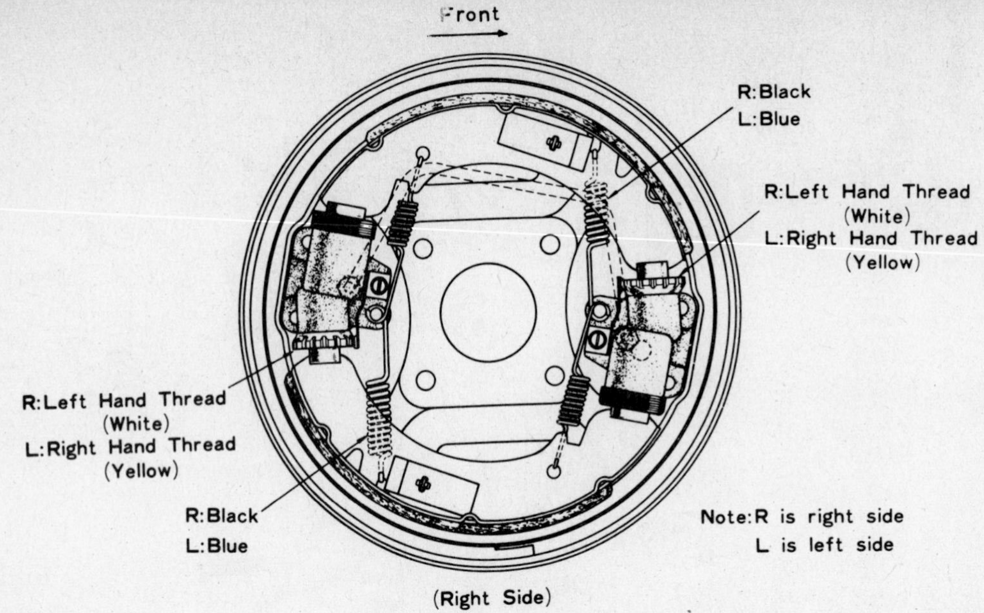

Corolla front brakes.

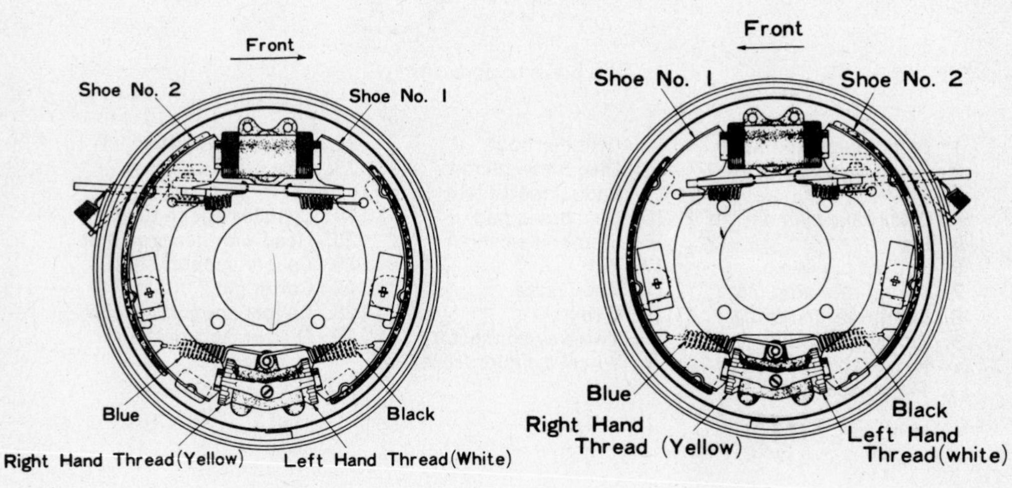

Corolla rear brakes.

Next, remove brake shoe retainers, self-adjusting cables, all springs and the shoes. Mark shoes for later identification(leading or trailing). Strip wheel cylinders and catch the escaping brake fluid. Cylinders need not be removed from backing plates for overhauling. On rear brakes, the parking brake lever must be disconnected to remove the shoes. Do not disengage the cable from its seat in the lever unless necessary.

Inspection

Check condition of lining and shoes; replace if worn to less than 30% of original thickness or if burnt, glazed or oily. (Burnt lining, although it still may retain its normal thickness, has lost its braking properties and will crack and peel off.) Check brake drums for uneven wear, scoring, bell-mouthed wear, glazing or hard spots. Factory drum refinishing limit is 0.080″ for all models except F series, which is 0.120″.

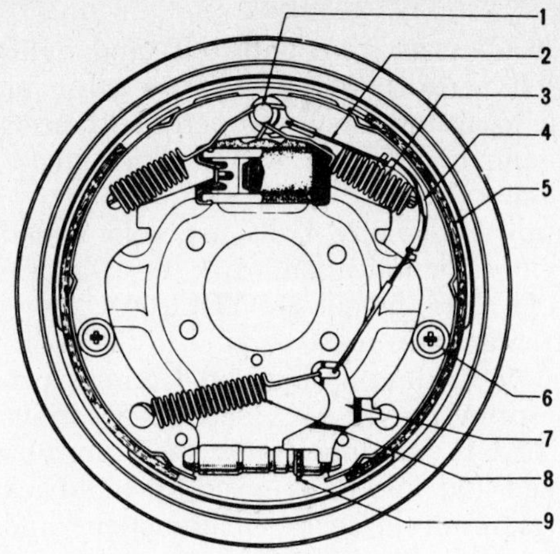

Left Front Brake

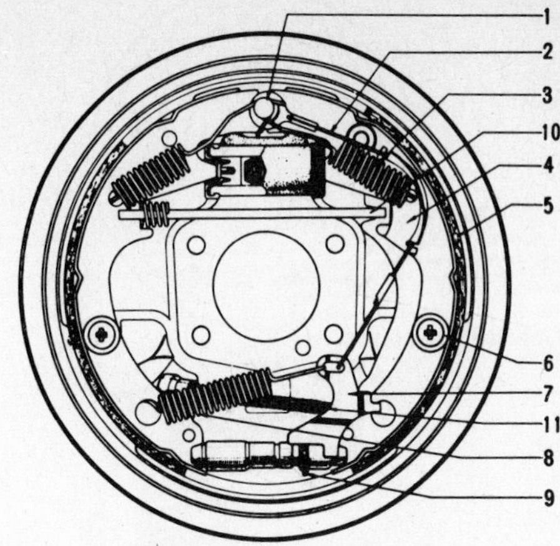

Left Rear Brake

Corona brakes with self-adjusters.

1. Anchor pin
2. Self-adjuster cable
3. Anchor pin-to-No. 2 shoe spring
4. Cable guide
5. No. 2 shoe assembly
6. Shoe hold-down spring cup
7. Self-adjuster lever
8. Adjuster spring
9. Adjusting screw
10. Parking brake shoe
11. Parking brake cable

Contour grind new brake shoes for a better fit. Check shoes closely and remove all sharp edges from metal which might contact the backing plate. Shoes are bonded and replacement lining must conform to federal safety standards.

Wheel Cylinders

Remove boots, pistons and cups and closely inspect bores for signs of wear, scoring and/or scuffing. When in doubt, replace or hone wheel cylinders with a special brake hone, using clean brake fluid as lubricant. Wash residue from bores using clean fluid; never use oil or any other solvent on any brake components. Blow dry with air and install with fresh brake fluid. General limit of honed cylinder is 0.005″ oversize. (Do not try to save money by reusing brake components such as cylinders and cups.) The self-adjuster screws should be taken apart and all dirt and rust removed with a wire brush. Lightly coat with Lubriplate before assembly; components should turn freely.

Installation

After cleaning the backing plates and applying a light coat of Lubriplate at the points of contact between shoes and plate, install the wheel cylinder (already assembled). Position the brake shoes and secure them with the hold-down springs and pins. Hook eye of spring onto anchor pin of rear shoe and hook other end to front shoe. *NOTE: With self-adjusters, coat cable guide with Lubriplate and install onto rear shoe.*

Adjustment

Brake shoes must be adjusted so that there will be slight contact with the drum but no binding or dragging of shoes.

Corolla Front

Remove plugs from backing plate and with adjusting tool or a thin screwdriver turn wheel cylinder adjusting nut until wheel locks (turn tool away from center of wheel), then back off about four notches until wheel rotates freely.

Corolla Rear

Move tool to tighten brakes (there are two adjusters on each front and rear wheel); back off four notches.

Crown Rear

Move adjusting tool *away* from center of wheel to tighten, then back off about nine notches.

Corona Front and Rear

Self-adjusting type.

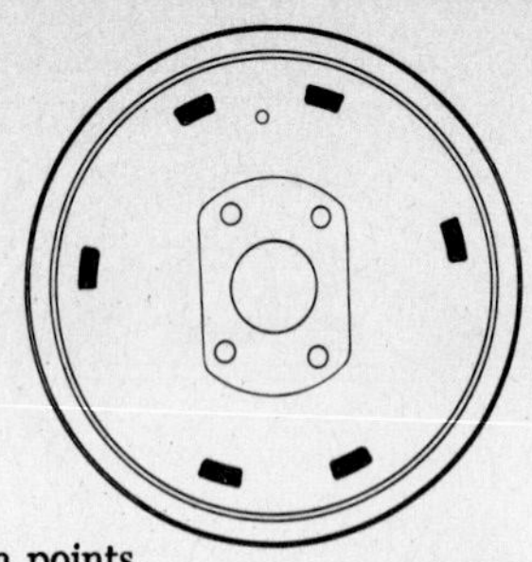
Lubrication points.

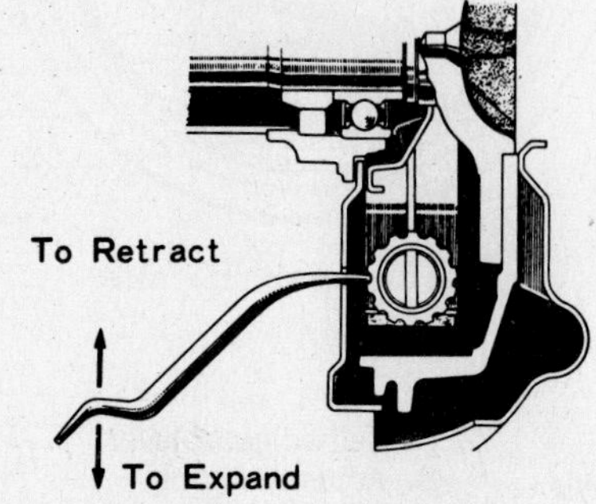

Front brake adjustment.

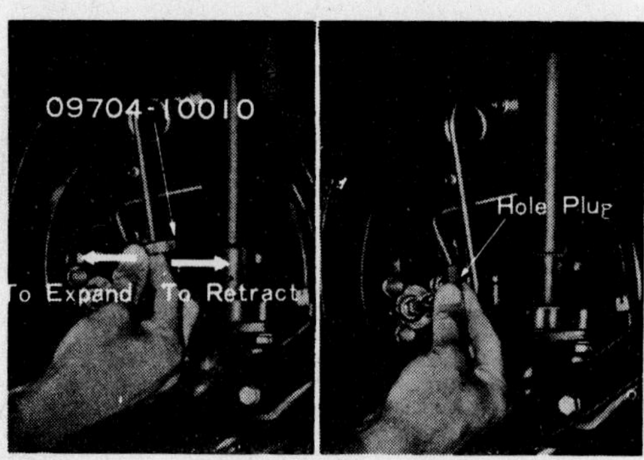

Rear brake adjustment.

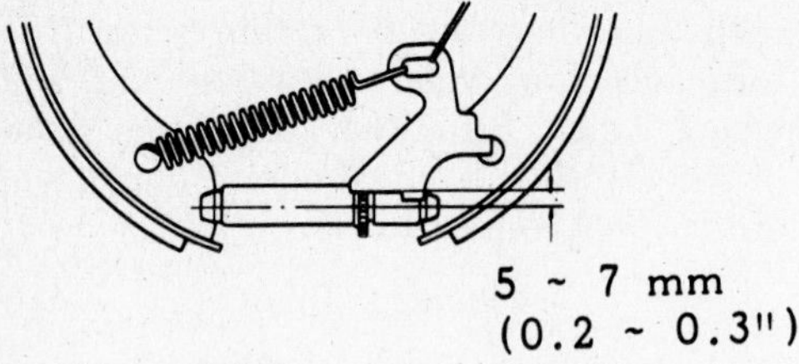

Self-adjuster lever position.

Land Cruiser Front

Each shoe must be adjusted separately (there are two adjusters per wheel). Tighten each shoe until locked, then back off five notches.

Self-Adjusters

Self-adjusters have both left- and right-handed threads and great care must be taken to install them correctly. Adjusters are stamped "L" and "R" for easier identification.

Corolla adjusting bolts are color-coded for easy identification; LH threads are WHITE, RH threads are YELLOW.

Attention also must be paid to the color-coded individual springs on Corona; primary springs are BLACK, secondary springs are BLUE. Springs must be carefully checked and installed; mixed up pull-back springs result in severe malfunctions and eventual failure.

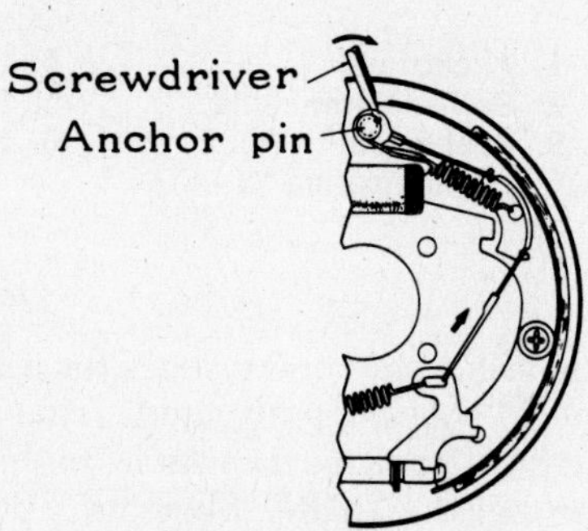

Checking self-adjuster action.

POWER BRAKES

All models except Corolla are equipped with a power booster. Manifold vacuum is utilized to operate a booster diaphragm, which assists braking by applying pressure to the wheel cylinders. The system consists of three separate components: vacuum booster, vacuum control valve and hydraulic cylinder. An additional check valve, located in the booster end plate, maintains maximum vacuum in the system at all times.

PARKING BRAKE

All passenger cars except the Corolla have a dash-mounted L-shaped handle which operates the parking brake. The Corolla employs a floor-mounted straight lever-type handle. Parking brake cables cannot be removed without first removing rear wheels and brake drums. Land Cruiser parking brake acts on the rear drive shaft by means of a special brake drum.

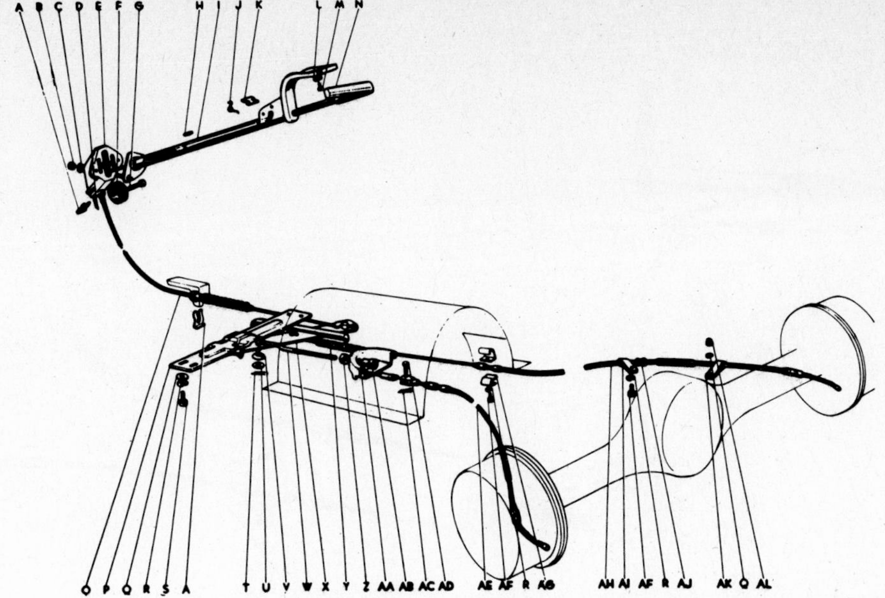

Corona and Crown parking brake components

A. Clip
B. Nut
C. Wave washer
D. Cotter pin
E. Pulley bracket
F. Wire pulley
G. W/hole pin
H. Parking brake plunger pin
I. Parking brake plunger guide
J. Torsion spring
K. Parking brake pawl
L. Toothed washer
M. Screw
N. Parking brake plunger
O. Parking brake No. 1 cable
P. Equalizer support bracket
Q. Plate washer
R. Spring washer
S. Bolt
T. Cotter pin
U. Plate washer
V. Wave washer
W. Parking brake pull rod
X. Parking brake intermediate lever
Y. Tension spring
Z. Nut
AA. Parking brake equalizer
AB. Nut
AC. Cotter pin
AD. W/hole pin
AE. Parking brake No. 3 cable
AF. Bolt
AG. Cable retainer
AH. Parking brake No. 2 cable
AI. Clamp
AJ. Bushing
AK. Cable guide
AL. Nut

Parking Brake Adjustment

Corolla

Remove the adjusting cap (plastic) and adjust cable so that there are at least five, but no more than nine, notches (teeth) of lever travel when the brake is fully applied.

Corona (all), Mark II, and Crown

Loosen the brake warning switch bracket and push parking brake lever all the way down. Reset the switch so that it will come *on* as soon as the lever is moved one notch. Release the parking brake lever fully, then loosen the parking brake pull rod locknut at the equalizer bar and adjust until the front cable has no more slack. Tighten locknut and test adjustment by pulling parking brake lever; it should have a little play at the start and should travel from eight to thirteen notches during application.

Land Cruiser

Jack up rear wheels. Turn the parking brake adjuster, located at the bottom of the brake plate, counterclockwise. When brake is fully locked, back off one or two notches so that the drum can rotate freely.

Hi-Lux

1. Loosen parking brake switch bracket until plunger interferes with pawl. Switch should be in off position.
2. Fully return brake plunger. Adjust cables to zero play. Accomplish this by turning adjusting nut on parking brake equalizer. Be sure brake does not drag.

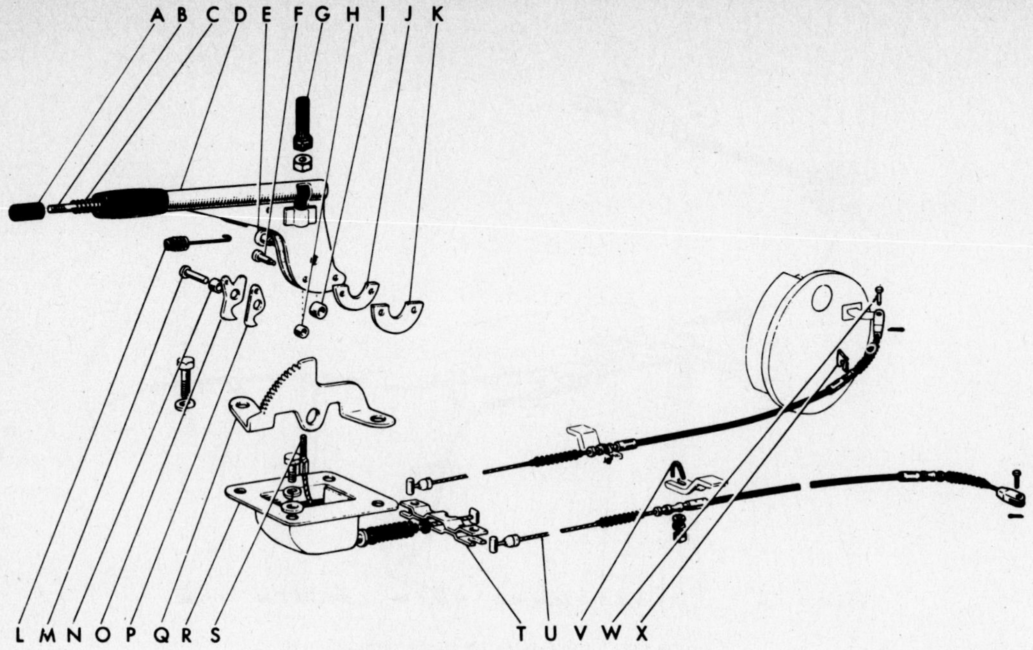

Parking brake components; Corolla.

A. Parking brake release rod knob
B. Parking brake pawl release rod
C. Compression spring
D. Parking brake lever
E. Lever pivot pin
F. Pin
G. Wire adjusting cap
H. Spacer
I. Spacer
J. Parking brake cable guide
K. Parking brake cable guide support
L. Tension spring
M. Pin
N. Spacer
O. Parking brake pawl No. 2
P. Parking brake pawl No. 1
Q. Parking brake lever sector
R. Parking brake lever boot
S. Parking brake cable No. 1
T. Parking brake equalizer
U. Parking brake cable No. 2
V. Cable clamp
W. Pin
X. Cable clip

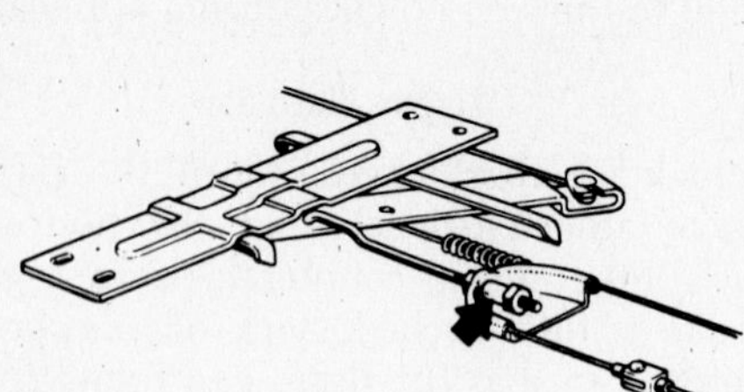

Corona parking brake adjusting bolt.

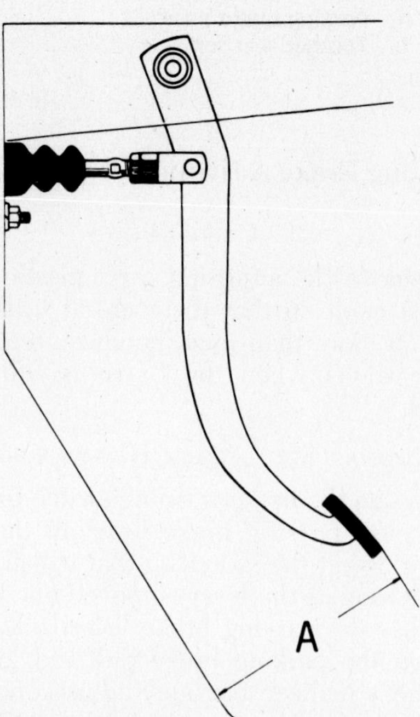

Brake pedal adjustment.

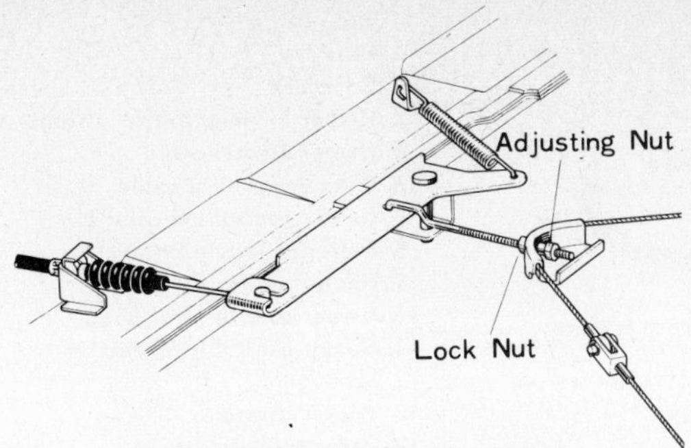

Hi-Lux parking brake adjustment

3. Pull parking brake handle. Some play is normal. Six to nine notches is the standard parking brake travel.

Stop Light Switch

Switches are of the mechanical type, actuated by the brake pedal. Adjust so that switch will come *on* as soon as pedal travel exceeds free-play. Make sure that some play is left for the master cylinder pushrod; at least 1/16″ but not more than 1/8″. To adjust, loosen locknut at clevis and turn pushrod until desired clearance is obtained between pushrod and master cylinder piston. Check the height of the pedal and adjust by setting the stoplight switch (which in this case acts as a pedal stop). All passenger

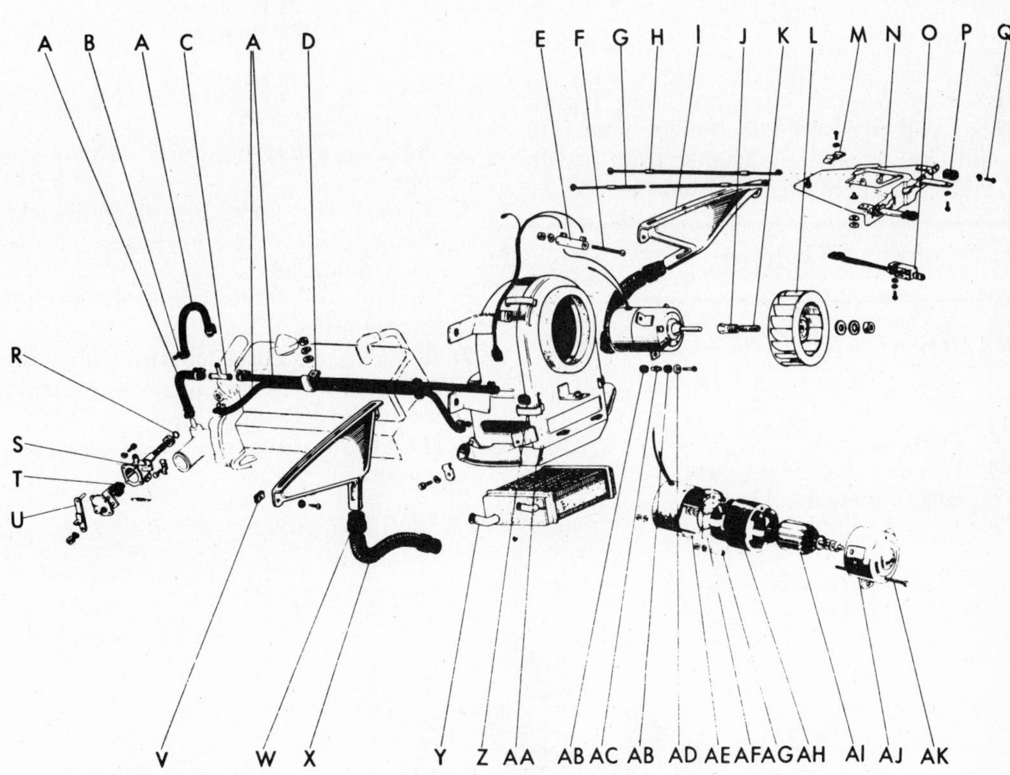

Corolla heater components

A	Hose	M	Heater control wire clamp	Y	Radiator
B	Hose clamp	N	Heater control box	Z	Heater case fastening spring
C	Water hose connector	O	Heater blower switch	AA	Heater case
D	Water hose retainer	P	Heater control lever knob	AB	Bushing
E	Resistance	Q	Screw	AC	Collar
F	Through bolt	R	O-ring	AD	Washer
G	Heater control cable	S	Water valve body	AE	Blower motor housing
H	Defroster control cable	T	Water valve controller	AF	Blower motor brush holder
I	Defroster nozzle	U	Water valve lever	AG	Bushing
J	Adaptor	V	Anchor nut	AH	Blower motor stator
K	Pipe	W	Defroster hose adaptor	AI	Blower motor armature
L	Blower fan	X	Defroster hose	AJ	Blower motor housing
				AK	Bolt

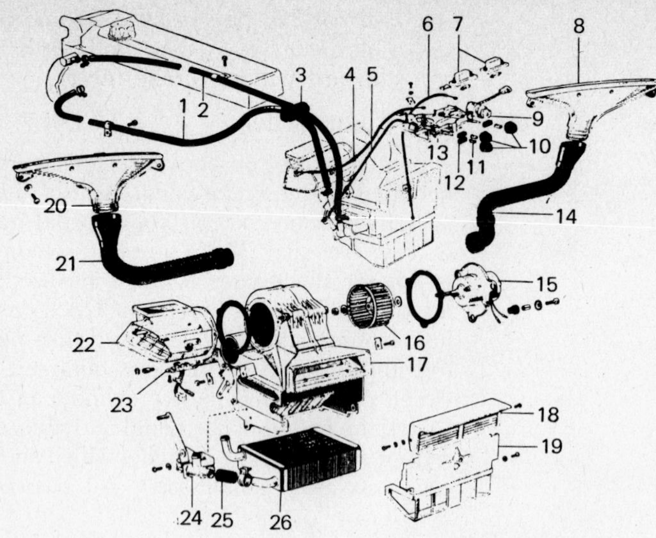

1 Hose
2 Hose
3 Grommet
4 Heater air inlet butterfly cable
5 Heater control cable
6 Defroster control cable
7 Heater control indicator lamp
8 Defroster nozzle RH
9 Heater blower switch
10 Heater control lever knob
11 Heater control lever retainer
12 Lever guide
13 Heater control
14 Defroster hose RH
15 Blower motor
16 Blower fan
17 Heater case
18 Ventilator louver
19 Cover
20 Defroster nozzle LH
21 Defroster hose LH
22 Air damper
23 Blower resistor
24 Water valve
25 Hose
26 Radiator unit

Corona heater assembly

cars have 5.5-6.0″ clearance from top of pedal pad to slanted section of floor. On Land Cruiser models, distance from pad to vertical section of firewall should be 6.7″.

Heater

REMOVAL AND INSTALLATION

Corolla

1. Drain radiator.
2. Remove heater control cable from heater control valve.
3. Remove water hose and valve assembly.
4. Remove tray under instrument panel.
5. Remove all defroster hoses with attached nozzles.
6. Remove inlet and outlet hoses from heater.
7. Remove defroster control cable and wiring connector. Remove attaching bolts and lift out heater.
8. To install heater, reverse removal procedure.

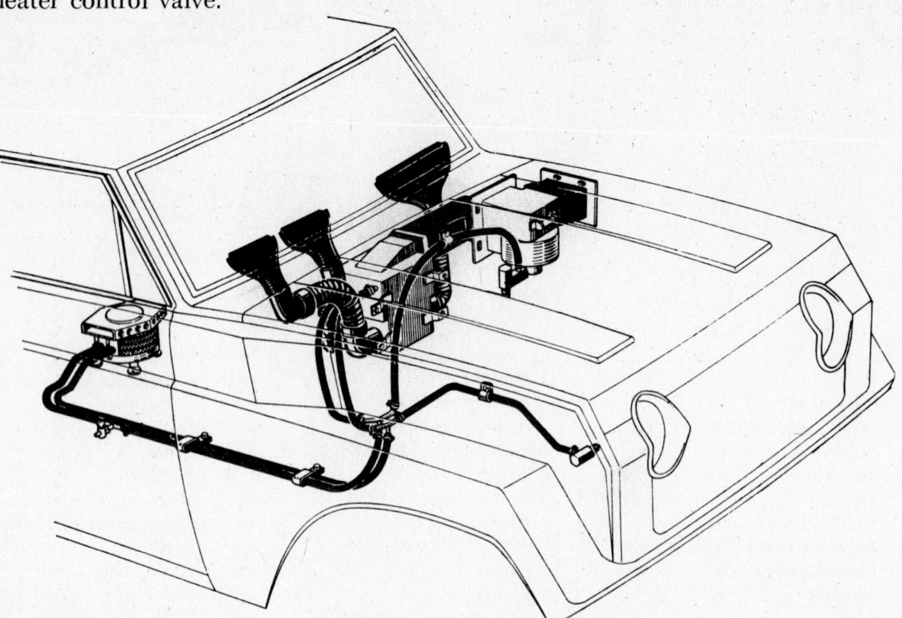

Land Cruiser heater location

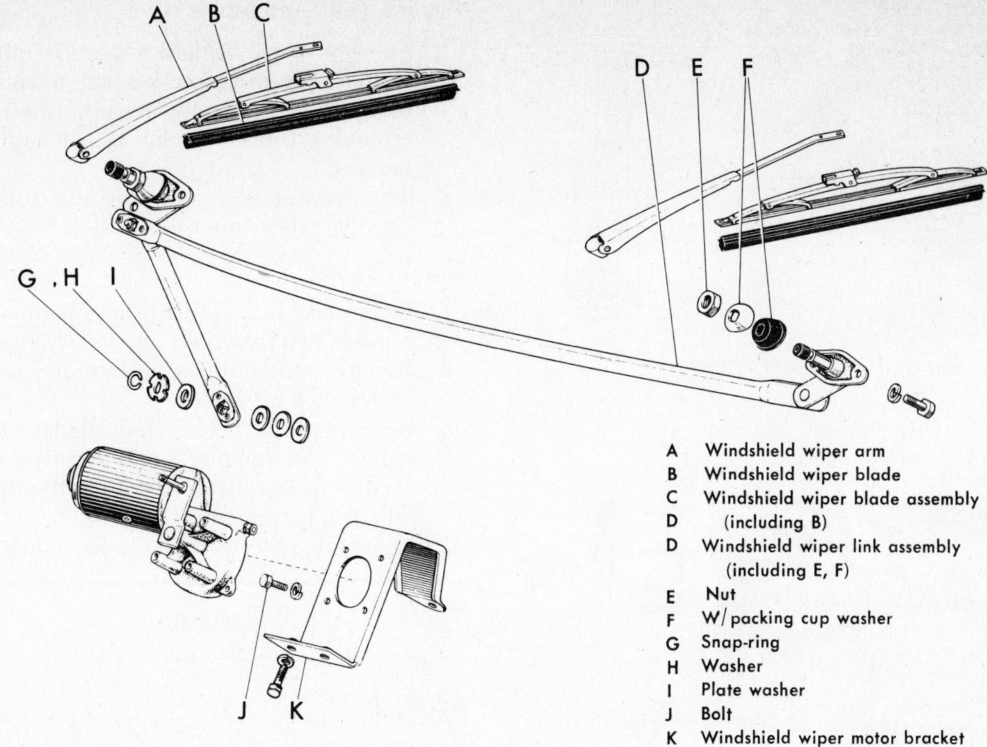

Corolla windshield wiper components

Corona (all) and Mark II

1. Follow Corolla heater removal procedures. In addition, remove the ash tray, cigarette lighter, and the radio securing bolt.
2. To install heater, reverse removal procedure. Be sure to install heater control wiring correctly.

HEATER BLOWER REMOVAL AND INSTALLATION

Land Cruiser

1. Loosen and remove air duct clamps with attaching bolts.
2. Remove air duct screen. Remove bolts and lift out blower.
3. To install, reverse removal procedures.

HEATER CORE REMOVAL AND INSTALLATION

Land Cruiser

1. Close water hose valve.
2. Disconnect heater inlet and outlet hoses from radiator.
3. Loosen air duct clamp. Disconnect defroster hoses.
4. Remove bolts and lift out radiator.
5. To install, reverse removal procedures.

REAR HEATER

1. Shut water hose valve.
2. Disconnect all inlet and outlet hoses.
3. Disconnect all wiring.
4. Remove bolts and lift out radiator.
5. To install, reverse removal procedures.

Windshield Wipers

REMOVAL

Corolla

1. Remove wiper arms and blade.
2. Remove all parts from wiper link pivot.
3. Remove wiring connector.
4. Remove speedometer drive cable with defroster nozzle.
5. Remove bolts holding motor and remove with bracket.
6. Wiper stop position should be .4-1.6″ from weatherstrip.
7. To install, reverse removal procedure.

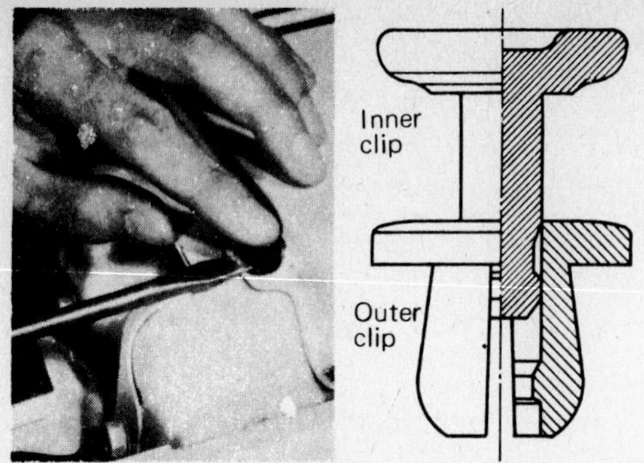

Cowl louver clip removal

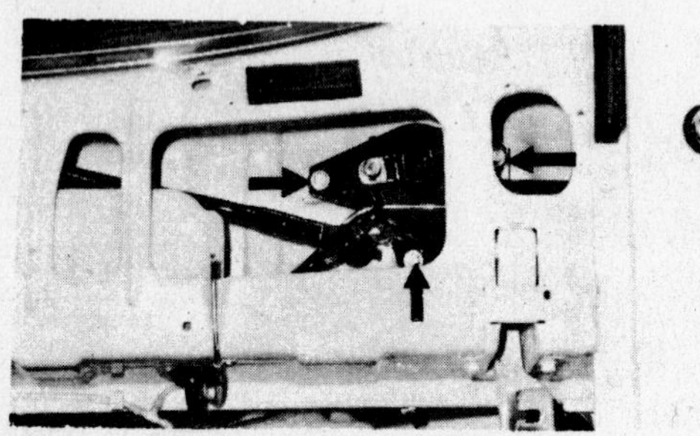

Corona wiper location

Corona (all) and Mark II

1. To remove windshield wiper assembly, the cowl ventilation louvers must be removed. This may be accomplished by removing the inner clip and lifting off louvers.
2. To disassemble and install, follow Corolla procedure.

Land Cruiser

1. Disconnect wiper blade at motor and remove two rear bolts.
2. Remove remaining wiper motor screws and detach all wiring.
3. Remove wiper arms and blades. Remove speedometer and instrument cluster. Loosen throttle wire if wiper link is to be removed.
4. To install, reverse removal procedure.

Radio

REMOVAL

Corolla and Corona

1. Disconnect battery.
2. Remove tray under instrument panel (if installed).
3. Remove ash tray and heater control assembly.
4. Disconnect all radio wiring. Pull off all radio knobs.
5. Remove radio mounting bolts and pull out radio.
6. To install, reverse removal procedure.

Mark II

1. Follow Corolla removal procedure. Note that clock must be removed with radio assembly.

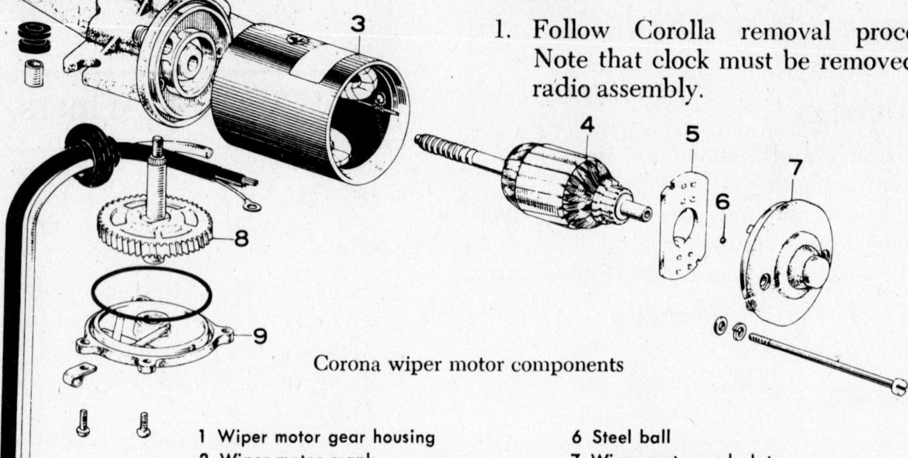

Corona wiper motor components

1 Wiper motor gear housing
2 Wiper motor crank
3 Wiper motor stator sub-assembly
4 Wiper motor armature
5 Wiper motor brush holder sub-assembly
6 Steel ball
7 Wiper motor end plate
8 Wiper drive shaft sub-assembly
9 Wiper motor crank housing cover

TRIUMPH SECTION

Index

Introduction

The TR-4 superseded the TR-3 in 1962 as the latest of the TR series of sports cars. Of straightforward mechanical design, the TR-4 combined rugged components with a reliable 2,138 cc. (130.5 cu. in.) overhead valve, four-cylinder engine to become one of America's most popular sports/racing cars of the 1960's.

The output of the TR-4 engine was increased from 100 to 104 bhp in 1965 with the introduction of the TR-4A. The TR-4A retained the basic design of the TR-4 and offered independent rear suspension as an option.

In 1968 the TR-250 (designated the TR-5 for the British home market) was introduced, combining the basic styling and independent rear suspension of the TR-4A with a 2,498 cc. (152 cu. in.) version of the GT6 six-cylinder engine.

The TR-6 susperseded the TR-250 in 1970. The TR-6 is mechanically identical to the TR-250 except for the addition of a front anti-roll bar and wider wheels. The engine develops 104 bhp.

The Spitfire roadster was introduced in 1964. This economy sports model was equipped with an 1,147 cc. (70 cu. in.) overhead valve, four-cylinder engine. The rear suspension was of the swing-axle type with a transverse leaf spring. The Spitfire Mark II appeared in 1965. This model is basically the same as the Spitfire 4 and is identified by its horizontal grille.

The Spitfire Mark III, introduced in 1968, featured a slightly larger engine. The bore was increased to provide 1,296 cc.'s (79.2 cu. in.) and 75 bhp. The Mark III can be recognized by its higher bumpers and one-piece grille.

In 1971, the Spitfire was restyled and the rear suspension improved. The Spitfire Mark IV engine was improved by the addition of larger rod bearings and journals. The dual SU carburetors were replaced with a single Stromberg CD emission control unit, lowering the power rating to 68 bhp. The transmission on the Mark IV is synchromesh in all four forward gears.

The GT6 was introduced in 1967. It shares the same basic chassis structure, front suspension and lower body structure with the Spitfire. The six-cylinder engine has a shorter stroke than its twin used in the TR models, displacing 1,998 cc. (122 cu. in.) and producing 84 bhp. The 1969-70 model, designated the GT6+, has 95 bhp and is distinguishable from earlier models by the high bumper and one-piece grille of the similar-bodied Spitfire Mark III. The GT6+ has fully independent rear suspension, with double-jointed halfshafts, lower A-arms and a top transverse leaf spring.

The GT6 Mark III, introduced in 1971, is mechanically the same as earlier models, but is slightly restyled. The Mark III is identified by its thin wrap-around front bumper and large horizontal tail lights.

Model Identification

TR-4

TR-4A

TR-250

TR-6

Spitfire MK II

Spitfire

Spitfire Mk III

Spitfire Mk IV

GT6 Mk III

Vehicle and Engine Serial Number Identification

CHASSIS NUMBER

The chassis number (commission number) is stamped on a plate located on the firewall under the hood on the left side.

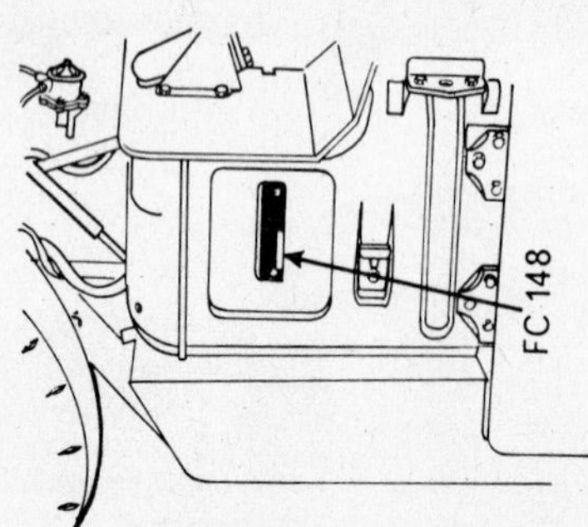

Chassis number location, Spitfire and GT6

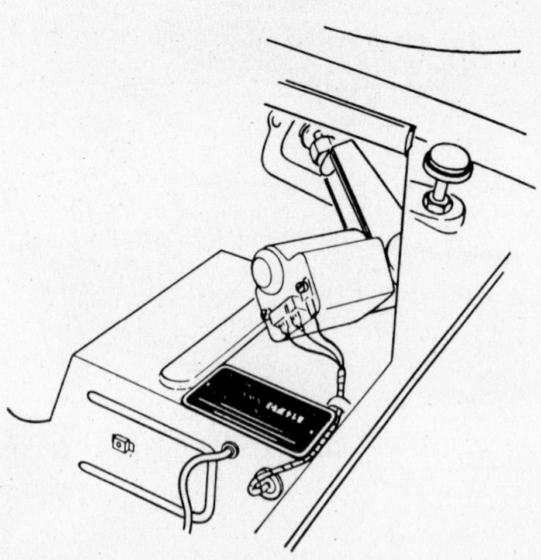
Location of chassis number, TR models.

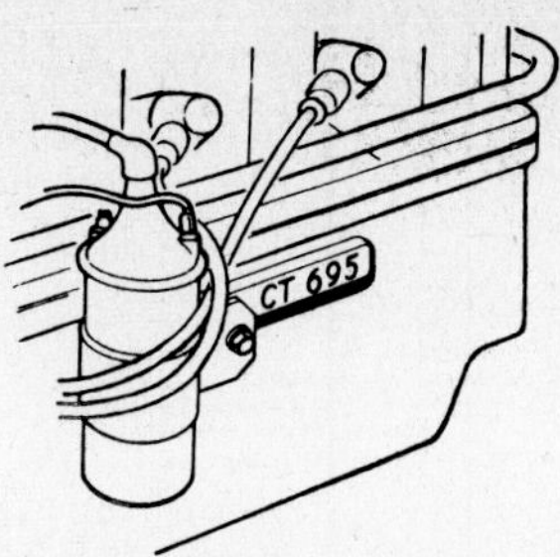

The engine serial number is stamped on the left side of the engine block.

ENGINE NUMBER

The engine number of all models is stamped on the left side of the engine block.

TRANSMISSION NUMBER

The transmission number is stamped on the left side of the clutch housing (TR models) or on the top face of the transmission case at the right side (GT6 and Spitfire).

REAR AXLE NUMBER

The rear axle number of all models is stamped on the housing flange.

Engine Identification

Number of Cylinders	*Cu. In. (cc.) Displacement*	*Type*	*Serial Number or Code (Model)*
4	130.5 (2,138)	OHV	CT (TR-4)
4	130.5 (2,138)	OHV	CTC (TR-4A)
6	152 (2,498)	OHV	(TR-250)
6	152 (2,498)	OHV	(TR-6)
4	70 (1,147)	OHV	FC . . . HE or FC . . . LE① (Spitfire 4 and MK II)
4	79.2 (1,296)	OHV	FD . . . HE or FD . . . LE① (Spitfire MK III and MK IV)
6	122 (1,998)	OHV	(GT6)

① HE: high compression; LE: low compression

General Engine Specifications

Year	Model	Cu. In. Displacement (cc.)	Carburetor	Developed bhp @ rpm	Developed Torque (ft. lbs.) @ rpm	Bore x Stroke (in.)	Compression Ratio	Maximum Oil Pressure (psi)
1962-64	TR-4	130.5 (2,138)	(2) SU H6	100 @ 4,600	125 @ 3,350	3.386 x 3.622	9:1	70
1965-68	TR-4A	130.5 (2,138)	(2) Stromberg 175 CD	104 @ 4,700	132.5 @ 3,000	3.386 x 3.622	9:1	70
1968-69	TR-250	152 (2,498)	(2) Stromberg 175 CDSE③	111 @ 4,500	152 @ 3,000	2.94 x 3.74	8.5:1	70
1970-71	TR-6	152 (2,498)	(2) Stromberg 175 CDSE③	104 @ 4,500	142 @ 3,000	2.94 x 3.74	8.5:1	70
1963-64	Spitfire 4	70 (1,147)	(2) SU HS2	63 @ 5,720①	67 @ 3,500①	2.728 x 2.992	9:1①	40-60
1965-67	Spitfire MK II	70 (1,147)	(2) SU HS2	67 @ 6,000①	67 @ 3,760①	2.728 x 2.992	9:1①	40-60
1968-70	Spitfire MK III	79.2 (1,296)	(2) SU HS2	68 @ 5,500	73.3 @ 3,000	2.900 x 2.992	8.5:1	40-60
1971	Spitfire MK IV	79.2 (1,296)	(1) Stromberg 150 CDSE③	58 @ 5,200	72 @ 3,000	2.900 x 2.992	9:1	40-60
1967-68	GT6	122 (1,998)	(2) Stromberg 150 CD	95 @ 5,000②	117.3 @ 3,000②	2.94 x 2.992	9.5:1②	45-55
1969-70	GT6+	122 (1,998)	(2) Stromberg 150 CDSE③	95 @ 4,700	117 @ 3,400	2.94 x 2.992	9.25:1	45-55
1971	GT6 MK III	122 (1,998)	(2) Stromberg 150 CDSE③	90 @ 4,700	116 @ 3,400	2.94 x 2.992	9.25:1	45-55

① High compression engines only. Low compression option for the Spitfire 4: 53 bhp @ 5,600 rpm, 60 ft. lbs. @ 3,500 rpm; for the Spitfire MK II: 57 bhp @ 5,800 rpm, 60 ft. lbs. @ 3,750 rpm. Compression ratio: 7:1.

② Conventional engines only. Emission controlled engine (U.S.): 84 bhp @ 4,600 rpm, 106 ft. lbs. @ 2,800 rpm, 8.5:1 compression ratio.

③ Emission control unit (US).

Tune-up Specifications

Year	Model	Spark Plugs Type*	Spark Plugs Gap (in.)	Distributor Dwell (deg.)	Distributor Point Gap (in.)	Static Ignition Timing (deg.)	Cranking Compression (psi)	Valves (in.) Intake	Valves (in.) Exhaust	Intake Opens (deg.)	Idle Speed (rpm)
1962-64	TR-4	UL-15Y①	.025	N.A.	.014-.016	4BTDC	②	.010	.010	17BTDC	500
1965-67	TR-4A	UL-15Y①	.025	N.A.	.014-.016	4BTDC	②	.010	.010	17BTDC	600-650
1968	TR-4A	UN-12Y	.025	57-63	.014-.016	TDC	②	.010	.010	17BTDC	850-900
1968-69	TR-250	UN-12Y	.025	32-38	.014-.016	10BTDC	②	.010	.010	10BTDC	800-850
1970-71	TR-6	UN-12Y	.025	32-38	.014-.016	10BTDC④	②	.010	.010	10BTDC	800-850
1963-64	Spitfire 4	UN-12Y	.025	35-37⑤	.014-.016	13BTDC	②	.010	.010	18BTDC	550
1965-67	Spitfire MKII	UN-12Y③	.025	35-37⑤	.014-.016	13BTDC	②	.010	.010	25BTDC	550
1968-70	Spitfire MKIII	UN-12Y	.025	40-42	.014-.016	6BTDC④	②	.010	.010	10BTDC	800-850
1971	Spitfire MKIV	UN-12Y	.025	40-42	.014-.016	6ATDC④	②	.010	.010	N.A.	800-850
1967-68	GT6	UN-12Y	.025	40-42	.014-.016	6BTDC④	②	.010	.010	10BTDC	600-650⑥
1969-70	GT6+	UN-12Y	.025	40-42	.014-.016	6BTDC④	②	.010	.010	10BTDC	800-850
1971	GT6 MKIII	UN-12Y	.025	40-42	.014-.016	6BTDC④	②	.010	.010	10BTDC	800-850
1972	All Models	See engine compartment stickers for tune-up specifications.									

* Champion
① Normal use. For high speed—L-7.
② Compression readings of all cylinders must be within 5 psi of each other.
③ After engine number FC64762F—L87Y.
④ Emission controlled (US only) appropriate static. Timing at idle—4ATDC.
⑤ @ 1,000 rpm.
⑥ 1968 emission controlled idle speed—800-850 rpm.

NOTE: All models imported to the United States during and since 1968 have been modified to comply with the federal exhaust emission standards. Particular care must be taken to follow the ignition timing and carburetor tuning instructions exactly to ensure reliable and efficient engine performance, as well as a safe and legal level of emissions. If the figures in the Tune-Up Chart do not agree with those on the engine compartment sticker, use the sticker figures.

Engine Rebuilding Specifications
Crankshaft

Model	Main Bearing Journals (in.)					Connecting Rod Bearing Journals (in.)			
	Diameter					Diameter			
	New	Undersize Min.	Oil Clearance	End-play	Thrust on No.	New	Min. Undersize	Oil Clearance	End-play
TR-4, TR-4A	2.4790-2.4795	2.4490	.0015-.0025①	.004-.006②	2	2.0861-2.0866	2.0561	.0028-.0040③	.007-.014
TR-250, GT6	2.0005-2.0010	2.0705	.0012-.0020	.006-.008	4	1.8750-1.8755	1.8450	.0010-.0027	.0086-.0125
TR-6	2.3110-2.3115	2.2810	.0015-.0025	.006-.008	4	1.8750-1.8755	1.8450	.0010-.0027	.007-.014
Spitfire 4, MKII	2.0005-2.0010	1.9605	.0005-.0032	.004-.008	3	1.6250-1.6255	1.5950	.0005-.0020	.0105-.0126
Spitfire MKIII	2.0005-2.0010	1.9605	.0010-.0020	.004-.008	3	1.6250-1.6255	1.5950	.0005-.0020	.0105-.0126

① Manufacturing and rebuilding limit only. Wear limit—.0031.
② Manufacturing and rebuilding only. Wear limit—.015.
③ Manufacturing and rebuilding only. Wear limit—.005.

Firing Order

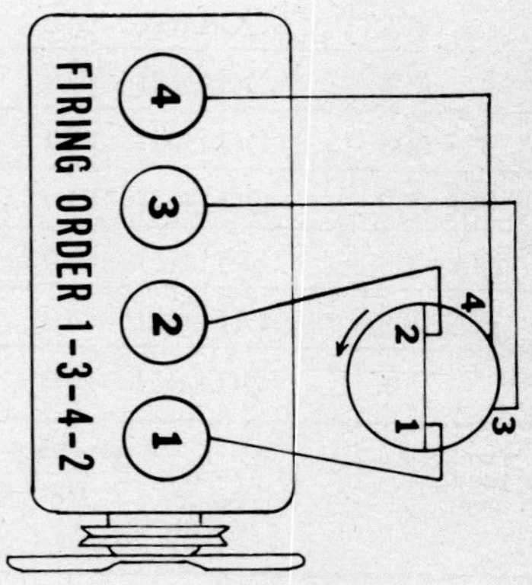

TR-4, TR-4A

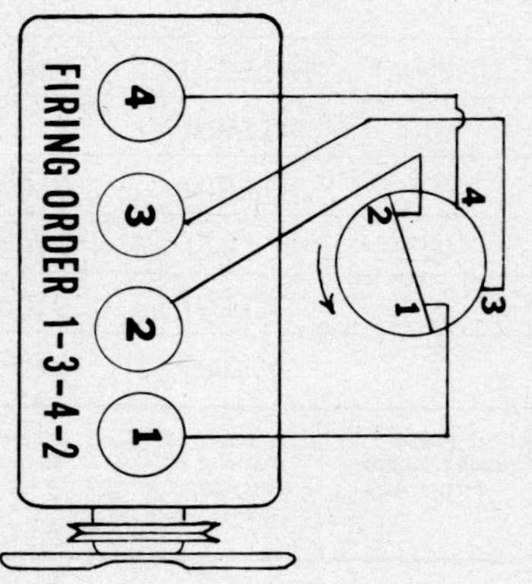

Spitfire

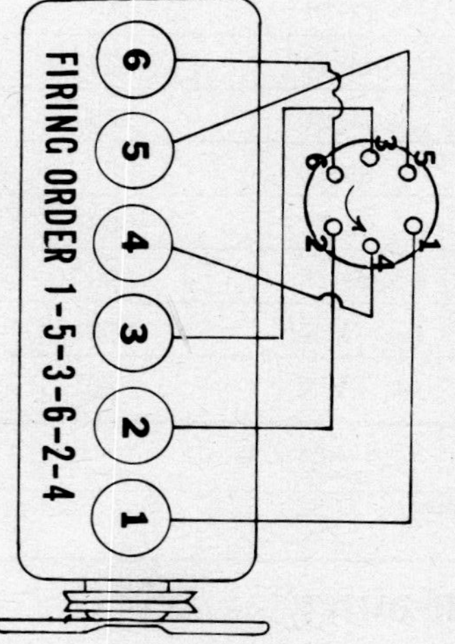

TR-250, TR-6, GT6

Spitfire 4 and MKII Pistons

Block			Piston (in.)				
Bore (in.)			Diameter			Clearance	
Grade	New	Maximum Oversize	Grade	Crown	Skirt	Crown	Skirt
F	2.7280-2.7283	①	F②	2.7250-2.7254	2.7268-2.7272	.0026-.0033	.0008-.0015
G	2.7284-2.7287	①	G②	2.7254-2.7258	2.7272-2.7276	.0026-.0033	.0008-.0015
H	2.7288-2.7291	①	H②	2.7258-2.7262	2.7276-2.7280	.0026-.0033	.0008-.0015
F	2.7280-2.7283	①	F③	2.7090-2.7120	2.7268-2.7271	.0160-.0193	.0009-.0015
G	2.7284-2.7287	①	G③	2.7090-2.7120	2.7272-2.7275	.0164-.0197	.0009-.0015
H	2.7288-2.7291	①	H③	2.7090-2.7120	2.7276-2.7279	.0168-.0201	.0009-.0015
F	2.7280-2.7283	①	F④	2.7242-2.7245	2.7268-2.7271	.0035-.0041	.0009-.0015
G	2.7284-2.7287	①	G④	2.7246-2.7249	2.7272-2.7275	.0035-.0041	.0009-.0015
H	2.7288-2.7291	①	H④	2.7250-2.7253	2.7276-2.7279	.0035-.0041	.0009-.0015

① .010, .020, and .030 in. oversize pistons are available.
② Manufactured by Automotive Engineering Co. Ltd.
③ Manufactured by British Piston Ring Co. Ltd.
④ Manufactured by Wellworthy

Spitfire MKIII Pistons

Block			Piston (in.)				
Bore (in.)			Diameter			Clearance	
Grade	New	Maximum oversize	Grade	Crown	Skirt	Crown	Skirt
F	2.899-2.900	①	F②	2.875-2.880	2.8976-2.8981	.019-.025	.0009-.0024
G	2.9001-2.9005	①	G②	2.875-2.880	2.8982-2.8987	.020-.026	.0014-.0023
F	2.899-2.900	①	F③	2.8752-2.8799	2.8976-2.8981	.019-.025	.0009-.0024
G	2.9001-2.9005	①	G③	2.8752-2.8799	2.8983-2.8987	.0202-.0253	.0014-.0022

① .010, .020, and .030 in. oversize pistons are available.
② Manufactured by Brico Co., Ltd.
③ Manufactured by Hepworth Co. Ltd.

TR-4 and TR-4A Pistons

Cylinder			Piston (in.)			
Bore (in.)			Diameter		Clearance	
Grade	New	Maximum Oversize	Crown	Skirt	Crown	Skirt
F	3.3854-3.3857	①	3.3803-3.3807	3.3818-3.3822	.0047-0054	.0032-.0039
G	3.3858-3.3861	①	3.3807-3.3811	3.3822-3.3826	.0047-0054	.0032-.0039
H	3.3862-3.3865	①	3.3811-3.3815	3.3826-3.3830	.0047-0054	.0032-.0039

① .010, .020, .030, and .040 in. oversize pistons are available.

TR-250 and GT6 Pistons

	Cylinder Bore (in.)		Piston (in.)			
			Diameter		Clearance	
Grade	New	Maximum Oversize	Crown	Skirt	Crown	Skirt
F	2.9405-2.9408	①	2.9366-2.9370	2.9384-2.9388	.0035-.0042	.0017-.0024
G	2.9409-2.9412	①	2.9370-2.9374	2.9388-2.9392	.0035-.0042	.0017-.0024
H	2.9413-2.9416	①	2.9374-2.9378	2.9392-2.9396	.0035-.0042	.0017-.0024

① .010, .020, .030, and .040 in. oversize pistons are available.

TR-6 Pistons

	Cylinder Bore (in.)		Piston (in.)			
			Diameter		Clearance	
Grade	New	Maximum Oversize	Crown	Skirt	Crown	Skirt
F	2.9405-2.9408	①	2.9363-2.9367	2.9380-2.9384	.0038-.0045	.0021-.0028
G	2.9409-2.9412	①	2.9367-2.9371	2.9384-2.9388	.0038-.0045	.0021-.0028
H	2.9413-2.9416	①	2.9371-2.9375	2.9388-2.9392	.0038-.0045	.0021-.0028

① .010, .020, and .030 in. oversize pistons are available.

Piston Rings

Model	Type	Side Clearance (in.)	End-Gap (in.)
TR-4, TR-4A	All	.0010-.0030①	.010-.015
TR-250	Compression	.0019-.0035	.008-.013
	Oil Control	.0007-.0027	.008-.013
TR-6	1st Compression	.0010-.0030	.012-.017
	2d Compression	.0010-.0030	.008-.013
	Oil (plain)	.0010-.0030	.015-.055
	Oil (scraper)	.0010-.0030	(ends butt)
Spitfire 4 & MKII	Compression	.0015-.0035	.008-.013
	Oil Control	.001-.004	.008-.013
Spitfire MKIII	Compression	.0015-.0035	.012-.022
	Oil Control	.0018-.0048	.012-.022
GT6	Compression	.0019-.0035	.008-.013
	Oil Control	.0007-.0027	.008-.013

① Wear limit—.0038.

Valves

Model	Seat Angle (deg.)	Valve Lift (in.)		Spring Pressure (lbs.)		Stem Diameter (in.)		Stem to Guide Clearance (in.)		Valve Guide Removable
		Intake	Exhaust	Intake	Exhaust	Intake	Exhaust	Intake	Exhaust	
TR-4, TR-4A	45	.260	.260	N.A.①	N.A.①	.310-.311	.3705-.3715	.001-.003②	.003-.005③	yes
TR-250, GT6	45	N.A.	N.A.	④	④	.3107-.3112	.3100-.3105	.0018-.0023	.0015-.0025	yes
TR-6	45	N.A.	N.A.	235⑤ lbs./in.	235⑤ lbs./in.	.3107-.3112	.3100-.3105	⑥	⑥	yes
Spitfire 4	45	N.A.	N.A.	32-42⑦	32-42⑦	.310-.311	.308-.309	.001-.003	.003-.005	yes
Spitfire MKII, MKIII, MKIV	45	N.A.	N.A.	32-42⑦	32-42⑦	.3100-.3112	.3100-.3105	.0008-.0023	.0015-.0025	yes

① Free length: auxiliary inner (exhaust only)—1.55 in.; inner—1.88 in.; outer—1.94 in.
② Wear limit—.0038 in.
③ Wear limit—.0063 in.
④ Pressure at fitted length: inner—11-14 lbs. @ 1.14 in.; outer—27-30 lbs. @ 1.386 in.
⑤ 117.5 lbs. compression required to close coils .5 in.
⑥ Check wear by installing a new valve, lifting it ⅛ in., and rocking it sideways. If the movement of the valve head across the seat exceeds .020 in., the guide must be replaced. Valve guides are pressed in.
⑦ Installed load.

Distributor Advance Specifications

Model	Distributor Identification	Centrifugal Advance: Start Degrees @ rpm	Intermediate Degrees @ rpm	Intermediate Degrees @ rpm	End Degrees @ rpm
Spitfire 4	DR 7952800 ST 209697	0-1.5@500	7.4-9.4@900	9.4-11.4@1,200	11-13@1,450
Spitfire MK II	DR 7953166 ST 212500	0-1.75@400	6-8@700	9-11@1,600	11.4-13.4 @ 2,300
Spitfire MK III (Early)	DR 7953577 DR 200	0-1@300	9.8-11.8@750	12.4-14.4@1,600	16@2,500
Spitfire MK III (Late), MK IV	DR 200	0-2@350	9.5-11.5@750	12.5-14.5@1,700	14-16@2,100
TR-4 (Early)	L-40795 ST 208972	0-2@350	5-7@600	9-11@800	9-11@1,200
TR-4 (Late)	L-40842 ST 209092	0-1@400	.5-2.5@700	4-6@1,350	7-9@1,900
TR-4A	DR 200 ST 214799	0-3.5@500	7-10.5@700	11-13@900	11-13@2,500
TR-250 (Early)	L-41202A ST 308371 L-22D6	0-1@450	5-7@900	10-12@850	12-14@2,300
TR-250 (Late)	L-41202B ST 308460	1-3@450	7-9@800	11-13@1,200	14-16@2,000
TR-6	L-22D6	0-1@450	4-6@850	6-8@1,500	9-11@2,500
GT6 (All)	DR D202	1-3@500	4.6-8@875	6.8-9.2@1,200	12-14@2,500

NOTE: *Specifications are given in distributor degrees and distributor rpm.*
L=Lucas
DR=Delco Remy
ST=Standard Triumph
NOTE: *Distributor retard unit should be serviced by a qualified mechanic only.*
Distributor rotation: counter-clockwise

Distributor Advance Specifications

Model	Distributor Identification	Vacuum Advance: Start Degrees @ in. Hg	Vacuum Advance: Intermediate Degrees @ in. Hg	Vacuum Advance: End Degrees @ in. Hg
Spitfire 4	DR 7952800 ST 209697	1.5@2.5	7-9@7	9-11@10
Spitfire MK II	DR 7953166 ST 212500	0-1@5	5.75-7.75@9	11-13@16
Spitfire MK III (Early)	DR 7953577 DR 200	0@4	5.5-7.7@10.7	7.5@20
Spitfire MK III (Late), MK IV	DR 200	0-3@6	4.5-7.5@10	5.5-7.5@20
TR-4 (Early)	L-40795 ST 208972	1@3	1.75@4	2.75@6
TR-4 (Late)	L-40842 ST 209092	1.5@3	4.5@7	10@8
TR-4A	DR 200 ST 214799	0-2.7@4	6.5-8.9@10	7-8.9@20
TR-250 (Early)	L-41202A ST 308371 L-22D6	.5@4	5.5-8@9	9-11@20
TR-250 (Late)	L-41202B ST 308460	0-.5@3	2.5-7@6	7-9@15
TR-6	L-22D6	0-.5@3	2.5@6	7@15
GT6 (All)	DR D202	0@4-6	4-6@11	11@20

NOTE: *Specifications are given in distributor degrees and distribuor rpm.*
L=Lucas
DR=Delco Remy
ST=Standard Triumph
NOTE: *Distributor retard unit should be serviced by a qualified mechanic only.*
Distributor rotation: counter-clockwise

Tightening Torques (ft. lbs.)

Model	Cylinder Head Bolts	Main Bearing Bolts	Rod Bearing Bolts	Crankshaft Pulley Bolt	Flywheel to Crankshaft Bolts	Manifold Intake	Manifold Exhaust
TR-4, TR-4A	100-105	85-90	55-60	N.A.	42-46	12-14	12-14
TR-250	65-70	55-60	38-42	90-100	55-60	①	①
TR-6	65-70	55-60	38-42	90-100	55-60	②	②
Spitfire	42-46	50-55	38-42	N.A.	42-46	24-26	24-26
GT6	42-46	55-60	38-42	90-100	42-46	14-16③	20-22

① Studs—24-26; bolts—18-20.
② Outer (2)—12-14; inner—16-18.
③ Exhaust/intake attaching bolt—20-22.

Tightening Sequences

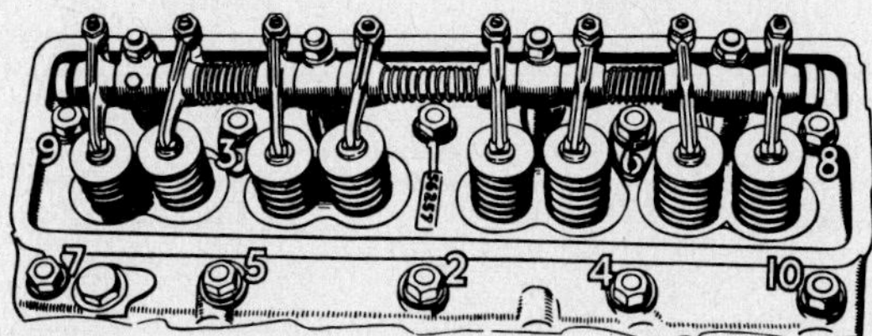

Cylinder head nut tightening sequence, TR–4, TR–4A engines.

Cylinder head tightening sequence, Spitfire engine, heads with four intake ports only.

Cylinder head nut tightening sequence, Spitfire engine. Heads with two intake ports only.

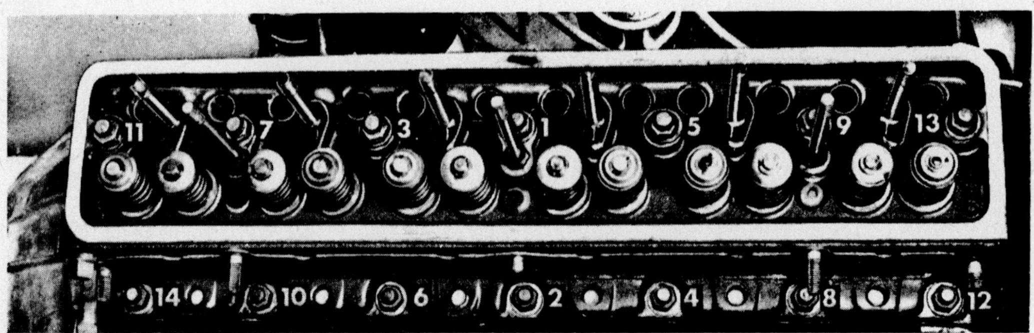

Cylinder head nut tightening sequence, six-cylinder engines.

Electrical Specifications—Battery and Starter

	Battery			*Starter*						
				Lock Test			*No Load Test*			
Model	*Capacity (amp. hrs.)*	*Voltage*	*Ground*	*Amps.*	*Volts*	*Torque (ft. lbs.)*	*Amps.*	*Volts*	*rpm*	*Brush Spring Tension (oz.)*
TR-4, TR-4A	58	12	Pos.	440-460	7.0-7.4	17	45	12	7,400-8,500	32-40
TR-250	57	12	Neg.	370	7.5-7.9	8.2	60	12	8,000-11,500	30-34
TR-6	60	12	Neg.	465	7.0	15	80	12	5,500-8,000	36
Spitfire 4, MKII, MKIII	43②	12	Pos.①	420-440	7.3-7.9	10	45	12	7,400-8,500	32-34
GT6	56	12	Neg.	370	7.5-7.9	8.2	60	12	8,000-11,500	30-34

① Spitfire MKIII and MKIV have negative ground systems.
② Spitfire MKIV is equipped with a 40 amp. hr. battery.

Generator/Alternator Specifications

Model	*Brush Spring Pressure (oz.)*	*Field Resistance (ohms)*	*Maximum Output (amps.)*
Spitfire (All)	22-25	6	22@2,050-2,250 rpm (load .61 ohms)
TR-4, TR-4A	22-25	6	22@2,050-2,250 rpm (load .61 ohms)
TR-250	7-10	4.3@20°C	25@2,870 rpm (14 volts)
TR-6	7-10 (Face flush with brushbox)	4.3@20°C (±) 5%	
GT6 (Early)	17-32	5-9 (±) .3	25@1,660 rpm (.54 resistance)
GT6 (Late)	7-10 (Face flush with brushbox)	4.3@20°C	25@2,870 rpm (14 volts)

NOTE: *C=Centigrade; 20 Degrees Centigrade=72 Degrees Farenheit*

Regulator Specifications

Model	*Cutout Relay (Volts to close)*	*Maximum Current (amps)*	*Voltage Regulator Setting*
Spitfire	12.6-13.4	22	13.5
TR-4, TR-4A	12.6-13.4	22	13.5
TR-250	12.7-13.3	25	15
TR-6	12.6-13.4	22	13.5
GT6 (All)	12.7-13.3	25	15

NOTE: *Regulated output may be exceeded when cold. Therefore, engine should be at operating temperature when tested.*

Capacities and Pressures

Model	Engine Crankcase Refill after draining (pts.)		Transmission Refill after draining (pts.)	
	With filter	Without filter	With Overdrive	Without Overdrive
Spitfire	9.6	8.4	2.85	1.8
TR-4, TR-4A	13.2	12	4.2	3.3
TR-6	9.64	8.4	4.2	3.3
TR-250	9.64	8.4	4.2	3.3
GT6 (All)	9.64	8.4	2.85	1.8

Model	Fuel Tank (gals.)	Normal Fuel Pressure (psi.)	Drive Axle (pts.)	Maximum Coolant Pressure (psi)	Cooling System with Heater (qts.)
Spitfire	10.0	1.5-2.5	1.2	7	11.4, Spitfire MK III, IV—9.6
TR-4, TR-4A	13.5	1.25-2.5	1.8	4	16.8
TR-6	13.5	1.25-2.5	3.0	4	13.2
TR-250	13.5	1.25-2.5	1.8	4	13.2
GT6 (All)	11.7	1.5-2.5	1.2	7	13.2

Brake Specifications

Model	Type: Front	Type: Rear	Brake Cylinder Bore (in.): Master Cylinder	Wheel Cylinder: Front	Wheel Cylinder: Rear	Brake Drum or Disc Diameter (in.): Front	Rear
TR-4, TR-4A, TR-250, TR-6	Disc	Drum	.70	N.A.	N.A.	10.9	9
Spitfire Series	Disc	Drum	N.A.	N.A.	N.A.	9	7
GT6 Series	Disc	Drum	N.A.	N.A.	N.A.	9.7	8

Chassis and Wheel Alignment Specifications

Model	Chassis (in.): Wheel-base	Track: Front	Track: Rear	Wheel Alignment: Caster (deg.)	Camber (deg.): Front	Camber (deg.): Rear	Toe-in (in.)	King Pin Inclina-tion (deg.)
Spitfire	83	48.94	48	+4	+2	−3	0-1/16	6¾
TR-4	88	Disc wheels-49, wire wheels—50	Disc—49, Wire—50	Up to CT6344, wire wheels; Up to CT6390, disc wheels: 0, all following: +3	+2	0	⅛ ①	7
TR-4A	88	Disc—49, Wire—49.75	IRS, Disc—48.5, Wire—49.25 LA—48.75	+2.66 ±.5	0 ±½	LA: 0, IRS: −1±½	0-1/16	9 ±¾
TR-250	88	Disc—49.25, Wire—49.75	Disc—48.75, Wire—49.25	+2.75 ±.5	0 ±½	+1 ±½	0-1/16	9 ±¾
TR-6	88	50.25	49.75	+2.75 ±.5	−¼ ±½	+1 ±½	0-1/16	9¼ ±¾
GT6	83	49	48	+4 ±.5	+2 ±½	−2½ ±½	0-1/16	6¾ ±¾

①—1/16 with radial tires.
IRS—Independent rear suspension
LA—Live axle

Light Bulb Specifications

Model	*Usage*	*Lucas Number*	*US Equivalent Number*	*Base*	*Wattage*
TR-4, TR-4A	Headlights	301			36/36
All other		54522231			50/40
TR-6	Front/rear flashers, backup lights	380			5/21
All other		382			21
TR-250	Front parking	989	57	1	6
TR-4, TR-4A		222	57	1	4
Spitfire, GT6		207	89	3	6
TR-6		380			5/21
TR-250	Front/rear markers	501			5
All other		222	57	1	4
All	Tail/stop	380			5/21
GT6	License plate	222	57	1	6
All other		207	89	3	6
All	Instrument, warning, glove compartment	987	1446	2	2.2
GT6	Interior	254			6
TR-6	Transmission tunnel	254			6
	Trunk	256			3

Wiring Diagrams

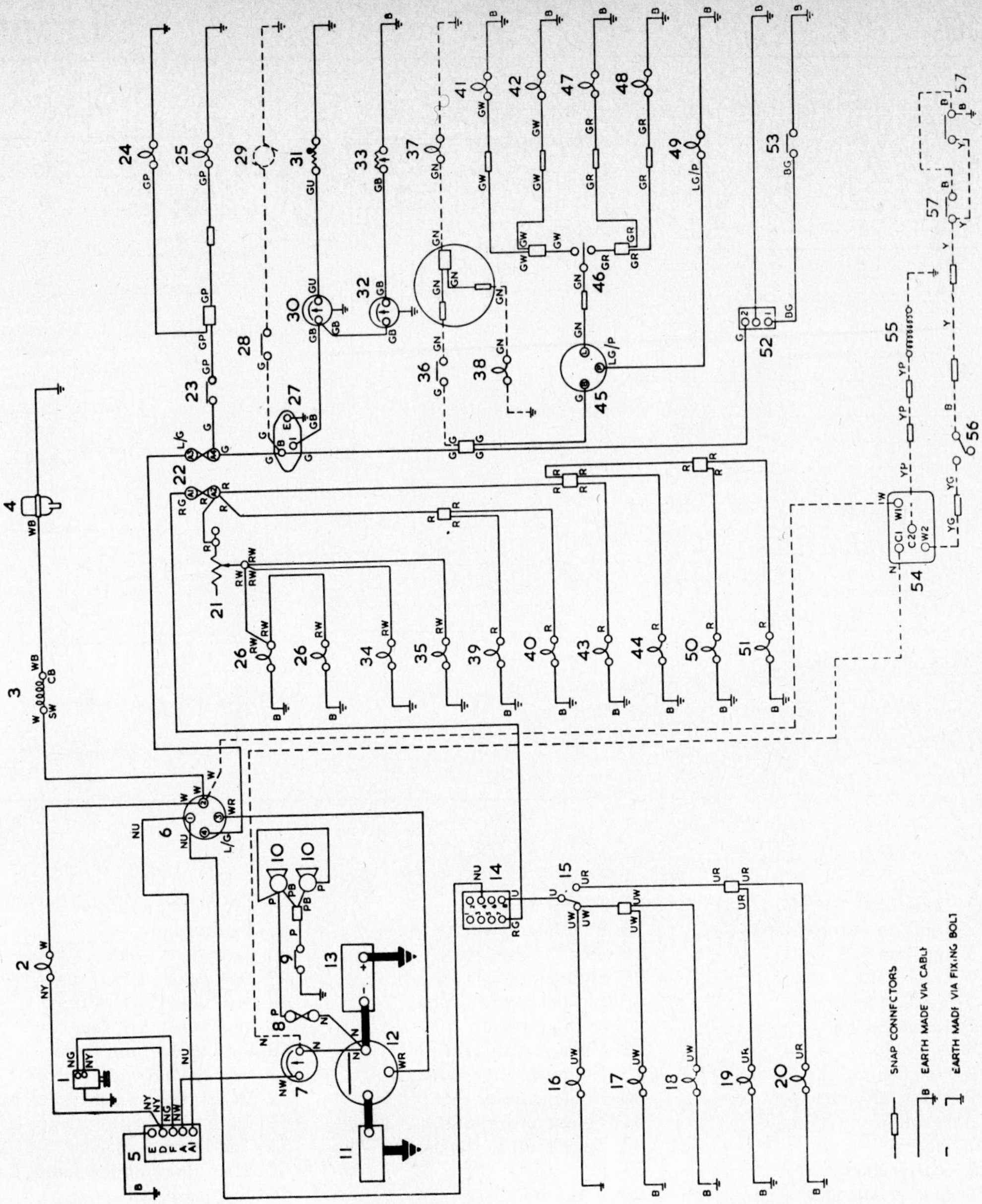

SNAP CONNECTORS
EARTH MADE VIA CABLE
EARTH MADE VIA FIXING BOLT

1 Generator
2 Ignition warning lamp
3 Ignition coil
4 Distributor
5 Voltage regulator
switch
7 Ammeter
8 Horn fuse
9 Horn button
10 Horns
11 Starter motor
12 Starter solenoid
13 Battery
14 Light switch
15 Dimmer switch
16 High beam indicator lamp
17 Headlamp high beam, R.H.
18 Headlamp high beam, L.H.
19 Headlamp low beam, R.H.
20 Headlamp low beam, L.H.
21 Instrument illumination
rheostat
22 Fuse unit
23 Stop lamp switch
24 Stop lamp, R.H.
25 Stop lamp, L.H.
26 Ammeter and gauges
illumination
27 Voltage stablizer
28 Heater blower motor switch
29 Heater blower motor
30 Temperature indicator gauge
31 Temperature transmitter
32 Fuel gauge
33 Tank unit
34 Speedometer illumination
35 Tachometer illumination
36 Backup lamp switch
37 Backup lamp
38 Backup lamp
} Optional Extra
39 Parking lamp, R.H.
40 Parking lamp, L.H.
41 Turn signal, R.H. Front
42 Turn signal, L.H. Front
43 Tail lamp, R.H.
44 Plate illumination lamp, R.H.
45 Flasher unit
46 Turn signal switch
47 Turn signal, R.H. Rear
48 Turn signal, L.H. Rear
49 Turn signal monitor lamp
50 Tail lamp, L.H.
51 Plate illumination almp, L.H.
52 Windshield wiper motor switch
53 Windshield wiper motor switch
54 Relay
55 Solenoid
56 Column control
57 Transmission switches
} Overdrive Optional Extras

CABLE COLOR CODE

B	Black	W	White
U	Blue	Y	Yellow
N	Brown	D	Dark
G	Green	L	Light
K	Pink	M	Medium
P	Purple		
R	Red		
S	Slate		

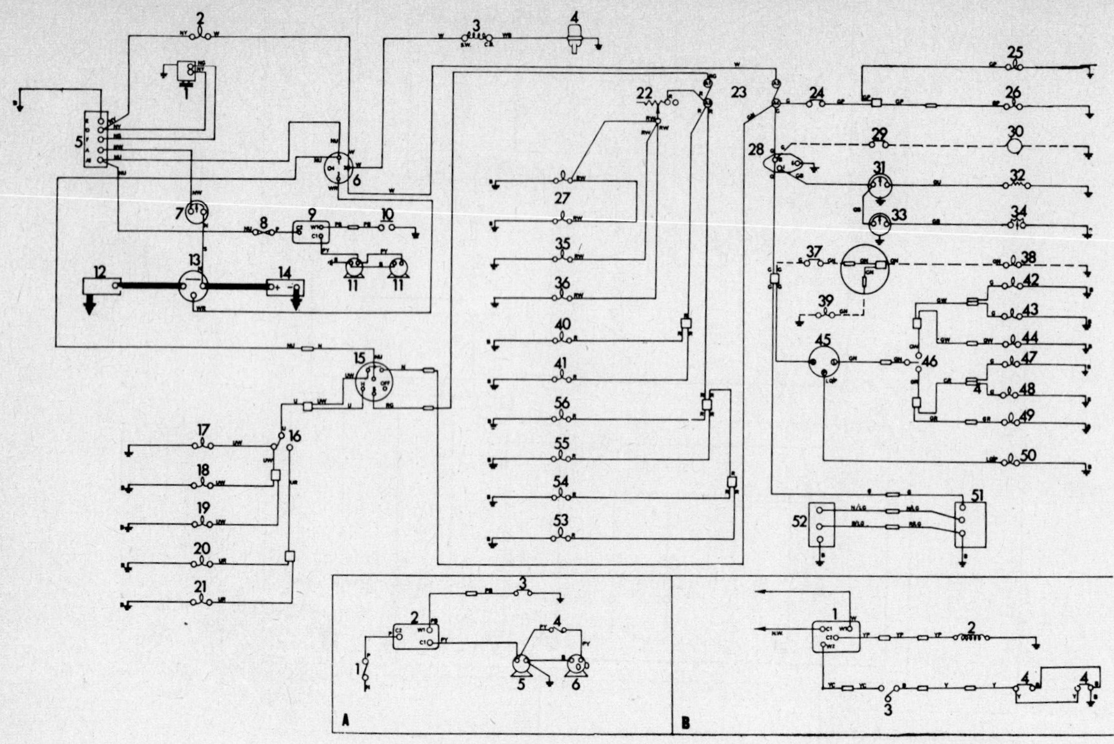

TR-4A

1 Generator
2 Ignition warning lamp
3 Ignition coil
4 Distributor
5 Voltage regulator
6 Ignition switch
7 Ammeter
8 Horn fuse
9 Horn relay
10 Horn button
11 Horns
12 Starter motor
13 Starter solenoid
14 Battery
15 Light switch
16 Dimmer switch
17 High beam indicator lamp
18 Headlamp high beam, R.H.
19 Headlamp high beam, L.H.
20 Headlamp low beam, R.H.
21 Headlamp low beam, L.H.
22 Instrument illumination rheostat
23 Fuse unit
24 Stop lamp switch
26 Stop lamp, R.H.
26 Stop lamp, L.H.
27 Ammeter and gauge illumination
28 Voltage stabilizer
29 Heater blower motor switch
30 Heater blower motor
31 Temperature indicator gauge
32 Temperature transmitter
33 Fuel gauge
34 Tank unit
35 Speedometer illumination
36 Tachometer illumination
37 Backup lamp switch
38 Backup lamp
39 Backup lamp
40 Parking lamp, R.H.
41 Parking lamp, L.H.
42 Turn signal, R.H. Front
43 Turn signal, L.H. Front Repeater
44 Turn signal, R.H. Rear
45 Flasher unit
46 Turn signal switch
47 Turn signal, L.H. Front
48 Turn signal, L.H. Front
49 Turn signal, L.H. Rear
50 Flasher warning lamp
51 Windshield wiper motor
52 Windshield wiper motor switch
53 Plate illumination lamp, L.H.
54 Tail lamp, R.H.
55 Plate illumination lamp, L.H.
56 Tail lamp, R.H.

CABLE COLOR CODE

B	Black	S	Slate
U	Blue	W	White
N	Brown	Y	Yellow
G	Green	D	Dark
K	Pink	L	Light
P	Purple	M	Medium
R	Red		

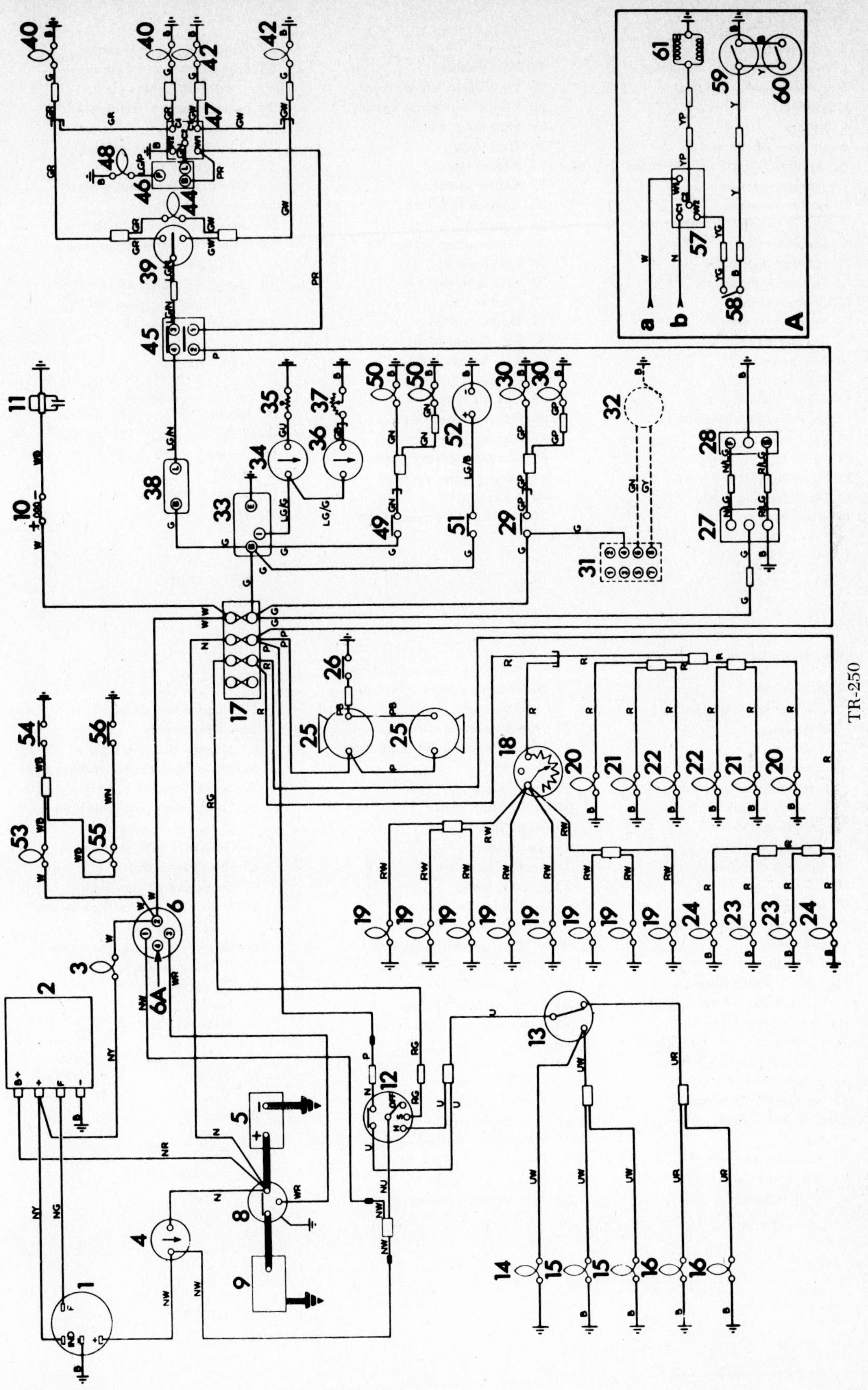
TR-250

TR-250 Wiring Diagram

1 Alternator
2 Alternator voltage regulator
3 Ignition warning light
4 Ammeter
5 Battery
6 Ignition/starter switch
6a Ignition/starter switch—radio supply connector
8 Starter solenoid
9 Starter motor
10 Ignition coil
11 Ignition distributor
12 Column light switch
13 Dimmer switch
14 High beam warning light
15 Dimmer beam
16 Low beam
17 Fuse box
18 Panel rheostat
19 Instrument illumination
20 Rear marker lamp
21 Tail lamp
22 Plate illumination lamp
23 Front parking lamp
24 Front marker lamp
25 Horn
26 Horn button
27 Windshield wiper motor
28 Windshield wiper switch
29 Stop lamp switch
30 Stop lamp
31 Heater motor
32 Heater motor
33 Voltage stablizer
34 Temperature indicator
35 Temperature transmitter
36 Fuel indicator
37 Fuel tank unit
38 Flasher unit
39 Flasher switch
40 L.H. flasher lamp
42 R.H. flasher lamp
44 Flasher warning light
45 Hazard switch
46 Hazard flasher unit
47 Hazard relay
48 Hazard warning light
49 Backup lamp switch
50 Backup lamp
51 Windshield washer switch
52 Windshield washer motor
53 Brake pressure differential warning light
54 Brake pressure differential switch
55 Oil pressure warning light
56 Oil pressure switch
A Overdrive (optional extra)
57 Overdrive relay
58 Overdrive column switch
59 Overdrive transmission switch—2nd gear ON
60 Overdrive transmission switch—3rd and 4th gear ON
61 Overdrive solenoid
a From fuse box
b From fuse box

COLOR CODE

N Brown
U Blue
P Purple
G Green
L/G Light Green
W White
Y Yellow
S Slate
B Black

TR-6 Wiring Diagram

1 Alternator
2 Ignition warning light
3 Ammeter
4 Battery
5 Ignition/starter switch
5A Ignition/starter switch radio supply connector
7 Starter motor
8 Ignition coil
9 Ignition distributor
10 Column light switch
11 Dimmer switch
12 High beam warning light
14 Low beam
15 Fuse box
16 Front parking lamp
17 Front marker lamp
18 Rear marker lamp
19 Tail lamp
20 Plate illumination lamp
21 Panel rheostat
22 Instrument illumination
23 Connector block
24 Horn
25 Horn button
26 Glove compartment illumination
27 Glove compartment illumination switch
28 Transmission tunnel lamp
29 Transmission tunnel lamp door switch
30 Trunk lamp
31 Trunk lamp switch
32 Stop lamp switch
33 Stop lamp
34 Backup lamp switch
35 Backup lamp
36 Windshield wiper switch
37 Windshield wiper motor
38 Windshield washer switch
39 Windshield washer pump
40 Voltage stabilizer
41 Temperature indicator
42 Temperature transmitter
43 Fuel indicator
44 Fuel tank unit
45 Heater switch
46 Heater motor
47 Turn signal flasher unit
48 Turn signal switch
49 L.H. flasher lamp
51 R.H. flasher lamp
53 Turn signal warning light
54 Hazard switch
55 Hazard flasher unit
56 Hazard relay
57 Hazard warning light
58 Brake line failure warning light
59 Brake line failure switch
60 Oil pressure warning light
61 Oil pressure switch
A Overdrive (optional extra)
62 Overdrive relay
63 Overdrive column switch
64 Overdrive transmission switch 2nd gear ON
65 Overdrive transmission switch 3rd and 4th gear ON
66 Overdrive solenoid
a From fuse box
b From fuse box

COLOR CODE

N Brown
U Blue
R Red
P Purple
G Green
LG Light Green
W White
Y Yellow
S Slate
B Black

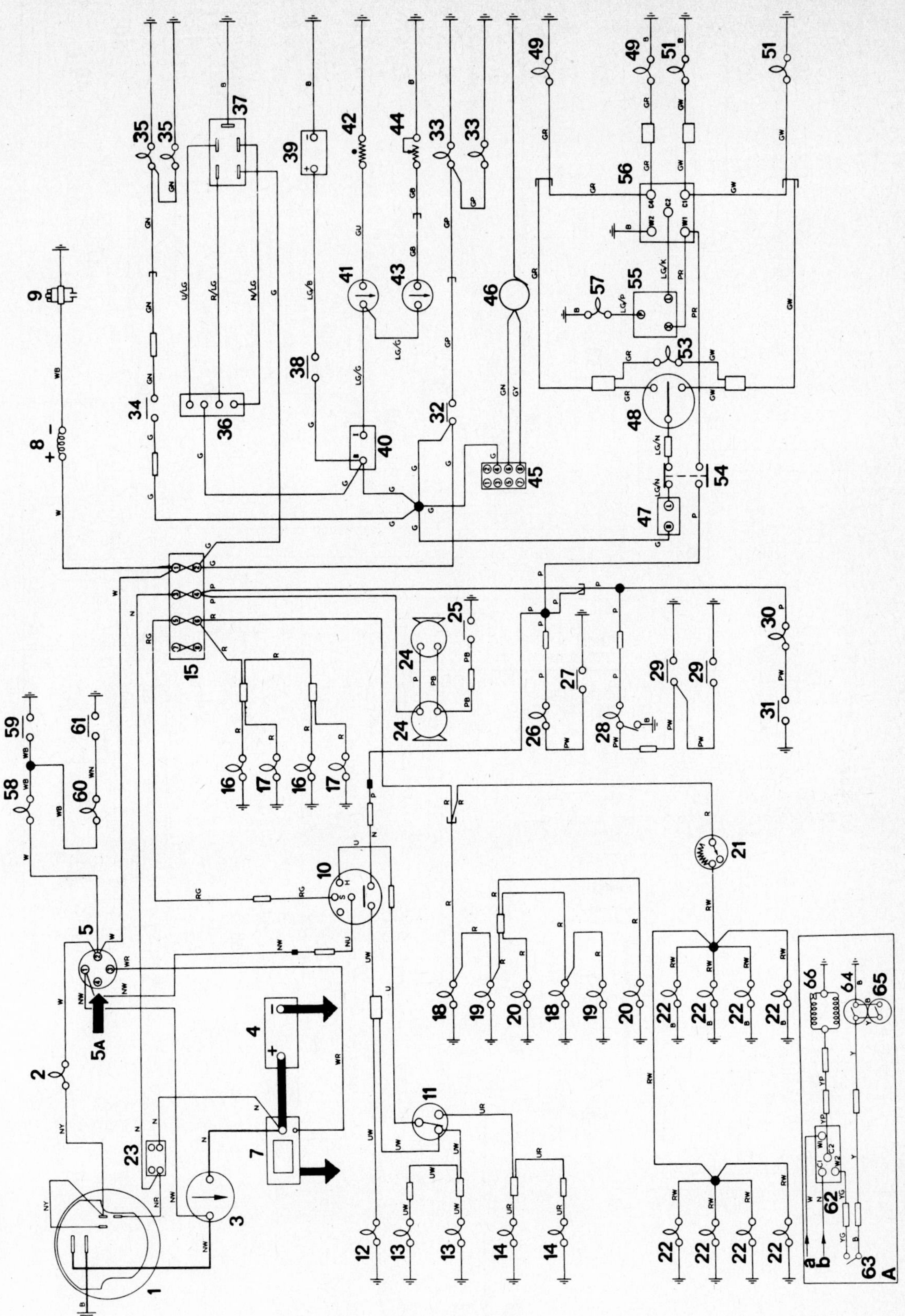

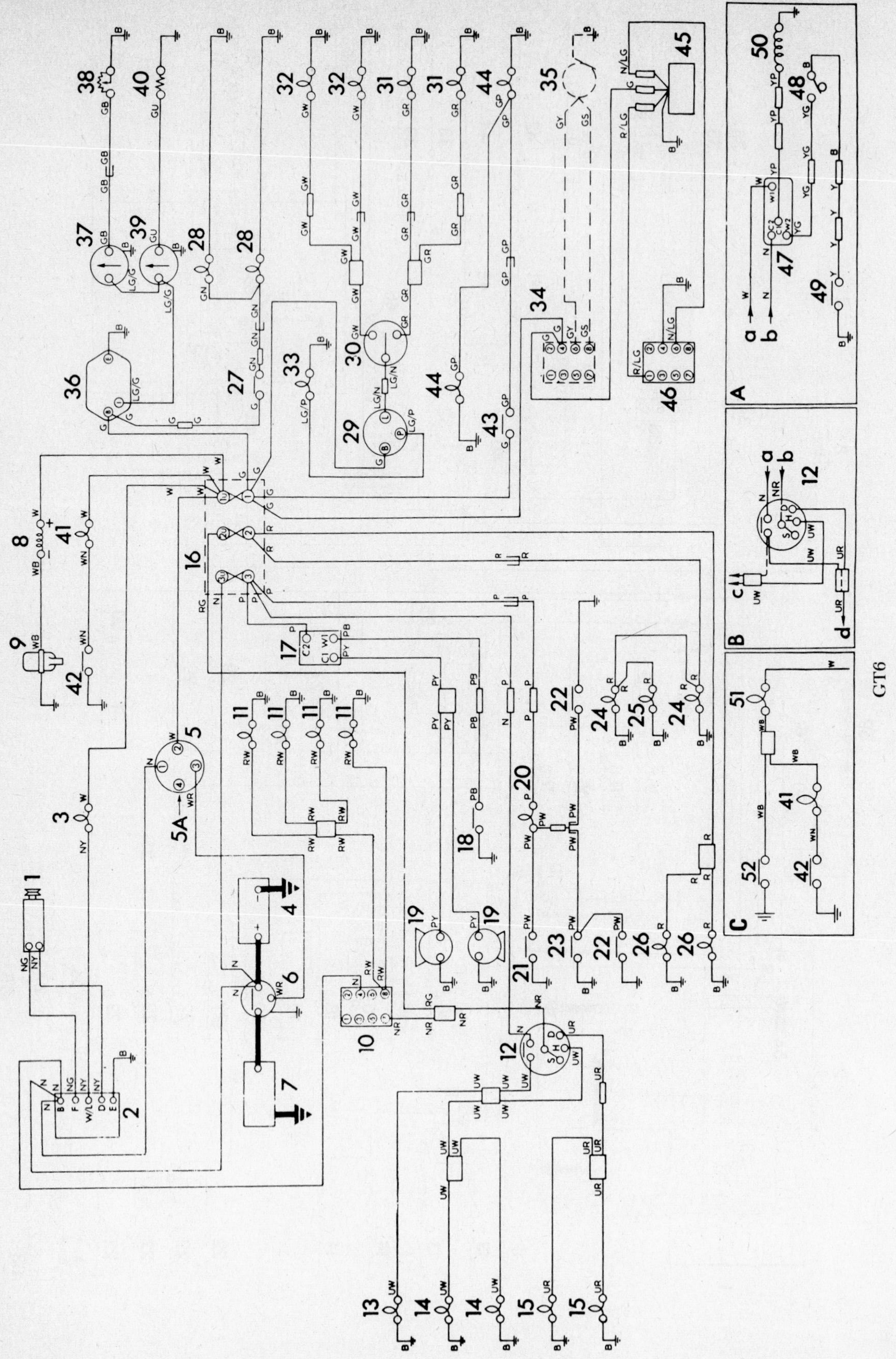
GT6

GT6 Wiring Diagram

1 Generator
2 Voltage regulator
3 Ignition warning light
4 Battery
5 Ignition/starter switch
5A Ignition/starter switch—radio supply connector
6 Starter solenoid
7 Starter motor
8 Ignition coil
9 Ignition distributor
10 Master light switch
11 Instrument illumination
12 Column light switch
13 High beam warning light
14 High beam
15 Low beam
16 Fuse assembly
17 Horn relay
18 Horn button
19 Horn
20 Interior lamp
21 Interior lamp tailgate switch
22. Interior lamp door switch
23 Interior lamp dashboard switch
24 Tail lamp
25 Plate illumination lamp
26 Front parking lamp
27 Backup lamp switch
28 Backup lamp
29 Flasher unit
30 Flasher switch
31 L.H. flasher lamp
32 R.H. flasher lamp
33 Flasher warning light
34 Heater switch
35 Heater motor
36 Voltage stabilizer
37 Fuel indicator
38 Fuel tank unit
39 Temperature indicator
40 Temperature transmitter
41 Oil pressure warning light
42 Oil pressure switch
43 Stop lamp switch
44 Stop lamp
45 Windshield wiper motor
46 Windshield wiper switch

A. Overdrive (optional extra)
47 Overdrive relay
48 Overdrive column switch
49 Overdrive transmission switch
50 Overdrive solenoid
(a) From ignition/starter switch——conector 2
(b) From ignition/starter switch——connector 1
C. GT6—Modifications to comply with U.S. Federal Standards
41 Oil pressure warning light
42 Oil pressure switch
51 Brake line failure warning light
52 Brake line failure switch

COLOR CODE

N	Brown	W	White
U	Blue	Y	Yellow
R	Red	S	Slate
P	Purple	B	Black
G	Green		
L/G	Light Green		

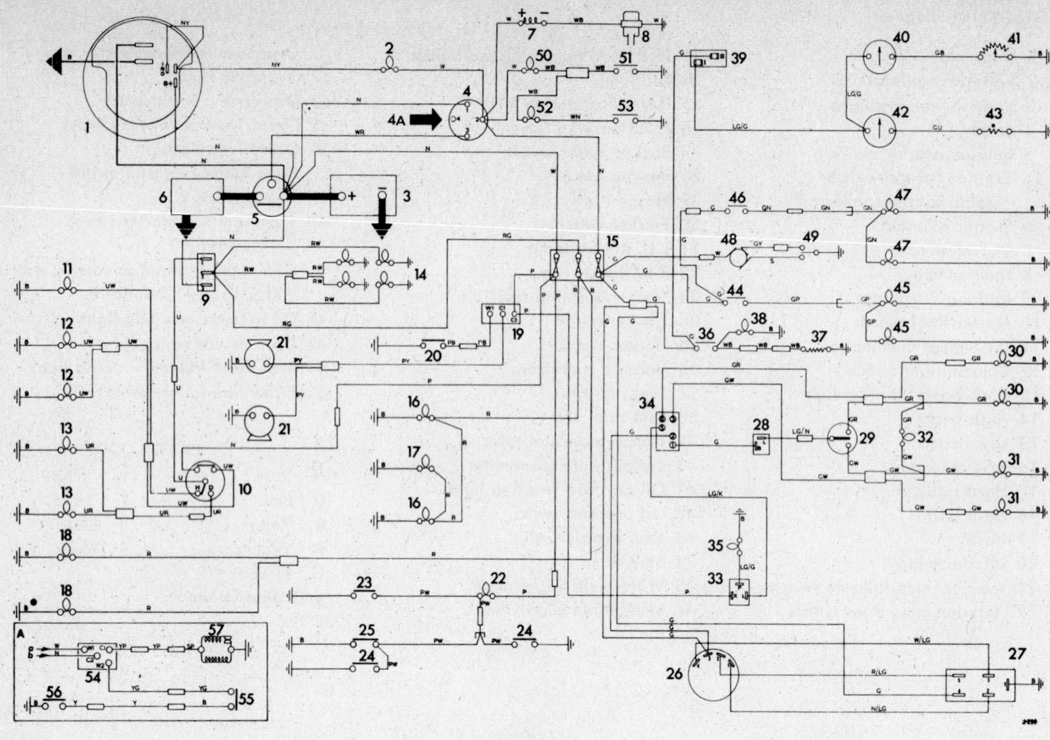

GT6+

1 Alternator
2 Ignition warning light
3 Battery
4 Ignition/starter switch
4A Ignition/starter switch—radio supply connector
5 Starter solenoid
6 Starter motor
7 Ignition coil
8 Ignition distributor
9 Master light switch
10 Column light switch
11 High beam warning light
12 High beam
13 Low beam
14 Instrument illumination
15 Fuse assembly
16 Tail lamp
17 Plate illumination lamp
18 Front parking lamp
19 Horn relay
20 Horn button
21 Horn
22 Interior lamp
23 Interior lamp tailgate switch
24 Interior lamp door switch
25 Interior lamp instrument panel switch
26 Windshield wiper switch
27 Windshileld wiper motor
28 Turn signal flasher unit
29 Turn signal flasher switch
30 L.H. Flasher lamp
31 R.H. Flasher lamp
32 Turn signal warning light
33 Hazard flasher unit
34 Hazard switch
35 Hazard warning light
36 Heated rear window switch
37 Heated rear window
38 Heated rear window warning light
39 Voltage stabilizer
40 Fuel indicator
41 Fuel tank unit
42 Temperature indicator
43 Temperature transmitter
44 Stop lamp switch
45 Stop lamp
46 Backup lamp switch
47 Backup lamp
48 Heater motor
49 Heater switch
50 Brake line failure warning light
51 Brake line failure switch
52 Oil pressure warning light
53 Oil pressure switch
A. Overdrive (optional extra)
54 Overdrive relay
55 Overdrive column switch
56 Overdrive transmission switch
57 Overdrive solenoid
(a) From ignition/starter switch—connector 2
(b) From ignition/starter switch—connector 1

COLOR CODE

N Brown
U Blue
R Red
P Purple
G Green
LG Light Green
W White
Y Yellow
B Black
S Slate

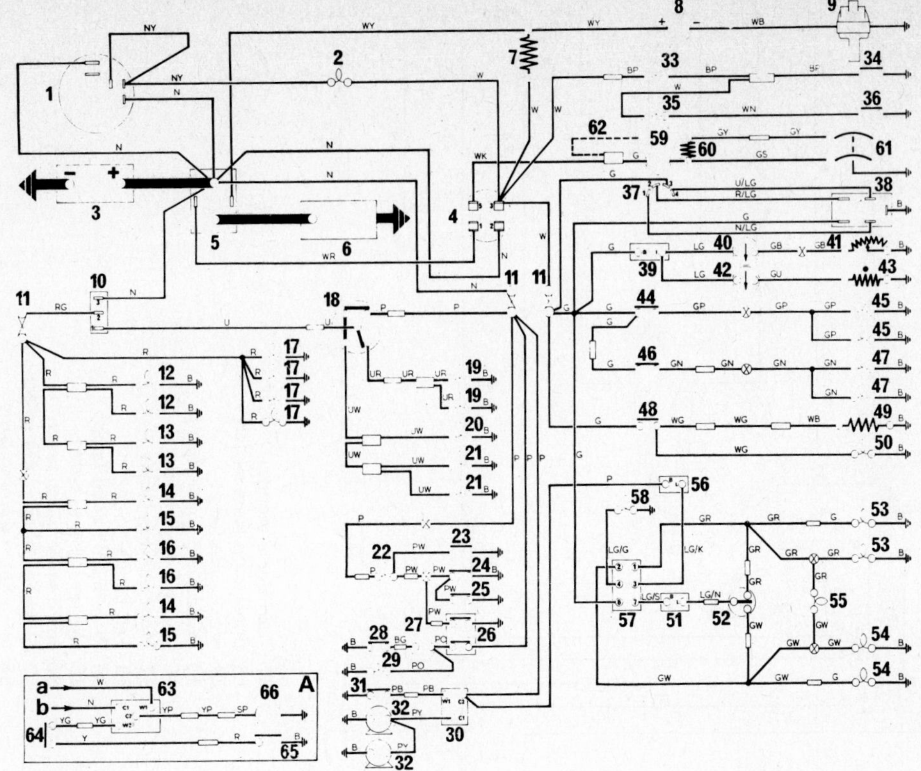

GT6 Mk III

1 Alternator
2 Ignition warning light
3 Battery
4 Ignition/starter switch
5 Starter solenoid
6 Starter motor
7 Ballast resistor
8 Ignition coil—6 volt
9 Ignition distributor
10 Master light switch
11 Fuse
12 Front parking lamp
13 Front marker lamp
14 Rear marker lamp
15 Tail lamp
16 Plate illumination lamp
17 Instrument illumination
18 Column light switch
19 Low beam
20 High beam warning light
21 High beam
22 Interior lamp
23 Tailgate switch
24 Instrument panel switch
25 R.H. door switch
26 L.H. door switch
27 Key warning buzzer
28 Key switch
29 Key courtesy light
30 Horn relay
31 Horn button
32 Horn
33 Brake warning light
34 Brake line failure switch
35 Oil pressure warning light
36 Oil pressure switch
37 Windshield wiper switch
38 Windshield wiper motor
39 Voltage stabilizer
40 Fuel indicator
41 Fuel tank unit
42 Temperature indicator
43 Temperature transmitter
44 Stop lamp switch
45 Stop lamp
46 Backup lamp switch
47 Backup lamp
48 Heated rear window switch
49 Heated rear window
50 Heated rear window warning light
51 Turn signal flasher unit
52 Turn signal switch
53 L.H. flasher lamp
54 R.H. flasher lamp
55 Turn signal warning light
56 Hazard flasher unit
57 Hazard switch
58 Hazard warning light
59 Heater motor
60 Heater rheostat
61 Heater switch
62 Radio
A Overdrive (optional extra)
63 Overdrive relay
64 Overdrive transmission switch
65 Overdrive gear lever switch
66 Overdrive solenoid
a From ignition/starter switch—terminal 3
b From ignition/starter switch—terminal 2

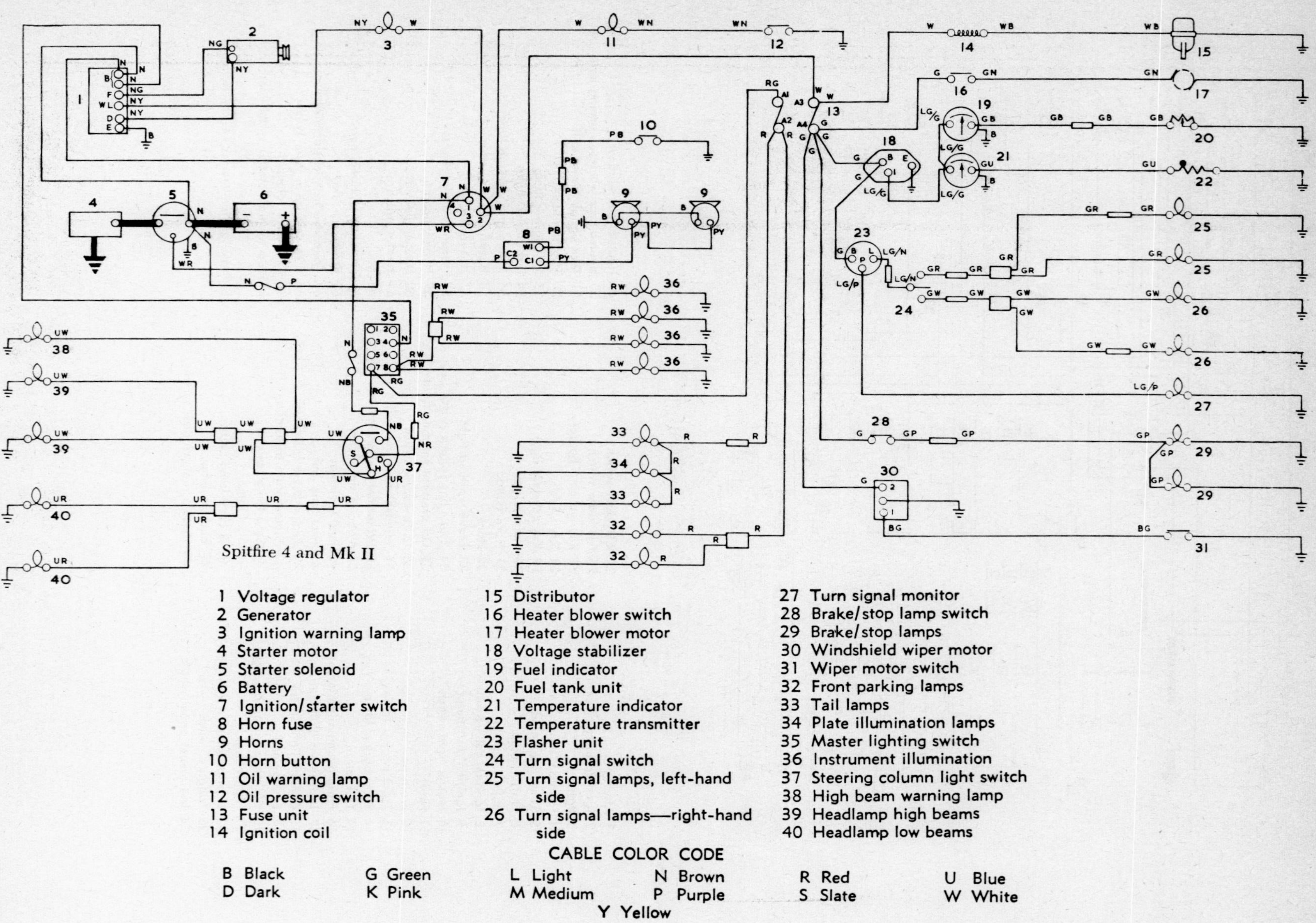
Spitfire 4 and Mk II

1 Voltage regulator
2 Generator
3 Ignition warning lamp
4 Starter motor
5 Starter solenoid
6 Battery
7 Ignition/starter switch
8 Horn fuse
9 Horns
10 Horn button
11 Oil warning lamp
12 Oil pressure switch
13 Fuse unit
14 Ignition coil
15 Distributor
16 Heater blower switch
17 Heater blower motor
18 Voltage stabilizer
19 Fuel indicator
20 Fuel tank unit
21 Temperature indicator
22 Temperature transmitter
23 Flasher unit
24 Turn signal switch
25 Turn signal lamps, left-hand side
26 Turn signal lamps—right-hand side
27 Turn signal monitor
28 Brake/stop lamp switch
29 Brake/stop lamps
30 Windshield wiper motor
31 Wiper motor switch
32 Front parking lamps
33 Tail lamps
34 Plate illumination lamps
35 Master lighting switch
36 Instrument illumination
37 Steering column light switch
38 High beam warning lamp
39 Headlamp high beams
40 Headlamp low beams

CABLE COLOR CODE

B Black
D Dark
G Green
K Pink
L Light
M Medium
N Brown
P Purple
R Red
S Slate
U Blue
W White
Y Yellow

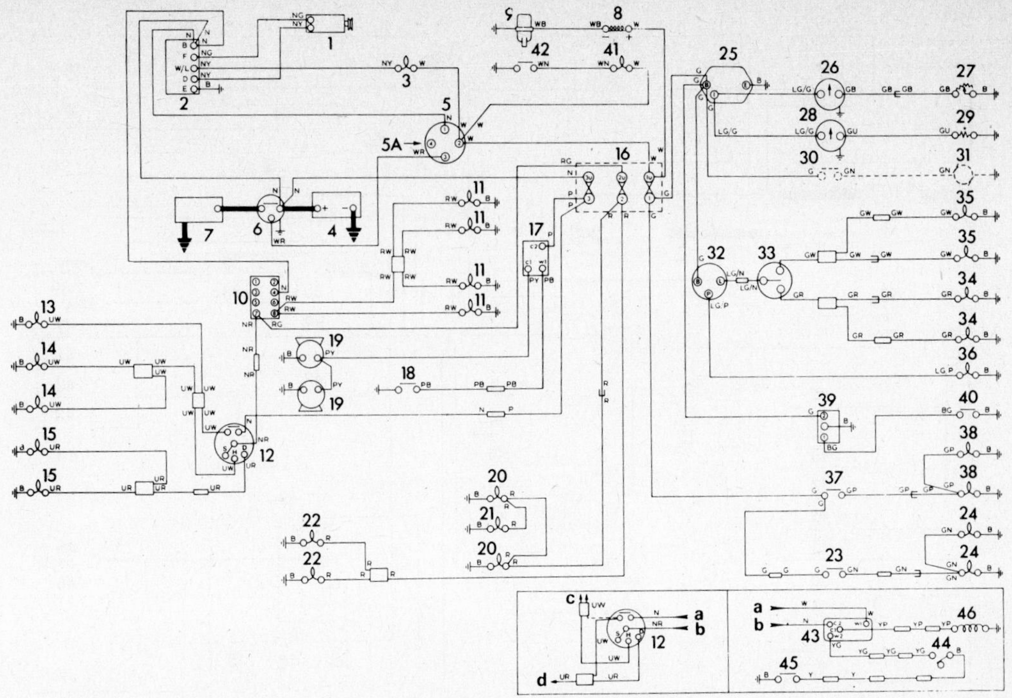

Spitfire Mk III

1 Generator
2 Voltage regulator
3 Ignition warning light
4 Battery
5 Ignition/starter switch
5a Ignition/starter switch—radio supply position
6 Starter solenoid
7 Starter motor
8 Ignition coil
9 Ignition distributor
10 Master light switch
11 Instrument illumination
12 Lights selector switch
13 High beam warning light
14 High beam
15 Low beam
16 Fuse assembly
17 Horn relay
18 Horn button
19 Horn
20 Tail lamp
21 Plate illumination lamp
22 Front parking lamp
23 Backup lamp switch
24 Backup lamp
25 Voltage stabilizer
26 Fuel indicator
27 Fuel tank unit
28 Temperature indicator
29 Temperature transmitter
30 Heater switch
31 Heater motor
32 Flasher unit
33 Direction indicator switch
34 L.H. direction indicator lamp
35 R.H. direction indicator lamp
36 Direction indicator warning light
37 Stop lamp switch
38 Stop lamp
39 Windshield wiper motor
40 Windshield wiper switch
41 Oil pressure warning light
42 Oil pressure switch

OVERDRIVE (OPTIONAL)

43 Overdrive relay
44 Overdrive column switch
45 Overdrive transmission switch
46 Overdrive solenoid
a From ignition starter switch—connector 2
b From ignition starter switch—connector 1

CABLE COLOR CODE

N	Brown	LG	Light Green
U	Blue	W	White
R	Red	Y	Yellow
P	Purple	B	Black
G	Green		

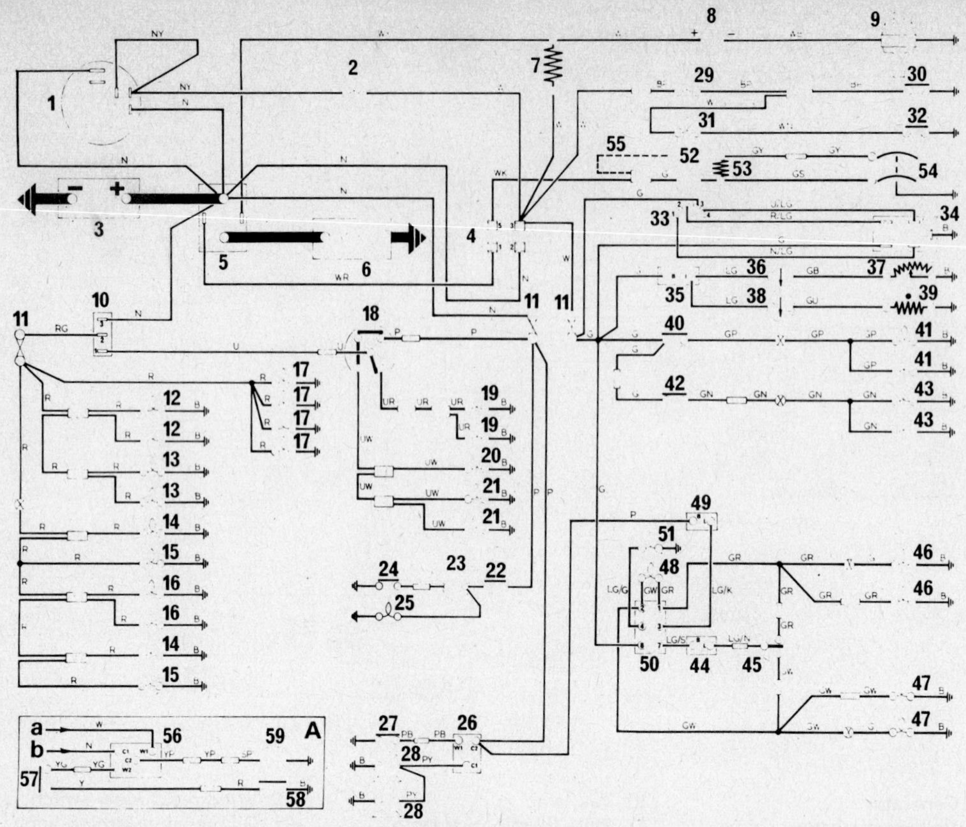

Spitfire MK IV

1 Alternator
2 Ignition warning light
3 Battery
4 Ignition starter switch
5 Starter solenoid
6 Starter motor
7 Ballast resistor
8 Ignition coil—6 volt
9 Ignition distributor
10 Master light switch
11 Fuse
12 Front parking lamp
13 Front marker lamp
14 Rear marker lamp
15 Tail lamp
16 Plate illumination lamp
17 Instrument illumination
18 Column light switch
19 Low beam
20 High beam warning light
21 High beam
22 Door switch
23 Key warning buzzer
24 Key switch
25 Courtesy light
26 Horn relay
27 Horn button
28 Horn
29 Brake warning light
30 Brake line failure switch
31 Oil pressure warning light
32 Oil pressure switch
33 Windshield wiper switch
34 Windshield wiper motor
35 Voltage stabilizer
36 Fuel indicator
37 Fuel tank unit
38 Temperature indicator
39 Temperature transmitter
40 Stop lamp switch
41 Stop lamp
42 Backup lamp switch
43 Backup lamp
44 Turn signal flasher unit
45 Turn signal switch
46 L.H. flasher lamp
47 R.H. flasher lamp
48 Turn signal warning light
49 Hazard flasher unit
50 Hazard switch
51 Hazard warning light
52 Heater motor
53 Heater switch
54 Radio
A Overdrive (optional extra)
55 Overdrive relay
56 Overdrive transmission switch
57 Overdrive gear lever switch

Engine Electrical

DISTRIBUTOR

CAUTION: *Before removing the distributor, be sure the tachometer drive is disconnected. When connecting the vacuum lines, be sure they are not reversed.*

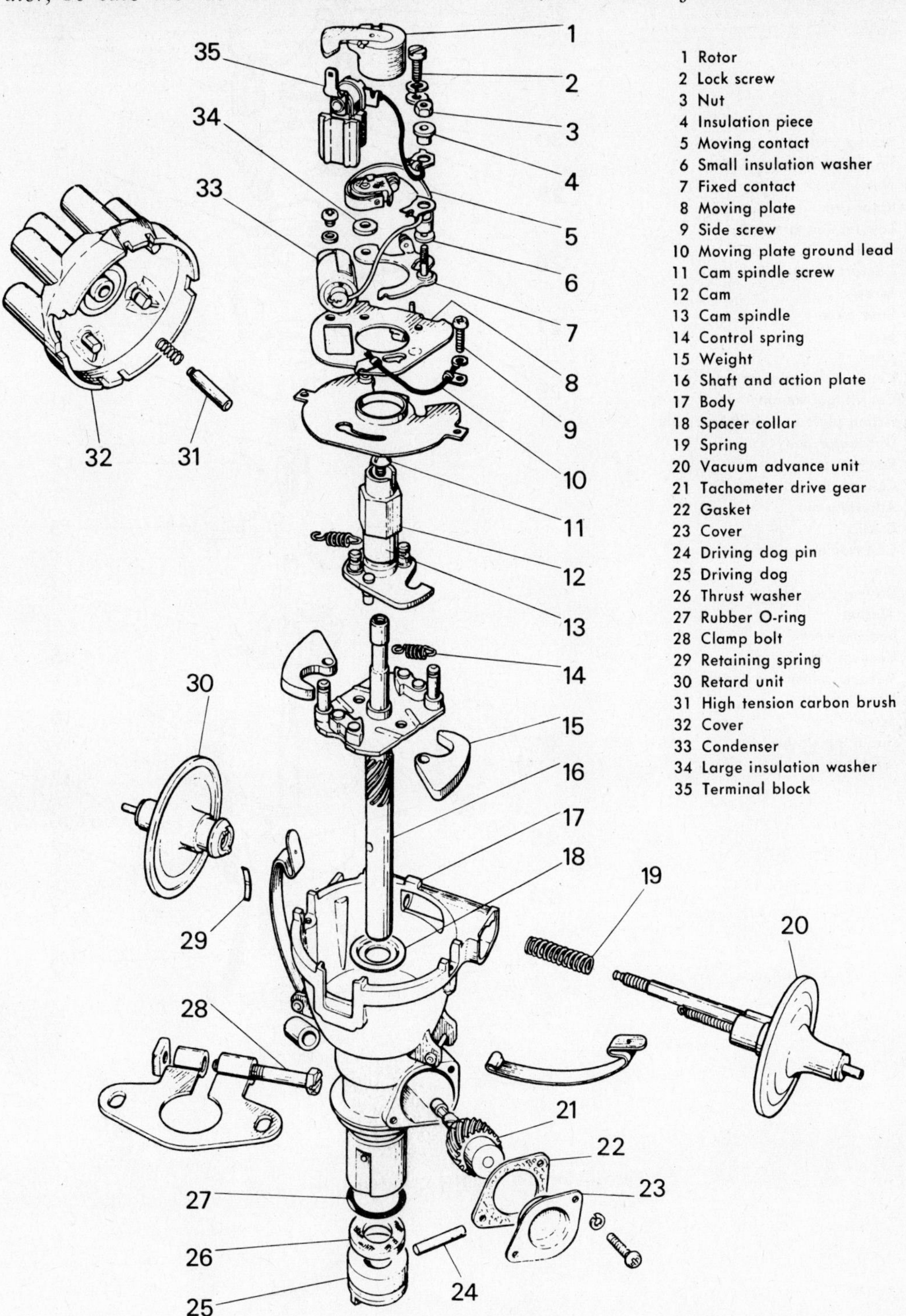

Lucas dual diaphragm distributor, TR-250 and TR-6

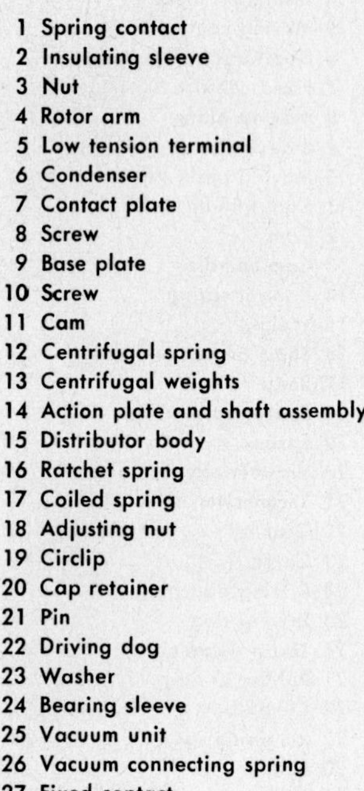

1 Spring contact
2 Insulating sleeve
3 Nut
4 Rotor arm
5 Low tension terminal
6 Condenser
7 Contact plate
8 Screw
9 Base plate
10 Screw
11 Cam
12 Centrifugal spring
13 Centrifugal weights
14 Action plate and shaft assembly
15 Distributor body
16 Ratchet spring
17 Coiled spring
18 Adjusting nut
19 Circlip
20 Cap retainer
21 Pin
22 Driving dog
23 Washer
24 Bearing sleeve
25 Vacuum unit
26 Vacuum connecting spring
27 Fixed contact
28 Screw
29 Insulating washer
30 Insulating washer

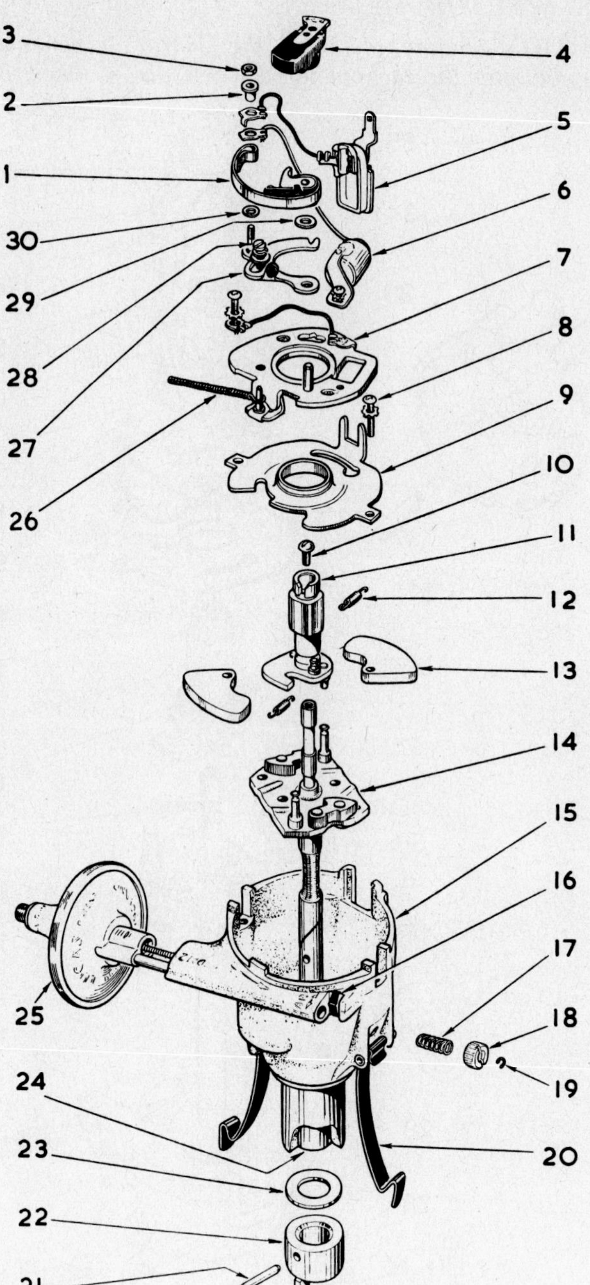

Distributor; TR-4, TR-4A, and Spitfire

1 Rotor
2 Rotor contact
3 Mounting plate lead
4 Side screw
5 Cap
6 Oil retaining felt
7 Cam
8 Cam spindle
9 Upper thrust washer
10 Short side screw
11 Housing
12 Oil retaining felt
13 Upper sintered iron bearing
14 Side screw
15 Vernier adjustment knob
16 Vacuum advance mechanism
17 Clamp bolt
18 Coupling
19 Coupling pin
20 Lower thrust washer
21 Rubber O-ring
22 Staked plug
23 Tachometer drive gear
24 Thrust washer
25 Shaft and centrifugal advance mechanism unit
26 Weight
27 Control spring
28 Mounting plate
29 Condenser
30 Eccentric screw
31 Fixed contact
32 Terminal stud inner nut
33 Moving contact
34 Terminal stud
35 Lock screw
36 Low tension wire

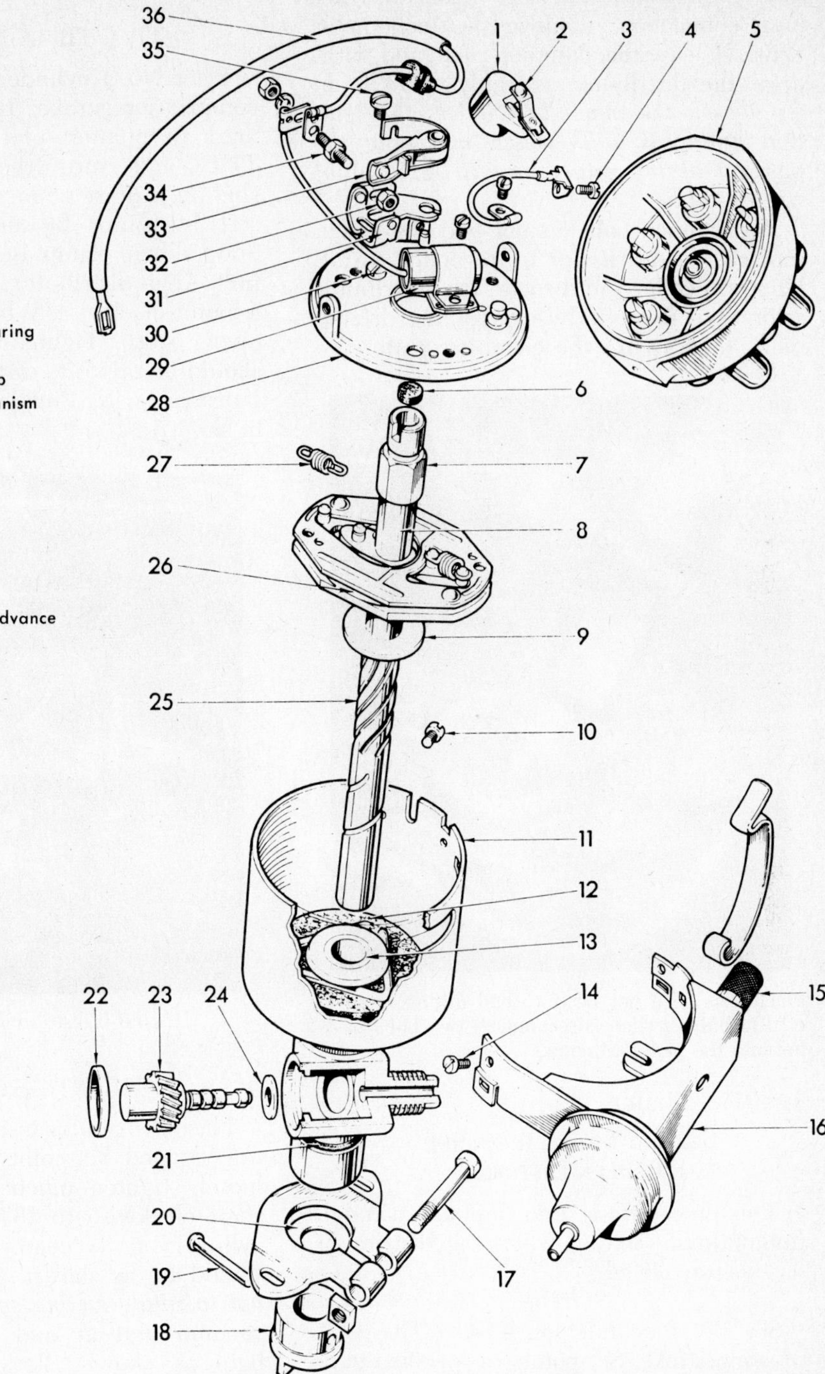

Delco Remy D202 distributor; GT6, GT6+, and GT6 MkIII

Distributor R&R

Detach the spring clips and remove the distributor cap, low tension wire, and vacuum connection. Remove the tachometer drive. Release the clamping plate and withdraw the distributor assembly. *NOTE: do not loosen the pinch bolt unless the ignition timing is to be reset, and note the position of the rotor prior to removal of the assembly.*

If the pinch bolt has not been loosened, replace the distributor by reversing installation procedure, and rotate the distributor rotor until it properly engages the driving shaft, then secure the clamping plate.

Pinch bolt need not be disturbed during removal of distributor, which is secured by two bolts passing into the pedestal below.

Ignition Timing

Setting Timing If Engine Has Been Disturbed

This procedure is used to obtain a rough initial timing setting when the distributor has been removed.

Spitfire

Set No. 1 cylinder on TDC of its compression stroke. Set points to specified gap. Place distributor and bracket in cylinder block. Be sure distributor gear is engaged.

On models without emission controls, set vacuum mechanism to fully retarded position. Turn distributor counter to direction of normal rotor rotation until points appear ready to open. Tighten pinch bolt on plate. Set final ignition timing.

On models with emission controls, start engine and accelerate to 800-850 rpm. Set final ignition timing.

TR-4, TR-4A, TR-250, TR-6

Place No. 1 cylinder at 10° BTDC on its compression stroke. If there is no timing mark or pointer, place No. 1 cylinder at TDC and turn the engine backward slightly. Adjust points to specifications. Insert distributor. Be sure gears are in mesh. Snug down clamp bracket. Loosen pinch bolt. Align distributor as shown. Rotate distributor clockwise. When points are seen to open, stop. Tighten pinch bolt. Rotor should be opposite distributor terminal No. 1 primary wire. Finalize timing with timing light.

TR-6 distributor alignment

GT6, GT6+, GT6 MK III

Place distributor in engine. Be sure gears are engaged. Set points to specified gap and loosely tighten pinch bolt. Rotate crankshaft clockwise to 13° BTDC with No. 1 cylinder on its compression stroke. Rotor should be as shown. *CAUTION: Be sure not to rotate engine counter-clockwise.* Set vacuum unit at mid scale. Connect test light as shown. Rotate distributor until points open (light goes out). Tighten down distributor. With light still attached, rotate engine until No. 6 cylinder comes up on its compression stroke. Note crankshaft pulley position when light goes out. Again rotate engine to TDC on No. 1. Note pulley position as above. Both readings should be 13° BTDC. Tighten distributor. Time engine with light to specified dynamic timing figure.

GT6 distributor in firing position for No. 1 cylinder

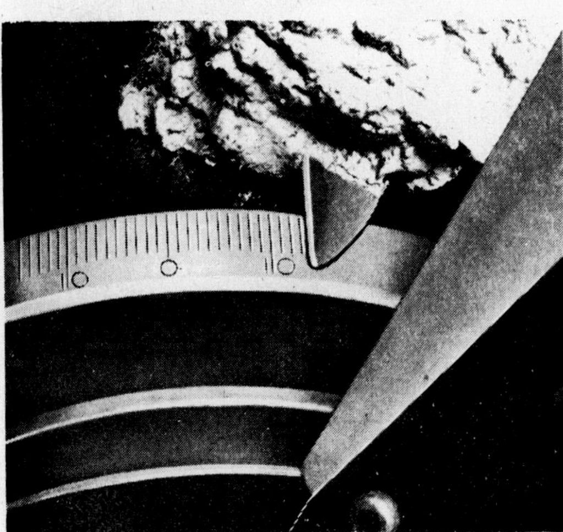

GT6 timing marks

Distributor test circuit

Final Ignition Timing

TR-4, TR-4A (Non Emission Controlled)

Ignition timing for these models is specified as 4° BTDC, static. With the hole in the crankshaft pulley flange lined up with the pointer on the timing cover (i.e., the TDC position), adjust the distributor setting so that the points are just beginning to open. Connect a test lamp to the small distributor wire leading to the coil and to ground. With the distributor set so that the points are just opening at the TDC position, rotate the micrometer ignition timing nut on the distributor counterclockwise until one extra division appears on the scale. The ignition timing will now be set at 4° BTDC.

Spitfire 4 and Mk II

The ignition timing for these models is 13° BTDC (static), and is adjusted as follows: rotate the adjusting screw on the distributor counterclockwise to fully retard the setting. Position the crankshaft so that number one cylinder is at TDC and ready to fire—the pointer on the timing cover will be lined up with the mark or hole on the rim of the crankshaft pulley. Rotate the distributor clockwise until the contact points just begin to open (a test lamp is helpful). Tighten the clamp bolt and rotate the adjusting screw clockwise 13 clicks to obtain the correct ignition timing. Each click of the adjusting screw will advance the ignition 1°.

TR-4A; Spitfire Mk III and IV
(Emission Controlled)

The TR-4A (emission controlled) has a hole on the inside face of the crankshaft pulley edge that lines up with a pointer on the timing cover when number one piston is at TDC. Static and stroboscopic timing are both specified at TDC. Time engine with strobe light at the idling speed of 850-900 rpm.

The Spitfire Mk III has two timing marks. When number one piston is at TDC, a *hole* on the inside face of the crankshaft pulley lines up with the pointer on the timing cover. When number one piston is 2° past TDC (i.e., 2° ATDC), the timing cover pointer aligns with a *mark* across the periphery of the crankshaft pulley. Timing specs are 6° ATDC (static) and 2° ATDC (stroboscopic). Time the engine with a strobe light at the idling speed of 800-850 RPM. During the initial static adjustment,

The Spitfire MK III has two timing marks: C indicates the TDC position when aligned with pointer A, while B is 2° ATDC.

When the TR-4 or TR-4A engine is at TDC, the hole in the crankshaft pulley will line up with the pointer on the timing cover.

the micrometer adjustor on the distributor should be set in the middle of its range. After the clamp bolt has been tightened, the timing should be rechecked.

GT6, GT6+, GT6 Mk III

GT6 models with emission control systems require a stroboscopic ignition timing setting for greater accuracy. On earlier models, there is no scale provided on the crankshaft pulley, necessitating the measurement of the advance and retard distances along the periphery of the pulley. When number one piston is at TDC, the timing cover pointer will line up with a white mark on the periphery of the crankshaft pulley. Set GT6 models at 6° BTDC static timing and 4° ATDC at 800-850 rpm using a timing light. The 6° BTDC timing point (static setting) is determined by measuring .3 in. to the right of the TDC mark already provided. Likewise, the 4° ATDC (*after* TDC) mark is determined by measuring .2 in. to the left of the TDC mark on the crankshaft pulley. Later models are provided with a scale that eliminates the necessity of the preceding measurements.

GT6 distributor vacuum lines. 1 is retard; 2 is advance line.

TR-250, TR-6

Ignition timing for these models is 10° BTDC (static) and 4° ATDC (stroboscopic, at 800-850 rpm). In the case of the TR-250, it may be necessary to measure off the distances from the TDC point and mark accordingly. On the TR-250 crankshaft pulley, 10° BTDC is .57 in. to the right of the TDC mark, while 4° ATDC is .23 in. to the left of TDC. As with the GT6, timing scales are provided on more recent models.

Distributor Lubrication

At 6000 mile intervals, the following service should be performed on early model distributors. *CAUTION: Be careful not to overlubricate components. Make sure points are oil free.*

Lubrication points for early distributors

1. Cam bearing—place a few drops of thin oil into the rotor arm spindle.
2. Pivot post—place a drop of clean engine oil on the tip of the post.
3. Centrifugal advance—place a few drops of clean engine oil through the opening at the edge of the contact breaker assembly. Some distributors may require oiling through the hole near the cam and opposite the contact breaker assembly.
4. Place a teaspoon of oil in the larger hole behind the condenser to lubricate the upper bearing.

LATE SPITFIRE, GT6, GT6+, GT6 MK III

Remove distributor cap and rotor. Lubricate parts 3, 4, and 6 with a few drops of clean engine oil. Place one teaspoon of oil through number 5.

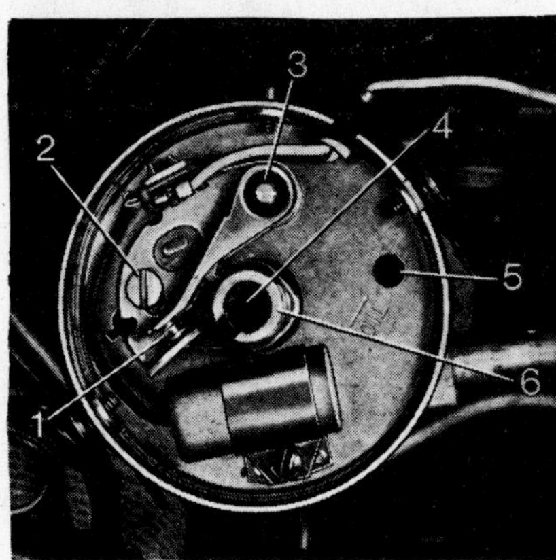

Late Spitfire and GT6 distributor lubrication points

TR-6

Remove distributor cap and rotor. Place a few drops of oil on the cam face, 5. Lightly lubricate the cam screw, 4. Place only one drop of lubricant on the breaker pivot, 6.

TR-6 distributor lubrication points

Distributor Contact Points R&R

If the contact points are badly burned or pitted, they should be replaced. Remove the wires from the connections at the post

On some distributors, point adjustment is facilitated by the provision of an eccentric adjusting screw, 2. After the locking screw, 1 has been tightened, point adjustment should always be rechecked.

that retains the spring of the movable point. Remove the screw holding the fixed point plate and remove the fixed point and plate.

To replace the points, reverse the procedure. The gap should be adjusted to .014–.016 in. (.36–.41 mm.) when the points are fully open. Adjustment is facilitated by the slot in the base plate of some units. After tightening the holding screw, recheck the point gap and adjust the ignition timing.

GENERATOR

While current Triumphs are equipped with alternators, models of recent years were provided with Lucas generators. In general, disassembly involves removing the through bolts, withdrawing the commutator end bracket, and lifting off the driving-end bracket and armature. During assembly, lubricate the porous bronze bushing with clean engine oil.

For the Lucas C40-1 generator used in the TR-4, TR-4A, and Spitfire, minimum brush length is specified as 11/32 in. (9 mm.), with spring tension on the brush 22-25 oz. The C40L generator of the GT6 should have brushes at least 9/32 in. (7.1 mm.) long under a tension of 17-32 oz. Maximum output of the C40-1 generator is 22 amperes at 2050-2250 rpm, while the C40L unit produces a maximum amperage of 25 at 2275 rpm.

Generator Testing

CAUTION: Observe correct polarity. Failure to do so will result in damage to the electrical system.

1. Remove all generator connections.
2. Connect generator terminals to jumper leads.
3. Place voltmeter (20 volt scale) between leads and ground.
4. Start engine. Accelerate to 730 rpm. Voltmeter should rise steadily and rapidly. (Do not exceed 20 volts). If generator fluctuates, or rise in voltage is not rapid, this indicates a need for repair or replacement.

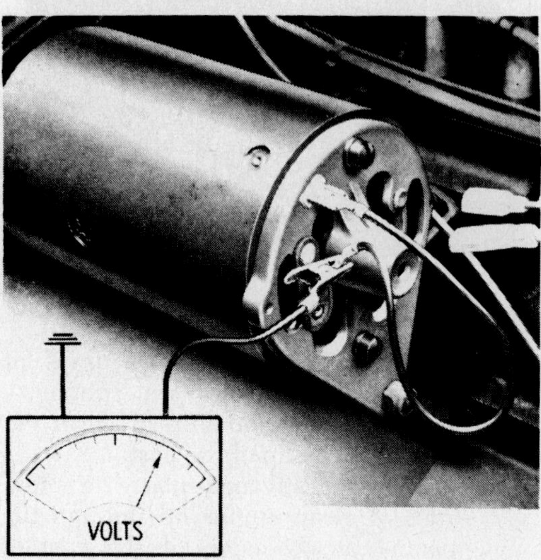

Generator test hookup

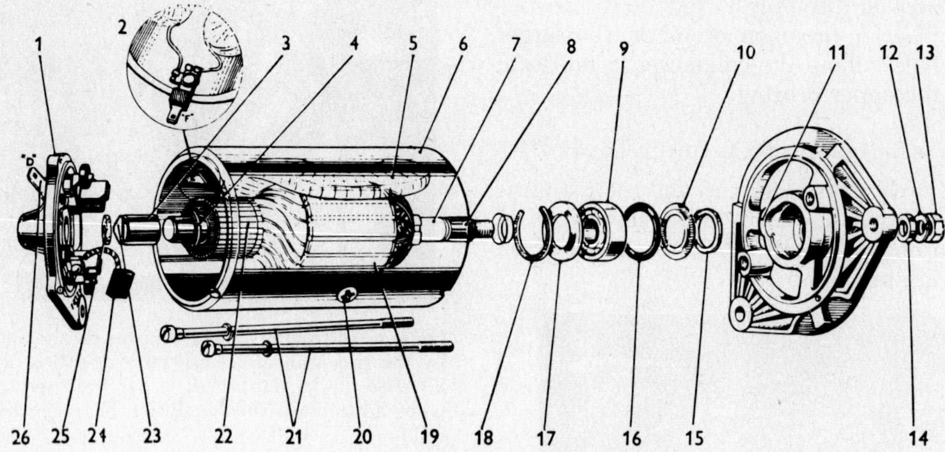

The C4OL generator used in the GT6

1 Commutator end bracket
2 Field connector and field winding ground lead
3 Porous bronze bearing bushing
4 Fiber thrust washer
5 Field winding
6 Yoke
7 Shaft
8 Key
9 Ballrace
10 Pressure ring and felt ring retaining plate
11 Drive end bracket
12 Washer
13 Shaft nut
14 Pulley spacer
15 Felt ring
16 Pressure ring
17 Bearing retaining plate
18 Circlip
19 Armature
20 Pole shoe screw
21 Through bolts
22 Commutator
23 Felt ring retainer
24 Brush
25 Felt ring
26 Output connector

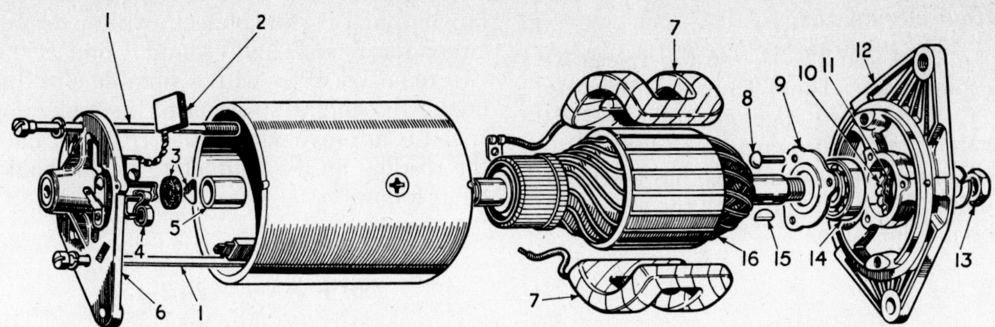

Exploded view of the C40-1 generator of the TR–4, TR–4A and Spitfire.

1 Bolts
2 Brush
3 Felt ring and aluminum sealing disc
4 Brush spring
5 Bearing bushing
6 Commutator end bracket
7 Field coils
8 Rivet
9 Bearing retainer plate
10 Corrugated washer
11 Felt washer
12 Driving end bracket
13 Pulley retainer nut
14 Bearing
15 Woodruff key
16 Armature

ALTERNATOR (AC GENERATOR)

All recent models are equipped with either Lucas 15AC (early) or 15ACR (later) alternators. Normally, this unit requires no service. If a malfunction is suspected, it is best to let maintenance be handled by a fully equipped repair shop.

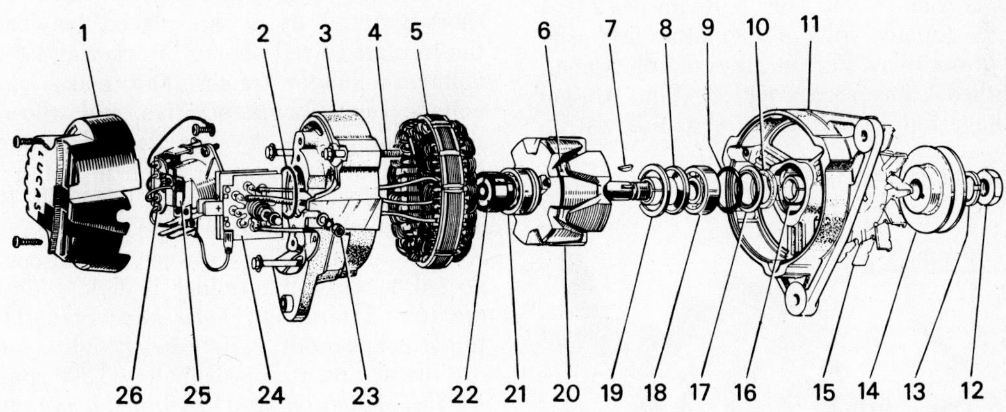

Exploded view Lucas 15 ACR alternator

1 Moulded cover
2 Rubber O-ring
3 Slip ring end bracket
4 Through bolt
5 Stator windings
6 Field winding
7 Key
8 Bearing retaining plate
9 Pressure ring
10 Felt ring
11 Drive end bracket
12 Nut
13 Spring washer
14 Pulley
15 Fan
16 Spacer
17 Pressure ring and felt ring retaining plate
18 Drive end bearing
19 Circlip
20 Rotor
21 Slip ring end bearing
22 Slip ring moulding
23 Nut
24 Rectifier pack
25 Brushbox assembly
26 Regulator unit

Voltage Regulator

The TR-4 and TR-4A use the Lucas RB 106/2 regulator. The GT6 and Spitfire use the Lucas RB-340 regulator. The TR-250 uses the Lucas 4TR regulator, and the TR-6, as well as all current models, has a voltage regulator that is integral with the alternator and non-adjustable.

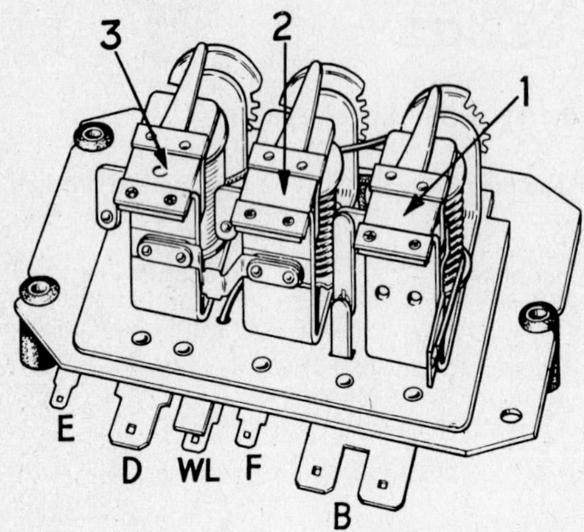

RB 340 control box, showing cutout, 1, current regulator, 2, and voltage regulator ,3.

THE RB-340 VOLTAGE REGULATOR

This voltage regulator is used in the GT6 and Spitfire, and contains three units: (1) a single-contact current regulator, (2) a single-contact voltage regulator, and (3) a cut-out relay. For purposes of adjustment, toothed cams are provided. The RB-340 voltage regulator is adjusted as follows:

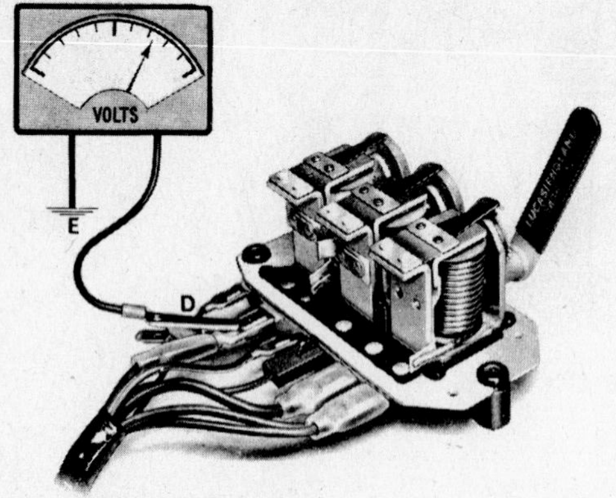

Circuitry of the voltage setting adjustment, RB 340 voltage regulator

Voltage Regulator Adjustment

Disconnect the wires from the control box terminal B and connect a voltmeter between terminal D and ground. Connect the two removed wires with a suitable clip. Increase the engine speed until the generator speed is approximately 3,000 rpm and note the reading on the voltmeter, which should be as follows:

Temperature	*Voltage Range*
50° F	14.9–15.5
68° F	14.7–15.3
86° F	14.5–15.1
104° F	14.3–14.9

If the reading of the voltmeter is outside the range specified, rotate the voltage adjustment cam clockwise to raise the voltage reading, counterclockwise to lower it. After adjusting the voltage, stop the engine, restart, and repeat the measurement procedure. *ÇAUTION: the voltage regulator adjustment and test should not be carried out for longer than 30 seconds or the heating of the shunt coil will result in false readings.*

Current Regulator Adjustment

To conduct the current regulator test, the voltage regulator contact must be short-circuited by a clip placed between the insulated fixed contact bracket and the voltage regulator frame. This makes the voltage regulator inoperative and allows the generator to develop its full output independent of the condition of the battery.

Disconnect the wires from terminals B, clip the two removed wires together, and connect an ammeter between the disconnected wires and terminal B. *CAUTION: the two B terminals must have only this single connection.* Switch on all lights and run the engine at approximately 3,300 rpm. *NOTE: switch on lights before starting engine or current may blow bulbs.* At this speed, the ammeter should register 24–26 amps for the C40L generator and 20–24 amps for the C40-1 unit. If the ammeter reading is outside these ranges, the current adjusting cam may be turned clockwise to raise the setting, counterclockwise to lower. *CAUTION: this test should also be limited to 30 seconds. The lights should not be turned on while the engine is running, but switched on before the engine is started.*

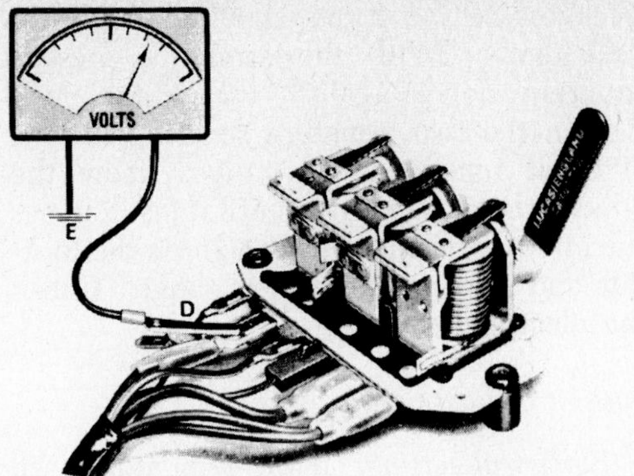

Circuitry of the cut-in voltage adjustment, RB 340 control box

Regulator Cut-in Adjustment

Connect a voltmeter between terminal D and ground. Switch on all lights and start the engine, slowly increasing its speed. While the engine is gradually accelerated, observe the voltmeter. The voltage should rise steadily and then drop slightly when the contacts close. The cut-in voltage is the figure reached just before the voltmeter pointer drops. If the headlights are turned on, the drop will be easier to spot. If the cut-in voltage is outside of the limits 12.7–13.3 volts, adjust by turning the adjusting cam clockwise to raise and counterclockwise to lower the setting. After each adjustment, repeat the test and complete within 30 seconds each time. After removing the voltmeter and replacing all disturbed components, check the drop-off voltage as follows:

Remove the wires from terminal B of the control box and connect them together.

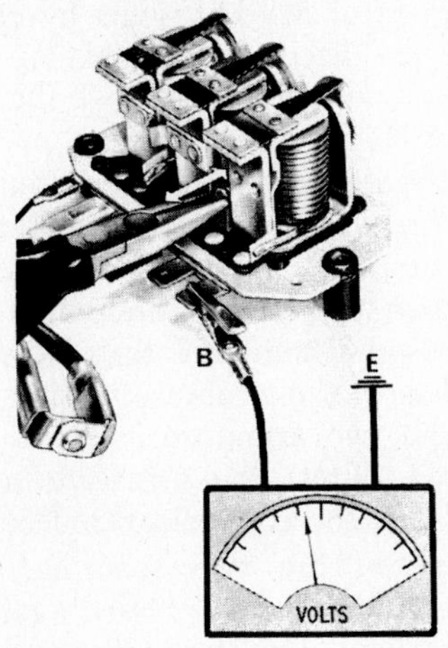

Circuitry of the drop-off voltage adjustment, RB 340 voltage regulato.

Connect a voltmeter between terminal B and ground. Start the engine and increase its speed until the cut-in speed is exceeded, then slowly decelerate the engine and observe the voltmeter needle. When the contacts open, the needle should drop to zero —this should happen between 9.5 and 11.0 volts. If adjustment is required, this is done by slightly bending the fixed contact. Closing the gap will raise the drop-off voltage, while opening it will reduce the voltage.

The RB 106/2 Voltage Regulator

The Lucas RB106/2 regulator contains two units: the voltage regulator and the cutout switch. The voltage regulator does the conventional job of controlling the generator output in accordance with the demands on the battery and its state of charge. The cutout switch connects and disconnects the battery with the generator in order that the battery will not discharge through the generator when the engine is stopped or running slowly. Adjustments to the RB 106/2 unit are the following:

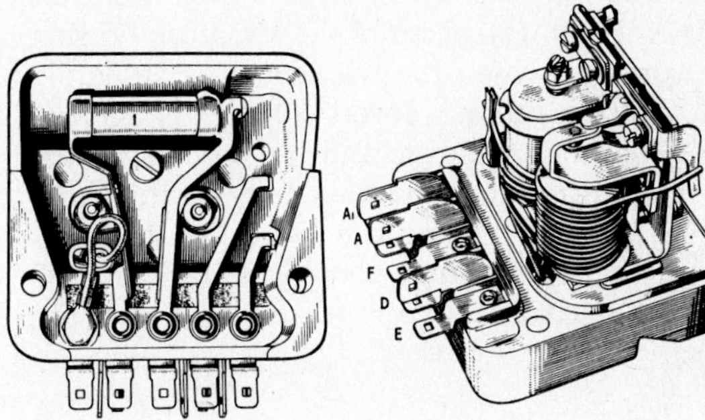

The RB 106/2 voltage regulator combines two units—a voltage regulator and a cutout switch.

Voltage Regulator Adjustments

Electrical setting: Remove the cover and place a thin piece of cardboard between the armature and the core face of the cutout in order to prevent the contacts from closing. Remove the wires from the terminals marked A and A1 at the control box and connect them together.

Connect the negative lead of a voltmeter to terminal D and the other lead to terminal E. Slowly increase the speed of the engine until the voltmeter needle flutters and then becomes steady (approximately 3,000 generator rpm). This should occur at the following range of voltages, depending on the temperature:

Ambient Temperature	*Voltage*
50° F.	16.1–16.7
68° F.	16.0–16.6
86° F.	15.9–16.5
104° F.	15.8–16.4

If the voltage indicated is outside of the above limits for the ambient temperature, stop the engine and remove the cover of the control box. Release the locknut that secures the regulator adjusting screw and turn the screw clockwise to raise the setting or counterclockwise to lower. The adjusting screw should be rotated only a small fraction of a turn at a time until the correct setting is achieved. During adjustment, do not speed the engine to more than half-throttle and make all adjustments as quickly as possible to guard against false readings due to temperature increases. Remove the cardboard from the armature and core face gap.

Mechanical setting: Loosen the locknut on the fixed contact and unscrew the contact until it is well clear of the moving contact. Loosen the voltage adjusting screw locknut and unscrew the adjuster until it is well clean of the armature tension spring. Loosen the two armature assembly securing screws. Insert a feeler gauge between the armature and the core shim. Be careful not to damage or turn up the shim. If a round separator is used, the thickness of the feeler gauge should be .015 in. (.38 mm.). If a square separator is in use, the thickness of the gauge should be .021 in. (.53 mm.). With the armature pressed squarely down against the gauge leaf, tighten the two armature securing screws. Without removing the gauge, screw the adjustable contact down until it just touches the armature contact, then tighten the locknut and remove the feeler gauge. Check the electrical setting.

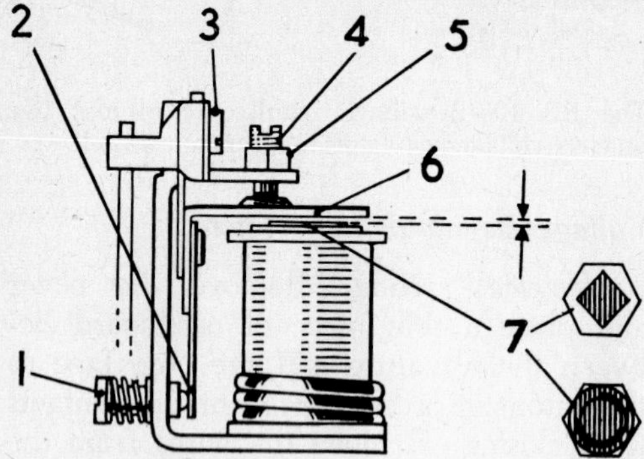

The RB 106/2 regulator air-gap setting depends on whether a square or round separator is used, as discussed in text.

1 Voltage adjusting screw
2 Armature tension spring
3 Armature securing screws
4 Fixed contact adjustment screw
5 Locknut
6 Armature
7 Core face and shim

Cutout Adjustments

Electrical setting: If the regulator is set, but the battery still is not being charged, the cutout is probably out of adjustment. Check the voltage at which the cutout operates as follows: Remove the cover of the control box and connect the voltmeter between terminals D and E. Start the engine and slowly increase its speed until the cutout contacts are observed to close, noting the voltage at which this occurs. The voltage observed should be between 12.7 and 13.3 volts. If it is not, adjust the setting as follows:

1. Loosen the locknut that secures the cutout adjusting screw and turn the screw in a clockwise direction to raise the setting or counterclockwise to lower. Turn the screw only a fraction of a turn at a time. Tighten the locknut.
2. Test after each adjustment by following the checking procedure outlined above, being careful to operate as quickly as possible to avoid false readings caused by increases in temperature.

Adjust the drop-off voltage, if necessary, to the range of 8.5–11.0 volts by carefully bending the fixed contact blade. If the cutout does not operate, remove the regulator for further examination.

Mechanical setting: If the cutout armature has been removed from the frame, adjust the mechanical setting upon reassembly. Loosen the locknut and unscrew the adjusting screw until the tip of the screw is well clear of the armature tension spring. Loosen the two armature assembly securing screws. Press the armature squarely down against the copper-covered core face and retighten the two securing screws. With the armature still pressed against the core face, bend the stop arm so that the gap between the armature stop arm and the armature tongue is .015 in. (.38 mm.).

Adjust the fixed contact blade so that it will be deflected .015 in. (.38 mm.) by the moving armature contact when the armature is pressed against the core face. Check the electrical cutout setting.

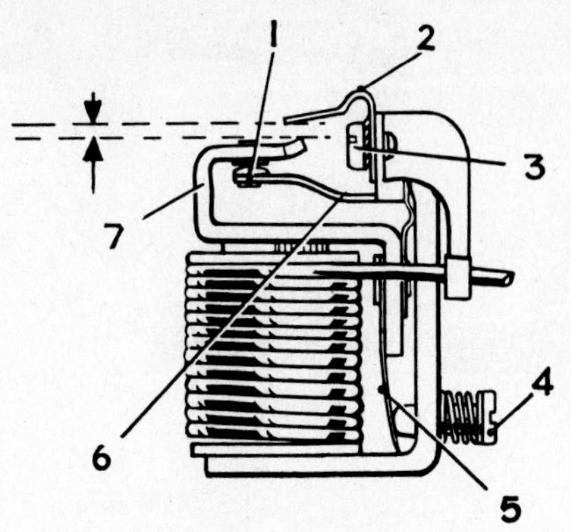

RB 106/2 cutout air-gap setting should be .015 in.

1 Follow through—.015 in. (.38mm.)
2 Stop arm
3 Armature securing screws
4 Cutout adjusting screw
5 Armature tension spring
6 Fixed contact blade
7 Armature tongue and moving contact

THE LUCAS 4TR VOLTAGE REGULATOR

The 4TR voltage regulator is used on the TR–250 which is equipped with an alternator in place of a DC generator. Because of this, the 4TR does not have a current regulator as alternators have inherent self-regulating current characteristics, and it does not have a cutout since diodes incorporated in the alternator perform this function. The only maintenance required is ensuring that the contacts, the multi-socket connector, and the cover remain clean and dry. This type of regulator is used on all current models.

BATTERY

Once a month–more frequently in hot weather–fill the battery with distilled or demineralized water to a level even with the tops of the separators between the cells.

The condition of the battery may be tested reliably with a hydrometer, which measures the specific gravity of acid in each cell. All cells should read approximately the same, and the readings should be adjusted (corrected) to reflect the specific gravity at 60° F (16° C). For every 5 F above 60° F, add .002 to the observed reading of the hydrometer. For each 5° F below the 60° F level, subtract .002 from the observed reading. Don't measure the temperature of the ambient air, but of the electrolyte itself. Compare the specific gravity of the electrolyte with the values given in the following table:

State of Battery	*Specific Gravity*
Fully Charged	1.270–1.290
Half Discharged	1.190–1.210
Fully Discharged	1.110–1.130

For climates above 90° F (32° C), subtract .040 from the above readings.

If corrosion forms in the area of the battery terminals, less efficient operation will result. To remove corrosion, a rag soaked in baking soda and water will prove effective. If baking soda is not available, ammonia will suffice. *CAUTION: Be careful not to drip either of the above solutions into the battery. Serious damage will result if this occurs.*

To prevent further deterioration of the battery terminals, coat them with some type of petroleum jelly or a commercial battery terminal preparation.

If it becomes necessary to jump start the vehicle, be sure cable polarity is correct. (positive to positive, and negative to negative). Otherwise, serious damage to electrical components will result.

STARTER

The GT6 and GT6+ are equipped with a Lucas M35G starter. The TR-4, TR-4A, TR-250, and TR-6 employ a Lucas M418G starter. Spitfires have the Lucas M35G. The Spitfire Mk IV is equipped with a Lucas M35J. The GT6 Mk III is equipped with a Lucas #25149 starter.

Starter Maintenance

The only maintenance normally required on starters is an occasional cleaning and checking of the brushes and commutator. To accomplish this, remove the starter motor, take off the metal band cover, and check that the brushes move freely in the brush holders by pulling gently on the flexible connection. If a brush has a tendency to stick, remove it from its holder and clean its sides with a cloth soaked in a safe solvent. Replace the brushes in their original positions. Brushes that will not bed prop-

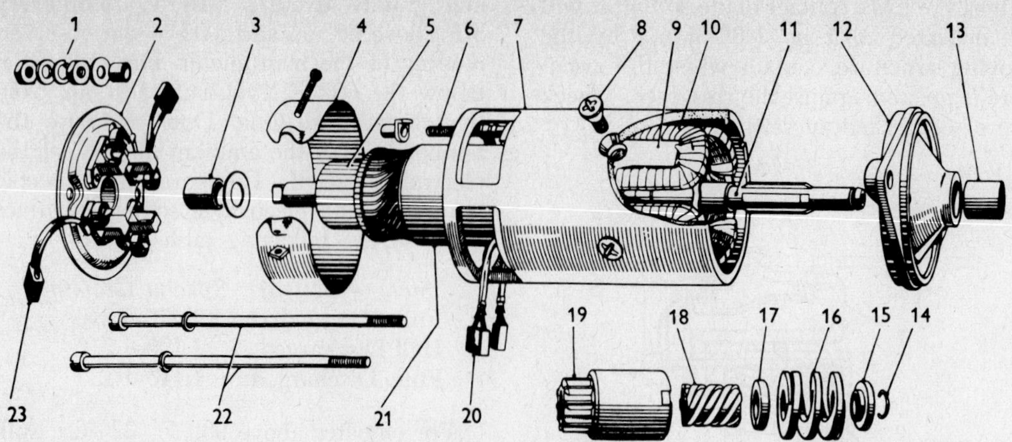

M35G starter, exploded view

1 Terminal post nuts and washers
2 Commutator end bracket
3 Commutator end bracket bearing bushing
4 Cover band
5 Commutator
6 Terminal post
7 Yoke
8 Pole shoe screw
9 Pole shoe
10 Field winding
11 Shaft
12 Drive end bracket
13 Drive end bracket bearing bushing
14 Ring
15 Shaft collar
16 Main spring
17 Buffer washer
18 Screwed sleeve
19 Pinion and barrel
20 Field winding brush
21 Armature
22 Through bolts
23 Ground brush

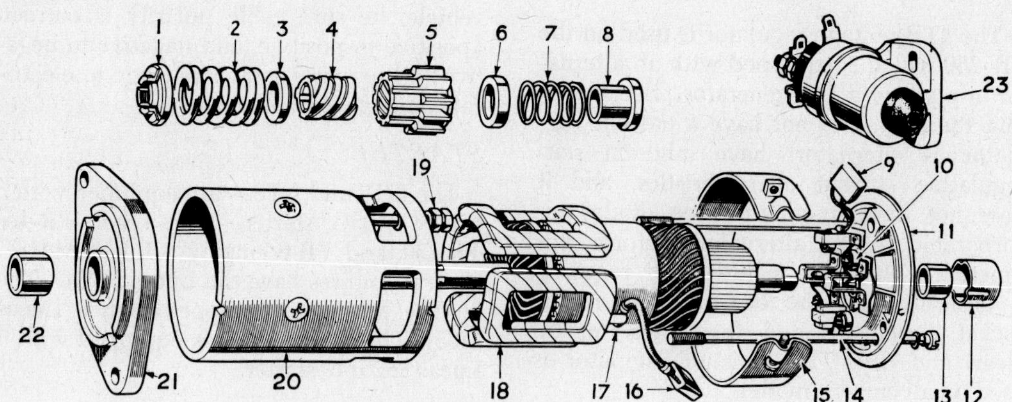

Exploded view of the components of the M418G starter of the TR–4, TR–4A and TR–6.

1 Starter drive nut
2 Starter drive spring
3 Thrust washer
4 Screwed sleeve
5 Pinion
6 Thrust washer
7 Spring
8 Collar
9 Brush
10 Brush spring
11 Commutator end bracket
12 Cover
13 Bushing
14 Bolt
15 Brush cover
16 Brush
17 Field coil connection
18 Field coil
19 Terminal
20 Yoke
21 Drive end cover
22 Bushing
23 Starter solenoid

erly on the commutator, or are less than the minimum specified length, should be replaced. Minimum length for brushes is 5/16 in. (8 mm.). While the starter is removed from the engine, check the brush spring tension, which should be 32-40 oz. for the Spitfire, TR-4 and TR-4A, 36 oz. for the TR-6, and 30-34 oz. for the TR-250 and GT6. Check the commutator for cleanliness and, if necessary, clean with a solvent moistened cloth. If the commutator is badly worn, it can be turned down slightly. The diameter must not be less than 1 9/32 in. (M35G) or 1 17/32 in. (M418G).

Typical starter solenoid used in Triumph provides a button that can be used for turning the engine from beneath the hood for tuning purposes such as a compression check.

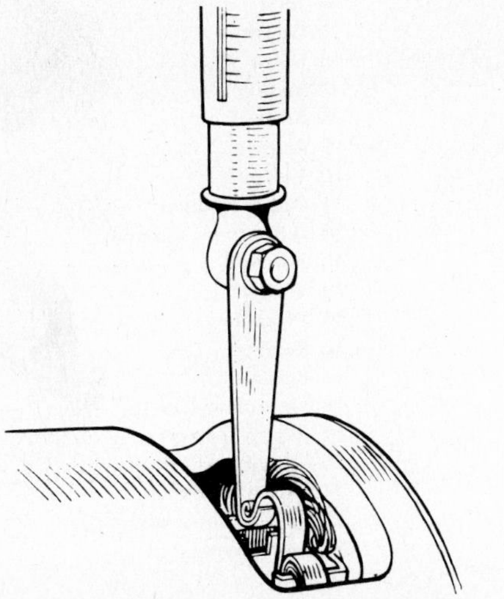

Using a spring scale to check the tension of the starter brush springs.

Starter Removal and Installation

Removal of the starter requires disconnecting all terminal connections and withdrawing all securing bolts. CAUTION: *Starter is very heavy. Be careful not to drop or damage.*

To install the starter, measure the distance between the flywheel ring gear (pinion side) and the starter mounting face. In addition, measure the distance from the starter face to the pinion end. End clearance from starter pinion to flywheel ring gear should be 3/32 to 5/32 in. (shims are available). Connect all cables. Be sure battery lead is connected last.

Fuel System

FUEL PUMP

All models are equipped with an AC mechanical diaphragm type fuel pump on the left side of the engine.

Fuel Pump R&R

To remove the fuel pump, disconnect fuel inlet and outlet lines. NOTE: *Gasoline will spill on the engine unless precautions are taken.* Unscrew attaching nuts. Pump will now be free, and can be removed.

Fuel Pump Disassembly

The mechanical fuel pumps shown in this section are disassembled in numerical order of their numbered components. When removing the diaphragm assembly, turn the assembly 90° counterclockwise before lifting it out of engagement with the link lever. When replacing the inlet and outlet valve assemblies, be sure that the valves are pointed in the proper directions. Fuel pump delivery pressure should be 1 1/2-2 1/2 pounds per square inch (psi). CAUTION: *Be certain fuel lines are snug to pump, but do not overtighten*

Fuel Pump Cleaning

Every 12,000 miles the fuel pump should be serviced. This may be accomplished by:

1. Removing top bolt and domed cover.
2. Removing gauze filter and thoroughly washing in a safe solvent.
3. Cleaning the sediment in fuel bowl with a small screw-driver. The preferred method for removing loosened sediment is compressed air. Wipe out interior of fuel bowl with soft, clean rag. CAUTION: *Interior of fuel bowl*

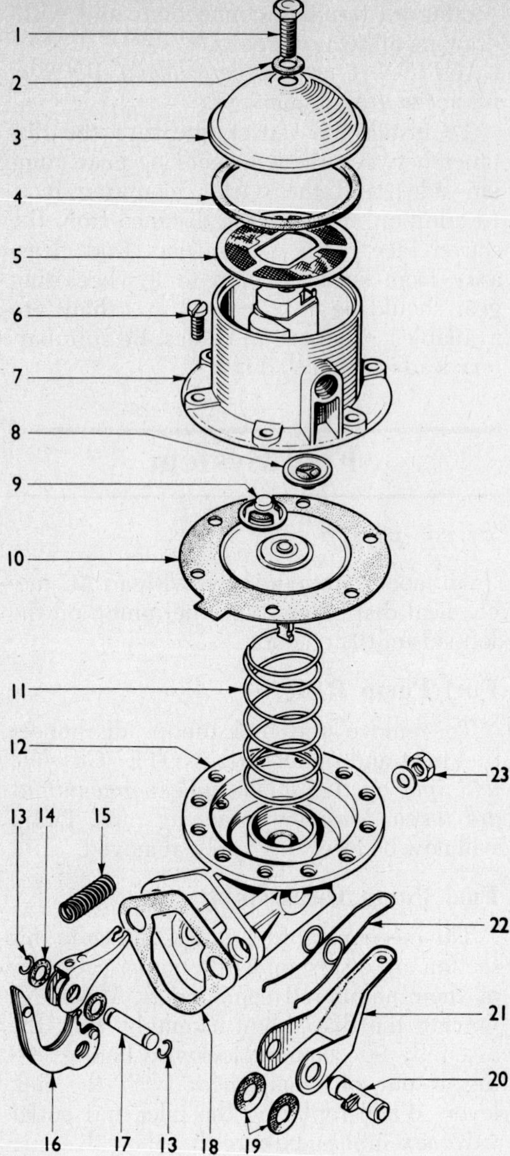

TR-6, GT6 MK III fuel pump

1 Retaining screw
2 Washer
3 Cover
4 Joint
5 Gauze
6 Screw
7 Body
8 Inlet valve
9 Outlet valve
10 Diaphragm assembly
11 Diaphragm spring
12 Lower body
13 Circlip
14 Spacer washer
15 Return spring
16 Rocker arm
17 Rocker arm pin
18 Gasket
19 Cork seals
10 Primer lever shaft
21 Primer lever
22 Primer lever spring
23 Pump retainer nut

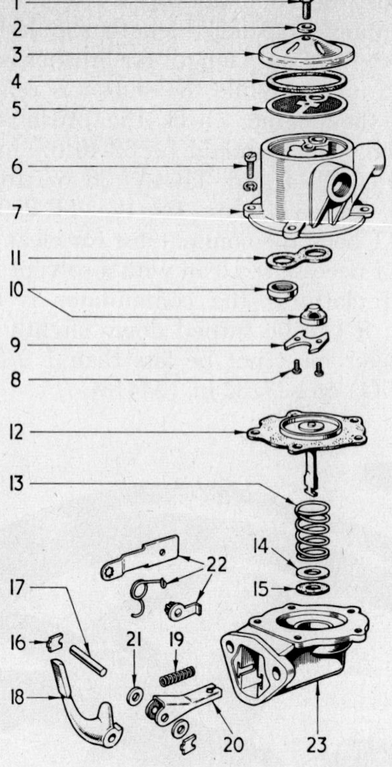

Spitfire series fuel pump

1 Retaining screw
2 Washer
3 Cover
4 Joint
5 Gauze
6 Screw
7 Body
8 Screws
9 Retainer
10 Valves
11 Upper retainer
12 Diaphragm assembly
13 Spring
14 Washer
15 Washer
16 Retainer
17 Spindle
18 Operating lever
19 Return spring
20 Operating fork
21 Distance washer
22 Priming lever assembly
23 Lower body

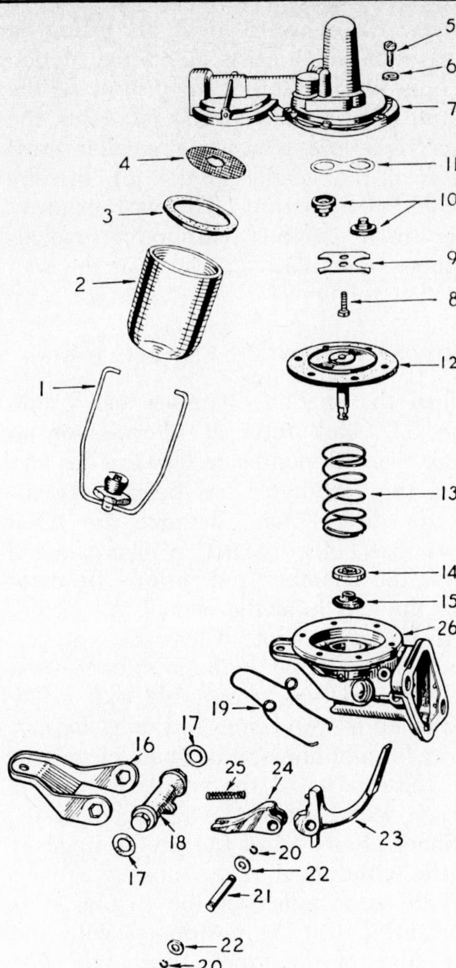

TR-4, TR-4A, TR-250 fuel pump

1 Stirrup
2 Glass sediment bowl
3 Cork seal
4 Gauze filter
5 Securing screw
6 Lock washer
7 Upper body
8 Screw for retaining plate
9 Valve retaining plate
10 Inlet and outlet valve assemblies
11 Valve gasket
12 Diaphragm assembly
13 Diaphragm spring
14 Oil seal retainer
15 Oil seal
16 Primer lever
17 Cork washer
18 Primer lever shaft
19 Hand primer spring
20 Circlip
21 Rocker arm pin
22 Washer
23 Rocker arm
24 Link lever
25 Rocker arm spring
26 Lower body

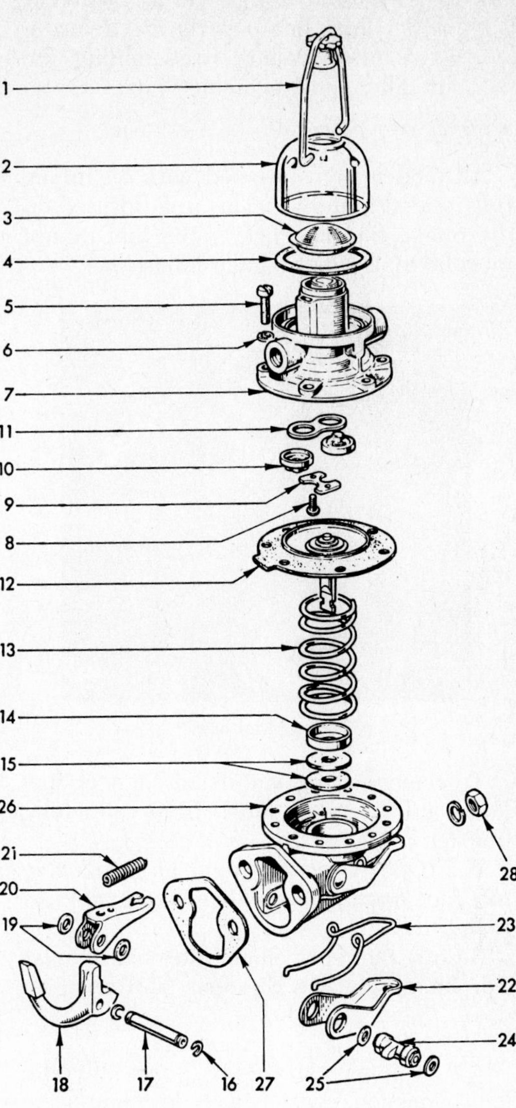

GT6, GT6+, GT6 MK III fuel pump

1 Stirrup
2 Sediment bowl
3 Filter gauze
4 Cork seal
5 Screw
6 Spring washer
7 Upper body
8 Retaining plate screw
9 Retaining plate
10 Valve assemblies
11 Valve gasket
12 Diaphragm assembly
13 Diaphragm spring
14 Cup
15 Washers
16 Circlip
17 Rocker arm pin
18 Rocker arm
19 Spacer washers
20 Link lever
21 Rocker arm spring
22 Primer lever
23 Primer lever spring
24 Primer lever shaft
25 Cork seals
26 Lower body
27 Pump gasket
28 Pump retainer nut

must be absolutely free of grease or lint.

4. Renewing the cork gasket if cracked or brittle. Fuel pump parts are delicate; use caution. When reassembling, be sure filter gauze is facing down.

FUEL FILTER

All models are equipped with an inline, fully sealed fuel filter. This unit, located on the intake fuel line before the fuel pump, must be replaced at regular intervals.

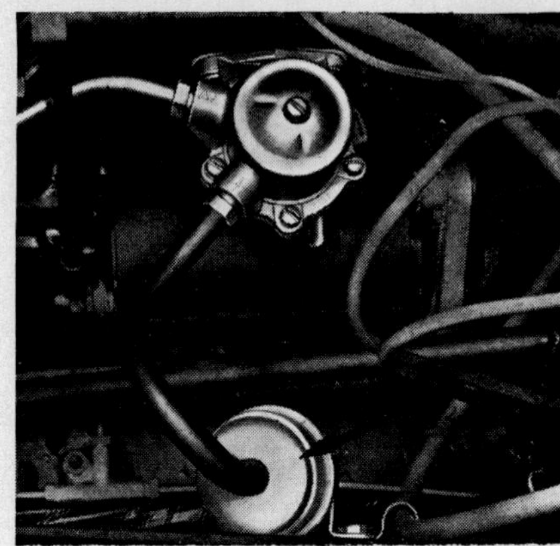

Typical fuel filter

To remove filter, simply disconnect fuel lines and remove filter from attaching bracket.

CAUTION: A small amount of gasoline in the fuel lines will spill when the filter is removed.

Be sure the replacement filter has its inlet side facing towards the floor (downward).

CARBURETORS

All Triumph carburetors, especially the later emission controlled type, should be considered precision instruments. Servicing procedures should not be undertaken unless one is fully prepared with the proper replacement gaskets and an adequate knowledge of carburetor workings. All original adjustments and positioning of various parts should be carefully noted.

S.U. Carburetors

The H6 and HS2 carburetors used in the TR-4 and Spitfire 4, Mk II and III are of very simple construction, and as a result require relatively little attention. The mixture of fuel and air is determined by the position of the tapered needle in its jet. The carburetor piston, to which the needle is attached, moves the needle along its upward-downward path according to the vacuum which exists above the suction disc built into the top of the piston. As the vacuum (and engine speed) increases, the piston rises and exposes a smaller cross section of the needle to the jet, thereby enriching the mixture. The vast majority of service to the S.U. carburetor involves the three operations discussed in the sections that follow:

Suction Chamber and Piston Cleaning

Clean the suction chamber and piston of an S.U. carburetor at intervals of no greater than 12 months or 12,000 miles and also if the carburetor has been disassembled for any reason. Remove the three screws that hold the suction chamber and remove the chamber and piston. Be careful of the needle at the end of the piston, for it is easily bent. Clean the suction chamber and piston with a solvent-moistened rag and then reassemble with a few drops of oil on the piston rod only. Do not use any form of abrasive or metal cleaner to clean these parts. If the needle is bent or loose, it will have to be replaced or repositioned. Removal of the needle involves only the withdrawal of the setscrew. When a needle is installed in the piston, it is important that it be positioned with the lower edge of the groove flush with the base of the piston.

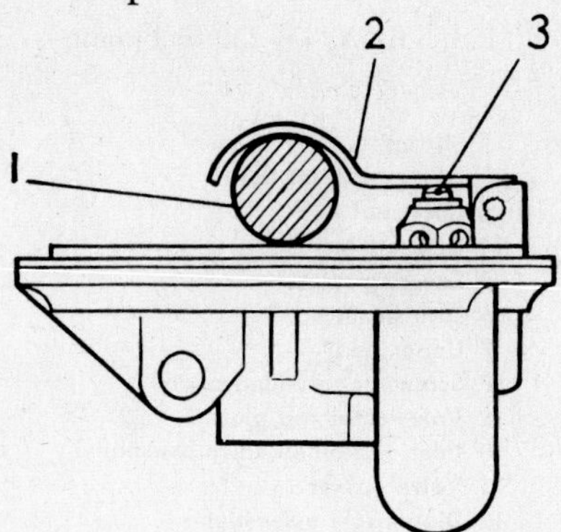

Checking the float level of the TR–4 carburetor. Lever should be bent only where curved portion intersects with straight section.

Float Level Adjustment

The float level setting of the S.U. carburetor should be closely adhered to. When the float level of the TR-4 H6 carburetor is correct, a 7⁄16 in. (11 mm.) test bar will just slide between the float lid face and the inside curve of the float lever fork when

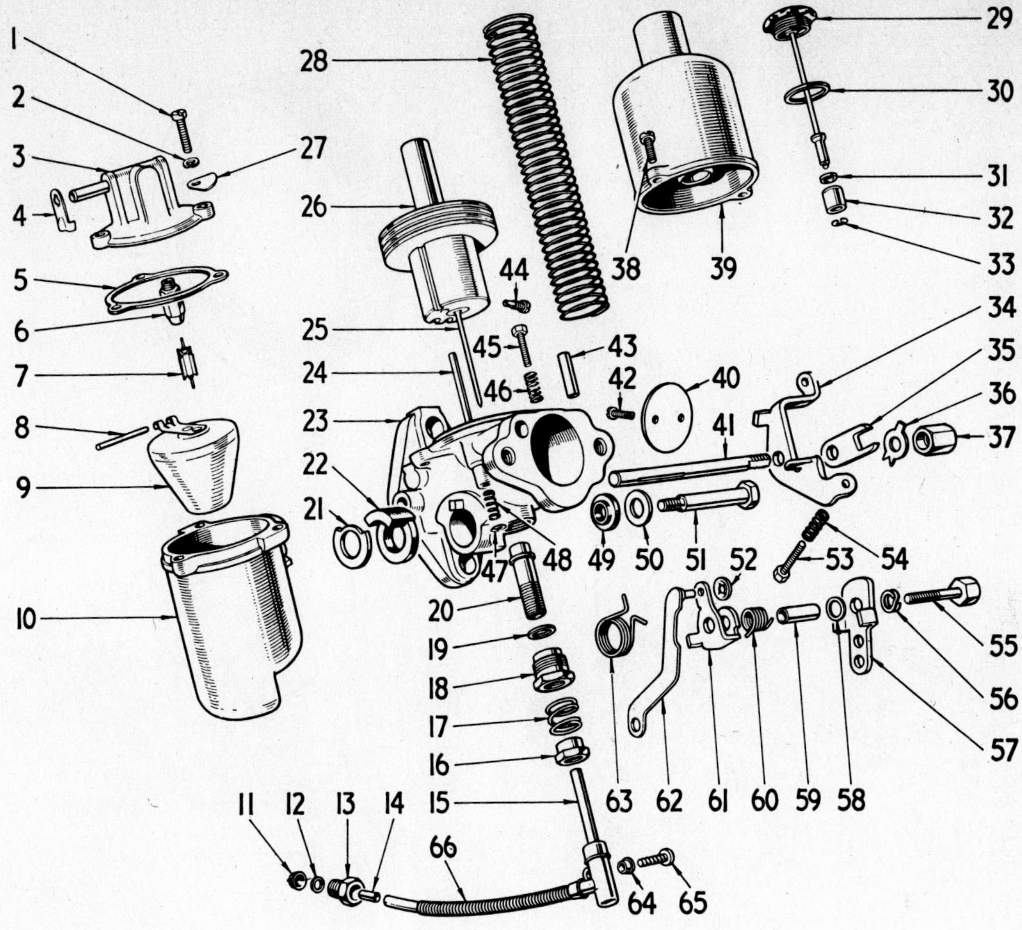

S.U. HS2 carburetor

1 Screw
2 Spring washer
3 Float chamber lid
4 Breather hole shroud
5 Gasket
6 Needle valve body
7 Needle valve
8 Float spindle
9 Float
10 Float chamber
11 Cup
12 Washer
13 Union nut
14 Sleeve
15 Jet
16 Adjusting nut
17 Spring
18 Gland nut
19 Washer
20 Jet holder
21 Washer
22 Rubber seal
23 Main body
24 Lifting pin
25 Needle
26 Piston
27 Identification plate
28 Spring
29 Cap
30 Washer
31 Washer
32 Piston
33 Circlip
34 Throttle adjusting bracket
35 Throttle fork
36 Lock tab
37 Nut
38 Screw
39 Vacuum chamber
40 Throttle disc
41 Throttle spindle
42 Screw
43 Mixture enrichment cable abutment
44 Needle retaining screw
45 Throttle adjusting screw
46 Spring
47 Circlip
48 Spring
49 Rubber seal
50 Plain washer
51 Bolt
52 Circlip
53 Throttle adjusting screw
54 Spring
55 Bolt
56 Spring washer
57 Cam lever
58 Distance washer
59 Tube
60 Return spring
61 Pick-up lever
62 Jet lever
63 Return spring
64 Shouldered washer
65 Screw
66 Flexible pipe

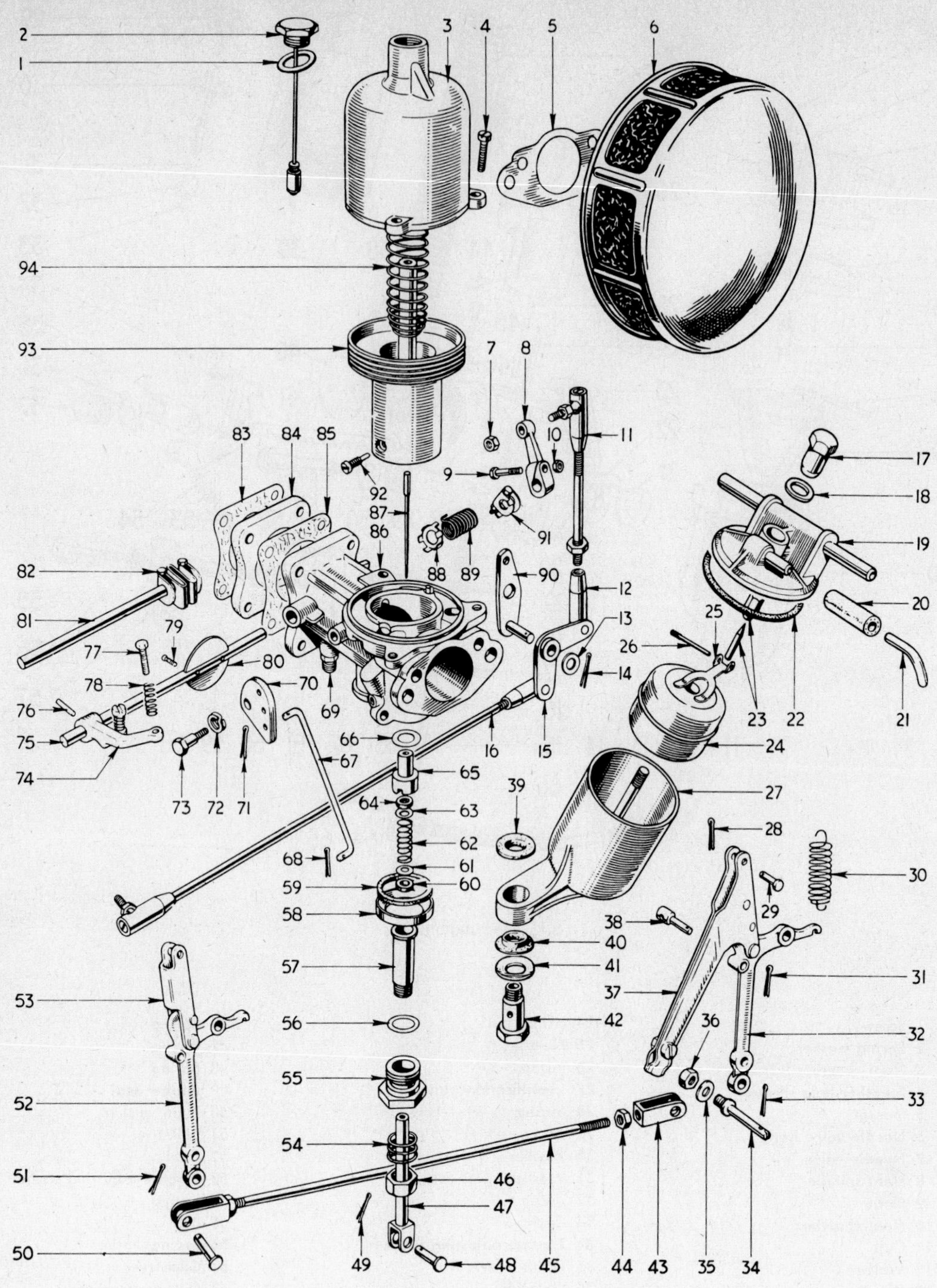

S.U. H6 carburetor

1 Filber washer
2 Damper assembly
3 Suction chamber
4 Screw
5 Gasket
6 Air cleaner
7 Nut
8 Throttle lever
9 Pinch bolt
10 Nut
11 Link rod coupling
12 Link rod coupling
13 Plain washer
14 Cotter pin
15 Relay lever
16 Link rod assembly
17 Cap nut
18 Washer
19 Front chamber cover
20 Fuel pipe coupling
21 Fuel pipe
22 Gasket
23 Needle valve
24 Float
25 Fork
26 Hinge pin
27 Float chamber
28 Cotter pin
29 Pin
30 Jet lever return spring
31 Cotter pin
32 Jet lever
33 Cotter pin
34 Choke cable connector
35 Washer
36 Nut
37 Jet link and choke cable support
38 Pin
39 Washer
40 Shouldered washer
41 Washer
42 Float chamber attachment bolt
43 Forked end
44 Nut
45 Jet control connecting link
46 Jet adjusting nut
47 Jet head
48 Pin
49 Pin
50 Pin
51 Cotter pin
52 Jet lever
53 Jet lever link
54 Loading spring
55 Jet locking nut
56 Washer
57 Bottom half, jet bearing
58 Sealing ring
59 Cork washer
60 Cork gland washer
61 Copper gland washer
62 Spring between gland washer
63 Copper gland washer
64 Cork gland washer
65 Top half, jet bearing
66 Washer
67 Choke/throttle interconnecting link
68 Cotten pin
69 Cotter pin
70 Lever cam
71 Cotter pin
72 Double spring washer
73 Shouldered bolt
74 Throttle stop
75 Throttle stop
76 Pin
77 Stop adjusting screw
78 Spring
79 Throttle butterfly screw
80 Butterfly
81 Throttle connecting rod
82 Coupling
83 Gasket
86 Carburetor body
87 Needle
88 Anchor plate
89 Return spring
90 Pivot lever
91 End clip
92 Needle locking screw
93 Piston
94 Piston spring

the needle valve is in the closed position. If the test bar does not fit snugly, bend the float lever in the necessary direction to bring about the proper level. Bend the lever only at the intersection of the curved and straight portions. Both prongs of the fork should be kept level, and the straight portion should be kept perfectly flat. Once the float level has been set correctly,

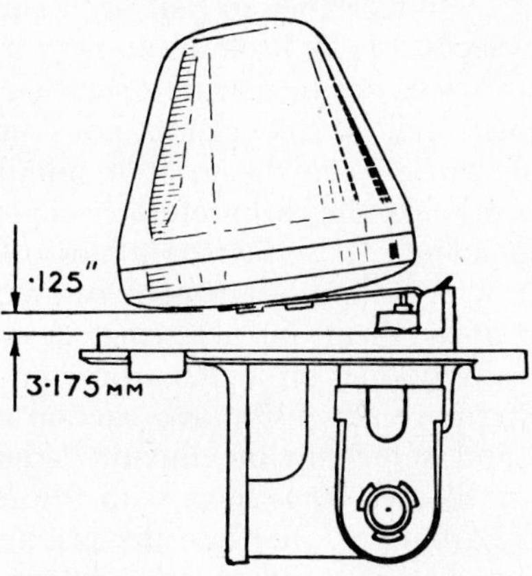

Float of Spitfire 4, Mk II and III should be as shown.

chances are that it won't have to be changed very often. Flooding will more likely be the result of a leaky float, excessive friction in the float lever, or a sticking needle valve.

Adjust the float level of the Spitfire 4 and Mk II HS2 carburetor in similar fashion. There should be ⅛ in. (3.18 mm.) clearance between the end of the float lever and the nearer lid face, as shown in the accompanying illustration.

Centering the Jet

NOTE: when performing the centering operation, be careful not to bend the needle. If the jet is correctly centered, the piston should fall freely and hit the jet bridge with a metallic click when the jet adjusting nut is in its uppermost position. If the metallic click is audible only when the jet is in its lowest position, the jet must be centralized. With the jet in its uppermost position (do not force the jet upward if it is impeded by the piston needle; temporarily remove the piston), loosen the jet locking nut and move the jet assembly laterally until the jet is concentric with the needle. Tighten the locking nut. The piston should now be able to fall freely and hit the jet bridge with a metallic click. Check the centering of the jet by noting the difference in sound when: (1) the piston drops onto the jet when the jet is in its highest position, and (2) when the piston is dropped when the jet is in its lowest position. If there is any difference in sound between conditions (1) and (2), the adjustment process will have to be repeated. When the operation is completed, top up the dampers and adjust the mixture setting of the carburetors.

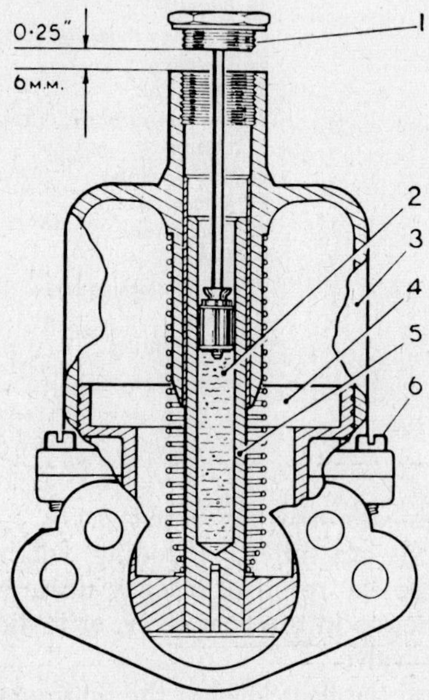

Damper of TR–4 carburetor should be filled with oil to a level where resistance is just felt when the damper cap is about ¼ inch above the top of the vacuum chamber.

1 Damper
2 Oil well
3 Suction chamber
4 Piston
5 Piston rod
6 Screw

Damper Assembly Lubrication

Every 3,000 miles, the damper reservoirs should be topped up with thin engine oil (SAE 20 or 30) to a level where resistance is felt when the damper cap is ¼ in. (6 mm.) above the top of the vacuum chamber. The damper assembly enriches the mixture during acceleration and cold starting. If the oil well does not have sufficient lubricant in it, the damper will not function.

Mixture is adjusted by rotating jet adjusting nuts (16) up or down. Other parts shown are jet (15) and throttle stop screw (45).

Tuning and Synchronization

Before tuning the carburetors, ascertain that all other engine adjustments, and the engine itself, are up to specifications. Carburetor tuning will be only as good as the engine adjustments that precede it. The tuning of the TR-4 and Spitfire 4 and Mk II carburetors is limited to the adjustment of the slow-speed (idle) mixture, the slow-speed synchronization, and the fast-idle speed.

In tuning the S.U. carburetors, first remove the air cleaner so that each carburetor is accessible by itself. Next, with the engine warmed up to normal operating temperature, release the clamp bolts on the couplings between the throttle spindles in order to make the carburetors mechanically independent. Close throttle plates fully by unscrewing idling adjustment screws, and then open them by screwing down 1½ turns. Working on one carburetor at a time, remove the piston and suction chambers and screw up the mixture adjusting nuts until each jet is flush with the bridge of its carburetor. Replace the pistons and suction chambers and check to be sure that each piston falls freely onto the bridge of its carburetor. Screw the jet adjusting nuts down by two turns (12 flats) for an initial setting. Start the engine and adjust to the desired idling speed of 500-550 rpm by moving each slow-running volume screw an equal amount. By listening to the hiss of the carburetors (or through the use of an air-flow measuring device such as the Uni-Syn), adjust the slow-running volume screws so that the intensity of the hiss (or the level of the Uni-Syn indicator) is the same for both carburetors while maintaining the desired idle speed. This will synchronize the volume of air flowing through the carburetors.

When the air flow has been synchronized, adjust the mixture by screwing the jet adjusting nuts up or down by the same amount until the fastest idle speed is obtained with even running of the engine being maintained. As the slow-running mixture is adjusted, the engine will probably run faster, and it may be necessary to reduce the idle speed by unscrewing the slow-running volume screws. Check the mixture adjustment by lifting the piston of the front carburetor by approximately 1/32 in. (.8 mm.) with a screwdriver. If:

(1) The engine speed increases and continues to run faster, the mixture is too rich.

(2) The engine speed immediately decreases, the mixture is too lean.

(3) The engine speed momentarily increases, then returns to the previous level, the mixture is correct.

Repeat this operation on the remaining carburetor and, after adjustment, check the front carburetor again since the carburetors are interdependent. Screwing the mixture adjusting nuts upward will lean the mixture, and screwing them downward will enrichen it. When the mixture is correct, the exhaust note will be regular and even. A colorless exhaust with a splashy misfire and an irregular note indicates that the mixture is too lean, while blackish exhaust together with a regular or rhythmical misfire is a clue that the mixture is too rich.

Adjust the fast-idle setting as follows:

TR–4: With the choke controls reconnected, but the choke not applied, adjust each fast-idle screw so that there is .062 in. (1.6 mm.) clearance between the end of the screw and the cam.

Spitfire: Check to see that the jet control linkage has about 1/16 in. (1.5 mm.) free movement before it begins to pull on the jet levers, then set the choke control knob as far out as possible before the jets begin to move. Adjust the fast-idle screws so that the engine speed is about 1,000 rpm when hot.

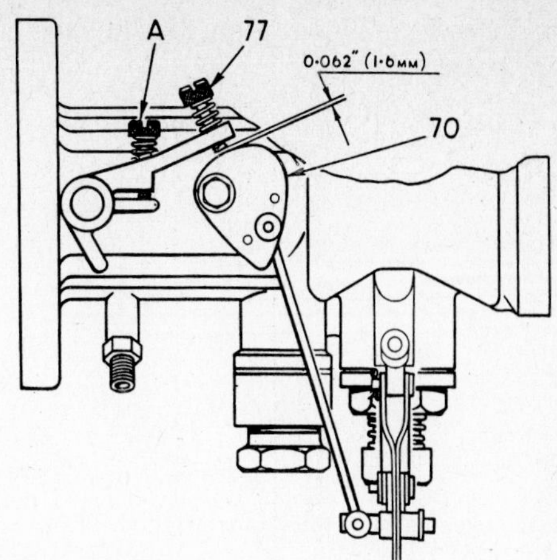

With the TR–4 choke fully in, and the engine idling, clearance between the screw and rocker lever (70) should be 1/16 in.

With the carburetor throttle coupling clamp bolts tightened (and the TR–4 connecting rod reinstalled), recheck the idle air flow volumes through the carburetors to ensure that synchronization has not been disturbed by the tightening of the clamp bolts. The throttle lever pins of the Spitfire HS2 should have approximately .015 in. (.38 mm.) between each pin and the bottom of its throttle lever fork.

S.U. Emission Control Carburetors

The S.U. emission control carburetors on the TR-4A and the Spitfire Mk III incorporate a number of changes from the previous S.U. units. A new needle is used to provide a leaner mixture. Jet adjustment restrictors are installed in each carburetor to restrict the range of adjustment of the mixture strength. After the correct mixture has been set at the factory, the restrictor is locked to prevent further enrichment; subsequent adjustment within the range of the restrictor will only lean the mixture. A modified piston damper is installed to provide a more immediate effect on the piston, thereby maintaining acceleration efficiency with the leaner needle. A throttle disc poppet valve is added to supplement the volume of fuel-air mixture when the vehicle is overrunning the engine with the throttle closed. Carburetor float level is

3⁄16 in. (4.8 mm.) between the lid face and float lever.

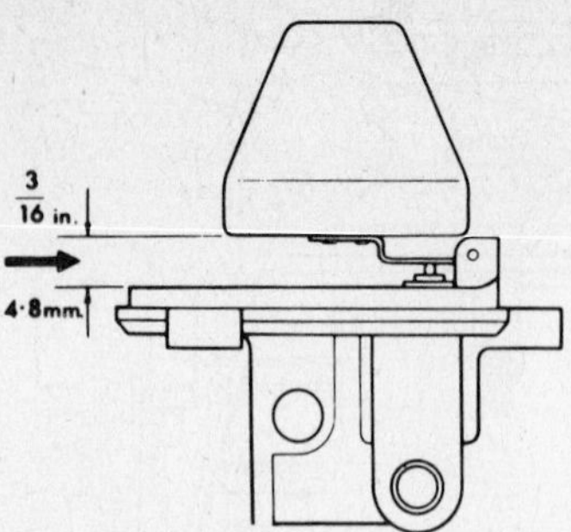

Correct float level, emission-controlled TR-4A and Spitfire Mk III

Tuning

Loosen both clamping bolts on the throttle coupling and unscrew both fast-idle screws until they are clear of their respective cams. Disconnect the jet control interconnection by loosening the clamping bolts. Disconnect the choke cable. Close the throttles by unscrewing the throttle adjusting screws fully, then open slightly by screwing each adjustment screw one-half turn in the open direction. Be sure that the carburetor piston dampers are filled up.

To stabilize engine temperature and air-fuel mixture requirements, observe the following *tuning conditions.*

Run the engine at a fast idle until normal operating temperature is reached. Ideal ambient temperature is between 60° and 80° F. The engine should be run for at least five minutes after the thermostat has opened. Run the engine for one-half minute at 2,500 rpm under no-load conditions. Start tuning adjustments and carry them out in the shortest possible time. If the time exceeds three minutes, run the engine once again at 2,500 rpm for one-half minute. Repeat this cleaning operation at three-minute intervals until tuning is completed. With this in mind, proceed as follows:

Adjust each throttle screw by the same amount to obtain the correct idle speed (800-850 rpm for Spitfire Mk III; 850-900 rpm for TR-4A). Using a Uni-Syn or other suitable air-flow meter, balance the carburetors while maintaining the given idle speed.

Adjust the mixture setting: *NOTE: each time the jet adjusting nut is moved, tap the neck of the suction chamber lightly with a screwdriver handle.* Turn each jet adjusting nut up (to lean) or down (to enrich) until the engine is running as fast as possible. Turn both adjusting nuts very slowly up to lean the mixture until the engine speed just starts to drop, then turn both adjusting nuts down by one-half flat to enrich the mixture. Adjust the idle speed, if necessary, ensuring that both carburetors remain balanced. Using an exhaust gas analyzer (carbon monoxide meter or air/fuel ratio meter), check that the percentage of CO or the air/fuel ratio is within the following limits:

Idle CO level, engine warm: 3.5–4.5%
Equiv. air/fuel ratio at idle: 13:1

If the meter reading falls outside the above limits, both adjusting nuts will have to be turned just enough to bring the reading within the limits. Holding the jet adjusting nut of each carburetor, rotate each adjustment restrictor until the vertical tag contacts the carburetor body on the left side as seen from the air cleaner flange. Bend the tag of the adjustment restrictor so that the restrictor locks to the nut. *NOTE: the preceding applies only if, for reasons such as carburetor replacement or reconditioning, new jet adjustment restrictors are being installed.*

Set the throttle interconnection clamping levers so that there is .015 in. (.38 mm.) clearance between the actuating pins and the lower edge of the fork. There should be a total of 1⁄32 in. end play between the interconnecting clamping levers and the throttle nuts. With both jet levers pressed to their lowest position, adjust the jet interconnection lever clamping bolts so that the jets begin to open at the same time. With the engine running at 1,500 rpm, use the air-flow meter to ensure that the carburetors are balanced. Reconnect the choke cable so that it has about 1⁄16 in. free movement before it begins to displace the jet levers. With the choke pulled out until the carburetor jets are about to drop, use the balancing meter to maintain equal adjustment while turning the fast idle screws to obtain the proper hot fast-idle speed—1,100 rpm.

Stromberg 175 CD Carburetors

Dual Stromberg 175 CD (non emission controlled) carburetors were installed on some TR4A models. As with S.U. carburetors, the damper oil well must be filled with light engine oil (SAE 20) periodically. The oil level is correct when it is within 1/4 in. of the top of the rod. The following services apply to all Stromberg 175 CD carburetors.

Carburetor damper

Float Chamber Fuel Level

To check the float level, remove the carburetor from the engine and the float cham-

Jet assembly (12) and mixture adjusting screw (13) of the Stromberg 175 CD carburetor used in the TR–4A.

ber from the carburetor. When the needle is against its seat, the highest point of the float should be .73 in. (18.5 mm.) above the face of the main body. The level must be reset by carefully bending the tag which contacts the end of the needle. Also, the installation of a thin fiber washer beneath the needle valve seat will appreciably lower the fuel level.

Centralizing the Jet

As with the S.U. carburetor, the needle of the Stromberg unit must be correctly centered in the jet opening. Centralize the jet as follows: Lift the air valve and fully tighten the jet assembly. Screw the adjusting screw up until the top of the orifice is just above the bridge. Loosen the jet assembly approximately one-half turn in order to release the orifice bushing. Let the air valve fall, allowing the needle to enter and centralize the orifice. Slowly tighten the assembly, at the same time checking to ensure that the needle is free in the orifice. Check by raising the air valve approximately ¼ in. (6.35 mm.) and allowing it to fall. The piston should stop firmly on the bridge. Adjust the engine idle speed.

Idle Speed Adjustments

The idle speed and mixture are adjusted by two screws. The speed is controlled by the throttle stop screw, while the mixture is governed by the jet-adjusting screw. Turning the jet-adjusting screw clockwise will lean the mixture strength, while turning the screw counterclockwise will enrich it. Screwing up the jet adjustment screw until the jet contacts the bottom of the air valve, then turning the screw down three turns, will result in an approximate jet position from which to proceed. With the engine warm, loosen the clamping bolts on the throttle couplings and use the throttle stop screws and an air-flow meter to balance the carburetors at an idle speed of 600-650 rpm. To check the idle mixture, lift the air valve a small amount (about $\frac{1}{32}$ in.). If the engine speed increases significantly, the mixture is too rich. If the engine speed drops, the mixture is too weak. When the mixture is properly adjusted, the engine speed will either remain constant or decrease only slightly when the valve is lifted. Set the fast-idle screws so that there is .062 in. (1.587 mm.) clearance between the end of the screw and the cam with the choke cable at the off position. With the throttle coupling clamp bolts retightened, check the synchronization of the carburetors and the idle speed. Replace the air cleaners and reconnect the choke control.

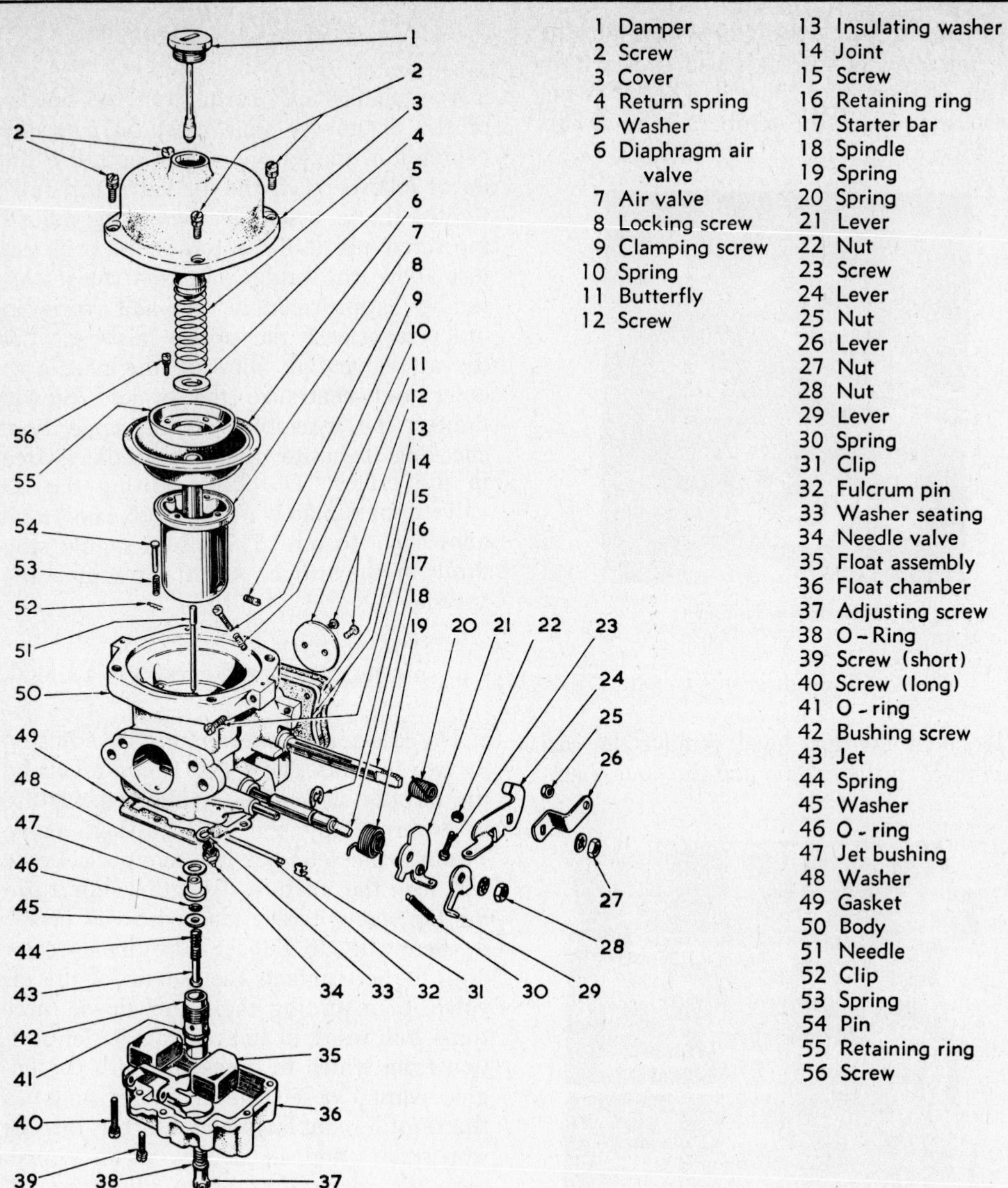

Stromberg 175 CD carburetor

Stromberg 175 CDSE Carburetors

These carburetors are used on the TR-250 and TR-6. They are also used on late TR-4A models. The letter E signifies that these are emission control carburetors.

Permissible adjustments are limited to the following: (1) idle speed (2) idle emission (controlled by trimming screw), and (3) fast idle. Idle speed is adjusted in the normal manner, which requires the use of a suitable air-flow meter to maintain the balance between the carburetors. The purpose of the idle trimming screw is to provide a very fine degree of adjustment to compensate for the difference between a new, stiff engine and one that has been broken in. It is not an idle mixture adjusting screw, as the amount of adjustment it provides is minimal and can only be detected by means of a CO or air/fuel meter.

In setting the fast idle, ensure that the choke lever on each carburetor is against its stop when the choke control is pushed fully in. If necessary, the cables should be adjusted. Pull the choke control out so that the cable pivot lines up with the center of the fast-idle screw and the center of the

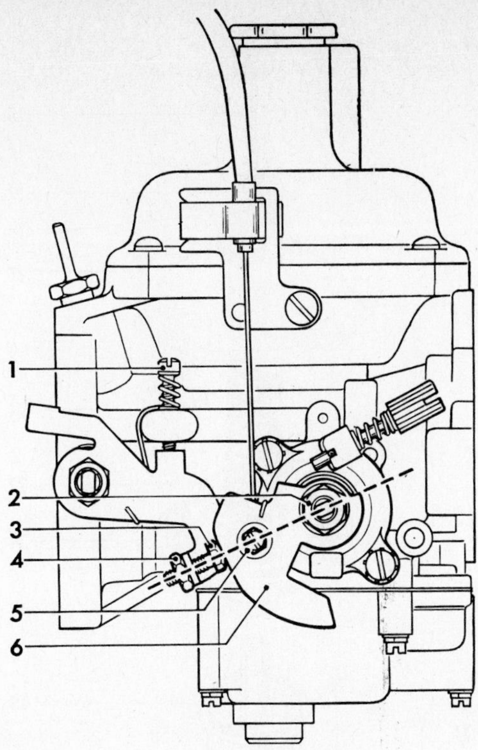

Position of the choke cam lever when making fast-idle adjustment of the Stromberg 175 CDSE carburetor. Components shown include the idling screw (1), starter box (2), fast-idle screw (3), locknut (4), cable trunnion (5) and cam lever (6).

cam pivot point. Loosen the locknuts and unscrew both idle screws until each is just contacting the cam. Start the engine and, while it is cold (68°-86° F), adjust the fast-idle screws an equal amount to provide an engine speed of 1,100 rpm. Tighten the locknuts and recheck the fast-idle speed.

Carburetor settings for the TR-4A and TR-250 are as follows:

Idle CO level: 2.5-3.5% (warm engine)
Equivalent air/fuel ratio: 13.5:1

Stromberg 175 CDSE (Emission Controlled)

1 Carburetor
2 Spring—idle trimming screw
3 Idle trimming screw
4 Gasket—by-pass valve
5 By-pass valve
6 Lockwasher under (7)
7 Screw—securing (5)
8 Temperature compensator unit
9 Lockwasher under (10)
10 Screw—securing (8)
11 Cover—temperature compensator
12 Screw—securing (11)
13 Seal—on compensator body
14 Seal—inside carburetor
15 Damper rod } damper assembly
16 Washer
17 Spacer sleeve
18 Circlip
19 Cover—air valve
20 Screws—securing (19)
21 Spring—air valve return
22 Ring—diaphragm attachment
23 Screw—securing (22) (24)
24 Diaphragm
25 Air valve
26 Screw—securing (27)
27 Needle assembly
28 Spring—idle adjusting screw
29 Idle adjusting screw
30 Throttle disc
31 Screw—securing (30)
32 Seal—throttle spindle
33 Throttle spindle
34 Spring—throttle return
35 Lever—throttle
36 Screw—fast idle
37 Locknut—securing (36)
38 Lockwasher—retaining (39)
39 Nut—throttle spindle
40 Coupling—throttle spindles
41 Connecting lever assembly
42 Clamping bolt
43 Washer—under (42)
44 Nut—securing (42)
45 Nut } Starter box assembly
46 Shakeproof washer
47 Washer
48 Lever
49 Screw—cable attachment
50 Return spring
51 Screw
52 Shakeproof washer
53 Starter box cover
54 Spring
55 Spindle
56 Retainer
57 Valve plate
58 Cable abutment bracket
59 Spring clip
60 Screw—securing (58)
61 Float pivot pin
62 Gasket—float chamber
63 Needle valve
64 Float assembly
65 Float chamber cover
66 Washer—under (68/69)
67 Spring washer—under (68/69)
68 Screw—securing (65)
69 Screw—securing (65)
70 Plug
71 Rubber O-ring—for (70)

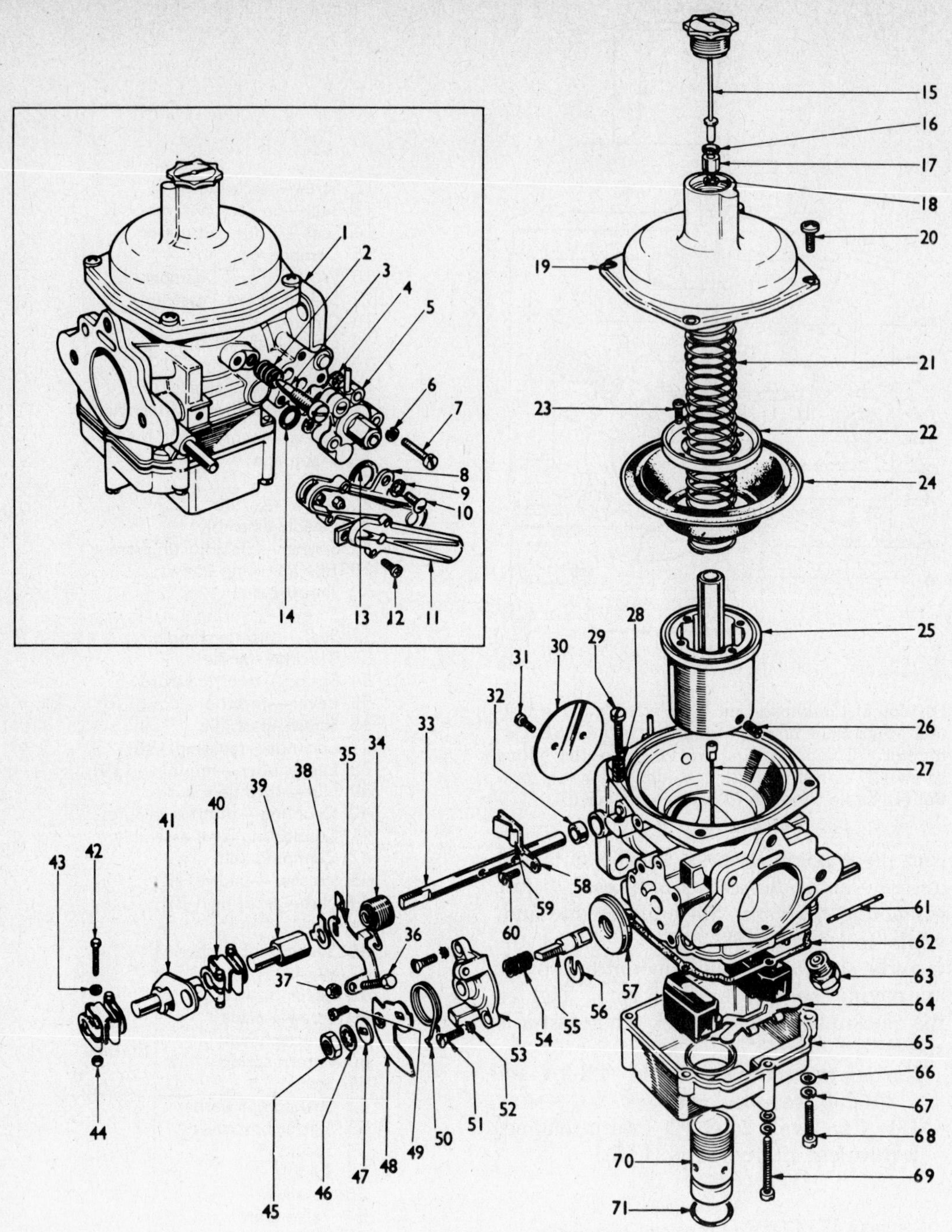

Stromberg 175 CDSE (Emission Controlled)

Disassembly and Service

(When carrying out the following operations, be careful to ensure that similar components are not switched to the wrong carburetors. Keep all parts of one carburetor separate from those of the other.)

Remove the carburetors from the manifold, position on a clean surface, and separate the units. Drain the fuel from each carburetor by unscrewing the brass plug Unscrew the damper and drain the oil from the well. Unscrew the retaining screws and withdraw the float chamber vertically from the carburetor body. Remove the float chamber gaskets, release the pivot pin, and remove the floats. Remove the needle valve and the O-ring. After cleaning all removed components, use a new washer in replacing the needle valve. Inspect the floats for damage, replace the float assembly, insert the pivot pin and clip the assembly into position. Check the fuel level by inverting the unit so that the float lever tag closes the needle valve, then measure the distance from the face of the cover (with gasket removed) to the highest point of each float. This distance should be between 16.0-17.0 mm.

Using a new gasket, replace the float chamber by tightening the screws from the center outward. Install a new O-ring to the center plug and install the plug. Use new gaskets when replacing both carburetors on the manifold. Top up the damper oil reservoirs to within ¼ in. of the top of the center rod and install the dampers. Reconnect the accelerator linkage controls and adjust the carburetors.

Service the air valve assembly as follows: Remove the damper assembly, remove the retaining screws and lift off the cover. Remove the air valve return spring, withdraw the air valve, and drain the oil from the guide rod. Loosen the metering needle clamping screw and withdraw the needle, being careful not to damage it. Remove the diaphragm retaining screws, remove the ring, and the diaphragm. Install the new diaphragm by locating its tag in the recess provided and install the ring and retaining screws. Check to ensure that spring action exists at the needle housing, then insert the needle into the base of the air valve until the flat portion is lined up with the locking screw. Use a straightedge to push the needle shoulder into the air valve until the straightedge aligns the shoulder with the flat face inside the flange on the outer edge of the air valve. The positioning of the needle is very critical. The locking screw should be tightened only lightly in order to avoid damage to the housing of the needle loading spring. When the needle is correctly installed, it will—unlike the needle of the S.U.—be spring-loaded towards the throttle. Be sure that the shoulder of the needle is flush with the face of the air valve. Install the air valve and diaphragm assembly to the main body, using a finger in the air intake to help guide the needle into the jet. The outer tag of the diaphragm should be located in the opening provided on top of the body. Looking through the center of the air valve, ensure that the two vacuum transfer holes are lined up with the throttle spindle. Also check to ensure that the needle is loaded toward the throttle. Replace the return spring of the air valve and install the cover with the damper ventilation boss toward the air intake. Replace the securing screws and check the air valve for freedom of movement. When released from its uppermost position, the air valve should fall to the bridge with a sharp metallic click.

Remove the retaining screws and remove the temperature compensator. Release the cover and check the freedom of movement of the valve. In order to compensate for thermal expansion, there should be a consistent radial clearance around the valve. If the valve is not centered, loosen the retaining screw and move the blade laterally until the valve is centralized. Check again that the valve moves freely, then replace the cover and tighten with the retaining screw. Using new seals, replace the inner seal in the carburetor body and the outer seal on the compensator. Replace the unit to the carburetor and secure with the two retaining screws.

Replace the throttle spindle seals as follows: Remove the screws and detach the bypass valve assembly and gasket. Unscrew the spindle nut, release the throttle spring and remove the lever and spring. Remove the old throttle spindle seals and replace with new seals. Removal is facilitated by a small hole provided in the face of the seal. With the spring and lever reassembled to the throttle spindle, tighten and lock the nut. Using a new gasket, replace the bypass valve to the body of the carburetor and tighten the three retaining screws.

STROMBERG 175 CD AND CDSE LINKAGE ADJUSTMENTS

1. Loosen bolts on spring couplings (both carburetor ends).
2. Adjust slow idle screw to fully closed position (both). At this point, rotate screws open exactly 1 1/2 turns. Make sure fast idle adjustment screw is clear of linkage cam. Be sure choke linkage is fully closed.
3. Start and warm engine to operating temperature. Adjust slow idle screw to set both carburetors to correct speed. Stop engine.
4. With linkage as shown, place 3/32 in. drill bit in space a. Be sure it is in the space between the lever tongue, b, and the lever slot edge. With bit in position, and putting pressure on stop cam, tighten spring bolts. Remove bit.
5. Place relay lever against stop screw. Loosen vacuum valve screws. Adjust valve to .030 in. clearance (between valve and lever).
6. Move linkage until tongue, b, nests in lever slot. Valve should be fully closed (throttle should be at point of opening).

STROMBERG 150 CD AND 150 CDSE CARBURETORS

The 150 CD is a non emission controlled carburetor used on the GT6. The 150 CDSE is an emission controlled unit used on the Spitfire Mk IV, GT6+, and GT6 Mk III.

Dampers

At 1,000 mile intervals, each carburetor damper chamber should be filled with SAE 20 oil to a point 1/4 in. above the dash pot.

Centralizing the Jet

Ascertain that the air valve moves freely by raising and allowing the valve to fall. Slow action may indicate the need for

Lifting the air valve to center the jet

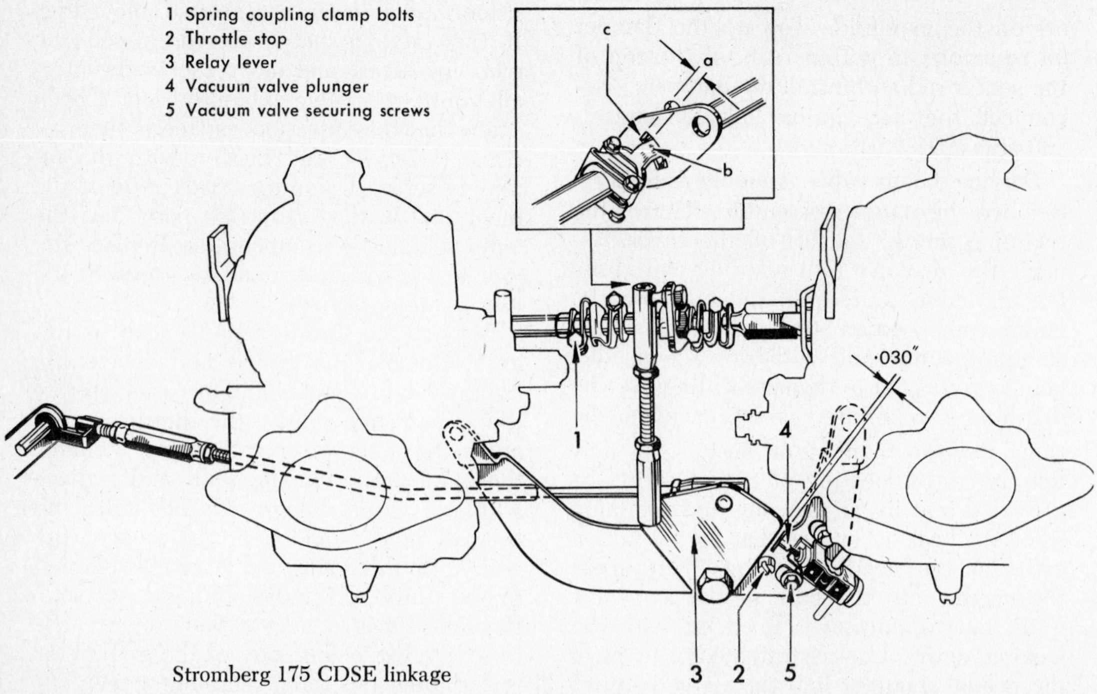

Stromberg 175 CDSE linkage

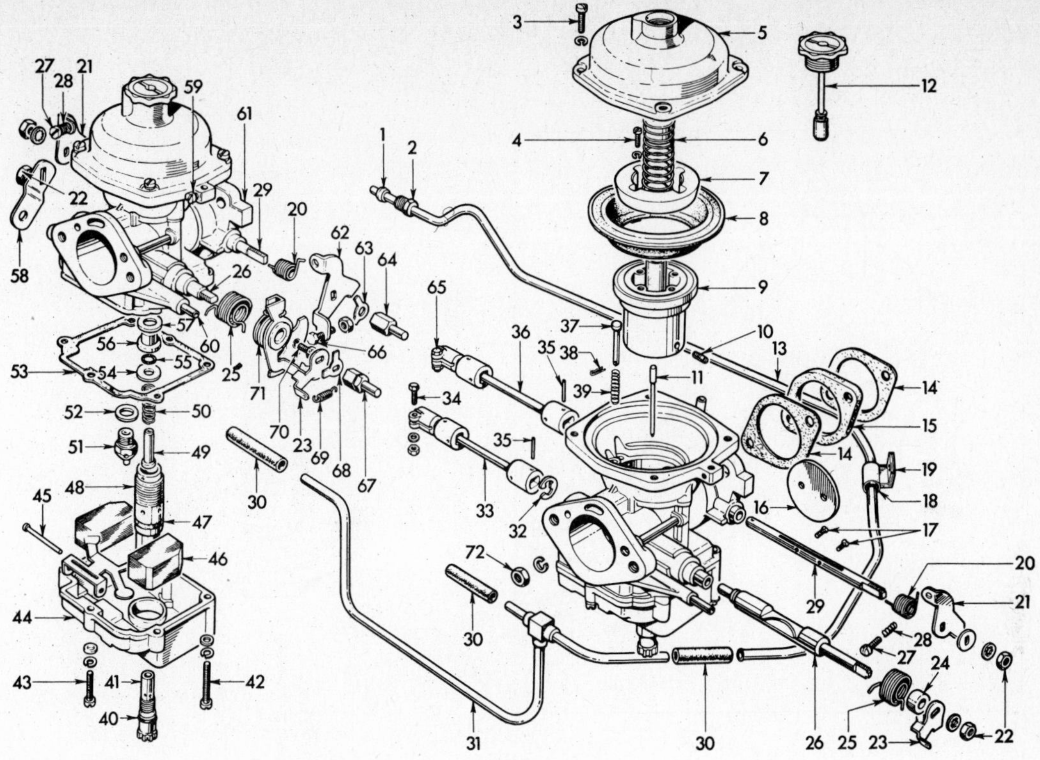

Stromberg 150 CD

1 Sleeve
2 Nut
3 Top cover screw
4 Screw
5 Top cover
6 Coil spring
7 Retaining ring
8 Diaphragm
9 Air valve
10 Locking screw
11 Needle
12 Damper
13 Pipe
14 Gasket
15 Insulator
16 Throttle butterfly valve
17 Screws
18 Grommet
19 Bracket
20 Spring
21 Throttle stop lever
22 Nuts
23 Lever
24 Bushing
25 Return spring
26 Starter bar spindle
27 Throttle stop screw
28 Spring
29 Throttle spindle
30 Fuel line connector
31 Line
32 Circlip
33 Coupling
34 Clamping bolt
35 Pin
36 Coupling
37 Air valve lifting pin
38 Spring clip
39 Spring
40 O-ring
41 Orifice adjusting screw
42 Screw (long)
43 Screw (short)
44 Float chamber cover
45 Fulcrum pin
46 Float assembly
47 O-ring
48 Bushing screw
49 Jet
50 Spring
51 Needle valve
52 Washer
53 Gasket
54 Washer
55 O-ring
56 Bushing
57 Washer
58 Connecting link
59 Screw
60 Fuel inlet
61 Body
62 Stop lever
63 Lock plate
64 Coupling nut
65 Clamping bolt
66 Cam screw
67 Coupling nut
68 Lock plate
69 Spring
70 Cam screw
71 Choke cam lever
72 Nut

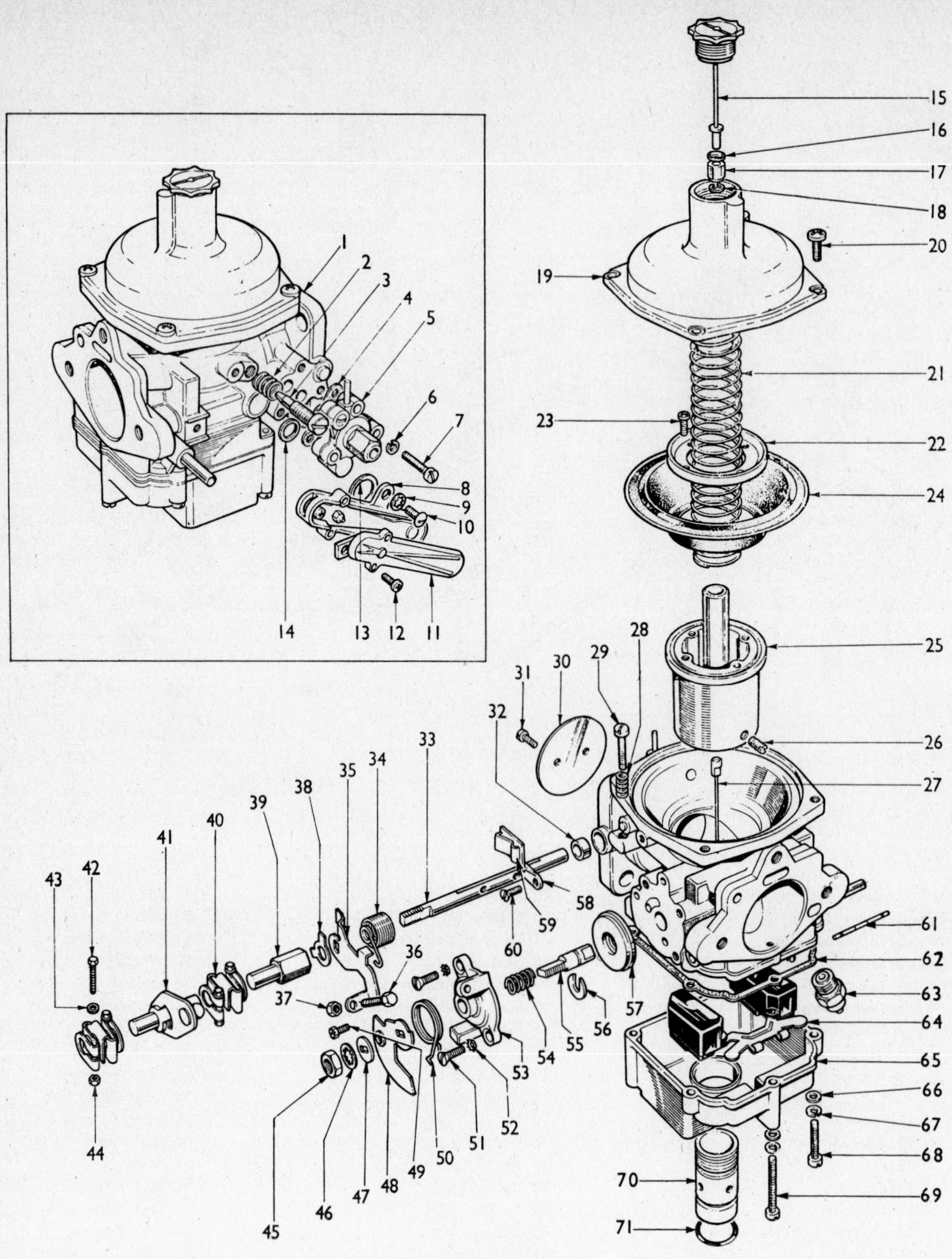

Stromberg 150 CDSE

1 Carburetor
2 Spring—idle trimming screw
3 Idle trimming screw
4 Gasket—by-pass valve
5 By-pass valve
6 Lockwasher under (7)
7 Screw—securing (5)
8 Temperature compensator unit
9 Lockwasher under (10)
10 Screw—securing (8)
11 Cover—temperature compensator
12 Screw—securing (11)
13 Seal—on compensator body
14 Seal—inside carburetor
15 Damper rod
16 Washer
17 Distance sleeve
18 Circlip
(15–18: Damper assembly)
19 Cover—air valve
20 Screws—securing (19)
21 Spring—air valve return
22 Ring—diaphragm attachment
23 Screw—securing (22) (24)
24 Diaphragm
25 Air valve
26 Screw—securing (27)
27 Needle assembly
28 Spring—idle adjusting screw
29 Idle adjusting screw
30 Throttle disc
31 Screw—securing (30)
32 Seal—throttle spindle
33 Throttle spindle
34 Spring—throttle return
35 Lever—throttle
36 Screw—fast idle
37 Locknut—securing (36)
38 Lockwasher—retaining (39)
39 Nut—throttle spindle
40 Coupling—throttle spindles
41 Connecting lever assembly
42 Clamping bolt
43 Washer—under (42)
44 Nut—securing (42)
45 Nut
46 Shakeproof washer
47 Washer
48 Lever
49 Screw—cable attachment
50 Return spring
51 Screw
52 Shakeproof washer
53 Starter box cover
54 Spring
55 Spindle
56 Retainer
57 Valve plate
(45–57: Starter box assembly)
58 Cable abutment bracket
59 Spring clip
60 Screw—securing (58)
61 Float pivot pin
62 Gasket—float chamber
63 Needle valve
64 Float assembly
65 Float chamber cover
66 Washer—under (68/69)
67 Spring washer—under (68/69)
68 Screw—securing (65)
69 Screw—securing (65)
70 Plug
71 Rubber O-ring for (70)

cleaning by removing and cleansing both bore and air valve with solvent.

If the jet is not centralized, it may be corrected as follows:

1. Raise air valve and tighten jet bushing screw. Tighten orifice adjusting screw until it is just above bridge.
2. Loosen jet bushing screw to release orifice bushing. Permit air valve to drop. This will align bushing. Tighten bushing screw to secure bushing and recheck. Repeat until piston falls freely.
3. Move adjusting screw until it barely touches air valve underside when resting on bridge. Three turns from this position (loose) gives a reasonable figure to use when synchronizing dual carburetors.

Stromberg 150 CD (Non Emission Controlled)

Disassembly

1. Remove nuts holding manifold and carburetor together.
2. Loosen clamping bolts and pull carburetor apart.
3. Remove dampers and drain dashpots.
4. Remove top cover screws. Mark on upper flanges. Remove cover and string. Separate air valve diaphragm.
5. Carefully remove air valve assembly.
6. Place carburetor on flange face. Remove bushing screw assembly.
7. Disassemble cover by removing six screws.
8. Remove jet assembly.
9. Remove pin. Pull out float assembly.
10. Loosen and remove needle valve with washer.

Synchronization and Idle Adjustments

Each carburetor has one mixture and one idle speed screw. The throttle stop screw adjustment controls the speed and the jet adjusting screw determines the proportion of fuel/air mixture entering the combustion chamber. When viewed from below, turn the jet adjusting screw clockwise to reduce mixture strength; turn counterclockwise to richen the mixture. The stop adjustment should be set to an idle speed of 600-650 rpm.

To check mixture, raise air valve slightly. To do this, use the piston lifting pin. Observe the effect this has upon the engine. If the engine stalls, the mixture is too lean. If the adjustment is correct, engine rpm will either fall slightly or stay the same when the air valve is lifted.

Adjust fast idle to give 1/16 in. clearance between face of cam and screw head.

Stromberg 150 CDSE Carburetors

There are only three permissible adjustments to this unit. They are:

1. Idle speed—screw adjustment
2. Idle emission—to be used only with a fuel/air ratio measuring device.
3. Fast idle—simple screw adjustment. Settings are as follow:

	GT6, GT6+	*GT6 MK III, Spitfire MK IV*
Idle CO level (engine hot)	2.5 to 3.5%	.5 to 2.5%
Idle air/fuel ratio	13.5:1	13.6-14.4:1

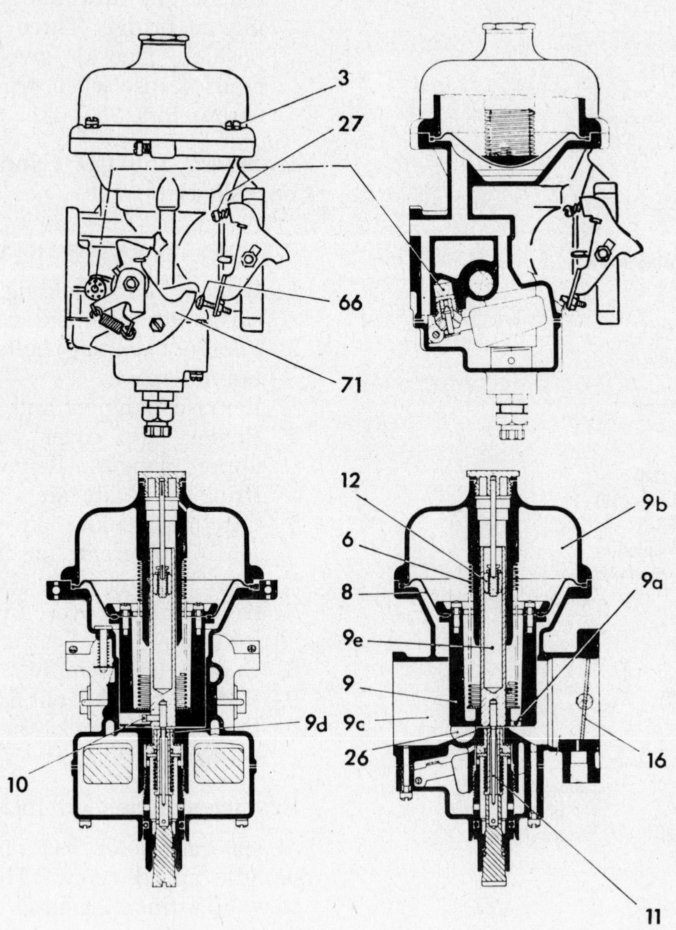

Stromberg 150 CD (cross section)

3 Top cover screw
6 Coil spring
8 Diaphragm
9 Air valve
10 Locking screw
11 Metering needle
12 Damper
16 Butterfly throttle
26 Starter bar
27 Throttle stop screw
66 Cam screw
71 Choke cam lever
9a Air valve drilling
9b Chamber
9c Bore
9d Jet orifice
9e Guide rod

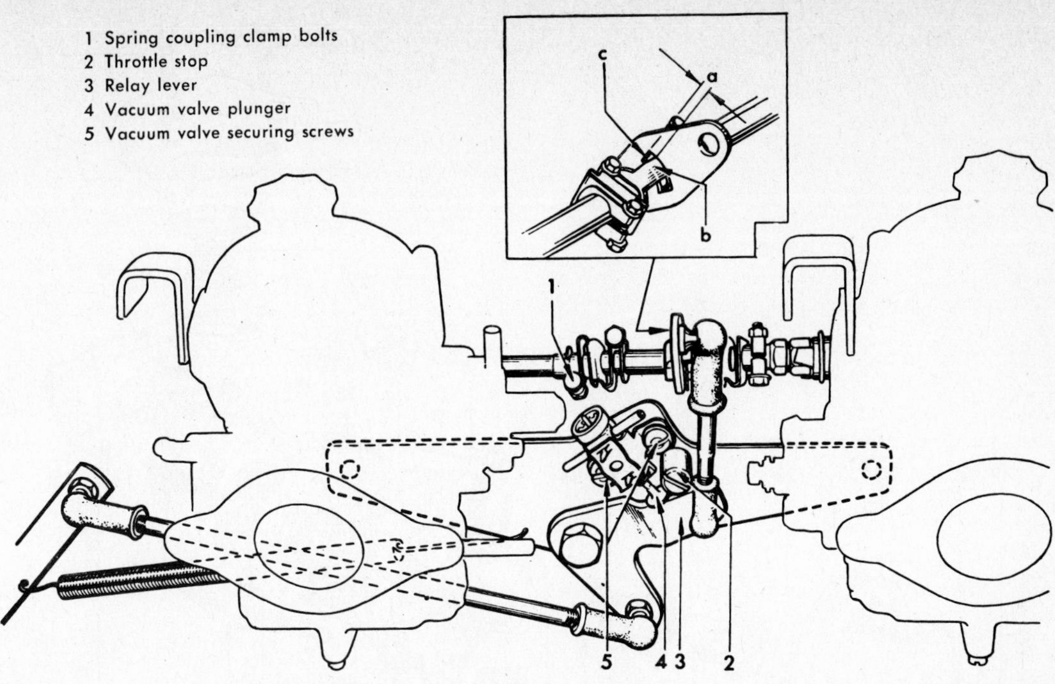

Stromberg 150 series linkage

Stromberg 150 CD and CDSE Linkage Adjustments

Follow Stromberg 175 CD and CDSE Linkage Adjustments Procedure with the following modifications:

1. Use a 1/16 in. drill bit in Step 4.
2. In Step 5, do not position relay lever against stop screw.

Cooling System

WATER PUMP

Removal and Installation

TR-4, TR-4A

Disconnect the battery, drain the cooling system, loosen the generator retaining nuts and remove the driving belt. Disconnect the pump hoses and remove the temperature sending wire. Remove the three bolts and detach the water pump from the cylinder block.

TR-250, TR-6, GT6, Spitfire

Disconnect the battery, drain the cooling system, loosen the generator (alternator) mounting bolts and remove the fan belt. Disconnect the radiator and water hoses at the thermostat housing and water pump, and disconnect the fuel supply line at the carburetors and fuel pump. Remove the temperature transmitter connection and the three bolts securing the water pump to the cylinder head. Remove the water pump. When replacing the pump, be sure that the cylinder head and pump mating surfaces are clean and install a new gasket.

FAN BELT

Adjustment and Replacement

On all models, the fan belt should have about ¾ in. of free movement along its longest run. Adjustment is accomplished by loosening the adjusting bolt and two mounting bolts and moving the generator (alternator) until the tension is correct. A too tight fan belt will wear out the water pump and generator bearings, and excessive slack will cause the belt to squeak, the generator to produce less than its quota of electricity, and the water pump to operate at less than full efficiency.

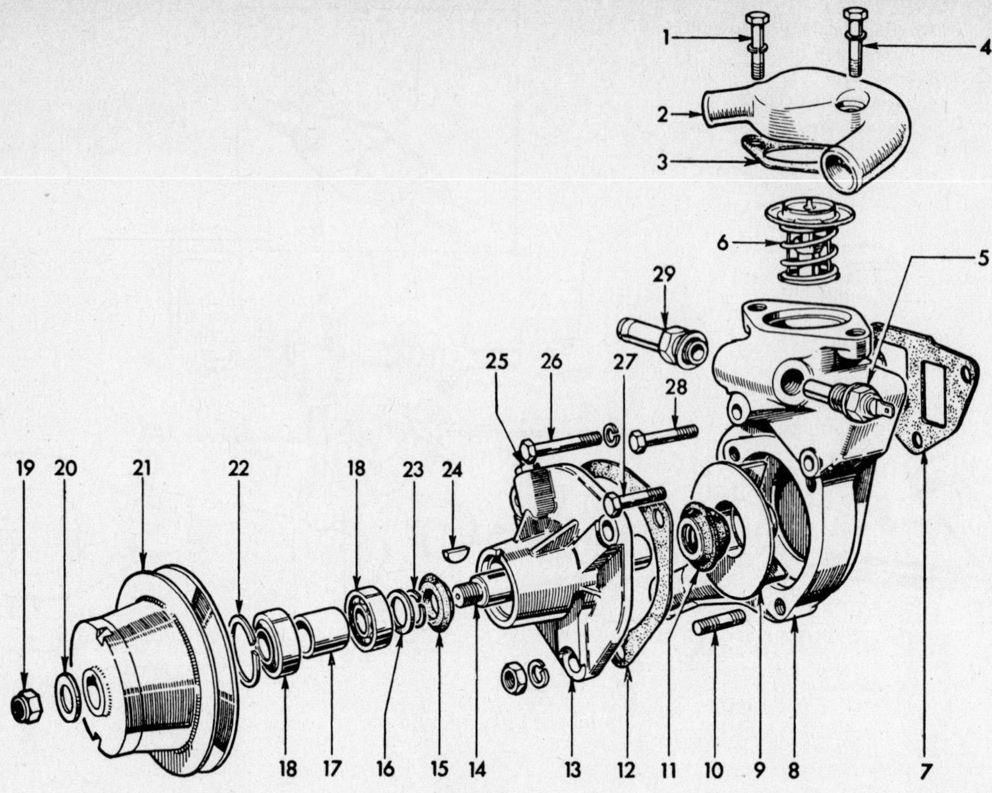

GT6, TR-250, TR-6 water pump

1 Bolt
2 Elbow
3 Gasket
4 Bolt
5 Temperature transmitter
6 Thermostat
7 Gasket
8 Body
9 Impeller
10 Stud
11 Seal
12 Gasket
13 Bearing housing
14 Spindle
15 Spinner
16 Washer
17 Spacer
18 Ball race
19 Nut
20 Washer
21 Pulley
22 Circlip
23 Circlip
24 Woodruff key
25 Grease plug
26 Bolt
27 Bolt
28 Bolt
29 Union

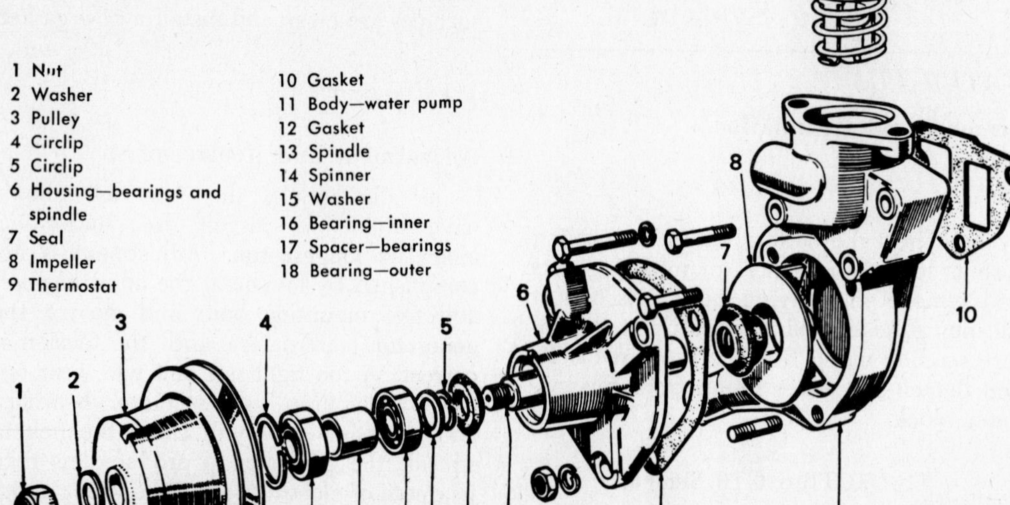

1 Nut
2 Washer
3 Pulley
4 Circlip
5 Circlip
6 Housing—bearings and spindle
7 Seal
8 Impeller
9 Thermostat
10 Gasket
11 Body—water pump
12 Gasket
13 Spindle
14 Spinner
15 Washer
16 Bearing—inner
17 Spacer—bearings
18 Bearing—outer

Spitfire water pump

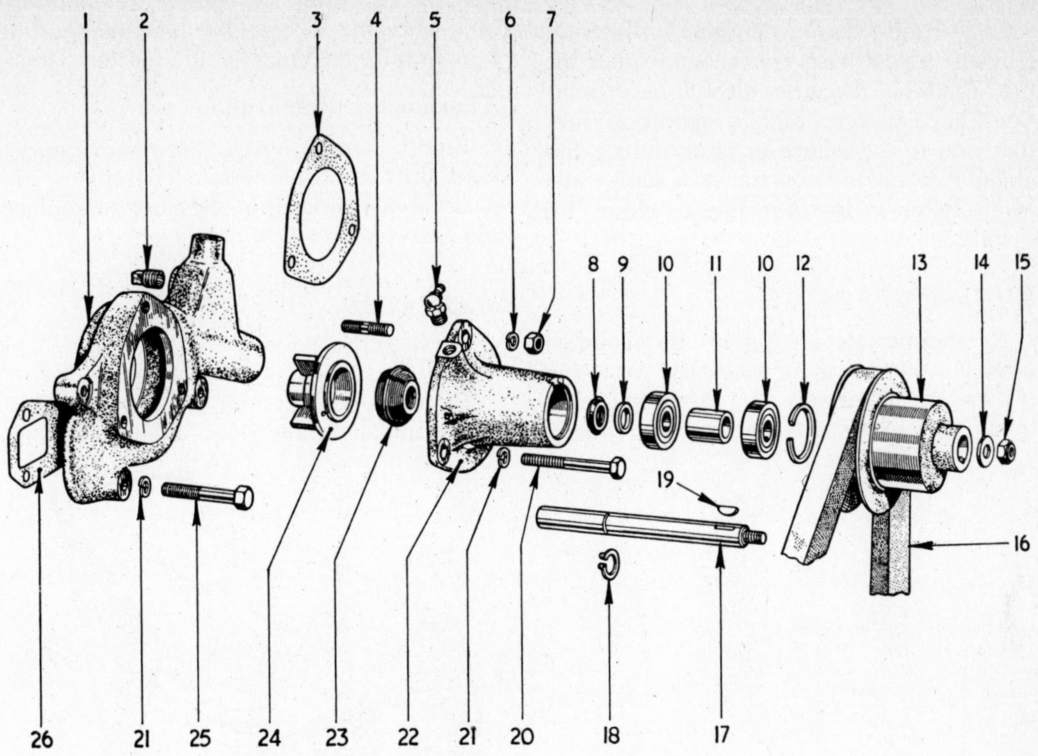

1 Body
2 Heater return pipe blanking plug
3 Gasket
4 Stud
5 Grease nipple
6 Spring washer
7 Nut
8 Spinner
9 Distance washer
10 Ball race
11 Distance tube
12 Circlip
13 Pulley
14 Plain washer
15 Nyloc nut
16 Driving belt
17 Shaft
18 Circlip
19 Woodruff key
20 Bolt
21 Spring washer
22 Bearing housing
23 Seal and bellows assembly
24 Impeller
25 Bolt
26 Gasket

ANTI-FREEZE

Only anti-freeze solutions with an ethylene glycol base are recommended for the Triumph, because alcohol-base solutions have a very high evaporation rate that can, in the course of time, reduce the amount of engine coolant to a dangerous level. Refer to the Anti-Freeze charts for details.

THERMOSTAT

All thermostats are pre-set at manufacture; no adjustment is necessary. Servicing is by replacement only. If a thermostat malfunction is suspected, it may be tested by placing in water of specific temperature and watching to see if unit functions at temperature marked on thermostat flange.

Thermostat Removal

Empty cooling system and remove outlet hose. Lift out thermostat. To replace, reverse above procedure. Be sure to replace old gasket with a new one.

RADIATOR

Removal

Empty cooling system. Remove air ducts, hoses, and overflow lines. Remove mount-

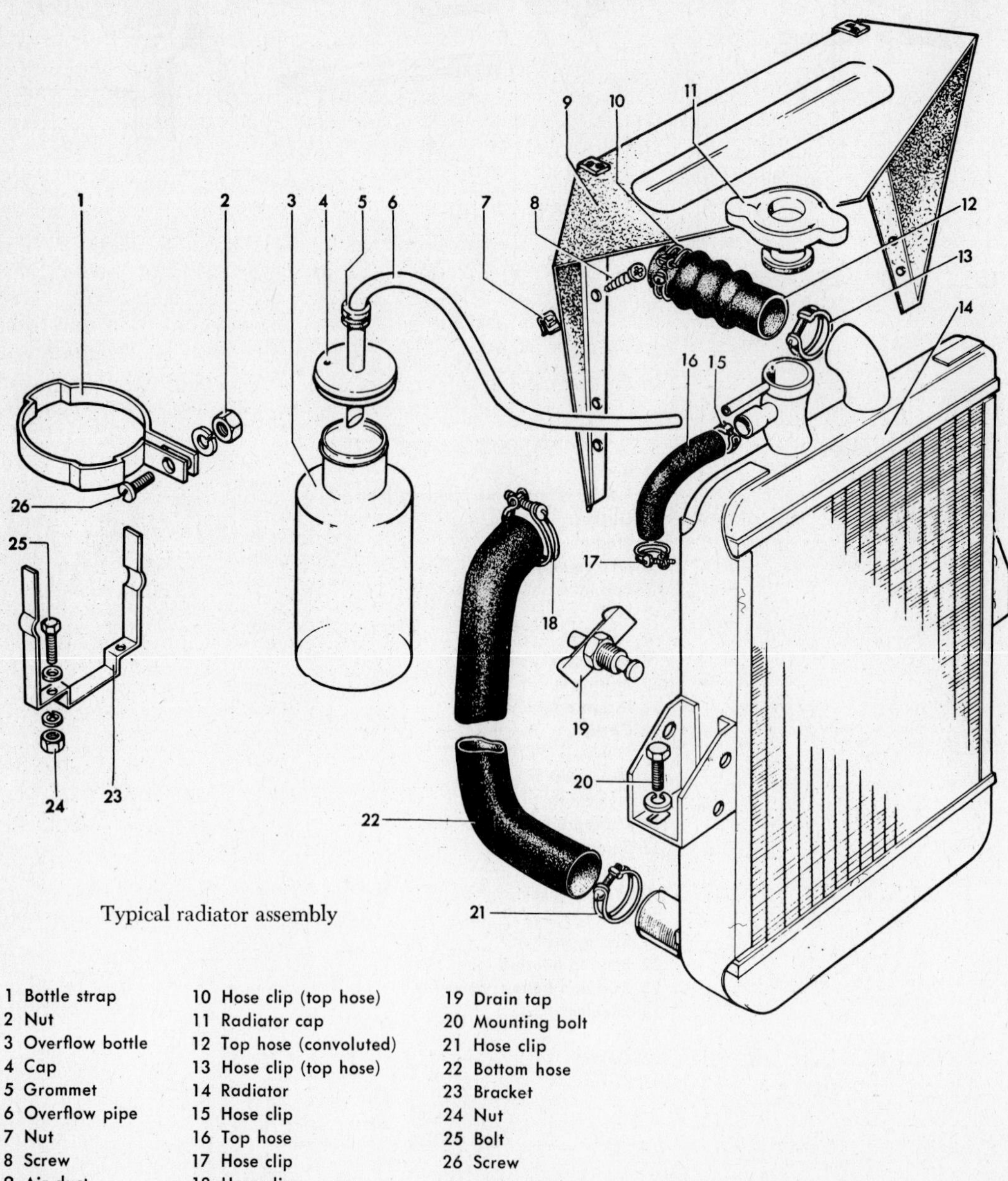

Typical radiator assembly

1 Bottle strap
2 Nut
3 Overflow bottle
4 Cap
5 Grommet
6 Overflow pipe
7 Nut
8 Screw
9 Air duct
10 Hose clip (top hose)
11 Radiator cap
12 Top hose (convoluted)
13 Hose clip (top hose)
14 Radiator
15 Hose clip
16 Top hose
17 Hose clip
18 Hose clip
19 Drain tap
20 Mounting bolt
21 Hose clip
22 Bottom hose
23 Bracket
24 Nut
25 Bolt
26 Screw

ing bolts. Lift out radiator. To replace, reverse above procedure. CAUTION: *Radiator will puncture easily. Use care when removing so core is not damaged.*

Engine

The engines are of conventional design and construction, incorporating pushrod operated overhead valves. The six-cylinder powerplants of the TR-250, TR-6, and GT6 are basically similar in design, with minor constructional and dimensional differences. The six-cylinder engines and the Spitfire's four-cylinder engine are of bore-in-block design, while that of the TR-4 and TR-4A uses four wet-type cylinder liners.

EMISSION CONTROL SYSTEM

With the advent of emission control laws, Triumphs were modified to comply. Due to the strictness of these laws, exhaust emission control systems should not be modified in any way. What follows is a brief rundown on the various modifications made to meet smog control specifications.

Carburetors

These are the main components of the emission control system. Generally, they were modified by using leaner jets and mixture. In the case of the Spitfire MK IV, a change was made from dual S.U. HS2 carburetors to a single Stromberg 150 CDSE. The tuning of carburetors to meet emission standards has, in general, reduced power considerably. Servicing procedures will be found in the Carburetor Section.

Distributors

All current models are now equipped with a vacuum retard unit. This assembly retards the spark during idling and deceleration, thereby reducing exhaust emissions.

Cylinder Head and Camshaft

These have been modified for cleaner burning in the case of the former and lower emissions at idle in the case of the latter. (The camshaft accomplishes this by reduced overlap.)

PCV Valve

The crankcase vent valve has been used for several years and remains virtually unchanged. This component requires the following service at 12,000 mile intervals:

Remove all connections. Loosen and remove spring clip and cover plate. Remove rubber diaphragm—note its exact position in relation to top of assembly. Thoroughly clean entire unit. NOTE: *Be certain all*

Distributor emission control system

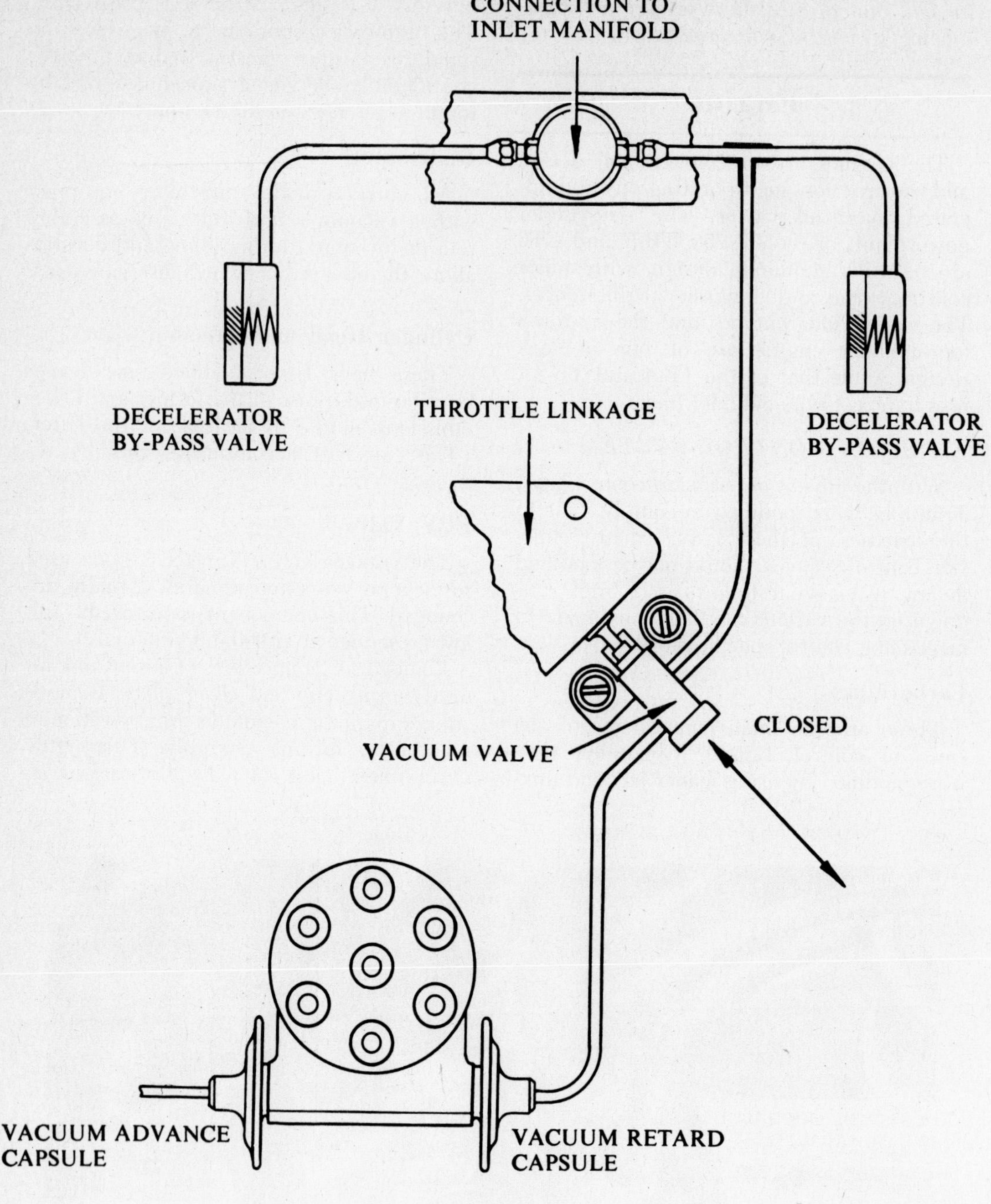

Typical emission control vacuum circuit. Deceleration valve opens during deceleration

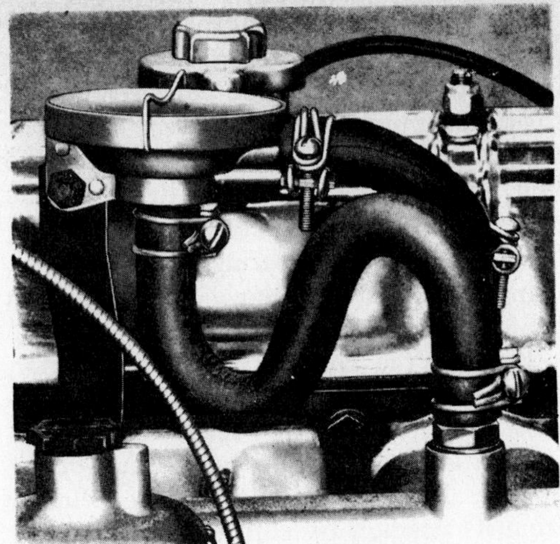

PCV valve assembly

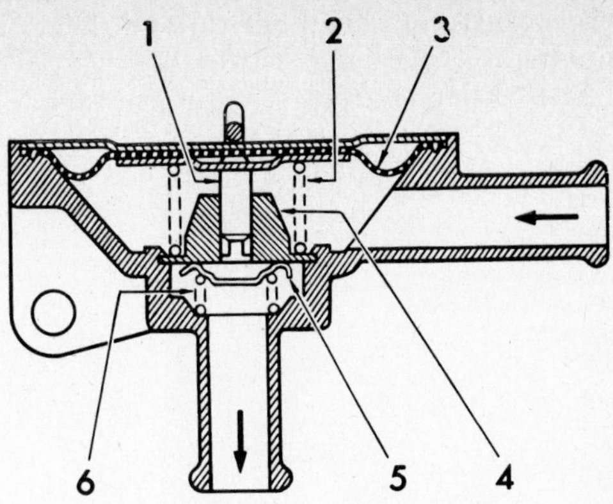

Cutaway of PCV valve

1 Valve pin
2 Spring
3 Diaphragm
4 Orifice plate
5 Plate valve
6 Spring

parts are cleaned in a safe solvent and are absolutely spotless. Be sure the valve plate moves freely and the retaining spring (located below valve) maintains upward position. When reassembling, make sure plunger is correctly positioned in mid-point of orifice plate.

Evaporation Control System

This closed fuel system prevents gasoline from escaping into the atmosphere. The following maintenance is required every 12,000 miles:

Remove all tubes from canister top. Loosen attachments and lift from bracket. Loosen base cover and remove; lift out the filter gauze and replace. Clean base and re-

1 Flame trap Filter
2 Pipe-Canister purge
3 Activated Carbon Canister
4 Pipe-overflow tank to Canister
5 Overflow Tank
6 Main Fuel Tank
7 Sealed Filler Cap
8 Pipe Filler to Overflow Tank

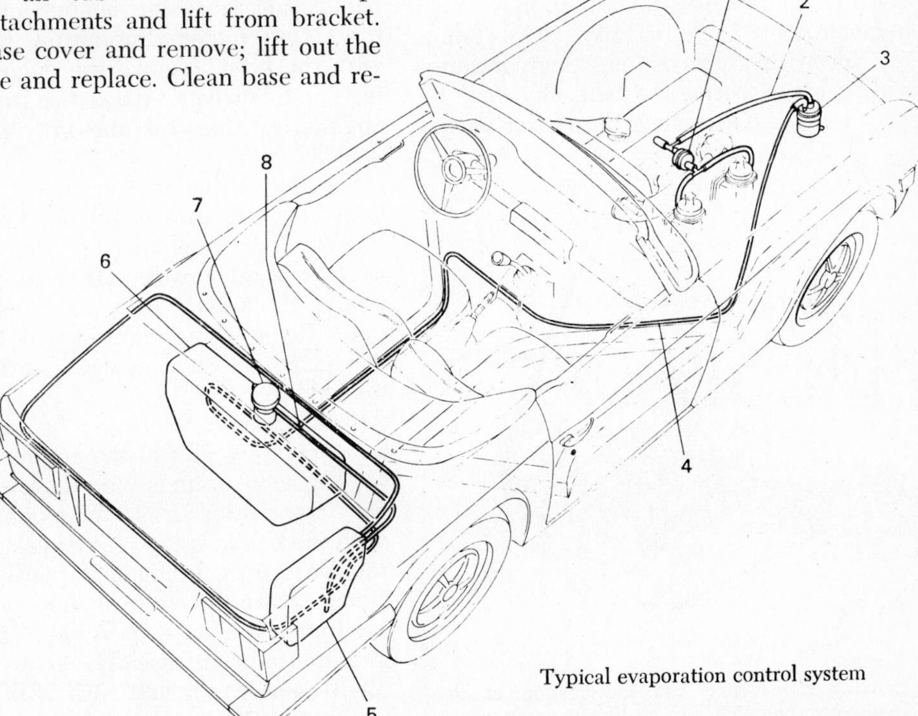

Typical evaporation control system

place. Make certain all lines are not bent or rubbing.

At 48,000 miles, replace entire canister.

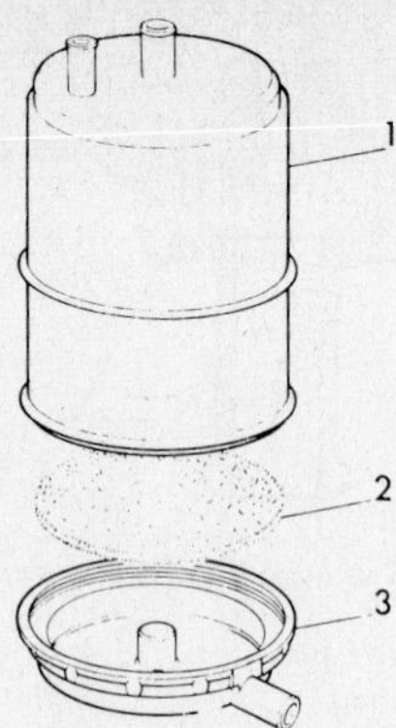

Evaporation control system carbon canister

1 Carbon Canister
2 Filter Gauze
3 Base Cap

ENGINE REMOVAL AND INSTALLATION

TR-4 and TR-4A

The engine and transmission of the TR–4 and TR–4A are removed as follows:

Remove the battery and drain the engine, transmission, and cooling system. Disconnect the oil pressure line, fuel lines, tachometer drive cable, vacuum connection, coil electrical connection, temperature sending cable, horns, fan belt, and engine ground strap. Disconnect the heater valve control, heater hoses, choke control cable, and accelerator linkage rod beneath the carburetors. Remove the carburetors and the exhaust pipe flange. Remove the lower coupling bolt of the steering column (the bolt nearest the steering box), release the two U-bolts on either side of the steering box and move the steering box as far forward as possible. Remove the front cross tube located above the steering box.

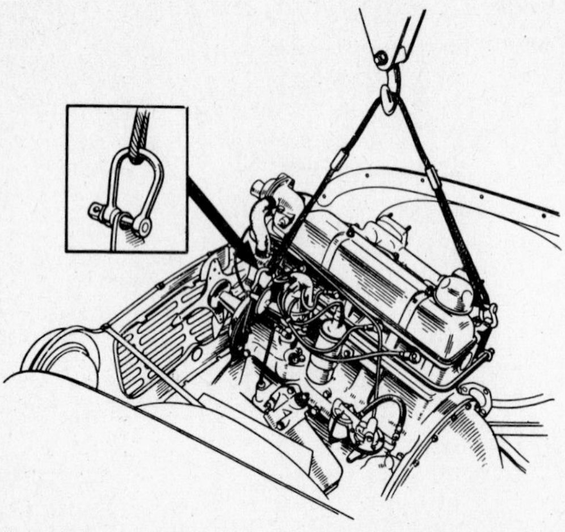

Removing the engine and transmission of the TR–4 with sling attached to lifting points.

Remove the front hood, starter motor, and the radiator and its air deflector. Remove the engine torque reaction arm from its position at the right front corner of the engine. Remove the clutch slave cylinder from its position beneath the car, allowing the cylinder to hang on its hose. From within the vehicle, remove the seat cushions and carpeting, the wishbone-shaped dashboard support, the center transmission hump cover, the speedometer cable, and the front end of the driveshaft. If the vehicle is equipped with overdrive, it will be necessary to remove the electrical connections to the overdrive solenoid.

At this point, it is possible to remove the engine either with or without the transmission, depending on the subsequent steps taken.

To remove the engine alone, support the transmission and attach a hoist to the engine lifting eyes. Disconnect the clutch bellhousing from the engine and remove the starter motor. Supporting the engine with the hoist, remove the engine mountings and brackets. Raise the front of the engine, pull forward and lift clear of the vehicle.

To remove the engine and transmission as a unit, proceed as follows: disconnect the clutch slave cylinder, speedometer drive cable, overdrive cables (if car is overdrive-equipped), and the front driveshaft connection. Remove the transmission top cover and place a section of cardboard over the opening to prevent entry of foreign matter. Attach a hoist to the engine lifting eyes and support the weight of the engine. Remove the engine mountings and brackets. Release the transmission from its mounting and, with the transmission rear extension raised, remove the mounting and plate from the frame. Raise the front of the engine, pulling forward as far as possible. Tilt the engine-transmission assembly at an angle of 30–40° and lift the unit clear of the vehicle.

Reverse the procedure for installation.

TR-250, TR-6

The six-cylinder engine is removed usually along with the transmission.

Disconnect the battery and remove it from the car. Remove the front hood. With the heater set to the HOT position and the radiator cap removed, drain the cooling system via the cylinder block and radiator taps. Disconnect the choke control cables, the throttle linkage at the cross-shaft lever, and the fuel supply line. Release the radiator overflow at the filler cap, the radiator hoses, the heater hoses, and the heater valve control cable. Remove the electrical connections of the starter motor solenoid, positive lead to coil, alternator, oil switch, ground strap, and water temperature sending unit. Disconnect the oil pressure pipe at the crankcase, tachometer drive at distributor, brake servo pipe and clip, ignition advance and retard lines, and the breather pipe from the air cleaner.

Remove the radiator air deflector attachments, air deflector, radiator support struts, and lift out the radiator. Remove the tubular crossmember beneath the radiator. Remove the air cleaner, the U-clamps attaching the steering box to the chassis, and the exhaust pipe from the exhaust manifold flange.

From within the car, remove the driver's and passenger's seats, console, carpeting, and the bolts securing the transmission cover. Remove the gearshift lever knob and rubber boot and withdraw the transmission cover from the right side of the car. Disconnect the backup light connection and the overdrive relay leads (if installed). Disconnect the driveshaft at the transmission flange, the exhaust bracket at the transmission mounting, and the clutch slave cylinder bracket from the bellhousing. Remove the pin from the slave cylinder actuating rod. Loosen the bolts securing the transmission rear mounting and support bracket. Disconnect the speedometer cable and remove the transmission cover.

With a hoisting cable attached to the engine lifting eyes, support the weight of the transmission rear extension and remove the engine front mounting next to the steering linkage and remove the two securing bolts from the opposite mount. Remove the transmission mounting and support plate, and maneuver the engine-transmission assembly clear of the car.

The engine may be removed alone leaving the transmission in place, although this is not recommended. To remove the engine alone, proceed as above until transmission cover is removed. Then support the transmission and attach the hoist to the lifting eyes. Disconnect the clutch housing from the engine and remove the starter motor. Support the engine using the hoist and remove engine mounting brackets. Raise front of engine, pull forward and lift clear of body.

To install engine reverse above procedure. *NOTE: Do not allow weight of engine and transmission to rest on transmission input shaft.*

GT6

Disconnect the battery, drain the cooling system, transmission, and engine sump, and remove the air cleaner. Remove the front hood assembly and radiator components. Remove the front support members at the side of the engine by removing the three bolts at the front and two bolts at the rear. Remove the seat cushions, seats, dashboard support bracket, safety belt anchor bolts, transmission tunnel screws, gear-shift lever knob, and carpeting.

Remove the 12 screws and plates and lift off the transmission cover. Disconnect the driveshaft from the transmission drive flange and detach the slave cylinder, speedometer drive cable, and exhaust pipe attachment. With first gear selected, remove the transmission top cover and extension assemblies. Place a cardboard cover over the transmission opening. Remove the rear transmission mounting bracket nuts and release the mounting bracket. Place a jack under the oil pan in order to support the engine.

Remove the fuel line from the fuel pump, disconnect the tachometer drive cable from the distributor, and release the oil pressure switch and generator wires. Remove the ignition lead wire from the coil. Disconnect the heater hoses and remove the cable from the heater control valve. Disconnect the choke and throttle controls, the electrical connection to the starter motor, and the ground strap from the bellhousing. Release the wire from the temperature sending unit at the thermostat housing. Disconnect the front exhaust pipe from the manifold flange and transmission, and remove the ground strap from the front engine plate.

Supporting the weight of the engine with a hoist, remove the nuts, bolts and shims from the engine mountings and raise the engine sufficiently to enable the positioning of a brake line protection plate (a special plate designed to protect the vulnerable brake line at the front from damage when the engine and transmission are removed). If this special tool is not available, a suitable substitute may be fabricated according to the dimensions and material described in the accompanying diagram. Raise the engine, at the same time tilting it to the rear and pulling it forward, and maneuver the engine-transmission assembly from the car.

In replacing the engine and transmission, the assembly is hoisted into position and suspended while the front and rear mountings are secured to the frame.

Spitfire

Remove engine and transmission of the Spitfire as follows:

Drain the cooling system, engine and transmission. Disconnect the battery and remove the hood. Disconnect and plug the fuel inlet line. Remove the air cleaners, choke and throttle controls, starter motor cable, heater hoses, and the exhaust pipe flange and bracket to the clutch housing. Remove the radiator and hoses and disconnect the coil cables, oil pressure switch cable, generator D and F cables, ground strap, fuel connect to the pump, and tachometer cable.

Remove the front seats and carpeting, transmission cover attaching screws, dashboard support bracket and transmission cover. Disconnect the speedometer cable, clutch slave cylinder, overdrive solenoid wires (if installed), and the front end of the driveshaft. Remove the transmission gear shift extension, installing a cardboard

Brake line protection plate in use on GT6

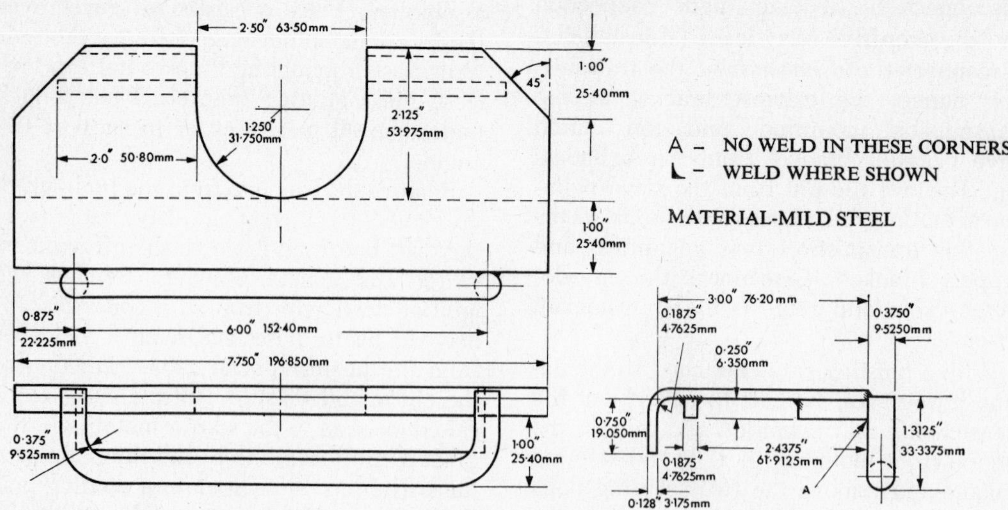

Brake line protection plate details

cover in its place. With the engine supported by a hoist attached to the lifting eyes, release the front and rear engine mountings and lift the engine and transmission assembly until the oil pan clears the chassis crossmember. Lift the assembly and push it forward until the transmission is clear of the vehicle.

To install engine reverse above procedure.

ENGINE DISASSEMBLY

After the engine and transmission have been removed from the chassis, the course of action depends on the reason the engine was removed from the car.

TR-4, TR-4A

After separating the engine from the transmission and placing the engine on a stand or bench, remove:

1. The heater pipe that runs around the left side of the engine; heater bypass hose; coil; oil filter and oil pressure line; fuel pump; spark plug leads; distributor and pedestal; and breather pipe.
2. Fan belt, adjusting link, water pump, generator and mounting bracket, manifolds, thermostat housing.
3. Rocker cover, rocket shaft assembly and pushrods, cylinder head nuts, lifting eye, washers, cylinder head and gasket.
4. Valves, distributor driving gear, distributor shaft, tappets, and dipstick.
5. Flywheel.
6. Fan and pulley assembly; timing cover and gasket; sprockets, chain, disc, sprocket shims and keys.
7. Camshaft, front engine support plate.
8. Oil pan and gasket, oil pump and gasket.
9. Connecting rod caps and bearing shells.
10. Cylinder liners and pistons, piston circlips, and piston pins.
11. Front sealing block and main bearing caps; thrust washers and lower oil seal.
12. Crankshaft, bearing shells, thrust washers, and upper oil seal.
13. Miscellaneous plugs, washers, studs and bearings.

Six-Cylinder Engines

Disassembly of the GT6 engine—which is similar to the TR-250 and TR-6 engines—follows:

Remove the clutch bellhousing bolts, lift out the starter motor and remove the transmission assembly. Remove the fuel pump, the distributor high and low tension wires, coil wires, and remove the distributor and its driving gear. Take out the spark plugs and remove the coil, oil filter, oil pressure switch, and dipstick. Release the domed nut and withdraw the oil pressure relief valve plunger and spring.

Remove the two pivot bolts and adjuster bolt and lift off the generator or alternator and fan belt. Withdraw the generator bracket and release the fuel and vacuum lines retaining clip. Disconnect the fuel and vacuum lines from the carburetors and from the engine. Release the water hose at the right front portion of the engine. Disconnect the water return pipe from the pump and remove the water pump assembly. Remove the center bolt and extract the fan and pulley assembly. Remove the emission-control hoses on all six-cylinder engines and the emission valve on GT6. Gradually loosen the four nuts and six clamps and remove the manifold assembly. Remove the engine mounting brackets, lifting eyes, and cylinder block coolant drain tap if present. Remove the clutch retaining bolts and withdraw the pressure plate assembly and center plate.

Unscrew the two nuts and lift off the rocker arm cover and gasket. Gradually loosen the rocker pedestal nuts, lift off the rocker assembly, and lift out the pushrods. Gradually release the cylinder head nuts in the sequence reverse of that for assembly. Remove the cylinder head, gasket and valve tappets. Use a spring compressor to facilitate the removal of the valve keepers, retainers, outer springs, inner springs, spring seats, and valves. Remove the timing cover and gasket.

Remove the camshaft sprocket and lift off the timing chain. After withdrawing the seal extension, oil slinger and sprocket, remove the key and shims. Remove the keeper plate and front engine plate, and withdraw the camshaft. Remove the retaining nut and washer and take out the spring and relief valve. Remove the oil pan and gasket. Unscrew the retaining bolts and remove the oil pump. Remove the connecting rod big-end cap bolts, take off the caps, and push the connecting rod and piston assem-

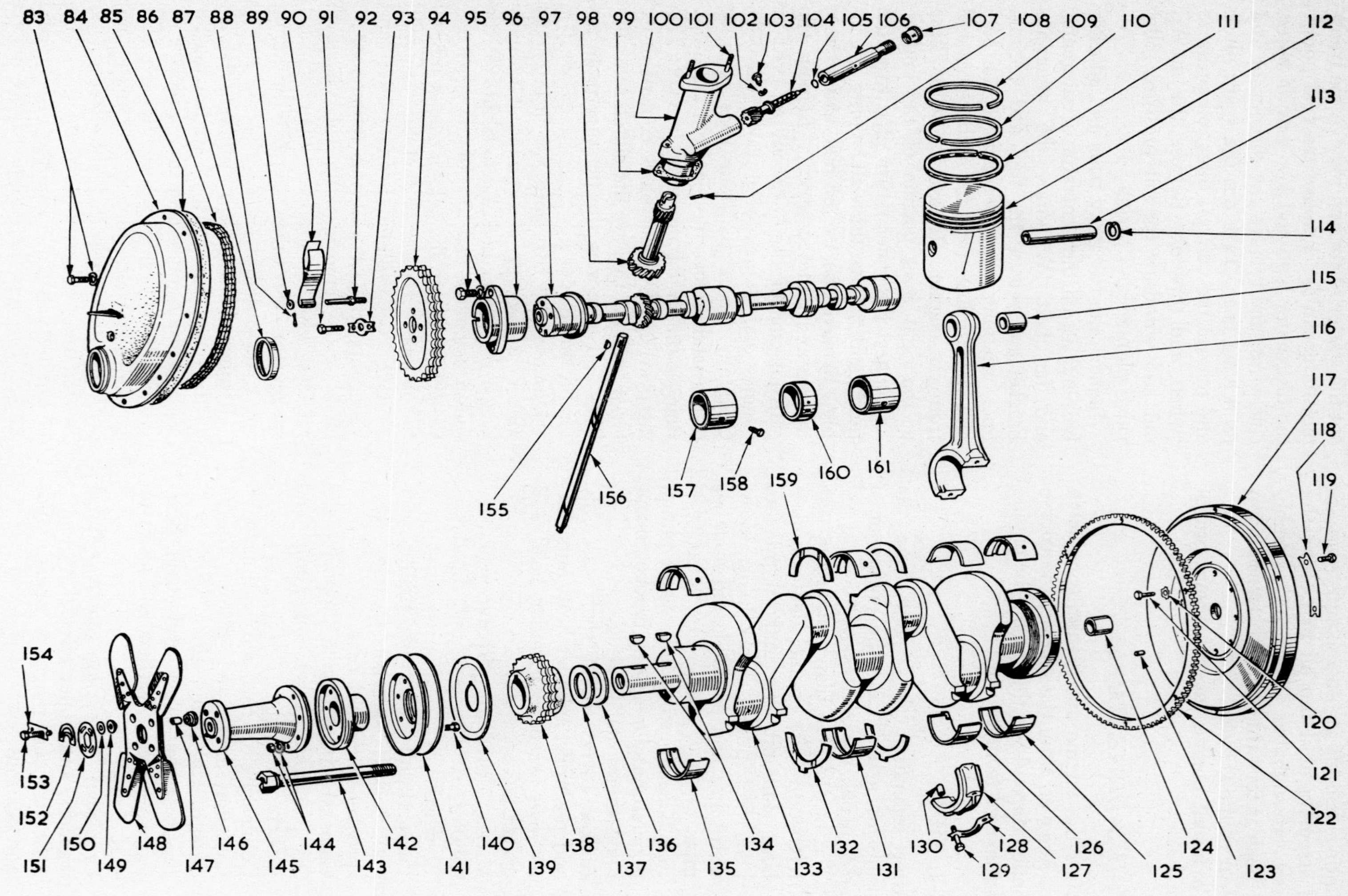

Internal components of TR-4 engine.

83 Bolt and spring washer
84 Timing cover
85 Gasket
86 Timing chain
87 Oil seal
88 Cotter pin
89 Washer
90 Tensioner blade
91 Bolt
92 Tensioner pin
93 Lockplate
94 Camshaft sprocket
95 Bolt and spring washer
96 Front camshaft bearing
97 Camshaft
98 Distributor drive gear
99 Gasket
100 Distributor pedestal
101 Stud
102 Spring washer
103 Peg bolt
104 Tachometer drive gear
105 Rubber O-ring
106 Drive gear housing
107 Cap
108 Pin
109 Compression ring (taper)
110 Compression ring (parallel)
111 Oil control ring
112 Piston
113 Piston pin
114 Circlip
115 Piston pin bushing
116 Connecting rod
117 Flywheel
118 Lockplate
119 Bolt
120 Tab washer
121 Bolt
122 Starter ring gear
123 Dowel
124 Spigot bearing
125 Rear main bearing shell
126 Con-rod bearing shell
127 Con-rod cap
128 Lockplate
129 Con-rod bolt
130 Dowel
131 Center main bearing shell
132 Lower thrust washer
133 Crankshaft
134 Woodruff keys
135 Front main bearing shell
136 Shim washer 0.004" (0.1mm.)
137 Shim washer 0.006" (0.15mm.)
138 Crankshaft sprocket
139 Oil thrower disc
140 Bolt
141 Pulley
142 Pulley hub
143 Starting handle dog bolt
144 Washer and nut
145 Fan extension
146 Rubber bushing
147 Spacer tube
148 Fan
149 Rubber bushing
150 Plain washer
151 Plate
152 Balancer
153 Bolt
154 Lockplate
155 Woodruff key
156 Oil pump drive shaft
157 Intermediate front camshaft bearing
158 Peg bolt
159 Upper thrust washer
160 Intermediate rear camshaft bearing
161 Rear camshaft bearing

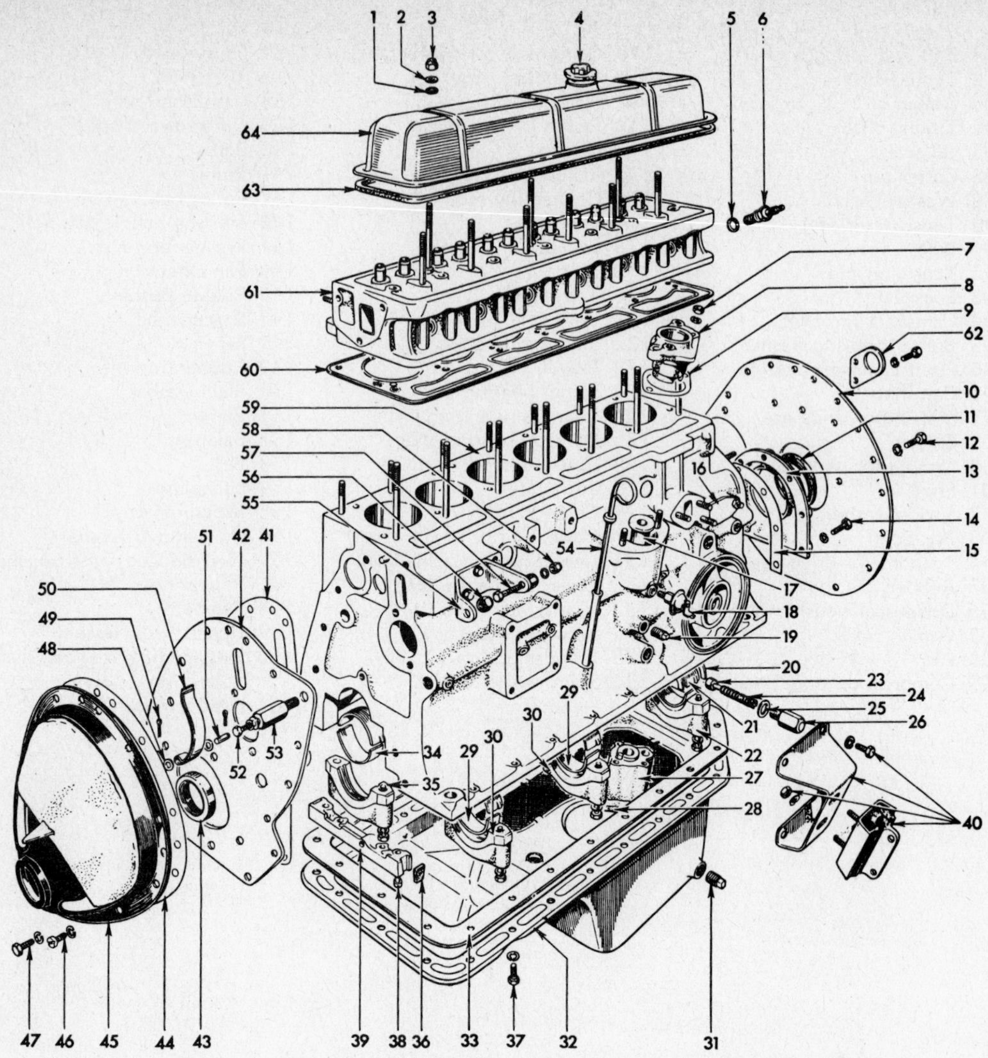

Stationary parts of GT6 engine

1 Fiber washer
2 Plain washer
3 Nyloc nut
4 Filler cap
5 Copper/asbestos washer
6 Spark plug
7 Nut
8 Adaptor
9 Gasket
10 Rear engine plate
11 Rear oil seal
12 Bolt
13 Rear oil seal housing
14 Bolt
15 Gasket
16 Banking plate
17 Oil pump drive shaft bushing
18 Oil pressure switch
19 Plug
20 Crankshaft thrust washer
21 Rear bearing shell
22 Rear bearing cap
23 Relief valve
24 Spring
25 Copper washer
26 Cap nut
27 Oil pump body
28 Oil pump end plate
29 Center bearing shell
30 Center main bearing cap
31 Drain plug
32 Oil pan
33 Oil pan gasket
34 Front bearing shell
35 Front main bearing cap
36 Sealing wedges
37 Oil pan bolt
38 Slotted screw
39 Front sealing block
40 Front engine mounting
41 Gasket
42 Front engine plate
43 Oil seal
44 Gasket
45 Front timing cover
46 Slotted setscrew
47 Bolt
48 Plain washer
49 Cotter pin
50 Chain tensioner
51 Pivot pin
52 Bolt
53 Generator pedestal
54 Dipstick
55 Bracket
56 Nyloc nut
57 Bolt
58 Nyloc nut
59 Cylinder block
60 Cylinder head gasket
61 Cylinder head
62 Lifting eye
63 Rocker cover gasket
64 Rocker cover

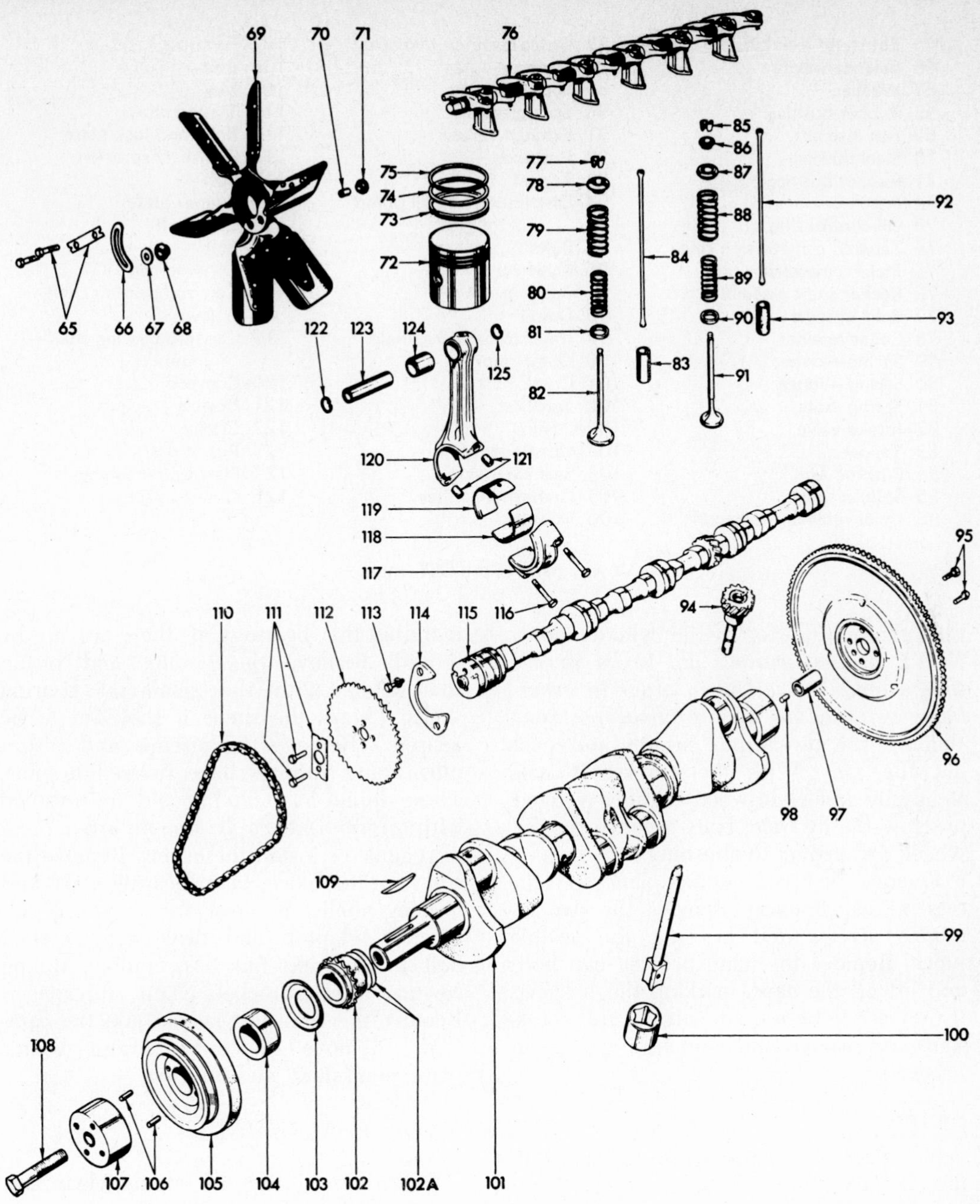

Moving parts of the GT6 engine

65 Bolts and lock tabs
66 Balance weight
67 Washer
68 Rubber bushing
69 Fan assembly
70 Steel bushing
71 Rubber bushing
72 Piston
73 Oil control ring
74 Tapered compression ring
75 Plain compression ring
76 Rocker shaft assembly
77 Split keepers
78 Collar retainer
79 Spring—outer
80 Spring—inner
81 Spring seats
82 Intake valve
83 Tappet
84 Pushrod
85 Split keepers
86 Inner retainer (exhaust)
87 Outer retainer (exhaust)
88 Spring—outer
89 Spring—inner
90 Spring seats
91 Exhaust valve)
92 Pushrod
93 Tappet
94 Distributor and oil pump drive gear
95 Bolts
96 Flywheel
97 Bushing
98 Dowel
99 Inner rotor and spindle
100 Outer rotor
101 Crankshaft
102 Sprocket
102A Shim
103 Oil slinger
104 Seal extension
105 Crankshaft pulley
106 Dowels
107 Fan boss
108 Bolt
109 Key
110 Timing chain
111 Bolts and lock plate
112 Camshaft sprocket
113 Bolt
114 Keeper plate
115 Camshaft
116 Bolt
117 Con-rod cap
118 Con-rod bearing shell—lower
119 Con-rod bearing shell—upper
120 Con-rod
121 Dowels
122 Circlip
123 Piston pin
124 Piston pin bushing
125 Circlip

Moving parts of the GT6 engine

blies through the top of the cylinder bores. *NOTE: if the bearings are to be reused, they should be marked in order to ensure being returned to their original positions.* Remove the piston pin circlips and push out the pins. With the crankshaft held steady by a block of wood suitably wedged, unscrew the flywheel bolts, remove the flywheel, and extract the bushing.

Remove the rear engine plate and the real oil seal housing. Remove the two retaining screws and tap out the sealing block. Remove the main bearing cap bolts and lift off the caps, marking the bearings if they are to be reused. Lift out the crankshaft and remove studs and sealing plugs as necessary.

Spitfire

The disassembly procedure for the Spitfire engine follows:

Remove the transmission and clutch assembly and take off the following: fan belt, water pump, generator and bracket, fuel and vacuum lines, coil, tachometer cable, distributor, spark plugs, fuel pump, oil filter, breather pipe, carburetors, manifolds, and dipstick.

Remove the rocker cover, rocker assembly, pushrods, cylinder head, gasket, tappets. Use a valve spring compressor to aid in disassembling the retainers and keepers, springs, spring seals, and valves. Remove the oil pan, gasket, and oil pump. Remove the connecting rod caps and bearing shells, marking the bearings if they are to be reused. Remove the circlips and piston rods along with the small-end bearing shells. (Mark the shells if they are to be reused.) Remove the circlips and piston pins. Some Spitfires have pressed in pins. These do not have circlips and are installed with an interference fit. Use an arbor press to remove or install these pins. Remove the front sealing block, main bearing caps, and bearing shells. Remove the flywheel, distributor adaptor, and drive gear, extract bolt or nut and fan boss, pulley, timing cover, gasket, sprocket, chain and spacer. Remove the camshaft keeper and the camshaft. Remove the engine front bearer plate, crankshaft, and bushing.

ENGINE ASSEMBLY

Before assembling the engine, clean and scrape all gasket material off sealing surfaces and install new gaskets. Degrease all engine components and clean the oil passages with compressed air. Assess the wear and serviceability of all components. Use new gaskets and tab washers and replace damaged studs, nuts, bolts, etc. Use a suitable sealing compound for all gasket joints and sealing block faces.

When installing the front sealing block, coat the ends with sealing compound and locate it in the cylinder block, partially tightening the retaining screws. Coat the wooden shims with sealing compound and

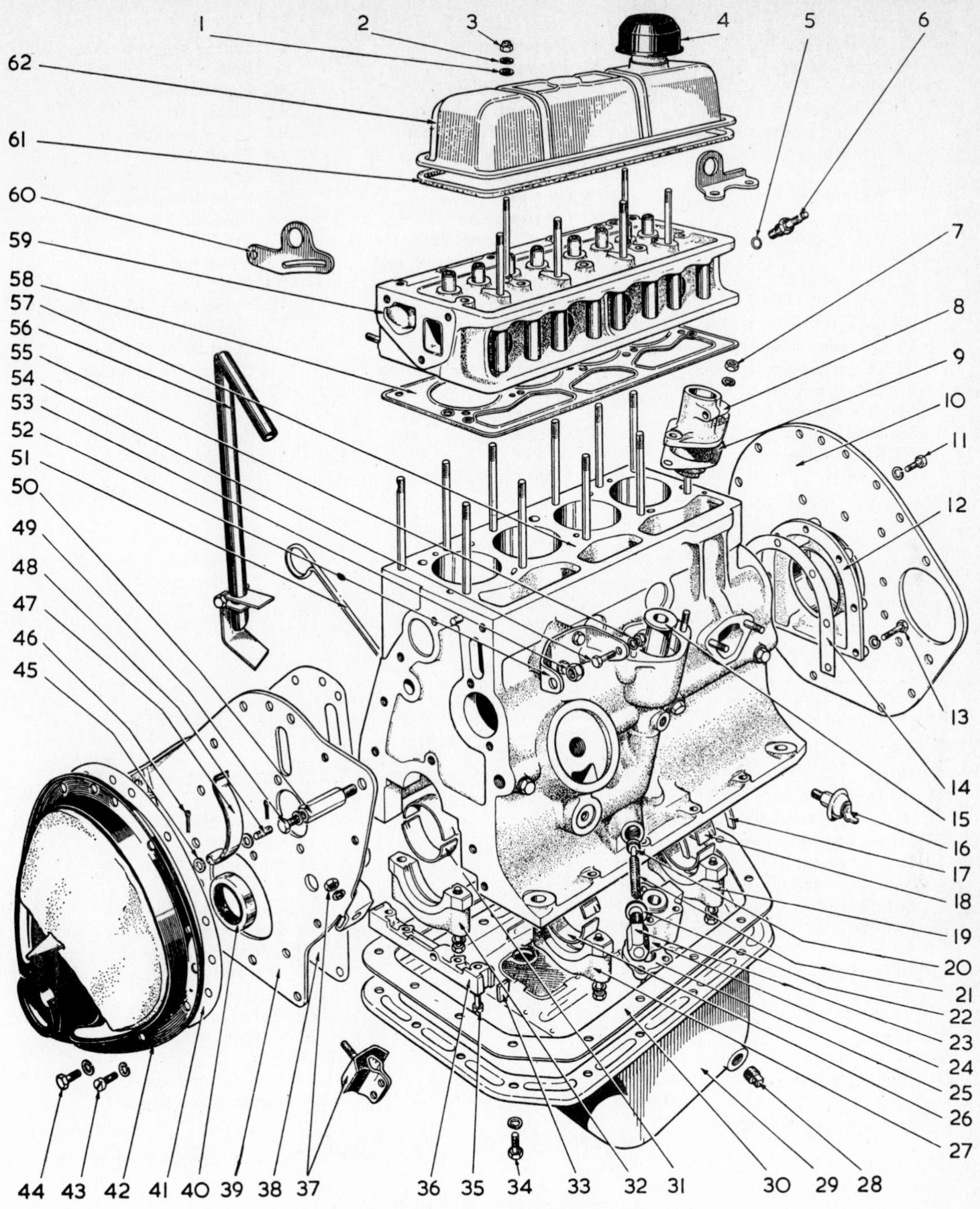

Fixed components of the Spitfire engine.

Fixed components of the Spitfire engine.

1 Fiber washer
2 Plain washer
3 Nyloc nut
4 Filler cap
5 Copper/asbestos washer
6 Spark plug
7 Nut
8 Adaptor
9 Gasket
10 Rear engine plate
11 Bolt
12 Rear oil seal
13 Bolt
14 Gasket
15 Oil pump drive shaft bushing
16 Oil pressure switch
17 Crankshaft thrust washer
18 Rear bearing shell
19 Rear bearing cap
20 Relief valve
21 Spring
22 Copper washer
23 Cap nut
24 Oil pump body
25 Oil pump end plate
26 Center bearing shell
27 Center main bearing cap
28 Drain plug
29 Oil pan
30 Oil pan gasket
31 Front bearing shell
32 Front main bearing cap
33 Sealing wedges
34 Sump bolt
35 Slotted screw
36 Front sealing block
37 Front engine mounting
38 Gasket
39 Front engine plate
40 Oil seal
41 Gasket
42 Front timing cover
43 Slotted setscrew
44 Bolt
45 Plain washer
46 Cotter pin
47 Chain tensioner
48 Pivot pin
49 Bolt
50 Generator pedestal
51 Dipstick
52 Bracket
53 Nyloc nut
54 Bolt
55 Nyloc nut
56 Breather pipe
57 Cylinder block
58 Cylinder head gasket
59 Cylinder head
60 Generator adjusting link
61 Rocker cover gasket
62 Rocker cover

Internal components of the Spitfire engine.

70 Piston
71 Oil control ring
72 Taper compression ring
73 Plain compression ring
74 Rocker assembly
80 Spring—outer
81 Spring—inner
82 Pushrod
83 Pushrod
86 Spring seats
87 Spring seats
88 Tappet
89 Tappet
90 Exhaust valve
91 Intake valve
92 Distributor and oil pump drive gear
93 Lock tab
94 Bolt
95 Flywheel
96 Bush
97 Dowel
98 Inner rotor and spindle
99 Outer rotor
100 Crankshaft
101 Key
102 Sprocket
103 Flinger
105 Crankshaft pulley
109 Timing chain
110 Bolts and lock tab
111 Camshaft sprocket
112 Bolt
113 Keeper plate
114 Camshaft
115 Bolt and locktab
116 Con-rod cap
117 Con-rod bearing shell—lower
118 Con-rod bearing shell—upper
119 Dowels
120 Con-rod
121 Circlip
122 Piston pin
123 Piston pin bushing
124 Nut
125 Retainer and keeper
126 Retainer and keeper

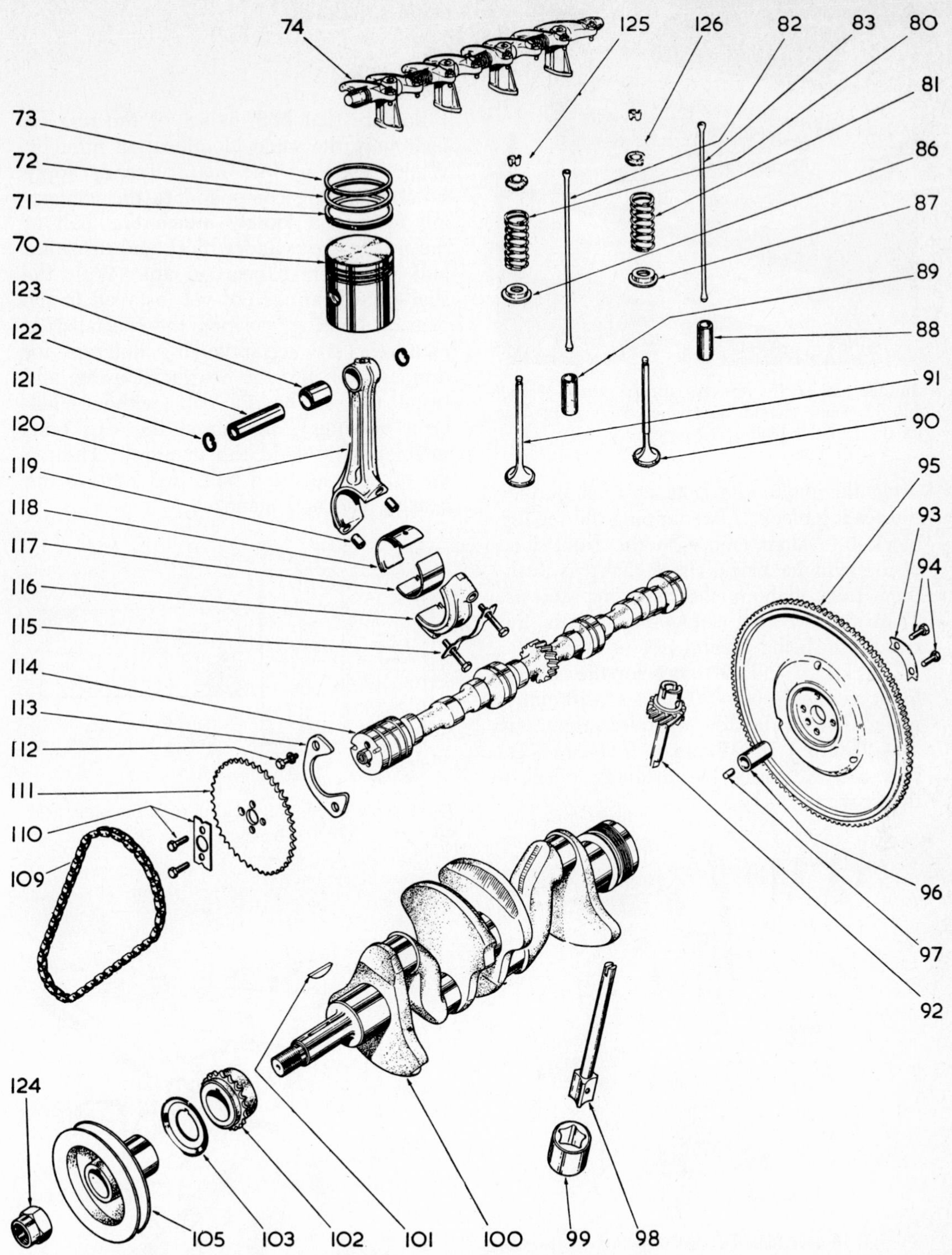

Internal components of the Spitfire engine.

Installation of the wedges of the front sealing block. Block should be aligned with front face of the cylinder block.

drive them into the slots at each end of the sealing block. After tapping the sealing block into alignment with the front face of the cylinder block, check that it is flush, then fully tighten the retaining screws. Trim the wooden shims flush with the crankcase, being careful not to undercut.

Crankshaft end clearance for the six-cylinder engines is .006–.008 in. (.16–.20 mm.), while that of the four-cylinder engines is .004–.006 in. (.10–.15 mm.). Reduce excessive end clearance by installing oversize thrust washers.

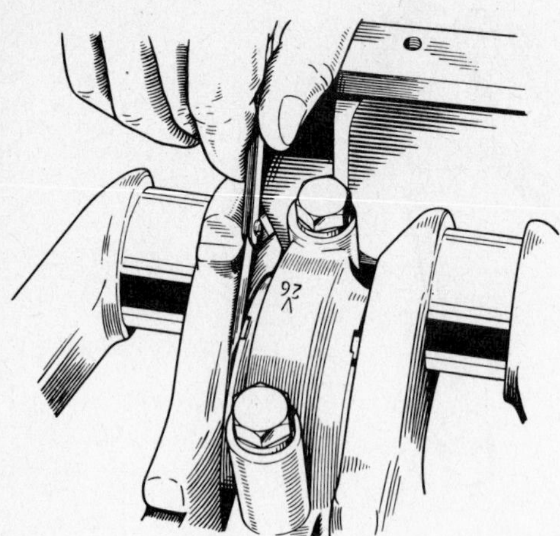

Crankshaft end clearance is .004–.006 in. for the four-cylinder engines and .006–.008 in. for six-cylinder models.

Camshaft end clearance is .004–.008 in. (.10–.20 mm.) for the six-cylinder engines and .003–.0075 in. (.108–.19 mm.) for the four-cylinder models.

Engine assembly notes for the specific engines follow:

TR-4, TR-4A

Be sure that both halves of the rear oil seal show the same identification number. When installing the rear oil seal, apply suitable sealing compound to the contacting faces and loosely attach one half of the seal to the cylinder block and the other half to the rear bearing cap. With the shell-type bearings not yet installed in the bearing housing, position the special-sized mandrel (see accompanying diagram for dimensions) into the bearing housing, and install the rear bearing cap (without shell-type bearings), tightening the cap bolts sufficiently to hold the mandrel. Tighten the oil seal securing bolts and remove the bearing cap and mandrel.

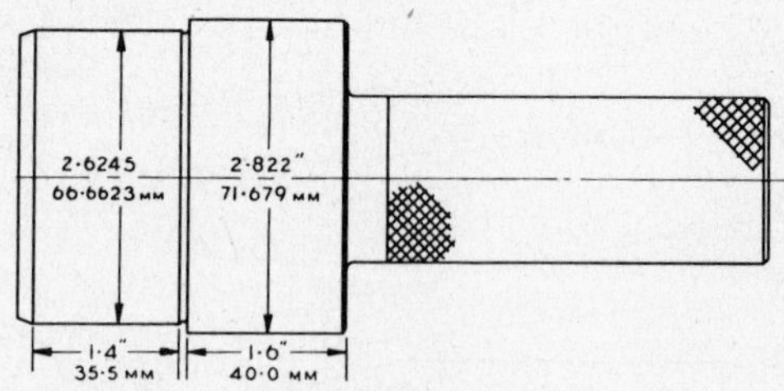

Dimensions of oil seal mandrel used to center rear oil seal of TR–4, TR–4A.

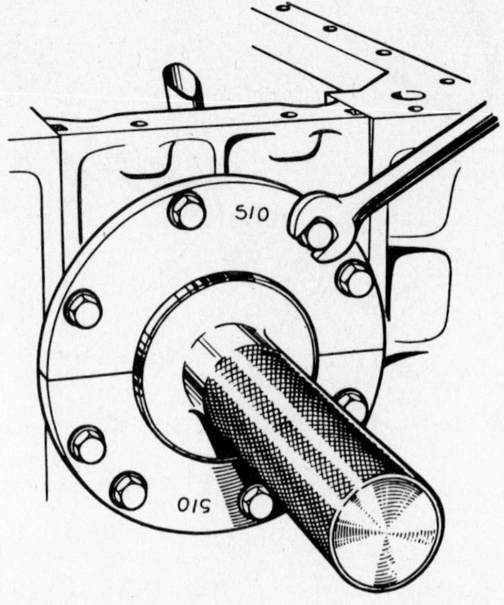

Using the special mandrel to centralize the TR–4, TR–4A rear oil seal.

When replacing the crankshaft and bearings, be sure that the locating taps engage the recesses provided. The white metal faces of the thrust washers should be against the thrust faces of the crankshaft. Upon installing the bearing caps into position, ensure that the markings on the caps are placed adjacent to corresponding identical markings on the crankcase.

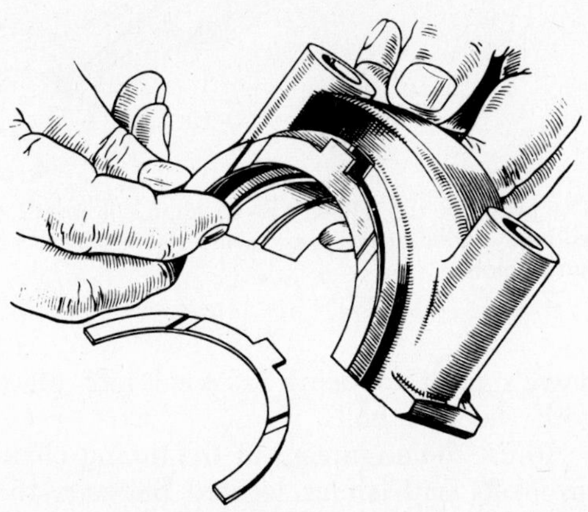

When installing thrust washers, the white metal faces of the thrust washers should be against the thrust faces of the crankshaft.

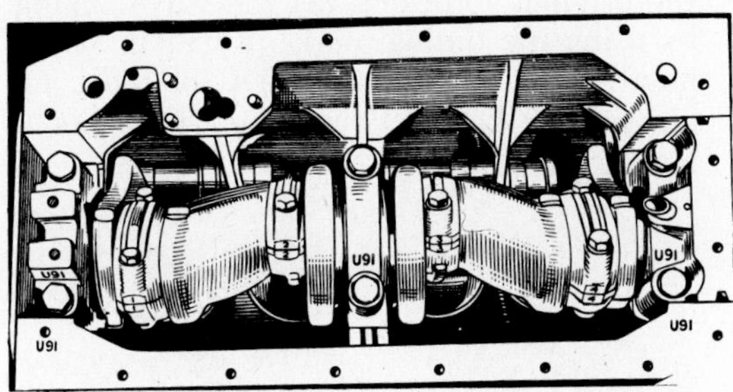

Main bearing caps and crankcase are stamped with corresponding numbers for reassembly.

Seal the rear bearing cap by ramming lengths of felt into the rear bearing cap slots. Excess felt should be trimmed with a knife.

Installation and measurement of the piston rings is carried out as shown in the accompanying illustrations, with the tapered compression ring installed with its taper towards the top. When measuring the piston ring gap, insert the ring into the liner and use a piston to push the ring about 1/4 in. into the bore.

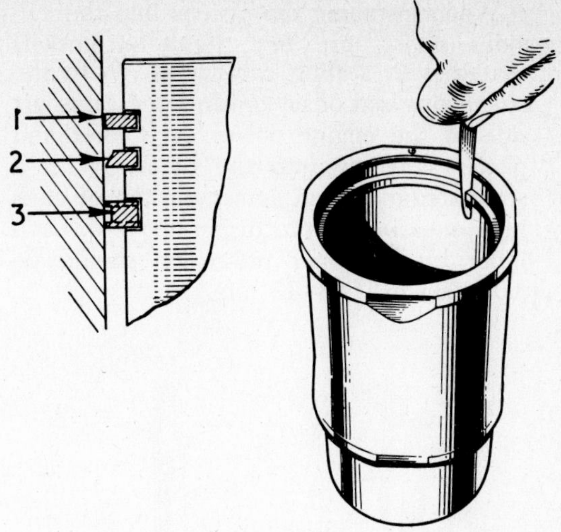

Piston ring location, plain compression (1), tapered compression (2), and oil control (3) rings. Illustration at right shows method of measuring piston ring gaps.

In choosing pistons or assessing their possible reuse, do not use a set in which the maximum variation in weight exceeds 7.09 grams. The piston must be heated in boiling water in order to assemble it onto the connecting rod. The accompanying illustration indicates the proper positioning of the components.

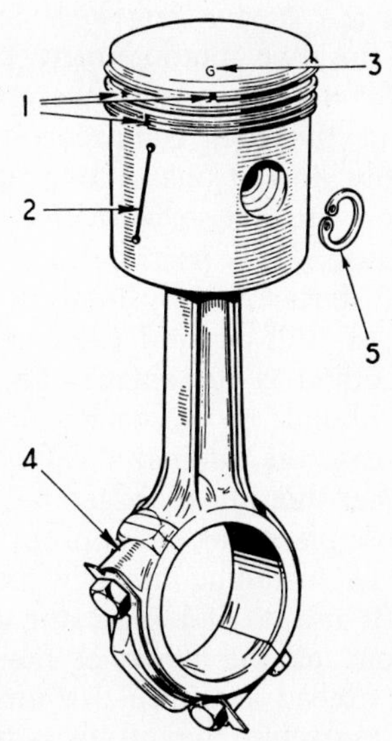

Proper relative positioning of piston on connecting rod of TR–4, TR–4A engine. Shown are: rings (1), piston slot (2), piston identification marking (3), connecting rod cap (4), and piston circlip (5).

When installing the pistons into the cylinder liners, use new figure 8 gaskets coated with sealing compound. With the connecting rod offset towards the camshaft side of the engine, lower each liner and piston assembly into the block. With a straightedge placed across the top of each liner, measure its protrusion above the cylinder block. Liner protrusion should be .003–.005 in. (.08–.13 mm.).

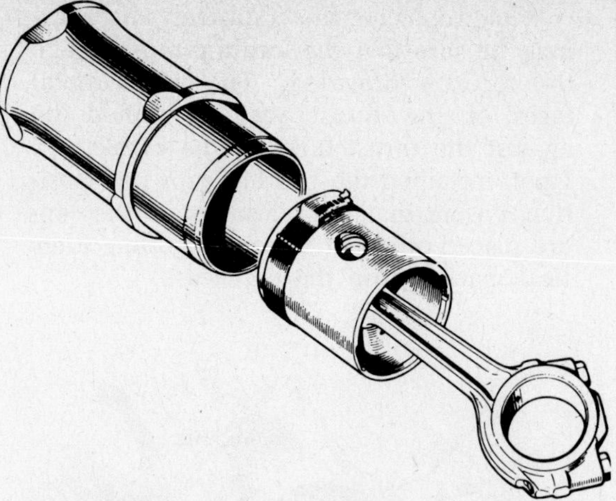

The piston of the TR–4, TR–4A engine is installed to the cylinder sleeve prior to the sleeve's insertion to the block.

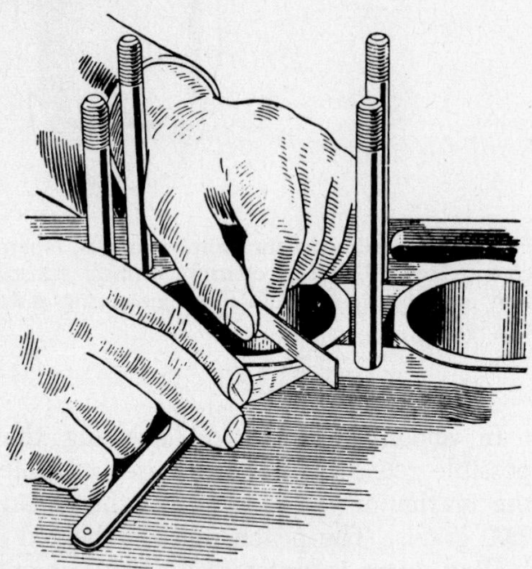

Measuring cylinder liner protrusion of the TR–4, TR–4A, which should be .003–.005 in. above the cylinder block.

Inspect the starter ring gear for excess wear at the two predominant points of starter pinion engagement (the crankshaft, because of the four compression strokes, will usually stop at one of two positions). If the teeth are not so worn that jamming will be caused, it is possible to extend the life of the starter ring by rotating the ring gear 60° or 120° around the flywheel. A second method is to replace the flywheel to the crankshaft on its second dowel hole, in which case the original T.D.C. arrow on the flywheel should be obliterated and another arrow placed at the appropriate position. When installing the flywheel to the crankshaft, use a dial indicator to check the run-out of the flywheel face, which must not exceed .003 in. (.076 mm.).

When replacing the oil pan, note that the breather pipe bracket is secured with a long bolt, while the front sealing block is retained by two short bolts. The front engine bearer plate is located by two dowels prior to being fastened into place with the five bolts.

Adjust the alignment of the timing chain sprockets with shims located between the crankshaft sprocket and a shoulder of the crankshaft. In aligning the sprockets, place a straightedge across both the crankshaft and camshaft sprockets, as shown. Remove or add shims as necessary. When replacing the original sprockets, set the valve timing by using the timing marks provided. When number one piston is at TDC of the compression stroke, the two scribed lines should be aligned as shown.

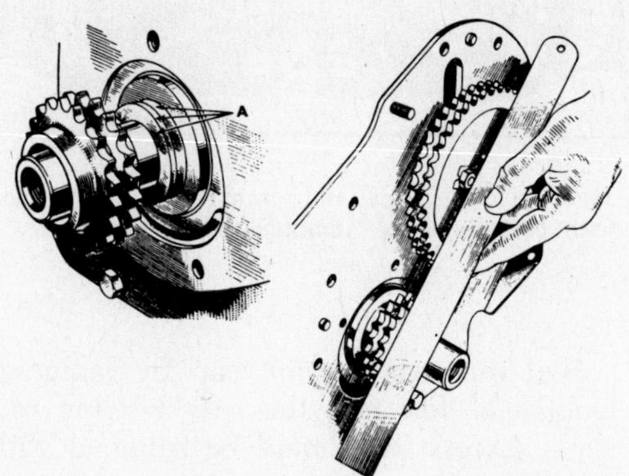

The timing sprockets are aligned by installation of shims (A). The alignment is checked with a straightedge, as shown at right.

If new sprockets are being installed, the following operations must be followed: Temporarily attach the camshaft sprocket and turn the camshaft until number one pushrod is at its highest point. Adjust number eight rocker clearance to .040 in. (1 mm.). Repeat the preceding, except with number two pushrod at its highest point and number seven rocker adjusted to .040 in. (1 mm.). Turn the camshaft until valves numbers seven and eight are rocking—i.e., one valve is about to open and the other is about to close. The exact point is obtained by moving the camshaft slowly until the clearances between the rockers and valve stems are equal for both valves. At this point, turn the crankshaft so as to bring pistons numbers one and four to the TDC position.

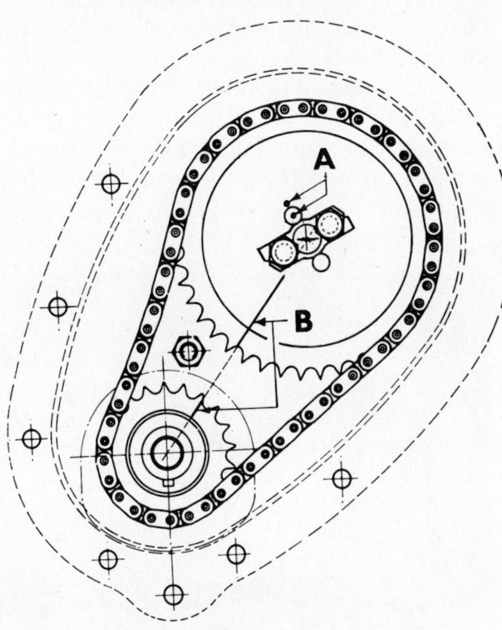

Relative positions of TR-4, TR-4A timing marks when No. 1 piston is at TDC of the compression stroke

Install the timing chain as follows: Remove the camshaft sprocket without disturbing the position of the camshaft, encircle both sprockets with the timing chain and install the camshaft sprocket to the camshaft. The sprocket may be maneuvered by skipping a link at a time or by reversing the sprocket until a pair of holes exactly coincide with those of the camshaft. Such action will probably have to be taken if a new sprocket is being used. Keep in mind:

The camshaft sprocket has four holes which are equally spaced, but which are offset from a tooth center. For

When No. 1 piston is at TDC, the distributor drive slot of the TR-4 and TR-4A should be as shown

this reason, a half-tooth adjustment may be obtained by rotating the sprocket 90° from its original position. Likewise, a quarter-tooth adjustment is obtained by turning the sprocket from front to back on the shaft. (When it is rotated 90° in the reversed position, a variation of three-quarters of a tooth results.)

After the sprocket has been secured, the

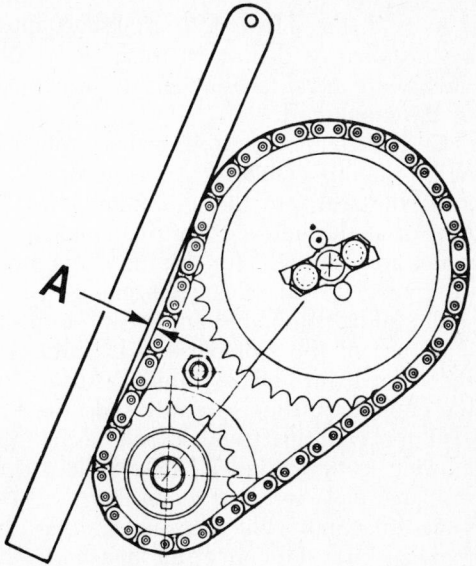

Using a straightedge to check the timing chain for wear. Dimension A should not be greater than .4 in.

timing should be rechecked to ensure that the camshaft has not been moved during the preceding operations. When number one piston is at TDC, rocker clearances of valves numbers seven and eight should be equal. Readjust the rocker clearances to .010 in. (.25 mm.). Check the timing chain for wear by lining up a straightedge as shown. Dimension A should not exceed .4 in. (10 mm.).

When installing the timing cover, replace worn or damaged oil seals or tensioners. The oil slinger should be positioned with its dished face outward, adjacent to the crankshaft sprocket. The distributor driving gear end clearance should be .003–.007 in. (.076–.178 mm.), and is adjusted by shims located underneath the distributor pedestal.

Adjust the oil pressure relief valve as follows: With the engine at normal operating temperature, slowly increase the engine speed and observe the oil pressure gauge. As the engine speed increases to 2,000 rpm, oil pressure should rise to 75 psi, then fall to 70 psi when 2,000 rpm is reached. If adjustment is necessary, loosen the relief valve locking nut and rotate the screw clockwise to increase the relief valve opening pressure or counterclockwise to lower it. After correct adjustment has been attained, tighten the locking nut.

GT6, TR-250, and TR-6

As with the TR–4, the crankshaft must be installed with thrust washers having their white metal faces against a thrust face of the crankshaft.

Centralize the rear oil seal as follows: With the lip of the seal facing forward press the seal into the aluminum housing. Note that the housing has two small holes which may be used for driving out a worn or damaged seal. Coat the paper gasket with sealing compound and locate it on the rear face of the cylinder block. Lubricate the oil seal lip and its running surface on the crankshaft, then carefully slide the seal over the crankshaft and loosely secure the housing to the cylinder block. Slide a centralizing tool over the crankshaft, at the same time move the housing so that the tool can enter the bore of the housing. With the centralizing tool in place, tighten the securing bolts, then withdraw the tool.

If replacement of the starter ring gear is necessary, a new gear may be installed by heating in boiling water and pressing onto the flywheel. The ring gear is an interference fit and is shrunk onto the flywheel assembly at the factory.

The run-out of the flywheel face is measured with a dial indicator, and must not exceed .003 in. (.076 mm.).

The maximum permissible variation between the heaviest and lightest connecting rod (or piston) in a set of six must not be greater than 7.09 grams for purposes of proper balance.

In assembling the pistons to the connecting rods, observe the Front or arrow identification on the piston crown and install the piston so that this mark points toward the timing cover.

When installing the original timing chain sprockets, the valve timing is set by utilizing the scribed marks on the sprockets, as shown in the accompanying illustration.

Relative position of the GT6 and TR-250 timing marks with No. 1 piston at TDC of the compression stroke

For the installation of new, unmarked sprockets, refer to the appropriate section below:

GT6, TR-250

With the camshaft sprocket temporarily attached, turn the camshaft until number twelve pushrod is at its highest point, then adjust number one rocker clearance to .040

in. (1 mm.). Repeat the preceding with number eleven pushrod and number two rocker. Next, turn the camshaft until valves number one and two are rocking, i.e., one valve is about to open and the other is about to close. Turn the crankshaft until pistons numbers one and six are at top dead center. Remove the timing sprocket without disturbing the position of the camshaft, encircle both sprockets with the chain, and install the camshaft sprocket to the camshaft. As with the TR-4 and TR-4A camshaft sprocket, that of the GT6 and GT-250 may be rotated 90° or reversed on the shaft in order to obtain half-tooth or quarter-tooth adjustment, respectively. After the sprocket is secured, the timing should be rechecked to ensure that the position of the camshaft has not been changed. With number one piston at top dead center, the clearances of rockers numbers one and two should be equal. After timing, readjust all rocker clearances to .010 in. (.25 mm.).

TR-6

The engine of the TR–6 incorporates a duplex timing chain with accompanying dual sprockets at the crankshaft and camshaft. Installation of new sprockets is as follows: In order that valves cannot strike the piston crowns when valve clearances are being adjusted in the absence of the timing chain, the engine should be rotated to approximately 45° BTDC. With the crankshaft in this position, adjust valve clearances of cylinders one through five to .010 in. (.25 mm.) by rotating the camshaft as necessary in the clockwise (as viewed from the timing case) direction. Adjust the valve clearances of number six cylinder to the valve timing checking clearance of .040 in. (1.02 mm.). With the flywheel at the TDC position, rotate the camshaft until valve number twelve – the exhaust valve of cylinder number six–is almost closed and valve number eleven is about to open. This position may be accurately obtained by using feeler gauges of equal thickness at each rocker. In replacing the timing chain, remove the camshaft sprocket, encircle both sprockets with the timing chain, and install the camshaft sprocket to the camshaft. As with the preceding models, a precise setting is made possible by the reversing of the camshaft sprocket or its rotation by 90°. After the camshaft sprocket has been secured, adjust the valves of number six cylinder to the normal clearance of .010 in. (.25 mm.).

Replace the timing cover oil seal, ensuring that the sealing lip is towards the rear of the engine. Replace the oil slinger on the crankshaft so that the dished face is towards the oil seal. Check the end clearance of the distributor drive gear and adjust, if necessary, by means of shims placed beneath the distributor pedestal. Distributor drive end float should be .003–.007 in. (.08–.18 mm.). Shim addition or removal is generally necessary only when new components are being installed.

Distributor drive gear is adjusted by means of shims (9) placed below the distributor pedestal (8).

Spitfire

The current Spitfires use a lip type seal which is installed in the same fashion as the seal on the six cylinder engines. Earlier engines use a scroll type seal which is installed as follows: Using a new gasket coated with sealing compound, secure the gasket and rear oil seal to the crankcase by tightening the bolts only slightly. A .003 in. (.076 mm.) feeler gauge may then be used, along with a soft-headed mallet, to centralize the oil seal on the rear of the crankshaft. The securing bolts should be fully tightened only after the oil seal has been centralized.

NOTE: From Chassis No. FC 2794, a cast iron housing has replaced the aluminum housing. With the cast iron housings the clearance is .002 in. (.05 mm.).

Installation of unmarked sprockets must be accompanied by a valve timing check and/or adjustment, carried out as follows:

With the camshaft sprocket temporarily attached, turn the camshaft until pushrod number one is at its highest position and adjust the clearance of number eight rocker to .040 in. (1 mm.). Repeat the preceding with number two pushrod and number seven rocker. Turn the camshaft until valves number seven and eight are rocking—i.e., one is about to open, the other is about to close. Move the camshaft to a point where the clearances between the rockers and valve stems are equal. This is the proper position for the camshaft. Next, turn the crankshaft until pistons numbers one and four are at TDC. Replace the timing chain as described in the TR-4, TR–4A section preceding, and adjust all rocker clearances to .010 in. (.25 mm.).

Check the distributor drive gear end float, which should be .003–.007 in. (.08–.18 mm.). This end float is adjustable by means of shims placed beneath the distributor pedestal.

CYLINDER HEAD

Removal and Installation

Disconnect the battery, drain the cooling system, and disconnect the cable of the cylinder head. Remove the air cleaner(s) and the intake and exhaust manifolds. Loosen the generator mounting bolts, pivot the generator toward the cylinder head and detach the belt from the water pump pulley. Remove the bolts securing the water pump to the cylinder head and remove the pump. Remove the rocker arm cover, the rocker assembly, and the push-rods. Be sure that all electrical and hose connections to the cylinder head have been disconnected. Remove the spark plugs. Loosen and remove cylinder head nuts in reverse order of the tightening sequence shown in this chapter for each model. Lift off the cylinder head. *NOTE: If the cylinder head does not lift readily, tap each side with a hammer, using a short piece of wood to help absorb the shock. Another method is to reinsert the spark plugs and crank the engine with the starter, using the engine's own compression pressure to supply the force needed to break the seal.*

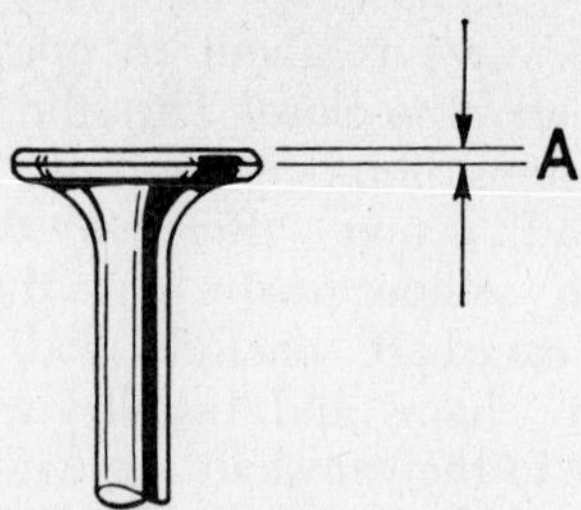

Valves with a head thickness less than 1/32 in. (dimension A) should be replaced.

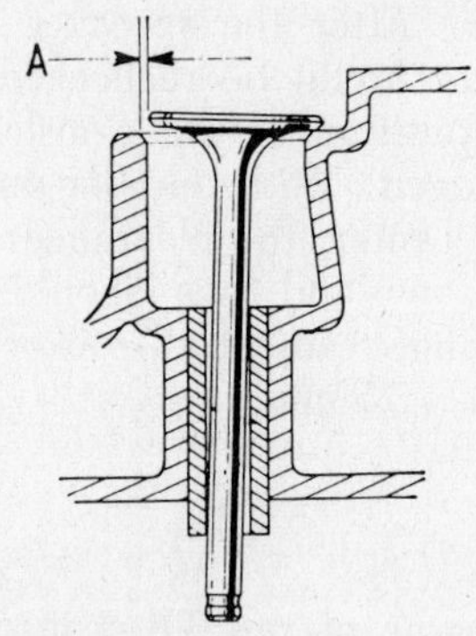

Maximum permissible movement of the valve head across the seat is .02 in.

Before replacing the cylinder head, be sure that the gasket surfaces of the head and block are perfectly clean and smooth. If any dirt is present, the gasket may leak when the head is installed. Check for the presence of dirt or carbon particles in the stud passages in the head. Also, inspect the valves and guides for wear and damage. Check valve stems for wear and distortion. Any valve with a head thickness less than 1/32 in. (.8 mm.) at the seat edge should be replaced. Valve guide wear may be checked by inserting a new valve into the guide, lifting it 1/8 in. (3.2 mm.) from its seat, and moving it sideways, as shown in the accompanying illustration. If the movement of the valve head across the seat exceeds .020 in. (.5 mm.), the guide should be replaced. Valve guides must protrude above the top face of the cylinder head as follows:

TR–4, TR–4A: .78 in. (19.84 mm.)
TR-250, GT6, Spitfire: .749-.751 in. (19.025–19.075 mm.)
TR–6: .63 in. (16 mm.)

Upon replacing the head gasket, note its markings and position it accordingly. After slipping the head gasket over the studs, lower the cylinder head into position. Tighten the cylinder head nuts finger tight, then gradually tighten them in the proper order.

Replace the valve rocker arm assembly and reverse the cylinder head removal sequence covered previously. Check the valve clearances before running the engine, then again after a brief running period when normal temperature is reached. Make a third check after a few hundred miles and at this time check the cylinder head nuts for tightness and tighten them to the specified torque. Although tightening down the cylinder head nuts will affect valve clearances slightly, the differences will not usually be enough to warrant resetting the valves. However, the clearances should be checked:

NOTE: the removal and replacement of a cylinder head is not difficult for any mechanically inclined person, and can result in significant savings if your car needs a valve job or upper cylinder reconditioning. Simply remove the cylinder head, complete with valves, take it to a workshop where valve and guide work is done, then replace the head at your convenience. This can reduce the cost of a valve job by about two-thirds.

Upper Cylinder Area Cleaning

Clean, or decarbonize, the upper cylinder area as follows: Remove the cylinder head, valves, and head gasket. Plug water passages with clean rags. In the absence of special equipment, use a blunt scraper to clean the carbon deposits from the piston crowns, cylinder block, and cylinder head. Allow a ring of carbon to remain around the periphery of the piston crown, and around the top of the cylinder bore. To facilitate this, place an old piston ring in the bore so that it rests on top of the piston.

Clean and gap the spark plugs and clean carbon deposits from the valve stems, valve ports, and combustion chamber surfaces. Use compressed air after cleaning to remove any remaining particles. Next, clean all components thoroughly with kerosene and permit to dry before reassembly. Replace the cylinder head and gasket as described in the preceding section.

ENGINE LUBRICATION

Oil Pump Removal and Installation

The oil pump is of the eccentric rotor type and consists of: the body, the driving spindle inner rotor, the outer rotor, the cover, and the main body. To remove the oil pump, remove the dipstick, drain the oil pan, remove the oil pan and remove the bolts securing the oil pump to the crankcase. Clean all components. With the oil pump assembled except for the top cover, measure the clearances between the inner and outer rotors, the outer rotor and the pump housing, and the inner rotor and the face of the pump housing as shown in the accompanying figures. Clearances should fall within the clearances in the table. In case of excessive clearances replace worn or damaged parts.

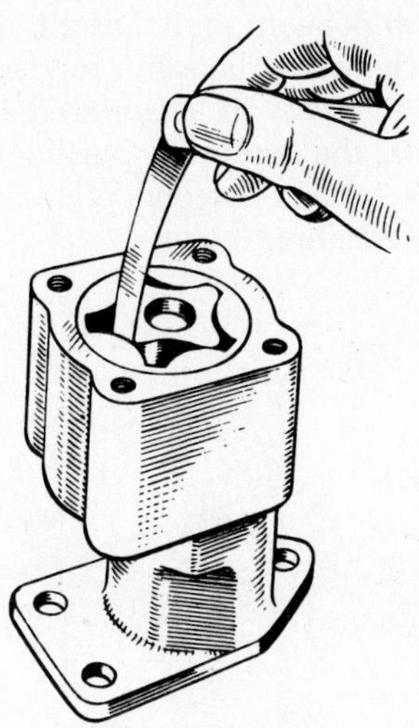

Using a feeler gauge to measure the clearance between the inner and outer oil pump rotors.

OIL PUMP CLEARANCES

Model	*Inner Rotor to Outer Rotor (in.)*		*Outer Rotor to Pump Housing (in.)*		*Inner Rotor to Housing Face (in.)*	
	min.	*max.*	*min.*	*max.*	*min.*	*max.*
TR–4		.010		.0100		.0040
Early Spitfire		.010		.0080	.0017	.0066
Late Spitfire		.010		.0075	.0015	.0035
Spitfire Mk III		.010		.0075	.0015	.0035
GT6	.001	.004		.0075		.0040
TR–250	.001	.004		.0075		.0040
TR–6	.001	.004		.0075		.0040

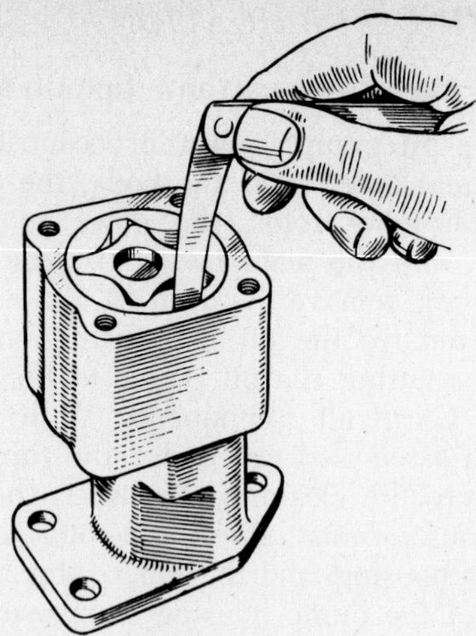

Measuring the clearance between the oil pump outer rotor and body.

When assembling the oil pump, replace worn components and install the inner rotor in the pump housing, followed by the outer rotor, with its chamfered face leading. With the assembly positioned in the crankcase, attach the end plate and secure with the retaining bolts.

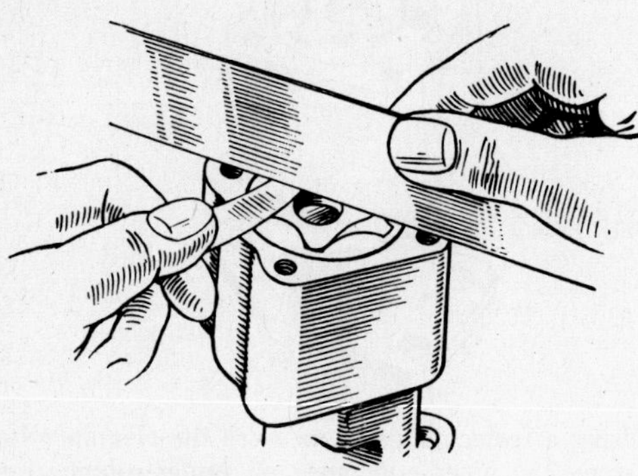

Using a straightedge and feeler gauge to measure rotor end clearance.

During installation of the oil pan, apply sealing compound to both faces of a new gasket. When installing the Spitfire oil pan, note that a long bolt is used to retain the breather pipe bracket, and two short bolts are used at the front sealing block.

Oil Filter

The oil filter is of the full flow type and has a replaceable element. A relief valve, located in the base of the filter, opens to allow the passage of unfiltered oil if the filter element becomes fouled and restricts the flow of oil. This serves as a safety outlet so that oil will be able to reach the bearings even if the filter element becomes completely clogged.

While the relief valve makes it possible to operate the car with a completely clogged oil filter element, this should not be done. The oil filter element should be changed at the recommended intervals. On some models, the filter and housing are replaced together, as a unit. On others, the element is replaced by removing the center bolt, filter body, and rubber sealing ring. When cleaning the inside of the filter body, use a safe solvent and allow the body to

The GT6 has a full flow oil filter of the replaceable element type.

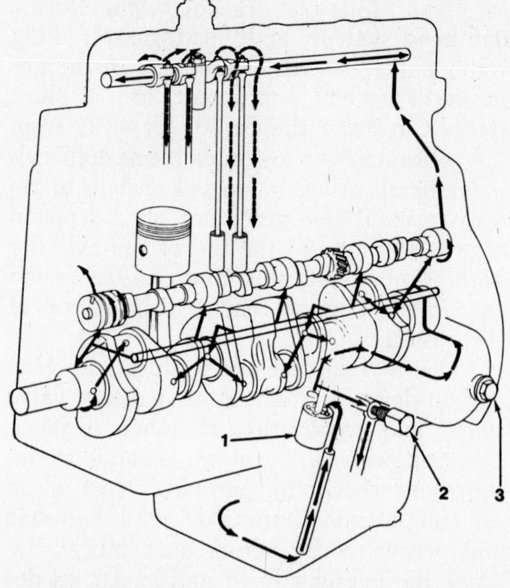

Engine oil circulation

dry before the new element is installed. When the filter body is reinstalled, apply a new rubber sealing ring to the groove between the body and the base of the filter. Be sure that the ring is seated properly before fully tightening the center bolt. Check for leakage after the engine has warmed up.

Clutch and Transmission

CLUTCH

The clutch is a single-plate, diaphragm-spring type and is operated hydraulically. Depression of the clutch pedal causes fluid pressure to be transmitted through the clutch master cylinder to the slave cylinder mounted on the clutch housing. At the slave cylinder, the pressure is transformed to mechanical force at the pushrod, which in turn causes the clutch withdrawal lever to pivot, and the clutch to release.

Bleeding Hydraulic System

If the clutch does not disengage fully, causing shifting difficulties, possibly air has entered the hydraulic system through a break in the system or because the level in the reservoir has fallen too low. In either case, it is necessary to bleed the system to remove the air.

Top up the clutch fluid reservoir to within 1/4 in. of the full level. Clean the bleed nipple on the slave cylinder and attach to it a short length of tubing. Allow the tubing to hang so that its end is below the fluid level in a clean glass container partially filled with hydraulic fluid. Unscrew the bleed nipple one complete turn. During the following operations, observe the precaution noted below:

NOTE: during the bleeding operation, the level of fluid in the reservoir will fall quickly. Constantly add new fluid to ensure that the reservoir is always at least half filled with fluid. If the reservoir should empty during the bleeding operation, air will be drawn into the system and the entire procedure will have to be repeated.

Depress the clutch pedal fully and allow it to return normally. Repeat this operation, allowing a slight pause between each depression of the pedal. Note the appearance of the fluid being discharged into the glass container. When no bubbles are observed, hold the clutch pedal down on the following depression. While the pedal is held down, tighten the bleed screw and remove the tubing from the nipple. Top up the master cylinder reservoir with hydraulic fluid and road test the car. After the bleeding operation has been completed, store left-over fluid in a sealed container. Exposure to the atmosphere will cause the hydraulic fluid to deteriorate.

Adjustment—TR-4

In order for pedal free play to be as specified, a small clearance is necessary at the clutch slave cylinder linkage between the clutch operating piston and the pushrod. Measure and adjust clearance as follows:

Adjustment of the TR–4 clutch free play is carried out by loosening the locknut (3) and rotating the pushrod (2) until the correct clearance between the nut and fork (4) is obtained.

Slacken the locking nut on the pushrod and unscrew the pushrod until all clearance between the pushrod and the cupped end of the operating piston (inside the slave cylinder body) is taken up. Adjust the position of the locking nut until a .1 in. (2.54 mm.) feeler gauge can just be inserted between the face of the nut and the operating fork. Without disturbing the position of the locking nut on the pushrod, screw the pushrod into the operating fork until the nut contacts the face of the fork, then lock the nut.

NOTE: All other models have a self-adjusting clutch.

Clutch and Transmission Removal

TR-4, TR-4A, TR-250, TR-6

The clutch and transmission of these cars are removed, with the engine remaining in

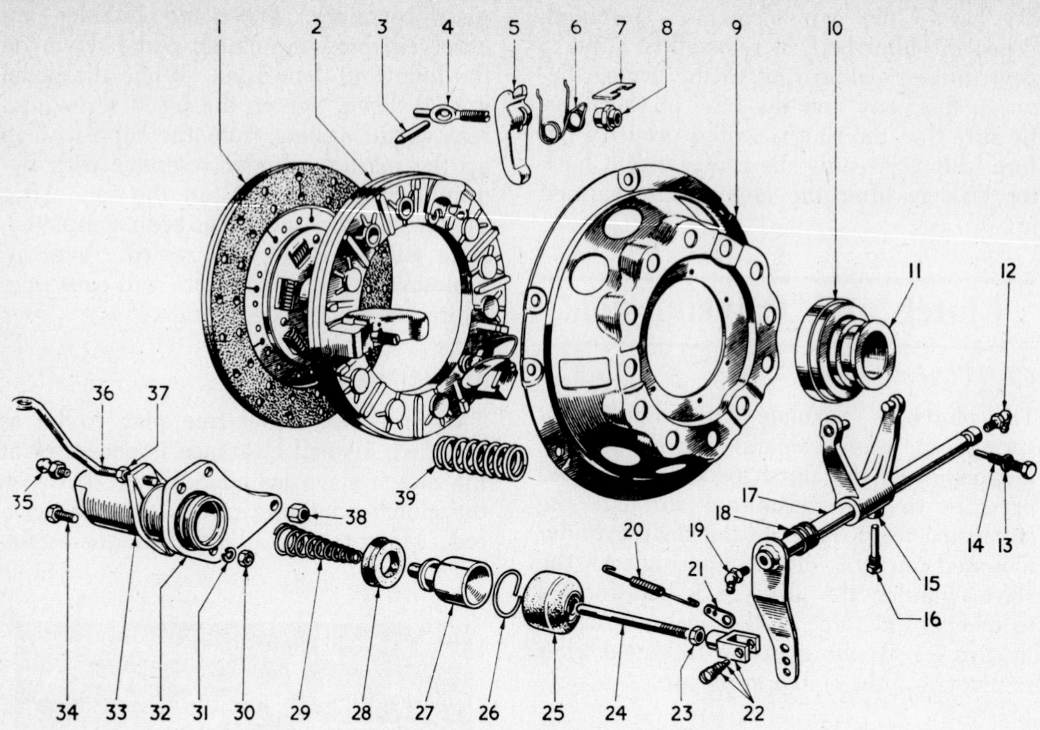

TR-4 clutch and slave cylinder

1 Driven plate assembly
2 Pressure plate
3 Release lever pin
4 Eyebolt
5 Release lever
6 Anti-rattle spring
7 Strut
8 Adjusting nut
9 Clutch cover
10 Release bearing
11 Bearing sleeve
12 Grease nipple
13 Washer
14 Shaft locating bolt
15 Clutch operating fork
16 Screwed taper pin
17 Clutch operating shaft
18 Fork return spring
19 Grease nipple
20 Pushrod return spring
21 Spring anchor plate
22 Clevis fork, spring and pin
23 Locknut
24 Pushrod
25 Rubber end cover
26 Circlip
27 Piston
28 Piston seal
29 Piston return spring
30 Nut
31 Spring washer
32 Slave cylinder bracket
33 Slave cylinder
34 Bolt
35 Bleed nipple
36 Support
37 Nut
38 Nut
39 Clutch thrust spring

position, as follows: With the vehicle raised by means of a ramp or axle stands, disconnect the battery, drain the transmission, and remove the seat cushions and carpets. Disconnect the cables from the heater control switch, the control cable from the heater unit, and the lower left control cable from the center control panel. Remove the dashboard support, which is secured by two bolts at the top and two bolts at each side of the bottom. Remove the headlight dimmer switch, leaving the electrical connections attached. Remove the bolts and washers securing the center floor cover and remove the cover. Disconnect and remove the driveshaft. Remove the retaining pin and bolts and remove the clutch slave cylinder, allowing it to hang by its flexible hose. Remove the clutch cover plate from the lower part of the clutch housing. Disconnect the speedometer cable and the overdrive connections (if installed).

With a block of wood protecting the oil pan, use a jack to support the weight of the engine and transmission. The jack should be placed as far as possible toward the rear of the oil pan. Release the exhaust pipe bracket next to the hand brake, then detach the rear mounting from the transmission and crossmember. Raise the engine and transmission, then remove the crossmember by sliding it forward. Remove the bolts, nuts, and washers attaching the clutch housing flange to the engine. Withdraw the transmission to the rear until it is clear of the clutch, then maneuver the clutch housing to the right and the rear section to the left, at the same time tilting the transmission case so that the clutch operating lever will clear the opening in the floor. Lift the transmission from the car. Replacement is the reverse of the preceding, except that it is important that the transmission not be allowed to hang on the clutch shaft while it is being attached to the engine. Fill the transmission with lubricant of the proper type and viscosity.

Aligning the clutch with a dummy shaft on installation to the flywheel

GT6

With the vehicle raised, disconnect the battery and drain the lubricant from the transmission. Remove the seat cushions, seats, and dashboard support bracket. Remove the safety belt anchoring bolts and the two small screws next to each, then take off the transmission tunnel side liners that they secure. Remove the gearshift lever knob and take out the carpeting. Release the retaining screws and plates and remove the transmission center cover.

Disconnect the driveshaft from the transmission driving flange and detach the slave cylinder, speedometer cable, and exhaust pipe attachment. With first gear selected, remove the transmission top cover and extension assemblies.

Fit a cardboard cover over the opening to prevent the entry of foreign matter. From beneath the vehicle, release the mounting bracket at the rear of the transmission. With a jack placed under the oil pan to support the weight of the engine, detach the clutch housing flange attachments and raise the engine until the transmission can be withdrawn. With the rear of the transmission raised, maneuver the clutch housing underneath the parcel shelf at the passenger side of the vehicle.

When replacing the transmission, be sure that the transmission does not hang on the input shaft during installation.

SPITFIRE

With the vehicle suitably supported on a ramp or stands, disconnect the battery, drain the transmission, and remove the front seats and carpets. Remove the dashboard support beneath the instruments and disconnect the tachometer drive cable. Remove the gearshift lever knob and rubber boot. Remove the screws and fasteners and lift off the transmission cover. Remove the securing nuts and pin and release the clutch slave cylinder, allowing it to hang on its pipe. Remove the retaining bolts and remove the driveshaft. Release the front exhaust pipe at its manifold and clutch housing. Remove the starter motor and remove the speedometer drive cable from the transmission extension. Remove the retaining nuts, lift off the transmission gearshift extension, and temporarily install a cardboard cover to prevent the entry of foreign matter.

Remove the nuts attaching the rear transmission mountings to the body crossmember, and jack up the engine until the transmission extension clears the mounting bracket, then remove the rear mountings. Release the bolts securing the clutch housing flange to the engine, and remove the transmission from the car. When replacing, do not allow the transmission to hang on the clutch shaft during installation.

Clutch Disassembly and Assembly

TR-4

After the clutch and transmission have been removed from the car, gradually loosen and remove the clutch attaching screws. Separate the cover assembly and driven plate from the flywheel face.

Disassemble the TR–4 clutch as follows: Mark the cover, the lugs on the pressure plate, and the release levers so that the parts may be reassembled in the same relative positions and thereby retain their balance. *NOTE: a special fixture is recommended for the disassembly and assembly of this clutch unit.* Clean the top of the fixture baseplate and place three spacers on the positions marked with D. Position the clutch cover assembly on the baseplate so that the release levers are directly above the spacers and the bolt holes of the cover are lined up with the tapped holes in the baseplate. Screw the actuator into the center hole and press the handle so as to clamp the cover housing to the baseplate.

Secure the cover to the fixture baseplate with the six bolts provided with the fixture,

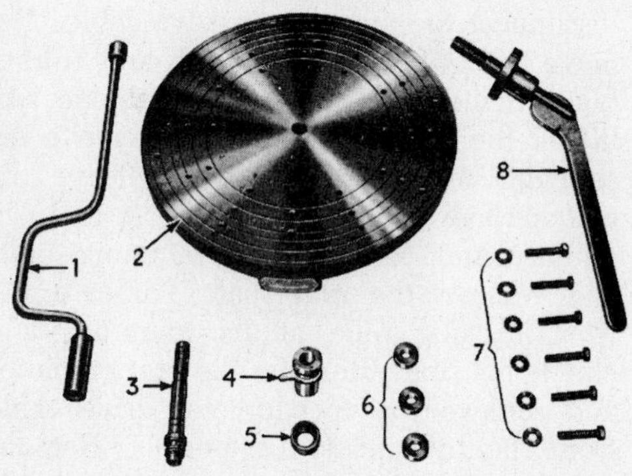

Components of clutch assembly fixture for TR-4 and Spitfire Mk I clutch disassembly and assembly: brace, 1; baseplate, 2; pillar ,3; gauge finger, 4; adaptor, 5; spacers, 6; washers and screws, 7; and actuator, 8.

then remove the actuator. Remove the three adjusting nuts, then remove the cover from the baseplate. Lift the nine thrust springs from the pressure plate and remove the three anti-rattle springs from the cover. Lift up the inner end of each release lever in order to disengage the strut. Gripping the end of the release lever and the eyebolt, lift each lever from the pressure plate. Remove the eyebolts from the release levers and take out the pins. Remove the struts from the pressure plate.

Prior to assembly, lubricate all bearing surfaces and observe the markings made previously in arranging the components in their same relative positions. Place a strut in position in a lug of the pressure plate. Assemble the pin to the eyebolt and insert the threaded portion through the release lever. With the strut in the pressure plate held to one side, insert the plain end of the eyebolt (assembled to the release lever) into the pressure plate. Place the strut into the groove in the outer end of the release lever. Repeat the preceding operations with the remaining release levers. Position the pressure plate and assembled release levers, with the release levers over the spacers, on the baseplate of the clutch fixture.

Install the springs to their seats on the pressure plate. Install the anti-rattle springs and position the cover over the pressure plate, allowing the lugs to protrude through the cover. Secure the cover to the baseplate, then screw on the adjuster nuts until their heads are flush with the tops of the eyebolts. Position the actuator in the center hole of the baseplate and operate the handle about six times in order to

Alternative setup to special clutch fixture assembly

settle the components. Remove the actuator and secure the pillar firmly into the center of the baseplate, assembling to it the adaptor (with its recessed side downward) and the gauge finger. Adjust the nuts to raise or lower the release levers so that the finger gauge is just contacted. Remove the pillar, replace the actuator, and operate the clutch a dozen or more times, rechecking with the finger gauge and making any adjustments necessary. Lock the adjusting nuts and remove the completed assembly from the baseplate.

Spitfire Mk I

In disassembling and assembling the Spitfire Mk I clutch, a special assembly fixture is recommended. Disassembly is as follows: With the spacers on the baseplate, place the clutch unit over the spacers so that the release levers are as close as possible over the spacers. Mark the pressure plate, cover, and release levers to facilitate replacement to their original positions. Position the actuator to the baseplate and clamp the clutch unit into position. Secure the unit to the baseplate and remove the actuator. Hold the release lever plate down and detach the retaining springs. Remove the release lever plate. Release the locking plates and remove the nuts, lockplates, bridge sections and release levers. Gradually and progressively loosen the bolts securing the cover to the baseplate and lift off the cover, retainers, springs, and pressure plate.

Reassembly is as follows: With the spacers positioned under the lever fulcrum studs, position the pressure plate on the baseplate. Install the springs, cups, and cover and tighten the cover to the baseplate. Install the release levers, bridge

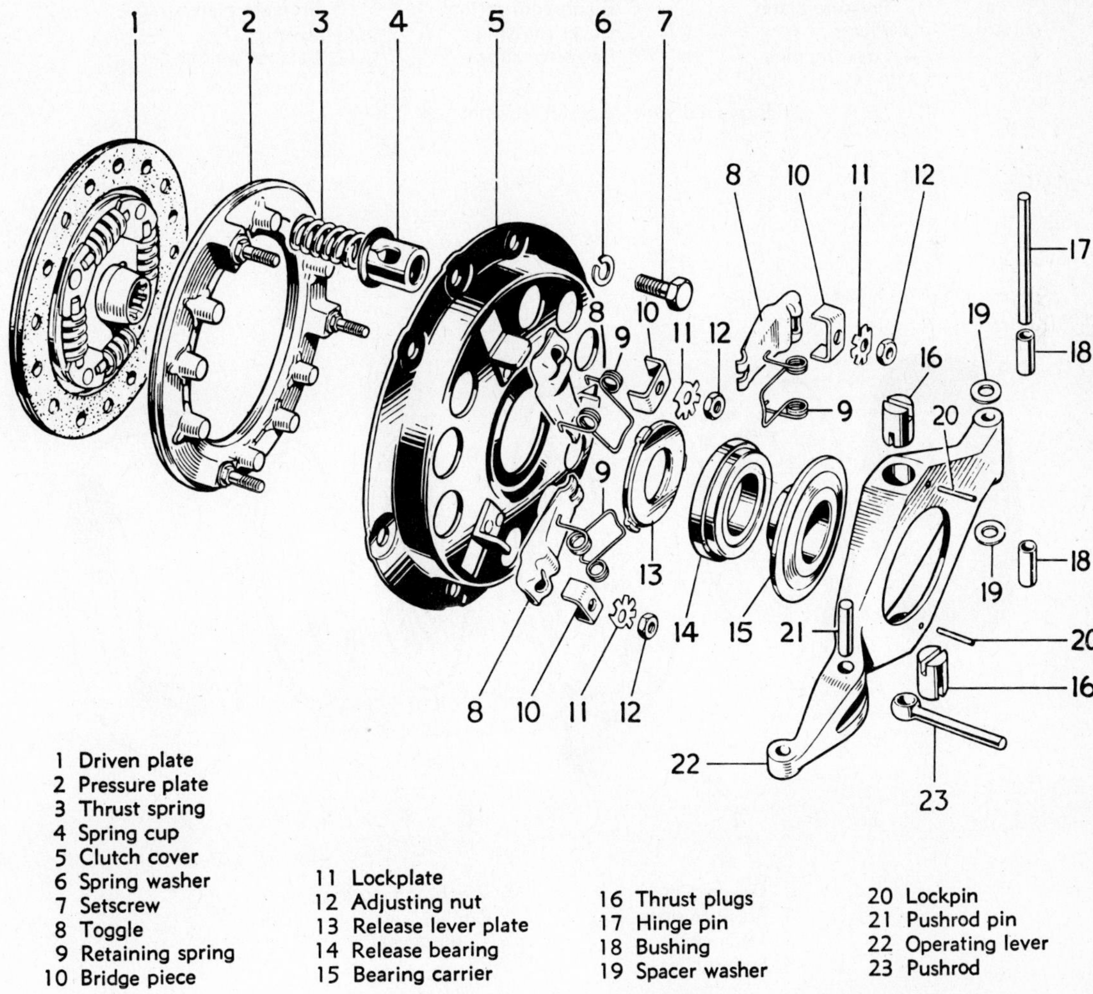

Spitfire Mk I clutch components

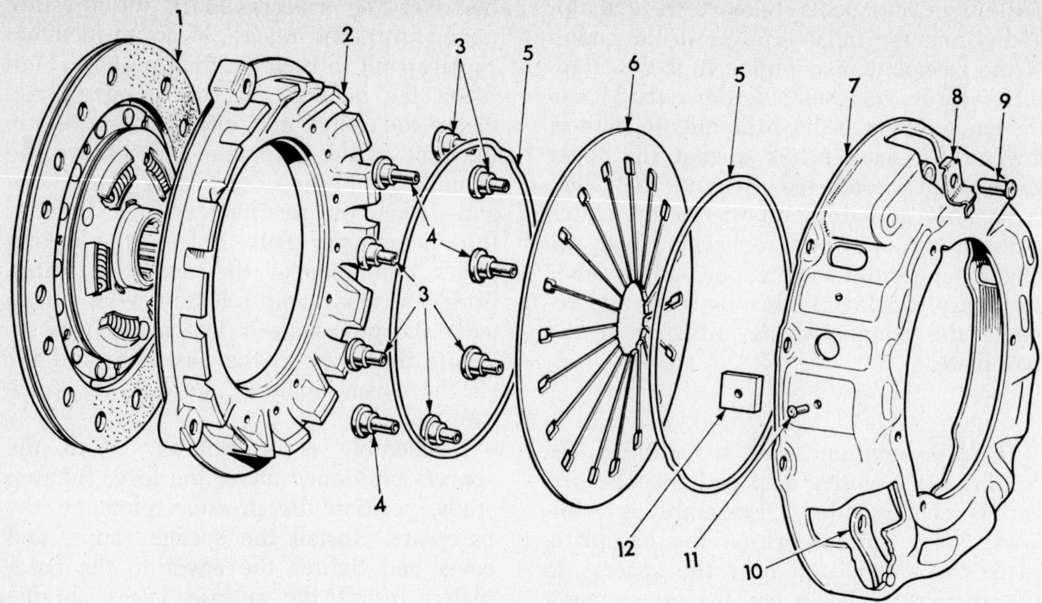

1 Driven plate
2 Pressure plate
3 Rivets
4 Locating pins
5 Fulcrum rings
6 Diaphragm spring
7 Cover pressing
8 Retractor clips
9 Rivet
10 Pressure plate strap
11 Rivet
12 Balance weight

Exploded view of clutch components, TR–4A.

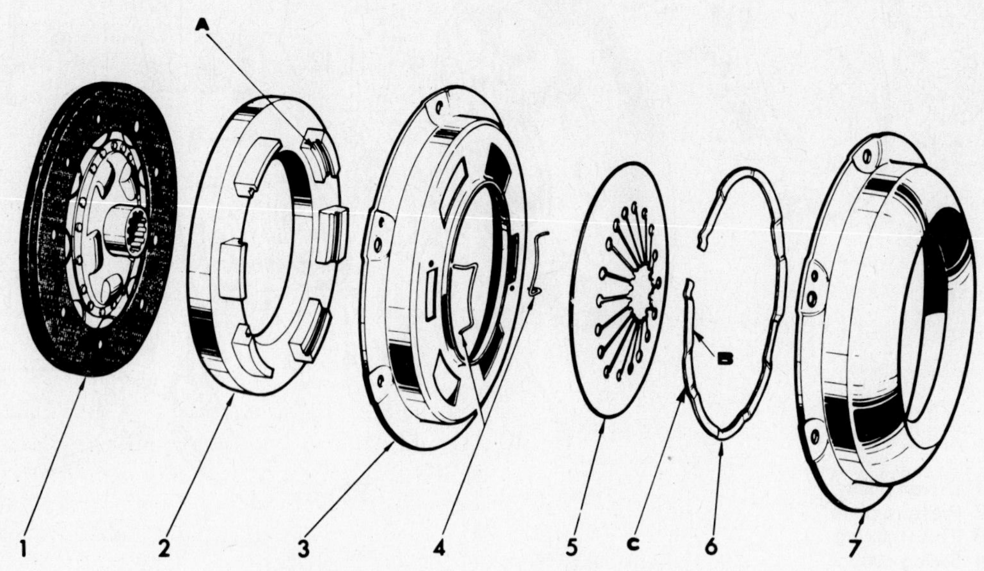

1 Driven plate
2 Pressure plate
3 Inner cover
4 Spring clips
5 Diaphragm spring
6 Circlip
7 Outer cover

Exploded view of clutch components, TR–250, TR–6.

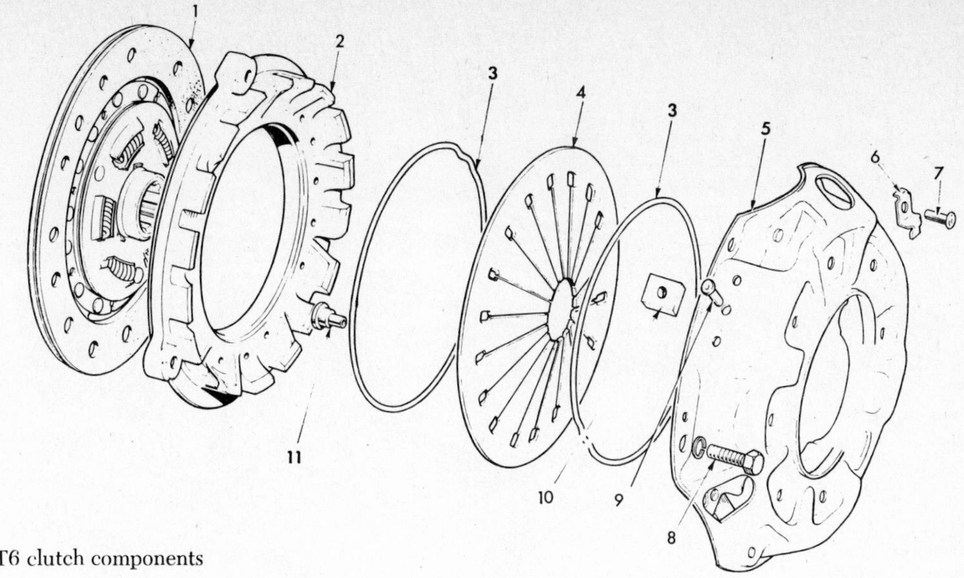

GT6 clutch components

1 Driven plate
2 Pressure plate
3 Fulcrum ring
4 Diaphragm spring
5 Cover pressing
6 Retractor clip
7 Rivet
8 Setscrew
9 Rivet
10 Balance weight
11 Rivet

sections, locking plates, and nuts. Install the gauge finger, with an adaptor, and adjust the nuts until the gauge finger just contacts the ends of each lever. Remove the gauge and stud, then install the actuator and operate the clutch several times. With the gauge and stud replaced, recheck the lever height and adjust if necessary. When the levers have been correctly adjusted, lock the nuts by bending up the locking plates. Install the release plate and secure with the retaining springs. Check the runout of the release plate with a suitable dial gauge. This measurement should not exceed .015 in. (.38 mm.). Remove the clutch from the baseplate.

TR-4A, TR-250, TR-6, GT6, and Spitfire Mk II, III, IV

The diaphragm spring clutch units installed in these models are a great deal simpler in construction than those of the TR-4 and Spitfire Mk I. It is recommended, in case a clutch problem should arise with these units, that a complete replacement assembly be installed.

TRANSMISSION

TR-4, TR-4A, TR-250, TR-6

Disassembly

The transmissions of these models involve the same disassembly/assembly operations, although they do differ slightly. The TR–250 and TR–6, however, differ from the TR–4 and TR–4A in the following ways:

TR–250 and TR–6 transmissions are provided with a countershaft hub modification that involves the addition of circlips in both ends of the countershaft hub in order to retain the needle roller bearings. In addition, a caged type needle roller bearing is installed on the mainshaft and countershaft, replacing the previous type. The gear lever assembly of the two more recent models has been modified to prevent gear lever rattle and transmitted noise. A rubber bushing has been added to the gear lever assembly, along with the addition of adjustable locating pins secured by locknuts. Other modifications include a molded (instead of steel) speedometer drive gear, a circular mainshaft flange, deletion of the clutch cross-shaft grease nipple, and a reduction in the length of the front cover nose.

Disassemble these transmissions as follows: (refer to the accompanying exploded views).

Disassemble the top cover as follows: Re-

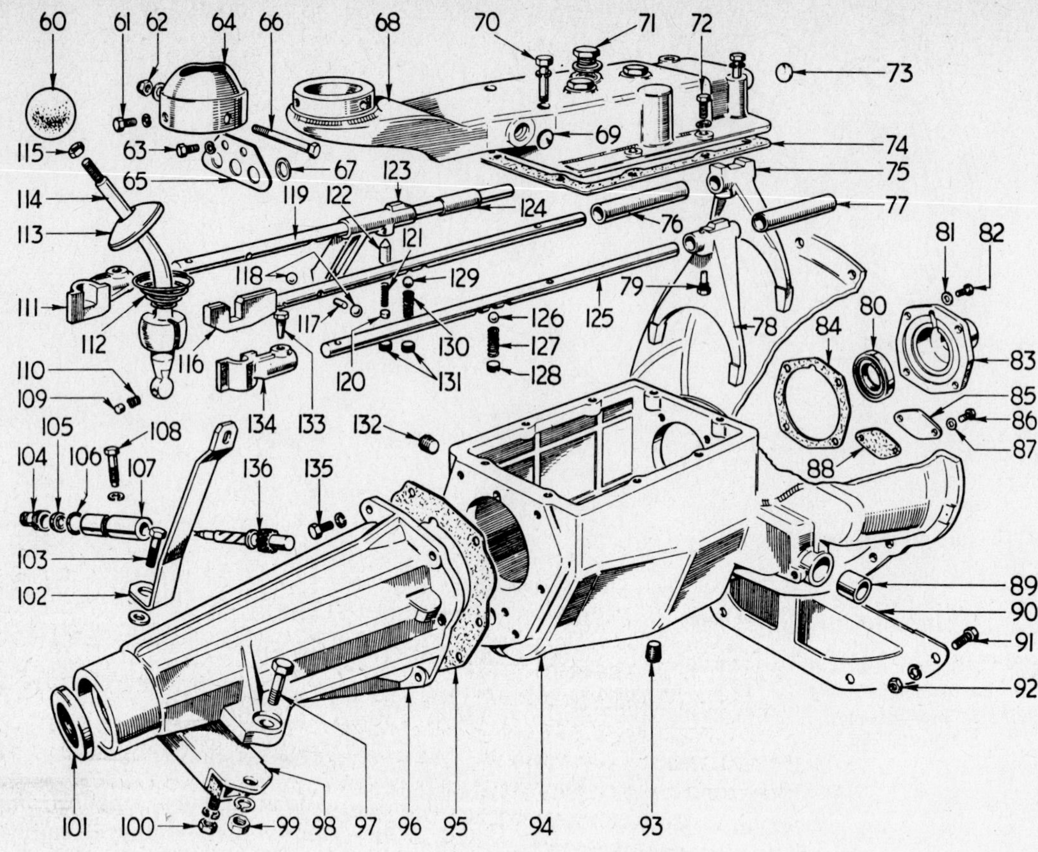

Stationary components of TR-4, TR-4A, TR-250, TR-6 transmission

60 Knob
61 Setscrew
62 Nyloc nut
63 Setscrew
64 Cap
65 End plate
66 Cross bolt
67 Rubber "O" ring
68 Top cover
69 Plug
70 Bolt
71 Plug
72 Bolt
73 Plug
74 Gasket
75 Top/3rd selector fork
76 Spacer tube
77 Spacer tube
78 2nd/1st selector fork
79 Peg bolt
80 Oil seal
81 Copper washer
82 Bolt
83 Front cover
84 Gasket
85 Countershaft end plate
86 Setscrew
87 Copper washer
88 Gasket
89 Bushing
90 Cover plate
91 Setscrew
92 Nut
93 Drain plug
94 Casing
95 Gasket
96 Extension housing
97 Bolt
98 Mounting
99 Nut
100 Nut
101 Oil seal
102 Support
103 Bolt
104 Speedometer cable adaptor
105 Seal
106 Rubber "O" ring
107 Housing
108 Peg bolt
109 Plunger—anti-rattle
110 Spring
111 Selector—reverse
112 Spring
113 Cap disc
114 Lever
115 Nut
116 Top/3rd selector shaft
117 Interlock plunger
118 Balls—interlock
119 Reverse selector shaft
120 Shim
121 Spring
122 Plunger
123 Reverse actuator
124 Spacer
125 2nd/1st selector shaft
126 Ball—detent
127 Spring
128 Plug
129 Ball—detent
130 Spring
131 Plug
132 Level/filler plug
133 Peg bolt
134 Selector 1st/2nd
135 Bolt
136 Speedo drive gear

move the bolts, washers, top cover, and paper gasket. Remove the nut, cross pin, cover, and withdraw the gear shift lever assembly from the top cover. With the cover inverted, remove the plugs, spacer, springs, plunger and balls. Detach the peg bolts. With the selector shafts in the neutral position, withdraw the 3rd/4th gear selector shaft, being careful to remove the interlock plunger and balls as they are released. Remove the 3rd/4th selector fork and spacer tube from the top cover. Repeat the preceding operation for the 1st/2nd and reverse gear selector shafts. Remove the retaining screws and take out the retaining plate. Remove the sealing rings from their recesses. If necessary, remove the peg bolts and remove the selectors from their shafts.

Disassemble the front cover: Remove the grease nipple (TR-4 and TR-4A), the tapered bolt, bolt and spring washer. *NOTE: See accompanying illustration for components.* Withdraw the cross-shaft along with the release spring, release bearing, sleeve and fork. Remove the retaining bolts and remove the front cover, bolts and plate.

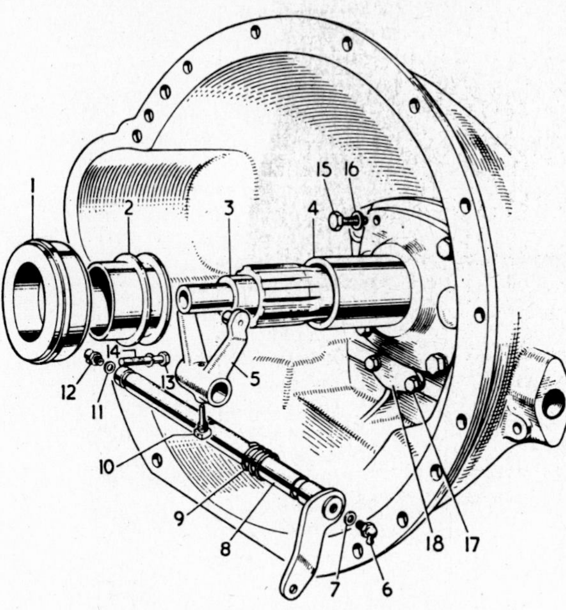

TR-4 front cover and clutch release mechanism

1 Release bearing
2 Sleeve
3 Input shaft
4 Front cover
5 Fork
6 Grease nipple
7 Fiber washer
8 Cross-shaft
9 Anti-rattle spring
10 Screwed taper pin
11 Fiber washer
12 Grease nipple
13 Cross-shaft locating
14 Spring washer
15 Bolts
16 Washers
17 Bolts
18 Plate

Disassemble the rear extension: Remove the peg bolt and withdraw the speedometer drive gear assembly. Remove the cotter pin, slotted nut and withdraw the flange. Remove the retaining bolts and detach the rear extension, using an extractor.

Remove the countershaft and reverse pinion shaft by removing the retaining screw and plate. Withdraw the input shaft assembly from the transmission. Remove circlips, spacer washer and withdraw the bearing. Detach the disc and, if necessary, remove the needle roller bearing.

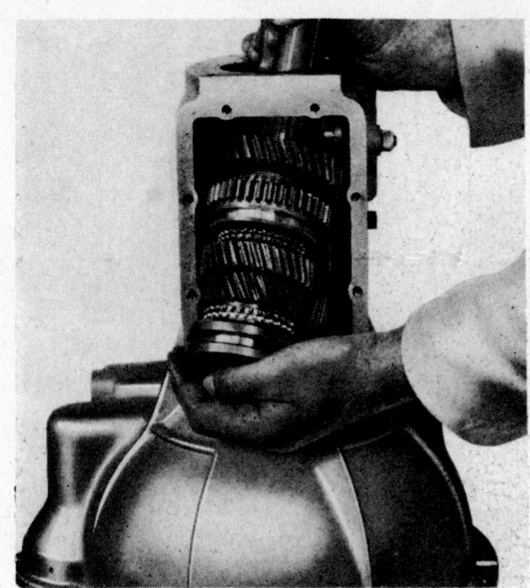

Mainshaft removal

Remove the circlip, spacer washer and circlip, and remove the mainshaft rear bearing. After maneuvering the mainshaft assembly through the transmission top cover opening, lift out the countershaft assembly, thrust washers, and reverse gear. Remove the countershaft gears from the hub and, if necessary, remove the needle roller assemblies from the hub bore. Remove the circlip by driving a special tool beneath the circlip and then levering the 3rd gear forward to remove the circlip from its groove. Remove all mainshaft components, and remove the 1st/2nd and 3rd/4th synchronizer inner hubs from the outer sleeves (being careful to catch the springs and balls).

After disassembly is completed, clean all components and inspect for wear. The transmission case should be washed with solvent and inspected for cracks and burrs. All items that have doubtful potential for reuse should be replaced.

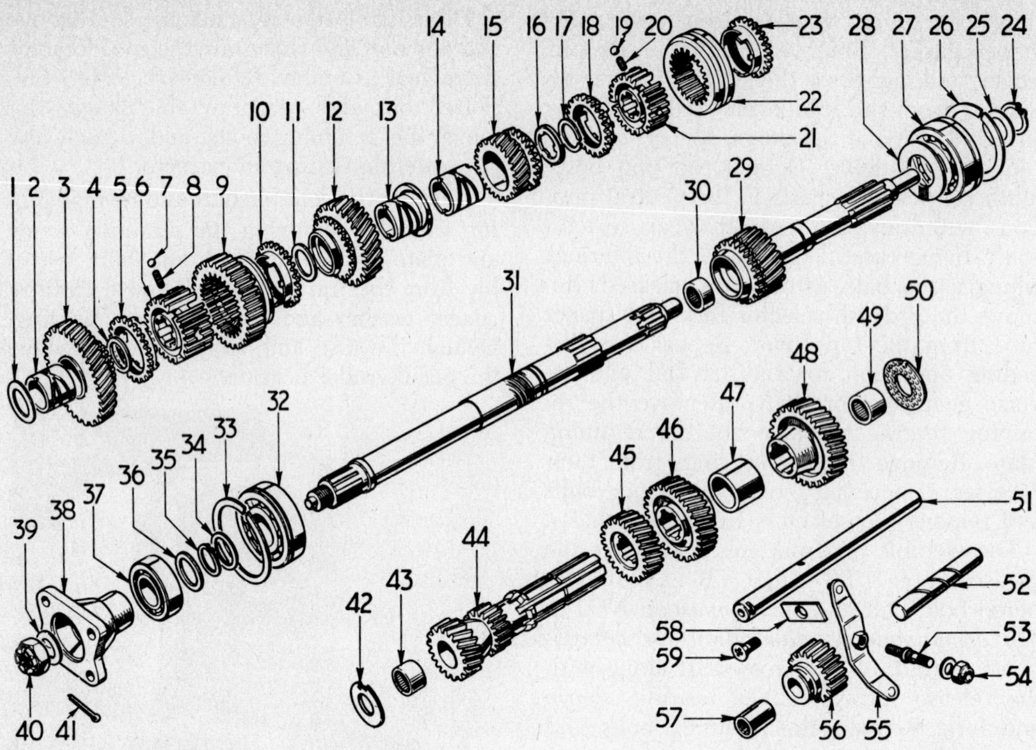

Moving components of TR-4, TR-4A, TR-250, TR-6 transmission

1 Thrust washer
2 Bushing—1st speed gear
3 1st speed gear
4 Thrust washer
5 1st speed synchro cup
6 1st/2nd speed synchro hub
7 Synchro ball
8 Spring
9 Reverse mainshaft gear and synchro outer sleeve
10 2nd speed synchro cup
11 Thrust washer
12 2nd speed gear
13 Bushing—2nd speed gear
14 Bushing—3rd speed gear
15 3rd speed gear
16 Thrust washer
17 Circlip
18 3rd speed synchro cup
19 Synchro ball
20 Spring
21 3rd/top synchro hub
22 Synchro sleeve
23 Top gear synchro cup
24 Circlip
25 Spacer washer
26 Circlip
27 Ball race
28 Oil deflector plate
29 Input shaft
30 Needle roller bearing
31 Mainshaft
32 Ball race
33 Circlip
34 Spacer washer
35 Circlip
36 Spacer washer
37 Rear ball race
38 Flange
39 Plain washer
40 Slotted nut
41 Cotter pin
42 Rear thrust washer
43 Needle roller bearing
44 Countershaft hub
45 2nd speed countershaft gear
46 3rd speed countershaft gear
47 Spacer piece
48 Countershaft gear
49 Needle roller bearing
50 Front thrust washer
51 Countershaft
52 Reverse gear shaft
53 Pivot stud
54 Nyloc nut and washer
55 Reverse gear operating lever
56 Reverse gear
57 Reverse gear bushing
58 Locating plate
59 Screw

Assembly

Install the reverse gear in the transmission, with the selector groove to the rear. Install the reverse gear shaft, securing it with string to prevent it from sliding into the transmission. Use a stepped drift to drive a new needle roller bearing (with lettered face outward) into each end of the countershaft hub. Install the gears, spacer, and gear to the countershaft hub. Using grease to retain the countershaft thrust washers, install the washers into the transmission and lower the gear cluster into position. With the countershaft temporarily installed, measure the cluster gear end float, which should be .007-.012 in. (.1778-.3048 mm.). End clearance may be adjusted to within this range through the use of thrust washers of larger or smaller thickness. Remove the countershaft and drop the gear cluster to the bottom of the transmission case.

Transmission case with countershaft and reverse gear in position.

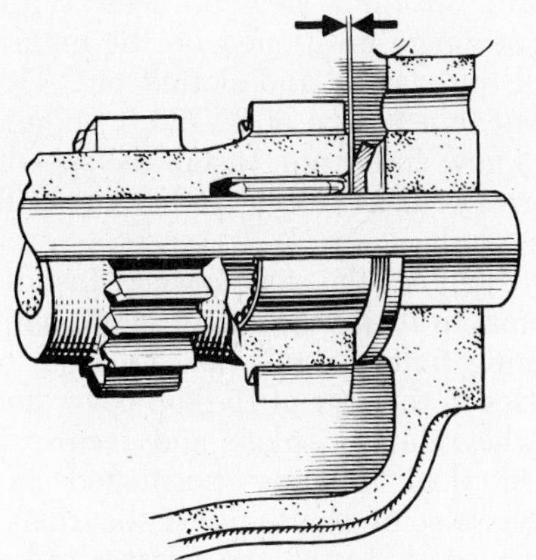

Clearance of the countershaft rear thrust washer should be .007–.012 in.

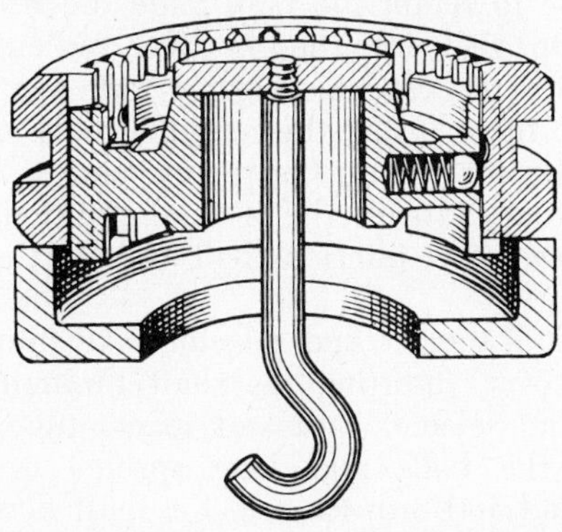

Using a spring balance to check synchronizer release load.

Assemble the synchronizer springs, balls and shims to the 3rd/4th synchronizer hub. Install the outer sleeve. Repeat the preceding operations with the 1st/2nd synchronizer unit. Check the axial release loads, as illustrated in the accompanying diagram. The points of release should be as follows:

3rd/4th: 19–21 lbs.
1st/2nd: 25–27 lbs.

If the actual release loads observed are greater or less than those specified above, the, correct loading may be achieved by adjusting the number of shims beneath each synchronizer spring.

Using a straightedge and a feeler gauge, measure the end clearance of each mainshaft gear on its bushing, as shown in the accompanying illustration. The end clearance measured should be .004–.006 in. (.1–.15 mm.), and may be increased by installing a new bushing and decreased by reducing bush length. In the preceding adjustments, take care, as reduction of bushing length will cause the end clearance of the bushings on the mainshaft to increase.

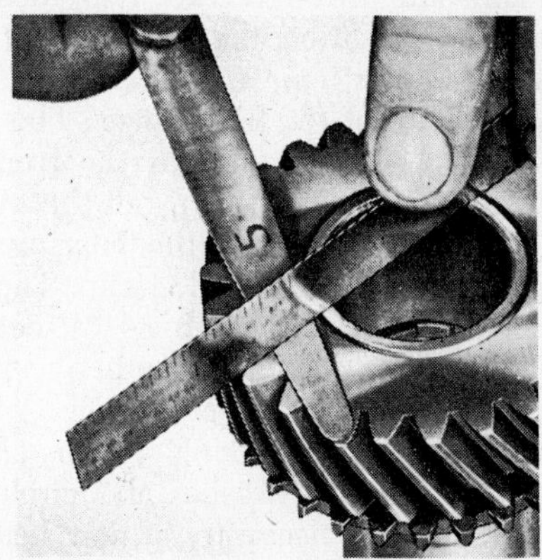

End clearance of gears on bushings should be .004–.006 in., measured as shown.

Install the thrust washer, bushings and thrust washer to the mainshaft, secure the assembly and measure the total end clearance of the bushings and thrust washers on the mainshaft. This measurement should be .003-.009 in. (.08-.23 mm.), and may be adjusted by using thrust washers available in the following thicknesses:

Color	*Thickness*
Plain	.119 in. (3.02 mm.)
Green	.122 in. (3.10 mm.)
Blue	.125 in. (3.18 mm.)
Orange	.128 in. (3.25 mm.)
Yellow	.133 in. (3.38 mm.)

Install the thrust washer, bushing, and thrust washer to the mainshaft. Using a special tool assemble the race into position and install the washer and circlip. The race should be driven towards the rear to ensure that it is firmly against the circlip. Measure the 1st gear end clearance by gauging the distance between the washer and bushing. The end clearance should be .003-.009 in. (.08-.23 mm.) and is adjustable by use of the various thrust washers described above. Prior to final assembly, all components should be removed from the mainshaft.

Assemble the mainshaft as follows: With the components placed in their proper relative positions, install them in the following order: thrust washer, gear and bushing, gear and bushing, thrust washer, a new circlip, 3rd/4th synchronizer unit with baulk ring at each side. Install a baulk ring to each side of the 1st/2nd synchronizer unit, slide the unit over the rear of the mainshaft and onto the larger splines. Install the washer, gear and bushing, and washer to the rear of the mainshaft. Pass the rear of the mainshaft through the rear bearing housing and position the shaft. With the mainshaft in position, a special tool is installed in place of the front cover. This tool consists of a plate that holds the front of the mainshaft in position. Install the circlip to the bearing and drive the bearing into position. Install washer and circlip. Tap the rear of the mainshaft with a soft-headed mallet to take up the clearance between the circlip, washer and bearing.

Install the disc, bearing (with circlip groove to the front), washer and circlip to the input shaft. If necessary, a new bearing should be installed to the bore of the input shaft, with the lettered face of the bearing facing outward. Install the circlip to the bearing and install the assembly. Install the front cover as follows: With the lip of the seal towards the gears, use a special tool to drive a new seal into the front cover. With a seal protector protecting the oil seal, install the gasket and cover and secure with the retaining washers and bolts.

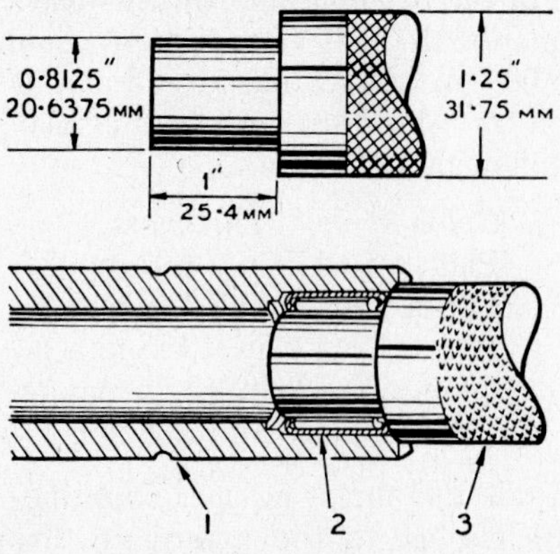

Countershaft bearing tool

With a tapered pilot tool inserted to align the countershaft gears and thrust washers, insert the countershaft, pushing out the pilot tool. With the ends of the countershaft and reverse gear shafts engaged at the retaining plate, secure with the Phillips head screw. Install and secure the countershaft cover gasket and cover plate.

Assemble the rear extension as follows: Install a new gasket and the rear extension to the transmission and secure with the retaining bolts. Install a spacer washer to the mainshaft and drive the extension ball bearing into position. With its sealing face forward, install a new oil seal. With the driving flange positioned on the mainshaft, install the washer and slotted nut. Tighten the nut to a torque of 80-120 ft. lb. and install a new cotter pin. Install the speedometer drive gear assembly, and secure with retaining bolt.

Reassemble the top cover: Install the selectors to their shafts and secure with the retaining bolts. Install new O-rings to the recesses in the rear of the top cover and install the retaining plate and secure. With the interlock plunger positioned in the 3d/4th selector shaft, insert the shaft into the top cover. Install the selector fork, spacer tube, and retaining bolt. Install the interlock ball between the bores of the reverse and 3rd/4th selector shafts, using grease to retain the ball. Slide the reverse selector shaft into the top cover and engage it with the reverse selector fork and distance tube. Install the retaining bolt to the selector fork. With the reverse and 3rd/4th selector shafts in the neutral position, install the other interlock ball, using grease to retain it.

Install the 1st/2nd selector shaft into the top cover, inserting the shaft through the 1st/2nd selector fork and spacer tube. Install the balls and long springs to the 1st/2nd and 3rd/4th selector shaft detents. The springs may be retained by screwing the plugs so that they are flush with the machined lower face of the top cover. *NOTE: From transmission number CT.9899, the 3rd/4th selector shaft ball and long spring have been replaced by a plunger and short spring identical to those of the reverse selector shaft.*

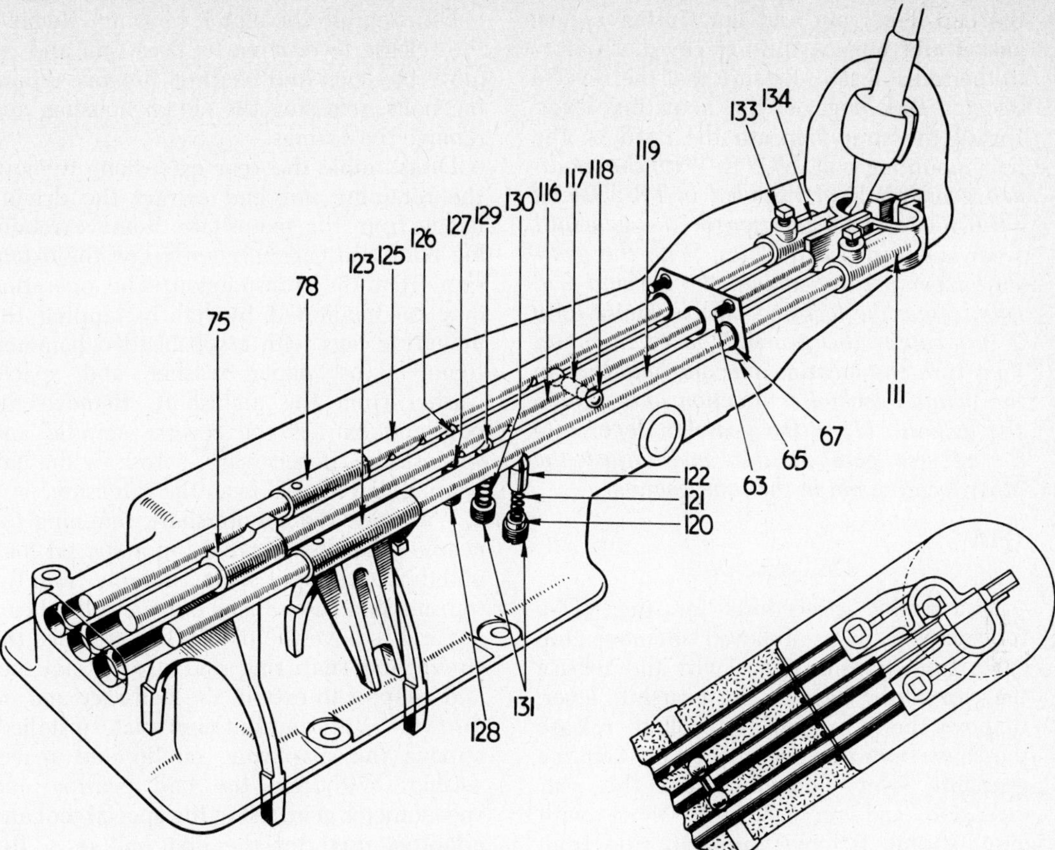

TR-4, TR-4A, TR-250, TR-6 top cover components. See illustration of stationary transmission components for identification of numbered components.

Install the plunger, short spring and shim to the reverse selector shaft detent, and use the plug to retain the assembly. Use a spring balance to check the selector shaft release loads, which should be as follows:

Selector Shaft	*Release Load*
1st/2nd	32–34 lbs.
3rd/4th	26–28 lbs.
Reverse	26–28 lbs.

If necessary, the spring loads may be adjusted by grinding the end of the spring (to reduce the release load) or by installing shims between the spring and plunger (to increase the load).

Replace the spring and plunger to the gearshift lever. Assemble the gearshift lever, spring and plate to the top cover, pressing the plunger with a screwdriver as the end of the gearshift lever engages the selectors. Retain the gearshift lever with

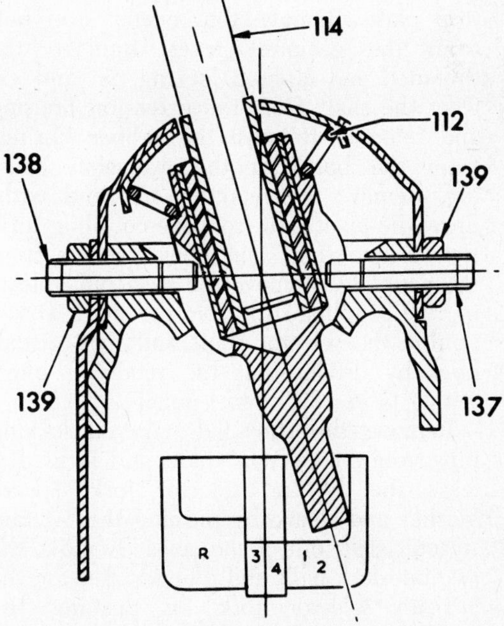

Cross-sectional view of gearshift lever modifications to TR-250 and TR-6 models, showing spring (112), lever assembly (114), locating pins (137 and 138) and locknuts (139).

the cap, cross pin and nut. Install a new gasket and replace the top cover assembly to the transmission. Be sure that the reverse selector fork engages the actuating lever. Install the strap beneath the head of the rear mounting bolt. *NOTE: With the modified gearshift lever installed in TR-250 and TR-6 models, the position of the gearshift lever is adjusted as follows: With the gearshift lever positioned into the 1st and 2nd gate, screw the locating pin clockwise until it just causes the gearshift lever to move, then turn the locating pin one-half turn in the counterclockwise direction and tighten the locknut. Move the gearshift lever into the reverse gate position and adjust the other locating pin in the same manner.*

GT6

Disassembly

Disassembly procedure for the GT-6 transmission is as follows: Remove top cover from transmission. Twist and release the cap at the base of the gearshift lever. Remove the nyloc nut and bolt to release the shaft from the gearshift lever. Lift the gearshift lever assembly from the rear extension and remove cups along with outer spring. Remove the snap ring from the gearshift lever, then remove the inner spring and the nylon ball. Remove the two retaining screws and take off the reverse stop plate. Remove the reverse stop bolt from the gearshift lever. Remove the threaded and tapered locking pin and extract the shaft from the extension housing and selector. Remove the rubber O-rings from the bores of the extension housing. Remove the retaining nut and withdraw the pivot bolt from the coupling fork. Extract the shaft and fiber washers from the coupling. Remove the steel pin, releasing the coupling fork from the shaft. Disassemble the selector shaft and fork assemblies by driving out the retaining plugs with a ⅛ in. (3.17 mm.) punch.

Remove the threaded, tapered locking pins from the selector shafts and forks. Release the 1st/2nd selector fork, spacer washer and sleeve by pushing the 1st/2nd selector shaft out of the cover. Remove the two interlock balls and plunger. Release the 3rd/4th selector fork by pushing the 3rd/4th selector shaft out of the cover. Release the reverse selector by pushing the reverse selector shaft out of the cover. Remove the detent plungers and springs from the cover.

Disassemble the clutch housing: Remove the release lever from its pivot pin and remove the lever and bearing. Remove retaining bolts, releasing the clutch housing, and remove the springs.

Disassemble the rear extension: Remove the retaining nut and extract the driving flange from the mainshaft. Remove retaining bolts and carefully withdraw the extension from the transmission. The operation may be facilitated by lightly tapping the mounting lugs with a soft-headed hammer. Remove the paper washer and spacer washer from the mainshaft. Remove the bolt and extract the reverse spindle and spacer tube. If necessary, withdraw the ball bearing and oil seal from the extension.

Withdraw the countershaft, retaining the needle roller bearings. Using a special tool, withdraw the input shaft assembly from the transmission case. Shake out the roller bearing and remove the baulk ring. Remove the circlip and snap ring and use special tool and adaptor to extract the ball race and oil thrower. With an abutment plate installed, remove the snap ring, circlip and spacer washer. Withdraw the ball bearing and speedometer gear, using the special tool and adaptors used for the first ball race. Remove the abutment plate, tilt the mainshaft assembly and maneuver it from the transmission case.

Disassemble the mainshaft as follows: Remove the 3rd/4th synchronizer unit, 3rd gear baulk ring, thrust washer, 1st gear and 1st gear baulk ring. Remove the circlip, washer, 3rd gear, bushing, thrust washer, 2nd gear, bushing, thrust washer, 2nd gear baulk ring, 1st/2nd synchronizer unit, and split collars. Disassemble each synchronizer unit by pressing the hub through the sleeve. During this operation, the synchronizer unit should be placed in a suitable container to prevent the loss of the spring-loaded balls. Withdraw the countershaft assembly from the case and lift out the thrust washers. The countershaft may be further disassembled by removing the needle rollers and the retaining rings. Disassemble the reverse idler gear and actuator by taking out the idler gear, removing the securing nut, and removing the actuator and pivot pin.

Assembly

Replace the needle rollers, smearing them with grease, and insert the retaining tube. With the steel face of the front thrust

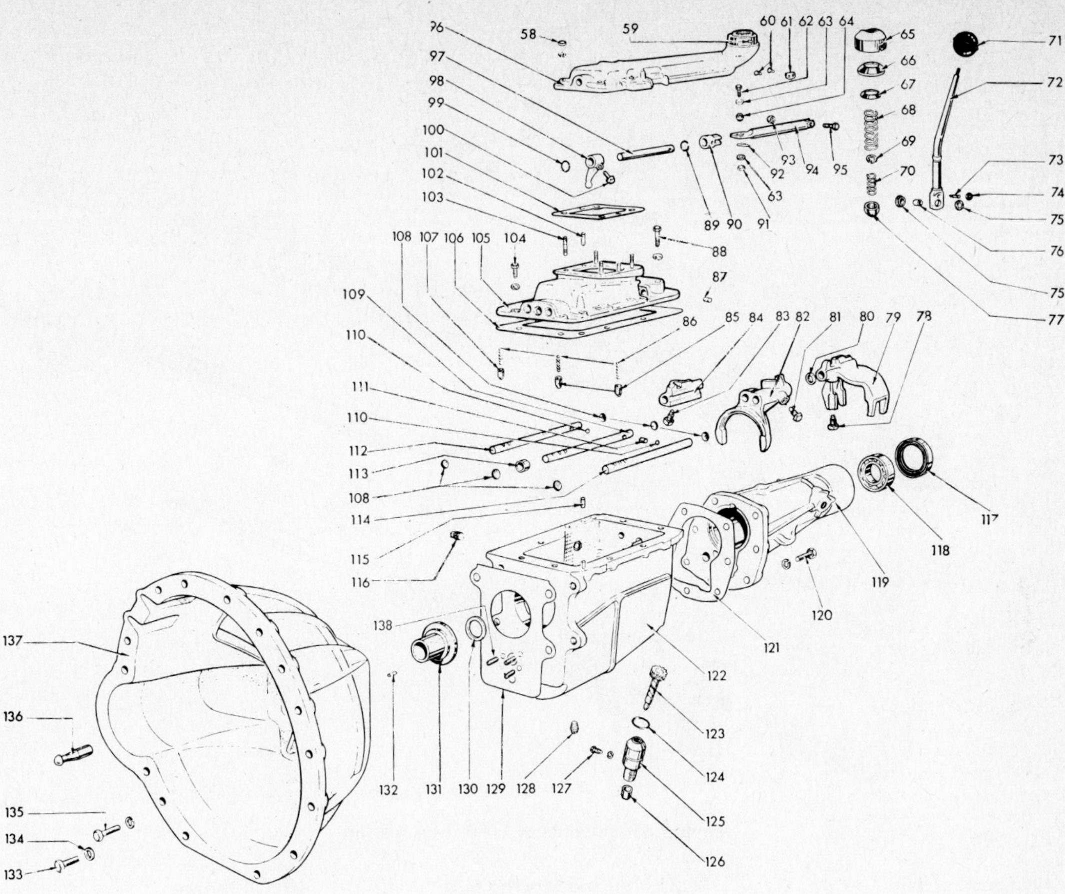

Stationary components of GT6 transmission

58 Nut
59 Locating pin
60 Screws
61 Reverse stop plate
62 Pivot bolt
63 Fiber washers
64 Bushing
65 Cap
66 Cup
67 Cup
68 Spring
69 Snap ring
70 Spring
71 Knob
72 Gear lever
73 Reverse stop bolt
74 Locknut
75 Nylon bushings
76 Spacer tube
77 Nylon ball
78 Taper locking pin
79 1st/2nd selector fork
80 Spacer washer
81 Taper locking pin
82 3rd/top selector fork
83 Taper locking pin
84 Reverse selector
85 Detent plungers
86 Springs
87 Plug
88 Bolt
89 Rubber O-ring
90 Coupling fork
91 Nyloc nut
92 Hollow pin
93 Nyloc nut
94 Gear lever shaft
95 Setscrew
96 Top cover extension housing
97 Gear lever shaft
98 Selector
99 Rubber O-ring
100 Taper locking pin
101 Gasket
102 Dowel
103 Stud
104 Bolt
105 Top cover housing
106 Gasket
107 Detent plunger
108 Plugs
109 1st/2nd selector shaft
110 Interlock balls
111 Interlock plunger
112 Reverse selector shaft
113 Sleeve
114 3rd/Top selector shaft
115 Dowel
116 Filler/level plug
117 Oil seal
118 Rear ballrace
119 Rear extension
120 Bolt
121 Gasket
122 Gear casing
123 Speedometer
123 Speedometer driven gear
124 Rubber O-ring
125 Bearing
126 Oil seal
127 Locating bolt
128 Drain plug
129 Gasket
130 Oil seal
131 Oil seal housing
132 Pin
133 Bolt
134 Copper washer
135 Bolt
136 Pivot pin
137 Clutch housing
138 Springs

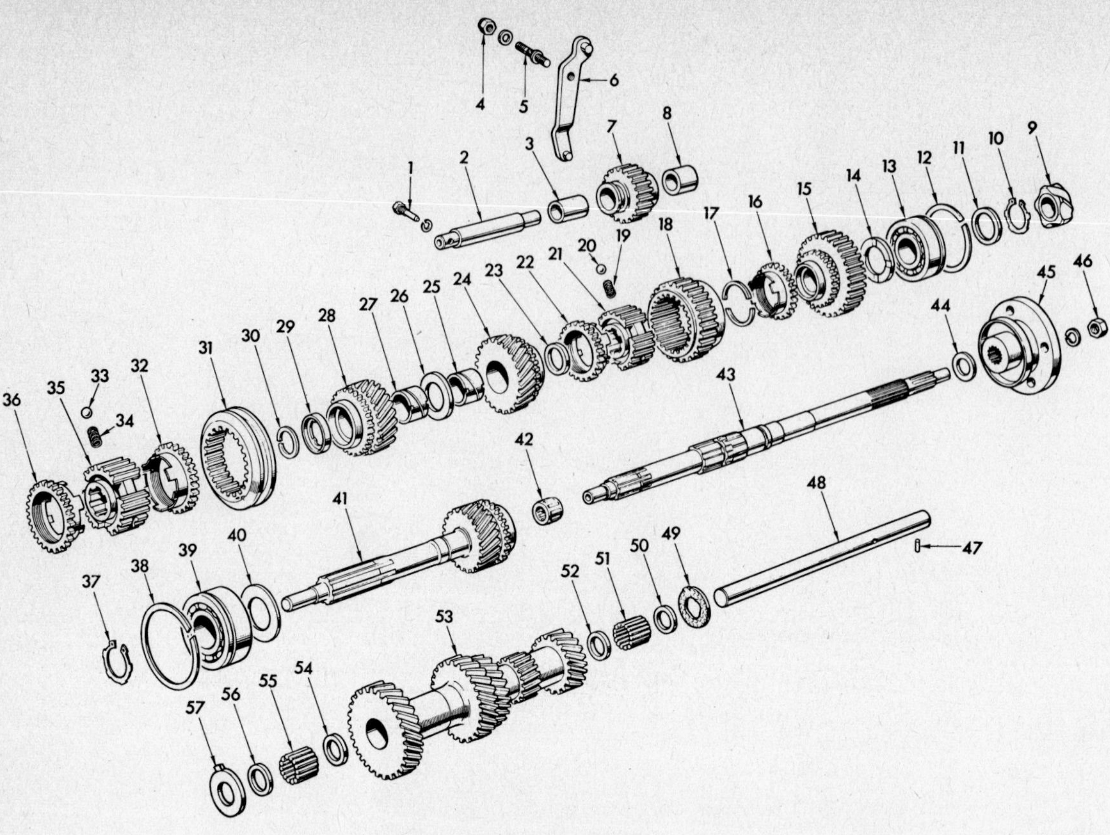

Moving components of GT6 transmission

1 Locating ball
2 Reverse idler spindle
4 Nyloc nut
5 Pivot pin
6 Reverse actuator
7 Reverse idler gear
8 Spacer tube
9 Speedometer driven gear
10 Circlip
11 Washer
12 Snap ring
13 Center ballrace
14 Thrust washer
15 1st speed gear
16 Baulk ring
17 Split collars
18 1st/2nd synchro sleeve
19 Spring
20 Ball
21 1st/2nd synchro hub
22 Baulk ring
23 Thrust washer
24 2nd speed gear
25 2nd gear bushing
26 Thrust washer
27 3rd gear bushing
28 3rd speed gear
29 Circlip washer
30 Circlip
31 3rd/Top synchro sleeve
32 Baulk ring
33 Ball
34 Spring
35 3rd/Top synchro hub
36 Baulk ring
37 Circlip
38 Snap ring
39 Front ballrace
40 Oil thrower
41 Input shaft
42 Roller bearing
43 Mainshaft
44 Thrust washer
45 Coupling flange
46 Nut
47 Pin
48 Countershaft spindle
49 Rear thrust washer
50 Retaining ring
51 Needle rollers
52 Retaining ring
53 Countershaft gear cluster
54 Retaining ring
55 Needle rollers
56 Retaining ring
57 Front thrust washer

washer smeared with grease, locate the washer in the transmission case. The tag should engage the recess provided. Insert the end of the countershaft spindle through the case to centralize the thrust washer. With the countershaft gear cluster assembly lowered into the case, install the rear thrust washer and insert the spindle. Measure the end clearance of the countershaft and adjust if necessary to .007-.013 in. (.178-.330 mm.) by using thrust washers of selected thickness. If the thickness of a thrust washer must be reduced, do not remove metal from the bronze face. Insert the needle roller retaining tube and remove the countershaft spindle. Allow the gear cluster assembly to drop to the bottom of the transmission case.

Assemble the reverse idle gear mechanism by screwing the pivot pin into the ac-

Measuring countershaft end play

tuator until a thread is seen to protrude through the boss of the lever. Install into the transmission case and secure with nut and washer. Position the reverse idler gear in the case. Install the synchronizer springs and balls to the 3rd/4th synchronizer hub and install the outer sleeve. Repeat the preceding with the 1st/2nd synchronizer unit and test the axial release loads, which should be between 19 and 21 pounds for each unit. The axial release load may be adjusted by the installation of new springs or the addition/subtraction of shims to/from the position beneath each synchronizer spring.

Measure the end clearance of each mainshaft gear on its respective bushing. Correct end clearance is .002–.006 in. (.05–.15 mm.). End clearance may be increased by the installation of a new bushing and decreased by the reduction of the length of the bushing. *NOTE: the reduction of bushing length will increase the end clearance of the bushings on the mainshaft.* Install the thrust washer, bushing, thrust washer, bushing and washer to the mainshaft. With the assembly secured with half a circlip, measure the total end clearance of the bushings and thrust washers on the mainshaft. The end clearance may be adjusted to the correct range of .004-.010 in. (.10-.25 mm.) through the use of thrust washers of various thicknesses.

Using feeler gauge to determine thickness of circlip washer, as described in text.

Determine the required thickness of the circlip washer by installing the split collars, 1st gear, thrust washer, bearing inner race or spacer tube, spacer washer and half a circlip to the mainshaft, then insert a feeler gauge as shown in the illustration. Use washers of proper thickness to obtain the correct clearance of .000-.002 in. (00-.50 mm.).

Install the following components on the mainshaft: 1st/2nd synchronizer unit, 2nd gear baulk ring, thrust washer, 2nd gear bushing, 2nd gear, thrust washer, 3rd gear bushing, 3rd gear, and washer. Use a special tool to install the circlip, and install the 3rd/4th synchronizer unit, split collars, 1st gear baulk ring, and 1st gear. Position the mainshaft assembly in the transmission case, install abutment plate tool or its equivalent, and install the thrust washer.

With the transmission positioned vertically, and the abutment plate held in a vise, install the snap ring to the ball bearing and position the ball bearing over the mainshaft. Being sure that the mainshaft is correctly located in the abutment plate, drive the ball bearing into position, using special tool and adaptor or their equivalents. Install the speedometer drive gear and remove the abutment plate from the transmission.

Proper positioning of 4th gear baulk ring (36) in 3rd/4th synchronizer unit.

Assemble the input shaft components: Position the 4th gear baulk ring into the

3rd/4th synchronizer unit, as shown in the illustration. Using special tool and adaptor or their equivalents, press the ball bearing and oil thrower onto the input shaft and secure the ball bearing with the circlip. Install the snap ring onto the ball bearing and place the roller bearing in the bore of the input shaft. Ensuring that the baulk ring is correctly located, drive the input shaft assembly into the transmission case. Assemble the countershaft by inverting the transmission, lining up the countershaft thrust washers and gear cluster, and inserting the spindle from the rear. With the reverse idler gear correctly positioned, insert the spindle and install the spacer tube.

Assemble the rear extension: Replace the ball bearing and seal to the rear extension. Install a new gasket at the rear of the transmission and place the washer over the end of the mainshaft. Install the rear extension assembly and secure with bolts. Replace and secure the driving flange. Torque nut to 90-100 ft.lbs. Assemble the bearing, oil seal, O-rings and driven gear and install the assembly to the extension housing, securing with the bolt. Insert the three springs into their holes in the front face of the transmission case. Replace, if necessary, the oil seal in the clutch housing and install a new gasket to the front face of the transmission. Secure the clutch housing with bolts and washers. Replace the clutch throw-out bearing and sleeve and release lever.

Replacement of interlock balls to top cover.

Reassemble the top cover as follows: Insert plungers and springs into the cover and slide the 3rd/4th selector shaft into the front end of the cover. While the shaft is being slid into position, press down on the selector plunger so that the shaft will be able to pass over it and through the selector fork. The shaft should be inserted until its middle indentation engages the plunger, achieving the neutral position. Repeat the above procedure with the reverse shaft and selector. With the interlock plunger inserted into the 1st/2nd selector shaft, install the selector fork, sleeve and washer into the cover in similar fashion, ensuring that the shaft also passes through the 3rd/4th selector fork. Before the 1st/2nd selector shaft is pushed to its neutral position, insert the two interlock balls into the transverse bore connecting the shaft bores at the rear of the casting (see accompanying illustration) and then push the shaft further into the cover until the selector plunger engages the middle indentation and the balls and plunger are retained by the shafts. Use new tapered locking pins to secure the selector and forks to the shafts. Use sealing compound around the edges of the plugs before driving them into the ends of the selector shaft bores. Use a new pin to secure the fork to the shaft. If necessary, replace the "Metalistik" bushing in the shaft. Using new fiber washers, secure the shaft to the

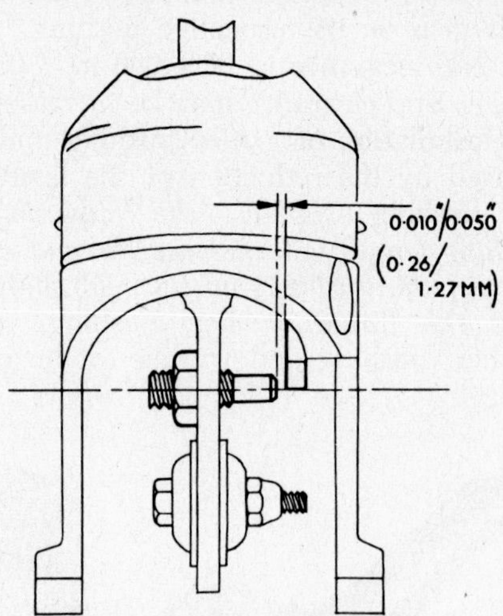

When adjustment of reverse stop plate and bolt is correct, clearance should be as shown.

fork with the bolt and nut. Install new O-rings to the case and install the shaft through the bores of the case and through the selector. Use a new tapered locking pin in securing the selector to the shaft. Install the reverse stop bolt, locknut, nylon ball, spring and snap ring to the gear shift lever.

Install the reverse stop plate to the cover and secure with the retaining screws. With the gearshift lever assembly positioned in the cover, install two new bushings to the lever, install the spacer tube, and secure the lever to the shaft with the retaining bolt and nut. Install the spring, cups and cap over the gearshift lever. Adjust the reverse stop plate and bolt with the gearshift lever in the neutral position of the 1st/2nd gate. The clearance between the reverse stop plate and bolt should be, as shown in the diagram, .010-.050 in. (.26-1.27 mm.). Reinstall top cover on transmission.

Spitfire

Disassembly

Disassemble the top cover as follows: Withdraw the retaining bolts and lift off the top cover and gasket. Remove the retaining nuts and washers and lift off the gearshift extension and gasket. Remove the nut and bolt to detach the shaft from the gearshift lever. Remove the gearshift lever knob. Remove the cap at the bottom of the gearshift lever and lift the lever assembly from the extension and remove cups and the outer spring. Remove the snap ring from the lever and remove the inner spring and nylon ball. Remove the retaining screws and detach the reverse stop plate. Remove the reverse stop bolt from the gearshift lever. Withdraw the threaded, tapered locking pin and extract the shaft from the extension case and selector. Remove the rubber O-rings from the extension case bore. Remove the locking nut and remove the pivot bolt from the coupling fork. Withdraw the shaft and fiber washers from the coupling. Remove the hollow spring steel pin and detach the coupling fork from the shaft. Disassemble the selector shaft and fork assemblies by driving out the plugs with a ⅛ in. (3.17 mm.) punch, taking care to see that the selector shafts are clear. Remove the threaded, tapered locking pins from the selector shafts and forks. Push the reverse selector shaft out of the cover, followed by the 1st/2nd selector shaft and the 3rd/4th selector shaft. Remove the two interlock balls, plunger, selector plungers and springs.

Disassemble the clutch housing by driving out the pivot pin, removing the operating lever assembly, and removing the slave cylinder bracket, four bolts and Wedgelock bolt.

Disassemble the rear extension: Remove the nut and spring washer and withdraw the driving flange from the mainshaft. Remove the six bolts and one longer bolt that secure the extension to the transmission. Remove the extension by pulling and lightly tapping the mounting lugs with a soft-headed hammer. Remove the paper gasket and spacer washer from the mainshaft. Remove the bolt and separate the housing from the extension. Remove the gear and shaft from the housing and take out the rubber O-ring. Detach the ball bearing and oil seal from the extension.

Withdraw the countershaft locating bolt and remove the countershaft, allowing the countershaft gear cluster to drop clear of the mainshaft. Withdraw the input shaft assembly from the transmission case. Remove the circlips, spacer washer and, using a press, extract the ball bearing and oil deflector. Drive the mainshaft to the rear until the rear ball bearing is clear of its housing. With the mainshaft assembly tilted, withdraw the synchronizer unit and the synchronizer cups. With the mainshaft repositioned, use a special extractor to remove the circlip. Drive the mainshaft to the rear and remove the components as they are released from the shaft. The mainshaft may be completely dismantled by removing the nylon speedometer driving gear, circlips, spacer washer and ball bearing.

Withdraw the reverse idler gear to the rear and remove the retaining bolt and the reverse idler gear shaft. Remove the rear thrust washer, lift the gear cluster from the case, and remove the front thrust washer and the rear rotating thrust washer. Remove the nut and remove the operating lever and pivot pin.

Disassemble the synchronizer units by withdrawing their outer sleeves. Because these sleeves retain the spring-loaded balls, perform this operation with the synchronizer units in a small container so that the balls are not lost. In addition to the synchronizer balls and springs, the 2nd gear synchronizer unit is provided with an interlock ball and plunger.

Assembly

Smear the steel face of the front countershaft thrust washer with grease and locate the washer in the transmission case so that its bronze face is towards the gear and its tag is engaged in the recess pro-

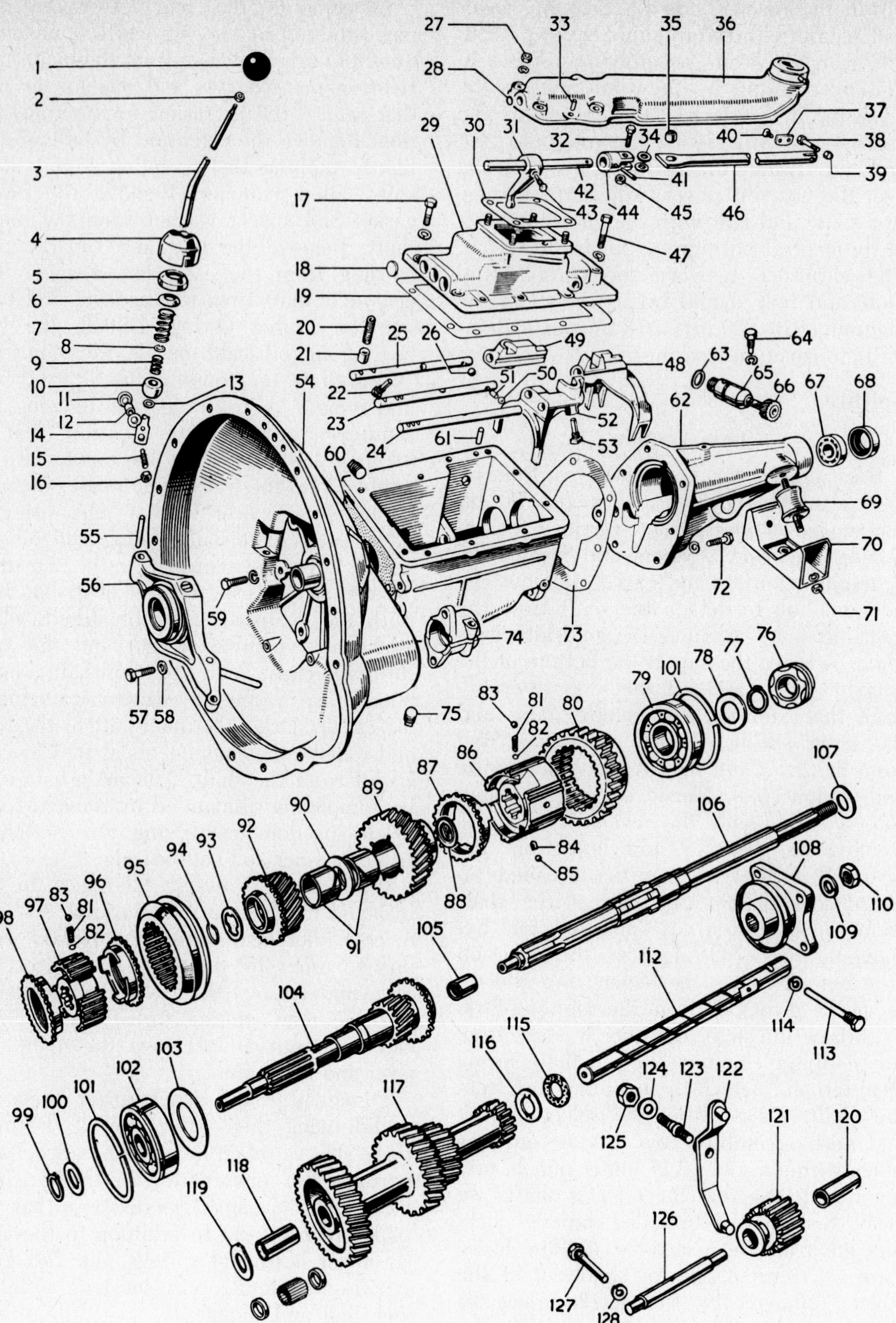

Exploded view of components of Spitfire transmission.

1 Knob
2 Locknut
3 Gearshift lever
4 Cover
5 Shield
6 Plate
7 Spring
8 Circlip
9 Spring
10 Nylon ball
11 Stepped nylon washer
12 Bushing
13 Washer
14 Lever end
15 Reverse stop pin
16 Locknut
17 Bolt
18 Welch plug
19 Gasket
20 Spring
21 Plunger
22 Taper locking pin
23 1st/2nd selector shaft
24 3rd/top selector shaft
25 Reverse selector shaft
26 Interlock ball
27 Nut
28 Rubber O-ring
29 Top cover
30 Gasket
31 Selector ball-end
32 Bolt
33 Dowel
34 Washer
35 Bonded rubber bushing
36 Gearshift extension
37 Reverse stop
38 Bolt
39 Nyloc nut
40 Screw
41 Pin
42 Remote control shaft (front)
43 Taper locking pin
44 Fork
45 Nut
46 Remote control shaft (rear)
47 Bolt
48 1st/2nd selector fork
49 Reverse selector
50 Interlock ball
51 Interlock plunger
52 Top/3rd selector fork
53 Taper locking pin
54 Clutch housing
55 Pin
56 Clutch release mechanism
57 Bolt
58 Plain washer
59 Bolt
60 Gasket
61 Dowel
62 Rear extension
63 Rubber O-ring
64 Peg bolt
65 Speedometer drive gear housing
66 Speedometer drive gear
67 Extension ball race
68 Oil seal
69 Gearbox mounting rubber
70 Mounting bracket
71 Nut
72 Bolt
73 Gasket
74 Clutch slave cylinder bracket
75 Sump plug
76 Speedometer driving gear
77 Circlip
78 Space washer
79 Ball race
80 1st speed gear
81 Spring
82 Shim
83 Synchromesh ball
84 Plunger
85 Ball
86 2nd speed synchro hub
87 2nd speed synchro cup
88 Thrust washer
89 2nd speed mainshaft gear
90 Thrust washer
91 Bushings
92 3rd speed mainshaft gear
93 Thrust washer
94 Circlip
95 3rd/top synchro sleeve
96 3rd speed synchro cup
97 3rd/top inner synchro hub
98 Top synchro cup
99 Circlip
100 Spacer washer
101 Circlip
102 Ball race
103 Oil deflector
104 Input shaft
105 Needle roller bearing
106 Mainshaft
107 Spacer washer
108 Driving flange
109 Spring washer
110 Nut
111 Countershaft
113 Peg bolt
114 Spring washer
115 Rear fixed thrust washer
116 Rear rotating thrust washer
116 Rear rotating thrust washer
117 Countershaft gear cluster
118 Countershaft bushing
119 Front fixed thrust washer
120 Reverse gear bushing
121 Reverse gear
122 Reverse gear actuator
123 Actuator pilot
124 Plain washer
125 Nyloc nut
126 Reverse gear shaft
127 Reverse shaft retaining bolt
128 Spring washer

vided. Centralize the washer by inserting the rear of the countershaft through the transmission case. Attach the rear rotating thrust washer in similar fashion, with its tags engaging the rear slotted face of the countershaft gear cluster. Lower the gear cluster assembly into the case. Push the gear cluster towards the front thrust washer as far as possible, then smear the rear thrust washer with grease and insert the washer between the transmission case and the rotating thrust washer, with its tag located in the recess provided. To measure the countershaft end clearance, line up the thrust washers and the gear cluster with the appropriate holes in the transmission case, then install the countershaft. Measure the end float with feeler gauges inserted between the rear fixed thrust washer and the adjacent rotating washer.

Permissible limits for the countershaft cluster gear end clearance are .0015–.0125 in. (.04–.31 mm.), but it is recommended that an end float of .006 in. be obtained by selective assembly of available thrust washers. If it is necessary to reduce the thickness of any thrust washer, do not remove metal from the bronze face of the washer. Remove the countershaft and let the cluster gear drop to allow the installation of the mainshaft assembly.

Screw the reverse idler gear pivot pin into the selector lever until a thread is seen to protrude through the boss on the lever. Secure the pin and lever assembly in the case with the nut and plain washer. With the reverse idler gear shaft positioned in the case and its locating hole aligned, secure the shaft with the locking pin and lock washer. Slide the reverse idler gear over its shaft so that its annular groove is engaged with the pin attached to the lower end of the operating lever.

Assemble the 3rd/4th synchronizer unit by installing the springs, balls and shims to the hub and adding the outer sleeve. Repeat the preceding with the 2nd gear synchronizer unit. Test the axial release load of the synchronizer units. Axial release should occur at 19-21 lbs. Adjust release by altering the number of shims beneath each synchronizer spring until the correct loading is achieved.

Measure the end clearance of each mainshaft gear on its respective bushing. End clearance on the bushing should be .002–.006 in. (.05–.1524 mm.) for both gears. Float may be increased by installing a new bushing and decreased by reducing the housing length. *NOTE: reduction of bushing length will increase the end clearance of the bushings on the mainshaft.* Check the overall end clearance of the bushings on the mainshaft as follows: With the thrust washer, bushing, washer, bushing and thrust washer assembled to the mainshaft, secure the assembly with a discarded half-circlip and measure the total end clearance of the bushings and thrust washers on the mainshaft. If necessary, adjust the end clearance to the recommended .004-.010 in. (.1016-.254 mm.) by the selective use of thrust washers of various thicknesses.

Assemble the mainshaft as follows: With the circlip groove to the rear, press the ball bearing onto the mainshaft. Install the spacer washer and circlip, ensuring that the circlip is correctly located in the groove of the mainshaft. Press the speedometer drive gear onto the mainshaft and install the large circlip into the groove of the ball bearing. Insert the mainshaft through the transmission case and install the components to the shaft in the following order (see accompanying illustration): 2nd gear synchronizer unit assembly, with gear portion forward (be sure that the interlock plug and ball are located correctly in the unit), 2nd gear synchronizer cup (be sure that the three lugs are located in the synchronizer hub), rear thrust washer, with scrolled face forward, and 2nd gear and bushing. Install the center thrust washer, 3rd gear and bushing, and the front thrust washer, with its scrolled face to the rear. Install the circlip. With the longer boss of the inner synchronizer member forward, slide the 3rd/4th synchronizer unit, baulk rings attached, over the mainshaft and drive the rear ball race into its housing.

Assemble the input shaft as follows: *NOTE: it is not possible to remove the needle roller bearing, and its replacement necessitates replacement of the input shaft.* Smear the oil deflector plate with grease and position it on the input shaft. Without disturbing the position of the plate, press the ball bearing onto the shaft. Secure the ball bearing with the spacer washer and circlip, ensuring that the latter is correctly located in the groove of the shaft. With the large circlip on the ball bearing outer race and the synchronizer cup over its cone on the input shaft, insert the assembly, simultaneously locating the baulk ring lugs into their respective slots in the synchronizer hub.

Line up the thrust washers and the countershaft gear cluster by pushing a .655 in. (16.64 mm.) diameter rod, tapered at one end, through the case and countershaft assembly. Push the countershaft through the case and countershaft assembly, forcing out the pilot rod. Be sure to maintain contact between the two shafts when the pilot rod is being driven out. Secure the countershaft by locking pin holes, inserting the locking pin and securing with the lockwasher.

Assemble the rear extension: Drive the ball bearing into its bore in the rear of the housing and insert the oil seal, with its sealing lip facing forward. Lubricate the speedometer drive shaft and insert into its housing. The rubber O-ring should be replaced if it is worn or damaged. With the drive gear assembly inserted into the rear extension, line up the location hole with the corresponding hole in the extension. Insert the retaining bolt and tighten. Install the spacer washer over the end of the mainshaft. Smear the gasket with grease and locate it on the rear face of the transmission case. Drive the rear ball bearing over the mainshaft, install the extension and secure with the retaining bolts and locking washers. Install the driving flange, washer and nut and tighten to a torque of 6-8 ft-lbs. To reassemble the clutch housing and release mechanism, reverse the removal procedure, except for the installation of a new copper-plated steel washer beneath the lower bolt to prevent oil leakage.

Assemble the top cover as follows: Insert the plungers and springs into the cover and slide the 3rd/4th selector shaft into the front end of the cover. While the 3rd/4th shaft is being pushed into position, depress the selector plunger to enable the shaft to pass over it and through the appropriate selector fork. Continue to insert the shaft until its middle indentation engages the plunger. This will be the neutral position. Repeat the preceding procedure with the reverse shaft and selector until it has also reached the neutral position. With the interlock plunger inserted into the 1st/2nd gear shaft, assemble these and the selector fork into the the cover in similar fashion, except that the shaft will also pass through the 3rd/4th selector fork. Before the shaft has been pushed to its neutral position, the two interlock balls must be inserted into the transverse bore that connects the shaft bores at the rear of the cover casting. The shaft should then be pushed further into the cover until its selector plunger engages the middle indentation and the interlock balls and plunger are retained by the shafts. Secure the forks and reverse selector with the threaded, tapered lockpins. Coat the edges of the plugs with sealing compound and drive these into the ends of the selector shaft bores. With all selectors and gears in the neutral position, install the gasket and top cover assembly over the two dowels on the transmission and secure with the retaining bolts and lock washers, with the longer bolts at the rear.

Driveshafts and U-Joints

DRIVESHAFT

Place vehicle on jackstands. Remove dashboard supports and transmission cover. Remove attaching nuts. Gently angle transmission/engine forward to remove driveshaft. Remove shaft to the rear. Models with sliding splines do not require movement of the engine/transmission assembly. To replace, reverse above procedure. If original nuts can be replaced with finger pressure, they must be replaced with new nyloc nuts.

U-JOINTS

Disassembly

Remove lock-ring from forked end of shaft. Tap lug until bearing cup is seen to protrude. Remove cup with pliers. Repeat operation on reverse side. Remove flange. Remove all remaining lock-rings. Rest shaft on block and gently tap out remaining components.

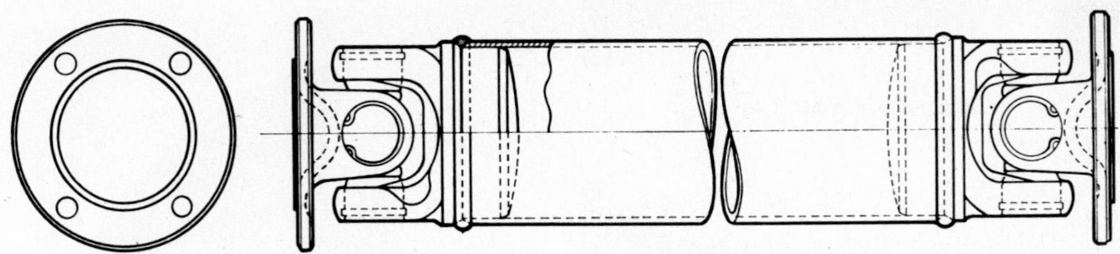

Solid type driveshaft

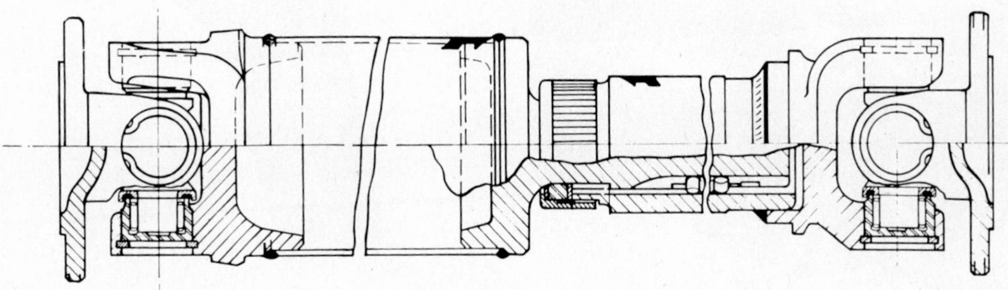

Sliding spline type driveshaft

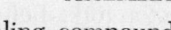

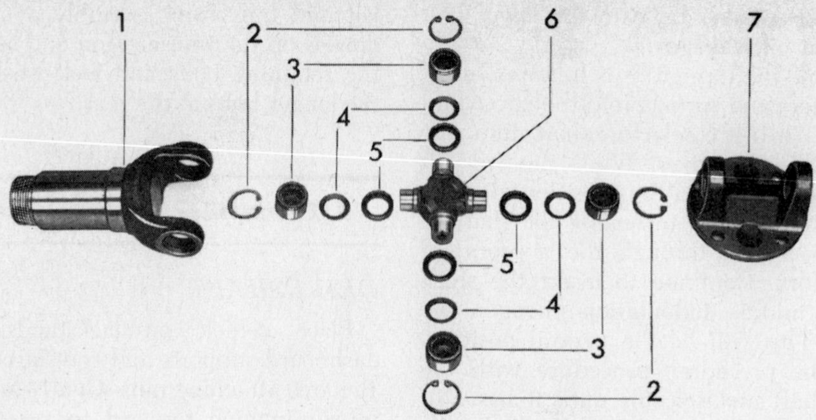

Universal Joint

1 Sliding yoke
2 Circlips
3 Bearing cups
4 Seals
5 Retainers
6 Spider
7 Flange

Replacing bearing cups

Assembly

Place sealing compound on shoulders of new spider journals. Fit oil seal retainers over trunnions with tubular drift. Fit oil seals. Place trunnion into bearing holes and fit bearing caps and lock-rings. Make sure they are properly seated. Fit spider with lubrication nipple toward driveshaft. Place other trunnion through bearing holes in forked end of driveshaft and fit cups and lock-rings. Repeat procedure on second universal joint.

CAUTION: *Do not disassemble sliding yoke for any reason.*

Spider replacement

Grease plug location

Drive Axle

NOTE: unless one has the special tools and experience, he should not attempt work on the rear axle assembly. The TR–4 rear axle is of conventional design, with hypoid bevel gears connected to semi-floating axle shafts. The TR–4A, TR–250 and TR–6 are equipped with a semi-trailing arm independent suspension (optional on TR-4A). The GT6 and Spitfire were equipped with a swing axle type rear end, but the latest models use a semi trailing arm independent rear suspension similar to that on the TR series.

REAR AXLE SPECIFICATIONS

Backlash between pinion and ring gears:
All: .004–.006 in. (.10–.15 mm.)
Pinion bearing preload, without oil seal:
TR-4, TR-4A, TR-250, TR-6: 15-18 in. lb
GT6 and Spitfire: 12-16 in. lb.
Differential bearing preload, measured over both bearings:
All: .003 in. (.076 mm.)
Axle shaft end clearance:
TR–4: .004–.006 in. (.10–.15 mm.)
NOTE: adjust by varying the shim thickness between the end of the axle case and the brake backing plate. To keep thrust block centered with the cross pin, change the shims at both sides an equal amount.

Maximum run-out of ring gear, when bolted to differential carrier:
All: .003 in. (.076 mm.)

REAR AXLE TORQUES

TR-4

Bearing caps to housing: 34–36 ft.lb.
Backing plate attachment: 26–28 ft.lb.
Ring gear to differential case: 35–40 ft.lb.
Hypoid pinion flange: 85–100 ft.lb.
Hub to axle shaft: 125–145 ft.lb.
Rear cover attachment: 16–18 ft.lb.

TR-4A, TR-250, TR-6

Ring gear to differential case: 40–45 ft.lb.
Inner driving flange to inner axle: 100–110 ft.lb.
Driveshaft flange to pinion; TR–250, TR–6: 90–100 ft.lb.

GT6, Spitfire

Hypoid pinion flange attachment:
(GT6) 90-100 ft. lb.
(Spitfire) 70–85 ft.lb.
Rear hub to axle shaft: 100–110 ft.lb.

DIFFERENTIAL TOOTH CONTACT CONDITIONS

By painting about ten teeth of the ring gear with special paint, then moving the pinion into mesh with the painted teeth, it is possible to obtain a good impression of how the teeth are making contact. The following tooth contact conditions, along with their remedies, are keyed to the accompanying diagrams:

Ideal Contact (a): The area of contact is distributed evenly over the tooth profile, and is closer to the toe than to the heel.

High Tooth Contact (b): The area of

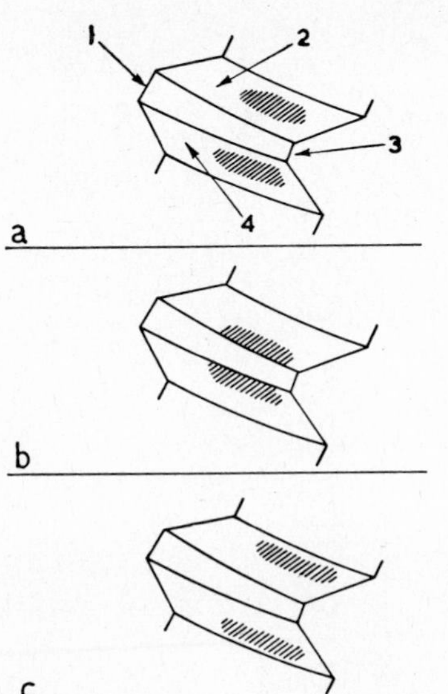

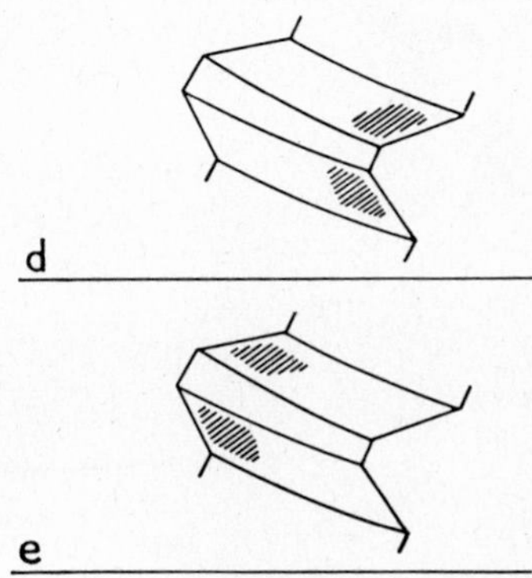

Gear tooth markings, as described in text. Numbered sections are heel (1), coasting side (2), toe (3) and drive side(4).

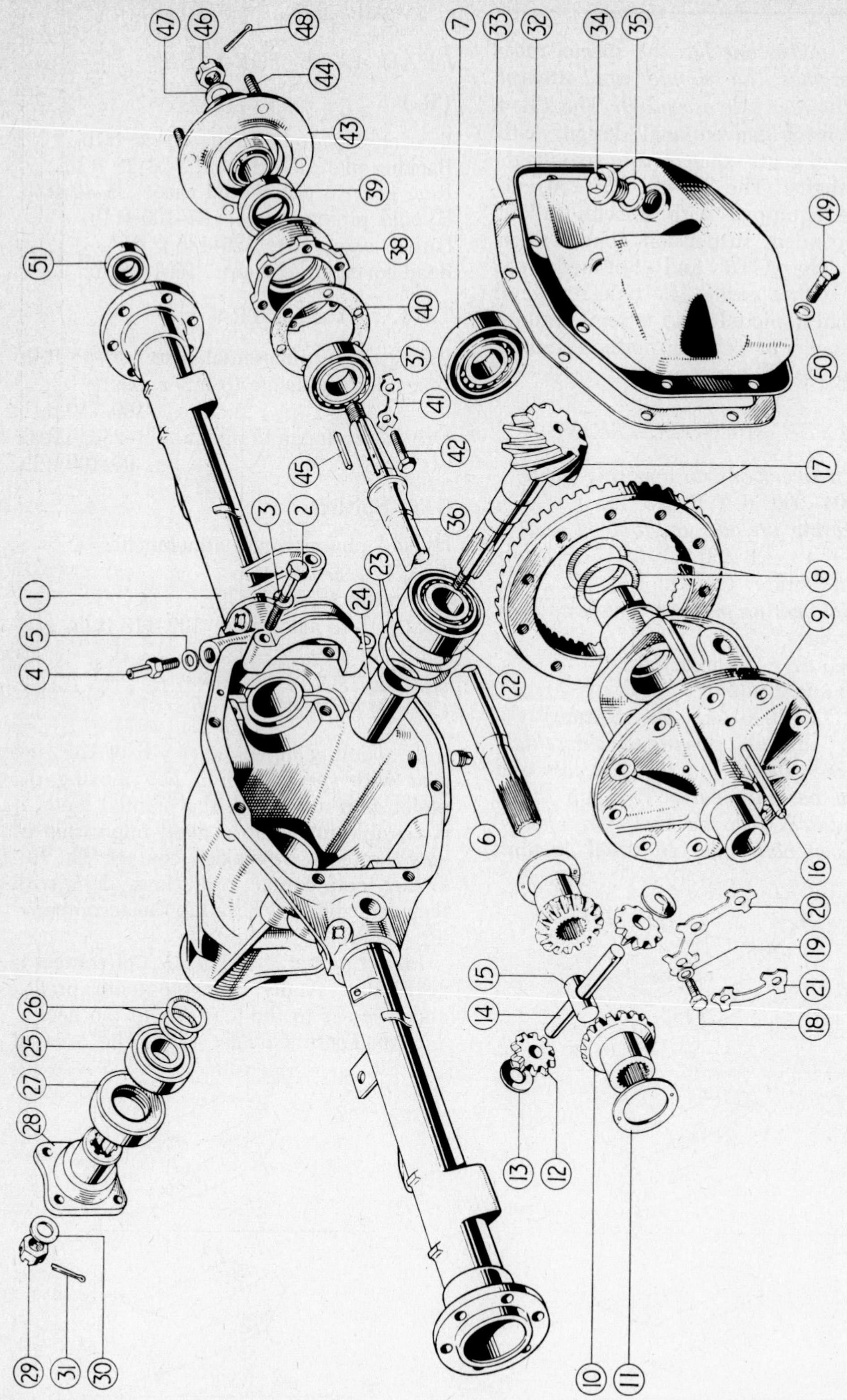

Exploded view of rear axle components, TR–4.

Exploded view of rear axle components, TR-4.

1 Axle casing assembly
2 Bearing cap setscrew
3 Spring washer
4 Axle case breather
5 Fiber washer
6 Drain plug
7 Differential bearing
8 Adjusting shims for (7)
9 Differential carrier
10 Differential sun gear
11 Thrust washer for (10)
12 Differential planet gear
13 Thrust washer for (12)
14 Cross pin
15 Thrust lock
16 Lockpin for securing (14)
17 Ring gear and pinion
18 Ring gear securing bolt
19 Spring washer for (18)
20 Three hole lockplate
21 Two hole lockplate
22 Pinion head bearing
23 Adjusting shims for (22)
24 Bearing spacer
25 Pinion tail bearing
26 Adjusting shims for (25)
27 Pinion shaft oil seal
28 Pinion driving flange
29 Driving flange securing nut
30 Plain washer for (29)
31 Cotter pin for (29)
32 Rear cover
33 Gasket for (32)
34 Oil filler plug
35 Fiber washer
36 Axle shaft
37 Hub bearing
38 Hub bearing housing
39 Oil seal for hub bearing housing
40 Adjusting shims for hub bearing
41 Lockplate
42 Setscrew for securing housing
43 Hub
44 Wheel attachment stud
45 Hub driving key
46 Hub securing nut
47 Plain washer for (46)
48 Cotter pin for (46)
49 Cover plate securing setscrew
50 Spring washer for (49)
51 Axle tube oil seal

Exploded view of swing axle components, GT6, spitfire swing axle is similar.

1 Shims
2 Differential side bearing
3 Thrust washer
4 Cross-shaft locking pin
5 Sun gear
6 Planet gear
7 Thrust washer
8 Gasket
9 Rear mounting bolt
10 Bushing
11 Hypoid rear casing
12 Circlip
13 Nyloc nut
14 Seal housing plate
15 Oil seal
16 Hexagon socket screw
17 Ball race
18 Differential carrier
19 Differential side bearing
20 Shims
21 Inner axle shaft
22 Nyloc nut
23 Bolt
24 Bolt
25 Shim
26 Rubber sealing ring
27 Nylon bushing
28 Shim
29 Stud
30 Hub
31 Nyloc nut
32 Grease trap
33 Outer seal housing
34 Seal
35 Ballrace
36 Gasket
37 Trunnion housing
38 Spacer tube
39 Grease plug
40 Needle roller bearing
41 Inner oil seal
42 Key
43 Outer axle shaft
44 Grease flinger
45 Universal joint assembly
46 Circlip
47 Bearing cap
48 Tubular dowel
49 Bolt
50 Mounting rubber
51 Nyloc nut
52 Plain washer
53 Rubber pad
54 Bolt
55 Cotter pin
56 Slotted nut
57 Coupling flange
58 Oil seal
59 Pinion tail bearing
60 Shims
61 Spacer
62 Mounting plate
63 Bolt
64 Hypoid nose piece casing
65 Pinion head bearing
66 Spacer
67 Pinion
68 Ring gear
69 Cross-shaft
70 Bolt
71 Lockplate
72 Brake backplate
73 Bolt
74 Nyloc nut
75 Vertical link

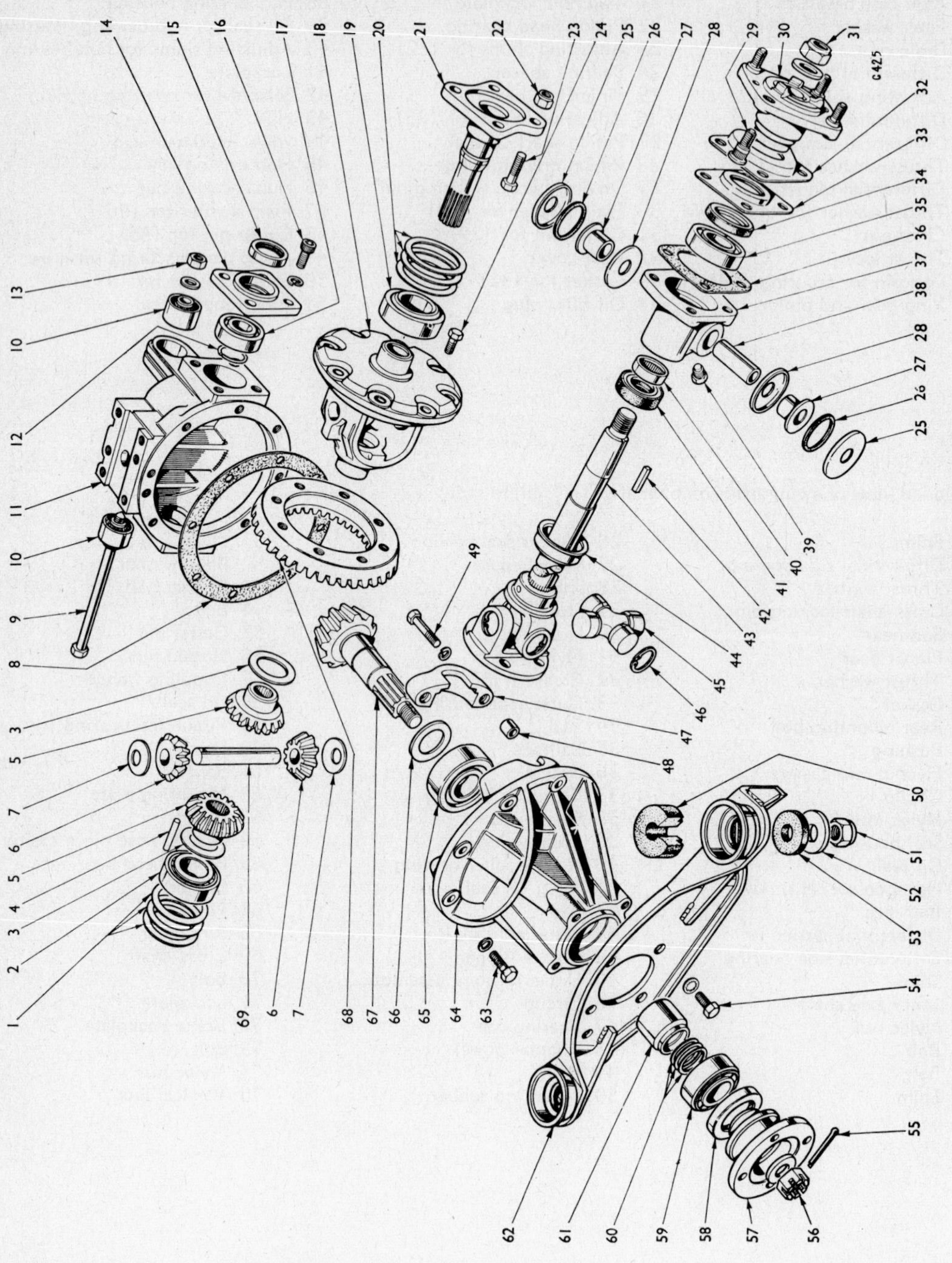

Exploded view of swing axle components, GT6, spitfire swing axle is similar.

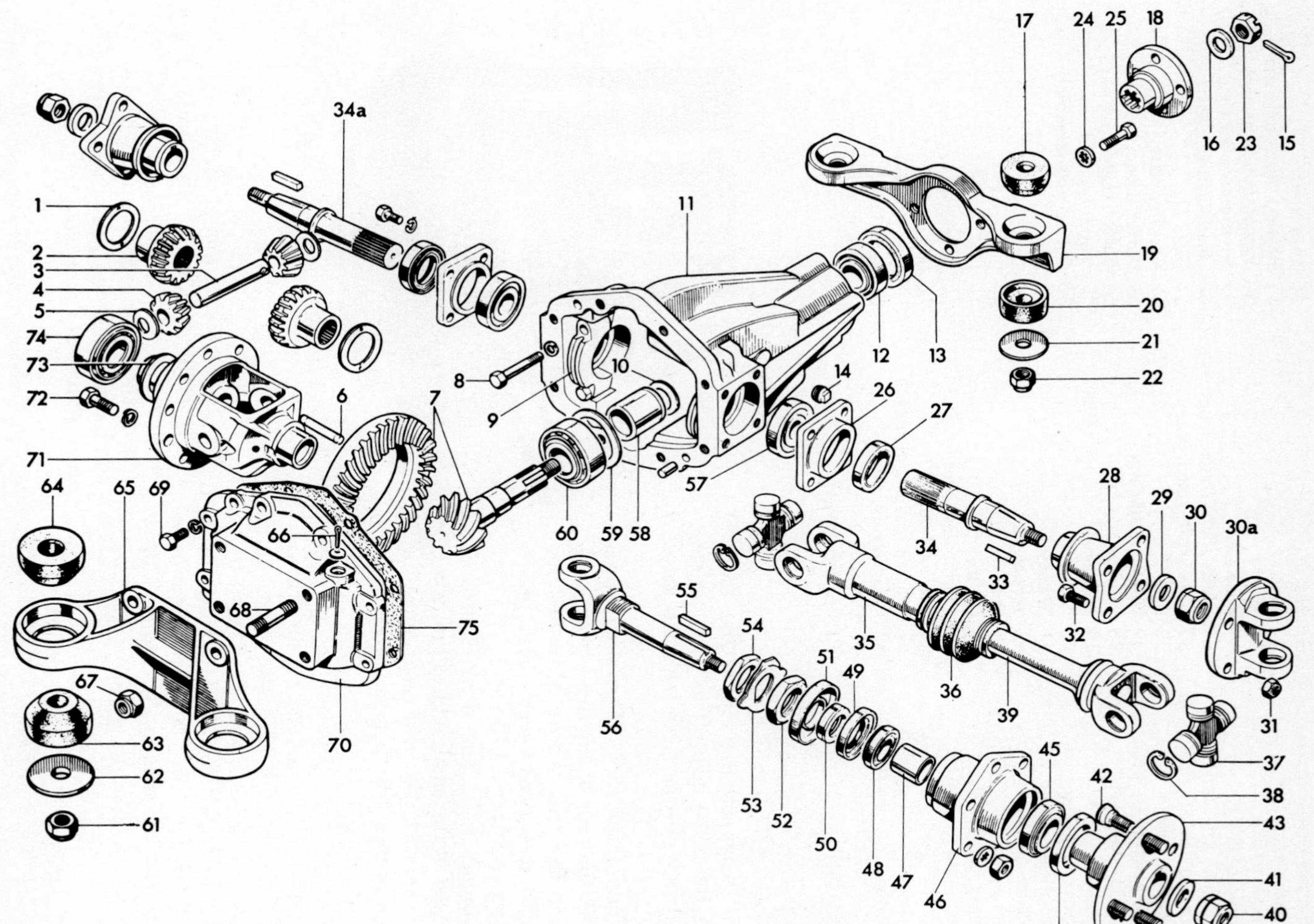

Exploded view of rear axle components, TR-4A, TR-250, TR-6.

Exploded view of rear axle components, TR–4A, TR–250, TR–6.

1 Thrust washer—sun gear
2 Sun gear
3 Cross shaft
4 Planet gear
5 Thrust washer—planet gear
6 Locking pin—cross shaft
7 Ring gear and pinion
8 Bolt, bearing cap
9 Bearing cap
10 Shim, pinion pre-loading
11 Axle casing
12 Tail bearing, pinion
13 Oil seal, pinion
14 Filler plug—oil level
15 Cotter pin
16 Washer
17 Rubber buffer, upper
18 Companion flange
19 Mounting, front
20 Rubber buffer, lower
21 Backing plate
22 Nyloc nut
23 Slotted nut
24 Lockwasher
25 Bolt
26 Bearing retainer
27 Oil seal
28 Flange
29 Washer
30 Nut
30a Yoke
31 Nut
32 Bolt
33 Key
34 Axle shaft, inner, short
34a Axle shaft, inner, long
35 Axle shaft, fixed, outer
36 Seal
37 Universal spider
38 Circlip
39 Axle shaft, sliding, outer
40 Nut
41 Washer
42 Wheel stud
43 Hub
44 Oil seal
45 Hub bearing, outer
46 Bearing housing
47 Bearing spacer, collapsible
48 Hub bearing, inner
49 Oil seal
50 Bearing spacer
51 Stone guard
52 Adjusting nut
53 Tab washer
54 Locknut
55 Key
56 Stub shaft
57 Bearing, inner axle shaft
58 Spacer, pinion bearing
59 Shim, pinion locating
60 Head bearing, pinion
61 Nut
62 Backing plate
63 Buffer, lower
64 Buffer, upper
65 Mounting, rear
66 Cotter pin—breather
67 Nut
68 Stud
69 Bolt
70 Rear cover
71 Differential cage
72 Bolt
73 Shim, pre-load
74 Bearing, differential cage
75 Gasket, rear cover

contact is heavy on the top of the tooth profile of the drive gear. The pinion must be moved into deeper mesh with the drive gear.

Low Tooth Contact (c): The contact area is heavy in the root of the drive gear tooth profile, and the pinion gear is meshed too deeply with the drive gear. The pinion must be moved away.

Toe Contact (d): The contact area is concentrated at the small end of the driven tooth. To correct, the ring gear must be moved out of mesh by increasing the backlash.

Heel Contact (e): The contact area is concentrated at the large end of the driven tooth. To correct, the ring gear must be moved into closer mesh with the pinion by decreasing the backlash. *CAUTION: when decreasing the backlash, be sure to maintain the minimum backlash of .004 in. (.10 mm.).*

AXLE COMPONENT SERVICE FOR VEHICLES WITH INDEPENDENT REAR SUSPENSION

Outer Axle Shaft and Hub Assembly

REMOVAL

Place vehicle on jack stands; remove

Brake linkage, D; radius arm bolt, E; shock absorber nut, H.

wheel and backing plate. Remove brake hose, attaching bracket, and brake line. Disconnect handbrake from attaching lever. Relieve shock absorber of load by use of jack. Remove bolt to release radius arm. Remove universal joint coupling bolts. Remove nut and washer from lower attaching eye; pull shock clear. Remove jack. While supporting brake drum by hand, remove spring eye nuts. Hub and axle shafts are now free.

INSTALLATION

Refit vertical link to spring attaching eye;

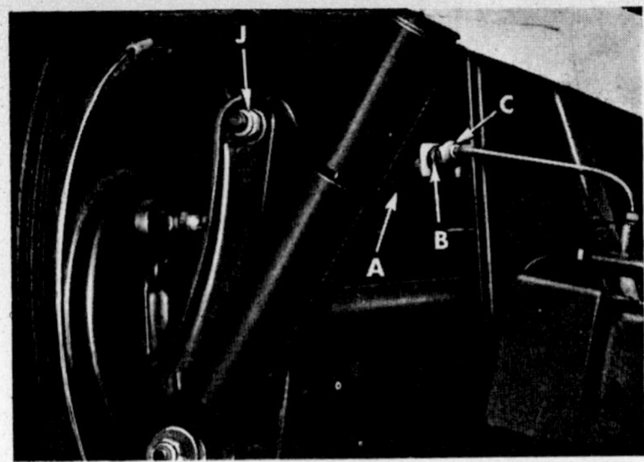

Brake line, A; brake line coupling, B and C; spring eye nut, J.

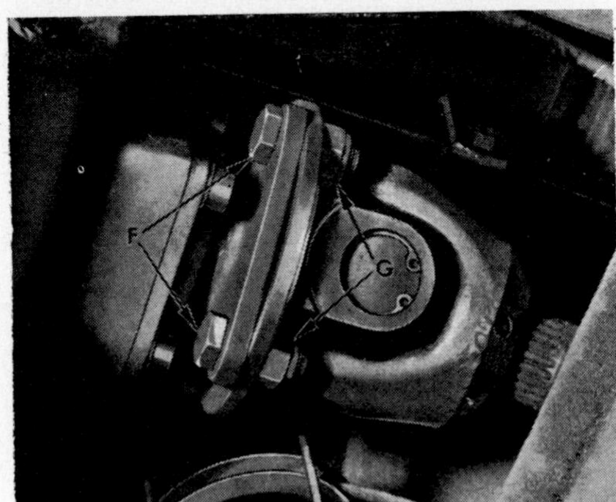

Axle shaft couplings

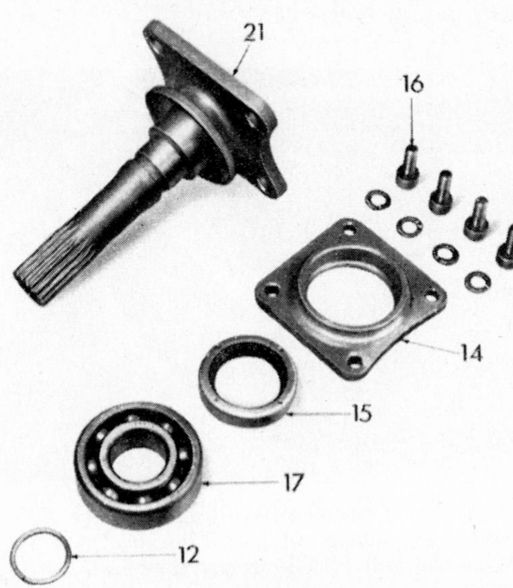

Inner axle shaft parts

12 Circlip
14 Seal housing plate
15 Oil seal
16 Allen screws
21 Inner axle shaft

leave nut loose. Using caution, jack up vertical link and affix extended shock absorber to lower attaching bracket. Refit radius arm to link; secure in position. Fasten inner and outer axle shafts together. Place a load of 300 lbs. in the front seats. Tighten securing nut to vertical link. Reverse removal procedures to complete installation.

Inner Axle Shaft Removal and Installation

Remove outer axle shaft as previously described. Drain rear axle. Using a 3/16 in. Allen wrench, remove Allen screws from differential housing. To install, reverse procedure.

Removing inner axle shaft

Pinion Oil Seal Replacement

Drain rear axle. Remove tailpipe and driveshaft. Remove split pin, nut, and flange. Remove old seal. Drive in new seal. To reassemble, reverse procedure.

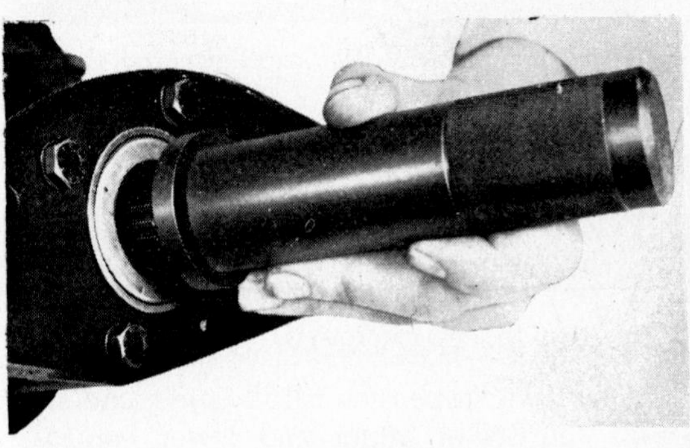

Replacing pinion oil seal

Differential Unit Removal

Place vehicle on jackstands and drain rear axle. Remove wheels and backing plate. Place supports under vertical links to remove load from shock absorbers. Remove shock absorber. Remove resonator and tailpipe. Disconnect driveshaft. Remove luggage compartment floor panel; remove spring access plate. Unscrew nuts and remove rear spring attachments. With assistant supporting weight of unit, cautiously release front mounts. Remove unit forward and down. To reassemble, reverse above procedures. Be sure to readjust brakes.

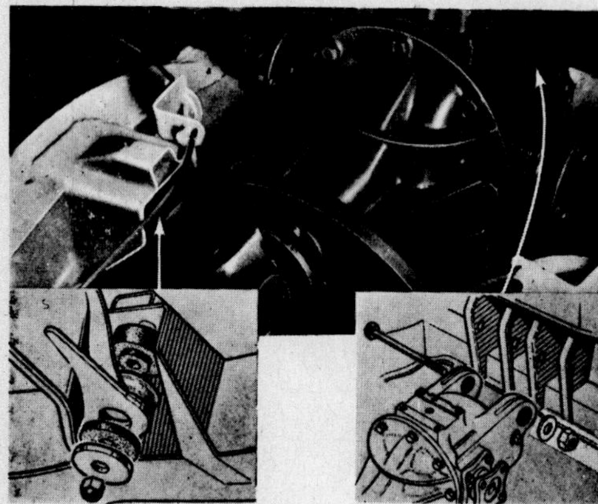

Differential attachment points

Luggage compartment floor panel removed showing spring mounting bolts

Suspension

FRONT SUSPENSION

The front suspension is fully independent and consists of upper and lower control arms at each side holding the spindles, coil springs, and hydraulic shock absorbers. The front wheel bearings are of the tapered roller design.

Ball Joint Removal and Replacement

Before starting work, be sure the handbrake is on. Remove ball joint stud washer and nut. Using a ball joint separator, pull ball joint from vertical link. Loosen and remove bolts holding ball joint to upper A-arm. *CAUTION: When removing ball joints, hub assembly must be supported.*

To replace: Make sure all parts are thoroughly cleaned. Attach ball joint to upper A-arm. Tighten bolts. Place ball joint stud into vertical link and tighten nut and washer. Replace stud nut with new nyloc nut. Tighten all remaining bolts.

Wheel Bearing Adjustment

The end float of the front wheel bearings should be .003–.005 in. (.08–.13 mm.), and may be checked by a suitable dial gauge. The front wheel hub nut is provided with slots to accomapny a securing cotter pin. In the event that a suitable gauge is not available, proceed as follows: While rotating the hub, tighten the nut only sufficiently to remove looseness (a torque of about 5 ft.lbs. should be sufficient for this purpose), then loosen the nut by one flat and secure with a new cotter pin.

End float of front wheel bearings should be .003–.005 in. Tightening nut to 5 ft.lb., then loosening by one flat will provide proper clearance.

Front End Alignment

The following suspension geometry angles and measurements apply to cars that are static laden, i.e. with the vehicle sta-

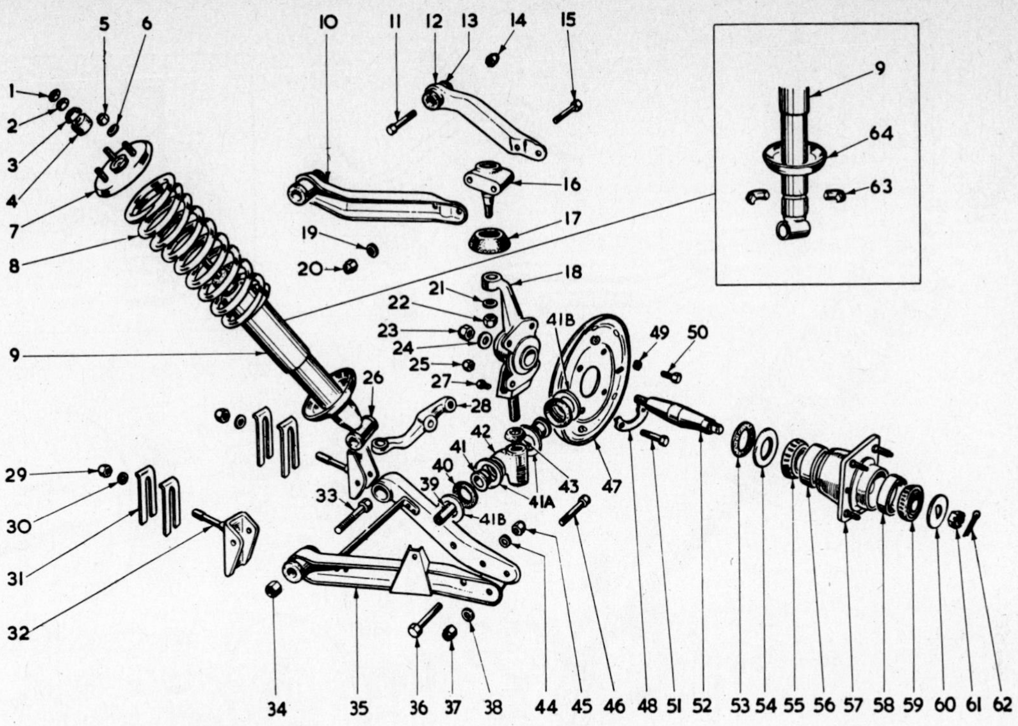

Spitfire front suspension

1 Locknut
2 Nut
3 Washer
4 Rubber bushing
5 Nyloc nut
6 Plain washer
7 Upper spring pan
8 Road spring
9 Damper
10 Front upper wishbone arm
11 Bolt
12 Rear upper wishbone arm
13 Rubber bushing
14 Nyloc nut
15 Bolt
16 Ball joint
17 Rubber gaiter
18 Vertical link
19 Plain washer
20 Nyloc nut
21 Plain washer
22 Nyloc nut
23 Nyloc nut
24 Plain Washer
25 Nyloc nut
26 Rubber bushing
27 Plug
28 Steering arm
29 Nyloc nut
30 Plain washer
31 Shim
32 Inner fulcrum bracket
33 Fulcrum bolt
34 Nyloc nut
35 Lower wishbone assembly
36 Suspension unit fulcrum bolt
37 Nyloc nut
38 Plain washer
39 Steel bushing
40 Rubber seal
41 Nylon bush
41A Washer
41B Washer
42 Lower trunnion
43 Rubber seal
44 Plain washer
45 Nyloc nut
46 Fulcrum bolt
47 Brake backplate
48 Locking plate
49 Spring washer
50 Setscrew
51 Bolt
52 Stub axle
53 Felt seal
54 Seal retainer
55 Taper roller bearing—inner
56 Roller bearing outer ring
57 Hub
58 Roller bearing outer ring
59 Taper roller bearing—outer
60 D washer
61 Slotted nut
62 Split pin
63 Spring retaining collet
64 Spring cup

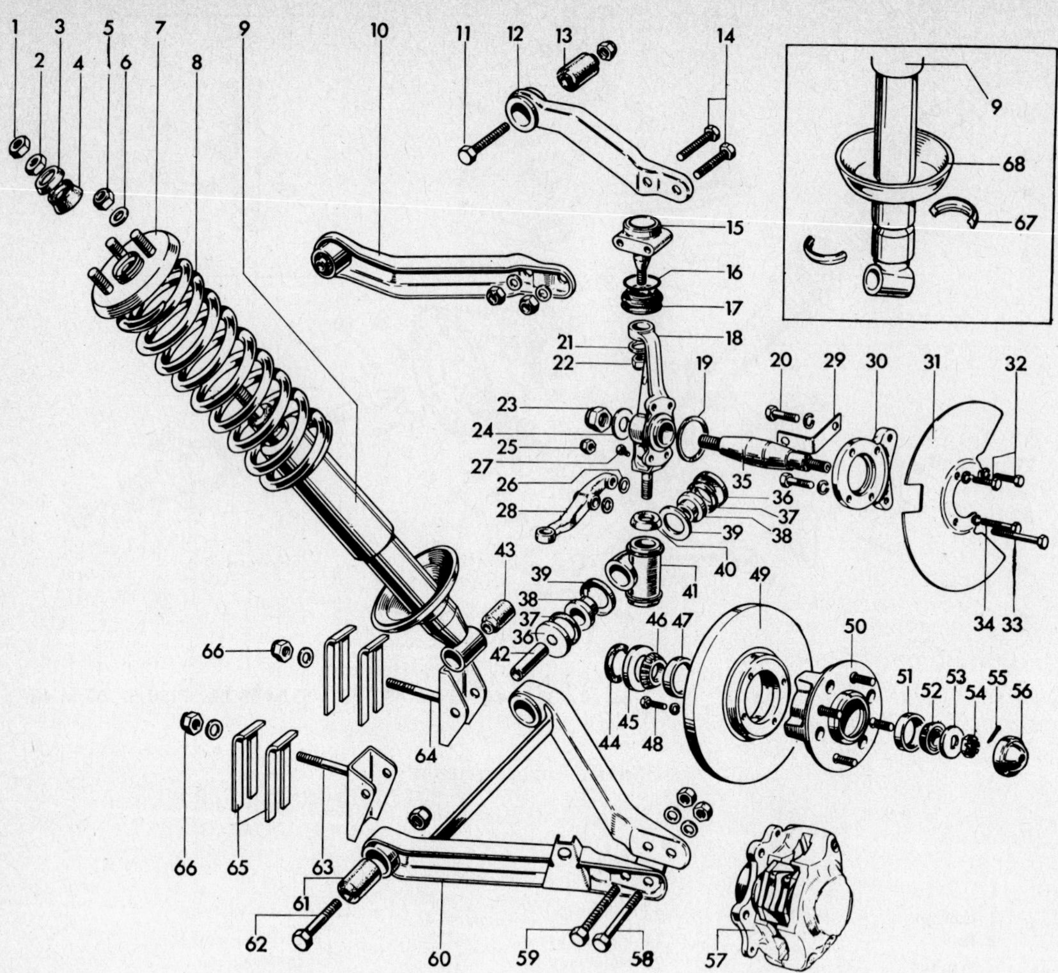

Exploded view of GT6 front suspension components

1 Nut
2 Nut
3 Washer
4 Mounting rubber
5 Nut
6 Washer
7 Upper spring pan
8 Road spring
9 Shock absorber
10 Top control arm
11 Fulcrum bolt
12 Top control arm
13 Fulcrum bushing
14 Bolt
15 Ball joint
16 Retainer
17 Rubber seal
18 Vertical link
19 Rubber seal
20 Bolt
21 Washer
22 Nut
23 Nut
24 Washer
25 Nut
26 Spacer
27 Plug
28 Steering arm
29 Bracket
30 Caliper bracket
31 Dust shield
32 Bolt
33 Bolt
34 Bolt
35 Spindle
36 Dust seal
37 Rubber ring
38 Nylon bushing
39 Dust seal
40 Rubber seal
41 Trunnion
42 Bushing
43 Fulcrum bushing
44 Felt seal
45 Seal holder
46 Inner race
47 Outer track
48 Bolt
49 Brake disc
50 Hub
51 Outer track
52 Inner race
53 Washer
54 Nut
55 Cotter pin
56 Grease cap
57 Brake caliper
58 Trunnion bolt
59 Shock absorber bolt
60 Lower control arm
61 Fulcrum bushing
62 Bolt
63 Front fulcrum bracket
64 Rear fulcrum bracket
65 Shim
66 Nut
67 Keeper
68 Lower spring pan

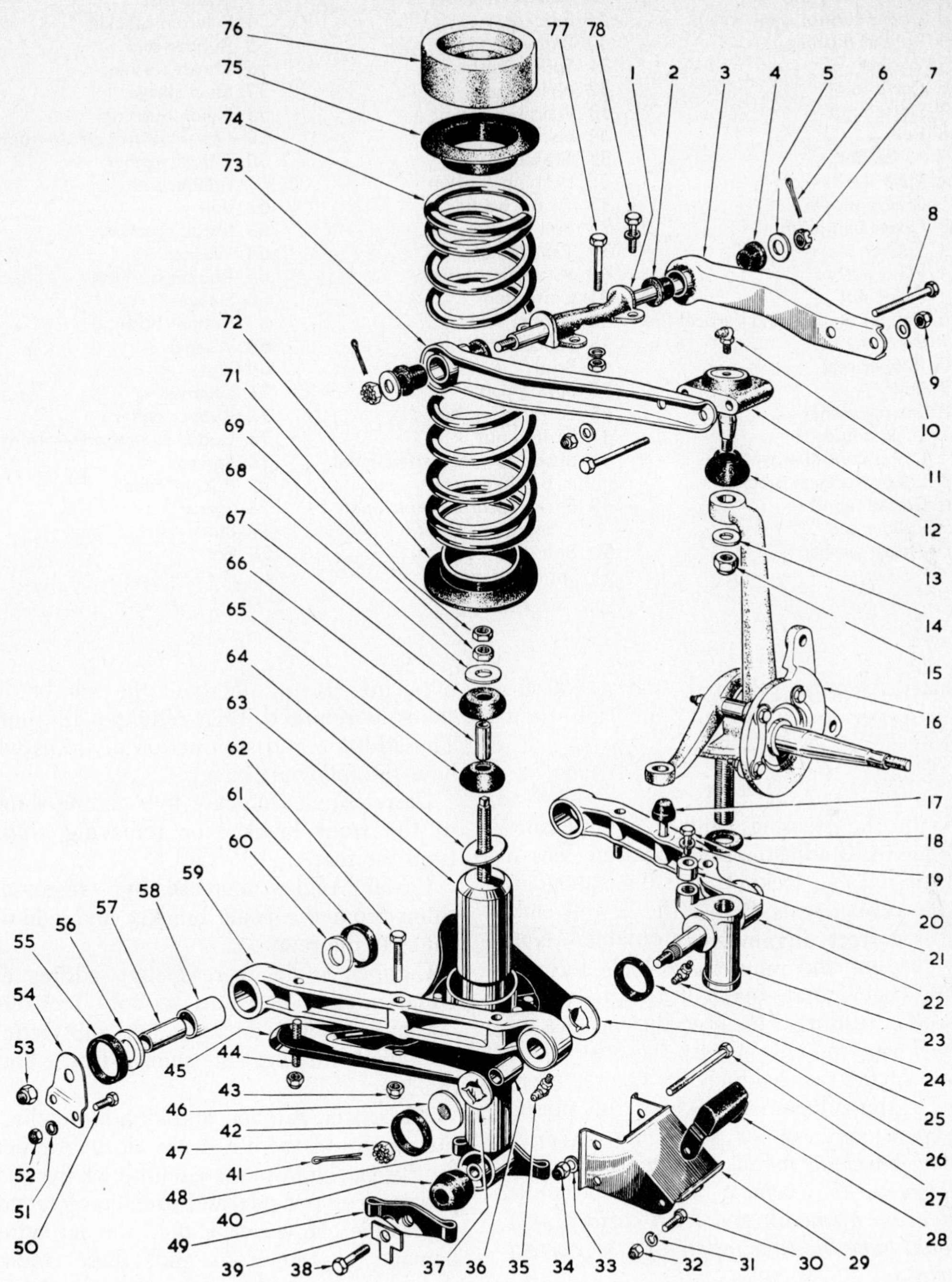

TR-4, front suspension; TR-4A, TR-250, TR-6 are similar

TR-4, front suspension; TR-4A, TR-250, TR-6 are similar

1 Upper inner fulcrum
2 Rubber bushing
3 Upper control arm—rear
4 Rubber bushing
5 Washer
6 Cotter pin
7 Slotted nut
8 Bolt
9 Nyloc nut
10 Plain washer
11 Grease nipple
12 Upper ball joint
13 Rubber seal
14 Plain washer
15 Nyloc nut
16 Caliper bracket and vertical link
17 Bump rubber
18 Rubber seal
19 Bolt
20 Spring washer
21 Lock stop collar
22 Lower control arm—rear
23 Lower trunnion bracket
24 Grease nipple
25 Rubber seal
26 Thrust washer
27 Bolt
28 Rebound rubber
29 Bracket
30 Bolt
31 Spring washer
32 Nyloc nut
33 Plain washer
34 Nyloc nut
35 Grease nipple
36 Bushing—nylon
37 Thrust washer
38 Bolt
39 Tab washer
40 Rubber bushing
41 Cotter pin
42 Rubber seal
43 Nyloc nut
44 Stud
45 Spring pan
46 Serrated washer
47 Slotted nut
48 Shock absorber attachment bracket—rear
49 Shock absorber attachment bracket—front
50 Bolt
51 Spring washer
52 Nut
53 Nyloc nut
54 Fulcrum bracket
55 Rubber seal
56 Thrust washer
57 Steel sleeve
58 Nylon bushing
59 Lower control arm—front
60 Thrust washer
61 Rubber seal
62 Bolt
63 Shock absorber
64 Washer
65 Rubber bushing
66 Sleeve
67 Rubber bushing
68 Washer
69 Nut
71 Locknut
72 Rubber collar
73 Upper control arm—front
74 Spring
75 Rubber collar
76 Spacer
77 Bolt
78 Bolt

tionary, steering centered, and a 150 lb. weight (or its equivalent) on each front seat.

Toe-in

With the steering centralized, measure the toe-in. If adjustment is required, loosen the tie-rod end locknuts and the outer clip of the rubber seals. Rotate the tie-rod ends until correct alignment is obtained. Note the reading and move the vehicle forward until wheels rotate one-half turn, then take a second reading. This procedure allows for wheel rim run-out. Adjust tie-rods to the mean of the two readings for greater accuracy. After adjustment, tighten the tie-rod locknuts and rubber seal clips. *NOTE: When checking toe-in, or other suspension geometry, the vehicle should be static laden, on a smooth and level surface, and should have the tires inflated to the correct pressure.*

Caster and Camber

Adjust the caster and camber angles of the TR-4A, TR-250, TR-6, GT6 and Spitfire front suspensions by altering the number of shims positioned between the chassis and the lower inner fulcrum brackets. When adjusting these angles, raise the vehicle, loosen the lower control arm mounting nuts, increase or decrease the number of shims as required, then retighten the nuts. The addition and subtraction of shims will have the following effects:

Caster Angle, increase by: adding shims to the front bracket or removing shims from the rear.

Caster Angle, decrease by: removing shims from the front bracket and adding shims to the rear.

Camber Angle, increase by: adding an equal number of shims to both brackets.

Camber Angle, decrease by: subtracting an equal number of shims, from both brackets.

The caster, camber, and king pin inclination angles of the TR–4 are all determined by the machining and assembly of the suspension components and are therefore not adjustable. However, should the car suffer damage to the front end, these angles should be checked to determine if replacement parts are necessary. Any damage to the upper and/or lower wishbone arms is likely to change the values of the caster, camber, and king pin angles.

REAR SUSPENSION

The rear suspension on the TR-4 and TR-4A uses a live (solid) axle and leaf springs. Independent rear suspension with coil springs was introduced as an option on the TR-4A and continued on the TR-250 and TR-6. The Spitfire uses swing axles with a transverse leaf spring. On the Spitfire MK IV, leaf spring modifications were used, resulting in a lower rear roll center and improved handling. The GT6 has a suspension system similar to that on the Spitfire, but uses a fully independent arrangement with sliding splined half-shafts.

Spring Removal and Replacement

Independent Rear with Leaf Spring

Disconnect brake lines (be careful not to spill fluid) and chassis bracket. Disconnect handbrake.

Jack up suspension vertical link. Disconnect axle shaft and couplings. On late GT6, remove radius arm mounting bolts from chassis. Remove shock absorber and lower vertical link. While supporting vertical link, remove eye bolt from spring eye. Remove luggage floor plate and slide spring from vehicle.

To replace spring: align spring in recess in differential casing. Make sure bolt is in correct hole. (Spring is marked Front to indicate proper position.) Replace studs in casing. Make sure the shorter threaded end is down. Replace spring clamp plate and fasten down. Refit luggage floor plate. Use appropriate body sealer. Fasten vertical link to spring eyes. Do not tighten spring eye nut. (Refit radius arms at this point, if

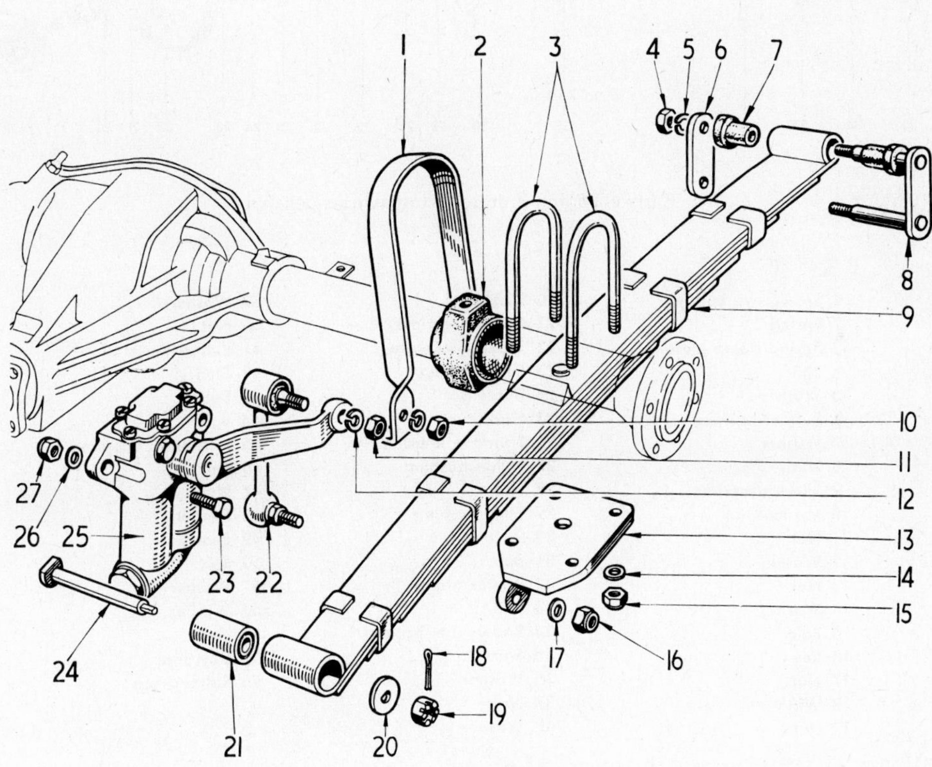

TR-4, TR-4A straight axle rear suspension

1 Bump strap
2 Bump and rebound rubber
3 U bolts
4 Nut
5 Spring washer
6 Shackle plate
7 Rubber bush
8 Shackle
9 Spring
10 Nut
11 Nut
12 Spring washer
13 Spring plate
14 Plain washer
15 Nyloc nut
16 Nyloc nut
17 Plain washer
18 Split pin
19 Slotted nut
20 Washer
21 Bush
22 Shock absorber link
23 Bolt
24 Shackle pin
25 Shock absorber
26 Plain washer
27 Nyloc nut

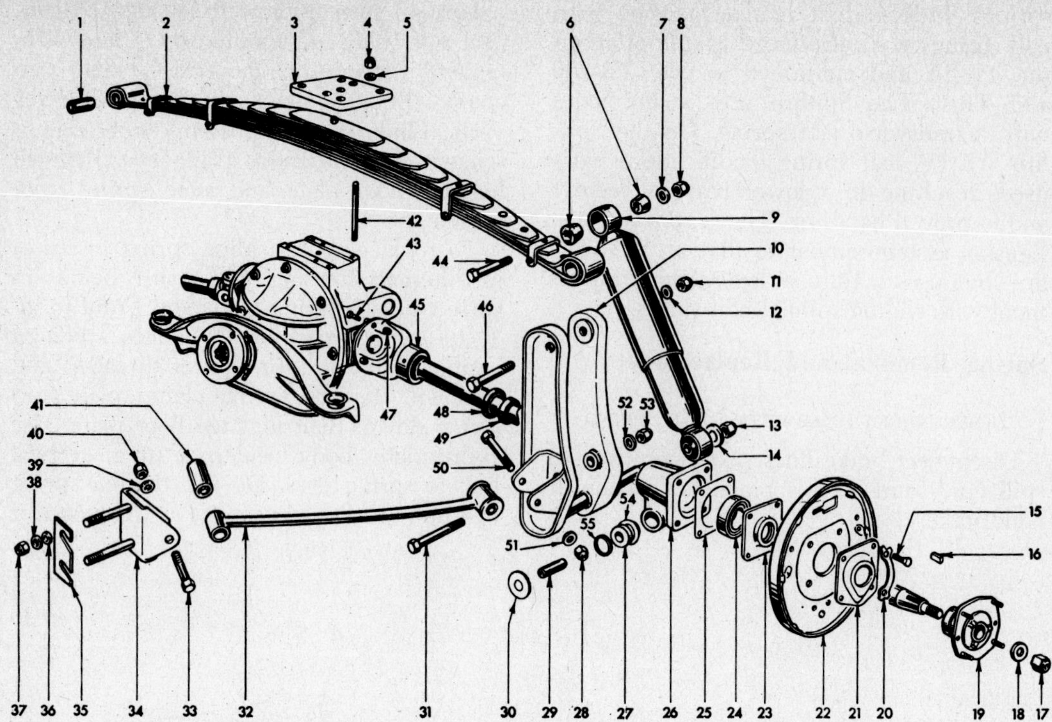

Early GT6 and Spitfire swing axle suspension

1 Spring eye bushing
2 Spring
3 Spring clamp plate
4 Nut
5 Washer
6 Rubber bushing
7 Washer
8 Nut
9 Shock absorber
10 Vertical link
11 Nut
12 Washer
13 Nut
14 Washer
15 Bolt
16 Key
17 Nut
18 Washer
19 Hub
20 Locktab
21 Grease retainer
22 Brake backplate
23 Seal housing
24 Bearing
25 Gasket
26 Trunnion housing
27 Nylon bushing
28 Nut
29 Steel bushing
30 Dust seal
31 Bolt
32 Radius arm
33 Bolt
34 Radius arm bracket
35 Shim
36 Washer
37 Nut
38 Washer
39 Washer
40 Nut
41 Rubber bushing
42 Stud
43 Bolt
44 Bolt
45 Axle shaft coupling
46 Bolt
47 Nut
48 Flinger
49 Seal
50 Bolt
51 Washer
52 Washer
53 Nut
54 Dust seal
55 Rubber ring

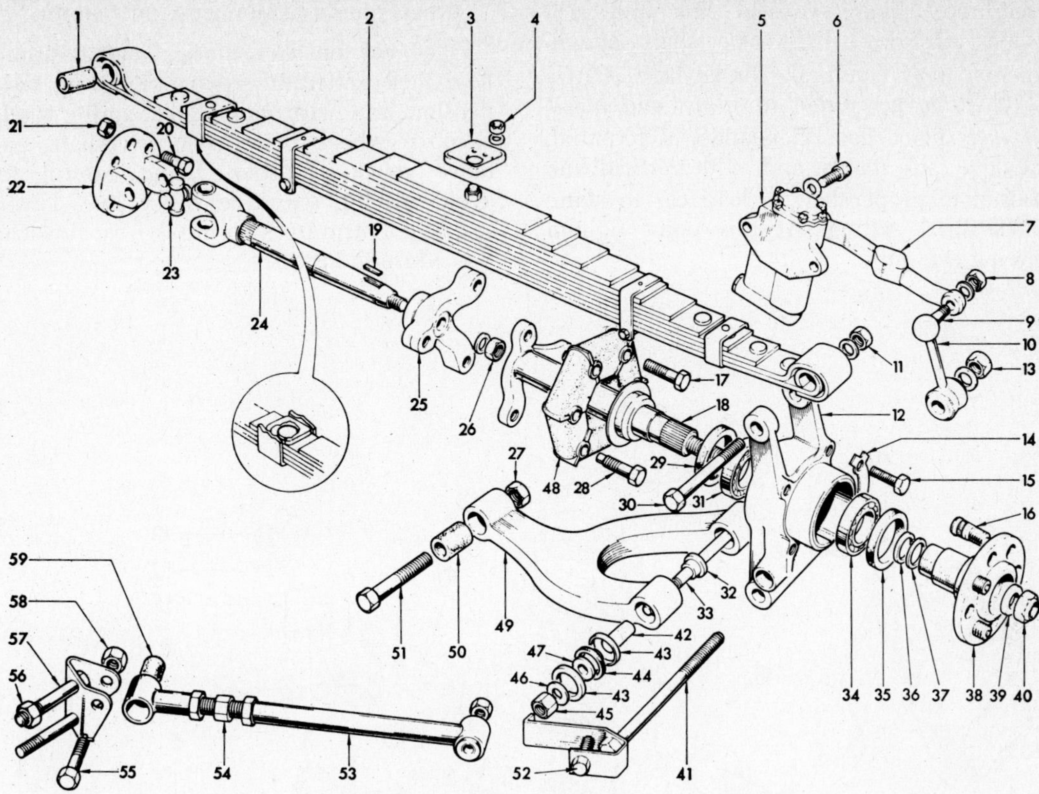

Late GT6 rear suspension

1 Rubber bushing—spring eye
2 Rear transverse road spring
3 Spring plate
4 Nyloc nut—spring plate to axle housing
5 Rear shock absorber—lever arm type
6 Screw—shock absorber to mounting bracket
7 Shock absorber arm
8 Nyloc nut—shock absorber arm to link
9 Ball end taper
10 Link assembly
11 Nyloc nut—rear spring ends to vertical link
12 Rear vertical link
13 Nyloc nut—shock absorber link to vertical link
14 Tab washer—vertical link to rear brake
15 Setscrew—vertical link to rear brake
16 Wheel stud
17 Bolt, outer drive shaft—rotoflex coupling
18 Outer drive shaft assembly
19 Key—intermediate shaft
20 Bolt—shaft joint to inner axle shaft
21 Nyloc nut—inner axle shaft
22 Flange yoke—coupling
23 Yoke
24 Intermediate drive shaft
25 Driven flange
26 Nyloc nut—driven flange to shaft
27 Nyloc nut—lower wishbone to chassis
28 Bolt—driven flange to rotoflex coupling
29 Inner oil seal
30 Bolt—rear spring ends to vertical link
31 Inner bearing
32 Outer bushing } wishbone to vertical link
33 Bolt }
34 Outer bearing
35 Outer oil seal
36 Spacer } outer drive shaft
37 Shim }
38 Rear hub and stud assembly
39 Washer
40 Nyloc nut—rear hub to outer drive shaft
41 Bracket—assembly mounting radius arm to vertical link
42 Distance piece }
43 Water shield } wishbone to vertical link
44 Dirt seal }
45 Nyloc nut }
46 Washer } wishbone to vertical link
47 Outer bushing }
48 Rotoflex wishbone assembly
49 Lower wishbone assembly
50 Lower wishbone—inner bushing
51 Bolt—wishbone to chassis
52 Bolt—radius arm to vertical link
53 Radius arm
54 Radius arm adjuster
55 Bolt—radius arm to bracket
56 Nyloc nut—radius arm to bracket
57 Bolt—radius arm support bracket
58 Nut—radius arm to bracket
59 Rubber bushing—radius arm

required.) Raise vertical link and refit shock absorber. Refit axle shaft attachments. Refit handbrake brake lines. *CAUTION: Do not forget to adjust and bleed brakes.* Place floor jack under differential, remove jack stands, and, with vertical link raised to proper height, load car to static (300 lbs.) setting. At this point tighten spring eye nuts.

Independent Rear with Coil Springs

Place car on jack stands and position floor jack under differential. Push up suspension arm with jack under spring well. Remove wheel, disconnect driveshaft, remove shock absorber. Being careful to avoid placing stress on brake line, lower suspension arm until spring is free. Reverse procedure to install.

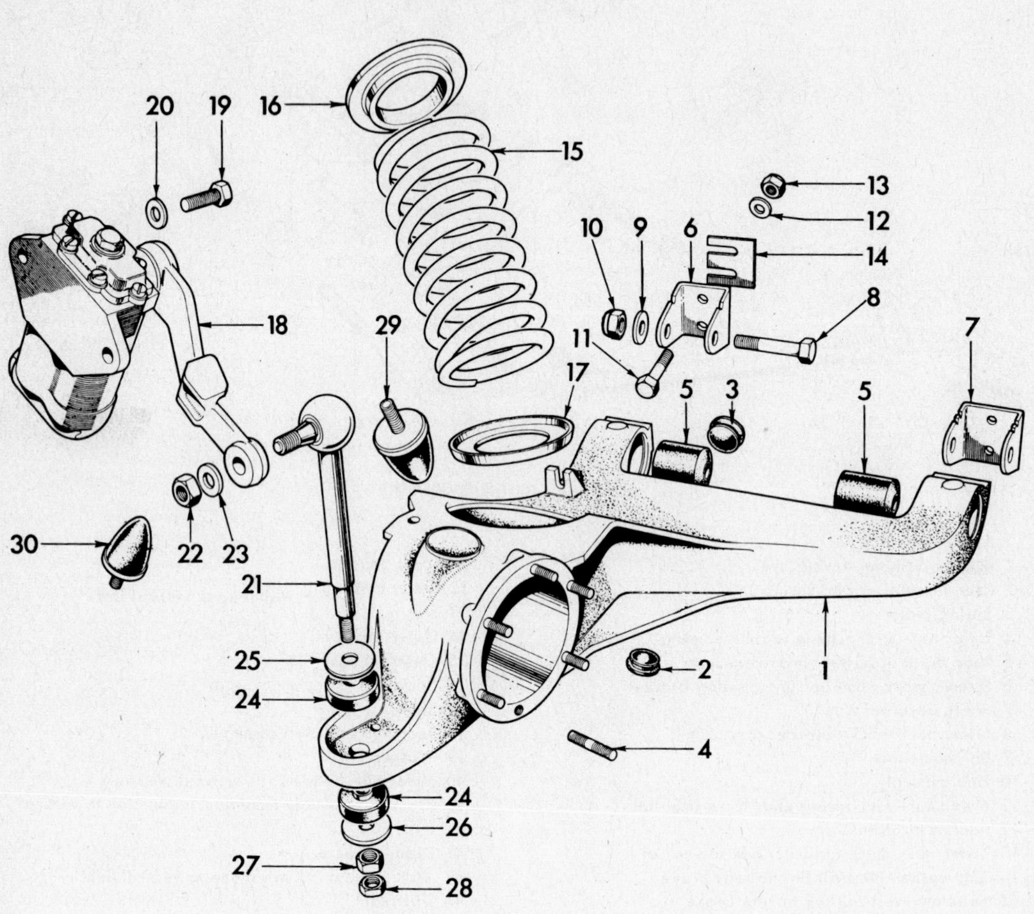

Coil spring independent rear suspension

1 Suspension arm	11 Bolt	21 Shock absorber link
2 Rubber plug	12 Plain washer	22 Nut
3 Rubber plug	13 Nyloc nut	23 Washer
4 Stud	14 Shim	24 Rubber buffer
5 Metalastik bushing	15 Road spring	25 Backing plate
6 Fulcrum bracket, inner	16 Rubber insulator	26 Backing plate
7 Fulcrum bracket, outer	17 Rubber insulator	27 Nut
8 Bolt	18 Shock absorber arm	28 Locknut
9 Plain washer	19 Bolt	29 Bump stop
10 Nyloc nut	20 Washer	30 Rebound rubber

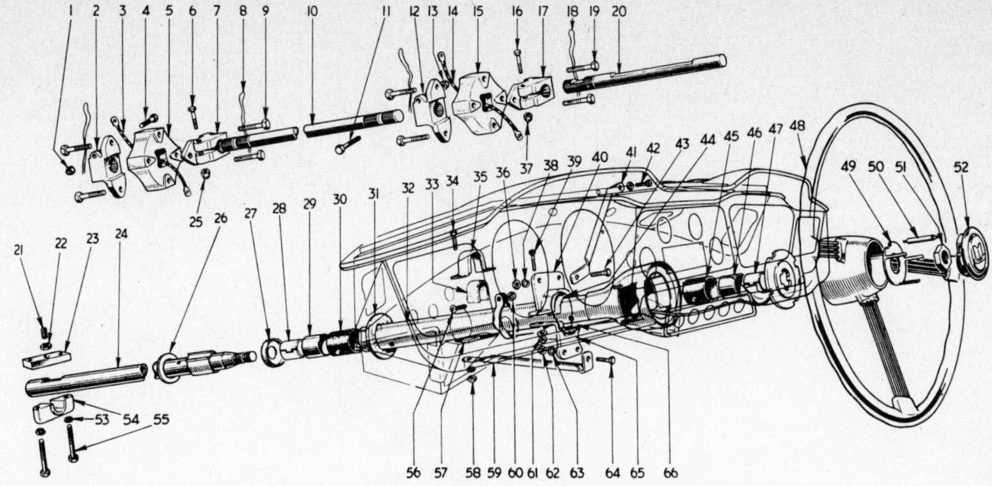

Steering column ;TR-4, TR-4A

1 Nyloc nut
2 Adapter
3 Ground cable
4 Pinch bolt
5 Rubber coupling
6 Pinch bolt
7 Adapter
8 Locking wire
9 Bolt
10 Lower steering column
11 Pinch bolt
12 Adapter
13 Nut
14 Ground cable
15 Rubber coupling
16 Pinch bolt
17 Adapter
18 Locking wire
19 Bolt
20 Lower column
21 Allen screw
22 Locknut
23 Impact clamp plate
24 Upper inner column
25 Nylon nut
26 Washer
27 Cap
28 Nylon bush
29 Steel bushing
30 Rubber bushing
31 Rubber grommet
32 Upper outer column
33 Felt
34 Bolt
35 Clamp
36 Nut
37 Nyloc nut
38 Spring washer
39 Bolt
40 Upper clamp
41 Stay
42 Bolt
43 Bolt
44 Felt
45 Rubber bushing
46 Steel bushing
47 Nylon bushing
48 Steering wheel
49 Clip
50 Horn brush
51 Nut
52 Horn button
53 Spring washer
54 Impact clamp
55 Bolt
56 Screw
57 Felt
58 Nut
59 Stay
60 Nut
61 Nut
62 Nut
63 Spring washer
64 Bolt
65 Bracket
66 Cable trough

Steering

STEERING GEAR

Adjustment

The steering gear is of the direct-acting rack and pinion type in which motion is transmitted from the steering wheel column through a pinion to the steering rack. First adjust the end clearance of the pinion shaft. This should be as little as possible with the pinion still able to rotate freely. There are shims available in thicknesses of .004 in. (.102 mm.) and .010 in. (.254 mm.) to obtain minimal end clearance with free rotation. The second adjustment involves the damper cap. With the pressure pad and cap nut installed to the rack tube, tighten the cap nut to eliminate all end clearance. Measure, with a feeler gauge the clearance between the nut and the housing, as shown in the accompanying illustration. Put to-

Using a feeler gauge to measure the clearance between the cap nut and housing in order to establish the thickness of shims required beneath the nut.

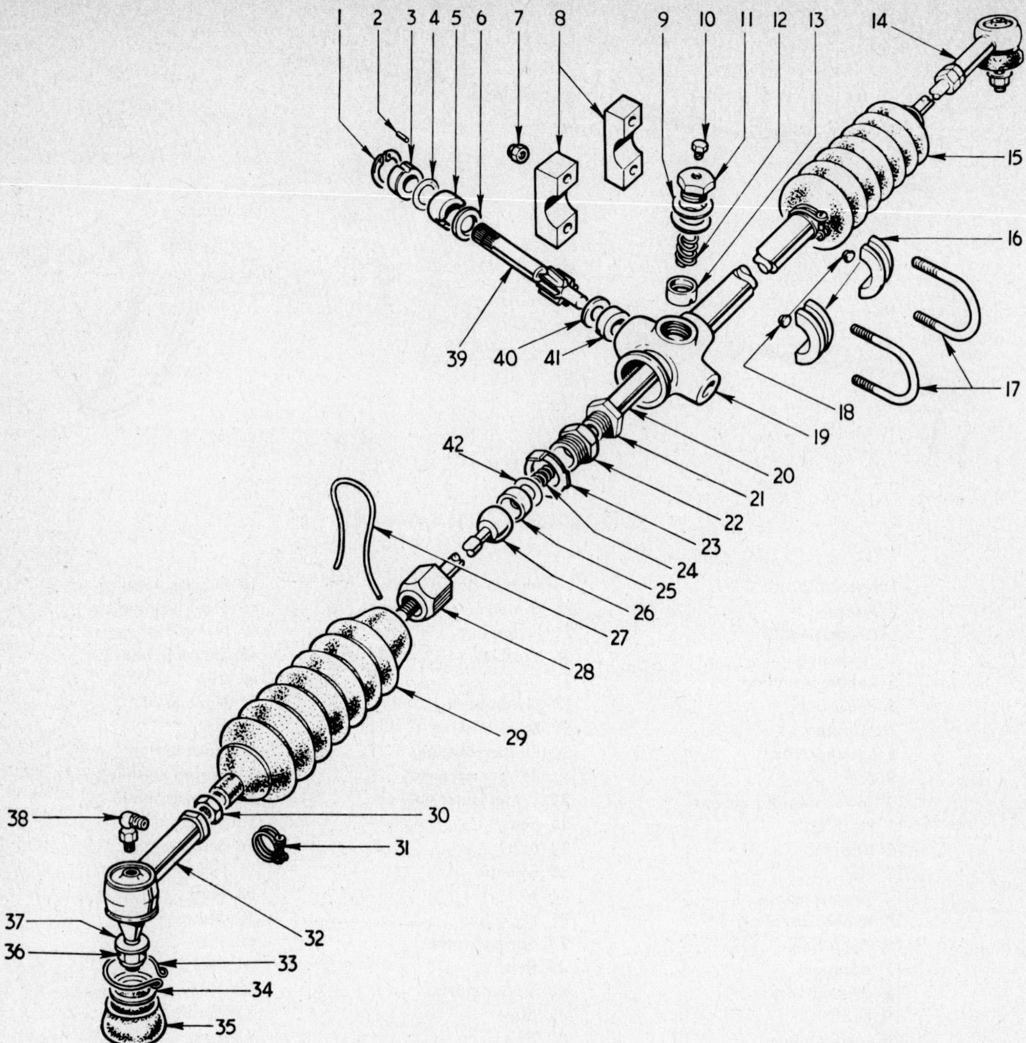

Exploded view of a typical rack and pinion steering system as used in the Triumph.

1 Circlip
2 Peg
3 Retainer
4 Shim
5 Bushing
6 Thrust washer
7 Nyloc nut
8 Packing pieces—rear
9 Shim
10 Plug
11 Cap
12 Spring
13 Thrust piece
14 Tie-rod ends
15 Rubber seal
16 Packing pieces—front
17 U bolts
18 Dowels
19 Rack tube
20 Rack
21 Locknut
22 Sleeve nut
23 Lockplate
24 Spring
25 Cup
26 Outer tie rod
27 Locking wire
28 Cup nut
29 Rubber seal
30 Locknut
31 Wire clip
32 Outer tie-rod end
33 Clip
34 Washer
35 Rubber seal
36 Nyloc nut
37 Washer
38 Grease nipple
39 Pinion
40 Thrust washer
41 Bushing
42 Shim

gether a shim package that is equal to the clearance between the cap nut and the housing plus .004 in. (.1 mm.) (i.e., pack-clearance + .004 in.) Pack the unit with grease and install the cap nut, shim pack, spring, and pressure pad to the housing and tighten the cap nut. When the cap nut is correctly adjusted, a force of 2 lb. on a radius of 8 in. (20.3 cm.) is required to rotate the pinion shaft. Check the unit and readjust if necessary by adding or subtracting shims from beneath the cap nut.

When the cap nut is properly adjusted, a 2 lb. load on an 8 in. radius (as shown) will be required to turn the pinion.

Removal

Place vehicle on jack stands and remove front wheels. Empty cooling system and remove bottom radiator hose. Loosen and remove bolt from steering shaft coupling. Remove steering rod end nuts. Pull ball joints from tie rod lever. Remove: nuts, U-bolts, and shims. Pull steering unit forward. Remove unit by pulling through wheelwell.

Disassembly

Pinch wire clips and slide bellows towards ball joints. Remove outer tie rods from rack. Remove spring, washer and nut and washer assembly from rack end. Remove nuts from rack ends. Loosen cap and remove spring, shims, and pad. Remove circlips and pull out pinion assembly. Be sure not to lose peg. Remove ring, shim, bushings, and thrust washer. Detach rubber O-ring. Pull rack from tube. Remove remaining parts from housing.

Installation

To reassemble steering gear, reverse above procedure. Be careful to note steering adjustments.

Replacement

Count number of pinion shaft turns required to move gear from lock to lock. Return shaft to central position and move steering wheel to straight ahead. Fit steering unit by placing splined pinion shaft into splined coupling. Place aluminum packing pieces behind rack and two front aluminum packing blocks into dowels. These fit into holes in rack tube. Replace U-bolts and nuts. Replace unit in car. Place taper pins of tie rod ball joints into steering levers and insert steering washers and nuts. Replace bolt and nut. *CAUTION: Check front end alignment.*

Removing steering wheel with puller

Brakes

MASTER CYLINDER

Early vehicles employed a single circuit master cylinder. With the advent of U.S. safety regulations, this was replaced by a dual circuit master cylinder. It consists of two independent cylinders, one each for the front and rear brakes. Both are supplied with fluid by a common reservoir divided by a partition. When replacing, be sure to use the correct parts; different cylinders have different front/rear volume ratios.

Removal

Remove both brake lines. Be careful not to let fluid drip out. Pull out rubber dust cover. Remove clevis pin. (This is secured by a cotter or split type pin.) Remove master cylinder attaching bolts and lift off the cylinder.

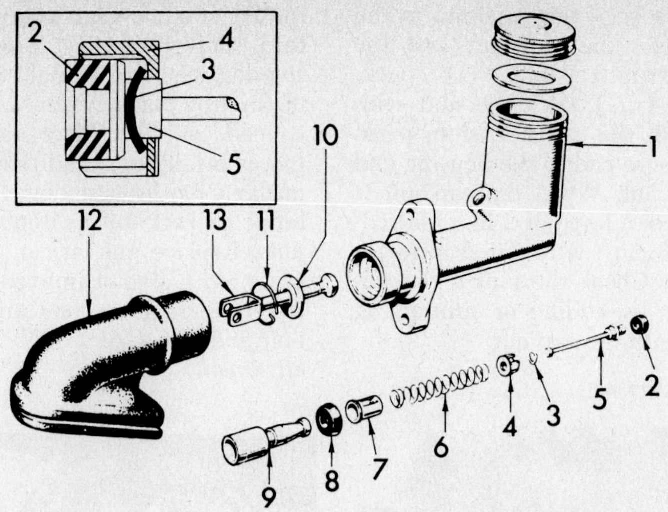

GT6 single circuit master cylinder

1 Master cylinder body
2 Seal (valve)
3 Spring (valve seal)
4 Distance piece
5 Valve
6 Plunger return spring
7 Retainer
8 Seal (plunger)
9 Plunger
10 Abutment plate
11 Circlip
12 Dust excluder
13 Pushrod

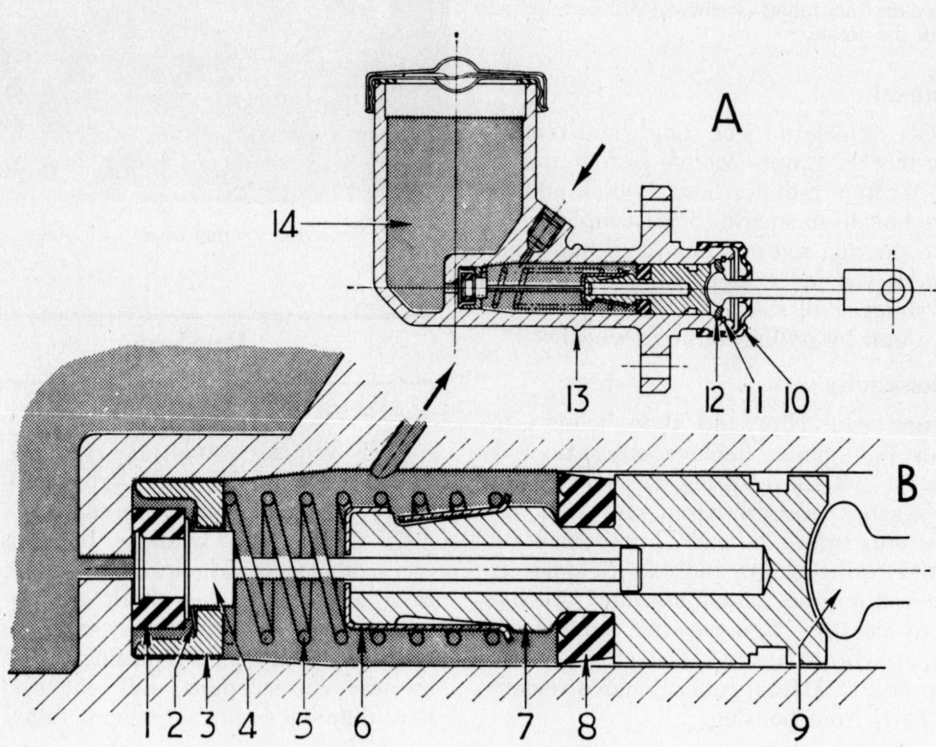

TR and Spitfire single circuit master cylinder

1 Valve seal
2 Spring (valve seal)
3 Distance piece
4 Valve shank
5 Plunger return spring
6 Spring retainer
7 Plunger
8 Plunger seal
9 Push rod
10 Dust cover
11 Circlip
12 Push rod stop
13 Identification ring(s)
14 Fluid reservoir

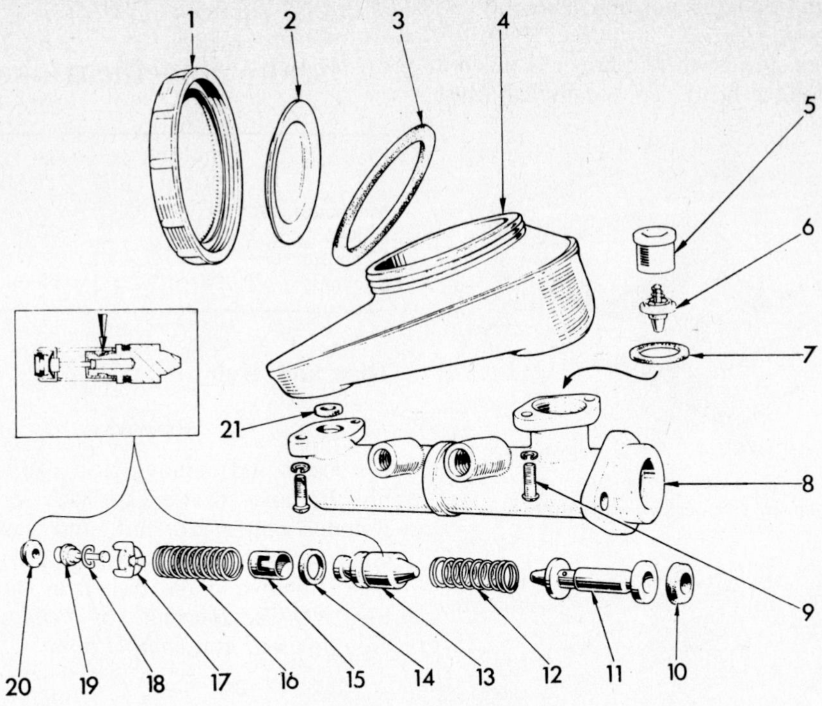

Dual circuit master cylinder

1 Cap
2 Baffle plate
3 Seal
4 Reservoir
5 Tipping valve securing nut
6 Tipping valve
7 Seal—reservoir to body
8 Body
9 Screw—reservoir to body
10 Seal
11 Primary plunger
12 Intermediate spring
13 Secondary plunger
14 Seal
15 Spring retainer
16 Secondary spring
17 Valve spacer
18 Spring washer
19 Valve
20 Seal
21 Seal—reservoir to body

Disassembly

This procedure applies to dual circuit master cylinders. Drain master cylinder and discard old fluid. Remove screws holding reservoir to body. Press down on push rod, remove circlip, and pull out push rod, abutment plate, and circlip. Using an Allen wrench, remove tipping valve nut and lift out seal. Depress plunger and remove tipping valve. Lightly shake body to remove internal parts. Pull intermediate spring and plunger apart.

Raise leaf spring of spring retainer and lift out valve assembly from plunger. Remove spring, valve spacer, and washer spring from valve stem.

Next, take valve seal from valve head end. Remove seals from both plungers. Take baffle and cap washer from cap.

Rebuilding

Replace all seals with new ones from rebuilding kit. Thoroughly clean all other parts in clean brake fluid. Check cylinder bore for any imperfections or coarseness. If any doubt exists as to condition, replace the cylinder.

Reassembly

Before assembling, lubricate all parts with clean brake fluid. Place seals on plungers.

Place valve seals, smaller end leading, on valve head. Place spring washer on stem of valve. It must be positioned with flare away from stem shoulder. Next, fit valve spacer, legs leading.

Place retainer on stem, keyway first. Put

spring over retainer; position assembly on plunger.

Compress spring while retainer is pushed behind plunger head. To accomplish this,

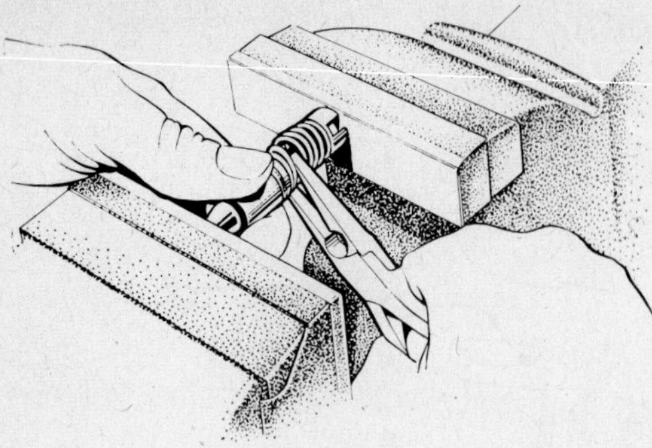

Pushing spring retainer behind plunger head

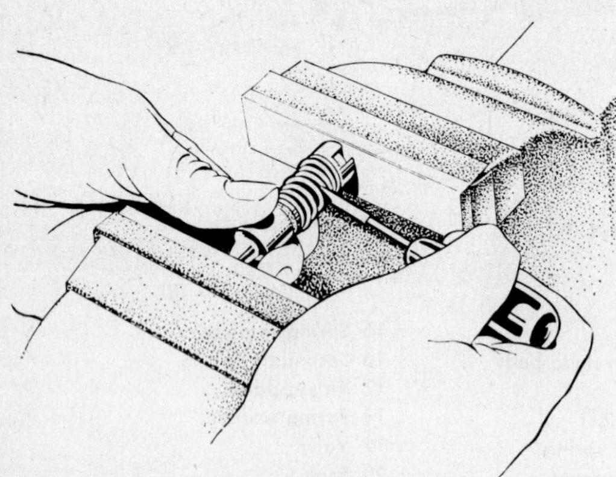

Depressing spring against secondary plunger

place subassembly in vice and place clean paper between each subassembly end and vise jaws to prevent contamination.

Close vise until spring is nearly coil bound. Using a small screwdriver, press spring retainer against secondary plunger. Using needle nose pliers, depress spring retainer leaf behind plunger head. Be certain retainer lead is properly aligned (straight) and is firmly located behind plunger.

Place spring between plungers. Lubricate plunger seals and bore of cylinder with clean brake fluid.

Fit plunger assembly in bore. Make sure valve end is leading. Use caution to avoid seal damage. Press plunger down into bore and put in tipping valve. Tighten seal to 35-40 ft. lbs.

Reassemble cap washer and baffle to cap. Place cap on reservoir. Assembly is now complete.

FRONT BRAKES (DISC)

Brake Specifications

	TR-4, TR-4A, TR-250, TR-6	GT6, GT6+, GT6 Mk III	Spitfire
Maximum disc runout	.002 in.	.006 in.	.004 in.
Minimum disc thickness	.440 in.	.460 in.	—

Disc and Hub

Removal

Loosen and remove disc caliper assembly. Remove grease cap with screwdriver. Remove cotter pin, nut, and washer. Pull out hub with outer race and part of inner race. Remove brake disc from hub assembly. *NOTE: Bearings, if needed, should only be fitted as a complete set.*

Replacement

Place outer bearing rings (taper outward) into proper position. Replace discs. Secure with washer and bolts. Put inner races together and fit hub with disc to stub axle. Put on washer and slotted nut while rotating hub, finger tighten only. Loosen nut to closest cotter pin hole and mark position by center punching end of stub axle and nut. Hub end float should be .003-.005 in.

If loosening nut gives excessive float, remove nut and file rear face. This will correct problem. Remove nut, washer, hub, and races. Pack hub with appropriate grease.

Place new hub seal in seal retainer. Use joining compound. Allow to dry. Then saturate seal in engine oil and squeeze out excess. Place races and seal retainer on hub. Be sure seal faces inward.

Replace hub assembly to axle. Refit washer and nut. Tighten nut till punch marks correspond; secure nuts with new cotter pin. Refit remaining parts. Be sure to replace any shims.

Replacing Disc Brake Friction Pads

Place car on jack stands and remove wheels. Remove spring retainers and pad

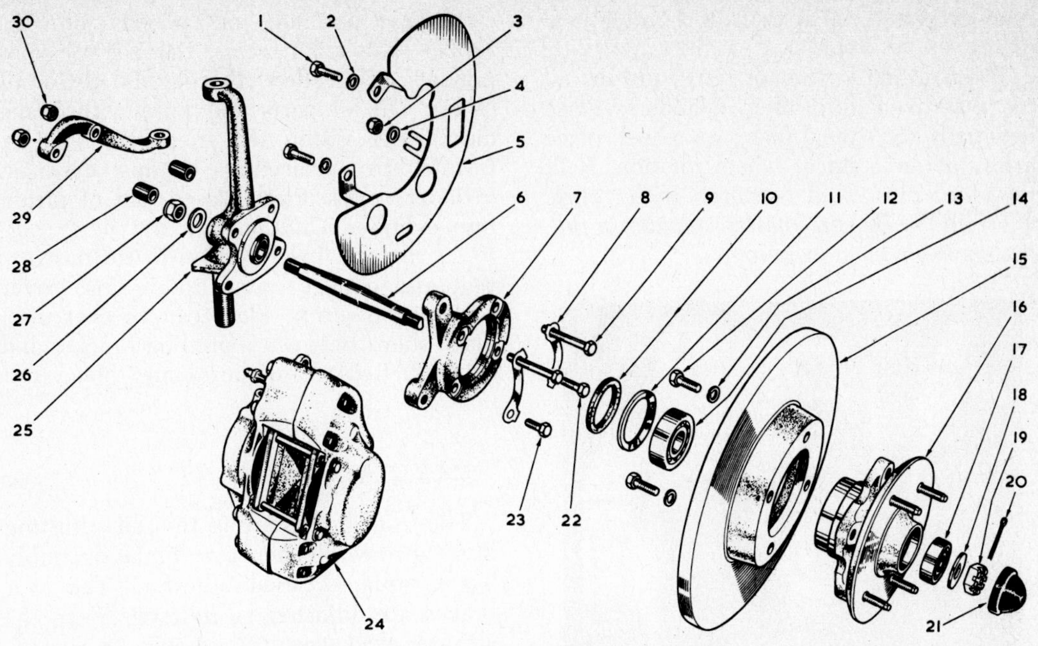

Disc and hub

1 Bolt
2 Spring washer
3 Nyloc nut
4 Plain washer
5 Dust shield
6 Stub axle
7 Caliper bracket
8 Tab plate
9 Bolt
10 Felt seal
11 Seal retainer
12 Bolt
13 Spring washer
14 Inner tapered race
15 Disc
16 Hub
17 Outer tapered race
18 Washer
19 Slotted nut
20 Cotter pin
21 Hub cap
22 Bolt
23 Bolt
24 Caliper unit
25 Vertical link
26 Plain washer
27 Nyloc nut
28 Distance pieces
29 Steering arm
30 Nyloc nut

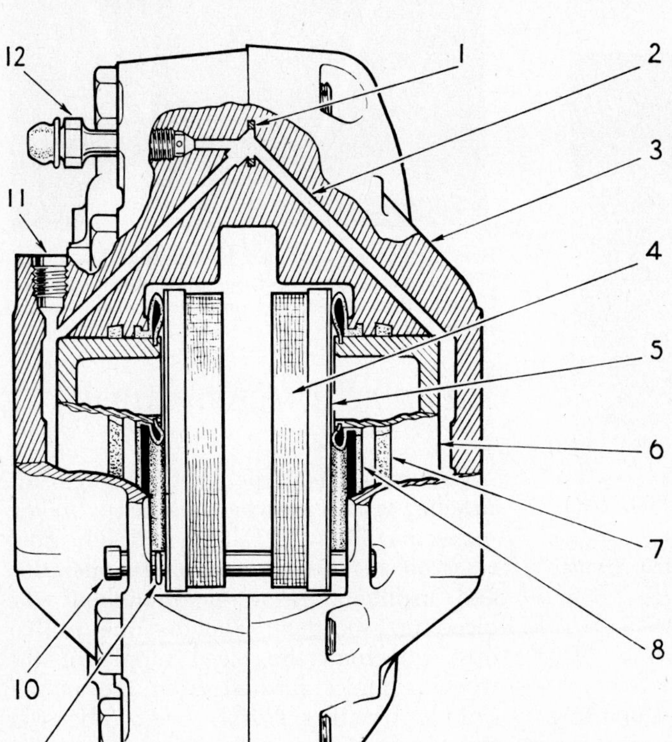

Disc brake side view

1 Rubber O-ring
2 Fluid transfer channels
3 Caliper body
4 Brake pad
5 Anti-squeal plate
6 Piston
7 Piston sealing ring
8 Dust cover
9 Retaining clip
10 Retaining pin
11 Flexible hose connection
12 Bleed nipple

retainer pins. Lift off pads and anti squeal plates.

When fitting new pads, push pistons all the way back into their cylinders. Place new pads and squeal plates on wheel; place arrow in direction of wheel rotation. Refit retainer pins and secure with clips. *CAUTION: Be sure master cylinder is full, system is bled and leakproof.*

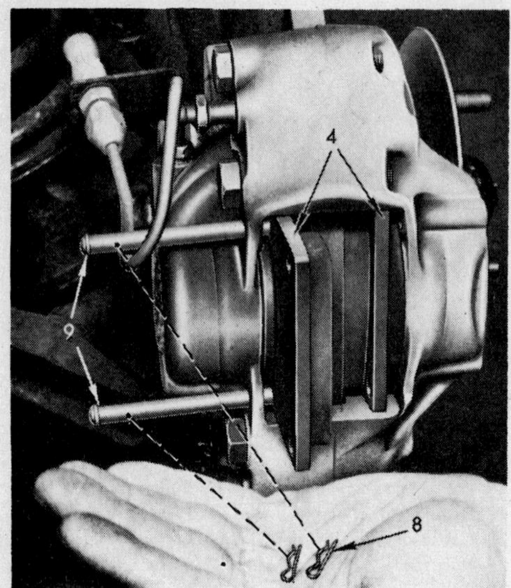

Disc brake pads, 4; pad retainer pins, 9; spring clips, 8.

When replacing TR–4 brake pads, be sure the anti-squeal plate arrow is pointing in the direction of forward wheel rotation.

Replacing Piston Seals

Remove line and locknut at supporting bracket. Remove flexible hose. Remove bolts holding caliper to support bracket; lift off caliper and take out pistons. Remove rubber seals from recess. Replace all components as needed; thoroughly clean all others. Oil all parts and bore with brake fluid. Place piston seal in cylinder recess. Locate lips (projecting) of dust cover in cylinder recess. Place closed end of piston into cylinder. *Caution: Do not harm polished surface.* Insert piston to furthest extent and engage outer lip of dust cover with piston recess. Place caliper over disc; place shims between mounting bracket and calipers. Replace all hoses and bleed system.

BRAKE ADJUSTMENT

The front brakes are of the self-adjusting disc type, while each rear brake assembly has a square-headed adjuster. The rear brakes are adjusted as follows: Turn the adjuster clockwise until the wheel is locked, then turn counterclockwise a notch at a time until the wheel is free to rotate. Be sure that the handbrake is not applied while the rear brakes are being adjusted.

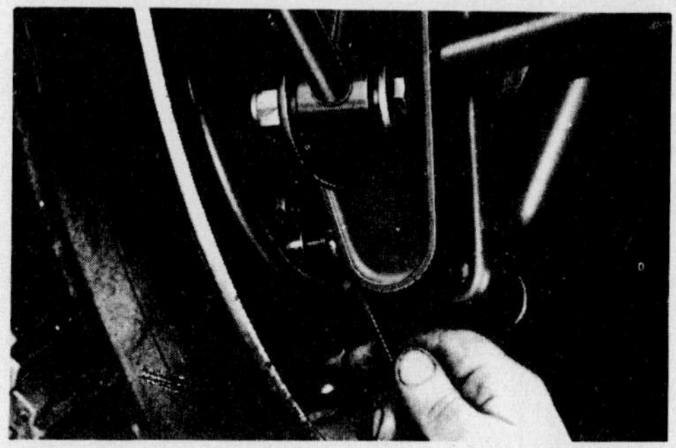

Rear brakes are adjusted by turning the square-headed adjuster clockwise until the wheel is locked, then loosening until the wheel rotates freely.

BLEEDING THE HYDRAULIC SYSTEM

For models equipped with a single hydraulic system serving all four brakes, proceed as follows: Fill the hydraulic fluid reservoir at the beginning of the operation and maintain the level throughout the bleeding procedure. Remove the rubber dust cap from the bleed nipple of the wheel cylinder farthest from the master cylinder. With a flexible bleed tube over the nipple, immerse the free end of the tube in a jar containing a small amount of brake fluid. Unscrew the nipple about ¾ turn and pump the brake pedal until the fluid entering the jar is free of air bubbles. With the pedal held in the fully depressed position, tighten the bleed nipple, remove the tube and replace the dust cap. Repeat the procedure for the other three wheels, finishing with the wheel cylinder nearest the master cylinder. Adjust the brakes and apply pressure to the brake pedal while checking for leaks at all connections.

For those recent models equipped with a dual braking system (one system serves the front brakes, the other serves the rear), proceed as follows: In bleeding the rear brakes, turn the brake adjusters so that the shoes are locked against the drums. Note that the front brakes must be bled as one system, and the rear brakes as another. Attach a tube to the system bleed nipple that is farthest from the master cylinder, allowing the other end of the tube to hang submerged in a jar containing a small amount of clean brakefluid. Unscrew the bleed nipple about half a turn to allow the fluid to be pumped out. Press the brake pedal *lightly* without pushing through to the end of the stroke. If the pedal is pushed heavily or fully through its stroke, the pressure differential switch could be actuated, causing the brake warning light to glow brightly until the actuating piston is recentralized. Pausing between each depression of the pedal, pump until no bubbles can be seen in the fluid being pumped into the jar. With the pedal depressed, tighten the bleed nipple and repeat on the other brake of the system.

If, by mistake, the brake warning light piston has been pushed off center, causing the brake warning light to glow, the following procedure will have to be followed to recentralize the piston: Attach a rubber tube to a bleed nipple at the opposite end of the car to that which was being bled when the piston was actuated. Open the bleed screw and turn the ignition to the "ON" position without starting the engine. The brake warning light will glow, but the oil pressure warning light will be out. Push steadily on the brake pedal until the brake light dims and the oil light glows. As the piston returns to mid-position, a click will be felt on the pedal. *NOTE: if the pedal is pushed too hard, the piston will move over to the other side, necessitating the*

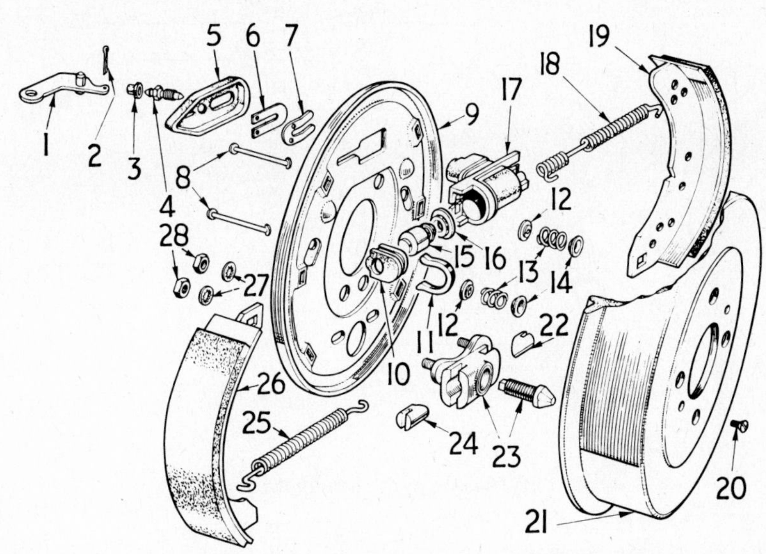

Rear brake

1 Handbrake lever
2 Cotter pin
3 Dust cap
4 Bleed nipple
5 Dust excluder
6 Retaining clip
7 Retaining clip
8 Steady pins
9 Backplate
10 Dust excluder
11 Clip
12 Steady pin cups
13 Springs
14 Steady pin cups
15 Piston
16 Seal
17 Wheel cylinder
18 Return spring
19 Brake shoe
20 Countersunk screw
21 Brake drum
22 Adjuster tappet
23 Adjuster wedge and body
24 Adjuster tappet
25 Return spring
26 Brake shoe
27 Shakeproof washers
28 Nuts

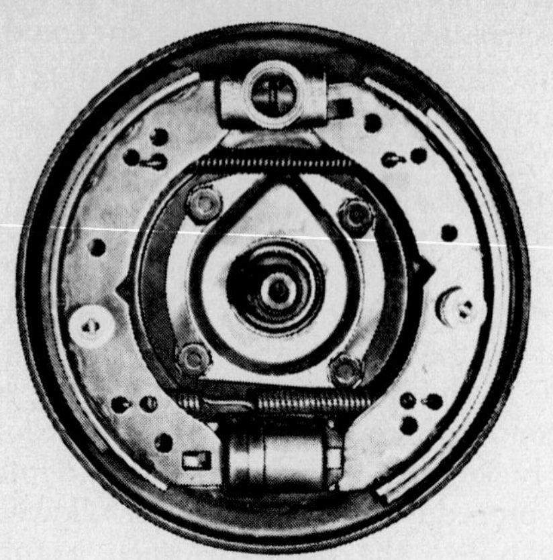

Rear brake outer view

repeat of the preceding operations at the other end of the car. Tighten the bleed screw.

HANDBRAKE

Adjustment

Adjust as follows: Lift rear wheels from ground. Lock brake drums by screwing each adjuster in to its fullest extent. Remove spring and clevis pin. Adjust clevis at each cable end by equal amounts to reduce play in cable. Cable is overly tightened when clevis pin cannot be inserted without straining cables. Secure clevis pin, hook up spring and adjust cable brackets to give slight spring tension.

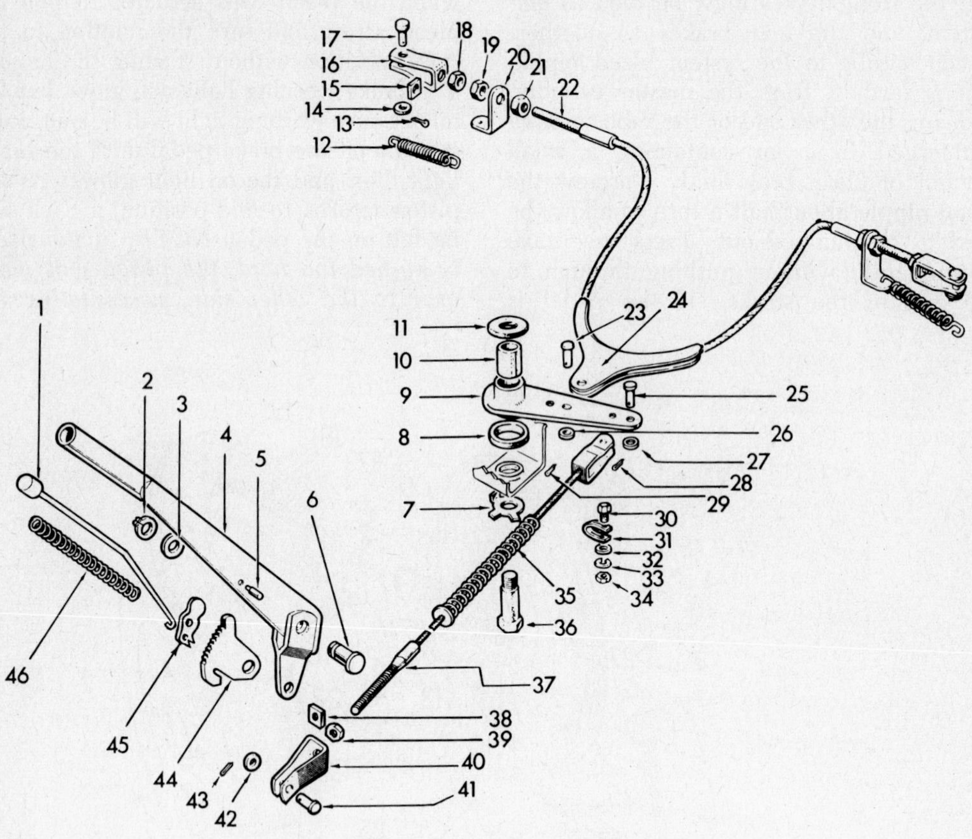

GT6 and Spitfire handbrake

1 Pawl release rod
2 Circlip
3 Plain washer
4 Handbrake lever
5 Pawl pivot pin
6 Pivot pin
7 Lock plate
8 Rubber seal
9 Relay lever
10 Bushing
11 Felt seal
12 Pull-off spring
13 Cotter pin
14 Plain washer
15 Square nut
16 Clevis
17 Clevis pin
18 Locknut
19 Adjusting nut
20 Adjustable spring anchor
21 Lock nut
22 Secondary cable
23 Clevis pin
24 Compensator sector
25 Clevis pin
26 Plain washer
27 Plain washer
28 Cotter pin
29 Cotter pin
30 Clamp bolt
31 Clamp
32 Plain washer
33 Spring washer
34 Nut
35 Spring
36 Pivot bolt
37 Primary cable
38 Square nut
39 Locknut
40 Clevis
41 Clevis pin
42 Plain washer
43 Cotter pin
44 Ratchet
45 Pawl
46 Pawl spring

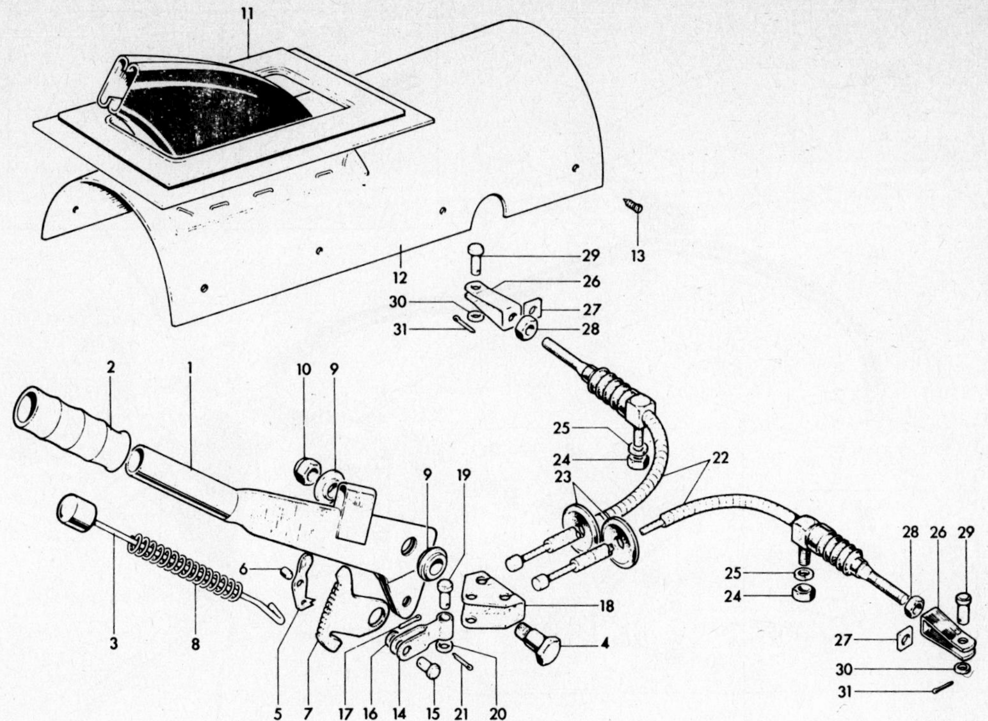

TR series handbrake

1 Handlever	17 Cotter pin
2 Rubber grip	18 Compensator
3 Operating rod, pawl	19 Clevis pin
4 Fulcrum pin, handlever	20 Washer
5 Pawl	21 Cotter pin
6 Pivot pin, pawl	22 Cable assembly
7 Ratchet	23 Rubber grommet
8 Spring	24 Nut
9 Nylon washer	25 Lockwasher
10 Nyloc nut	26 Fork end
11 Carpet trim	27 Nut
12 Cardboard cover	28 Locknut
13 Screw	29 Clevis pin
14 Link	30 Washer
15 Clevis pin	31 Cotter pin
16 Washer	

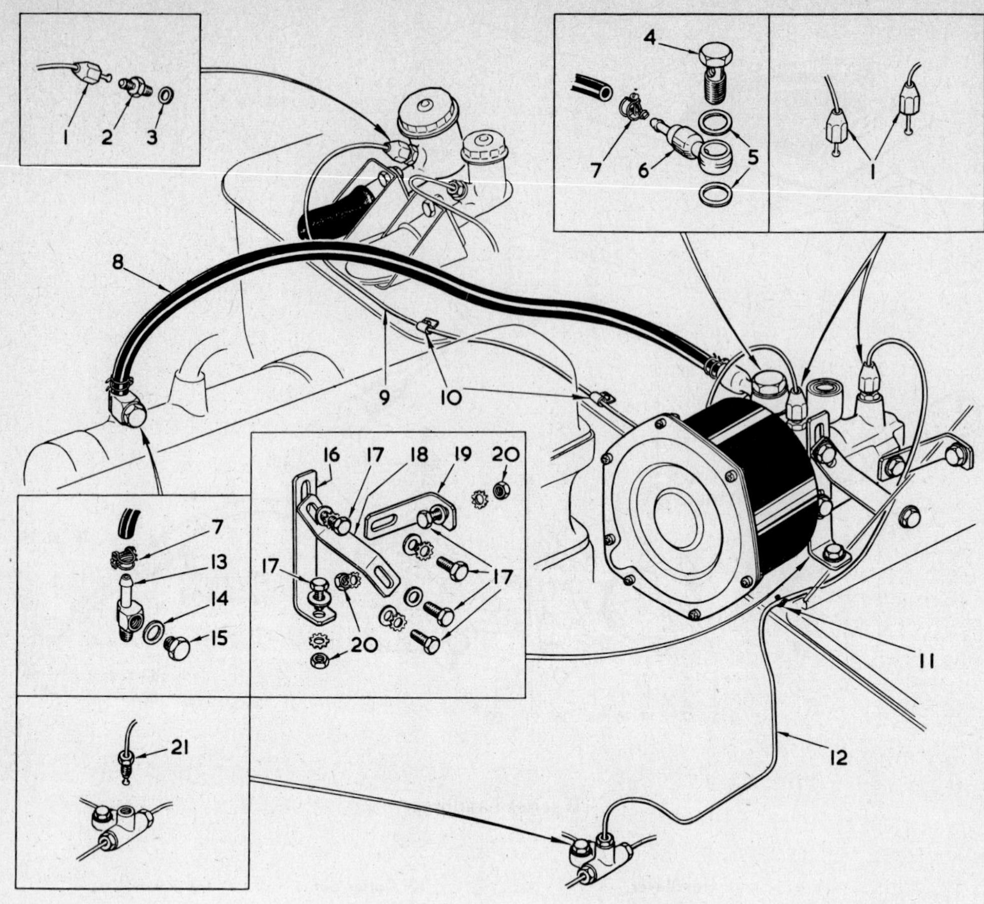

Girling Power Stop brake unit (GT6)

1 Unions (female)
2 Adapter
3 Copper washer
4 Banjo bolt
5 Copper washers
6 Non-return valve
7 Hose clips
8 Vacuum hose
9 Brake pipe
10 Pipe clips
11 Pipe clip
12 Brake pipe
13 Adaptor
14 Copper washer
15 Plug
16 Bracket
17 Bolts
18 Bracket
19 Bracket
20 Nuts
21 Union (male)

Heater

REMOVAL AND REPLACEMENT

Disconnect battery and empty cooling system. Remove heater hoses. Remove screws holding water valve mounting bracket to dash shelf. Push bracket and valve assembly away from dash. Inside car, remove dash board support bracket. Remove passenger and driver's side parcel shelf. Take off bracket holding choke and heater cable. Disconnect tachometer and speedometer cables from back of gauges. Pull cables into engine compartment. Be careful not to damage cables or grommet. (Remove bolts attaching heater box to dash. Plug heater lines to insure against water spillage. Lift out heater. To replace heater, reverse above procedure.

BLOWER MOTOR REMOVAL AND REPLACEMENT

Remove heater. Remove screws securing inner and outer heater assembly. Loosen large nut in center of impeller. Remove impeller from shaft. Remove exposed nut and lift out motor. To replace, reverse above procedure.

Heater blower motor removal

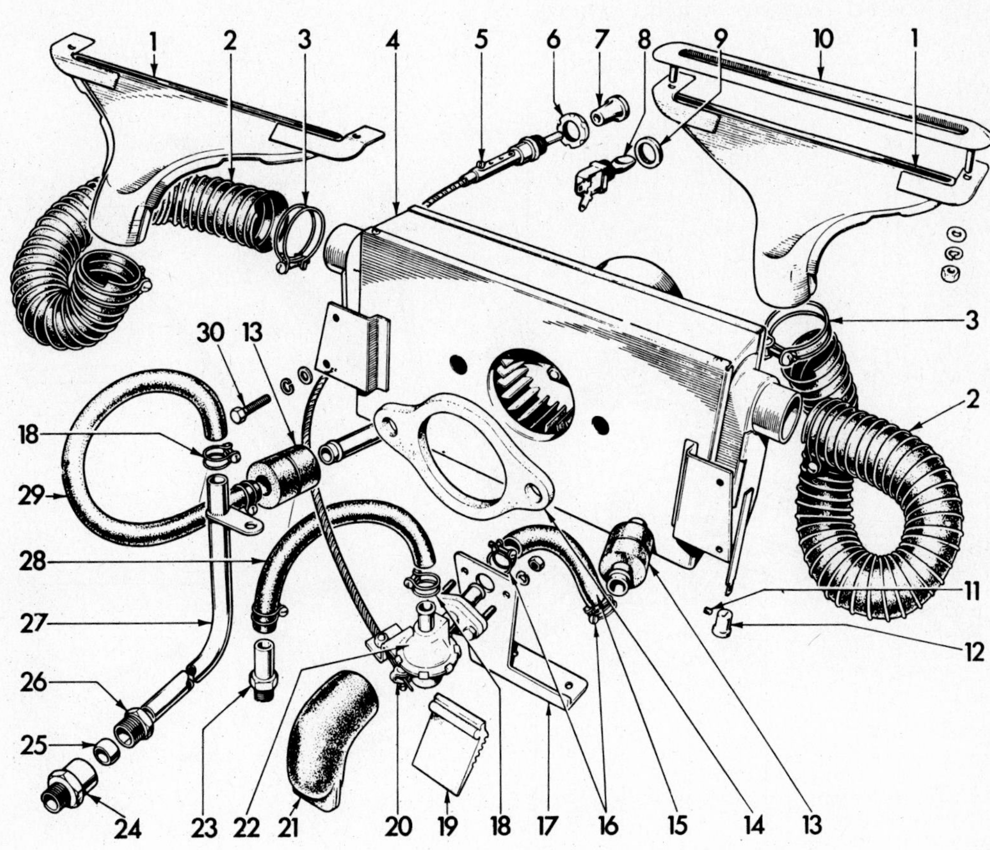

Typical heater assembly

1 Defroster nozzle
2 Air hose
3 Hose clip
4 Heater unit
5 Heat control assembly
6 Bezel
7 Control knob
8 Blower switch
9 Bezel
10 Demister finisher
11 Screw
12 Flap knob
13 Sponge packing
14 Sealing ring
15 Water hose
16 Hose clip
17 Mounting bracket
18 Hose clip
19 Drain flap (from April 1964)
20 Water valve lever
21 Drain elbow (up to April 1964)
22 Water control valve
23 Adapter—cylinder head
24 Adapter—water pump
25 Sealing ring
26 Nut
27 Water return pipe
28 Water hose
29 Water hose
30 Bolt—heater attachment

Windshield Wipers

The windshield wiper mechanism used on all models consists of a dual speed electric motor connected to a cable rack mechanism. A small gearbox unit is also employed.

Wiper motor in position

REMOVAL

Remove all electrical connections. Make mark on domed cover and gearbox cover. Remove four hold down screws. Move gearbox and cover clear. Remove exposed spring clip by pulling sideways. Take off moving contact limiting switch. Remove

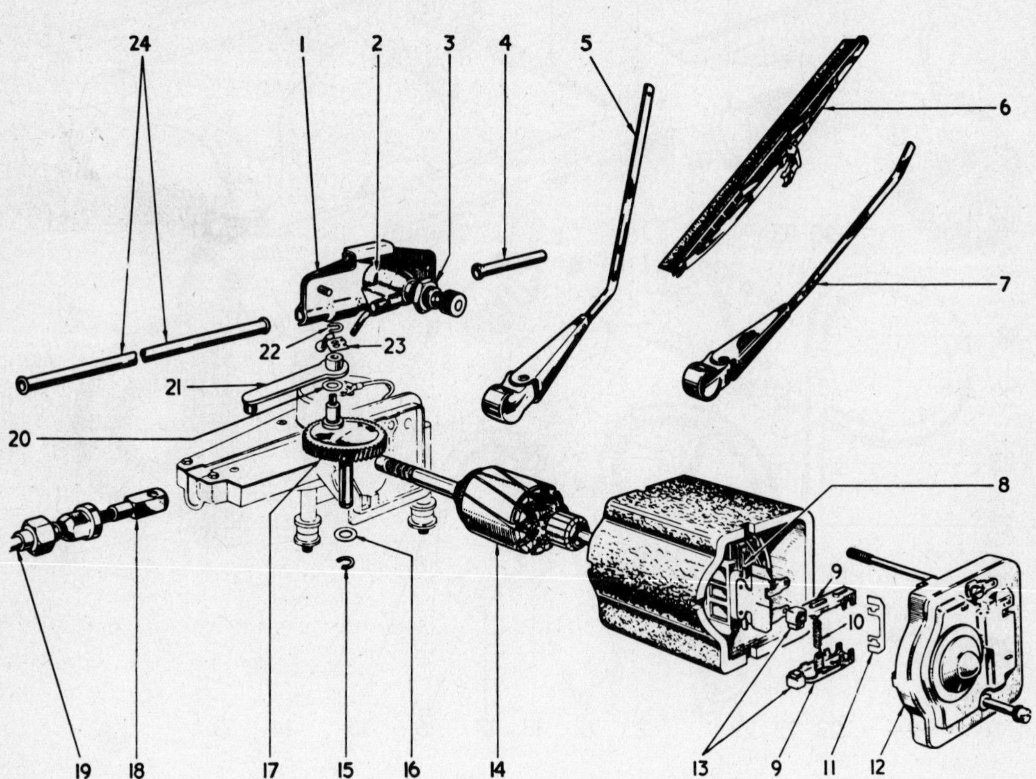

Typical wiper assembly

1 Wheel box
2 Jet and bushing assembly
3 Nut
4 Rigid tubing—right side
5 Wiper arm
6 Blade
7 Wiper arm
8 Field coil assembly
9 Brushgear
10 Tension spring and retainers
11 Brushgear retainer
12 End cove
13 Brushes
14 Armature
15 Circlip
16 Washer
17 Final drive wheel
18 Cable rack
19 Rigid tubing—left side
20 Spacer
21 Connecting rod
22 Circlip
23 Parking switch contact
24 Rigid tubing—centre section

connecting rod. Take mounting bracket from firewall. Move unit to allow vacuum assembly to be released. Remove mounting bracket.

ADJUSTING WIPER STOP (PARK POSITION)

Loosen four holding screws and rotate domed cover. Rotate cover either way till desired stop position is achieved. Replace cover and tighten down.

Adjustment for wiper stop (park) position

Fuses

A fuse that is burned out may be suspected when all electrical components in the particular circuit refuse to operate. A blown fuse may be identified by merely looking at the glass enclosed metal strip. If it is separated or burned, it must be replaced. NOTE: *It is imperative that a fuse be replaced by one of the same amperage.* If a fuse is replaced and immediately fails, the source of the trouble should be found before the vehicle is operated. Otherwise, serious and costly damage may result.

TR-250, TR-6

The fusebox is located on the left side of the inner fender panel at the rear of the engine compartment. It contains three 35 amp. operating fuses, one fuse for a possible accessory circuit, and two spares.

Fuse one (brown leads) protects the headlamp flasher, dash warning lights, and horn. Fuse two (red/green leads) protects the tail lights, front parking and marker lamp circuits, rear marker, dash board, and license plate lamps. Fuse three (white leads) protects all other electrical components.

GT6, GT6+, GT6 MKIII

This unit contains three operating fuses of 35 amp. capacity and provision for two spares. Brown leads denote the fuse which protects the following: horns, dash warning lights, headlamp flasher and the interior light. The fuse fed by a red and green wire protects the tail lamps, license plate, and front parking lights. The fuse fed by a white wire protects everything not specifically listed above.

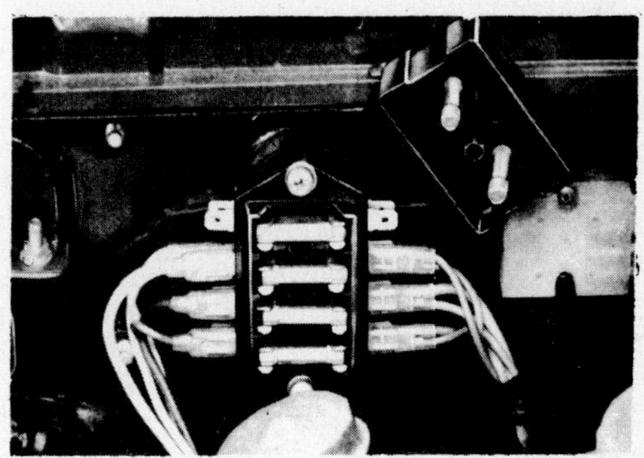

Fuse box

SPITFIRE

The fuse box for all Spitfire models is located under the dashboard on the left side. The unit contains two 35 amp. fuses. In addition, an inline fuse of the same rating is located adjacent to the main unit and protects the headlights and horn. Fuse one may be identified by red and green leads. It protects the tail and front parking lights. Fuse two can be readily distinguished by its white cable leads. It protects all instruments and accessory equipment.

TR-4, TR-4A

The fusebox is located in the engine compartment on the left inner fender panel at the rear, adjacent to the regulator. The housing contains two operating and two spare fuses. Fuse one (right, 25 amp. rating) protects items which may be used only when the engine is on. This includes gauges, windshield wipers, etc. Fuse two (left, 25 amp.) is connected to the side and license plate lamps. Horns operate on a separate, 35 amp., inline fuse located below the main box.

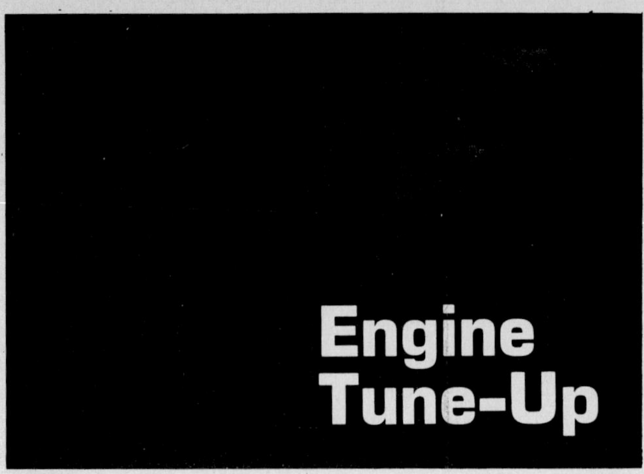

Engine tune-up is a procedure performed to restore engine performance, deteriorated due to normal wear and loss of adjustment. The three major areas considered in a routine tune-up are compression, ignition, and carburetion, although valve adjustment may be included.

A tune-up is performed in three steps: *analysis*, in which it is determined whether normal wear is responsible for performance loss, and which parts require replacement or service; *parts replacement or service*; and *adjustment*, in which engine adjustments are returned to original specifications. Since the advent of emission control equipment, precision adjustment has become increasingly critical, in order to maintain pollutant emission levels.

Analysis

The procedures below are used to indicate where adjustments, parts service or replacement are necessary within the realm of a normal tune-up. If, following these tests, all systems appear to be functioning properly, proceed to the Troubleshooting Section for further diagnosis.

—Remove all spark plugs, noting the cylinder in which they were installed. Remove the air cleaner, and position the throttle and choke in the full open position. Disconnect the coil high tension lead from the coil and the distributor cap. Insert a compression gauge into the spark plug port of each cylinder, in succession, and crank the engine with the starter to obtain the highest possible reading. Record the readings, and compare the highest to the lowest on the compression pressure limit chart. If the difference exceeds the limits on the chart, or if all readings are excessively low, proceed to a wet compression check (see Troubleshooting Section).

Maxi. Press. Lbs. Sq. In.	*Min. Press. Lbs. Sq. In.*	*Max. Press. Lbs. Sq. In.*	*Min. Press. Lbs. Sq. In.*
134	101	188	141
136	102	190	142
138	104	192	144
140	105	194	145
142	107	196	147
146	110	198	148
148	111	200	150
150	113	202	151
152	114	204	153
154	115	206	154
156	117	208	156
158	118	210	157
160	120	212	158
162	121	214	160
164	123	216	162
166	124	218	163
168	126	220	165
170	127	222	166
172	129	224	168
174	131	226	169
176	132	228	171
178	133	230	172
180	135	232	174
182	136	234	175
184	138	236	177
186	140	238	178

Compression pressure limits

—Evaluate the spark plugs according to the spark plug chart in the Troubleshooting Section, and proceed as indicated in the chart.

—Remove the distributor cap, and inspect it inside and out for cracks and/or carbon tracks, and inside for excessive wear or burning of the rotor contacts. If any of these faults are evident, the cap must be replaced.

—Check the breaker points for burning, pitting or wear, and the contact heel resting on the distributor cam for excessive wear. If defects are noted, replace the entire breaker point set.

—Remove and inspect the rotor. If the contacts are burned or worn, or if the rotor is excessively loose on the distributor shaft (where applicable), the rotor must be replaced.

—Inspect the spark plug leads and the coil high tension lead for cracks or brittleness. If any of the wires appear defective, the entire set should be replaced.

—Check the air filter to ensure that it is functioning properly.

Parts Replacement and Service

The determination of whether to replace or service parts is at the mechanic's discretion; however, it is suggested that any parts in questionable condition be replaced rather than reused.

—Clean and regap, or replace, the spark plugs as needed. Lightly coat the threads with engine oil and install the plugs. CAUTION: *Do not over-torque taper-seat spark plugs, or plugs being installed in aluminum cylinder heads.*

SPARK PLUG TORQUE

Thread size	*Cast-Iron Heads*	*Aluminum Heads*
10 mm.	14	11
14 mm.	30	27
18 mm.	34*	32
7/8 in.—18	37	35

* 17 ft. lbs. for tapered plugs using no gaskets.

—If the distributor cap is to be reused, clean the inside with a dry rag, and remove corrosion from the rotor contact points with fine emery cloth. Remove the spark plug wires one by one, and clean the wire ends and the inside of the towers. If the boots are loose, they should be replaced.

If the cap is to be replaced, transfer the wires one by one, cleaning the wire ends and replacing the boots if necessary.

—If the original points are to remain in service, clean them lightly with emery cloth, lubricate the contact heel with grease specifically designed for this purpose. Rotate the crankshaft until the heel rests on a high point of the distributor cam, and adjust the point gap to specifications.

When replacing the points, remove the original points and condenser, and wipe out the inside of the distributor housing with a clean, dry rag. Lightly lubricate the contact heel and pivot point, and install the points and condenser. Rotate the crankshaft until the heel rests on a high point of the distributor cam, and adjust the point gap to specifications. NOTE: *Always replace the condenser when changing the points.*

—If the rotor is to be reused, clean the contacts with solvent. Do not alter the spring tension of the rotor center contact. Install the rotor and the distributor cap.

—Replace the coil high tension lead and/or the spark plug leads as necessary.

—Clean the carburetor using a spray solvent (e.g., Gumout Spray). Remove the varnish from the throttle bores, and clean the linkage. Disconnect and plug the fuel line, and run the engine until it runs out of fuel. Partially fill the float chamber with solvent, and reconnect the fuel line. In extreme cases, the jets can be pressure flushed by inserting a rubber plug into the float vent, running the spray nozzle through it, and spraying the solvent until it squirts out of the venturi fuel dump.

—Clean and tighten all wiring connections in the primary electrical circuit.

Additional Services

The following services *should* be performed in conjunction with a routine tune-up to ensure efficient performance.

—Inspect the battery and fill to the proper level with distilled water. Remove the cable clamps, clean clamps and posts thoroughly, coat the posts lightly with petroleum jelly, reinstall and tighten.

—Inspect all belts, replace and/or adjust as necessary.

—Test the PCV valve (if so equipped), and clean or replace as indicated. Clean all crankcase ventilation hoses, or replace if cracked or hardened.

—Adjust the valves (if necessary) to manufacturer's specifications.

Adjustments

—Connect a dwell-tachometer between the distributor primary lead and ground. Remove the distributor cap and rotor (unless equipped with Delco externally adjustable distributor). With the ignition off, crank the engine with a remote starter switch and measure the point dwell angle. Adjust the dwell angle to specifications. NOTE: *Increasing the gap decreases the dwell angle and vice-versa.* Install the rotor and distributor cap.

—Connect a timing light according to the manufacturer's specifications. Identify the proper timing marks with chalk or paint. NOTE: *Luminescent (day-glo) paint is excellent for this purpose.* Start the engine, and run it until it reaches operating temperature. Disconnect and plug any distributor vacuum lines, and adjust idle to the speed required to adjust timing, according to specifications. Loosen the distributor clamp and adjust timing to specifications by rotating the distributor in the engine. NOTE: *To advance timing, rotate distributor opposite normal direction of rotor rotation, and vice-versa.*

—Synchronize the throttles and mixture of multiple carburetors (if so equipped) according to procedures given in the individual car sections.

—Adjust the idle speed, mixture, and idle quality, as specified in the car sections. Final idle adjustments should be made with the air cleaner installed. CAUTION: *Due to strict emission control requirements on 1969 and later models, special test equipment (CO meter, SUN Tester) may be necessary to properly adjust idle mixture to specifications.*

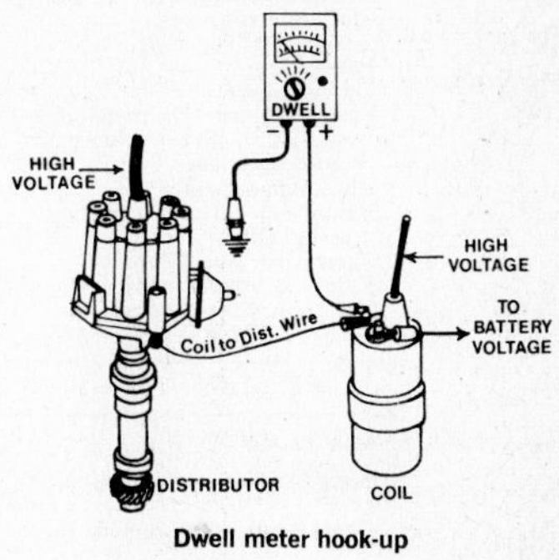

Dwell meter hook-up

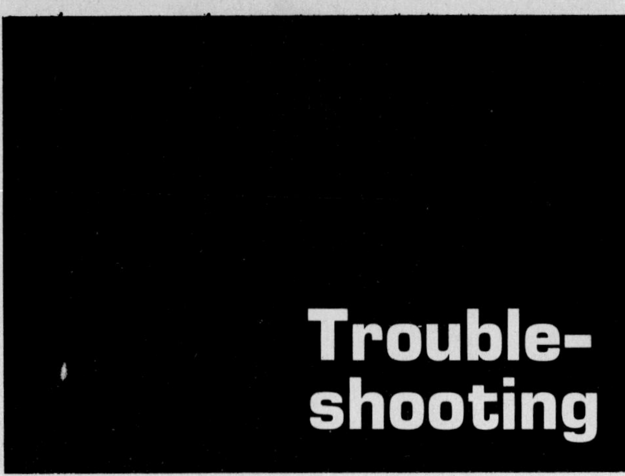

The following section is designed to aid in the rapid diagnosis of engine problems. The systematic format is used to diagnose problems ranging from engine starting difficulties to the need for engine overhaul. It is assumed that the user is equipped with basic hand tools and test equipment (tach-dwell meter, timing light, voltmeter, and ohmmeter).

Troubleshooting is divided into two sections. The first, *General Diagnosis*, is used to locate the problem area. In the second, *Specific Diagnosis*, the problem is systematically evaluated.

General Diagnosis

PROBLEM: Symptom	*Begin diagnosis at Section Two, Number ——*
Engine won't start:	
Starter doesn't turn	1.1, 2.1
Starter turns, engine doesn't	2.1
Starter turns engine very slowly	1.1, 2.4
Starter turns engine normally	3.1, 4.1
Starter turns engine very quickly	6.1
Engine fires intermittently	4.1
Engine fires consistently	5.1, 6.1
Engine runs poorly:	
Hard starting	3.1, 4.1, 5.1, 8.1
Rough idle	4.1, 5.1, 8.1
Stalling	3.1, 4.1, 5.1, 8.1
Engine dies at high speeds	4.1, 5.1
Hesitation (on acceleration from standing stop)	5.1, 8.1
Poor pickup	4.1, 5.1, 8.1
Lack of power	3.1, 4.1, 5.1, 8.1
Backfire through the carburetor	4.1, 8.1, 9.1
Backfire through the exhaust	4.1, 8.1, 9.1
Blue exhaust gases	6.1, 7.1
Black exhaust gases	5.1
Running on (after the ignition is shut off)	3.1, 8.1
Susceptible to moisture	4.1
Engine misfires under load	4.1, 7.1, 8.4, 9.1
Engine misfires at speed	4.1, 8.4
Engine misfires at idle	3.1, 4.1, 5.1, 7.1, 8.4

PROBLEM: Symptom	*Probable Cause*
Engine noises: ①	
Metallic grind while starting	Starter drive not engaging completely
Constant grind or rumble	*Starter drive not releasing, worn main bearings
Constant knock	Worn connecting rod bearings
Knock under load	Fuel octane too low, worn connecting rod bearings
Double knock	Loose piston pin
Metallic tap	*Collapsed or sticky valve lifter, excessive valve clearance, excessive end play in a rotating shaft
Scrape	*Fan belt contacting a stationary surface
Tick while starting	S.U. electric fuel pump (normal), starter brushes
Constant tick	*Generator brushes, shreaded fan belt
Squeal	*Improperly tensioned fan belt
Hiss or roar	*Steam escaping through a leak in the cooling system or the radiator overflow vent
Whistle	*Vacuum leak
Wheeze	Loose or cracked spark plug

①—It is extremely difficult to evaluate vehicle noises. While the above are general definitions of engine noises, those starred (*) should be considered as possibly originating elsewhere in the car. To aid diagnosis, the following list considers other potential sources of these sounds.

Metallic grind:
Throwout bearing; transmission gears, bearings, or synchronizers; differential bearings, gears; something metallic in contact with brake drum or disc.

Metallic tap:
U-joints; fan-to-radiator (or shroud) contact.

Scrape:
Brake shoe or pad dragging; tire to body contact; suspension contacting undercarriage or exhaust; something non-metallic contacting brake shoe or drum.

Tick:
Transmission gears; differential gears; lack of radio suppression; resonant vibration of body panels; windshield wiper motor or transmission; heater motor and blower.

Squeal:
Brake shoe or pad not fully releasing; tires (excessive wear, uneven wear, improper inflation); front or rear wheel alignment (most commonly due to improper toe-in).

Hiss or whistle:
Wind leaks (body or window); heater motor and blower fan.

Roar:
Wheel bearings; wind leaks (body and window).

Specific Diagnosis

This section is arranged so that following each test, instructions are given to proceed to another, until a problem is diagnosed.

INDEX

Group		Topic
1	*	Battery
2	*	Cranking system
3	*	Primary electrical system
4	*	Secondary electrical system
5	*	Fuel system
6	*	Engine compression
7	**	Engine vacuum
8	**	Secondary electrical system
9	**	Valve train
10	**	Exhaust system
11	**	Cooling system
12	**	Engine lubrication

*—The engine need not be running.
**—The engine must be running.

SAMPLE SECTION

Test and Procedure	*Results and Indications*	*Proceed to*
4.1—Check for spark: Hold each spark plug wire approximately ¼″ from ground with gloves or a heavy, dry rag. Crank the engine and observe the spark.	→ If no spark is evident: →	4.2
	→ If spark is good in some cases: →	4.3
	→ If spark is good in all cases: →	4.6

DIAGNOSIS

Test and Procedure	Results and Indications	Proceed to
1.1—Inspect the battery visually for case condition (corrosion, cracks) and water level.	If case is cracked, replace battery:	1.4
	If the case is intact, remove corrosion with a solution of baking soda and water (CAUTION: *do not get the solution into the battery*), and fill with water:	1.2
1.2—Check the battery cable connections: Insert a screwdriver between the battery post and the cable clamp. Turn the headlights on high beam, and observe them as the screwdriver is gently twisted to ensure good metal to metal contact.	If the lights brighten, remove and clean the clamp and post; coat the post with petroleum jelly, install and tighten the clamp:	1.4
	If no improvement is noted:	1.3

Testing battery cable connections using a screwdriver

Test and Procedure	Results and Indications	Proceed to
1.3—Test the state of charge of the battery using an individual cell tester or hydrometer.	If indicated, charge the battery. NOTE: *If no obvious reason exists for the low state of charge (i.e., battery age, prolonged storage), the charging system should be tested:*	1.4

Spec. Grav. Reading	*Charged Condition*
1.260-1.280	Fully Charged
1.230-1.250	Three Quarter Charged
1.200-1.220	One Half Charged
1.170-1.190	One Quarter Charged
1.140-1.160	Just About Flat
1.110-1.130	All The Way Down

State of battery charge

The effect of temperature on the specific gravity of battery electrolyte

Test and Procedure	*Results and Indications*	*Proceed to*
1.4- -Visually inspect battery cables for cracking, bad connection to ground, or bad connection to starter.	If necessary, tighten connections or replace the cables:	2.1

Tests in Group 2 are performed with coil high tension lead disconnected to prevent accidental starting.

Test and Procedure	*Results and Indications*	*Proceed to*
2.1—Test the starter motor and solenoid: Connect a jumper from the battery post of the solenoid (or relay) to the starter post of the solenoid (or relay).	If starter turns the engine normally:	2.2
	If the starter buzzes, or turns the engine very slowly:	2.4
	If no response, replace the solenoid (or relay).	3.1
	If the starter turns, but the engine doesn't, ensure that the flywheel ring gear is intact. If the gear is undamaged, replace the starter drive.	3.1
2.2—Determine whether ignition override switches are functioning properly (clutch start switch, neutral safety switch), by connecting a jumper across the switch(es), and turning the ignition switch to "start".	If starter operates, adjust or replace switch:	3.1
	If the starter doesn't operate:	2.3
2.3—Check the ignition switch "start" position: Connect a 12V test lamp between the starter post of the solenoid (or relay) and ground. Turn the ignition switch to the "start" position, and jiggle the key.	If the lamp doesn't light when the switch is turned, check the ignition switch for loose connections, cracked insulation, or broken wires. Repair or replace as necessary:	3.1
	If the lamp flickers when the key is jiggled, replace the ignition switch.	3.3
2.4—Remove and bench test the starter, according to specifications in the car section.	If the starter does not meet specifications, repair or replace as needed:	3.1
	If the starter is operating properly:	2.5
2.5—Determine whether the engine can turn freely: Remove the spark plugs, and check for water in the cylinders. Check for water on the dipstick, or oil in the radiator. Attempt to turn the engine using an 18″ flex drive and socket on the crankshaft pulley nut or bolt.	If the engine will turn freely only with the spark plugs out, and hydrostatic lock (water in the cylinders) is ruled out, check valve timing:	9.2
	If engine will not turn freely, and it is known that the clutch and transmission are free, the engine must be disassembled for further evaluation:	Next Chapter

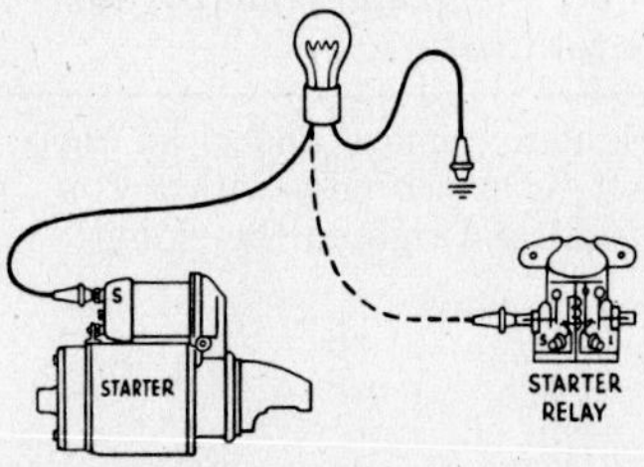

Checking the ignition switch "start" position

Tests and Procedures	*Results and Indications*	*Proceed to*
3.1—Check the ignition switch "on" position: Connect a jumper wire between the distributor side of the coil and ground, and a 12V test lamp between the switch side of the coil and ground. Remove the high tension lead from the coil. Turn the ignition switch on and jiggle the key.	If the lamp lights:	3.2
	If the lamp flickers when the key is jiggled, replace the ignition switch:	3.3
	If the lamp doesn't light, check for loose or open connections. If none are found, remove the ignition switch and check for continuity. If the switch is faulty, replace it:	3.3
Checking the ignition switch "on" position		
3.2—Check the ballast resistor or resistance wire for an open circuit, using an ohmmeter.	Replace the resistor or the resistance wire if the resistance is zero.	3.3
3.3—Visually inspect the breaker points for burning, pitting, or excessive wear. Gray coloring of the point contact surfaces is normal. Rotate the crankshaft until the contact heel rests on a high point of the distributor cam, and adjust the point gap to specifications.	If the breaker points are intact, clean the contact surfaces with fine emery cloth, and adjust the point gap to specifications. If pitted or worn, replace the points and condenser, and adjust the gap to specifications: NOTE: *Always lubricate the distributor cam according to manufacturer's recommendations when servicing the breaker points.*	3.4
3.4—Connect a dwell meter between the distributor primary lead and ground. Crank the engine and observe the point dwell angle.	If necessary, adjust the point dwell angle: NOTE: *Increasing the point gap decreases the dwell angle, and vice-versa.*	3.6
	If dwell meter shows little or no reading:	3.5
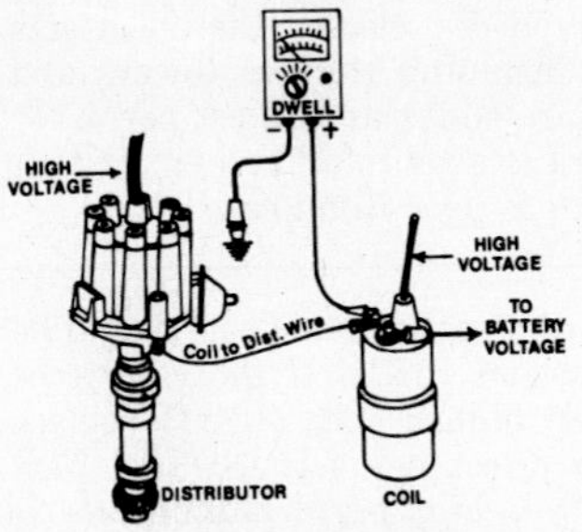 Dwell meter hook-up	Dwell angle	
3.5—Check the condenser for short: Connect an ohmmeter across the condenser body and the pigtail lead.	If any reading other than infinite resistance is noted, replace the condenser:	3.6
Checking the condenser for short		

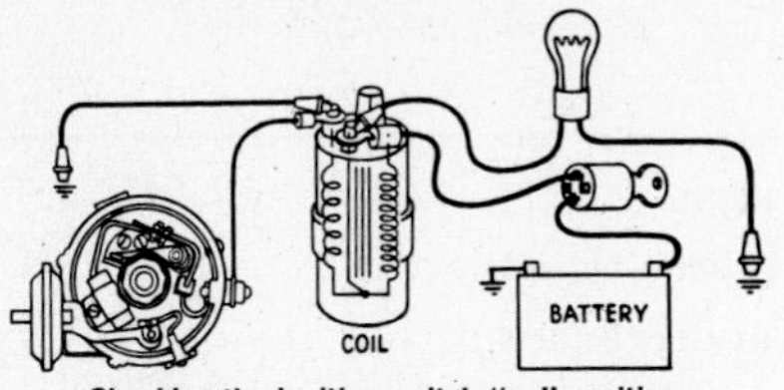

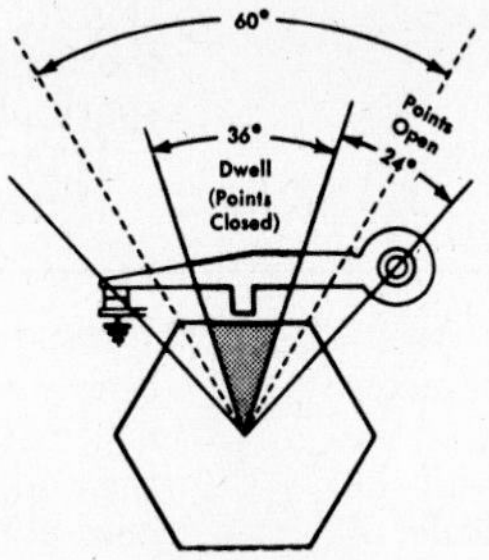

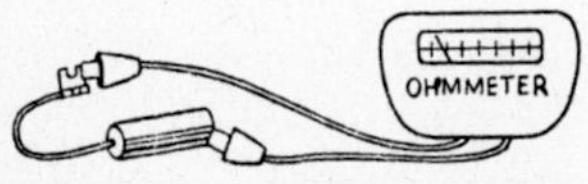

Test and Procedure	*Results and Indications*	*Proceed to*
3.6—Test the coil primary resistance: Connect an ohmmeter across the coil primary terminals, and read the resistance on the low scale. Note whether an external ballast resistor or resistance wire is utilized. 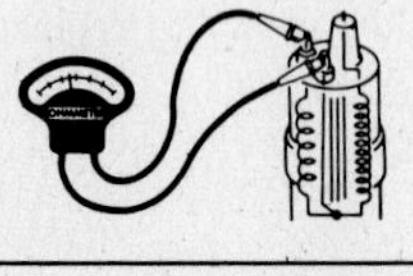	Coils utilizing ballast resistors or resistance wires should have approximately 1.0Ω resistance; coils with internal resistors should have approximately 4.0Ω resistance. If values far from the above are noted, replace the coil:	4.1

Testing the coil primary resistance

Test and Procedure	*Results and Indications*	*Proceed to*
4.1—Check for spark: Hold each spark plug wire approximately ¼″ from ground with gloves or a heavy, dry rag. Crank the engine, and observe the spark.	If no spark is evident:	4.2
	If spark is good in some cylinders:	4.3
	If spark is good in all cylinders:	4.6
4.2—Check for spark at the coil high tension lead: Remove the coil high tension lead from the distributor and position it approximately ¼″ from ground. Crank the engine and observe spark. CAUTION: *This test should not be performed on cars equipped with transistorized ignition.*	If the spark is good and consistent:	4.3
	If the spark is good but intermittent, test the primary electrical system starting at 3.3:	3.3
	If the spark is weak or non-existent, replace the coil high tension lead, clean and tighten all connections and retest. If no improvement is noted:	4.4
4.3—Visually inspect the distributor cap and rotor for burned or corroded contacts, cracks, carbon tracks, or moisture. Also check the fit of the rotor on the distributor shaft (where applicable).	If moisture is present, dry thoroughly, and retest per 4.1:	4.1
	If burned or excessively corroded contacts, cracks, or carbon tracks are noted, replace the defective part(s) and retest per 4.1:	4.1
	If the rotor and cap appear intact, or are only slightly corroded, clean the contacts thoroughly (including the cap towers and spark plug wire ends) and retest per 4.1:	
	If the spark is good in all cases:	4.6
	If the spark is poor in all cases:	4.5
4.4—Check the coil secondary resistance: Connect an ohmmeter across the distributor side of the coil and the coil tower. Read the resistance on the high scale of the ohmmeter. 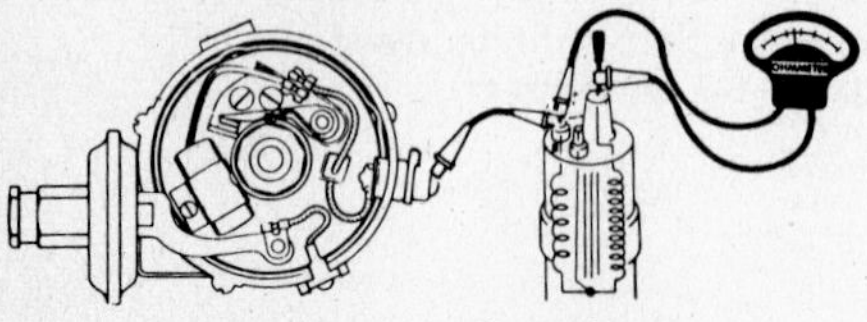	The resistance of a satisfactory coil should be between 4KΩ and 10KΩ. If the resistance is considerably higher (i.e., 40KΩ) replace the coil, and retest per 4.1: NOTE: *This does not apply to high performance coils.*	4.1

Testing the coil secondary resistance

Test and Procedure	*Results and Indications*	*Proceed to*
4.5—Visually inspect the spark plug wires for cracking or brittleness. Ensure that no two wires are positioned so as to cause induction firing (adjacent and parallel). Remove each wire, one by one, and check resistance with an ohmmeter.	Replace any cracked or brittle wires. If any of the wires are defective, replace the entire set. Replace any wires with excessive resistance (over 8000Ω per foot for suppression wire), and separate any wires that might cause induction firing.	4.6
4.6—Remove the spark plugs, noting the cylinders from which they were removed, and evaluate according to the chart below.	See below.	See below.

Condition	*Cause*	*Remedy*	*Proceed to*
Electrodes eroded, light brown deposits.	Normal wear. Normal wear is indicated by approximately .001″ wear per 1000 miles.	Clean and regap the spark plug if wear is not excessive: Replace the spark plug if excessively worn:	4.7
Carbon fouling (black, dry, fluffy deposits).	If present on one or two plugs:		
	Faulty high tension lead(s).	Test the high tension leads:	4.5
	Burnt or sticking valve(s).	Check the valve train: (Clean and regap the plugs in either case.)	9.1
	If present on most or all plugs: Overly rich fuel mixture, due to restricted air filter, improper carburetor adjustment, improper choke or heat riser adjustment or operation.	Check the fuel system:	5.1
Oil fouling (wet black deposits)	Worn engine components. NOTE: *Oil fouling may occur in new or recently rebuilt engines until broken in.*	Check engine vacuum and compression: Replace with new spark plug	6.1
Lead fouling (gray, black, tan, or yellow deposits, which appear glazed or cinder-like).	Combustion by-products.	Clean and regap the plugs: (Use plugs of a different heat range if the problem recurs.)	4.7

Condition	Cause	Remedy	Proceed to
Gap bridging (deposits lodged between the electrodes).	Incomplete combustion, or transfer of deposits from the combustion chamber.	Replace the spark plugs:	4.7
Overheating (burnt electrodes, and extremely white insulator with small black spots).	Ignition timing advanced too far.	Adjust timing to specifications:	8.2
	Overly lean fuel mixture.	Check the fuel system:	5.1
	Spark plugs not seated properly.	Clean spark plug seat and install a new gasket washer: (Replace the spark plugs in all cases.)	4.7
Fused spot deposits on the insulator.	Combustion chamber blow-by.	Clean and regap the spark plugs:	4.7
Pre-ignition (melted or severely burned electrodes, blistered or cracked insulators, or metallic deposits on the insulator).	Incorrect spark plug heat range.	Replace with plugs of the proper heat range:	4.7
	Ignition timing advanced too far.	Adjust timing to specifications:	8.2
	Spark plugs not being cooled efficiently.	Clean the spark plug seat, and check the cooling system:	11.1
	Fuel mixture too lean.	Check the fuel system:	5.1
	Poor compression.	Check compression:	6.1
	Fuel grade too low.	Use higher octane fuel:	4.7

Test and Procedure	Results and Indications	Proceed to
4.7—Determine the static ignition timing: Using the flywheel or crankshaft pulley timing marks as a guide, locate top dead center on the *compression* stroke of the No. 1 cylinder. Remove the distributor cap.	Adjust the distributor so that the rotor points toward the No. 1 tower in the distributor cap, and the points are just opening:	4.8
4.8—Check coil polarity: Connect a voltmeter negative lead to the coil high tension lead, and the positive lead to ground (NOTE: *reverse the hook-up for positive ground cars*). Crank the engine momentarily. (Checking coil polarity)	If the voltmeter reads up-scale, the polarity is correct:	5.1
	If the voltmeter reads down-scale, reverse the coil polarity (switch the primary leads):	5.1

Test and Procedure	*Results and Indications*	*Proceed to*
5.1—Determine that the air filter is functioning efficiently: Hold paper elements up to a strong light, and attempt to see light through the filter.	Clean permanent air filters in gasoline (or manufacturer's recommendation), and allow to dry. Replace paper elements through which light cannot be seen:	5.2
5.2—Determine whether a flooding condition exists: Flooding is identified by a strong gasoline odor, and excessive gasoline present in the throttle bore(s) of the carburetor.	If flooding is not evident:	5.3
	If flooding is evident, permit the gasoline to dry for a few moments and restart. If flooding doesn't recur:	5.6
	If flooding is persistant:	5.5
5.3—Check that fuel is reaching the carburetor: Detach the fuel line at the carburetor inlet. Hold the end of the line in a cup (not styrofoam), and crank the engine.	If fuel flows smoothly:	5.6
	If fuel doesn't flow (NOTE: *Make sure that there is fuel in the tank*), or flows erratically:	5.4
5.4—Test the fuel pump: Disconnect all fuel lines from the fuel pump. Hold a finger over the input fitting, crank the engine (with electric pump, turn the ignition or pump on), and feel for suction.	If suction is evident, blow out the fuel line to the tank with low pressure compressed air until bubbling is heard from the fuel filler neck. Also blow out the carburetor fuel line (both ends disconnected):	5.6
	If no suction is evident, replace or repair the fuel pump:	5.6
	NOTE: *Repeated oil fouling of the spark plugs, or a no-start condition, could be the result of a ruptured vacuum booster pump diaphragm, through which oil or gasoline is being drawn into the intake manifold (where applicable).*	
5.5—Check the needle and seat: Tap the carburetor in the area of the needle and seat.	If flooding stops, a gasoline additive (e.g., Gumout) will often cure the problem:	5.6
	If flooding continues, check the fuel pump for excessive pressure at the carburetor (according to specifications). If the pressure is normal, the needle and seat must be removed and checked, and/or the float level adjusted:	5.6
5.6—Test the accelerator pump by looking into the throttle bores while operating the throttle.	If the accelerator pump appears to be operating normally:	5.7
	If the accelerator pump is not operating, the pump must be reconditioned. Where possible, service the pump with the carburetor(s) installed on the engine. If necessary, remove the carburetor. Prior to removal:	5.7
5.7—Determine whether the carburetor main fuel system is functioning: Spray a commercial starting fluid into the carburetor while attempting to start the engine.	If the engine starts, runs for a few seconds, and dies:	5.8
	If the engine doesn't start:	6.1

Test and Procedures	*Results and Indications*	*Proceed to*
5.8—Uncommon fuel system malfunctions: See below:	If the problem is solved:	6.1
	If the problem remains, remove and recondition the carburetor.	

Condition	*Indication*	*Test*	*Usual Weather Conditions*	*Remedy*
Vapor lock	Car will not restart shortly after running.	Cool the components of the fuel system until the engine starts.	Hot to very hot	Ensure that the exhaust manifold heat control valve is operating. Check with the vehicle manufacturer for the recommended solution to vapor lock on the model in question.
Carburetor icing	Car will not idle, stalls at low speeds.	Visually inspect the throttle plate area of the throttle bores for frost.	High humidity, 32-40° F.	Ensure that the exhaust manifold heat control valve is operating, and that the intake manifold heat riser is not blocked.
Water in the fuel	Engine sputters and stalls; may not start.	Pump a small amount of fuel into a glass jar. Allow to stand, and inspect for droplets or a layer of water.	High humidity, extreme temperature changes.	For droplets, use one or two cans of commercial gas dryer (Dry Gas) For a layer of water, the tank must be drained, and the fuel lines blown out with compressed air.

Test and Procedure	*Results and Indications*	*Proceed to*
6.1—Test engine compression: Remove all spark plugs. Insert a compression gauge into a spark plug port, crank the engine to obtain the maximum reading, and record.	If compression is within limits on all cylinders:	7.1
	If gauge reading is extremely low on all cylinders:	6.2
	If gauge reading is low on one or two cylinders:	6.2
	(If gauge readings are identical and low on two or more adjacent cylinders, the head gasket must be replaced.)	

Testing compression
(© Chevrolet Div. G.M. Corp.)

Maxi. Press. Lbs. Sq. In.	*Min. Press. Lbs. Sq. In.*	*Maxi. Press. Lbs. Sq. In.*	*Min. Press. Lbs. Sq. In.*	*Max. Press. Lbs. Sq. In.*	*Min. Press. Lbs. Sq. In.*	*Max. Press. Lbs. Sq. In.*	*Min. Press. Lbs. Sq. In.*
134	101	162	121	188	141	214	160
136	102	164	123	190	142	216	162
138	104	166	124	192	144	218	163
140	105	168	126	194	145	220	165
142	107	170	127	196	147	222	166
146	110	172	129	198	148	224	168
148	111	174	131	200	150	226	169
150	113	176	132	202	151	228	171
152	114	178	133	204	153	230	172
154	115	180	135	206	154	232	174
156	117	182	136	208	156	234	175
158	118	184	138	210	157	236	177
160	120	186	140	212	158	238	178

Compression pressure limits
(© Buick Div. G.M. Corp.)

Test and Procedure	*Results and Indications*	*Proceed to*
6.2—Test engine compression (wet): Squirt approximately 30 cc. of engine oil into each cylinder, and retest per 6.1.	If the readings improve, worn or cracked rings or broken pistons are indicated:	Next Chapter
	If the readings do not improve, burned or excessively carboned valves or a jumped timing chain are indicated:	7.1
	NOTE: *A jumped timing chain is often indicated by difficult cranking.*	
7.1—Perform a vacuum check of the engine: Attach a vacuum gauge to the intake manifold beyond the throttle plate. Start the engine, and observe the action of the needle over the range of engine speeds.	See below.	See below

Reading	*Indications*	*Proceed to*
 Steady, from 17-22 in. Hg.	Normal.	8.1
 Low and steady.	Late ignition or valve timing, or low compression:	6.1
 Very low	Vacuum leak:	7.2
 Needle fluctuates as engine speed increases.	Ignition miss, blown cylinder head gasket, leaking valve or weak valve spring:	6.1, 8.3
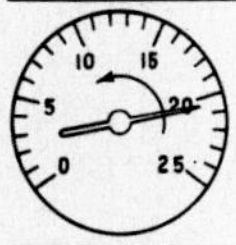 Gradual drop in reading at idle.	Excessive back pressure in the exhaust system:	10.1
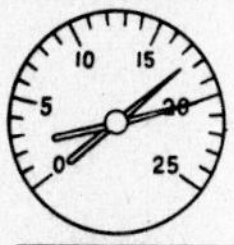 Intermittent fluctuation at idle.	Ignition miss, sticking valve:	8.3, 9.1
 Drifting needle.	Improper idle mixture adjustment, carburetors not synchronized (where applicable), or minor intake leak. Synchronize the carburetors, adjust the idle, and retest. If the condition persists:	7.2
 High and steady.	Early ignition timing:	8.2

Test and Procedure	*Results and Indications*	*Proceed to*
7.2—Attach a vacuum gauge per 7.1, and test for an intake manifold leak. Squirt a small amount of oil around the intake manifold gaskets, carburetor gaskets, plugs and fittings. Observe the action of the vacuum gauge.	If the reading improves, replace the indicated gasket, or seal the indicated fitting or plug:	8.1
	If the reading remains low:	7.3
7.3—Test all vacuum hoses and accessories for leaks as described in 7.2. Also check the carburetor body (dashpots, automatic choke mechanism, throttle shafts) for leaks in the same manner.	If the reading improves, service or replace the offending part(s):	8.1
	If the reading remains low:	6.1
8.1—Check the point dwell angle: Connect a dwell meter between the distributor primary wire and ground. Start the engine, and observe the dwell angle from idle to 3000 rpm.	If necessary, adjust the dwell angle. NOTE: *Increasing the point gap reduces the dwell angle and vice-versa.* If the dwell angle moves outside specifications as engine speed increases, the distributor should be removed and checked for cam accuracy, shaft endplay and concentricity, bushing wear, and adequate point arm tension (NOTE: *Most of these items may be checked with the distributor installed in the engine, using an oscilloscope*):	8.2
8.2—Connect a timing light (per manufacturer's recommendation) and check the dynamic ignition timing. Disconnect and plug the vacuum hose(s) to the distributor if specified, start the engine, and observe the timing marks at the specified engine speed.	If the timing is not correct, adjust to specifications by rotating the distributor in the engine: (Advance timing by rotating distributor opposite normal direction of rotor rotation, retard timing by rotating distributor in same direction as rotor rotation.)	8.3
8.3—Check the operation of the distributor advance mechanism(s): To test the mechanical advance, disconnect all but the mechanical advance, and observe the timing marks with a timing light as the engine speed is increased from idle. If the mark moves smoothly, without hesitation, it may be assumed that the mechanical advance is functioning properly. To test vacuum advance and/or retard systems, alternately crimp and release the vacuum line, and observe the timing mark for movement. If movement is noted, the system is operating.	If the systems are functioning:	8.4
	If the systems are not functioning, remove the distributor, and test on a distributor tester:	8.4
8.4—Locate an ignition miss: With the engine running, remove each spark plug wire, one by one, until one is found that doesn't cause the engine to roughen and slow down.	When the missing cylinder is identified:	4.1

Test and Procedure	*Results and Indications*	*Proceed to*
9.1—Evaluate the valve train: Remove the valve cover, and ensure that the valves are adjusted to specifications. A mechanic's stethoscope may be used to aid in the diagnosis of the valve train. By pushing the probe on or near push rods or rockers, valve noise often can be isolated. A timing light also may be used to diagnose valve problems. Connect the light according to manufacturer's recommendations, and start the engine. Vary the firing moment of the light by increasing the engine speed (and therefore the ignition advance), and moving the trigger from cylinder to cylinder. Observe the movement of each valve.	See below	See below

Observation	*Probable Cause*	*Remedy*	*Proceed to*
Metallic tap heard through the stethoscope.	Sticking hydraulic lifter or excessive valve clearance.	Adjust valve. If tap persists, remove and replace the lifter:	10.1
Metallic tap through the stethoscope, able to push the rocker arm (lifter side) down by hand.	Collapsed valve lifter.	Remove and replace the lifter:	10.1
Erratic, irregular motion of the valve stem.*	Sticking valve, burned valve.	Recondition the valve and/or valve guide:	Next Chapter
Eccentric motion of the pushrod at the rocker arm.*	Bent pushrod.	Replace the pushrod:	10.1
Valve retainer bounces as the valve closes.*	Weak valve spring or damper.	Remove and test the spring and damper. Replace if necessary:	10.1

*—When observed with a timing light.

Test and Procedure	*Results and Indications*	*Proceed to*
9.2—Check the valve timing: Locate top dead center of the No. 1 piston, and install a degree wheel or tape on the crankshaft pulley or damper with zero corresponding to an index mark on the engine. Rotate the crankshaft in its direction of rotation, and observe the opening of the No. 1 cylinder intake valve. The opening should correspond with the correct mark on the degree wheel according to specifications.	If the timing is not correct, the timing cover must be removed for further investigation:	

Test and Procedure	*Results and Indications*	*Proceed to*
10.1—Determine whether the exhaust manifold heat control valve is operating: Operate the valve by hand to determine whether it is free to move. If the valve is free, run the engine to operating temperature and observe the action of the valve, to ensure that it is opening.	If the valve sticks, spray it with a suitable solvent, open and close the valve to free it, and retest.	
	If the valve functions properly:	10.2
	If the valve does not free, or does not operate, replace the valve:	10.2
10.2—Ensure that there are no exhaust restrictions: Visually inspect the exhaust system for kinks, dents, or crushing. Also note that gasses are flowing freely from the tailpipe at all engine speeds, indicating no restriction in the muffler or resonator.	Replace any damaged portion of the system:	11.1
11.1—Visually inspect the fan belt for glazing, cracks, and fraying, and replace if necessary. Tighten the belt so that the longest span has approximately ½″ play at its midpoint under thumb pressure. 	Replace or tighten the fan belt as necessary: Checking the fan belt tension (© Nissan Motor Co. Ltd.)	11.2
11.2—Check the fluid level of the cooling system.	If full or slightly low, fill as necessary:	11.5
	If extremely low:	11.3
11.3—Visually inspect the external portions of the cooling system (radiator, radiator hoses, thermostat elbow, water pump seals, heater hoses, etc.) for leaks. If none are found, pressurize the cooling system to 14-15 psi.	If cooling system holds the pressure:	11.5
	If cooling system loses pressure rapidly, reinspect external parts of the system for leaks under pressure. If none are found, check dipstick for coolant in crankcase. If no coolant is present, but pressure loss continues:	11.4
	If coolant is evident in crankcase, remove cylinder head(s), and check gasket(s). If gaskets are intact, block and cylinder head(s) should be checked for cracks or holes.	
	If the gasket(s) is blown, replace, and purge the crankcase of coolant:	12.6
	NOTE: *Occasionally, due to atmospheric and driving conditions, condensation of water can occur in the crankcase. This causes the oil to appear milky white. To remedy, run the engine until hot, and change the oil and oil filter.*	

Test and Procedure	Results and Indication	Proceed to
11.4—Check for combustion leaks into the cooling system: Pressurize the cooling system as above. Start the engine, and observe the pressure gauge. If the needle fluctuates, remove each spark plug wire, one by one, noting which cylinder(s) reduce or eliminate the fluctuation. Radiator pressure tester (© American Motors Corp.)	Cylinders which reduce or eliminate the fluctuation, when the spark plug wire is removed, are leaking into the cooling system. Replace the head gasket on the affected cylinder bank(s).	
11.5—Check the radiator pressure cap: Attach a radiator pressure tester to the radiator cap (wet the seal prior to installation). Quickly pump up the pressure, noting the point at which the cap releases. Testing the radiator pressure cap (© American Motors Corp.)	If the cap releases within ± 1 psi of the specified rating, it is operating properly:	11.6
	If the cap releases at more than ± 1 psi of the specified rating, it should be replaced:	11.6
11.6—Test the thermostat: Start the engine cold, remove the radiator cap, and insert a thermometer into the radiator. Allow the engine to idle. After a short while, there will be a sudden, rapid increase in coolant temperature. The temperature at which this sharp rise stops is the thermostat opening temperature.	If the thermostat opens at or about the specified temperature:	11.7
	If the temperature doesn't increase: (If the temperature increases slowly and gradually, replace the thermostat.)	11.7
11.7—Check the water pump: Remove the thermostat elbow and the thermostat, disconnect the coil high tension lead (to prevent starting), and crank the engine momentarily.	If coolant flows, replace the thermostat and retest per 11.6:	11.6
	If coolant doesn't flow, reverse flush the cooling system to alleviate any blockage that might exist. If system is not blocked, and coolant will not flow, recondition the water pump.	—
12.1—Check the oil pressure gauge or warning light: If the gauge shows low pressure, or the light is on, for no obvious reason, remove the oil pressure sender. Install an accurate oil pressure gauge and run the engine momentarily.	If oil pressure builds normally, run engine for a few moments to determine that it is functioning normally, and replace the sender.	—
	If the pressure remains low:	12.2
	If the pressure surges:	12.3
	If the oil pressure is zero:	12.3

Test and Procedure	*Results and Indications*	*Proceed to*
12.2—Visually inspect the oil: If the oil is watery or very thin, milky, or foamy, replace the oil and oil filter.	If the oil is normal:	12.3
	If after replacing oil the pressure remains low:	12.3
	If after replacing oil the pressure becomes normal:	—
12.3—Inspect the oil pressure relief valve and spring, to ensure that it is not sticking or stuck. Remove and thoroughly clean the valve, spring, and the valve body. 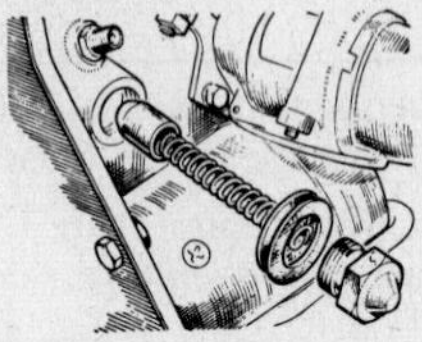 **Oil pressure relief valve** (© British Leyland Motors)	If the oil pressure improves:	—
	If no improvement is noted:	12.4
12.4—Check to ensure that the oil pump is not cavitating (sucking air instead of oil): See that the crankcase is neither over nor underfull, and that the pickup in the sump is in the proper position and free from sludge.	Fill or drain the crankcase to the proper capacity, and clean the pickup screen in solvent if necessary. If no improvement is noted:	12.5
12.5—Inspect the oil pump drive and the oil pump:	If the pump drive or the oil pump appear to be defective, service as necessary and retest per 12.1:	12.1
	If the pump drive and pump appear to be operating normally, the engine should be disassembled to determine where blockage exists:	Next Chapter
12.6—Purge the engine of ethylene glycol coolant: Completely drain the crankcase and the oil filter. Obtain a commercial butyl cellosolve base solvent, designated for this purpose, and follow the instructions precisely. Following this, install a new oil filter and refill the crankcase with the proper weight oil. The next oil and filter change should follow shortly thereafter (1000 miles).		

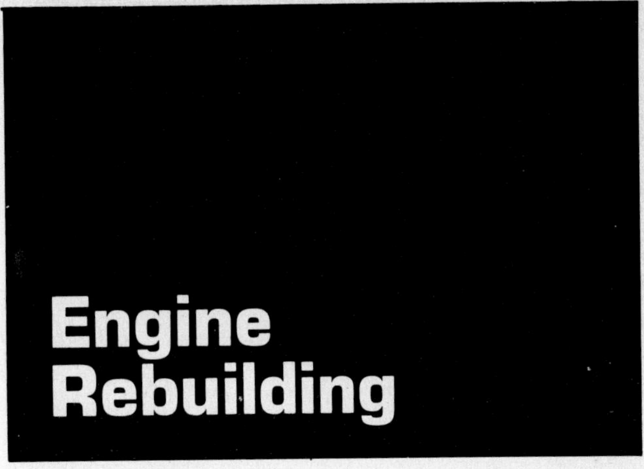

Engine Rebuilding

This chapter describes, in detail, the procedures involved in rebuilding a typical engine. The procedures specifically refer to an inline engine, however, they are basically identical to those used in rebuilding engines of nearly all design and configurations. Procedures for servicing atypical engines (i.e., horizontally opposed) are described in the individual car sections, although in most cases, cylinder head reconditioning procedures described in this chapter will apply.

The chapter is divided into two sections. The first, Cylinder Head Reconditioning, assumes that the cylinder head is removed from the engine, all manifolds are removed, and the cylinder head is on a workbench. The camshaft should be removed from overhead cam cylinder heads. The second section, Cylinder Block Reconditioning, covers the block, pistons, connecting rods and crankshaft. It is assumed that the engine is mounted on a work stand, and the cylinder head and all accessories are removed.

Procedures are identified as follows:

Unmarked—Basic procedures that must be performed in order to successfully complete the rebuilding process.

Starred (*)—Procedures that should be performed to ensure maximum performance and engine life.

Double starred (**)—Procedures that may be performed to increase engine performance and reliability. These procedures are usually reserved for extremely heavy-duty or competition usage.

In many cases, a choice of methods is also provided. Methods are identified in the same manner as procedures. The choice of method for a procedure is at the discretion of the user.

The tools required for the basic rebuilding procedure should, with minor exceptions, be those

TORQUE (ft. lbs.)*

U.S.

Bolt Diameter (inches)	Bolt Grade (SAE) 1 and 2	5	6	8	Wrench Size (inches) Bolt	Nut
1/4	5	7	10	10.5	3/8	7/16
5/16	9	14	19	22	1/2	9/16
3/8	15	25	34	37	9/16	5/8
7/16	24	40	55	60	5/8	3/4
1/2	37	60	85	92	3/4	13/16
9/16	53	88	120	132	7/8	7/8
5/8	74	120	167	180	15/16	1
3/4	120	200	280	296	1-1/8	1-1/8
7/8	190	302	440	473	1-5/16	1-5/16
1	282	466	660	714	1-1/2	1-1/2

Metric

Bolt Diameter (mm)	Bolt Grade 5D	8G	10K	12K	Wrench Size (mm) Bolt and Nut
6	5	6	8	10	10
8	10	16	22	27	14
10	19	31	40	49	17
12	34	54	70	86	19
14	55	89	117	137	22
16	83	132	175	208	24
18	111	182	236	283	27
22	182	284	394	464	32
24	261	419	570	689	36

*—Torque values are for lightly oiled bolts. CAUTION: Bolts threaded into aluminum require much less torque.

General Torque Specifications

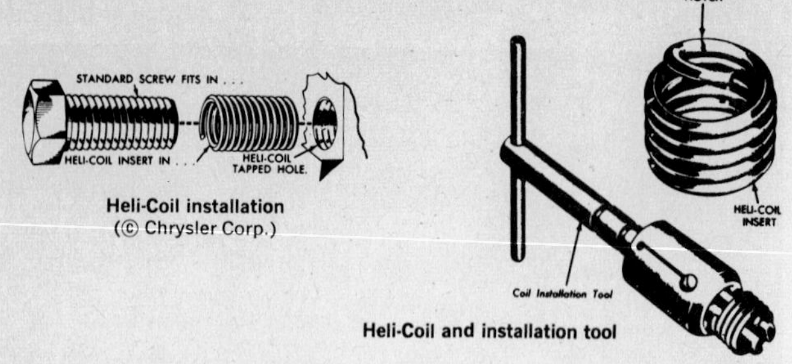

Heli-Coil installation
(© Chrysler Corp.)

Heli-Coil and installation tool

Heli-Coil Insert			*Drill*	*Tap*	*Insert. Tool*	*Extracting Tool*
Thread Size	*Part No.*	*Insert Length (In.)*	*Size*	*Part No.*	*Part No.*	*Part No.*
1/2 -20	1185-4	3/8	17/64(.266)	4 CPB	528-4N	1227-6
5/16-18	1185-5	15/32	Q(.332)	5 CPB	528-5N	1227-6
3/8 -16	1185-6	9/16	X(.397)	6 CPB	528-6N	1227-6
7/16-14	1185-7	21/32	29/64(.453)	7 CPB	528-7N	1227-16
1/2 -13	1185-8	3/4	33/64(.516)	8 CPB	528-8N	1227-16

Heli-Coil Specifications

included in a mechanic's tool kit. An accurate torque wrench, and a dial indicator (reading in thousandths) mounted on a universal base should be available. Bolts and nuts with no torque specification should be tightened according to size (see chart). Special tools, where required, all are readily available from the major tool suppliers (i.e., Craftsman, Snap-On, K-D). The services of a competent automotive machine shop must also be readily available.

When assembling the engine, any parts that will be in frictional contact must be pre-lubricated, to provide protection on initial start-up. Vortex Pre-Lube, STP, or any product specifically formulated for this purpose may be used. NOTE: *Do not use engine oil.* Where semi-permanent (locked but removable) installation of bolts or nuts is desired, threads should be cleaned and coated with Loctite. Studs may be permanently installed using Loctite Stud and Bearing Mount.

Aluminum has become increasingly popular for use in engines, due to its low weight and excellent heat transfer characteristics. The following precautions must be observed when handling aluminum engine parts:

—Never hot-tank aluminum parts.

—Remove all aluminum parts (identification tags, etc.) from engine parts before hot-tanking (otherwise they will be removed during the process).

—Always coat threads lightly with engine oil or anti-seize compounds before installation, to prevent seizure.

—Never over-torque bolts or spark plugs in aluminum threads. Should stripping occur, threads can be restored according to the following procedure, using Heli-Coil thread inserts:

Tap drill the hole with the stripped threads to the specified size (see chart). Using the specified tap (NOTE: *Heli-Coil tap sizes refer to the size thread being replaced, rather than the actual tap size*), tap the hole for the Heli-Coil. Place the insert on the proper installation tool (see chart). Apply pressure on the insert while winding it clockwise into the hole, until the top of the insert is one turn below the surface. Remove the installation tool, and break the installation tang from the bottom of the insert by moving it up and down. If the Heli-Coil must be removed, tap the removal tool firmly into the hole, so that it engages the top thread, and turn the tool counter-clockwise to extract the insert.

Snapped bolts or studs may be removed, using a stud extractor (unthreaded) or Vise-Grip pliers (threaded). Penetrating oil (e.g., Liquid Wrench) will often aid in breaking frozen threads. In cases where the stud or bolt is flush with, or below the surface, proceed as follows:

Drill a hole in the broken stud or bolt, approximately ½ its diameter. Select a screw extractor (e.g., Easy-Out) of the proper size, and tap it into the stud or bolt. Turn the extractor counter-clockwise to remove the stud or bolt.

Magnaflux and Zyglo are inspection techniques used to locate material flaws, such as stress cracks. Magnafluxing coats the part with fine magnetic particles, and subjects the part to a magnetic field. Cracks cause breaks

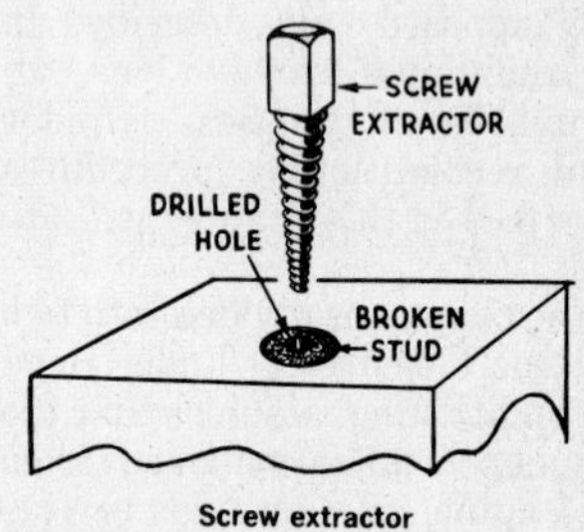

Screw extractor

in the magnetic field, which are outlined by the particles. Since Magnaflux is a magnetic process, it is applicable only to ferrous materials. The Zyglo process coats the material with a fluorescent dye penetrant, and then subjects it to blacklight inspection, under which cracks glow bright-

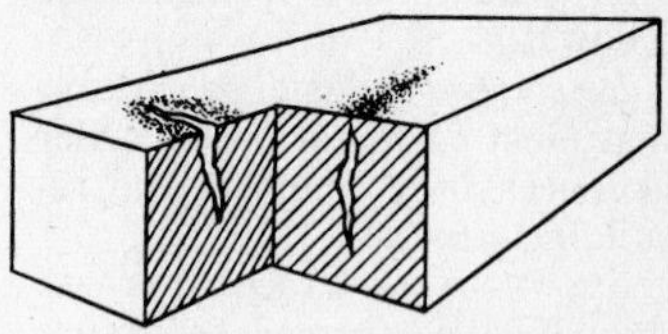

Magnaflux indication of cracks

ly. Parts made of any material may be tested using Zyglo. While Magnaflux and Zyglo are excellent for general inspection, and locating hidden defects, specific checks of suspected cracks may be made at lower cost and more readily using spot check dye. The dye is sprayed onto the suspected area, wiped off, and the area is then sprayed with a developer. Cracks then will show up brightly. Spot check dyes will only indicate surface cracks; therefore, structural cracks below the surface may escape detection. When questionable, the part should be tested using Magnaflux or Zyglo.

CYLINDER HEAD RECONDITIONING

Procedure	*Method*
Identify the valves: 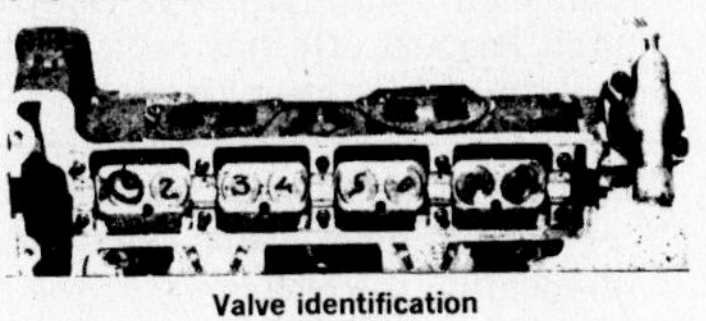 Valve identification (© SAAB)	Invert the cylinder head, and number the valve faces front to rear, using a permanent felt-tip marker.
Remove the rocker arms:	Remove the rocker arms with shaft(s) or balls and nuts. Wire the sets of rockers, balls and nuts together, and identify according to the corresponding valve.
Remove the valves and springs:	Using an appropriate valve spring compressor (depending on the configuration of the cylinder head), compress the valve springs. Lift out the keepers with needlenose pliers, release the compressor, and remove the valve, spring, and spring retainer.
Check the valve stem-to-guide clearance:  Checking the valve stem-to-guide clearance (© American Motors Corp.)	Clean the valve stem with lacquer thinner or a similar solvent to remove all gum and varnish. Clean the valve guides using solvent and an expanding wire-type valve guide cleaner. Mount a dial indicator so that the stem is at 90 to the valve stem, as close to the valve guide as possible. Move the valve off its seat, and measure the valve guide-to-stem clearance by moving the stem back and forth to actuate the dial indicator. Measure the valve stems using a micrometer, and compare to specifications, to determine whether stem or guide wear is responsible for excessive clearance.
De-carbon the cylinder head and valves: 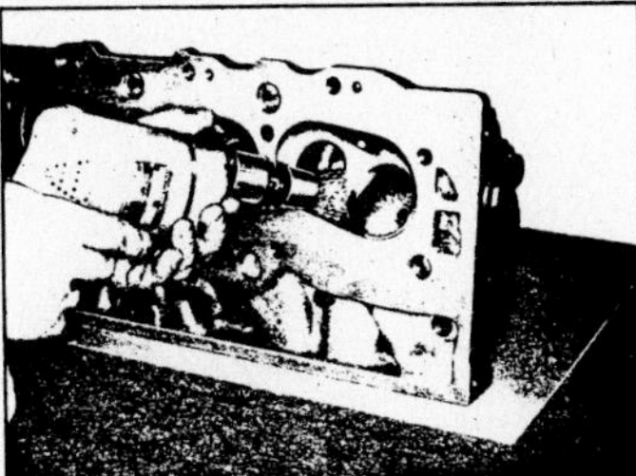 Removing carbon from the cylinder head (© Chevrolet Div. G.M. Corp.)	Chip carbon away from the valve heads, combustion chambers, and ports, using a chisel made of hardwood. Remove the remaining deposits with a stiff wire brush. NOTE: *Ensure that the deposits are actually removed, rather than burnished.*

Procedure	*Method*
Hot-tank the cylinder head:	Have the cylinder head hot-tanked to remove grease, corrosion, and scale from the water passages. NOTE: *In the case of overhead cam cylinder heads, consult the operator to determine whether the camshaft bearings will be damaged by the caustic solution.*
Degrease the remaining cylinder head parts:	Using solvent (i.e., Gunk), clean the rockers, rocker shaft(s) (where applicable), rocker balls and nuts, springs, spring retainers, and keepers. Do not remove the protective coating from the springs.
Check the cylinder head for warpage: 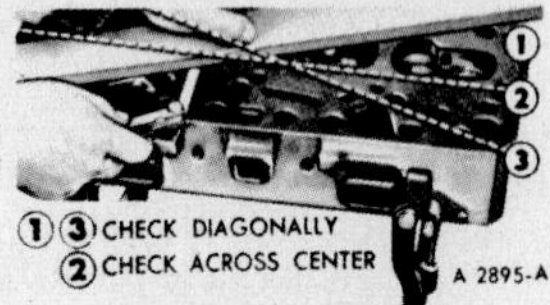 **Checking the cylinder head for warpage** (© Ford Motor Co.)	Place a straight-edge across the gasket surface of the cylinder head. Using feeler gauges, determine the clearance at the center of the straight-edge. Measure across both diagonals, along the longitudinal centerline, and across the cylinder head at several points. If warpage exceeds .003″ in a 6″ span, or .006″ over the total length, the cylinder head must be resurfaced. NOTE: *If warpage exceeds the manufacturers maximum tolerance for material removal, the cylinder head must be replaced.* When milling the cylinder heads of V-type engines, the intake manifold mounting position is altered, and must be corrected by milling the manifold flange a proportionate amount.
** Porting and gasket matching: 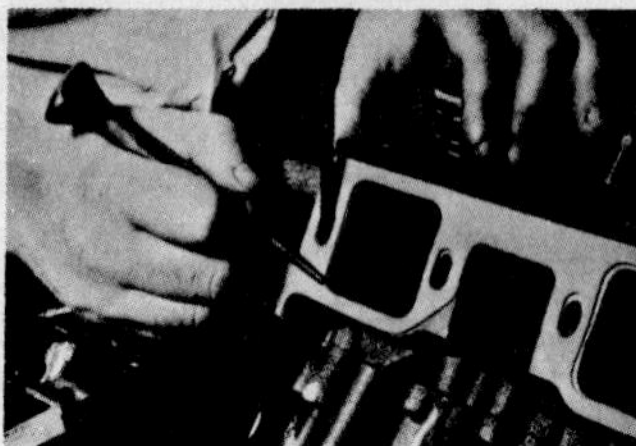 **Marking the cylinder head for gasket matching** (© Petersen Publishing Co.)  **Port configuration before and after gasket matching** (© Petersen Publishing Co.)	** Coat the manifold flanges of the cylinder head with Prussian blue dye. Glue intake and exhaust gaskets to the cylinder head in their installed position using rubber cement and scribe the outline of the ports on the manifold flanges. Remove the gaskets. Using a small cutter in a hand-held power tool (i.e., Dremel Moto-Tool), gradually taper the walls of the port out to the scribed outline of the gasket. Further enlargement of the ports should include the removal of sharp edges and radiusing of sharp corners. Do not alter the valve guides. NOTE: *The most efficient port configuration is determined only by extensive testing. Therefore, it is best to consult someone experienced with the head in question to determine the optimum alterations.* 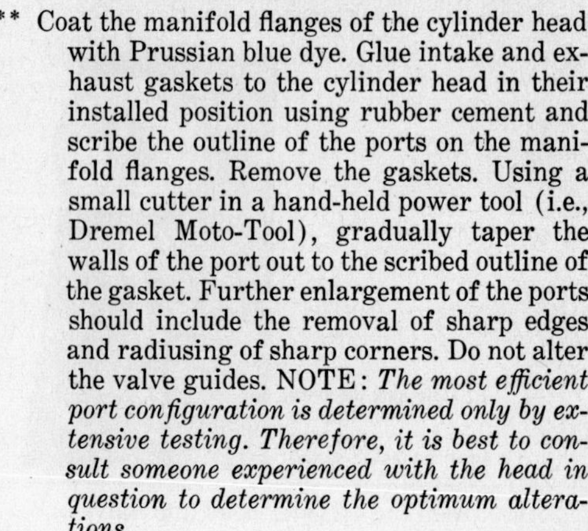

Procedure	*Method*
** Polish the ports:	** Using a grinding stone with the above mentioned tool, polish the walls of the intake and exhaust ports, and combustion chamber. Use progressively finer stones until all surface imperfections are removed. NOTE: *Through testing, it has been determined that a smooth surface is more effective than a mirror polished surface in intake ports, and vice-versa in exhaust ports.*

Relieved and polished ports
(© Petersen Publishing Co.)

Polished combustion chamber
(© Petersen Publishing Co.)

* Knurling the valve guides:	* Valve guides which are not excessively worn or distorted may, in some cases, be knurled rather than replaced. Knurling is a process in which metal is displaced and raised, thereby reducing clearance. Knurling also provides excellent oil control. The possibility of knurling rather than replacing valve guides should be discussed with a machinist.

Cut-away view of a knurled valve guide
(© Petersen Publishing Co.)

Replacing the valve guides: NOTE: *Valve guides should only be replaced if damaged or if an oversize valve stem is not available.*	Depending on the type of cylinder head, valve guides may be pressed, hammered, or shrunk in. In cases where the guides are shrunk into the head, replacement should be left to an equipped machine shop. In other cases, the guides are replaced as follows: Press or tap the valve guides out of the head using a stepped drift (see illustration). Determine the height above the boss that the guide must extend, and obtain a stack of washers, their I.D. similar to the guide's O.D., of that height. Place the stack of washers on the guide, and insert the guide into the boss. NOTE: *Valve guides are often tapered or beveled for installation.* Using the stepped installation tool (see illustration), press or tap the guides into position. Ream the guides according to the size of the valve stem.

B
A
A-VALVE GUIDE I.D.
B-SLIGHTLY SMALLER THAN VALVE GUIDE O.D.

Valve guide removal tool

WASHERS
B
A
A-VALVE GUIDE I.D.
B-LARGER THAN THE VALVE GUIDE O.D.

Valve guide installation tool (with washers used during installation)

Procedure	*Method*
Replacing valve seat inserts:	Replacement of valve seat inserts which are worn beyond resurfacing or broken, if feasible, must be done by a machine shop.
Resurfacing (grinding) the valve face:	Using a valve grinder, resurface the valves according to specifications. CAUTION: *Valve face angle is not always identical to valve seat angle.* A minimum margin of 1/32″ should remain after grinding the valve. The valve stem tip should also be squared and resurfaced, by placing the stem in the V-block of the grinder, and turning it while pressing lightly against the grinding wheel.

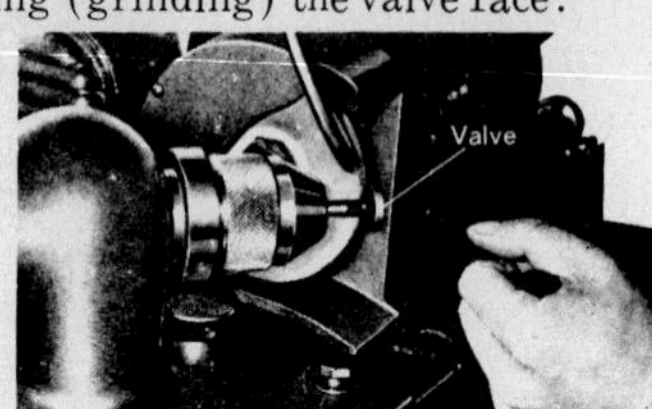

Grinding a valve (© Subaru)

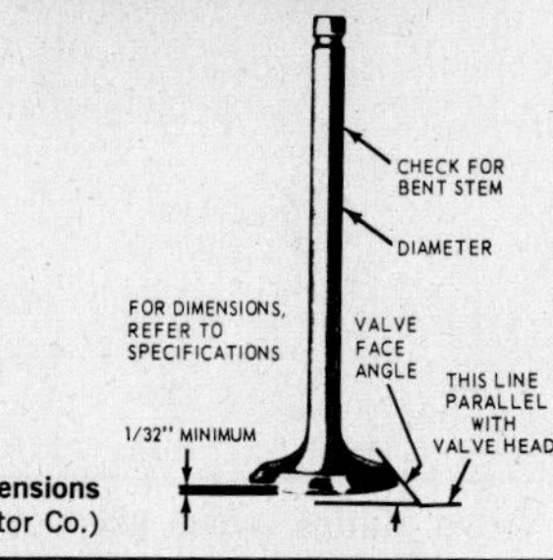

Critical valve dimensions (© Ford Motor Co.)

Procedure	*Method*
Resurfacing the valve seats using reamers:	Select a reamer of the correct seat angle, slightly larger than the diameter of the valve seat, and assemble it with a pilot of the correct size. Install the pilot into the valve guide, and using steady pressure, turn the reamer clockwise. CAUTION: *Do not turn the reamer counter-clockwise.* Remove only as much material as necessary to clean the seat. Check the concentricity of the seat (see below). If the dye method is not used, coat the valve face with Prussian blue dye, install and rotate it on the valve seat. Using the dye marked area as a centering guide, center and narrow the valve seat to specifications with correction cutters. NOTE: *When no specifications are available, minimum seat width for exhaust valves should be 5/64″, intake valves 1/16″.* After making correction cuts, check the position of the valve seat on the valve face using Prussian blue dye.

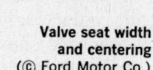

Reaming the valve seat (© S.p.A. Fiat)

Valve seat width and centering (© Ford Motor Co.)

Procedure	*Method*
* Resurfacing the valve seats using a grinder:	Select a pilot of the correct size, and a coarse stone of the correct seat angle. Lubricate the pilot if necessary, and install the tool in the valve guide. Move the stone on and off the seat at approximately two cycles per second, until all flaws are removed from the seat. Install a fine stone, and finish the seat. Center and narrow the seat using correction stones, as described above.

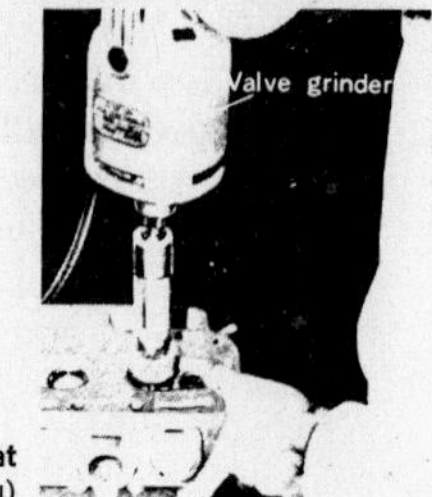

Grinding a valve seat (© Subaru)

Procedure	Method
Checking the valve seat concentricity:	Coat the valve face with Prussian blue dye, install the valve, and rotate it on the valve seat. If the entire seat becomes coated, and the valve is known to be concentric, the seat is concentric.
	* Install the dial gauge pilot into the guide, and rest the arm on the valve seat. Zero the gauge, and rotate the arm around the seat. Run-out should not exceed .002″.

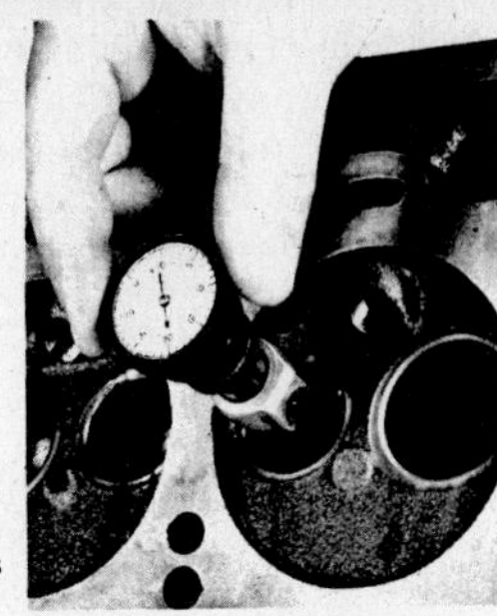

Checking the valve seat concentricity using a dial gauge (© American Motors Corp.)

Procedure	Method
* Lapping the valves: NOTE: *Valve lapping is done to ensure efficient sealing of resurfaced valves and seats. Valve lapping alone is not recommended for use as a resurfacing procedure.*	* Invert the cylinder head, lightly lubricate the valve stems, and install the valves in the head as numbered. Coat valve seats with fine grinding compound, and attach the lapping tool suction cup to a valve head (NOTE: *Moisten the suction cup*). Rotate the tool between the palms, changing position and lifting the tool often to prevent grooving. Lap the valve until a smooth, polished seat is evident. Remove the valve and tool, and rinse away all traces of grinding compound.
	** Fasten a suction cup to a piece of drill rod, and mount the rod in a hand drill. Proceed as above, using the hand drill as a lapping tool. CAUTION: *Due to the higher speeds involved when using the hand drill, care must be exercised to avoid grooving the seat.* Lift the tool and change direction of rotation often.

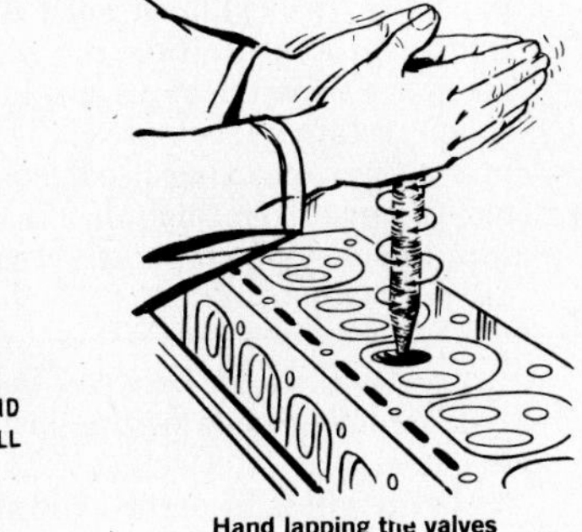

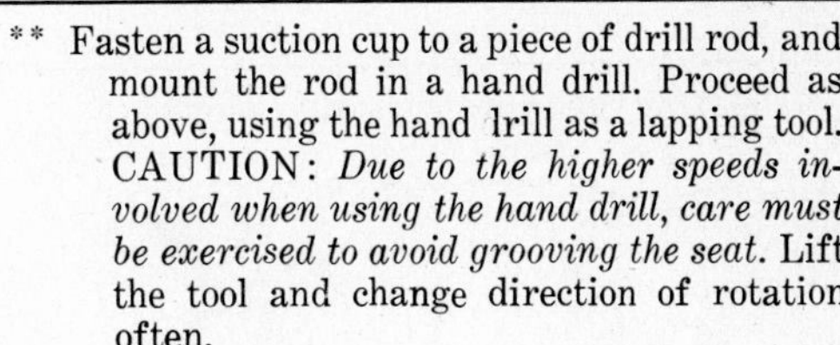

Hand lapping the valves

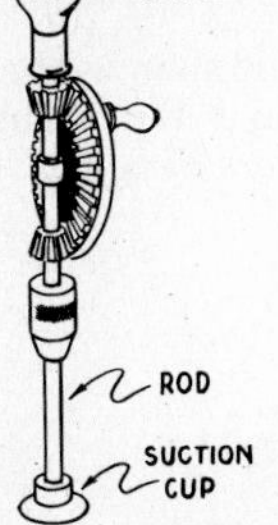

Home made mechanical valve lapping tool

Procedure	Method
Check the valve springs:	Place the spring on a flat surface next to a square. Measure the height of the spring, and rotate it against the edge of the square to measure distortion. If spring height varies (by comparison) by more than 1/16″ or if distortion exceeds 1/16″, replace the spring.
	** In addition to evaluating the spring as above, test the spring pressure at the installed and compressed (installed height minus valve lift) height using a valve spring tester. Springs used on small displacement engines (up to 3 liters) should be ± 1 lb. of all other springs in either position. A tolerance of ± 5 lbs. is permissible on larger engines.

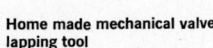

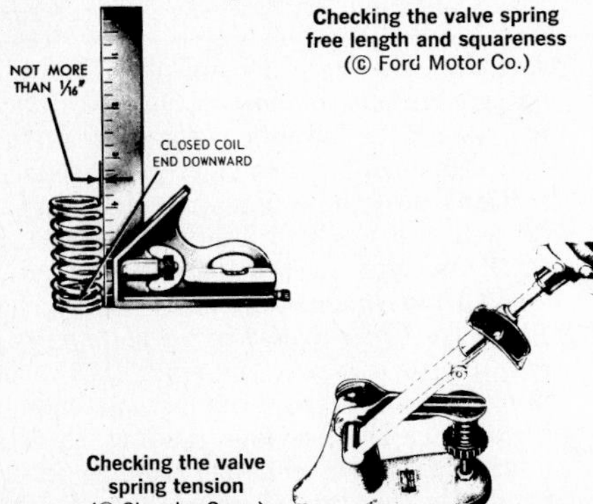

Checking the valve spring free length and squareness (© Ford Motor Co.)

Checking the valve spring tension (© Chrysler Corp.)

Procedure	*Method*
* Install valve stem seals:  **Valve stem seal installation** (© Ford Motor Co.)	* Due to the pressure differential that exists at the ends of the intake valve guides (atmospheric pressure above, manifold vacuum below), oil is drawn through the valve guides into the intake port. This has been alleviated somewhat since the addition of positive crankcase ventilation, which lowers the pressure above the guides. Several types of valve stem seals are available to reduce blow-by. Certain seals simply slip over the stem and guide boss, while others require that the boss be machined. Recently, Teflon guide seals have become popular. Consult a parts supplier or machinist concerning availability and suggested usages. NOTE: *When installing seals, ensure that a small amount of oil is able to pass the seal to lubricate the valve guides; otherwise, excessive wear may result.*
Install the valves:	Lubricate the valve stems, and install the valves in the cylinder head as numbered. Lubricate and position the seals (if used, see above) and the valve springs. Install the spring retainers, compress the springs, and insert the keys using needlenose pliers or a tool designed for this purpose. NOTE: *Retain the keys with wheel bearing grease during installation.*
Checking valve spring installed height: 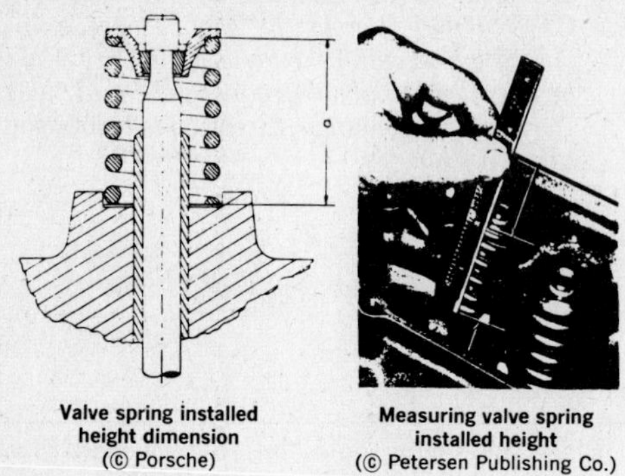 **Valve spring installed height dimension** (© Porsche) **Measuring valve spring installed height** (© Petersen Publishing Co.)	Measure the distance between the spring pad and the lower edge of the spring retainer, and compare to specifications. If the installed height is incorrect, add shim washers between the spring pad and the spring. CAUTION: *Use only washers designed for this purpose.*
** CC'ing the combustion chambers:	** Invert the cylinder head and place a bead of sealer around a combustion chamber. Install an apparatus designed for this purpose (burette mounted on a clear plate; see illustration) over the combustion chamber, and fill with the specified fluid to an even mark on the burette. Record the burette reading, and fill the combustion chamber with fluid. (NOTE: *A hole drilled in the plate will permit air to escape*). Subtract the burette reading, with the combustion chamber filled, from the previous reading, to determine combustion chamber volume in cc's. Duplicate this procedure in all combustion

Procedure	*Method*
 CC'ing the combustion chamber (© Petersen Publishing Co.)	chambers on the cylinder head, and compare the readings. The volume of all combustion chambers should be made equal to that of the largest. Combustion chamber volume may be increased in two ways. When only a small change is required (usually), a small cutter or coarse stone may be used to remove material from the combustion chamber. NOTE: *Check volume frequently.* Remove material over a wide area, so as not to change the configuration of the combustion chamber. When a larger change is required, the valve seat may be sunk (lowered into the head). NOTE: *When altering valve seat, remember to compensate for the change in spring installed height.*
Inspect the rocker arms, balls, studs, and nuts (where applicable):  Stress cracks in rocker nuts (© Ford Motor Co.)	Visually inspect the rocker arms, balls, studs, and nuts for cracks, galling, burning, scoring, or wear. If all parts are intact, liberally lubricate the rocker arms and balls, and install them on the cylinder head. If wear is noted on a rocker arm at the point of valve contact, grind it smooth and square, removing as little material as possible. Replace the rocker arm if excessively worn. If a rocker stud shows signs of wear, it must be replaced (see below). If a rocker nut shows stress cracks, replace it. If an exhaust ball is galled or burned, substitute the intake ball from the same cylinder (if it is intact), and install a new intake ball. NOTE: *Avoid using new rocker balls on exhaust valves.*
Replacing rocker studs:  Reaming the stud bore for oversize rocker studs (© Buick Div. G.M. Corp.)  Extracting a pressed in rocker stud (© Buick Div. G.M. Corp.)	In order to remove a threaded stud, lock two nuts on the stud, and unscrew the stud using the lower nut. Coat the lower threads of the new stud with Loctite, and install. Two alternative methods are available for replacing pressed in studs. Remove the damaged stud using a stack of washers and a nut (see illustration). In the first, the boss is reamed .005-.006″ oversize, and an oversize stud pressed in. Control the stud extension over the boss using washers, in the same manner as valve guides. Before installing the stud, coat it with white lead and grease. To retain the stud more positively, drill a hole through the stud and boss, and install a roll pin. In the second method, the boss is tapped, and a threaded stud installed. Retain the stud using Loctite Stud and Bearing Mount.

Procedure	*Method*
Inspect the rocker shaft(s) and rocker arms (where applicable): Disassembled rocker shaft parts arranged for inspection (© American Motors Corp.) 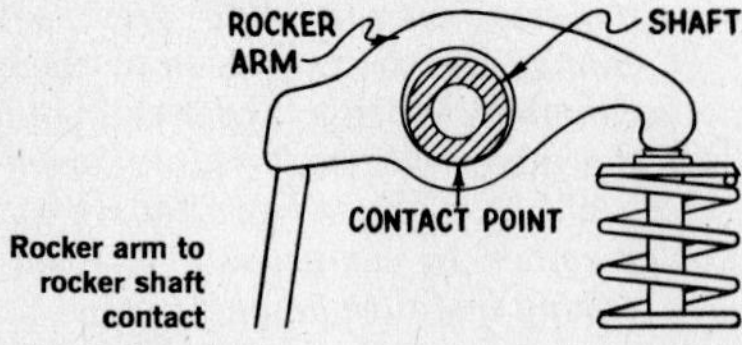 Rocker arm to rocker shaft contact	Remove rocker arms, springs and washers from rocker shaft. NOTE: *Lay out parts in the order they are removed.* Inspect rocker arms for pitting or wear on the valve contact point, or excessive bushing wear. Bushings need only be replaced if wear is excessive, because the rocker arm normally contacts the shaft at one point only. Grind the valve contact point of rocker arm smooth if necessary, removing as little material as possible. If excessive material must be removed to smooth and square the arm, it should be replaced. Clean out all oil holes and passages in rocker shaft. If shaft is grooved or worn, replace it. Lubricate and assemble the rocker shaft.
Inspect the camshaft bushings and the camshaft (overhead cam engines):	See next section.
Inspect the pushrods:	Remove the pushrods, and, if hollow, clean out the oil passages using fine wire. Roll each pushrod over a piece of clean glass. If a distinct clicking sound is heard as the pushrod rolls, the rod is bent, and must be replaced. * The length of all pushrods must be equal. Measure the length of the pushrods, compare to specifications, and replace as necessary.
Inspect the valve lifters:  Checking the lifter face (© American Motors Corp.)	Remove lifters from their bores, and remove gum and varnish, using solvent. Clean walls of lifter bores. Check lifters for concave wear as illustrated. If face is worn concave, replace lifter, and carefully inspect the camshaft. Lightly lubricate lifter and insert it into its bore. If play is excessive, an oversize lifter must be installed (where possible). Consult a machinist concerning feasibility. If play is satisfactory, remove, lubricate, and reinstall the lifter.
* Testing hydraulic lifter leak down: 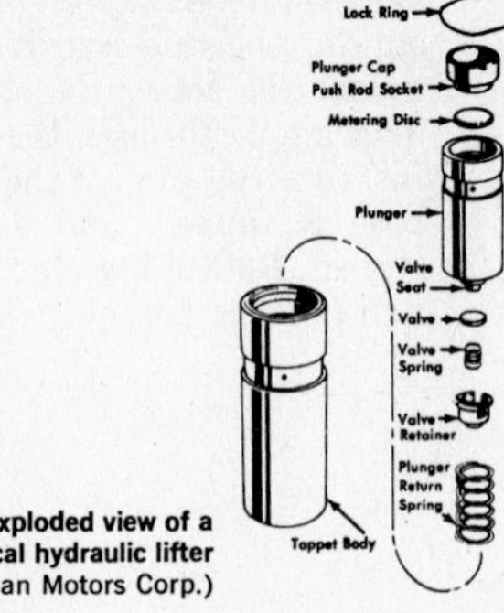 Exploded view of a typical hydraulic lifter (© American Motors Corp.)	Submerge lifter in a container of kerosene. Chuck a used pushrod or its equivalent into a drill press. Position container of kerosene so pushrod acts on the lifter plunger. Pump lifter with the drill press, until resistance increases. Pump several more times to bleed any air out of lifter. Apply very firm, constant pressure to the lifter, and observe rate at which fluid bleeds out of lifter. If the fluid bleeds very quickly (less than 15 seconds), lifter is defective. If the time exceeds 60 seconds, lifter is sticking. In either case, recondition or replace lifter. If lifter is operating properly (leak down time 15-60 seconds), lubricate and install it.

CYLINDER BLOCK RECONDITIONING

Procedure	*Method*

Checking the main bearing clearance:

Plastigage installed on main bearing journal
(© Chevrolet Div. G.M. Corp.)

Measuring Plastigage to determine main bearing clearance
(© Chevrolet Div. G.M. Corp.)

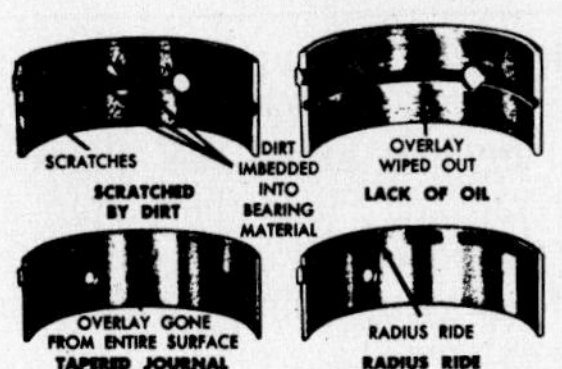

Causes of bearing failure
(© Ford Motor Co.)

Invert engine, and remove cap from the bearing to be checked. Using a clean, dry rag, thoroughly clean all oil from crankshaft journal and bearing insert. NOTE: *Plastigage is soluble in oil; therefore, oil on the journal or bearing could result in erroneous readings.* Place a piece of Plastigage along the full length of journal, reinstall cap, and torque to specifications. Remove bearing cap, and determine bearing clearance by comparing width of Plastigage to the scale on Plastigage envelope. Journal taper is determined by comparing width of the Plastigage strip near its ends. Rotate crankshaft 90° and retest, to determine journal eccentricity. NOTE: *Do not rotate crankshaft with Plastigage installed.* If bearing insert and journal appear intact, and are within tolerances, no further main bearing service is required. If bearing or journal appear defective, cause of failure should be determined before replacement.

* Remove crankshaft from block (see below). Measure the main bearing journals at each end twice (90° apart) using a micrometer, to determine diameter, journal taper and eccentricity. If journals are within tolerances, reinstall bearing caps at their specified torque. Using a telescope gauge and micrometer, measure bearing I.D. parallel to piston axis and at 30° on each side of piston axis. Subtract journal O.D. from bearing I.D. to determine oil clearance. If crankshaft journals appear defective, or do not meet tolerances, there is no need to measure bearings; for the crankshaft will require grinding and/or undersize bearings will be required. If bearing appears defective, cause for failure should be determined prior to replacement.

Checking the connecting rod bearing clearance:

Plastigage installed on connecting rod bearing journal
(© Chevrolet Div. G.M. Corp.)

Connecting rod bearing clearance is checked in the same manner as main bearing clearance, using Plastigage. Before removing the crankshaft, connecting rod side clearance also should be measured and recorded.

* Checking connecting rod bearing clearance, using a micrometer, is identical to checking main bearing clearance. If no other service

Procedure	*Method*

Measuring Plastigage to determine connecting rod bearing clearance (© Chevrolet Div. G.M. Corp.)

is required, the piston and rod assemblies need not be removed.

Removing the crankshaft:

Connecting rod matching marks (© Ford Motor Co.)

Using a punch, mark the corresponding main bearing caps and saddles according to position (i.e., one punch on the front main cap and saddle, two on the second, three on the third, etc.). Using number stamps, identify the corresponding connecting rods and caps, according to cylinder (if no numbers are present). Remove the main and connecting rod caps, and place sleeves of plastic tubing over the connecting rod bolts, to protect the journals as the crankshaft is removed. Lift the crankshaft out of the block.

Remove the ridge from the top of the cylinder:

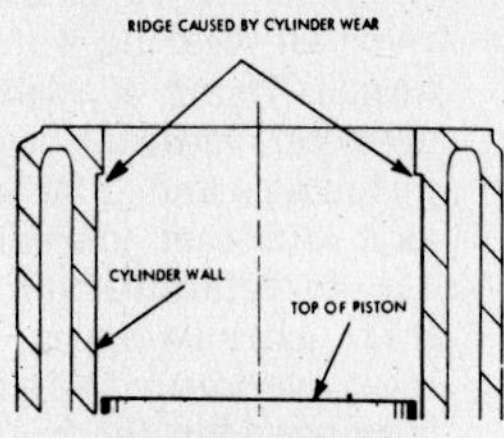

Cylinder bore ridge (© Pontiac Div. G.M. Corp.)

In order to facilitate removal of the piston and connecting rod, the ridge at the top of the cylinder (unworn area; see illustration) must be removed. Place the piston at the bottom of the bore, and cover it with a rag. Cut the ridge away using a ridge reamer, exercising extreme care to avoid cutting too deeply. Remove the rag, and remove cuttings that remain on the piston. CAUTION: *If the ridge is not removed, and new rings are installed, damage to rings will result.*

Removing the piston and connecting rod:

Removing the piston (© SAAB)

Invert the engine, and push the pistons and connecting rods out of the cylinders. If necessary, tap the connecting rod boss with a wooden hammer handle, to force the piston out. CAUTION: *Do not attempt to force the piston past the cylinder ridge* (see above).

Procedure	*Method*
Service the crankshaft:	Ensure that all oil holes and passages in the crankshaft are open and free of sludge. If necessary, have the crankshaft ground to the largest possible undersize.
	** Have the crankshaft Magnafluxed, to locate stress cracks. Consult a machinist concerning additional service procedures, such as surface hardening (e.g., nitriding, Tuftriding) to improve wear characteristics, cross drilling and chamfering the oil holes to improve lubrication, and balancing.
Removing freeze plugs:	Drill a hole in the center of the freeze plugs, and pry them out using a screwdriver or drift.
Remove the oil gallery plugs:	Threaded plugs should be removed using an appropriate (usually square) wrench. To remove soft, pressed in plugs, drill a hole in the plug, and thread in a sheet metal screw. Pull the plug out by the screw using pliers.
Hot-tank the block:	Have the block hot-tanked to remove grease, corrosion, and scale from the water jackets. NOTE: *Consult the operator to determine whether the camshaft bearings will be damaged during the hot-tank process.*
Check the block for cracks:	Visually inspect the block for cracks or chips. The most common locations are as follows: Adjacent to freeze plugs. Between the cylinders and water jackets. Adjacent to the main bearing saddles. At the extreme bottom of the cylinders. Check only suspected cracks using spot check dye (see introduction). If a crack is located, consult a machinist concerning possible repairs.
	** Magnaflux the block to locate hidden cracks. If cracks are located, consult a machinist about feasibility of repair.
Install the oil gallery plugs and freeze plugs:	Coat freeze plugs with sealer and tap into position using a piece of pipe, slightly smaller than the plug, as a driver. To ensure retention, stake the edges of the plugs. Coat threaded oil gallery plugs with sealer and install. Drive replacement soft plugs into block using a large drift as a driver.
	* Rather than reinstalling lead plugs, drill and tap the holes, and install threaded plugs.

Procedure	*Method*
Check the bore diameter and surface:	Visually inspect the cylinder bores for roughness, scoring, or scuffing. If evident, the cylinder bore must be bored or honed oversize to eliminate imperfections, and the smallest possible oversize piston used. The new pistons should be given to the machinist with the block, so that the cylinders can be bored or honed exactly to the piston size (plus clearance). If no flaws are evident, measure the bore diameter using a telescope gauge and micrometer, or dial gauge, parallel and perpendicular to the engine centerline, at the top (below the ridge) and bottom of the bore. Subtract the bottom measurements from the top to determine taper, and the parallel to the centerline measurements from the perpendicular measurements to determine eccentricity. If the measurements are not within specifications, the cylinder must be bored or honed, and an oversize piston installed. If the measurements are within specifications the cylinder may be used as is, with only finish honing (see below). NOTE: *Prior to submitting the block for boring, perform the following operation(s).*

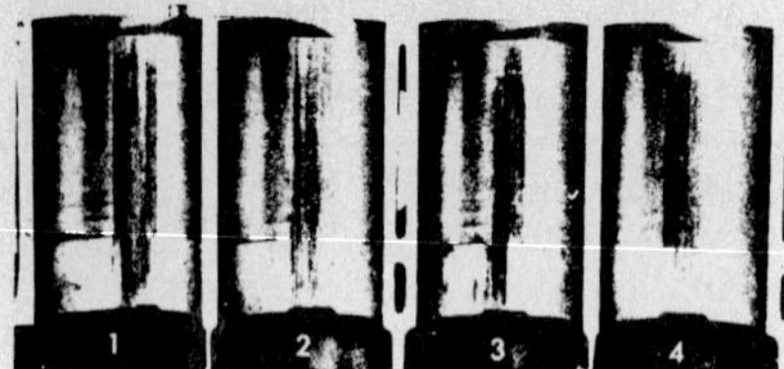

1, 2, 3 Piston skirt seizure resulted in this pattern. Engine must be rebored

4. Piston skirt and oil ring seizure caused this damage. Engine must be rebored

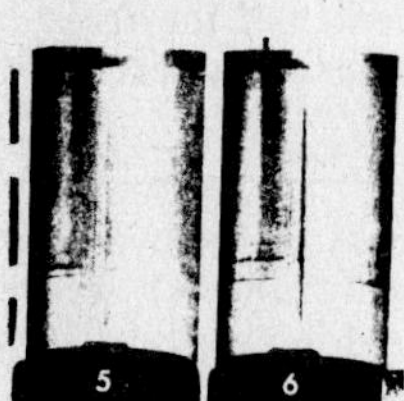

5, 6 Score marks caused by a split piston skirt. Damage is not serious enough to warrant reboring

7. Ring seized longitudinally, causing a score mark 1 3/16" wide, on the land side of the piston groove. The honing pattern is destroyed and the cylinder must be rebored

8. Result of oil ring seizure. Engine must be rebored

9. Oil ring seizure here was not serious enough to warrant reboring. The honing marks are still visible

Cylinder wall damage
(© Daimler-Benz A.G.)

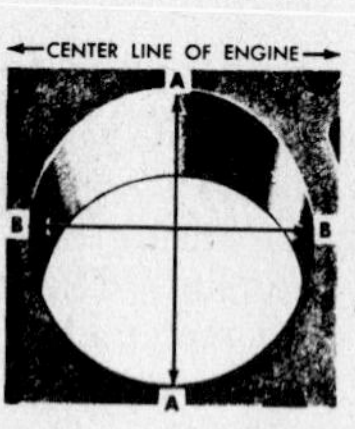

Cylinder bore measuring positions
(© Ford Motor Co.)

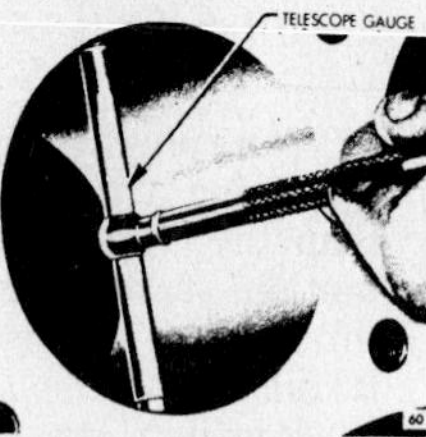

Measuring the cylinder bore with a telescope gauge
(© Buick Div. G.M. Corp.)

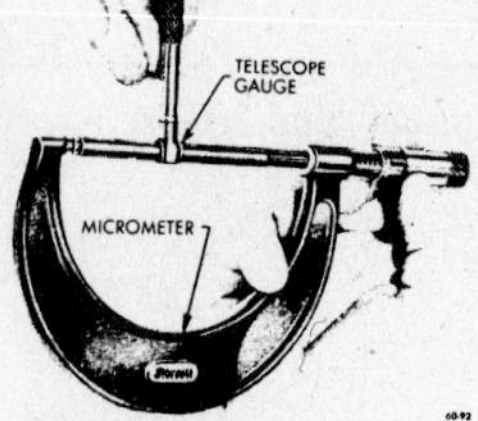

Determining the cylinder bore by measuring the telescope gauge with a micrometer
(© Buick Div. G.M. Corp.)

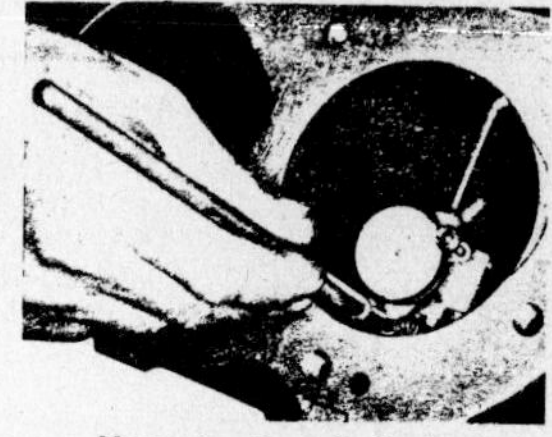

Measuring the cylinder bore with a dial gauge
(© Chevrolet Div. G.M. Corp.)

Procedure	*Method*
Check the block deck for warpage:	Using a straightedge and feeler gauges, check the block deck for warpage in the same manner that the cylinder head is checked (see Cylinder Head Reconditioning). If warpage exceeds specifications, have the deck resurfaced. NOTE: *In certain cases a specification for total material removal (Cylinder head and block deck) is provided. This specification must not be exceeded.*
* Check the deck height:	The deck height is the distance from the crankshaft centerline to the block deck. To measure, invert the engine, and install the crankshaft, retaining it with the center main cap. Measure the distance from the crankshaft journal to the block deck, parallel to the cylinder centerline. Measure the diameter of the end (front and rear) main journals, parallel to the centerline of the cylinders, divide the diameter in half, and subtract it from the previous measurement. The results of the front and rear measurements should be identical. If the difference exceeds .005″, the deck height should be corrected. NOTE: *Block deck height and warpage should be corrected concurrently.*
Check the cylinder block bearing alignment:  Checking main bearing saddle alignment (© Petersen Publishing Co.)	Remove the upper bearing inserts. Place a straightedge in the bearing saddles along the centerline of the crankshaft. If clearance exists between the straightedge and the center saddle, the block must be alignbored.
Clean and inspect the pistons and connecting rods:  Removing the piston rings (© Subaru)	Using a ring expander, remove the rings from the piston. Remove the retaining rings (if so equipped) and remove piston pin. NOTE: *If the piston pin must be pressed out, determine the proper method and use the proper tools; otherwise the piston will distort.* Clean the ring grooves using an appropriate tool, exercising care to avoid cutting too deeply. Thoroughly clean all carbon and varnish from the piston with solvent. CAUTION: *Do not use a wire brush or caustic solvent on pistons.* Inspect the pistons for scuffing, scoring, cracks, pitting, or excessive ring groove wear. If wear is evident, the piston must be replaced. Check the connecting rod length by measuring the rod from the inside of the large end to the inside of the small end using calipers (see

Procedure	Method
 Cleaning the piston ring grooves (© Ford Motor Co.) 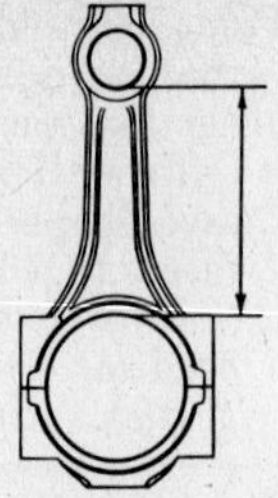 Connecting rod length checking dimension	illustration). All connecting rods should be equal length. Replace any rod that differs from the others in the engine.
	* Have the connecting rod alignment checked in an alignment fixture by a machinist. Replace any twisted or bent rods.
	* Magnaflux the connecting rods to locate stress cracks. If cracks are found, replace the connecting rod.
Fit the pistons to the cylinders: 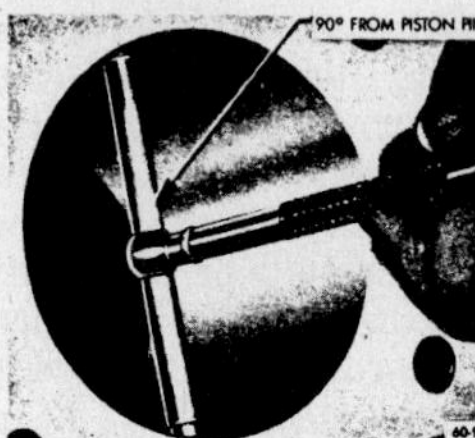 Measuring the cylinder with a telescope gauge for piston fitting (© Buick Div. G.M. Corp.)  Measuring the piston for fitting (© Buick Div. G.M. Corp.)	Using a telescope gauge and micrometer, or a dial gauge, measure the cylinder bore diameter perpendicular to the piston pin, 2½″ below the deck. Measure the piston perpendicular to its pin on the skirt. The difference between the two measurements is the piston clearance. If the clearance is within specifications or slightly below (after boring or honing), finish honing is all that is required. If the clearance is excessive, try to obtain a slightly larger piston to bring clearance within specifications. Where this is not possible, obtain the first oversize piston, and hone (or if necessary, bore) the cylinder to size.
Assemble the pistons and connecting rods:  Installing piston pin lock rings (© Nissan Motor Co., Ltd.)	Inspect piston pin, connecting rod small end bushing, and piston bore for galling, scoring, or excessive wear. If evident, replace defective part(s). Measure the I.D. of the piston boss and connecting rod small end, and the O.D. of the piston pin. If within specifications, assemble piston pin and rod. CAUTION: *If piston pin must be pressed in, determine the proper method and use the proper tools; otherwise the piston will distort.* Install the lock rings; ensure that they seat properly. If the parts are not within specifiçations, determine the service method for the type of engine. In some cases, piston and pin are serviced as an assembly when either is defective. Others specify reaming the piston and connecting rods for an oversize pin. If the connecting rod bushing is worn, it may in many cases be replaced. Reaming the piston and replacing the rod bushing are machine shop operations.

Procedure	*Method*

Clean and inspect the camshaft:

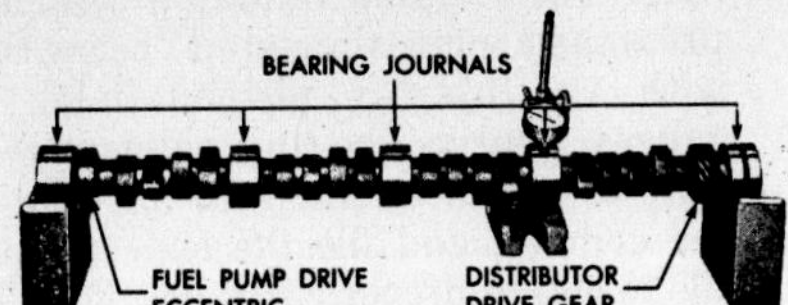

Checking the camshaft for straightness
(© Chevrolet Motor Div. G.M. Corp.)

Degrease the camshaft, using solvent, and clean out all oil holes. Visually inspect cam lobes and bearing journals for excessive wear. If a lobe is questionable, check all lobes as indicated below. If a journal or lobe is worn, the camshaft must be reground or replaced. NOTE: *If a journal is worn, there is a good chance that the bushings are worn.* If lobes and journals appear intact, place the front and rear journals in V-blocks, and rest a dial indicator on the center journal. Rotate the camshaft to check straightness. If deviation exceeds .001″, replace the camshaft.

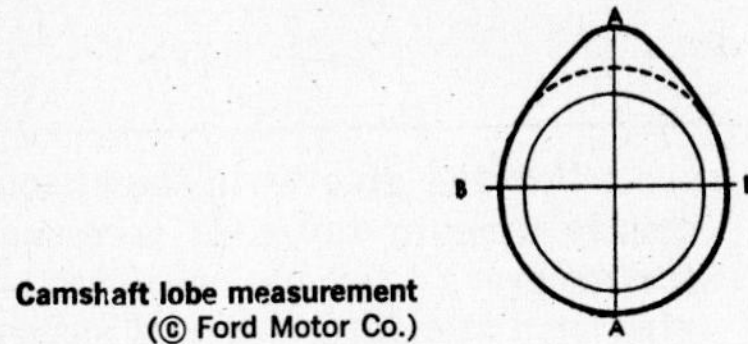

Camshaft lobe measurement
(© Ford Motor Co.)

* Check the camshaft lobes with a micrometer, by measuring the lobes from the nose to base and again at 90° (see illustration). The lift is determined by subtracting the second measurement from the first. If all exhaust lobes and all intake lobes are not identical, the camshaft must be reground or replaced.

Replace the camshaft bearings:

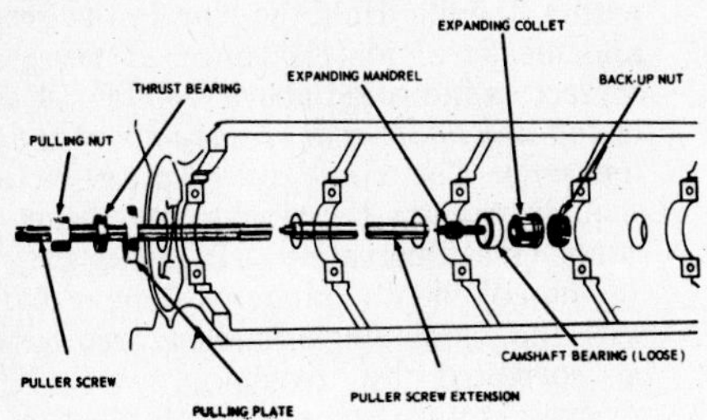

Camshaft removal and installation tool (typical)
(© Ford Motor Co.)

If excessive wear is indicated, or if the engine is being completely rebuilt, camshaft bearings should be replaced as follows: Drive the camshaft rear plug from the block. Assemble the removal puller with its shoulder on the bearing to be removed. Gradually tighten the puller nut until bearing is removed. Remove remaining bearings, leaving the front and rear for last. To remove front and rear bearings, reverse position of the tool, so as to pull the bearings in toward the center of the block. Leave the tool in this position, pilot the new front and rear bearings on the installer, and pull them into position. Return the tool to its original position and pull remaining bearings into position. NOTE: *Ensure that oil holes align when installing bearings.* Replace camshaft rear plug, and stake it into position to aid retention.

Finish hone the cylinders:

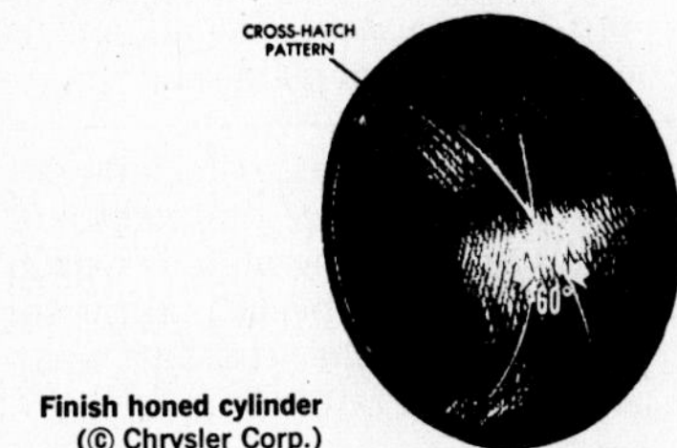

Finish honed cylinder
(© Chrysler Corp.)

Chuck a flexible drive hone into a power drill, and insert it into the cylinder. Start the hone, and move it up and down in the cylinder at a rate which will produce approximately a 60° cross-hatch pattern (see illustration). NOTE: *Do not extend the hone below the cylinder bore.* After developing the pattern, remove the hone and recheck piston fit. Wash the cylinders with a detergent and water solution to remove abrasive dust, dry, and wipe several times with a rag soaked in engine oil.

Procedure	*Method*
Check piston ring end-gap:  Checking ring end-gap (© Chevrolet Motor Div. G.M. Corp.)	Compress the piston rings to be used in a cylinder, one at a time, into that cylinder, and press them approximately 1″ below the deck with an inverted piston. Using feeler gauges, measure the ring end-gap, and compare to specifications. Pull the ring out of the cylinder and file the ends with a fine file to obtain proper clearance. CAUTION: *If inadequate ring end-gap is utilized, ring breakage will result.*
Install the piston rings: 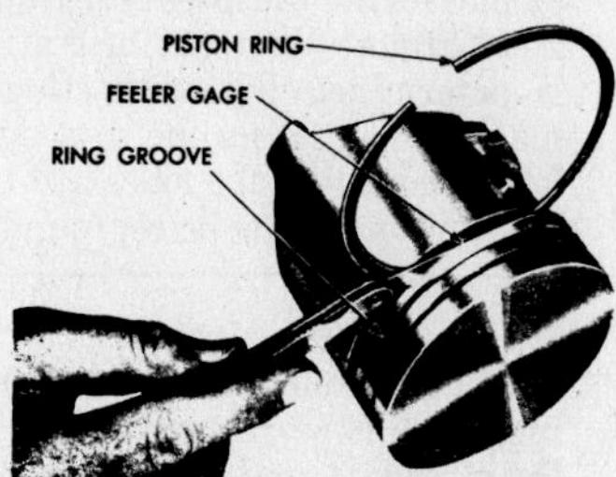 Checking ring side clearance (© Chrysler Corp.) 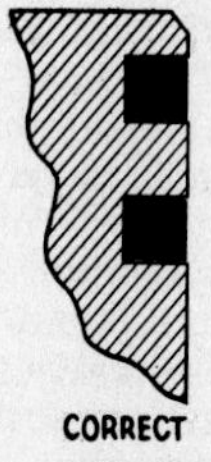 CORRECT 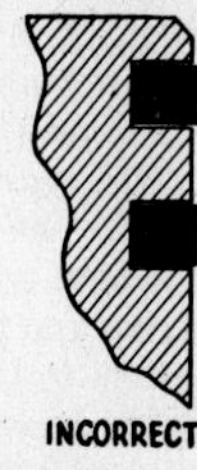 INCORRECT 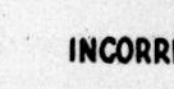 Piston groove depth Correct ring spacer installation	Inspect the ring grooves in the piston for excessive wear or taper. If necessary, recut the groove(s) for use with an overwidth ring or a standard ring and spacer. If the groove is worn uniformly, overwidth rings, or standard rings and spacers may be installed without recutting. Roll the outside of the ring around the groove to check for burrs or deposits. If any are found, remove with a fine file. Hold the ring in the groove, and measure side clearance. If necessary, correct as indicated above. NOTE: *Always install any additional spacers above the piston ring.* The ring groove must be deep enough to allow the ring to seat below the lands (see illustration). In many cases, a "go-no-go" depth gauge will be provided with the piston rings. Shallow grooves may be corrected by recutting, while deep grooves require some type of filler or expander behind the piston. Consult the piston ring supplier concerning the suggested method. Install the rings on the piston, lowest ring first, using a ring expander. NOTE: *Position the ring markings as specified by the manufacturer (see car section).*
Install the camshaft:	Liberally lubricate the camshaft lobes and journals, and slide the camshaft into the block. CAUTION: *Exercise extreme care to avoid damaging the bearings when inserting the camshaft.* Install and tighten the camshaft thrust plate retaining bolts.
Check camshaft end-play: 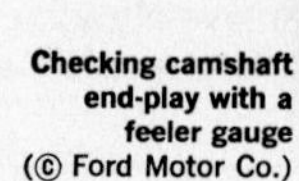 Checking camshaft end-play with a feeler gauge (© Ford Motor Co.) 	Using feeler gauges, determine whether the clearance between the camshaft boss (or gear) and backing plate is within specifications. Install shims behind the thrust plate, or reposition the camshaft gear (see car section), and retest end-play.

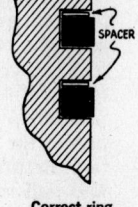

Procedure	*Method*
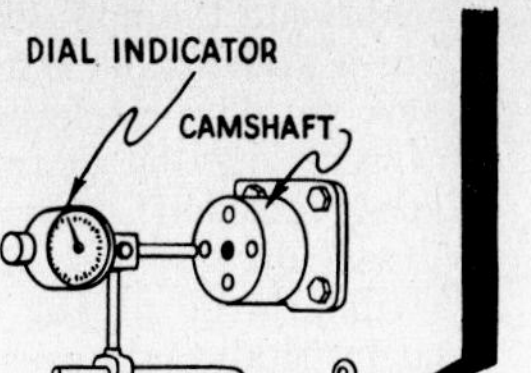 Checking camshaft end-play with a dial indicator	* Mount a dial indicator stand so that the stem of the dial indicator rests on the nose of the camshaft, parallel to the camshaft axis. Push the camshaft as far in as possible and zero the gauge. Move the camshaft outward to determine the amount of camshaft end-play. If the end-play is not within tolerance, install shims behind the thrust plate, or reposition the camshaft gear (see car section), and retest.
Install the rear main seal (where applicable):  Seating the rear main seal (© Buick Div. G.M. Corp.)	Position the block with the bearing saddles facing upward. Lay the rear main seal in its groove and press it lightly into its seat. Place a piece of pipe the same diameter as the crankshaft journal into the saddle, and firmly seat the seal. Hold the pipe in position, and trim the ends of the seal flush if required.
Install the crankshaft: 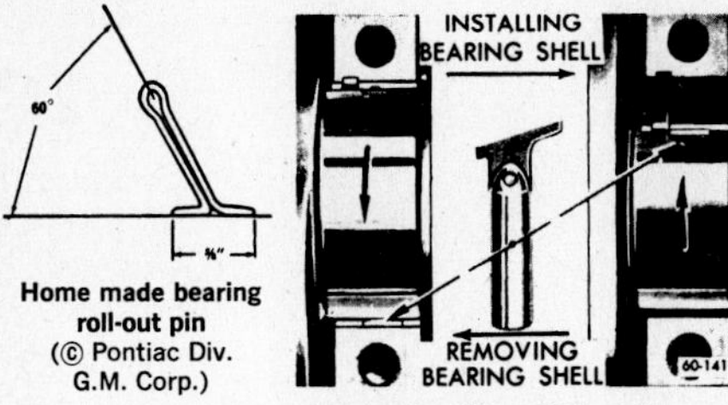 Home made bearing roll-out pin (© Pontiac Div. G.M. Corp.) Removal and installation of upper bearing insert using a roll-out pin (© Buick Div. G.M. Corp.)	Thoroughly clean the main bearing saddles and caps. Place the upper halves of the bearing inserts on the saddles and press into position. NOTE: *Ensure that the oil holes align.* Press the corresponding bearing inserts into the main bearing caps. Lubricate the upper main bearings, and lay the crankshaft in position. Place a strip of Plastigage on each of the crankshaft journals, install the main caps, and torque to specifications. Remove the main caps, and compare the Plastigage to the scale on the Plastigage envelope. If clearances are within tolerances, remove the Plastigage, turn the crankshaft 90°, wipe off all oil and retest. If all clearances are correct, remove all Plastigage, thoroughly

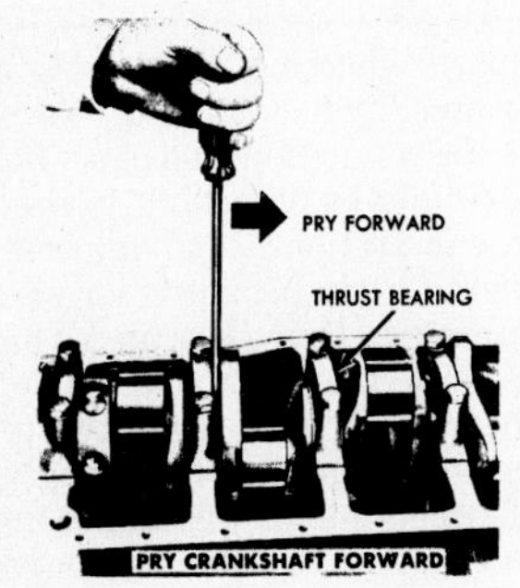

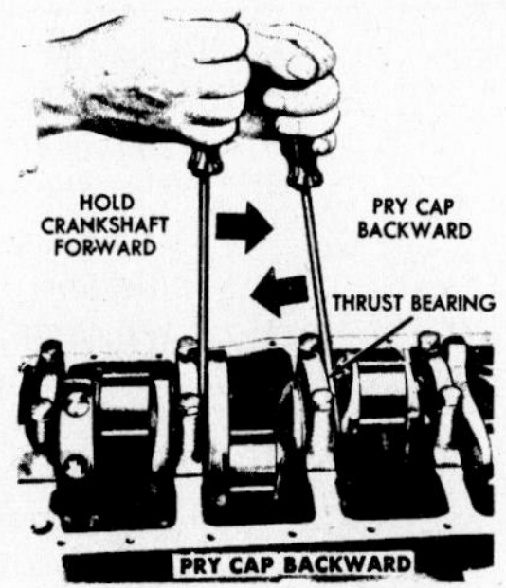

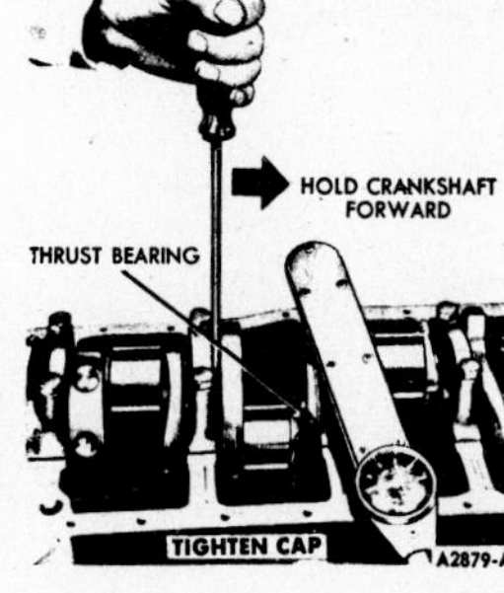

Aligning the thrust bearing
(© Ford Motor Co.)

Procedure	Method
	lubricate the main caps and bearing journals, and install the main caps. If clearances are not within tolerance, the upper bearing inserts may be removed, without removing the crankshaft, using a bearing roll out pin (see illustration). Roll in a bearing that will provide proper clearance, and retest. Torque all main caps, excluding the thrust bearing cap, to specifications. Tighten the thrust bearing cap finger tight. To properly align the thrust bearing, pry the crankshaft the extent of its axial travel several times, the last movement held toward the front of the engine, and torque the thrust bearing cap to specifications. Determine the crankshaft end-play (see below), and bring within tolerance with thrust washers.
Measure crankshaft end-play:  Checking crankshaft end-play with a dial indicator (© Ford Motor Co.) 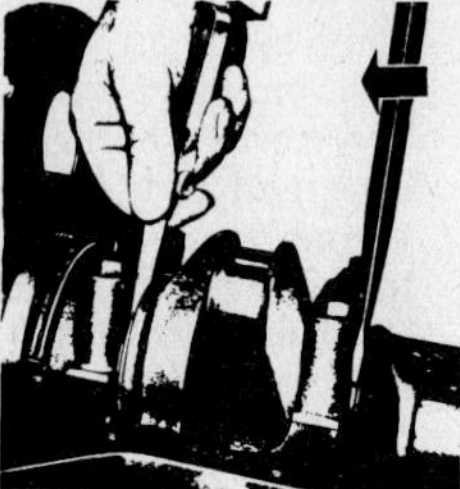 Checking crankshaft end-play with a feeler gauge (© Chevrolet Div. (G.M. Corp.)	Mount a dial indicator stand on the front of the block, with the dial indicator stem resting on the nose of the crankshaft, parallel to the crankshaft axis. Pry the crankshaft the extent of its travel rearward, and zero the indicator. Pry the crankshaft forward and record crankshaft end-play. NOTE: *Crankshaft end-play also may be measured at the thrust bearing, using feeler gauges* (see illustration).
Install the pistons:	Press the upper connecting rod bearing halves into the connecting rods, and the lower halves into the connecting rod caps. Position the piston ring gaps according to specifications (see car section), and lubricate the pistons. Install a ring compresser on a piston, and press two long (8″) pieces of plastic tubing over the rod bolts. Using the plastic tubes as a guide, press the pistons into the bores and onto the crankshaft with a wooden hammer handle. After seating the rod on the crankshaft journal, remove the tubes and install the cap finger tight. Install the remaining pistons in the same man-

Procedure	Method
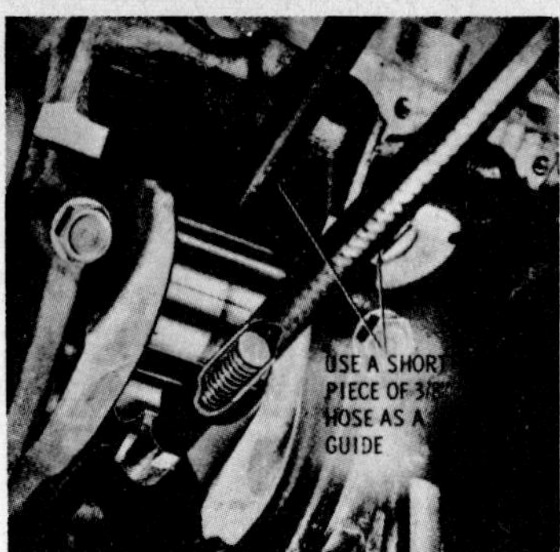 Tubing used as guide when installing a piston (© Oldsmobile Div. G.M. Corp.) 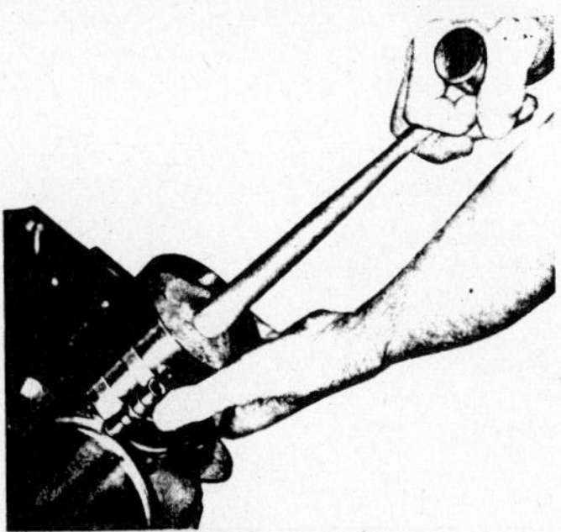 Installing a piston (© Chevrolet Div. G.M. Corp.)	ner. Invert the engine and check the bearing clearance at two points (90° apart) on each journal with Plastigage. NOTE: *Do not turn the crankshaft with Plastigage installed.* If clearance is within tolerances, remove *all* Plastigage, thoroughly lubricate the journals, and torque the rod caps to specifications. If clearance is not within specifications, install different thickness bearing inserts and recheck. CAUTION: *Never shim or file the connecting rods or caps.* Always install plastic tube sleeves over the rod bolts when the caps are not installed, to protect the crankshaft journals.
Check connecting rod side clearance:  Checking connecting rod side clearance (© Chevrolet Div. G.M. Corp.)	Determine the clearance between the sides of the connecting rods and the crankshaft, using feeler gauges. If clearance is below the minimum tolerance, the rod may be machined to provide adequate clearance. If clearance is excessive, substitute an unworn rod, and recheck. If clearance is still outside specifications, the crankshaft must be welded and reground, or replaced.
Inspect the timing chain:	Visually inspect the timing chain for broken or loose links, and replace the chain if any are found. If the chain will flex sideways, it must be replaced. Install the timing chain as specified in the car section. NOTE: *If the original timing chain is to be reused, install it in its original position.*

Procedure	Method
Check timing gear backlash and runout:	Mount a dial indicator with its stem resting on a tooth of the camshaft gear (as illustrated). Rotate the gear until all slack is removed, and zero the indicator. Rotate the gear in the opposite direction until slack is removed, and record gear backlash. Mount the indicator with its stem resting on the edge of the camshaft gear, parallel to the axis of the camshaft. Zero the indicator, and turn the camshaft gear one full turn, recording the runout. If either backlash or runout exceed specifications, replace the worn gear(s).

Checking camshaft gear backlash
(© Chevrolet Div. G.M. Corp.)

Checking camshaft gear runout
(© Chevrolet Div. G.M. Corp.)

Completing the Rebuilding Process

Following the above procedures, complete the rebuilding process as follows:

Fill the oil pump with oil, to prevent cavitating (sucking air) on initial engine start up. Install the oil pump and the pickup tube on the engine. Coat the oil pan gasket as necessary, and install the gasket and the oil pan. Mount the flywheel and the crankshaft vibrational damper or pulley on the crankshaft. NOTE: *Always use new bolts when installing the flywheel.* Inspect the clutch shaft pilot bushing in the crankshaft. If the bushing is excessively worn, remove it with an expanding puller and a slide hammer, and tap a new bushing into place.

Position the engine, cylinder head side up. Lubricate the lifters, and install them into their bores. Install the cylinder head, and torque it as specified in the car section. Insert the pushrods (where applicable), and install the rocker shaft(s) (if so equipped) or position the rocker arms on the pushrods. If solid lifters are utilized, adjust the valves to the "cold" specifications.

Mount the intake and exhaust manifolds, the carburetor(s), the distributor and spark plugs. Adjust the point gap and the static ignition timing. Mount all accessories and install the engine in the car. Fill the radiator with coolant, and the crankcase with high quality engine oil.

Break-in Procedure

Start the engine, and allow it to run at low speed for a few minutes, while checking for leaks. Stop the engine, check the oil level, and fill as necessary. Restart the engine, and fill the cooling system to capacity. Check the point dwell angle and adjust the ignition timing and the valves. Run the engine at low to medium speed (800-2500 rpm) for approximately ½ hour, and retorque the cylinder head bolts. Road test the car, and check again for leaks.

Follow the manufacturer's recommended engine break-in procedure and maintenance schedule for new engines.

Appendix

General Conversion Table

Multiply by	*To convert*	*To*	
2.54	Inches	Centimeters	.3937
30.48	Feet	Centimeters	.0328
.914	Yards	Meters	1.094
1.609	Miles	Kilometers	.621
.645	Square inches	Square cm.	.155
.836	Square yards	Square meters	1.196
16.39	Cubic inches	Cubic cm.	.061
28.3	Cubic feet	Liters	.0353
.4536	Pounds	Kilograms	2.2045
4.546	Gallons	Liters	.22
.068	Lbs./sq. in. (psi)	Atmospheres	14.7
.138	Foot pounds	Kg. m.	7.23
1.014	H.P. (DIN)	H.P. (SAE)	.9861
——	To obtain	From	Multiply by

Note: 1 cm. equals 10 mm.; 1 mm. equals .0394″.

Conversion—Common Fractions to Decimals and Millimeters

Inches			Inches			Inches		
Common Fractions	*Decimal Fractions*	*Millimeters (approx.)*	*Common Fractions*	*Decimal Fractions*	*Millimeters (approx.)*	*Common Fractions*	*Decimal Fractions*	*Millimeters (approx.)*
1/128	.008	0.20	11/32	.344	8.73	43/64	.672	17.07
1/64	.016	0.40	23/64	.359	9.13	11/16	.688	17.46
1/32	.031	0.79	3/8	.375	9.53	45/64	.703	17.86
3/64	.047	1.19	25/64	.391	9.92	23/32	.719	18.26
1/16	.063	1.59	13/32	.406	10.32	47/64	.734	18.65
5/64	.078	1.98	27/64	.422	10.72	3/4	.750	19.05
3/32	.094	2.38	7/16	.438	11.11	49/64	.766	19.45
7/64	.109	2.78	29/64	.453	11.51	25/32	.781	19.84
1/8	.125	3.18	15/32	.469	11.91	51/64	.797	20.24
9/64	.141	3.57	31/64	.484	12.30	13/16	.813	20.64
5/32	.156	3.97	1/2	.500	12.70	53/64	.828	21.03
11/64	.172	4.37	33/64	.516	13.10	27/32	.844	21.43
3/16	.188	4.76	17/32	.531	13.49	55/64	.859	21.83
13/64	.203	5.16	35/64	.547	13.89	7/8	.875	22.23
7/32	.219	5.56	9/16	.563	14.29	57/64	.891	22.62
15/64	.234	5.95	37/64	.578	14.68	29/32	.906	23.02
1/4	.250	6.35	19/32	.594	15.08	59/64	.922	23.42
17/64	.266	6.75	39/64	.609	15.48	15/16	.938	23.81
9/32	.281	7.14	5/8	.625	15.88	61/64	.953	24.21
19/64	.297	7.54	41/64	.641	16.27	31/32	.969	24.61
5/16	.313	7.94	21/32	.656	16.67	63/64	.984	25.00
21/64	.328	8.33						

Conversion—Millimeters to Decimal Inches

mm	*inches*	*mm*	*inches*	*mm*	*inches*	*mm*	*inches*	*mm*	*inches*
1	.039 370	31	1.220 470	61	2.401 570	91	3.582 670	210	8.267 700
2	.078 740	32	1.259 840	62	2.440 940	92	3.622 040	220	8.661 400
3	.118 110	33	1.299 210	63	2.480 310	93	3.661 410	230	9.055 100
4	.157 480	34	1.338 580	64	2.519 680	94	3.700 780	240	9.448 800
5	.196 850	35	1.377 949	65	2.559 050	95	3.740 150	250	9.842 500
6	.236 220	36	1.417 319	66	2.598 420	96	3.779 520	260	10.236 200
7	.275 590	37	1.456 689	67	2.637 790	97	3.818 890	270	10.629 900
8	.314 960	38	1.496 050	68	2.677 160	98	3.858 260	280	11.032 600
9	.354 330	39	1.535 430	69	2.716 530	99	3.897 630	290	11.417 300
10	.393 700	40	1.574 800	70	2.755 900	100	3.937 000	300	11.811 000
11	.433 070	41	1.614 170	71	2.795 270	105	4.133 848	310	12.204 700
12	.472 440	42	1.653 540	72	2.834 640	110	4.330 700	320	12.598 400
13	.511 810	43	1.692 910	73	2.874 010	115	4.527 550	330	12.992 100
14	.551 180	44	1.732 280	74	2.913 380	120	4.724 400	340	13.385 800
15	.590 550	45	1.771 650	75	2.952 750	125	4.921 250	350	13.779 500
16	.629 920	46	1.811 020	76	2.992 120	130	5.118 100	360	14.173 200
17	.669 290	47	1.850 390	77	3.031 490	135	5.314 950	370	14.566 900
18	.708 660	48	1.889 760	78	3.070 860	140	5.511 800	380	14.960 600
19	.748 030	49	1.929 130	79	3.110 230	145	5.708 650	390	15.354 300
20	.787 400	50	1.968 500	80	3.149 600	150	5.905 500	400	15.748 000
21	.826 770	51	2.007 870	81	3.188 970	155	6.102 350	500	19.685 000
22	.866 140	52	2.047 240	82	3.228 340	160	6.299 200	600	23.622 000
23	.905 510	53	2.086 610	83	3.267 710	165	6.496 050	700	27.559 000
24	.944 880	54	2.125 980	84	3.307 080	170	6.692 900	800	31.496 000
25	.984 250	55	2.165 350	85	3.346 450	175	6.889 750	900	35.433 000
26	1.023 620	56	2.204 720	86	3.385 820	180	7.086 600	1000	39.370 000
27	1.062 990	57	2.244 090	87	3.425 190	185	7.283 450	2000	78.740 000
28	1.102 360	58	2.283 460	88	3.464 560	190	7.480 300	3000	118.110 000
29	1.141 730	59	2.322 830	89	3.503 903	195	7.677 150	4000	157.480 000
30	1.181 100	60	2.362 200	90	3.543 300	200	7.874 000	5000	196.850 000

To change decimal millimeters to decimal inches, position the decimal point where desired on either side of the millimeter measurement shown and reset the inches decimal by the same number of digits in the same direction. For example, to convert .001 mm into decimal inches, reset the decimal behind the 1 mm (shown on the chart) to .001; change the decimal inch equivalent (.039" shown) to .00039").

Tap Drill Sizes

National Fine or S.A.E.

Screw & Tap Size	Threads Per Inch	Use Drill Number
No. 5	44	37
No. 6	40	33
No. 8	36	29
No. 10	32	21
No. 12	28	15
1/4	28	3
5/16	24	1
3/8	24	Q
7/16	20	W
1/2	20	29/64
9/16	18	33/64
5/8	18	37/64
3/4	16	11/16
7/8	14	13/16
1 1/8	12	1 3/64
1 1/4	12	1 11/64
1 1/2	12	1 27/64

National Coarse or U.S.S.

Screw & Tap Size	Threads Per Inch	Use Drill Number
No. 5	40	39
No. 6	32	36
No. 8	32	29
No. 10	24	25
No. 12	24	17
1/4	20	8
5/16	18	F
3/8	16	5/16
7/16	14	U
1/2	13	27/64
9/16	12	31/64
5/8	11	17/32
3/4	10	21/32
7/8	9	49/64
1	8	7/8
1 1/8	7	63/64
1 1/4	7	1 7/64
1 1/2	6	1 11/32

Decimal Equivalent Size of the Number Drills

Drill No.	Decimal Equivalent	Drill No.	Decimal Equivalent	Drill No.	Decimal Equivalent
80	.0135	53	.0595	26	.1470
79	.0145	52	.0635	25	.1495
78	.0160	51	.0670	24	.1520
77	.0180	50	.0700	23	.1540
76	.0200	49	.0730	22	.1570
75	.0210	48	.0760	21	.1590
74	.0225	47	.0785	20	.1610
73	.0240	46	.0810	19	.1660
72	.0250	45	.0820	18	.1695
71	.0260	44	.0860	17	.1730
70	.0280	43	.0890	16	.1770
69	.0292	42	.0935	15	.1800
68	.0310	41	.0960	14	.1820
67	.0320	40	.0980	13	.1850
66	.0330	39	.0995	12	.1890
65	.0350	38	.1015	11	.1910
64	.0360	37	.1040	10	.1935
63	.0370	36	.1065	9	.1960
62	.0380	35	.1100	8	.1990
61	.0390	34	.1110	7	.2010
60	.0400	33	.1130	6	.2040
59	.0410	32	.1160	5	.2055
58	.0420	31	.1200	4	.2090
57	.0430	30	.1285	3	.2130
56	.0465	29	.1360	2	.2210
55	.0520	28	.1405	1	.2280
54	.0550	27	.1440		

Decimal Equivalent Size of the Letter Drills

Letter Drill	Decimal Equivalent	Letter Drill	Decimal Equivalent	Letter Drill	Decimal Equivalent
A	.234	J	.277	S	.348
B	.238	K	.281	T	.358
C	.242	L	.290	U	.368
D	.246	M	.295	V	.377
E	.250	N	.302	W	.386
F	.257	O	.316	X	.397
G	.261	P	.323	Y	.404
H	.266	Q	.332	Z	.413
I	.272	R	.339		

ANTI-FREEZE INFORMATION

Freezing and Boiling Points of Solutions According to Percentage of Alcohol or Ethylene Glycol

Freezing Point of Solution	Alcohol Volume %	Alcohol Solution Boils at	Ethylene Glycol Volume %	Ethylene Glycol Solution Boils at
20°F.	12	196°F.	16	216°F.
10°F.	20	189°F.	25	218°F.
0°F.	27	184°F.	33	220°F.
–10°F.	32	181°F.	39	222°F.
–20°F.	38	178°F.	44	224°F.
–30°F.	42	176°F.	48	225°F.

Note: above boiling points are at sea level. For every 1,000 feet of altitude, boiling points are approximately 2°F. lower than those shown. For every pound of pressure exerted by the pressure cap, the boiling points are approximately 3°F. higher than those shown.

To Increase the Freezing Protection of Anti-Freeze Solutions Already Installed

Cooling System Capacity Quarts	Number of Quarts of **ALCOHOL** Anti-Freeze Required to Increase Protection													
	From +20°F. to					From +10°F. to					From 0°F. to			
	0°	−10°	−20°	−30°	−40°	0°	−10°	−20°	−30°	−40°	−10°	−20°	−30°	−40°
10	2	2¾	3½	4	4½	1	2	2⅓	3¼	3¾	1	1¾	2½	3
12	2½	3¼	4	4¾	5¼	1¼	2¼	3	3¾	4½	1¼	2	2¾	3½
14	3	4	4¾	5½	6	1½	2½	3½	4½	5	1¼	2½	3¼	4
16	3¼	4½	5½	6¼	7	1¾	3	4	5	5¾	1½	2¾	3¾	4¾
18	3¾	5	6	7	7¾	2	3¼	4½	5¾	6½	1¾	3	4¼	5¼
20	4	5½	6¾	7¾	8¾	2	3¼	5	6¼	7¼	1¾	3½	4¾	5¾
22	4½	6	7½	8½	9½	2¼	4	5½	6¾	8	2	3¾	5¼	6½
24	5	6¾	8	9¼	10½	2½	4½	6	7½	8¾	2¼	4	5½	7
26	5¼	7¼	8¾	10	11¼	2¾	4¾	6½	8	9½	2½	4½	6	7½
28	5¾	7¾	9½	11	12	3	5¼	7	8¾	10¼	2½	4¾	6½	8
30	6	8¼	10	11¾	13	3	5½	7½	9¼	10¾	2¾	5	7	8¾

Test radiator solution with proper tester. Determine from the table the number of quarts of solution to be drawn off from a full cooling system and replace with concentrated anti-freeze, to give the desired increased protection. For example, to increase protection of a 22-quart cooling system containing Alcohol anti-freeze, from +10°F. to −20°F. will require the replacement of 5½ quarts of solution with concentrated anti-freeze.

Cooling System Capacity Quarts	Number of Quarts of **ETHYLENE GLYCOL** Anti-Freeze Required to Increase Protection													
	From +20°F. to					From +10°F. to					From 0°F. to			
	0°	−10°	−20°	−30°	−40°	0°	−10°	−20°	−30°	−40°	−10°	−20°	−30°	−40°
10	1¾	2¼	3	3½	3¾	¾	1½	2¼	2¾	3¼	¾	1½	2	2½
12	2	2¾	3½	4	4½	1	1¾	2½	3¼	3¾	1	1¾	2½	3¼
14	2¼	3¼	4	4¾	5½	1¼	2	3	3¾	4½	1	2	3	3½
16	2½	3½	4½	5¼	6	1¼	2½	3½	4¼	5¼	1¼	2¼	3¼	4
18	3	4	5	6	7	1½	2¾	4	5	5¾	1½	2½	3¾	4¾
20	3¼	4½	5¾	6¾	7½	1¾	3	4¼	5½	6½	1½	2¾	4¼	5¼
22	3½	5	6¼	7¼	8¼	1¾	3¼	4¾	6	7¼	1¾	3¼	4½	5½
24	4	5½	7	8	9	2	3½	5	6½	7½	1¾	3½	5	6
26	4¼	6	7½	8¾	10	2	4	5½	7	8¼	2	3¾	5½	6¾
28	4½	6¼	8	9½	10½	2¼	4¼	6	7½	9	2	4	5¾	7¼
30	5	6¾	8½	10	11½	2½	4½	6½	8	9½	2¼	4¼	6¼	7¾

Test radiator solution with proper hydrometer. Determine from the table the number of quarts of solution to be drawn off from a full cooling system and replace with undiluted anti-freeze, to give the desired increased protection. For example, to increase protection of a 22-quart cooling system containing Ethylene Glycol (permanent type) anti-freeze, from +20°F. to −20°F. will require the replacement of 6¼ quarts of solution with undiluted anti-freeze.

ANTI-FREEZE CHART

Temperatures Shown in Degrees Fahrenheit
+32 is Freezing

Cooling System Capacity Quarts	Quarts of **ALCOHOL** Needed for Protection to Temperatures Shown Below												
	1	2	3	4	5	6	7	8	9	10	11	12	13
10	+23°	+11°	− 5°	−27°									
11	+25	+13	0	−18	−40°								
12		+15	+ 3	−12	−31								
13		+17	+ 7	− 7	−23								
14		+19	+ 9	− 3	−17	−34°							
15		+20	+11	+ 1	−12	−27							
16		+21	+13	+ 3	− 8	−21	−36°						
17		+22	+16	+ 6	− 4	−16	−29						
18		+23	+17	+ 8	− 1	−12	−25	−38°					
19		+24	+17	+ 9	+ 2	− 8	−21	−32					
20			+18	+11	+ 4	− 5	−16	−27	−39°				
21			+19	+12	+ 5	− 3	−12	−22	−34				
22			+20	+14	+ 7	0	− 9	−18	−29	−40°			
23			+21	+15	+ 8	+ 2	− 7	−15	−25	−36°			
24			+21	+16	+10	+ 4	− 4	−12	21	−31			
25			+22	+17	+11	+ 6	− 2	− 9	−18	−27	−37°		
26			+22	+17	+12	+ 7	+ 1	− 7	−14	−23	−32		
27			+23	+18	+13	+ 8	+ 3	− 5	−12	−20	−28	−39°	
28			+23	+19	+14	+ 9	+ 4	− 3	− 9	−17	−25	−34	
29			+24	+19	+15	+10	+ 6	− 1	− 7	−15	−22	−30	−39°
30			+24	+20	+16	+11	+ 7	+ 1	− 5	−12	−19	−27	−35

+ Figures are above Zero, but below Freezing.

− Figures are below Zero. Also below Freezing.

Cooling System Capacity Quarts	Quarts of **ETHYLENE GLYCOL** Needed for Protection to Temperatures Shown Below													
	1	2	3	4	5	6	7	8	9	10	11	12	13	14
10	+24°	+16°	+ 4°	−12°	−34°	−62°								
11	+25	+18	+ 8	− 6	−23	−47								
12	+26	+19	+10	0	−15	−34	−57°							
13	+27	+21	+13	+ 3	− 9	−25	−45							
14			+15	+ 6	− 5	−18	−34							
15			+16	+ 8	0	−12	−26							
16			+17	+10	+ 2	− 8	−19	−34	−52°					
17			+18	+12	+ 5	− 4	−14	−27	−42					
18			+19	+14	+ 7	0	−10	−21	−34	−50°				
19			+20	+15	+ 9	+ 2	− 7	−16	−28	−42		*		
20				+16	+10	+ 4	− 3	−12	−22	−34	−48°			
21				+17	+12	+ 6	0	− 9	−17	−28	−41			
22				+18	+13	+ 8	+ 2	− 6	−14	−23	−34	−47°		
23				+19	+14	+ 9	+ 4	− 3	−10	−19	−29	−40		
24				+19	+15	+10	+ 5	0	− 8	−15	−23	−34	−46°	
25				+20	+16	+12	+ 7	+ 1	− 5	−12	−20	−29	−40	−50°
26					+17	+13	+ 8	+ 3	− 3	− 9	−16	−25	−34	−44
27					+18	+14	+ 9	+ 5	− 1	− 7	−13	−21	−29	−39
28					+18	+15	+10	+ 6	+ 1	− 5	−11	−18	−25	−34
29					+19	+16	+12	+ 7	+ 2	− 3	− 8	−15	−22	−29
30					+20	+17	+13	+ 8	+ 4	− 1	− 6	−12	−18	−25

For capacities over 30 quarts divide true capacity by 3. Find quarts Anti-Freeze for the ⅓ and multiply by 3 for quarts to add.

* For capacities under 10 quarts multiply true capacity by 3. Find quarts Anti-Freeze for the tripled volume and divide by 3 for quarts to add.

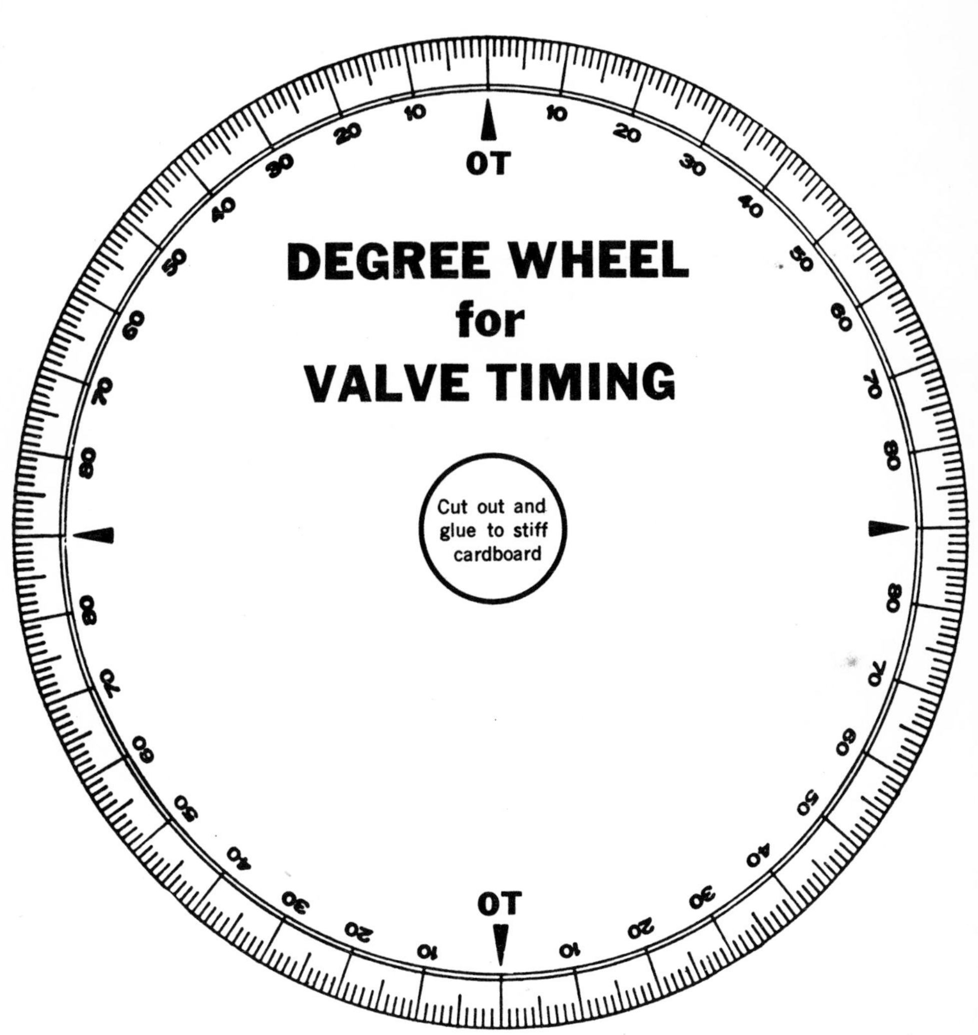

DEGREE WHEEL
for
VALVE TIMING
OT
OT
Cut out and glue to stiff cardboard
10
20
30
40
50
60
70
80